Anony

Census of England and Wales, 1881

Vol. III

Anonymous

Census of England and Wales, 1881

Vol. III

Reprint of the original, first published in 1883.

1st Edition 2024 | ISBN: 978-3-38531-465-8

Verlag (Publisher): Outlook Verlag GmbH, Zeilweg 44, 60439 Frankfurt, Deutschland
Vertretungsberechtigt (Authorized to represent): E. Roepke, Zeilweg 44, 60439 Frankfurt, Deutschland
Druck (Print): Books on Demand GmbH, In de Tarpen 42, 22848 Norderstedt, Deutschland

Table 13A.—NUMBER and COUNTRY of BIRTH of FOREIGNERS enumerated in the R

WHERE BORN.	REGISTRATION DISTRICTS.										
	LONDON.		1 KENSINGTON.		2 FULHAM.		3 CHELSEA.		4 ST. GEORGE, HANOVER SQ.		5 WE MINS
	Males.	Females.	Males.	Females.	Males.	Females.	Males.	Females.	Males.	Females.	Males.
TOTAL - - -	37,125	23,127	2,129	2,583	632	486	389	314	1,122	1,218	2,185
EUROPE.											
RUSSIA - - - - -	1,161	617	31	31	4	.	5	2	14	10	30
POLAND (RUSSIAN) - - - -	3,877	3,054	30	20	6	1	6	1	5	1	106
SWEDEN - - - - -	730	174	24	25	7	6	3	1	25	11	57
NORWAY - - - -	517	81	11	5	3	2	2	1	4	1	5
DENMARK - - - -	411	142	20	23	4	.	5	2	9	6	10
HOLLAND - - - -	2,295	1,898	57	59	21	15	8	5	19	16	47
BELGIUM - - - -	844	648	54	57	24	8	20	18	46	35	97
FRANCE - - - -	4,108	4,143	338	715	78	128	85	95	305	466	552
GERMANY - - - -	14,132	7,834	750	814	325	209	129	97	364	329	667
AUSTRIA - - - -	931	347	61	43	13	4	11	4	33	15	48
HUNGARY - - - -	189	58	16	4	3	.	5	1	12	9	7
SWITZERLAND - - - -	1,448	848	138	209	17	10	26	24	99	146	187
SPAIN - - - - -	322	151	44	24	18	9	3	3	6	10	17
PORTUGAL - - - -	92	59	16	9	2	5	3	.	1	1	4
ITALY - - - -	2,876	628	123	70	35	19	30	5	66	34	252
GREECE - - - -	181	47	41	20	3	1	1	1	9	4	1
SERVIA - - - - -	2	2	.	.	.	.	.	.	.	.	.
ROUMANIA - - - -	29	7	3	6	1	.	.	.	3	.	.
TURKEY - - - - -	130	73	47	40	2	2	1	.	6	2	9
ASIA.											
ARABIA - - - - -	22	1	.	.	.	.	.	.	1	.	1
PERSIA - - - - -	6	4	2	.	1	.	.	.	.	2	1
CHINA - - - - -	100	9	3	2	.	.	2	.	.	.	.
OTHER COUNTRIES - - -	77	24	27	13	3	.	.	2	.	1	3
AFRICA.											
EGYPT - - - - -	12	10	3	5	.	.	.	.	.	1	2
OTHER PARTS - - - -	53	23	7	3	1	.	1	.	1	3	2
AMERICA.											
UNITED STATES - - - -	2,255	2,046	221	318	54	60	39	51	83	99	67
MEXICO - - - - -	18	10	3	2	.	.	1	.	1	.	1
BRAZIL - - - - -	42	39	7	16	3	.	.	.	5	3	3
OTHER STATES - - - -	161	117	36	37	4	7	.	.	1	11	5
BORN ABROAD (COUNTRY NOT STATED)	47	22	16	6	.	.	2	.	4	2	3
BORN AT SEA - - - -	7	11	.	2	.	.	1	1	.	.	1

Table 13A *continued.*—NUMBER and COUNTRY of BIRTH OF FOREIGNERS enumerated in

WHERE BORN.	REGISTRATION DISTRICTS.											
	10 HACKNEY.		11 ST. GILES.		12 STRAND.		13 HOLBORN.		14 LONDON CITY.		15 SHOREDITCH.	
	Males.	Females.	Males.	Females.	Males.	Females.	Males.	Females.	Males.	Females.	Males.	Female
TOTAL	1,168	636	813	380	768	280	2,602	776	1,014	505	799	32
EUROPE.												
RUSSIA	26	3	19	5	7	.	16	8	42	29	21	[illegible]
POLAND (RUSSIAN)	19	7	42	29	14	7	30	14	227	167	58	[illegible]
SWEDEN	18	4	7	1	9	.	13	3	7	1	12	.
NORWAY	13	8	3	.	2	2	6	3	5	1	3	
DENMARK	22	7	7	2	4	3	12	3	4	1	10	.
HOLLAND	94	88	33	32	12	10	29	16	74	45	31	[illegible]
BELGIUM	37	29	32	20	23	17	25	16	18	10	11	[illegible]
FRANCE	91	82	127	76	127	91	204	125	50	20	37	[illegible]
GERMANY	636	291	295	122	201	68	683	238	345	141	489	[illegible]
AUSTRIA	32	9	24	3	18	5	56	17	21	11	30	.
HUNGARY	12	5	2	.	3	2	7	.	6	4	5	.
SWITZERLAND	40	11	33	13	116	16	82	24	58	16	17	[illegible]
SPAIN	13	9	9	1	6	3	8	3	10	2	4	
PORTUGAL	2	.	1	2	1	.	.	1	1	1	.	
ITALY	25	4	65	12	108	7	1,311	250	65	8	28	
GREECE	8	1	4	.	3	.	3	.	4	1	1	
SERVIA	.	.	.	.	.	.	1	.	.	.	.	
ROUMANIA	2	.	.	.	1	.	.	.	.	.	2	
TURKEY	4	2	8	.	1	.	4	1	7	1	1	
ASIA.												
ARABIA	.	.	.	.	.	.	.	.	.	.	.	
PERSIA	.	.	.	.	.	.	.	.	.	.	.	
CHINA	2	1	.	.	.	.	.	.	.	.	.	
OTHER COUNTRIES	2	.	2	.	4	.	.	.	1	.	.	
AFRICA.												
EGYPT	.	.	.	.	.	.	1	.	.	1	.	
OTHER PARTS	1	.	2	.	1	1	1	.	13	4	.	
AMERICA.												
UNITED STATES	56	64	83	56	103	48	91	51	49	32	39	[illegible]
MEXICO	.	.	.	.	.	.	1	.	4	3	.	
BRAZIL	4	.	.	.	.	.	3	.	.	2	.	
OTHER STATES	7	10	15	6	4	.	13	2	1	.	.	.
COUNTRY NOT STATED	.	.	.	.	.	.	2	1	2	4	.	.
AT SEA	.	1	.	.	.	.	.	.	.	.	.	.

B 4178.

D

Table 13A *continued.*—NUMBER and COUNTRY of BIRTH of FOREIGNERS enumerated

WHERE BORN.	REGISTRATION DIS										
	20 MILE END OLD TOWN.		21 POPLAR.		22 ST. SAVIOUR, SOUTHWARK.		23 ST. OLAVE, SOUTHWARK.		24 LAMBETH.		25
	Males.	Females.	Males.	Females.	Males.	Females.	Males.	Females.	Males.	Females.	M
TOTAL	1,718	1,147	1,279	299	775	327	786	188	1,170	668	
EUROPE.											
RUSSIA	86	50	54	5	10	1	10	.	11	7	
POLAND (RUSSIAN)	436	321	20	13	7	5	6	1	14	4	
SWEDEN	7	3	157	18	7		36	4	8	5	
NORWAY	3	5	119	3	1	.	154	6	5	3	
DENMARK	4	4	47	5	6	.	45	2	19	8	
HOLLAND	202	177	41	29	25	13	53	7	42	30	
BELGIUM	45	27	9	5	17	8	22	19	37	25	
FRANCE	18	81	87	14	137	92	24	16	140	154	
GERMANY	769	443	501	158	358	124	313	84	553	254	
AUSTRIA	65	39	14	2	11	6	26	4	23	6	
HUNGARY	5	8	3	.	2	.	1	.	7	1	
SWITZERLAND	5	4	8	1	21	2	2	.	69	21	
SPAIN	2	.	41	.	3	.	3	3	12	3	
PORTUGAL	2	1	2	.	.	1	2	.	3	.	
ITALY	5	.	37	.	39	11	22	3	65	11	
GREECE	.	1	11	1	4		8		7	1	
SERVIA	.	.	.	.	.	.	.	.	.	.	
ROUMANIA	4	.	.	.	.	.	.	.	1	1	
TURKEY	1	2	6	.	4		11	.	6	3	
ASIA.											
ARABIA	.	.	.	.	.	.		.	.	.	
PERSIA	.	.	.	.	.	.	.	.	.	.	
CHINA	.	.	35		1	.	.	.	2	.	
OTHER COUNTRIES	1	.	.		.	.		.	3	.	
AFRICA.											
EGYPT	1	.	.	.	.	.	.	.	.	.	
OTHER PARTS	1	.	.		1	.	.	.	2	.	
AMERICA.											
UNITED STATES	46	40	70	39	121	64	47	39	127	127	
MEXICO	.	.	1	.	.	.	.	.	1	.	
BRAZIL	.	.	2	.	.	.	.	.	.	.	
OTHER STATES	1	1	14	5	.	.	1	.	4	3	
BORN ABROAD (COUNTRY NOT STATED)	.	.	.	1	.	.	.	.			
BORN AT SEA	.	.	.	.	.			.		1	

Sanitary District.		All Ages. Persons.	All Ages. Males and Females.		Under 1 Year.	1–	2–	3–	4–	Under 5 Years.	5–	10–	15–	20–	25–	3
ABINGDON	Urban	5684	M.	2594	71	80	77	71	61	360	336	297	279	204	199	
			F.	3090	72	88	76	75	78	387	328	308	339	309	233	
ABINGDON	Rural	13550	M.	6897	200	182	194	205	203	984	864	865	797	523	353	
			F.	6653	197	162	187	163	190	899	848	743	524	506	455	
ALDERSHOT	Urban	20155	M.	12847	298	270	256	234	198	1251	869	636	1035	3096	1869	1
			F.	7308	316	290	250	250	222	1328	940	686	588	845	810	
ALRESFORD	Rural	6907	M.	3400	90	77	102	90	90	449	484	393	307	255	228	
			F.	3507	91	87	90	81	83	437	441	406	311	254		
ALTON	Urban	4497	M.	2110	55	60	67	56	67	305	263	248	226	149	124	
			F.	2387	78	63	61	60	65	327	280	270	214	216	171	
ALTON	Rural	10701	M.	5438	148	163	140	137	158	755	689	674	561	360	288	
			F.	5263	137	145	136	143	161	722	786	657	408	357	304	
ALVERSTOKE	Urban	21581	M.	11632	324	260	262	262	272	1389	1276	1045	1254	1478	1046	
			F.	9949	270	267	283	300	269	1389	1207	1033	851	830	785	
ANDOVER	Urban	5653	M.	2761	82	60	81	72	66	361	317	329	270	220	201	
			F.	2892	59	82	67	74	63	345	340	314	286	253	198	
ANDOVER	Rural	10047	M.	5082	116	136	141	106	128	621	617	623	521	373	318	
			F.	4965	128	130	134	133	132	657	591	589	421	351	312	
ARUNDEL	Urban	2748	M.	1357	30	39	20	25	40	163	177	154	125	116	101	
			F.	1391	37	32	28	36	31	164	188	164	134	119	100	
ASHFORD	Urban	9693	M.	4679	161	125	127	134	115	662	616	522	457	402	335	
			F.	5014	145	131	123	140	153	692	580	563	466	424	403	
BASINGSTOKE	Urban	6681	M.	3156	101	79	90	92	80	442	394	346	331	283	289	
			F.	3525	99	111	109	86	88	493	409	373	338	317	305	
BASINGSTOKE	Rural	12593	M.	6524	189	149	168	167	174	847	843	788	650	440	384	
			F.	6069	178	185	130	136	174	848	813	655	441	422	381	
BATTLE	Urban	3319	M.	1671	46	41	51	41	41	220	194	220	168	122	101	
			F.	1648	49	39	55	36	43	222	218	187	145	115	105	
BATTLE	Rural	11200	M.	5681	161	147	161	162	172	803	764	703	541	421	354	
			F.	5519	170	151	167	163	159	810	716	641	431	433	376	
BECKENHAM	Urban	13045	M.	5759	189	156	176	136	175	832	803	685	470	488	489	
			F.	7286	188	160	176	168	166	858	813	676	714	881	845	
BEXLEY	Urban	8793	M.	4007	127	127	111	112	123	600	509	448	368	315	250	
			F.	4786	128	106	127	110	114	585	495	581	486	483	369	
BLEAN	Rural	12498	M.	6249	177	180	165	160	177	868	851	857	656	381	351	
			F.	6244	189	166	183	168	181	887	852	750	557	399	372	
BOGNOR	Urban	3200	M.	1331	16	30	42	29	39	156	171	144	136	89	66	
			F.	1969	49	32	40	26	38	185	169	224	264	189	146	
BOURNEMOUTH	Urban	16858	M.	6304	178	178	172	164	160	847	703	667	608	594	583	
			F.	10554	200	171	169	171	164	875	812	731	1349	1493	1157	
BRADFIELD	Rural	17972	M.	9176	234	278	220	292	213	1257	1093	1064	1044	730	592	
			F.	8796	243	241	245	258	267	1254	1163	932	692	669	600	
BRIDGE	Rural	11319	M.	5594	147	139	150	154	146	736	689	587	501	369	367	
			F.	5725	158	136	174	166	133	767	682	581	429	425	422	
BRIGHTON	Urban	107546	M	47196	1384	1215	1225	1172	1217	6213	5658	5294	4480	4326	3878	3
			F	0350	1385	1270	1260	1282	1224	6371	5583	5447	6512	6398	5452	4
BROADSTAIRS	Urban	4322	M.	1887	60	45	47	60	58	265	290	248	158	106	115	
			F.	2435	53	60	45	60	66	284	260	289	259	221	168	
BROMLEY	Urban	15154	M.	6892	212	212	204	205	212	1045	848	735	607	643	571	
			F.	8262	218	207	191	201	216	1033	914	784	798	883	815	
BROMLEY	Rural	20773	M.	9804	267	270	280	274	258	1349	1221	1024	912	782	764	
			F.	10969	291	255	261	274	270	1351	1258	1183	1032	1055	917	
BURGESS HILL	Urban	3972	M.	1959	65	67	55	53	59	299	275	226	197	176	150	
			F.	2013	74	54	58	59	63	308	254	244	171	196	141	
CANTERBURY	Urban	21704	M.	10670	277	295	208	285	268	1383	1180	1092	1132	1060	897	
			F.	11034	275	242	278	265	257	1317	1249	1101	1000	968	878	

Note.—For the Parishes comprised in each Urban Sanitary District, *see* Vol. II., I

* The Hamlet of Penge, in the District of Croydon, forms part of the District of the Metropolitan Board of Works, and is therefore excluded

SANITARY DISTRICT.		ALL AGES. Persons.	ALL AGES. Males and Females.		Under 1 Year.	1–	2–	3–	4–	Under 5 Years.	5–	10–	15–	20–	25–
CATHERINGTON - - - -	Rural	2747	M. -	1387	36	28	38	22	38	162	173	164	159	101	73
			F. -	1360	45	30	33	33	38	179	140	160	134	106	89
CHAILEY - - - -	Rural	10373	M. -	5279	116	106	131	132	127	612	607	621	489	406	350
			F. -	5094	136	128	113	128	128	633	598	529	411	356	357
CHATHAM - - - -	Urban	26424	M. -	13670	365	338	357	342	350	1742	1522	1318	1467	1699	1121
			F. -	12754	382	330	370	340	376	1816	1627	1324	1207	1080	1058
CHERTSEY - - - -	Rural	27137	M. -	13258	365	366	341	361	372	1805	1736	1829	1257	956	909
			F. -	13879	356	384	370	368	376	1854	1668	1490	1179	1223	1070
CHICHESTER - - - -	Urban	8114	M. -	3683	94	98	100	107	97	496	461	437	383	265	245
			F. -	4431	108	98	87	90	105	488	484	461	474	371	325
CHICHESTER - - - -	Rural	829	M. -	594	12	11	9	13	14	59	33	26	162	100	61
			F. -	235	13	9	8	10	9	54	30	19	13	18	27
CHRISTCHURCH - - - -	Rural	12597	M. -	6115	209	189	182	181	176	928	809	701	579	441	443
			F. -	6482	187	194	180	153	178	892	757	654	588	563	564
COOKHAM - - - -	Rural	8725	M. -	4308	110	126	104	116	106	562	526	502	431	341	312
			F. -	4417	106	96	128	100	126	555	557	491	346	366	329
CRANBROOK - - - -	Rural	13774	M. -	6881	181	187	161	170	186	885	874	1104	731	468	427
			F. -	6893	184	170	196	174	168	892	862	854	612	521	447
CROYDON - - - -	Urban	78958	M. -	35210	1127	1026	998	992	1032	5175	4405	3754	3283	3043	2735
			F. -	43748	1184	988	1023	1041	1009	5245	4669	4313	4581	4815	3942
CROYDON - - - -	Rural	21570	M. -	10490	295	269	274	273	302	1413	1538	1474	979	857	701
			F. -	11080	319	247	267	301	265	1399	1456	1518	988	974	845
CUCKFIELD - - - -	Urban	1713	M. -	822	19	19	16	18	17	89	100	86	64	56	54
			F. -	891	25	25	18	27	19	114	95	105	83	74	77
CUCKFIELD - - - -	Rural	14887	M. -	7842	203	192	193	180	204	972	892	1130	873	572	504
			F. -	7045	189	208	182	197	179	955	951	820	581	553	516
DARTFORD - - - -	Urban	10163	M. -	5210	165	142	156	145	135	742	653	700	453	465	412
			F. -	4953	165	149	143	138	135	730	624	504	485	399	410
DARTFORD - - - -	Rural	24667	M. -	12791	360	309	331	293	325	1618	1701	1649	1648	1048	888
			F. -	11876	330	322	308	328	309	1597	1511	1296	1005	1018	843
DEAL - - - -	Urban	8500	M. -	3937	117	105	98	108	102	530	515	469	367	266	260
			F. -	4563	94	84	79	102	103	462	533	485	466	385	311
DORKING - - - -	Urban	6328	M. -	2979	88	78	71	80	92	409	361	331	265	226	202
			F. -	3349	74	66	73	77	82	372	352	352	314	276	244
DORKING - - - -	Rural	9124	M. -	4574	136	132	136	111	139	654	590	521	413	351	278
			F. -	4550	124	104	130	118	136	611	583	530	325	346	306
DOVER - - - -	Urban	30270	M. -	14548	426	398	371	365	372	1932	1724	1531	1481	1534	1064
			F. -	15722	403	409	400	359	357	1928	1772	1545	1613	1463	1238
DOVER - - - -	Rural	6543	M. -	3449	94	76	98	88	81	437	423	353	401	283	230
			F. -	3094	82	83	100	81	75	421	404	365	233	222	193
DROXFORD - - - -	Rural	11197	M. -	5566	148	135	138	122	142	685	634	620	552	418	384
			F. -	5631	138	141	153	159	143	736	681	640	438	415	391
EAST ASHFORD - - -	Rural	13697	M. -	7016	204	177	177	199	195	952	940	836	694	517	409
			F. -	6681	197	185	235	208	151	976	898	800	519	489	414
EASTBOURNE - - -	Urban	22014	M. -	10060	292	304	287	245	281	1409	1158	1217	1097	1015	875
			F. -	11954	318	289	292	274	245	1418	1109	1116	1456	1445	1107
EASTBOURNE - - -	Rural	5742	M. -	2925	69	72	64	81	69	355	353	340	280	258	197
			F. -	2817	86	64	86	71	77	384	340	328	246	209	200
EAST COWES - - - -	Urban	2512	M. -	1206	44	32	50	38	40	204	165	142	103	89	87
			F. -	1306	43	33	36	41	30	183	156	120	96	115	124
EAST GRINSTEAD - - -	Rural	18581	M. -	9575	248	281	249	246	267	1291	1235	1045	914	785	656
			F. -	9006	248	252	246	261	260	1267	1293	1149	750	634	665
EASTHAMPSTEAD - - -	Rural	12659	M. -	6769	155	166	136	164	142	763	704	858	1032	403	424
			F. -	5890	148	162	164	165	156	795	784	630	460	474	450
EAST MOLESEY - - -	Urban	3289	M. -	1393	41	34	31	40	39	185	150	129	132	128	123
			F. -	1896	53	63	57	41	51	254	194	157	186	227	170

Sanitary District.		All Ages. Persons.	All Ages. Males and Females.		Under 1 Year.	1–	2–	3–	4–	Under 5 Years.	5–	10–	15–	20–	25–
EAST PRESTON (WORTHING)	Rural	8025	M.	4065	122	112	101	117	92	544	518	425	426	304	239
			F.	3960	98	114	115	106	108	540	500	478	281	274	266
EASTRY	Rural	12419	M.	6194	159	155	163	172	163	812	805	718	539	391	359
			F.	6225	167	176	140	154	163	809	763	724	474	441	410
ELHAM	Rural	9218	M.	5211	138	122	111	107	132	610	532	476	671	728	393
			F.	1007	128	121	124	119	107	599	495	427	329	325	321
EPSOM	Urban	6916	M.	3380	74	76	91	75	73	389	365	410	401	288	249
			F.	3536	71	77	80	67	94	389	370	366	365	336	313
EPSOM	Rural	34191	M.	16338	415	393	424	407	417	2056	2362	2463	1353	1186	1110
			F.	17853	422	413	369	435	433	2072	2250	2022	1553	1601	1458
ERITH	Urban	9812	M.	4861	131	137	143	161	122	694	615	506	455	422	360
			F.	4951	153	121	142	114	138	668	608	535	492	451	407
FAREHAM	Urban	7183	M.	3334	82	82	70	82	79	401	373	343	290	226	203
			F.	3849	88	77	93	85	84	427	358	372	310	319	234
FAREHAM	Rural	9637	M.	4972	146	118	126	138	125	651	693	642	516	384	338
			F.	4665	127	98	119	129	123	596	575	552	375	347	330
FARINGDON	Rural	13676	M.	6778	178	183	185	192	194	937	861	811	693	465	341
			F.	6898	187	179	188	182	175	911	917	813	627	445	441
FARNHAM	Urban	4488	M.	2077	49	55	45	59	55	263	237	235	206	155	152
			F.	2411	50	54	60	54	46	272	264	238	244	224	186
FARNHAM	Rural	16752	M.	7777	237	183	237	231	217	1105	1022	973	741	526	500
			F.	7976	239	248	222	223	238	1170	1121	894	624	587	615
FAVERSHAM	Urban	8743	M.	4363	138	111	131	129	120	629	569	531	429	367	305
			F.	4380	137	141	113	135	107	633	541	457	403	390	305
FAVERSHAM	Rural	16213	M.	8385	251	245	230	231	251	1208	1076	1074	821	680	620
			F.	7828	283	237	277	238	231	1266	1046	928	680	587	532
FOLKESTONE	Urban	18816	M.	8189	255	247	233	215	222	1172	999	929	820	688	646
			F.	10627	239	209	236	224	221	1129	1077	1024	1190	1172	990
FORDINGBRIDGE	Rural	6234	M.	3165	80	76	91	85	89	421	403	382	323	217	189
			F.	3079	76	72	88	70	81	387	396	323	271	236	222
GILLINGHAM	Urban	20745	M.	11236	332	293	275	280	273	1453	1239	1052	938	1234	1084
			F.	9509	280	293	261	269	306	1409	1249	1027	836	707	739
GODALMING	Urban	2505	M.	1191	34	20	30	30	40	154	140	125	133	107	86
			F.	1314	34	31	40	24	37	166	146	118	177	112	83
GODSTONE	Rural	17692	M.	9295	213	205	206	207	236	1067	936	811	901	1001	746
			F.	8397	199	208	210	187	207	1011	964	788	678	685	686
GRAVESEND	Urban	23302	M.	11411	250	292	276	273	278	1408	1343	1268	1141	1167	945
			F.	11891	304	254	296	271	261	1385	1230	1283	1407	1117	929
GUILDFORD	Urban	10858	M.	4986	125	144	128	138	134	669	565	625	469	464	385
			F.	5873	150	124	117	130	121	642	633	593	628	589	463
GUILDFORD	Rural	29414	M.	15004	409	332	350	373	345	1809	1607	1914	1689	1202	1046
			F.	14410	351	358	363	349	340	1761	1669	1409	1102	1180	1141
HAILSHAM	Rural	13405	M.	6898	200	183	194	199	183	959	895	836	683	496	423
			F.	6507	221	196	174	180	194	965	898	746	519	446	446
HAMBLEDON	Rural	16272	M.	8514	206	193	211	230	245	1085	987	1072	917	707	590
			F.	7758	215	207	213	194	209	1038	983	848	629	644	664
HAM COMMON	Urban	1349	M.	537	10	14	16	15	22	77	80	62	47	37	35
			F.	812	25	17	20	18	14	94	113	147	112	60	61
HAMPTON WICK	Urban	2164	M.	992	52	21	29	23	28	133	132	107	82	97	68
			F.	1172	26	33	25	24	23	130	117	93	117	120	106
HARTLEY WINTNEY	Rural	21326	M.	12008	250	267	255	231	241	1244	1236	1277	1408	1935	1082
			F.	9318	272	230	264	238	245	1249	1203	1036	760	783	669
HASTINGS	Urban	42258	M.	17372	503	445	501	476	430	2366	2197	2081	1677	1404	1381
			F.	24886	531	472	486	461	452	2402	2148	2138	2662	2830	2305
HASTINGS	Rural	7871	M.	3836	126	126	132	121	114	618	518	440	390	269	254
			F.	4035	128	107	128	106	133	602	500	365	352	363	304

F 3

Table 6 *continued*.—AGES of MALES and FEMALES in SAN

SANITARY DISTRICT.		ALL AGES. Persons.	Males and Females.		Under 1 Year.	1–	2–	3–	4–	Under 5 Years.	5–	10–	15–	20–	25–
HAVANT	Urban	3032	M.	1484	49	43	47	34	37	210	183	201	130	97	83
			F.	1548	35	43	35	41	33	187	192	185	149	112	111
HAVANT	Rural	5640	M.	2651	85	68	60	68	78	359	333	354	217	176	147
			F.	2989	86	61	84	71	88	390	363	304	295	210	220
HAYWARD'S HEATH	Urban	1814	M.	838	24	31	18	35	19	127	118	102	79	66	69
			F.	976	28	27	20	35	25	135	114	114	100	88	73
HERNE BAY	Urban	2816	M.	1199	31	29	26	31	36	153	207	178	112	77	77
			F.	1617	31	26	24	32	30	143	201	218	196	154	108
HOLLINGBOURN	Rural	14040	M.	7170	192	183	173	193	195	936	857	887	770	505	460
			F.	6870	177	193	178	200	175	923	915	759	633	673	461
HOO	Rural	3405	M.	1891	63	51	54	56	49	273	245	165	180	136	144
			F.	1514	52	46	39	53	43	233	213	182	120	124	102
HORSHAM	Urban	6874	M.	3223	107	84	97	104	98	490	434	341	329	253	250
			F.	3651	94	87	107	85	109	482	442	403	347	297	277
HORSHAM	Rural	15426	M.	7915	216	215	219	234	202	1086	1053	949	771	551	463
			F.	7511	231	211	230	169	204	1045	991	888	629	668	518
HOVE	Urban	20804	M.	8113	233	199	199	193	196	1090	1000	964	778	839	691
			F.	12691	211	185	231	198	178	1003	902	1026	1557	1625	1313
HUNGERFORD	Rural	17802	M.	8988	241	242	253	200	227	1163	1134	1041	988	643	542
			F.	8814	232	231	227	236	221	1147	1135	998	692	642	537
HURSLEY	Rural	2753	M.	1384	28	38	31	35	32	164	196	184	126	84	74
			F.	1369	42	33	35	49	47	206	179	156	88	95	93
HYTHE	Urban	4173	M.	2152	62	54	62	65	53	276	243	180	170	199	207
			F.	2021	43	59	41	45	52	231	232	208	174	201	157
ISLE OF WIGHT	Rural	28008	M.	14428	378	324	364	373	353	1792	1689	1548	1294	1197	1044
			F.	13580	368	346	382	332	342	1770	1786	1496	1136	1044	945
KINGSCLERE	Rural	8524	M.	4287	115	100	109	111	125	560	577	503	451	280	239
			F.	4237	127	102	140	99	116	584	567	493	316	288	237
KINGSTON-ON-THAMES	Urban	20648	M.	9697	302	295	283	262	269	1411	1225	1104	867	824	670
			F.	10951	282	256	281	270	269	1357	1278	1096	1081	1013	890
KINGSTON-ON-THAMES	Rural	15114	M.	6951	189	180	194	190	193	937	877	767	682	622	497
			F.	8103	186	174	182	179	178	899	982	814	744	782	738
LEWES	Urban	6017	M.	2936	89	75	67	76	66	373	338	329	337	316	243
			F.	3081	80	69	64	82	68	363	347	353	296	274	232
LEWES	Rural	3866	M.	1972	54	44	45	43	56	242	217	208	189	232	150
			F.	1894	51	38	48	52	38	227	215	218	171	161	138
LINDFIELD	Urban	866	M.	392	10	9	10	12	9	50	36	48	44	35	35
			F.	474	17	7	16	14	6	59	63	34	41	35	39
LITTLEHAMPTON	Urban	3926	M.	1865	47	44	55	52	44	242	252	267	106	137	95
			F.	2061	51	54	50	49	48	252	236	218	228	176	143
LYMINGTON	Urban	4366	M.	1952	67	55	57	53	48	281	235	219	171	161	109
			F.	2414	66	42	46	54	56	264	244	230	286	192	185
LYMINGTON	Rural	8285	M.	4090	126	92	119	117	110	564	662	409	393	287	244
			F.	4195	108	112	105	106	110	541	504	506	353	335	253
MAIDENHEAD	Urban	8220	M.	3932	121	105	118	98	82	524	532	499	363	290	284
			F.	4288	103	107	113	110	100	533	463	480	448	371	353
MAIDSTONE	Urban	29623	M.	14246	399	381	377	352	393	1902	1659	1464	1507	1347	1131
			F.	15377	398	380	405	387	379	1949	1652	1520	1402	1438	1227
MAIDSTONE	Rural	15468	M.	7725	218	217	229	216	202	1082	1078	900	724	480	488
			F.	7743	218	218	224	203	251	1114	984	935	602	614	552
MALLING	Rural	22745	M.	11671	340	300	335	352	326	1662	1485	1328	1191	974	821
			F.	11074	355	348	337	357	319	1716	1476	1264	877	824	796
MARGATE	Urban	16030	M.	7391	190	168	179	205	163	905	1065	1429	660	516	460
			F.	8639	188	184	167	166	176	881	936	1101	1029	832	687
MEDWAY	Rural	236	M.	116	-	1	4	1	6	12	13	14	10	14	8
			F.	120	9	3	2	2	3	19	17	7	16	11	4

F 4

Sanitary District.		All Ages. Persons.	All Ages. Males and Females.		Under 1 Year.	1–	2–	3–	4–	Under 5 Years.	5–	10–	15–	20–	25–
MIDHURST	Rural	13933	M.	7170	179	212	195	183	189	958	002	859	672	508	480
			F.	6763	219	181	181	193	198	972	874	782	536	505	445
MILTON	Rural	11195	M.	5798	183	170	145	192	158	848	722	667	624	499	393
			F.	5397	168	186	178	170	161	863	687	637	484	454	389
MILTON-NEXT-SITTINGBOURNE	Urban	4219	M.	2204	58	54	62	63	65	302	270	244	239	160	154
			F.	2015	84	57	72	59	56	328	203	221	186	150	146
NEWBURY	Urban	10144	M.	4681	151	130	100	118	131	630	561	505	406	390	313
			F.	5463	131	131	144	114	116	636	617	608	597	480	370
NEWBURY	Rural	11183	M.	5527	125	144	150	119	142	680	600	679	548	413	310
			F.	5656	148	118	156	157	134	713	663	668	475	422	361
NEW FOREST	Rural	13221	M.	6609	161	160	160	162	174	817	885	749	664	532	408
			F.	6612	140	172	170	198	167	856	810	710	518	511	454
NEWHAVEN	Rural	8607	M.	4868	142	119	119	118	125	628	601	613	475	459	399
			F.	3739	124	121	101	104	116	566	570	440	292	265	290
NEW MALDEN	Urban	2538	M.	1182	39	28	42	25	33	167	163	149	120	96	75
			F.	1356	36	39	31	31	36	173	149	140	139	149	106
NEWPORT (Isle of Wight)	Urban	9357	M.	4436	135	111	134	123	103	606	532	488	394	347	327
			F.	4921	124	120	132	107	116	599	499	479	460	416	381
NEW SHOREHAM	Urban	3505	M.	1799	36	45	55	60	52	248	230	242	146	120	106
			F.	1706	55	33	38	39	40	210	204	214	161	108	103
NEW WINCHESTER	Rural	10617	M.	5386	141	110	151	107	139	648	640	703	504	420	280
			F.	5231	167	144	147	146	144	748	629	581	422	335	375
NORTH AYLESFORD	Rural	11580	M.	6445	191	141	166	166	168	832	712	622	677	595	532
			F.	5135	170	155	153	136	155	769	728	647	412	367	321
NORTHFLEET	Urban	8790	M.	4660	137	127	143	120	124	651	630	446	555	479	394
			F.	4130	139	150	118	138	116	661	529	470	330	349	336
OXFORD,* *part of*	Urban	1120	M.	565	18	14	15	10	19	76	86	60	52	50	47
			F.	555	19	19	20	21	20	99	78	55	43	38	44
PETERSFIELD	Rural	10255	M.	5097	166	125	126	140	136	692	638	530	402	392	309
			F.	5158	144	135	129	159	127	694	671	582	416	404	351
PETWORTH	Rural	9595	M.	4858	127	110	114	134	123	608	620	598	446	338	269
			F.	4737	113	144	132	137	121	647	625	538	374	323	298
PORTSEA ISLAND	Rural	33	M.	20	1	2	1	.	.	4	4	6	1	.	.
			F.	13	1	.	.	.	1	2	2	.	2	2	.
PORTSMOUTH	Urban	127989	M.	62397	1807	1653	1720	1685	1670	8625	7308	6391	6089	5910	5268
			F.	65592	1951	1644	1670	1591	1669	8525	7242	6566	6482	6273	5413
RAMSGATE	Urban	22683	M.	10376	307	266	287	272	277	1400	1319	1344	1171	853	738
			F.	12307	232	248	265	255	287	1337	1261	1243	1351	1247	986
READING	Urban	42054	M.	20556	653	627	606	585	542	3013	2417	2072	2066	2084	1790
			F.	21498	673	553	570	584	570	2950	2507	2186	2080	1997	1781
READING	Rural	1440	M.	637	16	18	18	15	23	90	90	57	63	49	49
			F.	803	17	12	18	10	13	70	77	70	103	92	67
REIGATE	Urban	18662	M.	8794	211	215	229	213	227	1095	1081	1112	1000	739	616
			F.	9868	206	236	228	213	221	1104	1087	1014	978	980	873
REIGATE	Rural	11697	M.	5827	159	161	151	161	171	803	735	638	610	460	379
			F.	5870	182	156	172	169	176	855	734	733	478	456	447
RICHMOND	Urban	19066	M.	7854	216	210	204	173	212	1015	895	812	740	786	650
			F.	11212	229	205	286	216	231	1117	935	963	1290	1333	1126
RICHMOND	Rural	14567	M.	6533	211	173	161	173	167	885	797	796	590	608	556
			F.	8034	206	201	222	217	150	1036	785	686	817	924	774
RINGWOOD	Rural	5488	M.	2710	74	76	78	82	64	374	356	301	250	190	176
			F.	2778	65	66	67	80	66	353	308	319	225	211	183
ROCHESTER	Urban	21307	M.	10664	304	256	262	253	282	1357	1346	1099	973	985	932
			F.	10643	323	276	279	272	261	1416	1247	1170	1121	929	776

The remainder of the Urban Sanitary District of Oxford is in Division III. (*see* Table 6) :—

	Persons.			Under 1 Year.	1–	2–	3–	4–	Under 5 Years.	5–	10–	15–	20–	25–
Entire Urban Sanitary District of Oxford	39186	M.	18119	541	512	491	475	464	2483	2168	1943	1853	1852	1432
		F.	21067	523	497	487	484	523	2514	2167	2114	2486	2008	1712

Sanitary District.		All Ages. Persons.	All Ages. Males and Females.		Under 1 Year.	1–	2–	3–	4–	Under 5 Years.	5–	10–	15–	20–	25–
ROMNEY MARSH	Rural	6959	M.	3297	87	88	89	91	81	436	360	344	304	288	248
			F.	2762	106	69	77	78	93	418	356	316	232	201	181
ROMSEY	Urban	4204	M.	2013	56	57	68	54	60	295	254	226	222	169	132
			F.	2191	60	69	59	51	48	287	236	240	213	199	144
ROMSEY	Rural	6396	M.	3267	93	83	92	90	68	426	393	394	326	230	184
			F.	3129	78	86	75	86	90	415	416	385	235	217	189
RYDE	Urban	11461	M.	4917	106	114	120	117	141	598	602	537	493	396	336
			F.	6544	125	131	139	117	115	627	577	551	724	642	575
RYE	Urban	4224	M.	2108	56	56	61	58	65	296	260	236	206	173	151
			F.	2116	55	53	43	63	56	270	269	234	185	129	159
RYE	Rural	7816	M.	3891	111	94	114	94	110	523	461	451	340	293	244
			F.	3925	118	110	112	102	119	561	471	474	305	259	282
ST. HELENS	Urban	4210	M.	1959	51	55	47	40	53	255	270	236	205	135	132
			F.	2251	57	40	54	63	63	236	272	218	201	231	161
ST. THOMAS-IN-THE-CLIFFE	Urban	1664	M.	837	23	19	19	20	19	100	120	102	75	89	53
			F.	827	19	20	15	23	20	97	96	104	80	58	53
SANDGATE	Urban	1669	M.	741	21	20	17	17	24	90	99	83	75	56	42
			F.	928	21	27	19	20	26	113	82	83	101	97	80
SANDOWN	Urban	3120	M.	1339	41	34	47	44	46	212	170	140	132	89	88
			F.	1781	29	26	35	32	37	159	160	160	210	211	150
SANDWICH	Urban	2846	M.	1382	25	42	37	34	32	170	163	176	134	93	76
			F.	1464	24	38	31	33	32	158	147	157	142	117	84
SEVENOAKS	Urban	6296	M.	2911	81	88	73	89	63	394	390	336	255	213	245
			F.	3385	81	87	85	94	75	422	325	359	355	326	310
SEVENOAKS	Rural	20894	M.	10565	282	274	306	260	274	1396	1327	1229	964	851	695
			F.	10329	271	280	279	240	310	1380	1314	1194	873	769	729
SHANKLIN	Urban	2740	M.	1157	40	22	28	40	26	156	166	123	125	74	80
			F.	1583	38	43	39	30	39	189	152	151	164	170	136
SHEERNESS	Urban	14286	M.	7760	216	184	197	202	179	978	770	672	713	993	879
			F.	6526	198	192	184	175	183	932	822	773	575	553	483
SHEPPEY	Rural	3918	M.	2157	73	61	57	67	51	290	269	214	263	136	142
			F.	1761	52	62	53	51	56	274	247	216	136	110	127
SHIRLEY	Urban	7143	M.	3187	111	81	84	87	79	442	428	419	323	202	230
			F.	3956	104	91	96	86	88	465	438	429	430	370	288
SITTINGBOURNE	Urban	7856	M.	3964	139	127	119	129	113	627	462	447	446	346	294
			F.	3892	142	114	157	107	120	620	548	436	337	346	284
SOUTH STONEHAM	Rural	27070	M.	13398	389	354	387	391	360	1881	1761	1470	1235	1241	1067
			F.	13672	419	372	386	387	341	1905	1660	1440	1154	1171	1074
SOUTHAMPTON	Urban	60051	M.	28382	841	795	762	774	746	3918	3426	3140	2720	2548	2108
			F.	31669	832	754	815	750	749	3900	3439	3316	3114	2937	2437
SOUTHBOROUGH	Urban	3870	M.	1729	36	56	46	49	47	234	246	228	175	124	101
			F.	2141	57	48	47	47	53	252	234	221	193	188	123
STEYNING	Rural	16325	M.	8401	229	221	241	245	244	1180	1084	1015	944	607	602
			F.	7924	257	246	235	239	219	1196	1029	806	660	586	586
STOCKBRIDGE	Rural	6972	M.	3580	88	87	106	91	96	468	419	444	398	256	180
			F.	3392	86	72	95	78	98	427	441	382	283	227	207
SURBITON	Urban	9406	M.	3672	122	99	90	100	90	501	487	375	328	290	285
			F.	5734	110	92	112	111	98	523	510	481	634	785	628
TEDDINGTON	Urban	6599	M.	2922	80	83	95	89	92	439	431	331	253	222	215
			F.	3677	95	92	80	96	82	445	407	352	358	420	336
TENTERDEN	Urban	3620	M.	1728	40	58	39	41	54	227	229	188	159	115	85
			F.	1892	47	48	62	43	44	244	241	270	169	124	126
TENTERDEN	Rural	6841	M.	3387	122	82	112	88	85	489	413	408	307	233	222
			F.	3454	100	79	110	96	105	[illegible]	476	398	207	[illegible]	193
THAKEHAM	Rural	6286	M.	4247	138	115	105	112	112	[illegible]	[illegible]	[illegible]	[illegible]	293	235
			F.	4038	[illegible]	[illegible]	[illegible]	[illegible]	[illegible]	[illegible]	[illegible]	[illegible]	[illegible]	[illegible]	[illegible]

R 4178.

G

Sanitary District.		All Ages. Persons.	Males and Females.		Under 1 Year.	1–	2–	3–	4–	Under 5 Years.	5–	10–	15–	20–	25–
THANET	Rural	7786	M.	3845	104	107	118	113	102	544	488	418	381	300	240
			F.	3941	127	99	119	101	97	543	482	432	306	322	254
TICEHURST	Rural	15871	M.	7962	234	249	206	235	206	1130	1104	943	767	593	526
			F.	7909	212	230	209	228	248	1127	1065	917	629	641	549
TUNBRIDGE	Urban	9317	M.	4472	128	113	124	122	128	615	547	589	524	350	295
			F.	4845	115	132	112	119	134	612	583	544	485	424	371
TUNBRIDGE	Rural	15360	M.	7730	224	201	250	235	222	1132	1034	1030	784	520	436
			F.	7630	215	201	215	208	194	1033	1071	914	612	593	505
TUNBRIDGE WELLS	Urban	24308	M.	10240	301	294	260	284	271	1410	1326	1152	995	760	770
			F.	14068	320	283	278	252	293	1426	1342	1279	1461	1496	1216
UCKFIELD	Urban	2146	M.	984	33	28	27	25	26	139	123	114	90	57	56
			F.	1162	25	21	37	26	29	138	132	132	107	92	78
UCKFIELD	Rural	17952	M.	9145	286	243	271	252	265	1317	1249	1080	949	709	550
			F.	8807	284	275	287	261	262	1369	1208	1115	706	644	635
VENTNOR	Urban	5504	M.	2244	60	40	55	52	57	264	265	209	181	215	186
			F.	3260	55	50	48	63	57	282	259	301	388	414	300
WALLINGFORD	Urban	2803	M.	1356	31	42	29	30	34	166	163	167	142	106	81
			F.	1447	32	27	28	29	30	146	155	168	155	133	82
WALLINGFORD	Rural	11690	M.	5893	158	138	162	161	189	808	752	753	528	366	325
			F.	5797	149	136	166	136	161	738	746	638	426	367	350
WALMER	Urban	4309	M.	2630	40	54	39	39	33	205	209	120	937	379	188
			F.	1679	42	38	48	41	43	212	172	180	155	171	127
WANTAGE	Urban	3488	M.	1683	50	54	37	39	47	227	222	216	197	119	104
			F.	1805	46	43	42	42	47	220	198	223	216	133	125
WANTAGE	Rural	13672	M.	7240	185	184	212	186	161	928	890	867	779	566	455
			F.	6432	199	182	156	191	168	896	866	730	476	455	407
WEST ASHFORD	Rural	8433	M.	4340	89	107	110	108	117	531	502	565	449	363	278
			F.	4093	131	82	100	112	111	536	549	461	357	306	276
WESTBOURNE	Rural	7420	M.	3742	116	104	93	102	107	522	465	427	368	263	207
			F.	3678	112	98	106	104	110	530	467	400	280	276	260
WEST COWES	Urban	6721	M.	3246	82	101	99	78	87	447	374	338	328	258	275
			F.	3475	74	86	85	88	93	426	389	365	333	327	278
WEST FIRLE	Rural	2369	M.	1246	30	43	34	26	34	167	146	139	111	112	85
			F.	1123	32	28	26	23	44	153	134	126	87	87	79
WESTHAMPNETT	Rural	15989	M.	8117	230	226	220	210	217	1103	1052	871	731	561	480
			F.	7872	199	207	210	236	214	1066	1004	873	560	527	486
WEST WORTHING	Urban	689	M.	276	10	7	10	10	7	44	31	69	19	16	17
			F.	413	4	4	6	11	2	27	38	42	52	64	49
WHITCHURCH	Rural	5458	M.	2761	83	74	76	73	77	383	348	297	290	234	178
			F.	2697	75	76	85	76	62	374	331	292	225	225	190
WIMBLEDON	Urban	15960	M.	7097	237	216	183	222	193	1051	904	701	708	711	579
			F.	8863	239	229	227	197	207	1099	863	843	986	1048	840
WINCHESTER	Urban	17780	M.	8719	230	209	208	211	199	1057	923	934	1227	901	696
			F.	9061	244	196	203	210	179	1032	904	892	1000	814	712
WINDSOR	Urban	12273	M.	6113	143	122	127	110	140	642	605	751	623	849	605
			F.	6160	123	127	128	134	123	635	621	581	678	593	502
WINDSOR	Rural	19719	M.	9769	270	256	271	254	271	1322	1157	1120	925	894	861
			F.	9950	260	248	263	251	251	1273	1172	1013	889	830	842
WOKINGHAM	Urban	3099	M.	1465	45	36	39	40	41	201	193	167	115	94	101
			F.	1634	40	43	50	33	39	205	206	163	136	119	117
WOKINGHAM	Rural	16919	M.	8374	271	222	232	212	212	1149	1156	996	865	633	531
			F.	8545	251	225	248	271	254	1249	1086	934	720	636	614
WORTHING	Urban	10976	M.	4701	159	122	132	117	147	677	667	578	467	380	334
			F.	6275	140	123	148	141	140	692	585	646	683	665	489
WROTHAM	Urban	3296	M.	1633	56	44	47	52	43	242	199	186	163	130	106
			F.	1663	57	48	40	45	46	245	211	154	166	126	119

Table 13.—NUMBER and COUNTRY of BIRTH of FOREIGNERS enumerated in COUNTIES, and in each exceeds 50,000 PERSONS.

WHERE BORN.	WHERE ENUMERA[TED]										
	SOUTH-EASTERN COUNTIES.		COUNTIES.								
			SURREY.		KENT.		SUSSEX.		HAMPSHIRE.		BE[RK]SH[IRE]
	Males.	Females.	Males.	Females.	Males.	Females.	Males.	Females.	Males.	Females.	Males.
TOTAL	9,235	6,460	5,127	3,258	2,239	1,463	956	896	712	639	201
EUROPE.											
DENMARK	174	41	99	24	41	13	10	2	22	2	2
NORWAY	303	47	179	26	78	11	3	4	43	5	.
SWEDEN	205	59	75	28	102	22	18	5	10	2	.
RUSSIA	132	30	40	15	40	11	13	5	14	7	7
POLAND (RUSSIAN)	116	57	44	16	24	16	13	9	31	16	4
AUSTRIA	167	67	107	28	36	23	13	11	8	3	3
HUNGARY	35	15	17	4	7	2	2	.	8	9	1
SWITZERLAND	410	418	227	149	83	102	33	76	42	65	5
GERMAN EMPIRE	3,476	2,313	2,209	1,266	803	556	253	270	164	170	47
HOLLAND	287	179	196	108	55	43	26	22	8	6	2
BELGIUM	327	210	170	123	123	45	22	21	10	13	2
FRANCE	1,621	1,626	714	753	355	319	337	209	147	181	68
PORTUGAL	22	11	13	5	5	2	1	1	2	2	1
SPAIN	89	43	46	23	15	4	15	10	7	5	6
ITALY	579	155	252	65	151	30	73	26	75	20	28
GREECE	75	18	44	11	7	1	1	.	23	1	.
TURKEY	49	17	34	6	8	6	4	4	2	1	1
SERVIA	.	.	.	.	.	.	.	.	.	.	.
ROUMANIA	6	3	1	2	1	.	3	1	1	.	.
ASIA.											
ARABIA	.	.	.	.	.	.	.	.	.	.	.
PERSIA	2	3	1	2	1	1	.	.	.	.	.
CHINA	10	10	6	5	1	3	1	2	1	.	1
OTHER COUNTRIES	26	5	13	3	9		1	1	3	1	.
AFRICA.											
EGYPT	3	5	2	5	1	.	.	.	.	.	.
OTHER PARTS	11	8	9	6	1	.	.	1	.	1	1
AMERICA.											
UNITED STATES	1,037	1,066	585	550	269	248	81	111	82	117	20
MEXICO	3	8	2	2	.	1	1	5	.	.	.
BRAZIL	20	16	11	11	3	2	2	2	4	.	.
OTHER STATES	38	22	18	11	9	2	7	6	3	3	1
COUNTRY NOT STATED	11	3	3	1	2	.	3	2	2	.	1
AT SEA	1	1	1	1	.	.		.	.	.	.

R 4178.

Sanitary District.		All Ages. Persons.	All Ages. Males and Females.		Under 1 Year.	1–	2–	3–	4–	Under 5 Years.	5–	10–	15–	20–	25–	30
ACTON	Urban	17126	M.	7864	300	290	269	276	243	1378	1037	803	648	728	652	5
			F.	9262	304	266	253	252	232	1312	1059	880	897	983	781	7
AMERSHAM	Rural	16684	M.	8138	237	224	235	257	224	1177	1107	958	756	572	477	4
			F.	8546	233	216	246	227	218	1140	1104	1032	711	628	541	5
AMPTHILL	Rural	16253	M.	7755	217	199	231	211	224	1082	1072	950	755	526	413	4
			F.	8498	236	223	211	218	234	1122	1080	939	606	678	539	5
AYLESBURY	Urban	7795	M.	3699	96	101	110	90	105	502	479	393	404	296	279	2
			F.	4096	111	93	119	96	103	522	489	418	417	353	294	2
AYLESBURY	Rural	16812	M.	8354	243	223	217	238	240	1161	1085	992	754	552	506	4
			F.	8458	189	217	229	212	236	1083	1095	931	628	602	592	4
BALDOCK	Urban	2326	M.	1075	27	36	35	28	42	168	147	115	106	64	70	
			F.	1251	34	24	26	29	25	138	146	155	104	93	105	
BANBURY	Urban	12072	M.	5753	175	143	140	155	161	774	747	704	600	444	359	3
			F.	6319	149	134	168	134	147	734	784	759	668	550	444	4
BANBURY	Rural	18048	M.	9137	243	205	240	223	227	1144	1114	1216	938	645	516	4
			F.	8911	237	213	237	249	239	1175	1128	1023	645	583	546	5
BARNET	Urban	4095	M.	2101	44	50	32	49	35	210	269	331	216	182	135	1
			F.	1994	43	52	40	51	41	227	203	229	105	153	144	1
BARNET	Rural	13003	M.	6133	160	152	149	151	128	740	606	726	545	471	454	4
			F.	6870	138	144	146	124	165	717	651	564	488	598	604	5
BEACONSFIELD	Urban	1635	M.	802	19	17	12	27	18	93	112	142	78	55	35	
			F.	833	30	22	21	21	23	117	102	102	75	72	46	
BEDFORD	Urban	19533	M.	8666	241	181	231	224	205	1082	1133	1157	021	715	591	5
			F.	10867	231	222	192	214	246	1105	1138	1175	1335	1098	861	7
BEDFORD	Rural	23399	M.	11699	321	266	301	311	313	1512	1483	1487	1353	820	650	6
			F.	11700	289	299	334	279	329	1530	1519	1257	029	916	751	7
BERKHAMPSTEAD	Rural	10737	M.	5095	140	155	135	156	148	734	699	619	519	345	336	2
			F.	5642	160	168	147	134	160	769	685	604	457	472	439	3
BICESTER	Urban	3306	M.	1632	50	42	48	46	34	220	189	183	172	140	112	
			F.	1674	42	28	44	36	45	195	185	178	173	151	119	
BICESTER	Rural	10851	M.	5435	128	150	164	126	152	720	654	626	551	430	341	2
			F.	5416	160	114	136	139	155	704	681	609	448	400	328	3
BIGGLESWADE	Rural	27378	M.	13339	348	322	381	349	376	1776	1784	1702	1386	889	737	7
			F.	14039	370	370	338	381	340	1805	1721	1553	1146	1044	961	9
BISHOP STORTFORD	Urban	6704	M.	3292	95	78	115	87	94	469	439	442	331	190	227	2
			F.	3412	96	79	86	78	105	444	384	345	336	310	268	2
BISHOP STORTFORD	Rural	15097	M.	7618	219	168	218	203	191	999	1002	958	795	508	441	4
			F.	7479	222	169	197	206	220	1014	1000	874	539	542	437	4
BRACKLEY	Rural	12340	M.	6197	174	168	152	166	162	822	769	783	641	445	329	3
			F.	6143	137	124	162	189	165	727	730	662	518	453	398	3
BRENTFORD	Urban	11810	M.	5848	190	186	182	165	165	883	760	560	565	523	481	4
			F.	5962	187	170	161	149	158	825	706	631	551	531	497	4
BRENTFORD	Rural	5825	M.	2811	81	69	75	73	91	389	575	500	201	176	158	1
			F.	3014	62	74	53	79	85	358	501	532	265	227	234	1
BRIXWORTH	Rural	13336	M.	6746	167	146	152	170	172	813	757	707	686	582	413	8
			F.	6590	180	171	162	173	167	853	799	705	500	471	439	8
BUCKINGHAM	Urban	3585	M.	1717	48	50	44	49	40	240	213	208	150	119	107	1
			F.	1868	37	38	50	40	39	204	216	181	189	139	126	1
BUCKINGHAM	Rural	8833	M.	4352	101	103	127	124	113	568	556	544	432	258	280	2
			F.	4481	97	90	111	104	122	533	530	506	358	330	293	3
BUNTINGFORD	Rural	6032	M.	3091	30	67	79	76	81	383	396	415	327	189	151	1
			F.	2941	71	74	79	83	73	380	407	328	233	192	163	1
CAMBRIDGE	Urban	35363	M.	16521	441	375	424	406	445	2091	1917	1781	1881	2034	1260	10
			F.	18342	479	397	397	446	380	2099	1989	1988	2133	1830	1530	12
CAXTON	Rural	10357	M.	5248	128	142	139	138	148	695	713	600	501	334	276	2
			F.	5109	157	131	140	142	148	718	757	586	366	310	316	2

M

Note.—For the Parishes comprised in each Urban Sanitary District, *see* Vol. II., Di

Table 6 *continued*.—Ages of Males and Females in Sanit

Sanitary District.		All Ages. Persons.	All Ages. Males and Females.		Under 1 Year.	1–	2–	3–	4–	Under 5 Years.	5–	10–	15–	20–	25–	30–
CHATTERIS	Urban	4712	M.	2323	67	59	41	65	63	295	291	279	222	193	149	118
			F.	2389	62	55	65	56	63	301	311	236	238	197	160	104
CHESHUNT	Urban	7735	M.	3673	118	99	90	112	105	524	459	382	353	291	264	216
			F.	4062	97	104	105	94	107	507	494	448	366	329	279	276
CHESTERTON	Urban	5706	M.	2796	111	69	86	68	81	415	388	319	243	220	188	185
			F.	2910	89	77	82	76	81	405	353	345	265	244	203	211
CHESTERTON	Rural	23343	M.	11732	318	284	307	304	330	1543	1561	1359	1202	838	709	709
			F.	11611	265	316	318	308	311	1518	1478	1312	856	817	748	704
CHIPPING NORTON	Urban	4167	M.	1989	55	54	57	58	68	292	264	225	190	180	140	115
			F.	2178	52	60	62	46	42	262	262	236	210	184	153	138
CHIPPING NORTON	Rural	13791	M.	6912	197	170	182	183	193	925	887	841	704	479	402	376
			F.	6879	197	205	202	217	176	907	967	784	567	481	358	444
CHIPPING WYCOMBE	Urban	10618	M.	5145	191	137	174	169	166	837	696	571	550	382	382	340
			F.	5473	177	147	131	154	174	783	731	599	580	485	444	331
CHISWICK	Urban	16075	M.	7383	229	262	203	202	224	1120	934	790	674	731	644	595
			F.	8692	260	215	206	231	201	1122	916	846	900	924	809	660
DAVENTRY	Urban	3859	M.	1899	46	48	62	43	44	243	239	211	180	148	113	102
			F.	1960	66	56	39	57	45	263	238	189	104	162	138	108
DAVENTRY	Rural	14655	M.	7497	179	181	192	173	176	901	849	768	715	668	509	434
			F.	7158	161	174	197	171	192	895	845	747	552	526	402	413
DUNSTABLE	Urban	4627	M.	1933	73	50	51	55	52	281	240	227	180	125	127	113
			F.	2694	46	49	46	51	55	247	240	263	290	258	202	192
EALING	Urban	15764	M.	6634	202	161	186	164	178	891	880	786	669	568	510	454
			F.	9130	208	171	181	168	202	930	844	807	1115	1169	856	685
EAST BARNET VALLEY	Urban	5809	M.	2541	85	66	58	73	87	369	311	359	229	195	173	161
			F.	3268	81	91	80	86	73	411	369	322	364	362	273	242
EDMONTON	Urban	23463	M.	11517	364	335	342	323	330	1684	1560	1351	967	842	795	763
			F.	11946	344	309	345	318	327	1643	1530	1234	1027	895	916	803
ELY	Urban	8171	M.	4068	110	94	94	102	117	517	482	469	484	328	268	258
			F.	4103	119	102	91	108	108	528	504	460	408	318	289	268
ELY	Rural	12531	M.	6289	150	149	170	165	153	787	852	757	584	457	349	312
			F.	6242	153	154	142	173	158	780	873	765	470	420	353	360
ENFIELD	Urban	19104	M.	9306	301	262	257	276	236	1332	1296	1115	836	817	659	614
			F.	9798	281	262	276	279	283	1381	1299	1129	882	882	712	683
ETON	Urban	3464	M.	1985	33	22	25	28	29	137	149	346	698	129	86	72
			F.	1479	26	24	33	24	23	130	104	132	170	180	106	127
ETON	Rural	19162	M.	9706	264	225	228	248	233	1198	1245	1440	1018	728	581	513
			F.	9456	259	238	260	243	275	1270	1236	1057	765	696	682	587
FINCHLEY	Urban	11191	M.	4997	156	150	161	156	132	755	638	571	545	418	363	356
			F.	6194	174	145	163	152	168	802	676	589	659	672	538	500
GODMANCHESTER	Urban	2188	M.	1037	21	27	23	24	19	114	124	150	98	62	49	64
			F.	1151	25	25	25	22	32	129	152	126	105	71	60	77
HARDINGSTONE	Urban	4866	M.	2556	77	87	74	79	85	402	322	269	246	268	203	209
			F.	2310	95	79	76	78	80	408	329	260	180	177	184	164
HARDINGSTONE	Rural	8672	M.	4368	118	109	127	103	130	587	551	476	434	330	271	240
			F.	4304	121	118	133	103	118	598	529	482	336	334	280	253
HARROW	Urban	5558	M.	2734	74	55	53	57	52	291	258	405	619	201	154	130
			F.	2824	60	53	65	60	58	296	312	279	323	336	229	206
HATFIELD	Rural	6502	M.	3220	81	68	100	92	91	442	426	359	315	253	230	204
			F.	3282	96	99	95	84	97	471	425	303	284	225	277	226
HEADINGTON	Rural	11543	M.	5905	153	159	167	125	168	772	705	812	617	466	381	340
			F.	5638	184	125	135	166	148	758	669	588	442	454	416	407
HEMEL HEMPSTEAD	Rural	14696	M.	6985	203	182	217	193	191	987	894	872	640	480	451	437
			F.	7611	201	176	180	182	197	936	905	825	691	607	582	511
HENDON	Urban	10484	M.	4851	127	124	131	117	129	620	585	579	490	447	406	341
			F.	5633	158	139	172	138	154	768	642	584	632	582	368	410

SANITARY DISTRICT.		ALL AGES. Persons.	Males and Females.		Under 1 Year.	1–	2–	3–	4–	Under 5 Years.	5–	10–	15–	20–	25–
HENDON	Rural	10987	M.	5272	132	139	139	130	134	674	694	839	471	395	368
			F.	5715	163	144	162	150	128	747	683	740	537	458	432
HENLEY	Urban	4604	M.	2164	62	50	58	70	49	298	301	235	200	181	143
			F.	2440	57	44	68	57	48	274	277	287	231	207	178
HENLEY	Rural	15388	M.	7785	227	180	204	213	213	1037	1051	956	896	540	460
			F.	7603	220	179	205	248	200	1047	1027	896	567	578	503
HERTFORD	Urban	7747	M.	3913	85	75	100	95	72	427	580	549	482	321	260
			F.	3834	91	90	110	77	92	460	429	476	397	301	254
HERTFORD	Rural	8987	M.	4584	114	120	139	108	133	614	619	626	458	290	238
			F.	4403	113	94	113	122	108	550	589	510	343	314	270
HESTON AND ISLEWORTH	Urban	22727	M.	11292	282	280	284	266	299	1411	1445	1602	1149	994	728
			F.	11435	335	279	271	303	278	1466	1390	1179	1059	982	810
HITCHIN	Urban	8434	M.	3872	119	109	118	110	103	559	516	467	368	260	243
			F.	4562	129	101	117	115	90	552	489	475	458	421	326
HITCHIN	Rural	13541	M.	6563	189	170	208	224	185	976	926	820	598	444	387
			F.	6978	203	201	188	153	183	928	934	795	618	572	488
HORNSEY	Urban	22485	M.	9938	341	310	295	297	293	1536	1316	1076	869	893	808
			F.	12547	299	293	302	283	294	1471	1294	1131	1641	1462	1175
HUNTINGDON	Urban	4228	M.	1997	50	51	43	41	31	216	229	231	232	181	134
			F.	2231	40	55	50	51	51	247	230	254	280	192	136
HUNTINGDON	Rural	8528	M.	4233	111	95	125	118	124	573	524	587	462	209	230
			F.	4245	123	106	128	102	134	593	578	489	362	276	245
KETTERING	Urban	11095	M.	5540	190	162	175	148	164	839	727	579	528	551	461
			F.	5555	201	169	190	175	159	894	736	593	541	499	452
KETTERING	Rural	14558	M.	7368	226	216	221	210	206	1079	937	773	725	611	485
			F.	7190	220	178	221	212	203	1034	936	803	636	559	474
LEIGHTON BUZZARD	Rural	18316	M.	8714	243	238	261	243	262	1247	1174	1074	880	504	521
			F.	9602	261	257	250	240	248	1265	1175	1066	910	781	686
LINTON	Rural	13015	M.	6424	171	168	183	166	193	881	856	743	722	468	379
			F.	6591	178	156	192	191	177	894	905	817	519	460	392
LUTON	Urban	23960	M.	10574	358	349	318	291	277	1593	1390	1214	1122	909	807
			F.	13386	360	302	314	340	319	1635	1365	1425	1557	1351	1161
LUTON	Rural	10913	M.	5188	166	126	151	155	151	749	711	647	508	336	285
			F.	5725	150	154	172	140	146	762	713	620	551	471	374
MARCH	Urban	6190	M.	3030	76	92	74	82	99	423	368	354	321	241	200
			F.	3160	85	75	88	89	75	412	431	375	297	220	211
NEWMARKET	Urban	5093	M.	2564	50	37	57	47	43	234	241	291	366	280	225
			F.	2529	48	60	51	64	51	274	265	228	317	263	210
NEWMARKET	Rural	23154	M.	11621	313	280	311	306	340	1550	1483	1415	1134	857	629
			F.	11533	342	262	320	328	324	1576	1501	1278	894	775	725
NEWPORT PAGNELL	Rural	24583	M.	12030	372	319	351	339	346	1727	1537	1361	1185	802	762
			F.	12553	347	334	383	293	355	1712	1628	1360	1062	935	840
NORTHAMPTON	Urban	51881	M.	25249	819	672	695	660	686	3541	3180	2740	2549	2270	2035
			F.	26632	828	726	773	760	709	3796	3295	2888	2515	2515	2139
NORTHAMPTON	Rural	9311	M.	4695	143	116	129	129	127	644	563	403	461	379	321
			F.	4616	116	130	129	134	109	618	552	483	357	354	329
NORTH WITCHFORD	Rural	4562	M.	2360	58	56	65	60	53	292	319	281	238	164	127
			F.	2202	57	62	48	74	79	320	288	281	182	132	121
OUNDLE	Urban	2890	M.	1452	24	36	44	33	37	174	165	234	175	99	77
			F.	1438	29	35	27	32	35	158	167	140	167	129	113
OUNDLE	Rural	11196	M.	5665	148	139	137	118	151	688	706	739	582	405	318
			F.	5531	140	136	147	171	134	737	714	665	433	353	322
OXFORD,* *Part of*	Urban	38066	M.	17554	523	498	476	465	445	2407	2082	1863	1801	1793	1385
			F.	20512	504	478	467	463	503	2415	2089	2059	2443	1970	1668

* The remainder of the Urban Sanitary District of Oxford is in Division II. (*see* Table 6) :—

	Persons			Under 1	1–	2–	3–	4–	Under 5	5–	10–	15–	20–	25–
Entire Urban Sanitary District of Oxford	39186	M.	18119	541	512	491	475	464	2483	2168	1943	1853	1852	1432
		F.	21067	523	497	487	484	523	2514	2167	2114	2486	2008	1712

M 2

Table 6 *continued.*—AGES of MALES and FEMALES in S[...]

SANITARY DISTRICT.		ALL AGES. Persons.	ALL AGES. Males and Females.		Under 1 Year.	1–	2–	3–	4–	Under 5 Years.	5–	10–	15–	20–	25–	
PETERBOROUGH	Urban	21228	M.	10383	319	347	285	313	284	1548	1345	1109	1016	974	837	
			F.	10845	312	266	303	286	295	1492	1326	1171	1105	903	893	
PETERBOROUGH	Rural	20276	M.	10141	267	245	301	275	307	1395	1281	1204	1071	774	644	
			F.	10135	311	253	288	262	292	1406	1344	1220	870	684	651	
POTTERSPURY	Rural	12231	M.	6156	193	145	168	163	164	833	773	742	665	479	397	
			F.	6075	160	162	191	170	153	836	745	860	521	470	406	
RAMSEY	Urban	4617	M.	2338	72	55	75	70	66	333	337	291	222	163	140	
			F.	2279	54	59	68	57	60	298	291	264	219	168	161	
ROYSTON	Rural	18623	M.	9459	260	230	268	246	284	1288	1295	1201	994	599	497	
			F.	9164	259	240	226	279	248	1252	1258	1101	716	548	539	
ST. ALBANS	Urban	10931	M.	5004	145	133	155	126	151	715	659	541	436	381	353	
			F.	5927	151	162	143	140	125	721	657	584	568	539	444	
ST. ALBANS	Rural	12365	M.	5959	173	174	182	155	169	853	839	709	575	419	365	
			F.	6406	179	158	170	176	198	881	793	681	531	506	473	
ST. IVES	Urban	3038	M.	1406	52	30	28	28	30	168	185	144	165	117	89	
			F.	1632	46	24	38	42	36	186	170	187	101	150	105	
ST. IVES	Rural	13717	M.	6781	170	104	170	105	101	680	870	[illegible]	675	440	[illegible]	
			F.	6936	183	167	173	188	173	884	924	832	511	407	378	
ST. NEOTS	Urban	4261	M.	1983	57	50	58	59	60	284	296	229	197	126	105	
			F.	2273	44	45	61	55	48	253	286	258	246	185	158	
ST. NEOTS	Rural	12646	M.	6242	157	157	183	159	169	825	838	784	637	419	316	
			F.	6404	171	146	161	163	160	801	325	757	490	467	396	
SLOUGH	Urban	5095	M.	2336	65	56	46	48	67	282	300	328	222	182	155	
			F.	2759	62	54	50	63	55	284	301	380	308	223	208	
SOUTH HORNSEY	Urban	14593	M.	6486	219	173	191	201	184	968	843	662	610	639	543	
			F.	8107	197	198	176	201	184	956	822	720	980	996	725	
STAINES	Urban	4628	M.	2222	81	64	67	61	52	325	302	237	212	155	174	
			F.	2406	56	51	58	63	72	300	295	248	223	261	184	
STAINES	Rural	19146	M.	9872	245	231	263	245	248	1232	1375	1836	1004	664	542	
			F.	9274	248	217	249	251	279	1244	1277	1163	768	695	646	
STEVENAGE	Urban	3116	M.	1493	41	41	33	36	48	199	212	213	162	97	78	
			F.	1623	39	39	46	43	45	212	194	179	152	114	112	
THAME	Urban	3267	M.	1658	53	37	43	48	46	227	202	236	181	118	102	
			F.	1609	41	32	33	27	38	171	184	198	147	144	108	
THAME	Rural	10595	M.	5237	128	143	141	134	140	686	717	671	507	350	286	
			F.	5358	156	136	139	143	156	730	713	630	392	375	320	
THRAPSTON	Rural	15115	M.	7615	233	181	217	214	214	1059	1006	892	779	561	481	
			F.	7500	219	191	230	239	206	1085	1035	853	647	524	513	
TOTTENHAM	Urban	46456	M.	22309	801	721	686	703	708	3619	2997	2512	1981	1936	1930	1
			F.	24147	812	708	751	691	647	3609	3080	2490	2303	2292	2093	1
TOWCESTER	Rural	12584	M.	6189	195	145	169	146	181	836	784	711	623	427	360	
			F.	6395	170	149	183	172	195	869	789	682	501	480	413	
TRING	Urban	4354	M.	2078	54	62	53	48	67	284	277	239	207	146	143	
			F.	2276	67	52	50	57	55	281	259	253	213	186	168	
TWICKENHAM	Urban	12479	M.	5707	169	163	159	136	166	793	779	724	623	418	368	
			F.	6772	166	150	147	160	146	769	702	685	647	747	615	
UXBRIDGE	Urban	7669	M.	3730	110	90	104	87	106	497	445	441	408	317	259	
			F.	3939	106	85	105	74	105	475	424	430	355	336	301	
UXBRIDGE	Rural	19881	M.	9805	259	240	226	289	262	1276	1190	1151	900	744	649	
			F.	10078	260	239	274	247	259	1279	1245	1059	702	755	719	
WALSOKEN	Urban	2697	M.	1273	37	25	42	25	41	170	173	167	111	89	67	
			F.	1424	40	23	38	38	41	180	178	152	110	89	89	
WALTHAM HOLY CROSS	Urban	5368	M.	2713	79	92	75	80	78	404	365	269	234	244	210	
			F.	2655	65	86	88	57	72	368	361	316	245	182	202	
WARE	Urban	5277	M.	2656	77	79	61	73	66	356	354	338	256	208	180	
			F.	2621	75	85	82	89	79	390	344	259	233	188	200	

Sanitary District.		All Ages. Persons.	Males and Females.		Under 1 Year.	1–	2–	3–	4–	Under 5 Years.	5–	10–	15–	20–	25–
WARE	Rural	13368	M.	6790	172	162	159	171	168	832	784	958	955	474	408
			F.	6578	184	157	161	161	161	824	782	780	564	524	449
WATFORD	Urban	10073	M.	4712	150	122	136	135	140	683	614	478	434	373	365
			F.	5361	146	151	137	140	149	723	620	555	509	446	421
WATFORD	Rural	21255	M.	10343	262	235	261	230	234	1222	1302	1538	923	728	684
			F.	10912	248	236	253	252	236	1215	1274	1286	874	805	761
WELLINGBOROUGH	Urban	13794	M.	6725	184	195	194	187	218	978	940	701	633	605	564
			F.	7069	223	208	198	197	189	1015	912	745	811	655	610
WELLINGBOROUGH	Rural	23148	M.	11650	354	326	306	310	317	1613	1462	1286	1285	1019	891
			F.	11498	355	333	320	335	312	1655	1610	1284	1146	920	856
WELWYN	Rural	2300	M.	1151	32	43	39	35	43	192	141	112	113	82	79
			F.	1149	44	42	30	33	33	182	120	104	97	85	85
WHEATLEY	Urban	1020	M.	542	17	12	14	16	16	75	80	57	48	38	24
			F.	478	10	13	13	13	16	65	75	52	32	32	27
WHITTLESEY	Urban	3682	M.	1703	37	35	44	51	49	216	215	208	160	91	76
			F.	1979	40	47	40	43	46	216	217	209	192	131	102
WHITTLESEY	Rural	2773	M.	1482	52	32	50	47	42	223	189	177	162	100	92
			F.	1291	34	32	38	44	45	188	180	157	105	66	104
WILLESDEN	Urban	27453	M.	12883	481	393	403	385	391	2053	1744	1369	1187	1184	1009
			F.	14570	412	369	381	395	398	1955	1692	1546	1381	1511	1313
WINSLOW	Rural	7943	M.	3876	108	88	87	93	99	475	534	495	374	276	198
			F.	4067	91	103	98	95	106	493	521	511	378	287	240
WISBECH	Urban	9249	M.	4195	114	103	105	104	111	537	476	528	468	280	239
			F.	5054	124	116	89	94	95	518	528	520	518	435	367
WISBECH	Rural	20516	M.	10274	292	263	281	302	302	1440	1414	1189	990	680	582
			F.	10242	288	253	279	260	284	1364	1365	1163	822	704	632
WITNEY	Urban	3017	M.	1448	51	34	44	36	45	210	195	169	139	99	86
			F.	1569	46	46	36	26	50	204	193	183	153	134	98
WITNEY	Rural	18519	M.	9223	258	202	261	244	276	1241	1201	1102	926	637	504
			F.	9296	245	230	268	255	253	1260	1224	1070	730	606	601
WOBURN	Rural	9880	M.	4708	133	120	109	128	122	612	622	551	483	308	241
			F.	5172	104	113	119	164	131	571	592	564	447	386	368
WOODSTOCK	Rural	13316	M.	6534	206	161	178	167	175	887	847	821	628	468	358
			F.	6782	186	172	175	187	194	914	862	777	530	527	447
W.YCOMBE	Rural	29660	M.	14656	406	413	405	412	432	2068	2007	1749	1384	1062	910
			F.	15004	408	424	421	401	448	2102	2015	1781	1203	1110	997

M 3

Table 13.—NUMBER and COUNTRY of BIRTH of FOREIGNERS enumerated in COUNTIES, and in each exceeds 50,000 PERSONS.

WHERE BORN.	WHERE ENUMERAT										
	SOUTH MIDLAND COUNTIES.		COUNTIES.								
			MIDDLE-SEX.		HERTFORD-SHIRE.		BUCKING-HAMSHIRE.		OXFORD-SHIRE.		NO AM SE
	Males.	Females.	Males.	Females.	Males.	Females.	Males.	Females.	Males.	Females.	Males.
TOTAL - - -	33,409	21,541	32,785	20,954	139	130	76	59	130	111	104
EUROPE.											
DENMARK - - - -	324	126	317	121	2	.	.	1	1	1	2
NORWAY - - - -	330	59	335	58	.	.	.	.	2	.	1
SWEDEN - - - - -	639	150	635	149	.	.	.	.	1	.	2
RUSSIA - - - - -	1112	608	1102	602	1	2	1	.	4	4	1
POLAND (RUSSIAN) - - - -	3357	3044	3846	3043	3	.	.	.	5	.	2
AUSTRIA - - - -	854	316	846	316	2	.	1	.	2	.	1
HUNGARY - - - - -	178	58	175	57	1	.	.	.	.	.	.
SWITZERLAND - - - -	1333	864	1316	804	5	20	2	3	3	7	2
GERMAN EMPIRE - - - -	12270	7024	12094	6840	46	52	9	16	44	48	31
HOLLAND - - - -	2144	1824	2132	1818	1	1	2	.	1	1	1
BELGIUM - - - - -	737	582	724	568	3	.	1	1	4	3	1
FRANCE - - - - -	3674	3853	3601	3761	20	19	12	9	22	22	10
PORTUGAL - - - - -	82	58	81	58	.	.	.	.	.	.	.
SPAIN - - - - -	306	147	296	146	4	.	2	1	4	.	.
ITALY - - - - -	2714	600	2664	586	10	5	4	3	12	.	3
GREECE - - - - -	139	40	138	40	.	.	1	.	.	.	.
TURKEY - - - - -	149	68	149	68	.		.	.	.	.	.
SERVIA - - - - -	2	2	2	2	.		.	.	.	.	.
ROUMANIA - - - - -	30	10	30	10	.		.	.	.	.	
ASIA.											
ARABIA - - - - - -	22	1	22	1	.	.	.	.	.	.	.
PERSIA - - - - -	6	3	6	3	.		.	.	.	.	.
CHINA - - - - -	98	7	97	7	.	.	.	.	.	.	.
OTHER COUNTRIES - - - -	67	24	65	23	.	.	.	.	2	.	.
AFRICA.											
EGYPT - - - - - -	12	10	12	10	.	.	.	.	.	.	.
OTHER PARTS - - - -	52	23	51	22	.	.	.	.	.	.	.
AMERICA.											
UNITED STATES - - - -	1980	1846	1781	1648	33	31	29	25	23	25	46
MEXICO - - - - - -	19	11	17	11	.	.	2	.	.	.	.
BRAZIL - - - - -	46	34	42	34	1	.	3	.	.	.	.
OTHER STATES - - - -	171	117	157	117	7	.	7	.	.	.	.
COUNTRY NOT STATED - - -	46	22	46	22	.	.	.	.	.	.	.
AT SEA - - - - - -	7	10	6	10	.	.	.	.	.	.	1

R 3

Sanitary District.		All Ages. Persons.		Males and Females.	Under 1 Year.	1–	2–	3–	4–	Under 5 Years.	5–	10–	15–	20–	25–
AYLSHAM	Rural	18057	M.	8972	252	215	224	243	201	1135	1125	1021	977	729	521
			F.	9085	248	221	244	208	240	1161	1072	1013	753	653	591
BECCLES	Urban	5721	M.	2764	81	63	75	70	78	367	392	385	250	231	178
			F.	2957	67	92	70	88	81	398	330	328	308	234	197
BILLERICAY	Rural	18331	M.	9176	223	205	211	213	214	1066	1151	1200	900	703	544
			F.	9155	234	281	238	252	247	1197	1166	1034	766	714	675
BLOFIELD	Rural	11618	M.	5647	124	146	166	113	117	666	694	603	516	478	375
			F.	5971	177	132	128	142	166	745	639	589	465	462	413
BLYTHING	Rural	23710	M.	11722	314	340	325	305	303	1587	1566	1423	1079	833	665
			F.	11988	368	304	306	287	314	1579	1506	1347	970	830	758
BOSMERE	Rural	15226	M.	7704	193	213	193	201	180	980	982	946	781	568	473
			F.	7522	210	200	226	195	109	1030	979	880	596	540	439
BRAINTREE	Urban	5182	M.	2336	79	54	68	58	61	320	295	265	230	168	141
			F.	2846	79	60	59	63	58	319	306	304	338	248	206
BRAINTREE	Rural	20480	M.	9909	263	255	248	244	272	1282	1293	1208	987	657	500
			F.	10571	268	236	200	270	278	1337	1304	1219	864	744	675
BURY ST. EDMUND'S	Urban	16111	M.	7574	205	185	195	184	195	964	935	880	911	647	530
			F.	8537	195	202	208	190	201	996	916	967	909	740	642
CHELMSFORD	Urban	9885	M.	4697	130	133	124	130	144	657	557	602	484	340	311
			F.	5188	136	127	120	135	113	637	582	537	539	407	385
CHELMSFORD	Rural	23086	M.	11709	317	300	357	295	317	1592	1518	1408	1137	795	636
			F.	11377	319	282	201	279	275	1446	1455	1312	880	704	727
COLCHESTER	Urban	28374	M.	13922	303	357	373	325	342	1790	1460	1406	1618	1585	1236
			F.	14452	378	352	345	337	347	1759	1849	1520	1523	1385	1179
COSFORD	Rural	12583	M.	6265	164	172	152	141	184	813	778	726	637	473	357
			F.	6318	190	143	185	150	159	827	831	748	529	452	393
DEPWADE	Rural	19736	M.	9705	240	263	269	242	235	1258	1222	1130	970	711	532
			F.	10031	278	239	237	237	278	1269	1231	1106	878	664	564
DISS	Urban	3846	M.	1740	40	47	48	44	50	230	230	196	158	120	99
			F.	2106	50	47	40	58	48	243	257	219	234	167	168
DOCKING	Rural	17510	M.	8633	226	208	214	233	250	1131	1077	1004	915	611	448
			F.	8877	223	198	214	209	213	1062	1075	980	749	641	554
DOWNHAM	Rural	16771	M.	8414	217	209	207	211	221	1065	1028	1056	877	598	609
			F.	8357	234	213	220	240	236	1143	1004	999	661	584	631
DOWNHAM MARKET	Urban	2633	M.	1271	32	19	31	24	19	125	146	169	140	93	81
			F.	1362	24	32	29	25	29	139	160	149	145	123	89
DUNMOW	Rural	17990	M.	9200	227	201	239	225	237	1129	1185	1201	961	606	402
			F.	8790	242	215	230	240	246	1173	1159	1024	681	543	519
EAST DEREHAM	Urban	5640	M.	2724	71	75	86	72	72	356	302	309	260	236	199
			F.	2916	69	84	69	75	67	364	293	301	318	253	209
EAST HAM	Urban	9713	M.	5436	159	152	136	145	160	752	707	1045	610	356	436
			F.	4277	166	169	138	164	139	706	615	540	277	315	349
EPPING	Rural	21754	M.	10703	273	260	253	272	286	1383	1376	1308	1089	836	630
			F.	11051	294	256	288	288	269	1395	1375	1246	1028	914	724
ERPINGHAM	Rural	17005	M.	8353	222	210	217	205	207	1061	1016	970	846	681	474
			F.	8652	213	205	210	231	240	1099	983	927	708	663	588
EYE	Urban	2296	M.	1107	29	29	19	32	32	141	112	137	108	63	51
			F.	1189	24	22	31	23	30	130	152	130	109	89	67
FLEGG	Rural	9714	M.	4778	160	129	130	138	127	623	660	553	415	339	282
			F.	4936	147	131	116	146	145	685	637	515	419	408	341
FOREHOE	Rural	11971	M.	5937	148	133	170	147	150	748	736	671	599	461	357
			F.	6034	156	137	146	137	148	724	727	659	503	429	380
FREEBRIDGE LYNN	Rural	12235	M.	6053	159	157	160	156	144	776	735	683	630	479	363
			F.	6182	172	136	106	165	167	806	700	687	520	396	422
GREAT YARMOUTH	Urban	46159	M.	21753	630	599	652	560	583	3030	2530	2344	2444	2043	1464
			F.	24406	652	640	600	576	552	2925	2605	2316	2533	2212	1896
GUILTCROSS	Rural	10563	M.	5305	144	145	145	144	122	700	623	624	559	392	298
			F.	5258	150	90	136	131	125	632	664	585	422	357	327

Note.—For the Parishes comprised in each Urban Sanitary District, *see* Vol. II.,

Sanitary District.		All Ages. Persons.	Males and Females.		Under 1 Year.	1–	2–	3–	4–	Under 5 Years.	5–	10–	15–	20–	25–
HADLEIGH	Urban	3237	M.	1536	38	40	44	42	41	205	174	174	157	100	101
			F.	1701	43	41	34	47	32	197	105	183	174	140	108
HALSTEAD	Urban	5804	M.	2557	72	55	61	54	74	316	310	315	288	174	141
			F.	3247	66	70	60	62	71	329	320	381	357	285	255
HALSTEAD	Rural	11201	M.	5330	114	185	165	129	154	697	725	673	497	322	237
			F.	5862	138	115	118	152	156	679	755	652	520	439	368
HARTISMERE	Rural	13495	M.	6867	203	185	183	186	185	941	920	891	681	477	357
			F.	6628	181	177	175	160	201	894	881	789	623	470	403
HARWICH	Urban	7842	M.	4243	117	107	107	100	98	529	439	342	437	497	416
			F.	3599	129	100	117	108	101	555	474	378	330	290	288
HAVERHILL	Urban	3685	M.	1742	68	58	57	62	46	291	238	194	196	134	117
			F.	1943	56	50	72	48	56	282	248	239	213	172	129
HENSTEAD	Rural	10636	M.	5278	141	133	129	128	135	666	634	587	530	437	333
			F.	5358	126	130	141	141	128	666	612	542	455	440	373
HOXNE	Rural	12601	M.	6355	173	160	167	161	172	833	790	767	664	470	351
			F.	6246	190	161	173	152	160	845	808	743	507	436	353
IPSWICH	Urban	50546	M.	23726	680	636	633	681	661	3300	2920	2616	2338	1881	1836
			F.	26820	681	666	613	628	565	3143	2968	2829	2783	2492	2096
IPSWICH	Rural	213	M.	105	3	3	5	3	3	17	13	16	9	9	6
			F.	108	3	2	4	4	1	14	10	15	8	5	7
KING'S LYNN	Urban	18539	M.	8784	249	209	229	234	228	1149	985	904	904	772	712
			F.	9755	257	238	208	209	196	1108	1035	927	975	878	765
KING'S LYNN	Rural	667	M.	346	10	5	11	12	15	53	44	44	34	23	24
			F.	321	9	8	9	12	9	47	42	30	18	22	22
LEXDEN	Rural	21775	M.	10933	302	287	303	287	330	1509	1501	1378	1008	721	544
			F.	10842	279	286	286	270	325	1455	1415	1269	851	757	658
LEYTON	Urban	27068	M.	12983	441	370	410	416	449	2095	2016	1623	1049	905	880
			F.	14085	385	390	416	398	390	1979	1862	1678	1434	1147	1051
LODDON	Rural	13702	M.	6687	216	164	168	173	190	911	860	802	566	465	366
			F.	7015	193	166	176	187	170	892	900	748	561	514	467
LOWESTOFT	Urban	19696	M.	9562	301	268	286	266	288	1409	1196	986	1103	992	733
			F.	10134	304	273	270	274	267	1388	1221	1054	1050	963	825
MALDON	Urban	5468	M.	2621	73	62	67	64	64	330	348	311	266	174	147
			F.	2847	71	69	74	60	90	364	364	299	264	201	202
MALDON	Rural	18344	M.	9405	272	290	259	255	284	1360	1269	1206	1004	552	474
			F.	8939	253	252	248	262	278	1293	1283	1103	686	551	538
MILDENHALL	Rural	8957	M.	4447	140	121	124	117	120	622	604	499	421	326	265
			F.	4510	135	117	133	148	131	664	593	514	340	311	290
MITFORD	Rural	21727	M.	10866	300	272	305	286	279	1442	1325	1239	1097	810	630
			F.	10861	297	257	257	265	252	1328	1358	1206	869	749	689
MUTFORD	Rural	10774	M.	5201	184	166	190	160	157	857	724	620	431	331	321
			F.	5573	188	163	156	164	172	843	760	604	429	417	359
NORTH WALSHAM	Urban	3234	M.	1578	37	45	40	43	36	201	185	213	162	138	106
			F.	1656	45	40	41	38	36	200	165	156	195	127	110
NORWICH	Urban	87842	M.	40288	1224	1050	1089	1021	1045	5438	4784	4601	4006	3548	2953
			F.	47554	1267	1120	1099	1080	1070	5636	4929	4724	5001	4650	3604
ONGAR	Rural	10671	M.	5529	170	89	126	130	118	642	712	740	547	364	327
			F.	5142	143	133	153	138	165	727	691	614	397	334	340
ORSETT	Rural	16480	M.	9309	249	263	230	230	233	1205	993	1496	1125	765	647
			F.	7171	233	234	250	217	239	1173	1007	839	530	532	478
PLOMESGATE	Rural	20479	M.	10161	264	243	273	275	275	1330	1234	1825	1029	760	645
			F.	10318	250	259	279	262	248	1298	1288	1079	944	753	654
RISBRIDGE	Rural	13549	M.	6706	209	168	192	185	182	936	921	899	685	431	356
			F.	6843	177	157	203	186	200	923	909	814	578	503	400
ROCHFORD	Rural	[illegible]	M.	9050	232	262	245	247	228	1914	1080	[illegible]	[illegible]	[illegible]	[illegible]

Sanitary District.		All Ages. Persons.		All Ages. Males and Females.	Under 1 Year.	1–	2–	3–	4–	Under 5 Years.	5–	10–	15–	20–	25–
ROMFORD	Rural	29874	M.	14662	451	409	460	433	437	2190	1961	1761	1522	1197	1028
			F.	15212	450	429	446	422	446	2193	2183	1938	1360	1193	1056
SAFFRON WALDEN	Urban	6060	M.	2835	73	58	73	71	66	341	359	379	269	208	161
			F.	3225	78	71	79	61	80	369	409	363	316	260	198
SAFFRON WALDEN	Rural	12523	M.	6365	187	130	174	151	185	827	845	789	654	449	361
			F.	6163	184	175	183	162	187	891	848	682	437	380	371
ST. FAITH'S	Rural	11418	M.	5600	154	135	167	166	135	757	675	620	561	458	358
			F.	6818	182	137	137	133	150	739	714	587	489	480	389
SAMFORD	Rural	11564	M.	5817	161	144	143	172	134	754	714	671	584	405	332
			F.	5747	169	151	146	147	148	761	685	640	448	396	366
SMALLBURGH	Rural	14348	M.	7139	203	180	197	199	168	947	876	850	602	527	435
			F.	7209	204	182	186	187	194	953	914	776	592	500	455
SOUTHEND	Urban	7979	M.	3646	100	99	104	100	95	408	452	364	350	300	302
			F.	4333	131	129	102	114	103	579	484	530	488	423	334
SOUTHWOLD	Urban	2107	M.	955	36	21	31	27	33	148	111	107	88	89	74
			F.	1152	28	28	30	22	27	135	115	122	101	105	86
STOW	Rural	16148	M.	8019	209	231	220	221	196	1077	1060	948	781	574	432
			F.	8124	224	210	211	219	223	1087	1064	967	642	577	504
STOWMARKET	Urban	4052	M.	1851	45	60	57	58	51	271	252	188	184	128	111
			F.	2201	64	71	55	62	57	309	275	245	223	166	142
SUDBURY	Urban	6584	M.	3087	80	63	68	65	64	340	368	357	323	227	182
			F.	3497	78	76	76	91	69	390	376	380	387	282	250
SUDBURY	Rural	23571	M.	11615	298	311	322	305	326	1562	1616	1385	1212	794	601
			F.	11956	311	278	334	306	314	1543	1533	1373	1012	885	770
SWAFFHAM	Urban	3643	M.	1701	44	41	65	41	48	239	215	187	159	101	117
			F.	1942	41	32	43	55	47	218	224	195	228	137	121
SWAFFHAM	Rural	9216	M.	4593	114	97	114	117	133	575	575	528	507	338	255
			F.	4623	121	125	123	131	141	641	586	626	349	330	277
TENDRING	Rural	24262	M.	12309	315	206	331	329	334	1605	1591	1525	1183	852	606
			F.	11953	335	336	319	328	296	1614	1535	1402	900	760	694
THETFORD	Urban	4032	M.	1981	60	49	56	54	51	270	256	229	200	131	104
			F.	2051	43	44	48	39	55	229	273	235	175	144	132
THETFORD	Rural	13598	M.	6826	183	181	186	198	209	960	886	772	621	490	300
			F.	6772	187	164	156	177	174	858	863	771	546	505	420
THINGOE	Rural	16386	M.	8195	217	187	215	218	228	1065	1060	941	855	528	479
			F.	8191	221	213	229	218	233	1114	1035	900	638	550	505
WALSINGHAM	Rural	17298	M.	8630	227	196	223	217	251	1114	1059	970	890	728	551
			F.	8668	236	201	218	223	203	1081	1020	963	753	653	566
WALTHAMSTOW	Urban	21715	M.	10344	369	352	333	349	304	1707	1377	1267	936	802	855
			F.	11371	396	348	348	363	325	1780	1475	1277	984	985	946
WALTON-ON-THE-NAZE	Urban	1371	M.	633	17	21	14	17	19	88	80	82	55	40	24
			F.	738	16	18	17	22	23	96	123	73	51	46	48
WANGFORD	Rural	8735	M.	4264	121	111	112	102	138	584	514	490	414	325	258
			F.	4471	115	105	120	121	109	570	553	491	393	326	273
WANSTEAD	Urban	5362	M.	2391	70	40	56	57	62	285	430	478	197	166	150
			F.	2071	42	53	56	42	53	246	305	309	358	395	228
WAYLAND	Rural	10716	M.	5351	148	138	157	135	124	702	644	583	563	326	234
			F.	5365	145	124	119	127	119	634	619	508	435	381	340
WELLS	Urban	2645	M.	1167	32	27	29	33	32	153	138	132	101	73	69
			F.	1478	43	34	40	33	37	187	165	147	124	116	102
WEST HAM	Urban	128953	M.	65410	2252	2073	2137	2111	2031	10604	8909	7080	5728	5624	5552
			F.	63543	2287	2121	2117	2008	1964	10497	8830	7031	6203	5021	5308
WEST HAM	Rural	993	M.	493	12	20	13	19	14	78	66	50	48	35	42
			F.	500	18	18	13	18	19	86	62	43	50	36	40
WITHAM	Urban	2966	M.	1357	50	34	38	40	32	203	152	157	127	96	81
			F.	1609	35	37	37	42	30	181	187	160	135	136	108
WOODBRIDGE	Rural	22516	M.	11087	302	303	268	306	297	1476	1306	1355	1060	701	610
			F.	11429	303	315	307	267	288	1480	1363	1222	943	843	753
WOODFORD	Urban	7154	M.	3151	91	91	96	94	86	458	432	311	307	268	243
			F.	4003	105	89	88	96	91	469	408	404	486	451	365

R 4

Table 13.—NUMBER and COUNTRY of BIRTH of FOREIGNERS enumerated in COUNTIES, and in ea[...] exceeds 50,000 PERSONS.

WHERE BORN.	WHERE ENUMER[...]							
	EASTERN COUNTIES.		COUNTIES.					
			ESSEX.		SUFFOLK.		NORFOLK	
	Males.	Females.	Males.	Females.	Males.	Females.	Males.	Fem[...]
TOTAL	1447	821	1115	553	150	126	182	14[...]
EUROPE.								
DENMARK	22	7	16	5	1	1	5	
NORWAY	48	7	13	4	24	1	11	
SWEDEN	44	8	28	7	6	.	10	
RUSSIA	28	9	18	6	7	2	8	
POLAND (RUSSIAN)	33	2	30	2	2	.	1	
AUSTRIA	14	8	9	5	2	1	3	
HUNGARY	4	.	2	.	2	.	.	
SWITZERLAND	16	55	11	24	.	13	5	
GERMAN EMPIRE	622	351	538	270	39	36	45	
HOLLAND	42	20	28	16	8	2	6	
BELGIUM	47	12	44	8	2	3	1	
FRANCE	116	111	90	70	11	24	15	
PORTUGAL	2	.	2	.	.	.	.	
SPAIN	7	5	7	4	.	1	.	
ITALY	67	15	43	9	17	5	7	
GREECE	3	1	2	.	.	.	1	
TURKEY	2	3	2	.	.	2	.	
SERVIA	.	.	.	.	.	.	.	
ROUMANIA	1	.	.	.	1	.	.	
ASIA.								
ARABIA	6	.	6	.	.	.	.	
PERSIA	.	.	.	.	.	.	.	
CHINA	3	1	3	1	.	.	.	
OTHER COUNTRIES	40	.	40	.	.	.	.	
AFRICA.								
EGYPT	1	1	1	.	.	1	.	
OTHER PARTS	32	.	32	.	.	.	.	
AMERICA.								
UNITED STATES	241	205	150	122	28	34	63	
MEXICO	.	.	.	.	.	.	.	
BRAZIL	1	.	.	.	.	.	1	
OTHER STATES	.	.	.	.	.	.	.	
COUNTRY NOT STATED	5	.	5	.	.	.	.	
AT SEA	.	.	.	.	.	.	.	

Table 6.—Ages of Males and Females in Sanitary

Sanitary District.		All Ages. Both Sexes.		All Ages. Males and Females.	Under 1 Year.	1–	2–	3–	4–	Under 5 Years.	5–	10–	15–	20–	25–
ALDERBURY	Rural	12433	M.	6262	149	150	171	153	151	774	758	737	636	467	354
			F.	6171	159	162	168	140	141	770	763	684	523	506	380
AMESBURY	Rural	7628	M.	3874	94	103	105	104	70	476	465	477	433	266	204
			F.	3754	84	108	90	101	91	478	454	434	336	256	235
AXBRIDGE	Rural	26053	M.	12624	302	328	337	339	322	1628	1663	1457	1210	881	745
			F.	13429	322	328	324	326	357	1657	1591	1495	1147	1071	870
AXMINSTER	Rural	15258	M.	7579	184	207	201	212	197	1001	947	975	763	564	400
			F.	7679	167	163	183	197	174	884	906	839	719	557	479
BAMPTON	Urban	1089	M.	567	12	13	13	12	13	63	65	56	46	43	55
			F.	522	6	12	8	14	10	50	62	69	41	42	34
BARNSTAPLE	Urban	12282	M.	5509	117	114	143	151	148	698	644	658	587	426	377
			F.	6773	172	131	138	138	130	709	712	628	743	614	489
BARNSTAPLE	Rural	18456	M.	9105	232	251	258	238	217	1196	1167	1085	907	692	516
			F.	9351	208	234	218	224	247	1131	1093	987	883	725	611
BATH	Urban	51814	M.	21020	519	492	536	561	500	2608	2478	2384	2163	1652	1467
			F.	30794	511	515	483	522	533	2572	2552	2669	3380	3229	2564
BATH	Rural	18812	M.	9104	263	239	267	224	251	1244	1164	1390	1022	632	569
			F.	9708	245	246	255	253	249	1247	1108	987	866	815	757
BEAMINSTER	Rural	11468	M.	5512	143	121	124	140	142	670	669	606	583	406	328
			F.	5956	146	153	116	137	150	732	731	623	552	434	360
BEDMINSTER	Rural	24405	M.	11627	325	338	324	336	326	1649	1548	1466	1124	864	730
			F.	12778	336	335	327	328	363	1689	1537	1387	1223	1051	920
BIDEFORD	Urban	6512	M.	2883	89	84	74	75	86	408	397	302	317	226	156
			F.	3629	77	93	95	73	77	415	372	347	398	372	237
BIDEFORD	Rural	7792	M.	3888	94	98	93	91	102	478	494	473	438	317	229
			F.	3904	110	95	111	98	108	522	465	448	344	327	257
BLANDFORD FORUM	Urban	3753	M.	1724	44	40	40	33	34	191	215	207	173	186	105
			F.	2029	43	35	44	45	40	207	210	217	207	212	127
BLANDFORD	Rural	9982	M.	4960	128	103	123	133	115	602	601	600	556	373	292
			F.	5022	119	110	126	128	144	627	601	513	444	382	338
BODMIN	Urban	5061	M.	2467	55	60	37	37	59	248	247	199	307	254	164
			F.	2594	47	45	41	50	31	214	242	239	240	223	168
BODMIN	Rural	14187	M.	6842	169	184	162	147	195	857	842	814	780	540	385
			F.	7345	171	154	190	165	165	845	842	772	717	554	508
BRADFORD-ON-AVON	Urban	4922	M.	2212	67	71	69	67	63	337	288	257	200	179	132
			F.	2710	88	58	70	71	66	353	286	270	289	257	204
BRADFORD-ON-AVON	Rural	5938	M.	2835	81	71	88	76	76	392	400	289	245	220	157
			F.	3103	84	59	82	84	84	393	363	327	300	217	229
BRIDGWATER	Urban	12007	M.	5781	191	159	143	161	162	816	721	685	673	473	361
			F.	6226	171	160	159	168	160	818	718	671	636	526	436
BRIDGWATER	Rural	21666	M.	10762	284	269	278	287	284	1402	1429	1337	1131	754	650
			F.	10904	267	262	287	295	277	1388	1328	1201	853	772	712
BRIDPORT	Urban	6795	M.	3108	98	84	79	92	73	426	402	403	308	217	179
			F.	3687	87	72	83	76	86	404	407	401	373	308	241
BRIDPORT	Rural	8016	M.	3879	113	100	101	94	108	516	507	505	414	242	224
			F.	4137	107	94	103	107	108	519	552	468	348	281	266
BRISTOL,* *part of*	Urban	38131	M.	18431	691	619	620	549	595	3074	2545	1958	1781	1560	1560
			F.	19700	671	597	609	567	586	3030	2596	2153	1663	1660	1592

* The remainder of the Urban Sanitary District of Bristol is in Division VI. (*see* Table 6):—

	Both Sexes		Males and Females	Under 1 Year	1–	2–	3–	4–	Under 5 Years	5–	10–	15–	20–	25–
Entire Urban Sanitary District of Bristol	206874	M.	93711	2928	2673	2710	2602	2587	13500	11973	11182	9572	7880	7464
		F.	113163	2983	2778	2733	2686	2743	13923	12210	11633	11846	11274	9455

Note.—For the Parishes comprised in each Urban Sanitary District, *see* Vol.

Table 6 *continued*.—AGES of MALES and FEMALES in SANI

SANITARY DISTRICT.		ALL AGES. Persons.	ALL AGES. Males and Females.		Under 1 Year.	1–	2–	3–	4–	Under 5 Years.	5–	10–	15–	20–	25–
BUDLEIGH SALTERTON	Urban	1908	M.	729	20	19	25	12	16	92	100	85	79	46	32
			F.	1179	14	21	18	17	23	93	94	114	132	124	86
BURNHAM	Urban	1904	M.	850	25	29	27	27	19	127	101	108	84	68	64
			F.	1054	23	29	21	24	21	118	87	129	123	87	78
CALNE	Urban	3405	M.	1605	44	36	43	45	51	219	222	218	148	110	77
			F.	1800	50	42	43	46	44	225	219	203	169	132	113
CALNE	Rural	5215	M.	2598	52	64	54	70	63	303	340	303	257	213	126
			F.	2617	64	71	61	69	62	327	311	380	206	173	163
CAMBORNE	Urban	13601	M.	6004	161	143	169	140	156	775	778	860	880	507	339
			F.	7597	155	131	161	145	142	734	821	765	881	714	531
CAMELFORD	Rural	7605	M.	3755	96	97	93	92	92	473	470	520	392	267	207
			F.	3850	90	97	93	80	97	457	478	417	344	281	250
CERNE	Rural	6496	M.	3257	92	79	94	89	69	423	396	386	362	264	202
			F.	3239	68	92	85	77	85	407	391	336	279	244	222
CHARD	Urban	2411	M.	1097	34	24	28	33	22	141	130	140	140	70	87
			F.	1314	38	32	34	37	22	163	105	110	168	135	116
CHARD	Rural	22942	M.	11004	303	305	301	336	317	1562	1461	1365	1190	821	619
			F.	11938	297	294	314	295	310	1510	1446	1380	1157	930	775
CHIPPENHAM	Urban	4495	M.	2122	57	46	52	60	58	263	266	270	212	165	155
			F.	2873	57	56	66	59	54	292	264	268	244	210	171
CHIPPENHAM	Rural	16716	M.	8339	214	213	216	225	221	1089	1047	1022	820	585	600
			F.	8377	219	208	232	233	162	1054	1024	900	613	569	535
CLEVEDON	Urban	4869	M.	1933	40	34	42	48	52	216	264	253	194	164	125
			F.	2936	53	52	53	38	34	230	263	294	337	295	264
CLUTTON	Rural	16119	M.	8116	209	203	217	226	215	1070	1026	1007	657	576	482
			F.	8003	220	198	201	200	203	1022	1008	915	604	578	494
CREDITON	Urban	4165	M.	1921	48	57	57	55	43	260	258	220	163	140	120
			F.	2244	64	48	43	62	58	279	260	215	199	166	156
CREDITON	Rural	13764	M.	6928	167	188	176	183	169	883	862	775	760	535	412
			F.	6836	147	171	208	184	169	879	866	750	590	523	431
CRICKLADE	Rural	11283	M.	5622	176	130	142	141	142	731	707	669	525	402	319
			F.	5661	138	141	164	156	159	758	724	691	446	398	334
DARTMOUTH	Urban	5725	M.	2819	75	78	76	57	69	355	386	409	249	221	202
			F.	2906	60	58	78	71	71	338	330	284	282	242	190
DAWLISH	Urban	3977	M.	1604	43	34	38	36	52	203	192	189	142	118	108
			F.	2373	43	27	43	44	37	194	187	196	244	263	214
DEVIZES	Urban	6645	M.	3117	93	106	85	94	80	458	333	321	321	233	224
			F.	3528	83	89	79	76	70	397	400	410	389	306	252
DEVIZES	Rural	13865	M.	7004	175	169	190	194	165	893	854	811	668	489	378
			F.	6861	155	181	163	163	158	820	861	686	517	453	446
DEVONPORT	Urban	48939	M.	24805	662	558	516	533	514	2783	2419	2165	4338	2560	2050
			F.	24134	651	536	522	568	500	2777	2446	2433	2282	2169	1934
DORCHESTER	Urban	7567	M.	3778	97	114	91	81	85	468	376	351	472	438	304
			F.	3789	92	88	95	96	101	472	396	359	419	345	338
DORCHESTER	Rural	10827	M.	5310	119	130	107	132	118	606	630	623	562	435	317
			F.	5517	116	120	125	129	149	639	627	608	473	438	351
DULVERTON	Rural	5453	M.	2802	70	51	63	70	62	316	377	351	206	218	136
			F.	2651	69	59	69	64	73	334	343	301	245	180	105
EAST STONEHOUSE	Urban	15041	M.	7145	247	210	183	194	173	1007	851	685	721	674	553
			F.	7896	221	237	215	212	160	1045	839	716	648	728	690
EXETER	Urban	37665	M.	16757	482	412	374	429	397	2094	1909	1880	1828	1483	1222
			F.	20908	464	432	393	365	389	2043	1944	1970	2314	2155	1709

Z 2

Table 6 *continued.*—AGES of MALES and FEMALES in SANIT

SANITARY DISTRICT.		ALL AGES. Persons.	Males and Females.		Under 1 Year.	1–	2–	3–	4–	Under 5 Years.	5–	10–	15–	20–	25–
EXETER	*	4	M.	2	.	.	.	.	.	.	.	.	.	1	.
			F.	2	.	.	.	.	.	.	.	1	.	.	.
EXMOUTH	Urban	6245	M.	2606	79	80	77	70	67	373	338	301	255	206	168
			F.	3639	69	67	69	66	65	336	357	324	378	340	281
FALMOUTH	Urban	5973	M.	3937	47	37	37	54	42	217	200	225	932	544	396
			F.	2036	45	43	49	42	42	221	204	185	198	206	163
FALMOUTH PARISH	Urban	6158	M.	2586	84	47	73	62	62	328	325	319	238	187	148
			F.	3572	55	64	76	72	52	319	345	361	393	365	277
FALMOUTH	Rural	9960	M.	4602	142	121	137	135	120	655	594	653	540	327	269
			F.	5358	111	113	125	107	105	561	577	500	523	474	397
FROME	Urban	9377	M.	4300	112	86	134	124	112	568	529	495	450	339	277
			F.	5077	139	106	103	111	111	570	535	499	511	469	356
FROME	Rural	13775	M.	6762	192	163	171	178	190	894	997	862	702	461	376
			F.	7013	160	197	191	195	184	933	859	828	601	480	458
GLASTONBURY	Urban	3719	M.	1765	44	38	59	48	59	246	225	211	192	132	97
			F.	1954	49	54	37	43	49	223	270	186	200	164	114
GREAT TORRINGTON	Urban	3445	M.	1468	55	37	34	30	40	196	211	188	138	98	88
			F.	1977	40	35	46	52	30	206	223	173	195	179	150
HAYLE	Urban	1089	M.	483	11	11	12	12	13	59	56	69	71	41	23
			F.	606	10	11	13	11	11	56	48	68	65	68	48
HELSTON	Urban	3432	M.	1456	43	33	35	26	19	158	190	194	160	115	56
			F.	1976	28	36	28	43	29	166	196	177	217	172	139
HELSTON	Rural	20249	M.	9354	252	240	236	218	231	1172	1121	1275	1140	701	586
			F.	10895	238	209	219	244	242	1152	1101	1135	1051	882	746
HIGHWORTH	Rural	13381	M.	6828	194	205	209	204	208	1020	849	780	741	509	401
			F.	6553	195	185	180	184	203	947	945	780	456	447	431
HOLSWORTHY	Rural	9008	M.	4538	115	108	114	110	113	560	565	575	495	371	283
			F.	4475	125	93	107	114	103	542	562	476	455	379	321
HONITON	Urban	3358	M.	1593	39	44	26	31	43	183	209	248	178	121	84
			F.	1765	38	44	36	38	37	193	183	203	191	142	127
HONITON	Rural	10274	M.	5066	125	126	112	126	134	625	650	596	500	401	281
			F.	5208	122	145	120	131	129	653	607	590	419	427	338
ILFRACOMBE	Urban	6255	M.	2785	74	46	62	55	54	291	298	292	327	279	211
			F.	3470	63	70	63	70	61	327	310	327	412	356	280
IVYBRIDGE	Urban	1587	M.	748	20	21	20	19	18	98	90	107	72	68	49
			F.	839	24	22	20	16	18	100	78	81	96	86	50
KEYNSHAM	Rural	25781	M.	12570	400	393	384	351	371	1899	1721	1446	1360	966	821
			F.	13211	371	346	362	388	393	1860	1727	1462	1198	1092	903
KINGSBRIDGE	Rural	16934	M.	8267	211	181	204	212	205	1013	1063	906	812	618	515
			F.	8667	227	197	203	213	209	1049	1068	884	743	665	593
LANGPORT	Rural	15574	M.	7571	211	196	194	194	170	965	973	915	835	487	453
			F.	8003	192	179	183	216	183	953	1005	868	652	532	559
LAUNCESTON	Urban	3808	M.	1737	58	46	54	50	42	250	222	222	169	124	110
			F.	2071	50	51	59	49	44	253	194	216	226	191	158
LAUNCESTON	Rural	12250	M.	6124	152	159	172	167	137	787	763	710	740	536	387
			F.	6126	136	156	143	155	134	724	747	716	614	509	390
LISKEARD	Urban	4536	M.	2041	48	39	40	46	39	212	268	270	235	152	128
			F.	2495	63	43	40	50	58	254	205	226	303	224	187
LISKEARD	Rural	24251	M.	11581	336	287	308	318	307	1556	1467	1441	1419	927	622
			F.	12670	307	267	305	333	296	1508	1546	1411	1280	1037	831
LOWER BRIXHAM	Urban	5866	M.	2426	83	83	96	80	78	420	360	325	209	165	139
			F.	2940	94	72	84	100	81	431	352	315	255	238	216

* Exeter Castle Yard appears to be neither included in a Rural nor in an Urba

Table 6 *continued.*—AGES of MALES and FEMALES in S

Z 3

SANITARY DISTRICT.		ALL AGES. Persons.	ALL AGES. Males and Females.		Under 1 Year.	1–	2–	3–	4–	Under 5 Years.	5–	10–	15–	20–	25–
LUDGVAN	Urban	2632	M.	1212	27	33	29	31	28	148	161	171	161	110	90
			F.	1420	34	27	38	25	32	156	136	164	153	140	93
LYME REGIS	Urban	2290	M.	992	21	18	25	18	18	100	122	131	110	73	46
			F.	1298	25	22	23	26	25	121	120	120	140	106	82
LYNTON	Urban	1213	M.	537	16	9	13	8	19	65	70	54	48	40	37
			F.	676	11	10	15	15	10	61	80	78	67	58	43
MADRON	Urban	2737	M.	1252	35	34	32	29	34	164	158	158	156	97	65
			F.	1485	25	33	35	31	28	152	153	147	149	139	114
MALMESBURY	Urban	3133	M.	1475	48	41	45	37	46	217	171	174	144	114	90
			F.	1658	45	34	47	40	40	206	222	185	162	120	106
MALMESBURY	Rural	10816	M.	5372	136	131	154	125	150	696	720	650	507	400	283
			F.	5444	136	164	152	144	154	750	686	636	438	364	360
MARLBOROUGH	Urban	3343	M.	1676	37	35	37	37	33	179	192	227	294	112	96
			F.	1667	30	36	45	28	38	186	173	173	209	165	115
MARLBOROUGH	Rural	[illegible]	M.	3418	90	54	80	60	90	[illegible]	281	[illegible]	[illegible]	106	[illegible]
			F.	2072	73	78	92	87	87	417	404	339	246	212	177
MELKSHAM	Urban	2178	M.	975	32	28	20	34	23	137	122	94	92	79	74
			F.	1203	21	28	24	26	26	125	128	134	115	124	85
MELKSHAM	Rural	4859	M.	2351	67	62	79	66	65	339	323	266	210	125	126
			F.	2508	58	73	73	75	70	349	301	266	211	150	190
MERE	Rural	7349	M.	3594	93	93	91	102	105	434	472	441	370	238	184
			F.	3755	85	98	86	81	80	439	474	417	318	270	243
MIDSOMER NORTON	Urban	4422	M.	2349	73	76	58	62	69	338	305	321	272	169	163
			F.	2073	63	63	60	77	66	334	260	245	183	141	132
NEWQUAY	Urban	1600	M.	693	16	14	29	13	36	108	112	84	51	58	39
			F.	907	20	27	23	19	11	100	118	94	96	87	66
NEWTON ABBOT	Rural	25711	M.	12265	327	318	363	324	347	1679	1512	1395	1209	806	747
			F.	13446	336	300	321	350	297	1604	1514	1369	1197	1156	914
NORTHAM	Urban	4454	M.	1951	55	49	44	47	56	251	297	318	249	105	90
			F.	2503	52	58	55	58	54	277	271	259	277	227	157
OKEHAMPTON	Urban	1695	M.	782	14	21	18	24	20	97	90	70	83	78	53
			F.	913	27	23	18	16	13	97	116	92	89	82	72
OKEHAMPTON	Rural	15267	M.	7646	187	180	179	176	190	918	964	940	845	591	446
			F.	7623	160	201	177	227	173	938	892	912	686	589	510
OLD SWINDON	Urban	4696	M.	2361	57	75	54	66	65	317	260	246	259	216	186
			F.	2335	65	72	62	72	67	341	279	251	231	227	171
OTTERY ST. MARY	Urban	3973	M.	1881	53	49	64	37	52	255	242	242	195	136	100
			F.	2092	54	41	52	43	42	237	226	227	166	166	129
PADSTOW	Urban	1749	M.	721	31	26	22	22	15	116	107	90	65	49	38
			F.	1028	21	26	25	25	26	123	114	100	89	81	74
PAIGNTON	Urban	4613	M.	2072	58	43	66	50	61	278	259	238	189	185	141
			F.	2541	56	59	62	51	44	272	260	255	259	232	219
PENRYN	Urban	3466	M.	1541	44	37	56	50	49	236	202	185	170	104	78
			F.	1925	49	50	40	52	48	243	230	192	171	141	142
PENZANCE	Urban	12409	M.	5961	129	104	124	106	137	600	592	572	791	613	526
			F.	6448	131	123	124	125	118	621	556	555	680	648	557
PENZANCE	Rural	25610	M.	12101	298	317	307	309	280	1511	1527	1498	1541	1133	697
			F.	13509	350	298	329	295	305	1572	1447	1433	1325	1175	870
PEWSEY	Rural	12403	M.	6288	173	142	161	160	162	798	811	746	639	448	355
			F.	6115	176	163	152	167	162	820	796	688	468	444	348
PHILLACK	Urban	3643	M.	1691	39	45	46	48	47	225	230	242	171	141	89
			F.	1952	55	57	52	42	41	247	202	201	104	160	135

Table 6 *continued*.—AGES of MALES and FEMALES in SA

SANITARY DISTRICT.		ALL AGES. Persons.	ALL AGES. Males and Females.		Under 1 Year.	1–	2–	3–	4–	Under 5 Years.	5–	10–	15–	20–	25–
PLYMOUTH	Urban	78704	M.	33750	1001	847	872	840	802	4362	3970	3564	3403	3050	2529
			F.	40044	980	883	860	874	749	4346	4001	3912	3935	3898	3227
PLYMOUTH	*	69	M.	57	1	.	.	1	.	2	.	.	9	15	15
			F.	12	1	.	1	.	.	2	2		1	5	.
PLYMPTON ST. MARY	Rural	22729	M.	10950	273	284	305	282	283	1427	1363	1320	1266	931	630
			F.	11779	297	276	252	240	257	1322	1378	1284	1139	1063	801
POOLE	Urban	12310	M.	5820	193	141	177	147	166	824	724	624	575	494	409
			F.	6490	184	178	175	149	165	851	730	724	606	506	489
POOLE	Rural	6392	M.	3200	106	109	105	103	102	525	434	874	330	216	200
			F.	3192	92	97	114	112	99	514	447	369	259	241	228
PORTLAND	Urban	10061	M.	6515	110	103	91	98	94	496	437	469	701	1016	855
			F.	3546	117	93	108	83	103	504	451	466	323	258	256
RADSTOCK	Urban	3074	M.	1626	45	62	43	54	55	259	245	188	172	133	84
			F.	1448	57	43	50	43	48	250	215	187	95	81	98
REDRUTH	Urban	9335	M.	3998	97	98	96	118	121	530	511	527	527	340	240
			F.	5337	117	107	114	101	103	542	490	513	509	511	422
REDRUTH	Rural	18938	M.	8410	254	179	224	210	212	1079	1152	1068	1160	710	503
			F.	10528	210	206	238	210	227	1091	1077	1004	1076	886	740
ST. AUSTELL	Urban	3582	M.	1543	38	84	33	38	25	168	186	190	183	103	87
			F.	2039	33	45	30	35	30	173	221	189	240	180	161
ST. AUSTELL	Rural	26604	M.	12818	343	317	379	353	347	1730	1715	1564	1571	1003	720
			F.	13786	359	319	355	371	330	1734	1635	1523	1209	1040	992
ST. COLUMB	Rural	12994	M.	6257	161	133	154	131	151	729	795	766	733	534	386
			F.	6737	176	154	165	146	165	806	793	725	598	558	458
ST. GERMANS	Rural	16730	M.	7775	198	190	199	204	185	976	916	1016	794	576	421
			F.	8955	205	199	176	217	192	989	1025	947	821	728	665
ST. IVES	Urban	6445	M.	2932	100	83	75	74	86	418	410	334	294	217	208
			F.	3518	73	70	86	70	63	362	371	329	364	291	250
ST. MARY CHURCH	Urban	5759	M.	2439	78	79	81	75	65	378	296	259	246	187	182
			F.	3320	66	63	76	61	70	341	392	361	300	324	261
ST. THOMAS THE APOSTLE	Urban	6161	M.	2939	92	78	88	76	92	426	353	309	269	244	225
			F.	3222	93	94	71	85	77	420	356	347	280	276	256
ST. THOMAS	Rural	33927	M.	16131	426	413	443	431	419	2137	2039	1877	1584	1200	1000
			F.	17796	459	422	382	459	433	2155	1975	1799	1494	1357	1286
SALCOMBE	Urban	1826	M.	744	25	18	27	17	29	116	134	114	41	32	39
			F.	1082	29	26	25	34	17	131	127	115	97	78	59
SALISBURY	Urban	14792	M.	6647	210	187	171	161	180	909	771	729	732	625	532
			F.	8145	178	190	163	187	168	886	839	880	969	839	634
SCILLY ISLANDS	Rural	2320	M.	1213	27	29	22	28	26	132	115	110	112	115	89
			F.	1107	19	25	18	30	35	127	115	97	98	72	80
SEATON	Urban	1221	M.	477	15	11	10	7	9	52	58	52	59	30	23
			F.	744	7	8	14	16	13	58	64	89	78	92	48
SHAFTESBURY	Urban	2312	M.	1051	27	24	27	47	36	161	121	117	133	62	58
			F.	1261	27	28	33	29	32	149	149	143	151	114	77
SHAFTESBURY	Rural	10350	M.	4982	128	120	146	134	136	664	633	603	407	361	285
			F.	5368	140	125	142	137	144	688	626	602	511	371	356
SHEPTON MALLET	Urban	5822	M.	2465	56	65	67	59	59	306	311	261	233	219	168
			F.	2857	79	60	61	65	61	326	345	320	291	252	184
SHEPTON MALLET	Rural	10457	M.	5154	138	132	115	117	148	650	681	594	561	386	313
			F.	5303	115	150	127	150	151	693	646	603	427	380	341
SHERBORNE	Urban	5053	M.	2415	52	56	60	52	61	281	267	388	361	163	114
			F.	2638	63	48	59	56	54	280	260	254	299	255	186

* Plymouth Lighthouses and Drake's Island appear to be neither included in a Rural n

Table 6 *continued*.—Ages of Males and Females in Sani

Sanitary District.		All Ages. Persons.	All Ages. Males and Females.		Under 1 Year.	1–	2–	3–	4–	Under 5 Years.	5–	10–	15–	20–	25–	30–
SHERBORNE	Rural	7642	M.	3665	93	87	85	86	104	455	475	450	386	269	213	[illegible]
			F.	3977	121	96	96	102	93	508	462	464	341	298	260	[illegible]
SIDMOUTH	Urban	3475	M.	1500	34	35	33	37	33	172	195	175	131	123	100	[illegible]
			F.	1975	36	34	37	40	47	194	158	168	204	178	141	[illegible]
SOUTH MOLTON	Urban	3340	M.	1518	37	42	41	42	33	195	199	165	141	96	93	[illegible]
			F.	1822	38	44	30	42	43	197	207	179	103	144	127	[illegible]
SOUTH MOLTON	Rural	13478	M.	6957	162	143	186	183	177	854	879	863	826	574	397	[illegible]
			F.	6521	167	162	172	179	164	844	805	711	613	464	474	[illegible]
STRATTON	Rural	7439	M.	3629	97	110	100	95	103	505	489	387	369	278	224	[illegible]
			F.	3810	90	110	73	97	75	445	446	433	374	326	241	[illegible]
STREET	Urban	2514	M.	1242	31	32	31	34	38	166	159	148	151	110	82	[illegible]
			F.	1272	30	33	37	35	36	180	150	129	130	119	99	[illegible]
STURMINSTER	Rural	10050	M.	4713	123	109	145	116	112	605	620	557	462	321	284	[illegible]
			F.	5337	125	140	136	133	138	672	607	611	485	436	377	[illegible]
SWANAGE	Urban	2357	M.	1144	30	39	32	28	23	154	108	190	114	111	88	[illegible]
			F.	1213	35	29	30	36	31	161	137	135	113	82	80	[illegible]
SWINDON NEW TOWN	Urban	17678	M.	9411	340	310	304	280	257	1491	1186	918	928	1074	983	[illegible]
			F.	8267	343	351	310	285	303	1592	1177	869	641	659	742	[illegible]
TAUNTON	Urban	16614	M.	7340	207	138	200	178	182	905	862	872	766	648	559	[illegible]
			F.	9274	211	195	186	201	189	982	895	962	1107	924	663	[illegible]
TAUNTON	Rural	19368	M.	9540	204	225	240	231	232	1132	1129	1296	1155	648	542	[illegible]
			F.	9828	232	223	237	225	258	1175	1146	1062	932	750	616	[illegible]
TAVISTOCK	Rural	29190	M.	14712	367	337	346	363	333	1746	1758	1684	1622	1217	990	[illegible]
			F.	14478	359	331	323	350	341	1704	1689	1640	1456	1212	1014	[illegible]
TEIGNMOUTH	Urban	7120	M.	2983	96	76	82	85	74	413	333	361	397	247	194	[illegible]
			F.	4137	87	72	74	78	76	387	400	330	435	448	341	[illegible]
TISBURY	Rural	9306	M.	4734	115	113	127	116	111	582	632	604	465	347	269	[illegible]
			F.	4572	125	103	119	134	111	592	591	547	345	332	267	[illegible]
TIVERTON	Urban	10462	M.	4872	143	141	121	107	106	618	609	536	532	425	281	[illegible]
			F.	5590	132	105	118	124	106	585	585	569	638	484	405	[illegible]
TIVERTON	Rural	16961	M.	8326	220	193	232	207	213	1065	1086	1014	838	554	526	[illegible]
			F.	8635	231	210	253	213	226	1133	1009	997	740	680	560	[illegible]
TORQUAY	Urban	24767	M.	10130	315	248	269	232	254	1318	1204	1119	980	832	752	[illegible]
			F.	14637	278	239	297	257	274	1345	1278	1197	1625	1665	1320	[illegible]
TORRINGTON	Rural	11375	M.	5633	139	121	150	134	148	692	674	739	689	434	340	[illegible]
			F.	5742	151	135	142	145	138	711	672	648	554	483	361	[illegible]
TOTNES	Urban	4089	M.	1857	44	48	35	39	58	224	219	242	196	127	89	[illegible]
			F.	2232	55	38	37	36	48	214	206	241	226	212	144	[illegible]
TOTNES	Rural	16730	M.	8115	222	223	197	222	222	1086	1074	957	831	586	483	[illegible]
			F.	8615	225	212	212	220	207	1085	1047	853	784	796	592	[illegible]
TROWBRIDGE	Urban	11040	M.	5057	154	137	143	153	138	725	677	618	504	337	337	[illegible]
			F.	5983	146	133	164	133	140	706	671	638	643	502	459	[illegible]
TRURO	Urban	10619	M.	4579	132	123	123	105	111	594	537	555	519	383	310	[illegible]
			F.	6040	112	101	122	85	121	541	534	564	662	619	518	[illegible]
TRURO	Rural	25363	M.	11720	299	241	249	270	279	1347	1409	1557	1603	864	896	[illegible]
			F.	13643	279	266	278	254	291	1368	1451	1442	1321	1121	950	[illegible]
WAREHAM	Urban	2112	M.	1035	31	33	18	17	31	130	127	116	94	80	87	[illegible]
			F.	1077	35	23	25	27	32	142	127	106	91	83	69	[illegible]
WAREHAM	Rural	12477	M.	6244	159	146	187	170	160	821	782	731	648	470	372	[illegible]
			F.	6233	168	168	168	156	165	825	790	694	524	468	391	[illegible]
WARMINSTER	Urban	5640	M.	2697	56	68	58	65	61	308	321	415	322	183	149	[illegible]
			F.	2943	64	65	55	70	65	319	327	331	314	232	186	[illegible]

Z 4

Table 6 *continued*.—Ages of Males and Females in San

Sanitary District.		All Ages. Persons.	All Ages. Males and Females.		Under 1 Year.	1–	2–	3–	4–	Under 5 Years.	5–	10–	15–	20–	25–
WARMINSTER	Rural	8200	M.	4086	102	96	99	117	111	526	488	452	462	203	230
			F.	4114	117	86	108	98	95	504	490	428	329	282	265
WELLINGTON	Urban	6300	M.	2030	97	81	75	58	71	382	373	358	208	230	197
			F.	3430	75	81	92	79	93	420	362	338	341	322	254
WELLINGTON	Rural	11210	M.	5604	142	158	154	142	153	740	723	693	549	417	297
			F.	5606	146	133	175	115	133	702	707	644	478	401	359
WELLS	Urban	4634	M.	2169	64	57	64	57	68	308	247	232	211	187	160
			F.	2465	71	57	50	67	55	290	241	221	236	230	192
WELLS	Rural	11146	M.	5411	127	129	188	147	141	682	610	592	541	380	310
			F.	5735	145	130	128	120	132	664	686	610	476	430	[illegible]
WESTBURY	Rural	10650	M.	5158	115	143	143	152	141	604	653	633	602	328	[illegible]
			F.	5492	147	129	127	138	154	696	689	616	444	380	[illegible]
WESTON-SUPER-MARE	Urban	12884	M.	5177	129	133	134	140	116	652	661	731	540	301	381
			F.	7707	137	141	134	136	142	690	687	718	990	906	[illegible]
WEYMOUTH AND MELCOMBE REGIS	Urban	13715	M.	6004	142	163	168	141	150	754	671	690	611	505	[illegible]
			F.	7711	151	138	145	160	154	738	697	704	907	815	630
WEYMOUTH	Rural	8246	M.	4046	124	104	111	116	98	553	532	500	415	290	[illegible]
			F.	4200	102	101	94	85	114	496	481	462	363	324	[illegible]
WILLITON	Rural	18685	M.	9204	267	237	229	238	250	1211	1195	1161	1025	640	497
			F.	9481	226	233	241	243	250	1192	1179	1101	844	653	589
WILTON	Urban	1326	M.	843	32	25	21	25	22	125	108	102	71	68	64
			F.	983	28	26	23	29	23	129	99	107	88	87	80
WILTON	Rural	8424	M.	4210	101	104	100	100	117	528	508	535	467	286	207
			F.	4214	111	97	97	101	113	519	566	488	354	281	241
WIMBORNE	Rural	16991	M.	8473	246	215	216	252	227	1156	1067	983	857	631	551
			F.	8518	215	212	219	215	186	1047	1080	904	748	608	631
WINCANTON	Rural	19770	M.	9461	235	262	262	260	248	1266	1232	1119	913	681	565
			F.	10306	224	257	263	235	249	1228	1210	1178	936	860	711
WIVELISCOMBE	Urban	1624	M.	763	15	26	16	23	21	101	102	99	92	48	37
			F.	861	19	20	9	14	16	78	108	129	90	64	38
WOLBOROUGH	Urban	7662	M.	3513	113	95	93	104	97	502	427	447	339	276	255
			F.	4149	108	86	99	102	104	491	449	409	400	399	350
YEOVIL	Urban	8479	M.	3831	112	111	102	111	97	533	511	451	387	308	[illegible]
			F.	4648	121	100	88	127	123	559	515	538	486	413	[illegible]
YEOVIL	Rural	19227	M.	9009	246	232	289	239	246	1262	1222	1176	989	604	459
			F.	10218	238	216	232	238	283	1207	1227	1179	932	767	679

Table 13.—NUMBER and COUNTRY of BIRTH of FOREIGNERS enumerated in COUNTIES, and in each exceeds 50,000 PERSONS.

WHERE BORN.	WHERE ENUMERATED								
	SOUTH-WESTERN COUNTIES.		COUNTIES.						
			WILTSHIRE.		DORSETSHIRE.		DEVONSHIRE.		CC
	Males	Females.	Males.	Females.	Males.	Females.	Males.	Females.	Ma
TOTAL	2322	1204	78	119	157	77	768	392	9'
EUROPE.									
DENMARK	97	5	.	.	5	.	28	1	
NORWAY	153	6	.	.	10	1	50	1	
SWEDEN	104	3	.	.	8	1	36	.	
RUSSIA	76	5	1	.	20	.	26	2	
POLAND (RUSSIAN)	12	5	1	.	1	.	8	4	
AUSTRIA	52	6	.	1	2	.	15	3	
HUNGARY	6	1	.	.	1	.	4	.	
SWITZERLAND	27	78	1	7	4	8	10	37	
GERMAN EMPIRE	478	209	19	27	49	18	154	77	1
HOLLAND	57	9	.	.	.	1	23	3	
BELGIUM	28	20	.	2	1	.	4	5	
FRANCE	405	184	9	18	22	25	141	75	[illegible]
PORTUGAL	7	2	.	.	.	1	3	1	
SPAIN	.	3	.	.	.	1	.	2	
ITALY	182	32	7	.	8	.	69	7	
GREECE	42	1	.	.	3	.	8	.	
TURKEY	8	.	.	.	.	.	1	.	
SERVIA	.	.	.	.	.	.	.	.	
ROUMANIA	.	.	.	.	.	.	.		
ASIA.									
ARABIA	.	.	.	.	.	.	.	.	
PERSIA	.	.	.	.	.	.	.	.	
CHINA	3	.	.	.	.	.	.	.	
OTHER COUNTRIES	1	.	1	.	.	.	.	.	
AFRICA.									
EGYPT	.	.	.	.	.	.	.	.	
OTHER PARTS	2	.	.	.	.	.	2	.	
AMERICA.									
UNITED STATES	575	632	38	64	23	21	179	171	2
MEXICO	1	.	.	.	.	.	.	.	
BRAZIL	1	1	.	.	.	.	.	.	
OTHER STATES	5	2	.	.	.	.	1	.	
COUNTRY NOT STATED	.	.	.	.	.	.	.	.	
AT SEA	1	.	1	.	.	.	.	.	

Table 6.—Ages of Males and Females in Sanitary I

Sanitary District.		All Ages. Persons.	All Ages. Males and Females.		Under 1 Year.	1–	2–	3–	4–	Under 5 Years.	5–	10–	15–	20–	25–
ALCESTER	Rural	17393	M.	8659	269	227	253	255	247	1251	1144	964	802	616	520
			F.	8734	225	198	261	241	217	1135	1112	1001	779	629	602
ASTON	Rural	17962	M.	8479	221	230	220	227	231	1129	1065	1076	770	663	643
			F.	9483	191	211	220	219	229	1070	1094	1958	1030	928	751
ASTON MANOR	Urban	53842	M.	25896	887	814	886	801	808	4196	3463	2980	2538	2253	2134
			F.	27946	838	858	883	839	817	4235	3622	2934	2883	2501	2392
ATCHAM	Rural	22155	M.	11128	265	260	276	276	279	1346	1332	1265	1104	785	682
			F.	11027	263	226	314	272	276	1351	1330	1241	959	783	711
ATHERSTONE	Rural	14419	M.	7338	211	218	210	220	211	1970	1009	840	776	595	574
			F.	7081	228	218	196	203	202	1047	902	784	658	557	539
AUDLEY	Urban	11215	M.	5945	209	186	184	181	194	954	840	708	595	530	440
			F.	5270	175	160	172	204	170	890	882	612	335	383	365
AWRE	Urban	1179	M.	557	20	16	17	15	14	82	58	62	47	32	38
			F.	622	18	10	19	18	12	77	63	54	63	54	62
BALSALL HEATH	Urban	22497	M.	10708	350	332	350	332	310	1704	1429	1231	1093	879	909
			F.	11789	368	326	354	365	347	1760	1409	1259	1216	1009	980
BARTON REGIS	Rural	13155	M.	6359	176	145	169	185	182	857	810	670	828	575	446
			F.	6786	204	178	185	166	159	892	786	673	667	628	572
BEWDLEY	Urban	3088	M.	1459	33	37	33	37	42	182	202	176	122	117	84
			F.	1633	56	39	46	50	44	235	178	192	154	130	120
BILSTON	Urban	22730	M.	11418	361	209	345	315	341	1661	1483	1309	1197	1059	848
			F.	11312	346	299	313	314	305	1577	1581	1306	1174	925	839
BIRMINGHAM	Urban	400774	M.	194540	6233	5682	5875	5572	5549	28911	24635	21067	19863	17608	16316
			F.	206234	6261	5720	5902	5673	5577	29133	24670	21563	20739	20348	17571
BISLEY	Urban	5169	M.	2404	69	66	71	58	83	347	289	283	259	195	148
			F.	2765	73	50	73	59	71	326	317	291	272	238	204
BRIDGNORTH	Urban	5885	M.	2734	65	46	68	69	64	312	359	326	258	215	164
			F.	3151	67	58	59	73	73	330	370	387	333	245	197
BRIDGNORTH	Rural	9394	M.	4739	120	109	129	102	139	599	632	508	459	367	285
			F.	4655	130	113	125	143	104	615	592	524	393	342	283
BRIERLEY HILL	Urban	11603	M.	5842	187	158	154	184	167	850	820	684	634	522	441
			F.	5761	192	177	151	164	183	867	789	639	570	496	448
BRISTOL* (*part of*)	Urban	168743	M.	75280	2237	2063	2081	2053	1992	10426	9428	9224	7791	6320	5904
			F.	93463	2312	2181	2124	2119	2157	10893	9614	9480	19183	9614	7863
BROMSGROVE	Rural	11177	M.	5552	163	148	137	165	162	775	76	681	565	[illegible]	351
			F.	5625	148	142	147	141	123	701	94	605	491	461	429
BROMSGROVE COUNTRY	Urban	4853	M.	2455	73	61	78	54	96	362	325	252	231	190	160
			F.	2398	91	67	75	81	75	389	321	261	200	178	188
BROMSGROVE TOWN	Urban	7960	M.	3997	116	117	117	122	89	561	487	517	433	288	252
			F.	3963	108	112	114	103	115	552	508	456	361	327	291
BROMYARD	Rural	11055	M.	5584	120	116	125	129	138	628	665	646	557	447	366
			F.	5471	134	138	150	131	154	707	712	617	432	423	325
BROSELEY	Urban	4458	M.	2242	76	77	65	50	70	338	324	260	238	171	150
			F.	2216	58	55	68	49	62	292	307	279	174	142	135
BROWNHILLS	Urban	11059	M.	5890	183	176	164	189	172	884	808	642	641	509	419
			F.	5169	178	155	207	200	186	926	837	646	371	357	355
BULKINGTON	Urban	1590	M.	812	20	13	16	18	15	82	117	119	77	51	51
			F.	778	16	18	15	22	21	92	100	74	59	64	47

* The remainder of the Urban Sanitary District of Bristol is in Division V. (see Table 6).

Entire Urban Sanitary District of Bristol		206874	M.	93711	2928	2673	2710	2602	2587	13500	11973	11182	9672	7880	7464
			F.	113163	2983	2778	2733	2686	2743	13923	12210	11633	11846	11274	9455

Ff 2

Table 6 *continued.*—Ages of Males and Females in Sa

Sanitary District.		All Ages. Persons.	All Ages. Males and Females.		Under 1 Year.	1–	2–	3–	4–	Under 5 Years.	5–	10–	15–	20–	25–
BURSLEM	Urban	26522	M.	13027	446	330	381	396	347	1809	1767	1676	1819	1142	1002
			F.	13495	435	391	446	401	373	2046	1754	1530	1389	1281	1044
BURTON ON TRENT	Urban	39238	M.	20676	691	646	617	597	568	3119	2557	2108	1951	2249	2116
			F.	18562	683	664	660	613	596	3216	2514	2100	1565	1537	1586
BURTON ON TRENT	Rural	31608	M.	16070	545	461	493	481	505	2488	2120	1880	1779	1328	1110
			F.	15532	486	504	488	504	482	2464	2160	1703	1326	1206	1131
CANNOCK	Urban	17125	M.	9149	323	283	339	274	333	1552	1277	1001	860	808	747
			F.	7976	312	297	300	319	276	1504	1261	974	577	567	613
CANNOCK	Rural	15451	M.	7859	231	194	224	220	213	1082	1017	908	740	647	535
			F.	7592	208	199	209	200	219	1035	996	831	657	552	513
CHARLTON KINGS	Urban	3950	M.	1783	58	41	40	60	41	249	226	189	178	115	113
			F.	2167	66	50	54	41	52	263	237	220	192	202	181
CHEADLE	Rural	21305	M.	10687	302	300	299	278	295	1474	1447	1389	1088	792	624
			F.	10618	294	307	296	293	306	1496	1428	1230	982	802	710
CHELTENHAM	Urban	43972	M.	18224	429	436	465	491	441	2262	2146	2355	2121	1372	1200
			F.	25748	472	424	468	475	402	2241	2192	2348	3046	2884	2062
CHELTENHAM	Rural	4082	M.	1884	41	39	47	39	48	208	208	206	190	141	100
			F.	2198	58	48	40	49	44	239	216	217	209	185	156
CHILVERS COTON	Urban	3005	M.	1440	47	43	32	42	45	209	194	182	124	111	101
			F.	1565	40	43	47	44	34	217	182	171	112	123	110
CHIPPING SODBURY	Rural	17523	M.	8816	225	196	200	230	211	1068	1110	1161	913	620	534
			F.	8707	248	198	248	233	220	1147	1097	949	610	603	560
CHURCH STRETTON	Rural	5672	M.	2913	65	60	71	63	82	341	319	356	297	209	160
			F.	2759	67	52	72	63	66	320	342	306	280	197	156
CIRENCESTER	Urban	7658	M.	3776	90	98	91	80	83	451	422	389	485	386	244
			F.	3882	100	80	91	104	77	452	408	419	424	353	270
CIRENCESTER	Rural	13652	M.	6845	164	139	171	103	189	826	874	783	764	519	417
			F.	6807	179	165	162	167	158	831	878	759	567	479	427
CLAINES	Urban	3814	M.	1788	61	45	50	46	51	253	231	202	190	126	132
			F.	2026	72	58	69	63	73	335	236	221	177	150	150
CLEOBURY MORTIMER	Rural	8138	M.	4208	97	102	116	110	105	530	501	476	431	310	264
			F.	3930	89	104	114	100	117	524	526	411	306	265	240
CLUN	Rural	10167	M.	5249	139	101	154	117	146	657	632	589	584	420	316
			F.	4918	128	107	132	138	133	638	640	555	449	365	341
COSELEY	Urban	21700	M.	11025	342	323	342	335	353	1695	1516	1232	1214	1005	898
			F.	10675	319	325	346	296	324	1610	1528	1281	966	821	765
COVENTRY	Urban	42111	M.	19961	678	510	546	543	545	2722	2449	2012	2011	1817	1548
			F.	22150	603	549	540	571	567	2830	2514	2242	2205	2144	1724
COVENTRY	Rural	3005	M.	1415	39	31	51	44	45	210	208	163	124	123	99
			F.	1590	55	35	46	27	45	208	200	182	155	148	131
DARLASTON	Urban	13563	M.	6769	234	166	210	192	227	1029	931	783	724	596	452
			F.	6794	251	189	193	200	183	1016	973	788	668	581	481
DAWLEY	Urban	9200	M.	4764	129	107	125	133	143	637	667	625	563	394	296
			F.	4436	134	104	132	137	153	660	676	536	341	262	241
DORE	Rural	8568	M.	4521	104	83	114	95	125	528	568	482	416	362	271
			F.	4047	90	88	102	103	105	488	485	506	335	293	253
DRESDEN	Urban	3094	M.	1483	54	34	52	32	52	224	217	177	164	148	100
			F.	1611	42	58	49	43	34	226	214	183	175	155	137
DROITWICH	Urban	3761	M.	1857	57	49	54	59	55	274	253	212	159	156	104
			F.	1904	55	48	49	56	58	266	237	198	159	170	129
DROITWICH	Rural	13737	M.	6828	189	178	201	183	183	934	886	793	699	485	438
			F.	6909	190	183	176	195	199	943	870	771	634	486	476
DUDLEY	Urban	46252	M.	22622	755	701	692	691	699	3538	3084	2585	2389	1928	1715
			F.	23630	765	711	742	736	715	3369	3195	2639	2260	2106	1674

Table 6 *continued*.—AGES of MALES and FEMALES in SANI[TARY DISTRICTS]

SANITARY DISTRICT.		ALL AGES. Persons.		ALL AGES. Males and Females.	Under 1 Year.	1–	2–	3–	4–	Under 5 Years.	5–	10–	15–	20–	25–	30–
DURSLEY	Rural	12550	M.	5910	153	142	143	138	146	722	762	760	566	399	320	30
			F.	6640	181	155	154	163	161	814	752	710	593	512	420	39
EAST VALE	Urban	1419	M.	689	25	21	28	22	14	110	92	89	70	66	54	4
			F.	730	27	28	17	25	18	115	115	70	62	74	55	4
ELLESMERE	Urban	1875	M.	854	19	15	26	17	25	102	103	92	79	75	60	4
			F.	1021	13	22	20	19	21	95	96	139	132	83	59	8
ELLESMERE	Rural	11833	M.	5897	147	143	162	164	136	752	667	618	634	465	377	29
			F.	5936	148	128	130	149	131	686	677	684	570	480	387	30
EVESHAM	Urban	5112	M.	2512	85	66	69	73	72	365	337	291	255	198	176	15
			F.	2600	76	67	69	68	71	341	259	295	243	270	213	18
EVESHAM	Rural	10158	M.	5129	113	125	125	146	125	634	663	662	407	354	269	27
			F.	5029	127	131	135	137	143	673	666	621	384	319	303	26
FENTON	Urban	13830	M.	6883	253	203	231	206	225	1118	945	793	652	600	576	46
			F.	6947	262	247	196	213	215	1132	964	838	643	634	564	41
FOLESHILL	Rural	18497	M.	8983	207	240	267	252	273	1329	1191	1033	888	669	602	49
			F.	9514	285	239	248	259	284	1315	1212	1011	808	791	665	50
GLOUCESTER	Urban	36521	M.	17608	507	478	522	484	424	2415	2172	1927	1864	1594	1379	117
			F.	18913	567	502	525	464	489	2547	2140	2023	1909	1774	1546	127
GLOUCESTER	Rural	10339	M.	5051	116	113	127	118	130	604	573	624	497	370	313	31
			F.	5288	122	106	110	118	114	570	613	545	440	465	372	33
GREAT MALVERN	Urban	5846	M.	2335	39	37	47	36	33	192	228	380	404	150	145	12
			F.	3511	44	46	39	47	51	227	236	297	481	501	320	26
HANDSWORTH	Urban	22896	M.	10211	321	289	288	281	286	1465	1250	1086	1088	946	816	71
			F.	12685	312	270	295	308	290	1484	1236	1268	1610	1485	1115	92
HANLEY	Urban	48361	M.	24139	845	696	724	708	661	3632	3104	2664	2520	2140	2080	165
			F.	24222	784	709	710	717	742	3662	3133	2716	2492	2256	1963	167
HARBORNE	Urban	6433	M.	2937	82	75	84	89	85	415	359	340	293	254	201	19
			F.	3496	104	87	75	73	85	424	398	377	396	343	259	24
HEREFORD	Urban	19821	M.	9349	276	204	240	217	228	1165	1068	1147	1065	774	685	57
			F.	10472	256	261	257	240	236	1253	1109	1082	1123	1018	832	60
HEREFORD	Rural	14705	M.	7197	186	170	197	182	194	929	890	863	705	478	420	38
			F.	7508	171	158	160	190	173	852	897	875	640	518	482	40
HORFIELD	Urban	4451	M.	2059	74	76	64	69	58	340	317	210	167	145	158	16
			F.	2392	59	64	71	75	75	344	305	216	230	183	196	19
KENILWORTH	Urban	4150	M.	1906	55	49	52	41	64	261	200	213	175	156	133	10
			F.	2244	47	52	55	55	43	252	248	214	212	200	149	14
KIDDERMINSTER	Urban	24270	M.	11527	388	317	325	342	359	1731	1421	1268	1146	996	949	74
			F.	12743	370	318	348	300	347	1683	1488	1282	1428	1370	1058	81
KIDDERMINSTER	Rural	10226	M.	4937	130	142	131	130	141	683	630	565	517	383	321	28
			F.	5289	137	126	155	130	111	659	632	581	513	411	367	33
KIDSGROVE	Urban	3994	M.	2125	49	53	51	60	50	263	282	216	245	208	189	14
			F.	1869	62	46	57	58	49	272	289	234	165	126	140	11
KINGS NORTON	Rural	19367	M.	9160	261	242	270	256	263	1292	1141	1014	939	773	713	55
			F.	10207	285	225	245	283	247	1285	1123	1061	1064	1164	890	63
KINGTON	Urban	2075	M.	1001	22	25	31	20	20	118	124	106	107	82	60	6
			F.	1074	22	20	24	24	29	119	106	115	110	70	84	7
KINGTON	Rural	10122	M.	5146	122	128	134	131	138	653	603	617	541	330	332	29
			F.	4976	140	100	145	123	118	626	630	594	448	381	308	30
LEAMINGTON	Urban	22979	M.	9498	293	240	233	219	257	1242	1087	1019	1021	789	670	58
			F.	13481	263	263	240	237	228	1240	1187	1160	1630	1461	1094	91
LECKHAMPTON	Urban	3501	M.	1458	36	31	32	36	24	158	198	188	156	109	87	9
			F.	2043	26	35	37	47	41	186	203	196	204	210	150	13

Ff3

Table 6 *continued.*—AGES of MALES and FEMALES in SA

SANITARY DISTRICT.		ALL AGES. Persons.	Males and Females.		Under 1 Year.	1–	2–	3–	4–	Under 5 Years.	5–	10–	15–	20–	25–
LEDBURY	Rural	12605	M.	6257	148	110	158	147	144	707	755	756	639	459	391
			F.	6348	143	156	163	142	142	746	744	672	526	459	429
LEEK	Urban	12863	M.	5888	168	148	162	168	175	821	780	692	560	487	386
			F.	6975	208	157	162	153	164	844	814	666	746	742	541
LEEK	Rural	13760	M.	6970	192	186	210	205	192	985	959	832	672	526	448
			F.	6790	205	187	223	206	197	1018	962	828	580	505	467
LEOMINSTER	Urban	6044	M.	2887	83	63	69	78	73	366	363	349	277	234	183
			F.	3157	67	70	81	76	70	364	364	362	349	262	198
LEOMINSTER	Rural	8604	M.	4408	107	98	107	106	119	537	555	539	428	304	214
			F.	4196	90	78	107	96	119	490	525	499	360	266	242
LICHFIELD	Urban	8349	M.	3929	94	126	92	126	111	549	490	433	339	306	277
			F.	4420	115	103	97	114	94	523	537	470	457	353	328
LICHFIELD	Rural	22372	M.	11714	304	304	305	309	317	1539	1459	1198	1324	1136	843
			F.	10658	331	292	349	308	314	1594	1470	1206	843	795	727
LILLINGTON	Urban	938	M.	283	7	6	3	3	3	22	24	25	33	18	24
			F.	655	4	3	2	5	7	21	31	37	72	111	96
LONGTON	Urban	18620	M.	9164	325	242	287	250	272	1376	1221	1138	895	761	772
			F.	9466	314	209	298	278	264	1453	1250	1162	967	858	716
LUDLOW	Urban	5035	M.	2368	51	72	46	55	70	294	306	270	243	187	146
			F.	2667	66	60	61	71	57	315	273	308	271	232	172
LUDLOW	Rural	13554	M.	6950	210	156	180	165	186	897	839	772	685	577	456
			F.	6604	179	150	189	195	174	887	861	753	540	483	444
MADELEY	Urban	9212	M.	4609	132	118	116	114	118	598	554	543	470	353	280
			F.	4603	111	106	127	118	124	586	555	529	376	312	285
MADELEY	Rural	2123	M.	1061	33	21	25	29	23	131	112	105	120	89	80
			F.	1062	24	21	28	24	29	126	127	122	88	75	63
MALVERN LINK	Urban	1800	M.	755	20	16	22	19	22	99	98	97	76	60	58
			F.	1045	25	14	21	16	18	94	85	119	129	120	75
MARKET DRAYTON	Rural	14849	M.	7370	175	173	203	173	214	938	950	871	772	560	442
			F.	7479	173	183	185	175	197	913	904	825	670	592	520
MARTLEY	Rural	14592	M.	7331	189	168	194	206	186	943	996	888	719	402	413
			F.	7261	186	144	181	192	173	876	917	788	591	519	448
MERIDEN	Rural	11025	M.	5555	133	136	132	146	132	679	663	826	536	400	341
			F.	5470	134	113	120	125	132	624	708	623	436	396	391
MITTON, LOWER	Urban	3358	M.	1648	65	58	45	43	53	264	200	190	168	149	119
			F.	1710	47	49	49	52	50	247	215	172	167	165	103
MILVERTON	Urban	2162	M.	747	27	19	15	21	14	96	64	77	69	44	63
			F.	1415	22	18	15	16	23	94	78	104	178	176	151
MUCH WENLOCK	Urban	2321	M.	1172	31	29	28	29	38	155	133	141	111	82	77
			F.	1149	26	31	22	19	31	129	140	139	104	90	65
NEWCASTLE UNDER LYME	Urban	17508	M.	8749	247	226	241	249	271	1234	1122	1039	857	731	634
			F.	8759	240	241	248	244	233	1206	1118	1048	914	760	649
NEWCASTLE UNDER LYME	Rural	663	M.	2876	99	67	72	64	86	388	370	321	291	254	223
			F.	2787	73	78	78	90	71	390	361	302	249	242	220
NEWENT	Rural	11030	M.	5496	133	125	137	134	151	680	678	683	535	370	303
			F.	5534	145	134	136	134	147	696	714	646	417	368	367
NEWNHAM	Urban	1455	M.	697	18	21	13	20	20	92	107	67	77	48	37
			F.	758	21	15	25	25	17	103	92	100	71	58	50
NEWPORT	Urban	3044	M.	1506	39	40	38	29	31	177	157	186	192	130	86
			F.	1538	33	33	32	28	42	168	169	194	175	119	98
NEWPORT	Rural	12308	M.	6201	167	138	159	182	169	815	792	725	634	508	390
			F.	6107	152	146	193	163	173	837	751	691	523	434	372

Sanitary District.		All Ages. Persons.	All Ages. Males and Females.		Under 1 Year.	1–	2–	3–	4–	Under 5 Years.	5–	10–	15–	20–	25–	30–
NORTHLEACH	Rural	9884	M.	5131	121	123	120	142	131	646	636	650	540	364	288	279
			F.	4753	105	117	104	129	134	589	607	540	393	261	280	276
NUNEATON	Urban	8465	M.	4041	125	100	118	117	128	597	500	454	410	337	324	246
			F.	4424	147	107	121	132	124	631	558	435	414	390	351	275
NUNEATON	Rural	641	M.	310	8	5	7	6	4	30	46	27	31	19	17	13
			F.	331	11	6	8	11	10	46	38	30	34	18	21	16
OLDBURY	Urban	18841	M.	9619	340	292	290	298	279	1503	1302	1145	981	850	744	625
			F.	9322	359	296	356	307	295	1613	1360	1101	816	777	688	624
OSWESTRY	Urban	7847	M.	3811	97	89	81	76	101	444	455	471	437	313	289	283
			F.	4036	96	102	92	110	81	481	453	465	455	352	267	244
OSWESTRY	Rural	19226	M.	9686	271	259	255	236	284	1305	1247	1061	985	741	635	537
			F.	9640	249	251	261	258	253	1272	1239	1120	827	684	648	561
PERSHORE	Rural	13560	M.	6740	177	177	169	138	174	835	854	724	707	603	397	347
			F.	6820	183	158	172	166	174	853	830	824	534	484	429	420
QUARRY BANK	Urban	6238	M.	3188	115	86	113	98	99	511	415	377	353	313	231	181
			F.	3050	108	88	97	89	112	494	421	377	268	261	208	195
REDDITCH	Urban	9961	M.	4603	163	143	147	129	132	714	574	505	460	417	346	310
			F.	5358	169	135	145	130	131	700	625	576	587	558	400	371
ROSS	Urban	3724	M.	1815	36	53	44	42	49	224	227	202	208	149	125	102
			F.	1909	52	46	44	35	37	214	239	200	208	134	144	109
ROSS	Rural	12645	M.	6304	175	153	153	165	162	808	815	759	584	460	358	344
			F.	6341	154	134	161	178	167	794	801	749	531	480	384	360
ROWLEY REGIS	Urban	27385	M.	13831	515	443	418	466	439	2271	2044	1640	1426	1206	978	830
			F.	13554	502	446	478	425	429	2280	1922	1577	1296	1164	988	900
RUGBY	Urban	9891	M.	5000	136	111	116	117	102	581	460	611	771	488	442	325
			F.	4891	118	114	116	127	128	603	539	468	511	494	461	337
RUGBY	Rural	17309	M.	8685	222	214	245	202	210	1093	1030	1035	857	683	574	490
			F.	8624	231	237	232	218	234	1152	1053	939	668	627	588	507
RUGELEY	Urban	4249	M.	2196	64	68	62	57	76	327	269	232	204	208	188	137
			F.	2053	54	71	63	54	71	313	251	224	179	166	163	130
ST. GEORGE	Urban	26433	M.	12917	485	447	418	453	429	2232	1915	1601	1293	991	967	825
			F.	13516	484	441	483	443	437	2288	1962	1549	1230	1093	991	851
SALTLEY	Urban	6422	M.	3348	119	91	116	90	84	500	406	375	417	340	253	234
			F.	3074	92	112	90	107	86	487	452	364	292	243	221	234
SEISDON	Rural	17712	M.	8604	202	207	226	224	232	1091	1059	975	923	690	615	502
			F.	9108	249	198	222	207	240	1116	1061	946	860	795	739	630
SHIFNAL	Rural	12821	M.	6382	161	164	155	161	182	823	818	775	702	463	402	338
			F.	6439	154	152	166	148	164	784	839	811	623	443	398	362
SHIPSTON ON STOUR	Rural	17874	M.	8913	235	245	264	214	240	1198	1147	1005	867	610	521	446
			F.	8961	227	198	226	227	249	1127	1111	1046	757	558	544	503
SHORT HEATH	Urban	2394	M.	1308	35	40	50	34	41	200	185	160	140	114	77	81
			F.	1086	41	28	33	40	40	182	173	146	74	85	69	84
SHREWSBURY	Urban	26478	M.	12821	327	312	325	316	298	1578	1413	1301	1407	1231	1086	876
			F.	13657	348	326	333	282	330	1619	1445	1328	1477	1288	1123	951
SMALLTHORNE	Urban	4615	M.	2368	87	64	82	70	76	379	357	285	226	209	152	140
			F.	2247	86	78	92	83	75	414	394	282	192	137	144	148
SMETHWICK	Urban	25084	M.	12641	460	413	430	403	382	2088	1737	1442	1267	1153	1013	880
			F.	12443	463	365	424	406	410	2068	1727	1383	1178	1031	1009	837
SOLIHULL	Rural	21377	M.	10183	273	264	298	311	298	1447	1281	1057	1007	788	654	624
			F.	11194	248	245	254	252	273	1272	1276	1179	1171	1041	906	720
SOUTHAM	Rural	10282	M.	5249	142	131	149	137	118	677	645	604	484	396	311	276
			F.	5033	133	116	138	155	154	698	659	553	395	334	308	282

Table 6 *continued*.—AGES of MALES and FEMALES in SAN

SANITARY DISTRICT		ALL AGES. Persons.	ALL AGES. Males and Females.		Under 1 Year.	1–	2–	3–	4–	Under 5 Years.	5–	10–	15–	20–	25–	3
STAFFORD	Urban	19977	M.	10155	296	280	273	297	278	1424	1244	1019	985	894	867	
			F.	9822	295	268	295	263	271	1392	1207	1046	988	927	758	
STAFFORD	Rural	10568	M.	5172	127	119	134	136	139	655	654	634	523	383	346	
			F.	5396	127	118	119	129	142	635	694	609	501	373	409	
STAPLETON	Urban	10833	M.	5223	133	130	140	129	135	674	610	712	414	315	302	
			F.	5610	161	122	117	128	111	639	626	649	550	449	391	
STOKE ON TRENT	Urban	19231	M.	9431	271	252	269	281	268	1341	1277	1082	956	834	700	
			F.	9830	315	259	291	264	262	1391	1246	1060	1011	934	817	
STOKE ON TRENT	Rural	4241	M.	2205	67	50	79	69	55	329	325	260	225	173	157	
			F.	2036	76	44	66	70	72	328	292	245	180	155	144	
STONE	Urban	5669	M.	2709	76	68	64	66	64	338	380	310	250	232	191	
			F.	2960	75	56	80	98	67	371	363	363	292	270	200	
STONE	Rural	20356	M.	9786	282	243	279	307	266	1377	1237	1060	976	807	709	
			F.	10570	270	287	273	287	268	1385	1307	1145	1068	965	827	
STOURBRIDGE	Urban	9757	M.	4672	153	120	136	121	138	668	591	513	447	403	355	
			F.	5080	129	118	134	142	129	663	561	577	542	483	582	
STOURBRIDGE	Rural	51998	M.	25805	809	780	781	762	768	3900	3652	3083	2581	2197	1849	1
			F.	26193	825	755	811	786	867	4044	3608	3027	2387	2188	1894	1
STOW ON THE WOLD	Urban	1636	M.	813	28	20	29	19	18	114	103	91	77	45	60	
			F.	823	23	20	19	17	18	97	84	84	83	79	53	
STOW ON THE WOLD	Rural	7493	M.	3759	96	109	95	78	93	471	465	452	380	265	221	
			F.	3734	88	85	84	103	110	470	494	388	294	269	225	
STRATFORD ON AVON	Urban	8054	M.	3890	101	103	89	111	119	523	474	470	405	302	281	
			F.	4164	110	107	107	103	99	526	474	403	409	376	304	
STRATFORD ON AVON	Rural	14442	M.	7220	183	173	187	193	179	915	956	853	688	477	415	
			F.	7222	177	185	207	198	208	975	959	791	570	487	439	
STROUD	Urban	7848	M.	3470	108	89	106	110	108	521	451	388	321	230	253	
			F.	4378	102	112	101	95	77	487	472	442	552	426	364	
STROUD	Rural	28328	M.	13174	385	324	365	342	399	1815	1746	1553	1302	956	827	
			F.	15154	364	344	347	344	350	1749	1709	1645	1444	1288	1133	
SWADLINCOTE	Urban	2982	M.	1507	50	43	37	54	42	226	203	152	165	120	132	
			F.	1475	64	50	47	41	67	269	217	148	138	127	118	
TAMWORTH	Urban	4891	M.	2351	82	72	70	69	58	351	297	254	249	198	182	
			F.	2540	68	79	67	82	69	365	303	279	268	216	212	
TAMWORTH	Rural	14509	M.	7325	202	245	230	217	203	1097	1009	858	737	574	546	
			F.	7184	226	219	240	223	238	1146	963	808	657	535	539	
TENBURY	Rural	7588	M.	3814	93	86	92	88	112	471	447	465	396	301	244	
			F.	3774	118	99	101	109	112	539	456	429	318	271	241	
TETBURY	Urban	2419	M.	1185	29	29	28	34	36	156	138	168	118	94	70	
			F.	1234	36	35	30	29	25	155	146	137	129	99	76	
TETBURY	Rural	3474	M.	1710	48	44	59	44	43	238	227	184	167	138	111	
			F.	1764	52	39	52	50	46	239	210	197	157	156	131	
TEWKESBURY	Urban	5100	M.	2445	71	64	49	64	72	320	303	298	256	193	156	
			F.	2655	73	63	59	72	56	323	278	270	291	220	182	
TEWKESBURY	Rural	7804	M.	3905	102	79	96	105	104	486	499	458	366	287	224	
			F.	3989	97	95	105	89	108	494	479	420	318	260	251	
THORNBURY	Rural	17088	M.	8465	204	184	249	210	225	1078	1076	978	838	646	524	
			F.	8623	249	224	252	227	240	1192	1099	968	652	635	565	
TIPTON	Urban	30013	M.	15277	515	490	499	425	428	2357	2210	1775	1526	1329	1165	
			F.	14736	496	438	472	409	460	2365	2106	1615	1334	1214	1086	
TUNSTALL	Urban	14244	M.	7160	240	194	210	208	213	1065	942	805	715	682	585	
			F.	7084	253	182	224	187	220	1076	939	875	754	646	551	

Table 6 *continued*.—AGES of MALES and FEMALES in SANI

SANITARY DISTRICT.		ALL AGES. Persons.	ALL AGES. Males and Females.		Under 1 Year.	1–	2–	3–	4–	Under 5 Years.	5–	10–	15–	20–	25–	3(
UPPER SEDGLEY	Urban	14874	M.	7293	223	217	187	226	236	1089	974	901	723	589	474	4
			F.	7581	219	204	240	248	216	1127	1066	840	738	623	521	4
UPTON ON SEVERN	Rural	17388	M.	8337	205	187	211	192	192	987	987	1019	794	614	528	3
			F.	9051	200	174	187	200	189	950	983	970	753	686	634	5
UTTOXETER	Rural	14073	M.	6873	171	169	198	174	193	905	856	768	669	553	467	4
			F.	7200	171	167	185	179	183	885	835	825	725	621	408	4
WALSALL	Urban	58795	M.	29336	944	874	927	839	920	4504	3943	3288	2942	2567	2273	19
			F.	29459	958	847	908	857	910	4480	4034	3362	3016	2388	2252	18
WALSALL	Rural	8507	M.	4344	143	113	124	136	116	632	666	606	467	395	303	2
			F.	4163	121	132	134	123	128	638	571	518	402	340	302	2
WARWICK	Urban	11800	M.	5810	154	157	177	160	131	779	642	611	597	441	428	3
			F.	5990	144	160	127	140	152	723	686	592	565	498	433	3
WARWICK	Rural	10845	M.	5419	127	117	140	126	128	638	624	560	551	370	354	3
			F.	5426	140	124	136	131	130	661	608	505	331	411	390	3
WEDNESBURY	Urban	24566	M.	12537	379	347	376	342	350	1794	1595	1403	1393	1213	983	7
			F.	12029	388	312	329	376	381	1783	1662	1347	1146	1074	865	7
WEDNESFIELD	Urban	4556	M.	2391	70	67	75	64	90	366	355	245	236	198	172	1
			F.	2165	72	71	79	82	81	385	331	271	159	138	147	1
WEDNESFIELD HEATH or HEATH TOWN	Urban	6245	M.	3174	137	100	119	110	107	582	411	357	311	268	255	1
			F.	3071	132	94	101	107	103	537	424	336	253	242	240	1
WELLINGTON	Urban	6217	M.	3058	98	78	69	88	89	422	380	366	337	228	212	1
			F.	3159	71	74	92	74	77	388	368	367	327	246	216	1
WELLINGTON	Rural	20267	M.	10447	310	264	303	350	306	1533	1482	1260	1085	807	647	5
			F.	9820	313	276	275	277	295	1436	1425	1203	734	614	633	5
WEM	Rural	10565	M.	5322	104	105	141	138	147	635	629	645	550	411	292	2
			F.	5243	115	132	129	126	118	620	637	564	486	381	344	2
WEOBLY	Rural	8179	M.	4056	106	81	126	92	89	494	533	439	412	263	239	2
			F.	4123	118	83	118	104	113	533	458	494	346	290	265	2
WEST BROMWICH	Urban	56295	M.	28285	989	874	833	903	845	4447	3874	3258	3026	2480	2176	17
			F.	28010	963	921	921	808	931	4634	4008	3205	2610	2403	2098	17
WEST BROMWICH	Rural	3565	M.	1780	55	49	61	63	44	272	244	210	175	158	119	
			F.	1785	42	59	55	48	52	256	288	211	163	139	119	1
WESTBURY ON SEVERN	Urban	2262	M.	1147	39	25	33	25	31	153	151	118	92	63	72	
			F.	1115	24	24	18	26	28	120	129	152	97	71	63	
WESTBURY ON SEVERN	Rural	18659	M.	9360	324	281	276	271	286	1438	1365	1162	997	741	608	5
			F.	8999	298	257	310	284	307	1456	1323	1072	646	677	623	5
WHEATENHURST	Rural	7353	M.	3538	75	104	85	90	112	466	477	428	352	244	199	1
			F.	3815	98	94	105	89	98	484	391	437	338	283	257	2
WHITCHURCH	Urban	3756	M.	1777	40	49	45	46	41	221	219	197	172	145	133	1
			F.	1979	49	30	43	37	49	217	203	197	221	169	162	1
WHITCHURCH	Rural	7490	M.	3723	100	89	102	89	99	479	470	418	307	306	231	2
			F.	3767	92	96	95	92	99	474	430	380	381	329	283	2
WILLENHALL	Urban	16067	M.	8221	248	236	267	277	230	1258	1092	951	928	718	600	5
			F.	7846	311	257	254	235	223	1280	1112	959	752	635	564	4
WINCHCOMB	Rural	9533	M.	4868	122	115	108	128	129	602	619	558	491	339	250	2
			F.	4665	127	112	114	126	113	592	578	530	390	334	305	2
WOLSTANTON	Rural	30995	M.	15906	465	443	484	459	414	2265	2339	1914	1645	1382	1003	10
			F.	15089	404	477	467	527	527	2402	2296	1805	1276	1250	1075	9
WOLVERHAMPTON	Urban	75766	M.	37827	1186	1024	1126	1077	1102	5515	4666	4277	3899	3424	3050	24
			F.	37989	1143	1014	1098	1082	1027	5363	4479	4124	3896	3530	3013	24
WORCESTER	Urban	33066	M.	15962	444	386	453	390	427	2100	1793	1728	1637	1479	1271	10
			F.	18004	486	380	439	391	396	2001	1880	1844	1935	1733	1434	11
WORCESTER	Rural	3106	M.	1487	40	39	35	30	41	183	226	183	166	95	98	
			F.	1619	37	33	57	35	31	196	101	155	162	158	120	1

Table 13.—NUMBER and COUNTRY of BIRTH of FOREIGNERS enumerated in COUNTIES, and in eac
exceeds 50.000 PERSONS.

WHERE BORN.	WHERE ENUME						
	WEST-MIDLAND COUNTIES.		GLOUCESTER-SHIRE.		HEREFORD-SHIRE.		SHROPSH
	Males.	Females.	Males.	Females.	Males.	Females.	Males.
TOTAL	2432	1876	706	427	41	65	56
EUROPE.							
DENMARK	19	7	9	.	1	1	.
NORWAY	66	6	60	4	.	.	.
SWEDEN	47	5	40	3	.	.	.
RUSSIA	61	25	12	4	.	.	.
POLAND (RUSSIAN)	171	113	42	27	.	.	1
AUSTRIA	51	7	23	4	1	.	.
HUNGARY	2	4	1	2	.	.	.
SWITZERLAND	71	96	17	35	2	8	.
GERMAN EMPIRE	580	372	120	100	13	14	13
HOLLAND	24	21	8	6	.	.	.
BELGIUM	31	37	7	11	1	2	1
FRANCE	231	241	99	85	4	4	6
PORTUGAL	3	.	1	.	.	.	.
SPAIN	15	1	3	.	.	1	1
ITALY	210	90	85	23	3	.	8
GREECE	5	1	1	.	.	.	.
TURKEY	3	2	1	.	.	.	.
SERVIA	.	.	.	.	.	.	.
ROUMANIA	9	1	.	.	.	.	.
ASIA.							
ARABIA	.	.	.	.	.	.	.
PERSIA	.	.	.	.	.	.	.
CHINA	1	1	.	.	.	.	.
OTHER COUNTRIES	1	.	1	.	.	.	.
AFRICA.							
EGYPT	1	.	.	.	1	.	.
OTHER PARTS	.	.	.	.	.	.	.
AMERICA.							
UNITED STATES	825	843	176	122	14	35	26
MEXICO	1	.	.	.	.	.	.
BRAZIL	1	2	.	1	.	.	.
OTHER STATES	3	.	.	.	1	.	.
COUNTRY NOT STATED	.	1	.	.	.	.	.
AT SEA	.	.	.	.	.	.	.

Table 13 *continued*.—NUMBER and COUNTRY of BIRTH of FOREIGNERS enumerated in COUNTIES, and i
exceeds 50,000 PERSONS.

WHERE BORN.	WHERE ENU… URBAN SANITAR… BRISTOL.		WOLVER-HAMPTON.		WALSALL.	
	Males.	Females.	Males.	Females.	Males.	Females.
TOTAL	398	207	67	47	48	25
EUROPE.						
DENMARK	6	.	2	.	1	.
NORWAY	13	.	.	.	.	.
SWEDEN	37	2	.	.	1	.
RUSSIA	8	3	4	1	.	.
POLAND (RUSSIAN)	9	9	10	11	4	1
AUSTRIA	18	1	.	.	.	.
HUNGARY	.	2	1	.	.	.
SWITZERLAND	11	17	6	1	.	.
GERMAN EMPIRE	67	45	16	3	5	3
HOLLAND	6	3	.	.	.	.
BELGIUM	4	7	1	1	1	.
FRANCE	58	48	1	3	4	3
PORTUGAL	2	.	.	.	.	.
SPAIN	3	.	.	.	.	.
ITALY	60	5	4	3	2	1
GREECE	.	1	.	.	.	.
TURKEY	.	.	.	.	.	.
SERVIA	.	.	.	.	.	.
ROUMANIA	.	.	.	.	.	.
ASIA.						
ARABIA	.	.	.	.	.	.
PERSIA	.	.	.	.	.	.
CHINA	.	.	.	.	.	.
OTHER COUNTRIES	1	.	.	.	.	.
AFRICA.						
EGYPT	.	.	.	.	.	.
OTHER PARTS	.	.	.	.	.	.
AMERICA.						
UNITED STATES	95	64	21	24	30	17
MEXICO	.	.	1	.	.	.
BRAZIL	.	.	.	.	.	.
OTHER STATES	.	.	.	.	.	.
COUNTRY NOT STATED	.	.	.	.	.	.
AT SEA	.	.	.	.	.	.

L 13

Table 6.—Ages of Males and Females in Sanitary

N n 3

Sanitary District.		All Ages. Persons.	All Ages. Males and Females.		Under 1 Year.	1–	2–	3–	4–	Under 5 Years.	5–	10–	15–	20–	25–	30
ALFRETON - - - -	Urban	4992	M. F.	2817 2175	78 76	71 81	81 79	69 93	72 68	371 397	324 302	245 224	210 170	204 192	195 140	1 1
ALVASTON AND BOULTON	Urban	1506	M. F.	785 771	21 30	29 22	22 35	21 19	21 24	114 130	88 94	88 80	68 62	72 74	69 60	
ARNOLD - - - -	Urban	5745	M. F.	2836 2909	108 94	69 83	77 90	84 95	66 80	404 451	390 420	273 331	295 283	245 254	184 231	1 1
ASHBORNE - - - -	Urban	3435	M. F.	1536 1899	36 55	45 36	33 46	42 55	44 43	200 235	192 212	189 199	163 213	113 160	131 159	 1
ASHBORNE - - - -	Rural	15156	M. F.	7542 7614	218 180	191 209	202 169	230 180	202 213	1043 951	919 936	832 782	797 716	593 657	462 525	4 4
ASHBY-DE-LA-ZOUCH -	Urban	4536	M. F.	2117 2419	66 47	57 69	47 59	48 75	61 48	279 318	263 279	208 265	211 261	177 230	180 188	1 1
ASHBY-DE-LA-ZOUCH -	Rural	22188	M. F.	11341 10847	[illegible] 326	[illegible] 343	[illegible] 335	[illegible] 356	307 344	1719 1705	1400 1496	1271 1211	1181 918	941 809	813 703	8 6
ASHBY WOULDS - - -	Urban	2929	M. F.	1522 1407	48 44	49 57	40 59	51 42	59 40	256 242	200 240	190 183	156 119	128 112	139 93	
BAKEWELL - - - -	Urban	2502	M. F.	1173 1324	37 29	25 29	26 33	26 35	42 31	156 157	159 156	134 143	112 143	98 122	94 102	
BAKEWELL - - - -	Rural	18557	M. F.	9221 9336	241 245	238 244	246 216	245 241	237 251	1207 1204	1093 1138	1030 944	876 868	786 803	624 627	5 5
BARROW UPON SOAR -	Rural	18244	M. F.	8954 9290	270 290	226 225	258 285	258 248	252 287	1284 1345	1184 1202	1082 994	897 798	667 743	595 646	5 5
BARTON UPON HUMBER -	Urban	5339	M. F.	2533 2806	73 72	67 67	94 79	65 77	83 68	382 363	333 378	287 309	227 272	205 227	174 200	1 1
BASFORD - - - -	Rural	48437	M. F.	25200 23237	810 852	752 724	795 752	769 764	744 775	3870 3867	3327 3407	2748 2578	2509 1829	2311 1963	2041 1778	15 14
BASLOW - - - -	Urban	843	M. F.	419 424	8 16	9 4	10 3	14 14	7 3	48 40	35 37	34 43	35 47	58 36	31 35	
BEESTON - - - -	Urban	4479	M. F.	2144 2335	65 72	69 63	61 73	62 65	66 47	323 330	255 248	238 230	201 256	190 244	205 203	1 1
BELGRAVE - - - -	Urban	7260	M. F.	3469 3791	144 128	109 94	132 128	106 137	112 117	603 604	475 532	415 435	356 341	267 321	243 299	2 2
BELPER - - - -	Urban	9875	M. F.	4812 5063	143 153	152 113	133 134	135 120	121 140	684 660	607 585	599 567	453 552	378 487	324 325	2 3
BELPER - - - -	Rural	31098	M. F.	15814 15284	477 474	468 461	465 440	477 467	467 425	2364 2267	2048 2011	1745 1788	1652 1322	1333 1304	1135 1075	9 8
BILLESDON - - - -	Rural	10073	M. F.	5146 4927	119 124	138 129	125 121	145 122	109 146	636 642	596 574	494 507	464 445	461 437	426 385	3 3
BINGHAM - - - -	Rural	14721	M. F.	7312 7409	179 189	181 185	204 179	197 170	201 200	962 923	877 875	842 772	704 640	558 597	432 487	3 4
BLABY - - - -	Rural	21853	M. F.	10847 11005	355 379	313 349	337 344	340 351	315 289	1640 1712	1380 1381	1143 1100	1190 927	869 997	803 850	6 7
BONSALL - - - -	Urban	1354	M. F.	631 723	12 16	15 21	12 25	15 25	22 15	76 103	85 94	64 85	59 79	50 52	44 52	
BOSTON - - - -	Urban	14941	M. F.	6924 8017	168 189	166 182	173 210	180 177	198 175	894 933	880 909	822 840	678 846	507 696	459 558	4 4

Note.—For the Parishes comprised in each Urban nitary District, see Vol. II.,

Table 6 *continued*.—Ages of Males and Females in Sani

Sanitary District.		All Ages. Persons.		All Ages. Males and Females.	Under 1 Year.	1–	2–	3–	4–	Under 5 Years.	5–	10–	15–	20–	25–	3
BOSTON	Rural	24469	M.	12337	337	294	318	344	299	1592	1566	1451	1209	892	751	6
			F.	12132	312	327	333	314	323	1609	1520	1327	1065	909	748	6
BOURN	Rural	18918	M.	9401	248	220	280	256	270	1274	1292	1076	941	642	578	4
			F.	9517	255	243	236	240	260	1234	1230	1088	852	669	614	5
BRAMPTON AND WALTON	Urban	7567	M.	3778	118	115	104	126	129	592	539	430	349	301	268	2
			F.	3789	118	108	115	111	124	574	519	437	399	331	274	2
BRIGG	Urban	3087	M.	1514	35	51	34	32	40	192	160	161	165	139	113	
			F.	1573	40	26	45	43	46	200	183	156	180	150	109	
BROUGHTON	Urban	1094	M.	564	15	18	12	26	17	88	68	58	50	41	43	
			F.	530	12	15	11	23	12	73	78	55	35	43	33	
BUXTON	Urban	6025	M.	2647	71	62	73	59	54	319	298	284	259	242	209	2
			F.	3378	63	77	71	67	64	342	319	310	407	423	298	2
CAISTOR	Rural	21219	M.	10760	283	261	222	321	276	1363	1322	1277	1166	833	626	5
			F.	10459	263	264	294	275	320	1416	1271	1193	993	840	648	5
CHAPEL-EN-LE-FRITH	Rural	11995	M.	6114	175	171	170	156	171	843	757	667	629	568	479	3
			F.	5881	155	159	184	150	167	815	724	661	582	496	463	3
CHESTERFIELD	Urban	12221	M.	6146	180	168	184	183	174	889	764	626	539	558	547	4
			F.	6075	192	156	160	165	143	816	717	667	688	560	465	3
CHESTERFIELD	Rural	54314	M.	28862	961	905	972	842	926	4606	3832	3214	2866	2655	2386	18
			F.	25452	1000	867	972	872	930	4641	3920	2971	1945	1869	1883	16
CLAY LANE	Urban	6879	M.	3676	145	118	123	133	102	621	499	414	355	329	281	2
			F.	3203	134	120	106	112	125	597	513	370	272	218	238	2
CLEETHORPES	Urban	2840	M.	1428	46	44	44	50	29	213	189	161	147	143	118	
			F.	1412	34	48	38	46	44	210	186	156	139	127	100	
CLEE WITH WEELSBY	Urban	11620	M.	6297	209	158	192	184	187	930	757	579	880	756	586	4
			F.	5323	182	173	202	148	209	914	738	621	521	401	444	3
DERBY	Urban	81168	M.	40033	1264	1179	1186	1114	1119	5862	4929	4086	3720	3829	3781	30
			F.	41135	1279	1185	1193	1180	1149	5986	5128	4133	4009	3944	3499	28
DERBY	Rural	995	M.	444	16	12	8	12	8	56	52	51	50	37	41	
			F.	551	7	15	7	14	8	51	56	64	61	57	39	
DRONFIELD	Urban	4331	M.	2278	73	78	92	85	76	404	329	214	200	219	193	1
			F.	2053	78	68	88	68	72	374	308	221	187	149	167	1
EAST RETFORD	Urban	9748	M.	4680	151	129	150	126	153	709	594	459	449	352	381	2
			F.	5068	142	145	154	153	117	711	610	546	464	438	388	3
EAST RETFORD	Rural	13523	M.	6749	205	148	186	185	171	895	753	723	727	530	356	3
			F.	6774	173	150	147	158	162	790	827	737	633	541	442	3
FAIRFIELD	Urban	1464	M.	731	23	21	18	15	17	94	85	82	71	74	67	
			F.	733	23	16	23	22	22	106	95	81	67	65	57	
GAINSBOROUGH	Urban	10873	M.	5464	172	153	154	157	162	798	598	521	461	617	575	4
			F.	5409	210	185	159	150	171	875	657	539	490	518	512	3
GAINSBOROUGH	Rural	19075	M.	9499	263	274	253	269	240	1299	1094	997	996	772	601	4
			F.	9576	267	236	243	263	231	1290	1184	1074	843	726	592	5
GLANFORD BRIGG	Rural	28737	M.	14590	466	379	463	416	418	2132	1905	1639	1345	1196	1002	9
			F.	14147	465	402	434	405	422	2128	1817	1579	1261	1055	1025	8
GLOSSOP	Urban	19574	M.	8872	266	241	226	229	254	1216	1019	976	981	843	652	5
			F.	10702	277	237	253	251	236	1254	1108	1067	1153	1062	931	7
GLOSSOP	Rural	3976	M.	1897	43	41	51	43	38	216	234	209	190	161	145	1
			F.	2079	60	58	53	53	57	281	233	204	202	194	148	1
GRANTHAM	Urban	16886	M.	8215	260	233	250	224	232	1199	1001	865	795	716	686	5
			F.	3671	260	254	256	222	193	1185	1023	993	598	819	678	5

Table 6 *continued*.—AGES of MALES and FEMALES in SAN

SANITARY DISTRICT.		ALL AGES. Persons.	ALL AGES. Males and Females.		Under 1 Year.	1–	2–	3–	4–	Under 5 Years.	5–	10–	15–	20–	25–	3
GRANTHAM	Rural	16793	M.	8540	215	212	237	229	222	1116	1087	985	877	661	552	
			F.	8253	224	138	206	205	229	1052	1017	916	695	644	627	
GREAT GRIMSBY	Urban	28503	M.	15005	431	397	417	430	410	2085	1510	1837	1838	1760	1516	1
			F.	13498	463	406	387	409	378	2043	1669	1302	1304	1397	1176	
HAYFIELD -	Rural	6182	M.	2990	77	70	79	70	74	370	363	326	326	251	217	
			F.	3192	77	85	91	74	80	407	372	326	340	290	237	
HEAGE - - - -	Urban	2405	M.	1225	86	34	46	36	53	205	162	146	127	93	77	
			F.	1130	44	26	38	32	39	179	181	145	111	104	71	
HEANOR - - - -	Urban	6822	M.	3583	116	117	100	123	111	567	513	379	358	321	295	
			F.	3239	104	113	117	126	110	570	464	364	282	276	255	
HINCKLEY - - -	Urban	7673	M.	3534	106	99	94	102	109	510	458	399	352	253	233	
			F.	4139	122	115	126	115	134	612	508	428	448	384	312	
HINCKLEY - - - - - -	Rural	9729	M.	4823	162	124	133	137	130	686	625	555	438	374	322	
			F.	4906	145	151	160	153	138	747	614	548	403	416	335	
HOLBEACH - - - -	Urban	5190	M.	2634	63	61	68	59	79	330	360	336	204	190	151	
			F.	2556	70	60	91	75	67	363	325	287	212	206	159	
HOLBEACH - - -	Rural	9158	M.	4596	133	113	111	140	146	643	650	631	455	273	275	
			F.	4562	144	129	164	126	134	697	606	553	385	285	285	
HORNCASTLE - - -	Urban	4818	M.	2245	48	49	62	60	65	284	255	237	242	155	144	
			F.	2573	62	67	40	61	51	281	268	271	267	237	184	
HORNCASTLE - - -	Rural	16694	M.	8439	194	202	209	220	191	1016	1053	958	880	638	543	
			F.	8255	222	203	212	189	227	1053	1026	960	773	629	523	
HUCKNALL TORKARD -	Urban	10023	M.	5429	198	180	177	156	162	873	807	521	508	539	508	
			F.	4594	198	154	169	181	178	880	709	546	319	386	366	
HUCKNALL UNDER HUTHWAITE - - - - - -	Urban	2028	M.	1079	22	31	34	35	36	158	143	120	97	102	97	
			F.	949	33	32	36	30	34	165	132	122	81	74	67	
ILKESTON - - -	Urban	14122	M.	7317	278	228	233	245	217	1196	1004	793	722	666	623	
			F.	6805	234	252	217	228	236	1167	1011	812	600	570	522	
LEICESTER - - -	Urban	122376	M.	57720	1910	1706	1645	1673	1596	8536	7219	6091	5746	5457	4973	4
			F.	64656	2020	1732	1682	1656	1644	8734	7487	6485	6942	6624	6657	4
LINCOLN - - - - - -	Urban	37313	M.	18382	549	534	500	507	490	2580	2187	1890	1749	1729	1602	1
			F.	18931	569	499	539	495	543	2645	2214	1960	1902	1719	1573	1
LINCOLN - - - -	Rural	27199	M.	13891	345	302	416	333	381	1776	1645	1556	1411	1088	908	
			F.	13308	368	329	373	337	348	1755	1795	1518	1107	946	852	
LONG EATON - -	Urban	6217	M.	3178	121	96	109	91	97	514	413	381	344	356	292	
			F.	3039	122	101	118	109	117	567	410	322	286	288	263	
LONG SUTTON - - -	Urban	2694	M.	1268	43	28	27	40	40	178	157	134	120	63	67	
			F.	1426	26	37	33	36	28	160	175	172	118	99	99	
LOUGHBOROUGH - -	Urban	14803	M.	6993	230	205	180	211	202	1028	858	812	734	604	531	
			F.	7810	240	227	234	206	182	1098	911	817	866	744	598	
LOUGHBOROUGH -	Rural	13080	M.	6501	178	177	180	163	188	886	827	774	656	472	414	
			F.	6579	189	186	165	173	171	884	830	732	588	530	426	
LOUTH - - - - -	Urban	10691	M.	4862	133	122	184	139	120	653	556	574	500	335	304	
			F.	5829	117	125	125	105	130	602	620	611	631	474	387	
LOUTH - - - - -	Rural	23161	M.	11798	324	287	316	341	312	1580	1477	1409	1199	939	692	
			F.	11363	265	283	311	285	328	1472	1416	1381	1005	893	726	
LUTTERWORTH -	Rural	13356	M.	6558	168	143	162	160	149	782	759	732	682	478	390	
			F.	6798	158	139	181	143	177	798	776	682	556	484	436	

N n 4

Table 6 *continued*.—AGES of MALES and FEMALES in SAN

SANITARY DISTRICT.		ALL AGES. Persons.	ALL AGES. Males and Females.		Under 1 Year.	1–	2–	3–	4–	Under 5 Years.	5–	10–	15–	20–	25–
MANSFIELD	Urban	13653	M.	6583	208	186	174	167	185	915	780	720	638	848	521
			F.	7070	211	179	199	184	204	977	857	740	747	688	506
MANSFIELD	Rural	16807	M.	8986	283	302	260	298	293	1436	1244	967	942	769	748
			F.	7821	322	277	287	298	288	1472	1257	831	576	606	584
MANSFIELD WOODHOUSE	Urban	2618	M.	1292	34	41	38	40	35	188	168	161	130	98	74
			F.	1326	32	23	41	30	33	159	150	137	152	132	99
MARKET BOSWORTH	Rural	14611	M.	7398	240	226	209	235	226	1136	940	810	707	598	485
			F.	7213	224	191	232	229	188	1064	985	779	537	554	503
MARKET HARBOROUGH	Urban	5351	M.	2554	77	77	84	69	71	378	320	236	243	223	209
			F.	2797	81	66	82	81	65	375	334	278	293	301	236
MARKET HARBOROUGH	Rural	10845	M.	5395	142	152	138	142	132	686	672	636	501	412	318
			F.	5450	145	106	142	108	127	628	651	586	475	404	351
MARKET RASEN	Urban	2612	M.	1219	26	31	33	30	32	152	125	130	125	94	81
			F.	1393	29	24	29	21	27	130	158	155	147	127	94
MATLOCK	Urban	4395	M.	2104	68	55	57	59	46	285	243	223	185	191	172
			F.	2291	68	57	52	57	59	293	241	216	217	247	193
MATLOCK BATH AND SCARTHIN NICK	Urban	1698	M.	726	14	13	26	22	17	92	92	69	58	56	51
			F.	972	22	20	17	13	14	86	89	89	122	115	78
MELTON MOWBRAY	Urban	5766	M.	2912	84	83	101	74	80	422	341	265	252	268	247
			F.	2854	82	82	76	71	69	380	333	297	238	280	237
MELTON MOWBRAY	Rural	14726	M.	7356	197	188	187	169	178	919	821	822	727	589	508
			F.	7370	198	179	187	186	201	951	850	777	625	604	519
NEWARK	Rural	16598	M.	8309	219	197	213	217	223	1069	1000	1022	817	640	446
			F.	8289	234	188	225	209	207	1063	905	873	766	635	497
NEWARK UPON TRENT	Urban	14018	M.	6805	200	179	201	180	185	945	833	690	740	660	540
			F.	7213	198	219	213	201	188	1019	842	775	717	703	530
NEWBOLD AND DUNSTON	Urban	6158	M.	3149	105	107	85	102	107	516	476	335	296	260	259
			F.	3009	97	106	112	96	106	517	407	332	281	258	219
NEW MILLS	Urban	6552	M.	3224	87	86	101	74	86	434	402	348	315	301	237
			F.	3328	91	88	105	76	83	443	432	374	302	291	259
NEW SLEAFORD	Urban	4965	M.	2404	68	62	64	61	59	314	263	211	241	219	194
			F.	2561	65	58	67	50	72	312	299	273	231	202	213
NORTH DARLEY	Urban	1848	M.	921	26	38	31	29	29	153	116	94	85	89	65
			F.	927	33	29	28	31	25	146	115	113	72	79	67
NOTTINGHAM	Urban	186575	M.	87633	2714	2411	2272	2332	2339	12068	10263	8888	8533	8473	7929
			F.	98942	2666	2354	2355	2446	2400	12281	10538	9657	11024	10754	8860
OAKHAM	Rural	10978	M.	5441	150	113	141	136	142	682	666	612	544	446	345
			F.	5537	138	145	127	133	140	683	721	591	502	436	362
QUORNDON	Urban	1816	M.	857	28	23	26	32	24	133	127	89	73	60	53
			F.	959	26	24	22	22	32	126	112	112	85	84	74
RIPLEY	Urban	6087	M.	3085	104	80	100	103	101	488	414	344	333	231	213
			F.	3002	94	93	103	92	82	464	441	385	259	233	228
ROXBY CUM RISBY	Urban	417	M.	210	7	4	4	6	4	25	28	27	26	21	10
			F.	207	4	5	7	9	3	28	25	25	19	25	11
RUSKINGTON	Urban	1191	M.	577	16	17	9	27	6	75	76	85	50	46	31
			F.	614	23	18	21	23	17	102	74	75	45	35	31
SHARDLOW	Rural	33967	M.	16807	518	417	482	455	488	2355	2055	1920	1727	1498	1211
			F.	17160	505	449	499	473	499	2425	2105	1850	1638	1442	1209

Table 6 *continued*.—AGES of MALES and FEMALES in SAN

SANITARY DISTRICT.		ALL AGES. Persons.	Males and Females.		Under 1 Year.	1–	2–	3–	4–	Under 5 Years.	5–	10–	15–	20–	25–
SLEAFORD	Rural	19564	M.	9990	271	256	229	252	257	1265	1281	1180	1103	788	612
			F.	9574	230	252	252	260	269	1263	1234	1183	840	723	620
SOUTH DARLEY	Urban	679	M.	340	12	8	8	11	5	44	39	45	37	22	22
			F.	339	4	9	12	7	9	41	43	36	34	29	21
SOUTHWELL	Rural	20351	M.	9916	247	212	245	277	245	1226	1211	1057	917	726	612
			F.	10435	266	239	258	236	269	1268	1187	1102	945	768	647
SPALDING	Urban	9260	M.	4413	117	123	101	107	122	570	564	494	441	303	264
			F.	4347	101	100	105	116	112	534	517	514	499	418	339
SPALDING	Rural	13701	M.	7030	191	177	195	206	185	954	893	907	752	498	430
			F.	6671	187	179	179	203	193	941	931	816	544	435	384
SPILSBY	Rural	27887	M.	13919	355	351	363	361	333	1763	1788	1668	1455	959	823
			F.	13968	343	367	333	371	329	1743	1660	1597	1305	1019	830
STAMFORD	Urban	8773	M.	4094	114	114	100	97	106	531	516	484	451	335	290
			F.	4679	110	99	100	102	119	530	490	405	508	477	277
STAMFORD	Rural	9571	M.	4797	120	113	105	140	125	603	574	536	506	384	287
			F.	4774	119	118	121	113	116	587	613	540	386	378	303
SUTTON BRIDGE	Urban	2207	M.	1111	37	41	27	28	35	168	133	117	113	91	82
			F.	1096	52	29	37	31	31	180	151	132	92	80	79
SUTTON IN ASHFIELD	Urban	8523	M.	4378	133	128	135	153	124	673	638	461	404	349	322
			F.	4145	123	116	135	126	137	637	561	403	385	348	288
THURMASTON	Urban	1545	M.	738	20	27	22	23	17	118	92	100	72	49	49
			F.	807	19	28	16	36	28	127	129	81	87	64	51
UPPINGHAM	Rural	12029	M.	6078	165	166	141	148	154	774	709	781	706	449	397
			F.	5951	145	145	152	139	134	715	717	614	540	457	412
WARSOP	Urban	1329	M.	687	15	17	12	17	24	85	92	84	66	47	40
			F.	642	23	17	20	13	15	88	93	74	47	58	37
WHITTINGTON	Urban	7271	M.	3834	147	100	140	122	129	638	560	370	353	335	347
			F.	3437	130	145	136	130	129	685	536	383	252	254	253
WHITWICK	Urban	3881	M.	2028	61	58	64	56	60	299	260	260	226	138	125
			F.	1853	55	64	62	64	55	300	254	226	156	138	127
WINTERTON	Urban	1601	M.	760	19	20	35	19	18	111	111	87	65	46	47
			F.	841	17	22	14	21	19	93	109	95	95	56	51
WIRKSWORTH	Urban	3678	M.	1794	55	48	47	52	40	242	244	195	162	143	116
			F.	1884	53	43	44	49	44	233	228	180	189	151	134
WORKSOP	Urban	11625	M.	5798	190	178	162	178	174	882	745	646	504	471	457
			F.	5827	175	186	165	201	191	918	805	628	504	440	417
WORKSOP	Rural	16897	M.	8655	281	240	251	226	250	1248	1115	963	852	731	647
			F.	8242	279	236	290	264	282	1351	1214	920	650	630	562

Table 13.—NUMBER and COUNTRY of BIRTH of FOREIGNERS enumerated in COUNTIES, and in each
exceeds 50,000 PERSONS.

WHERE BORN.	WHERE ENUMERAT[ED]								
	NORTH-MIDLAND COUNTIES.		COUNTIES.						
			LEICESTERSHIRE.		RUTLANDSHIRE.		LINCOLNSHIRE.		NOTT[ING]HAMSH[IRE]
	Males.	Females.	Males.	Females.	Males.	Females.	Males.	Females.	Males.
TOTAL - - -	1841	1057	192	147	16	22	1018	442	413
EUROPE.									
DENMARK	63	6	.	.	.	.	57	4	2
NORWAY	148	16	.	.	.	.	147	16	.
SWEDEN	57	9	1	.	.	.	52	4	3
RUSSIA	76	14	3	2	.	.	47	8	23
POLAND (RUSSIAN)	84	52	9	5	.	.	34	20	32
AUSTRIA	20	11	5	2	.	1	4	1	2
HUNGARY	4	1	1	.	.	.	2	1	1
SWITZERLAND	27	58	3	14	2	6	5	11	11
GERMAN EMPIRE	639	457	40	37	7	12	412	294	129
HOLLAND	102	8	5	3	.	.	89	2	6
BELGIUM	31	12	14	3	1	.	11	4	4
FRANCE	196	124	29	21	3	2	65	14	80
PORTUGAL	2	.	.	.	.	.	1	.	.
SPAIN	4	2	1	1	.	.	.	.	1
ITALY	86	20	22	7	.	.	21	3	28
GREECE	5	3	.	1	.	.	3	.	.
TURKEY	1	1	.	1	.	.	1	.	.
SERVIA	.	.	.	.	.	.	.	.	.
ROUMANIA	.	.	.	.	.	.	.	.	.
ASIA.									
ARABIA	.	.	.	.	.	.	.	.	.
PERSIA	.	.	.	.	.	.	.	.	.
CHINA	6	1	.	.	.	.	.	.	6
OTHER COUNTRIES	1	2	.	.	.	.	.	.	1
AFRICA.									
EGYPT	.	.	.	.	.	.	.	.	.
OTHER PARTS	2	1	.	.	.	.	1	.	1
AMERICA.									
UNITED STATES	284	255	59	50	3	1	63	48	83
MEXICO	.	.	.	.	.	.	.	.	.
BRAZIL	.	.	.	.	.	.	.	.	.
OTHER STATES	2	2	.	.	.	.	2	1	.
COUNTRY NOT STATED	1	2	.	.	.	.	1	2	.
AT SEA	.	.	.	.	.	.	.	.	.

Table 6.—Ages of Males and Females in Sanitary

Sanitary District.		All Ages. Persons.	All Ages. Males and Females.		Under 1 Year.	1–	2–	3–	4–	Under 5 Years.	5–	10–	15–	20–	25–	30–
ABRAM	Urban	2638	M.	1405	65	51	50	45	47	258	190	140	137	137	115	9
			F.	1233	35	45	42	45	51	218	201	173	109	93	87	8
ACCRINGTON	Urban	31435	M.	14964	464	409	427	446	423	2169	1833	1523	1482	1497	1272	108
			F.	16471	483	422	445	423	417	2195	1871	1686	1674	1668	1455	122
ADLINGTON	Urban	3258	M.	1592	44	52	43	47	53	239	271	199	166	131	91	8
			F.	1666	57	51	53	41	51	253	221	183	197	142	106	9
ALLERTON	Urban	830	M.	340	10	13	9	18	6	56	45	16	38	27	36	2
			F.	490	14	4	13	6	9	46	53	39	46	64	54	4
ALTRINCHAM	Urban	11250	M.	5244	198	155	158	129	146	784	736	577	503	448	385	35
			F.	6006	150	158	137	173	170	788	670	620	565	595	509	41
ALTRINCHAM	Rural	26454	M.	12749	324	325	335	356	303	1643	1511	1431	1228	1159	938	82
			F.	13705	326	338	303	338	349	1654	1536	1347	1434	1342	1154	91
ASHTON IN MAKERFIELD	Urban	9824	M.	5251	164	140	170	160	163	797	692	597	502	564	425	37
			F.	4573	160	134	145	135	150	724	701	502	461	389	337	30
ASHTON UNDER LYNE	Urban	37040	M.	17412	520	455	463	452	454	2347	2077	1823	1736	1568	1485	119
			F.	19628	500	440	460	477	448	2068	2100	1060	1050	1904	1790	110
ASHTON UNDER LYNE*	Rural	14042	M.	7077	226	199	191	179	194	989	878	761	778	652	587	46
			F.	6965	190	175	191	185	203	944	889	768	674	625	547	45
ASPULL	Urban	8113	M.	4178	138	119	144	125	102	628	579	472	474	419	354	25
			F.	3935	156	144	129	154	138	721	580	474	372	342	298	22
ASTLEY BRIDGE	Urban	5613	M.	2656	85	82	89	79	85	411	357	310	280	233	198	16
			F.	2957	75	80	73	80	70	378	326	300	331	282	262	21
ATHERTON	Urban	12602	M.	6209	257	181	187	191	206	1022	851	701	608	578	524	41
			F.	6393	233	211	217	192	182	1035	850	660	655	597	508	42
AUDENSHAW	Urban	5936	M.	2908	107	78	83	84	89	441	380	298	285	250	228	23
			F.	3028	81	83	71	80	88	403	352	337	294	256	265	22
BACUP	Urban	25034	M.	11860	340	324	326	314	288	1592	1334	1224	1274	1206	1063	86
			F.	13174	358	302	359	326	316	1661	1475	1304	1344	1385	1172	95
BARROW IN FURNESS	Urban	47100	M.	25488	814	747	808	775	792	3936	3148	2352	2170	2749	2768	230
			F.	21612	839	753	808	759	783	3942	3126	2357	1856	1901	1912	168
BARROW IN FURNESS	Rural	159	M.	87	4	1	2	3	2	12	12	6	13	9	6	
			F.	72	.	5	2	1	3	11	9	5	12	5	1	1
BARTON, ECCLES, WINTON, and MONTON	Urban	21786	M.	9821	312	288	299	300	302	1501	1255	1054	920	812	765	68
			F.	11965	307	280	296	284	286	1513	1306	1229	1259	1212	1004	87
BARTON UPON IRWELL	Rural	19195	M.	9260	290	269	261	268	266	1354	1187	1031	907	858	726	63
			F.	9935	293	245	251	287	272	1348	1241	1112	997	925	765	72
BILLINGE	Urban	3832	M.	1935	59	70	55	51	66	301	240	238	199	192	151	11
			F.	1897	55	61	57	69	60	302	239	217	174	179	125	10
BIRKDALE	Urban	8705	M.	3652	134	91	107	121	95	548	441	505	429	256	252	22
			F.	5053	100	106	105	116	92	519	475	522	508	549	497	36
BIRKENHEAD	Urban	84006	M.	41174	1309	1186	1244	1171	1171	6081	5125	4290	3840	3797	3561	313
			F.	42832	1283	1198	1208	1135	1189	6013	5096	4347	4151	4208	3743	315
BIRKENHEAD	Rural	391	M.	191	3	1	3	4	4	15	23	27	35	19	11	
			F.	200	4	7	7	1	5	24	16	24	29	29	14	1
BLACKBURN	Urban	104014	M.	49133	1647	1439	1475	1474	1350	7385	5991	5431	4866	4762	4090	337
			F.	54881	1527	1456	1445	1413	1384	7225	6202	5660	5749	5773	4827	393
BLACKBURN	Rural	12158	M.	5959	170	155	174	152	137	794	739	667	620	557	500	36
			F.	6199	187	166	165	181	143	842	720	630	630	619	531	43
BLACKPOOL	Urban	14229	M.	6393	205	189	169	170	170	903	767	730	505	490	537	44
			F.	7836	191	178	192	182	186	929	819	728	732	687	681	60

Note.—For the Parishes comprised in each Urban Sanitary District, see Vol. II., Division VIII., Table 5.

* The Urban Sanitary District of Stalybridge was extended by Act 44 & 45 Vict. c. 191, and embraces the Urban Sanitary District of Staley, dissolved by th Act did not come into operation until 11th August 1881, the figures given in this Table for Ashton under Lyne (Rural) and for Stalybridge (Urban) relate to t

Table 6 *continued.*—Ages of Males and Females in Sanit…

Sanitary District.		All Ages. Persons.	All Ages. Males and Females.		Under 1 Year.	1–	2–	3–	4–	Under 5 Years.	5–	10–	15–	20–	25–	30–
BLACKROD	Urban	4234	M.	2175	60	59	50	55	72	296	278	255	274	227	153	141
			F.	2059	58	79	56	70	65	328	327	256	195	177	140	11
BOLLINGTON	Urban	3963	M.	1824	51	53	58	54	57	273	256	211	188	119	131	12
			F.	2139	45	62	54	49	59	260	252	212	223	179	165	15
BOLTON	Urban	105414	M.	49962	1614	1407	1422	1389	1420	7261	6410	5382	5112	4653	4415	352
			F.	55462	1603	1526	1473	1514	1475	7591	6591	5865	5536	5453	4804	393
BOLTON	Rural	24679	M.	12067	364	333	319	361	354	1721	1558	1484	1262	1099	922	79
			F.	12612	356	334	342	312	342	1686	1519	1366	1212	1268	1119	88
BOOTLE CUM LINACRE	Urban	27374	M.	13959	440	430	402	386	370	2037	1674	1335	1205	1406	1418	107
			F.	13415	422	391	393	420	418	2044	1613	1330	1314	1268	1181	101
BOWDON	Urban	2559	M.	923	25	28	12	28	24	117	101	123	85	69	56	6
			F.	1636	23	17	16	21	30	117	119	119	182	236	204	19
BRADFORD	Urban	16121	M.	8027	321	305	255	278	230	1308	1179	890	753	632	663	63
			F.	8094	306	247	250	300	265	1368	1136	916	718	666	663	59
BREDBURY AND ROMILEY	Urban	5553	M.	2591	64	55	71	71	73	334	322	304	250	198	228	17
			F.	2962	87	69	87	68	90	401	365	328	275	247	226	21
BRIERFIELD	Urban	4088	M.	1951	63	47	60	58	49	277	253	222	211	265	154	13
			F.	2137	69	60	66	62	66	322	250	212	219	203	219	15
BROMBOROUGH	Urban	1335	M.	660	21	20	21	20	20	102	91	57	62	56	48	4
			F.	675	25	21	17	17	13	93	77	72	62	53	69	6
BUGLAWTON	Urban	1550	M.	678	20	20	18	28	22	108	106	72	57	42	10	4
			F.	872	20	18	20	27	14	99	104	93	106	72	67	7
BURNLEY	Urban	58751	M.	28398	907	870	803	781	778	4139	3420	3040	2817	2724	2441	214
			F.	30353	943	859	898	801	807	4308	3650	3102	3017	2998	2719	226
BURNLEY	Rural	21672	M.	10732	323	278	294	293	277	1465	1314	1160	1088	934	881	75
			F.	10940	337	315	293	315	275	1535	1306	1130	1015	1033	892	80
BURY	Urban	52213	M.	24693	751	677	703	688	661	3480	3002	2602	2386	2236	2176	186
			F.	27520	820	683	717	760	684	3664	3044	2676	2678	2678	2501	196
BURY	Rural	24719	M.	12206	363	339	337	325	346	1710	1538	1287	1331	1221	996	83
			F.	12513	367	313	334	313	326	1653	1492	1354	1259	1173	1060	85
CASTLETON BY ROCHDALE	Urban	4017	M.	1937	40	51	61	51	45	247	252	220	205	175	176	11
			F.	2080	49	46	51	51	58	258	232	212	200	232	189	131
CHADDERTON	Urban	16890	M.	8264	266	237	240	216	231	1220	1061	903	872	799	728	56
			F.	8636	282	239	241	262	233	1257	1114	969	851	800	726	58
CHESTER	Urban	36794	M.	17668	525	477	482	448	495	2427	2093	2091	1803	1628	1432	121
			F.	19126	516	473	437	431	446	2353	2127	2112	1937	1799	1488	1311
CHESTER	Rural	8723	M.	4459	108	96	94	104	110	506	466	433	556	459	332	24
			F.	4264	103	94	116	88	105	506	449	429	430	388	314	27
CHILDWALL	Urban	187	M.	78	1	.	2	[illegible]	2	7	7	6	5	6	11	[illegible]
			F.	109	[illegible]	4	3	3	1	13	8	4	10	12	16	[illegible]
CHORLEY (*Lanc.*)	Urban	19478	M.	9239	308	290	297	243	265	1403	1214	1030	907	848	721	594
			F.	10239	286	263	309	287	279	1424	1235	1092	1026	988	820	701
CHORLEY (*Cheshire*)	Urban	2067	M.	836	22	20	26	24	23	115	109	90	87	69	65	5
			F.	1231	28	30	23	25	16	120	118	113	121	164	148	9
CHORLEY	Rural	18242	M.	9020	253	236	281	243	257	1270	1091	995	932	829	654	56
			F.	9222	272	254	272	269	237	1304	1138	968	879	861	710	50
CHURCH	Urban	4850	M.	2337	66	87	71	64	63	351	272	264	266	239	191	16
			F.	2513	82	58	72	65	61	338	288	287	233	263	212	178
CLAYTON-LE-MOORS	Urban	6695	M.	3222	85	82	99	105	78	449	454	388	302	320	261	218
			F.	3473	112	94	104	101	79	490	436	376	340	327	323	218
CLITHEROE	Urban	10176	M.	4910	166	140	140	132	138	725	632	525	482	416	407	327
			F.	5266	129	145	144	145	167	720	577	574	526	529	423	375

Table 6 *continued.*—AGES of MALES and FEMALES in SANI

SANITARY DISTRICT.		ALL AGES. Persons.	ALL AGES. Males and Females.		Under 1 Year.	1–	2–	3–	4–	Under 5 Years.	5–	10–	15–	20–	25–
CLITHEROE	Rural	13326	M. F.	6921 6405	158 150	165 154	138 164	143 180	158 150	762 798	800 722	849 635	798 563	625 576	526 514
COLNE AND MARSDEN	Urban	11971	M. F.	5752 6219	190 173	145 172	164 164	158 171	172 159	829 839	702 709	568 624	599 638	530 597	503 558
CONGLETON	Urban	11116	M. F.	4977 6139	136 152	142 126	126 136	114 151	118 151	636 716	663 717	580 588	406 669	391 603	345 454
CONGLETON	Rural	19851	M. F.	10202 9649	323 289	266 237	277 200	297 270	316 240	1479 1335	1321 1268	1176 1136	1182 989	860 818	690 731
CREWE	Urban	24385	M. F.	12657 11728	359 400	364 371	387 364	367 365	354 374	1831 1883	1641 1671	1401 1473	1297 1012	1264 918	1038 847
CROMPTON	Urban	9797	M. F.	4610 5187	124 146	185 144	127 129	127 129	185 136	618 684	579 602	526 567	517 530	424 499	380 410
CROSTON	Urban	1791	M. F.	868 923	19 27	23 25	27 25	24 18	26 29	119 124	107 116	93 81	86 76	83 88	67 70
CRUMPSALL	Urban	8154	M. F.	3746 4408	102 96	85 78	76 69	82 84	79 67	424 394	324 314	287 291	240 319	272 420	357 411
DALTON IN FURNESS	Urban	13339	M. F.	7125 6214	241 284	203 246	242 217	225 261	231 284	1142 1192	1037 986	787 710	519 387	672 460	648 501
DENTON	Urban	7660	M. F.	3688 3972	120 98	110 125	91 104	93 104	105 108	519 539	492 478	463 434	352 412	334 345	269 331
DROYLSDEN	Urban	8687	M. F.	4153 4534	123 124	125 95	101 115	115 109	104 109	568 552	534 550	493 460	418 469	363 437	338 357
DUKINFIELD	Urban	16942	M. F.	7962 8980	240 241	243 248	230 256	237 227	233 267	1183 1239	1074 1113	948 939	835 869	684 785	588 756
FAILSWORTH	Urban	7912	M. F.	3865 4047	151 128	119 127	117 129	110 129	109 126	606 639	477 503	400 440	376 364	365 394	386 331
FARNWORTH	Urban	20708	M. F.	9878 10830	317 338	281 313	302 260	302 269	295 301	1497 1481	1285 1283	1127 1131	965 1083	873 1049	771 859
FLEETWOOD	Urban	6733	M. F.	3608 3125	112 113	86 95	100 90	98 94	76 85	472 477	407 442	373 325	473 298	397 253	327 286
FULWOOD	Urban	3725	M. F.	2199 1526	40 44	29 25	26 32	33 24	25 35	153 160	161 124	176 111	377 152	360 183	180 139
FYLDE	Rural	10807	M. F.	5331 5476	143 142	129 123	138 151	135 146	145 121	690 683	684 619	588 582	566 538	463 509	378 416
GARSTANG	Rural	12375	M. F.	6374 6001	184 157	164 166	174 178	163 188	149 148	834 837	733 759	772 627	743 587	544 497	453 446
GARSTON	Urban	10271	M. F.	5051 5220	107 147	142 139	164 148	147 147	147 125	767 706	656 625	484 540	474 507	524 518	456 509
GORTON	Urban	33086	M. F.	16587 16500	572 546	462 514	523 506	520 476	502 520	2579 2562	2133 2270	1776 1734	1592 1374	1673 1342	1504 1431
GRANGE	Urban	1150	M. F.	465 685	10 16	11 8	11 15	10 15	12 10	54 64	74 56	61 44	50 85	16 83	32 57
GREAT CROSBY	Urban	5033	M. F.	2156 2877	77 75	61 61	76 70	52 74	67 62	333 342	298 293	242 270	234 321	163 395	160 273
GREAT HARWOOD	Urban	6287	M. F.	3085 3202	112 86	81 73	94 90	69 82	75 73	431 404	380 368	331 367	313 375	301 324	255 247
HASLINGDEN	Urban	14333	M. F.	6773 7560	192 203	198 174	186 195	188 173	183 184	947 929	842 879	705 796	679 759	654 773	563 656
HASLINGDEN	Rural	21663	M. F.	10524 11139	314 319	309 293	314 315	321 298	302 279	1560 1504	1344 1317	1193 1195	1073 1104	968 1059	853 946
HAUGHTON	Urban	5051	M. F.	2436 2615	76 81	71 48	77 66	56 71	66 80	346 346	332 343	302 292	254 269	203 225	187 194

Table 6 *continued*.—AGES of MALES and FEMALES in SANI

Sanitary District.		All Ages. Persons.	All Ages. Males and Females.		Under 1 Year.	1–	2–	3–	4–	Under 5 Years.	5–	10–	15–	20–	25–	30–
HAWARDEN	Rural	15695	M.	8226	239	229	225	241	202	1136	1103	1057	834	647	560	469
			F.	7469	200	213	215	242	240	1110	1030	937	543	506	477	454
HAYDOCK	Urban	5863	M.	3110	108	82	105	92	93	480	446	333	297	273	269	225
			F.	2753	106	99	93	95	108	501	425	306	198	202	227	196
HEATON NORRIS	Urban	5797	M.	2574	63	57	67	54	71	302	304	514	272	167	163	155
			F.	3223	74	68	63	64	63	337	316	350	414	406	305	224
HEYWOOD	Urban	22979	M.	10644	299	296	279	300	298	1472	1309	1176	1147	947	880	716
			F.	12335	261	249	280	311	283	1384	1336	1289	1300	1173	1003	894
HIGHER BEBINGTON	Urban	1959	M.	1328	24	16	24	14	16	94	75	159	376	197	131	66
			F.	631	16	13	8	19	3	69	84	70	63	64	64	39
HINDLEY	Urban	14715	M.	7422	262	256	235	228	235	1216	1022	850	696	707	585	494
			F.	7293	240	228	234	221	232	1155	1034	862	759	631	572	447
HOLLINGWORTH	Urban	2658	M.	1222	25	33	38	28	26	150	134	152	127	109	87	77
			F.	1436	32	32	28	42	27	161	183	132	144	158	107	92
HOOLE	Urban	2899	M.	1421	25	40	41	35	31	172	181	198	115	104	116	93
			F.	1478	39	34	27	43	37	180	186	166	139	110	119	91
HORWICH	Urban	3761	M.	1799	52	50	62	45	62	271	209	198	162	154	158	112
			F.	1962	46	50	51	45	59	251	236	185	188	175	166	135
HURST	Urban	6384	M.	2987	80	93	71	90	78	412	416	329	306	279	253	203
			F.	3397	100	73	89	93	33	443	304	368	328	298	288	252
HUYTON WITH ROBY	Urban	4060	M.	1823	53	54	38	46	43	234	228	191	198	204	146	108
			F.	2237	54	43	43	59	63	262	232	208	249	270	236	134
HYDE	Urban	28630	M.	13247	421	394	379	389	379	1962	1729	1470	1282	1130	1082	900
			F.	15383	422	397	399	336	379	1973	1806	1520	1453	1405	1302	1052
INCE IN MAKERFIELD	Urban	16007	M.	8199	312	275	275	247	298	1407	1140	806	780	801	721	633
			F.	7808	294	288	256	275	254	1367	1122	911	713	704	637	546
KEARSLEY	Urban	7253	M.	3426	101	103	101	108	117	530	451	391	336	323	284	199
			F.	3827	111	109	115	115	104	554	511	440	385	351	297	248
KIRKHAM	Urban	3840	M.	1703	61	63	46	43	47	260	211	221	181	157	107	83
			F.	2134	52	43	42	40	56	233	230	195	205	206	177	169
LANCASTER	Urban	20663	M.	10146	272	263	234	251	227	1302	1051	1057	958	988	941	764
			F.	10517	267	257	255	269	267	1315	1143	1027	1026	1016	870	700
LANCASTER	Rural	16244	M.	8343	261	244	238	254	220	1217	1033	952	887	820	654	558
			F.	7901	237	248	242	240	218	1185	938	877	804	713	625	520
LATHOM	Urban	4161	M.	2081	69	49	71	69	59	317	266	210	204	230	152	138
			F.	2080	65	61	57	59	57	299	287	228	174	218	133	149
LEES	Urban	3511	M.	1662	51	46	48	50	39	234	203	199	178	140	147	111
			F.	1849	49	46	52	36	45	228	198	207	164	181	156	140
LEIGH	Urban	21734	M.	10558	363	303	308	279	321	1574	1371	1113	1081	1038	871	721
			F.	11176	373	316	332	319	351	1691	1402	1204	1098	1075	933	670
LEIGH	Rural	12028	M.	5808	169	156	189	164	179	857	774	683	600	546	421	356
			F.	6120	188	168	178	163	175	872	793	719	655	497	428	343
LEVENSHULME	Urban	3557	M.	1621	50	53	41	52	50	246	214	169	188	154	144	120
			F.	1936	68	56	52	52	49	271	225	184	210	221	177	130
LEYLAND	Urban	4961	M.	2325	85	62	52	68	74	341	284	286	251	208	168	142
			F.	2630	90	63	77	69	65	364	300	281	270	201	209	181
LITHERLAND	Urban	2426	M.	1108	30	31	34	30	28	154	161	129	105	91	76	90
			F.	1318	33	30	41	30	43	177	165	142	154	130	104	95
LITTLEBOROUGH	Urban	10406	M.	4909	128	92	146	112	124	602	584	577	543	453	427	350
			F.	5497	133	141	135	126	151	686	642	586	546	524	468	409
LITTLE CROSBY	Urban	553	M.	306	9	4	7	4	7	31	26	82	32	30	15	18
			F.	247	2	7	6	6	3	24	38	19	28	28	19	19

Table 6 *continued.*—AGES of MALES and FEMALES in SANI

SANITARY DISTRICT.		ALL AGES. Persons.	ALL AGES. Males and Females.		Under 1 Year.	1–	2–	3–	4–	Under 5 Years.	5–	10–	15–	20–	25–	30
LITTLE HULTON	Urban	5714	M.	2819	88	104	72	90	80	443	378	321	293	265	229	1[illegible]
			F.	2895	88	85	79	66	82	400	407	348	277	270	225	10
LITTLE LEVER	Urban	4413	M.	2143	51	71	51	63	68	304	272	227	262	201	148	15
			F.	2270	74	67	70	66	58	335	322	267	228	178	171	1[illegible]
LITTLE WOOLTON	Urban	1159	M.	481	14	13	15	10	11	63	61	45	56	42	34	4
			F.	678	20	8	17	18	18	81	64	57	66	82	60	5
LIVERPOOL	Urban	552508	M.	271996	8838	7445	7549	7309	7037	38178	32255	27697	25118	25843	24897	2138
			F.	280512	8583	7475	7086	7373	7378	38498	32309	27931	25498	26708	24615	214[illegible]
LOWER BEBINGTON	Urban	4050	M.	2049	62	59	52	57	53	283	220	235	332	168	175	12
			F.	2001	32	43	52	45	52	244	231	210	204	193	186	13
LUNESDALE	Rural	7132	M.	3568	97	90	74	92	77	430	437	387	387	320	250	1[illegible]
			F.	3564	87	91	92	95	96	461	411	371	350	338	284	21
LYMM	Urban	4665	M.	2248	55	63	65	73	65	321	288	252	204	226	166	13
			F.	2417	66	54	69	48	55	292	291	278	231	255	191	15
LYTHAM	Urban	4122	M.	1717	48	39	48	59	43	237	230	239	148	140	137	10
			F.	2405	54	51	55	60	47	257	221	203	242	243	242	19
MACCLESFIELD	Urban	37514	M.	17255	450	430	402	427	447	2216	1995	1928	1687	1374	1165	97
			F.	20259	515	459	432	489	490	2385	2102	1864	1948	1902	1630	13[illegible]
MACCLESFIELD	Rural	17589	M.	8587	224	226	229	221	226	1126	1054	900	945	736	571	52
			F.	9002	250	199	239	251	261	1200	1083	923	887	787	723	57
MANCHESTER	Urban	341414	M.	163475	4940	4405	4594	4363	4370	22681	19197	16975	16023	16250	15197	1273
			F.	177939	5078	4653	4550	4593	4367	23241	19574	17251	17314	18232	16323	133[illegible]
MARPLE	Urban	4421	M.	1980	52	44	44	43	42	225	224	228	221	178	156	11
			F.	2441	63	45	62	52	64	286	230	235	278	267	214	15
MIDDLETON AND TONGE	Urban	18953	M.	9141	263	237	219	229	249	1197	1097	987	918	868	757	65
			F.	9812	239	241	281	256	282	1299	1113	1028	965	932	800	69
MIDDLEWICH	Urban	3379	M.	1688	45	40	51	56	48	240	219	189	170	158	116	9
			F.	1691	53	65	40	49	41	248	229	211	165	137	110	10
MILNROW	Urban	7013	M.	3336	79	75	91	86	78	409	372	371	341	324	275	24
			F.	3677	84	65	89	80	87	405	395	385	354	340	338	24
*MOSSLEY (*part of*)	Urban	8993	M.	4174	136	105	117	119	102	579	523	465	441	382	374	28
			F.	4819	129	104	122	132	129	616	554	509	503	472	367	36
MOSS SIDE	Urban	18131	M.	8072	205	216	219	207	213	1060	919	859	887	758	762	68
			F.	10059	222	221	199	226	205	1073	999	964	1157	1218	1061	82
MOTTRAM IN LONGDENDALE	Urban	2913	M.	1367	37	30	37	37	30	171	173	162	124	126	105	9
			F.	1546	36	28	42	32	42	180	190	144	158	156	125	10
MUCH WOOLTON	Urban	4541	M.	2140	71	55	74	63	57	320	288	217	208	188	177	14
			F.	2401	63	53	55	66	50	287	292	226	244	211	187	16
NANTWICH	Urban	7495	M.	3649	127	85	115	90	83	500	459	419	371	292	245	23
			F.	3846	121	100	98	90	79	458	454	431	451	382	286	20
NANTWICH	Rural	27017	M.	13480	373	373	356	372	348	1822	1743	1536	1455	1114	898	72
			F.	13537	392	329	344	368	356	1789	1686	1580	1382	1163	954	79
NELSON	Urban	10381	M.	4092	195	133	150	136	150	764	623	572	521	464	430	36
			F.	5389	156	177	151	138	156	778	647	579	564	575	488	34
NESTON AND PARKGATE	Urban	3405	M.	1620	63	34	49	46	54	246	216	205	157	150	119	9
			F.	1785	51	44	56	45	51	247	228	190	180	163	129	10
NEWTON HEATH	Urban	29189	M.	14296	460	416	450	450	418	2194	1954	1570	1354	1259	1251	100
			F.	14893	494	418	450	458	407	2227	1878	1539	1460	1334	1214	103

* The remainder of the Urban Sanitary District of Mossley is in Division IX. (See Table 6.)

Entire Urban Sanitary District of Mossley		13372	M.	6121	204	154	174	172	158	862	747	690	646	564	555	40
			F.	7251	194	165	187	193	190	929	793	763	776	728	592	51

Table 6 *continued.*—Ages of Males and Females in Sanit

Sanitary District.		All Ages. Persons.		All Ages. Males and Females.	Under 1 Year.	1–	2–	3–	4–	Under 5 Years.	5–	10–	15–	20–	25–	30–
NEWTON IN MAKERFIELD	Urban	10580	M.	5638	176	157	172	158	171	834	709	607	621	533	510	4
			F.	4942	170	170	168	152	147	807	708	560	413	404	383	3
NORDEN	Urban	4043	M.	1935	52	47	46	54	46	244	218	203	202	191	150	1
			F.	2108	69	44	50	54	47	264	241	232	209	194	179	1
NORTHWICH	Urban	12246	M.	6307	209	200	188	187	173	957	764	707	647	550	497	38
			F.	5939	186	185	160	174	169	874	764	673	515	514	435	37
NORTHWICH	Rural	18380	M.	9420	250	269	267	258	238	1282	1212	1068	1027	849	691	51
			F.	8951	275	232	288	267	242	1304	1160	1096	790	772	633	54
OLDHAM	Urban	111343	M.	53536	1624	1457	1521	1484	1400	7486	6335	5688	5813	5038	4837	40
			F.	57807	1567	1507	1506	1503	1438	7521	6672	5895	5811	5833	5079	40
OPENSHAW	Urban	16153	M.	8047	306	257	246	226	229	1261	1014	848	754	742	738	6
			F.	8106	285	248	262	272	234	1296	1088	824	761	700	676	5
ORMSKIRK	Urban	6651	M.	3297	90	68	96	71	96	421	410	351	332	288	261	24
			F.	3354	99	76	103	82	80	440	418	341	326	297	223	21
ORMSKIRK	Rural	25782	M.	13013	374	384	370	428	335	1900	1607	1422	1331	1254	1004	81
			F.	12769	380	301	381	357	346	1864	1649	1354	1290	1158	934	8
ORRELL	Urban	4299	M.	2161	78	59	77	64	58	336	292	249	206	217	163	1
			F.	2138	78	66	65	73	55	337	292	216	223	198	169	1
OSWALDTWISLE	Urban	12206	M.	5904	186	155	171	208	161	881	706	677	662	588	507	8
			F.	6302	183	210	170	165	147	875	735	708	646	653	503	4
OVER DARWEN	Urban	29744	M.	13977	431	360	441	380	394	2006	1837	1672	1439	1268	1175	10
			F.	15767	426	389	384	407	418	2024	1956	1778	1698	1520	1377	11
PADIHAM AND HAPTON	Urban	8974	M.	4254	123	121	116	139	111	610	503	484	407	404	371	2
			F.	4720	124	110	118	115	126	602	526	461	461	484	435	3
PEMBERTON	Urban	13762	M.	6809	254	226	222	222	197	1121	1047	792	690	590	543	4
			F.	6953	246	216	216	189	242	1109	971	888	728	626	557	41
POULTON, BARE, AND TORRIS-HOLME	Urban	3931	M.	1773	55	46	57	45	54	257	203	186	169	167	120	11
			F.	2158	47	54	55	53	44	253	232	215	227	196	107	14
PRESCOT	Urban	6419	M.	3244	97	96	96	91	88	468	432	375	346	272	275	1
			F.	3175	112	85	103	100	99	499	416	376	273	258	243	1
PRESCOT	Rural	15698	M.	7903	212	221	259	247	199	1138	957	821	735	730	621	6
			F.	7705	223	232	214	235	218	1122	983	859	696	656	560	51
PRESTON	Urban	96537	M.	44264	1372	1254	1222	1277	1180	6305	5598	5138	4060	3893	3417	28
			F.	52273	1438	1298	1357	1240	1217	6550	5656	5343	5401	5269	4325	371
PRESTON	Rural	19612	M.	9594	253	230	221	227	229	1160	1112	1045	951	813	712	61
			F.	10018	243	223	217	236	207	1126	1091	996	852	905	820	7
PRESTWICH	Urban	8627	M.	3945	97	109	92	109	88	495	456	349	302	342	361	31
			F.	4682	99	97	98	97	79	470	427	401	408	475	461	3
PRESTWICH	Rural	17605	M.	8411	287	254	246	264	250	1301	1113	922	798	682	723	6
			F.	9195	320	249	277	269	258	1373	1094	964	907	856	764	7
RADCLIFFE	Urban	16267	M.	7793	237	245	232	224	214	1152	981	834	857	729	690	5
			F.	8474	251	236	230	227	223	1167	1062	883	840	833	741	6
RAINFORD	Urban	3745	M.	2004	63	49	80	40	54	295	227	213	231	218	180	1
			F.	1741	74	52	59	54	60	299	260	187	159	123	146	1
RAMSBOTTOM	Urban	5242	M.	2424	67	60	73	80	54	343	297	254	244	199	214	1
			F.	2818	88	65	51	72	80	356	300	295	268	271	262	2
RAWTENSTALL	Urban	12571	M.	5943	197	165	160	169	148	834	683	649	649	535	484	3
			F.	6628	179	161	191	181	165	877	733	681	696	634	509	4

T t 3

Table 6 *continued*.—AGES of MALES and FEMALES in SANI[illegible]

SANITARY DISTRICT.		ALL AGES. Persons.	ALL AGES. Males and Females.		Under 1 Year.	1–	2–	3–	4–	Under 5 Years.	5–	10–	15–	20–	25–	30
ROCHDALE	Urban	68866	M.	31985	852	822	829	852	841	4196	3960	3580	3234	2868	2643	218
			F.	36881	874	801	865	852	866	4258	3077	3661	3702	3661	3306	26
ROYTON	Urban	11433	M.	5450	174	150	142	132	128	726	657	594	582	515	501	3
			F.	5983	168	152	166	174	135	795	671	628	570	571	511	4
RUNCORN	Urban	15126	M.	7697	263	235	257	236	237	1228	1026	840	726	668	639	5
			F.	7429	261	237	244	216	236	1194	1021	798	689	603	570	4
RUNCORN	Rural	18897	M.	9748	282	254	277	250	258	1321	1188	1061	1009	998	671	6
			F.	9149	259	248	263	238	240	1248	1171	1068	912	778	609	5
RUSHOLME	Urban	11238	M.	4815	137	134	128	132	127	658	545	474	489	493	438	3
			F.	6423	144	122	161	119	122	668	575	520	761	863	693	5
ST. ANNE'S ON THE SEA	Urban	1179	M.	563	14	18	19	14	16	81	79	80	51	44	47	
			F.	616	10	14	18	13	11	66	68	88	81	60	52	
ST. HELENS	Urban	57403	M.	29797	1011	928	914	936	867	4656	3981	3221	2891	2939	2689	21
			F.	27606	979	949	962	893	885	4668	3908	3109	2596	2348	2157	18
SALE	Urban	7915	M.	3392	92	91	99	111	109	502	425	368	299	258	256	2
			F.	4523	101	92	97	120	88	498	454	434	504	527	434	3
SALFORD	Urban	176235	M.	84610	2916	2435	2585	2521	2443	12900	10854	9241	8128	7645	7416	65
			F.	91625	2820	2482	2636	2490	2517	12945	11017	9237	8494	8639	8130	71
SANDBACH	Urban	5493	M.	2732	75	83	84	74	66	382	347	290	259	243	190	1
			F.	2761	88	55	63	58	76	340	349	314	275	226	208	1
SKELMERSDALE	Urban	5707	M.	3065	112	98	100	99	83	492	407	331	321	296	275	2
			F.	2642	98	108	105	105	91	507	441	312	193	198	206	1
SOUTHPORT	Urban	32206	M.	13272	392	328	368	377	362	1827	1583	1516	1264	1131	1080	8
			F.	18934	373	351	376	368	374	1842	1623	1645	2028	2148	1816	14
STALYBRIDGE*	Urban	25977	M.	12097	405	333	321	342	332	1733	1505	1316	1211	1080	972	8
			F.	13880	383	321	333	352	324	1713	1518	1348	1353	1309	1166	9
STANDISH WITH LANGTREE	Urban	4261	M.	2146	65	76	60	72	68	341	317	232	207	193	176	1
			F.	2115	85	72	74	79	69	379	300	241	208	167	157	1
STOCKPORT	Urban	59553	M.	27567	790	755	754	747	778	3824	3216	2980	2732	2410	2365	19
			F.	31986	830	705	757	746	780	3818	3411	3181	3093	3187	2794	23
STOCKPORT	Rural	21935	M.	10236	320	275	291	293	280	1459	1260	1195	1006	892	826	6
			F.	11699	256	300	296	315	304	1501	1316	1168	1213	1225	1008	8
STRETFORD	Urban	19018	M.	8634	215	211	212	226	255	1119	1056	966	911	807	708	6
			F.	10384	245	230	249	225	225	1174	1018	997	1186	1206	993	8
SWINTON AND PENDLEBURY	Urban	18107	M.	8847	293	233	243	281	254	1304	1346	1204	870	787	695	5
			F.	9260	295	285	249	256	241	1326	1267	1164	920	848	726	5
TARPORLEY	Urban	2669	M.	1276	28	25	27	34	25	139	108	139	127	120	92	
			F.	1393	42	30	33	42	43	190	163	165	102	119	83	
TARVIN	Rural	11186	M.	5478	164	124	165	143	139	735	631	692	579	444	335	2
			F.	5708	141	150	145	136	152	724	708	663	580	476	396	3
TODMORDEN (*part of*)†	Urban	333	M.	169	2	4	1	3	6	16	24	8	20	16	12	
			F.	164	2	9	3	3	4	21	12	13	22	8	24	
TOXTETH PARK	Urban	10368	M.	4136	122	121	96	132	97	568	523	437	356	340	316	3
			F.	6232	114	110	127	127	103	581	545	495	741	882	706	5
TRAWDEN	Urban	2164	M.	1071	45	23	37	23	40	168	135	110	111	82	84	
			F.	1093	33	22	50	27	27	159	160	132	95	100	88	
TURTON	Urban	5653	M.	2645	86	78	72	78	62	376	339	300	287	270	214	1
			F.	3008	80	74	70	83	80	387	317	309	324	313	261	1

* The Urban Sanitary District of Stalybridge was extended by Act 44 and 45 Vict. c. 191, and embraces the Urban Sanitary District of Stayley, dissolved by this Act did not come into operation until 11th August 1881, the figures given in this Table for Stalybridge (Urban) and for Ashton-under-Lyne (Rural) rel[illegible]

† The remainder of the Urban Sanitary District of Todmorden is in Division IX. (*See* Table 6.)

	Persons		All Ages	Under 1	1–	2–	3–	4–	Under 5	5–	10–	15–	20–	25–	30
Entire Urban Sanitary District of Todmorden	23862	M.	11541	328	294	303	293	289	1507	1358	1149	1096	1089	952	9
		F.	12321	316	272	293	284	321	1486	1293	1173	1167	1208	1092	9

Table 6 *continued.*—Ages of Males and Females in San

Sanitary District.		All Ages. Persons.	All Ages. Males and Females.		Under 1 Year.	1–	2–	3–	4–	Under 5 Years.	5–	10–	15–	20–	25–	30
Tyldesley with Shakerley	Urban	9954	M.	4990	166	147	158	135	159	765	677	520	494	467	452	3
			F.	4964	164	140	153	162	146	765	701	518	484	455	349	8
Ulverston	Urban	10008	M.	4948	146	153	150	119	162	780	628	583	384	415	393	3
			F.	5060	160	151	151	132	140	734	629	509	400	435	429	5
Ulverston	Rural	19184	M.	9691	276	251	286	250	285	1348	1170	1077	1025	820	674	5
			F.	9493	261	270	264	272	272	1339	1169	1068	876	777	703	5
Upholland	Urban	4435	M.	2318	80	65	69	68	62	344	312	259	228	209	200	1
			F.	2117	63	72	53	74	68	335	292	235	205	182	163	1
Wallasey	Urban	21192	M.	10027	311	279	326	282	272	1470	1297	1081	931	860	818	7
			F.	11165	304	273	294	304	297	1472	1246	1091	1199	1178	1030	8
Walton-le-Dale	Urban	9286	M.	4268	141	105	123	122	116	612	528	516	502	399	325	2
			F.	5018	132	128	120	132	115	627	563	518	535	489	423	3
Walton on the Hill	Urban	18536	M.	8642	302	294	261	275	239	1371	1082	716	614	755	704	6
			F.	9894	290	278	281	266	247	1342	1033	839	932	1064	986	8
Warrington	Urban	41452	M.	20734	725	648	640	621	641	3275	2811	2353	1886	1876	1329	14
			F.	20718	759	671	664	665	664	3423	2705	2844	2045	1971	1617	13
Warrington	Rural	12323	M.	6602	203	174	172	188	167	903	780	669	830	797	505	4
			F.	5721	174	173	177	170	199	893	778	678	490	452	451	5
Waterloo with Seaforth	Urban	9118	M.	3782	101	115	125	100	111	552	494	408	345	371	301	2
			F.	5336	106	108	88	124	108	534	516	485	611	728	586	4
Wavertree	Urban	11097	M.	5119	136	162	152	169	149	818	691	494	493	465	418	3
			F.	5978	168	156	158	148	164	794	675	569	572	639	558	4
West Derby	Urban	33614	M.	14953	462	418	418	395	425	2118	1910	1778	1418	1346	1137	10
			F.	18661	438	433	451	466	447	2230	1935	1927	2160	2022	1622	13
West Derby	Rural	4550	M.	2219	61	58	43	41	50	258	254	234	257	265	169	1
			F.	2331	63	56	58	64	52	293	256	266	236	243	193	1
Westhoughton	Urban	9197	M.	4590	179	188	151	143	136	745	602	531	445	404	379	2
			F.	4607	139	119	156	139	148	701	638	525	429	393	369	2
Whitefield	Urban	9516	M.	4469	136	115	107	117	107	582	550	490	434	436	344	3
			F.	5047	144	127	108	129	121	629	588	520	509	479	424	3
Whitworth	Urban	11892	M.	5740	141	162	166	150	166	785	729	619	609	554	484	3
			F.	6152	159	130	176	152	173	790	676	664	646	638	514	4
Widnes	Urban	24935	M.	13450	502	398	477	438	407	2222	1774	1423	1065	1268	1340	10
			F.	11485	441	427	412	423	419	2122	1676	1324	999	941	907	8
Wigan	Urban	48194	M.	23508	800	651	708	676	674	3509	2987	2649	2284	2283	2012	16
			F.	24686	808	665	718	678	735	3594	3076	2715	2673	2422	1988	16
Wigan	Rural	5554	M.	2903	77	84	83	89	82	415	377	333	289	280	190	1
			F.	2651	89	92	74	68	79	422	366	277	240	223	199	1
Wilmslow	Urban	5664	M.	2671	75	64	63	63	73	338	351	325	256	214	166	1
			F.	2993	67	72	77	81	77	374	309	268	323	311	246	2
Winsford	Urban	10041	M.	5155	165	172	177	175	158	847	707	615	500	406	377	3
			F.	4886	186	156	171	178	143	834	734	628	418	344	342	3
Wirral	Rural	15016	M.	7294	214	227	201	221	214	1077	962	831	754	598	541	4
			F.	7722	201	198	225	199	197	1020	945	848	796	748	599	5
Withington	Urban	17109	M.	7446	203	188	217	183	190	981	873	831	622	622	592	4
			F.	9663	210	192	189	187	202	980	903	828	1000	1193	949	7
Wuerdle and Wardle	Urban	4640	M.	2286	45	50	53	54	51	253	289	259	204	178	156	1
			F.	2354	63	39	41	57	43	243	280	258	211	193	205	1
Yeardsley cum Whaley	Urban	1272	M.	634	17	20	15	17	20	89	81	70	69	47	53	
			F.	638	12	15	20	13	27	87	68	78	54	67	52	

Tt 4

Table 13.—NUMBER and COUNTRY of BIRTH of FOREIGNERS enumerated in COUNTIES, and in each U
exceeds 50,000 PERSONS.

WHERE BORN.	WHERE ENUMERA								
	NORTH-WESTERN COUNTIES.		COUNTIES.						
			33. CHESHIRE.		34. LANCASHIRE.		STOCKPORT.		BIR
	Males.	Females.	Males.	Females.	Males.	Females.	Males.	Females.	Mal
TOTAL - - -	11,102	5,647	1,206	593	9,896	5,054	45	40	5
EUROPE.									
DENMARK	189	35	17	.	172	35	1	.	
NORWAY	700	189	140	1	[illegible]	138	.	.	
SWEDEN	466	67	33	3	433	64	.	.	
RUSSIA	442	174	29	2	413	172	1	1	
POLAND (RUSSIAN)	831	558	6	4	825	554	.	.	
AUSTRIA	366	60	171	6	195	54	1	.	
HUNGARY	80	11	17	5	63	6	1	.	
SWITZERLAND	232	180	29	45	203	135	1	1	
GERMAN EMPIRE	2,713	1,259	211	141	2,502	1,118	8	2	1
HOLLAND	201	94	29	11	172	83	1	.	
BELGIUM	84	63	6	7	78	56	.	1	
FRANCE	432	361	39	49	393	312	4	.	
PORTUGAL	60	12	5	1	55	11	.	.	
SPAIN	626	91	167	3	459	88	.	.	1
ITALY	539	142	38	3	501	139	1	1	
GREECE	167	28	4	.	163	28	.	.	
TURKEY	200	52	7	6	193	46	.	.	
SERVIA	.	.	.	.	.	.	.	.	
ROUMANIA	15	13	2	.	13	13	.	.	
ASIA.									
ARABIA	3	.	.	.	3	.	.	.	
PERSIA	1	.	.	.	1	.	.	.	
CHINA	22	1	3	.	19	1	.	.	
OTHER COUNTRIES	41	17	19	2	22	15	.	.	
AFRICA.									
EGYPT	24	12	2	.	22	12	.	.	
OTHER PARTS	30	10	3	.	27	10	.	.	
AMERICA.									
UNITED STATES	2,502	2,218	208	290	2,294	1,928	26	34	
MEXICO	15	5	1	.	14	5	.	.	
BRAZIL	32	11	5	4	27	7	.	.	
OTHER STATES	50	28	13	10	37	18	.	.	
COUNTRY NOT STATED	5	3	1	.	4	3	.	.	
AT SEA	2	3	1	.	1	3	.	.	

Table 13 *continued*.—NUMBER and COUNTRY OF BIRTH of FOREIGNERS enumerated in COUNTIES, and ... exceeds 50,000 PERSONS.

WHERE BORN.	WHERE ENUME[RATED]							
	URBAN SANITARY [DISTRICTS]							
	BURY.		SALFORD.		MAN-CHESTER.		OLDHAM.	
	Males.	Females.	Males.	Females.	Males.	Females.	Males.	Females.
TOTAL	57	38	272		1,786	1,019	99	74
EUROPE.								
Denmark	.	1	.	.	14	.	.	.
Norway	.	.	1	.	3	.	.	.
Sweden	.	.	3	.	9	1	.	.
Russia	1	.	6	3	86	40	1	.
Poland (Russian)	1	.	7	2	423	339	2	.
Austria	.	.	7	6	63	28	1	.
Hungary	.	.	6	1	5	.	.	.
Switzerland	1	.	4	8	51	12	.	1
German Empire	12	12	63	40	468	223	15	7
Holland	.	.	11	4	28	8	.	.
Belgium	.	2	5	2	8	7	1	.
France	3	1	29	25	90	48	2	.
Portugal	.	.	.	.	8	3	.	.
Spain	.	.	2	.	20	1	2	.
Italy	5	1	10	4	154	73	1	.
Greece	.	.	14	11	30	6	.	.
Turkey	.	.	28	17	161	17	.	.
Servia	.	.	.	.	.	.	.	.
Roumania	.	.	2	5	9	8	.	.
ASIA.								
Arabia	.	.	.	.	2	.	.	.
Persia	.	.	.	.	1	.	.	.
China	.	.	.	.	.	.	.	.
Other Countries	.	.	3	3	1	.	.	.
AFRICA.								
Egypt	.	.	1	.	5	2	.	.
Other Parts	.	.	.	.	14	6	.	.
AMERICA.								
United States	34	21	67	96	188	196	74	66
Mexico	.	.	2	.	.	1	.	.
Brazil	.	.	1	.	2	.	.	.
Other States	.	.	.	.	3	.	.	.
Country not stated	.	.	.	.	.	.	.	.
At Sea	.	.	.	.	.	.	.	.

R 4178

Table 6.—AGES of MALES and FEMALES in SANITARY

SANITARY DISTRICT.		ALL AGES. Persons.	ALL AGES. Males and Females.		Under 1 Year.	1–	2–	3–	4–	Under 5 Years.	5–	10–	15–	20–	25–
ALLERTON	Urban	3685	M.	1698	50	44	57	33	49	233	188	204	198	143	132
			F.	1987	56	44	54	57	54	265	225	194	231	203	177
ALTOFTS	Urban	3172	M.	1692	61	48	55	55	59	278	248	198	146	153	106
			F.	1480	63	61	48	56	57	285	238	175	97	107	121
ASKERN	Urban	548	M.	240	5	4	8	4	3	24	21	49	23	18	10
			F.	308	7	5	2	7	7	28	29	48	82	28	15
AUSTONLEY	Urban	1662	M.	791	29	30	25	13	23	120	92	77	77	77	68
			F.	871	19	22	23	19	21	104	116	87	79	85	84
AYSGARTH	Rural	5482	M.	2793	69	70	88	65	73	360	315	335	254	248	216
			F.	2689	86	69	60	56	61	332	285	280	271	242	197
BAILDON	Urban	5430	M.	2638	88	68	67	66	72	361	320	302	256	259	231
			F.	2792	76	68	73	54	76	347	306	276	296	292	236
BARKISLAND	Urban	2102	M.	989	25	21	28	30	30	134	153	111	80	84	84
			F.	1113	34	46	27	29	28	164	125	129	121	112	89
BARNSLEY	Urban	29790	M.	14979	472	465	404	449	452	2243	1796	1536	1408	1379	1321
			F.	14811	496	409	455	446	434	2240	1936	1524	1443	1403	1228
BARNSLEY	Rural	20616	M.	11114	375	353	336	360	345	1769	1479	1188	1079	1115	1015
			F.	9502	357	365	357	337	364	1780	1486	1085	673	689	750
BATLEY	Urban	27505	M.	12907	426	318	377	369	393	1883	1689	1491	1291	1141	1041
			F.	14598	332	308	411	381	302	1934	1807	1575	1569	1477	1200
BEDALE	Rural	6518	M.	3249	67	92	93	102	87	441	381	373	332	255	201
			F.	3269	97	78	73	74	87	404	378	351	300	277	239
BEVERLEY	Urban	11425	M.	5335	161	148	137	147	161	754	686	554	468	373	403
			F.	6090	156	157	154	155	141	763	732	646	548	486	455
BEVERLEY	Rural	11075	M.	5904	153	142	157	147	162	761	626	564	702	619	402
			F.	5171	135	158	107	154	147	696	645	509	461	383	362
BINGLEY	Urban	9465	M.	4528	119	114	102	133	146	614	537	515	483	412	344
			F.	4937	130	130	123	123	129	635	557	511	526	473	414
BINGLEY IMPROVEMENT DISTRICT	Urban	8972	M.	4120	118	119	114	118	120	580	526	454	414	367	305
			F.	4852	121	113	116	110	114	574	535	487	469	505	412
BIRKENSHAW	Urban	2699	M.	1281	26	30	30	36	34	156	168	134	142	130	102
			F.	1418	43	34	39	34	32	182	170	153	142	140	113
BIRSTAL	Urban	676[illegible]	M.	3172	109	88	97	96	102	492	342	334	338	274	261
			F.	3594	116	89	96	84	90	475	422	382	372	354	320
BRADFORD	Urban	183032	M.	85211	2714	2295	2282	2399	2357	12047	10636	9346	8512	7524	7051
			F.	97821	2651	2337	2501	2430	2422	12341	10676	9717	10091	10071	8830
BRIDLINGTON	Urban	8343	M.	3713	110	100	109	103	95	517	468	392	317	255	232
			F.	4630	123	94	122	123	103	565	491	460	500	400	317
BRIDLINGTON	Rural	8419	M.	4432	130	112	110	101	110	563	506	473	577	419	407
			F.	3987	116	96	125	129	105	571	513	432	404	306	291
BRIGHOUSE	Urban	7965	M.	3862	130	107	94	98	95	524	491	422	414	361	335
			F.	4103	120	111	112	115	108	560	510	439	439	378	352
BROTTON	Urban	4184	M.	2284	78	52	74	61	65	330	305	231	207	225	213
			F.	1900	75	77	80	62	81	375	267	227	166	148	144
BURLEY	Urban	2550	M.	1177	38	33	35	33	36	175	150	122	107	98	85
			F.	1373	31	39	34	28	41	173	145	162	140	140	104
CALVERLEY	Urban	3772	M.	1762	48	55	43	44	47	237	216	208	167	132	130
			F.	2010	54	45	34	53	47	233	252	205	200	171	170

Note.—For the Parishes comprised in each Urban Sanitary District, see Vol. II., I

SANITARY DISTRICT.		ALL AGES. Persons.	Males and Females.		Under 1 Year.	1–	2–	3–	4–	Under 5 Years.	5–	–10	15–	20–	25–
CARTWORTH - - - - - -	Urban	2037	M. -	1059	32	39	24	21	28	144	134	113	106	93	90
			F. -	978	33	22	24	35	18	132	139	107	94	84	82
CASTLEFORD - - - - - -	Urban	10530	M. -	5530	205	176	173	181	169	904	744	600	629	493	639
			F. -	6000	186	170	185	195	188	924	743	584	387	383	439
CHURWELL - - - -	Urban	1973	M. -	974	39	29	20	24	28	140	131	111	112	73	82
			F. -	999	24	31	26	20	29	130	140	90	95	108	72
CLAYTON - - -	Urban	4301	M. -	2166	49	45	54	54	54	256	276	239	234	167	156
			F. -	2135	69	57	49	40	66	271	206	239	208	208	193
CLAYTON WEST - - - -	Urban	1435	M. -	705	26	19	27	19	16	107	81	96	78	50	45
			F. -	730	14	7	16	17	18	71	79	87	82	61	68
CLECKHEATON - - -	Urban	10653	M. -	6138	148	158	138	138	144	726	617	620	560	462	398
			F. -	6515	141	122	131	155	165	714	667	585	590	542	450
COTTINGHAM - - -	Urban	6228	M. -	2874	92	79	85	84	84	424	393	390	265	223	204
			F. -	3354	81	70	79	93	90	413	403	381	332	329	271
CROWLE - - - - - -	Urban	3353	M. -	1636	41	37	30	41	47	205	204	202	149	117	81
			F. -	1717	39	46	36	32	41	194	230	203	176	119	103
CUMBERWORTH - - -	Urban	1471	M. -	743	16	23	21	23	16	98	93	80	78	69	45
			F. -	728	29	18	15	17	19	98	90	99	70	70	45
DARTON - - -	Urban	6014	M. -	3117	95	98	79	87	94	453	425	379	300	272	230
			F. -	2897	108	103	101	94	130	536	442	341	222	210	196
DENBY - - - - - - -	Urban	1559	M. -	784	28	26	20	24	20	118	88	71	70	77	65
			F. -	775	21	22	21	17	32	113	85	77	78	69	57
DENHOLME GATE - - -	Urban	3549	M. -	1761	47	49	41	49	38	224	193	186	185	147	163
			F. -	1788	53	40	36	45	40	214	203	188	181	144	146
DEWSBURY - - -	Urban	29637	M. -	14179	423	396	395	397	351	1962	1786	1521	1473	1284	1170
			F. -	15458	459	379	382	400	417	2037	1719	1573	1611	1655	1361
DODWORTH - - - - - -	Urban	2989	M. -	1618	66	51	41	60	56	274	236	202	151	120	123
			F. -	1371	44	40	51	44	48	231	229	160	101	94	99
DONCASTER - - - -	Urban	21139	M. -	10445	336	266	253	262	260	1376	1213	1138	1001	1004	834
			F. -	10694	317	243	259	251	245	1315	1156	1191	1068	1000	834
DONCASTER - - -	Rural	24182	M. -	12231	362	320	376	334	313	1705	1545	1260	1196	1073	904
			F. -	11951	366	359	340	342	327	1734	1526	1363	1047	943	888
DRIFFIELD - - - - - -	Rural	14130	M. -	7388	196	153	209	199	173	930	877	789	889	689	523
			F. -	6742	227	188	192	203	201	1011	885	731	608	543	453
DRIGHLINGTON - - -	Urban	4214	M. -	2094	51	64	54	56	63	277	263	245	211	200	167
			F. -	2120	51	60	58	72	47	288	285	227	206	213	184
EASINGWOLD - - -	Rural	9533	M. -	4897	120	128	125	113	133	619	544	627	600	443	319
			F. -	4636	126	106	120	131	103	586	558	506	473	402	301
ECCLESALL BIERLOW - -	Rural	5400	M. -	2708	78	86	80	65	85	394	366	298	236	212	199
			F. -	2692	75	56	79	76	92	378	364	317	243	229	187
ECCLESHILL - - - -	Urban	7037	M. -	3380	120	98	96	96	104	514	376	394	318	282	240
			F. -	3657	101	99	95	101	93	489	419	393	330	360	313
ELLAND - - -	Urban	8278	M. -	3940	116	121	114	84	97	632	438	478	446	374	324
			F. -	4338	129	99	130	103	115	576	485	444	465	400	369
EMLEY - - - - - - -	Urban	1289	M. -	662	17	12	10	19	12	70	71	75	89	58	48
			F. -	627	19	15	15	21	10	80	87	77	55	52	36
FARNLEY TYAS - - -	Urban	614	M. -	323	6	10	9	8	8	41	36	40	28	36	23
			F. -	291	6	15	6	7	8	41	31	26	26	22	15
FARSLEY - - -	Urban	4434	M. -	2090	67	64	49	45	44	269	234	230	219	198	173
			F. -	2344	67	46	67	39	60	269	235	233	251	240	213

Table 6 *continued*.—AGES of MALES and FEMALES in SAN

SANITARY DISTRICT.		ALL AGES. Persons.	Males and Females.		Under 1 Year.	1–	2–	3–	4–	Under 5 Years.	5–	10–	15–	20–	25–	30
FEATHERSTONE	Urban	5901	M.	3171	110	98	114	106	115	543	431	361	277	270	273	
			F.	2730	120	108	110	95	100	542	502	322	140	157	281	
FILEY	Urban	2337	M.	1036	39	23	40	32	27	161	150	120	75	69	62	
			F.	1301	32	25	45	24	43	169	130	142	132	116	87	
FLOCKTON	Urban	1180	M.	620	26	13	22	20	18	99	87	77	58	49	42	
			F.	560	18	17	19	19	12	85	89	78	42	39	41	
FULSTONE	Urban	1906	M.	934	31	20	27	34	26	138	126	105	91	97	83	
			F.	972	28	25	30	21	25	129	114	126	116	86	84	
GILDERSOME	Urban	3470	M.	1741	50	48	43	56	52	249	212	241	201	144	122	
			F.	1729	59	43	40	58	56	256	225	204	177	158	139	
GOLCAR	Urban	7653	M.	3746	120	93	102	104	114	533	453	408	415	380	336	
			F.	3907	115	98	108	112	95	528	482	449	401	372	383	
GOMERSAL	Urban	3988	M.	1849	56	52	59	41	50	258	211	197	218	160	164	
			F.	2139	58	57	50	56	43	264	234	219	219	219	198	
GOOLE	Urban	10418	M.	5282	184	166	166	171	138	825	660	512	463	462	486	
			F.	5136	163	142	168	151	152	776	705	575	475	425	407	
GOOLE	Rural	9140	M.	4520	126	121	110	115	123	595	525	503	580	386	283	
			F.	4620	116	126	126	109	118	535	562	484	416	369	313	
GREASBROUGH	Urban	2914	M.	1522	45	38	47	47	44	221	213	175	167	129	122	
			F.	1392	46	44	48	36	44	218	203	188	117	84	94	
GREAT DRIFFIELD	Urban	5937	M.	2887	77	77	78	89	84	405	368	382	266	233	203	
			F.	3050	72	81	77	91	86	407	342	334	298	280	219	
GREAT OUSEBURN	Rural	11955	M.	5928	142	166	156	173	141	773	740	648	593	500	394	
			F.	6027	155	142	137	159	165	758	745	668	589	515	382	
GREETLAND	Urban	4166	M.	1953	47	47	61	57	46	258	241	221	208	168	151	
			F.	2213	71	54	55	32	49	261	268	234	208	206	184	
GUISBROUGH	Urban	6616	M.	3452	116	103	91	108	124	542	524	375	292	248	275	
			F.	3164	122	113	102	111	87	535	484	381	269	273	238	
GUISBROUGH	Rural	8251	M.	4281	123	112	115	115	135	600	527	468	429	411	321	
			F.	3970	128	115	126	117	149	635	587	492	324	319	292	
GUISELEY	Urban	3706	M.	1831	48	53	45	53	55	254	260	218	186	145	109	
			F.	1875	60	44	47	53	45	249	254	235	167	157	129	
GUNTHWAITE AND INGBIRCH-WORTH	Urban	405	M.	214	6	9	6	3	9	33	24	12	19	31	18	
			F.	191	8	5	6	5	11	35	19	22	18	13	13	
HALIFAX	Urban	73630	M.	34634	1014	886	918	879	883	4580	4160	3718	3352	3122	2938	
			F.	38996	1052	840	919	948	925	4684	4228	3804	3845	3829	3504	
HALIFAX	Rural	9256	M.	4526	134	111	118	129	123	615	589	514	408	419	353	
			F.	4730	149	116	131	131	136	663	591	504	464	411	401	
HANDSWORTH	Urban	7645	M.	4062	145	107	132	131	133	648	562	436	402	380	335	
			F.	3583	134	109	122	110	128	603	549	421	293	273	248	
HARROGATE	Urban	9482	M.	3964	107	100	95	110	84	496	456	539	416	208	281	
			F.	5518	91	93	93	110	96	483	469	490	726	692	496	
HAWORTH	Urban	3816	M.	1781	48	54	39	57	47	245	194	180	198	159	133	
			F.	2035	54	48	55	50	34	241	195	237	218	231	177	
HEATON	Urban	3107	M.	1460	57	41	42	50	46	236	207	159	142	99	110	
			F.	1647	41	35	48	39	49	212	179	168	163	187	139	
HEBDEN BRIDGE	Urban	5007	M.	2388	62	83	57	76	61	338	290	247	220	248	214	
			F.	2619	69	47	48	65	44	273	242	235	269	282	248	
HECKMONDWIKE	Urban	9282	M.	4464	155	139	128	129	117	668	548	466	421	417	368	
			F.	4818	122	109	113	131	141	616	578	481	517	490	414	

Table 6 *continued*.—AGES of MALES and FEMALES in SAN

SANITARY DISTRICT.		ALL AGES. Persons.	ALL AGES. Males and Females.		Under 1 Year.	1–	2–	3–	4–	Under 5 Years.	5–	10–	15–	20–	25–	3(
HEDON	Urban	966	M.	437	15	12	11	13	9	60	50	53	34	31	23	
			F.	529	11	11	15	15	17	69	65	63	40	44	27	
HELMSLEY	Rural	5919	M.	3151	86	66	68	81	70	371	351	386	410	260	207	1
			F.	2768	85	78	63	85	53	364	359	317	293	233	168	1
HEMSWORTH	Rural	11106	M.	5935	168	165	162	163	156	814	640	708	578	593	480	4
			F.	5171	151	151	148	151	133	734	683	616	443	435	383	3
HEPWORTH	Urban	1047	M.	550	22	13	21	17	14	87	77	65	64	53	36	
			F.	497	21	10	17	13	21	82	68	60	53	48	32	
HINDERWELL	Urban	2467	M.	1239	40	44	31	34	39	188	157	170	96	108	84	
			F.	1228	37	37	43	26	35	178	103	141	110	102	81	
HIPPERHOLME	Urban	2934	M.	1302	45	41	36	38	35	195	159	132	107	121	118	1
			F.	1632	45	42	46	38	45	216	192	147	173	157	165	1
HOLME	Urban	678	M.	354	7	10	9	6	16	48	38	44	34	38	25	
			F.	324	7	4	7	5	12	35	45	40	30	35	21	
HONLEY	Urban	5070	M.	2451	62	65	57	59	57	300	284	253	251	219	193	1
			F.	2619	65	56	65	66	65	317	277	274	252	235	230	1
HORBURY	Urban	5050	M.	2384	73	78	79	84	77	391	304	273	248	206	171	1
			F.	2666	69	62	70	76	60	337	341	298	320	290	184	1
HORNSEA	Urban	1836	M.	777	22	14	28	22	28	114	91	73	68	66	44	
			F.	1059	17	38	20	27	28	130	117	102	117	107	73	
HORSFORTH	Urban	6346	M.	3046	98	95	82	84	88	447	398	357	280	245	246	1
			F.	3300	104	92	80	94	85	455	434	322	332	301	276	[illegible]
HOWDEN	Rural	12182	M.	6282	137	133	158	149	159	736	749	803	746	473	409	[illegible]
			F.	5900	173	150	155	170	147	795	693	662	534	473	343	[illegible]
HOYLAND-SWAINE	Urban	750	M.	396	16	12	15	16	8	67	46	36	39	30	27	
			F.	354	13	13	11	12	7	56	60	42	20	26	27	
HUDDERSFIELD	Urban	81841	M.	38957	1125	990	1013	1045	984	5157	4670	4373	3887	3614	3367	2[illegible]
			F.	42884	1046	1027	1045	988	1030	5136	4840	4354	4456	4534	3788	3[illegible]
HUNSLET	Rural	5687	M.	2871	89	78	105	83	96	451	375	304	274	251	215	1
			F.	2816	94	75	87	86	83	425	397	308	231	201	232	1
HUNSWORTH	Urban	1516	M.	752	27	14	16	16	25	98	93	74	84	74	53	
			F.	764	15	20	21	21	16	93	83	93	77	69	60	
IDLE	Urban	6643	M.	3181	96	77	91	103	77	444	395	365	314	280	238	1
			F.	3462	95	83	82	93	90	443	427	392	333	302	293	[illegible]
ILKLEY	Urban	4736	M.	2050	64	65	57	65	61	312	244	188	156	166	208	1
			F.	2686	59	58	63	47	56	283	237	223	325	360	278	[illegible]
KEIGHLEY	Urban	25247	M.	12085	307	318	321	319	333	1598	1516	1364	1284	1124	989	[illegible]
			F.	13162	342	331	335	316	330	1654	1488	1373	1325	1403	1155	[illegible]
KEIGHLEY	Rural	5416	M.	2550	48	79	67	68	60	322	321	258	270	211	187	1
			F.	2866	78	64	68	71	71	352	326	275	205	256	268	[illegible]
KINGSTON UPON HULL	Urban	154240	M.	75746	2313	2102	2140	2183	2182	10920	9119	8039	6889	6600	6606	58
			F.	78494	2353	2184	2139	2260	2125	11070	9465	7888	7230	7273	6603	57
KIRKBY MOORSIDE	Rural	5514	M.	2823	76	70	76	63	76	361	333	337	291	227	184	1
			F.	2691	73	59	86	53	63	334	333	300	280	227	162	1
KIRKBURTON	Urban	3407	M.	1622	39	41	36	37	39	192	225	174	163	127	107	1
			F.	1785	38	36	45	48	42	209	226	194	196	140	152	1
KIRKHEATON	Urban	2747	M.	1365	50	34	36	35	41	196	148	123	133	135	108	
			F.	1382	45	44	44	38	32	203	154	134	131	120	126	
KIRKLEATHAM	Urban	3898	M.	1859	52	52	57	50	62	273	257	237	152	159	140	1
			F.	2039	47	48	39	46	52	232	253	209	274	208	172	1

Table 6 *continued*.—Ages of Males and Females in Sa

Sanitary District.		All Ages. Persons.	All Ages. Males and Females.		Under 1 Year.	1–	2–	3–	4–	Under 5 Years.	5–	10–	15–	20–	25–
KIRKLINGTON CUM UPSLAND	Urban	249	M.	120	3	3	9	5	1	21	13	8	16	9	6
			F.	129	5	2	4	2	3	16	14	15	11	11	9
KNARESBOROUGH	Urban	5000	M.	2339	55	60	55	70	59	299	278	241	188	179	170
			F.	2661	75	56	68	46	62	307	312	284	225	225	183
KNARESBOROUGH	Rural	8153	M.	4137	112	95	108	118	106	537	502	562	436	307	292
			F.	4016	116	100	118	104	122	560	471	425	365	308	310
LEEDS	Urban	309119	M.	149844	4771	4836	4280	4146	4195	21728	18497	15948	14392	13309	13039
			F.	159275	4960	4829	4407	4302	4269	22267	18876	16571	15634	14941	13729
LEEDS	Rural	2159	M.	1041	30	28	39	34	29	158	138	123	102	88	75
			F.	1118	34	28	32	20	31	145	161	128	90	107	91
LEPTON	Urban	3019	M.	1509	28	36	28	29	41	162	180	198	140	134	107
			F.	1510	32	43	33	42	30	180	188	173	162	141	97
LEYBURN	Rural	7653	M.	3734	85	95	103	94	100	477	401	477	405	308	252
			F.	3919	91	89	99	84	92	455	452	391	369	353	286
LINTHWAITE	Urban	6068	M.	2954	92	66	84	86	98	426	368	340	293	287	219
			F.	3114	103	81	64	80	64	392	389	334	308	297	265
LIVERSEDGE	Urban	12757	M.	6233	173	169	159	174	172	847	753	769	714	576	487
			F.	6524	193	164	186	188	187	918	794	719	709	576	488
LOFTUS	Urban	6699	M.	3553	121	99	116	124	125	585	534	349	276	271	304
			F.	3146	132	107	115	107	126	587	491	371	243	239	254
LONGWOOD	Urban	4661	M.	2294	55	61	55	86	73	330	312	272	230	209	191
			F.	2367	65	47	73	67	65	317	294	266	227	230	206
LUDDENDEN FOOT	Urban	2891	M.	1395	44	39	32	36	35	186	195	149	173	127	98
			F.	1496	40	37	50	47	32	206	180	147	143	139	123
MALTON	Urban	8754	M.	4242	134	116	123	119	127	619	528	461	389	341	308
			F.	4512	121	108	115	115	130	589	506	494	480	425	372
MALTON	Rural	14277	M.	7380	185	168	183	194	184	914	861	804	936	647	463
			F.	6897	205	176	211	195	178	965	842	767	666	578	472
MARSDEN IN ALMONDBURY	Urban	2633	M.	1242	21	34	32	35	34	156	146	144	124	118	113
			F.	1391	38	31	32	29	26	156	163	156	139	150	99
MARSDEN IN HUDDERSFIELD	Urban	686	M.	336	9	10	6	4	4	33	33	50	41	31	21
			F.	350	7	5	9	8	13	42	36	34	44	41	25
MASHAM	Urban	2174	M.	1096	24	30	26	26	26	132	110	136	110	101	59
			F.	1078	17	21	27	22	23	110	109	101	117	95	77
MELTHAM	Urban	4529	M.	2082	64	45	44	45	64	262	250	229	222	190	150
			F.	2447	62	49	68	59	52	290	230	255	246	237	204
METHLEY	Urban	4074	M.	2143	82	66	78	82	64	372	272	218	217	188	191
			F.	1931	75	60	74	64	54	327	306	236	143	133	154
MEXBOROUGH	Urban	6319	M.	3324	108	90	115	107	107	522	462	377	322	275	301
			F.	2995	139	97	106	113	98	553	420	352	251	232	244
MIDDLESBROUGH	Urban	55934	M.	29175	937	784	848	841	896	4306	3743	3103	2580	2577	2653
			F.	26759	911	794	946	846	898	4395	3347	3134	2594	2346	2081
MIDDLESBROUGH	Rural	7878	M.	4410	114	89	110	115	107	535	533	440	495	512	405
			F.	3468	135	111	107	143	90	586	501	366	354	309	234
MIDGLEY	Urban	2939	M.	1362	33	33	36	30	48	186	150	147	110	131	97
			F.	1577	30	27	30	43	29	159	165	146	151	161	147
MIRFIELD	Urban	11508	M.	5585	146	141	143	163	159	752	670	706	674	538	451
			F.	5923	165	144	141	147	140	746	717	638	618	563	518
MONK BRETTON	Urban	2918	M.	1549	40	54	49	62	39	244	191	173	159	129	145
			F.	1369	59	50	52	48	60	264	218	161	103	99	122

8 C 3

SANITARY DISTRICT.		ALL AGES. Persons.	ALL AGES. Males and Females.		Under 1 Year.	1–	2–	3–	4–	Under 5 Years.	5–	10–	15–	20–	25–
MORLEY	Urban	15011	M.	7274	256	194	238	224	213	1124	985	805	719	640	628
			F.	7737	251	243	236	238	227	1195	1003	868	802	734	688
*MOSSLEY, *part of*	Urban	4379	M.	1947	68	49	57	53	56	283	218	225	205	182	181
			F.	2432	65	61	65	61	61	313	239	244	273	256	225
NETHER SOOTHILL	Urban	5240	M.	2537	76	75	71	69	63	354	322	282	273	215	201
			F.	2703	70	78	87	65	75	375	313	279	299	248	217
NETHERTHONG	Urban	936	M.	451	8	5	14	12	5	44	63	55	55	38	26
			F.	485	8	10	6	11	11	46	37	54	48	58	40
NEWINGTON	Urban	7986	M.	3952	123	126	128	150	111	638	550	438	327	299	325
			F.	4034	138	126	146	132	139	681	634	480	310	249	317
NORMANBY	Urban	7714	M.	4324	137	101	143	143	132	656	476	377	373	490	434
			F.	3390	138	114	127	119	126	624	521	391	285	276	278
NORMANTON	Urban	8038	M.	4309	172	147	151	158	147	775	622	474	360	411	414
			F.	3729	170	135	156	154	142	757	632	429	212	291	334
NORTHALLERTON	Urban	3692	M.	1833	45	47	56	55	53	256	236	206	177	146	141
			F.	1859	55	55	52	54	46	262	205	197	192	157	136
NORTHALLERTON	Rural	8192	M.	4156	129	88	119	96	110	542	500	473	452	361	262
			F.	4036	103	105	119	117	116	560	438	424	406	356	309
NORTH BIERLEY	Urban	20935	M.	10024	292	258	261	275	286	1372	1215	1055	1064	1034	801
			F.	10911	321	309	284	282	274	1470	1262	1144	1099	1038	933
NORTHOWRAM	Urban	3294	M.	1670	41	47	51	43	52	234	193	176	160	160	142
			F.	1624	43	39	47	46	42	217	194	155	151	142	148
OAKWORTH	Urban	5762	M.	2769	73	72	57	73	66	341	344	321	292	215	214
			F.	2993	62	81	53	72	72	340	301	295	320	311	258
ORMESBY	Urban	7719	M.	4112	151	133	140	120	120	673	584	459	376	337	339
			E.	3607	148	113	118	127	140	646	542	438	287	302	288
OSSETT CUM GAWTHORPE	Urban	10957	M.	5232	161	138	144	153	148	744	658	629	581	453	401
			F.	5725	132	162	125	154	138	711	668	638	622	578	493
OTLEY	Urban	6806	M.	3318	114	102	99	85	100	500	421	364	280	254	272
			F.	3488	105	100	95	88	101	489	442	346	318	313	279
OVENDEN	Urban	7487	M.	3669	97	84	85	94	98	458	413	414	401	301	284
			F.	3818	79	88	87	80	110	444	425	397	375	335	319
OXENHOPE	Urban	2443	M.	1221	31	26	28	26	21	132	129	138	113	93	113
			F.	1222	33	30	25	34	32	154	133	114	102	110	111
PATELEY BRIDGE	Rural	8944	M.	4536	123	121	123	123	128	618	576	479	452	390	325
			F.	4408	132	122	126	107	112	599	518	494	413	364	323
PATRINGTON	Rural	8758	M.	4355	123	100	100	130	102	555	482	448	440	386	275
			F.	4403	123	104	133	108	97	565	540	463	422	373	288
PENISTONE	Urban	2254	M.	1179	42	28	44	43	45	202	132	120	107	104	126
			F.	1075	49	22	48	26	32	177	156	126	92	87	101
PENISTONE	Rural	5886	M.	3075	100	68	86	85	82	421	374	331	333	307	234
			F.	2811	91	97	86	89	94	457	393	344	221	227	188
PICKERING	Urban	3959	M.	2018	53	58	61	62	66	300	259	232	189	138	129
			F.	1941	58	48	47	66	49	268	266	236	162	143	128
PICKERING	Rural	6719	M.	3406	88	92	89	70	91	430	435	400	344	246	225
			F.	3313	90	93	96	12	88	459	434	373	305	266	211

* The remainder of the Urban Sanitary District of Mossley is in Division VIII. (See Table 6.)

					Under 1 Year.	1–	2–	3–	4–	Under 5 Years.	5–	10–	15–	20–	25–
Entire Urban Sanitary District of Mossley		13372	M.	6121	204	154	174	172	158	862	747	696	646	564	555
			F.	7251	194	165	187	193	190	929	793	753	776	728	592

3 C 4

Table 6 *continued.*—AGES of MALES and FEMALES in SANI

SANITARY DISTRICT.		ALL AGES. Persons.	Males and Females.		Under 1 Year.	1–	2–	3–	4–	Under 5 Years.	5–	10–	15–	20–	25–
POCKLINGTON	Rural	15461	M.	7979	238	183	188	206	186	1001	860	870	1000	681	406
			F.	7482	203	170	185	212	174	944	922	881	740	632	468
PONTEFRACT	Urban	8798	M.	4535	135	133	126	129	113	636	511	435	506	476	410
			F.	4263	146	120	119	114	119	618	543	468	412	408	356
PONTEFRACT	Rural	14471	M.	7368	258	227	223	197	210	1115	914	872	715	632	539
			F.	7103	204	188	218	207	196	1013	936	764	639	605	536
PUDSEY	Urban	15459	M.	7386	236	192	199	194	182	1002	903	817	757	613	599
			F.	8073	206	221	188	214	197	1026	882	866	808	730	652
QUEENSBURY	Urban	6824	M.	3243	90	89	92	81	102	454	403	370	365	284	258
			F.	3581	112	76	92	74	76	430	438	366	378	337	294
QUICKMERE	Urban	3660	M.	1727	40	51	29	41	53	223	221	200	191	152	140
			F.	1933	57	48	55	56	52	268	239	202	193	175	148
RASTRICK	Urban	8039	M.	3861	129	110	128	121	118	606	498.	391	413	340	310
			F.	4178	121	110	112	97	100	540	499	456	419	379	363
RAVENSTHORPE	Urban	4364	M.	2110	57	55	67	72	61	312	224	248	219	221	182
			F.	2254	69	71	57	56	59	312	261	251	254	222	189
RAWDON	Urban	3407	M.	1650	37	47	49	40	45	218	192	343	133	111	101
			F.	1757	47	38	43	47	42	217	207	177	172	167	183
RAWMARSH	Urban	10179	M.	5331	183	174	156	185	177	875	745	609	538	470	458
			F.	4848	184	184	164	181	174	887	810	562	372	340	351
REDCAR	Urban	2458	M.	1181	41	34	36	45	41	197	169	141	92	70	81
			F.	1277	33	36	34	43	35	181	165	147	127	99	93
REETH	Rural	4717	M.	2370	56	50	69	59	57	291	309	279	227	198	154
			F.	2347	70	62	63	56	57	308	298	229	207	104	155
RICHMOND	Urban	4502	M.	2127	60	51	53	51	46	261	250	234	253	193	129
			F.	2375	60	62	51	66	53	292	231	273	262	224	200
RICHMOND	Rural	8956	M.	4531	125	133	121	111	114	604	540	543	451	387	296
			F.	4425	116	116	123	121	122	598	533	461	419	391	336
RIPON	Urban	7390	M.	3343	103	96	80	97	84	460	417	375	290	244	247
			F.	4047	104	85	86	92	69	436	479	410	449	405	313
RIPON	Rural	9057	M.	4536	107	106	140	103	107	563	515	497	505	382	298
			F.	4521	115	108	105	114	120	562	504	449	430	393	331
RISHWORTH	Urban	1110	M.	563	11	17	12	17	9	66	65	100	73	46	37
			F.	547	14	19	13	12	17	75	89	65	48	48	36
ROTHERHAM	Urban	34782	M.	17758	602	562	530	573	574	2850	2399	1915	1627	1553	1477
			F.	17024	621	561	533	596	524	2835	2350	1900	1448	1414	1341
ROTHERHAM	Rural	17124	M.	8884	267	245	274	283	262	1331	1224	980	876	762	674
			F.	8240	265	279	266	256	274	1340	1218	960	646	625	577
ROTHWELL	Urban	5105	M.	2485	91	63	79	74	88	395	314	303	253	187	200
			F.	2620	93	84	85	95	92	449	379	326	235	206	186
SADDLEWORTH	Rural	12876	M.	6363	152	160	159	135	161	767	748	689	681	547	462
			F.	6513	180	162	160	180	143	825	777	671	643	575	523
SALTBURN BY THE SEA	Urban	1646	M.	747	22	24	25	23	27	121	102	76	66	58	47
			F.	899	20	14	28	24.	18	104	98	115	113	98	61
SANDAL MAGNA	Urban	4264	M.	2093	99	72	68	69	79	387	285	206	197	151	175
			F.	2171	85	66	65	69	61	346	275	230	185	209	195
SCAMMONDEN	Urban	607	M.	284	7	4	6	3	6	25	32	35	36	27	16
			F.	323	11	4	7	5	7	34	33	35	36	38	20
SCARBOROUGH	Urban	30504	M.	13548	371	355	384	360	341	1811	1682	1544	1283	1099	1058
			F.	16956	378	396	328	378	354	1834	1624	1536	1824	1793	1421

Table 6 *continued.*—Ages of Males and Females in Sa

Sanitary District.		All Ages. Persons.	All Ages. Males and Females.		Under 1 Year.	1–	2–	3–	4–	Under 5 Years.	5–	10–	15–	20–	25–
SCARBOROUGH	Rural	10424	M.	5425	155	124	141	153	149	722	643	616	628	455	367
			F.	4999	138	117	150	135	141	690	631	577	489	422	323
SCHOLES	Urban	1182	M.	580	20	16	14	14	12	76	76	66	64	47	43
			F.	602	20	15	18	14	22	89	72	58	63	52	46
SCULCOATES	Rural	8670	M.	4089	115	125	131	108	117	596	490	389	396	380	298
			F.	4581	114	117	110	101	107	549	520	482	469	484	357
SEDBERGH	Rural	4079	M.	2074	59	46	51	51	53	260	241	223	283	135	146
			F.	2005	61	43	52	53	51	260	215	207	195	169	148
SELBY	Urban	6046	M.	2900	86	70	80	75	81	392	385	333	289	225	214
			F.	3146	82	83	84	60	96	405	390	366	269	270	229
SELBY	Rural	9769	M.	4909	136	116	129	123	149	653	598	563	493	305	295
			F.	4860	135	105	144	112	110	606	579	544	466	383	327
SETTLE	Rural	13800	M.	6848	197	224	197	152	167	937	754	756	721	588	513
			F.	6952	193	154	165	201	161	874	836	688	674	704	556
SHEFFIELD	Urban	284508	M.	141298	4538	4119	3988	4073	3884	20602	17481	15156	13770	12710	12160
			F.	143210	4646	4208	4035	4075	4045	21009	18134	15859	14260	13187	11797
SHELF	Urban	2754	M.	1282	39	34	38	26	29	161	138	138	138	128	91
			F.	1472	34	25	29	30	42	160	154	151	146	136	120
SHELLEY	Urban	1687	M.	823	30	17	21	23	19	110	78	97	80	68	65
			F.	864	22	20	28	24	20	114	92	81	92	82	62
SHEPLEY	Urban	1593	M.	770	15	24	27	22	21	109	95	90	92	71	60
			F.	823	25	26	20	24	20	115	100	99	99	69	67
SHIPLEY	Urban	15093	M.	6995	188	201	179	179	185	932	912	876	702	586	545
			F.	8098	229	184	184	216	192	1005	895	874	925	825	721
SILSDEN	Urban	3329	M.	1611	42	37	45	45	40	209	178	157	163	141	127
			F.	1718	42	51	56	36	43	228	196	178	133	157	153
SKELMANTHORPE	Urban	3120	M.	1532	43	48	49	34	51	225	214	189	142	126	101
			F.	1588	57	38	45	44	51	235	216	204	148	135	105
SKELTON IN CLEVELAND	Urban	9374	M.	5035	172	165	194	159	167	857	696	509	440	433	425
			F.	4339	171	135	169	190	170	835	707	501	314	333	350
SKIPTON	Urban	9091	M.	4312	132	154	120	123	122	651	548	464	388	412	350
			F.	4779	129	141	102	134	142	648	574	483	400	483	406
SKIPTON	Rural	24700	M.	12158	332	321	345	313	321	1632	1399	1249	1251	1103	909
			F.	12542	342	305	315	309	305	1576	1422	1319	1228	1211	1027
SKIRLAUGH	Rural	7959	M.	4075	121	94	94	100	95	504	477	421	490	374	270
			F.	3884	113	90	119	121	115	558	532	408	363	305	257
SLAITHWAITE	Urban	3882	M.	1906	62	45	41	52	45	245	216	205	167	178	153
			F.	1976	47	50	40	36	49	231	207	221	190	189	163
SOUTH CAVE AND WALLINGFEN	Urban	2065	M.	1078	30	24	29	24	20	127	126	120	103	98	76
			F.	987	27	28	25	22	24	126	115	105	99	88	59
SOUTH CROSLAND	Urban	3048	M.	1436	37	27	30	31	42	167	164	161	153	106	122
			F.	1612	41	27	44	31	40	183	173	186	152	138	125
SOUTHOWRAM	Urban	3036	M.	1500	52	46	47	40	39	224	208	203	152	90	125
			F.	1536	53	43	28	43	40	207	197	169	153	122	131
*SOUTH STOCKTON (*part of*)	Urban	10608	M.	5723	194	154	186	176	173	883	804	617	522	495	515
			F.	4885	190	157	180	197	162	886	756	549	443	380	380

* The remainder of the Urban Sanitary District of South Stockton is in Division X. (See Table 6.)

Entire Urban Sanitary District of South Stockton		10665	M.	5756	195	154	188	176	174	887	809	622	525	408	516
			F.	4909	191	159	180	197	163	890	760	550	444	381	381

B 4178.

3 D

Table 6 *continued*.—Ages of Males and Females in Sani

Sanitary District.		All Ages. Persons.	All Ages. Males and Females.		Under 1 Year.	1–	2–	3–	4–	Under 5 Years.	5–	10–	15–	20–	25–	30
SOWERBY	Urban	6179	M.	2947	86	69	71	65	82	373	368	312	290	266	230	
			F.	3232	81	75	87	74	77	394	343	301	331	302	277	
SOWERBY BRIDGE	Urban	8724	M.	4177	112	117	111	98	111	549	520	461	426	367	355	
			F.	4547	115	106	95	118	109	543	532	419	460	439	362	
SOYLAND	Urban	3467	M.	1666	35	33	42	42	40	192	216	206	194	139	118	
			F.	1801	46	45	37	49	56	283	200	217	175	150	140	
STAINLAND	Urban	4933	M.	2343	67	55	70	57	66	315	207	278	216	223	182	
			F.	2590	71	79	65	64	71	350	306	250	274	241	201	
STOCKSBRIDGE	Urban	4660	M.	2428	77	72	73	74	92	388	318	275	277	231	221	
			F.	2232	95	70	64	64	72	365	301	290	248	193	153	
STOKESLEY	Rural	12009	M.	5975	164	129	155	149	161	758	741	677	627	477	413	
			F.	6034	149	150	168	161	144	772	715	681	628	572	427	
SWINTON	Urban	7612	M.	3908	161	147	137	137	124	706	536	407	368	329	346	
			F.	3704	143	139	126	129	145	682	604	413	285	280	298	
TADCASTER	Rural	23955	M.	12342	383	328	363	355	375	1804	1496	1332	1304	1057	960	
			F.	11613	349	343	362	300	347	1701	1613	1319	942	929	882	
THIRSK	Rural	12848	M.	6317	171	182	172	177	180	882	801	646	632	519	409	
			F.	6531	175	183	199	169	174	900	774	726	677	496	465	
THORNE	Rural	12828	M.	6408	160	150	181	173	160	824	763	762	619	486	385	
			F.	6420	179	147	169	155	150	800	764	742	583	462	400	
THORNHILL	Urban	8843	M.	4356	150	131	135	138	123	677	546	502	470	423	362	
			F.	4487	134	150	138	115	131	668	610	503	400	442	370	
THORNTON	Urban	6084	M.	2941	89	84	85	63	75	396	363	301	326	290	219	
			F.	3143	73	77	81	78	85	394	366	338	335	310	280	
THURLSTONE	Urban	2851	M.	1469	49	43	43	45	42	222	195	180	148	122	116	
			F.	1382	48	43	33	59	45	228	195	185	117	113	100	
THURSTONLAND	Urban	997	M.	506	19	11	15	14	13	72	84	64	46	34	27	
			F.	401	21	6	15	21	6	69	60	50	45	41	39	
TICKHILL	Urban	1684	M.	816	17	18	23	25	28	111	105	98	65	52	52	
			F.	868	27	22	16	13	19	97	103	95	66	67	46	
*TODMORDEN (*part of*)	Urban	23529	M.	11372	326	290	302	290	283	1491	1334	1141	1076	1073	940	
			F.	12157	314	263	290	281	317	1465	1281	1160	1145	1200	1068	
TODMORDEN	Rural	6991	M.	3335	87	90	90	90	80	437	367	333	301	295	264	
			F.	3656	102	91	74	84	89	440	362	341	364	319	308	
TONG	Urban	5591	M.	2745	69	69	77	63	74	352	366	333	329	245	193	
			F.	2846	71	78	83	65	77	374	369	308	283	241	232	
UPPER MILL	Urban	1384	M.	656	17	16	21	15	16	85	82	64	68	69	51	
			F.	728	23	15	18	14	26	96	80	73	86	64	62	
UPPER SOOTHILL	Urban	5155	M.	2522	84	66	72	80	69	371	305	265	281	256	225	
			F.	2633	91	78	75	81	84	409	322	297	270	268	213	
UPPERTHONG	Urban	2436	M.	1141	31	31	22	29	26	139	119	144	117	87	83	
			F.	1295	31	27	26	47	33	164	155	121	139	125	111	
UPPER WHITLEY	Urban	909	M.	494	11	10	18	13	11	63	64	63	68	48	38	
			F.	415	18	10	11	15	15	69	41	53	37	49	32	
WAKEFIELD	Urban	30854	M.	15377	498	411	442	407	420	2178	1805	1621	1434	1491	1400	11
			F.	15477	472	386	416	448	414	2136	1742	1619	1632	1498	1315	10

* The remainder of the Urban Sanitary District of Todmorden is in Division VIII. (See Table 6.)

Entire Urban Sanitary District of Todmorden	23862	M.	11541	328	294	303	293	289	1507	1358	1149	1096	1086	952	91
		F.	12321	316	272	293	284	21	1486	1293	1173	1167	1208	1093	94

Table 6 *continued*.—Ages of Males and Females in S

Sanitary District.		All Ages. Persons.	All Ages. Males and Females.		Under 1 Year.	1–	2–	3–	4–	Under 5 Years.	5–	10–	15–	20–	25–	3
WAKEFIELD	Rural	35266	M.	18146	574	550	529	563	537	2753	2390	1957	1740	1610	1440	1
			F.	17120	603	566	558	573	537	2837	2345	1864	1433	1336	1339	1
WARLEY	Urban	3211	M.	1525	45	40	42	32	47	206	184	182	170	130	105	
			F.	1686	48	31	34	38	45	191	177	186	188	165	133	
WATH UPON DEARNE	Urban	2904	M.	1477	47	57	36	57	51	248	214	150	133	139	109	
			F.	1427	51	47	48	43	44	233	206	152	117	113	103	
WETHERBY	Rural	16194	M.	8046	208	197	195	177	204	981	920	1103	308	645	514	
			F.	8148	194	130	212	202	198	905	935	850	733	679	599	
WHARFEDALE	Rural	7190	M.	3789	90	87	96	88	92	453	366	422	442	296	277	
			F.	3401	88	87	91	90	73	429	418	342	306	340	267	
WHITBY	Urban	14086	M.	6561	222	156	185	183	176	922	834	700	590	522	553	
			F.	7525	205	190	198	191	211	905	858	733	762	634	577	
WHITBY	Rural	9921	M.	5034	157	126	136	116	146	681	642	568	502	417	318	
			F.	4887	152	120	137	137	134	680	598	563	464	405	327	
WHITWOOD	Urban	4102	M.	2197	79	78	61	72	84	374	319	241	216	190	168	
			F.	1905	67	67	69	74	64	341	318	234	148	118	141	
WILSDEN	Urban	2966	M.	1380	37	40	35	28	42	182	164	133	151	125	107	
			F.	1586	26	44	44	44	36	194	174	161	155	146	130	
WINDHILL	Urban	6732	M	3228	101	103	111	97	94	506	441	380	284	269	243	
			F.	3504	110	107	82	104	92	405	448	338	314	315	242	
WOMBWELL	Urban	8451	M.	4515	160	149	145	163	137	754	594	505	424	438	415	
			F.	3936	151	141	135	155	166	748	666	459	294	298	277	
WOOLDALE	Urban	4387	M.	2142	81	60	52	64	67	324	239	222	227	202	171	
			F.	2245	59	63	61	47	52	282	250	340	250	221	197	
WORSBROUGH	Urban	8443	M.	4506	146	140	149	140	154	729	623	520	429	418	405	
			F.	3937	171	145	165	143	159	783	611	469	265	272	316	
WORTLEY	Rural	31848	M.	16388	487	488	485	470	516	2446	2072	1835	1639	1472	1354	1
			F.	15460	582	493	482	475	486	2518	2126	1806	1250	1166	1132	1
YEADON	Urban	6534	M.	3127	105	91	107	92	78	473	363	339	334	282	261	
			F.	3407	107	112	74	95	83	471	412	553	357	344	292	
YORK	Urban	49530	M.	23957	706	606	629	647	613	3201	2809	2552	2395	2198	2019	1
			F.	25573	698	603	671	597	631	3200	2875	2652	2613	2338	2078	1
YORK	Rural	27165	M.	14134	418	359	335	355	328	1795	1469	1524	1600	1604	1143	
			F.	13031	383	313	336	318	368	1668	1454	1289	1242	1297	1091	

Table 13.—NUMBER and COUNTRY of BIRTH OF FOREIGNERS enumerated in YORKSHIRE, and in ea exceeds 50,000 PERSONS.

WHERE BORN.	WHERE ENUMERA								
	COUNTY.		URBAN SANI						
	YORKSHIRE.		HUDDERSFIELD.		HALIFAX.		BRADFORD.		L
	Males.	Females.	Males.	Females.	Males.	Females.	Males.	Females.	Males
TOTAL	4843	3240	100	48	54	50	367	256	1189
EUROPE.									
DENMARK	121	30	.	.	.	.	1	1	9
NORWAY	210	76	.	.	.	.	.	.	7
SWEDEN	208	59	.	1	.	.	3	1	3
RUSSIA	377	234	6	1	.	.	2	.	197
POLAND (RUSSIAN)	790	624	6	.	2	.	4	1	565
AUSTRIA	76	17	1	.	.	.	11	2	13
HUNGARY	19	9	.	.	.	.	.	.	12
SWITZERLAND	60	59	7	5	.	1	22	3	6
GERMAN EMPIRE	1591	1082	29	16	11	10	211	170	184
HOLLAND	95	54	2	.	.	1	6	2	9
BELGIUM	49	34	1	.	.	.	2	2	6
FRANCE	182	141	8	1	3	4	14	4	30
PORTUGAL	11	4	.	.	.	.	1	.	1
SPAIN	17	6	1	.	.	.	1	2	.
ITALY	220	43	3	2	3	3	15	2	43
GREECE	39	1	.	.	.	.	.	.	1
TURKEY	5	1	.	.	.	.	.	.	1
SERVIA	.	.	.	.	.	.	.	.	.
ROUMANIA	3	.	.	.	.	.	1	.	.
ASIA.									
ARABIA	.	.	.	.	.	.	.	.	.
PERSIA	.	.	.	.	.	.	.	.	.
CHINA	1	1	.	.	.	.	.	.	.
OTHER COUNTRIES	.	3	.	.	.	.	.	.	.
AFRICA.									
EGYPT	.	1	.	.	.	.	.	.	.
OTHER PARTS	2	2	.	.	.	.	.	.	.
AMERICA.									
UNITED STATES	746	745	37	22	32	31	72	64	102
MEXICO	.	.	.	.	.	.	1	.	.
BRAZIL	3	3	.	.	.	.	.	2	.
OTHER STATES	12	7	.	.	.	.	.	.	.
COUNTRY NOT STATED	2	3	.	.	.	.	.	.	.
AT SEA	4	1	.	.	.	.	.	.	.

Table 6.—Ages of Males and Females in Sanitai

Sanitary District.		All Ages. Persons.	All Ages. Males and Females.		Under 1 Year.	1–	2–	3–	4–	Under 5 Years.	5–	10–	15–	20–	25–	3(
ALNWICK AND CANONGATE	Urban	6693	M.	3189	96	80	100	85	76	437	399	352	346	240	214	2
			F.	3504	81	58	101	69	102	411	379	363	332	295	251	2
ALNWICK	Rural	12609	M.	6145	164	148	154	159	147	772	733	675	663	553	443	3
			F.	6464	134	144	179	146	138	741	748	660	641	609	502	4
ALSTON	Rural	4621	M.	2253	62	49	49	54	55	269	274	271	245	183	169	1
			F.	2368	46	48	51	63	57	265	283	266	245	190	164	1
AMBLE	Urban	2016	M.	1076	45	28	25	30	25	153	122	94	113	112	108	
			F.	940	37	20	29	30	28	144	123	90	84	79	80	
AUCKLAND	Rural	58854	M.	30852	1016	831	942	908	913	4610	4239	3547	3276	2764	2449	20
			F.	28002	1027	893	868	888	945	4621	4293	3547	2619	2300	2054	17
BARNARD CASTLE	Urban	4544	M.	2132	63	41	58	52	58	272	273	248	210	156	139	
			F.	2412	58	46	45	60	60	269	291	259	251	221	181	1
BEDLINGTONSHIRE	Urban	14510	M	7579	258	212	235	236	223	1164	1058	858	808	633	554	4
			F.	6931	260	178	237	195	238	1108	1082	825	558	543	488	4
BELFORD	Rural	5737	M.	2727	78	65	57	58	76	334	328	323	304	250	195	1
			F.	3010	64	68	80	55	66	333	317	294	325	305	231	2
BELLINGHAM	Rural	6107	M.	3022	79	74	75	72	72	372	364	307	250	241	205	1
			F.	3085	81	73	77	88	70	389	346	349	285	241	247	1
BENFIELDSIDE	Urban	5703	M.	2911	92	84	94	73	83	426	361	342	318	284	209	1
			F.	2792	84	75	74	98	78	409	394	321	302	247	202	1
BENWELL AND FENHAM	Urban	4893	M.	2472	93	69	76	76	88	402	346	269	229	197	206	1
			F.	2421	74	79	82	93	75	403	303	286	207	204	181	1
BERWICK UPON TWEED	Urban	13998	M.	6722	204	160	217	176	191	948	835	755	691	593	471	4
			F.	7276	196	184	208	158	171	917	807	747	671	569	540	4
BERWICK	Rural	7050	M.	3384	82	80	96	88	93	439	410	401	369	296	231	1
			F.	3666	84	89	92	87	80	432	440	387	372	336	267	2
BISHOP AUCKLAND	Urban	10097	M.	5059	158	131	115	132	134	670	632	546	489	442	460	3
			F.	5038	147	117	136	159	138	697	575	582	580	544	395	3
BLAYDON	Urban	10687	M.	5597	164	162	161	150	158	795	745	641	564	535	469	3
			F.	5090	182	161	173	154	154	824	707	590	505	458	363	2
BOOTLE	Rural	5997	M.	3120	79	68	87	66	79	379	348	330	358	287	228	2
			F.	2877	69	96	82	72	82	401	313	301	337	217	229	1
BOWNESS	Urban	1855	M.	851	20	16	28	12	21	97	106	99	84	70	69	
			F.	1004	25	16	12	18	21	92	101	109	96	127	95	
BRAMPTON	Rural	10565	M.	5354	148	106	135	121	122	632	614	621	573	468	389	6
			F.	5211	125	109	130	100	125	589	572	532	522	504	387	3
BRANDON AND BYSHOTTLES	Urban	10850	M.	5825	188	156	175	160	188	865	808	673	673	563	446	3
			F.	5025	188	144	161	177	175	845	746	667	486	403	352	2
CARLISLE	Urban	35884	M.	17224	532	457	472	460	477	2428	2033	1875	1807	1635	1504	11
			F.	18660	526	481	508	451	452	2418	2081	1892	1864	1798	1673	12
CARLISLE	Rural	16878	M.	8081	207	208	235	209	167	1026	950	895	802	596	559	5
			F.	8847	204	182	201	183	215	985	966	873	865	778	689	5
CASTLE WARD	Rural	15594	M.	8064	204	194	211	203	239	1051	984	900	921	682	555	5
			F.	7530	219	218	193	211	217	1063	953	800	736	663	541	4
CHESTER-LE-STREET	Rural	43352	M.	22630	717	586	670	694	721	3388	2989	2606	2429	2086	1769	14
			F.	20722	728	617	663	635	633	3276	3038	2446	1965	1761	1528	12
CLEATOR MOOR	Urban	10420	M.	5428	170	158	167	167	184	846	708	586	571	578	488	4
			F.	4992	184	152	154	189	173	852	753	621	478	436	339	3
COCKERMOUTH	Urban	5353	M.	2532	88	65	63	65	72	353	316	288	219	190	198	1
			F.	2821	65	69	62	78	71	345	314	313	268	220	173	1
COCKERMOUTH	Rural	26782	M.	13686	428	421	429	393	364	2035	1777	1507	1320	1288	1054	8
			F.	13096	451	372	395	488	387	2043	1776	1488	1169	1080	959	7

Note.—For the Parishes comprised in each Urban Sanitary District, see Vol. II

3 H 4

Table 6 *continued.*—AGES of MALES and FEMALES in SAN

SANITARY DISTRICT.		ALL AGES. Persons.	ALL AGES. Males and Females.		Under 1 Year.	1–	2–	3–	4–	Under 5 Years.	5–	10–	15–	20–	25–
CONSETT	Urban	7163	M.	3894	111	107	103	113	87	521	473	401	362	452	386
			F.	3269	110	96	102	99	118	525	487	386	348	294	224
COWPEN	Urban	5065	M.	2493	92	67	74	93	76	402	336	261	229	226	213
			F.	2572	88	74	74	71	78	385	329	291	239	235	214
CRAMLINGTON	Urban	5744	M.	3067	81	88	91	88	93	441	391	362	319	349	256
			F.	2677	108	80	80	87	100	455	399	302	226	224	182
DARLINGTON	Urban	35104	M.	17401	555	453	519	512	539	2578	2392	1880	1679	1531	1400
			F.	17703	549	439	405	533	529	2545	2230	1948	1968	1634	1396
DARLINGTON	Rural	12572	M.	6118	171	180	183	175	182	896	774	702	620	482	424
			F.	6454	154	182	188	186	171	881	817	735	648	568	455
DAWDON	Urban	7714	M.	3872	109	116	122	129	97	573	539	444	373	341	319
			F.	3842	134	97	117	132	120	600	613	436	361	347	275
DURHAM	Urban	14932	M.	7240	173	210	160	176	166	885	784	749	722	*742	601
			F.	7692	187	175	167	196	158	883	846	746	907	849	613
DURHAM	Rural	38539	M.	20027	664	576	623	619	575	3057	2815	2324	1986	1711	1656
			F.	18512	656	544	633	584	603	3020	2764	2233	1819	1529	1365
EASINGTON	Rural	33384	M.	[illegible]	574	560	[illegible]	554	564	2714	2523	1948	1793	1545	1343
			F.	16048	582	537	492	543	507	2661	2517	1997	1463	1309	1175
EAST WARD	Rural	14515	M.	7276	197	176	178	165	197	913	830	812	697	537	502
			F.	7239	204	212	192	193	183	984	789	781	693	625	529
EGREMONT	Urban	5976	M.	3124	108	90	82	97	91	468	426	348	277	290	288
			F.	2852	103	105	105	96	84	403	411	314	223	243	234
FELLING	Urban	16376	M.	8466	281	251	238	233	279	1282	1139	907	894	707	668
			F.	7910	251	260	258	263	266	1298	1092	962	722	609	583
GATESHEAD	Urban	65803	M.	32991	1140	1018	1001	1001	1049	5209	4403	3586	3142	2785	2737
			F.	32812	1092	952	1050	1047	957	5098	4844	3684	3071	2870	2591
GLENDALE	Rural	10933	M.	5195	134	111	129	133	119	626	625	621	581	450	357
			F.	5738	113	130	133	143	126	645	647	628	580	530	451
GRASMERE	Urban	684	M.	305	13	3	8	7	4	35	32	40	26	26	28
			F.	379	8	13	7	7	6	41	44	42	33	34	37
HALTWHISTLE	Rural	7902	M.	4001	121	117	111	116	108	572	471	452	407	342	308
			F.	3901	121	111	95	113	106	546	489	425	404	339	295
HARTLEPOOL	Urban	12361	M.	6169	210	165	212	180	189	956	795	692	590	482	481
			F.	6192	196	178	160	190	190	914	827	664	647	583	456
HARTLEPOOL	Rural	2167	M.	1094	21	31	27	20	34	133	122	141	125	98	62
			F.	1073	27	25	27	27	26	132	143	106	120	94	67
HEBBURN	Urban	11302	M.	6496	217	199	191	217	183	1007	845	655	637	653	610
			F.	5306	215	223	193	187	199	1017	802	635	446	444	410
HEXHAM	Urban	5919	M.	2733	68	80	77	88	71	384	319	316	262	213	210
			F.	3186	82	76	62	77	78	375	336	324	342	338	228
HEXHAM	Rural	28167	M.	14168	383	378	345	368	367	1841	1762	1604	1503	1290	1067
			F.	13999	371	368	378	379	381	1877	1710	1481	1410	1276	1094
HOLME CULTRAM	Urban	4230	M.	2082	43	59	51	56	60	268	242	222	221	183	141
			F.	2148	57	57	61	57	50	282	241	242	203	180	157
HOUGHTON-LE-SPRING	Urban	6041	M.	3043	95	83	89	88	101	456	371	383	285	258	231
			F.	2998	107	77	93	76	85	438	416	323	316	279	239
HOUGHTON-LE-SPRING	Rural	28104	M.	14681	512	446	463	450	438	2309	2010	1644	1632	1368	1163
			F.	13423	613	439	453	409	446	2260	1969	1575	1199	1094	989
HOWDON	Urban	1099	M.	550	21	16	21	13	14	85	76	67	57	36	38
			F.	549	20	21	15	23	16	95	83	68	42	33	40
JARROW	Urban	25469	M.	13505	467	398	377	377	386	2026	1702	1427	1231	1330	1224
			F.	11964	465	364	436	416	402	2083	1778	1356	1118	962	897

Sanitary District.		All Ages. Persons.	All Ages. Males and Females.		Under 1 Year.	1–	2–	3–	4–	Under 5 Years.	5–	10–	15–	20–	25–	30–
KENDAL - - - -	Urban	13696	M. -	6500	202	188	173	173	166	902	874	751	630	528	403	432
			F. -	7196	212	196	165	189	180	942	883	768	725	637	566	481
KENDAL - - - -	Rural	22337	M. -	11050	296	291	299	292	290	1467	1363	1257	1183	943	766	667
			F. -	11287	299	275	300	299	284	1457	1338	1364	1159	965	824	687
KESWICK - - - -	Urban	3220	M. -	1448	41	46	48	36	38	209	175	160	140	107	107	94
			F. -	1772	37	37	42	42	37	195	184	191	199	154	133	116
KIRKBY LONSDALE - -	Urban	1733	M. -	841	29	24	23	30	36	142	113	99	73	53	54	64
			F. -	892	24	27	22	17	26	116	103	87	86	81	76	6[illegible]
LANCHESTER - - -	Rural	40519	M. -	21622	712	593	658	641	632	3236	2900	2499	2378	2112	1718	1397
			F. -	18897	710	567	654	642	678	3251	2939	2294	1805	1567	1315	1154
LEADGATE - - -	Urban	4271	M. -	2299	87	60	104	67	81	389	281	228	228	234	206	14[illegible]
			F. -	1972	61	64	62	54	74	315	288	207	204	178	162	10[illegible]
LONGTOWN - - - -	Rural	7711	M. -	3916	104	80	90	95	96	465	476	408	409	342	238	24[illegible]
			F. -	3795	89	88	102	96	105	480	415	413	377	336	267	22[illegible]
MARYPORT - - -	Urban	8126	M. -	3893	132	126	106	113	110	586	553	397	353	373	303	26[illegible]
			F. -	4233	136	122	115	144	117	684	527	431	405	399	328	251
MIDDLETON IN STRANTON	Urban	1195	M. -	622	17	17	16	16	16	82	75	56	57	63	49	5[illegible]
			F. -	573	15	24	22	14	22	97	85	65	64	36	35	3[illegible]
MILLOM - - - -	Urban	6228	M. -	3269	144	101	109	122	97	573	460	325	295	273	300	287
			F. -	2959	115	120	120	114	106	575	416	306	222	264	225	20[illegible]
MORPETH - - -	Urban	6115	M. -	2986	87	75	75	79	66	382	314	339	301	234	229	18[illegible]
			F. -	3129	71	54	77	64	86	355	333	314	308	273	233	20[illegible]
MORPETH - - - -	Rural	14064	M. -	7221	220	187	184	217	222	1030	1008	769	769	673	562	47[illegible]
			F. -	6843	225	221	197	232	228	1103	947	804	629	659	486	47[illegible]
NEWBIGGIN - - -	Urban	1388	M. -	658	20	17	16	17	20	90	84	75	65	60	34	3[illegible]
			F. -	730	20	18	14	24	17	93	91	93	70	63	41	3[illegible]
NEWCASTLE UPON TYNE	Urban	145359	M. -	71100	2224	2074	1947	2032	1944	10221	8843	7454	6820	6614	6291	5194
			F. -	74259	2213	2031	2084	1981	2027	10336	8878	7718	7664	7425	6088	504[illegible]
PENRITH - - -	Urban	9268	M. -	4340	160	104	129	107	122	622	532	500	417	355	312	25[illegible]
			F. -	4928	128	126	115	123	120	612	556	506	465	465	388	333
PENRITH - - - -	Rural	13974	M. -	7185	182	169	163	177	153	844	900	776	828	613	484	389
			F. -	6789	161	171	185	158	143	813	760	727	708	627	497	393
ROTHBURY - - - -	Rural	6709	M. -	3261	69	65	82	78	88	382	393	332	327	320	238	189
			F. -	3448	86	78	99	80	76	419	369	379	376	314	233	229
RYTON - - - -	Urban	4568	M. -	2204	62	60	63	75	69	329	290	246	211	205	170	130
			F. -	2364	72	67	71	71	78	359	329	277	231	181	168	156
SEATON CAREW - - -	Urban	925	M. -	402	15	13	8	14	12	62	55	44	37	33	34	30
			F. -	523	8	11	15	16	13	63	56	36	61	65	52	37
SEDGEFIELD - - -	Rural	17103	M. -	8914	260	244	280	266	258	1308	1126	936	808	786	759	633
			F. -	8189	275	239	230	272	278	1294	1170	989	718	679	634	515
SEGHILL - - - -	Urban	2131	M. -	1170	37	36	29	38	45	185	160	111	135	120	92	72
			F. -	961	40	34	29	32	22	157	132	118	82	91	78	57
SHILDON AND EAST THICKLEY	Urban	8704	M. -	4583	156	120	138	136	118	668	658	536	454	406	387	299
			F. -	4121	159	119	124	116	165	683	596	477	375	300	338	276
SOUTH BLYTH - - -	Urban	1983	M. -	902	26	19	21	27	26	119	100	102	105	76	63	55
			F. -	1081	25	28	24	36	31	144	140	103	116	105	65	46
SOUTH GOSFORTH - -	Urban	4126	M. -	1915	64	54	51	51	52	272	246	196	165	159	143	135
			F. -	2211	58	51	50	63	49	271	247	222	244	228	178	169
SOUTH SHIELDS - - -	Urban	56875	M. -	28373	973	864	931	869	884	4511	3718	3033	2630	2416	2315	2114
			F. -	28502	1008	809	911	834	815	4377	3710	3129	2740	2511	2267	1954
SOUTH SHIELDS - -	Rural	9053	M. -	4653	139	115	172	149	138	713	653	400	423	390	349	314
			F. -	4400	132	126	132	126	127	643	609	490	423	391	334	293

SANITARY DISTRICT.		All Ages. Persons.		All Ages. Males and Females.	Under 1 Year.	1–	2–	3–	4–	Under 5 Years.	5–	10–	15–	20–	25–	30
*SOUTH STOCKTON (*part of*)	Urban	57	M.	33	1	.	2	.	1	4	5	5	3	3	1	
			F.	24	1	2	.	.	1	4	4	1	1	1	1	
SOUTHWICK	Urban	8178	M.	4234	144	135	152	130	129	690	606	440	436	364	381	3
			F.	3894	130	127	126	134	113	630	563	451	320	346	318	2
SPENNYMOOR	Urban	5917	M.	3061	91	89	89	109	114	492	409	355	235	248	260	2
			F.	2856	101	90	101	92	75	459	430	338	277	235	220	2
STANHOPE	Urban	1840	M.	932	25	22	20	23	19	109	120	89	100	89	73	[illegible]
			F.	908	31	13	30	27	24	125	95	114	95	79	86	[illegible]
STOCKTON-ON-TEES	Urban	41015	M.	21465	617	609	692	586	613	3117	2654	2136	1989	2080	2056	18
			F.	19550	714	594	613	603	635	3159	2727	2145	1367	1783	1589	14
STOCKTON	Rural	10137	M.	5176	132	148	167	122	158	727	705	576	493	453	404	3
			F.	4981	160	140	135	155	158	738	643	591	489	430	387	3
SUNDERLAND	Urban	116548	M.	57133	1804	1711	1719	1737	1611	8582	7576	6201	5581	4976	4722	41
			F.	59415	1829	1682	1708	1727	1073	8614	7536	6102	6130	5472	4918	39
SUNDERLAND	Rural	14562	M.	7729	259	202	215	218	231	1125	1017	885	851	771	627	5
			F.	6833	239	210	227	193	223	1092	1035	889	091	558	479	4
TEESDALE	Rural	16233	M.	8173	233	195	197	215	219	1059	989	1027	899	710	557	4
			F.	8060	198	175	216	211	230	1030	968	930	837	750	576	4
THROSTON	Urban	3442	M.	1086	69	54	59	69	69	307	291	310	188	158	187	1
			F.	1608	55	62	51	48	65	281	268	141	148	132	130	1
TOW LAW	Urban	5005	M.	2634	76	52	68	73	70	344	323	283	324	271	240	1
			F.	2371	93	61	100	80	80	419	305	298	227	182	180	1
TYNEMOUTH	Urban	44118	M.	21825	626	595	610	601	586	3018	2751	2412	2054	1879	1860	15
			F.	22293	649	569	565	587	584	2954	2675	2275	2305	2129	1791	14
TYNEMOUTH	Rural	31405	M.	16340	584	461	483	466	544	2538	2238	1872	1631	1434	1304	10
			F.	15065	539	423	497	481	511	2451	2292	1809	1295	1128	1084	9
WALKER	Urban	9527	M.	5159	189	141	167	155	143	795	695	521	492	490	421	4
			F.	4368	160	137	129	168	147	741	621	512	401	312	314	3
WALLSEND	Urban	6351	M.	3384	123	85	88	99	98	493	462	353	359	316	280	2
			F.	2967	89	110	106	107	104	516	447	330	275	217	203	1
WEARDALE	Rural	10902	M.	5585	139	147	115	158	153	712	685	609	609	500	383	3
			F.	5317	129	127	142	136	130	664	670	655	550	454	383	3
WEST HARTLEPOOL	Urban	28523	M.	14745	505	453	462	474	427	2321	1946	1530	1437	1328	1266	10
			F.	13778	485	430	426	430	429	2200	1918	1475	1447	1246	1085	9
WEST WARD	Rural	8225	M.	4195	104	94	111	92	108	509	507	507	412	360	281	2
			F.	4030	98	95	100	90	101	484	478	446	387	337	305	2
WHICKHAM	Urban	7976	M.	4019	132	123	120	140	130	645	549	427	373	332	323	2
			F.	3957	118	118	129	120	141	626	561	485	362	314	285	2
WHITEHAVEN	Urban	19295	M.	9432	301	250	255	288	263	1357	1241	1016	914	795	800	6
			F.	9863	335	274	280	264	264	1417	1184	1006	983	848	765	6
WHITEHAVEN	Rural	23601	M.	12116	380	339	385	371	355	1830	1556	1388	1190	1098	1010	8
			F.	11485	338	341	354	397	363	1843	1569	1315	1029	978	822	7
WHITLEY AND MONKSEATON	Urban	1800	M.	757	31	22	25	23	20	121	93	83	50	59	62	5
			F.	1043	22	24	26	20	20	112	120	102	132	118	89	[illegible]
WIGTON	Urban	3948	M.	1768	51	46	53	46	47	243	223	179	166	141	134	9
			F.	2180	59	40	58	50	55	262	223	233	206	210	170	12
WIGTON	Rural	15262	M.	7631	219	200	199	205	186	1009	888	881	817	584	549	47
			F.	7631	189	185	214	192	188	968	921	801	692	630	564	47
WILLINGTON QUAY	Urban	4974	M.	2617	105	77	89	85	84	440	322	253	236	238	224	1
			F.	2357	86	88	74	77	67	392	331	279	199	215	174	1
WINDERMERE	Urban	1269	M.	567	13	11	14	20	12	70	75	85	57	43	40	3
			F.	702	21	20	14	18	13	86	89	65	69	61	65	4
WORKINGTON	Urban	13308	M.	6914	205	191	205	204	202	1007	804	701	588	789	768	5
			F.	6394	244	194	215	179	218	1050	847	651	562	507	531	4

* The remainder of the Urban Sanitary District of South Stockton is in Division IX. (See Table 6.)

Entire Urban Sanitary District of South Stockton		10665	M.	5756	195	154	188	176	174	887	809	622	525	498	516	47
			F.	4909	191	159	180	197	163	890	760	550	444	381	381	33

Table 13.—NUMBER and COUNTRY of BIRTH of FOREIGNERS enumerated in COUNTIES, and in each exceeds 50,000 PERSONS.

3 M

WHERE BORN.	WHERE ENUMER.									
	NORTHERN COUNTIES.		COUNTIES.							
			DURHAM.		NORTHUM-BERLAND.		CUMBERLAND.		WESTM LANI	
	Males.	Females.	Males.	Females.	Males.	Females.	Males.	Females.	Males.	Fe
TOTAL - -	4012	1209	2060	585	1822	525	106	70	24	
EUROPE.										
DENMARK	341	71	84	15	255	56	2	.	.	
NORWAY	546	81	277	40	267	39	2	1	.	
SWEDEN	594	51	381	19	263	31	.	.	.	
RUSSIA	217	20	131	15	82	5	4	.	.	
POLAND (RUSSIAN)	113	66	55	28	55	38	3	.	.	
AUSTRIA	84	13	8	5	74	8	2	.	.	
HUNGARY	12	.	1	.	10	.	1	.	.	
SWITZERLAND	29	25	15	7	8	9	4	6	2	
GERMAN EMPIRE	918	386	545	200	338	154	34	23	6	
HOLLAND	119	42	73	21	46	21	.	.	.	
BELGIUM	43	21	17	9	25	10	1	2	.	
FRANCE	198	87	107	31	75	38	10	14	6	
PORTUGAL	6	1	3	.	3	1	.	.	.	
SPAIN	14	4	2	1	11	3	1	.	.	
ITALY	204	26	71	9	119	14	12	1	2	
GREECE	58	.	28	.	30	.	.	.	.	
TURKEY	18	.	4	.	14	.	.	.	.	
SERVIA	.	.	.	.	.	.	.	.	.	
ROUMANIA	.	.	.	.	.	.	.	.	.	
ASIA.										
ARABIA	1	.	.	.	.	.	1	.	.	
PERSIA	1	.	1	.	.	.	.	.	.	
CHINA	27	.	1	.	26	.	.	.	.	
OTHER COUNTRIES	3	1	.	.	3	1	.	.	.	
AFRICA.										
EGYPT	5	.	5	.	.	.	.	.	.	
OTHER PARTS	5	.	3	.	2	.	.	.	.	
AMERICA.										
UNITED STATES	408	299	279	180	92	90	29	20	8	
MEXICO	1	1	1	.	.	.	.	1	.	
BRAZIL	2	1	2	.	.	1	.	.	.	
OTHER STATES	13	6	8	2	5	2	.	2	.	
COUNTRY NOT STATED	32	6	8	3	24	3	.	.	.	
AT SEA	.	1	.	.	.	1	.	.	.	

Sanitary District.		All Ages. Persons.		All Ages. Males and Females.	Under 1 Year.	1–	2–	3–	4–	Under 5 Years.	5–	10–	15–	20–	25–	30–
Aberavon	Urban	4859	M.	2466	72	79	64	63	66	344	350	285	298	224	186	143
			F.	2393	62	76	64	71	61	334	314	266	259	251	173	141
Aberayron	Rural	11218	M.	4792	135	124	140	122	140	661	647	670	477	301	240	190
			F.	6426	153	133	136	129	140	691	665	656	588	466	436	426
Aberdare	Urban	33804	M.	17446	518	423	467	493	456	2357	2293	2067	1830	1048	1420	1170
			F.	16358	539	464	505	435	490	2433	2303	1965	1507	1838	1248	1031
Abergavenny	Urban	6941	M.	3320	97	98	90	116	87	488	402	362	291	234	263	264
			F.	3621	102	102	82	96	90	472	398	351	338	347	298	205
Abergavenny	Rural	8345	M.	4207	95	86	102	72	102	457	434	456	404	330	280	275
			F.	4138	84	75	95	98	90	446	467	439	371	304	275	224
Abergele and Pensarn	Urban	1916	M.	875	21	25	24	22	25	117	113	88	67	58	55	65
			F.	1041	29	20	19	22	30	120	90	104	76	87	84	67
Abersychan	Urban	13496	M.	7000	186	181	203	193	220	983	989	876	705	602	486	375
			F.	6496	209	191	194	208	202	1004	1003	830	558	450	390	350
Abertillery	Urban	6003	M.	3196	93	92	83	97	92	457	469	347	360	329	262	214
			F.	2807	96	102	107	88	100	493	437	327	282	208	197	189
Aberystwith	Urban	7088	M.	3119	94	57	73	84	87	395	373	377	411	254	106	165
			F.	3969	82	77	69	86	65	379	356	410	473	427	291	235
Aberystwith	Rural	18518	M.	8733	211	218	228	218	243	1118	1178	1149	989	650	549	418
			F.	9785	239	165	225	269	234	1102	1134	1121	967	788	682	547
Anglesey	Rural	15182	M.	7127	163	154	168	169	166	820	829	810	716	515	430	350
			F.	8055	169	163	168	188	176	864	840	767	752	509	509	520
Bala	Urban	1653	M.	829	12	13	17	14	13	69	96	95	73	96	64	4[illegible]
			F.	824	19	16	16	12	19	82	77	73	71	69	76	50
Bala	Rural	5087	M.	2669	55	42	53	52	47	249	266	261	283	277	192	186
			F.	2418	67	57	62	59	58	303	283	278	204	203	148	140
Bangor	Urban	8247	M.	3830	100	92	86	79	96	453	418	392	387	359	302	270
			F.	4417	124	87	92	100	69	472	421	435	470	415	358	303
Bangor	Rural	19016	M.	9374	220	203	245	199	231	1098	1017	1196	964	680	689	533
			F.	9642	218	214	231	224	202	1089	1057	1038	887	792	656	598
Barmouth	Urban	1512	M.	638	18	21	21	26	22	108	76	67	46	46	43	47
			F.	874	22	13	25	16	15	91	78	81	81	76	91	61
Beaumaris	Urban	2239	M.	1055	16	23	26	20	26	111	84	107	113	106	84	7[illegible]
			F.	1184	25	23	18	23	15	104	101	97	127	128	94	8[illegible]
Bedwelty	Rural	13204	M.	6862	208	161	180	188	203	940	923	771	742	595	582	436
			F.	6342	200	195	224	209	209	1037	947	700	576	451	441	379
Bethesda	Urban	6969	M.	3543	112	95	107	107	82	503	399	394	319	286	278	264
			F.	3426	110	78	99	106	88	481	393	369	271	261	284	241
Blaenavon	Urban	9451	M.	4997	114	130	126	119	139	628	630	589	544	429	363	337
			F.	4454	148	131	144	148	143	714	665	546	346	317	295	252
Brecknock	Urban	6372	M.	3204	87	78	87	67	69	388	359	379	381	330	240	186
			F.	3168	86	60	76	70	79	371	312	314	339	301	266	195
Brecknock	Rural	10806	M.	5374	128	118	138	127	115	626	639	605	589	446	358	341
			F.	5432	122	99	111	144	144	620	616	656	561	454	390	313
Bridgend	Urban	4153	M.	1997	55	53	66	51	48	273	219	198	189	175	152	154
			F.	2156	52	61	56	64	71	304	256	218	235	203	170	150
Bridgend	Rural	28535	M.	14876	403	367	430	403	365	1968	1830	1546	1475	1388	1190	1048
			F.	13659	395	362	392	388	378	1915	1813	1533	1200	1141	1022	898
Briton Ferry	Urban	6061	M.	3092	86	92	95	92	90	455	376	336	333	267	276	219
			F.	2969	119	69	97	92	98	475	404	327	308	255	212	189
Brynmawr	Urban	5347	M.	2749	79	64	80	72	91	386	358	289	240	256	229	173
			F.	2598	75	69	74	57	86	361	357	306	230	205	191	174
Builth	Urban	1424	M.	660	24	13	19	23	20	99	88	74	40	48	41	44
			F.	764	21	27	12	24	22	106	69	83	102	67	67	46

Note.—For the Parishes comprised in each Urban Sanitary District, see Vol. II., I

Table 6 *continued*.—AGES of MALES and FEMALES in SA[NITARY DISTRICTS]

SANITARY DISTRICT.		ALL AGES. Persons.	Males and Females.		Under 1 Year.	1–	2–	3–	4–	Under 5 Years.	5–	10–	15–	20–	25–
BUILTH	Rural	6758	M.	3355	66	76	102	77	96	439	417	374	344	256	223
			F.	3403	89	80	87	78	93	427	419	414	332	293	255
CAERLEON	Urban	1099	M.	527	15	10	8	6	18	57	84	102	44	36	32
			F.	572	16	10	8	16	11	61	78	87	38	38	43
CARDIFF	Urban	82761	M.	42316	1204	1198	1123	1227	1165	5919	4887	4185	4184	4810	4049
			F.	40445	1276	1240	1151	1192	1110	5672	4738	4169	4189	4235	3616
CARDIFF	Rural	17175	M.	8626	198	208	228	210	194	1047	1094	1012	898	712	632
			F.	8549	237	218	230	207	221	1122	1078	988	902	769	552
CARDIGAN	Urban	3669	M.	1597	39	37	48	46	42	212	200	175	180	116	95
			F.	2072	60	26	41	27	40	194	182	188	167	180	159
CARDIGAN	Rural	13946	M.	5986	127	147	197	177	170	818	811	783	588	390	289
			F.	7960	155	156	167	171	165	814	807	772	783	596	554
CARMARTHEN	Urban	10514	M.	4833	116	102	114	106	129	597	556	541	535	453	345
			F.	5681	118	102	99	123	109	551	553	547	604	576	428
CARMARTHEN	Rural	24561	M.	11484	320	312	335	314	323	1604	1583	1487	1141	875	718
			F.	13077	317	295	326	315	300	1553	1403	1377	1313	1217	996
CARNARVON	Urban	10258	M.	4911	108	107	115	129	113	572	521	512	545	515	408
			F.	5347	118	124	97	120	119	578	534	511	587	522	475
CARNARVON	Rural	33739	M.	17147	519	429	479	494	441	2362	2172	1969	1683	1406	1318
			F.	16592	460	432	488	488	473	2350	1941	1816	1460	1219	1283
CHEPSTOW	Urban	3591	M.	1750	56	46	42	53	36	233	209	189	174	128	134
			F.	1841	51	34	55	42	51	233	209	199	172	154	138
CHEPSTOW	Rural	15110	M.	7711	215	180	202	190	206	993	928	907	724	609	512
			F.	7399	197	178	198	228	182	973	949	881	631	540	493
CHRISTCHURCH	Urban	3114	M.	1460	41	44	58	37	44	224	199	157	142	110	112
			F.	1654	50	42	51	56	46	245	196	179	175	129	133
COLEFORD	Urban	2709	M.	1359	35	35	32	43	38	183	169	170	133	100	63
			F.	1350	34	36	36	38	48	192	185	156	95	79	77
CONWAY	Urban	3254	M.	1651	51	28	44	46	29	198	168	188	181	164	150
			F.	1603	49	40	47	39	39	214	158	143	135	159	131
CONWAY	Rural	8146	M.	4009	106	105	112	104	95	522	476	475	405	318	288
			F.	4137	103	98	90	104	86	485	444	470	465	323	288
CORWEN	Rural	13710	M.	6962	161	155	182	184	155	837	861	773	700	595	472
			F.	6748	199	170	172	195	166	902	892	780	553	514	426
CRICCIETH	Urban	1108	M.	475	15	18	21	20	20	94	50	56	38	26	27
			F.	633	23	16	19	12	17	87	64	65	65	39	46
CRICKHOWELL	Rural	7710	M.	3825	111	78	105	94	95	483	485	385	346	292	234
			F.	3885	90	74	104	93	112	473	462	435	359	294	250
DENBIGH	Urban	6535	M.	3074	74	56	62	67	73	332	315	329	301	249	203
			F.	3461	81	73	84	60	65	363	344	359	375	295	257
DOLGELLY[1]	Urban	2455	M.	1117	30	29	22	22	25	128	131	104	117	89	70
			F.	1338	35	21	25	28	36	145	132	142	126	105	82
DOLGELLY	Rural	11213	M.	5518	130	147	151	173	134	735	682	632	510	398	384
			F.	5695	130	139	142	151	151	713	717	676	509	417	404
DWYGYFYLCH[1]	Urban	2122	M.	1015	20	32	23	32	30	146	121	116	93	74	75
			F.	1107	26	32	24	19	26	127	105	121	119	98	96
EBBW VALE	Urban	14700	M.	7900	240	198	193	219	204	1054	963	797	858	798	675
			F.	6800	214	192	184	233	210	1033	1002	783	619	555	519
FESTINIOG	Urban	11274	M.	6015	195	180	159	173	156	863	722	574	552	618	585
			F.	5259	170	168	158	202	166	864	646	583	431	427	454
FESTINIOG	Rural	12745	M.	6506	178	161	173	158	178	848	806	699	622	602	492
			F.	6239	147	173	161	191	149	821	768	730	547	487	444
FLINT	Urban	5096	M.	2683	74	64	80	78	64	360	321	306	273	219	215
			F.	2413	51	72	67	78	76	344	326	272	216	166	158

Table 6 *continued*.—AGES of MALES and FEMALES in SANIT[illegible]

SANITARY DISTRICT.		ALL AGES. Persons.	ALL AGES. Males and Females.		Under 1 Year.	1–	2–	3–	4–	Under 5 Years.	5–	10–	15–	20–	25–	30
FORDEN	Rural	12250	M.	6372	164	144	154	145	145	752	806	742	630	524	432	33
			F.	5878	153	126	158	179	149	765	768	650	504	448	377	33
GOWER	Rural	7615	M.	3735	106	111	94	115	111	537	491	388	374	292	270	20
			F.	3880	117	123	95	106	103	544	489	420	363	292	290	26
HAVERFORDWEST	Urban	6398	M.	2914	67	61	59	70	74	331	325	347	369	244	181	13
			F.	3484	77	68	73	71	65	354	340	364	398	323	230	20
HAVERFORDWEST	Rural	23581	M.	11038	294	313	327	305	302	1541	1371	1369	1168	934	830	[illegible]
			F.	12543	317	291	310	320	303	1541	1420	1340	1203	1055	855	72
HAY	Urban	1916	M.	880	28	19	24	28	22	121	109	115	77	59	60	5
			F.	1027	28	26	18	31	25	128	120	104	90	106	74	7
HAY	Rural	8306	M.	4139	93	89	104	95	117	408	463	475	412	305	277	[illegible]
			F.	4167	110	101	90	88	116	505	500	450	394	330	279	[illegible]
HOLYHEAD	Urban	8679	M.	4436	137	107	116	111	84	[illegible]	505	453	395	394	391	[illegible]
			F.	4243	115	105	123	120	129	592	463	430	350	327	320	31
HOLYHEAD	Rural	11280	M.	5627	111	127	152	153	130	673	631	582	593	441	382	31
			F.	5653	113	128	130	128	130	634	591	540	520	403	414	34
HOLYWELL	Urban	3090	M.	1477	47	41	35	35	28	186	186	170	138	105	106	10
			F.	1613	54	29	41	38	30	201	183	176	162	132	106	9
HOLYWELL	Rural	33268	M.	16928	438	432	436	459	460	2225	2183	1936	1759	1385	1234	10[illegible]
			F.	16340	450	421	419	428	455	2173	2216	2032	1289	1084	1052	9[illegible]
KNIGHTON	Urban	1720	M.	836	16	20	29	19	21	106	91	102	97	72	58	4
			F.	884	20	13	18	23	15	89	92	97	94	93	66	4
KNIGHTON	Rural	10062	M.	5221	118	107	136	132	133	626	605	613	538	477	358	3[illegible]
			F.	4841	116	131	117	127	117	608	618	600	480	379	336	2[illegible]
LAMPETER	Urban	1443	M.	713	16	14	20	17	10	86	75	81	78	94	57	[illegible]
			F.	730	20	15	13	11	14	73	82	76	85	72	52	[illegible]
LAMPETER	Rural	8644	M.	3958	102	121	84	111	111	529	495	494	403	294	252	2[illegible]
			F.	4686	99	111	112	118	121	561	515	516	415	371	321	2[illegible]
LLANDILO	Urban	1533	M.	704	15	22	18	10	23	88	88	89	61	60	56	4
			F.	829	12	14	13	11	16	66	89	80	88	76	77	6
LLANDILOFAWR	Rural	17266	M.	8328	224	248	236	255	252	1215	1190	1002	863	599	529	4[illegible]
			F.	8938	237	205	235	252	227	1156	1124	973	826	775	630	5[illegible]
LLANDOVERY	Urban	2035	M.	990	24	20	21	16	22	103	119	145	151	50	55	4
			F.	1045	19	20	24	34	25	122	110	100	99	99	70	[illegible]
LLANDOVERY	Rural	10730	M.	5110	118	132	110	144	123	632	653	651	496	404	308	2[illegible]
			F.	5614	123	125	115	113	165	641	630	569	603	558	399	3[illegible]
LLANDUDNO	Urban	4839	M.	2056	44	43	54	61	52	254	234	219	212	185	139	1[illegible]
			F.	2783	63	62	63	61	47	296	243	241	314	339	272	1[illegible]
LLANELLY	Urban	19760	M.	9744	303	290	291	264	298	1441	1311	1132	1044	944	802	6[illegible]
			F.	10016	321	291	289	297	278	1476	1380	1188	1080	952	673	6[illegible]
LLANELLY	Rural	24856	M.	12290	416	326	378	408	372	1900	1829	1548	1303	1019	785	7[illegible]
			F.	12566	404	363	347	406	369	1889	1742	1408	1218	1042	894	80
LLANFAIRFECHAN	Urban	2041	M.	990	14	21	30	22	26	113	133	130	101	76	66	4
			F.	1051	26	19	21	21	18	105	121	117	98	98	71	[illegible]
LLANFYLLIN	Rural	18883	M.	9406	208	205	208	256	219	1096	1148	1089	980	766	575	51
			F.	9387	247	214	2[illegible]9	228	227	1145	1152	1100	913	677	581	52
LLANGOLLEN	Urban	3123	M.	1476	35	25	35	38	42	175	162	179	133	120	90	[illegible]
			F.	1647	38	34	26	37	40	175	188	167	157	144	117	[illegible]
LLANIDLOES	Urban	3421	M.	1614	62	43	51	50	64	260	229	228	139	105	98	8
			F.	1807	45	44	57	53	40	239	248	182	163	118	110	11
LLANRWST	Rural	14109	M.	7081	179	171	186	199	179	914	799	717	679	627	535	47
			F.	7028	181	167	179	173	158	853	776	750	713	601	508	48
MACHYNLLETH	Rural	9152	M.	4465	106	108	105	130	105	554	544	557	482	342	273	24
			F.	4687	93	103	114	113	116	539	588	540	458	375	314	28

Table 6 *continued.*—AGES of MALES and FEMALES in SANI

SANITARY DISTRICT.		ALL AGES. Persons.	ALL AGES. Males and Females.		Under 1 Year.	1–	2–	3–	4–	Under 5 Years.	5–	10–	15–	20–	25–
MAESTEG	Urban	8310	M.	4250	126	113	134	125	134	632	606	471	440	353	307
			F.	4060	127	114	110	115	124	590	602	485	397	326	287
MERTHYR TYDFIL	Urban	48861	M.	25056	688	602	639	644	670	3243	3100	2731	2713	2450	1989
			F.	23805	692	579	692	699	633	3350	3166	2676	2343	2013	1758
MERTHYR TYDFIL	Rural	17047	M.	8984	242	231	276	254	247	1250	1140	993	950	831	725
			F.	8063	246	215	250	229	222	1162	1140	978	762	683	568
MILFORD	Urban	3812	M.	2204	48	26	42	29	50	195	184	202	279	238	212
			F.	1608	48	41	50	37	44	220	174	158	160	149	107
MOLD	Urban	4320	M.	2129	65	43	77	46	59	290	253	229	228	166	155
			F.	2191	53	50	56	54	54	267	267	244	231	157	159
MONMOUTH	Urban	6111	M.	3008	84	71	69	77	67	388	358	382	321	226	191
			F.	3103	89	69	68	64	79	349	348	313	333	289	246
MONMOUTH	Rural	21520	M.	11010	270	273	317	336	295	1491	1507	1336	1126	800	677
			F.	10510	292	287	318	304	286	1486	1467	1234	794	693	690
MOUNTAIN ASH	Urban	10295	M.	5652	164	157	124	162	142	749	736	602	599	688	504
			F.	4643	155	135	144	147	129	710	689	589	418	393	323
NARBERTH	Rural	19541	M.	9149	253	235	270	243	279	1285	1196	1174	945	661	557
			F.	10392	254	210	280	251	285	1280	1173	1090	948	913	747
NEATH	Urban	10409	M.	5088	140	118	146	143	152	708	661	562	532	462	375
			F.	5321	139	137	118	123	173	690	683	604	530	514	373
NEATH	Rural	28670	M.	14504	457	430	394	430	423	2134	1963	1710	1503	1269	1125
			F.	14166	424	407	408	454	414	2107	2001	1711	1395	1199	936
NEWCASTLE IN EMLYN	Rural	19014	M.	8643	232	230	228	229	231	1150	1152	1079	918	639	526
			F.	10371	213	200	231	236	241	1121	1106	1028	979	894	735
NEWPORT	Urban	35313	M.	17503	543	433	516	508	491	2495	2120	1708	1749	1667	1583
			F.	17810	555	519	498	488	414	2474	2132	1942	1809	1335	1445
NEWPORT	Rural	25476	M.	12917	378	352	358	381	332	1301	1746	1442	1276	1058	895
			F.	12559	328	328	390	352	386	1784	1688	1511	1223	966	920
NEW QUAY	Urban	1325	M.	486	16	17	14	14	14	75	83	70	45	21	18
			F.	839	19	12	20	16	18	85	94	54	63	74	51
NEWTOWN AND LLANLLWCHAIARN	Urban	7170	M.	3495	99	94	95	86	102	476	385	377	401	327	253
			F.	3675	81	96	97	86	96	456	390	342	418	376	274
NEWTOWN	Rural	14848	M.	7623	177	174	224	197	205	977	960	1004	816	596	494
			F.	7225	208	186	216	228	191	1029	1013	876	698	575	426
OYSTERMOUTH	Urban	3487	M.	1564	32	41	50	47	49	219	249	214	127	88	93
			F.	1923	38	63	39	51	46	237	247	194	179	172	137
PANTEG	Urban	3321	M.	1770	52	44	60	63	50	259	268	216	179	144	145
			F.	1551	58	56	52	48	34	248	202	170	134	131	114
PEMBROKE	Urban	14156	M.	7175	205	185	194	164	176	924	834	705	820	722	512
			F.	6981	166	198	180	187	171	902	834	727	725	655	501
PEMBROKE	Rural	11441	M.	5689	176	151	157	152	157	793	740	715	620	502	353
			F.	5752	167	140	163	147	148	765	671	659	616	512	393
PENARTH	Urban	6228	M.	3186	109	77	100	83	101	470	395	313	312	300	309
			F.	3042	100	96	100	97	94	487	407	310	315	328	236
PONTARDAWE	Rural	20186	M.	10116	331	268	318	284	335	1531	1466	1255	1084	849	730
			F.	10069	290	290	324	303	313	1520	1474	1210	993	802	759
PONTYPOOL	Urban	5244	M.	2552	79	69	72	68	52	340	294	269	270	230	201
			F.	2692	74	75	96	74	74	392	355	295	284	274	212
PONTYPOOL	Rural	6464	M.	3340	77	72	87	91	72	399	403	375	361	275	238
			F.	3124	83	75	69	74	86	387	399	364	312	240	225
PONTYPRIDD	Urban	12317	M.	6400	186	172	181	176	203	918	782	662	644	635	569
			F.	5917	197	160	179	163	157	856	799	683	584	639	462
PONTYPRIDD	Rural	16978	M.	8690	247	231	211	233	215	1137	1124	991	842	753	626
			F.	8288	223	245	228	274	245	1210	1163	988	775	661	565

Sanitary District.		All Ages. Persons.	All Ages. Males and Females.		Under 1 Year.	1–	2–	3–	4–	Under 5 Years.	5–	10–	15–	20–	25–	30–
PWLLHELI	Urban	3242	M.	1498	40	30	50	38	36	194	199	102	123	109	89	7
			F.	1744	48	42	48	44	39	221	181	159	133	156	137	10
PWLLHELI	Rural	18561	M.	9188	223	239	250	246	216	1174	1034	1011	926	784	617	58
			F.	9373	236	184	231	227	224	1102	973	902	818	792	645	58
RHAYADER	Rural	6741	M.	3347	84	78	90	87	80	423	435	383	301	294	215	21
			F.	3394	96	84	89	87	88	444	394	397	329	289	253	20
RHYL	Urban	6029	M.	2503	74	70	61	58	60	323	294	320	230	177	178	16
			F.	3526	71	53	57	59	70	310	324	367	435	384	303	23
RHYMNEY	Urban	8663	M.	4723	116	85	116	112	114	543	541	475	484	400	391	36
			F.	3940	100	86	118	121	115	540	528	484	353	345	271	27
RISCA	Urban	5540	M.	2790	96	80	80	94	79	429	394	338	289	242	209	17
			F.	2750	85	81	90	90	79	425	420	351	289	223	184	15
RUTHIN	Urban	3033	M.	1461	50	41	31	30	43	195	142	164	157	105	101	8
			F.	1572	29	34	32	39	46	180	180	155	135	117	135	8
RUTHIN	Rural	10377	M.	5547	136	118	121	130	145	650	597	635	624	481	354	29
			F.	5330	120	115	118	136	116	605	612	625	506	427	332	29
ST. ASAPH	Rural	13283	M.	7085	180	169	167	198	191	910	859	919	803	589	507	48
			F.	7048	170	193	198	169	193	918	870	794	693	560	538	47
SWANSEA	Urban	65597	M.	32222	1024	378	958	931	951	4742	4092	3381	3202	3068	2772	243
			F.	33375	1098	848	1023	874	909	4752	4106	3623	3408	3244	2752	224
SWANSEA	Rural	29404	M.	14985	407	415	506	410	465	2302	2163	1854	1624	1295	1164	104
			F.	14419	481	476	461	430	455	2306	2149	1752	1353	1183	1075	94
TENBY	Urban	4750	M.	1916	60	61	46	61	60	288	240	203	168	149	134	12
			F.	2834	54	49	61	56	43	263	266	250	327	334	236	22
TOWYN	Urban	3365	M.	1615	26	42	38	41	36	183	189	180	171	154	125	8
			F.	1750	37	35	41	35	41	189	169	191	179	174	112	10
TREDEGAR	Urban	18771	M.	9008	283	242	284	295	277	1381	1311	1159	1036	820	771	63
			F.	8868	299	254	276	260	300	1389	1276	1050	805	692	646	54
TREGARON	Rural	10272	M.	4690	116	126	127	132	128	629	640	591	501	319	278	25
			F.	5582	124	119	131	127	138	639	640	558	534	450	408	37
UPPER LLANVRECHVA	Urban	4177	M.	2243	77	66	80	65	57	345	309	234	231	198	138	1
			F.	1934	45	68	63	67	67	310	291	219	140	178	151	1
USK	Urban	1470	M.	708	18	14	14	22	21	89	68	60	82	56	44	4
			F.	762	18	15	14	19	19	85	73	86	72	77	68	4
WELSHPOOL	Urban	7107	M.	3615	83	71	95	87	90	426	429	407	410	302	240	1
			F.	3492	84	94	89	70	77	414	378	403	343	283	228	2
WREXHAM	Urban	10978	M.	5437	151	143	155	149	154	752	607	519	638	557	406	37
			F.	5541	154	179	170	147	149	799	652	641	575	495	474	38
WREXHAM	Rural	44180	M.	22888	642	570	619	626	658	3115	3011	2781	2418	1823	1622	14
			F.	21292	622	558	698	633	621	3127	2981	2601	1671	1390	1422	13
YNYSCYNHAIARN	Urban	5506	M.	2620	69	72	98	71	83	393	360	297	202	227	162	16
			F.	2886	76	75	81	85	73	390	335	289	235	231	209	21
YSTRADYFODWG	Urban	55632	M.	30877	1013	803	892	856	880	4444	3805	3045	3143	3063	3161	24
			F.	24755	955	769	866	790	861	4241	3606	2907	2227	2257	2097	17

Table 13.—NUMBER and COUNTRY of BIRTH of FOREIGNERS enumerated in COUNTIES, and in each U
exceeds 50,000 PERSONS.

WHERE BORN.	WHERE ENUMERAT								
	MONMOUTH-SHIRE AND WALES.		COU						
			MONMOUTH.		GLAMORGAN.		CARMAR-THEN.		PEM
	Males.	Females.	Males.	Females.	Males.	Females.	Males.	Females.	Males.
TOTAL	3454	879	589	107	2272	457	41	37	78
EUROPE.									
DENMARK	66	4	14	.	48	3	1	1	3
NORWAY	198	24	44	2	140	21	.	.	4
SWEDEN	186	5	28	.	132	3	.	.	8
RUSSIA	118	22	22	10	91	11	1	.	3
POLAND (RUSSIAN)	90	61	24	16	59	43	2	.	.
AUSTRIA	173	6	27	1	137	4	.	.	1
HUNGARY	2	.	.	.	2	.	.	.	.
SWITZERLAND	27	24	3	5	11	3	1	.	1
GERMAN EMPIRE	427	134	52	18	288	63	13	5	14
HOLLAND	33	2	17	.	10	2	.	.	.
BELGIUM	73	21	7	.	58	20	.	.	1
FRANCE	720	93	147	13	400	49	2	5	14
PORTUGAL	9	.	2	.	7	.	.	.	.
SPAIN	50	3	22	.	17	3	.	.	6
ITALY	543	37	87	2	429	26	1	.	6
GREECE	71	3	8	.	61	2	.	.	.
TURKEY	18	2	1	.	17	2	.	.	.
SERVIA	.	.	.	.	.	.	.	.	.
ROUMANIA	.	.	.	.	.	.	.	.	.
ASIA.									
ARABIA	.	.	.	.	.	.	.	.	.
PERSIA	.	.	.	.	.	.	.	.	.
CHINA	9	.	.	.	9	.	.	.	.
OTHER COUNTRIES	1	.	.	.	1	.	.	.	.
AFRICA.									
EGYPT	1	1	.	.	.	1	.	.	.
OTHER PARTS	1	.	.	.	1	.	.	.	.
AMERICA.									
UNITED STATES	628	432	83	40	387	198	20	26	17
MEXICO	.	.	.	.	.	.	.	.	.
BRAZIL	5	.	.	.	.	.	.	.	.
OTHER STATES	3	4	1	.	1	2	.	.	.
COUNTRY NOT STATED	1	1	.	.	1	1	.	.	.
AT SEA	1	.	.	.	1	.	.	.	.

Table 13 *continued.*—NUMBER and COUNTRY of BIRTH of FOREIGNERS enumerated in COUNTIES, and in
exceeds 50,000 PERSONS.

WHERE BORN.	WHERE ENUMERAT									
	COUNTIES.									
	MONT-GOMERY.		FLINT.		DENBIGH.		MERIONETH.		CARNARVON	
	Males.	Females.	Males.	Females.	Males.	Females.	Males.	Females.	Males.	Females.
TOTAL	13	15	141	44	31	42	111	38	87	54
EUROPE.										
DENMARK	.	.	.	.	.	.	.	.	.	.
NORWAY	.	.	.	.	.	.	.	.	3	1
SWEDEN	.	.	.	.	.	1	.	1	4	.
RUSSIA	.	.	.	.	.	.	.	.	1	1
POLAND (RUSSIAN)	.	.	.	.	.	.	.	.	3	1
AUSTRIA	.	.	1	.	2	.	.	.	2	.
HUNGARY	.	.	.	.	.	.	.	.	.	.
SWITZERLAND	.	2	4	1	.	3	3	1	2	2
GERMAN EMPIRE	4	2	24	6	7	7	5	2	9	7
HOLLAND	.	.	2	.	.	.	1	.	2	.
BELGIUM	.	.	2	.	1	1	1	.	2	.
FRANCE	.	1	77	5	2	5	72	4	2	4
PORTUGAL	.	.	.	.	.	.	.	.	.	.
SPAIN	.	.	1	.	.	.	3	.	1	.
ITALY	1	1	5	.	5	3	2	.	3	1
GREECE	.	.	.	1	.	.	.	.	.	.
TURKEY	.	.	.	.	.	.	.	.	.	.
SERVIA	.	.	.	.	.	.	.	.	.	.
ROUMANIA	.	.	.	.	.	.	.	.	.	.
ASIA.										
ARABIA	.	.	.	.	.	.	.	.	.	.
PERSIA	.	.	.	.	.	.	.	.	.	.
CHINA	.	.	.	.	.	.	.	.	.	.
OTHER COUNTRIES	.	.	.	.	.	.	.	.	.	.
AFRICA.										
EGYPT	.	.	1	.	.	.	.	.	.	.
OTHER PARTS	.	.	.	.	.	.	.	.	.	.
AMERICA.										
UNITED STATES	8	9	20	31	14	22	24	30	51	35
MEXICO	.	.	.	.	.	.	.	.	.	.
BRAZIL	.	.	4	.	.	.	.	.	1	.
OTHER STATES	.	.	.	.	.	.	.	.	1	2
COUNTRY NOT STATED	.	.	.	.	.	.	.	.	.	.
AT SEA	.	.	.	.	.	.	.	.	.	.

E 8516.

TABLE 14.—ENGLAND AND WALES.—ENUMERATED POPULATION (PERSONS, MALES, and FEMALES,)

AGES.	1841.			1851.			1861.		
	PERSONS.	Males.	Females.	PERSONS.	Males.	Females.	PERSONS.	Males.	Females
All ages -	15,914,148	7,777,586	8,136,562	17,927,609	8,781,225	9,146,384	20,066,224	9,776,259	10,289.96
0— -	2,106,295	1,048,242	1,058,053	2,348,107	1,176,253	1,171,354	2,700,782	1,354,907	1,345,87
5— -	1,904,913	953,111	951,802	2,092,359	1,050,228	1,042,131	2,344,066	1,172,960	1,171,10
10— -	1,732,284	880,548	851,736	1,913,357	963,995	949,362	2,105,176	1,059,889	1,045,28
15— -	1,156,850	781,679	805,171	1,757,189	873,236	883,953	1,932,642	957,930	974,71
20— -	1,550,418	723,490	826,928	1,666,607	795,455	871,152	1,829,493	860,210	969,28
25— -	2,449,879	1,175,700	1,274,179	2,746,601	1,317,234	1,429,367	2,955,942	1,395,977	1,559,96
35— -	1,772,583	870,729	901,854	2,057,178	1,006,891	1,050,287	2,358,669	1,141,338	1,217,33
45— -	1,273,000	620,639	652,361	1,507,790	738,986	768,804	1,737,403	845,506	891,89
55— -	831,549	398,738	432,811	1,007,597	482,132	525,465	1,170,244	564,536	605,70
65— -	483,844	224,780	259,064	577,681	266,370	311,311	657,917	303,966	353,95
75— -	190,341	86,719	103,622	219,942	96,706	123,236	240,299	106,036	134,26
85 and upwards	32,192	13,211	18,981	33,201	13,239	19,962	33,591	13,004	20,58

TABLE 15.—ENGLAND AND WALES.—PROPORTION of MALES and FEMALES at TWELVE GROUPS last FIVE CENSUSES.

AGES.	PROPORTION PER 1,000,000					
	1841.		1851.		1861.	
	Males.	Females.	Males.	Females.	Males.	Fem
All ages - -	488,721	511,279	489,816	510,184	487,200	512
0— - -	65,869	66,485	65,639	65,338	67,522	67
5— - -	59,891	59,809	58,582	58,130	58,454	58
10— - -	55,331	53,521	53,772	52,955	52,820	52
15— - -	49,118	50,595	48,709	49,307	47,738	48
20— - -	45,462	51,962	44,370	48,593	42,869	48
25— - -	73,878	80,064	73,476	79,730	69,568	77
35— - -	54,714	56,670	56,164	58,585	56,879	60
45— - -	38,999	40,993	41,221	42,884	42,136	44
55— - -	25,055	27,197	26,893	29,310	28,134	30
65— - -	14,125	16,279	14,858	17,365	15,148	17
75— - -	5,449	6,511	5,394	6,874	5,284	6
85— - -	830	1,193	738	1,113	648	1

M

THREE EXAMPLES of the MODE OF FILLING UP THE HOUSEHOLDER'S SCHEDULE.

		Name and Surname.	Relation to Head of Family.	Condition as to Marriage.	Sex.	Age last Birth-day.	Rank, Profession, or Occupation.	Where Born.	If (1) Deaf and Dumb. (2) Blind. (3) Imbecile or Idiot. (4) Lunatic.
1.	1	George Wood	Head of Family	Married.	M.	48	Farmer (of 317 acres, employing 8 labourers and 3 boys).	Surrey, Godstone	—
	2	Maria Wood	Wife	Married	F.	44	Farmer's Wife	Scotland	—
	3	Alan Wood	Son	Unmarried	M.	20	Farmer's Son	Surrey, Godstone	—
	4	Flora Jane Wood	Daughter		F.	12	Scholar	Kent, Ramsgate	—
	5	Ellen Wood	Mother	Widow	F.	71	Annuitant	Canada	Lunatic.
	6	Eliza Edwards	Servant	Unmarried	F.	24	General Servant (Domestic)	Middlesex, Paddington	—
	7	Ann Young	Servant	Unmarried	F.	22	Dairymaid	Surrey Croydon	—
	8	Thomas Jones	Servant	Unmarried	M.	21	Farm Servant	Essex, Epping	—
2.	1	Janet Cox	Head of Family	Widow	F.	40	Staymaker	Scotland	—
	2	William Cox	Son	Unmarried	M.	28	Basketmaker	Surrey, Lambeth	Blind from Birth.
	3	Sophia Cox	Daughter	Unmarried	F.	24	Dressmaker	Middlesex, Poplar	—
	4	Alexander Wilson	Grandson		M.	11Mths.		Middlesex, Shoreditch	—
	5	Margaret Cox.	Mother-in-Law	Widow	F.	73	Formerly Laundress	Ireland	—
	6	John Butler	Boarder	Widower	M.	42	Printer—Compositor	France (British Subject)	—
	7	James Smith	Visitor	Unmarried	M.	36	Copper Miner	Cornwall, Truro	—
	1	Walter Johnson	Lodger	Unmarried	M.	23	Ship Carpenter	Durham, Sunderland	—

CENSUS
OF
ENGLAND AND WALES, 1881.

No.__________

HOUSEHOLDER'S SCHEDULE.

Prepared under the direction of the Local Government Board, pursuant to the Act of 43 and 44 Vict. c. 37.

☞ The following compartments to be filled up by the Enumerator.

Parish or Township.	
City, Town, Village, or Hamlet.	
Street, Square, &c. or Road.	
Name or No. of House.	
Name of Occupier.	

TO THE OCCUPIER.

You are requested to insert the particulars specified on the other side, in compliance with an Act passed during the last Session of Parliament, and which received the Royal assent on the 7th September 1880.

This Paper will be CALLED FOR on MONDAY, APRIL 4th, by the appointed Enumerator,

and it is desirable that you should have the *answers* written in the proper columns by the *morning of that day* in order that his progress may not be delayed. It will be his duty, under the Act, to complete the return if it be defective, and to correct it if erroneous. Any person authorized by you may write in the particulars if you are yourself unable to do so.

Persons who refuse to give INFORMATION, or who wilfully give FALSE INFORMATION, as to any of the required particulars, are liable, on summary conviction before Justices, to a *Penalty of Five Pounds.*

The Return is required to enable the Local Government Board to complete the NINTH CENSUS; which is to show the exact numbers, ages, and condition of the people—their arrangement by families in different ranks, professions, and trades—their distribution over the country in villages, towns, and cities—their increase and progress during the last ten years. The facts will be published in General Abstracts only, *and strict care will be taken that the returns are not used for the gratification of curiosity.*

BRYDGES P. HENNIKER,
Registrar-General.

Approved by the Local Government Board.
J. G. DODSON, *President.*

This Paper to be filled
If a house is let or sub
LODGER must make
SCHEDULE.

INSTRUCTIONS for

A person following n
t

1. The Titles of PEERS and othe to be inserted, as well as any im hold.

2. MEMBERS OF PARLIAM ALDERMEN, and other importar their profession or occupation, if rank or title.

3. All persons serving in the state their rank and the branch of belong. Officers to state whether List;-Chelsea, Greenwich, and ot designated.

4. All persons in the CIVIL rank, and the department or bran those retired or superannuated to

5. MINISTERS OF RELIGIC Church of England to return them "*Vicar of*——," "*Curate of*— *cure of souls.*" They are requ indefinite term "*Clerk.*" ROMA and Ministers of Foreign Churche such, and to state the name of the in which they officiate. DISSENT themselves as "*Independent Mini* "*Wesleyan Minister of*—— occasional preachers must retur *tions*; but may add "Local Meth

6. LEGAL PROFESSION.—I whether or not they are in actua tion *Solicitor* to be confined to actually on the Roll. *Barristers'* themselves. Clerks in Solicito whether they are *Solicitors Mana Clerk.* Officers of any Court to sta and the name of the Court.

7. Members of the MEDICAL whether they practise as *Phys Oculist, General Practitioner, As* practising." They must also stat Society of which they are Graduat

8. PROFESSORS, TEACHER AUTHORS and SCIENTIFIC ticular branch of Science or Liter ARTISTS, the art which they should enter their degrees in this

9. STUDENTS of *Theology, Lau graduates* of any University, to b

10. SCHOLARS.—Children or y School, or receiving regular inst returned as "*Scholars.*"

11. FARMERS to state the num the number of men, women, anc farm at the time of the Census.—*A Acres, employing 8 Labourers* Daughters employed at home o returned—"*Farmer's Son,*" "*Fa* employed on the farm and sleepi must be described in the schedule

12. AGRICULTURAL LABO and others employed on Farms Farmer's house, must be descril *bourers, Shepherds, &c.*

13. PERSONS ENGAGED IN chants, Brokers, Agents, &c., to ticular branch of Commerce in w

NOTE.—Examples of th

LIST of the MEMBERS of this FAMILY, of VISITORS, of BOARDERS, and of SERVANTS, who SLEPT or ABODE in

	NAME and SURNAME.	RELATION to Head of Family.	CONDITION as to Marriage.	SEX.	AGE Last Birthday.	RANK, PROFESSION, or OCC
	No Persons ABSENT *on the Night of Sunday April 3rd, to be entered here;* EXCEPT *those who may be* TRAVELLING *or out of* WORK *during that Night, and who* RETURN HOME ON MONDAY, APRIL 4TH. Write after the Name of the Head of the Family the Names of his Wife, Children, and other Relatives; then Visitors, Boarders, and Servants.	State whether Head, or Wife, Son, Daughter, or other Relative, Visitor, Boarder, or Servant.	Write either "*Married*," "*Widower*," "*Widow*," or "*Unmarried*," opposite the Names of all Persons, except Young Children.	Write "*M*" opposite Males, and "*F*" opposite Females.	For *Infants under One Year*, state the Age in *Months*, writing "*Under 1 Month*," "*1 Month*," "*2 Months*," &c.	*Before filling up this Column* *requested to read th* *Instructions on the other*
1						
2						
3						
4						
5						
6						
7						
8						
9						
10						
11						
12						
13						
14						
15						

I declare the foregoing to be a true Return, according to the best of my knowledge

Witness my Hand,

CENSUS OF ENGLAND AND WALES.

(43 & 44 Vict. c. 37.)

1881.

Volume III.

AGES, CONDITION AS TO MARRIAGE, OCCUPATIONS, AND BIRTH-PLACES OF THE PEOPLE.

Presented to both Houses of Parliament by Command of Her Majesty.

LONDON:
PRINTED BY EYRE AND SPOTTISWOODE.

To be purchased, either directly or through any Bookseller, from any of the following Agents, viz., Messrs. Hansard and Son, 13, Great Queen Street, W.C., and 32, Abingdon Street, Westminster; Messrs. Eyre and Spottiswoode, East Harding Street, Fleet Street, and Sale Office, House of Lords; Messrs. Adam and Charles Black, of Edinburgh; Messrs. Alexander Thom and Co., or Messrs. Hodges, Figgis, and Co., of Dublin.

1883.

CENSUS OF ENGLAND AND WALES.

(43 & 44 VICT. c. 37.)

1881.

VOLUME III.

AGES, CONDITION AS TO MARRIAGE, OCCUPATIONS, AND BIRTH-PLACES OF THE PEOPLE.

Presented to both Houses of Parliament by Command of Her Majesty.

LONDON:
PRINTED BY EYRE AND SPOTTISWOODE.

To be purchased, either directly or through any Bookseller, from any of the following Agents, viz.,
Messrs. HANSARD and SON, 13, Great Queen Street, W.C., and 32, Abingdon Street, Westminster;
Messrs. EYRE and SPOTTISWOODE, East Harding Street, Fleet Street, and Sale Office, House of Lords;
Messrs. ADAM and CHARLES BLACK, of Edinburgh;
Messrs. ALEXANDER THOM and Co., or Messrs. HODGES, FIGGIS, and Co., of Dublin.

1883.

[C.-3722.] *Price 6s.*

SUMMARY TABLES.

SUMMARY TABLES.

Table 1.—AGES of MALES and FEMALES enumerated in ENGLAND AND WALES.

AGES.	Persons.	Males.	Females.	AGES.	Persons.	Males.	Females.
ALL AGES -	25974439	12639902	13334537	30- - -	1745469	840259	905210
				35- - -	1541399	744924	796475
0- - -	753113	376890	376223	40- - -	1399354	672971	726383
1- - -	684412	341434	342978	45- - -	1151371	547508	603863
2- - -	704409	351616	352793	50- - -	1022075	485758	536317
3- - -	691695	344788	346907	55- - -	806464	381998	424466
4- - -	687235	342929	344306	60- - - -	727622	340555	387067
Under 5 years -	3520864	1757657	1763207	65- - -	502469	231549	270920
5- - -	3147396	1568579	1578817	70- - - -	349955	158333	191622
10- -	2800331	1402230	1398101	75-	202322	89847	112475
15- - -	2547232	1268269	1278963	80- - -	95750	41171	54579
20- - -	2328226	1112354	1215872	85- -	29987	11929	18058
25- - -	2047992	981278	1066714	90- -	6790	2330	4460
				95- - -	1230	359	871
				100 and upwards -	141	44	97

Table 2.—AGES of MALES and FEMALES in URBAN and in RURAL SANITARY DISTRICTS.*

AGES.	URBAN.			RURAL.		
	Males.	Females.	Persons.	Persons.	Males.	Females.
ALL AGES - - -	8467334	9169830	17637164	8337275	4172568	4164707
0- -	261594	261513	523107	230006	115296	114710
1- -	234450	236029	470479	213933	106984	106949
2- -	237937	239986	477923	226486	113679	112807
3- -	232924	235274	468198	223497	111864	111633
4- -	230719	232014	462733	224502	112210	112292
Under 5 years	1197624	1204816	2402440	1118424	560033	558391
5-	1039359	1052477	2091836	1055560	529220	526340
10- - -	910897	931919	1842816	957515	491333	466182
15- - -	838272	912697	1750969	796263	429997	366266
20- -	780399	888116	1668515	659711	331955	327756
25- - -	707016	777334	1484350	563642	274262	289380
30- - -	599532	650487	1250019	495450	240727	254723
35-	523407	563961	1087368	454031	221517	232514
40- - -	466576	509173	975749	423605	206395	217210
45- - -	364857	410433	775290	376081	182651	193430
50- - -	315105	359703	674808	347267	170653	176614
55- -	235230	273133	508363	298101	146768	151333
60- - -	204031	248527	452558	275064	136524	138540
65- - -	129456	165379	294835	207634	102093	105541
70- - -	85013	114729	199742	150213	73320	76893
75- - -	44716	64402	109118	93204	45131	48073
80- -	19425	30125	49550	46200	21746	24454
85- - -	5191	9585	14776	15211	6738	8473
90- - -	1028	2279	3307	3483	1302	2181
95- - -	180	493	673	557	179	378
100 and upwards	20	62	82	59	24	35

Table 3.—CONDITION as to MARRIAGE and AGES of MALES and FEMALES enumerated in ENGLAND AND WALES.

AGES.	MALES.			FEMALES.		
	Unmarried.	Married.†	Widowed.	Unmarried.	Married.†	Widowed.
ALL AGES - -	7828210	4376898	434794	7897529	4437962	999046
0- - -	4728466	-	-	4740125	-	-
15- -	1262311	5860	98	1246329	32416	218
20- - -	864402	245466	2486	809001	402019	4852
25- - -	577349	1217714	26474	576103	1343802	52019
35- - -	195427	1170779	51689	233820	1164949	124089
45- - -	99498	859840	73928	136080	810420	193680
55- - -	59865	562693	99995	88401	471321	251811
65 and upwards .	40892	314546	180124	67670	213035	372377

* The total population of the Urban Sanitary Districts in this table will be found to differ slightly from that given in other parts of the Report, owing to the population of the extended District of Stalybridge (Div. VIII.) having been included here, although the Act by which it was extended did not come into operation until shortly after the day of the Census.

† In a few cases, persons described as "Married" were stated to be under 15 years of age. These have been classed with married persons aged "15 and under 20 years."

Table 4.—OCCUPATIONS of MALES and FEMALES in ENGLAND and WALES, in CLASSES, ORDERS, and SUB-ORDERS.

	CLASSES, ORDERS, AND SUB-ORDERS.	PERSONS.	MALES.	FEMALES.
	TOTAL - -	25974439	12639902	13334537
	CLASSES.			
	I. PROFESSIONAL CLASS - - -	647075	450955	196120
	II. DOMESTIC CLASS - - -	1803810	258508	1545302
	III. COMMERCIAL CLASS - - -	980128	960661	19467
	IV. AGRICULTURAL CLASS - - -	1383184	1318344	64840
	V. INDUSTRIAL CLASS - - -	6373367	4795178	1578189
	VI. INDEFINITE AND NON-PRODUCTIVE CLASS - - - - - - -	14786875	4856256	9930619
	ORDERS AND SUB-ORDERS.			
CLASS I.	1. PERSONS ENGAGED IN THE GENERAL OR LOCAL GOVERNMENT OF THE COUNTRY - - -	104592	97222	7370
	1. National Government -	50859	46506	4353
	2. Local Government -	53493	50476	3017
	3. East India and Colonial Service	240	240	—
	2. PERSONS ENGAGED IN THE DEFENCE OF THE COUNTRY - -	124580	124530	50*
	1. Army (at Home) - - -	87185	87168	17
	2. Navy (Ashore or in Port) -	37395	37362	33
	3. PERSONS ENGAGED IN PROFESSIONAL OCCUPATIONS, WITH THEIR IMMEDIATE SUBORDINATES -	417903	229203	188700
	1. Clerical profession	51120	43958	7162
	2. Legal profession	43641	43541	100
	3. Medical profession	64548	26638	37910†
	4. Teachers - -	171831	47836	123995
	5. Literary and Scientific persons	8394	7780	614
	6. Engineers and Surveyors	14809	14809	—
	7. Artists	58517	40164	18353
	8. Persons engaged in exhibitions, shows, games, &c. -	5043	4477	566
CLASS II.	4. PERSONS ENGAGED IN DOMESTIC OFFICES OR SERVICES - -	1803810	258508	1545302
	1. Domestic service	1502676	244391	1258285
	2. Other service -	301134	14117	287017
CLASS III.	5. PERSONS ENGAGED IN COMMERCIAL OCCUPATIONS - -	316865	308391	8474
	1. Merchants and agents -	285138	277000	8138
	2. Dealers in money -	16659	16570	89
	3. Persons occupied in insurance -	15068	14821	247

* Consisting of Army and Navy Pensioners.

† Including midwives and sick nurses.

Table 4 *continued.*—OCCUPATIONS of MALES and FEMALES in ENGLAND and WALES, in CLASSES, ORDERS, and SUB-ORDERS.

	CLASSES, ORDERS, AND SUB-ORDERS.	PERSONS.	MALES.	FEMALES.
CLASS III.—*cont.*	6. PERSONS ENGAGED IN CONVEYANCE OF MEN, GOODS, AND MESSAGES -	663263	652270	10993
	1. On railways - - -	139408	138760	648
	2. On roads - - -	167232	165854	1378
	3. On canals, rivers, and seas	183984	183034	950
	4. In storage	32026	27847	4179
	5. In conveying messages, porterage, &c.	140613	136775	3838
CLASS IV.	7. PERSONS ENGAGED IN AGRICULTURE -	1278624	1214453	64171
	1. In fields and pastures -	1196836	1135763	61073
	2. In woods -	8151	8151	—
	3. In gardens	73637	70539	3098
	8. PERSONS ENGAGED ABOUT ANIMALS -	104560	103891	669
	1. About animals -	104560	103891	669
CLASS V.	9. PERSONS WORKING AND DEALING IN BOOKS, PRINTS, AND MAPS -	105042	89130	15912
	1. Books -	98321	82722	15599
	2. Prints and Maps -	6721	6408	313
	10. PERSONS WORKING AND DEALING IN MACHINES AND IMPLEMENTS -	267976	253994	13982
	1. Machines - -	160797	159735	1062
	2. Tools and implements -	48556	39631	8925
	3. Clocks, watches, and philosophical instruments - - -	32064	30848	1216
	4. Surgical instruments	1511	1181	330
	5. Arms and ordnance -	8227	8003	224
	6. Musical instruments - -	9249	9008	241
	7. Type, dies, medals, coins	2708	2693	85
	8. Tackle for sports and games	4364	2965	1899
	11. PERSONS WORKING AND DEALING IN HOUSES, FURNITURE, AND DECORATIONS - -	786660	768283	18377
	1. Houses - -	666738	665350	1388
	2. Furniture and Fittings	101066	89197	11869
	3. House decorations - -	18856	13736	5120
	12. PERSONS WORKING AND DEALING IN CARRIAGES AND HARNESS -	87174	84692	2482
	1. Carriages - - -	63308	62861	447
	2. Harness	23866	21831	2035
	13. PERSONS WORKING AND DEALING IN SHIPS AND BOATS - - -	54080	53967	113
	1. Hull - -	45671	45632	39
	2. Masts, rigging, &c.	8409	8335	74

Table 4 *continued*.—OCCUPATIONS of MALES and FEMALES in ENGLAND and WALES, in CLASSES, ORDERS, and SUB-ORDERS.

CLASSES, ORDERS, AND SUB-ORDERS.		PERSONS.	MALES.	FEMALES.
CLASS V.—*cont.*	14. PERSONS WORKING AND DEALING IN CHEMICALS AND COMPOUNDS	43015	38597	4418
	1. Colouring matter	3261	2715	546
	2. Explosives	3616	1607	2009
	3. Drugs and other chemicals and compounds	36138	34275	1863
	15. PERSONS WORKING AND DEALING IN TOBACCO AND PIPES	22175	12862	9313
	1. Tobacco and pipes	22175	12862	9313
	16. PERSONS WORKING AND DEALING IN FOOD AND LODGING	629371	503344	126027
	1. Board and lodging	115655	67392	48263
	2. Spirituous drinks	65052	60177	4875
	3. Food	448664	375775	72889
	17. PERSONS WORKING AND DEALING IN TEXTILE FABRICS	1053648	463024	590624
	1. Wool and worsted	233256	108371	124885
	2. Silk	63577	21455	42122
	3. Cotton and flax	586470	231147	355323
	4. Hemp and other fibrous materials	22471	14070	8401
	5. Mixed or unspecified materials	147874	87981	59893
	18. PERSONS WORKING AND DEALING IN DRESS	981105	364680	616425
	1. Dress	981105	364680	616425
	19. PERSONS WORKING AND DEALING IN VARIOUS ANIMAL SUBSTANCES	68202	53564	14638
	1. In grease, gut, bone, horn, ivory, and whalebone	10401	9266	1135
	2. In skins	39748	34262	5486
	3. In hair and feathers	18053	10036	8017
	20. PERSONS WORKING AND DEALING IN VARIOUS VEGETABLE SUBSTANCES	166745	130580	36165
	1. In oils, gums, and resins	20509	16639	3870
	2. In cane, rush, and straw	17909	15334	2575
	3. In wood and bark	75338	71417	3921
	4. In paper	52989	27190	25799

Table 4 *continued.*—OCCUPATIONS of MALES and FEMALES in ENGLAND and WALES, in CLASSES, ORDERS, and SUB-ORDERS.

Classes, Orders, and Sub-Orders.		Persons.	Males.	Females.
Class V.—*cont.*	21. PERSONS WORKING AND DEALING IN VARIOUS MINERAL SUBSTANCES -	1277592	1212491	65101
	1. Miners - -	441272	435497	5775
	2. Coal, coal gas, &c. -	58044	56734	1310
	3. Stone, clay, and road making -	193083	189783	3300
	4. Earthenware and glass	74407	52917	21490
	5. Salt -	2982	2823	159
	6. Water -	2673	2653	20
	7. Precious metals and jewellery -	29632	23622	6010
	8. Iron and steel -	361343	348029	13314
	9. Copper	7348	7298	50
	10. Tin and zinc -	39188	34633	4555
	11. Lead - -	2460	2319	141
	12. In other, mixed, or unspecified metals -	65160	56183	8977
	22. PERSONS WORKING AND DEALING IN GENERAL OR UNSPECIFIED COMMODITIES -	816243	753285	62958
	1. Makers and dealers (general or undefined) - -	121407	76118	45289
	2. Mechanics and labourers (general or undefined) - -	694836	677167	17669
	23. PERSONS WORKING AND DEALING IN REFUSE MATTERS - -	14339	12685	1654
	1. Refuse matters	14339	12685	1654
Class VI.	24. PERSONS WITHOUT SPECIFIED OCCUPATIONS - - - -	14786875	4856256	9930619
	1. Persons returned by property, rank, &c., and not by special occupation, including all Children under 5 years of age -	14786875	4856256	9930619

Table 5.—OCCUPATIONS of MALES and FEMALES in ENGLAND and WALES, at SEVEN GROUPS of AGES.

Ages of Males: Under 5 years.	5-	15-	20-	25-	45-	65 and upwards.	All Ages.	OCCUPATIONS.	Ages of Females: All Ages.	Under 5 years.	5-	15-	20-	25-	45-	65 and upwards.
1757657	2970809	1268269	1112354	3239432	1755819	535561	12639902	TOTAL - - -	13334537	1763207	2976918	1278963	1215872	3404782	1961713	653308
								I. PROFESSIONAL CLASS.								
								1. PERSONS ENGAGED IN THE GENERAL OR LOCAL GOVERNMENT OF THE COUNTRY.								
								1. *National Government.*								
.	.	2	10	194	285	123	614	Peer, M.P., Privy Councillor (not otherwise described) - - -	.	.	.	.	.	.	.	.
.	99	1827	3373	10263	5835	938	22332	Civil Service (officers and clerks) - -	3216	.	28	423	643	1098	735	300
.	1051	4666	3391	7140	2326	447	19027	Civil Service (messengers, &c.)	656	.	92	94	60	140	171	10
.	2	5	63	1822	1010	24	2913	Prison Officer, &c. - - - -	584	.	1	6	36	412	126	3
								2. *Local Government.*								
.	.	142	5440	22473	4353	100	32508	Police - - - - - -	.	.	.	.	.	.	.	.
.	27	312	732	5223	4309	1292	11895	Municipal, Parish, Union, District, Officer	3017	.	6	76	388	1688	775	85
.	8	114	182	1717	2548	1504	6075	Other Local or County Official - -	.	.	.	.	.	.	.	.
								3. *East Indian and Colonial Service.*								
.	.	6	27	135	60	12	240	East Indian and Colonial Service -	.	.	.	.	.	.	.	.
								2. PERSONS ENGAGED IN THE DEFENCE OF THE COUNTRY.								
								1. *Army (at Home).*								
.	.	667	913	3989	4073	1272	10914	Army Officer (effective or retired) -	.	.	.	.	.	.	.	.
.	287	9173	12904	26887	856	28	50135	Soldier and Non-commissioned Officer -	.	.	.	.	.	.	.	.
.	48	3555	2132	3546	1378	88	10747	Militia, Yeomanry, Volunteers - -	.	.	.	.	.	.	.	.
.	.	1	25	2562	4413	1571	8572	Army Pensioner - - - -	17	.	.	.	.	5	9	3
								2. *Navy (ashore or in port).*								
.	111	86	136	1570	1490	529	3921	Navy Officer (effective or retired) -	.	.	.	.	.	.	.	.
.	52	4774	3590	7512	857	26	16811	Seaman, R.N. - - - - -	.	.	.	.	.	.	.	.
.	19	1339	2016	4140	185	21	7720	Royal Marines (officers and men) - -	.	.	.	.	.	.	.	.
.	.	1	33	1908	4729	2239	8910	Navy Pensioner - - - -	33	.	.	.	1	5	10	17
								3. PERSONS ENGAGED IN PROFESSIONAL OCCUPATIONS (WITH THEIR IMMEDIATE SUBORDINATES).								
								1. *Clerical Profession.*								
.	.	.	401	9307	8686	3269	21663	Clergyman (Established Church) - -	.	.	.	.	.	.	.	.
.	.	.	46	1247	644	149	2089	Roman Catholic Priest - - - -	.	.	.	.	.	.	.	.
.	.	11	326	5306	3122	969	9734	Minister, Priest, of other religious bodies	.	.	.	.	.	.	.	.
.	1	26	287	1366	1045	290	2965	Missionary, Scripture Reader, Itinerant Preacher - - -	1660	.	3	67	126	604	754	106
								Nun, Sister of Charity - - -	3795	.	11	141	430	2223	849	121
.	3	332	1507	1072	11	.	2925	Theological Student - - - -	.	.	.	.	.	.	.	.
.	118	53	94	1372	1940	1010	4582	Church, Chapel, Cemetery—Officer, Servant - - - - -	1707	.	.	19	51	422	887	328
								2. *Legal Profession.*								
.	.	.	994	9771	5044	1577	17386	Barrister, Solicitor - - -	.	.	.	.	.	.	.	.
.	4	409	792	433	15	.	1653	Law Student - - - -	.	.	.	.	.	.	.	.
.	953	6800	5841	8295	2263	850	24602	Law Clerk, and others connected with Law - - - - -	100	.	1	23	39	31	5	1
								3. *Medical Profession.*								
.	.	.	810	8300	4455	1546	15091	Physician, Surgeon, General Practitioner	25	.	.	1	.	20	4	.
.	46	417	565	1792	671	93	3583	Dentist - - - - - -	.	.	.	.	.	.	.	.
.	11	1687	2500	1663	119	12	5992	Medical Student, Assistant -	64	.	1	10	20	28	5	.
.	.	.	.	.	.	.	.	Midwife - - - - -	2646	.	.	1	9	485	1379	772
.	10	176	190	753	658	190	1977	Subordinate Medical Service -	35175	.	22	228	714	7634	19259	7318
								4. *Teachers.*								
.	1871	11481	7893	13945	4009	539	39738	Schoolmaster - - - - -	94241	.	5152	29056	21172	28653	8684	1524
.	22	334	896	3162	1585	334	6336	Teacher, Professor, Lecturer - -	29605	.	84	3399	8638	13665	2564	255
.	7	35	59	962	630	69	1762	School Service, and others concerned in Teaching - - - -	1149	.	5	38	66	567	424	51
								5. *Literary and Scientific Persons.*								
.	2	45	237	1684	840	154	2962	Author, Editor, Journalist -	452	.	1	11	30	250	134	26
.	15	413	607	1292	235	40	2602	Reporter, Short-hand Writer - -	15	.	.	4	5	4	2	.
.	16	144	246	523	205	52	1186	Persons engaged in Scientific Pursuits -	14	.	.	.	2	5	5	2
.	5	42	106	460	280	57	950	Literary, Scientific, Institution, Service, &c. - - -	133	.	.	6	10	72	38	7
								6. *Engineers and Surveyors.*								
.	17	613	1035	3448	1727	284	7124	Civil Engineer - - - -	.	.	.	.	.	.	.	.
.	7	196	398	1062	541	87	2291	Mining Engineer - - - -	.	.	.	.	.	.	.	.
.	45	516	771	2289	1402	371	5394	Land, House, Ship, Surveyor - -	.	.	.	.	.	.	.	.
								7. *Artists.*								
.	37	380	767	2815	1634	449	6082	Painter (artist) - - - -	1880	.	10	199	456	931	243	41
.	57	376	323	893	443	107	2201	Engraver (artist) - - -	64	.	3	15	14	18	12	2
.	2	57	198	416	105	38	816	Sculptor - - - - -	16	.	.	.	.	12	4	.
.	28	847	1378	3187	1261	212	6898	Architect - - - - -	.	.	.	.	.	.	.	.
.	193	1180	1884	7451	3005	457	14170	Musician, Music Master - - -	11370	.	131	1813	2939	5117	1252	124
.	33	858	345	97	3	1	1337	Art Student - - - - -	1059	.	12	410	411	217	6	3
.	121	753	749	2544	1100	85	5352	Photographer - - - -	1309	.	37	381	387	416	83	5
.	17	138	384	1306	316	36	2197	Actor - - - - -	2308	.	84	439	739	987	109	10
.	13	76	120	574	260	68	1111	Art, Music, Theatre, Service -	281	.	6	52	52	126	40	5

NOTE.—Persons returned as engaged in more than one occupation have been referred to the one that appeared to be of most importance; or, if there was no difference in this respect, to the one first given by the person in his or her return. In some cases special rules have been followed; *e.g.*, "Clergyman and Schoolmaster" in combination has always been referred to "Schoolmaster"; a Member of Parliament or Peer engaged in any branch of commerce or industry has always been referred to this latter, not to "Peer, M.P."

The numbers returned under any heading include Labourers, Apprentices, and Assistants, as well as Masters, but not Clerks, Messengers, Errand boys, Porters, or Watchmen, for which occupations there are special headings. Civil, Military, and Naval Clerks, Law, Bank, Insurance, and Railway Clerks, and Government and Railway Porters, are, however, exceptions to this rule. Many young persons, being Apprentices or Assistants, have therefore been referred to occupations usually followed by adults. Women also, chiefly widows or orphans carrying on the business of their deceased husbands or fathers, will sometimes be found under occupations commonly followed by men only.

Persons returned as *retired* from any business have not been referred to that business. Inmates of workhouses have been referred to their trades, unless their age or infirmities showed that they were past work. But persons who might be supposed to be only temporarily separated from their usual employment, such as Prisoners, and Patients in General Hospitals, have been classed under their usual occupations.

In some cases, for convenience of space, the male designation, *e.g.*, "Schoolmaster," alone is given, instead of "Schoolmaster, Schoolmistress."

Table 5. *cont.*—OCCUPATIONS of MALES and FEMALES in ENGLAND and WALES, at SEVEN GROUPS of AGES.

Ages of Males: Under 5 years.	5-	15-	20-	25-	45-	65 and upwards.	All Ages.	OCCUPATIONS.	Ages of Females: All Ages.	Under 5 years.	5-	15-	20-	25-	45-	65 and upwards.
								8. *Persons engaged in Exhibitions, Shows, Games, &c.*								
.	73	136	212	686	223	31	1361	Performer, Showman, Exhibition, Service	520	.	52	102	114	181	51	10
.	161	744	590	1265	323	30	3113	Billiard, Cricket, & other Games, Service	46	.	1	10	11	12	9	3
								II. DOMESTIC CLASS.								
								4. PERSONS ENGAGED IN DOMESTIC OFFICES OR SERVICES.								
								1. *Domestic Service.*								
.	1638	9615	12116	33891	12772	1735	73167	Domestic Coachman, Groom	.	.	.	.	.	.	.	.
.	1461	7834	8841	23446	20818	6798	74603	Domestic Gardener	45	.	1	5	4	9	20	6
.	4341	14480	9886	10393	6538	1124	56202	Domestic Indoor Servant	1230406	.	98190	430177	301474	295302	88506	16757
.	12	98	96	447	762	328	1383	Lodge, Gate, Park, Keeper (not Government)	748	.	2	12	15	185	303	231
.	1038	8628	9092	13800	2900	375	35823	Inn, Hotel, Servant	26487	.	694	7341	9400	7740	728	89
.	66	899	409	1281	612	86	2853	College, Club, Service	590	.	3	11	35	258	261	33
								2. *Other Service.*								
.	6	28	33	768	835	213	1883	Office Keeper (not Government)	4301	.	18	121	252	1491	2015	404
.	29	240	485	1581	485	55	2875	Cook (not domestic)	1753	.	1	29	118	730	709	177
.	.	.	.	.	.	.	.	Charwoman	92474	.	170	1803	3674	34886	42028	9913
.	37	285	281	1383	1116	276	3408	Washing and Bathing Service	176670	.	1318	12953	16232	64655	65805	15897
.	17	127	525	2545	928	128	4270	Hospital and Institution Service	11526	.	22	569	2724	5711	2102	308
.	227	511	117	454	286	86	1681	Others engaged in Service	293	.	4	27	32	56	110	34
								III. COMMERCIAL CLASS.								
								5. PERSONS ENGAGED IN COMMERCIAL OCCUPATIONS.								
								1. *Merchants and Agents.*								
.	21	355	649	5297	3406	580	10308	Merchant	51	.	.	8	2	24	17	5
.	36	1017	2264	15764	9835	1781	30697	Broker, Agent, Factor	511	.	2	18	23	187	239	42
.	21	416	762	4574	3400	843	10016	Auctioneer, Appraiser, Valuer, House Agent	59	.	1	2	5	12	31	8
.	24	320	1164	6045	3151	813	11517	Accountant	89	.	.	14	16	41	13	5
.	11	316	702	1666	424	37	3156	Salesman, Buyer (not otherwise described)	1439	.	2	292	447	595	94	9
.	31	976	4135	21801	7683	852	35478	Commercial Traveller	.	.	.	.	.	.	.	.
.	6193	43624	39109	65400	16489	2053	173468	Commercial Clerk	5989	.	130	1488	1809	2192	331	39
.	.	4	14	208	116	18	360	Officer of Commercial Company, Guild, Society, &c.	.	.	.	.	.	.	.	.
								2. *Dealers in Money.*								
.	1	5	60	474	398	114	1052	Banker	5	.	.	.	.	2	3	.
.	83	2016	3644	7077	1037	207	14914	Bank Service	84	.	.	12	21	41	7	3
.	3	15	47	321	187	31	604	Bill Discounter, Bill Broker, Finance Agent	.	.	.	.	.	.	.	.
								3. *Persons occupied in Insurance.*								
.	91	1221	2132	7967	2992	418	14821	Life, House, Ship, &c., Insurance Service	247	.	.	25	58	99	54	11
								6. PERSONS ENGAGED IN CONVEYANCE OF MEN, GOODS, AND MESSAGES.								
								1. *On Railways.*								
.	25	916	4623	14394	2897	101	22956	Railway Engine Driver, Stoker	.	.	.	.	.	.	.	.
.	71	362	1196	7415	1225	37	10286	Railway Guard	.	.	.	.	.	.	.	.
.	15	393	1310	3217	943	216	6094	Pointsman, Level Crossing Man	171	.	3	4	10	61	80	13
.	1743	16471	20041	47443	12645	1231	99574	Other Railway Officials and Servants	477	.	1	34	52	186	174	30
								2. *On Roads.*								
.	13	16	24	186	317	161	717	Toll Collector, Turnpike Gate Keeper	387	.	4	10	23	117	165	68
.	23	120	430	3277	2324	373	6547	Omnibus, Coach, Cab, Owner—Livery Stable Keeper	240	.	1	4	4	73	116	42
.	216	1666	4328	16953	6456	873	30492	Cabman, Flyman, Coachman (not domestic)	.	.	.	.	.	.	.	.
.	2751	14626	20037	60065	23761	3431	124671	Carman, Carrier, Carter, Haulier	731	.	3	37	34	146	367	144
.	53	402	497	1404	271	17	2644	Tramway Companies' Service	6	.	.	3	1	2	.	.
.	4	25	31	272	404	107	843	Wheel Chair Proprietor, Attendant, &c.	14	.	.	.	1	2	7	4
								3. *On Canals, Rivers and Seas.*								
.	27	107	189	982	954	310	2569	Inland Navigation Service	50	.	.	.	1	14	23	12
.	762	3750	4237	12982	6670	1469	29870	Bargeman, Lighterman, Waterman	353	.	32	72	46	107	71	25
.	4	44	81	760	881	237	2007	Navigation Service (on shore)	91	.	.	1	.	17	45	28
.	749	9593	14205	48979	18786	2781	95093	Seaman (Merchant Service)	.	.	.	.	.	.	.	.
.	15	157	180	1276	1148	215	2991	Pilot	.	.	.	.	.	.	.	.
.	111	1220	1072	3228	718	82	6431	Ship Steward, Cook	386	.	2	9	39	241	90	5
.	15	124	145	630	481	175	1570	Boatman on Seas	.	.	.	.	.	.	.	.
.	194	2827	4858	21401	11591	1612	42483	Harbour, Dock, Wharf, Lighthouse, Service	70	.	.	7	11	33	17	2
								4. *In Storage.*								
.	367	3832	4773	12241	4837	640	26690	Warehouseman (not Manchester)	4179	.	122	1040	1184	1400	335	98
.	19	55	85	497	403	98	1157	Meter, Weigher	.	.	.	.	.	.	.	.
								5. *In conveying Messages, Porterage, &c.*								
.	45144	35068	8832	23594	14050	2873	129561	Messenger, Porter, Watchman (neither Railway nor Government)	1610	.	888	483	41	77	81	40
.	617	2473	1494	2373	245	12	7214	Telegraph, Telephone, Service	2228	.	59	677	778	683	31	.

Table 5.—Occupations of Males and Females in England and Wales, at Seven Groups of Ages.

Ages of Males.								Occupations.	Ages of Females.							
Under 5 years.	5–	15–	20–	25–	45–	65 and upwards.	All Ages.		All Ages.	Under 5 years.	5–	15–	20–	25–	45–	65 and upwards.
1757637	2970809	1268269	1112554	3239452	1755819	535565	12639902	TOTAL	13334537	1769207	2976918	1278963	1215872	3494782	1951713	65308
								I. PROFESSIONAL CLASS.								
								1. Persons engaged in the General or Local Government of the Country.								
								1. *National Government.*								
.	.	2	10	194	285	123	614	Peer, M.P., Privy Councillor (not otherwise described)	.	.	.	.	.	.	.	.
.	99	1827	3376	10283	5835	933	22352	Civil Service (officers and clerks)	3216	.	28	423	642	1088	736	300
.	1831	4086	3391	7146	2626	447	20627	Civil Service (messengers, &c.)	563	.	22	94	69	148	161	69
.	2	5	50	1822	1610	54	2913	Prison Officer, &c.	584	.	1	6	56	411	120	3
								2. *Local Government.*								
.	.	142	5440	22475	4353	98	32508	Police	.	.	.	.	.	.	.	.
.	27	312	732	5223	4309	1292	11895	Municipal, Parish, Union, District, Officer	3017	.	5	76	388	1688	775	85
.	8	114	182	1717	2548	1604	6075	Other Local or County Official	.	.	.	.	.	.	.	.
								3. *East Indian and Colonial Service.*								
.	.	6	27	135	60	12	240	East Indian and Colonial Service	.	.	.	.	.	.	.	.
								2. Persons engaged in the Defence of the Country.								
								1. *Army (at Home).*								
.	.	867	918	3989	4075	1272	10914	Army Officer (effective or retired)	.	.	.	.	.	.	.	.
.	287	9173	19964	26687	856	28	56935	Soldier and Non-commissioned Officer	.	.	.	.	.	.	.	.
.	48	3555	2132	3546	1378	88	10747	Militia, Yeomanry, Volunteers	.	.	.	.	.	.	.	.
.	.	1	25	2562	4413	1571	8572	Army Pensioner	17	.	.	.	.	5	9	3
								2. *Navy (ashore or in port).*								
.	111	88	125	1570	1490	529	3921	Navy Officer (effective or retired)	.	.	.	.	.	.	.	.
.	62	4774	3590	7612	857	26	16811	Seaman, R.N.	.	.	.	.	.	.	.	.
.	19	1339	2010	4146	185	21	7720	Royal Marines (officers and men)	.	.	.	.	.	.	.	.
.	.	1	38	1908	4729	2230	8916	Navy Pensioner	33	.	.	.	1	5	10	17
								3. Persons engaged in Professional Occupations (with their immediate Subordinates).								
								1. *Clerical Profession.*								
.	.	.	401	9307	8888	3263	21863	Clergyman (Established Church)	.	.	.	.	.	.	.	.
.	.	.	49	1247	644	149	2089	Roman Catholic Priest	.	.	.	.	.	.	.	.
.	.	11	326	5308	3122	969	9784	Minister, Priest, of other religious bodies	.	.	.	.	.	.	.	.
.	1	26	237	1368	1045	290	2965	Missionary, Scripture Reader, Itinerant Preacher	1680	.	3	67	126	604	754	106
.	.	.	.	.	.	.	.	Nun, Sister of Charity	3795	.	11	141	450	2223	849	121
.	3	332	1507	1072	11	.	2925	Theological Student	.	.	.	.	.	.	.	.
.	113	53	94	1372	1940	1010	4582	Church, Chapel, Cemetery—Officer, Servant	1707	.	.	10	51	422	887	328
								2. *Legal Profession.*								
.	.	.	994	9771	5044	1577	17386	Barrister, Solicitor	.	.	.	.	.	.	.	.
.	4	409	792	433	15	.	1653	Law Student	.	.	.	.	.	.	.	.
.	933	6800	6841	8205	2263	350	24502	Law Clerk, and others connected with Law	100	.	1	29	29	31	9	1
								3. *Medical Profession.*								
.	.	.	810	8300	4435	1546	15091	Physician, Surgeon, General Practitioner	25	.	.	1	.	20	4	.
.	45	417	565	1792	671	93	3583	Dentist	.	.	.	.	.	.	.	.
.	11	1687	2500	1863	119	12	5902	Medical Student, Assistant	64	.	1	10	20	28	6	.
.	.	.	.	.	.	.	.	Midwife	2646	.	.	1	9	485	1373	772
.	10	176	190	753	655	196	1972	Subordinate Medical Service	35175	.	22	228	714	7034	10259	7318
								4. *Teachers.*								
.	1871	11481	7893	13945	4009	539	39738	Schoolmaster	94241	.	5152	30056	21172	28553	8684	1024
.	22	334	899	3102	1585	334	6336	Teacher, Professor, Lecturer	28605	.	84	3399	8638	13665	2564	255
.	7	55	59	902	680	69	1762	School Service, and others concerned in Teaching	1149	.	6	30	66	567	424	51
								5. *Literary and Scientific Persons.*								
.	2	45	257	1684	840	164	2982	Author, Editor, Journalist	452	.	1	11	30	250	134	26
.	15	413	687	1262	235	49	2662	Reporter, Short-hand Writer	15	.	.	4	5	4	2	.
.	16	144	246	523	205	52	1186	Persons engaged in Scientific Pursuits	14	.	.	.	2	5	5	2
.	5	42	106	460	280	57	950	Literary, Scientific, Institution, Service, &c.	133	.	.	6	10	72	38	7
								6. *Engineers and Surveyors.*								
.	17	613	1055	3443	1727	269	7124	Civil Engineer	.	.	.	.	.	.	.	.
.	7	196	308	1062	541	87	2201	Mining Engineer	.	.	.	.	.	.	.	.
.	45	616	771	2289	1402	871	5994	Land, House, Ship, Surveyor	.	.	.	.	.	.	.	.
								7. *Artists.*								
.	37	380	767	2815	1634	449	6082	Painter (artist)	1839	.	10	190	450	931	248	41
.	57	376	325	893	443	107	2201	Engraver (artist)	84	.	3	16	14	18	12	2
.	2	67	108	410	193	38	818	Sculptor	16	.	.	.	.	12	4	.
.	23	847	1378	3187	1251	212	6898	Architect	.	.	.	.	.	.	.	.
.	193	1180	1884	7451	3005	457	14170	Musician, Music Master	11378	.	131	1813	2939	5117	1252	124
.	83	858	345	97	3	1	1337	Art Student	1059	.	12	416	411	217	6	3
.	121	753	740	2544	1109	85	5352	Photographer	1309	.	37	381	367	438	83	5
.	17	135	384	1306	316	39	2197	Actor	2388	.	84	439	739	987	109	10
.	13	76	120	574	260	68	1111	Art, Music, Theatre, Service	281	.	8	62	62	120	40	5

* Note.—Persons returned as engaged in more than one occupation have been referred to the one that appeared to be of most importance; or, if there was no difference in this respect, to the one first given by the person in his or her return. In some cases special rules have been followed; *e.g.*, "Clergymen and Schoolmaster" in combination has always been referred to "Schoolmaster"; a Member of Parliament or Peer engaged in any branch of commerce or industry has always been referred to this latter, not to "Peer, M.P."

The numbers returned under any heading include Labourers, Apprentices, and Assistants as well as Masters, but not Clerks, Messengers, Errand boys, Porters, or Watchmen, for which occupations there are special headings. Civil, Military, and Naval Clerks, Law, Bank, Insurance, and Railway Clerks, and Government and Railway Porters, are, however, exceptions to this rule. Many young persons, being Apprentices or Assistants, have therefore been referred to occupations usually followed by adults. Women also, chiefly widows or orphans carrying on the business of their deceased husbands or fathers, will sometimes be found under occupations commonly followed by men only.

Persons returned as *retired* from any business have not been referred to that business. Inmates of workhouses have been referred to their trades, unless their age or infirmities showed that they were past work. But persons who might be supposed to be only temporarily separated from their usual employment, such as Prisoners, and Patients in General Hospitals, have been classed under their usual occupations.

In some cases, for convenience of space, the male designation, *e.g.*, "Schoolmaster," alone is given, instead of "Schoolmaster, Schoolmistress."

Table 5. *cont.*—OCCUPATIONS of MALES and FEMALES in ENGLAND and WALES, at SEVEN GROUPS of AGES.

Ages of Males.								Occupations.	Ages of Females.							
Under 5 years.	5-	15-	20-	25-	45-	65 and upwards.	All Ages.		All Ages.	Under 5 years.	5-	15-	20-	25-	45-	65 and upwards.
								8. *Persons engaged in Exhibitions, Shows, Games, &c.*								
.	73	136	212	686	223	31	1361	Performer, Showman, Exhibition, Service	520	.	52	102	114	191	51	10
.	161	744	590	1268	323	30	3116	Billiard, Cricket, & other Games, Service	46	.	1	10	11	12	9	3
								II. DOMESTIC CLASS.								
								4. Persons engaged in Domestic Offices or Services.								
								1. *Domestic Service.*								
.	1058	9615	12110	35891	12772	1735	73167	Domestic Coachman, Groom	.	.	.	.	.	.	.	.
.	1461	7834	8341	29446	20813	6703	74603	Domestic Gardener	45	.	1	5	4	9	20	6
.	4841	14480	9886	19393	6538	1124	56262	Domestic Indoor Servant	1230406	.	98150	430177	301474	295302	88506	16757
.	12	98	36	447	762	328	1683	Lodge, Gate, Park, Keeper (not Government)	748	.	2	12	15	185	303	231
.	1038	8528	6092	13800	2990	375	35823	Inn, Hotel, Servant	26487	.	604	7841	9400	7740	723	89
.	66	399	409	1281	612	86	2853	College, Club, Service	599	.	8	11	35	256	261	33
								2. *Other Service.*								
.	6	28	33	768	835	213	1883	Office Keeper (not Government)	4301	.	18	121	252	1491	2015	404
.	29	240	485	1581	485	55	2875	Cook (not domestic)	1753	.	1	29	116	730	700	177
.	.	.	.	.	.	.	.	Charwoman	92474	.	170	1808	3674	34886	42028	9913
.	37	285	261	1383	1116	276	3408	Washing and Bathing Service	176670	.	1318	12953	15242	64655	66605	15897
.	17	127	525	2545	928	128	4270	Hospital and Institution Service	11526	.	22	569	2724	5711	2192	308
.	227	511	117	454	286	86	1681	Others engaged in Service	293	.	4	27	32	96	110	34
								III. COMMERCIAL CLASS.								
								5. Persons engaged in Commercial Occupations.								
								1. *Merchants and Agents.*								
.	21	355	649	5297	3406	580	10309	Merchant	51	.	.	3	2	24	17	5
.	96	1017	2264	15704	9835	1781	30697	Broker, Agent, Factor	511	.	2	18	23	187	239	42
.	21	416	762	4574	3400	843	10016	Auctioneer, Appraiser, Valuer, House Agent	59	.	1	2	5	12	31	8
.	24	520	1164	6045	3151	613	11517	Accountant	89	.	.	14	16	41	13	5
.	11	316	702	1666	424	37	3156	Salesman, Buyer (not otherwise described)	1439	.	2	292	447	595	94	9
.	31	976	4135	21801	7683	852	35478	Commercial Traveller	.	.	.	.	.	.	.	.
.	6193	45624	39109	65400	16489	2653	175468	Commercial Clerk	5989	.	130	1488	1809	2192	331	39
.	.	4	14	208	116	18	360	Officer of Commercial Company, Guild, Society, &c.	.	.	.	.	.	.	.	.
								2. *Dealers in Money.*								
.	1	5	60	474	398	114	1052	Banker	5	.	.	.	.	2	3	.
.	33	2016	3644	7077	1937	207	14914	Bank Service	84	.	.	12	21	41	7	3
.	3	15	47	321	187	31	604	Bill Discounter, Bill Broker, Finance Agent	.	.	.	.	.	.	.	.
								3. *Persons occupied in Insurance.*								
.	91	1221	2132	7967	2992	418	14821	Life, House, Ship, &c., Insurance Service	247	.	.	25	58	99	54	11
								6. Persons engaged in Conveyance of Men, Goods, and Messages.								
								1. *On Railways.*								
.	25	916	4523	14394	2897	101	22856	Railway Engine Driver, Stoker	.	.	.	.	.	.	.	.
.	71	352	1196	7415	1225	37	10296	Railway Guard	.	.	.	.	.	.	.	.
.	15	333	1310	3217	943	216	6034	Pointsman, Level Crossing Man	171	.	3	4	10	81	60	13
.	1743	16471	20041	47443	12645	1231	99574	Other Railway Officials and Servants	477	.	1	34	52	186	174	30
								2. *On Roads.*								
.	13	16	24	186	317	161	717	Toll Collector, Turnpike Gate Keeper	387	.	4	16	23	117	165	62
.	23	120	430	3277	2324	373	6547	Omnibus, Coach, Cab, Owner—Livery Stable Keeper	240	.	1	4	4	73	116	42
.	216	1666	4328	16053	6456	873	30192	Cabman, Flyman, Coachman (not domestic)	.	.	.	.	.	.	.	.
.	2751	14626	20037	60005	23761	3431	124611	Carman, Carrier, Carter, Haulier	731	.	3	37	34	146	367	144
.	53	402	497	1404	271	17	2644	Tramway Companies' Service	6	.	.	3	1	2	.	.
.	4	25	31	272	404	107	843	Wheel Chair Proprietor, Attendant, &c.	14	.	.	.	1	2	7	4
								3. *On Canals, Rivers and Seas.*								
.	27	107	169	982	954	310	2549	Inland Navigation Service	50	.	.	.	1	14	23	12
.	782	3750	4237	12982	6670	1469	29870	Bargeman, Lighterman, Waterman	353	.	32	72	46	107	71	25
.	4	44	81	760	881	237	2007	Navigation Service (on shore)	91	.	.	1	.	17	45	28
.	749	9593	14205	48979	18786	2781	95093	Seaman (Merchant Service)	.	.	.	.	.	.	.	.
.	15	157	180	1276	1148	215	2991	Pilot	.	.	.	.	.	.	.	.
.	111	1220	1072	3228	718	32	6381	Ship Steward, Cook	386	.	2	9	39	241	90	5
.	15	124	145	630	461	175	1570	Boatman on Seas	.	.	.	.	.	.	.	.
.	194	2827	4858	21491	11591	1612	42573	Harbour, Dock, Wharf, Lighthouse, Service	70	.	.	7	11	33	17	2
								4. *In Storage.*								
.	367	3832	4773	12241	4837	640	26690	Warehouseman (not Manchester)	4179	.	122	1040	1184	1400	395	38
.	19	55	85	497	403	98	1157	Meter, Weigher	.	.	.	.	.	.	.	.
								5. *In conveying Messages, Porterage, &c.*								
.	45144	35068	8532	23594	14050	2873	129561	Messenger, Porter, Watchman (neither Railway nor Government)	1610	.	888	483	41	77	81	40
.	617	2473	1494	2373	245	12	7214	Telegraph, Telephone, Service	2228	.	59	677	778	683	31	.

Table 5 *cont.*—OCCUPATIONS of MALES and FEMALES in ENGLAND and WALES, at SEVEN GROUPS of AGES.

Ages of Males: Under 5 years.	5-	15-	20-	25-	45-	65 and upwards.	All Ages.	OCCUPATIONS.	Ages of Females: All Ages.	Under 5 years.	5-	15-	20-	25-	45-	65 and upwards.
								IV. AGRICULTURAL CLASS.								
								7. PERSONS ENGAGED IN AGRICULTURE.								
								1. *In Fields and Pastures.*								
.	21	916	4906	71512	91528	34446	203329	Farmer, Grazier	20614	.	2	50	156	2735	10449	7222
.	155	27921	21592	23414	1952	183	75197	Farmer's, Grazier's—Son, Grandson, Brother, Nephew*	.	.	.	.	.	.	.	.
.	4	159	927	8360	8496	1811	19377	Farm Bailiff	.	.	.	.	.	.	.	.
.	87054	154596	97730	232028	186029	70171	807608	Agricultural Labourer, Farm Servant, Cottager	40346	.	2054	8907	6362	11006	9120	2897
.	941	1809	1484	8618	8089	1903	23844	Shepherd	.	.	.	.	.	.	.	.
.	15	121	194	676	598	93	1695	Land Drainage Service (not in towns)	.	.	.	.	.	.	.	.
.	32	242	521	2257	1074	96	4222	Agricultural Machine—Proprietor, Attendant	38	.	.	1	.	12	21	4
.	13	372	280	60	2	1	728	Agricultural Student, Pupil	.	.	.	.	.	.	.	.
.	14	64	77	330	206	72	763	Others engaged in, or connected with, Agriculture	75	.	3	6	6	30	23	7
								2. *In Woods.*								
.	121	543	656	2700	3037	1095	8151	Woodman	.	.	.	.	.	.	.	.
								3. *In Gardens.*								
.	206	815	855	2818	1873	459	7021	Nurseryman, Seedsman, Florist	734	.	23	151	137	247	130	44
.	1519	6267	6127	22170	18983	7552	63518	Gardener (not domestic)	2364	.	42	253	178	549	934	408
								8. PERSONS ENGAGED ABOUT ANIMALS.								
								1. *About Animals.*								
.	9	108	267	1111	628	110	2228	Horse Proprietor, Breeder, Dealer	5	.	.	.	.	3	2	.
.	1150	6280	6928	17073	7429	1309	40819	Groom, Horse-keeper, Horse-breaker	44	.	2	2	5	22	9	4
.	26	614	941	3640	1785	505	7511	Veterinary Surgeon, Farrier	.	.	.	.	.	.	.	.
.	23	207	514	2461	2057	527	5729	Cattle, Sheep, Pig—Dealer, Salesman	25	.	.	1	2	8	9	5
.	35	192	282	1121	749	207	2588	Drover	.	.	.	.	.	.	.	.
.	87	643	991	6287	3630	693	12633	Gamekeeper	.	.	.	.	.	.	.	.
.	71	119	119	418	342	87	1156	Dog, Bird, Animal—Keeper, Dealer	212	.	2	8	12	72	83	35
.	21	86	71	323	472	266	1219	Vermin destroyer	4	.	.	1	.	1	2	.
.	807	5355	5258	11532	4998	1454	29402	Fisherman	294	.	18	76	39	81	59	21
.	21	58	78	309	124	18	608	Knacker, Catsmeat Dealer, &c., &c.	85	.	2	10	8	37	23	5
								V. INDUSTRIAL CLASS.								
								9. PERSONS WORKING AND DEALING IN BOOKS, PRINTS, AND MAPS.								
								1. *Books.*								
.	281	1165	1094	3650	1943	390	8472	Publisher, Bookseller, Librarian	1438	.	27	256	233	511	335	76
.	20	166	158	547	276	33	1206	Music—Publisher, Seller, Printer	234	.	5	62	39	72	43	13
.	368	1920	1632	3808	1514	263	9505	Bookbinder	10592	.	767	3923	2370	2506	814	122
.	4409	16397	9671	21799	6855	957	59988	Printer	2202	.	314	1089	361	297	120	21
.	355	493	311	1681	1239	307	4386	Newspaper Agent, News Room Keeper	1129	.	20	76	72	383	456	122
.	2	4	7	36	12	4	65	Others	4	.	.	.	.	3	.	1
								2. *Prints and Maps.*								
.	180	1167	871	2550	729	66	5546	Lithographer, Lithographic Printer	135	.	27	59	16	25	4	4
.	1	40	57	131	133	41	403	Copper Plate and Steel Plate Printer	12	.	.	3	.	7	2	.
.	4	48	55	192	129	31	459	Map and Print—Colourer, Seller	166	.	3	34	40	47	30	12
								10. PERSONS WORKING AND DEALING IN MACHINES AND IMPLEMENTS.								
								1. *Machines.*								
.	646	5904	5498	17403	7820	909	38180	Engine, Machine, Maker	301	.	13	84	61	108	33	2
.	50	613	791	3033	2063	381	6940	Millwright	.	.	.	.	.	.	.	.
.	1096	10359	12278	30856	9309	855	64663	Fitter, Turner (Engine and Machine)	.	.	.	.	.	.	.	.
.	606	3751	3958	13196	4328	333	26170	Boiler Maker	.	.	.	.	.	.	.	.
.	720	3117	2761	8440	3655	496	19209	Spinning and Weaving Machine Maker	687	.	52	207	136	195	82	91
.	99	586	571	1693	937	180	4066	Agricultural Machine and Implement Maker	58	.	2	4	6	23	15	8
.	15	67	58	237	111	19	507	Domestic Machinery—Maker, Dealer	21	.	.	8	3	4	2	4
								2. *Tools and Implements.*								
.	177	1224	1407	4130	1906	318	9162	Tool Maker, Dealer	191	.	6	54	35	54	32	10
.	645	2233	2109	7210	3682	672	16551	Cutler, Scissors Maker	1583	.	98	531	329	436	165	23
.	255	1086	1109	3619	1477	215	7761	File Maker	1206	.	55	267	247	494	140	3
.	54	240	246	859	548	90	2016	Saw Maker	100	.	1	28	19	39	13	.
.	16	43	26	82	55	12	234	Pin Maker	495	.	65	203	113	90	21	3
.	180	379	345	914	474	89	2381	Needle Maker	2074	.	124	425	328	768	379	50
.	7	46	18	89	49	11	220	Steel Pen Maker	2303	.	93	804	865	778	157	6
.	2	39	18	47	43	10	159	Pencil Maker (Wood)	73	.	4	35	20	12	3	1
.	58	191	147	393	217	41	1047	Domestic Implement Maker	700	.	37	204	168	233	50	8
								3. *Watches and Philosophical Instruments.*								
.	410	2985	3322	9539	5124	1196	22576	Watch Maker, Clock Maker	775	.	43	230	188	184	109	21
.	56	463	471	1510	710	175	3385	Philosophical Instrument Maker, Optician	220	.	11	47	45	72	38	7
.	37	343	445	1278	371	23	2496	Electrical Apparatus Maker	26	.	5	9	5	5	1	1
.	59	318	306	1096	510	102	2391	Weighing and Measuring Apparatus Maker	195	.	10	86	60	29	8	2

* Only male relatives living with the farmer or grazier, and therefore presumably engaged in agriculture, are included above.

Table 5 *cont.*—OCCUPATIONS of MALES and FEMALES in ENGLAND and WALES, at SEVEN GROUPS of AGES.

AGES OF MALES.								OCCUPATIONS.	AGES OF FEMALES.							
Under 5 years.	5-	15-	20-	25-	45-	65 and upwards.	All Ages.		All Ages.	Under 5 years.	5-	15-	20-	25-	45-	65 and upwards.
								4. *Surgical Instruments.*								
.	20	148	196	510	250	57	1181	Surgical Instrument Maker	330	.	12	75	72	103	59	9
								5. *Arms and Ordnance.*								
.	185	806	726	3420	2056	331	7522	Gunsmith, Gun Manufacturer	219	.	4	41	25	88	53	8
.	.	21	20	141	81	4	267	Ordnance Manufacturer	1	.	.	.	.	1	.	.
.	4	19	29	78	46	10	186	Sword, Bayonet—Maker, Cutler	4	.	.	.	1	2	1	.
.	.	1	2	10	11	4	28	Others	.	.	.	.	.	.	.	.
								6. *Musical Instruments.*								
.	166	1281	1443	3993	1801	324	9008	Musical Instrument Maker, Dealer	241	.	8	50	45	86	48	10
								7. *Type, Dies, Medals, Coins.*								
.	60	236	150	400	261	30	1137	Type Cutter, Founder	33	.	1	13	10	7	1	.
.	55	267	222	633	251	60	1486	Die, Seal, Coin, Medal, Maker	53	.	3	14	17	14	4	1
								8. *Tackle for Sports and Games.*								
.	34	131	105	453	297	79	1099	Toy Maker, Dealer	1293	.	16	184	126	467	391	109
.	55	154	116	338	188	47	898	Fishing Rod, Tackle, Maker, Dealer	563	.	51	140	109	179	69	15
.	19	148	151	437	191	32	968	Apparatus for other Games, Maker, Dealer	103	.	4	28	25	26	16	4
								11. PERSONS WORKING AND DEALING IN HOUSES, FURNITURE, AND DECORATIONS.								
								1. *Houses.*								
.	212	1974	2074	13944	10441	1919	30564	Builder	135	.	.	3	5	28	71	28
.	3054	33613	34671	105500	48523	12656	238017	Carpenter, Joiner	216	.	6	36	25	68	65	18
.	1880	14294	21035	56632	24715	4761	125055	Bricklayer	85	.	5	18	16	28	13	5
.	1556	11385	13968	44702	21112	4710	97432	Mason	108	.	4	11	18	48	22	10
.	103	905	1196	3455	1484	326	7469	Slater, Tiler	14	.	1	4	1	1	6	1
.	463	3787	4447	13777	5385	1001	28860	Plasterer, Whitewasher	41	.	1	6	1	19	10	4
.	99	665	630	2048	638	77	4177	Paperhanger	95	.	.	9	9	30	38	8
.	1209	8485	6199	16274	5305	698	37160	Plumber	240	.	4	13	17	68	109	29
.	1434	12316	14213	40502	19686	2526	90678	Painter, Glazier	454	.	10	81	67	154	119	23
								2. *Furniture and Fittings.*								
.	840	7579	7718	22918	10488	2218	51761	Cabinet Maker, Upholsterer	7985	.	153	1295	1227	2686	2126	498
.	168	1215	1409	3796	1353	142	8083	French Polisher	2029	.	78	546	460	704	225	16
.	48	308	430	2368	1592	277	5023	Furniture Broker, Dealer	955	.	6	81	81	326	373	88
.	304	1232	933	2859	1582	436	7348	Locksmith, Bellhanger	362	.	14	128	74	72	58	16
.	263	1858	1913	5937	2224	225	12420	Gas Fitter	147	.	15	77	18	20	13	4
.	50	344	416	1418	503	84	2815	House and Shop Fittings—Maker, Dealer	206	.	7	46	34	71	40	6
.	19	152	194	686	540	110	1701	Funeral Furniture Maker, Undertaker	192	.	5	33	30	56	49	19
.	1	5	4	28	12	2	52	Others	3	.	.	.	.	2	1	.
								3. *House Decorations.*								
.	56	372	413	1530	629	80	3080	Wood Carver	28	.	.	5	6	10	7	.
.	136	1094	1160	3498	1639	287	7814	Carver, Gilder	330	.	19	83	62	93	60	13
.	4	56	97	531	297	66	1051	Dealer in Works of Art	109	.	1	14	13	45	30	6
.	7	63	49	164	81	21	385	Figure, Image—Maker, Dealer	33	.	2	7	3	8	9	4
.	5	53	47	292	209	80	686	Animal, Bird, &c., Preserver, Naturalist	159	.	13	54	33	38	20	1
.	15	81	88	317	198	21	720	Artificial Flower Maker	4461	.	228	977	1024	1676	516	40
								12. PERSONS WORKING AND DEALING IN CARRIAGES AND HARNESS.								
								1. *Carriages.*								
.	385	3424	3350	11025	4690	896	23750	Coachmaker	216	.	3	30	33	60	63	27
.	138	1058	1161	3740	1277	114	7512	Railway Carriage, Railway Wagon, Maker	58	.	1	23	17	11	6	.
.	403	4141	3904	11376	6607	2114	28635	Wheelwright	97	.	1	10	2	18	46	20
.	39	251	255	446	61	7	1059	Bicycle, Tricycle,—Maker, Dealer	13	.	1	5	6	1	.	.
.	26	306	325	797	369	82	1905	Others	63	.	3	11	15	21	13	.
								2. *Harness.*								
.	545	3398	2948	9214	4504	1222	21831	Saddler, Harness, Whip, Maker	2035	.	87	600	393	612	282	7
								13. PERSONS WORKING AND DEALING IN SHIPS AND BOATS.								
								1. *Hull.*								
.	627	3688	3288	10206	3522	471	21792	Ship, Boat, Barge, Builder	39	.	3	5	4	12	11	.
.	164	1965	2534	11082	7171	1013	23930	Shipwright, Ship Carpenter (ashore)	.	.	.	.	.	.	.	.
								2. *Masts, Rigging, &c.*								
.	30	184	128	600	396	81	1419	Mast, Yard, Oar, Block, Maker	.	.	.	.	.	.	.	.
.	26	144	156	1316	1084	109	2834	Ship Rigger, Chandler, Fitter	27	.	.	3	1	8	10	.
.	108	569	434	1767	1015	189	4082	Sail Maker	47	.	.	5	6	17	18	.

Table 5 *cont.*—OCCUPATIONS of MALES and FEMALES in ENGLAND and WALES, at SEVEN GROUPS of AGES.

Ages of Males.								Occupations.	Ages of Females.							
Under 5 years.	5-	15-	20-	25-	45-	65 and upwards.	All Ages.		All Ages.	Under 5 years.	5-	15-	20-	25-	45-	65 and upwards.
								14 PERSONS WORKING AND DEALING IN CHEMICALS AND COMPOUNDS.								
								1 *Colouring Matter.*								
.	25	191	192	747	416	67	1638	Dye, Paint, Manufacture	389	.	13	139	87	95	48	7
.	54	190	154	405	230	44	1077	Ink, Blacking, Colouring Substance, Manufacture	157	.	4	64	37	24	23	5
								2 *Explosives.*								
.	10	89	71	260	186	29	637	Gunpowder, Guncotton, Explosive Substance Manufacture	122	.	3	39	25	39	11	5
.	105	340	104	259	132	20	960	Fusee, Fireworks, Explosive Article, Manufacture	1887	.	133	858	475	352	59	10
								3 *Drugs and other Chemicals and Compounds.*								
.	267	3283	2777	7906	3551	585	18369	Chemist, Druggist	651	.	17	153	100	194	146	41
.	199	1232	1724	6459	2860	369	12843	Manufacturing Chemist	1128	.	62	419	269	254	93	31
.	28	188	325	1188	386	28	2142	Alkali Manufacture	7	.	.	3	.	2	2	.
.	8	95	112	450	227	28	920	Drysalter	97	.	4	26	20	38	8	1
								15 PERSONS WORKING AND DEALING IN TOBACCO AND PIPES.								
								1 *Tobacco and Pipes.*								
.	343	1394	1521	5298	2273	330	11159	Tobacco Manufacturer, Tobacconist	8575	.	796	3304	1828	1819	757	116
.	27	187	155	685	543	106	1703	Tobacco Pipe, Snuff Box, &c., Maker	738	.	21	146	103	252	182	35
								16 PERSONS WORKING AND DEALING IN FOOD AND LODGING.								
								1 *Board and Lodging.*								
.	28	328	1680	26878	22918	3585	57397	Innkeeper, Hotel Keeper, Publican	12709	.	10	95	831	4034	6362	1877
.	4	18	56	1508	2194	711	4480	Lodging, Boarding House, Keeper	32890	.	15	277	711	10135	16767	4985
.	21	155	516	3044	1765	208	5709	Coffee, Eating House, Keeper	2664	.	30	132	243	1205	915	141
								2 *Spirituous Drinks.*								
.		14	34	200	152	28	428	Hop—Merchant, Dealer	10	.	.	.	2	2	2	4
.	44	484	1182	4671	2553	539	9473	Maltster	58	.	.	2	3	11	29	13
.	162	1536	3058	12690	5830	925	24196	Brewer	371	.	4	12	22	93	180	60
.	25	114	370	6411	5071	864	12855	Beerseller. Ale, Porter, Cider, Dealer	3728	.	2	33	77	1145	1905	566
.	138	787	974	3001	780	78	5758	Cellarman	286	.	6	76	56	94	49	5
.	36	428	659	3757	2245	368	7467	Wine, Spirit—Merchant, Agent	422	.	.	18	49	186	140	29
								3 *Food.*								
.	1120	8278	2700	6457	4670	1137	24362	Milkseller, Dairyman	4443	.	186	591	437	1324	1531	424
.	80	647	681	1843	984	91	4326	Cheesemonger, Butterman	353	.	4	26	29	110	143	41
.	2124	13670	12583	32023	14420	2806	78206	Butcher, Meat Salesman	4096	.	39	407	378	1910	1100	263
.	128	970	1128	5306	3163	540	11235	Provision Curer, Dealer	5329	.	76	436	374	1863	2076	504
.	30	314	403	1298	780	130	2923	Poulterer, Game Dealer	668	.	8	61	57	194	271	77
.	271	1709	1923	7373	3662	556	15494	Fishmonger	2412	.	48	346	283	892	683	159
.	85	748	987	4289	2615	511	9183	Corn, Flour, Seed—Merchant, Dealer	783	.	5	83	111	227	261	96
.	453	2980	3148	9798	5710	1061	23162	Corn Miller	300	.	5	12	20	74	140	49
.	2482	12701	9932	24437	11571	2276	63399	Baker	7833	.	100	1389	1095	2025	2209	745
.	535	1977	1624	5271	2810	468	12483	Confectioner, Pastrycook	13051	.	329	2584	2287	4286	2867	899
.	529	2286	2300	10124	6374	1146	22759	Greengrocer, Fruiterer	6855	.	131	733	644	2303	2372	672
.	36	111	91	341	211	35	825	Mustard, Vinegar, Spice, Pickle—Maker, Dealer	684	.	28	201	150	172	110	23
.	41	319	492	1440	584	66	2951	Sugar Refiner	119	.	4	21	13	43	27	11
.	3506	20103	15353	28656	20825	4682	103396	Grocer, Tea, Coffee, Chocolate—Maker, Dealer	26422	.	899	2505	2361	8244	9738	3175
.	158	754	723	1957	846	89	4335	Ginger Beer, Mineral Water—Manufacturer, Dealer	337	.	9	88	44	85	83	28
.	.	1	9	7	8	1	26	Others dealing in Food	4	.	1	.	.	1	1	1
								17 PERSONS WORKING AND DEALING IN TEXTILE FABRICS.								
								1 *Wool and Worsted.*								
.	50	222	335	1071	717	151	2546	Woolstapler	28	.	1	5	4	8	6	4
.	4647	10206	7240	20146	11028	3141	57307	Woollen Cloth Manufacture	58501	.	4373	16876	13099	18714	4821	618
.	108	300	399	1223	695	102	2754	Wool, Woollen goods—Dyer, Printer	44	.	15	7	4	9	8	1
.	7787	7150	3941	10168	5337	1053	35436	Worsted, Stuff, Manufacture	63801	.	10888	17883	12987	18023	3898	195
.	24	73	63	218	200	78	656	Flannel Manufacture	470	.	11	105	105	154	75	20
.	30	93	112	494	454	130	1313	Blanket Manufacture	1374	.	63	492	370	389	73	8
.	84	318	366	1093	538	90	2498	Fuller	17	.	1	4	3	7	2	.
.	33	635	831	2697	1166	171	5533	Cloth, Worsted, Stuff, Flannel, Blanket, Dealer	80	.	.	14	16	22	21	7
.	53	45	49	180	85	16	428	Others	570	.	60	131	157	184	34	4
								2 *Silk.*								
.	1528	2193	1664	4817	5265	2188	17655	Silk, Silk goods, Manufacture	39694	.	3581	9072	6875	11727	6914	1525
.	46	185	214	569	454	94	1562	Silk Dyer, Printer	118	.	10	45	23	28	9	3
.	4	38	42	269	351	174	878	Ribbon Manufacture	1188	.	13	123	131	483	372	134
.	1	10	16	80	59	10	178	Crape, Gauze, Manufacture	1006	.	37	209	202	363	175	20
.	14	139	144	531	315	41	1184	Silk Merchant, Dealer	118	.	2	21	30	44	21	.

Table 5 *cont.*—OCCUPATIONS of MALES and FEMALES in ENGLAND and WALES, at SEVEN GROUPS of AGES.

Ages of Males: Under 5 years.	5-	15-	20-	25-	45-	65 and upwards.	All Ages.	OCCUPATIONS.	Ages of Females: All Ages.	Under 5 years.	5-	15-	20-	25-	45-	65 and upwards.
								3. Cotton and Flax								
.	28439	38662	27336	60648	26218	4108	185410	Cotton, Cotton goods, Manufacture	302387	.	38593	79778	65015	97768	19708	1195
.	2074	4587	3361	7601	4177	960	22760	Cotton, Calico—Printer, Dyer, Bleacher	3032	.	601	1534	894	861	168	16
.	55	276	413	1560	764	107	3175	Cotton, Calico—Warehouseman, Dealer	379	.	6	54	56	188	78	3
.	261	465	399	1821	1186	369	4212	Flax, Linen—Manufacturer, Dealer	7853	.	582	2314	1708	2454	716	79
.	747	2861	1804	3685	2012	460	11359	Lace Manufacturer, Dealer	32785	.	2803	8967	4642	10195	6668	2510
.	277	466	443	1191	512	112	3011	Fustian Manufacturer, Dealer	5176	.	528	1416	1185	1577	423	47
.	46	92	90	312	165	27	732	Tape Manufacturer, Dealer	1159	.	84	414	225	296	115	21
.	71	119	72	128	98	10	498	Thread Manufacturer, Dealer	1672	.	128	489	376	532	129	16
								4. Hemp and other Fibrous Materials.								
.	157	262	134	408	193	26	1181	Hemp, Jute, Cocoa Fibre, Manufacture	2297	.	224	943	579	430	114	7
.	1345	1702	841	2852	2337	981	9058	Rope, Twine, Cord—Maker, Dealer	2093	.	154	695	446	485	247	67
.	73	281	306	778	298	71	1800	Mat Maker, Seller	479	.	29	112	85	159	84	19
.	4	19	24	113	56	36	252	Net Maker	1481	.	68	373	237	428	283	92
.	12	27	42	121	135	37	374	Canvas, Sailcloth, Manufacture	274	.	15	79	58	63	54	5
.	16	70	54	210	170	55	575	Sacking, Sack, Bag—Maker, Dealer	1594	.	57	323	289	521	353	51
.	6	26	17	105	66	10	230	Others working and dealing in Hemp	183	.	2	35	14	59	68	15
								5. Mixed or Unspecified Materials.								
.	51	224	226	690	659	371	2230	Weaver (undefined)	2811	.	139	558	547	970	322	75
.	392	1804	1854	4014	2428	499	11796	Dyer, Printer, Scourer, Bleacher, Calenderer (undefined)	1849	.	65	378	386	607	330	94
.	1447	1600	604	1300	637	109	5697	Factory hand (Textile, undefined)	7817	.	968	2742	1590	1908	530	72
.	16	64	62	206	88	23	446	Felt Manufacture	45	.	1	7	21	12	4	.
.	586	1351	1179	3340	1950	359	8795	Carpet, Rug, Manufacture	5190	.	530	1627	1204	1400	370	59
.	14	465	559	642	182	6	1868	Manchester Warehouseman	16	.	1	1	8	5	1	.
.	1458	11627	10434	21765	7278	1039	53581	Draper, Linen Draper, Mercer	28781	.	564	8447	8181	8522	2609	458
.	36	176	198	604	272	47	1388	Fancy Goods (Textile), Manufacturer, Worker, Dealer	6188	.	249	1360	1041	2136	1080	313
.	95	248	170	642	377	79	1611	Trimming Maker, Dealer	4888	.	250	1314	1028	1703	525	68
.	1	18	15	51	23	2	110	Embroiderer	2311	.	139	591	494	718	320	49
.	12	42	73	171	112	46	456	Others	209	.	4	39	48	71	42	5
								18. PERSONS WORKING AND DEALING IN DRESS.								
								1. Dress.								
.	469	1990	1926	5784	2647	891	13617	Hatter, Hat Manufacture (not straw)	9072	.	769	2423	1795	3026	912	148
.	122	418	370	1366	688	98	3061	Straw—Hat, Bonnet, Plait, Manufacture	27383	.	1939	4943	3835	10583	5985	1396
.	1813	11762	12615	41524	30976	8780	107668	Tailor	52980	.	1620	11162	9760	19173	9663	1672
.	51	369	391	1418	606	112	2937	Milliner, Dressmaker, Staymaker	357995	.	9170	84234	76007	129673	51738	7173
.	6	26	28	84	51	13	208	Shawl Manufacture	408	.	78	101	69	113	34	13
.	41	183	217	673	236	29	1379	Shirt Maker, Seamstress	81865	.	1568	11519	11537	27631	21538	8072
.	626	2172	2048	6326	5784	1906	18862	Hosiery Manufacture	21510	.	1402	4062	3681	6573	3768	1434
.	87	736	777	2190	932	157	4879	Hosier, Haberdasher	4686	.	187	1047	943	1614	736	159
.	126	232	218	895	594	198	2263	Glover, Glove Maker	13261	.	725	2120	1892	5213	2734	577
.	109	258	331	952	561	75	2286	Button Maker, Dealer	4121	.	309	1196	886	1206	461	63
.	4915	20759	19732	68890	51269	15409	18068	Shoe, Boot—Maker, Dealer	35672	.	2354	9667	7154	11483	4813	801
.	329	1321	1097	3174	1263	255	7429	Patten, Clog, Maker	74	.	3	10	8	17	32	4
.	620	2462	2101	5668	2677	687	14165	Wig Maker, Hairdresser	708	.	19	146	145	294	134	30
.	196	617	499	1767	880	179	4118	Umbrella, Parasol, Stick—Maker, Dealer	4112	.	388	1263	813	1181	484	83
.	11	41	53	134	94	12	345	Accoutrement Maker	255	.	6	49	51	93	49	7
.	7	29	50	234	250	69	639	Old Clothes Dealer, and others	1663	.	8	66	91	635	710	153
								19. PERSONS WORKING AND DEALING IN VARIOUS ANIMAL SUBSTANCES.								
								1. In Grease, Gut, Bone, Horn, Ivory, and Whalebone.								
.	99	296	318	1194	881	227	3013	Tallow Chandler, Candle, Grease, Manufacture	222	.	11	55	29	65	48	14
.	71	398	285	831	430	62	2047	Soap Boiler, Maker	279	.	11	131	79	44	14	.
.	29	93	51	206	103	15	497	Glue, Size, Gelatine, Isinglass—Maker, Dealer	158	.	2	55	39	38	22	2
.	14	89	112	552	339	62	1168	Manure Manufacture	56	.	.	5	8	25	14	3
.	61	214	224	721	398	102	1710	Bone, Horn, Ivory, Tortoise-shell—Worker, Dealer	155	.	8	47	23	52	23	2
.	21	47	46	175	205	90	584	Comb Maker	171	.	11	65	34	43	16	2
.	3	18	33	117	60	16	247	Others	95	.	3	16	26	36	14	1
								2. In Skins.								
.	110	557	691	2284	879	162	4683	Furrier, Skinner	3465	.	110	820	725	1190	518	102
.	150	1056	1278	4598	2549	526	10157	Tanner, Fellmonger	91	.	4	17	10	24	28	8
.	256	1812	2353	6733	3462	675	14891	Currier	506	.	29	138	103	148	161	27
.	108	582	563	1874	772	125	4024	Leather Goods, Portmanteau, Bag, Strap, &c.—Maker, Dealer	1346	.	94	439	280	377	135	21
.	17	55	60	163	90	22	407	Parchment, Vellum—Maker, Dealer	24	.	1	5	8	4	5	1
								3. In Hair and Feathers.								
.	51	113	110	367	217	35	893	Hair, Bristle—Worker, Dealer	1746	.	92	349	369	718	193	22
.	354	1306	1202	3548	1867	437	8714	Brush, Broom, Maker	4185	.	170	1147	897	1412	477	82
.	6	67	61	200	84	11	429	Quill, Feather—Dresser, Dealer	2089	.	154	784	418	597	143	23

Table 5 *cont.*—OCCUPATIONS of MALES and FEMALES in ENGLAND and WALES, at SEVEN GROUPS of AGES.

Ages of Males: Under 5 years.	5-	15-	20-	25-	45-	65 and upwards.	All Ages.	OCCUPATIONS.	Ages of Females: All Ages.	Under 5 years.	5-	15-	20-	25-	45-	65 and upwards.
								20. PERSONS WORKING AND DEALING IN VARIOUS VEGETABLE SUBSTANCES.								
								1. *In Oils, Gums, and Resins.*								
.	49	592	763	2089	867	128	4488	Oil Miller, Oil Cake—Maker, Dealer	102	.	.	18	12	36	38	.
.	115	700	614	1981	746	102	4257	Oil and Colourman	381	.	3	62	60	139	96	19
.	32	204	175	596	239	26	1312	Floor Cloth, Oil Cloth, Manufacture	22	.	.	1	8	4	9	2
.	28	176	172	579	333	71	1359	Japanner	1539	.	71	476	816	462	187	27
.	173	560	468	1671	698	89	3817	India Rubber, Gutta Percha—Worker, Dealer	1440	.	137	618	322	306	67	8
.	63	215	241	521	189	34	1233	Waterproof Goods—Maker, Dealer	350	.	7	114	88	105	35	1
.	18	48	60	230	142	26	533	Others	28	.	1	6	5	9	5	2
								2. *In Cane, Rush, and Straw.*								
.	198	975	1092	3614	2359	779	9017	Willow, Cane, Rush—Worker, Dealer, Basketmaker	2525	.	125	518	392	841	514	137
.	38	142	234	1143	854	192	2603	Hay, Straw (not plait), Chaff—Cutter, Dealer	54	.	1	7	4	13	19	6
.	122	298	250	1062	1304	674	3710	Thatcher	.	.	.	.	.	.	.	.
								3. *In Wood and Bark.*								
.	300	1289	1217	5074	3214	735	11795	Timber, Wood—Merchant, Dealer	978	.	71	257	102	301	203	44
.	388	2220	2695	9958	7731	1782	24712	Sawyer	.	.	.	.	.	.	.	.
.	61	362	388	1210	659	236	2919	Lath, Wooden Fence, Hurdle, Maker	18	.	1	6	2	7	2	.
.	559	2484	1619	4401	2236	614	11382	Wood Turner, Box Maker	2596	.	215	784	528	775	251	46
.	265	1890	2258	8634	4465	1094	18596	Cooper, Hoop Maker, Bender	103	.	1	9	9	23	44	17
.	58	189	172	793	434	85	1741	Cork, Bark—Cutter, Worker, Dealer	187	.	9	60	35	43	36	4
.	9	37	31	91	71	33	272	Others	40	.	3	6	6	8	12	5
								4. *In Paper.*								
.	692	1811	1446	4112	1920	372	10352	Paper Manufacture	8277	.	455	2518	1709	2364	1109	129
.	22	57	24	58	14	.	175	Envelope Maker	1933	.	175	778	469	408	100	3
.	303	1847	1443	4283	1833	271	9980	Stationer, Law Stationer	5261	.	197	1331	1129	1604	845	155
.	47	242	215	522	160	33	1209	Card, Pattern Card, Maker	440	.	29	172	104	102	29	4
.	238	444	223	575	298	45	1822	Paper Stainer	445	.	23	118	95	143	64	3
.	92	258	140	442	205	44	1187	Paper Box, Paper Bag, Maker	8718	.	771	3072	2170	2210	431	64
.	52	147	64	237	120	22	643	Ticket, Label, Writer	498	.	53	106	99	109	40	10
.	32	161	243	748	533	146	1863	Others	227	.	22	77	46	58	21	3
								21. PERSONS WORKING AND DEALING IN VARIOUS MINERAL SUBSTANCES.								
								1. *Miners.*								
.	23361	66085	61779	158965	60945	7589	378664	Coal Miner	3099	.	148	1017	671	966	266	32
.	726	3293	4156	12954	4379	871	26379	Ironstone Miner	231	.	15	81	44	70	18	3
.	193	776	647	1116	978	184	3894	Copper Miner	257	.	28	111	56	54	15	3
.	971	2530	1704	2971	1876	347	10499	Tin Miner	1903	.	267	719	345	441	126	11
.	423	1604	1441	4480	2674	400	11022	Lead Miner	204	.	11	78	37	68	20	.
.	79	260	201	898	447	86	2061	Miner in other, or undefined, Minerals	41	.	1	12	3	12	6	7
.	10	51	208	1501	1563	239	3572	Mine Service	30	.	.	.	2	8	16	4
								2. *Coal, Coal Gas, &c.*								
.	155	717	1876	8507	6855	1643	19253	Coal Merchant, Dealer	1168	.	10	85	61	360	487	166
.	347	1286	1624	6786	8281	499	18723	Coalheaver	.	.	.	.	.	.	.	.
.	101	362	690	2735	1294	153	5243	Coke, Charcoal, Peat—Cutter, Burner, Dealer	142	.	5	57	22	32	23	3
.	64	746	1927	10680	4659	489	18533	Gas Works Service	.	.	.	.	.	.	.	.
								3. *Stone, Clay, and Road Making.*								
.	625	2968	4417	13635	8639	986	28870	Stone Quarrier	.	.	.	.	.	.	.	.
.	110	721	910	3215	1509	292	6847	Stone Cutter, Dresser, Dealer	.	.	.	.	.	.	.	.
.	367	2148	2172	6811	2788	614	14900	Slate Quarrier	.	.	.	.	.	.	.	.
.	61	158	154	494	238	47	1140	Slate Worker, Dealer	32	.	1	14	4	6	5	2
.	103	316	362	1276	860	253	3270	Limeburner	39	.	.	9	4	7	13	7
.	214	723	716	1885	904	189	4722	Clay, Sand, Gravel, Chalk—Labourer, Dealer	122	.	3	28	11	34	34	12
.	24	99	197	389	70	4	686	Fossil, Coprolite—Digger, Dealer	19	.	.	7	3	5	3	1
.	3	41	119	740	469	81	1460	Well Sinker, Borer	.	.	.	.	.	.	.	.
.	96	478	617	1643	778	122	3634	Plaster, Cement, Manufacture	46	.	1	5	14	8	6	8
.	2685	8475	6493	19192	9236	1656	47337	Brick, Tile—Maker, Burner, Dealer	2738	.	75	978	841	656	164	24
.	32	325	568	1978	1095	152	4150	Paviour	.	.	.	.	.	.	.	.
.	2	10	41	435	651	180	1326	Road Contractor, Surveyor, Inspector	.	.	.	.	.	.	.	.
.	115	409	554	2776	4547	2551	10947	Road Labourer	.	.	.	.	.	.	.	.
.	9	37	154	684	248	30	1162	Railway Contractor	.	.	.	.	.	.	.	.
.	32	755	2835	11478	6295	602	21997	Platelayer	.	.	.	.	.	.	.	.
.	803	2641	5432	18435	8995	1044	36850	Railway Labourer, Navvy	.	.	.	.	.	.	.	.
.	18	64	46	193	116	28	465	Others	304	.	17	84	54	79	58	12
								4. *Earthenware and Glass.*								
.	2404	5200	3792	11918	4709	597	28719	Earthenware, China, Porcelain, Manufacture	17877	.	1835	5685	3689	5053	1425	192
.	1176	4097	3011	8363	2941	370	19938	Glass Manufacture	1692	.	62	695	392	404	136	13
.	59	346	395	1967	1315	244	4260	Earthenware, China, Glass, Dealer	1921	.	22	211	236	686	595	172
								5. *Salt.*								
.	24	248	387	1375	718	126	2823	Salt Maker, Dealer	159	.	3	36	27	47	37	9

Table 5 *cont.*—OCCUPATIONS of MALES and FEMALES in ENGLAND and WALES, at SEVEN GROUPS of AGES.

Ages of Males.								Occupations.	Ages of Females.							
Under 5 years.	5-	15-	20-	25-	45-	65 and upwards.	All Ages.		All Ages.	Under 5 years.	5-	15-	20-	25-	45-	65 and upwards.
								6. *Water.*								
.	12	87	210	1324	770	114	2517	Waterworks Service	8	.	.	.	.	4	2	2
.	4	3	11	66	42	16	136	Others	12	.	.	3	.	5	4	.
								7. *Precious Metals and Jewellery.*								
.	938	3353	3372	9453	3249	597	20062	Goldsmith, Silversmith, Jeweller	3753	.	259	1273	563	1083	273	43
.	9	100	85	255	175	28	651	Gold, Silver, Beater	.	.	.	.	.	.	.	.
.	63	182	234	722	192	18	1411	Lapidary	280	.	26	93	60	73	10	.
.	8	58	68	280	156	18	588	Others	1977	.	131	711	474	536	112	13
								8. *Iron and Steel.*								
.	3116	16916	13861	46773	24902	5588	112176	Blacksmith	347	.	2	13	15	69	162	86
.	172	1349	1089	3513	1833	256	8212	Whitesmith	41	.	1	4	9	11	15	1
.	443	1226	973	3351	2723	687	9003	Nail Manufacture	9138	.	344	1952	1677	3377	1561	267
.	178	489	511	1726	967	167	4038	Anchor, Chain, Manufacture	991	.	63	235	207	375	104	7
.	5667	29733	30698	93767	34964	3907	198786	Other Iron and Steel Manufactures	1891	.	72	683	455	401	196	24
.	299	3397	2527	6265	2556	480	15214	Ironmonger, Hardware Dealer, Merchant	906	.	12	115	103	310	283	83
								9. *Copper.*								
.	194	1125	1043	3195	1487	254	7298	Copper, Copper goods—Manufacturer, Worker, Dealer	50	.	2	13	5	16	9	3
								10. *Tin and Zinc.*								
.	1720	7315	5316	12539	4620	882	32392	Tin, Tin Plate, Tin goods—Manufacturer, Worker, Dealer	4531	.	345	2377	1066	570	157	16
.	42	365	336	1103	342	33	2241	Zinc, Zinc Goods—Manufacturer, Worker, Dealer	24	.	2	5	5	9	3	.
								11. *Lead.*								
.	28	158	247	1170	622	85	2310	Lead, Leaden goods—Manufacturer, Worker, Dealer	141	.	.	41	37	46	13	4
								12. *In Other, Mixed, or Unspecified, Metals.*								
.	117	701	633	1936	756	73	4216	Metal Refiner, Worker, Turner, Dealer	300	.	9	104	76	79	31	1
.	1035	6059	4643	10763	3615	557	26692	Brass, Bronze, Manufacture, Brazier	982	.	59	334	251	252	80	6
.	19	118	84	198	42	17	478	Metal Burnisher, Lacquerer	2209	.	106	738	566	636	148	15
.	190	805	747	2107	818	124	4791	White Metal, Plated Ware, Manufacture, Pewterer	838	.	44	246	201	252	87	8
.	348	1544	1369	3735	1480	246	8722	Wire Maker, Worker, Weaver, Drawer	521	.	31	167	117	136	63	7
.	513	1152	801	2361	763	83	5673	Bolt, Nut, Rivet, Screw, Staple, Maker	2344	.	112	917	503	585	159	8
.	100	542	443	1054	338	64	2541	Lamp, Lantern, Candlestick, Maker	503	.	25	184	147	114	31	2
.	54	148	118	304	211	48	883	Clasp, Buckle, Hinge, Maker	479	.	30	170	142	108	25	4
.	23	63	43	134	65	14	342	Fancy Chain, Gilt Toy, Maker	700	.	57	250	185	175	30	3
.	80	443	344	615	184	30	1696	Others	101	.	5	42	29	19	5	1
								22. PERSONS WORKING AND DEALING IN GENERAL OR UNSPECIFIED COMMODITIES.								
								1. *Makers and Dealers (General or Undefined).*								
.	669	3111	2963	11016	8370	2119	29088	General Shopkeeper, Dealer	25772	.	436	3176	2870	8024	8818	2448
.	466	2072	1245	2663	1073	162	7681	Pawnbroker	1278	.	54	281	227	420	262	48
.	1006	2611	2779	11614	8700	2741	29451	Costermonger, Huckster, Street Seller	17660	.	340	1484	1650	6625	5888	1673
.	46	347	559	3344	2279	310	6884	Manufacturer, Manager, Superintendent (undefined)	552	.	1	38	80	320	101	12
.	5	83	178	1382	1193	173	3014	Contractor (undefined)	27	.	1	1	1	10	13	1
								2. *Mechanics and Labourers (General or Undefined).*								
.	13097	71710	73185	235433	137069	36382	566876	General Labourer	2893	.	95	500	320	972	793	213
.	494	5086	9325	35443	14375	1414	66137	Engine Driver, Stoker, Fireman (not railway, marine, nor agricultural)	.	.	.	.	.	.	.	.
.	1380	5680	4924	11361	4710	737	28777	Artizan, Mechanic (undefined)	2255	.	181	766	462	581	218	46
.	764	2858	184	13	5	1	3825	Apprentice (undefined)	789	.	219	514	19	5	1	1
.	1409	4165	2464	5943	2524	402	16907	Factory Labourer (undefined)	4238	.	468	2133	819	619	175	24
.	181	851	699	1935	867	112	4645	Machinist, Machine Worker (undefined)	7524	.	224	2302	1983	2650	350	15
								23. PERSONS WORKING AND DEALING IN REFUSE MATTERS.								
								1. *Refuse Matters.*								
.	22	82	124	649	416	70	1363	Town Drainage Service	.	.	.	.	.	.	.	.
.	96	706	843	3220	1613	253	6740	Chimney Sweep, Soot Merchant	77	.	.	4	4	20	34	15
.	50	170	212	878	1007	377	2694	Scavenger, Crossing Sweeper	174	.	3	41	22	48	50	12
.	32	165	201	691	619	180	1888	Rag Gatherer, Dealer	1403	.	54	244	235	475	346	49
								VI. UNOCCUPIED CLASS.								
								24. PERSONS WITHOUT SPECIFIED OCCUPATIONS								
1757651	2649514	124012	32171	62560	87632	142716	4856256	Persons returned by Property, Rank, &c., and not by special occupation, including all Children under 5 years of age	9630019	1763207	2765392	408435	535277	2481037	1442594	633677

TABLE 6.—OCCUPATIONS of MALES and FEMALES, enumerated in England and Wales, arranged in Alphabetical Order.

RANK OR OCCUPATION.	PERSONS.	M.	F.	Reference to Classified Arrangement. Order.	Sub-order.
Accountant	11606	11517	89	5	1
Accoutrement Maker	600	343	255	18	1
Actor	4565	2197	2368	3	7
Agent, Broker, Factor	31208	30697	511	5	1
Agricultural Labourer, Farm Servant, Cottager	847954	807608	40346	7	1
Agricultural Machine and Implement Maker	4119	4066	53	10	1
Agricultural Machine—Proprietor, Attendant	4266	4228	38	7	1
Agricultural Student, Pupil	728	728	.	7	1
Ale, Porter, Cider Dealer. Beerseller	16583	12855	3728	16	2
Alkali Manufacture	2150	2143	7	14	3
Anchor, Chain, Manufacture	5029	4038	991	21	8
Animal, Bird, &c., Preserver. Naturalist	845	686	159	11	3
Appraiser. Auctioneer, Valuer, House Agent	10075	10016	59	5	1
Apprentice (undefined)	4584	3825	759	22	2
Architect	6898	6898	.	3	7
Army Officer (effective or retired)	10914	10914	.	2	1
Army Pensioner	8589	8572	17	2	1
Art, Dealer in Works of	1160	1051	109	11	3
Art, Music, Theatre, Service	1392	1111	281	3	7
Art Student	2396	1337	1059	3	7
Artificial Flower Maker	5181	720	4461	11	3
Artizan, Mechanic (undefined)	31032	28777	2255	22	2
Auctioneer, Appraiser, Valuer, House Agent	10075	10016	59	5	1
Author, Editor, Journalist	3434	2982	452	3	5
Bag (Paper), Paper Box, Maker	9905	1187	8718	20	4
Bag, Portmanteau, Strap, &c. Leather Goods—Maker, Dealer	5370	4024	1346	19	2
Bag, Sacking, Sack—Maker, Dealer	2169	575	1594	17	4
Bailiff, Farm	19377	19377	.	7	1
Baker	71032	63399	7633	16	3
Bank Service	14998	14914	84	5	2
Banker	1057	1052	5	5	2
Barge, Ship, Boat, Builder	21741	21702	39	13	1
Bargeman, Lighterman, Waterman	30223	29870	353	6	3
Bark, Cork—Cutter, Worker, Dealer	1928	1741	187	20	3
Barrister, Solicitor	17386	17386	.	3	2
Basketmaker. Willow, Cane, Rush—Worker, Dealer	11542	9017	2525	20	2
Bathing and Washing Service	180078	3108	176970	4	2
Bayonet, Sword,—Maker. Cutler	190	186	4	10	5
Beerseller, Ale, Porter, Cider, Dealer	16583	12855	3728	16	2
Bellhanger, Locksmith	7694	7342	352	11	2
Bicycle, Tricycle—Maker, Dealer	1072	1059	13	12	1
Bill Discounter, Bill Broker, Finance Agent	604	604	.	5	2
Billiard, Cricket, and other Games, Service	3162	3116	46	3	8
Bird, Animal, &c. Preserver. Naturalist	845	686	159	11	3
Bird, Dog, Animal—Keeper, Dealer	1368	1156	212	8	1
Blacking, Ink, Colouring Substance Manufacture	1234	1077	157	14	1
Blacksmith	112523	112176	347	21	8
Blanket, Cloth, Worsted, Stuff, Flannel, Dealer	5613	5533	80	17	1
Blanket Manufacture	2687	1313	1374	17	1
Bleacher, Dyer, Printer, Scourer, Calenderer (undefined)	13639	11799	1840	17	5
Boarding House, Lodging, Keeper	37376	4486	32890	16	1
Boat, Barge, Ship, Builder	21741	21702	39	13	1
Boatman on Seas	1570	1570	.	6	3
Boiler Maker	26170	26170	.	10	1
Bolt, Nut, Rivet, Screw, Staple, Maker	8017	5673	2344	21	12
Bone, Horn, Ivory, Tortoise-shell—Worker, Dealer	1865	1710	155	19	1
Bonnet, Hat, Plait Manufacture (Straw)	30984	3001	27983	18	1
Bookbinder	20097	9505	10592	9	1
Bookseller, Publisher, Librarian	9910	8472	1438	9	1
Boot, Shoe—Maker, Dealer	216556	180884	35672	18	1
Box Maker, Wood Turner	13977	11382	2595	20	3
Box (Paper), Paper Bag, Maker	9905	1187	8718	20	4
Brass, Bronze, Manufacture. Brazier	27874	26892	982	21	12
Brewer	24567	24196	371	16	2
Bricklayer	125140	125055	85	11	1
Brick, Tile—Maker, Burner, Dealer	50075	47337	2738	21	3
Bristle, Hair—Worker, Dealer	2636	893	1743	19	3
Broker, Agent, Factor	31208	30697	511	5	1
Broker (Bill), Bill Discounter, Finance Agent	604	604	.	5	2
Bronze, Brass, Manufacture—Brazier	27874	26892	982	21	12

RANK OR OCCUPATION.	PERSONS.	M.	F.	Reference to Classified Arrangement. Order.	Sub-order.
Broom, Brush—Maker	12899	8714	4185	19	3
Buckle, Clasp, Hinge—Maker	1412	933	479	21	12
Builder	30699	30564	135	11	1
Burnisher (Metal), Lacquerer	2687	478	2209	21	12
Butcher, Meat Salesman	81702	78206	3496	16	3
Butterman, Cheesemonger	4379	4026	353	16	3
Button—Maker, Dealer	6407	2286	4121	13	1
Buyer, Salesman (not otherwise described)	4595	3156	1439	5	1
Cab, Coach, Omnibus, Owner—Livery Stable Keeper	6787	6547	240	6	2
Cabinet Maker, Upholsterer	59746	51761	7985	11	2
Cabman, Flyman, Coachman (not domestic)	30492	30492	.	6	2
Cake (Oil), Oil Miller—Maker, Dealer	4530	4428	102	20	1
Calenderer, Dyer, Printer, Scourer, Bleacher (undefined)	13639	11799	1840	17	5
Calico, Cotton—Printer, Dyer, Bleacher	26682	22750	3932	17	3
Calico, Cotton—Warehouseman, Dealer	3554	3175	379	17	3
Candle, Grease, Manufacture. Tallow Chandler	3235	3013	222	19	1
Candlestick, Lamp, Lantern, Maker	3044	2541	503	21	12
Cane, Willow, Rush—Worker, Dealer. Basket-maker	11542	9017	2525	20	2
Canvas, Sailcloth, Manufacture	648	874	274	17	4
Card, Pattern Card, Maker	1649	1209	440	20	4
Carman, Carrier, Carter, Haulier	125342	124611	731	6	2
Carpenter, Joiner	235233	235017	216	11	1
Carpet, Rug, Manufacture	13986	8795	5190	17	5
Carrier, Carman, Carter, Haulier	125342	124611	731	6	2
Carver, Gilder	8144	7814	330	11	3
Carver (Wood)	3108	3090	22	11	3
Catsmeat Dealer, Knacker, &c.	693	608	85	8	1
Cattle, Sheep, Pig—Dealer, Salesman	5754	5729	25	8	1
Cellarman	6044	5758	286	16	2
Cement, Plaster, Manufacture	3680	3634	46	21	5
Cemetery, Church, Chapel—Officer, Servant	6289	4582	1707	3	1
Chaff, Hay, Straw (not plait)—Cutter, Dealer	2648	2598	50	20	2
Chain, Anchor, Manufacture	5029	4038	991	21	8
Chain (Fancy) Gilt Toy—Maker	1042	342	700	21	12
Chair (Wheel) Proprietor, Attendant, &c.	857	843	14	8	2
Chalk, Clay, Sand, Gravel—Labourer, Dealer	4844	4722	122	21	3
Chandler, Ship Rigger, Fitter	2861	2834	27	13	2
Chapel, Church, Cemetery—Officer, Servant	6289	4582	1707	3	1
Charcoal, Coke, Peat—Cutter, Burner, Dealer	5385	5243	142	21	2
Charwoman	92474	.	92474	4	2
Cheesemonger, Butterman	4379	4026	353	16	3
Chemist, Druggist	19990	18309	681	14	3
Chemist, Manufacturing	13971	12843	1128	14	3
Chimney Sweep, Soot Merchant	6817	6740	77	23	1
China, Earthenware, Glass, Dealer	6181	4260	1921	21	4
China, Earthenware, Porcelain, Manufacture	46596	28719	17877	21	4
Chocolate, Tea, Coffee—Maker, Dealer. Grocer	129818	103396	26422	16	3
Church, Chapel, Cemetery—Officer, Servant	6289	4582	1707	3	1
Cider, Ale, Porter—Dealer. Beerseller	16583	12855	3728	16	2
Civil Engineer	7124	7124	.	3	6
Civil Service (messengers, &c.)	21180	20627	553	1	1
Civil Service (Officers and Clerks)	25868	22352	3210	1	1
Clasp, Buckle, Hinge, Maker	1412	933	479	21	12
Clay, Sand, Gravel, Chalk—Labourer, Dealer	4844	4722	122	21	3
Clergyman (Established Church)	21663	21663	.	3	1
Clerk, Commercial	181457	175468	5989	5	1
Clock Maker, Watch Maker	23351	22576	775	10	3
Clog, Patten—Maker	7503	7429	74	18	1
Cloth (Oil, Floor) Manufacture	1334	1312	22	20	1
Cloth, Worsted, Stuff, Flannel, Blanket, Dealer	5613	5533	80	17	1
Clothes (Old), Dealer	2302	639	1663	18	1
Club, College, Service	3452	2853	599	4	1
Coach, Omnibus, Cab, Owner—Livery Stable Keeper	6787	6547	240	6	2
Coachmaker	23966	23750	216	12	1
Coachman (not domestic), Cabman, Flyman	30492	30492	.	6	2
Coachman, Groom (domestic)	73167	73167	.	4	1
Coalheaver	13723	13723	.	21	5
Coal Merchant, Dealer	20401	19233	1168	21	2

TABLE 6 *cont.*—OCCUPATIONS of MALES and FEMALES, enumerated in England and Wales, arranged in Alphabetical Order.

RANK OR OCCUPATION.	PERSONS.	M.	F.	Reference to Classified Arrangement. Order.	Sub-order.
Coal Miner	381763	378664	3099	21	1
Cocoa Fibre, Hemp, Jute—Manufacture	3478	1181	2297	17	4
Coffee, Eating, House, Keeper	8173	5509	2664	16	1
Coffee, Tea, Chocolate—Maker, Dealer, Grocer	129818	103386	26432	16	3
Coin, Die, Seal, Medal—Maker	1539	1486	53	10	7
Coke, Charcoal, Peat—Cutter, Burner, Dealer	5385	5243	142	21	2
Collector (Toll), Turnpike Gate Keeper	1104	717	387	6	2
College, Club, Service	3452	2853	599	4	1
Colonial and East Indian Service	240	240	.	1	3
Colour and Oilman	4638	4257	381	20	1
Comb Maker	755	584	171	19	1
Commercial Clerk	181457	175468	5989	5	1
Commercial Company, Guild, Society, &c. (Officer of)	360	360	.	5	1
Commercial Traveller	35478	35478	.	5	1
Confectioner, Pastrycook	25534	12483	13051	16	3
Contractor (Railway)	1182	1182	.	21	3
Contractor, Surveyor, Inspector (Road)	1326	1326	.	21	3
Contractor (undefined)	3041	3014	27	22	1
Cook (not domestic)	4628	2875	1753	4	2
Cook, Steward (Ship)	6767	6381	386	8	3
Cooper, Hoop Maker, Bender	18699	18596	103	20	3
Copper, Copper Goods—Manufacturer, Worker, Dealer	7348	7298	50	21	9
Copper Miner	4067	3800	267	21	1
Copper Plate and Steel Plate Printer	415	403	12	9	2
Coprolite, Fossil — Digger, Dealer	705	686	19	21	3
Cord, Rope, Twine—Maker, Dealer	11751	9658	2093	17	4
Cork, Bark—Cutter, Worker, Dealer	1928	1741	187	20	3
Corn, Flour, Seed—Merchant, Dealer	9966	9183	783	16	3
Corn Miller	23462	23162	300	16	3
Costermonger, Huckster, Street Seller	47111	29451	17660	22	1
Cottager, Agricultural Labourer, Farm Servant	847954	807608	40346	7	1
Cotton, Calico—Printer, Dyer, Bleacher	26682	22750	3932	17	3
Cotton, Calico—Warehouseman, Dealer	3554	3175	379	17	3
Cotton, Cotton Goods, Manufacture	487777	185410	302367	17	3
Crape, Gauze, Manufacture	1182	176	1006	17	2
Cricket, Billiard, and other Games, Service	3162	3116	46	3	8
Crossing Sweeper, Scavenger	2868	2694	174	23	1
Currier	15651	14991	660	19	2
Cutler, Scissors Maker	12234	10651	1583	10	2
Dairyman, Milkseller	25805	21362	4443	16	3
Dealer (General), Shopkeeper	54860	29088	25772	22	1
Dentist	3583	3583	.	3	3
Die, Seal, Coin, Medal—Maker	1539	1486	53	10	7
Discounter (Bill), Bill Broker Finance Agent	604	604	.	5	2
District, Municipal, Parish, Union—Officer	14912	11895	3017	1	2
Dock, Harbour, Wharf, Lighthouse—Service	42648	42578	70	6	3
Dog, Bird, Animal—Keeper, Dealer	1368	1156	212	3	1
Domestic Coachman, Groom	73167	73167	.	4	1
Domestic Gardener	74648	74603	45	4	1
Domestic Indoor Servant	1286668	56262	1230406	4	1
Drainage Service, Land (not in towns)	1695	1695	.	7	1
Drainage Service (Town)	1363	1363		23	1
Draper, Linen Draper, Mercer	82362	53581	28781	17	5
Dressmaker, Milliner, Staymaker	360032	2037	357995	18	1
Driver, Stoker (Railway Engine)	22856	22856	.	6	1
Drover	2586	2586	.	8	1
Druggist, Chemist	19000	18369	631	14	3
Drysalter	1017	920	97	14	3
Dye, Paint, Manufacture	2027	1638	389	14	1
Dyer, Printer, Scourer, Bleacher, Calenderer (undefined)	13639	11799	1840	17	3
Earthenware, China, Glass, Dealer	6181	4260	1921	21	4
Earthenware, China, Porcelain, Manufacture	46596	28719	17877	21	4
East Indian and Colonial Service	240	240	.	1	3
Eating, Coffee, House, Keeper	8173	5509	2664	16	1
Editor, Author, Journalist	3434	2982	452	3	5
Electrical Apparatus Maker	2522	2496	26	10	3
Embroiderer	2421	110	2311	17	5
Engine (Railway) Driver, Stoker	22856	22856	.	6	1
Engine Driver, Stoker, Fireman (neither railway, marine, nor agricultural)	66137	66137	.	22	2
Engine and Machine Fitter, Turner	64663	64663	.	10	1
Engine, Machine, Maker	38481	38180	301	10	1
Engineer, Civil	7124	7124	.	3	6
Engineer, Mining	2291	2291	.	3	6
Engraver (artist)	2265	2201	64	3	7
Envelope Maker	2108	175	1933	2	4
Exhibition Service, Showman, Performer	1881	1361	520	3	8
Explosive Article, Fusee, Fireworks, Manufacture	2837	950	1887	14	2
Explosive Substance, Gunpowder, Guncotton, Manufacture	779	657	122	14	2
Factor, Broker, Agent	31308	30697	611	5	1
Factory Labourer (undefined)	21143	16907	4236	22	2
Farm Bailiff	19377	19377	.	7	1
Farm Servant, Agricultural Labourer, Cottager	847954	807608	40346	7	1
Farmer, Grazier	223943	203329	20614	7	1
Farmer, Grazier—Son, Grandson, Brother, Nephew	75197	75197	*.	7	1
Fancy Chain, Gilt Toy, Maker	1042	342	700	21	12
Fancy Goods (Textile)—Manufacturer, Worker, Dealer	7573	1388	6185	17	5
Farrier, Veterinary Surgeon	7511	7511	.	8	1
Feather, Quill—Dresser, Dealer	2518	429	2089	19	3
Fellmonger, Tanner	10248	10157	91	19	2
Felt Manufacture	491	446	45	17	5
Figure, Image—Maker, Dealer	418	385	33	11	3
File Maker	8967	7761	1206	10	2
Finance Agent, Bill Discounter, Bill Broker	604	604	.	5	2
Fireman, Engine Driver, Stoker (neither railway, marine, nor agricultural)	66137	66137	.	22	2
Fireworks, Fusee, Explosive Article Manufacture	2837	950	1887	14	2
Fisherman	29696	29402	294	8	1
Fishing Rod, Tackle—Maker, Dealer	1401	898	503	10	8
Fishmonger	17906	15494	2412	16	3
Fitter, Turner (Engine and Machine)	64663	64663	.	10	1
Flannel, Cloth, Worsted, Stuff, Blanket—Dealer	5613	5533	80	17	1
Flannel Manufacture	1126	656	470	17	1
Flax, Linen — Manufacturer, Dealer	12065	4212	7853	17	3
Floor Cloth, Oil Cloth, Manufacture	1334	1312	22	20	1
Florist, Nurseryman, Seedsman	7755	7021	734	7	3
Flour, Corn, Seed—Merchant, Dealer	9966	9183	783	16	3
Flower Maker, Artificial	5181	720	4461	11	3
Flyman, Cabman, Coachman, (not domestic)	30492	30492	.	6	2
Fossil, Coprolite—Digger, Dealer	705	686	19	21	3
French Polisher	10112	8083	2029	11	3
Fruiterer, Greengrocer	29614	22759	6855	16	3
Fuller	2515	2498	17	17	1
Funeral Furniture Maker, Undertaker	1893	1701	192	11	2
Furniture Broker, Dealer	5978	5023	955	11	2
Furrier, Skinner	8148	4683	3465	19	2
Fusee, Fireworks, Explosive Article Manufacture	2837	950	1887	14	2
Fustian Manufacturer, Dealer	8187	3011	5176	17	3
Game Dealer, Poulterer	3591	2923	668	16	3
Gamekeeper	12633	12633	.	8	1
Games, Apparatus for, Maker of	1071	968	103	10	8
Gardener, Domestic	74648	74603	45	4	1
Gardener (not domestic)	65852	63518	2334	7	3
Gas Fitter	12567	12420	147	11	2
Gas Works Service	18535	18535	.	21	2
Gate Keeper (Turnpike) Toll Collector	1104	717	387	6	2
Gate, Lodge, Park, Keeper (not Government)	2431	1683	748	4	1
Gauze, Crape, Manufacture	1182	176	1006	17	2
Gelatine, Glue, Size, Isinglass,—Maker, Dealer	655	497	158	19	1
General Labourer	559769	556876	2893	22	2
General Practitioner, Physician, Surgeon	15116	15091	25	3	3
General Shopkeeper, Dealer	54860	29088	25772	22	1
Gilder, Carver	8144	7814	330	11	3
Gilt Toy, Fancy Chain, Maker	1042	342	700	21	12
Ginger Beer, Mineral Water—Manufacturer, Dealer	4662	4325	337	16	3
Glass, Earthenware, China, Dealer	6181	4260	1921	21	4
Glass Manufacture	21680	19938	1742	21	4
Glazier, Painter	100130	99675	4	11	1

* The corresponding Female relatives were not abstracted.

TABLE 6 *cont.*—OCCUPATIONS of MALES and FEMALES, enumerated in England and Wales, arranged in Alphabetical Order.

RANK OR OCCUPATION.	PERSONS.	M.	F.	Reference to Classified Arrangement. Order.	Sub-order.
Glover, Glove Maker	15524	2263	13261	18	1
Glue, Size, Gelatine, Isinglass, Maker, Dealer	655	497	158	19	1
Gold, Silver, Beater	661	661	.	21	7
Goldsmith, Silversmith, Jeweller	24715	20962	3753	21	7
Gravel, Clay, Sand, Chalk—Labourer, Dealer	4844	4722	122	21	3
Grazier, Farmer	223943	203329	20614	7	1
Grease, Candle—Manufacture	3235	3013	222	19	1
Greengrocer, Fruiterer	29614	22759	6855	16	3
Grocer, Tea, Coffee, Chocolate—Maker, Dealer	129818	103396	26422	16	3
Groom, Coachman (domestic)	73167	73167	.	4	1
Groom, Horse Keeper, Horse-Breaker	40863	40819	44	8	1
Guard, Railway	10296	10296	.	6	1
Guild, Commercial Company, Society, &c. (Officer of)	360	360	.	5	1
Gunpowder, Guncotton, Explosive Substance, Manufacture	779	657	122	14	2
Gunsmith, Gun Manufacturer	7741	7522	219	10	5
Gutta Percha, India Rubber—Worker, Dealer	4965	3517	1448	20	1
Haberdasher, Hosier	9565	4879	4686	18	1
Hair, Bristle—Worker, Dealer	2636	893	1743	19	3
Hairdresser, Wig Maker	14933	14165	768	18	1
Harbour, Dock, Wharf, Lighthouse, Service	42643	42573	70	6	3
Hardware Dealer, Merchant, Ironmonger	16120	15214	906	21	8
Harness, Whip, Maker, Saddler	23866	21831	2035	12	2
Hat, Bonnet, Plait Manufacture (Straw)	30984	3001	27983	18	1
Hatter, Hat Manufacture (not Straw)	22689	13617	9072	18	1
Haulier, Carman, Carrier, Carter	125342	124611	731	6	2
Hay, Straw (not plait), Chaff—Cutter, Dealer	2646	2596	50	20	2
Hemp, Jute, Cocoa Fibre, Manufacture	3478	1181	2297	17	4
Hinge, Clasp, Buckle, Maker	1412	933	479	21	12
Hoop Maker, Bender—Cooper	18699	18596	103	20	3
Hop—Merchant, Dealer	436	426	10	16	2
Horn, Bone, Ivory, Tortoise-shell—Worker, Dealer	1865	1710	155	19	1
Horse-breaker, Groom, Horse-keeper	40863	40819	44	8	1
Horse Proprietor, Breeder, Dealer	2233	2228	5	8	1
Hosier, Haberdasher	9565	4879	4686	18	1
Hosiery Manufacture	40372	18862	21510	18	1
Hospital and Institution Service	15796	4270	11526	4	2
Hotel, Inn, Servant	62310	35823	26487	4	1
Hotel Keeper, Innkeeper, Publican	70106	57397	12709	16	1
House Agent, Auctioneer, Appraiser, Valuer	10675	10616	59	5	1
House and Shop Fittings—Maker, Dealer	3021	2815	206	11	2
House, Land, Ship—Surveyor	5394	5394	.	3	6
House, Life, Ship, &c., Insurance Service	15068	14821	247	5	3
Huckster, Costermonger, Street Seller	47111	29451	17660	22	1
Hurdle, Lath, Wooden Fence, Maker	2937	2919	18	20	3
Image, Figure—Maker, Dealer	418	385	33	11	3
Implement Maker (domestic)	1747	1047	700	10	2
India Rubber, Gutta Percha—Worker, Dealer	4965	3517	1448	20	1
Ink, Blacking, Colouring Substance Manufacture	1234	1077	157	14	1
Inn, Hotel, Servant	62310	35823	26487	4	1
Innkeeper, Hotel Keeper, Publican	70106	57397	12709	16	1
Inland Navigation Service	2599	2549	50	6	3
Inspector, Contractor, Surveyor (Road)	1826	1826	.	21	3
Institution and Hospital Service	15796	4270	11526	4	2
Institution, Literary, Scientific, Service, &c.	1083	950	133	3	5
Insurance Service (Life, House, Ship, &c.)	15068	14821	247	5	3
Iron and Steel (other than Nail, Anchor, and Chain), Manufactures	200677	198786	1891	21	8
Ironmonger, Hardware—Dealer, Merchant	16122	15214	906	21	8
Ironstone Miner	26110	25879	231	21	1

RANK OR OCCUPATION.	PERSONS.	M.	F.	Reference to Classified Arrangement. Order.	Sub-order.
Isinglass, Glue, Size, Gelatine—Maker, Dealer	655	497	158	19	1
Ivory, Bone, Horn, Tortoise-shell—Worker, Dealer	1865	1710	155	19	1
Japanner	2898	1359	1539	20	1
Jeweller, Goldsmith, Silversmith	24715	20962	3753	21	7
Joiner, Carpenter	235233	235017	216	11	1
Journalist, Author, Editor	3434	2982	452	3	6
Jute, Hemp, Cocoa Fibre, Manufacture	3478	1181	2297	17	4
Knacker, Catsmeat Dealer, &c., &c.	693	608	85	8	1
Label, Ticket, Writer	1140	642	498	20	4
Labourer, Factory (undefined)	21145	16907	4238	22	2
Labourer (General)	559769	556876	2893	22	2
Labourer (Railway), Navvy	36850	36850	.	21	3
Labourer (Road)	10947	10947	.	21	3
Lace Manufacturer, Dealer	44144	11359	32785	17	3
Lacquerer, Metal Burnisher	2687	478	2209	21	12
Lamp, Lantern, Candlestick Maker	3044	2541	503	21	12
Land Drainage Service (not in towns)	1695	1695	.	7	1
Land, House, Ship, Surveyor	5394	5394	.	3	6
Lantern, Lamp, Candlestick, Maker	3044	2541	503	21	12
Lapidary	1691	1411	280	21	7
Lath, Wooden Fence, Hurdle, Maker	2937	2919	18	20	3
Law Clerk, and others connected with Law	24602	24502	100	3	2
Law Stationer, Stationer	15241	9980	5261	20	4
Law Student	1653	1653	.	3	2
Lead, Leaden goods—Manufacturer, Worker, Dealer	2460	2319	141	21	11
Lead Miner	11226	11022	204	21	1
Leather Goods, Portmanteau, Bag, Strap, &c.—Maker, Dealer	5370	4024	1346	19	2
Lecturer, Teacher, Professor	34941	6336	28605	3	4
Level Crossing Man, Pointsman	6205	6034	171	6	1
Librarian, Publisher, Bookseller	9910	8472	1438	9	1
Life, House, Ship, &c., Insurance Service	15068	14821	247	5	3
Lighterman, Bargeman, Waterman	30223	29870	353	6	3
Lighthouse, Harbour, Dock, Wharf Service	42643	42573	70	6	3
Limeburner	3309	3270	39	21	3
Linen Draper, Draper, Mercer	82362	53581	28781	17	5
Linen, Flax,—Manufacturer, Dealer	12065	4212	7853	17	5
Literary, Scientific, Institution, Service, &c.	1083	950	133	3	5
Lithographer, Lithographic Printer	5681	5546	135	9	2
Livery Stable Keeper—Omnibus, Coach, Cab, Owner	6787	6547	240	6	2
Locksmith, Bellhanger	7694	7342	352	11	2
Lodge, Gate, Park Keeper (not Government)	2431	1683	748	4	1
Lodging, Boarding House, Keeper	37376	4486	32890	16	1
Machine, Agricultural—Proprietor, Attendant	4260	4222	38	7	1
Machine, Engine, Maker	38481	38180	301	10	1
Machinery (domestic), Maker, Dealer	528	507	21	10	1
Machinist, Machine Worker, (undefined)	12169	4645	7524	22	2
Maltster	9531	9473	58	16	2
Manchester Warehouseman	1884	1868	16	17	5
Manufacturer, Manager, Superintendent (undefined)	7436	6884	552	22	1
Manure Manufacture	1223	1168	55	19	1

TABLE 6 *cont.*—OCCUPATIONS of MALES and FEMALES, enumerated in England and Wales, arranged in Alphabetical Order.

RANK OR OCCUPATION.	PERSONS.	M.	F.	Reference to Classified Arrangement.	
				Order.	Sub-order.
Map and Print—Colourer, Seller	625	459	166	9	2
Mason	97540	97432	108	11	1
Mast, Yard, Oar, Block—Maker	1419	1419	.	13	2
Mat Maker, Seller	2279	1800	479	17	4
Measuring and Weighing Apparatus Maker	2586	2391	195	10	3
Meat Salesman, Butcher	81702	78206	3496	16	3
Mechanic, Artisan (undefined)	31032	28777	2255	22	2
Medal, Die, Seal, Coin—Maker	1539	1486	53	10	7
Medical Service (Subordinate)	37147	1972	35175	3	3
Medical Student, Assistant	6056	5992	64	3	3
Mercer, Draper, Linen Draper	82362	53581	28781	17	3
Merchant	10359	10308	51	5	1
Messenger, Porter, Watchman (neither Railway nor Government)	131171	129561	1610	6	3
Metal Burnisher, Lacquerer	2687	478	2209	21	12
Metal Refiner, Worker, Turner, Dealer	4515	4215	300	21	12
Meter, Weigher	1157	1157	.	6	4
Midwife	2646	.	2646	3	3
Militia, Yeomanry, Volunteers	10747	10747	.	2	1
Milkseller, Dairyman	25805	21362	4443	16	3
Miller (Corn)	23468	23162	306	16	3
Miller (Oil), Oil Cake—Maker, Dealer	4530	4428	102	20	1
Milliner, Dressmaker, Staymaker	360932	2937	357995	18	1
Millwright	6940	6940	.	10	1
Mine Service	3602	3572	30	21	1
Miner in undefined Minerals	2102	2061	41	21	1
Mineral Water, Ginger Beer—Manufacturer, Dealer	4662	4325	337	16	3
Mining Engineer	2391	2391	.	3	6
Minister, Priest, other than of the Established or Roman Catholic Churches	9734	9734	.	3	1
Missionary, Scripture Reader, Itinerant Preacher	4625	2965	1660	3	1
Municipal, Parish, Union, District—Officer	14912	11895	3017	1	2
Music, Art, Theatre, Service	1302	1111	221	3	7
Music,—Publisher, Seller, Printer	1440	1206	234	9	1
Musical Instrument Maker, Dealer	9249	9008	241	10	6
Musician, Music Master	25546	14170	11376	3	7
Mustard, Vinegar, Spice, Pickle,—Maker, Dealer	1509	825	684	16	3
Nail Manufacture	18741	9603	9138	21	8
Naturalist. Animal, Bird, &c., Preserver	845	686	159	11	3
Navigation Service (Inland)	2599	2549	50	6	3
Navigation Service (on shore)	2098	2007	91	6	3
Navvy, Railway Labourer	36850	36850	.	21	3
Navy Officer (effective or retired)	3921	3921	.	2	2
Navy Pensioner	8943	8910	33	2	2
Needle Maker	4455	2381	2074	10	2
Net Maker	1783	292	1491	17	4
News Room Keeper, Newspaper Agent	5515	4386	1129	9	1
Non-commissioned Officer and Soldier	56936	56935	.	2	1
Nun, Sister of Charity	3795	.	3795	3	1
Nurseryman, Seedsman, Florist	7755	7021	734	7	3
Nut, Bolt, Rivet, Screw Staple—Maker	8017	5673	2344	21	12
Oar, Yard, Mast, Block—Maker	1419	1419	.	13	2
Office Keeper (not Government)	6184	1853	4391	4	2
Officer, Army (effective or retired)	10914	10914		2	1
Officer, Navy (effective or retired)	3921	3921	.	2	2
Officer of Commercial Company, Guild, Society, &c.	360	360	.	5	1
Oil and Colourman	4638	4257	381	20	1
Oil Cloth, Floor Cloth, Manufacture	1334	1312	22	20	1
Oil Miller, Oil Cake—Maker, Dealer	4530	4428	102	20	1
Omnibus, Coach, Cab Owner—Livery Stable Keeper	6787	6547	240	6	2
Optician, Philosophical Instrument Maker	3605	3385	220	10	3
Ordnance Manufacturer	268	267	1	10	5
Paint, Dye, Manufacture	2027	1638	389	14	1
Painter (Artist)	7962	6082	1880	3	7
Painter, Glazier	100130	99676	454	11	1
Paper Box, Paper Bag, Maker	9906	1187	8718	20	4
Paper Manufacture	18629	10352	8277	20	4
Paper Stainer	2267	1822	445	20	4
Paperhanger	4272	4177	95	11	1
Parasol, Umbrella, Stick—Maker, Dealer	8230	4118	4112	18	1
Parchment, Vellum,—Maker, Dealer	431	407	24	19	2
Parish, Municipal, Union, District—Officer	14912	11895	3017	1	2
Park, Lodge, Gate Keeper (not Government)	2431	1683	748	4	1
Pastrycook, Confectioner	25534	12483	13051	16	3
Patten, Clog—Maker	7503	7429	74	18	1
Paviour	4150	4150	.	21	3
Pawnbroker	8960	7681	1279	22	1
Peat, Coke, Charcoal—Cutter, Burner, Dealer	5385	5243	142	21	2
Peer, M.P., Privy Councillor (not otherwise described)	614	614	.	1	1
Pen Maker (Steel)	2733	230	2503	10	2
Pencil Maker (Wood)	232	159	73	10	2
Pensioner, Army	8589	8572	17	2	1
Pensioner, Navy	8943	8910	33	2	2
Performer, Showman, Exhibition Service	1881	1363	520	3	8
Pewterer, White Metal, Plated Ware, Manufacture	5629	4791	838	21	12
Philosophical Instrument Maker, Optician	3605	3385	220	10	3
Photographer	6661	5352	1309	3	7
Physician, Surgeon, General Practitioner	15116	15091	25	3	3
Pickle, Spice, Mustard, Vinegar Maker, Dealer	1509	825	684	16	3
Pig, Cattle, Sheep—Dealer, Salesman	5754	5729	25	8	1
Pilot	2991	2991	.	6	3
Pin Maker	729	234	495	10	2
Plait, Hat, Bonnet, Manufacture (Straw)	30934	3001	27933	18	1
Plaster, Cement, Manufacture	3680	3634	46	21	3
Plasterer, Whitewasher	28841	28800	41	11	1
Plated Ware, White Metal, Manufacture, Pewterer	5629	4791	838	21	12
Platelayer, Railway	21997	21997	.	21	3
Plumber	37400	37160	240	11	1
Pointsman, Level Crossing Man	6205	6034	171	6	1
Police	32508	32508	.	1	2
Porcelain, Earthenware, China, Manufacture	46596	28719	17877	21	4
Porter, Messenger, Watchman (neither Railway nor Government	131171	129561	1610	6	3
Portmanteau, Bag, Strap, &c. Leather Goods — Maker, Dealer	5370	4024	1346	19	2
Poulterer, Game Dealer	3591	2923	668	16	3
Preacher (Itinerant), Missionary, Scripture Reader	4625	2965	1660	3	1
Priest, Minister, other than of the Established or Roman Catholic Churches	9734	9734	.	3	1
Priest, Roman Catholic	2089	2089	.	3	1
Print and Map—Colourer, Seller	625	459	166	9	2
Printer	61290	59088	2202	9	1
Prison Officer, &c.	3497	2913	584	1	1
Professor, Teacher, Lecturer	34941	6336	28605	3	4
Property, Rank, &c. (Persons returned by), and not by special occupation	14786875	4856256	9930619	24	1
Provision Curer, Dealer	16584	11255	5329	16	3
Publican, Innkeeper, Hotel Keeper	70106	57397	12709	16	1
Publisher, Bookseller, Librarian	9910	8472	1438	9	1
Quarrier (Slate)	14900	14900	.	21	3
Quarrier (Stone)	28870	28870	.	21	3
Quill, Feather — Dresser, Dealer	2518	429	2089	19	5
Rag Gatherer, Dealer	3291	1888	1403	23	1
Railway Carriage, Railway Waggon, Maker	7570	7512	58	12	1
Railway Contractor	1182	1182	.	21	3
Railway Engine Driver, Stoker	22856	22856	.	6	1
Railway Guard	10296	10296	.	6	1
Railway Labourer, Navvy	36850	36850	.	21	3
Railway Officials and Servants (other than above)	100051	99574	477	6	1

TABLE 6 *cont.*—OCCUPATIONS of MALES and FEMALES, enumerated in England and Wales, arranged in Alphabetical Order.

RANK OR OCCUPATION.	PERSONS.	M.	F.	Reference to Classified Arrangement.	
				Order.	Sub-order.
Rank, Property, &c. (Persons returned by), and not by special occupation	14780875	4850256	9930619	24	1
Refiner, Worker, Turner, Dealer (Metal)	4515	4215	300	21	12
Reporter, Short-hand Writer	2677	2662	15	3	5
Ribbon Manufacture	2064	878	1186	17	2
Rivet, Bolt, Nut, Screw, Staple—Maker	8017	5673	2344	21	12
Road Contractor, Surveyor, Inspector	1020	1020	.	21	6
Road Labourer	10947	10947	.	21	3
Roman Catholic Priest	2089	2089	.	3	1
Rope, Twine, Cord—Maker, Dealer	11751	9658	2093	17	4
Royal Marines (officers and men)	7720	7720	.	2	3
Rug, Carpet, Manufacture	13985	8795	5190	17	5
Rush, Willow, Cane—Worker, Dealer, Basketmaker	11548	9017	2523	20	2
Sacking, Sack, Bag—Maker, Dealer	2169	575	1594	17	4
Saddler, Harness, Whip Maker	23866	21831	2035	12	2
Sail Maker	4129	4082	47	13	2
Salesman, Buyer (not otherwise described)	4595	3166	1429	5	1
Salt Maker, Dealer	2982	2823	159	21	3
Sand, Clay, Gravel, Chalk—Labourer, Dealer	4844	4722	122	21	3
Saw Maker	2116	2016	100	10	2
Sawyer	24712	24712	.	20	3
Scavenger, Crossing Sweeper	2868	2694	174	23	1
School Service, and others concerned in Teaching	2911	1762	1149	3	4
Schoolmaster	133079	38738	94241	3	4
Scientific, Literary, Institution, Service, &c.	1083	950	133	3	8
Scientific Pursuits (Persons engaged in)	1200	1186	14	3	5
Scissors Maker, Cutler	18234	16651	1583	10	2
Scourer, Dyer, Printer, Bleacher, Calenderer, (undefined)	15639	13799	1840	17	5
Screw, Bolt, Nut, Rivet, Staple—Maker	8017	5673	2344	21	12
Scripture Reader, Missionary, Itinerant Preacher	3925	2265	1660	3	1
Sculptor	832	816	16	3	7
Seal, Die, Coin, Medal—Maker	1539	1486	53	10	7
Seaman (Merchant Service)	85093	85093	.	6	3
Seaman, R.N.	16811	16811	.	2	2
Seamstress, Shirt Maker	83244	1379	81865	18	1
Seed, Corn, Flour—Merchant, Dealer	9696	8913	783	16	3
Seedsman, Nurseryman, Florist	7755	7021	734	7	3
Servant, Domestic Indoor	1280668	50262	1230406	4	1
Servant, Inn, Hotel	62310	35823	26487	4	1
Shawl Manufacture	616	208	408	18	1
Sheep, Cattle, Pig—Dealer, Salesman	5754	5729	25	8	1
Shepherd	22844	22844	.	7	1
Ship, Boat, Barge—Builder	21741	21702	39	13	1
Ship Carpenter, Shipwright (ashore)	23930	23930	.	13	1
Ship, Land, House—Surveyor	5394	5394	.	3	6
Ship, Life, House, &c., Insurance Service	15068	14821	247	5	3
Ship Rigger, Chandler, Fitter	2861	2834	27	13	2
Ship Steward, Cook	6767	6381	386	6	3
Shipwright, Ship Carpenter (ashore)	23930	23930	.	13	1
Shirt Maker, Seamstress	83244	1379	81865	18	1
Shoe, Boot—Maker, Dealer	216556	180884	35672	18	1
Shop and House Fittings,—Maker, Dealer	3021	2815	206	11	2
Shopkeeper (General), Dealer	54860	29088	25772	22	1
Short-hand Writer, Reporter	2677	2662	15	3	5
Showman, Performer, Exhibition Service	1881	1361	520	3	8
Silk Dyer, Printer	1630	1512	118	17	2
Silk Merchant, Dealer	1302	1184	118	17	2
Silk, Silk Goods, Manufacture	57349	17655	39694	17	2
Silver, Gold, Beater	663	663	.	21	7
Silversmith, Goldsmith, Jeweller	24715	20962	3753	21	7
Sister of Charity, Nun	3795	.	3795	3	1
Size, Glue, Gelatine, Isinglass,—Maker, Dealer	655	497	158	19	1
Skinner, Furrier	8148	4683	3465	19	2
Slate Quarrier	14900	14900	.	21	3
Slate Worker, Dealer	1172	1140	32	21	3
Slater, Tiler	7483	7469	14	11	1
Snuff Box, Tobacco Pipe, &c., Maker	2441	1703	738	15	1
Soap Boiler, Maker	2326	2047	279	19	1
Soldier and Non-commissioned Officer	56936	56936	.	2	1
Solicitor, Barrister	17386	17386	.	3	2
Soot Merchant, Chimney Sweep	6817	6740	77	23	1

RANK OR OCCUPATION.	PERSONS.	M.	F.	Reference to Classified Arrangement.	
				Order.	Sub-order.
Spice, Mustard, Vinegar, Pickle Maker, Dealer	1509	825	684	16	3
Spinning and Weaving Machine Maker	19896	19209	687	10	1
Spirit, Wine—Merchant, Agent	7889	7467	422	16	2
Stable Keeper (Livery),—Omnibus, Coach, Cab, Owner	6787	6547	240	6	2
Stainer (Paper)	2267	1822	445	20	4
Staple, Bolt, Nut, Rivet, Screw—Maker	8017	5673	2344	21	12
Stationer, Law Stationer	15241	9980	5261	20	4
Staymaker, Milliner, Dressmaker	360232	2637	357595	18	1
Steel and Iron (other than Nail, Anchor, and Chain) Manufacture	200677	198786	1891	21	8
Steel Pen Maker	2723	220	2503	10	2
Steel Plate and Copper Plate Printer	415	403	12	9	2
Steward, Cook (Ship)	6767	6381	386	6	3
Stick, Umbrella, Parasol,—Maker, Dealer	8230	4118	4112	15	1
Stoker, Driver (Railway Engine)	22856	22856	.	6	1
Stoker, Engine Driver, Fireman (neither railway, marine, nor agricultural)	66137	66137	.	22	2
Stone Cutter, Dresser, Dealer	6847	6847	.	21	3
Stone Quarrier	23870	23870	.	21	3
Strap, Portmanteau, Bag, &c. (Leather Goods)—Maker, Dealer	5370	4024	1346	19	2
Straw Hat, Bonnet, Plait, Manufacture	30984	3001	27983	18	1
Straw (not plait) Hay, Chaff—Cutter, Dealer	2648	2598	50	20	2
Stuff, Worsted, Cloth, Flannel, Blanket—Dealer	3613	3533	80	17	1
Stuff, Worsted, Manufacture	99237	35436	63801	17	1
Sugar Refiner	3070	2951	119	16	3
Superintendent, Manufacturer Manager (undefined)	7436	6884	552	22	1
Surgeon, Physician, General Practitioner	15116	15091	25	3	3
Surgical Instrument Maker	1511	1181	330	10	4
Surveyor, Contractor, Inspector (Road)	1326	1326	.	21	3
Sweep (Chimney), Soot Merchant	6817	6740	77	23	1
Sweeper (Crossing), Scavenger	2868	2694	174	23	1
Sword, Bayonet,—Maker, Cutler	190	186	4	10	5
Tackle (Fishing), Rod, &c. Maker	1461	898	563	10	8
Tailor	160648	107668	52980	18	1
Tallow Chandler, Candle, Grease, Manufacture	3235	3013	222	19	1
Tanner, Fellmonger	10248	10157	91	19	2
Tape Manufacturer, Dealer	1891	732	1159	17	3
Tea, Coffee, Chocolate,—Maker, Dealer, Grocer	129818	103396	26422	16	3
Teacher, Professor, Lecturer	34941	6336	28605	3	4
Telegraph, Telephone, Service	9442	7214	2228	6	5
Textile, Fancy Goods—Manufacturer, Worker, Dealer	7573	1388	6185	17	5
Thatcher	3710	3710	.	20	2
Theatre, Art, Music, Service	1392	1111	281	8	7
Theological Student	2925	2925	.	3	1
Thread Manufacturer, Dealer	2170	498	1672	17	3
Ticket, Label, Writer	1140	642	498	20	4
Tile, Brick—Maker, Burner, Dealer	50075	47337	2738	21	4
Tiler, Slater	7483	7469	14	11	1
Timber, Wood—Merchant, Dealer	12773	11795	978	20	3
Tin Miner	12402	10499	1903	21	1
Tin, Tin Plate, Tin Goods—Manufacturer, Worker, Dealer	36923	32392	4531	21	10
Tobacco Manufacturer, Tobacconist	19734	11159	8575	15	1
Tobacco Pipe, Snuff Box, &c., Maker	2441	1703	738	15	1
Toll Collector, Turnpike Gate Keeper	1104	717	387	6	3
Tool Maker, Dealer	9353	9162	191	10	2
Tortoise-shell, Ivory, Bone, Horn—Worker, Dealer	1865	1710	155	19	1
Town Drainage Service	1363	1363	.	23	1
Toy (Gilt), Fancy Chain, Maker	1042	342	700	21	12
Toy Maker, Dealer	2332	1099	1233	10	8
Tramway Companies' Service	2650	2644	6	6	2
Traveller, Commercial	35478	35478	.	5	1
Tricycle, Bicycle—Maker, Dealer	1072	1059	13	12	1
Trimming Maker, Dealer	6499	1611	4888	17	5
Turner, Fitter (Engine and Machine)	64663	64663	.	10	1
Turner (Wood), Box Maker	13977	11382	2595	20	3

Table 6 *cont.*—OCCUPATIONS of MALES and FEMALES, enumerated in England and Wales, arranged in Alphabetical Order.

RANK OR OCCUPATION.	PERSONS.	M.	F.	Reference to Classified Arrangement. Order.	Sub-order.
Turnpike Gate Keeper, Toll Collector	1104	717	387	6	2
Twine, Rope, Cord—Maker, Dealer	11751	9658	2093	17	4
Type Cutter, Founder	1189	1137	52	10	7
Umbrella, Parasol, Stick—Maker, Dealer	8230	4118	4112	18	1
Undertaker, Funeral Furniture Maker	1893	1701	192	11	2
Union, Municipal, Parish, District—Officer	14812	11895	3017	1	2
Unoccupied Class—Persons returned by Property, Rank, &c., and not by special occupation	14786875	4856256	9930619	24	1
Upholsterer, Cabinet Maker	59746	51761	7985	11	2
Valuer, Auctioneer, Appraiser, House Agent	10075	10016	59	5	1
Vellum, Parchment—Maker, Dealer	431	407	24	19	2
Vermin Destroyer	1223	1219	4	8	1
Veterinary Surgeon, Farrier	7511	7511	.	8	1
Vinegar, Mustard, Spice, Pickle—Maker, Dealer	1509	825	684	16	3
Volunteers, Militia, Yeomanry	10747	10747	.	2	1
Warehouseman (not Manchester)	30869	26699	4170	6	4
Washing and Bathing Service	180078	3408	176670	4	2
Watch Maker, Clock Maker	23351	22576	775	10	3
Watchman, Messenger, Porter (neither Railway nor Government)	131171	129561	1610	6	5
Waterman, Bargeman, Lighterman	30823	30490	333	6	3
Waterproof Goods — Maker, Dealer	1583	1233	350	20	1
Waterworks Service	2525	2517	8	21	6
Weaver (undefined)	4841	2230	2611	17	5
Weaving and Spinning Machine Maker	19896	19209	687	10	1
Weigher, Meter	1157	1157	.	6	4
Weighing and Measuring Apparatus Maker	2586	2401	185	16	3
Well Sinker, Borer	1490	1490	.	21	3
Wharf, Harbour, Dock, Lighthouse, Service	42643	42573	70	6	3
Wheel Chair Proprietor, Attendant, &c.	857	843	14	6	2
Wheelwright	28732	28635	97	12	1
Whip, Harness, Maker, Saddler	23866	21831	2035	12	2
White Metal, Plated Ware, Manufacture, Pewterer	5629	4791	838	21	12
Whitesmith	8253	8212	41	21	8
Whitewasher, Plasterer	29841	29800	41	11	1
Wig Maker, Hairdresser	14933	14165	768	18	1
Willow, Cane, Rush—Worker, Dealer, Basketmaker	11542	9017	2525	20	2
Wine, Spirit—Merchant, Agent	7889	7467	422	16	2
Wire Maker, Worker, Weaver, Drawer	9243	8722	521	21	12
Wood Carver	3108	3080	28	11	3
Wood, Timber — Merchant, Dealer	12773	11795	978	20	3
Wood Turner, Box Maker	13977	11392	2585	20	3
Wooden Fence, Lath, Hurdle, Maker	2937	2919	18	20	3
Woodman	8151	8151	.	7	2
Wool, Woollen Goods—Dyer, Printer	2798	2754	44	17	1
Woollen Cloth Manufacture	115808	57307	58501	17	1
Woolstapler	2474	2446	28	17	1
Worsted, Cloth, Stuff, Flannel, Blanket—Dealer	5613	5533	80	17	1
Worsted, Stuff, Manufacture	99237	35436	63801	17	1
Writer (Ticket, Label)	1140	644	496	20	4
Yard, Mast, Oar, Block, Maker	1419	1419	.	13	2
Yeomanry, Militia, Volunteers	10747	10747	.	2	1
Zinc, Zinc Goods—Manufacturer, Worker, Dealer	2265	2241	24	21	10

Table 7.—Country of Birth of Males and Females, enumerated in England and Wales.

Where Born.	1881.			1871.		
	Males.	Females.	Persons.	Persons.	Males.	Females.
TOTAL ENUMERATED IN ENGLAND AND WALES	12639902	13334537	25974439	22712266	11058934	11653332
ENGLAND	11387256	12094797	23482053	20272886	9841436	10431440
WALES	668027	705742	1373769	1419280	692077	727203
SCOTLAND	132483	121045	253528	213254	113889	99365
IRELAND	290468	271906	562374	566540	283231	283309
ISLANDS IN THE BRITISH SEAS	13151	16165	29316	25655	11413	14242
BRITISH COLONIES OR DEPENDENCIES	42981	51418	94399	70812	31724	39088
FOREIGN PARTS:						
British Subjects	29285	27088	56373	38807	20073	18734
Foreign Subjects	74681	43318	117999	100638	63623	37015
AT SEA:						
British Subjects	2154	2442	4596	4395	2066	2329
Foreign Subjects	16	16	32	*	*	*

Table 8.—County of Birth of enumerated Natives of England and Wales.

County of Birth.	Persons.	Males.	Females.
TOTAL BORN AND ENUMERATED IN ENGLAND AND WALES	24855822	12055283	12800539
LONDON	2986655	1418006	1568649
Middlesex (*Intra-metropolitan*)	2127560	1005969	1121591
Surrey (*Intra-metropolitan*)	661525	317581	343944
Kent (*Intra-metropolitan*)	197570	94456	103114
SOUTH-EASTERN COUNTIES	2304673	1115882	1188791
Surrey (*Extra-metropolitan*)	335150	162399	172751
Kent (*Extra-metropolitan*)	703131	340342	362789
Sussex	464409	226830	237579
Hampshire	565988	271772	294216
Berkshire	236015	114539	121476
SOUTH-MIDLAND COUNTIES	1725340	840228	885112
Middlesex (*Extra-metn.*)	275372	131764	143608
Hertfordshire	226110	109200	116910
Buckinghamshire	220049	108089	111960
Oxfordshire	222867	108769	114098
Northamptonshire	298398	147006	151392
Huntingdonshire	78305	38574	40731
Bedfordshire	173985	85567	88418
Cambridgeshire	229254	111259	117995
EASTERN COUNTIES	1551899	752956	798943
Essex	550769	267669	283100
Suffolk	445785	216854	228931
Norfolk	555345	268333	287012
SOUTH-WESTERN COUNTIES	2189938	1036256	1153682
Wiltshire	329908	159955	169953
Dorsetshire	234883	112859	122024
Devonshire	687749	324329	363420
Cornwall	386898	176796	210102
Somersetshire	550500	262317	288183
WEST-MIDLAND COUNTIES	3135026	1528676	1606350
Gloucestershire	606641	292410	314231
Herefordshire	146944	71601	75343
Shropshire	313531	153073	160458
Staffordshire	977353	480511	496842
Worcestershire	393847	191951	201896
Warwickshire	696710	339130	357580
NORTH-MIDLAND COUNTIES	1738320	857157	881163
Leicestershire	332902	163660	169242
Rutlandshire	28606	14170	14436
Lincolnshire	537137	263863	273274
Nottinghamshire	381226	188440	192786
Derbyshire	458449	227024	231425
NORTH-WESTERN COUNTIES	3440142	1673071	1767071
Cheshire	608589	298738	309851
Lancashire	2831553	1374333	1457220
YORKSHIRE	2684925	1315767	1369158
NORTHERN COUNTIES	1454786	715500	739286
Durham	694258	342801	351457
Northumberland	427891	210208	217683
Cumberland	254898	124018	130880
Westmorland	77759	38473	39286
MONMOUTHSHIRE AND WALES	1568214	763286	804928
Monmouthshire	194445	95259	99186
Glamorganshire	375153	184069	191084
Carmarthenshire	149235	72271	76964
Pembrokeshire	112238	53009	59229
Cardiganshire	87063	41007	46056
Brecknockshire	66197	32846	33351
Radnorshire	33794	16878	16916
Montgomeryshire	81828	40349	41479
Flintshire	88495	43893	44602
Denbighshire	120986	59943	61043
Merionethshire	51125	25227	25898
Carnarvonshire	113241	54628	58613
Anglesey	61722	29842	31880
Wales (*County not stated*)	32692	14065	18627
ENGLAND (*County not stated*)	75904	38498	37406

Table 9.—Country of Birth of all Foreigners enumerated in England and Wales.

Country of Birth.	Persons.	Males.	Females.
TOTAL FOREIGNERS ENUMERATED IN ENGLAND AND WALES	118031	74097	43934
EUROPE.			
Denmark	1748	1416	332
Norway	3203	2742	461
Sweden	2966	2550	416
Russia	3789	2639	1150
Poland (Russian)	10679	6097	4582
Austria	2368	1857	511
Hungary	441	342	99
Switzerland	4089	2232	1857
German Empire	37301	23714	13587
Holland	5357	3104	2253
Belgium	2462	1450	1012
France	14596	7775	6821
Portugal	332	244	88
Spain	1433	1128	305
Italy	6504	5344	1160
Greece	695	604	91
Turkey	599	453	146
Servia	4	2	2
Roumania	91	64	27
Total of European Foreigners	98617	63717	34900
ASIA.			
Arabia	33	32	1
Persia	16	10	6
China	202	180	22
Other Countries	233	181	52
Total Asian Foreigners	484	403	81
AFRICA.			
Egypt	77	47	30
Other Parts	181	137	44
Total African Foreigners	258	184	74
AMERICA.			
United States	17767	9226	8541
Mexico	65	40	25
Brazil	179	111	68
Other States	485	297	188
Total American Foreigners	18496	9674	8822
Country not stated	144	103	41
Born at Sea	32	16	16

Table 10.—DISTRIBUTION in COUNTIES of enumerated NATIVES of SCOTLAND, IRELAND, and FOREIGN COUNTRIES.

COUNTY IN WHICH ENUMERATED.	SCOTCH.			IRISH.			FOREIGNERS.		
	Persons.	Males.	Females.	Persons.	Males.	Females.	Persons.	Males.	Females.
TOTAL ENUMERATED IN ENGLAND AND WALES	253528	132483	121045	562374	290468	271906	118031	74097	43934
LONDON	49554	26037	23517	80778	37173	43605	60252	37125	23127
MIDDLESEX (*Intra-metropolitan*)	35650	18615	16985	56273	25888	30935	52111	31921	20190
SURREY (*Intra-metropolitan*)	10186	5414	4754	18879	8603	8876	6528	4241	2285
KENT (*Intra-metropolitan*)	3788	2008	1780	7626	3832	3794	1615	963	652
I. SOUTH-EASTERN COUNTIES	18068	9946	8122	29579	16158	13421	7554	4031	3523
SURREY (*Extra-metropolitan*)	3699	1798	1901	4821	2101	2720	1859	886	973
KENT (*Extra-metropolitan*)	4840	2894	1946	8272	4436	3833	2087	1276	811
SUSSEX	2737	1186	1571	3374	1508	1078	1852	956	896
HAMPSHIRE	5747	3537	2210	11441	7231	4210	1351	712	839
BERKSHIRE	1045	551	494	1471	789	682	405	201	204
II. SOUTH-MIDLAND COUNTIES	7375	3739	3636	9131	4339	4792	2839	1488	1351
MIDDLESEX (*Extra-metropolitan*)	3609	1788	1821	5045	2260	2785	1628	864	764
HERTFORDSHIRE	941	469	472	793	410	383	289	139	130
BUCKINGHAMSHIRE	593	297	296	501	260	241	139	76	63
OXFORDSHIRE	582	315	267	562	289	273	241	130	111
NORTHAMPTONSHIRE	715	371	344	1073	547	526	221	104	117
HUNTINGDONSHIRE	120	62	58	153	71	82	33	17	16
BEDFORDSHIRE	416	207	209	494	232	262	131	60	71
CAMBRIDGESHIRE	399	230	169	510	270	240	181	98	83
IV. EASTERN COUNTIES	6360	3522	2838	6948	3562	3386	2268	1447	821
ESSEX	4367	2384	1983	4958	2597	2361	1668	1115	553
SUFFOLK	952	522	430	988	471	407	276	150	126
NORFOLK	1041	616	425	1022	494	528	324	182	142
V. SOUTH-WESTERN COUNTIES	5994	3306	2688	12426	6463	5963	3526	2322	1204
WILTSHIRE	554	280	274	775	378	397	197	78	119
DORSETSHIRE	719	448	271	1431	850	581	234	157	77
DEVONSHIRE	2798	1576	1222	6256	3430	2826	1160	768	392
CORNWALL	843	598	245	1693	928	765	1270	977	293
SOMERSETSHIRE	1280	604	676	2271	877	1394	665	342	323
VI. WEST-MIDLAND COUNTIES	10944	5692	5252	32744	17298	15446	4308	2432	1876
GLOUCESTERSHIRE	2336	1171	1165	5330	2422	2908	1133	706	427
HEREFORDSHIRE	396	197	199	583	250	333	106	41	65
SHROPSHIRE	812	413	399	1860	1034	826	143	56	87
STAFFORDSHIRE	3324	1824	1500	13100	7572	5528	911	494	417
WORCESTERSHIRE	1168	580	588	2243	1143	1100	286	154	132
WARWICKSHIRE	2908	1507	1401	9628	4877	4751	1629	951	678
VII. NORTH-MIDLAND COUNTIES	5327	2850	2477	11336	6230	5106	2898	1841	1057
LEICESTERSHIRE	1036	549	487	1856	967	889	339	192	147
RUTLANDSHIRE	94	50	44	85	55	30	38	16	22
LINCOLNSHIRE	1201	621	580	1921	1100	821	1460	1018	442
NOTTINGHAMSHIRE	1380	713	667	2255	1151	1104	687	413	274
DERBYSHIRE	1616	917	699	5219	2957	2262	374	202	172
VIII. NORTH-WESTERN COUNTIES	63701	32151	31550	235965	117396	118569	16749	11102	5647
CHESHIRE	7869	3883	3986	23615	12108	11507	1799	1266	533
LANCASHIRE	55832	28268	27564	212350	105288	107062	14950	9896	5054
IX. YORKSHIRE	19386	9903	9483	56878	30264	26614	8083	4843	3240
X. NORTHERN COUNTIES	61379	32059	29320	63717	38490	25227	5221	4012	1209
DURHAM	24714	13478	11236	36764	22846	13918	2645	2060	585
NORTHUMBERLAND	23413	12153	11260	12480	7195	5204	2347	1822	525
CUMBERLAND	12207	5922	6285	14093	8255	5838	176	106	70
WESTMORLAND	1045	506	539	371	194	177	53	24	29
XI. MONMOUTHSHIRE AND WALES	5440	3278	2162	22872	13095	9777	4333	3454	879
MONMOUTHSHIRE	677	431	246	5218	2930	2288	696	589	107
GLAMORGANSHIRE	2019	1309	710	11958	6832	5126	2729	2272	457
CARMARTHENSHIRE	239	148	91	362	196	166	78	41	37
PEMBROKESHIRE	305	200	105	991	669	322	106	78	28
CARDIGANSHIRE	109	55	54	103	65	38	41	23	18
BRECKNOCKSHIRE	203	116	87	444	263	181	46	24	22
RADNORSHIRE	43	22	21	47	28	19	11	3	8
MONTGOMERYSHIRE	190	113	77	199	117	82	28	13	15
FLINTSHIRE	399	191	208	1394	786	608	185	141	44
DENBIGHSHIRE	550	266	284	973	528	445	73	31	42
MERIONETHSHIRE	112	64	48	136	95	41	149	111	38
CARNARVONSHIRE	443	261	182	621	313	308	141	87	54
ANGLESEY	151	102	49	426	273	153	50	41	9

Table 11.—DISTRIBUTION in COUNTIES of EUROPEAN FOREIGNERS enumerated in ENGLAND and WALES.

COUNTY IN WHICH ENUMERATED.	COUNTRY OF BIRTH.									
	All European Countries.	Denmark.	Norway.	Sweden.	Russia.	Poland (Russian).	Austria.	Hungary.	Switzerland.	German Empire.
ENGLAND AND WALES	98617	1748	3203	2966	3789	10679	2368	441	4089	87301
I. LONDON	55136	553	598	904	1776	6931	1278	247	2296	21966
MIDDLESEX (*Intra-metropolitan*)	48224	425	387	772	1694	6867	1139	225	1299	18364
SURREY (*Intra-metropolitan*)	5540	108	190	88	54	55	112	16	924	2805
KENT (*Intra-metropolitan*)	1372	20	21	44	28	9	27	6	73	797
II. SOUTH-EASTERN COUNTIES	6471	87	139	132	87	109	95	28	531	2187
SURREY (*Extra-metropolitan*)	1585	15	15	15	8	5	23	5	152	670
KENT (*Extra-metropolitan*)	1777	34	68	80	32	31	32	3	112	562
SUSSEX	1626	12	7	23	18	22	24	2	129	523
HAMPSHIRE	1134	24	48	12	21	47	11	17	107	334
BERKSHIRE	349	2	1	2	8	4	5	1	31	98
III. SOUTH-MIDLAND COUNTIES	2095	25	11	17	26	34	31	11	198	930
MIDDLESEX (*Extra-metropolitan*)	1308	13	6	12	10	22	23	7	121	570
HERTFORDSHIRE	197	2	.	.	3	3	2	1	25	98
BUCKINGHAMSHIRE	69	1	.	.	1	.	1	.	5	25
OXFORDSHIRE	191	2	2	1	8	5	2	.	10	92
NORTHAMPTONSHIRE	130	3	1	2	1	3	1	.	12	61
HUNTINGDONSHIRE	12	.	.	.	.	1	.	.	1	6
BEDFORDSHIRE	90	.	1	1	1	.	1	1	19	38
CAMBRIDGESHIRE	98	4	1	1	2	.	1	2	5	40
IV. EASTERN COUNTIES	1732	29	55	52	37	35	22	4	71	973
ESSEX	1308	21	17	35	19	32	14	2	35	808
SUFFOLK	213	2	25	6	9	2	3	2	13	75
NORFOLK	211	6	13	11	9	1	5	.	23	90
V. SOUTH-WESTERN COUNTIES	2302	102	158	107	81	17	58	7	105	687
WILTSHIRE	93	.	.	.	1	1	1	.	8	46
DORSETSHIRE	190	5	11	9	20	1	2	1	12	67
DEVONSHIRE	807	29	57	36	28	12	18	4	47	231
CORNWALL	808	63	87	59	27	.	33	2	5	201
SOMERSETSHIRE	404	5	3	3	5	3	4	.	33	142
VI. WEST-MIDLAND COUNTIES	2628	26	72	52	86	284	58	6	167	952
GLOUCESTERSHIRE	833	9	64	43	16	69	27	3	52	220
HEREFORDSHIRE	55	2	.	.	.	.	1	.	10	27
SHROPSHIRE	84	.	.	.	.	1	.	.	15	34
STAFFORDSHIRE	408	9	3	1	8	46	9	3	25	173
WORCESTERSHIRE	163	1	1	.	2	3	2	.	16	73
WARWICKSHIRE	1085	5	4	8	60	165	19	.	49	425
VII. NORTH-MIDLAND COUNTIES	2339	69	164	66	90	136	31	5	85	1096
LEICESTERSHIRE	230	.	.	1	5	14	7	1	17	77
RUTLANDSHIRE	34	.	.	.	.	.	1	.	8	19
LINCOLNSHIRE	1342	61	163	56	55	63	5	3	16	706
NOTTINGHAMSHIRE	521	3	.	5	27	50	7	1	24	206
DERBYSHIRE	212	5	1	4	3	9	11	.	20	88
VIII. NORTH-WESTERN COUNTIES	11714	224	871	533	616	1389	426	91	412	3972
CHESHIRE	1237	17	141	36	31	10	177	22	74	352
LANCASHIRE	10477	207	730	497	585	1379	249	69	338	3620
IX. YORKSHIRE	6547	151	286	267	611	1414	93	28	119	2673
X. NORTHERN COUNTIES	4408	412	627	645	237	179	97	12	54	1304
DURHAM	2152	99	317	380	146	33	13	1	22	745
NORTHUMBERLAND	2097	311	306	264	87	143	82	10	17	487
CUMBERLAND	123	2	3	.	4	3	2	1	10	57
WESTMORLAND	36	.	1	1	.	.	.	.	5	15
XI. MONMOUTHSHIRE AND WALES	3245	70	222	191	140	151	179	2	51	561
MONMOUTHSHIRE	572	14	46	28	32	40	28	.	8	70
GLAMORGANSHIRE	2156	51	161	135	102	102	141	2	14	345
CARMARTHENSHIRE	32	2	.	.	1	2	.	.	1	18
PEMBROKESHIRE	83	3	4	8	3	.	2	.	6	24
CARDIGANSHIRE	18	.	4	3	.	.	1	.	1	5
BRECKNOCKSHIRE	11	.	.	.	.	3	.	.	.	8
RADNORSHIRE	5	.	.	.	.	.	.	.	1	3
MONTGOMERYSHIRE	12	.	.	.	.	.	.	.	2	6
FLINTSHIRE	129	.	.	.	.	.	1	.	5	30
DENBIGHSHIRE	37	.	.	1	.	.	2	.	3	14
MERIONETHSHIRE	95	.	.	1	.	.	.	.	4	7
CARNARVONSHIRE	51	.	4	4	2	4	2	.	4	16
ANGLESEY	45	.	3	11	.	.	2	.	3	15

Table 11 *continued*.—DISTRIBUTION in COUNTIES of EUROPEAN FOREIGNERS enumerated IN ENGLAND and WALES.

COUNTY IN WHICH ENUMERATED.	COUNTRY OF BIRTH. Holland.	Belgium.	France.	Portugal.	Spain.	Italy.	Greece.	Turkey.	Servia.	Roumania.
ENGLAND AND WALES	5357	2462	14596	292	1433	6504	695	599	4	91
I. LONDON	4193	1492	8251	151	473	3504	228	253	4	36
MIDDLESEX (*Intra-metropolitan*)	3893	1252	7025	134	417	3202	175	214	4	33
SURREY (*Intra-metropolitan*)	262	216	1039	12	48	225	49	35	.	3
KENT (*Intra-metropolitan*)	38	24	187	5	8	77	4	4	.	.
II. SOUTH-EASTERN COUNTIES	166	297	2021	16	76	432	35	27	.	6
SURREY (*Extra-metropolitan*)	48	77	428	6	21	92	6	5	.	.
KENT (*Extra-metropolitan*)	60	144	487	2	11	104	4	16	.	1
SUSSEX	48	43	636	2	25	99	1	5	.	4
HAMPSHIRE	14	23	328	4	12	104	24	3	.	1
BERKSHIRE	2	10	142	2	7	33	.	1	.	.
III. SOUTH-MIDLAND COUNTIES	75	67	503	6	36	112	4	3	.	7
MIDDLESEX (*Extra-metropolitan*)	57	40	337	5	24	48	3	3	.	7
HERTFORDSHIRE	2	8	29	.	4	15	.	.	.	.
BUCKINGHAMSHIRE	2	2	21	.	3	7	1	.	.	.
OXFORDSHIRE	2	7	44	.	4	12	.	.	.	.
NORTHAMPTONSHIRE	2	8	29	.	1	6	.	.	.	.
HUNTINGDONSHIRE	.	.	2	1	.	1	.	.	.	.
BEDFORDSHIRE	8	2	16	.	.	7	.	.	.	.
CAMBRIDGESHIRE	7	5	14	.	.	16	.	.	.	.
IV. EASTERN COUNTIES	62	59	227	2	12	82	4	5	.	1
ESSEX	44	52	160	2	11	52	2	2	.	.
SUFFOLK	10	5	35	.	1	22	.	2	.	1
NORFOLK	8	2	32	.	.	8	2	1	.	.
V. SOUTH-WESTERN COUNTIES	66	48	589	9	3	214	43	8	.	.
WILTSHIRE	.	2	27	.	.	7	.	.	.	.
DORSETSHIRE	1	1	47	1	1	8	3	.	.	.
DEVONSHIRE	26	9	219	4	2	76	8	1	.	.
CORNWALL	26	14	201	3	.	49	31	7	.	.
SOMERSETSHIRE	13	22	95	1	.	74	1	.	.	.
VI. WEST-MIDLAND COUNTIES	45	68	472	3	16	300	6	5	.	10
GLOUCESTERSHIRE	14	18	184	1	3	108	1	1	.	.
HEREFORDSHIRE	.	3	8	.	1	3	.	.	.	.
SHROPSHIRE	1	2	10	.	1	11	.	.	.	.
STAFFORDSHIRE	5	13	70	.	2	36	3	.	.	2
WORCESTERSHIRE	3	1	49	1	1	8	.	2	.	.
WARWICKSHIRE	22	31	142	1	8	134	2	2	.	8
VII. NORTH-MIDLAND COUNTIES	110	43	320	2	6	106	8	2	.	.
LEICESTERSHIRE	8	17	50	.	2	29	1	1	.	.
RUTLANDSHIRE	.	1	5	.	.	.	.	.	.	.
LINCOLNSHIRE	91	15	79	1	.	24	3	1	.	.
NOTTINGHAMSHIRE	8	8	144	.	1	36	1	.	.	.
DERBYSHIRE	3	2	42	1	3	17	3	.	.	.
VIII. NORTH-WESTERN COUNTIES	295	147	793	72	717	681	195	252	.	28
CHESHIRE	40	13	88	6	170	41	4	13	.	2
LANCASHIRE	255	134	705	66	547	640	191	239	.	26
IX. YORKSHIRE	149	83	323	15	23	263	40	6	.	3
X. NORTHERN COUNTIES	161	64	285	7	18	230	58	18	.	.
DURHAM	94	26	138	3	3	80	28	4	.	.
NORTHUMBERLAND	67	35	113	4	14	133	30	14	.	.
CUMBERLAND	.	3	24	.	1	13	.	.	.	.
WESTMORLAND	.	.	10	.	.	4	.	.	.	.
XI. MONMOUTHSHIRE AND WALES	35	94	813	9	53	580	74	20	.	.
MONMOUTHSHIRE	17	7	169	2	22	89	5	1	.	.
GLAMORGANSHIRE	12	78	440	7	20	455	68	19	.	.
CARMARTHENSHIRE	.	.	7	.	.	1	.	.	.	.
PEMBROKESHIRE	.	1	17	.	6	9	.	.	.	.
CARDIGANSHIRE	.	.	3	.	.	1	.	.	.	.
BRECKNOCKSHIRE	.	.	.	.	.	.	.	.	.	.
RADNORSHIRE	.	.	1	.	.	.	.	.	.	.
MONTGOMERYSHIRE	.	.	1	.	.	2	.	.	.	.
FLINTSHIRE	2	2	82	.	1	5	1	.	.	.
DENBIGHSHIRE	.	2	7	.	.	8	.	.	.	.
MERIONETHSHIRE	1	1	76	.	3	2	.	.	.	.
CARNARVONSHIRE	2	2	6	.	1	4	.	.	.	.
ANGLESEY	1	1	4	.	.	4	2	.	.	.

Table 12.—Country of Birth and Ages of European Foreigners, Males and Females, enumerated in England and Wales.

Where Born.	All Ages.			Under 15 Years.	15–	20–	25–	45–	65 and upwards.
	Both Sexes.	Males and Females.							
TOTAL NATIVES OF EUROPEAN STATES	98617	M.	63717	3241	5376	9838	32027	10733	1539
		F.	34900	3084	3214	5906	16321	5439	346
DENMARK	1748	M.	1416	28	75	269	844	178	22
		F.	332	30	16	58	175	43	10
NORWAY	3203	M.	2742	60	349	617	1489	219	8
		F.	461	76	42	88	213	35	7
SWEDEN	2966	M.	2550	35	188	569	1514	224	19
		F.	416	28	30	97	217	36	2
RUSSIA	3789	M.	2639	194	237	609	1275	280	44
		F.	1150	195	130	202	479	128	16
POLAND (RUSSIAN)	10679	M.	6097	673	556	974	2847	882	165
		F.	4582	663	564	740	1963	565	87
AUSTRIA	2368	M.	1857	74	131	295	1196	236	25
		F.	511	66	45	84	244	65	7
HUNGARY	441	M.	342	8	17	52	185	66	14
		F.	99	17	10	16	43	13	.
SWITZERLAND	4089	M.	2232	55	188	470	1202	266	51
		F.	1857	55	223	502	882	163	32
GERMAN EMPIRE	37301	M.	23714	896	1779	3653	12208	4532	565
		F.	13587	900	1131	2309	6698	2257	301
HOLLAND	5357	M.	3104	142	209	296	1522	803	132
		F.	2253	157	148	194	991	606	157
BELGIUM	2462	M.	1450	129	69	157	731	326	38
		F.	1012	100	76	117	460	220	39
FRANCE	14596	M.	7775	832	836	837	3693	1522	255
		F.	6821	568	602	1129	3230	1061	231
PORTUGAL	292	M.	204	11	16	29	103	35	10
		F.	88	14	10	6	38	14	6
SPAIN	1433	M.	1128	58	188	143	620	101	18
		F.	305	47	36	50	131	36	5
ITALY	6504	M.	5344	210	487	763	2859	867	158
		F.	1160	132	123	135	525	155	30
GREECE	695	M.	604	7	28	83	364	116	6
		F.	91	3	5	13	49	18	3
TURKEY	599	M.	453	23	38	67	238	76	9
		F.	146	19	15	32	64	14	12
SERVIA	4	M.	2	.	.	.	2	.	.
		F.	2	.	.	1	1	.	.
ROUMANIA	91	M.	64	4	6	15	35	4	.
		F.	27	14	2	2	8	1	.

Table 13.—OCCUPATIONS and COUNTRY of BIRTH of EUROPEAN FOREIGNERS, MALES and FEMALES, enumerated in ENGLAND and WALES.

Denmark.		Norway.		Sweden.		Russia.		Poland (Russian).		OCCUPATIONS.	Austria.		Hungary.		Switzerland.		German Empire.	
M.	F.	M.	F.	M.	F.	M.	F.	M.	F.		M.	F.	M.	F.	M.	F.	M.	F.
1416	332	2742	461	2550	416	6339	1150	6067	4582	TOTAL - -	1557	511	342	99	2232	1867	23714	13587
										I. PROFESSIONAL CLASS.								
										1. PERSONS ENGAGED IN THE GENERAL OR LOCAL GOVERNMENT OF THE COUNTRY.								
										1. *National Government.*								
.	.	.	.	.	.	.	.	.	.	Peer, M.P., Privy Councillor (not otherwise described) - -	.	.	.	.	.	.	.	.
.	.	.	.	1	.	.	.	.	.	Civil Service (officers and clerks) -	.	.	.	.	.	.	1	.
.	.	.	.	.	.	.	.	.	.	Civil Service (messengers, &c.) -	.	.	.	.	.	.	9	.
.	.	.	.	2	.	.	.	.	.	Prison Officer, &c. - - -	.	.	.	.	.	.	1	1
										2. *Local Government.*								
1	.	1	.	1	.	.	.	.	.	Police - - - -	.	.	.	.	1	.	12	.
.	1	.	.	.	.	.	.	.	.	Municipal, Parish, Union, District, Officer	.	.	.	.	.	.	3	.
.	.	.	.	.	.	.	.	.	.	Other Local or County Official - -	.	.	.	.	.	.	.	.
										3. *East Indian and Colonial Service.*								
.	.	.	.	.	.	.	.	.	.	East Indian and Colonial Service -	.	.	.	.	.	.	.	.
										2. PERSONS ENGAGED IN THE DEFENCE OF THE COUNTRY.								
										1. *Army (at Home).*								
.	.	.	.	4	.	.	.	.	.	Army Officer (effective or retired) -	.	.	.	.	1	.	4	.
.	.	.	.	1	.	.	.	.	.	Soldier and Non-commissioned Officer -	.	.	.	.	1	.	7	.
.	.	.	.	.	.	.	.	.	.	Militia, Yeomanry, Volunteers - -	.	.	.	.	.	.	1	.
.	.	.	.	.	.	.	.	.	.	Army Pensioner - - -	.	.	.	.	.	.	.	.
										2. *Navy (ashore or in port).*								
.	.	1	.	.	.	1	.	.	.	Navy Officer (effective or retired) - -	.	.	.	.	.	.	.	.
.	.	.	.	1	.	.	.	.	.	Seaman, R.N. - - - -	.	.	.	.	.	.	2	.
.	.	.	.	.	.	.	.	.	.	Royal Marines (officers and men) -	.	.	.	.	.	.	.	.
.	.	.	.	.	.	.	.	.	.	Navy Pensioner - - - -	.	.	.	.	.	.	3	.
										3. PERSONS ENGAGED IN PROFESSIONAL OCCUPATIONS (WITH THEIR IMMEDIATE SUBORDINATES).								
										1. *Clerical Profession.*								
.	.	2	.	.	.	7	.	3	.	Clergyman (Established Church) -	4	.	.	.	4	.	18	.
.	.	.	.	.	.	.	.	.	.	Roman Catholic Priest - - -	6	.	.	.	8	.	105	.
4	.	3	.	4	.	20	.	21	.	Minister, Priest, of other religious bodies	1	.	.	.	2	.	21	.
.	.	7	.	3	1	16	.	5	.	Missionary, Scripture Reader, Itinerant Preacher - - -	3	1	.	.	1	.	9	.
.	1	.	.	.	1	.	.	.	4	Nun, Sister of Charity - - -	.	3	.	.	.	6	.	75
.	.	.	.	.	.	.	.	2	.	Theological Student - - - -	.	.	1	.	7	.	32	.
.	.	.	.	.	.	3	.	4	.	Church, Chapel, Cemetery—Officer, Servant - - - -	.	.	.	.	.	3	.	1
										2. *Legal Profession.*								
.	.	.	.	.	.	.	.	1	.	Barrister, Solicitor - - - -	1	.	1	.	.	.	9	.
.	.	.	.	.	.	.	.	.	.	Law Student - - - -	.	.	.	.	.	.	.	.
.	.	1	.	.	.	.	.	.	.	Law Clerk, and others connected with Law - - - - -	.	.	.	.	.	.	2	.
										3. *Medical Profession.*								
3	.	1	.	2	.	7	.	3	.	Physician, Surgeon, General Practitioner	3	.	1	.	6	.	52	.
1	.	.	.	1	.	1	.	2	.	Dentist - - - - -	1	.	.	.	3	.	9	.
.	.	.	.	.	.	.	.	.	.	Medical Student, Assistant -	2	.	.	.	.	.	4	.
.	.	.	.	.	.	.	.	.	1	Midwife - - - -	.	.	.	.	.	.	.	.
.	.	.	.	.	.	.	1	2	3	Subordinate Medical Service -	2	.	1	.	1	1	18	2
										4. *Teachers.*								
.	.	.	.	.	1	1	.	14	1	Schoolmaster - - - -	2	1	1	.	18	15	42	35
.	15	1	4	6	25	28	30	63	6	Teacher, Professor, Lecturer - - -	23	45	6	6	98	427	325	1625
.	.	.	.	.	.	.	.	1	.	School Service, and others concerned in Teaching - - -	.	.	.	.	.	.	1	.
										5. *Literary and Scientific Persons.*								
1	1	.	.	.	.	3	.	1	.	Author, Editor, Journalist - -	8	.	2	.	7	.	28	8
.	.	.	.	1	.	1	.	1	.	Reporter, Short-hand Writer -	1	.	.	.	.	.	4	.
.	.	.	.	.	.	1	.	1	.	Persons engaged in Scientific Pursuits -	3	.	.	.	.	.	12	.
5	.	5	.	8	.	5	.	4	.	Literary, Scientific, Institution, Service, &c. - - - -	6	.	1	.	5	1	41	4
										6. *Engineers and Surveyors.*								
9	.	4	.	15	.	4	.	2	.	Civil Engineer - - -	7	.	.	.	7	.	68	.
.	.	1	.	.	.	.	.	.	.	Mining Engineer - - -	.	.	.	.	.	.	8	.
.	.	5	.	.	.	1	.	.	.	Land, House, Ship, Surveyor - -	.	.	.	.	1	.	6	.
										7. *Artists.*								
7	.	1	.	4	2	8	1	4	.	Painter (artist) - - - -	15	3	2	.	4	2	98	10
1	.	.	.	.	.	.	.	1	.	Engraver (artist) - - -	3	.	.	.	3	.	12	1
.	.	.	.	.	.	.	.	1	.	Sculptor - - -	1	.	.	.	3	.	11	.
1	.	.	.	1	.	.	.	.	.	Architect - - -	.	.	.	.	3	.	4	.
5	2	4	.	6	5	7	5	8	.	Musician, Music Master - -	25	6	6	1	17	8	786	94
.	.	.	.	.	.	.	.	.	.	Art Student - - -	.	.	.	.	.	1	2	1
1	.	2	.	1	.	3	.	9	.	Photographer - - -	2	.	.	.	2	.	41	3
.	.	.	.	.	.	1	2	3	2	Actor - - -	.	1	.	1	.	.	18	7
.	.	.	1	1	.	1	.	1	.	Art, Music, Theatre, Service - -	1	.	.	.	3	1	6	1

Table 13 *continued*.—OCCUPATIONS and COUNTRY of BIRTH of EUROPEAN FOREIGNERS, MALES and FEMALES, enumerated in ENGLAND and WALES.

Denmark.		Norway.		Sweden.		Russia.		Poland (Russian).		OCCUPATIONS.	Austria.		Hungary.		Switzer-land.		German Empire.	
M.	F.	M.	F.	M.	F.	M.	F.	M.	F.		M.	F.	M.	F.	M.	F.	M.	F.
										8. *Persons engaged in Exhibitions, Shows, Games, &c.*								
.	.	1	.	1	.	.	.	1	.	Performer, Showman, Exhibition, Service	10	1	.	.	.	.	4	6
.	.	.	.	2	.	.	.	.	.	Billiard, Cricket, & other Games, Service	1	.	.	.	1	.	5	.
										II. DOMESTIC CLASS.								
										4. PERSONS ENGAGED IN DOMESTIC OFFICES OR SERVICES.								
										1. *Domestic Service.*								
1	.	.	.	2	.	1	.	1	.	Domestic Coachman, Groom	.	.	.	.	2	.	15	.
15	.	3	.	3	.	.	.	.	.	Domestic Gardener	3	.	.	.	10	.	85	.
6	71	11	91	9	129	3	38	10	110	Domestic Indoor Servant	45	61	6	11	256	807	431	2553
.	.	.	.	.	.	.	.	.	.	Lodge, Gate, Park, Keeper (not Government)	.	.	.	.	.	.	1	.
9	1	3	1	14	1	4	2	2	.	Inn, Hotel, Servant	80	1	7	.	251	3	849	28
.	.	.	.	1	.	.	.	1	.	College, Club, Service	.	.	.	.	.	.	16	.
										2. *Other Service.*								
.	.	.	.	1	.	.	.	.	.	Office Keeper (not Government)	.	.	.	.	1	.	3	.
3	12	.	25	.	28	1	6	2	8	Cook (not domestic)	3	4	1	1	90	22	80	446
.	1	.	2	.	.	.	.	.	6	Charwoman	.	.	.	.	.	.	.	37
.	2	1	3	.	8	.	.	.	14	Washing and Bathing Service	.	.	.	.	3	4	12	105
.	1	.	.	.	.	.	.	.	.	Hospital and Institution Service	.	.	.	.	1	1	12	21
.	.	.	.	1	.	.	.	.	.	Others engaged in Service	5	.	.	.	21	.	24	1
										III. COMMERCIAL CLASS.								
										5. PERSONS ENGAGED IN COMMERCIAL OCCUPATIONS.								
										1. *Merchants and Agents.*								
36	.	28	.	30	.	27	.	20	.	Merchant	52	.	12	.	86	.	969	3
35	.	47	.	40	.	21	.	30	1	Broker, Agent, Factor	51	.	10	.	51	.	464	2
.	.	.	.	.	.	.	.	1	.	Auctioneer, Appraiser, Valuer, House Agent	1	.	.	.	.	.	5	.
4	.	.	.	.	.	.	.	.	.	Accountant	2	.	.	.	1	.	17	.
5	.	.	.	1	.	2	.	3	.	Salesman, Buyer (not otherwise described)	.	.	.	.	1	.	15	3
8	.	3	.	9	.	102	.	107	.	Commercial Traveller	41	.	11	.	19	.	296	.
101	2	77	.	100	.	56	1	21	.	Commercial Clerk	94	.	37	.	221	3	1781	14
.	.	.	.	.	.	.	.	.	.	Officer of Commercial Company, Guild, Society, &c.	.	.	.	.	.	.	.	.
										2. *Dealers in Money.*								
1	.	.	.	.	.	.	.	.	.	Banker	3	.	.	.	5	.	16	.
.	.	.	.	.	.	3	.	.	.	Bank Service	2	.	.	.	11	.	47	.
.	.	.	.	.	.	4	.	10	.	Bill Discounter, Bill Broker, Finance Agent	2	.	.	.	2	.	6	.
										3. *Persons occupied in Insurance.*								
1	.	.	.	2	.	.	.	1	.	Life, House, Ship, &c., Insurance Service	4	.	.	.	3	.	15	.
										6. PERSONS ENGAGED IN CONVEYANCE OF MEN, GOODS, AND MESSAGES.								
										1. *On Railways.*								
.	.	.	.	.	.	.	.	1	.	Railway Engine Driver, Stoker	.	.	.	.	.	.	.	.
.	.	.	.	.	.	.	.	.	.	Railway Guard	.	.	.	.	.	.	1	.
.	.	.	.	.	.	.	.	.	.	Pointsman, Level Crossing Man	.	.	.	.	.	.	.	.
2	.	2	.	3	.	1	.	1	.	Other Railway Officials and Servants	.	.	.	.	.	.	15	.
										2. *On Roads.*								
.	.	.	.	.	.	.	.	.	.	Toll Collector, Turnpike Gate Keeper	.	.	.	.	.	.	1	.
1	.	.	.	.	.	.	.	.	.	Omnibus, Coach, Cab, Owner—Livery Stable Keeper	.	.	.	.	.	.	4	.
.	.	.	.	.	.	.	.	1	.	Cabman, Flyman, Coachman (not domestic)	.	.	.	.	.	.	22	.
1	.	4	.	3	.	3	.	.	.	Carman, Carrier, Carter, Haulier	.	.	.	.	5	.	23	.
.	.	.	.	.	.	.	.	.	.	Tramway Companies' Service	.	.	.	.	.	.	1	.
.	.	.	.	.	.	.	.	2	.	Wheel Chair Proprietor, Attendant, &c.	.	.	.	.	.	.	3	.
										3. *On Canals, Rivers, and Seas.*								
.	.	.	.	.	.	.	.	.	.	Inland Navigation Service	.	.	.	.	.	.	1	.
.	.	2	.	1	.	.	.	.	.	Bargeman, Lighterman, Waterman	.	.	.	.	.	.	1	.
1	.	4	.	.	.	.	.	.	.	Navigation Service (on shore)	.	.	.	.	.	.	5	.
635	.	1922	.	1473	.	506	.	11	.	Seaman (Merchant Service)	342	.	15	.	11	.	1725	.
.	.	.	.	.	.	.	.	.	.	Pilot	.	.	.	.	.	.	1	.
46	2	94	1	60	15	12	.	.	.	Ship Steward, Cook	12	.	.	.	1	.	130	4
.	.	1	.	2	.	.	.	.	.	Boatman on Seas	.	.	.	.	.	.	3	.
10	.	14	.	11	.	6	.	4	.	Harbour, Dock, Wharf, Lighthouse, Service	4	.	.	.	1	.	70	.
										4. *In Storage.*								
3	.	.	.	.	.	2	.	4	.	Warehouseman (not Manchester)	2	.	.	.	3	.	51	.
.	.	.	.	.	.	.	.	.	.	Meter, Weigher	.	.	.	.	.	.	.	.
										5. *In conveying Messages, Porterage, &c.*								
5	.	5	.	7	.	9	.	20	.	Messenger, Porter, Watchman (neither Railway nor Government)	6	.	1	.	54	.	129	.
10	.	1	1	1	.	1	.	.	.	Telegraph, Telephone, Service	1	.	.	.	1	.	13	.

Table 13 *continued*.—Occupations and Country of Birth of European Foreigners, Males and Females, enumerated in England and Wales.

Denmark.		Norway.		Sweden.		Russia.		Poland (Russian).		Occupations.	Austria.		Hungary.		Switzerland.		German Empire.	
M.	F.	M.	F.	M.	F.	M.	F.	M.	F.		M.	F.	M.	F.	M.	F.	M.	F.
										IV. Agricultural Class.								
										7. Persons engaged in Agriculture.								
										1. *In Fields and Pastures.*								
6	.	.	.	10	.	11	.	4	.	Farmer, Grazier	1	.	.	.	11	.	68	.
.	.	.	.	.	.	.	.	.	.	Farmer's, Grazier's—Son, Grandson, Brother, Nephew	.	.	.	.	.	.	7	.
.	.	.	.	.	.	.	.	.	.	Farm Bailiff	.	.	.	.	.	.	1	.
.	.	21	.	32	2	.	.	20	3	Agricultural Labourer, Farm Servant, Cottager	14	.	.	.	11	.	28	.
.	.	.	.	1	.	.	.	.	.	Shepherd	.	.	.	.	.	.	.	.
.	.	.	.	.	.	.	.	.	.	Land Drainage Service (not in towns)	.	.	.	.	.	.	.	.
.	.	.	.	.	.	.	.	.	.	Agricultural Machine—Proprietor, Attendant	.	.	.	.	.	.	.	.
.	.	.	.	.	.	.	.	.	.	Agricultural Student, Pupil	.	.	.	.	.	.	3	.
.	.	.	.	.	.	.	.	.	.	Others engaged in, or connected with, Agriculture	.	.	.	.	.	.	6	.
										2. *In Woods.*								
.	.	.	.	.	.	.	.	.	.	Woodman	.	.	.	.	.	.	.	.
										3. *In Gardens.*								
1	.	.	.	1	.	.	.	2	.	Nurseryman, Seedsman, Florist	2	.	.	.	7	.	25	2
.	.	.	.	.	.	.	.	.	.	Gardener (not domestic)	.	.	.	.	.	.	1	2
										8. Persons engaged about Animals.								
										1. *About Animals.*								
.	.	.	.	.	.	1	.	1	.	Horse Proprietor, Breeder, Dealer	.	.	.	.	.	.	7	.
1	.	.	.	1	.	5	.	2	.	Groom, Horse-keeper, Horse-breaker	.	.	3	.	.	.	4	.
.	.	.	.	.	.	.	.	1	.	Veterinary Surgeon, Farrier	.	.	.	.	.	.	4	.
10	.	.	.	.	.	.	.	.	.	Cattle, Sheep, Pig—Dealer, Salesman	.	.	.	.	.	.	20	.
.	.	.	.	.	.	.	.	.	.	Drover	.	.	.	.	.	.	1	.
.	.	.	.	.	.	.	.	.	.	Gamekeeper	.	.	.	.	.	.	.	.
.	.	.	.	.	.	.	.	1	.	Dog, Bird, Animal—Keeper, Dealer	.	.	.	.	.	.	7	.
.	.	.	.	.	.	.	.	.	.	Vermin destroyer	.	.	.	.	.	.	.	.
13	.	16	.	5	.	4	.	1	.	Fisherman	.	.	.	.	.	.	15	.
.	.	.	.	.	.	.	.	.	.	Knacker, Catsmeat Dealer, &c., &c.	.	.	.	.	1	.	.	.
										V. Industrial Class.								
										9. Persons working and dealing in Books, Prints, and Maps.								
										1. *Books.*								
.	.	.	.	.	.	2	.	6	.	Publisher, Bookseller, Librarian	2	.	.	.	2	.	31	1
.	.	.	.	.	.	.	.	.	.	Music—Publisher, Seller, Printer	1	.	.	.	.	.	15	1
.	.	.	.	1	.	3	.	5	.	Bookbinder	3	.	1	.	2	.	28	2
1	.	2	.	4	.	11	.	12	.	Printer	3	.	1	.	17	.	75	1
3	.	.	.	.	.	.	.	1	.	Newspaper Agent, News Room Keeper	.	.	.	.	1	.	6	1
.	.	.	.	.	.	.	.	.	.	Others	.	.	.	.	.	.	.	.
										2. *Prints and Maps.*								
.	.	.	.	1	.	2	.	.	.	Lithographer, Lithographic Printer	2	.	.	1	.	1	39	.
.	.	.	.	.	.	.	.	.	.	Copper Plate and Steel Plate Printer	.	.	.	.	.	.	.	.
.	.	.	.	1	.	.	.	.	.	Map and Print—Colourer, Seller	1	.	.	.	.	.	8	1
										10. Persons working and dealing in Machines and Implements.								
										1. *Machines.*								
10	.	12	.	17	.	15	.	3	.	Engine, Machine, Maker	15	.	1	.	18	.	127	1
.	.	.	.	.	.	.	.	.	.	Millwright	1	.	.	.	.	.	.	.
10	.	23	.	12	.	9	.	8	.	Fitter, Turner (Engine and Machine)	5	.	.	.	8	.	72	.
.	.	.	.	.	.	.	.	.	.	Boiler Maker	.	.	.	.	.	.	4	.
.	.	.	.	.	.	.	.	.	.	Spinning and Weaving Machine Maker	.	.	.	.	.	.	1	.
.	.	.	.	.	.	.	.	.	.	Agricultural Machine and Implement Maker	.	.	.	.	.	.	1	.
.	.	.	.	.	.	.	.	.	.	Domestic Machinery—Maker, Dealer	.	.	.	.	.	.	.	.
										2. *Tools and Implements.*								
.	.	.	.	.	.	.	.	.	.	Tool Maker, Dealer	1	.	.	.	.	1	5	.
.	.	.	.	.	.	.	.	.	.	Cutler, Scissors Maker	2	.	.	.	1	.	8	.
.	.	.	.	.	.	.	.	.	.	File Maker	.	.	.	.	.	.	3	.
.	.	.	.	.	.	.	.	.	.	Saw Maker	1	.	.	.	.	.	.	.
.	.	.	.	.	.	.	.	.	.	Pin Maker	.	.	.	.	.	.	.	.
.	.	.	.	.	.	.	.	.	.	Needle Maker	.	.	.	.	.	.	1	.
.	.	.	.	.	.	.	.	.	.	Steel Pen Maker	.	.	.	.	.	.	.	1
.	.	.	.	.	.	.	.	.	.	Pencil Maker (Wood)	.	.	.	.	.	.	1	.
.	.	.	.	.	.	.	.	.	.	Domestic Implement Maker	.	.	.	.	.	.	.	.
										3. *Watches and Philosophical Instruments.*								
16	.	10	.	11	.	16	.	27	.	Watch Maker, Clock Maker	13	.	4	.	61	.	885	3
1	.	2	.	.	.	1	.	1	.	Philosophical Instrument Maker, Optician	1	.	2	.	2	.	20	.
7	.	.	.	8	.	2	.	.	.	Electrical Apparatus Maker	5	.	.	.	5	.	28	.
.	.	.	.	.	.	.	.	2	.	Weighing and Measuring Apparatus Maker	.	.	.	.	.	.	4	.

Table 13 *continued*.—OCCUPATIONS and COUNTRY of BIRTH of EUROPEAN FOREIGNERS, MALES and FEMALES, enumerated in ENGLAND and WALES.

Denmark.		Norway.		Sweden.		Russia.		Poland (Russian).		OCCUPATIONS.	Austria.		Hungary.		Switzerland.		German Empire.	
M.	F.	M.	F.	M.	F.	M.	F.	M.	F.		M.	F.	M.	F.	M.	F.	M.	F.
										4. Surgical Instruments.								
.	.	.	.	1	.	1	.	1	.	Surgical Instrument Maker	2	.	2	.	1	.	27	.
										5. Arms and Ordnance.								
1	.	.	.	.	.	.	.	.	.	Gunsmith, Gun Manufacturer	1	.	.	.	.	.	7	.
.	.	.	.	.	.	.	.	.	.	Ordnance Manufacturer	.	.	.	.	.	.	.	.
.	.	.	.	.	.	.	.	.	.	Sword, Bayonet—Maker, Cutler	.	.	.	.	.	.	.	.
.	.	.	.	.	.	.	.	.	.	Others	.	.	.	.	.	.	.	.
										6. Musical Instruments.								
3	.	4	.	.	.	1	.	6	.	Musical Instrument Maker, Dealer	2	.	3	1	4	.	90	1
										7. Type, Dies, Medals, Coins.								
.	.	.	.	.	.	.	.	.	.	Type Cutter, Founder	.	.	.	.	1	.	4	.
.	.	.	.	.	.	1	.	1	.	Die, Seal, Coin, Medal, Maker	1	.	.	.	1	.	3	.
										8. Tackle for Sports and Games.								
.	.	.	.	.	.	.	.	.	.	Toy Maker, Dealer	.	.	1	.	1	.	11	2
.	.	.	.	.	.	.	.	.	.	Fishing Rod, Tackle, Maker, Dealer	.	.	.	.	.	.	.	.
.	.	.	.	.	.	.	.	.	.	Apparatus for other Games, Maker, Dealer	.	.	.	.	.	.	.	.
										11. PERSONS WORKING AND DEALING IN HOUSES, FURNITURE AND DECORATIONS.								
										1. Houses.								
1	.	.	.	1	.	.	.	2	.	Builder	.	.	.	.	1	.	8	.
16	.	22	.	19	.	17	.	35	.	Carpenter, Joiner	10	.	.	.	4	.	128	.
.	.	.	.	.	.	.	.	2	.	Bricklayer	1	.	.	.	1	.	14	.
.	.	.	.	.	.	1	.	1	.	Mason	.	.	.	.	2	.	25	.
.	.	.	.	.	.	.	.	.	.	Slater, Tiler	.	.	.	.	.	.	5	.
.	.	.	.	.	.	.	.	1	1	Plasterer, Whitewasher	.	.	.	.	.	.	1	.
.	.	1	.	.	.	1	.	5	.	Paperhanger	.	.	.	.	.	.	4	1
.	.	.	.	2	.	1	.	7	.	Plumber	1	.	1	.	3	.	10	.
6	.	7	.	7	.	134	.	315	.	Painter, Glazier	18	.	4	.	9	.	142	1
										2. Furniture and Fittings.								
23	.	8	.	13	1	58	.	110	.	Cabinet Maker, Upholsterer	36	.	9	1	27	.	579	7
.	.	.	.	.	.	.	.	1	.	French Polisher	.	.	.	.	.	.	6	.
1	.	1	.	.	.	5	.	6	.	Furniture Broker, Dealer	2	.	.	.	1	.	8	2
1	.	.	.	.	.	1	.	1	.	Locksmith, Bellhanger	.	.	.	.	1	.	18	1
.	.	1	.	.	.	1	.	1	.	Gas Fitter	.	.	1	.	.	.	7	.
1	.	.	.	.	.	.	.	.	.	House and Shop Fittings—Maker, Dealer	1	.	.	.	.	.	10	.
.	.	.	.	1	.	.	.	.	.	Funeral Furniture Maker, Undertaker	.	.	1	.	.	.	1	.
.	.	.	.	.	.	.	.	.	.	Others	.	.	.	.	.	.	.	.
										3. House Decorations.								
1	.	2	.	.	.	1	.	2	.	Wood Carver	.	.	.	.	1	.	20	.
.	.	.	.	.	.	14	.	24	.	Carver, Gilder	5	.	2	.	5	1	76	1
3	.	.	.	.	.	8	1	8	2	Dealer in Works of Art	1	1	2	.	1	.	41	1
.	.	.	.	.	.	.	.	.	.	Figure, Image—Maker, Dealer	.	.	.	.	1	.	.	.
1	.	.	.	.	.	.	.	.	.	Animal, Bird, &c., Preserver, Naturalist	.	.	.	.	.	.	5	.
.	.	.	.	.	.	.	.	.	.	Artificial Flower Maker	.	.	.	.	1	.	.	6
										12. PERSONS WORKING AND DEALING IN CARRIAGES AND HARNESS.								
										1. Carriages.								
3	.	.	.	.	.	.	.	3	.	Coachmaker	1	.	.	.	1	.	22	.
.	.	.	.	1	.	.	.	1	.	Railway Carriage, Railway Wagon, Maker	.	.	.	.	.	.	2	.
.	.	1	.	1	.	.	.	2	.	Wheelwright	.	.	.	.	1	.	5	.
.	.	.	.	.	.	.	.	.	.	Bicycle, Tricycle—Maker, Dealer	.	.	.	.	.	.	.	.
.	.	.	.	.	.	.	.	.	.	Others	.	.	.	.	.	.	1	.
										2. Harness.								
.	.	1	.	1	.	.	.	4	.	Saddler, Harness, Whip, Maker	.	.	.	.	4	.	10	.
										13. PERSONS WORKING AND DEALING IN SHIPS AND BOATS.								
										1. Hull.								
8	.	1	.	1	1	2	.	.	.	Ship, Boat, Barge, Builder	.	.	.	.	.	.	4	.
5	.	10	.	11	.	6	.	.	.	Shipwright, Ship Carpenter (ashore)	.	.	.	.	.	.	36	.
										2. Masts, Rigging, &c.								
.	.	.	.	.	.	.	.	.	.	Mast, Yard, Oar, Block, Maker	.	.	.	.	.	.	6	.
11	.	7	.	13	.	4	.	.	.	Ship Rigger, Chandler, Fitter	5	.	.	.	.	.	27	.
1	.	4	.	.	.	1	.	1	.	Sail Maker	.	.	.	.	.	.	14	.

Table 13 *continued*.—OCCUPATIONS and COUNTRY of BIRTH of EUROPEAN FOREIGNERS, MALES and FEMALES, enumerated in ENGLAND and WALES.

Denmark.		Norway.		Sweden.		Russia.		Poland (Russian).		OCCUPATIONS.	Austria.		Hungary.		Switzerland.		German Empire.	
M.	F.	M.	F.	M.	F.	M.	F.	M.	F.		M.	F.	M.	F.	M.	F.	M.	F.
										14. PERSONS WORKING AND DEALING IN CHEMICALS AND COMPOUNDS.								
										1. *Colouring Matter.*								
.	.	.	.	.	.	.	.	.	.	Dye, Paint, Manufacture	.	.	.	.	.	.	3	.
.	.	.	.	.	.	.	.	.	.	Ink, Blacking, Colouring Substance, Manufacture	.	.	.	.	2	.	1	.
										2. *Explosives.*								
.	.	.	.	.	.	.	.	.	.	Gunpowder, Guncotton, Explosive Substance, Manufacture	.	.	.	.	.	.	1	.
.	.	.	.	.	.	.	.	.	.	Fusee, Fireworks, Explosive Article, Manufacture	.	.	.	.	.	.	4	.
										3. *Drugs and other Chemicals and Compounds.*								
.	.	2	.	.	.	2	.	.	.	Chemist, Druggist	1	.	.	.	11	.	54	.
1	.	.	.	.	.	1	.	2	1	Manufacturing Chemist	3	.	.	.	1	.	26	.
.	.	.	.	.	.	.	.	7	.	Alkali Manufacture	.	.	.	.	.	.	.	.
.	.	.	.	.	.	.	.	.	.	Drysalter	.	.	.	.	2	.	3	.
										15. PERSONS WORKING AND DEALING IN TOBACCO AND PIPES.								
										1. *Tobacco and Pipes.*								
2	.	3	.	1	.	44	1	72	6	Tobacco Manufacturer, Tobacconist	7	1	5	.	8	1	133	9
.	.	.	.	.	.	1	.	1	.	Tobacco Pipe, Snuff Box, &c., Maker	7	.	.	.	.	.	7	.
										16. PERSONS WORKING AND DEALING IN FOOD AND LODGING.								
										1. *Board and Lodging.*								
6	.	2	.	10	.	3	.	1	.	Innkeeper, Hotel Keeper, Publican	8	.	2	1	25	3	162	5
7	.	9	3	9	2	5	1	2	1	Lodging, Boarding House, Keeper	9	.	.	1	13	5	51	37
4	1	2	.	2	.	4	1	4	.	Coffee, Eating House, Keeper	4	1	1	.	54	1	51	5
										2. *Spirituous Drinks.*								
.	.	.	.	.	.	.	.	.	.	Hop—Merchant, Dealer	1	.	.	.	.	.	11	.
1	.	.	.	.	.	.	.	.	.	Maltster	.	.	.	.	.	.	2	.
1	.	1	.	.	.	.	.	.	.	Brewer	.	.	.	.	3	.	12	.
.	.	.	.	3	.	.	.	.	.	Beerseller, Ale, Porter, Cider, Dealer	.	.	.	.	.	.	24	1
1	.	.	.	.	.	1	.	.	.	Cellarman	.	.	.	.	4	.	24	1
.	.	1	.	4	.	3	.	.	.	Wine, Spirit—Merchant, Agent	5	.	1	.	4	.	68	.
										3. *Food.*								
.	.	.	.	.	.	2	.	3	.	Milkseller, Dairyman	.	.	.	.	.	.	6	1
2	.	.	.	.	.	.	.	.	.	Cheesemonger, Butterman	.	.	1	.	.	.	4	.
3	.	1	.	6	.	7	.	23	.	Butcher, Meat Salesman	4	.	2	.	2	.	730	13
4	.	1	.	3	.	.	.	8	.	Provision Curer, Dealer	3	.	2	.	3	.	45	1
.	.	1	.	.	.	1	.	1	.	Poulterer, Game Dealer	.	.	.	.	.	.	1	2
.	.	1	.	.	.	.	.	4	1	Fishmonger	.	.	.	.	.	.	.	.
7	.	.	.	.	.	.	.	1	.	Corn, Flour, Seed—Merchant, Dealer	.	.	6	.	9	.	17	.
1	.	.	.	.	.	.	.	.	.	Corn Miller	1	.	2	.	1	.	35	.
3	.	.	1	.	.	13	.	22	.	Baker	8	.	.	.	8	.	2020	23
1	.	2	.	.	.	1	.	8	3	Confectioner, Pastrycook	5	.	1	.	168	14	92	10
.	.	1	.	1	.	.	.	1	2	Greengrocer, Fruiterer	.	.	1	.	2	.	43	6
.	.	.	.	.	.	.	.	.	.	Mustard, Vinegar, Spice, Pickle—Maker, Dealer	.	.	.	.	.	.	1	.
2	.	2	.	3	.	6	.	48	.	Sugar Refiner	4	.	17	.	2	.	443	1
2	.	3	.	5	.	12	.	23	2	Grocer, Tea, Coffee, Chocolate—Maker, Dealer	3	.	.	.	13	.	73	6
.	.	.	.	.	.	.	.	.	.	Ginger Beer, Mineral Water—Manufacturer, Dealer	.	.	.	.	1	.	4	1
.	.	.	.	.	.	.	.	.	.	Others dealing in Food	.	.	.	.	.	.	.	.
										17. PERSONS WORKING AND DEALING IN TEXTILE FABRICS.								
										1. *Wool and Worsted.*								
.	.	.	.	.	.	.	.	.	.	Woolstapler	1	.	.	.	2	.	24	.
.	.	.	.	.	.	.	.	.	.	Woollen Cloth Manufacture	.	.	.	.	.	.	5	1
.	.	.	.	.	.	.	.	.	.	Wool, Woollen goods—Dyer, Printer	.	.	.	.	.	.	.	.
.	.	.	.	.	.	.	.	.	.	Worsted, Stuff, Manufacture	.	.	.	.	.	.	2	3
.	.	.	.	.	.	.	.	.	.	Flannel Manufacture	.	.	.	.	.	.	.	.
.	.	.	.	.	.	.	.	.	.	Blanket Manufacture	.	.	.	.	.	.	.	.
.	.	.	.	.	.	.	.	.	.	Fuller	.	.	.	.	.	.	.	.
.	.	.	.	.	.	.	.	3	.	Cloth, Worsted, Stuff, Flannel, Blanket, Dealer	.	.	.	.	2	.	26	.
.	.	.	.	.	.	.	.	.	.	Others	.	.	.	.	.	.	.	.
										2. *Silk.*								
.	.	.	.	.	.	.	.	.	1	Silk, Silk goods, Manufacture	1	.	.	.	1	.	15	1
.	.	.	.	.	.	.	.	.	.	Silk Dyer, Printer	.	.	.	.	.	.	1	1
.	.	.	.	.	.	.	.	.	.	Ribbon Manufacture	.	.	.	.	.	.	.	.
.	.	.	.	.	.	.	.	.	.	Crape, Gauze, Manufacture	.	.	.	.	.	.	.	.
.	.	.	.	.	.	.	.	1	1	Silk Merchant, Dealer	1	.	.	.	7	.	11	.

Table 13 *continued*.—OCCUPATIONS and COUNTRY of BIRTH of EUROPEAN FOREIGNERS, MALES and FEMALES, enumerated in ENGLAND and WALES.

Denmark.		Norway.		Sweden.		Russia.		Poland (Russian).		OCCUPATIONS.	Austria.		Hungary.		Switzerland.		German Empire.	
M.	F.	M.	F.	M.	F.	M.	F.	M.	F.		M.	F.	M.	F.	M.	F.	M.	F.
										3. Cotton and Flax.								
				1						Cotton, Cotton goods, Manufacture					3		4	4
										Cotton, Calico—Printer, Dyer, Bleacher					1		2	
										Cotton, Calico—Warehouseman, Dealer	2				1		17	
		1								Flax, Linen—Manufacturer, Dealer					1		1	
										Lace Manufacturer, Dealer					6		16	2
										Fustian Manufacturer, Dealer								
										Tape Manufacturer, Dealer							1	
										Thread Manufacturer, Dealer								
										4. Hemp and other Fibrous Materials.								
										Hemp, Jute, Cocoa Fibre, Manufacture							1	
1				1			1			Rope, Twine, Cord—Maker, Dealer							5	
						1				Mat Maker, Seller							1	
										Net Maker							1	
										Canvas, Sailcloth, Manufacture								
										Sacking, Sack, Bag—Maker, Dealer	7						20	1
								1		Others working and dealing in Hemp							1	1
										5. Mixed or Unspecified Materials.								
										Weaver (undefined)							4	6
						2		2		Dyer, Printer, Scourer, Bleacher, Calenderer (undefined)	1				1		42	1
										Factory hand (Textile, undefined)							4	4
										Felt Manufacture							2	
								3		Carpet, Rug, Manufacture							1	
										Manchester Warehouseman								
6		6		2		18		10	2	Draper, Linen Draper, Mercer	1		1		2	1	30	6
					1			1		Fancy Goods (Textile), Manufacturer, Worker, Dealer						1	2	6
						3		7		Trimming Maker, Dealer	6	2					12	8
	1									Embroiderer					9	3	8	6
								1		Others							1	1
										18. PERSONS WORKING AND DEALING IN DRESS.								
										1. Dress.								
		1				30	1	117	3	Hatter, Hat Manufacture (not straw)	20		1				53	
										Straw—Hat, Bonnet, Plait, Manufacture					1		1	
32	4	36	4	135	5	464	64	2274	472	Tailor	104	12	44	1	28		1484	235
	6		14		10	5	15	3	52	Milliner, Dressmaker, Staymaker	4	12	3	1	1	39	32	245
										Shawl Manufacture								
	1		1		2		7	1	55	Shirt Maker, Seamstress		2		1		5	3	70
										Hosiery Manufacture							1	4
								2		Hosier, Haberdasher					2		7	4
1										Glover, Glove Maker							2	
		1					2			Button Maker, Dealer	1						6	
11		9		21		127		510	15	Shoe, Boot—Maker, Dealer	32		8		11		878	25
										Patten, Clog, Maker								
6		1		8	1	14	1	82	6	Wig Maker, Hairdresser	15		4		23	1	375	8
2						10		38		Umbrella, Parasol, Stick—Maker, Dealer	9						111	4
										Accoutrement Maker							1	
								2	4	Old Clothes Dealer, and others							7	5
										19. PERSONS WORKING AND DEALING IN VARIOUS ANIMAL SUBSTANCES.								
										1. In Grease, Gut, Bone, Horn, Ivory, and Whalebone.								
								1		Tallow Chandler, Candle, Grease, Manufacture							6	
										Soap Boiler, Maker			1		1		13	
										Glue, Size, Gelatine, Isinglass—Maker, Dealer								
										Manure Manufacture							3	
										Bone, Horn, Ivory, Tortoise-shell—Worker, Dealer	1		1		1		19	
										Comb Maker							1	
						2	1	11		Others							16	1
										2. In Skins.								
3				1	1	70	14	110	57	Furrier, Skinner	47	13	15	3	2		432	16
										Tanner, Fellmonger							7	
2						2		6		Currier	3		1				38	
				3		5		5		Leather Goods, Portmanteau, Bag, Strap, &c., Maker, Dealer	1				2		57	1
										Parchment, Vellum—Maker, Dealer								
										3. In Hair and Feathers.								
										Hair, Bristle—Worker, Dealer							6	
1										Brush, Broom, Maker							9	1
						1		2		Quill, Feather—Dresser, Dealer							4	2

Table 13 *continued*.—OCCUPATIONS and COUNTRY of BIRTH of EUROPEAN FOREIGNERS, MALES and FEMALES, enumerated in ENGLAND and WALES.

Denmark.		Norway.		Sweden.		Russia.		Poland (Russian).		OCCUPATIONS.	Austria.		Hungary.		Switzerland.		German Empire.	
M.	F.	M.	F.	M.	F.	M.	F.	M.	F.		M.	F.	M.	F.	M.	F.	M.	F.
										20. PERSONS WORKING AND DEALING IN VARIOUS VEGETABLE SUBSTANCES.								
										1. *In Oils, Gums, and Resins.*								
.	.	.	.	.	.	.	.	.	.	Oil Miller, Oil Cake—Maker, Dealer	.	.	.	.	1	.	6	.
.	.	.	.	1	.	.	.	.	.	Oil and Colourman	.	.	.	.	.	.	4	.
.	.	.	.	.	.	.	.	.	.	Floor Cloth, Oil Cloth, Manufacture	1	.	.	.	.	.	.	.
1	.	.	.	.	.	.	.	1	.	Japanner	.	.	.	.	.	.	1	.
.	.	.	.	.	.	.	.	3	.	India Rubber, Gutta Percha—Worker, Dealer	2	1	.	.	.	.	.	.
.	.	.	.	.	.	9	2	40	7	Waterproof Goods—Maker, Dealer	8	.	.	.	.	.	8	.
1	.	.	.	.	.	.	.	.	.	Others	.	.	.	.	.	.	2	.
										2. *In Cane, Rush, and Straw.*								
1	.	.	.	2	.	.	.	2	.	Willow, Cane, Rush—Worker, Dealer, Basketmaker	.	.	.	.	1	.	36	2
.	.	.	.	.	.	.	.	.	.	Hay, Straw (not plait), Chaff—Cutter, Dealer	.	.	.	.	1	.	1	.
.	.	.	.	.	.	.	.	.	.	Thatcher	.	.	.	.	.	.	.	.
										3. *In Wood and Bark.*								
2	.	4	.	4	.	1	.	.	.	Timber, Wood—Merchant, Dealer	.	.	.	.	.	.	10	.
.	.	1	.	1	.	.	.	2	.	Sawyer	1	.	.	.	.	.	1	.
.	.	.	.	.	.	.	.	.	.	Lath, Wooden Fence, Hurdle, Maker	.	.	.	.	.	.	5	.
.	.	.	.	.	.	.	.	3	.	Wood Turner, Box Maker	2	.	.	.	.	.	14	.
1	.	.	.	.	.	.	.	.	.	Cooper. Hoop Maker, Bender	1	.	.	.	.	.	61	.
.	.	.	.	.	.	.	.	.	.	Cork, Bark—Cutter, Worker, Dealer	1	.	.	.	.	.	2	.
.	.	.	.	.	.	.	.	.	.	Others	.	.	.	.	.	.	.	.
										4. *In Paper.*								
.	.	.	.	1	.	.	.	1	.	Paper Manufacture	1	.	.	.	1	.	14	.
.	.	.	.	.	.	.	.	.	.	Envelope Maker	.	.	.	.	.	.	.	.
.	.	.	.	.	.	.	.	2	1	Stationer, Law Stationer	3	.	1	.	2	1	13	.
.	.	.	.	.	.	.	.	.	.	Card, Pattern Card, Maker	.	.	.	.	.	.	2	.
.	.	.	.	.	.	.	.	1	.	Paper Stainer	.	.	.	.	.	.	.	.
1	.	.	.	1	.	.	.	.	.	Paper Box, Paper Bag, Maker	.	.	.	.	2	.	7	5
.	.	.	.	.	.	.	.	.	.	Ticket, Label, Writer	.	.	.	.	.	.	1	.
.	.	.	.	.	.	.	.	.	.	Others	.	.	.	.	.	.	1	.
										21. PERSONS WORKING AND DEALING IN VARIOUS MINERAL SUBSTANCES.								
										1. *Miners.*								
2	.	3	.	1	.	.	.	1	.	Coal Miner	.	.	.	.	.	.	34	.
.	.	.	.	2	.	.	.	.	.	Ironstone Miner	.	.	.	.	.	.	3	.
.	.	.	.	.	.	.	.	.	.	Copper Miner	.	.	.	.	.	.	.	.
.	.	.	.	.	.	.	.	.	.	Tin Miner	.	.	.	.	.	.	.	.
.	.	.	.	.	.	.	.	.	.	Lead Miner	.	.	.	.	.	.	.	.
2	.	.	.	2	.	.	.	.	.	Miner in other, or undefined, Minerals	2	.	.	.	.	.	29	2
.	.	.	.	.	.	.	.	.	.	Mine Service	.	.	.	.	.	.	.	.
										2. *Coal, Coal Gas, &c.*								
3	.	2	.	1	.	1	.	2	.	Coal Merchant, Dealer	.	.	1	.	.	.	11	.
1	.	4	.	2	.	.	.	.	.	Coalheaver	.	.	.	.	.	.	2	.
.	.	1	.	.	.	.	.	.	.	Coke, Charcoal, Peat—Cutter, Burner, Dealer	.	.	.	.	.	.	5	.
1	.	1	.	1	.	.	.	1	.	Gas Works Service	.	.	.	.	.	.	51	.
										3. *Stone, Clay, and Road Making.*								
.	.	.	.	.	.	.	.	.	.	Stone Quarrier	.	.	.	.	.	.	.	.
.	.	.	.	.	.	.	.	.	.	Stone Cutter, Dresser, Dealer	.	.	.	.	.	.	1	.
.	.	.	.	.	.	.	.	.	.	Slate Quarrier	.	.	.	.	.	.	.	.
.	.	.	.	.	.	.	.	.	.	Slate Worker, Dealer	.	.	.	.	.	.	.	.
1	.	.	.	.	.	.	.	.	.	Limeburner	.	.	.	.	.	.	.	.
.	.	.	.	.	.	.	.	.	.	Clay, Sand, Gravel, Chalk—Labourer, Dealer	.	.	.	.	.	.	.	.
.	.	.	.	.	.	.	.	.	.	Fossil, Coprolite—Digger, Dealer	.	.	.	.	.	.	.	.
.	.	.	.	.	.	.	.	.	.	Well Sinker, Borer	.	.	.	.	.	.	3	.
.	.	.	.	.	.	.	.	.	.	Plaster, Cement, Manufacture	.	.	.	.	.	.	.	.
.	.	.	.	.	.	.	.	.	.	Brick, Tile—Maker, Burner, Dealer	.	.	.	.	1	.	1	.
.	.	1	.	1	.	.	.	.	.	Paviour	.	.	.	.	.	.	4	.
.	.	.	.	.	.	.	.	.	.	Road Contractor, Surveyor, Inspector	.	.	.	.	.	.	.	.
.	.	.	.	.	.	.	.	.	.	Road Labourer	.	.	.	.	.	.	.	.
.	.	.	.	.	.	.	.	.	.	Railway Contractor	.	.	.	.	.	.	.	.
.	.	.	.	2	.	.	.	1	.	Platelayer	.	.	.	.	.	.	.	.
1	.	.	.	.	.	.	.	.	.	Railway Labourer, Navvy	1	.	.	.	1	.	3	.
.	.	.	.	.	.	.	.	.	.	Others	.	.	.	.	.	.	.	.
										4. *Earthenware and Glass.*								
.	.	2	.	.	.	1	.	.	.	Earthenware, China, Porcelain, Manufacture	.	.	.	.	1	.	12	1
.	.	.	.	.	.	.	.	6	1	Glass Manufacture	22	.	.	.	1	.	38	.
.	.	.	.	.	.	4	.	11	.	Earthenware, China, Glass, Dealer	2	.	.	.	.	.	17	1
										5. *Salt.*								
1	.	.	.	.	.	.	.	.	.	Salt Maker, Dealer	70	.	7	.	1	.	9	.

Table 13 *continued*.—OCCUPATIONS and COUNTRY of BIRTH of EUROPEAN FOREIGNERS, MALES and FEMALES, enumerated in ENGLAND and WALES.

Denmark.		Norway.		Sweden.		Russia.		Poland (Russian).		OCCUPATIONS.	Austria.		Hungary.		Switzerland.		German Empire.	
M.	F.	M.	F.	M.	F.	M.	F.	M.	F.		M.	F.	M.	F.	M.	F.	M.	F.
										6. Water.								
.	.	.	.	.	.	.	.	.	.	Waterworks Service	.	.	.	.	.	.	.	.
.	.	.	.	.	.	.	.	.	.	Others	.	.	.	.	2	.	.	.
										7. Precious Metals and Jewellery.								
7	.	1	.	1	.	25	.	78	1	Goldsmith, Silversmith, Jeweller	59	2	10	.	21	.	257	4
.	.	.	.	.	.	.	.	.	.	Gold, Silver, Beater	.	.	.	.	.	.	.	.
.	.	.	.	.	.	.	.	.	.	Lapidary	.	.	.	.	.	.	2	.
.	.	.	.	.	.	.	.	.	.	Others	.	.	.	.	.	.	1	.
										8. Iron and Steel.								
1	.	8	.	5	.	1	.	5	.	Blacksmith	.	.	.	.	1	.	34	.
1	.	.	.	.	.	.	.	.	.	Whitesmith	.	.	.	.	.	.	1	.
.	.	.	.	.	.	.	.	.	.	Nail Manufacture	.	.	.	.	.	.	2	.
.	.	.	.	.	.	.	.	.	.	Anchor, Chain, Manufacture	.	.	.	.	.	.	.	.
1	.	1	.	8	.	1	.	7	.	Other Iron and Steel Manufactures	.	.	1	.	.	.	64	.
1	.	1	.	2	.	8	.	.	.	Ironmonger, Hardware Dealer, Merchant	1	.	.	.	5	.	13	.
										9. Copper.								
.	.	1	.	.	.	.	.	.	.	Copper, Copper goods—Manufacturer, Worker, Dealer	2	.	.	.	1	.	12	.
										10. Tin and Zinc.								
1	.	.	.	1	.	2	.	20	.	Tin, Tin Plate, Tin goods—Manufacturer, Worker, Dealer	2	.	.	.	2	.	51	.
1	.	.	.	.	.	2	.	2	.	Zinc, Zinc Goods—Manufacturer, Worker, Dealer	.	.	.	.	.	.	15	.
										11. Lead.								
.	.	.	.	.	.	.	.	1	.	Lead, Leaden goods—Manufacturer Worker, Dealer	.	.	.	.	.	.	1	.
										12. In Other, Mixed, or Unspecified, Metals.								
.	.	.	.	.	.	.	.	2	.	Metal Refiner, Worker, Turner, Dealer	3	.	.	.	1	.	16	.
1	.	.	.	2	.	.	.	.	.	Brass, Bronze, Manufacture. Brazier	8	.	.	.	1	.	20	.
.	.	.	.	.	.	.	.	.	.	Metal Burnisher, Lacquerer	.	.	.	.	.	.	.	.
1	.	.	.	.	.	.	.	.	.	White Metal, Plated Ware, Manufacture. Pewterer	1	.	.	.	.	.	2	.
.	.	.	.	.	.	.	.	1	.	Wire Maker, Worker, Weaver, Drawer	.	.	.	.	.	.	8	.
.	.	.	.	.	.	.	.	.	.	Bolt, Nut, Rivet, Screw, Staple, Maker	.	.	.	.	.	.	2	.
.	.	.	.	1	.	.	.	.	.	Lamp, Lantern, Candlestick, Maker	.	.	.	.	1	.	8	1
.	.	.	.	.	.	.	.	.	.	Clasp, Buckle, Hinge, Maker	.	.	.	.	.	.	.	.
.	.	.	.	.	.	.	.	.	.	Fancy Chain, Gilt Toy, Maker	.	.	.	.	.	.	.	.
.	.	.	.	.	.	.	.	.	.	Others	.	.	.	.	.	.	1	.
										22. PERSONS WORKING AND DEALING IN GENERAL OR UNSPECIFIED COMMODITIES.								
										1. *Makers and Dealers (General or Undefined).*								
5	.	3	1	9	.	51	2	101	17	General Shopkeeper, Dealer	8	1	2	.	15	3	194	39
.	.	.	.	.	.	15	2	42	3	Pawnbroker	1	.	1	.	.	.	28	3
3	.	.	.	1	.	76	1	92	7	Costermonger, Huckster, Street Seller	13	.	.	.	5	.	40	6
6	1	3	.	2	1	3	.	7	.	Manufacturer, Manager, Superintendent (undefined)	11	.	2	.	18	8	103	4
.	.	.	.	1	.	.	.	.	.	Contractor (undefined)	.	.	.	.	.	.	4	.
										2. *Mechanics and Labourers (General or Undefined).*								
32	.	24	.	87	.	40	.	55	.	General Labourer	55	.	24	.	23	.	592	2
4	.	3	.	12	.	8	.	5	.	Engine Driver, Stoker, Fireman (not railway, marine, nor agricultural)	21	.	2	.	2	.	108	.
5	.	6	.	12	.	13	.	8	2	Artisan, Mechanic (undefined)	12	.	4	.	11	1	69	.
.	.	1	.	1	.	1	.	10	1	Apprentice (undefined)	1	.	.	.	3	.	14	1
.	.	.	.	1	.	2	.	1	.	Factory Labourer (undefined)	.	.	.	.	1	.	13	.
.	.	2	2	.	.	21	5	66	28	Machinist, Machine Worker (undefined)	2	.	.	.	.	1	11	38
										23. PERSONS WORKING AND DEALING IN REFUSE MATTERS.								
										1. *Refuse Matters.*								
.	.	.	.	.	.	.	.	.	.	Town Drainage Service	.	.	.	.	.	.	.	.
.	.	.	.	.	.	.	.	.	.	Chimney Sweep, Soot Merchant	.	.	.	.	.	.	2	.
.	.	.	.	.	.	.	.	2	.	Scavenger, Crossing Sweeper	.	.	.	.	.	.	1	.
.	.	.	.	.	.	4	.	19	.	Rag Gatherer, Dealer	2	.	.	.	.	.	6	.
										VI. UNOCCUPIED CLASS.								
										24. PERSONS WITHOUT SPECIFIED OCCUPATIONS.								
75	206	173	306	101	173	286	948	966	3669	Persons returned by Property, Rank, &c., and not by special occupation, including all children under 5 years of age	160	336	27	68	145	466	1806	7589

Table 13 *continued*.—OCCUPATIONS and COUNTRY of BIRTH of EUROPEAN FOREIGNERS, MALES and FEMALES, enumerated in ENGLAND and WALES.

Holland.		Belgium.		France.		Portugal.		Spain.		OCCUPATIONS.	Italy.		Greece.		Turkey.		Servia.		Roumania.	
M.	F.	M.	F.	M.	F.	M.	F.	M.	F.		M.	F.	M.	F.	M.	F.	M.	F.	M.	F.
3104	2253	1450	1612	7775	6821	204	86	1128	305	TOTAL	5344	1166	604	91	453	148	2	2	84	27
										I. PROFESSIONAL CLASS.										
										1. PERSONS ENGAGED IN THE GENERAL OR LOCAL GOVERNMENT OF THE COUNTRY.										
										1. *National Government.*										
.	.	.	.	.	.	.	.	.	.	Peer, M.P., Privy Councillor (not otherwise described)	.	.	.	.	.	.	.	.	.	.
4	.	.	.	2	1	.	.	1	.	Civil Service (officers and clerks)	.	.	1	.	.	.	.	.	.	.
1	.	.	.	2	.	.	.	.	.	Civil Service (messengers, &c.)	.	.	.	.	.	.	.	.	.	.
.	.	.	.	.	.	.	.	.	.	Prison Officer, &c.	.	.	.	.	.	.	.	.	.	.
										2. *Local Government.*										
1	.	.	.	.	.	.	.	.	.	Police	.	.	.	.	.	.	.	.	.	.
.	.	.	.	.	.	.	.	.	.	Municipal, Parish, Union, District, Officer	.	.	.	.	.	.	.	.	.	.
.	.	.	.	1	.	.	.	.	.	Other Local or County Official	.	.	.	.	.	.	.	.	.	.
										3. *East Indian and Colonial Service.*										
.	.	.	.	.	.	.	.	.	.	East Indian and Colonial Service	.	.	.	.	.	.	.	.	.	.
										2. PERSONS ENGAGED IN THE DEFENCE OF THE COUNTRY.										
										1. *Army (at Home).*										
.	.	.	.	5	.	1	.	2	.	Army Officer (effective or retired)	.	.	.	.	.	.	.	.	.	.
1	.	.	.	6	.	.	.	.	.	Soldier and Non-commissioned Officer	2	.	.	.	.	.	.	.	.	.
.	.	.	.	.	.	.	.	.	.	Militia, Yeomanry, Volunteers	.	.	.	.	.	.	.	.	.	.
.	.	.	.	.	.	.	.	.	.	Army Pensioner	.	.	.	.	.	.	.	.	.	.
										2. *Navy (ashore or in port).*										
.	.	.	.	1	.	.	.	1	.	Navy Officer (effective or retired)	.	.	.	.	.	.	.	.	.	.
.	.	.	.	.	.	.	.	.	.	Seaman, R.N.	.	.	.	.	.	.	.	.	.	.
.	.	.	.	.	.	.	.	.	.	Royal Marines (officers and men)	.	.	.	.	.	.	.	.	.	.
.	.	.	.	.	.	.	.	.	.	Navy Pensioner	.	.	.	.	.	.	.	.	.	.
										3. PERSONS ENGAGED IN PROFESSIONAL OCCUPATIONS (WITH THEIR IMMEDIATE SUBORDINATES).										
										1. *Clerical Profession.*										
4	.	1	.	5	.	.	.	.	.	Clergyman (Established Church)	3	.	.	.	.	.	.	.	.	.
28	.	67	.	119	.	.	.	10	.	Roman Catholic Priest	45	.	2	.	2	.	.	.	.	.
2	.	1	.	6	.	.	.	.	.	Minister, Priest, of other religious bodies	3	.	2	.	2	.	.	.	.	.
.	.	2	.	1	.	.	.	.	.	Missionary, Scripture Reader, Itinerant Preacher	3	.	.	.	2	.	.	.	2	.
.	12	.	37	.	269	.	.	.	3	Nun, Sister of Charity	.	3	.	.	.	.	.	.	.	.
5	.	7	.	14	.	.	.	12	.	Theological Student	5	.	.	.	.	.	.	.	.	.
9	2	.	.	.	.	.	.	.	.	Church, Chapel, Cemetery—Officer, Servant	1	.	1	.	1	.	.	.	.	.
										2. *Legal Profession.*										
1	.	1	.	12	.	.	.	1	.	Barrister, Solicitor	4	.	1	.	.	.	.	.	.	.
.	.	.	.	1	.	.	.	.	.	Law Student	1	.	.	.	.	.	.	.	.	.
.	.	.	.	3	.	.	.	.	.	Law Clerk, and others connected with Law	2	.	.	.	.	.	.	.	.	.
										3. *Medical Profession.*										
2	.	.	.	22	.	.	.	2	.	Physician, Surgeon, General Practitioner	7	.	1	.	3	.	.	.	.	.
1	.	.	.	2	.	.	.	.	.	Dentist	2	.	.	.	.	.	.	.	.	.
.	.	1	.	1	.	3	.	1	.	Medical Student, Assistant	2	.	6	.	.	.	.	.	.	.
.	.	.	1	.	3	.	.	.	.	Midwife	.	.	.	.	.	.	.	.	.	.
8	2	.	1	3	7	.	.	.	1	Subordinate Medical Service	.	.	.	.	.	1	.	.	.	.
										4. *Teachers.*										
9	3	2	3	32	30	.	.	.	1	Schoolmaster	.	1	.	.	.	1	.	.	.	.
27	51	30	90	467	1118	1	.	14	5	Teacher, Professor, Lecturer	61	47	9	11	5	8	.	.	.	1
1	.	.	.	.	.	.	.	.	.	School Service, and others concerned in Teaching	.	.	.	.	.	.	.	.	.	.
										5. *Literary and Scientific Persons.*										
2	.	1	.	11	2	1	.	1	.	Author, Editor, Journalist	5	.	3	.	.	.	.	.	.	.
1	.	.	.	5	.	.	.	.	.	Reporter, Short-hand Writer	.	.	.	.	.	.	.	.	.	.
.	.	.	.	.	.	.	.	.	.	Persons engaged in Scientific Pursuits	.	.	1	.	.	.	.	.	.	.
10	.	8	.	39	13	2	.	3	.	Literary, Scientific, Institution, Service, &c.	20	1	2	.	4	.	1	.	.	.
										6. *Engineers and Surveyors.*										
2	.	7	.	21	.	2	.	4	.	Civil Engineer	2	.	2	.	.	.	.	.	.	.
.	.	3	.	1	.	.	.	.	.	Mining Engineer	.	.	.	.	.	.	.	.	.	.
.	.	.	.	1	.	.	.	.	.	Land, House, Ship, Surveyor	.	.	.	.	.	.	.	.	.	.
										7. *Artists.*										
16	4	33	6	111	22	1	.	6	1	Painter (artist)	42	2	2	.	.	1	.	.	.	.
4	.	2	.	11	1	.	.	.	.	Engraver (artist)	3	.	.	.	.	.	.	.	.	.
.	.	9	.	14	1	.	.	.	.	Sculptor	34	.	.	.	.	.	.	.	.	.
.	.	.	.	4	.	.	.	.	.	Architect	.	.	.	.	.	.	.	.	.	.
45	7	40	11	74	44	7	.	4	.	Musician, Music Master	1017	223	.	2	1	.	.	.	.	.
.	.	.	1	1	1	.	.	1	.	Art Student	.	.	.	.	.	.	.	.	.	.
1	.	1	.	12	1	.	.	1	.	Photographer	9	1	.	.	.	.	.	.	.	.
3	.	.	1	13	9	.	.	.	2	Actor	2	3	1	.	.	.	.	.	.	.
2	.	1	.	2	1	.	.	.	.	Art, Music, Theatre, Service	10	2	.	.	.	.	.	.	.	.

Table 13 *continued*.—Occupations and Country of Birth of European Foreigners, Males and Females, enumerated in England and Wales.

Holland.		Belgium.		France.		Portugal.		Spain.		Occupations.	Italy.		Greece.		Turkey.		Servia.		Roumania.	
M.	F.	M.	F.	M.	F.	M.	F.	M.	F.		M.	F.	M.	F.	M.	F.	M.	F.	M.	F.
										8. Persons engaged in Exhibitions, Shows, Games, &c.										
2		1	1	8	3	.	.	2	.	Performer, Showman, Exhibition, Service	13	5	.	.	1	.	.	.	.	.
1		1	.	3	.	.	.	.	.	Billiard, Cricket, and other games, Service	4	.	.	.	.	.	.	.	.	.
										II. DOMESTIC CLASS.										
										4. Persons engaged in Domestic Offices or Services.										
										1. Domestic Service.										
2	.	2	.	10	.	.	.	.	.	Domestic Coachman, Groom	3	.	.	.	1	.	.	.	.	.
4	.	8	.	19	.	.	.	.	.	Domestic Gardener	3	.	.	.	.	.	.	.	.	.
14	153	52	131	227	1233	4	10	7	46	Domestic Indoor Servant	144	130	5	18	6	12	.	.	.	1
.	.	.	.	.	.	.	.	.	.	Lodge, Gate, Park, Keeper (not Government)	.	.	.	.	.	.	.	.	.	.
14	1	17	2	86	14	.	.	1	.	Inn, Hotel, Servant	224	7	2	.	3	.	.	.	1	.
.	.	.	.	3	.	.	.	.	.	College, Club, Service	.	.	.	.	.	.	.	.	.	.
										2. Other Service.										
.	.	.	.	.	.	1	.	.	.	Office Keeper (not Government)	1	.	.	.	.	.	.	.	.	.
11	18	18	21	385	181	.	.	2	3	Cook (not domestic)	116	14	6	1	1	1	.	.	.	.
.	11	.	1	.	3	.	.	.	3	Charwoman	.	4	.	.	.	1	.	.	.	.
1	16	9	22	16	107	.	1	.	3	Washing and Bathing Service	2	8	.	.	.	.	.	.	.	.
1	1	7	2	.	6	.	.	.	.	Hospital and Institution Service	.	.	.	.	.	.	.	.	.	.
5	.	4	.	7	.	1	.	3	.	Others engaged in Service	18	.	1	.	.	.	.	.	.	.
										III. COMMERCIAL CLASS.										
										5. Persons engaged in Commercial Occupations.										
										1. Merchants and Agents.										
71	1	20	.	163	1	10	.	59	.	Merchant	58	1	77	.	115	.	.	.	12	.
60	2	29	.	128	.	2	.	18	.	Broker, Agent, Factor	50	.	35	.	43	.	.	.	3	.
5	.	.	.	4	.	.	.	.	.	Auctioneer, Appraiser, Valuer, House Agent	1	.	.	.	.	.	.	.	.	.
1	.	6	.	12	.	1	.	.	.	Accountant	3	1	.	.	3	.	.	.	.	.
8	.	.	.	9	1	.	.	1	.	Salesman, Buyer (not otherwise described)	2	1	.	.	2	.	.	.	.	.
76	.	14	.	95	.	.	.	5	.	Commercial Traveller	23	.	2	.	4	.	.	.	3	.
137	2	78	4	351	9	25	.	65	.	Commercial Clerk	88	1	42	1	33	.	.	.	3	.
.	.	.	.	.	.	.	.	.	.	Officer of Commercial Company, Guild, Society, &c.	.	.	.	.	.	.	.	.	.	.
										2. Dealers in Money.										
3	.	.	.	9	.	.	.	.	.	Banker	.	.	.	.	1	.	.	.	.	.
4	.	2	.	72	.	.	.	.	.	Bank Service	4	.	.	.	2	.	.	.	.	.
1	.	.	.	2	.	2	.	3	.	Bill Discounter, Bill Broker, Finance Agent	2	.	3	.	.	.	.	.	.	.
										3. Persons occupied in Insurance.										
5	.	.	.	3	.	1	.	1	.	Life, House, Ship, &c., Insurance Service	2	.	.	.	.	.	.	.	.	.
										6. Persons engaged in Conveyance of Men, Goods, and Messages.										
										1. On Railways.										
.	.	.	.	.	.	.	.	.	.	Railway Engine Driver, Stoker	1	.	.	.	.	.	.	.	.	.
.	.	.	.	.	.	.	.	.	.	Railway Guard	.	.	.	.	.	.	.	.	.	.
.	.	.	.	.	.	.	.	.	.	Pointsman, Level Crossing Man	.	.	.	.	.	.	.	.	.	.
3	.	.	.	6	.	.	.	.	.	Other Railway Officials and servants	2	.	1	.	.	.	.	.	.	.
										2. On Roads.										
.	.	.	.	.	.	.	.	.	.	Toll Collector, Turnpike Gate Keeper	.	.	.	.	.	.	.	.	.	.
.	.	.	.	2	.	.	.	.	.	Omnibus, Coach, Cab, Owner—Livery Stable Keeper	.	.	1	.	.	.	.	.	.	.
1	.	1	.	3	.	.	.	.	.	Cabman, Flyman, Coachman (not domestic)	2	.	.	.	.	.	.	.	.	.
5	.	.	.	12	.	.	.	1	.	Carman, Carrier, Carter, Haulier	7	.	.	.	.	.	.	.	.	.
.	.	.	.	1	.	.	.	.	.	Tramway Companies' Service	.	.	.	.	.	.	.	.	.	.
.	.	.	.	1	.	.	.	.	.	Wheel Chair Proprietor, Attendant, &c.	1	.	.	.	.	.	.	.	.	.
										3. On Canals, Rivers, and Seas.										
.	.	.	.	.	.	.	.	.	.	Inland Navigation Service	.	.	.	.	.	.	.	.	.	.
1	.	1	.	.	.	.	.	.	.	Bargeman, Lighterman, Waterman	.	.	.	.	.	.	.	.	.	.
2	.	1	.	2	.	.	.	.	.	Navigation Service (on shore)	.	.	.	.	.	.	.	.	.	.
369	.	148	.	1222	.	48	.	548	.	Seaman (Merchant Service)	734	.	243	.	54	.	.	.	.	.
7	.	6	.	7	.	.	.	4	.	Pilot	1	.	.	.	.	.	.	.	.	.
27	2	6	2	56	1	8	.	29	.	Ship Steward, Cook	36	.	12	.	2	.	.	.	.	.
1	.	.	.	.	.	.	.	.	.	Boatman on Seas	.	.	.	.	.	.	.	.	.	.
11	.	4	.	3	.	3	.	5	.	Harbour, Dock, Wharf, Lighthouse, Service	4	.	.	.	.	.	.	.	.	.
										4. In Storage.										
4	.	1	.	27	.	.	.	.	.	Warehouseman,—(not Manchester)	3	.	1	.	2	.	.	.	.	.
.	.	.	.	.	.	.	.	.	.	Meter, Weigher	.	.	1	.	.	.	.	.	.	.
										5. In conveying Messages, Porterage, &c.										
23	.	11	.	46	3	.	.	.	.	Messenger, Porter, Watchman (neither Railway nor Government)	23	.	6	.	3	.	.	.	1	.
7	.	.	.	11	.	.	.	.	.	Telegraph, Telephone, Service	.	.	.	.	.	.	.	.	.	.

Table 13 *continued*.—OCCUPATIONS and COUNTRY of BIRTH of EUROPEAN FOREIGNERS, MALES and FEMALES, enumerated in ENGLAND and WALES.

Holland. M.	Holland. F.	Belgium. M.	Belgium. F.	France. M.	France. F.	Portugal. M.	Portugal. F.	Spain. M.	Spain. F.	OCCUPATIONS.	Italy. M.	Italy. F.	Greece. M.	Greece. F.	Turkey. M.	Turkey. F.	Servia. M.	Servia. F.	Roumania. M.	Roumania. F.
										IV. AGRICULTURAL CLASS.										
										7. PERSONS ENGAGED IN AGRICULTURE.										
										1. *In Fields and Pastures.*										
.	.	1	.	6	.	.	.	2	.	Farmer, Grazier	3	.	.	.	1	.	.	.	.	.
.	.	.	.	1	.	.	.	.	.	Farmer's, Grazier's—Son, Grandson, Brother, Nephew	.	.	.	.	.	.	.	.	.	.
.	.	.	.	.	.	.	.	.	.	Farm Bailiff	.	.	.	.	.	.	.	.	.	.
2	.	.	.	2	.	1	.	.	.	Agricultural Labourer, Farm Servant, Cottager	9	.	.	.	.	.	.	.	.	.
.	.	.	.	.	.	.	.	.	.	Shepherd	.	.	.	.	.	.	.	.	.	.
.	.	.	.	.	.	.	.	.	.	Land Drainage Service (not in towns)	.	.	.	.	.	.	.	.	.	.
.	.	.	.	.	.	.	.	.	.	Agricultural Machine—Proprietor, Attendant	.	.	.	.	.	.	.	.	.	.
.	.	.	.	.	.	.	.	.	.	Agricultural Student, Pupil	.	.	.	.	.	.	.	.	.	.
2	.	.	.	2	.	1	.	.	.	Others engaged in, or connected with, Agriculture	.	.	.	.	.	.	.	.	.	.
										2. *In Woods.*										
.	.	.	.	.	.	.	.	.	.	Woodman	.	.	.	.	.	.	.	.	.	.
										3. *In Gardens.*										
6	1	2	2	9	3	.	.	.	.	Nurseryman, Seedsman, Florist	.	.	.	.	.	.	.	.	.	.
.	.	1	.	1	.	.	.	.	.	Gardener (not domestic)	.	.	.	.	.	.	.	.	.	.
										8. PERSONS ENGAGED ABOUT ANIMALS.										
										1. *About Animals.*										
2	.	2	.	.	.	.	.	.	.	Horse Proprietor, Breeder, Dealer	.	.	.	.	.	.	.	.	.	.
1	.	1	.	6	.	.	.	.	.	Groom, Horse-keeper, Horse breaker	3	1	1	.	.	.	.	.	.	.
1	.	.	.	.	.	.	.	.	.	Veterinary Surgeon, Farrier	.	.	.	.	.	.	.	.	.	.
26	.	1	.	.	.	.	.	.	.	Cattle, Sheep, Pig—Dealer, Salesman	.	.	.	.	.	.	.	.	.	.
5	.	.	.	.	.	1	.	.	.	Drover	.	.	.	.	.	.	.	.	.	.
1	.	.	.	.	.	.	.	.	.	Gamekeeper	.	.	.	.	.	.	.	.	.	.
.	.	.	.	2	.	.	.	.	.	Dog, Bird, Animal—Keeper, Dealer	4	.	.	.	.	.	.	.	.	.
.	.	.	.	.	.	.	.	.	.	Vermin destroyer	.	.	.	.	.	.	.	.	.	.
3	.	2	.	71	.	.	.	.	.	Fisherman	2	.	.	.	.	.	.	.	.	.
.	.	.	.	.	.	.	.	.	.	Knacker, Catsmeat Dealer, &c., &c.	.	.	.	.	.	.	.	.	.	.
										V. INDUSTRIAL CLASS.										
										9. PERSONS WORKING AND DEALING IN BOOKS, PRINTS, AND MAPS.										
										1. *Books.*										
.	.	.	.	8	2	.	.	.	.	Publisher, Bookseller, Librarian	.	.	.	.	2	.	.	.	.	.
.	.	1	.	3	.	.	.	.	.	Music—Publisher, Seller, Printer	.	.	.	.	.	.	.	.	.	.
4	1	1	.	11	2	.	.	.	.	Bookbinder	1	.	.	.	1	.	.	.	1	.
12	.	8	.	29	1	.	.	3	.	Printer	5	.	.	.	4	.	.	.	1	.
1	1	3	.	3	1	.	.	.	.	Newspaper Agent, News Room Keeper	1	.	.	.	.	.	.	.	.	.
.	.	.	.	.	.	.	.	.	.	Others	.	.	.	.	.	.	.	.	.	.
										2. *Prints and Maps.*										
1	.	1	.	14	.	.	.	.	.	Lithographer, Lithographic Printer	3	.	.	.	.	.	.	.	.	.
.	.	.	.	.	.	.	.	.	.	Copper Plate and Steel Plate Printer	.	.	.	.	.	.	.	.	.	.
.	.	.	.	8	.	.	.	.	.	Map and Print—Colourer, Seller	1	.	.	.	.	.	.	.	.	.
										10. PERSONS WORKING AND DEALING IN MACHINES AND IMPLEMENTS.										
										1. *Machines.*										
5	.	12	.	66	1	.	.	11	.	Engine, Machine, Maker	17	.	3	.	1	.	.	.	.	.
.	.	.	.	.	.	.	.	.	.	Millwright	.	.	.	.	.	.	.	.	.	.
5	.	19	.	27	.	.	.	7	.	Fitter, Turner (Engine and Machine)	2	.	2	.	1	.	.	.	.	.
.	.	.	.	8	.	.	.	.	.	Boiler Maker	.	.	.	.	.	.	.	.	.	.
.	.	.	.	.	.	.	.	.	.	Spinning and Weaving Machine Maker	.	.	.	.	.	.	.	.	.	.
.	.	.	.	.	.	.	.	.	.	Agricultural Machine and Implement Maker	.	.	.	.	.	.	.	.	.	.
.	.	.	.	.	.	.	.	.	.	Domestic Machinery—Maker, Dealer	.	.	.	.	.	.	.	.	.	.
										2. *Tools and Implements.*										
1	.	.	.	5	.	.	.	.	.	Tool Maker, Dealer	.	.	1	.	.	.	.	.	.	.
1	.	.	.	3	.	.	.	.	.	Cutler, Scissors Maker	5	.	.	.	.	.	.	.	.	.
.	.	.	.	1	.	.	.	.	.	File Maker	.	.	1	.	.	.	.	.	.	.
.	.	.	.	1	.	.	.	.	.	Saw Maker	.	.	.	.	.	.	.	.	.	.
.	.	.	.	.	.	.	.	.	.	Pin Maker	.	.	.	.	.	.	.	.	.	.
.	.	.	.	.	.	.	.	.	.	Needle Maker	.	.	.	.	.	.	.	.	.	.
1	.	.	.	.	1	.	.	.	.	Steel Pen Maker	.	.	.	.	.	.	.	.	.	.
.	.	.	.	.	.	.	.	.	.	Pencil Maker (Wood)	.	.	.	.	.	.	.	.	.	.
.	.	.	.	.	.	.	.	.	.	Domestic Implement Maker	.	.	.	.	.	.	.	.	.	.
										3. *Watches and Philosophical Instruments.*										
10	.	6	.	81	1	.	.	3	.	Watch Maker, Clock Maker	8	.	1	.	1	.	.	.	.	.
3	.	.	.	21	.	1	.	.	.	Philosophical Instrument Maker, Optician	15	.	.	.	.	.	.	.	.	.
.	.	1	.	8	.	.	.	.	.	Electrical Apparatus Maker	2	.	.	.	.	.	.	.	.	.
.	.	.	.	.	.	.	.	.	.	Weighing and Measuring Apparatus Maker	.	.	.	.	.	.	.	.	.	.

Table 13 *continued*.—OCCUPATIONS and COUNTRY of BIRTH of EUROPEAN FOREIGNERS, MALES and FEMALES, enumerated in ENGLAND and WALES.

Holland.		Belgium.		France.		Portugal.		Spain.		OCCUPATIONS.	Italy.		Greece.		Turkey.		Servia.		Roumania.	
M.	F.	M.	F.	M.	F.	M.	F.	M.	F.		M.	F.	M.	F.	M.	F.	M.	F.	M.	F.
										4. *Surgical Instruments.*										
.	.	.	.	6	.	.	.	1	.	Surgical Instrument Maker	.	.	.	.	.	.	.	.	.	.
										5. *Arms and Ordnance.*										
.	.	3	.	4	.	.	.	.	.	Gunsmith, Gun Manufacturer	.	.	.	.	.	.	.	.	.	.
.	.	.	.	.	.	.	.	.	.	Ordnance Manufacturer	.	.	.	.	.	.	.	.	.	.
.	.	.	.	.	.	.	.	.	.	Sword, Bayonet—Maker, Cutler	.	.	.	.	.	.	.	.	.	.
.	.	.	.	.	.	.	.	.	.	Others	.	.	.	.	.	.	.	.	.	.
										6. *Musical Instruments.*										
4	.	8	.	27	1	.	.	2	.	Musical Instrument Maker, Dealer	31	1	.	.	.	.	.	.	.	.
										7. *Type, Dies, Medals, Coins.*										
.	.	.	.	7	1	.	.	.	.	Type Cutter, Founder	.	.	.	.	.	.	.	.	.	.
1	.	.	.	5	.	.	.	.	.	Die, Seal, Coin, Medal, Maker	1	.	.	.	.	.	.	.	.	.
										8. *Tackle for Sports and Games.*										
.	1	.	.	5	2	.	.	.	.	Toy Maker, Dealer	1	.	.	.	.	.	.	.	.	.
.	.	.	.	.	.	.	.	.	.	Fishing Rod, Tackle, Maker, Dealer	.	.	.	.	.	.	.	.	.	.
.	.	.	.	.	.	.	.	.	.	Apparatus for other Games, Maker, Dealer	.	.	.	.	.	.	.	.	.	.
										11. PERSONS WORKING AND DEALING IN HOUSES, FURNITURE, AND DECORATIONS.										
										1. *Houses.*										
2	.	.	.	4	.	.	.	1	.	Builder	1	.	.	.	.	.	.	.	.	.
20	.	24	.	26	.	2	.	3	.	Carpenter, Joiner	33	.	.	.	1	.	.	.	.	.
1	.	1	.	5	.	.	.	1	.	Bricklayer	7	.	1	.	.	.	.	.	.	.
6	.	13	.	14	.	.	.	.	.	Mason	24	.	.	.	.	.	.	.	.	.
.	.	.	.	.	.	.	.	.	.	Slater, Tiler	.	.	.	.	.	.	.	.	.	.
2	.	.	.	3	.	.	.	.	.	Plasterer, Whitewasher	15	.	.	.	.	.	.	.	.	.
.	.	2	.	1	.	.	.	.	.	Paperhanger	.	.	.	.	.	.	.	.	.	.
3	.	1	.	4	.	.	.	.	.	Plumber	3	.	.	.	.	.	.	.	.	.
17	.	17	.	53	.	.	.	.	.	Painter, Glazier	13	.	1	.	.	.	.	.	.	.
										2. *Furniture and Fittings.*										
48	1	60	1	102	4	.	.	4	.	Cabinet Maker, Upholsterer	78	.	.	.	2	.	.	.	1	.
4	.	2	.	5	2	.	.	.	.	French Polisher	4	.	.	.	.	.	.	.	.	.
1	.	2	.	1	.	.	.	.	.	Furniture Broker, Dealer	7	.	.	.	.	.	.	.	.	.
.	.	1	.	2	.	.	.	.	.	Locksmith, Bellhanger	2	.	.	.	.	.	.	.	1	.
.	.	.	.	3	.	.	.	.	.	Gas Fitter	.	.	.	.	.	.	.	.	.	.
2	.	.	.	3	.	.	.	.	.	House and Shop Fittings—Maker, Dealer	1	.	.	.	.	.	.	.	.	.
.	1	.	.	1	.	.	.	.	.	Funeral Furniture Maker, Undertaker	1	.	.	.	.	.	.	.	.	.
.	.	.	.	.	.	.	.	.	.	Others	.	.	.	.	.	.	.	.	.	.
										3. *House Decorations.*										
5	.	4	.	4	.	.	.	.	.	Wood Carver	2	.	.	.	.	.	.	.	.	.
8	.	.	.	26	2	.	.	2	.	Carver, Gilder	134	.	1	.	.	.	.	.	.	.
13	.	2	.	7	.	.	.	.	.	Dealer in Works of Art	9	1	1	.	.	.	.	.	1	.
.	.	.	.	.	.	.	.	.	.	Figure, Image—Maker, Dealer	243	2	.	.	.	.	.	.	.	.
.	.	.	.	1	.	.	.	.	.	Animal, Bird, &c., Preserver, Naturalist	1	.	.	.	.	.	.	.	.	.
.	.	.	1	15	7	.	.	.	.	Artificial Flower Maker	4	.	.	.	.	.	.	.	.	.
										12. PERSONS WORKING AND DEALING IN CARRIAGES AND HARNESS.										
										1. *Carriages.*										
1	.	6	.	8	.	.	.	.	.	Coachmaker	1	.	.	.	.	.	.	.	.	.
.	.	.	.	1	.	.	.	.	.	Railway Carriage, Railway Wagon, Maker	.	.	.	.	.	.	.	.	.	.
.	.	.	.	2	.	.	.	.	.	Wheelwright	.	.	.	.	.	.	.	.	.	.
.	.	.	.	1	.	.	.	.	.	Bicycle, Tricycle—Maker, Dealer	.	.	.	.	.	.	.	.	.	.
.	.	.	.	.	.	.	.	.	.	Others	.	.	.	.	.	.	.	.	.	.
										2. *Harness.*										
1	.	1	.	1	1	.	.	.	.	Saddler, Harness, Whip, Maker	.	.	.	.	.	.	.	.	.	.
										13. PERSONS WORKING AND DEALING IN SHIPS AND BOATS.										
										1. *Hull.*										
.	.	.	.	1	.	.	.	3	.	Ship, Boat, Barge, Builder	3	.	.	.	.	.	.	.	.	.
4	.	1	.	5	.	1	.	1	.	Shipwright, Ship Carpenter (ashore)	1	.	.	.	.	.	.	.	.	.
										2. *Masts, Rigging, &c.*										
.	.	.	.	.	.	.	.	.	.	Mast, Yard, Oar, Block, Maker	5	.	.	.	.	.	.	.	.	.
5	.	2	.	5	.	2	.	2	.	Ship Rigger, Chandler, Fitter	11	.	.	.	.	.	.	.	.	.
2	.	1	.	4	.	.	.	.	.	Sail Maker	2	.	.	.	.	.	.	.	.	.

Table 13 *continued*.—Occupations and Country of Birth of European Foreigners, Males, and Females, enumerated in England and Wales.

Holland.		Belgium.		France.		Portugal.		Spain.		Occupations.	Italy.		Greece.		Turkey.		Servia.		Roumania.	
M.	F.	M.	F.	M.	F.	M.	F.	M.	F.		M.	F.	M.	F.	M.	F.	M.	F.	M.	F.
										14. Persons working and dealing in Chemicals and Compounds.										
										1. *Colouring Matter.*										
1	.	.	.	.	.	.	.	.	.	Dye, Paint, Manufacture	.	.	.	.	.	.	.	.	.	.
3	.	.	.	.	.	.	.	.	.	Ink, Blacking, Colouring Substance, Manufacture	.	.	.	.	.	.	.	.	.	.
										2. *Explosives.*										
.	.	.	.	.	.	.	.	.	.	Gunpowder, Guncotton, Explosive Substance, Manufacture	.	.	.	.	.	.	.	.	.	.
.	.	.	.	.	.	.	.	.	.	Fusee, Fireworks, Explosive Article, Manufacture	.	.	.	.	.	.	.	.	.	.
										3. *Drugs and other Chemicals and Compounds.*										
3	.	2	.	16	.	2	.	1	.	Chemist, Druggist	2	.	.	.	.	.	.	.	1	.
3	.	.	.	11	1	.	.	1	.	Manufacturing Chemist	.	.	.	.	.	.	.	.	.	.
.	.	.	.	.	.	.	.	.	.	Alkali Manufacture	.	.	.	.	.	.	.	.	.	.
2	.	.	.	.	.	.	.	.	.	Drysalter	.	.	.	.	.	.	.	.	.	.
										15. Persons working and dealing in Tobacco and Pipes.										
										1. *Tobacco and Pipes.*										
616	18	83	1	17	6	3	.	4	.	Tobacco Manufacturer, Tobacconist	4	.	13	.	14	.	.	.	3	.
1	.	.	.	5	1	.	.	.	.	Tobacco Pipe, Snuff Box, &c., Maker	.	.	.	.	.	.	.	.	.	.
										16. Persons working and dealing in Food and Lodging.										
										1. *Board and Lodging.*										
9	.	7	1	31	4	1	.	2	.	Innkeeper, Hotel Keeper, Publican	36	1	4	.	.	.	.	.	.	.
8	7	2	2	18	17	1	1	2	2	Lodging, Boarding House, Keeper	39	19	8	.	1	.	.	.	2	1
7	.	4	1	29	3	.	.	1	.	Coffee, Eating House, Keeper	41	2	8	.	3	.	.	.	.	.
										2. *Spirituous Drinks.*										
.	.	.	.	.	.	.	.	.	.	Hop—Merchant, Dealer	.	.	.	.	.	.	.	.	.	.
.	.	.	.	.	.	.	.	.	.	Malster	.	.	.	.	.	.	.	.	.	.
3	.	1	.	8	.	.	.	.	.	Brewer	.	.	.	.	.	.	.	.	.	.
.	.	1	.	3	.	.	.	.	.	Beerseller. Ale, Porter, Cider, Dealer	2	.	8	.	.	.	.	.	.	.
.	.	2	.	28	.	.	.	.	.	Cellarman	.	.	.	.	.	.	.	.	.	.
7	.	6	.	82	3	8	.	13	.	Wine, Spirit—Merchant, Agent	11	.	.	.	.	.	.	.	.	.
										3. *Food.*										
6	1	.	.	1	2	.	.	.	.	Milkseller, Dairyman	2	.	1	.	.	.	.	.	.	.
11	2	3	.	5	.	.	.	.	.	Cheesemonger, Butterman	2	.	.	.	.	.	.	.	.	.
28	.	6	1	15	1	.	.	3	.	Butcher, Meat Salesman	1	.	.	.	.	.	.	.	.	.
17	2	1	.	25	4	.	.	.	.	Provision Curer, Dealer	11	.	.	.	.	.	.	.	.	.
2	.	.	.	4	.	.	.	.	.	Poulterer, Game Dealer	.	.	.	.	.	.	.	.	.	.
11	.	1	.	13	1	.	.	.	.	Fishmonger	7	.	1	.	.	.	.	.	.	.
.	.	1	.	6	.	.	.	.	.	Corn, Flour, Seed—Merchant, Dealer	1	.	2	.	1	.	.	.	.	.
.	.	.	.	1	.	.	.	.	.	Corn Miller	2	.	.	.	.	.	.	.	.	.
12	.	1	.	22	5	.	.	.	.	Baker	10	.	.	.	.	.	.	.	.	.
34	2	11	.	63	11	.	.	2	.	Confectioner, Pastrycook	191	7	4	.	4	.	.	.	.	.
13	6	1	1	13	2	1	.	4	.	Greengrocer, Fruiterer	7	1	5	.	3	.	.	.	.	.
3	.	.	.	.	.	.	.	.	.	Mustard, Vinegar, Spice, Pickle—Maker, Dealer	.	.	.	.	.	.	.	.	.	.
5	.	.	.	4	.	.	.	.	.	Sugar Refiner	.	.	.	.	.	.	.	.	.	.
13	1	3	1	18	.	.	.	.	1	Grocer. Tea, Coffee, Chocolate—Maker, Dealer	16	.	1	.	4	.	.	.	.	.
.	.	.	.	3	.	.	.	.	.	Ginger Beer, Mineral Water—Manufacturer, Dealer	15	.	.	.	.	.	.	.	.	.
.	.	.	.	.	.	.	.	.	.	Others dealing in Food	.	.	.	.	.	.	.	.	.	.
										17. Persons working and dealing in Textile Fabrics.										
										1. *Wool and Worsted.*										
.	.	2	.	3	.	.	.	.	.	Woolstapler	1	.	.	.	.	.	.	.	.	.
.	.	.	.	3	.	.	.	.	.	Woollen Cloth Manufacture	1	.	.	.	.	.	.	.	.	.
.	.	.	.	.	.	.	.	.	.	Wool, Woollen goods—Dyer, Printer	.	.	.	.	.	.	.	.	.	.
1	.	.	.	.	.	.	.	.	.	Worsted, Stuff, Manufacture	.	.	.	.	.	.	.	.	.	.
.	.	.	.	.	.	.	.	.	.	Flannel Manufacture	.	.	.	.	.	.	.	.	.	.
.	.	.	.	.	.	.	.	.	.	Blanket Manufacture	.	.	.	.	.	.	.	.	.	.
.	.	.	.	.	.	.	.	.	.	Fuller	.	.	.	.	.	.	.	.	.	.
.	.	.	.	6	.	.	.	.	.	Cloth, Worsted, Stuff, Flannel, Blanket Dealer	.	.	.	.	2	.	.	.	.	.
.	.	.	.	.	.	.	.	.	.	Others	.	.	.	.	.	.	.	.	.	.
										2. *Silk.*										
.	.	.	.	7	1	.	.	.	.	Silk, Silk goods, Manufacture	.	.	.	.	.	.	.	.	.	.
.	.	.	.	3	.	.	.	.	.	Silk Dyer, Printer	.	.	.	.	.	.	.	.	.	.
.	.	.	.	.	.	.	.	.	.	Ribbon Manufacture	.	.	.	.	.	.	.	.	.	.
.	.	.	.	.	.	.	.	.	.	Crape, Gauze, Manufacture	.	.	.	.	.	.	.	.	.	.
.	.	.	.	12	1	.	.	.	.	Silk Merchant, Dealer	4	.	.	.	.	.	.	.	.	.

Table 13 *continued.*—OCCUPATIONS and COUNTRY of BIRTH of EUROPEAN FOREIGNERS, MALES and FEMALES, enumerated in ENGLAND and WALES.

Holland.		Belgium.		France.		Portugal.		Spain.		OCCUPATIONS.	Italy.		Greece.		Turkey.		Servia.		Roumania.	
M.	F.	M.	F.	M.	F.	M.	F.	M.	F.		M.	F.	M.	F.	M.	F.	M.	F.	M.	F.
										3. Cotton and Flax.										
		1		3		1			1	Cotton, Cotton goods, Manufacture			3							
1				1						Cotton, Calico—Printer, Dyer, Bleacher										
1										Cotton, Calico—Warehouseman, Dealer			8		4					
		2		1						Flax, Linen—Manufacturer, Dealer										
		2	3	27	13					Lace Manufacturer, Dealer		1								
										Fustian Manufacturer, Dealer										
										Tape Manufacturer, Dealer										
										Thread Manufacturer, Dealer										
										4. Hemp and other Fibrous Materials.										
										Hemp, Jute, Cocoa Fibre, Manufacture										
				1						Rope, Twine, Cord—Maker, Dealer										
										Mat Maker, Seller										
										Net Maker										
										Canvas, Sailcloth, Manufacture										
					1					Sacking, Sack, Bag—Maker, Dealer										
										Others working and dealing in Hemp										
										5. Mixed or Unspecified Materials.										
			1	1						Weaver (undefined)		1								
2		1		18	4					Dyer, Printer, Scourer, Bleacher, Calenderer (undefined)	1									
				1					1	Factory hand (Textile, undefined)										
										Felt Manufacture										
1				1						Carpet, Rug, Manufacture	1				2		1			
										Manchester Warehouseman										
12	4	2	3	19	5			3		Draper, Linen Draper, Mercer	3				1					
	1		1	2	2					Fancy Goods (Textile), Manufacturer, Worker, Dealer										
			1	6	2					Trimming Maker, Dealer										
	2			2	29				1	Embroiderer										
				20	5					Others										
										18. PERSONS WORKING AND DEALING IN DRESS.										
										1. Dress.										
17		3		33				1		Hatter, Hat Manufacture (not straw)	7	1								
				1						Straw—Hat, Bonnet, Plait, Manufacture	2									
142	103	34	11	106	38	2		10	6	Tailor	49	6	2		2				1	
3	70	2	66	27	621		2	1	14	Milliner, Dressmaker, Staymaker	1	25		2		2				
										Shawl Manufacture										
	12	3	10	4	31		2		2	Shirt Maker, Seamstress	1	3								
1	2									Hosiery Manufacture										
1				4		1				Hosier, Haberdasher	1									
		2	1	3	1					Glover, Glove Maker										
		1		2						Button Maker, Dealer										
82	3	23	1	88	4	1		6		Shoe, Boot—Maker, Dealer	24				3				1	
										Patten, Clog, Maker										
10		16	2	119	7			8		Wig Maker, Hairdresser	17	1			2				2	
4		1		6	1					Umbrella, Parasol, Stick—Maker, Dealer	2									
										Accoutrement Maker										
1		1		5						Old Clothes Dealer, and others										
										19. PERSONS WORKING AND DEALING IN VARIOUS ANIMAL SUBSTANCES.										
										1. In Grease, Gut, Bone, Horn, Ivory, and Whalebone.										
2				1						Tallow Chandler, Candle, Grease, Manufacture										
				1						Soap Boiler, Maker										
										Glue, Size, Gelatine, Isinglass—Maker, Dealer										
										Manure Manufacture										
		1		12	1					Bone, Horn, Ivory, Tortoise-shell—Worker, Dealer									1	
										Comb Maker										
								1		Others			6		2					
										2. In Skins.										
9	5	3		14	8					Furrier, Skinner										
		1								Tanner, Fellmonger									1	
3		2		10						Currier	3				1					
1		1		9						Leather Goods, Portmanteau, Bag, Strap, &c.—Maker, Dealer	1									
										Parchment, Vellum—Maker, Dealer										
										3. In Hair and Feathers.										
1				2						Hair, Bristle—Worker, Dealer										
2				5						Brush, Broom, Maker	7									
	2		1	6	8					Quill, Feather—Dresser, Dealer										

Table 13 *continued*.—OCCUPATIONS and COUNTRY of BIRTH of EUROPEAN FOREIGNERS, MALES and FEMALES, enumerated in ENGLAND and WALES.

Holland.		Belgium.		France.		Portugal.		Spain.		OCCUPATIONS.	Italy.		Greece.		Turkey.		Servia.		Roumania.	
M.	F.	M.	F.	M.	F.	M.	F.	M.	F.		M.	F.	M.	F.	M.	F.	M.	F.	M.	F.
										20. PERSONS WORKING AND DEALING IN VARIOUS VEGETABLE SUBSTANCES.										
										1. *In Oils, Gums, and Resins.*										
1	.	2	.	1	.	.	.	.	.	Oil Miller, Oil Cake—Maker, Dealer	.	.	.	.	.	.	.	.	.	.
1	.	.	.	6	.	.	.	.	.	Oil and Colourman	1	.	.	.	.	.	.	.	.	.
.	.	.	.	.	.	.	.	.	.	Floor Cloth, Oil Cloth, Manufacture	.	.	.	.	.	.	.	.	.	.
.	.	.	.	.	.	.	.	.	.	Japanner	.	.	.	.	.	.	.	.	.	.
1	.	.	.	3	.	.	.	.	.	India Rubber, Gutta Percha—Worker, Dealer	.	.	.	.	.	.	.	.	.	.
.	.	.	.	1	1	.	.	.	.	Waterproof Goods—Maker, Dealer	.	.	.	.	.	.	.	.	.	.
.	.	.	.	2	.	.	.	.	.	Others	.	.	.	.	.	.	.	.	.	.
										2. *In Cane, Rush, and Straw.*										
10	1	2	.	36	.	.	.	.	.	Willow, Cane, Rush—Worker, Dealer. Basket maker	4	.	.	.	.	.	.	.	.	.
.	.	.	.	1	.	.	.	.	.	Hay, Straw (not plait), Chaff—Cutter Dealer	.	.	.	.	.	.	.	.	.	.
.	.	.	.	.	.	.	.	.	.	Thatcher	.	.	.	.	.	.	.	.	.	.
										3. *In Wood and Bark.*										
5	.	2	.	1	.	.	.	.	.	Timber, Wood—Merchant, Dealer	.	.	.	.	.	.	.	.	.	.
.	.	.	.	8	.	.	.	.	.	Sawyer	1	.	.	.	.	.	.	.	.	.
.	.	.	.	.	.	.	.	.	.	Lath, Wooden Fence, Hurdle, Maker	.	.	.	.	.	.	.	.	.	.
.	.	.	.	2	.	.	.	.	.	Wood Turner, Box Maker	1	.	.	.	.	.	.	.	.	.
2	.	2	.	2	.	.	.	.	.	Cooper, Hoop Maker, Bender	2	.	.	.	.	.	.	.	.	.
.	.	.	.	4	.	.	.	3	.	Cork, Bark—Cutter, Worker, Dealer	.	.	.	.	.	.	.	.	.	.
.	.	.	.	.	.	.	.	.	.	Others	.	.	.	.	.	.	.	.	.	.
										4. *In Paper.*										
2	.	1	.	1	.	.	.	.	.	Paper Manufacture	.	.	.	.	.	.	.	.	.	.
.	.	.	.	.	.	.	.	.	.	Envelope Maker	.	.	.	.	.	.	.	.	.	.
1	1	.	.	4	1	.	.	.	.	Stationer, Law Stationer	1	.	.	.	.	.	.	.	.	.
1	.	.	.	1	.	.	.	.	.	Card, Pattern Card, Maker	.	.	.	.	.	.	.	.	.	.
1	.	1	.	16	.	.	.	.	.	Paper Stainer	1	.	.	.	.	.	.	.	.	.
.	1	1	.	1	1	.	.	.	.	Paper Box, Paper Bag, Maker	.	.	.	.	.	.	.	.	.	.
6	.	.	.	1	.	.	.	.	.	Ticket, Label, Writer	.	.	.	.	.	.	.	.	.	.
.	.	.	.	.	.	.	.	.	.	Others	1	.	.	.	.	.	.	.	.	.
										21. PERSONS WORKING AND DEALING IN VARIOUS MINERAL SUBSTANCES.										
										1. *Miners.*										
.	.	1	.	6	.	.	.	2	.	Coal Miner	2	.	.	.	.	.	.	.	.	.
.	.	.	.	.	.	.	.	1	.	Ironstone Miner	.	.	.	.	.	.	.	.	.	.
.	.	.	.	.	.	.	.	.	.	Copper Miner	1	.	.	.	.	.	.	.	.	.
.	.	.	.	.	.	.	.	.	.	Tin Miner	.	.	.	.	.	.	.	.	.	.
.	.	.	.	.	.	.	.	.	.	Lead Miner	.	.	.	.	.	.	.	.	.	.
.	.	1	.	.	.	.	.	.	.	Miner in other, or undefined, Minerals	2	.	.	.	.	.	.	.	.	.
.	.	.	.	1	.	.	.	.	.	Mine Service	.	.	.	.	.	.	.	.	.	.
										2. *Coal, Coal Gas, &c.*										
2	.	1	.	4	.	1	.	.	.	Coal Merchant, Dealer	4	.	.	.	.	.	.	.	.	.
.	.	.	.	.	.	.	.	.	.	Coalheaver	.	.	.	.	1	.	.	.	.	.
.	.	1	.	.	.	.	.	.	.	Coke, Charcoal, Peat—Cutter, Burner, Dealer	.	.	.	.	.	.	.	.	.	.
2	.	4	.	1	.	.	.	.	.	Gas Works Service	6	.	.	.	.	.	.	.	.	.
										3. *Stone, Clay and Road Making.*										
.	.	.	.	.	.	.	.	.	.	Stone Quarrier	1	.	.	.	.	.	.	.	.	.
1	.	.	.	3	.	.	.	.	.	Stone Cutter, Dresser, Dealer	1	.	.	.	.	.	.	.	.	.
.	.	.	.	.	.	.	.	.	.	Slate Quarrier	.	.	.	.	.	.	.	.	.	.
.	.	.	.	.	.	.	.	.	.	Slate Worker, Dealer	.	.	.	.	.	.	.	.	.	.
.	.	.	.	.	.	.	.	.	.	Limeburner	.	.	.	.	.	.	.	.	.	.
.	.	.	.	1	.	.	.	.	.	Clay, Sand, Gravel, Chalk—Labourer, Dealer	.	.	.	.	.	.	.	.	.	.
.	.	.	.	.	.	.	.	.	.	Fossil, Coprolite—Digger, Dealer	.	.	.	.	.	.	.	.	.	.
.	.	.	.	.	.	.	.	.	.	Well Sinker, Borer	.	.	.	.	.	.	.	.	.	.
.	.	.	.	.	.	.	.	.	.	Plaster, Cement, Manufacture	.	.	.	.	.	.	.	.	.	.
1	.	3	.	4	.	.	.	.	.	Brick, Tile—Maker, Burner, Dealer	1	.	.	.	.	.	.	.	.	.
1	.	.	.	4	.	.	.	.	.	Paviour	107	.	.	.	.	.	.	.	.	.
.	.	.	.	.	.	.	.	.	.	Road Contractor, Surveyor, Inspector	.	.	.	.	.	.	.	.	.	.
.	.	.	.	.	.	.	.	.	.	Road Labourer	.	.	.	.	.	.	.	.	.	.
.	.	.	.	.	.	.	.	.	.	Railway Contractor	.	.	.	.	.	.	.	.	.	.
.	.	.	.	.	.	.	.	.	.	Platelayer	2	.	.	.	.	.	.	.	.	.
.	.	1	.	.	.	.	.	.	.	Railway Labourer, Navvy	.	.	.	.	.	.	.	.	.	.
.	.	.	.	.	.	.	.	.	.	Others	.	.	.	.	.	.	.	.	.	.
										4. *Earthenware and Glass.*										
2	.	1	.	10	.	.	.	.	.	Earthenware, China, Porcelain, Manufacture	24	.	.	.	1	.	.	.	.	.
1	.	3	.	16	.	.	.	.	.	Glass Manufacture	3	.	.	.	.	.	.	.	.	.
.	.	1	.	7	.	.	.	.	.	Earthenware, China, Glass, Dealer	1	.	.	.	.	.	.	.	.	.
										5. *Salt.*										
1	.	.	.	.	.	.	.	.	.	Salt Maker, Dealer	1	.	.	.	.	.	.	.	.	.

Table 13 *continued*.—OCCUPATIONS and COUNTRY of BIRTH of EUROPEAN FOREIGNERS, MALES and FEMALES, enumerated in ENGLAND and WALES.

Holland.		Belgium.		France.		Portugal.		Spain.		OCCUPATIONS.	Italy.		Greece.		Turkey.		Servia.		Roumania.	
M.	F.	M.	F.	M.	F.	M.	F.	M.	F.		M.	F.	M.	F.	M.	F.	M.	F.	M.	F.
										6. Water.										
.	.	.	.	.	.	.	.	.	.	Waterworks Service	.	.	.	.	.	.	.	.	.	.
.	.	.	.	1	.	.	.	.	.	Others	3	.	.	.	.	.	.	.	.	.
										7. Precious Metals and Jewellery.										
96	2	9	.	140	10	.	.	1	.	Goldsmith, Silversmith, Jeweller	42	.	1	.	3	.	.	.	1	.
.	.	.	.	.	.	.	.	.	.	Gold, Silver, Beater	.	.	.	.	.	.	.	.	.	.
.	.	.	.	.	.	.	.	.	.	Lapidary	2	.	.	.	.	.	.	.	.	.
.	.	.	.	1	.	.	.	.	.	Others	.	.	.	.	.	.	.	.	.	.
										8. Iron and Steel.										
2	.	6	.	5	.	.	.	.	.	Blacksmith	3	.	.	.	.	.	.	.	.	.
.	.	.	.	.	.	.	.	.	.	Whitesmith	.	.	.	.	.	.	.	.	.	.
.	.	.	.	.	.	.	.	.	.	Nail Manufacture	.	.	.	.	.	.	.	.	.	.
.	.	.	.	1	.	.	.	.	.	Anchor, Chain, Manufacture	.	.	.	.	.	.	.	.	.	.
8	.	13	.	25	.	.	.	1	.	Other Iron and Steel Manufactures	4	.	.	.	.	.	.	.	.	.
1	.	.	.	1	.	.	.	.	.	Ironmonger. Hardware Dealer, Merchant	2	.	.	.	.	.	.	.	.	.
										9. Copper.										
.	.	3	.	.	.	.	.	.	.	Copper, Copper goods,—Manufacturer, Worker, Dealer	1	.	.	.	.	.	.	.	.	.
										10. Tin and Zinc.										
1	.	.	.	12	.	.	.	.	.	Tin, Tin Plate, Tin goods,—Manufacturer, Worker, Dealer	1	.	.	.	.	.	.	.	.	.
1	.	25	.	6	.	.	.	.	.	Zinc, Zinc Goods — Manufacturer, Worker, Dealer	.	.	.	.	.	.	.	.	.	.
										11. Lead.										
.	.	.	.	.	.	.	.	.	.	Lead, Leaden goods,—Manufacturer, Worker, Dealer	.	.	.	.	.	.	.	.	.	.
										12. In Other, Mixed, or Unspecified, Metals.										
4	.	5	.	6	.	.	.	.	.	Metal Refiner, Worker, Turner, Dealer	1	.	.	.	.	.	.	.	.	.
.	.	2	.	19	.	.	.	1	.	Brass, Bronze, Manufacture. Brazier	.	.	.	.	.	.	.	.	.	.
.	.	.	.	.	.	.	.	.	.	Metal Burnisher, Lacquerer	.	.	.	.	.	.	.	.	.	.
.	.	.	.	1	.	.	.	2	.	White Metal, Plated Ware, Manufacture. Pewterer	.	.	.	.	.	.	.	.	.	.
2	.	.	.	4	.	.	.	.	.	Wire Maker, Worker, Weaver, Drawer	14	.	.	.	.	.	.	.	.	.
.	.	.	.	.	.	.	.	.	.	Bolt, Nut, Rivet, Screw, Staple Maker	.	.	.	.	.	.	.	.	.	.
.	.	.	.	8	.	.	.	.	.	Lamp, Lantern, Candlestick, Maker	.	.	.	.	.	.	.	.	.	.
.	.	.	.	.	.	.	.	.	.	Clasp, Buckle, Hinge, Maker	.	.	.	.	.	.	.	.	.	.
.	.	.	.	.	.	.	.	.	.	Fancy Chain, Gilt Toy, Maker	.	.	.	.	.	.	.	.	.	.
.	.	.	.	.	.	.	.	.	.	Others	1	.	.	.	.	.	.	.	.	.
										22. PERSONS WORKING AND DEALING IN GENERAL OR UNSPECIFIED COMMODITIES.										
										1. *Makers and Dealers (General or Undefined).*										
23	12	5	3	63	10	.	.	2	.	General Shopkeeper, Dealer	67	2	1	.	9	.	.	.	.	.
1	.	.	.	.	.	.	.	.	.	Pawnbroker	.	.	.	.	.	.	.	.	.	.
48	5	.	.	8	3	.	.	.	.	Costermonger, Huckster, Street Seller	327	29	.	.	2	.	.	.	.	.
14	.	10	.	40	3	1	.	1	.	Manufacturer, Manager, Superintendent (undefined)	11	1	1	.	.	.	.	.	.	.
.	.	.	.	2	.	.	.	.	.	Contractor (undefined)	.	.	.	.	.	.	.	.	.	.
										2. *Mechanics and Labourers (General or Undefined).*										
43	.	21	.	39	1	3	.	6	.	General Labourer	237	4	4	.	.	.	.	.	1	.
2	.	.	.	8	.	.	.	1	.	Engine Driver, Stoker, Fireman (neither railway, marine, nor agricultural)	12	.	6	.	.	.	.	.	.	.
3	.	8	.	79	4	.	.	4	1	Artizan, Mechanic (undefined)	10	.	.	.	1	.	.	.	.	.
5	.	.	.	1	.	.	.	1	.	Apprentice (undefined)	1	.	2	.	.	.	.	.	.	.
5	.	1	.	3	.	.	.	.	.	Factory Labourer (undefined)	6	.	.	.	2	.	.	.	.	.
3	11	.	7	3	9	.	.	.	3	Machinist, Machine Worker (undefined)	1	1	.	.	1	.	.	.	.	.
										23. PERSONS WORKING AND DEALING IN REFUSE MATTERS.										
										1. *Refuse Matters.*										
.	.	.	.	.	.	.	.	.	.	Town Drainage Service	.	.	.	.	.	.	.	.	.	.
.	.	.	.	.	.	.	.	.	.	Chimney Sweep, Soot Merchant	.	.	.	.	.	.	.	.	.	.
.	.	.	.	1	.	.	.	.	.	Scavenger, Crossing Sweeper	1	.	.	.	.	.	.	.	.	.
7	.	.	.	.	.	.	.	.	.	Rag Gatherer, Dealer	2	.	.	.	.	.	.	.	.	.
										VI. UNOCCUPIED CLASS.										
										24. PERSONS WITHOUT SPECIFIED OCCUPATIONS.										
289	[illegible]	218	162	1486	2650	59	63	180	203	Persons returned by Property, Rank, &c., and not by special occupation, including all children under 5 years of age	321	604	40	56	74	119	.	3	22	24

Table 14.—Number and Ages of Males and Females returned as Blind, Blind from Birth, Deaf and Dumb, Idiots or Imbeciles, and Lunatics.

Returned as	All Ages.			0–	5–	15–	20–	25–	45–	65 and upwards.
	Both Sexes.	Males and Females.								
BLIND (*including Blind from Birth*)	22832	M.	12048	302	927	570	546	2591	3418	3694
		F.	10784	284	783	419	437	1728	2808	4325
BLIND FROM BIRTH	1958	M.	981	182	239	103	90	197	130	40
		F.	977	134	246	94	81	241	136	55
DEAF AND DUMB	13295	M.	7111	294	1862	778	760	2027	1066	324
		F.	6184	204	1046	658	621	1800	913	342
IDIOTS OR IMBECILES	32717	M.	16105	275	2868	2208	1936	5040	2616	1162
		F.	16612	176	2002	1704	1690	5635	3624	1781
LUNATICS	51786	M.	23684	5	83	371	1153	10684	8830	2558
		F.	28102	6	81	380	1087	10893	11641	4008

Table 15.—Number and Ages of Males and Females returned as Suffering from Combined Infirmities.

Returned as	All Ages.			0–	5–	15–	20–	25–	45–	65 and upwards.
	Both Sexes.	Males and Females.								
IDIOT AND DUMB	368	M.	214	2	55	34	35	61	20	1
		F.	154	3	41	17	8	46	32	7
IDIOT AND BLIND	151	M.	85	2	18	9	5	26	21	4
		F.	66	1	4	9	14	17	10	11
IDIOT, DUMB, AND BLIND	13	M.	5	.	3	1	.	.	.	1
		F.	8	1	2	.	1	2	2	.
LUNATIC AND DUMB	93	M.	52	.	2	4	2	25	14	5
		F.	41	.	4	3	1	24	7	2
LUNATIC AND BLIND	204	M.	110	.	2	1	4	43	43	18
		F.	94	1	2	.	2	15	37	37
LUNATIC, DUMB, AND BLIND	4	M.	4	.	.	.	.	1	3	.
		F.	.	.		.	.	.	.	.
DUMB AND BLIND	59	M.	28	2	10	2	4	4	4	2
		F.	31		7	3	1	7	8	4

Table 16.—Total Number of Persons returned as Blind, Deaf and Dumb, Idiots or Imbeciles, and Lunatics in Registration Divisions and Counties.

Registration Division and County.	Blind.			Deaf and Dumb.	Mentally Deranged.		
	From Birth.	Others.	Total.		Idiots.	Lunatics.	Total.
ENGLAND AND WALES	1958	20874	22832	13295	32717	51786	84503
LONDON	252	2962	3214	1972	2081	3951	6032
MIDDLESEX (*Intra-metropolitan*)	137	1956	2093	1377	1408	1731	3139
SURREY (*Intra-metropolitan*)	105	813	918	477	548	2190	2738
KENT (*Intra-metropolitan*)	10	193	203	118	125	30	155
SOUTH-EASTERN COUNTIES	156	1869	2025	1436	5536	9481	15017
SURREY (*Extra-metropolitan*)	16	320	336	243	2114	3984	6098
KENT (*Extra-metropolitan*)	45	504	549	536	1598	2278	3876
SUSSEX	41	386	427	286	604	1096	1700
HAMPSHIRE	38	454	492	259	821	1276	2097
BERKSHIRE	16	205	221	122	399	847	1246
SOUTH-MIDLAND COUNTIES	119	1315	1434	823	3032	8504	11536
MIDDLESEX (*Extra-metropolitan*)	27	255	282	186	285	4367	4652
HERTFORDSHIRE	17	170	187	125	1030	1258	2288
BUCKINGHAMSHIRE	15	147	162	79	267	374	641
OXFORDSHIRE	13	195	208	100	328	500	828
NORTHAMPTONSHIRE	20	219	239	134	445	830	1275
HUNTINGDONSHIRE	3	56	59	20	62	7	69
BEDFORDSHIRE	14	113	127	79	305	835	1140
CAMBRIDGESHIRE	10	160	170	116	310	333	643
EASTERN COUNTIES	127	1181	1308	654	1960	2800	4760
ESSEX	41	381	422	231	767	931	1698
SUFFOLK	40	331	371	198	586	680	1266
NORFOLK	46	469	515	225	607	1189	1796
SOUTH-WESTERN COUNTIES	174	2180	2354	1058	2868	4194	7062
WILTSHIRE	14	224	238	127	506	1090	1596
DORSETSHIRE	20	205	225	98	289	460	749
DEVONSHIRE	63	705	768	374	837	1118	1955
CORNWALL	29	535	564	200	369	605	974
SOMERSETSHIRE	48	511	559	261	867	921	1788
WEST-MIDLAND COUNTIES	267	2647	2914	1690	4407	5915	10322
GLOUCESTERSHIRE	72	602	674	331	923	1325	2248
HEREFORDSHIRE	13	132	145	76	259	290	549
SHROPSHIRE	29	259	288	130	460	538	998
STAFFORDSHIRE	62	760	822	481	1172	1763	2935
WORCESTERSHIRE	37	378	415	301	486	725	1211
WARWICKSHIRE	64	506	570	371	1107	1274	2381
NORTH-MIDLAND COUNTIES	129	1300	1429	705	2039	1882	3921
LEICESTERSHIRE	29	268	297	114	438	604	1042
RUTLANDSHIRE	2	17	19	6	17	2	19
LINCOLNSHIRE	41	374	415	205	652	596	1248
NOTTINGHAMSHIRE	42	358	400	171	550	621	1171
DERBYSHIRE	15	283	298	209	382	59	441
NORTH-WESTERN COUNTIES	317	2687	3004	1872	4467	6731	11198
CHESHIRE	42	408	450	268	758	1250	2008
LANCASHIRE	275	2279	2554	1604	3709	5481	9190
YORKSHIRE	223	2071	2294	1481	2903	3862	6765
WEST RIDING	163	1439	1602	1197	2255	2529	4784
EAST RIDING	39	368	407	163	365	1309	1674
NORTH RIDING	21	264	285	121	283	24	307
NORTHERN COUNTIES	112	1147	1259	770	1394	2202	3596
DURHAM	47	565	612	355	614	1098	1712
NORTHUMBERLAND	40	316	356	269	486	654	1140
CUMBERLAND	17	215	232	113	209	438	647
WESTMORLAND	8	51	59	33	85	12	97
MONMOUTHSHIRE AND WALES	82	1515	1597	834	2030	2264	4294
MONMOUTHSHIRE	12	242	254	98	296	533	829
GLAMORGANSHIRE	20	456	476	270	382	688	1070
CARMARTHENSHIRE	3	113	116	66	234	494	728
PEMBROKESHIRE	1	90	91	40	102	32	134
CARDIGANSHIRE	3	117	120	51	173	44	217
BRECKNOCKSHIRE	3	60	63	33	57	11	68
RADNORSHIRE	1	17	18	14	39	5	44
MONTGOMERYSHIRE	3	84	87	31	105	18	123
FLINTSHIRE	7	51	58	29	40	7	47
DENBIGHSHIRE	6	94	100	61	247	370	617
MERIONETHSHIRE	7	61	68	37	111	19	130
CARNARVONSHIRE	7	106	113	52	175	34	209
ANGLESEY	3	30	33	26	69	9	78

THE BLIND.

TABLE XVII.—OCCUPATIONS of MALES and FEMALES returned as BLIND.*

	Occupations.	Males.	Females.
	TOTAL	12048	10784
	I. Professional Class.		
1.	Civil Service (officers and clerks)	12	2
	Civil Service (messengers, &c.)	12	.
	Prison Officer, &c.	2	.
	Police	4	.
	Municipal Parish, Union, District, Officer	14	2
	Other Local or County Official	3	.
2.	Army Officer (effective or retired)	5	.
	Soldier and Non-Commissioned Officer	19	.
	Army Pensioner	4	.
	Navy Officer (effective or retired)	2	.
	Seamen, R.N.	7	.
3.	Clergyman (Established Church)	23	.
	Minister, Priest, of other religious bodies	10	.
	Missionary, Scripture Reader, Itinerant Preacher	28	1
	Theological Student	3	.
	Church, Chapel, Cemetery—Officer, Servant	7	2
	Barrister, Solicitor	15	.
	Law Clerk, and others connected with Law	3	.
	Physician, Surgeon, General Practitioner	13	.
	Dentist	2	.
	Medical Student, Assistant	2	.
	Midwife	.	3
	Subordinate Medical Service	.	40
	Schoolmaster	17	16
	Teacher, Professor, Lecturer	36	31
	Author, Editor, Journalist	.	1
	Literary, Scientific, Institution, Service, &c.	1	.
	Civil Engineer	4	.
	Land, House, Ship, Surveyor	2	.
	Painter (artist)	6	.
	Architect	2	.
	Musician, Music Master	496	70
	Photographer	1	.
	Actor	1	.
	Art, Music, Theatre Service	9	.
	Performer, Showman, Exhibition Service	1	.
	Billiard, Cricket, and other games, Service	2	.
	II. Domestic Class.		
4.	Domestic Coachman, Groom	29	.
	Domestic Gardener	62	.
	Domestic Indoor Servant	23	317
	Lodge, Gate, Park, Keeper (not Government)	3	1
	Inn, Hotel, Servant	6	2
	College, Club, Service	1	.
	Office Keeper (not Government)		1
	Charwoman		76
	Washing and Bathing Service	16	140
	Hospital and Institution Service	2	3
	Others engaged in Service	8	.
	III. Commercial Class.		
5.	Merchant	9	.
	Broker, Agent, Factor	17	1
	Auctioneer, Appraiser, Valuer, House Agent	4	.
	Accountant	5	.
	Salesman, Buyer, (not otherwise described)	1	.
	Commercial Traveller	16	.
	Commercial Clerk	20	.
	Banker	2	.
	Bank Service	3	.
	Bill Discounter, Bill Broker, Finance Agent	1	.
	Life, House, Ship, &c., Insurance Service	3	.
6.	Railway Guard	3	.
	Other Railway Officials and Servants	12	.
6.—cont.	Toll Collector, Turnpike Gate Keeper	2	.
	Omnibus, Coach, Cab, Owner, Livery Stable Keeper	3	.
	Cabman, Flyman, Coachman (not domestic)	5	.
	Carman, Carrier, Carter, Haulier	65	.
	Wheel Chair Proprietor, Attendant, &c.	2	.
	Bargeman, Lighterman, Waterman	23	.
	Navigation Service (on shore)	2	.
	Seaman (Merchant Service)	83	.
	Pilot	5	.
	Boatman on Seas	1	.
	Harbour, Dock, Wharf, Lighthouse, Service	18	.
	Warehouseman (not Manchester)	10	1
	Messenger, Porter, Watchman (neither Railway nor Government)	37	.
	IV. Agricultural Class.		
7.	Farmer, Grazier	332	46
	Farm Bailiff	6	.
	Agricultural Labourer, Farm Servant, Cottager	674	21
	Shepherd	11	.
	Woodman	3	.
	Nurseryman, Seedsman, Florist	2	1
	Gardener (not domestic)	9	1
8.	Horse proprietor, Breeder, Dealer	3	.
	Groom, Horse-keeper, Horsebreaker	26	.
	Veterinary Surgeon, Farrier	3	.
	Cattle, Sheep, Pig—Dealer, Salesman	4	.
	Drover	3	.
	Gamekeeper	7	.
	Vermin Destroyer	2	.
	Fisherman	21	1
	V. Industrial Class.		
9.	Publisher, Bookseller, Librarian	12	2
	Music—Publisher, Seller, Printer	4	.
	Bookbinder	2	3
	Printer	25	.
	Newspaper Agent, News-room Keeper	43	3
	Map and Print—Colourer, Seller		1
10.	Engine, Machine, Maker	8	.
	Millwright	2	.
	Fitter, Turner (Engine and Machine)	22	.
	Boiler Maker	9	.
	Spinning and Weaving Machine Maker	1	.
	Agricultural Machine and Implement Maker	1	.
	Domestic Machinery—Maker, Dealer	1	.
	Tool Maker, Dealer	7	.
	Cutler, Scissors Maker	15	.
	File Maker	4	.
	Domestic Implement Maker	1	.
	Watch Maker, Clock Maker	9	.
	Philosophical Instrument Maker, Optician	2	.
	Electrical Apparatus Maker, Worker (not Govt.)	.	1
	Weighing and Measuring Apparatus Maker	2	.
	Gunsmith, Gun Manufacturer	3	1
	Musical Instrument Maker, Dealer	41	.
	Die, Seal, Coin, Medal, Maker	1	.
	Toy Maker, Dealer	3	.
	Fishing Rod, Tackle, Maker	1	.
11.	Builder	15	1
	Carpenter, Joiner	120	.
	Bricklayer	66	.
	Mason	58	.
	Slater, Tiler	4	.
	Plasterer, Whitewasher	14	.
	Paperhanger	1	.
	Plumber	8	.
11.—cont.	Painter, Glazier	46	.
	Cabinet Maker, Upholsterer	30	12
	French Polisher	3	.
	Furniture Broker, Dealer	3	.
	Locksmith, Bellhanger	3	1
	Gas Fitter	1	.
	Funeral Furniture Maker, Undertaker	1	.
	Carver, Gilder	4	.
	Dealer in Works of Art	2	.
	Artificial Flower Maker	1	2
12.	Coachmaker	12	.
	Wheelwright	21	.
	Others	3	.
	Saddler, Harness, Whip, Maker	5	.
13.	Ship, Boat, Barge, Builder	4	.
	Shipwright, Ship Carpenter (ashore)	27	.
	Mast, Yard, Oar, Block, Maker	1	.
	Ship Rigger, Chandler, Fitter	2	.
	Sail Maker	5	.
14.	Dye, Paint Manufacturer	1	1
	Ink, Blacking, Colouring, Substance, Manufacture	1	.
	Chemist, Druggist	12	.
	Manufacturing Chemist	3	.
	Drysalter	1	.
15.	Tobacco Manufacturer, Tobacconist	7	1
	Tobacco Pipe, Snuff Box, &c. Maker	2	.
16.	Innkeeper, Hotel Keeper, Publican	65	20
	Lodging, Boarding House, Keeper	14	11
	Coffee, Eating House, Keeper	1	.
	Maltster	7	.
	Brewer	16	.
	Beerseller, Ale, Porter, Cider, Dealer	12	4
	Cellarman	1	.
	Wine, Spirit—Merchant, Agent	4	.
	Milkseller, Dairyman	17	4
	Cheesemonger, Butterman	3	.
	Butcher, Meat Salesman	36	1
	Provision Curer, Dealer	11	2
	Poulterer, Game Dealer	3	.
	Fishmonger	26	1
	Corn, Flour, Seed—Merchant, Dealer	12	1
	Corn Miller	19	1
	Baker	44	.
	Confectioner, Pastrycook	14	2
	Greengrocer, Fruiterer	48	7
	Mustard, Vinegar, Spice, Pickle, Maker, Dealer	2	
	Sugar Refiner	3	.
	Grocer, Tea, Coffee, Chocolate—Maker, Dealer	177	15
	Ginger Beer, Mineral Water—Manufacturer, Dealer	6	.
17.	Woolstapler	4	.
	Woollen Cloth Manufacture	24	11
	Wool, Woollen Goods—Dyer, Printer	2	.
	Worsted, Stuff Manufacture	5	4
	Blanket Manufacture	2	.
	Others	1	.
	Silk, Silk Goods Manufacture	23	17
	Ribbon Manufacture	2	2
	Cotton, Cotton Goods Manufacture	34	34
	Cotton, Calico—Printer, Dyer, Bleacher	7	
	Cotton, Calico—Warehouseman, Dealer	1	.
	Flax, Linen Manufacturer, Dealer	4	2
	Lace Manufacturer, Dealer	8	14
	Hemp, Jute, Cocoa Fibre, Manufacture	9	1
	Rope, Twine, Cord—Maker, Dealer	12	3
	Mat Maker, Seller	158	5
	Net Maker	6	1
	Canvas, Sailcloth, Manufacture		1
	Sacking, Sack, Bag—Maker, Dealer	3	3

* Including those returned as Blind from Birth, also given separately in Table 18. Blind persons returned as *retired* from any business have nevertheless been referred to that business.

THE BLIND—*continued.*

TABLE XVII *continued.*—OCCUPATIONS of MALES and FEMALES returned as BLIND.

OCCUPATIONS.	Males.	Females.
17.—*cont.*		
Others working and dealing in Hemp	1	.
Weaver (undefined)	17	11
Dyer, Printer, Scourer, Bleacher, Calenderer (undefined)	9	1
Factory Hand (Textile) undefined	6	15
Felt Manufacture	1	.
Carpet and Rug Manufacture	11	.
Draper, Linen Draper, Mercer	26	3
Fancy Goods (Textile) Manufacturer, Worker, Dealer	3	173
Trimming Maker, Dealer	2	.
18. Hatter, Hat Manufacturer (not Straw)	9	1
Straw, Hat, Bonnet, Plait, Manufacture	3	12
Tailor	80	19
Milliner, Dressmaker, Staymaker	.	89
Shirtmaker, Seamstress	.	65
Hosiery Manufacture	11	28
Hosier, Haberdasher	7	1
Glover, Glove Maker	2	2
Button Maker, Dealer	2	2
Shoe, Boot—Maker, Dealer	165	9
Patten, Clog, Maker	4	.
Wig Maker, Hairdresser	6	.
Umbrella, Parasol, Stick—Maker, Dealer	6	1
Old Clothes Dealer, and others	.	1
19. Tallow Chandler, Candle, Grease Manufacture	5	.
Manure Manufacture	1	.
Comb Maker	2	.
Furrier, Skinner	.	2
Tanner, Fellmonger	10	.
Currier	9	.
Leather Goods, Portmanteau, Bag, Strap, &c. Maker, Dealer	2	.
Hair, Bristle—Worker, Dealer	2	1
Brush, Broom, Maker	143	41
20. Oil Miller, Oil Cake—Maker, Dealer	4	.
Oil and Colourman	2	.
India Rubber, Gutta Percha—Worker, Dealer	1	.
Others	.	1

OCCUPATIONS.	Males.	Females.
20.—*cont.*		
Willow, Cane, Rush—Worker Dealer, Basketmaker	772	91
Hay, Straw, (not plait), Chaff—Cutter, Dealer	7	.
Thatcher	6	.
Timber, Wood—Merchant, Dealer	32	1
Sawyer	21	.
Lath, Wooden Fence, Hurdle, Maker	4	.
Wood Turner, Box Maker	12	.
Cooper, Hoop Maker, Bender	18	.
Cork, Bark—Cutter, Worker, Dealer	2	.
Paper Manufacture	2	.
Stationer, Law Stationer	7	1
Card, Pattern Card, Maker	1	.
Paper Stainer	1	.
Paper Box, Paper Bag, Maker	1	7
Others	1	.
21. Coal Miner	192	1
Ironstone Miner	24	.
Copper Miner	22	.
Tin Miner	36	.
Lead Miner	27	.
Miner in other, or undefined Minerals	41	.
Mine Service	2	.
Coal Merchant, Dealer	43	2
Coalheaver	18	.
Coke, Charcoal, Peat—Cutter, Burner, Dealer	1	.
Gas Works Service	6	.
Stone Quarrier	36	.
Stone Cutter, Dresser, Dealer	6	.
Slate Quarrier	4	.
Limeburner	3	.
Clay, Sand, Gravel, Chalk—Labourer, Dealer	1	.
Well Sinker, Borer	2	.
Brick, Tile—Maker, Burner, Dealer	19	1
Paviour	4	.
Road Labourer	11	.
Platelayer	5	.
Railway Labourer, Navvy	14	.
Earthenware, China, Porcelain Manufacture	16	3
Glass Manufacture	11	.
Earthenware, China, Glass, Dealer	5	4
Others	1	.
Goldsmith, Silversmith, Jeweller	10	1
Gold, Silver, Beater	2	.

OCCUPATIONS.	Males.	Females.
21.—*cont.*		
Lapidary	2	.
Others	2	.
Blacksmith	104	1
Whitesmith	2	.
Nail Manufacture	8	1
Anchor, Chain, Manufacture	9	.
Other Iron and Steel Manufactures	91	.
Ironmonger, Hardware Dealer, Merchant	7	1
Copper, Copper goods—Manufacturer, Worker, Dealer	4	.
Tin, Tin Plate, Tin goods—Manufacturer, Worker, Dealer	18	.
Zinc, Zinc goods—Manufacturer, Worker, Dealer	1	.
Metal Refiner, Worker, Turner, Dealer	2	.
Brass, Bronze, Manufacture, Brazier	6	.
Metal Burnisher, Lacquerer	.	1
White Metal, Plated Ware, Manufacture, Pewterer	3	.
Wire Maker, Worker, Weaver, Drawer	5	.
Bolt, Nut, Rivet, Screw, Staple, Maker	2	2
Others	.	1
22. General Shopkeeper, Dealer	76	9
Pawnbroker	2	.
Costermonger, Huckster, Street Seller	266	39
Manufacturer, Manager, Superintendent (undefined)	5	.
Contractor (undefined)	3	.
General Labourer	497	1
Engine Driver, Stoker, Fireman (neither Railway, Marine, nor Agricultural)	24	.
Artizan, Mechanic (undefined)	25	2
Factory Labourer (undefined)	16	1
Machinist, Machine Worker (undefined)	.	1
23. Chimney Sweep, Soot Merchant	13	.
Scavenger, Crossing Sweeper	3	.
Rag Gatherer, Dealer	7	.
VI. UNOCCUPIED CLASS.		
24. Persons returned by Property, Rank, &c., and not by special occupation, including all children under 5 years of age	4997	9158

TABLE XVIII.—OCCUPATIONS of MALES and FEMALES returned as BLIND from BIRTH.

OCCUPATIONS.	Males.	Females.
TOTAL	981	977
I. PROFESSIONAL CLASS.		
Civil Service (Letter Carrier)	1	.
Town Crier	2	.
Nonconformist Minister	1	.
Missionary, Scripture Reader	3	.
Schoolmistress	.	8
Teacher	1	5
Musician, Music Master	82	21
Piano Tuner	7	.
Organ Blower	1	.
II. DOMESTIC CLASS.		
Domestic Servant	2	9
Charwoman	.	1
Washerwoman	.	4
Shoeblack	1	.
Night-caller	2	.
III. COMMERCIAL CLASS.		
Messenger, Porter (neither Railway nor Government)	2	.

OCCUPATIONS.	Males.	Females.
IV. AGRICULTURAL CLASS.		
Farmer	.	2
Agricultural Labourer	7	.
Horse Proprietor	1	.
Ostler	1	.
Fisherman	1	.
V. INDUSTRIAL CLASS.		
Newspaper Agent, Newsroom Keeper	4	.
Cutler	1	.
Carpenter	1	.
Upholsterer	1	.
Mattress Maker	1	.
Innkeeper	1	.
Greengrocer, Fruiterer	3	.
Tea Dealer	1	.
Flax Reeler	.	1
Cocoa Fibre, Manufacturer	4	.
Sash-line Maker	.	1
Mat Maker	23	.
Net Maker	1	.
Weaver	.	1
Knitter (Hosiery, Fancy Goods)	.	44

OCCUPATIONS.	Males.	Females.
V.—*cont.*		
Dressmaker	.	2
Shirtmaker, Seamstress	.	1
Haberdasher	1	.
Shoemaker	2	.
Patten, Clog, Maker	1	.
Brush and Broom Maker	19	6
Basket Maker	89	6
Chair-caner	3	11
Sawyer	2	.
Wood Worker	1	.
Coal Miner	6	.
Ironstone Miner	1	.
Miner (undefined)	1	.
Coal Dealer	1	.
Iron Manufacturer	2	.
Coppersmith	1	.
General Shopkeeper	2	.
Costermonger, Huckster, Street Seller	15	3
General Labourer	12	.
VI. UNOCCUPIED CLASS.		
Persons returned by Property, Rank, &c., and not by special occupation, including all children under 5 years of age	666	856

THE DEAF AND DUMB.

TABLE XIX.—OCCUPATIONS of MALES and FEMALES returned as DEAF and DUMB.

OCCUPATIONS.	Males.	Females.
TOTAL	7111	6184
I.—PROFESSIONAL CLASS.		
1. Civil Service (Officers and Clerks)	1	.
Civil Service (Messengers, &c.)	2	1
2. Soldier and Non-commissioned Officer	1	.
3. Minister, Priest, of other religious bodies	1	.
Missionary, Scripture Reader, Itinerant Preacher	8	1
Church, Chapel, Cemetery—Officer, Servant	.	2
Law Clerk, and others connected with law	8	.
Dentist	3	.
Subordinate Medical Service	.	3
Schoolmaster	.	1
Teacher, Professor, Lecturer	2	12
Civil Engineer	2	.
Land, House, Ship Surveyor	1	.
Painter (Artist)	34	1
Engraver (Artist)	23	.
Sculptor	5	.
Architect	1	.
Art Student	.	1
Photographer	1	.
Art, Music, Theatre Service	8	.
Billiard, Cricket, and other Games, Service	.	1
II.—DOMESTIC CLASS.		
4. Domestic Coachman, Groom	1	.
Domestic Gardener	37	1
Domestic Indoor Servant	18	315
Inn, Hotel, Servant	7	2
Office Keeper (not Gov.)	.	1
Charwoman	.	74
Washing and Bathing Service	8	158
Hospital and Institution Service	.	3
Others engaged in Service	11	.
III.—COMMERCIAL CLASS.		
5. Broker, Agent, Factor	2	.
Accountant	2	.
Commercial Traveller	4	.
Commercial Clerk	20	.
6. Other Railway Officials and Servants	2	.
Cabman, Flyman, Coachman, (not domestic)	1	.
Carm., Carr., Carter, Haulier	9	.
Bargeman, Lighterman, Waterman	9	.
Seaman (Merchant Service)	8	.
Harbour, Dock, Wharf, Lighthouse, Service	13	.
Warehouseman (not Manchester)	7	1
Meter, Weigher	1	.
Messenger, Porter, Watchman (neither Railway nor Government)	28	.
IV.—AGRICULTURAL CLASS.		
7. Farmer, Grazier	37	3
Farmer's, Grazier's Son, Grandson, Brother, Nephew	8	.
Farm Bailiff	3	.
Agricultural Labourer, Farm Servant, Cottager	403	10
Shepherd	4	.
Woodman	4	.
Nurseryman, Seedsman, Florist	1	1
Gardener (not domestic)	10	1
8. Groom, Horse-keeper, Horse-breaker	13	.
Veterinary Surgeon, Farrier	2	.
Drover	3	.
Game-keeper	2	.
Dog, Bird, Animal-keeper, Dealer	1	.
Vermin Destroyer	1	.
Fisherman	10	.
V.—INDUSTRIAL CLASS.		
9. Publisher, Bookseller, Librarian	1	.
Bookbinder	40	22
Printer	55	1
Newspaper Agent, News Room Keeper	2	.
Lithographer, Lithographic Printer	26	.
Map and Print-colourer, Seller	4	.
10. Engine and Machine Maker	7	1
Fitter and Turner (Engine and Machine)	28	.
Boiler Maker	9	.
Spinning and Weaving Machine Maker	0	1
Agricultural Machine and Implement Maker	6	.
Tool Maker, Dealer	4	.
Cutler, Scissors Maker	8	9
File Maker	6	.
Saw Maker	1	.
Needle Maker	1	1
Steel Pen Maker	1	1
Domestic Implement Maker	1	.
Watch Maker, Clock Maker	11	.
Philosophical Instrument Maker, Optician	1	.
Electrical Apparatus Maker	3	.
Weighing and Measuring Apparatus Maker	2	.
Gunsmith, Gun Manufacturer	1	.
Musical Instrument Maker, Dealer	3	.
Die, Seal, Coin, Medal, Maker	4	.
Toy Maker, Dealer	1	.
11. Builder	7	.
Carpenter, Joiner	137	.
Bricklayer	41	.
Mason	61	.
Plasterer, Whitewasher	7	.
Paperhanger	1	.
Plumber	6	.
Painter, Glazier	85	.
Cabinet Maker, Upholsterer	75	7
French Polisher	21	1
Furniture Broker, Dealer	3	.
Locksmith, Bellhanger	1	.
Gas Fitter	1	.
House and Shop Fittings-maker, Dealer	5	.
Funeral Furniture Maker, Undertaker	1	.
Wood Carver	22	.
Carver, Gilder	12	.
Animal, Bird, &c., Preserver, Naturalist	1	.
Artificial Flower Maker	1	1
12. Coachmaker	12	.
Wheelright	15	.
Others	4	.
Saddler, Harness, Whip, Maker	43	.
13. Ship, Boat, Barge, Builder	8	.
Shipwright, Ship Carpenter (ashore)	4	.
Mast, Yard, Oar, Block, Maker	4	.
Sail Maker	6	.
14. Dye, Paint, Manufacture	3	1
Fusee, Fireworks, Explosive Article Manufacture	1	1
Manufacturing Chemist	2	.
Alkali Manufacture	1	.
15. Tobacco Manufacturer, Tobacconist	7	5
Tobacco Pipe, Snuff Box, &c., Maker	.	1
16. Innkeeper, Hotel Keeper, Publican	5	.
Lodging, Boarding House, Keeper	.	.
Malster	1	.
Brewer	5	.
Beerseller, Ale, Porter, Cider, Dealer	1	.
Cellarman	3	.
Wine and Spirit—Merchant, Agent	1	.
Milkseller, Dairyman	6	.
Butcher, Meat Salesman	17	1
Provision Curer, Dealer	1	.
Corn, Flour, Seed—Merchant, Dealer	1	.
Corn Miller	9	.
Baker	19	.
Confectioner, Pastrycook	4	1
Greengrocer, Fruiterer	4	1
Mustard, Vinegar, Spice, Pickle—Maker, Dealer	.	1
Grocer, Tea, Coffee, Chocolate—Maker, Dealer	3	3
Ginger Beer, Mineral Water, Manufacturer, Dealer	1	2
17. Woolstapler	1	.
Woollen Cloth Manufacture	32	15
Worsted, Stuff Manufacture	9	16
Flannel Manufacture	.	1
Blanket Manufacture	3	.
Fuller	1	.
Silk, Silk Goods, Manufacture	6	12
Silk Dyer, Printer	1	.
Ribbon Manufacture	2	.
Cotton, Cotton Goods, Manufacture	57	134
Cotton, Calico—Printer, Dyer, Bleacher	3	.
Cotton, Calico, Warehouseman, Dealer	3	.
Flax, Linen Manufacturer, Dealer	5	7
Lace Manufacturer, Dealer	4	23
Fustian Manufacturer, Dealer	1	4
Tape Manufacturer, Dealer	.	3
Hemp, Jute, Cocoa Fibre, Manufacture	2	1
Rope, Twine, Cord, Maker, Dealer	2	.
Mat Maker, Seller	3	1
Net Maker	1	.
Sacking, Sack, Bag—Maker, Dealer	.	1
Weaver (undefined)	2	6
Dyer, Printer, Scourer, Bleacher, Calenderer (undefined)	7	1
Factory Hand (Textile), undefined	6	8
Carpet, Rug, Manufacture	7	1
Draper, Linen Draper, Mercer	.	1
Fancy Goods (Textile), Manufacturer, Worker, Dealer	3	2
Trimming Maker, Dealer	1	2
Others	.	1
18. Hatter, Hat Manufacture (not Straw)	7	5
Straw—Hat, Bonnet, Plait, Manufacture	.	23
Tailor	344	75
Milliner, Dressmaker, Staymaker	1	557
Shawl Manufacture	.	2
Shirtmaker, Seamstress	2	97
Hosiery Manufacture	4	8
Hosier, Haberdasher	1	2
Glover, Glove Maker	2	12
Button Maker, Dealer	3	3
Shoe, Boot—Maker, Dealer	507	19
Pattern, Clog, Maker	23	.
Wig Maker, Hair Dresser	10	.
Umbrella, Parasol, Stick—Maker, Dealer	3	2
Accoutrement Maker	.	1

THE DEAF AND DUMB—*continued.*

TABLE XIX *continued.*—OCCUPATIONS of MALES and FEMALES returned as DEAF and DUMB.

Occupations.	Males.	Females.
Tallow Chandler, Candle, Grease Manufacturer	1	.
Soap Boiler, Maker	.	2
Manure Manufacture	1	.
Bone, Horn, Ivory, Tortoise-shell—Worker, Dealer	2	.
Furrier, Skinner	1	.
Tanner, Fellmonger	7	.
Currier	8	1
Leather Goods, Portmanteau, Bag, Strap, &c., Maker, Dealer	4	1
Hair, Bristle—Worker, Dealer	1	.
Brush, Broom, Maker	10	6
Quill, Feather—Dresser, Dealer	.	1
20. Oil Miller, Oil Cake—Maker, Dealer	4	.
Japanner	3	.
Waterproof Goods—Maker, Dealer	2	.
Willow, Cane, Rush—Worker, Dealer. Basketmaker	29	2
Thatcher	1	.
Timber, Wood—Merchant, Dealer	6	.
Sawyer	13	.
Lath, Wooden Fence, Hurdle, Maker	1	.
Wood Turner, Box Maker	18	2
Cooper, Hoop Maker, Bender	23	.
Cork, Bark—Cutter, Worker, Dealer	1	.
Paper Manufacture	1	4
Envelope Maker	.	1
Stationer, Law Stationer	4	.
Card, Pattern Card, Maker	.	1
Paper Stainer	.	1
Paper Box, Paper Bag, Maker	5	8
Ticket, Label, Writer	2	.
Others	.	1
21. Coal Miner	71	1
Ironstone Miner	1	.
Copper Miner	.	1
Tin Miner	1	1
Lead Miner	4	1
Miner in other, or undefined minerals	12	.
Coal Merchant, Dealer	3	.
Coalheaver	6	.
Coke, Charcoal, Peat—Cutter, Burner, Dealer	2	.
Gas Works Service	7	.
Stone Quarrier	14	.
Stone Cutter, Dresser, Dealer	4	.
Slate Quarrier	1	.
Slate Worker, Dealer	1	.
Clay, Sand, Gravel, Chalk—Labourer, Dealer	1	.
Plaster, Cement, Manufacture	1	.
Brick, Tile—Maker, Burner, Dealer	22	2
Paviour	1	.
Road Labourer	9	.
Platelayer	3	.
Railway Labourer, Navy	3	.
Others	1	.
Earthenware, China, Porcelain Manufacture	22	9
Glass Manufacture	20	.
Salt Maker, Dealer	2	.
Waterworks Service	1	.
Goldsmith, Silversmith, Jeweller	11	1
Gold, Silver, Beater	1	.
Others	.	1
Blacksmith	55	.
Nail Manufacture	6	3
Anchor, Chain, Manufacture	5	.
Other Iron and Steel Manufactures	65	.
Ironmonger, Hardware Dealer, Merchant	1	.
Copper, Copper Goods—Manufacturer, Worker, Dealer	3	.
Tin, Tin Plate, Tin Goods—Manufacturer, Worker, Dealer	14	1
21.—*cont.*		
Metal Refiner, Worker, Turner, Dealer	3	.
Brass, Bronze Manufacture, Brazier	18	.
Metal Burnisher, Lacquerer	1	2
Wire Maker, Worker, Weaver, Drawer	6	1
Bolt, Nut, Rivet, Screw, Staple, Maker	8	.
Others	2	1
22. General Shopkeeper, Dealer	4	.
Pawnbroker	2	.
Costermonger, Huckster, Street Seller	14	.
Manufacturer, Manager, Superintendent (undefined)	1	.
General Labourer	360	2
Engine Driver, Stoker, Fireman (neither railway, marine, nor agricultural)	11	.
Artizan, Mechanic (undefined)	30	.
Apprentice (undefined)	5	1
Factory Labourer (undefined)	11	.
Mechinist, Machine Worker (und.)	1	5
23. Chimney Sweep, Soot Merchant	1	.
Scavenger, Crossing Sweeper	3	.
Rag Gatherer, Dealer	2	.
VI.—UNOCCUPIED CLASS.		
24. Persons returned by property, Rank, &c., and not by special occupation, including all children under 5 years of age	3280	4408

END OF SUMMARY TABLES.

AGES,

CONDITION AS TO MARRIAGE,

OCCUPATIONS, AND BIRTH-PLACES

OF THE PEOPLE;

WITH THE

NUMBERS AND AGES OF THE BLIND, DEAF AND DUMB,
IDIOTS OR IMBECILES, AND LUNATICS.

DIVISION I.—LONDON;

MIDDLESEX (*Intra-metropolitan*),
SURREY (*Intra-metropolitan*),
KENT (*Intra-metropolitan*).

TABLES IN DIVISION I.—LONDON.

AGES.

Table

1.—AGES of MALES and FEMALES in the LONDON DIVISION and its REGISTRATION COUNTIES.

2.—AGES of MALES and FEMALES in REGISTRATION DISTRICTS.

3.—AGES of MALES and FEMALES in REGISTRATION SUB-DISTRICTS.

4.—MALE and FEMALE CHILDREN at *each Year of Age* under 5 in the LONDON DIVISION and its REGISTRATION COUNTIES.

5.—MALE and FEMALE CHILDREN at *each Year of Age* under 5 in REGISTRATION DISTRICTS.

6.—AGES of MALES and FEMALES in SANITARY DISTRICT.

CONDITION AS TO MARRIAGE.

7.—CONDITION as to MARRIAGE and AGES of MALES and FEMALES in the LONDON DIVISION and its REGISTRATION COUNTIES.

8.—CONDITION as to MARRIAGE and AGES of MALES and FEMALES in REGISTRATION DISTRICTS.

9.*

OCCUPATIONS.

10.—OCCUPATIONS of MALES and FEMALES in the LONDON DIVISION and its REGISTRATION COUNTIES.

BIRTH-PLACES.

11.—BIRTH-PLACES of MALES and FEMALES enumerated in COUNTIES.

12.—DISTRIBUTION of enumerated NATIVES of COUNTIES.

13.—NUMBER and COUNTRY of BIRTH of FOREIGNERS enumerated in the LONDON DIVISION and its REGISTRATION COUNTIES.

13A.—NUMBER and COUNTRY of BIRTH of FOREIGNERS enumerated in the REGISTRATION DISTRICTS OF LONDON.

THE BLIND, DEAF AND DUMB, IDIOTS OR IMBECILES, AND LUNATICS.

14.—NUMBER and AGES of MALES and FEMALES returned as BLIND or BLIND from BIRTH in the LONDON DIVISION and its REGISTRATION COUNTIES.

15.—NUMBER and AGES of MALES and FEMALES returned as BLIND in the LONDON DIVISION and its REGISTRATION COUNTIES.

16.—NUMBER and AGES of MALES and FEMALES returned as BLIND from BIRTH in the LONDON DIVISION and its REGISTRATION COUNTIES.

17.—NUMBER and AGES of MALES and FEMALES returned as DEAF and DUMB in the LONDON DIVISION and its REGISTRATION COUNTIES.

18.—NUMBER and AGES of MALES and FEMALES returned as IDIOTS or IMBECILES, and LUNATICS in the LONDON DIVISION and its REGISTRATION COUNTIES.

19.—NUMBER and AGES of MALES and FEMALES returned as IDIOTS or IMBECILES in the LONDON DIVISION and its REGISTRATION COUNTIES.

20.—NUMBER and AGES of MALES and FEMALES returned as LUNATICS in the LONDON DIVISION and its REGISTRATION COUNTIES.

21.—NUMBER of the BLIND, of the DEAF and DUMB, of IDIOTS or IMBECILES, and of LUNATICS in the LONDON DIVISION and its REGISTRATION COUNTIES and DISTRICTS.

* Table 9 is omitted in this Division as the Metropolis contains no Urban Sanitary Districts as constituted by the Public Health Act of 1872; the numbers of the other tables have, however, been left unaltered, in order to preserve uniformity in the numbering of these tables in the eleven Registration Divisions.

AGES.

DIVISION I.—LONDON.*

Table 1.—Ages of Males and Females in the London Division and its Registration Counties.

Registration County.	All Ages. Persons.	All Ages. Males and Females.	Under 5† Years.	5–	10–	15–	20–	25–	30–	35–	40–	45–	50–	55–	60–	65–	70–	75–	80–	85–	90–	95–	100‡ and upw^{ds}.
I.—LONDON	3816483	M. 1797486	248819	208193	179485	171569	176186	160710	136375	118650	103867	79874	67742	46979	42913	23385	15464	8369	3508	986	192	32	3
		F. 2018997	248485	211547	186628	196909	209050	188073	136187	132583	116131	92315	80590	56944	55985	36244	25432	14314	6791	2186	534	110	10
MIDDLESEX (*Intra-metropolitan*)	2550556	M. 1192885	160411	133306	115099	114023	120030	109678	91976	79267	69213	53487	45961	32783	29284	17548	11176	5674	2355	658	123	22	2
		F. 1357671	160283	136110	120835	134038	143701	130423	106533	90535	78843	63066	55488	40377	38355	24769	17306	9079	4523	1477	376	76	8
SURREY (*Intra-metropolitan*)	980522	M. 468890	63254	57890	48704	44327	42978	40410	33335	30090	26732	20281	16701	11649	10375	6147	3975	2023	848	232	50	8	1
		F. 511632	69122	58553	50783	47061	48525	45139	38561	33606	28917	22589	19200	14243	13552	8761	6161	3506	1718	534	125	24	—
KENT (*Intra-metropolitan*)	285405	M. 135711	18964	17097	15590	13308	13269	10624	9102	8293	7902	6130	5060	3647	3254	1990	1303	672	305	96	26	2	—
		F. 149694	19070	16884	15060	14970	14761	12581	11073	9451	8371	6680	5851	4329	4078	2714	1985	1070	550	175	53	10	2

* The boundaries of "London" for Census and Registration purposes are identical, and are conterminous with those of the District of the Metropolitan Board of Works, with the following exceptions:—the Hamlet of Penge in the Registration District of Croydon is within the District of the Metropolitan Board, but is *not included* within Registration London; and the Hamlet of Mottingham in the Registration District of Lewisham, is within Registration London, but is *not included* within the District of the Metropolitan Board.

† For the Number of Children at each Year of Age under 5, see Table 4.

‡ One of these Males was stated to be 101, and two 103 years of age. Three of these Females were stated to be 100 years of age, three 101, one 103, one 104, one 105, and one 106 years of age.

Table 2.—Ages of Males and Females in Registration Districts.

Registration District.	All Ages. Persons.	All Ages. Males and Females.	Under 5* Years.	5–	10–	15–	20–	25–	30–	35–	40–	45–	50–	55–	60–	65–	70–	75–	80–	85–	90–	95–	100 and upw^{ds}.
MIDDLESEX (*Intra-metropolitan*).†																							
WEST DISTRICTS.																							
1 KENSINGTON	276309	M. 1[illegible]133	14147	11909	9828	[illegible]	10903	9990	8336	7372	6259	4961	4345	3291	2796	1894	1150	596	266	79	11	2	.
		F. 162136	14137	12584	11738	17202	21546	18705	14892	11401	9701	7724	6608	4848	4557	2982	2026	1156	552	167	48	15	.
2 FULHAM	114839	M. 53174	8293	6736	5319	4647	4831	4768	4507	3698	3923	2120	1778	1192	998	659	428	340	95	32	8	1	.
		F. 61665	8272	6792	5870	6931	6103	5703	4826	4109	3335	2630	2344	1595	1397	1068	813	414	194	70	15	3	1
3 CHELSEA	88123	M. 41830	6267	4783	4129	3549	4188	3980	3280	2825	2383	1625	1488	1153	1000	634	440	250	93	25	11	2	1
		F. 46293	5870	4537	4112	3341	4415	4505	3841	3206	2998	2233	1889	1400	1361	862	598	370	157	48	8	2	1
4 ST. GEORGE HANOVER SQUARE	149748	M. 67855	7051	5892	5211	6311	8517	7442	5757	4872	4307	3389	2570	2080	1904	1131	740	325	149	52	5	1	.
		F. 81893	7096	6070	5524	8407	10210	9231	7417	6152	5261	4235	3609	2703	2528	1677	1110	599	280	101	32	7	1
5 WESTMINSTER	46540	M. 22877	2353	1976	1916	2389	2528	2318	1545	1497	1402	1217	1039	729	693	412	234	110	58	7	4	1	.
		F. 23674	2350	2017	1934	2517	2042	2324	1585	1081	1103	1221	1050	720	685	447	275	164	89	24	3	2	.
NORTH DISTRICTS.																							
6 MARYLEBONE	154910	M. 67895	7974	6597	5813	6569	7445	8451	8316	7842	4192	3305	2865	2026	2014	1177	791	425	175	47	10	4	.
		F. 87015	7928	6790	6315	9532	10555	9282	7330	6105	5525	4403	4014	3876	2737	1817	1350	771	363	103	25	2	2
7 HAMPSTEAD	45452	M. 17569	2301	2167	1941	1703	1036	1402	1230	1103	1018	784	669	586	424	308	190	105	30	12	.		1
		F. 27883	2381	2226	2487	3622	4050	3071	2221	1770	1370	1095	1005	726	686	338	309	179	85	31	8	3	1
8 PANCRAS	236258	M. 112516	14002	12023	10372	10551	11792	10916	8967	7804	6852	5106	4298	3041	2721	1692	1130	650	230	48	15	1	.
		F. 123742	14489	12475	10934	11322	12805	11943	9794	8232	7322	5977	5163	3343	3664	2414	1676	980	439	158	45	3	.
9 ISLINGTON	282865	M. 132580	19030	15748	13072	12064	13091	12345	10471	8845	7411	6409	4783	3275	2903	1748	1161	594	241	80	16	2	.
		F. 150285	18613	15824	13646	14877	16375	14842	11718	9838	8438	6407	5976	4325	4128	2765	1880	1120	641	172	43	4	.
10 HACKNEY	186462	M. 83808	12452	10453	9739	7893	7684	7172	6294	5396	4464	3517	2949	2189	1967	1184	788	419	188	53	5	1	.
		F. 102654	12707	10808	9724	11452	10038	9190	7558	6225	5536	4271	3820	2311	2838	1900	1451	790	378	121	31	3	.
CENTRAL DISTRICTS.																							
11 ST. GILES	45382	M. 22088	2429	2014	1886	2001	2392	2150	1810	1403	1467	1183	1003	749	695	306	248	117	53	10	3	.	.
		F. 23294	2398	2066	1907	2384	2008	2341	1893	1547	1473	1161	1029	734	704	435	290	135	68	23	4	.	.
12 STRAND	35582	M. 15799	1556	1330	1311	1703	2087	1702	1484	1233	1137	957	789	533	471	286	148	57	29	3	1	.	.
		F. 16783	1596	1456	1348	1780	2009	1641	1383	1183	1073	901	785	574	502	359	167	91	30	13	6	.	.
13 HOLBORN	151835	M. 76056	9715	7984	7091	8081	8044	7235	5900	4803	4550	3568	3068	2106	1888	938	561	201	106	30	4	1	.
		F. 75779	9675	8071	7361	7283	7509	6842	5632	4864	4530	3089	3291	2219	2130	1216	880	432	181	59	7	6	2
14 LONDON CITY	51439	M. 25593	2164	2140	2735	3463	3704	2237	1670	1551	1420	1097	1073	731	893	424	257	108	54	9	3	.	.
		F. 25876	2146	2032	2176	3087	3043	2239	1821	1679	1556	1385	1297	969	919	686	446	258	105	33	6	2	.
EAST DISTRICTS.																							
15 SHOREDITCH	126591	M. 61685	9213	7203	6032	5859	5925	5827	4586	3839	3235	2953	2185	1629	1537	943	588	280	120	37	4		.
		F. 64906	9434	7297	6170	5768	6193	5875	4710	3985	3447	2919	2464	1891	1847	1217	860	480	251	80	14	3	.
16 BETHNAL GREEN	120961	M. 56546	9731	8179	6778	6107	6156	5425	4113	3739	3312	2451	2194	1608	1339	864	610	337	129	25	4		.
		F. 64415	9649	8072	6953	5996	5755	5279	4520	3758	3430	2710	2408	1834	1639	1096	741	399	178	49	15	3	.
17 WHITECHAPEL	71363	M. 36718	4407	3968	3522	3089	3951	3322	2867	2431	2219	1723	1532	1072	972	491	298	156	50	14	2	3	.
		F. 34646	4599	4015	3598	3791	3283	2758	2357	2114	2006	1600	1409	996	936	507	329	200	84	30	18	5	.
18 ST. GEORGE IN THE EAST	47157	M. 23611	3230	2627	2306	2172	2346	2143	1847	1515	1399	1113	967	644	580	342	253	82	32	5	1	.	.
		F. 23546	3264	2891	2368	2123	2239	1959	1651	1484	1352	1128	1033	548	686	386	293	144	56	23	5	2	.
19 STEPNEY	58543	M. 29394	4040	3545	3356	2920	2667	2409	2112	1893	1703	1322	1230	823	700	374	175	80	24	12	5	.	.
		F. 29149	4089	3548	3094	2728	2513	2308	2095	1870	1711	1347	1250	854	757	447	270	150	76	28	7	1	.
20 MILE END OLD TOWN	105613	M. 50938	7573	6331	5440	4812	4772	4334	3770	3228	2764	2100	1857	1345	1158	718	413	190	95	28	8	3	.
		F. 54675	7685	6318	5344	4994	4948	4680	3980	3300	3014	2496	2215	1625	1609	1043	718	402	188	63	21	8	.
21 POPLAR	156510	M. 79090	11928	10131	8450	7527	6598	6474	5709	5334	4719	3522	2963	2040	1677	963	598	287	129	40	5	.	.
		F. 77420	12018	10048	8293	8599	6317	6395	5801	4933	4344	3414	2916	2016	1836	1153	747	441	223	76	17	4	.

Note.—The Registration Districts of this Division are co-extensive with the Poor Law Districts, with the following exception:—Kensington Registration District contains the two Parishes and Poor Law Districts of Kensington and Paddington.

For the Parishes comprised in each Registration District, see Vol. II., Division I., Table 4.

The Districts are arranged topographically under the Registration Counties, and are numbered consecutively, commencing with the Metropolitan Districts, Division I.

* For the Number of Children at each Year of Age under 5, see Table 3.

† For the Extra-Metropolitan Districts of Middlesex, see Division III., Table 2.

Table 2 *continued*.—AGES of MALES and FEMALES in REGISTRATION DISTRICTS.

REGISTRATION DISTRICT.	ALL AGES. Persons.	ALL AGES. Males and Females.	Under 5 Years.	5–	10–	15–	20–	25–	30–	35–	40–	45–	50–	55–	60–	65–	70–	75–	80–	85–	90–	95–	100 and upwards.
SOUTH DISTRICTS.																							
SURREY (*Intra-metropolitan*).*																							
22 ST. SAVIOUR SOUTHWARK	195164	M. - 96498	13541	10815	9340	9286	9543	8781	7508	6429	5581	4418	3639	2451	2321	1385	854	419	140	51	9	2	1
		F. - 98666	13593	11130	9585	8655	9047	8721	7477	6636	5651	4490	3889	2827	2814	1737	1202	890	330	103	34	5	.
23 ST. OLAVE SOUTHWARK	134632	M. - 67566	10291	8423	7241	6621	5126	5652	4900	4292	3826	2880	2369	1721	1468	807	563	240	108	31	4	1	.
		F. - 67066	10163	8409	7137	5831	5620	5433	4772	4290	3343	2361	2596	1839	1671	1076	746	420	182	58	18	1	.
24 LAMBETH	253699	M. 119176	16737	14090	12033	10926	11343	10902	9169	8017	6831	5136	4293	3147	2877	1723	1085	575	227	54	12	.	.
		F. 134523	16979	14330	12512	12942	13698	12827	10265	8852	7617	6052	5138	3951	3948	2514	1736	1055	501	141	29	6	.
25 WANDSWORTH	210434	M. - 98159	[illegible]	[illegible]	10382	9270	8635	8664	7010	6606	5608	4064	[illegible]	[illegible]	1919	1161	799	415	176	44	11	9	.
		F. 112275	14898	12707	11620	10077	11014	10106	8565	7444	6313	4845	3942	2946	2080	1791	1239	728	314	120	23	3	.
26 CAMBERWELL	186593	M. - 87491	13086	11731	9788	8235	7271	6091	6357	5587	4362	3567	3040	2016	1767	1081	761	374	198	62	14	3	.
		F. - 99102	13469	11837	9879	9556	9246	8552	7482	6474	5408	4221	3695	2680	2430	1643	1238	675	391	112	21	9	.
KENT (*Intra-metropolitan*).†																							
27 GREENWICH	131233	M. - 63403	9086	8092	7750	6085	5497	4814	4237	3870	3569	2663	2353	1737	1657	933	632	303	134	48	16	2	.
		F. - 67830	9210	7933	7054	5472	6102	5497	4891	4298	3743	2998	2680	1077	1876	1266	949	592	256	88	30	4	2
28 LEWISHAM	73327	M. - 31301	4455	4060	3501	3042	2687	2496	2183	1951	1767	1370	1166	836	695	466	316	202	80	19	5	.	.
		F. - 42026	4478	3948	3850	4485	3243	4032	3219	2700	2279	1795	1096	1112	1053	751	557	306	155	40	13	.	.
29 WOOLWICH	80845	M. - 41007	5413	4985	4359	4175	4085	3314	2722	2472	2566	2103	1656	1074	1002	501	365	167	91	29	4	.	.
		F. - 39838	5382	4837	4146	3586	3446	3052	2963	2453	2349	1693	1575	1235	1140	717	490	262	137	47	19	6	.

* For the Extra-Metropolitan Districts of Surrey, see Division II., Table 2.
† For the Extra-Metropolitan Districts of Kent, see Division II., Table 2.

Table 3.—AGES of MALES and FEMALES in REGISTRATION SUB-DISTRICTS.

REGISTRATION SUB-DISTRICT.	ALL AGES. Persons.	ALL AGES. Males and Females.	Under 5 Years.	5–	10–	15–	20–	25–	30–	35–	40–	45–	50–	55–	60–	65–	70–	75–	80–	85–	90–	95–	100 and upwards.
MIDDLESEX (*Intra-metropolitan*).																							
1 KENSINGTON.																							
1 ST. MARY PADDINGTON. (W. H.[2])	69888	M. - 29503	3048	3155	2718	2709	3005	2889	2337	2019	1700	1344	1130	802	680	473	330	146	62	17	4	2	.
		F. - 40385	3066	3281	3338	4170	5030	4814	3343	2715	2447	1928	1684	1266	1262	840	550	317	167	44	16	4	
2 ST. JOHN PADDINGTON. (H.)	37330	M. - 13279	1373	1249	918	1210	1548	1271	1030	931	861	673	630	489	417	302	191	186	47	11	.	.	
		F. - 24051	1437	1272	1329	2578	3506	3135	2387	1841	1493	1298	1077	744	601	441	341	309	90	25	6	3	
3 KENSINGTON TOWN. (W. H[3]. B.)	120141	M. - 50007	6969	6030	4050	4640	4566	4371	3605	3331	3073	2130	1940	1392	1277	841	409	274	112	30	7	.	
		F. - 70134	6962	6825	5816	7135	8506	7180	5973	4852	4144	3293	2738	2011	1937	1278	890	481	220	62	17	5	
4 BROMPTON. (H. L. B.)	43010	M. - 15444	1863	1473	1048	1433	1814	1559	1298	1071	928	865	645	518	432	278	180	71	45	16	.	.	
		F. - 27566	1891	1645	1575	3896	4445	3718	2620	1933	1617	1206	1103	837	677	413	315	189	75	25	10	3	
2 FULHAM.																							
1 ST. PETER HAMMERSMITH (L.)	7599	M. - 3342	466	407	328	324	275	252	281	232	172	165	109	96	79	62	48	24	7	3	1	.	
		F. - 4257	514	463	372	448	439	307	326	259	220	187	167	131	120	108	72	57	23	3	1	1	
2 ST. PAUL HAMMERSMITH. (H. L. P. R.)	64340	M. - 29409	4487	3662	3003	2654	2693	2674	2399	2075	1668	1159	1011	675	546	331	203	118	66	18	3	1	
		F. - 34931	4470	3779	3358	3572	3982	3247	2673	2308	1616	1425	1286	928	931	619	404	228	94	40	9	2	
3 FULHAM. (W.[2] L.[5] P. R.)	42900	M. - 20423	3302	2651	1991	1686	1863	1867	1624	1391	1192	805	658	422	373	256	180	98	32	12	4	.	
		F. - 22477	3308	2523	2149	1911	2186	2088	1827	1533	1249	973	791	636	540	341	271	149	77	22	6	1	
3 CHELSEA.																							
1 CHELSEA SOUTH. (H.[4] R.[2] B.)	30396	M. - 15247	1963	1514	1756	1285	1661	1415	1114	1003	819	709	567	457	400	249	203	92	40	10	6	1	
		F. - 15149	1894	1565	1370	1321	1456	1390	1218	1046	870	750	612	488	498	293	201	99	37	14	3	.	
2 CHELSEA NORTH-WEST. (W. H.[4])	24925	M. - 11281	1574	1209	986	1008	1065	994	908	718	670	512	452	348	321	224	144	106	27	10	4	1	
		F. - 13644	1559	1363	1196	1185	1241	1279	1100	948	782	705	583	459	461	260	229	178	86	16	5	2	
3 CHELSEA NORTH-EAST (L. R.)	32807	M. - 15362	2468	1830	1446	1255	1452	1571	1258	1104	894	604	479	348	288	151	90	58	26	5	1	.	
		F. - 17445	2435	1909	1546	1335	1724	1839	1633	1214	1046	763	644	453	422	269	168	98	34	18	.	.	
4 ST. GEORGE HANOVER SQUARE.																							
1 HANOVER SQUARE. (H.)	16862	M. - 7109	604	508	510	739	964	766	614	560	462	379	342	268	210	119	83	36	17	5	1	.	
		F. 9753	577	557	544	1149	1409	1196	937	687	656	512	443	319	299	176	96	85	24	10	8	2	
2 MAYFAIR. (W.[2])	13491	M. - 5704	339	247	229	500	766	719	464	441	358	280	254	205	301	235	179	117	36	13	1	.	
		F. - 7787	312	228	294	841	1285	1042	747	606	458	369	331	228	311	265	215	134	58	21	10	1	
3 BELGRAVE. (H.[2] B.)	59220	M. - 25256	2890	2195	1962	2287	2900	2777	2226	1840	1611	1278	1074	785	664	383	230	131	59	21	2	1	
		F. - 33964	2786	2369	2108	3476	4310	3951	3127	2962	2179	1765	1584	1145	1008	686	423	215	124	47	8	2	
4 ST. JOHN WESTMINSTER. (H.[4] P.)	35490	M. - 18149	2204	1786	1617	1625	2116	1863	1474	1280	1029	956	729	507	482	238	127	62	18	6	.	2	
		F. - 17356	2194	1873	1573	1348	1536	1580	1428	1196	1134	902	803	575	545	311	207	89	44	11	4	2	
5 ST. MARGARET WESTMINSTER. (H. P. B.[5])	24679	M. - 11646	1117	961	993	1150	1771	1367	940	817	670	516	471	325	297	186	121	49	19	7	1	.	
		F. - 13033	1146	918	945	1283	1590	1450	1208	1046	844	638	558	438	305	259	189	98	30	12	5	.	
5 WESTMINSTER.																							
1 GOLDEN SQUARE. (W. H.)	11608	M. - 5486	633	455	445	690	613	563	396	342	359	264	255	192	192	131	70	45	33	3	3	1	
		F. 6122	484	420	487	649	738	590	419	405	386	317	299	187	193	149	121	90	50	15	2	2	
2 BERWICK STREET (H.)	18333	M. - 9287	792	678	694	1017	1119	982	816	703	620	324	425	308	280	107	92	41	17	4	1	.	
		F. - 9046	805	750	607	1024	1204	933	742	647	631	457	396	288	256	119	83	41	17	5	1	.	
3 ST. ANNE SOHO. (H.[5])	16608	M. - 8104	926	845	777	782	896	773	634	652	483	420	358	229	212	114	62	24	8	.	.	.	
		F. - 8504	971	847	809	843	916	801	674	589	526	447	355	254	236	139	71	33	22	4	.	.	

Note.—For the Parishes comprised in each Registration Sub-District, see Vol. I., Division I., Table 4.
(W.) denotes that a Workhouse, and (WS.) that a Workhouse School belonging to the District is situated within the Sub-District; (w.) denotes a Workhouse and (ws.) a Workhouse School, not belonging to the District; (H.) a Hospital or Infirmary; (L.) a Lunatic Asylum; (P.) a Prison or Convict Establishment; (R.) a certified Reformatory or Industrial School; (B.) Barracks, &c.; (S.) H. M. Ships. A figure appended to any of these letters denotes the number of institutions of a similar class situated within the Sub-District. The names of the institutions thus indicated, and the number of inmates enumerated therein, will be found in Vol. II., Division, I. Table 6.

Table 3 *continued.*—AGES of MALES and FEMALES in REGISTRATION SUB-DISTRICTS.

REGISTRATION SUB-DISTRICT.	ALL AGES. Persons.	ALL AGES. Males and Females.	Under 5 Years	5-	10-	15-	20-	25-	30-	35-	40-	45-	50-	55-	60-	65-	70-	75-	80-	85-	90-	95-	100 and upw.
MIDDLESEX (*Intra-metropolitan*) —*cont.*																							
6 MARYLEBONE.																							
1 ALL SOULS. (H.[6] R.)	26739	M. - 12201	1414	1073	961	1178	1466	1282	1008	851	742	674	520	401	342	202	97	80	21	4	3	.	.
		F. - 14403	1340	1151	1020	1398	1709	1600	1271	1031	956	800	720	515	436	299	175	87	38	6	3	1	.
2 CAVENDISH SQUARE. (H.[3])	14831	M. - 5904	483	403	388	362	918	676	600	449	396	273	287	178	173	104	75	32	11	8	.	.	.
		F. - 8927	518	487	395	1120	1501	1172	847	705	563	465	373	250	203	110	117	49	14	5	2	.	.
3 RECTORY. (W.[2] H. R.)	24899	M. - 10663	1199	928	878	980	1085	959	899	706	705	569	487	328	411	260	206	123	75	13	2	.	.
		F. - 14236	1171	1045	952	1432	1658	1374	1081	922	808	734	703	322	538	408	338	212	105	30	10	3	.
4 ST. MARY. (H.[4])	21118	M. - 9152	1083	837	778	838	1066	913	707	622	620	465	398	209	261	145	83	53	17	8	1	1	2
		F. - 11966	1017	856	781	1130	1398	1281	1005	881	811	677	575	427	378	273	202	113	50	18	1	.	.
5 CHRISTCHURCH. (H.[5])	38700	M. - 18551	1946	1602	1461	1628	1679	1380	1161	1062	995	704	623	432	390	240	153	69	38	8	4	.	.
		F. - 18149	1987	1658	1633	1695	1823	1788	1423	1330	1182	918	709	517	358	319	212	144	57	17	5	1	.
6 ST. JOHN. (H.[3] B.)	33633	M. - 14384	1950	1884	1351	1280	1371	1294	1102	884	811	660	597	473	417	226	175	80	38	10	.	.	.
		F. - 19249	1874	1618	1459	1941	2473	2077	1575	1224	1118	901	838	613	619	378	275	147	93	26	4	.	.
7 HAMPSTEAD.																							
1 HAMPSTEAD. (W.[3] H.[3] R.[3])	45452	M. - 17569	2801	2187	1941	1708	1880	1402	1250	1103	1018	781	689	536	524	308	196	105	30	12	.	.	1
		F. - 27883	2361	2220	2437	3622	4060	3071	2221	1770	1578	1005	1009	730	636	395	309	170	84	31	8	3	1
8 PANCRAS.																							
1 REGENT'S PARK. (H. R. E.)	39115	M. - 18278	2370	1837	1478	1769	2028	1882	1684	1309	1345	832	721	514	484	374	164	84	37	6	1	.	.
		F. - 20837	2221	1983	1950	1991	2306	2103	1728	1434	1296	1098	861	617	640	400	259	180	68	27	5	.	.
2 TOTTENHAM COURT. (w. H.[4] R.)	27729	M. - 13099	1442	1184	1066	1379	1538	1411	1066	914	806	652	545	471	434	207	138	55	21	8	1	.	.
		F. - 14630	1424	1261	1147	1262	1705	1371	1228	1061	912	758	671	484	477	271	160	80	44	18	5	.	.
3 GRAY'S INN LANE. (H.[3])	30047	M. - 14304	1735	1381	1328	1428	1636	1532	1159	1000	805	652	587	411	372	205	141	41	20	4	3	.	.
		F. - 15743	1713	1471	1409	1454	1721	1582	1284	1034	906	744	683	483	396	270	258	33	49	14	3	.	.
4 SOMERS TOWN. (H.)	34369	M. - 16563	2207	1823	1636	1604	1597	1468	1244	1079	983	738	690	544	518	330	161	64	21	5	.	.	.
		F. - 17806	2252	1022	1686	1487	1703	1407	1328	1157	1055	889	804	580	536	371	244	129	59	24	6	.	.
5 CAMDEN TOWN. (W. H.)	17311	M. - 8331	1048	755	687	674	865	786	608	477	481	389	309	241	278	232	197	144	67	14	4	1	.
		F. - 8980	1074	832	716	673	701	794	681	624	500	420	354	299	373	323	269	217	80	33	10	2	.
6 KENTISH TOWN. (W. w. H.)	87487	M. - 41741	6008	4943	4230	3753	4121	3945	3296	2830	2372	1793	1470	1032	877	524	329	162	71	13	6	.	.
		F. - 45746	5798	5005	4320	4826	4928	4304	3545	3087	2612	2008	1775	1377	1188	770	535	309	133	45	14	1	.
9 ISLINGTON.																							
1 ISLINGTON WEST. (H.[4] P.[4])	121152	M. - 58049	8386	6777	5653	5480	5935	5608	4736	4126	3348	2508	2073	1456	1230	680	430	180	68	33	3	1	.
		F. - 62803	8177	6852	5902	5962	6444	6082	4897	4158	3542	2768	2467	1741	1576	1015	640	307	179	56	10	.	.
2 ISLINGTON EAST. (W. w.[2] WS. H.)	161413	M. - 73931	10514	8071	7389	6634	7136	6737	5755	4819	4063	3061	2719	1810	1725	1008	711	414	173	54	13	1	.
		F. - 87482	10438	8072	7743	8515	9132	8184	6926	5686	4894	3725	3415	2051	2532	1750	1234	783	302	116	32	4	.
10. HACKNEY.																							
1 STOKE NEWINGTON. (H. L.)	22781	M. - 9910	1546	1202	1138	827	906	951	808	703	510	388	337	214	202	140	88	49	29	11	.	.	.
		F. - 12871	1549	1190	1039	1486	1511	1280	1017	820	659	453	468	358	364	243	204	94	41	16	3	1	.
2 STAMFORD HILL	9277	M. - 3886	834	466	392	365	378	300	267	226	207	106	134	102	92	71	41	17	9	3	1	.	.
		F. - 5391	539	577	451	643	670	638	416	331	251	225	172	150	127	92	59	81	11	4	4	1	.
3 WEST HACKNEY	37610	M. - 16974	2406	2058	1967	1556	1681	1304	1311	1118	993	713	615	435	307	253	134	60	33	10	2	.	.
		F. - 20636	2495	2075	1830	2370	2592	1858	1533	1316	1417	816	821	594	590	306	278	154	69	30	5	1	.
4 HACKNEY. (W. w.[3] H. L. R.)	72911	M. - 34765	5040	4215	3674	3246	3331	3303	2560	2234	1773	1458	1194	927	825	529	363	252	90	18	2	1	.
		F. - 38146	5210	4107	4066	4377	4332	3775	3105	2514	2254	1804	1379	1261	1188	814	469	374	184	55	10	.	.
5 SOUTH HACKNEY. (R.)	39883	M. - 18385	2876	2473	2034	1907	1758	1698	1294	1124	1082	718	615	421	441	101	102	86	27	11	.	.	.
		F. - 21898	2871	2556	2373	2357	2277	1734	1450	1140	1176	741	790	629	569	314	241	157	70	18	3	.	.
11 ST. GILES.																							
1 ST. GEORGE BLOOMSBURY	16081	M. - 7925	780	614	616	737	915	778	692	590	488	353	330	273	232	182	73	48	20	2	1	.	.
		F. - 9156	766	620	620	988	1277	1031	775	617	603	449	408	290	238	173	119	50	38	12	1	.	.
2 ST. GILES SOUTH. (W. H.)	14861	M. - 7814	827	696	637	850	734	703	639	589	545	471	395	282	277	158	97	44	28	6	1	.	.
		F. - 7039	781	718	658	840	687	686	575	457	451	386	301	328	271	149	101	33	29	3	1	.	.
3 ST. GILES NORTH	13837	M. - 6739	813	673	616	608	723	478	560	424	447	368	271	212	198	126	58	28	7	2	1	.	.
		F. - 7098	801	689	590	736	784	724	619	473	391	316	320	216	193	111	79	50	11	4	2	.	.
12 STRAND.																							
1 ST. MARTIN IN THE FIELDS. (H.[2] B.)	17508	M. - 8863	799	851	622	890	1184	922	787	632	601	489	343	266	245	149	97	33	11	2	1	.	.
		F. - 8645	754	713	656	962	1036	979	754	678	587	480	398	360	215	158	78	46	10	5	5	.	.
2 ST. MARY-LE-STRAND	7515	M. - 3707	364	316	322	397	409	294	231	301	258	212	172	126	88	70	36	11	11	.	.	.	.
		F. - 3808	412	344	311	432	453	335	180	257	229	175	177	125	123	56	40	21	11	5	1	.	.
3 ST. CLEMENT DANES. (H. S.)	8559	M. - 4229	351	384	386	416	464	497	347	269	275	227	187	138	118	57	36	13	7	1	.	.	.
		F. - 4330	287	309	331	452	410	514	294	265	287	246	210	140	134	76	54	30	9	5	.	.	.
13 HOLBORN.																							
1 ST. GEORGE THE MARTYR. (H.[6])	15671	M. - 9118	985	856	739	639	950	847	764	682	623	460	480	301	219	135	78	45	18	3	2	.	.
		F. - 8553	1037	847	853	914	990	875	784	651	571	481	474	316	343	214	121	67	31	10	.	1	1
2 ST. ANDREW EASTERN. (W.)	10706	M. - 5732	873	640	559	635	878	571	443	506	382	316	278	164	100	72	36	30	9	.	.	.	.
		F. - 4974	509	635	541	590	479	352	313	344	339	288	239	157	163	81	33	38	12	4	1	.	1
3 SAFFRON HILL. (H.)	6538	M. - 3390	328	329	307	415	292	259	220	224	223	185	181	111	114	61	34	24	12	7	.	.	.
		F. - 3144	363	316	304	332	336	229	229	207	211	147	157	97	99	45	37	20	10	3	.	.	.
4 ST. JAMES CLERKENWELL. (P.)	17712	M. - 8888	1244	1084	910	928	885	742	640	562	518	411	327	231	195	101	52	41	7	8	1	.	.
		F. - 8628	1192	997	908	830	792	745	650	542	516	425	363	233	186	122	95	34	13	7	.	1	.
5 AMWELL. (P.)	19251	M. - 10220	1219	936	852	1173	1347	1037	831	656	584	430	343	211	199	118	98	26	9	1	.	.	.
		F. - 9031	1165	996	862	858	970	817	710	601	531	422	351	230	225	130	98	22	19	3	1	1	.
6 PENTONVILLE	14773	M. - 7349	1033	848	776	744	701	628	582	463	452	352	262	105	163	80	47	25	13	1	.	.	.
		F. - 7424	1014	839	762	691	675	648	570	510	433	334	253	225	174	127	71	41	15	7	.	1	.
7 GOSWELL STREET	17506	M. - 8486	1128	987	779	871	858	833	680	557	500	383	396	264	213	97	60	34	10	5	1	.	.
		F. - 9020	1089	909	753	856	947	880	604	594	559	418	394	278	260	163	124	55	21	10	1	.	.
8 OLD STREET. (H.)	11541	M. - 5631	830	678	514	568	633	610	429	375	280	229	210	154	118	52	42	18	6	4	.	.	.
		F. - 5910	819	648	520	497	684	596	437	363	322	271	235	160	161	106	58	26	8	2	.	.	.
9 CITY ROAD. (H.[2] L.)	18628	M. - 8993	1342	1095	851	917	854	878	657	531	477	394	348	221	212	91	68	31	12	3	1	.	.
		F. - 9635	1402	1008	938	874	953	827	675	540	586	472	402	308	278	176	103	60	37	10	1	1	.
10 WHITECROSS STREET	9217	M. - 4508	636	559	535	512	420	373	312	247	263	212	179	117	136	53	43	8	6	1	.	.	.
		F. - 4709	637	563	548	474	455	313	388	273	280	218	212	138	165	75	55	19	3	2	2	.	.
11 FINSBURY. (H. B.)	7463	M. - 3652	394	346	298	408	429	327	276	237	243	196	175	105	111	48	28	14	5	2	.	1	.
		F. - 3811	393	351	349	457	586	335	289	240	234	207	179	111	138	65	42	34	8	1	1	1	.

Table 3 *continued*.—Ages of Males and Females in Registration Sub-Districts.

Registration Sub-District.	All Ages. Persons.	Males and Females.		Under 5 Years.	5–	10–	15–	20–	25–	30–	35–	40–	45–	50–	55–	60–	65–	70–	75–	80–	85–	90–	95–	100 and upw^ds.
MIDDLESEX (*Intra-metropolitan*)—*cont.*																								
14 LONDON CITY.																								
1 St. Botolph. (H.)	11174	M.	5316	636	602	594	633	558	449	324	295	319	247	223	126	140	80	58	20	8	4	.	.	.
		F.	5858	607	580	576	615	600	541	351	370	351	282	272	208	218	162	114	64	23	11	2	.	.
2 Cripplegate	7193	M.	3624	364	360	354	465	551	310	241	206	168	150	140	83	83	60	48	25	6	2	.	.	.
		F.	3569	344	283	325	393	373	283	235	228	217	185	158	120	146	108	96	51	19	3	2	.	.
3 St. Sepulchre. (H. P.)	5365	M.	2656	231	237	243	346	266	233	193	193	159	110	119	82	67	37	36	21	7	.	1	.	.
		F.	2709	240	266	300	300	288	241	214	198	166	133	130	81	80	61	28	27	9	3	.	1	.
4 St. Bride. (W.)	8396	M.	4504	323	318	289	619	686	483	387	338	282	220	222	162	130	78	30	22	14	1	.	.	.
		F.	3892	338	291	294	399	503	380	276	261	229	215	206	166	117	109	61	31	22	4	.	.	.
5 Castle Baynard	9985	M.	5430	280	253	358	1085	1101	464	282	247	217	182	178	122	116	68	40	11	8	1	1	.	.
		F.	4555	277	273	306	641	667	484	362	291	276	250	221	157	143	92	32	36	14	4	.	.	.
6 Allhallows Barking	3661	M.	1636	138	134	125	187	221	136	118	113	117	82	73	71	65	42	19	8	6	.	1	.	.
		F.	2025	123	127	166	261	221	173	152	141	137	122	116	108	68	56	22	20	10	2	1	1	.
7 Broad Street. (H.)	5652	M.	2377	216	236	232	308	251	162	140	160	158	117	118	86	92	50	26	12	5	1	.	.	.
		F.	3275	208	219	287	478	384	226	228	200	180	189	188	131	140	93	73	29	8	6	1	.	.
15 SHOREDITCH.																								
1 Holywell	7376	M.	3685	412	333	324	420	417	354	295	224	217	205	145	117	111	60	34	12	5	.	.	.	.
		F.	3691	430	376	354	388	376	338	276	245	214	180	167	130	117	50	29	8	12	5	1	1	.
2 St. Leonard. (L.)	14967	M.	7417	1088	979	781	729	606	626	503	407	462	323	270	196	139	69	33	17	5	4	.	.	.
		F.	7550	1126	960	853	733	639	660	538	449	462	335	274	198	162	90	59	41	15	6	1	.	.
3 Hoxton New Town. (W.)	29937	M.	14508	2031	1539	1285	1294	1391	1464	1126	906	751	577	518	393	470	316	219	110	53	13	2	.	.
		F.	15429	2174	1567	1302	1308	1538	1416	1142	947	780	633	632	469	551	370	277	163	87	38	5	1	.
4 Hoxton Old Town	28036	M.	13531	2082	1671	1373	1273	1321	1288	1053	862	708	603	496	348	276	165	80	39	15	3	.	.	.
		F.	14505	2101	1638	1549	1246	1445	1321	1098	925	768	679	556	461	379	256	158	87	36	12	1	1	.
5 Haggerston. (W. H.²)	46275	M.	22544	3570	2781	2268	2073	2166	2005	1608	1373	1142	945	756	575	541	333	220	102	42	17	8	.	.
		F.	23731	3603	2813	2312	2090	2195	2140	1656	1397	1225	1072	855	643	638	442	337	131	101	25	6	.	.
16 BETHNAL GREEN.																								
Hackney Road. (H.)	28738	M.	14689	2315	1936	1541	1414	1343	1218	1114	916	789	593	614	372	303	166	97	80	21	3	1	.	.
		F.	14049	2361	1837	1606	1423	1366	1296	1043	918	803	637	544	425	322	209	132	68	28	8	3	.	.
Green. (W. H. L.)	47932	M.	23401	3633	3002	2496	2280	2130	1802	1552	1416	1234	916	839	603	587	468	307	215	79	17	3	.	.
		F.	24531	3437	2930	2611	2227	2201	2073	1763	1395	1290	1063	940	688	716	440	367	225	103	27	9	3	.
Church	29981	M.	14796	2423	1959	1627	1303	1340	1274	1048	867	786	538	486	384	315	161	123	54	13	5	.	.	.
		F.	15185	2404	2010	1657	1358	1547	1102	1074	913	789	605	539	440	380	212	144	70	36	11	2	.	.
Town	19310	M.	9660	1460	1282	1111	1011	845	731	692	547	503	374	365	249	204	120	83	38	16	3	.	.	.
		F.	9650	1447	1246	1076	908	841	718	666	521	648	405	385	301	241	145	98	39	11	4	1	.	.
17 WHITECHAPEL.																								
Spitalfields. (H.)	22585	M.	11884	1376	1214	1020	1126	1283	1160	984	770	800	586	585	380	347	143	86	46	19	5	.	1	.
		F.	10701	1364	1217	1084	1162	1043	910	746	672	608	527	424	333	292	146	86	51	17	12	8	1	.
Mile End New Town. (W. R.)	15473	M.	7848	1080	900	709	686	696	386	555	500	465	394	332	228	227	137	94	50	21	4	2	2	.
		F.	7625	1177	942	803	751	612	570	499	431	422	366	281	195	182	144	105	69	25	11	7	3	.
Whitechapel North (W. R.)	10001	M.	5073	619	649	624	563	553	419	353	308	276	207	167	115	108	62	26	14	9	1	.	.	.
		F.	4928	685	598	503	555	485	364	383	363	282	216	204	137	134	66	35	23	19	1	.	1	.
Whitechapel Church (H.)	7489	M.	3665	398	385	344	389	383	319	298	229	233	176	145	110	96	59	35	13	2	1	.	.	.
		F.	3824	415	421	347	442	430	346	297	222	218	171	170	90	123	56	40	18	11	3	1	.	.
Goodmans Fields (R.)	9713	M.	4879	620	543	556	539	547	412	330	307	254	213	209	123	101	60	28	22	7	3	.	.	.
		F.	4834	529	560	470	668	494	348	305	209	308	236	208	150	117	62	39	29	9	1	2	.	.
Aldgate (B.)	6102	M.	3369	288	277	270	376	490	328	314	207	201	148	144	110	93	39	19	11	1	.	.	.	.
		F.	2733	331	317	294	318	210	201	186	187	170	146	122	91	88	40	25	11	3	2	.	.	.
18 ST. GEORGE IN THE EAST.																								
St. Mary	18125	M.	9018	1297	1023	922	876	909	787	702	578	543	394	363	234	190	100	58	17	8	.	.	.	.
		F.	9107	1270	1128	906	880	920	743	672	578	517	413	379	260	218	103	71	28	10	6	.	.	.
St. Paul	20622	M.	10317	1192	1156	1092	925	1018	955	851	670	619	538	416	283	242	117	85	22	10	3	.	.	.
		F.	10305	1439	1222	975	918	984	913	722	660	599	505	451	276	286	159	98	60	15	6	3	1	.
St. John. (W.)	8410	M.	4276	531	413	378	308	419	401	294	267	232	187	188	127	148	116	110	43	14	3	1	.	.
		F.	4134	532	451	387	316	395	303	257	246	236	210	203	122	183	125	124	59	31	11	3	1	.
19 STEPNEY.																								
Shadwell. (H.)	10395	M.	5324	734	647	538	493	513	442	401	341	307	269	232	144	134	64	30	20	9	4	2	.	.
		F.	5071	679	619	526	459	454	419	366	333	324	253	225	145	112	83	46	21	12	3	2	.	.
Ratcliff	16107	M.	8168	1042	968	1048	850	708	682	591	511	474	347	331	234	198	102	50	19	9	3	1	.	.
		F.	7939	1089	937	797	745	617	641	587	524	479	387	346	257	221	144	96	57	30	10	2	.	.
Limehouse	32041	M.	15902	2334	1930	1770	1677	1448	1285	1126	1047	922	706	667	445	368	208	95	41	6	5	.	.	.
		F.	16139	2321	1992	1771	1524	1442	1248	1153	1013	908	727	686	452	425	220	138	72	34	15	3	1	.
20 MILE END OLD TOWN.																								
Mile End Old Town Western.	37960	M.	18454	2761	2095	1730	1732	1861	1771	1400	1207	1094	763	675	487	414	233	142	51	33	3	1	1	.
		F.	19506	2798	2173	1729	1707	1877	1789	1474	1222	1076	897	837	594	592	334	224	111	46	19	6	1	.
Mile End Old Town Eastern. (WS. w.² H. L. R.)	67653	M.	32484	4812	4236	3710	3080	2911	2563	2280	2017	1760	1337	1182	858	744	485	274	130	62	25	7	2	.
		F.	35169	4897	4148	3615	3287	3072	2891	2812	2087	1968	1596	1378	1081	1017	709	494	291	142	44	15	5	.
21 POPLAR.																								
Bow. (L. R.)	37074	M.	18323	2819	2422	2074	1817	1474	1406	1238	1265	1074	800	645	426	380	198	98	54	21	12	.	.	.
		F.	18751	2890	2447	2077	1788	1548	1545	1380	1154	1016	763	690	482	407	253	189	86	46	13	1	.	.
Bromley. (w.² H.)	64359	M.	32296	5216	4209	3507	2960	2562	2850	2313	2162	1875	1348	1121	793	673	374	280	139	66	24	4	.	.
		F.	32063	5189	4323	3429	2553	2589	2705	2428	2075	1731	1387	1100	766	703	436	304	213	105	37	8	2	.
Poplar. (WS.)	55077	M.	28471	3893	3410	2860	2750	2362	2398	2008	1903	1770	1374	1197	821	674	391	220	94	42	4	1	.	.
		F.	26606	3939	3278	2787	2258	2200	2145	1823	1704	1597	1294	1126	768	725	458	254	142	72	26	8	2	.

Table 3 *continued*.—AGES of MALES and FEMALES in REGISTRATION SUB-DISTRICTS.

Registration Sub-District.	All Ages. Persons.		All Ages. Males and Females.	Under 5 Years.	5–	10–	15–	20–	25–	30–	35–	40–	45–	50–	55–	60–	65–	70–	75–	80–	85–	90–	95–	100 and upw^ds.
SURREY (*Intra-metropolitan.*)																								
22 ST. SAVIOUR SOUTHWARK.																								
1 Christchurch Southwark. (W. H.)	13603	M.	7101	839	614	598	622	704	671	567	470	428	347	280	207	251	188	176	98	32	12		1	1
		F.	6502	845	635	570	614	637	620	468	437	371	312	293	105	212	100	84	60	28	6	2		
2 St. Saviour Southwark. (H.)	14999	M.	7605	988	890	821	882	721	633	532	534	417	346	293	215	198	107	61	20	7	2			
		F.	7394	1049	926	715	731	621	546	512	529	420	356	281	245	218	119	64	40	8	3	3		
3 Kent Road	21381	M.	10790	1541	1315	1087	1077	1060	983	864	684	678	460	412	270	241	161	59	26	9	3	1		
		F.	10591	1466	1315	1144	1022	951	985	768	705	604	428	393	275	259	162	102	37	15	6	2	2	
4 Borough Road (W. H.)	15953	M.	8265	1094	831	693	770	770	751	704	561	544	417	386	235	268	156	66	31	7	1	1	1	
		F.	7688	985	811	738	622	728	691	605	503	458	387	321	217	245	163	115	52	37	6	4		
5 London Road. (H. L.)	21818	M.	10878	1381	1046	1098	1076	1096	906	720	675	610	474	420	281	250	180	70	46	15	2	1		
		F.	10940	1344	1167	1176	1013	1046	943	838	686	701	541	468	321	303	192	110	63	24	8	4		
6 Trinity Newington	26672	M.	13187	1886	1448	1247	1256	1451	1246	1026	807	777	616	466	310	282	162	89	41	16	7	1		
		F.	13485	1892	1585	1318	1169	1309	1173	1049	932	759	638	497	376	338	198	130	73	52	9	3		
7 St. Peter Walworth. (W.)	59556	M.	28866	4434	3561	2853	2689	2652	2605	2215	1939	1613	1251	1022	663	687	378	241	109	40	19	4		
		F.	30690	4550	3621	2917	2788	2655	2674	2312	2065	1696	1306	1177	886	925	585	458	276	144	51	11	3	
8 St. Mary Newington	21623	M.	10307	1416	1167	948	950	1051	976	868	726	674	513	370	261	196	132	82	54	14	5	1		
		F.	11316	1462	1161	1007	907	1115	1128	925	755	633	522	469	314	314	209	133	39	44	14	5		
23 ST. OLAVE SOUTHWARK.																								
1 St. Olave Southwark. (H.)	3028	M.	1504	115	143	135	206	161	140	105	110	97	99	68	49	42	20	17	3	3	1			
		F.	1524	151	128	134	176	165	157	122	96	109	79	65	35	43	30	23	9	4	4			
2 St. John Horsleydown. (W.)	8928	M.	4428	583	508	492	476	424	370	273	278	262	188	165	140	131	73	38	17	8	1	1		
		F.	4500	610	582	467	412	380	353	282	266	247	227	231	149	138	96	86	38	16	9	1		
3 Leather Market	16300	M.	8243	1146	1043	964	867	789	640	535	491	455	353	293	195	204	96	53	19	4	1			
		F.	8057	1211	1070	886	761	686	608	511	490	488	392	312	214	208	113	60	29	18	7		1	
4 St. Mary Magdalen. (W.)	15669	M.	7866	1168	882	861	745	709	697	520	503	417	340	325	234	207	119	99	50	24	13	2		
		F.	7803	1118	905	769	665	658	626	518	469	434	364	334	261	242	103	130	104	36	15	2		
5 St. James Bermondsey	54683	M.	27154	4484	3643	2919	2500	2411	2256	2102	1720	1544	1117	888	590	612	248	192	73	34	6		1	
		F.	27529	4312	3478	2889	2304	2358	2338	2027	1809	1593	1192	1028	750	606	306	273	143	55	12	10		
6 Rotherhithe (W.)	36024	M.	18371	2794	2304	1980	1737	1646	1641	1355	1190	1051	789	626	504	372	251	164	78	35	9	1		
		F.	17653	2761	2366	2002	1613	1279	1368	1312	1076	972	747	626	440	434	278	188	97	53	11	5		
24 LAMBETH.																								
1 Waterloo Road First. (H.)	15195	M.	7695	1114	870	754	740	778	762	566	529	454	338	298	201	182	83	46	21	10				
		F.	7500	1081	913	716	638	696	670	558	511	452	330	272	218	225	160	66	41	9	6	3	1	
2 Waterloo Road Second. (H.)	16951	M.	8308	1061	878	750	786	958	836	672	592	467	367	327	225	198	103	58	32	9	2			
		F.	8643	1063	851	732	770	839	723	608	598	462	378	318	218	191	126	82	39	19	4	2		
3 Lambeth Church First. (H.)	19876	M.	9927	1385	1129	986	967	942	929	758	660	589	468	286	261	244	141	73	27	10	2			
		F.	9949	1368	1148	971	898	894	931	755	673	588	476	394	268	298	155	87	52	21	5			
4 Lambeth Church Second. (W.²)	39859	M.	19870	2902	2293	1931	1791	1807	1802	1490	1317	1096	877	728	531	559	360	216	122	47	7	1		
		F.	19989	2934	2272	1953	1463	1725	1769	1624	1262	1178	962	767	461	682	424	283	170	37	18	5	1	
5 Kennington First	45232	M.	21447	2883	2458	2043	2031	2198	1933	1671	1463	1215	930	816	697	603	298	139	109	33	13	4		
		F.	23785	3058	2625	2209	2218	2237	2174	1774	1575	1356	1129	978	782	720	463	296	189	78	30	4		
6 Kennington Second	39332	M.	19904	2186	1973	1756	1610	1410	1370	1124	1012	829	678	547	427	403	244	177	88	39	7	4		
		F.	19428	2161	1857	1708	2017	2045	1646	1471	1382	1134	928	797	671	611	394	314	207	113	28	1	4	
7 Brixton. (W². L. P.)	62837	M.	27460	4065	3279	2585	2337	2541	2662	2299	1956	1607	1112	899	699	624	394	246	132	60	20	8		
		F.	35377	4061	3572	3084	3917	4675	3449	2825	2243	1899	1455	1238	978	960	686	484	269	137	38	8		
8 Norwood. (WS. H. L.)	19027	M.	8565	1222	1224	1218	749	705	648	579	498	465	346	292	206	167	110	70	44	19	3			
		F.	10462	1233	1192	1119	1080	1093	965	786	663	578	454	374	255	261	177	124	79	28	12	6		
25 WANDSWORTH.																								
1 Clapham. (H. B.)	36380	M.	15935	2216	1943	1641	1635	1488	1268	1101	1071	916	705	582	437	396	260	134	90	36	12	2		
		F.	20445	2131	1858	1968	2342	2256	1911	1602	1363	1155	967	864	634	581	399	285	161	88	28	3	1	
2 Battersea. (WS. H.)	107262	M.	52665	8701	7418	5834	4699	4340	4262	3836	3544	2961	2246	1672	1088	854	509	309	167	70	15	3	2	
		F.	54597	8583	7346	6135	4526	4400	4594	4179	3696	3094	2272	1731	1298	1088	715	404	260	120	37	6	2	
3 Wandsworth. (H. L.² P. R.)	28004	M.	13328	1771	1518	1299	1465	1304	1146	956	893	802	633	504	349	315	179	108	63	29	6			
		F.	14676	1756	1527	1476	1469	1522	1188	1061	989	871	715	596	429	430	285	186	119	46	17	3		
4 Putney (L.)	13235	M.	5406	736	630	478	563	587	489	425	359	315	239	199	139	123	91	41	34	12	9	2		
		F.	7829	734	659	701	998	1048	830	656	487	400	320	276	200	209	134	89	47	24	13	7		
5 Streatham (P.)	25553	M.	10825	1572	1313	1149	980	967	919	835	698	608	432	403	304	251	172	130	61	29	7	4		
		F.	14728	1634	1318	1340	1642	1791	1583	1177	909	795	631	535	395	370	258	186	161	36	25	2		
26 CAMBERWELL.																								
1 Dulwich	5590	M.	2103	206	245	294	284	183	133	119	129	110	96	98	64	56	30	31	16	8	2			
		F.	3487	212	250	209	471	584	413	298	238	202	177	148	82	78	36	31	21	3	4	3	1	
2 Camberwell. (W. L.²)	59104	M.	26561	4086	3421	2781	2308	2241	2246	1967	1777	1617	1164	898	885	568	394	232	120	60	25	10	1	
		F.	32543	3968	3645	3022	3476	3322	2992	2528	2135	1738	1569	1206	918	825	601	458	287	146	42	10	5	
3 Peckham. (W. L.)	71089	M.	33833	5318	4593	3758	3130	2774	2681	2512	2220	1883	1370	1183	745	672	423	322	164	67	18	3	2	
		F.	37256	6436	4610	3836	3391	3194	3077	2773	2434	2020	1559	1407	1008	957	613	490	243	151	44	6	3	
4 St. George	50810	M.	24994	4076	3472	2960	2423	2075	1931	1769	1661	1372	937	861	522	452	234	176	74	43	7	1		
		F.	25816	3874	3432	2813	2218	2146	2076	1883	1667	1603	1136	934	672	570	367	259	144	85	22	2		
KENT (*Intra-metropolitan*).																								
27 GREENWICH.																								
1 St. Paul Deptford (W.)	76752	M.	36788	5519	4841	4076	3465	3229	2989	2589	2359	2123	1630	1320	1061	771	468	285	184	61	19	10		
		F.	39964	5626	4783	4065	3936	3677	3306	2598	2578	2187	1682	1499	1106	1015	672	473	222	108	32	14	3	
2 St. Nicholas Deptford	7901	M.	4048	557	522	478	467	386	270	228	232	244	185	177	117	94	55	32	10	1	2	1		
		F.	3853	583	524	492	328	231	226	234	244	217	204	176	111	93	60	39	28	11	3			
3 Greenwich West	21972	M.	10302	1414	1324	1191	977	914	769	698	809	549	436	421	311	204	182	129	67	24	12	1		
		F.	11670	1488	1349	1192	1121	1019	919	923	711	742	567	502	383	375	246	218	117	63	30	5		
4 Greenwich East. (W. H. R.)	24608	M.	12265	1596	1465	2605	1186	968	786	742	670	683	503	446	308	398	248	186	102	48	15	4	2	
		F.	12343	1619	1383	1315	1088	1125	1048	836	765	687	529	503	377	303	288	21	138	76	23	11	1	2

Table 3 *continued*.—AGES of MALES and FEMALES in REGISTRATION SUB-DISTRICTS.

REGISTRATION SUB-DISTRICT.	ALL AGES. Persons.	Males and Females.	Under 5 Years.	5-	10-	15-	20-	25-	30-	35-	40-	45-	50-	55-	60-	65-	70-	75-	80-	85-	90-	95-	100 and upwards.
KENT (*Intra-metropolitan*)—*cont.*																							
28 LEWISHAM.																							
ELTHAM. (H. R.)	5827	M. - 2486	325	307	255	245	200	159	166	160	158	118	107	85	72	50	26	31	13	.	.	.	.
		F. 3341	332	318	372	361	388	313	255	196	175	169	139	103	84	61	44	17	16	8	1	.	.
LEE	21559	M. - 8597	1098	1137	1082	809	742	672	555	473	445	386	332	228	220	139	108	58	19	3	4	.	.
		F. - 12962	1135	1945	1075	1685	1870	1310	970	865	664	573	518	365	312	231	190	116	48	11	7	.	.
LEWISHAM. (W. H.)	19805	M. - 8907	1282	1147	949	799	736	758	637	580	528	369	509	231	195	116	31	65	24	7	2	.	.
		F. - 10898	1379	1158	1031	1200	1120	955	803	692	803	455	408	264	260	206	162	73	49	12	3	.	.
SYDENHAM. (H.)	26076	M 11251	1058	1460	1011	1162	980	907	809	790	620	497	417	300	296	101	61	46	24	0	.	.	.
		F. - 14825	1632	1427	1382	1690	1859	1445	1141	947	847	598	540	390	377	234	161	100	42	11	2	.	.
29 WOOLWICH.																							
CHARLTON. (H. B.)	10930	M. - 5124	579	585	543	453	603	460	382	342	277	203	184	149	146	106	58	25	16	3	.	.	.
		F. - 5806	582	530	501	615	744	569	438	369	305	253	247	135	183	111	71	38	26	7	1	1	.
WOOLWICH DOCKYARD (B.)	17617	M. - 9713	1154	1012	909	989	1280	1045	711	589	508	406	258	211	204	125	78	26	13	7	1	.	.
		F. 7904	1149	1030	778	636	606	586	586	477	474	374	395	235	232	157	108	40	29	5	1	2	.
WOOLWICH ARSENAL. (H.[3] B.[4])	19048	M. - 9708	1269	1100	995	1092	985	749	601	675	657	464	403	254	242	130	72	32	12	7	2	.	.
		F. - 9340	1233	1160	971	823	830	657	763	611	567	479	368	290	268	161	90	57	24	11	3	.	.
PLUMSTEAD WEST (H.)	14009	M. - 6656	938	872	727	643	527	446	406	409	437	371	317	190	192	87	64	22	18	4	1	.	.
		F. - 7353	903	877	760	756	632	569	522	448	440	315	304	232	241	130	72	40	27	5	1	1	.
PLUMSTEAD EAST. (W.)	19241	M. - 9806	1482	1376	1205	989	746	611	532	526	697	539	304	279	218	137	86	64	32	8	.	.	.
		F. - 9435	1625	1339	1136	735	606	607	654	548	554	472	351	308	235	158	119	78	31	19	4	2	.

Table 4.—MALE and FEMALE CHILDREN at *each Year of Age* under 5 in the LONDON DIVISION and its REGISTRATION COUNTIES.

REGISTRATION COUNTY.	TOTAL UNDER 5 YEARS. Persons.	Males and Females.	Under 1 Year.	1-	2-	3-	4-
1 LONDON.	497044	M. - 248619	55889	49268	49243	47190	46439
		F. - 248425	55704	50046	49229	47414	46032
1 MIDDLESEX (*Intra-metropolitan*)	320644	M. 160411	36370	32182	31656	30291	29912
		F. - 160233	36073	32252	31688	30743	29482
2 SURREY (*Intra-metropolitan*)	138376	M. - 69254	15423	13888	13811	13240	12883
		F. - 69122	15436	13980	13831	12949	12897
3 KENT (*Intra-metropolitan*)	38024	M. - 18954	4006	3788	3776	3650	3644
		F. - 19070	4175	3806	3715	3722	3653

Table 5.—MALE and FEMALE CHILDREN at *each Year of Age* under 5 in REGISTRATION DISTRICTS.

REGISTRATION DISTRICT.	Total under 5 Years. Persons.	Males and Females.	Under 1 Year.	1-	2-	3-	4-
IDDLESEX (*Intra-metropolitan*).							
ENSINGTON	25284	M. - 14147	3142	2830	2748	2796	2631
		F. - 14137	3098	2855	2742	2772	2670
ULHAM	16574	M. - 8282	1947	1715	1548	1548	1524
		F. - 8292	1873	1705	1684	1545	1485
HELSEA	11879	M. - 6000	1361	1226	1207	1174	1032
		F. - 5879	1302	1184	1173	1143	1074
T. GEORGE HANOVER SQUARE	14090	M. - 7084	1678	1419	1339	1347	1301
		F. - 7006	1558	1453	1409	1285	1301
ESTMINSTER	4618	M. - 2258	566	400	420	429	425
		F. - 2360	601	356	419	441	443
ARYLEBONE	15900	M. - 7974	1806	1561	1562	1480	1466
		F. - 7926	1807	1512	1552	1522	1433
AMPSTEAD	4662	M. - 2301	505	442	458	451	445
		F. - 2361	596	457	456	452	470
ANCRAS	29361	M. - 14902	3361	3096	3017	2805	2673
		F. - 14459	3323	2961	2839	2767	2569
SLINGTON	37613	M. - 19000	4293	3884	3069	3478	3676
		F. - 18613	4101	3775	3686	3693	3358
HACKNEY	25159	M. - 12452	2783	2430	2494	2344	2451
		F. - 12707	2758	2493	2547	2524	2385
T. GILES	4827	M. - 2429	536	508	402	451	472
		F. - 2398	567	484	416	468	450
STRAND	3152	M. - 1556	347	301	306	302	300
		F. - 1596	367	320	303	317	289
HOLBORN	19390	M. - 9715	2273	1975	1921	1764	1782
		F. - 9675	2194	1964	1905	1826	1787
LONDON CITY	4310	M. - 2164	438	400	447	435	435
		F. - 2146	465	475	381	468	407
SHOREDITCH	18647	M. - 9213	2099	1852	1830	1769	1663
		F. - 9434	2190	1916	1873	1739	1716
BETHNAL GREEN	19380	M. - 9731	2158	1936	2015	1811	1809
		F. 9649	2141	1912	1927	1842	1827
MIDDLESEX (*Intra-metropolitan*)—*cont.*							
17 WHITECHAPEL	9036	M. - 4437	958	844	878	896	861
		F. 4599	1062	902	886	876	873
18 ST. GEORGE IN THE EAST	6494	M. - 3230	752	631	637	585	625
		F. - 3264	763	617	693	612	579
19 STEPNEY	8129	M. - 4040	929	801	818	733	759
		F. - 4089	913	867	792	756	761
20 MILE END OLD TOWN	15268	M. - 7573	1738	1542	1459	1433	1401
		F. - 7695	1777	1456	1615	1433	1414
21 POPLAR	23946	M. - 11928	2667	2419	2402	2256	2184
		F. - 12018	2774	2408	2352	2323	2161
SURREY (*Intra-metropolitan*).							
22 ST. SAVIOUR SOUTHWARK	27137	M. - 13544	3050	2791	2680	2590	2433
		F. - 13593	3083	2742	2746	2404	2598
23 ST. OLAVE SOUTHWARK	20454	M. - 10291	2370	2074	2000	1954	1893
		F. - 10163	2300	2104	2038	1919	1803
24 LAMBETH	33716	M. - 16737	3733	3347	3412	3176	3069
		F. - 16979	3853	3462	3363	3171	3130
25 WANDSWORTH	28794	M. - 14096	3274	2908	3057	2871	2986
		F. - 14698	3283	2920	3010	2812	2873
26 CAMBERWELL	27375	M. - 13886	2998	2708	2662	2653	2867
		F. - 13489	2967	2761	2674	2553	2594
KENT (*Intra-metropolitan*).							
27 GREENWICH	18296	M. - 9086	2006	1801	1807	1760	1712
		F. - 9210	2105	1811	1773	1786	1735
28 LEWISHAM	8933	M. - 4455	924	903	913	868	847
		F. - 4478	956	901	877	873	871
29 WOOLWICH	10800	M. - 5418	1186	1084	1056	1022	1085
		F. - 5382	1114	1093	1065	1063	1047

Table 6.—Ages of Males and Females in Sanitary District.

LEWISHAM.—Rural.

Ages.	Males.	Females.	Ages.	Males.	Females.	Ages.	Males.	Females.	Ages.	Males.	Females.
All ages	363	416	5-	52	48	40-	24	16	75-	3	—
Under 1 year	11	19	10-	43	43	45-	8	20	80-	—	1
1-	7	14	15-	30	38	50-	16	15	85-	—	—
2-	12	9	20-	25	46	55-	8	11	90-	—	—
3-	11	18	25-	24	31	60-	9	12	95-	—	—
4-	17	9	30-	24	20	65-	13	8	100 and upwds.	—	—
Under 5 years	58	64	35-	23	27	70-	2	7			

Note.—As the district of the Metropolitan Board of Works was excluded from the operation of the Public Health Act of 1872 Division I. contains no urban or rural sanitary districts as defined by those Acts, with the single exception of the hamlet of Mottingham, which, not being included in the district of the Metropolitan Board of Works, constitutes the rural sanitary district of Lewisham.

Table 7.—Condition as to Marriage and Ages of Males and Females in the London Division and its Registration Counties.

Registration County.		All Ages.	Under 15 Years.	15-	20-	25-	35-	45-	55-	65 and upwards.
I.—LONDON.										
Unmarried	Males	1098840	630295	170722	137127	98526	30452	14110	7371	4242
	Females	1192263	646600	191250	141093	118727	45310	25297	16091	11985
Married	Males	641808	—	924	38708	194781	183796	122158	69656	31791
	Females	653601	—	5674	66053	210966	177851	109925	54438	19694
Widowed	Males	56833	—	13	361	3778	8175	11348	13965	19203
	Females	173143	—	45	1604	16487	25503	37692	44400	58962
MIDDLESEX (*Intra-metropolitan*).										
Unmarried	Males	728302	468716	113403	94874	70361	21996	10344	5424	3184
	Females	803638	417178	130207	100834	83514	33516	18503	11489	8397
Married	Males	423890	—	611	25813	128745	120987	81324	46977	21343
	Females	433875	—	3801	44241	145792	110825	73380	36403	13133
Widowed	Males	38783	—	9	252	2548	5497	7780	9666	13031
	Females	120458	—	30	989	7820	18028	26671	30840	36080
SURREY (*Intra-metropolitan*).										
Unmarried	Males	285717	178638	44068	32491	21625	6461	2914	1477	808
	Females	298546	178408	46483	30790	22498	8842	5152	3582	2791
Married	Males	169025	—	256	10400	53015	40176	31231	17152	7786
	Females	172077	—	1467	17488	58865	47730	27977	13626	4914
Widowed	Males	14148	—	3	78	1005	2165	2807	3396	4698
	Females	41669	—	11	247	2337	5951	3670	10607	13186
KENT (*Intra-metropolitan*).										
Unmarried	Males	84826	51641	13251	9762	6540	2055	852	470	255
	Females	90069	51014	14560	10389	7715	2952	1612	1050	797
Married	Males	46983	—	57	2486	13021	13627	9603	5527	2662
	Females	47949	—	406	4324	15309	13296	8568	4398	1647
Widowed	Males	3902	—	1	21	225	513	761	904	1477
	Females	11676	—	4	68	630	1574	2351	53	4096

Note.—In a few cases, persons described as "Married" were stated to be under 15 years of age. These have been classed with married persons aged "15 and under 20 years."

Table 8.—Condition as to Marriage and Ages of Males and Females in Registration Districts.

Registration District.	All Ages.	Under 15 Years.	15–	20–	25–	35–	45–	55–	65 and upw^ds.
MIDDLESEX (*Intra-metropolitan.*)									
WEST DISTRICTS.									
1 KENSINGTON:									
Unmarried M.	65240	35684	9952	9126	6856	1941	902	474	314
Unmarried F.	108502	38419	17029	18128	18334	7222	3740	2220	1401
Married M.	35001	.	16	1887	11959	11606	7801	4733	2444
Married F.	41519	.	202	3356	13706	11048	7481	3768	1893
Widowed M.	3333	.	.	16	205	471	823	780	1230
Widowed F.	14116	.	4	62	987	2232	3155	3473	4222
2 FULHAM:									
Unmarried M.	32338	23397	4020	3592	2654	620	236	135	84
Unmarried F.	36659	20924	5753	4047	2996	1262	715	522	442
Married M.	19471	.	27	1233	6357	5598	3341	1755	860
Married F.	20082	.	178	2151	7229	5627	3023	1442	352
Widowed M.	1365	.	.	6	69	202	270	301	497
Widowed F.	4924	.	.	25	303	696	1058	1228	1584
3 CHELSEA:									
Unmarried M.	25403	14743	3528	3381	2318	701	365	233	184
Unmarried F.	26315	14848	3722	2851	2478	1044	632	425	318
Married M.	15096	.	23	862	4854	4320	2718	1664	758
Married F.	15709	.	118	1537	5666	4233	2320	1240	465
Widowed M.	1391	.	.	5	88	187	230	365	516
Widowed F.	4214	.	1	27	258	629	910	1116	1263
4 ST. GEORGE HANOVER SQUARE:									
Unmarried M.	42072	17977	6202	7440	6680	2083	908	470	322
Unmarried F.	50056	18800	7917	8106	6488	3568	1780	944	623
Married M.	23391	.	17	1066	6400	6727	4895	2561	1328
Married F.	23762	.	139	2011	7641	6574	4358	2262	777
Widowed M.	2392	.	2	11	169	323	456	603	826
Widowed F.	8045	.	1	43	552	1275	1736	2025	2418
5 WESTMINSTER:									
Unmarried M.	14412	6146	2389	2357	2117	754	370	255	134
Unmarried F.	15954	6231	2452	2227	1680	646	344	224	150
Married M.	7580	.	8	368	1995	2105	1708	937	410
Married F.	7446	.	65	702	2348	2116	1880	648	212
Widowed M.	876	.	1	5	51	140	177	230	272
Widowed F.	2272	.	.	19	166	362	567	542	602
NORTH DISTRICTS.									
6 MARYLEBONE:									
Unmarried M.	40797	20294	6530	6128	4760	1632	769	408	269
Unmarried F.	52836	21031	8378	8104	7805	3417	1984	1136	893
Married M.	24550	.	20	1308	6882	6877	4901	3056	1494
Married F.	25470	.	294	2406	8181	6887	4642	2332	940
Widowed M.	2548	.	.	1	145	286	520	639	866
Widowed F.	8700	.	7	45	628	1414	1581	2139	2600
7 HAMPSTEAD:									
Unmarried M.	11006	6469	1695	1391	1035	299	124	70	87
Unmarried F.	12632	7077	3599	3504	3255	1185	619	353	189
Married M.	6009	.	1	244	1575	1725	1223	730	413
Married F.	6105	.	2	483	1934	1818	1109	560	255
Widowed M.	494	.	.	1	26	63	106	100	196
Widowed F.	1850	.	1	18	105	337	372	400	508
8 PANCRAS:									
Unmarried M.	67750	37297	10506	9248	7026	2017	801	440	831
Unmarried F.	70873	37398	11009	8425	6826	2746	1556	1080	842
Married M.	46970	.	51	2615	12505	11619	7766	4350	2042
Married F.	41727	.	315	4822	14185	11216	7017	3437	1301
Widowed M.	3781	.	.	21	264	525	747	923	1293
Widowed F.	11572	.	1	60	784	1660	2556	2990	3570
9 ISLINGTON:									
Unmarried M.	80595	47820	11906	10151	7127	2022	821	411	247
Unmarried F.	88951	48082	14484	10669	6196	3336	1951	1254	960
Married M.	46150	.	57	2916	15444	13783	8742	4920	2268
Married F.	48886	.	391	4852	17028	13142	7844	3908	1426
Widowed M.	3865	.	1	24	245	551	780	912	1333
Widowed F.	12748	.	2	67	732	1776	2678	3363	4132
10 HACKNEY:									
Unmarried M.	51355	31635	7863	6051	3912	1028	430	253	175
Unmarried F.	63520	33239	11244	7969	5717	2350	1816	948	754
Married M.	23993	.	30	1606	9361	8528	5571	3303	1499
Married F.	30851	.	207	2942	10601	8282	5161	2634	1023
Widowed M.	2586	.	.	20	182	324	466	590	964
Widowed F.	8283	.	1	43	439	1122	1614	2167	2906
CENTRAL DISTRICTS.									
11 ST. GILES:									
Unmarried M.	13792	6329	1986	1966	1846	762	474	289	141
Unmarried F.	13534	6371	318	1929	1574	642	350	214	136
Married M.	7349	.	15	421	2067	2958	1408	908	380
Married F.	7421	.	66	752	2510	1398	1251	640	204
Widowed M.	940	.	.	6	67	140	214	247	286
Widowed F.	2369	.	.	17	166	380	689	584	613
MIDDLESEX (*Intra-metropolitan*)—*cont.*									
CENTEAL DISTRICTS—cont.									
12 STRAND:									
Unmarried M.	10031	4197	1006	1795	1710	667	350	175	71
Unmarried F.	9863	4400	1723	1518	1281	484	270	137	85
Married M.	5605	.	7	268	1409	1608	1235	679	298
Married F.	5248	.	61	481	1672	1509	977	490	158
Widowed M.	633	.	.	4	47	97	161	170	154
Widowed F.	1672	.	2	13	121	263	439	449	385
13 HOLBORN:									
Unmarried M.	46473	34750	8019	6017	4663	1560	846	390	130
Unmarried F.	41796	25107	6934	4218	2939	1199	696	412	203
Married M.	27096	.	60	2008	8282	7495	5232	2913	1106
Married F.	26832	.	347	3234	8863	7021	4570	2112	686
Widowed M.	2487	.	2	19	196	388	555	682	645
Widowed F.	7148	.	1	54	476	1174	1714	1826	1904
14 LONDON CITY:									
Unmarried M.	17068	7039	3481	3337	2092	611	290	139	60
Unmarried F.	15853	6354	3059	2483	1918	711	413	242	103
Married M.	7671	.	12	360	1759	2240	1681	1070	549
Married F.	7319	.	47	549	1982	2048	1537	826	330
Widowed M.	834	.	.	7	56	111	199	215	246
Widowed F.	3204	.	1	11	161	478	732	826	1013
EAST DISTRICTS.									
15 SHOREDITCH:									
Unmarried M.	36292	22448	5806	4033	2579	728	342	222	134
Unmarried F.	35540	22901	5497	3112	2965	798	504	340	323
Married M.	28113	.	55	1873	7715	6043	4063	2347	999
Married F.	23412	.	266	3643	8193	5776	3661	1858	618
Widowed M.	2280	.	.	19	118	290	413	597	821
Widowed F.	5954	.	2	35	327	838	1258	1540	1973
16 BETHNAL GREEN:									
Unmarried M.	37792	24688	6080	3850	2081	618	275	140	39
Unmarried F.	36321	24874	5731	2976	1651	570	363	236	140
Married M.	22811	.	46	1793	7226	6199	3996	2384	1167
Married F.	23659	.	265	2741	7828	3885	3835	1962	743
Widowed M.	1943	.	1	15	131	259	344	470	723
Widowed F.	5035	.	.	38	326	728	1150	1306	1608
17 WHITECHAPEL:									
Unmarried M.	23722	11927	3650	3167	2672	1192	649	353	142
Unmarried F.	19980	12242	3659	1975	1158	450	244	142	110
Married M.	11700	.	38	807	3433	3251	2328	1355	558
Married F.	11597	.	131	1286	3732	3146	2013	994	295
Widowed M.	1236	.	1	7	74	207	283	336	328
Widowed F.	3068	.	1	22	205	524	752	796	768
18 ST. GEORGE IN THE EAST:									
Unmarried M.	14270	8163	2161	1670	1354	480	205	111	57
Unmarried F.	12520	8333	1994	1061	631	226	120	75	66
Married M.	8460	.	11	667	2574	2292	1640	886	379
Married F.	8634	.	129	1136	2816	2216	1459	659	219
Widowed M.	881	.	.	9	62	133	172	226	280
Widowed F.	2392	.	.	22	163	400	582	800	626
19 STEPNEY:									
Unmarried M.	18139	10941	2908	2034	1402	491	226	102	35
Unmarried F.	16091	10731	2634	1362	814	273	135	62	80
Married M.	10367	.	12	622	3050	2973	2113	1163	438
Married F.	10874	.	92	1138	3436	2968	1880	907	253
Widowed M.	868	.	.	11	69	138	213	252	309
Widowed F.	2384	.	2	13	155	340	582	642	682
20 MILE END OLD TOWN:									
Unmarried M.	30722	19344	4792	3415	2119	609	231	151	61
Unmarried F.	30409	19637	4788	2758	1768	755	434	305	246
Married M.	18603	.	20	1341	5871	6162	3415	1953	841
Married F.	19261	.	204	2160	6608	4838	3233	1592	646
Widowed M.	1613	.	.	16	114	217	311	399	555
Widowed F.	4085	.	2	31	292	630	1054	1537	1649
21 POPLAR:									
Unmarried M.	46335	30509	7476	4596	3406	1227	520	184	115
Unmarried F.	48201	30359	6313	3301	1868	618	349	219	179
Married M.	28306	.	50	1685	8632	8465	5483	2903	1138
Married F.	28869	.	261	2978	9792	7965	4779	2193	782
Widowed M.	2449	.	1	15	145	357	632	680	769
Widowed F.	5589	.	5	38	341	734	1232	1439	1730

Table 8 *continued.*—CONDITION as to MARRIAGE and AGES of MALES and FEMALES in REGISTRATION DISTRICTS.

REGISTRATION DISTRICT.		ALL AGES.	Under 15 Years.	15–	20–	25–	35–	45–	55–	65 and upw^ds^.
SURREY (*Intra-metropolitan*).										
SOUTH DISTRICTS.										
22 St. SAVIOUR SOUTHWARK:										
UNMARRIED	M.	57089	33899	9186	6807	4766	1647	837	434	223
	F.	53798	34358	8224	4787	3312	1361	769	570	427
MARRIED	M.	35441	.	81	2621	11232	9834	6513	3495	1665
	F.	35974	.	427	4203	12404	8572	5669	2772	927
WIDOWED	M.	3808	.	2	23	229	528	797	843	1033
	F.	8894	.	4	57	482	1364	1941	2299	2747
23 ST. OLAVE SOUTHWARK:										
UNMARRIED	M.	41275	25965	6576	4620	2791	821	353	161	98
	F.	37456	23799	5601	2963	1714	668	331	204	175
MARRIED	M.	24148	.	51	1594	7592	6964	4463	2490	989
	F.	24320	.	226	2021	8305	6619	4078	1910	665
WIDOWED	M.	2148	.	.	12	109	333	439	588	657
	F.	5285	.	2	36	280	756	1148	1596	1661
24 LAMBETH:										
UNMARRIED	M.	71863	42869	10875	8811	6218	1765	727	381	217
	F.	78626	43821	12567	9088	6707	2706	1622	1143	873
MARRIED	M.	43509	.	51	2612	13575	12528	7869	4722	2152
	F.	44458	.	371	4446	13215	12129	7157	3733	1407
WIDOWED	M.	3805	.	.	20	268	556	733	921	1307
	F.	11539	.	4	64	679	1656	2411	3023	3702
25 WANDSWORTH:										
UNMARRIED	M.	69692	38210	9224	6733	4338	1209	670	271	137
	F.	69096	39225	10790	7798	6057	2316	1305	902	686
MARRIED	M.	35010	.	48	1947	10875	10618	6536	3439	1543
	F.	35807	.	230	3178	12150	10336	5662	2747	1014
WIDOWED	M.	2457	.	.	15	181	375	464	602	840
	F.	7673	.	1	48	464	1105	1560	1977	2518
SURREY (*Intra-metropolitan*)—*cont.*										
SOUTH DISTRICTS—cont.										
26 CAMBERWELL:										
UNMARRIED	M.	54198	35205	8207	5530	3512	959	427	230	128
	F.	59672	35205	9356	6164	4708	1602	1095	733	630
MARRIED	M.	30922	.	27	1735	9678	9237	5738	3012	1497
	F.	31812	.	221	3040	10891	9074	5211	2474	901
WIDOWED	M.	2371	.	1	5	168	373	434	541	858
	F.	7618	.	.	42	435	1061	1610	1912	2558
KENT (*Intra-metropolitan*).										
SOUTH DISTRICTS—cont.										
27 GREENWICH:										
UNMARRIED	M.	39341	24028	6056	4186	2508	869	372	230	111
	F.	39686	24203	6254	3922	2783	1106	629	428	331
MARRIED	M.	22180	.	29	1293	6369	6314	4275	2806	1223
	F.	22643	.	217	2150	7319	6187	3972	2041	757
WIDOWED	M.	1962	.	.	12	113	263	374	464	734
	F.	5631	.	1	30	286	748	1071	1384	2111
28 LEWISHAM:										
UNMARRIED	M.	19560	12016	3031	2198	1548	405	188	112	63
	F.	27731	12286	4850	4848	3431	1357	713	434	312
MARRIED	M.	10838	.	14	486	3083	3196	2187	1238	694
	F.	11268	.	59	875	3661	3203	2039	1062	419
WIDOWED	M.	843	.	.	3	53	113	161	181	332
	F.	3037	.	.	20	159	419	639	729	1071
29 WOOLWICH:										
UNMARRIED	M.	25925	14697	4164	3378	2399	786	292	128	81
	F.	22882	14525	3656	2099	1361	489	270	188	154
MARRIED	M.	13985	.	14	701	3578	4117	3141	1686	745
	F.	14948	.	130	1299	4329	3906	2567	1356	471
WIDOWED	M.	1097	.	1	8	58	155	228	259	411
	F.	3108	.	3	18	183	407	641	840	1014

Table 9 is omitted in this Division, as the Metropolis contains no Urban Sanitary Districts as constituted by the Public Health Act of 1872; the numbers of the other Tables have, however, been left unaltered in order to preserve uniformity in the numbering of these Tables in the eleven Registration Divisions.

Table 10.—Occupations of Males and Females in the London Division and its Registration Counties.

Occupations.	London.		Registration Counties. Middlesex. (*Intra-metn.*)		Surrey. (*Intra-metn.*)		Kent. (*Intra-metn.*)	
	Males.	Females.	Males.	Females.	Males.	Females.	Males.	Females.
TOTAL	1797486	2018997	1192885	1357671	468890	511632	135711	149694
I. PROFESSIONAL CLASS.								
1. Persons engaged in the General or Local Government of the Country.								
1. *National Government.*								
Peer, M.P., Privy Councillor (not otherwise described)	366	.	363	.	2	.	1	.
Civil Service (officers and clerks)	8359	572	5324	386	2271	136	764	50
Civil Service (messengers, &c.)	6940	51	4608	43	1970	7	362	1
Prison Officer, &c.	609	139	456	138	149	1	4	.
2. *Local Government.*								
Police	9354	.	6744	.	1995	.	615	.
Municipal, Parish, Union, District, Officer	2150	624	1376	467	591	109	183	48
Other Local or County Official	796	.	667	.	87	.	42	.
3. *East Indian and Colonial Service.*								
East Indian and Colonial Service	118	.	94	.	16	.	8	.
2. Persons engaged in the Defence of the Country.								
1. *Army (at Home).*								
Army Officer (effective or retired)	3191	.	2362	.	202	.	627	.
Soldier and Non-commissioned Officer	8990	.	4885	.	228	.	3877	.
Militia, Yeomanry, Volunteers	508	.	400	.	74	.	34	.
Army Pensioner	1991	3	1311	2	336	1	344	.
2. *Navy (ashore or in port).*								
Navy Officer (effective or retired)	770	.	429	.	95	.	246	.
Seaman, R.N.	210	.	144	.	37	.	29	.
Royal Marines (officers and men)	82	.	54	.	10	.	18	.
Navy Pensioner	654	6	252	5	148	1	254	.
3. Persons engaged in Professional Occupations (with their immediate Subordinates).								
1. *Clerical Profession.*								
Clergyman (Established Church)	1961	.	1437	.	378	.	146	.
Roman Catholic Priest	346	.	291	.	43	.	12	.
Minister, Priest, of other religious bodies	788	.	520	.	190	.	78	.
Missionary, Scripture Reader, Itinerant Preacher	750	552	494	413	187	113	69	26
Nun, Sister of Charity	.	1131	.	833	.	284	.	14
Theological Student	597	.	392	.	190	.	15	.
Church, Chapel, Cemetery—Officer, Servant	605	631	448	461	112	128	45	42
2. *Legal Profession.*								
Barrister, Solicitor	5905	.	4748	.	845	.	312	.
Law Student	750	.	616	.	106	.	28	.
Law Clerk, and others connected with Law	8540	76	5562	46	2626	23	352	7
3. *Medical Profession.*								
Physician, Surgeon, General Practitioner	3705	10	2801	8	699	2	205	.
Dentist	1122	.	890	.	184	.	48	.
Medical Student, Assistant	2381	40	1679	35	554	3	148	2
Midwife	.	307	.	208	.	70	.	29
Subordinate Medical Service	421	10176	299	7086	91	2485	31	605
4. *Teachers.*								
Schoolmaster	4347	13616	2486	7765	1447	4188	464	1663
Teacher, Professor, Lecturer	1854	5880	1373	5097	356	539	125	244
School Service, and others concerned in Teaching	458	211	279	43	135	50	44	18
5. *Literary and Scientific Persons.*								
Author, Editor, Journalist	1485	237	1005	86	406	37	74	14
Reporter, Short-hand Writer	1005	10	570	5	391	5	44	.
Persons engaged in Scientific Pursuits	382	1	255	.	59	1	68	.
Literary, Scientific, Institution, Service, &c.	490	50	381	1	93	8	16	1
6. *Engineers and Surveyors.*								
Civil Engineer	2223	.	1399	.	642	.	182	.
Mining Engineer	115	.	85	.	23	.	7	.
Land, House, Ship, Surveyor	1173	.	669	.	393	.	111	.
7. *Artists.*								
Painter (artist)	2799	922	2176	684	535	200	88	38
Engraver (artist)	1129	87	819	32	273	4	37	1
Sculptor	328	12	225	12	96	.	7	.
Architect	2067	.	1454	.	464	.	149	.
Musician, Music Master	4198	3684	3070	2407	341	927	187	200
Art Student	452	651	327	581	93	81	32	20
Photographer	1192	335	747	207	327	83	118	45
Actor	788	1090	563	732	208	348	17	15
Art, Music, Theatre, Service	564	183	404	120	147	62	13	8

Note.—Persons returned as engaged in more than one occupation have been referred to the one that appeared to be of most importance; or, if there was no difference in this respect, to the one first given by the person in his or her return. In some cases special rules have been followed: *e.g.*, "Clergyman and Schoolmaster" in combination has always been referred to "Schoolmaster"; a Member of Parliament or Peer engaged in any branch of commerce or industry has always been referred to this latter, not to "Peer, M.P."

The numbers returned under any heading include Labourers, Apprentices, and Assistants, as well as Masters, but not Clerks, Messengers, Errand boys, Porters, or Watchmen, for which occupations there are special headings. Civil, Military, and Naval Clerks, Law, Bank, Insurance, and Railway Clerks, and Government and Railway Porters are, however, exceptions to this rule. Many young persons, being Apprentices or Assistants, have therefore been referred to occupations usually followed by adults. Women also, chiefly widows or orphans carrying on the business of their deceased husbands or fathers, will sometimes be found under occupations commonly followed by men only.

Persons returned as *retired* from any business have not been referred to that business. Inmates of workhouses have been referred to their trades, unless their age or infirmities showed that they were past work. But persons who might be supposed to be only temporarily separated from their usual employment, such as Prisoners, and Patients in General Hospitals, have been classed under their usual occupations.

In some cases, for convenience of space, the male designation, *e.g.*, "Schoolmaster," alone is given, instead of "Schoolmaster, Schoolmistress."

Table 10 *continued*.—OCCUPATIONS of MALES and FEMALES in the LONDON DIVISION and its REGISTRATION COUNTIES.

OCCUPATIONS.	LONDON.		REGISTRATION COUNTIES.					
			MIDDLESEX. (*Intra-metn.*)		SURREY. (*Intra-metn.*)		KENT. (*Intra-metn.*)	
	Males.	Females.	Males.	Females.	Males.	Females.	Males.	Females.
8. *Persons engaged in Exhibitions, Shows, Games, &c.*								
Performer, Showman, Exhibition, Service	343	167	197	112	131	52	15	3
Billiard, Cricket, & other Games, Service	804	10	589	3	188	7	27	.
II. DOMESTIC CLASS.								
4. PERSONS ENGAGED IN DOMESTIC OFFICES OR SERVICES.								
1. *Domestic Service.*								
Domestic Coachman, Groom	14224	.	11536	.	2083	.	605	.
Domestic Gardener	4230	2	794	1	2508	.	928	1
Domestic Indoor Servant	18576	240133	16399	175498	1630	45523	547	19112
Lodge, Gate, Park, Keeper (not Government)	540	18	381	8	125	8	34	2
Inn, Hotel, Servant	15842	6621	11700	4878	3589	1408	553	335
College, Club, Service	969	33	852	21	101	9	16	3
2. *Other Service.*								
Office Keeper (not Government)	1073	2336	969	2212	85	115	19	9
Cook (not domestic)	1895	417	1388	198	456	182	51	37
Charwoman	.	19334	.	14468	.	3876	.	990
Washing and Bathing Service	1704	48559	1202	32566	433	12708	69	3285
Hospital and Institution Service	846	3340	542	2338	243	854	61	148
Others engaged in Service	951	45	776	26	102	14	13	5
III. COMMERCIAL CLASS.								
5. PERSONS ENGAGED IN COMMERCIAL OCCUPATIONS.								
1. *Merchants and Agents.*								
Merchant	4022	17	2957	9	706	8	359	.
Broker, Agent, Factor	7947	62	5339	48	1987	11	621	3
Auctioneer, Appraiser, Valuer, House Agent	1818	13	1220	8	452	4	141	1
Accountant	2980	37	1881	33	859	3	240	1
Salesman, Buyer (not otherwise described)	1138	462	805	356	286	92	47	14
Commercial Traveller	11654	.	7421	.	3655	.	578	.
Commercial Clerk	58278	2327	37410	1679	16988	541	3880	107
Officer of Commercial Company, Guild, Society, &c.	160	.	100	.	51	.	9	.
2. *Dealers in Money.*								
Banker	330	1	277	1	39	.	14	.
Bank Service	4548	57	2783	52	1261	3	504	2
Bill Discounter, Bill Broker, Finance Agent	235	.	150	.	67	.	18	.
3. *Persons occupied in Insurance.*								
Life, House, Ship, &c., Insurance Service	3319	105	1955	56	1049	40	315	9
6. PERSONS ENGAGED IN CONVEYANCE OF MEN, GOODS, AND MESSAGES.								
1. *On Railways.*								
Railway Engine Driver, Stoker	2398	.	1298	.	860	.	240	.
Railway Guard	1714	.	1028	.	514	.	172	.
Pointsman, Level Crossing Man	233	.	155	.	62	.	16	.
Other Railway Officials and Servants	17606	137	11358	77	5132	47	1116	13
2. *On Roads.*								
Toll Collector, Turnpike Gate Keeper	54	2	40	1	12	1	2	.
Omnibus, Coach, Cab, Owner—Livery Stable Keeper	1882	74	1423	53	383	20	76	1
Cabman, Flyman, Coachman (not domestic)	13509	.	10473	.	2693	.	343	.
Carman, Carrier, Carter, Haulier	32086	58	21368	40	9419	17	1302	1
Tramway Companies' Service	803	4	454	2	255	2	94	.
Wheel Chair Proprietor, Attendant, &c.	135	2	122	1	11	1	2	.
3. *On Canals, Rivers and Seas.*								
Inland Navigation Service	151	.	114	.	31	.	6	.
Bargeman, Lighterman, Waterman	6482	24	3231	11	2323	12	928	1
Navigation Service (on shore)	203	3	147	2	29	1	27	.
Seaman (Merchant Service)	10110	.	6794	.	1932	.	1384	.
Pilot	167	.	82	.	41	.	44	.
Ship Steward, Cook	883	70	608	41	184	21	91	8
Boatman on Seas	7	.	7	.	.	.	.	.
Harbour, Dock, Wharf, Lighthouse, Service	12109	9	9062	7	2475	1	562	1
4. *In Storage.*								
Warehouseman (not Manchester)	9139	282	5811	214	2802	65	356	3
Meter, Weigher	196	.	94	.	76	.	26	.
5. *In conveying Messages, Porterage, &c.*								
Messenger, Porter, Watchman (not Railway nor Government)	46984	391	34470	324	11180	62	1305	5
Telegraph, Telephone, Service	1735	798	804	582	590	188	142	28

Table 10 *continued*.—Occupations of Males and Females in the London Division and its Registration Counties.

Occupations.	London.		Registration Counties. Middlesex. (*Intra-metn.*)		Surrey. (*Intra-metn.*)		Kent. (*Intra-metn.*)	
	Males.	Females.	Males.	Females.	Males.	Females.	Males.	Females.
IV. AGRICULTURAL CLASS								
7. Persons engaged in Agriculture.								
1. *In Fields and Pastures.*								
Farmer, Grazier	358	25	242	20	73	3	43	2
Farmer's, Grazier's—Son, Grandson, Brother, Nephew*	64	.	36	.	16	.	12	.
Farm Bailiff	64	.	24	.	16	.	24	.
Agricultural Labourer, Farm Servant, Cottager	1583	183	654	111	302	17	627	55
Shepherd	25	.	14	.	6	.	5	.
Land Drainage Service (not in towns)	13	.	5	.	1	.	7	.
Agricultural Machine—Proprietor, Attendant	2	.	.	.	2	.	.	.
Agricultural Student, Pupil	7	.	5	.	2	.	.	.
Others engaged in, or connected with, Agriculture	90	4	78	2	8	2	4	.
2. *In Woods.*								
Woodman	89	.	60	.	27	.	2	.
3. *In Gardens.*								
Nurseryman, Seedsman, Florist	1142	349	698	293	277	46	167	10
Gardener (not domestic)	5765	215	3474	74	1252	33	1039	108
8. Persons engaged about Animals.								
1. *About Animals.*								
Horse Proprietor, Breeder, Dealer	355	3	269	3	65	.	11	.
Groom, Horse-keeper, Horse-breaker	7903	20	5898	17	1715	3	290	.
Veterinary Surgeon, Farrier	2720	.	1912	.	690	.	118	.
Cattle, Sheep, Pig—Dealer, Salesman	337	2	276	2	43	.	18	.
Drover	596	.	464	.	60	.	72	.
Gamekeeper	33	.	17	.	7	.	9	.
Dog, Bird, Animal—Keeper, Dealer	220	31	163	26	44	5	13	.
Vermin destroyer	20	1	13	1	6	.	1	.
Fisherman	167	1	38	.	20	1	109	.
Knacker, Catsmeat Dealer, &c., &c.	387	76	264	55	97	20	26	1
V. INDUSTRIAL CLASS.								
9. Persons working and dealing in Books, Prints, and Maps.								
1. *Books.*								
Publisher, Bookseller, Librarian	3159	264	2092	179	936	73	131	12
Music—Publisher, Seller, Printer	600	73	490	46	100	22	10	5
Bookbinder	5639	7293	3921	5006	1607	2240	111	47
Printer	25595	631	16002	407	8925	213	668	11
Newspaper Agent, News Room Keeper	1462	311	950	244	427	60	85	7
Others	50	2	39	2	11	.	.	.
2. *Prints and Maps.*								
Lithographer, Lithographic Printer	2353	26	1619	15	666	9	68	2
Copper Plate and Steel Plate Printer	288	8	215	6	68	2	5	.
Map and Print—Colourer, Seller	339	129	212	108	113	20	14	1
10. Persons working and dealing in Machines and Implements.								
1. *Machines.*								
Engine, Machine, Maker	6778	68	3044	42	2532	16	1202	10
Millwright	419	.	213	.	134	.	72	.
Fitter, Turner (Engine and Machine)	7830	.	3512	.	2638	.	1680	.
Boiler Maker	2434	.	1193	.	600	.	641	.
Spinning and Weaving Machine Maker	52	6	41	6	11	.	.	.
Agricultural Machine and Implement Maker	76	10	55	9	21	1	.	.
Domestic Machinery—Maker, Dealer	169	8	95	5	59	1	15	2
2. *Tools and Implements.*								
Tool Maker, Dealer	563	18	402	16	117	.	44	2
Cutler, Scissors Maker	450	18	332	13	97	5	21	.
File Maker	138	4	65	2	68	.	5	2
Saw Maker	245	8	177	7	52	1	16	.
Pin Maker	17	17	6	8	11	9	.	.
Needle Maker	8	3	4	1	4	2	.	.
Steel Pen Maker	20	9	11	5	8	4	1	.
Pencil Maker (Wood)	41	36	26	8	15	28	.	.
Domestic Implement Maker	57	5	49	3	7	2	1	.
3. *Watches and Philosophical Instruments.*								
Watch Maker, Clock Maker	4865	91	3979	81	699	7	187	3
Philosophical Instrument Maker, Optician	1735	62	1329	45	295	17	111	.
Electrical Apparatus Maker	1321	16	503	15	161	1	657	.
Weighing and Measuring Apparatus Maker	753	6	541	3	194	3	18	.

* Only male relatives living with the farmer or grazier, and, therefore, presumably engaged in agriculture, are included above.

Table 10 *continued*.—OCCUPATIONS of MALES and FEMALES in the LONDON DIVISION and its REGISTRATION COUNTIES.

OCCUPATIONS.	LONDON.		REGISTRATION COUNTIES.					
			MIDDLESEX. (*Intra-metn.*)		SURREY. (*Intra-metn.*)		KENT. (*Intra-metn.*)	
	Males.	Females.	Males.	Females.	Males.	Females.	Males.	Females.
4. *Surgical Instruments.*								
Surgical Instrument Maker	629	190	472	149	151	40	6	1
5. *Arms and Ordnance.*								
Gunsmith, Gun Manufacturer	927	19	673	16	185	3	69	.
Ordnance Manufacturer	98	1	5	1	1	.	92	.
Sword, Bayonet—Maker, Cutler	69	1	61	1	8	.	.	.
Others	4	.	4	.	.	.	.	.
6. *Musical Instruments.*								
Musical Instrument Maker, Dealer	5873	168	5178	153	653	15	42	
7. *Type, Dies, Medals, Coins.*								
Type Cutter, Founder	841	6	747	5	92	1	2	.
Die, Seal, Coin, Medal, Maker	405	20	310	17	90	3	5	.
8. *Tackle for Sports and Games.*								
Toy Maker, Dealer	602	430	455	317	135	80	12	24
Fishing Rod, Tackle, Maker, Dealer	151	46	118	40	31	6	2	.
Apparatus for other Games, Maker, Dealer	561	73	234	86	164	11	103	26
11. PERSONS WORKING AND DEALING IN HOUSES, FURNITURE, AND DECORATIONS.								
1. *Houses.*								
Builder	7319	23	4494	18	2307	6	518	.
Carpenter, Joiner	38103	41	24185	25	11161	16	2646	.
Bricklayer	23322	9	13986	2	7221	4	2075	3
Mason	7502	12	4584	2	3609	3	509	1
Slater, Tiler	754	.	429	.	306	.	25	.
Plasterer, Whitewasher	6699	7	4326	6	1899	1	474	.
Paperhanger	1797	11	1249	5	457	2	91	4
Plumber	7477	26	4875	12	1997	12	605	2
Painter, Glazier	38084	97	19541	68	6897	24	1646	5
2. *Furniture and Fittings.*								
Cabinet Maker, Upholsterer	19007	2950	16022	2500	3044	378	541	72
French Polisher	4295	472	3654	462	589	27	52	3
Furniture Broker, Dealer	1673	142	1262	110	340	26	71	6
Locksmith, Bellhanger	689	14	549	14	123	.	17	.
Gas Fitter	4636	18	3115	16	1238	2	283	.
House and Shop Fittings—Maker, Dealer	1497	121	1076	101	342	20	79	.
Funeral Furniture Maker, Undertaker	959	39	699	32	217	7	43	.
Others	40	1	35	1	5	.	.	.
3. *House Decorations.*								
Wood Carver	1632	12	1453	11	177	1	2	.
Carver, Gilder	4908	141	3404	105	559	28	45	8
Dealer in Works of Art	602	57	491	44	94	11	17	2
Figure, Image—Maker, Dealer	181	21	140	12	31	9	1	.
Animal, Bird, &c., Preserver, Naturalist	206	116	172	110	29	6	5	.
Artificial Flower Maker	671	3986	492	3490	77	481	2	17
12. PERSONS WORKING AND DEALING IN CARRIAGES AND HARNESS.								
1. *Carriages.*								
Coachmaker	5685	60	4180	46	1341	13	164	1
Railway Carriage, Railway Wagon, Maker	271	1	152	1	109	.	10	.
Wheelwright	3069	12	1779	5	1004	4	286	3
Bicycle, Tricycle—Maker, Dealer	181	2	61	1	33	1	7	.
Others	194	27	107	18	84	9	3	.
2. *Harness.*								
Saddler, Harness, Whip, Maker	3264	175	2642	134	818	38	104	3
13. PERSONS WORKING AND DEALING IN SHIPS AND BOATS.								
1. *Hull.*								
Ship, Boat, Barge, Builder	2025	1	1126	1	588	.	311	.
Shipwright, Ship Carpenter (ashore)	2525	.	1089	.	361	.	475	.
2. *Masts, Rigging, &c.*								
Mast, Yard, Oar, Block, Maker	264	.	164	.	84	.	16	.
Ship Rigger, Chandler, Fitter	488	2	445	3	23	.	20	.
Sail Maker	594	10	451	14	63	3	50	.

Table 10 *continued*.—OCCUPATIONS of MALES and FEMALES in the LONDON DIVISION and its REGISTRATION COUNTIES.

OCCUPATIONS.	LONDON.		REGISTRATION COUNTIES. MIDDLESEX. (*Intra-metn.*)		SURREY. (*Intra-metn.*)		KENT. (*Intra-metn.*)	
	Males.	Females.	Males.	Females.	Males.	Females.	Males.	Females.
14. PERSONS WORKING AND DEALING IN CHEMICALS AND COMPOUNDS.								
1. *Colouring Matter.*								
Dye, Paint, Manufacture	464	48	315	43	109	3	40	2
Ink, Blacking, Colouring Substance, Manufacture	551	30	353	28	149	8	9	.
2. *Explosives.*								
Gunpowder, Guncotton, Explosive Substance, Manufacture	28,	12	9	8	2	1	17	3
Fusee, Fireworks, Explosive Article, Manufacture	471	763	157	692	77	69	237	2
3. *Drugs and other Chemicals and Compounds.*								
Chemist, Druggist	3762	162	2542	124	920	33	200	5
Manufacturing Chemist	1399	459	906	320	380	127	113	12
Alkali Manufacture	16	.	14	.	2	.	.	.
Drysalter	139	16	91	11	42	5	6	.
15. PERSONS WORKING AND DEALING IN TOBACCO AND PIPES.								
1. *Tobacco and Pipes.*								
Tobacco Manufacturer, Tobacconist	5694	2001	4693	1504	882	438	119	59
Tobacco Pipe, Snuff Box, &c., Maker	642	220	508	183	104	34	30	3
16. PERSONS WORKING AND DEALING IN FOOD AND LODGING.								
1. *Board and Lodging.*								
Innkeeper, Hotel Keeper, Publican	6783	948	4813	720	1502	166	468	62
Lodging, Boarding House, Keeper	1069	5798	994	4897	57	682	18	219
Coffee, Eating House, Keeper	2791	895	2115	656	574	192	102	47
2. *Spirituous Drinks.*								
Hop—Merchant, Dealer	245	6	48	4	164	2	33	.
Maltster	136	.	77	.	48	.	11	.
Brewer	2392	15	1955	7	835	7	102	1
Beerseller. Ale, Porter, Cider, Dealer	2012	306	1347	175	592	109	173	22
Cellarman	2726	145	1885	103	780	42	61	.
Wine, Spirit—Merchant, Agent	2169	91	1469	70	517	13	183	8
3. *Food.*								
Milkseller, Dairyman	6597	1219	4369	1008	1669	176	559	37
Cheesemonger, Butterman	3132	144	2207	112	776	28	150	4
Butcher, Meat Salesman	12698	321	8550	226	3165	73	983	22
Provision Curer, Dealer	2071	430	1447	320	522	95	102	15
Poulterer, Game Dealer	738	35	537	25	181	1	20	9
Fishmonger	4937	393	3237	236	1424	107	276	30
Corn, Flour, Seed—Merchant, Dealer	2014	212	1170	148	695	47	149	17
Corn Miller	777	3	262		346	3	169	.
Baker	12291	1458	8448	842	3543	522	1099	94
Confectioner, Pastrycook	3333	2387	2419	1738	764	539	150	110
Greengrocer, Fruiterer	6651	1087	4355	768	1794	240	302	79
Mustard, Vinegar, Spice, Pickle—Maker, Dealer	331	356	166	244	147	104	18	8
Sugar Refiner	878	11	726	8	67	3	85	.
Grocer. Tea, Coffee, Chocolate—Maker, Dealer	11967	1131	7526	719	3488	323	953	84
Ginger Beer, Mineral Water—Manufacturer, Dealer	924	79	608	42	287	36	29	1
Others dealing in Food	13	.	8	.	5	.	.	.
17. PERSONS WORKING AND DEALING IN TEXTILE FABRICS.								
1. *Wool and Worsted.*								
Woolstapler	257	4	164	3	63	1	30	.
Woollen Cloth Manufacture	686	39	517	29	128	9	13	.
Wool, Woollen goods—Dyer, Printer	25	.	18	.	7	.	2	1
Worsted, Stuff, Manufacture	70	54	49	39	21	11	.	.
Flannel Manufacture	10	2	9	2	.	.	1	4
Blanket Manufacture	2	.	.	.	2	.	.	.
Fuller	1	1	1	.	.	1	.	.
Cloth, Worsted, Stuff, Flannel, Blanket, Dealer	482	18	267	14	195	4	20	.
Others	23	7	12	7	10	.	1	.
2. *Silk.*								
Silk, Silk goods, Manufacture	1802	2004	1705	1916	8	63	9	36
Silk Dyer, Printer	128	18	68	3	5	15	2	.
Ribbon Manufacture	22	11	14	8		3	2	.
Crape, Gauze, Manufacture	15	23	12	14	2	9	1	.
Silk Merchant, Dealer	446	42	275	87	131	4	40	1

Table 10 *continued*.—OCCUPATIONS of MALES and FEMALES in the LONDON DIVISION and its REGISTRATION COUNTIES.

OCCUPATIONS.	LONDON.		REGISTRATION COUNTIES. MIDDLESEX. (*Intra-metn.*)		SURREY. (*Intra-metn.*)		KENT. (*Intra-metn.*)	
	Males.	Females.	Males.	Females.	Males.	Females.	Males.	Females.
3. Cotton and Flax								
Cotton, Cotton goods, Manufacture	205	224	157	204	41	16	7	5
Cotton, Calico—Printer, Dyer, Bleacher	43	8	32	4	10	4	1	.
Cotton, Calico—Warehouseman, Dealer	71	5	41	2	25	2	5	1
Flax, Linen—Manufacturer, Dealer	127	29	87	22	33	6	7	1
Lace Manufacturer, Dealer	297	791	204	619	76	156	17	16
Fustian Manufacturer, Dealer	.	.	.	.	.	.	.	.
Tape Manufacturer, Dealer	3	3	2	3	1	.	.	.
Thread Manufacturer, Dealer	7	4	6	3	1	.	.	1
4. Hemp and other Fibrous Materials.								
Hemp, Jute, Cocoa Fibre, Manufacture	200	54	124	36	73	18	3	.
Rope, Twine, Cord—Maker, Dealer	1225	179	928	151	256	27	41	1
Mat Maker, Seller	408	105	236	49	160	56	12	.
Net Maker	14	45	9	31	4	13	1	.
Canvas, Sailcloth, Manufacture	20	36	13	27	6	9	1	1
Sacking, Sack, Bag—Maker, Dealer	194	609	108	309	77	297	9	3
Others working and dealing in Hemp	77	105	47	72	26	32	4	1
5. Mixed or Unspecified Materials.								
Weaver (undefined)	232	163	193	142	35	17	4	5
Dyer, Printer, Scourer, Bleacher, Calenderer (undefined)	1253	615	823	426	385	166	45	23
Factory hand (Textile, undefined)	27	145	18	94	9	47	.	4
Felt Manufacture	86	8	67	6	18	2	1	.
Carpet, Rug, Manufacture	572	76	386	36	178	37	14	.
Manchester Warehouseman	1027	10	888	1	109	9	30	4
Draper, Linen Draper, Mercer	11257	6470	8877	4555	2327	1458	353	457
Fancy Goods (Textile), Manufacturer, Worker, Dealer	604	1610	493	1146	98	387	13	77
Trimming Maker, Dealer	679	2079	597	1909	68	157	14	13
Embroiderer	76	1138	58	890	15	289	3	19
Others	22	14	15	13	7	1	.	.
18. PERSONS WORKING AND DEALING IN DRESS.								
1. Dress.								
Hatter, Hat Manufacture (not straw)	2868	1999	1338	593	1150	690	80	10
Straw—Hat, Bonnet, Plait, Manufacture	203	486	172	401	30	58	1	13
Tailor	22744	18477	18411	13991	3464	2191	849	265
Milliner, Dressmaker, Staymaker	1481	70476	1034	51258	347	15322	40	3836
Shawl Manufacture	19	9	9	8	1	1	9	.
Shirt Maker, Seamstress	866	26461	526	18344	308	6772	32	1285
Hosiery Manufacture	125	95	89	75	35	19	4	1
Hosier, Haberdasher	1829	2878	1275	2180	480	685	74	33
Glover, Glove Maker	294	274	148	117	102	158	14	1
Button Maker, Dealer	155	292	123	277	30	13	2	2
Shoe, Boot—Maker, Dealer	30655	6682	23718	5751	5676	840	1267	91
Patten, Clog, Maker	65	8	35	3	27	5	3	.
Wig Maker, Hairdresser	3447	225	2477	240	802	48	163	7
Umbrella, Parasol, Stick—Maker, Dealer	1873	1543	1633	1314	203	115	37	11
Accoutrement Maker	214	104	113	127	90	58	15	9
Old Clothes Dealer, and others	239	362	159	411	57	139	13	21
19. PERSONS WORKING AND DEALING IN VARIOUS ANIMAL SUBSTANCES.								
1. In Grease, Gut, Bone, Horn, Ivory, and Whalebone.								
Tallow Chandler, Candle, Grease, Manufacture	786	73	255	30	493	43	38	.
Soap Boiler, Maker	531	21	304	17	148	3	79	1
Glue, Size, Gelatine, Isinglass—Maker, Dealer	119	53	48	7	68	52	3	.
Manure Manufacture	90	4	44	1	40	3	6	.
Bone, Horn, Ivory, Tortoise-shell—Worker, Dealer	746	37	630	34	104	3	12	.
Comb Maker	145	28	93	26	50	2	2	.
Others	141	74	127	71	12	2	2	1
2. In Skins.								
Furrier, Skinner	2655	2793	1852	1793	760	1056	43	14
Tanner, Fellmonger	1577	12	58	5	1500	7	19	.
Currier	3890	120	1027	55	2734	58	129	7
Leather Goods, Portmanteau, Bag, Strap, &c.—Maker, Dealer	2394	620	1706	509	649	109	39	2
Parchment, Vellum—Maker, Dealer	161	13	78	3	83	5	.	.
3. In Hair and Feathers.								
Hair, Bristle—Worker, Dealer	352	102	303	168	48	23	1	1
Brush, Broom, Maker	2732	1910	1893	1385	855	318	35	10
Quill, Feather—Dresser, Dealer	233	1531	231	1312	53	205	4	14

Table 10 *continued*.—Occupations of Males and Females in the London Division and its Registration Counties.

Occupations.	London. Males.	London. Females.	Middlesex (Intra-metn.) Males.	Middlesex (Intra-metn.) Females.	Surrey (Intra-metn.) Males.	Surrey (Intra-metn.) Females.	Kent (Intra-metn.) Males.	Kent (Intra-metn.) Females.
20. Persons working and dealing in various Vegetable Substances.								
1. In Oils, Gums, and Resins.								
Oil Miller, Oil Cake—Maker, Dealer	545	39	349	34	165	2	31	3
Oil and Colourman	3117	283	2046	190	862	81	209	12
Floor Cloth, Oil Cloth, Manufacture	377	9	112	6	241	3	24	.
Japanner	446	93	286	72	157	20	1	1
India Rubber, Gutta Percha—Worker, Dealer	434	153	246	71	132	78	56	4
Waterproof Goods—Maker, Dealer	357	190	287	166	60	24	10	.
Others	210	13	132	11	71	2	16	.
2. In Cane, Rush, and Straw.								
Willow, Cane, Rush—Worker, Dealer, Basketmaker	1491	718	849	472	570	220	72	26
Hay, Straw (not plait), Chaff—Cutter, Dealer	372	1	249	.	88	1	35	.
Thatcher	7	.	.	.	4	.	3	.
3. In Wood and Bark.								
Timber, Wood—Merchant, Dealer	3212	601	1850	247	954	203	408	151
Sawyer	3213	.	1847	.	1028	.	338	.
Lath, Wooden Fence, Hurdle, Maker	479	3	299	.	148	3	32	.
Wood Turner, Box Maker	3050	1713	2335	1303	608	407	107	3
Cooper. Hoop Maker, Bender	4481	20	2804	15	1440	5	237	.
Cork, Bark—Cutter, Worker, Dealer	765	93	520	57	232	34	13	2
Others	63	5	44	4	15	.	4	1
4. In Paper.								
Paper Manufacture	880	542	600	276	264	264	16	2
Envelope Maker	135	1552	95	997	38	538	2	17
Stationer, Law Stationer	5119	2001	3546	1421	1373	510	200	70
Card, Pattern Card, Maker	417	303	334	252	83	48	.	3
Paper Stainer	961	200	759	169	140	31	2	.
Paper Box, Paper Bag, Maker	631	3873	558	3169	68	701	5	3
Ticket, Label, Writer	343	282	271	222	49	58	3	2
Others	444	127	333	112	96	13	16	2
21. Persons working and dealing in various Mineral Substances.								
1. Miners.								
Coal Miner	133	9	90	9	39	.	4	.
Ironstone Miner	.	.	.	.	.	.	.	.
Copper Miner	10	.	8	.	1	.	1	.
Tin Miner	4	.	3	.	.	.	1	.
Lead Miner	.	.	.	.	.	.	.	.
Miner in other, or undefined, Minerals	51	.	30	.	3	.	7	.
Mine Service	62	2	51	2	9	.	2	.
2. Coal, Coal Gas, &c.								
Coal Merchant, Dealer	1379	99	991	74	289	20	99	5
Coalheaver	3243	.	2270	.	729	.	244	.
Coke, Charcoal, Peat—Cutter, Burner, Dealer	179	11	120	7	48	4	11	.
Gas Works Service	3851	.	2283	.	1166	.	412	.
3. Stone, Clay, and Road Making.								
Stone Quarrier	35	.	19	.	15	.	1	.
Stone Cutter, Dresser, Dealer	853	.	487	.	321	.	48	.
Slate Quarrier	6	.	3	.	2	.	1	.
Slate Worker, Dealer	136	4	55	1	77	3	4	.
Limeburner	86	2	50	.	23	2	13	.
Clay, Sand, Gravel, Chalk—Labourer, Dealer	55	5	23	3	24	.	9	2
Fossil, Coprolite—Digger, Dealer	.	1	.	1	.	.	.	.
Well Sinker, Borer	50	.	29	.	16	.	5	.
Plaster, Cement, Manufacture	197	8	88	4	64	5	45	.
Brick, Tile—Maker, Burner, Dealer	1343	9	863	6	227	2	253	1
Paviour	852	.	579	.	216	.	57	.
Road Contractor, Surveyor, Inspector	41	.	22	.	18	.	1	.
Road Labourer	607	.	376	.	174	.	58	.
Railway Contractor	195	.	81	.	101	.	13	.
Platelayer	1113	.	686	.	206	.	152	.
Railway Labourer, Navvy	1924	.	1145	.	614	.	165	.
Others	145	10	45	14	94	2	6	.
4. Earthenware and Glass.								
Earthenware, China, Porcelain, Manufacture	1163	263	347	122	761	134	55	7
Glass Manufacture	2650	113	1824	90	784	22	48	1
Earthenware, China, Glass, Dealer	1220	334	854	240	293	71	73	23
5. Salt.								
Salt Maker, Dealer	32	13	23	9	7	4	2	.

Table 10 *continued.*—OCCUPATIONS of MALES and FEMALES in the LONDON DIVISION and its REGISTRATION COUNTIES.

OCCUPATIONS.	LONDON.		REGISTRATION COUNTIES. MIDDLESEX. (*Intra-metn.*)		SURREY. (*Intra-metn.*)		KENT. (*Intra-metn.*)	
	Males.	Females.	Males.	Females.	Males.	Females.	Males.	Females.
6. Water.								
Waterworks Service	584	.	386	.	157	.	41	.
Others	49	6	32	4	15	2	2	.
7. Precious Metals and Jewellery.								
Goldsmith, Silversmith, Jeweller	6918	425	5908	362	889	48	121	15
Gold, Silver, Beater	346	.	302	.	43	.	1	.
Lapidary	155	56	140	52	13	4	2	.
Others	298	458	223	382	52	34	23	42
8. Iron and Steel.								
Blacksmith	8521	12	5192	9	2212	3	1117	.
Whitesmith	1223	2	804	2	328	.	91	.
Nail Manufacture	68	20	41	3	10	16	8	1
Anchor, Chain, Manufacture	40	.	32	.	7	.	1	.
Other Iron and Steel Manufactures	6585	24	3398	18	1785	4	1402	2
Ironmonger, Hardware Dealer, Merchant	2546	89	1663	66	707	21	176	8
9. Copper.								
Copper, Copper goods—Manufacturer, Worker, Dealer	942	8	526	8	284	.	132	
10. Tin and Zinc.								
Tin, Tin Plate, Tin goods—Manufacturer, Worker, Dealer	3719	181	2436	157	1121	23	162	1
Zinc, Zinc Goods—Manufacturer, Worker, Dealer	976	9	684	9	221	.	71	.
11. Lead.								
Lead, Leaden goods—Manufacturer, Worker, Dealer	363	43	255	40	96	2	12	1
12. In Other, Mixed, or Unspecified, Metals.								
Metal Refiner, Worker, Turner, Dealer	893	15	581	14	173	1	139	.
Brass, Bronze, Manufacture, Brazier	4671	11	3176	8	1183	3	312	.
Metal Burnisher, Lacquerer	87	184	81	161	6	22	.	1
White Metal, Plated Ware, Manufacture, Pewterer	573	11	435	9	122	3	16	.
Wire Maker, Worker, Weaver, Drawer	1071	86	755	46	249	28	67	6
Bolt, Nut, Rivet, Screw, Staple, Maker	109	4	73	2	28	2	8	.
Lamp, Lantern, Candlestick, Maker	418	14	328	9	63	4	2	1
Clasp, Buckle, Hinge, Maker	17	1	12	1	5	.	.	.
Fancy Chain, Gilt Toy, Maker	35	9	35	6	.	3	.	.
Others	79	16	58	14	20	2	1	.
22. PERSONS WORKING AND DEALING IN GENERAL OR UNSPECIFIED COMMODITIES.								
1. Makers and Dealers (General or Undefined).								
General Shopkeeper, Dealer	8957	4919	6361	3555	2136	1104	460	260
Pawnbroker	2335	43	1588	25	611	13	136	5
Costermonger, Huckster, Street Seller	5504	3060	3789	2282	1473	582	242	196
Manufacturer, Manager, Superintendent (undefined)	1968	291	1234	212	500	71	234	8
Contractor (undefined)	465	10	290	6	136	4	39	.
2. Mechanics and Labourers (General or Undefined).								
General Labourer	77796	319	45762	194	21878	85	10156	40
Engine Driver, Stoker, Fireman (not railway, marine, nor agricultural)	6045	.	3605	.	1823	.	617	
Artisan, Mechanic (undefined)	5182	407	3965	310	930	88	287	9
Apprentice (undefined)	748	273	530	218	155	48	63	7
Factory Labourer (undefined)	3762	1079	2438	761	1101	301	223	17
Machinist, Machine Worker (undefined)	370	5104	356	3145	186	1612	128	347
23. PERSONS WORKING AND DEALING IN REFUSE MATTERS.								
1. Refuse Matters.								
Town Drainage Service	316	.	203	.	81	.	32	.
Chimney Sweep, Soot Merchant	1427	30	1039	24	303	5	85	1
Scavenger, Crossing Sweeper	915	139	739	84	149	54	27	1
Rag Gatherer, Dealer	485	242	345	126	113	112	27	4
VI. UNOCCUPIED CLASS.								
24. PERSONS WITHOUT SPECIFIED OCCUPATIONS								
Persons returned by Property, Rank, &c., and not by special occupation	431193	1177346	277134	765098	117026	317981	37033	94267
Children under 5 years of age	248619	248425	160411	160283	69254	69122	18954	19670

Table 11.—BIRTH-PLACES of MALES and FEMALES enumerated in COUNTIES.

WHERE BORN.	WHERE ENUMERATED.							
			METROPOLITAN PARTS OF COUNTIES.*					
	LONDON.		MIDDLESEX. (*Intra-metn.*)		SURREY. (*Intra-metn.*)		KENT. (*Intra-metn.*)	
	Males.	Females.	Males.	Females.	Males.	Females.	Males.	Females.
TOTAL OF INHABITANTS	1797486	2018997	1192885	1357671	477039	520651	127562	140675
LONDON	1147063	1254892	756337	834072	314136	337001	76567	83349
MIDDLESEX (*Intra-metropolitan*)	797652	877724	711761	778237	74319	84592	11581	14495
SURREY (*Intra-metropolitan*)	275152	296173	36725	45247	231386	242536	7041	8290
KENT (*Intra-metropolitan*)	74259	80995	7851	10588	8463	9853	57945	60564
SOUTH-EASTERN COUNTIES	127697	161511	67124	91674	44378	51746	16195	18091
SURREY (*Extra-metropolitan*)	28411	34873	13099	17439	13015	14666	2239	3768
KENT (*Extra-metropolitan*)	48234	53271	20408	27982	13384	16038	8382	9236
SUSSEX	19505	24896	10712	14980	6657	7604	2136	2312
HAMPSHIRE	23773	29921	13565	18530	7653	8706	2553	2665
BERKSHIRE	13774	18550	9280	12778	3669	4087	885	1090
SOUTH-MIDLAND COUNTIES	112228	136678	83274	102616	23775	27796	5179	6266
MIDDLESEX (*Extra-metropolitan*)	44635	52881	35210	41561	8151	9506	1494	1814
HERTFORDSHIRE	16088	19705	11898	14737	3344	3964	849	1004
BUCKINGHAMSHIRE	12026	14756	8691	10564	3197	3469	638	723
OXFORDSHIRE	9469	12904	6564	9281	2411	2977	494	646
NORTHAMPTONSHIRE	7995	9578	5786	6981	1767	2067	442	525
HUNTINGDONSHIRE	3077	4315	2177	3159	703	903	197	253
BEDFORDSHIRE	7568	8109	5561	5991	1593	1666	414	452
CAMBRIDGESHIRE	10650	14435	7300	10342	2609	3244	651	849
EASTERN COUNTIES	84715	111153	57186	76890	20795	25798	6734	8465
ESSEX	39981	52572	27320	36652	9271	11683	3381	4237
SUFFOLK	23168	30148	15105	20415	6146	7484	1827	2249
NORFOLK	21566	28433	14662	19823	5378	6631	1526	1979
SOUTH-WESTERN COUNTIES	73255	95287	48152	65443	19919	23348	5184	6496
WILTSHIRE	13066	18261	8338	12407	3939	4767	778	1087
DORSETSHIRE	8046	10168	4923	6660	2502	2774	621	734
DEVONSHIRE	26577	32379	17567	23099	6927	7871	2083	2409
CORNWALL	7104	9430	4712	6414	1812	2232	580	784
SOMERSETSHIRE	18473	25049	12812	17863	4739	5704	1122	1482
WEST-MIDLAND COUNTIES	43317	51965	30079	36844	10688	12194	2550	2927
GLOUCESTERSHIRE	16292	18843	10564	13432	3899	4432	829	979
HEREFORDSHIRE	2643	4031	1798	2898	698	905	147	231
SHROPSHIRE	2878	3987	2019	2890	678	853	181	244
STAFFORDSHIRE	6132	9639	4135	4570	1490	1623	457	437
WORCESTERSHIRE	4190	6845	2793	3696	1129	1328	268	311
WARWICKSHIRE	12182	13120	3720	9352	2794	3043	668	725
NORTH-MIDLAND COUNTIES	19900	21666	13747	15256	4831	5137	1322	1273
LEICESTERSHIRE	4204	4163	2958	2018	977	1014	269	231
RUTLANDSHIRE	872	842	526	646	113	161	33	35
LINCOLNSHIRE	8034	9676	5086	6844	1956	2248	318	584
NOTTINGHAMSHIRE	3949	3926	2699	2742	965	968	285	215
DERBYSHIRE	3021	3060	1984	2100	820	746	217	208
NORTH-WESTERN COUNTIES	17157	16962	11366	11418	4563	4369	1228	1175
CHESHIRE	2977	3100	1994	2086	772	780	211	234
LANCASHIRE	14180	13862	9372	9332	3791	3589	1017	941
YORKSHIRE	16409	15814	10972	10608	4214	4111	1223	1095
NORTHERN COUNTIES	10291	10021	6917	6843	2540	2368	834	810
DURHAM	4029	4041	2572	2657	1065	1000	392	384
NORTHUMBERLAND	3817	3961	2623	2720	895	983	299	308
CUMBERLAND	1815	1546	1282	1043	433	359	100	94
WESTMORLAND	630	473	440	373	147	76	43	24
MONMOUTHSHIRE AND WALES	11829	16216	8500	11952	2656	3278	673	986
MONMOUTHSHIRE	1730	2762	1187	2008	427	594	122	160
GLAMORGANSHIRE	1869	2427	1308	1760	425	513	136	154
CARMARTHENSHIRE	818	784	612	581	169	163	37	40
PEMBROKESHIRE	1246	1586	835	1129	284	295	127	162
CARDIGANSHIRE	1176	1176	907	891	235	247	34	38
BRECKNOCKSHIRE	487	718	359	530	108	122	24	47
RADNORSHIRE	270	388	193	282	67	91	10	15
MONTGOMERYSHIRE	639	1022	454	809	146	171	20	42
FLINTSHIRE	373	373	256	270	100	83	18	20
DENBIGHSHIRE	508	604	381	459	110	135	17	30
MERIONETHSHIRE	221	337	169	263	48	62	4	12
CARNARVONSHIRE	354	450	263	315	74	85	17	30
ANGLESEY	186	250	133	182	43	41	12	17
WALES (*County not stated*)	1934	3364	1398	2463	470	676	86	225
ENGLAND (*County not stated*)	9019	9480	6683	7073	1877	1942	439	465
OTHER PARTS OF BRITISH EMPIRE	77381	84868	53288	59965	16369	17035	7724	7868
ISLANDS in the BRITISH SEAS	2388	3069	1570	2032	612	687	806	290
SCOTLAND	26037	23617	18615	16985	5414	4752	2008	1780
IRELAND	37173	43605	25338	30935	8003	8878	3832	3794
BRITISH COLONIES or DEPENDENCIES	11783	14737	7765	10013	2340	2720	1678	2004
FOREIGN COUNTRIES	46676	31780	38900	26522	6147	4002	1629	1256
British Subjects	9558	8664	6983	6342	1907	1718	666	604
Foreigners	37118	23116	31915	20180	4240	2284	963	652
AT SEA	549	704	360	495	128	146	61	63
British Subjects	542	696	354	485	127	145	61	63
Foreigners	7	11	6	10	1	1	—	—

* The Counties *proper*, and not the Registration Counties are referred to in this Table.

Table 12.—DISTRIBUTION of the enumerated NATIVES of COUNTIES.

WHERE ENUMERATED.	WHERE BORN.							
	LONDON.		MIDDLESEX. (*Intra-metn.*)		SURREY. (*Intra-metn.*)		KENT. (*Intra-metn.*)	
	Males.	Females.	Males.	Females.	Males.	Females.	Males.	Females.
TOTAL ENUMERATED NATIVES	1418006	1568649	1005969	1121591	317581	343944	94456	103114
LONDON	1147063	1254892	797652	877724	275152	296173	74259	80995
MIDDLESEX (*Intra-metropolitan*)	756337	834072	711761	778237	38725	46247	7851	10588
SURREY (*Intra-metropolitan*)	314159	337381	74310	84992	231386	242536	8463	9853
KENT (*Intra-metropolitan*)	76567	83439	11581	14495	7041	8200	57945	60554
SOUTH-EASTERN COUNTIES	84808	105821	55571	71803	19805	23354	9432	10665
SURREY (*Extra-metropolitan*)	28049	37527	17080	23480	9461	11116	2408	2931
KENT (*Extra-metropolitan*)	25488	29150	15916	18667	5889	6038	4183	4446
SUSSEX	13322	20700	9878	15758	2380	3301	1064	1443
HAMPSHIRE	12549	12939	9008	9410	1920	1938	1534	1591
BERKSHIRE	4500	5505	3668	4487	655	761	243	257
SOUTH MIDLAND COUNTIES	62160	71939	52155	60394	7858	9113	2147	2482
MIDDLESEX (*Extra-metropolitan*)	44041	50807	37287	42984	5470	6356	1284	1473
HERTFORDSHIRE	6765	8085	5675	6808	785	989	300	347
BUCKINGHAMSHIRE	3036	3286	2482	2925	434	506	130	155
OXFORDSHIRE	2002	2419	1587	1932	311	369	104	111
NORTHAMPTONSHIRE	2454	2717	1997	2264	329	324	128	129
HUNTINGDONSHIRE	451	608	372	479	56	83	23	41
BEDFORDSHIRE	1637	2066	1297	1644	349	300	91	122
CAMBRIDGESHIRE	1779	2013	1458	1658	224	251	97	104
EASTERN COUNTIES	47074	51192	38493	42114	5751	6084	2830	2994
ESSEX	40380	42946	33033	35406	4958	5096	2389	2444
SUFFOLK	3392	4189	2730	3391	412	510	250	288
NORFOLK	3302	4057	2730	3317	381	478	191	202
SOUTH-WESTERN COUNTIES	13575	16058	10421	12735	1997	1952	1157	1371
WILTSHIRE	1983	2678	1511	2136	364	381	108	161
DORSETSHIRE	1832	1630	1416	1290	286	242	130	107
DEVONSHIRE	5687	6227	4207	4743	826	735	655	749
CORNWALL	1066	1153	824	953	145	113	97	107
SOMERSETSHIRE	3007	4361	2463	3633	377	481	167	247
WEST-MIDLAND COUNTIES	17699	20927	14797	17643	1915	2224	987	1060
GLOUCESTERSHIRE	4456	5961	3631	4932	536	670	279	329
HEREFORDSHIRE	683	914	577	773	78	69	33	42
SHROPSHIRE	801	995	674	837	87	113	46	45
STAFFORDSHIRE	3315	3571	2741	2987	383	368	189	216
WORCESTERSHIRE	1878	2415	1518	1996	254	302	100	117
WARWICKSHIRE	6566	7071	5636	6097	590	663	340	311
NORTH-MIDLAND COUNTIES	9019	9350	7194	7559	1034	1033	861	758
LEICESTERSHIRE	1885	2229	1563	1821	218	236	104	172
RUTLANDSHIRE	268	225	165	186	21	28	22	11
LINCOLNSHIRE	3126	2584	2286	1987	330	310	510	287
NOTTINGHAMSHIRE	2006	2328	1658	1928	239	235	109	163
DERBYSHIRE	1794	1984	1452	1637	226	224	116	123
NORTH-WESTERN COUNTIES	15527	16809	12871	14084	1740	1694	916	1031
CHESHIRE	2443	2718	1994	2233	295	321	156	164
LANCASHIRE	13082	14091	10877	11851	1445	1373	760	867
YORKSHIRE	10796	11499	8638	9376	1283	1276	875	847
NORTHERN COUNTIES	5629	5385	4483	4308	567	586	579	491
DURHAM	3064	2819	2436	2238	293	304	335	277
NORTHUMBERLAND	1881	1737	1483	1383	201	182	197	172
CUMBERLAND	522	582	431	483	49	66	42	33
WESTMORLAND	162	247	133	204	24	34	5	9
MONMOUTHSHIRE AND WALES	4656	4727	3764	3852	479	455	413	420
MONMOUTHSHIRE	711	728	605	622	67	55	39	51
GLAMORGANSHIRE	1819	1775	1491	1445	188	207	140	120
CARMARTHENSHIRE	193	195	155	167	23	17	15	11
PEMBROKESHIRE	568	443	352	236	60	39	156	148
CARDIGANSHIRE	159	187	141	158	10	18	8	11
BRECKNOCKSHIRE	180	171	143	131	29	14	8	6
RADNORSHIRE	60	102	50	89	4	7	6	6
MONTGOMERYSHIRE	122	162	103	143	14	11	5	8
FLINTSHIRE	171	242	141	203	25	26	5	13
DENBIGHSHIRE	229	270	196	233	19	23	14	14
MERIONETHSHIRE	66	117	55	102	11	9	[illegible]	6
CARNARVONSHIRE	215	232	182	195	24	19	5	18
ANGLESEY	163	103	150	85	5	10	8	8

Table 13.—Number and Country of Birth of Foreigners enumerated in the London Division and its Registration Counties.

Where Born.	Where Enumerated.							
	London.		Counties.					
			Middlesex (*Intra-metn*).		Surrey (*Intra-metn*).		Kent (*Intra-metn*).	
	Males.	Females.	Males.	Females.	Males.	Females.	Males.	Females.
TOTAL - - -	37125	23127	31921	20190	4241	2285	963	652
EUROPE.								
Denmark - -	411	142	307	118	92	16	12	8
Norway - - -	517	81	330	57	172	18	16	6
Sweden - - -	730	174	626	146	67	21	37	7
Russia - - -	1161	617	1097	597	41	15	23	5
Poland (Russian) - -	3877	3054	3830	3037	39	16	8	1
Austria - - - - -	931	347	896	313	96	22	15	12
Hungary - -	189	58	172	55	13	3	4	2
Switzerland - - -	1448	848	1254	745	156	68	38	35
German Empire -	14132	7834	11761	6603	1890	915	481	316
Holland - -	2295	1898	2093	1800	177	85	25	13
Belgium - - -	844	648	701	551	124	92	19	5
France - - -	4108	4143	3471	3554	559	480	78	109
Portugal - - - -	92	59	78	56	10	2	4	1
Spain - -	322	151	283	134	33	15	6	2
Italy - -	2878	628	2625	577	190	33	61	16
Greece - -	181	47	136	39	42	7	3	1
Turkey - - - -	180	73	140	68	31	4	3	1
Servia - - - - - -	2	2	2	2	.	.	.	.
Roumania - -	29	7	28	6	1	2	.	.
ASIA.								
Arabia - -	22	1	22	1	.	.	.	.
Persia - - -	6	4	6	3	.	.	.	1
China - -	109	9	97	7	3	2	.	.
Other Countries - - - -	77	24	63	23	7	1	7	.
AFRICA.								
Egypt - - - -	12	10	10	9	1	1	1	.
Other Parts - - -	53	23	50	22	3	1	.	.
AMERICA.								
United States - - -	2255	2046	1653	1483	484	463	118	110
Mexico - - - -	18	10	17	10	1	.	.	.
Brazil - - -	42	39	38	34	4	5	.	.
Other States - - - -	161	117	148	111	9	5	4	1
Country not stated - - -	47	22	45	22	1	.	1	.
At Sea - - - - -	7	11	6	10	1	1	.	.

Table 14.—NUMBER and AGES of MALES and FEMALES returned as BLIND or BLIND FROM BIRTH in the LONDON DIVISION and its REGISTRATION COUNTIES.

REGISTRATION COUNTY.	ALL AGES.		0–	5–	15–	20–	25–	45–	65 and upwards.
	Both Sexes.	Males and Females.							
I. LONDON - -	3214	M. 1551	41	160	93	75	332	479	371
		F. 1663	44	129	75	72	256	485	602
MIDDLESEX (*Intra-metropoln.*)	2093	M. - 997	26	88	46	29	220	335	253
		F. - 1096	31	88	38	40	173	345	381
SURREY (*Intra-metropolitan*) -	918	M. - 450	11	66	44	40	91	114	84
		F. - 468	12	36	36	28	74	115	167
KENT (*Intra-metropolitan*) -	203	M. - 104	4	6	3	6	21	30	34
		F. - 99	1	5	1	4	9	25	54

Table 15.—NUMBER and AGES of MALES and FEMALES returned as BLIND in the LONDON DIVISION and its REGISTRATION COUNTIES.

REGISTRATION COUNTY.	ALL AGES.		0–	5–	15–	20–	25–	45–	65 and upwards.
	Both Sexes.	Males and Females.							
I. LONDON - -	2962	M. 1426	20	122	84	65	299	469	367
		F. 1536	24	98	55	61	229	473	595
MIDDLESEX (*Intra-metropoln.*)	1956	M. - 934	14	70	44	26	200	329	251
		F. - 1022	18	72	32	36	155	335	375
SURREY (*Intra-metropolitan*) -	813	M. - 395	5	48	38	34	78	110	82
		F. - 418	5	23	23	32	66	113	166
KENT (*Intra-metropolitan*) -	193	M. - 97	1	4	2	5	21	30	34
		F. 96	1	3	1	4	8	25	54

Table 16.—NUMBER and AGES of MALES and FEMALES returned as BLIND FROM BIRTH in the LONDON DIVISION and its REGISTRATION COUNTIES.

REGISTRATION COUNTY.	ALL AGES.		0–	5–	15–	20–	25–	45–	65 and upwards.
	Both Sexes.	Males and Females.							
I. LONDON -	252	M. 125	21	38	9	10	33	10	4
		F. 127	20	31	19	11	27	12	7
MIDDLESEX (*Intra-metropoln.*)	137	M. - 63	12	18	2	3	20	6	2
		F. - 74	13	16	6	5	18	10	6
SURREY (*Intra-metropolitan*) -	105	M. - 55	6	18	6	6	13	4	2
		F. - 50	7	13	13	6	8	2	1
KENT (*Intra-metropolitan*) -	10	M. - 7	3	2	1	1	.	.	.
		F. - 3	.	2	.	.	1	.	.

Table 17.—NUMBER and AGES of MALES and FEMALES returned as DEAF AND DUMB in the LONDON DIVISION and its REGISTRATION COUNTIES.

REGISTRATION COUNTY.	ALL AGES.		0–	5–	15–	20–	25–	45–	65 and upwards.
	Both Sexes.	Males and Females.							
I. LONDON -	1972	M. 1075	54	257	107	127	337	149	44
		F. 897	31	231	160	88	269	137	41
MIDDLESEX (*Intra-metropoln.*)	1377	M. - 756	38	181	77	97	238	92	33
		F. - 621	25	159	60	66	182	99	24
SURREY (*Intra-metropolitan*) -	477	M. - 258	12	68	20	20	86	43	9
		F. - 219	6	57	26	19	73	25	13
KENT (*Intra-metropolitan*)	118	M. - 61	4	8	10	10	13	14	2
		F. - 57	.	15	8	3	14	13	4

Table 18.—NUMBER and AGES of MALES and FEMALES returned as IDIOTS or IMBECILES, and LUNATICS, in the LONDON DIVISION and its REGISTRATION COUNTIES.

REGISTRATION COUNTY.	ALL AGES. Both Sexes.	ALL AGES. Males and Females.	0–	5–	15–	20–	25–	45–	65 and upwards.
I. LONDON	6032	M. 2758	42	237	157	207	1186	671	258
		F. 3274	29	183	152	220	1109	1032	549
MIDDLESEX (*Intra-metropoln.*)	3139	M. 1587	31	147	88	110	705	347	159
		F. 1552	21	126	90	108	438	440	329
SURREY (*Intra-metropolitan*)	2738	M. 1090	9	71	61	87	462	313	87
		F. 1648	6	48	56	103	653	577	205
KENT (*Intra-metropolitan*)	155	M. 81	2	19	8	10	19	11	12
		F. 74	2	9	6	9	18	15	15

Table 19.—NUMBER and AGES of MALES and FEMALES returned as IDIOTS or IMBECILES in the LONDON DIVISION and its REGISTRATION COUNTIES.

REGISTRATION COUNTY.	ALL AGES. Both Sexes.	ALL AGES. Males and Females.	0–	5–	15–	20–	25–	45–	65 and upwards.
I. LONDON	2081	M. 1024	42	229	132	115	251	137	118
		F. 1057	28	176	107	93	244	181	228
MIDDLESEX (*Intra-metropoln.*)	1408	M. 668	31	143	78	72	162	91	91
		F. 740	20	121	69	61	163	125	181
SURREY (*Intra-metropolitan*)	548	M. 290	9	69	46	33	75	38	20
		F. 258	6		32	24	65	47	38
KENT (*Intra-metropolitan*)	125	M. 66	2	17	8	10	14	8	7
		F. 59	2	9	6	8	16	9	9

Table 20.—NUMBER and AGES of MALES and FEMALES returned as LUNATICS in the LONDON DIVISION and its REGISTRATION COUNTIES.

REGISTRATION COUNTY.	ALL AGES. Both Sexes.	ALL AGES. Males and Females.	0–	5–	15–	20–	25–	45–	65 and upwards.
I. LONDON	3951	M. 1734	.	8	25	92	935	534	140
		F. 2217	1	7	45	127	865	851	321
MIDDLESEX (*Intra-metropoln.*)	1731	M. 919	.	4	10	38	543	256	68
		F. 812	1	5	21	47	275	315	148
SURREY (*Intra-metropolitan*)	2190	M. 800	.	2	15	54	387	275	67
		F. 1390	.	2	24	79	588	530	167
KENT (*Intra-metropolitan*)	30	M. 15	.	2	.	.	5	3	5
		F. 15	.	.	.	1	2	6	6

Table 21.—Number of the Blind, of the Deaf and Dumb, of Idiots or Imbeciles, and of Lunatics in the London Division and its Registration Counties and Districts.

Registration County and District.	Blind.			Deaf and Dumb.	Mentally Deranged.		
	From Birth.	Others.	Total.		Idiots.	Lunatics.	Total.
1. LONDON	252	2962	3214	1972	2081	3951	6032
MIDDLESEX (*Intra metropolitan*)	137	1956	2093	1377	1408	1731	3139
SURREY (*Intra-metropolitan*)	105	813	918	477	548	2190	2738
KENT (*Intra-metropolitan*)	10	193	203	118	135	30	165
MIDDLESEX (*Intra-metropolitan*).							
1 KENSINGTON	4	155	159	154	87	48	135
2 FULHAM	6	77	83	64	88	114	202
3 CHELSEA	2	73	75	38	52	24	76
4 ST. GEORGE, HANOVER SQUARE	7	133	140	54	67	23	90
5 WESTMINSTER	1	36	37	21	60	7	67
6 MARYLEBONE	12	139	151	92	52	16	68
7 HAMPSTEAD	3	114	117	8	11	6	17
8 PANCRAS	18	130	148	104	109	36	145
9 ISLINGTON	16	179	195	135	134	54	198
10 HACKNEY	16	99	115	124	90	157	247
11 ST. GILES	4	62	66	35	30	6	36
12 STRAND	2	22	24	7	10	2	12
13 HOLBORN	8	97	105	103	105	221	326
14 LONDON CITY	6	67	73	27	21	4	25
15 SHOREDITCH	3	98	101	83	69	163	232
16 BETHNAL GREEN	12	105	117	87	97	359	456
17 WHITECHAPEL	2	93	95	55	54	19	73
18 ST. GEORGE IN THE EAST	1	42	43	42	64	6	70
19 STEPNEY	1	33	34	27	82	3	85
20 MILE END OLD TOWN	5	75	80	49	57	9	66
21 POPLAR	10	127	137	68	119	444	563
SURREY (*Intra-metropolitan*).							
22 ST. SAVIOUR, SOUTHWARK	55	279	334	160	83	261	344
23 ST. OLAVE, SOUTHWARK	8	93	101	68	84	19	103
24 LAMBETH	17	160	177	120	99	37	136
25 WANDSWORTH	13	160	173	75	185	1030	1215
26 CAMBERWELL	12	121	133	54	99	853	952
KENT (*Intra-metropolitan*).							
27 GREENWICH	3	94	97	53	68	18	6
28 LEWISHAM	2	37	39	30	25	8	33
29 WOOLWICH	5	62	67	35	32	4	36

AGES,

CONDITION AS TO MARRIAGE,

OCCUPATIONS, AND BIRTH-PLACES

OF THE PEOPLE:

WITH THE

NUMBERS AND AGES OF THE BLIND, DEAF AND DUMB,
IDIOTS OR IMBECILES, AND LUNATICS.

DIVISION II.—SOUTH-EASTERN COUNTIES;

SURREY (*Extra-metropolitan*),
KENT (*Extra-metropolitan*),
SUSSEX,
HAMPSHIRE,
BERKSHIRE.

TABLES IN DIVISION II.—SOUTH-EASTERN COUNTIES.

AGES.

Table.

1.—Ages of Males and Females in the South-eastern Division and its Registration Counties.

2.—Ages of Males and Females in Registration Districts.

3.—Ages of Males and Females in Registration Sub-districts.

4.—Male and Female Children at *each Year of Age* under 5 in the South-Eastern Division and its Registration Counties.

5.—Male and Female Children at *each Year of Age* under 5 in Registration Districts.

6.—Ages of Males and Females in Sanitary Districts.

CONDITION AS TO MARRIAGE.

7.—Condition as to Marriage and Ages of Males and Females in the South-eastern Division and its Registration Counties.

8.—Condition as to Marriage and Ages of Males and Females in Registration Districts.

9.—Condition as to Marriage and Ages of Males and Females in each Urban Sanitary District of which the Population exceeds 50,000 Persons.

OCCUPATIONS.

10.—Occupations of Males and Females in the South-eastern Division and its Registration Counties, and in each Urban Sanitary District of which the Population exceeds 50,000 Persons.

BIRTH-PLACES.

11.—Birth-places of Males and Females enumerated in Counties, and in each Urban Sanitary District of which the Population exceeds 50.000 Persons.

12.—Distribution of the enumerated Natives of Counties.

13.—Number and Country of Birth of Foreigners enumerated in Counties, and in each Urban Sanitary District of which the Population exceeds 50,000 Persons

THE BLIND, DEAF AND DUMB, IDIOTS OR IMBECILES, AND LUNATICS.

14.—Number and Ages of Males and Females returned as Blind or Blind from Birth in the South-eastern Division and its Registration Counties.

15.—Number and Ages of Males and Females returned as Blind in the South-eastern Division and its Registration Counties.

16.—Number and Ages of Males and Females returned as Blind from Birth in the South-eastern Division and its Registration Counties.

17.—Number and Ages of Males and Females returned as Deaf and Dumb in the South-eastern Division and its Registration Counties.

18.—Number and Ages of Males and Females returned as Idiots or Imbeciles, and Lunatics in the South-eastern Division and its Registration Counties.

19.—Number and Ages of Males and Females returned as Idiots or Imbeciles in the South-eastern Division and its Registration Counties.

20.—Number and Ages of Males and Females returned as Lunatics in the South-Eastern Division and its Registration Counties.

21.—Number of the Blind, of the Deaf and Dumb, of Idiots or Imbeciles, and of Lunatics in the South-eastern Division and its Registration Counties and Districts.

AGES.

DIVISION II.—SOUTH EASTERN COUNTIES.

Table 1.—Ages of Males and Females in the South-Eastern Division and its Registration Counties.

Registration County.	All Ages. Persons.	Males and Females.	Under 5* Years.	5–	10–	15–	20–	25–	30–	35–	40–	45–	50–	55–	60–	65–	70–	75–	80–	85–	90–	95–	100† and upw^ds^.
II.—SOUTH EASTERN COUNTIES	2487076	M. 1208550	161461	148548	137625	121495	105415	88745	77717	70238	63893	52787	46584	38354	35226	25111	17815	10584	5259	1522	317	50	6
		F. 1278526	161612	147369	134641	120442	115173	100535	87344	75621	70083	59308	52718	42498	39394	28732	20770	12380	6220	2073	522	105	11
1 SURREY (*Extra-metropolitan*)	461054	M. 219076	29072	26788	25156	21328	20417	16859	14837	13545	11934	9438	8164	6358	5762	3899	2761	1554	763	185	47	7	—
		F. 241978	29408	27253	24658	23255	24117	20846	17451	15112	13364	11085	9562	7532	6604	4785	3308	2012	1006	327	61	18	1
2 KENT (*Extra-metropolitan*)	708527	M. 350615	47184	43324	39784	35935	30423	25780	22268	20154	18790	16241	13258	10888	10112	7214	5068	3108	1552	479	104	17	3
		F. 357912	46028	43724	38872	33607	31086	27306	25754	20989	19189	16393	14385	11623	10941	7960	5888	3559	1856	622	191	50	4
3 SUSSEX	494194	M. 234248	31523	29309	27354	23079	19279	16708	14960	13317	11984	10079	9288	7597	7045	5091	3760	2283	1118	335	72	9	1
		F. 259946	31670	28549	26936	25154	23880	20832	17914	15495	14538	12058	10954	8920	8182	6048	4413	2618	1258	430	122	19	—
4 HAMPSHIRE	575409	M. 281310	37210	33830	30982	28008	24978	20795	18071	16436	14984	12522	11118	8671	8447	6037	4223	2423	1228	360	65	14	2
		F. 294099	37235	33606	30673	27404	26009	22491	20031	17696	16221	13893	12507	10146	9588	6914	4769	2877	1413	439	98	32	3
5 BERKSHIRE	247892	M. 123301	16472	15037	14347	12935	10316	8628	7581	6786	6201	5487	4756	3946	3860	2880	2013	1214	598	157	29	3	1
		F. 124591	16311	15187	13482	11022	10075	9060	8194	7326	6776	5034	5310	4283	4069	3015	2302	1314	687	195	50	6	5

Note.—Registration Counties consist of groups of Registration Districts, which are generally co-extensive with the Poor Law Unions. Those Registration Districts which extend into two or more Counties are included in that Registration County in which the principal town of the District or the greater part of the population is located. The boundaries of Registration Counties, therefore, differ more or less from the boundaries of Counties. For such differences in Division II., see Vol. II., Table 11.

* For the number of Children at each Year of Age under 5, see Table 4.

† Two of these Males were stated to be 100 years of age, one 101, one 102, and two 103 years of age. Eight of these Females were stated to be 100 years of age, one 102, one 103, and one 105 years of age.

Table 2.—Ages of Males and Females in Registration Districts.

Registration District.	All Ages. Persons.	Males and Females.	Under 5* Years.	5–	10–	15–	20–	25–	30–	35–	40–	45–	50–	55–	60–	65–	70–	75–	80–	85–	90–	95–	100 and upw^ds^.
1. SURREY (*Ex.-metropolitan*).																							
30 EPSOM	41107	M. - 19718	2445	2727	2873	1754	1473	1359	1276	1145	1072	831	711	582	585	387	259	145	75	13	5	1	.
		F. - 21389	2461	2620	2388	1918	1935	1771	1465	1328	1296	994	889	732	606	460	297	193	91	34	4	1	.
31 CHERTSEY	27137	M. - 13258	1805	1736	1829	1257	955	909	833	747	679	564	522	403	377	267	168	119	49	15	8	1	.
		F. - 13879	1854	1658	1480	1179	1223	1070	1014	836	778	641	570	442	407	284	225	120	57	14	6	2	.
32 GUILDFORD	42696	M. - 21139	2624	2308	2560	2284	1772	1515	1382	1312	1201	947	879	717	591	478	298	183	78	10	5	.	.
		F. - 21557	2561	2444	2115	1905	1879	1685	1577	1339	1300	1097	1014	838	682	470	315	180	100	28	11	2	.
33 FARNHAM	40395	M. - 22701	2619	2123	1844	2582	3776	2621	1778	1434	1108	804	610	474	386	271	181	111	56	16	2	.	
		F. - 17694	2770	2325	1788	1456	1656	1611	1209	1031	913	709	628	466	397	254	176	106	72	25	5	.	.
34 HAMBLEDON	16353	M. - 8555	1093	991	1076	924	708	592	478	431	423	395	364	290	287	219	155	76	41	9	3	.	.
		F. - 7798	1046	987	853	631	646	566	491	440	412	402	331	317	253	188	114	63	43	14	1	.	.
35 DORKING	15452	M. - 7553	1063	941	852	678	577	480	516	416	379	339	315	273	257	180	153	80	35	8	2	.	.
		F. - 7899	953	935	882	639	622	560	582	534	433	357	345	275	247	225	141	93	37	16	3	.	.
36 REIGATE	30359	M. - 14621	1898	1816	1750	1610	1208	995	945	829	708	698	615	477	385	281	200	126	52	13	5	.	.
		F. - 15738	1959	1821	1747	1486	1430	1320	1085	935	894	750	640	498	437	312	225	121	60	18	2	3	.
37 GODSTONE	17692	M. - 9295	1067	936	811	901	1001	746	674	593	542	458	427	341	318	211	136	78	46	5	5	.	.
		F. - 8397	1011	904	788	678	685	686	601	554	484	427	389	364	275	205	147	84	46	18	.	1	.
38 CROYDON	119173	M. - 53406	7657	7074	6240	4950	4517	3089	3589	3309	3013	2307	1930	1456	1330	750	651	333	165	45	9	2	.
		F. - 65767	7696	7206	6837	6931	7185	5804	4727	4091	3561	2896	2405	1788	1692	1196	888	516	340	80	17	4	.
39 KINGSTON	77057	M. - 34443	4901	4439	3715	3249	3036	2547	2358	2291	2010	1490	1271	943	866	564	401	213	121	40	6	2	
		F. - 42614	4974	4613	4131	4255	4594	3883	3144	2783	2353	1891	1576	1231	1114	911	585	339	176	56	7	3	
40 RICHMOND	33633	M. - 14387	1900	1692	1608	1339	1394	1206	1028	948	799	625	520	402	377	277	129	90	39	11	2	1	.
		F. - 19246	2153	1720	1639	2107	2257	1900	1466	1199	1030	872	763	616	554	387	285	187	78	26	5	3	.
2. KENT (*Extra-metropolitan*).																							
41 BROMLEY	48972	M. - 22455	3276	2872	2394	1989	1913	1824	1591	1459	1326	982	802	614	589	354	241	137	66	20	5	.	1
		F. - 26517	3237	2980	2343	2594	2819	2577	1952	1742	1466	1179	930	674	636	407	354	173	112	33	6	3	.
42 DARTFORD	53435	M. - 26869	3654	3538	3303	2924	2250	1860	1581	1449	1408	1160	1008	767	732	518	363	225	96	27	6	.	.
		F. - 26566	3580	3238	2868	2528	2351	2029	1774	1514	1464	1167	1075	858	772	557	416	199	126	41	9	1	1
43 GRAVESEND	23302	M. - 11411	1408	1343	1268	1141	1167	945	820	735	601	497	385	346	297	210	125	94	35	13	3	.	.
		F. - 11891	1385	1230	1283	1407	1117	929	770	694	640	530	461	405	368	266	199	126	66	20	10	1	.
44 NORTH AYLESFORD	27437	M. - 14683	1988	1723	1473	1580	1371	1184	956	920	926	670	530	403	543	256	169	107	46	17	4	2	1
		F. - 12754	1996	1695	1529	1073	987	902	825	756	672	554	446	350	528	270	181	133	49	13	4	1	
45 HOO	3405	M. - 1891	273	245	165	180	186	144	135	129	130	84	75	67	50	32	26	19	8	3	.	.	.
		F. - 1514	233	213	182	120	124	102	86	94	72	64	67	40	34	37	23	18	5	.	.	.	.
46 MEDWAY	61644	M. - 32107	4059	3639	3078	3040	3535	2857	2310	2055	1965	1455	1230	902	770	497	348	182	135	35	13	2	.
		F. - 29537	4104	3602	3116	2858	2456	2331	1981	1783	1614	1887	1224	896	835	545	401	355	118	59	18	4	.

Note.—The Registration Districts of Division II. are co-extensive with the Poor Law Unions of the same name, with the following exceptions:—The Lewes District (76) comprises the four Poor Law Unions of Lewes, Chailey, West Firle, and Newhaven; and the Winchester District (101) comprises the two Unions of New Winchester and Hursley. Canterbury (57) Chichester (84) and Southampton (97) Districts are Incorporations under Local Acts; and the Parish of Brighton (77) is also under a Local Act.

For the Parishes comprised in each Registration District, see Vol. II., Division II., Table 4.

The Districts are arranged topographically under the Registration Counties, and are numbered consecutively, commencing with the Metropolitan Districts, Division I.

For the Metropolitan Districts of Surrey and Kent, see Division I., London.

* For the Number of Children at each Year of age under 5, see Table 5.

Table 2 *continued*.—Ages of Males and Females in Registration Districts.

Registration District.	All Ages. Persons.	All Ages. Males and Females.	Under 5 Years.	5-	10-	15-	20-	25-	30-	35-	40-	45-	50-	55-	60-	65-	70-	75-	80-	85-	90-	95-	100 and upwards.
2 KENT (*Extra-metropolitan*)—*cont.*																							
47 MALLING	26041	M. - 13304	1904	1684	1514	1354	1104	927	776	738	691	598	480	390	407	295	210	146	53	39	6	1	.
		F. - 12737	1961	1636	1418	1043	966	915	822	707	675	586	512	397	357	305	196	117	66	17	3	1	.
48 SEVENOAKS	27190	M. - 13476	1730	1717	1565	1249	1064	940	841	804	724	571	547	479	422	325	201	130	79	21	6	1	.
		F. - 13714	1811	1639	1555	1228	1095	1039	921	846	780	699	545	473	411	318	208	141	74	15	7	1	.
49 TUNBRIDGE	51507	M. - 23675	3328	3098	2965	2425	1708	1569	1444	1380	1179	1012	913	786	699	491	362	198	104	28	4	1	.
		F. - 27832	3270	3170	2876	2664	2588	2124	1978	1703	1569	1400	1191	969	840	605	443	260	129	40	19	4	.
50 MAIDSTONE	45091	M. - 21971	2934	2737	2304	2231	1883	1619	1361	1277	1162	954	878	721	633	440	361	220	109	23	2	2	.
		F. - 23120	3063	2636	2465	2604	1952	1779	1587	1359	1287	1079	951	807	768	522	412	239	136	56	16	1	1
51 HOLLINGBOURN	14040	M. - 7170	936	857	887	770	505	460	409	342	362	317	313	299	242	174	138	101	42	24	2	.	.
		F. 6870	923	915	759	633	573	461	393	355	358	330	299	269	211	138	105	88	49	20	4	.	.
52 CRANBROOK	13774	M. - 6861	985	874	904	781	468	427	374	343	334	306	288	256	232	177	149	75	42	11	2	.	.
		F. 6898	992	862	854	612	521	447	413	366	305	310	283	257	241	194	111	70	42	11	6	.	.
53 TENTERDEN	10461	M. 5115	716	633	606	466	348	307	276	300	250	233	189	216	201	156	95	64	45	11	3	.	.
		F. 5346	784	722	607	466	391	315	334	301	276	245	216	176	180	141	115	77	33	9	3	1	.
54 WEST ASHFORD	18126	M. - 9019	1193	1118	1087	906	765	618	568	453	455	401	343	341	267	211	166	80	39	12	1	.	.
		F. 9107	1228	1129	1034	823	730	679	555	511	477	418	355	320	264	238	160	117	46	17	2	.	.
55 EAST ASHFORD	13897	M. - 7016	952	940	836	694	517	409	383	353	345	335	276	244	237	197	138	87	42	18	3	.	.
		F. 6881	976	898	803	519	489	414	354	374	348	324	242	224	222	170	147	88	36	12	2	1	.
56 BRIDGE	12405	M. - 6123	814	757	643	548	495	411	361	325	333	290	296	232	232	190	144	85	42	15	2	.	.
		F. - 6282	842	736	654	481	455	463	376	343	334	322	316	236	243	171	189	95	44	19	4	.	.
57 CANTERBURY	17060	M. - 8476	1053	968	827	907	934	745	555	486	469	341	306	263	240	176	135	72	40	17	1	1	
		F. 8584	986	965	859	801	743	678	584	510	446	400	359	282	296	244	169	112	68	23	8	1	
58 BLEAN	18867	M. - 9113	1278	1282	1244	948	548	536	490	493	456	385	349	271	298	213	152	101	57	22	3	.	
		F. 9754	1276	1233	1137	899	726	640	604	558	480	428	398	367	334	248	191	127	57	19	9	1	
59 FAVERSHAM	24956	M. - 12748	1837	1645	1606	1260	1047	825	759	681	648	523	509	391	377	243	191	131	64	18	8	1	
		F. - 12208	1899	1587	1385	1083	977	837	780	673	687	522	509	390	341	255	181	114	62	28	6	1	
60 MILTON	23270	M. - 11966	1777	1463	1358	1309	996	841	734	680	616	552	466	328	317	236	133	94	32	14	.	.	
		F. - 11304	1811	1498	1294	1007	950	819	688	628	589	478	439	390	302	218	144	75	44	17	2	.	
61 SHEPPEY	18204	M. - 9917	1277	1039	886	976	1129	1021	665	601	604	406	368	332	221	107	86	48	21	9	1	.	
		F. 8287	1206	1060	989	711	653	610	579	407	477	365	282	234	255	143	100	68	27	10	4	.	
62 THANET	50821	M. - 23499	3123	3162	3439	2370	1775	1563	1467	1253	1153	864	822	661	695	489	343	190	102	26	10	2	
		F. - 27322	3046	2939	3065	2944	2622	2129	1852	1574	1396	1200	1061	933	940	640	477	208	144	60	11	5	
63 EASTRY	28074	M. - 14143	1717	1692	1478	1977	1129	883	812	733	684	581	524	507	484	397	267	174	83	29	5	1	
		F. - 13931	1641	1615	1546	1287	1114	988	931	745	714	673	647	529	546	403	506	184	122	25	15	.	
64 DOVER	36813	M. - 17997	2360	2147	1984	1882	1817	1294	1252	1027	928	813	665	509	491	385	258	166	87	22	9	.	
		F. - 18816	2340	2176	1910	1846	1688	1426	1206	1104	1018	898	767	605	609	482	358	229	102	33	15	.	
65 ELHAM	33769	M. - 16234	2148	1867	1658	1734	1667	1283	1129	971	841	684	548	448	478	292	238	140	79	23	8	3	
		F. - 17535	2062	1881	1730	1790	1792	1543	1239	1081	922	857	692	547	486	366	283	143	85	20	6	1	
66 ROMNEY MARSH	6166	M. - 3356	445	386	355	306	292	258	210	212	213	164	137	117	101	93	39	34	14	5	2	.	
		F. - 2810	428	380	319	236	204	156	151	171	138	128	115	87	112	79	48	29	15	5	.	2	
3 SUSSEX.																							
67 RYE	12040	M. - 5999	819	721	687	564	466	375	367	364	262	204	243	232	197	187	108	68	37	11	4	.	
		F. - 6041	881	749	708	490	558	441	374	336	298	291	251	243	215	175	134	75	29	16	5	1	
68 HASTINGS	50129	M. - 21208	2978	2715	2521	2067	1763	1635	1384	1211	1080	870	827	602	571	420	296	154	91	19	9	.	
		F. - 28921	3304	2648	2533	3214	3193	2609	2198	1837	1694	1357	1280	1027	852	610	429	276	113	38	11	3	
69 BATTLE	14519	M. - 7352	1028	958	923	704	543	458	433	396	345	335	301	241	281	157	148	80	27	13	2	1	
		F. - 7167	1032	934	828	576	548	480	484	406	366	302	296	257	258	159	126	67	40	9	2	.	
70 EASTBOURNE	27756	M. - 12985	1764	1511	1557	1377	1273	1072	897	749	671	470	454	353	318	200	158	84	58	9	5	1	
		F. - 14771	1802	1449	1444	1702	1864	1307	1086	808	861	631	545	429	411	268	192	106	53	17	6	2	
71 HAILSHAM	13405	M. - 6898	989	895	836	683	496	423	408	347	343	263	295	243	227	182	156	92	35	12	1	.	
		F. - 6507	963	898	746	519	446	446	414	368	335	281	268	224	220	163	106	70	30	16	3	.	
72 TICEHURST	17219	M. - 8458	1163	1161	977	829	639	559	506	450	395	342	344	298	249	210	180	85	45	13	3	.	
		F. - 8761	1180	1125	999	716	754	639	543	527	469	394	337	311	232	225	143	95	46	18	5	.	
73 UCKFIELD	20098	M. - 10129	1456	1372	1194	1039	766	608	589	526	477	397	405	321	364	245	159	112	57	25	5	.	
		F. - 9969	1497	1340	1247	813	736	713	592	519	526	426	373	347	297	251	135	100	41	10	4	2	
74 EAST GRINSTEAD	18581	M. - 9075	1291	1238	1045	914	765	636	650	537	525	470	386	308	281	213	141	109	37	15	7	.	
		F. - 9506	1267	1203	1149	750	634	665	600	618	463	417	357	272	262	182	136	88	32	15	1	.	
75 CUCKFIELD	23252	M. - 11853	1537	1421	1587	1257	905	803	756	647	574	506	477	388	336	252	226	111	47	14	9	.	
		F. - 11399	1571	1477	1317	976	946	846	758	626	614	504	460	369	341	256	181	89	46	17	5	.	
76 LEWES	32896	M. - 17138	2117	2029	2012	1676	1614	1280	1085	992	880	740	689	575	529	374	275	109	87	21	2	1	
		F. - 15758	2039	1959	1768	1346	1201	1140	1045	926	904	754	676	570	474	371	291	164	76	37	7	1	
77 BRIGHTON	99091	M. - 43418	5661	5212	4836	4122	3922	3406	3036	2617	2320	1968	1773	1372	1170	759	581	362	172	88	7	2	
		F. - 55673	5766	5101	5050	6011	5885	4669	4108	3519	3267	2687	2496	1930	1781	1232	952	546	281	76	19	4	
78 STEYNING	49089	M. - 22091	3000	2755	2470	2226	1963	1779	1464	1254	1160	939	793	649	601	412	294	178	83	28	2	2	
		F. - 26998	3314	2567	2533	2888	2632	2496	2069	1662	1580	1244	1118	867	839	554	426	238	116	42	9	.	
79 HORSHAM	22300	M. - 11138	1576	1487	1230	1100	894	713	649	604	506	498	446	307	360	271	190	108	55	11	.	.	
		F. - 11162	1527	1433	1291	967	863	795	676	663	611	517	465	382	335	261	187	116	59	17	7	2	
80 PETWORTH	9595	M. 4858	608	620	598	446	338	269	260	265	257	249	197	185	201	130	106	85	32	12	.	.	
		F. - 4737	647	625	538	374	323	298	288	255	242	237	209	170	181	133	123	57	20	14	3	.	
81 THAKEHAM	8283	M. - 4247	582	550	465	460	298	255	270	224	200	177	196	154	171	108	75	45	28	6	.	.	
		F. - 4036	558	531	476	307	300	264	258	210	221	189	152	159	125	119	82	48	19	8	3	.	
82 EAST PRESTON (WORTHING).	26364	M. - 12264	1670	1643	1459	1232	963	786	713	608	614	520	467	377	396	287	191	138	65	28	5	.	
		F. - 14100	1675	1491	1550	1378	1297	1047	942	904	783	622	592	479	442	365	258	156	82	26	9	2	
83 WESTHAMPNETT	19653	M. - 9617	1283	1236	1032	877	654	561	583	542	500	463	415	342	363	297	217	124	79	18	4	.	
		F. - 10036	1271	1194	1118	842	726	645	600	578	569	471	462	324	373	332	228	122	80	26	13	2	
84 CHICHESTER	8569	M. - 4108	531	481	446	485	351	291	269	287	225	173	144	126	112	93	57	35	15	5	2	.	
		F. 4461	522	488	459	469	379	339	303	263	259	206	183	127	166	121	88	58	33	11	3	.	
85 MIDHURST	13933	M. - 7170	968	992	859	672	508	480	413	385	394	329	288	284	242	178	135	85	43	10	3	2	
		F. - 6763	972	874	752	536	505	445	412	377	347	326	289	241	222	174	121	90	34	11	5	.	
86 WESTBOURNE	7420	M. - 3742	522	465	427	388	263	207	198	208	196	170	164	150	115	116	81	52	29	9	2	.	
		F. - 3678	530	467	400	280	276	250	224	199	209	182	155	123	112	94	76	57	28	11	2	.	
4 HAMPSHIRE.																							
87 HAVANT	8672	M. - 4135	569	516	555	247	273	235	269	230	217	181	171	155	149	119	71	45	23	9	1	.	
		F. - 4537	577	645	289	444	322	331	287	268	239	193	222	148	154	133	90	51	35	7	2	.	
88 PORTSEA ISLAND	128022	M. - 62417	8629	7312	6397	5990	5816	5268	4371	3997	3645	2796	2341	1950	1607	1006	673	314	140	57	14	.	
		F. - 65605	8527	7244	6566	6484	6275	5413	4718	4071	3709	2870	[illegible]	2061	1997	1333	843	470	210	95	19	7	
89 ALVERSTOKE	21581	M. - 11632	1380	1276	1045	1254	1473	1046	875	745	601	489	[illegible]	344	289	202	117	78	46	17	2	3	
		F. - 9949	1388	1207	1033	881	836	786	691	607	533	445	[illegible]	309	312	257	140	83	61	12	4	.	

Table 2 *continued*.—AGES of MALES and FEMALES in REGISTRATION DISTRICTS.

REGISTRATION DISTRICT.	ALL AGES. Persons.	ALL AGES. Males and Females.	Under 5 Years.	5-	10-	15-	20-	25-	30-	35-	40-	45-	50-	55-	60-	65-	70-	75-	80-	85-	90-	95-	100 and upw.
MPSHIRE—*cont.*																							
EHAM	16820	M. - 8306	1052	966	985	800	605	541	475	471	477	393	369	345	288	213	169	102	45	17	3	.	2
		F. - 8514	1093	992	924	685	667	584	589	524	453	472	418	327	337	224	167	127	51	21	4	.	.
I OF WIGHT	73633	M. - 34842	4534	4204	3761	3255	2809	2555	2379	2203	1870	1627	1418	1233	1058	830	568	311	170	42	9	5	.
		F. - 38791	4521	4330	3841	3720	3576	3059	2705	2462	2135	1936	1607	1313	1233	912	666	389	205	60	15	3	.
IINGTON	12651	M. - 6042	846	707	718	564	443	353	327	297	289	312	242	231	206	150	118	89	42	10	5	.	.
		F. 6609	805	748	736	639	527	468	452	337	350	341	318	233	247	193	139	75	53	4	6	1	.
ISTCHURCH	29455	M. - 12419	1775	1512	1383	1187	1035	1026	863	747	630	499	464	409	340	242	172	85	48	16	2	.	.
		F. - 17036	1767	1569	1385	1947	2956	1711	1370	1071	909	804	634	551	496	360	207	123	45	22	1	1	.
GWOOD	5488	M. - 2710	374	356	301	259	190	176	140	154	141	118	102	109	98	94	65	25	31	7	1	1	.
		F. 2778	383	369	310	293	211	190	169	161	115	148	118	110	107	71	57	39	19	3	1	.	.
DINGBRIDGE	6234	M. - 3155	421	403	382	323	217	189	190	142	136	105	144	139	123	102	84	46	16	8	1	.	.
		F. - 3079	387	390	323	271	236	222	166	132	169	144	143	139	131	97	70	40	11	6	1	1	.
V FOREST	13221	M. - 6609	817	885	749	604	552	408	413	372	299	290	278	232	235	179	126	69	45	14	1	1	.
		F. 6612	836	810	710	518	511	454	411	411	338	529	294	260	258	196	129	88	37	14	2	1	.
THAMPTON	52989	M. - 25099	3419	2990	2720	2397	2387	1962	1753	1472	1420	1196	1077	775	708	426	273	177	74	16	6	1	2
		F. - 27890	3397	2968	2881	2773	2624	2177	1966	1690	1646	1373	1173	885	884	623	401	271	149	30	6	4	.
TH STONEHAM	41275	M. - 19868	2822	2625	2309	1891	1704	1503	1192	1146	1078	934	689	632	601	399	270	147	78	18	1	.	.
		F. - 21407	2873	2569	2304	1934	1854	1622	1426	1379	1180	905	859	721	637	425	324	193	89	43	5	6	.
ISEY	10609	M. - 5280	721	647	620	548	399	316	286	256	272	328	247	211	203	137	99	67	26	5	1	1	.
		F. - 5329	702	652	625	446	416	333	336	273	287	267	234	209	202	132	106	53	34	13	1	1	.
CKBRIDGE	6972	M. - 3580	468	419	444	308	256	180	198	183	177	171	166	130	149	103	57	42	27	10	2	.	.
		F. - 3392	427	441	382	283	227	207	191	218	169	191	150	141	110	96	61	44	22	6	.	1	.
ICHESTER	31150	M. - 15489	1869	1720	1821	1917	1406	1050	946	891	784	643	580	516	504	341	240	148	66	13	2	.	.
		F. - 15661	1986	1703	1629	1610	1204	1180	1090	942	817	760	623	590	545	404	302	164	80	29	8	1	1
IXFORD	11197	M. - 5566	685	684	620	552	418	394	390	293	264	261	234	226	228	198	128	84	41	13	3	.	.
		F. - 5631	736	681	640	436	415	391	341	301	276	269	230	216	234	167	119	74	42	8	2	1	.
HERINGTON	2747	M. - 1387	168	173	164	150	101	78	76	59	72	79	55	60	40	42	33	19	15	5	.	.	.
		F. - 1360	179	146	166	134	106	89	83	76	57	63	71	54	49	33	32	13	12	6	.	.	.
ERSFIELD	10255	M. - 5097	692	638	530	462	392	390	303	296	234	231	204	200	191	154	102	64	31	12	1	1	.
		F. - 5158	694	671	582	416	404	351	304	301	267	226	232	191	181	147	98	69	27	5	1	.	.
LESFORD	6967	M. - 3460	449	434	393	307	255	228	198	200	163	152	175	141	121	90	74	45	25	9	1	.	.
		F. - 3507	437	441	466	311	254	214	211	106	195	146	158	138	115	100	50	50	13	11	1	.	.
TON	15198	M. - 7548	1060	992	917	787	509	412	481	424	403	358	319	251	256	177	148	81	41	15	4	.	.
		F. 7650	1049	1016	927	617	573	475	456	437	437	347	298	269	255	191	151	73	48	15	4	.	.
RTLEY - WINTNEY	21328	M. - 12009	1244	1236	1277	1408	1935	1082	723	574	505	422	418	336	299	227	153	96	59	12	1	.	.
		F. - 9318	1249	1203	1036	760	783	633	598	486	528	439	425	326	322	208	148	81	35	19	5	1	.
INGSTOKE	19274	M. - 9680	1289	1237	1134	981	723	623	611	522	515	417	376	350	277	233	175	129	48	16	4	.	.
		F. - 9594	1341	1232	1028	779	799	686	610	567	489	442	384	341	300	287	136	108	58	18	4	.	.
ITCHURCH	5358	M. 2751	333	348	307	290	234	178	152	136	114	119	119	103	99	81	66	31	20	2	.	.	.
		F. 2607	374	331	292	225	225	190	159	125	136	115	128	108	97	87	47	37	12	5	1	3	.
DOVER	15700	M. - 7843	982	934	932	791	693	510	405	414	361	401	370	324	294	196	152	89	41	16	.	.	.
		F. 7857	1002	931	903	707	604	510	464	417	400	412	370	320	285	200	158	103	40	20	3	.	.
IGSCLERE	8524	M. - 4287	560	577	503	451	280	239	212	213	208	201	202	185	134	116	100	46	32	7	.	1	.
		F. - 4237	584	587	403	315	283	237	248	258	213	208	203	170	133	128	70	62	32	7	.	.	.
ERKSHIRE.																							
WBURY	21327	M. - 10208	1510	1251	1184	1013	812	623	574	586	508	463	442	396	364	305	214	134	61	13	4	1	.
		F. - 11119	1349	1283	1276	1072	902	731	672	588	694	560	475	391	394	327	257	157	76	21	7	.	.
NGERFORD	17802	M. - 8988	1163	1134	1041	988	643	542	452	450	411	421	392	357	361	252	190	125	78	16	2	.	.
		F. 8814	1147	1135	998	692	642	537	458	444	483	454	404	375	345	273	200	128	68	25	3	.	.
INGDON	13676	M. - 6778	937	861	811	693	465	341	368	351	357	312	206	232	251	210	157	86	36	9	2	.	.
		F. 6898	911	917	813	527	446	441	377	391	336	344	337	289	263	217	134	89	38	13	1	2	.
NGDON	20354	M. - 10056	1410	1286	1228	1128	786	609	576	473	459	427	374	340	334	264	197	115	59	15	2	.	.
		F. - 10298	1335	1254	1106	935	853	732	662	561	540	440	439	376	368	267	211	109	64	14	4	.	.
NTAGE	17160	M. - 8923	1155	1112	1083	976	675	659	510	433	417	394	346	326	340	246	174	112	45	16	4	.	.
		F. - 8237	1116	1064	953	692	588	582	482	458	414	391	361	343	289	218	189	104	45	12	6	.	.
LLINGFORD	14493	M. - 7249	974	915	920	670	472	406	404	336	406	344	316	262	245	210	162	104	45	11	.	.	.
		F. - 7244	884	901	806	681	500	432	437	422	434	364	362	305	276	212	167	88	40	13	1	.	.
ADFIELD	17972	M. 9176	1257	1098	1084	1044	730	592	528	500	443	414	347	281	317	238	154	105	35	14	2	.	.
		F. 8796	1254	1123	982	692	669	600	659	494	498	361	387	303	287	211	161	107	48	15	4	.	1
ADING	43494	M. - 21193	3103	2607	2129	2129	2133	1848	1516	1270	1119	936	715	531	483	365	208	112	69	15	3	.	1
		F. - 22301	3030	2584	2256	2183	2089	1848	1610	1339	1215	1009	845	613	526	432	330	192	95	30	9	2	.
KINGHAM	20018	M. - 9839	1360	1349	1163	960	727	632	633	557	402	429	370	335	277	203	149	89	54	21	.	.	.
		F. - 10179	1444	1202	1037	856	756	751	700	621	547	404	437	392	298	220	167	83	49	15	4	.	.
OKHAM	16945	M. - 8240	1089	1058	1001	794	637	506	508	409	368	348	331	277	256	184	137	77	30	10	4	.	.
		F. 8705	1088	1020	971	794	786	682	554	628	436	424	349	293	286	213	167	73	45	12	2	2	.
THAMPSTEAD	12659	M. - 6769	763	704	858	1032	493	424	406	309	367	319	269	199	230	138	78	60	24	8	1	1	.
		F. - 5890	795	784	639	460	474	450	428	300	323	312	248	184	153	105	83	45	19	4	3	.	.
NDSOR	31992	M. - 15882	1664	1762	1871	1648	1743	1406	1196	944	824	650	561	414	416	256	193	96	54	9	3	1	.
		F. - 16110	1909	1793	1594	1567	1423	1341	1216	1110	895	781	675	469	508	320	240	160	72	21	6	.	2

TABLE 3.—AGES of MALES and FEMALES in REGISTRATION SUB-DISTRICTS.

Registration Sub-District	All Ages. Persons.	All Ages. Males and Females.	Under 5 Years.	5-	10-	15-	20-	25-	30-	35-	40-	45-	50-	55-	60-	65-	70-	75-	80-	85-	90-	9
1 SURREY (*Extra-metropolitan*).																						
30 EPSOM.																						
1 Carshalton. (w. s. L².)	21118	M. - 9932	1221	1473	1565	750	707	680	865	598	561	523	327	281	270	185	105	46	20	6	1	
		F. - 11186	1222	1418	1299	967	1040	996	765	695	637	533	468	336	300	225	150	94	27	16	1	
2 Epsom. (W. w. s. H. L.)	11975	M. - 5779	694	742	778	602	450	417	361	506	293	224	231	163	196	129	98	64	26	4	2	
		F. - 6196	684	724	673	612	896	517	416	379	352	281	237	186	181	142	95	66	41	12	2	
3 Leatherhead	8014	M. - 4007	530	512	510	362	316	232	250	244	228	184	143	138	119	73	65	35	21	3	2	
		F. - 4007	553	476	416	330	291	328	234	251	217	180	184	150	126	93	52	34	23	6	1	
31 CHERTSEY.																						
1 Walton. (H.)	9599	M. - 4369	678	578	471	380	370	338	321	263	248	186	182	130	121	88	59	36	18	4	1	
		F. - 5230	616	521	505	498	542	478	432	324	288	244	219	178	143	107	85	33	21	2	3	
2 Chertsey. (W. H. R.²)	10819	M. - 5338	737	647	758	521	362	366	351	308	263	231	212	157	163	107	66	58	20	9	2	
		F. - 5481	792	746	632	428	436	388	366	328	294	240	227	155	174	114	81	52	25	8	2	
3 Chobham	6719	M. - 3551	476	511	600	356	223	205	181	176	168	147	128	116	98	75	68	25	11	2	.	
		F. - 3168	452	397	338	253	245	204	216	184	106	157	132	114	90	63	49	35	12	4	1	
32 GUILDFORD.																						
1 Woking. (L. P².)	10992	M. - 5409	639	566	515	412	408	435	387	406	399	310	271	222	169	132	90	54	13	1	.	
		F. - 5583	620	563	476	327	420	444	474	468	433	361	314	241	164	115	80	36	19	4	4	
2 Ripley	2590	M. - 1306	192	154	193	120	97	75	33	67	76	62	48	47	36	19	21	12	4	2	1	
		F. - 1284	174	177	150	100	99	96	79	67	62	51	59	44	51	25	24	9	13	1	1	
3 Albury	5133	M. - 2572	364	310	286	262	215	160	140	152	124	110	108	101	78	75	36	36	15	1	.	
		F. - 2561	325	320	286	232	190	186	156	145	145	127	112	102	72	74	36	32	13	5	1	
4 Guildford. (W. H. B.)	14143	M. - 6727	849	740	670	727	682	507	469	435	360	275	272	218	170	161	97	55	34	3	3	
		F. 7416	844	813	789	784	731	614	541	481	425	342	321	225	234	158	126	74	50	13	2	
5 Godalming. (H².)	9838	M. - 5125	900	551	894	763	370	338	298	232	242	190	186	129	138	86	54	27	12	3	1	
		F. - 4713	568	571	461	492	489	348	327	278	237	216	208	191	141	94	49	30	25	6	3	
33 FARNHAM.																						
1 Frimley. (H. B².)	27009	M. - 16217	1748	1303	1044	1933	3326	2105	1564	1075	786	497	328	248	202	128	70	37	14	4	.	
		F. - 10792	1786	1414	1056	887	1109	1114	876	656	528	383	335	232	181	108	76	31	19	8	.	
2 Farnham. (W.)	13386	M. - 6484	871	825	890	640	461	416	414	359	322	307	282	226	184	143	106	74	42	12	2	
		F. - 6902	984	911	732	569	547	407	439	376	386	325	293	234	216	146	100	76	63	15	6	
34 HAMBLEDON.																						
1 Witley. (W.)	7231	M. - 3696	471	415	379	360	317	270	227	183	187	198	166	138	139	91	79	37	25	6	3	
		F. - 3535	467	407	386	284	275	254	241	194	181	184	167	154	118	97	64	31	27	4	1	
2 Cranleigh. (H.)	9122	M. - 4860	622	576	697	474	391	322	251	248	236	190	190	135	148	128	76	89	16	3	.	
		F. - 4262	579	539	467	347	371	312	250	246	231	218	164	163	133	91	59	32	16	10	.	
35 DORKING.																						
1 Capel. (H.)	4491	M. - 2322	309	304	252	216	183	156	170	117	125	97	95	93	82	65	41	26	12	1	.	
		F. - 2169	285	289	254	157	169	154	150	148	116	88	84	87	54	63	41	27	15	5	1	
2 Dorking. (W. H.)	10961	M. - 5231	754	637	600	462	305	345	346	289	254	242	220	180	175	124	112	64	22	7	2	
		F. - 5730	648	646	628	482	453	416	432	386	317	269	261	188	193	160	166	66	22	11	2	
36 REIGATE.																						
1 Reigate. (W. w. s. H³. L. R.)	22946	M. - 10858	1361	1342	1227	1206	924	767	721	602	581	628	647	352	268	197	138	89	41	10	4	
		F. - 12088	1417	1865	1294	1173	1150	1062	842	729	696	576	512	374	328	230	171	98	46	12	1	
2 Horley. (H.)	7463	M. - 3763	337	471	423	404	284	228	224	227	177	170	168	128	120	84	62	37	18	3	1	
		F. - 3700	542	456	493	283	277	268	243	205	199	174	137	124	100	82	54	33	14	6	1	
37 GODSTONE.																						
1 Godstone. (W. H². L. R.)	17692	M. - 9295	1067	936	811	961	1001	746	674	363	542	468	427	341	318	211	136	78	48	6	5	
		F. - 8397	1011	964	788	678	686	636	591	554	484	427	380	364	275	206	147	84	46	18	.	
38 CROYDON.																						
1 Croydon. (W. w. s. H³.)	101241	M. - 44792	6461	5835	5024	4141	3840	3420	5060	2936	2559	1940	1615	1213	1094	828	553	283	146	37	6	
		F. - 56449	6530	5987	5682	6095	6366	5088	4182	3515	3056	2472	2084	1537	1450	1028	789	453	206	69	17	
2 Mitcham. (w. s. H.)	17932	M. - 8614	1196	1239	1218	800	677	589	629	463	454	387	316	243	236	122	98	60	20	8	3	
		F. - 9318	1168	1219	1255	836	817	716	575	576	506	424	321	251	242	171	129	63	40	11	.	
39 KINGSTON.																						
1 Wimbledon. (B².)	15860	M. - 7007	1061	904	701	708	711	579	506	476	407	292	234	171	168	89	83	29	15	3	.	
		F. - 8853	1090	863	848	985	1048	840	672	801	490	341	313	242	197	135	92	52	32	8	2	
2 Kingston. (W. H². B.)	36354	M. - 16236	2301	2101	1817	1418	1352	1148	1101	1068	979	716	695	465	401	294	197	103	67	19	3	
		F. - 20118	2291	2191	1996	2088	2148	1819	1432	1272	1136	887	749	603	522	403	289	171	91	27	2	
3 Esher. (H.)	11214	M. - 5038	692	677	527	482	462	398	338	355	260	199	213	107	138	86	81	62	20	3	2	
		F. - 6176	741	722	587	561	618	558	456	394	296	317	260	176	181	156	87	54	27	13	2	
4 Hampton. (H² L. B².)	13539	M. - 6072	857	857	670	561	511	422	306	392	354	288	229	150	159	95	70	29	19	10	1	
		F. - 7467	843	837	705	721	789	666	684	518	432	346	253	210	214	137	117	62	26	10	1	
40 RICHMOND.																						
1 Richmond. (W. H.)	21302	M. - 8718	1102	991	886	831	892	742	684	587	434	393	309	262	224	179	85	61	28	6	2	
		F. - 12584	1268	1036	1048	1473	1520	1278	960	826	688	666	480	425	374	260	203	138	69	19	3	
2 Mortlake	12331	M. - 5669	768	701	722	508	502	464	364	361	315	232	211	150	163	98	44	29	11	6	.	
		F. 6662	905	684	591	634	787	622	516	383	342	307	283	191	180	127	82	49	19	7	2	
1 KENT (*Extra-metropolitan*).																						
41 BROMLEY.																						
1 Bromley. (H². L.)	32960	M. - 15009	2243	1941	1603	1276	1289	1239	1097	996	891	658	534	396	365	222	146	72	34	8	2	
		F. - 17951	2184	2010	1711	1711	1965	1856	1366	1231	1011	776	631	423	409	268	222	114	61	19	2	
2 Chislehurst. (W. H.)	16012	M. - 7446	1033	931	791	714	624	685	494	463	436	326	268	218	224	132	96	66	32	12	3	
		F. - 8566	1053	970	932	883	854	741	586	511	406	403	299	251	227	139	132	59	51	14	4	1

Note.—For the Parishes comprised in each Registration Sub-district, *see* Vol. II., Division II., Table 4.
(W.) denotes that a Workhouse, and (W S.) that a Workhouse School, belonging to the District is situated within the Sub-district; (w.) denotes a house and (w s.) a Workhouse School, not belonging to the District, (H.) a Hospital or Infirmary, (L.) a Lunatic Asylum, (P.) a Prison or Convict Esta ment, (R.) a certified Reformatory or Industrial School, (B.) Barracks, &c., (S.) H.M. Ships. A figure appended to any of these letters denotes the num Institutions of a similar class situated within the Sub-district. The names of the Institutions thus indicated, and the number of inmates enumerated there be found in Vol. II., Division II., Table 6.

Table 3 *continued*.—AGES of MALES and FEMALES in REGISTRATION SUB-DISTRICTS.

REGISTRATION SUB-DISTRICT.	ALL AGES. Persons.	ALL AGES. Males and Females.	Under 5 Years.	5–	10–	15–	20–	25–	30–	35–	40–	45–	50–	55–	60–	65–	70–	75–	80–	85–	90–	95–	100 and upwᵈˢ.
NT (*Extra-litan*)—*cont.*																							
ARTFORD.																							
(H.)	24134	M. - 11642	1691	1507	1284	1096	960	796	685	639	610	520	476	372	323	245	179	121	42	11	3	.	.
		F. - 12492	1626	1478	1374	1182	1139	961	841	714	719	538	519	467	385	365	205	84	53	15	7	1	1
RD. (W. L.² R.)	22246	M. - 11472	1499	1423	1453	1458	964	823	699	597	612	481	376	301	294	202	150	72	34	12	3	.	.
		F. - 10774	1463	1315	1105	1065	943	842	758	643	566	485	400	331	302	226	153	92	50	19	2	.	.
GHAM	7055	M. - 3755	464	545	560	500	337	241	197	193	196	169	163	91	115	71	48	32	20	4	.	.	.
		F. - 3300	461	445	387	281	269	226	195	167	195	144	150	120	86	66	58	25	23	7	.	.	.
RAVESEND.																							
END. (W. H. R.)	23802	M. - 11411	1408	1348	1268	1141	1167	945	826	718	601	497	393	346	297	210	125	94	35	13	3	.	.
		F. - 11891	1385	1230	1233	1407	1117	929	770	694	640	539	451	465	388	266	190	120	66	23	10	1	.
H AYLESFORD.																							
FLEET. (H. B.)	12768	M. - 6676	929	782	673	752	635	511	417	393	418	292	240	184	161	137	64	46	27	9	1	1	1
		F. - 6092	923	793	701	815	487	442	404	384	333	249	218	180	164	144	92	63	31	6	3	1	.
(W. P. B.³)	14669	M. - 8007	1059	941	798	821	736	673	539	527	508	578	209	218	188	110	105	61	23	8	3	1	.
		F. - 6662	1064	602	628	560	493	406	421	492	389	505	228	170	154	136	80	68	18	7	1	.	.
46 HOO. W. B.³)	3405	M. - 1891	273	245	165	180	136	144	135	129	120	84	75	67	66	32	26	19	8	3	.	.	.
		F. - 1514	223	213	182	120	124	102	86	94	72	64	67	40	34	37	23	18	5	.	.	.	.
MEDWAY.																							
TER. (H². P. B. S.)	19346	M. - 9561	1188	1188	917	836	916	870	697	610	586	432	340	282	248	186	124	83	53	12	6	1	.
		F. - 9785	1227	1096	1031	1076	893	784	633	593	512	429	378	303	306	207	154	109	61	25	6	3	.
GHAM. (W. H². .)	42298	M. - 22546	2871	2451	2165	2184	2619	2017	1613	1446	1379	1023	850	620	522	311	234	119	62	25	7	1	.
		F. - 19752	2877	2506	2085	1783	1573	1367	1348	1139	1102	968	846	593	529	338	247	146	67	34	12	1	.
MALLING.																							
ORD	12745	M. - 6695	1604	847	748	694	587	547	493	387	368	291	224	182	146	112	71	49	16	6	1	.	.
		F. - 6050	1627	870	606	463	478	453	395	347	316	256	216	154	143	121	77	42	21	4	1	.	.
BCNHAM (W. L.)	7420	M. - 3684	487	465	431	358	292	198	182	184	189	174	143	115	104	115	84	66	25	8	3	1	.
		F. - 3736	510	442	448	311	263	256	238	199	194	189	160	148	116	112	69	42	25	5	2	1	.
AM	5876	M. - 2925	413	372	335	302	226	182	161	170	136	148	113	102	97	63	56	31	12	6	2	.	.
		F. - 2951	424	374	304	269	219	206	189	161	165	150	106	100	98	72	33	33	20	8	.	.	.
SEVENOAKS.																							
HAM	6420	M. - 3203	436	391	373	278	259	210	192	207	187	150	129	109	93	76	54	34	21	2	2	.	.
		F. - 3217	451	433	387	250	236	269	209	194	192	155	127	95	94	73	56	35	15	4	1	.	.
OAKS. (W. H³.)	13255	M. - 6439	852	829	712	586	486	487	440	350	357	256	258	227	109	143	100	60	34	9	4	1	.
		F. - 6816	877	753	730	635	577	567	482	456	351	239	269	231	107	155	97	73	43	6	4	.	.
UEST	7515	M. - 3834	502	497	480	385	319	243	209	208	190	166	160	145	130	106	47	36	24	10	.	.	.
		F. - 3681	483	453	436	343	292	263	230	202	207	165	140	140	120	90	56	30	16	5	2	1	.
TUNBRIDGE.																							
IDGE WELLS. (H.)	30352	M. - 13206	1859	1745	1562	1285	959	946	879	837	664	556	496	426	302	247	184	107	53	9	1	1	.
		F. - 17146	1853	1753	1698	1699	1739	1382	1254	1112	998	906	763	581	501	374	286	166	76	25	13	3	.
IDGE. (W. B.)	14690	M. - 7256	1013	908	950	791	592	463	404	400	342	298	280	270	196	167	112	70	39	14	3	.	.
		F. - 7434	971	946	865	678	625	531	516	430	392	355	314	249	218	147	110	71	31	9	1	.	.
RLEY	6465	M. - 3212	456	443	444	349	217	166	161	143	173	163	139	98	102	77	56	21	12	5	.	.	.
		F. - 3253	446	471	463	287	224	211	214	171	179	145	114	126	71	84	47	23	22	6	5	1	.
MAIDSTONE.																							
NG	4687	M. - 2365	324	353	280	231	150	151	133	134	112	[illegible]	80	86	86	58	33	22	16	2	.	1	.
		F. - 2322	352	292	283	170	156	147	171	141	113	111	80	93	79	51	37	17	17	6	.	.	.
EN. (W.)	4856	M. - 2505	379	327	258	202	157	155	145	128	120	105	103	98	110	72	70	43	32	5	1	.	.
		F. - 2351	360	291	377	192	163	182	137	123	129	91	107	82	76	63	64	37	36	7	4	.	.
(W. S.)	5925	M. - 2855	379	388	362	281	179	182	133	151	137	150	110	102	90	74	67	38	10	5	.	1	.
		F. - 3070	462	401	375	240	195	223	184	168	153	148	115	108	103	84	56	23	19	4	4	.	.
MAIDSTONE. (L.)	14201	M. - 6631	854	735	652	817	667	536	461	436	380	298	280	107	223	118	91	64	27	7	1	.	.
		F. - 7570	863	758	699	690	704	605	564	469	444	343	305	273	258	136	118	72	28	17	4	.	.
MAIDSTONE. (H³.)	15422	M. - 7415	1048	924	812	690	620	625	480	434	413	308	290	238	186	118	100	63	24	4	.	.	.
		F. - 8007	1086	894	821	712	734	622	531	458	448	396	343	251	252	108	137	85	46	22	4	1	1
HOLLINGBOURN.																							
NGBOURN. (W.)	4810	M. - 2478	310	292	299	248	190	172	143	111	120	113	101	103	84	68	47	43	15	11	.	.	.
		F. - 2332	312	290	237	201	231	174	144	119	119	111	98	97	55	40	33	27	13	10	2	.	.
AM. (H.)	3628	M. - 1887	251	239	213	199	126	112	114	97	102	94	85	71	61	48	32	22	14	6	1	.	.
		F. 1741	230	236	215	165	133	106	85	82	112	81	74	61	61	41	29	29	10	1	1	.	.
CORN	5612	M. - 2805	356	326	375	323	183	176	152	134	146	129	127	115	97	58	59	37	13	7	1	.	.
		F. - 2807	381	389	307	267	209	181	164	154	127	138	127	109	105	48	42	32	28	9	1	.	.
CRANBROOK.																							
BROOK. (W.)	6743	M. - 3387	408	409	470	285	234	194	170	171	169	168	147	119	112	82	60	43	23	5	.	.	.
		F. - 3356	422	453	431	297	244	188	169	172	205	156	138	127	120	92	51	34	21	5	1	.	.
HURST. (H. L².)	7031	M. - 3494	477	465	454	346	234	233	204	172	165	143	141	137	120	95	69	32	19	6	2	.	.
		F. - 3537	470	409	423	315	277	259	214	194	190	154	151	130	121	102	60	36	21	6	5	.	.
TENTERDEN.																							
NDEN	4060	M. - 1994	295	248	241	167	134	116	104	126	96	96	73	89	73	60	33	21	18	2	2	.	.
		F. - 2066	293	296	250	168	152	106	122	121	104	97	77	66	73	62	45	30	12	6	1	1	.
RDEN. (W.)	6401	M. - 3121	427	385	365	299	214	191	172	174	154	137	116	127	128	96	62	43	27	9	1	.	.
		F. - 3280	441	426	357	298	239	213	212	180	172	148	139	116	107	89	70	47	21	3	2	.	.
WEST ASHFORD.																							
ILL. (W.)	5553	M. - 2813	362	333	316	285	236	182	170	138	145	118	118	110	87	80	63	40	23	7	.	.	.
		F. - 2740	369	365	321	247	206	180	160	144	122	121	124	106	75	76	60	47	11	6	.	.	.
RD. (W. H². R.)	12573	M. - 6206	831	785	771	621	529	431	398	315	310	283	225	231	180	131	103	40	16	5	1	.	.
		F. - 6367	859	764	713	576	524	499	393	367	355	292	231	224	189	162	100	70	34	11	2	.	.

Table 3 *continued*—Ages of Males and Females in Registration Sub-Districts.

Registration Sub-District.	All Ages. Persons.	All Ages. Males and Females.		Under 5 Years.	5-	10-	15-	20-	25-	30-	35-	40-	45-	50-	55-	60-	65-	70-	75-	80-	85-	90-	9
2 KENT (*Extra-metropolitan*)—*cont.*																							
55 EAST ASHFORD.																							
1 Aldington	2570	M.	1362	206	174	166	148	95	86	74	61	68	56	40	44	59	43	27	14	6	2	.	.
		F.	1208	163	132	150	108	103	65	76	60	58	59	48	46	40	29	28	23	5	1	.	.
2 Brabourne. (W.)	5057	M.	2548	346	335	300	347	199	149	134	132	130	117	114	163	76	61	53	38	13	6	1	.
		F.	2509	401	357	312	167	158	158	140	156	140	135	88	80	71	51	61	28	14	8	2	.
3 Wye	6070	M.	3106	401	431	370	304	228	174	175	169	147	163	122	97	103	93	58	50	23	10	2	.
		F.	2964	412	369	338	244	230	197	168	158	145	130	117	98	121	90	83	38	17	8	.	
56 BRIDGE.																							
1 Chartham. (L.)	6461	M.	3178	418	386	329	297	222	212	208	174	186	148	165	120	108	86	61	44	16	4	.	.
		F.	3283	421	362	340	244	256	245	222	186	192	180	165	123	136	80	67	51	19	8	2	.
2 Barham. (W.)	5844	M.	2945	396	371	314	251	163	199	153	151	147	147	131	112	124	104	83	89	27	11	2	.
		F.	2899	421	384	314	237	205	217	154	157	142	142	151	118	113	91	72	44	25	11	2	.
57 CANTERBURY.																							
1 Canterbury. (W. H. P. B[2])	17060	M.	8476	1053	908	827	967	984	745	555	486	469	341	306	263	240	176	135	72	40	17	1	
		F.	8584	986	995	859	801	743	678	584	510	446	400	359	382	296	244	189	112	68	28	8	
58 BLEAN.																							
1 Sturry. (H.)	6753	M.	3367	466	421	489	391	191	194	178	165	167	154	140	112	109	85	57	26	20	7	.	.
		F.	3386	464	469	344	277	266	240	227	196	165	145	148	150	131	89	71	51	19	7	2	.
2 Herne. (W. w. s. H.)	6832	M.	3749	373	422	372	258	169	157	135	148	138	115	92	76	91	72	57	41	21	8	2	.
		F.	3083	355	415	389	300	246	176	164	175	155	122	115	117	102	95	60	45	21	5	5	
3 Whitstable	6282	M.	2997	447	419	373	297	188	185	191	186	131	118	117	83	98	56	38	34	16	7	1	.
		F.	3285	457	429	404	322	222	224	193	193	160	161	138	100	101	64	60	31	17	7	2	.
59 FAVERSHAM.																							
1 Boughton	5769	M.	3008	432	404	417	286	221	157	167	158	136	133	125	90	96	81	63	32	18	4	.	.
		F.	2761	436	343	307	245	211	182	166	157	133	117	130	98	81	70	54	26	12	6	.	.
2 Faversham. (W.)	13887	M.	6994	1635	918	839	695	598	474	425	367	380	282	268	207	184	105	86	63	54	11	8	.
		F.	6893	1670	908	778	684	554	460	447	304	346	305	277	219	180	124	90	68	51	12	5	.
3 Teynham	5330	M.	2776	379	328	340	269	233	194	167	159	132	118	110	94	97	57	42	36	12	8	.	.
		F.	2554	308	336	300	284	212	175	167	122	108	100	108	76	86	59	37	20	19	10	3	.
60 MILTON.																							
1 Milton. (W.)	23270	M.	11906	1777	1463	1358	1309	996	841	734	666	616	552	466	328	317	286	153	84	52	14	.	.
		F.	11364	1811	1498	1394	1607	960	819	688	628	589	478	439	308	302	218	144	75	44	17	2	.
61 SHEPPEY.																							
1 Minster. (W. H. B.[2] S.[8])	16640	M.	9078	1150	914	814	868	1084	962	605	540	571	428	338	301	201	164	78	89	17	8	1	.
		F.	7562	1086	965	895	651	612	557	539	454	438	343	264	211	234	128	91	57	25	7	3	.
2 Eastchurch	1564	M.	839	127	125	72	108	45	50	60	32	35	38	35	31	20	15	8	9	4	.	.	.
		F.	725	118	164	94	60	51	58	40	43	39	25	18	28	21	15	9	6	2	3	1	.
62 THANET.																							
1 Minster. (W.)	4925	M.	2469	330	315	272	240	180	122	137	130	146	97	95	82	107	71	70	40	24	7	4	.
		F.	2456	352	318	271	190	183	135	156	129	122	115	106	85	89	61	54	46	29	10	1	1
2 Margate. (w.[2] H.[3])	18226	M.	8418	1062	1198	1538	764	807	553	536	458	392	369	274	206	203	143	69	56	24	9	2	.
		F.	9808	1019	1062	1232	1125	847	892	668	677	488	418	351	368	305	202	139	101	49	26	5	1
3 Ramsgate. (H.[3])	27670	M.	12612	1731	1640	1639	1366	998	878	800	865	615	458	483	371	385	276	184	64	54	10	4	2
		F.	15058	1674	1559	1562	1629	1402	1180	1043	868	786	687	604	542	646	377	284	146	66	24	5	3
63 EASTRY.																							
1 Sandwich. (W. H.)	8855	M.	4359	521	567	549	372	298	232	222	233	248	198	186	187	181	160	101	78	42	14	2	.
		F.	4496	587	615	504	577	337	285	277	228	230	217	223	171	176	134	103	82	54	10	3	.
2 Wingham	2927	M.	1464	192	175	182	140	92	96	83	82	84	70	63	81	58	46	25	22	10	5	2	1
		F.	1463	172	139	157	111	101	105	88	89	74	68	69	64	69	37	31	18	15	2	4	.
3 Eythorne	2669	M.	1611	122	136	110	98	67	52	66	63	54	65	49	46	35	36	25	14	6	1	.	.
		F.	1058	95	122	147	91	65	65	62	54	55	54	44	45	44	33	27	12	8	4	1	.
4 Deal. (H.[3] B.[4])	14253	M.	7909	982	824	657	1370	682	504	442	565	308	258	224	213	210	171	106	62	25	5	1	.
		F.	6344	787	789	738	668	611	503	504	374	356	334	311	249	254	190	140	73	46	9	7	.
64 DOVER.																							
1 St. James. (H.[3] B.[8])	14844	M.	6897	962	873	768	691	635	446	433	421	381	291	276	196	196	163	98	69	30	6	5	.
		F.	7947	913	877	756	804	743	507	503	503	486	401	348	273	266	217	156	87	51	13	4	.
2 St Mary. (H.)	9623	M.	4637	802	556	448	488	877	357	349	246	275	257	201	160	123	83	61	82	20	8	1	.
		F.	4986	596	558	476	581	495	402	320	274	263	235	197	163	159	129	86	63	20	9	7	.
3 Hougham. (W. H. P. B.[3])	12356	M.	6473	865	724	676	706	785	491	470	357	269	265	188	168	172	137	99	65	37	8	3	.
		F.	5883	840	760	675	491	447	427	377	327	319	262	222	172	184	136	117	77	31	11	4	.
65 ELHAM.																							
1 Folkestone. (H.[3] B.[8])	23463	M.	10832	1476	1333	1117	1207	1198	875	780	661	559	418	344	279	294	168	118	67	36	8	3	2
		F.	12631	1455	1291	1314	1358	1877	1186	953	800	647	604	491	381	333	207	172	85	58	13	2	.
2 Elham. (W.)	3732	M.	1991	253	246	209	207	175	125	91	94	87	93	87	87	87	54	50	37	22	5	8	1
		F.	1741	237	220	201	143	126	110	99	88	86	85	74	65	62	62	38	16	15	6	1	.
3 Hythe. (B.[2])	6574	M.	3411	419	389	332	320	294	288	238	218	196	174	117	162	97	80	65	36	21	10	2	
		F.	3163	370	370	324	289	290	229	187	193	190	168	127	101	91	97	73	42	17	1	3	1
66 ROMNEY MARSH.																							
1 New Romney. (W. B.[2])	2766	M.	1423	199	168	157	126	108	91	85	85	85	63	62	49	49	44	26	19	5	4	.	.
		F.	1343	219	167	155	165	97	91	77	84	66	51	51	39	63	45	19	10	8	4	.	1
2 Lydd. (B.)	3400	M.	1933	246	198	196	180	184	162	135	127	128	102	75	68	53	40	14	15	9	1	2	.
		F.	1467	218	193	164	181	107	96	74	87	72	74	64	48	49	34	29	19	7	1	.	1
3 SUSSEX.																							
67 RYE.																							
1 Rye. (W.)	6657	M.	3363	461	364	389	328	271	207	208	198	183	173	132	136	103	104	60	41	20	9	2	.
		F.	3294	441	417	366	263	208	252	211	186	170	168	139	134	122	89	79	35	17	10	4	.
2 Beckley. (B.)	5383	M.	2636	368	337	298	226	196	168	159	166	109	121	114	102	94	83	48	27	17	2	2	.
		F.	2747	390	323	343	227	180	180	163	156	128	128	112	119	93	86	56	40	12	6	1	1
68 HASTINGS.																							
1 Ore. (W. H.)	5224	M.	2574	420	332	294	250	174	178	166	114	124	93	109	85	80	81	60	23	19	.	2	.
		F.	2650	461	338	256	223	247	126	187	154	140	99	99	87	77	61	46	30	11	7	4	.
2 All Saints. (H.)	9236	M.	4413	623	554	496	424	391	313	232	258	257	186	180	122	123	88	78	38	19	2	.	.
		F.	4823	684	567	487	359	411	364	346	302	267	230	205	195	151	101	75	48	22	7	2	1
3 St. Mary in the Castle. (H.[5])	35669	M.	14221	1886	1833	1731	1398	1198	1144	936	839	699	591	538	396	368	276	170	103	58	17	7	.
		F.	21448	1919	1746	1798	2332	2635	2049	1565	1381	1297	1019	978	746	824	448	306	203	60	19	5	2

Table 3 *continued*.—AGES of MALES and FEMALES in REGISTRATION SUB-DISTRICTS.

[RE]GISTRATION [SU]B-DISTRICT.	ALL AGES. Persons.	ALL AGES. Males and Females.	Under 5 Years.	5-	10-	15-	20-	25-	30-	35-	40-	45-	50-	55-	60-	65-	70-	75-	80-	85-	90-	95-	100 and upw^ds.
[SU]SSEX—*cont.*																							
[BATTLE.]																							
[...]LL. (B.)	6381	M. - 3202	442	439	402	287	249	198	195	184	162	148	134	166	109	60	62	21	9	5	.	.	.
		F. - 3179	460	397	373	248	240	225	230	188	173	127	128	112	108	65	51	32	18	4	.	.	.
[...]EST	2743	M. - 1406	208	174	168	147	101	97	74	66	67	68	76	38	61	30	23	17	8	2	1	1	.
		F. 1337	106	186	136	115	127	82	76	63	72	59	56	43	47	23	34	8	9	1	1	.	.
[...]E. (W.)	5395	M. - 2744	376	345	363	270	133	180	164	147	125	119	97	87	91	67	60	51	12	6	1	.	.
		F. 2651	370	361	320	213	181	173	178	152	181	116	113	102	98	68	41	27	16	4	1	.	.
[E]ASTBOURNE.																							
[...]HAM. (B.[4])	3283	M. - 1648	204	209	188	164	136	117	109	90	86	70	75	64	51	33	28	22	9	3	1	.	.
		F. - 1635	257	219	192	119	123	127	106	88	94	69	55	48	48	41	23	16	13	3	3	1	.
[...]OURNE. (W.H.[4]B.)	24473	M. - 11337	1506	1302	1989	1223	1137	965	788	659	586	409	379	289	267	168	130	62	44	6	4	1	.
		F. - 13136	1545	1230	1252	1583	1531	1186	980	718	787	571	490	381	363	327	170	90	40	14	3	1	.
HAILSHAM.																							
[...]SHAM	6703	M. - 3409	474	426	380	350	258	229	204	191	170	135	143	118	112	91	67	45	12	4	.	.	.
		F. - 3294	471	440	334	266	250	237	208	191	152	148	142	103	116	87	48	36	14	9	2	.	.
[...]INGLY. (W.)	6702	M. - 3489	465	400	456	333	238	194	204	156	173	128	153	125	115	91	89	47	23	8	1	.	1
		F. - 3213	494	458	362	253	196	219	266	177	173	133	126	121	104	76	87	34	16	7	1	.	.
TICEHURST.																							
[...]URST. (W. L.[2])	5292	M. - 2594	352	332	306	251	177	172	158	120	120	112	121	105	80	78	64	29	18	1	1	.	.
		F. 2698	359	335	302	219	240	191	136	154	139	114	122	104	73	82	51	28	13	10	4	.	.
[...]URST. (H. L.)	3364	M. - 1740	259	250	222	173	129	111	98	96	83	60	53	54	48	34	39	24	7	1	.	.	.
		F. - 1624	233	250	194	126	128	108	101	84	98	73	60	54	49	42	17	19	7	3	.	.	.
[...]URST	5082	M. - 2531	378	378	279	227	192	165	166	140	112	92	97	80	72	66	40	16	9	7	1	.	.
		F. - 2551	410	350	301	201	192	172	151	156	127	109	96	81	56	61	43	29	15	1	.	.	.
[...]T. (H.[3])	3481	M. - 1593	204	201	170	169	141	111	87	95	80	69	73	59	49	38	20	16	11	4	1	.	.
		F. 1888	198	190	202	170	194	168	135	133	105	98	69	72	54	43	32	19	11	4	1	.	.
UCKFIELD.																							
[...]ERFIELD	7246	M. - 3640	531	480	437	390	274	228	206	202	169	137	139	113	118	82	71	39	19	5	.	.	.
		F. - 3606	563	461	478	307	272	259	209	167	202	139	136	111	101	92	45	25	16	2	1	1	.
[...]FIELD	3726	M. - 1906	268	271	252	196	136	91	108	89	99	80	83	71	52	55	34	22	16	4	1	.	.
		F. - 1820	299	257	220	139	122	131	99	90	106	89	65	60	47	38	24	17	6	3	.	.	.
[...]LD. (W.)	2897	M. - 1380	195	170	163	131	93	74	79	80	72	63	45	40	60	33	43	13	7	8	2	.	.
		F. 1517	186	179	172	142	128	98	107	87	60	71	60	57	54	42	25	29	7	3	3	1	.
[...]FIELD	6229	M. - 3203	464	442	362	322	263	213	108	140	137	117	138	97	124	75	41	38	15	8	2	.	.
		F. - 3026	450	423	368	225	217	235	177	166	149	127	112	120	95	79	41	29	12	2	.	.	.
[EA]ST GRINSTEAD.																							
[...]YTHAM	3708	M. - 1880	241	234	211	197	122	119	131	100	99	83	73	67	70	57	36	19	4	6	1	.	.
		F. 1828	267	251	224	133	109	121	123	114	86	85	76	68	57	39	34	25	7	1	.	.	.
[...] GRINSTEAD. (W.)	9755	M. - 5005	651	606	540	470	424	361	353	283	291	269	188	161	149	95	76	62	22	5	4	.	.
		F. - 4750	657	615	600	434	366	365	303	264	243	199	186	129	147	90	73	44	17	0	1	.	.
[...]TH	5118	M. - 2696	399	375	294	247	219	176	166	154	165	118	110	90	72	61	29	28	11	4	2	.	.
		F. 2428	348	337	323	178	160	179	174	135	134	136	95	75	58	44	29	19	8	5	.	.	.
[C]UCKFIELD.																							
[...]FIELD	5671	M. 3168	356	382	323	343	231	220	199	169	160	126	146	104	190	69	64	22	6	3	2	.	.
		F. 2503	369	345	265	214	186	175	171	137	137	106	97	85	81	64	45	19	9	6	2	.	.
[...]FIELD. (W.)	8399	M. - 4177	551	510	487	411	324	282	288	241	213	198	160	167	123	88	82	49	23	7	3	.	.
		F. 4222	587	534	481	362	341	332	273	245	226	197	162	132	112	97	66	45	22	8	.	.	.
[...]STPIERPOINT	9182	M. - 4508	630	579	665	503	350	301	269	247	201	182	171	147	113	104	80	40	18	4	4	.	.
		F. - 4674	615	598	581	400	419	330	314	246	251	201	201	162	148	95	68	25	15	3	3	.	.
[...] LEWES.																							
[...]HLING. (W. L.[2])	5198	M. - 2524	282	283	268	217	186	181	157	184	142	129	126	105	75	75	53	32	17	5	.	.	.
		F. - 2674	316	292	251	203	185	190	201	188	172	172	163	115	69	82	48	26	5	6	1	.	.
[...]LEY. (H. R.)	5175	M. - 2755	330	324	353	272	213	169	167	131	136	127	134	104	102	76	54	38	22	3	.	.	.
		F. - 2420	317	306	278	308	171	167	154	131	126	131	115	81	77	57	58	23	13	4	3	.	.
[...]ES. (W. H.[1] P.[3] B.[2])	11547	M. - 5745	715	675	680	601	637	446	349	311	280	223	210	195	164	118	86	59	30	7	.	.	.
		F. 5802	687	657	673	556	493	423	385	358	333	256	213	205	176	138	121	73	33	16	3	1	.
[...]T FIRLE. (W.)	2369	M. - 1246	167	146	139	111	112	85	61	62	59	65	63	40	48	38	32	12	7	3	1	.	.
		F. - 1123	163	134	126	87	87	79	70	67	46	53	56	53	41	29	20	10	5	7	.	.	.
[...]HAVEN. (W. B.[2])	5558	M. - 3275	408	346	304	325	367	317	274	233	203	139	110	87	84	47	29	16	5	1	.	.	.
		F. 2283	370	319	223	192	174	192	161	143	138	73	79	80	58	32	17	18	11	3	.	.	.
[...]TINGDEAN. (w.a. H.[2])	3049	M. - 1593	215	256	300	156	102	82	73	71	69	68	46	44	47	20	21	12	6	2	1	1	.
		F. - 1456	196	231	217	100	91	98	74	69	87	69	50	36	33	33	27	15	9	1	.	.	.
[...] BRIGHTON.																							
[...]P TOWN. (H.[5])	15489	M. - 5967	681	722	673	616	490	452	415	332	339	288	272	204	185	101	85	66	36	15	1	.	.
		F. 9532	716	717	798	1244	1135	878	608	568	507	316	465	362	316	219	100	92	46	9	2	1	.
[...]PETER. (W. H.[2])	62437	M. - 29518	4168	3638	3270	2788	2056	2302	2061	1805	1550	1229	1126	868	775	507	376	233	105	36	4	1	.
		F. - 32919	4246	3585	3299	2985	2918	2753	2401	2067	1882	1518	1308	1061	1006	716	553	312	174	38	11	.	.
[...] PALACE. (H.[3])	21165	M. - 7943	812	852	993	748	776	654	563	480	441	351	375	300	210	131	130	63	37	7	2	1	.
		F. - 13222	804	799	983	1782	1832	1328	1009	884	788	659	627	516	460	207	239	142	62	32	6	3	.
[...] STEYNING.																							
[...]BHAM. (W. B.[2])	42987	M. - 19015	2546	2358	2112	1925	1787	1591	1286	1122	1003	804	674	551	488	328	234	147	61	25	1	2	.
		F. - 23972	2503	2156	2201	2031	2687	2290	1848	1503	1304	1111	986	761	711	484	374	196	101	29	7	.	.
[...]NING	6102	M. - 3076	454	397	367	301	206	188	178	162	157	135	119	98	113	84	60	31	22	3	1	.	.
		F. - 3026	421	411	332	287	205	205	161	180	166	158	128	106	128	70	62	42	15	13	2	.	.
[...] HORSHAM.																							
[...]H HORSHAM	4083	M. - 2177	300	291	254	233	161	117	129	114	104	97	90	81	68	70	32	30	8	2	.	.	.
		F. - 1906	271	255	245	188	150	121	118	104	98	78	71	76	63	59	30	14	11	2	.	1	.
[...]TH HORSHAM. (W.)	14277	M. - 6944	900	915	786	687	529	476	412	347	357	318	273	223	215	150	128	54	37	7	.	.	.
		F. - 7333	987	915	825	669	587	540	436	446	404	347	306	243	218	163	114	74	38	16	6	1	.
[...]T HORSHAM	3940	M. - 2017	286	281	246	180	124	120	128	103	105	83	83	91	67	51	36	24	13	2	.	.	.
		F. - 1923	260	263	221	140	126	134	122	104	108	92	56	63	56	59	43	20	19	.	1	.	.

Table 3 *continued*.—AGES of MALES and FEMALES in REGISTRATION SUB-DISTRICTS.

Registration Sub-District.	All Ages. Persons.	All Ages. Males and Females.		Under 5 Years.	5–	10–	15–	20–	25–	30–	35–	40–	45–	50–	55–	60–	65–	70–	75–	80–	85–	90–	95–
3 SUSSEX—*cont.*																							
80 PETWORTH.																							
1 Petworth Northern. (W. W. B.)	4160	M.	2178	266	238	267	219	133	127	122	122	112	113	86	98	82	54	48	37	19	2	.	.
		F.	1982	296	263	231	139	185	119	119	101	108	122	90	74	64	51	43	24	10	7	3	.
2 Petworth Southern. (W. H².)	5435	M.	2680	348	357	331	227	205	142	138	148	145	136	111	93	119	76	58	48	13	10	.	.
		F.	2755	361	364	307	235	188	170	169	154	139	115	110	96	117	82	80	33	16	7	.	.
81 THAKEHAM.																							
1 Pulborough	3888	M.	2016	281	273	223	195	136	106	129	109	98	80	102	79	84	48	37	33	13	5	.	.
		F.	1872	251	230	225	135	136	126	112	97	107	90	87	80	60	54	35	25	11	8	2	.
2 Washington. (W.)	4397	M.	2231	301	277	242	268	158	120	141	125	106	97	94	75	87	62	38	22	13	3	.	.
		F.	2166	207	301	261	172	164	138	146	122	114	83	66	79	68	65	47	23	8	5	1	.
82 EAST PRESTON.																							
1 Worthing. (H.)	14576	M.	6406	886	873	788	646	538	438	344	392	304	258	209	207	179	148	100	65	25	10	2	.
		F.	8170	923	779	882	846	838	636	579	541	438	346	334	275	202	212	147	85	46	12	3	1
2 Littlehampton. (W. B¹.)	7679	M.	3815	517	502	480	392	256	204	245	200	213	170	161	115	133	84	59	48	28	15	3	.
		F.	3864	498	479	427	347	300	202	243	240	237	179	157	128	125	92	71	46	22	10	4	.
3 Arundel	4110	M.	2044	267	268	215	194	165	144	124	108	97	94	97	57	84	60	32	27	12	1	.	.
		F.	2066	254	233	241	185	164	149	120	123	108	97	101	79	65	61	40	25	14	4	2	1
83 WESTHAMPNETT.																							
1 Manhood	3473	M.	1801	264	257	174	147	128	108	109	107	94	73	81	54	57	63	33	17	19	3	1	.
		F.	1672	239	226	200	96	93	108	111	100	83	76	73	82	58	62	41	14	13	6	2	.
2 Wyke	3112	M.	1530	193	184	162	139	108	108	86	67	96	75	67	49	81	43	34	23	15	5	1	.
		F.	1582	199	191	155	135	97	92	100	88	93	72	73	77	72	50	60	18	12	6	2	1
3 South Bersted. (H.)	4166	M.	1777	208	228	188	182	120	113	118	112	94	96	80	67	58	46	38	22	13	4	.	.
		F.	2389	250	229	268	289	122	166	148	127	134	121	112	87	78	75	48	20	14	3	3	.
4 Yapton	2949	M.	1475	206	165	178	134	104	74	94	84	68	71	69	67	57	47	32	24	10	6	1	.
		F.	1474	208	168	159	122	124	81	76	84	74	74	75	56	56	49	28	20	14	4	2	.
5 Boxgrove. (W.)	4374	M.	2237	308	291	251	199	154	132	141	119	107	105	88	76	93	76	63	32	17	.	1	.
		F.	2137	241	278	249	151	151	151	121	131	143	89	90	88	90	75	46	39	22	7	3	1
6 Singleton	1579	M.	797	109	106	79	76	63	51	45	55	41	37	30	37	20	23	16	6	5	.	.	.
		F.	782	114	102	116	48	39	47	48	48	42	29	39	25	19	21	16	11	5	1	1	.
84 CHICHESTER.																							
1 Chichester. (W. H. B⁴.)	8569	M.	4108	531	481	446	436	351	291	269	267	229	173	144	126	112	93	57	35	16	5	2	.
		F.	4461	522	493	460	469	379	339	308	263	239	206	185	127	163	121	83	58	33	11	3	.
85 MIDHURST.																							
1 Midhurst. (W.)	6541	M.	3340	480	389	392	317	259	241	206	182	193	131	141	133	128	73	61	46	23	4	.	2
		F.	3201	431	405	354	278	245	205	189	181	162	153	146	122	119	88	64	39	20	7	3	.
2 Fernhurst	2435	M.	1271	179	165	166	117	86	77	81	67	60	64	59	58	24	33	16	15	9	1	1	.
		F.	1164	188	167	137	77	69	82	71	78	71	52	40	39	30	27	19	17	3	1	1	.
3 Harting	4967	M.	2569	349	343	361	238	163	162	132	138	141	134	97	91	95	70	58	26	11	5	2	.
		F.	2398	353	302	291	181	101	158	162	123	114	121	103	80	73	59	48	34	11	3	1	.
86 WESTBOURNE.																							
1 Westbourne. (W.)	7020	M.	3742	522	465	427	358	263	207	198	208	196	176	164	160	115	116	81	52	20	9	2	.
		F.	3278	530	467	466	280	278	250	224	193	209	182	158	123	112	94	76	57	28	11	2	.
4 HAMPSHIRE.																							
87 HAVANT.																							
1 Havant. (W. R. B.)	8672	M.	4135	569	516	555	347	273	235	269	230	217	181	171	165	140	119	71	45	23	9	1	.
		F.	4537	577	546	489	444	322	331	287	268	239	193	222	148	154	133	90	51	35	7	2	.
88 PORTSEA ISLAND.																							
1 Kingston. (W. H². L. P. B.)	39127	M.	18739	3033	2515	2278	1640	1278	1195	1113	1098	1033	855	746	617	498	361	220	117	54	22	6	.
		F.	20388	2901	2533	2147	1808	1676	1602	1458	1260	1174	841	825	628	591	422	278	144	77	27	7	2
2 Portsea Town. (H². P⁵. B². S⁸.)	17183	M.	10306	864	682	644	986	1874	1376	927	788	641	463	367	208	202	99	81	26	16	4	2	.
		F.	6877	857	732	672	690	720	877	563	456	392	327	265	195	169	128	75	47	21	13	2	1
3 Portsmouth Town. (B⁶. S³.)	7591	M.	4580	328	312	290	799	587	552	501	372	200	189	169	96	80	47	32	14	8	2	1	.
		F.	3011	366	304	287	347	298	277	206	175	193	133	129	102	81	54	26	23	7	2	.	.
4 Landport. (H⁴. B⁴.)	64121	M.	28792	4466	3809	3185	2865	2221	2140	1830	1730	1651	1289	1009	960	827	499	340	157	62	29	3	.
		F.	35329	4408	3667	3460	3639	3581	2357	2056	2190	1950	1369	1443	1165	1126	728	466	265	105	63	10	4
89 ALVERSTOKE.																							
1 Alverstoke. (W. H². P. B¹⁰. S³.)	21581	M.	11632	1389	1276	1045	1254	1473	1046	878	745	661	489	368	344	259	202	117	78	46	17	2	3
		F.	9949	1339	1207	1033	831	830	785	691	607	538	443	408	300	312	267	149	83	61	12	4	.
90 FAREHAM.																							
1 Fareham. (W. L. B³.)	10961	M.	5272	671	606	530	475	377	349	318	321	331	264	242	228	200	136	108	71	35	9	2	.
		F.	5689	651	585	594	452	460	373	396	362	315	325	290	216	237	160	129	89	48	12	1	.
2 Titchfield. (B³.)	5859	M.	3034	381	360	446	331	232	192	158	166	146	141	117	117	88	77	51	31	10	8	1	.
		F.	2825	372	348	330	283	208	191	105	162	143	147	128	111	100	65	38	38	8	9	3	.
91 ISLE OF WIGHT.																							
1 Cowes. (P. S.)	13012	M.	6427	896	763	682	617	409	496	412	404	378	300	270	230	202	120	86	35	25	6	1	2
		F.	6585	877	782	713	578	568	506	461	404	336	329	276	228	200	137	91	59	22	11	2	1
2 Newport. (W. P. B.)	14148	M.	7279	841	762	746	619	650	574	501	467	400	337	314	260	235	201	150	80	37	10	3	2
		F.	6869	834	777	609	632	353	527	467	401	354	360	299	237	231	133	158	93	53	17	6	1
3 Ryde. (H. L. B⁷.)	28359	M.	12708	1702	1642	1421	1267	942	870	783	772	714	589	609	446	368	235	102	109	68	16	3	1
		F.	15651	1728	1642	1470	1360	1814	1273	1099	1005	923	779	707	540	494	367	287	150	78	29	5	.
4 Godshill. (H³.)	11718	M.	5266	673	644	547	447	460	386	376	339	299	247	199	195	161	126	85	54	20	6	2	.
		F.	6452	686	698	629	673	683	574	458	439	384	305	261	201	213	142	79	53	31	8	1	.
5 Calbourne. (B⁸.)	6396	M.	3252	422	363	365	306	249	226	217	221	179	154	126	101	92	89	55	33	20	6	.	.
		F.	3144	465	421	359	277	250	179	190	214	188	162	124	103	86	73	51	29	26	4	1	1
92 LYMINGTON.																							
1 Lymington. (W. H.)	8376	M.	3929	555	501	455	365	312	230	197	195	187	200	162	150	146	94	82	56	32	6	4	.
		F.	4447	527	489	470	466	355	296	288	226	237	229	215	160	177	123	96	51	36	3	5	1
2 Milford. (B.)	4275	M.	2113	290	296	263	199	136	123	130	102	102	112	80	81	59	56	36	33	10	4	1	.
		F.	2162	278	259	266	173	172	142	144	112	119	113	98	74	70	67	42	24	7	1	1	.

Table 3 *continued*.—AGES of MALES and FEMALES in REGISTRATION SUB-DISTRICTS.

REGISTRATION SUB-DISTRICT.	ALL AGES. Persons.	ALL AGES. Males and Females.	Under 5 Years.	5–	10–	15–	20–	25–	30–	35–	40–	45–	50–	55–	60–	65–	70–	75–	80–	85–	90–	95–	100 and upw^ds.
AMPSHIRE—*cont.*																							
HRISTCHURCH.																							
ISTCHURCH. (W. . S. H.* B.)	29455	M. 12419	1775	1512	1388	1187	1835	1026	853	747	630	400	464	406	346	242	172	88	46	16	2		
		F. 17036	1707	1569	1385	1937	2036	1711	1876	1071	966	884	654	551	496	366	207	123	45	22	1	1	
RINGWOOD.																							
GWOOD. (W.)	5488	M. 2710	374	326	301	259	190	176	140	152	141	118	102	109	98	64	65	25	31	7	1	1	
		F. 2778	353	368	319	225	211	183	160	151	145	142	116	112	107	74	57	30	19	5	1		
ORDINGBRIDGE.																							
ADINGBRIDGE. (W.)	6231	M. 3152	491	400	300	320	217	180	180	142	136	166	149	130	123	105	84	40	16	8	1		
		F. 3079	487	396	323	271	236	222	166	132	169	144	143	133	131	97	70	40	11	6	1	1	
NEW FOREST.																							
NDHURST	3294	M. 1629	208	214	204	155	119	90	110	91	87	77	70	56	48	37	32	16	10	3	1		
		F. 1665	215	186	168	136	138	127	111	109	84	71	88	70	62	41	35	26	5	4			
WLEY	3889	M. 1913	254	273	193	184	132	122	118	116	78	98	73	75	76	49	37	22	12	5			
		F. 1976	249	240	197	164	147	128	124	131	101	111	71	70	86	75	42	24	16	3	1	1	
ING. (W. H. R. B.)	6538	M. 3067	355	378	352	325	281	196	187	165	134	117	135	161	110	93	57	31	23	6		1	
		F. 2871	362	384	350	218	226	207	176	171	151	144	146	120	107	70	52	39	16	7	1		
SOUTHAMPTON.																							
UTHAMPTON. (W.H.² B. S.)	52989	M. 25699	3419	2990	2720	2597	2287	1902	1783	1473	1420	1196	1077	775	760	426	273	177	74	16	5	1	2
		F. 27290	3397	2968	2891	2773	2824	2177	1996	1699	1646	1373	1178	985	864	399	401	271	149	39	6	4	
SOUTH STONEHAM.																							
. MARY EXTRA. (H.S.)	10586	M. 5540	743	682	568	488	679	548	394	364	310	194	163	131	110	66	56	28	14	5			
		F. 5046	761	652	541	445	484	406	362	351	276	194	184	148	112	68	60	38	25	7	1	1	
UTH STONEHAM. (W.)	14048	M. 6719	1002	880	816	626	508	481	402	371	351	311	245	224	195	152	160	65	30	7			
		F. 7329	975	901	820	624	610	516	464	484	395	347	235	266	224	165	111	79	34	16	1	2	
ILLBROOK	16639	M. 7609	1071	1063	925	769	517	524	896	411	415	329	269	277	266	171	120	54	34	7	1		
		F. 9030	1137	1016	943	865	810	700	608	535	509	424	379	312	311	193	153	86	31	20	3	3	
99 ROMSEY.																							
OMSEY. (W.)	6527	M. 3181	452	395	387	327	242	193	169	157	153	132	155	123	120	76	50	36	11	1	1	1	
		F. 3346	440	391	382	305	269	223	209	189	189	166	125	131	129	75	64	34	18	6	1		
ICHELMERSH	4073	M. 2099	269	263	225	221	157	123	117	99	110	96	92	88	83	61	39	31	15	4			
		F. 1974	262	261	243	143	147	116	127	84	98	101	109	72	73	57	42	21	16	7		1	
100 STOCKBRIDGE.																							
BROUGHTON	3436	M. 1750	224	185	238	208	114	105	98	84	78	96	86	66	77	49	26	20	7	8	1		
		F. 1686	222	226	172	145	113	107	103	95	85	100	76	61	82	36	32	20	10	3			
TOCKBRIDGE. (W.)	3534	M. 1830	244	234	216	199	142	75	100	69	99	85	80	64	72	54	31	22	20	2	1		
		F. 1704	205	216	210	140	114	100	89	118	119	82	74	80	48	40	29	24	13	3		1	
101 WINCHESTER.																							
MICHELDEVER	2257	M. 1174	121	138	135	136	100	62	61	62	56	45	61	64	45	41	23	9	4	1			
		F. 1083	150	134	125	82	69	74	66	53	50	60	46	54	42	42	18	4	8	6			
THE WORTHYS	2869	M. 1465	196	174	149	168	112	81	97	90	71	62	56	49	57	41	28	23	8	3			
		F. 1404	225	194	156	124	101	112	107	83	73	65	57	57	56	38	28	14	6				
WINCHESTER. (W. H. P. R.* B.)	19652	M. 9150	1103	978	1027	1271	935	715	570	542	445	361	302	254	261	170	116	66	35	5			
		F. 9603	1086	941	936	1042	875	759	639	589	503	468	368	328	323	218	193	108	52	17	7	1	
TWYFORD	4528	M. 2316	285	273	326	216	174	118	130	125	118	111	92	95	94	54	49	26	13	3	1		
		F. 2212	319	264	256	174	154	142	140	136	119	91	104	97	81	57	39	26	6	3	1		1
HURSLEY. (W. H.)	2753	M. 1384	164	196	184	126	84	74	79	65	84	64	69	48	47	35	30	24	6	1	1		
		F. 1369	206	170	156	88	95	93	88	79	72	78	53	64	43	47	24	12	8	3			
102 DROXFORD.																							
BISHOPS WALTHAM	3616	M. 1773	210	184	201	189	150	132	93	88	70	81	81	71	69	63	36	27	6	2	2		
		F. 1843	240	214	210	161	129	130	95	96	105	95	89	72	68	53	40	22	14	4			
WESTMEON	2152	M. 1098	128	122	116	105	83	84	69	68	51	52	42	46	50	46	22	17	7	1			
		F. 1054	119	114	134	78	80	76	66	58	52	52	64	43	39	33	34	10	8		1	1	
HAMBLEDON. (W. H.)	5429	M. 2695	343	328	303	238	186	168	138	142	134	128	111	109	109	80	70	40	28	10	1		
		F. 2734	377	353	296	201	206	191	180	147	119	132	137	101	117	78	45	42	26	4	1		
103 CATHERINGTON.																							
HORNDEAN. (W.)	2747	M. 1387	162	173	164	139	101	73	76	59	72	79	56	60	40	42	33	19	15	5			
		F. 1360	179	140	160	134	106	69	88	76	57	68	74	54	40	33	32	13	12	6			
104 PETERSFIELD.																							
PETERSFIELD. (W. H.)	7463	M. 3635	470	454	367	333	301	230	234	226	172	163	150	140	134	121	89	37	23	9			
		F. 3828	510	491	410	328	300	236	226	227	190	177	175	142	126	109	65	41	21	3	1		
EASTMEON	2772	M. 1442	222	184	163	157	91	79	69	70	62	68	54	60	57	33	33	27	8	3	1	1	
		F. 1330	184	180	172	90	104	61	78	74	77	49	39	40	55	38	33	19	6	2			
105 ALRESFORD.																							
ROPLEY	3409	M. 1748	223	234	199	157	138	116	94	103	78	73	85	76	58	50	39	31	9	4			
		F. 1661	220	206	179	135	118	119	104	95	90	67	73	64	66	51	28	19	9	5			
ALRESFORD. (W. R.)	3561	M. 1715	226	210	194	150	127	112	104	97	87	79	90	65	63	40	35	14	16	5	1		
		F. 1846	208	235	287	176	136	90	107	101	96	79	85	74	49	49	27	31	4	0	1		
106 ALTON.																							
ALTON. (W. H. L.)	9082	M. 4474	632	548	517	475	310	257	244	249	248	208	196	140	146	101	88	47	26	9	3		
		F. 4608	647	587	522	387	373	282	270	271	259	210	177	151	161	119	85	53	28	11	2		
BINSTED	6166	M. 3114	438	404	400	312	196	155	187	175	180	148	123	111	110	76	60	34	15	8	1		
		F. 3052	402	429	405	236	190	193	196	166	178	137	121	118	92	72	63	35	20	4	2		
107 HARTLEY-WINTNEY.																							
ODIHAM. (W. S.)	7030	M. 3535	424	503	481	336	246	188	178	176	170	152	160	149	130	93	72	39	23	4	1		
		F. 3495	421	470	412	286	260	210	213	188	187	171	171	141	134	95	53	34	17	11	2		
FARNBOROUGH. (B.)	9369	M. 5066	503	437	438	830	1524	787	409	255	219	148	141	100	76	53	25	25	14	2			
		F. 3344	520	427	366	509	323	295	238	166	196	148	138	72	87	47	37	13	7	3	1	1	
HARTLEY-WINTNEY. (W.)	4987	M. 2508	317	296	248	233	165	137	138	143	116	122	117	86	93	81	56	32	22	6			
		F. 2479	308	306	266	205	180	164	147	132	145	120	116	113	101	63	56	34	14	6	2		

Table 3 *continued*.—Ages of Males and Females in Registration Sub-Districts.

Registration Sub-District.	All Ages. Persons.		All Ages. Males and Females.	Under 5 Years.	5-	10-	15-	20-	25-	30-	35-	40-	45-	50-	55-	60-	65-	70-	75-	80-	85-	90-	95-
4 HAMPSHIRE— *cont.*																							
108 BASINGSTOKE.																							
1 Basingstoke. (W.H.)	9970	M.	4869	669	627	557	499	469	382	340	273	205	192	175	150	123	111	78	58	23	4	3	.
		F.	5101	734	610	535	447	431	405	357	303	251	226	179	160	153	140	88	51	22	8	1	.
Bramley	4759	M.	2490	337	320	315	237	172	162	137	117	127	116	102	101	90	70	52	37	12	6	.	.
		F.	2269	261	322	243	154	150	151	137	131	126	107	105	94	73	83	63	23	19	3	2	.
3 Dummer	4545	M.	2321	283	290	262	265	151	139	134	132	123	109	99	99	64	72	46	34	13	6	1	.
		F.	2224	328	299	250	178	155	130	126	135	111	109	100	87	74	64	35	29	17	7	1	.
109 WHITCHURCH.																							
1 Whitchurch. (W.)	5458	M.	2761	383	348	297	290	234	178	152	138	114	118	118	105	99	81	56	31	26	2	.	.
		F.	2697	374	331	292	225	225	190	159	126	136	115	128	108	97	87	47	37	12	5	1	3
110 ANDOVER.																							
1 Longparish	4185	M.	2116	286	281	261	227	142	126	100	112	96	126	160	83	74	56	40	18	10	4	.	.
		F.	2069	279	259	241	180	147	136	97	115	105	120	97	99	67	48	35	33	11	5	1	.
2 Amport	2684	M.	1356	167	154	163	142	103	84	78	72	69	80	65	50	50	30	22	11	6	4	.	.
		F.	1328	183	157	174	98	115	86	81	66	67	77	64	42	33	38	22	18	5	2	.	.
3 Andover. (W.H.²)	6884	M.	3378	422	384	416	317	266	251	188	187	149	162	162	136	129	79	67	38	18	7	.	.
		F.	3506	413	405	382	359	230	237	236	192	177	165	169	142	130	86	70	42	18	12	.	.
4 Hurstbourne Tarrant	1947	M.	993	127	115	112	105	32	58	39	43	50	39	52	46	41	31	23	21	7	1	.	.
		F.	954	127	110	106	90	52	58	50	44	51	49	40	37	55	34	30	12	6	1	3	.
111 KINGSCLERE.																							
1 Highclere	3112	M.	1537	188	214	169	161	96	90	80	78	76	70	75	73	54	45	33	15	14	3	.	1
		F.	1575	208	202	163	106	104	106	94	116	84	78	80	62	51	49	32	30	13	2	.	.
2 Kingsclere. (W.)	5412	M.	2750	372	382	334	226	184	149	132	138	132	131	127	112	100	71	65	31	18	4	.	.
		F.	2662	381	385	330	209	184	131	164	142	129	150	123	108	81	79	38	32	19	5	2	.
5 BERKSHIRE.																							
112 NEWBURY.																							
1 Thatcham	5768	M.	2846	394	386	353	247	209	171	149	164	130	143	119	111	101	73	47	41	12	5	.	.
		F.	2920	419	372	333	220	221	193	182	154	169	156	120	81	87	76	76	34	16	7	1	.
2 Newbury. (W. H.)	7940	M.	3784	408	438	419	401	312	259	243	182	193	158	162	130	129	78	89	44	26	4	1	1
		F.	4156	474	483	456	439	364	296	253	214	213	206	168	163	154	133	93	60	28	8	3	.
3 Speen. (H.)	7621	M.	3578	418	427	412	365	300	292	182	190	185	162	161	149	134	134	78	40	25	4	3	.
		F.	4043	456	425	487	413	327	272	237	226	222	198	187	154	153	118	88	45	32	8	3	.
113 HUNGERFORD.																							
1 Kintbury	3884	M.	1982	283	260	228	209	137	111	106	96	90	91	94	83	79	52	45	19	17	3	.	.
		F.	1902	247	241	224	155	138	127	99	92	102	93	93	71	88	51	52	19	13	8	.	.
2 Hungerford. (W.)	8967	M.	4495	574	565	514	402	307	268	268	221	233	236	185	176	185	125	88	72	44	8	2	.
		F.	4472	567	549	513	360	321	271	225	220	253	224	208	210	170	142	104	77	33	13	3	.
3 Lambourn	5011	M.	2571	326	319	299	287	199	163	139	113	118	122	113	98	87	75	67	34	17	5	.	.
		F.	2440	333	345	261	168	183	139	140	132	128	137	103	94	95	89	44	32	22	4	.	.
114 FARINGDON.																							
1 Shrivenham	3818	M.	1910	262	243	239	209	127	79	85	97	104	92	95	71	73	60	41	18	8	5	2	.
		F.	1908	248	256	234	149	119	119	110	115	100	99	105	69	75	58	35	24	18	3	1	.
2 Faringdon. (W.)	5521	M.	2674	361	335	322	279	174	167	161	140	144	129	99	85	89	82	62	40	14	1	.	.
		F.	2847	382	374	341	234	176	177	164	161	139	141	129	109	119	87	60	33	23	5	.	2
3 Buckland	4337	M.	2194	314	283	250	208	164	105	122	114	109	91	102	76	92	69	54	38	14	3	.	.
		F.	2143	281	287	238	153	150	145	123	115	97	104	103	102	83	72	39	31	15	5	.	.
115 ABINGDON.																							
1 Fyfield	1683	M.	861	122	105	87	104	72	56	46	36	47	42	21	36	28	32	16	15	6	2	.	.
		F.	822	115	99	91	65	53	63	33	51	44	31	34	42	31	29	22	14	4	.	1	.
2 Abingdon. (W.)	9022	M.	4283	576	540	543	514	364	277	256	216	180	163	151	148	148	109	84	51	28	3	1	.
		F.	4739	597	632	592	468	440	335	310	257	252	199	199	169	163	136	93	47	36	6	3	.
3 Cumnor	3249	M.	1681	246	225	195	184	153	96	101	78	87	67	81	56	42	37	36	11	8	3	1	.
		F.	1568	219	234	165	124	118	112	116	92	82	66	55	54	56	34	23	13	7	3	.	.
4 Nuneham Courtney	2300	M.	1138	163	121	141	109	84	72	52	65	56	69	67	43	45	23	18	14	7	2	.	.
		F.	1162	171	145	128	97	96	72	68	71	58	58	61	38	30	23	27	3	4	2	.	.
5 Sutton Courtney	4100	M.	2093	313	296	256	217	173	116	111	84	95	96	74	59	61	67	43	24	10	5	.	.
		F.	2007	283	240	219	154	156	180	130	89	115	94	98	72	82	46	40	27	19	3	.	.
116 WANTAGE.																							
1 Wantage. (W.)	7496	M.	3758	517	509	472	383	262	268	197	185	179	178	118	133	147	105	79	52	25	8	1	.
		F.	3738	512	457	438	361	259	248	236	209	180	164	154	157	126	87	83	51	16	3	4	.
2 Ilsley	5205	M.	2772	331	328	325	326	228	187	168	127	124	122	117	108	96	84	52	36	9	5	1	.
		F.	2433	339	315	271	162	182	144	141	114	119	118	122	103	98	74	61	39	21	7	2	.
3 Hendred	4459	M.	2393	307	275	286	267	185	164	145	121	114	94	111	85	97	57	43	24	11	5	2	.
		F.	2066	265	292	244	168	147	150	111	115	106	109	85	83	65	57	45	14	8	2	.	.
117 WALLINGFORD.																							
1 Cholsey. (L.)	6980	M.	3536	486	455	411	319	296	198	207	196	198	187	166	138	126	98	74	42	14	5	.	.
		F.	3444	414	437	387	240	219	197	237	213	217	173	170	163	140	91	75	41	23	7	.	.
2 Wallingford. (W.H.)	7513	M.	3713	465	480	509	351	246	208	197	186	210	157	156	116	126	118	88	62	31	6	.	.
		F.	3800	470	464	419	341	281	235	230	209	207	181	192	142	138	121	92	47	26	6	1	.
118 BRADFIELD.																							
1 Bucklebury. (W.)	5630	M.	2898	369	334	364	386	206	188	148	143	133	143	126	98	112	85	73	40	18	4	.	.
		F.	2732	371	339	288	223	200	160	171	134	139	126	125	86	87	68	80	43	25	6	1	.
2 Mortimer	4961	M.	2453	378	367	263	270	179	146	157	183	111	117	107	70	92	87	40	30	8	7	1	.
		F.	2508	345	319	291	173	195	179	149	157	138	98	120	95	91	77	39	33	6	3	.	.
3 Tilehurst. (H. B.)	7381	M.	3825	510	457	447	488	351	260	223	233	199	164	114	115	113	76	41	35	11	3	1	.
		F.	3556	538	445	403	290	274	201	239	203	201	137	142	122	109	86	62	33	17	6	3	.

Table 3 *continued*.—AGES of MALES and FEMALES in REGISTRATION SUB-DISTRICTS.

REGISTRATION SUB-DISTRICT.	ALL AGES. Persons.	Males and Females.	Under 5 Years.	5–	10–	15–	20–	25–	30–	35–	40–	45–	50–	55–	60–	65–	70–	75–	80–	85–	90–	–95	100 and upw^{d}.
BERKSHIRE—*cont.*																							
119 READING.																							
. MARY. (W.)	17262	M. - 8228	1182	1003	916	709	772	696	587	473	428	349	290	226	200	164	94	60	38	5	2	.	1
		F. - 9034	1202	1031	909	891	817	748	629	544	475	402	366	243	256	198	149	95	58	14	6	1	
. LAWRENCE (W. P.)	4674	M. - 2379	301	245	216	253	274	228	184	146	135	126	31	53	51	33	23	10	9	1	.	.	.
		F. - 2295	279	240	223	268	216	191	194	128	136	114	95	68	64	46	34	10	7	6	1	.	.
. GILES. (H^{2}.)	21558	M. - 10586	1650	1250	898	1105	1057	924	745	651	958	462	334	258	234	166	91	33	21	9	1	.	.
		F. - 10972	1539	1313	1124	1024	1026	909	847	667	603	483	384	302	276	186	142	87	31	11	2	1	.
120 WOKINGHAM.																							
OKINGHAM. (W.)	8824	M. - 4335	586	572	497	388	311	271	274	238	217	209	184	177	138	106	81	49	20	8	.	.	.
		F. - 4489	651	525	441	390	316	332	314	284	281	224	208	162	150	116	93	40	10	11	2	.	.
ARGRAVE. (W. S.)	11194	M. - 5504	764	777	666	692	416	361	359	319	276	250	186	158	139	96	68	40	25	13	.	.	.
		F. - 5690	823	707	656	466	433	399	395	337	316	270	220	190	146	104	74	43	30	4	2	.	.
121 COOKHAM.																							
RAY	8259	M. - 4027	540	527	486	390	303	291	247	256	192	156	160	140	113	96	70	32	14	3	2	.	
		F. - 4232	535	520	409	347	331	332	265	263	254	193	158	147	132	107	57	41	23	7	2	.	.
OOKHAM. (W. H.)	8686	M. - 4213	537	531	515	404	334	306	261	243	206	192	171	137	143	88	67	46	25	7	2	.	.
		F. - 4473	553	461	502	447	405	360	289	255	231	231	182	146	154	106	70	32	22	5		2	.
EASTHAMPSTEAD.																							
ACKNELL. (W. H. L. B.)	8464	M. - 4175	536	518	495	404	333	304	258	242	213	185	165	132	160	94	62	48	18	6	1	1	.
		F. - 4289	589	565	472	336	340	344	311	266	216	215	164	133	125	85	68	42	12	4	2	.	.
NDHURST	4195	M. - 2594	228	186	303	628	160	120	138	160	154	134	111	66	70	44	16	12	6	2	.	.	.
		F. - 1601	206	219	168	124	134	106	117	125	167	97	84	51	27	29	15	3	7	.	1	.	.
123 WINDSOR.																							
HAM. (H. B.)	13362	M. - 6663	909	757	683	635	688	620	491	408	342	296	241	182	177	114	70	43	18	3	2	1	.
		F. - 6699	889	821	671	563	568	648	629	467	309	312	237	207	201	113	86	62	22	8	3	.	2
INDSOR. (W. H^{2}. B^{2}.)	18630	M. - 9219	1066	1006	1208	913	1055	840	615	636	482	354	320	232	239	142	123	56	30	6	5	.	.
		F. - 9411	1019	962	923	1004	855	796	687	653	505	469	438	262	307	207	160	98	56	13	3	.	.

Table 4.—MALE and FEMALE CHILDREN at *each Year of Age* under 5 in the SOUTH-EASTERN DIVISION and its REGISTRATION COUNTIES.

REGISTRATION COUNTY.	TOTAL UNDER 5 YEARS. Persons.	Males and Females.	Under 1 Year.	1–	2–	3–	4–
II SOUTH-EASTERN COUNTIES.	323073	M. - 161461	34167	31658	32156	31729	31751
		F. 161612	34126	31591	32492	31650	31754
1 SURREY (*Extra-metropolitan*)	58540	M. - 29072	6135	5686	5712	5695	5850
		F. - 29468	6217	5787	5866	5805	5804
2 KENT (*Extra-metropolitan*)	94112	M. - 47184	9948	9260	9359	9380	9233
		F. - 46928	9907	9179	9474	9140	9228
3 SUSSEX	63193	M. - 31623	6646	6211	6278	6181	6213
		F. - 31570	6710	6244	6307	6104	6215
4 HAMPSHIRE	74445	M. - 37210	7970	7147	7522	7286	7285
		F. - 37235	7915	7251	7549	7251	7269
5 BERKSHIRE	32783	M. - 16472	3478	3364	3285	3187	3170
		F. - 16311	3376	3150	3307	3209	3238

Table 5.—MALE and FEMALE CHILDREN at *each Year of Age* under 5 in REGISTRATION DISTRICTS.

REGISTRATION DISTRICT.	Total under 5 Years. Persons.	Males and Females.	Under 1 Year.	1–	2–	3–	4–
SURREY (*Extra-metropolitan*).							
EPSOM	4906	M. - 2445	489	469	515	482	490
		F. - 2461	493	490	449	502	527
CHERTSEY	3659	M. - 1805	365	366	341	361	372
		F. - 1854	368	384	378	368	376
GUILDFORD	5185	M. - 2624	608	495	566	541	515
		F. - 2561	531	511	519	505	497
FARNHAM	5389	M. - 2619	584	508	533	524	465
		F. 2770	614	592	632	627	505
HAMBLEDON	2139	M. - 1093	200	194	214	230	249
		F. - 1046	219	209	214	194	210
DORKING	2046	M. 1063	224	210	207	191	231
		F. 983	198	170	203	195	217
REIGATE	3857	M. - 1898	370	376	380	374	398
		F. - 1959	388	392	400	382	397
GODSTONE	2078	M. - 1067	213	205	206	207	236
		F. - 1011	199	208	210	187	207
CROYDON	15353	M. - 7657	1646	1504	1478	1473	1556
		F. - 7696	1733	1442	1485	1547	1489
KINGSTON	9875	M. - 4901	1043	970	963	966	959
		F. - 4974	1061	983	1016	967	968
RICHMOND	4053	M. - 1900	427	383	365	346	379
		F. - 2153	435	406	453	433	421

REGISTRATION DISTRICT.	Total under 5 Years. Persons.	Males and Females.	Under 1 Year.	1–	2–	3–	4–
2 KENT (*Extra-metropolitan*).							
41 BROMLEY	6513	M. - 3276	568	638	660	665	645
		F. 3237	692	622	628	643	652
42 DARTFORD	7234	M. - 3654	783	715	740	711	705
		F. - 3580	775	808	720	690	696
43 GRAVESEND	2793	M. - 1408	290	292	270	273	273
		F. - 1385	304	254	295	271	261
44 NORTH AYLESFORD	3974	M. - 1988	446	363	413	376	397
		F. - 1986	438	404	392	373	379
45 HOO	606	M. - 273	43	51	54	56	49
		F. - 283	52	46	30	53	43
46 MEDWAY	8163	M. - 4059	879	703	704	787	806
		F. 4104	879	803	800	793	838
47 MALLING	3865	M. - 1904	405	344	382	404	369
		F. - 1961	412	396	386	409	358
48 SEVENOAKS	3601	M. - 1790	363	362	379	340	357
		F. - 1811	352	367	364	343	385
49 TUNBRIDGE	6598	M. - 3328	674	654	668	676	656
		F. - 3270	698	649	644	626	653
50 MAIDSTONE	6047	M. - 2984	617	598	606	568	595
		F. - 3063	616	598	629	590	630
51 HOLLINGBOURNE	1860	M. - 936	192	183	173	193	195
		F. - 925	177	193	178	206	175

Table 5 *cont.*—Male and Female Children at *each Year of Age* under 5 in Registration Districts.

Registration District.	Total under 5 Years. Persons.		Males and Females.	Under 1 Year.	1–	2–	3–	4–
2 KENT (*Extra-metropolitan*)—*cont.*								
52 CRANBROOK	1777	M.	885	181	187	161	170	186
		F.	892	184	170	196	174	168
53 TENTERDEN	1450	M.	716	102	135	151	129	139
		F.	734	147	127	172	139	149
54 WEST ASHFORD	2421	M.	1193	250	232	237	242	232
		F.	1228	276	213	223	262	264
55 EAST ASHFORD	1928	M.	952	204	177	177	199	195
		F.	976	197	186	235	208	151
56 BRIDGE	1656	M.	814	198	152	165	172	159
		F.	842	171	156	189	174	152
57 CANTERBURY	2039	M.	1053	202	226	200	224	201
		F.	986	215	178	206	195	192
58 BLEAN	2554	M.	1278	264	266	244	243	262
		F.	1276	267	236	264	252	257
59 FAVERSHAM	3736	M.	1837	389	356	361	360	371
		F.	1899	420	378	390	373	338
60 MILTON	3588	M.	1777	380	351	328	384	336
		F.	1811	394	357	387	330	337
61 SHEPPEY	2483	M.	1277	289	245	254	259	230
		F.	1206	250	254	237	226	239
62 THANET	6108	M.	3123	661	586	631	650	595
		F.	3045	650	591	596	582	626
63 EASTRY	3358	M.	1717	341	356	337	353	330
		F.	1641	327	336	307	330	341
64 DOVER	4718	M.	2369	520	474	469	453	463
		F.	2349	485	492	500	440	432
65 ELHAM	4210	M.	2148	473	442	411	393	429
		F.	2062	430	405	419	404	404
66 ROMNEY MARSH	873	M.	445	90	80	91	92	83
		F.	428	107	71	78	77	95
3 SUSSEX.								
67 RYE	1650	M.	810	167	160	176	152	175
		F.	851	178	183	155	165	176
68 HASTINGS	5977	M.	2973	629	570	633	597	544
		F.	3004	659	579	614	567	585
69 BATTLE	2055	M.	1023	207	188	212	203	213
		F.	1032	219	190	222	199	202
70 EASTBOURNE	3565	M.	1764	361	376	351	326	350
		F.	1802	404	353	378	345	322
71 HAILSHAM	1924	M.	959	200	183	194	199	183
		F.	965	221	196	174	180	194
72 TICEHURST	2373	M.	1193	240	233	218	249	216
		F.	1180	221	245	217	234	263
73 UCKFIELD	2963	M.	1466	310	271	295	277	291
		F.	1497	309	296	324	277	291
74 EAST GRINSTEAD	2658	M.	1291	248	281	249	246	267
		F.	1267	248	252	246	261	260
75 CUCKFIELD	3108	M.	1537	321	318	292	298	308
		F.	1571	333	321	293	332	292
76 LEWES	4156	M.	2117	454	406	415	415	427
		F.	2039	442	404	367	412	414
77 BRIGHTON	11427	M.	5661	1273	1104	1121	1056	1107
		F.	5766	1227	1159	1141	1137	1102
78 STEYNING	6014	M.	3000	609	576	599	614	602
		F.	3014	651	580	623	571	559
79 HORSHAM	3103	M.	1576	323	299	316	338	300
		F.	1527	325	298	337	254	313
80 PETWORTH	1255	M.	608	127	110	114	134	123
		F.	647	113	144	132	137	121
81 THAKEHAM	1140	M.	582	138	115	106	112	112
		F.	558	100	112	105	122	119
82 EAST PRESTON	3345	M.	1670	368	324	327	321	330
		F.	1675	330	327	347	342	329
83 WESTHAMPNETT	2554	M.	1283	243	260	267	244	263
		F.	1271	255	245	252	265	254
84 CHICHESTER	1053	M.	531	103	105	104	115	104
		F.	522	119	103	93	97	112
85 MIDHURST	1930	M.	958	179	212	196	183	180
		F.	972	219	181	181	193	198
86 WESTBOURNE	1052	M.	522	116	104	93	102	107
		F.	530	112	98	105	104	110

Registration District.	Total under 5 Years. Persons.		Males and Females.	Under 1 Year.	1–	2–	3–
4 HAMPSHIRE.							
87 HAVANT	1146	M.	569	124	111	107	192
		F.	577	121	104	110	112
88 PORTSEA ISLAND	17156	M.	8629	1808	1655	1721	1685
		F.	8527	1952	1644	1670	1591
89 ALVERSTOKE	2778	M.	1389	324	259	262	282
		F.	1389	270	257	283	309
90 FAREHAM	2075	M.	1052	227	200	201	220
		F.	1023	215	175	212	214
91 ISLE OF WIGHT	9356	M.	4834	937	833	944	914
		F.	4521	918	893	980	978
92 LYMINGTON	1650	M.	845	193	147	176	170
		F.	805	174	154	151	160
93 CHRISTCHURCH	3542	M.	1775	337	353	354	345
		F.	1767	387	365	346	324
94 RINGWOOD	727	M.	374	74	76	78	82
		F.	353	65	66	67	89
95 FORDINGBRIDGE	808	M.	421	80	76	91	86
		F.	387	76	72	88	70
96 NEW FOREST	1673	M.	817	161	160	169	162
		F.	856	149	172	170	198
97 SOUTHAMPTON	6816	M.	3419	720	696	685	678
		F.	3397	783	667	669	652
98 SOUTH STONEHAM	5695	M.	2822	611	534	568	574
		F.	2873	619	550	598	571
99 ROMSEY	1423	M.	721	149	146	160	144
		F.	702	138	155	134	137
100 STOCKBRIDGE	895	M.	468	88	87	106	91
		F.	427	86	72	93	78
101 WINCHESTER	3855	M.	1869	390	367	390	353
		F.	1986	453	373	355	405
102 DROXFORD	1421	M.	685	148	135	136	122
		F.	736	138	141	153	159
103 CATHERINGTON	341	M.	162	54	28	38	22
		F.	179	45	30	33	33
104 PETERSFIELD	1386	M.	692	166	125	125	140
		F.	694	144	135	129	130
105 ALRESFORD	886	M.	449	90	77	102	90
		F.	437	91	67	90	81
106 ALTON	2109	M.	1060	203	223	216	193
		F.	1049	210	213	197	203
107 HARTLEY WINTNEY	2493	M.	1244	250	267	256	231
		F.	1249	272	230	264	233
108 BASINGSTOKE	2630	M.	1289	296	228	258	259
		F.	1341	272	296	289	242
109 WHITCHURCH (HANTS)	757	M.	383	83	74	76	73
		F.	374	75	76	85	76
110 ANDOVER	1984	M.	982	197	190	222	178
		F.	1002	187	212	201	207
111 KINGSCLERE	1144	M.	560	115	106	109	111
		F.	584	127	102	140	93
5 BERKSHIRE.							
112 NEWBURY	2659	M.	1310	275	274	250	237
		F.	1349	279	240	300	271
113 HUNGERFORD	2310	M.	1163	241	219	253	200
		F.	1147	232	231	227	259
114 FARINGDON	1848	M.	937	178	188	186	192
		F.	911	187	170	188	182
115 ABINGDON	2795	M.	1410	289	276	286	280
		F.	1385	288	269	283	257
116 WANTAGE	2271	M.	1156	235	238	240	225
		F.	1115	246	225	198	231
117 WALLINGFORD	1858	M.	974	189	169	191	191
		F.	884	181	163	184	163
118 BRADFIELD	2511	M.	1257	254	278	229	262
		F.	1254	243	231	245	258
119 READING	6123	M.	3103	669	645	634	660
		F.	3020	690	565	598	594
120 WOKINGHAM	2804	M.	1350	316	258	271	232
		F.	1454	291	293	298	304
121 COOKHAM	2174	M.	1086	231	231	222	215
		F.	1088	209	203	241	210
122 EASTHAMPSTEAD	1558	M.	763	165	166	136	164
		F.	795	148	162	164	165
123 WINDSOR	3872	M.	1964	413	378	398	384
		F.	1908	383	378	391	385

Table 7.—CONDITION as to MARRIAGE and AGES of MALES and FEMALES in the SOUTH-EASTERN DIVISION a[illegible] REGISTRATION COUNTIES.

REGISTRATION COUNTY.		ALL AGES.	Under 15 Years.	15–	20–	25–	35–	45–	55–	up[illegible]
II.—SOUTH-EASTERN COUNTIES.										
UNMARRIED	Males	768339	447434	121124	86501	60081	21051	10806	6514	
	Females	772188	443592	117968	81576	63847	27429	16380	11370	
MARRIED	Males	407903	.	361	18752	104417	108688	82051	57638	[illegible]
	Females	414221	.	2456	32970	119506	108236	78390	48393	[illegible]
WIDOWED	Males	42308	.	10	160	1964	4892	6514	9428	[illegible]
	Females	92117	.	18	327	4526	11044	16656	22123	[illegible]
1 SURREY (*Extra-metropolitan*).										
UNMARRIED	Males	140460	81018	21447	17293	12244	4519	2098	1214	
	Females	151948	81419	22883	18387	15230	6204	3684	2322	[illegible]
MARRIED	Males	71697	.	57	3099	18111	20654	14414	9314	[illegible]
	Females	73155	.	367	5665	22201	20007	13653	7708	[illegible]
WIDOWED	Males	6913	.	4	25	341	806	1115	1592	[illegible]
	Females	16875	.	5	65	857	2268	3260	4166	[illegible]
2 KENT (*Extra-metropolitan*).										
UNMARRIED	Males	219627	130292	38779	24664	16800	6986	3004	1810	[illegible]
	Females	214424	128524	32787	20999	15583	6717	4283	3025	[illegible]
MARRIED	Males	118755	.	105	6707	30757	31680	23623	16406	[illegible]
	Females	118626	.	816	9997	34294	30641	22160	13086	[illegible]
WIDOWED	Males	12233	.	1	52	576	1278	1872	2784	[illegible]
	Females	24862	.	4	90	1183	2820	4340	5853	[illegible]
3 SUSSEX.										
UNMARRIED	Males	145512	88246	22989	15269	10583	3843	2250	1344	[illegible]
	Females	169856	87155	24691	17570	14691	6806	4297	2814	[illegible]
MARRIED	Males	79081	.	88	3974	20668	20616	15806	11430	[illegible]
	Females	81126	.	462	6255	23244	21079	16275	9746	[illegible]
WIDOWED	Males	8755	.	2	36	415	848	1312	1868	[illegible]
	Females	18964	.	1	61	911	2349	3440	4492	[illegible]
4 HAMPSHIRE.										
UNMARRIED	Males	175850	102622	27987	20862	15042	4960	2448	1478	[illegible]
	Females	172045	101514	26779	17856	13041	5504	3246	2236	[illegible]
MARRIED	Males	95638	.	74	4087	25385	25439	19638	14355	[illegible]
	Females	99305	.	617	8066	28251	25665	19020	11963	[illegible]
WIDOWED	Males	9822	.	3	29	439	1031	1564	2185	[illegible]
	Females	22740	.	8	87	1236	2748	4134	5529	[illegible]
5 BERKSHIRE.										
UNMARRIED	Males	75890	45856	12958	8413	5516	1053	1011	668	[illegible]
	Females	73918	44980	10828	7064	5393	2399	1470	979	[illegible]
MARRIED	Males	41832	.	37	1885	10499	10606	8571	6133	[illegible]
	Females	42006	.	194	2987	11516	10844	8282	5230	[illegible]
WIDOWED	Males	4579	.	.	18	194	429	661	999	[illegible]
	Females	8667	.	.	24	346	869	1482	2083	[illegible]

Note.—In a few cases, persons described as "Married" were stated to be under 15 years of age. These have been classed with married persons aged "15 and [illegible] 20 years."

Table 8.—CONDITION as to MARRIAGE and AGES of MALES and FEMALES in REGISTRATION DISTRICTS.

REGISTRATION DISTRICT.		ALL AGES.	Under 15 Years.	15–	20–	25–	35–	45–	55–	65 and upw^ds.
RREY (*Extra-metropolitan*).										
OM:										
NMARRIED	M.	12949	8046	1744	1240	900	453	229	144	98
	F.	13741	7469	1894	1528	1302	620	423	249	165
ARRIED	M.	6059	.	7	228	1609	1608	1190	855	406
	F.	6175	.	24	407	1789	1716	1174	734	331
IDOWED	M.	710	.	3	2	36	68	114	188	321
	F.	1473	.	.	1	65	193	283	365	586
RTSEY:										
NMARRIED	M.	8473	5370	1254	788	620	204	119	66	62
	F.	8605	5002	1161	913	814	325	196	116	78
ARRIED	M.	4384	.	3	167	1102	1178	960	615	392
	F.	4342	.	18	307	1233	1175	848	503	259
IDOWED	M.	421	.	.	.	20	46	58	99	198
	F.	931	.	.	3	37	114	178	230	371
LDFORD:										
NMARRIED	M.	13439	7492	2282	1491	1153	401	257	166	87
	F.	12838	7120	1869	1401	1188	556	340	203	161
ARRIED	M.	6306	.	2	279	1677	1932	1446	978	594
	F.	7024	.	23	473	1902	1887	1421	850	369
IDOWED	M.	794	.	.	2	37	96	123	176	366
	F.	1695	.	.	5	52	246	380	426	586
NHAM:										
NMARRIED	M.	16035	6591	2082	3521	2416	628	106	84	47
	F.	10269	6383	1391	897	636	209	118	71	66
ARRIED	M.	6122	.	.	252	1862	1851	1147	647	378
	F.	6415	.	65	752	2213	1677	1043	332	233
IDOWED	M.	544	.	.	3	81	83	101	129	217
	F.	1010	.	.	7	71	158	177	200	337
IBLEDON:										
NMARRIED	M.	5462	3160	920	608	419	146	94	64	51
	F.	4548	2886	621	426	333	120	82	53	24
ARRIED	M.	2743	.	4	100	640	672	615	438	274
	F.	2739	.	10	219	702	581	571	382	174
IDOWED	M.	350	.	.	.	11	36	60	75	178
	F.	511	.	.	1	22	51	80	132	225
KING:										
NMARRIED	M.	4726	2850	678	403	383	139	74	53	59
	F.	4862	2800	633	480	442	224	119	81	83
ARRIED	M.	2518	.	.	83	604	631	540	333	258
	F.	2516	.	5	138	675	678	501	330	189
IDOWED	M.	309	.	.	1	9	25	40	86	148
	F.	521	.	1	4	15	65	82	111	243
GATE:										
NMARRIED	M.	9394	5464	1606	1039	746	249	141	93	66
	F.	10018	5527	1438	1148	1015	388	246	151	105
ARRIED	M.	4755	.	4	168	1183	1243	1090	672	395
	F.	4783	.	17	284	1355	1320	989	561	257
IDOWED	M.	472	.	.	1	11	45	82	100	233
	F.	937	.	1	4	35	121	164	223	389
STONE:										
NMARRIED	M.	6363	2814	898	697	778	423	284	173	96
	F.	5203	2763	660	608	524	293	212	157	86
ARRIED	M.	2609	.	2	102	825	683	544	412	240
	F.	2723	.	18	176	728	691	536	380	184
IDOWED	M.	323	.	1	1	17	29	57	74	144
	F.	471	.	.	1	25	54	68	102	221
YDON:										
NMARRIED	M.	33452	20971	4027	3634	2418	772	378	260	152
	F.	42394	21739	6837	6077	4314	1705	953	628	841
ARRIED	M.	18417	.	23	875	5084	5438	3598	2250	1149
	F.	18748	.	91	1400	5966	5350	3398	1708	756
IDOWED	M.	1537	.	.	8	78	202	261	336	654
	F.	4625	.	3	16	262	597	950	1144	1653
GSTON:										
NMARRIED	M.	21337	13055	3243	2463	1561	547	240	120	103
	F.	27198	13718	4305	3590	3022	1182	669	386	317
ARRIED	M.	12078	.	6	569	3267	3612	2358	1433	833
	F.	12346	.	59	980	3829	3558	2203	1185	561
IDOWED	M.	1028	.	.	4	67	142	154	250	411
	F.	3070	.	.	15	176	416	589	774	1100
HMOND:										
NMARRIED	M.	8830	5260	1333	1113	740	267	102	55	20
	F.	12272	6512	2074	1810	1559	582	325	224	186
ARRIED	M.	5129	.	6	278	1468	1418	966	624	304
	F.	5343	.	33	439	1730	1594	989	537	241
IDOWED	M.	431	.	.	3	26	62	75	100	165
	F.	1631	.	.	8	77	263	341	400	543

REGISTRATION DISTRICT.		ALL AGES.	Under 15 Years.	15–	20–	25–	35–	45–	55–	65 and upw^ds.
2 KENT (*Extra-metropolitan*).										
41 BROMLEY:										
UNMARRIED	M.	13904	8542	1982	1639	1129	373	175	102	60
	F.	17005	8960	2560	2216	1963	694	377	203	132
MARRIED	M.	7859	.	7	306	2246	2319	1488	930	494
	F.	7888	.	34	595	2474	2314	1423	717	381
WIDOWED	M.	632	.	.	8	41	93	119	162	259
	F.	1624	.	.	8	92	200	300	390	625
42 DARTFORD:										
UNMARRIED	M.	17112	10405	2921	1751	1102	421	224	107	91
	F.	16996	9684	2479	1555	1140	468	287	204	169
MARRIED	M.	8860	.	3	497	2306	2334	1799	1194	727
	F.	8826	.	49	785	2566	2312	1630	1016	466
WIDOWED	M.	897	.	.	2	33	102	145	198	417
	F.	1746	.	.	8	82	198	325	411	715
43 GRAVESEND:										
UNMARRIED	M.	7215	4019	1137	985	691	217	90	39	37
	F.	7189	3898	1375	781	860	213	136	115	111
MARRIED	M.	3861	.	4	781	1061	1061	741	511	302
	F.	3654	.	32	330	1088	983	686	371	184
WIDOWED	M.	335	.	.	1	13	36	51	93	141
	F.	1048	.	.	8	51	138	175	287	387
44 NORTH AYLESFORD:										
UNMARRIED	M.	9079	5184	1599	1073	608	203	136	67	59
	F.	7419	5210	1027	519	288	150	75	71	78
MARRIED	M.	5115	.	11	285	1423	1400	985	671	340
	F.	4834	.	46	465	1400	1102	780	434	228
WIDOWED	M.	489	.	.	4	19	63	88	113	203
	F.	781	.	.	3	28	81	138	173	340
45 HOO:										
UNMARRIED	M.	1222	683	180	99	112	80	36	26	8
	F.	831	628	111	48	24	10	6	3	1
MARRIED	M.	596	.	.	37	164	102	115	78	40
	F.	580	.	9	76	163	148	106	48	30
WIDOWED	M.	73	.	.	.	3	7	9	14	40
	F.	103	.	.	.	1	8	19	23	52
46 MEDWAY:										
UNMARRIED	M.	20128	10776	3026	3011	2150	711	251	119	82
	F.	18721	10822	2771	1481	866	317	214	138	122
MARRIED	M.	10989	.	14	521	2982	3164	2248	1339	721
	F.	10728	.	87	972	3329	2818	1925	1120	477
WIDOWED	M.	992	.	.	3	66	146	183	214	379
	F.	2088	.	.	3	127	262	422	473	801
47 MALLING:										
UNMARRIED	M.	8374	6102	1362	976	554	224	110	95	53
	F.	7537	5065	1099	573	425	196	126	80	64
MARRIED	M.	4505	.	2	225	1134	1152	879	596	407
	F.	4412	.	34	376	1283	1115	832	490	282
WIDOWED	M.	635	.	.	5	15	50	89	115	272
	F.	788	.	.	1	23	72	140	184	368
48 SEVENOAKS:										
UNMARRIED	M.	8402	6672	1249	886	676	274	141	92	62
	F.	8881	6003	1213	811	673	311	165	107	92
MARRIED	M.	4480	.	.	177	1081	1204	905	699	414
	F.	4406	.	14	279	1246	1217	851	576	277
WIDOWED	M.	544	.	.	1	24	50	72	110	287
	F.	873	.	1	5	35	98	138	201	395
49 TUNBRIDGE:										
UNMARRIED	M.	14797	9389	3429	1378	889	312	164	108	87
	F.	17498	9316	2628	2027	1632	796	620	327	218
MARRIED	M.	8145	.	5	328	2088	2172	1646	1168	738
	F.	8313	.	36	565	2371	2243	1682	961	475
WIDOWED	M.	783	.	.	2	36	75	116	202	353
	F.	2003	.	.	6	90	239	380	521	800
50 MAIDSTONE:										
UNMARRIED	M.	13536	8085	2223	1437	958	390	222	138	83
	F.	13878	8154	1952	1275	1003	506	307	213	169
MARRIED	M.	7547	.	8	391	1979	1970	1477	1058	864
	F.	7799	.	62	669	2276	1942	1433	961	506
WIDOWED	M.	888	.	.	3	43	79	133	218	410
	F.	1743	.	.	8	88	198	300	401	748
51 HOLLINGBOURN:										
UNMARRIED	M.	4462	2680	765	417	308	102	75	51	54
	F.	4047	2597	617	377	251	86	64	44	32
MARRIED	M.	2386	.	5	87	549	569	517	408	251
	F.	2396	.	18	196	606	588	498	339	164
WIDOWED	M.	332	.	.	1	12	33	38	72	176
	F.	427	.	.	1	17	40	67	86	216

Table 8 *continued.*—CONDITION as to MARRIAGE and AGES of MALES and FEMALES in REGISTRATION DISTRICTS.

REGISTRATION DISTRICT.		ALL AGES.	Under 15 Years.	15–	20–	25–	35–	45–	55–	65 and upw^{ds}
2 KENT (*Extra-metropolitan*)—*cont.*										
52 CRANBROOK:										
UNMARRIED	M.	4274	2863	731	381	271	96	66	28	39
	F.	4164	2608	603	380	276	126	75	56	34
MARRIED	M.	2310	.	.	85	510	585	501	351	261
	F.	2302	.	5	135	573	594	460	340	176
WIDOWED	M.	297	.	.	2	11	28	31	69	155
	F.	427	.	.	.	11	41	58	83	224
53 TENTERDEN:										
UNMARRIED	M.	3106	1956	465	272	188	91	54	43	38
	F.	3232	2063	458	282	202	84	66	43	54
MARRIED	M.	1775	.	1	76	389	440	342	311	216
	F.	1709	.	8	128	441	466	342	240	174
WIDOWED	M.	234	.	.	.	6	15	26	63	120
	F.	315	.	.	1	10	27	53	73	151
54 WEST ASHFORD:										
UNMARRIED	M.	5542	3398	905	614	374	107	71	39	35
	F.	5237	3301	708	473	366	126	75	54	60
MARRIED	M.	3118	.	1	151	786	767	617	481	315
	F.	3144	.	25	252	854	801	502	402	218
WIDOWED	M.	358	.	.	.	31	34	66	68	159
	F.	626	.	.	5	20	61	101	138	301
55 EAST ASHFORD:										
UNMARRIED	M.	4266	2728	692	408	236	76	65	40	42
	F.	3838	2674	502	283	178	66	40	44	30
MARRIED	M.	2463	.	2	100	540	609	514	377	312
	F.	2467	.	17	206	613	622	475	317	217
WIDOWED	M.	257	.	.	.	7	22	32	55	141
	F.	379	.	.	.	7	28	48	95	200
56 BRIDGE:										
UNMARRIED	M.	3708	2214	548	324	280	139	96	52	49
	F.	3643	2232	471	295	280	126	98	82	59
MARRIED	M.	2102	.	.	81	487	496	459	369	265
	F.	2208	.	10	170	536	510	477	290	206
WIDOWED	M.	263	.	.	.	4	25	31	53	142
	F.	431	.	.	.	22	41	63	98	207
57 CANTERBURY:										
UNMARRIED	M.	5413	2788	993	615	594	164	72	40	37
	F.	5072	2840	783	516	412	170	125	108	118
MARRIED	M.	2784	.	4	114	695	764	528	388	276
	F.	2776	.	18	227	812	710	505	304	200
WIDOWED	M.	309	.	.	5	11	37	53	74	129
	F.	730	.	.	.	38	76	129	166	327
58 BLEAN:										
UNMARRIED	M.	6732	3784	948	437	299	111	69	46	41
	F.	5767	3668	872	305	328	132	75	86	94
MARRIED	M.	3071	.	1	110	791	802	626	468	353
	F.	3294	.	27	223	837	832	631	461	243
WIDOWED	M.	310	.	.	1	15	36	39	66	159
	F.	703	.	.	.	29	74	120	106	315
59 FAVERSHAM:										
UNMARRIED	M.	7892	5087	1248	762	449	151	84	52	59
	F.	7072	4871	1045	523	314	127	85	55	52
MARRIED	M.	4422	.	7	284	1109	1143	876	622	386
	F.	4443	.	37	440	1279	1077	818	506	277
WIDOWED	M.	434	.	.	1	26	35	72	94	206
	F.	636	.	1	3	24	26	119	172	318
60 MILTON:										
UNMARRIED	M.	7408	4598	1302	724	440	177	117	62	58
	F.	6529	4608	963	474	252	105	51	46	35
MARRIED	M.	4061	.	7	271	1108	1057	816	492	310
	F.	4164	.	44	474	1228	1030	752	413	214
WIDOWED	M.	447	.	.	1	27	42	25	51	201
	F.	611	.	.	2	22	73	114	149	251
61 SHEPPEY:										
UNMARRIED	M.	6307	3242	974	907	751	217	83	58	25
	F.	4664	3504	678	362	197	64	43	33	23
MARRIED	M.	3324	.	1	131	917	950	606	421	298
	F.	3122	.	33	297	968	843	532	323	126
WIDOWED	M.	286	.	1	1	18	38	52	74	102
	F.	501	.	.	4	23	67	75	133	190
62 THANET:										
UNMARRIED	M.	14241	9724	2358	1354	828	276	144	86	71
	F.	17163	9049	2895	1940	1457	707	457	367	296
MARRIED	M.	7909	.	12	416	2148	2065	1438	1091	739
	F.	8010	.	40	671	2413	1981	1430	1004	462
WIDOWED	M.	749	.	.	5	44	65	104	179	352
	F.	2144	.	.	11	102	282	374	502	873
63 EASTRY:										
UNMARRIED	M.	8686	4887	1974	966	613	229	135	92	90
	F.	8127	4892	1203	785	553	266	205	149	136
MARRIED	M.	4643	.	3	182	1060	1154	996	785	567
	F.	4732	.	34	326	1245	1083	963	681	400
WIDOWED	M.	514	.	.	1	10	31	64	114	285
	F.	1072	.	.	3	41	110	154	245	519
64 DOVER:										
UNMARRIED	M.	11466	6400	1877	1517	1046	337	142	113	64
	F.	11252	6436	1792	1128	835	306	291	130	177
MARRIED	M.	5924	.	5	296	1467	1555	1240	776	586
	F.	6103	.	64	652	1718	1670	1144	671	394
WIDOWED	M.	677	.	.	5	33	60	96	111	272
	F.	[illegible]								

REGISTRATION DISTRICT.		ALL AGES.	Under 15 Years.	15–	20–	25–	35–	45–	55–
2 KENT (*Extra-metropolitan*)—*cont.*									
65 ELHAM:									
UNMARRIED	M.	10303	6673	1728	1390	870	340	136	79
	F.	10802	5682	1733	1232	1021	447	297	180
MARRIED	M.	5421	.	6	207	1518	1418	1064	733
	F.	5454	.	35	408	1672	1585	993	666
WIDOWED	M.	510	.	.	1	24	48	72	114
	F.	1299	.	2	5	59	171	269	278
66 ROMNEY MARSH:									
UNMARRIED	M.	2063	1164	305	242	185	72	37	28
	F.	1611	1107	220	116	79	37	15	12
MARRIED	M.	1165	.	1	50	278	329	241	161
	F.	1016	.	7	98	252	256	205	138
WIDOWED	M.	138	.	.	.	9	24	23	29
	F.	181	.	.	2	6	10	20	48
3 SUSSEX.									
67 RYE:									
UNMARRIED	M.	3644	2227	563	381	238	100	68	34
	F.	3461	2270	477	282	214	91	70	35
MARRIED	M.	2007	.	1	83	408	501	435	341
	F.	2115	.	12	136	579	404	405	310
WIDOWED	M.	268	.	.	2	6	16	34	54
	F.	465	.	1	.	20	43	62	113
68 HASTINGS:									
UNMARRIED	M.	13007	8209	2058	1338	859	254	105	79
	F.	18783	8165	3178	2543	2258	1111	744	465
MARRIED	M.	7315	.	9	418	2113	1968	1418	962
	F.	7865	.	36	630	2424	2094	1396	866
WIDOWED	M.	680	.	.	7	47	72	114	132
	F.	2283	.	.	11	125	326	407	548
69 BATTLE:									
UNMARRIED	M.	4579	2904	700	440	290	102	62	39
	F.	4314	2794	561	371	312	106	67	58
MARRIED	M.	2489	.	4	97	583	816	534	408
	F.	2464	.	16	176	644	637	477	357
WIDOWED	M.	284	.	.	.	15	23	40	60
	F.	380	.	.	1	8	31	54	95
70 EASTBOURNE:									
UNMARRIED	M.	8221	4832	1565	984	674	213	73	47
	F.	9516	4695	1678	1245	963	400	250	152
MARRIED	M.	4368	.	9	286	1275	1158	784	544
	F.	4302	.	24	405	1372	1130	729	451
WIDOWED	M.	306	.	.	3	20	40	76	70
	F.	953	.	.	4	58	128	188	237
71 HAILSHAM:									
UNMARRIED	M.	4271	2690	681	379	259	105	79	37
	F.	3774	2609	506	265	197	78	54	38
MARRIED	M.	2319	.	2	117	557	564	440	370
	F.	2321	.	13	180	642	583	440	307
WIDOWED	M.	306	.	.	.	15	21	46	63
	F.	412	.	.	1	21	32	65	99
72 TICEHURST:									
UNMARRIED	M.	5311	3351	819	525	334	130	76	48
	F.	5403	3304	698	557	413	177	107	63
MARRIED	M.	2825	.	1	114	717	683	670	447
	F.	2841	.	18	168	747	762	546	377
WIDOWED	M.	322	.	.	.	14	32	40	57
	F.	517	.	.	2	22	67	78	97
73 UCKFIELD:									
UNMARRIED	M.	6348	4322	1034	660	387	144	80	62
	F.	6015	4034	784	453	350	140	98	61
MARRIED	M.	3348	.	5	164	846	810	652	527
	F.	3403	.	29	282	932	855	635	429
WIDOWED	M.	433	.	.	2	18	43	61	86
	F.	551	.	.	1	17	44	56	154
74 EAST GRINSTEAD:									
UNMARRIED	M.	6181	3571	911	655	507	240	155	91
	F.	5484	3619	740	444	309	140	87	54
MARRIED	M.	3051	.	3	108	784	763	640	426
	F.	3049	.	10	190	885	785	607	367
WIDOWED	M.	343	.	.	2	15	30	41	32
	F.	473	.	.	.	11	51	80	113
75 CUCKFIELD:									
UNMARRIED	M.	7660	4548	1252	736	567	240	162	100
	F.	6874	4365	954	855	516	218	130	75
MARRIED	M.	3759	.	5	174	948	947	770	529
	F.	3730	.	22	278	1057	938	721	468
WIDOWED	M.	434	.	.	1	23	34	61	95
	F.	686	.	.	3	31	84	113	167
76 LEWES:									
UNMARRIED	M.	10982	6158	1672	1356	978	261	230	134
	F.	9448	5766	1318	816	724	311	233	158
MARRIED	M.	5499	.	4	256	1363	1439	1100	818
	F.	6231	.	28	381	1415	1407	1016	684
WIDOWED	M.	687	[illegible]						

Table 8 *continued.*—CONDITION as to MARRIAGE and AGES of MALES and FEMALES in REGISTRATION DISTRICTS.

REGISTRATION DISTRICT.		ALL AGES.	Under 15 Years.	15–	20–	25–	35–	45–	55–	65 and upw^ds.
SUSSEX—*cont.*										
BRIGHTON:										
UNMARRIED	M.	28975	15809	4062	2887	1844	634	326	206	133
	F.	34302	15917	5881	4369	3802	1750	1184	770	620
MARRIED	M.	15771	.	28	1026	4464	4114	3047	1974	1131
	F.	16425	.	139	1501	5009	4318	2980	1707	783
WIDOWED	M.	1572	.	2	9	36	192	308	868	647
	F.	4946	.	.	16	256	712	1013	1243	1707
STEYNING:										
UNMARRIED	M.	13627	8234	2219	1625	1015	314	143	99	78
	F.	17022	8114	2563	2180	1921	865	518	335	235
MARRIED	M.	7837	.	7	438	2190	2070	1472	1027	633
	F.	7983	.	38	646	2470	2059	1467	687	400
WIDOWED	M.	627	.	.	.	38	60	117	124	288
	F.	2013	.	.	7	113	267	392	484	759
HORSHAM:										
UNMARRIED	M.	7636	4853	1097	653	479	167	138	82	61
	F.	6766	4251	936	604	489	199	127	86	56
MARRIED	M.	3702	.	3	159	800	964	749	563	383
	F.	3742	.	29	269	1096	977	748	462	242
WIDOWED	M.	406	.	.	1	13	39	57	102	194
	F.	720	.	.	.	27	88	105	149	351
PETWORTH:										
UNMARRIED	M.	2987	1820	446	283	280	94	64	40	25
	F.	2771	1810	366	287	170	73	42	43	24
MARRIED	M.	1632	.	.	54	212	416	347	304	199
	F.	1627	.	3	84	300	395	359	247	138
WIDOWED	M.	239	.	.	1	9	12	35	42	141
	F.	339	.	.	2	11	29	45	61	191
THAKEHAM:										
UNMARRIED	M.	2639	1597	457	257	192	68	46	26	18
	F.	2380	1565	297	219	152	72	33	24	18
MARRIED	M.	1390	.	3	35	305	357	300	244	140
	F.	1378	.	10	79	358	344	273	191	123
WIDOWED	M.	198	.	.	1	8	11	21	55	102
	F.	230	.	.	2	12	24	35	69	138
EAST PRESTON:										
UNMARRIED	M.	7389	4796	1231	706	462	179	113	68	55
	F.	8733	4716	1367	995	702	369	230	168	130
MARRIED	M.	4725	.	1	188	1029	1098	807	617	394
	F.	4266	.	11	298	1172	1174	801	528	282
WIDOWED	M.	480	.	.	.	17	35	57	98	283
	F.	1101	.	.	4	55	144	187	225	486
WESTHAMPNETT:										
UNMARRIED	M.	5797	3551	876	660	431	171	98	89	51
	F.	5868	3883	832	511	403	213	130	98	98
MARRIED	M.	3375	.	1	102	721	836	721	559	435
	F.	3414	.	10	213	820	868	684	486	335
WIDOWED	M.	445	.	.	2	22	38	58	77	253
	F.	754	.	.	2	22	78	119	163	370
CHICHESTER:										
UNMARRIED	M.	2697	1458	484	308	247	112	47	24	17
	F.	2793	1474	462	303	249	112	82	58	52
MARRIED	M.	1235	.	1	42	309	353	249	172	118
	F.	1273	.	7	78	377	352	231	138	89
WIDOWED	M.	175	.	.	1	13	27	21	42	72
	F.	398	.	.	.	10	38	76	96	178
MIDHURST:										
UNMARRIED	M.	4471	2719	671	418	358	159	87	58	30
	F.	3967	2328	624	339	222	108	68	43	35
MARRIED	M.	2397	.	1	88	546	633	482	388	259
	F.	2377	.	12	185	617	583	494	317	189
WIDOWED	M.	302	.	.	2	11	26	38	70	157
	F.	419	.	.	1	18	33	53	103	211
WESTBOURNE:										
UNMARRIED	M.	2306	1414	308	229	153	58	39	22	23
	F.	2148	1397	277	200	138	50	37	19	30
MARRIED	M.	1247	.	.	34	248	336	269	204	156
	F.	1284	.	3	75	393	336	262	163	122
WIDOWED	M.	189	.	.	.	4	10	26	39	110
	F.	246	.	.	1	13	22	41	53	116
HAMPSHIRE.										
HAVANT:										
UNMARRIED	M.	2523	1048	347	225	156	67	39	25	26
	F.	2720	1611	438	220	205	92	59	38	48
MARRIED	M.	1446	.	.	48	340	381	256	248	168
	F.	1462	.	6	83	404	375	298	191	98
WIDOWED	M.	164	.	.	.	8	19	27	36	74
	F.	355	.	.	.	9	40	58	73	175
PORTSEA ISLAND:										
UNMARRIED	M.	39174	22838	5964	4866	3856	1265	509	240	136
	F.	36882	22337	6236	3892	2340	924	466	377	301
MARRIED	M.	21408	.	25	1047	5680	6134	4293	2863	1387
	F.	23975	.	246	2350	7394	6024	3938	2283	540
WIDOWED	M.	1835	.	1	7	114	243	335	454	681
	F.	5848	.	2	33	388	832	1128	1418	1847
ALVERSTOKE:										
UNMARRIED	M.	7985	3710	1251	1865	1121	292	87	50	39
	F.	5627	3629	799	468	329	110	82	40	70
MARRIED	M.	3367	.	3	118	789	997	708	478	264
	F.	3552	.	32	357	1080	932	626	363	183
WIDOWED	M.	370	.	.	.	14	57	62	75	182
	F.	846	.	.	5	57	163	148	210	313

REGISTRATION DISTRICT.		ALL AGES.	Under 15 Years.	15–	20–	25–	35–	45–	55–	65 and upw^ds.
4 **HAMPSHIRE**—*cont.*										
90 FAREHAM:										
UNMARRIED	M.	5250	3008	806	524	492	210	114	91	67
	F.	4986	2826	675	476	408	202	167	107	82
MARRIED	M.	2724	.	.	85	508	710	590	469	302
	F.	2868	.	10	191	710	716	614	398	211
WIDOWED	M.	332	.	.	.	11	22	41	82	170
	F.	672	.	.	.	27	64	119	159	301
91 ISLE OF WIGHT:										
UNMARRIED	M.	21211	12408	3242	2356	1576	600	280	203	146
	F.	23475	12592	3681	2707	2166	1012	589	380	320
MARRIED	M.	12456	.	13	439	2297	3462	2358	1820	1167
	F.	12370	.	39	805	3482	3201	2149	1480	792
WIDOWED	M.	1265	.	.	5	61	111	198	268	622
	F.	2855	.	.	7	147	345	523	677	1147
92 LYMINGTON:										
UNMARRIED	M.	3693	2300	583	377	219	73	62	28	21
	F.	3952	2260	630	375	327	138	70	65	56
MARRIED	M.	2072	.	1	71	461	461	460	351	247
	F.	2132	.	9	181	514	511	477	261	170
WIDOWED	M.	277	.	.	.	10	22	42	57	146
	F.	525	.	.	1	23	45	98	126	222
93 CHRISTCHURCH:										
UNMARRIED	M.	7650	4675	1184	839	574	163	82	48	44
	F.	11255	4721	1916	1780	1538	632	412	183	123
MARRIED	M.	4488	.	3	202	1277	1165	813	626	352
	F.	4619	.	29	620	1470	1233	823	534	217
WIDOWED	M.	381	.	.	3	28	49	68	66	167
	F.	1162	.	1	6	73	166	221	330	365
94 RINGWOOD:										
UNMARRIED	M.	1666	1031	208	164	112	43	22	18	15
	F.	1696	1040	220	183	97	46	44	25	11
MARRIED	M.	932	.	1	36	201	237	184	162	111
	F.	941	.	4	57	243	231	186	141	78
WIDOWED	M.	122	.	.	.	3	8	14	29	68
	F.	201	.	.	1	3	10	28	53	97
95 FORDINGBRIDGE:										
UNMARRIED	M.	1916	1209	323	171	108	34	29	20	25
	F.	1748	1106	266	154	109	47	29	25	12
MARRIED	M.	1098	.	.	46	235	228	209	212	148
	F.	1102	.	4	82	270	244	223	180	103
WIDOWED	M.	141	.	.	.	6	16	11	30	78
	F.	229	.	1	.	9	14	35	59	111
96 NEW FOREST:										
UNMARRIED	M.	4095	2451	863	418	387	181	63	35	27
	F.	3818	2376	568	369	279	132	99	48	37
MARRIED	M.	2251	.	1	83	505	546	460	385	276
	F.	2281	.	16	141	565	569	471	387	188
WIDOWED	M.	263	.	.	1	9	25	30	47	132
	F.	513	.	.	1	21	49	80	133	232
97 SOUTHAMPTON:										
UNMARRIED	M.	15270	9129	2385	1769	1182	411	218	109	67
	F.	15591	9240	2791	1635	1017	429	227	178	163
MARRIED	M.	8963	.	12	518	2432	2360	1884	1160	577
	F.	9842	.	79	977	2985	2600	1816	982	412
WIDOWED	M.	860	.	.	5	41	108	171	210	331
	F.	2457	.	2	12	141	316	508	684	894
98 SOUTH STONEHAM:										
UNMARRIED	M.	12456	7786	1878	1398	914	287	114	62	47
	F.	12697	7746	1888	1501	871	337	204	159	101
MARRIED	M.	6820	.	3	305	1757	1884	1319	985	578
	F.	7225	.	46	547	2092	2008	1328	817	382
WIDOWED	M.	586	.	.	1	24	51	81	146	283
	F.	1575	.	.	6	80	205	291	392	601
99 ROMSEY:										
UNMARRIED	M.	3243	1983	548	319	193	73	56	47	25
	F.	3110	1979	415	272	197	80	47	55	35
MARRIED	M.	1814	.	.	78	404	433	385	320	184
	F.	1824	.	3	148	467	443	398	265	122
WIDOWED	M.	225	.	.	2	5	22	30	47	117
	F.	386	.	.	1	15	37	66	82	185
100 STOCKBRIDGE:										
UNMARRIED	M.	2199	1351	307	213	118	55	37	23	25
	F.	1931	1250	277	157	121	54	34	16	22
MARRIED	M.	1230	.	.	43	256	293	276	225	137
	F.	1232	.	6	79	268	387	282	182	37
WIDOWED	M.	151	.	1	.	4	12	24	31	79
	F.	229	.	.	.	9	21	25	53	121
101 WINCHESTER:										
UNMARRIED	M.	10026	5449	1914	1199	845	310	155	90	64
	F.	9353	5818	1490	946	789	350	180	160	124
MARRIED	M.	4951	.	3	204	1130	1314	996	817	487
	F.	6036	.	19	846	1421	1260	991	685	318
WIDOWED	M.	512	.	.	2	21	51	72	107	259
	F.	1272	.	1	3	60	149	211	300	548

Table 8 *continued.*—Condition as to Marriage and Ages of Males and Females in Registration Districts.

Registration District.		All Ages.	Under 15 Years.	15–	20–	25–	35–	45–	55–	65 and upw^{ds}.
4 HAMPSHIRE —*cont.*										
102 DROXFORD:										
Unmarried	M.	3379	1939	531	347	271	97	50	58	57
	F.	3279	2057	422	232	243	96	65	46	58
Married	M.	1972	.	1	71	408	433	404	363	292
	F.	1980	.	16	123	480	446	422	320	192
Widowed	M.	218	.	.	.	5	27	32	33	118
	F.	368	.	.	.	9	25	72	74	173
103 CATHERINGTON:										
Unmarried	M.	856	499	159	86	59	28	13	5	7
	F.	799	479	133	80	62	22	11	5	7
Married	M.	470	.	.	15	86	89	113	82	75
	F.	478	.	1	26	108	103	109	79	52
Widowed	M.	61	.	.	.	4	4	8	13	32
	F.	83	.	.	.	2	8	17	19	37
104 PETERSFIELD:										
Unmarried	M.	3094	1860	402	329	207	93	50	38	34
	F.	3022	1947	416	261	202	96	48	26	32
Married	M.	1790	.	.	79	397	429	359	304	238
	F.	1788	.	6	141	436	440	359	263	143
Widowed	M.	215	.	.	.	8	17	28	40	113
	F.	348	.	.	2	17	32	51	83	183
105 ALRESFORD:										
Unmarried	M.	2129	1276	367	222	156	57	48	34	29
	F.	2102	1344	305	175	137	57	34	26	23
Married	M.	1187	.	.	33	267	291	267	187	142
	F.	1183	.	6	78	278	316	239	165	102
Widowed	M.	144	.	.	.	3	15	12	41	73
	F.	222	.	.	.	10	19	31	62	100
106 ALTON:										
Unmarried	M.	4668	2929	787	486	268	108	61	44	35
	F.	4527	2092	610	344	261	119	62	57	42
Married	M.	2580	.	.	101	558	600	540	401	280
	F.	2614	.	6	183	646	712	510	340	214
Widowed	M.	310	.	.	2	7	34	54	62	151
	F.	506	.	1	3	21	43	73	125	243
107 HARTLEY-WINTNEY:										
Unmarried	M.	8238	3757	1404	1800	990	205	80	46	47
	F.	5449	3487	737	507	371	139	92	64	52
Married	M.	3303	.	4	135	803	842	694	609	316
	F.	3288	.	23	273	853	815	685	462	190
Widowed	M.	367	.	.	.	14	32	57	79	185
	F.	581	.	.	5	37	65	100	122	253
108 BASINGSTOKE:										
Unmarried	M.	6032	3660	981	592	444	153	91	61	51
	F.	5636	3591	765	526	339	168	87	56	50
Married	M.	3266	.	.	130	779	852	647	481	366
	F.	3271	.	14	213	881	826	656	430	251
Widowed	M.	383	.	.	1	11	33	55	75	208
	F.	687	.	.	.	25	61	83	153	367
109 WHITCHURCH:										
Unmarried	M.	1704	1068	238	183	118	31	25	16	18
	F.	1560	987	219	144	102	35	28	20	15
Married	M.	935	.	1	51	210	212	191	158	112
	F.	943	.	8	81	233	236	186	146	79
Widowed	M.	122	.	1	.	2	7	18	29	65
	F.	194	.	.	.	8	20	23	39	98
110 ANDOVER:										
Unmarried	M.	4809	2868	788	481	340	126	90	57	40
	F.	4620	2836	699	433	299	124	93	65	73
Married	M.	2693	.	3	102	569	626	643	473	277
	F.	2603	.	8	171	653	655	612	403	185
Widowed	M.	347	.	.	.	15	23	47	88	168
	F.	544	.	.	.	22	38	79	131	274
111 KINGSCLERE:										
Unmarried	M.	2632	1640	451	221	183	64	50	33	21
	F.	2460	1064	509	196	153	68	44	14	12
Married	M.	1467	.	.	52	277	340	334	275	182
	F.	1479	.	6	91	323	377	324	227	131
Widowed	M.	186	.	.	.	11	17	30	31	98
	F.	258	.	.	1	9	26	43	61	158
5 BERKSHIRE.										
112 NEWBURY:										
Unmarried	M.	6120	3745	1010	655	372	127	85	51	56
	F.	6630	3905	1050	643	477	233	134	99	92
Married	M.	3636	.	3	156	892	872	763	509	441
	F.	3672	.	16	258	885	902	773	508	329
Widowed	M.	452	.	.	1	17	35	54	110	235
	F.	817	.	.	1	41	57	128	187	403

Registration District.		All Ages	Under 15 Years	15–	20–	25–	35–	45–	55–	65 and upw^{ds}.
5 BERKSHIRE —*cont.*										
113 HUNGERFORD:										
Unmarried	M.	5490	3338	987	511	240	136	73	44	[illegible]
	F.	5016	3280	683	417	268	142	96	59	[illegible]
Married	M.	3123	.	1	127	648	684	683	573	[illegible]
	F.	3130	.	9	222	602	728	672	607	[illegible]
Widowed	M.	345	.	.	2	11	21	51	81	[illegible]
	F.	662	.	.	3	13	57	90	157	[illegible]
114 FARINGDON:										
Unmarried	M.	4166	2609	881	378	238	105	64	43	[illegible]
	F.	4005	2641	515	313	254	123	70	46	[illegible]
Married	M.	2316	.	2	86	463	577	505	385	[illegible]
	F.	2350	.	12	130	551	565	533	362	[illegible]
Widowed	M.	296	.	.	1	8	26	49	63	[illegible]
	F.	534	.	.	2	13	39	78	146	[illegible]
115 ABINGDON:										
Unmarried	M.	6227	3918	1123	603	323	119	65	43	[illegible]
	F.	6111	3746	892	635	415	186	98	79	[illegible]
Married	M.	3378	.	5	183	836	772	682	528	[illegible]
	F.	3387	.	14	214	847	836	657	474	[illegible]
Widowed	M.	461	.	.	.	16	41	64	93	[illegible]
	F.	809	.	.	3	32	88	124	190	[illegible]
116 WANTAGE:										
Unmarried	M.	5592	3350	974	546	308	137	92	60	[illegible]
	F.	4739	3133	674	396	282	115	64	42	[illegible]
Married	M.	2950	.	2	126	662	678	600	523	[illegible]
	F.	2916	.	18	190	716	693	600	444	[illegible]
Widowed	M.	381	.	.	.	9	35	58	83	[illegible]
	F.	582	.	.	2	16	44	88	146	[illegible]
117 WALLINGFORD:										
Unmarried	M.	4520	2809	667	390	325	144	88	56	[illegible]
	F.	4238	2591	565	377	304	168	98	54	61
Married	M.	2413	.	3	82	475	622	538	381	318
	F.	2470	.	16	121	578	640	517	368	[illegible]
Widowed	M.	310	.	.	.	10	26	34	59	181
	F.	536	.	.	2	17	48	101	129	239
118 BRADFIELD:										
Unmarried	M.	5773	3419	1043	603	400	142	82	47	[illegible]
	F.	5192	3399	677	448	347	160	81	53	[illegible]
Married	M.	3088	.	1	125	709	781	634	489	340
	F.	3080	.	15	221	793	799	597	410	[illegible]
Widowed	M.	315	.	.	2	11	29	45	62	[illegible]
	F.	524	.	.	.	10	43	70	127	[illegible]
119 READING:										
Unmarried	M.	13077	7739	2120	1695	971	290	134	75	[illegible]
	F.	13364	7880	2145	1387	935	408	283	173	[illegible]
Married	M.	7478	.	9	432	2356	2026	1401	731	[illegible]
	F.	7467	.	38	699	2449	1974	1292	669	[illegible]
Widowed	M.	653	.	.	6	37	79	116	150	[illegible]
	F.	1460	.	.	3	74	175	279	337	[illegible]
120 WOKINGHAM:										
Unmarried	M.	6120	3862	977	583	374	144	73	55	[illegible]
	F.	6005	3843	840	534	480	181	120	86	[illegible]
Married	M.	3387	.	3	143	877	880	713	490	[illegible]
	F.	3438	.	16	221	986	927	682	410	[illegible]
Widowed	M.	332	.	.	1	14	25	43	64	[illegible]
	F.	640	.	.	.	24	60	129	162	[illegible]
121 COOKHAM:										
Unmarried	M.	5086	3148	792	504	371	136	81	51	[illegible]
	F.	5273	3078	778	537	441	196	108	88	[illegible]
Married	M.	2853	.	2	132	725	736	575	418	[illegible]
	F.	2843	.	16	198	770	755	563	337	204
Widowed	M.	302	.	.	1	8	27	46	64	[illegible]
	F.	589	.	.	1	25	62	93	164	[illegible]
122 EASTHAMPSTEAD:										
Married	M.	4473	2325	1030	421	322	164	101	68	[illegible]
	F.	3567	2209	454	334	315	115	71	41	[illegible]
Unmarried	M.	2043	.	2	71	409	675	440	360	[illegible]
	F.	2010	.	6	140	549	561	419	221	[illegible]
Widowed	M.	250	.	.	1	9	26	44	61	[illegible]
	F.	323	.	.	.	14	39	70	75	[illegible]
123 WINDSOR:										
Unmarried	M.	10260	5597	1544	1518	1076	300	104	55	[illegible]
	F.	9675	5296	1549	1043	910	394	247	138	[illegible]
Married	M.	5155	.	4	222	1452	1409	1037	658	[illegible]
	F.	5241	.	16	373	1583	1464	977	590	[illegible]
Widowed	M.	467	.	.	3	44	59	70	109	[illegible]
	F.	1194	.	.	7	57	147	232	289	462

'able 9.—CONDITION as to MARRIAGE and AGES of MALES and FEMALES in each URBAN SANITARY DISTRICT of which the POPULATION EXCEEDS 50,000 PERSONS.

[U]RBAN SANITARY DISTRICT.		ALL AGES.	Under 15 Years.	15–	20–	25–	35–	45–	55–	65 and upw^{ds}.
[..]DON:										
UNMARRIED	M.	21662	13334	3265	2425	1599	830	250	140	113
	F.	27980	14227	4517	3762	2912	1117	659	416	370
MARRIED	M.	12462	.	13	612	3534	3695	2369	1476	758
	F.	12679	.	82	1041	4110	3590	2271	1116	489
WIDOWED	M.	1080	.	.	6	52	136	186	236	470
	F.	3084	.	2	12	156	491	640	757	1116
[..]HTON:										
UNMARRIED	M.	28291	17160	4449	3178	2147	671	340	209	137
	F.	37096	17361	6377	4727	4049	1874	1253	811	648
MARRIED	M.	17255	.	29	1139	4979	4478	3292	2114	1224
	F.	17980	.	135	1054	5606	4679	3222	1850	835
WIDOWED	M.	1650	.	2	9	91	207	278	384	679
	F.	5280	.	.	17	273	752	1077	1327	1834

URBAN SANITARY DISTRICT.		ALL AGES.	Under 15 Years.	15–	20–	25–	35–	45–	55–	65 and upw^{ds}.
PORTSMOUTH:										
UNMARRIED	M.	39158	22324	3903	4856	3866	1265	600	230	136
	F.	36874	22333	6234	3891	2348	924	466	377	301
MARRIED	M.	21404	.	25	1047	5659	6131	4292	2863	1387
	F.	23071	.	246	2349	7393	6022	3988	2283	840
WIDOWED	M.	1885	.	1	7	114	243	335	454	681
	F.	5647	.	2	32	388	832	1128	1418	1846
SOUTHAMPTON:										
UNMARRIED	M.	17314	10484	2708	1971	1287	440	235	115	74
	F.	17831	10655	3034	1852	1150	482	271	203	184
MARRIED	M.	10116	.	12	572	2722*	2722	2109	1312	667
	F.	11072	.	78	1073	3327	2971	3042	1112	469
WIDOWED	M.	952	.	.	5	45	118	189	231	363
	F.	2766	.	2	12	154	359	571	664	1004

Table 10.—OCCUPATIONS of MALES and FEMALES in the SOUTH-EASTERN DIVISION and its REGISTRATION COUNTIES, and in each URBAN SANITARY DISTRICT of which the POPULATION exceeds 50,000 PERSONS.

OCCUPATIONS.	SOUTH-EASTERN COUNTIES.		REGISTRATION COUNTIES. 1. SURREY. (Extra-metn.)		2. KENT. (Extra-metn.)		3. SUSSEX.		4. HAMPSHIRE.	
	Males.	Females.	Males.	Females.	Males.	Females.	Males.	Females.	Males.	Females.
TOTAL	1208550	1278826	219076	241978	350615	367912	234248	259946	281810	294099
I. PROFESSIONAL CLASS.										
1. PERSONS ENGAGED IN THE GENERAL OR LOCAL GOVERNMENT OF THE COUNTRY.										
1. National Government.										
Peer, M.P., Privy Councillor (not otherwise described)	80	.	14	.	19	.	26	.	16	.
Civil Service (officers and clerks)	2787	379	765	65	874	101	293	45	693	101
Civil Service (messengers, &c.)	2119	29	485	5	517	4	415	8	456	7
Prison Officer, &c.	861	117	107	93	284	8	41	4	358	8
2. Local Government.										
Police	3184	.	789	.	922	.	506	.	755	.
Municipal, Parish, Union, District, Officer	1237	344	190	47	325	96	286	79	295	88
Other Local or County Official	881	.	123	.	225	.	197	.	220	.
3. East Indian and Colonial Service.										
East Indian and Colonial Service	85	.	22	.	21	.	10	.	8	.
2. PERSONS ENGAGED IN THE DEFENCE OF THE COUNTRY.										
1. Army (at Home).										
Army Officer (effective or retired)	3765	.	859	.	833	.	478	.	1009	.
Soldier and Non-commissioned Officer	25527	.	7959	.	7561	.	468	.	8154	.
Militia, Yeomanry, Volunteers	2548	.	454	.	646	.	458	.	735	.
Army Pensioner	1479	3	201	1	414	2	190	.	546	.
2. Navy (ashore or in port).										
Navy Officer (effective or retired)	1508	.	96	.	301	.	101	.	775	.
Seaman, R.N.	7184	.	11	.	2030	.	444	.	4695	.
Royal Marines (officers and men)	5565	.	8	.	2531	.	47	.	2976	.
Navy Pensioner	3696	8	88	.	777	6	286	.	2571	2
3. PERSONS ENGAGED IN PROFESSIONAL OCCUPATIONS (WITH THEIR IMMEDIATE SUBORDINATES).										
1. Clerical Profession.										
Clergyman (Established Church)	3182	.	401	.	801	.	736	.	735	.
Roman Catholic Priest	204	.	30	.	60	.	49	.	37	.
Minister, Priest, of other religious bodies	890	.	156	.	236	.	190	.	222	.
Missionary, Scripture Reader, Itinerant Preacher	297	142	42	37	96	31	52	26	76	38
Nun, Sister of Charity	.	548	.	91	.	97	.	165	.	50
Theological Student	212	.	64	.	69	.	28	.	25	.
Church, Chapel, Cemetery—Officer, Servant	508	136	80	38	137	42	97	23	119	23
2. Legal Profession.										
Barrister, Solicitor	2309	.	887	.	545	.	474	.	336	.
Law Student	179	.	54	.	44	.	36	.	25	.
Law Clerk, and others connected with Law	1832	6	440	2	443	1	397	.	322	3
3. Medical Profession.										
Physician, Surgeon, General Practitioner	1834	2	380	1	485	.	435	.	388	1
Dentist	855	.	79	.	76	.	108	.	67	.
Medical Student, Assistant	513	4	158	2	132	1	99	1	102	.
Midwife	.	248	.	37	.	78	.	26	.	69
Subordinate Medical Service	151	4632	32	889	45	1331	29	957	33	1007
4. Teachers.										
Schoolmaster	4414	11412	828	1757	1229	2859	801	2784	902	2813
Teacher, Professor, Lecturer	1089	4812	243	1586	209	1528	344	868	182	628
School Service, and others concerned in Teaching	120	202	25	62	35	69	27	26	23	10
5. Literary and Scientific Persons.										
Author, Editor, Journalist	316	70	118	18	63	15	70	23	44	12
Reporter, Short-hand Writer	620	1	51	.	35	1	51	.	46	.
Persons engaged in Scientific Pursuits	82	.	31	.	18	.	13	.	16	.
Literary, Scientific, Institution, Service, &c.	84	18	28	8	25	2	12	7	11	1
6. Engineers and Surveyors.										
Civil Engineer	788	.	282	.	209	.	189	.	94	.
Mining Engineer	19	.	8	.	7	.	2	.	3	.
Land, House, Ship, Surveyor	760	.	183	.	125	.	118	.	275	.
7. Artists.										
Painter (artist)	643	217	252	65	103	32	136	67	110	85
Engraver (artist)	119	8	30	1	18	.	9	.	49	1
Sculptor	46	.	18	.	10	.	10	.	4	.
Architect	834	.	209	.	158	.	179	.	131	.
Musician, Music Master	1540	1253	308	241	350	321	431	309	331	297
Art Student	143	89	37	39	20	12	27	22	40	14
Photographer	801	201	161	54	194	35	207	66	182	51
Actor	116	120	27	35	26	22	32	35	24	21
Art, Music, Theatre, Service	54	16	6	.	2	5	24	3	15	6

NOTE.—Persons returned as engaged in more than one occupation have been referred to the one that appeared to be of most importance; or, if there was no difference in this respect, to the one first given by the person in his or her return. In some cases special rules have been followed; e.g., "Clergyman and Schoolmaster" in combination has always been referred to "Schoolmaster"; a Member of Parliament or Peer engaged in any branch of commerce or industry has always been referred to this latter, not to "Peer, M.P."

The numbers returned under any heading include Labourers, Apprentices, and Assistants, as well as Masters, but not Clerks, Messengers, Errand boys, Porters, or Watchmen, for which occupations there are special headings. Civil, Military, and Naval Clerks, Law, Bank, Insurance, and Railway Clerks, and Government and Railway Porters, are, however, exceptions to this rule. Many young persons, being Apprentices or Assistants, have therefore been referred to occupations usually followed by adults. Women also, chiefly widows or orphans carrying on the business of their deceased husbands or fathers, will sometimes be found under occupations commonly followed by men only.

Persons returned as *retired* from any business have not been referred to that business. Inmates of workhouses have been referred to their trades, unless their age or infirmities showed that they were past work. But persons who might be supposed to be only temporarily separated from their usual employment, such as Prisoners, and Patients in General Hospitals, have been classed under their usual occupations.

In some cases, for convenience of space, the male designation, e.g., "Schoolmaster," alone is given, instead of "Schoolmaster, Schoolmistress."

Table 10 *continued*.—OCCUPATIONS of MALES and FEMALES in the SOUTH-EASTERN DIVISION and its REGISTRATION COUNTIES, and in each URBAN SANITARY DISTRICT of which the POPULATION exceeds 50,000 PERSONS.

OCCUPATIONS.	SOUTH-EASTERN COUNTIES.		REGISTRATION COUNTIES. 1. SURREY. (*Extra-metn.*)		2. KENT. (*Extra-metn.*)		3. SUSSEX.		4. HAMPSHIRE.	
	Males.	Females.	Males.	Females.	Males.	Females.	Males.	Females.	Males.	Females.
8. *Persons engaged in Exhibitions, Shows, Games, &c.*										
Performer, Showman, Exhibition, Service	106	31	24	9	19	4	27	8	24	10
Billiard, Cricket, & other Games, Service	310	6	77	3	66	.	70	1	66	1
II. DOMESTIC CLASS.										
4. PERSONS ENGAGED IN DOMESTIC OFFICES OR SERVICES.										
1. *Domestic Service.*										
Domestic Coachman, Groom	11835	.	2622	.	2778	.	2565	.	2422	.
Domestic Gardener	13086	3	3910	2	4425	.	2084	.	2194	1
Domestic Indoor Servant	9723	163948	2144	37588	2138	40272	2165	37405	2080	33935
Lodge, Gate, Park, Keeper (not Government)	178	146	46	42	44	26	26	33	26	21
Inn, Hotel, Servant	3645	2859	709	481	990	782	940	771	609	606
College, Club, Service	257	30	58	8	35	14	36	4	44	8
2. *Other Service.*										
Office Keeper (not Government)	80	89	18	11	25	23	10	25	24	22
Cook (not domestic)	270	360	50	155	46	8	78	113	69	76
Charwoman	.	7734	.	1278	.	2245	.	1738	.	1785
Washing and Bathing Service	465	27621	100	6533	89	6150	182	6085	73	6143
Hospital and Institution Service	735	1600	195	506	199	412	108	276	129	291
Others engaged in Service	138	33	64	21	20	2	17	5	25	3
III. COMMERCIAL CLASS.										
5. PERSONS ENGAGED IN COMMERCIAL OCCUPATIONS.										
1. *Merchants and Agents.*										
Merchant	1076	3	534	2	229	.	204	.	83	1
Broker, Agent, Factor	2297	39	1082	4	569	9	356	14	265	8
Auctioneer, Appraiser, Valuer, House Agent	1106	10	238	2	250	3	267	3	239	2
Accountant	863	15	283	3	195	3	106	4	152	.
Salesman, Buyer (not otherwise described)	79	52	25	15	17	8	15	15	20	5
Commercial Traveller	1714	.	538	.	339	.	324	.	565	.
Commercial Clerk	10022	607	3530	149	2104	158	1560	181	1900	83
Officer of Commercial Company, Guild, Society, &c.	34	.	10	.	7	.	7	.	8	.
2. *Dealers in Money.*										
Banker	173	3	40	.	44	.	41	.	30	3
Bank Service	1563	8	638	5	329	2	220	1	286	.
Bill Discounter, Bill Broker, Finance Agent	60	.	20	.	11	.	15	.	12	.
3. *Persons occupied in Insurance.*										
Life, House, Ship, &c., Insurance Service	1162	13	480	2	320	3	148	3	207	5
6. PERSONS ENGAGED IN CONVEYANCE OF MEN, GOODS, AND MESSAGES.										
1. *On Railways.*										
Railway Engine Driver, Stoker	1240	.	220	.	344	.	306	.	260	.
Railway Guard	569	.	130	.	142	.	152	.	91	.
Pointsman, Level Crossing Man	260	24	45	3	46	4	61	16	55	1
Other Railway Officials and Servants	7258	64	1773	13	1809	22	1309	13	1618	16
2. *On Roads.*										
Toll Collector, Turnpike Gate Keeper	71	29	6	2	11	5	6	7	40	12
Omnibus, Coach, Cab, Owner—Livery Stable Keeper	1081	36	180	12	296	4	356	7	223	8
Cabman, Flyman, Coachman (not domestic)	3739	.	978	.	836	.	988	.	797	.
Carman, Carrier, Carter, Haulier	7852	56	1984	9	2039	18	1604	5	1549	9
Tramway Companies' Service	133	.	15	.	.	.	.	.	101	.
Wheel Chair Proprietor, Attendant, &c.	337	8	8	1	70	.	222	6	36	1
3. *On Canals, Rivers and Seas.*										
Inland Navigation Service	101	8	25	1	25	5	11	1	3	.
Bargeman, Lighterman, Waterman	2758	7	258	3	1919	2	150	.	314	1
Navigation Service (on shore)	176	19	37	1	72	8	86	3	29	7
Seaman (Merchant Service)	13387	.	158	.	6454	.	1429	.	5313	.
Pilot	532	.	1	.	406	.	39	.	83	.
Ship Steward, Cook	774	57	10	1	253	17	57	12	452	26
Boatman on Seas	683	.	.	.	304	.	205	.	174	.
Harbour, Dock, Wharf, Lighthouse, Service	1402	3	39	.	464	2	170	.	711	1
4. *In Storage.*										
Warehouseman (not Manchester)	609	8	207	3	200	.	81	2	95	1
Meter, Weigher	85	.	.	.	39	.	14	.	32	.
5. *In conveying Messages, Porterage, &c.*										
Messenger, Porter, Watchman (not Railway nor Government)	10486	44	1708	9	2291	9	2701	12	2736	9
Telegraph, Telephone, Service	533	165	115	27	138	43	103	43	144	34

Table 10 *continued*.—Occupations of Males and Females in the South-eastern Division and its Registration Counties, and in each Urban Sanitary District of which the Population exceeds 50,000 Persons.

Occupations.	South-Eastern Counties.		Registration Counties. 1. Surrey. (*Extra-metn.*)		2. Kent. (*Extra-metn.*)		3. Sussex.		4. Hampshire.	
	Males.	Females.	Males.	Females.	Males.	Females.	Males.	Females.	Males.	Females.
IV. Agricultural Class.										
7. Persons engaged in Agriculture.										
1. *In Fields and Pastures.*										
Farmer, Grazier	13223	845	1275	75	4068	276	3348	291	2961	203
Farmer's, Grazier's—Son, Grandson, Brother, Nephew*	4015	.	377	.	1256	.	1102	.	831	.
Farm Bailiff	3024	.	485	.	1329	.	796	.	597	.
Agricultural Labourer, Farm Servant, Cottager	124824	3485	13646	412	38901	1147	28654	273	24065	402
Shepherd	4658	.	290	.	958	.	964	.	1481	.
Land Drainage Service (not in towns)	67	.	15	.	21	.	7	.	10	.
Agricultural Machine—Proprietor, Attendant	807	6	41	.	193	.	157	3	265	1
Agricultural Student, Pupil	127	.	8	.	38	.	24	.	46	.
Others engaged in, or connected with, Agriculture	141	9	41	1	21	.	18	1	25	6
2. *In Woods.*										
Woodman	1556	.	101	.	263	.	204	.	735	.
3. *In Gardens.*										
Nurseryman, Seedsman, Florist	1437	83	488	20	337	20	254	27	166	12
Gardener (not domestic)	16247	213	4556	62	3622	70	3319	24	3349	32
8. Persons engaged about Animals.										
1. *About Animals.*										
Horse Proprietor, Breeder, Dealer	185	.	25	.	53	.	34	.	36	.
Groom, Horse-keeper, Horse-breaker	4867	5	983	.	741	2	1092	3	1128	.
Veterinary Surgeon, Farrier	698	.	186	.	168	.	133	.	110	.
Cattle, Sheep, Pig—Dealer, Salesman	436	3	62	.	82	2	58	1	160	.
Drover	200	.	34	.	49	.	37	.	50	.
Gamekeeper	2155	.	351	.	431	.	549	.	548	.
Dog, Bird, Animal—Keeper, Dealer	139	17	20	4	31	2	48	8	28	2
Vermin destroyer	79	.	6	.	31	.	22	.	12	.
Fisherman	3746	5	34	1	1681	3	1471	2	527	.
Knacker, Catsmeat Dealer, &c., &c.	45	.	19	.	10	.	6	.	8	.
V. Industrial Class.										
9. Persons working and dealing in Books, Prints, and Maps.										
1. *Books.*										
Publisher, Bookseller, Librarian	869	227	232	32	217	66	183	50	175	64
Music—Publisher, Seller, Printer	93	20	12	8	22	3	30	4	20	2
Bookbinder	238	108	40	21	81	18	67	36	85	17
Printer	3546	45	815	15	848	8	814	11	750	6
Newspaper Agent, News Room Keeper	328	71	89	17	54	16	73	11	89	22
Others	3	.	2	.	1	.	.	.	.	.
2. *Prints and Maps.*										
Lithographer, Lithographic Printer	113	1	30	.	38	1	18	.	19	.
Copper Plate and Steel Plate Printer	20	.	3	.	4	.	5	.	7	.
Map and Print—Colourer, Seller	36	1	4	.	3	.	4	.	27	1
10. Persons working and dealing in Machines and Implements.										
1. *Machines.*										
Engine, Machine, Maker	2907	10	203	4	778	1	260	2	634	2
Millwright	566	.	82	.	212	.	77	.	155	.
Fitter, Turner (Engine and Machine)	3590	.	194	.	1401	.	422	.	1136	.
Boiler Maker	1476	.	83	.	320	.	209	.	658	.
Spinning and Weaving Machine Maker	3	.	.	.	1	.	.	.	2	.
Agricultural Machine and Implement Maker	189	1	8	.	30	.	26	.	47	1
Domestic Machinery—Maker, Dealer	6	.	3	.	2	.	1	.	.	.
2. *Tools and Implements.*										
Tool Maker, Dealer	53	4	7	.	14	4	8	.	18	.
Cutler, Scissors Maker	173	11	21	1	42	2	32	3	61	4
File Maker	7	.	1	.	1	.	5	.	.	.
Saw Maker	39	.	5	.	8	.	13	.	9	.
Pin Maker	.	.	.	.	.	.	.	.	.	.
Needle Maker	.	.	.	.	.	.	.	.	.	.
Steel Pen Maker	.	.	.	.	.	.	.	.	.	.
Pencil Maker (Wood)	2	.	.	.	2	.	.	.	.	.
Domestic Implement Maker	14	7	9	6	1	1	2	.	2	.
3. *Watches and Philosophical Instruments.*										
Watch Maker, Clock Maker	1757	92	345	2	400	11	366	9	394	66
Philosophical Instrument Maker, Optician	712	3	42	.	29	.	15	3	23	.
Electrical Apparatus Maker	144	1	44	1	56	.	10	.	29	.
Weighing and Measuring Apparatus Maker	87	.	11	.	26	.	9	.	9	.

* Only male relatives living with the farmer or grazier, and therefore presumably engaged in agriculture, are included above.

Table 10 *continued.*—OCCUPATIONS of MALES and FEMALES in the SOUTH-EASTERN DIVISION and its REGISTRATION COUNTIES, and in each URBAN SANITARY DISTRICT of which the POPULATION exceeds 50,000 PERSONS.

OCCUPATIONS.	SOUTH-EASTERN COUNTIES.		REGISTRATION COUNTIES. 1. SURREY. (*Extra-metn.*)		2. KENT. (*Extra-metn.*)		3. SUSSEX.		4. HAMPSHIRE.	
	Males.	Females.	Males.	Females.	Males.	Females.	Males.	Females.	Males.	Females.
4. Surgical Instruments.										
Surgical Instrument Maker	28	6	16	1	5	1	3	3	3	.
5. Arms and Ordnance.										
Gunsmith, Gun Manufacturer	158	5	23	.	48	1	21	1	88	2
Ordnance Manufacturer	20	.	.	.	12	.	.	.	8	.
Sword, Bayonet—Maker, Cutler	8	.	.	.	.	.	4	.	4	.
Others	9	.	.	.	3	.	1	.	4	.
6. Musical Instruments.										
Musical Instrument Maker, Dealer	330	8	65	2	82	2	108	1	57	2
7. Type, Dies, Medals, Coins.										
Type Cutter, Founder	16	.	4	.	5	.	2	.	.	.
Die, Seal, Coin, Medal, Maker	34	.	7	.	3	.	2	.	6	.
8. Tackle for Sports and Games.										
Toy Maker, Dealer	77	168	7	24	15	58	20	37	29	31
Fishing Rod, Tackle, Maker, Dealer	9	5	4	2	.	2	1	.	3	1
Apparatus for other Games, Maker, Dealer	227	6	8	.	208	4	4	.	6	1
11. PERSONS WORKING AND DEALING IN HOUSES, FURNITURE, AND DECORATIONS.										
1. Houses.										
Builder	4493	29	1038	5	1092	4	1069	6	893	12
Carpenter, Joiner	27101	25	5453	8	6691	3	5971	5	6289	6
Bricklayer	22081	9	4761	.	5346	3	5816	3	4166	3
Mason	3430	8	636	3	561	1	506	1	1018	2
Slater, Tiler	231	1	63	.	23	.	41	.	89	1
Plasterer, Whitewasher	3377	4	819	3	620	.	1100	.	531	1
Paperhanger	501	1	107	.	99	1	181	.	86	1
Plumber	3911	27	980	5	1037	8	809	4	736	7
Painter, Glazier	11330	33	2652	8	2737	8	2475	10	2521	5
2. Furniture and Fittings.										
Cabinet Maker, Upholsterer	3269	678	535	142	753	129	750	168	880	159
French Polisher	451	8	72	2	82	.	114	3	136	1
Furniture Broker, Dealer	533	73	102	13	120	14	141	16	131	26
Locksmith, Bellhanger	133	1	21	.	42	.	24	1	26	.
Gas Fitter	1102	4	251	1	257	1	308	.	285	2
House and Shop Fittings—Maker, Dealer	174	4	48	1	28	.	69	1	23	2
Funeral Furniture Maker, Undertaker	107	4	26	4	21	.	32	.	23	.
Others	.	.	.	.	.	.	.	.	.	.
3. House Decorations.										
Wood Carver	84	1	11	.	21	1	26	.	10	.
Carver, Gilder	329	13	54	5	72	1	113	1	77	5
Dealer in Works of Art	61	3	10	1	9	.	20	1	10	1
Figure, Image—Maker, Dealer	31	1	6	1	7	.	8	.	3	.
Animal, Bird, &c., Preserver, Naturalist	101	17	18	2	27	1	30	12	21	1
Artificial Flower Maker	14	33	3	9	4	9	4	10	2	5
12. PERSONS WORKING AND DEALING IN CARRIAGES AND HARNESS.										
1. Carriages.										
Coachmaker	2698	15	497	2	696	7	633	1	556	3
Railway Carriage, Railway Wagon, Maker	227	5	1	.	143	5	67	.	5	.
Wheelwright	3107	11	516	2	970	3	728	3	579	3
Bicycle, Tricycle—Maker, Dealer	68	.	15	.	9	.	16	.	5	.
Others	7	2	1	.	1	1	.	.	1	1
2. Harness.										
Saddler, Harness, Whip, Maker	1865	42	344	7	468	12	378	2	421	16
13. PERSONS WORKING AND DEALING IN SHIPS AND BOATS.										
1. Hull.										
Ship, Boat, Barge, Builder	1335	2	116	.	289	.	90	1	758	1
Shipwright, Ship Carpenter (ashore)	4759	.	11	.	2023	.	223	.	2490	.
2. Masts, Rigging, &c.										
Mast, Yard, Oar, Block, Maker	110	.	7	.	39	.	4	.	67	.
Ship Rigger, Chandler, Fitter	355	4	1	.	131	3	.	.	223	1
Sail Maker	501	6	11	1	194	2	56	1	240	2

Table 10 *continued*.—OCCUPATIONS of MALES and FEMALES in the SOUTH-EASTERN DIVISION and its REGISTRATION COUNTIES, and in each URBAN SANITARY DISTRICT of which the POPULATION exceeds 50,000 PERSONS.

OCCUPATIONS.	SOUTH-EASTERN COUNTIES.		REGISTRATION COUNTIES. 1. SURREY (*Extra-metn.*)		2. KENT. (*Extra-metn.*)		3 SUSSEX.		4. HAMPSHIRE.	
	Males.	Females.	Males.	Females.	Males.	Females.	Males.	Females.	Males.	Females.
14. PERSONS WORKING AND DEALING IN CHEMICALS AND COMPOUNDS.										
1. *Colouring Matter.*										
Dye, Paint, Manufacture	35	10	17	2	15	4	4	3	9	1
Ink, Blacking, Colouring Substance, Manufacture	13	2	6	2	2	.	2	.	.	.
2. *Explosives.*										
Gunpowder, Guncotton, Explosive Substance, Manufacture	274	45	20	.	230	45	.	.	24	.
Fusee, Fireworks, Explosive Article, Manufacture	57	43	47	54	5	9	2	.	3	.
3. *Drugs and other Chemicals and Compounds.*										
Chemist, Druggist	1678	37	317	3	447	9	376	18	397	6
Manufacturing Chemist	178	16	76	6	34	1	24	3	43	5
Alkali Manufacture	8	.	1	.	1	.	1	.	5	.
Drysalter	10	.	4	.	2	.	1	.	3	.
15. PERSONS WORKING AND DEALING IN TOBACCO AND PIPES.										
1. *Tobacco and Pipes.*										
Tobacco Manufacturer, Tobacconist	584	218	150	56	159	61	102	36	110	46
Tobacco Pipe, Snuff Box, &c., Maker	122	13	24	3	56	6	24	.	15	3
16. PERSONS WORKING AND DEALING IN FOOD AND LODGING.										
1. *Board and Lodging.*										
Innkeeper, Hotel Keeper, Publican	6790	1166	1122	182	2076	316	1158	198	1605	326
Lodging, Boarding House, Keeper	1073	6872	59	428	236	1792	617	2351	248	1263
Coffee, Eating House, Keeper	488	230	105	60	116	64	107	47	121	62
2. *Spirituous Drinks.*										
Hop—Merchant, Dealer	76	.	31	.	34	.	6	.	5	.
Maltster	605	3	82	.	128	1	115	.	143	1
Brewer	8112	27	486	3	851	5	601	5	749	11
Beerseller, Ale, Porter, Cider, Dealer	1746	482	312	56	536	131	344	103	454	156
Cellarman	592	3	118	.	105	.	146	2	156	1
Wine, Spirit—Merchant, Agent	910	37	308	19	192	9	201	4	139	5
3. *Food.*										
Milkseller, Dairyman	2962	415	634	46	792	67	676	62	706	305
Cheesemonger, Butterman	107	4	49	2	16	.	24	1	12	.
Butcher, Meat Salesman	7400	243	1403	83	2213	73	1631	48	1498	72
Provision Curer, Dealer	827	51	91	5	57	9	80	18	72	19
Poulterer, Game Dealer	879	45	76	8	85	6	128	15	57	14
Fishmonger	1655	150	293	14	481	56	380	29	322	42
Corn, Flour, Seed—Merchant, Dealer	1257	75	284	14	319	24	237	11	260	12
Corn Miller	2714	26	246	8	749	4	872	8	573	5
Baker	11176	972	1708	136	2561	235	1765	174	2322	175
Confectioner, Pastrycook	1086	761	182	101	236	205	260	206	238	179
Greengrocer, Fruiterer	2379	700	507	88	729	227	521	169	472	171
Mustard, Vinegar, Spice, Pickle—Maker, Dealer	25	9	13	1	4	1	.	.	.	.
Sugar Refiner	138	3	27	1	21	.	18	.	69	1
Grocer, Tea, Coffee, Chocolate—Maker, Dealer	12285	1873	2214	277	3867	412	2730	364	2382	427
Ginger Beer, Mineral Water—Manufacturer, Dealer	481	26	95	1	118	6	143	9	103	4
Others dealing in Food	2	1	1	.	.	.	.	.	1	1
17. PERSONS WORKING AND DEALING IN TEXTILE FABRICS.										
1. *Wool and Worsted.*										
Woolstapler	115	.	14	.	37	.	22	.	39	.
Woollen Cloth Manufacture	34	7	18	3	5	2	4	.	6	.
Wool, Woollen goods—Dyer, Printer	8	.	5	.	3	.	.	.	.	.
Worsted, Stuff, Manufacture	6	17	1	4	1	.	3	.	1	13
Flannel Manufacture	3	.	1	.	2	.	.	.	.	.
Blanket Manufacture	.	.	.	.	.	.	.	.	.	.
Fuller	.	.	.	.	.	.	.	.	.	.
Cloth, Worsted, Stuff, Flannel, Blanket, Dealer	85	2	42	.	13	.	12	.	11	1
Others	2	7	.	.	2	1	.	.	.	1
2. *Silk.*										
Silk, Silk goods, Manufacture	49	30	29	7	61	1	3	2	9	19
Silk Dyer, Printer	183	64	34	.	149	64	.	.	.	.
Ribbon Manufacture	2	3	1	1	15	1	.	.	.	1
Crape, Gauze, Manufacture	2	.	1	.	[illegible]	.	1	.	.	.
Silk Merchant, Dealer	111	16	40	.	33	7	12	1	2	2

Table 10 *continued*.—OCCUPATIONS of MALES and FEMALES in the SOUTH-EASTERN DIVISION and its REGISTRATION COUNTIES, and in each URBAN SANITARY DISTRICT of which the POPULATION exceeds 50,000 Persons.

OCCUPATIONS.	SOUTH-EASTERN COUNTIES.		REGISTRATION COUNTIES. 1. SURREY. (*Extra-metn.*)		2. KENT. (*Extra-metn.*)		3. SUSSEX.		4. HAMPSHIRE.	
	Males.	Females.	Males.	Females.	Males.	Females.	Males.	Females.	Males.	Females.
3. *Cotton and Flax*										
Cotton, Cotton goods, Manufacture	55	45	19	38	11	8	4	.	20	5
Cotton, Calico—Printer, Dyer, Bleacher	15	3	5	.	8	3	1	.	1	.
Cotton, Calico—Warehouseman, Dealer	12	.	7	.	2	.	1	.	1	.
Flax, Linen—Manufacturer, Dealer	89	35	8	.	20	1	7	.	30	24
Lace Manufacturer, Dealer	39	146	12	28	11	24	4	38	11	38
Fustian Manufacturer, Dealer	1	.	1	.	.	.	.	.	.	.
Tape Manufacturer, Dealer	.	.	.	.	.	.	.	.	.	.
Thread Manufacturer, Dealer	.	.	.	.	.	.	.	.	.	.
4. *Hemp and other Fibrous Materials.*										
Hemp, Jute, Cocoa Fibre, Manufacture	34	15	8	.	5	5	15	.	3	7
Rope, Twine, Cord—Maker, Dealer	489	41	17	1	156	21	113	10	164	6
Mat Maker, Seller	43	4	12	1	14	.	8	1	4	2
Net Maker	13	13	2	1	7	7	3	1	.	3
Canvas, Sailcloth, Manufacture	51	8	3	1	1	.	2	.	43	7
Sacking, Sack, Bag—Maker, Dealer	40	22	4	1	12	7	14	.	8	10
Others working and dealing in Hemp	14	5	7	.	2	1	1	.	2	2
5. *Mixed or Unspecified Materials.*										
Weaver (undefined)	34	12	8	1	15	2	5	3	3	8
Dyer, Printer, Scourer, Bleacher, Calenderer (undefined)	297	146	67	29	69	40	65	39	72	21
Factory hand (Textile, undefined)	5	53	1	31	1	7	.	.	3	.
Felt Manufacture	10	3	8	3	2	.	.	.	.	.
Carpet, Rug, Manufacture	69	1	6	1	41	.	10	.	11	.
Manchester Warehouseman	33	.	23	.	7	.	2	.	.	.
Draper, Linen Draper, Mercer	5280	3334	984	558	1463	987	1208	668	1115	809
Fancy Goods (Textile), Manufacturer, Worker, Dealer	79	550	20	130	20	134	25	138	11	118
Trimming Maker, Dealer	12	7	5	1	5	.	2	2	.	4
Embroiderer	2	63	.	11	2	7	.	22	.	9
Others	1	.	1	.	.	.	.	.	.	.
18. PERSONS WORKING AND DEALING IN DRESS.										
1. *Dress.*										
Hatter, Hat Manufacture (not straw)	228	46	51	7	47	4	57	7	68	27
Straw—Hat, Bonnet, Plait, Manufacture	11	157	3	16	2	34	3	31	3	56
Tailor	8146	2738	1367	150	2121	707	1667	255	2073	1041
Milliner, Dressmaker, Staymaker	158	31382	35	8539	18	8162	30	6683	174	9016
Shawl Manufacture	2	.	2	.	.	.	.	.	.	.
Shirt Maker, Seamstress	52	7209	12	1047	14	1884	8	1237	17	1824
Hosiery Manufacture	64	27	57	5	3	.	3	9	.	13
Hosier, Haberdasher	271	77	63	15	70	26	71	13	44	19
Glover, Glove Maker	53	107	9	5	16	14	16	7	7	74
Button Maker, Dealer	8	8	5	2	.	.	.	.	3	1
Shoe, Boot—Maker, Dealer	11681	716	2131	141	3056	157	2943	127	2879	224
Patten, Clog, Maker	10	2	1	1	4	.	4	1	1	.
Wig Maker, Hairdresser	1138	65	322	10	283	16	261	20	267	16
Umbrella, Parasol, Stick—Maker, Dealer	199	73	68	12	50	8	27	24	38	21
Accoutrement Maker	5	7	3	2	.	.	.	.	2	5
Old Clothes Dealer, and others	36	115	11	26	10	33	5	23	9	28
19. PERSONS WORKING AND DEALING IN VARIOUS ANIMAL SUBSTANCES.										
1. *In Grease, Gut, Bone, Horn, Ivory, and Whalebone.*										
Tallow Chandler, Candle, Grease, Manufacture	204	4	40	.	73	3	61	1	23	.
Soap Boiler, Maker	56	1	20	1	14	.	13	.	8	.
Glue, Size, Gelatine, Isinglass—Maker, Dealer	6	3	2	2	3	1	.	.	1	.
Manure Manufacture	30	.	3	.	11	.	5	.	14	.
Bone, Horn, Ivory, Tortoise-shell—Worker, Dealer	30	2	16	.	6	1	6	1	1	.
Comb Maker	3	.	2	.	.	.	1	.	.	.
Others	5	.	1	.	2	.	1	.	1	.
2. *In Skins.*										
Furrier, Skinner	134	36	93	3	12	7	13	13	12	11
Tanner, Fellmonger	837	4	146	.	318	.	168	2	103	1
Currier	820	6	247	1	143	1	79	1	106	3
Leather Goods, Portmanteau, Bag, Strap, &c.—Maker, Dealer	85	8	26	3	14	2	20	.	24	3
Parchment, Vellum—Maker, Dealer	69	.	.	.	.	.	9	.	29	.
3. *In Hair and Feathers.*										
Hair, Bristle—Worker, Dealer	11	3	3	.	2	.	8	3	.	.
Brush, Broom, Maker	366	64	83	5	51	24	59	3	130	25
Quill, Feather—Dresser, Dealer	17	36	4	3	7	11	4	7	2	13

Table 10 *continued*.—Occupations of Males and Females in the South-eastern Division and its Registration Counties, and in each Urban Sanitary District of which the Population exceeds 50,000 Persons.

Occupations.	South-Eastern Counties.		Registration Counties. 1. Surrey. (*Extra-metn.*)		2. Kent. (*Extra-metn.*)		3. Sussex.		4. Hampshire.	
	Males.	Females.	Males.	Females.	Males.	Females.	Males.	Females.	Males.	Females.
20. Persons working and dealing in various Vegetable Substances.										
1. *In Oils, Gums, and Resins.*										
Oil Miller, Oil Cake—Maker, Dealer	315	4	22	.	195	1	30	1	63	2
Oil and Colourman	380	28	136	10	129	3	50	9	39	6
Floor Cloth, Oil Cloth, Manufacture	137	1	109	1	1	.	2	.	1	.
Japanner	22	6	8	1	6	.	5	.	1	.
India Rubber, Gutta Percha—Worker, Dealer	49	7	28	4	8	2	4	.	8	.
Waterproof Goods—Maker, Dealer	34	2	6	.	12	.	10	2	5	.
Others	37	1	25	.	4	.	1	1	4	.
2. *In Cane, Rush, and Straw.*										
Willow, Cane, Rush—Worker, Dealer, Basketmaker	820	160	89	20	271	45	183	28	162	38
Hay, Straw (not plait), Chaff—Cutter, Dealer	143	3	28	1	49	1	19	.	30	.
Thatcher	520	.	21	.	128	.	89	.	210	.
3. *In Wood and Bark.*										
Timber, Wood—Merchant, Dealer	1494	43	242	5	379	21	427	7	336	5
Sawyer	2022	.	387	.	676	.	614	.	846	.
Lath, Wooden Fence, Hurdle, Maker	616	2	86	.	115	1	140	1	105	.
Wood Turner, Box Maker	387	12	54	3	72	3	80	2	105	8
Cooper. Hoop Maker, Bender	1807	13	166	3	839	6	371	.	311	3
Cork, Bark—Cutter, Worker, Dealer	83	6	12	.	12	.	11	4	44	5
Others	13	2	5	2	2	.	3	.	1	.
4. *In Paper.*										
Paper Manufacture	1762	2098	169	197	1819	1723	10	12	118	137
Envelope Maker	8	5	1	1	1	3	1	1	.	.
Stationer, Law Stationer	726	441	193	112	170	111	180	101	125	88
Card, Pattern Card, Maker	14	.	3	.	3	.	4	.	4	.
Paper Stainer	12	1	5	1	1	.	3	.	1	.
Paper Box, Paper Bag, Maker	21	117	6	7	5	20	7	14	3	70
Ticket, Label, Writer	31	1	4	1	5	.	12	.	9	.
Others	125	2	23	.	87	1	22	1	30	.
21. Persons working and dealing in various Mineral Substances.										
1. *Miners.*										
Coal Miner	175	.	16	.	51	.	8	.	96	.
Ironstone Miner	3	.	2	.	.	.	.	.	.	.
Copper Miner	1	.	.	.	.	.	.	.	1	.
Tin Miner	.	.	.	.	.	.	.	.	.	.
Lead Miner	.	.	.	.	.	.	.	.	.	.
Miner in other, or undefined, Minerals	68	.	14	.	14	.	38	.	5	1
Mine Service	32	1	11	.	6	.	8	.	6	.
2. *Coal, Coal Gas, &c.*										
Coal Merchant, Dealer	1485	59	228	13	392	7	286	7	353	13
Coalheaver	1145	.	190	.	417	.	170	.	266	.
Coke, Charcoal, Peat—Cutter, Burner, Dealer	140	3	13	1	56	.	43	2	25	.
Gas Works Service	1533	.	302	.	463	.	345	.	287	.
3. *Stone, Clay, and Road Making.*										
Stone Quarrier	233	.	24	.	165	.	20	.	17	.
Stone Cutter, Dresser, Dealer	225	.	40	.	55	.	58	.	43	.
Slate Quarrier	13	.	12	.	1	.	2	.	.	.
Slate Worker, Dealer	16	.	6	.	1	.	2	.	3	.
Limeburner	561	3	132	2	270	1	76	.	73	.
Clay, Sand, Gravel, Chalk—Labourer, Dealer	496	7	65	.	319	6	108	.	8	1
Fossil, Coprolite—Digger, Dealer	.	1	.	.	.	1	.	.	.	.
Well Sinker, Borer	71	.	18	.	23	.	18	.	10	.
Plaster, Cement, Manufacture	2062	11	7	.	1034	9	12	2	100	.
Brick, Tile—Maker, Burner, Dealer	8244	102	831	3	4209	81	1485	2	1096	9
Paviour	63	.	17	.	18	.	14	.	11	.
Road Contractor, Surveyor, Inspector	102	.	28	.	33	.	21	.	14	.
Road Labourer	912	.	139	.	285	.	235	.	131	.
Railway Contractor	67	.	13	.	23	.	6	.	6	.
Platelayer	1824	.	863	.	598	.	830	.	347	.
Railway Labourer, Navvy	4798	.	1052	.	921	.	1678	.	479	.
Others	29	5	25	1	4	1	.	2	.	1
4. *Earthenware and Glass.*										
Earthenware, China, Porcelain, Manufacture	376	6	82	1	101	.	92	3	62	.
Glass Manufacture	97	2	34	1	21	.	14	.	18	.
Earthenware, China, Glass, Dealer	391	197	85	60	83	42	76	34	103	45
5. *Salt.*										
Salt Maker, Dealer	4	1	.	.	.	.	3	.	1	1

Table 10 *continued.*—OCCUPATIONS of MALES and FEMALES in the SOUTH-EASTERN DIVISION and its REGISTRATION COUNTIES, and in each URBAN SANITARY DISTRICT of which the POPULATION exceeds 50,000 Persons.

OCCUPATIONS.	SOUTH-EASTERN COUNTIES.		REGISTRATION COUNTIES.							
			1. SURREY. (*Extra-metn.*)		2. KENT. (*Extra-metn.*)		3. SUSSEX.		4. HAMPSHIRE.	
	Males.	Females.	Males.	Females.	Males.	Females.	Males.	Females.	Males.	Females.
6. *Water.*										
Waterworks Service	273	.	104	.	61	.	56	.	57	.
Others	14	1	1	.	5	.	2	1	3	.
7. *Precious Metals and Jewellery.*										
Goldsmith, Silversmith, Jeweller	645	68	123	5	144	11	201	20	137	25
Gold, Silver, Beater	21	.	1	.	10	.	7	.	3	.
Lapidary	9	2	.	.	.	.	4	2	4	.
Others	6	3	2	1	3	2	.	.	.	.
8. *Iron and Steel.*										
Blacksmith	10120	71	1308	13	3039	22	1871	13	2777	13
Whitesmith	1264	6	835	4	241	.	264	.	278	2
Nail Manufacture	21	3	1	3	6	.	.	.	5	.
Anchor, Chain, Manufacture	8	.	2	.	3	.	1	.	2	.
Other Iron and Steel Manufactures	2652	3	187	.	870	.	364	1	783	1
Ironmonger, Hardware Dealer, Merchant	1715	63	355	16	455	14	332	14	389	18
9. *Copper.*										
Copper, Copper goods—Manufacturer, Worker, Dealer	364	.	40	.	111	.	34	.	169	.
10. *Tin and Zinc.*										
Tin, Tin Plate, Tin goods—Manufacturer, Worker, Dealer	1082	34	114	2	199	2	127	.	219	1
Zinc, Zinc Goods—Manufacturer, Worker, Dealer	76	1	25	1	18	.	21	.	4	.
11. *Lead.*										
Lead, Leaden goods—Manufacturer, Worker, Dealer	26	.	5	.	7	.	2	.	9	.
12. *In Other, Mixed, or Unspecified, Metals.*										
Metal Refiner, Worker, Turner, Dealer	96	3	20	.	48	3	10	.	6	.
Brass, Bronze, Manufacture. Brazier	449	.	88	.	109	.	85	.	153	.
Metal Burnisher, Lacquerer	.	5	.	1	.	1	.	3	.	.
White Metal, Plated Ware, Manufacture. Pewterer	22	2	3	.	4	1	10	1	4	.
Wire Maker, Worker, Weaver, Drawer	76	2	22	1	14	.	12	.	16	.
Bolt, Nut, Rivet, Screw, Staple, Maker	35	1	1	.	10	1	9	.	10	.
Lamp, Lantern, Candlestick, Maker	12	.	4	.	5	.	2	.	1	.
Clasp, Buckle, Hinge, Maker	1	.	1	.	.	.	.	.	.	.
Fancy Chain, Gilt Toy, Maker	1	.	.	.	.	.	.	.	1	.
Others	5	.	1	.	.	.	.	.	2	.
22. PERSONS WORKING AND DEALING IN GENERAL OR UNSPECIFIED COMMODITIES.										
1. *Makers and Dealers (General or Undefined).*										
General Shopkeeper, Dealer	8314	1691	573	293	983	490	478	348	1045	411
Pawnbroker	375	38	76	2	113	12	52	3	112	19
Costermonger, Huckster, Street Seller	2855	1562	515	325	745	556	761	320	613	263
Manufacturer, Manager, Superintendent (undefined)	376	25	89	3	130	5	66	10	78	6
Contractor (undefined)	271	4	78	2	70	2	62	.	30	.
2. *Mechanics and Labourers (General or Undefined).*										
General Labourer	63487	195	12352	19	18952	54	10459	17	15892	71
Engine Driver, Stoker, Fireman (not railway, marine, nor agricultural)	3043	.	471	.	1233	.	430	.	659	.
Artizan, Mechanic (undefined)	976	44	291	1	374	5	77	24	201	13
Apprentice (undefined)	295	81	38	9	53	29	65	13	112	24
Factory Labourer (undefined)	575	86	110	45	155	26	31	8	108	7
Machinist, Machine Worker (undefined)	185	304	42	.	42	1	39	60	33	143
23. PERSONS WORKING AND DEALING IN REFUSE MATTERS.										
1. *Refuse Matters.*										
Town Drainage Service	112	.	18	.	70	.	9	.	13	.
Chimney Sweep, Soot Merchant	836	11	192	1	215	2	102	3	179	3
Scavenger, Crossing Sweeper	137	.	23	.	44	.	30	.	25	.
Rag Gatherer, Dealer	115	36	9	11	39	6	18	7	31	12
VI. UNOCCUPIED CLASS.										
24. PERSONS WITHOUT SPECIFIED OCCUPATIONS										
Persons returned by Property, Rank, &c., and not by special occupation	318853	810743	61913	149006	92840	233097	61497	160590	71369	189066
Children under 5 years of age	161461.	161612	29072	29468	47184	46928	31523	31670	37210	37235

Table 10 *continued*.—Occupations of Males and Females in the South-eastern Division and its Registration Counties, and in each Urban Sanitary District of which the Population exceeds 50,000 Persons.

Occupations.	Registration County.		Urban Sanitary Districts.							
	5. Berkshire.		Croydon.		Brighton.		Portsmouth.		Southampton.	
	Males.	Females.	Males.	Females.	Males.	Females.	Males.	Females.	Males.	Females.
TOTAL	123301	124591	35210	43743	47196	60350	63397	65592	28382	31069
I. PROFESSIONAL CLASS.										
1. Persons engaged in the General or Local Government of the Country.										
1. *National Government.*										
Peer, M.P., Privy Councillor (not otherwise described)	5	.	1	.	5	.	.	.	.	.
Civil Service (officers and clerks)	142	67	176	2	63	.	233	6	176	3
Civil Service (messengers, &c.)	246	7	84	.	96	1	66	.	44	.
Prison Officer, &c.	11	4	.	.	.	.	198	3	.	.
2. *Local Government.*										
Police	262	.	90	.	147	.	253	.	80	.
Municipal, Parish, Union, District, Officer	131	34	50	15	50	17	46	22	32	3
Other Local or County Official	110	.	10	.	46	.	20	.	5	.
3. *East Indian and Colonial Service.*										
East Indian and Colonial Service	4	.	6	.	2	.	3	.	1	.
2. Persons engaged in the Defence of the Country.										
1. *Army (at Home).*										
Army Officer (effective or retired)	588	.	60	.	126	.	273	.	43	.
Soldier and Non-Commissioned Officer	1195	.	7	.	71	.	2152	.	67	.
Militia, Yeomanry, Volunteers	268	.	10	.	17	.	31	.	7	.
Army Pensioner	120	.	22	.	52	.	211	.	30	.
2. *Navy (ashore or in port).*										
Navy Officer (effective or retired)	35	.	9	.	18	.	497	.	19	.
Seaman, R.N.	4	.	1	.	7	.	3575	.	44	.
Royal Marines (officers and men)	6	.	.	.	.	.	1358	.	2	.
Navy Pensioner	21	.	12	.	40	.	1847	2	40	.
3. Persons engaged in Professional Occupations (with their immediate Subordinates).										
1. *Clerical Profession.*										
Clergyman (Established Church)	389	.	50	.	148	.	58	.	40	.
Roman Catholic Priest	28	.	6	.	7	.	5	.	4	.
Minister, Priest, of other religious bodies	86	.	35	.	48	.	34	.	10	.
Missionary, Scripture Reader, Itinerant Preacher	32	12	11	7	16	13	16	13	4	4
Nun, Sister of Charity	.	139	.	74	.	54	.	1	.	.
Theological Student	26	.	3	.	3	.	7	.	5	.
Church, Chapel, Cemetery—Officer, Servant	75	12	16	7	28	12	10	7	7	6
2. *Legal Profession.*										
Barrister, Solicitor	146	.	153	.	146	.	55	.	37	.
Law Student	19	.	8	.	11	.	4	.	3	.
Law Clerk, and others connected with Law	169	.	107	1	121	.	72	2	67	.
3. *Medical Profession.*										
Physician, Surgeon, General Practitioner	143	.	71	.	129	.	69	.	38	.
Dentist	27	.	26	.	63	.	16	.	15	.
Medical Student, Assistant	36	.	26	1	28	.	35	.	10	.
Midwife	.	38	.	.	.	16	.	17	.	6
Subordinate Medical Service	21	448	5	184	9	324	3	233	12	138
4. *Teachers.*										
Schoolmaster	564	1189	105	288	144	738	159	588	79	299
Teacher, Professor, Lecturer	81	404	47	333	146	186	46	71	12	38
School Service, and others concerned in Teaching	10	35	9	8	11	9	10	.	3	2
5. *Literary and Scientific Persons.*										
Author, Editor, Journalist	21	2	20	1	34	9	15	.	10	.
Reporter, Short-hand Writer	17	.	12	.	23	.	18	.	7	.
Persons engaged in Scientific Pursuits	4	.	6	.	4	.	.	.	2	.
Literary, Scientific, Institution, Service, &c.	8	.	6	.	4	4	.	.	6	1
6. *Engineers and Surveyors.*										
Civil Engineer	44	.	57	.	56	.	20	.	6	.
Mining Engineer	2	.	2	.	1	.	.	.	.	.
Land, House, Ship, Surveyor	68	.	47	.	27	.	11	.	122	.
7. *Artists.*										
Painter (artist)	46	18	45	14	50	29	26	5	23	7
Engraver (artist)	7	1	10	.	2	.	1	.	45	.
Sculptor	7	.	3	.	8	.	.	.	.	.
Architect	67	.	77	.	58	.	27	.	17	.
Musician, Music Master	120	85	61	57	221	140	119	129	45	40
Art Student	19	2	8	12	5	5	.	4	4	2
Photographer	57	10	37	7	100	39	39	16	27	13
Actor	7	4	3	4	11	16	12	17	8	2
Art, Music, Theatre, Service	1	1	3	.	17	1	4	1	5	4

Table 10 *continued*.—OCCUPATIONS of MALES and FEMALES in the SOUTH-EASTERN DIVISION and its REGISTRATION COUNTIES, and in each URBAN SANITARY DISTRICT of which the POPULATION exceeds 50,000 PERSONS.

OCCUPATIONS.	REGISTRATION COUNTY.		URBAN SANITARY DISTRICTS.							
	5. BERKSHIRE.		CROYDON.		BRIGHTON.		PORTSMOUTH.		SOUTHAMPTON.	
	Males.	Females.	Males.	Females.	Males.	Females.	Males.	Females.	Males.	Females.
8. *Persons engaged in Exhibitions, Shows, Games, &c.*										
Performer, Showman, Exhibition, Service	12	7	9	.	11	3	12	3	2	.
Billiard, Cricket, & other Games, Service	25	1	12	.	35	1	19	.	8	.
II. DOMESTIC CLASS.										
4. PERSONS ENGAGED IN DOMESTIC OFFICES OR SERVICES.										
1. *Domestic Service.*										
Domestic Coachman, Groom	1448	.	140	.	470	.	141	.	67	.
Domestic Gardener	1393	.	158	.	69	.	52	.	42	.
Domestic Indoor Servant	1196	14744	194	7164	452	9445	198	5606	66	3123
Lodge, Gate, Park, Keeper (not Government)	36	18	2	5	2	.	3	1	4	2
Inn, Hotel, Servant	307	210	130	86	446	330	153	148	111	118
College, Club, Service	84	1	5	1	18	3	12	3	3	.
2. *Other Service.*										
Office Keeper (not Government)	3	8	8	.	4	18	8	2	4	10
Cook (not domestic)	27	8	7	41	50	60	23	22	21	8
Charwoman	.	743	.	217	.	706	.	628	.	258
Washing and Bathing Service	14	2710	19	1223	91	2456	14	1224	5	497
Hospital and Institution Service	104	115	5	32	14	102	23	66	.	39
Others engaged in Service	12	2	7	6	7	2	5	.	10	1
III. COMMERCIAL CLASS.										
5. PERSONS ENGAGED IN COMMERCIAL OCCUPATIONS.										
1. *Merchants and Agents.*										
Merchant	26	.	128	.	89	.	7	1	15	.
Broker, Agent, Factor	96	4	314	4	143	5	53	2	78	.
Auctioneer, Appraiser, Valuer, House Agent	108	.	53	1	89	2	47	1	32	.
Accountant	67	5	83	.	84	1	26	.	30	.
Salesman, Buyer (not otherwise described)	2	9	3	4	11	10	5	1	9	1
Commercial Traveller	156	.	196	.	202	.	124	.	61	.
Commercial Clerk	919	33	1160	35	706	89	448	15	570	11
Officer of Commercial Company, Guild, Society, &c.	7	.	4	.	4	.	3	.	.	.
2. *Dealers in Money.*										
Banker	18	.	3	.	6	.	7	1	3	.
Bank Service	112	.	229	.	62	.	65	.	39	.
Bill Discounter, Bill Broker, Finance Agent	2	.	3	.	8	.	7	.	3	.
3. *Persons occupied in Insurance.*										
Life, House, Ship, &c., Insurance Service	57	.	146	.	47	.	76	3	36	1
6. PERSONS ENGAGED IN CONVEYANCE OF MEN, GOODS, AND MESSAGES.										
1. *On Railways.*										
Railway Engine Driver, Stoker	110	.	34	.	166	.	76	.	115	.
Railway Guard	64	.	18	.	80	.	33	.	24	.
Pointsman, Level Crossing Man	53	.	16	.	21	.	7	1	6	.
Other Railway Officials and Servants	659	.	333	6	406	3	234	1	307	2
2. *On Roads.*										
Toll Collector, Turnpike Gate Keeper	8	3	.	.	2	1	5	.	4	.
Omnibus, Coach, Cab, Owner—Livery Stable Keeper	56	1	38	3	192	5	66	2	43	2
Cabman, Flyman, Coachman (not domestic)	282	.	304	.	425	.	111	.	128	.
Carman, Carrier, Carter, Haulier	735	15	460	.	473	1	386	1	154	.
Tramway Companies' Service	17	.	13	.	.	.	89	.	22	.
Wheel Chair Proprietor, Attendant, &c.	1	.	2	1	110	4	19	.	2	1
3. *On Canals, Rivers and Seas.*										
Inland Navigation Service	37	1	.	.	1	.	.	.	.	.
Bargeman, Lighterman, Waterman	123	1	5	1	20	.	240	1	36	.
Navigation Service (on shore)	2	.	8	.	5	.	1	1	11	5
Seaman (Merchant Service)	35	.	41	.	89	.	1240	.	583	.
Pilot	1	.	.	.	1	.	15	.	22	.
Ship Steward, Cook	2	1	3	1	3	3	54	1	235	21
Boatman on Seas	.	.	.	.	101	.	21	.	8	.
Harbour, Dock, Wharf, Lighthouse, Service	18	.	6	.	3	.	47	1	508	.
4. *In Storage.*										
Warehouseman (not Manchester)	17	.	72	1	26	2	39	.	18	1
Meter, Weigher	.	.	.	.	2	.	8	.	16	.
5. *In conveying Messages, Porterage, &c.*										
Messenger, Porter, Watchman (not Railway nor Government)	1650	5	347	2	1264	6	626	.	574	1
Telegraph, Telephone, Service	33	16	36	2	41	9	29	2	38	5

Table 10 *continued*.—OCCUPATIONS of MALES and FEMALES in the SOUTH-EASTERN DIVISION and its REGISTRATION COUNTIES, and in each URBAN SANITARY DISTRICT of which the POPULATION exceeds 50,000 PERSONS.

OCCUPATIONS.	REGISTRATION COUNTY. 5. BERKSHIRE. Males.	Females.	URBAN SANITARY DISTRICTS. CROYDON. Males.	Females.	BRIGHTON. Males.	Females.	PORTSMOUTH. Males.	Females.	SOUTHAMPTON. Males.	Females.
IV. AGRICULTURAL CLASS.										
7. PERSONS ENGAGED IN AGRICULTURE.										
1. *In Fields and Pastures.*										
Farmer, Grazier	1551	90	32	1	34	.	27	.	7	.
Farmer's, Grazier's—Son, Grandson, Brother, Nephew*	449	.	4	.	4	.	4	.	.	.
Farm Bailiff	417	.	18	.	1	.	3	.	4	.
Agricultural Labourer, Farm Servant, Cottager	18638	1162	382	37	197	5	300	3	25	.
Shepherd	980	.	3	.	1	.	3	.	.	.
Land Drainage Service (not in towns)	14	.	.	.	.	.	.	.	.	.
Agricultural Machine—Proprietor, Attendant	151	2	1	.	.	.	.	.	.	.
Agricultural Student, Pupil	12	.	1	.	1	.	2	.	.	.
Others engaged in, or connected with, Agriculture	36	1	5	.	5	.	1	.	1	.
2. *In Woods.*										
Woodman	253	.	5	.	.	.	2	.	1	.
3. *In Gardens.*										
Nurseryman, Seedsman, Florist	192	4	42	1	28	1	18	1	20	.
Gardener (not domestic)	2002	25	206	11	361	4	175	.	155	.
8. PERSONS ENGAGED ABOUT ANIMALS.										
1. *About Animals.*										
Horse Proprietor, Breeder, Dealer	37	.	7	.	7	.	8	.	5	.
Groom, Horse-keeper, Horse-breaker	918	.	144	.	207	3	96	.	87	.
Veterinary Surgeon, Farrier	101	.	22	.	31	.	10	.	19	.
Cattle, Sheep, Pig—Dealer, Salesman	74	.	9	.	11	.	25	.	8	.
Drover	39	.	9	.	7	.	18	.	7	.
Gamekeeper	281	.	7	.	6	.	3	.	1	.
Dog, Bird, Animal—Keeper, Dealer	12	1	2	.	11	.	3	.	1	.
Vermin destroyer	5		2	.	1	.	2	.	.	.
Fisherman	55		.	.	273	1	100	.	9	.
Knacker, Catsmeat Dealer, &c., &c.	2	.	12	.	6	.	6	.	1	.
V. INDUSTRIAL CLASS.										
9. PERSONS WORKING AND DEALING IN BOOKS, PRINTS, AND MAPS.										
1. *Books.*										
Publisher, Bookseller, Librarian	62	15	46	9	77	19	42	15	29	16
Music—Publisher, Seller, Printer	8	3	9	.	12	2	8	.	2	.
Bookbinder	35	16	11	8	39	23	26	9	20	5
Printer	319	5	171	8	384	4	210	1	160	.
Newspaper Agent, News Room Keeper	23	3	25	4	37	6	40	5	7	2
Others	.	.	.	.	.	.	.	.	.	.
2. *Prints and Maps.*										
Lithographer, Lithographic Printer	8	.	11	.	11	.	2	.	9	.
Copper Plate and Steel Plate Printer	1	.	.	.	5	.	2	.	6	.
Map and Print—Colourer, Seller	.	.	.	.	4	.	1	.	7	.
10. PERSONS WORKING AND DEALING IN MACHINES AND IMPLEMENTS.										
1. *Machines.*										
Engine, Machine, Maker	193	1	39	2	168	1	227	1	171	.
Millwright	40	.	27	.	16	.	87	.	5	.
Fitter, Turner (Engine and Machine)	347	.	41	.	296	.	650	.	230	.
Boiler Maker	56	.	2	.	150	.	308	.	236	.
Spinning and Weaving Machine Maker	.	.	.	.	.	.	1	.	.	.
Agricultural Machine and Implement Maker	48	.	.	.	2	.	.	.	.	.
Domestic Machinery—Maker, Dealer	.	.	1	.	1	.	.	.	.	.
2. *Tools and Implements.*										
Tool Maker, Dealer	6	.	2	.	6	.	6	.	1	.
Cutler, Scissors Maker	17	1	1	1	12	2	19	.	7	2
File Maker	.	.	.	.	.	.	.	.	.	.
Saw Maker	4	.	2	.	5	.	5	.	.	.
Pin Maker	.	.	.	.	.	.	.	.	4	.
Needle Maker	.	.	.	.	.	.	.	.	.	.
Steel Pen Maker	.	.	.	.	.	.	.	.	.	.
Pencil Maker (Wood)	.	.	.	.	.	.	.	.	.	.
Domestic Implement Maker	.	.	.	.	1	.	.	.	.	.
3. *Watches and Philosophical Instruments.*										
Watch Maker, Clock Maker	162	4	109	1	133	5	95	2	66	.
Philosophical Instrument Maker, Optician	3	1	28	.	8	2	6	.	13	.
Electrical Apparatus Maker	5	.	16	.	6	.	5	.	7	.
Weighing and Measuring Apparatus Maker	12	.	5	.	8	.	5	.	3	.

Table 10 *continued.*—OCCUPATIONS of MALES and FEMALES in the SOUTH-EASTERN DIVISION and its REGISTRATION COUNTIES, and in each URBAN SANITARY DISTRICT of which the POPULATION exceeds 50,000 PERSONS.

OCCUPATIONS.	REGISTRATION COUNTY.		URBAN SANITARY DISTRICTS.							
	5. BERKSHIRE.		CROYDON.		BRIGHTON.		PORTSMOUTH.		SOUTHAMPTON.	
	Males.	Females.	Males.	Females.	Males.	Females.	Males.	Females.	Males.	Females.
4. Surgical Instruments.										
Surgical Instrument Maker	.	.	5	.	1	3	3	.	.	.
5. Arms and Ordnance.										
Gunsmith, Gun Manufacturer	25	1	5	.	4	1	11	.	6	.
Ordnance Manufacturer	.	.	.	.	.	.	.	.	.	.
Sword, Bayonet—Maker, Cutler	.	.	.	.	4	.	1	.	3	.
Others	1	.	.	.	1	.	4	.	.	.
6. Musical Instruments.										
Musical Instrument Maker, Dealer	24	1	18	.	32	.	19	2	17	.
7. Type, Dies, Medals, Coins.										
Type Cutter, Founder	5	.	.	.	2	.	.	.	.	.
Die, Seal, Coin, Medal, Maker	6	.	2	.	1	.	4	.	.	.
8. Tackle for Sports and Games.										
Toy Maker, Dealer	6	18	.	8	14	14	10	11	7	5
Fishing Rod, Tackle, Maker, Dealer	1	.	.	.	.	.	.	.	.	.
Apparatus for other Games, Maker, Dealer	1	1	1	.	2	.	2	.	1	.
11. PERSONS WORKING AND DEALING IN HOUSES, FURNITURE, AND DECORATIONS.										
1. Houses.										
Builder	401	3	211	.	239	.	174	.	103	2
Carpenter, Joiner	2817	2	1060	3	1332	1	1444	.	682	2
Bricklayer	2193	.	867	.	1323	.	993	1	838	.
Mason	729	1	148	.	114	.	256	.	87	.
Slater, Tiler	16	.	30	.	18	.	33	.	38	.
Plasterer, Whitewasher	237	.	247	2	390	.	199	.	98	.
Paperhanger	54	.	80	.	103	.	28	.	25	.
Plumber	349	5	269	.	207	.	215	1	111	.
Painter, Glazier	941	2	642	.	982	2	672	2	464	.
2. Furniture and Fittings.										
Cabinet Maker, Upholsterer	352	80	130	27	308	97	217	36	161	36
French Polisher	47	2	25	1	65	2	45	1	36	.
Furniture Broker, Dealer	37	4	28	4	84	7	62	15	20	3
Locksmith, Bellhanger	18	.	6	.	12	1	7	.	6	.
Gas Fitter	91	.	72	.	160	.	94	.	40	.
House and Shop Fittings—Maker, Dealer	6	.	27	.	47	1	6	.	8	2
Funeral Furniture Maker, Undertaker	3	.	8	1	26	.	8	.	6	.
Others	.	.	.	.	.	.	.	.	.	.
3. House Decorations.										
Wood Carver	16	.	1	.	14	.	1	.	3	.
Carver, Gilder	34	1	18	1	73	1	23	.	21	1
Dealer in Works of Art	8	.	2	.	10	1	5	.	.	.
Figure, Image—Maker, Dealer	7	.	3	1	5	.	.	.	1	.
Animal, Bird, &c., Preserver, Naturalist	5	1	7	1	15	4	6	.	3	.
Artificial Flower Maker	1	.	.	3	2	6	1	2	.	1
12. PERSONS WORKING AND DEALING IN CARRIAGES AND HARNESS.										
1. Carriages.										
Coachmaker	316	2	119	1	370	.	161	1	122	1
Railway Carriage, Railway Wagon, Maker	11	.	.	.	66	.	.	.	2	.
Wheelwright	314	.	71	1	76	.	89	.	35	.
Bicycle, Tricycle—Maker, Dealer	23	.	7	.	14	.	2	.	1	.
Others	4	.	.	.	.	.	.	.	.	.
2. Harness.										
Saddler, Harness, Whip, Maker	264	5	40	1	63	.	48	1	27	.
13. PERSONS WORKING AND DEALING IN SHIPS AND BOATS.										
1. Hull.										
Ship, Boat, Barge, Builder	84	.	4	.	14	.	178	.	116	.
Shipwright, Ship Carpenter (ashore)	3	.	3	.	10	.	1704	.	290	.
2. Masts, Rigging, &c.										
Mast, Yard, Oar, Block, Maker	2	.	.	.	1	.	26	.	16	.
Ship Rigger, Chandler, Fitter	.	.	1	.	.	.	186	.	11	1
Sail Maker	1	.	1	.	14	.	71	.	42	.

Table 10 *continued.*—Occupations of Males and Females in the South-eastern Division and its Registration Counties, and in each Urban Sanitary District of which the Population exceeds 50,000 Persons.

Occupations.	Registration County.		Urban Sanitary Districts.							
	5. Berkshire.		Croydon.		Brighton.		Portsmouth.		Southampton.	
	Males.	Females.	Males.	Females.	Males.	Females.	Males.	Females.	Males.	Females.
14. Persons working and dealing in Chemicals and Compounds.										
1. *Colouring Matter.*										
Dye, Paint, Manufacture	.	.	2	.	2	5	1	.	3	.
Ink, Blacking, Colouring Substance, Manufacture	3	.	2	.	2	.	.	.	.	.
2. *Explosives.*										
Gunpowder, Guncotton, Explosive Substance, Manufacture	.	.	.	.	.	.	.	.	.	.
Fusee, Fireworks, Explosive Article, Manufacture	.	.	22	6	2	.	1	.	1	.
3. *Drugs and other Chemicals and Compounds.*										
Chemist, Druggist	142	3	77	1	137	10	106	1	60	.
Manufacturing Chemist	1	1	15	5	2	1	7	.	3	3
Alkali Manufacture	.	.	.	.	.	.	.	.	.	.
Drysalter	.	.	5	.	1	.	2	.	.	.
15. Persons working and dealing in Tobacco and Pipes.										
1. *Tobacco and Pipes.*										
Tobacco Manufacturer, Tobacconist	54	20	30	10	46	16	57	25	16	8
Tobacco Pipe, Snuff Box, &c., Maker	3	1	8	.	16	.	7	.	.	1
16. Persons working and dealing in Food and Lodging.										
1. *Board and Lodging.*										
Innkeeper, Hotel Keeper, Publican	829	144	126	12	281	52	304	53	186	43
Lodging, Boarding House, Keeper	13	123	9	86	203	890	57	396	29	151
Coffee, Eating House, Keeper	39	17	21	17	52	20	41	15	26	3
2. *Spirituous Drinks.*										
Hop—Merchant, Dealer	.	.	10	.	1	.	.	.	.	.
Maltster	142	1	8	.	28	.	6	.	6	.
Brewer	425	5	65	.	130	1	151	.	52	.
Beerseller. Ale, Porter, Cider, Dealer	120	36	69	6	137	40	250	69	53	28
Cellarman	40	.	21	.	65	.	38	.	27	.
Wine, Spirit—Merchant, Agent	70	.	73	6	73	2	37	1	10	1
3. *Food.*										
Milkseller, Dairyman	156	35	168	6	236	18	184	23	76	18
Cheesemonger, Butterman	6	1	17	1	15	.	10	.	.	.
Butcher, Meat Salesman	684	17	285	9	438	11	382	27	214	9
Provision Curer, Dealer	27	1	20	1	55	16	34	3	8	6
Poulterer, Game Dealer	24	2	16	.	49	4	12	2	7	.
Fishmonger	79	9	65	1	148	19	109	11	54	10
Corn, Flour, Seed—Merchant, Dealer	148	14	74	1	59	2	40	3	60	2
Corn Miller	354	3	40	.	76	.	17	.	8	.
Baker	2830	263	295	21	557	48	525	28	248	22
Confectioner, Pastrycook	102	70	46	19	112	76	94	64	46	34
Greengrocer, Fruiterer	159	45	144	19	256	81	235	82	63	33
Mustard, Vinegar, Spice, Pickle—Maker, Dealer	8	7	3	.	.	.	.	.	.	.
Sugar Refiner	8	1	1	.	8	.	1	.	40	.
Grocer. Tea, Coffee, Chocolate—Maker, Dealer	1002	193	391	46	533	62	505	73	277	29
Ginger Beer, Mineral Water—Manufacturer, Dealer	22	6	34	.	75	8	32	5	19	.
Others dealing in Food	.	.	.	.	.	.	.	.	.	.
17. Persons working and dealing in Textile Fabrics.										
1. *Wool and Worsted.*										
Woolstapler	3	.	4	.	.	.	.	.	.	.
Woollen Cloth Manufacture	1	2	.	.	.	.	2	.	.	.
Wool, Woollen goods—Dyer, Printer	.	.	.	.	.	.	.	.	.	.
Worsted, Stuff, Manufacture	.	.	.	.	.	.	.	.	.	.
Flannel Manufacture	.	.	.	.	.	.	.	16	1	3
Blanket Manufacture	.	.	.	.	.	.	.	.	.	.
Fuller	.	.	.	.	.	.	.	.	.	.
Cloth, Worsted, Stuff, Flannel, Blanket, Dealer	7	1	16	.	2	.	3	.	.	.
Others	.	5	.	.	.	.	.	.	.	.
2. *Silk.*										
Silk, Silk goods, Manufacture	2	1	6	2	3	1	3	.	.	.
Silk Dyer, Printer	.	.	.	.	.	.	.	.	.	.
Ribbon Manufacture	.	.	1	.	.	.	.	.	.	.
Crape, Gauze, Manufacture	.	.	.	.	.	.	.	1	.	.
Silk Merchant, Dealer	15	.	19	.	2	1	1	.	.	.

Table 10 *continued*.—OCCUPATIONS of MALES and FEMALES in the SOUTH-EASTERN DIVISION and its REGISTRATION COUNTIES, and in each URBAN SANITARY DISTRICT of which the POPULATION exceeds 50,000 PERSONS.

OCCUPATIONS.	REGISTRATION COUNTY. 5. BERKSHIRE.		URBAN SANITARY DISTRICTS. CROYDON.		BRIGHTON.		PORTSMOUTH.		SOUTHAMPTON.	
	Males.	Females.	Males.	Females.	Males.	Females.	Males.	Females.	Males.	Females.
3. Cotton and Flax										
Cotton, Cotton goods Manufacture	1	.	.	.	1	1	6	4	.	.
Cotton, Calico—Printer, Dyer, Bleacher	.	.	.	.	.	.	1	.	.	.
Cotton, Calico—Warehouseman, Dealer	.	.	1	.	.	.	.	.	.	.
Flax, Linen—Manufacturer, Dealer	24	10	6	.	8	.	2	.	.	2
Lace Manufacturer, Dealer	1	17	5	10	2	26	2	9	.	.
Fustian Manufacturer, Dealer	.	.	.	.	.	.	.	.	.	.
Tape Manufacturer, Dealer	.	.	.	.	.	.	.	.	.	.
Thread Manufacturer, Dealer	.	.	.	.	.	.	.	.	.	.
4. Hemp and other Fibrous Materials.										
Hemp, Jute, Cocoa Fibre, Manufacture	3	3	1	.	1	.	.	6	.	.
Rope, Twine, Cord—Maker, Dealer	39	4	.	.	4	1	66	3	35	2
Mat Maker, Seller	7	.	7	.	5	1	1	1	.	.
Net Maker	1	1	1	.	3	1	.	1	.	.
Canvas, Sailcloth, Manufacture	.	.	3	.	2	.	.	.	1	.
Sacking, Sack, Bag—Maker, Dealer	4	4	1	.	4	.	.	2	8	2
Others working and dealing in Hemp	2	2	3	.	.	.	1	.	.	2
5. Mixed or Unspecified Materials.										
Weaver (undefined)	5	3	1	1	1	1	2	.	.	.
Dyer, Printer, Scourer, Bleacher, Calenderer (undefined)	24	17	21	8	28	22	21	8	22	6
Factory hand (Textile, undefined)	.	15	.	3	.	.	.	.	.	.
Felt Manufacture	.	.	.	.	.	.	.	.	.	.
Carpet, Rug, Manufacture	1	.	4	.	7	.	7	.	1	.
Manchester Warehouseman	1	.	9	.	3	.	.	.	.	.
Draper, Linen Draper, Mercer	520	299	293	172	432	227	242	244	183	108
Fancy Goods (Textile), Manufacturer, Worker, Dealer	3	34	9	27	10	67	4	20	5	14
Trimming Maker, Dealer	.	.	1	.	.	1	.	2	.	1
Embroiderer	.	14	.	6	.	17	.	5	.	.
Others	.	.	.	.	.	.	.	.	.	.
18. PERSONS WORKING AND DEALING IN DRESS.										
1. Dress.										
Hatter, Hat Manufacture (not straw)	21	1	22	2	39	6	34	14	3	1
Straw—Hat, Bonnet, Plait, Manufacture	1	20	1	4	1	10	2	15	.	4
Tailor	928	585	247	42	643	141	689	407	266	278
Milliner, Dressmaker, Staymaker	1	2762	9	1105	19	2648	159	3461	5	1142
Shawl Manufacture	.	.	1	.	.	.	.	.	.	.
Shirt Maker, Seamstress	7	1217	4	156	2	582	5	741	.	232
Hosiery Manufacture	1	.	1	.	1	7	.	10	.	1
Hosier, Haberdasher	23	4	17	8	40	5	14	8	14	3
Glover, Glove Maker	5	7	3	5	3	3	.	1	1	2
Button Maker, Dealer	.	.	4	1	.	.	2	.	.	.
Shoe, Boot—Maker, Dealer	1822	67	407	46	664	65	711	81	388	68
Patten, Clog, Maker	.	.	.	.	.	.	1	.	.	.
Wig Maker, Hairdresser	106	3	63	7	123	13	83	3	63	6
Umbrella, Parasol, Stick—Maker, Dealer	16	7	12	3	16	12	12	11	7	2
Accoutrement Maker	.	.	2	.	.	.	2	6	.	.
Old Clothes Dealer, and others	1	4	5	7	4	10	6	18	2	3
19. PERSONS WORKING AND DEALING IN VARIOUS ANIMAL SUBSTANCES.										
1. In Grease, Gut, Bone, Horn, Ivory, and Whalebone.										
Tallow Chandler, Candle, Grease, Manufacture	17	.	2	.	23	.	6	.	5	.
Soap Boiler, Maker	1	.	1	.	10	.	6	.	1	.
Glue, Size, Gelatine, Isinglass—Maker, Dealer	.	.	.	.	.	.	1	.	.	.
Manure Manufacture	5	.	1	.	1	.	.	.	.	.
Bone, Horn, Ivory, Tortoise-shell—Worker, Dealer	2	.	3	.	3	1	1	.	.	.
Comb Maker	.	.	.	.	.	.	.	.	.	.
Others	.	.	.	.	.	.	.	.	.	.
2. In Skins.										
Furrier, Skinner	4	2	9	.	5	10	2	2	1	4
Tanner, Fellmonger	97	1	7	.	3	.	3	.	1	.
Currier	65	.	37	.	9	1	35	1	18	1
Leather Goods, Portmanteau, Bag, Strap, &c.—Maker, Dealer	7	.	9	.	17	.	15	8	5	.
Parchment, Vellum—Maker, Dealer	21	.	.	.	.	.	.	.	.	.
3. In Hair and Feathers.										
Hair, Bristle—Worker, Dealer	1	.	2	.	3	3	.	.	.	.
Brush, Broom, Maker	43	7	8	1	15	2	23	5	34	18
Quill, Feather—Dresser, Dealer	.	2	1	.	2	5	2	7	.	4

Table 10 *continued.*—Occupations of Males and Females in the South-eastern Division and its Registration Counties, and in each Urban Sanitary District of which the Population exceeds 50,000 Persons.

Occupations.	Registration County.		Urban Sanitary Districts.							
	5. Berkshire.		Croydon.		Brighton.		Portsmouth.		Southampton.	
	Males.	Females.	Males.	Females.	Males.	Females.	Males.	Females.	Males.	Females.
20. Persons working and dealing in various Vegetable Substances.										
1. *In Oils, Gums, and Resins.*										
Oil Miller, Oil Cake—Maker, Dealer	5	.	4	.	9	.	4	1	46	.
Oil and Colourman	26	1	45	5	28	3	12	.	19	5
Floor Cloth, Oil Cloth, Manufacture	24	.	7	.	.	.	.	.	.	.
Japanner	2	5	1	.	5	.	1	.	.	.
India Rubber, Gutta Percha—Worker, Dealer	1	.	6	.	3	.	4	.	3	.
Waterproof Goods—Maker, Dealer	1	.	4	.	7	.	.	.	.	.
Others	3	.	2	.	.	1	1	.	.	.
2. *In Cane, Rush, and Straw.*										
Willow, Cane, Rush—Worker, Dealer, Basketmaker	116	22	16	3	50	13	28	5	18	1
Hay, Straw (not plait), Chaff—Cutter, Dealer	17	1	3	.	11	.	4	.	1	.
Thatcher	81	.	.	.	.	.	.	.	.	.
3. *In Wood and Bark.*										
Timber, Wood—Merchant, Dealer	110	5	43	.	81	.	58	1	32	1
Sawyer	400	.	54	.	62	.	133	.	107	.
Lath, Wooden Fence, Hurdle, Maker	61	.	20	.	15	.	20	.	11	.
Wood Turner, Box Maker	76	1	12	2	46	2	30	3	15	.
Cooper, Hoop Maker, Bender	120	1	16	.	39	.	44	.	38	2
Cork, Bark—Cutter, Worker, Dealer	4	.	7	.	5	2	83	.	1	.
Others	2	.	5	.	.	.	.	.	1	.
4. *In Paper.*										
Paper Manufacture	146	59	.	1	2	1	5	2	1	.
Envelope Maker	.	.	.	.	.	1	.	.	.	.
Stationer, Law Stationer	58	29	53	28	82	27	31	19	74	9
Card, Pattern Card, Maker	.	.	.	.	1	.	2	.	1	.
Paper Stainer	2	.	1	.	2	.	.	1	1	.
Paper Box, Paper Bag, Maker	.	6	4	.	3	14	3	63	.	2
Ticket, Label, Writer	1	.	.	.	9	.	3	.	5	.
Others	13	.	5	.	13	.	8	.	4	.
21. Persons working and dealing in various Mineral Substances.										
1. *Miners.*										
Coal Miner	4	.	1	.	3	.	65	.	1	.
Ironstone Miner	.	.	1	.	.	.	.	.	.	.
Copper Miner	.	.	.	.	.	.	.	.	.	.
Tin Miner	.	.	.	.	.	.	.	.	.	.
Lead Miner	.	.	.	.	.	.	.	.	.	.
Miner in other, or undefined, Minerals	.	.	1	.	2	.	1	.	.	.
Mine Service	7	.	6	.	2	.	.	.	.	1
2. *Coal, Coal Gas, &c.*										
Coal Merchant, Dealer	176	19	45	2	86	2	89	8	40	1
Coalheaver	102	.	29	.	63	.	44	.	114	.
Coke, Charcoal, Peat—Cutter, Burner, Dealer	3	.	1	.	1	.	6	.	2	.
Gas Works Service	134	.	55	.	74	.	81	.	65	.
3. *Stone, Clay, and Road Making.*										
Stone Quarrier	7	.	.	.	.	.	4	.	.	.
Stone Cutter, Dresser, Dealer	29	.	10	.	12	.	9	.	7	.
Slate Quarrier	.	.	.	.	.	.	.	.	.	.
Slate Worker, Dealer	3	.	1	.	.	.	1	.	2	.
Limeburner	8	.	1	.	1	.	1	.	6	.
Clay, Sand, Gravel, Chalk—Labourer, Dealer	3	.	7	.	2	.	2	.	.	.
Fossil, Coprolite—Digger, Dealer	.	.	.	.	.	.	.	.	.	.
Well Sinker, Borer	2	.	1	.	2	.	1	.	.	.
Plaster, Cement, Manufacture	9	.	1	.	6	.	6	.	36	.
Brick, Tile—Maker, Burner, Dealer	623	7	111	1	24	.	226	1	34	.
Paviour	3	.	2	.	8	.	6	.	.	.
Road Contractor, Surveyor, Inspector	6	.	7	.	4	.	.	.	2	.
Road Labourer	102	.	17	.	47	.	52	.	7	.
Railway Contractor	19	.	2	.	4	.	.	.	2	.
Platelayer	186	.	56	.	29	.	17	.	21	.
Railway Labourer, Navvy	668	.	83	.	189	.	65	.	24	.
Others	.	.	1	.	.	.	.	.	.	.
4. *Earthenware and Glass.*										
Earthenware, China, Porcelain, Manufacture	39	2	6	.	8	2	3	.	1	.
Glass Manufacture	10	1	9	.	7	.	6	.	3	.
Earthenware, China, Glass, Dealer	44	18	22	21	33	13	40	14	21	6
5. *Salt.*										
Salt Maker, Dealer	1	.	.	.	1	.	1	1	.	.

Table 10 *continued*.—OCCUPATIONS of MALES and FEMALES in the SOUTH-EASTERN DIVISION and its REGISTRATION COUNTIES, and in each URBAN SANITARY DISTRICT of which the POPULATION exceeds 50,000 PERSONS.

OCCUPATIONS.	REGISTRATION COUNTY.		URBAN SANITARY DISTRICTS.							
	5. BERKSHIRE.		CROYDON.		BRIGHTON.		PORTSMOUTH.		SOUTHAMPTON.	
	Males.	Females.	Males.	Females.	Males.	Females.	Males.	Females.	Males.	Females.
6. Water.										
Waterworks Service	16	.	11	.	13	.	30	.	5	.
Others	3	.	.	.	2	.	1	.	.	.
7. Precious Metals and Jewellery.										
Goldsmith, Silversmith, Jeweller	40	7	32	1	108	12	48	10	25	2
Gold, Silver, Beater	.	.	.	.	7	.	3	.	.	.
Lapidary	1	.	.	.	1	2	1	.	.	.
Others	1	.	.	.	.	.	.	.	.	.
8. Iron and Steel.										
Blacksmith	1125	10	179	.	300	3	778	1	242	.
Whitesmith	146	.	53	.	111	.	48	.	41	.
Nail Manufacture	9	.	.	.	.	.	3	.	.	.
Anchor, Chain, Manufacture	.	.	1	.	1	.	1	.	1	.
Other Iron and Steel Manufactures	348	1	41	.	219	1	214	.	308	.
Ironmonger, Hardware Dealer, Merchant	184	7	66	2	88	2	76	6	49	2
9. Copper.										
Copper, Copper goods—Manufacturer, Worker, Dealer	10	.	2	.	23	.	94	.	38	.
10. Tin and Zinc.										
Tin, Tin Plate, Tin goods—Manufacturer, Worker, Dealer	423	28	21	.	65	.	35	.	53	1
Zinc, Zinc Goods—Manufacturer, Worker, Dealer	8	.	15	.	17	.	.	.	2	.
11. Lead.										
Lead, Leaden goods—Manufacturer, Worker, Dealer	3	.	.	.	1	.	1	.	8	.
12. In Other, Mixed, or Unspecified, Metals.										
Metal Refiner, Worker, Turner, Dealer	12	.	5	.	6	.	2	.	1	.
Brass, Bronze, Manufacture. Brazier	24	.	22	.	77	.	63	.	37	.
Metal Burnisher, Lacquerer	.	.	.	1	.	2	.	.	.	.
White Metal, Plated Ware, Manufacture. Pewterer	1	.	.	.	7	.	1	.	1	.
Wire Maker, Worker, Weaver, Drawer	12	1	7	1	8	.	5	.	10	.
Bolt, Nut, Rivet, Screw, Staple, Maker	5	.	.	.	9	.	2	.	4	.
Lamp, Lantern, Candlestick, Maker	.	.	.	.	1	.	.	.	.	.
Clasp, Buckle, Hinge, Maker	.	.	.	.	.	.	.	.	.	.
Fancy Chain, Gilt Toy, Maker	.	.	.	.	.	.	.	.	.	.
Others	2	.	.	.	.	.	2	.	.	.
22. PERSONS WORKING AND DEALING IN GENERAL OR UNSPECIFIED COMMODITIES.										
1. Makers and Dealers (General or Undefined).										
General Shopkeeper, Dealer	235	149	161	76	141	140	399	61	147	95
Pawnbroker	23	2	24	.	31	2	70	15	26	1
Costermonger, Huckster, Street Seller	221	99	108	38	273	143	184	57	125	58
Manufacturer, Manager, Superintendent (undefined)	13	1	25	1	26	2	40	2	14	.
Contractor (undefined)	11	.	18	1	14	.	13	.	6	.
2. Mechanics and Labourers (General or Undefined).										
General Labourer	5832	34	2974	7	1673	2	3142	4	1766	4
Engine Driver, Stoker, Fireman (not railway, marine, nor agricultural)	248	.	87	.	117	.	204	.	165	.
Artizan, Mechanic (undefined)	33	3	53	1	43	.	77	.	74	4
Apprentice (undefined)	27	15	11	1	25	5	26	2	34	8
Factory Labourer (undefined)	146	2	12	.	20	2	49	.	29	.
Machinist, Machine Worker (undefined)	29	.	12	.	25	49	9	30	9	52
23. PERSONS WORKING AND DEALING IN REFUSE MATTERS.										
1. Refuse Matters.										
Town Drainage Service	2	.	2	.	4	.	4	.	2	.
Chimney Sweep, Soot Merchant	88	2	33	.	40	.	23	2	17	1
Scavenger, Crossing Sweeper	15	.	12	.	15	.	4	.	1	.
Rag Gatherer, Dealer	18	.	3	11	7	4	14	5	2	7
VI. UNOCCUPIED CLASS.										
24. PERSONS WITHOUT SPECIFIED OCCUPATIONS										
Persons returned by Property, Rank, &c., and not by special occupation	31234	78984	10067	26449	12724	33169	15584	41767	7126	20444
Children under 5 years of age	16472	16311	5175	5245	6213	6371	8625	8525	3918	3900

Table 11.—BIRTH-PLACES of MALES and FEMALES enumerated in COUNTIES, and in each URBAN SANITARY DISTRICT of which the POPULATION EXCEEDS 50,000 PERSONS.

WHERE BORN.	WHERE ENUMERATED.									
	SOUTH-EASTERN COUNTIES.		COUNTIES.†							
			SURREY.*		KENT.*		SUSSEX.		HAMPSHIRE.	
	Males.	Females.	Males.	Females.	Males.	Females.	Males.	Females.	Males.	Females.
TOTAL OF INHABITANTS	1795693	1921250	683228	753671	478653	499053	232331	258174	293050	300420
LONDON	475532	526641	343108	374908	102047	111689	13322	20700	12549	12939
MIDDLESEX (*Intra-metropolitan*)	141462	171289	91390	108472	27497	33162	9878	15758	9095	9410
SURREY (*Intra-metropolitan*)	258232	274280	240847	253652	12430	14428	2380	3501	1920	1938
KENT (*Intra-metropolitan*)	75838	81072	10871	12784	62120	64099	1064	1441	1534	1591
SOUTH-EASTERN COUNTIES	946410	983210	174484	186051	288797	296727	190180	197551	213584	225023
SURREY (*Extra-metropolitan*)	134437	138736	118028	119766	6482	7239	4977	6144	3441	3925
KENT (*Extra-metropolitan*)	293707	308179	19747	23926	261433	267004	8122	10580	3488	3752
SUSSEX	203450	208996	18237	16914	12107	12925	170027	172097	5291	6339
HAMPSHIRE	229244	243189	14623	16917	6385	6855	6087	7305	198908	207519
BERKSHIRE	85572	86112	6849	8529	2270	2704	987	1475	3236	3403
SOUTH-MIDLAND COUNTIES	67592	80261	35500	42573	12933	14716	4831	7258	5146	5088
MIDDLESEX (*Ex-metropolitan*)	19814	22377	12361	15057	3270	3939	1172	1753	1072	1030
HERTFORDSHIRE	8778	10753	4034	5271	2081	2373	735	1182	632	691
BUCKINGHAMSHIRE	10169	11364	4839	5465	1734	1879	585	885	714	711
OXFORDSHIRE	11976	14386	3824	4824	1516	1741	602	1021	1068	1086
NORTHAMPTONSHIRE	5384	6143	2634	3091	1243	1371	610	802	582	627
HUNTINGDONSHIRE	1853	2356	973	1275	472	546	154	255	174	189
BEDFORDSHIRE	4468	4641	2313	2408	1116	1079	430	565	440	363
CAMBRIDGESHIRE	6150	7792	3432	4432	1601	1788	543	805	464	591
EASTERN COUNTIES	53603	66413	27836	36116	16760	19062	3665	5554	4014	4078
ESSEX	26240	31334	12645	16533	8637	9801	1768	2584	1749	1746
SUFFOLK	15124	18620	8272	10059	4407	4985	992	1478	1072	1130
NORFOLK	13230	16459	7019	9924	3716	4276	905	1492	1193	1202
SOUTH-WESTERN COUNTIES	75585	90420	27404	33692	12400	14697	5028	6997	24713	28231
WILTSHIRE	19481	22960	6863	7290	1988	2532	1061	1378	6994	7068
DORSETSHIRE	15884	18373	3745	4808	1051	1830	992	1200	8083	10493
DEVONSHIRE	20176	24135	9067	10865	4771	5394	1338	2009	4207	4092
CORNWALL	5541	7115	2292	3008	1578	1737	399	646	1333	1543
SOMERSETSHIRE	14353	17837	6447	8221	3012	3214	1238	1758	3229	3545
WEST-MIDLAND COUNTIES	31961	35707	14497	17349	6990	7083	2819	4116	5064	4392
GLOUCESTERSHIRE	11265	13074	5216	6185	2164	2353	969	1380	1721	1767
HEREFORDSHIRE	2045	2831	995	1371	437	636	233	360	240	303
SHROPSHIRE	2319	2718	976	1348	679	867	217	323	384	327
STAFFORDSHIRE	4973	4831	2022	2302	1223	1039	446	639	966	606
WORCESTERSHIRE	3587	3982	1575	1941	747	818	292	479	515	463
WARWICKSHIRE	7978	8271	3713	4202	1860	1081	663	935	1238	926
NORTH-MIDLAND COUNTIES	15354	15136	6810	7553	3614	3275	1641	2110	2586	1574
LEICESTERSHIRE	3266	3021	1449	1656	709	596	379	402	599	311
RUTLANDSHIRE	484	548	208	209	120	123	70	84	61	50
LINCOLNSHIRE	5790	6429	2728	3284	1430	1440	609	577	801	589
NOTTINGHAMSHIRE	3076	2767	1297	1346	715	601	321	397	601	331
DERBYSHIRE	2718	2371	1134	1099	640	515	262	350	524	293
NORTH-WESTERN COUNTIES	14961	12542	6199	6193	3714	2777	1214	1459	3272	1647
CHESHIRE	2067	2556	1087	1180	638	556	258	349	539	302
LANCASHIRE	12294	9986	5112	5013	3076	2221	956	1110	2733	1285
YORKSHIRE	13288	11825	5763	5724	3430	2685	1273	1577	2192	1451
NORTHERN COUNTIES	8638	7670	3368	3344	2614	2046	702	787	1720	1272
DURHAM	4176	3448	1400	1382	1391	1021	294	279	992	701
NORTHUMBERLAND	2770	2623	1140	1259	809	698	219	206	514	376
CUMBERLAND	1239	1171	588	560	311	240	125	166	166	147
WESTMORLAND	463	368	232	143	103	87	64	76	48	48
MONMOUTHSHIRE AND WALES	8164	9960	3524	4667	2007	2334	663	1105	1495	1363
MONMOUTHSHIRE	1402	1744	611	853	206	348	128	205	255	262
GLAMORGANSHIRE	1404	1636	607	744	347	374	123	192	311	228
CARMARTHENSHIRE	449	436	217	228	93	98	43	85	72	46
PEMBROKESHIRE	1291	1476	322	439	558	521	67	124	328	237
CARDIGANSHIRE	434	422	268	284	76	68	23	29	62	32
BRECKNOCKSHIRE	338	422	151	196	73	96	27	57	54	43
RADNORSHIRE	754	236	84	128	19	38	20	33	17	18
MONTGOMERYSHIRE	369	519	191	271	77	106	46	64	33	46
FLINTSHIRE	303	282	130	140	66	55	34	33	31	34
DENBIGHSHIRE	317	390	162	202	58	68	19	37	58	51
MERIONETHSHIRE	126	156	68	88	35	30	5	14	10	10
CAERNARVONSHIRE	245	307	106	152	61	71	19	42	49	28
ANGLESEY	130	157	51	62	38	45	12	15	31	30
WALES (*County not stated*)	1131	1703	566	878	220	421	97	195	101	208
ENGLAND (*County not stated*)	8487	8531	4754	5180	1721	1332	907	1027	706	641
OTHER PARTS OF BRITISH EMPIRE	60653	59826	22083	24273	17648	16634	4414	6032	14455	11065
ISLANDS in the BRITISH SEAS	2037	3230	786	998	608	653	247	318	968	1170
SCOTLAND	17368	14054	7212	6663	4602	3726	1166	1671	3537	2210
IRELAND	27993	26091	10104	11596	8271	7627	1598	1976	7231	4210
BRITISH COLONIES or DEPENDENCIES	12635	15851	3981	5026	3867	4628	1403	2167	2735	3475
FOREIGN COUNTRIES	14975	12568	7706	5837	3757	2944	1639	1834	1469	1555
British Subjects	5741	6109	2580	2580	1518	1481	683	938	757	916
Foreigners	9234	6459	5126	3257	2239	1463	956	896	712	639
AT SEA	490	540	192	211	165	152	33	67	85	96
British Subjects	489	539	191	210	165	152	33	67	85	96
Foreigners	1	1	1	1						

Table 11 *continued.*—BIRTH-PLACES of MALES and FEMALES enumerated in COUNTIES, and in each URBAN SANITARY DISTRICT of which the POPULATION EXCEEDS 50,000 PERSONS.

WHERE BORN.	WHERE ENUMERATED.									
	COUNTY.		URBAN SANITARY DISTRICTS.							
	BERKSHIRE.		CROYDON.		BRIGHTON.		PORTSMOUTH.		SOUTHAMPTON.	
	Males.	Females.	Males.	Females.	Males.	Females.	Males.	Females.	Males.	Females.
TOTAL OF INHABITANTS	108431	109932	35210	43743	47196	60350	62397	65592	28382	31669
LONDON	4500	505	7735	10484	4468	6893	3717	3267	1152	1321
MIDDLESEX (*Intra-metropolitan*)	3602	1487	4053	5870	3371	5375	2403	2066	879	1020
SURREY (*Intra-metropolitan*)	655	761	3025	3688	776	1083	571	455	183	198
KENT (*Intra-metropolitan*)	243	257	657	926	322	435	743	746	90	103
SOUTH-EASTERN COUNTIES	79365	77853	18492	20649	35158	42001	42543	49125	20617	23162
SURREY (*Extra-metropolitan*)	1509	1661	13729	14650	888	1362	406	476	171	187
KENT (*Extra-metropolitan*)	857	968	1888	2460	1178	1701	1200	1201	280	316
SUSSEX	628	720	1706	1028	31783	37051	1837	2193	352	333
HAMPSHIRE	4141	4503	742	1020	1089	1485	38816	45011	19671	22177
BERKSHIRE	72230	69911	427	596	220	402	284	244	143	149
SOUTH-MIDLAND COUNTIES	9182	10626	1978	2754	1243	2138	872	761	355	427
MIDDLESEX (*Ex-metropolitan*)	740	898	572	790	320	534	196	145	70	97
HERTFORDSHIRE	396	486	333	461	191	328	193	97	49	60
BUCKINGHAMSHIRE	2207	2624	235	346	152	276	114	82	47	68
OXFORDSHIRE	4996	5713	236	389	148	205	146	146	69	92
NORTHAMPTONSHIRE	315	362	207	254	159	236	112	108	45	37
HUNTINGDONSHIRE	89	91	45	58	41	63	30	41	17	17
BEDFORDSHIRE	169	186	153	180	103	149	23	68	28	24
CAMBRIDGESHIRE	210	266	107	287	134	263	78	74	30	32
EASTERN COUNTIES	1328	1603	1666	2650	978	1619	1016	917	288	335
ESSEX	541	670	817	1343	443	746	411	429	124	137
SUFFOLK	381	468	473	743	293	435	294	261	68	81
NORFOLK	406	465	376	564	242	438	311	227	96	117
SOUTH-WESTERN COUNTIES	6040	6803	1370	2019	1178	1877	5126	5411	3186	3859
WILTSHIRE	3665	4094	318	441	270	378	675	697	778	956
DORSETSHIRE	463	533	169	214	210	286	1406	1500	1280	1514
DEVONSHIRE	743	996	416	647	300	531	1680	1889	506	609
CORNWALL	139	182	143	215	79	146	548	614	200	291
SOMERSETSHIRE	1030	1099	294	502	319	536	727	621	416	489
WEST-MIDLAND COUNTIES	2591	2767	803	1077	754	1246	1317	885	387	414
GLOUCESTERSHIRE	1305	1389	287	360	280	430	496	403	172	208
HEREFORDSHIRE	140	161	76	117	48	104	60	48	21	30
SHROPSHIRE	163	163	60	98	55	95	85	50	19	16
STAFFORDSHIRE	317	246	97	125	113	189	224	184	55	48
WORCESTERSHIRE	258	281	87	118	75	138	106	77	43	31
WARWICKSHIRE	508	527	197	260	183	290	346	182	77	84
NORTH-MIDLAND COUNTIES	703	624	449	588	413	573	556	269	141	125
LEICESTERSHIRE	150	156	99	126	91	103	114	56	38	23
RUTLANDSHIRE	33	22	18	23	12	21	9	7	5	4
LINCOLNSHIRE	222	239	182	267	146	247	200	91	45	49
NOTTINGHAMSHIRE	142	93	67	73	90	113	122	68	31	18
DERBYSHIRE	156	114	83	100	74	89	111	47	27	31
NORTH-WESTERN COUNTIES	562	466	325	409	338	422	1081	348	148	134
CHESHIRE	145	109	56	89	76	114	175	71	16	35
LANCASHIRE	417	357	275	320	262	308	906	277	132	99
YORKSHIRE	580	388	378	375	362	460	583	303	165	104
NORTHERN COUNTIES	234	221	185	233	166	218	481	246	171	118
DURHAM	90	65	87	98	64	69	246	138	110	69
NORTHUMBERLAND	79	84	53	74	58	86	179	83	46	30
CUMBERLAND	49	58	37	48	38	47	48	17	12	17
WESTMORLAND	16	14	8	13	9	16	8	8	4	2
MONMOUTHSHIRE AND WALES	475	491	167	295	150	314	553	430	142	132
MONMOUTHSHIRE	162	91	35	65	23	61	64	41	18	36
GLAMORGANSHIRE	106	98	28	51	24	51	100	67	43	28
CARMARTHENSHIRE	24	13	8	10	11	20	23	9	5	2
PEMBROKESHIRE	39	55	26	34	15	23	208	185	16	23
CARDIGANSHIRE	25	9	5	11	9	12	16	4	13	7
BRECKNOCKSHIRE	28	28	10	16	4	14	14	7	.	3
RADNORSHIRE	14	19	2	5	5	3	7	6	.	2
MONTGOMERYSHIRE	22	32	10	18	11	16	8	7	3	2
FLINTSHIRE	12	20	6	15	3	9	23	8	4	5
DENBIGHSHIRE	20	32	7	19	5	9	20	3	3	4
MERIONETHSHIRE	2	8	1	2	4	4	3	3	2	.
CARNARVONSHIRE	10	14	10	11	8	15	10	5	4	1
ANGLESEY	4	5	2	.	2	6	8	11	7	4
WALES (*County not stated*)	67	61	17	38	27	71	59	75	35	17
ENGLAND (*County not stated*)	399	351	146	157	96	162	237	162	75	83
OTHER PARTS OF BRITISH EMPIRE	2053	1822	1068	1574	1310	1777	3879	3128	1254	1248
ISLANDS in the BRITISH SEAS	64	91	35	67	63	107	264	314	286	352
SCOTLAND	551	494	358	390	339	479	895	471	375	302
IRELAND	789	682	420	606	507	628	1798	1248	393	371
BRITISH COLONIES OR DEPENDENCIES	640	555	275	511	401	563	922	1095	200	223
FOREIGN COUNTRIES	404	398	414	465	572	623	404	303	297	200
British Subjects	203	194	191	214	273	313	197	193	129	131
Foreigners	201	204	223	251	299	310	207	110	168	69
AT SEA	15	14	14	14	10	27	32	37	4	7
British Subjects	15	14	14	14	10	27	32	37	4	7
Foreigners	.	.	.	.	.	.	.	.	.	.

Table 12.—Distribution of the enumerated Natives of Counties.

Where enumerated.	Where born.											
	South-Eastern Counties.		Surrey.*		Kent.*		Sussex.		Hampshire.		Berkshire.	
	Males.	Females.	Males.	Females.	Males.	Females.	Males.	Females.	Males.	Females.	Males.	Females.
TOTAL ENUMERATED NATIVES OF EACH COUNTY	1527919	1635849	479980	516675	434798	465903	226830	237579	271772	294216	114539	121476
LONDON	477106	538679	303563	331046	116491	134266	19505	24896	23773	29921	13774	18550
Middlesex (*Intra-metropolitan*)	111760	147509	49824	62686	28319	38520	10712	14080	13565	18550	9280	12773
Surrey (*Intra-metropolitan*)	284227	304130	244399	257202	21847	29936	6657	7604	7655	8706	3669	4687
Kent (*Intra-metropolitan*)	81179	87038	9340	11152	66325	69810	2136	2312	2553	2665	825	1090
SOUTH-EASTERN COUNTIES	915074	947392	138930	144635	281373	291505	194657	199079	219036	231818	81•78	80335
Surrey (*Extra-metropolitan*)	141975	148352	114476	116216	8771	10773	8580	9310	6068	8211	3180	3842
Kent (*Extra-metropolitan*)	282174	289119	9677	10509	257294	262193	10031	10618	3832	4190	1445	1614
Sussex	193624	202493	7357	9645	9136	11971	170027	172697	6087	7305	967	1475
Hampshire	217035	228557	5361	5863	5022	5343	5391	6239	198008	207519	3256	3493
Berkshire	80268	78871	2164	2427	1100	1225	628	720	4141	4593	72230	69911
SOUTH-MIDLAND COUNTIES	39640	47848	14072	16456	7568	9438	3172	3880	5301	6398	9527	11676
Middlesex (*Extra-metropolitan*)	21108	25565	9718	11464	4250	5482	1714	2162	2674	3340	2743	3161
Hertfordshire	3775	4514	1410	1596	1017	1226	384	405	585	664	379	533
Buckinghamshire	4166	4715	922	989	577	701	283	305	547	658	1837	2062
Oxfordshire	6012	7643	627	746	418	516	217	202	662	792	4088	5327
Northamptonshire	1890	2097	548	590	541	600	223	238	371	377	212	282
Huntingdonshire	354	417	90	146	83	135	24	40	58	51	44	39
Bedfordshire	1211	1563	380	486	321	427	148	194	227	297	126	159
Cambridgeshire	1174	1334	373	427	342	398	179	177	182	219	98	113
EASTERN COUNTIES	22068	23851	7389	8438	8459	8826	1824	2086	2843	3201	1053	1300
Essex	17397	18313	6550	6839	6670	6833	1351	1473	2070	2266	750	902
Suffolk	2514	2879	734	827	1006	1062	235	308	377	484	162	198
Norfolk	2157	2659	605	772	777	931	238	305	396	451	141	200
SOUTH-WESTERN COUNTIES	20861	23051	3421	3573	4030	4523	1821	1764	8533	9670	3056	3521
Wiltshire	5737	6611	664	697	398	526	231	262	2491	2964	1958	2162
Dorsetshire	4034	4319	521	464	541	463	196	260	2453	2715	187	197
Devonshire	6346	6636	1311	1273	2062	2197	688	615	2006	2103	330	448
Cornwall	1473	1239	226	213	415	366	307	149	455	440	70	71
Somersetshire	3271	4432	699	926	679	971	399	408	1092	1448	502	649
WEST-MIDLAND COUNTIES	13974	16291	3339	3817	3426	4062	1485	1756	3154	3829	2570	2827
Gloucestershire	4304	5611	944	1177	949	1211	425	573	1045	1460	941	1190
Herefordshire	565	653	149	180	136	161	58	85	116	140	106	87
Shropshire	692	828	147	201	184	242	80	82	178	178	103	125
Staffordshire	2761	2723	663	641	705	742	303	308	654	650	436	381
Worcestershire	1558	1910	443	528	373	506	155	213	324	384	263	279
Warwickshire	4094	4868	993	1090	1079	1198	464	495	837	1017	721	765
NORTH-MIDLAND COUNTIES	7584	7747	1904	1902	2630	2699	818	837	1496	1633	736	676
Leicestershire	1404	1765	419	408	400	556	137	188	359	390	179	172
Rutlandshire	191	161	53	45	63	45	26	22	22	30	21	19
Lincolnshire	2697	2343	554	558	1279	946	278	258	419	423	167	153
Nottinghamshire	1599	1791	456	422	442	614	204	212	345	389	152	151
Derbyshire	1693	1687	422	410	440	538	173	157	351	401	217	181
NORTH-WESTERN COUNTIES	11590	12462	2862	2833	3553	4078	1191	1224	3016	3326	968	1001
Cheshire	2155	2268	548	579	614	680	231	211	568	622	194	177
Lancashire	9435	10194	2314	2265	2939	3398	960	1013	2448	2704	774	824
YORKSHIRE	9509	9441	2191	2185	3346	3244	1068	1065	1975	2087	929	860
NORTHERN COUNTIES	5694	4614	928	918	2447	1852	742	494	1330	1115	247	235
Durham	3644	2649	497	486	1547	1113	456	257	884	670	130	123
Northumberland	1555	1341	297	276	764	552	173	150	318	303	63	60
Cumberland	453	455	93	102	155	146	39	54	106	111	40	42
Westmorland	142	169	41	54	41	41	24	33	22	31	14	10
MONMOUTHSHIRE AND WALES	4819	4473	881	832	1475	1410	547	498	1315	1218	601	495
Monmouthshire	781	727	154	132	198	262	101	87	200	205	122	98
Glamorganshire	1355	1073	334	342	511	446	218	179	603	562	289	204
Carmarthenshire	200	183	43	37	50	44	35	29	45	52	32	21
Pembrokeshire	826	644	102	59	407	350	89	50	213	151	41	34
Cardiganshire	79	99	18	26	22	35	9	10	21	16	11	12
Brecknockshire	175	173	56	40	39	38	18	31	32	46	27	18
Radnorshire	62	61	9	17	21	14	4	7	10	12	8	8
Montgomeryshire	96	113	22	32	25	31	15	10	19	22	12	13
Flintshire	153	182	42	50	30	42	15	16	37	44	20	30
Denbighshire	216	256	40	44	71	33	26	36	54	72	25	27
Merionethshire	52	60	13	16	8	14	9	14	10	11	16	5
Carnarvonshire	149	200	35	34	52	68	16	10	36	61	10	21
Anglesey	91	102	13	23	27	42	19	12	28	21	4	4

* The figures in this column relate to the entire county, including that portion situated [illegible]

Table 14.—Number and Ages of Males and Females returned as Blind or Blind from Birth in the South eastern Division and its Registration Counties.

Registration County.	All Ages. Both Sexes.	All Ages. Males and Females.	0–	5–	15–	20–	25–	45–	65 and upwards.
II. SOUTH-EASTERN COUNTIES.	2025	M. 1022	26	79	47	40	189	299	342
		F. 1003	18	74	43	23	142	242	461
1 SURREY (*Extra-metropolitan*)	336	M. 179	3	21	18	12	33	45	47
		F. 157	3	16	5	4	25	31	72
2 KENT (*Extra-metropolitan*)	549	M. 267	12	18	6	7	50	93	81
		F. 282	6	13	14	4	37	75	133
3 SUSSEX	427	M. 222	8	25	11	10	38	60	70
		F. 205		19	11	8	28	40	90
4 HAMPSHIRE	492	M. 239	1	11	11	5	51	66	94
		F. 253	4	22	11	6	87	61	111
5 BERKSHIRE	221	M. 115	2	4	1	6	17	35	50
		F. 106	2	3	4	1	15	26	55

Table 15.—Number and Ages of Males and Females returned as Blind in the South-eastern Division and its Registration Counties.

Registration County.	All Ages. Both Sexes.	All Ages. Males and Females.	0–	5–	15–	20–	25–	45–	65 and upwards.
II. SOUTH-EASTERN COUNTIES.	1869	M. 956	12	62	36	33	180	293	340
		F. 913	12	49	33	18	119	227	455
1 SURREY (*Extra-metropolitan*)	320	M. 174	1	19	18	11	33	46	47
		F. 146	1	13	1	4	22	34	72
2 KENT (*Extra-metropolitan*)	504	M. 247	7	14	3	6	47	90	80
		F. 257	4	8	12	2	28	73	130
3 SUSSEX	386	M. 199	3	18	5	9	36	50	69
		F. 187	3	12	7	8	25	43	89
4 HAMPSHIRE	454	M. 228	.	9	9	2	48	66	94
		F. 226	3	13	9	3	32	56	110
5 BERKSHIRE	205	M. 108	1	2	1	5	16	33	66
		F. 97	1	3	4	1	12	22	64

Table 16.—Number and Ages of Males and Females returned as Blind from Birth in the South-eastern Division and its Registration Counties.

Registration County.	All Ages. Both Sexes.	All Ages. Males and Females.	0–	5–	15–	20–	25–	45–	65 and upwards.
II. SOUTH-EASTERN COUNTIES.	156	M. 66	14	17	11	7	9	6	2
		F. 90	6	25	10	5	23	15	6
1 SURREY (*Extra-metropolitan*)	16	M. 5	2	3	.	1	.	.	.
		F. 11	2	3	2	.	8	1	.
2 KENT (*Extra-metropolitan*)	45	M. 20	5	4	3	1	3	3	1
		F. 25	2	5	2	2	9	2	3
3 SUSSEX	41	M. 23	5	7	6	1	2	1	1
		F. 18	.	7	4	.	3	3	1
4 HAMPSHIRE	38	M. 11	1	2	2	3		.	.
		F. 27	1	10	2	3	6	5	1
5 BERKSHIRE	16	M. 7	1	2	.	1	1	2	.
		F. 9	1	.	.	.	3	4	1

Table 17.—Number and Ages of Males and Females returned as Deaf and Dumb in the South-eastern Division and its Registration Counties.

Registration County.	All Ages. Both Sexes.	All Ages. Males and Females.	0–	5–	15–	20–	25–	45–	65 and upwards.
II. SOUTH-EASTERN COUNTIES.	1436	M. 761	31	256	82	52	187	104	49
		F. 675	22	240	65	50	166	95	37
1 SURREY (*Extra-metropolitan*)	243	M. 130	5	15	16	14	53	19	8
		F. 113	6	16	11	10	46	16	10
2 KENT (*Extra-metropolitan*)	526	M. 270	9	169	26	6	41	16	13
		F. 256	4	149	17	11	44	21	10
3 SUSSEX	286	M. 155	4	49	21	12	35	35	9
		F. 131	5	31	12	16	36	22	10
4 HAMPSHIRE	259	M. 140	10	22	12	18	38	29	11
		F. 119	6	28	18	9	28	24	6
5 BERKSHIRE	122	M. 66	3	11	7	2	20	16	8
		F. 56	1	17	7	.	[illegible]	[illegible]	[illegible]

Table 18.—NUMBER and AGES of MALES and FEMALES returned as IDIOTS or IMBECILES, and LUNATICS in the SOUTH-EASTERN DIVISION and its REGISTRATION COUNTIES.

REGISTRATION COUNTY.	ALL AGES. Both Sexes.	ALL AGES. Males and Females.	0-	5-	15-	20-	25-	45-	65 and upwards.
II. SOUTH-EASTERN COUNTIES.	15017	M. 7049	41	615	507	547	2740	1951	648
		F. 7968	26	363	374	441	2840	2844	1080
1 SURREY (*Extra-metropolitan*)	6048	M. - 2847	8	192	187	290	1193	739	236
		F. - 3201	5	92	97	154	1180	1247	467
2 KENT (*Extra-metropolitan*) -	3876	M. - 1712	14	266	178	108	474	438	134
		F. - 2164	14	166	168	122	716	705	273
3 SUSSEX -	1700	M. - 762	7	57	56	49	302	204	87
		F. - 938	6	39	59	62	338	325	118
4 HAMPSHIRE -	2097	M. - 996	8	71	65	74	380	288	101
		F. - 1101	1	46	42	67	393	384	168
5 BERKSHIRE - -	1246	M. - 732	4	29	21	26	280	282	90
		F. - 514	.	20	17	38	264	183	54

Table 19.—NUMBER and AGES of MALES and FEMALES returned as IDIOTS or IMBECILES in the SOUTH-EASTERN DIVISION and its REGISTRATION COUNTIES.

REGISTRATION COUNTY.	ALL AGES. Both Sexes.	ALL AGES. Males and Females.	0-	5-	15-	20-	25-	45-	65 and upwards.
II. SOUTH-EASTERN COUNTIES.	5536	M. 2616	40	610	447	340	748	313	118
		F. 2920	26	355	327	287	942	635	348
1 SURREY (*Extra-metropolitan*)	2114	M. - 937	8	192	168	195	227	79	17
		F. - 1177	5	92	89	106	441	227	147
2 KENT (*Extra-metropolitan*) -	1598	M. - 750	14	260	167	68	147	62	26
		F. - 848	14	165	151	73	208	145	92
3 SUSSEX - - - -	604	M. - 286	7	55	43	26	92	45	19
		F. 318	6	37	36	37	99	67	36
4 HAMPSHIRE - -	821	M. 421	7	68	49	53	137	93	34
		F. - 400	1	43	36	48	128	91	53
5 BERKSHIRE - -	399	M. 222	4	29	21	18	85	43	23
		F. 177	.	18	15	23	66	35	20

Table 20.—NUMBER and AGES of MALES and FEMALES returned as LUNATICS in the SOUTH-EASTERN DIVISION and its REGISTRATION COUNTIES.

REGISTRATION COUNTY.	ALL AGES. Both Sexes.	ALL AGES. Males and Females.	0-	5-	15-	20-	25-	45-	65 and upwards.
II. SOUTH-EASTERN COUNTIES.	9481	M. 4433	1	5	60	207	1992	1638	530
		F. 5048	.	8	47	154	1898	2209	732
1 SURREY (*Extra-metropolitan*)	3984	M. - 1910	.	.	19	96	908	669	219
		F. - 2074	.	.	8	48	748	960	320
2 KENT (*Extra-metropolitan*) -	2278	M. - 962	.	.	11	40	427	376	108
		F. - 1316	.	1	17	49	508	560	181
3 SUSSEX - -	1096	M. - 476	.	2	14	23	219	159	68
		F. - 620	.	2	14	23	239	258	82
4 HAMPSHIRE - - -	1276	M. - 575	1	3	16	41	252	195	67
		F. - 701	.	3	6	19	265	293	115
5 BERKSHIRE - -	847	M. 510	.	.	.	8	105	239	68
		F. - 337	.	2	3	13	138	148	34

Table 21.—NUMBER of the BLIND, of the DEAF AND DUMB, of IDIOTS or IMBECILES, and of LUNATICS in the SOUTH-EASTERN DIVISION and its REGISTRATION COUNTIES and DISTRICTS.

Registration County and District.	Blind. From Birth.	Blind. Others.	Blind. Total.	Deaf and Dumb.	Mentally Deranged. Idiots.	Mentally Deranged. Lunatics.	Mentally Deranged. Total.
II. SOUTH-EASTERN COUNTIES.	156	1869	2025	1436	5536	9481	15017
1 SURREY (*Extra-metropolitan*)	16	320	336	242	2114	3984	6098
2 KENT (*Extra-metropolitan*)	45	504	549	526	1598	2278	3876
3 SUSSEX	41	386	427	286	664	1096	1760
4 HAMPSHIRE	38	454	492	259	821	1276	2097
5 BERKSHIRE	16	205	221	122	399	847	1246
1 SURREY (*Extra-metropolitan*).							
30 EPSOM	.	24	24	18	194	1550	1744
31 CHERTSEY	2	15	17	6	20	3	23
32 GUILDFORD	.	31	31	28	140	1156	1296
33 FARNHAM	1	16	17	19	39	1	40
34 HAMBLEDON	.	7	7	1	27	1	28
35 DORKING	.	10	10	10	6	2	8
36 REIGATE	2	16	18	18	586	4	590
37 GODSTONE	.	45	45	46	793	1244	2037
38 CROYDON	.	102	102	46	84	9	93
39 KINGSTON	8	32	40	37	188	13	201
40 RICHMOND	3	22	25	14	37	1	38
2 KENT (*Extra-metropolitan*).							
41 BROMLEY	1	28	29	10	46	3	49
42 DARTFORD	.	49	49	22	761	367	1128
43 GRAVESEND	2	13	15	4	25	.	25
44 NORTH AYLESFORD	1	18	19	9	29	2	31
45 HOO	.	.	.	1	5	.	5
46 MEDWAY	9	46	55	19	76	2	78
47 MALLING	.	15	15	8	28	21	49
48 SEVENOAKS	2	18	20	11	29	1	30
49 TUNBRIDGE	1	44	45	19	55	4	59
50 MAIDSTONE	1	37	38	16	135	1218	1353
51 HOLLINGBOURN	1	9	10	4	19	.	19
52 CRANBROOK	.	12	12	3	18	26	44
53 TENTERDEN	.	6	6	1	23	1	24
54 WEST ASHFORD	1	14	15	8	20	1	21
55 EAST ASHFORD	1	11	12	5	20	2	22
56 BRIDGE	.	11	11	6	80	608	688
57 CANTERBURY	1	17	18	8	19	5	24
58 BLEAN	1	12	13	11	19	5	24
59 FAVERSHAM	3	13	16	8	21	2	23
60 MILTON	3	20	23	9	17	.	17
61 SHEPPEY	2	8	10	8	15	.	15
62 THANET	5	36	41	297	50	4	54
63 EASTRY	2	15	17	15	30	2	32
64 DOVER	4	31	35	8	29	2	31
65 ELHAM	4	18	22	11	23	2	25
66 ROMNEY MARSH	.	3	3	2	6	.	6
3 SUSSEX.							
67 RYE	.	12	12	1	23	2	
68 HASTINGS	1	38	39	14	28	2	
69 BATTLE	.	6	6	9	15	6	
70 EASTBOURNE	4	19	23	16	24	10	
71 HAILSHAM	1	6	7	10	27	2	
72 TICEHURST	1	12	13	6	33	72	
73 UCKFIELD	.	10	10	11	54	5	
74 EAST GRINSTEAD	.	9	9	11	34	3	
75 CUCKFIELD	1	9	10	6	25	3	
76 LEWES	1	27	28	24	47	861	
77 BRIGHTON	20	114	134	122	81	106	
78 STEYNING	3	38	41	17	43	13	
79 HORSHAM	3	13	16	8	33	1	
80 PETWORTH	.	9	9	6	25	2	
81 THAKEHAM	1	10	11	5	9	.	
82 EAST PRESTON	1	15	16	9	37	1	
83 WESTHAMPNETT	3	16	19	5	30	3	
84 CHICHESTER	.	6	6	1	8	.	
85 MIDHURST	.	12	12	3	21	.	
86 WESTBOURNE	1	5	6	2	18	2	
4 HAMPSHIRE.							
87 HAVANT	.	7	7	6	11	.	
88 PORTSEA ISLAND	17	113	130	46	111	480	
89 ALVERSTOKE	3	21	24	9	19	21	
90 FAREHAM	.	24	24	12	167	667	
91 ISLE OF WIGHT	2	37	39	27	62	12	
92 LYMINGTON	.	14	14	13	15	3	
93 CHRISTCHURCH	1	16	17	6	24	.	
94 RINGWOOD	1	4	5	2	12	.	
95 FORDINGBRIDGE	.	5	5	7	12	.	
96 NEW FOREST	1	12	13	6	20	.	
97 SOUTHAMPTON	3	40	43	13	81	3	
98 SOUTH STONEHAM	.	30	30	23	28	51	
99 ROMSEY	.	12	12	4	21	.	
100 STOCKBRIDGE	.	8	8	5	9	1	
101 WINCHESTER	3	23	26	14	29	1	
102 DROXFORD	1	7	8	5	15	6	
103 CATHERINGTON	.	2	2	2	7	1	
104 PETERSFIELD	.	3	3	8	6	1	
105 ALRESFORD	1	8	9	4	6	.	
106 ALTON	1	9	10	1	30	26	
107 HARTLEY WINTNEY	.	19	19	13	38	.	
108 BASINGSTOKE	.	16	16	20	48	.	
109 WHITCHURCH	.	3	3	3	10	.	
110 ANDOVER	4	13	17	11	24	1	
111 KINGSCLERE	.	9	9	9	71	2	
5 BERKSHIRE.							
112 NEWBURY	1	18	19	17	19	2	
113 HUNGERFORD	1	22	23	8	23	.	
114 FARINGDON	3	23	26	10	14	3	
115 ABINGDON	2	21	23	12	28	3	
116 WANTAGE	3	12	15	6	27	2	
117 WALLINGFORD	1	19	20	12	107	356	
118 BRADFIELD	1	12	13	9	16	.	
119 READING	.	29	29	16	46	3	
120 WOKINGHAM	1	17	18	11	25	.	
121 COOKHAM	2	8	10	4	42	1	
122 EASTHAMPSTEAD	.	10	10	10	21	474	
123 WINDSOR	1	14	15	7	31	3	

AGES,

CONDITION AS TO MARRIAGE, OCCUPATIONS, AND BIRTH-PLACES OF THE PEOPLE:

WITH THE

NUMBERS AND AGES OF THE BLIND, DEAF AND DUMB, IDIOTS OR IMBECILES, AND LUNATICS.

DIVISION III.—SOUTH-MIDLAND COUNTIES;

MIDDLESEX (*Extra-metropolitan*),
HERTFORDSHIRE,
BUCKINGHAMSHIRE,
OXFORDSHIRE,
NORTHAMPTONSHIRE,
HUNTINGDONSHIRE,
BEDFORDSHIRE,
CAMBRIDGESHIRE.

TABLES IN DIVISION III.—SOUTH-MIDLAND COUNTIES.

AGES

Table.

1.—Ages of Males and Females in the South-Midland Division and its Registration Counties.

2.—Ages of Males and Females in Registration Districts.

3.—Ages of Males and Females in Registration Sub-districts.

4.—Male and Female Children at *each Year of Age* under 5 in the South-Midland Division and its Re tration Counties.

5.—Male and Female Children at *each Year of Age* under 5 in Registration Districts.

6.—Ages of Males and Females in Sanitary Districts.

CONDITION AS TO MARRIAGE.

7.—Condition as to Marriage and Ages of Males and Females in the South Midland Division and its Re tration Counties.

8.—Condition as to Marriage and Ages of Males and Females in Registration Districts.

9.—Condition as to Marriage and Ages of Males and Females in each Urban Sanitary District of wl the Population exceeds 50,000 Persons.

OCCUPATIONS.

10.—Occupations of Males and Females in the South-Midland Division and its Registration Counties, an each Urban Sanitary District of which the Population exceeds 50,000 Persons.

BIRTH-PLACES.

11.—Birth-places of Males and Females enumerated in Counties, and in each Urban Sanitary District of wh the Population exceeds 50,000 Persons.

12.—Distribution of the enumerated Natives of Counties.

13.—Number and Country of Birth of Foreigners enumerated in Counties, and in each Urban Sanitary Distr of which the Population exceeds 50,000 Persons.

THE BLIND, DEAF AND DUMB, IDIOTS OR IMBECILES, AND LUNATICS.

14.—Number and Ages of Males and Females returned as Blind or Blind from Birth in the South-Midla Division and its Registration Counties.

15.—Number and Ages of Males and Females returned as Blind in the South-Midland Division and its Reg tration Counties.

16.—Number and Ages of Males and Females returned as Blind from Birth in the South-Midland Divisi and its Registration Counties.

17.—Number and Ages of Males and Females returned as Deaf and Dumb in the South-Midland Division a its Registration Counties.

18.—Number and Ages of Males and Females returned as Idiots or Imbeciles, and Lunatics in the South-Midla Division and its Registration Counties.

19.—Number and Ages of Males and Females returned as Idiots or Imbeciles in the South-Midland Divisi and its Registration Counties.

20.—Number and Ages of Males and Females returned as Lunatics in the South-Midland Division and Registration Counties.

21.—Number of the Blind, of the Deaf and Dumb, of Idiots or Imbeciles, and of Lunatics, in the South-Midla Division and its Registration Counties and Districts.

AGES.

DIVISION III.—SOUTH MIDLAND COUNTIES.

Table 1.—Ages of Males and Females in the South Midland Division and its Registration Counties.

Registration County.	All Ages. Persons.	All Ages. Males and Females.	Under 5* Years.	5–	10–	15–	20–	25–	30–	35–	40–	45–	50–	55–	60–	65–	70–	75–	80–	85–	90–	95–	100† and upw[d].
III.—SOUTH MIDLAND COUNTIES.	1590259	M. 770926	106387	100382	93596	78380	60784	51246	46763	43242	39651	36670	33020	26573	23801	17514	12221	7523	3470	990	174	21	.
		F. 820333	106592	100010	89786	75520	68208	59702	53390	48062	44255	37787	34470	28241	26677	19622	14008	8708	4210	1396	328	60	5
MIDDLESEX (Extra-metropolitan)	380814	M. 180622	25985	28508	22036	17205	15173	13450	12425	11011	9785	7471	6509	4847	4962	2910	1982	1168	561	147	30	3	.
		F. 200192	26925	28467	20781	19516	19920	16634	14581	12960	10011	8710	7865	5701	6330	3740	2815	1636	799	304	73	11	2
HERTFORDSHIRE	203375	M. 98963	13382	13121	12607	9094	6800	9184	8089	6806	5002	3736	4035	3472	3183	2401	1776	1034	490	132	22	.	.
		F. 104412	13020	12094	11531	9001	7556	7241	9700	9326	5000	4040	4401	3606	3600	2000	1047	1171	501	109	51	3	1
BUCKINGHAMSHIRE	155869	M. 76796	10369	10020	9527	8095	5503	4708	4226	4151	3805	3467	3110	2487	2523	1885	1381	894	272	114	28	1	.
		F. 79073	10378	10071	8990	6844	6043	5418	4854	4598	4292	3687	3470	2876	2668	2013	1406	872	436	132	30	8	1
OXFORDSHIRE	181570	M. 88009	11916	11286	10737	9098	6955	5599	5020	4795	4306	3025	3750	3079	3043	2268	1046	1016	430	136	10	3	.
		F. 92983	11965	11215	10360	8378	7376	6344	5700	6251	5947	4353	4014	3447	3249	2489	1737	1045	470	167	29	3	.
NORTHAMPTONSHIRE	277030	M. 138091	18935	17356	15507	13974	11590	9709	8552	7587	7947	6250	5531	4647	4176	3089	2083	1265	533	161	21	6	.
		F. 138941	19529	17441	15222	12930	11168	10081	8631	7847	7802	6376	5665	4782	4630	3224	2241	1394	653	201	48	6	.
HUNTINGDONSHIRE	53223	M. 26067	3404	3469	3216	2686	1815	1423	1354	1317	1339	1216	1138	1069	941	725	492	346	161	66	7	2	.
		F. 27156	3391	3466	3187	2404	1916	1630	1531	1577	1416	1277	1206	1060	1054	798	566	402	222	68	20	1	1
BEDFORDSHIRE	154259	M. 72570	9934	9699	9009	7588	5222	4372	4079	3945	3658	3193	2857	2561	2394	1745	1225	749	340	82	17	1	.
		F. 81683	10042	9543	8602	7861	6983	5393	5399	4612	4488	3962	2348	2987	2600	1926	1382	782	355	111	17	.	.
CAMBRIDGESHIRE	191114	M. 93903	12900	11928	10997	6708	7603	5815	5437	6224	4690	3843	3620	3281	3326	2471	1656	1085	501	171	32	6	.
		F. 97211	12231	12123	10872	8692	7412	5652	5852	6572	5136	4440	4058	3605	3648	2746	1823	1341	682	243	60	13	.

Note.—Registration Counties consist of groups of Registration Districts, which are generally co-extensive with the Poor Law Unions. Those Registration Districts which extend into two or more Counties are included in that Registration County in which the principal town of the District or the greater part of the population is located. The boundaries of Registration Counties, therefore, differ more or less from the boundaries of Counties. For such differences in Division III., see Vol. II., Table 11.

* For the number of Children at each Year of Age under 5, see Table 4.

† Four of these Females were stated to be 100, and one 101 years of age.

Table 2.—Ages of Males and Females in Registration Districts.

Registration District.	All Ages. Persons.	All Ages. Males and Females.	Under 5* Years.	5–	10–	15–	20–	25–	30–	35–	40–	45–	50–	55–	60–	65–	70–	75–	80–	85–	90–	95–	100 and upw[d].
MIDDLESEX (Ex.-metropolitan)																							
STAINES	23774	M. - 12094	1557	1677	2073	1218	819	716	661	683	578	461	450	350	311	226	172	82	44	13	4	1	.
		F. - 11680	1544	1572	1411	998	958	830	760	688	616	508	482	353	339	225	178	131	62	26	4	.	.
UXBRIDGE	27550	M. - 13535	1773	1638	1592	1308	1061	908	901	776	792	637	585	450	425	303	202	109	52	21	2	.	.
		F. - 14015	1754	1669	1469	1057	1091	1020	933	863	813	723	800	592	507	347	277	143	78	31	6	2	1
BRENTFORD	101706	M. - 47539	6870	6410	5825	4629	4138	3641	3283	2823	2484	1808	1713	1173	1131	771	565	274	155	30	9	.	.
		F. - 54167	6782	6118	5589	5434	5553	4301	3944	3285	2935	2397	2124	1312	1466	988	717	473	208	66	17	6	1
HENDON	54482	M. - 25740	3647	3281	3192	2767	2127	1937	1759	1541	1423	1040	801	712	672	354	226	128	55	16	1	1	.
		F. - 28742	3706	3329	3149	2873	2887	2432	2128	1745	1651	1230	1083	771	662	463	291	146	92	31	13	1	.
BARNET	34098	M. - 15772	2074	1854	1987	1535	1266	1125	1115	990	945	697	652	500	460	262	188	114	87	18	2	1	.
		F. - 18326	2157	1899	1704	1706	1785	1559	1473	1221	1104	872	779	585	511	387	286	173	76	38	9	2	.
EDMONTON	139204	M. - 65942	10067	8638	7357	6850	5692	5209	4706	4180	3563	2741	2246	1690	1423	934	694	454	228	48	12	.	.
		F. - 73262	9965	8850	7408	7144	7635	6102	5343	4496	3703	2060	2537	1338	1820	1320	1086	658	263	113	24	3	.
HERTFORDSHIRE.																							
WARE	18635	M. - 9434	1187	1136	1228	1211	681	596	589	457	436	418	358	321	290	230	160	100	32	16	5	.	.
		F. - 9130	1213	1124	1039	787	712	648	596	532	460	440	373	310	314	261	150	103	71	24	8	.	.
BISHOPSTORTFORD	21801	M. - 10910	1408	1441	1480	1126	693	668	618	560	514	474	484	394	392	395	219	121	61	15	2	.	.
		F. - 10891	1455	1384	1219	875	852	708	663	880	608	550	462	392	371	511	226	128	67	21	11	1	.
ROYSTON	24655	M. - 12550	1671	1691	1616	1521	788	648	649	674	636	589	516	407	438	326	263	163	85	21	1	.	.
		F. - 12105	1638	1665	1420	940	740	702	754	684	643	586	527	504	440	321	248	190	71	28	8	2	.
HITCHIN	27417	M. - 13003	1302	1801	1615	1234	865	778	740	650	509	555	599	453	424	323	224	140	63	13	3	.	.
		F. - 14414	1830	1763	1604	1832	1200	1031	909	842	742	673	608	408	485	330	275	171	72	26	9	.	.
HERTFORD	16754	M. - 8509	1042	1292	1177	949	612	498	468	439	418	353	332	279	256	190	148	100	39	7	1	.	.
		F. - 8245	1011	1020	988	740	615	525	529	481	426	403	348	309	284	209	182	105	59	18	3	.	.
HATFIELD	8802	M. - 4371	634	537	471	428	335	309	281	214	205	190	192	170	124	95	80	43	24	6	2	.	.
		F. - 4431	653	545	467	381	310	362	305	250	231	183	181	147	135	92	82	47	25	5	.	1	.
ST. ALBANS	23296	M. - 10963	1568	1408	1250	1011	800	718	667	648	590	442	433	377	337	252	138	97	53	16	1	.	.
		F. - 12333	1692	1450	1255	1069	1045	917	878	737	707	546	518	430	394	319	215	125	53	22	7	3	1
WATFORD	31328	M. - 15055	1905	1918	2016	1307	1101	1049	881	983	848	712	851	523	468	319	247	119	63	13	4	.	.
		F. - 16273	1938	1994	1841	1383	1251	1182	1086	1041	939	815	793	613	548	416	223	162	76	30	6	3	.
HEMEL HEMPSTEAD	14696	M. - 6905	987	894	672	640	483	461	437	369	394	292	272	232	253	189	113	73	29	9	1	.	.
		F. 7811	936	995	825	791	697	562	511	420	448	373	339	282	270	213	121	63	38	6	3	.	.
BERKHAMPSTEAD	15091	M. - 7173	1018	976	836	726	491	479	409	393	356	278	297	256	216	180	109	78	35	16	2	.	.
		F. 7918	1050	944	857	679	658	507	509	472	456	368	323	291	262	207	135	89	32	7	2	.	.
BUCKINGHAMSHIRE.																							
AMERSHAM	18319	M. - 8940	1270	1219	1100	834	627	512	514	468	412	391	391	342	300	221	177	93	44	18	1	.	.
		F. - 9379	1257	1206	1134	786	700	587	582	537	474	462	401	336	354	263	180	111	57	9	3	.	.
ETON	27721	M. - 14027	1612	1694	2114	1938	1039	822	724	779	685	629	554	405	369	263	207	126	53	11	3	.	.
		F. - 13694	1684	1640	1509	1243	1102	996	906	871	793	695	602	465	420	231	205	121	56	30	3	1	.
WYCOMBE	40278	M. - 19801	2905	2703	2320	1934	1444	1292	1122	1040	995	910	835	634	570	442	332	207	90	19	7	.	.
		F. - 20477	2885	2746	2380	1783	1896	1441	1232	1150	1112	906	854	621	608	461	324	178	104	25	7	5	.
AYLESBURY	24607	M. - 12053	1653	1564	1585	1158	848	785	700	646	631	535	472	447	433	296	230	150	75	23	6	.	.
		F. - 12554	1605	1584	1349	1045	955	886	723	740	703	637	577	476	429	357	237	167	62	23	8	1	.
WINSLOW	7943	M. - 3876	475	534	495	374	276	198	176	158	208	175	150	138	175	120	90	47	14	11	1	.	.
		F. 4067	493	521	511	378	287	240	232	225	214	198	138	143	173	105	85	55	22	5	1	.	.
NEWPORT PAGNELL	24583	M. - 12030	1727	1537	1381	1185	892	702	661	672	679	541	480	453	445	373	199	146	58	13	5	1	.
		F. - 12553	1712	1628	1390	1089	935	849	745	732	621	563	581	501	431	328	232	167	76	25	4	.	1
BUCKINGHAM	12418	M. - 6069	898	769	752	582	377	337	328	348	286	256	228	240	231	210	126	93	37	19	3	.	.
		F. - 6349	737	748	587	547	483	419	434	334	345	286	302	270	253	208	143	85	58	15	4	1	.

Note.—The Registration Districts of Division III. are co-extensive with the Poor Law Unions of the same name, with the following exceptions:—The Royston District (132) comprises the two Poor Law Unions of Royston and Buntingford; and the Hatfield District (136) comprises the two Unions of Hatfield and Welwyn. The Oxford District (156) is an Incorporation under a Local Act.

Table 2 *continued.*—Ages of Males and Females in Registration Districts.

Registration District.	All Ages. Persons.	All Ages. Males and Females.	Under 5 Years.	5–	10–	15–	20–	25–	30–	35–	40–	45–	50–	55–	60–	65–	70–	75–	80–	85–	90–	9[cut off]
9 OXFORDSHIRE.																						
147 HENLEY	19992	M. - 9949	1335	1362	1191	1096	721	603	597	526	518	400	391	321	336	224	168	108	36	17	3	
		F. - 10043	1321	1304	1163	798	785	631	632	588	524	489	410	360	375	239	176	94	61	22	1	
148 THAME	13862	M. - 6896	913	919	947	668	468	388	370	337	303	288	297	259	262	181	149	103	43	16	3	
		F. - 6967	961	902	828	839	519	428	423	393	338	324	315	292	273	203	147	83	46	18	1	
149 HEADINGTON	28723	M. - 13426	1860	1663	1638	1344	1125	936	866	780	681	667	504	466	397	304	200	153	61	21	.	
		F. - 15297	1873	1645	1580	1639	1395	1162	1098	894	884	657	623	407	489	383	251	147	73	27	3	
150 OXFORD	21902	M. - 10573	1304	1204	1113	1122	1172	864	710	697	521	471	435	302	254	195	122	84	35	8	.	
		F. - 11322	1365	1186	1119	1278	1060	950	759	685	634	554	453	364	320	266	169	97	35	12	5	
151 BICESTER	14157	M. - 7067	940	843	800	723	670	453	330	332	316	351	320	290	264	230	144	98	48	18	1	
		F. - 7090	899	865	797	621	551	447	396	378	374	354	326	209	260	226	141	103	40	19	1	
152 WOODSTOCK	13320	M. - 6536	887	847	822	638	468	358	340	335	327	296	298	231	260	176	129	78	31	12	4	
		F. - 6784	914	862	777	530	528	447	393	362	373	324	307	265	231	209	124	83	40	8	4	
153 WITNEY	21536	M. - 10671	1451	1396	1271	1065	730	590	423	529	548	474	473	388	398	367	260	153	65	21	.	
		F. - 10865	1464	1417	1253	953	740	609	500	610	618	519	483	393	399	338	233	156	74	22	5	
154 CHIPPING NORTON	17958	M. - 8901	1217	1151	1066	864	609	542	491	515	424	393	383	314	298	255	189	93	53	10	4	
		F. - 9057	1259	1169	1089	777	665	541	582	482	600	425	389	335	324	214	182	112	39	13	4	
155 BANBURY	30120	M. - 14890	1918	1861	1920	1538	1089	878	786	779	734	674	658	568	577	366	275	176	69	23	4	
		F. - 15230	1909	1862	1782	1313	1133	990	918	846	827	745	701	632	578	415	314	170	63	26	5	
10 NORTHAMPTONSHIRE.																						
156 BRACKLEY	12340	M. - 6197	822	769	783	641	445	320	311	319	329	289	248	257	235	156	122	78	30	11	1	
		F. - 6143	727	730	692	616	453	398	366	355	340	342	268	269	220	203	131	103	42	12	2	
157 TOWCESTER	12584	M. - 6189	836	784	711	623	427	360	356	327	295	302	275	246	224	170	114	90	35	12	1	
		F. - 6395	860	780	632	501	480	413	394	328	355	328	307	260	232	166	154	88	39	19	2	
158 POTTERSPURY	12231	M. - 6156	833	773	792	665	479	397	376	317	293	269	266	215	177	154	105	55	32	11	2	
		F. 6075	836	745	690	621	479	406	403	376	282	285	267	250	191	153	116	72	26	11	2	
159 HARDINGSTONE	10486	M. - 5348	725	637	565	534	400	358	321	298	266	267	212	184	178	148	101	62	25	4	1	
		F. 5138	730	641	570	401	339	348	324	276	300	228	223	213	176	140	81	48	24	7	1	
160 NORTHAMPTON	64244	M. - 31520	4448	[illegible]	3413	3156	2787	2473	2233	1826	1801	1602	1197	984	749	520	318	161	76	18	1	
		F. - 32724	4630	3674	3533	3367	2961	2593	2157	1955	1730	1416	1221	934	864	638	387	206	113	35	7	
161 DAVENTRY	18514	M. - 9396	1144	1068	979	875	811	622	536	536	507	438	449	369	372	255	203	115	58	17	.	
		F. - 9118	1148	1083	936	746	688	600	621	511	478	438	448	420	357	202	205	127	66	21	7	
162 BRIXWORTH	13336	M. - 6740	813	787	787	696	582	413	347	331	317	297	348	292	285	193	140	89	41	11	1	
		F. 6596	803	790	705	500	471	459	357	354	327	376	332	304	292	198	147	92	32	9	3	
163 WELLINGBOROUGH	36942	M. - 18375	2391	2402	1987	1918	1624	1455	1209	986	931	785	676	556	602	325	223	131	49	13	3	
		F. - 18567	2670	2422	2029	1957	1575	1466	1170	1008	933	798	658	530	496	354	246	144	64	14	2	
164 KETTERING	25053	M. - 12308	1918	1684	1352	1253	1162	946	842	706	612	629	486	441	378	247	197	121	37	16	2	
		F. - 12745	1928	1672	1336	1177	1058	926	840	718	625	531	491	404	366	250	160	109	43	11	3	
165 THRAPSTON	15115	M. - 7615	1069	1006	892	779	561	481	441	435	376	382	362	268	229	175	102	88	29	8	2	
		F. - 7500	1065	1035	853	647	524	518	427	428	416	353	295	226	232	187	134	95	30	13	1	
166 OUNDLE	14086	M. - 7117	862	871	973	737	504	595	348	363	321	340	285	275	289	224	153	94	39	18	2	1
		F. 6969	895	881	835	600	482	435	386	387	344	343	309	276	288	213	148	98	62	23	4	.
167 PETERBOROUGH	41604	M. - 20524	2848	2686	2313	2067	1748	1481	1232	1124	1000	889	798	681	581	456	304	187	82	27	5	.
		F. - 20080	2886	2670	2391	1978	1687	1544	1346	1161	1169	921	839	687	606	489	326	216	116	35	14	1
11 HUNTINGDONSHIRE.																						
168 HUNTINGDON	19561	M. - 9655	1241	1214	1259	1014	710	553	523	409	499	434	394	356	316	261	184	127	51	20	1	.
		F. - 9906	1267	1251	1133	966	707	602	553	584	488	458	423	384	361	291	186	139	87	21	5	.
169 ST. IVES	16755	M. - 8187	1061	1061	944	840	560	449	462	466	448	405	377	320	303	250	163	135	50	26	1	2
		F. - 8568	1070	1094	1019	702	537	453	473	524	461	419	378	337	358	268	197	142	73	19	6	.
170 ST. NEOTS	16907	M. - 8225	1100	1134	1013	854	645	421	486	411	412	376	367	383	322	214	145	84	56	16	5	.
		F. - 8682	1054	1111	1015	736	652	554	506	460	471	460	405	339	335	242	133	121	62	18	9	1
12 BEDFORDSHIRE.																						
171 BEDFORD	42933	M. - 20966	2594	2616	2644	2274	1535	1241	1110	1095	1066	928	722	710	700	494	365	217	97	21	3	1
		F. - 22367	2635	2667	2462	2384	2014	1612	1441	1328	1218	1095	880	898	761	585	407	242	124	35	4	.
172 BIGGLESWADE	27378	M. - 13339	1776	1784	1702	1386	889	737	748	727	608	605	560	471	432	338	235	156	67	15	6	.
		F. - 14039	1805	1721	1563	1146	1044	961	835	849	765	728	606	451	500	360	255	176	74	24	1	.
173 AMPTHILL	16253	M. - 7755	1082	1072	950	755	526	413	401	386	302	354	333	308	272	214	134	94	55	10	4	.
		F. - 8498	1122	1080	939	636	678	539	528	433	470	308	332	320	353	205	159	86	34	12	4	.
174 WOBURN	9880	M. - 4708	612	622	551	483	308	241	269	242	193	205	220	215	185	133	115	87	26	11	1	.
		F. - 5172	671	609	604	447	356	358	332	305	276	282	242	170	234	135	117	82	37	14	5	.
175 LEIGHTON BUZZARD	18316	M. - 8714	1247	1174	1074	880	594	521	535	400	484	349	317	288	304	213	134	90	42	10	.	.
		F. - 9602	1265	1175	1068	919	781	686	635	678	532	413	272	378	306	220	167	72	42	8	2	.
176 LUTON	39500	M. - 17695	2623	2341	2088	1816	1370	1219	1024	1005	945	752	705	550	494	351	224	116	67	15	3	.
		F. - 21805	2644	2318	2408	2308	2030	1737	1525	1868	1238	1046	863	701	652	420	278	153	74	18	1	.
13 CAMBRIDGESHIRE.																						
177 CAXTON	10357	M. - 5248	695	713	690	601	334	276	299	273	200	246	205	194	197	144	115	65	39	9	3	.
		F. - 5109	718	757	585	[illegible]	310	316	249	[illegible]	[illegible]	217	278	185	192	162	160	72	40	17	3	.
178 CHESTERTON	29049	M. - 14528	1958	1949	1678	1445	1067	897	894	877	708	568	540	541	512	340	231	189	104	29	.	1
		F. - 14521	1923	1831	1657	1121	1061	951	915	893	776	682	610	569	510	379	282	208	101	38	11	3
179 CAMBRIDGE	35363	M. - 16521	2091	1917	1781	1861	2434	1260	1035	931	826	615	552	479	424	282	211	113	70	16	2	1
		F. - 18842	2090	1989	1986	2128	1830	1530	1235	1124	1011	818	760	627	663	465	320	255	96	30	8	3
180 LINTON	13615	M. - 6424	981	856	743	722	468	379	317	304	319	276	263	227	220	179	137	91	29	12	1	.
		F. - [illegible]	894	905	817	510	460	322	338	326	348	275	279	228	245	222	140	113	46	19	8	1
181 NEWMARKET	28247	M. - 14185	1784	1724	1706	1500	1137	864	810	702	706	580	580	511	520	397	263	107	69	27	6	2
		F. - 14062	1850	1766	1506	1211	1638	935	810	789	754	665	612	565	649	403	276	212	135	47	5	1
182 ELY	20702	M. - 10357	1304	1334	1216	1068	785	617	565	539	551	422	440	388	407	305	202	126	67	21	5	1
		F. - 10345	1308	1377	1225	878	730	642	628	587	497	402	438	396	446	260	216	136	61	23	3	2
183 NORTH WITCHFORD	15494	M. - 7713	1010	978	914	781	598	476	450	458	493	367	297	279	294	220	128	85	53	20	2	.
		F. - 7761	1033	1030	892	717	540	422	401	463	427	341	305	256	299	215	144	91	58	17	6	.
184 WHITTLESEY	6455	M. - 3185	439	404	385	331	191	168	170	173	135	142	140	126	139	93	67	39	26	7	4	1
		F. - 3270	404	397	368	297	197	206	165	169	173	163	140	134	140	106	71	62	27	9	5	.
185 WISBECH	32462	M. - 15742	2142	2063	1884	1569	1049	888	917	898	792	682	613	543	613	451	302	180	114	36	9	.
		F. - 16720	2062	2071	1885	1454	1228	1388	1003	852	896	792	703	677	661	533	344	242	123	43	13	3

TABLE 3.—AGES of MALES and FEMALES in REGISTRATION SUB-DISTRICTS.

REGISTRATION SUB-DISTRICT.	ALL AGES. Persons.	ALL AGES. Males and Females.	Under 5 Years.	5-	10-	15-	20-	25-	30-	35-	40-	45-	50-	55-	60-	65-	70-	75-	80-	85-	90-	95-	100 and upw^ds.
IIDDLESEX xtra-metropo- ta).																							
124 STAINES.																							
BURY. (ws.L.R.)	11585	M. - 6083	688	870	1411	612	329	308	316	311	250	220	213	188	140	90	63	33	16	5	.	.	.
		F. - 5502	705	780	746	460	437	415	367	304	287	200	316	176	148	98	97	47	19	9	2	.	.
NES. (W.)	12089	M. - 6011	860	867	632	604	450	468	345	379	325	241	237	182	171	130	109	69	28	8	4	1	.
		F. - 6078	839	793	865	497	519	414	300	384	328	248	266	197	191	134	80	84	33	16	2	.	.
125 UXBRIDGE.																							
LINGDON. (W.H.L.)	10609	M. - [illegible]	727	611	616	656	426	328	340	291	292	265	202	166	162	137	78	65	23	12	.	.	.
		F. - [illegible]	742	602	610	458	472	415	348	320	281	250	233	135	167	153	118	48	26	15	2	.	1
RIDGE	5225	M. - 2884	312	323	340	310	220	200	180	131	146	113	102	94	85	81	38	12	13	3	1	.	.
		F. - 2341	306	291	292	230	211	175	160	107	156	113	118	89	98	52	43	34	15	6	2	.	.
VES. (ws.H.L.[2])	11028	M. - 5558	704	701	638	448	415	380	401	354	354	261	278	197	174	115	88	29	16	6	1	.	.
		F. - 5465	706	688	587	363	423	430	425	410	373	360	306	252	266	143	116	69	37	16	2	2	.
126 BRENTFORD.																							
WORTH. (W.L.B.)	22727	M. - 11292	1411	1445	1602	1149	904	728	701	698	624	435	413	286	298	218	144	93	53	8	3	.	.
		F. - 11435	1466	1399	1179	1059	682	810	801	704	672	535	477	364	338	256	194	139	64	19	4	1	.
OXENHAM. (H.[2]L.B.)	12479	M. - 5707	763	770	724	623	418	388	303	348	281	231	213	152	160	101	59	31	17	8	2	.	.
		F. - 6772	769	702	685	647	747	615	480	444	349	334	277	179	225	120	35	63	37	13	4	1	.
NTFORD. (H.L.)	27649	M. - 12522	1787	1647	1349	1238	1092	393	908	705	651	530	485	324	304	191	144	77	36	7	4	.	.
		F. - 15127	1738	1554	1445	1067	1708	1362	1006	889	830	726	590	443	414	258	236	120	52	22	5	2	.
SWICK. (L.)	15975	M. - 7383	1129	934	790	674	721	644	505	415	394	289	262	138	165	105	67	20	11	3	.	.	.
		F. - 8592	1132	916	848	960	984	804	635	519	453	361	316	239	200	136	86	67	19	6	6	1	.
ON. (ws. H.L.)	22876	M. - 10635	1759	1605	1360	845	903	809	688	657	536	370	340	256	197	156	91	44	18	4	.	.	.
		F. - 12241	1687	1556	1405	1161	1287	1010	902	703	660	471	434	307	204	218	116	88	36	6	9	1	1
127 HENDON.																							
ROW. (B.[3])	12796	M. - 6133	753	698	932	926	461	404	346	327	314	231	211	138	138	95	63	33	21	1	1	.	.
		F. - 6663	799	760	836	714	654	519	481	359	372	282	267	205	163	111	70	45	26	10	1	.	.
WARE. (H.)	3749	M. - 1873	212	259	312	164	145	118	123	96	94	80	73	67	38	33	19	13	8	2	.	.	.
		F. - 1876	244	235	194	146	140	142	132	125	115	86	80	65	64	59	29	15	8	7	1	.	.
LLESDEN	27453	M. - 12883	2053	1744	1369	1187	1184	1099	950	828	773	531	402	315	268	145	83	45	13	4	.	.	.
		F. - 14570	1955	1692	1546	1381	1811	1312	1185	911	884	658	549	360	237	108	137	51	43	3	8	.	.
NDON. (W.WS.L.R.)	10484	M. - 4851	639	585	579	496	447	466	311	280	242	208	173	137	120	81	61	37	13	9	.	1	.
		F. - 5633	768	642	584	632	582	469	410	320	301	204	138	141	148	104	55	34	17	5	3	1	.
128 BARNET.																							
TH MIMMS. (B.)	6391	M. - 3148	434	372	433	256	217	216	194	187	172	138	134	118	93	72	47	36	10	5	.	.	.
		F. - 3243	418	396	358	249	225	242	246	198	170	176	128	104	110	91	99	41	22	10	1	.	.
RNET. (W.R.)	10092	M. - 4761	574	610	763	461	395	300	274	278	261	182	200	113	126	78	69	42	12	8	1	1	.
		F. - 5331	638	587	549	575	544	433	383	317	304	213	216	150	134	112	73	55	24	14	4	1	.
CHLEY. (H.L.)	17615	M. - 7868	1066	882	791	708	654	606	647	664	503	377	318	275	181	112	67	36	15	5	1	.	.
		F. - 9747	1119	910	797	882	1016	884	850	706	630	483	418	326	287	184	144	77	36	14	4	1	.
129 EDMONTON.																							
RNSEY. (H.)	37078	M. - 16924	2304	2159	1738	1479	1532	1341	1230	1150	910	708	538	413	299	194	99	71	32	7	1	.	.
		F. - 20154	2427	2116	1851	2621	2408	1900	1572	1266	1077	845	671	531	476	341	240	142	64	23	2	1	.
TTENHAM. (H.[2])	46466	M. - 22380	3619	2907	2512	1981	1936	1980	1700	1452	1189	820	712	445	434	253	161	102	43	19	4	.	.
		F. - 24147	3609	3081	2400	2303	2202	2193	1894	1491	1242	983	791	570	655	337	277	187	78	27	7	1	.
MONTON. (W.w.ws.H.)	23463	M. - 11517	1684	1590	1351	967	842	716	793	680	530	474	439	293	295	288	241	177	105	22	4	.	.
		F. - 11946	1043	1539	1234	1027	865	918	843	737	620	615	422	329	352	307	364	178	91	37	8	.	.
FIELD. (WS.H.B.)	19104	M. - 9308	1332	1306	1115	836	817	559	614	852	526	485	310	283	209	148	94	51	29	4	.	.	.
		F. - 9796	1381	1295	1129	382	382	712	682	570	521	419	363	232	244	168	124	72	38	13	6	1	.
LTHAM ABBEY. (H.)	5368	M. - 2712	404	365	260	234	246	210	174	131	193	127	106	80	76	48	45	19	8	1	1	.	.
		F. - 2656	368	361	316	345	189	202	170	106	127	132	94	78	81	57	41	32	19	5	.	.	.
ESHUNT	7735	M. - 3673	524	459	382	353	291	264	216	203	225	168	143	147	110	78	56	34	13	5	2	.	.
		F. - 4062	537	495	418	366	324	279	276	248	206	198	196	126	149	99	80	49	22	8	1	.	.
HERTFORDSHIRE.																							
130 WARE.																							
DDESDON	6718	M. - 3408	399	375	325	373	232	203	192	164	146	156	110	105	84	61	42	22	10	7	2	.	.
		F. - 3310	406	385	357	291	304	246	232	206	177	170	137	108	95	77	40	38	24	7	4	.	.
ANSTEAD	2719	M. - 1371	175	170	168	145	99	88	79	63	69	73	62	50	59	30	30	15	3	3	1	.	.
		F. - 1348	176	163	155	121	107	84	83	81	71	73	36	50	48	42	17	13	12	3	.	.	.
ARE. (W.)	6212	M. - 3105	424	402	409	295	235	203	198	152	152	127	103	101	100	82	56	46	11	3	2	.	.
		F. - 3107	456	448	326	282	222	226	190	168	149	184	125	85	111	83	65	30	22	10	3	.	.
ANDON	2976	M. - 1550	189	188	160	198	115	92	75	78	69	64	93	65	58	48	32	17	8	3	.	.	.
		F. - 1426	187	168	191	93	79	93	82	77	72	63	80	60	60	59	29	15	13	4	1	.	.
BISHOP STORTFORD.																							
WBRIDGEWORTH	4675	M. - 2373	310	329	279	253	192	145	112	123	139	109	120	88	83	65	40	20	16	2	.	.	.
		F. - 2302	281	327	274	182	179	127	127	134	139	126	89	88	73	65	41	26	7	4	4	.	.
ANSTED	5157	M. - 2551	335	339	322	267	168	138	137	136	193	163	113	97	103	70	53	28	11	4	1	.	.
		F. - 2606	370	348	293	160	182	156	154	180	146	119	127	88	85	76	59	32	22	6	1	.	.
SHOP STORTFORD. (W.L.)	9350	M. - 4638	641	595	609	472	289	317	294	237	223	191	172	149	143	125	106	41	29	5	.	.	.
		F. - 4712	920	542	403	418	406	348	315	240	259	232	193	168	131	129	97	32	30	8	4	1	.
AUGHING	2619	M. - 1348	162	178	190	134	79	75	76	64	57	65	50	60	53	35	30	23	5	4	1	.	.
		F. - 1271	187	186	148	76	86	74	67	79	65	73	53	46	55	41	29	18	8	3	2	.	.
132 ROYSTON.																							
NTINGFORD. (W.)	6132	M. - 3091	383	396	415	327	189	151	151	148	144	140	153	134	114	91	67	51	27	7	.	.	.
		F. - 3041	386	407	328	233	192	163	160	140	163	147	142	139	110	78	64	51	23	13	2	.	.
YSTON. (H.)	9549	M. - 4822	649	682	591	535	298	255	250	246	264	231	193	162	171	120	84	61	26	6	.	.	.
		F. - 4729	646	635	553	384	292	302	295	268	241	236	108	207	171	116	91	68	20	16	3	.	.
LBOURN. (W.)	9081	M. - 4927	639	613	610	469	303	248	245	283	328	218	170	161	151	114	112	48	32	8	1	.	.
		F. - 4154	606	638	548	332	256	287	209	240	242	202	187	158	159	123	93	77	28	3	3	2	.
133 HITCHIN.																							
LDOCK	9147	M. - 4358	620	692	563	441	289	329	262	211	208	178	266	170	160	112	86	35	20	5	1	.	.
		F. - 4789	598	605	679	416	346	334	289	203	248	208	216	183	186	129	80	44	23	14	.	.	.
TCHIN. (W. H.)	18270	M. - 8645	1273	1209	1062	763	590	549	478	446	391	377	399	284	264	211	138	107	49	8	2	.	.
		F. - 9625	1242	1158	1025	918	854	697	[illegible]	546	406	465	392	315	380	222	186	127	40	12	3	.	.

te.—For the Parishes comprised in each Registration Sub-district, see Vol. II., Division III., Table 4.
.) denotes that a Workhouse and (WS.) that a Workhouse School belonging to the District is situated within the Sub-district; (w.) denotes a Workhouse (ws.) a Workhouse School not belonging to the District, (H.) a Hospital or Infirmary, (L.) a Lunatic Asylum, (P.) a Prison or Convict Establishment (R.) a sed Reformatory or Industrial School, (B.) Barracks, &c., (S.) H.M. Ships. A figure appended to any of these letters denotes the number of Institutions of a ar class situated within the Sub-district. The names of the Institutions thus indicated, and the number of Inmates enumerated herein, will be found in II., Division III., Table 6.

TABLE 3 *continued*.—AGES of MALES and FEMALES in REGISTRATION SUB-DISTRICTS.

REGISTRATION SUB-DISTRICT.	ALL AGES. Persons.		Males and Females.	Under 5 Years.	5–	10–	15–	20–	25–	30–	35–	40–	45–	50–	55–	60–	65–	70–	75–	80–	85–	90–	9
7 HERTFORDSHIRE—*cont.*																							
134 HERTFORD.																							
1 Watton	3887	M.	1947	245	290	261	180	115	103	92	99	91	100	76	80	88	43	38	29	6	3	.	
		F.	1940	267	271	236	165	117	103	106	108	111	95	86	80	70	55	30	27	11	4	.	
2 Hertford. (W.H.[2]R.)	12867	M.	6562	797	912	818	754	497	395	376	340	327	255	256	199	168	159	110	71	34	4	1	
		F.	6305	744	749	750	585	498	422	423	373	316	310	259	229	208	156	146	78	48	9	3	
135 HATFIELD.																							
1 Hatfield. (W.)	6502	M.	3220	442	426	359	315	253	230	204	166	136	138	143	115	89	65	58	35	18	6	2	
		F.	3282	471	425	363	284	225	277	226	181	177	135	135	102	95	68	61	54	18	4	.	
2 Welwyn. (W.)	2300	M.	1151	192	141	112	113	82	79	77	46	49	52	50	55	35	30	22	8	6	.	.	
		F.	1149	182	120	104	97	85	85	79	78	54	58	56	45	40	24	21	13	7	1	.	
136 ST. ALBANS.																							
1 Harpenden. (L.)	8491	M.	3993	502	591	475	384	260	240	225	219	216	160	156	128	118	99	73	33	20	5	1	
		F.	4498	598	532	473	379	362	322	292	265	260	193	164	154	139	128	73	47	16	9	1	
2 St. Albans. (W.H.P.)	14895	M.	6970	976	907	775	627	540	478	442	429	380	283	277	249	221	153	125	64	33	11	.	
		F.	7925	1004	918	792	720	683	595	586	472	447	363	354	276	255	191	142	78	37	13	6	
137 WATFORD.																							
1 Bushey	6621	M.	3159	426	439	421	366	216	179	192	165	173	156	134	112	92	65	51	26	15	.	.	
		F.	3462	431	465	384	327	259	252	197	224	205	164	140	113	104	78	60	31	17	8	2	
2 Watford. (W.[2] ws.)	15507	M.	7333	837	891	1069	596	558	558	449	477	421	340	313	249	218	164	109	54	30	8	2	
		F.	8174	854	854	964	672	651	604	575	546	489	400	386	351	298	216	185	88	38	17	4	
3 Rickmansworth	6211	M.	3111	416	382	359	340	217	238	148	170	175	152	140	126	93	61	62	26	12	3	2	
		F.	3100	420	364	336	275	223	218	184	186	199	179	135	115	101	84	52	34	13	4	.	
4 Abbots Langley	2989	M.	1452	226	213	177	115	110	84	92	81	79	64	64	36	36	29	25	13	6	2	.	
		F.	1537	224	211	158	109	118	108	129	85	76	72	72	64	45	32	26	9	8	1	.	
138 HEMEL HEMPSTEAD.																							
1 Kings Langley	2758	M.	1312	191	172	140	117	89	89	85	63	70	60	57	51	48	39	26	13	6	2	.	
		F.	1446	182	193	149	122	112	93	91	84	76	74	67	53	56	41	28	11	10	4	.	
2 Hemel Hempstead. (W. H[2].)	9564	M.	4863	607	560	571	390	396	278	264	231	256	184	167	137	164	117	71	39	22	5	1	
		F.	4701	570	515	508	429	374	371	324	237	294	239	212	170	169	137	70	36	22	2	2	
3 Flamstead	2784	M.	1320	189	162	161	124	98	96	88	72	68	48	58	44	41	39	21	21	1	2	.	
		F.	1464	184	197	168	140	121	98	96	79	76	60	66	59	45	36	23	16	6	.	1	
139 BERKHAMPSTEAD.																							
1 Berkhampstead. (W.)	7104	M.	3351	470	457	412	361	230	223	185	182	173	134	129	129	92	85	42	34	15	8	.	
		F.	3753	498	437	406	292	329	295	294	214	204	187	158	129	138	97	66	37	15	6	1	
2 Tring	7987	M.	3822	548	519	446	375	261	266	224	211	183	144	168	127	124	95	67	44	20	8	2	
		F.	4165	562	507	461	378	329	312	254	258	252	181	165	162	124	110	69	32	17	1	1	
8 BUCKINGHAMSHIRE.																							
140 AMERSHAM.																							
1 Missenden	2292	M.	1099	164	156	124	91	90	75	68	48	54	47	49	48	38	28	17	12	5	2	.	
		F.	1193	151	164	154	101	92	64	76	73	52	47	53	58	48	38	19	12	6	.	.	
2 Chesham. (H.)	6953	M.	3344	513	455	379	327	238	202	200	171	164	163	138	122	91	69	62	22	12	5	1	
		F.	3609	486	440	421	310	270	243	222	188	222	144	142	108	112	89	74	33	14	3	1	
3 Amersham. (W.)	3001	M.	1440	193	190	182	120	98	80	72	82	66	58	71	64	59	39	33	29	14	4	.	
		F.	1561	190	229	179	126	105	96	98	90	71	72	76	61	69	38	39	26	20	4	.	
4 Chalfont. (H.)	3108	M.	1552	214	209	190	143	95	75	100	90	64	67	61	75	60	48	32	17	7	6	.	
		F.	1556	199	187	182	122	111	98	107	94	81	58	70	72	64	56	32	12	8	2	2	
5 Beaconsfield	3065	M.	1505	186	209	225	143	106	80	83	77	64	56	2	50	53	45	27	21	6	2	.	
		F.	1560	231	197	198	127	122	87	87	87	58	81	60	57	61	42	17	28	9	1	.	
141 ETON.																							
1 Iver. (H.)	6489	M.	3258	359	372	462	331	206	229	172	188	176	155	169	116	94	82	56	32	9	.	.	
		F.	3231	327	383	320	277	253	270	198	206	174	175	132	118	105	87	63	34	12	9	.	
2 Eton. (W.)	13634	M.	6016	784	785	982	1214	513	377	357	375	323	297	247	187	169	110	93	60	31	7	3	
		F.	7618	774	784	838	665	594	498	478	441	415	341	315	223	210	134	99	59	37	15	3	1
3 Burnham	7398	M.	3853	469	537	689	308	260	218	195	276	186	177	138	102	106	71	56	34	13	4	.	
		F.	3545	483	475	411	391	255	234	240	224	204	184	155	122	105	70	43	28	7	6	.	
142 WYCOMBE.																							
1 High Wycombe. (H.)	16718	M.	8155	1284	1119	929	823	593	534	516	480	408	380	314	237	193	139	112	60	24	6	1	
		F.	8563	1227	1140	968	858	706	640	521	488	478	349	322	269	216	165	116	49	37	6	2	2
2 Great Marlow	5519	M.	2630	331	336	312	299	224	156	149	127	149	125	123	95	71	57	40	39	22	3	1	
		F.	2889	364	332	317	250	254	216	162	146	168	147	144	89	97	77	55	20	19	3	1	
3 West Wycombe	7620	M.	3847	505	554	487	386	259	249	193	193	188	173	155	124	118	88	55	43	18	4	3	
		F.	3773	572	548	467	294	269	238	245	206	190	158	158	113	122	79	47	37	21	5	3	1
4 Wendover	4738	M.	2322	312	313	258	223	182	154	117	121	111	105	104	91	90	66	48	31	12	3	1	
		F.	2416	329	318	300	176	177	154	142	142	123	109	103	103	92	62	49	30	11	4	.	1
5 Prince's Risborough. (W. WS.)	5685	M.	2849	395	381	334	249	206	179	147	140	141	127	139	87	98	81	77	43	14	3	1	
		F.	2836	402	388	328	207	189	168	182	158	155	143	127	107	81	78	57	33	16	5	1	1
143 AYLESBURY.																							
1 Haddenham	3875	M.	1897	235	252	224	178	117	106	92	98	99	96	77	91	72	58	51	32	17	2	1	
		F.	1978	252	285	233	128	135	114	100	102	107	112	101	89	78	68	46	34	13	3	.	
2 Aylesbury. (W. H. L.)	10086	M.	4816	665	591	450	409	398	356	301	288	264	199	179	161	162	111	78	60	31	9	4	
		F.	5270	632	612	504	495	431	387	328	354	283	248	258	209	181	158	100	56	24	7	2	1
3 Aston Clinton. (P.)	5746	M.	2889	408	419	368	268	208	167	187	150	181	122	118	97	100	56	45	30	14	2	1	
		F.	2867	404	382	346	239	212	204	175	159	186	139	115	83	88	54	38	32	10	8	5	
4 Waddesdon	4900	M.	2451	369	303	313	213	165	168	140	160	107	118	98	98	99	71	56	33	14	10	.	
		F.	2449	317	325	288	183	177	181	120	125	147	138	103	95	98	77	53	35	15	5	1	
144 WINSLOW.																							
1 Winslow. (W.)	7943	M.	3876	475	534	495	374	276	198	176	198	208	175	160	159	175	120	90	47	14	11	1	
		F.	4067	493	521	511	378	287	240	232	226	214	195	153	148	173	105	85	53	22	5	1	
145 NEWPORT PAGNELL.																							
1 Fenny Stratford	11224	M.	5546	828	691	631	536	396	384	313	321	278	240	210	197	191	130	88	51	26	4	3	
		F.	5678	804	796	825	488	413	369	374	330	318	287	229	203	193	138	95	56	32	2	2	
2 Newport Pagnell. (W.)	3686	M.	1760	238	226	188	182	142	118	106	88	87	78	86	64	57	53	31	40	8	3	1	1
		F.	1926	240	207	197	182	163	165	108	118	97	83	88	86	63	64	34	38	17	8	2	
3 Olney	9664	M.	4724	656	625	542	487	364	260	242	253	214	218	195	192	197	130	89	55	24	6	1	
		F.	4940	688	825	578	464	359	325	263	286	236	223	234	212	175	122	108	78	27	8	.	
146 BUCKINGHAM.																							
1 Leckhampstead	3631	M.	1809	219	234	220	192	119	94	92	114	78	86	73	80	73	61	36	20	14	8	.	
		F.	1822	205	208	211	136	142	115	135	92	88	84	94	75	80	55	42	28	24	5	2	
2 Buckingham. (W.)	5678	M.	2745	383	347	339	247	183	168	183	161	138	127	100	93	103	84	58	45	17	8	2	
		F.	2933	341	346	322	282	218	208	196	159	173	131	131	117	106	95	63	38	23	6	1	
3 Tingewick	3109	M.	1515	206	193	196	143	75	77	73	73	81	73	55	77	55	65	34	22	6	5	1	
		F.	1594	191	198	174	120	109	98	102	83	84	71	77	84	67	58	32	19	11	4	1	1

Table 3 *continued*.—AGES of MALES and FEMALES in REGISTRATION SUB-DISTRICTS.

REGISTRATION SUB-DISTRICT.	ALL AGES. Persons.	ALL AGES. Males and Females.	Under 5 Years.	5–	10–	15–	20–	25–	30–	35–	40–	45–	50–	55–	60–	65–	70–	75–	80–	85–	90–	95–	100 and upw'
KFORDSHIRE.																							
147 HENLEY. NLEY. (W.)	16083	M. - 7984	1085	1084	979	881	594	502	481	431	418	322	299	249	248	107	127	79	28	9	3	.	.
		F. - 8099	1974	1063	929	663	654	568	517	481	422	406	322	270	292	152	127	77	44	17	1	.	.
TLINGTON. (H.)	3909	M. - 1965	250	268	212	215	127	101	110	94	98	87	92	72	87	67	41	29	11	8	.	.	.
		F. - 1944	247	241	254	136	131	123	118	107	102	84	88	96	93	67	49	17	17	6	.	.	.
148 THAME. WKNOR	3500	M. - 1778	233	258	234	183	114	98	86	100	88	73	64	65	51	60	42	23	9	5	2	.	.
		F. 1722	242	236	215	133	116	97	111	89	96	90	74	72	57	56	18	19	8	4	.	.	.
AME. (W.)	5506	M. - 2747	379	351	370	276	193	160	107	121	115	119	119	96	104	66	58	36	20	4	1	1	.
		F. - 2759	334	337	318	223	220	183	182	103	120	114	119	120	112	70	68	31	20	9	1	.	.
ILL	4856	M. - 2370	301	310	308	229	181	130	117	110	100	105	114	98	107	63	46	44	14	7	.	.	.
		F. - 2486	326	340	295	177	174	148	130	141	117	120	122	100	104	77	61	33	17	5	.	.	.
49 HEADINGTON. BEATLEY	3613	M. - 1886	258	246	213	173	102	112	113	102	76	102	67	64	68	43	35	28	11	3	.	1	.
		F. - 1727	225	244	194	136	118	108	139	89	98	68	83	56	71	35	35	14	10	4	.	.	.
CLEMENT. (W. ws. H.[3] L.[2] B.)	25110	M. - 11540	1592	1417	1425	1172	963	824	753	687	546	465	437	342	339	261	185	123	50	18	.	.	.
		F. - 13570	1648	1401	1386	1503	1277	1044	959	801	766	585	540	451	418	248	216	183	63	23	3	1	.
150 OXFORD. FORD. (P.)	21902	M. - 10573	1594	1204	1113	1123	1172	854	710	597	521	471	435	302	254	195	122	84	35	8	.	.	.
		F. - 11329	1363	1188	1119	1278	1069	959	759	685	634	554	458	364	320	266	169	97	35	12	6	2	.
151 BICESTER. TCHINGTON	6572	M. - 3280	411	391	396	340	281	191	166	164	138	177	144	143	118	118	74	41	16	6	1	.	.
		F. 3292	443	416	380	274	230	194	177	168	171	162	166	133	119	117	60	63	21	7	1	.	.
CESTER. (W.)	7585	M. - 3787	529	452	413	383	309	252	179	178	178	177	176	147	146	112	70	47	27	2	.	.	.
		F. - 3798	456	450	407	347	321	253	218	210	203	192	163	166	141	109	81	50	19	12	.	.	.
152 WOODSTOCK. IDDINGTON	6152	M. - 3003	406	397	375	303	204	182	163	149	163	130	138	95	118	83	61	34	6	5	2	.	.
		F. 3149	435	410	378	240	241	220	170	170	180	159	126	122	100	97	54	37	18	1	1	1	.
OODSTOCK. (W.)	7168	M. - 3533	481	450	447	326	264	190	177	186	164	186	160	136	142	93	73	44	25	7	2	.	.
		F. 3635	485	462	398	290	287	227	223	192	193	195	181	143	131	112	70	46	24	7	3	2	.
153 WITNEY. SHAM	4890	M. - 2453	353	361	306	230	184	117	121	129	125	94	97	77	84	67	60	32	16	5	.	.	.
		F. - 2445	344	343	235	186	154	173	133	148	145	100	88	83	81	85	49	29	15	5	1	.	.
MPTON	4835	M. - 2445	336	294	209	267	159	133	136	107	114	115	111	98	97	84	44	39	16	6	.	1	.
		F. - 2390	324	322	262	179	158	162	109	136	138	119	115	98	82	85	42	41	16	5	.	.	.
TNEY. (W.)	7246	M. - 3545	402	471	431	344	226	197	171	180	197	157	167	124	137	105	101	56	20	9	.	.	.
		F. 3701	476	467	437	329	272	223	207	193	224	178	163	127	131	106	81	40	28	7	4	.	.
RFORD. (H.)	4556	M. - 2228	300	270	241	234	167	143	95	113	107	109	98	89	77	81	59	28	18	2	.	.	.
		F. - 2328	320	285	269	189	155	142	115	133	111	122	117	85	105	62	61	37	15	5	.	.	.
CHIPPING NORTON. ARLBURY	8332	M. - 4102	537	518	513	426	271	224	235	230	178	181	181	160	145	123	103	46	26	6	.	.	.
		F. 4230	596	570	488	353	304	235	260	205	216	202	189	168	151	106	94	60	22	8	2	1	.
IPPING NORTON. (W.)	9626	M. - 4799	600	633	563	478	338	318	276	285	248	212	202	154	152	132	86	47	28	4	4		.
		F. - 4827	693	590	562	424	361	306	322	277	284	221	206	167	173	104	88	52	17	5	2		.
155 BANBURY. LOXHAM	5998	M. - 3040	393	354	430	319	190	196	162	149	125	117	132	119	125	92	54	44	10	5	1	.	.
		F. 2958	434	390	316	197	199	194	188	153	142	150	130	134	126	84	69	35	15	8	2	1	.
WALCLIFFE	5427	M. - 2772	345	348	352	265	208	163	127	133	145	126	127	119	113	70	64	41	18	10	2	.	.
		F. - 2655	349	316	317	187	173	149	138	153	148	156	131	127	97	83	66	38	19	5	.	.	.
ROPREDY	3856	M. - 1959	238	234	250	204	144	98	93	94	93	115	89	87	72	54	55	26	11	1	1	.	.
		F. 1897	227	245	218	157	125	118	94	109	103	98	87	97	68	68	47	25	3	3	.	.	.
ANBURY. (W. H.)	14839	M. - 7119	942	925	862	759	580	418	400	404	371	316	310	243	206	150	102	65	30	6	.	.	.
		F. - 7720	899	911	937	772	636	529	498	431	429	343	353	274	287	175	133	72	27	12	3	.	.
0 NORTHAMPTONSHIRE.																							
156 BRACKLEY. BRACKLEY. (W. H.)	7600	M. - 3776	539	507	444	393	294	294	202	189	183	172	134	148	128	98	73	45	16	6	1	.	.
		F. - 3824	484	446	427	340	299	256	242	217	213	192	154	158	127	118	77	63	26	4	1	.	.
ULGRAVE. (L.)	4740	M. - 2421	283	260	339	248	151	125	109	121	146	117	114	109	107	88	50	33	14	5	.		.
		F. 2319	243	284	235	178	154	142	144	138	127	150	114	111	93	87	54	40	16	8	1	.	.
157 TOWCESTER. RTHORPE	4746	M. - 2302	288	295	255	207	144	127	141	129	97	109	116	102	112	60	57	43	17	5	.	1	.
		F. - 2444	339	292	252	174	150	144	159	119	140	128	126	111	110	71	77	32	16	4	1	.	.
TOWCESTER. (W.R.)	7838	M. - 3887	548	489	456	416	283	233	215	198	193	193	159	145	112	110	57	40	18	7	1	.	.
		F. 3951	530	497	450	327	321	269	244	209	216	200	181	140	122	96	77	64	24	6	1	.	.
158 POTTERSPURY. POTTERSPURY. (W.[2]H.)	12231	M. - 6156	833	773	742	665	479	397	378	317	298	269	256	216	177	164	105	55	32	11	2	.	.
		F. - 6075	836	743	660	521	470	406	403	376	285	285	287	250	191	153	116	79	26	11	2	.	.
59 HARDINGSTONE. BRAFIELD	3414	M. - 1680	225	212	193	164	132	77	84	101	87	81	67	71	62	54	38	23	8	1	.	.	.
		F. - 1734	256	212	210	131	141	98	104	82	98	74	93	60	59	52	35	13	9	1	1	.	.
HARDINGSTONE	4135	M. - 2146	285	280	226	232	208	162	142	123	107	109	76	59	63	43	33	20	8	1	1	.	.
		F. - 1989	272	259	212	183	140	136	133	119	126	95	70	81	53	50	21	20	11	1		.	.
MILTON. (W.)	2937	M. - 1522	216	195	146	138	120	110	95	75	66	67	69	54	51	51	30	19	9	2	.	.	.
		F. - 1415	202	170	148	87	109	117	88	76	76	61	60	63	64	47	25	13	4	5	.	.	.
160 NORTHAMPTON. ST. GILES. (W. H[3]. L.[2]P.R.B.)	42039	M. - 20326	2854	2594	2243	2073	1826	1577	1406	1184	1168	946	767	558	446	323	190	104	47	9	1	2	.
		F. - 21713	3077	2627	2371	2366	2056	1702	1440	1322	1122	912	784	673	532	347	239	130	68	23	6	1	.
ALL SAINTS	18140	M. - 9139	1339	1148	971	897	798	751	684	518	522	444	331	246	224	129	77	43	15	3	.	.	.
		F. - 9001	1369	1156	990	874	764	741	581	515	489	393	332	248	224	134	100	54	31	7	.	2	.
BUGBROOKE. (L.)	4065	M. - 2055	255	217	199	186	163	144	143	124	111	113	99	81	79	68	42	14	14	3	.	.	.
		F. - 2010	244	191	172	147	161	160	127	118	119	111	105	110	108	57	48	22	14	5	1	.	.
161 DAVENTRY. WEEDON. (B.)	5065	M. - 2642	334	291	248	247	305	217	168	141	118	167	126	92	96	69	49	30	10	3	.	.	.
		F. - 2423	319	292	246	176	190	163	128	127	121	129	126	91	95	76	66	38	17	6	3	.	.
DAVENTRY. (W.)	7871	M. - 3898	491	474	443	356	264	215	177	287	220	202	175	140	160	132	104	54	26	10	.	.	.
		F. - 3973	486	478	415	330	291	261	216	233	208	196	191	191	148	136	93	51	30	6	1	.	.
LONG BUCKBY	5578	M. - 2856	319	328	288	272	242	190	191	152	169	129	145	128	107	84	59	29	22	4	.	.	.
		F. - 2722	343	313	276	231	198	170	174	151	140	130	131	147	114	80	46	38	19	9	3	.	.
162 BRIXWORTH. SPRATTON	4837	M. - 2476	284	288	296	263	221	135	144	115	108	100	124	103	107	87	53	37	13	8	.	.	.
		F. - 2361	273	281	264	185	174	163	122	137	102	127	124	113	107	79	51	43	13	2	1	.	.
MOULTON. (L.)	4489	M. - 2227	317	283	254	215	181	148	116	105	105	97	128	93	94	56	47	22	15	2	1	.	.
		F. - 2262	302	268	233	171	161	143	121	118	117	139	118	108	99	63	57	27	9	3	2	.	.
BRIXWORTH. (W.)	4010	M. - 2043	212	238	247	218	180	132	87	111	104	100	96	96	84	56	40	30	13	1	.	.	.
		F. - 1967	278	250	208	144	136	130	114	89	108	110	90	83	86	56	39	22	10	4	.	.	.

Table 3 *continued*.—Ages of Males and Females in Registration Sub-Districts.

Registration Sub-District	All Ages: Persons	All Ages: Males and Females	Under 5 Years	5-	10-	15-	20-	25-	30-	35-	40-	45-	50-	55-	60-	65-	70-	75-	80-	85-	90-	95-
10 NORTHAMPTONSHIRE—*cont.*																						
163 WELLINGBOROUGH.																						
1 Earls Barton	7183	M. - 3568	513	383	409	380	279	225	197	185	132	180	136	119	123	60	51	32	13	4	1	.
		F. - 3615	506	436	422	346	263	237	219	137	193	184	154	117	121	82	56	30	19	3	1	.
2 Higham Ferrers	10790	M. - 5514	761	656	602	636	557	469	358	292	261	220	205	171	164	98	56	36	17	5	1	.
		F. - 5276	788	685	690	625	440	434	323	289	240	236	187	153	164	99	62	[illegible]	20	8	1	.
3 Wellingborough. (W.H.)	18969	M. - 9893	1327	1253	976	926	808	761	654	528	488	385	336	265	218	167	116	64	19	4	1	1
		F. - 9676	1377	1231	1017	1086	872	795	688	622	491	398	347	260	221	173	128	73	25	8	.	1
164 KETTERING.																						
1 Kettering. (W. H.)	14339	M. - 7202	1082	961	788	696	687	570	524	400	341	363	249	223	181	106	83	53	14	5	.	.
		F. 7137	1119	937	770	678	623	554	516	403	353	278	247	202	175	136	83	44	18	4	.	.
2 Rothwell	7335	M. - 3655	572	462	302	344	316	254	209	201	191	156	144	132	118	88	57	33	11	7	.	.
		F. - 3620	564	486	409	367	308	253	215	212	176	146	142	121	113	74	49	32	14	1	.	1
3 Corby	3979	M. - 2051	264	241	232	213	183	122	110	105	80	111	92	86	79	63	51	35	12	4	2	.
		F. - 1928	246	252	217	132	127	119	109	106	96	107	102	81	78	71	34	33	11	6	3	.
165 THRAPSTON.																						
1 Thrapston. (W.)	8087	M. - 4073	563	534	446	418	328	263	260	234	195	185	166	138	119	96	62	49	18	8	1	.
		F. - 4014	500	529	425	354	288	291	239	220	223	183	163	120	125	106	76	61	24	8	.	.
2 Raunds	7028	M. - 3542	496	472	446	381	233	218	191	221	181	177	136	150	110	79	46	39	11	.	1	.
		F. - 3486	495	506	428	338	236	222	198	208	198	170	132	109	107	82	58	34	12	5	1	.
166 OUNDLE.																						
1 Oundle. (W.)	6149	M. - 3100	357	373	453	341	226	174	180	170	124	137	116	112	136	99	65	42	13	5	1	1
		F. - 3049	365	375	327	308	245	205	166	174	148	140	131	129	120	82	59	39	27	9	.	.
2 Weldon	2113	M. - 1073	125	131	137	113	80	61	64	46	68	61	51	49	39	28	28	12	11	3	1	.
		F. 1040	123	146	107	82	72	70	65	47	58	54	47	44	47	29	24	14	9	2	.	.
3 Fotheringhay	5824	M. - 2944	380	367	383	303	199	160	139	152	139	152	119	114	114	97	65	40	15	8	.	.
		F. - 2880	407	360	371	210	165	160	155	166	138	140	131	103	121	102	65	45	16	13	4	.
167 PETERBOROUGH.																						
1 Stilton	5400	M. - 2669	366	324	337	296	194	148	138	132	116	115	134	102	83	78	48	33	21	3	1	.
		F. - 2731	385	342	309	240	193	172	171	125	149	119	115	101	84	92	56	33	21	4	3	.
2 Peterborough. (W.H.)	26679	M. - 13105	1946	1712	1422	1360	1165	1012	961	768	645	600	463	392	291	248	168	97	41	12	2	.
		F. - 13574	1902	1702	1808	1321	1085	1039	934	781	766	572	517	401	340	285	190	115	60	19	7	1
3 Crowland	7370	M. - 3705	492	448	450	371	296	244	181	175	181	167	164	126	156	113	76	47	17	9	2	.
		F. - 3665	466	603	444	296	232	242	151	199	203	182	162	149	148	106	69	53	29	8	4	.
4 Thorney	2065	M. - 1045	139	142	104	120	163	77	52	49	58	47	37	41	31	17	12	10	3	3	.	.
		F. - 1010	146	119	130	121	75	71	59	46	53	48	39	36	26	8	11	12	6	5	.	.
11 HUNTINGDONSHIRE.																						
168 HUNTINGDON.																						
1 Ramsey	5206	M. - 2620	374	375	329	248	186	161	130	149	117	104	102	94	98	69	44	31	12	3	.	.
		F. 2586	340	349	301	243	187	174	143	150	118	104	107	80	105	74	44	38	10	8	2	.
2 Sawtry	2177	M. - 1109	158	148	102	107	72	52	53	55	62	46	44	38	42	25	24	16	8	3	.	.
		F. 1068	161	141	136	83	74	57	47	67	51	53	61	40	30	22	20	14	9	3	.	.
3 Spaldwick	2893	M. - 1434	202	175	177	162	87	74	76	68	74	66	63	84	62	44	34	17	8	3	1	.
		F. - 1459	212	214	168	118	88	84	63	83	68	65	63	70	57	45	25	12	16	5	1	.
4 Huntingdon. (W.H.P.B.)	9285	M. - 4492	607	516	601	487	361	290	264	289	246	218	193	160	130	123	82	63	25	11	.	.
		F. - 4793	640	556	629	527	338	287	300	284	255	266	192	179	169	150	97	75	45	7	2	.
169 ST. IVES.																						
1 Warboys	2834	M. - 1382	167	174	171	127	96	73	78	80	76	67	68	50	65	37	23	21	11	4	.	.
		F. 1452	167	230	169	136	83	72	73	83	81	68	59	49	51	57	29	23	12	2	1	.
2 Somersham	3601	M. - 1788	227	220	226	160	132	86	96	71	101	93	82	81	68	62	35	31	18	3	.	2
		F. - 1813	217	213	293	157	123	63	100	114	83	103	63	96	82	54	35	35	15	5	1	.
3 Swavesey	3154	M. - 1593	204	214	189	175	94	79	80	84	88	83	75	68	61	53	34	23	12	5	.	.
		F. - 1561	195	213	204	98	63	85	87	109	93	92	76	65	68	45	33	30	11	6	2	.
4 St. Ives. (W.)	7166	M. - 3424	466	453	396	369	244	211	196	168	183	163	152	121	119	96	71	60	14	8	1	.
		F. - 3742	471	438	443	347	289	233	226	218	184	166	180	127	157	99	80	40	35	8	2	.
170 ST. NEOTS.																						
1 St. Neots	8928	M. - 4321	604	615	628	436	280	231	242	237	214	189	194	186	146	87	68	37	21	4	3	.
		F. 4607	571	597	516	419	372	307	292	263	257	213	213	156	169	106	97	72	35	8	4	.
2 Kimbolton. (W.)	7919	M. 3904	605	519	485	398	256	200	188	178	198	187	173	147	176	127	77	47	29	12	2	.
		F. - 4015	483	514	490	317	280	247	213	206	214	187	192	183	166	130	86	49	37	10	5	1
12 BEDFORDSHIRE.																						
171 BEDFORD.																						
1 Riseley	2409	M. - 1198	151	158	149	121	75	69	68	56	67	51	55	46	52	41	24	8	5	4	.	.
		F. - 1211	170	150	148	99	78	61	68	76	69	65	62	45	66	41	16	14	11	3	.	.
2 Sharnbrook	2619	M. - 1304	171	157	162	119	90	78	71	62	72	61	53	45	50	39	21	15	8	.	.	.
		F. - 1315	163	170	133	111	94	95	76	72	70	67	50	44	50	50	25	17	12	1	.	.
3 Harrold	2944	M. - 1433	180	182	166	143	97	79	79	66	78	65	64	64	52	43	47	20	8	2	.	.
		F. 1511	192	174	161	107	120	98	87	98	91	70	74	72	51	37	38	24	11	1	.	.
4 Turvey. (R.)	2118	M. - 1052	127	132	139	148	62	44	49	44	46	57	37	53	43	51	14	16	6	1	.	.
		F. - 1066	124	149	108	80	75	50	75	61	64	50	49	35	40	34	23	13	8	.	.	.
5 Bedford and Kempston. (W.L.P.B.)	15395	M. - 7187	868	931	968	892	672	474	383	369	304	298	227	207	231	189	113	85	43	9	3	1
		F. - 8208	920	868	873	1029	812	618	506	436	420	306	296	233	251	117	146	94	47	21	2	.
6 Bedford and Cardington. (H.L.)	14845	M. 6911	901	887	930	725	532	434	416	405	372	332	232	240	216	130	103	57	19	4	.	.
		F. 7934	896	951	875	837	780	581	549	469	446	379	289	276	248	170	149	69	27	5	2	.
7 Barford	2632	M. - 1310	160	169	160	112	91	63	64	63	72	64	43	55	53	43	34	16	10	1	.	.
		F. 1322	171	194	128	107	102	67	77	63	63	74	64	53	60	66	33	11	8	5	.	.
172 BIGGLESWADE.																						
1 Potton	9542	M. - 4710	642	822	628	495	316	270	248	207	225	199	179	171	160	109	96	61	22	7	3	.
		F. - 4832	657	635	551	383	320	338	303	252	269	244	208	193	165	118	97	63	29	6	.	.
2 Biggleswade. (W.H. L.R.)	17836	M. - 8629	1134	1162	1074	801	578	467	500	470	448	406	381	300	279	220	169	95	45	8	3	.
		F. - 9207	1148	1066	1002	763	724	832	632	678	508	464	308	356	335	242	158	107	45	18	1	.
173 AMPTHILL.																						
1 Shillington	4566	M. - 2151	315	302	254	192	138	125	120	120	195	104	105	79	75	56	35	17	9	.	1	.
		F. - 2415	324	310	276	230	200	154	142	151	124	135	107	86	100	43	34	16	7	4	.	.
2 Ampthill. (W.)	8404	M. - 3989	560	531	492	407	271	182	203	195	213	178	161	164	142	115	73	56	31	8	2	.
		F. - 4415	661	544	478	340	346	281	300	256	258	221	200	168	192	113	82	55	16	8	4	.
3 Cranfield	3284	M. - 1615	220	219	204	150	117	90	78	71	74	72	68	85	55	45	26	21	16	2	1	.
		F. - 1669	247	226	182	126	132	104	86	86	88	72	75	66	61	47	43	16	11	.	.	.
174 WOBURN.																						
1 Woburn. (W.)	5569	M. - 2630	334	317	298	267	169	117	137	130	100	123	132	138	112	77	63	68	20	9	1	.
		F. - 2939	291	325	326	241	238	197	191	169	148	161	138	125	151	77	68	51	26	11	6	.
2 Toddington	4311	M. - 2078	278	305	253	216	139	98	128	112	63	82	88	77	73	56	50	26	8	2	.	.
		F. - 2233	280	267	238	206	148	161	141	138	122	121	104	74	83	58	40	31	11	3	.	.

Table 3 *continued.*—AGES of MALES and FEMALES in REGISTRATION SUB-DISTRICTS.

REGISTRATION SUB-DISTRICT.	ALL AGES. Persons.		ALL AGES. Males and Females.	Under 5 Years.	5-	10-	15-	20-	25-	30-	35-	40-	45-	50-	55-	60-	65-	70-	75-	80-	85-	90-	95-	100 and upwards
BEDFORDSHIRE—*cont.*																								
175 LEIGHTON BUZZARD.																								
1 Leighton Buzzard. (W.)	10684	M.	4840	680	656	559	450	350	316	316	303	245	188	168	185	168	104	60	46	23	8	-	-	-
		F.	5844	720	653	604	529	454	406	300	330	285	228	214	214	160	131	101	47	25	5	-	-	-
2 Wing	2425	M.	1197	174	150	155	113	88	76	64	60	79	44	47	38	61	32	19	12	7	1	-	-	-
		F.	1228	178	162	137	107	107	86	66	73	64	46	48	49	37	33	19	6	8	-	-	-	-
3 Ivinghoe	2724	M.	1352	154	134	163	136	66	42	61	48	56	51	56	33	39	34	23	13	8	-	-	-	-
		F.	1372	127	138	123	95	78	78	71	64	70	52	47	39	38	19	18	8	5	1	1	-	-
4 Edlesborough	3383	M.	1625	230	233	191	171	101	87	82	78	86	64	66	67	55	46	26	19	2	1	-	-	-
		F.	1758	246	236	202	179	142	116	89	109	105	87	63	76	53	27	29	11	4	2	1	-	-
176 LUTON.																								
1 Dunstable. (W.)	9407	M.	4172	601	565	514	390	251	247	218	250	212	178	170	177	151	110	71	46	15	5	1	-	-
		F.	5235	567	581	534	546	457	363	377	317	363	279	232	214	193	144	80	45	17	7	-	-	-
2 Luton. (W.H.)	30093	M.	13523	2022	1776	1574	1420	1119	972	806	755	733	574	535	382	343	241	153	64	42	10	2	-	-
		F.	16570	2077	1757	1774	1883	1683	1374	1151	1051	935	767	631	487	450	276	198	58	57	11	1	-	-
13 CAMBRIDGESHIRE.																								
177 CAXTON.																								
1 Caxton. (W.)	10357	M.	5248	605	713	620	591	334	276	290	273	250	246	205	184	197	144	115	69	39	9	3	-	-
		F.	5109	718	757	586	366	310	316	289	309	257	217	213	185	192	102	109	72	40	17	3	-	-
178 CHESTERTON.																								
1 Willingham	9586	M.	4803	638	629	565	489	351	310	264	265	231	208	193	184	182	122	71	73	35	12	-	-	-
		F.	4783	622	612	545	351	355	295	277	295	246	235	206	219	163	137	96	77	40	12	3	2	-
2 Fulbourn. (W.L.P.)	11536	M.	5772	892	773	645	517	437	358	388	376	272	217	218	214	196	125	118	58	47	10	-	1	-
		F.	5764	775	713	640	461	413	386	388	384	332	258	289	292	194	148	108	74	31	14	4	1	-
3 Shelford	7927	M.	3953	518	547	478	438	279	229	242	236	206	143	120	143	134	93	41	58	33	7	-	-	-
		F.	3974	896	506	472	309	293	270	250	238	198	189	145	148	151	97	79	57	30	12	4	-	-
179 CAMBRIDGE.																								
1 St. Andrew the Less. (W.)	21078	M.	9900	1515	1364	1130	913	813	703	674	619	489	320	319	283	239	180	105	64	39	11	1	1	-
		F.	11178	1552	1356	1257	1044	923	904	763	680	602	437	418	328	308	240	172	110	47	15	5	3	-
2 St. Mary the Great. (H.)	4361	M.	2101	144	138	202	372	477	180	105	91	77	86	67	73	57	29	31	13	6	-	1	-	-
		F.	2260	122	151	199	300	295	204	186	122	145	114	104	84	70	52	45	25	20	3	-	-	-
3 St. Andrew the Great	5696	M.	2598	209	232	242	347	404	135	150	127	122	103	93	81	77	64	29	25	13	3	-	-	-
		F.	3098	220	286	270	459	367	249	198	173	159	160	145	134	110	91	66	41	16	8	3	-	-
4 St. Giles	4228	M.	1922	223	183	207	240	250	142	106	94	108	85	78	60	61	46	26	11	12	2	-	-	-
		F.	2306	190	246	262	270	245	173	141	147	105	112	93	81	86	63	37	20	13	4	-	-	-
180 LINTON.																								
1 Duxford	5027	M.	2478	331	325	297	294	166	140	129	117	132	110	103	89	75	61	37	35	9	2	-	-	-
		F.	2549	232	262	298	213	187	154	166	126	145	150	107	78	94	83	49	40	21	4	1	-	-
2 Linton. (W.)	4524	M.	2189	290	283	250	239	153	158	112	103	103	97	89	71	78	64	61	35	8	6	-	-	-
		F.	2335	334	312	253	184	173	184	123	110	111	95	113	77	79	76	49	44	14	7	3	-	-
3 Balsham	3464	M.	1757	240	248	196	180	149	92	79	84	84	69	71	50	67	54	39	21	11	4	1	-	-
		F.	1707	228	231	226	122	100	100	77	90	94	80	59	73	72	64	42	29	11	8	2	1	-
181 NEWMARKET.																								
1 Cheveley. (H.)	6686	M.	3360	414	407	409	362	283	205	217	150	161	138	126	130	112	93	53	47	18	3	2	-	-
		F.	3326	414	424	365	298	244	231	203	170	181	148	160	123	133	111	60	41	29	10	1	-	-
2 Newmarket. (W.)	6949	M.	3528	399	396	406	426	328	264	198	213	170	134	122	117	119	102	73	45	33	6	2	1	-
		F.	3421	467	403	358	333	294	264	180	212	182	169	108	102	114	72	58	43	41	8	2	1	-
3 Bottisham	3112	M.	1596	205	229	191	167	100	80	82	63	95	65	70	51	61	51	33	19	9	1	1	-	-
		F.	1516	227	200	169	109	86	80	96	69	89	70	75	43	73	58	52	20	9	5	-	-	-
4 Gazeley	3142	M.	1585	220	192	204	157	118	71	90	70	77	74	71	64	68	34	36	26	16	1	-	-	-
		F.	1557	184	214	168	119	107	108	97	90	93	67	74	86	56	46	29	31	13	7	1	-	-
5 Soham	8358	M.	4116	549	507	496	388	307	234	238	228	204	168	191	149	170	117	79	60	23	16	1	1	-
		F.	4242	558	525	456	352	307	265	224	223	219	205	195	169	193	121	97	68	43	17	1	-	-
182 ELY.																								
1 Haddenham	3584	M.	1783	231	218	206	171	128	103	94	96	102	81	81	68	77	56	34	21	8	5	1	-	-
		F.	1801	246	263	210	120	122	87	107	94	86	108	74	67	92	60	38	27	8	3	-	1	-
2 Sutton	3401	M.	1731	208	227	221	182	139	87	76	102	86	65	75	60	76	65	35	29	14	3	1	-	-
		F.	1670	208	225	209	120	117	88	102	115	81	89	58	65	81	48	41	21	8	6	-	-	-
3 Ely. (W.H.)	8124	M.	4042	611	479	457	481	325	267	251	192	236	129	153	143	144	101	77	37	30	7	1	1	-
		F.	4082	523	502	457	467	318	287	267	270	264	171	178	142	153	87	83	51	25	7	1	-	-
4 Littleport	5593	M.	2801	354	410	330	254	183	160	144	148	137	117	131	112	110	83	56	30	15	6	2	-	-
		F.	2792	351	393	358	222	182	170	152	150	127	158	126	110	114	65	54	36	20	8	2	1	-
183 NORTH WITCHFORD.																								
1 Chatteris. (W.)	8185	M.	4155	527	535	498	397	322	230	210	233	187	181	191	151	172	117	74	52	35	18	1	-	-
		F.	4030	529	533	436	378	293	253	197	216	222	193	169	154	171	126	70	58	29	8	6	-	-
2 March	7279	M.	3558	483	443	416	344	276	257	211	190	216	126	160	128	122	102	64	33	18	2	1	-	-
		F.	3721	504	497	406	335	256	239	204	237	205	148	136	132	122	90	74	33	24	9	-	-	-
184 WHITTLESEY.																								
1 Whittlesey. (W.)	6455	M.	3185	429	404	385	331	191	168	170	173	135	117	140	120	139	93	67	39	26	7	4	1	-
		F.	3270	404	397	368	297	197	200	195	165	173	162	140	134	149	106	71	62	27	9	6	-	-
185 WISBECH.																								
1 Leverington	5439	M.	2724	381	383	320	261	190	165	154	165	136	127	114	91	100	71	35	36	11	4	-	-	-
		F.	2715	386	378	329	210	175	158	164	178	133	136	103	93	80	90	46	34	8	6	-	-	-
2 Wisbech. (W.H.²)	9249	M.	4195	537	476	528	482	280	233	257	248	196	173	167	152	156	124	90	50	42	10	2	-	-
		F.	5054	518	528	520	518	436	387	291	271	258	246	232	208	212	186	126	86	48	17	4	5	-
3 Walpole St. Peter	2684	M.	1345	190	177	163	125	80	79	75	79	65	74	51	46	57	40	22	6	12	4	-	-	-
		F.	1339	187	179	166	98	85	84	84	73	74	59	45	56	49	41	27	23	7	4	3	-	-
4 Terrington St. Clement.	4947	M.	2492	347	312	273	247	168	157	137	121	150	101	98	80	106	74	75	34	17	2	3	-	-
		F.	2455	318	331	242	193	185	145	146	120	149	118	101	104	110	74	46	36	22	6	2	-	-
5 Walsoken	5493	M.	2662	366	361	337	255	179	183	143	154	130	116	97	88	92	87	45	32	22	5	-	-	-
		F.	2831	365	354	327	216	190	186	177	172	158	130	115	116	107	93	58	39	19	7	2	-	-
6 Upwell	4650	M.	2324	326	354	263	213	152	128	151	131	115	91	86	84	102	55	35	22	10	5	4	-	-
		F.	2326	288	381	261	299	188	148	139	129	124	108	107	100	94	69	42	26	19	3	2	-	-

Table 4.—MALE and FEMALE CHILDREN at *each Year of Age* under 5 in the SOUTH MIDLAND DIVISION and its REGISTRATION COUNTIES.

REGISTRATION COUNTY.	TOTAL UNDER 5 YEARS. Persons.	Males and Females.		Under 1 Year.	1–	2–	3–	4–
III. SOUTH MIDLAND COUNTIES.	212979	M.	106387	22423	20316	21393	20671	21384
		F.	106592	22259	20415	21458	21108	21354
6 MIDDLESEX (*Extra-metropolitan*)	51026	M.	25988	5620	5158	5080	5074	5056
		F.	25938	5532	5014	5220	5056	5116
7 HERTFORDSHIRE	26705	M.	13382	2728	2615	2511	2827	2701
		F.	13323	2808	2587	2696	2613	2879
8 BUCKINGHAMSHIRE	20833	M.	10460	2183	1987	2061	2117	2112
		F.	10373	2067	2004	2152	1973	2177
9 OXFORDSHIRE	23820	M.	11915	2626	2240	2323	2309	2408
		F.	11905	2488	2218	2388	2403	2410
10 NORTHAMPTONSHIRE	38324	M.	18895	4051	3664	3800	3655	3825
		F.	19329	4073	3658	3969	3871	3758
11 HUNTINGDONSHIRE	6795	M.	3404	690	629	711	684	690
		F.	3391	686	627	794	680	694
12 BEDFORDSHIRE	19076	M.	9934	2100	1851	2034	1967	1982
		F.	10042	2047	1989	1976	1976	2054
13 CAMBRIDGESHIRE	24600	M.	12309	2525	2263	2473	2438	2610
		F.	12291	2568	2318	2413	2534	2456

Table 5.—MALE and FEMALE CHILDREN at *each Year of Age* under 5 in REGISTRATION DISTRICTS.

REGISTRATION DISTRICT.	Total under 5 Years. Persons.	Males and Females.		Under 1 Year.	1–	2–	3–	4–
6 MIDDLESEX (*Extra-metropolitan*).								
124 STAINES	3101	M.	1557	326	296	330	306	300
		F.	1544	304	268	307	314	351
125 UXBRIDGE	3527	M.	1773	369	330	330	376	368
		F.	1754	366	324	379	321	364
126 BRENTFORD	13602	M.	6870	1463	1411	1358	1282	1356
		F.	6732	1431	1325	1282	1342	1352
127 HENDON	7413	M.	3647	814	712	726	689	706
		F.	3766	809	705	780	743	729
128 BARNET	4231	M.	2074	445	418	400	429	382
		F.	2157	436	432	429	413	447
129 EDMONTON	20003	M.	10067	2213	1992	1936	1992	1934
		F.	9936	2095	1960	2043	1923	1914
7 HERTFORDSHIRE.								
130 WARE	2400	M.	1187	249	240	220	244	234
		F.	1213	269	242	243	230	239
131 BISHOP STORTFORD	2926	M.	1468	314	246	333	290	285
		F.	1458	318	246	283	284	325
132 ROYSTON	3303	M.	1671	340	297	347	322	365
		F.	1632	330	314	305	362	321
133 HITCHIN	3732	M.	1902	376	352	394	398	378
		F.	1830	405	365	377	340	343
134 HERTFORD	2053	M.	1042	199	198	239	203	205
		F.	1011	204	184	223	199	201
135 HATFIELD	1287	M.	634	123	111	139	127	134
		F.	653	140	141	125	117	130
136 ST. ALBANS	3170	M.	1568	318	312	337	281	320
		F.	1602	330	320	313	316	323
137 WATFORD	3843	M.	1905	412	357	397	365	374
		F.	1938	384	377	390	392	385
138 HEMEL HEMPSTEAD	1923	M.	987	203	183	217	193	191
		F.	936	201	176	180	182	197
139 BERKHAMPSTEAD	2068	M.	1018	194	217	188	204	215
		F.	1050	227	220	197	191	215
8 BUCKINGHAMSHIRE.								
140 AMERSHAM	2527	M.	1270	256	241	247	284	242
		F.	1257	263	238	267	248	241
141 ETON	3296	M.	1612	352	298	299	319	329
		F.	1684	347	311	343	330	353
142 WYCOMBE	5790	M.	2903	597	550	679	581	598
		F.	2886	586	571	652	555	622
143 AYLESBURY	3268	M.	1663	339	324	327	228	345
		F.	1605	300	310	348	308	330
144 WINSLOW	968	M.	475	108	88	87	93	99
		F.	493	91	103	98	95	106
145 NEWPORT PAGNELL	3439	M.	1727	372	319	361	330	346
		F.	1712	347	334	383	293	355
146 BUCKINGHAM	1545	M.	808	140	162	171	178	153
		F.	737	134	137	161	144	161
9 OXFORDSHIRE.								
147 HENLEY	2656	M.	1335	280	329	262	283	262
		F.	1321	277	223	273	300	248
148 THAME	1814	M.	913	181	180	184	182	186
		F.	901	197	168	172	170	194
149 HEADINGTON	3733	M.	1860	387	359	366	346	372
		F.	1873	408	339	360	381	385
150 OXFORD	2759	M.	1394	296	310	271	260	257
		F.	1365	290	277	285	261	282
151 BICESTER	1839	M.	940	178	192	212	172	186
		F.	899	202	142	180	175	200
152 WOODSTOCK	1801	M.	887	206	161	178	167	175
		F.	914	186	172	178	187	155
153 WITNEY	2915	M.	1451	309	236	[illegible]	289	321
		F.	1464	291	285	304	281	303
154 CHIPPING NORTON	2476	M.	1217	252	224	239	241	261
		F.	1259	249	265	264	263	218
155 BANBURY	3827	M.	1918	418	348	368	378	388
		F.	1909	386	347	405	385	386

REGISTRATION DISTRICT.	Total under 5 Years. Persons.	Males and Females.		Under 1 Year.	1–	2–	3–	4–
10 NORTHAMPTONSHIRE.								
156 BRACKLEY	1549	M.	822	174	168	152	166	[illegible]
		F.	727	137	124	162	130	[illegible]
157 TOWCESTER	1706	M.	836	196	145	169	146	[illegible]
		F.	869	170	149	183	172	[illegible]
158 POTTERSPURY	1669	M.	833	193	146	168	162	[illegible]
		F.	836	160	162	191	170	[illegible]
159 HARDINGSTONE	1456	M.	726	147	141	150	131	[illegible]
		F.	730	164	145	154	136	[illegible]
160 NORTHAMPTON	9138	M.	4448	1010	843	875	940	[illegible]
		F.	4690	1006	908	957	944	[illegible]
161 DAVENTRY	2292	M.	1144	225	229	254	218	[illegible]
		F.	1148	217	230	236	238	[illegible]
162 BRIXWORTH	1686	M.	813	167	146	152	176	[illegible]
		F.	863	180	171	162	173	[illegible]
163 WELLINGBOROUGH	5261	M.	2591	538	621	500	497	[illegible]
		F.	2670	678	641	518	532	[illegible]
164 KETTERING	3846	M.	1918	416	378	386	358	[illegible]
		F.	1928	421	347	411	387	[illegible]
165 THRAPSTON	2144	M.	1059	233	151	217	224	[illegible]
		F.	1085	219	191	230	230	[illegible]
166 OUNDLE	1757	M.	862	167	175	181	181	[illegible]
		F.	895	178	171	174	208	[illegible]
167 PETERBOROUGH	5841	M.	2943	686	592	586	538	[illegible]
		F.	2898	653	519	691	548	[illegible]
11 HUNTINGDONSHIRE.								
168 HUNTINGDON	2508	M.	1241	254	228	266	252	[illegible]
		F.	1267	242	245	271	232	[illegible]
169 ST. IVES	2124	M.	1054	222	194	204	213	[illegible]
		F.	1070	229	191	211	230	[illegible]
170 ST. NEOTS	2163	M.	1109	214	207	241	218	[illegible]
		F.	1054	215	191	242	218	[illegible]
12 BEDFORDSHIRE.								
171 BEDFORD	5229	M.	2594	562	447	532	535	[illegible]
		F.	2635	520	621	528	462	[illegible]
172 BIGGLESWADE	3581	M.	1776	345	322	381	349	[illegible]
		F.	1805	370	370	338	381	[illegible]
173 AMPTHILL	2204	M.	1082	217	199	231	211	[illegible]
		F.	1122	236	223	211	218	[illegible]
174 WOBURN	1183	M.	612	133	120	109	126	[illegible]
		F.	571	104	113	119	104	[illegible]
175 LEIGHTON BUZZARD	2512	M.	1247	243	236	261	245	[illegible]
		F.	1265	261	257	250	246	[illegible]
176 LUTON	5267	M.	2623	597	525	620	501	[illegible]
		F.	2644	556	505	632	631	[illegible]
13 CAMBRIDGESHIRE.								
177 CAXTON	1413	M.	696	128	142	139	138	[illegible]
		F.	718	157	131	140	145	[illegible]
178 CHESTERTON	3881	M.	1958	429	363	393	372	[illegible]
		F.	1923	464	393	400	384	[illegible]
179 CAMBRIDGE	4190	M.	2091	441	375	424	406	[illegible]
		F.	2099	479	397	397	446	[illegible]
180 LINTON	1776	M.	881	171	186	183	166	[illegible]
		F.	894	178	186	192	161	[illegible]
181 NEWMARKET	3634	M.	1784	363	317	368	358	[illegible]
		F.	1850	390	322	371	369	[illegible]
182 ELY	2612	M.	1304	260	248	264	287	[illegible]
		F.	1308	272	258	283	281	[illegible]
183 NORTH WITCHFORD	2043	M.	1010	201	207	180	207	[illegible]
		F.	1033	204	192	201	219	[illegible]
184 WHITTLESEY	843	M.	439	89	67	94	98	[illegible]
		F.	404	74	79	73	87	[illegible]
185 WISBECH	4209	M.	2147	443	391	428	431	[illegible]
		F.	2062	482	302	406	393	[illegible]

Table 7.—Condition as to Marriage and Ages of Males and Females in the South Midland Division and its Registration Counties.

Registration County.		All Ages.	Under 15 Years.	15–	20–	25–	35–	45–	55–	65 and upwards.
III. SOUTH MIDLAND COUNTIES.										
Unmarried	Males	477006	300255	77091	46772	28913	11000	6203	3876	2782
	Females	485303	236387	74120	47322	36313	15517	9246	6300	4781
Married	Males	263548	.	355	13885	67703	69250	53823	33247	24067
	Females	271931		1302	20700	76398	70530	62390	34255	17307
Widowed	Males	28673	.	4	124	1323	2630	4282	6232	14046
	Females	59600		14	186	2481	6359	10031	14283	26346
6 MIDDLESEX (*Extra-metropolitan*).										
Unmarried	Males	134237	71717	17139	11852	7043	2727	1469	823	538
	Females	123786	70186	19163	13873	10460	4368	2681	1701	1314
Married	Males	61071	.	65	3296	17606	17443	11620	7077	3075
	Females	61988	.	341	5388	19909	17013	10867	5805	2685
Widowed	Males	3614	.	1	25	323	827	801	1209	2238
	Females	14418	.	1	54	746	1830	2527	3630	5439
7 HERTFORDSHIRE.										
Unmarried	Males	61560	39070	9939	6263	3746	1526	981	594	444
	Females	62129	37549	8706	5677	4759	2230	1378	1067	763
Married	Males	33510	.	35	1588	7987	8472	6826	5188	3413
	Females	33768	.	139	5292	8965	8719	6761	4487	2415
Widowed	Males	3803	.	.	6	144	364	505	826	1988
	Females	7822	.	2	22	266	749	1241	1702	3492
8 BUCKINGHAMSHIRE.										
Unmarried	Males	46023	30097	7058	4187	2520	1036	599	341	275
	Females	46032	29434	6701	4147	3117	1426	602	568	440
Married	Males	26760	.	47	1303	6288	6674	5563	4201	2674
	Females	26845	.	141	1890	6925	6934	5494	3620	1836
Widowed	Males	3123	.	.	13	125	246	415	668	1658
	Females	5336	.	2	6	230	523	961	1353	2231
9 OXFORDSHIRE.										
Unmarried	Males	55003	33838	9069	5605	3408	1346	737	563	329
	Females	53194	33479	8226	5285	3934	1309	1064	823	374
Married	Males	30286	.	28	1335	7081	7369	6376	4786	3331
	Females	30675	.	160	2070	7918	7769	6210	4255	2286
Widowed	Males	3319	.	1	18	133	299	571	776	1893
	Females	6963	.	2	21	252	703	1129	1018	3198
10 NORTHAMPTONSHIRE.										
Unmarried	Males	83616	51858	13888	8805	5126	1850	1076	906	417
	Females	80457	51095	12616	7060	4697	1617	1079	739	547
Married	Males	49238	.	84	2865	12855	12216	9664	7044	4231
	Females	49528	.	310	4072	13708	12423	9643	6165	3257
Widowed	Males	5217	.	2	30	280	529	830	1113	2488
	Females	9860	.	4	34	367	909	1442	2198	4263
11 HUNTINGDONSHIRE.										
Unmarried	Males	16690	10029	2677	1420	771	348	215	118	114
	Females	15852	10014	2369	1295	901	460	229	172	132
Married	Males	9308	.	11	291	1974	2247	1989	1605	1091
	Females	9419	.	43	616	2300	2363	1933	1455	807
Widowed	Males	1069	.	.	4	32	83	149	227	573
	Females	2185	.	.	5	69	174	321	427	1128
12 BEDFORDSHIRE.										
Unmarried	Males	43616	28552	7530	3621	2083	810	431	283	181
	Females	48939	28447	7752	4930	3938	1806	1007	599	441
Married	Males	26294	.	52	1690	6246	6650	5286	4068	2613
	Females	26760	.	107	1892	7081	6915	5250	3679	1766
Widowed	Males	2766	.	.	11	122	234	333	604	1468
	Females	5965	.	3	22	273	679	1050	1509	2429
13 CAMBRIDGESHIRE.										
Unmarried	Males	57331	35244	9766	6139	3321	1311	695	488	377
	Females	56183	35286	8583	5011	3497	1612	1006	693	646
Married	Males	32871	.	33	1520	7766	8286	8230	5288	3568
	Females	33262	.	159	2381	8612	8403	6333	4764	2611
Widowed	Males	3701	.	.	14	165	317	498	830	1877
	Females	7706	.	1	30	278	696	1160	1706	3815

Note.—In a few cases, persons described as "Married" were stated to be under 15 years of age. These have been classed with married persons aged "15 and under 20 years."

Table 8.—CONDITION as to MARRIAGE and AGES of MALES and FEMALES in REGISTRATION DISTRICTS.

REGISTRATION DISTRICT.		ALL AGES.	Under 15 Years.	15-	20-	25-	35-	45-	55-	65 and upw.
MIDDLESEX (*Extra-metropolitan*).										
TAINES:										
UNMARRIED	M.	8060	5307	1214	662	429	184	115	71	68
	F.	7187	4527	974	678	626	202	138	70	72
MARRIED	M.	3630	.	2	156	960	1036	740	504	314
	F.	3696	.	22	270	1028	1018	717	433	202
WIDOWED	M.	359	.	.	1	18	38	56	86	160
	F.	787	.	.	2	36	83	135	109	342
XBRIDGE:										
UNMARRIED	M.	8659	5000	1307	860	662	374	222	146	99
	F.	8495	4912	1038	758	670	404	283	210	130
MARRIED	M.	4394	.	1	195	1127	1146	918	628	379
	F.	4476	.	19	330	1233	1167	866	563	278
WIDOWED	M.	502	.	.	6	20	48	82	108	238
	F.	1134	.	.	8	56	125	214	266	476
RENTFORD:										
UNMARRIED	M.	30176	19105	4503	3191	2084	645	362	172	114
	F.	33582	18460	6332	4032	2962	1221	759	453	363
MARRIED	M.	16073	.	25	940	4653	4206	3006	1828	1114
	F.	16427	.	102	1566	5357	4404	2839	1484	715
WIDOWED	M.	1291	.	1	7	87	156	240	304	496
	F.	4158	.	.	23	216	575	903	1041	1398
RENDON:										
UNMARRIED	M.	16398	10120	2760	1740	1087	331	174	102	74
	F.	18065	10244	2845	2079	1589	620	361	205	122
MARRIED	M.	8674	.	7	476	2559	2537	1608	1023	464
	F.	8727	.	28	801	2859	2495	1554	774	286
WIDOWED	M.	668	.	.	2	50	96	119	158	243
	F.	1880	.	.	7	112	281	398	454	628
BARNET:										
UNMARRIED	M.	9966	5915	1532	1019	810	344	193	101	52
	F.	11472	5760	1677	1401	1317	601	356	209	151
MARRIED	M.	5336	.	3	247	1308	1535	1067	699	367
	F.	5316	.	23	382	1641	1549	1038	582	296
WIDOWED	M.	470	.	.	.	32	65	69	106	198
	F.	1338	.	.	2	74	176	257	305	524
EDMONTON:										
UNMARRIED	M.	41008	26270	5823	4371	2870	849	403	231	191
	F.	46075	26283	7502	4930	3398	1320	784	554	506
MARRIED	M.	22910	.	27	1232	6929	6679	4261	2385	1387
	F.	23076	.	141	2093	7791	6381	3813	1969	888
WIDOWED	M.	2024	.	.	9	116	224	325	447	903
	F.	6111	.	1	15	258	660	920	1265	2069
HERTFORDSHIRE.										
WARE:										
UNMARRIED	M.	6096	3614	1209	545	386	137	98	54	56
	F.	5525	3376	776	408	467	189	95	71	64
MARRIED	M.	2968	.	2	135	724	719	606	472	308
	F.	2968	.	11	211	776	754	611	398	213
WIDOWED	M.	372	.	.	1	16	37	54	85	179
	F.	698	.	1	3	17	58	112	155	352
BISHOP STORTFORD:										
UNMARRIED	M.	6324	4309	1124	568	481	161	93	75	53
	F.	6393	4061	855	608	422	184	120	84	56
MARRIED	M.	3665	.	2	129	846	891	775	588	422
	F.	3680	.	17	240	920	934	755	517	297
WIDOWED	M.	433	.	.	1	9	22	65	93	243
	F.	818	.	.	4	26	70	137	169	412
ROYSTON:										
UNMARRIED	M.	7708	4878	1317	617	386	179	102	67	62
	F.	6979	4726	933	502	374	178	122	83	61
MARRIED	M.	4280	.	4	171	898	1084	928	718	477
	F.	4243	.	16	238	1063	1069	885	639	343
WIDOWED	M.	562	.	.	.	13	47	75	108	319
	F.	883	.	.	.	29	59	105	222	468
ITCHIN:										
UNMARRIED	M.	7868	5318	1226	629	364	146	106	70	39
	F.	8721	5197	1311	879	649	270	184	132	99
MARRIED	M.	4602	.	8	235	1138	1978	963	715	465
	F.	4633	.	21	318	1249	1196	900	610	339
WIDOWED	M.	513	.	.	1	26	31	85	102	268
	F.	1060	.	.	3	42	118	197	241	459
ERTFORD:										
UNMARRIED	M.	5548	3421	898	509	373	149	81	46	28
	F.	4968	3017	728	447	385	181	101	77	81
MARRIED	M.	2348	.	4	105	575	680	559	427	294
	F.	2085	.	11	168	667	676	547	375	192
WIDOWED	M.	318	.	.	.	18	22	47	62	169
	F.	612	.	.	.	22	61	100	141	288
7 HERTFORDSHIRE—*cont.*										
135 HATFIELD:										
UNMARRIED	M.	2735	1672	428	271	139	63	61	34	19
	F.	2607	1605	373	220	221	86	46	32	24
MARRIED	M.	1457	.	.	64	385	345	297	230	138
	F.	1451	.	8	88	433	366	291	180	85
WIDOWED	M.	179	.	.	.	6	13	25	40	95
	F.	313	.	.	2	13	38	47	70	143
136 ST. ALBANS:										
UNMARRIED	M.	6632	4316	1006	567	409	160	86	73	45
	F.	7409	4317	1082	744	636	318	192	121	99
MARRIED	M.	3806	.	5	240	909	1038	726	549	378
	F.	3928	.	17	298	1129	1017	722	494	251
WIDOWED	M.	415	.	.	2	17	46	64	92	194
	F.	906	.	.	3	50	109	160	209	395
137 WATFORD:										
UNMARRIED	M.	9638	5837	1354	870	725	363	256	125	99
	F.	10093	6073	1367	896	897	501	333	256	170
MARRIED	M.	4876	.	3	218	1189	1336	1011	695	424
	F.	5025	.	16	362	1328	1347	1023	608	351
WIDOWED	M.	541	.	.	4	16	40	96	143	242
	F.	1155	.	.	3	43	132	192	297	488
138 HEMEL HEMPSTEAD:										
UNMARRIED	M.	4200	2753	638	350	259	96	42	26	37
	F.	4517	2666	684	433	340	151	113	78	52
MARRIED	M.	2536	.	2	130	621	637	482	409	255
	F.	2558	.	6	172	712	661	503	330	174
WIDOWED	M.	259	.	.	.	8	27	40	50	134
	F.	636	.	1	2	21	54	90	144	213
139 BERKHAMPSTEAD:										
UNMARRIED	M.	4306	2852	721	329	221	74	53	34	22
	F.	4737	2861	654	450	308	172	82	73	57
MARRIED	M.	2586	.	5	162	652	656	478	387	246
	F.	2634	.	16	206	694	700	514	338	168
WIDOWED	M.	271	.	.	.	15	19	44	51	142
	F.	547	.	.	3	23	56	95	144	227
8 BUCKINGHAMSHIRE.										
140 AMERSHAM:										
UNMARRIED	M.	5419	3589	831	460	254	129	80	41	35
	F.	5555	3597	768	472	382	169	80	72	65
MARRIED	M.	3155	.	3	105	759	719	658	527	324
	F.	3188	.	13	227	812	792	636	460	244
WIDOWED	M.	366	.	.	2	13	32	44	61	194
	F.	636	.	.	1	25	50	88	158	314
141 ETON:										
UNMARRIED	M.	9228	5420	1932	865	554	219	129	64	45
	F.	8384	4893	1226	838	710	334	193	109	81
MARRIED	M.	4335	.	6	172	974	1206	972	602	403
	F.	4348	.	17	263	1144	1220	924	525	265
WIDOWED	M.	464	.	.	2	18	39	82	108	215
	F.	962	.	.	1	48	110	183	240	371
142 WYCOMBE:										
UNMARRIED	M.	11041	7928	1920	1021	584	253	129	71	65
	F.	12026	8011	1737	1016	667	267	149	101	78
MARRIED	M.	7106	.	14	420	1794	1744	1511	981	645
	F.	7142	.	45	578	1944	1865	1412	870	428
WIDOWED	M.	761	.	.	3	36	68	106	152	387
	F.	1310	.	1	2	62	130	190	318	568
143 AYLESBURY:										
UNMARRIED	M.	7298	4612	1146	670	448	199	112	62	46
	F.	7362	4538	1034	686	508	277	149	90	71
MARRIED	M.	4228	.	9	177	1018	1034	837	598	454
	F.	4234	.	21	268	1066	1075	904	586	314
WIDOWED	M.	527	.	.	1	19	44	58	119	286
	F.	968	.	.	1	35	91	161	220	460
144 WINSLOW:										
UNMARRIED	M.	2336	1504	372	215	131	53	23	15	20
	F.	2436	1525	367	197	177	73	42	27	28
MARRIED	M.	1345	.	2	61	241	339	272	260	161
	F.	1334	.	10	89	281	340	290	226	98
WIDOWED	M.	196	.	.	.	2	14	28	50	102
	F.	297	.	1	1	14	27	40	69	146
145 NEWPORT PAGNELL:										
UNMARRIED	M.	7120	4626	1176	665	362	129	76	57	40
	F.	7261	4700	1037	609	425	194	114	105	77
MARRIED	M.	4398	.	9	222	1046	1082	880	736	423
	F.	4405	.	26	326	1142	1113	872	612	315
WIDOWED	M.	512	.	.	5	26	40	65	106	272
	F.	887	.	.	.	27	70	128	215	441

Table 8 *continued*.—CONDITION as to MARRIAGE and AGES of MALES and FEMALES in REGISTRATION DISTRICTS.

REGISTRATION DISTRICT.		ALL AGES.	Under 15 Years.	15–	20–	25–	35–	45–	55–	65 and upw.
8 BUCKINGHAMSHIRE—*cont.*										
146 BUCKINGHAM:										
UNMARRIED	M.	3582	2329	578	291	197	84	48	31	24
	F.	3619	2170	542	330	298	111	75	33	40
MARRIED	M.	2180	.	4	86	455	560	633	587	254
	F.	2194	.	5	199	536	529	451	352	182
WIDOWED	M.	307	.	.	.	12	9	33	53	200
	F.	536	.	.	.	19	39	62	124	292
9 OXFORDSHIRE.										
147 HENLEY:										
UNMARRIED	M.	6229	3878	1096	568	361	153	87	67	39
	F.	5966	3808	787	559	382	171	106	89	64
MARRIED	M.	3359	.	.	140	820	868	673	515	334
	F.	3389	.	11	226	606	865	682	478	221
WIDOWED	M.	381	.	.	4	19	46	49	75	183
	F.	688	.	.	.	25	76	111	168	308
148 THAME:										
UNMARRIED	M.	4249	2739	683	360	240	90	53	42	33
	F.	4124	2631	522	382	285	118	75	67	43
MARRIED	M.	2367	.	5	107	596	523	498	410	383
	F.	2331	.	15	138	548	567	451	383	204
WIDOWED	M.	289	.	.	1	13	19	36	60	100
	F.	512	.	2	4	17	51	73	115	250
149 HEADINGTON:										
UNMARRIED	M.	8475	5101	1341	911	592	205	126	76	61
	F.	9575	5056	1620	1648	885	402	233	156	133
MARRIED	M.	4440	.	5	211	1188	1142	855	622	419
	F.	4673	.	10	348	1311	1222	831	554	250
WIDOWED	M.	813	.	.	3	22	38	90	105	280
	F.	1140	.	.	1	54	130	216	296	462
150 OXFORD:										
UNMARRIED	M.	8687	5711	1112	978	531	187	87	62	19
	F.	6870	3672	1267	758	590	280	154	105	54
MARRIED	M.	3539	.	10	192	1012	895	741	413	276
	F.	3558	.	21	298	1030	691	670	371	177
WIDOWED	M.	347	.	.	2	21	38	78	81	129
	F.	901	.	.	4	38	108	188	208	356
151 BICESTER:										
UNMARRIED	M.	4328	2592	721	404	294	108	70	51	38
	F.	4198	2502	608	397	260	117	74	55	36
MARRIED	M.	2424	.	2	108	491	528	555	420	312
	F.	2448	.	13	152	553	662	536	372	217
WIDOWED	M.	315	.	.	.	7	17	49	73	169
	F.	534	.	.	2	18	38	72	132	277
152 WOODSTOCK:										
UNMARRIED	M.	3951	2506	627	364	298	93	46	32	32
	F.	4010	2553	518	384	278	117	64	54	42
MARRIED	M.	2296	.	1	101	482	540	409	401	281
	F.	2285	.	12	143	545	573	480	333	190
WIDOWED	M.	200	.	.	3	4	29	49	58	147
	F.	489	.	.	1	17	45	78	109	239
153 WITNEY:										
UNMARRIED	M.	6467	4118	1081	585	330	152	98	79	56
	F.	6320	4134	873	508	346	187	107	82	84
MARRIED	M.	3791	.	3	151	763	879	759	608	510
	F.	3748	.	10	230	896	962	778	532	336
WIDOWED	M.	563	.	1	.	20	41	72	98	271
	F.	802	.	.	2	18	79	117	178	408
154 CHIPPING NORTON:										
UNMARRIED	M.	5410	3434	892	489	327	131	64	44	40
	F.	5804	3478	758	440	306	138	86	63	35
MARRIED	M.	3130	.	2	119	696	789	670	488	376
	F.	3162	.	19	223	734	783	632	459	242
WIDOWED	M.	361	.	.	2	11	28	62	80	188
	F.	661	.	.	2	25	81	94	137	284
155 BANBURY:										
UNMARRIED	M.	9209	5699	1536	897	531	242	129	108	77
	F.	8917	5553	1283	899	593	276	165	162	88
MARRIED	M.	5641	.	2	189	1115	1215	1028	892	620
	F.	6056	.	30	319	1273	1274	1101	773	326
WIDOWED	M.	646	.	.	3	15	60	105	145	318
	F.	1217	.	.	5	42	128	180	285	585
10 NORTHAMPTONSHIRE.										
156 BRACKLEY:										
UNMARRIED	M.	3744	2374	639	355	170	94	39	46	27
	F.	3464	2119	512	326	245	109	61	54	44
MARRIED	M.	2167	.	2	30	452	517	462	380	266
	F.	2266	.	6	133	507	549	472	328	201
WIDOWED	M.	286	.	.	1	18	28	36	66	137
	F.	474	.	.	.	12	46	67	109	250
10 NORTHAMPTONSHIRE—*cont.*										
157 TOWCESTER:										
UNMARRIED	M.	3631	2331	618	329	184	57	42	36	74
	F.	3610	2340	495	326	210	53	50	47	41
MARRIED	M.	2289	.	5	98	521	532	400	398	255
	F.	2313	.	6	154	573	562	505	339	174
WIDOWED	M.	239	.	.	.	11	23	46	46	144
	F.	472	.	.	.	15	38	71	106	242
158 POTTERSPURY:										
UNMARRIED	M.	3760	2348	660	373	230	71	43	16	9
	F.	3495	2241	512	313	226	94	49	26	34
MARRIED	M.	2164	.	4	104	537	523	440	330	226
	F.	2171	.	9	155	564	531	480	329	103
WIDOWED	M.	242	.	1	3	8	21	42	48	134
	F.	409	.	.	2	19	33	64	94	193
159 HARDINGSTONE:										
UNMARRIED	M.	3133	1948	532	345	184	69	35	14	16
	F.	2859	1941	393	240	134	54	31	33	23
MARRIED	M.	1991	.	2	113	485	481	407	290	213
	F.	1977	.	3	150	528	490	384	282	135
WIDOWED	M.	234	.	.	2	10	17	27	65	113
	F.	301	.	.	.	11	22	36	74	148
160 NORTHAMPTON:										
UNMARRIED	M.	19071	11820	3122	1924	1216	478	294	147	70
	F.	19236	12197	3286	1778	1087	423	235	162	71
MARRIED	M.	11433	.	34	856	3408	3121	2213	1273	598
	F.	11416	.	101	1194	3558	3011	2014	1101	437
WIDOWED	M.	1016	.	.	7	81	128	192	213	395
	F.	2072	.	1	11	105	251	388	535	781
161 DAVENTRY:										
UNMARRIED	M.	5678	3211	871	679	470	226	114	63	44
	F.	5061	3167	726	465	343	150	98	72	40
MARRIED	M.	3274	.	4	131	676	770	710	578	405
	F.	3291	.	20	230	747	779	710	527	278
WIDOWED	M.	444	.	.	1	12	41	68	100	221
	F.	706	.	.	3	31	60	97	187	328
162 BRIXWORTH:										
UNMARRIED	M.	4021	2367	681	463	277	101	53	49	30
	F.	3650	2357	487	320	224	107	76	42	37
MARRIED	M.	2423	.	5	118	474	628	550	455	193
	F.	2440	.	13	149	557	530	594	428	169
WIDOWED	M.	302	.	.	1	9	19	42	73	158
	F.	500	.	.	2	15	44	68	126	245
163 WELLINGBOROUGH:										
UNMARRIED	M.	11090	6980	1908	1169	806	214	112	61	40
	F.	10934	7121	1902	944	529	194	125	67	52
MARRIED	M.	6675	.	9	463	2027	1636	1241	861	438
	F.	6622	.	53	623	2063	1632	1209	718	320
WIDOWED	M.	610	.	1	2	31	78	106	135	257
	F.	1011	.	2	8	44	115	152	243	446
164 KETTERING:										
UNMARRIED	M.	7880	4934	1245	835	487	160	91	72	44
	F.	7456	4696	1146	618	381	162	81	56	47
MARRIED	M.	4552	.	8	323	1287	1118	856	631	329
	F.	4570	.	31	437	1350	1120	828	536	268
WIDOWED	M.	487	.	.	4	34	40	67	98	246
	F.	589	.	.	3	26	61	113	179	307
165 THRAPSTON:										
UNMARRIED	M.	4503	2957	776	427	268	117	53	34	24
	F.	4336	2973	624	316	225	89	51	33	25
MARRIED	M.	2654	.	3	131	639	677	568	403	243
	F.	2650	.	22	207	608	720	614	314	164
WIDOWED	M.	298	.	.	3	15	37	50	60	133
	F.	505	.	1	1	17	35	83	111	267
166 OUNDLE:										
UNMARRIED	M.	4301	2706	755	421	257	101	68	52	31
	F.	4038	2561	588	348	276	103	63	49	56
MARRIED	M.	2380	.	2	81	473	555	497	444	324
	F.	2393	.	12	188	542	586	508	400	237
WIDOWED	M.	340	.	.	2	13	23	60	68	174
	F.	533	.	.	1	9	42	80	115	285
167 PETERBOROUGH:										
UNMARRIED	M.	12575	7382	2081	1375	777	201	129	76	54
	F.	12287	7359	1946	1075	724	240	162	99	83
MARRIED	M.	7250	.	6	388	1890	1847	1460	991	682
	F.	7271	.	29	507	2102	1922	1581	879	461
WIDOWED	M.	699	.	.	5	40	78	98	155	325
	F.	1428	.	.	5	63	149	227	315	663
11 HUNTINGDONSHIRE.										
168 HUNTINGDON:										
UNMARRIED	M.	5876	3714	1010	560	306	129	71	46	41
	F.	5711	3851	945	464	305	152	82	62	50
MARRIED	M.	3334	.	4	149	756	833	708	542	342
	F.	3423	.	21	248	828	853	682	512	277
WIDOWED	M.	385	.	.	1	13	36	49	85	201
	F.	772	.	.	1	24	57	117	171	402

Table 8 *continued.*—CONDITION as to MARRIAGE and AGES of MALES and FEMALES in REGISTRATION DISTRICTS.

REGISTRATION DISTRICT.		ALL AGES.	Under 15 Years.	15–	20–	25–	35–	45–	55–	65 and upwds.
HUNTING-NSHIRE—*cont.*										
T. IVES:										
UNMARRIED	M.	4906	3059	836	452	256	120	97	43	44
	F.	4848	3183	689	336	279	148	70	54	32
MARRIED	M.	2919	.	4	107	388	709	630	602	379
	F.	2978	.	15	163	636	785	629	407	285
WIDOWED	M.	382	.	.	1	8	21	55	78	198
	F.	742	.	.	1	21	62	98	174	386
T. NEOTS:										
UNMARRIED	M.	4908	3256	851	408	210	97	47	30	29
	F.	4893	3180	725	438	317	150	77	56	50
MARRIED	M.	2995	.	3	136	830	705	651	561	310
	F.	3018	.	11	211	718	785	622	476	245
WIDOWED	M.	322	.	.	2	11	25	45	64	175
	F.	671	.	.	3	24	65	106	142	341
2 BEDFORD-SHIRE.										
BEDFORD:										
UNMARRIED	M.	12386	7854	2204	1166	624	247	97	81	53
	F.	13474	7724	2234	1516	1033	453	236	146	180
MARRIED	M.	7204	.	10	308	1698	1793	1462	1157	716
	F.	7290	.	29	462	1940	1900	1404	1016	513
WIDOWED	M.	775	.	.	1	20	61	91	172	421
	F.	1794	.	1	6	80	208	335	485	729
BIGGLESWADE:										
UNMARRIED	M.	8141	5263	1381	629	417	206	125	77	41
	F.	8300	5079	1128	741	621	321	213	124	73
MARRIED	M.	4646	.	5	257	1047	1149	972	724	492
	F.	4720	.	17	301	1230	1180	950	669	373
WIDOWED	M.	552	.	.	3	21	40	68	109	311
	F.	1019	.	1	2	45	104	171	258	438
AMPTHILL:										
UNMARRIED	M.	4527	3104	751	332	170	79	47	28	16
	F.	4976	3141	683	484	341	170	101	60	46
MARRIED	M.	2870	.	4	193	828	672	607	469	300
	F.	2946	.	13	240	704	742	597	445	204
WIDOWED	M.	349	.	.	1	16	27	33	83	189
	F.	577	.	.	4	22	51	82	188	250
WOBURN:										
UNMARRIED	M.	2746	1785	483	230	140	35	26	27	20
	F.	3000	1727	438	285	270	113	84	48	35
MARRIED	M.	1729	.	.	76	354	392	368	323	226
	F.	1766	.	9	97	411	417	383	298	151
WIDOWED	M.	233	.	.	2	10	18	31	50	122
	F.	406	.	.	4	9	45	57	87	204
LEIGHTON BUZ-ZARD:										
UNMARRIED	M.	5335	3495	873	400	260	92	54	28	27
	F.	5736	3806	901	337	484	174	89	60	46
MARRIED	M.	3131	.	7	167	773	814	663	483	304
	F.	3199	.	9	242	864	867	581	447	189
WIDOWED	M.	348	.	.	1	21	38	49	81	158
	F.	667	.	.	2	33	69	115	171	277
LUTON:										
UNMARRIED	M.	10431	7052	1784	838	472	160	82	42	31
	F.	13473	7270	2368	1456	1249	595	284	139	92
MARRIED	M.	6705	.	20	509	1746	1746	1314	902	468
	F.	6846	.	30	620	1932	1809	1336	804	310
WIDOWED	M.	509	.	.	3	25	50	61	109	261
	F.	1493	.	.	4	84	202	290	390	522
CAMBRIDGE-SHIRE.										
CAXTON:										
UNMARRIED	M.	3224	2098	400	275	166	77	52	37	20
	F.	2965	2061	357	210	149	79	46	35	28
MARRIED	M.	1801	.	2	58	399	438	370	301	235
	F.	1802	.	9	89	447	449	346	279	170
WIDOWED	M.	223	.	.	1	10	10	29	53	120
	F.	342	.	.	1	9	38	35	63	196
13 CAMBRIDGE-SHIRE—*cont.*										
178 CHESTERTON:										
UNMARRIED	M.	8874	5585	1112	853	534	218	100	73	69
	F.	8275	5411	1005	706	466	238	143	101	90
MARRIED	M.	5095	.	3	212	1226	1320	933	849	547
	F.	5184	.	28	352	1335	1437	907	741	394
WIDOWED	M.	559	.	.	2	31	47	70	131	278
	F.	1062	.	.	3	36	94	152	237	538
179 CAMBRIDGE:										
UNMARRIED	M.	10689	6789	1875	1725	772	246	123	90	66
	F.	11758	6076	2111	1359	1063	491	317	190	151
MARRIED	M.	5202	.	6	307	1488	1451	974	692	384
	F.	5571	.	22	465	1516	1440	951	598	279
WIDOWED	M.	540	.	.	2	32	60	70	131	245
	F.	1713	.	.	5	89	204	305	422	687
180 LINTON:										
UNMARRIED	M.	3929	2480	720	365	196	80	34	36	28
	F.	3801	2618	510	277	205	82	41	36	32
MARRIED	M.	2240	.	2	110	492	526	469	357	293
	F.	2264	.	9	152	529	563	437	319	225
WIDOWED	M.	255	.	.	3	8	17	45	54	128
	F.	525	.	.	1	14	29	76	115	290
181 NEWMARKET:										
UNMARRIED	M.	8624	5214	1493	909	546	214	109	72	67
	F.	7935	5122	1177	678	480	189	133	92	64
MARRIED	M.	4977	.	7	225	1098	1232	965	847	603
	F.	4969	.	34	358	1230	1217	997	731	422
WIDOWED	M.	584	.	.	3	20	52	86	112	311
	F.	1138	.	.	2	35	107	147	249	598
182 ELY:										
UNMARRIED	M.	6172	3864	1065	609	325	145	88	53	35
	F.	5859	3910	856	438	293	122	83	72	55
MARRIED	M.	3751	.	3	176	842	909	722	639	460
	F.	3773	.	22	250	944	902	735	599	321
WIDOWED	M.	454	.	.	.	15	35	54	98	232
	F.	713	.	.	1	33	69	110	165	344
183 NORTH WITCH-FORD:										
UNMARRIED	M.	4633	2902	778	460	235	117	59	41	37
	F.	4426	2955	700	349	294	94	65	38	24
MARRIED	M.	2742	.	3	136	649	689	497	446	323
	F.	2771	.	17	203	676	735	500	412	227
WIDOWED	M.	338	.	.	2	18	35	48	87	148
	F.	554	.	.	.	13	50	81	135	275
184 WHITTLESEY:										
UNMARRIED	M.	1864	1223	329	141	81	35	21	19	7
	F.	1816	1167	293	133	98	40	24	31	20
MARRIED	M.	1163	.	2	46	253	259	248	215	139
	F.	1160	.	3	62	253	274	237	197	133
WIDOWED	M.	158	.	.	1	4	13	18	31	91
	F.	286	.	1	2	9	19	42	55	157
185 WISBECH:										
UNMARRIED	M.	9322	6094	1564	790	459	179	111	68	48
	F.	9348	5968	1435	814	511	268	154	96	102
MARRIED	M.	5810	.	5	250	1319	1463	1106	953	714
	F.	5959	.	15	410	1642	1485	1129	888	470
WIDOWED	M.	610	.	.	.	27	42	78	133	324
	F.	1433	.	.	4	38	95	212	354	730

Table 9.—CONDITION as to MARRIAGE and AGES of MALES and FEMALES in each URBAN SANITARY DISTRICT of which the POPULATION EXCEEDS 50,000 PERSONS.

URBAN SANITARY DISTRICT.		ALL AGES.	Under 15 Years.	15–	20–	25–	35–	45–	55–	65 and upwards.
NORTHAMPTON:										
UNMARRIED	M.	15238	9461	2518	1571	969	346	212	109	53
	F.	15811	9889	2834	1529	899	321	181	116	42
MARRIED	M.	9209	.	31	692	2805	2480	1765	980	456
	F.	9138	.	80	978	2940	2483	1586	815	316
WIDOWED	M.	802	.	.	7	67	103	158	171	296
	F.	1683	.	1	8	93	214	334	427	606

Table 10.—Occupations of Males and Females in the South-Midland Division and its Registration Counties, and in each Urban Sanitary District of which the Population exceed 50,000 Persons.

Occupations.	South-Midland Counties.		Registration Counties. 6. Middlesex. (Extra-metn.)		7. Hertfordshire.		8. Buckinghamshire.		9. Oxfordshire.	
	Males.	Females.	Males.	Females.	Males.	Females.	Males.	Females.	Males.	Females.
TOTAL	775926	820333	180622	200192	98063	103412	76796	79073	88908	92682
I. PROFESSIONAL CLASS.										
1. Persons engaged in the General or Local Government of the Country.										
1. National Government.										
Peer, M.P., Privy Councillor (not otherwise described)	30	.	7	.	9	.	7	.	4	.
Civil Service (officers and clerks)	1562	274	958	51	107	35	71	29	93	44
Civil Service (messengers, &c.)	1205	52	406	4	175	8	108	3	141	4
Prison Officer, &c.	89	21	3	2	12	3	14	2	11	3
2. Local Government.										
Police	2094	.	1026	.	191	.	134	.	146	.
Municipal, Parish, Union, District, Officer	631	167	146	17	81	21	63	12	77	27
Other Local or County Official	374	.	58	.	52	.	50	.	51	.
3. East Indian and Colonial Service.										
East Indian and Colonial Service	16	.	6	.	3	.	6	.	1	.
2. Persons engaged in the Defence of the Country.										
1. Army (at Home).										
Army Officer (effective or retired)	554	.	234	.	53	.	40	.	76	.
Soldier and Non-commissioned Officer	1569	.	720	.	28	.	26	.	144	.
Militia, Yeomanry, Volunteers	1062	.	348	.	266	.	48	.	40	.
Army Pensioner	544	.	140	.	71	.	49	.	85	.
2. Navy (ashore or in port).										
Navy Officer (effective or retired)	86	.	45	.	12	.	8	.	12	.
Seaman, R.N.	23	.	14	.	3	.	1	.	1	.
Royal Marines (officers and men)	5	.	1	.	1	.	.	.	.	.
Navy Pensioner	107	.	27	.	10	.	9	.	17	.
3. Persons engaged in Professional Occupations (with their immediate Subordinates).										
1. Clerical Profession.										
Clergyman (Established Church)	2050	.	277	.	278	.	243	.	356	.
Roman Catholic Priest	72	.	24	.	13	.	3	.	13	.
Minister, Priest, of other religious bodies	836	.	127	.	86	.	58	.	58	.
Missionary, Scripture Reader, Itinerant Preacher	172	92	58	43	17	19	13	3	26	3
Nun, Sister of Charity	.	218	.	115	.	2	.	.	.	68
Theological Student	182	.	84	.	27	.	3	.	27	.
Church, Chapel, Cemetery—Officer, Servant	395	84	106	30	43	13	36	6	54	7
2. Legal Profession.										
Barrister, Solicitor	1303	.	568	.	161	.	83	.	161	.
Law Student	141	.	61	.	16	.	11	.	17	.
Law Clerk, and others connected with Law	1377	6	627	2	112	.	68	.	144	.
3. Medical Profession.										
Physician, Surgeon, General Practitioner	960	1	336	.	118	.	86	.	98	.
Dentist	148	.	78	.	8	.	6	.	12	.
Medical Student, Assistant	297	1	122	.	28	.	11	.	21	.
Midwife	.	179	.	25	.	23	.	19	.	35
Subordinate Medical Service	79	2074	25	869	7	330	3	232	0	283
4. Teachers.										
Schoolmaster	2811	7325	682	1748	348	1028	304	711	301	891
Teacher, Professor, Lecturer	673	2412	202	939	47	318	61	164	126	300
School Service, and others concerned in Teaching	94	116	48	22	15	18	6	32	2	15
5. Literary and Scientific Persons.										
Author, Editor, Journalist	189	34	115	18	10	3	8	4	12	4
Reporter, Short-hand Writer	161	.	88	.	11	.	8	.	16	.
Persons engaged in Scientific Pursuits	74	2	31	2	11	.	.	.	15	.
Literary, Scientific, Institution, Service, &c.	84	13	23	7	6	3	2	2	31	1
6. Engineers and Surveyors.										
Civil Engineer	415	.	249	.	45	.	11	.	20	.
Mining Engineer	14	.	9	.	.	.	1	.	1	.
Land, House, Ship, Surveyor	485	.	146	.	35	.	29	.	53	.
7. Artists.										
Painter (artist)	234	121	186	71	23	14	19	8	17	11
Engraver (artist)	69	1	65	1	1	.	1	.	1	.
Sculptor	81	.	15	.	3	.	.	.	8	.
Architect	404	.	227	.	41	.	15	.	37	.
Musician, Music Master	633	675	203	301	63	63	37	38	98	58
Art Student	80	53	45	37	10	7	4	1	7	3
Photographer	402	107	168	57	36	4	23	15	67	11
Actor	62	38	21	9	1	.	12	4	1	2
Art, Music, Theatre, Service	35	3	16	5	.	.	.	.	7	.

Note.—Persons returned as engaged in more than one occupation have been referred to the one that appeared to be of most importance; or, if there was no difference in this respect, to the one first given by the person in his or her return. In some cases special rules have been followed: *e.g.*, "Clergyman and Schoolmaster" in combination has always been referred to "Schoolmaster"; a Member of Parliament or Peer engaged in any branch of commerce or industry has always been referred to this latter, not to "Peer, M.P."

The numbers returned under any heading include Labourers, Apprentices, and Assistants, as well as Masters, but not Clerks, Messengers, Errand boys, Porters, or Watchmen, for which occupations there are special headings. Civil, Military, and Naval Clerks, Law, Bank, Insurance, and Railway Clerks, and Government and Railway Porters, are, however, exceptions to this rule. Many young persons, being Apprentices or Assistants, have therefore been referred to occupations usually followed by adults. Women also, chiefly widows or orphans carrying on the business of their deceased husbands or fathers, will sometimes be found under occupations commonly followed by men only.

Persons returned as *retired* from any business have not been referred to that business. Inmates of workhouses have been referred to their trades, unless their age or infirmities showed that they were past work. But persons who might be supposed to be only temporarily separated from their usual employment, such as Prisoners, and Patients in General Hospitals, have been classed under their usual occupations.

In some cases, for convenience of space, the male designation, *e.g.*, "Schoolmaster," alone is given, instead of "Schoolmaster, Schoolmistress."

Table 10 *continued.*—OCCUPATIONS of MALES and FEMALES in the SOUTH-MIDLAND DIVISION and its REGISTRATION COUNTIES, and in each URBAN SANITARY DISTRICT of which the POPULATION exceeds 50,000 PERSONS.

OCCUPATIONS.	SOUTH-MIDLAND COUNTIES.		REGISTRATION COUNTIES. 6. MIDDLESEX. (*Extra-metn*).		7. HERTFORDSHIRE.		8. BUCKINGHAMSHIRE.		9. OXFORDSHIRE.	
	Males.	Females.	Males.	Females.	Males.	Females.	Males.	Females.	Males.	Females.
8. *Persons engaged in Exhibitions, Shows, Games, &c.*										
Performer, Showman, Exhibition, Service	45	19	9	4	3	2	1	.	1	.
Billiard, Cricket, & other Games, Service	194	1	36	.	11	.	8	.	55	.
II. DOMESTIC CLASS.										
4. PERSONS ENGAGED IN DOMESTIC OFFICES OR SERVICES.										
1. *Domestic Service.*										
Domestic Coachman, Groom	7028	.	1710	.	1086	.	796	.	927	.
Domestic Gardener	12775	2	4895	1	2114	.	1299	.	1361	1
Domestic Indoor Servant	4825	81654	1069	25867	890	10165	598	7055	823	10196
Lodge, Gate, Park, Keeper (not Government)	194	65	38	19	13	10	13	5	10	9
Inn, Hotel, Servant	1529	1141	567	333	171	121	92	109	168	138
College, Club, Service	893	314	11	1	.	.	7	2	486	32
2. *Other Service.*										
Office Keeper (not Government)	56	37	15	6	8	6	3	4	7	5
Cook (not domestic)	132	62	27	18	3	5	3	3	36	13
Charwoman	.	4876	.	1177	.	655	.	393	.	536
Washing and Bathing Service	393	15469	346	5919	14	1716	13	1377	7	1936
Hospital and Institution Service	418	1069	186	614	47	101	24	34	11	74
Others engaged in Service	91	10	51	1	9	5	2	.	12	1
III. COMMERCIAL CLASS.										
5. PERSONS ENGAGED IN COMMERCIAL OCCUPATIONS.										
1. *Merchants and Agents.*										
Merchant	548	.	409	.	97	.	23	.	10	.
Broker, Agent, Factor	1486	30	914	10	121	2	48	1	63	2
Auctioneer, Appraiser, Valuer, House Agent	636	5	295	.	81	1	48	.	64	1
Accountant	514	3	314	1	44	.	8	1	35	.
Salesman, Buyer (not otherwise described)	86	17	56	7	1	4	9	1	4	.
Commercial Traveller	1543	.	792	.	99	.	81	.	112	.
Commercial Clerk	7165	259	4405	138	490	18	210	15	410	28
Officer of Commercial Company, Guild, Society, &c.	11	.	9	.	.	.	.	.	1	.
2. *Dealers in Money.*										
Banker	87	.	26	.	19	.	8	.	8	.
Bank Service	1039	.	588	.	83	.	51	.	75	.
Bill Discounter, Bill Broker, Finance Agent	39	.	20	.	.	.	.	.	1	.
3. *Persons occupied in Insurance.*										
Life, House, Ship, &c., Insurance Service	683	9	405	6	55	1	37	.	28	1
6. PERSONS ENGAGED IN CONVEYANCE OF MEN, GOODS, AND MESSAGES.										
1. *On Railways.*										
Railway Engine Driver, Stoker	1454	.	169	.	118	.	111	.	61	.
Railway Guard	604	.	123	.	56	.	23	.	45	.
Pointsman, Level Crossing Man	316	18	32	.	18	3	20	.	24	6
Other Railway Officials and Servants	6596	26	2086	5	847	5	377	2	401	3
2. *On Roads.*										
Toll Collector, Turnpike Gate Keeper	31	9	3	.	5	4	1	2	3	.
Omnibus, Coach, Cab, Owner—Livery Stable Keeper	229	15	136	7	27	.	18	.	53	2
Cabman, Flyman, Coachman (not domestic)	751	.	403	.	56	.	27	.	93	.
Carman, Carrier, Carter, Haulier	4803	69	3061	3	524	9	350	8	459	16
Tramway Companies' Service	45	.	26	.	.	.	3	.	1	.
Wheel Chair Proprietor, Attendant, &c.	12	1	4	1	.	.	.	.	7	.
3. *On Canals, Rivers and Seas.*										
Inland Navigation Service	393	9	139	2	58	2	84	1	38	3
Bargeman, Lighterman, Waterman	1321	43	474	14	283	1	75	8	143	7
Navigation Service (on shore)	27	.	19	.	3	.	.	.	.	.
Seaman (Merchant Service)	326	.	148	.	24	.	6	.	13	.
Pilot	1	.	.	.	.	.	.	.	.	.
Ship Steward, Cook	18	1	9	1	5	.	.	.	1	.
Boatman on Seas	1	.	1	.	.	.	.	.	.	.
Harbour, Dock, Wharf, Lighthouse, Service	121	1	59	.	10	.	9	.	26	1
4. *In Storage.*										
Warehouseman (not Manchester)	690	4	367	7	27	.	16	.	21	.
Meter, Weigher	10	.	2	.	3	.	.	.	1	.
5. *In conveying Messages, Porterage, &c.*										
Messenger, Porter, Watchman (not Railway nor Government)	5439	58	1541	7	634	6	387	3	770	5
Telegraph, Telephone Service	312	122	100	56	47	11	19	10	24	1

Table 10 *continued*.—OCCUPATIONS of MALES and FEMALES in the SOUTH-MIDLAND DIVISION and its REGISTRATION COUNTIES, and in each URBAN SANITARY DISTRICT of which the POPULATION exceeds 50,000 PERSONS.

OCCUPATIONS.	SOUTH-MIDLAND COUNTIES.		REGISTRATION COUNTIES. 6. MIDDLESEX. (*Extra-metn.*)		7. HERTFORDSHIRE.		8. BUCKINGHAMSHIRE.		9. OXFORDSHIRE.	
	Males.	Females.	Males.	Females.	Males.	Females.	Males.	Females.	Males.	Females.
IV. AGRICULTURAL CLASS.										
7. PERSONS ENGAGED IN AGRICULTURE.										
1. *In Fields and Pastures.*										
Farmer, Grazier	12560	853	654	44	1308	95	1605	112	1652	130
Farmer's, Grazier's—Son, Grandson, Brother, Nephew*	3810	.	177	.	442	.	553	.	520	.
Farm Bailiff	2068	.	183	.	391	.	222	.	291	.
Agricultural Labourer, Farm Servant, Cottager	115309	3294	6367	232	16877	178	13277	191	17084	667
Shepherd	3701	.	69	.	525	.	394	.	823	.
Land Drainage Service (not in towns)	53	.	2	.	11	.	9	.	10	.
Agricultural Machine—Proprietor, Attendant	624	7	20	.	163	.	46	.	83	.
Agricultural Student, Pupil	50	.	2	.	9	.	3	.	20	.
Others engaged in, or connected with, Agriculture	201	18	19	1	92	9	24	3	12	2
2. *In Woods.*										
Woodman	567	.	30	.	104	.	122	.	124	.
3. *In Gardens.*										
Nurseryman, Seedsman, Florist	1073	81	654	20	119	2	32	7	76	9
Gardener (not domestic)	3604	569	1207	452	333	11	362	10	288	23
8. PERSONS ENGAGED ABOUT ANIMALS.										
1. *About Animals.*										
Horse Proprietor, Breeder, Dealer	190	.	38	.	24	.	14	.	44	.
Groom, Horse-keeper, Horse-breaker	4116	3	661	2	631	.	248	.	360	.
Veterinary Surgeon, Farrier	610	.	258	.	89	.	63	.	60	.
Cattle, Sheep, Pig—Dealer, Salesman	460	1	70	1	45	.	60	.	66	.
Drover	241	.	54	.	24	.	27	.	13	.
Gamekeeper	1106	.	79	.	301	.	179	.	175	.
Dog, Bird, Animal—Keeper, Dealer	138	16	17	.	26	1	34	3	4	4
Vermin destroyer	117	2	0	.	12	.	10	.	9	.
Fisherman	120	.	53	.	4	.	16	.	18	.
Knacker, Catsmeat Dealer, &c., &c.	34	2	11	2	6	.	.	.	1	.
V. INDUSTRIAL CLASS.										
9. PERSONS WORKING AND DEALING IN BOOKS, PRINTS, AND MAPS.										
1. *Books.*										
Publisher, Bookseller, Librarian	311	83	195	17	38	16	26	6	92	7
Music—Publisher, Seller, Printer	56	15	31	5	3	1	2	.	8	2
Bookbinder	330	146	92	39	19	5	15	14	98	43
Printer	2622	116	744	18	227	5	239	50	519	34
Newspaper Agent, News Room Keeper	176	33	92	12	14	1	6	.	18	5
Others	5	.	5	.	.	.	.	.	.	.
2. *Prints and Maps.*										
Lithographer, Lithographic Printer	101	1	71	.	12	.	1	.	1	.
Copper Plate and Steel Plate Printer	10	.	8	.	1	.	.	.	.	.
Map and Print—Colourer, Seller	20	5	8	1	1	.	1	.	4	.
10. PERSONS WORKING AND DEALING IN MACHINES AND IMPLEMENTS.										
1. *Machines.*										
Engine, Machine, Maker	802	5	283	2	84	1	61	1	58	.
Millwright	306	.	41	.	61	.	46	.	30	.
Fitter, Turner (Engine and Machine)	1382	.	368	.	98	.	100	.	108	.
Boiler Maker	236	.	73	.	4	.	25	.	9	.
Spinning and Weaving Machine Maker	10	2	0	1	.	.	.	.	2	.
Agricultural Machine and Implement Maker	130	4	17	.	12	.	27	.	20	.
Domestic Machinery—Maker, Dealer	6	.	4	.	.	.	.	.	.	.
2. *Tools and Implements.*										
Tool Maker, Dealer	66	1	38	.	16	.	2	.	1	.
Cutler, Scissors Maker	83	2	18	.	10	.	3	1	15	1
File Maker	10	1	6	.	1	.	.	.	.	.
Saw Maker	23	.	3	.	4	.	4	.	1	.
Pin Maker	.	.	.	.	.	.	.	.	.	.
Needle Maker	4	.	.	.	.	.	1	.	3	.
Steel Pen Maker	.	.	.	.	.	.	.	.	.	.
Pencil Maker (Wood)	2	1	2	1	.	.	.	.	.	.
Domestic Implement Maker	20	.	8	.	2	.	7	.	1	.
3. *Watches and Philosophical Instruments.*										
Watch Maker, Clock Maker	961	17	327	7	123	4	76	.	100	.
Philosophical Instrument Maker, Optician	107	1	90	1	3	.	.	.	2	.
Electrical Apparatus Maker	72	.	46	.	7	.	7	.	1	.
Weighing and Measuring Apparatus Maker	37	1	21	.	2	.	1	1	5	.

* Only male relatives living with the farmer or grazier, and, therefore, presumably engaged in agriculture, are included above.

Table 10 *continued*.—OCCUPATIONS of MALES and FEMALES in the SOUTH-MIDLAND DIVISION and its REGISTRATION COUNTIES, and in each URUAN SANITARY DISTRICT of which the POPULATION exceeds 50,000 PERSONS.

OCCUPATIONS.	SOUTH-MIDLAND COUNTIES.		REGISTRATION COUNTIES. 6. MIDDLESEX (*Extra-metn.*)		7. HERTFORDSHIRE.		8. BUCKINGHAMSHIRE.		9. OXFORDSHIRE.	
	Males.	Females.	Males.	Females.	Males.	Females.	Males.	Females.	Males.	Females.
4. Surgical Instruments.										
Surgical Instrument Maker	20	8	18	5	1	1	.	.	1	.
5. Arms and Ordnance.										
Gunsmith, Gun Manufacturer	646	5	590	2	8	1	3	.	13	.
Ordnance Manufacturer	20	.	1	.	.	.	.	.	.	.
Sword, Bayonet—Maker, Cutler	4	.	4	.	.	.	.	.	.	.
Others	.	.	.	.	.	.	.	.	.	.
6. Musical Instruments.										
Musical Instrument Maker, Dealer	353	3	239	1	11	.	3	1	28	.
7. Type, Dies, Medals, Coins.										
Type Cutter, Founder	32	.	21	.	1	.	.	.	10	.
Die, Seal, Coin, Medal, Maker	14	1	13	1	.	.	.	.	1	.
8. Tackle for Sports and Games.										
Toy Maker, Dealer	36	70	12	29	4	9	6	1	6	4
Fishing Rod, Tackle, Maker, Dealer	12	2	9	.	.	.	3	2	.	.
Apparatus for other Games, Maker, Dealer	47	1	9	1	1	.	12	.	21	.
11. PERSONS WORKING AND DEALING IN HOUSES, FURNITURE, AND DECORATIONS.										
1. Houses.										
Builder	2809	9	1117	6	317	.	197	1	342	1
Carpenter, Joiner	15261	2	4658	.	1903	.	1317	.	1846	3
Bricklayer	11587	2	3794	.	1670	.	1117	1	738	.
Mason	3107	6	570	1	141	1	261	1	1086	1
Slater, Tiler	205	1	73	.	10	.	4	.	83	1
Plasterer, Whitewasher	1542	1	921	1	71	.	47	.	234	.
Paperhanger	272	1	122	1	9	.	6	.	26	.
Plumber	2809	28	748	4	248	5	183	4	215	3
Painter, Glazier	5427	18	2286	2	648	5	376	2	528	3
2. Furniture and Fittings.										
Cabinet Maker, Upholsterer	3017	244	538	78	147	23	2283	18	364	34
French Polisher	277	33	89	.	7	.	110	7	24	1
Furniture Broker, Dealer	236	31	89	6	23	3	20	6	23	3
Locksmith, Bellhanger	63	1	23	1	3	.	4	.	6	.
Gas Fitter	609	2	398	1	46	.	45	.	73	.
House and Shop Fittings—Maker, Dealer	56	3	46	3	5	.	1	.	1	.
Funeral Furniture Maker, Undertaker	34	1	23	.	2	.	.	.	1	.
Others	2	.	2	.	.	.	.	.	.	.
3. House Decorations.										
Wood Carver	86	4	26	.	.	1	6	1	16	1
Carver, Gilder	187	3	99	1	11	.	8	1	31	.
Dealer in Works of Art	50	4	32	2	2	.	4	.	3	.
Figure, Image—Maker, Dealer	8	1	3	1	.	.	.	.	4	.
Animal, Bird, &c., Preserver, Naturalist	45	.	11	.	10	.	6	.	3	.
Artificial Flower Maker	31	65	23	60	3	1	9	1	.	2
12. PERSONS WORKING AND DEALING IN CARRIAGES AND HARNESS.										
1. Carriages.										
Coachmaker	1748	20	400	2	233	2	158	1	166	2
Railway Carriage, Railway Wagon, Maker	526	11	79	.	.	.	277	10	8	.
Wheelwright	2301	15	417	6	364	1	296	1	209	.
Bicycle, Tricycle—Maker, Dealer	22	.	8	.	1	.	1	.	.	.
Others	28	.	2	.	1	.	1	.	.	.
2. Harness.										
Saddler, Harness, Whip, Maker	1468	29	275	5	212	7	148	1	191	6
13. PERSONS WORKING AND DEALING IN SHIPS AND BOATS.										
1. Hull.										
Ship, Boat, Barge, Builder	332	.	166	.	27	.	14	.	63	.
Shipwright, Ship Carpenter (ashore)	20	.	9	.	1	.	.	.	2	.
2. Masts, Rigging, &c.										
Mast, Yard, Oar, Block, Maker	2	.	1	.	.	.	.	.	.	.
Ship Rigger, Chandler, Fitter	3	.	2	.	.	.	.	.	.	.
Sail Maker	26	6	14	6	.	.	1	.	4	.

Table 10 *continued.*—Occupations of Males and Females in the South-Midland Division and its Registration Counties, and in each Urban Sanitary District of which the Population exceeds 50,000 Persons.

Occupations.	South-Midland Counties.		Registration Counties.							
			6. Middlesex. (*Extra-metn*).		7. Hertfordshire.		8. Buckinghamshire.		9. Oxfordshire.	
	Males.	Females.	Males.	Females.	Males.	Females.	Males.	Females.	Males.	Females.
14. Persons working and dealing in Chemicals and Compounds.										
1. *Colouring Matter.*										
Dye, Paint, Manufacture	31	1	22	1	2	.	2	.	4	.
Ink, Blacking, Colouring Substance, Manufacture	37	.	26	.	.	.	4	.	3	.
2. *Explosives.*										
Gunpowder, Guncotton, Explosive Substance, Manufacture	66	20	56	20	.	.	.	.	.	.
Fusee, Fireworks, Explosive Article, Manufacture	22	64	21	64	.	.	.	.	.	.
3. *Drugs and other Chemicals and Compounds.*										
Chemist, Druggist	877	27	261	8	85	3	70	4	98	2
Manufacturing Chemist	138	13	74	8	22	.	4	.	4	1
Alkali Manufacture	5	.	2	.	3	.	.	.	.	.
Drysalter	11	.	6	.	1	.	.	.	.	.
15. Persons working and dealing in Tobacco and Pipes.										
1. *Tobacco and Pipes.*										
Tobacco Manufacturer, Tobacconist	258	99	137	46	25	4	15	6	30	9
Tobacco Pipe, Snuff Box, &c., Maker	85	15	17	7	6	.	.	1	3	.
16. Persons working and Dealing in Food and Lodging.										
1. *Board and Lodging.*										
Innkeeper, Hotel Keeper, Publican	4620	933	846	115	747	144	623	106	526	138
Lodging, Boarding House, Keeper	98	862	15	153	1	53	7	51	42	212
Coffee, Eating House, Keeper	169	71	89	53	11	7	8	3	18	5
2. *Spirituous Drinks.*										
Hop—Merchant, Dealer	18	.	4	.	2	.	3	.	2	.
Maltster	876	4	37	.	467	2	48	.	66	.
Brewer	2164	42	368	5	409	7	199	3	309	8
Beerseller. Ale, Porter, Cider, Dealer	865	321	347	82	137	68	77	43	54	86
Cellarman	199	1	73	.	23	.	11	.	23	.
Wine, Spirit—Merchant, Agent	417	22	260	10	53	2	18	1	45	6
3. *Food.*										
Milkseller, Dairyman	1266	233	598	62	107	43	80	24	129	12
Cheesemonger, Butterman	142	13	119	5	1	.	7	.	.	1
Butcher, Meat Salesman	5287	196	1177	32	607	21	556	28	625	24
Provision Curer, Dealer	285	78	107	22	9	4	45	2	15	6
Poulterer, Game Dealer	194	23	44	5	15	2	23	3	34	5
Fishmonger	781	55	304	22	97	6	58	8	71	6
Corn, Flour, Seed—Merchant, Dealer	765	54	206	18	160	5	73	6	85	4
Corn Miller	2078	16	95	.	351	1	188	1	259	7
Baker	6143	508	1317	117	801	77	667	40	878	68
Confectioner, Pastrycook	583	380	162	68	40	32	53	40	71	55
Greengrocer, Fruiterer	1004	223	543	65	90	39	90	29	56	22
Mustard, Vinegar, Spice, Pickle—Maker, Dealer	94	.	18	.	.	.	.	.	.	.
Sugar Refiner	46	9	13	.	4	1	.	.	2	1
Grocer. Tea, Coffee, Chocolate—Maker, Dealer	6128	1456	1528	181	831	184	599	160	742	184
Ginger Beer, Mineral Water—Manufacturer, Dealer	242	17	50	3	23	3	87	2	25	6
Others dealing in Food	.	.	.	.	.	.	.	.	.	.
17. Persons working and dealing in Textile Fabrics.										
1. *Wool and Worsted.*										
Woolstapler	49	.	12	.	3	.	4	.	16	.
Woollen Cloth Manufacture	226	336	31	6	3	8	1	.	179	308
Wool, Woollen goods—Dyer, Printer	17	.	1	.	.	.	.	4	15	.
Worsted, Stuff, Manufacture	25	4	6	.	.	.	.	.	19	4
Flannel Manufacture	1	.	1	.	.	.	.	.	.	.
Blanket Manufacture	137	83	.	.	.	.	.	.	137	83
Fuller	8	.	.	.	.	.	.	.	8	.
Cloth, Worsted, Stuff, Flannel, Blanket, Dealer	45	.	38	.	.	.	1	.	3	.
Others	16	.	.	.	.	.	1	.	9	.
2. *Silk.*										
Silk, Silk goods, Manufacture	202	507	52	19	151	395	11	85	2	.
Silk Dyer, Printer	8	.	7	.	.	.	1	.	.	.
Ribbon Manufacture	1	4	.	.	.	.	.	.	.	.
Crape, Gauze, Manufacture	29	72	29	72	.	.	.	.	.	.
Silk Merchant, Dealer	65	.	35	.	.	.	5	.	.	.

Table 10 *continued*.—OCCUPATIONS of MALES and FEMALES in the SOUTH-MIDLAND DIVISION and its REGISTRATION COUNTIES, and in each URBAN SANITARY DISTRICT of which the POPULATION exceeds 50,000 PERSONS.

OCCUPATIONS.	SOUTH-MIDLAND COUNTIES.		REGISTRATION COUNTIES. 6. MIDDLESEX. (*Extra-metn.*)		7. HERTFORDSHIRE.		8. BUCKINGHAMSHIRE.		9. OXFORDSHIRE.	
	Males.	Females.	Males.	Females.	Males.	Females.	Males.	Females.	Males.	Females.
3. Cotton and Flax										
Cotton, Cotton goods, Manufacture	38	31	9	14	25	2	.	3	3	6
Cotton, Calico—Printer, Dyer, Bleacher	2	1	2	1	.	.	.	.	.	.
Cotton, Calico—Warehouseman, Dealer	11	1	10	.	.	.	1	.	.	.
Flax, Linen—Manufacturer, Dealer	38	21	15	2	.	1	.	.	.	1
Lace Manufacturer, Dealer	78	13193	33	34	2	28	14	4442	2	298
Fustian Manufacturer, Dealer	.	.	.	.	.	.	.	.	.	.
Tape Manufacturer, Dealer	.	.	.	.	.	.	.	.	.	.
Thread Manufacturer, Dealer	3	1	1	.	.	.	.	.	.	.
4. Hemp and other Fibrous Materials.										
Hemp, Jute, Cocoa Fibre, Manufacture	49	187	42	187	2	.	4	.	.	.
Rope, Twine, Cord—Maker, Dealer	266	8	30	1	44	.	35	.	60	3
Mat Maker, Seller	120	7	51	1	5	1	19	.	6	.
Net Maker	4	3	.	.	.	.	.	.	1	2
Canvas, Sailcloth, Manufacture	16	.	.	.	16	.	.	.	.	.
Sacking, Sack, Bag—Maker, Dealer	25	32	8	9	4	1	2	1	1	.
Others working and dealing in Hemp	18	14	4	.	1	.	1	3	9	9
5. Mixed or Unspecified Materials.										
Weaver (undefined)	26	49	6	23	2	.	.	.	14	21
Dyer, Printer, Scourer, Bleacher, Calenderer (undefined)	175	52	85	15	15	8	1	.	29	18
Factory hand (Textile, undefined)	7	119	3	28	.	5	.	8	1	14
Felt Manufacture	.	.	.	.	.	.	.	.	.	.
Carpet, Rug, Manufacture	32	21	26	.	1	.	1	.	5	2
Manchester Warehouseman	34	.	31	.	2	.	.	.	.	.
Draper, Linen Draper, Mercer	2059	1760	915	527	366	217	268	138	342	184
Fancy Goods (Textile), Manufacturer, Worker, Dealer	26	234	20	83	1	38	4	22	1	37
Trimming Maker, Dealer	21	25	18	15	1	.	1	8	.	.
Embroiderer	9	80	7	37	.	4	2	31	.	5
Others	42	3	.	.	.	.	.	.	42	3
18. PERSONS WORKING AND DEALING IN DRESS.										
1. Dress.										
Hatter, Hat Manufacture (not straw)	178	12	66	2	14	4	8	1	25	2
Straw—Hat, Bonnet, Plait, Manufacture	2713	24593	24	49	339	7543	87	1654	4	41
Tailor	5378	1178	883	151	624	26	417	59	894	274
Milliner, Dressmaker, Staymaker	93	19641	46	4012	6	2942	3	1861	4	2307
Shawl Manufacture	.	8	.	1	.	.	.	.	.	7
Shirt Maker, Seamstress	39	3973	23	852	1	502	.	516	7	646
Hosiery Manufacture	9	62	4	4	1	2	1	6	.	11
Hosier, Haberdasher	157	87	84	58	3	1	4	6	16	5
Glover, Glove Maker	174	1426	9	9	1	.	2	5	150	1383
Button Maker, Dealer	9	1	6	.	.	1	1	.	.	.
Shoe, Boot—Maker, Dealer	24211	8529	1429	103	1172	88	1582	243	1002	99
Patten, Clog, Maker	10	.	2	.	1	.	1	.	.	.
Wig Maker, Hairdresser	686	36	101	8	74	5	48	7	86	5
Umbrella, Parasol, Stick—Maker, Dealer	123	35	63	15	13	5	9	2	10	4
Accoutrement Maker	10	1	10	1	.	.	.	.	.	.
Old Clothes Dealer, and others	11	51	5	17	.	4	.	1	2	8
19. PERSONS WORKING AND DEALING IN VARIOUS ANIMAL SUBSTANCES.										
1. In Grease, Gut, Bone, Horn, Ivory, and Whalebone.										
Tallow Chandler, Candle, Grease, Manufacture	79	19	28	10	11	4	2	1	16	1
Soap Boiler, Maker	69	15	64	15	.	.	.	.	.	.
Glue, Size, Gelatine, Isinglass—Maker, Dealer	9	.	4	.	.	.	.	.	.	.
Manure Manufacture	20	.	4	.	9	.	2	.	2	.
Bone, Horn, Ivory, Tortoise-shell—Worker, Dealer	34	9	31	9	1	.	1	.	.	.
Comb Maker	5	1	4	1	.	.	.	.	1	.
Others	10	6	5	6	.	.	1	.	.	.
2. In Skins.										
Furrier, Skinner	162	25	44	14	8	.	21	8	10	.
Tanner, Fellmonger	349	7	24	.	57	7	30	.	32	.
Currier	1295	8	93	2	39	.	33	1	52	.
Leather Goods, Portmanteau, Bag, Strap, &c.—Maker, Dealer	55	10	43	6	3	.	.	.	8	.
Parchment, Vellum—Maker, Dealer	117	2	92	1	7	.	25	1	4	.
3. In Hair and Feathers.										
Hair, Bristle—Worker, Dealer	23	2	17	.	4	1	2	.	.	1
Brush, Broom, Maker	243	278	64	22	65	69	79	180	5	1
Quill, Feather—Dresser, Dealer	18	69	15	19	.	.	.	.	.	4

Table 10 *continued*.—OCCUPATIONS of MALES and FEMALES in the SOUTH-MIDLAND DIVISION and its REGISTRATION COUNTIES, and in each URBAN SANITARY DISTRICT of which the POPULATION exceeds 50,000 PERSONS.

OCCUPATIONS.	SOUTH-MIDLAND COUNTIES.		REGISTRATION COUNTIES. 6. MIDDLESEX. (*Extra-metn.*)		7. HERTFORDSHIRE.		8. BUCKINGHAMSHIRE.		9. OXFORDSHIRE.	
	Males.	Females.	Males.	Females.	Males.	Females.	Males.	Females.	Males.	Females.
20. PERSONS WORKING AND DEALING IN VARIOUS VEGETABLE SUBSTANCES.										
1. *In Oils, Gums, and Resins.*										
Oil Miller, Oil Cake—Maker, Dealer	166	2	56	2	63	.	1	.	.	.
Oil and Colourman	205	12	150	8	22	2	2	.	5	1
Floor Cloth, Oil Cloth, Manufacture	297	1	294	1	.	.	3	.	.	.
Japanner	16	1	16	1	.	.	.	.	.	.
India Rubber, Gutta Percha—Worker, Dealer	186	144	177	117	.	.	.	.	1	.
Waterproof Goods—Maker, Dealer	50	19	10	5	1	2	2	1	4	.
Others	27	.	21	.	.	.	5	.	.	.
2. *In Cane, Rush, and Straw.*										
Willow, Cane, Rush—Worker, Dealer, Basketmaker	642	885	12	192	62	86	86	619	77	24
Hay, Straw (not plait), Chaff—Cutter, Dealer	382	7	133	.	101	2	68	2	13	2
Thatcher	451	.	8	.	65	.	83	.	65	.
3. *In Wood and Bark.*										
Timber, Wood—Merchant, Dealer	664	28	142	4	86	1	68	3	107	3
Sawyer	1724	.	248	.	275	.	330	.	243	.
Lath, Wooden Fence, Hurdle, Maker	255	8	62	1	54	.	46	.	65	1
Wood Turner, Box Maker	520	5	60	2	62	.	273	1	21	1
Cooper, Hoop Maker, Bender	332	10	187	4	83	2	36	2	78	1
Cork, Bark—Cutter, Worker, Dealer	27	1	14	.	1	.	.	.	5	.
Others	44	.	8	.	.	.	1	.	.	.
4. *In Paper.*										
Paper Manufacture	1126	1114	65	15	376	286	368	285	85	111
Envelope Maker	27	129	3	6	23	52	.	1	.	.
Stationer, Law Stationer	384	218	263	96	21	28	13	16	24	21
Card, Pattern Card, Maker	34	16	6	1	27	15	1	.	.	.
Paper Stainer	72	22	60	1	12	21	.	.	.	.
Paper Box, Paper Bag, Maker	18	75	11	25	3	13	.	1	3	10
Ticket, Label, Writer	7	19	5	2	.	.	.	17	.	.
Others	67	.	21	.	7	.	4	.	10	.
21. PERSONS WORKING AND DEALING IN VARIOUS MINERAL SUBSTANCES.										
1. *Miners.*										
Coal Miner	17	.	9	.	1	.	1	.	1	.
Ironstone Miner	1417	.	.	.	.	.	.	.	7	.
Copper Miner	2	.	.	.	.	.	.	.	.	.
Tin Miner	.	.	.	.	.	.	.	.	.	.
Lead Miner	2	.	2	.	.	.	.	.	.	.
Miner in other, or undefined, Minerals	13	.	6	.	3	.	.	.	1	.
Mine Service	25	.	8	.	1	.	2	.	1	.
2. *Coal, Coal Gas, &c.*										
Coal Merchant, Dealer	1273	46	226	12	140	8	150	4	170	8
Coalheaver	695	.	178	.	96	.	58	.	86	.
Coke, Charcoal, Peat—Cutter, Burner, Dealer	22	.	8	.	2	.	3	.	2	.
Gas Works Service	908	.	349	.	101	.	57	.	111	.
3. *Stone, Clay, and Road Making.*										
Stone Quarrier	62	.	.	.	1	.	4	.	33	.
Stone Cutter, Dresser, Dealer	160	.	41	.	4	.	51	.	30	.
Slate Quarrier	1	.	.	.	.	.	1	.	.	.
Slate Worker, Dealer	17	.	7	.	.	.	.	.	9	.
Limeburner	131	1	13	.	36	1	2	.	6	.
Clay, Sand, Gravel, Chalk—Labourer, Dealer	88	4	31	2	20	2	3	.	2	.
Fossil, Coprolite—Digger, Dealer	660	15	.	.	309	.	4	.	.	.
Well Sinker, Borer	82	.	19	.	16	.	6	.	3	.
Plaster, Cement, Manufacture	55	1	24	.	4	1	.	.	.	.
Brick, Tile—Maker, Burner, Dealer	4079	44	1463	28	375	.	389	3	244	7
Paviour	70	.	12	.	11	.	1	.	10	.
Road Contractor, Surveyor, Inspector	122	.	12	.	9	.	4	.	78	.
Road Labourer	780	.	132	.	109	.	76	.	120	.
Railway Contractor	93	.	50	.	13	.	4	.	2	.
Platelayer	1907	.	411	.	297	.	166	.	101	.
Railway Labourer, Navvy	3060	.	362	.	329	.	233	.	131	.
Others	13	2	4	.	7	2	.	.	.	.
4. *Earthenware and Glass.*										
Earthenware, China, Porcelain, Manufacture	162	2	89	.	19	.	17	1	21	.
Glass Manufacture	87	1	70	1	5	.	2	.	1	.
Earthenware, China, Glass, Dealer	204	73	72	28	24	8	15	13	33	7
5. *Salt.*										
Salt Maker, Dealer	2	1	1	.	.	.	.	.	.	.

Table 10 *continued.*—OCCUPATIONS of MALES and FEMALES in the SOUTH MIDLAND DIVISION and its REGISTRATION COUNTIES, and in each URBAN SANITARY DISTRICT of which the POPULATION exceeds 50,000 PERSONS.

OCCUPATIONS.	SOUTH-MIDLAND COUNTIES.		REGISTRATION COUNTIES. 6. MIDDLESEX. (*Extra-metn.*)		7. HERTFORDSHIRE		8. BUCKINGHAMSHIRE.		9. OXFORDSHIRE.	
	Males.	Females.	Males.	Females.	Males.	Females.	Males.	Females.	Males.	Females.
6. *Water.*										
Waterworks Service	135	.	99	.	7	.	9	.	3	.
Others	5	2	1	2	.	.	.	.	3	.
7. *Precious Metals and Jewellery.*										
Goldsmith, Silversmith, Jeweller	526	34	367	11	24	4	25	1	48	3
Gold, Silver, Beater	9	.	9	.	.	.	.	.	.	.
Lapidary	6	1	6	1	.	.	.	.	.	.
Others	15	1	14	1	1	.	.	.	.	.
8. *Iron and Steel.*										
Blacksmith	5599	42	841	4	810	7	585	7	706	4
Whitesmith	563	.	137	.	88	.	51	.	68	.
Nail Manufacture	18	2	.	.	1	.	2	.	14	2
Anchor, Chain, Manufacture	5	.	4	.	.	.	.	.	.	.
Other Iron and Steel Manufactures	2204	2	203	.	131	.	64	.	174	.
Ironmonger. Hardware Dealer, Merchant	967	46	234	10	124	5	69	5	148	6
9. *Copper.*										
Copper, Copper goods—Manufacturer, Worker, Dealer	63	1	18	1	10	.	2	.	7	.
10. *Tin and Zinc.*										
Tin, Tin Plate, Tin goods—Manufacturer, Worker, Dealer	618	22	133	.	83	.	55	21	69	.
Zinc, Zinc Goods—Manufacturer, Worker, Dealer	51	.	46	.	3	.	.	.	1	.
11. *Lead.*										
Lead, Leaden goods—Manufacturer, Worker, Dealer	12	.	12	.	.	.	.	.	.	.
12. *In Other, Mixed, or Unspecified, Metals.*										
Metal Refiner, Worker, Turner, Dealer	46	.	38	.	2	.	.	.	2	.
Brass, Bronze, Manufacture. Brazier	360	2	106	1	21	1	27	.	14	.
Metal Burnisher, Lacquerer	2	2	1	1	.	.	.	.	.	1
White Metal, Plated Ware, Manufacture, Pewterer	18	.	17	.	.	.	.	.	1	.
Wire Maker, Worker, Weaver, Drawer	51	3	17	.	13	.	4	.	4	1
Bolt, Nut, Rivet, Screw, Staple, Maker	20	.	3	.	1	.	6	.	2	.
Lamp, Lantern, Candlestick, Maker	40	.	15	.	.	.	5	.	.	.
Clasp, Buckle, Hinge, Maker	.	1	.	1	.	.	.	.	.	.
Fancy Chain, Gilt Toy, Maker	1	1	1	.	.	.	.	.	.	1
Others	3	.	2	.	.	.	.	.	1	.
22. PERSONS WORKING AND DEALING IN GENERAL OR UNSPECIFIED COMMODITIES.										
1. *Makers and Dealers (General or Undefined).*										
General Shopkeeper, Dealer	2009	1135	476	241	240	114	210	88	213	169
Pawnbroker	190	15	107	1	16	1	6	1	8	2
Costermonger, Huckster, Street Seller	1554	481	248	109	206	64	155	30	196	60
Manufacturer, Manager, Superintendent (undefined)	223	19	110	13	26	1	9	.	8	2
Contractor (undefined)	116	3	58	.	6	.	8	1	5	1
2. *Mechanics and Labourers (General or Undefined).*										
General Labourer	37129	177	10691	46	5189	20	4194	29	3706	25
Engine Driver, Stoker, Fireman (not railway, marine, nor agricultural)	1675	.	466	.	201	.	152	.	137	.
Artizan, Mechanic (undefined)	944	21	440	6	79	1	128	1	107	9
Apprentice (undefined)	159	39	41	8	17	1	8	5	20	3
Factory Labourer (undefined)	608	98	228	47	44	18	77	12	83	9
Machinist, Machine Worker (undefined)	266	163	89	80	25	21	17	6	24	48
23. PERSONS WORKING AND DEALING IN REFUSE MATTERS.										
1. *Refuse Matters.*										
Town Drainage Service	28	.	6	.	5	.	8	.	2	.
Chimney Sweep, Soot Merchant	555	6	138	2	73	3	54	.	75	1
Scavenger, Crossing Sweeper	62	2	12	1	4	.	7	.	5	.
Rag Gatherer, Dealer	160	17	20	3	12	1	6	2	14	8
VI. UNOCCUPIED CLASS.										
24. PERSONS WITHOUT SPECIFIED OCCUPATIONS										
Persons returned by Property, Rank, &c., and not by special occupation	206618	499632	54482	125897	27426	62198	26109	49901	22675	57808
Children under 5 years of age	106387	104592	25968	25938	13382	13323	10460	10373	11915	11905

Table 10 *continued*.—OCCUPATIONS of MALES and FEMALES in the SOUTH-MIDLAND DIVISION and its REGISTRATION COUNTIES, and in each URBAN SANITARY DISTRICT of which the POPULATION exceeds 50,000 PERSONS.

OCCUPATIONS.	REGISTRATION COUNTIES.								URBAN SANITARY DISTRICT.	
	10. NORTHAMPTONSHIRE.		11. HUNTINGDONSHIRE.		12. BEDFORDSHIRE.		13. CAMBRIDGESHIRE.		NORTHAMPTON.	
	Males.	Females.	Males.	Females.	Males.	Females.	Males.	Females.	Males.	Females.
TOTAL	138091	138944	28067	27156	72576	61683	93903	97211	25249	26632
I. PROFESSIONAL CLASS.										
1. PERSONS ENGAGED IN THE GENERAL OR LOCAL GOVERNMENT OF THE COUNTRY.										
1. *National Government.*										
Peer, M.P., Privy Councillor (not otherwise described)	8	.	.	.	3	.	1	.	.	.
Civil Service (officers and clerks)	119	62	32	9	77	23	105	23	24	1
Civil Service (messengers, &c.)	162	3	34	1	86	1	95	8	25	.
Prison Officer, &c.	14	5	9	2	15	4	11	.	12	4
2. *Local Government.*										
Police	214	.	46	.	143	.	192	.	63	.
Municipal, Parish, Union, District, Officer	95	29	24	10	64	20	84	31	19	6
Other Local or County Official	70	.	18	.	36	.	30	.	17	.
3. *East Indian and Colonial Service.*										
East Indian and Colonial Service	1	.	.	.	.	.	.	.	.	.
2. PERSONS ENGAGED IN THE DEFENCE OF THE COUNTRY.										
1. *Army (at Home).*										
Army Officer (effective or retired)	59	.	10	.	72	.	10	.	15	.
Soldier and Non-Commissioned Officer	464	.	11	.	148	.	28	.	59	.
Militia, Yeomanry, Volunteers	55	.	40	.	230	.	35	.	44	.
Army Pensioner	75	.	24	.	49	.	51	.	15	.
2. *Navy (ashore or in port).*										
Navy Officer (effective or retired)	3	.	.	.	11	.	5	.	.	.
Seaman, R.N.	1	.	.	.	1	.	2	.	1	.
Royal Marines (officers and men)	.	.	.	.	2	.	1	.	.	.
Navy Pensioner	13	.	6	.	18	.	7	.	2	.
3. PERSONS ENGAGED IN PROFESSIONAL OCCUPATIONS (WITH THEIR IMMEDIATE SUBORDINATES).										
1. *Clerical Profession.*										
Clergyman (Established Church)	360	.	86	.	156	.	308	.	29	.
Roman Catholic Priest	8	.	1	.	3	.	7	.	4	.
Minister, Priest, of other religious bodies	111	.	36	.	72	.	87	.	23	.
Missionary, Scripture Reader, Itinerant Preacher	26	5	6	.	13	2	14	13	6	6
Nun, Sister of Charity	.	38	.	.	.	.	.	.	.	38
Theological Student	5	.	.	.	8	.	30	.	8	.
Church, Chapel, Cemetery—Officer, Servant	53	3	13	3	35	7	53	15	9	.
2. *Legal Profession.*										
Barrister, Solicitor	106	.	33	.	53	.	98	.	29	.
Law Student	3	.	2	.	2	.	23	.	1	.
Law Clerk, and others connected with Law	158	3	44		76	1	148	.	48	.
3. *Medical Profession.*										
Physician, Surgeon, General Practitioner	128	.	28	.	78	.	98	1	27	.
Dentist	25	.	1	.	8	.	10	.	12	.
Medical Student, Assistant	27	.	2	.	30	.	66	1	3	.
Midwife	.	44	.	6	.	12	.	15	.	9
Subordinate Medical Service	14	450	.	130	7	217	14	445	4	112
4. *Teachers.*										
Schoolmaster	431	1153	90	251	232	671	273	372	78	208
Teacher, Professor, Lecturer	21	255	2	70	25	128	199	238	6	10
School Service, and others concerned in Teaching	11	12	1	4	6	7	5	10	6	2
5. *Literary and Scientific Persons.*										
Author, Editor, Journalist	18	1	1	.	6	3	12	1	6	1
Reporter, Short-hand Writer	22	.	.	.	4	.	17	.	13	.
Persons engaged in Scientific Pursuits	5	.	.	.	1	.	11	.	.	.
Literary, Scientific, Institution, Service, &c.	1	.	.	.	1	.	20	.	1	.
6. *Engineers and Surveyors.*										
Civil Engineer	32	.	7	.	17	.	14	.	13	.
Mining Engineer	1	.	.	.	1	.	1	.	.	.
Land, House, Ship, Surveyor	40	.	13	.	44	.	45	.	7	.
7. *Artists.*										
Painter (artist)	15	4	1	.	10	8	15	8	6	3
Engraver (artist)	.	.	.	.	.	.	1	.	.	.
Sculptor	.	.	.	.	1	.	4	.	.	.
Architect	39	.	7	.	18	.	21	.	14	.
Musician, Music Master	77	81	17	7	74	50	64	77	33	29
Art Student	5	2	2	1	3	.	3	2	2	.
Photographer	32	6	4	1	32	4	46	2	12	5
Actor	10	14	.	.	7	6	1	9	15	11
Art, Music, Theatre, Service	6	.	1	.	3	.	8	.	2	.

Table 10 *continued.*—OCCUPATIONS of MALES and FEMALES in the SOUTH-MIDLAND DIVISION and its REGISTRATION COUNTIES, and in each URBAN SANITARY DISTRICT of which the POPULATION exceeds 50,000 PERSONS.

OCCUPATIONS.	REGISTRATION COUNTIES.								URBAN SANITARY DISTRICT.	
	10. NORTHAMPTON-SHIRE.		11. HUNTINGDON-SHIRE.		12. BEDFORD-SHIRE.		13. CAMBRIDGE-SHIRE.		NORTHAMPTON.	
	Males.	Females.	Males.	Females.	Males.	Females.	Males.	Females.	Males.	Females.
8. *Persons engaged in Exhibitions, Shows, Games, &c.*										
Performer, Showman, Exhibition, Service	14	7	1	.	8	4	8	2	12	8
Billiard, Cricket, & other Games, Service	26	.	3	.	12	.	45	1	11	.
II. DOMESTIC CLASS.										
4. PERSONS ENGAGED IN DOMESTIC OFFICES OR SERVICES.										
1. *Domestic Service.*										
Domestic Coachman, Groom	930	.	221	.	607	.	689	.	34	.
Domestic Gardener	1027	.	305	.	636	.	1064	.	14	.
Domestic Indoor Servant	573	11076	121	2583	295	5741	413	8987	47	1963
Lodge, Gate, Park, Keeper (not Government)	14	8	1	2	9	9	6	2	1	.
Inn, Hotel, Servant	143	214	19	37	74	94	105	95	31	64
College, Club, Service	5	1	1	.	2	.	381	278	2	1
2. *Other Service.*										
Office Keeper (not Government)	4	4	2	3	5	2	12	7	2	2
Cook (not domestic)	6	5	.	.	1	6	86	13	3	3
Charwoman	.	812	.	221	.	350	.	727	.	196
Washing and Bathing Service	4	1861	.	304	7	1083	8	1472	1	368
Hospital and Institution Service	72	98	1	7	54	79	11	62	12	50
Others engaged in Service	11	2	.	.	1	.	5	1	6	.
III. COMMERCIAL CLASS.										
5. PERSONS ENGAGED IN COMMERCIAL OCCUPATIONS.										
1. *Merchants and Agents.*										
Merchant	15	.	7	.	15	.	22	.	2	.
Broker, Agent, Factor	185	7	28	3	66	1	70	5	58	2
Auctioneer, Appraiser, Valuer, House Agent	91	3	22	.	49	.	56	.	30	3
Accountant	39	1	4	.	29	.	41	.	16	.
Salesman, Buyer (not otherwise described)	3	4	1	1	2	.	4	.	3	4
Commercial Traveller	242	.	15	.	111	.	91	.	108	.
Commercial Clerk	744	24	93	8	336	11	438	22	382	7
Officer of Commercial Company, Guild, Society, &c.	1	.	.	.	.	.	.	.	1	.
2. *Dealers in Money.*										
Banker	3	.	5	.	7	.	12	.	.	.
Bank Service	97	.	10	.	52	.	77	.	32	.
Bill Discounter, Bill Broker, Finance Agent	4	.	1	.	2	.	2	.	2	.
3. *Persons occupied in Insurance.*										
Life, House, Ship, &c., Insurance Service	66	1	12	.	54	.	50	.	25	.
6. PERSONS ENGAGED IN CONVEYANCE OF MEN, GOODS, AND MESSAGES.										
1. *On Railways.*										
Railway Engine Driver, Stoker	700	.	6	.	58	.	141	.	21	.
Railway Guard	260	.	1	.	36	.	64	.	8	.
Pointsman, Level Crossing Man	110	.	8	.	10	2	85	8	4	.
Other Railway Officials and Servants	1472	8	125	.	449	1	839	2	95	1
2. *On Roads.*										
Toll Collector, Turnpike Gate Keeper	4	2	.	.	1	.	14	1	1	.
Omnibus, Coach, Cab, Owner—Livery Stable Keeper	26	2	2	.	7	.	30	4	15	.
Cabman, Flyman, Coachman (not domestic)	64	.	10	.	19	.	79	.	43	.
Carman, Carrier, Carter, Haulier	535	15	86	5	219	8	260	5	74	1
Tramway Companies' Service	3	.	.	.	.	.	12	.	1	.
Wheel Chair Proprietor, Attendant, &c.	.	.	.	.	1	.	.	.	.	.
3. *On Canals, Rivers and Seas.*										
Inland Navigation Service	41	.	1	.	13	.	19	1	2	.
Bargeman, Lighterman, Waterman	162	14	39	.	29	.	123	3	16	2
Navigation Service (on shore)	4	.	.	.	1	.	.	.	.	.
Seaman (Merchant Service)	25	.	.	.	23	.	86	.	3	.
Pilot	.	.	.	.	.	.	1	.	.	.
Ship Steward, Cook	3	.	.	.	.	.	.	.	3	.
Boatman on Seas	.	.	.	.	.	.	.	.	.	.
Harbour, Dock, Wharf, Lighthouse, Service	10	.	1	.	6	.	8	.	.	.
4. *In Storage.*										
Warehouseman (not Manchester)	65	.	.	.	75	1	20	.	37	.
Meter, Weigher	1	.	.	.	3	.	.	.	.	.
5. *In conveying Messages, Porterage, &c.*										
Messenger, Porter, Watchman (not Railway nor Government)	705	16	118	8	554	6	650	7	332	1
Telegraph, Telephone, Service	60	15	5	5	27	12	30	4	11	.

Table 10 *continued.*—Occupations of Males and Females in the South-Midland Division and its Registration Counties, and in each Urban Sanitary District of which the Population exceeds 50,000 Persons.

Occupations.	Registration Counties.								Urban Sanitary District.	
	10. Northamptonshire.		11. Huntingdonshire.		12. Bedfordshire.		13. Cambridgeshire.		Northampton.	
	Males.	Females.	Males.	Females.	Males.	Females.	Males.	Females.	Males.	Females.
IV. Agricultural Class.										
7. Persons engaged in Agriculture.										
1. *In Fields and Pastures.*										
Farmer, Grazier	2170	155	819	48	1209	93	3143	174	11	.
Farmer's, Grazier's—Son, Grandson, Brother, Nephew*	682	.	215	.	428	.	863	.	1	.
Farm Bailiff	286	.	127	.	177	.	301	.	3	.
Agricultural Labourer, Farm Servant, Cottager	19909	236	6782	286	14740	79	20004	1425	138	1
Shepherd	834	.	166	.	318	.	581	.	.	.
Land Drainage Service (not in towns)	5	.	3	.	8	.	7	.	.	.
Agricultural Machine—Proprietor, Attendant	102	1	53	1	67	1	150	4	2	.
Agricultural Student, Pupil	19	.	4	.	7	.	5	.	.	.
Others engaged in, or connected with, Agriculture	2	.	6	2	4	.	43	1	.	.
2. *In Woods.*										
Woodman	104	.	21	.	42	.	20	.	.	.
3. *In Gardens.*										
Nurseryman, Seedsman, Florist	72	4	23	4	42	1	64	6	17	.
Gardener (not domestic)	442	12	106	6	592	14	272	41	193	5

Occupations.	Northamptonshire Males.	Northamptonshire Females.	Huntingdonshire Males.	Huntingdonshire Females.	Bedfordshire Males.	Bedfordshire Females.	Cambridgeshire Males.	Cambridgeshire Females.	Northampton Males.	Northampton Females.
8. Persons engaged about Animals.										
1. *About Animals.*										
Horse Proprietor, Breeder, Dealer	23	.	14	.	17	.	25	.	3	.
Groom, Horse-keeper, Horse-breaker	633	.	158	.	252	.	1174	1	128	.
Veterinary Surgeon, Farrier	62	.	18	.	27	.	66	.	7	.
Cattle, Sheep, Pig—Dealer, Salesman	71	.	52	.	56	.	81	.	3	.
Drover	54	.	22	.	20	.	27	.	13	.
Gamekeeper	163	.	33	.	131	.	106	.	.	.
Dog, Bird, Animal—Keeper, Dealer	8	2	3	1	22	1	24	4	1	.
Vermin destroyer	16	.	14	1	16	.	34	1	.	.
Fisherman	5	.	6	.	1	.	17	.	1	.
Knacker, Catsmeat Dealer, &c., &c.	4	.	8	.	.	.	7	.	2	.

Occupations.	Northamptonshire Males.	Northamptonshire Females.	Huntingdonshire Males.	Huntingdonshire Females.	Bedfordshire Males.	Bedfordshire Females.	Cambridgeshire Males.	Cambridgeshire Females.	Northampton Males.	Northampton Females.
V. Industrial Class.										
9. Persons working and dealing in Books, Prints, and Maps.										
1. *Books.*										
Publisher, Bookseller, Librarian	45	18	4	8	25	7	86	7	26	7
Music—Publisher, Seller, Printer	4	1	1	.	3	.	6	6	1	1
Bookbinder	57	25	2	.	9	.	43	22	47	17
Printer	246	5	41	.	179	3	427	1	114	1
Newspaper Agent, News Room Keeper	26	4	1	.	5	2	14	9	11	1
Others	.	.	.	.	.	.	.	.	.	.
2. *Prints and Maps.*										
Lithographer, Lithographic Printer	3	1	.	.	12	.	1	.	3	1
Copper Plate and Steel Plate Printer	1	.	.	.	.	.	.	.	1	.
Map and Print—Colourer, Seller	3	.	.	.	.	.	3	2	3	.

Occupations.	Northamptonshire Males.	Northamptonshire Females.	Huntingdonshire Males.	Huntingdonshire Females.	Bedfordshire Males.	Bedfordshire Females.	Cambridgeshire Males.	Cambridgeshire Females.	Northampton Males.	Northampton Females.
10. Persons working and dealing in Machines and Implements.										
1. *Machines.*										
Engine, Machine, Maker	141	1	16	.	107	.	54	.	37	.
Millwright	30	.	15	.	19	.	64	.	5	.
Fitter, Turner (Engine and Machine)	442	.	28	.	153	.	86	.	46	.
Boiler Maker	74	.	2	.	22	.	27	.	19	.
Spinning and Weaving Machine Maker	2	1	.	.	.	.	.	.	.	.
Agricultural Machine and Implement Maker	42	.	8	1	46	.	18	3	2	.
Domestic Machinery—Maker, Dealer	2	.	.	.	.	.	.	.	.	.
2. *Tools and Implements.*										
Tool Maker, Dealer	8	.	.	.	6	1	1	.	7	.
Cutler, Scissors Maker	29	.	5	.	1	.	11	.	9	.
File Maker	1	1	1	.	1	.	.	.	1	.
Saw Maker	4	.	.	.	2	.	5	.	1	.
Pin Maker	.	.	.	.	.	.	.	.	.	.
Needle Maker	.	.	.	.	.	.	.	.	.	.
Steel Pen Maker	.	.	.	.	.	.	.	.	.	.
Pencil Maker (Wood)	.	.	.	.	.	.	.	.	.	.
Domestic Implement Maker	1	.	.	.	1	.	.	.	.	.
3. *Watches and Philosophical Instruments.*										
Watch Maker, Clock Maker	127	3	83	.	74	2	101	1	31	1
Philosophical Instrument Maker, Optician	3	.	.	.	1	.	8	.	1	.
Electrical Apparatus Maker	3	.	3	.	3	.	2	.	1	.
Weighing and Measuring Apparatus Maker	1	.	2	.	1	.	4	.	1	.

* Only male relatives living with the farmer or grazier, and therefore presumably engaged in agriculture, are included above.

Table 10 *continued*.—OCCUPATIONS of MALES and FEMALES in the SOUTH-MIDLAND DIVISION and its REGISTRATION COUNTIES, and in each URBAN SANITARY DISTRICT of which the POPULATION exceeds 50,000 PERSONS.

OCCUPATIONS.	REGISTRATION COUNTIES.								URBAN SANITARY DISTRICT.	
	10. NORTH-AMPTON-SHIRE.		11. HUNT-INGDON SHIRE.		12. BED-FORD-SHIRE.		13. CAM-BRIDGE-SHIRE.		NORTH-AMPTON.	
	Males.	Females.	Males.	Females.	Males.	Females.	Males.	Females.	Males.	Females.
4. Surgical Instruments.										
Surgical Instrument Maker	4	1	.	.	.	.	1	1	3	1
5. Arms and Ordnance.										
Gunsmith, Gun Manufacturer	16	1	1	.	6	.	9	1	4	1
Ordnance Manufacturer	16	.	3	.	.	.	.	.	.	.
Sword, Bayonet—Maker, Cutler	.	.	.	.	.	.	.	.	.	.
Others	.	.	.	.	.	.	.	.	.	.
6. Musical Instruments.										
Musical Instrument Maker, Dealer	25	1	3	.	16	.	28	.	10	
7. Type, Dies, Medals, Coins.										
Type Cutter, Founder	.	.	.	.	.	.	.		.	
Die, Seal, Coin, Medal, Maker	.	.	.	.	.	.	.	.	.	.
8. Tackle for Sports and Games.										
Toy Maker, Dealer	4	8	.	4	1	3	3	8	3	1
Fishing Rod, Tackle, Maker, Dealer	.	.	.	.	.	.	.	.	.	.
Apparatus for other Games, Maker, Dealer	.	.	.	.	.	.	4	.	.	.
11. PERSONS WORKING AND DEALING IN HOUSES, FURNITURE, AND DECORATIONS.										
1. Houses.										
Builder	376	.	62	.	174	.	224	2	75	.
Carpenter, Joiner	2398	.	432	.	1203	.	1445	.	408	.
Bricklayer	1615	1	282	.	1173	.	1171	.	209	.
Mason	743	1	33	.	159	.	174	1	74	.
Slater, Tiler	24	.	.	.	.	.	11	.	1	.
Plasterer, Whitewasher	140	.	2	.	42	.	85	.	54	.
Paperhanger	21	.	4	.	16	.	18	.	11	.
Plumber	309	4	47	.	161	1	208	2	72	.
Painter, Glazier	617	1	86	.	466	1	420	4	209	.
2. Furniture and Fittings.										
Cabinet Maker, Upholsterer	257	33	35	9	113	16	188	32	65	22
French Polisher	20	25	1	.	7	1	19	4	11	3
Furniture Broker, Dealer	35	5	4	1	24	4	19	4	20	4
Locksmith, Bellhanger	7	.	4	.	3	.	7	.	1	.
Gas Fitter	55	.	16	.	35	1	28	.	13	.
House and Shop Fittings—Maker, Dealer	1	.	1	.	1	.	.	.	.	.
Funeral Furniture Maker, Undertaker	4	1	.	.	3	.	1	.	2	1
Others	.	.	.	.	.	.	.	.	.	.
3. House Decorations.										
Wood Carver	9	1	1	.	7	.	21	.	5	1
Carver, Gilder	18	.	1	.	6	.	19	1	15	.
Dealer in Works of Art	2	2	.	.	.	.	7	.	1	.
Figure, Image—Maker, Dealer	.	.	.	.	.	.	2	.	.	.
Animal, Bird, &c., Preserver, Naturalist	4	.	.	.	4	.	7	.	1	.
Artificial Flower Maker	1	.	.	.	.	1	2	.	1	.
12. PERSONS WORKING AND DEALING IN CARRIAGES AND HARNESS.										
1. Carriages.										
Coachmaker	403	19	140	.	158	2	92	1	82	.
Railway Carriage, Railway Wagon, Maker	216	1	.	.	8	.	.	.	2	1
Wheelwright	378	2	101	2	231	1	315	2	33	.
Bicycle, Tricycle—Maker, Dealer	3	.	.	.	6	.	2	.	3	.
Others	22	.	1	.	1	.	.	.	3	.
2. Harness.										
Saddler, Harness, Whip, Maker	262	4	66	.	168	.	300	6	48	.
13. PERSONS WORKING AND DEALING IN SHIPS AND BOATS.										
1. Hull.										
Ship, Boat, Barge, Builder	27	.	5	.	0	.	38	.	.	.
Shipwright, Ship Carpenter (ashore)	2	.	1	.	.	.	5	.	1	.
2. Masts, Rigging, &c.										
Mast, Yard, Oar, Block, Maker	.	.	.	.	.	.	1	.	.	.
Ship Rigger, Chandler, Fitter	.	.	.	.	.	.	1	.	.	.
Sail Maker	1	.	.	.	.	.	3	.	1	.

Table 10 *continued*.—OCCUPATIONS of MALES and FEMALES in the SOUTH-MIDLAND DIVISION and its REGISTRATION COUNTIES, and in each URBAN SANITARY DISTRICT of which the POPULATION exceeds 50,000 PERSONS.

OCCUPATIONS.	REGISTRATION COUNTIES.								URBAN SANITARY DISTRICT.	
	10. NORTHAMPTONSHIRE.		11. HUNTINGDONSHIRE.		12. BEDFORDSHIRE.		13. CAMBRIDGESHIRE.		NORTHAMPTON.	
	Males.	Females.	Males.	Females.	Males.	Females.	Males.	Females.	Males.	Females.
14. PERSONS WORKING AND DEALING IN CHEMICALS AND COMPOUNDS.										
1. *Colouring Matter.*										
Dye, Paint, Manufacture	.	.	.	.	1	.	.	.	.	.
Ink, Blacking, Colouring Substance, Manufacture	5	.	1	.	.	.	.	.	3	.
2. *Explosives.*										
Gunpowder, Guncotton, Explosive Substance, Manufacture	.	.	.	.	.	.	.	.	.	.
Fusee, Fireworks, Explosive Article, Manufacture	.	.	.	.	.	.	1	.	.	.
3. *Drugs and other Chemicals and Compounds.*										
Chemist, Druggist	136	5	27	.	81	3	119	2	31	2
Manufacturing Chemist	4	1	1	.	8	2	23	1	2	1
Alkali Manufacture	.	.	.	.	.	.	.	.	.	.
Drysalter	1	.	.	.	3	.	.	.	1	.
15. PERSONS WORKING AND DEALING IN TOBACCO AND PIPES.										
1. *Tobacco and Pipes.*										
Tobacco Manufacturer, Tobacconist	19	14	1	2	7	3	34	8	14	11
Tobacco Pipe, Snuff Box, &c., Maker	.	3	.	.	2	.	7	2	.	.
16. PERSONS WORKING AND DEALING IN FOOD AND LODGING.										
1. *Board and Lodging.*										
Innkeeper, Hotel Keeper, Publican	640	132	184	54	487	58	567	146	83	15
Lodging, Boarding House, Keeper	7	80	.	9	4	66	22	238	4	21
Coffee, Eating House, Keeper	11	11	.	3	15	3	18	6	2	4
2. *Spirituous Drinks.*										
Hop—Merchant, Dealer	1	.	.	.	.	.	1	.	.	.
Maltster	83	1	53	.	62	1	89	.	11	.
Brewer	312	2	105	1	169	4	302	12	108	1
Beerseller, Ale, Porter, Cider, Dealer	146	40	18	7	35	13	54	32	73	14
Cellarman	25	.	3	.	9	.	28	1	13	.
Wine, Spirit—Merchant, Agent	45	3	5	.	23	.	30	.	15	1
3. *Food.*										
Milkseller, Dairyman	147	22	28	11	68	10	100	29	60	4
Cheesemonger, Butterman	1	.	5	4	3	.	8	3	.	.
Butcher, Meat Salesman	1008	28	185	13	589	25	590	27	232	8
Provision Curer, Dealer	61	33	4	.	88	4	16	7	33	23
Poulterer, Game Dealer	16	2	11	1	21	.	30	5	2	.
Fishmonger	86	8	20	.	73	3	82	11	39	5
Corn, Flour, Seed—Merchant, Dealer	99	3	43	1	79	3	161	14	21	.
Corn Miller	354	3	158	1	246	1	407	3	21	.
Baker	1056	75	283	21	646	55	567	35	179	9
Confectioner, Pastrycook	95	62	14	10	60	27	49	46	39	28
Greengrocer, Fruiterer	99	36	23	7	73	17	71	28	20	12
Mustard, Vinegar, Spice, Pickle—Maker, Dealer	1	.	.	.	.	.	5	.	.	.
Sugar Refiner	12	3	3	.	3	.	9	4	4	.
Grocer, Tea, Coffee, Chocolate—Maker, Dealer	852	278	186	62	543	182	757	219	183	24
Ginger Beer, Mineral Water—Manufacturer, Dealer	38	2	13	.	27	1	27	.	20	.
Others dealing in Food	.	.	.	.	.	.	.	.	.	.
17. PERSONS WORKING AND DEALING IN TEXTILE FABRICS.										
1. *Wool and Worsted.*										
Woolstapler	3	.	4	.	5	.	2	.	1	.
Woollen Cloth Manufacture	9	14	2	2	1	.	.	.	1	.
Wool, Woollen goods—Dyer, Printer	.	.	.	.	1	.	.	.	.	.
Worsted, Stuff, Manufacture	.	.	.	.	.	.	.	.	.	.
Flannel Manufacture	.	.	.	.	.	.	.	.	.	.
Blanket Manufacture	.	.	.	.	.	.	.	.	.	.
Fuller	.	.	.	.	.	.	.	.	.	.
Cloth, Worsted, Stuff, Flannel, Blanket, Dealer	3	.	.	.	.	.	.	.	2	.
Others	.	.	.	.	.	.	.	.	.	.
2. *Silk.*										
Silk, Silk goods, Manufacture	4	7	.	.	1	.	1	1	.	1
Silk Dyer, Printer	.	.	.	.	.	.	.	.	.	.
Ribbon Manufacture	1	4	.	.	.	.	.	.	.	.
Crape, Gauze, Manufacture	.	.	.	.	.	.	.	.	.	2
Silk Merchant, Dealer	5	.	.	.	.	.	2	.	2	.

Table 10 *continued*.—OCCUPATIONS of MALES and FEMALES in the SOUTH-MIDLAND DIVISION and its REGISTRATION COUNTIES, and in each URBAN SANITARY DISTRICT of which the POPULATION exceeds 50,000 PERSONS.

OCCUPATIONS.	REGISTRATION COUNTIES.								URBAN SANITARY DISTRICT.	
	10. NORTH-AMPTON-SHIRE.		11. HUNT-INGDON-SHIRE.		12. BED-FORD-SHIRE.		13. CAM-BRIDGE-SHIRE.		NORTH-AMPTON.	
	Males.	Females.	Males.	Females.	Males.	Females.	Males.	Females.	Males.	Females.
3. Cotton and Flax										
Cotton, Cotton goods, Manufacture	.	5	.	.	1	1	.	.	.	.
Cotton, Calico—Printer, Dyer, Bleacher	.	.	.	.	.	.	.	.	.	.
Cotton, Calico—Warehouseman, Dealer	.	.	.	.	.	.	.	1	.	.
Flax, Linen—Manufacturer, Dealer	2	.	.	.	.	.	21	17	.	.
Lace Manufacturer, Dealer	11	3231	2	370	12	4780	.	11	2	90
Fustian Manufacturer, Dealer	.	.	.	.	.	.	.	.	.	.
Tape Manufacturer, Dealer	.	.	.	.	.	.	.	.	.	.
Thread Manufacturer, Dealer	1	1	.	.	1	.	.	.	.	.
4. Hemp and other Fibrous Materials.										
Hemp, Jute, Cocoa Fibre, Manufacture	1	.	.	.	.	.	.	.	.	.
Rope, Twine, Cord—Maker, Dealer	43	1	16	.	35	.	47	8	6	.
Mat Maker, Seller	20	5	1	.	16	.	5	.	.	.
Net Maker	2	1	.	.	1	.	.	.	.	.
Canvas, Sailcloth, Manufacture	.	.	.	.	.	.	.	.	.	.
Sacking, Sack, Bag—Maker, Dealer	3	9	.	4	5	1	2	7	1	3
Others working and dealing in Hemp	1	2	.	.	1	.	1	.	.	.
5. Mixed or Unspecified Materials.										
Weaver (undefined)	4	3	.	.	.	1	.	1	1	.
Dyer, Printer, Scourer, Bleacher, Calenderer (undefined)	7	.	5	3	23	3	10	5	5	.
Factory hand (Textile, undefined)	2	37	.	2	1	.	.	25	.	.
Felt Manufacture	.	.	.	.	.	.	.	.	.	.
Carpet, Rug, Manufacture	3	1	.	.	.	.	2	18	.	.
Manchester Warehouseman	.	.	.	.	.	.	1	.	.	.
Draper, Linen Draper, Mercer	477	238	109	62	301	187	283	207	168	74
Fancy Goods (Textile), Manufacturer, Worker, Dealer	.	38	.	7	.	10	.	10	.	6
Trimming Maker, Dealer	.	1	.	1	1	.	.	.	.	.
Embroiderer	.	1	.	.	.	2	.	.	.	.
Others	.	.	.	.	.	.	.	.	.	1
18. PERSONS WORKING AND DEALING IN DRESS.										
1. Dress.										
Hatter, Hat Manufacture (not straw)	23	2	.	.	25	.	17	1	17	1
Straw—Hat, Bonnet, Plait, Manufacture	.	47	.	12	2268	15068	1	101	.	13
Tailor	976	361	212	14	517	59	855	234	204	104
Milliner, Dressmaker, Staymaker	28	3704	1	719	1	2327	4	2409	7	823
Shawl Manufacture	.	.	.	.	.	.	.	.	.	.
Shirt Maker, Seamstress	2	440	.	94	.	531	1	403	1	69
Hosiery Manufacture	3	20	.	7	.	3	.	9	.	1
Hosier, Haberdasher	22	8	1	.	4	5	23	6	14	5
Glover, Glove Maker	2	8	1	1	3	3	6	17	1	3
Button Maker, Dealer	.	.	1	.	1	.	.	.	.	.
Shoe, Boot—Maker, Dealer	10546	7831	338	10	973	100	1110	46	6988	3473
Patten, Clog, Maker	1	.	.	.	2	.	3	.	.	.
Wig Maker, Hairdresser	121	2	28	.	50	1	82	8	42	1
Umbrella, Parasol, Stick—Maker, Dealer	5	2	1	1	10	2	12	6	1	1
Accoutrement Maker	.	.	.	.	.	.	.	.	.	.
Old Clothes Dealer, and others	3	10	.	2	1	2	.	7	3	7
19. PERSONS WORKING AND DEALING IN VARIOUS ANIMAL SUBSTANCES.										
1. In Grease, Gut, Bone, Horn, Ivory, and Whalebone.										
Tallow Chandler, Candle, Grease, Manufacture	13	.	1	.	6	2	5	1	6	.
Soap Boiler, Maker	1	.	.	.	.	.	4	.	.	.
Glue, Size, Gelatine, Isinglass—Maker, Dealer	.	.	.	.	5	.	.	.	.	.
Manure Manufacture	3	.	5	.	.	.	6	.	.	.
Bone, Horn, Ivory, Tortoise-shell—Worker, Dealer	1	.	.	.	.	.	.	.	.	.
Comb Maker	.	.	.	.	.	.	.	.	.	.
Others	4	.	.	.	.	.	.	.	2	.
2. In Skins.										
Furrier, Skinner	10	.	1	.	11	1	50	2	2	.
Tanner, Fellmonger	149	.	11	.	34	.	22	.	72	.
Currier	950	5	17	.	68	.	63	.	404	2
Leather Goods, Portmanteau, Bag, Strap, &c.—Maker, Dealer	.	3	.	.	1	.	.	1	.	.
Parchment, Vellum—Maker, Dealer	8	.	9	.	9	.	33	.	.	.
3. In Hair and Feathers.										
Hair, Bristle—Worker, Dealer	.	.	.	.	.	.	.	.	.	.
Brush, Broom, Maker	20	3	.	.	8	8	4	.	5	1
Quill, Feather—Dresser, Dealer	2	3	.	.	2	4	1	30	.	3

Table 10 *continued.*—OCCUPATIONS of MALES and FEMALES in the SOUTH-MIDLAND DIVISION and its REGISTRATION COUNTIES, and in each URBAN SANITARY DISTRICT of which the POPULATION exceeds 50,000 PERSONS.

OCCUPATIONS.	REGISTRATION COUNTIES.								URBAN SANITARY DISTRICT.	
	10. NORTHAMPTONSHIRE.		11. HUNTINGDONSHIRE.		12. BEDFORDSHIRE.		13. CAMBRIDGESHIRE.		NORTHAMPTON.	
	Males.	Females.	Males.	Females.	Males.	Females.	Males.	Females.	Males.	Females.
20. PERSONS WORKING AND DEALING IN VARIOUS VEGETABLE SUBSTANCES.										
1. *In Oils, Gums, and Resins.*										
Oil Miller, Oil Cake—Maker, Dealer	12	.	12	.	15	.	7	.	9	.
Oil and Colourman	2	.	3	.	8	.	6	1	2	.
Floor Cloth, Oil Cloth, Manufacture	.	.	.	.	.	.	.	.	.	.
Japanner	.	.	.	.	.	.	.	.	.	.
India Rubber, Gutta Percha—Worker, Dealer	7	27	.	.	1	.	.	.	.	.
Waterproof Goods—Maker, Dealer	32	11	.	.	.	.	1	.	.	.
Others	1	.	.	.	.	.	.	.	.	.
2. *In Cane, Rush, and Straw.*										
Willow, Cane, Rush—Worker, Dealer, Basketmaker	86	5	36	1	86	50	97	5	14	.
Hay, Straw (not plait), Chaff—Cutter, Dealer	6	.	10	.	39	1	12	.	.	.
Thatcher	58	.	33	.	31	.	138	.	.	.
3. *In Wood and Bark.*										
Timber, Wood—Merchant, Dealer	160	13	3	.	41	2	48	2	28	7
Sawyer	319	.	36	.	130	.	121	.	80	.
Lath, Wooden Fence, Hurdle, Maker	39	.	5	.	44	.	46	.	.	.
Wood Turner, Box Maker	64	.	.	.	22	.	12	1	8	.
Cooper, Hoop Maker, Bender	65	1	14	.	35	.	34	.	25	.
Cork, Bark—Cutter, Worker, Dealer	5	.	.	.	.	.	2	1	4	.
Others	2	.	.	.	33	.	.	.	.	.
4. *In Paper.*										
Paper Manufacture	48	53	62	237	.	1	122	126	.	10
Envelope Maker	1	29	.	.	.	1	.	.	.	.
Stationer, Law Stationer	13	22	4	2	16	15	31	18	.	3
Card, Pattern Card, Maker	.	.	.	.	.	.	.	.	.	.
Paper Stainer	.	.	.	.	.	.	.	.	.	.
Paper Box, Paper Bag, Maker	.	20	.	3	1	8	.	.	.	15
Ticket, Label, Writer	.	.	1	.	.	.	1	.	.	.
Others	13	.	2	.	5	.	7	.	4	.
21. PERSONS WORKING AND DEALING IN VARIOUS MINERAL SUBSTANCES.										
1. *Miners.*										
Coal Miner	2	.	.	.	3	.	.	.	.	.
Ironstone Miner	1457	.	.	.	3	.	.	.	1	.
Copper Miner	1	.	.	.	1	.	.	.	.	.
Tin Miner	.	.	.	.	.	.	.	.	.	.
Lead Miner	.	.	.	.	.	.	.	.	.	.
Miner in other, or undefined, Minerals	.	.	1	.	.	.	2	.	.	.
Mine Service	11	.	.	.	1	.	1	.	.	.
2. *Coal, Coal Gas, &c.*										
Coal Merchant, Dealer	249	6	49	1	126	2	157	8	44	.
Coalheaver	110	.	13	.	60	.	83	.	16	.
Coke, Charcoal, Peat—Cutter, Burner, Dealer	1	.	.	.	.	.	6	.	.	.
Gas Works Service	116	.	18	.	68	.	86	.	31	.
3. *Stone, Clay, and Road Making.*										
Stone Quarrier	15	.	.	.	6	.	3	.	.	.
Stone Cutter, Dresser, Dealer	38	.	2	.	10	.	4	.	6	.
Slate Quarrier	.	.	.	.	.	.	.	.	.	.
Slate Worker, Dealer	.	.	.	.	.	.	1	.	.	.
Limeburner	40	.	.	.	14	.	20	.	.	.
Clay, Sand, Gravel, Chalk—Labourer, Dealer	2	.	4	.	15	.	11	.	.	.
Fossil, Coprolite—Digger, Dealer	.	.	.	.	30	11	317	4	.	.
Well Sinker, Borer	3	.	.	.	2	.	3	.	.	.
Plaster, Cement, Manufacture	.	.	.	.	23	.	4	.	.	.
Brick, Tile—Maker, Burner, Dealer	696	5	171	.	462	.	369	1	34	.
Paviour	21	.	.	.	6	.	9	.	14	.
Road Contractor, Surveyor, Inspector	15	.	4	.	3	.	7	.	.	.
Road Labourer	183	.	46	.	47	.	79	.	7	.
Railway Contractor	16	.	2	.	1	.	5	.	1	.
Platelayer	364	.	86	.	195	.	293	.	11	.
Railway Labourer, Navvy	1465	.	40	.	296	.	184	.	76	.
Others	.	.	.	.	2	.	.	.	.	.
4. *Earthenware and Glass.*										
Earthenware, China, Porcelain, Manufacture	8	1	3	.	2	.	1	.	1	.
Glass Manufacture	4	.	.	.	2	.	3	.	.	.
Earthenware, China, Glass, Dealer	26	8	6	2	15	5	14	2	5	.
5. *Salt.*										
Salt Maker, Dealer	4	.	.	.	1	.	.	1	.	.

Table 10 *continued.*—OCCUPATIONS of MALES and FEMALES in the SOUTH-MIDLAND DIVISION and its REGISTRATION COUNTIES, and in each URBAN SANITARY DISTRICT of which the POPULATION exceeds 50,000 PERSONS.

OCCUPATIONS.	REGISTRATION COUNTIES.								URBAN SANITARY DISTRICT.	
	10. NORTHAMPTONSHIRE.		11. HUNTINGDONSHIRE.		12. BEDFORDSHIRE.		13. CAMBRIDGESHIRE.		NORTHAMPTON.	
	Males.	Females.	Males	Females	Males.	Females.	Males.	Females.	Males.	Females.
6. Water.										
Waterworks Service	9	.	1	.	3	.	5	.	6	.
Others	.	.	1	.	.	.	.	.	.	.
7. Precious Metals and Jewellery.										
Goldsmith, Silversmith, Jeweller	27	5	6	2	21	4	28	4	14	3
Gold, Silver, Beater	.	.	.	.	.	.	.	.	.	.
Lapidary	.	.	.	.	.	.	.	.	.	.
Others	.	.	.	.	.	.	.	.	.	.
8. Iron and Steel.										
Blacksmith	1065	7	245	1	571	4	786	8	89	.
Whitesmith	57	.	4	.	61	.	97	.	22	.
Nail Manufacture	1	.	.	.	.	.	.	.	.	.
Anchor, Chain, Manufacture	1	.	.	.	.	.	.	.	.	.
Other Iron and Steel Manufactures	1089	.	38	.	330	1	66	1	171	.
Ironmonger. Hardware Dealer, Merchant	158	8	43	1	111	4	110	7	68	5
9. Copper.										
Copper, Copper goods—Manufacturer, Worker, Dealer	18	.	.	.	3	.	5	.	4	
10. Tin and Zinc.										
Tin, Tin Plate, Tin goods—Manufacturer, Worker, Dealer	109	1	21	.	70	.	69	.	25	.
Zinc, Zinc Goods—Manufacturer, Worker, Dealer	1	.	.	.	1	.	.	.	.	.
11. Lead.										
Lead, Leaden goods—Manufacturer, Worker, Dealer	.	.	.	.	.	.	.	.	.	.
12. In Other, Mixed, or Unspecified, Metals.										
Metal Refiner, Worker, Turner, Dealer	5	.	.	.	.	.	1	.	.	.
Brass, Bronze, Manufacture. Brazier	58	.	9	.	118	.	17	.	9	.
Metal Burnisher, Lacquerer	.	.	.	.	1	.	.	.	.	.
White Metal, Plated Ware, Manufacture. Pewterer	.	.	.	.	.	.	.	.	.	.
Wire Maker, Worker, Weaver, Drawer	7	1	1	.	1	1	5	.	2	.
Bolt, Nut, Rivet, Screw, Staple, Maker	4	.	.	.	4	.	.	.	.	1
Lamp, Lantern, Candlestick, Maker	20	.	.	.	.	.	.	.	.	.
Clasp, Buckle, Hinge, Maker	.	.	.	.	.	.	.	.	1	.
Fancy Chain, Gilt Toy, Maker	.	.	.	.	.	.	.	.	.	.
Others	.	.	.	.	.	.	.	.	.	.
22. PERSONS WORKING AND DEALING IN GENERAL OR UNSPECIFIED COMMODITIES.										
1. Makers and Dealers (General or Undefined).										
General Shopkeeper, Dealer	367	229	87	40	258	88	261	160	55	59
Pawnbroker	25	7	1	.	13	1	18	2	14	5
Costermonger, Huckster, Street Seller	319	82	86	30	190	47	190	50	57	16
Manufacturer, Manager, Superintendent (undefined)	38	1	3	.	21	1	8	1	6	1
Contractor (undefined)	18	.	.	.	3	.	10	.	8	.
2. Mechanics and Labourers (General or Undefined).										
General Labourer	5881	14	995	1	3117	3	3350	40	751	3
Engine Driver, Stoker, Fireman (not railway, marine, nor agricultural)	308	.	60	.	106	.	248	.	46	.
Artisan, Mechanic (undefined)	102	3	13	.	40	1	35	.	26	.
Apprentice (undefined)	34	3	.	1	10	4	23	11	2	.
Factory Labourer (undefined)	111	6	4	1	27	2	34	3	19	.
Machinist, Machine Worker (undefined)	52	1	3	.	28	1	50	.	1	.
23. PERSONS WORKING AND DEALING IN REFUSE MATTERS.										
1. Refuse Matters.										
Town Drainage Service	9	.	.	.	.	.	.	.	.	.
Chimney Sweep, Soot Merchant	56	.	23	.	81	.	69	.	17	.
Scavenger, Crossing Sweeper	9	.	1	.	3	.	21	1	2	.
Rag Gatherer, Dealer	17	1	11	.	4	.	16	2	4	.
VI. UNOCCUPIED CLASS.										
24. PERSONS WITHOUT SPECIFIED OCCUPATIONS										
Persons returned by Property, Rank, &c., and not by special occupation	32426	85384	6265	17842	16676	38963	24864	64637	6128	14677
Children under 5 years of age	18995	18929	3404	3891	9934	10642	12309	12291	3541	3796

Table 11.—Birth-Places of Males and Females enumerated in Counties, and in each Urban Sanitary District of which the Population exceeds 50,000 Persons.

Where Born.	Where Enumerated.									
	SOUTH-MIDLAND COUNTIES.		Counties.†							
			MIDDLESEX.*		HERTFORDSHIRE.		BUCKINGHAMSHIRE.		OXFORDSHIRE.	
	Males.	Females.	Males.	Females.	Males.	Females.	Males.	Females.	Males.	Females.
TOTAL OF INHABITANTS	1967837	2178712	1367692	1552793	98792	104277	86840	89483	88025	91
LONDON	[illegible]	906061	800278	894879	6760	8085	3086	3286	2002	9
Middlesex (*Intra-metropolitan*)	768916	838631	749048	821221	5675	6808	2482	2625	1587	
Surrey (*Intra-metropolitan*)	44583	54360	42195	61597	785	930	484	506	311	
Kent (*Intra-metropolitan*)	9998	13070	9135	19963	300	347	120	155	104	
SOUTH-EASTERN COUNTIES	96759	127927	81478	109416	2690	3237	3612	4054	5597	7
Surrey (*Extra-metropolitan*)	19313	24782	17347	22558	626	666	488	483	316	
Kent (*Extra-metropolitan*)	26839	34888	23443	31891	717	879	457	540	314	
Sussex	13884	18860	12426	17148	384	405	283	305	217	
Hampshire	18866	24948	16289	21890	585	654	547	658	662	
Berkshire	18507	24449	12023	15934	379	533	1837	2062	4088	5
SOUTH-MIDLAND COUNTIES	669402	701739	164867	185956	78269	80202	73602	75041	71578	709
Middlesex (*Ex-metropolitan*)	101523	111869	101075	107776	1353	2067	780	990	262	
Hertfordshire	91944	97878	17594	20842	69104	69708	1283	1441	218	
Buckinghamshire	87753	91171	12084	14795	2579	2933	65092	65092	2057	2
Oxfordshire	80420	83634	8309	11119	373	510	2335	3338	67449	65
Northamptonshire	116313	112837	6329	8012	474	609	1451	2044	1948	1
Huntingdonshire	30765	32486	2012	3083	258	340	52	108	51	
Bedfordshire	71462	75613	7202	7493	2629	2692	1631	1805	202	
Cambridgeshire	80033	90871	8811	11936	1013	1303	178	228	96	
EASTERN COUNTIES	80850	106209	65627	87865	4313	5156	741	1016	540	7
Essex	37279	49076	31865	42333	2970	3585	328	427	228	
Suffolk	21306	27364	17227	23112	681	815	212	299	143	
Norfolk	22166	29169	16535	22420	662	753	201	290	169	
SOUTH-WESTERN COUNTIES	60633	81662	54507	74059	1186	1603	1336	1445	1602	21
Wiltshire	11734	16778	9869	14520	272	360	445	401	629	
Dorsetshire	6486	8594	5686	7667	186	233	140	176	163	
Devonshire	21148	26527	18538	24634	359	455	305	319	285	
Cornwall	5643	7748	6224	7186	90	131	71	77	83	
Somersetshire	15887	22015	14240	20952	279	434	366	382	443	
WEST-MIDLAND COUNTIES	45689	56142	34245	42069	1158	1431	1426	1628	3900	53
Gloucestershire	15069	19154	11958	15248	306	419	345	422	1715	22
Herefordshire	2001	3797	2076	3321	64	78	65	82	97	1
Shropshire	2887	4090	2308	3549	93	163	109	127	101	1
Staffordshire	6429	7186	4813	5330	216	241	248	243	252	3
Worcestershire	4872	5517	3215	4284	115	157	131	148	448	5
Warwickshire	14871	16298	9875	10537	370	378	528	608	1287	19
NORTH-MIDLAND COUNTIES	27073	30672	15729	17655	887	1046	616	603	480	51
Leicestershire	6349	6835	3361	3853	183	207	173	198	144	1
Rutlandshire	1593	1903	613	736	50	63	32	38	19	
Lincolnshire	11679	14005	6362	7930	408	464	187	175	102	1
Nottinghamshire	4128	4329	3122	3196	133	167	88	78	90	1
Derbyshire	3324	3540	2271	2431	170	145	136	114	75	
NORTH-WESTERN COUNTIES	15795	15601	12954	13106	509	460	483	418	371	83
Cheshire	2996	3000	2327	2427	134	123	128	114	93	
Lancashire	12799	12602	10627	10679	385	337	355	304	278	2
YORKSHIRE	15953	15419	12517	12256	560	472	388	338	356	36
NORTHERN COUNTIES	8905	8800	7799	7733	213	228	133	148	135	13
Durham	3846	3402	2907	2999	72	79	56	51	50	
Northumberland	3303	3371	2954	3049	72	75	42	42	53	
Cumberland	1644	1475	1440	1256	47	46	23	35	22	
Westmorland	609	552	498	435	22	28	12	20	10	1
MONMOUTHSHIRE AND WALES	10559	14734	9354	13256	196	291	216	244	257	33
Monmouthshire	1541	2543	1348	2272	36	48	38	35	48	7
Glamorganshire	1675	2129	1472	1971	30	35	27	34	51	7
Carmarthenshire	745	712	668	848	19	10	18	15	7	
Pembrokeshire	1071	1415	959	1271	24	35	20	21	16	2
Cardiganshire	1065	986	650	943	9	8	3	8	17	
Brecknockshire	463	708	395	616	17	15	11	11	22	
Radnorshire	260	369	213	311	11	10	6	6	19	
Montgomeryshire	584	1019	560	894	12	31	9	17	13	
Flintshire	342	364	299	304	10	19	7	14	4	
Denbighshire	504	581	419	489	8	15	20	23	16	1
Merionethshire	207	314	188	288	3	4	6	4	6	
Carnarvonshire	328	415	287	361	4	12	8	8	13	
Anglesey	172	281	148	208	1	4	8	4	4	
Wales (*County not stated*)	1672	2858	1518	2680	27	30	29	44	21	
ENGLAND (*County not stated*)	10773	11618	8682	9581	465	521	275	251	87	8
OTHER PARTS OF BRITISH EMPIRE	64599	72249	58707	66399	1305	1260	792	838	886	84
Islands in the British Seas	1900	2494	1708	2258	41	51	22	36	41	51
SCOTLAND	22354	20021	20403	18806	469	472	297	296	315	26
IRELAND	29677	35727	27508	33720	410	383	260	241	369	27
British Colonies or Dependencies	10668	13407	8998	11615	385	304	213	265	241	22
FOREIGN COUNTRIES	41693	29247	40450	28001	273	269	176	164	223	212
British Subjects	8291	7716	7671	7057	134	139	100	105	93	10
Foreigners	33402	21531	32779	20944	139	130	76	59	130	11
AT SEA	456	629	398	562	8	16	8	9	11	8
British Subjects	449	619	392	552	8	16	8	9	11	8
Foreigners	7	10	6	10	.	.	.	.	.	.

* The figures in this Column relate to the entire county of Middlesex. The Metropolitan portion of this county is separately dealt with in Table 11, Division I., p. 20.

† The Counties *proper*, and not the Registration Counties are referred to in this Table.

Table 11 *continued*.—BIRTH-PLACES of MALES and FEMALES enumerated in COUNTIES, and in each URBAN SANITARY DISTRICT of which the POPULATION EXCEEDS 50,000 PERSONS.

WHERE BORN.	WHERE ENUMERATED. COUNTIES. NORTHAMPTONSHIRE.		HUNTINGDONSHIRE.		BEDFORDSHIRE.		CAMBRIDGESHIRE.		URBAN SANITARY DISTRICT. NORTHAMPTON.	
	Males.	Females.	Males.	Females.	Males.	Females.	Males.	Females.	Males.	Females.
TOTAL OF INHABITANTS	135662	136893	29195	30296	70354	79119	91277	94317	25249	26632
LONDON	2454	2717	451	603	1637	2066	1779	2013	878	863
MIDDLESEX (*Intra-metropolitan*)	1997	2264	372	470	1297	1644	1458	1658	714	737
SURREY (*Intra-metropolitan*)	329	324	50	83	246	300	324	251	132	99
KENT (*Intra-metropolitan*)	128	129	28	41	91	122	97	104	32	27
SOUTH-EASTERN COUNTIES	1433	1644	225	293	871	1141	853	979	384	436
SURREY (*Extra-metropolitan*)	214	275	34	66	140	186	149	176	47	59
KENT (*Extra-metropolitan*)	413	471	70	97	230	365	248	294	117	142
SUSSEX	228	239	24	40	148	194	179	177	61	55
HAMPSHIRE	371	377	53	51	227	297	182	219	112	127
BERKSHIRE	213	282	44	39	126	159	98	113	47	53
SOUTH-MIDLAND COUNTIES	115166	114860	26383	26809	62703	69948	76835	77993	20501	22076
MIDDLESEX (*Ex-metropolitan*)	202	212	38	45	145	270	170	187	55	42
HERTFORDSHIRE	468	432	109	139	2483	3365	775	877	98	89
BUCKINGHAMSHIRE	2348	2585	79	86	1373	2050	143	143	712	751
OXFORDSHIRE	1566	2111	20	46	227	365	98	91	174	193
NORTHAMPTONSHIRE	104062	102736	1177	1393	852	1460	625	763	18687	20248
HUNTINGDONSHIRE	2519	2765	22396	22654	844	1424	2037	2435	176	153
BEDFORDSHIRE	2749	2609	857	1081	56067	59619	633	711	486	488
CAMBRIDGESHIRE	1278	1428	1698	2285	612	875	72364	72766	148	112
EASTERN COUNTIES	1498	1431	563	656	725	847	6843	8517	328	316
ESSEX	350	359	124	143	266	336	1248	1577	75	73
SUFFOLK	393	332	160	188	229	248	2260	2771	103	92
NORFOLK	755	740	279	325	230	263	3335	4169	150	151
SOUTH-WESTERN COUNTIES	1074	1108	134	157	507	689	487	467	275	255
WILTSHIRE	278	278	30	36	115	163	86	89	61	48
DORSETSHIRE	153	134	15	23	38	83	76	62	34	34
DEVONSHIRE	275	326	44	40	172	206	165	154	76	78
CORNWALL	69	96	14	17	45	72	47	46	19	23
SOMERSETSHIRE	299	274	31	47	117	165	113	116	85	72
WEST-MIDLAND COUNTIES	3548	4080	172	215	729	887	511	497	862	875
GLOUCESTERSHIRE	430	479	29	45	152	192	110	122	120	120
HEREFORDSHIRE	127	161	12	8	31	23	29	27	26	19
SHROPSHIRE	149	184	8	21	85	61	64	47	46	34
STAFFORDSHIRE	690	722	34	48	140	163	106	112	192	191
WORCESTERSHIRE	315	304	14	23	82	118	53	57	80	74
WARWICKSHIRE	1817	2290	75	69	279	329	149	132	398	487
NORTH-MIDLAND COUNTIES	6071	6915	666	926	893	1024	1729	1984	738	749
LEICESTERSHIRE	2013	2387	80	89	241	275	154	170	386	375
RUTLANDSHIRE	746	839	42	94	37	39	54	82	44	53
LINCOLNSHIRE	2513	2705	433	635	296	375	1329	1514	161	164
NOTTINGHAMSHIRE	380	486	63	77	138	152	111	192	75	64
DERBYSHIRE	419	438	48	48	184	183	81	96	79	93
NORTH-WESTERN COUNTIES	744	646	82	73	283	299	369	269	230	175
CHESHIRE	177	145	14	15	60	60	73	53	48	38
LANCASHIRE	567	501	68	58	223	239	296	216	183	137
YORKSHIRE	1065	976	192	197	360	339	515	476	224	161
NORTHERN COUNTIES	278	284	47	48	89	110	211	122	73	54
DURHAM	98	101	22	13	34	45	107	56	19	9
NORTHUMBERLAND	72	79	14	18	33	40	66	37	15	20
CUMBERLAND	65	77	8	9	14	17	25	17	22	18
WESTMORLAND	43	27	3	8	8	8	13	12	17	8
MONMOUTHSHIRE AND WALES	309	293	22	43	105	163	100	105	78	71
MONMOUTHSHIRE	45	52	3	10	15	29	16	18	12	16
GLAMORGANSHIRE	37	36	5	10	14	22	21	20	9	6
CARMARTHENSHIRE	36	18	1	4	8	9	7	4	7	1
PEMBROKESHIRE	28	26	9	7	12	18	9	11	13	12
CARDIGANSHIRE	10	6		.	10	7	6	6	4	
BRECKNOCKSHIRE	12	24	1	2	1	8	4	7	3	3
RADNORSHIRE	8	17	.	1	1	1	3	5	.	4
MONTGOMERYSHIRE	20	25	3	1	4	15	3	12	8	5
FLINTSHIRE	13	15	2	.	5	14	2	2	6	6
DENBIGHSHIRE	16	21		.	13	18	6	4	4	8
MERIONETHSHIRE	1	8	.	2	1	2	2	2	.	1
CARNARVONSHIRE	9	17	3	.	4	2	11	2	.	1
ANGLESEY	19	3	1	1	3	1	2	3	3	2
WALES (*County not stated*)	54	31	4	5	10	17	9	11	9	6
ENGLAND (*County not stated*)	579	499	29	30	517	548	139	102	164	122
OTHER PARTS OF BRITISH EMPIRE	1205	1212	192	201	783	874	729	620	438	418
ISLANDS in the BRITISH SEAS	27	42	4	5	22	28	35	23	9	14
SCOTLAND	371	344	62	58	207	209	230	169	116	38
IRELAND	547	526	71	82	232	262	270	240	213	232
BRITISH COLONIES or DEPENDENCIES	260	300	55	56	322	375	194	188	100	114
FOREIGN COUNTRIES	222	219	35	45	142	170	172	167	71	60
British Subjects	119	102	18	29	82	99	74	84	44	32
Foreigners	103	117	17	16	60	71	98	83	27	28
AT SEA	16	9	2	5	8	14	5	6	5	1
British Subjects	15	9	2	5	8	14	5	6	5	1
Foreigners	1	.	.	.	.	.	.	.	.	.

Table 12.—DISTRIBUTION of the enumerated NATIVES of COUNTIES.

WHERE ENUMERATED.	WHERE BORN.									
	SOUTH MIDLAND COUNTIES.		MIDDLESEX *		HERTFORDHAMSHIRE.		BUCKINGSHIRE.		OXFORDSHIRE.	
	Males.	Females.	Males.	Females.	Males.	Females.	Males.	Females.	Males.	Females.
TOTAL ENUMERATED NATIVES OF EACH COUNTY	1846197	2006703	1137733	1265199	109200	116910	108089	111960	108769	114098
LONDON	909880	1014402	842507	930605	16088	19705	12526	14756	9469	12904
MIDDLESEX (*Intra-metropolitan*)	705035	880353	746971	810798	11895	14737	8691	10564	6564	9281
SURREY (*Intra-metropolitan*)	98085	113788	82461	94498	3344	3964	3197	3469	2411	2977
KENT (*Intra-metropolitan*)	16760	20761	13075	16309	849	1004	638	723	494	646
SOUTH-EASTERN COUNTIES	94209	118001	64740	83159	4525	5735	6334	7372	9071	10762
SURREY (*Extra-metropolitan*)	25805	38257	21480	29031	1590	2007	1642	1936	1413	1847
KENT (*Extra-metropolitan*)	23670	27117	17692	20798	1332	1369	1096	1136	1022	1095
SUSSEX	14709	23016	11050	17511	735	1182	585	885	602	1081
HAMPSHIRE	14241	14498	10167	10440	632	691	714	711	1068	1086
BERKSHIRE	12784	15113	4351	5385	396	486	2297	2624	4966	5713
SOUTH-MIDLAND COUNTIES	638283	659517	121470	130702	80049	82641	79064	80607	73857	74256
MIDDLESEX (*Extra-metropolitan*)	118869	126324	103152	109199	5909	6165	3908	4231	1786	2138
HERTFORDSHIRE	83944	87010	7528	8865	60104	69708	2570	2933	373	510
BUCKINGHAMSHIRE	76084	77986	9262	9615	1283	1441	65092	65092	2335	3338
OXFORDSHIRE	73164	73862	1349	2384	218	274	3057	2887	67440	65657
NORTHAMPTONSHIRE	117163	117124	3199	2476	463	432	2348	2585	1580	2111
HUNTINGDONSHIRE	26763	27288	410	524	159	139	79	86	29	46
BEDFORDSHIRE	64000	71502	1442	1914	2483	3565	1873	2950	327	365
CAMBRIDGESHIRE	78293	79651	1638	1825	775	977	143	143	98	91
EASTERN COUNTIES	56401	62256	41670	45619	3327	3780	1082	1191	826	994
ESSEX	44298	47773	35700	38393	2886	3237	849	880	584	707
SUFFOLK	5655	6930	2967	3656	244	204	135	164	133	163
NORFOLK	6446	7584	2943	3570	197	240	98	147	109	124
SOUTH-WESTERN COUNTIES	15457	18612	11329	13876	581	695	700	764	1316	1571
WILTSHIRE	2876	3698	1081	2338	117	138	219	221	554	592
DORSETSHIRE	2098	1042	1502	1411	86	80	79	92	142	139
DEVONSHIRE	5725	6467	4543	5175	203	215	188	192	245	316
CORNWALL	1148	1239	898	1013	40	39	42	33	48	63
SOMERSETSHIRE	3690	5350	2705	3936	185	223	172	226	327	461
WEST-MIDLAND COUNTIES	38770	42004	16216	19146	1148	1226	2691	2518	8976	8960
GLOUCESTERSHIRE	7075	9233	3971	5389	210	230	394	391	1791	2305
HEREFORDSHIRE	1028	1307	626	844	27	31	66	77	146	159
SHROPSHIRE	1260	1497	752	914	35	61	68	67	116	141
STAFFORDSHIRE	7854	7168	3008	3290	314	266	836	651	1380	1090
WORCESTERSHIRE	3866	4285	1673	2166	114	150	235	256	1045	917
WARWICKSHIRE	17687	18319	6184	6633	418	439	1168	1076	4498	4452
NORTH-MIDLAND COUNTIES	30151	30235	7776	8301	1217	1051	1523	1356	1250	1107
LEICESTERSHIRE	8515	9631	1711	1995	281	221	468	417	414	425
RUTLANDSHIRE	827	1170	179	207	20	28	26	37	35	21
LINCOLNSHIRE	9036	8565	2468	2152	337	293	186	168	186	166
NOTTINGHAMSHIRE	5744	5098	1849	2151	350	293	280	265	254	209
DERBYSHIRE	6029	5171	1569	1796	279	216	573	469	371	288
NORTH-WESTERN COUNTIES	25501	26684	13825	15005	744	788	2040	1828	1525	1507
CHESHIRE	4361	4610	2134	2389	150	185	786	657	257	263
LANCASHIRE	21140	22074	11601	12616	594	603	1254	1171	1268	1245
YORKSHIRE	24182	22549	9367	10084	1027	898	1511	1091	1573	1307
NORTHERN COUNTIES	7218	6588	4737	4554	192	192	307	255	287	250
DURHAM	4209	3641	2597	2370	100	99	172	142	163	128
NORTHUMBERLAND	2032	1858	1566	1454	54	55	75	58	34	62
CUMBERLAND	701	749	454	508	23	22	40	38	51	44
WESTMORLAND	276	335	140	222	15	16	20	17	19	16
MONMOUTHSHIRE AND WALES	6144	5817	4096	4148	242	199	311	222	619	480
MONMOUTHSHIRE	1023	987	653	676	37	24	56	41	138	102
GLAMORGANSHIRE	2875	2121	1618	1552	77	77	128	79	270	190
CARMARTHENSHIRE	261	247	171	183	17	7	11	5	25	27
PEMBROKESHIRE	543	379	404	290	31	13	33	6	23	19
CARDIGANSHIRE	195	196	143	167	3	2	11	7	15	8
BRECKNOCKSHIRE	262	258	163	164	15	16	14	11	33	23
RADNORSHIRE	92	136	51	81	8	6	2	4	17	10
MONTGOMERYSHIRE	171	203	115	153	1	6	8	7	13	12
FLINTSHIRE	264	335	150	218	14	13	14	12	28	26
DENBIGHSHIRE	354	383	221	250	19	14	14	20	27	34
MERIONETHSHIRE	115	156	66	197	4	3	2	3	10	4
CARNARVONSHIRE	281	325	191	213	11	12	23	23	13	19
ANGLESEY	208	123	152	96	15	6	5	4	7	1

* The figures in this column relate to the entire County, including that portion situated in the London Registration Division.

Table 12 *continued*.—DISTRIBUTION of the enumerated NATIVES of COUNTIES.

WHERE ENUMERATED.	WHERE BORN.							
	NORTHAMPTONSHIRE.		HUNTINGDONSHIRE.		BEDFORDSHIRE.		CAMBRIDGESHIRE.	
	Males.	Females.	Males.	Females.	Males.	Females.	Males.	Females.
TOTAL ENUMERATED NATIVES OF EACH COUNTY	147006	151392	38574	40731	85567	88418	111259	117995
LONDON	7995	9573	3077	4315	7568	8109	10650	14435
MIDDLESEX (*Intra-metropolitan*)	5786	6981	2177	3159	5561	5991	7390	10342
SURREY (*Intra-metropolitan*)	1767	2067	703	903	1593	1636	2609	3244
KENT (*Intra-metropolitan*)	442	525	197	253	414	482	651	849
SOUTH-EASTERN COUNTIES	3175	3551	953	1200	2461	2523	2890	3699
SURREY (*Extra-metropolitan*)	867	1014	270	372	720	802	823	1188
KENT (*Extra-metropolitan*)	801	846	276	293	702	627	850	939
SUSSEX	610	802	154	235	430	555	543	805
HAMPSHIRE	582	527	174	189	440	353	464	501
BERKSHIRE	315	362	30	91	169	186	210	266
SOUTH-MIDLAND COUNTIES	110727	111856	28578	29307	65891	69622	78648	80529
MIDDLESEX (*Extra-metropolitan*)	843	1031	435	594	1641	1502	1421	1394
HERTFORDSHIRE	474	609	253	340	2620	2692	1013	1353
BUCKINGHAMSHIRE	1451	2044	82	103	1381	1805	178	228
OXFORDSHIRE	1243	1620	51	62	202	203	86	118
NORTHAMPTONSHIRE	104062	102728	2510	2765	2740	2600	1276	1420
HUNTINGDONSHIRE	1177	1523	22396	21654	837	1081	1698	2235
BEDFORDSHIRE	832	1480	844	1424	55667	59019	612	875
CAMBRIDGESHIRE	625	763	2037	2435	633	711	72354	72706
EASTERN COUNTIES	1144	1279	782	876	1035	948	6535	7609
ESSEX	693	704	387	414	771	722	2468	2716
SUFFOLK	195	236	130	133	124	103	1627	2190
NORFOLK	256	339	265	329	140	123	2440	2703
SOUTH-WESTERN COUNTIES	632	682	138	172	357	366	404	486
WILTSHIRE	133	135	36	30	63	60	73	94
DORSETSHIRE	83	97	20	28	47	53	69	48
DEVONSHIRE	219	231	41	78	139	176	147	164
CORNWALL	45	32	10	16	30	19	35	24
SOMERSETSHIRE	152	187	31	40	78	118	80	156
WEST-MIDLAND COUNTIES	6790	7210	511	533	1330	1274	1108	1137
GLOUCESTERSHIRE	420	477	49	68	146	208	164	215
HEREFORDSHIRE	74	71	23	31	31	49	35	49
SHROPSHIRE	143	106	28	19	50	74	44	55
STAFFORDSHIRE	1447	1206	154	125	407	289	311	277
WORCESTERSHIRE	474	495	56	60	134	113	130	128
WARWICKSHIRE	4232	4735	201	230	562	541	424	413
NORTH-MIDLAND COUNTIES	9370	10475	2008	1974	3160	2457	3847	3514
LEICESTERSHIRE	4363	5204	274	393	657	624	407	442
RUTLANDSHIRE	440	699	60	88	34	20	43	70
LINCOLNSHIRE	2151	2426	871	866	597	435	2240	2058
NOTTINGHAMSHIRE	1146	1158	415	417	778	603	672	602
DERBYSHIRE	1270	988	388	300	1094	775	485	342
NORTH-WESTERN COUNTIES	2655	2742	890	906	1107	1061	2715	2847
CHESHIRE	522	552	100	115	211	195	201	255
LANCASHIRE	2133	2190	790	791	896	866	2514	2592
YORKSHIRE	3657	3283	1365	1240	2110	1646	3572	3000
NORTHERN COUNTIES	456	382	201	148	369	263	669	539
DURHAM	273	227	154	108	256	177	504	390
NORTHUMBERLAND	82	70	25	25	71	36	115	98
CUMBERLAND	61	57	11	11	27	38	34	31
WESTMORLAND	40	28	11	4	15	12	16	20
MONMOUTHSHIRE AND WALES	405	359	71	60	179	149	221	200
MONMOUTHSHIRE	69	71	13	6	21	30	36	35
GLAMORGANSHIRE	117	85	18	12	68	50	81	67
CARMARTHENSHIRE	12	13	4	1	5	5	16	6
PEMBROKESHIRE	28	28	5	2	14	7	25	14
CARDIGANSHIRE	16	7	1	2	2	1	4	2
BRECKNOCKSHIRE	23	14	2	10	7	10	5	10
RADNORSHIRE	4	6	4	3	2	.	4	6
MONTGOMERYSHIRE	21	12	2	2	9	1	2	10
FLINTSHIRE	30	39	8	4	7	15	13	15
DENBIGHSHIRE	34	30	8	9	18	11	13	15
MERIONETHSHIRE	18	12	4	1	7	3	4	3
CARNARVONSHIRE	19	36	2	6	10	7	12	10
ANGLESEY	14	7	.	.	9	2	6	7

Table 14.—NUMBER and AGES of MALES and FEMALES returned as BLIND or BLIND FROM BIRTH in the SOUTH-MIDLAND DIVISION and its REGISTRATION COUNTIES.

REGISTRATION COUNTY.	ALL AGES.		0–	5–	15–	20–	25–	45–	65 and upwards.
	Both Sexes.	Males and Females.							
III. SOUTH-MIDLAND COUNTIES.	1434	M. 694	24	46	30	31	121	197	245
		F. 740	15	52	19	28	116	176	334
6 MIDDLESEX (*Extra-metropolitan*)	282	M. 113	3	11	4	6	21	22	46
		F. 169	1	14	1	3	36	41	73
7 HERTFORDSHIRE	187	M. 96	1	4	3	2	21	30	35
		F. 91	2	7	5	3	19	23	32
8 BUCKINGHAMSHIRE	162	M. 80	2	9	6	5	8	28	22
		F. 82	1	2	2	6	7	21	43
9 OXFORDSHIRE	208	M. 110	2	4	8	8	19	33	36
		F. 98	2	6	3	2	14	21	50
10 NORTHAMPTONSHIRE	239	M. 121	8	7	2	5	18	32	49
		F. 118	2	8	4	5	12	27	60
11 HUNTINGDONSHIRE	59	M. 28	1	1	.	2	4	9	11
		F. 31	1	2	1	3	6	4	14
12 BEDFORDSHIRE	127	M. 65	3	4	3	2	12	22	19
		F. 62	3	4	.	3	8	18	26
13 CAMBRIDGESHIRE	170	M. 81	4	6	4	1	18	21	27
		F. 89	3	9	3	3	14	21	36

Table 15.—NUMBER and AGES of MALES and FEMALES returned as BLIND in the SOUTH-MIDLAND DIVISION and its REGISTRATION COUNTIES.

REGISTRATION COUNTY.	ALL AGES.		0–	5–	15–	20–	25–	45–	65 and upwards.
	Both Sexes.	Males and Females.							
III. SOUTH-MIDLAND COUNTIES.	1315	M. 636	16	36	19	23	112	188	242
		F. 679	5	34	17	22	103	171	327
6 MIDDLESEX (*Extra-metropolitan*)	255	M. 102	2	9	3	5	18	19	46
		F. 153	.	6	.	2	33	41	71
7 HERTFORDSHIRE	170	M. 89	.	3	2	1	19	29	35
		F. 81	.	5	5	3	17	22	29
8 BUCKINGHAMSHIRE	147	M. 72	2	8	5	3	7	27	20
		F. 75	.	2	1	4	6	20	42
9 OXFORDSHIRE	195	M. 104	1	3	5	8	18	33	36
		F. 91	.	5	3	1	12	20	50
10 NORTHAMPTONSHIRE	219	M. 110	7	4	1	3	16	30	48
		F. 109	1	4	4	5	10	26	59
11 HUNTINGDONSHIRE	56	M. 27	1	1	.	1	4	9	11
		F. 29	.	2	1	5	5	4	14
12 BEDFORDSHIRE	113	M. 55	.	3	.	1	12	20	19
		F. 58	2	4	.	2	7	17	26
13 CAMBRIDGESHIRE	160	M. 77	3	5	3	1	18	21	26
		F. 83	2	6	3	2	13	21	36

Table 16.—NUMBER and AGES of MALES and FEMALES returned as BLIND FROM BIRTH in the SOUTH-MIDLAND DIVISION and its REGISTRATION COUNTIES.

REGISTRATION COUNTY.	ALL AGES.		0–	5–	15–	20–	25–	45–	65 and upwards.
	Both Sexes.	Males and Females.							
III. SOUTH-MIDLAND COUNTIES.	119	M. 58	8	10	11	8	9	9	3
		F. 61	10	18	2	6	13	5	7
6 MIDDLESEX (*Extra-metropolitan*)	27	M. 11	1	2	1	1	3	3	.
		F. 16	1	8	1	1	3	.	2
7 HERTFORDSHIRE	17	M. 7	1	1	1	1	2	1	.
		F. 10	2	2	.	.	2	1	3
8 BUCKINGHAMSHIRE	15	M. 8	.	1	1	2	1	1	2
		F. 7	1		1	2	1	1	1
9 OXFORDSHIRE	13	M. 6	1	1	3	.	1	.	.
		F. 7	2	1	.	1	2	1	.
10 NORTHAMPTONSHIRE	20	M. 11	1	3	1	2	2	2	.
		F. 9	1	4	.	.	2	1	1
11 HUNTINGDONSHIRE	3	M. 1	.	.	.	1	.	.	.
		F. 2	1	.	.	.	1	.	.
12 BEDFORDSHIRE	14	M. 10	3	1	3	1	.	2	.
		F. 4	1	.	.	1	1	1	.
13 CAMBRIDGESHIRE	10	M. 4	1	1	1	.	.	.	1
		F. 6	1	3	.	1	1	.	.

Table 17.—Number and Ages of Males and Females returned as Deaf and Dumb in the South Midland Division and its Registration Counties.

Registration County.	All Ages. Both Sexes.	All Ages. Males and Females.	0–	5–	15–	20–	25–	45–	65 and upwards.
III. SOUTH-MIDLAND COUNTIES.	823	M. 418	18	91	51	38	114	79	27
		F. 405	13	79	48	42	120	67	36
6 MIDDLESEX (*Extra-metropolitan*)	186	M. 96	4	28	5	9	29	17	4
		F. 90	4	21	7	12	28	9	9
7 HERTFORDSHIRE	125	M. 68	.	9	8	11	22	12	6
		F. 57	3	8	6	4	19	16	1
8 BUCKINGHAMSHIRE	79	M. 29	2	8	4	4	3	6	3
		F. 50	1	9	13	3	12	9	3
9 OXFORDSHIRE	100	M. 52	4	10	6	2	16	12	2
		F. 48	2	9	6	5	16	7	3
10 NORTHAMPTONSHIRE	124	M. 67	5	9	11	5	18	12	7
		F. 57	1	8	5	7	20	8	8
11 HUNTINGDONSHIRE	20	M. 12	.	5	1	2	3	1	.
		F. 8	.	2	2	.	1	2	1
12 BEDFORDSHIRE	79	M. 37	2	8	3	1	11	10	2
		F. 42	.	10	5	7	11	7	2
13 CAMBRIDGESHIRE	110	M. 57	1	14	13	4	12	10	3
		F. 53	2	13	4	4	13	9	8

Table 18.—Number and Ages of Males and Females returned as Idiots or Imbeciles, and Lunatics in the South Midland Division and its Registration Counties.

Registration County.	All Ages. Both Sexes.	All Ages. Males and Females.	0–	5–	15–	20–	25–	45–	65 and upwards.
III. SOUTH MIDLAND COUNTIES.	11536	M. 5148	27	172	222	344	2130	1739	514
		F. 6388	8	135	146	330	2455	2458	856
6 MIDDLESEX (*Extra-metropolitan*)	4652	M. 1941	4	33	44	90	893	735	142
		F. 2711	2	30	42	116	1121	1066	334
7 HERTFORDSHIRE	2288	M. 1041	6	24	40	121	435	298	108
		F. 1247	2	14	20	79	423	488	212
8 BUCKINGHAMSHIRE	641	M. 283	1	16	20	16	109	78	43
		F. 358	.	14	14	18	137	127	48
9 OXFORDSHIRE	828	M. 369	2	20	21	19	117	130	60
		F. 459	.	12	15	26	158	180	68
10 NORTHAMPTONSHIRE	1275	M. 645	9	22	27	43	247	223	74
		F. 630	1	21	17	37	239	240	75
11 HUNTINGDONSHIRE	69	M. 27	1	4	4	3	7	3	5
		F. 42	1	7	1	3	14	12	4
12 BEDFORDSHIRE	1140	M. 537	2	26	36	33	200	183	45
		F. 603	1	17	11	38	241	230	71
13 CAMBRIDGESHIRE	643	M. 305	2	27	31	19	115	80	37
		F. 338	1	20	17	10	122	115	44

Table 19.—Number and Ages of Males and Females returned as Idiots or Imbeciles in the South Midland Division and its Registration Counties.

Registration County.	All Ages. Both Sexes.	All Ages. Males and Females.	0–	5–	15–	20–	25–	45–	65 and upwards.
III. SOUTH MIDLAND COUNTIES.	3032	M. 1521	27	169	185	197	574	265	104
		F. 1511	8	127	102	165	614	382	113
6 MIDDLESEX (*Extra-metropolitan*)	285	M. 150	4	31	27	12	39	18	18
		F. 135	2	28	12	14	28	27	24
7 HERTFORDSHIRE	1080	M. 500	6	24	46	99	237	77	11
		F. 580	2	14	29	72	263	136	19
8 BUCKINGHAMSHIRE	267	M. 136	1	16	18	12	53	22	14
		F. 131	.	14	11	8	58	33	7
9 OXFORDSHIRE	328	M. 162	2	20	21	12	58	33	16
		F. 166	.	11	11	17	64	48	15
10 NORTHAMPTONSHIRE	445	M. 229	9	22	23	26	77	47	25
		F. 216	1	21	16	18	80	60	20
11 HUNTINGDONSHIRE	62	M. 26	1	4	4	3	6	3	5
		F. 36	1	5	1	3	14	9	3
12 BEDFORDSHIRE	305	M. 163	2	26	26	19	53	33	4
		F. 142	1	14	8	20	51	38	10
13 CAMBRIDGESHIRE	310	M. 155	2	26	20	14	49	32	12
		F. 155	1	20	14	13	50	34	17

Table 20.—NUMBER and AGES of MALES and FEMALES returned as LUNATICS in the SOUTH-MIDLAND DIVISION and its REGISTRATION COUNTIES.

REGISTRATION COUNTY.	ALL AGES. Both Sexes.	ALL AGES. Males and Females.	0–	5–	15–	20–	25–	45–	65 and upwards.
III. SOUTH-MIDLAND COUNTIES.	8504	M. 3627	.	3	37	147	1556	1474	410
		F. 4877	.	8	44	165	1841	2076	743
6 MIDDLESEX (*Extra-metropolitan*)	4367	M. - 1791	.	2	17	78	854	717	123
		F. - 2576	.	2	69	102	1063	1030	310
7 HERTFORDSHIRE	1258	M. - 541	.	.	3	22	198	221	97
		F. - 717	.	.	.	7	160	352	198
8 BUCKINGHAMSHIRE	374	M. - 147	.	.	3	4	54	56	31
		F. - 227	.	.	3	10	79	94	41
9 OXFORDSHIRE	500	M. - 207	.	.	.	7	59	97	44
		F. - 293	.	1	4	9	94	135	50
10 NORTHAMPTONSHIRE	830	M. - 416	.	.	4	17	170	176	49
		F. - 414	.	.	1	18	159	180	55
11 HUNTINGDONSHIRE	7	M. - 1	.	.	.	.	1	.	.
		F. 6	.	2	.	.	.	3	1
12 BEDFORDSHIRE	835	M. - 374	.	.	10	14	156	153	41
		F. - 461	.	2	3	12	190	193	61
13 CAMBRIDGESHIRE	333	M. - 150	.	1	1	5	64	54	25
		F. - 183	.	.	3	6	66	81	27

Table 21.—NUMBER of the BLIND, of the DEAF AND DUMB, of IDIOTS or IMBECILES, and of LUNATICS in the SOUTH-MIDLAND DIVISION and its REGISTRATION COUNTIES and DISTRICTS.

Registration County and District.	Blind. From Birth.	Blind. Others.	Blind. Total.	Deaf and Dumb.	Mentally Deranged. Idiots.	Mentally Deranged. Lunatics.	Mentally Deranged. Total.
SOUTH MIDLAND COUNTIES.	119	1315	1434	823	3032	8504	11536
MIDDLESEX (*Extra-metropolitan*)	27	255	282	186	285	4367	4652
HERTFORDSHIRE	17	170	187	125	1030	1258	2288
BUCKINGHAMSHIRE	15	147	162	79	267	374	641
OXFORDSHIRE	13	195	208	100	328	500	828
NORTHAMPTONSHIRE	20	219	239	124	445	830	1275
HUNTINGDONSHIRE	3	56	59	20	62	7	69
BEDFORDSHIRE	14	113	127	79	305	835	1140
CAMBRIDGESHIRE	10	160	170	116	310	333	643
6 MIDDLESEX (*Extra-metropolitan*).							
124 STAINES	1	15	16	16	22	21	43
125 UXBRIDGE	3	43	46	15	52	1934	1986
126 BRENTFORD	7	54	61	49	57	327	384
127 HENDON	4	30	34	36	31	16	47
128 BARNET	4	28	32	20	42	2154	2196
129 EDMONTON	8	85	93	60	81	15	96
7 HERTFORDSHIRE.							
130 WARE	2	12	14	9	29	2	31
131 BISHOP STORTFORD	1	22	23	11	32	16	48
132 ROYSTON	3	11	14	16	43	1	44
133 HITCHIN	2	21	23	18	45	2	47
134 HERTFORD	3	19	22	6	25	.	25
135 HATFIELD	1	3	4	2	8	1	9
136 ST. ALBANS	.	13	13	12	28	5	33
137 WATFORD	4	41	45	42	795	1227	2022
138 HEMEL HEMPSTEAD	1	16	17	4	16	.	16
139 BERKHAMPSTEAD	.	12	12	5	15	4	19

Table 21 *continued*.—NUMBER of the BLIND, of the DEAF AND DUMB, of IDIOTS or IMBECILES, an[d] LUNATICS in the SOUTH-MIDLAND DIVISION and its REGISTRATION COUNTIES and DISTRICTS.

Registration County and District.	Blind.			Deaf and Dumb.	Mentally Deranged.		
	From Birth.	Others.	Total.		Idiots.	Lunatics.	Total.
8 BUCKINGHAMSHIRE.							
140 AMERSHAM	2	17	19	10	30	1	31
141 ETON	1	27	28	10	26	1	27
142 WYCOMBE	6	28	34	23	50	4	54
143 AYLESBURY	2	26	28	8	93	364	457
144 WINSLOW	2	6	8	6	12	1	13
145 NEWPORT PAGNELL	1	30	31	12	41	1	42
146 BUCKINGHAM	1	13	14	10	15	2	17
9 OXFORDSHIRE.							
147 HENLEY	1	14	15	10	27	1	28
148 THAME	4	17	21	12	36	3	39
149 HEADINGTON	.	35	35	10	114	484	598
150 OXFORD	2	23	25	8	8	2	10
151 BICESTER	1	14	15	9	23	.	23
152 WOODSTOCK	1	17	18	6	33	.	33
153 WITNEY	3	25	28	19	18	4	22
154 CHIPPING NORTON	1	26	27	6	23	4	27
155 BANBURY	.	24	24	20	46	2	48
10 NORTHAMPTONSHIRE.							
156 BRACKLEY	1	12	13	5	9	2	11
157 TOWCESTER	3	18	21	7	21	3	24
158 POTTERSPURY	.	8	8	10	13	6	19
159 HARDINGSTONE	1	5	5	5	17	1	18
160 NORTHAMPTON	5	54	59	35	162	785	947
161 DAVENTRY	1	11	12	12	23	8	31
162 BRIXWORTH	.	18	18	4	33	19	52
163 WELLINGBOROUGH	.	20	20	16	37	3	40
164 KETTERING	1	21	22	10	28	.	28
165 THRAPSTON		13	13	6	24	1	25
166 OUNDLE	.	15	15	7	31	1	32
167 PETERBOROUGH	8	24	32	7	47	1	48

Registration County and District.	Blind.			Deaf and Dumb.	Me[ntally] De[ranged].	
	From Birth.	Others.	Total.		Idiots.	
11 HUNTINGDONSHIRE.						
168 HUNTINGDON	1	18	20	7	17	
169 ST. IVES	2	20	22	6	26	
170 ST. NEOTS	.	18	18	7	19	
12 BEDFORDSHIRE.						
171 BEDFORD	5	31	36	20	40	
172 BIGGLESWADE	3	29	32	16	165	7
173 AMPTHILL	4	10	14	9	29	
174 WOBURN	1	4	5	10	15	
175 LEIGHTON BUZZARD	.	8	8	11	26	
176 LUTON	1	31	32	13	80	
13 CAMBRIDGESHIRE.						
177 CAXTON	.	8	6	9	15	
178 CHESTERTON	4	17	21	14	67	31[illegible]
179 CAMBRIDGE	1	39	40	18	26	[illegible]
180 LINTON	.	8	8	9	28	
181 NEWMARKET	1	23	24	26	54	
182 ELY	2	26	28	14	35	[illegible]
183 NORTH WITCHFORD	.	8	8	6	30	1
184 WHITTLESEY	.	9	9	2	8	[illegible]
185 WISBECH	2	24	26	12	51	4

AGES,

CONDITION AS TO MARRIAGE,

OCCUPATIONS, AND BIRTH-PLACES

OF THE PEOPLE;

WITH THE

NUMBERS AND AGES OF THE BLIND, DEAF AND DUMB
IDIOTS OR IMBECILES, AND LUNATICS.

DIVISION IV.—EASTERN COUNTIES;

ESSEX,
SUFFOLK,
NORFOLK.

TABLES IN DIVISION IV.—EASTERN COUNTIES.

AGES.

Table

1.—AGES of MALES and FEMALES in the EASTERN DIVISION and its REGISTRATION COUNTIES.

2.—AGES of MALES and FEMALES in REGISTRATION DISTRICTS.

3.—AGES of MALES and FEMALES in REGISTRATION SUB-DISTRICTS.

4.—MALE and FEMALE CHILDREN at *each Year of Age* under 5 in the EASTERN DIVISION and its REGI COUNTIES.

5.—MALE and FEMALE CHILDREN at *each Year of Age* under 5 in REGISTRATION DISTRICTS.

6.—AGES of MALES and FEMALES in SANITARY DISTRICTS.

CONDITION AS TO MARRIAGE.

7.—CONDITION as to MARRIAGE and AGES of MALES and FEMALES in the EASTERN DIVISION and its REG COUNTIES.

8.—CONDITION as to MARRIAGE and AGES of MALES and FEMALES in REGISTRATION DISTRICTS.

9.—CONDITION as to MARRIAGE and AGES of MALES and FEMALES in each URBAN SANITARY DISTRICT the POPULATION exceeds 50,000 PERSONS.

OCCUPATIONS.

10.—OCCUPATIONS of MALES and FEMALES in the EASTERN DIVISION and its REGISTRATION COUNTIES, an URBAN SANITARY DISTRICT of which the POPULATION exceeds 50,000 PERSONS.

BIRTH-PLACES.

11.—BIRTH-PLACES of MALES and FEMALES enumerated in COUNTIES, and in each URBAN SANITARY D which the POPULATION exceeds 50,000 PERSONS.

12.—DISTRIBUTION of the enumerated NATIVES of COUNTIES.

13.—NUMBER and COUNTRY of BIRTH of FOREIGNERS enumerated in COUNTIES, and in each URBAN DISTRICT of which the POPULATION exceeds 50,000 PERSONS.

THE BLIND, DEAF AND DUMB, IDIOTS OR IMBECILES, AND LUNATICS.

14.—NUMBER and AGES of MALES and FEMALES returned as BLIND or BLIND from BIRTH in the EASTERN and its REGISTRATION COUNTIES.

15.—NUMBER and AGES of MALES and FEMALES returned as BLIND in the EASTERN DIVISION and its REGI COUNTIES.

16.—NUMBER and AGES of MALES and FEMALES returned as BLIND from BIRTH in the EASTERN DIVISI REGISTRATION COUNTIES.

17.—NUMBER and AGES of MALES and FEMALES returned as DEAF and DUMB in the EASTERN DIVISIO REGISTRATION COUNTIES.

18.—NUMBER and AGES of MALES and FEMALES returned as IDIOTS or IMBECILES, and LUNATICS in the DIVISION and its REGISTRATION COUNTIES.

19.—NUMBER and AGES of MALES and FEMALES returned as IDIOTS or IMBECILES in the EASTERN DIVI its REGISTRATION COUNTIES.

20.—NUMBER and AGES of MALES and FEMALES returned as LUNATICS in the EASTERN DIVISION and i TRATION COUNTIES.

21.—NUMBER of the BLIND, of the DEAF and DUMB, of IDIOTS or IMBECILES, and of LUNATICS in the DIVISION and its REGISTRATION COUNTIES and DISTRICTS.

AGES.

DIVISION IV.—EASTERN COUNTIES.

Table 1.—Ages of Males and Females in the Eastern Division and its Registration Counties.

Registration County.	All Ages. Persons.		All Ages. Males and Females.	Under 5* Years.	5–	10–	15–	20–	25–	30–	35–	40–	–	50–	55–	60–	65–	70–	75–	80–	85–	90–	95–	100 and upw
V. EASTERN COUNTIES.	1343524	M.	660710	90676	83864	77832	65880	51606	45220	39094	35646	32615	28404	27044	22901	22005	16042	11418	7347	3748	1128	205	40	5
		F.	682814	90468	84672	75440	60890	53736	47705	42010	38890	35811	31458	29200	24562	23407	17098	12410	8273	4387	1556	463	70	2
ESSEX	552268	M.	276176	39256	36000	33300	26973	21664	19200	17569	16003	14311	11634	10420	8634	8065	5605	3775	2263	1125	306	65	9	1
		F.	276092	39214	36318	31571	24060	21536	20920	18272	16289	14557	12068	10758	8528	8305	5798	4060	2574	1301	484	114	14	1
SUFFOLK	353545	M.	172728	23565	22158	20499	17497	12954	10606	9649	8746	8039	7466	7317	6261	6200	4653	3460	2182	1126	368	50	13	—
		F.	180817	23463	22251	20133	16246	14036	12147	10903	9726	9311	8501	7928	6788	6598	4949	3575	2311	1287	480	134	20	—
NORFOLK	437711	M.	211806	27356	25606	24123	21410	16988	13414	11876	10897	10265	9304	9607	8006	7740	5784	4183	2962	1497	455	81	18	4
		F.	225905	27791	25073	23745	20593	18164	15536	13455	12575	11943	10880	10604	8946	8564	6351	4775	3388	1799	648	155	36	1

Note.—Registration Counties consist of groups of Registration Districts, which are generally co-extensive with the Poor Law Unions. Those Registration Districts which extend into two or more Counties, are included in that Registration County in which the principal town of the District, or the greater part of the population is located. The boundaries of Registration Counties, therefore, differ more or less from the boundaries of Counties. For such differences in Division IV., see Vol. II Table 11.

* For the Number of Children at each Year of Age under 5, see Table 4.

† Two of these Males were stated to be 100, two 101, and one 111 years of age. One of these Females was stated to be 103, and one 105 years of age.

Table 2.—Ages of Males and Females in Registration Districts.

Registration District.	All Ages. Persons.		All Ages. Males and Females.	Under 5* Years.	5–	10–	15–	20–	25–	30–	35–	40–	45–	50–	55–	60–	65–	70–	75–	80–	85–	90–	95–	100 and upw
14. ESSEX.																								
86 WEST HAM	200958	M.	100208	15979	13943	11864	8875	8151	8158	7466	6528	5483	3952	3264	2365	1837	1083	706	343	166	25	9	3	1
		F.	100750	15823	13656	11377	8887	8350	8287	7675	6357	5410	3864	3306	2435	2225	1394	911	557	243	73	26	3	1
87 EPPING	21754	M.	10703	1383	1376	1303	1089	836	630	606	605	572	509	437	370	374	251	171	110	56	21	4		.
		F.	11051	1395	1375	1246	1028	914	724	697	649	605	538	463	408	348	273	185	109	67	21	5	1	.
88 ONGAR	10671	M.	5529	642	712	740	547	384	327	326	266	284	262	238	203	203	170	131	63	37	11	8		.
		F.	5142	727	691	614	397	334	340	276	281	263	255	214	179	198	135	116	76	30	15	2	1	.
89 ROMFORD	37050	M.	18185	2093	2373	2146	1836	1561	1271	1068	1084	948	767	669	524	521	331	200	157	78	17	1	.	.
		F.	18865	2640	2645	2361	1692	1505	1294	1139	1115	980	802	710	546	516	358	278	149	92	33	8	.	.
90 ORSETT	16480	M.	9309	1205	993	1496	1125	765	647	537	433	469	386	328	256	259	170	128	73	28	9	2	.	.
		F.	7171	1173	1007	830	530	632	478	497	429	350	313	266	231	210	147	86	55	22	9	2	1	.
91 BILLERICAY	18331	M.	9176	1006	1151	1200	990	703	544	598	492	485	380	364	311	319	227	170	116	35	18	5	2	.
		F.	9155	1197	1166	1034	763	714	675	599	546	487	403	413	291	303	219	151	99	70	16	6	1	.
92 CHELMSFORD	32971	M.	16406	2249	2075	2010	1621	1134	947	901	837	820	752	674	656	632	462	300	203	103	34	2	.	.
		F.	16565	2083	2037	1849	1428	1201	1112	1021	984	844	792	755	645	622	487	319	230	108	44	13	1	.
93 ROCHFORD	24406	M.	12696	1712	1621	1314	1216	1163	1025	848	778	727	560	489	402	362	209	195	98	50	10	1	.	.
		F.	11710	1762	1520	1422	1044	943	893	730	653	626	473	454	354	352	231	167	98	57	13	6	3	.
94 MALDON	23812	M.	12026	1690	1614	1517	1270	726	621	606	613	564	635	463	475	457	412	238	135	65	19	6	.	.
		F.	11786	1657	1647	1402	950	752	740	639	638	605	593	431	489	433	329	213	142	56	19	2	.	.
95 TENDRING	33475	M.	17185	2222	2119	1949	1675	1395	1136	987	975	868	780	729	642	628	447	296	204	100	28	4	.	.
		F.	16290	2266	2132	1853	1371	1096	1030	1008	921	868	791	687	641	575	427	291	196	95	37	6	.	.
96 COLCHESTER	28374	M.	13922	1790	1460	1406	1018	1585	1236	945	805	695	531	501	373	389	218	196	92	60	20	4	.	.
		F.	14452	1759	1649	1620	1523	1385	1179	962	875	723	604	590	478	452	291	221	130	86	20	6	.	.
97 LEXDEN	21775	M.	10933	1509	1501	1378	1098	721	544	573	635	507	463	484	397	424	319	229	136	75	25	10	2	.
		F.	10842	1455	1415	1269	851	757	658	658	596	584	535	483	414	390	299	222	144	72	23	8	.	.
98 HALSTEAD	17005	M.	7896	1013	1035	988	785	496	375	437	402	378	363	390	345	342	218	152	111	58	8	1	.	.
		F.	9109	1008	1075	1053	877	724	623	548	496	500	464	427	380	354	228	187	101	56	20	7	1	.
99 BRAINTREE	28628	M.	13602	1805	1740	1630	1344	921	722	782	630	674	624	583	572	567	420	270	165	77	21	4	1	.
		F.	15026	1837	1887	1682	1332	1128	989	864	793	794	750	680	594	563	453	322	208	101	48	5	.	.
100 DUNMOW	17990	M.	9200	1120	1183	1201	961	606	409	416	505	421	305	418	385	384	296	208	119	72	16	3	1	.
		F.	8790	1173	1159	1084	631	643	619	475	463	428	463	443	383	385	204	196	143	81	22	5	.	.
101 SAFFRON WALDEN	18588	M.	9200	1168	1204	1168	923	657	522	479	466	418	385	389	366	357	286	190	135	65	17	6	.	.
		F.	9388	1260	1257	1045	753	658	569	524	488	484	446	427	361	370	283	204	147	66	28	9	2	.

Note.—The Registration Districts of Division IV. are co-extensive with the Poor Law Unions of the same name. The Bury St. Edmund's District (206), Mutford (218), Flegg (220), and Forehoe (226), are Incorporations under Local Acts.

For the Parishes comprised in each Registration District, see Vol. II., Division IV., Table 4.

The Districts are arranged topographically under the Registration Counties, and are numbered consecutively, commencing with the Metropolitan District Division I.

* For the Number of Children at each Year of Age under 5, see Table 5.

Table 2 *continued*.—AGES of MALES and FEMALES in REGISTRATION DISTRICTS.

REGISTRATION DISTRICT.	ALL AGES. Persons.		ALL AGES. Males and Females.	Under 5 Years.	5–	10–	15–	20–	25–	30–	35–	40–	45–	50–	55–	60–	65–	70–	75–	80–	85–	90–
15. SUFFOLK.																						
202 RISBRIDGE	17234	M.	8448	1227	1159	1083	880	565	473	404	398	360	353	341	308	302	225	177	108	57	12	2
		F.	8786	1206	1157	1053	791	675	529	505	459	353	428	361	336	347	190	170	103	52	24	5
203 SUDBURY	30155	M.	14702	1902	1984	1742	1535	1021	783	777	712	677	702	675	591	643	401	310	200	111	33	3
		F.	15453	1933	1909	1753	1399	1147	1020	890	805	872	791	682	642	844	482	291	178	103	61	10
204 COSFORD	15820	M.	7801	1018	952	900	794	573	458	409	358	350	378	361	326	277	250	195	114	66	23	1
		F.	8019	1024	1026	981	703	592	501	449	367	416	400	365	329	284	233	197	116	57	21	6
205 THINGOE	16386	M.	8195	1065	1090	951	855	526	479	451	431	377	346	374	333	309	255	171	139	54	23	3
		F.	8191	1114	1036	909	638	650	505	490	419	464	373	385	323	326	261	185	110	73	20	9
206 BURY ST. EDMUND'S	16111	M.	7574	964	985	880	911	647	530	466	428	360	298	275	240	226	169	144	62	23	5	4
		F.	8537	996	916	967	909	740	648	552	613	439	374	353	277	284	223	107	108	62	17	4
207 MILDENHALL	8957	M.	4447	622	694	499	481	326	265	235	251	184	183	185	182	178	123	99	55	40	13	2
		F.	4510	664	593	514	349	311	290	248	258	217	203	185	166	187	129	97	65	30	9	2
208 STOW	20195	M.	9870	1348	1312	1136	965	702	548	575	478	478	428	430	371	390	259	211	197	83	22	2
		F.	10325	1396	1359	1212	806	743	646	597	541	514	481	465	386	403	282	189	151	77	28	7
209 HARTISMERE	15791	M.	7974	1082	1032	1028	789	540	508	429	326	356	342	348	313	326	240	197	127	65	23	2
		F.	7817	1094	1033	919	632	559	470	466	387	372	386	339	331	316	228	176	109	67	25	7
210 HOXNE	12601	M.	6365	833	790	767	684	470	351	348	254	279	271	269	236	269	196	164	115	55	23	5
		F.	6240	845	808	743	607	438	333	325	290	301	312	276	241	298	170	150	105	52	25	8
211 BOSMERE	15402	M.	7796	963	961	906	733	680	581	363	396	369	369	346	278	310	217	184	91	64	14	1
		F.	7606	1045	994	886	600	550	446	429	400	389	376	339	309	258	218	157	107	65	20	9
212 SAMFORD	11598	M.	5832	766	716	672	686	406	332	279	313	286	249	308	260	245	136	111	88	30	14	2
		F.	5766	763	687	646	449	397	367	326	312	329	223	280	274	206	177	117	86	46	14	2
213 IPSWICH	50320	M.	23608	3287	2909	2612	2318	1982	1826	1537	1376	1144	1048	966	775	758	456	329	179	87	30	4
		F.	26712	3129	2654	2827	2773	2474	2087	1800	1533	1396	1268	1197	897	858	642	417	254	142	51	10
214 WOODBRIDGE	22745	M.	11203	1492	1410	1364	1075	706	618	600	563	543	506	473	461	480	340	259	180	91	34	7
		F.	11542	1401	1379	1233	956	854	761	678	657	603	557	533	479	470	330	256	165	95	35	18
215 PLOMESGATE	20479	M.	10161	1330	1234	1325	1029	760	646	556	489	440	472	397	382	365	326	237	162	89	26	9
		F.	10318	1298	1288	1079	954	783	654	622	540	533	484	447	406	409	322	227	172	96	33	12
216 BLYTHING	25817	M.	12677	1735	1677	1530	1167	892	739	694	621	683	567	566	423	462	403	276	214	95	43	9
		F.	13140	1714	1711	1469	1071	941	844	786	700	628	593	588	501	526	408	307	196	98	47	12
217 WANGFORD	14466	M.	7028	961	906	881	664	556	486	365	367	346	310	280	220	255	214	150	87	43	13	1
		F.	7438	968	883	819	701	660	470	425	427	371	338	311	281	280	242	148	98	65	33	5
218 MUTFORD	39478	M.	19057	2961	2488	2083	2081	1700	1339	1178	1003	878	677	733	802	609	384	255	127	77	18	2
		F.	20421	2854	2589	2179	1959	1754	1562	1320	1129	1065	874	824	609	603	448	325	184	106	29	18
16. NORFOLK.																						
219 YARMOUTH	37151	M.	17459	2338	1962	1867	1927	1666	1179	1106	1036	935	775	746	560	520	365	237	147	74	18	5
		F.	19692	2302	2017	1796	2053	1838	1518	1299	1218	1091	936	937	721	715	473	354	221	135	58	7
220 FLEGG	9714	M.	4778	653	660	553	475	330	282	253	245	212	211	206	188	170	136	108	63	32	10	3
		F.	4936	685	637	515	419	408	341	284	258	242	229	212	187	163	127	96	70	38	18	7
221 SMALLBURGH	14348	M.	7139	947	876	850	692	527	436	309	403	319	298	321	268	260	203	173	114	68	18	6
		F.	7209	953	914	776	592	500	455	419	397	404	344	362	288	251	204	140	114	65	25	6
222 ERPINGHAM	20239	M.	9931	1262	1201	1183	1008	709	580	556	442	440	447	457	303	390	287	248	162	77	28	6
		F.	10308	1299	1148	1083	903	790	698	589	544	523	504	571	416	428	323	247	155	96	43	7
223 AYLSHAM	18057	M.	8972	1135	1125	1021	977	729	521	460	412	427	407	392	385	329	249	203	133	79	23	3
		F.	9085	1161	1072	1013	783	653	591	467	484	491	452	410	396	329	204	246	156	78	29	9
224 ST. FAITH'S	11418	M.	5600	757	675	620	581	458	358	293	270	279	246	282	158	204	172	106	87	42	9	2
		F.	5818	789	714	587	489	480	330	323	310	348	294	274	224	218	172	125	94	48	13	5
225 NORWICH	87842	M.	40288	5438	4784	4601	4095	3548	2953	2546	2215	1938	1787	1765	1417	1236	818	590	425	156	56	10
		F.	47554	5630	4989	4724	5001	4550	3604	3062	2700	2491	2203	2236	1770	1563	1166	864	617	325	92	23
226 FOREHOE	11971	M.	5937	748	785	671	599	461	337	280	288	290	284	265	236	236	174	127	108	60	17	1
		F.	6034	724	727	659	603	429	380	345	317	359	293	293	248	240	195	134	100	58	21	3
227 HENSTEAD	10636	M.	5278	696	634	587	530	437	353	262	254	246	210	245	218	200	169	128	97	47	14	2
		F.	5358	666	612	542	455	440	373	308	280	267	252	272	207	215	167	146	95	50	10	2
228 BLOFIELD	11618	M.	5647	666	694	608	516	478	375	303	206	294	261	264	237	225	170	125	82	51	17	1
		F.	5971	745	639	589	465	462	413	380	341	384	313	349	231	261	171	121	99	46	16	5
229 LODDON	13702	M.	6687	911	860	802	566	465	366	378	310	312	296	315	204	273	193	169	115	67	15	2
		F.	7015	892	960	748	561	614	467	390	339	383	273	358	302	248	229	146	100	61	20	2
230 DEPWADE	23582	M.	11445	1488	1452	1332	1128	840	631	615	565	537	479	535	461	462	386	249	179	104	23	7
		F.	12137	1512	1488	1415	1112	831	732	672	626	598	595	537	485	436	382	318	192	104	43	9
231 GUILTCROSS	10563	M.	5305	700	625	624	559	392	298	272	242	254	245	219	204	217	168	135	79	40	21	3
		F.	5258	632	694	585	482	357	327	286	306	271	267	248	235	214	165	106	87	58	21	7
232 WAYLAND	10716	M.	5351	702	644	583	563	396	294	278	255	250	247	248	219	231	206	103	72	40	15	3
		F.	5365	634	619	598	436	361	340	302	311	306	281	244	230	253	175	123	76	42	10	8
233 MITFORD	27367	M.	13590	1798	1627	1548	1386	1040	829	734	678	617	574	619	538	558	398	271	218	108	38	5
		F.	13777	1692	1626	1507	1167	1002	808	806	713	795	687	627	645	595	405	338	230	137	52	7
234 WALSINGHAM	19943	M.	9797	1267	1197	1102	991	801	620	482	481	480	448	418	374	382	266	219	162	88	31	3
		F.	10146	1268	1155	1110	877	769	668	552	550	555	480	456	440	397	316	226	184	76	25	11
235 DOCKING	17510	M.	8633	1131	1077	1004	915	611	448	459	417	454	412	365	340	312	270	185	146	61	14	3
		F.	8877	1062	1075	980	749	641	554	497	504	510	442	411	387	338	258	206	153	71	31	7
236 FREEBRIDGE LYNN	12235	M.	6053	778	735	683	630	479	383	328	331	289	248	253	248	221	184	122	84	49	17	1
		F.	6182	806	790	687	520	398	482	347	356	322	320	289	245	215	158	138	89	48	24	10
237 KING'S LYNN	19256	M.	9180	1202	1029	948	938	795	736	698	518	409	370	356	326	298	223	176	91	44	13	.
		F.	10076	1168	1077	957	993	900	787	650	593	497	447	470	364	403	268	228	164	87	25	4
238 DOWNHAM	19404	M.	9685	1190	1174	1225	1017	691	590	511	486	493	413	423	354	407	297	185	125	70	26	6
		F.	9719	1282	1164	1148	806	707	620	561	528	487	481	455	388	421	263	171	138	67	27	12
239 SWAFFHAM	12859	M.	6294	814	796	715	686	439	372	354	281	307	311	246	225	281	180	149	96	46	14	4
		F.	6565	859	819	721	577	467	398	370	386	338	291	305	263	262	200	147	116	42	20	5
240 THETFORD	17630	M.	8807	1230	1142	1001	821	621	464	459	483	415	390	397	366	319	281	187	123	66	18	5
		F.	8823	1087	1136	1006	721	649	561	542	493	465	405	384	375	346	271	187	132	67	22	4

Table 3.—Ages of Males and Females in Registration Sub-Districts.

Registration Sub-District.	All Ages. Persons.	All Ages. Males and Females.	Under 5 Years	5–	10–	15–	20–	25–	30–	35–	40–	45–	50–	55–	60–	65–	70–	75–	80–	85–	90–	95–	100 and upw^ds^.
14 ESSEX.																							
186 WEST HAM.																							
ratford	33606	M. - 19480	3114	2436	1988	1806	1940	1816	1468	1240	1026	692	660	487	372	207	126	63	27	6	1		
		F. - 19126	3110	2429	1964	1680	1698	1655	1406	1209	939	734	671	519	456	252	167	84	49	12	5		
est Ham. (ws². H.R¹.)	101053	M. - 51869	8320	7246	6287	4580	4075	4214	3908	3518	3048	2148	1724	1114	812	456	264	115	63	4	3	1	
		F. - 49194	8239	7087	6653	4045	3874	4042	3738	3304	2707	1904	1609	1068	838	595	382	240	70	25	7	2	
eyton. (W. ws. L².)	32430	M. - 15374	2380	2402	2101	1246	1071	1030	1034	931	734	664	462	386	378	264	106	100	68	8	3		
		F. - 17056	2225	2287	2077	1797	1542	1279	1256	1012	894	584	536	445	423	288	208	155	54	22	5	1	
'althamstow. (H.²R.)	28869	M. - 13495	2186	1859	1578	1248	1065	1098	976	833	674	548	418	318	280	184	111	66	35	7	2	2	1
		F. - 15374	2239	1832	1681	1470	1436	1311	1065	952	770	582	531	403	408	259	172	118	64	14	5		1
187 EPPING.																							
higwell. (H.)	10544	M. - 4991	680	639	686	502	396	308	313	295	269	249	206	185	174	96	58	42	17	8	1		
		F. - 5553	734	640	597	587	627	419	376	320	292	258	222	173	147	117	66	45	26	8			
pping. (W.H.)	5564	M. - 2812	349	349	368	257	210	164	138	138	163	138	111	107	110	72	69	36	26	7			
		F. - 2752	356	366	305	223	200	153	170	157	157	135	125	125	82	77	65	30	24	6	1	1	
arlow	5646	M. - 2900	354	368	359	330	230	168	165	172	150	122	121	108	90	83	46	32	13	6	3		
		F. - 2746	311	369	344	218	187	182	161	172	156	145	118	110	119	79	55	34	17	7	4		
188 ONGAR.																							
obbingworth	5027	M. - 2565	331	333	315	268	165	154	148	128	122	110	118	92	163	76	68	32	16	4	1		
		F. - 2462	267	244	307	175	164	140	130	128	120	129	94	90	87	70	53	40	13	9	1	1	
hipping Ongar. (W.)	5644	M. - 2964	311	379	425	279	209	173	178	137	162	162	120	111	100	94	73	31	21	7	2		
		F. - 2680	360	347	307	222	170	151	140	153	143	135	120	80	111	65	43	36	17	4	1		
189 ROMFORD.																							
omford. (W.)	12898	M. - 6401	934	816	719	608	541	422	390	394	325	265	252	209	198	126	65	73	38	7	1		
		F. - 6497	875	871	774	558	511	430	429	397	325	274	275	216	202	140	117	56	34	8	5		
ford	7645	M. - 3650	543	526	438	389	298	239	229	202	189	155	136	98	96	63	27	34	10	3			
		F. - 3995	529	660	644	334	267	259	220	222	194	168	133	107	97	61	51	35	13	10	1		
arking Town	9203	M. - 4462	723	572	632	467	398	358	284	287	229	184	145	101	97	56	27	17	14	1			
		F. - 4741	700	624	562	493	468	341	380	283	256	220	142	112	101	63	45	26	18	8			
ornchurch. (B².)	7304	M. - 3672	493	459	457	372	289	252	196	201	205	185	136	116	130	86	61	33	16	6			
		F. - 3632	536	490	381	307	309	264	210	213	211	141	160	110	116	94	62	32	27	7	2		
190 ORSETT.																							
rays. (R⁴.B.)	10485	M. - 5871	786	814	1097	816	496	423	343	265	267	229	189	122	119	85	62	29	10	1	2		
		F. - 4614	781	640	633	331	373	311	305	207	227	196	153	117	121	74	41	28	10	6	2	1	
rsett. (W.B².)	5995	M. - 3338	419	379	399	309	209	224	194	168	202	157	139	124	140	86	60	44	18	8			
		F. - 2657	392	367	306	199	159	167	192	162	123	118	113	114	89	73	39	20	12	3			
191 BILLERICAY.																							
rentwood. (W.S. L.R.B.)	11909	M. - 5946	686	748	795	706	493	379	408	329	309	238	215	188	169	129	93	46	10	10	2	1	
		F. - 5963	724	700	685	545	503	477	400	370	314	270	273	180	192	138	95	52	40	7	4		
reat Burstead. (W.)	4711	M. - 2341	265	297	306	204	158	115	135	116	117	101	114	80	121	70	60	56	17	7	1	1	
		F. - 2370	348	339	260	165	164	143	161	129	123	100	105	73	87	61	43	39	27	6	1	1	
ickford	1711	M. - 895	135	100	99	80	52	50	55	47	59	41	35	43	29	28	17	14	2	1	2		
		F. - 816	125	127	89	56	57	55	38	47	56	33	35	53	24	20	13	8	3	3			
192 CHELMSFORD.																							
ngatestone	6016	M. - 3114	427	421	374	294	192	169	191	123	171	138	130	128	117	101	65	45	23	9			
		F. - 2902	365	357	349	240	182	182	188	161	147	143	147	115	108	90	60	34	18	8	2		
helmsford. (W. H.R.)	10185	M. - 4846	678	674	619	504	347	322	256	259	226	236	175	183	166	122	85	64	30		2		
		F. - 5339	654	600	553	630	424	394	333	318	221	251	211	197	205	141	101	56	37	16	7	1	
rittle	4959	M. - 2512	360	342	323	235	186	129	124	132	131	123	116	88	87	72	60	19	11	5			
		F. - 2447	318	347	250	182	186	153	143	148	114	115	114	83	96	69	30	36	10	6	2		
reat Waltham	5243	M. - 2649	366	339	314	264	167	129	124	145	128	134	114	115	129	74	49	34	18	8			
		F. - 2594	339	360	312	179	164	155	167	161	121	130	120	124	91	73	58	35	17	7	1		
reat Baddow (P.)	6508	M. - 3285	428	308	380	334	242	198	206	172	164	181	140	136	134	93	61	41	21	5			
		F. - 3223	404	383	355	277	245	228	200	196	171	148	163	126	122	114	61	69	20	10	1		
193 ROCHFORD.																							
ayleigh	4887	M. - 2597	348	334	314	257	184	130	135	134	162	129	114	97	92	71	65	24	9	4			
		F. - 2290	346	345	255	180	153	122	142	124	144	118	89	68	81	68	49	27	16	4			
rittlewell. (H.)	10510	M. - 5132	671	683	507	633	460	444	387	335	271	243	207	103	120	102	68	38	14	3			
		F. - 5378	734	600	655	575	404	406	340	291	297	217	221	163	163	95	66	41	21	5	2	3	
ochford. (W.)	3881	M. - 2030	279	273	227	184	161	140	98	123	104	73	80	71	84	67	51	26	16	3	1		
		F. - 1851	282	248	241	162	126	94	109	115	98	72	76	63	60	45	34	20	12	3	2		
reat Wakering. (B.)	5128	M. - 2967	428	331	266	243	309	293	248	186	190	105	88	71	67	59	26	11	11	6			
		F. - 2161	400	327	271	167	170	181	140	123	97	66	58	60	48	33	19	10	9	1	1		
194 MALDON.																							
outhminster	4680	M. - 2387	358	304	305	251	153	136	104	119	96	105	99	96	93	80	51	23	10	3	1		
		F. - 2293	351	325	259	168	151	142	132	107	103	117	87	100	90	60	50	36	14	2			
radwell	2690	M. - 1375	206	185	185	143	83	60	61	58	71	61	60	48	57	46	30	8	10	3	1		
		F. - 1315	193	190	183	106	67	78	77	58	76	58	43	43	66	23	20	18	8	4			
ll Saints. (W.)	4387	M. - 2287	275	294	286	215	147	119	124	126	102	100	86	89	87	108	69	44	17	3			
		F. - 2100	273	256	218	204	150	129	124	109	124	105	91	89	87	62	44	23	8	3	1		
. Peter. (W.)	8464	M. - 4164	558	582	504	457	256	236	232	220	104	198	154	164	162	114	65	42	16	9	2		
		F. - 4300	581	603	524	341	279	270	263	262	213	228	156	181	159	114	70	63	13	9	1		
ollesbury	3591	M. - 1813	294	249	238	204	87	71	85	90	101	71	64	78	59	64	26	18	12	1	2		
		F. - 1778	259	264	218	131	105	121	103	112	89	86	54	76	81	56	29	12	12	1			

ote.—For the Parishes comprised in each Registration Sub-District, see Vol. II., Division IV., Table 4. (W.) denotes that a Workhouse, and (WS.) that a Workhouse School belonging to the district is situated within the Sub-district, (w.) denotes a Workhouse and (ws.) a Workhouse School not belonging to the district. (H.) a Hospital or Infirmary, (L.) a Lunatic Asylum, (P.) a Prison or Convict Establishment, (R.) a certified Reformatory or Industrial School, (B.) Barracks, &c., (S.) H.M. Ships. A figure appended to any of these letters denotes the number of institutions of a similar class situated within the Sub-district. The names of the Institutions thus indicated, and the number of inmates enumerated therein, will be found in Vol. II., Division IV., Table 6.

Table 3 *continued*.—Ages of Males and Females in Registration Sub-Districts.

Registration Sub-District	All Ages: Persons		All Ages: Males and Females	Under 5 Years	5-	10-	15-	20-	25-	30-	35-	40-	45-	50-	55-	60-	65-	70-	75-	80-	85-	90-
14 ESSEX—*cont.*																						
195 TENDRING.																						
1 Thorpe. (W.)	9667	M.	5008	683	628	617	476	337	260	258	246	225	249	232	264	202	157	104	72	40	15	2
		F.	4659	622	626	492	366	294	281	282	248	274	237	205	201	187	143	94	56	40	11	1
2 Harwich. (H.B[t].S[t].)	7342	M.	4243	529	439	342	437	497	416	331	323	258	169	159	167	113	66	52	16	7	2	.
		F.	3699	556	474	378	330	300	288	240	241	171	143	111	110	103	58	48	38	12	2	1
3 Manningtree. (L.)	6123	M.	3043	372	388	380	296	216	170	161	162	140	150	125	137	113	90	64	48	23	6	2
		F.	3080	422	386	369	244	262	162	176	176	168	152	153	129	114	91	73	47	16	6	1
4 Ardleigh	9843	M.	4891	638	664	610	466	345	290	237	242	245	212	213	194	200	154	96	68	30	7	.
		F.	4952	666	646	624	431	310	290	364	256	255	259	218	201	171	135	76	56	27	15	3
196 COLCHESTER.																						
1 Colchester First Ward. (W.H[s].B[s].)	14039	M.	7180	829	830	602	880	1028	776	540	449	348	249	223	139	179	161	100	52	34	10	3
		F.	6859	829	738	634	720	690	624	467	423	340	283	277	226	210	140	118	67	44	14	6
2 Colchester Second Ward. (L.)	7021	M.	3318	483	406	411	340	274	212	217	160	172	133	133	108	108	53	53	23	15	6	.
		F.	3703	454	454	414	376	353	287	219	216	176	161	164	117	119	89	43	37	21	3	.
3 Colchester Third Ward	7314	M.	3424	478	421	393	389	283	240	179	194	178	149	145	126	102	64	43	17	11	5	1
		F.	3890	476	467	472	437	342	268	266	226	207	160	158	136	123	62	60	26	21	3	.
197 LEXDEN.																						
1 Wivenhoe	2280	M.	1108	151	174	139	111	66	67	63	58	59	47	43	36	40	26	24	8	2	1	2
		F.	1172	146	136	142	94	90	77	83	64	69	61	46	36	51	32	17	19	6	3	1
2 Peldon	5079	M.	2549	368	369	397	250	167	131	126	126	129	129	116	90	75	81	39	20	15	10	3
		F.	2530	356	344	302	196	160	164	161	139	131	119	108	133	85	60	48	34	12	5	3
3 Stanway. (W.)	5677	M.	2877	386	402	386	280	194	137	162	133	117	118	137	92	140	90	77	46	29	4	2
		F.	2800	361	369	319	230	204	163	184	138	157	131	133	96	100	88	61	31	24	10	2
4 Fordham	4506	M.	2311	330	327	305	229	159	106	110	116	112	90	98	80	91	69	34	38	13	4	.
		F.	2194	327	313	255	169	150	126	118	120	117	119	82	83	79	61	39	28	11	4	1
5 Dedham	4234	M.	2088	274	239	291	228	135	113	113	102	90	79	98	60	78	53	55	24	16	6	3
		F.	2146	265	253	261	172	153	129	112	129	110	105	114	97	84	58	57	32	20	1	1
198 HALSTEAD.																						
1 Halstead. (W.R.)	10973	M.	5020	646	632	616	511	343	244	305	263	255	236	243	202	212	129	98	72	38	9	.
		F.	5953	666	574	653	591	489	436	306	340	322	308	250	228	226	136	119	70	36	14	4
2 Hedingham	6032	M.	2876	365	403	372	274	163	134	132	139	141	153	147	141	130	89	57	39	20	6	1
		F.	3156	353	401	380	286	235	187	182	156	178	166	141	152	128	92	68	31	26	6	3
199 BRAINTREE.																						
1 Finchingfield	4337	M.	2131	299	289	209	200	125	108	119	109	103	98	81	90	90	70	44	19	17	3	1
		F.	2206	296	336	267	173	161	138	115	113	112	107	84	77	88	69	41	28	16	5	1
2 Bocking (W.H.)	5116	M.	2400	311	288	288	220	158	115	187	109	117	106	89	106	107	94	61	40	30	5	.
		F.	2716	294	332	306	242	200	186	170	143	151	128	120	111	106	76	68	60	21	5	1
3 Coggeshall	4162	M.	1910	220	259	224	200	121	95	109	84	86	111	93	84	88	56	40	30	16	3	1
		F.	2252	283	271	262	201	163	144	125	120	104	118	125	81	75	76	52	34	16	6	2
4 Kelvedon	2227	M.	1117	132	145	144	122	84	60	49	50	53	55	56	53	48	26	18	16	6	1	1
		F.	1110	144	146	110	81	69	67	76	47	66	68	52	46	46	32	22	19	10	8	1
5 Witham. (L.)	5534	M.	2682	397	326	299	274	198	152	158	135	132	106	120	117	110	77	46	25	12	5	1
		F.	2842	360	305	308	301	225	188	172	168	137	136	139	136	117	78	49	37	28	6	.
6 Braintree	7252	M.	3352	468	429	406	319	235	192	190	193	165	158	144	122	118	67	62	35	13	4	.
		F.	3900	469	453	431	434	320	266	226	202	224	191	154	143	136	108	89	40	10	13	.
200 DUNMOW.																						
1 Stebbing	4596	M.	2410	272	297	378	316	169	123	93	115	89	97	98	107	90	70	45	30	12	8	.
		F.	2186	319	279	256	145	154	116	116	116	101	123	91	111	90	66	40	40	17	6	.
2 Dunmow. (W.)	5265	M.	2627	335	344	301	237	155	153	131	149	128	104	126	106	115	90	76	43	29	5	.
		F.	2638	324	328	309	212	183	158	163	136	122	113	140	118	126	83	60	43	22	9	2
3 Hatfield. (H.)	4256	M.	2178	274	283	246	217	161	130	163	126	103	111	93	87	91	57	47	28	18	2	1
		F.	2078	299	287	232	123	112	144	111	110	109	103	107	74	92	62	53	34	20	4	2
4 Thaxted	3874	M.	1985	248	259	276	191	131	86	83	115	91	83	101	55	88	73	35	18	13	6	2
		F.	1889	231	267	227	151	94	101	95	102	96	114	105	80	78	53	43	26	22	3	1
201 SAFFRON WALDEN.																						
1 Newport	4850	M.	2442	321	334	326	264	159	180	111	124	119	89	113	88	100	68	49	33	18	6	3
		F.	2408	331	346	269	166	161	162	127	127	146	114	89	103	91	69	56	42	21	7	2
2 Saffron Walden. (W.H.)	9627	M.	4646	587	670	606	461	342	271	265	240	202	206	182	182	192	153	92	77	32	6	2
		F.	4981	609	663	647	447	377	320	262	273	239	228	248	175	209	132	104	75	35	13	4
3 Radwinter	4111	M.	2112	280	360	247	218	186	121	103	102	97	90	94	99	66	66	49	26	15	5	1
		F.	1999	320	248	229	140	130	97	115	93	100	106	96	83	70	82	44	30	10	8	3
15 SUFFOLK.																						
202 RISBRIDGE.																						
1 Haverhill. (W.)	8258	M.	3990	632	506	478	391	289	247	197	195	177	168	161	139	129	85	86	40	19	8	.
		F.	4268	599	544	586	434	350	347	206	214	183	195	151	183	164	81	82	35	22	8	1
2 Wickhambrook	4238	M.	2148	279	305	288	226	121	129	102	163	101	81	106	76	77	68	49	29	13	2	1
		F.	2090	303	279	246	159	144	130	117	111	92	111	87	86	79	58	27	29	15	0	2
3 Clare	4738	M.	2310	316	289	331	263	165	97	105	95	107	94	90	93	96	73	42	30	25	5	1
		F.	2428	303	334	271	198	172	148	128	134	118	122	123	90	164	51	61	30	15	10	2
203 SUDBURY.																						
1 Bulmer	4263	M.	2098	244	301	238	241	129	162	106	100	88	92	97	95	91	74	44	34	13	5	1
		F.	2165	255	251	244	202	184	128	128	150	108	118	92	99	97	70	36	32	16	7	.
2 Bures	4908	M.	2438	336	330	279	217	177	115	122	129	107	166	111	95	118	76	55	37	21	12	1
		F.	2470	306	320	260	199	168	153	147	139	137	165	99	126	80	86	65	33	22	14	3
3 Sudbury. (W.H.)	8607	M.	4109	483	434	482	442	300	233	216	205	220	222	195	169	128	120	90	67	38	9	.
		F.	4488	513	497	562	474	337	309	272	226	278	245	209	153	157	130	75	48	23	16	3
4 Melford	5898	M.	2871	390	383	355	290	217	174	164	128	129	140	120	111	103	64	53	30	23	2	.
		F.	3027	398	398	346	253	240	214	169	153	163	157	158	101	89	75	48	29	20	0	1
5 Hartest	6489	M.	3186	449	476	388	345	108	169	160	160	133	142	147	121	103	83	62	42	16	5	1
		F.	3303	461	443	401	271	241	216	174	157	188	166	133	133	112	71	67	36	22	8	3

Table 3 *continued.*—AGES of MALES and FEMALES in REGISTRATION SUB-DISTRICTS.

REGISTRATION SUB-DISTRICT.	ALL AGES. Persons.		ALL AGES. Males and Females.	Under 5 Years.	5–	10–	15–	20–	25–	30–	35–	40–	45–	50–	55–	60–	65–	70–	75–	80–	85–	90–	95–	100 and upw[ds].
SUFFOLK— …nt.																								
…04 COSFORD.																								
…enham	7231	M.	3559	455	445	415	374	279	197	174	158	171	170	174	146	125	110	72	49	31	13	1	.	.
		F.	3672	467	496	453	310	260	224	210	157	201	180	160	132	131	109	87	50	24	7	4	1	.
…leigh. (W.)	8589	M.	4242	588	507	485	420	294	267	235	200	179	205	187	180	152	140	123	65	55	16	.	1	.
		F.	4347	557	530	498	383	332	277	233	210	215	211	205	177	153	124	110	68	33	14	2	1	.
205 THINGOE.																								
…igham	5338	M.	2731	355	300	338	307	166	152	140	134	119	127	123	96	115	94	60	42	12	10	.	.	.
		F.	2607	364	332	271	213	161	161	161	138	157	119	122	111	100	100	67	40	26	8	4	1	.
…nham	5447	M.	2675	357	339	292	271	185	156	161	144	136	102	124	111	107	70	45	45	19	5	3	.	.
		F.	2772	385	355	304	219	200	182	174	156	144	111	120	103	108	74	56	37	23	6	4	1	.
…forth	5551	M.	2789	373	361	616	277	177	170	150	153	122	117	127	127	87	91	63	62	17	8	.	1	.
		F.	2762	367	347	334	256	183	162	155	125	155	148	134	100	116	87	59	62	24	6	1	1	.
…URY ST. EDMUND'S.																								
…ry St. Edmund's. (W.H. L.B.)	16111	M.	7574	964	935	880	911	637	580	473	423	396	298	275	240	226	162	144	62	23	5	4	1	.
		F.	8537	996	910	967	909	740	642	562	512	438	374	353	277	231	223	167	193	62	17	4	.	.
… MILDENHALL.																								
…rlington	3367	M.	1667	224	254	195	139	116	100	92	87	67	72	62	57	67	44	38	22	9	5	2	.	.
		F.	1700	253	227	191	122	111	116	80	102	82	73	72	68	70	40	42	18	10	4	.	.	.
…kenheath. (W.H.)	5590	M.	2780	398	350	304	302	210	165	143	164	117	111	123	105	111	79	66	55	31	8	.	.	.
		F.	2810	411	385	328	227	200	174	153	156	135	125	111	103	117	80	55	47	20	5	2	.	.
208 STOW.																								
…lsham-le-Willows	5201	M.	2560	334	321	311	266	183	147	140	103	120	108	100	115	99	75	70	37	27	10	.	.	.
		F.	2641	325	318	336	214	205	140	138	124	132	136	136	102	119	88	51	40	21	8	2	1	.
…ttlesden. (W.)	6184	M.	3094	486	426	348	291	218	153	170	111	150	133	129	118	135	85	66	42	37	6	1	.	.
		F.	3090	425	415	353	237	209	200	182	164	167	187	127	120	123	90	65	38	25	9	3	1	.
…wmarket	8804	M.	4210	548	565	477	408	301	243	205	214	208	187	201	158	131	99	78	58	25	6	1	.	.
		F.	4594	646	611	523	414	320	267	277	253	215	214	202	164	161	106	73	64	31	11	2	1	.
…9 HARTISMERE																								
…ndlesham (L.)	5194	M.	2652	374	350	332	265	188	143	140	100	123	113	115	101	111	76	61	53	18	15	.	.	.
		F.	2542	378	338	283	190	183	148	148	117	133	101	123	108	104	70	51	35	22	8	3	1	.
…tesdale. (W.S.H.)	4685	M.	2377	301	347	314	235	166	115	153	99	91	57	92	105	103	71	60	26	25	.	1	.	.
		F.	2308	279	294	295	188	163	141	139	117	105	123	90	88	86	72	54	34	24	4	2	.	.
…e. (W.R.)	5912	M.	2945	407	335	389	309	186	151	156	127	141	132	141	107	114	93	80	48	27	8	1	.	.
		F.	2967	367	401	342	245	213	181	178	163	134	132	136	125	126	86	71	46	21	13	2	.	.
210 HOXNE.																								
…radbroke	6532	M.	3280	425	393	393	345	236	162	166	133	162	129	146	127	162	95	83	46	30	11	2	.	.
		F.	3252	425	447	407	274	230	177	172	151	153	165	150	123	154	85	87	47	29	12	5	1	.
…nnington	6079	M.	3116	498	395	374	319	234	189	178	121	127	142	124	109	106	101	81	67	26	12	3	1	.
		F.	2963	420	361	336	283	206	176	153	135	140	147	126	118	144	85	63	58	23	18	3	.	.
211 BOSMERE.																								
…ddenham (W.)	7666	M.	3880	517	474	471	386	274	233	175	210	195	166	167	144	161	116	95	55	37	9	1	.	.
		F.	3786	515	471	465	298	275	221	210	205	190	183	166	154	129	111	76	62	63	14	6	.	.
…edham Market	7736	M.	3916	476	517	486	415	306	243	188	186	174	203	170	134	149	101	89	56	27	5	.	.	.
		F.	3820	530	523	421	332	275	225	219	204	193	193	173	155	120	107	81	45	30	6	3	.	.
212 SAMFORD.																								
…pel St. Mary	5837	M.	2907	380	334	343	293	190	167	140	180	136	131	140	125	118	100	65	44	16	10	1	.	.
		F.	2930	361	320	308	241	210	191	185	156	176	148	142	135	107	107	68	50	26	9	1	.	.
…lbrook. (W.B.)	5761	M.	2925	376	381	329	287	207	165	139	158	150	118	138	126	131	95	40	41	10	4	1	.	.
		F.	2836	402	358	392	208	197	176	161	156	163	145	138	139	90	70	49	36	10	5	1	2	.
213 IPSWICH.																								
…. Matthew. (W.R.B.)	21661	M.	10232	1460	1282	1116	984	910	863	671	583	473	433	414	322	322	201	140	86	43	19	2	.	.
		F.	11429	1352	1242	1158	1106	1114	907	753	615	606	623	502	398	350	282	191	114	60	22	5	1	.
…. Clement. (L.)	10710	M.	5102	680	608	493	408	420	400	355	331	254	256	231	179	163	106	89	37	16	5	2	.	.
		F.	5608	666	652	576	537	502	417	407	332	275	280	257	192	261	130	78	57	34	11	4	.	.
…. Margaret. (W.S.H.P.B.)	17949	M.	8284	1127	1069	1003	836	648	623	511	476	417	389	321	274	278	149	112	67	28	6	.	.	.
		F.	9665	1111	1066	1096	1037	858	763	640	556	515	480	478	307	296	236	148	83	48	18	1	2	.
…14 WOODBRIDGE.																								
…rlford. (L.)	8775	M.	4393	568	523	525	448	290	230	252	193	233	197	198	183	204	145	75	72	38	13	1	.	.
		F.	4382	525	519	453	341	324	289	362	227	246	228	213	107	193	140	110	66	83	11	5	.	.
…lneis. (W.H.B.)	6507	M.	3235	440	447	426	253	179	173	168	189	164	141	129	181	111	95	38	40	26	7	2	.	.
		F.	3272	468	454	380	265	216	210	185	191	168	161	135	113	121	99	43	44	25	4	2	.	.
…oodbridge and Wilford	7463	M.	3575	485	440	413	384	228	215	172	178	166	168	140	145	195	109	106	61	27	14	4	1	.
		F.	3888	478	466	421	350	314	262	231	220	189	198	187	169	136	120	102	55	37	18	8	.	.
…15 PLOMESGATE.																								
…rl Soham	2239	M.	1134	158	140	146	109	93	46	66	43	56	58	41	36	46	32	32	10	9	3	1	.	.
		F.	1105	134	157	115	85	71	63	66	58	55	63	48	41	43	30	26	16	13	2	.	.	.
…amlingham	3581	M.	1805	204	198	310	231	114	95	79	71	75	67	63	86	65	53	31	30	18	8	3	.	.
		F.	1776	202	184	193	161	125	110	98	69	81	91	74	77	69	62	48	37	20	6	4	1	.
…ford. (W.)	7330	M.	3670	433	434	410	346	318	207	195	193	161	171	169	151	181	113	92	65	33	7	2	.	.
		F.	3660	499	460	352	312	262	237	219	187	190	175	154	136	147	117	60	56	25	12	2	.	.
…deburgh	4316	M.	2129	297	207	301	200	129	128	120	107	96	94	89	72	65	78	47	23	13	4	2	.	.
		F.	2187	285	273	295	290	162	142	136	123	122	86	111	72	80	59	57	35	17	8	6	.	.
…xmundham	3013	M.	1423	183	186	158	143	109	65	91	76	54	72	56	56	45	49	35	28	16	8	1	.	.
		F.	1590	178	215	168	146	121	96	104	78	81	69	69	77	60	64	28	26	20	5	1	.	.
216 BLYTHING.																								
…estleton. (W.H.)	9995	M.	4996	601	694	598	462	338	273	262	233	236	228	199	182	179	151	110	89	38	20	4	1	.
		F.	4999	652	706	568	389	332	327	300	280	262	215	218	187	192	155	102	70	34	10	2	.	.
…alesworth	7395	M.	3638	471	496	457	348	271	217	210	183	159	148	168	102	118	123	67	65	27	12	1	.	.
		F.	3757	510	467	425	317	270	236	221	207	169	166	166	140	166	120	98	54	29	12	4	.	.
…enhaston	8427	M.	4043	573	487	476	362	283	240	222	205	189	181	189	139	165	123	94	69	30	11	4	.	.
		F.	4384	552	538	476	385	359	281	265	224	207	212	214	174	107	133	107	72	35	16	6	1	.

TABLE 3 *continued*.—AGES of MALES and FEMALES in REGISTRATION SUB-DISTRICTS.

REGISTRATION SUB-DISTRICT.	ALL AGES. Persons.	ALL AGES. Males and Females.	Under 5 Years.	5-	10-	15-	20-	25-	30-	35-	40-	45-	50-	55-	60-	65-	70-	75-	80-	85-
15. SUFFOLK—*cont.*																				
217 WANGFORD.																				
1 BUNGAY	5855	M. - 2791	386	313	320	285	218	173	125	137	144	136	120	101	110	98	56	37	21	5
		F. - 3064	374	356	374	290	237	199	139	168	162	141	146	109	141	92	73	46	27	12
2 BECCLES. (W.H.)	8601	M. - 4237	465	593	561	379	338	269	227	226	202	174	180	119	145	116	94	50	22	8
		F. - 4364	504	527	485	411	323	271	266	261	209	177	166	172	139	150	75	52	41	21
218 MUTFORD.																				
1 KESSINGLAND	7463	M. - 3448	590	511	429	268	215	216	186	172	138	147	138	113	127	90	49	38	21	3
		F. - 4015	578	535	419	353	343	209	263	213	221	185	164	125	140	92	44	48	20	7
2 LOWESTOFT. (W. H.[3])	20752	M. - 10214	1487	1264	1043	1172	1030	777	690	570	469	337	389	322	242	200	119	62	29	10
		F. - 10538	1493	1305	1124	1020	951	841	664	560	636	437	431	319	302	221	169	90	58	12
3 GORLESTON (B.)	11263	M. - 5395	884	713	611	611	455	546	300	261	271	193	206	157	140	94	87	32	27	5
		F. - 5868	763	726	626	586	460	482	403	354	328	252	229	166	161	129	112	46	28	10
16. NORFOLK																				
219 YARMOUTH.																				
1 YARMOUTH SOUTHERN (H.[2] L.B.)	16576	M. - 7815	1073	905	841	925	721	529	475	468	438	345	314	244	201	162	90	57	18	5
		F. - 8761	1087	940	812	897	786	662	599	562	487	413	409	295	301	195	142	95	54	21
2 YARMOUTH NORTHERN (W.H.)	20675	M. - 9644	1262	1097	1026	1002	945	850	631	568	405	430	432	316	319	203	147	90	56	13
		F. - 10031	1215	1077	983	1156	1052	856	700	656	604	523	528	426	414	278	212	126	81	37
220 FLEGG.																				
1 EAST FLEGG	5020	M. - 2443	356	348	297	220	167	140	128	123	104	107	110	57	87	53	57	35	14	7
		F. - 2577	359	333	268	205	221	182	149	147	132	110	120	89	84	63	47	35	21	8
2 WEST FLEGG. (W.)	4694	M. - 2335	338	312	256	196	172	142	125	119	108	104	96	101	85	83	51	28	18	3
		F. - 2359	326	302	247	214	187	159	135	111	110	119	92	98	79	64	43	35	17	10
221 SMALLBURGH.																				
1 LUDHAM	3594	M. - 1838	281	224	201	178	134	105	95	165	75	65	73	80	64	60	38	32	10	5
		F. - 1756	233	229	194	150	113	114	101	101	92	86	93	64	57	45	34	29	18	7
2 SMALLBURGH. (W.)	4235	M. - 2123	270	284	244	207	158	135	97	92	100	92	101	66	82	54	65	26	37	9
		F. 2112	267	245	216	186	141	143	122	104	119	110	119	82	80	70	39	28	29	7
3 STALHAM	4103	M. - 1997	251	225	253	165	144	126	119	126	92	85	84	80	63	63	47	27	13	3
		F. 2106	310	287	230	143	153	109	124	121	121	92	86	98	71	59	41	33	12	7
4 BACTON	2416	M. - 1181	145	143	122	112	91	69	63	80	52	66	63	43	41	36	23	27	8	1
		F. 1235	148	162	127	113	93	89	72	71	72	56	64	44	43	29	26	24	5	2
222 ERPINGHAM.																				
1 NORTH WALSHAM	7145	M. - 3802	452	426	440	353	262	230	180	155	182	140	156	131	130	97	65	57	18	6
		F. - 3343	400	408	366	334	272	240	225	195	175	171	172	140	141	106	90	55	40	17
2 CROMER. (W.H.)	7233	M. - 3635	458	425	486	354	284	194	193	175	187	170	166	159	151	99	88	59	20	14
		F. - 3598	453	426	403	334	301	249	199	204	188	183	168	145	161	99	73	41	25	15
3 HOLT	5861	M. - 2894	352	359	327	301	222	156	177	112	121	137	135	103	109	91	95	53	33	6
		F. - 2967	356	313	314	235	217	209	165	146	160	150	141	131	126	118	84	59	31	11
223 AYLSHAM.																				
1 EYNSFORD	8485	M. - 4305	542	514	523	470	302	259	234	201	182	204	191	173	179	122	99	69	39	9
		F. - 4180	547	480	449	320	315	264	225	206	258	215	188	178	187	127	115	80	29	10
2 BUXTON. (W.R.)	9572	M. - 4667	593	611	558	507	367	262	228	211	245	203	201	182	150	127	104	64	40	14
		F. - 4905	614	592	564	433	338	327	242	278	263	237	222	217	172	137	131	76	49	19
224 ST. FAITH'S.																				
1 ST. FAITH'S. (W.)	5161	M. - 2555	345	222	290	256	200	154	121	121	112	112	130	77	98	85	80	47	20	3
		F. - 2606	347	337	272	229	200	164	123	148	129	122	113	101	87	81	73	48	21	3
2 SPROWSTON. (L[2].)	6257	M. - 3045	412	353	321	305	258	204	172	149	167	134	132	121	106	87	56	40	22	6
		F. - 3212	392	377	316	260	280	225	194	168	187	172	161	122	131	91	52	46	27	8
225 NORWICH.																				
1 COSLANY.	14193	M. 6760	1049	850	767	661	547	474	418	365	338	287	294	201	191	125	95	62	10	7
		F. - 7433	961	821	789	773	672	537	406	433	384	330	317	274	224	173	109	69	39	12
2 EAST WYMER (B.)	14082	M. - 6495	673	775	699	645	570	464	410	329	287	264	281	270	203	135	101	98	50	18
		F. - 7587	872	810	770	773	734	577	446	384	365	370	379	252	286	190	161	128	74	27
3 CONISFORD (W.S.)	13549	M. - 6342	833	774	818	620	563	455	392	377	255	269	300	206	187	118	80	47	8	8
		F. 7207	841	790	785	718	673	555	452	414	376	346	523	229	244	174	126	101	41	9
4 MANCROFT. (H.L.P.)	15714	M. - 6959	838	753	771	733	709	510	408	363	368	327	307	283	235	161	98	81	32	9
		F. - 8755	950	807	851	1031	943	640	546	406	467	409	434	364	293	212	153	108	51	12
5 WEST WYMER. (W.H.[3]L.)	30304	M. - 13732	1845	1626	1546	1549	1189	1047	910	781	666	609	573	487	417	279	216	137	77	14
		F. - 16572	2026	1761	1549	[illegible]	[illegible]	1298	1113	979	870	[illegible]	773	651	541	416	315	211	121	31
226 FOREHOE.																				
1 COSTESSEY	3831	M. - 1919	248	254	229	177	130	109	87	102	89	102	85	79	80	57	44	27	14	6
		F. - 1912	248	246	202	146	133	119	98	112	128	91	86	75	70	68	36	31	19	3
2 WYMONDHAM. (W.)	8140	M. - 4018	500	481	442	422	331	218	193	188	201	162	180	157	176	117	83	81	46	11
		F. - 4122	476	481	457	357	296	261	247	205	231	202	207	173	170	127	98	75	30	18
227 HENSTEAD.																				
1 HUMBLEYARD. (W.)	5441	M. - 2678	350	309	319	250	225	174	139	127	136	104	121	111	97	88	69	50	26	6
		F. - 2763	347	315	255	246	238	181	167	166	125	140	128	107	109	86	70	57	26	8
2 HENSTEAD	5195	M. - 2600	330	325	268	280	212	150	123	127	110	106	124	105	112	71	59	47	27	8
		F. - 2595	318	297	287	209	202	192	139	124	142	112	144	100	106	81	76	58	24	2
228 BLOFIELD.																				
1 BLOFIELD. (W. L.)	6061	M. - 2898	329	331	288	259	235	195	164	153	168	130	140	132	120	89	75	35	34	10
		F. - 3163	333	325	281	247	236	223	217	188	207	175	204	129	141	107	65	54	34	6
2 SOUTH WALSHAM	5557	M. - 2749	357	365	315	257	243	180	130	142	120	121	115	105	105	81	48	47	17	7
		F. - 2808	472	314	308	218	226	190	163	153	127	138	138	102	120	64	58	45	21	9

Table 3 *continued*.—AGES of MALES and FEMALES in REGISTRATION SUB-DISTRICTS.

REGISTRATION SUB-DISTRICT.	ALL AGES. Persons.	Males and Females.	Under 5 Years.	5-	10-	15-	20-	25-	30-	35-	40-	45-	50-	55-	60-	65-	70-	75-	80-	85-	90-	95-	100 and upw^ds.
5 NORFOLK—*cont.*																							
229 LODDON.																							
LDEBY	4026	M. - 2426	343	304	298	176	140	145	166	116	123	110	104	104	100	70	53	44	16	8	1	.	.
		F. - 2600	351	333	262	186	101	163	128	123	138	134	107	112	103	80	52	56	21	8	.	1	.
ODDON. (W.)	4771	M. - 2312	310	281	267	218	186	121	118	101	98	99	121	101	88	62	69	42	23	6	1	1	.
		F. - 2459	303	320	248	208	197	146	137	117	128	134	133	108	82	77	53	39	25	8	.	1	.
OODTON. (H.)	4005	M. - 1949	258	275	237	172	183	100	101	96	91	87	90	89	76	65	37	29	18	2	.	1	.
		F. - 2056	258	242	242	172	158	138	125	90	117	105	98	82	65	72	41	25	15	4	2	.	.
230 DEPWADE.																							
ARLESTON	5568	M. - 2684	365	352	332	262	173	147	184	121	133	106	126	110	105	95	62	41	24	4	3	.	.
		F. - 2884	372	336	341	271	185	168	164	155	140	133	141	107	112	92	83	49	27	6	2	.	.
ISS	7422	M. - 3507	465	468	393	337	306	181	227	180	176	140	157	138	132	102	83	40	22	9	.	1	.
		F. - 3915	472	434	429	386	283	280	234	211	175	195	168	153	141	105	87	68	20	14	3	.	.
TRATTON. (W.)	5457	M. - 2678	336	396	318	251	197	157	129	100	120	128	120	114	100	111	73	57	34	7	2	.	.
		F. - 2779	329	348	310	231	183	164	130	158	148	135	136	122	83	98	82	42	34	10	2	1	.
ORNCETT	5135	M. - 2576	321	326	289	288	204	138	125	139	109	99	132	92	106	78	81	41	24	5	2	1	.
		F. - 2559	309	310	356	224	175	130	144	132	135	132	93	105	111	87	64	48	14	13	2	1	.
231 GUILTCROSS.																							
ANHAM	5190	M. - 2605	328	312	338	265	188	140	128	115	123	129	109	91	108	88	67	41	24	9	2	.	.
		F. - 2585	311	322	282	210	159	155	138	180	141	141	119	124	99	98	54	33	30	13	1	.	.
ENNINGHALL. (W.)	5373	M. - 2700	372	311	286	294	204	158	144	127	131	116	110	113	109	90	68	58	25	12	1	1	.
		F. - 2673	381	342	308	212	198	172	148	156	130	126	129	111	115	72	52	44	28	8	6	.	.
232 WAYLAND.																							
TTLEBOROUGH. (W.)	5177	M. - 2580	338	311	289	265	194	126	142	123	126	111	125	112	111	92	53	31	22	11	1	.	.
		F. - 2597	315	291	302	194	187	160	143	153	154	144	116	119	112	84	56	34	28	3	.	2	.
ATTON	5539	M. - 2771	364	333	294	298	202	171	136	132	124	136	123	107	120	114	50	41	18	4	2	1	1
		F. - 2768	319	328	286	241	194	180	159	158	102	137	128	111	141	91	67	42	14	7	3	.	.
233 MITFORD.																							
HIPDHAM	2632	M. - 1304	176	160	140	125	102	71	81	68	66	58	59	47	86	43	26	15	9	2	.	.	.
		F. - 1328	154	154	158	102	85	81	84	73	74	56	65	51	77	41	30	26	14	5	.	.	.
ATTISHALL	3907	M. - 1938	282	246	212	179	144	115	121	99	73	89	88	89	88	90	39	38	30	8	.	.	.
		F. - 1969	231	239	199	147	133	132	116	114	83	98	110	85	87	74	48	36	24	10	4	.	.
AWDESWELL	2974	M. - 1467	204	171	154	151	104	92	65	72	69	63	73	64	62	54	28	36	12	3	.	.	.
		F. - 1507	178	189	156	121	98	86	92	85	75	88	67	57	85	31	51	25	19	4	.	.	.
AST DEREHAM. (W.)	8601	M. - 4218	530	494	479	428	342	280	219	228	204	168	187	169	162	120	92	63	29	13	2	.	.
		F. - 4383	562	494	451	425	340	302	268	222	258	225	190	166	171	115	86	71	42	16	1	.	.
ITCHAM. (H.)	4848	M. - 2420	322	292	279	261	196	138	124	121	108	106	164	104	112	59	39	28	12	5	1	.	.
		F. - 2428	282	307	286	217	183	158	128	113	128	126	116	107	110	60	48	35	20	7	1	.	.
ORTH ELMHAM	4355	M. - 2193	275	274	284	242	180	135	124	90	97	90	93	75	78	92	47	40	16	10	2	.	.
		F. - 2162	286	273	257	175	158	139	125	106	102	102	89	79	83	64	56	40	18	10	1	.	.
234 WALSINGHAM.																							
KENHAM (R.)	7702	M. - 3849	472	468	449	368	365	265	195	196	198	171	148	146	146	74	69	53	26	9	1	.	.
		F. - 3853	469	465	431	379	310	263	214	197	204	174	171	144	141	111	82	54	26	12	4	.	.
ALSINGHAM. (W.)	6258	M. - 3149	422	393	335	327	254	200	156	148	155	132	143	94	128	107	77	68	34	6	.	.	.
		F. - 3109	396	354	354	239	228	198	170	184	172	149	126	145	128	101	76	68	19	10	1	.	.
ELLS	5983	M. - 2799	373	366	318	266	182	155	151	157	127	140	127	134	108	75	73	41	28	16	2	.	.
		F. - 3184	403	366	325	259	234	207	168	169	179	157	159	151	128	104	68	58	29	3	6	1	.
235 DOCKING.																							
RNHAM	5669	M. - 2819	377	350	322	303	182	132	139	146	143	121	138	114	112	98	68	50	26	6	2	.	.
		F. - 2850	350	358	318	220	188	152	181	172	178	139	134	131	120	80	75	57	23	8	.	.	.
ETTISHAM. (H.)	6942	M. - 3336	447	445	395	348	256	183	190	161	185	154	129	130	121	96	55	42	18	8	.	.	.
		F. - 3607	431	430	399	330	273	252	210	204	189	179	164	150	138	99	72	51	23	16	5	1	.
OCKING. (W.)	4889	M. - 2478	307	282	287	264	194	133	130	110	126	137	98	105	70	86	62	54	20	3	1	.	.
		F. - 2411	281	292	263	199	180	150	126	128	143	133	113	106	80	79	59	45	25	7	2	.	.
236 FREEBRIDGE LYNN.																							
ILLINGTON	4267	M. - 2159	267	229	245	219	170	136	119	104	113	93	98	98	90	68	46	31	20	3	.	.	.
		F. - 2108	252	260	230	174	141	143	107	110	121	102	92	102	82	53	60	33	25	8	3	.	1
AXTON. (W.)	3910	M. - 1933	245	246	225	209	145	112	114	101	82	77	94	66	69	53	39	28	15	11	.	2	.
		F. - 1977	285	244	218	180	128	139	123	105	87	110	92	74	73	46	35	29	14	6	4	.	.
IDDLETON	2092	M. - 998	134	118	90	104	79	56	80	65	49	59	28	46	50	41	18	21	9	1	.	.	.
		F. - 1094	141	135	127	100	65	69	60	72	60	56	57	36	32	30	27	18	3	5	1	.	.
STLE RISING	1966	M. - 963	150	119	123	98	76	50	45	61	55	32	39	41	32	23	19	4	5	2	1	.	.
		F. - 1003	128	151	112	86	62	71	51	59	54	52	48	33	28	30	16	9	6	5	2	.	.
237 KING'S LYNN.																							
NG'S LYNN NORTH	11629	M. - 5543	702	619	559	600	499	448	364	332	306	230	224	175	184	134	91	40	22	5	.	.	.
		F. - 6086	690	628	617	644	549	473	388	365	236	270	280	218	217	162	122	95	47	13	1	1	.
NG'S LYNN SOUTH. (W.H.)	7877	M. - 3887	500	410	389	338	396	238	254	189	163	140	132	151	114	80	88	42	22	8	.	.	.
		F. - 3990	465	446	340	349	361	314	262	234	191	177	180	148	186	106	106	60	40	12	3	.	.
238 DOWNHAM.																							
GGENHALL	6002	M. - 3055	413	369	386	311	213	192	177	150	134	127	129	105	128	102	59	39	18	7	3	2	.
		F. - 2947	369	352	344	239	196	196	196	157	130	149	151	131	123	94	45	42	18	11	6	2	.
WNHAM. (W.)	8873	M. - 4407	509	558	562	491	327	270	231	230	238	173	181	156	180	129	70	56	32	13	1	.	.
		F. - 4466	601	537	639	585	353	279	248	240	226	211	197	149	193	104	79	62	31	8	4	1	.
CHAM	4529	M. - 2223	268	257	277	215	151	128	103	106	121	113	113	93	9	68	66	30	19	6	2	.	.
		F. - 2306	312	275	245	182	158	146	107	131	131	121	107	100	106	85	47	34	21	8	2	.	.
239 SWAFFHAM.																							
AFFHAM. (W.)	12859	M. - 6294	814	790	715	668	489	372	354	281	307	311	246	225	281	190	149	90	46	14	4	.	.
		F. - 6564	859	810	721	677	407	398	376	336	336	291	306	263	262	200	147	116	42	20	5	3	.
240 THETFORD.																							
THWOLD	8644	M. - 4274	614	564	478	368	306	254	233	236	224	205	169	172	150	126	90	61	34	6	.	.	.
		F. - 4370	541	561	515	368	[illegible]	292	[illegible]	243	233	181	181	160	164	128	86	56	32	8	2	.	.
TFORD. (W.)	8986	M. - 4533	618	578	526	455	316	240	226	247	191	185	228	184	160	155	107	62	31	12	5	.	.
		F. - 4453	646	575	491	363	317	269	256	245	222	224	203	209	182	143	81	76	35	14	2	.	.

Table 4.—MALE and FEMALE CHILDREN at *each Year of Age* under 5 in the EASTERN DIVISION and its REGISTRATION COUNTIES.

REGISTRATION COUNTY.	TOTAL UNDER 5 YEARS.		Under 1 Year.	1–	2–	3–	4–
	Persons.	Males and Females.					
IV. EASTERN COUNTIES.	181144	M. 90676 F. 90468	18032 19199	17541 17602	18362 18039	17859 17797	17982 17831
14 ESSEX	78469	M. 39255 F. 39214	8183 8230	7574 7723	7942 7887	7720 7722	7836 7702
15 SUFFOLK	47028	M. 23565 F. 23463	4852 4920	4626 4586	4694 4777	4671 4570	4716 4610
16 NORFOLK	55647	M. 27856 F. 27791	5891 6049	5841 5293	5726 5425	5463 5505	5450 5519

Table 5.—MALE and FEMALE CHILDREN at *each Year of Age* under 5 in REGISTRATION DISTRICTS

REGISTRATION DISTRICT.	Total under 5 Years.		Under 1 Year.	1–	2–	3–	4–
	Persons.	Males and Females.					
14 ESSEX.							
186 WEST HAM	31802	M. 15979 F. 15823	3304 3390	3107 3178	3181 3176	3191 3089	3106 2981
187 EPPING	2778	M. 1883 F. 1895	273 291	260 258	283 298	279 298	288 269
188 ONGAR	1369	M. 642 F. 727	170 143	89 138	126 153	139 138	118 156
189 ROMFORD	5833	M. 2893 F. 2940	541 558	509 615	561 526	549 512	633 534
190 ORSETT	2378	M. 1205 F. 1173	249 233	263 234	230 250	230 217	233 239
191 BILLERICAY	2263	M. 1066 F. 1197	223 234	205 231	211 233	213 252	214 247
192 CHELMSFORD	4332	M. 2249 F. 2083	447 435	439 400	481 417	421 444	461 385
193 ROCHFORD	3494	M. 1712 F. 1782	388 373	351 370	349 332	347 364	383 323
194 MALDON	3347	M. 1690 F. 1657	345 344	362 321	346 322	319 322	348 308
195 TENDRING	4487	M. 2222 F. 2265	449 480	424 454	452 453	446 458	451 420
196 COLCHESTER	3549	M. 1790 F. 1759	308 378	357 352	378 345	325 337	342 347
197 LEXDEN	2964	M. 1509 F. 1455	302 279	287 286	303 288	287 279	330 325
198 HALSTEAD	2021	M. 1013 F. 1008	196 204	198 195	206 178	183 214	228 227
199 BRAINTREE	3642	M. 1805 F. 1837	302 377	343 332	351 366	351 375	365 386
200 DUNMOW	2302	M. 1129 F. 1173	227 243	231 215	239 230	205 240	227 240
201 SAFFRON WALDEN	2428	M. 1168 F. 1260	266 262	188 246	247 262	222 223	261 267
15 SUFFOLK.							
202 RISBRIDGE	2432	M. 1227 F. 1205	277 233	220 207	246 275	247 284	228 206
203 SUDBURY	3885	M. 1902 F. 1983	378 389	374 354	390 410	370 397	390 383
204 COSFORD	2042	M. 1018 F. 1024	202 233	212 184	196 219	183 197	225 191
205 THINGOE	2179	M. 1065 F. 1114	217 221	187 213	215 229	218 218	228 233
206 BURY ST. EDMUND'S	1960	M. 964 F. 996	205 195	186 202	195 208	184 190	[illegible] 201
207 MILDENHALL	1286	M. 622 F. 664	140 135	121 117	124 133	117 148	120 131
208 STOW	2744	M. 1348 F. 1396	254 288	291 281	277 266	270 281	247 280
209 HARTISMERE	2106	M. 1082 F. 1024	232 205	214 199	208 206	217 183	217 231
210 HOXNE	1678	M. 833 F. 845	173 190	160 161	167 173	161 162	172 169
211 BOSMERE	2038	M. 993 F. 1045	197 215	214 204	196 278	204 198	182 200
212 SAMFORD	1518	M. 755 F. 763	161 169	145 151	143 146	172 148	134 140
213 IPSWICH	6416	M. 3287 F. 3129	685 675	633 652	632 613	678 626	659 563

REGISTRATION DISTRICT.	Total under 5 Years.		Under 1 Year.	1–	2
	Persons.	Males and Females.			
15 SUFFOLK—*cont.*					
214 WOODBRIDGE	2983	M. 1492 F. 1491	306 307	307 317	2 3
215 PLOMESGATE	2628	M. 1330 F. 1298	264 250	243 259	2 2
216 BLYTHING	3449	M. 1735 F. 1714	350 396	361 332	3 3
217 WANGFORD	1919	M. 951 F. 968	202 182	174 197	1 1
218 MUTFORD	5815	M. 2961 F. 2854	610 637	578 556	6 6
16 NORFOLK.					
219 YARMOUTH	4687	M. 2385 F. 2302	499 507	454 486	5 4
220 FLEGG	1378	M. 693 F. 685	160 147	129 131	1 1
221 SMALLBURGH	1900	M. 947 F. 953	208 204	180 182	1 1
222 ERPINGHAM	2561	M. 1262 F. 1299	239 258	256 245	25 25
223 AYLSHAM	2296	M. 1135 F. 1161	252 248	215 221	22 24
224 ST. FAITH'S	1496	M. 757 F. 739	154 182	126 137	16 13
225 NORWICH	11074	M. 5438 F. 5636	1224 1267	1089 1120	108 100
226 FOREHOE	1472	M. 748 F. 724	148 156	133 137	17 14
227 HENSTEAD	1332	M. 666 F. 666	141 128	133 130	12 14
228 BLOFIELD	1411	M. 666 F. 745	124 177	146 132	16 12
229 LODDON	1803	M. 911 F. 892	216 173	164 168	16 17
230 DEPWADE	3000	M. 1489 F. 1512	295 328	316 293	31 27
231 GUILTCROSS	1332	M. 700 F. 632	144 150	145 96	14 13
232 WAYLAND	1336	M. 702 F. 634	148 145	138 124	16 11
233 MITFORD	3490	M. 1798 F. 1692	371 306	347 341	37 38
234 WALSINGHAM	2535	M. 1267 F. 1268	259 279	223 235	23 23
235 DOCKING	2193	M. 1131 F. 1062	229 228	208 198	21 21
236 FREEBRIDGE LYNN	1582	M. 776 F. 806	159 172	157 136	16 16
237 KING'S LYNN	2357	M. 1202 F. 1155	259 266	214 246	24 21
238 DOWNHAM	2472	M. 1190 F. 1282	249 258	228 245	23 24
239 SWAFFHAM	1673	M. 814 F. 859	158 162	138 157	17 16
240 THETFORD	2817	M. 1230 F. 1087	248 230	230 208	24 20

TABLE 7.—CONDITION as to MARRIAGE and AGES of MALES and FEMALES in the EASTERN DIVISION REGISTRATION COUNTIES.

REGISTRATION COUNTY.		ALL AGES.	Under 15 years.	15–	20–	25–	35–	45–	55–
IV.—EASTERN COUNTIES.									
UNMARRIED	Males	393693	252362	65609	39469	23309	8246	4743	3322
	Females	394791	256489	59494	34546	24106	10778	6743	4792
MARRIED	Males	236385	—	263	12038	57887	57862	47268	36806
	Females	238085	—	1306	18016	64161	56736	46337	31048
WIDOWED	Males	24732	—	8	99	1124	2159	3442	5279
	Females	50018	—	9	174	2646	4843	8008	11694
14. ESSEX.									
UNMARRIED	Males	171388	108565	26859	16781	10853	3876	2040	1411
	Females	162468	107103	23406	13470	9848	4054	2258	1617
MARRIED	Males	95449	—	169	4831	26447	25484	18578	13143
	Females	95349	—	560	7987	28065	24824	17371	11663
WIDOWED	Males	9339	—	5	52	469	954	1441	2145
	Females	18275	—	4	79	879	1888	3197	4453
15. SUFFOLK.									
UNMARRIED	Males	103487	66152	17438	9845	5461	1939	1176	829
	Females	104818	65877	15910	9396	6374	2844	1851	1500
MARRIED	Males	62214	—	59	3092	14484	14275	12717	10161
	Females	62964	—	332	4916	16181	14967	12616	9011
WIDOWED	Males	7627	—	—	17	310	571	890	1471
	Females	13535	—	4	56	495	1226	2082	3075
16. NORFOLK.									
UNMARRIED	Males	124718	77675	21312	12843	6995	2425	1527	1092
	Females	128006	77509	20178	11986	8384	3900	2634	1875
MARRIED	Males	78722	—	35	4115	17550	18103	15973	13001
	Females	79092	—	414	6119	19015	18989	16110	11462
WIDOWED	Males	8566	—	3	30	345	634	1111	1603
	Females	18208	—	1	59	672	1629	2749	4168

Note.—In a few cases persons described as "married" were stated to be under 15 years of age. These have been classed with the married persons aged under 20 years."

Table 8.—CONDITION as to MARRIAGE and AGES of MALES and FEMALES in REGISTRATION DISTRICT

REGISTRATION DISTRICT.		ALL AGES.	Under 15 Years.	15–	20–	25–	35–	45–	55–	65 and upw^ds.
14 ESSEX.										
186 WEST HAM:										
UNMARRIED	M.	62645	41770	8220	6092	3946	1160	590	264	138
	F.	58588	40856	8609	4733	2060	1184	689	385	282
MARRIED	M.	35149	.	64	2163	11470	10479	6231	3394	1418
	F.	35246	.	276	3584	12522	9762	5347	2733	1022
WIDOWED	M.	2414	.	1	16	298	363	485	504	777
	F.	3906	.	2	33	380	821	1224	1542	1004
187 EPPING:										
UNMARRIED	M.	6637	4062	1087	681	440	192	106	78	51
	F.	6638	4016	1010	673	503	200	131	91	64
MARRIED	M.	3574	.	2	155	774	945	770	583	345
	F.	3803	.	18	240	892	978	744	484	247
WIDOWED	M.	432	.	.	.	22	40	70	83	217
	F.	780	.	.	1	28	76	126	181	350
188 ONGAR										
UNMARRIED	M.	3498	2094	547	300	271	121	69	59	44
	F.	3816	2632	288	222	137	79	39	46	23
MARRIED	M.	1792	.	.	63	373	407	396	316	237
	F.	1769	.	9	111	411	437	375	260	157
WIDOWED	M.	239	.	.	1	9	22	35	38	134
	F.	366	.	.	1	13	28	55	71	193

REGISTRATION DISTRICT.		ALL AGES.	Under 15 Years.	15–	20–	25–	35–	45–
14 ESSEX—*cont.*								
189 ROMFORD:								
UNMARRIED	M.	11426	7212	1831	1129	694	265	140
	F.	11325	7646	1642	919	675	254	141
MARRIED	M.	6161	.	5	368	1616	1700	1198
	F.	6236	.	46	579	1790	1691	1124
WIDOWED	M.	508	.	.	4	29	67	98
	F.	1310	.	1	7	68	156	247
190 ORSETT:								
UNMARRIED	M.	6141	3634	1121	597	395	139	89
	F.	4088	3019	512	257	173	50	35
MARRIED	M.	2884	.	4	165	774	735	577
	F.	2695	.	18	271	782	688	476
WIDOWED	M.	284	.	.	3	16	22	46
	F.	378	.	.	4	26	32	66
191 BILLERICAY:								
UNMARRIED	M.	8807	3417	988	604	406	184	134
	F.	6661	3397	749	618	433	206	119
MARRIED	M.	2930	.	2	98	697	772	567
	F.	2090	.	17	192	809	769	577
WIDOWED	M.	349	.	.	1	9	21	43
	F.	604	.	.	4	32	58	220

Table 8 *continued*.—CONDITION as to MARRIAGE and AGES of MALES and FEMALES in REGISTRATION DISTRICTS.

REGISTRATION DISTRICT.		ALL AGES.	Under 15 Years.	15–	20–	25–	35–	45–	55–	65 and upw.
SSEX—*cont.*										
ELMSFORD:										
UNMARRIED	M.	10114	6334	1615	908	609	340	173	132	103
	F.	9725	5960	1599	862	705	345	178	145	122
MARRIED	M.	5833	.	8	224	1219	1365	1164	987	668
	F.	5609	.	20	338	1380	1380	1185	840	442
WIDOWED	M.	659	.	.	2	20	52	89	163	333
	F.	1231	.	.	1	39	97	154	282	628
CHFORD:										
UNMARRIED	M.	7915	4547	1209	870	691	305	131	102	60
	F.	7002	4704	959	571	342	178	94	63	51
MARRIED	M.	4350	.	4	229	1164	1155	855	556	387
	F.	3970	.	45	368	1104	1013	710	442	231
WIDOWED	M.	431	.	3	4	18	45	53	96	212
	F.	738	.	.	7	27	88	123	201	292
LDON:										
UNMARRIED	M.	7444	4821	1264	570	365	186	106	86	81
	F.	6791	4706	921	432	343	129	93	72	46
MARRIED	M.	4099	.	6	153	808	987	827	732	536
	F.	4225	.	29	269	1058	1041	821	662	345
WIDOWED	M.	483	.	.	3	11	34	63	114	258
	F.	770	.	.	1	28	73	110	188	370
NDRING:										
UNMARRIED	M.	10215	6290	1668	1120	644	224	128	83	58
	F.	9128	6250	1332	657	412	192	112	93	78
MARRIED	M.	6256	.	7	274	1456	1559	1291	1015	654
	F.	6074	.	38	435	1577	1499	1206	858	461
WIDOWED	M.	714	.	.	1	23	61	90	172	367
	F.	1090	.	1	4	49	98	180	265	313
LCHESTER:										
UNMARRIED	M.	9008	4656	1614	1353	882	267	96	68	72
	F.	8748	4928	1482	924	670	320	175	133	107
MARRIED	M.	4503	.	3	231	1279	1187	859	588	356
	F.	4607	.	41	456	1398	1124	830	525	233
WIDOWED	M.	411	.	1	1	20	44	77	106	162
	F.	1077	.	.	5	54	134	198	272	414
EXDEN:										
UNMARRIED	M.	6646	4388	1096	567	290	131	78	46	50
	F.	6128	4138	808	561	339	136	93	44	59
MARRIED	M.	3821	.	2	152	809	830	810	678	490
	F.	3941	.	25	253	935	976	861	614	337
WIDOWED	M.	466	.	.	2	18	31	59	97	259
	F.	773	.	.	3	42	68	124	155	381
ALSTEAD:										
UNMARRIED	M.	4554	3036	784	364	189	76	50	32	23
	F.	5477	3116	871	542	472	216	126	77	57
MARRIED	M.	2962	.	1	129	616	876	847	560	333
	F.	2999	.	6	181	678	752	680	492	230
WIDOWED	M.	380	.	.	3	10	26	56	83	192
	F.	633	.	.	1	21	48	85	165	313
RAINTREE:										
UNMARRIED	M.	7979	5175	1336	689	405	151	79	97	47
	F.	8838	5407	1307	802	834	289	161	124	121
MARRIED	M.	5012	.	8	228	1071	1148	1058	883	616
	F.	5042	.	25	322	1201	1229	1094	753	418
WIDOWED	M.	611	.	.	4	28	55	70	159	295
	F.	1148	.	.	4	38	78	175	280	573
UNMOW:										
UNMARRIED	M.	5687	3513	959	488	307	142	86	74	58
	F.	4949	3386	618	362	292	113	85	67	56
MARRIED	M.	3134	.	2	115	579	750	664	598	426
	F.	3117	.	13	180	684	726	720	527	267
WIDOWED	M.	469	.	.	3	16	34	63	97	226
	F.	724	.	.	1	18	52	91	174	388
AFFRON WALDEN:										
UNMARRIED	M.	5582	3540	929	509	296	114	73	74	56
	F.	5400	3562	741	445	290	143	87	76	47
MARRIED	M.	3189	.	3	144	692	739	659	540	403
	F.	3341	.	12	211	775	773	681	504	385
WIDOWED	M.	429	.	.	4	13	31	48	100	239
	F.	747	.	.	2	19	61	107	151	407
5 SUFFOLK.										
ISBRIDGE:										
UNMARRIED	M.	5101	3479	876	383	187	98	40	25	43
	F.	5173	3415	775	410	273	161	76	82	41
MARRIED	M.	2968	.	4	182	683	679	586	500	334
	F.	2988	.	16	253	736	688	821	446	218
WIDOWED	M.	359	.	.	.	7	34	48	85	185
	F.	625	.	.	2	25	63	92	157	286

REGISTRATION DISTRICT.		ALL AGES.	Under 15 Years.	15–	20–	25–	35–	45–	55–	65 and upw.
15 SUFFOLK—*cont.*										
203 SUDBURY:										
UNMARRIED	M.	8739	5628	1527	773	405	147	125	84	53
	F.	8986	5595	1376	799	601	286	166	110	93
MARRIED	M.	5290	.	8	247	1132	1134	1180	966	622
	F.	5326	.	25	346	1272	1328	1127	808	422
WIDOWED	M.	684	.	.	1	26	58	72	124	383
	F.	1131	.	.	2	37	93	180	268	551
204 COSFORD:										
UNMARRIED	M.	4531	2870	791	419	232	77	68	38	36
	F.	4643	2981	681	353	241	103	75	50	54
MARRIED	M.	2865	.	2	154	616	604	622	491	375
	F.	2886	.	22	239	688	635	608	443	256
WIDOWED	M.	405	.	.	.	19	27	46	74	239
	F.	590	.	.	.	26	40	82	120	322
205 THINGOE:										
UNMARRIED	M.	4881	3066	854	424	277	119	62	40	39
	F.	4591	3058	636	354	286	109	64	46	38
MARRIED	M.	2961	.	1	101	637	664	615	521	422
	F.	2968	.	2	196	695	705	621	467	278
WIDOWED	M.	353	.	.	3	16	25	43	81	185
	F.	632	.	.	.	13	58	73	136	354
206 BURY ST. EDMUNDS:										
UNMARRIED	M.	4746	2779	911	514	298	113	51	43	36
	F.	5204	2879	890	531	416	205	120	88	75
MARRIED	M.	2559	.	.	133	678	654	486	364	244
	F.	2578	.	19	207	747	670	465	299	165
WIDOWED	M.	270	.	.	.	20	27	38	59	128
	F.	753	.	1	2	31	70	142	174	333
207 MILDENHALL:										
UNMARRIED	M.	2641	1725	419	239	135	55	32	19	17
	F.	2569	1771	341	174	142	61	29	25	23
MARRIED	M.	1614	.	2	85	360	383	319	277	208
	F.	1608	.	5	135	382	306	313	243	134
WIDOWED	M.	192	.	.	2	5	17	17	44	107
	F.	332	.	.	2	10	18	44	83	175
208 STOW:										
UNMARRIED	M.	5842	3796	963	518	294	123	64	39	45
	F.	5960	3947	885	468	334	131	116	65	53
MARRIED	M.	3607	.	2	184	808	796	748	622	447
	F.	3594	.	10	274	898	840	724	552	300
WIDOWED	M.	421	.	.	.	16	37	46	100	222
	F.	762	.	.	.	21	78	106	172	384
209 HARTISMERE:										
UNMARRIED	M.	4781	3142	782	385	210	99	83	56	50
	F.	4450	2976	603	356	321	118	79	56	60
MARRIED	M.	2847	.	7	155	614	565	583	520	403
	F.	2827	.	29	201	764	588	586	470	279
WIDOWED	M.	348	.	.	.	13	16	44	71	202
	F.	531	.	.	3	17	53	80	121	284
210 HOXNE:										
UNMARRIED	M.	3757	2390	664	356	197	82	40	25	23
	F.	3528	2306	495	268	177	85	56	33	24
MARRIED	M.	2296	.	.	113	482	643	471	434	353
	F.	2285	.	12	165	488	488	464	405	243
WIDOWED	M.	302	.	.	1	15	28	29	46	183
	F.	483	.	.	3	13	18	84	101	244
211 BOSMERE:										
UNMARRIED	M.	4686	2946	791	440	268	95	71	56	31
	F.	4326	2925	587	345	206	98	73	51	41
MARRIED	M.	2772	.	9	139	504	660	584	466	367
	F.	2747	.	13	205	647	651	577	402	252
WIDOWED	M.	338	.	.	1	12	20	60	72	173
	F.	533	.	.	.	22	49	65	114	283
212 SAMFORD:										
UNMARRIED	M.	3440	2142	584	338	186	76	48	43	24
	F.	3206	2090	439	268	205	87	50	31	36
MARRIED	M.	2137	.	2	68	416	501	477	394	279
	F.	2154	.	10	128	475	520	466	363	192
WIDOWED	M.	255	.	.	.	9	22	32	62	130
	F.	406	.	.	1	13	84	67	86	215
213 IPSWICH:										
UNMARRIED	M.	14139	8808	2309	1818	904	293	146	92	69
	F.	15604	8910	2727	1701	1145	498	333	204	176
MARRIED	M.	9650	.	9	461	2403	2139	1734	1241	663
	F.	9673	.	45	763	2651	2198	1740	1022	454
WIDOWED	M.	819	.	.	3	56	82	134	200	344
	F.	2145	.	1	16	91	283	292	524	889

Table 8 *continued.*—Condition as to Marriage and Ages of Males and Females in Registration Districts.

Registration District.		All Ages.	Under 15 Years.	15–	20–	25–	35–	45–	55–	65 and upw.
15 SUFFOLK—*cont.*										
214 WOODBRIDGE:										
Unmarried	M.	6632	4263	1075	559	377	144	96	75	43
	F.	6575	4105	940	579	441	211	132	38	70
Married	M.	4026	.	.	148	924	950	923	743	580
	F.	4074	.	16	278	966	956	929	658	378
Widowed	M.	[illegible]	.	.	1	17	32	61	105	300
	F.	893	.	.	2	32	73	129	200	457
215 PLOMESGATE:										
Unmarried	M.	6093	3859	1028	609	316	106	65	47	33
	F.	5910	3665	980	510	384	166	112	78	60
Married	M.	3654	.	1	149	789	794	780	822	583
	F.	3661	.	14	243	874	844	765	696	381
Widowed	M.	414	.	.	2	19	29	45	68	251
	F.	757	.	.	.	18	64	114	146	415
216 BLYTHING:										
Unmarried	M.	7495	4942	1167	694	392	177	75	55	53
	F.	7444	4894	1053	613	414	174	125	96	75
Married	M.	4670	.	.	168	1026	1048	909	745	685
	F.	4735	.	18	328	1185	1082	940	702	480
Widowed	M.	512	.	.	.	16	39	69	85	303
	F.	961	.	.	.	31	72	116	228	514
217 WANGFORD:										
Unmarried	M.	4253	2738	658	439	223	74	46	39	36
	F.	4326	2670	688	367	258	128	79	74	67
Married	M.	2468	.	6	116	557	606	503	373	307
	F.	2479	.	13	191	626	622	474	349	204
Widowed	M.	307	.	.	1	11	23	41	63	168
	F.	623	.	.	2	16	48	96	138	323
218 MUTFORD:										
Unmarried	M.	11731	7532	2030	1237	563	172	85	67	36
	F.	11805	7602	1896	994	635	309	172	115	83
Married	M.	6801	.	12	461	1919	1654	1258	922	576
	F.	7190	.	62	753	2162	1741	1266	795	411
Widowed	M.	525	.	.	2	33	55	67	112	256
	F.	1426	.	2	7	85	164	260	302	606
16. NORFOLK.										
219 YARMOUTH:										
Unmarried	M.	10433	6164	1911	1219	586	247	176	83	47
	F.	11129	6114	2093	1226	782	387	281	189	139
Married	M.	6463	.	15	445	1650	1676	1253	873	545
	F.	6673	.	60	607	1931	1708	1241	786	372
Widowed	M.	563	.	1	2	43	46	92	124	255
	F.	1909	.	.	6	104	219	351	481	741
220 FLEGG:										
Unmarried	M.	2822	1906	410	264	134	43	35	19	13
	F.	2723	1837	406	228	132	49	27	31	16
Married	M.	1785	.	5	75	394	397	361	304	249
	F.	1888	.	14	179	471	419	365	265	175
Widowed	M.	171	.	.	.	7	18	23	35	88
	F.	325	.	.	3	22	32	49	54	165
221 SMALLBURGH:										
Unmarried	M.	4161	2678	687	385	218	80	42	43	32
	F.	3993	2643	565	297	230	123	75	29	31
Married	M.	2685	.	5	146	573	615	542	434	370
	F.	2691	.	27	208	625	643	648	307	250
Widowed	M.	293	.	.	2	12	27	36	41	176
	F.	525	.	.	.	19	35	86	113	273
222 ERPINGHAM:										
Unmarried	M.	6815	3846	1004	597	372	106	61	42	43
	F.	5788	3630	833	513	378	162	111	83	78
Married	M.	3673	.	4	170	792	752	800	661	494
	F.	3772	.	20	272	882	835	790	602	364
Widowed	M.	443	.	.	2	16	30	43	80	272
	F.	798	.	.	5	26	70	108	159	430
223 AYLSHAM:										
Unmarried	M.	5378	3281	972	569	277	116	82	37	44
	F.	5088	3246	739	405	293	180	101	68	76
Married	M.	3260	.	5	160	686	701	689	579	440
	F.	3295	.	14	244	751	795	683	524	314
Widowed	M.	334	.	.	.	8	22	28	68	208
	F.	702	.	.	4	14	50	78	162	394
224 ST. FAITH'S:										
Unmarried	M.	3274	2056	559	347	164	55	46	30	21
	F.	3280	2040	476	315	195	111	75	38	30
Married	M.	2098	.	2	110	477	463	427	343	276
	F.	2118	.	13	163	504	487	436	309	204
Widowed	M.	228	.	.	1	10	31	35	29	122
	F.	422	.	.	2	13	28	57	95	227

Registration District.		All Ages.	Under 15 Years.	15–	20–	25–	35–	45–	55–
16 NORFOLK—*cont.*									
225 NORWICH:									
Unmarried	M.	23441	14823	3971	2437	1310	404	241	146
	F.	27700	15289	4885	3021	2018	912	670	478
Married	M.	16371	.	33	1100	4106	3818	3085	2106
	F.	15726	.	115	1512	4486	3829	2973	1897
Widowed	M.	1479	.	1	11	88	131	216	211
	F.	4129	.	1	17	162	450	783	989
226 FOREHOE:									
Unmarried	M.	3502	2154	697	375	197	64	51	30
	F.	3377	2110	498	293	266	84	54	39
Married	M.	2158	.	1	86	430	602	490	396
	F.	2169	.	5	135	467	654	465	335
Widowed	M.	277	.	1	.	10	12	28	67
	F.	488	.	.	1	12	38	67	114
227 HENSTEAD:									
Unmarried	M.	3052	1887	528	324	160	59	36	30
	F.	2952	1820	448	285	201	74	45	46
Married	M.	1985	.	2	111	426	424	388	346
	F.	1980	.	7	155	465	482	419	294
Widowed	M.	241	.	.	2	9	17	31	59
	F.	426	.	.	.	13	41	64	83
228 BLOFIELD:									
Unmarried	M.	3277	1963	615	346	215	95	61	45
	F.	3298	1973	446	273	240	153	106	61
Married	M.	2170	.	3	132	467	478	430	383
	F.	2222	.	19	189	523	481	474	332
Widowed	M.	205	.	.	.	6	19	34	30
	F.	451	.	.	.	21	41	78	98
229 LODDON:									
Unmarried	M.	3880	2573	566	361	197	66	46	46
	F.	4007	2540	552	363	243	107	86	68
Married	M.	2547	.	1	103	535	593	536	465
	F.	2552	.	9	150	602	671	580	380
Widowed	M.	260	.	.	1	8	23	30	54
	F.	460	.	.	1	12	44	66	104
230 DEPWADE:									
Unmarried	M.	6789	4272	1125	663	382	122	94	66
	F.	6934	4416	1095	577	396	181	111	86
Married	M.	4206	.	3	175	851	942	885	743
	F.	4240	.	17	251	980	1000	908	645
Widowed	M.	480	.	.	4	13	28	66	94
	F.	833	.	.	3	29	73	113	211
231 GUILTCROSS:									
Unmarried	M.	3178	1947	569	315	188	91	37	37
	F.	2922	1891	414	247	193	74	52	37
Married	M.	1880	.	.	77	372	418	397	307
	F.	1902	.	8	109	410	471	415	321
Widowed	M.	248	.	.	.	12	17	30	47
	F.	434	.	.	1	10	32	50	91
232 WAYLAND:									
Unmarried	M.	3093	1929	561	292	154	82	81	35
	F.	2891	1851	421	235	182	86	54	42
Married	M.	2052	.	2	104	409	433	432	372
	F.	2058	.	14	144	447	496	420	347
Widowed	M.	206	.	.	.	9	10	25	43
	F.	416	.	.	2	13	35	51	84
233 MITFORD:									
Unmarried	M.	8064	4973	1384	828	452	162	100	85
	F.	7706	4855	1165	661	477	203	148	119
Married	M.	4987	.	2	217	1094	1088	1008	911
	F.	4987	.	22	339	1186	1138	1042	777
Widowed	M.	539	.	.	1	17	45	76	100
	F.	1084	.	.	2	41	77	129	221
234 WALSINGHAM:									
Unmarried	M.	5837	3568	989	646	352	118	72	67
	F.	5778	3563	806	519	355	201	111	96
Married	M.	3620	.	2	166	732	823	724	626
	F.	3518	.	11	248	829	834	718	551
Widowed	M.	440	.	.	1	18	20	65	73
	F.	852	.	.	2	36	70	107	190
235 DOCKING:									
Unmarried	M.	5122	3212	912	438	262	108	58	41
	F.	5015	3117	739	470	312	162	97	80
Married	M.	3136	.	8	113	686	737	869	563
	F.	3171	.	10	170	717	797	672	409
Widowed	M.	378	.	.	.	9	28	60	67
	F.	801	.	.	1	22	65	84	146
236 FREEBRIDGE LYNN:									
Unmarried	M.	3572	2184	629	377	212	78	38	31
	F.	3489	2283	613	269	225	95	58	29
Married	M.	2252	.	1	102	475	548	441	390
	F.	2266	.	7	137	535	546	490	346
Widowed	M.	229	.	.	.	4	9	27	48
	F.	427	.	.	.	9	36	45	98

Table 8 *continued*.—CONDITION as to MARRIAGE and AGES of MALES and FEMALES in REGISTRATION DISTRICTS.

REGISTRATION DISTRICT.		ALL AGES.	Under 15 Years.	15–	20–	25–	35–	45–	55–	65 and upw^s.
NORFOLK—cont.										
KING'S LYNN:										
UNMARRIED	M.	5354	3179	938	603	398	113	67	32	29
	F.	5764	3189	883	607	405	222	151	103	104
MARRIED	M.	3414	.	.	191	924	845	608	514	335
	F.	3386	.	10	288	969	805	639	422	233
WIDOWED	M.	362	.	.	1	17	29	54	78	183
	F.	928	.	.	5	43	69	127	242	446
DOWNHAM:										
UNMARRIED	M.	5734	3589	1014	553	330	119	62	46	35
	F.	5529	3594	800	460	340	132	92	59	52
MARRIED	M.	3529	.	3	132	765	831	718	636	444
	F.	3597	.	6	248	811	837	749	576	302
WIDOWED	M.	402	.		.	6	29	56	79	232
	F.	663	.		1	20	40	95	174	327
16 NORFOLK—cont.										
239 SWAFFHAM:										
UNMARRIED	M.	3715	2319	667	355	212	55	44	37	28
	F.	3738	2300	671	318	216	108	52	46	37
MARRIED	M.	2341	.	1	83	504	516	486	421	330
	F.	2343	.	6	147	545	560	482	375	227
WIDOWED	M.	238	.	.	1	16	17	27	48	135
	F.	485	.	.	2	13	34	63	104	209
240 THETFORD:										
UNMARRIED	M.	5249	3373	819	484	279	105	75	57	48
	F.	4965	3429	711	417	367	114	85	67	35
MARRIED	M.	3204	.	2	136	657	765	661	549	434
	F.	3219	.	10	231	768	783	620	510	290
WIDOWED	M.	353	.	.	1	17	28	51	69	197
	F.	646	.	.	1	28	51	84	144	338

Table 9.—CONDITION as to MARRIAGE and AGES of MALES and FEMALES in each URBAN SANITARY DISTRICT of which the POPULATION EXCEEDS 50,000 PERSONS.

URBAN SANITARY DISTRICT.		ALL AGES.	Under 15 Years.	15–	20–	25–	35–	45–	55–	65 and upwards.
WEST HAM:										
UNMARRIED	M.	40364	26593	5981	4078	2863	831	321	144	53
	F.	36427	26367	5099	2455	1454	523	246	161	122
MARRIED	M.	23607	.	46	1537	7825	7128	4187	2121	763
	F.	23579	.	198	2951	8468	6519	3869	1691	583
WIDOWED	M.	1439	.	1	9	149	253	333	316	378
	F.	3637	.	1	15	258	543	780	938	1602
IPSWICH:										
UNMARRIED	M.	14191	8836	2329	1520	907	292	140	89	69
	F.	15747	8940	2737	1710	1146	499	335	205	175
MARRIED	M.	8705	.	9	463	2415	2149	1744	1254	668
	F.	8927	.	45	772	2069	2201	1747	1039	454
WIDOWED	M.	830	.	.	3	56	83	134	203	351
	F.	2146	.	1	10	90	254	394	528	869
NORWICH:										
UNMARRIED	M.	23441	14823	3971	2437	1310	404	241	146	169
	F.	27700	15289	4885	3621	2918	912	670	472	433
MARRIED	M.	15371	.	33	1100	4108	3618	3006	2186	1284
	F.	15725	.	115	1512	4486	3629	2973	1897	913
WIDOWED	M.	1476	.	1	11	83	131	216	341	693
	F.	4129	.	1	17	152	456	786	969	1748

Table 10.—Occupations of Males and Females in the Eastern Division and its Registration Counties, and in each Urban Sanitary District of which the Population exceeds 50,000 Persons.

Occupations.	Eastern Division.		Registration Counties. 14. Essex.		15. Suffolk.		16. Norfolk.	
	Males.	Females.	Males.	Females.	Males.	Females.	Males.	Females.
TOTAL	660710	682814	276176	276092	178728	180817	211806	225668
I. PROFESSIONAL CLASS.								
1. Persons engaged in the General or Local Government of the Country.								
1. National Government.								
Peer, M.P., Privy Councillor (not otherwise described)	13	.	1	.	4	.	8	.
Civil Service (officers and clerks)	931	255	484	116	223	53	224	86
Civil Service (messengers, &c.)	923	37	408	12	236	7	279	18
Prison Officer, &c.	46	12	23	4	13	5	10	3
2. Local Government.								
Police	1467	.	774	.	289	.	404	.
Municipal, Parish, Union, District, Officer	619	215	274	89	145	52	200	74
Other Local or County Official	262	.	95	.	72	.	95	.
3. East Indian and Colonial Service.								
East Indian and Colonial Service	6	.	1	.	2	.	3	.
2. Persons engaged in the Defence of the Country.								
1. Army (at Home).								
Army Officer (effective or retired)	374	.	233	.	75	.	66	.
Soldier and Non-commissioned Officer	4172	.	3146	.	834	.	192	.
Militia, Yeomanry, Volunteers	389	.	67	.	88	.	234	.
Army Pensioner	356	1	216	.	140	.	199	1
2. Navy (ashore or in port).								
Navy Officer (effective or retired)	99	.	50	.	29	.	20	.
Seaman, R.N.	634	.	408	.	111	.	115	.
Royal Marines (officers and men)	17	.	14	.	3	.	.	.
Navy Pensioner	319	1	183	1	65	.	71	.
3. Persons engaged in Professional Occupations (with their immediate Subordinates).								
1. Clerical Profession.								
Clergyman (Established Church)	1784	.	547	.	538	.	709	.
Roman Catholic Priest	56	.	35	.	11	.	9	.
Minister, Priest, of other religious bodies	503	.	188	.	142	.	183	.
Missionary, Scripture Reader, Itinerant Preacher	113	71	53	37	10	15	51	19
Nun, Sister of Charity	.	116	.	85	.	.	.	31
Theological Student	5	.	33	.	7	.	10	.
Church, Chapel, Cemetery—Officer, Servant	262	66	101	47	67	8	94	11
2. Legal Profession.								
Barrister, Solicitor	637	.	260	.	154	.	223	.
Law Student	42	.	24	.	7	.	11	.
Law Clerk, and others connected with Law	1041	2	475	2	184	.	382	.
3. Medical Profession.								
Physician, Surgeon, General Practitioner	688	.	247	.	133	.	198	.
Dentist	84	.	21	.	23	.	40	.
Medical Student, Assistant	167	1	90	.	34	.	43	1
Midwife	.	116	.	36	.	23	.	57
Subordinate Medical Service	97	2677	42	1066	15	753	40	858
4. Teachers.								
Schoolmaster	1895	5083	802	2155	474	1546	619	1382
Teacher, Professor, Lecturer	154	1957	71	785	43	546	40	626
School Service, and others concerned in Teaching	56	66	36	30	7	10	13	26
5. Literary and Scientific Persons.								
Author, Editor, Journalist	62	11	38	7	7	.	17	4
Reporter, Short-hand Writer	82	.	34	.	17	.	31	.
Persons engaged in Scientific Pursuits	37	1	15	.	10	.	12	1
Literary, Scientific, Institution, Service, &c.	23	4	15	2	4	2	4	.
6. Engineers and Surveyors.								
Civil Engineer	201	.	109		44	.	48	.
Mining Engineer	5	.	2	.	2	.	1	.
Land, House, Ship, Surveyor	330	.	110		92	.	118	.
7. Artists.								
Painter (artist)	135	45	75	23	26	9	34	13
Engraver (artist)	57	1	46	.	.	.	11	1
Sculptor	11	.	6	.	3	.	2	.
Architect	198	.	122	.	43	.	33	.
Musician, Music Master	438	479	167	213	87	136	184	130
Art Student	40	11	20	7	9	2	11	2
Photographer	212	18	82	6	52	4	78	8
Actor	54	35	19	14	8	2	27	19
Art, Music, Theatre, Service	25	4	9	.	2	.	14	4

Note.—Persons returned as engaged in more than one occupation have been referred to the one that appeared to be of most importance; or, if there was no difference in this respect, to the one first given by the person in his or her return. In some cases special rules have been followed: *e.g.*, "Clergyman and Schoolmaster" in combination has always been referred to "Schoolmaster"; a Member of Parliament or Peer engaged in any branch of commerce or industry has always been referred to this latter, not to "Peer, M.P."

The numbers returned under any heading include Labourers, Apprentices, and Assistants, as well as Masters, but not Clerks, Messengers, Errand boys, Porters, or Watchmen, for which occupations there are special headings. Civil, Military, and Naval Clerks, Law, Bank, Insurance, and Railway Clerks, and Government and Railway Porters, are, however, exceptions to this rule. Many young persons, being Apprentices or Assistants, have therefore been referred to occupations usually followed by adults. Women also, chiefly widows or orphans carrying on the business of their deceased husbands or fathers, will sometimes be found under occupations commonly followed by men only.

Persons returned as *retired* from any business have not been referred to that business. Inmates of workhouses have been referred to their trades, unless their age or infirmities showed that they were past work. But persons who might be supposed to be only temporarily separated from their usual employment, such as Prisoners, and Patients in General Hospitals, have been classed under their usual occupations.

In some cases, for convenience of space, the male designation, *e.g.*, "Schoolmaster," alone is given, instead of "Schoolmaster, Schoolmistress."

Table 10 *continued.*—OCCUPATIONS of MALES and FEMALES in the EASTERN DIVISION and its REGISTRATION COUNTIES, and in each URBAN SANITARY DISTRICT of which the POPULATION exceeds 50,000 PERSONS.

OCCUPATIONS.	EASTERN DIVISION.		REGISTRATION COUNTIES.					
			14. ESSEX.		15. SUFFOLK.		16. NORFOLK.	
	Males.	Females.	Males.	Females.	Males.	Females.	Males.	Females.
8. *Persons engaged in Exhibitions, Shows, Games, &c.*								
Performer, Showman, Exhibition, Service	45	13	18	10	.	1	27	2
Billiard, Cricket, & other Games, Service	93	.	36	.	22	.	35	.
II. DOMESTIC CLASS.								
4. PERSONS ENGAGED IN DOMESTIC OFFICES OR SERVICES.								
1. *Domestic Service.*								
Domestic Coachman, Groom	4903	.	1902	.	1336	.	1645	.
Domestic Gardener	5066	.	2178	.	1282	.	1606	.
Domestic Indoor Servant	2298	60432	924	23527	600	10631	774	20274
Lodge, Gate, Park, Keeper (not Government)	65	35	36	10	13	14	16	11
Inn, Hotel, Servant	1282	1120	729	515	287	275	266	330
College, Club, Service	19	8	6	1	6	1	7	6
2. *Other Service.*								
Office Keeper (not Government)	24	45	11	13	4	12	9	20
Cook (not domestic)	73	17	61	8	4	8	8	1
Charwoman	.	5042	.	1431	.	1396	.	2212
Washing and Bathing Service	68	9196	42	3745	11	2475	15	2976
Hospital and Institution Service	224	454	79	211	47	108	98	140
Others engaged in Service	13	2	8	2	2	.	3	.
III. COMMERCIAL CLASS.								
5. PERSONS ENGAGED IN COMMERCIAL OCCUPATIONS.								
1. *Merchants and Agents.*								
Merchant	293	1	175	.	41	.	77	1
Broker, Agent, Factor	854	11	554	6	110	2	190	3
Auctioneer, Appraiser, Valuer, House Agent	421	1	168	.	109	.	144	1
Accountant	398	3	226	1	65	1	107	1
Salesman, Buyer (not otherwise described)	59	13	51	8	5	1	3	4
Commercial Traveller	1087	.	614	.	184	.	289	.
Commercial Clerk	6301	156	4350	79	790	38	1152	39
Officer of Commercial Company, Guild, Society, &c.	21	.	17	.	1	.	3	.
2. *Dealers in Money.*								
Banker	38	.	16	.	10	.	12	.
Bank Service	716	.	383	.	136	.	197	.
Bill Discounter, Bill Broker, Finance Agent	8	.	7	.	1	.	.	.
3. *Persons occupied in Insurance.*								
Life, House, Ship, &c., Insurance Service	516	6	268	4	66	1	182	1
6. PERSONS ENGAGED IN CONVEYANCE OF MEN, GOODS, AND MESSAGES.								
1. *On Railways.*								
Railway Engine Driver, Stoker	861	.	506	.	138	.	218	.
Railway Guard	348	.	216	.	58	.	74	.
Pointsman, Level Crossing Man	203	83	97	5	54	5	52	23
Other Railway Officials and Servants	4235	16	2407	8	802	3	1026	6
2. *On Roads.*								
Toll Collector, Turnpike Gate Keeper	16	7	5	1	2	2	9	4
Omnibus, Coach, Cab, Owner—Livery Stable Keeper	225	5	103	3	45	1	77	1
Cabman, Flyman, Coachman (not domestic)	773	.	386	.	140	.	233	.
Carman, Carrier, Carter, Haulier	4124	27	2134	7	911	7	1079	13
Tramway Companies' Service	77	.	57	.	18	.	2	.
Wheel Chair Proprietor, Attendant, &c.	4	.	.	.	2	.	2	.
3. *On Canals, Rivers and Seas.*								
Inland Navigation Service	42	7	28	7	6	.	8	.
Bargeman, Lighterman, Waterman	1078	3	603	2	109	.	367	1
Navigation Service (on shore)	174	12	53	3	53	7	62	2
Seaman (Merchant Service)	7502	.	4898	.	1204	.	1400	.
Pilot	167	.	51	.	82	.	34	.
Ship Steward, Cook	433	78	350	13	17	3	36	2
Boatman on Seas	276	.	16	.	42	.	218	.
Harbour, Dock, Wharf, Lighthouse, Service	2575	8	2200	7	166	.	209	1
4. *In Storage.*								
Warehouseman (not Manchester)	660	13	421	1	70	.	169	9
Meter, Weigher	113	.	46	.	35	.	33	.
5. *In conveying Messages, Porterage, &c.*								
Messenger, Porter, Watchman (not Railway nor Government)	4659	48	2813	17	1145	17	1521	14
Telegraph, Telephone, Service	206	89	113	53	44	14	49	22

Table 10 *continued.*—Occupations of Males and Females in the Eastern Division and it Registration Counties, and in each Urban Sanitary District of which the Populatio exceeds 50,000 Persons.

Occupations.	Eastern Division.		Registration Counties. 14. Essex.		15. Suffolk.		16. Norfolk.	
	Males.	Females.	Males.	Females.	Males.	Females.	Males.	Females.
IV. AGRICULTURAL CLASS.								
7. Persons engaged in Agriculture.								
1. *In Fields and Pastures.*								
Farmer, Grazier	12527	904	3083	220	4028	325	5418	369
Farmer's, Grazier's—Son, Grandson, Brother, Nephew*	3463	.	803	.	1164	.	1436	.
Farm Bailiff	2971	.	1012	.	934	.	1025	.
Agricultural Labourer, Farm Servant, Cottager	112588	3084	37742	638	38515	710	36331	1736
Shepherd	2327	.	436	.	769	.	1122	.
Land Drainage Service (not in towns)	142	1	20	.	33	1	89	.
Agricultural Machine—Proprietor, Attendant	588	5	210	2	224	1	254	2
Agricultural Student, Pupil	58	.	17	.	20	.	21	.
Others engaged in, or connected with, Agriculture	27	1	10	1	7	.	10	.
2. *In Woods.*								
Woodman	582	.	102	.	231	.	249	.
3. *In Gardens.*								
Nurseryman, Seedsman, Florist	504	32	285	17	103	7	116	8
Gardener (not domestic)	4377	126	1705	57	1196	20	1476	49
8. Persons engaged about Animals.								
1. *About Animals.*								
Horse Proprietor, Breeder, Dealer	144	1	45	1	38	.	61	.
Groom, Horse-keeper, Horse-breaker	2977	4	1020	1	870	1	1087	2
Veterinary Surgeon, Farrier	494	.	216	.	133	.	146	.
Cattle, Sheep, Pig—Dealer, Salesman	549	3	141	1	188	1	220	1
Drover	328	.	81	.	71	.	178	.
Gamekeeper	1422	.	198	.	512	.	712	.
Dog, Bird, Animal—Keeper, Dealer	199	31	28	8	63	16	108	7
Vermin destroyer	389	.	69	.	104	.	215	.
Fisherman	6604	37	973	7	2761	2	2870	28
Knacker, Catsmeat Dealer, &c., &c.	38	1	18	1	12	.	8	.
V. INDUSTRIAL CLASS.								
9. Persons working and dealing in Books, Prints, and Maps.								
1. *Books.*								
Publisher, Bookseller, Librarian	275	66	123	23	60	27	92	16
Music—Publisher, Seller, Printer	27	7	7	1	7	5	13	1
Bookbinder	264	134	122	37	53	47	89	50
Printer	2115	123	777	11	656	105	682	7
Newspaper Agent, News Room Keeper	133	48	68	26	35	11	30	11
Others	1	.	1	.	.	.	.	.
2. *Prints and Maps.*								
Lithographer, Lithographic Printer	104	.	55	.	17	.	32	.
Copper Plate and Steel Plate Printer	8	.	7	.	1	.	.	.
Map and Print—Colourer, Seller	11	1	8	.	1	.	2	1
10. Persons working and dealing in Machines and Implements.								
1. *Machines.*								
Engine, Machine, Maker	1547	5	930	2	319	3	298	.
Millwright	305	.	92	.	115	.	98	.
Fitter, Turner (Engine and Machine)	2487	.	1368	.	635	.	484	.
Boiler Maker	786	.	571	.	136	.	79	.
Spinning and Weaving Machine Maker	24	19	15	2	1	.	8	17
Agricultural Machine and Implement Maker	218	1	43	.	124	.	46	1
Domestic Machinery—Maker, Dealer	12	.	5	.	3	.	4	.
2. *Tools and Implements.*								
Tool Maker, Dealer	59	2	28	.	6	.	25	3
Cutler, Scissors Maker	102	.	32	.	25	.	45	.
File Maker	11	1	9	1	2	.	.	.
Saw Maker	29	.	18	.	7	.	9	.
Pin Maker	1	.	1	.	.	.	.	.
Needle Maker	1	.	.	.	.	.	.	.
Steel Pen Maker	.	.	.	.	.	.	1	.
Pencil Maker (Wood)	.	.	.	.	.	.	.	.
Domestic Implement Maker	8	.	5	.	1	.	2	.
3. *Watches and Philosophical Instruments.*								
Watch Maker, Clock Maker	809	22	306	7	215	3	289	12
Philosophical Instrument Maker, Optician	78	3	71	2	3	.	4	1
Electrical Apparatus Maker	138	.	124	.	22	.	12	.
Weighing and Measuring Apparatus Maker	37	.	24	.	6	.	7	.

* Only male relatives living with the farmer or grazier, and, therefore, presumably engaged in agriculture, are included above.

Table 10 *continued.*—OCCUPATIONS of MALES and FEMALES in the EASTERN DIVISION and its REGISTRATION COUNTIES, and in each URBAN SANITARY DISTRICT of which the POPULATION exceeds 50,000 PERSONS.

OCCUPATIONS.	EASTERN DIVISION.		REGISTRATION COUNTIES. 14. ESSEX.		15. SUFFOLK.		16. NORFOLK.	
	Males.	Females.	Males.	Females.	Males.	Females.	Males.	Females.
4. Surgical Instruments.								
Surgical Instrument Maker	11	5	9	4	.	.	2	1
5. Arms and Ordnance.								
Gunsmith, Gun Manufacturer	110	1	47	1	25	.	38	.
Ordnance Manufacturer	6	.	5	.	.	.	1	.
Sword, Bayonet—Maker, Cutler	3	.	3	.	.	.	.	.
Others	.	.	.	.	.	.	.	.
6. Musical Instruments.								
Musical Instrument Maker, Dealer	160	2	80	.	34	1	46	1
7. Type, Dies, Medals, Coins.								
Type Cutter, Founder	19	.	19	.	.	.	.	.
Die, Seal, Coin, Medal, Maker	11	.	9	.	1	.	1	.
8. Tackle for Sports and Games.								
Toy Maker, Dealer	38	49	28	28	6	13	4	8
Fishing Rod, Tackle, Maker, Dealer	4	.	3	.	.	.	1	.
Apparatus for other Games, Maker, Dealer	11	1	10	1	1	.	.	.
11. PERSONS WORKING AND DEALING IN HOUSES, FURNITURE, AND DECORATIONS.								
1. Houses.								
Builder	1725	13	914	5	421	6	390	2
Carpenter, Joiner	12825	11	5433	1	3158	1	4234	9
Bricklayer	10452	6	4290	2	2566	2	3596	2
Mason	1066	5	512	2	203	1	351	2
Slater, Tiler	80	.	45	.	7	.	28	.
Plasterer, Whitewasher	667	.	488	.	63	.	116	.
Paperhanger	123	.	64	.	22	.	37	.
Plumber	1524	9	690	1	380	3	454	5
Painter, Glazier	3718	10	1819	2	851	3	1048	5
2. Furniture and Fittings.								
Cabinet Maker, Upholsterer	1639	253	791	55	336	72	582	126
French Polisher	181	4	93	3	14	.	74	1
Furniture Broker, Dealer	190	20	77	7	56	1	57	12
Locksmith, Bellhanger	47	1	20	1	13	.	14	.
Gas Fitter	404	1	230	1	67	.	107	.
House and Shop Fittings—Maker, Dealer	72	2	55	1	3	.	14	1
Funeral Furniture Maker, Undertaker	37	.	30	.	7	.	.	.
Others	.	.	.	.	.	.	.	.
3. House Decorations.								
Wood Carver	78	.	31	.	8	.	34	.
Carver, Gilder	171	3	66	1	45	1	60	1
Dealer in Works of Art	27	2	9	.	8	2	13	.
Figure, Image—Maker, Dealer	6	.	4	.	.	.	2	.
Animal, Bird, &c., Preserver, Naturalist	41	8	18	6	9	1	14	1
Artificial Flower Maker	18	33	15	20	.	.	3	5
12. PERSONS WORKING AND DEALING IN CARRIAGES AND HARNESS.								
1. Carriages.								
Coachmaker	1449	12	489	2	437	3	523	6
Railway Carriage, Railway Wagon, Maker	266	.	260	.	5	.	1	.
Wheelwright	2453	13	887	6	769	5	797	8
Bicycle, Tricycle—Maker, Dealer	15	.	7	.	1	.	7	.
Others	4	.	1	.	.	.	3	.
2. Harness.								
Saddler, Harness, Whip, Maker	1360	30	497	14	369	9	494	7
13. PERSONS WORKING AND DEALING IN SHIPS AND BOATS.								
1. Hull.								
Ship, Boat, Barge, Builder	559	3	257	1	127	1	176	1
Shipwright, Ship Carpenter (ashore)	952	.	461	.	294	.	197	.
2. Masts, Rigging, &c.								
Mast, Yard, Oar, Block, Maker	124	.	24	.	52	.	48	.
Ship Rigger, Chandler, Fitter	79	2	39	2	25	.	15	.
Sail Maker	338	3	80	2	138	.	120	1

Table 10 *continued*.—OCCUPATIONS of MALES and FEMALES in the EASTERN DIVISION an[d] REGISTRATION COUNTIES, and in each URBAN SANITARY DISTRICT of which the POPULA[TION] exceeds 50,000 Persons.

OCCUPATIONS.	EASTERN DIVISION.		REGISTRATION COUNTIES.					
			14. ESSEX.		15. SUFFOLK.		16. NORFO[LK.]	
	Males.	Females.	Males.	Females.	Males.	Females.	Males.	Fem[ales.]
14. PERSONS WORKING AND DEALING IN CHEMICALS AND COMPOUNDS.								
1. *Colouring Matter.*								
Dye, Paint, Manufacture	43	22	33	2	.	.	10	
Ink, Blacking, Colouring Substance, Manufacture	29	.	24	.	.	.	5	
2. *Explosives.*								
Gunpowder, Guncotton, Explosive Substance, Manufacture	18	7	7	1	11	6	.	
Fusee, Fireworks, Explosive Article, Manufacture	25	53	23	53	1	.	1	
3. *Drugs and other Chemicals and Compounds.*								
Chemist, Druggist	787	21	315	7	188	7	284	
Manufacturing Chemist	760	133	423	15	94	3	243	
Alkali Manufacture	12	.	6	.	3	.	3	
Drysalter	12	.	12	.	.	.	.	
15. PERSONS WORKING AND DEALING IN TOBACCO AND PIPES.								
1. *Tobacco and Pipes.*								
Tobacco Manufacturer, Tobacconist	302	103	141	38	81	22	60	
Tobacco Pipe, Snuff Box, &c., Maker	65	10	22	5	10	1	33	
16. PERSONS WORKING AND DEALING IN FOOD AND LODGING.								
1. *Board and Lodging.*								
Innkeeper, Hotel Keeper, Publican	3778	646	1301	201	910	162	1567	2[illegible]
Lodging, Boarding House, Keeper	87	1184	23	395	28	307	36	[illegible]
Coffee, Eating House, Keeper	188	76	115	42	33	17	40	[illegible]
2. *Spirituous Drinks.*								
Hop—Merchant, Dealer	14	.	9	.	4	.	1	
Maltster	1558	3	327	1	765	1	466	
Brewer	1478	22	654	8	294	6	530	.
Beerseller, Ale, Porter, Cider, Dealer	720	208	432	120	204	57	84	[illegible]
Cellarman	180	3	98	1	27	2	55	
Wine, Spirit—Merchant, Agent	321	20	168	10	62	5	91	
3. *Food.*								
Milkseller, Dairyman	848	79	490	38	152	24	197	1
Cheesemonger, Butterman	94	4	75	3	3	1	16	
Butcher, Meat Salesman	3898	248	1611	51	998	88	1289	10[illegible]
Provision Curer, Dealer	174	57	92	12	44	14	38	3[illegible]
Poulterer, Game Dealer	132	27	79	7	25	9	27	1[illegible]
Fishmonger	1254	136	421	32	356	38	477	[illegible]
Corn, Flour, Seed—Merchant, Dealer	691	51	271	19	215	19	205	1[illegible]
Corn Miller	2601	17	701	6	1053	7	937	
Baker	4103	417	2048	143	817	121	1238	15[illegible]
Confectioner, Pastrycook	546	431	232	223	109	108	205	19[illegible]
Greengrocer, Fruiterer	725	218	478	64	117	61	130	2[illegible]
Mustard, Vinegar, Spice, Pickle—Maker, Dealer	166	42	6	3	2	.	148	3[illegible]
Sugar Refiner	549	14	498	5	5	1	46	[illegible]
Grocer, Tea, Coffee, Chocolate—Maker, Dealer	5086	936	2010	343	1414	319	1662	3[illegible]
Ginger Beer, Mineral Water—Manufacturer, Dealer	162	10	53	1	41	1	68	[illegible]
Others dealing in Food	.	.	.	.	.	.	.	
17. PERSONS WORKING AND DEALING IN TEXTILE FABRICS.								
1. *Wool and Worsted.*								
Woolstapler	44	.	35	.	6	.	15	.
Woollen Cloth Manufacture	53	7	12	4	6	2	35	1
Wool, Woollen goods—Dyer, Printer	3	.	.	.	.	.	3	.
Worsted, Stuff, Manufacture	31	6	2	.	4	.	25	[illegible]
Flannel Manufacture	.	.	.	.	.	.	.	.
Blanket Manufacture	.	.	.	.	.	.	.	.
Fuller	.	.	.	.	.	.	.	.
Cloth, Worsted, Stuff, Flannel, Blanket, Dealer	61	.	42	.	10	.	9	.
Others	8	2	.	1	.	.	3	1
2. *Silk.*								
Silk, Silk goods, Manufacture	1042	4716	306	1825	416	754	320	2137
Silk Dyer, Printer	21	.	15	.	2	.	4	.
Ribbon Manufacture	1	.	1	.	.	.	.	.
Crape, Gauze, Manufacture	98	742	79	392	.	3	19	147
Silk Merchant, Dealer	[illegible]	.	[illegible]	.	8	1	1	5

Table 10 *continued.*—OCCUPATIONS of MALES and FEMALES in the EASTERN DIVISION and its REGISTRATION COUNTIES, and in each URBAN SANITARY DISTRICT of which the POPULATION exceeds 50,000 Persons.

OCCUPATIONS.	EASTERN DIVISION.		REGISTRATION COUNTIES. 14. ESSEX.		15. SUFFOLK.		16. NORFOLK.	
	Males.	Females.	Males.	Females.	Males.	Females.	Males.	Females.
3. Cotton and Flax								
Cotton, Cotton goods, Manufacture	65	375	38	168	29	64	7	146
Cotton, Calico—Printer, Dyer, Bleacher	4	.	4	.	.	.	.	.
Cotton, Calico—Warehouseman, Dealer	4	.	3	.	.	.	1	.
Flax, Linen—Manufacturer, Dealer	145	23	5	1	86	19	54	3
Lace Manufacturer, Dealer	14	226	9	213	2	7	3	6
Fustian Manufacturer, Dealer	.	.	.	.	.	.	.	.
Tape Manufacturer, Dealer	.	.	.	.	.	.	.	.
Thread Manufacturer, Dealer	1	.	1	.	.	.	.	.
4. Hemp and other Fibrous Materials.								
Hemp, Jute, Cocoa Fibre, Manufacture	380	932	274	928	98	2	8	2
Rope, Twine, Cord—Maker, Dealer	585	18	101	6	132	5	352	3
Mat Maker, Seller	800	109	87	14	559	50	154	45
Net Maker	33	728	4	3	13	469	16	256
Canvas, Sailcloth, Manufacture	2	2	.	2	2	.	.	.
Sacking, Sack, Bag—Maker, Dealer	45	238	23	208	14	29	8	6
Others working and dealing in Hemp	6	2	4	1	.	.	2	1
5. Mixed or Unspecified Materials.								
Weaver (undefined)	97	191	24	32	2	9	71	150
Dyer, Printer, Scourer, Bleacher, Calenderer (undefined)	128	61	27	17	26	17	75	27
Factory hand (Textile, undefined)	54	297	19	54	23	31	12	212
Felt Manufacture	3	.	3	.	.	.	.	.
Carpet, Rug, Manufacture	21	2	12	1	4	1	5	.
Manchester Warehouseman	19	.	14	.	.	.	5	.
Draper, Linen Draper, Mercer	2078	1976	884	701	518	453	676	822
Fancy Goods (Textile), Manufacturer, Worker, Dealer	27	288	12	94	1	58	14	136
Trimming Maker, Dealer	17	38	16	34	.	.	1	4
Embroiderer	4	34	3	24	.	8	1	2
Others	11	30	.	1	5	19	6	10
18. PERSONS WORKING AND DEALING IN DRESS.								
1. Dress.								
Hatter, Hat Manufacture (not straw)	128	19	67	8	19	3	42	8
Straw—Hat, Bonnet, Plait, Manufacture	13	1769	8	922	5	776	.	71
Tailor	4124	5100	1335	2169	1283	1581	1506	1350
Milliner, Dressmaker, Staymaker	79	17727	38	5409	38	5412	3	6906
Shawl Manufacture	2	5	.	.	.	.	2	5
Shirt Maker, Seamstress	33	3444	27	1681	2	941	4	822
Hosiery Manufacture	3	26	2	4	.	9	1	13
Hosier, Haberdasher	117	70	73	44	16	8	28	18
Glover, Glove Maker	76	172	18	32	28	69	30	71
Button Maker, Dealer	4	4	4	4	.	.	.	.
Shoe, Boot—Maker, Dealer	11464	2493	2751	241	2872	325	5841	1927
Patten, Clog, Maker	23	1	8	.	3	1	12	.
Wig Maker, Hairdresser	497	23	228	7	134	9	135	7
Umbrella, Parasol, Stick—Maker, Dealer	98	33	59	19	18	8	21	6
Accoutrement Maker	.	.	.	.	.	.	.	.
Old Clothes Dealer, and others	18	65	7	18	2	18	9	29
19. PERSONS WORKING AND DEALING IN VARIOUS ANIMAL SUBSTANCES.								
1. In Grease, Gut, Bone, Horn, Ivory, and Whalebone.								
Tallow Chandler, Candle, Grease, Manufacture	154	4	93	4	27	.	34	.
Soap Boiler, Maker	112	1	91	1	18	.	3	.
Glue, Size, Gelatine, Isinglass—Maker, Dealer	45	10	42	.	3	10	.	.
Manure Manufacture	238	4	118	2	84	1	36	1
Bone, Horn, Ivory, Tortoise-shell—Worker, Dealer	50	7	49	7	.	.	1	.
Comb Maker	8	1	6	.	2	1	.	.
Others	3	.	2	.	.	.	1	.
2. In Skins.								
Furrier, Skinner	144	208	114	23	5	8	25	177
Tanner, Fellmonger	395	1	91	.	196	.	108	1
Currier	491	18	173	4	141	10	177	4
Leather Goods, Portmanteau, Bag, Strap, &c.—Maker, Dealer	95	68	61	29	25	38	9	1
Parchment, Vellum—Maker, Dealer	1	.	1	.	.	.	.	.
3. In Hair and Feathers.								
Hair, Bristle—Worker, Dealer	225	1008	4	4	126	699	95	305
Brush, Broom, Maker	611	413	183	60	47	18	381	335
Quill, Feather—Dresser, Dealer	10	10	10	8	.	2	.	.

Tables 10 *continued*.—Occupations of Males and Females in the Eastern Division and its Registration Counties, and in each Urban Sanitary District of which the Population exceeds 50,000 Persons.

Occupations.	Eastern Division.		Registration Counties. 14. Essex.		15. Suffolk.		16. Norfolk.	
	Males.	Females.	Males.	Females.	Males.	Females.	Males.	Females.
20. Persons working and dealing in various Vegetable Substances.								
1. In Oils, Gums, and Resins.								
Oil Miller, Oil Cake—Maker, Dealer	285	1	76	.	66	1	141	.
Oil and Colourman	191	19	160	19	23	.	8	.
Floor Cloth, Oil Cloth, Manufacture	42	2	42	1	.	.	.	1
Japanner	9	.	3	.	1	.	5	.
India Rubber, Gutta Percha—Worker, Dealer	120	10	118	8	.	.	2	2
Waterproof Goods—Maker, Dealer	51	5	43	5	1	.	9	.
Others	28	1	27	1	1	.	.	.
2. In Cane, Rush, and Straw.								
Willow, Cane, Rush—Worker, Dealer, Basketmaker	632	54	155	26	141	2	336	26
Hay, Straw (not plait), Chaff—Cutter, Dealer	181	2	88	1	33	.	60	1
Thatcher	949	.	348	.	428	.	173	.
3. In Wood and Bark.								
Timber, Wood—Merchant, Dealer	487	15	223	9	92	4	172	2
Sawyer	1234	.	491	.	362	.	381	.
Lath, Wooden Fence, Hurdle, Maker	280	.	109	.	95	.	76	.
Wood Turner, Box Maker	246	38	103	34	24	3	119	1
Cooper, Hoop Maker, Bender	989	1	473	.	200	.	307	1
Cork, Bark—Cutter, Worker, Dealer	88	3	36	.	11	1	38	2
Others	3	.	1	.	.	.	2	.
4. In Paper.								
Paper Manufacture	165	102	48	9	10	4	107	89
Envelope Maker	1	10	1	10	.	.	.	.
Stationer, Law Stationer	325	161	200	68	53	50	72	43
Card, Pattern Card, Maker	18	4	16	4	.	.	2	.
Paper Stainer	15	1	15	1	.	.	.	.
Paper Box, Paper Bag, Maker	28	254	13	38	6	30	9	186
Ticket, Label, Writer	11	8	5	5	1	.	5	3
Others	87	.	19	.	21	.	47	.
21. Persons working and dealing in various Mineral Substances.								
1. Miners.								
Coal Miner	22	.	8	.	6	.	8	.
Ironstone Miner	2	.	.	.	.	.	2	.
Copper Miner	.	.	.	.	.	.	.	.
Tin Miner	1	.	1	.	.	.	.	.
Lead Miner	2	.	.	.	1	.	1	.
Miner in other, or undefined, Minerals	9	.	6	.	.	.	3	.
Mine Service	1	.	.	.	1	.	.	.
2. Coal, Coal Gas, &c.								
Coal Merchant, Dealer	686	31	240	15	169	5	277	11
Coalheaver	1161	.	670	.	187	.	304	.
Coke, Charcoal, Peat—Cutter, Burner, Dealer	25	1	22	.	1	.	2	1
Gas Works Service	1089	.	802	.	119	.	168	.
3. Stone, Clay, and Road Making.								
Stone Quarrier	14	.	2	.	1	.	11	.
Stone Cutter, Dresser, Dealer	125	.	64	.	29	.	32	.
Slate Quarrier	.	.	.	.	.	.	.	.
Slate Worker, Dealer	14	1	10	.	2	.	2	1
Limeburner	176	1	40	.	56	.	80	1
Clay, Sand, Gravel, Chalk—Labourer, Dealer	170	4	134	.	12	4	24	.
Fossil, Coprolite—Digger, Dealer	22	.	.	.	17	.	5	.
Well Sinker, Borer	53	.	21	.	4	.	28	.
Plaster, Cement, Manufacture	351	7	297	1	47	5	7	1
Brick, Tile—Maker, Burner, Dealer	3207	18	1381	9	944	5	932	4
Paviour	53	.	26	.	11	.	16	.
Road Contractor, Surveyor, Inspector	25	.	14	.	6	.	3	.
Road Labourer	226	.	99	.	57	.	70	.
Railway Contractor	61	.	33	.	12	.	16	.
Platelayer	1107	.	505	.	266	.	338	.
Railway Labourer, Navvy	1482	.	537	.	214	.	711	.
Others	10	2	9	.	1	1	.	1
4. Earthenware and Glass.								
Earthenware, China, Porcelain, Manufacture	147	2	48	1	42	.	57	1
Glass Manufacture	64	2	57	.	3	1	4	1
Earthenware, China, Glass, Dealer	129	104	64	35	22	26	43	43
5. Salt.								
Salt Maker, Dealer	4	.	2		2	.	.	.

Table 10 *continued*.—OCCUPATIONS of MALES and FEMALES in the EASTERN DIVISION and its REGISTRATION COUNTIES, and in each URBAN SANITARY DISTRICT of which the POPULATION exceeds 50,000 Persons.

OCCUPATIONS.	EASTERN DIVISION.		REGISTRATION COUNTIES.					
			14. ESSEX.		15. SUFFOLK.		16. NORFOLK.	
	Males.	Females.	Males.	Females.	Males.	Females.	Males.	Females.
6. *Water.*								
Waterworks Service	90	.	49	.	7	.	34	.
Others	5	.	1	.	.	.	4	.
7. *Precious Metals and Jewellery.*								
Goldsmith, Silversmith, Jeweller	222	10	122	5	30	6	70	5
Gold, Silver, Beater	2	.	2	.	.	.	.	.
Lapidary	4	2	2	.	.	.	2	2
Others	3	.	3	.	.	.	.	.
8. *Iron and Steel.*								
Blacksmith	6368	35	2189	14	1877	13	2302	8
Whitesmith	446	.	129	.	120	.	197	.
Nail Manufacture	4	.	1	.	1	.	2	.
Anchor, Chain, Manufacture	1	.	1	.	.	.	.	.
Other Iron and Steel Manufactures	2781	10	288	4	1935	1	558	5
Ironmonger. Hardware Dealer, Merchant	812	43	297	11	230	13	285	19
9. *Copper.*								
Copper, Copper goods—Manufacturer, Worker, Dealer	69	.	34	.	19	.	16	.
10. *Tin and Zinc.*								
Tin, Tin Plate, Tin goods—Manufacturer, Worker, Dealer	638	14	217	11	123	2	298	1
Zinc, Zinc Goods—Manufacturer, Worker, Dealer	35	.	31	.	3	.	1	.
11. *Lead.*								
Lead, Leaden goods—Manufacturer, Worker, Dealer	15	2	15	2	.	.	.	.
12. *In Other, Mixed, or Unspecified, Metals.*								
Metal Refiner, Worker, Turner, Dealer	26	.	21	.	2	.	3	.
Brass, Bronze, Manufacture. Brazier	346	3	171	1	61	2	114	.
Metal Burnisher, Lacquerer	.	.	.	.	.	.	.	.
White Metal, Plated Ware, Manufacture. Pewterer	12	.	10	.	2	.	.	.
Wire Maker, Worker, Weaver, Drawer	62	3	31	3	17	.	14	.
Bolt, Nut, Rivet, Screw, Staple, Maker	54	.	39	.	14	.	1	.
Lamp, Lantern, Candlestick, Maker	25	.	24	.	.	.	1	.
Clasp, Buckle, Hinge, Maker	.	.	.	.	.	.	.	.
Fancy Chain, Gilt Toy, Maker	.	.	.	.	.	.	.	.
Others	.	.	.	.	.	.	.	.
22. PERSONS WORKING AND DEALING IN GENERAL OR UNSPECIFIED COMMODITIES.								
1. *Makers and Dealers (General or Undefined).*								
General Shopkeeper, Dealer	2216	1624	769	517	604	406	843	701
Pawnbroker	219	10	124	2	43	1	52	7
Costermonger, Huckster, Street Seller	1620	449	490	162	380	99	750	188
Manufacturer, Manager, Superintendent (undefined)	257	8	158	6	17	1	82	1
Contractor (undefined)	94	1	74	1	10	.	10	.
2. *Mechanics and Labourers (General or Undefined).*								
General Labourer	28079	75	15439	29	4033	10	8607	36
Engine Driver, Stoker, Fireman (not railway, marine, nor agricultural)	1901	.	1215	.	308	.	378	.
Artisan, Mechanic (undefined)	533	45	283	8	83	10	167	27
Apprentice (undefined)	172	35	56	11	35	6	81	18
Factory Labourer (undefined)	520	150	375	103	74	17	71	30
Machinist, Machine Worker (undefined)	211	1	80	1	72	.	59	.
23. PERSONS WORKING AND DEALING IN REFUSE MATTERS.								
1. *Refuse Matters.*								
Town Drainage Service	37	.	13	.	12	.	12	.
Chimney Sweep, Soot Merchant	395	4	147	4	114	.	134	.
Scavenger, Crossing Sweeper	94	1	27	.	31	.	36	1
Rag Gatherer, Dealer	49	36	29	8	11	18	9	10
VI. UNOCCUPIED CLASS.								
24. PERSONS WITHOUT SPECIFIED OCCUPATIONS								
Persons returned by Property, Rank, &c., and not by special occupation	165961	446093	72574	183632	43083	117644	51304	145817
Children under 5 years of age	90676	90468	39235	39214	23585	23463	27856	27791

Table 10 *continued*.—Occupations of Males and Females in the Eastern Division and its Registration Counties, and in each Urban Sanitary District of which the Population exceeds 50,000 Persons.

Occupations.	Urban Sanitary Districts.					
	West Ham.		Ipswich.		Norwich.	
	Males.	Females.	Males.	Females.	Males.	Females.
TOTAL - - -	63410	63543	23736	26820	40258	47554
I. PROFESSIONAL CLASS.						
1. Persons engaged in the General or Local Government of the Country.						
1. *National Government.*						
Peer, M.P., Privy Councillor (not otherwise described)	.	.	.	.	1	.
Civil Service (officers and clerks)	162	3	83	.	70	3
Civil Service (messengers, &c.)	101	.	42	.	77	1
Prison Officer, &c.	.	.	11	2	10	8
2. *Local Government.*						
Police	173	.	60	.	108	.
Municipal, Parish, Union, District, Officer	43	.	30	5	50	10
Other Local or County Official	12	.	9	.	14	.
3. *East Indian and Colonial Service.*						
East Indian and Colonial Service	.	.	1	.	.	.
2. Persons engaged in the Defence of the Country.						
1. *Army (at Home).*						
Army Officer (effective or retired)	4	.	14	.	11	.
Soldier and Non-Commissioned Officer	20	.	280	.	114	.
Militia, Yeomanry, Volunteers	12	.	13	.	68	.
Army Pensioner	35	.	35	.	72	1
2. *Navy (ashore or in port).*						
Navy Officer (effective or retired)	4	.	13	.	.	.
Seaman, R.N.	4	.	6	.	1	.
Royal Marines (officers and men)	.	.	2	.	.	.
Navy Pensioner	34	.	8	.	3	.
3. Persons engaged in Professional Occupations (with their immediate Subordinates).						
1. *Clerical Profession.*						
Clergyman (Established Church)	34	.	30	.	71	.
Roman Catholic Priest	14	.	3	.	5	.
Minister, Priest, of other religious bodies	25	.	20	.	34	.
Missionary, Scripture Reader, Itinerant Preacher	20	12	5	4	22	10
Nun, Sister of Charity	.	15	.	.	.	4
Theological Student	23	.	1	.	1	.
Church, Chapel, Cemetery—Officer, Servant	13	14	8	5	22	5
2. *Legal Profession.*						
Barrister, Solicitor	26	.	31	.	79	.
Law Student	1	.	4	.	4	.
Law Clerk, and others connected with Law	83	.	53	.	177	.
3. *Medical Profession.*						
Physician, Surgeon, General Practitioner	40	.	28	.	36	.
Dentist	7	.	12	.	29	.
Medical Student, Assistant	28	.	5	.	13	.
Midwife	.	12	.	5	.	8
Subordinate Medical Service	19	280	5	163	19	201
4. *Teachers.*						
Schoolmaster	165	377	84	257	132	426
Teacher, Professor, Lecturer	14	107	11	104	23	143
School Service, and others concerned in Teaching	17	8	2	3	9	14
5. *Literary and Scientific Persons.*						
Author, Editor, Journalist	9	.	8	.	10	.
Reporter, Short-hand Writer	13	.	11	.	15	.
Persons engaged in Scientific Pursuits	4	.	2	.	5	.
Literary, Scientific, Institution, Service, &c.	2	1	2	.	3	.
6. *Engineers and Surveyors.*						
Civil Engineer	34	.	19	.	18	.
Mining Engineer	.	.	.	.	.	.
Land, House, Ship, Surveyor	37	.	32	.	21	.
7. *Artists.*						
Painter (artist)	16	2	13	4	22	3
Engraver (artist)	12	.	.	.	9	.
Sculptor	2	.	2	.	2	.
Architect	44	.	23	.	18	.
Musician, Music Master	56	64	29	48	79	51
Art Student	3	2	6	1	8	1
Photographer	25	.	15	1	24	7
Actor	11	4	.	.	3	1
Art, Music, Theatre, Service	.	.	1	.	4	2

Table 10 *continued*.—OCCUPATIONS of MALES and FEMALES in the EASTERN DIVISION and its REGISTRATION COUNTIES, and in each URBAN SANITARY DISTRICT of which the POPULATION exceeds 50,000 Persons.

OCCUPATIONS.	URBAN SANITARY DISTRICTS.					
	WEST HAM.		IPSWICH.		NORWICH.	
	Males.	Females.	Males.	Females.	Males.	Females.
8. *Persons engaged in Exhibitions, Shows, Games, &c.*						
Performer, Showman, Exhibition, Service	5	3	.	1	16	2
Billiard, Cricket, & other Games, Service	8	.	10	.	9	.
II. DOMESTIC CLASS.						
4. PERSONS ENGAGED IN DOMESTIC OFFICES OR SERVICES.						
1. *Domestic Service.*						
Domestic Coachman, Groom	51	.	117	.	187	.
Domestic Gardener	62	.	127	.	326	.
Domestic Indoor Servant	26	3463	47	2638	102	3982
Lodge, Gate, Park, Keeper (not Government)	15	.	2	.	4	1
Inn, Hotel, Servant	268	150	70	76	80	92
College, Club, Service	1	.	4	1	5	3
2. *Other Service.*						
Office Keeper (not Government)	6	6	2	9	7	7
Cook (not domestic)	31	.	1	5	4	.
Charwoman	.	272	.	281	.	737
Washing and Bathing Service	9	706	3	484	5	879
Hospital and Institution Service	5	21	19	40	20	72
Others engaged in Service	3	.	.	.	1	.
III. COMMERCIAL CLASS.						
5. PERSONS ENGAGED IN COMMERCIAL OCCUPATIONS.						
1. *Merchants and Agents.*						
Merchant	14	.	4	.	11	.
Broker, Agent, Factor	139	.	38	.	68	1
Auctioneer, Appraiser, Valuer, House Agent	39	.	26	.	37	.
Accountant	72	.	32	.	80	.
Salesman, Buyer (not otherwise described)	26	7	4	1	.	3
Commercial Traveller	275	.	81	.	182	.
Commercial Clerk	1816	31	350	10	586	15
Officer of Commercial Company, Guild, Society, &c.	7	.	.	.	1	.
2. *Dealers in Money.*						
Banker	.	.	4	.	.	.
Bank Service	67	.	39	.	76	.
Bill Discounter, Bill Broker, Finance Agent	4	.	1	.	.	.
3. *Persons occupied in Insurance.*						
Life, House, Ship, &c., Insurance Service	81	1	23	.	116	.
6. PERSONS ENGAGED IN CONVEYANCE OF MEN, GOODS, AND MESSAGES.						
1. *On Railways.*						
Railway Engine Driver, Stoker	398	.	64	.	131	.
Railway Guard	138	.	27	.	99	.
Pointsman, Level Crossing Man	52	.	12	.	9	.
Other Railway Officials and Servants	1183	5	216	1	286	2
2. *On Roads.*						
Toll Collector, Turnpike Gate Keeper	4	.	.	1	.	1
Omnibus, Coach, Cab, Owner—Livery Stable Keeper	9	1	20	1	27	.
Cabman, Flyman, Coachman (not domestic)	127	.	54	.	123	.
Carman, Carrier, Carter, Haulier	705	.	134	.	367	1
Tramway Companies' Service	54	.	7	.	.	.
Wheel Chair Proprietor, Attendant, &c.	.	.	.	.	.	.
3. *On Canals, Rivers and Seas.*						
Inland Navigation Service	2	.	.	.	.	.
Bargeman, Lighterman, Waterman	274	1	22	.	76	.
Navigation Service (on shore)	6	.	6	.	.	.
Seaman (Merchant Service)	1870	.	369	.	80	.
Pilot	17	.	10	.	.	.
Ship Steward, Cook	241	5	5	1	1	.
Boatman on Seas	.	.	.	.	.	.
Harbour, Dock, Wharf, Lighthouse, Service	1903	7	96	.	6	.
4. *In Storage.*						
Warehouseman (not Manchester)	189	.	26	.	133	7
Meter, Weigher	30	.	19	.	1	.
5. *In conveying Messages, Porterage, &c.*						
Messenger, Porter, Watchman (not Railway nor Government)	719		418	2	673	4
Telegraph, Telephone, Service	53		21	.	26	.

Table 10 *continued.*—OCCUPATIONS of MALES and FEMALES in the EASTERN DIVISION and its REGISTRATION COUNTIES, and in each URBAN SANITARY DISTRICT of which the POPULATION exceeds 50,000 PERSONS.

OCCUPATIONS.	URBAN SANITARY DISTRICTS.					
	WEST HAM.		IPSWICH.		NORWICH.	
	Males.	Females.	Males.	Females.	Males.	Females.
IV. AGRICULTURAL CLASS.						
7. PERSONS ENGAGED IN AGRICULTURE.						
1. *In Fields and Pastures.*						
Farmer, Grazier	14	1	39	3	40	2
Farmer's, Grazier's—Son, Grandson, Brother, Nephew*	1	.	10	.	5	.
Farm Bailiff	6	.	16	.	10	.
Agricultural Labourer, Farm Servant, Cottager	133	22	346	5	401	18
Shepherd	1	.	13	.	7	.
Land Drainage Service (not in towns)	1	.	.	.	.	.
Agricultural Machine—Proprietor, Attendant	.	.	3	.	2	.
Agricultural Student, Pupil	.	.	1	.	.	.
Others engaged in, or connected with, Agriculture	.	1	.	.	1	.
2. *In Woods.*						
Woodman	1	.	6	.	2	.
3. *In Gardens.*						
Nurseryman, Seedsman, Florist	20	2	30	1	39	5
Gardener (not domestic)	148	19	245	.	233	9
8. PERSONS ENGAGED ABOUT ANIMALS.						
1. *About Animals.*						
Horse Proprietor, Breeder, Dealer	10	.	9	.	17	.
Groom, Horse-keeper, Horse-breaker	133	.	93	.	192	.
Veterinary Surgeon, Farrier	47	.	11	.	16	.
Cattle, Sheep, Pig—Dealer, Salesman	14	1	20	.	16	.
Drover	5	.	15	.	54	.
Gamekeeper	2	.	4	.	3	.
Dog, Bird, Animal—Keeper, Dealer	1	.	13	3	13	3
Vermin destroyer	3	.	.	.	3	.
Fisherman	2	.	20	.	10	.
Knacker, Catsmeat Dealer, &c., &c.	1	1	3	.	1	.
V. INDUSTRIAL CLASS.						
9. PERSONS WORKING AND DEALING IN BOOKS, PRINTS, AND MAPS.						
1. *Books.*						
Publisher, Bookseller, Librarian	31	2	22	4	58	3
Music—Publisher, Seller, Printer	2	1	2	2	8	1
Bookbinder	57	26	32	18	64	45
Printer	288	7	237	4	428	2
Newspaper Agent, News Room Keeper	17	13	19	7	17	5
Others	.	.	.	.	.	.
2. *Prints and Maps.*						
Lithographer, Lithographic Printer	20	.	15	.	30	.
Copper Plate and Steel Plate Printer	4	.	1	.	.	.
Map and Print—Colourer, Seller	5	.	.	.	1	1
10. PERSONS WORKING AND DEALING IN MACHINES AND IMPLEMENTS.						
1. *Machines.*						
Engine, Machine, Maker	608	1	144	3	127	.
Millwright	30	.	19	.	32	.
Fitter, Turner (Engine and Machine)	901	.	358	.	239	.
Boiler Maker	479	.	94	.	37	.
Spinning and Weaving Machine Maker	6	.	.	.	8	15
Agricultural Machine and Implement Maker	.	.	77	.	17	.
Domestic Machinery—Maker, Dealer	.	.	.	.	5	.
2. *Tools and Implements.*						
Tool Maker, Dealer	12	.	5	.	21	2
Cutler, Scissors Maker	7	.	5	.	19	.
File Maker	8	1	2	.	.	.
Saw Maker	11	.	5	.	4	.
Pin Maker	1	.	.	.	.	.
Needle Maker	.	.	.	.	1	.
Steel Pen Maker	.	.	.	.	.	.
Pencil Maker (Wood)	.	.	.	.	.	.
Domestic Implement Maker	4	.	.	.	.	.
3. *Watches and Philosophical Instruments.*						
Watch Maker, Clock Maker	90	4	48	.	94	6
Philosophical Instrument Maker, Optician	38	1	1	.	2	.
Electrical Apparatus Maker	86	.	14	.	10	.
Weighing and Measuring Apparatus Maker	10	.	6	.	3	.

* Only male relatives living with the farmer or grazier, and therefore [illegible]

Table 10 *continued*.—OCCUPATIONS of MALES and FEMALES in the EASTERN DIVISION and its REGISTRATION COUNTIES, and in each URBAN SANITARY DISTRICT of which the POPULATION exceeds 50,000 PERSONS.

OCCUPATIONS.	URBAN SANITARY DISTRICTS.					
	WEST HAM.		IPSWICH.		NORWICH.	
	Males.	Females.	Males.	Females.	Males.	Females.
4. Surgical Instruments.						
Surgical Instrument Maker	3	4	.	.	1	.
5. Arms and Ordnance.						
Gunsmith, Gun Manufacturer	7	.	7	.	11	.
Ordnance Manufacturer	.	.	.	.	.	.
Sword, Bayonet—Maker, Cutler	2	.	.	.	.	.
Others	.	.	.	.	.	.
6. Musical Instruments.						
Musical Instrument Maker, Dealer	18	.	18	.	32	1
7. Type, Dies, Medals, Coins.						
Type Cutter, Founder	10	.	.	.	.	.
Die, Seal, Coin, Medal, Maker	5	.	.	.	1	.
8. Tackle for Sports and Games.						
Toy Maker, Dealer	5	8	3	3	3	2
Fishing Rod, Tackle, Maker, Dealer	.	.	.	.	.	.
Apparatus for other Games, Maker, Dealer	2	1	1	.	.	.
11. PERSONS WORKING AND DEALING IN HOUSES, FURNITURE, AND DECORATIONS.						
1. Houses.						
Builder	235	.	102	1	88	.
Carpenter, Joiner	1565	1	594	.	979	1
Bricklayer	1682	2	496	.	964	1
Mason	219	.	74	.	127	.
Slater, Tiler	35	.	6	.	5	.
Plasterer, Whitewasher	239	.	26	.	78	.
Paperhanger	28	.	11	.	26	.
Plumber	238	.	114	1	135	.
Painter, Glazier	641	.	284	1	411	1
2. Furniture and Fittings.						
Cabinet Maker, Upholsterer	158	15	114	28	327	83
French Polisher	29	1	6	.	55	.
Furniture Broker, Dealer	26	2	24	1	36	6
Locksmith, Bellhanger	6	.	6	.	6	.
Gas Fitter	120	.	25	.	67	.
House and Shop Fittings—Maker, Dealer	19	1	1	.	6	1
Funeral Furniture Maker, Undertaker	19	.	6	.	.	.
Others	.	.	.	.	.	.
3. House Decorations.						
Wood Carver	5	.	5	.	29	.
Carver, Gilder	27	1	12	1	36	1
Dealer in Works of Art	3	.	6	1	7	.
Figure, Image—Maker, Dealer	2	.	.	.	2	.
Animal, Bird, &c., Preserver, Naturalist	6	2	2	.	9	1
Artificial Flower Maker	9	11	.	.	2	4
12. PERSONS WORKING AND DEALING IN CARRIAGES AND HARNESS.						
1. Carriages.						
Coachmaker	129	1	164	1	216	2
Railway Carriage, Railway Wagon, Maker	251	.	5	.	1	.
Wheelwright	111	.	45	.	69	.
Bicycle, Tricycle—Maker, Dealer	.	.	1	.	.	.
Others	.	.	.	.	3	.
2. Harness.						
Saddler, Harness, Whip, Maker	68	5	49	.	91	2
13. PERSONS WORKING AND DEALING IN SHIPS AND BOATS.						
1. Hull.						
Ship, Boat, Barge, Builder	165	.	17	.	19	.
Shipwright, Ship Carpenter (ashore)	186	.	79	.	.	.
2. Masts, Rigging, &c.						
Mast, Yard, Oar, Block, Maker	7	.	6	.	.	.
Ship Rigger, Chandler, Fitter	27	.	4	.	.	.
Sail Maker	11	.	9	.	3	1

Table 10 *continued.*—Occupations of Males and Females in the Eastern Division and its Registration Counties, and in each Urban Sanitary District of which the Population exceeds 50,000 Persons.

Occupations.	Urban Sanitary Districts.					
	West Ham.		Ipswich.		Norwich.	
	Males.	Females.	Males.	Females.	Males.	Females.
14. Persons working and dealing in Chemicals and Compounds.						
1. *Colouring Matter.*						
Dye, Paint, Manufacture	26	2	.	.	9	19
Ink, Blacking, Colouring Substance, Manufacture	21	.	.	.	.	.
2. *Explosives.*						
Gunpowder, Guncotton, Explosive Substance, Manufacture	1	.	.	.	.	.
Fusee, Fireworks, Explosive Article, Manufacture	17	50	1	.	1	.
3. *Drugs and other Chemicals and Compounds.*						
Chemist, Druggist	89	1	55	4	96	.
Manufacturing Chemist	341	12	6	.	196	114
Alkali Manufacture	6	.	1	.	.	.
Drysalter	5	.	.	.	.	.
15. Persons working and dealing in Tobacco and Pipes.						
1. *Tobacco and Pipes.*						
Tobacco Manufacturer, Tobacconist	66	22	58	4	65	41
Tobacco Pipe, Snuff Box, &c., Maker	8	4	7	1	7	4
16. Persons working and dealing in Food and Lodging.						
1. *Board and Lodging.*						
Innkeeper, Hotel Keeper, Publican	167	16	142	18	375	91
Lodging, Boarding House, Keeper	5	50	6	20	3	149
Coffee, Eating House, Keeper	58	19	10	5	17	8
2. *Spirituous Drinks.*						
Hop—Merchant, Dealer	1	.	2	.	1	.
Maltster	4	.	96	.	86	.
Brewer	54	.	51	.	261	4
Beerseller. Ale, Porter, Cider, Dealer	107	21	33	12	4	1
Cellarman	46	1	8	2	26	.
Wine, Spirit—Merchant, Agent	45	2	22	1	29	1
3. *Food.*						
Milkseller, Dairyman	195	17	50	11	62	8
Cheesemonger, Butterman	54	1	2	.	3	.
Butcher, Meat Salesman	461	6	172	34	254	34
Provision Curer, Dealer	44	7	15	2	21	22
Poulterer, Game Dealer	13	.	5	1	6	4
Fishmonger	139	11	39	1	124	18
Corn, Flour, Seed—Merchant, Dealer	54	7	65	11	53	2
Corn Miller	47	.	64	.	55	.
Baker	403	21	234	24	360	50
Confectioner, Pastrycook	126	120	42	31	138	33
Greengrocer, Fruiterer	187	11	48	20	58	39
Mustard, Vinegar, Spice, Pickle—Maker, Dealer	3	3	.	.	142	39
Sugar Refiner	466	3	.	.	26	3
Grocer. Tea, Coffee, Chocolate—Maker, Dealer	378	36	241	34	370	34
Ginger Beer, Mineral Water—Manufacturer, Dealer	5	.	19	1	23	1
Others dealing in Food	.	.	.	.	.	.
17. Persons working and dealing in Textile Fabrics.						
1. *Wool and Worsted.*						
Woolstapler	4	.	5	.	11	.
Woollen Cloth Manufacture	1	4	3	.	32	1
Wool. Woollen goods—Dyer, Printer	.	.	.	.	2	.
Worsted, Stuff, Manufacture	.	.	.	.	23	6
Flannel Manufacture	.	.	.	.	.	.
Blanket Manufacture	.	.	.	.	.	.
Fuller	.	.	.	.	.	.
Cloth, Worsted, Stuff, Flannel, Blanket, Dealer	8	.	6	.	6	.
Others	.	1	.	.	3	1
2. *Silk.*						
Silk, Silk goods, Manufacture	12	40	.	2	263	1202
Silk Dyer, Printer	10	.	.	.	4	.
Ribbon Manufacture	.	.	.	.	.	.
Crape, Gauze, Manufacture	.	.	.	.	17	108
Silk Merchant, Dealer	10	.	7	4	9	5

Table 10 *continued*.—OCCUPATIONS of MALES and FEMALES in the EASTERN DIVISION and its REGISTRATION COUNTIES, and in each URBAN SANITARY DISTRICT of which the POPULATION exceeds 50,000 PERSONS.

OCCUPATIONS.	URBAN SANITARY DISTRICTS.					
	WEST HAM.		IPSWICH.		NORWICH.	
	Males.	Females.	Males.	Females.	Males.	Females.
3. Cotton and Flax						
Cotton, Cotton goods, Manufacture	34	150	1	1	4	131
Cotton, Calico—Printer, Dyer, Bleacher	3	·	·	·	·	·
Cotton, Calico—Warehouseman, Dealer	1	·	·	·	·	·
Flax, Linen—Manufacturer, Dealer	3	1	·	·	·	·
Lace Manufacturer, Dealer	1	18	1	2	2	3
Fustian Manufacturer, Dealer	·	·	·	·	·	·
Tape Manufacturer, Dealer	·	·	·	·	·	·
Thread Manufacturer, Dealer	·	·	·	·	·	·
4. Hemp and other Fibrous Materials.						
Hemp, Jute, Cocoa Fibre, Manufacture	98	374	·	·	6	·
Rope, Twine, Cord—Maker, Dealer	15	2	8	·	40	·
Mat Maker, Seller	31	13	6	2	9	7
Net Maker	1	·	·	·	1	3
Canvas, Sailcloth, Manufacture	·	2	·	·	·	·
Sacking, Sack, Bag—Maker, Dealer	9	87	7	28	4	6
Others working and dealing in Hemp	·	·	·	·	2	1
5. Mixed or Unspecified Materials.						
Weaver (undefined)	6	24	·	·	65	142
Dyer, Printer, Scourer, Bleacher, Calenderer (undefined)	10	8	9	6	64	16
Factory hand (Textile, undefined)	3	4	·	·	9	292
Felt Manufacture	1	·	·	·	·	·
Carpet, Rug, Manufacture	7	·	·	·	3	·
Manchester Warehouseman	5	·	·	·	5	·
Draper, Linen Draper, Mercer	218	183	138	114	252	294
Fancy Goods (Textile), Manufacturer, Worker, Dealer	7	27	·	6	6	65
Trimming Maker, Dealer	7	19	·	·	1	3
Embroiderer	1	16	·	4	1	1
Others	·	1	·	·	·	·
18. PERSONS WORKING AND DEALING IN DRESS.						
1. Dress.						
Hatter, Hat Manufacture (not straw)	31	5	13	1	21	4
Straw—Hat, Bonnet, Plait, Manufacture	3	8	·	11	·	11
Tailor	247	167	327	512	568	894
Milliner, Dressmaker, Staymaker	15	1429	34	1659	·	1909
Shawl Manufacture	·	·	·	·	1	5
Shirt Maker, Seamstress	15	854	·	231	3	254
Hosiery Manufacture	·	1	·	1	1	·
Hosier, Haberdasher	38	16	9	3	14	8
Glover, Glove Maker	3	8	5	13	7	20
Button Maker, Dealer	1	3	·	·	·	·
Shoe, Boot—Maker, Dealer	480	41	765	185	3286	1772
Patten, Clog, Maker	6	·	·	·	11	·
Wig Maker, Hairdresser	91	1	35	4	41	1
Umbrella, Parasol, Stick—Maker, Dealer	18	10	3	4	11	5
Accoutrement Maker	·	·	·	·	·	·
Old Clothes Dealer, and others	5	9	2	10	5	17
19. PERSONS WORKING AND DEALING IN VARIOUS ANIMAL SUBSTANCES.						
1. In Grease, Gut, Bone, Horn, Ivory, and Whalebone.						
Tallow Chandler, Candle, Grease, Manufacture	51	·	8	·	16	·
Soap Boiler, Maker	86	1	12	·	2	·
Glue, Size, Gelatine, Isinglass—Maker, Dealer	4	·	·	·	·	·
Manure Manufacture	94	2	30	1	5	1
Bone, Horn, Ivory, Tortoise-shell—Worker, Dealer	17	·	·	·	·	·
Comb Maker	3	·	·	·	·	·
Others	1	·	·	·	·	·
2. In Skins.						
Furrier, Skinner	69	17	1	3	4	14
Tanner, Fellmonger	2	·	20	·	20	·
Currier	26	4	64	3	109	2
Leather Goods, Portmanteau, Bag, Strap, &c.—Maker, Dealer	41	12	7	38	5	1
Parchment, Vellum—Maker, Dealer	1	·	·	·	·	·
3. In Hair and Feathers.						
Hair, Bristle—Worker, Dealer	1	2	·	1	87	178
Brush, Broom, Maker	93	36	4	1	268	278
Quill, Feather—Dresser, Dealer	5	7	·	1	·	3

Table 10 *continued*.—OCCUPATIONS of MALES and FEMALES in the EASTERN DIVISION and its REGISTRATION COUNTIES, and in each URBAN SANITARY DISTRICT of which the POPULATION exceeds 50,000 PERSONS.

OCCUPATIONS.	URBAN SANITARY DISTRICTS.					
	WEST HAM.		IPSWICH.		NORWICH.	
	Males.	Females.	Males.	Females.	Males.	Females.
20. PERSONS WORKING AND DEALING IN VARIOUS VEGETABLE SUBSTANCES.						
1. *In Oils, Gums, and Resins.*						
Oil Miller, Oil Cake—Maker, Dealer	38	.	44	.	10	.
Oil and Colourman	85	17	14	.	1	.
Floor Cloth, Oil Cloth, Manufacture	36	1	.	.	.	.
Japanner	.	.	1	.	2	.
India Rubber, Gutta Percha—Worker, Dealer	101	7	.	.	2	2
Waterproof Goods—Maker, Dealer	28	5	.	.	1	.
Others	18	1	.	.	.	.
2. *In Cane, Rush, and Straw.*						
Willow, Cane, Rush—Worker, Dealer, Basketmaker	28	8	16	1	73	18
Hay, Straw (not plait), Chaff—Cutter, Dealer	6	.	9	.	28	1
Thatcher	2		3	.	4	.
3. *In Wood and Bark.*						
Timber, Wood—Merchant, Dealer	87	8	23	2	55	1
Sawyer	143	.	80	.	126	.
Lath, Wooden Fence, Hurdle, Maker	19	.	8	.	10	.
Wood Turner, Box Maker	38	36	14	.	90	1
Cooper, Hoop Maker, Bender	217	.	24	.	109	.
Cork, Bark—Cutter, Worker, Dealer	15	.	3	.	15	1
Others	.	.	.	.	.	.
4. *In Paper.*						
Paper Manufacture	6	3	2	.	62	43
Envelope Maker	.	6	.	.	.	.
Stationer, Law Stationer	66	10	34	13	45	14
Card, Pattern Card, Maker	6	.	.	.	.	.
Paper Stainer	8	1	.	.	.	.
Paper Box, Paper Bag, Maker	5	19	6	50	9	179
Ticket, Label, Writer	1	2	1	.	8	2
Others	4	.	8	.	18	.
21. PERSONS WORKING AND DEALING IN VARIOUS MINERAL SUBSTANCES.						
1. *Miners.*						
Coal Miner	2	.	.	.	2	.
Ironstone Miner	.	.	.	.	.	.
Copper Miner	.	.	.	.	.	.
Tin Miner	1	.	.	.	.	.
Lead Miner	.	.	.	.	1	.
Miner in other, or undefined, Minerals	4	.	.	1	1	.
Mine Service	.	.	1	.	.	.
2. *Coal, Coal Gas, &c.*						
Coal Merchant, Dealer	56	5	40	.	63	.
Coalheaver	378	.	45	.	117	.
Coke, Charcoal, Peat—Cutter, Burner, Dealer	13	.	1	.	.	1
Gas Works Service	348	.	38	.	92	.
3. *Stone, Clay, and Road Making.*						
Stone Quarrier	.	.	.	.	.	.
Stone Cutter, Dresser, Dealer	28	.	11	.	16	.
Slate Quarrier	.	.	.	.	.	.
Slate Worker, Dealer	10	.	1	.	.	.
Limeburner	8	.	8	.	26	.
Clay, Sand, Gravel, Chalk—Labourer, Dealer	.	.	1	.	7	.
Fossil, Coprolite—Digger, Dealer	.	.	.	.	.	.
Well Sinker, Borer	3	.	.	.	5	.
Plaster, Cement, Manufacture	2	.	7	2	1	1
Brick, Tile—Maker, Burner, Dealer	94	.	138	.	121	1
Paviour	18	.	4	.	9	.
Road Contractor, Surveyor, Inspector	1	.	.	.	1	.
Road Labourer	20	.	4	.	17	.
Railway Contractor	30	.	1	.	1	.
Platelayer	133	.	27	.	25	.
Railway Labourer, Navvy	220	.	59	.	47	.
Others	8	.	.	.	.	.
4. *Earthenware and Glass.*						
Earthenware, China, Porcelain, Manufacture	7	1	9	.	8	.
Glass Manufacture	23	.	.	.	3	.
Earthenware, China, Glass, Dealer	21	8	8	11	18	6
5. *Salt.*						
Salt Maker, Dealer	1	.	.	.	.	.

Table 10 *continued.*—OCCUPATIONS of MALES and FEMALES in the EASTERN DIVISION and its REGISTRATION COUNTIES, and in each URBAN SANITARY DISTRICT of which the POPULATION exceeds 50,000 PERSONS.

OCCUPATIONS.	URBAN SANITARY DISTRICTS.					
	WEST HAM.		IPSWICH.		NORWICH.	
	Males.	Females.	Males.	Females.	Males.	Females.
6. Water.						
Waterworks Service	12	.	2	.	23	.
Others	.	.	.	.	2	.
7. Precious Metals and Jewellery.						
Goldsmith, Silversmith, Jeweller	60	1	14	2	36	4
Gold, Silver, Beater	.	.	.	.	.	.
Lapidary	1	.	.	.	.	.
Others	.	.	.	.	.	.
8. Iron and Steel.						
Blacksmith	448	.	302	1	272	.
Whitesmith	21	.	38	.	107	.
Nail Manufacture	1	.	.	.	2	.
Anchor, Chain, Manufacture	1	.	.	.	.	.
Other Iron and Steel Manufactures	662	4	605	1	300	3
Ironmonger. Hardware Dealer, Merchant	63	4	71	2	99	2
9. Copper.						
Copper, Copper goods—Manufacturer, Worker, Dealer	58	.	12	.	11	.
10. Tin and Zinc.						
Tin, Tin Plate, Tin goods—Manufacturer, Worker, Dealer	103	6	25	1	164	.
Zinc, Zinc Goods—Manufacturer, Worker, Dealer	17	.	.	.	1	.
11. Lead.						
Lead, Leaden goods—Manufacturer, Worker, Dealer	5	2	.	.	.	
12. In Other, Mixed, or Unspecified, Metals.						
Metal Refiner, Worker, Turner, Dealer	12	.	2	.	1	
Brass, Bronze, Manufacture. Brazier	96	1	22	2	45	
Metal Burnisher, Lacquerer	.	.	.	.		.
White Metal, Plated Ware, Manufacture, Pewterer	5	.	3	.	.	.
Wire Maker, Worker, Weaver, Drawer	22	2	9	.	109	.
Bolt, Nut, Rivet, Screw, Staple, Maker	24	.	12	.	1	.
Lamp, Lantern, Candlestick, Maker	13	.	.	.	1	.
Clasp, Buckle, Hinge, Maker	.	.	.	.	.	.
Fancy Chain, Gilt Toy, Maker	.	.	.	.	.	.
Others	.	.	.	.	.	.
22. PERSONS WORKING AND DEALING IN GENERAL OR UNSPECIFIED COMMODITIES.						
1. Makers and Dealers (General or Undefined).						
General Shopkeeper, Dealer	179	130	106	93	242	309
Pawnbroker	76	2	21	.	27	2
Costermonger, Huckster, Street Seller	108	42	99	26	330	48
Manufacturer, Manager, Superintendent (undefined)	83	1	7	.	33	1
Contractor (undefined)	50	.	3	.	6	.
2. Mechanics and Labourers (General or Undefined).						
General Labourer	6073	17	1170	5	1886	4
Engine Driver, Stoker, Fireman (not railway, marine, nor agricultural)	652	.	73	.	126	.
Artizan, Mechanic (undefined)	94	5	18	.	78	11
Apprentice (undefined)	14	3	5	3	31	6
Factory Labourer (undefined)	149	84	22	8	50	37
Machinist, Machine Worker (undefined)	20	.	19	.	20	.
23. PERSONS WORKING AND DEALING IN REFUSE MATTERS.						
1. Refuse Matters.						
Town Drainage Service	6	.	10	.	11	.
Chimney Sweep, Soot Merchant	21	2	14	.	36	.
Scavenger, Crossing Sweeper	14	.	19	.	10	.
Rag Gatherer, Dealer	11	6	3	4	6	7
VI. UNOCCUPIED CLASS.						
24. PERSONS WITHOUT SPECIFIED OCCUPATIONS						
Persons returned by Property, Rank, &c., and not by special occupation	10645	45104	6089	16073	9382	20734
Children under 5 years of age	10604	10407	3300	3143	5438	5636

Table 11.—Birth-Places of Males and Females enumerated in Counties, and in each Urban District of which the Population exceeds 50,000 Persons.

Where Born.	Where Enumerated.							
	EASTERN COUNTIES.		Counties.*					
			ESSEX.		SUFFOLK.		NORFOLK.	
	Males.	Females.	Males.	Females.	Males.	Females.	Males.	Females.
TOTAL OF INHABITANTS	678052	700024	288180	288254	174606	182287	215266	229483
LONDON	47074	51192	40380	42946	3392	4189	3302	4057
Middlesex (*Intra-metropolitan*)	38493	42114	33036	36406	2730	3391	2730	3317
Surrey (*Intra-metropolitan*)	5751	6084	4956	5096	412	510	381	478
Kent (*Intra-metropolitan*)	2830	2994	2388	2444	250	288	191	262
SOUTH-EASTERN COUNTIES	13487	14773	10050	10773	1852	2081	1585	1919
Surrey (*Extra-metropolitan*)	2138	2354	1592	1743	322	317	224	294
Kent (*Extra-metropolitan*)	5629	5832	4287	4389	756	774	686	669
Sussex	1824	2086	1351	1473	235	308	238	305
Hampshire	2843	3201	2070	2266	377	484	386	461
Berkshire	1053	1300	760	902	162	198	141	200
SOUTH-MIDLAND COUNTIES	17908	20182	11365	12367	2825	3548	3718	4267
Middlesex (*Extra-metropolitan*)	3177	3505	2727	2987	237	265	213	253
Hertfordshire	3327	3780	2886	3237	244	294	197	249
Buckinghamshire	1082	1191	849	880	135	164	98	147
Oxfordshire	826	994	564	707	133	163	109	124
Northamptonshire	1144	1279	693	704	195	236	256	339
Huntingdonshire	782	876	387	414	130	133	265	329
Bedfordshire	1035	948	771	722	124	103	140	123
Cambridgeshire	6535	7608	2468	2716	1627	2190	2440	2703
EASTERN COUNTIES	560928	576487	201431	199412	160610	166073	198887	211002
Essex	192965	191694	187872	185385	4058	6144	1035	1135
Suffolk	164778	168437	9831	10237	147918	150122	7029	8078
Norfolk	203185	215856	3728	3790	8634	10807	190823	200728
SOUTH-WESTERN COUNTIES	6267	7031	4612	5015	890	1068	765	948
Wiltshire	987	1236	761	908	119	179	107	148
Dorsetshire	894	927	646	602	129	159	119	168
Devonshire	2260	2437	1637	1700	373	417	249	320
Cornwall	690	797	486	574	102	113	103	110
Somersetshire	1437	1634	1083	1230	167	200	187	204
WEST-MIDLAND COUNTIES	4729	4980	3293	3311	711	883	725	786
Gloucestershire	1294	1428	918	1008	174	211	202	209
Herefordshire	270	333	196	226	36	66	37	51
Shropshire	320	379	190	242	64	74	66	65
Staffordshire	1040	986	728	629	172	186	140	171
Worcestershire	592	599	398	388	96	133	98	73
Warwickshire	1213	1265	864	818	167	223	182	214
NORTH-MIDLAND COUNTIES	4054	4280	1822	1810	672	708	1560	1762
Leicestershire	672	639	376	342	125	118	171	179
Rutlandshire	119	130	60	76	20	13	30	41
Lincolnshire	2175	2420	789	840	304	373	1082	1216
Nottinghamshire	520	666	298	300	100	94	122	172
Derbyshire	568	516	299	252	114	110	155	154
NORTH-WESTERN COUNTIES	2642	2443	1671	1465	465	363	506	615
Cheshire	523	416	326	246	79	68	118	102
Lancashire	2119	2027	1345	1219	386	295	388	513
YORKSHIRE	3454	3044	1613	1303	664	577	1177	1164
NORTHERN COUNTIES	2322	2212	1298	1073	341	430	683	709
Durham	1265	1193	716	550	183	241	372	402
Northumberland	739	741	403	340	115	147	221	245
Cumberland	219	195	128	129	32	32	59	41
Westmorland	99	83	57	52	11	10	31	21
MONMOUTHSHIRE AND WALES	1219	1303	873	890	160	210	186	203
Monmouthshire	216	230	168	179	23	22	25	29
Glamorganshire	275	267	190	189	46	35	40	43
Carmarthenshire	69	59	48	40	6	11	5	8
Pembrokeshire	169	180	108	105	19	33	42	42
Cardiganshire	59	29	35	24	10	3	14	2
Brecknockshire	65	40	42	30	10	16	3	3
Radnorshire	13	33	8	21	1	3	4	9
Montgomeryshire	45	51	35	29	3	16	5	6
Flintshire	48	41	25	22	10	10	6	9
Denbighshire	45	49	30	28	8	8	7	13
Merionethshire	20	16	11	12	2	4	7	.
Carnarvonshire	59	46	47	29	3	12	9	6
Anglesey	31	30	27	22	3	6	1	2
Wales (*County not stated*)	132	223	99	160	17	31	16	32
ENGLAND (*County not stated*)	1766	1739	1079	952	367	420	320	367
OTHER PARTS OF BRITISH EMPIRE	9669	8581	6830	5755	1347	1442	1492	1384
Islands in the British Seas	353	364	274	266	28	69	61	41
SCOTLAND	3622	2836	2384	1983	522	430	616	475
IRELAND	3562	3386	2597	2361	471	497	494	528
British Colonies or Dependencies	2232	1983	1675	1146	328	457	331	300
FOREIGN COUNTRIES	2438	1688	1808	1126	296	281	334	281
British Subjects	991	867	693	573	146	155	162	139
Foreigners	1447	821	1115	553	150	126	182	142
AT SEA	95	89	55	56	14	14	26	19
British Subjects	95	89	55	56	14	14	26	19
Foreigners	.	.	.	.	.	.	.	.

Table 11 *continued*.—BIRTH-PLACES of MALES and FEMALES enumerated in COUNTIES, and in each URBAN SANITARY DISTRICT of which the POPULATION EXCEEDS 50,000 PERSONS.

WHERE BORN.	WHERE ENUMERATED.					
	URBAN SANITARY DISTRICTS.					
	WEST HAM.		IPSWICH.		NORWICH.	
	Males.	Females.	Males.	Females.	Males.	Females.
TOTAL OF INHABITANTS	65410	63543	23726	26820	40288	47554
LONDON	18756	19722	845	979	932	1131
MIDDLESEX (*Intra-metropolitan*)	15380	16207	665	783	786	946
SURREY (*Intra-metropolitan*)	2247	2274	110	118	97	117
KENT (*Intra-metropolitan*)	1129	1151	72	78	49	68
SOUTH-EASTERN COUNTIES	3607	3757	381	417	345	399
SURREY (*Extra-metropolitan*)	538	572	65	64	46	57
KENT (*Extra-metropolitan*)	1429	1507	152	166	129	153
SUSSEX	540	521	44	54	45	57
HAMPSHIRE	847	878	96	107	77	88
BERKSHIRE	253	279	24	26	48	44
SOUTH-MIDLAND COUNTIES	3818	3620	367	431	464	532
MIDDLESEX (*Extra-metropolitan*)	910	934	35	35	66	67
HERTFORDSHIRE	750	688	55	60	52	51
BUCKINGHAMSHIRE	342	312	22	26	21	28
OXFORDSHIRE	197	231	29	28	28	38
NORTHAMPTONSHIRE	278	270	46	50	71	69
HUNTINGDONSHIRE	162	172	13	23	32	40
BEDFORDSHIRE	268	214	33	25	27	22
CAMBRIDGESHIRE	911	799	134	185	167	217
EASTERN COUNTIES	28469	27526	20689	23632	36852	43669
ESSEX	25039	24445	1079	1251	256	293
SUFFOLK	1783	1569	18882	21524	1179	1622
NORFOLK	1647	1512	728	857	35417	41754
SOUTH-WESTERN COUNTIES	1818	1926	207	186	188	213
WILTSHIRE	279	320	29	23	27	32
DORSETSHIRE	250	209	22	20	26	33
DEVONSHIRE	645	663	72	73	54	69
CORNWALL	216	264	30	21	27	27
SOMERSETSHIRE	428	470	54	39	54	52
WEST-MIDLAND COUNTIES	1549	1368	188	180	197	198
GLOUCESTERSHIRE	418	362	48	40	66	56
HEREFORDSHIRE	58	64	9	9	9	9
SHROPSHIRE	72	91	17	15	9	11
STAFFORDSHIRE	402	326	46	35	27	38
WORCESTERSHIRE	219	172	24	27	20	15
WARWICKSHIRE	380	373	44	54	66	69
NORTH-MIDLAND COUNTIES	671	630	166	166	192	236
LEICESTERSHIRE	134	124	37	35	40	40
RUTLANDSHIRE	13	12	6	2	4	4
LINCOLNSHIRE	320	308	85	94	97	125
NOTTINGHAMSHIRE	98	96	18	17	25	45
DERBYSHIRE	106	90	20	18	26	22
NORTH-WESTERN COUNTIES	726	649	118	93	182	218
CHESHIRE	132	98	15	17	33	32
LANCASHIRE	594	551	103	76	149	186
YORKSHIRE	569	484	149	118	225	238
NORTHERN COUNTIES	556	456	71	65	91	95
DURHAM	296	239	42	36	44	40
NORTHUMBERLAND	199	163	18	25	33	40
CUMBERLAND	48	43	9	4	11	13
WESTMORLAND	13	11	2	.	3	2
MONMOUTHSHIRE AND WALES	337	352	39	33	26	37
MONMOUTHSHIRE	71	91	5	3	6	9
GLAMORGANSHIRE	76	81	12	14	7	8
CARMARTHENSHIRE	17	15	3	3	2	4
PEMBROKESHIRE	42	41	4	3	1	4
CARDIGANSHIRE	15	12	.	1	1	.
BRECKNOCKSHIRE	6	5	7	.	1	.
RADNORSHIRE	1	6	1	.	.	2
MONTGOMERYSHIRE	12	6	.	.	3	2
FLINTSHIRE	6	7	3	1	3	2
DENBIGHSHIRE	18	4	1	.	.	1
MERIONETHSHIRE	4	2	.	.	.	.
CARNARVONSHIRE	12	7	.	2	.	.
ANGLESEY	10	3	1	2	.	1
WALES (*County not stated*)	49	72	2	4	2	4
ENGLAND (*County not stated*)	231	203	54	95	33	49
OTHER PARTS OF BRITISH EMPIRE	3209	2305	376	361	458	439
ISLANDS IN THE BRITISH SEAS	120	120	8	12	8	11
SCOTLAND	1221	1001	167	116	185	140
IRELAND	1065	944	125	120	157	176
BRITISH COLONIES OR DEPENDENCIES	803	240	76	113	108	112
FOREIGN COUNTRIES	1079	513	70	62	97	89
British Subjects	363	243	39	28	53	40
Foreigners	716	270	31	34	44	49
AT SEA	15	12	6	2	6	11
British Subjects	15	12	6	2	6	11
Foreigners	.	.	.	.	.	.

Table 12.—Distribution of the enumerated Natives of Counties.

Where Enumerated.	Where Born.							
	EASTERN COUNTIES.		ESSEX.		SUFFOLK.		NORFOLK.	
	Males.	Females.	Males.	Females.	Males.	Females.	Males.	Females.
TOTAL ENUMERATED NATIVES OF EACH COUNTY	752956	798943	267669	283100	216954	228831	268333	287012
LONDON	84715	111153	39981	52572	23168	30148	21566	28433
Middlesex (*Intra-metropolitan*)	57186	76890	27329	36652	15196	20415	14662	19823
Surrey (*Intra-metropolitan*)	20786	25798	9271	11683	6146	7484	5378	6631
Kent (*Intra-metropolitan*)	6734	8465	3381	4237	1827	2249	1526	1979
SOUTH-EASTERN COUNTIES	26074	32150	12588	15414	7151	8887	6335	7849
Surrey (*Extra-metropolitan*)	7041	10318	3274	4850	2126	3075	1641	2303
Kent (*Extra-metropolitan*)	10026	10507	5256	5564	2580	2736	2190	2297
Sussex	3665	5554	1738	2584	902	1478	905	1492
Hampshire	4014	4078	1749	1746	1072	1130	1193	1202
Berkshire	1328	1693	541	670	381	468	406	465
SOUTH-MIDLAND COUNTIES	23664	29319	10050	12424	6110	7549	7504	9346
Middlesex (*Extra-metropolitan*)	8441	10975	4536	5681	2032	2697	1873	2597
Hertfordshire	4313	5156	2970	3585	681	818	662	753
Buckinghamshire	741	1016	328	427	212	299	201	290
Oxfordshire	540	721	228	318	143	196	169	209
Northamptonshire	1498	1431	350	359	393	332	755	740
Huntingdonshire	563	656	124	142	160	188	279	325
Bedfordshire	735	847	266	336	239	248	230	263
Cambridgeshire	6848	8517	1248	1677	2260	2771	3335	4169
EASTERN COUNTIES	560928	576487	192965	191694	164778	169437	203185	215356
Essex	201431	199412	187872	185385	9831	10237	3728	3790
Suffolk	160610	166073	4058	5144	147918	150122	8634	10807
Norfolk	198887	211002	1035	1165	7029	9078	190823	200759
SOUTH-WESTERN COUNTIES	4029	3766	1363	1586	1482	1024	1184	1156
Wiltshire	518	651	184	264	155	181	179	206
Dorsetshire	548	481	241	182	152	145	155	154
Devonshire	1371	1296	503	551	424	344	444	401
Cornwall	862	300	153	135	532	84	177	81
Somersetshire	730	1038	282	454	219	276	229	374
WEST-MIDLAND COUNTIES	5790	5967	1643	1993	2058	1857	2089	2117
Gloucestershire	1140	1463	380	539	347	443	404	461
Herefordshire	191	265	52	97	76	99	63	69
Shropshire	366	396	108	99	127	137	131	160
Staffordshire	1804	1336	388	480	842	475	574	461
Worcestershire	579	642	178	215	184	196	217	231
Warwickshire	1710	1635	528	613	482	507	700	715
NORTH-MIDLAND COUNTIES	9712	8335	2134	1900	2347	1829	5231	4606
Leicestershire	1164	1187	330	332	296	304	538	551
Rutlandshire	120	124	24	28	27	30	69	68
Lincolnshire	5200	4149	1154	332	916	625	3130	2592
Nottinghamshire	1568	1530	296	310	450	394	822	826
Derbyshire	1660	1345	330	298	658	476	672	571
NORTH-WESTERN COUNTIES	7991	8233	1753	1780	2471	2507	3767	3946
Cheshire	1041	1114	306	318	297	321	439	480
Lancashire	6950	7119	1448	1467	2174	2186	3328	3466
YORKSHIRE	17621	14559	2511	1858	4718	3704	10392	8997
NORTHERN COUNTIES	10656	7703	2070	1366	2247	1516	6539	4821
Durham	8043	5589	1536	988	1755	1149	4752	3452
Northumberland	2558	1846	459	294	415	290	1684	1262
Cumberland	168	188	57	58	51	50	80	80
Westmorland	87	80	18	26	26	27	23	27
MONMOUTHSHIRE AND WALES	1576	1271	611	513	424	373	541	385
Monmouthshire	223	263	80	80	65	64	78	59
Glamorganshire	581	451	230	194	150	134	201	123
Carmarthenshire	67	43	30	17	14	12	23	14
Pembrokeshire	200	137	73	64	62	31	65	48
Cardiganshire	38	27	12	8	9	8	15	11
Brecknockshire	70	62	24	25	13	8	33	19
Radnorshire	15	25	6	13	3	8	6	6
Montgomeryshire	35	32	13	13	9	10	13	9
Flintshire	51	68	15	21	15	19	21	28
Denbighshire	102	104	24	36	38	35	40	33
Merionethshire	30	33	11	10	9	14	10	9
Carnarvonshire	99	61	46	12	27	23	26	26
Anglesey	67	35	47	20	10	9	10	6

Table 14.—Number and Ages of Males and Females returned as Blind or Blind from Birth in the Eastern Division and its Registration Counties.

Registration County.	All Ages. Both Sexes.	All Ages. Males and Females.	0–	5–	15–	20–	25–	45–	65 and upwards.
IV. EASTERN COUNTIES.	1308	M. 673	14	48	25	23	123	194	246
		F. 635	14	27	26	20	69	159	320
14 ESSEX	422	M. 212	4	21	7	7	38	62	73
		F. 210	6	16	5	5	30	51	103
15 SUFFOLK	371	M. 196	5	14	5	4	38	56	74
		F. 175	4	7	9	5	15	54	81
16 NORFOLK	516	M. 266	5	13	13	12	47	76	99
		F. 250	4	10	12	10	24	64	136

Table 15.—Number and Ages of Males and Females returned as Blind in the Eastern Division and its Registration Counties.

Registration County.	All Ages. Both Sexes.	All Ages. Males and Females.	0–	5–	15–	20–	25–	45–	65 and upwards.
IV. EASTERN COUNTIES.	1181	M. 607	8	34	21	19	108	179	238
		F. 574	7	12	20	18	57	142	318
14 ESSEX	381	M. 194	4	17	5	6	33	56	73
		F. 187	4	7	2	4	22	45	103
15 SUFFOLK	331	M. 172	1	9	5	3	32	51	71
		F. 159	1	1	6	5	14	51	81
16 NORFOLK	469	M. 241	3	8	11	10	43	72	94
		F. 228	2	4	12	9	21	46	134

Table 16.—Number and Ages of Males and Females returned as Blind from Birth in the Eastern Division and its Registration Counties.

Registration County.	All Ages. Both Sexes.	All Ages. Males and Females.	0–	5–	15–	20–	25–	45–	65 and upwards.
IV. EASTERN COUNTIES.	127	M. 66	6	14	4	4	15	15	8
		F. 61	7	15	6	2	12	17	2
14 ESSEX	41	M. 18	·	4	2	1	5	6	·
		F. 23	2	3	3	1	8	6	·
15 SUFFOLK	40	M. 24	4	5	·	1	6	5	3
		F. 16	3	6	3	·	1	3	·
16 NORFOLK	46	M. 24	2	5	2	2	4	4	5
		F. 22	2	6	·	1	3	8	2

Table 17.—Number and Ages of Males and Females returned as Deaf and Dumb in the Eastern Division and its Registration Counties.

Registration County.	All Ages. Both Sexes.	All Ages. Males and Females.	0–	5–	15–	20–	25–	45–	65 and upwards.
IV. EASTERN COUNTIES.	654	M. 348	12	70	43	35	111	60	17
		F. 306	18	67	31	29	92	40	29
14 ESSEX	231	M. 121	5	36	16	11	39	18	2
		F. 110	12	23	16	17	27	14	7
15 SUFFOLK	198	M. 101	4	17	10	11	36	20	4
		F. 97	3	23	13	6	30	11	11
16 NORFOLK	225	M. 126	5	33	17	13	37	22	11
		F. 99	3	21	8	6	35	15	11

Table 18.—NUMBER and AGES of MALES and FEMALES returned as IDIOTS or IMBECILES, and LUNATICS in the EASTERN DIVISION and its REGISTRATION COUNTIES.

REGISTRATION COUNTY.	ALL AGES. Both Sexes	ALL AGES. Males and Females.	0–	5–	15–	20–	25–	45–	65 and upwards.
IV. EASTERN COUNTIES.	4760	M. 2176	18	194	154	140	794	646	230
		F. 2584	8	156	138	165	905	846	366
14 ESSEX - - -	1698	M. - 768	8	102	70	53	265	196	74
		F. - 930	4	69	63	68	352	257	117
15 SUFFOLK - - -	1266	M. - 570	3	43	44	40	215	161	64
		F. - 696	1	42	36	34	240	246	97
16 NORFOLK - - -	1796	M. - 838	7	49	40	47	314	289	92
		F. - 958	3	45	39	63	313	343	152

Table 19.—NUMBER and AGES of MALES and FEMALES returned as IDIOTS or IMBECILES in the EASTERN DIVISION and its REGISTRATION COUNTIES.

REGISTRATION COUNTY.	ALL AGES. Both Sexes.	ALL AGES. Males and Females.	0–	5–	15–	20–	25–	45–	65 and upwards.
IV. EASTERN COUNTIES.	1960	M. 935	17	188	134	91	274	152	79
		F. 1025	8	151	117	89	317	213	130
14 ESSEX - - -	767	M. - 391	8	100	62	43	108	47	23
		F. - 376	4	67	52	37	114	63	39
15 SUFFOLK - -	586	M. - 278	2	40	40	30	87	46	33
		F. - 308	1	42	34	25	98	74	34
16 NORFOLK - -	607	M. 266	7	48	32	18	79	59	23
		F. 341	3	42	31	27	105	76	57

Table 20.—NUMBER and AGES of MALES and FEMALES returned as LUNATICS in the EASTERN DIVISION and its REGISTRATION COUNTIES.

REGISTRATION COUNTY.	ALL AGES. Both Sexes.	ALL AGES. Males and Females.	0–	5–	15–	20–	25–	45–	65 and upwards.
IV. EASTERN COUNTIES.	2800	M. 1241	1	6	20	49	520	494	151
		F. 1559	.	5	21	76	588	633	236
14 ESSEX - -	931	M. - 377	.	2	8	10	157	149	51
		F. - 554	.	2	11	31	238	194	78
15 SUFFOLK - -	680	M. - 292	1	3	4	10	128	115	31
		F. 388	.	.	2	9	142	172	63
16 NORFOLK - - -	1189	M. - 572	.	1	8	29	235	230	69
		F. - 617	.	3	8	36	208	267	95

Table 21.—NUMBER of the BLIND, of the DEAF and DUMB, of IDIOTS or IMBECILES, and of LUNAT in the EASTERN DIVISION and its REGISTRATION COUNTIES and DISTRICTS.

Registration County and District.	Blind.			Deaf and Dumb.	Mentally Deranged.		
	From Birth.	Others.	Total.		Idiots.	Lunatics.	Total.
IV. EASTERN COUNTIES.	127	1181	1308	654	1960	2800	4760
14 ESSEX	41	381	422	231	767	931	1698
15 SUFFOLK	40	331	371	198	586	680	1266
16 NORFOLK	46	469	515	225	607	1189	1796
14 ESSEX.							
186 WEST HAM	9	90	99	71	152	52	204
187 EPPING	5	17	22	11	32	3	35
188 ONGAR	2	11	13	6	16	.	16
189 ROMFORD	4	28	32	12	24	2	26
190 ORSETT	.	8	8	6	23	2	25
191 BILLERICAY	2	10	12	8	61	777	838
192 CHELMSFORD	3	28	31	26	49	.	49
193 ROCHFORD	1	24	25	11	26	2	28
194 MALDON	2	17	19	8	20	3	23
195 TENDRING	6	35	41	14	38	53	91
196 COLCHESTER	1	20	21	10	144	5	149
197 LEXDEN	.	18	18	7	40	1	41
198 HALSTEAD	3	19	22	12	29	1	30
199 BRAINTREE	.	23	23	8	54	21	75
200 DUNMOW	.	15	15	9	20	8	28
201 SAFFRON WALDEN	3	18	21	12	39	1	40

Registration County and District.	Blind.			Deaf and Dumb.	M. Dei
	From Birth.	Others.	Total.		Idiots.
15 SUFFOLK.					
202 RISBRIDGE	.	13	13	5	38
203 SUDBURY	6	26	32	19	63
204 COSFORD	3	19	22	11	39
205 THINGOE	.	15	15	12	33
206 BURY ST. EDMUNDS	5	12	17	5	25
207 MILDENHALL	.	6	6	7	16
208 STOW	3	21	24	10	43
209 HARTISMERE	5	14	19	15	34
210 HOXNE	3	18	21	7	31
211 BOSMERE	1	18	19	9	18
212 SAMFORD	.	7	7	13	16
213 IPSWICH	3	48	51	18	83
214 WOODBRIDGE	2	36	38	14	34
215 PLOMESGATE	2	22	24	13	27
216 BLYTHING	1	22	23	13	28
217 WANGFORD	1	16	17	6	31
218 MUTFORD	5	18	23	21	34
16 NORFOLK.					
219 YARMOUTH	4	41	45	28	45
220 FLEGG	.	8	8	4	17
221 SMALLBURGH	1	15	16	10	8
222 ERPINGHAM	1	18	19	13	18
223 AYLSHAM	6	22	28	17	32
224 ST. FAITH'S	.	9	9	8	24
225 NORWICH	16	102	118	25	92
226 FOREHOE	2	15	17	2	20
227 HENSTEAD	2	6	8	14	16
228 BLOFIELD	.	13	13	3	47
229 LODDON	3	6	9	.	23
230 DEPWADE	2	28	30	12	48
231 GUILTCROSS	1	15	16	7	23
232 WAYLAND	1	13	14	5	17
233 MITFORD	1	26	27	24	44
234 WALSINGHAM	1	21	22	8	21
235 DOCKING	1	26	27	5	10
236 FREEBRIDGE LYNN	.	16	16	10	11
237 KING'S LYNN	2	22	24	7	28
238 DOWNHAM	.	21	21	10	31
239 SWAFFHAM	.	4	4	10	15
240 THETFORD	2	22	24	3	17

AGES,

CONDITION AS TO MARRIAGE, OCCUPATIONS, AND BIRTH-PLACES OF THE PEOPLE;

WITH THE

NUMBERS AND AGES OF THE BLIND, DEAF AND DUMB, IDIOTS OR IMBECILES, AND LUNATICS.

DIVISION V.—SOUTH-WESTERN COUNTIES;

WILTSHIRE,
DORSETSHIRE,
DEVONSHIRE,
CORNWALL,
SOMERSETSHIRE.

TABLES IN DIVISION V.—SOUTH-WESTERN COUNTIES.

AGES.

Table.

1.—Ages of Males and Females in the South-western Division and its Registration Counties.

2.—Ages of Males and Females in Registration Districts.

3.—Ages of Males and Females in Registration Sub-districts.

4.—Male and Female Children at *each Year of Age* under 5 in the South-western Division and Registration Counties.

5.—Male and Female Children at *each Year of Age* under 5 in Registration Districts.

6.—Ages of Males and Females in Sanitary Districts.

CONDITION AS TO MARRIAGE.

7.—Condition as to Marriage and Ages of Males and Females in the South-western Division and Registration Counties.

8.—Condition as to Marriage and Ages of Males and Females in Registration Districts.

9.—Condition as to Marriage and Ages of Males and Females in each Urban Sanitary District which the Population exceeds 50,000 Persons.

OCCUPATIONS.

10.—Occupations of Males and Females in the South-western Division and its Registration Counti and in each Urban Sanitary District of which the Population exceeds 50,000 Persons.

BIRTH-PLACES.

11.—Birth-places of Males and Females enumerated in Counties, and in each Urban Sanitary Distri of which the Population exceeds 50,000 Persons.

12.—Distribution of the enumerated Natives of Counties.

13.—Number and Country of Birth of Foreigners enumerated in Counties, and in each Urban Sanita District of which the Population exceeds 50,000 Persons.

THE BLIND, DEAF AND DUMB, IDIOTS OR IMBECILES, AND LUNATICS.

14.—Number and Ages of Males and Females returned as Blind, or Blind from Birth, in the Sout western Division and its Registration Counties.

15.—Number and Ages of Males and Females returned as Blind in the South-western Division a its Registration Counties.

16.—Number and Ages of Males and Females returned as Blind from Birth in the South-western Divisi and its Registration Counties.

17.—Number and Ages of Males and Females returned as Deaf and Dumb in the South-western Divisi and its Registration Counties.

18.—Number and Ages of Males and Females returned as Idiots or Imbeciles, and Lunatics in the Sout western Division and its Registration Counties.

19.—Number and Ages of Males and Females returned as Idiots or Imbeciles in the South-western Divisi and its Registration Counties.

20.—Number and Ages of Males and Females returned as Lunatics in the South-western Division and Registration Counties.

21.—Number of the Blind, of the Deaf and Dumb, of Idiots or Imbeciles, and of Lunatics in the Sou western Division and its Registration Counties and Districts.

AGES.

DIVISION V.—SOUTH-WESTERN COUNTIES.

ıble I.—AGES of MALES and FEMALES in the SOUTH-WESTERN DIVISION and its REGISTRATION COUNTIES.

REGISTRATION COUNTY.	ALL AGES. Persons.	Males and Females.		Under 5* Years.	5–	10–	15–	20–	25–	30–	35–	40–	45–	50–	55–	60–	65–	70–	75–	80–	85–	90–	95–
—SOUTH-WESTERN COUNTIES.	1859013	M.	885471	114096	109838	104470	97337	70709	56805	49182	45098	43285	38438	36263	31707	29696	22473	16684	10330	4089	1598	329	43
		F.	973542	114631	109540	102265	92868	82379	69634	59693	54982	51287	45082	48765	37812	35941	27352	20948	13183	6678	3378	808	116
LTSHIRE	248664	M.	122766	16370	15435	14537	12823	9340	7639	7107	6350	6024	5430	5208	4527	4164	3064	2385	1305	603	231	32	3
		F.	125898	16419	15606	13976	11018	9603	8469	7578	6989	6618	6073	5668	4908	4550	3318	2559	1592	735	262	65	12
RSETSHIRE	184372	M.	90235	11481	10820	10403	9524	7524	6120	5406	4889	4582	4162	3721	3309	2953	2330	1748	1078	541	145	34	4
		F.	94137	11582	10899	10152	8802	7647	6607	5749	5401	4809	4640	4238	3801	3453	2628	2002	1238	827	205	46	9
VONSHIRE	608400	M.	287461	36798	34645	32658	31669	23683	19982	16043	16046	14278	12537	11687	10582	9807	7574	5553	3251	1571	605	102	13
		F.	320939	36475	34595	32528	20942	28653	23786	20050	18250	17219	15506	14558	12489	12129	9189	6976	4378	2225	770	211	46
RNWALL	326375	M.	153016	19070	18998	18745	18083	12830	9223	7044	7692	7149	6448	5998	5546	5066	3861	2947	1809	856	264	57	8
		F.	173360	18855	18753	17900	17390	14727	12270	10308	9826	9434	6716	7783	7136	6661	5159	4014	2485	1282	464	105	18
IERSETSHIRE	490602	M.	231394	31367	29830	28127	24268	17326	14769	12984	12209	11252	9852	9449	7762	7706	5656	4251	2697	1328	453	104	15
		F.	259208	31290	29696	27609	24606	21749	18098	16011	14614	14067	12151	11610	9681	9248	7065	5397	3490	1809	665	176	31

.—Registration Counties consist of groups of Registration Districts, which are generally co-extensive with the Poor Law Unions. Those Registr ts which extend into two or more Counties are included in that Registration County in which the principal town of the District or the greater part o tion is located. The boundaries of Registration Counties, therefore, differ more or less from the boundaries of Counties. For such differences in Divisic l. II., Table 11.

r the number of Children at each Year of Age under 5, see Table 4.

ıe of these Males was stated to be 100 and one 104 years of age. Two of these Females were stated to be 100, two 102, one 103, and one 104 years of age.

Table 2.—AGES of MALES and FEMALES in REGISTRATION DISTRICTS.

REGISTRATION DISTRICT.	ALL AGES. Persons.	Males and Females.		Under 5* Years.	5–	10–	15–	20–	25–	30–	35–	40–	45–	50–	55–	60–	65–	70–	75–	80–	85–	90–	95–
WILTSHIRE.																							
IGHWORTH	35755	M.	18600	2828	2295	1949	1958	1790	1675	1366	1087	914	716	584	437	426	286	199	105	58	15	3	.
		F.	17155	2880	2401	1900	1528	1338	1344	1213	1033	868	722	601	432	418	293	193	118	40	27	2	.
RICKLADE	11283	M.	5622	731	767	669	525	402	319	290	260	273	269	223	214	230	164	144	79	43	10	1	.
		F.	5661	758	724	691	448	338	324	293	294	310	278	235	202	211	166	139	86	30	18	4	1
ALMESBURY	13949	M.	6847	912	891	824	651	514	373	370	342	367	293	263	244	267	177	161	97	59	19	3	.
		F.	7102	958	908	821	600	484	466	403	416	347	325	292	282	275	190	154	101	58	22	4	.
HIPPENHAM	21211	M.	10461	1362	1313	1292	1032	750	635	593	581	527	462	427	346	405	252	241	130	72	19	1	1
		F.	10750	1376	1358	1168	857	779	706	667	573	584	548	478	432	400	247	210	162	75	20	9	1
ALNE	8620	M.	4203	522	562	521	403	382	203	221	199	205	221	198	162	160	106	86	63	26	9	2	.
		F.	4417	552	530	533	376	308	276	237	234	223	246	221	183	179	133	88	56	37	8	3	.
ARLBOROUGH	9733	M.	5094	551	573	755	923	307	268	258	193	241	216	225	184	135	118	67	51	24	7	.	.
		F.	4639	603	577	512	455	377	292	251	268	227	243	238	162	165	114	76	50	23	10	.	1
EVIZES	20530	M.	10121	1351	1237	1132	989	747	692	583	560	516	474	462	413	393	275	191	131	53	17	5	.
		F.	10409	1217	1261	1096	908	739	698	634	568	549	542	482	444	438	290	256	165	69	33	6	2
ELKSHAM	18077	M.	8383	1201	1122	978	805	641	537	500	475	387	355	359	292	291	205	153	105	57	15	2	2
		F.	9694	1180	1100	1038	969	776	734	628	550	480	440	457	391	330	212	193	118	66	17	5	1
RADFORD - ON AVON	10660	M.	5047	719	668	546	445	396	289	296	256	251	204	213	225	170	118	98	72	18	7	3	
		F.	5613	746	649	597	529	474	433	343	323	263	253	249	286	213	145	113	73	35	15	5	
ESTBURY	10620	M.	5158	694	683	633	502	328	261	272	271	263	221	246	228	186	148	129	68	36	14	.	
		F.	5462	696	689	616	434	380	298	328	308	290	279	253	248	233	161	141	72	32	7	9	
ARMINSTER	13840	M.	6783	853	809	867	774	476	388	332	306	315	306	318	296	268	204	146	92	41	17	5	.
		F.	7057	823	817	789	648	514	451	403	381	370	370	341	332	296	216	172	107	41	18	2	1
EWSEY	12403	M.	6288	708	811	746	639	448	355	353	274	278	294	292	258	234	196	164	80	44	21	8	.
		F.	6115	820	796	868	468	444	348	347	328	276	298	298	262	256	180	147	107	40	13	1	1
MESBURY	7623	M.	3869	476	465	477	433	266	234	212	187	185	175	221	163	153	98	74	46	24	9	1	.
		F.	3754	478	464	434	336	255	235	220	210	184	198	200	154	145	97	84	39	28	5	2	-
LDERBURY	27225	M.	12909	1683	1529	1465	1368	1092	886	790	694	668	608	502	401	386	307	243	107	61	18	1	.
		F.	14316	1656	1602	1564	1492	1346	1014	892	770	763	675	610	529	482	380	268	149	66	22	6	2
ILTON	10250	M.	5053	563	616	637	538	354	271	254	264	228	240	228	236	183	148	103	66	28	6	.	.
		F.	5197	548	665	595	442	368	330	264	287	271	242	255	213	203	170	113	70	40	11	3	1
SBURY	9396	M.	4734	582	632	604	465	347	269	232	231	232	240	213	211	147	121	99	60	28	12	.	.
		F.	4672	592	601	547	345	332	267	249	244	278	236	223	189	167	123	101	54	20	4	1	.
ERE	7339	M.	3584	484	472	441	370	238	184	176	161	169	146	199	137	135	125	87	43	21	7	2	.
		F.	3755	439	474	417	318	270	243	206	267	215	186	160	165	141	105	94	68	22	12	3	1

ı.—The Registration Districts of Division V. are co-extensive with the Poor Law Unions of the same name, with the following exceptions:—The Dorc ct (265) comprises the two Poor Law Unions of Dorchester and Cerne; the Scilly Islands (302), being still under 43 Eliz., are not included in any Unic hey a Workhouse, but each Island maintains its own poor; Lundy Island, in the Bideford District (287), and Steep Holme Island, in the Axl t (315), are likewise not included in any Union. The Plymouth District (277) is an Incorporation under a Local Act. The Stoke Damerel District (27 under a Local Act.

the Parishes comprised in each Registration District, see Vol. II., Division V., Table 4.

Districts are arranged topographically under the Registration Counties, and are numbered consecutively, commencing with the Metropolitan Dis on I.

r the Number of Children at each Year of Age under 5, see Table 5.

Table 2 *continued*.—AGES of MALES and FEMALES in REGISTRATION DISTRICTS.

REGISTRATION DISTRICT.	ALL AGES. Persons.	ALL AGES. Males and Females.	Under 5 Years.	5–	10–	15–	20–	25–	30–	35–	40–	45–	50–	55–	60–	65–	70–	75–	80–	85–	90–
18 DORSETSHIRE.																					
258 SHAFTESBURY	12662	M. - 6033	825	754	717	630	428	323	321	313	285	296	258	230	222	158	139	78	48	10	3
		F. - 6629	837	775	745	662	485	453	378	368	339	323	297	247	224	178	167	91	62	22	3
259 STURMINSTER	10050	M. - 4713	605	650	557	452	321	284	267	250	207	213	212	197	164	136	111	65	40	9	3
		F. - 5337	672	667	611	435	436	377	348	294	229	255	256	204	215	136	87	76	46	8	6
260 BLANDFORD	13735	M. - 6684	793	816	807	725	529	397	336	329	321	322	289	286	266	167	152	85	43	12	3
		F. - 7051	834	811	730	651	504	465	411	373	356	352	370	287	323	190	151	96	49	13	5
261 WIMBORNE	16991	M. - 8473	1156	1067	983	867	621	561	467	417	362	365	385	354	271	268	176	116	65	13	6
		F. - 8518	1047	1032	904	748	608	631	464	472	410	462	361	369	353	207	153	106	43	19	5
262 POOLE	18702	M. - 9020	1349	1158	998	905	710	609	565	568	482	403	355	308	253	166	122	80	34	15	.
		F. - 9682	1365	1177	1053	865	807	717	617	582	504	444	384	321	280	214	144	93	50	19	6
263 WAREHAM	16946	M. - 8423	1105	1041	970	836	661	546	481	421	435	374	352	305	270	222	185	131	62	18	5
		F. - 8523	1128	1064	935	728	693	540	530	463	426	413	383	346	288	225	196	119	68	25	2
264 WEYMOUTH	32022	M. - 16565	1803	1640	1599	1727	1820	1535	1237	1067	980	759	633	507	458	334	234	126	59	22	5
		F. - 15457	1738	1629	1636	1568	1367	1214	962	935	818	749	673	528	533	402	333	178	96	25	3
265 DORCHESTER	24890	M. - 12345	1497	1404	1360	1282	1152	823	764	648	592	598	482	460	410	324	230	146	67	16	3
		F. - 12545	1518	1404	1353	1170	1027	611	778	742	633	602	573	515	467	374	285	174	78	25	8
266 SHERBORNE	12605	M. - 6090	736	746	836	717	432	327	308	312	304	282	231	210	185	176	114	68	50	18	2
		F. - 6515	788	722	718	640	563	440	382	398	331	288	307	270	220	197	136	92	40	19	4
267 BEAMINSTER	11468	M. - 5512	670	[illegible]	666	583	466	326	321	279	267	248	246	188	203	175	133	77	43	12	2
		F. - 5956	752	731	622	562	434	380	345	321	325	289	276	215	224	198	177	98	46	10	3
268 BRIDPORT	14811	M. - 6987	942	969	908	722	469	463	349	327	347	297	298	257	251	204	152	106	47	5	2
		F. - 7824	923	969	889	721	589	507	484	433	378	463	358	290	276	241	173	117	67	20	4
19 DEVONSHIRE.																					
269 AXMINSTER	18769	M. - 9048	1153	1121	1168	932	667	469	474	470	403	424	373	465	354	274	200	136	67	24	4
		F. - 9721	1073	1077	1048	937	755	609	521	542	466	502	516	469	394	313	224	152	82	25	9
270 HONITON	21080	M. - 10040	[illegible]	1216	1301	1044	781	660	521	478	457	438	425	393	384	286	205	161	86	23	4
		F. - 11040	1277	1174	1175	980	913	735	652	578	570	376	526	443	493	356	273	176	80	33	8
271 ST. THOMAS	48241	M. - 22405	3028	2820	2572	2147	1605	1425	1333	1177	1072	965	894	822	808	633	481	294	141	38	7
		F. - 25836	3004	2788	2584	2284	2097	1909	1616	1504	1457	1219	1277	1034	1005	738	616	370	194	83	17
272 EXETER	37069	M. - 16759	2094	1969	1880	1523	1484	1223	1030	1023	839	734	680	569	483	378	286	164	83	21	3
		F. - 20310	2043	1944	1971	2314	2153	1700	1460	1240	1120	1003	929	786	693	575	406	278	141	37	13
273 NEWTON ABBOT	74996	M. - 32934	4482	3864	3710	3232	2556	2236	1869	1773	1639	1463	1345	1231	1141	896	626	363	170	53	11
		F. - 42062	4302	4220	3802	4102	3245	3400	2818	2561	2311	2122	1941	1668	1560	1161	815	514	273	97	20
274 TOTNES	36574	M. - 17329	2354	2226	2177	1677	1290	1039	954	882	860	714	707	662	568	473	352	214	88	33	3
		F. - 19245	2343	2106	1952	1809	1632	1364	1211	1032	1070	926	805	705	756	542	412	288	140	50	12
275 KINGSBRIDGE	18844	M. - 9042	1133	1209	1024	858	680	598	402	520	496	371	336	344	353	289	208	139	57	18	8
		F. - 9802	1188	1261	1062	852	750	609	565	553	517	448	420	387	397	364	259	172	81	24	7
276 PLYMPTON ST. MARY	24181	M. - 11627	1520	1442	1417	1333	968	672	586	595	544	517	486	371	392	319	211	127	78	21	8
		F. - 12554	1413	1449	1358	1225	1140	821	771	753	600	546	662	401	431	352	260	157	100	24	9
277 PLYMOUTH	73863	M. - 33807	4364	3970	3564	3412	3074	2544	2095	1909	1804	1574	1528	1275	1044	747	505	263	132	25	6
		F. - 40056	4348	4003	3912	3936	3903	3227	2892	2359	2248	2024	1536	1502	1308	1036	749	462	229	70	18
278 EAST STONEHOUSE	15041	M. - 7145	1007	851	685	721	674	563	444	514	463	325	234	200	173	134	98	48	21	15	.
		F. - 7896	1045	839	716	648	728	690	647	568	463	342	293	269	252	166	125	63	46	16	3
279 STOKE DAMEREL	48939	M. - 24805	2783	2419	2163	4338	2593	2059	1464	1234	1248	1112	975	785	642	456	292	178	69	25	3
		F. - 24134	2777	2446	2423	2282	2169	1954	1615	1388	1415	1208	1009	938	875	626	447	278	129	42	8
280 TAVISTOCK	29190	M. - 14712	1748	1758	1684	1652	1247	999	812	728	688	713	671	621	484	413	273	158	63	30	1
		F. - 14478	1794	1639	1640	1466	1212	1015	790	789	679	675	652	579	462	428	312	204	79	38	9
281 OKEHAMPTON	16962	M. - 8427	1015	1064	1010	928	609	490	437	404	379	373	337	311	334	276	191	111	54	28	6
		F. - 8535	1035	1068	1004	775	671	584	458	442	300	388	368	402	302	270	199	118	79	31	5
282 CREDITON	17929	M. - 8849	1143	1140	995	892	675	532	445	420	308	334	389	353	384	267	214	120	67	23	3
		F. - 9080	1158	1126	968	789	689	587	509	459	417	430	428	373	390	306	216	132	82	20	13
283 TIVERTON	28512	M. - 13765	1746	1770	1636	1416	1022	862	723	721	687	638	563	567	513	420	301	178	94	29	3
		F. - 14747	1768	1626	1685	1419	1206	909	862	750	723	680	686	603	592	461	380	216	101	41	9
284 SOUTH MOLTON	16818	M. - 8475	1049	1078	1028	967	670	497	441	400	398	334	331	296	312	251	219	138	57	16	10
		F. - 8343	1041	1012	890	806	696	602	471	445	413	398	344	324	341	252	198	128	44	19	7
285 BARNSTAPLE	38206	M. - 17936	2250	2179	2089	1959	1437	1141	940	990	923	793	708	646	640	479	308	258	122	51	7
		F. - 20270	2228	2185	2020	2105	1753	1423	1181	1506	1120	981	917	770	782	638	507	315	180	61	16
286 TORRINGTON	14820	M. - 7101	888	885	927	827	532	423	331	322	317	258	297	286	268	205	152	106	55	12	5
		F. - 7719	914	895	821	746	602	511	415	409	387	338	371	310	311	219	187	133	68	21	7
287 BIDEFORD	18758	M. - 8722	1137	1188	1093	1004	848	475	441	400	407	374	391	300	318	245	170	128	69	16	8
		F. - 10036	1214	1108	1051	1019	928	651	588	523	531	451	416	333	350	282	240	183	71	33	10
288 HOLSWORTHY	9008	M. - 4533	560	585	576	495	371	283	228	212	223	153	182	152	162	133	104	69	25	5	6
		F. - 4475	542	502	478	455	379	321	254	247	193	213	178	172	155	127	95	66	33	10	2
20 CORNWALL.																					
289 STRATTON	7439	M. - 3629	505	480	387	369	278	224	177	177	169	176	129	119	118	117	98	61	35	8	2
		F. - 3810	445	649	433	374	320	241	224	206	189	180	170	154	118	119	106	60	24	7	2
290 CAMELFORD	7605	M. - 3755	473	470	520	392	267	207	192	193	160	170	144	137	137	121	80	63	21	7	3
		F. - 3850	457	478	417	304	281	256	230	216	169	182	166	144	180	125	83	58	20	16	4
291 LAUNCESTON	16058	M. - 7861	1037	985	932	918	639	497	370	331	368	329	315	314	269	214	158	92	69	17	6
		F. - 8197	977	941	932	840	700	648	458	428	411	422	335	331	259	234	178	98	72	19	9
292 ST. GERMANS	16730	M. - 7775	976	916	1016	794	576	421	356	300	389	336	342	331	304	252	193	118	47	15	2
		F. - 8955	989	1025	947	821	728	605	544	490	459	436	397	368	376	305	225	132	74	29	5
293 LISKEARD	28787	M. - 13622	1768	1725	1711	1684	1079	755	633	592	605	580	571	524	495	380	204	188	65	26	14
		F. - 15165	1762	1751	1687	1583	1261	1018	829	811	777	744	660	604	677	452	333	228	97	41	8
294 BODMIN	19248	M. - 9309	1103	1089	1013	1087	794	549	473	517	402	414	393	369	332	281	241	146	75	12	7
		F. - 9939	1068	1084	1041	986	777	676	594	558	538	498	436	430	460	384	265	161	75	41	8
295 ST. COLUMB	16543	M. - 7871	953	1014	940	849	641	463	371	397	345	310	318	284	257	195	164	111	44	13	2
		F. - 8672	1029	1025	919	783	728	598	568	462	464	392	358	355	334	229	190	130	78	25	9
296 ST. AUSTELL	30186	M. - 14361	1907	1901	1754	1754	1106	807	748	694	626	591	552	566	486	381	281	148	78	24	3
		F. - 15825	1907	1896	1712	1539	1220	1153	913	892	895	742	690	643	590	452	350	211	96	38	6
297 TRURO	35982	M. - 16299	1941	2006	2112	2122	1347	906	748	736	726	716	680	656	598	452	318	202	94	34	7
		F. - 19683	1909	1985	2006	1969	1740	1468	1194	1073	1071	1005	936	788	830	606	467	298	157	54	10
298 FALMOUTH	25557	M. - 12666	1436	1321	1282	1240	1162	886	764	773	701	559	482	415	356	268	188	125	61	22	3
		F. - 12891	1344	1336	1298	1288	1186	979	789	757	744	685	597	480	452	382	291	163	88	28	9

Table 2 *continued*.—AGES of MALES and FEMALES in REGISTRATION DISTRICTS.

REGISTRATION DISTRICT.	ALL AGES. Persons.	Males and Females.	Under 5 Years.	5–	10–	15–	20–	25–	30–	35–	40–	45–	50–	55–	60–	65–	70–	75–	80–	85–	90–	95–	100 and up
CORNWALL—*cont.*																							
LISTON	23681	M. - 10810	1328	1311	1409	1300	906	644	511	622	503	464	391	384	356	246	236	131	77	26	1	.	
		F. - 12871	1318	1387	1312	1268	1064	885	762	728	757	654	587	567	485	408	310	213	117	44	10	1	
REDRUTH	46128	M. - 20364	2538	2695	2733	2777	1818	1183	895	944	922	820	815	641	661	367	272	167	73	16	1	.	
		F. - 25764	2540	2624	2517	2798	2308	1866	1671	1820	1514	1571	1399	1639	978	741	642	385	172	50	10	2	
PENZANCE	50311	M. - 23680	2871	2850	2767	2373	2186	1537	1310	1232	1183	918	823	708	752	650	447	247	111	39	6	1	.
		F. - 26631	2867	2686	2662	2688	2424	1903	1613	1615	1464	1345	1212	1057	1038	760	612	345	201	69	16	2	.
SCILLY ISLANDS	2320	M. - 1213	132	115	110	112	113	89	86	84	61	59	43	34	53	45	31	19	19	5	1	.	.
		F. - 1107	127	115	97	99	79	80	75	78	57	64	36	36	40	45	44	26	13	5	.	.	.
SOMERSETSHIRE.																							
WILLITON	18685	M. - 9204	1211	1196	1161	1026	640	497	448	411	456	427	390	343	354	269	181	118	72	22	7	.	
		F. - 9481	1192	1179	1101	844	653	589	495	506	587	433	449	400	364	298	201	151	78	25	5	1	
DULVERTON	5453	M. - 2802	316	377	351	296	218	130	137	152	132	128	128	102	85	94	74	48	19	5	.	.	
		F. - 2651	334	343	361	245	180	165	133	127	140	135	115	114	101	88	59	38	18	8	.	.	
WELLINGTON	19194	M. 9297	1232	1198	1160	939	695	531	476	428	458	393	379	363	337	266	240	128	67	20	6	2	
		F. 9897	1290	1167	1111	909	787	651	579	447	529	454	451	413	388	314	230	153	78	29	6	1	
TAUNTON	35582	M. - 16389	2087	1901	2168	1821	1296	1161	911	881	782	786	685	661	678	440	328	213	87	33	8	1	
		F. - 19193	2157	2041	2014	2639	1674	1309	1205	986	1003	848	847	735	744	556	407	339	131	47	18	4	
BRIDGWATER	33673	M. - 16543	2218	2150	2022	1804	1227	1011	858	824	776	693	702	600	587	398	306	208	102	38	10	1	
		F. - 17130	2206	2046	1872	1489	1298	1148	1023	834	896	818	709	716	641	471	352	237	150	41	13	1	
LANGPORT	15674	M. - 7671	965	973	915	835	487	453	397	372	358	330	353	270	305	216	164	102	46	24	5	1	
		F. - 8003	953	1005	868	652	532	550	438	448	427	417	378	341	318	200	190	133	55	31	7	1	
CHARD	25353	M. - 12151	1703	1561	1511	1339	891	708	663	598	613	532	462	369	438	312	246	120	75	11	9	.	
		F. - 13202	1673	1551	1506	1325	1065	891	707	752	714	594	630	478	462	380	284	167	96	26	8	.	
YEOVIL	27706	M. - 12900	1785	1733	1627	1576	912	764	639	691	599	538	538	425	416	311	220	163	77	23	1	2	
		F. - 14806	1766	1742	1717	1408	1180	1019	939	867	786	714	647	532	514	378	228	195	94	30	5	1	
WINCANTON	19770	M. - 9461	1296	1232	1119	913	681	595	524	522	479	465	382	343	341	262	202	112	61	14	6	2	
		F. - 10309	1228	1210	1178	926	850	711	594	579	539	456	461	386	392	307	237	126	67	35	8	.	
FROME	23152	M. - 11062	1462	1436	1257	1162	800	653	591	598	603	478	496	412	389	279	210	130	81	30	5	.	
		F. - 12090	1506	1484	1327	1112	940	814	691	677	626	618	564	482	451	325	250	126	85	41	9	2	
SHEPTON MALLET	15779	M. - 7619	956	992	864	794	585	470	408	416	377	328	341	275	276	188	150	106	55	23	6	.	
		F. - 8160	1019	991	923	718	632	525	439	386	438	358	406	310	292	233	187	126	64	19	6	2	
WELLS	22013	M. - 10587	1402	1241	1188	1095	818	685	663	600	551	470	476	380	357	290	227	127	89	18	4	1	
		F. - 11426	1367	1347	1146	1042	993	767	709	662	641	508	503	438	429	323	248	133	86	28	8	2	
AXBRIDGE	40841	M. - 18651	2407	2425	2296	1843	1540	1190	1077	1002	932	893	766	640	656	464	357	261	114	46	9	3	
		F. - 22190	2465	2365	2342	2260	2064	1606	1341	1264	1146	1035	926	836	831	633	470	323	154	73	14	3	
CLUTTON	23615	M. - 12091	1607	1679	1516	1301	878	729	617	611	597	562	459	520	438	302	249	143	80	26	8	1	
		F. - 11524	1606	1402	1347	852	800	724	676	583	620	536	518	473	451	325	261	138	82	45	14	1	
BATH	70626	M. - 30124	3852	3642	3774	3185	2284	2036	1823	1632	1548	1285	1246	983	994	711	519	385	151	63	11	.	
		F. - 40502	3819	3660	3853	4246	4044	3351	2751	2440	2367	2076	1844	1642	1594	1186	938	567	215	101	29	7	
KEYNSHAM	25781	M. - 12570	1899	1721	1445	1350	960	821	741	673	577	524	484	369	380	346	199	128	67	19	4	.	
		F. - 13211	1860	1727	1452	1198	1092	993	823	705	652	661	556	438	416	302	235	146	87	38	8	2	
BEDMINSTER	67405	M. - 31991	4039	4357	3677	3098	2588	2415	2064	1838	1594	1321	1140	871	770	675	378	225	96	40	5	1	
		F. - 35414	4049	4396	3834	3223	3066	2776	2423	2170	1951	1564	1348	1077	884	711	500	359	106	61	18	3	

Table 3.—AGES of MALES and FEMALES in REGISTRATION SUB-DISTRICTS.

REGISTRATION SUB-DISTRICT.	ALL AGES. Persons.	Males and Females.	Under 5 Years.	5–	10–	15–	20–	25–	30–	35–	40–	45–	50–	55–	60–	65–	70–	75–	80–	85–	90–	95–
WILTSHIRE.																						
[...]1. HIGHWORTH																						
HIGHWORTH. (W.)	10261	M. - 5252	847	716	667	529	368	348	339	306	268	209	149	133	144	106	82	56	32	10	.	.
		F. - 5009	815	757	654	347	347	366	315	303	282	218	187	127	153	103	67	52	23	16	2	.
SWINDON. (H.)	25494	M. - 13348	1981	1579	1342	1429	1411	1227	1027	787	646	567	435	314	282	180	117	50	26	5	3	.
		F. - 12146	2065	1644	1346	981	939	978	808	730	580	509	414	305	285	190	126	64	26	11	.	.
[...]2 CRICKLADE.																						
WOOTTON BASSETT	5720	M. - 2834	391	369	336	291	197	167	140	132	138	136	111	121	117	80	74	40	22	11	1	.
		F. - 2886	388	386	345	230	197	172	147	147	149	145	127	106	112	79	75	38	20	10	4	.
CRICKLADE (WH.)	5563	M. - 2788	350	398	333	264	205	152	180	137	135	124	112	93	113	84	70	39	21	8	.	.
		F 2775	370	338	346	297	201	162	146	147	161	133	153	96	99	77	64	47	19	8	.	1
[...] MALMESBURY.																						
MALMESBURY, EASTERN. (H.)	7009	M. - 3420	458	459	378	328	260	178	200	159	192	159	144	116	132	95	81	50	29	9	2	.
		F. - 3589	477	464	408	299	235	246	207	199	182	176	146	145	140	90	75	55	32	12	2	.
MALMESBURY, WESTERN. (W.)	6940	M. - 3427	454	432	446	323	264	195	170	183	175	142	139	128	136	82	80	47	30	10	1	.
		F. - 3513	479	444	413	301	249	220	198	217	165	149	147	137	133	100	79	46	26	16	2	.

[...]*te*.—For the Parishes comprised in each Registration Sub-district, *see* Vol. II., Division V., Table 4.
[(W].) denotes that a Workhouse, and (WS.) that a Workhouse School belonging to the District is situated within the Sub-district; (w.) denotes a Workho[...] (ws.) a Workhouse School not belonging to the District, (H.) a Hospital or Infirmary, (L.) a Lunatic Asylum, (P.) a Prison or Convict Establi[...] (R.) a certified Reformatory or Industrial School, (B.) Barracks, &c., (S.) H.M. Ships. A figure appended to any of these letters denotes the num[...] [in]stitutions of a similar class situated within the Sub-district. The names of the institutions thus indicated, and the number of inmates enumerated there[...] be found in Vol. II., Division V., Table 6.

Table 3 *continued*.—Ages of Males and Females in Registration Sub-Districts.

Registration Sub-District.	All Ages. Persons.	Males and Females.	Under 5 Years.	5-	10-	15-	20-	25-	30-	35-	40-	45-	50-	55-	60-	65-	70-	75-	80-	85-	90-
17 WILTSHIRE—*cont.*																					
244 CHIPPENHAM.																					
1 Castle Combe	2793	M. - 1403	177	165	163	141	104	73	65	63	70	65	66	66	66	46	38	21	7	3	.
		F. - 1390	164	179	150	95	88	90	82	62	72	89	63	64	60	57	35	36	11	2	.
2 Corsham. (L.)	7893	M. - 3821	530	609	472	369	273	259	222	237	204	161	138	117	117	84	68	29	27	4	1
		F. - 3872	524	540	412	278	273	274	230	233	219	186	168	134	118	120	80	49	26	7	5
3 Chippenham. (W.)	7947	M. - 3867	473	467	463	397	288	226	220	214	182	171	172	123	155	95	90	55	25	9	.
		F. - 4080	407	462	457	378	322	267	269	210	216	203	181	172	155	113	72	66	27	6	9
4 Christian Malford	2778	M. - 1370	172	162	164	135	85	97	66	67	71	65	61	46	67	36	48	25	13	3	.
		F. - 1408	191	177	149	106	96	75	80	78	77	76	66	62	67	52	23	21	11	5	2
245 CALNE.																					
1 Calne. (W.)	8620	M. - 4203	522	562	521	406	332	283	221	199	206	221	198	162	160	106	86	62	26	9	2
		F. - 4417	552	530	533	375	305	276	237	234	223	246	221	183	179	133	86	86	37	8	3
246 MARLBOROUGH.																					
1 Marlborough. (W.H.)	9733	M. - 5094	551	573	755	823	807	268	258	193	241	216	225	184	135	116	67	51	24	7	.
		F. - 4639	663	577	618	455	377	292	261	268	227	243	238	162	165	114	76	59	23	10	.
247 DEVIZES.																					
1 Devizes. (W.H². L.P.B.)	11213	M. - 5477	712	651	638	563	444	352	329	330	280	270	244	199	190	139	93	58	21	6	2
		F. - 5736	802	642	615	553	467	398	374	365	309	311	258	246	221	135	124	76	34	17	3
2 Lavington. (L.)	4764	M. - 2408	334	307	283	242	150	190	119	114	138	171	103	127	101	65	54	36	15	7	1
		F. 2356	268	316	262	169	144	128	137	132	138	124	104	103	107	61	81	56	19	7	1
3 Bromham	4553	M. - 2236	315	279	236	184	163	144	135	116	98	96	105	87	102	71	38	37	17	4	2
		F. - 2317	297	303	218	184	148	182	123	131	102	107	120	95	110	90	50	33	13	9	2
248 MELKSHAM.																					
1 Melksham. (W. H.)	5861	M. - 2767	461	360	286	244	178	165	160	153	125	94	128	115	104	91	71	47	25	11	1
		F. - 3094	383	368	329	267	236	233	176	172	141	132	157	137	122	89	69	47	32	10	5
2 Trowbridge. (H.B.)	12216	M. - 5616	800	762	693	662	365	372	351	322	262	261	231	177	187	114	82	58	32	4	1
		F. - 6603	797	732	709	702	580	501	452	378	346	308	300	254	208	123	124	71	24	7	2
249 BRADFORD ON AVON.																					
1 Bradford, South-eastern. (W.R.)	7101	M. - 3293	479	454	340	283	262	197	189	170	173	126	157	160	111	75	84	51	11	2	2
		F. - 3808	496	413	392	347	383	289	228	219	171	150	164	189	138	94	74	45	23	10	4
2 Bradford, North-western	3759	M. - 1754	249	234	206	162	137	92	107	86	78	78	86	75	59	43	34	21	7	5	1
		F. 2005	259	236	225	182	171	144	115	104	92	94	95	96	76	51	39	28	12	5	1
250 WESTBURY.																					
1 Bradley	2192	M. - 1075	143	141	143	113	79	48	63	48	47	56	62	47	30	28	28	14	4	3	.
		F. - 1117	146	155	111	93	85	67	63	58	48	53	59	45	39	39	27	23	7	1	2
2 Edington	3100	M. - 1517	186	174	175	161	95	81	78	84	80	77	69	71	54	40	30	28	16	2	.
		F. - 1583	196	171	187	129	116	88	90	83	80	80	72	82	71	51	63	22	8	4	2
3 Westbury. (W.)	5358	M. - 2656	365	338	316	228	154	182	131	139	141	108	115	110	102	71	64	28	16	9	.
		F. - 2702	354	363	318	230	178	143	175	167	165	146	122	123	123	71	63	27	17	2	5
251 WARMINSTER.																					
1 Warminster. (W.H.R.)	6994	M. - 3366	326	398	491	380	330	186	182	190	148	142	144	136	107	95	79	45	21	8	3
		F. - 3628	411	406	468	353	260	233	219	201	178	185	169	164	130	105	91	61	19	8	1
2 Longbridge-Deverill	3226	M. - 1589	210	184	178	169	108	96	69	71	77	73	80	82	65	53	28	27	8	3	1
		F. - 1637	184	198	170	130	105	110	81	82	97	96	88	88	76	53	39	21	15	9	1
3 Heytesbury	3620	M. - 1826	237	227	188	216	158	106	84	75	92	91	89	78	71	50	29	20	12	6	1
		F. - 1794	228	219	181	160	140	106	103	98	101	80	84	86	70	58	42	26	7	1	.
252 PEWSEY.																					
1 Netheravon. (W.)	6971	M. - 3536	489	448	432	336	257	209	214	141	152	144	140	150	144	114	91	41	22	11	1
		F. - 3435	468	439	360	281	266	210	207	139	150	152	166	140	153	90	74	52	20	7	1
2 Collingbourne	5432	M. - 2752	319	363	314	303	191	146	139	133	126	150	143	108	99	82	73	39	22	10	2
		F. - 2680	352	357	319	187	168	138	140	129	128	141	132	122	103	90	73	55	20	6	.
253 AMESBURY.																					
1 Orcheston	2230	M. - 1130	142	163	135	126	68	52	46	62	56	50	72	47	52	21	18	15	7	3	.
		F. - 1100	128	131	129	104	71	61	66	67	60	64	58	42	55	30	24	11	4	1	.
2 Amesbury. (W.)	3535	M. - 1828	213	231	228	198	125	94	27	87	92	80	84	68	67	58	42	21	10	6	.
		F. - 1707	220	206	198	158	184	101	106	94	86	94	87	72	59	34	33	16	16	5	1
3 Winterbourne	1849	M. - 911	128	81	104	99	75	58	89	39	43	36	55	48	34	19	14	10	7	.	1
		F. 938	130	117	107	70	60	73	55	48	38	38	55	40	32	24	21	12	6	1	1
254 ALDERBURY.																					
1 Alderbury	4055	M. - 2071	267	266	267	224	147	103	121	93	97	100	82	87	73	70	46	28	11	4	.
		F. - 1984	220	233	245	186	138	109	115	109	128	68	97	84	78	66	46	20	4	7	.
2 Downton	4713	M. - 2361	298	290	296	245	176	123	129	131	118	121	109	90	79	55	64	18	13	6	.
		F. - 2352	280	286	270	187	173	155	149	115	131	126	116	105	93	62	44	35	11	2	2
3 Britford. (W. H. L.²)	9573	M. - 4380	607	523	469	417	393	326	299	255	226	212	148	162	131	86	68	37	18	3	.
		F. - 5193	814	535	488	588	552	420	363	382	270	238	199	173	154	120	102	42	19	4	1
4 Salisbury. (R.)	8854	M. - 4067	511	459	444	482	376	234	260	315	227	175	163	152	103	86	65	29	19	6	1
		F. - 4787	513	408	661	561	482	330	275	244	234	243	207	167	157	132	96	52	32	9	3
255 WILTON.																					
1 Wilton. (W.)	5871	M. - 2878	584	343	380	290	208	168	136	145	124	139	183	129	109	74	49	36	17	3	.
		F. - 2993	377	365	340	243	234	205	157	162	156	137	150	123	125	35	55	39	22	9	.
2 Bishopstone	4379	M. - 2175	269	271	257	230	146	163	118	119	104	101	95	107	74	74	64	30	11	3	.
		F. - 2204	271	300	256	199	134	125	107	125	115	105	105	91	78	81	68	31	18	2	3

Table 3 *continued*.—AGES of MALES and FEMALES in REGISTRATION SUB-DISTRICTS.

-ISTRATION -DISTRICT.	ALL AGES. Persons.		Males and Females.	Under 5 Years.	5–	10–	15–	20–	25–	30–	35–	40–	45–	50–	55–	60–	65–	70–	75–	80–	85–	90–	95–	100 and upw-
-LTSHIRE— *cont.*																								
TISBURY.																								
-AD - -	3694	M.	1869	217	252	220	190	145	104	90	95	93	83	79	99	70	60	33	23	9	7			
		F.	1825	235	227	204	159	148	100	93	106	103	95	102	83	59	50	31	22	10	1			
-TY. (W.) - -	3260	M.	1628	207	221	217	147	103	93	77	82	97	77	82	67	43	44	35	19	10	5			
		F.	1632	205	225	211	116	120	94	98	80	110	72	68	63	65	36	39	20	6	3	1		
-N - - -	2352	M.	1237	158	159	167	128	99	70	65	54	42	79	52	46	34	27	31	18	9				
		F.	1115	152	149	132	70	93	73	58	58	65	69	63	43	44	28	31	12	4				
-97 MERE.																								
(W.) -	7340	M.	3504	484	472	443	370	238	184	176	161	169	145	190	137	135	123	87	43	21	7	2		
		F.	3756	459	474	417	318	270	243	206	207	215	186	169	165	141	105	94	68	22	12	3	1	
-DORSET-SHIRE.																								
-HAFTESBURY.																								
-SBURY. (W. H.)	4855	M.	2256	336	270	260	241	143	114	132	126	103	116	89	84	79	61	50	28	16	3			
		F.	2599	318	328	313	262	196	163	159	144	134	128	104	83	82	71	63	28	21	9	1	1	
-ELL - -	3085	M.	1460	186	160	172	145	111	92	78	68	62	72	73	51	63	45	37	20	14	2	1		
		F.	1625	210	143	173	138	109	107	81	80	79	72	75	68	67	47	43	28	7	7		1	
-GHAM - -	4802	M.	2207	304	294	285	244	163	117	111	110	120	108	94	93	80	54	52	30	18	5	2		
		F.	2595	309	304	259	252	180	163	147	144	126	123	118	96	88	60	61	35	24	6	2	1	
TURMINSTER.																								
-BRIDGE - -	4145	M.	1880	334	204	222	180	124	90	109	113	83	91	91	81	60	53	41	23	15	2	2		
		F.	2265	288	245	288	208	189	150	132	124	92	121	90	74	68	64	39	34	16	3	2	1	
-MINSTER. (W.) -	5905	M.	2833	371	356	335	272	201	188	158	137	124	122	121	116	104	85	70	42	25	7	1		
		F.	3072	389	362	323	277	241	221	216	170	137	134	160	130	117	72	48	42	24	5	4		
BLANDFORD.																								
-ON AREAS. (H.R.)	6575	M.	2784	346	322	345	339	190	174	120	133	117	123	133	126	112	80	64	40	19	2	1	1	
		F.	2791	374	341	290	233	211	180	157	129	127	132	172	118	126	81	59	34	14	6	2		
-DFORD. (W.) -	8150	M.	3900	447	494	402	399	339	228	210	166	204	199	156	160	154	87	88	45	24	10	2	1	
		F.	4250	460	470	440	413	383	285	254	244	229	220	198	169	187	109	92	62	35	7	3		
WIMBORNE.																								
-BORNE - -	6740	M.	3490	404	439	419	356	274	183	182	169	141	165	163	182	113	122	74	45	24	3	2		
		F.	3250	428	432	351	247	233	213	171	180	139	182	143	159	132	110	48	30	14	7	2		
-HAMPTON -	4313	M.	2135	270	279	240	222	144	136	140	101	106	87	87	108	77	73	62	24	9	6			
		F.	2178	274	263	263	159	162	131	130	122	98	107	93	96	108	69	42	31	15	6	1	1	
-BORNE (W.) -	5938	M.	2848	422	349	315	279	212	232	166	147	121	113	115	102	81	73	40	47	25	4	4		
		F.	3090	345	335	300	342	303	267	183	161	155	133	125	115	113	88	63	39	14	6	2	1	
-262 POOLE.																								
-FORD -	4852	M.	2419	411	341	295	238	160	160	139	144	121	112	83	72	61	30	22	19	8	4			
		F.	2433	393	355	289	206	191	184	141	156	120	113	81	65	57	30	20	19	6	3	2		
-R. (W.H.R.) -	11642	M.	5484	769	673	586	544	473	385	357	310	308	231	233	186	164	101	82	50	23	9			
		F.	6158	702	691	679	583	549	461	496	392	338	280	248	210	201	149	88	67	36	14	4		
-CHEST - - -	2208	M.	1117	169	144	117	123	77	64	70	54	33	30	39	50	28	35	18	11	3	2			
		F.	1091	178	131	125	76	67	72	70	64	46	51	56	46	28	35	27	10	8	2			
-63 WAREHAM.																								
-NAGE - - -	4158	M.	2056	266	242	222	213	186	143	120	114	114	85	88	61	59	45	46	29	12	3	2		
		F.	2102	292	249	236	177	160	143	142	115	110	100	80	84	71	54	47	23	15	7		1	
-E CASTLE - -	2339	M.	1187	130	144	134	121	88	71	86	54	61	57	48	47	41	34	24	21	6				
		F.	1152	139	156	128	88	98	59	75	67	40	65	47	46	37	28	29	17	3	1	1		
-EHAM. (W.) -	5897	M.	2913	358	306	328	296	229	193	148	158	132	135	119	123	92	73	70	45	18	10	2		
		F.	2984	368	367	309	278	224	196	185	182	140	141	144	124	94	85	60	40	23	9			
-E REGIS - -	4552	M.	2267	331	289	280	229	158	136	121	95	108	97	97	74	78	70	45	38	16	2	1		
		F.	2283	316	282	262	185	161	142	128	119	118	107	112	92	86	58	66	37	21	8	1		
WEYMOUTH.																								
-AY - - -	4767	M.	2167	274	271	292	221	176	129	96	106	139	105	83	69	82	63	45	24	14	7	1		
		F.	2600	248	246	253	282	242	213	196	172	123	135	134	100	90	86	58	42	17	3			
-MOUTH. (W.H⁵.B².)	15255	M.	6873	884	795	762	700	501	494	439	385	379	308	278	232	237	160	131	65	26	11	1		
		F.	8382	872	811	800	931	826	681	846	488	460	409	366	302	307	230	191	92	57	16	2		
-LAND. (H.P.B.S⁴.)	10061	M.	6515	496	497	609	701	1616	855	642	547	442	312	227	176	107	70	35	24	11		2		
		F.	3546	504	451	466	323	258	266	231	221	193	163	130	94	97	54	59	25	16	4	1		
-TSBURY - -	1939	M.	1010	149	137	116	105	67	57	60	40	50	34	45	30	32	30	23	13	8	4	1		
		F.	929	114	121	104	67	71	64	59	54	42	42	43	32	39	28	25	19	5	2			
DORCHESTER.																								
-CHESTER.(W.H.P.B².)	8668	M.	4321	543	457	413	519	482	335	312	243	223	190	156	142	97	87	59	39	17	6	1		
		F.	4347	531	482	420	471	397	371	281	254	220	199	130	148	124	113	75	40	27	3	2		
-LETOWN - -	4041	M.	1965	240	232	223	242	170	116	106	93	80	88	83	80	79	60	32	23	7	1			
		F.	2076	253	245	248	183	156	138	124	117	91	97	104	80	70	70	45	35	14	6			
-EN NEWTON. (L.)	5685	M.	2802	291	310	338	273	216	170	163	160	151	150	121	122	115	82	67	41	20	2	1		
		F.	2883	327	296	299	258	230	180	177	189	152	159	155	138	102	102	78	42	14	7			
-E. (W.) - -	6496	M.	3257	423	396	388	352	264	202	183	180	138	165	122	116	119	95	72	43	23	7	1		
		F.	3239	407	381	336	278	244	222	196	182	170	147	134	149	131	89	89	43	25	9	3	1	

Table 3 *continued*.—Ages of Males and Females in Registration Sub-Districts.

Registration Sub-District.	All Ages. Persons.		Males and Females.	Under 5 Years	5–	10–	15–	20–	25–	30–	35–	40–	45–	50–	55–	60–	65–	70–	75–	80–	85–	90–
18 DORSETSHIRE—*cont.*																						
266 SHERBORNE.																						
1 Yetminster	3972	M.	1884	225	220	232	200	138	126	103	98	96	81	76	64	79	63	34	18	22	10	
		F.	2088	256	236	217	185	175	139	119	128	109	89	91	96	87	63	50	34	10	4	
2 Sherborne. (W.H.)	5717	M.	2752	325	322	438	394	183	180	183	132	140	127	91	90	58	78	54	[illegible]	16	6	
		F.	2965	328	301	296	336	275	212	173	186	182	136	136	124	81	96	52	39	20	10	
3 Bradford Abbas	3006	M.	1444	186	200	168	153	111	71	72	92	69	74	64	56	48	35	26	17	12	.	
		F.	1562	204	186	206	125	102	95	96	84	100	60	80	51	52	44	34	23	19	5	
267 BEAMINSTER.																						
1 Evershot	2729	M.	1316	151	143	157	140	112	79	71	66	60	63	56	57	42	45	33	17	7	3	
		F.	1413	174	189	143	148	111	88	77	86	74	65	58	57	46	38	27	21	14	3	
2 Netherbury. (W.)	5470	M.	2648	321	327	335	279	171	150	155	146	141	114	109	80	109	81	68	35	23	4	
		F.	2822	309	359	288	247	200	166	196	169	160	126	138	95	104	91	107	44	16	3	
3 Beaminster	3269	M.	1548	198	190	174	155	123	97	95	67	66	69	78	40	52	49	32	25	13	5	
		F.	1721	199	183	191	157	123	106	102	82	91	88	80	63	75	67	49	33	15	4	
268 BRIDPORT.																						
1 Burton Bradstock	4331	M.	2062	260	273	262	215	140	129	126	80	119	86	86	76	63	56	47	36	13	2	
		F.	2269	306	295	247	196	162	157	143	116	99	111	105	80	71	69	56	34	19	3	
2 Bridport. (W. H.)	7212	M.	3327	462	433	437	353	225	194	165	174	151	154	130	113	123	92	69	42	26	1	
		F.	3885	423	430	423	390	328	256	242	236	187	199	179	141	150	114	79	57	32	9	
3 Whitchurch Canonicorum.	3268	M.	1598	220	203	209	174	94	80	68	73	77	57	73	68	65	36	36	25	14	2	
		F.	1670	195	234	190	126	99	93	99	82	92	68	74	75	55	61	38	26	16	8	
19 DEVONSHIRE.																						
269 AXMINSTER.																						
1 Lyme. (H³.)	3826	M.	1705	195	190	201	187	129	93	81	89	72	85	66	80	84	60	44	27	17	6	
		F.	2121	261	192	200	216	171	146	114	128	97	114	124	102	91	80	66	41	17	11	
2 Axminster. (W.)	5186	M.	2609	335	348	306	265	219	142	143	118	117	123	104	110	82	68	51	32	18	8	
		F.	2577	304	308	297	253	180	171	144	131	147	127	126	95	88	76	45	34	25	3	
3 Chardstock	3249	M.	1688	186	207	243	188	110	75	71	71	75	80	89	70	87	55	46	30	10	5	
		F.	1561	189	174	157	138	108	86	74	93	81	87	81	71	88	52	36	23	12	6	
4 Colyton	6528	M.	3056	417	376	408	294	209	159	139	182	145	136	120	145	101	91	66	47	22	9	
		F.	3472	379	416	394	330	290	207	189	193	171	174	185	141	127	99	78	54	28	6	
270 HONITON.																						
1 Honiton. (W.)	9712	M.	4745	566	616	683	489	362	249	240	216	212	200	216	161	177	130	132	82	44	9	
		F.	4967	609	566	567	443	416	327	279	232	249	247	244	171	191	154	125	91	42	16	
2 Ottery St. Mary. (H.)	11368	M.	5295	669	680	628	515	419	316	281	262	245	229	209	205	207	156	138	81	42	14	
		F.	6073	668	614	621	537	497	408	373	346	327	329	282	272	302	202	150	85	38	17	
271 ST. THOMAS.																						
1 East Budleigh	4742	M.	2081	283	293	206	218	128	105	111	96	85	95	91	74	52	75	36	23	16	2	
		F.	2661	271	280	256	257	246	179	107	166	144	158	129	117	96	75	63	37	22	12	
2 Exmouth	8294	M.	3517	316	457	412	331	265	222	204	196	150	125	145	122	117	110	78	47	25	3	
		F.	4777	475	472	414	486	440	381	296	303	271	196	234	191	204	106	116	81	41	18	
3 Woodbury	3417	M.	1622	240	218	199	132	104	83	69	88	61	72	51	61	70	58	40	22	9	2	
		F.	1795	236	228	243	147	125	102	149	113	95	84	84	59	65	60	37	27	11	8	
4 Broad Clist	3151	M.	1578	201	196	175	175	96	101	84	70	70	67	72	78	54	58	25	34	9	3	
		F.	1573	212	165	159	143	105	121	76	71	88	78	86	79	71	51	38	22	11	4	
5 Topsham	4011	M.	1841	225	228	236	183	136	104	107	77	76	78	74	75	78	41	48	27	13	5	
		F.	2170	252	243	222	192	187	138	134	100	124	107	140	99	89	62	56	35	24	7	
6 Heavitree. (H.L.B.)	6302	M.	2882	396	380	282	281	261	240	173	168	147	138	104	92	87	60	51	29	15	6	
		F.	3420	422	368	323	311	292	302	235	215	177	148	163	125	164	85	72	47	18	9	
7 St. Thomas. (W.R.)	7512	M.	3620	512	497	396	349	293	265	251	191	189	181	124	131	112	91	72	51	19	4	
		F.	3892	501	441	418	336	317	295	270	217	213	188	189	129	140	[illegible]	84	64	22	11	
8 Alphington	3656	M.	1833	233	234	198	199	151	104	100	101	102	77	68	62	59	47	37	34	9	4	
		F.	1823	261	222	192	161	122	134	94	109	109	87	77	63	60	61	43	16	8	5	
9 Christow	1475	M.	746	83	91	72	84	71	53	43	35	29	32	36	34	22	18	26	20	2	1	1
		F.	729	81	83	81	65	55	32	47	21	34	39	43	35	36	25	17	13	4	2	
10 Kenton. (L³.R.)	5651	M.	2686	305	327	324	229	190	148	177	163	137	130	120	96	120	78	66	37	24	8	
		F.	2965	293	283	315	196	208	200	192	180	183	172	177	159	131	117	89	47	33	7	
272 EXETER.																						
1 Exeter Eastern. (W.H³.R.)	23054	M.	10120	1307	1194	1130	1053	859	719	641	618	535	420	389	330	303	246	194	110	55	16	
		F.	12934	1292	1203	1169	1412	1286	1035	875	775	746	621	560	472	452	389	336	180	107	21	8
2 Exeter Western. (P.B.)	14615	M.	6639	787	715	700	775	625	563	398	405	404	314	291	229	186	132	92	54	28	5	
		F.	7976	751	742	808	902	869	674	525	467	434	382	363	314	241	186	159	98	44	16	
273 NEWTON ABBOT.																						
1 Teignmouth. (H².)	12884	M.	5378	738	618	628	519	417	341	309	299	306	246	227	224	204	143	103	57	36	9	1
		F.	7506	682	684	628	706	794	636	488	458	426	304	354	313	319	235	151	96	56	18	
2 Chudleigh	6426	M.	3060	404	377	374	306	212	196	157	158	123	129	141	124	117	94	76	51	16	5	
		F.	3366	374	373	349	302	271	253	182	178	178	196	165	124	123	112	92	57	33	12	2
3 Moreton Hampstead	2708	M.	1355	169	174	149	132	107	78	71	69	73	57	58	56	58	47	27	26	16	4	1
		F.	1353	188	146	143	129	103	85	87	76	77	61	45	53	65	31	22	27	12	3	1
4 Ashburton. (H.)	5797	M.	2771	373	323	314	288	195	161	132	125	128	139	146	131	107	91	66	31	24	4	
		F.	3026	363	315	320	254	258	164	181	112	140	153	148	128	125	95	67	58	26	15	3
5 Newton Abbot. (W.H.)	14233	M.	6715	969	828	822	644	515	467	373	357	301	265	220	238	208	174	146	79	28	13	1
		F.	7518	949	856	731	656	711	579	488	406	360	357	315	279	275	157	143	89	44	22	10
6 Torquay. (H³.)	32868	M.	13665	1838	1644	1483	1343	1109	995	827	767	748	633	583	464	452	347	208	119	62	18	8
		F.	19203	1806	1870	1686	1969	2108	1683	1303	1246	1124	960	914	775	649	501	340	187	102	27	7

Table 3 *continued.*—AGES of MALES and FEMALES in REGISTRATION SUB-DISTRICTS.

REGISTRATION SUB-DISTRICT.	ALL AGES. Persons.		ALL AGES. Males and Females.	Under 5 Years.	5-	10-	15-	20-	25-	30-	35-	40-	45-	50-	55-	60-	65-	70-	75-	80-	85-	90-	95-
EVONSHIRE —*cont.*																							
74 TOTNES.																							
STON	5704	M.	2636	353	342	298	236	231	168	148	142	135	103	100	99	98	78	57	32	12	6	.	.
		F.	3128	358	337	310	305	275	265	193	170	186	152	121	110	108	98	71	35	25	7	2	.
HAM	7664	M.	3541	580	560	456	306	255	197	182	178	161	122	123	141	121	87	70	37	13	5	1	.
		F.	4123	572	607	440	361	317	288	259	294	241	185	156	151	171	112	78	54	26	7	2	1
MOUTH. (S.)	6729	M.	3291	422	373	458	296	255	235	192	210	192	149	139	116	78	68	59	33	12	3	1	.
		F.	3438	392	396	340	308	254	222	229	218	208	160	151	125	135	90	72	50	26	9	8	
ES (W.)	5832	M.	2704	329	354	346	270	183	132	147	127	130	125	117	105	100	90	69	50	17	7	.	.
		F.	3129	333	318	332	301	254	201	187	163	170	173	140	132	121	84	87	49	23	16	2	.
KPASTLEIGH	4161	M.	1971	263	232	237	230	130	128	103	94	94	86	84	75	78	61	42	19	18	6	1	.
		F.	2190	271	240	193	228	201	157	142	109	114	99	94	78	98	65	47	38	11	7	2	.
OBOUGH	3774	M.	1871	244	227	224	191	143	123	112	74	93	78	98	74	71	55	28	30	9	5	.	.
		F.	1903	235	231	192	182	130	124	136	84	94	95	85	75	89	40	32	32	15	3	1	.
BBETON	2649	M.	1315	173	192	160	142	91	76	70	57	64	57	51	52	42	34	30	13	9	2	.	.
		F.	1834	179	167	145	123	102	97	74	84	57	53	58	36	53	42	25	21	11	5	1	1
KINGSBRIDGE.																							
KAWTON	2449	M.	1142	164	147	100	119	76	74	65	57	59	48	40	48	50	41	28	21	10	2	1	.
		F.	1390	166	161	118	115	98	104	87	65	58	55	60	62	58	31	35	17	13	2	3	.
ENHAM	3865	M.	2049	247	233	199	189	163	167	140	128	111	89	72	79	75	47	42	32	11	3	2	.
		F.	1816	238	232	208	134	135	134	100	87	100	80	76	77	73	52	37	33	13	6	1	1
ALVINGTON (W.)	4667	M.	2117	278	316	267	156	134	111	92	127	113	78	74	69	104	78	65	45	10	6	.	1
		F.	2550	292	310	269	216	195	164	156	188	135	114	101	200	163	93	74	39	22	5	2	.
SBRIDGE	4287	M.	1961	229	255	255	213	135	108	94	115	110	83	71	70	72	65	35	23	11	5	.	.
		F.	2326	263	275	227	222	198	137	144	114	136	125	91	98	91	75	67	48	15	5	.	.
URY	3583	M.	1773	215	226	203	172	152	96	100	93	82	87	79	78	82	58	33	18	15	2	2	.
		F.	1810	236	223	185	164	131	130	98	101	82	78	83	60	68	63	46	34	15	6	1	.
PLYMPTON ST. MARY.																							
MPTON. (B.)	9900	M.	4928	665	602	595	403	438	302	274	278	242	214	199	153	140	141	88	58	38	7	3	.
		F.	4972	577	610	588	457	415	297	296	285	266	236	190	185	187	153	105	71	66	10	3	1
PTON (W.H.L.B.)	14281	M.	6699	855	840	822	840	560	370	312	317	302	303	287	218	252	178	123	71	40	14	5	.
		F.	7582	836	889	770	768	725	554	475	468	404	307	363	360	264	199	155	85	44	14	4	1
PLYMOUTH.																							
LES (W.P.)	27213	M.	12082	1575	1440	1394	1168	1090	822	700	640	575	554	560	506	405	322	222	121	56	12	5	1
		F.	15131	1619	1890	1485	1505	1346	1135	966	856	808	780	685	589	593	430	345	282	123	23	11	.
NDREW (H.B.S.)	46650	M.	21725	2729	2524	2170	2244	2074	1722	1395	1269	1229	1020	968	770	641	425	283	132	58	13	1	.
		F.	24925	3729	3413	2437	2431	2557	2092	1726	1503	1437	1235	1145	913	915	606	464	250	106	47	7	2
ST STONEHOUSE.																							
STONEHOUSE (W.H.B.)	15041	M.	7145	1037	851	835	721	674	553	444	514	453	325	234	200	173	134	93	48	21	15	.	.
		F.	7896	1045	830	716	648	728	690	647	568	453	342	236	260	252	166	125	68	40	16	3	2
STOKE DAMEREL.																							
AUBYN (H.B.)	15786	M.	7749	968	863	748	722	825	604	548	428	456	350	290	263	236	170	103	57	23	8	.	.
		F.	8037	996	796	760	674	740	664	560	479	479	394	367	309	311	206	146	91	33	11	2	1
ICE (H.P.B.S.)	10657	M.	6468	475	435	418	2282	750	537	298	246	237	207	206	146	99	52	48	23	6	3	1	.
		F.	4089	474	468	424	388	361	306	277	213	241	213	206	162	154	87	75	37	18	5	2	2
E (W.H.)	9597	M.	4025	534	479	451	372	315	208	211	182	195	230	209	163	155	115	67	48	22	7	1	.
		F.	5572	522	504	637	621	663	448	317	292	315	278	263	217	200	199	104	71	41	15	1	1
AR. (S.)	12990	M.	6563	806	680	552	902	670	568	407	370	358	316	261	213	152	119	74	60	18	7	1	.
		F.	6423	785	678	612	602	698	537	452	404	380	323	263	269	211	174	132	76	37	11	3	.
TAVISTOCK.																							
STOCK	8415	M.	4119	554	552	484	529	371	251	171	149	171	175	188	168	109	116	68	51	12	5	1	3
		F.	4296	527	526	525	426	369	282	223	218	167	192	191	171	167	104	91	58	16	9	3	2
STOCK (W.P.)	13390	M.	6948	748	714	745	704	691	530	452	391	374	361	323	313	266	189	139	69	34	19	.	1
		F.	6459	696	712	696	691	582	473	363	397	311	308	361	227	247	194	133	100	42	22	3	2
TON ABBOT	3781	M.	1591	216	249	226	213	152	112	104	95	65	94	88	74	70	66	39	23	9	4	.	.
		F.	1890	238	216	296	183	141	131	103	119	91	96	77	87	83	71	40	26	6	2	2	.
TON	3595	M.	1762	229	240	229	176	133	97	85	95	78	83	70	66	55	42	42	24	8	2	.	.
		F.	1833	243	236	213	174	120	128	101	114	80	79	83	64	55	58	48	20	16	.	1	.
OKEHAMPTON.																							
TTON CLOVELLY	1973	M.	995	121	133	116	100	89	55	62	40	51	52	42	29	21	26	25	13	7	.	1	.
		F.	978	115	126	109	107	75	64	85	42	48	50	48	41	26	25	14	13	7	2	.	1
KERLEIGH	3385	M.	1656	213	195	195	194	141	82	74	79	68	68	95	61	62	77	31	20	6	6	1	.
		F.	1729	192	205	228	154	148	106	98	92	58	76	81	89	67	85	34	30	10	4	2	.
HAMPTON (W.)	4858	M.	2409	300	304	272	233	186	168	139	124	109	105	102	87	105	68	50	32	18	9	1	.
		F.	2449	308	295	275	220	188	182	129	150	127	98	104	113	85	73	56	34	16	14	.	.
SFORD	2666	M.	1361	142	172	156	159	102	91	71	62	65	62	64	55	54	42	33	24	11	5	1	.
		F.	1335	145	146	153	110	101	161	74	59	53	71	58	79	47	58	47	18	17	8	2	.
TH TAWTON	4050	M.	2006	239	250	271	222	151	110	106	90	88	95	64	79	92	68	43	22	12	5	1	.
		F.	2044	275	236	239	184	159	129	92	119	119	93	82	80	77	61	48	23	27	8	1	1
2 CREDITON.																							
CHARD BISHOP	3950	M.	1984	242	243	269	215	161	126	84	76	87	70	71	90	97	55	68	18	18	3	1	.
		F.	1966	248	235	209	192	150	137	105	87	94	81	99	79	82	63	42	25	14	2	2	.
	2940	M.	1506	188	196	166	175	118	82	95	76	71	55	74	77	67	42	28	21	9	3	.	.
		F.	1440	172	198	178	111	108	78	78	63	68	80	58	59	61	41	32	21	13	3	1	.
ITON (W.)	6452	M.	3075	403	429	341	299	212	194	168	187	133	120	127	104	127	90	77	47	25	9	2	1
		F.	3377	445	398	322	249	262	233	223	180	148	162	169	136	146	107	64	49	28	9	6	.
ITON-FITZPAINE	4578	M.	2284	312	272	219	243	189	130	128	111	105	89	107	92	93	80	51	40	15	5	.	.
		F.	2294	293	205	266	187	169	139	123	169	107	107	111	99	91	75	58	57	27	6	4	1

V 9

Table 3 *continued*.—Ages of Males and Females in Registration Sub-Districts.

Registration Sub-District.	All Ages. Persons.		All Ages. Males and Females.	Under 5 Years.	5-	10-	15-	20-	25-	30-	35-	40-	45-	50-	55-	60-	65-	70-	75-	80-	85-	90-
19 DEVONSHIRE —*cont.*																						
283 TIVERTON.																						
1 Silverton	4631	M.	2270	306	301	261	219	156	148	123	110	108	89	93	99	89	75	48	27	13	5	.
		F.	2361	296	282	278	193	181	154	144	127	109	119	116	103	98	67	44	39	13	3	2
2 Cullompton	3896	M.	1908	242	267	202	174	196	138	102	120	74	66	75	96	82	59	34	24	18	7	2
		F.	1988	276	184	202	175	181	139	110	100	86	79	91	97	102	71	32	32	20	8	3
3 Uffculme	4601	M.	2193	270	284	290	225	131	127	98	117	116	79	96	87	86	83	50	32	16	3	.
		F.	2408	317	298	288	214	167	150	124	120	117	108	102	98	99	87	64	48	17	8	.
4 Tiverton (W.H.)	10402	M.	4872	618	609	566	592	425	281	284	228	242	211	195	179	169	124	108	62	33	9	.
		F.	5600	585	586	569	638	484	405	344	297	281	271	282	208	203	151	147	77	38	19	4
5 Washfield	2327	M.	1203	152	151	152	138	83	72	48	63	50	42	40	56	45	36	34	15	7	6	.
		F.	1124	130	139	132	104	99	70	75	46	58	55	56	45	46	26	27	8	8	2	.
6 Bampton	2595	M.	1319	157	168	156	133	91	96	79	83	59	51	55	50	42	43	30	18	7	.	1
		F.	1276	164	179	171	95	94	75	65	60	73	48	53	52	44	49	32	17	5	1	.
284 SOUTH MOLTON.																						
1 Witheridge	4714	M.	2464	321	341	254	237	211	154	129	112	110	85	101	75	111	65	64	47	16	6	5
		F.	2250	291	272	271	197	140	160	119	129	116	116	97	83	96	68	46	27	4	6	3
2 Chulmleigh (H.)	4063	M.	2064	223	247	207	261	178	108	109	93	103	90	69	80	66	66	54	26	16	3	1
		F.	2019	240	255	214	222	189	158	119	104	110	94	86	76	78	57	38	39	8	5	2
3 South Molton (W.)	8021	M.	3947	506	490	507	443	281	208	203	190	175	169	162	141	135	120	101	65	25	7	4
		F.	4074	510	505	405	387	320	288	233	212	187	187	162	166	167	127	114	62	32	8	2
285 BARNSTAPLE.																						
1 Barnstaple (W.H.)	11583	M.	5342	701	627	618	556	424	371	292	280	299	242	217	182	188	120	125	80	36	12	.
		F.	6241	649	669	599	663	558	445	390	338	377	286	280	243	238	101	170	80	48	20	4
2 Paracombe (H.)	2710	M.	1284	162	147	144	124	98	86	67	74	65	57	48	42	55	42	32	23	10	8	1
		F.	1426	154	171	153	139	112	91	84	75	74	75	69	51	57	52	34	21	16	6	2
3 Combmartin	3237	M.	1617	186	209	198	190	120	80	74	79	78	62	63	67	63	52	38	26	14	7	3
		F.	1620	191	178	186	148	110	97	81	98	82	74	70	73	64	63	46	30	19	8	.
4 Ilfracombe (H.)	7881	M.	3615	403	406	384	418	360	265	218	187	215	167	188	128	120	94	57	44	22	14	.
		F.	4266	446	397	401	480	425	360	227	219	249	208	203	156	153	130	96	71	43	16	4
5 Braunton	6695	M.	3248	427	431	386	353	242	170	180	155	148	132	127	113	113	104	79	52	18	7	2
		F.	3447	445	403	373	338	244	202	220	182	176	176	143	125	129	112	81	58	31	6	3
6 Bishops Tawton	6100	M.	2830	362	359	364	323	203	171	118	131	148	133	110	114	101	67	87	33	22	3	1
		F.	3270	343	377	308	337	310	237	179	166	172	162	102	120	139	90	80	55	33	6	3
286 TORRINGTON.																						
1 High Bickington	2535	M.	1239	160	160	164	147	80	86	58	64	53	51	49	62	43	34	29	13	14	2	.
		F.	1206	198	152	162	120	106	88	61	74	61	49	69	38	48	36	26	18	12	.	1
2 Winkleigh	2053	M.	1013	110	108	123	120	79	61	52	57	43	40	43	50	40	35	23	22	9	.	.
		F.	1040	126	119	118	94	83	48	62	46	48	50	47	54	43	37	35	15	10	5	2
3 Dolton	2544	M.	1260	167	162	158	131	97	80	67	56	61	32	61	62	56	36	27	24	11	1	.
		F.	1284	180	144	125	119	110	92	78	72	48	58	62	56	55	33	33	31	9	3	1
4 Shebbear	2516	M.	1299	165	144	132	181	105	75	46	51	56	56	59	50	47	34	28	9	2	1	2
		F.	1217	127	146	146	127	90	87	57	55	67	51	62	61	50	38	25	21	8	5	.
5 Great Torrington (W.)	5172	M.	2290	296	311	298	242	171	136	108	104	102	85	95	82	80	67	45	38	19	8	8
		F.	2882	312	334	276	280	271	193	182	162	163	134	140	106	115	75	68	48	19	8	3
287 BIDEFORD.																						
1 Bideford (W.H.)	6596	M.	2923	413	404	367	322	229	159	154	159	135	135	108	92	113	92	59	41	13	5	2
		F.	3673	423	375	347	463	378	243	215	215	196	174	169	110	131	101	100	52	23	16	3
2 Northam	5231	M.	2334	302	340	383	287	131	107	100	90	107	84	72	79	76	62	42	26	20	5	3
		F.	2897	325	314	290	315	200	186	175	174	161	158	109	100	100	72	65	45	22	8	2
3 Parkham	2443	M.	1183	169	154	139	126	90	70	71	60	68	47	34	60	49	28	25	18	12	1	1
		F.	1260	195	137	154	99	96	100	81	62	51	64	56	46	65	44	28	20	9	4	1
4 Hartland	3756	M.	1908	212	244	215	223	183	118	89	107	101	92	69	61	66	48	33	37	17	6	2
		F.	1848	251	234	219	167	153	93	99	96	197	79	77	63	86	61	49	32	16	4	3
5 Beaworthy	732	M.	374	40	37	49	47	45	21	18	14	16	16	18	8	15	15	5	6	3	1	.
		F.	358	49	48	41	35	27	20	28	16	10	16	11	14	14	7	7	4	3	1	1
288 HOLSWORTHY.																						
1 Milton Damerel	2128	M.	1098	122	127	140	130	103	74	54	39	53	44	60	56	37	27	24	17	6	.	1
		F.	1030	117	123	108	106	99	76	52	52	60	60	40	47	31	24	22	16	9	2	.
2 Holsworthy (W.)	2650	M.	1325	109	161	157	146	121	82	75	70	57	58	47	40	43	50	30	16	8	2	3
		F.	1325	150	153	139	148	114	97	75	73	54	63	47	58	43	42	30	24	9	6	1
3 Black Torrington	1751	M.	863	115	125	103	79	59	59	37	45	42	38	34	29	35	23	18	16	6	2	2
		F.	888	122	120	91	77	62	64	60	46	44	34	38	30	33	26	21	9	4	2	1
4 Broadwoodwidger	849	M.	445	63	53	74	61	28	11	27	12	35	13	13	15	16	15	11	8	.	.	.
		F.	404	48	59	43	43	34	18	26	23	24	18	11	13	14	14	4	8	4	.	.
5 Clawton	1630	M.	802	102	99	101	89	60	57	37	46	36	30	38	18	31	19	21	13	5	1	.
		F.	828	105	107	96	81	70	64	41	53	33	36	38	24	32	21	18	9	7	.	.
20 CORNWALL.																						
289 STRATTON.																						
1 Kilkhampton	1785	M.	892	125	130	104	91	66	62	36	44	46	42	26	25	28	25	22	16	8	6	.
		F.	893	102	105	120	80	76	64	44	53	42	37	41	32	32	26	19	15	2	3	.
2 Stratton (W.H.)	3282	M.	1517	223	201	158	142	97	[illegible]	[illegible]	79	67	82	56	50	38	60	40	29	16	2	1
		F.	1765	192	195	177	190	146	163	117	103	88	87	81	80	61	57	56	20	13	2	1
3 Week St. Mary	2372	M.	1220	157	149	125	136	115	86	50	34	56	52	48	44	52	32	36	16	11	.	1
		F.	1152	151	140	135	104	99	74	61	55	62	56	43	42	35	30	31	16	9	2	1

Table 3 *continued.*—AGES of MALES and FEMALES in REGISTRATION SUB-DISTRICTS.

REGISTRATION SUB-DISTRICT.	ALL AGES. Persons.		Males and Females.	Under 5 Years.	5–	10–	15–	20–	25–	30–	35–	40–	45–	50–	55–	60–	65–	70–	75–	80–	85–	90–	95–
ORNWALL—*cont.*																							
CAMELFORD.																							
ASTLE	2293	M.	1130	139	135	160	124	77	72	61	67	40	52	47	35	14	30	19	17	5	3	.	.
		F.	1163	145	139	109	118	97	68	64	66	65	47	41	39	63	42	29	15	7	7	2	.
ELFORD (W.)	5312	M.	2625	334	337	360	268	100	135	141	126	111	118	97	102	38	85	61	48	16	4	2	.
		F.	2687	312	320	308	240	184	182	160	150	124	135	115	105	117	83	54	48	13	0	2	.
LAUNCESTON																							
ARNON	2194	M.	1101	151	139	121	110	93	70	59	50	32	45	50	47	43	28	18	24	10	3	.	.
		F.	1093	107	122	126	115	88	72	60	50	53	36	48	40	39	43	25	19	11	5	.	.
TH PETHERWIN	2090	M.	1064	148	134	127	129	91	79	40	41	55	35	58	30	40	26	18	8	8	2	.	.
		F.	1026	124	134	121	95	100	68	50	57	47	55	55	42	20	24	20	12	4	3	1	2
STEPHEN	3459	M.	1752	217	222	220	198	131	106	84	73	89	64	84	80	49	50	38	13	10	2	3	.
		F.	1707	210	266	213	171	137	112	90	61	88	107	65	69	50	42	34	15	9	1	3	1
NCESTON. (W.H.)	3791	M.	1819	230	190	182	168	182	102	85	74	77	77	57	57	52	50	42	71	14	3	1	.
		F.	1972	240	185	192	220	187	140	112	120	98	95	77	78	63	57	51	20	17	5	.	.
THILL	4724	M.	2325	281	296	273	304	203	140	96	93	106	108	86	91	85	59	44	36	17	7	2	.
		F.	2399	296	295	283	236	188	147	128	114	126	118	111	96	78	68	48	34	31	5	5	1
ST. GERMANS.																							
ONY. (W.L.B.[4])	7290	M.	3311	433	413	367	290	248	179	149	161	172	178	150	147	136	108	87	61	25	6	2	1
		F.	3979	440	450	423	353	236	209	245	217	201	201	261	156	151	141	109	67	26	11	2	1
GERMANS	2869	M.	1332	177	168	140	134	109	67	58	70	78	48	60	53	46	53	30	24	7	1	.	.
		F.	1537	185	184	152	129	116	93	92	74	78	75	58	66	83	51	49	26	17	7	.	.
TASH. (R.)	6571	M.	3132	366	335	500	370	219	175	140	159	139	110	132	131	122	93	76	33	16	8	.	.
		F.	3439	355	391	372	389	318	243	207	190	177	160	138	134	142	113	67	39	31	11	3	2
93 LISKEARD.																							
LINGTON	7678	M.	3716	503	446	461	485	321	202	173	151	150	173	168	141	127	98	53	43	17	8	5	.
		F.	3962	461	489	461	388	335	252	202	209	180	194	196	169	147	112	83	50	17	16	4	1
KEARD. (W.)	11737	M.	5526	660	726	728	691	420	299	239	231	247	229	235	231	197	161	117	67	32	10	6	.
		F.	6211	707	679	662	704	503	423	316	336	349	315	273	224	245	189	126	95	54	12	2	1
IE	5662	M.	2682	374	334	317	299	211	184	134	124	130	90	93	103	102	83	52	37	8	7	1	1
		F.	2980	342	353	309	296	252	211	200	158	143	143	113	127	100	95	73	41	14	7	1	.
RIN	3710	M.	1698	237	219	215	179	127	85	87	88	69	79	75	40	60	37	42	38	8	1	2	.
		F.	2012	262	230	205	195	172	135	111	108	93	92	78	74	85	56	40	42	12	6	1	.
204 BODMIN.																							
LIVERY	4548	M.	2207	280	280	271	241	172	122	95	115	85	88	77	84	90	80	45	49	20	2	4	1
		F.	2341	267	277	248	254	175	161	128	134	117	93	118	93	90	73	62	43	14	8	2	.
MABYN	2818	M.	1355	182	163	160	151	119	72	60	71	57	65	56	48	64	49	30	22	14	2	.	.
		F.	1463	177	170	148	136	104	109	81	57	84	74	72	68	59	43	32	29	13	5	2	.
MIN. (W.H.L.P.B.)	7079	M.	3446	387	361	322	442	324	228	203	202	170	163	100	141	98	92	108	45	26	7	2	.
		F.	3633	315	364	381	362	302	220	223	225	212	190	174	140	153	140	104	46	30	18	2	.
LOSHAYLE	4803	M.	2301	300	289	230	253	179	127	115	129	90	98	100	96	95	70	58	31	13	1	1	.
		F.	2502	309	273	234	284	196	176	162	142	123	126	100	123	98	72	67	37	18	10	2	.
05 ST. COLUMB.																							
OSTOW	6086	M.	2861	373	364	342	315	242	190	137	138	135	116	118	105	100	75	52	40	17	1	1	.
		F.	3225	394	375	320	288	270	224	230	154	156	140	141	143	134	88	77	48	28	11	3	.
COLUMB. (W.)	7006	M.	3279	388	453	422	245	281	188	143	172	145	139	144	134	103	90	85	56	16	6	1	.
		F.	3727	422	427	400	355	315	252	228	215	228	172	146	143	138	98	82	55	36	12	2	.
WLYN	3251	M.	1551	192	217	176	180	118	87	91	87	67	55	58	65	54	30	27	15	11	4	.	.
		F.	1720	213	223	199	137	141	122	110	93	82	80	71	69	62	48	31	26	12	2	4	.
06 ST. AUSTELL.																							
WEY. (H.)	6785	M.	3169	423	431	383	393	231	162	166	149	146	109	130	128	104	106	67	26	14	6	2	.
		F.	3616	413	385	365	366	277	273	202	203	198	180	180	149	161	128	98	48	25	10	2	.
AUSTELL. (W.)	14202	M.	6660	910	867	829	823	600	350	364	331	280	296	244	231	212	137	124	67	34	11	1	.
		F.	7542	908	932	833	762	573	530	455	451	367	314	306	294	278	212	158	88	44	16	3	1
VAGISSEY	4227	M.	2042	251	264	247	225	156	132	94	93	85	91	90	75	81	57	39	32	20	4	.	.
		F.	2185	262	213	236	205	160	152	127	116	108	120	107	102	86	65	51	40	19	8	1	.
AMPOUND	4972	M.	2480	323	330	295	313	215	163	124	115	121	95	88	112	66	42	51	19	8	3	.	.
		F.	2492	329	326	276	216	294	189	126	122	132	119	117	98	75	52	52	35	8	4	.	.
297 TRURO.																							
BUS	3618	M.	1789	216	218	242	228	136	92	87	80	65	72	68	60	67	52	38	22	10	3	.	.
		F.	1829	210	182	192	177	168	148	109	98	105	83	78	82	71	48	40	25	17	3	2	.
JUST	4332	M.	2067	247	231	259	248	144	125	108	103	91	82	85	87	80	63	55	30	14	7	2	.
		F.	2265	239	256	234	223	173	166	136	120	109	105	110	99	99	76	58	36	25	4	1	2
AGNES	7481	M.	3382	368	458	469	528	239	156	146	138	136	158	187	136	119	74	47	35	9	1	1	.
		F.	4099	381	455	466	382	361	255	239	215	243	224	208	198	170	129	89	53	25	10	3	.
CLEMENT. (W.)	7338	M.	3232	423	382	362	372	274	221	163	166	138	139	135	114	132	84	60	45	24	9	2	.
		F.	4106	370	359	378	480	402	346	259	222	217	197	191	186	181	112	84	67	41	13	2	.
WYN. (H.)	8686	M.	3790	487	466	456	463	315	227	184	170	172	175	148	150	130	107	75	46	21	12	1	.
		F.	4896	463	460	469	494	456	393	316	270	259	285	219	210	211	167	128	69	34	20	1	1
	4627	M.	2139	230	251	235	293	120	85	64	89	107	96	77	100	75	72	41	25	7	2	1	.
		F.	2488	246	269	267	227	202	160	141	148	147	128	124	113	104	75	68	48	15	5	1	.
98 FALMOUTH.																							
LOR	3309	M.	1458	217	158	175	164	98	84	56	71	65	64	59	64	58	38	26	24	8	4	1	.
		F.	1851	183	207	177	189	154	141	103	114	86	103	99	77	65	58	56	24	13	3	.	.
MOUTH. (W.H[2].B.S.[3])	14619	M.	7676	716	667	684	1305	808	606	513	618	461	334	275	237	198	143	85	68	28	14	1	1
		F.	6943	976	600	654	711	706	548	443	403	426	377	307	240	241	185	137	92	44	14	8	.
RYN	4503	M.	2098	306	261	236	216	137	108	132	105	112	66	92	68	57	57	29	16	18	1	1	3
		F.	2405	311	293	254	222	103	181	144	140	146	122	112	90	90	70	60	20	23	3	1	.
STANTINE	3126	M.	1624	197	205	188	195	124	88	74	87	73	65	56	48	43	28	26	17	7	3	.	.
		F.	1502	174	166	183	183	133	109	99	92	88	83	79	55	56	49	33	21	8	6	.	.

Table 3 *continued*.—AGES of MALES and FEMALES in REGISTRATION SUB-DISTRICTS.

REGISTRATION SUB-DISTRICT.	ALL AGES. Persons.	ALL AGES. Males and Females.	Under 5 Years.	5–	10–	15–	20–	25–	30–	35–	40–	45–	50–	55–	60–	65–	70–	75–	80–	85–	90–
20 CORNWALL—*cont.*																					
299 HELSTON.																					
1 WENDRON	7914	M. - 3759	304	456	546	462	316	251	170	168	189	160	126	132	88	68	66	27	15	2	1
		F. - 4184	471	474	449	419	349	302	231	227	248	208	171	179	152	108	74	68	33	8	1
2 HELSTON. (W.)	4908	M. - 2143	240	267	277	239	174	100	108	132	98	93	81	69	81	68	56	39	21	10	.
		F. - 2765	239	285	259	315	240	180	165	173	171	134	141	108	96	63	80	51	24	13	2
3 ST. KEVERNE	4661	M. - 2179	277	280	285	225	166	139	113	112	113	77	80	86	83	60	58	34	23	8	.
		F. - 2482	295	259	231	238	209	177	107	146	132	103	99	114	85	97	64	33	28	12	4
4 BREAGE	3605	M. - 1569	161	193	247	216	138	77	65	52	60	78	67	56	68	33	34	20	11	5	.
		F. - 2036	164	210	219	176	152	119	107	108	127	129	115	111	102	72	59	36	18	10	2
5 CROWAN	2593	M. - 1169	146	135	132	158	112	77	57	58	53	56	37	45	35	27	22	11	7	1	.
		F. - 1424	149	159	154	120	104	107	102	75	79	80	61	64	48	45	36	25	14	1	1
300 REDRUTH.																					
1 GWENNAP	8032	M. 3477	447	486	442	408	299	201	141	167	154	131	136	129	109	72	52	27	13	3	1
		F. - 4555	483	448	456	427	369	324	283	274	287	225	209	213	206	163	114	96	44	13	4
2 REDRUTH. (H.)	9335	M. - 3998	530	511	527	527	340	240	184	180	192	190	166	106	122	80	50	38	17	2	.
		F. - 5337	542	469	613	599	511	422	323	311	324	309	236	190	200	137	113	72	27	6	2
3 ILLOGAN. (W.)	8723	M. - 3905	401	538	607	541	326	248	183	166	181	138	161	120	96	79	62	30	15	3	.
		F. 4818	537	519	446	528	416	332	301	231	272	240	232	193	186	122	106	70	28	8	1
4 CAMBORNE	13691	M. - 6094	775	778	860	880	597	339	263	256	258	243	259	178	156	81	52	31	14	4	.
		F. 7597	734	821	765	881	714	531	418	444	468	399	383	297	266	200	129	76	54	16	1
5 PHILLACK	6437	M. - 2980	395	383	396	381	251	166	138	100	137	124	102	108	82	74	56	41	13	4	.
		F. - 3457	404	346	337	363	308	257	186	200	183	195	139	138	120	119	80	51	19	7	2
301 PENZANCE.																					
1 UNY-LELANT	6401	M. - 3011	383	396	411	404	276	190	130	110	140	112	101	109	87	67	55	26	12	2	.
		F. 3390	358	338	375	338	327	206	139	120	197	186	147	155	118	103	75	41	25	6	3
2 ST. IVES	7690	M. - 3513	478	481	406	376	278	242	192	156	144	137	118	114	136	87	81	32	17	7	1
		F. 4177	454	446	422	417	347	288	292	251	231	199	193	172	152	133	105	60	29	6	.
3 MARAZION	3231	M. - 1430	178	177	179	198	120	89	82	56	70	54	64	69	39	47	27	15	9	2	.
		F. - 1801	176	160	162	165	163	139	102	102	100	92	97	92	84	76	44	24	17	4	1
4 PENZANCE. (W.H².)	22774	M. - 10863	1245	1212	1132	1353	1034	833	662	637	595	437	378	326	349	241	197	123	63	21	3
		F. - 11911	1287	1150	1111	1231	1131	940	724	707	647	632	542	467	468	294	272	139	89	33	6
5 ST. JUST IN PENWITH	7530	M. - 3529	425	447	460	474	341	178	180	168	167	115	122	113	108	83	59	38	15	3	1
		F. - 4001	474	453	437	395	327	262	214	213	219	173	185	169	172	163	95	60	29	18	2
6 ST. BURYAN	2685	M. - 1334	164	157	150	170	143	73	69	69	66	63	50	38	43	27	28	13	6	4	1
		F. - 1351	168	159	152	142	129	67	85	92	70	63	48	42	44	41	21	21	12	2	3
302 SCILLY ISLANDS.																					
1 SCILLY ISLANDS	2320	M. 1213	132	116	110	112	115	89	86	84	61	59	43	34	58	46	31	19	19	5	1
		F. - 1107	127	115	97	98	72	80	75	73	57	54	35	55	40	45	44	23	13	5	.
21 SOMERSETSHIRE.																					
303 WILLITON.																					
1 MINEHEAD	3467	M. - 1658	205	187	191	196	116	116	80	73	78	71	76	68	71	53	33	22	15	6	1
		F. - 1809	186	224	196	173	124	125	100	86	92	84	90	93	76	60	46	35	16	6	1
2 DUNSTER. (H.)	3717	M. - 1816	218	231	234	198	128	96	82	68	104	84	79	71	78	62	30	23	25	2	.
		F. - 1901	246	254	206	179	147	103	106	68	100	74	103	79	82	38	30	24	9	3	1
3 WILLITON. (W.)	5827	M. - 2882	410	383	372	342	190	150	141	137	130	132	129	93	93	67	55	54	14	7	3
		F. - 2945	388	340	352	202	217	191	163	109	169	140	125	111	111	65	56	49	31	8	2
4 STOGURSEY	2319	M. - 1136	149	168	145	95	76	59	57	59	51	60	49	45	50	39	20	14	4	3	2
		F. - 1183	172	139	128	103	69	72	56	59	64	58	55	50	38	54	34	16	7	5	.
5 STOGUMBER	3356	M. - 1713	229	226	219	194	130	85	55	74	73	80	60	66	62	48	37	25	14	4	1
		F. - 1643	202	216	219	127	96	100	80	94	97	79	76	67	57	51	35	27	16	3	1
304 DULVERTON.																					
1 DULVERTON. (W.)	5453	M. - 2802	316	377	351	296	218	136	137	152	132	128	128	106	85	94	74	48	19	6	.
		F. - 2651	334	343	301	246	180	105	133	127	140	135	115	114	101	56	59	38	18	8	.
305 WELLINGTON.																					
1 WIVELISCOMBE	3301	M. - 1598	219	214	201	176	107	93	75	72	70	67	66	65	62	47	30	27	10	4	1
		F. 1703	184	207	237	169	124	89	95	77	70	98	74	75	54	52	47	30	14	7	1
2 MILVERTON	3518	M. - 1740	228	226	[illegible]	[illegible]	135	82	66	73	88	75	56	68	72	41	50	29	14	2	.
		F. 1778	202	213	192	144	120	108	120	76	92	88	86	70	83	65	46	36	19	7	.
3 WELLINGTON. (W.)	8476	M. - 3957	526	499	492	338	303	248	216	186	201	162	153	153	124	115	106	50	29	9	4
		F. - 4519	553	488	463	437	411	328	277	207	268	184	205	185	175	133	96	63	29	13	5
4 CULMSTOCK	3899	M. - 2002	279	259	236	204	150	118	98	97	90	89	80	77	79	62	54	23	14	6	1
		F. - 1897	261	259	219	169	126	126	83	87	99	84	86	88	76	64	43	25	16	2	.
306 TAUNTON.																					
1 PITMINSTER	4440	M. - 2270	244	253	264	221	158	111	112	102	94	94	92	82	86	62	45	36	8	5	1
		F. - 2170	238	296	232	213	171	147	139	105	96	113	109	91	92	81	45	44	13	5	1
2 NORTH CURRY	5546	M. - 2706	317	347	226	304	187	175	147	139	126	116	104	110	121	73	62	34	21	6	1
		F. - 2840	300	325	334	257	194	150	160	146	139	123	123	112	136	87	68	52	29	9	5
3 TAUNTON ST. MARY MAGDALENE. (W.H².P².)	10450	M. - 4563	552	526	592	502	401	339	269	234	225	181	200	160	154	124	91	49	25	6	1
		F. - 5887	588	545	585	734	614	448	387	296	329	237	242	204	220	161	123	106	43	16	8
4 TAUNTON ST. JAMES (H.)	12074	M. - 5625	755	658	745	601	441	402	296	316	268	236	219	196	204	125	98	70	22	11	2
		F. - 6449	747	710	661	873	567	471	430	336	344	291	294	250	223	167	126	108	36	11	3
5 BISHOPS-LYDEARD	3472	M. - 1716	219	208	211	193	109	74	87	91	76	72	71	83	73	56	43	24	11	6	3
		F. - 1756	194	225	222	162	128	93	87	91	95	84	79	78	73	60	47	30	11	6	1

Table 3 *continued.*—AGES of MALES and FEMALES in REGISTRATION SUB-DISTRICTS.

REGISTRATION SUB-DISTRICT.	ALL AGES. Persons.	ALL AGES. Males and Females.		Under 5 Years	5-	10-	15-	20-	25-	30-	35-	40-	45-	50-	55-	60-	65-	70-	75-	80-	85-	90-	95-
SOMERSETSHIRE — *cont.*																							
BRIDGWATER.																							
...WEY. (R.)	4535	M.	2274	300	289	317	231	146	132	110	111	95	89	101	85	88	69	41	30	22	4	2	.
		F.	2261	254	266	243	186	148	140	132	127	109	115	98	125	104	82	65	35	23	7	2	.
...TH PETHERTON	4844	M.	2372	290	314	295	229	189	156	118	111	97	91	101	94	100	83	44	20	8	9	1	1
		F.	2471	290	326	270	197	171	170	137	129	123	118	110	76	100	80	46	41	24	9	2	.
...IDLEZOY	2198	M.	1091	123	145	109	110	94	58	58	67	45	40	56	33	57	34	29	18	9	3	1	.
		F.	1107	133	135	127	78	83	80	73	57	60	61	44	47	46	35	39	22	7	2	1	.
...DGWATER. (W.H.)	14737	M.	7106	1003	910	849	818	550	434	382	358	340	338	277	242	211	140	118	93	37	9	5	.
		F.	7631	1000	850	815	749	632	541	464	430	309	360	323	288	238	103	129	90	60	19	6	1
...NTSPILL	4167	M.	2097	290	290	235	204	142	133	102	110	111	90	96	82	72	47	36	12	18	3	.	.
		F.	2070	256	258	228	162	140	147	135	106	112	94	110	80	59	59	34	27	15	1	2	.
...DEN HILL	3202	M.	1602	186	212	197	163	106	91	83	80	82	55	72	73	86	47	38	24	13	10	1	.
		F.	1600	192	181	180	121	114	88	82	81	88	73	78	77	95	46	48	22	21	3	.	.
308 LANGPORT.																							
...ERTON	4895	M.	2350	288	286	288	258	135	132	137	117	110	106	123	90	96	61	61	31	18	10	2	.
		F.	2545	306	341	297	197	174	178	115	149	133	131	134	106	95	83	52	41	21	6	2	.
...GPORT. (W.)	6114	M.	3049	480	403	382	307	163	180	115	143	139	132	137	101	119	89	69	50	17	10	1	1
		F.	3065	338	373	342	258	192	214	171	189	166	148	154	129	127	108	74	56	19	7	.	1
...RY-RIVEL. (L.)	4565	M.	2172	279	284	245	245	153	132	115	112	109	97	88	70	90	63	44	21	13	4	2	.
		F.	2393	309	291	279	197	186	197	122	110	128	138	90	108	92	60	64	36	15	8	4	.
309 CHARD.																							
...INSTER	7843	M.	3876	486	455	453	358	241	177	166	170	164	149	123	118	115	78	63	36	19	4	3	.
		F.	3967	483	481	489	461	320	260	197	223	205	172	183	148	136	111	87	45	20	8	1	.
...IBE ST. NICHOLAS	3005	M.	1526	213	200	172	158	119	73	81	64	81	61	52	44	73	57	42	18	15	2	1	.
		F.	1479	199	180	177	135	93	86	66	89	84	67	83	46	68	53	37	14	7	2	1	.
...RD. (W.)	6854	M.	3309	447	406	423	377	234	210	154	176	107	140	142	107	124	87	65	30	21	2	1	.
		F.	3545	432	398	347	360	310	253	200	214	198	154	145	148	116	77	60	51	29	9	3	.
...WKERNE. (H.)	8151	M.	3890	567	530	463	437	297	246	196	188	201	182	136	102	126	90	78	38	20	3	4	.
		F.	4261	553	483	493	439	342	280	232	226	227	201	209	139	142	118	80	57	40	7	3	.
310 YEOVIL.																							
...ER	5663	M.	2709	377	372	358	299	185	142	167	134	111	117	141	98	90	66	63	32	22	6	1	.
		F.	2954	339	362	370	264	224	182	158	133	162	148	142	123	97	74	90	44	22	6	3	.
...TH PETHERTON	3742	M.	1772	230	244	230	208	115	87	82	99	96	58	68	59	56	53	30	27	14	5	.	1
		F.	1970	218	262	228	187	130	115	133	132	132	67	99	74	82	50	46	23	16	3	1	.
...RTOCK	5783	M.	2590	307	319	331	270	185	143	138	128	100	114	103	86	92	68	44	32	11	3	.	.
		F.	3193	381	379	354	330	264	230	182	186	155	106	132	125	108	78	66	49	23	7	1	.
...OVIL. (W.H.)	10425	M.	4786	658	635	584	486	371	310	276	278	261	201	186	147	142	105	75	39	25	6	.	1
		F.	5639	698	629	650	574	478	416	401	337	277	270	225	173	183	141	104	58	22	12	1	1
...HESTER	2093	M.	993	114	133	120	107	75	72	56	52	41	48	41	37	35	19	18	17	6	3	.	.
		F.	1100	130	135	108	93	84	82	65	57	64	65	54	37	44	38	22	21	9	2	.	.
311 WINCANTON.																							
...STLE CARY	5415	M.	2572	358	348	270	238	199	159	165	148	122	110	114	105	91	73	46	26	8	2	3	.
		F.	2843	325	317	318	257	229	218	161	142	151	130	129	121	106	94	73	37	18	14	4	.
...LBORNE PORT	5426	M.	2596	367	347	294	241	195	178	139	146	140	129	106	90	82	84	51	22	18	5	1	.
		F.	2830	343	358	307	240	253	196	175	159	145	127	120	108	88	63	55	25	19	10	1	.
...NCANTON. (W.)	5738	M.	2755	352	342	364	274	173	155	151	147	132	106	115	84	111	80	72	53	27	4	2	1
		F.	2983	331	355	378	273	239	187	176	165	158	142	127	98	129	103	67	32	15	8	3	.
...UTON	3191	M.	1538	195	194	191	157	114	133	69	81	85	66	53	64	67	48	33	17	8	2	.	1
		F.	1653	224	180	175	160	133	108	82	103	85	60	86	58	67	48	42	25	15	3	.	.
312 FROME.																							
...INNEY	4228	M.	2060	277	251	267	223	136	111	93	128	91	102	102	82	61	57	32	24	10	5	.	.
		F.	2168	276	254	276	268	151	126	125	117	103	115	93	72	78	67	53	24	18	12	1	.
...OME. (W.H.)	11443	M.	5280	698	641	611	663	407	315	293	287	253	201	227	191	185	146	112	67	37	13	4	.
		F.	6163	703	673	625	628	552	444	353	329	338	303	291	240	247	159	115	96	41	18	6	2
...AD	3143	M.	1507	175	231	198	154	95	59	65	71	72	79	71	54	76	39	37	21	11	5	.	.
		F.	1636	191	189	215	147	103	95	70	105	93	98	89	71	70	65	40	17	11	4	.	.
...LMERSDON	4338	M.	2215	312	323	281	212	102	138	137	112	98	96	93	85	67	37	29	18	14	7	1	.
		F.	2123	336	318	210	186	148	140	133	126	102	104	111	89	56	44	39	23	15	7	2	.
SHEPTON MALLET.																							
...EPTON MALLET. (W.H.P.)	11160	M.	5377	679	665	609	561	440	329	306	304	258	233	230	182	203	113	104	75	40	18	6	.
		F.	5783	723	713	548	579	468	379	358	250	319	296	273	221	208	144	133	87	48	13	5	2
...ERCREECH	4619	M.	2242	277	296	250	235	165	147	102	112	119	93	111	93	72	70	46	31	15	5	.	.
		F.	2377	296	278	273	194	194	146	131	130	119	122	126	95	89	63	54	39	16	6	1	.
314 WELLS.																							
...ELLS. (W.H.L.)	11504	M.	5476	712	665	599	508	396	347	368	298	313	258	251	181	194	148	146	70	40	8	2	1
		F.	6028	672	666	803	596	502	427	376	379	350	275	335	238	231	176	136	83	47	10	5	1
...ASTONBURY	10509	M.	5111	690	593	584	587	422	308	306	261	238	212	225	179	192	153	82	57	40	10	2	.
		F.	5398	685	679	543	538	441	370	330	274	282	233	238	198	198	145	112	50	42	18	3	1
315 AXBRIDGE.																							
...DMORE	5460	M.	2644	309	345	312	251	180	147	137	149	143	132	118	99	108	80	54	53	21	4	1	1
		F.	2816	357	363	281	213	200	173	148	159	128	151	127	102	108	102	81	43	19	9	1	.
...RNHAM	6806	M.	3296	451	444	359	331	270	207	174	261	199	132	186	104	91	79	53	40	19	5	.	.
		F.	3510	430	370	420	325	377	230	189	220	175	174	169	133	126	94	77	66	33	8	3	2
...TWELL. (H.)	17646	M.	7441	959	954	999	797	538	513	457	375	352	330	278	244	246	162	116	73	30	10	5	.
		F.	10205	1002	979	1009	1209	1120	824	647	582	343	464	433	378	365	264	187	119	57	27	4	1
...BRIDGE. (W.)	5704	M.	2758	353	349	337	257	167	168	168	139	118	98	112	107	114	106	83	46	18	13	1	1
		F.	2946	348	359	346	249	240	160	183	156	142	112	140	120	109	98	75	51	22	9	2	.
...GDON	5226	M.	2513	332	330	289	227	183	155	141	137	120	113	131	86	95	87	51	32	26	12	3	1
		F.	2713	318	292	292	243	227	186	160	138	158	134	117	103	113	78	59	39	23	20	4	.

Table 3 *continued*.—AGES of MALES and FEMALES in REGISTRATION SUB-DISTRICTS.

REGISTRATION SUB-DISTRICT.	ALL AGES. Persons.	ALL AGES. Males and Females.	Under 5 Years.	5-	10-	15-	20-	25-	30-	35-	40-	45-	50-	55-	60-	65-	70-	75-	80-	85-	90-
21 SOMERSETSHIRE — *cont.*																					
316 CLUTTON.																					
1 HARPTREE	2991	M. - 1517	173	184	209	152	104	76	64	83	65	69	78	63	67	44	28	35	13	4	.
		F. - 1474	162	160	166	125	108	93	93	69	70	76	80	58	62	41	48	23	12	11	4
2 CHEW MAGNA	3302	M. - 1919	262	347	229	181	114	118	104	93	97	80	82	86	77	61	46	24	14	4	3
		F. - 1383	226	240	238	152	162	110	106	110	114	88	100	78	88	78	47	31	11	6	2
3 CLUTTON. (W.H.)	6331	M. - 3196	439	406	356	348	237	203	160	152	120	123	130	113	121	90	66	36	22	14	2
		F. - 3135	420	425	365	336	206	204	178	148	165	163	132	125	113	106	71	42	27	16	5
4 MIDSOMER NORTON. (L.)	10391	M. - 5459	787	740	695	620	423	332	290	282	246	230	190	164	168	107	89	48	31	4	3
		F. - 4932	798	687	690	339	324	317	299	250	264	215	206	202	168	103	95	42	32	12	3
317 BATH.																					
1 TWERTON. (R.)	8880	M. 4560	637	645	643	418	350	337	252	234	228	168	138	125	114	94	71	50	15	10	1
		F. - 4320	702	533	429	330	315	336	301	285	236	176	163	139	144	90	81	32	19	8	2
2 BATHWICK. (H.[a])	7323	M. - 2793	310	315	376	341	183	175	159	146	128	103	124	109	117	79	40	40	21	10	.
		F. - 4530	288	318	387	492	562	386	302	274	280	238	229	188	137	143	94	82	45	14	4
3 LYNCOMBE. (W.B.)	12277	M. - 5547	787	694	657	528	430	418	368	308	204	234	217	168	167	133	103	64	30	6	3
		F. - 6730	771	724	633	673	595	564	470	360	375	336	272	224	245	185	140	104	48	18	6
4 WALCOT. (H.[a] R.)	20871	M. - 8789	1090	1034	986	932	731	600	593	494	504	385	408	287	235	178	183	94	35	19	3
		F. - 12082	1058	1061	1167	1345	1167	992	815	680	713	514	553	494	317	348	309	145	75	26	10
5 LANSDOWN. (H.)	13512	M. - 4905	552	567	533	493	388	333	281	283	277	226	213	197	184	148	109	84	34	12	1
		F. - 8607	577	566	615	973	1009	731	602	681	512	519	405	356	344	312	280	143	97	24	6
6 BATHEASTON. (L.)	7763	M. - 3530	416	397	400	472	212	203	180	167	147	169	146	100	117	81	54	44	16	6	3
		F. - 4233	423	458	435	453	306	323	261	254	245	203	220	146	147	103	84	58	31	11	2
318 KEYNSHAM.																					
1 BITTON	5814	M. - 2791	422	402	302	292	226	180	173	136	117	122	118	73	69	46	35	33	12	3	1
		F. - 3023	448	412	335	271	235	216	189	152	145	118	121	107	102	60	56	38	17	7	2
2 OLDLAND. (R.)	12948	M. - 6466	1023	912	787	761	492	411	376	361	209	240	220	160	159	107	72	45	30	10	1
		F. - 6482	955	892	773	581	516	426	339	352	331	250	263	197	192	127	101	57	48	18	3
3 NEWTON	2150	M. - 1041	139	124	114	109	70	62	66	60	48	40	48	54	33	25	16	17	12	1	1
		F. - 1109	148	127	108	104	82	66	77	44	45	62	60	49	41	32	28	21	9	5	.
4 KEYNSHAM. (W.L.)	4869	M. - 2272	315	283	242	206	178	189	126	116	113	115	98	79	69	68	56	33	13	5	1
		F. - 2597	309	296	246	242	259	136	158	157	130	131	106	85	86	90	50	34	15	10	3
319 BEDMINSTER.																					
1 BEDMINSTER. (H[a].P.R.)	44759	M. - 21509	3588	2991	2306	2069	1806	1737	1501	1270	1088	867	686	495	432	270	121	26	32	16	1
		F. - 23250	3570	3632	2565	2060	1268	1855	1663	1447	1266	987	882	619	403	386	250	163	68	26	6
2 LONG ASHTON (W.)	6181	M. 3061	381	366	401	316	238	172	146	160	132	129	131	118	110	111	68	53	22	6	2
		F. - 3120	380	372	326	261	271	230	203	168	163	136	133	125	103	79	63	39	32	13	3
3 YATTON. (H.)	9811	M. - 4212	518	654	517	413	331	263	223	285	193	197	187	157	135	136	98	45	28	13	.
		F. - 5399	523	562	544	550	499	445	320	344	310	261	213	218	194	150	122	84	48	16	5
4 ST. GEORGE. (H.)	6854	M. - 3203	452	446	463	301	213	183	194	173	181	135	136	101	87	53	51	31	12	5	2
		F. - 3648	476	440	399	346	281	240	237	211	212	181	165	115	94	96	65	53	18	6	4

Table 4.—MALE and FEMALE CHILDREN at *each Year of Age* under 5 in the SOUTH-WESTERN DIVISI[ON] and its REGISTRATION COUNTIES.

REGISTRATION COUNTY.	TOTAL UNDER 5 YEARS. Persons.	TOTAL UNDER 5 YEARS. Males and Females.	Under 1 Year.	1-	2-	3-	4-
V. SOUTH-WESTERN COUNTIES.	229627	M. - 114996	23399	22405	23207	22757	22628
		F. - 114631	23015	22477	22958	22981	22605
17 WILTSHIRE	32789	M. - 16370	3343	3208	3317	3278	3224
		F. - 16419	3336	3271	3204	3236	3232
18 DORSETSHIRE	23063	M. - 11481	2407	2202	2327	2301	2244
		F. - 11582	2358	2240	2351	2265	2373
19 DEVONSHIRE	73183	M. - 36708	7337	7184	7355	7179	7153
		F. - 36475	7722	7162	7235	7422	6934
20 CORNWALL	37935	M. - 19070	4019	3650	3867	3748	3780
		F. - 18865	3864	3667	3872	3778	3684
21 SOMERSETSHIRE	62887	M. - 31687	6333	6161	6341	6251	6221
		F. - 31200	6340	6137	6201	6230	6382

Table 5.—MALE and FEMALE CHILDREN at *each Year of Age* under 5 in REGISTRATION DISTRICTS.

EGISTRATION DISTRICT.	Total under 5 Years. Persons.		Total under 5 Years. Males and Females.	Under 1 Year.	1–	2–	3–	4–
7 WILTSHIRE.								
IGHWORTH	5708	M.	2828	591	580	567	550	530
		F.	2880	606	608	552	541	573
RICKLADE	1489	M.	731	176	130	142	141	142
		F.	758	138	141	164	156	160
ALMESBURY	1868	M.	912	153	172	199	162	196
		F.	956	184	198	199	184	195
HIPPENHAM	2728	M.	1352	271	250	268	275	270
		F.	1376	276	264	298	292	246
ALNE	1074	M.	522	98	100	97	113	114
		F.	552	114	113	104	115	106
IARLBOROUGH	1184	M.	581	127	89	117	96	122
		F.	603	112	114	137	115	125
DEVIZES	2568	M.	1351	258	274	278	288	245
		F.	1217	238	270	248	239	228
IELKSHAM	2381	M.	1201	263	227	242	253	226
		F.	1180	225	234	251	236	230
RADFORD-ON-AVON	1465	M.	719	138	142	157	143	139
		F.	746	173	117	152	155	150
VESTBURY	1389	M.	694	118	143	143	152	141
		F.	695	147	129	127	138	154
VARMINSTER	1656	M.	833	158	164	157	182	172
		F.	823	181	151	163	168	164
EWSEY	1618	M.	798	173	142	161	160	162
		F.	820	176	163	152	167	162
MESBURY	954	M.	476	94	103	146	164	70
		F.	478	84	103	99	101	91
LDERBURY	3339	M.	1683	359	337	342	314	331
		F.	1656	337	342	329	336	312
VILTON	1301	M.	653	138	129	127	125	139
		F.	648	139	123	120	130	136
ISBURY	1174	M.	582	115	113	127	116	111
		F.	592	125	108	119	134	111
IERE	923	M.	484	93	93	91	102	105
		F.	439	85	98	86	81	89
DORSETSHIRE.								
HAFTESBURY	1662	M.	825	135	144	173	161	172
		F.	837	167	153	175	166	176
STURMINSTER	1277	M.	605	123	109	145	116	112
		F.	672	125	140	130	133	136
BLANDFORD	1627	M.	793	173	143	163	166	149
		F.	834	162	140	170	173	184
WIMBORNE	2203	M.	1156	236	218	216	252	227
		F.	1047	210	212	219	215	185
POOLE	2714	M.	1349	299	250	282	250	268
		F.	1365	276	275	280	261	264
WAREHAM	2233	M.	1105	229	210	237	215	214
		F.	1128	238	220	223	219	228
WEYMOUTH	3541	M.	1803	376	360	370	355	342
		F.	1738	376	332	347	318	371
DORCHESTER	3015	M.	1497	308	323	292	302	272
		F.	1518	276	300	305	302	335
SHERBORNE	1524	M.	736	145	143	145	138	165
		F.	788	184	144	155	158	147
BEAMINSTER	1402	M.	670	143	121	124	140	142
		F.	732	148	153	148	137	150
BRIDPORT	1865	M.	942	211	184	180	186	181
		F.	923	194	166	186	183	194
19 DEVONSHIRE.								
AXMINSTER	2226	M.	1153	220	236	236	237	224
		F.	1073	199	193	230	239	212
HONITON	2512	M.	1235	251	256	235	231	262
		F.	1277	259	264	251	257	255
ST. THOMAS	6032	M.	3028	617	595	633	589	594
		F.	3004	635	604	540	627	598
EXETER	4137	M.	2094	482	412	374	429	397
		F.	2043	464	432	383	365	399
NEWTON ABBOT	8855	M.	4403	972	850	926	856	889
		F.	4452	910	792	910	892	858
TOTNES	4707	M.	2364	480	477	470	449	488
		F.	2343	461	439	472	450	451
KINGSBRIDGE	2319	M.	1153	239	[illegible]	232	230	234
		F.	1166	257	224	230	247	228
PLYMPTON ST. MARY	2933	M.	1520	293	303	324	299	301
		F.	1413	313	297	271	253	273
PLYMOUTH	8712	M.	4364	1002	867	872	841	802
		F.	4348	931	883	861	874	749
EAST STONEHOUSE	2052	M.	1007	247	210	183	194	173
		F.	1045	221	237	215	212	160
STOKE DAMEREL	5560	M.	2783	682	658	516	533	514
		F.	2777	651	536	522	568	506
TAVISTOCK	3450	M.	1746	367	337	346	363	333
		F.	1704	359	331	323	350	341

REGISTRATION DISTRICT.	Total under 5 Years. Persons.		Total under 5 Years. Males and Females.	Under 1 Year.	1–	2–	3–
19 DEVONSHIRE—*cont.*							
281 OKEHAMPTON	2050	M.	1015	201	207	197	200
		F.	1035	187	224	196	243
282 CREDITON	2301	M.	1143	216	245	233	238
		F.	1158	218	219	251	246
283 TIVERTON	3514	M.	1746	375	347	306	326
		F.	1768	369	327	379	351
284 SOUTH MOLTON	2090	M.	1049	199	168	227	225
		F.	1041	205	206	202	221
285 BARNSTAPLE	4478	M.	2250	405	420	476	432
		F.	2228	454	448	434	417
286 TORRINGTON	1802	M.	888	194	158	184	164
		F.	914	181	170	188	197
287 BIDEFORD	2351	M.	1137	238	231	211	21
		F.	1214	239	245	261	22
288 HOLSWORTHY	1162	M.	565	115	108	114	11
		F.	542	125	93	107	11
20 CORNWALL.							
289 STRATTON	930	M.	505	97	110	109	9
		F.	415	94	118	73	9
290 CAMELFORD	930	M.	473	96	97	96	9
		F.	457	90	87	93	8
291 LAUNCESTON	2014	M.	1037	216	246	226	21
		F.	977	183	207	202	20
292 ST. GERMANS	1965	M.	976	198	190	199	20
		F.	989	205	193	176	21
293 LISKEARD	3530	M.	1768	384	326	348	3
		F.	1762	370	310	345	38
294 BODMIN	2173	M.	1105	224	244	199	18
		F.	1068	218	199	240	21
295 ST. COLUMB	1982	M.	953	208	172	205	1
		F.	1029	217	207	216	19
296 ST. AUSTELL	3814	M.	1907	381	351	412	39
		F.	1907	392	364	385	40
297 TRURO	3850	M.	1941	402	364	372	38
		F.	1909	391	367	400	3
298 FALMOUTH	2770	M.	1436	317	242	303	3
		F.	1344	260	279	290	2
299 HELSTON	2640	M.	1322	295	273	271	2
		F.	1318	266	245	247	2
300 REDRUTH	5284	M.	2638	555	473	539	5
		F.	2646	543	507	575	5
301 PENZANCE	5758	M.	2871	526	574	575	5
		F.	2887	617	551	615	5
302 SCILLY ISLANDS	259	M.	132	27	29	22	
		F.	127	19	23	18	
21 SOMERSETSHIRE.							
303 WILLITON	2403	M.	1211	237	237	229	2
		F.	1192	225	233	241	2
304 DULVERTON	650	M.	316	70	81	63	
		F.	334	68	59	60	
305 WELLINGTON	2432	M.	1232	254	265	245	2
		F.	1200	240	234	276	2
306 TAUNTON	4244	M.	2087	411	413	440	4
		F.	2157	443	418	423	4
307 BRIDGWATER	4424	M.	2218	475	428	421	4
		F.	2206	438	422	445	4
308 LANGPORT	1918	M.	965	211	196	194	1
		F.	953	192	178	183	2
309 CHARD	3376	M.	1703	337	329	329	3
		F.	1673	335	326	348	3
310 YEOVIL	3551	M.	1785	358	343	391	3
		F.	1766	369	315	320	3
311 WINCANTON	2494	M.	1266	235	262	252	2
		F.	1228	224	257	263	2
312 FROME	2962	M.	1462	304	249	305	3
		F.	1500	308	303	294	3
313 SHEPTON MALLET	1975	M.	956	194	197	182	1
		F.	1019	184	210	188	2
314 WELLS	2759	M.	1402	266	254	292	2
		F.	1357	304	283	252	2
315 AXBRIDGE	4872	M.	2407	456	490	408	5
		F.	2465	482	493	479	4
316 CLUTTON	3273	M.	1667	327	341	318	3
		F.	1606	346	309	320	3
317 BATH	7671	M.	3852	782	731	803	7
		F.	3819	756	760	748	7
318 KEYNSHAM	3759	M.	1899	400	393	384	3
		F.	1860	371	346	362	3
319 BEDMINSTER	9888	M.	4869	1056	982	995	9
		F.	4949	1060	984	983	9

le 7.—CONDITION as to MARRIAGE and AGES of MALES and FEMALES in the SOUTH-WESTERN DIVISION its REGISTRATION COUNTIES.

REGISTRATION COUNTY.		ALL AGES.	Under 15 Years.	15–	20–	25–	35–	45–	55–	… upw
SOUTH-WESTERN COUNTIES.										
ARRIED	Males	543900	329304	97054	56748	34037	11830	6587	4545	
	Females	572538	326445	91279	60260	44822	19857	12705	9188	
RIED	Males	308432	.	278	13839	70690	74854	63731	49719	3
	Females	316942	.	1378	21830	81396	78759	64180	44572	2
OWED	Males	38139	.	5	122	1258	2690	4383	7138	1
	Females	84062	.	1	289	3109	8353	13862	19993	3
17 WILTSHIRE.										
ARRIED	Males	74927	46342	12782	7448	4522	1734	962	634	
	Females	73372	46001	10819	6662	4712	2136	1307	955	
IED	Males	42987	.	40	1880	10056	10348	9053	7014	
	Females	43332	.	194	2904	11060	10594	8987	6261	
WED	Males	4852	.	1	12	168	392	832	1083	
	Females	9194	.	.	27	285	777	1451	2259	
18 DORSETSHIRE.										
ARRIED	Males	55360	32704	9568	6003	3976	1392	745	482	
	Females	55436	32643	8680	5517	4158	1759	1131	819	
IED	Males	31864	.	28	1411	7420	7765	6637	5012	
	Females	31409	.	125	2113	7861	7794	6447	4449	
WED	Males	3611	.	.	20	180	314	501	759	
	Females	7292	.	.	17	231	657	1200	1689	
19 DEVONSHIRE.										
ARRIED	Males	175990	104211	31588	19292	11872	4028	2194	1574	1
	Females	188224	103598	30471	21072	15496	6854	4391	3396	1
IED	Males	100578	.	78	4359	22810	24414	20792	16376	1
	Females	104458	.	471	7410	27156	25619	20942	14600	
WED	Males	10896	.	3	38	421	884	1438	2419	
	Females	28257	.	.	111	1184	2996	4743	6622	1
20 CORNWALL.										
ARRIED	Males	96502	56723	18944	10675	5825	1920	1030	723	
	Females	101240	55518	17154	11245	8539	3755	2293	1505	1
IED	Males	51086	.	39	2132	10638	12392	10715	8761	
	Females	54271	.	236	3494	13389	13701	11200	7931	
WED	Males	6427	.	.	23	204	439	701	1128	2
	Females	17840	.	.	58	647	1806	3000	4361	7
21 SOMERSETSHIRE.										
ERRIED	Males	141121	89324	24172	13240	7848	2768	1658	1132	
	Females	154266	88685	24155	15764	11917	5333	3589	2530	2
IED	Males	81920	.	95	4057	19566	20035	16534	12556	9
	Females	83472	.	552	5908	21840	21051	16904	11301	6
WED	Males	8353	.	1	29	335	661	1111	1779	4
	Females	21470	.	1	76	762	2117	3468	5062	9

—In a few cases, persons described as "Married" were stated to be under 15 years of age. These have been classed with married persons aged "15 and s."

Table 8.—Condition as to Marriage and Ages of Males and Females in Registration Districts

Registration District.		All Ages.	Under 15 Years.	15–	20–	25–	35–	45–	55–	65 and upw^ds.
17 WILTSHIRE.										
241 HIGHWORTH: Unmarried	M.	11720	7072	1949	1439	814	254	96	44	52
	F.	9941	7181	1283	713	415	171	73	53	52
Married	M.	6376	.	9	360	2095	1678	1127	710	397
	F.	6327	.	45	815	2096	1637	1063	588	284
Widowed	M.	504	.	.	.	32	69	77	109	217
	F.	887	.	.	3	47	93	187	209	346
242 CRICKLADE: Unmarried	M.	5559	2167	526	319	188	78	32	82	27
	F.	3257	2173	435	272	164	84	62	35	32
Married	M.	2001	.	.	91	412	450	432	343	273
	F.	1983	.	11	124	450	494	427	294	183
Widowed	M.	262	.	.	1	9	14	19	69	150
	F.	421	.	.	2	13	26	69	84	237
243 MALMESBURY: Unmarried	M.	4169	2627	650	414	241	163	59	39	35
	F.	4173	2635	589	344	235	122	59	51	38
Married	M.	2258	.	1	98	493	580	474	404	208
	F.	2388	.	11	140	573	591	484	367	222
Widowed	M.	320	.	.	2	9	26	43	68	172
	F.	641	.	.	.	11	50	74	137	269
244 CHIPPENHAM: Unmarried	M.	6351	3957	1027	597	412	185	71	46	56
	F.	6189	3909	840	657	441	196	121	82	70
Married	M.	3699	.	5	152	821	900	705	598	468
	F.	3736	.	17	238	909	883	769	571	344
Widowed	M.	411	.	.	1	15	23	63	107	272
	F.	925	.	.	4	24	78	136	179	410
245 CALNE: Unmarried	M.	2499	1605	404	264	119	34	30	28	15
	F.	2590	1615	371	223	159	60	52	39	81
Married	M.	1534	.	1	68	303	356	368	265	174
	F.	1545	.	4	82	347	372	368	246	130
Widowed	M.	170	.	.	.	2	15	21	29	103
	F.	322	.	.	.	7	25	47	81	162
246 MARLBOROUGH: Unmarried	M.	3379	1879	925	269	167	69	43	18	29
	F.	2774	1092	448	283	191	68	44	37	21
Married	M.	1554	.	.	45	353	348	372	269	167
	F.	1555	.	7	93	345	392	393	218	117
Widowed	M.	161	.	.	2	6	17	26	32	78
	F.	300	.	.	1	7	30	44	82	136
247 DEVIZES: Unmarried	M.	6109	3720	986	589	391	191	117	75	40
	F.	5964	3874	891	534	409	203	147	111	95
Married	M.	3507	.	3	167	782	854	741	632	398
	F.	3595	.	15	294	897	843	754	559	383
Widowed	M.	445	.	.	1	12	31	68	99	234
	F.	859	.	.	1	26	71	128	212	417
248 MELKSHAM: Unmarried	M.	4661	3301	804	395	260	95	56	25	35
	F.	5749	3318	959	569	438	190	180	80	65
Married	M.	3088	.	2	146	767	746	619	475	333
	F.	3179	.	10	203	900	778	620	451	217
Widowed	M.	314	.	.	.	10	21	59	73	171
	F.	766	.	.	4	24	71	147	190	330
249 BRADFORD-ON-AVON: Unmarried	M.	2942	1853	442	279	128	51	49	24	21
	F.	3411	1992	579	321	242	115	66	65	31
Married	M.	1921	.	2	120	435	443	370	334	197
	F.	1966	.	10	151	556	439	376	311	138
Widowed	M.	184	.	1	.	7	13	28	37	98
	F.	462	.	.	2	9	33	70	122	217
250 WESTBURY: Unmarried	M.	3021	1980	501	254	140	55	34	28	25
	F.	3068	2000	486	264	174	76	50	49	19
Married	M.	1985	.	1	74	338	465	406	351	250
	F.	1975	.	3	115	438	495	424	321	174
	M.	202	.	.	.	5	15	27	35	120
	F.	449	.	.	1	14	36	58	111	229
251 WARMINSTER: Unmarried	M.	4094	2509	770	582	245	79	38	37	34
	F.	4016	2389	639	386	281	180	78	50	53
Married	M.	2412	.	4	93	471	523	541	408	312
	F.	2461	.	4	128	555	570	642	427	235
Widowed	M.	277	.	.	1	4	19	40	54	159
	F.	580	.	.	.	18	51	91	151	269

Registration District.		All Ages.	Under 15 Years.	15–	20–	25–	35–	45–
17 WILTSHIRE—*cont.*								
252 PEWSEY: Unmarried	M.	3810	2356	636	374	268	84	34
	F.	3591	2304	460	317	200	92	54
Married	M.	2182	.	3	72	440	449	514
	F.	2190	.	8	126	485	490	481
Widowed	M.	290	.	.	2	10	19	38
	F.	424	.	.	1	12	24	56
253 AMESBURY: Unmarried	M.	2356	1418	432	226	140	67	36
	F.	2155	1368	331	198	128	62	26
Married	M.	1326	.	1	41	268	294	338
	F.	1314	.	5	59	319	304	328
Widowed	M.	187	.	.	.	8	11	22
	F.	285	.	.	.	8	28	42
254 ALDERBURY: Unmarried	M.	7973	4678	1564	885	569	216	131
	F.	8768	4822	1472	1006	670	310	214
Married	M.	4422	.	4	206	1092	1096	910
	F.	4463	.	20	336	1192	1119	914
Widowed	M.	514	.	.	1	24	50	69
	F.	1080	.	.	4	44	104	166
255 WILTON: Unmarried	M.	3067	1900	537	292	178	62	55
	F.	3001	1908	435	258	193	89	48
Married	M.	1763	.	1	61	246	415	393
	F.	1786	.	7	110	366	441	394
Widowed	M.	223	.	.	1	6	15	20
	F.	410	.	.	.	5	28	55
256 TISBURY: Unmarried	M.	2930	1818	464	296	170	74	45
	F.	2676	1740	337	241	160	84	48
Married	M.	1538	.	1	52	317	372	394
	F.	1591	.	8	91	346	420	366
Widowed	M.	216	.	.	.	5	17	23
	F.	305	.	.	.	10	18	49
257 MERE: Unmarried	M.	2167	1397	368	194	103	33	36
	F.	2179	1330	314	198	162	84	54
Married	M.	1261	.	2	94	253	280	289
	F.	1279	.	4	70	280	321	284
Widowed	M.	166	.	.	.	4	17	19
	F.	297	.	.	2	7	17	37
18 DORSETSHIRE.								
258 SHAFTESBURY: Unmarried	M.	3613	2296	629	324	180	73	50
	F.	3900	2357	655	369	240	118	61
Married	M.	2172	.	1	98	450	502	469
	F.	2201	.	7	116	556	551	466
Widowed	M.	248	.	.	3	8	23	35
	F.	528	.	.	.	15	38	94
259 STURMINSTER: Unmarried	M.	2890	1782	452	245	167	61	39
	F.	3166	1890	478	320	262	97	56
Married	M.	1717	.	.	75	380	385	365
	F.	1789	.	7	108	458	403	374
Widowed	M.	196	.	.	1	4	11	21
	F.	412	.	.	2	15	23	81
260 BLANDFORD: Unmarried	M.	3999	2416	728	429	241	75	44
	F.	4122	2375	641	458	315	121	86
Married	M.	2416	.	1	100	456	567	626
	F.	2428	.	10	135	549	568	555
Widowed	M.	270	.	.	.	6	18	41
	F.	501	.	.	1	12	40	81
261 WIMBORNE: Unmarried	M.	5063	3206	856	434	283	87	65
	F.	4837	2981	744	463	357	131	75
Married	M.	3038	.	1	147	709	668	609
	F.	3044	.	4	236	741	704	620
Widowed	M.	382	.	.	.	16	24	56
	F.	687	.	.	.	17	47	86
262 POOLE: Unmarried	M.	5465	3595	901	538	281	113	62
	F.	5747	3635	853	524	368	153	96
Married	M.	3246	.	4	172	881	846	641
	F.	3283	.	12	281	968	865	609
Widowed	M.	309	.	.	.	12	31	65
	F.	652	.	.	2	18	68	123

Table 8 *continued*.—CONDITION as to MARRIAGE and AGES of MALES and FEMALES in REGISTRATION DISTRICTS.

REGISTRATION DISTRICT.		ALL AGES.	Under 15 Years.	15–	20–	25–	35–	45–	55–	65 and upw.
DORSET-HIRE—*cont.*										
AREHAM:										
UNMARRIED	M.	5114	3116	853	524	321	140	83	34	43
	F.	4965	3117	711	422	327	148	117	61	62
MARRIED	M.	2958	.	8	133	694	691	594	473	365
	F.	2942	.	17	211	727	707	590	426	264
WIDOWED	M.	356	.	.	4	8	25	49	68	202
	F.	616	.	.	.	16	54	89	147	310
EYMOUTH:										
UNMARRIED	M.	10379	5042	1723	1566	1298	417	160	86	91
	F.	9204	4909	1554	1049	821	312	260	152	147
MARRIED	M.	5590	.	4	220	1441	1579	1131	735	480
	F.	4914	.	29	343	1343	1305	944	606	344
WIDOWED	M.	587	.	.	5	33	71	96	144	239
	F.	1249	.	.	5	42	136	218	303	545
ORCHESTER:										
UNMARRIED	M.	7688	4261	1385	945	610	211	108	93	75
	F.	7368	4225	1149	740	589	271	152	124	118
MARRIED	M.	4145	.	1	182	962	977	900	660	463
	F.	4200	.	21	281	1068	1008	872	588	362
WIDOWED	M.	512	.	.	5	18	50	77	117	248
	F.	977	.	.	6	32	96	151	230	462
HERBORNE:										
UNMARRIED	M.	3764	2316	743	338	194	77	38	35	23
	F.	3969	2228	636	422	343	154	79	56	51
MARRIED	M.	2086	.	4	93	432	524	450	309	274
	F.	2070	.	4	131	471	564	416	312	172
WIDOWED	M.	230	.	.	1	9	15	25	51	129
	F.	546	.	.	.	14	51	100	122	259
EAMINSTER:										
UNMARRIED	M.	3393	2096	582	335	207	63	50	31	30
	F.	3452	2085	546	322	225	115	69	45	45
MARRIED	M.	1961	.	1	71	450	460	413	315	272
	F.	1966	.	6	112	460	495	420	276	197
WIDOWED	M.	248	.	.	.	10	24	31	43	140
	F.	538	.	.	.	20	36	76	118	288
RIDPORT:										
UNMARRIED	M.	4182	2759	716	345	194	75	40	30	23
	F.	4566	2751	713	428	331	139	80	72	52
MARRIED	M.	2532	.	6	113	549	577	539	411	337
	F.	2582	.	8	160	636	604	582	360	232
WIDOWED	M.	273	.	.	1	9	22	16	67	158
	F.	678	.	.	1	30	68	98	138	340
DEVONSHIRE.										
XMINSTER:										
UNMARRIED	M.	5456	3432	931	532	272	108	77	51	53
	F.	5693	3211	923	577	426	210	147	106	93
MARRIED	M.	3183	.	1	114	620	696	683	611	458
	F.	3261	.	14	174	687	786	736	532	332
WIDOWED	M.	389	.	.	1	11	35	42	97	203
	F.	767	.	.	4	17	62	135	165	384
HONITON:										
UNMARRIED	M.	6091	3792	1004	921	359	196	71	69	49
	F.	6545	3630	971	704	556	243	172	156	104
MARRIED	M.	3560	.	.	160	713	787	750	607	545
	F.	3613	.	9	207	794	841	800	582	380
WIDOWED	M.	389	.	.	.	14	22	42	74	237
	F.	882	.	.	2	37	70	130	198	445
ST. THOMAS:										
UNMARRIED	M.	13658	8430	2152	1357	881	373	193	154	118
	F.	13371	6370	2257	1627	1354	669	456	347	291
MARRIED	M.	7875	.	5	334	1849	1806	1587	1298	996
	F.	8167	.	27	457	2084	2031	1676	1169	723
WIDOWED	M.	842	.	.	4	30	70	79	178	481
	F.	2298	.	.	13	81	241	374	523	1066
EXETER:										
UNMARRIED	M.	9879	5833	1822	1174	551	251	113	71	64
	F.	12646	5958	2288	1650	1240	562	373	301	284
MARRIED	M.	6110	.	6	308	1570	1642	1201	820	563
	F.	6203	.	26	469	1783	1660	1212	682	371
WIDOWED	M.	670	.	.	2	40	69	100	161	308
	F.	2041	.	.	6	86	218	347	406	888
NEWTON ABBOT:										
UNMARRIED	M.	19069	12227	3219	2022	1253	386	252	170	140
	F.	25836	12444	4068	3395	2741	1296	845	625	420
MARRIED	M.	12947	.	11	829	2806	2927	2481	1930	1368
	F.	12578	.	34	842	3294	3142	2590	1707	967
WIDOWED	M.	1218	.	2	4	49	99	175	266	623
	F.	3950	.	.	8	183	432	828	895	1604
OTNES:										
UNMARRIED	M.	10639	6767	1676	1040	608	235	139	100	79
	F.	11357	6401	1783	1192	853	407	232	221	178
MARRIED	M.	6045	.	1	246	1383	1466	1201	1004	742
	F.	6279	.	26	432	1649	1540	1240	800	592
[illegible]	M.	845	.	.	2	27	50	81	146	539
	F.	[illegible]	[illegible]	[illegible]	[illegible]	[illegible]	[illegible]	[illegible]	[illegible]	[illegible]

REGISTRATION DISTRICT.		ALL AGES.	Under 15 Years.	15–	20–	25–	35–	45–	55–
19 DEVONSHIRE —*cont.*									
275 KINGSBRIDGE:									
UNMARRIED	M.	5494	3357	854	547	332	148	81	78
	F.	5750	3389	836	572	440	179	128	104
MARRIED	M.	3161	.	1	101	655	807	588	574
	F.	3224	.	16	177	773	801	632	494
WIDOWED	M.	387	.	.	2	11	31	38	78
	F.	928	.	.	1	28	92	108	180
276 PLYMPTON ST. MARY:									
UNMARRIED	M.	7317	4379	1331	828	460	141	91	87
	F.	7535	4220	1210	859	611	278	148	108
MARRIED	M.	3886	.	2	161	725	900	887	618
	F.	3992	.	15	263	983	1028	819	682
WIDOWED	M.	424	.	.	1	13	38	55	88
	F.	1027	.	.	8	48	109	141	252
277 PLYMOUTH:									
UNMARRIED	M.	20157	11898	3391	2414	1510	460	269	131
	F.	22496	12963	3813	2636	1863	749	479	354
MARRIED	M.	12496	.	20	658	3062	3126	2647	1907
	F.	13459	.	123	1243	3859	3294	2553	1665
WIDOWED	M.	1154	.	1	4	67	127	196	281
	F.	4191	.	.	24	197	581	822	991
278 EAST STONEHOUSE:									
UNMARRIED	M.	4370	2543	718	565	344	125	41	28
	F.	4234	2309	624	458	280	130	87	39
MARRIED	M.	2558	.	3	107	639	620	486	301
	F.	2382	.	24	287	1006	796	435	285
WIDOWED	M.	217	.	.	2	14	22	32	44
	F.	690	.	.	3	42	95	133	188
279 STOKE DAMEREL:									
UNMARRIED	M.	18135	7365	4330	2216	1562	386	145	74
	F.	12967	7066	2209	1359	829	330	224	192
MARRIED	M.	7046	.	8	342	1936	2032	1817	1158
	F.	8756	.	73	797	2594	2193	1660	1008
WIDOWED	M.	726	.	.	2	25	64	125	195
	F.	2411	.	.	13	146	280	423	814
280 TAVISTOCK:									
UNMARRIED	M.	9202	5168	1619	1060	745	251	140	114
	F.	8418	5033	1428	887	591	205	95	82
MARRIED	M.	4916	.	3	187	1034	1123	1123	989
	F.	4782	.	18	320	1169	1133	1010	746
WIDOWED	M.	504	.	.	.	23	42	112	122
	F.	1278	.	.	5	44	110	222	303
281 OKEHAMPTON:									
UNMARRIED	M.	5240	3079	927	558	338	136	81	63
	F.	5027	3047	771	493	364	139	93	82
MARRIED	M.	2807	.	1	109	882	619	600	507
	F.	2848	.	4	177	868	656	592	477
WIDOWED	M.	380	.	.	2	11	28	43	78
	F.	663	.	.	1	8	53	81	144
282 CREDITON:									
UNMARRIED	M.	5399	3278	930	652	332	116	68	63
	F.	5297	3249	782	510	360	142	92	82
MARRIED	M.	3057	.	2	123	637	674	612	[illegible]
	F.	3077	.	7	178	725	679	673	[illegible]
WIDOWED	M.	393	.	.	.	8	36	43	[illegible]
	F.	706	.	.	1	21	55	63	[illegible]
283 TIVERTON:									
UNMARRIED	M.	8335	5152	1412	813	524	193	96	[illegible]
	F.	8608	5059	1409	885	609	239	109	[illegible]
MARRIED	M.	4858	.	4	206	1048	1146	934	[illegible]
	F.	4882	.	10	319	1220	1105	995	[illegible]
WIDOWED	M.	572	.	.	3	19	30	72	[illegible]
	F.	1257	.	.	2	32	109	212	[illegible]
284 SOUTH MOLTON:									
UNMARRIED	M.	5317	3155	966	556	343	111	64	[illegible]
	F.	4912	2943	802	444	376	143	78	[illegible]
MARRIED	M.	2792	.	1	104	570	663	563	[illegible]
	F.	2814	.	4	164	679	671	578	[illegible]
WIDOWED	M.	366	.	.	.	9	24	38	[illegible]
	F.	617	.	.	.	18	44	84	[illegible]
285 BARNSTAPLE:									
UNMARRIED	M.	10762	6518	1953	1146	628	238	125	[illegible]
	F.	12127	6443	2089	1327	986	400	306	[illegible]
MARRIED	M.	6456	.	6	290	1435	1537	1312	[illegible]
	F.	6433	.	16	421	1580	1540	1316	[illegible]
WIDOWED	M.	704	.	.	2	23	64	64	[illegible]
	F.	1710	.	.	5	68	166	276	[illegible]
286 TORRINGTON:									
UNMARRIED	M.	4394	2700	825	436	233	69	58	[illegible]
	F.	4704	2630	741	518	370	103	123	[illegible]
MARRIED	M.	2416	.	2	94	520	551	460	[illegible]
	F.	2447	.	8	142	539	592	492	42
WIDOWED	M.	292	.	.	3	6	19	37	7
	F.	568	.	.	2	17	41	94	10

Table 8 *continued*.—CONDITION as to MARRIAGE and AGES of MALES and FEMALES in REGISTRATION DISTRICTS.

REGISTRATION DISTRICT.		ALL AGES.	Under 15 Years.	15–	20–	25–	35–	45–	55–	65 and upw^{ds}.
19 DEVONSHIRE —*cont.*										
287 BIDEFORD:										
UNMARRIED	M.	5459	3418	1064	526	281	106	53	42	35
	F.	6054	3373	1010	716	444	204	140	65	82
MARRIED	M.	2934	.	.	124	628	693	585	504	309
	F.	3153	.	9	206	761	806	616	447	308
WIDOWED	M.	425	.	.	4	7	6	60	72	262
	F.	849	.	.	4	54	64	141	177	409
288 HOLSWORTHY										
UNMARRIED	M.	2847	1700	494	309	181	69	39	29	26
	F.	2677	1580	447	273	205	76	34	31	31
MARRIED	M.	1480	.	1	62	322	349	298	249	199
	F.	1493	.	8	105	364	335	317	238	136
WIDOWED	M.	206	.	.	.	8	17	28	36	117
	F.	305	.	.	1	16	29	40	58	161
20 CORNWALL										
289 STRATTON:										
UNMARRIED	M.	2228	1372	368	223	133	51	31	22	28
	F.	2246	1318	371	228	155	73	46	33	23
MARRIED	M.	1239	.	1	55	284	285	237	190	187
	F.	1253	.	3	91	304	294	263	183	125
WIDOWED	M.	162	.	.	.	4	10	17	25	106
	F.	301	.	.	1	4	28	42	56	170
290 CAMELFORD:										
UNMARRIED	M.	2359	1463	392	220	129	56	45	25	29
	F.	2213	1352	361	190	160	59	39	34	18
MARRIED	M.	1226	.	.	47	265	277	248	216	169
	F.	1265	.	3	90	306	307	249	197	113
WIDOWED	M.	170	.	.	.	1	20	21	33	95
	F.	372	.	.	1	14	39	50	93	175
291 LAUNCESTON:										
UNMARRIED	M.	4961	2984	918	576	308	81	37	51	46
	F.	4895	2860	831	539	351	137	79	55	53
MARRIED	M.	2601	.	.	89	550	587	578	459	338
	F.	2642	.	9	158	633	634	582	381	245
WIDOWED	M.	299	.	.	1	12	21	29	73	163
	F.	660	.	.	3	22	68	97	154	316
292 ST. GERMANS:										
UNMARRIED	M.	4707	2808	790	499	296	96	54	29	35
	F.	5116	2967	816	539	376	161	108	85	65
MARRIED	M.	2715	.	4	76	472	663	581	535	384
	F.	2987	.	6	188	736	714	598	460	286
WIDOWED	M.	353	.	.	1	9	20	45	71	209
	F.	858	.	.	1	37	71	127	199	423
293 LISKEARD:										
UNMARRIED	M.	8589	5204	1651	965	448	144	80	77	77
	F.	8858	5180	1558	926	670	242	135	89	88
MARRIED	M.	4551	.	3	175	928	1017	1006	828	596
	F.	4919	.	25	331	1145	1202	1033	736	447
WIDOWED	M.	485	.	.	1	7	36	66	114	262
	F.	1388	.	.	4	32	144	238	346	626
294 BODMIN:										
UNMARRIED	M.	5882	3297	1065	692	428	181	108	71	62
	F.	5848	3163	956	597	497	265	148	123	101
MARRIED	M.	3074	.	4	106	580	712	643	559	476
	F.	3202	.	10	177	737	748	680	510	340
WIDOWED	M.	403	.	.	2	14	26	56	71	234
	F.	886	.	.	3	36	85	128	197	444
295 ST. COLUMB:										
UNMARRIED	M.	4820	2977	847	582	309	86	50	38	31
	F.	5202	2973	776	590	437	180	110	71	65
MARRIED	M.	2554	.	2	86	512	622	556	445	345
	F.	2697	.	7	130	699	684	525	425	228
WIDOWED	M.	297	.	.	3	13	28	42	58	153
	F.	773	.	.	6	30	62	112	192	371
296 ST. AUSTELL:										
UNMARRIED	M.	9057	5562	1749	912	464	169	82	60	59
	F.	9189	5475	1511	923	678	266	143	100	67
MARRIED	M.	4809	.	5	191	1066	1117	1000	854	576
	F.	5201	.	28	287	1344	1293	1061	782	405
WIDOWED	M.	465	.	.	3	25	34	61	118	254
	F.	1455	.	.	4	44	138	228	350	691
297 TRURO:										
UNMARRIED	M.	10199	6659	2118	1056	575	151	106	78	59
	F.	11467	6900	1964	1414	1122	429	288	204	146
MARRIED	M.	5488	.	4	190	1058	1267	1217	1051	701
	F.	6050	.	19	323	1468	1403	1303	980	464
WIDOWED	M.	612	.	.	1	21	44	73	128	345
	F.	166	.	.	3	72	222	344	540	985
20 CORNWALL —*cont.*										
298 FALMOUTH:										
UNMARRIED	M.	7949	4039	1877	966	646	282	79	63	47
	F.	7671	3998	1269	925	677	316	231	119	144
MARRIED	M.	4567	.	3	174	884	1210	909	626	461
	F.	3967	.	16	254	1023	1062	838	522	254
WIDOWED	M.	416	.	.	0	20	42	65	92	201
	F.	1253	.	.	9	68	129	215	291	541
299 HELSTON:										
UNMARRIED	M.	6960	4108	1399	777	421	156	90	53	56
	F.	7543	4017	1245	796	687	339	210	132	107
MARRIED	M.	3466	.	1	127	722	832	720	617	447
	F.	3845	.	19	256	914	994	776	558	329
WIDOWED	M.	384	.	.	2	12	37	45	73	215
	F.	1423	.	.	3	46	152	256	354	673
300 REDRUTH:										
UNMARRIED	M.	13312	8066	2774	1420	631	206	109	60	47
	F.	14715	7787	2744	1699	1256	597	331	172	138
MARRIED	M.	6580	.	3	387	1431	1639	1453	1044	623
	F.	7806	.	54	597	2018	2075	1629	987	446
WIDOWED	M.	472	.	.	8	20	41	79	101	225
	F.	3240	.	.	12	104	362	610	849	1398
301 PENZANCE:										
UNMARRIED	M.	14870	8618	2066	1768	975	306	151	106	82
	F.	15680	8235	2652	1819	1419	665	419	263	208
MARRIED	M.	7985	.	9	417	1896	2032	1476	1265	890
	F.	8653	.	36	598	1069	2115	1595	1153	587
WIDOWED	M.	825	.	.	1	42	77	114	160	481
	F.	2898	.	.	7	131	299	543	719	1199
302 SCILLY ISLANDS:										
UNMARRIED	M.	662	357	112	95	65	16	8	4	5
	F.	620	339	97	56	55	34	7	12	13
MARRIED	M.	491	.	.	20	106	126	91	72	76
	F.	374	.	1	15	92	96	67	65	57
WIDOWED	M.	60	.	.	.	4	3	3	11	39
	F.	113	.	.	1	7	9	15	21	60
21 SOMERSETSHIRE.										
303 WILLITON:										
UNMARRIED	M.	5763	3567	1024	532	332	109	80	58	55
	F.	5572	3472	841	490	387	142	69	83	68
MARRIED	M.	3059	.	1	101	602	708	689	563	395
	F.	3129	.	3	161	675	824	684	489	292
WIDOWED	M.	382	.	.	1	8	30	48	75	219
	F.	780	.	.	2	22	67	139	192	358
304 DULVERTON:										
UNMARRIED	M.	1781	1044	296	103	116	47	36	27	22
	F.	1544	978	241	140	91	39	23	19	13
MARRIED	M.	906	.	.	25	154	230	206	146	145
	F.	907	.	4	89	293	217	195	130	99
WIDOWED	M.	115	.	.	.	3	7	14	18	73
	F.	200	.	.	1	4	20	32	46	97
305 WELLINGTON:										
UNMARRIED	M.	5648	3680	938	529	304	105	71	55	66
	F.	5797	3478	897	558	410	162	114	98	94
MARRIED	M.	3292	.	1	165	696	758	646	579	447
	F.	3309	.	12	226	791	754	685	540	301
WIDOWED	M.	367	.	.	1	7	23	45	60	231
	F.	791	.	.	2	29	60	106	168	426
306 TAUNTON:										
UNMARRIED	M.	10351	6246	1913	996	661	238	188	95	74
	F.	11462	6212	2011	1252	938	388	258	107	146
MARRIED	M.	5954	.	8	297	1335	1389	1193	1010	732
	F.	6036	.	28	418	1519	1455	1184	915	517
WIDOWED	M.	565	.	.	3	26	36	61	134	305
	F.	1684	.	.	4	55	146	253	387	832
307 BRIDGWATER:										
UNMARRIED	M.	10179	6860	1801	978	663	191	108	74	74
	F.	9829	6124	1468	901	650	281	176	122	107
MARRIED	M.	5755	.	3	247	1236	1356	1188	966	665
	F.	5925	.	21	394	1486	1418	1203	907	496
WIDOWED	M.	629	.	.	2	20	53	98	132	324
	F.	1876	.	.	3	35	131	206	328	673
308 LANGPORT:										
UNMARRIED	M.	4611	2853	833	399	290	111	59	41	25
	F.	4584	2826	648	395	355	160	99	50	51
MARRIED	M.	2654	.	2	88	543	598	584	482	357
	F.	2698	.	4	136	621	663	624	435	245
WIDOWED	M.	306	.	.	.	17	21	40	62	176
	F.	721	.	.	1	21	52	102	174	371
309 CHARD:										
UNMARRIED	M.	7448	4895	1323	658	367	124	77	51	48
	F.	7330	4724	1308	766	530	242	162	129	69
MARRIED	M.	4226	.	7	235	923	1056	853	689	463
	F.	4279	.	17	295	1031	1130	889	578	353
WIDOWED	M.	427	.	.	3	9	31	55	87	232
	F.	1048	.	.	4	37	88	163	233	518

able 8 *continued.*—CONDITION as to MARRIAGE and AGES of MALES and FEMALES in REGISTRATION DISTRICTS.

TRATION TRICT.		ALL AGES.	Under 15 Years.	15–	20–	25–	35–	45–	55–	65 and upw^{ds}.
MERSET- E—*cont.*										
L:										
RRIED	M.	7855	6145	1375	681	380	129	85	41	39
	F.	8950	5225	1401	888	600	322	196	114	123
IED	M.	4566	.	1	229	1037	1126	950	709	514
	F.	4687	.	17	290	1222	1199	958	647	369
WED	M.	419	.	.	2	16	35	41	91	234
	F.	1220	.	.	2	46	126	212	285	549
NTON:										
RRIED	M.	5735	3617	909	544	378	128	83	41	35
	F.	6111	3616	925	627	471	183	130	81	78
IED	M.	3358	.	4	137	733	841	662	562	414
	F.	3349	.	11	220	814	860	661	492	291
WED	M.	378	.	.	.	8	32	43	81	210
	F.	849	.	.	8	20	75	129	211	411
E:										
RRIED	M.	6662	4255	1151	611	516	127	92	60	60
	F.	7081	4207	1099	647	489	229	152	104	94
IED	M.	3966	.	1	188	918	939	833	646	441
	F.	4081	.	13	297	936	982	852	571	300
WED	M.	434	.	.	1	10	35	40	95	244
	F.	978	.	.	5	30	94	143	228	478
TON MALLET:										
ARRIED	M.	4590	2803	792	484	272	97	61	38	43
	F.	4782	2933	708	472	308	121	164	74	67
RIED	M.	2727	.	2	121	695	660	575	452	318
	F.	2724	.	10	159	687	660	586	381	241
OWED	M.	302	.	.	.	17	27	31	60	167
	F.	654	.	.	1	24	43	108	153	330
S:										
ARRIED	M.	6484	3828	1068	654	417	195	116	82	51
	F.	6765	3850	1029	692	528	269	174	118	105
RIED	M.	3725	.	2	164	886	869	766	551	407
	F.	3760	.	13	250	952	941	781	507	316
OWED	M.	428	.	.	.	15	27	64	84	238
	F.	901	.	.	1	23	84	146	237	410

REGISTRATION DISTRICT.		ALL AGES.	Under 15 Years.	15–	20–	25–	35–	45–	55–	65 and upw^{ds}.
21 SOMERSETSHIRE—*cont.*										
315 AXBRIDGE:										
UNMARRIED	M.	11277	7128	1836	1044	851	264	135	98	91
	F.	13603	7172	2236	1637	1167	485	354	242	210
MARRIED	M.	6705	.	7	293	1554	1617	1362	1005	817
	F.	6799	.	24	422	1728	1785	1334	954	607
WIDOWED	M.	660	.	.	3	32	53	84	138	364
	F.	1888	.	.	5	57	180	323	461	862
316 CLUTTON:										
UNMARRIED	M.	7422	4759	1296	689	363	184	89	58	54
	F.	6433	4445	832	490	327	133	98	72	66
MARRIED	M.	4232	.	5	206	972	977	851	898	523
	F.	4244	.	20	307	1052	998	858	684	377
WIDOWED	M.	437	.	.	3	11	37	51	109	232
	F.	817	.	.	3	21	72	100	198	423
317 BATH:										
UNMARRIED	M.	16012	11268	3165	1715	1044	344	202	151	123
	F.	25201	11136	4190	3240	2844	1429	969	753	731
MARRIED	M.	10958	.	19	564	2764	2748	2171	1572	1120
	F.	11194	.	55	788	3074	2908	2216	1436	714
WIDOWED	M.	1164	.	1	5	51	88	168	254	597
	F.	4017	.	1	16	154	470	732	947	1697
318 KEYNSHAM:										
UNMARRIED	M.	7758	5066	1346	688	372	113	75	49	51
	F.	7848	5049	1167	707	442	193	133	82	75
MARRIED	M.	4398	.	15	277	1164	1103	872	566	401
	F.	4434	.	31	382	1253	1066	846	550	288
WIDOWED	M.	414	.	.	1	28	54	81	91	211
	F.	929	.	.	8	31	79	183	221	462
319 BEDMINSTER:										
UNMARRIED	M.	19695	12978	3082	1864	1016	309	140	118	8
	F.	20805	13179	3154	1851	1235	575	359	298	13
MARRIED	M.	11454	.	17	720	3404	3031	2143	1306	83
	F.	11967	.	69	1125	3751	3210	2073	1146	58
WIDOWED	M.	942	.	.	4	56	92	169	222	39
	F.	3642	.	.	20	153	330	476	613	105

le 9.—CONDITION as to MARRIAGE and AGES of MALES and FEMALES in each URBAN SANITARY DISTRICT of which the POPULATION EXCEEDS 50,000 PERSONS.

URBAN SANITARY DISTRICT.		ALL AGES.	Under 15 Years.	15–	20–	25–	35–	45–	55–	65 and upwards
TH:										
MARRIED	Males	20110	11896	3382	2400	1497	461	259	131	94
	Females	22460	12259	3812	2655	1863	749	479	384	339
RRIED	Males	12487	.	20	665	3058	3123	2046	1907	1078
	Females	13458	.	123	1239	3858	3293	2553	1665	722
DOWED	Males	1153	.	1	4	67	127	195	281	478
	Females	4101	.	.	24	107	561	822	991	1506
MARRIED	Males	12331	7470	2151	1270	783	277	153	119	103
	Females	19493	7793	3348	2656	2350	1203	840	655	648
RIED	Males	7806	.	12	377	1982	1942	1576	1126	791
	Females	7988	.	86	553	2190	2067	1625	1018	403
OWED	Males	883	.	.	5	38	80	119	202	430
	Females	3318		1	14	132	385	598	787	1896

f the City of Bristol is situated in Division 5 (in Bedminster District of Somersetshire), but the "Condition as to Marriage and Ages of Males and Females" in the entire City will be found in Table 9 of Division 6, the greater part of the City being situated in Gloucestershire.

Table 10.—Occupations of Males and Females in the South-western Division and its Registration Counties, and in each Urban Sanitary District of which the Population exceeds 50,000 Persons.

Occupations.	South-Western Counties.		Registration Counties. 17. Wiltshire.		18. Dorsetshire.		19. Devonshire.	
	Males.	Females.	Males.	Females.	Males.	Females.	Males.	Females.
TOTAL	885471	973542	122769	125998	90835	94127	287461	320839
I. PROFESSIONAL CLASS.								
1. Persons engaged in the General or Local Government of the Country.								
1. *National Government.*								
Peer, M.P., Privy Councillor (not otherwise described)	25	.	6	.	7	.	8	.
Civil Service (officers and clerks)	1268	363	128	59	119	44	564	114
Civil Service (messengers, &c.)	1516	112	196	6	148	7	640	24
Prison Officer, &c.	618	31	16	8	258	4	189	9
2. *Local Government.*								
Police	1871	.	214	.	178	.	751	.
Municipal, Parish, Union, District, Officer	875	263	124	48	105	36	274	72
Other Local or County Official	608	.	77	.	79	.	271	.
3. *East Indian and Colonial Service.*								
East Indian and Colonial Service	9	.	.	.	.	.	4	.
2. Persons engaged in the Defence of the Country.								
1. *Army (at Home).*								
Army Officer (effective or retired)	1147	.	74	.	124	.	552	.
Soldier and Non-commissioned Officer	4461	.	311	.	1112	.	2462	.
Militia, Yeomanry, Volunteers	1193	.	52	.	259	.	593	.
Army Pensioner	919	.	148	.	77	.	374	.
2. *Navy (ashore or in port).*								
Navy Officer (effective or retired)	1253	.	13	.	87	.	937	.
Seaman, R.N.	7594	.	9	.	696	.	5801	.
Royal Marines (officers and men)	1781	.	14	.	132	.	1560	.
Navy Pensioner	3378	18	77	.	171	.	2301	10
3. Persons engaged in Professional Occupations (with their immediate Subordinates).								
1. *Clerical Profession.*								
Clergyman (Established Church)	2038	.	400	.	316	.	822	.
Roman Catholic Priest	128	.	8	.	15	.	44	.
Minister, Priest, of other religious bodies	902	.	105	.	65	.	290	.
Missionary, Scripture Reader, Itinerant Preacher	221	106	24	7	21	3	76	42
Nun, Sister of Charity	.	406	.	31	.	59	.	171
Theological Student	233	.	49	.	9	.	93	.
Church, Chapel, Cemetery—Officer, Servant	326	121	63	15	37	3	98	44
2. *Legal Profession.*								
Barrister, Solicitor	1034	.	105	.	77	.	405	.
Law Student	62	.	2	.	6	.	27	.
Law Clerk, and others connected with Law	1407	.	194	.	140	.	432	.
3. *Medical Profession.*								
Physician, Surgeon, General Practitioner	1122	.	129	.	101	.	420	.
Dentist	190	.	14	.	8	.	99	.
Medical Student, Assistant	254	1	32	.	20	1	100	.
Midwife	.	163	.	28	.	21	.	44
Subordinate Medical Service	176	3510	21	407	10	281	58	1371
4. *Teachers.*								
Schoolmaster	3285	8089	334	1148	295	856	1178	2652
Teacher, Professor, Lecturer	339	2609	29	365	25	284	134	871
School Service, and others concerned in Teaching	42	70	3	10	3	7	12	19
5. *Literary and Scientific Persons.*								
Author, Editor, Journalist	101	22	11	2	8	.	45	9
Reporter, Short-hand Writer	124	.	15	.	9	.	54	.
Persons engaged in Scientific Pursuits	43	3	3	3	4	.	19	.
Literary, Scientific, Institution, Service, &c.	24	9	4	1	1	2	5	4
6. *Engineers and Surveyors.*								
Civil Engineer	325	.	46	.	21	.	128	.
Mining Engineer	189	.	1	.	1	.	36	.
Land, House, Ship, Surveyor	340	.	55	.	21	.	92	.
7. *Artists.*								
Painter (artist)	246	81	15	3	11	4	126	32
Engraver (artist)	44	.	.	.	2	.	22	.
Sculptor	32	1	.	.	5	.	11	1
Architect	254	.	33	.	21	.	127	.
Musician, Music Master	718	577	67	47	63	45	311	215
Art Student	69	35	3	4	4	1	38	13
Photographer	401	74	20	8	37	7	156	32
Actor	65	53	5	3	1	1	23	22
Art, Music, Theatre, Service	33	1	3	.	3	.	15	.

Note.—Persons returned as engaged in more than one occupation have been referred to the one that appeared to be of most importance; or, if there was no difference in this respect, to the one first given by the person in his or her return. In some cases special rules have been followed: *e.g.*, "Clergyman and Schoolmaster" in combination has always been referred to "Schoolmaster"; a Member of Parliament or Peer engaged in any branch of commerce or industry has always been referred to this latter, not to "Peer, M.P."

The numbers returned under any heading include Labourers, Apprentices, and Assistants, as well as Masters, but not Clerks, Messengers, Errand boys, Porters, or Watchmen, for which occupations there are special headings. Civil, Military, and Naval Clerks, Law, Bank, Insurance, and Railway Clerks, and Government and Railway Porters are, however, exceptions to this rule. Many young persons, being Apprentices or Assistants, have therefore been referred to occupations usually followed by adults. Women also, chiefly widows or orphans carrying on the business of their deceased husbands or fathers, will sometimes be found under occupations commonly followed by men only.

Persons returned as *retired* from any business have not been referred to that business. Inmates of workhouses have been referred to their trades, unless their age or infirmities showed that they were past work. But persons who might be supposed to be only temporarily separated from their usual employment, such as Prisoners, and Patients in General Hospitals, have been classed under their usual occupations.

ble 10 *continued.*—OCCUPATIONS of MALES and FEMALES in the SOUTH-WESTERN DIVISION and its REGISTRATION COUNTIES, and in each URBAN SANITARY DISTRICT of which the POPULATION exceeds 50,000 PERSONS.

OCCUPATIONS.	SOUTH-WESTERN COUNTIES.		REGISTRATION COUNTIES. 17. WILTSHIRE.		18. DORSETSHIRE.		19. DEVONSHIRE.	
	Males.	Females.	Males.	Females.	Males.	Females.	Males.	Females.
8. *Persons engaged in Exhibitions, Shows, Games, &c.*								
erformer, Showman, Exhibition, Service	53	10	10	8	16	1	19	1
illiard, Cricket, & other Games, Service	154	1	11	.	12	.	73	1
II. DOMESTIC CLASS.								
4. PERSONS ENGAGED IN DOMESTIC OFFICES OR SERVICES.								
1. *Domestic Service.*								
omestic Coachman, Groom	4677	.	788	.	674	.	1473	.
omestic Gardener	4586	3	602	.	411	.	1439	.
omestic Indoor Servant	3828	100132	574	11888	518	8825	1436	30458
odge, Gate, Park, Keeper (not Government)	58	71	8	17	14	6	18	21
nn, Hotel, Servant	1391	1487	105	214	133	136	479	521
ollege, Club, Service	70	23	29	4	6	2	23	12
2. *Other Service.*								
ffice Keeper (not Government)	26	74	2	8	2	3	11	26
ook (not domestic)	50	24	3	1	4	3	37	11
harwoman	.	8208	.	502	.	462	.	3185
Vashing and Bathing Service	80	17106	6	2062	7	1908	26	6708
lospital and Institution Service	364	724	68	132	21	58	143	242
thers engaged in Service	46	11	4	.	6	.	25	4
III. COMMERCIAL CLASS.								
5. PERSONS ENGAGED IN COMMERCIAL OCCUPATIONS.								
1. *Merchants and Agents.*								
Merchant	273	2	4	.	16	.	119	.
roker, Agent, Factor	775	20	40	1	48	3	302	5
uctioneer, Appraiser, Valuer, House Agent	561	.	76	.	63	.	179	.
ccountant	1114	23	48	.	86	3	424	18
alesman, Buyer (not otherwise described)	27	18	1	1	1	.	10	5
ommercial Traveller	1309	.	119	.	86	.	588	.
ommercial Clerk	4075	190	465	25	338	28	1347	72
fficer of Commercial Company, Guild, Society, &c.	12	.	.	.	.	.	6	.
2. *Dealers in Money.*								
anker	132	11	3	.	9	.	46	1
ank Service	943	.	150	.	102	.	346	1
ill Discounter, Bill Broker, Finance Agent	13	.	1	.	.	.	7	.
3. *Persons occupied in Insurance.*								
ife, House, Ship, &c., Insurance Service	568	9	48	1	40	1	210	4
6. PERSONS ENGAGED IN CONVEYANCE OF MEN, GOODS, AND MESSAGES.								
1. *On Railways.*								
ailway Engine Driver, Stoker	353	.	221	.	71	.	270	.
ailway Guard	476	.	95	.	48	.	137	.
ointsman, Level Crossing Men	180	14	48	1	28	3	30	4
ther Railway Officials and Servants	4958	19	929	3	447	2	1539	2
2. *On Roads.*								
oll Collector, Turnpike Gate Keeper	82	56	1	1	9	8	62	31
mnibus, Coach, Cab, Owner—Livery Stable Keeper	483	21	16	1	15	.	252	8
abman, Flyman, Coachman (not domestic)	1812	.	149	.	104	.	740	.
arman, Carrier, Carter, Haulier	4646	79	702	19	533	12	1032	9
ramway Companies' Service	71	.	.	.	.	.	27	.
Wheel Chair Proprietor, Attendant, &c.	158	1	1	.	25	.	11	1
3. *On Canals, Rivers and Seas.*								
nland Navigation Service	84	1	37	.	.	.	17	.
argeman, Lighterman, Waterman	279	6	55	1	23	2	447	3
avigation Service (on shore)	118	13	2	.	6	.	70	9
eaman (Merchant Service)	11253	.	36	.	1066	.	4714	.
ilot	388	.	.	.	38	.	105	.
hip Steward, Cook	334	20	2	.	56	1	330	11
oatman on Seas	408	.	.	.	44	.	161	.
arbour, Dock, Wharf, Lighthouse, Service	715	5	11	1	67	.	353	2
4. *In Storage.*								
Varehouseman (not Manchester)	437	12	15	1	31	1	199	7
eter, Weigher	40	.	1	.	7	.	11	.
. *In conveying Messages, Porterage, &c.*								
essenger, Porter, Watchman (not Railway nor Government)	6953	104	825	11	594	4	2778	51
elegraph, Telephone, Service	342	102	39	14	22	10	136	38

Table 10 *continued*.—Occupations of Males and Females in the South-Western Division and its Registration Counties, and in each Urban Sanitary District of which the Population exceeds 50,000 Persons.

Occupations.	South-Western Counties.		Registration Counties.					
			17. Wiltshire.		18. Dorsetshire.		19. Devonshire.	
	Males.	Females.	Males.	Females.	Males.	Females.	Males.	Females.
IV. AGRICULTURAL CLASS.								
7. Persons engaged in Agriculture.								
1. *In Fields and Pastures.*								
Farmer, Grazier	29001	2071	2869	202	2163	177	9229	525
Farmer's, Grazier's—Son, Grandson, Brother, Nephew*	11827	.	962	.	662	.	4382	.
Farm Bailiff	1626	.	378	.	266	.	402	.
Agricultural Labourer, Farm Servant, Cottager	106987	6820	21611	1884	14822	787	29282	1196
Shepherd	2963	.	1277	.	759	.	310	.
Land Drainage Service (not in towns)	162	.	18	.	17	.	61	.
Agricultural Machine—Proprietor, Attendant	366	3	131	1	73	.	58	.
Agricultural Student, Pupil	101	.	30	.	13	.	23	.
Others engaged in, or connected with, Agriculture	137	36	6	1	3	.	13	.
2. *In Woods.*								
Woodman	1142	.	318	.	404	.	123	.
3. *In Gardens.*								
Nurseryman, Seedsman, Florist	556	39	85	4	65	5	198	10
Gardener (not domestic)	9295	322	1410	22	1103	15	3174	52
8. Persons engaged about Animals.								
1. *About Animals.*								
Horse Proprietor, Breeder, Dealer	141	.	35	.	26	.	33	.
Groom, Horse-keeper, Horse-breaker	3250	4	967	.	607	1	754	5
Veterinary Surgeon, Farrier	435	.	68	.	61	.	133	.
Cattle, Sheep, Pig—Dealer, Salesman	563	1	80	.	91	.	134	.
Drover	184	.	27	.	20	.	52	.
Gamekeeper	1464	.	284	.	284	.	384	.
Dog, Bird, Animal—Keeper, Dealer	122	27	22	3	17	5	31	7
Vermin destroyer	47	.	10	.	3	.	16	.
Fisherman	9544	13	2	.	367	3	1822	4
Knacker, Catsmeat Dealer, &c., &c.	10	2	.	.	.	.	1	2
V. INDUSTRIAL CLASS.								
9. Persons working and dealing in Books, Prints, and Maps.								
1. *Books.*								
Publisher, Bookseller, Librarian	461	133	50	7	40	15	166	61
Music—Publisher, Seller, Printer	36	23	4	4	4	4	13	10
Bookbinder	252	202	23	3	21	.	61	58
Printer	2393	38	255	.	222	1	972	12
Newspaper Agent, News Room Keeper	266	38	32	3	38	4	114	19
Others	.	.	.	.	.	.	.	.
2. *Prints and Maps.*								
Lithographer, Lithographic Printer	119	.	5	.	1	.	49	.
Copper Plate and Steel Plate Printer	5	.	1	.	.	.	2	.
Map and Print—Colourer, Seller	2	.	.	.	.	.	1	.
10. Persons working and dealing in Machines and Implements.								
1. *Machines.*								
Engine, Machine, Maker	1967	9	664	1	109	.	623	7
Millwright	342	.	58	.	22	.	141	.
Fitter, Turner (Engine and Machine)	2961	.	1138	.	129	.	858	.
Boiler Maker	835	.	296	.	27	.	297	.
Spinning and Weaving Machine Maker	96	3	22	2	18	.	4	.
Agricultural Machine and Implement Maker	190	4	22	2	17	.	76	.
Domestic Machinery—Maker, Dealer	.	.	.	.	.	.	.	.
2. *Tools and Implements.*								
Tool Maker, Dealer	152	1	21	.	3	.	30	1
Cutler, Scissors Maker	128	11	27	6	11	1	40	2
File Maker	3	.	.	.	.	.	1	.
Saw Maker	11	.	3	.	.	.	3	.
Pin Maker	5	1	.	.	.	.	.	.
Needle Maker	3	1	1	.	.	.	1	1
Steel Pen Maker	.	.	.	.	.	.	.	.
Pencil Maker (Wood)	.	.	.	.	.	.	.	.
Domestic Implement Maker	1	.	1	.	.	.	.	.
3. *Watches and Philosophical Instruments.*								
Watch Maker, Clock Maker	1162	28	132	2	117	2	488	12
Philosophical Instrument Maker, Optician	53	2	3	.	3	.	30	2
Electrical Apparatus Maker	49	.	10	.	5	.	17	.
Weighing and Measuring Apparatus Maker	43	.	.	.	1	.	18	.

* Only male relatives living with the farmer or grazier, and, therefore, presumably [illegible]

Table 10 *continued.*—OCCUPATIONS of MALES and FEMALES in the SOUTH-WESTERN DIVISION and its REGISTRATION COUNTIES, and in each URBAN SANITARY DISTRICT of which the POPULATION exceeds 50,000 PERSONS.

OCCUPATIONS.	SOUTH-WESTERN COUNTIES.		REGISTRATION COUNTIES. 17. WILT-SHIRE.		18. DORSET-SHIRE.		19. DEVON-SHIRE.	
	Males.	Females.	Males.	Females.	Males.	Females.	Males.	Females.
4. Surgical Instruments.								
Surgical Instrument Maker	15	9	.	.	.	.	7	3
5. Arms and Ordnance.								
Gunsmith, Gun Manufacturer	78	3	14	.	6	.	31	1
Ordnance Manufacturer	32	.	.	.	1	.	31	.
Sword, Bayonet—Maker, Cutler	.	.	.	.	.	.	.	.
Others	3	.	.	.	.	.	3	.
6. Musical Instruments.								
Musical Instrument Maker, Dealer	239	3	21	.	12	1	98	1
7. Type, Dies, Medals, Coins.								
Type Cutter, Founder	5	.	.	.	2	.	1	.
Die, Seal, Coin, Medal, Maker	4	.	.	.	.	.	.	.
8. Tackle for Sports and Games.								
Toy Maker, Dealer	18	70	2	6	1	8	9	32
Fishing Rod, Tackle, Maker, Dealer	15	6	1	.	1	.	12	6
Apparatus for other Games, Maker, Dealer	7	1	1	.	.	.	4	1
11. PERSONS WORKING AND DEALING IN HOUSES, FURNITURE, AND DECORATIONS.								
1. Houses.								
Builder	2189	7	251	4	344	.	861	2
Carpenter, Joiner	19390	20	2411	5	2014	2	6978	5
Bricklayer	2649	.	934	.	888	.	472	.
Mason	17069	4	1814	.	1287	2	6270	1
Slater, Tiler	97	.	49	.	13	.	9	.
Plasterer, Whitewasher	1884	1	315	1	158	.	722	.
Paperhanger	86	6	8	.	8	.	34	1
Plumber	2023	19	249	7	140	3	955	4
Painter, Glazier	5826	12	674	.	458	.	2068	5
2. Furniture and Fittings.								
Cabinet Maker, Upholsterer	2737	527	292	47	186	30	1078	255
French Polisher	282	26	20	14	12	.	106	9
Furniture Broker, Dealer	168	51	24	5	5	3	70	25
Locksmith, Bellhanger	72	1	11	.	7	.	30	.
Gas Fitter	474	2	58	.	59	.	108	1
House and Shop Fittings—Maker, Dealer	28	1	.	.	.	.	8	1
Funeral Furniture Maker, Undertaker	17	.	.	.	.	.	5	.
Others	3	.	.	.	.	.	.	.
3. House Decorations.								
Wood Carver	152	.	5	.	3	.	70	.
Carver, Gilder	221	6	15	.	12	.	100	5
Dealer in Works of Art	16	7	.	.	5	.	8	3
Figure, Image—Maker, Dealer	12	1	1	.	1	.	5	.
Animal, Bird, &c., Preserver, Naturalist	43	6	9	.	4	1	17	3
Artificial Flower Maker	2	14	.	1	.	.	1	3
12. PERSONS WORKING AND DEALING IN CARRIAGES AND HARNESS.								
1. Carriages.								
Coachmaker	1591	10	212	.	181	.	537	4
Railway Carriage, Railway Wagon, Maker	684	11	602	11	.	.	8	.
Wheelwright	2095	3	236	1	171	1	915	1
Bicycle, Tricycle—Maker, Dealer	9	.	4	.	2	.	1	.
Others	3	.	.	.	.	.	2	.
2. Harness.								
Saddler, Harness, Whip, Maker	1641	37	276	6	164	4	505	17
13. PERSONS WORKING AND DEALING IN SHIPS AND BOATS.								
1. Hull.								
Ship, Boat, Barge, Builder	648	1	.	.	39	.	419	.
Shipwright, Ship Carpenter (ashore)	2791	.	1	.	78	.	1844	.
2. Masts, Rigging, &c.								
Mast, Yard, Oar, Block, Maker	83	.	.	.	3	.	53	.
Ship Rigger, Chandler, Fitter	188	3	.	.	3	.	148	1
Sail Maker	388	4	2	2	22	.	195	2

Table 10 *continued.*—OCCUPATIONS of MALES and FEMALES in the SOUTH-WESTERN DIVISION and its REGISTRATION COUNTIES, and in each URBAN SANITARY DISTRICT of which the POPULATION exceeds 50,000 PERSONS.

OCCUPATIONS.	SOUTH-WESTERN COUNTIES.		REGISTRATION COUNTIES. 17. WILT-SHIRE.		18. DORSET-SHIRE.		19. DEVON-SHIRE.	
	Males.	Females.	Males.	Females.	Males.	Females.	Males.	Females.
14. PERSONS WORKING AND DEALING IN CHEMICALS AND COMPOUNDS.								
1. *Colouring Matter.*								
Dye, Paint, Manufacture	53	8	3	.	.	.	12	7
Ink, Blacking, Colouring Substance, Manufacture	33	31	.	.	.	.	6	29
2. *Explosives.*								
Gunpowder, Guncotton, Explosive Substance, Manufacture	63	7	.	.	.	.	25	.
Fusee, Fireworks, Explosive Article, Manufacture	18	182		.	.	.	1	.
3. *Drugs and other Chemicals and Compounds.*								
Chemist, Druggist	1065	17	107	2	80	.	437	4
Manufacturing Chemist	113	23	3	1	.	.	43	13
Alkali Manufacture	17	.	.	.	.	.	5	.
Drysalter	8	.	.	.	.	.	3	.
15. PERSONS WORKING AND DEALING IN TOBACCO AND PIPES.								
1. *Tobacco and Pipes.*								
Tobacco Manufacturer, Tobacconist	219	188	28	29	9	5	80	33
Tobacco Pipe, Snuff Box, &c., Maker	31	23	1	.	3	.	14	8
16. PERSONS WORKING AND DEALING IN FOOD AND LODGING.								
1. *Board and Lodging.*								
Innkeeper, Hotel Keeper, Publican	4127	1039	596	108	473	124	1439	356
Lodging, Boarding House, Keeper	352	2530	6	80	31	159	162	1178
Coffee, Eating House, Keeper	189	198	27	25	21	10	77	104
2. *Spirituous Drinks.*								
Hop—Merchant, Dealer	6	.	2	.	.	.	5	.
Maltster	722	2	291	1	86	.	193	1
Brewer	1521	34	331	6	219	3	304	4
Beerseller. Ale, Porter, Cider, Dealer	454	183	87	30	44	20	142	48
Cellarman	250	3	23	.	25	.	100	1
Wine, Spirit—Merchant, Agent	442	38	37	1	38	2	194	12
3. *Food.*								
Milkseller, Dairyman	1982	299	199	21	631	9	600	137
Cheesemonger, Butterman	119	33	24	1	15	1	11	13
Butcher, Meat Salesman	5185	328	621	42	537	20	1619	123
Provision Curer, Dealer	291	178	57	70	19	10	113	61
Poulterer, Game Dealer	186	105	21	2	12	4	84	51
Fishmonger	674	251	44	8	63	74	263	129
Corn, Flour, Seed—Merchant, Dealer	581	53	92	4	56	5	190	17
Corn Miller	2091	55	377	6	291	6	848	18
Baker	6100	840	991	161	708	58	2133	381
Confectioner, Pastrycook	590	454	72	53	56	29	203	167
Greengrocer, Fruiterer	662	585	70	37	44	25	216	289
Mustard, Vinegar, Spice, Pickle—Maker, Dealer	6	3	.	.	.	.	1	3
Sugar Refiner	71	7	2	.	1	.	22	4
Grocer. Tea, Coffee, Chocolate—Maker, Dealer	6187	3193	885	304	723	250	1832	871
Ginger Beer, Mineral Water—Manufacturer, Dealer	183	12	27	2	27	1	74	3
Others dealing in Food	.	.	.	.	.	.	.	.
17. PERSONS WORKING AND DEALING IN TEXTILE FABRICS.								
1. *Wool and Worsted.*								
Woolstapler	160	2	49	2	12	.	46	.
Woollen Cloth Manufacture	2620	4246	1440	2446	6	.	300	680
Wool, Woollen goods—Dyer, Printer	160	3	99	.	.	.	13	.
Worsted, Stuff, Manufacture	26	122	5	1	1	.	17	83
Flannel Manufacture	.	.	.	.	.	.	.	.
Blanket Manufacture	21	2	.	.	1	.	6	.
Fuller	20	1	2	.	.	.	5	.
Cloth, Worsted, Stuff, Flannel, Blanket, Dealer	48	5	13	.	.	.	22	1
Others	9	2	.	.	.	.	7	2
2. *Silk.*								
Silk, Silk goods, Manufacture	276	1556	108	560	33	182	25	51
Silk Dyer, Printer	6	1	.	.	3	.	3	.
Ribbon Manufacture	.	2	.	2	.	.	.	.
Crape, Gauze, Manufacture	7	86	.	.	.	.	.	4
Silk Merchant, Dealer	34	25	2	.	2	7	15	16

Table 10 *continued.*—OCCUPATIONS of MALES and FEMALES in the SOUTH-WESTERN DIVISION and its REGISTRATION COUNTIES, and in each URBAN SANITARY DISTRICT of which the POPULATION exceeds 50,000 PERSONS.

OCCUPATIONS.	SOUTH-WESTERN COUNTIES.		REGISTRATION COUNTIES.					
			17. WILTSHIRE.		18. DORSETSHIRE.		19. DEVONSHIRE.	
	Males.	Females.	Males.	Females.	Males.	Females.	Males.	Females.
3. Cotton and Flax								
Cotton, Cotton goods, Manufacture	66	75	1	1	28	7	20	8
Cotton, Calico—Printer, Dyer, Bleacher	5	.	.	.	3	.	2	.
Cotton, Calico—Warehouseman, Dealer	11	6	.	1	.	.	11	1
Flax, Linen—Manufacturer, Dealer	267	239	9	7	44	55	20	10
Lace Manufacturer, Dealer	613	3457	.	17	1	20	355	3073
Fustian Manufacturer, Dealer	.	.	.	.	.	.	.	.
Tape Manufacturer, Dealer	.	.	.	.	.	.	.	.
Thread Manufacturer, Dealer	3	43	.	.	1	41	.	1
4. Hemp and other Fibrous Materials.								
Hemp, Jute, Cocoa Fibre, Manufacture	72	109	13	12	11	.	.	.
Rope, Twine, Cord—Maker, Dealer	1525	696	82	15	554	564	363	36
Mat Maker, Seller	65	20	30	6	.	.	11	3
Net Maker	118	524	1	1	104	391	1	14
Canvas, Sailcloth, Manufacture	139	101	.	1	32	25	18	7
Sacking, Sack, Bag—Maker, Dealer	41	48	18	7	7	11	10	13
Others working and dealing in Hemp	8	1	4		1	.	2	1
5. Mixed or Unspecified Materials.								
Weaver (undefined)	54	76	7	1	1		5	20
Dyer, Printer, Scourer, Bleacher, Calenderer (undefined)	151	85	10	5	8	3	68	49
Factory hand (Textile, undefined)	80	117	6	6	16	45	38	6
Felt Manufacture	27	2	26	1	.	.	.	1
Carpet, Rug, Manufacture	125	132	55	82	3	4	10	2
Manchester Warehouseman	4	.	.	.	.	.	.	.
Draper, Linen Draper, Mercer	3389	4152	379	317	328	336	1197	1604
Fancy Goods (Textile), Manufacturer, Worker, Dealer	8	433	.	52	1	43	2	160
Trimming Maker, Dealer	2	9	.	1	1		1	4
Embroiderer	1	21	.	2	.	.	1	7
Others	140	86	4	1	3	3	1	.
18. PERSONS WORKING AND DEALING IN DRESS.								
1. Dress.								
Hatter, Hat Manufacture (not straw)	201	63	13	3	10	1	78	21
Straw—Hat, Bonnet, Plait, Manufacture	5	178	.	27	.	24	1	40
Tailor	7381	4607	726	320	683	281	3168	1540
Milliner, Dressmaker, Staymaker	113	33228	3	2700	.	3044	12	13427
Shawl Manufacture	.	.	.	.	.	.	.	.
Shirt Maker, Seamstress	95	6938	1	535	2	834	21	2806
Hosiery Manufacture	9	110	.	.	1	3	5	30
Hosier, Haberdasher	78	82	13	8	1	1	27	60
Glover, Glove Maker	921	7812	15	180	38	2142	59	1188
Button Maker, Dealer	6	2	1	1	2	1	1	.
Shoe, Boot—Maker, Dealer	13857	1962	1365	82	1175	58	4701	623
Patten, Clog, Maker	11	1	1	.	1	.	3	.
Wig Maker, Hairdresser	705	37	72	6	67	4	270	15
Umbrella, Parasol, Stick—Maker, Dealer	103	73	17	7	10	7	45	38
Accoutrement Maker	1	.	.	.	.	.	1	.
Old Clothes Dealer, and others	11	52	1	4	2	3	6	21
19. PERSONS WORKING AND DEALING IN VARIOUS ANIMAL SUBSTANCES.								
1. In Grease, Gut, Bone, Horn, Ivory, and Whalebone.								
Tallow Chandler, Candle, Grease, Manufacture	152	8	24	1	11	.	87	5
Soap Boiler, Maker	63	5	6	.	9	.	40	5
Glue, Size, Gelatine, Isinglass—Maker, Dealer	29	1	.		.	.	3	1
Manure Manufacture	145	4	4	.	1	.	62	3
Bone, Horn, Ivory, Tortoise-shell—Worker, Dealer	6	.	.	.	.	.	3	.
Comb Maker	2		1	.	.	.	.	.
Others	10	.	2	.	.	.	2	.
2. In Skins.								
Furrier, Skinner	55	34	16	1	2	1	13	15
Tanner, Fellmonger	1248	11	36	5	74	.	531	4
Currier	788	14	121	3	34	.	246	6
Leather Goods, Portmanteau, Bag, Strap, &c.—Maker, Dealer	89	17	6	.	5	2	35	8
Parchment, Vellum—Maker, Dealer	13	.	9	.	.	.	.	.
3. In Hair and Feathers.								
Hair, Bristle—Worker, Dealer	76	195	12	5	.	1	.	4
Brush, Broom, Maker	536	152	72	12	57	11	155	43
Quill, Feather—Dresser, Dealer	3	27	1	2	.	1	2	18

Table 10 *continued*.—Occupations of Males and Females in the South-western Division and its Registration Counties, and in each Urban Sanitary District of which the Population exceeds 50,000 Persons.

Occupations.	South-Western Counties.		Registration Counties. 17. Wiltshire.		18. Dorsetshire.		19. Devonshire.	
	Males.	Females.	Males.	Females.	Males.	Females.	Males.	Females.
20. Persons working and dealing in various Vegetable Substances.								
1. In Oils, Gums, and Resins.								
Oil Miller, Oil Cake—Maker, Dealer	70	2	9	.	5	1	16	1
Oil and Colourman	76	5	3	.	8	.	29	4
Floor Cloth, Oil Cloth, Manufacture	65	1	.	.	.	.	.	.
Japanner	11	2	.	.	1	.	4	2
India Rubber, Gutta Percha—Worker, Dealer	60	10	53	7	.	.	5	.
Waterproof Goods—Maker, Dealer	15	2	1	.	.	1	3	1
Others	16	.	.	.	.	.	.	.
2. In Cane, Rush, and Straw.								
Willow, Cane, Rush—Worker, Dealer, Basketmaker	828	136	96	18	85	7	278	40
Hay, Straw (not plait), Chaff—Cutter, Dealer	105	1	13	.	11	.	14	.
Thatcher	1488	.	201	.	246	.	603	.
3. In Wood and Bark.								
Timber, Wood—Merchant, Dealer	565	23	73	3	52	1	181	6
Sawyer	2029	.	444	.	256	.	882	.
Lath, Wooden Fence, Hurdle, Maker	277	.	77	.	67	.	42	.
Wood Turner, Box Maker	299	9	30	4	12	.	108	1
Cooper, Hoop Maker, Bender	917	3	85	.	82	.	257	3
Cork, Bark—Cutter, Worker, Dealer	57	2	4	.	1	.	35	2
Others	5	.	.	.	.	.	.	.
4. In Paper.								
Paper Manufacture	338	890	26	24	15	11	416	369
Envelope Maker	2	18	.	.	.	.	.	2
Stationer, Law Stationer	205	311	52	23	22	28	92	129
Card, Pattern Card, Maker	4	6	.	.	.	.	1	.
Paper Stainer	18	.	.	.	.	.	13	.
Paper Box, Paper Bag, Maker	42	176	3	.	.	1	10	60
Ticket, Label, Writer	14	2	1	.	1	.	6	2
Others	131	.	18	.	9	.	42	.
21. Persons working and dealing in various Mineral Substances.								
1. Miners.								
Coal Miner	5182	9	.	.	58	.	46	.
Ironstone Miner	591	4	8	.	.	.	158	.
Copper Miner	3266	283	1	.	.	.	1363	85
Tin Miner	10409	1903	.	.	.	.	156	3
Lead Miner	486	16	.	.	.	.	43	1
Miner in other, or undefined, Minerals	472	33	8	.	7	.	197	14
Mine Service	112	2	2	.	.	.	15	1
2. Coal, Coal Gas, &c.								
Coal Merchant, Dealer	1125	71	171	14	108	.	351	23
Coalheaver	760	.	93	.	79	.	290	.
Coke, Charcoal, Peat—Cutter, Burner, Dealer	37	.	8	.	1	.	12	.
Gas Works Service	599	.	76	.	58	.	220	.
3. Stone, Clay, and Road Making.								
Stone Quarrier	2855	.	896	.	677	.	436	.
Stone Cutter, Dresser, Dealer	957	.	63	.	42	.	261	.
Slate Quarrier	516	.	.	.	.	.	75	.
Slate Worker, Dealer	159	1	1	.	.	.	75	1
Limeburner	350	6	30	3	30	.	90	1
Clay, Sand, Gravel, Chalk—Labourer, Dealer	2030	38	7	.	268	.	401	3
Fossil, Coprolite—Digger, Dealer	2	1	.	1	.	.	2	.
Well Sinker, Borer	26	.	5	.	6	.	4	.
Plaster, Cement, Manufacture	65	.	15	.	12	.	19	.
Brick, Tile—Maker, Burner, Dealer	2133	17	272	4	356	.	369	4
Paviour	44	.	.	.	4	.	29	.
Road Contractor, Surveyor, Inspector	400	.	42	.	29	.	157	.
Road Labourer	1115	.	153	.	98	.	198	.
Railway Contractor	61	.	13	.	3	.	25	.
Platelayer	838	.	154	.	96	.	324	.
Railway Labourer, Navvy	2811	.	655	.	223	.	848	.
Others	12	21	.	3	2	4	3	4
4. Earthenware and Glass.								
Earthenware, China, Porcelain, Manufacture	613	86	7	.	221	4	232	66
Glass Manufacture	55	1	2	.	6	.	18	1
Earthenware, China, Glass, Dealer	261	131	29	14	25	14	118	52
5. Salt.								
Salt Maker, Dealer	8	2	.	.	2	.	3	.

Table 10 *continued.*—OCCUPATIONS of MALES and FEMALES in the SOUTH-WESTERN DIVISION and its REGISTRATION COUNTIES, and in each URBAN SANITARY DISTRICT of which the POPULATION exceeds 50,000 PERSONS.

OCCUPATIONS.	SOUTH-WESTERN COUNTIES.		REGISTRATION COUNTIES. 17. WILTSHIRE.		18. DORSETSHIRE.		19. DEVONSHIRE.	
	Males.	Females.	Males.	Females.	Males.	Females.	Males.	Females.
6. Water.								
Waterworks Service	79	1	9	.	4	.	39	1
Others	18	2	8	.	2	.	3	.
7. Precious Metals and Jewellery.								
Goldsmith, Silversmith, Jeweller	475	61	31	5	41	2	211	35
Gold, Silver, Beater	.	.	.	.	.	.	.	.
Lapidary	34	8	.	.	.	.	4	2
Others	.	1	.	.	.	.	.	1
8. Iron and Steel.								
Blacksmith	9644	30	1218	8	941	6	3140	4
Whitesmith	306	.	88	.	44	.	148	.
Nail Manufacture	41	2	8	.	.	.	4	.
Anchor, Chain, Manufacture	7	.	2	.	.	.	1	.
Other Iron and Steel Manufactures	2497	3	866	1	175	1	465	1
Ironmonger, Hardware Dealer, Merchant	1272	89	161	3	125	3	507	44
9. Copper.								
Copper, Copper goods—Manufacturer, Worker, Dealer	143	1	36	.	5	.	67	.
10. Tin and Zinc.								
Tin, Tin Plate, Tin goods—Manufacturer, Worker, Dealer	968	12	116	2	87	.	231	2
Zinc, Zinc Goods—Manufacturer, Worker, Dealer	6	5	1	.	.	.	3	.
11. Lead.								
Lead, Leaden goods—Manufacturer, Worker, Dealer	72	1	1	.		.	10	1
12. In Other, Mixed, or Unspecified, Metals.								
Metal Refiner, Worker, Turner, Dealer	66	1	18	.	3	.	6	.
Brass, Bronze, Manufacture. Brazier	482	2	49	.	16	.	174	1
Metal Burnisher, Lacquerer	1	2	.	.	.	.	1	2
White Metal, Plated Ware, Manufacture. Pewterer	34	1	7	.	4	.	4	.
Wire Maker, Worker, Weaver, Drawer	65	3	1	.	16	1	20	1
Bolt, Nut, Rivet, Screw, Staple, Maker	31	2	20	.	3	1	1	.
Lamp, Lantern, Candlestick, Maker	11	.	3	.	.	.	7	.
Clasp, Buckle, Hinge, Maker	1	.	.	.	1	.	.	.
Fancy Chain, Gilt Toy, Maker	.	.	.	.	.	.	.	.
Others	2	.	.	.	.	.	.	.
22. PERSONS WORKING AND DEALING IN GENERAL OR UNSPECIFIED COMMODITIES.								
1. Makers and Dealers (General or Undefined).								
General Shopkeeper, Dealer	1694	2177	244	199	200	193	538	821
Pawnbroker	166	46	11	.	6	.	78	26
Costermonger, Huckster, Street Seller	1764	940	257	101	269	76	381	377
Manufacturer, Manager, Superintendent (undefined)	125	7	7	2	12	1	65	2
Contractor (undefined)	113	1	7	.	21	.	44	1
2. Mechanics and Labourers (General or Undefined).								
General Labourer	37140	269	6271	72	4206	43	11511	23
Engine Driver, Stoker, Fireman (not railway, marine, nor agricultural)	2194	.	207	.	140	.	392	.
Artisan, Mechanic (undefined)	391	25	45	1	25	.	158	18
Apprentice (undefined)	274	71	35	3	28	8	110	27
Factory Labourer (undefined)	1138	132	929	11	26	2	88	61
Machinist, Machine Worker (undefined)	120	2	23	.	13	.	51	2
23. PERSONS WORKING AND DEALING IN REFUSE MATTERS.								
1. Refuse Matters.								
Town Drainage Service	5	.	.	.	.	.	1	.
Chimney Sweep, Soot Merchant	410	4	62	.	57	.	144	.
Scavenger, Crossing Sweeper	94	.	9	.	9	.	34	.
Rag Gatherer, Dealer	54	79	12	1	7	19	16	49
VI. UNOCCUPIED CLASS.								
24. PERSONS WITHOUT SPECIFIED OCCUPATIONS								
Persons returned by Property, Rank, &c., and not by special occupation	229493	611776	30776	81146	23063	59016	74844	199444
Children under 5 years of age	114996	114631	16370	16419	11481	11582	36768	35475

Table 10 *continued.*—OCCUPATIONS of MALES and FEMALES in the SOUTH-WESTERN DIVISION and its REGISTRATION COUNTIES, and in each URBAN SANITARY DISTRICT of which the POPULATION exceeds 50,000 PERSONS.

OCCUPATIONS.	REGISTRATION COUNTIES.				URBAN SANITARY DISTRICTS.*			
	20. CORNWALL.		21. SOMERSETSHIRE.		PLYMOUTH.		BATH.	
	Males.	Females.	Males.	Females.	Males.	Females.	Males.	Females.
TOTAL	153015	173360	231394	259208	33750	40044	21020	30794
2. PROFESSIONAL CLASS.								
1. PERSONS ENGAGED IN THE GENERAL OR LOCAL GOVERNMENT OF THE COUNTRY.								
1. *National Government.*								
Peer, M.P., Privy Councillor (not otherwise described)	2	.	2	.	.	.	1	.
Civil Service (officers and clerks)	178	60	289	86	130	4	48	2
Civil Service (messengers, &c.)	226	42	406	83	76	.	71	.
Prison Officer, &c.	12	4	43	11	8	5	.	2
2. *Local Government.*								
Police	254	.	404	.	98	.	85	.
Municipal, Parish, Union, District Officer	130	45	242	62	39	9	29	8
Other Local or County Official	84	.	187	.	23	.	42	.
3. *East Indian and Colonial Service.*								
East Indian and Colonial Service	1	.	4	.	.	.	1	.
2. PERSONS ENGAGED IN THE DEFENCE OF THE COUNTRY.								
1. *Army (at Home).*								
Army Officer (effective or retired)	67	.	330	.	67	.	162	.
Soldier and Non-Commissioned Officer	345	.	231	.	608	.	11	.
Militia, Yeomanry, Volunteers	236	.	143	.	11	.	46	.
Army Pensioner	86	.	234	.	78	.	38	.
2. *Navy (ashore or in port).*								
Navy Officer (effective or retired)	153	.	63	.	114	.	21	.
Seaman, R.N.	1051	.	37	.	449	.	.	.
Royal Marines (officers and men)	56	.	19	.	53	.	2	.
Navy Pensioner	711	2	108	6	594	1	13	.
3. PERSONS ENGAGED IN PROFESSIONAL OCCUPATIONS (WITH THEIR IMMEDIATE SUBORDINATES).								
1. *Clerical Profession.*								
Clergyman (Established Church)	312	.	788	.	38	.	109	.
Roman Catholic Priest	7	.	54	.	5	.	13	.
Minister, Priest, of other religious bodies	190	.	252	.	22	.	31	.
Missionary, Scripture Reader, Itinerant Preacher	28	20	72	25	18	14	8	8
Nun, Sister of Charity	.	18	.	127	.	14	.	.
Theological Student	27	.	55	.	13	.	17	.
Church, Chapel, Cemetery—Officer, Servant	36	15	96	44	7	16	11	14
2. *Legal Profession.*								
Barrister, Solicitor	136	.	321	.	52	.	74	.
Law Student	8	.	19	.	5	.	8	.
Law Clerk, and others connected with Law	211	.	430	.	72	.	77	.
3. *Medical Profession.*								
Physician, Surgeon, General Practitioner	158	.	314	.	43	.	66	.
Dentist	19	.	50	.	26	.	18	.
Medical Student, Assistant	38	.	64	.	10	.	13	.
Midwife	.	25	.	48	.	5	.	7
Subordinate Medical Service	10	460	22	971	11	181	5	204
4. *Teachers.*								
Schoolmaster	586	1155	832	2278	100	408	85	253
Teacher, Professor, Lecturer	27	277	124	812	26	63	37	151
School Service, and others concerned in Teaching	10	5	15	32	3	.	3	8
5. *Literary and Scientific Persons.*								
Author, Editor, Journalist	12	1	25	10	11	1	10	2
Reporter, Short-hand Writer	8	.	38	.	7	.	11	.
Persons engaged in Scientific Pursuits	6	.	11	.	4	.	3	.
Literary, Scientific, Institution, Service, &c.	6	.	8	2	2	1	4	1
6. *Engineers and Surveyors.*								
Civil Engineer	57	.	73	.	25	.	17	.
Mining Engineer	118	.	33	.	3	.	.	.
Land, House, Ship, Surveyor	78	.	100	.	10	.	22	.
7. *Artists.*								
Painter (artist)	34	13	60	29	32	6	33	13
Engraver (artist)	2	.	18	.	3	.	7	.
Sculptor	4	.	12	.	3	1	2	.
Architect	24	.	49	.	13	.	10	.
Musician, Music Master	67	69	210	201	76	53	86	78
Art Student	4	16	20	7	6	2	5	4
Photographer	39	5	110	22	33	7	46	5
Actor	17	10	19	17	8	8	11	11
Art, Music, Theatre, Service	3	1	9	.	6	.	4	.

* A portion of the City of Bristol is situated in this Division, but the Occupations for the entire City are returned in Division VI.

Table 10 *continued*.—OCCUPATIONS of MALES and FEMALES in the SOUTH-WESTERN DIVISION and its REGISTRATION COUNTIES, and in each URBAN SANITARY DISTRICT of which the POPULATION exceeds 50,000 PERSONS.

OCCUPATIONS.	REGISTRATION COUNTIES.				URBAN SANITARY DISTRICTS.			
	20. CORNWALL.		21. SOMERSETSHIRE.		PLYMOUTH.		BATH.	
	Males.	Females.	Males.	Females.	Males.	Females.	Males.	Females.
8. *Persons engaged in Exhibitions, Shows, Games, &c.*								
Performer, Showman, Exhibition, Service	1	.	7	5	5	1	.	.
Billiard, Cricket, & other Games, Service	20	.	39	.	16	1	12	.
IX. DOMESTIC CLASS.								
4. PERSONS ENGAGED IN DOMESTIC OFFICES OR SERVICES.								
1. *Domestic Service.*								
Domestic Coachman, Groom	487	.	1305	.	71	.	176	.
Domestic Gardener	385	.	1639	3	105	.	213	.
Domestic Indoor Servant	357	15477	943	27499	56	3870	200	3984
Lodge, Gate, Park, Keeper (not Government)	4	6	14	21	3	1	2	.
Inn, Hotel, Servant	133	208	351	413	71	79	83	94
College, Club, Service	.	.	18	5	4	3	10	.
2. *Other Service.*								
Office Keeper (not Government)	3	20	8	17	3	7	4	5
Cook (not domestic)	2	2	13	7	6	2	7	4
Charwoman	.	2184	.	1905	.	646	.	413
Washing and Bathing Service	3	974	38	6453	6	668	13	1007
Hospital and Institution Service	38	70	94	227	6	37	11	63
Others engaged in Service	3	1	8	6	2	1	2	2
III. COMMERCIAL CLASS.								
5. PERSONS ENGAGED IN COMMERCIAL OCCUPATIONS.								
1. *Merchants and Agents.*								
Merchant	80	2	54	.	20	.	13	.
Broker, Agent, Factor	143	2	233	9	86	2	41	3
Auctioneer, Appraiser, Valuer, House Agent	86	.	157	.	16	.	34	.
Accountant	224	2	338	2	106	3	74	.
Salesman, Buyer (not otherwise described)	6	2	9	10	5	2	5	2
Commercial Traveller	117	.	456	.	213	.	122	.
Commercial Clerk	411	17	1514	48	393	23	224	19
Officer of Commercial Company, Guild, Society, &c.	1	.	5	.	3	.	1	.
2. *Dealers in Money.*								
Banker	35	.	37	.	2	.	7	.
Bank Service	137	.	207	.	44	.	42	.
Bill Discounter, Bill Broker, Finance Agent	1	.	4	.	5	.	.	.
3. *Persons occupied in Insurance.*								
Life, House, Ship, &c., Insurance Service	105	3	185	3	50	1	21	.
6. PERSONS ENGAGED IN CONVEYANCE OF MEN, GOODS, AND MESSAGES.								
1. *On Railways.*								
Railway Engine Driver, Stoker	71	.	320	.	70	.	16	.
Railway Guard	47	.	148	.	35	.	3	.
Pointsman, Level Crossing Man	17	6	87	.	6	.	3	.
Other Railway Officials and Servants	363	2	1677	9	231	1	146	.
2. *On Roads.*								
Toll Collector, Turnpike Gate Keeper	3	9	17	7	3	.	3	1
Omnibus, Coach, Cab, Owner—Livery Stable Keeper	67	5	133	7	32	1	53	4
Cabman, Flyman, Coachman (not domestic)	258	.	587	.	141	.	181	.
Carman, Carrier, Carter, Haulier	587	11	1732	28	242	1	201	.
Tramway Companies' Service	.	.	44	.	21	.	12	.
Wheel Chair Proprietor, Attendant, &c.	.	.	121	.	1	.	85	.
3. *On Canals, Rivers and Seas.*								
Inland Navigation Service	6	.	34	1	4	.	2	1
Bargeman, Lighterman, Waterman	206	.	141	.	127	1	51	.
Navigation Service (on shore)	25	2	10	2	15	.	2	.
Seaman (Merchant Service)	4372	.	1075	.	1547	.	12	.
Pilot	198	.	47	.	20	.	.	.
Ship Steward, Cook	200	4	27	4	107	3	3	1
Boatman on Seas	125	.	75	.	29	.	.	.
Harbour, Dock, Wharf, Lighthouse, Service	176	1	208	1	147	.	4	.
4. *In Storage.*								
Warehouseman (not Manchester)	44	.	148	3	69	1	8	.
Meter, Weigher	12	.	9	.	8	.	.	.
5. *In conveying Messages, Porterage, &c.*								
Messenger, Porter, Watchman (not Railway nor Government)	533	21	2223	17	693	1	715	7
Telegraph, Telephone, Service	81	18	71	22	37		10	.

Table 10 *continued*.—OCCUPATIONS of MALES and FEMALES in the SOUTH-WESTERN DIVISION and its REGISTRATION COUNTIES, and in each URBAN SANITARY DISTRICT of which the POPULATION exceeds 50,000 PERSONS.

OCCUPATIONS.	REGISTRATION COUNTIES.				URBAN SANITARY DISTRICTS.			
	20. CORNWALL.		21. SOMERSETSHIRE.		PLYMOUTH.		BATH.	
	Males.	Females.	Males.	Females.	Males.	Females.	Males.	Females.
IV. AGRICULTURAL CLASS.								
7. PERSONS ENGAGED IN AGRICULTURE.								
1. *In Fields and Pastures.*								
Farmer, Grazier	7722	863	7078	502	21	2	25	2
Farmer's, Grazier's—Son, Grandson, Brother, Nephew*	3097	.	2724	.	7	.	7	.
Farm Bailiff	193	.	387	.	2	.	2	.
Agricultural Labourer, Farm Servant, Cottager	15393	1291	26479	1662	71	8	175	13
Shepherd	73	.	544	.	.	.	1	.
Land Drainage Service (not in towns)	11	.	55	.	.	.	.	.
Agricultural Machine—Proprietor, Attendant	22	.	82	2	.	.	.	.
Agricultural Student, Pupil	16	.	19	.	.	.	.	.
Others engaged in, or connected with, Agriculture	1	.	114	35	.	.	.	.
2. *In Woods.*								
Woodman	158	.	134	.	.	.	.	.
3. *In Gardens.*								
Nurseryman, Seedsman, Florist	47	3	161	17	15	1	30	4
Gardener (not domestic)	1179	182	2427	73	50	1	307	
8. PERSONS ENGAGED ABOUT ANIMALS.								
1. *About Animals.*								
Horse Proprietor, Breeder, Dealer	.	.	47	.	5	.	3	.
Groom, Horse-keeper, Horse-breaker	233	.	629	1	107	.	75	1
Veterinary Surgeon, Farrier	46	.	157	.	12	.	22	.
Cattle, Sheep, Pig—Dealer, Salesman	71	1	187	.	7	.	1	.
Drover	11	.	74	.	19	.	4	.
Gamekeeper	116	.	336	.	.	.	.	.
Dog, Bird, Animal—Keeper, Dealer	12	4	40	8	2	.	8	1
Vermin destroyer	4	.	14	.	.	.	.	.
Fisherman	4394	6	59	.	497	2	1	.
Knacker, Catsmeat Dealer, &c., &c.	6	.	3	.	.	.	1	.
V. INDUSTRIAL CLASS.								
9. PERSONS WORKING AND DEALING IN BOOKS, PRINTS, AND MAPS.								
1. *Books.*								
Publisher, Bookseller, Librarian	45	16	146	34	36	5	54	8
Music—Publisher, Seller, Printer	.	.	15	5	2	2	9	.
Bookbinder	77	3	110	138	34	30	27	7
Printer	311	2	933	23	279	2	173	1
Newspaper Agent, News Room Keeper	9	2	73	11	27	2	13	3
Others	.		.	.	.	.	.	.
2. *Prints and Maps.*								
Lithographer, Lithographic Printer	2	.	62	.	22	.	4	.
Copper Plate and Steel Plate Printer	.	.	2	.	1	.	1	.
Map and Print—Colourer, Seller	1	.	.	.	.	.	.	.
10. PERSONS WORKING AND DEALING IN MACHINES AND IMPLEMENTS.								
1. *Machines.*								
Engine, Machine, Maker	226	.	345	1	64	1	44	.
Millwright	53	.	68	.	10	.	2	.
Fitter, Turner (Engine and Machine)	325	.	516	.	101	.	52	.
Boiler Maker	111	.	114	.	35	.	10	.
Spinning and Weaving Machine Maker	.	.	52	1	.	.	.	.
Agricultural Machine and Implement Maker	25	.	50	2	.	.	4	1
Domestic Machinery—Maker, Dealer	.	.	.	.	.	.	.	.
2. *Tools and Implements.*								
Tool Maker, Dealer	4	.	94	.	3	.	1	.
Cutler, Scissors Maker	14	1	27	1	11	1	6	1
File Maker	.	.	2	.	1	.	.	.
Saw Maker	1	.	2	.	3	.	.	.
Pin Maker	.	.	5	1	.	.	1	.
Needle Maker	.	.	1	.	.	.	.	.
Steel Pen Maker	.	.	.	.	.	.	.	.
Pencil Maker (Wood)	.	.	.	.	.	.	.	.
Domestic Implement Maker	.	.	.	.	.	.	.	.
3. *Watches and Philosophical Instruments.*								
Watch Maker, Clock Maker	156	5	290	7	86	3	74	2
Philosophical Instrument Maker, Optician	4	.	13	.	14	.	4	.
Electrical Apparatus Maker	5	.	12	.	4	.	.	.
Weighing and Measuring Apparatus Maker		.	22	.		.	4	

* Only male relatives living with the farmer or grazier, and, therefore, presumably engaged in agriculture, are included above.

ble 10 *continued.*—OCCUPATIONS of MALES and FEMALES in the SOUTH-WESTERN DIVISION and its REGISTRATION COUNTIES, and in each URBAN SANITARY DISTRICT of which the POPULATION exceeds 50,000 PERSONS.

OCCUPATIONS.	REGISTRATION COUNTIES.				URBAN SANITARY DISTRICTS.			
	20. CORNWALL.		21. SOMERSETSHIRE.		PLYMOUTH.		BATH.	
	Males.	Females.	Males.	Females.	Males.	Females.	Males.	Females.
4. *Surgical Instruments.*								
urgical Instrument Maker	2	.	6	6	3	1	4	2
5. *Arms and Ordnance.*								
unsmith, Gun Manufacturer	1	.	26	2	10	.	5	.
rdnance Manufacturer	.	.	.	.	.	.	.	.
word, Bayonet—Maker, Cutler	.	.	.	.	.	.	.	.
thers	.	.	.	.	.	.	.	.
6. *Musical Instruments.*								
usical Instrument Maker, Dealer	18	.	90	1	35	1	41	.
7. *Type, Dies, Medals, Coins.*								
ype Cutter, Founder	.	.	2	.	.	.	2	.
ie, Seal, Coin, Medal, Maker	1	.	3	.	.	.	.	.
8. *Tackle for Sports and Games.*								
oy Maker, Dealer	2	3	4	21	1	2	1	13
ishing Rod, Tackle, Maker, Dealer	.	.	1	.	1	.	.	.
pparatus for other Games, Maker, Dealer	1	.	1	.	1	.	.	.
11. PERSONS WORKING AND DEALING IN HOUSES, FURNITURE, AND DECORATIONS.								
1. *Houses.*								
Builder	312	1	521	.	110	.	47	.
Carpenter, Joiner	3084	4	4055	3	881	.	463	1
Bricklayer	16	.	339	.	21	.	18	.
Mason	3445	1	4753	.	644	.	593	.
Slater, Tiler	.	.	26	.	.	.	1	.
Plasterer, Whitewasher	66	.	624	.	223	.	101	.
Paperhanger	.	3	36	2	7	.	14	1
Plumber	187	3	402	2	192	2	84	.
Painter, Glazier	426	2	1700	5	382	.	491	.
2. *Furniture and Fittings.*								
Cabinet Maker, Upholsterer	266	34	915	161	188	58	304	69
French Polisher	9	.	135	3	35	6	84	.
Furniture Broker, Dealer	5	3	62	15	18	10	21	4
Locksmith, Bellhanger	1	.	23	1	8	.	8	.
Gas Fitter	24	.	225	1	18	.	94	.
House and Shop Fittings—Maker, Dealer	1	.	19	.	1	.	13	.
Funeral Furniture Maker, Undertaker	1	.	11	.	1	.	4	.
Others	.	.	3	.	.	.	2	.
3. *House Decorations.*								
Wood Carver	8	.	66	.	23	.	36	.
Carver, Gilder	14	.	80	1	33	2	44	1
Dealer in Works of Art	.	.	3	4	1	.	2	3
Figure, Image—Maker, Dealer	1	.	4	1	1	.	2	.
Animal, Bird, &c., Preserver, Naturalist	2	.	11	2	2	1	4	1
Artificial Flower Maker	.	1	1	8	.	1	.	6
12. PERSONS WORKING AND DEALING IN CARRIAGES AND HARNESS.								
1. *Carriages.*								
Coachmaker	220	1	471	5	78	.	154	1
Railway Carriage, Railway Wagon, Maker	10	.	64	.	.	.	.	.
Wheelwright	247	.	536	.	59	.	41	.
Bicycle, Tricycle—Maker, Dealer	.	.	2	.	1	.	.	.
Others	1	.	.	.	.	.	.	.
2. *Harness.*								
Saddler, Harness, Whip, Maker	241	2	455	8	41	1	44	2
13. PERSONS WORKING AND DEALING IN SHIPS AND BOATS.								
1. *Hull.*								
Ship, Boat, Barge, Builder	144	.	35	1	60	.	6	.
Shipwright, Ship Carpenter (ashore)	703	.	165	.	348	.	.	.
2. *Masts, Rigging, &c.*								
Mast, Yard, Oar, Block, Maker	16	.	11	.	19	.	.	.
Ship Rigger, Chandler, Fitter	33	2	10	.	37	1	.	.
Sail Maker	122	.	42	.	61	.	.	.

Table 10 *continued*.—OCCUPATIONS of MALES and FEMALES in the SOUTH-WESTERN DIVISION and its REGISTRATION COUNTIES, and in each URBAN SANITARY DISTRICT of which the POPULATION exceeds 50,000 PERSONS.

OCCUPATIONS.	REGISTRATION COUNTIES.				URBAN SANITARY DISTRICTS.			
	20. CORNWALL.		21. SOMERSETSHIRE.		PLYMOUTH.		BATH.	
	Males.	Females.	Males.	Females.	Males.	Females.	Males.	Females.
14. PERSONS WORKING AND DEALING IN CHEMICALS AND COMPOUNDS.								
1. *Colouring Matter.*								
Dye, Paint, Manufacture	1	.	37	1	2	5	.	.
Ink, Blacking, Colouring Substance, Manufacture	1	1	26	1	6	27	1	.
2. *Explosives.*								
Gunpowder, Guncotton, Explosive Substance, Manufacture	38	7	.	.	.	.	.	.
Fusee, Fireworks, Explosive Article, Manufacture	15	180	2	2	1	.	.	.
3. *Drugs and other Chemicals and Compounds.*								
Chemist, Druggist	159	2	272	9	73	.	74	.
Manufacturing Chemist	9	3	53	6	38	13	3	2
Alkali Manufacture	10	.	8	.	5	.	.	.
Drysalter	.	.	5	.	2	.	1	.
15. PERSONS WORKING AND DEALING IN TOBACCO AND PIPES.								
1. *Tobacco and Pipes.*								
Tobacco Manufacturer, Tobacconist	8	7	94	109	10	9	24	11
Tobacco Pipe, Snuff Box, &c., Maker	2	4	11	11	4	.	6	6
16. PERSONS WORKING AND DEALING IN FOOD AND LODGING.								
1. *Board and Lodging.*								
Innkeeper, Hotel Keeper, Publican	503	175	1114	276	178	37	142	29
Lodging, Boarding House, Keeper	22	817	131	796	10	182	80	337
Coffee, Eating House, Keeper	27	27	37	32	20	12	13	5
2. *Spirituous Drinks.*								
Hop—Merchant, Dealer	.	.	1	.	.		1	.
Maltster	53	.	192	.	11	.	11	.
Brewer	68	2	590	9	44	1	58	.
Beerseller. Ale, Porter, Cider, Dealer	15	15	166	70	53	15	32	8
Cellarman	26	1	76	1	32	.	29	1
Wine, Spirit—Merchant, Agent	43	6	132	15	38	.	33	3
3. *Food.*								
Milkseller, Dairyman	134	60	413	82	112	29	72	16
Cheesemonger, Butterman	10	2	59	16	2	.	8	4
Butcher, Meat Salesman	793	67	1615	74	232	20	250	23
Provision Curer, Dealer	20	13	86	24	84	11	25	1
Poulterer, Game Dealer	13	24	58	24	7	9	21	2
Fishmonger	157	74	147	28	71	38	43	4
Corn, Flour, Seed—Merchant, Dealer	92	11	151	16	50	.	20	4
Corn Miller	575	12	600	13	32	.	37	.
Baker	844	114	1082	146	323	48	253	24
Confectioner, Pastrycook	41	57	218	148	50	31	56	48
Greengrocer, Fruiterer	134	189	179	105	59	65	49	31
Mustard, Vinegar, Spice, Pickle—Maker, Dealer	.	.	5	.	.	3	.	.
Sugar Refiner	7	2	39	1	16	.	1	.
Grocer. Tea, Coffee, Chocolate—Maker, Dealer	1105	1100	1642	668	304	86	247	53
Ginger Beer, Mineral Water—Manufacturer, Dealer	11	8	44	4	27	1	13	1
Others dealing in Food	.	.	.	.	.	.	.	.
17. PERSONS WORKING AND DEALING IN TEXTILE FABRICS.								
1. *Wool and Worsted.*								
Woolstapler	15	.	23	.	5			
Woollen Cloth Manufacture	12	91	862	1019	1	.	.	.
Wool, Woollen goods—Dyer, Printer	.	.	48	3	.	2	11	.
Worsted, Stuff, Manufacture	1	2	4	36	.	.	1	.
Flannel Manufacture	.	.	.	.	.	.	1	.
Blanket Manufacture	.	.	14	2	.	.	.	.
Fuller	1	.	12	1	.	.	.	.
Cloth, Worsted, Stuff, Flannel, Blanket, Dealer	5	.	8	4	7	.	2	.
Others	1	.	1	.	.	.	.	.
2. *Silk.*								
Silk, Silk goods, Manufacture	.	.	110	762	.	1	.	2
Silk Dyer, Printer	.	1	.	.	1	.	.	.
Ribbon Manufacture	.	.	.	.	.	.	.	.
Crape, Gauze, Manufacture	.	.	7	82	.	.	.	1
Silk Merchant, Dealer	.	.	15	1	1	.	11	1

Table 10 *continued.*—OCCUPATIONS of MALES and FEMALES in the SOUTH-WESTERN DIVISION and its REGISTRATION COUNTIES, and in each URBAN SANITARY DISTRICT of which the POPULATION exceeds 50,000 PERSONS.

OCCUPATIONS.	REGISTRATION COUNTIES.				URBAN SANITARY DISTRICTS.			
	20. CORNWALL.		21. SOMERSETSHIRE.		PLYMOUTH.		BATH.	
	Males.	Females.	Males.	Females.	Males.	Females.	Males.	Females.
3. Cotton and Flax								
Cotton, Cottongoods, Manufacture	3	5	14	35	.	1	.	.
Cotton, Calico—Printer, Dyer, Bleacher	.	.	.	.	1	.	.	.
Cotton, Calico—Warehouseman, Dealer	.	.	.	4	.	.	.	.
Flax, Linen—Manufacturer, Dealer	.	6	194	161	5	.	.	.
Lace Manufacturer, Dealer	1	7	256	340	.	14	6	18
Fustian Manufacturer, Dealer	.	.	.	.	.	.	.	.
Tape Manufacturer, Dealer	.	.	.	.	.	.	.	.
Thread Manufacturer, Dealer	.	.	1	1	.	.	.	.
4. Hemp and other Fibrous Materials.								
Hemp, Jute, Cocoa Fibre, Manufacture	2	11	46	86	.	.	.	.
Rope, Twine, Cord—Maker, Dealer	190	15	334	66	87	8	3	1
Mat Maker, Seller	2	.	22	11	4	.	.	1
Net Maker	11	115	1	3	.	3	.	.
Canvas, Sailcloth, Manufacture	.	.	89	68	5	2	.	.
Sacking, Sack, Bag—Maker, Dealer	3	.	5	17	4	7	.	.
Others working and dealing in Hemp	.	.	1	.	.	1	.	.
6. Mixed or Unspecified Materials.								
Weaver (undefined)	.	.	41	55	2	3	1	4
Dyer, Printer, Scourer, Bleacher, Calenderer (undefined)	7	6	58	28	27	22	28	10
Factory hand (Textile, undefined)	1	.	37	60	1	2	1	2
Felt Manufacture	.	.	1	.	.	1	.	.
Carpet, Rug, Manufacture	1	.	56	44	3	.	3	.
Manchester Warehouseman	.	.	4	.	.	.	.	.
Draper, Linen Draper, Mercer	385	922	870	373	195	281	179	205
Fancy Goods (Textile), Manufacturer, Worker, Dealer	.	53	3	125	1	20	.	59
Trimming Maker, Dealer	.	.	.	4	.	1	.	3
Embroiderer	.	1	.	11	.	2	.	8
Others	.	.	131	82	.	.	.	.
18. PERSONS WORKING AND DEALING IN DRESS.								
1. Dress.								
Hatter, Hat Manufacture (not straw)	21	11	81	17	23	7	16	1
Straw—Hat, Bonnet, Plait, Manufacture	1	10	3	72	.	6	2	25
Tailor	934	1233	1830	1433	350	475	348	166
Milliner, Dressmaker, Staymaker	3	8984	93	9073	2	1831	17	1792
Shawl Manufacture	.	.	.	.	.	.	.	.
Shirt Maker, Seamstress	.	772	71	2502	2	443	.	369
Hosiery Manufacture	1	35	2	32	1	2	.	2
Hosier, Haberdasher	3	3	32	16	10	15	16	5
Glover, Glove Maker	1	2	808	4105	.	.	4	17
Button Maker, Dealer	.	.	2	.	.	.	.	.
Shoe, Boot—Maker, Dealer	2116	193	4800	1190	551	93	323	43
Patten, Clog, Maker	.	.	6	1	2	.	.	.
Wig Maker, Hairdresser	116	2	180	11	68	1	51	3
Umbrella, Parasol, Stick—Maker, Dealer	7	6	26	25	11	7	12	5
Accoutrement Maker	.	.	.	.	.	.	.	.
Old Clothes Dealer, and others	.	6	2	19	3	7	.	15
19. PERSONS WORKING AND DEALING IN VARIOUS ANIMAL SUBSTANCES.								
1. In Grease, Gut, Bone, Horn, Ivory, and Whalebone.								
Tallow Chandler, Candle, Grease, Manufacture	29	.	40	2	22	1	3	.
Soap Boiler, Maker	.	.	15	.	34	5	.	.
Glue, Size, Gelatine, Isinglass—Maker, Dealer	.	.	26	.	.	1	.	.
Manure Manufacture	19	.	29	1	28	2	.	.
Bone, Horn, Ivory, Tortoise-shell—Worker, Dealer	1	.	2	.	.	.	.	.
Comb Maker	.	.	1	.	.	.	1	.
Others	1	.	5	.	.	.	.	.
2. In Skins.								
Furrier, Skinner	1	4	23	13	7	3	3	7
Tanner, Fellmonger	154	.	389	2	33	.	1	.
Currier	10	3	288	2	32	2	14	.
Leather Goods, Portmanteau, Bag, Strap, &c.—Maker, Dealer	.	1	42	6	10	2	17	4
Parchment, Vellum—Maker, Dealer	.	.	4	.	.	.	.	.
3. In Hair and Feathers.								
Hair, Bristle—Worker, Dealer	.	.	64	135	.	.	1	2
Brush, Broom, Maker	29	14	223	72	54	12	9	3
Quill, Feather—Dresser, Dealer	.	.	.	6	.	7	.	5

Table 10 *continued.*—OCCUPATIONS of MALES and FEMALES in the SOUTH-WESTERN DIVISION and its REGISTRATION COUNTIES, and in each URBAN SANITARY DISTRICT of which the POPULATION exceeds 50,000 PERSONS.

OCCUPATIONS.	REGISTRATION COUNTIES.				URBAN SANITARY DISTRICTS.			
	20. CORNWALL.		21. SOMERSETSHIRE.		PLYMOUTH.		BATH	
	Males.	Females.	Males.	Females.	Males.	Females.	Males.	Females.
20. PERSONS WORKING AND DEALING IN VARIOUS VEGETABLE SUBSTANCES.								
1. In Oils, Gums, and Resins.								
Oil Miller, Oil Cake—Maker, Dealer	3	.	44	.	2	.	1	.
Oil and Colourman	4	.	32	1	8	.	9	.
Floor Cloth, Oil Cloth, Manufacture	.	.	55	1	.	.	.	.
Japanner	.	.	6	.	2	.	1	.
India Rubber, Gutta Percha—Worker, Dealer	1	.	2	3	3	.	.	.
Waterproof Goods—Maker, Dealer	8	.	3	.	2	1	.	.
Others	.	.	10	.	.	.	.	.
2. In Cane, Rush, and Straw.								
Willow, Cane, Rush—Worker, Dealer, Basketmaker	103	31	207	40	56	5	29	28
Hay, Straw (not plait), Chaff—Cutter, Dealer	1	.	66	1	7	.	6	.
Thatcher	36	.	402	.	.	.	2	.
3. In Wood and Bark.								
Timber, Wood—Merchant, Dealer	43	.	206	13	32	2	19	7
Sawyer	323	.	724	.	136	.	49	.
Lath, Wooden Fence, Hurdle, Maker	12	.	79	.	12	.	4	.
Wood Turner, Box Maker	14	1	135	3	23	1	28	1
Cooper, Hoop Maker, Bender	172	1	301	.	43	1	15	.
Cork, Bark—Cutter, Worker, Dealer	1	.	16	.	11	.	3	.
Others	.	.	5	.	.	.	.	.
4. In Paper.								
Paper Manufacture	6	9	370	477	2	3	1	14
Envelope Maker	.	.	3	16	.	.	.	.
Stationer, Law Stationer	27	30	92	101	28	38	28	26
Card, Pattern Card, Maker	1	.	2	6	.	.	.	.
Paper Stainer	.	.	3	.	14	.	.	.
Paper Box, Paper Bag, Maker	2	.	27	115	9	18	1	6
Ticket, Label, Writer	.	.	6	.	4	1	4	.
Others	9	.	53	.	10	.	8	.
21. PERSONS WORKING AND DEALING IN VARIOUS MINERAL SUBSTANCES.								
1. Miners.								
Coal Miner	8	.	5070	9	4	.	8	.
Ironstone Miner	221	3	204	1	2	.	.	.
Copper Miner	1839	168	3	.	3	.	.	.
Tin Miner	10263	1901	.	.	8	1	.	.
Lead Miner	392	15	51	.	1	.	.	.
Miner in other, or undefined, Minerals	280	19	10	.	5	.	1	.
Mine Service	27	1	68	.	1	.	2	.
2. Coal, Coal Gas, &c.								
Coal Merchant, Dealer	146	9	349	25	74	5	70	10
Coalheaver	158	.	141	.	111	.	13	.
Coke, Charcoal, Peat—Cutter, Burner, Dealer	1	.	18	.	2	.	.	.
Gas Works Service	57	.	188	.	54	.	28	.
3. Stone, Clay, and Road Making.								
Stone Quarrier	187	.	652	.	63	.	38	.
Stone Cutter, Dresser, Dealer	184	.	497	.	46	.	20	.
Slate Quarrier	427	.	14	.	.	.	.	.
Slate Worker, Dealer	59	.	24	.	3	1	.	.
Limeburner	46	1	182	1	11	.	3	.
Clay, Sand, Gravel, Chalk—Labourer, Dealer	1847	35	7	.	2	.	.	.
Fossil, Coprolite—Digger, Dealer	.	.	.	.	.	.	.	.
Well Sinker, Borer	.	.	11	.	2	.	3	.
Plaster, Cement, Manufacture	1	.	18	.	12	.	1	.
Brick, Tile—Maker, Burner, Dealer	70	1	1066	8	9	.	3	.
Paviour	2	.	9	.	16	.	.	.
Road Contractor, Surveyor, Inspector	33	.	139	.	.	.	1	.
Road Labourer	284	.	372	.	.	.	10	.
Railway Contractor	2	.	18	.	.	.	.	.
Platelayer	74	.	291	.	16	.	8	.
Railway Labourer, Navvy	330	.	695	.	38	.	4	.
Others	1	6	6	4	.	2	1	.
4. Earthenware and Glass.								
Earthenware, China, Porcelain, Manufacture	14	1	139	14	6	1	4	.
Glass Manufacture	3	.	26	.	4	.	.	.
Earthenware, China, Glass, Dealer	27	13	52	33	13	11	13	5
5. Salt.								
Salt Maker, Dealer	.	.	3	2	1	.	.	.

Table 10 *continued.*—OCCUPATIONS of MALES and FEMALES in the SOUTH-WESTERN DIVISION and its REGISTRATION COUNTIES, and in each URBAN SANITARY DISTRICT of which the POPULATION exceeds 50,000 PERSONS.

OCCUPATIONS.	REGISTRATION COUNTIES.				URBAN SANITARY DISTRICTS.			
	20. CORNWALL.		21. SOMERSETSHIRE.		PLYMOUTH.		BATH.	
	Males.	Females.	Males.	Females.	Males.	Females.	Females.	Males.
6. Water.								
Waterworks Service	6	.	22	.	8	.	4	.
Others	5	2	.	.	3	.	.	.
7. Precious Metals and Jewellery.								
Goldsmith, Silversmith, Jeweller	53	8	139	10	45	6	39	3
Gold, Silver, Beater	.	.	.	.	.	.	.	.
Lapidary	29	6	1	.	.	.	1	.
Others	.	.	.	.	.	1	.	.
8. Iron and Steel.								
Blacksmith	2101	6	2144	8	277	.	138	1
Whitesmith	4	.	42	.	9	.	6	.
Nail Manufacture	.	.	29	2	1	.	1	.
Anchor, Chain, Manufacture	3	.	1	.	1	.	.	.
Other Iron and Steel Manufactures	340	.	681	.	52	1	45	.
Ironmonger. Hardware Dealer, Merchant	185	30	294	17	74	4	44	3
9. Copper.								
Copper, Copper goods—Manufacturer, Worker, Dealer	13	.	23	1	.	.	2	.
10. Tin and Zinc.								
Tin, Tin Plate, Tin goods—Manufacturer, Worker, Dealer	229	7	206	1	30	.	19	1
Zinc, Zinc Goods—Manufacturer, Worker, Dealer	.	.	3	.	.	.	2	.
11. Lead.								
Lead, Leaden goods—Manufacturer, Worker, Dealer	14	.	47	.	5	1	.	.
12. In Other, Mixed, or Unspecified, Metals.								
Metal Refiner, Worker, Turner, Dealer	17	.	22	1	2	.	4	.
Brass, Bronze, Manufacture. Brazier	7	.	166	1	43	.	22	.
Metal Burnisher, Lacquerer	.	.	.	.	.	1	.	.
White Metal, Plated Ware, Manufacture. Pewterer	.	.	19	1	3	.	5	1
Wire Maker, Worker, Weaver, Drawer	5	.	80	1	4	1	7	.
Bolt, Nut, Rivet, Screw, Staple, Maker	.	.	7	1	.	.	.	.
Lamp, Lantern, Candlestick, Maker	.	.	1	.	.	.	.	.
Clasp, Buckle, Hinge, Maker	.	.	.	.	.	.	.	.
Fancy Chain, Gilt Toy, Maker	.	.	.	.	.	.	.	.
Others	2	.	.	.	.	.	.	.
22. PERSONS WORKING AND DEALING IN GENERAL OR UNSPECIFIED COMMODITIES.								
1. Makers and Dealers (General or Undefined).								
General Shopkeeper, Dealer	210	364	392	600	127	228	75	32
Pawnbroker	11	11	60	8	31	9	23	1
Costermonger, Huckster, Street Seller	280	140	437	246	133	166	84	87
Manufacturer, Manager, Superintendent (undefined)	3	1	38	1	21	1	5	.
Contractor (undefined)	13	.	28	.	13	1	.	.
2. Mechanics and Labourers (General or Undefined).								
General Labourer	3729	26	11423	105	2156	8	751	1
Engine Driver, Stoker, Fireman (not railway, marine, nor agricultural)	798	.	648	.	91	.	39	.
Artizan, Mechanic (undefined)	53	3	82	3	48	2	19	1
Apprentice (undefined)	17	3	84	30	19	7	25	5
Factory Labourer (undefined)	16	29	79	29	34	38	6	2
Machinist, Machine Worker (undefined)	17	.	16	.	6	1	5	.
23. PERSONS WORKING AND DEALING IN REFUSE MATTERS.								
1. Refuse Matters.								
Town Drainage Service	1	.	3	.	.	.	.	.
Chimney Sweep, Soot Merchant	15	.	131	4	24	.	37	3
Scavenger, Crossing Sweeper	13	.	29	.	10	.	10	.
Rag Gatherer, Dealer	9	9	10	19	6	33	.	2
VI. UNOCCUPIED CLASS.								
24. PERSONS WITHOUT SPECIFIED OCCUPATIONS								
Persons returned by Property, Rank, &c., and not by special occupation	39129	116129	61691	158741	8567	24847	5677	16184
Children under 5 years of age	19079	18865	31387	31290	4362	4346	2608	3722

Table 11.—Birth-Places of Males and Females enumerated in Counties, and in each Urban Sanitary District of which the Population exceeds 50,000 Persons.

Where Born.	Where Enumerated.							
	South-Western Counties.		Counties.*					
			Wiltshire.		Dorsetshire.		Devonshire.	
	Males.	Females.	Males.	Females.	Males.	Females.	Males.	Females.
TOTAL OF INHABITANTS	882887	970496	128114	130851	93736	97292	285340	318255
LONDON	13575	16058	1983	2678	1832	1639	5687	6227
Middlesex (*Intra-metropolitan*)	10421	12735	1511	2136	1416	1290	4207	4743
Surrey (*Intra-metropolitan*)	1997	1952	364	381	286	242	825	735
Kent (*Intra-metropolitan*)	1157	1371	108	161	130	107	655	749
SOUTH-EASTERN COUNTIES	17707	19728	5265	6069	3618	3770	4866	5146
Surrey (*Extra-metropolitan*)	1424	1621	300	316	235	292	486	558
Kent (*Extra-metropolitan*)	2873	3152	285	365	411	356	1347	1448
Sussex	1821	1764	231	262	296	280	688	615
Hampshire	8533	9670	2491	2964	2489	2715	2006	2103
Berkshire	3056	3521	1958	2162	187	197	339	442
SOUTH-MIDLAND COUNTIES	5036	5877	1365	1472	612	658	1518	1724
Middlesex (*Extra-metropolitan*)	908	1141	170	202	86	121	336	432
Hertfordshire	581	895	117	158	86	80	203	278
Buckinghamshire	700	764	219	221	79	92	188	198
Oxfordshire	1316	1571	554	592	142	139	245	316
Northamptonshire	632	682	133	135	83	97	219	231
Huntingdonshire	138	172	36	30	20	28	41	58
Bedfordshire	357	366	63	90	47	53	130	116
Cambridgeshire	404	486	73	94	69	48	147	164
EASTERN COUNTIES	4029	3766	518	651	548	481	1371	1296
Essex	1363	1586	184	264	241	182	503	551
Suffolk	1482	1024	155	181	152	145	424	344
Norfolk	1184	1156	179	206	155	154	444	401
SOUTH-WESTERN COUNTIES	783099	862566	110593	110734	81617	86603	253088	286356
Wiltshire	111422	112862	103554	102029	1393	2164	656	811
Dorsetshire	82625	87457	2214	2579	74487	77391	1719	1971
Devonshire	251977	281506	777	908	1038	2106	234152	260954
Cornwall	148228	177054	144	181	261	300	10788	16437
Somersetshire	188849	203687	3904	5037	3638	4642	5747	6203
WEST-MIDLAND COUNTIES	21663	25758	4542	5090	954	934	3517	3558
Gloucestershire	16100	19643	3483	3937	407	488	1627	1720
Herefordshire	705	881	155	184	46	66	210	213
Shropshire	533	656	105	191	61	63	187	207
Staffordshire	1399	1488	223	248	159	130	520	509
Worcestershire	1189	1352	253	280	100	75	336	371
Warwickshire	1737	1738	323	340	201	117	631	545
NORTH-MIDLAND COUNTIES	2429	2379	349	385	376	243	902	869
Leicestershire	560	528	84	92	38	80	198	197
Rutlandshire	66	77	16	17	5	9	24	24
Lincolnshire	772	776	99	114	131	108	271	275
Nottinghamshire	543	461	78	80	77	41	221	180
Derbyshire	548	537	72	82	75	35	188	193
NORTH-WESTERN COUNTIES	3936	3235	381	384	651	239	1631	1246
Cheshire	760	720	72	98	109	59	325	265
Lancashire	3176	2515	309	286	542	180	1306	981
YORKSHIRE	2852	2406	357	312	509	212	1055	916
NORTHERN COUNTIES	1677	1490	183	158	233	136	637	577
Durham	771	634	69	69	102	65	298	219
Northumberland	515	476	74	56	87	44	204	206
Cumberland	302	280	28	22	24	21	109	109
Westmorland	89	100	12	11	20	6	26	43
MONMOUTHSHIRE AND WALES	6151	6823	888	1001	335	331	1701	1677
Monmouthshire	1685	2087	306	429	78	74	812	202
Glamorganshire	1910	2099	253	250	93	83	537	539
Carmarthenshire	268	253	24	24	23	17	77	70
Pembrokeshire	632	778	53	64	35	53	261	306
Cardiganshire	210	98	8	5	11	9	53	20
Brecknockshire	169	200	40	43	11	7	38	40
Radnorshire	67	84	15	15	10	11	17	22
Montgomeryshire	86	91	20	20	18	15	20	27
Flintshire	107	95	11	10	8	13	39	24
Denbighshire	110	106	17	22	8	8	54	33
Merionethshire	59	29	8	6	2	8	15	6
Carnarvonshire	177	67	5	3	5	1	50	36
Anglesey	118	49	4	4	2	1	49	28
Wales (*County not stated*)	553	824	69	106	34	28	179	235
ENGLAND (*County not stated*)	2245	2304	445	516	315	338	742	621
OTHER PARTS OF BRITISH EMPIRE	14599	15135	1035	1143	1853	1499	7233	6951
Islands in the British Seas	1252	1482	57	91	192	213	631	705
SCOTLAND	3306	2688	280	274	448	271	1576	1222
IRELAND	6463	5963	378	397	850	581	3430	2828
British Colonies or Dependencies	3578	5002	320	381	363	434	1596	2196
FOREIGN COUNTRIES	3748	2813	201	246	272	198	1320	1018
British Subjects	1427	1609	124	127	115	121	552	626
Foreigners	2321	1204	77	119	157	77	768	392
AT SEA	141	158	9	12	11	11	72	73
British Subjects	140	158	8	12	11	11	72	73
Foreigners	1	.	1	.	.	.	.	.

* The Counties *proper*, and not the Registration Counties are referred to in this Table.

Table 11 *continued.*—BIRTH-PLACES of MALES and FEMALES enumerated in COUNTIES, and in each URBAN SANITARY DISTRICT of which the POPULATION EXCEEDS 50,000 PERSONS.

WHERE BORN.	WHERE ENUMERATED.							
	COUNTIES.				* URBAN SANITARY DISTRICTS.			
	CORNWALL.		SOMERSETSHIRE.		PLYMOUTH.		BATH.	
	Males.	Females.	Males.	Females.	Males.	Females.	Males.	Females.
TOTAL OF INHABITANTS	155115	175571	220582	248527	33750	40044	21020	30794
LONDON	1066	1153	3007	4361	795	798	683	1187
MIDDLESEX (*Intra-metropolitan*)	824	933	2463	3633	581	618	555	972
SURREY (*Intra-metropolitan*)	145	113	377	481	120	87	91	142
KENT (*Intra-metropolitan*)	97	107	167	247	94	93	37	73
SOUTH-EASTERN COUNTIES	1231	1019	2727	3724	844	723	537	996
SURREY (*Extra-metropolitan*)	81	100	322	445	60	39	61	123
KENT (*Extra-metropolitan*)	318	239	512	724	265	228	108	184
SUSSEX	307	140	299	458	178	87	75	146
HAMPSHIRE	455	440	1092	1448	302	332	191	355
BERKSHIRE	70	71	502	649	39	37	102	188
SOUTH-MIDLAND COUNTIES	324	306	1217	1717	159	135	233	489
MIDDLESEX (*Extra-metropolitan*)	74	80	242	306	35	27	46	100
HERTFORDSHIRE	40	39	135	223	21	9	30	80
BUCKINGHAMSHIRE	43	33	172	226	18	12	29	51
OXFORDSHIRE	48	63	327	461	23	28	62	114
NORTHAMPTONSHIRE	45	32	102	187	23	21	30	[illegible]
HUNTINGDONSHIRE	10	16	31	40	4	6	10	16
BEDFORDSHIRE	30	19	78	118	16	13	13	30
CAMBRIDGESHIRE	35	24	86	156	10	18	13	40
EASTERN COUNTIES	862	300	730	1038	286	147	149	289
ESSEX	153	135	282	451	61	63	65	122
SUFFOLK	532	84	219	270	131	38	46	79
NORFOLK	177	81	229	314	94	46	38	88
SOUTH-WESTERN COUNTIES	145095	168005	192706	210868	28316	35593	16653	22847
WILTSHIRE	116	101	5463	7757	82	60	1423	2963
DORSETSHIRE	209	232	4055	5264	135	129	206	358
DEVONSHIRE	7828	8087	7532	9471	24817	30108	467	834
CORNWALL	136336	159160	702	976	2905	4895	89	178
SOMERSETSHIRE	606	425	174054	187380	377	401	14468	18464
WEST-MIDLAND COUNTIES	682	546	11968	15630	469	372	1217	2241
GLOUCESTERSHIRE	325	262	10267	13241	235	206	941	1716
HEREFORDSHIRE	36	30	258	388	26	10	52	103
SHROPSHIRE	35	28	145	257	26	17	38	78
STAFFORDSHIRE	97	81	405	527	84	45	45	84
WORCESTERSHIRE	64	59	436	567	47	26	64	118
WARWICKSHIRE	125	86	457	650	51	63	77	142
NORTH-MIDLAND COUNTIES	200	192	602	690	106	75	115	177
LEICESTERSHIRE	37	41	159	148	31	13	24	37
RUTLANDSHIRE	3	2	18	25	1	-	4	11
LINCOLNSHIRE	65	72	146	207	39	25	31	54
NOTTINGHAMSHIRE	46	25	121	135	16	23	25	35
DERBYSHIRE	49	52	153	175	19	14	31	40
NORTH-WESTERN COUNTIES	519	366	754	1000	246	167	134	220
CHESHIRE	87	59	167	239	38	38	22	46
LANCASHIRE	432	307	587	761	208	123	112	174
YORKSHIRE	292	236	639	730	179	108	131	182
NORTHERN COUNTIES	301	237	323	382	139	97	41	84
DURHAM	160	118	142	163	77	44	18	30
NORTHUMBERLAND	68	70	82	100	44	36	15	14
CUMBERLAND	68	46	73	82	16	12	4	27
WESTMORLAND	5	3	26	37	2	5	4	13
MONMOUTHSHIRE AND WALES	881	485	2346	3329	319	208	292	506
MONMOUTHSHIRE	81	67	851	1205	49	31	82	155
GLAMORGANSHIRE	188	154	889	1073	72	56	96	120
CARMARTHENSHIRE	66	24	78	118	11	7	12	28
PEMBROKESHIRE	134	63	149	287	49	44	37	70
CARDIGANSHIRE	81	12	37	41	19	5	6	9
BRECKNOCKSHIRE	7	9	73	101	5	4	13	17
RADNORSHIRE	8	1	20	35	2	2	8	11
MONTGOMERYSHIRE	7	6	21	25	3	2	8	8
FLINTSHIRE	34	13	15	25	19	2	·	7
DENBIGHSHIRE	13	13	18	30	36	2	3	6
MERIONETHSHIRE	25	4	14	10	6	3	3	2
CARNARVONSHIRE	101	8	16	29	16	5	3	6
ANGLESEY	50	11	18	5	11	4	3	2
WALES (*County not stated*)	89	100	182	345	27	43	23	65
ENGLAND (*County not stated*)	308	354	435	475	49	65	62	84
OTHER PARTS OF BRITISH EMPIRE	2006	1676	2472	3866	1459	1380	613	1280
ISLANDS in the BRITISH SEAS	225	179	147	244	211	205	17	40
SCOTLAND	398	245	604	676	314	137	119	185
IRELAND	928	765	877	1394	692	739	210	454
BRITISH COLONIES or DEPENDENCIES	455	487	844	1552	242	299	267	601
FOREIGN COUNTRIES	1325	671	630	680	365	159	158	201
British Subjects	348	378	288	357	136	107	78	116
Foreigners	977	293	342	323	229	52	80	85
AT SEA	23	25	26	37	19	17	2	11
British Subjects	23	25	26	37	19	17	2	11
Foreigners	·	·	·	·	·	·	·	·

* ... situated in this Division, but the Birth-Places for the entire City are returned in Division VI.

Table 12.—Distribution of the enumerated Natives of Counties.

Where Enumerated.	Where Born. South-Western Counties.		Wiltshire.		Dorsetshire.		Devonshire.		Cornwall.		Somersetshire.	
	Males.	Females.	Males.	Females.	Males.	Females.	Males.	Females.	Males.	Females.	Males.	Females.
TOTAL ENUMERATED NATIVES OF EACH COUNTY	1036256	1153682	159955	16995[illegible]	112859	122024	324329	363420	176796	210102	262317	288183
LONDON	73255	95287	13055	18261	8046	10168	26577	32379	7104	9430	18473	25049
Middlesex (*Intra-metropolitan*)	48512	55443	8338	12407	4923	6660	17567	22096	4712	5414	12612	17863
Surrey (*Intra-metropolitan*)	19919	23348	3939	4767	2502	2774	6927	7871	1812	2232	4739	5704
Kent (*Intra-metropolitan*)	5184	6496	778	1087	621	734	2083	2409	580	784	1122	1482
SOUTH-EASTERN COUNTIES	50482	60576	14764	17106	12711	14865	11166	13855	3149	4099	8692	10651
Surrey (*Extra-metropolitan*)	7485	10344	1924	2523	1243	1584	2130	2904	480	778	1738	2517
Kent (*Extra-metropolitan*)	7216	8201	1210	1445	1030	1096	2588	2975	798	953	1190	1732
Sussex	5028	6907	1061	1376	902	1209	1338	2002	309	646	1238	1758
Hampshire	24713	28231	6904	7068	8933	10433	4257	4082	1333	1542	3228	3545
Berkshire	6040	6803	3665	4094	463	633	743	895	139	182	1030	1099
SOUTH-MIDLAND COUNTIES	12681	16219	3386	4371	1513	1934	3576	4428	931	1334	3275	4152
Middlesex (*Extra-metropolitan*)	6355	8818	1531	2113	713	1007	1971	2535	512	772	1628	2180
Hertfordshire	1185	1603	272	350	186	233	259	455	90	131	279	434
Buckinghamshire	1336	1645	445	491	149	176	305	319	71	77	386	392
Oxfordshire	1602	2184	629	857	163	216	285	393	88	123	442	516
Northamptonshire	1074	1108	278	278	153	131	275	321	69	98	299	274
Huntingdonshire	134	157	30	30	15	22	44	40	14	17	31	47
Bedfordshire	507	689	115	163	58	83	172	206	45	72	117	185
Cambridgeshire	487	487	88	89	76	62	165	154	47	46	113	116
EASTERN COUNTIES	6267	7031	987	1266	894	927	2259	2437	690	797	1437	1634
Essex	4612	5015	761	906	646	692	1687	1700	486	574	1083	1230
Suffolk	890	1068	119	179	129	139	373	417	102	113	167	200
Norfolk	765	948	107	149	118	166	249	320	103	110	187	204
SOUTH-WESTERN COUNTIES	783099	862506	111422	112868	82625	87457	251977	281506	148226	177054	188849	203687
Wiltshire	110598	110734	105554	102020	2214	2579	777	908	144	181	3904	5087
Dorsetshire	81617	86603	1533	2164	74437	77891	168-	2106	261	300	3638	4842
Devonshire	243388	283356	606	811	1710	1971	281152	280684	10783	18437	5747	6233
Cornwall	145995	168085	118	101	209	232	7826	8087	126336	159166	692	425
Somersetshire	192706	210863	5463	7757	4955	5284	7532	9471	702	976	174954	187380
SOUTH-MIDLAND COUNTIES	37813	46781	8134	9545	1988	2243	7837	9085	1753	2277	18601	23631
Gloucestershire	23517	34966	5805	7297	1002	1266	4104	5863	823	1244	14425	19305
Herefordshire	989	905	206	213	86	96	231	263	58	56	339	367
Shropshire	592	759	128	143	74	87	141	217	63	72	186	254
Staffordshire	3351	3153	746	607	299	262	779	811	388	358	1139	1107
Worcestershire	2123	2370	465	491	146	172	469	578	100	138	948	971
Warwickshire	4280	4629	784	794	331	368	1258	1347	321	399	1541	1627
NORTH-MIDLAND COUNTIES	5558	5530	939	896	647	574	1665	1775	622	717	1685	1568
Leicestershire	1027	1032	260	181	156	115	313	326	193	117	255	296
Rutlandshire	88	101	17	22	10	11	16	23	17	25	28	22
Lincolnshire	1280	1273	165	169	169	143	502	521	162	178	291	263
Nottinghamshire	1447	1502	175	204	140	139	438	438	123	148	571	527
Derbyshire	1716	1622	332	321	181	160	396	421	217	251	540	461
NORTH-WESTERN COUNTIES	16326	17670	1463	1487	1665	1658	5014	5310	4681	5378	3503	3837
Cheshire	2278	2479	256	280	266	298	808	826	415	478	533	597
Lancashire	14048	15191	1207	1207	1399	1286	4206	4484	4286	4906	2970	3240
YORKSHIRE	9554	9552	1323	1251	830	764	3128	3214	1999	2118	2224	2205
NORTHERN COUNTIES	8377	7112	385	357	393	325	2711	2334	3663	3192	1195	904
Durham	4717	3965	253	203	229	170	1494	1231	1910	1721	885	610
Northumberland	1720	1470	78	84	109	90	672	623	603	548	168	146
Cumberland	1811	1535	44	45	29	36	567	463	1064	903	107	84
Westmorland	129	142	10	21	25	25	38	37	20	20	35	33
MONMOUTHSHIRE AND WALES	32844	25358	4097	2581	1497	1109	8919	7097	3948	3700	14383	10865
Monmouthshire	6087	5981	1481	890	345	221	1442	1116	302	336	4407	3473
Glamorganshire	21384	16519	2185	1381	887	680	5458	5058	2850	2751	8994	6651
Carmarthenshire	583	419	81	44	37	37	138	122	115	81	174	134
Pembrokeshire	858	697	82	53	54	47	387	308	154	121	211	188
Cardiganshire	130	148	15	14	9	4	29	11	62	62	21	22
Brecknockshire	621	471	127	81	38	25	121	78	26	35	309	231
Radnorshire	66	55	14	15	7	1	12	11	12	8	21	21
Montgomeryshire	145	144	20	16	7	12	41	37	47	36	30	41
Flintshire	237	232	12	14	47	41	60	63	54	58	54	56
Denbighshire	251	238	32	29	38	27	73	71	74	64	36	39
Merionethshire	97	91	14	9	12	5	38	38	10	15	23	29
Carnarvonshire	208	202	19	33	13	15	74	74	125	10	35	40
Anglesey	130	91	15	2	5	2	48	45	47	31	15	11

Table 14.—NUMBER and AGES of MALES AND FEMALES returned as BLIND or BLIND FROM BIRTH in the SOUTH-WESTERN DIVISION and its REGISTRATION COUNTIES.

REGISTRATION COUNTY.	ALL AGES. Both Sexes.	ALL AGES. Males and Females.	0–	5–	15–	20–	25–	45–	65 and upwards.
V. SOUTH-WESTERN COUNTIES.	2354	M. 1257	20	50	31	58	262	365	471
		F. 1097	21	54	31	84	179	239	589
17 WILTSHIRE	238	M. 114	5	4	2	2	16	34	51
		F. 124	2	4	6	5	16	34	57
18 DORSETSHIRE	225	M. 119	1	9	3	1	23	36	46
		F. 106	3	7	1	3	15	21	56
19 DEVONSHIRE	768	M. 432	4	15	16	31	106	104	156
		F. 336	7	15	13	12	52	79	157
20 CORNWALL	564	M. 315	5	10	5	8	72	113	102
		F. 249	2	8	5	5	40	42	147
21 SOMERSETSHIRE	559	M. 277	5	12	5	16	45	78	116
		F. 282	7	13	6	9	66	63	122

Table 15.—NUMBER and AGES of MALES and FEMALES returned as BLIND in the SOUTH-WESTERN DIVISION and its REGISTRATION COUNTIES.

REGISTRATION COUNTY.	ALL AGES. Both Sexes.	ALL AGES. Males and Females.	0–	5–	15–	20–	25–	45–	65 and upwards.
V. SOUTH-WESTERN COUNTIES.	2180	M. 1172	12	32	28	48	234	353	465
		F. 1008	12	30	21	27	152	230	536
17 WILTSHIRE	224	M. 111	4	4	2	3	15	34	50
		F. 113	1	2	6	4	12	31	57
18 DORSETSHIRE	205	M. 107	.	3	3	1	20	35	45
		F. 98	2	4	1	2	13	20	56
19 DEVONSHIRE	705	M. 393	.	9	16	25	90	98	155
		F. 312	5	11	7	9	44	79	157
20 CORNWALL	535	M. 305	4	7	4	7	72	111	100
		F. 230	1	2	3	5	34	40	148
21 SOMERSETSHIRE	511	M. 256	4	9	3	13	37	75	115
		F. 255	3	11	4	7	49	60	121

Table 16.—NUMBER and AGES of MALES and FEMALES returned as BLIND FROM BIRTH in the SOUTH-WESTERN DIVISION and its REGISTRATION COUNTIES.

REGISTRATION COUNTY.	ALL AGES. Both Sexes.	ALL AGES. Males and Females.	0–	5–	15–	20–	25–	45–	65 and upwards.
V. SOUTH-WESTERN COUNTIES.	174	M. 85	8	18	3	10	28	12	6
		F. 89	9	24	10	7	27	9	3
17 WILTSHIRE	14	M. 3	1	.	.	.	1	.	1
		F. 11	1	2	.	1	4	3	.
18 DORSETSHIRE	20	M. 12	1	6	.	.	3	1	1
		F. 8	1	3	.	1	2	1	.
19 DEVONSHIRE	63	M. 39	4	6	.	6	16	6	1
		F. 24	2	5	6	3	8	.	.
20 CORNWALL	29	M. 10	1	3	1	1	.	2	2
		F. 19	1	6	2	.	6	2	2
21 SOMERSETSHIRE	48	M. 21	1	3	2	3	8	3	1
		F. 27	4	8	2	2	7	3	1

Table 17.—NUMBER and AGES of MALES and FEMALES returned as DEAF AND DUMB in the SOUTH-WESTERN DIVISION and its REGISTRATION COUNTIES.

REGISTRATION COUNTY.	ALL AGES. Both Sexes.	ALL AGES. Males and Females.	0–	5–	15–	20–	25–	45–	65 and upwards.
V. SOUTH-WESTERN COUNTIES.	1058	M. 548	19	107	51	65	171	106	29
		F. 510	10	110	57	56	138	103	36
17 WILTSHIRE	127	M. 68	4	11	8	8	18	16	3
		F. 59	1	12	10	7	15	11	3
18 DORSETSHIRE	96	M. 48	2	7	2	6	18	9	4
		F. 48	.	10	4	1	15	15	3
19 DEVONSHIRE	374	M. 208	5	53	23	21	57	41	8
		F. 166	3	48	23	13	45	28	16
20 CORNWALL	200	M. 101	4	14	10	15	38	15	5
		F. 99	3	17	5	17	32	21	4
21 SOMERSETSHIRE	261	M. 123	4	22	8	15	40	25	9
		F. 138	4	28	15	19	31	30	11

Table 18.—NUMBER and AGES of MALES and FEMALES returned as IDIOTS or IMBECILES, and LUNATICS in the SOUTH-WESTERN DIVISION and its REGISTRATION COUNTIES.

REGISTRATION COUNTY.	ALL AGES. Both Sexes.	ALL AGES. Males and Females.	0-	5-	15-	20-	25-	45-	65 and upwards.
V. SOUTH-WESTERN COUNTIES.	7062	M. 3207 F. 3855	15 26	252 173	206 168	229 238	1134 1271	981 1411	390 568
17. WILTSHIRE	1596	M. - 722 F. - 874	2 5	32 26	28 46	49 46	297 311	247 330	67 110
18. DORSETSHIRE	749	M. - 349 F. - 400	1 3	25 12	18 14	25 33	123 123	111 145	46 70
19. DEVONSHIRE	1955	M. - 893 F. - 1062	2 9	100 57	75 45	73 53	287 337	246 391	110 170
20. CORNWALL	974	M. - 426 F. - 548	1 4	23 17	36 22	31 34	157 179	133 201	45 91
21. SOMERSETSHIRE	1788	M. - 817 F. - 971	9 5	72 61	49 41	51 72	270 321	244 344	122 127

Table 19.—NUMBER and AGES of MALES and FEMALES returned as IDIOTS or IMBECILES in the SOUTH-WESTERN DIVISION and its REGISTRATION COUNTIES.

REGISTRATION COUNTY.	ALL AGES. Both Sexes.	ALL AGES. Males and Females.	0-	5-	15-	20-	25-	45-	65 and upwards.
V. SOUTH-WESTERN COUNTIES.	2868	M. 1424 F. 1444	15 26	248 168	182 143	162 157	443 472	262 327	112 151
17. WILTSHIRE	506	M. - 237 F. - 269	2 5	31 26	22 36	27 24	96 98	44 57	15 23
18. DORSETSHIRE	289	M. - 151 F. - 138	1 3	24 12	14 12	20 21	55 41	25 31	12 18
19. DEVONSHIRE	837	M. - 441 F. - 396	2 9	98 52	70 40	52 37	116 129	77 88	26 41
20. CORNWALL	369	M. - 173 F. - 196	1 4	23 17	32 20	23 28	50 59	32 49	12 19
21. SOMERSETSHIRE	867	M. - 422 F. - 445	9 5	72 61	44 36	40 47	126 145	84 102	47 50

Table 20.—NUMBER and AGES of MALES and FEMALES returned as LUNATICS in the SOUTH-WESTERN DIVISION and its REGISTRATION COUNTIES.

REGISTRATION COUNTY.	ALL AGES. Both Sexes.	ALL AGES. Males and Females.	0-	5-	15-	20-	25-	45-	65 and upwards.
V. SOUTH-WESTERN COUNTIES.	4194	M. 1783 F. 2411	. .	4 5	24 25	67 81	691 799	719 1084	378 417
17. WILTSHIRE	1090	M. - 485 F. - 605	. .	1 .	6 10	22 22	201 213	203 273	52 87
18. DORSETSHIRE	460	M. - 198 F. - 262	. .	1 .	4 2	5 12	68 82	86 114	34 52
19. DEVONSHIRE	1118	M. - 452 F. - 666	. .	2 5	5 5	21 16	171 208	169 303	84 129
20. CORNWALL	605	M. - 253 F. - 352	. .	. .	4 2	8 6	107 120	101 152	33 72
21. SOMERSETSHIRE	921	M. - 395 F. - 526	. .	. .	5 6	11 25	144 176	160 242	75 77

Table 21.—Number of the Blind, of the Deaf and Dumb, of Idiots or Imbeciles, and of Lunatics in the South-western Division and its Registration Counties and Districts.

Registration County and District.	Blind. From Birth.	Blind. Others.	Blind. Total.	Deaf and Dumb.	Mentally Deranged. Idiots.	Mentally Deranged. Lunatics.	Mentally Deranged. Total.
V. SOUTH-WESTERN COUNTIES.	174	2180	2354	1056	2868	4194	7062
17 WILTSHIRE	14	224	238	127	506	1090	1596
18 DORSETSHIRE	20	205	225	96	289	460	749
19 DEVONSHIRE	63	705	768	374	837	1118	1955
20 CORNWALL	29	535	564	200	369	605	974
21 SOMERSETSHIRE	48	511	559	261	867	921	1788
17 WILTSHIRE.							
241 HIGHWORTH	2	29	31	7	31	2	33
242 CRICKLADE	.	10	10	4	16	2	18
243 MALMESBURY	1	11	12	4	26	.	26
244 CHIPPENHAM	2	20	22	6	51	29	80
245 CALNE	.	8	8	0	20	2	22
246 MARLBOROUGH	.	5	5	7	17	8	25
247 DEVIZES	1	17	18	8	110	542	652
248 MELKSHAM	2	24	26	13	23	6	29
249 BRADFORD-ON-AVON	.	11	11	8	24	4	28
250 WESTBURY	1	10	11	3	11	2	13
251 WARMINSTER	.	13	13	12	22	7	29
252 PEWSEY	1	17	18	9	23	.	23
253 AMESBURY	.	7	7	5	13	.	13
254 ALDERBURY	.	23	23	17	58	480	538
255 WILTON	2	6	8	8	21	5	26
256 TISBURY	1	10	11	6	20	1	21
257 MERE	1	3	4	4	20	.	20
18 DORSETSHIRE.							
258 SHAFTESBURY	3	18	21	9	20	1	21
259 STURMINSTER	.	7	7	4	10	1	11
260 BLANDFORD	1	17	18	3	18	4	22
261 WIMBORNE	2	26	28	14	18	2	20
262 POOLE	1	23	24	4	18	22	40
263 WAREHAM	.	15	15	11	26	.	26
264 WEYMOUTH	2	35	37	16	33	2	35
265 DORCHESTER	5	27	32	14	79	425	504
266 SHERBORNE	2	11	13	4	20	1	21
267 BEAMINSTER	2	12	14	10	31	.	31
268 BRIDPORT	2	14	16	7	16	2	18
19 DEVONSHIRE.							
269 AXMINSTER	2	19	21	10	31	2	33
270 HONITON	2	23	25	14	27	10	37
271 ST. THOMAS	3	63	66	39	174	894	1068
272 EXETER	6	85	91	58	27	45	72
19 DEVONSHIRE—*continued.*							
273 NEWTON ABBOT	8	81	89	32	57	10	67
274 TOTNES	3	41	44	16	48	8	56
275 KINGSBRIDGE	1	20	21	8	25	4	29
276 PLYMPTON ST. MARY	3	22	25	16	25	47	72
277 PLYMOUTH	14	87	101	53	74	43	117
278 EAST STONEHOUSE	1	12	13	8	11	2	13
279 STOKE DAMEREL	10	52	62	23	40	27	70
280 TAVISTOCK	.	38	38	16	48	8	50
281 OKEHAMPTON	3	18	21	9	28	3	31
282 CREDITON	2	17	19	8	34	.	34
283 TIVERTON	1	30	31	23	42	1	43
284 SOUTH MOLTON	.	19	19	7	28	2	30
285 BARNSTAPLE	1	42	43	10	36	1	37
286 TORRINGTON	.	14	14	5	33	4	37
287 BIDEFORD	3	15	18	10	28	4	32
288 HOLSWORTHY	.	7	7	8	12	3	15
20 CORNWALL.							
289 STRATTON	.	5	5	3	6	1	7
290 CAMELFORD	1	15	16	7	17	.	17
291 LAUNCESTON	.	26	26	8	11	1	12
292 ST. GERMANS	1	15	16	8	14	2	16
293 LISKEARD	1	44	45	23	28	2	30
294 BODMIN	.	26	26	12	32	570	602
295 ST. COLUMB	1	25	26	6	11	7	18
296 ST. AUSTELL	5	50	55	20	42	1	43
297 TRURO	4	62	66	17	52	2	54
298 FALMOUTH	6	28	34	16	22	1	23
299 HELSTON	2	55	57	20	34	5	39
300 REDRUTH	5	101	106	27	50	5	55
301 PENZANCE	3	80	83	29	47	7	54
302 SCILLY ISLANDS	.	3	3	4	3	1	4
21 SOMERSETSHIRE.							
303 WILLITON	.	21	21	9	50	2	52
304 DULVERTON	.	6	6	7	18	.	18
305 WELLINGTON	1	20	21	5	63	3	66
306 TAUNTON	3	39	42	28	35	6	41
307 BRIDGWATER	7	39	46	13	29	20	49
308 LANGPORT	1	13	14	13	46	9	55
309 CHARD	1	18	19	10	43	6	49
310 YEOVIL	4	28	32	27	47	5	52
311 WINCANTON	1	23	24	8	29	2	31
312 FROME	2	38	40	12	67	1	68
313 SHEPTON MALLET	2	14	16	8	34	2	36
314 WELLS	1	23	24	8	70	694	764
315 AXBRIDGE	4	37	41	20	47	8	55
316 CLUTTON	2	13	15	10	45	2	47
317 BATH	13	97	110	45	119	73	192
318 KEYNSHAM	1	20	21	13	64	80	144
319 BEDMINSTER	5	62	67	23	61	8	69

AGES,

CONDITION AS TO MARRIAGE,

OCCUPATIONS, AND BIRTH-PLACES

OF THE PEOPLE:

WITH THE

NUMBERS AND AGES OF THE BLIND, DEAF AND DUMB,
IDIOTS OR IMBECILES, AND LUNATICS.

DIVISION VI.—WEST-MIDLAND COUNTIES;

GLOUCESTERSHIRE,
HEREFORDSHIRE,
SHROPSHIRE,
STAFFORDSHIRE,
WORCESTERSHIRE,
WARWICKSHIRE.

TABLES IN DIVISION VI.—WEST-MIDLAND COUNTIES.

AGES.

Table.

1.—Ages of Males and Females in the West-Midland Division and its Registration Counties.

2.—Ages of Males and Females in Registration Districts.

3.—Ages of Males and Females in Registration Sub-districts.

4. Male and Female Children at *each Year of Age* under 5 in the West-Midland Division and its Registration Counties.

5.—Male and Female Children at *each Year of Age* under 5 in Registration Districts.

6.—Ages of Males and Females in Sanitary Districts.

CONDITION AS TO MARRIAGE.

7.—Condition as to Marriage and Ages of Males and Females in the West-Midland Division and its Registration Counties

8.—Condition as to Marriage and Ages of Males and Females in Registration Districts.

9.—Condition as to Marriage and Ages of Males and Females in each Urban Sanitary District of which the Population exceeds 50,000 Persons.

OCCUPATIONS.

10.—Occupations of Males and Females in the West-Midland Division and its Registration Counties, and in each Urban Sanitary District of which the Population exceeds 50,000 Persons.

BIRTH-PLACES.

11.—Birth-places of Males and Females enumerated in Counties, and in each Urban Sanitary District of which the Population exceeds 50,000 Persons.

12.—Distribution of the enumerated Natives of Counties.

13.—Number and Country of Birth of Foreigners enumerated in Counties, and in each Urban Sanitary District of which the Population exceeds 50,000 Persons.

THE BLIND, DEAF AND DUMB, IDIOTS OR IMBECILES, AND LUNATICS.

14.—Number and Ages of Males and Females returned as Blind or Blind from Birth in the West-Midland Division and its Registration Counties.

15.—Number and Ages of Males and Females returned as Blind in the West-Midland Division and its Registration Counties.

16.—Number and Ages of Males and Females returned as Blind from Birth in the West-Midland Division and its Registration Counties.

17.—Number and Ages of Males and Females returned as Deaf and Dumb in the West-Midland Division and its Registration Counties.

18.—Number and Ages of Males and Females returned as Idiots or Imbeciles, and Lunatics in the West-Midland Division and its Registration Counties.

19.—Number and Ages of Males and Females returned as Idiots or Imbeciles in the West-Midland Division and its Registration Counties.

20.—Number and Ages of Males and Females returned as Lunatics in the West-Midland Division and its Registration Counties.

21.—Number of the Blind, of the Deaf and Dumb, of Idiots or Imbeciles, and of Lunatics in the West-Midland Division and its Registration Counties and Districts.

AGES.

DIVISION VI.—WEST-MIDLAND COUNTIES.

1.—Ages of Males and Females in the West-Midland Division and its Registration Counties.

ATION ITY.	All Ages. Persons.	Males and Females.	Under 5* Years.	5-	10-	15-	20-	25-	30-	35-	40-	45-	50-	55-	60-	65-	70-	75-	80-	85-	90-	95-	100† and upw^{ds}.
EST-AND TIES	3029504	M. 1481685	209897	190192	169890	151078	124191	108708	92694	82471	77388	64387	58867	49018	40728	27858	19520	10024	5027	1309	297	56	3
		F. 1547010	211357	191467	168978	140413	126721	117266	99900	87642	82711	69471	62810	49167	44899	29196	22775	17351	6404	2109	573	104	10
STER	525167	M. 245627	33137	31174	29534	25459	19287	16983	15050	13022	12684	10599	9565	7988	7634	5304	3883	2306	1095	331	70	12	.
		F. 279540	33095	31254	29330	27645	25222	21357	18188	16143	15108	13150	12032	9600	9138	6828	5030	3171	1506	562	144	32	1
ORD	118147	M. 58325	7165	7165	6805	5932	4302	3644	3328	3216	3166	2840	2669	2213	2139	1520	1161	661	328	91	24	3	1
		F. 59822	7180	7070	6764	5408	4534	3946	3559	3301	3367	2941	2731	2287	2180	1647	1279	811	408	150	48	15	2
HIRE	265890	M. 132992	17050	16481	15301	13946	10536	8690	7349	7175	6948	6487	5965	4757	4624	3192	2587	1435	665	202	37	8	1
		F. 132898	16763	16474	15046	12209	10016	8848	7880	7504	7239	6275	5948	4841	4632	3631	2746	1561	848	321	77	7	.
RDSHIRE	1096768	M. 504874	75089	67037	57470	51797	44330	38582	32090	27982	26097	21276	18808	14557	13248	7958	5256	2765	1217	315	86	12	.
		F. 591894	75842	67731	56918	48038	43189	37799	31879	27382	26238	21388	18764	14422	12600	8746	5706	3151	1486	433	110	17	6
STER	383011	M. 184016	23860	23470	21361	18816	16236	13243	11324	10130	9417	8050	7461	5929	5114	3664	2583	1451	668	196	40	8	1
		F. 198995	26023	23570	21301	19795	18069	15481	12866	11208	10500	8641	8163	6326	5733	4223	3063	1865	931	319	92	20	3
CKSHIRE	730581	M. 356501	51407	46865	39329	36023	30410	27617	23597	20360	19118	15530	13609	10568	9069	6211	4130	2285	1054	294	51	7	1
		F. 374080	51343	45358	39519	36322	34161	29904	24927	22087	20715	16904	14942	11714	10406	7123	4901	2777	1245	419	162	13	1

Registration Counties consist of groups of Registration Districts, which are generally co-extensive with the Poor Law Unions. Those Registration which extend into two or more Counties are included in that Registration County in which the principal town of the District or the greater part of the n is located. The boundaries of Registration Counties, therefore, differ more or less from the boundaries of Counties. For such differences in Division VI., I., Table 11.

he number of Children at each year of age under 5, see Table 4.

three Males were stated to be each 100 years of age. Nine of these Females were stated to be 100 years of age, two 101, two 102, two 103, one 104, one 105, 06 years of age.

Table 2.—Ages of Males and Females in Registration Districts.

STRATION STRICT.	All Ages. Persons.	Males and Females.	Under 5* Years.	5-	10-	15-	20-	25-	30-	35-	40-	45-	50-	55-	60-	65-	70-	75-	80-	85-	90-	95-	100 and upw^{ds}
LOUCES-SHIRE.																							
OL	57479	M. - 26661	3457	2081	3346	2705	2323	2138	1787	1866	1406	1214	1031	813	742	464	289	162	68	16	2	1	.
		F. - 30818	3494	3030	3098	3268	3048	2535	2030	1901	1772	1460	1330	986	967	754	549	320	140	49	14	4	.
ON REGIS	166136	M. - 75187	11073	10000	9071	7788	6023	5629	4989	4687	3827	3125	2628	1937	1851	1276	840	470	201	64	11	4	.
		F. - 90949	11562	10183	9469	9601	6910	7478	6241	5344	4840	4016	3480	2651	2567	1868	1319	790	408	141	42	13	1
PING SOD-Y	17523	M. - 8816	1068	1110	1151	913	626	584	487	441	433	387	380	352	333	232	193	111	52	25	7	1	.
		F. - 8707	1147	1007	949	616	603	560	502	483	454	467	445	354	368	244	224	123	63	17	2	.	.
NBURY	17088	M. - 8465	1078	1076	978	838	646	524	501	465	496	384	347	318	307	214	180	107	48	11	7	.	.
		F. - 8623	1102	1099	968	652	635	565	522	464	478	403	384	340	304	230	177	117	59	23	8	.	.
LEY	12550	M. - 5910	722	762	760	566	399	328	301	291	302	250	262	238	237	173	153	104	47	14	2	1	.
		F. - 6640	814	752	710	595	512	420	390	343	347	311	203	314	262	197	162	128	51	12	7	2	.
BURY ON ERN	23555	M. - 12061	1765	1681	1409	1213	884	815	702	685	565	466	473	399	387	251	180	112	56	13	4	.	.
		F. - 11494	1750	1607	1378	876	760	798	606	504	572	581	468	440	365	292	176	103	57	21	5	.	.
NT	11030	M. - 5496	680	678	683	535	370	303	298	240	285	257	259	222	242	173	143	80	36	11	4	.	.
		F. - 5534	696	714	646	417	368	357	291	281	250	302	281	205	220	169	139	90	45	20	4	.	.
CESTER	46860	M. - 22659	3019	2745	2451	2301	1973	1723	1401	1334	1280	990	888	744	636	434	308	169	81	23	3	1	.
		F. - 24201	3117	2753	2868	2349	2239	1918	1606	1413	1288	1137	1029	725	719	547	383	234	117	47	9	3	.
TENHURST	7353	M. - 3538	466	477	428	332	246	189	191	172	168	146	156	133	124	107	82	61	22	7	2	.	.
		F. - 3815	484	391	437	338	286	257	240	192	213	170	185	153	162	129	83	56	27	9	3	.	.
UD	41345	M. - 19046	2683	2486	2269	1882	1390	1228	1113	977	993	822	794	672	603	420	321	233	121	38	4	.	.
		F. - 22207	2562	2408	2378	2268	1952	1791	1413	1233	1237	1003	1050	863	731	520	421	303	108	46	9	2	.
URY	5893	M. - 2895	304	365	342	285	232	187	153	141	130	136	129	106	117	78	52	33	15	5	1	.	.
		F. - 2998	394	356	334	286	255	207	191	150	127	149	136	122	118	67	54	30	16	4	2	.	.
CESTER	21310	M. - 10621	1277	1296	1172	1240	905	661	578	514	530	458	411	419	397	299	217	151	65	23	8	.	.
		F. - 10689	1283	1286	1178	991	832	697	658	633	562	523	493	405	384	319	213	126	76	22	5	2	.
HLEACH	9884	M. - 5131	648	636	650	540	364	288	278	273	243	240	215	235	174	121	98	71	40	7	6	2	.
		F. - 4753	589	667	540	393	261	280	276	269	264	261	243	197	168	132	102	68	28	15	3	.	.
ON THE D	9129	M. - 4572	585	568	543	466	310	281	245	239	219	208	206	167	165	147	110	64	41	6	2	.	.
		F. - 4557	567	578	472	377	348	278	264	267	231	231	233	198	177	141	97	58	31	10	.	1	.
HCOMB	9533	M. - 4868	602	619	588	491	369	250	243	234	259	227	254	197	203	119	98	80	44	10	1	.	.
		F. - 4665	602	578	526	360	334	305	233	281	240	247	252	210	172	142	95	64	38	12	3	1	.
TENHAM	55505	M. - 23349	2877	2793	2937	2658	1767	1518	1363	1281	1216	976	874	782	779	588	468	254	125	43	13	2	.
		F. - 32156	2929	2848	2981	3651	2400	2558	2226	1908	1831	1595	1409	1191	1193	888	682	407	251	80	24	4	.
ESBURY	12994	M. - 6350	806	802	786	622	460	550	352	353	293	326	260	272	237	169	144	74	33	15	2	.	.
		F. - 6644	817	757	899	609	480	433	400	387	383	342	332	267	241	180	160	107	41	24	5	.	.

The Registration Districts of Division VI. are co-extensive with the Poor Law Unions of the same name, with the following exceptions:—The Hereford (339) comprises the two Poor Law Unions of Hereford and Dore; and Wolverhampton District (371) comprises the two Unions of Wolverhampton and Bristol (320), Oswestry (352), and Coventry (392) Districts are Incorporations under Local Acts; and the Parish of Birmingham (386) is also under a

Parishes comprised in each Registration District, see Vol. II., Division VI., Table 4.

stricts are arranged topographically under the Registration Counties, and are numbered consecutively, commencing with the Metropolitan Districts, I.

he Number of Children at each Year of Age under 5, see Table 5.

Table 2 *continued*.—Ages of Males and Females in Registration Districts.

Registration District.	All Ages. Persons.	All Ages. Males and Females.	Under 5 Years.	5–	10–	15–	20–	25–	30–	35–	40–	45–	50–	55–	60–	65–	70–	75–	80–	85–	90–	95–	100 and upwards.
23. HEREFORDSHIRE.																							
337 LEDBURY	12605	M. - 6257	707	756	56	630	459	391	364	317	322	312	297	236	235	175	136	75	40	8	3	.	.
		F. - 6348	746	744	72	526	459	425	372	375	357	328	318	268	252	181	176	98	57	20	9	2	1
338 ROSS	16369	M. - 8119	1032	1042	961	792	609	485	446	461	432	389	345	304	299	248	170	87	47	8	4	.	.
		F. - 8250	1008	1040	919	739	614	528	469	488	450	362	369	294	340	224	175	103	60	25	13	.	.
339 HEREFORD	43094	M. - 21067	2620	2526	2482	2189	1614	1376	1201	1211	1173	998	916	777	720	625	557	219	122	32	9	.	1
		F. - 22027	2593	2491	2462	2208	1829	1667	1370	1265	1211	1068	965	801	780	690	446	300	130	51	17	7	1
340 WEOBLY	8179	M. - 4056	484	538	439	412	263	239	205	231	220	221	201	167	182	109	65	53	19	7	1	2	.
		F. - 4123	536	458	494	346	290	285	212	281	251	221	299	183	147	137	89	65	41	16	1	.	.
341 BROMYARD	11055	M. - 5584	628	665	648	567	447	366	321	298	306	278	270	236	218	123	117	72	63	10	5	.	.
		F. - 5471	707	712	617	432	423	325	326	267	328	258	245	229	210	148	112	76	46	14	3	2	.
342 LEOMINSTER	14648	M. - 7296	908	917	885	706	639	397	459	365	387	371	341	234	282	198	140	87	37	12	.	.	.
		F. - 7352	854	889	861	709	528	449	430	389	425	396	344	290	268	216	153	194	49	12	6	1	.
343 KINGTON	12197	M. - 6147	771	727	723	648	462	392	361	315	316	276	297	230	235	159	121	76	31	14	2	1	.
		F. - 6050	745	736	709	658	451	392	380	326	286	315	281	242	213	151	143	68	37	17	.	3	.
24. SHROPSHIRE.																							
344 LUDLOW	18589	M. - 9318	1191	1144	1042	928	764	602	549	539	519	418	434	312	316	217	180	108	66	14	1	.	.
		F. - 9271	1262	1134	1059	811	716	616	671	515	527	405	419	309	316	256	196	125	61	29	6	.	.
345 CLUN	10167	M. - 5249	657	682	589	584	420	316	300	263	258	228	225	190	193	136	133	75	33	11	5	2	.
		F. - 4918	638	640	555	449	365	341	255	266	231	247	182	193	179	129	110	39	30	19	.	.	.
346 CHURCH STRETTON	5672	M. - 2913	341	319	356	287	209	160	133	154	161	156	149	112	131	80	80	30	28	5	2	1	.
		F. - 2759	320	312	308	280	197	156	137	155	146	144	152	119	97	78	69	41	29	8	2	.	.
347 CLEOBURY MORTIMER	8138	M. - 4208	530	561	478	431	319	266	223	214	231	189	216	167	165	115	89	59	27	7	2	.	.
		F. - 3930	524	625	441	506	266	240	210	211	210	186	211	149	162	107	94	56	31	8	3	.	.
348 BRIDGNORTH	15279	M. - 7473	911	982	834	717	682	449	418	404	371	312	342	311	338	194	148	88	52	16	3	1	.
		F. - 7806	945	962	911	728	587	480	467	412	438	335	349	291	290	241	170	112	52	25	4	.	.
349 SHIFNAL	12821	M. - 6382	823	818	778	702	483	402	338	329	332	296	307	226	221	148	114	60	20	12	1	.	.
		F. - 6439	784	859	811	613	443	358	362	379	364	305	296	227	299	174	116	98	39	11	2	.	.
350 MADELEY	27314	M. - 13848	1859	1789	1674	1502	1089	892	698	696	690	631	637	465	452	309	238	134	63	18	2	.	.
		F. - 13466	1798	1906	1606	1078	881	789	790	708	738	671	682	625	449	372	281	130	74	57	7	1	.
351 ATCHAM	48033	M. - 23949	2924	2746	2658	2611	2016	1768	1470	1419	1382	1106	1041	810	772	542	459	221	84	22	2	.	.
		F. - 24084	2970	2775	2689	2427	2071	1834	1588	1498	1372	1133	1071	870	827	675	606	297	141	43	17	2	.
352 OSWESTRY	27073	M. - 13497	1749	1702	1532	1422	1354	924	770	739	686	641	588	462	464	291	247	141	56	23	6	.	.
		F. - 13576	1753	1602	1575	1282	1038	916	805	736	721	651	596	474	495	331	239	152	94	29	9	1	.
353 ELLESMERE	13708	M. - 6751	854	770	719	713	546	427	338	367	343	309	300	298	264	216	167	85	38	13	2	.	.
		F. - 6957	781	773	803	711	672	446	367	386	364	331	319	282	282	217	159	32	52	18	1	1	.
354 WEM	10565	M. - 5322	636	629	645	550	411	292	273	292	297	241	260	229	222	155	120	75	36	7	2	.	.
		F. - 5243	620	637	654	486	381	344	275	299	271	234	255	236	208	179	106	72	37	16	3	1	.
355 WHITCHURCH	11246	M. - 5500	700	698	615	589	451	364	310	262	273	247	227	195	200	158	100	64	34	11	1	1	.
		F. - 5746	691	633	577	602	498	445	349	325	270	261	240	218	201	138	139	74	48	29	2	.	.
356 MARKET DRAYTON	14849	M. - 7370	938	956	871	772	556	442	400	377	385	355	315	270	256	181	158	95	41	12	.	1	1
		F. - 7479	913	964	825	670	592	520	474	427	420	375	324	236	287	208	153	85	42	10	9	.	.
357 WELLINGTON	26484	M. - 13505	1965	1862	1615	1422	1035	958	737	716	661	616	682	415	390	267	195	104	63	15	6	.	.
		F. - 12979	1824	1792	1670	1061	950	854	753	784	741	587	573	409	362	294	248	146	68	26	6	.	.
358 NEWPORT	15352	M. - 7707	992	949	911	826	633	478	594	383	396	343	352	284	251	190	168	92	45	16	2	2	.
		F. - 7645	1005	920	885	698	553	470	449	404	406	381	329	311	257	213	165	112	64	22	6	1	.
25. STAFFORDSHIRE.																							
359 STAFFORD	30545	M. - 15327	2070	1898	1653	1608	1277	1213	1045	923	803	664	582	440	436	288	228	133	68	16	4	.	.
		F. - 15218	2027	1901	1666	1489	1300	1167	1015	930	839	685	594	448	407	300	243	142	67	15	4	.	.
360 STONE	29134	M. - 13984	1939	1836	1548	1390	1187	1001	867	743	756	632	590	471	377	255	188	129	53	19	3	1	.
		F. - 15150	1982	1884	1692	1537	1390	1164	919	822	820	652	623	473	432	387	227	132	70	16	4	2	.
361 NEWCASTLE UNDER LYME	34661	M. - 17724	2398	2350	2085	1767	1529	1313	1123	1016	964	737	[illegible]	[illegible]	423	272	203	80	52	5	1	.	.
		F. - 16937	2506	2375	1968	1542	1394	1231	1120	894	926	740	638	541	424	273	198	112	40	17	5	.	.
362 WOLSTANTON	75465	M. - 38058	5470	5361	4493	3909	3400	2912	2559	2281	2039	1625	1398	980	789	429	277	120	47	7	2	.	.
		F. - 37407	5838	5264	4446	3568	3294	2703	2253	2053	1929	1603	1455	992	845	487	321	165	65	14	1	2	1
363 STOKE UPON TRENT	104313	M. - 51812	7796	6872	5937	5248	4508	4285	3441	3221	2899	2265	1831	1301	1084	680	359	108	72	15	1	.	.
		F. - 52501	7296	6885	6021	5294	4736	4204	3371	3068	2705	2270	1810	1437	1175	771	463	285	98	21	6	.	.
364 LEEK	31238	M. - 15226	2185	2096	1809	1468	1202	996	984	838	774	668	627	472	451	337	206	125	49	11	3	.	.
		F. - 16012	2276	2170	1776	1518	1384	1152	1036	914	856	669	594	480	421	339	215	128	64	18	4	.	.
365 CHEADLE	22724	M. - 11376	1584	1539	1478	1158	858	678	649	662	684	502	409	339	364	263	183	104	57	11	4	.	.
		F. - 11348	1611	1543	1800	1044	878	705	657	596	617	522	441	381	352	292	180	102	51	11	6	.	.
366 UTTOXETER	14073	M. - 6873	905	866	758	689	653	417	408	335	334	321	292	254	259	177	140	78	40	21	4	2	.
		F. - 7200	885	835	825	725	621	498	428	382	357	297	327	285	227	208	160	89	37	19	5	.	.
367 BURTON UPON TRENT	73878	M. - 38309	5833	4880	4090	3895	3697	3484	2689	2303	1982	1494	1287	968	741	491	352	201	87	25	4	1	.
		F. - 35569	5049	4891	3957	3029	2869	2785	2418	2037	1914	1435	1219	936	818	550	402	218	109	31	6	1	.
368 TAMWORTH	19400	M. - 9676	1448	1306	1112	956	772	728	535	493	507	417	358	290	260	206	136	73	36	9	.	.	.
		F. - 9724	1511	1206	1087	925	751	751	605	515	507	408	384	307	276	193	123	77	42	12	5	.	.
369 LICHFIELD	39241	M. - 20096	2762	2539	2194	2096	1843	1471	1248	1162	1088	878	771	678	583	418	280	157	96	25	4	1	.
		F. - 19145	2801	2561	2171	1617	1451	1361	1266	1067	1055	839	762	605	550	441	290	181	106	32	11	.	.
370 CANNOCK	36122	M. - 18946	2955	2556	2102	1838	1622	1420	1160	1081	983	796	709	593	441	303	200	184	57	15	4	1	.
		F. - 17176	2831	2529	1997	1346	1229	1235	1133	959	949	730	670	484	410	289	181	107	70	22	3	.	.
371 WOLVERHAMPTON	145470	M. - 72943	10673	9251	8274	7584	6471	5617	4588	3888	3048	3019	2918	2295	1977	1279	798	400	151	61	12	4	.
		F. - 72527	10440	9381	8088	7157	6330	5616	4623	3871	3733	3251	2907	2188	1956	1303	886	474	223	69	14	4	.
372 WALSALL	84107	M. - 42144	6401	5666	4780	4306	3707	3146	2682	2339	2708	1809	1594	1211	991	616	398	202	77	17	3	.	.
		F. - 41963	6397	5840	4851	4207	3719	3148	2635	2273	2204	1751	1478	1087	927	646	497	228	89	24	4	3	1
373 WEST BROMWICH	126163	M. - 62332	9481	8265	7114	6076	5617	4844	3930	3331	3124	3099	2286	1685	1396	945	590	262	117	34	6	1	.
		F. - 63831	9773	8609	7132	6346	5878	4885	4116	3428	3280	2671	2309	1710	1532	1010	649	307	148	46	16	2	1
374 DUDLEY	140224	M. - 70048	10950	9828	8133	7278	6957	5146	4229	3473	3464	2835	2676	2075	1670	1091	721	362	151	34	11	1	.
		F. - 70176	11061	9817	7962	6094	5948	5034	4834	3610	3578	2860	2574	2101	1808	1282	836	453	192	84	16	3	2

Table 2 *continued*.—AGES of MALES and FEMALES in REGISTRATION DISTRICTS.

ISTRATION ISTRICT.	ALL AGES. Persons.	ALL AGES. Males and Females.	Under 5 Years.	5–	10–	15–	20–	25–	30–	35–	40–	45–	50–	55–	60–	65–	70–	75–	80–	85–	90–	95–	100 and upw
RCESTER-HIRE.																							
EBRIDGE -	79596	M. - 39507	5920	5378	4657	4015	3435	2876	2401	2013	1899	1575	1541	1171	992	733	409	254	183	32	4	.	.
		F. - 40089	6068	5452	4620	3767	3398	2832	2540	2129	1298	1718	1545	1174	1024	769	510	275	119	41	9	.	1
ERMINSTER -	40942	M. - 19562	2860	2453	2199	1953	1045	1473	1232	1026	989	849	759	630	594	366	278	187	08	19	0	.	.
		F. - 21380	2824	2513	2227	2202	2070	1648	1351	1160	1095	934	889	665	628	443	315	200	107	43	11	.	1
IURY - -	7588	M. - 3814	471	447	405	396	301	244	206	193	209	194	174	174	136	81	67	32	16	4	1	.	.
		F. - 3774	530	456	429	318	271	241	221	184	217	178	164	143	135	110	86	44	21	7	6	.	.
TLEY - - -	16392	M. - 8086	1042	1004	993	795	552	471	444	424	421	412	356	298	289	217	145	85	42	17	1	1	.
		F. - 8306	970	1002	907	730	630	523	511	401	470	419	415	328	290	229	191	127	68	25	9	2	.
CESTER -	32294	M. - 15258	1975	1772	1669	1573	1364	1202	905	887	850	737	618	480	411	305	199	115	61	18	3	2	1
		F. - 17036	1940	1754	1736	1844	1630	1836	1092	1029	979	824	759	609	524	389	290	162	106	37	8	4	.
N ON SEVERN	23234	M. - 10672	1170	1215	1390	1198	773	678	521	508	503	642	513	442	357	274	198	127	79	16	6	1	.
		F. - 12562	1177	1219	1207	1254	1187	354	781	720	760	652	653	497	467	340	298	169	87	34	13	4	1
HAM -	15270	M. - 7641	909	1000	963	732	552	445	433	432	408	323	309	289	218	175	109	95	45	12	5	.	.
		F. - 7629	1014	925	916	627	589	516	449	420	416	343	326	231	257	222	155	96	43	20	8	1	.
SHORE - -	13560	M. - 6740	836	804	724	707	503	397	347	410	377	331	329	237	235	206	122	99	49	17	.	.	.
		F. - 6820	853	839	824	635	484	429	420	384	356	371	308	247	241	203	152	104	47	14	6	2	.
TWICH - -	25080	M. - 12654	1760	1617	1458	1278	977	841	756	748	682	533	547	439	354	270	190	96	61	20	3	1	.
		F. - 12426	1891	1633	1463	1248	1065	974	843	706	769	606	570	473	401	242	254	149	83	31	3	.	.
MSGROVE -	31914	M. - 15655	2267	1949	1851	1578	1248	1039	944	812	748	704	665	535	501	341	251	148	56	12	4	3	.
		F. - 16259	2224	2016	1700	1521	1415	1268	1077	847	854	749	868	625	493	344	254	143	59	15	3	.	.
S NORTON -	90141	M. - 44427	6334	6091	5910	4505	3896	3582	3025	2617	2251	1847	1643	1243	988	696	415	243	108	29	7	1	.
		F. - 45714	6523	6764	5156	4743	5750	4661	3578	3113	2882	2148	1832	1360	1276	912	510	341	180	48	16	7	.
ARWICK-SHIRE.																							
MINGHAM -	246353	M. 120364	17262	14911	12036	12498	11145	10063	8424	7181	6768	5344	4434	3203	2094	1705	1065	408	186	59	14	.	
		F. 125989	17592	14061	13237	12708	12260	10508	8570	7530	7121	5629	4971	3563	3107	1917	1272	653	257	74	17	5	
ON -	209887	M. 102918	16433	13027	11360	10197	8892	8437	7404	6230	5509	4199	3519	2464	2017	1217	707	394	177	48	8	2	
		F. 106969	16351	13830	11636	10339	9609	8904	7386	6374	5739	4414	3693	2789	2318	1547	1023	548	216	67	13	2	
IDEN -	11925	M. - 6455	679	633	826	536	400	341	257	274	264	235	205	216	190	102	108	77	42	12	.	2	
		F. - 5470	624	708	623	436	590	301	313	290	312	275	273	212	215	102	104	76	52	12	6	1	
ERSTONE -	14419	M. - 7338	1070	1009	846	778	585	574	453	322	332	293	242	202	223	141	109	61	35	13	1	.	
		F. - 7081	1047	902	784	658	537	520	428	411	342	236	284	221	222	148	105	81	37	15	10	.	
EATON -	13701	M. - 6603	618	856	732	642	518	433	408	318	312	287	280	251	216	152	99	77	29	8	2	.	
		F. - 7098	985	878	710	619	595	335	438	387	408	298	315	278	252	151	122	66	31	12	8	.	
ESHILL -	18497	M. - 8983	1329	1191	1035	889	669	602	498	437	471	361	390	348	295	204	174	105	48	34	4	.	
		F. - 9514	1315	1212	1011	808	701	608	590	502	504	394	425	375	331	214	180	99	49	12	6	1	
ENTRY -	45116	M. - 21376	2932	2657	2175	2135	1940	1647	1345	1143	1165	970	807	634	619	466	370	167	87	16	2	.	
		F. - 23740	3038	2714	2424	2300	2232	1855	1486	1293	1327	1154	1019	841	608	529	374	208	92	32	3	.	
BY - -	27206	M. - 13683	1674	1490	1640	1628	1171	1016	815	786	674	601	565	491	427	328	220	135	64	12	2	.	
		F. - 13515	1755	1682	1467	1179	1121	1049	844	801	721	683	590	563	475	318	241	154	75	28	3	.	
IHULL -	21377	M. - 10183	1447	1281	1057	1007	788	654	624	503	556	498	439	317	319	251	100	99	39	18	2	.	
		F. - 11194	1274	1270	1171	1171	1041	905	720	697	625	548	442	358	339	257	187	95	49	18	3	1	
WICK -	52874	M. - 23663	3038	2701	2505	2446	1817	1672	1442	1281	1331	1138	1064	901	811	639	448	278	112	34	9	1	
		F. - 29211	2961	2838	2812	3008	2837	2316	1053	1767	1703	1451	1329	1243	1123	834	538	363	168	70	16	1	
ATFORD ON ON -	22496	M. - 11110	1488	1430	1323	1003	779	698	590	539	577	563	488	457	385	307	199	125	79	18	3	1	
		F. - 11386	1501	1483	1194	976	805	743	640	658	638	552	514	478	413	308	210	142	61	26	7	1	
ESTER -	19430	M. - 9611	1396	1257	1068	916	694	590	575	542	487	410	401	329	361	232	181	122	34	12	1	.	
		F. - 9819	1253	1246	1132	897	738	702	615	581	543	458	367	371	318	250	178	96	49	19	7	1	
PSTON ON OUR -	17874	M. - 8913	1198	1147	1005	867	610	521	446	455	488	415	414	387	330	257	183	138	55	19	2	1	
		F. - 8961	1127	1111	1046	757	555	544	503	500	473	436	447	323	330	290	226	131	60	23	5	.	
THAM -	10282	M. - 5249	677	645	604	484	396	311	278	294	284	220	244	227	180	106	117	71	37	6	1	.	
		F. - 5033	698	659	553	395	334	308	282	295	259	237	257	197	186	192	131	69	37	12	3	.	

TABLE 3.—AGES of MALES and FEMALES in REGISTRATION SUB-DISTRICTS.

EGISTRATION UB-DISTRICT.	ALL AGES. Persons.	ALL AGES. Males and Females.	Under 5 Years.	5–	10–	15–	20–	25–	30–	35–	40–	45–	50–	55–	60–	65–	70–	75–	80–	85–	90–	95–	1.. a.. u..
OUCESTER-SHIRE.																							
BRISTOL.																							
IARY REDCLIFF.) -	9602	M. - 4533	520	547	534	453	360	321	288	282	275	215	173	157	142	98	73	23	11	.	.	.	
		F. 5069	625	562	481	562	419	340	340	308	320	222	225	108	173	137	117	55	20	10	3	2	
E PRECINCTS. P.R.S.) -	6748	M. - 3543	282	268	618	372	387	393	224	224	230	185	145	117	92	56	29	14	10	4	.	.	
		F. - 3205	290	274	291	419	374	270	205	171	194	170	134	119	99	86	47	38	15	7	1	.	
UL -	18643	M. - 8682	1317	1082	955	807	740	721	852	556	484	378	290	239	220	131	81	59	20	4	.	.	
		F. - 9961	1303	1067	963	890	891	850	718	648	539	487	301	299	309	240	182	100	45	22	4	8	
MES. (H[2].) -	8420	M. - 3730	474	418	412	407	319	328	245	225	210	183	148	105	120	70	35	17	8	2	.	.	
		F. - 4690	488	465	470	486	608	404	296	290	272	207	253	164	155	110	64	46	25	6	1	.	
GUSTINE. (H[3].R[2].)	14066	M. - 6173	794	668	827	664	537	462	378	379	317	253	266	196	168	115	79	48	13	6	2	1	
		F. - 7893	788	722	879	931	856	671	479	484	447	333	347	248	231	181	139	81	35	4	5	.	

-For the Parishes comprised in each Registration Sub-district, *see* Vol. II., Division VI., Table 4.
lenotes that a Workhouse and (W S.) that a Workhouse School belonging to the District is situated within the Sub-district; (w.) denotes a W. d (ws.) a Workhouse School not belonging to the District, (H.) a Hospital or Infirmary, (L.) a Lunatic Asylum, (P.) a Prison or Convict Establishment, d Reformatory or Industrial School, (B.) Barracks, &c., (S.) H.M. Ships. A figure appended to any of these letters denotes the number of Institutions class situated within the Sub-district. The names of the Institutions thus indicated, and the number of inmates enumerated therein, will be foun Division VI., Table 6.

TABLE 3 *continued*.—AGES of MALES and FEMALES in REGISTRATION SUB-DISTRICTS.

Registration Sub-District.	All Ages. Persons.	All Ages. Males and Females.	Under 5 Years.	5–	10–	15–	20–	25–	30–	35–	40–	45–	50–	55–	60–	65–	70–	75–	80–	85–	90–	95–	100 and upw^ds.
22 GLOUCESTERSHIRE—*cont.*																							
321 BARTON REGIS.																							
1 Clifton. (H^s. R. B^s.)	28695	M. - 11177	1370	1377	1632	1447	811	773	673	632	527	475	372	360	309	247	138	77	39	15	3	.	.
		F. - 17518	1458	1261	1466	2076	2174	1702	1296	1107	968	894	785	597	587	453	305	219	119	34	15	2	.
2 Ashley	24853	M. - 10968	1509	1522	1232	1216	976	873	769	654	565	426	337	276	236	166	121	60	20	8	2	.	.
		F. - 13885	1591	1655	1516	1661	1230	991	921	801	693	549	473	403	385	297	209	108	60	28	3	2	.
3 St. George	26433	M. - 12917	2232	1915	1601	1298	961	967	825	758	680	520	377	266	248	146	81	49	20	7	.	.	.
		F. - 13516	2288	1962	1640	1230	1093	991	851	789	743	564	442	319	269	182	125	69	34	12	3	1	.
4 St. Philip and Jacob	50108	M. - 24435	3899	3328	2744	2302	2086	2000	1711	1473	1236	1008	819	601	524	284	139	94	35	7	1	2	.
		F. - 25673	4119	3357	2686	2257	2173	2064	1774	1518	1366	1087	977	677	676	413	303	134	75	16	9	1	1
5 Westbury (R.)	21425	M. - 9633	1122	1081	1045	843	712	611	591	513	495	371	331	239	244	184	125	76	36	10	3	1	.
		F. - 12792	1210	1101	1089	1043	1646	1189	932	732	661	594	475	399	383	309	207	128	63	24	6	3	.
6 Stapleton. (W.w.H.L.)	14622	M. - 7057	940	876	917	597	445	416	420	357	368	325	287	195	295	249	186	114	51	17	2	1	.
		F. - 7565	896	844	863	734	802	541	467	397	428	328	337	251	267	214	176	134	85	27	6	4	.
322 CHIPPING SODBURY.																							
1 Chipping Sodbury	4773	M. - 2388	272	282	310	272	182	130	123	137	106	112	124	90	86	62	54	26	12	5	3	.	.
		F. - 2385	285	290	254	214	180	146	138	143	125	124	130	96	99	57	53	29	16	5	1	.	.
2 Marshfield	3696	M. - 1881	232	229	245	203	135	118	103	79	100	85	71	77	74	49	41	28	3	4	.	.	.
		F. - 1815	249	228	206	111	130	129	100	102	88	90	86	68	76	55	50	31	11	5	.	.	.
3 Hawkesbury	3743	M. - 1874	230	245	221	183	131	109	102	83	103	84	69	81	76	63	40	30	14	7	2	1	.
		F. - 1869	249	247	224	114	117	110	101	99	106	99	89	73	86	40	58	26	18	4	.	.	.
4 Iron Acton. (W. L.)	5311	M. - 2673	334	354	375	265	178	177	139	142	124	106	116	104	97	58	58	27	18	9	2	.	.
		F. - 2638	364	332	266	177	176	175	163	139	136	144	140	117	107	83	63	36	18	3	1	.	.
323 THORNBURY.																							
1 Almondsbury	5671	M. - 2802	334	326	316	301	253	177	169	158	146	133	116	88	105	59	55	43	16	4	3	.	.
		F. - 2869	413	374	297	223	225	179	176	143	162	142	149	120	84	74	43	34	19	9	3	.	.
2 Thornbury. (W.)	5421	M. - 2643	341	347	326	228	175	145	144	127	127	129	113	117	104	89	61	42	19	5	2	.	.
		F. - 2778	363	338	303	204	183	189	148	149	181	124	122	125	132	76	76	48	24	10	3	.	.
3 Berkeley. (H.)	5996	M. - 3020	403	403	336	309	218	202	186	180	163	122	113	113	98	66	64	22	13	2	2	.	.
		F. - 2976	416	387	368	228	227	197	198	172	156	140	113	95	88	80	68	35	16	4	2	.	.
324 DURSLEY.																							
1 Wotton under Edge	5101	M. - 2338	270	281	288	233	156	127	127	106	137	94	99	104	99	78	61	48	23	5	1	1	.
		F. - 2763	284	295	282	276	217	182	152	144	135	125	132	148	136	88	73	65	26	5	2	1	.
2 Uley	2157	M. - 1076	160	134	146	96	75	48	58	46	57	44	51	47	44	27	23	22	3	1	.	.	.
		F. - 1081	142	142	111	87	72	54	66	57	64	57	49	46	43	40	26	17	5	1	3	.	.
3 Dursley. (W.)	5292	M. - 2496	292	347	332	237	168	151	121	139	108	112	112	87	94	68	69	34	16	8	1	.	.
		F. - 2796	388	315	317	230	223	184	172	142	148	129	112	126	103	69	63	46	20	6	2	1	.
325 WESTBURY ON SEVERN.																							
1 Newnham	18623	M. - 9601	1458	1385	1130	1007	737	662	556	530	450	373	346	282	270	190	110	68	38	9	4	.	.
		F. - 9022	1450	1320	1090	671	584	646	344	461	455	410	351	315	263	217	115	69	38	12	3	.	.
2 Huntley. (W.)	4932	M. - 2460	307	296	279	206	147	183	146	129	115	93	127	108	117	91	70	54	18	4	.	.	.
		F. - 2472	297	287	279	205	176	152	181	143	117	121	117	125	102	75	61	34	19	9	2	.	.
326 NEWENT.																							
1 Newent. (W.)	6164	M. - 3094	389	382	391	295	215	173	163	137	168	128	148	130	123	91	85	47	19	9	1	.	.
		F. 3070	390	403	352	218	203	197	164	153	168	166	140	114	128	85	78	60	27	12	3	.	.
2 Redmarley	4866	M. - 2402	291	296	292	240	155	130	132	103	117	129	111	92	119	82	58	33	17	2	3	.	.
		F. 2464	306	311	298	199	165	170	127	128	112	136	132	91	92	84	61	30	18	6	1	.	.
327 GLOUCESTER.																							
1 Kingsholm. (L^s. P.)	9354	M. - 4589	555	527	458	462	375	323	288	279	282	223	190	191	150	118	97	44	16	9	2	.	.
		F. 4765	633	603	447	412	444	397	395	260	277	243	250	166	171	140	103	50	39	16	4	.	.
2 St. Nicholas. (W. H.)	8342	M. - 4072	561	473	428	415	332	337	270	240	258	172	171	134	125	90	50	48	21	5	.	.	.
		F. 4270	538	470	462	483	403	359	275	225	218	206	166	119	129	113	66	61	25	7	1	.	.
3 St. John the Baptist } H.	7391	M. - 3418	403	373	400	382	337	251	216	196	196	162	144	133	105	82	43	14	10	1	.	.	.
		F. - 3973	412	370	420	510	456	312	250	228	217	190	176	123	107	74	69	37	15	10	2	1	.
4 South Hamlet } H.	21773	M. - 10580	1580	1372	1165	1102	929	811	717	619	555	433	383	280	255	174	110	65	34	8	1	1	.
		F. - 11193	1634	1416	1229	1004	931	890	776	670	576	498	435	317	312	220	145	80	38	14	2	2	.
328 WHEATENHURST.																							
1 Haresfield (R.)	3135	M. - 1554	193	196	198	174	115	98	97	80	62	59	68	61	52	46	35	20	9	3	1	.	.
		F. 1581	213	170	171	130	117	109	99	60	82	77	65	60	86	58	39	27	13	.	1	.	.
2 Frampton. (W.)	4218	M. - 1984	273	283	230	178	131	103	94	92	106	86	88	82	72	61	47	41	13	4	1	.	.
		F. - 2234	271	221	266	268	169	148	141	112	131	93	120	103	82	71	44	29	14	9	2	.	.
329 STROUD.																							
1 Stonehouse. (H.)	5154	M. - 2344	306	307	261	287	180	142	158	105	134	111	104	81	81	57	42	26	10	5	1	.	.
		F. - 2810	305	292	286	328	284	204	168	152	153	127	127	120	88	59	56	34	17	4	3	.	.
2 Painswick	5016	M. - 2330	318	289	266	224	175	161	134	119	125	109	100	84	77	52	47	28	11	11	.	.	.
		F. 2686	309	317	291	240	213	212	182	128	161	122	137	107	98	71	49	31	16	5	1	.	.
3 Bisley	5169	M. - 2404	347	289	283	259	195	148	138	124	117	104	93	87	74	62	46	21	15	2	.	.	.
		F. - 2765	326	317	291	272	238	204	179	149	149	142	117	95	77	68	60	44	12	4	1	1	.
4 Stroud. (W. H^s.)	11112	M. - 5012	772	669	574	460	346	351	280	301	269	182	216	180	147	88	61	64	36	9	1	.	.
		F. - 6100	724	673	640	712	586	491	387	349	350	235	282	197	196	125	98	66	25	11	2	1	.
5 Rodborough	5779	M. - 2666	332	330	335	276	194	160	162	120	128	138	101	76	80	58	45	25	17	6	.	.	.
		F. - 3113	363	337	361	280	245	237	211	179	167	130	156	129	106	57	69	46	10	6	2	.	.
6 Minchinhampton (H.)	4561	M. - 2128	270	291	274	207	145	132	120	109	103	87	85	81	62	63	38	37	15	1	2	.	.
		F. - 2433	275	270	242	200	215	192	164	131	135	121	101	104	93	76	45	41	13	8	.	.	.
7 Horsley	4555	M. - 2164	309	261	276	220	139	134	112	90	117	91	85	83	82	52	41	32	17	3	.	.	.
		F. - 2391	257	292	287	224	173	161	143	145	122	117	120	101	78	63	54	42	15	7	.	.	.
330 TETBURY.																							
1 Didmarton	1252	M. - 628	90	78	62	55	57	37	38	30	26	38	32	24	19	17	9	9	3	4	.	.	.
		F. - 624	83	83	62	47	44	53	48	29	31	32	33	19	22	13	11	11	3	.	.	.	.
2 Tetbury. (W.H.)	4641	M. - 2267	304	287	280	230	175	150	115	111	104	92	97	82	98	61	48	24	12	1	1	.	.
		F. - 2374	311	273	272	239	211	154	148	121	96	117	103	103	96	54	43	25	7	4	2	.	.

Table 3 *continued*.—AGES of MALES and FEMALES in REGISTRATION SUB-DISTRICTS.

STRATION DISTRICT.	ALL AGES. Persons.	ALL AGES. Males and Females.	Under 5 Years.	5–	10–	15–	20–	25–	30–	35–	40–	45–	50–	55–	60–	65–	70–	75–	80–	85–	90–	95–	100 and upw^s
UCESTER-RE—*cont.*																							
ENCESTER.																							
D	3584	M. - 1799	237	226	182	208	136	123	94	87	94	87	62	72	71	56	35	26	9	1	8	.	.
		F. 1785	225	251	198	131	118	113	109	114	83	97	81	86	67	83	32	22	16	2	1	.	.
STER. (W.H.³B.)	12208	M. - 6046	711	730	654	736	565	572	340	307	295	256	233	204	211	168	109	76	38	10	2	.	.
		F. 6162	731	699	670	619	528	599	388	364	351	238	287	216	217	161	114	67	37	13	4	2	.
D. (H. L².)	5518	M. - 2776	308	350	336	305	204	166	135	126	141	116	116	134	115	75	73	49	18	12	3	.	.
		F. - 2742	324	336	310	241	186	185	161	155	122	128	125	130	100	106	67	37	23	7	.	.	.
RTHLEACH.																							
(W.)	4928	M. - 2485	329	291	315	265	186	159	126	117	108	125	102	114	88	66	49	35	26	4	4	.	.
		F. 2443	268	356	294	207	126	140	141	127	137	139	129	91	90	77	58	34	17	11	1	.	.
RTH. (W.L.)	4956	M. - 2646	317	345	336	272	178	140	154	156	135	115	116	121	86	61	49	39	14	3	2	2	.
		F. - 2310	321	311	246	186	135	140	136	142	127	122	114	103	78	55	44	34	9	4	1	.	.
OW ON THE WOLD.																							
ON THE (H.)	5144	M. - 2949	291	289	267	243	151	120	124	119	100	103	106	81	79	73	40	34	22	1	.	.	.
		F. - 2195	287	296	232	177	140	136	129	136	122	126	99	96	76	74	37	30	13	4	.	1	.
THE WOLD.	[illegible]	M. - 2323	294	288	276	223	159	168	121	120	110	105	100	86	88	74	70	30	19	5	2	.	.
		F. - 2302	300	283	210	290	202	142	135	131	110	105	134	100	101	67	60	28	18	6	.	.	.
NCHCOMB.																							
(W.)	5674	M. - 2873	368	313	345	290	232	146	149	141	114	132	162	122	124	64	58	40	27	5	1	.	.
		F. - 2801	356	367	258	204	211	189	136	166	120	151	134	128	100	84	47	37	21	11	2	.	.
	3859	M. - 1995	244	276	343	291	137	104	94	93	115	95	102	75	70	56	40	29	17	5	.	.	.
		F. - 1864	206	211	228	146	123	116	97	116	111	96	98	83	72	58	48	27	17	1	1	1	.
ELTENHAM.																							
ON KINGS. (H.)	11533	M. - 5125	615	647	582	532	395	309	290	279	275	240	237	203	191	136	99	51	28	14	4	2	.
		F. - 6408	688	636	633	606	606	496	419	371	358	352	280	255	235	186	130	83	41	19	5	.	.
HAM. (W. H².)	43972	M. - 18224	2262	2146	2355	2121	1372	1209	1073	961	941	736	737	574	588	482	359	203	97	29	9	.	.
		F. - 25748	2281	2102	2348	3046	2884	2062	1817	1537	1473	1243	1129	936	968	703	552	374	160	61	18	4	.
WKESBURY.																							
BURY. (W. H.)	10341	M. - 5095	645	633	616	522	378	312	280	208	244	255	283	205	178	134	116	62	23	13	1	.	.
		F. - 5246	648	581	551	591	400	302	311	307	272	273	261	190	194	148	118	84	39	18	3	.	.
RY	2653	M. - 1255	161	169	140	100	82	61	72	85	49	65	57	67	59	35	28	12	10	9	1	.	.
		F. - 1398	169	176	148	108	80	81	89	89	91	99	71	67	47	37	42	23	12	6	2	.	.
EREFORD-HIRE.																							
EDBURY.																							
T. (W. H.)	8646	M. - 4267	479	520	531	442	313	271	243	232	216	209	198	186	161	115	97	52	25	5	2	.	.
		F. 4379	509	519	442	258	321	302	256	266	252	237	224	184	150	130	117	71	29	15	6	1	.
LL	3959	M. 1990	247	255	225	107	140	129	121	115	107	103	90	70	74	60	39	23	15	3	1	.	.
		F. 1969	237	234	230	168	138	127	115	119	106	91	94	84	73	51	59	25	8	5	4	1	.
S ROSS.																							
HOPE	3423	M. - 1690	295	217	290	157	118	95	82	98	102	75	81	70	65	57	31	20	14	2	1	.	.
		F. - 1733	200	238	291	147	129	98	93	106	93	85	92	57	81	41	36	22	10	3	2	.	.
W. H.)	9651	M. - 4749	609	610	553	489	309	313	261	250	248	225	189	172	138	140	107	43	24	5	3	.	.
		F. - 4902	589	594	544	468	377	346	287	292	266	204	208	180	186	139	105	61	39	18	3	.	.
NARDS	3205	M. - 1590	218	215	208	136	122	73	106	103	82	89	84	62	66	51	32	24	9	1	.	.	.
		F. - 1615	219	208	204	134	108	84	89	91	91	73	69	57	73	44	34	20	11	4	2	.	.
EREFORD.																							
RCH	4524	M. - 2272	284	288	304	223	153	126	119	137	108	124	98	91	87	67	28	19	11	5	1	.	.
		F. - 2252	274	274	300	189	156	149	141	119	128	106	99	79	84	62	51	31	12	4	3	1	.
RE	[illegible]	M. - [illegible]	350	335	304	260	175	145	135	145	147	150	115	107	88	70	63	29	13	3	.	.	.
		F. - 3028	347	358	334	296	259	226	176	160	176	141	135	125	101	62	62	52	17	5	3	1	.
LL. (L.)	7306	M. - 3625	402	444	443	377	236	240	197	216	214	183	160	126	127	84	54	29	19	3	2	.	.
		F. - 3681	415	415	401	311	252	283	228	232	241	194	180	145	156	121	82	46	20	9	.	2	.
RD CITY. P. R.)	17044	M. - 8025	998	891	949	910	688	595	512	451	449	334	329	263	251	163	120	81	38	11	2	.	.
		F. - 9019	1071	959	922	1067	878	706	586	506	455	430	383	282	301	230	167	112	56	19	7	2	.
	2768	M. - 1430	167	192	177	139	101	75	78	89	85	67	59	60	51	46	24	17	10	4	.	.	.
		F. - 1338	172	171	173	97	89	74	91	81	59	67	68	31	48	47	19	23	10	5	1	.	.
URCH. (W.)	3503	M. - 1867	212	242	158	168	159	115	93	93	119	87	82	92	78	57	49	28	16	5	2	.	.
		F. 1636	191	204	197	165	108	106	94	91	99	77	78	79	50	39	38	24	11	6	1	.	.
	2297	M. - 1224	147	134	117	118	102	81	69	89	60	53	63	49	41	38	38	16	15	1	2	.	.
		F. - 1073	125	119	135	85	98	73	56	66	51	48	45	40	45	39	21	12	10	3	2	1	.
WEOBLY.																							
(W.)	4809	M. - 2397	286	302	272	257	154	138	112	139	134	119	122	91	112	68	41	33	12	3	.	2	.
		F. - 2412	308	279	308	184	178	155	116	121	138	132	123	87	80	62	47	39	25	12	.	.	.
	3370	M. - 1659	208	231	167	155	109	101	93	92	88	102	79	66	70	41	24	23	7	4	1	.	.
		F. - 1711	229	179	180	162	114	110	96	80	113	89	86	66	67	56	33	26	16	4	1	.	.
ROMYARD.																							
RD. (H.)	3423	M. - 1745	195	212	186	177	145	111	99	85	104	93	63	75	81	41	33	21	9	5	.	.	.
		F. - 1678	198	209	180	157	142	104	111	86	100	85	79	67	66	46	35	20	11	.	1	.	.
FROME	4058	M. - 2056	238	217	237	210	177	148	124	111	102	106	93	93	64	47	30	33	10	4	3	.	.
		F. - 2002	252	255	230	141	163	127	111	97	135	96	93	69	78	62	43	25	21	8	.	2	.
MPTON. (W.)	3574	M. - 1783	195	236	223	170	125	107	98	102	100	89	94	67	68	35	40	18	13	1	2	.	.
		F. - 1791	257	268	207	134	119	94	104	104	93	79	73	73	56	40	34	32	16	6	2	.	.
OMINSTER.																							
TER. (W.)	6617	M. - 3221	461	393	391	332	270	187	206	157	170	156	129	122	108	85	55	44	16	2	.	.	.
		F. 3396	386	414	394	290	263	224	209	175	180	162	166	104	118	101	64	42	29	4	2	.	.
AM	3755	M. - 1925	235	256	224	177	124	103	106	82	115	99	114	83	73	48	46	20	9	7	.	.	.
		F. 1830	224	220	225	166	121	92	105	96	112	116	89	88	65	45	39	28	7	5	1	1	.
ND	4276	M. - 2149	267	263	273	196	144	107	118	120	112	116	100	79	101	57	41	33	13	3	.	.	.
		F. 2127	244	255	242	193	144	124	116	118	124	124	93	88	85	79	50	34	13	3	2	.	.

Table 3 *continued*.—Ages of Males and Females in Registration Sub-Districts.

Registration Sub-District.	All Ages. Persons.		Males and Females.	Under 5 Years.	5-	10-	15-	20-	25-	30-	35-	40-	45-	50-	55-	60-	65-	70-	75-	80-	85-	90-	95-	100 and upwards.
23 HEREFORDSHIRE—*cont.*																								
343 KINGTON.																								
1 Brilley	1865	M.	967	98	122	105	117	62	63	56	50	47	45	37	46	28	24	23	10	4	1	.	.	.
		F.	898	104	102	114	80	76	48	60	48	41	45	46	44	40	21	16	13	2	2	.	.	.
2 Radnor	3256	M.	1663	222	174	206	106	134	110	88	85	83	82	79	47	79	41	30	21	11	3	1	1	.
		F.	1593	211	220	180	137	142	106	97	86	80	71	69	60	47	36	28	18	14	1	.	.	.
3 Kington. (W.)	5868	M.	2891	366	363	332	317	180	170	173	145	150	125	151	112	106	75	57	34	11	7	.	.	.
		F.	2977	356	347	364	282	197	196	187	163	152	163	140	112	108	79	79	31	18	14	.	2	.
4 Kinsham	1208	M.	636	80	78	80	48	57	41	44	25	27	24	30	15	22	19	11	11	5	3	1	.	.
		F.	572	74	61	65	60	36	45	36	30	20	32	27	27	18	15	20	8	3	.	.	1	.
24 SHROPSHIRE.																								
344 LUDLOW.																								
1 Leintwardine	2311	M.	1162	126	140	133	98	106	77	69	66	68	62	57	58	41	31	17	16	11	1	.	.	.
		F.	1149	145	142	135	107	80	66	71	69	61	37	43	48	47	35	18	11	6	7	1	.	.
2 Ludlow. (W.)	9462	M.	4583	574	506	513	460	348	271	276	258	263	196	234	153	139	111	102	45	29	9	1	.	.
		F.	4879	598	559	566	446	395	325	290	278	293	215	245	169	163	132	99	76	41	18	2	.	.
3 Cainham	2651	M.	1417	181	174	163	154	135	93	90	97	76	57	44	39	53	27	25	11	1	1	.	.	.
		F.	1234	177	189	146	83	85	91	85	73	65	53	47	33	42	37	35	15	5	2	1	.	.
4 Munslow	1825	M.	950	138	95	100	88	83	76	50	61	42	43	45	30	42	23	15	14	7	2	.	.	.
		F.	875	116	128	89	80	61	69	41	45	46	38	42	33	31	21	18	14	4	2	2	.	.
5 Diddlebury	2340	M.	1206	172	140	133	119	92	85	73	74	61	69	64	31	40	26	21	18	7	1	.	.	.
		F.	1134	166	171	123	96	94	65	84	52	62	42	42	35	33	31	25	9	6	.	.	.	.
345 CLUN.																								
1 Clun	3931	M.	2018	250	253	208	190	154	133	122	112	101	85	80	77	74	65	54	37	18	6	1	2	.
		F.	1913	257	243	215	160	130	142	121	101	95	86	68	76	85	40	52	18	18	9	.	.	.
2 Bishops Castle. (W.)	2797	M.	1429	178	146	168	179	116	79	80	79	81	65	58	43	56	33	39	19	7	6	1	.	.
		F.	1368	159	178	144	135	103	94	77	80	77	69	49	52	44	46	23	12	12	5	.	.	.
3 Norbury	1609	M.	865	97	116	116	118	78	47	44	36	40	29	37	32	36	23	18	9	4	.	1	.	.
		F.	744	168	110	98	68	53	47	40	32	40	34	33	35	17	10	18	2	6	2	.	.	.
4 Lydbury	1836	M.	937	123	121	97	97	78	57	54	36	36	40	56	38	37	24	22	10	6	.	2	.	.
		F.	899	114	100	106	77	70	58	47	44	30	58	45	30	33	32	17	7	3	3	.	.	.
346 CHURCH STRETTON.																								
1 Church Stretton. (W. L.)	3688	M.	1879	245	208	223	170	188	101	92	95	111	94	102	75	76	53	48	31	20	3	2	1	.
		F.	1809	196	235	189	184	130	107	88	115	97	98	98	61	60	56	37	33	15	7	1	.	.
2 Wall	1981	M.	1031	116	111	133	118	71	59	41	59	56	62	47	37	56	25	32	8	8	2	.	.	.
		F.	950	124	117	117	98	67	49	49	40	49	54	54	38	37	22	22	8	5	1	1	.	.
347 CLEOBURY MORTIMER.																								
1 Cleobury Mortimer (W.)	5448	M.	2772	332	334	324	275	212	171	130	150	165	126	144	108	102	74	57	43	19	5	2	.	.
		F.	2676	346	357	297	213	170	168	134	143	180	125	140	102	113	73	74	64	23	7	3	.	.
2 Stottesden	2690	M.	1436	198	167	152	158	107	96	84	64	76	63	72	50	53	41	23	16	8	2	.	.	.
		F.	1254	178	108	144	92	89	78	78	68	71	60	62	48	39	34	20	22	8	1	.	.	.
348 BRIDGNORTH.																								
1 Chetton	4433	M.	2301	294	252	240	230	190	136	134	124	113	98	103	90	103	51	85	29	15	5	.	1	.
		F.	2132	293	283	245	172	161	127	121	161	128	84	107	66	81	66	48	30	17	8	3	.	.
2 Bridgnorth. (W. H.)	5848	M.	2671	312	318	258	251	223	108	162	152	131	116	128	116	123	83	54	34	21	6	3	.	.
		F.	3177	342	341	341	341	261	204	206	174	168	146	138	126	126	98	82	52	18	12	1	.	.
3 Worfield. (W.S.)	4995	M.	2501	298	372	327	236	169	145	122	128	127	98	106	96	112	60	59	25	16	5	.	.	.
		F.	2494	310	338	325	218	165	140	140	137	142	165	164	99	83	83	49	30	17	5	.	.	.
349 SHIFNAL.																								
1 Albrighton	4129	M.	2008	271	246	242	193	141	137	111	113	103	90	88	76	69	47	31	26	6	1	.	.	.
		F.	2121	242	268	265	215	129	145	138	121	114	101	89	76	64	55	43	28	11	2	.	.	.
2 Shifnal. (W.)	8692	M.	4374	502	475	523	509	322	245	227	214	229	208	219	156	152	96	83	35	15	11	1	.	.
		F.	4318	542	591	546	498	284	253	229	218	250	204	207	181	136	119	73	38	28	9	2	.	..
350 MADELEY.																								
1 Dawley	9458	M.	4898	661	676	658	575	496	308	228	215	226	211	244	142	145	94	75	32	16	3	.	.	.
		F.	4560	686	689	543	349	268	284	285	188	245	243	213	170	129	132	88	36	10	9	1	.	.
2 Madeley. (W.)	10626	M.	5026	646	605	683	516	303	321	265	269	256	248	229	197	184	129	96	68	32	6	.	.	.
		F.	5600	629	700	571	407	340	361	275	277	280	252	243	192	191	189	118	44	33	15	2	.	.
3 Broseley	5509	M.	2772	307	376	312	306	209	186	144	172	147	112	103	98	84	58	39	19	8	3	.	.	.
		F.	2737	350	376	346	218	183	169	168	175	153	116	111	122	86	71	49	27	14	9	3	.	.
4 Much Wenlock	2321	M.	1172	155	132	141	111	82	77	61	59	61	66	61	48	39	28	29	15	4	6	2	.	.
		F.	1149	129	140	139	104	96	65	62	66	68	60	66	40	43	33	31	13	8	4	1	1	.
351 ATCHAM.																								
1 Condover. (W.)	5736	M.	2952	337	341	367	287	207	169	161	140	167	187	124	120	120	101	87	64	19	8	1	.	.
		F.	2784	334	353	368	240	180	170	164	162	143	158	116	94	107	86	72	50	21	11	2	1	.
2 Pontesbury	3507	M.	1784	259	227	197	184	125	114	96	90	84	84	78	68	62	45	36	14	9	2	1	.	.
		F.	1723	253	230	197	130	115	119	98	59	78	73	96	61	59	49	34	18	8	4	3	.	.
3 Westbury	2224	M.	1127	138	138	134	116	86	81	65	56	65	55	60	34	39	32	22	11	3	1	.	.	.
		F.	1097	148	135	137	81	79	68	66	68	53	55	46	36	36	35	27	20	4	1	.	.	.
4 Alberbury	2056	M.	1047	125	113	124	109	79	71	44	58	64	58	39	38	41	36	23	19	5	1	.	.	.
		F.	1009	124	115	108	120	77	65	54	50	55	35	47	37	39	46	24	14	5	.	.	.	.
5 Montford	1172	M.	579	79	96	59	57	33	29	26	45	26	31	20	16	22	17	16	5	4	1	.	.	.
		F.	593	75	79	78	51	38	29	29	36	46	23	24	21	21	17	13	9	7	.	.	.	.
6 Battlefield	1935	M.	973	113	121	116	101	61	51	55	52	55	46	48	42	39	36	22	18	4	1	.	.	.
		F.	962	120	127	111	73	69	49	59	53	66	53	37	46	41	33	13	11	2	2	1	.	.
7 Atcham	1533	M.	764	87	87	100	73	52	40	48	43	48	37	34	24	30	26	13	10	8	1	.	.	.
		F.	769	89	94	68	64	56	66	38	54	43	41	31	33	31	29	17	14	5	1	1	.	.
8 St. Mary Shrewsbury. (H. & L. P.)	20346	M.	9707	1213	1067	1051	1006	896	825	685	580	574	445	408	318	289	178	144	68	15	4	.	.	.
		F.	10639	1204	1143	1025	1078	956	876	744	642	613	482	465	383	327	262	267	93	57	15	6	1	.
9 St. Chad Shrewsbury (B.)	10124	M.	5016	573	564	528	585	477	388	320	340	309	212	224	147	121	82	90	30	17	3	.	.	.
		F.	5108	563	499	537	567	498	302	334	331	291	213	215	159	107	130	99	65	32	9	4	.	.

Table 3 *continued*.—AGES of MALES and FEMALES in REGISTRATION SUB-DISTRICTS.

STRATION DISTRICT.	ALL AGES. Persons.	ALL AGES. Males and Females.	Under 5 Years.	5–	10–	15–	20–	25–	30–	35–	40–	45–	50–	55–	60–	65–	70–	75–	80–	85–	90–	95–	100 and upw.
OPSHIRE —*cont.*																							
SWESTRY.																							
I -	4134	M. - 1998	281	248	204	210	144	120	105	115	108	80	82	72	80	53	45	19	12	3	1	.	.
		F. - 2136	268	275	236	189	148	145	122	115	122	90	91	74	82	51	48	31	18	1	.	.	.
IN -	3919	M. - 2001	248	241	215	230	140	143	107	90	89	96	88	84	76	47	43	23	8	3	1	.	.
		F. - 1918	237	237	210	183	140	132	100	87	96	95	84	62	78	51	45	25	17	2	2	.	.
TY. (W.H.)	11923	M. - 5875	719	729	726	620	454	407	329	321	320	308	267	173	204	120	59	46	21	13	4	.	.
		F. - 6048	732	682	691	542	501	408	360	346	307	318	275	226	294	146	80	63	40	17	3	1	.
TIN -	7097	M. - 3323	501	464	392	362	307	248	228	201	171	148	151	133	104	71	60	42	15	4	.	.	.
		F. - 3474	506	498	400	268	246	239	224	187	202	148	146	112	111	83	54	38	10	9	4	.	.
LLESMERE.																							
N -	1401	M. - 695	77	73	65	73	53	45	43	42	42	36	24	40	31	21	14	8	4	4	.	.	.
		F. - 706	72	93	94	70	47	60	44	45	42	40	31	37	28	32	17	10	5	1	.	1	.
-	2372	M. - 1184	159	125	123	148	92	84	51	68	58	52	52	50	34	33	33	14	7	1	.	.	.
		F. - 1188	132	128	135	95	111	99	54	64	54	51	56	45	51	42	25	16	10	4	.	.	.
ERE. (W.)	6256	M. - 3060	387	349	325	311	254	194	155	160	152	136	148	124	123	104	76	35	18	8	2	.	.
		F. - 3196	351	346	378	303	261	192	174	176	154	164	150	131	127	95	73	42	25	11	1	.	.
RCH -	3619	M. - 1812	231	223	197	181	141	104	87	97	90	65	76	84	73	57	44	28	11	.	.	.	.
		F. - 1807	205	206	196	191	153	96	93	103	114	86	83	69	76	48	44	22	12	2	.	.	.
& WEM.																							
(W.) -	7215	M. - 3611	437	431	429	370	283	215	190	199	177	165	161	144	140	112	82	52	17	7	1	.	.
		F. - 3604	429	431	375	333	277	239	191	216	185	180	171	151	135	121	73	63	25	6	3	.	.
- - -	3350	M. - 1711	198	198	216	180	128	77	74	93	90	80	89	76	82	43	38	23	19	.	1	.	.
		F. - 1639	191	206	179	153	104	105	84	83	88	81	84	76	73	57	33	19	12	10	.	1	.
HITCHURCH.																							
URCH. (W.L.) -	7826	M. - 3816	501	501	422	381	304	261	213	204	187	172	152	132	134	108	66	43	23	7	.	.	.
		F. - 4010	473	438	393	429	349	323	243	231	192	179	172	146	138	112	109	45	26	12	.	.	.
- -	3420	M. - 1684	199	187	193	188	147	103	92	78	81	75	75	63	60	50	34	21	11	4	1	1	.
		F. - 1736	218	195	184	173	140	122	106	94	78	82	68	72	65	46	30	29	17	8	2	.	.
KET DRAYTON.																							
ON SAY -	3900	M. - 1938	242	236	224	188	154	137	99	102	107	100	95	69	60	49	38	26	10	.	.	1	1
		F. - 1962	246	237	217	185	157	142	111	102	106	105	86	69	74	58	29	20	12	3	3	.	.
T DRAYTON. (W.)	5954	M. - 2889	390	382	340	299	219	197	170	148	145	145	113	93	94	58	57	44	12	6	.	.	.
		F. - 3065	381	357	341	287	246	221	208	174	167	130	135	67	118	70	72	38	23	4	5	.	.
T - -	4995	M. - 2543	306	325	307	285	177	138	151	127	133	110	107	108	102	74	63	25	19	6	.	.	.
		F. - 2452	286	310	267	198	189	157	155	151	153	114	103	99	100	80	52	27	7	3	1	.	.
ELLINGTON.																							
MAGNA. -	3043	M. - 1589	200	196	207	134	114	91	82	81	73	68	74	57	80	58	44	22	11	3	2	.	.
		F. - 1454	185	174	134	110	107	100	82	81	70	62	69	71	56	40	43	24	7	7	3	.	.
NGTON. (W.) -	15273	M. - 7727	1093	1025	893	855	591	504	417	402	308	357	336	249	218	186	117	56	36	11	4	.	.
		F. - 7546	1004	1018	937	651	512	485	422	455	461	345	342	225	240	135	138	60	42	15	1	.	.
IDGE -	8168	M. - 4189	602	641	509	433	330	264	238	233	198	191	172	109	92	63	34	26	6	1	.	.	.
		F. - 3979	635	601	469	300	241	240	240	248	210	182	132	115	86	86	17	31	19	4	2	.	.
NEWPORT.																							
RT. (W.) -	10764	M. - 5377	691	675	650	587	453	316	309	267	279	243	240	194	154	134	118	53	30	8	.	2	.
		F. - 5387	675	677	639	504	396	335	320	289	278	275	229	198	176	150	112	73	42	16	2	1	.
L -	4588	M. - 2330	298	274	252	239	180	169	125	118	117	100	112	90	97	54	50	30	15	8	2	.	.
		F. - 2258	330	243	246	194	167	135	129	115	122	106	100	113	81	63	53	39	22	6	4	.	.
TAFFORD-SHIRE.																							
STAFFORD.																							
RD. (W.H.I.P.)	26470	M. - 13344	1837	1650	1419	1258	1135	1079	939	826	745	566	508	382	306	233	192	109	55	14	4	.	.
		F. - 13126	1790	1632	1421	1297	1163	1008	900	819	722	576	504	306	333	236	182	114	44	13	3	.	.
IH -	4075	M. - 1983	242	248	234	223	142	134	106	99	118	98	74	67	70	53	30	24	13	2	.	.	.
		F. 2092	237	260	234	192	137	159	115	111	117	109	90	83	69	54	61	28	13	3	1	.	.
O STONE.																							
(W. H.) -	10316	M. - 4918	624	646	578	402	393	323	266	246	278	231	238	204	147	110	75	58	25	7	3	1	.
		F. - 5398	653	645	630	535	480	382	303	281	306	246	247	188	172	123	83	59	26	7	3	2	.
HALL -	5715	M. - 2817	365	376	310	273	215	182	161	133	140	124	129	103	105	72	56	35	18	11	.	.	.
		F. 2898	323	344	310	291	238	193	168	158	136	142	120	89	106	73	57	38	24	7	.	.	.
IAM -	13103	M. - 6249	950	813	660	655	679	493	440	364	329	277	222	164	125	73	57	34	10	1	.	.	.
		F. - 6854	943	895	743	711	663	389	448	383	358	264	256	196	155	110	77	35	20	4	1	.	.
EWCASTLE DER LYME.																							
ORE -	1084	M. - 540	78	61	61	57	44	28	40	26	31	27	14	19	22	14	8	5	4	1	.	.	.
		F. - 544	66	74	67	41	47	42	34	26	34	25	16	25	19	9	9	3	4	2	1	.	.
STLE UNDER (W. B.)	20998	M. - 10539	1481	1350	1241	1043	890	784	655	631	616	465	438	294	255	180	132	48	27	2	1	.	.
		F. - 10459	1462	1351	1232	1050	912	779	662	572	582	472	384	323	270	170	117	72	30	10	3	.	.
- -	12579	M. - 6645	1089	933	788	667	595	501	430	359	317	245	223	216	146	78	63	27	21	2	.	.	.
		F. - 5934	978	960	669	451	435	430	424	296	309	243	238	163	135	88	87	37	15	5	1	.	.
OLSTANTON.																							
NTON -	17541	M. - 8894	1302	1317	1072	911	754	611	507	526	489	361	246	226	193	86	66	21	12	2	1	.	.
		F. - 8647	1458	1285	994	728	741	636	518	498	471	389	325	228	174	96	61	44	15	3	.	1	.
LL. (W.) -	29675	M. - 15252	2149	2093	1736	1560	1418	1181	1015	902	840	648	535	441	333	189	118	43	19	5	.	.	.
		F. - 14423	2188	2198	1808	1374	1294	1055	877	764	746	602	571	308	318	190	129	54	26	5	1	.	.
M - -	28249	M. - 13912	2019	1891	1687	1423	1228	1120	937	833	739	616	497	332	263	164	93	53	16	.	1	.	.
		F. - 14337	2180	1871	1649	1466	1349	1102	838	801	712	632	559	366	353	199	131	67	22	8	.	1	1

Table 3 *continued.*—Ages of Males and Females in Registration Sub-Districts.

Registration Sub-District.	All Ages. Persons.	Males and Females.	Under 5 Years.	5–	10–	15–	20–	25–	30–	35–	40–	45–	50–	55–	60–	65–	70–	75–	80–	85–	90–	95–	100 and upwards.
25 STAFFORDSHIRE—*cont.*																							
363 STOKE UPON TRENT.																							
1 Hanley	26089	M. 13108	1982	1748	1407	1369	1176	1092	894	885	657	551	468	311	230	144	84	46	20	6	1	.	.
		F. 12983	2005	1746	1469	1271	1195	1042	831	724	673	566	436	375	273	189	164	67	22	4	1	.	.
2 Shelton	28196	M. 14049	2091	1767	1501	1452	1229	1224	936	903	801	622	528	366	312	141	87	41	14	4	.	.	.
		F. 14147	2111	1737	1570	1491	1313	1151	935	824	705	615	525	364	337	163	117	89	28	6	1	.	.
3 Stoke upon Trent. (W. H².)	17272	M. 8453	1208	1169	989	869	724	612	527	448	469	406	301	237	214	128	76	54	19	3	.	.	.
		F. 8819	1247	1116	961	903	832	722	563	505	447	418	285	263	208	152	95	73	25	5	2	.	.
4 Fenton	14136	M. 7050	1139	937	812	663	618	585	472	449	363	285	248	184	132	82	42	22	8	2	.	.	.
		F. 7086	1150	937	880	638	639	573	421	461	366	283	260	179	138	103	50	35	12	2	1	.	.
5 Longton. (H.)	18620	M. 9154	1376	1221	1138	895	761	772	592	583	519	391	297	203	106	105	69	35	11	.	.	.	.
		F. 9466	1453	1250	1162	987	886	713	571	524	514	393	304	236	219	144	88	31	13	4	1	.	.
364 LEEK.																							
1 Norton	10430	M. 5327	848	779	642	501	440	387	354	233	274	213	181	131	113	83	46	16	10	3	1	.	.
		F. 5103	922	837	630	411	561	375	329	230	252	177	150	122	116	63	43	15	12	6	2	.	.
2 Leek. (W. H².)	15094	M. 6999	965	930	805	699	561	471	428	380	344	318	308	221	224	160	94	70	23	8	1	.	.
		F. 8095	1005	956	803	851	840	617	546	405	442	352	320	254	226	190	111	69	36	9	2	.	.
3 Leek Frith	1757	M. 881	124	122	101	87	63	47	51	36	48	44	47	38	31	23	14	8	3	.	.	.	.
		F. 876	122	138	99	93	60	47	52	51	45	46	29	23	22	22	16	12	2	.	.	.	.
4 Longnor	3357	M. 2019	248	268	283	171	128	111	101	101	108	98	91	82	83	71	80	31	13	.	1	.	.
		F. 1988	227	242	244	163	133	115	107	108	115	94	86	81	57	73	45	32	14	3	.	.	.
365 CHEADLE.																							
1 Alton	2994	M. 1607	194	186	306	232	95	86	78	78	78	56	48	48	49	35	51	15	7	2	.	.	.
		F. 1387	206	192	146	111	90	97	80	75	80	60	51	53	56	42	23	11	9	4	1	.	.
2 Ipstones	5418	M. 2760	365	308	333	262	197	159	155	134	142	139	114	103	91	71	56	19	17	5	.	.	.
		F. 2658	325	335	325	224	177	176	157	123	159	122	113	89	76	76	50	32	12	2	1	.	.
3 Dilhorne. (R.)	7152	M. 3609	521	502	405	382	312	224	210	186	186	161	125	127	87	61	35	28	12	2	2	.	.
		F. 3543	516	514	411	314	290	246	208	201	130	172	119	106	85	66	46	29	7	1	.	.	.
4 Cheadle. (W.)	7160	M. 3400	504	463	345	331	231	200	206	164	183	147	125	116	137	98	61	42	21	2	2	.	.
		F. 3760	604	452	418	369	219	253	217	197	208	169	158	131	133	198	61	30	23	4	4	.	.
366 UTTOXETER.																							
1 Uttoxeter. (W.)	7932	M. 3834	525	490	420	346	307	285	231	177	189	167	159	147	141	107	60	32	18	12	2	1	.
		F. 4098	529	453	446	415	377	292	248	218	207	167	187	166	131	103	78	42	19	10	4	.	.
2 Abbots Bromley	2690	M. 1307	181	159	147	127	111	63	71	72	54	67	64	39	45	25	37	25	15	4	1	.	.
		F. 1383	164	189	187	143	101	93	70	68	60	59	59	48	47	47	23	28	14	3	1	.	.
3 Sudbury	3451	M. 1732	199	128	191	196	136	119	106	86	91	87	69	68	73	46	34	21	7	5	1	1	.
		F. 1719	192	223	198	162	143	113	116	93	90	71	81	71	49	52	45	21	4	6	.	.	.
367 BURTON UPON TRENT.																							
1 Tutbury	7569	M. 3733	583	487	408	377	331	236	237	209	170	167	126	126	118	75	66	37	19	2	2	.	.
		F. 3836	654	502	418	371	306	287	251	199	203	164	149	119	115	81	58	31	28	5	.	.	.
2 Repton. (L.)	6587	M. 3394	377	361	429	309	256	224	196	174	184	141	119	136	104	73	60	32	16	3	.	.	.
		F. 3193	376	330	315	295	272	248	203	182	201	123	160	143	118	101	64	50	25	7	.	.	.
3 Gresley	19747	M. 10137	1741	1488	1107	1039	843	794	672	576	494	390	333	250	186	121	72	54	20	7	.	.	.
		F. 9610	1795	1485	1062	778	732	705	607	522	485	329	328	244	196	120	83	49	20	9	1	.	.
4 Burton upon Trent. (W. H.²)	39975	M. 21045	3162	2594	2151	1970	2267	2108	1584	1353	1134	796	629	457	333	222	154	78	37	13	2	1	.
		F. 18930	3224	2571	2162	1582	1559	1660	1352	1134	1025	754	587	430	389	248	195	108	41	10	5	1	.
368 TAMWORTH.																							
1 Tamworth. (W.H.L.)	9650	M. 4742	665	626	541	480	363	338	256	238	254	216	158	166	137	118	82	38	22	8	.	.	.
		F. 4908	684	612	577	477	378	368	299	271	262	213	204	163	148	91	73	47	28	9	2	.	.
2 Fazeley	9750	M. 4934	723	680	571	497	409	390	279	255	253	138	168	124	129	88	54	35	13	7	.	.	.
		F. 4816	827	654	510	448	373	383	306	244	245	136	160	142	127	102	59	30	14	8	3	.	.
369 LICHFIELD.																							
1 Lichfield. (W. L.B.)	24442	M. 12603	1692	1362	1270	1419	1216	928	903	728	605	555	479	320	361	254	160	94	57	16	2	1	.
		F. 11839	1627	1531	1385	1080	927	874	734	670	623	536	437	371	330	283	185	98	57	18	5	.	.
2 Yoxall. (H.)	4374	M. 2147	257	260	261	181	160	116	115	130	116	117	97	87	81	72	49	23	17	6	2	.	.
		F. 2227	295	281	276	177	148	121	116	103	141	108	111	98	80	94	45	33	20	6	1	.	.
3 Rugeley. (H².)	10375	M. 5346	835	717	573	406	467	427	327	307	277	201	195	171	141	90	71	46	24	9		.	.
		F. 5029	809	689	643	410	376	366	356	278	218	215	213	141	140	94	70	50	28	8	5	.	.
370 CANNOCK.																							
1 Penkridge	4246	M. 2122	297	287	227	207	155	143	117	108	116	88	74	83	72	66	44	26	11	1	.	.	.
		F. 2124	288	252	226	199	157	128	124	119	135	107	98	91	67	57	39	19	13	3	2	.	.
2 Brewood	5771	M. 2821	366	338	344	242	230	166	160	156	145	132	141	110	94	71	50	38	21	6	1	1	.
		F. 2950	364	382	317	262	209	230	191	161	157	121	146	101	111	86	53	29	22	7	1	.	.
3 Cannock. (W.)	26105	M. 14003	2272	1939	1581	1389	1228	1111	883	817	722	576	491	400	275	166	106	70	25	8	3	.	.
		F. 12102	2179	1895	1464	885	863	877	818	679	650	511	426	292	232	146	83	56	35	12	.	.	.
371 WOLVERHAMPTON.																							
1 Tettenhall	7992	M. 3832	476	480	456	428	314	260	213	209	168	183	162	163	112	91	63	30	14	5	2	.	.
		F. 4160	406	482	448	405	306	323	294	231	196	189	191	142	125	123	69	40	22	7	2	1	.
2 Kinver	4019	M. 2031	257	259	220	207	169	154	109	100	91	87	92	67	79	65	47	12	10	4	3	.	.
		F. 1988	283	255	203	171	143	156	121	113	98	98	88	69	67	53	38	24	11	5	.	.	.
3 Wombourn. (W.)	5711	M. 2741	358	320	239	288	207	201	180	140	125	101	121	115	123	65	44	25	20	6	3	.	.
		F. 2970	332	344	295	274	286	250	215	170	144	135	142	96	165	82	56	21	13	4	3	.	.
4 Wolverhampton Western	37156	M. 17864	2646	2219	2034	1648	1592	1439	1230	1022	987	718	685	500	409	275	104	90	26	10	.	.	.
		F. 19292	2648	2311	2129	2100	1861	1576	1283	1096	1000	810	740	540	480	330	220	118	57	16	3	2	.
5 Wolverhampton Eastern. (W. H.)	38610	M. 19963	2860	2447	2243	2051	1832	1611	1261	1056	1011	799	811	617	600	376	204	112	43	14	4	2	.
		F. 18647	2715	2368	1996	1786	1660	1442	1182	936	1027	841	803	561	541	328	206	108	56	20	3	1	.
4 Willenhall	29262	M. 15094	2406	2043	1713	1615	1268	1104	913	761	742	631	545	480	360	245	136	77	26	9	.	1	.
		F. 14168	2384	2046	1712	1238	1100	1020	881	731	690	583	560	415	340	247	162	81	30	13	1	.	.
5 Bilston	22730	M. 11418	1663	1483	1309	1197	1059	848	682	597	574	520	499	353	285	172	108	55	12	3	.	1	.
		F. 11312	1577	1581	1306	1174	925	830	644	575	578	555	443	362	208	206	133	76	34	4	2	.	.

Table 3 *continued*.—AGES of MALES and FEMALES in REGISTRATION SUB-DISTRICTS.

STRATION DISTRICT.	ALL AGES. Persons.	ALL AGES. Males and Females.	Under 5 Years.	5-	10-	15-	20-	25-	30-	35-	40-	45-	50-	55-	60-	65-	70-	75-	80-	85-	90-	95-	100 and upw
AFFORD-RE—*cont.*																							
VALSALL.																							
ON	13900	M. 6941	1049	953	804	736	615	487	431	398	356	306	261	194	178	107	68	26	16	6	.	.	.
		F. 6959	1046	994	812	691	592	492	426	381	373	315	228	187	172	122	84	41	16	2	.	2	.
JS	13180	M. 6869	1021	1000	817	688	560	491	407	308	379	278	270	219	137	104	66	32	16	3	2	.	.
		F. 6311	1036	1004	786	541	458	407	410	314	387	281	216	153	142	111	57	37	18	3	1	.	.
L. (W.H¹.)	44959	M. 22243	3384	2925	2417	2253	1967	1746	1485	1218	1162	968	868	636	524	361	206	116	55	6	1	.	.
		F. 22716	3357	2970	2576	2402	2157	1777	1408	1215	1160	928	804	677	497	323	217	118	42	14	2	1	1
DE	12068	M. 6091	944	786	632	629	550	452	360	337	304	259	246	162	157	104	63	28	11	2	.	.	.
		F. 5977	964	866	677	583	512	472	547	329	305	227	231	170	160	84	40	32	13	5	1	.	.
T BROMWICH.																							
WORTH	24251	M. 10856	1564	1385	1158	1141	1007	869	754	616	571	455	430	313	256	178	106	53	19	16	.	.	.
		F. 13395	1870	1414	1858	1674	1540	1169	967	766	692	548	481	353	354	220	145	88	49	15	8	.	.
Y	21061	M. 10664	1676	1461	1292	1103	927	819	685	588	501	433	268	258	237	152	86	33	15	4	2	1	.
		F. 10397	1783	1525	1222	915	855	753	704	538	528	385	371	220	227	161	114	45	17	3	1	.	.
BROMWICH WEST. (H.)	28803	M. 14598	2328	1966	1675	1599	1328	1110	908	740	731	624	496	378	318	186	109	52	25	9	.	.	.
		F. 14205	2464	2029	1561	1288	1240	1096	850	781	681	603	476	375	327	202	131	58	24	4	1	1	.
BROMWICH EAST. (W.W.S.)	27402	M. 13597	2384	1888	1583	1429	1152	1060	824	737	680	523	458	356	317	256	174	84	44	8	4	.	.
		F. 13805	2170	1979	1611	1354	1157	1002	842	728	699	567	466	378	343	249	141	83	38	19	5	1	1
WBURY	25357	M. 12537	1794	1595	1496	1396	1218	986	758	620	671	574	520	388	273	173	115	38	14	3	.	.	.
		F. 12820	1786	1602	1347	1146	1074	865	743	615	656	570	515	364	311	188	118	53	20	5	1	.	.
DUDLEY.																							
REGIS	27385	M. 13831	2271	2044	1640	1426	1266	978	830	710	627	550	458	391	289	201	128	67	23	4	2	.	.
		F. 13554	2280	1923	1677	1280	1184	968	860	671	635	517	488	368	297	206	130	67	36	10	3	.	.
(H.)	30013	M. 15277	2357	2216	1775	1526	1329	1165	936	785	724	658	567	431	382	242	131	67	24	6	2	.	.
		F. 14736	2366	2106	1615	1334	1214	1096	880	790	770	627	529	442	407	248	170	95	33	11	5	1	1
Y. (W.)	36574	M. 18318	2784	2400	2183	1937	1504	1282	1016	873	892	752	721	595	477	303	244	145	64	13	3	.	.
		F. 18256	2737	2594	2121	1704	1444	1286	1058	861	969	778	682	603	518	387	253	136	65	23	6	2	1
T. (H.)	46252	M. 22622	3538	3084	2585	2380	1928	1715	1447	1167	1161	915	838	656	549	347	218	90	40	11	4	1	.
		F. 23630	3660	3195	2639	2300	2106	1674	1406	1268	1204	938	875	603	588	434	264	145	58	20	4	.	.
ORCESTER-SHIRE.																							
OURBRIDGE.																							
WEN	16264	M. 7998	1283	1122	971	805	641	584	472	411	409	322	295	224	169	135	81	51	18	5	1	.	.
		F. 8266	1268	1228	919	804	697	570	544	429	396	349	288	210	166	138	79	43	22	8	.	.	.
BRIDGE	27565	M. 13445	1942	1768	1583	1283	1198	1001	870	717	686	589	532	426	371	251	176	68	33	16	2	.	.
		F. 14120	2008	1771	1678	1375	1280	1075	884	771	708	602	566	414	369	275	191	98	36	17	5	.	1
INFORD. (W.L.)	36767	M. 18994	2702	2488	2104	1927	1536	1291	1059	885	804	715	714	537	455	347	242	135	50	12	1	.	.
		F. 17703	2692	2433	2026	1588	1442	1287	1112	929	894	707	691	512	489	350	241	134	41	16	4	.	.
DERMINSTER.																							
SLEY CORBETT	2239	M. 1093	196	126	124	124	77	66	64	55	51	50	47	38	49	30	21	19	5	2	.	.	.
		F. 1146	161	140	123	99	67	65	75	57	75	68	67	36	39	36	26	14	12	7	.	.	.
RLEY	3641	M. 1822	238	258	219	204	155	106	101	88	95	84	94	58	58	39	23	7	4	1	1	.	.
		F. 1819	211	234	224	173	140	112	118	106	98	80	94	69	66	40	23	13	15	4	.	.	.
MINSTER. (W.H.)	27675	M. 13086	1057	1618	1443	1289	1111	1073	846	700	653	567	487	414	390	223	163	99	46	11	2	.	.
		F. 14589	1929	1675	1460	1628	1549	1219	929	781	713	638	561	438	381	267	185	125	68	26	5	.	.
MITTON	3358	M. 1648	264	200	190	198	140	110	108	82	86	64	54	54	47	28	21	9	3	1	1	.	.
		F. 1710	247	215	172	167	166	193	119	67	95	70	71	51	65	37	30	15	6	2	3	.	.
EY	4029	M. 1913	256	250	223	166	153	110	119	103	104	81	87	66	50	46	50	9	7	4	2	.	.
		F. 2116	293	249	230	186	164	145	110	119	115	89	86	71	80	63	50	28	9	4	3	.	1
TENBURY.																							
Y. (W.H.)	4657	M. 2306	282	261	284	243	180	155	121	130	124	116	100	108	83	61	39	20	5	3	1	.	.
		F. 2351	333	274	283	201	170	165	136	122	146	93	95	84	96	72	56	22	18	5	1	.	.
TON	2981	M. 1508	186	180	181	153	121	89	85	90	85	78	74	68	53	30	28	12	11	1	.	.	.
		F. 1423	206	182	161	117	101	76	85	62	71	56	61	59	45	38	29	22	10	2	5	.	.
MARTLEY.																							
Y. (W.R.)	2905	M. 1537	195	183	190	162	97	78	91	80	76	71	63	52	61	48	46	25	13	5	1	.	.
		F. 1368	173	195	124	106	90	90	78	82	63	61	61	38	62	41	43	22	13	8	2	.	.
	3272	M. 1645	208	219	193	132	117	84	81	91	89	90	81	66	65	50	33	13	7	6	.	.	.
		F. 1627	226	204	187	116	107	95	76	101	101	87	79	62	54	47	53	32	12	4	3	2	.
	3709	M. 1813	238	261	215	174	120	165	101	90	99	69	73	65	69	50	22	19	9	4	.	1	.
		F. 1896	213	233	220	138	154	121	122	92	113	99	90	73	68	53	42	25	21	7	3	.	.
(H.)	6506	M. 3392	401	431	382	307	218	204	171	154	157	102	139	115	85	69	44	32	13	2	.	.	.
		F. 3114	358	379	367	360	288	217	235	186	191	109	185	146	166	88	76	48	18	6	2	.	.
ORCESTER.																							
ORCESTER	9872	M. 4730	618	586	546	477	393	345	303	291	281	222	208	142	126	85	54	24	15	8	.	.	.
		F. 5142	693	575	534	544	462	422	316	308	296	235	234	178	163	111	76	46	23	11	4	1	.
WORCESTER .P.)	9861	M. 4632	548	479	444	493	440	367	308	298	234	231	137	156	138	116	85	54	30	11	3	1	.
		F. 5229	520	466	508	561	548	494	344	314	312	267	245	178	181	133	113	58	45	15	1	3	.
WORCESTER	12571	M. 5606	789	707	670	693	525	460	381	328	345	254	228	183	147	164	69	37	12	1	.	1	1
		F. 6965	817	683	694	729	625	509	432	407	371	322	280	255	180	145	102	63	38	11	3	1	.
N ON SEVERN.																							
CASTLE (H.L.)	14362	M. 6295	835	682	870	772	448	424	310	338	349	320	321	292	206	142	97	88	39	10	5	1	.
		F. 8067	646	677	747	869	856	657	516	396	517	421	456	311	301	179	182	98	47	22	7	3	1
N SEVERN. (W.)	5478	M. 2721	317	338	331	265	211	140	132	141	136	143	111	112	103	86	68	45	28	4	1	.	.
		F. 2757	329	333	332	202	200	185	166	125	150	129	157	102	105	95	70	44	22	8	3	1	.
Y	3464	M. 1666	227	195	139	161	114	100	70	89	108	79	81	78	48	46	33	24	12	2	.	.	.
		F. 1798	202	200	188	163	132	112	100	100	99	102	80	84	61	66	46	27	18	6	3	.	.

Table 3 *continued.*—Ages of Males and Females in Registration Sub-Districts.

Registration Sub-District.	All Ages. Persons.	All Ages. Males and Females.	Under 5 Years.	5–	10–	15–	20–	25–	30–	35–	40–	45–	50–	55–	60–	65–	70–	75–	80–	85–	90–	95–	100 and upwards
26 WORCESTERSHIRE—*cont.*																							
381 EVESHAM.																							
1 Evesham. (W.H.)	8321	M. - 4180	556	326	494	418	327	278	238	252	207	167	166	163	133	84	87	49	26	6	3	.	.
		F. - 4141	520	464	457	360	376	323	267	215	204	186	188	159	136	113	87	45	23	12	8	.	.
2 Broadway	6949	M. - 3461	443	474	459	334	225	167	196	180	201	159	140	123	115	91	82	46	19	6	2	.	.
		F. - 3488	494	461	450	267	213	193	182	205	215	157	140	122	121	109	68	51	20	8	8	1	.
382 PERSHORE.																							
1 Eckington	3828	M. - 1844	232	219	205	191	147	107	196	102	84	94	90	84	61	58	22	23	18	6	.	.	.
		F. 1984	244	241	224	151	144	130	131	97	95	126	93	80	67	63	40	20	22	4	3	.	.
2 Pershore. (W.B.)	6734	M. - 3359	421	438	343	353	246	201	171	225	209	152	160	104	108	90	64	48	20	6	.	.	.
		F. - 3375	432	403	409	271	233	223	205	207	181	170	151	112	125	95	79	43	18	11	3	2	.
3 Upton Snodsbury	2098	M. - 1537	182	107	176	163	110	89	70	83	64	85	79	49	56	58	36	28	7	5	.	.	.
		F. 1461	177	196	131	112	107	76	84	80	80	75	64	65	40	45	33	30	7	1	.	.	.
383 DROITWICH.																							
1 Claines. (H.)	12839	M. - 6100	846	767	695	630	401	434	379	331	350	274	237	214	161	107	61	31	22	10	.	.	.
		F. 6739	971	791	715	657	541	626	443	406	383	310	269	207	183	115	115	56	36	13	2	.	.
2 Ombersley	5831	M. - 2869	394	385	342	280	210	198	178	155	131	108	146	93	105	68	51	24	23	5	2	1	.
		F. 2962	418	360	319	253	225	207	187	150	149	126	120	126	103	60	72	40	21	9	.	.	.
3 Droitwich. (W.H.)	7410	M. - 3685	523	495	421	368	276	209	219	202	181	181	164	126	178	95	78	31	16	5	1	.	.
		F. - 3726	502	479	419	333	290	241	218	201	237	171	152	149	115	67	67	53	26	6	1	.	.
384 BROMSGROVE.																							
1 Bromsgrove. (W.H[2].R.)	15222	M. - 7717	1113	972	955	803	577	498	430	308	376	339	315	265	254	176	142	77	28	6	3	1	.
		F. - 7505	1093	987	853	663	601	506	467	393	400	354	282	224	218	167	127	76	38	9	2	.	.
2 Belbroughton	5391	M. - 2581	353	324	310	253	185	160	158	127	119	137	111	80	106	70	42	35	13	2	.	1	.
		F. - 2810	344	318	310	248	218	228	202	157	164	129	126	103	88	84	44	29	15	3	.	.	.
3 Tardebigg	11301	M. - 5357	801	653	586	522	486	381	352	287	253	228	230	190	161	95	67	26	16	4	1	.	.
		F. - 5944	787	711	603	610	606	474	408	297	290	266	260	196	157	113	53	38	11	3	1	.	.
385 KINGS NORTON.																							
1 Kings Norton	34074	M. - 15746	2455	2119	1841	1665	1360	1354	1090	977	887	674	590	437	381	260	150	86	40	10	2	.	.
		F. - 18328	2509	2434	1916	1953	1841	1581	1205	1150	1008	733	651	471	439	350	181	105	58	21	4	3	.
2 Edgbaston. (W.)	29950	M. - 12503	1576	1476	1367	1350	1110	1014	847	700	630	589	526	397	356	236	172	80	31	8	3	1	.
		F. - 17447	1622	1595	1480	2219	2536	1812	1292	1034	878	767	658	512	474	319	211	126	76	20	9	1	.
3 Harborne	31617	M. - 15678	2603	2096	1782	1550	1407	1214	1079	931	754	684	528	400	272	210	143	74	29	11	2	.	.
		F. - 15939	2492	2125	1760	1574	1374	1268	1081	923	796	648	573	400	363	234	164	105	46	7	5	3	.
27 WARWICKSHIRE.																							
386 BIRMINGHAM.																							
1 Lady Wood. (H.)	50863	M. - 24793	3768	3183	2507	2516	2223	2116	1813	1452	1303	1000	874	624	459	298	147	77	31	4	.	.	.
		F. - 26070	3791	3221	2756	2812	2464	2253	1792	1552	1442	1184	1087	729	593	368	211	99	48	10	4	2	.
2 St. Thomas. (H[2].)	39031	M. - 19007	2586	2356	2018	1968	1812	1667	1333	1097	1103	836	696	641	434	296	162	67	25	8	2	.	.
		F. - 20024	2592	2269	2034	2021	2096	1680	1377	1208	1149	845	920	611	564	323	219	98	43	16	2	.	1
3 St. Martin. (R.)	41828	M. - 20579	2718	2394	2189	2160	2011	1765	1459	1284	1254	956	833	634	407	264	163	68	29	8	1	.	.
		F. - 21249	3002	2469	2218	2142	2060	1772	1422	1239	1246	1011	826	600	524	316	205	99	38	8	2	1	4
4 St. George. (H.)	64915	M. - 31459	4699	3962	3386	3365	2909	2502	2115	1872	1794	1421	1138	875	712	376	258	88	38	2	4	.	.
		F. - 33456	4656	3949	3590	3538	3261	2658	2275	1925	1916	1472	1330	964	872	472	310	172	68	17	2	1	.
5 All Saints (W.H[2].L.P.)	49716	M. - 24526	3591	3016	2556	2469	2194	1971	1674	1476	1314	1066	888	684	593	471	326	178	75	17	7	.	.
		F. - 25190	3547	3053	2564	2492	2300	2139	1704	1580	1368	1117	940	659	608	440	318	186	70	23	7	1	.
387 ASTON.																							
1 Deritend. (R.)	76413	M. - 37475	6217	5122	4110	3726	3147	3068	2702	2311	2078	1503	1108	887	663	401	222	95	47	12	1	1	.
		F. - 38938	6155	5008	4238	3697	3486	3291	2765	2354	2133	1626	1288	959	816	531	357	184	75	19	4	.	.
2 Duddeston. (R.)	55248	M. - 27720	4397	3568	3019	2602	2489	2439	2029	1883	1463	1158	976	660	591	364	169	82	41	9	1	.	.
		F. - 27528	4404	3654	3042	2448	2451	2240	1947	1665	1465	1134	984	688	621	363	243	108	48	11	3	.	.
3 Erdington. (W.R.)	69644	M. - 33726	6291	4467	3979	3378	2941	2605	2419	2045	1761	1315	1176	796	629	407	253	161	64	24	6	1	.
		F. - 35918	5275	4680	3887	3667	3280	2994	2633	2095	1916	1463	1251	934	738	546	346	203	78	28	4	2	.
4 Sutton Coldfield	8582	M. - 3997	534	470	452	307	315	202	257	211	207	214	170	151	134	105	63	26	25	3	1	.	.
		F. 4585	517	488	469	538	482	370	291	265	226	189	200	148	143	107	76	51	17	9	2	.	.
388 MERIDEN.																							
1 Coleshill. (W.R.)	5122	M. - 2527	323	354	371	235	177	165	115	126	112	103	109	85	79	74	48	33	15	3	.	.	.
		F. 2595	315	366	322	226	183	178	142	139	133	118	114	87	69	66	43	32	27	1	2	.	.
2 Meriden. (W.R.)	5903	M. - 3028	356	309	465	391	223	170	142	148	152	132	156	131	117	88	60	44	27	9	.	2	.
		F. - 2875	309	342	301	210	211	213	171	151	179	157	150	125	116	86	61	43	25	11	4	1	.
389 ATHERSTONE.																							
1 Atherstone. (W.)	14419	M. - 7338	1070	1009	840	776	505	374	453	322	332	298	242	252	223	141	100	91	36	13	1	.	.
		F. - 7081	1047	962	784	668	567	530	428	411	342	286	284	221	222	148	109	81	37	15	10	.	.
390 NUNEATON.																							
1 Nuneaton. (W.)	13701	M. - 6603	918	856	732	642	518	493	408	318	312	287	286	251	216	152	99	77	28	8	2	.	.
		F. - 7098	985	978	710	615	596	535	468	367	408	298	315	278	282	186	122	66	31	12	3	.	.
391 FOLESHILL.																							
1 Foleshill. (W.)	14439	M. - 7005	1082	940	805	698	508	477	403	323	344	275	291	251	214	166	139	78	35	8	3	.	.
		F. - 7434	1050	969	794	650	621	517	480	398	388	298	312	253	253	179	136	75	39	7	5	.	.
2 Sowe	4058	M. - 1978	267	251	228	190	166	125	95	98	67	86	99	97	81	48	35	25	13	6	1	.	.
		F. - 2080	265	243	217	158	170	148	180	104	116	96	113	92	78	65	44	24	10	5	1	1	.
392 COVENTRY.																							
1 St John. (W.R.B.)	23092	M. - 11029	1492	1376	1126	1116	937	861	680	693	567	516	427	349	312	287	205	103	53	7	2	.	.
		F. - 12063	1589	1400	1246	1209	1168	967	735	683	679	578	497	390	327	253	200	109	58	15	2	.	.
2 Holy Trinity. (H[2].R.)	22024	M. - 10347	1440	1281	1049	1010	943	788	685	540	568	484	440	346	307	218	165	64	34	9	.	.	.
		F. - 11677	1469	1314	1178	1151	1124	868	751	630	657	676	632	442	371	267	174	99	36	17	3	.	.

Table 3 *continued*.—AGES of MALES and FEMALES in REGISTRATION SUB-DISTRICTS.

[REGIS]TRATION [SUB-D]ISTRICT.	ALL AGES. Persons.	Males and Females.	Under 5 Years.	5–	10–	15–	20–	25–	30–	35–	40–	45–	50–	55–	60–	65–	70–	75–	80–	85–	90–	95–	100 and upw^ds.
[WA]RWICK[SHIR]E—*cont.*																							
[R]UGBY.																							
(W.H².)	16589	M. - 8359	994	880	1014	1118	774	655	516	459	394	341	336	271	232	152	111	70	30	2	1	.	.
		F. - 8230	1069	961	825	767	747	709	545	490	432	382	350	286	246	165	134	76	35	11	2	.	.
- -	5274	M. - 2705	344	304	307	265	228	160	161	159	149	121	85	104	102	96	56	24	16	4	.	.	.
		F. - 2569	336	322	281	208	179	179	136	140	151	120	119	97	110	76	53	24	20	8	1	.	.
[...]rch -	5337	M. - 2621	336	297	316	245	169	181	138	118	131	139	134	116	93	80	55	41	18	6	1	.	.
		F. - 2716	360	309	301	204	198	161	163	162	138	161	127	120	119	79	54	54	20	9	.	.	.
[S]OLIHULL.																							
[...]l. (W.H².)	15235	M. - 7136	1031	912	733	703	577	485	456	447	399	329	295	213	193	168	105	61	20	9	.	.	.
		F. - 8090	927	934	827	918	799	673	538	519	456	366	312	234	221	168	119	63	28	11	2	1	2
(L.) -	3121	M. - 1511	219	182	169	136	108	76	98	75	75	87	50	57	56	41	38	15	9	1	1	.	.
		F. - 1610	162	173	176	139	124	119	95	105	83	92	71	73	77	50	33	17	11	4	.	.	.
[...]th -	3021	M. - 1536	197	187	158	168	105	94	76	71	82	82	85	67	70	42	26	23	10	3	1	.	.
		F. - 1485	183	169	176	114	127	113	87	73	86	86	52	51	55	39	29	15	16	3	1	.	.
[W]ARWICK.																							
[...]k (W.H.L.P.B.)	16646	M. - 8170	1044	896	833	782	603	591	516	478	511	391	370	318	309	233	157	98	40	12	2	1	.
		F. - 8476	1000	935	788	714	783	618	567	522	615	447	364	377	319	243	161	120	45	25	8	.	.
[...]ton. (H².)	25141	M. - 10245	1338	1151	1096	1090	833	733	646	566	369	504	463	337	303	270	189	160	46	13	4	.	.
		F. - 14896	1334	1298	1264	1698	1637	1245	1015	914	841	730	654	602	586	411	298	163	96	31	4	1	.
[...]rth (H.)	6546	M. - 3123	421	413	346	312	230	200	172	139	141	137	143	139	113	73	58	45	16	5	2	.	.
		F. - 3423	379	375	351	303	286	240	211	198	211	156	182	168	118	92	65	53	23	9	3	.	.
[...] (R.) -	4541	M. - 2125	238	241	230	202	152	139	108	104	119	101	88	107	86	64	44	37	10	4	1	.	.
		F. - 2416	278	263	209	183	231	215	160	133	136	109	120	96	106	82	44	27	10	4	1	.	.
[STR]ATFORD ON [A]VON.																							
[...] -	2302	M. - 1155	136	149	143	117	87	66	63	63	60	51	48	64	33	27	21	16	8	3	.	.	.
		F. - 1147	150	166	121	101	88	75	62	65	57	43	50	53	38	21	17	10	13	4	.	.	.
[...]bourne -	2853	M. - 1418	167	201	138	131	97	77	74	74	76	79	69	65	46	50	24	13	14	3	.	.	.
		F. - 1435	164	170	167	122	91	93	76	83	74	75	76	62	63	37	27	12	10	3	.	.	.
[...]rd on Avon.	6338	M. - 3099	387	377	382	355	232	219	162	153	135	146	121	129	104	84	54	35	22	.	1	1	.
		F. - 3239	397	379	320	306	275	219	195	177	199	157	123	148	119	90	66	42	10	9	2	.	.
[...]atford. (W.) -	7250	M. - 3569	507	473	411	243	227	236	186	182	194	168	161	116	153	96	72	40	20	4	.	.	.
		F. - 3681	611	471	396	302	274	252	212	231	201	181	166	127	124	93	71	49	16	10	3	1	.
[...]n Wawen. (L².)	3753	M. - 1869	241	230	229	147	136	98	105	97	112	109	89	83	60	50	28	21	15	8	2	.	.
		F. - 1884	249	247	190	148	135	104	104	124	107	96	98	88	69	52	35	29	12	3	2	.	.
[A]LCESTER.																							
[...] -	5259	M. - 2571	387	297	280	284	213	174	103	148	161	127	113	70	72	40	33	18	9	1	.	.	.
		F. - 2688	324	333	293	278	284	208	178	151	152	141	90	108	78	43	37	25	9	3	2	.	.
[...]r. (W.H.) -	5290	M. - 2664	379	371	303	228	200	153	143	147	131	108	103	96	115	76	59	37	15	3	.	.	.
		F. - 2626	351	336	299	237	181	182	163	188	148	113	97	115	84	71	48	23	19	3	2	1	.
[...]ham -	6145	M. - 3021	457	397	384	277	205	167	180	182	154	128	118	105	101	76	61	44	18	4	1	.	.
		F. 3124	404	408	386	271	233	218	196	187	154	147	120	96	100	88	61	39	14	10	1	.	.
[...]d -	2736	M. - 1355	173	192	151	132	72	76	86	70	71	53	68	49	56	36	29	23	14	4	.	.	.
		F. - 1381	174	177	155	111	96	94	81	75	94	57	66	54	56	42	32	17	7	3	2	.	.
[SH]IPSTON ON STOUR.																							
[...]n -	4590	M. - 2322	300	319	253	220	156	133	127	123	108	102	101	104	75	85	36	29	10	4	1	.	.
		F. - 2268	290	286	271	203	131	134	137	136	112	114	112	92	83	64	60	28	15	3	1	.	.
[...]on. (H.) -	5350	M. - 2623	363	343	296	268	177	141	125	131	140	123	113	113	111	63	56	37	29	3	.	.	.
		F. 2727	345	336	299	238	179	166	144	144	157	139	131	107	103	98	73	30	22	7	.	.	.
[...]on on Stour.	4530	M. - 2269	205	282	243	216	161	155	114	117	117	98	110	96	83	58	62	30	14	8	1	1	.
		F. 2261	271	270	253	190	148	159	127	135	113	117	119	95	87	61	59	36	13	5	4	.	.
[...]rd - -	3404	M. - 1699	234	203	183	154	116	92	80	84	93	92	90	88	67	46	39	33	11	4	.	.	.
		F. - 1705	221	219	223	128	100	85	95	91	91	90	86	71	57	67	38	28	10	7	.	.	.
SOUTHAM.																							
[...]m. (W.) -	10282	M. - 5249	677	645	604	484	396	311	270	294	284	226	244	227	180	106	117	71	37	6	1	.	.
		F. - 5033	668	655	563	395	334	308	282	295	259	237	237	197	185	152	101	69	37	12	3	.	.

[T]able 4.—MALE and FEMALE CHILDREN *at each Year of Age* under 5 in the WEST-MIDLAND DIVISION and its REGISTRATION COUNTIES.

REGISTRATION COUNTY.	TOTAL UNDER 5 YEARS. Persons.	Males and Females.	Under 1 Year.	1–	2–	3–	4–
VI WEST-MIDLAND COUNTIES.	421164	M. - 209807	44341	40173	42473	41241	41579
		F. - 211357	44373	40580	42778	41862	41764
22 GLOUCESTERSHIRE -	67192	M. - 33137	6916	6391	6670	6631	6583
		F. - 33295	7232	6579	6822	6708	6654
23 HEREFORDSHIRE - -	14344	M. - 7156	1485	1289	1408	1404	1479
		F. - 7189	1431	1332	1512	1451	1463
24 SHROPSHIRE -	33822	M. - 17059	3468	3166	3463	3377	3585
		F. - 16763	3358	3147	3489	3340	3429
25 STAFFORDSHIRE - - -	150881	M. - 76039	16059	14861	15088	14768	14783
		F. 75842	15966	14597	15830	15063	14877
26 WORCESTERSHIRE - -	51883	M. - 26880	5434	4978	5213	5055	5180
		F. - 26023	5542	4821	5259	5132	5268
27 WARWICKSHIRE -	103042	M. - 51497	10979	9988	10535	10006	9989
		F. - 51545	10844	10103	10357	10168	10073

Table 5.—Male and Female Children *at each Year of Age* under 5 in Registration Districts.

Registration District.	Total under 5 years. Persons.	Males and Females.	Under 1 Year.	1–	2–	3–	4–
22 GLOUCESTERSHIRE.							
320 BRISTOL	6951	M. - 3457 F. - 3494	724 732	723 685	693 690	654 712	663 675
321 BARTON REGIS	22934	M. - 11072 F. - 11862	2381 2488	2137 2301	2185 2296	2235 2219	2134 2264
322 CHIPPING SODBURY	2215	M. - 1068 F. - 1147	225 248	196 198	206 248	230 233	211 220
323 THORNBURY	2270	M. - 1078 F. - 1192	204 249	184 224	249 262	216 227	225 240
324 DURSLEY	1606	M. - 792 F. - 814	183 181	142 155	143 164	138 163	140 161
325 WESTBURY ON SEVERN	3521	M. - 1765 F. - 1756	401 361	343 366	333 372	331 363	351 364
326 NEWENT	1376	M. - 680 F. - 696	133 145	125 134	137 135	134 134	151 147
327 GLOUCESTER	6136	M. - 3019 F. - 3117	623 659	691 608	649 635	602 652	554 563
328 WHEATENHURST	950	M. - 466 F. - 484	75 96	104 94	85 105	90 89	112 98
329 STROUD	5245	M. - 2683 F. - 2562	562 539	479 506	542 521	510 498	590 498
330 TETBURY	788	M. - 394 F. 394	77 88	73 74	67 82	78 79	79 71
331 CIRENCESTER	2560	M. - 1277 F. - 1283	254 279	237 245	262 253	252 271	272 235
332 NORTHLEACH	1235	M. - 646 F. - 589	121 105	123 117	129 104	142 129	131 134
333 STOW ON THE WOLD	1152	M. - 585 F. - 567	124 111	129 105	124 103	97 120	111 128
334 WINCHCOMB	1194	M. - 602 F. - 592	122 127	115 112	136 114	128 126	129 113
335 CHELTENHAM	5206	M. - 2877 F. - 2329	504 622	547 557	693 599	625 612	548 539
336 TEWKESBURY	1623	M. - 806 F. - 817	173 170	143 168	145 164	169 161	176 164
23 HEREFORDSHIRE.							
337 LEDBURY	1453	M. - 707 F. - 746	148 143	130 156	158 162	147 142	144 142
338 ROSS	2040	M. - 1032 F. - 1008	211 206	206 180	197 206	207 213	211 204
339 HEREFORD	5213	M. - 2620 F. - 2593	566 511	462 607	551 519	494 542	547 514
340 WEOBLY	1030	M. - 494 F. - 536	108 118	81 83	126 118	92 104	89 113
341 BROMYARD	1335	M. - 628 F. - 707	120 134	116 138	125 150	129 131	138 154
342 LEOMINSTER	1757	M. - 893 F. - 864	190 157	161 148	176 188	184 172	192 189
343 KINGTON	1516	M. - 771 F. - 745	144 163	153 120	165 169	161 147	158 147
24 SHROPSHIRE.							
344 LUDLOW	2393	M. - 1191 F. - 1202	261 246	228 210	226 260	220 266	250 231
345 CLUN	1295	M. - 657 F. - 638	139 128	101 107	154 132	117 138	146 133
346 CHURCH STRETTON	661	M. - 341 F. - 320	65 67	60 52	71 72	63 63	82 66
347 CLEOBURY MORTIMER	1054	M. - 530 F. - 524	97 89	102 104	116 114	110 100	105 117
348 BRIDGNORTH	1856	M. - 911 F. - 945	185 197	165 171	197 184	171 215	203 177
349 SHIFNAL	1607	M. - 823 F. - 784	161 154	164 152	155 166	161 148	182 164
350 MADELEY	3652	M. - 1859 F. - 1793	401 353	352 317	369 377	355 347	392 399
351 ATCHAM	5394	M. - 2924 F. - 2470	592 611	562 552	601 647	582 654	577 606
352 OSWESTRY	3502	M. - 1749 F. 1753	368 345	348 353	336 353	312 368	385 334
353 ELLESMERE	1635	M. - 864 F. - 771	166 161	158 150	188 150	181 168	161 152
354 WEM	1255	M. - 635 F. - 620	104 115	105 132	141 129	138 126	147 118
355 WHITCHURCH	1391	M. - 700 F. - 691	140 141	138 135	147 138	135 129	140 148
356 MARKET DRAYTON	1851	M. - 938 F. - 913	175 173	173 183	203 185	173 175	214 197
357 WELLINGTON	3779	M. - 1955 F. - 1824	408 384	342 350	372 367	438 351	395 372
358 NEWPORT	1997	M. - 992 F. - 1005	208 196	178 179	197 225	211 191	200 215

Registration District.	Total under 5 years. Persons.	Males and Females.	Under 1 Year.	1–	2–	3–	4–
25 STAFFORDSHIRE.							
359 STAFFORD	4106	M. - 2079 F. - 2027	423 422	399 380	467 414	433 392	4 4
360 STONE	3921	M. - 1939 F. - 1982	412 387	315 371	305 402	406 423	3 3
361 NEWCASTLE UNDER LYNE	5104	M. - 2598 F. - 2506	560 438	489 402	500 501	497 542	5 4
362 WOLSTANTON	11306	M. - 5470 F. - 5836	1199 1209	1010 1092	1123 1191	1119 1179	16 11
363 STOKE UPON TRENT	15762	M. - 7796 F. - 7966	1761 1751	1462 1868	1690 1660	1512 1542	14 16
364 LEEK	4461	M. - 2185 F. - 2276	447 409	398 422	464 477	443 442	4 4
365 CHEADLE	3195	M. - 1584 F. - 1611	327 321	321 335	327 313	306 318	3 3
366 UTTOXETER	1790	M. - 905 F. - 885	171 171	169 167	198 185	174 179	1 1
367 BURTON UPON TRENT	11782	M. - 5833 F. - 5949	1236 1233	1160 1218	1147 1196	1136 1158	11 114
368 TAMWORTH	2959	M. - 1448 F. - 1511	284 294	317 298	300 307	286 306	26 34
369 LICHFIELD	5563	M. - 2762 F. - 2801	538 565	557 583	528 501	580 559	57 65
370 CANNOCK	5766	M. - 2935 F. - 2831	615 579	533 548	613 569	655 585	66 65
371 WOLVERHAMPTON	21113	M. - 10673 F. - 10440	2239 2293	1082 1961	2208 2100	2101 2087	214 201
372 WALSALL	12798	M. - 6401 F. - 6397	1367 1384	1214 1204	1306 1300	1211 1231	130 127
373 WEST BROMWICH	19254	M. - 9481 F. 9773	2084 2034	1861 1858	1854 1966	1888 1937	180 185
374 DUDLEY	22001	M. - 10950 F. - 11051	2350 2301	2174 2124	2158 2278	2138 2204	218 214
26 WORCESTERSHIRE.							
375 STOURBRIDGE	11997	M. - 5929 F. - 6068	1264 1254	1144 1149	1184 1183	1185 1181	117 1261
376 KIDDERMINSTER	5684	M. - 2860 F. - 2824	625 610	664 582	534 598	582 532	580 552
377 TENBURY	1010	M. - 477 F. - 533	93 118	86 99	92 101	88 109	112 113
378 MARTLEY	2012	M. - 1042 F. - 970	209 211	184 158	216 202	225 208	208 193
379 WORCESTER	3915	M. - 1975 F. 1940	423 441	365 349	417 426	397 371	405 363
380 UPTON-ON-SEVERN	2356	M. - 1179 F. - 1177	244 244	224 220	258 236	228 247	218 199
381 EVESHAM	2013	M. - 999 F. - 1014	198 203	191 198	194 204	210 195	193 214
382 PERSHORE	1688	M. - 835 F. 853	177 187	177 158	169 172	138 166	176 174
383 DROITWICH	3660	M. - 1769 F. 1891	368 390	332 356	374 364	341 369	354 407
384 BROMSGROVE	4491	M. - 2267 F. - 2224	476 468	446 434	446 408	447 426	451 438
385 KINGS NORTON	13057	M. - 6534 F. - 6523	1357 1411	1276 1169	1330 1315	1288 1318	1288 1310
27 WARWICKSHIRE.							
386 BIRMINGHAM	34850	M. - 17262 F. - 17588	3734 3838	3352 3445	3500 3521	3333 3389	3346 3465
387 ASTON	32790	M. - 16439 F. - 16351	3522 3353	3251 3290	3401 3347	3182 3258	3113 3106
388 MERIDEN	1303	M. - 679 F. - 624	133 134	136 113	132 130	146 125	132 132
389 ATHERSTONE	2117	M. - 1070 F. - 1047	211 228	218 218	210 196	220 203	211 202
390 NUNEATON	1903	M. - 918 F. - 985	200 223	170 173	173 191	183 209	182 189
391 FOLESHILL	2844	M. - 1529 F. - 1315	297 285	240 239	207 248	252 259	273 254
392 COVENTRY	5970	M. - 2932 F. - 3038	617 652	541 584	597 588	569 598	590 612
393 RUGBY	3429	M. - 1674 F. - 1755	357 349	326 361	381 348	319 345	312 362
394 SOLIHULL	2719	M. - 1447 F. - 1272	278 248	264 245	298 254	311 252	298 273
395 WARWICK	6029	M. - 3038 F. - 2991	663 620	568 580	620 584	570 584	597 585
396 STRATFORD ON AVON	2939	M. - 1438 F. - 1501	284 287	276 292	276 314	304 301	298 307
397 ALCESTER	2649	M. - 1396 F. - 1253	308 258	251 220	287 274	278 263	272 238
398 SHIPSTON ON STOUR	2325	M. - 1198 F. - 1127	235 227	245 198	264 226	214 227	240 249
399 SOUTHAM	1375	M. - 677 F. - 698	142 136	131 115	149 138	137 165	135 159

Table 7.—CONDITION as to MARRIAGE and AGES of MALES and FEMALES in the WEST-MIDLAND DIVISION and its REGISTRATION COUNTIES.

REGISTRATION COUNTY.		ALL AGES.	Under 15 years.	15–	20–	25–	35–	45–	55–	65 and upwards
VI.—WEST-MIDLAND COUNTIES.										
UNMARRIED	Males	919025	563889	151269	95345	59717	20506	11065	7115	5056
	Females	929881	571692	146299	90038	59806	23171	13707	9829	7846
MARRIED	Males	512069	.	708	28587	138032	133845	103216	68242	33541
	Females	518440	.	3109	45207	151986	135671	98226	67562	[illegible]
WIDOWED	Males	49563	.	11	259	2753	5505	8173	11381	21481
	Females	108598	.	12	486	4833	12091	20151	27486	43480
22 GLOUCESTERSHIRE.										
UNMARRIED	Males	150109	93096	25311	14670	9251	3378	1800	1130	857
	Females	167896	94570	27128	18177	13518	5902	3778	2571	2242
MARRIED	Males	86844	.	145	4672	22350	22036	17136	12494	8011
	Females	89215	.	516	7050	25070	22068	17429	10707	5535
WIDOWED	Males	8584	.	3	45	432	806	1218	1898	4122
	Females	22429	.	1	95	967	2441	3975	5460	9500
23 HEREFORDSHIRE.										
UNMARRIED	Males	36898	21215	5930	3764	2970	1265	788	559	407
	Females	35215	21023	5347	3600	2643	1090	685	493	428
MARRIED	Males	19290	.	9	619	3021	4891	4373	3264	2215
	Females	19424	.	50	1074	4731	5086	4216	2757	1251
WIDOWED	Males	2337	.	.	9	81	226	353	629	1139
	Females	4983	.	2	11	131	432	771	1197	2439
24 SHROPSHIRE.										
UNMARRIED	Males	84096	48841	13923	9075	6477	2448	1473	1083	776
	Females	79122	48283	13059	7410	5786	2275	1582	970	957
MARRIED	Males	43669	.	23	1448	9233	11194	9818	7166	4738
	Females	43870	.	146	2577	10628	11821	9321	6147	3428
WIDOWED	Males	5227	.	.	13	218	489	761	1132	2614
	Females	9906	.	2	29	314	847	1520	2356	4838
25 STAFFORDSHIRE.										
UNMARRIED	Males	317502	199646	51503	33239	19789	6638	3451	2105	1331
	Females	298041	200401	46723	25597	14641	5029	2702	1643	1218
MARRIED	Males	171781	.	288	10992	40851	45877	33781	21078	10814
	Females	172871	.	1311	17425	53438	44080	31379	17212	7136
WIDOWED	Males	15591	.	6	90	1028	1940	2852	3622	6044
	Females	30972	.	2	167	1893	3616	6046	8176	11272
26 WORCESTERSHIRE.										
UNMARRIED	Males	113966	70691	18725	11890	7225	2478	1381	878	681
	Females	120377	70894	19466	13140	9147	3406	2053	1225	1046
MARRIED	Males	64017	.	85	3359	17036	16449	13207	8752	5129
	Females	64891	.	325	5312	18623	16969	12506	7363	3613
WIDOWED	Males	6093	.	.	27	306	623	923	1413	2801
	Females	13817	.	2	57	574	1434	2485	3468	5797
27 WARWICKSHIRE.										
UNMARRIED	Males	217352	135691	35869	22847	14006	4408	2172	1360	1004
	Females	220230	136422	35576	22205	14071	5460	3107	1920	1460
MARRIED	Males	126468	.	153	7497	36481	33711	24901	15488	8237
	Females	128259	.	743	11769	39496	34007	23285	13366	[illegible]
WIDOWED	Males	11731	.	2	66	688	1361	2066	2787	4761
	Females	26403	.	3	127	1324	3321	5354	6328	9954

Note.—In a few cases persons described as "Married" were stated to be under 15 years of age. These have been classed with married persons aged "15 and under 20 years."

ble 8.—CONDITION as to MARRIAGE and AGES of MALES and FEMALES in REGISTRATION DISTRICTS.

…TRATION …RICT.		ALL AGES.	Under 15 Years.	15–	20–	25–	35–	45–	55–	65 and upw^d.
…CESTER-…RE.										
…L:										
…RRIED	M.	16018	9784	2680	1729	1143	378	170	89	48
	F.	17721	9682	3182	2116	1359	662	340	229	260
…IED	M.	9706	.	26	685	2726	2640	1940	1264	618
	F.	10025	.	85	914	3063	2654	1848	983	447
…WED	M.	847	.	.	9	66	117	135	202	328
	F.	3072	.	1	18	162	417	618	741	1123
…N REGIS:										
…RRIED	M.	46315	30242	7715	4237	2008	802	393	228	190
	F.	56271	31214	9395	6214	4587	1978	1267	874	742
…IED	M.	26680	.	70	1767	7962	7147	4905	3067	1742
	F.	27789	.	206	2671	8789	7383	4881	2646	1264
…WED	M.	2212	.	3	19	148	265	356	493	934
	F.	6898	.	.	34	343	832	1567	1098	2634
…ING SOD-…										
…RRIED	M.	5380	3329	911	603	353	139	59	47	39
	F.	4881	3193	608	416	340	131	87	66	51
…IED	M.	3094	.	2	122	636	707	670	566	392
	F.	3137	.	8	187	609	742	714	490	297
…WED	M.	342	.	.	1	12	28	38	73	190
	F.	689	.	.	.	23	64	101	177	324
…BURY:										
…RRIED	M.	5153	3132	837	606	359	147	79	65	28
	F.	5011	3259	641	439	322	148	93	68	46
…IED	M.	2985	.	1	139	658	729	607	492	359
	F.	2962	.	11	194	741	739	590	423	264
…WED	M.	327	.	.	1	8	25	45	68	180
	F.	650	.	.	2	24	60	107	153	304
…EY:										
…RRIED	M.	3514	2244	504	307	190	89	48	43	34
	F.	3900	2276	581	389	279	165	85	75	60
…IED	M.	2127	.	2	91	428	487	423	372	314
	F.	2155	.	12	122	515	493	457	364	212
…WED	M.	269	.	.	1	9	17	36	60	146
	F.	585	.	.	1	16	42	82	157	287
…BURY ON …RN:										
…RRIED	M.	7963	4855	1209	699	468	163	74	58	57
	F.	6573	4741	846	426	292	102	75	84	37
…IED	M.	4106	.	4	185	1040	1042	808	628	399
	F.	4170	.	30	332	1172	1001	827	530	278
…WED	M.	392	.	.	.	19	35	57	91	190
	F.	751	.	.	2	20	63	97	221	339
…NT:										
…RRIED	M.	3352	2041	534	316	234	92	64	41	30
	F.	3180	2035	413	265	228	95	56	33	37
…IED	M.	1915	.	1	55	360	412	442	356	289
	F.	1899	.	4	103	417	436	465	283	190
…WED	M.	229	.	.	.	4	20	10	67	128
	F.	455	.	.	.	15	30	61	109	240
…CESTER:										
…RRIED	M.	14100	8215	2548	1802	1071	478	295	114	77
	F.	14382	8458	2300	1565	1032	430	293	193	141
…IED	M.	7813	.	13	470	2093	2054	1465	1105	643
	F.	8099	.	49	672	2425	2079	1568	839	467
…WED	M.	716	.	.	1	49	91	118	161	296
	F.	1720	.	.	12	67	192	305	412	782
…TENHURST:										
…RRIED	M.	2192	1371	350	211	141	49	36	23	17
	F.	2191	1312	337	218	166	68	42	23	25
…IED	M.	1213	.	2	35	245	284	260	210	177
	F.	1308	.	1	68	324	312	272	209	122
…WED	M.	133	.	.	.	4	7	11	24	87
	F.	316	.	.	.	7	25	41	83	160
…D:										
…RRIED	M.	11424	7488	1871	1094	677	229	134	78	63
	F.	13372	7438	2243	1480	1126	446	288	192	159
…IED	M.	6934	.	11	350	1728	1695	1377	1061	712
	F.	7176	.	25	466	1913	1842	1467	990	474
…WED	M.	690	.	.	6	36	46	95	136	371
	F.	1745	.	.	6	75	183	298	402	785
…RY:										
…RRIED	M.	1781	1101	286	190	113	38	24	18	12
	F.	1815	1084	270	195	140	41	37	22	17
…IED	M.	981	.	.	42	225	220	213	178	103
	F.	989	.	7	65	249	218	219	162	75
…WED	M.	133	.	.	.	2	13	22	27	69
	F.	194	.	.	1	9	18	29	36	81

REGISTRATION DISTRICT.		ALL AGES.	Under 15 Years.	15–	20–	25–	35–	45–	55–	65 and upw^d.
22 GLOUCESTERSHIRE—*cont.*										
331 CIRENCESTER:										
UNMARRIED	M.	6527	3745	1248	752	437	143	83	66	[illegible]
	F.	6334	3747	977	611	466	232	137	88	76
MARRIED	M.	3696	.	1	153	783	858	736	629	43[illegible]
	F.	3597	.	14	219	872	893	769	520	31[illegible]
WIDOWED	M.	498	.	.	.	19	43	50	112	27[illegible]
	F.	768	.	.	2	17	70	110	182	37[illegible]
332 NORTHLEACH:										
UNMARRIED	M.	3202	1932	546	315	226	84	51	29	[illegible]
	F.	2717	1796	388	180	173	71	59	27	[illegible]
MARRIED	M.	1711	.	.	47	333	414	370	338	20[illegible]
	F.	1711	.	5	89	379	414	394	270	13[illegible]
WIDOWED	M.	218	.	.	2	8	18	37	42	11[illegible]
	F.	325	.	.	1	4	18	51	68	18[illegible]
333 STOW ON THE WOLD:										
UNMARRIED	M.	2720	1696	404	259	157	56	45	23	[illegible]
	F.	2690	1617	387	246	159	86	54	35	[illegible]
MARRIED	M.	1638	.	2	89	357	381	330	273	[illegible]
	F.	1633	.	10	106	378	396	369	251	[illegible]
WIDOWED	M.	214	.	.	1	12	21	30	36	[illegible]
	F.	334	.	.	2	5	22	51	87	[illegible]
334 WINCHCOMB:										
UNMARRIED	M.	2889	1809	401	303	160	82	61	44	[illegible]
	F.	2673	1696	367	219	187	75	56	48	[illegible]
MARRIED	M.	1660	.	.	64	325	392	389	307	[illegible]
	F.	1642	.	5	112	342	418	369	263	[illegible]
WIDOWED	M.	220	.	.	2	8	19	31	49	[illegible]
	F.	350	.	.	5	9	28	54	71	[illegible]
335 CHELTENHAM:										
UNMARRIED	M.	14101	8607	2643	1350	857	304	138	118	[illegible]
	F.	20475	8758	3613	2860	2390	1162	715	604	4[illegible]
MARRIED	M.	8372	.	10	415	1838	2062	1702	1249	9[illegible]
	F.	8652	.	38	619	2253	2247	1740	1157	5[illegible]
WIDOWED	M.	876	.	.	2	29	80	110	194	4[illegible]
	F.	3029	.	.	11	142	330	543	723	12[illegible]
336 TEWKESBURY:										
UNMARRIED	M.	3869	2364	621	367	267	114	57	46	
	F.	3810	2273	601	348	274	131	94	61	
MARRIED	M.	2213	.	1	93	486	511	480	400	[illegible]
	F.	2280	.	8	132	540	572	502	327	[illegible]
WIDOWED	M.	268	.	.	.	9	21	43	63	[illegible]
	F.	564	.	.	.	10	47	78	120	[illegible]
23 HEREFORDSHIRE.										
337 LEDBURY:										
UNMARRIED	M.	3909	2218	638	386	342	147	73	54	
	F.	3690	2162	517	348	323	148	86	60	
MARRIED	M.	2118	.	1	72	406	503	504	362	[illegible]
	F.	2097	.	8	108	471	539	480	310	[illegible]
WIDOWED	M.	230	.	.	1	7	19	32	66	[illegible]
	F.	561	.	1	3	7	48	80	130	[illegible]
338 ROSS:										
UNMARRIED	M.	5074	3035	788	521	383	148	95	40	
	F.	4827	2997	727	468	324	142	72	57	
MARRIED	M.	2731	.	4	88	538	704	591	404	[illegible]
	F.	2758	.	11	145	657	738	567	412	[illegible]
WIDOWED	M.	314	.	.	.	8	31	48	70	[illegible]
	F.	695	.	1	1	10	58	92	165	[illegible]
339 HEREFORD:										
UNMARRIED	M.	13336	7628	2183	1366	1042	406	273	205	[illegible]
	F.	13205	7546	2082	1412	1064	438	278	246	[illegible]
MARRIED	M.	6901	.	3	246	1503	1800	1605	1111	[illegible]
	F.	6970	.	16	413	1884	1842	1450	902	[illegible]
WIDOWED	M.	830	.	.	3	32	88	135	184	[illegible]
	F.	1852	.	.	4	49	186	300	463	[illegible]
340 WEOBLY:										
UNMARRIED	M.	2601	1466	412	225	191	80	54	42	
	F.	2401	1488	344	221	162	83	54	23	
MARRIED	M.	1362	.	.	37	244	352	334	241	[illegible]
	F.	1366	.	2	68	303	352	310	211	[illegible]
WIDOWED	M.	203	.	.	1	9	10	34	56	
	F.	366	.	.	1	6	17	66	66	[illegible]
341 BROMYARD:										
UNMARRIED	M.	3506	1939	557	386	305	133	87	61	
	F.	3190	2036	426	308	294	74	58	41	
MARRIED	M.	1853	.	.	89	377	446	431	334	[illegible]
	F.	1852	.	6	116	438	481	387	281	[illegible]
WIDOWED	M.	226	.	.	2	6	25	30	51	[illegible]
	F.	429	.	.	.	9	46	58	107	[illegible]

Table 8 *continued*.—Condition as to Marriage and Ages of Males and Females in Registration Districts.

Registration District.		All Ages.	Under 15 Years	15–	20–	25–	35–	45–	55–	65 and upwards
23 HEREFORDSHIRE—*cont.*										
342 LEOMINSTER:										
Unmarried	M.	4619	2708	704	459	370	131	114	81	82
	F.	4314	2604	701	403	304	113	79	61	51
Married	M.	2382	.	1	73	449	602	554	425	273
	F.	2415	.	8	127	542	665	659	331	183
Widowed	M.	294	.	.	1	8	27	47	60	151
	F.	674	.	.	1	24	46	102	155	346
343 KINGTON:										
Unmarried	M.	3964	2271	548	482	337	121	92	67	46
	F.	3589	2190	550	352	272	95	58	34	37
Married	M.	1953	.	.	30	404	484	454	337	235
	F.	1978	.	8	98	480	479	463	310	138
Widowed	M.	240	.	.	1	12	26	27	51	123
	F.	486	.	.	1	20	37	73	111	244
24 SHROPSHIRE.										
344 LUDLOW:										
Unmarried	M.	5929	3377	926	662	489	206	119	83	71
	F.	5544	3305	700	544	389	165	106	78	89
Married	M.	3011	.	3	99	653	812	627	458	319
	F.	3024	.	12	187	779	825	612	372	237
Widowed	M.	378	.	.	3	12	31	86	86	180
	F.	703	.	.	4	19	52	107	176	346
345 CLUN:										
Unmarried	M.	3373	1878	584	377	282	114	63	40	35
	F.	2953	1833	444	270	229	80	38	42	27
Married	M.	1625	.	.	43	328	392	375	278	200
	F.	1629	.	5	95	386	412	348	248	135
Widowed	M.	251	.	.	.	6	15	25	55	150
	F.	350	.	.	.	11	25	43	82	165
346 CHURCH STRETTON:										
Unmarried	M.	1878	1016	297	181	162	85	53	41	33
	F.	1690	968	278	166	106	47	35	24	26
Married	M.	918	.	.	28	127	204	222	180	134
	F.	924	.	2	43	184	238	229	143	87
Widowed	M.	189	.	.	.	4	6	30	22	68
	F.	195	.	.	.	3	16	32	49	95
347 CLEOBURY MORTIMER:										
Unmarried	M.	2828	1507	431	281	205	66	53	50	32
	F.	2249	1400	297	184	124	60	42	30	22
Married	M.	1411	.	.	85	274	337	324	235	156
	F.	1404	.	8	81	322	345	317	206	125
Widowed	M.	169	.	.	.	10	12	28	37	82
	F.	277	.	.	.	4	16	37	68	152
348 BRIDGNORTH:										
Unmarried	M.	4573	2727	717	513	340	140	78	82	46
	F.	4722	2818	721	451	342	147	91	63	89
Married	M.	2477	.	.	68	497	569	540	479	294
	F.	2470	.	6	133	582	644	523	380	213
Widowed	M.	324	.	.	1	10	27	36	88	162
	F.	605	.	.	4	23	69	70	138	311
349 SHIFNAL:										
Unmarried	M.	4074	2419	701	405	294	98	60	51	49
	F.	3901	2434	617	343	254	108	72	37	36
Married	M.	2099	.	1	87	432	543	503	348	212
	F.	2099	.	6	100	486	588	470	300	149
Widowed	M.	209	.	.	1	14	29	28	48	98
	F.	439	.	.	.	20	47	59	90	223
350 MADELEY:										
Unmarried	M.	8724	5313	1601	981	460	192	114	69	44
	F.	7764	5303	1069	502	449	139	87	62	63
Married	M.	4614	.	1	157	1008	1141	1070	767	472
	F.	4665	.	19	288	1122	1179	1041	663	356
Widowed	M.	510	.	.	1	24	62	84	101	248
	F.	1033	.	.	3	28	98	175	240	483
351 ATCHAM:										
Unmarried	M.	15197	8328	2505	1748	1387	537	320	210	166
	F.	14969	8314	2408	1570	1330	560	526	226	245
Married	M.	7825	.	6	268	1800	2148	1685	1164	754
	F.	7703	.	16	497	2018	2136	1505	996	534
Widowed	M.	927	.	.	.	51	116	141	208	411
	F.	1902	.	1	4	72	194	313	476	902
352 OSWESTRY:										
Unmarried	M.	8623	4983	1418	921	705	258	131	108	79
	F.	8178	5020	1264	778	594	208	129	102	83
Married	M.	4346	.	4	131	969	1106	1009	697	430
	F.	4377	.	16	254	1039	1146	944	613	301
Widowed	M.	528	.	.	2	20	81	69	121	255
	F.	1021	.	.	4	27	100	174	254	462
353 ELLESMERE:										
Unmarried	M.	4198	2334	713	469	341	144	94	60	43
	F.	4168	2357	704	443	330	130	97	40	47
Married	M.	2252	.	.	70	411	543	476	440	312
	F.	2271	.	7	129	469	576	461	306	215
Widowed	M.	391	.	.	1	11	23	89	62	165
	F.	518	.	.	.	14	35	72	119	278
24 SHROPSHIRE—*cont.*										
354 WEM:										
Unmarried	M.	3308	1909	549	351	250	95	69	48	[illegible]
	F.	3090	1811	479	298	283	91	63	46	[illegible]
Married	M.	1781	.	1	60	297	450	308	344	[illegible]
	F.	1778	.	7	96	340	401	403	306	[illegible]
Widowed	M.	238	.	.	.	9	14	33	60	[illegible]
	F.	378	.	.	2	7	18	63	99	[illegible]
355 WHITCHURCH:										
Unmarried	M.	3418	2013	599	363	258	84	50	45	[illegible]
	F.	3428	1901	593	388	288	107	67	58	[illegible]
Married	M.	1838	.	.	86	410	450	390	236	[illegible]
	F.	1863	.	8	110	491	449	381	257	[illegible]
Widowed	M.	244	.	.	2	6	21	31	54	[illegible]
	F.	455	.	1	.	15	39	63	104	[illegible]
356 MARKET DRAYTON:										
Unmarried	M.	4594	2759	772	469	324	124	66	45	[illegible]
	F.	4451	2642	606	453	380	139	80	50	[illegible]
Married	M.	2489	.	.	81	510	622	559	421	[illegible]
	F.	2517	.	4	135	601	669	542	342	[illegible]
Widowed	M.	287	.	.	.	6	16	45	30	[illegible]
	F.	511	.	.	4	13	46	77	130	[illegible]
357 WELLINGTON:										
Unmarried	M.	9017	5432	1417	858	519	160	108	83	[illegible]
	F.	7587	5187	1040	600	406	158	92	46	[illegible]
Married	M.	4454	.	6	181	1054	1170	1019	638	383
	F.	4613	.	21	293	1159	1296	920	586	289
Widowed	M.	434	.	.	1	25	47	71	86	206
	F.	909	.	.	1	42	71	148	229	435
358 NEWPORT:										
Unmarried	M.	4678	2832	824	548	335	136	82	58	43
	F.	4500	2810	690	389	322	107	68	55	49
Married	M.	2532	.	2	84	525	617	579	423	303
	F.	2561	.	8	151	681	656	545	396	251
Widowed	M.	297	.	.	1	10	28	35	64	109
	F.	584	.	.	2	10	42	97	123	303
25 STAFFORDSHIRE.										
359 STAFFORD:										
Unmarried	M.	9684	5630	1508	1061	800	310	170	115	[illegible]
	F.	9364	5533	1474	939	671	293	175	97	[illegible]
Married	M.	5086	.	4	215	1421	1417	987	633	[illegible]
	F.	4930	.	15	367	1467	1300	922	534	[illegible]
Widowed	M.	537	.	1	3	37	61	89	119	[illegible]
	F.	978	.	.	3	44	116	182	224	[illegible]
360 STONE:										
Unmarried	M.	9610	5322	1383	899	580	189	110	73	[illegible]
	F.	9217	5058	1510	946	640	242	140	96	[illegible]
Married	M.	4883	.	7	287	1255	1245	1018	657	[illegible]
	F.	4897	.	27	443	1309	1292	957	627	[illegible]
Widowed	M.	541	.	.	1	34	65	94	118	[illegible]
	F.	1036	.	.	1	38	108	178	288	[illegible]
361 NEWCASTLE UNDER LYME:										
Unmarried	M.	11291	7033	1760	1169	718	289	124	[illegible]	[illegible]
	F.	9906	6849	1592	777	446	145	87	54	[illegible]
Married	M.	5931	.	7	367	1684	1602	1176	746	349
	F.	5968	.	40	602	1859	1439	1074	607	247
Widowed	M.	592	.	.	3	56	89	112	187	215
	F.	1063	.	.	15	66	135	217	274	350
362 WOLSTANTON:										
Unmarried	M.	23932	15264	3866	2429	1472	496	235	128	[illegible]
	F.	21878	15546	3422	1759	741	208	102	58	[illegible]
Married	M.	13042	.	53	965	3904	3653	2558	1412	517
	F.	13186	.	145	1517	4172	3465	2326	1177	379
Widowed	M.	1084	.	2	6	96	171	230	248	[illegible]
	F.	2346	.	1	18	143	322	569	667	[illegible]
363 STOKE-UPON-TRENT:										
Unmarried	M.	32316	20606	5205	3122	2038	714	375	163	[illegible]
	F.	30806	20872	5093	2596	1405	413	222	134	[illegible]
Married	M.	17871	.	42	1363	5644	5046	3356	1636	[illegible]
	F.	18016	.	200	2123	4914	4800	3008	1487	[illegible]
Widowed	M.	1626	.	1	10	144	271	355	384	[illegible]
	F.	3680	.	.	17	206	530	830	991	[illegible]
364 LEEK:										
Unmarried	M.	9617	5000	1442	888	408	208	147	112	[illegible]
	F.	9802	5222	1486	883	654	248	150	88	[illegible]
Married	M.	5109	.	16	312	1311	1323	1068	635	[illegible]
	F.	5178	.	32	404	1480	1406	927	571	[illegible]
Widowed	M.	609	.	.	2	41	76	72	136	[illegible]
	F.	1035	.	.	7	45	115	177	242	[illegible]
365 CHEADLE:										
Unmarried	M.	7172	4631	1147	648	398	158	99	74	[illegible]
	F.	6759	4454	1010	568	347	160	96	79	[illegible]
Married	M.	3762	.	11	207	908	966	740	571	[illegible]
	F.	3791	.	34	309	1041	973	748	433	[illegible]
Widowed	M.	442	.	.	3	21	37	63	105	[illegible]
	F.	798	.	.	1	84	80	125	216	[illegible]

able 8 *continued.*—CONDITION as to MARRIAGE and AGES of MALES and FEMALES in REGISTRATION DISTRICTS.

ISTRATION ISTRICT.		ALL AGES.	Under 15 Years	15–	20–	25–	35–	45–	55–	65 and upw^{ds}.
TAFFORD-RE—*cont.*										
)XETER:										
MARRIED	M.	4320	2519	666	471	336	127	91	50	51
	F.	4398	2545	719	471	620	133	82	60	64
RRIED	M.	2275	.	3	81	526	525	486	393	261
	F.	2364	.	6	148	588	558	462	305	197
DOWED	M.	278	.	.	1	13	17	36	61	150
	F.	538	.	.	2	18	43	80	138	257
TON UPON ENT:										
MARRIED	M.	24454	14808	3863	2884	1707	627	245	137	78
	F.	24122	14727	2028	1560	957	414	220	133	115
RRIED	M.	12654	.	11	863	4149	3492	2238	1532	629
	F.	12538	.	109	1305	4123	3321	2081	1137	465
DOWED	M.	1201	.	1	10	107	196	218	240	469
	F.	1909	.	1	4	112	216	353	484	739
WORTH:										
MARRIED	M.	6477	3808	935	612	358	112	61	37	40
	F.	5913	3864	910	514	341	146	59	48	37
RRIED	M.	3258	.	1	150	894	861	658	480	260
	F.	3248	.	15	234	937	881	614	386	178
DOWED	M.	346	.	.	1	11	27	54	89	164
	F.	568	.	.	3	28	48	99	153	239
HFIELD:										
MARRIED	M.	13856	7405	2090	1514	1005	403	205	185	99
	F.	11427	7533	1577	922	707	293	176	124	95
RRIED	M.	6588	.	6	323	1676	1790	1335	876	530
	F.	6471	.	40	526	1843	1794	1241	737	380
IDOWED	M.	792	.	.	4	35	57	104	156	352
	F.	1247	.	.	8	67	115	203	234	375
NOCK:										
NMARRIED	M.	11909	7652	1824	1282	756	253	142	81	69
	F.	10096	7357	1298	665	424	158	93	50	51
ARRIED	M.	6407	.	14	386	1702	1750	1285	818	412
	F.	6232	.	48	561	1906	1669	1175	941	270
IDOWED	M.	540	.	.	4	32	61	75	135	583
	F.	798	.	.	3	38	74	188	208	342
LVERHAMPTON:										
NMARRIED	M.	45737	28138	7599	4088	2029	923	516	378	206
	F.	42341	27899	6979	3082	2281	723	401	210	184
ARRIED	M.	24830	.	34	1472	7137	6317	4983	3318	1569
	F.	25088	.	175	2429	7731	6293	4798	2587	1072
IDOWED	M.	2376	.	1	11	139	296	435	576	918
	F.	4898	.	.	19	327	536	909	1344	1913
LSALL:										
NMARRIED	M.	26591	16847	4288	2745	1589	473	296	158	105
	F.	25968	17088	4095	2193	1103	299	125	85	68
ARRIED	M.	14481	.	18	935	4179	3927	2860	1764	778
	F.	14583	.	112	1502	4652	3905	2520	1392	500
IDOWED	M.	1162	.	.	7	60	147	238	280	430
	F.	2322	.	.	22	128	273	454	587	828
ST BROMWICH:										
NMARRIED	M.	39494	24860	6632	4277	2394	643	302	182	114
	F.	38648	25514	6301	3692	2070	610	287	159	107
ARRIED	M.	21279	.	34	1355	6272	5611	4286	2512	1200
	F.	21577	.	144	2178	6740	5656	3944	2093	812
IDOWED	M.	1658	.	.	15	105	201	309	387	641
	F.	3614	.	.	18	190	408	729	998	1269
DLEY:										
NMARRIED	M.	43723	28011	7231	4253	2051	618	333	224	122
	F.	41177	28820	6519	3230	1528	588	268	170	104
ARRIED	M.	24448	.	47	1792	7200	6063	4750	3085	1511
	F.	24357	.	175	2687	7621	6208	4414	2648	1104
IDOWED	M.	1877	.	.	12	118	198	348	454	747
	F.	4142	.	.	31	219	442	752	1091	1607
VORCESTER-SHIRE.										
DURBRIDGE:										
NMARRIED	M.	24655	15064	3892	2569	1313	395	197	129	96
	F.	23853	16140	3692	2077	1190	371	192	113	80
ARRIED	M.	13673	.	25	861	3903	3397	2752	1700	977
	F.	13875	.	85	1311	4153	3526	2032	1461	677
IDOWED	M.	1179	.	.	5	61	120	167	274	552
	F.	2361	.	.	10	90	230	440	625	967
DERMINSTER:										
NMARRIED	M.	11906	7512	1043	1228	688	229	137	104	65
	F.	12714	7564	2229	1389	838	291	175	127	101
ARRIED	M.	7050	.	10	416	1988	1725	1308	959	555
	F.	7184	.	31	680	2096	1816	1359	823	385
IDOWED	M.	606	.	.	2	29	60	53	161	271
	F.	1482	.	3	7	65	145	289	340	634
VBURY:										
NMARRIED	M.	2451	1383	396	267	193	95	65	34	18
	F.	2251	1424	315	194	161	62	38	31	26
ARRIED	M.	1212	.	.	34	253	297	280	230	118
	F.	1207	.	3	74	294	306	257	170	109
IDOWED	M.	151	.	.	.	4	13	23	46	69
	F.	[illegible]				7	36	39	77	100

REGISTRATION DISTRICT.		ALL AGES.	Under 15 Years	15–	20–	25–	35–	45–	55–
26 WORCESTER-SHIRE—*cont.*									
378 MARTLEY:									
UNMARRIED	M.	5038	3121	794	468	316	147	88	58
	F.	4820	2670	711	484	348	149	125	68
MARRIED	M.	2750	.	1	84	584	681	846	449
	F.	2730	.	9	155	638	711	508	408
WIDOWED	M.	298	.	.	.	15	17	34	71
	F.	727	.	.	1	29	71	113	150
379 WORCESTER:									
UNMARRIED	M.	9128	5407	1564	1058	685	325	189	75
	F.	10806	5450	1788	1134	754	347	249	161
MARRIED	M.	5525	.	19	354	1504	1480	1109	679
	F.	5508	.	41	495	1606	1481	1048	582
WIDOWED	M.	605	.	.	2	30	62	187	137
	F.	1523	.	.	6	67	180	295	303
380 UPTON ON SEVERN:									
UNMARRIED	M.	6882	*3793	1194	651	507	251	142	93
	F.	7803	*3683	1326	369	864	430	307	177
MARRIED	M.	3596	.	4	120	673	874	853	630
	F.	3687	.	8	197	634	945	859	531
WIDOWED	M.	394	.	.	2	14	34	60	80
	F.	1072	.	.	1	37	111	198	286
381 EVESHAM:									
UNMARRIED	M.	4744	2952	740	448	282	127	76	62
	F.	4478	2865	615	403	302	122	78	55
MARRIED	M.	2987	.	3	101	586	688	595	415
	F.	2985	.	12	181	639	674	582	365
WIDOWED	M.	310	.	.	2	10	29	51	67
	F.	568	.	.	5	24	43	91	118
382 PERSHORE:									
UNMARRIED	M.	4108	2418	786	419	271	138	81	48
	F.	3934	2516	525	332	282	107	78	47
MARRIED	M.	2347	.	1	83	468	600	538	358
	F.	2358	.	9	130	552	600	535	307
WIDOWED	M.	285	.	.	1	7	25	41	56
	F.	528	.	.	2	15	33	66	134
383 DROITWICH:									
UNMARRIED	M.	7728	4844	1277	779	464	107	89	58
	F.	7976	4974	1226	772	489	217	137	81
MARRIED	M.	4497	.	1	195	1136	1193	921	672
	F.	4547	.	17	292	1283	1234	875	550
WIDOWED	M.	431	.	.	5	17	56	70	87
	F.	943	.	.	1	45	84	156	243
384 BROMSGROVE:									
UNMARRIED	M.	9571	6067	1570	894	539	201	132	99
	F.	9605	6806	1404	946	713	236	136	90
MARRIED	M.	5484	.	5	348	1416	1290	1155	795
	F.	5526	.	27	464	1594	1308	1090	656
WIDOWED	M.	600	.	.	6	28	64	82	151
	F.	1058	.	.	5	32	97	192	273
385 KINGS NORTON:									
UNMARRIED	M.	27897	17735	4058	3118	1938	605	235	137
	F.	32830	17443	5660	4421	3197	1074	587	276
MARRIED	M.	15296	.	15	764	4527	4206	3060	1806
	F.	15614	.	63	1313	4884	4311	2963	1518
WIDOWED	M.	1234	.	.	4	92	157	265	287
	F.	3261	.	.	16	135	416	619	865
27 WARWICK-SHIRE.									
386 BIRMINGHAM:									
UNMARRIED	M.	73989	45128	12438	8278	5127	1631	725	403
	F.	73142	45756	12405	7674	4354	1467	779	410
MARRIED	M.	48496	.	59	2850	13103	11752	9280	4509
	F.	43144	.	297	4530	14142	11099	7546	3709
WIDOWED	M.	3879	.	1	18	252	506	775	999
	F.	5743	.	3	55	579	1485	2275	2511
387 ASTON:									
UNMARRIED	M.	63657	41626	10439	6513	3727	996	306	213
	F.	63307	41817	10086	5829	3254	1119	622	307
MARRIED	M.	36606	.	48	2562	11800	10371	6765	3620
	F.	37391	.	204	3836	12815	10154	6150	8061
WIDOWED	M.	2656	.	.	17	214	378	548	642
	F.	6271	.	.	34	371	849	1306	1669
388 MERIDEN:									
UNMARRIED	M.	2478	2168	534	339	236	86	41	35
	F.	3199	1955	433	302	282	94	64	43
MARRIED	M.	1842	.	2	59	359	439	430	320
	F.	1834	.	3	93	414	465	419	279
WIDOWED	M.	285	.	.	2	3	13	39	57
	F.	437	.	.	1	8	48	65	105
389 ATHERSTONE:									
UNMARRIED	M.	4347	2919	775	444	255	59	48	33
	F.	4142	2733	640	327	224	100	52	37
MARRIED	M.	2533	.	1	148	759	672	458	373
	F.	2409	.	18	270	725	604	450	310
WIDOWED	M.	258	.	.	3	13	23	37	69
	F.	440	.	.	.	18	49	68	90

Table 8 *continued*.—Condition as to Marriage and Ages of Males and Females in Registration Districts.

Registration District.	All Ages.	Under 15 Years.	15–	20–	25–	35–	45–	55–	65 and upw.
27 WARWICKSHIRE—*cont.*									
390 NUNEATON:									
Unmarried M.	3838	2506	636	353	206	52	44	21	21
Unmarried F.	4053	2573	605	396	226	105	60	52	28
Married M.	2481	.	8	180	687	682	490	387	209
Married F.	2527	.	14	199	726	625	454	337	172
Widowed M.	274	.	1	6	8	26	30	50	136
Widowed F.	518	.	.	1	21	45	90	141	220
391 FOLESHILL:									
Unmarried M.	5240	3563	883	438	216	84	36	35	24
Unmarried F.	5358	3638	794	485	292	122	64	39	24
Married M.	3417	.	5	229	872	759	675	540	346
Married F.	3483	.	14	306	942	816	656	485	265
Widowed M.	317	.	.	2	12	18	40	68	177
Widowed F.	673	.	.	1	21	68	99	182	302
392 COVENTRY:									
Unmarried M.	12493	7764	2121	1416	710	225	123	64	61
Unmarried F.	13762	8176	2321	1630	966	380	234	126	90
Married M.	8148	.	14	621	2240	2010	1596	1077	590
Married F.	8241	.	39	752	2348	2042	1597	1010	453
Widowed M.	735	.	.	3	33	63	118	172	346
Widowed F.	1737	.	.	10	87	196	352	404	685
393 RUGBY:									
Unmarried M.	8516	4810	1826	968	648	211	116	74	64
Unmarried F.	7928	4754	1169	801	603	266	150	98	87
Married M.	4658	.	3	201	1159	1148	956	736	455
Married F.	4683	.	10	312	1265	1176	938	664	395
Widowed M.	512	.	.	2	24	51	85	108	242
Widowed F.	904	.	.	8	32	80	161	216	407
394 SOLIHULL:									
Unmarried M.	6301	3785	1004	676	464	174	91	58	49
Unmarried F.	6912	3727	1160	845	643	254	132	94	57
Married M.	3505	.	3	111	800	938	791	510	352
Married F.	3549	.	11	195	859	1009	704	441	230
Widowed M.	377	.	.	1	14	37	55	98	172
Widowed F.	733	.	.	1	23	50	140	176	325
27 WARWICKSHIRE—*cont.*									
395 WARWICK:									
Unmarried M.	14118	8244	2441	1442	1051	395	238	164	148
Unmarried F.	18039	8441	2973	2296	1037	964	582	474	393
Married M.	9614	.	6	971	2071	2107	1600	1064	894
Married F.	8635	.	29	555	2239	2271	1788	1262	503
Widowed M.	937	.	.	4	52	82	127	184	482
Widowed F.	2487	.	.	6	93	236	412	640	1101
396 STRATFORD ON AVON:									
Unmarried M.	6746	4191	1090	637	444	144	106	80	55
Unmarried F.	6687	4128	965	613	464	216	144	74	83
Married M.	3851	.	3	141	826	969	880	547	418
Married F.	3800	.	14	246	630	1016	797	605	284
Widowed M.	614	.	.	1	17	43	76	115	262
Widowed F.	839	.	.	4	29	76	125	212	394
397 ALCESTER:									
Unmarried M.	6803	3721	912	510	328	130	79	68	48
Unmarried F.	5725	3639	878	496	387	145	72	73	60
Married M.	3408	.	4	160	813	880	689	530	323
Married F.	3451	.	19	238	917	902	681	477	237
Widowed M.	400	.	.	2	24	19	50	82	223
Widowed F.	648	.	.	4	19	77	92	139	312
398 SHIPSTON ON STOUR:									
Unmarried M.	6481	3350	867	506	383	169	84	72	48
Unmarried F.	5752	3284	782	395	349	169	104	70	67
Married M.	3035	.	.	93	572	719	689	565	391
Married F.	3062	.	5	161	683	760	696	458	299
Widowed M.	397	.	.	3	12	26	66	69	221
Widowed F.	717	.	.	2	15	50	106	167	378
399 SOUTHAM:									
Unmarried M.	3138	1928	484	318	201	77	48	40	44
Unmarried F.	2834	1910	389	217	156	68	37	24	33
Married M.	1864	.	.	76	379	484	393	304	228
Married F.	1850	.	6	117	426	469	401	278	153
Widowed M.	247	.	.	2	7	17	59	65	125
Widowed F.	349	.	.	.	8	17	56	86	188

Table 9.—Condition as to Marriage and Ages of Males and Females in each Urban Sanitary District of which the Population exceeds 50,000 Persons.

Urban-Sanitary District.	All Ages.	Under 15 Years.	15–	20–	25–	35–	45–	55–	65 and upw.
BRISTOL*:									
Unmarried M.	57094	36655	9490	7615	3482	1021	448	257	150
Unmarried F.	68216	37760	11576	7725	5467	2306	1465	1012	916
Married M.	33997	.	76	2240	10185	9124	6383	3959	2076
Married F.	36538	.	269	3492	11394	9437	6280	3292	1464
Widowed M.	2020	.	1	25	197	563	471	600	963
Widowed F.	9408	.	1	57	628	1231	1687	2311	3364
WOLVERHAMPTON.									
Unmarried M.	23629	14458	3878	2612	1638	499	262	179	112
Unmarried F.	22266	14162	3798	2180	1252	410	241	127	76
Married M.	12914	.	26	804	3824	3363	2501	1642	760
Married F.	12088	.	97	1328	4095	3312	2412	1264	480
Widowed M.	1284	.	1	8	79	173	256	305	468
Widowed F.	2695	.	.	16	139	366	641	731	912
WALSALL:									
Unmarried M.	18463	11735	2881	1906	1142	332	216	117	66
Unmarried F.	17638	11878	2949	1597	795	220	96	63	6
Married M.	10687	.	11	858	3010	2745	1937	1212	614
Married F.	10167	.	76	1077	3246	2781	1716	916	328
Widowed M.	788	.	.	4	40	94	166	185	297
Widowed F.	1654	.	.	19	99	202	343	422	569
WEST BROMWICH:									
Unmarried M.	18022	11679	3010	1816	1002	296	167	94	71
Unmarried F.	16781	11847	2546	1328	678	132	100	54	36
Married M.	9479	.	18	660	2856	2483	1834	1099	534
Married F.	9631	.	84	1065	3032	2523	1875	918	314
Widowed M.	784	.	.	4	50	82	131	171	346
Widowed F.	1898	.	.	10	82	174	327	421	467
BIRMINGHAM:									
Unmarried M.	119850	74613	19764	13062	8083	2396	1008	569	368
Unmarried F.	121525	75366	20249	12941	7779	2681	1376	714	428
Married M.	68950	.	98	4617	21640	19190	13280	7172	3047
Married F.	70188	.	487	7322	23278	19070	12074	5962	1976
Widowed M.	5740	.	1	29	400	837	1166	1482	1835
Widowed F.	14641	.	3	86	873	2142	3293	3886	4259
ASTON MANOR:									
Unmarried M.	16066	10642	2629	1854	907	182	70	38	24
Unmarried F.	16809	10791	2821	1637	912	316	183	98	58
Married M.	9260	.	9	594	3059	2686	1689	655	388
Married F.	9490	.	82	948	3367	2688	1568	737	252
Widowed M.	581	.	.	6	61	88	128	129	176
Widowed F.	1647	.	.	6	103	231	368	421	523

* A portion of the City of Bristol is situated in the Bedminster District of Somersetshire (Division 6), but the condition as to Marriage, and Ages, &c. for the entire City are returned here.

Table 10.—OCCUPATIONS of MALES and FEMALES in the WEST MIDLAND DIVISION and its REGISTRATION COUNTIES, and in each URBAN SANITARY DISTRICT of which the POPULATION exceeds 50,000 PERSONS.

OCCUPATIONS.	WEST-MIDLAND COUNTIES.		REGISTRATION COUNTIES. 22. GLOUCESTER-SHIRE.		23. HEREFORD-SHIRE.		24. SHROP-SHIRE.		25. STAFFORD-SHIRE.	
	Males.	Females.	Males.	Females.	Males.	Females.	Males.	Females.	Males.	Females.
TOTAL	1481585	1547919	245027	279540	58525	59622	182932	132898	504874	501884
I. PROFESSIONAL CLASS.										
1. PERSONS ENGAGED IN THE GENERAL OR LOCAL GOVERNMENT OF THE COUNTRY.										
1. *National Government.*										
Peer, M.P., Privy Councillor (not otherwise described)	31	.	6	.	2	.	8	.	4	.
Civil Service (officers and clerks)	1586	426	478	100	62	40	174	69	407	96
Civil Service (messengers, &c.)	1902	71	435	16	132	5	239	9	378	24
Prison Officer, &c.	186	72	28	11	15	2	16	4	44	14
2. *Local Government.*										
Police	2740	.	594	.	106	.	190	.	755	
Municipal, Parish, Union, District, Officer	1268	281	244	73	72	14	141	34	336	57
Other Local or County Official	845	.	217	.	55	.	107	.	162	.
3. *East Indian and Colonial Service.*										
East Indian and Colonial Service	15	.	12	.	1	.	1	.	.	.
2. PERSONS ENGAGED IN THE DEFENCE OF THE COUNTRY.										
1. *Army (at Home).*										
Army Officer (effective or retired)	707	.	351	.	40	.	50	.	66	
Soldier and Non-commissioned Officer	1819	.	426	.	29	.	338	.	417	
Militia, Yeomanry, Volunteers	1362	.	471	.	75	.	59	.	571	.
Army Pensioner	665	.	220	.	22	.	54	.	126	.
2. *Navy (ashore or in port).*										
Navy Officer (effective or retired)	191	.	63	.	3	.	6	.	8	.
Seaman, R.N.	53	.	41	.	1	.	1	.	3	.
Royal Marines (officers and men)	33	.	16	.	2	.	1	.	5	.
Navy Pensioner	169	.	91	.	10	.	8	.	19	.
3. PERSONS ENGAGED IN PROFESSIONAL OCCUPATIONS (WITH THEIR IMMEDIATE SUBORDINATES).										
1. *Clerical Profession.*										
Clergyman (Established Church)	2038	.	679	.	248	.	403	.	568	
Roman Catholic Priest	233	.	35		14	.	12	.	69	
Minister, Priest, of other religious bodies	860	.	219	.	47	.	105	.	139	.
Missionary, Scripture Reader, Itinerant Preacher	292	147	93	47	7	6	20	4	61	22
Nun, Sister of Charity	.	562		83	.	142	.	2	.	114
Theological Student	254	.	69	.	85	.	6		66	.
Church, Chapel, Cemetery—Officer, Servant	456	191	96	71	18	8	42	19	127	31
2. *Legal Profession.*										
Barrister, Solicitor	1567	.	391	.	91	.	172	.	348	.
Law Student	103	.	22	.	2	.	4	.	30	.
Law Clerk, and others connected with Law	2221	2	501	2	107	.	179	.	551	.
3. *Medical Profession.*										
Physician, Surgeon, General Practitioner	1491	6	347	1	73	.	153	.	338	.
Dentist	346	.	123	.	11	.	14	.	69	
Medical Student, Assistant	447	6	88	2	21	.	44	.	135	
Midwife	.	412	.	61	.	26	.	49	.	114
Subordinate Medical Service	185	3063	36	968	6	101	10	206	66	534
4. *Teachers.*										
Schoolmaster	4665	10056	838	2152	201	387	440	832	1498	3091
Teacher, Professor, Lecturer	549	4372	201	1161	20	241	37	426	105	963
School Service, and others concerned in Teaching	173	143	25	38	2	4	9	3	48	29
5. *Literary and Scientific Persons.*										
Author, Editor, Journalist	190	24	39	8	7	3	19	4	42	4
Reporter, Short-hand Writer	210	1	50	1	12	.	16	.	54	.
Persons engaged in Scientific Pursuits	76	3	18	.	2	.	2	.	30	1
Literary, Scientific, Institution, Service, &c.	35	11	6	2	2	1	2	1	5	2
6. *Engineers and Surveyors.*										
Civil Engineer	538	.	119	.	21		33	.	164	.
Mining Engineer	435	.	34	.	2		32	.	297	.
Land, House, Ship, Surveyor	570	.	117	.	32	.	71	.	167	.
7. *Artists.*										
Painter (artist)	540	163	118	40	9	5	22	3	119	24
Engraver (artist)	216	11	25	.	.	.	.	1	88	1
Sculptor	84	1	29	1	14	.	2	.	11	.
Architect	555	.	116	.	18	.	33	.	160	.
Musician, Music Master	1379	1090	308	291	37	19	74	52	358	249
Art Student	123	61	32	23	5	.	4	2	32	17
Photographer	408	153	148	43	18	2	39	9	94	25
Actor	265	200	54	47	6	6	6	6	52	53
Art, Music, Theatre, Service	85	15	18	6	.	.	3	2	20	2

NOTE.—Persons returned as engaged in more than one occupation have been referred to the one that appeared to be of most importance; or, if there was no difference in this respect, to the one first given by the person in his or her return. In some cases special rules have been followed: *e.g.*, "Clergyman and Schoolmaster" in combination has always been referred to "Schoolmaster"; a Member of Parliament or Peer engaged in any branch of commerce or industry has always been referred to this latter, not to "Peer, M.P."

The numbers returned under any heading include Labourers, Apprentices, and Assistants, as well as Masters, but not Clerks, Messengers, Errand boys, Porters, or Watchmen, for which occupations there are special headings. Civil, Military, and Naval Clerks, Law, Bank, Insurance, and Railway Clerks, and Government and Railway Porters, are, however, exceptions to this rule. Many young persons, being Apprentices or Assistants, have therefore been referred to occupations usually followed by adults. Women also, chiefly widows or orphans carrying on the business of their deceased husbands or fathers, will sometimes be found under occupations commonly followed by men only.

Persons returned as *retired* from any business have not been referred to that business. Inmates of workhouses have been referred to their trades, unless their age or infirmities showed that they were past work. But persons who might be supposed to be only temporarily separated from their usual employment, such as Prisoners, and Patients in General Hospitals, have been classed under their usual occupations.

male designation, *e.g.*, "Schoolmaster," alone is given, instead of "Schoolmaster, Schoolmistress."

Table 10 *continued*.—Occupation of Males and Females in the West-Midland Division and its Registration Counties, and in each Urban Sanitary District of which the Population exceeds 50,000 Persons.

Occupations.	West Midland Counties.		Registration Counties. 22. Gloucestershire.		23. Herefordshire.		24. Shropshire.		25. Staffordshire.	
	Males.	Females.	Males.	Females.	Males.	Females.	Males.	Females.	Males.	Females.
8. Persons engaged in Exhibitions, Shows, Games, &c.										
Performer, Showman, Exhibition, Service	125	43	10	3	3	.	1	2	35	18
Billiard, Cricket, & other Games, Service	206	1	66	.	10	.	10	.	66	.
XX. DOMESTIC CLASS.										
4. Persons engaged in Domestic Offices or Services.										
1. Domestic Service.										
Domestic Coachman, Groom	8590	.	2248	.	271	.	1521	.	2031	.
Domestic Gardener	7822	13	1793	.	680	.	1109	6	2207	2
Domestic Indoor Servant	5544	154647	1315	30084	386	6824	821	15189	965	34728
Lodge, Gate, Park, Keeper (not Government)	143	121	29	22	5	23	9	14	42	20
Inn, Hotel, Servant	2533	3463	493	659	92	124	265	283	534	650
College, Club, Service	83	26	18	5	2	2	1	.	17	7
2. Other Service.										
Office Keeper (not Government)	113	126	13	35	1	6	4	6	23	18
Cook (not domestic)	62	344	14	127	1	8	2	28	3	53
Charwoman	.	9701	.	2534	.	459	.	798	.	2694
Washing and Bathing Service	143	20695	46	6361	5	1019	4	1413	22	3340
Hospital and Institution Service	435	1234	125	340	23	31	36	74	125	322
Others engaged in Service	48	57	11	11	1	1	2	2	5	7
XXI. COMMERCIAL CLASS.										
5. Persons engaged in Commercial Occupations.										
1. Merchants and Agents.										
Merchant	504	6	67	.	5	.	15	1	110	.
Broker, Agent, Factor	2951	69	507	12	41	1	137	.	979	22
Auctioneer, Appraiser, Valuer, House Agent	1016	5	192	1	45	1	127	.	257	1
Accountant	1257	3	512	.	38	1	97	.	290	.
Salesman, Buyer (not otherwise described)	102	49	29	11	4	.	5	.	17	1
Commercial Traveller	3943	.	936	.	49	.	112	.	839	.
Commercial Clerk	17540	823	3107	123	187	21	637	18	5774	110
Officer of Commercial Company, Guild, Society, &c.	20	.	4	.	.	.	2	.	4	.
2. Dealers in Money.										
Banker	61	.	23	.	6	.	12	.	3	.
Bank Service	1336	3	279	.	59	.	123	.	356	1
Bill Discounter, Bill Broker, Finance Agent	63	.	11	.	.	.	.	.	18	.
3. Persons occupied in Insurance.										
Life, House, Ship, &c., Insurance Service	1281	26	256	.	18	.	70	1	420	8
6. Persons engaged in Conveyance of Men, Goods, and Messages.										
1. On Railways.										
Railway Engine Driver, Stoker	2562	.	324	.	33	.	236	.	921	.
Railway Guard	958	.	153	.	31	.	85	.	348	.
Pointsman, Level Crossing Man	900	16	98	4	37	1	130	3	410	.
Other Railway Officials and Servants	10077	51	1432	5	363	.	902	3	3276	18
2. On Roads.										
Toll Collector, Turnpike Gate Keeper	97	35	15	7	1	1	8	3	40	17
Omnibus, Coach, Cab, Owner—Livery Stable Keeper	338	16	157	6	13	1	22	.	79	3
Cabman, Flyman, Coachman (not domestic)	2006	.	344	.	46	.	58	.	253	.
Carman, Carrier, Carter, Haulier	11006	133	2240	30	216	15	581	18	4073	30
Tramway Companies' Service	222	.	114	.	1	.	.	.	66	.
Wheel Chair Proprietor, Attendant, &c.	131	.	92	.	.	.	.	.	2	.
3. On Canals, Rivers and Seas.										
Inland Navigation Service	555	7	47	3	3	.	49	.	284	1
Bargeman, Lighterman, Waterman	4441	106	632	6	12	.	110	3	2189	60
Navigation Service (on shore)	42	1	36	3	1	.	.	.	5	.
Seaman (Merchant Service)	1689	.	1517	.	17	.	20	.	48	.
Pilot	82	.	81	.	.	.	1	.	.	.
Ship Steward, Cook	76	8	63	6	2	.	3	.	8	.
Boatman on Seas	18	.	18	.	.	.	.	.	.	.
Harbour, Dock, Wharf, Lighthouse, Service	1112	8	779	3	1	.	6	2	254	3
4. In Storage.										
Warehouseman (not Manchester)	2032	2515	323	10	4	.	25	.	514	428
Meter, Weigher	30	.	12	.	.	.	3	.	15	.
5. In conveying Messages, Porterage, &c.										
Messenger, Porter, Watchman (not Railway nor Government)	14587	245	3477	37	314	3	691	4	2591	33
Telegraph, Telephone, Service	615	160	129	44	14	7	62	8	150	43

Table 10 *continued.*—OCCUPATIONS of MALES and FEMALES in the WEST MIDLAND DIVISION and its REGISTRATION COUNTIES, and in each URBAN SANITARY DISTRICT of which the POPULATION exceeds 50,000 PERSONS.

OCCUPATIONS.	WEST MIDLAND COUNTIES.		REGISTRATION COUNTIES. 22. GLOUCESTERSHIRE.		23. HEREFORDSHIRE.		24. SHROPSHIRE.		25. STAFFORDSHIRE.	
	Males.	Females.	Males.	Females.	Males.	Females.	Males.	Females.	Males.	Females.
IV. AGRICULTURAL CLASS.										
7. PERSONS ENGAGED IN AGRICULTURE.										
1. *In Fields and Pastures.*										
Farmer, Grazier	22315	2423	3279	328	2901	327	4840	626	5856	617
Farmer's, Grazier's—Son, Grandson, Brother, Nephew*	7394	.	1299	.	1061	.	1818	.	1707	.
Farm Bailiff	2251	.	368	.	304	.	458	.	392	.
Agricultural Labourer, Farm Servant, Cottager	94009	4817	18650	1150	11123	453	18159	689	15686	678
Shepherd	2333	.	688	.	229	.	325	.	251	.
Land Drainage Service (not in towns)	358	.	30	.	59	.	162	.	42	.
Agricultural Machine—Proprietor, Attendant	419	2	87	.	45	.	87	1	67	1
Agricultural Student, Pupil	147	.	82	.	14	.	19	.	13	.
Others engaged in, or connected with, Agriculture	49	2	34	.	.	.	14	.	.	2
2. *In Woods.*										
Woodman	959	.	193	.	145	.	247	.	197	.
3. *In Gardens.*										
Nurseryman, Seedsman, Florist	645	48	165	12	58	5	46	.	107	4
Gardener (not domestic)	9472	319	2380	96	376	10	720	16	896	34
8. PERSONS ENGAGED ABOUT ANIMALS.										
1. *About Animals.*										
Horse Proprietor, Breeder, Dealer	286	1	90	1	7	.	29	.	79	.
Groom, Horse-keeper, Horse-breaker	4836	2	965	.	159	.	396	.	804	2
Veterinary Surgeon, Farrier	562	.	150	.	43	.	83	.	186	.
Cattle, Sheep, Pig—Dealer, Salesman	570	1	136	.	40	.	114	.	178	.
Drover	398	.	105	.	4	.	29	.	73	.
Gamekeeper	1443	.	218	.	150	.	484	.	300	.
Dog, Bird, Animal—Keeper, Dealer	76	26	19	3	8	1	11	4	9	2
Vermin destroyer	129	.	8	.	19	.	52	.	31	.
Fisherman	175	.	105	.	15	.	14	.	3	.
Knacker, Catsmeat Dealer, &c., &c.	21	2	4	1	.	.	.	.	8	.
V. INDUSTRIAL CLASS.										
9. PERSONS WORKING AND DEALING IN BOOKS, PRINTS, AND MAPS.										
1. *Books.*										
Publisher, Bookseller, Librarian	636	207	192	68	23	13	45	20	118	30
Music—Publisher, Seller, Printer	88	20	25	4	2	2	8	2	18	4
Bookbinder	497	474	138	120	7	2	31	3	85	95
Printer	4731	263	1019	34	148	3	290	6	919	45
Newspaper Agent, News Room Keeper	370	151	102	29	8	1	21	2	74	36
Others	1	.	1	.	.	.	.	.	.	.
2. *Prints and Maps.*										
Lithographer, Lithographic Printer	624	8	150	2	4	.	7	.	58	.
Copper Plate and Steel Plate Printer	15	2	6	1	.	.	.	.	3	.
Map and Print—Colourer, Seller	7	2	.	.	.	.	.	.	.	.
10. PERSONS WORKING AND DEALING IN MACHINES AND IMPLEMENTS.										
1. *Machines.*										
Engine, Machine, Maker	5674	57	477	7	39	.	185	1	1260	10
Millwright	582	.	141	.	12	.	33	.	197	.
Fitter, Turner (Engine and Machine)	7094	.	954	.	57	.	394	.	2779	.
Boiler Maker	2336	.	310	.	5	.	125	.	1374	.
Spinning and Weaving Machine Maker	215	17	37	3	.	.	6	.	10	2
Agricultural Machine and Implement Maker	1426	15	73	.	45	1	29	3	426	5
Domestic Machinery—Maker, Dealer	168	6	2	.	.	.	1	.	91	.
2. *Tools and Implements.*										
Tool Maker, Dealer	4247	83	38	.	3	.	.	.	1525	36
Cutler, Scissors Maker	212	17	42	2	6	2	18	.	65	1
File Maker	701	23	7	.	.	.	1	.	358	9
Saw Maker	112	6	13	.	.	.	7	.	15	2
Pin Maker	182	450	73	110	.	.	.	3	3	1
Needle Maker	1959	1007	.	.	1	.	.	.	5	1
Steel Pen Maker	191	2485	2	3	.	1	.	.	7	23
Pencil Maker (Wood)	8	27	.	.	.	.	.	.	.	.
Domestic Implement Maker	380	449	13	.	.	.	4	.	275	22
3. *Watches and Philosophical Instruments.*										
Watch Maker, Clock Maker	5787	391	304	8	80	.	136	1	393	11
Philosophical Instrument Maker, Optician	665	99	25	2	2	.	4	.	173	19
Electrical Apparatus Maker	150	1	15	.	2	.	2	.	22	.
Weighing and Measuring Apparatus Maker	868	169	43	.	1	.	.	.	78	22

* … the farmer or grazier, and, therefore, presumably engaged in agriculture, are included above.

Table 10 *continued.*—Occupations of Males and Females in the West Midland Division and its Registration Counties, and in each Urban Sanitary District of which the Population exceeds 50,000 Persons.

Occupations.	West Midland Counties.		Registration Counties. 22. Gloucestershire.		23. Herefordshire.		24. Shropshire.		25. Staffordshire.	
	Males.	Females.	Males.	Females.	Males.	Females.	Males.	Females.	Males.	Females.
4. Surgical Instruments.										
Surgical Instrument Maker	51	12	16	5	.	.	.	.	3	.
5. Arms and Ordnance.										
Gunsmith, Gun Manufacturer	5164	179	38	1	4	.	18	1	555	16
Ordnance Manufacturer	.	.	.	.	.	.	.	.	.	.
Sword, Bayonet—Maker, Cutler	89	3	.	.	.	.	.	.	3	.
Others	7	.	.	.	.	.	.	.	3	.
6. Musical Instruments.										
Musical Instrument Maker, Dealer	475	25	142	6	6	.	10	.	108	2
7. Type, Dies, Medals, Coins.										
Type Cutter, Founder	40	1	1	.	1	.	.	.	5	.
Die, Seal, Coin, Medal, Maker	603	21	8	2	.	1	.	2	123	6
8. Tackle for Sports and Games.										
Toy Maker, Dealer	86	100	12	16	3	6	.	7	4	17
Fishing Rod, Tackle, Maker, Dealer	621	404	3	5	1	.	4	1	8	1
Apparatus for other Games, Maker, Dealer	20	8	4	1	1	.	.	.	2	2
11. Persons working and dealing in Houses, Furniture, and Decorations.										
1. Houses.										
Builder	3253	21	694	4	188	.	281	2	740	5
Carpenter, Joiner	22847	33	4935	18	1205	.	2068	.	6158	6
Bricklayer	17183	29	936	.	377	.	1906	1	6387	17
Mason	7772	27	3874	10	640	.	620	2	1023	5
Slater, Tiler	686	2	167	1	15	.	39	.	152	.
Plasterer, Whitewasher	2788	9	1131	7	84	.	109	.	454	.
Paperhanger	300	7	100	1	5	1	7	.	30	1
Plumber	2893	30	752	11	90	1	226	1	778	3
Painter, Glazier	10260	147	2946	11	268	.	727	3	2735	27
2. Furniture and Fittings.										
Cabinet Maker, Upholsterer	4375	778	1262	257	52	28	283	38	682	118
French Polisher	492	804	218	16	6	1	22	2	68	58
Furniture Broker, Dealer	463	162	127	33	5	3	14	3	123	32
Locksmith, Bellhanger	5841	328	32	.	6	.	18	.	5487	316
Gas Fitter	2519	22	245	.	13	.	54	.	1255	10
House and Shop Fittings—Maker, Dealer	363	46	40	4	3	.	.	.	62	1
Funeral Furniture Maker, Undertaker	194	79	23	.	1	.	.	.	33	3
Others	5	.	4	.	.	.	.	.	1	.
3. House Decorations.										
Wood Carver	253	8	76	6	3	.	6	.	21	.
Carver, Gilder	746	77	190	6	3	.	17	2	82	10
Dealer in Works of Art	53	9	17	4	.	1	1	.	4	3
Figure, Image—Maker, Dealer	33	4	10	.	.	.	.	.	3	.
Animal, Bird, &c., Preserver, Naturalist	61	4	15	2	2	.	9	.	6	.
Artificial Flower Maker	18	39	5	13	.	1	1	1	9	5
12. Persons working and dealing in Carriages and Harness.										
1. Carriages.										
Coachmaker	3414	42	556	6	73	1	246	2	1050	13
Railway Carriage, Railway Wagon, Maker	1565	6	167	.	7	.	112	.	301	1
Wheelwright	4324	8	632	2	330	.	722	1	1419	5
Bicycle, Tricycle—Maker, Dealer	719	10	10	.	.	.	.	.	120	.
Others	233	11	93	1	.	.	.	.	91	.
2. Harness.										
Saddler, Harness, Whip, Maker	5539	1602	422	25	87	2	269	15	3081	1050
13. Persons working and dealing in Ships and Boats.										
1. Hull.										
Ship, Boat, Barge, Builder	620	1	70	.	2	.	25	.	341	1
Shipwright, Ship Carpenter (ashore)	341	.	322	.	.	.	3	.	9	.
2. Masts, Rigging, &c.										
Mast, Yard, Oar, Block, Maker	18	.	18	.	.	.	.	.	1	.
Ship Rigger, Chandler, Fitter	47	.	38	.	.	.	.	.	6	.
Sail Maker	77	2	58	1	2	.	3	.	2	1

Table 10 *continued.*—OCCUPATIONS of MALES and FEMALES in the WEST MIDLAND DIVISION an its REGISTRATION COUNTIES, and in each URBAN SANITARY DISTRICT of which the POPULATIO exceeds 50,000 PERSONS.

OCCUPATIONS.	WEST MIDLAND COUNTIES.		REGISTRATION COUNTIES. 22. GLOUCESTERSHIRE.		23. HEREFORDSHIRE.		24. SHROPSHIRE.		25. STAFFORDSHIRE.	
	Males.	Females.	Males.	Females.	Males.	Females.	Males.	Females.	Males.	Females.
14. PERSONS WORKING AND DEALING IN CHEMICALS AND COMPOUNDS.										
1. *Colouring Matter.*										
Dye, Paint, Manufacture	144	46	32	14	.	.	1	2	75	13
Ink, Blacking, Colouring Substance, Manufacture	58	17	9	2	.	.	2	.	23	3
2. *Explosives.*										
Gunpowder, Guncotton, Explosive Substance, Manufacture	8	12	1	.	.	.	.	.	2	.
Fuses, Fireworks, Explosive Article, Manufacture	152	457	40	69	.	.	.	.	17	18
3. *Drugs and other Chemicals and Compounds.*										
Chemist, Druggist	2929	72	396	9	67	3	172	3	546	86
Manufacturing Chemist	669	120	192	14	13	.	12	.	296	86
Alkali Manufacture	77	.	9	.	.	.	.	.	60	.
Drysalter	75	14	16	10	.	.	.	.	21	2
15. PERSONS WORKING AND DEALING IN TOBACCO AND PIPES.										
1. *Tobacco and Pipes.*										
Tobacco Manufacturer, Tobacconist	609	901	171	280	7	4	22	8	117	95
Tobacco Pipe, Snuff Box, &c., Maker	133	215	22	79	.	.	14	39	36	24
16. PERSONS WORKING AND DEALING IN FOOD AND LODGING.										
1. *Board and Lodging.*										
Innkeeper, Hotel Keeper, Publican	7379	1805	1213	328	299	119	733	212	2489	528
Lodging, Boarding House, Keeper	326	2174	150	821	6	63	14	117	31	926
Coffee, Eating House, Keeper	379	353	104	104	4	10	12	21	75	59
2. *Spirituous Drinks.*										
Hop—Merchant, Dealer	34	3	4	.	.	2	.	.	6	1
Maltster	1893	25	233	.	26	2	215	7	835	6
Brewer	5341	69	517	8	62	2	144	4	3234	17
Beerseller, Ale, Porter, Cider, Dealer	1588	600	334	132	27	6	92	33	662	221
Cellarman	376	15	171	3	8	.	12	2	58	.
Wine, Spirit—Merchant, Agent	718	69	202	13	23	2	70	9	174	17
3. *Food.*										
Milkseller, Dairyman	1850	440	467	87	39	3	32	18	436	137
Cheesemonger, Butterman	56	26	23	12	.	.	9	5	11	8
Butcher, Meat Salesman	8348	510	1514	113	332	7	896	31	2907	137
Provision Curer, Dealer	982	661	215	32	20	7	103	65	236	163
Poulterer, Game Dealer	265	98	63	23	12	8	20	17	64	16
Fishmonger	1072	204	210	30	26	6	62	11	283	61
Corn, Flour, Seed—Merchant, Dealer	702	74	262	22	21	5	40	4	127	29
Corn Miller	2731	40	584	12	233	3	438	5	541	6
Baker	7447	796	1828	198	233	25	345	37	1721	177
Confectioner, Pastrycook	1388	1132	357	245	24	13	88	92	308	239
Greengrocer, Fruiterer	2330	981	370	229	32	21	69	38	752	326
Mustard, Vinegar, Spice, Pickle—Maker, Dealer	88	73	26	25	2	.	.	.	3	.
Sugar Refiner	230	13	172	2	.	1	4	.	41	3
Grocer, Tea, Coffee, Chocolate—Maker, Dealer	11050	3272	2160	766	384	119	1092	293	3812	1117
Ginger Beer, Mineral Water—Manufacturer, Dealer	409	48	106	11	4	1	21		113	13
Others dealing in Food	.	2	.	2	.	.	.		.	.
17. PERSONS WORKING AND DEALING IN TEXTILE FABRICS.										
1. *Wool and Worsted.*										
Woolstapler	35	7	21	1	4	1	17	1	8	5
Woollen Cloth Manufacture	1735	2875	1625	2778	6	.	36	5	14	9
Wool, Woollen goods—Dyer, Printer	84	3	72	1	.	.	1	2	1	.
Worsted, Stuff, Manufacture	102	294	6	48	.	.	14	65	5	7
Flannel Manufacture	2	11	1	11	.	.	.	.	.	.
Blanket Manufacture	1		.	.	.	.	.	.	1	.
Fuller	10	.	10	.	.	.	.	.	.	.
Cloth, Worsted, Stuff, Flannel, Blanket, Dealer	94	9	40	.	.	.	.	.	13	2
Others	1	13	.	2	.	.	.	.	.	8
2. *Silk.*										
Silk, Silk goods, Manufacture	3001	8364	82	439	.	.	.	2	1443	2328
Silk Dyer, Printer	498	16	6	12	.	.	1	.	213	2
Ribbon Manufacture	744	1127	.	.	.	.	.	.	9	8
Crape, Gauze, Manufacture	1	1	.	.	.	.	.	.	1	.
Silk Merchant, Dealer	40	4	2	1	1	.	15	3	1	.

Table 10 *continued*.—Occupations of Males and Females in the West Midland Division and its Registration Counties, and in each Urban Sanitary District of which the Population exceeds 50,000 Persons.

Occupations.	West Midland Counties.		Registration Counties. 22. Gloucestershire.		23. Herefordshire.		24. Shropshire.		25. Staffordshire.	
	Males.	Females.	Males.	Females.	Males.	Females.	Males.	Females.	Males.	Females.
3. Cotton and Flax										
Cotton, Cotton goods, Manufacture	710	2870	228	1093	.	.	9	6	245	536
Cotton, Calico—Printer, Dyer, Bleacher	31	3	2	4	.	.	.	.	14	.
Cotton, Calico—Warehouseman, Dealer	8	7	1	3	.	.	.	.	3	1
Flax, Linen—Manufacturer, Dealer	87	110	43	65	.	1	14	5	8	16
Lace Manufacturer, Dealer	22	133	7	31	1	3	1	1	1	23
Fustian Manufacturer, Dealer	1	66	.	.	.	.	.	2	1	64
Tape Manufacturer, Dealer	212	714	.	.	.	.	.	.	198	631
Thread Manufacturer, Dealer	105	138	.	.	.	.	105	137	.	1
4. Hemp and other Fibrous Materials.										
Hemp, Jute, Cocoa Fibre, Manufacture	34	11	10	.	1	.	.	.	8	.
Rope, Twine, Cord—Maker, Dealer	749	151	149	16	14	3	47	2	171	24
Mat Maker, Seller	39	11	13	3	3	.	6	.	5	2
Net Maker	17	17	.	2	1	.	3	.	5	1
Canvas, Sailcloth, Manufacture	7	5	3	4	.	.	.	.	.	1
Sacking, Sack, Bag—Maker, Dealer	37	95	19	29	1	1	.	1	6	42
Others working and dealing in Hemp	25	6	2	1	.	.	.	.	11	.
5. Mixed or Unspecified Materials.										
Weaver (undefined)	92	133	15	70	1	.	1	1	14	11
Dyer, Printer, Scourer, Bleacher, Calenderer (undefined)	380	129	135	39	5	1	18	6	72	19
Factory hand (Textile, undefined)	92	199	38	126	.	.	23	26	4	19
Felt Manufacture	27	3	5	1	.	.	.	.	5	.
Carpet, Rug, Manufacture	3842	3072	19	1	1	1	132	49	8	1
Manchester Warehouseman	33	1	24	1	.	.	.	.	4	.
Draper, Linen Draper, Mercer	5167	2674	1111	1105	191	123	508	122	1384	444
Fancy Goods (Textile), Manufacturer, Worker, Dealer	87	618	10	109	.	8	3	31	34	145
Trimming Maker, Dealer	243	1034	2	8	.	.	.	2	65	54
Embroiderer	.	65	.	15	.	.	.	1	.	16
Others	37	12	.	.	.	.	.	.	6	12
18. Persons working and dealing in Dress.										
1. Dress.										
Hatter, Hat Manufacture (not straw)	1333	715	330	181	8	.	16	2	141	17
Straw—Hat, Bonnet, Plait, Manufacture	10	259	4	78	1	6	1	14	.	73
Tailor	10640	7272	2307	3308	509	56	1127	45	2630	1595
Milliner, Dressmaker, Staymaker	308	38537	90	9367	3	1426	4	2992	24	9033
Shawl Manufacture	1	.	.	.	.	.	.	.	.	.
Shirt Maker, Seamstress	70	7287	15	2263	1	243	1	317	29	1279
Hosiery Manufacture	65	112	38	45	1	.	.	2	6	22
Hosier, Haberdasher	480	508	72	39	2	5	28	38	120	100
Glover, Glove Maker	576	3218	2	318	4	196	.	.	.	9
Button Maker, Dealer	1933	3625	5	4	.	.	.	.	33	48
Shoe, Boot—Maker, Dealer	22215	5270	5705	1992	771	49	1609	73	7172	1910
Patten, Clog, Maker	288	9	14	2	6	.	40	1	190	3
Wig Maker, Hairdresser	1594	107	294	27	42	2	109	1	469	20
Umbrella, Parasol, Stick—Maker, Dealer	687	1250	395	322	9	·1	14	5	43	15
Accoutrement Maker	111	50	.	.	.	.	.	.	5	.
Old Clothes Dealer, and others	50	247	16	27	1	2	1	6	12	66
19. Persons working and dealing in various Animal Substances.										
1. In Grease, Gut, Bone, Horn, Ivory, and Whalebone.										
Tallow Chandler, Candle, Grease, Manufacture	295	23	61	7	12	1	26	2	98	2
Soap Boiler, Maker	190	34	148	4	.	.	.	.	3	22
Glue, Size, Gelatine, Isinglass—Maker, Dealer	106	42	9	5	.	.	.	.	6	4
Manure Manufacture	119	14	29	1	4	.	16	1	53	18
Bone, Horn, Ivory, Tortoise-shell—Worker, Dealer	455	40	32	6	.	.	.	.	35	3
Comb Maker	62	6	30	3	.	.	.	.	.	.
Others	15	6	4	.	.	.	.	.	1	.
2. In Skins.										
Furrier, Skinner	252	57	20	17	21	.	60	.	33	11
Tanner, Fellmonger	333	15	217	8	75	1	91	3	179	4
Currier	1542	92	307	13	38	.	66	6	566	24
Leather Goods, Portmanteau, Bag, Strap, &c.—Maker, Dealer	436	379	73	7	2	.	3	.	33	9
Parchment, Vellum—Maker, Dealer	23	5	6	.	.	.	.	.	.	.
3. In Hair and Feathers.										
Hair, Bristle—Worker, Dealer	60	148	6	10	.	.	1	10	.	2
Brush, Broom, Maker	1244	641	289	58	6	.	10	4	347	133
Quill, Feather—Dresser, Dealer	11	45	2	11	.	.	.	.	.	3

Table 10 *continued*.—OCCUPATIONS of MALES and FEMALES in the WEST MIDLAND DIVISION and its REGISTRATION COUNTIES, and in each URBAN SANITARY DISTRICT of which the POPULATION exceeds 50,000 PERSONS.

OCCUPATIONS.	WEST MIDLAND COUNTIES.		REGISTRATION COUNTIES. 22. GLOUCESTERSHIRE.		23. HEREFORDSHIRE.		24. SHROPSHIRE.		25. STAFFORDSHIRE.	
	Males.	Females.	Males.	Females.	Males.	Females.	Males.	Females.	Males.	Females.
20. PERSONS WORKING AND DEALING IN VARIOUS VEGETABLE SUBSTANCES.										
1. *In Oils, Gums, and Resins.*										
Oil Miller, Oil Cake—Maker, Dealer	252	15	130	5	.	.	7	.	76	8
Oil and Colourman	115	11	71	3	.	.	.	.	8	.
Floor Cloth, Oil Cloth, Manufacture	68	1	29	.	.	.	2	.	2	.
Japanner	722	1308	22	4	.	.	.	3	389	677
India Rubber, Gutta Percha—Worker, Dealer	355	186	91	66	.	.	1	.	12	5
Waterproof Goods—Maker, Dealer	104	15	4	.	.	1	4	.	11	2
Others	125	7	10	.	.	.	.	.	50	4
2. *In Cane, Rush, and Straw.*										
Willow, Cane, Rush—Worker, Dealer, Basketmaker	901	180	241	37	50	3	77	8	185	31
Hay, Straw (not plait), Chaff—Cutter, Dealer	342	11	78	2	4	.	11	.	127	5
Thatcher	175	.	78	.	54	.	17	.	1	.
3. *In Wood and Bark.*										
Timber, Wood—Merchant, Dealer	1130	752	326	88	45	3	108	2	244	9
Sawyer	3384	.	830	.	220	.	430	.	851	.
Lath, Wooden Fence, Hurdle, Maker	316	4	141	2	37	.	32	.	48	2
Wood Turner, Box Maker	1449	140	353	56	24	3	67	2	267	16
Cooper, Hoop Maker, Bender	2734	17	420	2	103	1	98	1	1546	6
Cork, Bark—Cutter, Worker, Dealer	127	16	52	4	.	.	3	1	27	2
Others	50	21	3	1	.	1	14	4	28	8
4. *In Paper.*										
Paper Manufacture	417	382	51	78	.	.	16	9	115	72
Envelope Maker	.	60	.	13	.	.	.	.	.	1
Stationer, Law Stationer	682	587	304	179	15	19	22	22	131	72
Card, Pattern Card, Maker	14	35	.	1	.	.	.	.	1	4
Paper Stainer	10	67	.	.	.	.	.	.	.	.
Paper Box, Paper Bag, Maker	138	1802	17	321	.	.	.	.	26	88
Ticket, Label, Writer	62	76	22	5	.	.	.	.	5	3
Others	207	57	41	4	4	.	10	.	65	1
21. PERSONS WORKING AND DEALING IN VARIOUS MINERAL SUBSTANCES.										
1. *Miners.*										
Coal Miner	50320	544	3901	11	236	.	4032	207	37200	314
Ironstone Miner	4286	175	384	.	26	.	874	153	3037	22
Copper Miner	11	.	2	.	.	.	4	.	3	.
Tin Miner	19	.	4	.	1	.	.	.	1	.
Lead Miner	306	2	2	.	1	.	300	2	2	.
Miner in other, or undefined, Minerals	214	.	2	.	1	.	8	.	175	.
Mine Service	710	3	37	.	3	.	169		466	3
2. *Coal, Coal Gas, &c.*										
Coal Merchant, Dealer	3128	244	383	33	70	2	195	21	980	90
Coalheaver	1611	.	136	.	20	.	68	.	275	.
Coke, Charcoal, Peat—Cutter, Burner, Dealer	339	27	19	.	8	.	32	.	211	24
Gas Works Service	2100	.	476	.	24	.	112	.	627	.
3. *Stone, Clay, and Road Making.*										
Stone Quarrier	1844	.	332	.	38	.	456	.	623	.
Stone Cutter, Dresser, Dealer	686	.	239	.	21	.	68	.	180	.
Slate Quarrier	2	.	1	.	.	.	1	.	.	.
Slate Worker, Dealer	61	15	39	11	.	.	3	.	1	1
Limeburner	303	7	70	1	35	.	63	3	189	.
Clay, Sand, Gravel, Chalk—Labourer, Dealer	446	9	14	.	.	.	67	.	125	3
Fossil, Coprolite—Digger, Dealer	1	.	.	.	.	.	.	.	.	.
Well Sinker, Borer	323	.	11	.	4	.	40	.	246	.
Plaster, Cement, Manufacture	189	1	1	.	.	.	4	.	39	.
Brick, Tile—Maker, Burner, Dealer	7370	1749	686	4	165	12	986	47	3864	1009
Paviour	267	.	27	.	1	.	21	.	102	.
Road Contractor, Surveyor, Inspector	106	.	36	.	4	.	12	.	13	.
Road Labourer	1782	.	274	.	166	.	296	.	386	.
Railway Contractor	138	.	10	.	6	.	7	.	57	.
Platelayer	2232	.	319	.	128	.	365	.	774	.
Railway Labourer, Navvy	3652	.	522	.	209	.	517	.	1063	.
Others	37	94	4	4	1	.	8	7	3	17
4. *Earthenware and Glass.*										
Earthenware, China, Porcelain, Manufacture	21868	16281	276	89	.	.	305	143	20536	15694
Glass Manufacture	4777	453	224	3	.	.	11	.	1067	54
Earthenware, China, Glass, Dealer	440	289	95	43	13	3	44	21	129	56
5. *Salt.*										
Salt Maker, Dealer	391	87	19	.	.	.	4	1	27	1

Table 10 *continued*.—OCCUPATIONS of MALES and FEMALES in the WEST MIDLAND DIVISION and its REGISTRATION COUNTIES, and in each URBAN SANITARY DISTRICT of which the POPULATION exceeds 50,000 PERSONS.

OCCUPATIONS.	WEST MIDLAND COUNTIES.		REGISTRATION COUNTIES. 22. GLOUCESTERSHIRE.		23. HEREFORDSHIRE.		24. SHROPSHIRE.		25. STAFFORDSHIRE.	
	Males.	Females.	Males.	Females.	Males.	Females.	Males.	Females.	Males.	Females.
6. Water.										
Waterworks Service	174	.	29	.	2	.	6	.	63	.
Others	7	1	.	1	1	.	.	.	4	.
7. Precious Metals and Jewellery.										
Goldsmith, Silversmith, Jeweller	8875	2632	203	30	10	5	36	4	619	83
Gold, Silver, Beater	198	.	8	.	.	.	.	.	2	.
Lapidary	189	187	1	2	.	.	.	.	7	2
Others	69	437	1	1	.	.	.	1	.	8
8. Iron and Steel.										
Blacksmith	14637	58	2118	12	681	5	1665	4	5099	8
Whitesmith	1111	20	74	2	14	.	54	.	605	9
Nail Manufacture	8556	8670	104	5	39	3	209	14	1636	4257
Anchor, Chain, Manufacture	3008	986	15	.	.	.	21	.	2009	717
Other Iron and Steel Manufactures	47374	1292	1612	17	66	1	3349	16	29689	769
Ironmonger, Hardware Dealer, Merchant	2629	143	382	22	95	5	176	2	563	47
9. Copper.										
Copper, Copper goods—Manufacturer, Worker, Dealer	642	11	59	.	1	.	5	.	157	2
10. Tin and Zinc.										
Tin, Tin Plate, Tin goods—Manufacturer, Worker, Dealer	4560	921	390	45	102	8	123	1	1710	180
Zinc, Zinc Goods—Manufacturer, Worker, Dealer	325	8	7	.	.	.	.	.	38	1
11. Lead.										
Lead, Leaden goods—Manufacturer, Worker, Dealer	164	13	85	1	.	.	53	2	4	2
12. In Other, Mixed, or Unspecified, Metals.										
Metal Refiner, Worker, Turner, Dealer	1776	189	19	.	.	.	2	.	184	9
Brass, Bronze, Manufacture, Brazier	13512	891	257	2	10	.	35	.	1809	104
Metal Burnisher, Lacquerer	368	1933	.	.	.	.	.	.	42	99
White Metal, Plated Ware, Manufacture, Pewterer	2826	573	29	1	2	.	.	.	670	23
Wire Maker, Worker, Weaver, Drawer	2180	156	85	9	1	.	153	.	189	8
Bolt, Nut, Rivet, Screw, Staple, Maker	8121	2156	58	1	.	.	2	1	2062	1059
Lamp, Lantern, Candlestick, Maker	1887	475	7	1	.	.	2	.	105	18
Clasp, Buckle, Hinge, Maker	702	469	1	1	.	.	.	.	368	312
Fancy Chain, Gilt Toy, Maker	283	680	2	.	.	.	.	.	17	9
Others	1283	78	.	.	.	.	1	.	273	11
22. PERSONS WORKING AND DEALING IN GENERAL OR UNSPECIFIED COMMODITIES.										
1. Makers and Dealers (General or Undefined).										
General Shopkeeper, Dealer	2357	3282	802	715	95	133	196	180	514	775
Pawnbroker	690	515	134	16	5	.	8	3	254	197
Costermonger, Huckster, Street Seller	2869	1899	628	503	55	61	221	138	653	444
Manufacturer, Manager, Superintendent (undefined)	824	54	79	11	3	1	18	.	204	7
Contractor (undefined)	360	1	41	.	4	.	15	.	127	1
2. Mechanics and Labourers (General or Undefined).										
General Labourer	67315	523	13875	89	3519	24	7201	35	21873	120
Engine Driver, Stoker, Fireman (not railway, marine, nor agricultural)	8548	.	986	.	118	.	603	.	4504	.
Artizan, Mechanic (undefined)	5058	724	208	8	15	.	78	4	1920	156
Apprentice (undefined)	417	57	111	21	21	5	23	7	120	12
Factory Labourer (undefined)	2218	1188	180	42	12	.	121	4	953	194
Machinist, Machine Worker (undefined)	1164	35	89	1	21	.	46	.	155	.
23. PERSONS WORKING AND DEALING IN REFUSE MATTERS.										
1. Refuse Matters.										
Town Drainage Service	183	.	22	.	2	.	24	.	53	.
Chimney Sweep, Soot Merchant	867	6	176	3	26	1	73	.	181	.
Scavenger, Crossing Sweeper	151	12	38	4	1	.	6	.	57	1
Rag Gatherer, Dealer	141	185	26	110	2	3	8	6	63	40
VI. UNOCCUPIED CLASS.										
24. PERSONS WITHOUT SPECIFIED OCCUPATIONS										
Persons returned by Property, Rank, &c., and not by special occupation	374685	953005	65320	168796	15158	39125	33886	88890	126765	323045
Children under 5 years of age	209807	211357	35197	33993	7155	7189	17059	16763	75030	75842

Table 10 *continued*.—OCCUPATIONS of MALES and FEMALES in the WEST MIDLAND DIVISION and its REGISTRATION COUNTIES, and in each URBAN SANITARY DISTRICT of which the POPULATION exceeds 50,000 PERSONS.

OCCUPATIONS.	REGISTRATION COUNTIES.				URBAN SANITARY DISTRICTS.			
	26. WORCESTERSHIRE.		27. WARWICKSHIRE.		BRISTOL.*		WOLVERHAMPTON.	
	Males.	Females.	Males.	Females.	Males.	Females.	Males.	Females.
TOTAL - - -	184010	198995	355551	374980	63711	113163	37827	37989
I. PROFESSIONAL CLASS.								
1. PERSONS ENGAGED IN THE GENERAL OR LOCAL GOVERNMENT OF THE COUNTRY.								
1. *National Government.*								
Peer, M.P., Privy Councillor (not otherwise described)	6	.	5	.	.	.	.	.
Civil Service (officers and clerks)	303	56	262	66	238	23	44	7
Civil Service (messengers, &c.)	236	10	187	7	204	1	30	.
Prison Officer, &c.	20	10	47	31	16	9	.	.
2. *Local Government.*								
Police	292	.	803	.	383	.	72	.
Municipal, Parish, Union, District Officer	178	30	297	73	66	10	24	12
Other Local or County Official	127	.	177	.	55	.	19	.
3. *East Indian and Colonial Service.*								
East Indian and Colonial Service	.	.	1	.	1	.	.	.
2. PERSONS ENGAGED IN THE DEFENCE OF THE COUNTRY.								
1. *Army (at Home).*								
Army Officer (effective or retired)	80	.	120	.	84	.	2	.
Soldier and Non-Commissioned Officer	173	.	436	.	83	.	13	.
Militia, Yeomanry, Volunteers	80	.	106	.	12	.	8	.
Army Pensioner	59	.	164	.	81	.	10	.
2. *Navy (ashore or in port).*								
Navy Officer (effective or retired)	12	.	14	.	33	.	.	.
Seaman, R.N.	1	.	6	.	44	.	.	.
Royal Marines (officers and men)	6	.	3	.	7	.	1	.
Navy Pensioner	20	.	24	.	52	.	.	.
3. PERSONS ENGAGED IN PROFESSIONAL OCCUPATIONS (WITH THEIR IMMEDIATE SUBORDINATES).								
1. *Clerical Profession.*								
Clergyman (Established Church)	377	.	428	.	183	.	35	.
Roman Catholic Priest	40	.	78	.	12	.	6	.
Minister, Priest, of other religious bodies	115	.	135	.	78	.	16	.
Missionary, Scripture Reader, Itinerant Preacher	33	20	78	48	62	33	6	9
Nun, Sister of Charity	.	83	.	138	.	23	.	28
Theological Student	28	.	56	.	44	.	.	.
Church, Chapel, Cemetery—Officer, Servant	86	18	87	51	32	51	5	6
2. *Legal Profession.*								
Barrister, Solicitor	339	.	226	.	148	.	31	.
Law Student	10	.	26	.	7	.	5	.
Law Clerk, and others connected with Law	379	.	504	.	236	.	63	.
3. *Medical Profession.*								
Physician, Surgeon, General Practitioner	242	2	338	3	153	1	36	.
Dentist	40	.	89	.	68	.	12	.
Medical Student, Assistant	54	.	102	4	48	1	9	.
Midwife	.	68	.	94	.	21	.	7
Subordinate Medical Service	21	409	46	845	17	481	9	50
4. *Teachers.*								
Schoolmaster	609	1469	1080	2125	299	870	97	276
Teacher, Professor, Lecturer	71	845	115	935	93	485	11	88
School Service, and others concerned in Teaching	26	19	63	45	14	13	4	3
5. *Literary and Scientific Persons.*								
Author, Editor, Journalist	38	5	48	2	23	1	8	.
Reporter, Short-hand Writer	23	.	55	.	28	.	8	.
Persons engaged in Scientific Pursuits	11	1	75	1	9	.	4	1
Literary, Scientific, Institution, Service, &c.	8	3	12	2	4	1	.	.
6. *Engineers and Surveyors.*								
Civil Engineer	73	.	108	.	57	.	20	.
Mining Engineer	43	.	27	.	20	.	3	.
Land, House, Ship, Surveyor	81	.	102	.	53	.	5	.
7. *Artists.*								
Painter (artist)	103	38	169	59	93	33	13	1
Engraver (artist)	21	.	76	9	24	.	1	.
Sculptor	10	.	18	.	9	1	2	.
Architect	118	.	101	.	65	.	12	.
Musician, Music Master	101	147	414	341	164	161	20	31
Art Student	31	16	19	9	15	15	1	2
Photographer	58	17	130	37	75	29	15	8
Actor	31	27	56	70	32	19	10	16
Art, Music, Theatre, Service	10	.	34	5	10	5	2	1

* A portion of the Urban Sanitary District of Bristol is situated in Division V., but the occupations for the entire District are returned in this Division.

Table 10 *continued*.—Occupations of Males and Females in the West Midland Division and its Registration Counties, and in each Urban Sanitary District of which the Population exceeds 50,000 Persons.

Occupations.	Registration Counties.				Urban Sanitary Districts.			
	26. Worcestershire.		27. Warwickshire.		Bristol.		Wolverhampton.	
	Males.	Females.	Males.	Females.	Males.	Females.	Males.	Females.
8. Persons engaged in Exhibitions, Shows, Games, &c.								
Performer, Showman, Exhibition, Service	29	9	47	17	13	3	3	.
Billiard, Cricket, & other Games, Service	34	.	61	1	34	.	8	.
II. DOMESTIC CLASS.								
4. Persons engaged in Domestic Offices or Services.								
1. Domestic Service.								
Domestic Coachman, Groom	1087	.	1341	.	529	.	154	.
Domestic Gardener	1137	.	806	5	394	1	96	.
Domestic Indoor Servant	742	26326	1095	27502	271	11980	32	2308
Lodge, Gate, Park, Keeper (not Government)	15	20	43	22	9	2	3	2
Inn, Hotel, Servant	240	405	909	1132	220	326	78	96
College, Club, Service	11	2	34	4	7	4	3	3
2. Other Service.								
Office Keeper (not Government)	8	25	64	36	6	13	4	2
Cook (not domestic)	7	37	33	31	16	69	.	3
Charwoman	.	1168	.	2628	.	1349	.	306
Washing and Bathing Service	27	3278	44	3279	19	2146	5	316
Hospital and Institution Service	30	131	87	330	28	161	7	46
Others engaged in Service	2	14	27	22	4	.	2	1
III. COMMERCIAL CLASS.								
5. Persons engaged in Commercial Occupations.								
1. Merchants and Agents.								
Merchant	168	1	149	4	41	.	5	.
Broker, Agent, Factor	509	11	778	40	339	5	126	6
Auctioneer, Appraiser, Valuer, House Agent	169	.	233	2	79	1	23	.
Accountant	197	.	213	2	371	.	20	.
Salesman, Buyer (not otherwise described)	14	9	42	28	10	6	6	.
Commercial Traveller	635	.	1372	.	663	.	167	.
Commercial Clerk	2740	113	5095	431	2137	66	773	16
Officer of Commercial Company, Guild, Society, &c.	1	.	9	.	1	.	1	.
2. Dealers in Money.								
Banker	7	.	10	.	10	.	.	.
Bank Service	274	2	265	.	143	.	27	.
Bill Discounter, Bill Broker, Finance Agent	11	.	15	.	9	.	6	.
3. Persons occupied in Insurance.								
Life, House, Ship, &c., Insurance Service	169	7	328	10	188	2	46	1
6. Persons engaged in Conveyance of Men, Goods, and Messages.								
1. On Railways.								
Railway Engine Driver, Stoker	169	.	859	.	198	.	262	.
Railway Guard	72	.	280	.	105	.	89	.
Pointsman, Level Crossing Man	56	4	169	.	27	.	36	.
Other Railway Officials and Servants	1061	2	2983	28	732	5	466	1
2. On Roads.								
Toll Collector, Turnpike Gate Keeper	15	4	9	1	6	.	2	.
Omnibus, Coach, Cab, Owner—Livery Stable Keeper	99	5	168	1	83	3	6	.
Cabman, Flyman, Coachman (not domestic)	519	.	988	.	202	.	51	.
Carman, Carrier, Carter, Haulier	1053	14	2842	26	1239	6	418	4
Tramway Companies' Service	16	.	31	.	101	.	21	.
Wheel Chair Proprietor, Attendant, &c.	.	.	37	.	31	.	.	.
3. On Canals, Rivers and Seas.								
Inland Navigation Service	87	2	135	1	3	.	9	.
Bargeman, Lighterman, Waterman	742	12	756	25	164	.	244	11
Navigation Service (on shore)	1	.	.	.	18	3	.	.
Seaman (Merchant Service)	33	.	54	.	1325	.	2	.
Pilot	.	.	.	.	10	.	.	.
Ship Steward, Cook	1	.	4	2	49	7	1	.
Boatman on Seas	.	.	.	.	15	.	.	.
Harbour, Dock, Wharf, Lighthouse, Service	31	.	41	.	465	2	6	.
4. In Storage.								
Warehouseman (not Manchester)	930	174	910	1903	349	10	88	109
Meter, Weigher	.	.	.	.	7	.	.	.
5. In conveying Messages, Porterage, &c.								
Messenger, Porter, Watchman (not Railway nor Government)	1303	14	4056	154	2183	52	377	3
Telegraph, Telephone, Service	63	33	198	25	69	25	21	9

Table 10 *continued*.—Occupations of Males and Females in the West Midland Division and its Registration Counties, and in each Urban Sanitary District of which the Population exceeds 50,000 Persons.

Occupations.	Registration Counties.				Urban Sanitary Districts.			
	26. Worcestershire.		27. Warwickshire.		Bristol.		Wolverhampton.	
	Males.	Females.	Males.	Females.	Males.	Females.	Males.	Females.
IV. AGRICULTURAL CLASS.								
7. Persons engaged in Agriculture.								
1. *In Fields and Pastures.*								
Farmer, Grazier	3450	270	3087	246	27	2	10	2
Farmer's, Grazier's—Son, Grandson, Brother, Nephew*	706	.	823	.	4	.	4	.
Farm Bailiff	835	.	393	.	2	.	5	.
Agricultural Labourer, Farm Servant, Cottager	13820	1237	16851	610	100	3	168	26
Shepherd	247	.	598	.	2	.	1	.
Land Drainage Service (not in towns)	46	.	18	.	.	.	.	.
Agricultural Machine—Proprietor, Attendant	55	.	70	.	2	.	3	.
Agricultural Student, Pupil	6	.	13	.	1	.	.	.
Others engaged in, or connected with, Agriculture	.	.	1	.	.	.	.	.
2. *In Woods.*								
Woodman	69	.	106	.	2	.	.	.
3. *In Gardens.*								
Nurseryman, Seedsman, Florist	172	6	99	23	42	3	13	.
Gardener (not domestic)	2591	142	2489	27	210	11	36	.
8. Persons engaged about Animals.								
1. *About Animals.*								
Horse Proprietor, Breeder, Dealer	41	.	46	.	21	.	18	.
Groom, Horse-keeper, Horse-breaker	601	.	1361	.	231	.	82	.
Veterinary Surgeon, Farrier	79	.	102	.	71	.	9	.
Cattle, Sheep, Pig—Dealer, Salesman	63	1	99	.	30	.	13	.
Drover	40	.	86	.	78	.	21	.
Gamekeeper	150	.	151	.	.	.	1	.
Dog, Bird, Animal—Keeper, Dealer	17	9	17	5	8	1	.	.
Vermin destroyer	8	.	11	.	.	.	.	.
Fisherman	36	.	3	.	5	.	1	.
Knacker, Catsmeat Dealer, &c., &c.	1	.	7	1	3	.	2	.
V. INDUSTRIAL CLASS.								
9. Persons working and dealing in Books, Prints, and Maps.								
1. *Books.*								
Publisher, Bookseller, Librarian	87	32	186	44	102	49	17	3
Music—Publisher, Seller, Printer	18	2	17	6	7	2	2	2
Bookbinder	67	24	169	230	121	112	15	38
Printer	584	18	1802	159	711	33	186	9
Newspaper Agent, News Room Keeper	47	15	118	68	66	24	14	9
Others	.	.	.	.	1	.	.	.
2. *Prints and Maps.*								
Lithographer, Lithographic Printer	80	.	316	6	169	1	14	.
Copper Plate and Steel Plate Printer	1	.	5	1	2	1	2	.
Map and Print—Colourer, Seller	8	.	4	2	.	.	.	.
10. Persons working and dealing in Machines and Implements.								
1. *Machines.*								
Engine, Machine, Maker	514	6	1193	33	306	5	219	2
Millwright	60	.	109	.	20	.	23	.
Fitter, Turner (Engine and Machine)	929	.	1981	.	548	.	487	.
Boiler Maker	242	.	280	.	203	.	125	.
Spinning and Weaving Machine Maker	106	1	56	11	.	.	1	.
Agricultural Machine and Implement Maker	554	3	299	1	16	.	47	.
Domestic Machinery—Maker, Dealer	41	.	33	6	.	.	71	.
2. *Tools and Implements.*								
Tool Maker, Dealer	378	9	2206	38	21	.	382	10
Cutler, Scissors Maker	18	1	63	11	28	2	4	1
File Maker	48	1	287	12	6	.	91	3
Saw Maker	13	.	64	3	7	.	2	.
Pin Maker	18	38	97	309	.	.	.	.
Needle Maker	729	926	1284	1170	.	.	.	.
Steel Pen Maker	27	48	155	2419	.	.	.	.
Pencil Maker (Wood)	.	.	8	27	.	.	.	.
Domestic Implement Maker	33	3	236	414	9	.	29	18
3. *Watches and Philosophical Instruments.*								
Watch Maker, Clock Maker	223	3	4811	308	181	5	30	4
Philosophical Instrument Maker, Optician	63	7	396	71	24	.	106	7
Electrical Apparatus Maker	29	.	90	1	6	.	1	.
Weighing and Measuring Apparatus Maker	84	2	656	135	46	.	18	.

* Only male relatives living with the farmer or grazier, and therefore, presumably engaged in agriculture, are included above.

Table 10 *continued.*—OCCUPATIONS of MALES and FEMALES in the WEST-MIDLAND DIVISION and its REGISTRATION COUNTIES, and in each URBAN SANITARY DISTRICT of which the POPULATION exceeds 50,000 PERSONS.

OCCUPATIONS.	REGISTRATION COUNTIES.				URBAN SANITARY DISTRICTS.			
	26. WORCESTERSHIRE.		27. WARWICKSHIRE.		BRISTOL.		WOLVERHAMPTON.	
	Males.	Females.	Males.	Females.	Males.	Females.	Males.	Females.
4. Surgical Instruments.								
Surgical Instrument Maker	6	1	32	6	8	8	2	.
5. Arms and Ordnance.								
Gunsmith, Gun Manufacturer	194	9	4355	152	27	.	40	1
Ordnance Manufacturer	.	.	.	.	.	.	.	.
Sword, Bayonet—Maker, Cutler	4	.	82	3	.	.	.	.
Others	.	.	5	.	.	.	.	.
6. Musical Instruments.								
Musical Instrument Maker, Dealer	57	1	156	16	96	3	6	.
7. Type, Dies, Medals, Coins.								
Type Cutter, Founder	2	.	31	1	1	.	.	.
Die, Seal, Coin, Medal, Maker	43	.	429	10	6	1	14	5
8. Tackle for Sports and Games.								
Toy Maker, Dealer	1	18	37	36	5	11	.	.
Fishing Rod, Tackle, Maker, Dealer	428	374	177	113	1	.	.	.
Apparatus for other Games, Maker, Dealer	3	8	11	3	3	1	1	.
11. PERSONS WORKING AND DEALING IN HOUSES, FURNITURE, AND DECORATIONS.								
1. Houses.								
Builder	472	4	978	6	247	.	81	.
Carpenter, Joiner	2778	2	5708	7	1876	8	463	.
Bricklayer	2458	3	3122	8	142	.	478	6
Mason	454	1	962	9	1695	4	90	1
Slater, Tiler	39	.	274	1	10	.	14	.
Plasterer, Whitewasher	278	.	712	2	326	2	62	.
Paperhanger	23	.	135	.	44	1	12	.
Plumber	294	4	752	10	383	4	61	.
Painter, Glazier	1210	7	3076	90	1328	7	317	8
2. Furniture and Fittings.								
Cabinet Maker, Upholsterer	428	75	1628	262	773	153	155	27
French Polisher	34	35	144	692	168	13	22	36
Furniture Broker, Dealer	46	14	148	57	73	21	24	8
Locksmith, Bellhanger	45	.	263	13	20	.	1406	76
Gas Fitter	223	.	729	12	145	.	141	.
House and Shop Fittings—Maker, Dealer	86	4	172	37	38	1	15	1
Funeral Furniture Maker, Undertaker	12	1	126	75	22	.	9	.
Others	.	.	.	.	3	.	1	.
3. House Decorations.								
Wood Carver	40	2	107	.	62	.	6	.
Carver, Gilder	84	4	372	53	126	6	16	6
Dealer in Works of Art	9	.	22	1	11	.	1	2
Figure, Image—Maker, Dealer	1	1	19	3	10	.	.	.
Animal, Bird, &c., Preserver, Naturalist	6	.	23	2	8	1	.	.
Artificial Flower Maker	.	.	3	19	6	13	1	1
12. PERSONS WORKING AND DEALING IN CARRIAGES AND HARNESS.								
1. Carriages.								
Coachmaker	388	2	1151	18	298	5	153	1
Railway Carriage, Railway Wagon, Maker	308	.	670	5	33	.	10	.
Wheelwright	474	.	747	.	200	.	64	.
Bicycle, Tricycle—Maker, Dealer	6	.	583	10	8	.	94	.
Others	6	.	87	10	17	.	.	.
2. Harness.								
Saddler, Harness, Whip, Maker	353	52	1327	458	226	16	57	1
13. PERSONS WORKING AND DEALING IN SHIPS AND BOATS.								
1. Hull.								
Ship, Boat, Barge, Builder	72	.	110	.	59	1	27	.
Shipwright, Ship Carpenter (ashore)	3	.	4	.	280	.	1	.
2. Masts, Rigging, &c.								
Mast, Yard, Oar, Block, Maker	.	.	4	.	17	.	.	.
Ship Rigger, Chandler, Fitter	1	.	2	.	25	.	3	.
Sail Maker	4	.	8	.	48	1	.	.

Table 10 *continued*.—OCCUPATIONS of MALES and FEMALES in the WEST MIDLAND DIVISION and its REGISTRATION COUNTIES, and in each URBAN SANITARY DISTRICT of which the POPULATION exceeds 50,000 PERSONS.

OCCUPATIONS.	REGISTRATION COUNTIES.				URBAN SANITARY DISTRICTS.			
	26. WORCESTERSHIRE.		27. WARWICKSHIRE.		BRISTOL.		WOLVERHAMPTON.	
	Males.	Females.	Males.	Females.	Males.	Females.	Males.	Females.
14. PERSONS WORKING AND DEALING IN CHEMICALS AND COMPOUNDS.								
1. *Colouring Matter.*								
Dye, Paint, Manufacture	12	3	24	8	31	12	8	3
Ink, Blacking, Colouring Substance, Manufacture	9	1	15	11	14	2	2	1
2. *Explosives.*								
Gunpowder, Guncotton, Explosive Substance, Manufacture	.	1	5	11	1	.	.	.
Fusee, Fireworks, Explosive Article, Manufacture	2	2	93	368	2	4	.	.
3. *Drugs and other Chemicals and Compounds.*								
Chemist, Druggist	260	9	588	22	219	14	73	6
Manufacturing Chemist	60	11	90	16	56	14	27	3
Alkali Manufacture	4	.	4	.	7	.	.	.
Drysalter	12	.	26	2	17	8	3	.
15. PERSONS WORKING AND DEALING IN TOBACCO AND PIPES.								
1. *Tobacco and Pipes.*								
Tobacco Manufacturer, Tobacconist	65	52	227	462	174	341	15	16
Tobacco Pipe, Snuff Box, &c., Maker	7	14	54	33	16	73	6	1
16. PERSONS WORKING AND DEALING IN FOOD AND LODGING.								
1. *Board and Lodging.*								
Innkeeper, Hotel Keeper, Publican	1012	283	1633	383	448	134	192	44
Lodging, Boarding House, Keeper	52	295	72	452	96	425	2	78
Coffee, Eating House, Keeper	56	52	148	107	59	59	11	5
2. *Spirituous Drinks.*								
Hop—Merchant, Dealer	24	.	.	.	2	.	.	1
Maltster	219	5	355	5	100	.	55	.
Brewer	365	8	1019	30	251	2	81	2
Beerseller, Ale, Porter, Cider, Dealer	141	72	311	136	204	71	63	29
Cellarman	34	1	98	9	108	3	12	.
Wine, Spirit—Merchant, Agent	115	5	134	12	124	6	22	3
3. *Food.*								
Milkseller, Dairyman	239	55	827	140	299	89	62	29
Cheesemonger, Butterman	5	1	8	.	10	2	.	.
Butcher, Meat Salesman	1076	89	2331	136	842	61	259	19
Provision Curer, Dealer	89	79	319	315	182	29	45	26
Poulterer, Game Dealer	20	9	86	25	26	6	16	.
Fishmonger	191	26	390	79	96	22	48	14
Corn, Flour, Seed—Merchant, Dealer	126	5	207	18	110	11	12	4
Corn Miller	378	8	587	6	121	1	21	.
Baker	866	101	2464	258	714	56	173	30
Confectioner, Pastrycook	148	111	465	433	258	193	52	25
Greengrocer, Fruiterer	317	105	790	262	222	141	64	33
Mustard, Vinegar, Spice, Pickle—Maker, Dealer	32	25	25	23	18	.	1	.
Sugar Refiner	3	1	19	6	157	1	1	.
Grocer, Tea, Coffee, Chocolate—Maker, Dealer	1276	343	2336	634	927	309	299	82
Ginger Beer, Mineral Water—Manufacturer, Dealer	41	.	124	21	69	10	13	1
Others dealing in Food	.	.	.	.	.	1	.	.
17. PERSONS WORKING AND DEALING IN TEXTILE FABRICS.								
1. *Wool and Worsted.*								
Woolstapler	30	1	11	1	3	.	3	.
Woollen Cloth Manufacture	23	7	37	76	7	12	5	1
Wool, Woollen goods—Dyer, Printer	7	.	3	.	2	.	.	.
Worsted, Stuff, Manufacture	33	6	62	168	1	6	.	.
Flannel Manufacture	1	.	.	.	.	.	.	.
Blanket Manufacture	.	.	.	.	.	.	.	.
Fuller	.	.	.	.	.	.	.	.
Cloth, Worsted, Stuff, Flannel, Blanket, Dealer	21	.	20	7	24	1	.	.
Others	.	.	1	2	.	2	.	.
2. *Silk.*								
Silk, Silk goods, Manufacture	12	14	1464	3791	4	2	.	.
Silk Dyer, Printer	.	.	186	2	2	.	.	1
Ribbon Manufacture	.	1	735	1218	.	.	.	1
Crape, Gauze, Manufacture	.	.	.	1	.	.	.	.
Silk Merchant, Dealer	4	.	17	.	2	.	.	.

Table 10 *continued*.—Occupations of Males and Females in the West Midland Division and its Registration Counties, and in each Urban Sanitary District of which the Population exceeds 50,000 Persons.

Occupations.	Registration Counties.				Urban Sanitary Districts.			
	26. WORCESTERSHIRE.		27. WARWICKSHIRE.		BRISTOL.		WOLVERHAMPTON.	
	Males.	Females.	Males.	Females.	Males.	Females.	Males.	Females.
3. Cotton and Flax								
Cotton, Cotton goods, Manufacture	6	19	225	966	124	518	.	2
Cotton, Calico—Printer, Dyer, Bleacher	1	.	14	3	.	.	.	.
Cotton, Calico—Warehouseman, Dealer	3	.	3	3	1	.	2	1
Flax, Linen—Manufacturer, Dealer	13	14	9	15	45	64	.	2
Lace Manufacturer, Dealer	7	19	5	57	3	16	.	1
Fustian Manufacturer, Dealer	.	.	.	.	.	.	.	.
Tape Manufacturer, Dealer	.	.	14	83	.	.	.	.
Thread Manufacturer, Dealer	.	.	.	.	.	.	.	1
4. Hemp and other Fibrous Materials.								
Hemp, Jute, Cocoa Fibre, Manufacture	7	.	8	11	6	.	2	.
Rope, Twine, Cord—Maker, Dealer	94	10	265	97	108	17	47	18
Mat Maker, Seller	6	2	6	4	9	2	1	.
Net Maker	2	2	6	12	.	1	2	.
Canvas, Sailcloth, Manufacture	.	.	4	.	3	3	.	.
Sacking, Sack, Bag—Maker, Dealer	1	7	10	13	7	14	1	4
Others working and dealing in Hemp	8	2	10	3	1	.	7	.
5. Mixed or Unspecified Materials.								
Weaver (undefined)	4	11	67	40	9	18	.	.
Dyer, Printer, Scourer, Bleacher, Calenderer (undefined)	26	10	84	54	36	31	6	3
Factory hand (Textile, undefined)	3	.	34	35	1	61	1	.
Felt Manufacture	8	2	9	.	2	.	.	.
Carpet, Rug, Manufacture	3060	2999	22	21	12	9	4	1
Manchester Warehouseman	3	.	2	.	22	1	.	.
Draper, Linen Draper, Mercer	595	273	1378	607	572	607	153	51
Fancy Goods (Textile), Manufacturer, Worker, Dealer	14	83	26	243	5	51	.	11
Trimming Maker, Dealer	8	3	173	987	2	5	.	.
Embroiderer	.	7	.	26	.	6	.	.
Others	.	.	31	.	.	.	.	.
18. Persons working and dealing in Dress.								
1. Dress.								
Hatter, Hat Manufacture (not straw)	45	7	793	508	331	160	19	3
Straw—Hat, Bonnet, Plait, Manufacture	1	30	3	60	2	25	.	2
Tailor	1109	480	2868	1728	1026	2689	264	138
Milliner, Dressmaker, Staymaker	32	4827	65	9994	119	4487	5	599
Shawl Manufacture	.	.	1	.	.	.	.	.
Shirt Maker, Seamstress	3	1064	21	2121	3	1294	1	153
Hosiery Manufacture	5	10	15	33	1	.	.	.
Hosier, Haberdasher	73	47	176	319	48	22	21	41
Glover, Glove Maker	563	3440	7	255	1	12	.	1
Button Maker, Dealer	153	170	1737	3403	1	.	.	1
Shoe, Boot—Maker, Dealer	2183	383	4685	927	3324	1447	561	164
Patten, Clog, Maker	9	.	29	4	12	3	8	.
Wig Maker, Hairdresser	130	12	500	45	170	18	68	2
Umbrella, Parasol, Stick—Maker, Dealer	31	30	195	889	23	27	6	5
Accoutrement Maker	15	2	91	48	.	.	.	.
Old Clothes Dealer, and others	2	16	33	140	11	18	3	16
19. Persons working and dealing in various Animal Substances.								
1. In Grease, Gut, Bone, Horn, Ivory, and Whalebone.								
Tallow Chandler, Candle, Grease, Manufacture	25	2	72	9	37	5	8	1
Soap Boiler, Maker	13	.	36	8	127	4	.	.
Glue, Size, Gelatine, Isinglass—Maker, Dealer	13	3	80	27	38	5	.	.
Manure Manufacture	9	.	15	.	27	1	16	2
Bone, Horn, Ivory, Tortoise-shell—Worker, Dealer	49	2	346	39	14	.	7	1
Comb Maker	18	.	14	3	20	3	.	.
Others	.		10	4	6	.	.	.
2. In Skins.								
Furrier, Skinner	78	10	50	10	7	13	2	1
Tanner, Fellmonger	117	.	154	.	342	5	4	.
Currier	267	16	298	83	239	6	17	2
Leather Goods, Portmanteau, Bag, Strap, &c.—Maker, Dealer	37	40	288	323	27	5	3	1
Parchment, Vellum—Maker, Dealer	17	.	.	3	7	.	.	.
3. In Hair and Feathers.								
Hair, Bristle—Worker, Dealer	31	69	32	57	6	16	.	.
Brush, Broom, Maker	136	97	525	349	131	70	13	6
Quill, Feather—Dresser, Dealer	2	13	7	17	1	10	.	2

Table 10 *continued*.—OCCUPATIONS of MALES and FEMALES in the WEST MIDLAND DIVISION and its REGISTRATION COUNTIES, and in each URBAN SANITARY DISTRICT of which the POPULATION exceeds 50,000 PERSONS.

OCCUPATIONS.	REGISTRATION COUNTIES.				URBAN SANITARY DISTRICTS.			
	26. WORCESTERSHIRE.		27. WARWICKSHIRE.		BRISTOL.		WOLVERHAMPTON.	
	Males.	Females.	Males.	Females.	Males.	Females.	Males.	Females.
20. PERSONS WORKING AND DEALING IN VARIOUS VEGETABLE SUBSTANCES.								
1. *In Oils, Gums, and Resins.*								
Oil Miller, Oil Cake—Maker, Dealer	14	2	25	2	100	5	5	2
Oil and Colourman	10	2	26	6	64	1	2	.
Floor Cloth, Oil Cloth, Manufacture	.	.	25	1	69	1	1	.
Japanner	48	42	272	582	19	3	246	296
India Rubber, Gutta Percha—Worker, Dealer	20	6	431	100	7	.	1	.
Waterproof Goods—Maker, Dealer	43	4	42	8	1	.	.	2
Others	9	.	36	3	12	.	35	3
2. *In Cane, Rush, and Straw.*								
Willow, Cane, Rush—Worker, Dealer, Basketmaker	150	82	282	98	108	23	21	4
Hay, Straw (not plait), Chaff—Cutter, Dealer	45	2	77	2	21	.	17	.
Thatcher	51	.	12	.	.	.	.	.
3. *In Wood and Bark.*								
Timber, Wood—Merchant, Dealer	148	6	249	41	125	71	32	5
Sawyer	376	.	477	.	305	.	86	.
Lath, Wooden Fence, Hurdle, Maker	15	.	47	.	50	1	17	.
Wood Turner, Box Maker	128	18	610	45	122	3	41	.
Cooper, Hoop Maker, Bender	182	3	385	4	306	2	124	3
Cork, Bark—Cutter, Worker, Dealer	7	1	38	8	39	5	2	.
Others	10	5	1	2	.	.	4	1
4. *In Paper.*								
Paper Manufacture	76	43	150	180	21	25	5	1
Envelope Maker	.	19	.	26	2	29	.	.
Stationer, Law Stationer	91	53	219	242	146	163	25	10
Card, Pattern Card, Maker	1	3	12	27	1	1	.	.
Paper Stainer	3	.	7	67	1	.	.	.
Paper Box, Paper Bag, Maker	20	103	75	1290	19	318	1	9
Ticket, Label, Writer	8	86	29	26	18	3	2	.
Others	19	1	68	51	18	3	12	1
21. PERSONS WORKING AND DEALING IN VARIOUS MINERAL SUBSTANCES.								
1. *Miners.*								
Coal Miner	1977	11	2974	1	590	4	263	11
Ironstone Miner	48	.	37	.	4	.	6	.
Copper Miner	2	.	.	.	2	.	.	.
Tin Miner	13	.	.	.	.	.	.	.
Lead Miner	1	.	.	.	.	.	.	.
Miner in other, or undefined, Minerals	11	.	17	.	.	.	.	.
Mine Service	65	.	30	.	9	.	4	.
2. *Coal, Coal Gas, &c.*								
Coal Merchant, Dealer	451	29	1049	69	106	14	122	7
Coalheaver	114	.	398	.	63	.	15	.
Coke, Charcoal, Peat—Cutter, Burner, Dealer	59	2	10	1	17	.	6	.
Gas Works Service	167	.	694	.	285	.	64	.
3. *Stone, Clay, and Road Making.*								
Stone Quarrier	88	.	310	.	106	.	.	.
Stone Cutter, Dresser, Dealer	38	.	142	.	86	.	13	.
Slate Quarrier	.	.	.	.	.	.	.	.
Slate Worker, Dealer	2	1	16	2	16	8	.	.
Limeburner	21	.	225	3	18	.	2	.
Clay, Sand, Gravel, Chalk—Labourer, Dealer	290	6	11	1	4	.	.	.
Fossil, Coprolite—Digger, Dealer	1	.	.	.	.	.	.	.
Well Sinker, Borer	36	.	47	.	5	.	9	.
Plaster, Cement, Manufacture	1	.	144	1	1	.	.	.
Brick, Tile—Maker, Burner, Dealer	926	660	1279	17	189	1	137	21
Paviour	10	.	106	.	25	.	6	.
Road Contractor, Surveyor, Inspector	18	.	24	.	1	.	.	.
Road Labourer	207	.	463	.	17	.	35	.
Railway Contractor	38	.	15	.	2	.	10	.
Platelayer	238	.	408	.	41	.	21	.
Railway Labourer, Navvy	400	.	941	.	92	.	96	.
Others	5	6	16	10	3	.	.	.
4. *Earthenware and Glass.*								
Earthenware, China, Porcelain, Manufacture	444	253	107	96	202	90	7	4
Glass Manufacture	1890	199	1555	107	104	2	4	.
Earthenware, China, Glass, Dealer	61	36	107	68	52	31	5	11
5. *Salt.*								
Salt Maker, Dealer	334	85	7	.	4	.	8	1

Table 10 *continued*.—OCCUPATIONS of MALES and FEMALES in the WEST MIDLAND DIVISION and its REGISTRATION COUNTIES, and in each URBAN SANITARY DISTRICT of which the POPULATION exceeds 50,000 PERSONS.

OCCUPATIONS.	REGISTRATION COUNTIES.				URBAN SANITARY DISTRICTS.			
	26. WORCESTERSHIRE.		27. WARWICKSHIRE.		BRISTOL.		WOLVERHAMPTON.	
	Males.	Females.	Males.	Females.	Males.	Females.	Males.	Females.
6. *Water.*								
Waterworks Service	16	.	58	.	21	.	5	.
Others	1	.	1	.	.	.	1	.
7. *Precious Metals and Jewellery.*								
Goldsmith, Silversmith, Jeweller	328	31	7179	2519	138	13	31	6
Gold, Silver, Beater	26	.	162	.	7	.	.	.
Lapidary	8	.	173	183	1	1	.	1
Others	5	8	62	421	1	1	.	.
8. *Iron and Steel.*								
Blacksmith	1836	13	3238	11	688	3	578	1
Whitesmith	68	.	296	9	15	.	79	1
Nail Manufacture	3613	3926	905	485	90	1	69	170
Anchor, Chain, Manufacture	921	258	42	11	13	.	11	.
Other Iron and Steel Manufactures	6683	114	6076	375	958	9	3474	337
Ironmonger. Hardware Dealer, Merchant	304	9	502	58	196	7	59	7
9. *Copper.*								
Copper, Copper goods—Manufacturer, Worker, Dealer	132	.	388	9	42	.	14	.
10. *Tin and Zinc.*								
Tin, Tin Plate, Tin goods—Manufacturer, Worker, Dealer	599	96	1636	691	146	4	974	113
Zinc, Zinc Goods—Manufacturer, Worker, Dealer	30	1	240	6	4	.	8	1
11. *Lead.*								
Lead, Leaden goods—Manufacturer, Worker, Dealer	3	2	17	6	50	1	.	.
12. *In Other, Mixed, or Unspecified, Metals.*								
Metal Refiner, Worker, Turner, Dealer	314	12	1257	168	16	1	26	.
Brass, Bronze, Manufacture. Brazier	1058	20	10283	765	316	2	748	44
Metal Burnisher, Lacquerer	31	80	295	1745	.	.	17	29
White Metal, Plated Ware, Manufacture. Pewterer	199	12	2026	537	30	1	80	5
Wire Maker, Worker, Weaver, Drawer	286	6	1526	133	56	7	43	6
Bolt, Nut, Rivet, Screw, Staple, Maker	443	336	377	759	8	.	138	92
Lamp, Lantern, Candlestick, Maker	203	20	1570	439	6	1	11	4
Clasp, Buckle, Hinge, Maker	56	2	277	145	1	.	98	31
Fancy Chain, Gilt Toy, Maker	15	72	247	608	2	.	10	.
Others	175	21	834	46	.	.	15	.
22. PERSONS WORKING AND DEALING IN GENERAL OR UNSPECIFIED COMMODITIES.								
1. *Makers and Dealers (General or Undefined).*								
General Shopkeeper, Dealer	313	495	637	984	325	432	59	103
Pawnbroker	60	49	229	250	109	9	23	29
Costermonger, Huckster, Street Seller	235	171	849	592	332	309	67	67
Manufacturer, Manager, Superintendent (undefined)	194	9	266	28	50	6	29	1
Contractor (undefined)	31	.	42	.	22	.	11	.
2. *Mechanics and Labourers (General or Undefined).*								
General Labourer	8817	146	12030	59	5584	38	994	10
Engine Driver, Stoker, Fireman (not railway, marine, nor agricultural)	777	.	1460	.	422	.	161	.
Artizan, Mechanic (undefined)	364	40	2478	516	135	6	107	54
Apprentice (undefined)	65	7	78	5	52	14	12	.
Factory Labourer (undefined)	244	47	699	901	108	51	97	63
Machinist, Machine Worker (undefined)	109	4	744	30	40	.	13	.
23. PERSONS WORKING AND DEALING IN REFUSE MATTERS.								
1. *Refuse Matters.*								
Town Drainage Service	13	.	70	.	12	.	6	.
Chimney Sweep, Soot Merchant	102	2	249	.	86	1	24	.
Scavenger, Crossing Sweeper	5	7	44	.	36	2	4	.
Rag Gatherer, Dealer	17	5	26	21	12	82	18	6
VI. UNOCCUPIED CLASS.								
24. PERSONS WITHOUT SPECIFIED OCCUPATIONS								
Persons returned by Property, Rank, &c., and not by special occupation	47177	117961	85609	217188	24908	64458	9453	24419
Children under 5 years of age	25860	26023	51497	51546	13509	15923	5515	5368

Table 10 *continued*.—OCCUPATIONS of MALES and FEMALES in the WEST MIDLAND DIVISION and its REGISTRATION COUNTIES, and in each URBAN SANITARY DISTRICT of which the POPULATION exceeds 50,000 PERSONS.

OCCUPATIONS.	URBAN SANITARY DISTRICTS.							
	WALSALL.		WEST BROMWICH.		BIRMINGHAM.		ASTON MANOR.	
	Males.	Females.	Males.	Females.	Males.	Females.	Males.	Females.
TOTAL	29936	29459	26285	28010	194540	206234	34806	27946
I. PROFESSIONAL CLASS.								
1. PERSONS ENGAGED IN THE GENERAL OR LOCAL GOVERNMENT OF THE COUNTRY.								
1. *National Government.*								
Peer, M.P., Privy Councillor (not otherwise described)	.	.	.	.	.	.	.	.
Civil Service (officers and clerks)	23	1	16	3	131	18	34	.
Civil Service (messengers, &c.)	18	.	26	.	277	2	19	.
Prison Officer, &c.	.	.	.	.	32	10	.	.
2. *Local Government.*								
Police	49	.	33	.	498	.	52	.
Municipal, Parish, Union, District, Officer	14	2	13	3	148	49	19	.
Other Local or County Official	16	.	3	.	69	.	4	.
3. *East Indian and Colonial Service.*								
East Indian and Colonial Service	.	.	.	.	.	.	.	.
2. PERSONS ENGAGED IN THE DEFENCE OF THE COUNTRY.								
1. *Army (at Home).*								
Army Officer (effective or retired)	.	.	.	.	17	.	4	.
Soldier and Non-Commissioned Officer	9	.	6	.	188	.	9	.
Militia, Yeomanry, Volunteers	.	.	.	.	9	.	.	.
Army Pensioner	11	.	3	.	73	.	13	.
2. *Navy (ashore or in port).*								
Navy Officer (effective or retired)	.	.	.	.	1	.	.	.
Seaman, R.N.	.	.	.	.	4	.	1	.
Royal Marines (officers and men)	.	.	.	.	1	.	.	.
Navy Pensioner	2	.	3	.	14	.	2	.
3. PERSONS ENGAGED IN PROFESSIONAL OCCUPATIONS (WITH THEIR IMMEDIATE SUBORDINATES).								
1. *Clerical Profession.*								
Clergyman (Established Church)	18	.	15	.	73	.	13	.
Roman Catholic Priest	3	.	1	.	22	.	2	.
Minister, Priest, of other religious bodies	16	.	11	.	56	.	14	.
Missionary, Scripture Reader, Itinerant Preacher	2	2	2	1	44	28	6	2
Nun, Sister of Charity	.	.	.	.	.	30	.	34
Theological Student	3	.	2	.	11	.	3	.
Church, Chapel, Cemetery—Officer, Servant	5	2	9	2	31	40	9	
2. *Legal Profession.*								
Barrister, Solicitor	16	.	10	.	138	.	7	.
Law Student	1	.	1	.	10	.	.	.
Law Clerk, and others connected with Law	40	.	19	.	297	.	64	.
3. *Medical Profession.*								
Physician, Surgeon, General Practitioner	15	.	13	.	176	3	17	.
Dentist	4	.	5	.	59	.	8	.
Medical Student, Assistant	11	.	7	.	68	3	12	.
Midwife	.	4	.	6	.	51	.	7
Subordinate Medical Service	6	32	6	26	33	439	3	61
4. *Teachers.*								
Schoolmaster	64	137	77	179	388	951	111	238
Teacher, Professor, Lecturer	9	59	4	23	80	428	13	60
School Service, and others concerned in Teaching	3	1	5	3	44	16	11	1
5. *Literary and Scientific Persons.*								
Author, Editor, Journalist	2	.	1	.	31	2	4	.
Reporter, Short-hand Writer	5	.	2	.	23	.	12	.
Persons engaged in Scientific Pursuits	.	.	1	.	8	1	.	.
Literary, Scientific, Institution, Service, &c.	.	.	1	.	8	1	1	.
6. *Engineers and Surveyors.*								
Civil Engineer	8	.	10	.	83	.	14	.
Mining Engineer	28	.	19	.	5	.	4	.
Land, House, Ship, Surveyor	3	.	9	.	43	.	15	.
7. *Artists.*								
Painter (artist)	4	1	1	.	138	40	23	5
Engraver (artist)	1	.	.	.	86	9	11	.
Sculptor	.	.	.	.	8	.	5	.
Architect	9	.	6	.	75	.	13	.
Musician, Music Master	23	22	14	15	282	235	28	37
Art Student	3	.	4	.	10	8	1	2
Photographer	5	.	4	1	73	44	14	10
Actor	4	6	3	4	43	69	2	2
Art, Music, Theatre, Service	4	.	.	.	25	3	4	.

Table 10 *continued*.—Occupations of Males and Females in the West Midland Division and its Registration Counties, and in each Urban Sanitary District of which the Population exceeds 50,000 Persons.

Occupations.	Urban Sanitary Districts.							
	Walsall.		West Bromwich.		Birmingham.		Aston Manor.	
	Males.	Females.	Males.	Females.	Males.	Females.	Males.	Females.
8. *Persons engaged in Exhibitions, Shows, Games, &c.*								
Performer, Showman, Exhibition, Service	9	1	.	.	80	17	1	.
Billiard, Cricket, & other Games, Service	7	.	4	.	63	.	8	.
II. DOMESTIC CLASS.								
4. Persons engaged in Domestic Offices or Services.								
1. *Domestic Service.*								
Domestic Coachman, Groom	48	.	58	.	309	.	19	.
Domestic Gardener	2	.	62	.	273	.	7	.
Domestic Indoor Servant	15	1886	17	1603	165	13123	9	1547
Lodge, Gate, Park, Keeper (not Government)	.	.	4	1	21	7	5	.
Inn, Hotel, Servant	15	69	26	34	645	744	33	48
College, Club, Service	7	.	1	.	31	1	.	.
2. *Other Service.*								
Office Keeper (not Government)	8	2	.	.	54	30	2	1
Cook (not domestic)	.	2	.	.	26	56	.	.
Charwoman	.	130	.	108	.	1471	.	79
Washing and Bathing Service	2	223	3	133	30	2398	3	251
Hospital and Institution Service	.	5	2	10	45	195	1	7
Others engaged in Service	1	.	.	.	21	14	2	.
III. COMMERCIAL CLASS.								
5. Persons engaged in Commercial Occupations.								
1. *Merchants and Agents.*								
Merchant	10	.	1	.	158	1	6	.
Broker, Agent, Factor	57	1	54	.	668	33	118	2
Auctioneer, Appraiser, Valuer, House Agent	12	1	14	.	112	2	20	.
Accountant	8	.	13	.	168	.	37	.
Salesman, Buyer (not otherwise described)	2	.	5	.	35	31	6	.
Commercial Traveller	33	.	37	.	974	.	256	.
Commercial Clerk	314	16	323	1	3709	349	791	58
Officer of Commercial Company, Guild, Society, &c.	1	.	.	.	8	.	.	.
2. *Dealers in Money.*								
Banker	.	.	.	.	1	.	.	.
Bank Service	18	.	9	.	178	1	13	.
Bill Discounter, Bill Broker, Finance Agent	1	.	.	.	15	.	1	.
3. *Persons occupied in Insurance.*								
Life, House, Ship, &c., Insurance Service	26	1	22	.	226	5	40	1
6. Persons engaged in Conveyance of Men, Goods, and Messages.								
1. *On Railways.*								
Railway Engine Driver, Stoker	117	.	3	.	401	.	7	.
Railway Guard	45	.	1	.	163	.	1	.
Pointsman, Level Crossing Man	28	.	16	.	99	.	4	.
Other Railway Officials and Servants	175	2	88	.	1779	16	110	3
2. *On Roads.*								
Toll Collector, Turnpike Gate Keeper	1	.	3	.	4	.	.	.
Omnibus, Coach, Cab, Owner—Livery Stable Keeper	3	.	8	1	98	1	14	.
Cabman, Flyman, Coachman (not domestic)	18	.	11	.	657	.	104	.
Carman, Carrier, Carter, Haulier	218	.	246	.	2019	8	150	.
Tramway Companies' Service	.	.	1	.	22	.	5	.
Wheel Chair Proprietor, Attendant, &c.	.	.	.	.	2	.	.	.
3. *On Canals, Rivers and Seas.*								
Inland Navigation Service	17	.	17	.	44	.	6	.
Bargeman, Lighterman, Waterman	108	3	209	5	427	8	31	.
Navigation Service (on shore)	.	.	.	.	.	.	.	.
Seaman (Merchant Service)	4	.	1	.	39	.	1	.
Pilot	.	.	.	.	.	.	.	.
Ship Steward, Cook	.	.	.	.	3	.	.	.
Boatman on Seas	.	.	.	.	.	.	.	.
Harbour, Dock, Wharf, Lighthouse, Service	.	.	36	.	22	.	1	.
4. *In Storage.*								
Warehouseman (not Manchester)	49	113	38	61	714	1601	98	240
Meter, Weigher	7	.	1	.	5	.	1	.
5. *In conveying Messages, Porterage, &c.*								
Messenger, Porter, Watchman (not Railway nor Government)	339	3	156	1	2810	138	270	7
Telegraph, Telephone, Service	9	.	2	.	734	9	19	3

Table 10 *continued*.—OCCUPATIONS of MALES and FEMALES in the WEST MIDLAND DIVISION and its REGISTRATION COUNTIES, and in each URBAN SANITARY DISTRICT of which the POPULATION exceeds 50,000 PERSONS.

OCCUPATIONS.	URBAN SANITARY DISTRICTS.							
	WALSALL.		WEST BROMWICH.		BIRMINGHAM.		ASTON MANOR.	
	Males.	Females.	Males.	Females.	Males.	Females.	Males.	Females.
IV. AGRICULTURAL CLASS.								
7. PERSONS ENGAGED IN AGRICULTURE.								
1. *In Fields and Pastures.*								
Farmer, Grazier	42	4	27	1	47	4	2	.
Farmer's, Grazier's—Son, Grandson, Brother, Nephew*	10	.	7	.	5	.	.	.
Farm Bailiff	5	.	7	.	7	.	3	.
Agricultural Labourer; Farm Servant, Cottager	246	29	118	12	236	14	25	.
Shepherd	4	.	3	.	.	.	.	.
Land Drainage Service (not in towns)	.	.	.	.	.	.	.	.
Agricultural Machine—Proprietor, Attendant	.	.	.	.	.	.	.	.
Agricultural Student, Pupil	.	.	.	.	.	.	.	.
Others engaged in, or connected with, Agriculture	.	.	.	.	.	.	.	.
2. *In Woods.*								
Woodman	.	.	.	.	.	.	.	.
3. *In Gardens.*								
Nurseryman, Seedsman, Florist	4	.	2	.	35	5	2	.
Gardener (not domestic)	80	.	1	.	402	2	87	.
8. PERSONS ENGAGED ABOUT ANIMALS.								
1. *About Animals.*								
Horse Proprietor, Breeder, Dealer	8	.	5	.	23	.	2	.
Groom, Horse-keeper, Horse-breaker	68	.	40	.	588	.	59	.
Veterinary Surgeon, Farrier	4	.	3	.	37	.	3	.
Cattle, Sheep, Pig—Dealer, Salesman	2	.	1	.	47	.	1	.
Drover	.	.	7	.	55	.	.	.
Gamekeeper	1	.	1	.	2	.	2	.
Dog, Bird, Animal—Keeper, Dealer	.	.	.	.	9	4	.	.
Vermin destroyer	.	.	.	.	2	.	1	.
Fisherman	.	.	.	.	.	1	.	.
Knacker, Catsmeat Dealer, &c., &c.	.	.	.	.	6	.	.	.
V. INDUSTRIAL CLASS.								
9. PERSONS WORKING AND DEALING IN BOOKS, PRINTS, AND MAPS.								
1. *Books.*								
Publisher, Bookseller, Librarian	5	2	6	1	113	18	20	.
Music—Publisher, Seller, Printer	1	1	.	1	13	8	1	.
Bookbinder	7	8	1	2	120	201	13	11
Printer	52	8	43	3	1280	148	154	6
Newspaper Agent, News Room Keeper	16	5	3	1	69	52	9	7
Others	.	.	.	.	.	.	.	.
2. *Prints and Maps.*								
Lithographer, Lithographic Printer	6	.	2	.	278	4	32	2
Copper Plate and Steel Plate Printer	.	.	.	.	3	.	1	.
Map and Print—Colourer, Seller	.	.	.	.	3	2	.	.
10. PERSONS WORKING AND DEALING IN MACHINES AND IMPLEMENTS.								
1. *Machines.*								
Engine, Machine, Maker	59	.	80	3	934	30	98	1
Millwright	3	.	13	.	62	.	3	.
Fitter, Turner (Engine and Machine)	76	.	133	.	1506	.	149	.
Boiler Maker	32	.	130	.	235	.	10	.
Spinning and Weaving Machine Maker	.	.	1	.	7	6	.	2
Agricultural Machine and Implement Maker	2	.	5	.	158	1	86	.
Domestic Machinery—Maker, Dealer	.	.	12	.	30	3	1	1
2. *Tools and Implements.*								
Tool Maker, Dealer	247	4	37	1	1740	29	434	4
Cutler, Scissors Maker	3	.	1	.	42	10	3	.
File Maker	34	1	6	.	249	10	29	2
Saw Maker	.	.	.	.	50	2	8	1
Pin Maker	.	.	.	.	68	281	29	23
Needle Maker	3	.	1	.	5	6	.	5
Steel Pen Maker	.	3	.	2	144	2232	15	186
Pencil Maker (Wood)	.	.	.	.	5	27	.	.
Domestic Implement Maker	3	2	6	3	214	396	20	17
3. *Watches and Philosophical Instruments.*								
Watch Maker, Clock Maker	24	1	11	.	693	146	137	15
Philosophical Instrument Maker, Optician	28	9	11	1	329	63	86	8
Electrical Apparatus Maker	.	.	.	.	59	1	1	.
Weighing and Measuring Apparatus Maker	.	.	32	6	609	127	47	6

Table 10 *continued*.—Occupations of Males and Females in the West Midland Division and its Registration Counties, and in each Urban Sanitary District of which the Population exceeds 50,000 Persons.

Occupations.	Urban Sanitary Districts.							
	Walsall.		West Bromwich.		Birmingham.		Aston Manor.	
	Males.	Females.	Males.	Females.	Males.	Females.	Males.	Females.
4. Surgical Instruments.								
Surgical Instrument Maker	1	.	.	.	52	6	.	.
5. Arms and Ordnance.								
Gunsmith, Gun Manufacturer	12	1	33	1	3391	188	877	12
Ordnance Manufacturer	.	.	.	.	.	.	.	.
Sword, Bayonet—Maker, Cutler	.	.	1	.	70	2	6	1
Others	.	.	.	.	4	.	1	.
6. Musical Instruments.								
Musical Instrument Maker, Dealer	23	2	4	.	111	12	22	.
7. Type, Dies, Medals, Coins.								
Type Cutter, Founder	.	.	1	.	24	1	8	.
Die, Seal, Coin, Medal, Maker	18	.	4	1	330	7	85	1
8. Tackle for Sports and Games.								
Toy Maker, Dealer	1	.	.	.	29	32	5	1
Fishing Rod, Tackle, Maker, Dealer	1	.	.	.	41	13	8	.
Apparatus for other Games, Maker, Dealer	1	.	.	.	7	1	2	.
11. Persons working and dealing in Houses, Furniture, and Decorations.								
1. Houses.								
Builder	32	1	31	.	553	5	72	.
Carpenter, Joiner	288	.	208	.	2821	7	469	.
Bricklayer	397	.	284	.	2829	6	308	.
Mason	33	.	23	.	476	4	99	3
Slater, Tiler	20	.	16	.	227	1	11	.
Plasterer, Whitewasher	48	.	31	.	462	2	43	.
Paperhanger	.	.	4	.	96	4	11	.
Plumber	20	.	25	.	406	3	30	.
Painter, Glazier	188	3	129	3	1976	38	206	8
2. Furniture and Fittings.								
Cabinet Maker, Upholsterer	56	10	19	6	1206	178	109	9
French Polisher	2	12	4	2	109	665	4	23
Furniture Broker, Dealer	12	5	8	.	110	41	10	5
Locksmith, Bellhanger	441	66	33	3	198	11	34	1
Gas Fitter	189	.	83	2	593	11	46	.
House and Shop Fittings—Maker, Dealer	1	.	28	.	148	39	18	.
Funeral Furniture Maker, Undertaker	4	1	3	.	110	73	12	2
Others	.	.	.	.	.	.	.	.
3. House Decorations.								
Wood Carver	.	.	1	.	81	.	6	.
Carver, Gilder	13	1	4	.	325	52	19	3
Dealer in Works of Art	.	.	.	1	23	1	3	.
Figure, Image—Maker, Dealer	.	.	.	.	20	4	.	.
Animal, Bird, &c., Preserver, Naturalist	.	.	.	.	13	2	1	.
Artificial Flower Maker	.	.	.	.	3	19	.	.
12. Persons working and dealing in Carriages and Harness.								
1. Carriages.								
Coachmaker	49	.	223	5	854	11	98	1
Railway Carriage, Railway Wagon, Maker	2	.	27	.	431	1	18	.
Wheelwright	49	.	39	.	255	.	20	.
Bicycle, Tricycle—Maker, Dealer	1	.	3	.	119	6	38	1
Others	5	.	.	.	34	7	2	3
2. Harness.								
Saddler, Harness, Whip, Maker	2490	1002	52	1	1065	441	80	11
13. Persons working and dealing in Ships and Boats.								
1. Hull.								
Ship, Boat, Barge, Builder	17	.	42	.	55	.	16	.
Shipwright, Ship Carpenter (ashore)	1	.	.	.	2	.	1	.
2. Masts, Rigging, &c.								
Mast, Yard, Oar, Block, Maker	.	.	.	.	4	.	.	.
Ship Rigger, Chandler, Fitter	.	.	.	.	1	.	.	.
Sail Maker	.	.	.	.	5	.	.	.

Table 10 *continued*.—OCCUPATIONS of MALES and FEMALES in the WEST MIDLAND DIVISION and its REGISTRATION COUNTIES, and in each URBAN SANITARY DISTRICT of which the POPULATION exceeds 50,000 PERSONS.

OCCUPATIONS.	URBAN SANITARY DISTRICTS.							
	WALSALL.		WEST BROMWICH.		BIRMINGHAM.		ASTON MANOR.	
	Males.	Females.	Males.	Females.	Males.	Females.	Males.	Females.
14. PERSONS WORKING AND DEALING IN CHEMICALS AND COMPOUNDS.								
1. *Colouring Matter.*								
Dye, Paint, Manufacture	.	.	2	.	[illegible]	6	1	.
Ink, Blacking, Colouring Substance, Manufacture	.	.	5	.	17	11	.	.
2. *Explosives.*								
Gunpowder, Guncotton, Explosive Substance, Manufacture	.	.	.	.	2	10	3	
Fusee, Fireworks, Explosive Article, Manufacture	.	.	.	.	36	133	82	162
3. *Drugs and other Chemicals and Compounds.*								
Chemist, Druggist	20	.	22	.	319	15	48	2
Manufacturing Chemist	2	1	30	73	84	13	9	1
Alkali Manufacture	.	.	13	.	4	.	.	.
Drysalter	.	.	.	.	22	3	1	.
15. PERSONS WORKING AND DEALING IN TOBACCO AND PIPES.								
1. *Tobacco and Pipes.*								
Tobacco Manufacturer, Tobacconist	7	12	6	2	158	315	20	26
Tobacco Pipe, Snuff Box, &c., Maker	7	14	2	4	42	36	6	2
16. PERSONS WORKING AND DEALING IN FOOD AND LODGING.								
1. *Board and Lodging.*								
Innkeeper, Hotel Keeper, Publican	134	32	124	28	748	158	80	18
Lodging, Boarding House, Keeper	5	28	1	8	30	231	.	21
Coffee, Eating House, Keeper	6	2	6	1	117	80	9	2
2. *Spirituous Drinks.*								
Hop—Merchant, Dealer	.	.	.	.	1	.	.	.
Maltster	38	.	24	.	159	1	48	.
Brewer	40	.	50	3	707	29	98	1
Beerseller. Ale, Porter, Cider, Dealer	35	8	42	15	225	85	20	18
Cellarman	5	.	2	.	71	7	8	1
Wine, Spirit—Merchant, Agent	14	4	6	1	64	7	5	.
3. *Food.*								
Milkseller, Dairyman	32	4	42	3	377	112	53	10
Cheesemonger, Butterman	1	.	.	.	4	.	2	.
Butcher, Meat Salesman	141	15	140	15	1258	102	142	6
Provision Curer, Dealer	8	21	14	15	228	218	23	27
Poulterer, Game Dealer	6	4	.	1	70	17	2	.
Fishmonger	13	4	12	3	200	81	10	3
Corn, Flour, Seed—Merchant, Dealer	7	.	16	3	133	9	17	2
Corn Miller	20	.	16	.	130	.	42	.
Baker	127	15	71	9	1237	142	151	12
Confectioner, Pastrycook	29	13	7	17	336	320	25	30
Greengrocer, Fruiterer	52	19	57	15	563	105	66	15
Mustard, Vinegar, Spice, Pickle—Maker, Dealer	.	.	.	.	17	21	6	1
Sugar Refiner	1	1	2	.	16	2	1	3
Grocer. Tea, Coffee, Chocolate—Maker, Dealer	233	47	184	25	1271	314	218	54
Ginger Beer, Mineral Water—Manufacturer, Dealer	7	.	11	3	58	11	19	2
Others dealing in Food	.	.	.	.	.	.	.	.
17. PERSONS WORKING AND DEALING IN TEXTILE FABRICS.								
1. *Wool and Worsted.*								
Woolstapler	.	2	.	.	2	.	.	.
Woollen Cloth Manufacture	3	.	.	.	9	23	1	.
Wool, Woollen goods—Dyer, Printer	.	.	.	.	.	.	.	.
Worsted, Stuff, Manufacture	3	2	.	.	1	4	.	.
Flannel Manufacture	.	.	.	.	5	.	.	.
Blanket Manufacture	.	.	.	.	.	.	.	.
Fuller	.	.	.	.	.	.	.	.
Cloth, Worsted, Stuff, Flannel, Blanket, Dealer	.	.	.	1	25	5	.	.
Others	.	.	.	.	.	.	.	.
2. *Silk.*								
Silk, Silk goods, Manufacture	.	4	.	1	8	44	.	3
Silk Dyer, Printer	.	.	.	.	2	.	1	.
Ribbon Manufacture	.	1	1	1	6	13	.	5
Crape, Gauze, Manufacture	.	.	.	.	.	.	.	.
Silk Merchant, Dealer	.	.	.	.	4	.	1	.

Table 10 *continued.*—OCCUPATIONS of MALES and FEMALES in the WEST MIDLAND DIVISION and its REGISTRATION COUNTIES, and in each URBAN SANITARY DISTRICT of which the POPULATION exceeds 50,000 PERSONS.

OCCUPATIONS.	URBAN SANITARY DISTRICTS.							
	WALSALL.		WEST BROMWICH.		BIRMINGHAM.		ASTON MANOR.	
	Males.	Females.	Males.	Females.	Males.	Females.	Males.	Females.
3. Cotton and Flax								
Cotton, Cotton goods, Manufacture	1	5	1	1	1	32	1	
Cotton, Calico—Printer, Dyer, Bleacher	.	.	.	.	2	.	.	.
Cotton, Calico Warehouseman, Dealer	.	.	.	.	9	9	.	.
Flax, Linen—Manufacturer, Dealer	.	.	.	1	1	11	.	.
Lace Manufacturer, Dealer	.	.	.	1	3	31	.	3
Fustian Manufacturer, Dealer	.	.	.	.	.	.	.	.
Tape Manufacturer, Dealer	.	2	.	.	.	2	.	1
Thread Manufacturer, Dealer	.	.	.	.	.	.	.	.
4. Hemp and other Fibrous Materials.								
Hemp, Jute, Cocoa Fibre, Manufacture	2	.	.	.	7	11	1	.
Rope, Twine, Cord—Maker, Dealer	13	.	11	.	207	87	4	.
Mat Maker, Seller	1	1	.	.	5	3	.	.
Net Maker	1	.	.	.	1	2	.	.
Canvas, Sailcloth, Manufacture	.	.	.	.	2	.	1	.
Sacking, Sack, Bag—Maker, Dealer	.	.	.	.	7	11	.	1
Others working and dealing in Hemp	1	.	.	.	6	3	.	.
5. Mixed or Unspecified Materials.								
Weaver (undefined)	1	4	.	1	5	21	.	7
Dyer, Printer, Scourer, Bleacher, Calenderer (undefined)	6	1	.	1	49	45	8	2
Factory hand (Textile, undefined)	.	3	.	.	4	7	3	.
Felt Manufacture	1	.	.	.	7	.	2	.
Carpet, Rug, Manufacture	1	.	1	.	15	18	1	.
Manchester Warehouseman	1	.	.	.	1	.	.	.
Draper, Linen Draper, Mercer	87	44	62	17	816	332	95	40
Fancy Goods (Textile), Manufacturer, Worker, Dealer	14	48	.	3	16	163	3	16
Trimming Maker, Dealer	.	.	.	.	7	23	1	1
Embroiderer	.	1	.	.	.	22	.	2
Others	2	3	.	.	3	.	.	.
18. PERSONS WORKING AND DEALING IN DRESS.								
1. Dress.								
Hatter, Hat Manufacture (not straw)	13	1	5	.	100	19	5	.
Straw—Hat, Bonnet, Plait, Manufacture	.	7	.	1	3	30	.	1
Tailor	178	212	111	63	1700	1429	108	88
Milliner, Dressmaker, Staymaker	2	552	.	448	46	5150	5	827
Shawl Manufacture	.	.	.	.	.	.	.	.
Shirt Maker, Seamstress	25	231	.	59	14	1273	.	140
Hosiery Manufacture	.	3	.	2	4	15	.	5
Hosier, Haberdasher	9	9	8	5	119	138	9	6
Glover, Glove Maker	.	2	.	1	4	18	.	2
Button Maker, Dealer	.	1	.	1	1491	3087	231	209
Shoe, Boot—Maker, Dealer	319	57	150	26	2769	764	207	35
Patten, Clog, Maker	2	.	3	.	25	4	1	.
Wig Maker, Hairdresser	20	.	20	2	546	26	24	3
Umbrella, Parasol, Stick—Maker, Dealer	5	.	3	1	164	838	6	23
Accoutrement Maker	2	.	.	.	86	88	6	10
Old Clothes Dealer, and others	1	13	.	6	23	121	2	2
19. PERSONS WORKING AND DEALING IN VARIOUS ANIMAL SUBSTANCES.								
1. In Grease, Gut, Bone, Horn, Ivory, and Whalebone.								
Tallow Chandler, Candle, Grease, Manufacture	6	.	3	.	44	9	4	.
Soap Boiler, Maker	.	.	1	20	16	4	7	3
Glue, Size, Gelatine, Isinglass—Maker, Dealer	2	2	2	2	5	3	.	1
Manure Manufacture	1	.	.	.	7	.	2	.
Bone, Horn, Ivory, Tortoise-shell—Worker, Dealer	8	.	1	.	330	26	10	4
Comb Maker	.	.	.	.	4	3	.	.
Others	.	.	.	.	5	4	.	.
2. In Skins.								
Furrier, Skinner	.	.	.	.	35	18	1	.
Tanner, Fellmonger	37	1	.	.	30	.	2	.
Currier	360	12	11	1	240	33	13	1
Leather Goods, Portmanteau, Bag, Strap, &c.—Maker, Dealer	5	2	2	1	230	364	42	33
Parchment, Vellum—Maker, Dealer	.	.	.	.	.	2	.	.
3. In Hair and Feathers.								
Hair, Bristle—Worker, Dealer	.	.	.	.	21	56	.	1
Brush, Broom, Maker	208	108	8	.	459	314	38	29
Quill, Feather—Dresser, Dealer	.	2	.	.	4	14	1	1

Table 10 *continued*.—OCCUPATIONS of MALES and FEMALES in the WEST MIDLAND DIVISION and its REGISTRATION COUNTIES, and in each URBAN SANITARY DISTRICT of which the POPULATION exceeds 50,000 PERSONS.

OCCUPATIONS.	URBAN SANITARY DISTRICTS.							
	WALSALL.		WEST BROMWICH.		BIRMINGHAM.		ASTON MANOR.	
	Males.	Females.	Males.	Females.	Males.	Females.	Males.	Females.
20. PERSONS WORKING AND DEALING IN VARIOUS VEGETABLE SUBSTANCES.								
1. *In Oils, Gums, and Resins.*								
Oil Miller, Oil Cake—Maker, Dealer	1	.	7	.	15	2	2	.
Oil and Colourman	1	.	.	.	27	4	2	.
Floor Cloth, Oil Cloth, Manufacture	.	.	.	.	23	1	2	.
Japanner	20	60	5	18	232	548	32	22
India Rubber, Gutta Percha—Worker, Dealer	12	1	.	.	26	18	3	.
Waterproof Goods—Maker, Dealer	.	.	.	.	39	8	1	.
Others	.	.	1	1	41	3	6	.
2. *In Cane, Rush, and Straw.*								
Willow, Cane, Rush—Worker, Dealer, Basketmaker	19	1	4	3	168	56	3	.
Hay, Straw (not plait), Chaff—Cutter, Dealer	8	1	4	.	46	1	3	.
Thatcher	.	.	.	.	.	.	.	.
3. *In Wood and Bark.*								
Timber, Wood—Merchant, Dealer	19	1	13	.	156	37	18	1
Sawyer	31	.	44	.	322	.	33	.
Lath, Wooden Fence, Hurdle, Maker	4	.	8	.	25	.	1	.
Wood Turner, Box Maker	18	3	19	.	496	42	39	3
Cooper, Hoop Maker, Bender	31	1	14	.	242	3	46	.
Cork, Bark—Cutter, Worker, Dealer	.	.	.	.	30	7	.	1
Others	.	.	1	.	.	.	.	1
4. *In Paper.*								
Paper Manufacture	.	.	.	.	103	147	16	6
Envelope Maker	.	.	.	.	.	1	.	1
Stationer, Law Stationer	9	3	2	7	161	165	21	14
Card, Pattern Card, Maker	.	.	.	.	11	24	1	3
Paper Stainer	.	.	.	.	8	39	1	.
Paper Box, Paper Bag, Maker	2	6	2	.	43	1078	7	105
Ticket, Label Writer	.	.	.	1	23	25	3	1
Others	5	.	1	.	44	8	8	9
21. PERSONS WORKING AND DEALING IN VARIOUS MINERAL SUBSTANCES.								
1. *Miners.*								
Coal Miner	1618	22	1401	16	42	.	.	.
Ironstone Miner	64	.	14	.	1	.	.	.
Copper Miner	.	.	.	.	.	.	.	.
Tin Miner	.	.	.	.	.	.	.	.
Lead Miner	.	.	.	.	.	.	.	.
Miner in other, or undefined, Minerals	26	.	.	.	9	.	.	.
Mine Service	23	.	23	.	5	.	.	.
2. *Coal, Coal Gas, &c.*								
Coal Merchant, Dealer	72	10	97	10	520	39	103	10
Coalheaver	25	.	28	.	283	.	17	.
Coke, Charcoal, Peat—Cutter, Burner, Dealer	2	2	28	6	5	1	2	.
Gas Works Service	45	.	143	.	439	.	33	.
3. *Stone, Clay, and Road Making.*								
Stone Quarrier	4	.	.	.	2	.	.	.
Stone Cutter, Dresser, Dealer	6	.	2	.	96	.	7	.
Slate Quarrier	.	.	.	.	.	.	.	.
Slate Worker, Dealer	.	.	.	.	14	2	2	.
Limeburner	24	.	5	.	9	.	.	.
Clay, Sand, Gravel, Chalk—Labourer, Dealer	1	.	6	.	8	1	.	.
Fossil, Coprolite—Digger, Dealer	.	.	.	.	.	.	.	.
Well Sinker, Borer	18	.	16	.	35	.	3	.
Plaster, Cement, Manufacture	.	.	3	.	6	1	2	.
Brick, Tile—Maker, Burner, Dealer	77	21	291	136	357	8	13	.
Paviour	5	.	4	.	85	.	15	.
Road Contractor, Surveyor, Inspector	1	.	.	.	4	.	1	.
Road Labourer	18	.	19	.	263	.	14	.
Railway Contractor	2	.	1	.	7	.	.	.
Platelayer	58	.	22	.	90	.	5	.
Railway Labourer, Navvy	92	.	33	.	332	.	24	.
Others	.	1	.	.	14	6	.	.
4. *Earthenware and Glass.*								
Earthenware, China, Porcelain, Manufacture	1	1	1	.	68	94	8	9
Glass Manufacture	30	7	417	33	1302	177	158	18
Earthenware, China, Glass, Dealer	6	2	7	5	60	49	19	4
5. *Salt.*								
Salt Maker, Dealer	.	.	.	.	4	.	.	.

Table 10 *continued*.—Occupations of Males and Females in the West Midland Division and its Registration Counties, and in each Urban Sanitary District of which the Population exceeds 50,000 Persons.

Occupations.	Urban Sanitary Districts.							
	Walsall.		West Bromwich.		Birmingham.		Aston Manor.	
	Males.	Females.	Males.	Females.	Males.	Females.	Males.	Females.
6. *Water.*								
Waterworks Service	6	.	1	.	47	.	7	.
Others	.	.	.	.	1	.	.	.
7. *Precious Metals and Jewellery.*								
Goldsmith, Silversmith, Jeweller	7	3	3	3	5423	2331	1665	188
Gold, Silver, Beater	1	.	1	.	161	.	10	.
Lapidary	.	.	.	.	148	162	23	21
Others	.	.	.	.	56	364	3	57
8. *Iron and Steel.*								
Blacksmith	195	1	337	.	1921	6	154	.
Whitesmith	4	.	188	1	155	9	6	.
Nail Manufacture	26	6	66	112	706	425	81	33
Anchor, Chain, Manufacture	353	9	17	.	38	10	1	1
Other Iron and Steel Manufactures	1528	36	4742	83	5071	357	836	18
Ironmonger, Hardware Dealer, Merchant	63	2	45	3	847	46	40	2
9. *Copper.*								
Copper, Copper goods—Manufacturer, Worker, Dealer	.		8	1	265	9	18	.
10. *Tin and Zinc.*								
Tin, Tin Plate, Tin goods—Manufacturer, Worker, Dealer	47	.	65	2	1376	559	145	30
Zinc, Zinc Goods—Manufacturer, Worker, Dealer	1	.	5	.	212	5	36	1
11. *Lead.*								
Lead, Leaden goods—Manufacturer, Worker, Dealer	.	.	.	.	15	5	2	1
12. *In Other, Mixed, or Unspecified, Metals.*								
Metal Refiner, Worker, Turner, Dealer	44	1	16	1	1033	180	154	12
Brass, Bronze, Manufacture. Brazier	433	14	59	11	9235	711	940	52
Metal Burnisher, Lacquerer	19	25	1	6	273	1585	25	165
White Metal, Plated Ware, Manufacture. Pewterer	428	4	2	2	1717	478	313	58
Wire Maker, Worker, Weaver, Drawer	4	.	11	1	1261	119	129	9
Bolt, Nut, Rivet, Screw, Staple, Maker	9	5	165	224	523	742	43	10
Lamp, Lantern, Candlestick, Maker	24	5	7	1	1459	406	182	32
Clasp, Buckle, Hinge, Maker	148	253	45	13	241	142	26	8
Fancy Chain, Gilt Toy, Maker	1	.	.	.	202	553	38	74
Others	83	2	1	7	805	42	29	5
22. Persons working and dealing in General or Unspecified Commodities.								
1. *Makers and Dealers (General or Undefined).*								
General Shopkeeper, Dealer	38	47	37	37	343	639	39	78
Pawnbroker	15	32	16	27	178	215	17	27
Costermonger, Huckster, Street Seller	37	33	10	17	582	486	15	8
Manufacturer, Manager, Superintendent (undefined)	17	3	16	.	209	19	35	3
Contractor (undefined)	7	.	5	.	19		3	.
2. *Mechanics and Labourers (General or Undefined).*								
General Labourer	940	12	1622	17	5286	25	463	1
Engine Driver, Stoker, Fireman (not railway, marine, nor agricultural)	226		257	.	538	.	104	.
Artizan, Mechanic (undefined)	348	32	456	9	2061	507	273	7
Apprentice (undefined)	9		10	.	36	4	10	.
Factory Labourer (undefined)	124	22	50	5	609	711	51	165
Machinist, Machine Worker (undefined)	6	.	16	.	391	25	98	1
23. Persons working and dealing in Refuse Matters.								
1. *Refuse Matters.*								
Town Drainage Service	.		1	.	54		6	
Chimney Sweep, Soot Merchant	14	.	3	.	142	.	8	.
Scavenger, Crossing Sweeper	5	.	9	.	80	.	2	.
Rag Gatherer, Dealer	2	2	7	3	20	18	.	.
VI. UNOCCUPIED CLASS.								
24. Persons without Specified Occupations								
Persons returned by Property, Rank, &c., and not by special occupation	7814	18787	7475	19377	46691	116892	6356	17359
Children under 5 years of age	4504	4480	4447	4634	28911	29133	4196	4285

Table 11.—BIRTH-PLACES of MALES and FEMALES enumerated in COUNTIES, and in each URBAN SANITARY DISTRICT of which the POPULATION EXCEEDS 50,000 PERSONS.

WHERE BORN.	WHERE ENUMERATED.									
	WEST-MIDLAND COUNTIES.		COUNTIES.*							
			GLOUCESTERSHIRE.		HEREFORDSHIRE.		SHROPSHIRE.		STAFFORDSHIRE.	
	Males.	Females.	Males.	Females.	Males.	Females.	Males.	Females.	Males.	Females.
TOTAL OF INHABITANTS	1486796	1553348	269470	302963	59809	61253	124157	123857	492009	489004
LONDON	17699	20927	4456	5961	683	914	801	995	3315	3571
MIDDLESEX (*Intra-metropolitan*)	14797	17648	3651	4953	577	773	674	837	2741	2967
SURREY (*Intra-metropolitan*)	1915	2224	526	679	73	99	87	113	385	368
KENT (*Intra-metropolitan*)	987	1060	279	329	33	42	40	45	189	210
SOUTH-EASTERN COUNTIES	11072	13007	3499	4603	459	512	565	670	2187	2139
SURREY (*Extra-metropolitan*)	1424	1593	418	498	76	81	60	58	278	273
KENT (*Extra-metropolitan*)	2439	3092	870	882	103	119	144	197	516	527
SUSSEX	1485	1756	425	573	58	85	89	82	303	308
HAMPSHIRE	3154	3829	1045	1460	116	140	179	178	554	600
BERKSHIRE	2570	2337	941	1190	106	87	103	125	486	381
SOUTH-MIDLAND COUNTIES	23973	24361	3424	4380	451	534	586	660	5113	4176
MIDDLESEX (*Ex.-metropolitan*)	1419	1503	320	436	49	71	78	77	304	218
HERTFORDSHIRE	1148	1226	210	230	27	31	65	61	314	255
BUCKINGHAMSHIRE	2691	2518	324	391	66	77	62	67	836	651
OXFORDSHIRE	8076	5960	1791	2305	146	155	116	141	1380	1090
NORTHAMPTONSHIRE	6790	7210	420	477	74	71	143	166	1447	1266
HUNTINGDONSHIRE	511	533	49	68	23	31	28	19	154	125
BEDFORDSHIRE	1330	1274	146	208	31	49	50	74	407	289
CAMBRIDGESHIRE	1108	1137	164	215	35	49	44	55	311	277
EASTERN COUNTIES	5790	5967	1140	1463	191	265	366	396	1804	1366
ESSEX	1643	1993	389	539	52	97	108	90	388	430
SUFFOLK	2058	1857	347	443	76	99	127	137	842	475
NORFOLK	2089	2117	404	481	63	69	131	169	574	461
SOUTH-WESTERN COUNTIES	37813	46781	26517	34965	950	995	592	769	3351	3153
WILTSHIRE	8134	9845	5805	7297	226	213	128	143	746	607
DORSETSHIRE	1988	2243	1002	1200	86	96	74	85	299	262
DEVONSHIRE	7237	9086	4464	5863	231	263	141	215	779	819
CORNWALL	1753	2277	823	1240	58	56	63	72	388	358
SOMERSETSHIRE	18801	23631	14423	19366	329	367	186	254	1139	1107
WEST-MIDLAND COUNTIES	1270567	1319089	213646	230760	51253	51205	107576	105614	431282	433919
GLOUCESTERSHIRE	223804	238128	203864	217720	2476	2702	512	531	3532	2863
HEREFORDSHIRE	58945	57790	2378	2544	44116	43558	1601	1762	1798	1574
SHROPSHIRE	122738	121298	473	654	1577	1639	98645	95638	15835	15367
STAFFORDSHIRE	409869	420973	1114	1426	406	462	4340	4897	373956	378600
WORCESTERSHIRE	169022	176967	3669	4647	2227	2275	1559	1687	17059	17549
WARWICKSHIRE	280039	303935	2148	2769	451	569	928	1099	17102	17966
NORTH-MIDLAND COUNTIES	24291	25083	1320	1570	282	227	672	698	11299	11175
LEICESTERSHIRE	9342	9173	342	398	75	61	247	194	3303	2867
RUTLANDSHIRE	376	422	46	47	11	8	6	18	123	106
LINCOLNSHIRE	2466	2585	283	398	74	56	142	142	729	691
NOTTINGHAMSHIRE	3156	3217	296	310	48	37	99	118	1131	1087
DERBYSHIRE	8951	9686	353	417	74	65	178	221	6013	6424
NORTH-WESTERN COUNTIES	23587	23565	1608	1835	409	418	3100	3490	12422	11480
CHESHIRE	11125	10674	296	365	105	107	1776	1975	7568	6718
LANCASHIRE	12462	12891	1312	1470	304	311	1324	1515	4854	4762
YORKSHIRE	8584	8618	1179	1239	196	219	561	529	2888	2778
NORTHERN COUNTIES	3348	3573	577	739	79	94	243	260	1226	1174
DURHAM	1409	1485	254	335	24	24	84	74	371	659
NORTHUMBERLAND	940	1048	168	195	19	17	50	71	327	324
CUMBERLAND	686	750	112	158	21	33	61	78	224	308
WESTMORLAND	313	290	43	51	15	20	48	37	104	83
MONMOUTHSHIRE AND WALES	24194	28935	5201	7866	4022	4934	6766	7668	4512	4175
MONMOUTHSHIRE	5206	6750	2423	3823	1162	1475	147	168	619	570
GLAMORGANSHIRE	2472	3286	1347	1963	182	248	98	107	325	365
CARMARTHENSHIRE	549	673	252	332	80	64	34	42	70	73
PEMBROKESHIRE	701	1035	358	650	60	63	55	61	80	96
CARDIGANSHIRE	364	341	95	99	34	37	69	64	57	36
BRECKNOCKSHIRE	981	1340	214	312	386	620	83	90	88	64
RADNORSHIRE	3325	3868	78	144	1883	2179	769	888	253	254
MONTGOMERYSHIRE	4099	5187	63	98	107	123	3330	3720	732	744
FLINTSHIRE	1611	1549	20	47	14	11	601	669	744	611
DENBIGHSHIRE	2130	2325	49	79	24	22	1198	1359	625	532
MERIONETHSHIRE	277	293	10	15	8	13	155	171	50	42
CARNARVONSHIRE	301	331	37	43	10	5	78	97	88	89
ANGLESEY	131	135	12	17	2	6	24	22	53	50
WALES (*County not stated*)	1547	1832	243	416	40	68	124	170	726	649
ENGLAND (*County not stated*)	4525	3912	531	494	177	113	522	406	1606	1253
OTHER PARTS OF BRITISH EMPIRE	26726	25515	5174	6178	561	690	1663	1513	9978	7732
ISLANDS in the BRITISH SEAS	494	698	201	262	10	17	26	42	85	128
SCOTLAND	5692	5252	1171	1165	197	199	418	309	1824	1509
IRELAND	17398	15446	2422	2908	250	333	1034	526	7573	5528
BRITISH COLONIES OF DEPENDENCIES	3242	4119	1380	1843	104	141	190	246	497	576
FOREIGN COUNTRIES	4431	3827	1158	943	93	127	130	183	963	873
British Subjects	1999	1951	452	516	52	62	74	96	469	456
Foreigners	2432	1876	706	427	41	65	56	87	494	417
AT SEA	196	186	40	67	3	6	14	11	63	40
British Subjects	196	186	40	67	3	6	14	11	63	40
Foreigners	-	-	-	-	-	-	-	-	-	-

s proper, and not the Registration Counties, are referred to in this Table.

Table 11 *continued.*—Birth-places of Males and Females enumerated in Counties, and in each Urban Sanitary District of which the Population exceeds 50,000 Persons.

Where Born.	Where Enumerated.							
	Counties.				Urban Sanitary Districts.			
	WORCESTERSHIRE.		WARWICKSHIRE.		BRISTOL.*		WOLVERHAMPTON.	
	Males.	Females.	Males.	Females.	Males.	Females.	Males.	Females.
TOTAL OF INHABITANTS	184205	196078	357146	380193	93711	113163	37827	37939
LONDON	1878	2415	6568	7071	2163	2706	396	395
Middlesex (*Intra-metropolitan*)	1518	1996	5636	6097	1770	2251	332	324
Surrey (*Intra-metropolitan*)	254	302	390	663	255	326	47	53
Kent (*Intra-metropolitan*)	106	117	540	311	138	129	17	18
SOUTH-EASTERN COUNTIES	1198	1491	3164	3592	1465	1897	219	209
Surrey (*Extra-metropolitan*)	139	226	433	427	149	176	27	24
Kent (*Extra-metropolitan*)	267	389	739	888	288	462	46	58
Sussex	155	213	464	495	154	222	28	25
Hampshire	324	384	887	1017	575	737	62	61
Berkshire	263	279	721	766	299	360	56	46
SOUTH-MIDLAND COUNTIES	2348	2289	12051	12422	743	1015	504	417
Middlesex (*Extra-metropolitan*)	160	170	548	536	136	179	38	25
Hertfordshire	114	150	418	489	68	87	26	13
Buckinghamshire	235	256	1168	1076	101	182	75	56
Oxfordshire	1046	917	4498	4462	169	208	139	131
Northamptonshire	474	405	4233	4735	143	178	143	118
Huntingdonshire	36	60	201	230	15	20	12	11
Bedfordshire	134	115	562	541	57	74	48	36
Cambridgeshire	130	128	424	418	54	80	23	30
EASTERN COUNTIES	579	642	1710	1835	462	642	112	115
Essex	178	215	528	613	152	244	33	44
Suffolk	184	196	482	507	128	189	27	33
Norfolk	217	231	700	715	182	209	52	38
SOUTH-WESTERN COUNTIES	2123	2370	4280	4529	26591	32890	341	338
Wiltshire	465	491	784	794	1985	2856	76	75
Dorsetshire	146	172	381	368	698	881	36	33
Devonshire	469	578	1253	1347	3742	4766	35	77
Cornwall	100	158	321	393	597	840	15	13
Somersetshire	943	971	1541	1627	19574	23803	129	140
WEST-MIDLAND COUNTIES	166943	177162	299867	320431	54307	63985	32746	33386
Gloucestershire	5413	6161	8057	8151	52606	61870	404	311
Herefordshire	3825	4622	2327	2780	262	395	252	205
Shropshire	2799	3341	5418	4459	115	135	2084	2190
Staffordshire	16273	12983	17780	22605	879	473	27384	27909
Worcestershire	129820	133171	14697	17638	284	443	1260	1297
Warwickshire	14822	16884	253588	264846	571	646	1446	1474
NORTH-MIDLAND COUNTIES	1733	1752	8985	9666	520	539	447	368
Leicestershire	627	578	4748	5075	166	155	138	110
Rutlandshire	35	39	165	204	6	8	7	7
Lincolnshire	289	318	949	980	106	146	53	34
Nottinghamshire	290	307	1292	1358	105	90	75	65
Derbyshire	492	510	1841	2049	137	140	174	152
NORTH-WESTERN COUNTIES	1429	1664	4619	4678	744	752	708	622
Cheshire	355	394	1025	1015	117	124	285	239
Lancashire	1074	1270	3594	3663	627	628	423	383
YORKSHIRE	1090	1113	2670	2740	447	429	243	238
NORTHERN COUNTIES	373	453	850	853	271	330	91	91
Durham	157	200	319	298	105	158	41	53
Northumberland	94	136	282	305	101	92	29	20
Cumberland	86	84	182	189	52	58	18	16
Westmorland	36	33	67	66	13	22	3	2
MONMOUTHSHIRE AND WALES	1336	1520	2357	2772	2455	4092	607	537
Monmouthshire	333	376	502	538	935	1671	94	82
Glamorganshire	102	205	327	308	525	1258	38	43
Carmarthenshire	52	57	87	75	118	161	11	10
Pembrokeshire	40	59	99	96	222	404	12	12
Cardiganshire	22	26	87	79	77	61	16	5
Brecknockshire	90	95	120	156	85	157	10	10
Radnorshire	142	107	150	206	19	31	29	26
Montgomeryshire	110	125	257	357	16	22	164	172
Flintshire	57	63	175	148	7	14	35	30
Denbighshire	73	78	161	215	11	20	86	57
Merionethshire	13	18	41	34	8	16	4	8
Carnarvonshire	23	24	65	93	17	22	12	5
Anglesey	8	4	32	38	9	10	4	5
Wales (*County not stated*)	152	190	260	341	111	251	93	77
ENGLAND (*County not stated*)	726	702	963	944	130	157	98	65
OTHER PARTS OF BRITISH EMPIRE	2054	2130	7296	7272	2754	3250	1176	1031
Islands in the British Seas	46	73	126	176	129	150	10	14
SCOTLAND	580	588	1507	1401	591	543	239	151
IRELAND	1143	1100	4877	4751	1434	1770	890	815
British Colonies or Dependencies	285	369	786	944	600	787	37	51
FOREIGN COUNTRIES	368	352	1719	1349	645	455	132	104
British Subjects	184	170	768	651	247	248	65	57
Foreigners	184	182	951	698	398	207	67	47
AT SEA	27	23	49	39	14	44	7	3
British Subjects	27	23	49	39	14	44	7	3
Foreigners	-	-	-	-	-	-	-	-

* A portion of the Urban Sanitary District of Bristol is situated in Division V., but the Birth-Places for the entire District are returned here.

Table 11 *continued.*—BIRTH-PLACES of MALES and FEMALES enumerated in COUNTIES, and in each URBAN SANITARY DISTRICT of which the POPULATION EXCEEDS 50,000 PERSONS.

WHERE BORN.	WHERE ENUMERATED.							
	URBAN SANITARY DISTRICTS.							
	WALSALL.		WEST BROMWICH.		BIRMINGHAM.		ASTON MANOR.	
	Males.	Females.	Males.	Females.	Males.	Females.	Males.	Females.
TOTAL OF INHABITANTS	29336	29459	28285	28010	194540	206234	25896	27946
LONDON	264	264	149	160	3901	4040	575	567
MIDDLESEX (*Intra-metropolitan*)	218	222	121	138	3403	3515	486	480
SURREY (*Intra-metropolitan*)	29	23	16	10	321	370	45	50
KENT (*Intra-metropolitan*)	17	19	12	12	177	155	44	37
SOUTH-EASTERN COUNTIES	121	113	123	112	1529	1636	213	240
SURREY (*Extra-metropolitan*)	15	10	11	9	185	197	31	19
KENT (*Extra-metropolitan*)	20	27	16	25	371	442	60	75
SUSSEX	30	18	12	10	211	204	37	53
HAMPSHIRE	31	33	43	35	440	481	43	51
BERKSHIRE	25	25	41	33	322	312	42	42
SOUTH-MIDLAND COUNTIES	391	322	419	310	4827	4303	555	529
MIDDLESEX (*Extra-metropolitan*)	21	19	8	8	297	202	45	43
HERTFORDSHIRE	15	15	15	19	180	180	17	28
BUCKINGHAMSHIRE	54	53	122	89	531	435	64	62
OXFORDSHIRE	102	65	131	85	1772	1524	183	157
NORTHAMPTONSHIRE	138	113	118	87	1478	1340	170	172
HUNTINGDONSHIRE	9	8	4	2	93	104	15	7
BEDFORDSHIRE	32	27	10	13	257	230	34	34
CAMBRIDGESHIRE	20	22	11	7	219	198	27	26
EASTERN COUNTIES	81	87	59	49	865	794	115	122
ESSEX	21	23	22	21	255	244	39	47
SUFFOLK	31	30	14	16	228	216	25	25
NORFOLK	29	34	23	12	382	334	51	50
SOUTH-WESTERN COUNTIES	237	247	183	174	2696	2686	335	322
WILTSHIRE	51	45	34	30	456	489	62	56
DORSETSHIRE	12	18	9	9	176	138	50	31
DEVONSHIRE	43	45	35	53	817	828	96	82
CORNWALL	13	16	14	11	220	229	24	26
SOMERSETSHIRE	118	123	91	71	1025	1022	103	127
WEST-MIDLAND COUNTIES	25807	26438	25959	25942	163637	175959	22167	24193
GLOUCESTERSHIRE	252	235	294	232	5226	4862	488	459
HEREFORDSHIRE	125	104	151	112	1781	2080	193	188
SHROPSHIRE	611	671	521	548	2458	3184	298	352
STAFFORDSHIRE	22639	23147	22086	22181	11708	14857	1883	2456
WORCESTERSHIRE	782	806	1719	1720	9885	11679	984	1181
WARWICKSHIRE	1408	1475	1188	1150	132579	139297	18324	19556
NORTH-MIDLAND COUNTIES	559	482	275	233	4149	4054	510	520
LEICESTERSHIRE	255	199	129	108	1738	1682	243	216
RUTLANDSHIRE	9	10	4	1	63	82	6	11
LINCOLNSHIRE	31	35	16	13	466	459	66	71
NOTTINGHAMSHIRE	66	73	37	33	848	816	77	28
DERBYSHIRE	198	165	89	78	991	1,018	118	194
NORTH-WESTERN COUNTIES	294	303	256	239	2629	2717	380	357
CHESHIRE	82	87	62	59	544	546	96	71
LANCASHIRE	212	216	194	180	2085	2171	284	286
YORKSHIRE	204	185	166	159	1595	1599	215	228
NORTHERN COUNTIES	63	64	59	68	496	436	60	72
DURHAM	29	29	39	43	192	166	26	26
NORTHUMBERLAND	16	19	11	13	176	182	12	19
CUMBERLAND	10	10	7	12	93	79	15	21
WESTMORLAND	8	6	2	.	35	29	7	6
MONMOUTHSHIRE AND WALES	171	172	208	195	1575	1742	257	290
MONMOUTHSHIRE	28	31	40	38	361	364	33	37
GLAMORGANSHIRE	17	20	19	21	237	278	28	42
CARMARTHENSHIRE	3	2	4	4	53	46	24	5
PEMBROKESHIRE	6	6	.	2	65	55	7	7
CARDIGANSHIRE	2	.	3	2	46	52	31	13
BRECKNOCKSHIRE	2	7	6	6	85	112	6	11
RADNORSHIRE	15	15	14	23	114	130	13	32
MONTGOMERYSHIRE	38	24	63	46	175	224	36	47
FLINTSHIRE	9	12	8	8	91	63	20	14
DENBIGHSHIRE	13	6	12	12	98	104	16	35
MERIONETHSHIRE	1	5	4	1	26	20	6	2
CARNARVONSHIRE	.	3	5	2	36	48	1	6
ANGLESEY	1	1	.	1	19	12	3	1
WALES (*County not stated*)	36	40	31	34	109	234	38	37
ENGLAND (*County not stated*)	85	49	75	75	496	552	56	43
OTHER PARTS OF BRITISH EMPIRE	882	687	306	241	4828	4816	358	386
ISLANDS IN THE BRITISH SEAS	4	6	5	5	65	79	16	21
SCOTLAND	148	116	72	38	912	755	102	113
IRELAND	716	536	209	166	3488	3584	187	181
BRITISH COLONIES OR DEPENDENCIES	14	29	20	32	363	398	53	71
FOREIGN COUNTRIES	69	44	45	52	1288	859	95	74
British Subjects	21	19	25	24	565	429	47	32
Foreigners	48	25	20	28	723	430	48	42
AT SEA	8	2	3	1	29	21	5	3
British Subjects	8	2	3	1	29	21	5	3
Foreigners	.	.	.	.	.	.		

Table 12.—Distribution of the enumerated Natives of Counties.

Where Enumerated.	Where Born.							
	West Midland Counties.		Gloucestershire.		Herefordshire.		Shropshire.	
	Males.	Females.	Males.	Females.	Males.	Females.	Males.	Females.
Total enumerated Natives in each County	1528676	1606350	292410	314231	71601	75343	153073	160458
London	48317	51965	15292	18843	2643	4031	2878	3987
Middlesex (*Intra-metropolitan*)	30079	36844	10534	13432	1798	2865	2019	2890
Surrey (*Intra-metropolitan*)	10688	12194	3899	4432	698	905	678	853
Kent (*Intra-metropolitan*)	2550	2987	829	979	147	231	181	244
South-Eastern Counties	18723	20586	6537	7663	1200	1695	1454	1621
Surrey (*Extra-metropolitan*)	3809	5155	1817	1752	297	466	298	495
Kent (*Extra-metropolitan*)	4440	4156	1325	1374	290	405	363	313
Sussex	2819	4116	969	1380	233	360	217	323
Hampshire	5064	4392	1721	1767	340	503	384	327
Berkshire	2591	2767	1205	1389	140	161	163	163
South-Midland Counties	15610	19298	4495	5722	703	902	868	1200
Middlesex (*Extra-metropolitan*)	4166	5225	1394	1816	276	426	289	459
Hertfordshire	1158	1431	300	410	64	78	92	183
Buckinghamshire	1426	1628	345	422	65	82	109	127
Oxfordshire	3900	5335	1715	2227	97	147	101	158
Northamptonshire	3546	4090	450	479	127	101	149	184
Huntingdonshire	172	215	29	45	13	8	6	21
Bedfordshire	729	887	152	102	31	83	55	61
Cambridgeshire	511	497	110	122	29	27	64	47
Eastern Counties	4729	4980	1294	1428	270	333	320	379
Essex	3293	3311	918	1008	195	226	190	242
Suffolk	711	882	174	211	38	56	64	74
Norfolk	725	786	202	209	37	51	66	63
South-Western Counties	21663	25758	16109	19643	705	881	533	656
Wiltshire	4542	5090	3463	3987	155	164	106	101
Dorsetshire	354	934	407	483	46	66	61	63
Devonshire	3517	3558	1027	1720	210	213	157	207
Cornwall	682	546	325	262	36	30	35	28
Somersetshire	11968	15830	10267	13241	258	388	145	257
West-Midland Counties	1270567	1319091	223854	238128	56045	57790	122738	121298
Gloucestershire	213646	230760	203864	217720	2378	3544	473	654
Herefordshire	51253	51205	2476	2702	44116	48558	1577	1629
Shropshire	107576	105614	512	531	1601	1762	98345	95638
Staffordshire	491282	433910	3532	2863	1798	1574	15835	15367
Worcestershire	186848	177182	5413	8181	3825	4622	2790	3541
Warwickshire	299987	320431	8057	8151	2327	2780	3418	4469
North-Midland Counties	29368	30768	2816	2504	589	639	1764	1824
Leicestershire	7298	8406	659	608	146	155	250	301
Rutlandshire	152	145	34	28	7	15	13	11
Lincolnshire	1697	1740	203	284	84	93	152	181
Nottinghamshire	5482	5628	779	723	124	148	495	475
Derbyshire	14759	14840	1051	863	228	224	874	856
North-Western Counties	57223	71361	5332	5768	1811	2350	12830	19525
Cheshire	14209	18182	836	952	385	476	3971	5317
Lancashire	43014	53179	4496	4816	1448	1874	8859	14208
Yorkshire	28767	27993	3711	3263	891	952	3008	3465
Northern Counties	8855	7409	1152	961	216	211	885	736
Durham	6220	5032	725	570	117	107	617	476
Northumberland	1428	1307	226	214	58	40	138	122
Cumberland	1009	786	153	116	30	36	109	91
Westmorland	198	284	48	57	11	19	23	47
Monmouthshire and Wales	29854	27141	11818	10308	6528	5559	5795	5767
Monmouthshire	9597	8480	4994	4427	2994	2590	389	337
Glamorganshire	9237	7644	5996	4886	1603	1088	309	302
Carmarthenshire	495	424	197	161	80	88	51	81
Pembrokeshire	451	407	215	191	44	54	35	33
Cardiganshire	225	311	48	73	24	35	74	83
Brecknockshire	1675	1385	319	264	960	844	187	126
Radnorshire	1348	1310	45	55	713	668	469	450
Montgomeryshire	2056	2107	54	80	77	93	1649	1671
Flintshire	1414	1597	65	50	24	35	858	768
Denbighshire	2416	2336	89	80	50	49	1570	1482
Merionethshire	317	301	28	25	35	15	145	164
Carnarvonshire	493	701	60	72	24	40	151	232
Anglesey	186	129	8	11	16	14	40	40

Table 12 *continued*.—DISTRIBUTION of the enumerated NATIVES of COUNTIES.

WHERE ENUMERATED.	WHERE BORN.					
	STAFFORDSHIRE.		WORCESTERSHIRE.		WARWICKSHIRE.	
	Males.	Females.	Males.	Females.	Males.	Females.
TOTAL ENUMERATED NATIVES IN EACH COUNTY	480511	496842	191951	201896	339130	357580
LONDON	6132	6639	4190	5345	12182	13120
MIDDLESEX (*Intra-metropolitan*)	4185	4879	2793	3696	8720	9352
SURREY (*Intra-metropolitan*)	1490	1623	1129	1338	2794	3043
KENT (*Intra-metropolitan*)	457	437	268	311	668	725
SOUTH-EASTERN COUNTIES	3026	2771	1990	2333	4516	4503
SURREY (*Extra-metropolitan*)	532	679	446	603	919	1159
KENT (*Extra-metropolitan*)	766	601	479	507	1188	956
SUSSEX	445	639	292	479	663	935
HAMPSHIRE	960	606	515	463	1238	926
BERKSHIRE	317	246	258	281	508	527
SOUTH-MIDLAND COUNTIES	2314	2607	1579	1921	5651	6946
MIDDLESEX (*Extra-metropolitan*)	628	751	422	588	1155	1185
HERTFORDSHIRE	216	241	115	157	370	373
BUCKINGHAMSHIRE	348	243	131	146	628	608
OXFORDSHIRE	252	320	448	628	1287	1969
NORTHAMPTONSHIRE	696	722	315	304	1817	2290
HUNTINGDONSHIRE	34	49	14	23	75	69
BEDFORDSHIRE	140	163	81	118	270	326
CAMBRIDGESHIRE	100	112	53	57	149	132
EASTERN COUNTIES	1040	986	592	599	1213	1255
ESSEX	728	629	398	388	864	818
SUFFOLK	172	186	96	133	167	223
NORFOLK	140	171	98	78	182	214
SOUTH-WESTERN COUNTIES	1390	1488	1189	1352	1737	1738
WILTSHIRE	223	248	253	280	323	340
DORSETSHIRE	139	130	100	75	201	117
DEVONSHIRE	526	502	336	371	631	545
CORNWALL	97	81	64	59	125	86
SOMERSETSHIRE	405	527	436	567	467	650
WEST-MIDLAND COUNTIES	409869	420973	169022	176967	289039	303935
GLOUCESTERSHIRE	1114	1476	3669	4647	2148	2769
HEREFORDSHIRE	406	462	2297	2275	451	569
SHROPSHIRE	4340	4897	1550	1687	928	1099
STAFFORDSHIRE	375956	378600	17089	17649	17102	17906
WORCESTERSHIRE	10273	12983	129820	183171	14822	16684
WARWICKSHIRE	17780	22605	14697	17638	253588	264848
NORTH-MIDLAND COUNTIES	13032	13990	2610	2536	8557	9275
LEICESTERSHIRE	1692	2009	501	616	3990	4713
RUTLANDSHIRE	35	38	13	12	50	42
LINCOLNSHIRE	454	485	265	232	469	475
NOTTINGHAMSHIRE	2062	2170	459	474	1543	1638
DERBYSHIRE	8789	9288	1312	1212	2505	2406
NORTH-WESTERN COUNTIES	24388	29477	4532	5101	8330	9140
CHESHIRE	6917	9005	745	910	1377	1522
LANCASHIRE	17471	20472	3787	4191	6953	7618
YORKSHIRE	12344	11616	3548	3459	5265	5238
NORTHERN COUNTIES	4281	3598	1223	970	1098	933
DURHAM	3216	2631	916	724	629	524
NORTHUMBERLAND	590	557	160	128	258	237
CUMBERLAND	422	333	116	85	179	131
WESTMORLAND	53	77	31	33	32	41
MONMOUTHSHIRE AND WALES	2695	2697	1476	1313	1542	1497
MONMOUTHSHIRE	478	485	446	279	296	272
GLAMORGANSHIRE	644	592	472	400	323	416
CARMARTHENSHIRE	77	74	45	33	45	37
PEMBROKESHIRE	67	45	32	37	58	46
CARDIGANSHIRE	34	47	19	26	26	42
BRECKNOCKSHIRE	71	68	101	63	67	40
RADNORSHIRE	44	57	57	57	20	34
MONTGOMERYSHIRE	147	140	70	55	53	88
FLINTSHIRE	451	475	79	84	139	167
DENBIGHSHIRE	400	496	83	90	134	140
MERIONETHSHIRE	46	33	26	31	35	35
CARNARVONSHIRE	120	163	33	44	105	150
ANGLESEY	26	34	11	12	41	28

Table 14.—Number and Ages of Males and Females returned as Blind or Blind from Birth in the West-Midland Division and its Registration Counties.

Registration County.	All Ages. Both Sexes.	All Ages. Males and Females.	0–	5–	15–	20–	25–	45–	65 and upwards.
VI. WEST-MIDLAND COUNTIES.	2914	M. 1606	39	108	99	61	313	430	556
		F. 1308	38	85	51	65	223	282	569
22 GLOUCESTERSHIRE	674	M. 342	7	23	28	13	62	84	125
		F. 332	6	13	16	24	61	64	148
23 HEREFORDSHIRE	145	M. 85	.	2	1	4	14	29	35
		F. 60	.	4	1	3	10	9	33
24 SHROPSHIRE	288	M. 151	2	6	2	2	24	41	74
		F. 137	4	4	1	4	21	35	68
25 STAFFORDSHIRE	822	M. 477	12	28	21	14	101	138	163
		F. 345	8	25	10	15	69	76	142
26 WORCESTERSHIRE	415	M. 252	5	31	35	15	35	60	71
		F. 163	4	16	18	10	23	34	63
27 WARWICKSHIRE	570	M. 299	13	18	12	13	77	78	88
		F. 271	11	23	10	9	39	64	115

Table 15.—Number and Ages of Males and Females returned as Blind in the West-Midland Divisionand its Registration Counties.

Registration County.	All Ages. Both Sexes.	All Ages. Males and Females.	0–	5–	15–	20–	25–	45–	65 and upwards.
VI. WEST-MIDLAND COUNTIES.	2647	M. 1468	26	78	85	50	274	403	547
		F. 1184	18	59	42	52	186	262	565
22 GLOUCESTERSHIRE	602	M. 312	6	15	24	12	53	77	125
		F. 290	1	5	11	17	50	59	147
23 HEREFORDSHIRE	132	M. 76	.	1	1	3	12	28	31
		F. 56	.	3	1	3	8	9	32
24 SHROPSHIRE	259	M. 138	1	2	2	1	22	36	74
		F. 121	2	1	1	2	16	31	68
25 STAFFORDSHIRE	760	M. 443	8	10	18	10	91	136	161
		F. 317	5	21	8	12	57	73	141
26 WORCESTERSHIRE	388	M. 230	4	27	32	13	30	55	69
		F. 158	3	14	12	10	23	33	63
27 WARWICKSHIRE	506	M. 264	7	14	8	11	66	71	87
		F. 242	7	15	9	8	32	57	114

Table 16.—Number and Ages of Males and Females returned as Blind from Birth in the West-Midland Division and its Registration Counties.

Registration County.	All Ages. Both Sexes.	All Ages. Males and Females.	0–	5–	15–	20–	25–	45–	65 and upwards.
VI. WEST-MIDLAND COUNTIES.	267	M. 143	13	30	14	11	39	27	9
		F. 124	15	26	9	13	37	20	4
22 GLOUCESTERSHIRE	72	M. 30	1	8	4	1	9	7	.
		F. 42	5	8	5	7	11	5	1
23 HEREFORDSHIRE	13	M. 9	.	1	.	1	2	1	4
		F. 4	.	1	.	.	2	.	1
24 SHROPSHIRE	29	M. 13	1	4		1	2	5	.
		F. 16	2	3	.	2	5	4	.
25 STAFFORDSHIRE	62	M. 34	4	9	3	4	10	2	2
		F. 28	3	4	2	3	12	3	1
26 WORCESTERSHIRE	27	M. 22	1	4	3	2	5	5	2
		F. 5	1	2	1	.	.	1	.
27 WARWICKSHIRE	64	M. 35	6	4	4	2	11	7	1
		F. 29	4	8	1	1	7	7	1

Table 17.—NUMBER and AGES of MALES and FEMALES returned as DEAF AND DUMB in the WEST-MIDLAND DIVISION and its REGISTRATION COUNTIES.

REGISTRATION COUNTY.	ALL AGES.		0–	5–	15–	20–	25–	45–	65 and upwards.
	Both Sexes.	Males and Females.							
VI. WEST-MIDLAND COUNTIES.	1690	M. 933	42	256	109	104	241	127	44
		F. 757	22	205	84	70	208	122	46
22 GLOUCESTERSHIRE	331	M. - 189	8	50	20	18	45	33	15
		F. 142	3	40	18	10	35	22	14
23 HEREFORDSHIRE - -	76	M. - 45	.	5	7	4	15	12	2
		F. - 31	.	1	2	3	14	8	3
24 SHROPSHIRE - - -	130	M. - 60	3	13	5	6	21	7	5
		F. - 70	2	9	6	7	18	19	9
25 STAFFORDSHIRE - -	481	M. - 264	14	62	37	37	68	36	10
		F. - 217	11	64	21	21	58	33	9
26 WORCESTERSHIRE -	301	M. - 159	1	74	19	14	35	14	2
		F. 142	1	52	21	12	28	19	9
27 WARWICKSHIRE - -	371	M. - 216	16	52	21	23	57	35	10
		F. 155	5	39	16	17	55	21	2

Table 18.—NUMBER and AGES of MALES and FEMALES returned as IDIOTS or IMBECILES, and LUNATICS in the WEST-MIDLAND DIVISION and its REGISTRATION COUNTIES.

REGISTRATION COUNTY.	ALL AGES.		0–	5–	15–	20–	25–	45–	65 and upwards.
	Both Sexes.	Males and Females.							
VI. WEST-MIDLAND COUNTIES.	10322	M. 4924	34	388	327	379	1887	1442	467
		F. 5398	16	265	329	344	2004	1758	682
22 GLOUCESTERSHIRE	2248	M. - 1034	10	76	58	68	378	328	116
		F. - 1214	1	46	77	75	410	432	173
23 HEREFORDSHIRE - -	549	M. - 255	2	14	18	17	101	82	21
		F. 294	1	11	11	14	107	99	51
24 SHROPSHIRE -	998	M. - 459	4	33	31	41	180	127	44
		F. - 539	4	24	23	33	186	170	90
25 STAFFORDSHIRE -	2935	M. - 1500	10	121	94	126	604	432	109
		F. - 1420	4	87	104	97	570	420	138
26 WORCESTERSHIRE -	1211	M. - 538	2	39	40	43	190	164	51
		F. 673	2	29	34	45	240	231	94
27 WARWICKSHIRE - -	2381	M. - 1132	6	106	86	84	435	289	126
		F. - 1249	4	70	80	92	482	397	124

Table 19.—NUMBER and AGES of MALES and FEMALES returned as IDIOTS or IMBECILES in the WEST-MIDLAND DIVISION and its REGISTRATION COUNTIES.

REGISTRATION COUNTY.	ALL AGES.		0–	5–	15–	20–	25–	45–	65 and upwards.
	Both Sexes.	Males and Females.							
VI. WEST-MIDLAND COUNTIES.	4407	M. 2164	34	368	264	251	686	392	169
		F. 2243	16	253	266	213	764	521	210
22 GLOUCESTERSHIRE -	923	M. - 424	10	74	48	42	121	84	42
		F. 499	1	43	59	52	145	138	66
23 HEREFORDSHIRE - -	259	M. - 127	2	13	15	15	40	31	4
		F. 132	1	11	11	12	57	26	14
24 SHROPSHIRE -	460	M. - 230	4	32	29	32	82	39	12
		F. - 230	4	23	31	21	94	62	16
25 STAFFORDSHIRE -	1172	M. - 593	10	111	76	78	175	111	32
		F. - 579	4	83	82	58	200	113	44
26 WORCESTERSHIRE -	486	M. - 219	2	38	26	25	77	39	12
		F. - 267	3	27	29	29	89	74	17
27 WARWICKSHIRE - -	1107	M. - 571	6	100	73	61	179	88	67
		F. 536	4	67	64	46	189	113	53

Table 20.—Number and Ages of Males and Females returned as Lunatics in the West-Midland Division and its Registration Counties.

Registration County.	All Ages. Both Sexes.	All Ages. Males and Females.	0–	5–	15–	20–	25–	45–	65 and upwards.
VI. WEST-MIDLAND COUNTIES.	5915	M. 2760	.	20	68	128	1201	1050	298
		F. 3155	.	12	63	131	1240	1237	472
22 GLOUCESTERSHIRE	1325	M. - 610	.	2	10	26	254	244	74
		F. 715	.	1	18	35	263	290	109
23 HEREFORDSHIRE -	290	M. - 128	.	1	3	4	52	51	17
		F. 162	.	-	.	2	58	73	37
24 SHROPSHIRE	538	M. - 229	.	.	2	9	98	88	32
		F. 309	.	2	2	12	102	117	74
25 STAFFORDSHIRE	1763	M. - 913	.	10	18	48	419	341	77
		F. 850	.	4	22	44	379	307	94
26 WORCESTERSHIRE	725	M. - 319	.	1	14	18	122	125	39
		F. 406	.	2	5	14	151	157	77
27 WARWICKSHIRE	1274	M. - 561	.	6	16	23	256	201	59
		F. 713	.	3	16	36	298	284	81

Table 21.—Number of the Blind, of the Deaf and Dumb, of Idiots or Imbeciles, and of Lunatics in the West-Midland Division and its Registration Counties and Districts.

Registration County and District.	Blind. From Birth.	Blind. Others.	Blind. Total.	Deaf and Dumb.	Mentally Deranged. Idiots.	Mentally Deranged. Lunatics.	Mentally Deranged. Total.
VI. WEST MIDLAND COUNTIES.	267	2647	2914	1690	4407	5915	10322
22 GLOUCESTERSHIRE	72	602	674	331	923	1325	2248
23 HEREFORDSHIRE	13	132	145	76	259	290	549
24 SHROPSHIRE -	29	259	288	130	460	538	998
25 STAFFORDSHIRE -	62	760	822	481	1172	1763	2935
26 WORCESTERSHIRE -	27	388	415	301	486	725	1211
27 WARWICKSHIRE	64	506	570	371	1107	1274	2381
22 GLOUCESTERSHIRE.							
320 BRISTOL - -	17	117	134	67	50	—	50
321 BARTON REGIS - -	19	144	163	82	329	436	765
322 CHIPPING SODBURY -	1	26	27	6	27	44	71
323 THORNBURY -	2	20	22	10	37	6	43
324 DURSLEY - -	1	15	16	0	26	—	26
22 GLOUCESTERSHIRE—cont.							
325 WESTBURY-ON-SEVERN	4	24	28	15	41	4	45
326 NEWENT - -	3	13	16	10	21	5	26
327 GLOUCESTER -	2	48	50	31	82	729	811
328 WHEATENHURST - -	1	10	11	4	24	—	24
329 STROUD -	4	43	47	29	100	5	105
330 TETBURY -	—	5	5	3	5	2	7
331 CIRENCESTER -	3	23	26	21	34	39	73
332 NORTHLEACH -	2	7	9	2	14	25	39
333 STOW-ON-THE-WOLD -	2	11	13	2	19	—	19
334 WINCHCOMB - -	1	8	9	5	18	3	21
335 CHELTENHAM - -	8	70	78	30	69	25	94
336 TEWKESBURY - -	2	18	20	8	27	2	29
23 HEREFORDSHIRE.							
337 LEDBURY - -	1	10	11	8	21	—	21
338 ROSS -	—	13	13	13	27	3	30
339 HEREFORD - -	2	61	63	20	147	283	304
340 WEOBLY - -	1	11	12	7	8	—	8
341 BROMYARD - -	3	12	15	7	15	1	16
342 LEOMINSTER - -	5	16	21	11	26	1	27
343 KINGTON -	1	9	10	10	15	2	17

21 *continued.*—NUMBER of the BLIND, of the DEAF and DUMB, of IDIOTS or IMBECILES, and of LUNATIC in the WEST-MIDLAND DIVISION and its REGISTRATION COUNTIES and DISTRICTS.

Registration County and District.	Blind.			Deaf and Dumb.	Mentally Deranged.		
	From Birth.	Others.	Total.		Idiots.	Lunatics.	Total.
SHROPSHIRE.							
UDLOW	3	16	19	13	27	1	28
LUN	1	9	10	6	10	2	12
HURCH STRETTON	.	4	4	6	37	40	77
LEOBURY MORTIMER	3	10	13	2	17	1	18
RIDGNORTH	4	21	25	7	21	.	21
HIFNAL	.	5	5	5	26	1	27
IADELEY	3	36	36	20	38	2	40
TCHAM	7	49	56	20	104	473	577
SWESTRY	1	28	29	11	39	4	43
LLESMERE	.	7	7	10	22	1	23
VEM	.	13	13	3	15	1	16
WHITCHURCH	1	12	13	4	21	3	24
MARKET DRAYTON	1	13	14	10	29	1	30
WELLINGTON	1	22	23	3	28	6	34
NEWPORT	4	15	19	10	26	2	28
STAFFORDSHIRE.							
STAFFORD	3	23	26	12	56	781	837
STONE	2	14	16	17	28	3	31
NEWCASTLE-UNDER-LYME	4	19	23	11	26	2	28
WOLSTANTON	5	39	44	32	44	7	51
STOKE-UPON-TRENT	4	81	85	60	131	10	141
LEEK	3	19	22	16	46	5	51
CHEADLE	3	22	25	16	33	5	38
UTTOXETER	.	13	13	4	21	4	25
BURTON-UPON-TRENT	2	43	45	34	115	331	446
TAMWORTH	1	11	12	9	16	3	19
LICHFIELD	3	27	30	18	77	496	573
CANNOCK	1	15	16	20	40	3	43
WOLVERHAMPTON	13	132	145	71	164	14	178
WALSALL	2	65	67	30	61	8	69
WEST BROMWICH	9	88	97	56	147	6	153
DUDLEY	7	149	156	73	167	85	252
26 WORCESTERSHIRE.							
375 STOURBRIDGE	2	59	61	54	94	28	122
376 KIDDERMINSTER	3	42	45	14	41	4	45
377 TENBURY	.	10	10	1	13	1	14
378 MARTLEY	9	10	19	9	27	1	28
379 WORCESTER	2	51	53	14	28	.	28
380 UPTON-ON-SEVERN	2	25	27	18	121	671	792
381 EVESHAM	.	15	15	8	15	7	22
382 PERSHORE	.	20	20	7	22	.	22
383 DROITWICH	1	15	16	19	19	4	23
384 BROMSGROVE	2	26	28	16	37	2	39
385 KINGS NORTON	6	115	121	141	69	7	76
27 WARWICKSHIRE.							
386 BIRMINGHAM	27	192	219	148	487	673	1160
387 ASTON	10	76	86	85	153	12	165
388 MERIDEN	2	4	6	8	14	1	15
389 ATHERSTONE	.	8	8	6	24	1	25
390 NUNEATON	.	9	9	8	14	.	14
391 FOLESHILL	3	20	23	17	26	1	27
392 COVENTRY	4	44	48	20	56	4	60
393 RUGBY	4	28	32	19	23	2	25
394 SOLIHULL	2	14	16	16	58	2	60
395 WARWICK	3	44	47	33	161	539	700
396 STRATFORD-ON-AVON	3	23	26	6	18	30	48
397 ALCESTER	4	12	16	3	30	7	37
398 SHIPSTON-ON-STOUR	2	14	16	7	26	.	26
399 SOUTHAM	.	16	16	6	17	2	19

AGES,

CONDITION AS TO MARRIAGE, OCCUPATIONS, AND BIRTH-PLACES OF THE PEOPLE:

WITH THE

NUMBERS AND AGES OF THE BLIND, DEAF AND DUMB, IDIOTS OR IMBECILES, AND LUNATICS.

DIVISION VII.—NORTH-MIDLAND COUNTIES:

LEICESTERSHIRE,
RUTLANDSHIRE,
LINCOLNSHIRE,
NOTTINGHAMSHIRE,
DERBYSHIRE.

TABLES IN DIVISION VII.—NORTH-MIDLAND COUNTIES.

AGES.

CONDITION AS TO MARRIAGE.

OCCUPATIONS.

BIRTH-PLACES.

THE BLIND, DEAF AND DUMB, IDIOTS OR IMBECILES, AND LUNATICS.

AGES.

DIVISION VII.—NORTH MIDLAND COUNTIES.

Table 1.—Ages of Males and Females in the North-Midland Division and its Registration Counties.

Registration County.	All Ages. Persons.	All Ages. Males and Females.	Under 5* Years.	5–	10–	15–	20–	25–	30–	35–	40–	45–	50–	55–	60–	65–	70–	75–	80–	85–	90–	95–
I.—NORTH-MIDLAND COUNTIES	1637865	M. 810473	114511	100871	88344	81092	70131	61010	51160	43408	40800	36137	31548	25626	23202	16753	12087	7252	3342	990	179	[illegible]
		F. 827392	115341	102193	88505	78861	73042	62382	55503	46842	42700	37021	32500	27036	24058	17950	12896	7042	3800	1236	201	[illegible]
LEICESTERSHIRE	326641	M. 158763	22629	19886	17354	15602	13458	12066	10181	8652	7865	6883	6204	6064	4601	3199	2287	1400	661	194	34	
		F. 167878	23333	20480	17523	16108	15259	13125	11008	9456	8737	7439	6526	5311	4773	2506	2571	1444	718	253	47	
RUTLANDSHIRE	23037	M. 11518	1490	1373	1393	1251	806	742	605	563	514	535	466	424	408	292	247	150	76	17	2	
		F. 11493	1398	1438	1208	1051	864	771	678	683	462	605	482	448	420	324	245	181	86	23	5	
LINCOLNSHIRE	463061	M. 231710	31127	28374	25737	23530	19464	16217	13817	12022	11585	10293	8892	7858	7646	5618	4150	2511	1224	382	79	
		F. 231351	30980	28565	25761	21555	18774	16025	14821	13148	11870	10631	9109	8077	7613	5581	4246	2738	1467	489	138	1
NOTTINGHAMSHIRE	438642	M. 216371	30332	26761	22755	21108	19324	17158	13872	12198	10895	9355	8305	6581	5728	4116	2908	1884	508	242	40	
		F. 223271	31087	27305	23465	21906	21010	17763	14383	12560	11801	9760	8752	6917	6054	4458	3237	1873	880	286	55	1
DERBYSHIRE	386514	M. 193110	25397	24475	21615	18932	17333	15437	12594	11071	9844	8221	7375	5702	4982	3534	2420	1361	583	155	34	
		F. 193404	28467	24505	20761	19230	17936	14796	12504	10926	9906	8350	7601	6083	5108	3673	2597	1309	656	185	46	

Note.—Registration Counties consist of groups of Registration Districts, which are generally co-extensive with the Poor Law Unions. Those Reg[istration Di]stricts which extend into two or more Counties are included in that Registration County in which the principal town of the District or the greater [po]pulation is located. The boundaries of Registration Counties, therefore, differ more or less from the boundaries of Counties. For such differences in Divi[sions, see] Vol. II., Table 11.

* For the number of Children at each Year of Age under 5, see Table 4.

† Two of those Males were stated to be 101 and one 102 years of age. Three of these Females were stated to be 100, and one 102 years of age.

Table 2.—Ages of Males and Females in Registration Districts.

Registration District.	All Ages. Persons.	All Ages. Males and Females.	Under 5* Years.	5–	10–	15–	20–	25–	30–	35–	40–	45–	50–	55–	60–	65–	70–	75–	80–	85–	90–	95–
28. LEICESTERSHIRE.																						
0 LUTTERWORTH	13356	M. 6558	782	770	732	682	478	360	324	397	294	326	333	321	315	217	171	85	46	16	.	
		F. 6798	736	774	692	550	484	436	408	370	372	330	352	368	297	225	172	93	49	23	9	
1 MARKET HARBOROUGH	16196	M. 7949	1064	902	872	744	655	527	445	415	430	302	319	317	273	208	176	109	40	13	6	
		F. 8247	1063	985	864	769	705	587	530	454	462	409	343	366	270	211	175	95	50	26	6	
2 BILLESDON	10073	M. 5146	636	596	484	464	461	426	357	308	290	232	243	274	149	108	75	52	23	8	1	
		F. 4927	642	574	557	455	437	385	355	282	271	241	220	183	164	89	85	48	20	7	2	
3 BLABY	21853	M. 10847	1600	1392	1183	1108	905	803	674	623	549	413	364	335	297	230	162	99	35	17	3	
		F. 11006	1712	1381	1100	927	957	836	784	651	560	421	393	349	262	243	169	95	43	18	2	
4 HINCKLEY	17402	M. 8357	1196	1083	954	798	927	855	528	397	391	338	364	312	281	210	160	100	44	17	2	
		F. 9045	1339	1122	976	851	799	847	545	427	445	417	360	319	274	191	151	93	54	15	2	
5 MARKET BOSWORTH	14611	M. 7398	1150	940	810	707	618	498	420	352	334	311	300	265	256	174	133	82	47	10	3	
		F. 7213	1064	585	779	687	554	503	436	353	371	310	307	240	243	206	133	93	55	14	.	
6 ASHBY-DE-LA-ZOUCH	33334	M. 17008	2546	2212	1929	1774	1387	1257	1029	845	820	702	664	534	460	361	233	148	72	21	3	
		F. 16326	2500	2271	1885	1454	1289	1201	973	835	904	730	610	530	462	356	254	122	56	23	4	
7 LOUGHBOROUGH	27883	M. 13494	1914	1685	1586	1380	1076	945	795	682	633	591	677	439	403	301	238	145	70	21	4	
		F. 14389	1982	1741	1549	1464	1274	1024	804	769	733	665	525	502	420	326	240	134	74	23	3	
8 BARROW UPON SOAR	28865	M. 14018	2118	1858	1680	1398	1043	940	830	763	684	594	534	439	415	275	210	141	34	17	1	
		F. 14847	2202	1975	1622	1311	1212	1070	902	874	777	671	576	486	496	294	224	142	64	31	7	
9 LEICESTER	122376	M. 57720	8656	7219	6091	5746	5457	4973	4153	3390	2922	2456	2017	1516	1367	880	661	259	139	35	0	
		F. 64656	8734	7487	6485	6042	6024	5857	4551	3557	3306	2696	2321	1833	1573	1096	788	402	167	55	6	
0 MELTON MOWBRAY	20492	M. 10268	1341	1162	1087	975	827	765	621	564	516	480	409	373	381	265	185	140	71	10	3	
		F. 10224	1331	1183	1074	863	884	758	651	518	536	452	454	465	366	268	196	127	66	18	6	
29. RUTLANDSHIRE.																						
1 OAKHAM	10978	M. 5441	682	665	612	544	440	346	298	277	305	269	220	200	196	146	121	73	37	8	1	
		F. 5537	663	721	591	502	436	362	303	324	306	302	236	194	204	142	108	70	42	10	2	
2 UPPINGHAM	12029	M. 6078	774	709	781	706	445	387	313	288	308	288	246	224	213	146	120	83	39	8	1	
		F. 5951	715	717	614	549	457	412	375	335	297	303	247	254	216	182	137	81	43	13	3	

Note.—The Registration Districts of Division VII. are co-extensive with the Poor Law Unions of the same name, with the following exception:—The [Di]strict (442) comprises the two Poor Law Unions of Glossop and Hayfield.
[F]or the Parishes comprised in each Registration District, see Vol. II., Division VII., Table 4.
[T]he Districts are arranged topographically under the Registration Counties, and are numbered consecutively, commencing with the Metropolitan [Di]vision 1.
* For the Number of Children at each Year of Age under 5, see Table 5.

Table 2 *continued.*—AGES of MALES and FEMALES in REGISTRATION DISTRICTS.

REGISTRATION DISTRICT.	ALL AGES. Persons.		ALL AGES. Males and Females.	Under 5 Years.	5–	10–	15–	20–	25–	30–	35–	40–	45–	50–	55–	60–	65–	70–	75–	80–	85–	90–	95–	100 and upwards.
30. LINCOLNSHIRE.																								
13 STAMFORD	18344	M.	8891	1134	1099	1020	957	719	577	538	488	469	402	359	262	277	247	191	97	46	11	5	2	.
		F.	9453	1117	1102	1036	894	855	646	598	531	510	480	373	314	301	266	212	134	60	20	9	2	.
14 BOURN	18918	M.	9401	1274	1232	1076	941	642	578	479	488	480	451	366	302	350	287	194	119	56	23	4	.	.
		F.	9517	1234	1230	1088	832	669	614	543	509	485	442	400	350	337	301	188	122	88	31	8	.	.
15 SPALDING	22961	M.	11443	1524	1457	1401	1193	861	694	655	584	547	528	403	419	414	353	228	148	75	16	3	.	.
		F.	11518	1475	1448	1230	1043	858	723	628	688	608	524	465	411	448	362	254	145	97	23	12	1	.
16 HOLBEACH	19249	M.	9600	1319	1309	1118	932	637	575	551	552	474	423	337	324	381	270	190	128	77	12	9	.	.
		F.	9649	1400	1257	1144	807	670	602	598	515	517	400	363	351	330	270	175	133	69	17	5	.	.
17 BOSTON	39416	M.	19261	2466	2446	2273	1887	1599	1210	1131	1066	994	850	734	699	693	535	448	246	134	28	18	.	.
		F.	20140	2542	2429	2167	1911	1605	1306	1179	1144	1068	917	798	709	736	616	438	296	109	54	12	1	1
18 SLEAFORD	25720	M.	12971	1654	1650	1476	1394	1065	837	694	706	654	569	548	478	435	360	257	148	61	27	6	.	.
		F.	12749	1677	1607	1531	1166	960	864	659	720	623	615	511	502	438	358	236	158	79	35	9	1	.
19 GRANTHAM	33679	M.	16755	2314	2068	1850	1672	1377	1238	966	936	841	736	665	603	563	375	291	159	70	29	3	.	.
		F.	16924	2237	2040	1909	1513	1463	1205	1019	940	828	772	727	605	542	433	290	196	87	32	8	.	.
20 LINCOLN	64512	M.	32273	4360	3882	3446	3160	2617	2510	2146	2032	1872	1417	1260	984	969	668	458	262	123	37	3	1	.
		F.	32239	4400	4009	3478	3069	2695	2425	2136	1978	1703	1418	1239	1040	1025	702	523	303	157	34	8	2	1
21 HORNCASTLE	21512	M.	10934	1300	1308	1195	1128	753	687	660	557	512	486	464	423	406	334	251	149	79	23	8	.	.
		F.	10578	1331	1254	1231	1040	866	707	674	590	540	580	424	408	381	319	218	170	76	26	9	2	.
22 SPILSBY	27887	M.	13919	1763	1758	1698	1455	952	823	736	724	656	684	594	532	524	353	284	175	93	34	3	1	.
		F.	13968	1743	1660	1507	1305	1019	830	818	786	736	719	587	535	541	419	290	212	103	50	16	1	.
23 LOUTH	33852	M.	16660	2238	2033	1953	1628	1274	996	879	895	856	769	722	615	602	428	312	230	93	32	3	.	.
		F.	17192	2074	2056	1992	1658	1367	1115	983	936	947	874	744	674	550	475	345	228	141	51	14	3	1
24 CAISTOR	66980	M.	34750	4749	3909	3492	4169	3581	2930	2364	1954	1750	1455	1183	994	862	573	424	245	116	31	8	.	.
		F.	32230	4717	4929	3454	3110	2867	2564	2162	1533	1650	1375	1162	914	844	603	405	256	133	47	8	.	.
25 GLANFORD BRIGG	40170	M.	20120	2924	2599	2251	1874	1643	1386	1204	1104	997	836	780	697	641	446	353	232	110	42	5	.	.
		F.	20050	2881	2533	2212	1858	1581	1426	1191	[illegible]	[illegible]	963	827	602	617	401	366	245	134	28	12	3	.
26 GAINSBOROUGH	28948	M.	14063	2097	1862	1516	1457	1389	1176	914	847	747	615	587	491	400	356	284	167	91	35	2	1	.
		F.	14885	2165	1841	1613	1334	1244	1104	898	844	707	618	[illegible]	516	474	395	320	180	92	32	8	.	.
31. NOTTINGHAMSHIRE.																								
27 EAST RETFORD	23271	M.	11429	1604	1347	1182	1176	882	737	644	600	554	522	522	415	411	304	234	168	83	30	5	.	.
		F.	11842	1501	1437	1283	1097	979	830	703	644	641	541	499	434	401	330	245	150	90	27	4	.	.
28 WORKSOP	28522	M.	14453	2139	1860	1699	1356	1202	1104	940	828	727	644	562	451	382	302	174	112	55	14	1	.	.
		F.	14069	2268	2019	1548	1154	1070	979	909	763	767	544	489	461	362	276	245	127	63	29	3	2	.
29 MANSFIELD	44058	M.	23005	3455	3074	2519	2277	1913	1802	1458	1306	1127	909	855	666	615	419	302	200	73	26	2	.	.
		F.	21053	3498	3053	2397	1988	1886	1581	1323	1196	1102	898	853	617	608	429	278	170	65	32	6	.	.
30 BASFORD	116040	M.	56098	9300	8096	6456	5880	5481	4982	3851	3270	2871	2308	2116	1979	1308	970	714	428	175	39	14	2	1
		F.	59942	9830	8058	6463	4971	5014	4489	3522	3124	2701	2214	2029	1899	1328	926	656	376	148	45	9	2	.
31 NOTTINGHAM	159263	M.	74144	10001	8469	7385	7238	7264	6808	5341	4603	4059	3440	3003	2107	1770	1131	835	459	177	55	6	.	1
		F.	85119	10216	8709	8117	[illegible]	9458	7754	5965	5204	4657	3903	3432	2475	2080	1317	1060	560	245	66	12	2	.
32 SOUTHWELL	20401	M.	9916	1226	1211	1057	917	726	612	496	496	490	461	456	440	407	365	255	172	95	31	3	1	.
		F.	10485	1268	1187	1102	945	768	647	645	566	503	490	434	442	445	348	262	176	93	43	8	2	.
33 NEWARK	30616	M.	15114	2014	1859	1712	1557	1309	986	847	792	726	681	645	545	465	405	285	164	93	29	6	1	.
		F.	15502	2082	1837	1648	1463	1313	1027	906	820	785	718	643	502	562	440	307	192	107	37	7	2	.
34 BINGHAM	14721	M.	7312	[illegible]	877	842	704	[illegible]	432	395	345	303	340	346	281	279	214	169	133	55	18	3	1	.
		F.	7409	923	875	772	640	597	487	410	373	415	362	350	329	262	222	183	116	69	17	6	1	.
32. DERBYSHIRE.																								
35 SHARDLOW	44673	M.	22207	3236	2782	2505	2261	2047	1792	1394	1269	994	904	724	663	569	418	345	212	92	31	5	.	.
		F.	22466	3384	2845	2413	2109	1933	1675	1486	1108	1106	950	662	703	626	498	369	208	107	25	9	2	.
36 DERBY	78631	M.	38681	5647	4721	3923	3640	3734	2683	2947	2467	2056	1636	1365	900	816	552	323	175	80	21	3	.	.
		F.	39950	5735	4920	4036	3939	3857	3383	2771	2382	2049	1757	1481	1146	964	668	453	232	102	28	10	.	.
37 BELPER	58184	M.	29356	4362	3820	3312	2945	2392	2069	1791	[illegible]	[illegible]	1287	1210	959	840	642	444	271	119	25	6	1	.
		F.	28828	4292	3776	3279	2622	2486	1985	1704	1625	1431	1298	1183	923	827	602	461	260	116	36	10	.	.
38 ASHBORNE	19985	M.	9750	1319	1190	1085	1019	766	697	530	482	435	448	441	369	341	299	199	123	56	10	4	1	.
		F.	10235	1289	1242	1086	1008	849	730	563	577	408	470	402	408	366	288	231	130	65	22	5	.	.
39 CHESTERFIELD	98741	M.	51723	8269	7008	5609	4458	4600	4281	3445	2831	2564	2106	1847	1369	1095	744	457	250	95	34	2	2	.
		F.	47018	8204	6920	5331	4024	3639	3501	3020	2551	2272	1927	1635	1265	1046	714	472	257	106	40	3	.	1
40 BAKEWELL	30522	M.	14909	1635	1777	1629	1588	1300	1059	898	846	755	645	664	550	513	344	287	159	72	18	2	.	.
		F.	15613	1967	1819	1584	1561	1431	1123	1090	870	860	736	671	631	525	370	273	142	85	29	5	.	.
41 CHAPEL-EN-LE-FRITH	19484	M.	9492	1256	1140	1033	949	884	765	577	540	520	435	409	294	266	189	126	65	36	8	.	.	.
		F.	9992	1263	1138	1052	1096	984	818	602	553	502	474	404	307	274	178	113	52	33	7	2	.	.
42 HAYFIELD	36284	M.	16983	2238	2015	1859	1762	1550	1251	1003	984	822	778	716	584	466	351	245	96	33	8	2	.	.
		F.	19301	2335	2145	1971	1997	1837	1576	1297	1162	1108	954	863	637	371	360	235	122	41	13	2	.	.

Table 3.—AGES of MALES and FEMALES in REGISTRATION SUB-DISTRICTS.

REGISTRATION SUB-DISTRICT.	ALL AGES. Persons.	Males and Females.	Under 5 Years.	5–	10–	15–	20–	25–	30–	35–	40–	45–	50–	55–	60–	65–	70–	75–	80–	85–	90–	95–
LEICESTER-SHIRE.																						
LUTTERWORTH.																						
TTERWORTH. (W.)	13356	M. - 6558	782	759	732	682	478	390	384	297	394	326	338	321	315	217	171	86	46	16	.	.
		F. - 6798	798	776	682	561	484	436	408	376	372	380	352	305	297	223	172	93	49	23	9	2
1 MARKET HARBOROUGH.																						
RKET HARBOROUGH. (W.)	16196	M. - 7949	1064	992	872	741	635	527	443	415	430	362	319	317	276	208	176	109	40	13	6	.
		F. - 8247	1098	985	884	763	718	587	530	451	409	400	341	330	270	211	175	83	50	20	6	.
402 BILLESDON.																						
LLESDON. (W. L.)	10073	M. - 5146	636	596	494	461	461	426	357	308	209	232	243	214	140	108	75	52	23	8	1	.
		F. - 4927	642	571	507	443	487	335	335	282	281	241	220	163	164	89	95	43	20	7	2	.
403 BLABY.																						
IGSTON (B.)	13885	M. - 6849	1065	872	706	794	595	533	440	418	333	268	224	184	164	142	93	48	19	6	3	.
		F. - 7036	1105	880	684	671	668	575	406	461	326	258	235	191	178	152	112	54	20	9	1	.
NDERBY. (W. H.)	7908	M. - 3938	595	508	437	391	393	270	234	265	297	147	160	171	133	88	57	51	25	11	.	.
		F. - 3970	607	501	416	316	328	294	288	200	204	166	158	158	124	91	57	39	23	9	1	.
404 HINCKLEY.																						
URBAGE	4941	M. - 2467	341	337	282	211	192	184	156	117	114	108	98	92	95	68	53	27	10	2	.	.
		F. - 2474	357	304	259	203	198	177	170	122	118	117	114	99	83	54	46	29	22	4	1	.
INCKLEY. (W.)	8869	M. - 4026	595	514	456	391	240	268	283	183	189	177	191	159	112	84	69	47	30	10	2	.
		F. - 4843	680	576	475	482	440	350	268	208	235	214	177	159	133	98	82	40	21	10	1	.
ARL SHILTON	3792	M. - 1864	260	232	216	188	155	133	89	97	88	71	75	61	74	55	29	26	8	5	.	.
		F. - 1928	233	243	246	160	161	120	105	97	92	86	69	70	58	30	26	15	11	1	.	.
405 MARKET BOSWORTH.																						
ARKET BOSWORTH. (W.)	6349	M. - 3196	408	407	372	202	227	191	158	150	126	152	145	131	138	91	68	40	25	5	2	.
		F. - 3146	408	404	307	251	267	214	169	150	162	144	155	133	128	107	58	56	27	12	.	.
BSTOCK (R.)	8269	M. - 4202	668	533	438	415	371	294	262	221	209	189	155	134	118	83	70	42	22	5	1	.
		F. - 4067	662	581	472	286	387	280	267	233	209	175	152	127	115	99	75	37	28	2	.	.
406 ASHBY-DE-LA-ZOUCH.																						
MEASHAM	3887	M. - 1964	272	255	230	190	129	135	105	94	103	92	96	62	69	55	42	19	7	2	.	.
		F. - 1923	282	252	191	172	130	135	110	114	109	90	91	78	87	53	39	18	11	2	1	.
HARTSHORN	7061	M. - 3609	580	468	385	375	303	252	238	186	182	157	128	115	104	75	52	34	17	4	3	.
		F. - 3452	549	409	382	261	252	230	193	179	184	155	138	92	120	81	53	29	11	7	2	.
ASHBY-DE-LA-ZOUCH. (W.)	9024	M. - 4413	650	547	473	435	362	378	237	220	203	187	175	143	124	99	72	42	22	6	.	.
		F. - 4611	680	628	529	449	399	389	275	219	246	197	158	187	132	101	78	28	14	4	1	.
WHITWICK (R.)	13562	M. - 7022	1083	925	883	769	593	438	421	343	332	208	260	214	181	182	67	47	20	9	2	.
		F. - 6540	1079	899	785	572	518	457	393	332	365	288	228	203	153	120	93	47	30	10	.	.
7 LOUGHBOROUGH.																						
LOUGHBOROUGH. (W.H.)	22194	M. - 10698	1571	1338	1254	1116	889	772	682	557	494	467	439	313	292	215	164	100	47	17	2	.
		F. - 11496	1613	1401	1241	1324	1050	840	717	615	586	518	451	376	325	227	158	88	56	16	1	.
LEAKE	5683	M. - 2800	343	349	332	273	187	173	133	120	139	134	147	120	111	86	78	45	23	4	2	.
		F. - 2883	360	340	308	230	224	175	177	145	148	148	141	126	95	99	82	46	18	7	3	.
408 BARROW UPON SOAR.																						
BARROW UPON SOAR	5757	M. - 2868	415	377	306	272	215	197	172	146	184	118	118	84	88	61	49	38	17	2	.	.
		F. - 2889	431	387	306	217	215	203	148	163	140	125	130	108	94	66	51	34	17	4	3	.
QUORNDON (H.)	5778	M. - 2801	438	395	330	280	204	197	132	152	188	126	108	102	82	56	44	26	12	4	1	.
		F. - 2977	409	384	329	271	240	213	167	179	153	152	116	103	90	62	48	32	18	11	.	.
ROTHLEY. (W.)	11304	M. - 5488	884	728	636	561	429	378	344	312	296	211	187	145	141	94	72	48	20	4	.	.
		F. - 5816	981	771	652	512	498	446	398	355	316	248	201	162	135	106	68	39	10	8	3	.
SYSTON	6026	M. - 2861	414	360	354	285	185	178	167	154	121	139	121	107	107	61	45	31	15	7	.	.
		F. - 3165	431	433	341	311	259	194	196	179	162	149	120	116	87	90	57	37	15	8	8	.
409 LEICESTER.																						
EAST LEICESTER. (W.)	79305	M. - 37462	5635	4724	3918	3904	3478	3315	2745	2318	1869	1608	1259	947	802	534	363	186	90	24	3	.
		F. - 41843	5811	4874	4142	4306	4158	3670	2914	2499	2155	1721	1464	1113	990	658	472	246	104	38	5	.
WEST LEICESTER. (H. L. P.)	43571	M. - 20258	2901	2468	2173	2082	1979	1695	1408	1168	1053	863	738	568	495	328	198	113	49	11	3	.
		F. - 23313	2923	2613	2343	2635	2406	1981	1637	1383	1204	977	867	730	583	430	286	160	83	22	1	.
MELTON MOWBRAY.																						
SOMERBY	3890	M. - 1923	241	237	202	181	164	142	112	106	95	93	82	70	62	57	42	23	14	4	.	.
		F. - 1967	247	246	133	159	178	139	122	104	106	103	78	81	62	53	43	29	13	8	1	.
MELTON MOWBRAY. (W.)	7695	M. - 3892	551	431	378	367	347	318	265	240	194	178	135	127	128	84	55	48	23	6	1	.
		F. - 3803	512	441	413	312	351	317	262	221	209	170	153	111	131	77	60	37	21	5	.	.
CLAWSON	5292	M. - 2658	325	281	292	254	219	196	145	125	134	117	168	109	108	68	48	36	22	6	2	.
		F. - 2634	320	282	280	241	217	166	174	127	129	139	132	125	99	79	58	41	22	9	3	.
WALTHAM	3615	M. - 1795	218	203	215	167	127	104	99	99	98	92	84	74	82	56	40	33	12	3	.	.
		F. - 1820	252	214	198	150	128	114	93	106	92	80	91	88	74	39	37	29	10	3	2	.
29 RUTLAND-SHIRE.																						
411 OAKHAM.																						
OAKHAM (W.)	10078	M. - 5441	682	686	612	544	446	343	292	277	305	269	220	200	195	146	121	73	37	9	1	.
		F. - 5537	683	721	591	502	436	362	303	324	305	302	235	194	204	142	108	70	42	10	2	.

Note.—For the Parishes comprised in each Registration Sub-district, *see* Vol. II., Division VII., Table 4.
(W.) denotes that a Workhouse and (WS.) that a Workhouse School belonging to the District is situated within the Sub-district, (w.) denotes a W d (ws.) a Workhouse School not belonging to the District, (H.) a Hospital or Infirmary, (L.) a Lunatic Asylum, (P.) a Prison or Convict Establish certified Reformatory or Industrial School, (B.) Barracks, &c. (S.) H.M. Ships. A figure appended to any of these letters denotes the number of Instit cular class situated within the Sub-district. The names of the Institutions thus indicated, and the number of inmates enumerated therein, will be found Division VII., Table 6.

Table 3 *continued*.—Ages of Males and Females in Registration Sub-Districts.

Registration Sub-District.	All Ages. Persons.		All Ages. Males and Females.	Under 5 Years.	5–	10–	15–	20–	25–	30–	35–	40–	45–	50–	55–	60–	65–	70–	75–	80–	85–	90–	95–
29 RUTLANDSHIRE—*cont.*																							
412 UPPINGHAM.																							
1 Uppingham. (W.)	5389	M.	2773	310	291	422	443	203	167	128	120	140	116	101	95	83	58	54	35	21	5	1	.
		F.	2616	281	285	277	276	223	167	158	147	137	148	107	112	93	81	59	35	24	7	1	.
2 Great Easton	3058	M.	1491	213	194	164	139	113	95	96	75	39	68	60	52	54	30	29	20	9	3	.	.
		F.	1567	202	216	140	123	129	115	100	82	78	77	64	60	60	46	31	23	7	2	1	.
3 Barrowden	3582	M.	1814	251	227	195	153	133	135	89	93	80	82	85	77	76	58	43	28	9	.	.	.
		F.	1768	232	216	188	144	105	130	117	106	83	80	74	82	63	61	47	23	12	4	1	1
30 LINCOLNSHIRE.																							
413 STAMFORD.																							
1 Stamford. (W.H.)	13273	M.	6373	870	791	740	655	509	414	396	362	349	274	248	182	191	179	136	73	37	6	5	2
		F.	6900	801	789	745	665	685	485	420	413	382	341	257	220	214	196	156	100	43	12	8	2
2 Barnack	5071	M.	2518	304	299	280	302	210	163	142	126	120	128	116	81	86	68	65	24	9	5	.	.
		F.	2553	316	313	296	329	200	153	160	120	128	139	116	94	87	70	62	34	17	8	6	.
414 BOURN.																							
1 Corby	3048	M.	1543	218	188	190	162	108	92	98	76	84	79	64	63	46	46	22	12	7	8	2	.
		F.	1505	223	232	158	120	100	89	83	56	78	70	65	53	50	36	39	21	15	4	.	.
2 Aslackby	4533	M.	2256	299	304	253	217	157	139	118	100	115	121	94	88	88	71	44	27	13	4	.	.
		F.	2277	293	302	271	192	172	158	154	121	104	120	85	84	86	68	29	31	20	7	3	.
3 Bourn. (W.)	7121	M.	3583	482	477	397	346	262	235	174	195	189	157	135	121	131	111	84	50	26	9	2	.
		F.	3538	432	412	428	344	269	288	196	205	193	148	140	125	137	120	69	46	27	10	1	.
4 Deeping	4218	M.	2019	254	263	236	216	117	121	99	114	92	94	82	93	90	59	44	30	10	5	.	.
		F.	2199	280	294	231	196	128	139	130	97	110	104	101	94	85	79	60	25	26	10	4	.
415 SPALDING.																							
1 Pinchbeck	3146	M.	1612	209	197	192	183	117	97	77	87	78	92	67	50	52	59	24	20	7	3	1	.
		F.	1534	218	228	187	117	93	79	88	89	93	79	63	50	67	41	19	10	13	2	.	.
2 Donington	2566	M.	1279	158	187	158	128	82	66	64	61	69	61	42	37	81	53	22	17	12	1	.	.
		F.	1287	178	168	164	108	71	69	83	70	75	46	33	59	56	44	31	19	10	3	1	.
3 Gosberton	3045	M.	1544	205	178	222	174	90	98	88	78	62	81	52	57	41	45	35	25	14	3	1	.
		F.	1501	207	214	177	118	102	90	74	93	74	54	68	46	50	49	41	29	11	1	3	.
4 Spalding. (W.H.P.)	9746	M.	4659	606	593	525	460	315	284	307	240	213	192	173	198	187	138	102	72	37	7	1	.
		F.	5087	360	348	547	517	434	551	293	303	257	233	227	193	209	172	103	68	49	16	7	1
5 Moulton	3094	M.	1577	236	218	213	161	105	90	75	99	95	70	47	52	62	51	29	9	4	2	.	.
		F.	1517	211	216	178	133	101	83	79	101	57	65	54	44	57	46	34	13	11	1	1	.
6 Deeping St. Nicholas	1364	M.	772	116	89	91	87	92	59	44	40	30	32	22	25	21	12	6	5	1	.	.	.
		F.	592	98	84	77	50	52	40	31	40	22	27	20	19	10	13	6	.	3	.	.	.
416 HOLBEACH.																							
1 Gedney Hill	2742	M.	1371	197	184	148	122	78	93	79	77	63	69	48	51	56	47	32	14	7	4	4	.
		F.	1371	199	188	159	180	99	88	83	77	78	57	55	58	52	36	23	10	6	4	1	.
2 Long Sutton	8805	M.	4327	635	553	482	429	312	262	255	252	225	187	138	147	178	104	76	52	36	6	3	.
		F.	4478	656	589	546	396	315	296	267	227	244	162	160	159	162	125	87	67	27	8	3	.
3 Holbeach. (W.)	7702	M.	3911	487	501	458	382	240	220	217	233	186	167	151	126	152	119	82	62	36	2	2	.
		F.	3791	551	480	439	323	256	224	248	211	196	181	148	139	136	115	65	47	37	5	1	.
417 BOSTON.																							
1 Kirton in Holland	5403	M.	2723	380	377	346	289	168	141	146	146	135	118	104	103	101	84	55	40	19	2	1	.
		F.	2680	369	339	312	239	265	166	143	156	136	124	106	104	104	80	57	20	17	4	.	.
2 Bennington	6974	M.	3629	471	458	410	334	276	235	208	203	186	168	133	135	131	117	81	46	35	4	5	.
		F.	3345	457	424	356	262	237	197	180	176	179	164	145	134	134	121	79	51	28	10	2	.
3 Sibsey	3668	M.	1910	248	226	224	175	161	129	110	98	116	82	71	89	65	53	35	22	11	2	2	.
		F.	1758	221	237	105	159	134	100	103	111	92	93	73	92	70	42	31	22	13	4	.	.
4 Boston. (W.H.)	18345	M.	8460	1077	1055	1007	826	622	554	530	488	410	373	320	286	320	199	211	98	58	16	10	.
		F.	9885	1160	1161	998	1041	677	694	622	561	528	430	380	362	357	286	223	163	81	30	10	1
5 Swineshead	5020	M.	2539	330	333	287	272	178	151	137	121	149	109	106	95	78	82	60	40	11	4	1	.
		F.	2481	335	329	305	219	152	140	142	140	131	110	94	107	71	88	48	34	21	6	.	.
418 SLEAFORD.																							
1 Billinghay	5574	M.	2802	359	364	328	321	219	164	129	168	157	129	103	97	90	64	63	42	14	8	1	.
		F.	2772	381	389	342	240	198	169	134	170	125	134	107	93	81	99	51	32	16	3	2	.
2 Sleaford. (W.)	9217	M.	4562	615	544	479	485	389	329	268	265	221	194	191	160	129	123	76	42	22	12	4	.
		F.	4655	619	670	524	445	365	346	250	266	222	222	169	197	153	117	91	54	28	19	4	1
3 Leadenham	3566	M.	1826	226	233	223	194	132	106	86	96	95	81	82	73	81	73	36	25	7	5	.	.
		F.	1740	248	215	198	134	139	118	84	119	89	88	77	74	62	49	31	31	5	2	3	.
4 Heckington	4563	M.	2296	289	311	294	236	175	139	118	122	112	96	98	73	79	50	49	25	12	4	.	.
		F.	2278	291	282	306	226	177	142	121	112	125	103	96	74	79	52	89	32	18	7	1	.
5 Aswarby	3000	M.	1491	170	108	152	162	139	99	79	65	69	69	74	70	73	41	32	19	6	8	.	.
		F.	1509	138	181	161	113	92	89	65	62	71	68	72	64	63	41	24	10	12	4	.	.
419 GRANTHAM.																							
1 Colsterworth	5648	M.	2851	306	374	380	281	200	171	151	148	154	118	112	109	121	68	63	25	12	9	.	.
		F.	2797	396	356	338	212	185	178	188	162	130	110	122	115	94	79	59	43	17	5	2	.
2 Denton	6865	M.	3537	429	404	390	312	264	226	168	151	158	175	156	137	121	90	78	40	23	9	2	.
		F.	3328	393	405	363	279	287	196	171	175	155	201	175	151	126	101	86	54	27	3	.	.
3 Grantham. (W.H.B.)	21386	M.	10587	1487	1290	1131	1079	904	841	647	639	629	443	397	366	321	217	155	84	35	11	1	.
		F.	10799	1445	1279	1208	1102	901	838	669	604	532	461	430	339	322	253	165	99	43	24	6	.
420 LINCOLN.																							
1 Lincoln, South-West	13827	M.	7222	860	828	824	755	577	488	424	418	418	326	341	257	248	188	129	80	48	13	.	.
		F.	6605	828	888	770	587	455	389	387	398	347	323	277	243	259	177	152	98	55	13	3	1
2 Lincoln Home. (W.H. L^A. P.B.)	42546	M.	20999	2948	2482	2161	1978	1922	1777	1615	1407	1238	910	745	567	534	380	254	131	49	13	2	1
		F.	21547	2978	2540	2236	2108	1687	1774	1530	1346	1136	924	781	657	653	442	387	151	94	18	5	1
3 Lincoln, North-East	8089	M.	4002	548	522	461	432	318	246	207	207	216	181	174	150	127	100	75	51	26	11	1	.
		F.	4087	594	581	472	334	328	262	219	235	220	165	171	140	113	83	84	60	28	3	.	.

Table 3 *continued.*—AGES of MALES and FEMALES in REGISTRATION SUB-DISTRICTS.

EGISTRATION JB-DISTRICT.	All Ages. Persons.		All Ages. Males and Females.	Under 5 Years.	5–	10–	15–	20–	25–	30–	35–	40–	45–	50–	55–	60–	65–	70–	75–	80–	85–	90–	95–
LINCOLN- IRE—*cont.*																							
IORNCASTLE.																							
BY - - -	4088	M. -	2068	263	268	212	238	163	165	117	108	82	91	83	75	66	56	48	27	16	4	2	.
		F. -	1970	235	239	216	229	169	138	123	109	83	95	87	61	60	47	28	23	13	5	1	.
CASTLE. (W.) -	8519	M. -	4094	475	483	404	425	302	249	216	217	217	192	195	160	154	136	92	62	37	9	2	.
		F. -	4425	509	504	488	420	386	255	240	244	232	235	174	157	143	130	80	83	37	11	4	1
BLO - -	3763	M. -	1905	234	249	200	144	100	110	107	110	100	94	80	78	69	6[illegible]	63	25	9	4	5	.
		F. -	1858	246	236	212	164	133	125	105	114	99	88	75	61	68	47	46	22	10	4	1	1
EBSHALL - -	5192	M. -	2617	328	308	299	279	193	167	140	116	118	119	120	108	116	87	80	55	17	8	1	.
		F. -	2575	324	316	314	227	178	131	146	123	126	102	108	99	100	80	65	42	16	5	3	.
22 SPILSBY.																							
CNEY - -	2488	M. -	1306	180	174	190	131	75	77	70	58	69	61	52	39	56	33	30	16	12	4	.	.
		F.	1182	180	133	123	98	64	88	68	56	68	60	46	44	45	36	24	18	15	5	.	.
FLEET - -	5285	M. -	2673	330	344	335	299	184	130	133	152	118	139	117	116	77	81	67	24	18	9	1	.
		F. -	2612	337	327	320	257	169	144	131	138	148	135	112	105	93	74	45	41	12	10	2	.
BY. (W.) - -	7082	M. -	3512	438	451	416	364	230	189	185	178	182	164	166	132	135	104	87	62	28	12	.	1
		F. -	3570	411	422	408	382	277	204	198	217	174	197	150	149	136	132	75	57	30	13	4	1
H - - -	5522	M. -	2771	338	384	305	275	198	199	154	153	125	148	105	101	118	79	42	30	16	3	.	.
		F. -	2751	348	323	311	236	221	173	165	130	158	134	124	112	117	71	30	48	21	10	4	.
RD - - -	7510	M. -	3657	400	435	452	365	275	228	194	180	171	172	164	154	138	96	78	48	19	6	2	.
		F. -	3853	467	455	440	382	297	241	233	219	188	193	135	145	140	106	102	53	25	12	6	.
423 LOUTH.																							
CERN. (H.) -	4412	M. -	2261	318	306	270	210	172	132	123	111	102	102	108	75	80	65	45	26	13	6	2	.
		F.	2151	254	267	234	265	165	139	131	115	115	114	91	83	73	44	38	22	21	10	2	.
H. (W. H.) - -	14763	M. -	6976	909	803	844	732	508	441	369	378	371	335	304	237	261	172	134	110	35	13	.	.
		F. -	7787	864	800	857	803	827	513	438	460	465	394	355	298	231	249	170	115	60	21	5	.
BROOKE - -	4151	M. -	2146	313	282	240	235	183	122	117	119	105	83	88	73	67	48	38	23	15	2	.	.
		F. -	2005	273	245	289	161	166	128	124	103	106	98	84	58	48	42	38	25	13	2	2	1
FLEET - -	5323	M. -	2672	343	327	330	248	201	161	137	146	141	134	124	124	111	75	40	36	11	7	1	.
		F. -	2651	323	329	326	227	208	178	146	116	128	145	114	103	110	81	52	36	19	10	3	.
BY - -	5263	M. -	2665	655	315	323	234	210	140	133	141	137	115	109	106	85	73	55	43	19	5	.	.
		F.	2598	380	335	307	240	201	159	146	137	133	128	100	104	97	89	52	30	28	8	2	2
424 CAISTOR.																							
AT GRIMSBY. (W. H².)	48613	M. -	25551	3611	2800	2375	3166	2871	2391	1870	1502	1299	974	798	830	547	327	202	129	47	10	3	.
		F. -	23062	3585	2945	2374	2225	2232	1884	1658	1363	1171	943	763	594	520	335	231	142	70	24	4	.
TOR. (W.) - -	8793	M. -	4485	549	540	544	488	354	287	227	227	224	224	176	164	151	123	105	52	39	9	2	.
		F. -	4308	554	526	524	416	367	270	230	242	246	190	177	162	140	110	84	48	29	9	4	.
KET RASEN. (H.) -	9498	M. -	4734	689	569	573	506	356	252	207	225	227	253	214	200	164	123	117	64	30	12	3	.
		F. -	4769	598	556	536	489	378	310	274	228	233	243	228	169	184	158	90	66	34	14	.	.
LANFORD BRIGG.																							
IG. (W.)	12243	M. -	6107	858	733	667	609	512	427	361	301	297	260	225	231	224	192	122	75	30	15	3	.
		F.	6136	868	754	636	576	502	450	346	307	295	262	247	258	207	160	135	65	47	13	3	2
TERTON - -	13523	M. -	6906	1066	911	773	621	579	502	452	390	326	253	271	207	177	123	99	72	38	14	.	.
		F.	6617	1024	912	738	605	501	445	414	395	290	298	276	191	100	141	104	74	35	12	4	.
TON - -	14404	M. -	7107	1011	955	811	694	552	457	391	413	374	285	284	259	240	155	132	85	44	18	2	.
		F. -	7297	991	917	808	675	548	531	481	430	395	343	304	228	230	180	136	106	52	13	3	1
GAINSBOROUGH.																							
TON - - -	4022	M. -	1980	243	231	227	195	143	118	91	104	93	94	96	89	82	64	58	29	18	7	1	.
		F. -	2042	241	232	217	175	142	110	116	112	106	101	104	96	77	68	72	40	23	2	2	.
TER - -	4258	M. -	2158	290	230	221	258	184	130	112	120	109	97	83	78	78	68	51	34	14	5	1	.
		F. -	2100	292	263	236	205	158	122	115	132	104	89	89	68	68	64	36	34	20	4	1	.
TERTON - -	3414	M. -	1693	262	292	172	157	137	100	90	103	84	64	67	67	73	40	31	22	8	5	.	.
		F. -	1721	250	240	218	121	136	113	98	89	87	59	74	82	53	55	27	20	13	5	1	.
NSBOROUGH. (W. H.)	12307	M. -	6162	907	695	590	651	562	635	464	303	301	228	189	148	140	99	58	46	15	12	.	1
		F. -	6145	990	746	617	544	576	569	419	334	265	230	200	160	166	118	100	47	23	12	3	.
LINGHAM. (H.) -	3982	M. -	2039	284	239	216	233	181	132	103	82	99	85	58	73	81	53	51	23	24	5	.	.
		F. -	1944	274	233	216	182	157	117	90	107	95	99	82	80	77	43	55	25	14	5	.	.
TON - - -	1967	M. -	933	114	104	92	100	82	54	54	45	51	42	42	38	36	23	17	13	12	1	.	.
		F.	1034	138	127	109	106	73	73	62	50	50	40	53	32	38	27	24	14	9	4	1	.
NOTTING- IAMSHIRE.																							
EAST RETFORD.																							
NGLEY -	3115	M. -	1594	222	201	176	162	127	84	81	78	73	71	63	61	67	40	30	31	18	3	.	.
		F. -	1521	175	194	171	135	113	94	92	79	83	65	74	62	62	39	30	19	16	8	2	.
SBOROUGH. (W.) -	6290	M. -	3165	454	389	327	290	210	200	180	180	159	130	144	119	110	97	74	58	22	10	2	.
		F. -	3125	469	380	351	291	238	209	191	191	168	134	131	113	104	99	68	53	27	8	.	.
RETFORD - -	9560	M. -	4544	665	530	443	495	376	356	271	282	211	218	191	144	142	99	67	44	27	11	2	.
		F. -	5016	669	609	539	493	457	384	308	262	262	219	184	165	144	119	91	54	28	7	2	.
FORD - - -	4306	M. -	2136	263	227	236	229	169	97	112	99	111	103	124	91	92	62	63	35	16	6	1	.
		F.	2170	268	254	222	208	171	143	113	112	108	123	110	94	91	73	47	30	19	4	.	.
28 WORKSOP.																							
KSOP. (W. H.) -	11697	M. -	5830	884	740	650	509	473	466	357	325	301	274	236	196	151	122	65	43	25	7	.	.
		F. -	5867	920	807	636	510	448	423	380	321	307	220	217	198	156	115	117	55	26	11	1	.
LTON - -	3416	M. -	1635	212	213	181	154	119	119	86	98	82	69	73	75	58	44	30	30	5	.	1	.
		F. -	1781	232	209	189	149	158	125	108	92	98	80	63	68	56	49	36	29	9	10	.	1
TON. (H.) - -	5838	M. -	3048	465	408	368	293	239	230	230	176	149	128	106	82	64	59	28	16	8	2	.	.
		F. -	2790	472	441	333	230	197	102	170	153	154	98	87	78	55	63	38	19	8	3	1	.
BURTON - -	7571	M. -	3920	509	495	410	400	371	289	267	229	195	173	147	98	109	77	45	24	17	5	.	.
		F.	3651	640	502	398	265	267	239	240	196	198	148	122	117	95	59	54	24	20	6	1	1

Table 3 *continued*.—AGES of MALES and FEMALES in REGISTRATION SUB-DISTRICTS.

REGISTRATION SUB-DISTRICT.	All Ages. Persons.	Males and Females.	Under 5 Years.	5–	10–	15–	20–	25–	30–	35–	40–	45–	50–	55–	60–	65–	70–	75–	80–	85–	90–	9[5–]
31 NOTTINGHAMSHIRE—*cont.*																						
429 MANSFIELD.																						
1 Warsop. (H.)	3982	M. 2002	275	262	246	204	146	114	107	100	84	83	98	86	60	55	45	26	7	5	.	
		F. 1980	249	246	212	261	170	136	108	95	100	86	95	73	67	54	45	29	9	5	.	
2 Pleasley	3231	M. 1720	234	226	171	196	133	128	105	88	106	78	68	63	43	32	21	14	9	3	.	
		F. 1511	236	232	144	137	108	117	86	81	78	68	62	48	34	32	23	20	6	4	2	
3 Blackwell	9961	M. 5320	896	731	562	542	483	463	370	312	240	204	171	116	99	51	34	29	12	4	1	
		F. 4641	919	798	509	307	366	349	273	255	216	161	180	110	83	51	38	16	8	3	.	
4 Sutton in Ashfield	12957	M. 6752	1042	993	740	623	552	539	427	364	350	307	241	177	140	104	84	48	18	7	1	
		F. 6205	1038	856	734	551	610	439	395	309	340	264	215	150	158	111	68	44	15	6	2	
5 Mansfield. (W.)	13653	M. 6583	815	789	720	638	548	621	417	369	336	270	257	199	241	157	100	74	28	7	.	
		F. 7070	977	857	740	747	688	596	426	466	344	292	274	216	245	168	86	54	28	13	2	
6 Blidworth	1174	M. 628	93	73	75	68	51	47	32	27	29	27	20	24	23	20	8	9	2	.	.	
		F. 546	80	84	58	45	44	34	35	26	29	27	30	20	21	13	8	6	3	1	.	
430 BASFORD.																						
1 Greasley	27188	M. 14236	2283	1936	1563	1434	1291	1141	919	786	685	550	478	378	314	197	151	81	44	6	4	
		F. 12952	2274	2026	1451	971	1025	898	838	703	589	408	462	353	283	201	186	78	35	14	.	
2 Ilkeston	22333	M. 11628	1841	1608	1258	1164	1061	904	734	614	530	451	433	314	249	164	134	81	21	4	2	
		F. 10705	1828	1565	1259	944	811	822	617	576	471	407	390	281	242	170	115	65	25	5	3	
3 Basford. (W.)	23328	M. 11291	1670	1523	1289	1111	991	949	713	621	579	441	398	338	267	216	140	101	30	10	3	
		F. 12037	1688	1441	1324	1286	1206	977	760	658	648	471	433	349	291	198	164	100	26	12	1	
4 Bulwell	21212	M. 11203	1788	1610	1124	1080	1007	1008	798	640	575	398	338	253	188	137	92	48	22	6	1	
		F. 10009	1809	1539	1139	782	863	774	653	602	482	374	312	231	190	119	79	44	22	3	1	
5 Arnold	10301	M. 5212	753	678	518	518	455	385	334	280	220	213	211	203	163	123	86	48	21	4	2	
		F. 5089	811	727	563	445	486	411	266	264	238	204	180	179	153	88	70	32	17	2	1	
6 Carlton	6476	M. 3332	538	399	346	301	331	316	203	160	149	118	134	86	93	52	53	34	23	5	2	
		F. 3144	483	401	329	270	319	272	203	163	132	124	119	106	75	59	36	35	12	5	1	
7 Wilford	6132	M. 3096	434	441	357	269	255	225	150	163	138	140	129	106	94	91	58	33	14	4	.	
		F. 3036	437	391	334	273	252	218	185	168	141	136	133	90	94	82	56	29	11	4	2	
431 NOTTINGHAM.																						
1 Lenton	9346	M. 4344	620	561	445	483	419	360	283	248	233	186	157	109	98	83	48	31	16	5	1	
		F. 5002	677	591	537	559	506	407	315	287	245	193	192	116	105	80	49	29	13	2	2	
2 Radford. (W.)	14346	M. 6851	1006	833	706	683	672	612	456	418	348	322	252	186	164	100	73	34	7	3	1	
		F. 7495	1098	865	742	747	780	620	487	440	301	361	286	207	168	133	87	49	12	3	1	
3 Hyson Green	6608	M. 3131	480	391	344	278	282	308	208	211	144	118	108	81	73	52	22	24	3	2	1	
		F. 3477	545	447	348	338	372	326	239	184	168	140	103	84	75	48	36	14	8	2	.	
4 Sneinton. (L.)	15478	M. 7308	1084	898	744	678	632	690	500	440	395	324	300	207	181	118	60	53	13	6	.	.
		F. 8170	1062	915	807	848	826	706	595	613	477	352	326	221	209	161	103	40	23	4	1	.
5 Sherwood	18620	M. 7882	808	811	787	831	856	712	518	479	446	424	348	247	215	143	120	42	27	5	2	.
		F. 10738	865	865	1002	1527	1452	940	623	664	584	515	467	370	286	213	170	63	37	14	1	.
6 St. Mary	6302	M. 2930	309	339	207	264	246	207	239	200	182	131	116	85	74	49	41	23	6	8	.	
		F. 3372	433	348	304	341	350	278	241	232	195	160	141	103	91	60	45	26	17	4	1	1
7 St. Ann. (W. H. L². P.)	34626	M. 16359	2162	1960	1650	1537	1581	1458	1208	982	989	704	664	459	569	270	216	120	48	13	.	
		F. 18267	2193	1842	1782	1981	1389	1757	1228	1133	968	943	740	539	429	390	228	131	61	18	3	1
8 Byron	19285	M. 9042	1225	1058	909	967	834	781	670	563	481	396	391	288	245	137	103	63	11	5	.	.
		F. 10243	1241	1080	989	1104	1034	856	785	650	595	493	437	326	283	160	128	58	20	5	.	.
9 Exchange	18520	M. 9155	1226	981	840	867	1021	998	744	585	545	397	346	227	210	77	68	22	18	4	.	.
		F. 9365	1207	982	871	1003	1098	920	704	590	538	411	377	243	193	128	102	67	28	6	.	.
10 Castle. (H.)	9331	M. 4389	580	480	419	440	472	445	323	302	206	195	179	115	76	58	40	18	10	4	1	.
		F. 4942	601	500	427	531	584	500	349	289	293	220	215	134	124	73	52	30	13	4	3	.
11 Park. (H³.)	6906	M. 2758	301	277	283	313	300	207	102	174	140	163	142	108	65	65	41	23	13	5	.	.
		F. 4148	291	271	358	645	658	411	203	233	215	197	158	132	117	72	60	39	18	4	.	.
432 SOUTHWELL.																						
1 Southwell. (W.)	11161	M. 5355	678	640	576	484	370	331	254	266	264	241	241	244	228	212	148	86	51	15	1	1
		F. 5806	663	630	600	538	459	372	389	312	311	279	277	242	232	201	161	93	51	29	3	1
2 Kneesal	9200	M. 4571	553	542	481	483	356	301	242	236	235	210	215	196	179	153	107	76	44	16	2	
		F. 4629	608	557	502	412	309	275	286	254	192	211	217	200	212	147	102	83	42	14	5	1
433 NEWARK.																						
1 North Collingham	4886	M. 2411	296	282	300	256	183	131	124	106	101	105	116	114	97	72	54	44	15	6	8	.
		F. 2475	306	274	259	254	204	156	134	118	118	106	131	111	100	78	59	43	18	5	1	.
2 Bassingham	3256	M. 1652	201	186	210	172	152	86	86	66	83	83	69	58	64	66	36	21	15	4	.	.
		F. 1604	193	201	179	157	123	75	96	78	85	71	73	64	84	46	42	17	15	2	1	1
3 Newark. (W. H. B.)	14083	M. 6843	949	840	697	741	666	545	429	407	388	307	269	217	153	124	88	47	23	6	1	1
		F. 7240	1027	844	776	729	712	551	429	421	370	332	250	209	194	187	108	70	36	11	3	1
4 Bennington	4339	M. 2112	289	275	239	186	147	111	111	116	110	97	91	71	85	71	68	25	18	8	1	.
		F. 2227	309	273	221	164	176	143	119	110	116	106	101	93	94	69	54	38	19	2	1	.
5 Claypole. (W.)	4052	M. 2096	279	260	260	202	182	113	103	97	97	80	100	83	94	72	46	27	24	7	1	.
		F. 1956	256	245	218	152	128	122	128	93	89	190	86	83	96	60	44	26	19	7	1	.
434 BINGHAM.																						
1 Bingham. (W.)	7002	M. 3493	427	401	399	336	281	203	185	150	170	168	159	134	154	114	91	76	33	9	1	.
		F. 3509	431	403	344	310	277	233	168	188	171	102	183	174	124	114	98	63	33	10	3	.
2 Ratcliffe upon Trent	7719	M. 3819	533	76	443	368	277	229	207	190	193	172	187	147	125	100	78	58	22	9	2	1
		F. 3900	492	472	428	330	320	254	222	185	244	200	187	155	138	108	85	53	36	7	3	1
32 DERBYSHIRE.																						
435 SHARDLOW.																						
1 Castle Donington	6186	M. 2969	482	361	348	299	211	176	164	166	149	135	131	118	89	75	48	35	20	11	.	.
		F. 3217	381	382	391	334	252	208	188	175	164	176	148	118	106	68	56	48	23	3	1	.
2 Melbourne	4921	M. 2360	335	286	275	244	207	164	123	125	104	80	83	87	87	63	46	32	16	4	.	.
		F. 2561	386	317	261	245	206	183	147	120	136	88	97	97	83	93	53	23	14	3	.	.
3 Shardlow. (W. B.)	8774	M. 4445	627	544	464	447	433	374	316	276	225	177	186	128	95	64	60	46	18	8	1	.
		F. 4329	678	581	436	367	391	344	318	258	201	178	161	126	103	77	65	40	19	5	2	1
4 Stapleford	16467	M. 8343	1294	1080	983	883	829	705	646	482	359	317	227	209	175	120	100	50	20	6	3	.
		F. 8124	1248	1059	840	776	727	680	568	409	412	318	278	214	204	151	99	62	24	6	3	1
5 Spondon	8346	M. 4111	568	518	520	418	370	283	246	220	157	186	147	128	113	91	85	43	18	2	1	.
		F. 4235	592	506	485	381	357	295	275	226	103	185	180	146	130	109	96	45	27	8	3	.

Table 3 *continued*.—AGES of MALES and FEMALES in REGISTRATION SUB-DISTRICTS.

REGISTRATION SUB-DISTRICT.	ALL AGES. Persons.		ALL AGES. Males and Females.	Under 5 Years.	5–	10–	15–	20–	25–	30–	35–	40–	45–	50–	55–	60–	65–	70–	75–	80–	85–	90–	95–
ERBYSHIRE —*cont.*																							
ISS DERBY.																							
Y. (Ht. P.)	78631	M.	38681	5647	4723	3923	3640	3734	3883	[illegible]	2457	2056	1838	1365	900	816	552	523	175	80	21	3	.
		F.	39950	5753	4920	4065	3930	3857	3383	2771	2282	2080	1757	1481	1146	964	668	405	232	102	28	10	.
37 BELPER.																							
IELD. (W. H.)	6814	M.	3369	417	391	369	361	274	229	151	167	149	162	145	128	120	113	111	68	21	5	.	.
		F.	3445	376	375	418	345	318	289	197	182	199	156	166	127	134	98	75	42	33	6	3	.
LEY. (H.)	6090	M.	3468	524	452	420	354	232	222	184	199	165	135	138	134	101	73	62	35	16	2	1	.
		F.	[illegible]	496	475	398	367	307	[illegible]	181	178	167	108	127	110	70	69	61	20	10	9	1	.
ER. (W. H.)	9875	M.	4812	684	607	599	453	378	324	267	261	258	202	198	160	139	136	71	47	23	4	1	.
		F.	5063	660	586	567	552	487	325	313	299	264	198	221	172	157	120	81	40	19	3	.	.
EY	14800	M.	7476	1186	901	882	803	590	504	453	369	353	350	334	246	205	140	90	47	27	5	1	.
		F.	7324	1113	1043	823	699	598	520	397	407	306	341	299	218	158	139	100	67	21	12	4	.
ETON	13885	M.	7232	1150	1031	763	677	843	584	403	413	338	295	246	192	168	198	73	51	21	4	2	.
		F.	6653	1200	975	738	481	552	466	416	306	308	282	216	178	158	110	89	46	20	2	1	.
KSWORTH. (H.)	6120	M.	2982	401	384	320	297	245	206	173	160	134	132	168	90	104	70	47	33	11	5	1	1
		F.	3138	375	373	340	318	273	221	200	154	176	153	144	111	111	72	60	53	16	4	1	.
ASHBOURNE.																							
ASFORD	2697	M.	1412	183	182	195	157	122	92	71	76	60	62	54	40	49	45	29	21	7	1	1	.
		F.	1285	150	139	143	118	121	77	84	74	56	57	49	40	46	48	27	12	10	1	.	.
FIELD	3601	M.	1720	230	323	212	182	129	120	91	93	60	82	74	50	69	50	26	18	5	4	.	.
		F.	1881	244	225	191	197	179	146	84	112	92	85	79	66	65	49	36	21	7	3	.	.
ORNE. (W.)	4884	M.	2296	307	259	255	234	169	176	137	100	101	113	98	85	89	71	58	27	14	1	1	1
		F.	2538	308	289	232	286	215	199	150	145	117	119	102	96	98	69	60	39	15	7	3	.
ON	2955	M.	1449	209	169	154	171	116	63	77	77	72	64	62	68	45	41	24	22	12	1	1	.
		F.	1506	172	177	160	145	120	103	79	95	73	78	64	69	56	34	43	25	11	2	1	.
INGTON	1487	M.	764	114	81	72	32	62	42	41	28	32	37	46	31	32	25	18	9	9	2	1	.
		F.	723	91	86	85	54	65	48	35	30	30	38	27	42	29	22	18	6	5	2	.	.
SINGTON	4371	M.	2118	270	286	237	193	167	139	122	105	101	90	108	81	66	67	44	26	9	1	.	.
		F.	2253	315	298	236	213	169	153	122	112	121	103	81	87	72	66	43	27	18	7	1	.
CHESTERFIELD.																							
VER. (H.)	17116	M.	8944	1603	1391	995	827	777	694	587	504	432	326	298	224	180	148	89	52	23	7	.	1
		F.	8172	1485	1343	979	631	534	608	531	429	422	321	253	232	174	125	83	51	17	7	2	.
TERFIELD. (W.H.B.)	46528	M.	23950	3807	3279	2407	2212	2120	2089	1624	1386	1230	975	899	622	518	549	196	197	35	13	.	1
		F.	22578	3829	3183	2480	2044	1902	1698	1182	1240	1094	925	832	572	510	545	220	130	64	34	1	.
OVER	3114	M.	1612	227	202	147	165	163	103	103	98	77	64	70	52	48	41	28	19	6	3	1	.
		F.	1502	204	204	177	131	110	104	102	93	79	75	61	52	43	37	19	12	7	1	.	.
NGTON	22120	M.	12033	1866	1592	1408	1269	1138	991	767	657	677	499	408	311	240	139	106	56	19	8	1	.
		F.	10087	1817	1543	1206	817	741	756	614	553	483	428	323	283	224	136	110	41	17	5	.	.
FIELD	9858	M.	5184	863	737	662	405	462	404	304	291	248	175	172	160	108	68	38	22	12	3	.	.
		F.	4674	869	747	559	381	322	340	291	267	203	178	163	127	94	73	50	23	11	3	.	.
BAKEWELL.																							
EWELL. (W.)	11052	M.	5453	712	659	588	497	499	399	368	321	250	230	271	227	194	129	129	50	32	8	.	.
		F.	5599	699	670	563	569	494	408	362	309	280	254	230	245	101	154	100	59	33	7	2	.
LOCK	11929	M.	5706	809	698	599	600	408	467	336	330	298	241	247	213	194	130	81	54	20	3	.	.
		F.	6223	772	707	625	590	690	482	419	351	301	291	259	222	199	138	106	44	36	10	2	.
SWELL	7541	M.	3750	465	429	443	391	303	253	202	195	210	174	186	137	125	85	77	55	20	7	2	.
		F.	3791	496	442	396	363	337	233	219	214	219	191	182	164	135	78	67	39	16	3	1	.
CHAPEL-EN-LE-FRITH.																							
TON. (H. L.)	9101	M.	4242	523	507	465	483	383	343	313	309	245	221	183	116	102	60	34	19	11	3	.	.
		F.	4859	585	512	470	535	561	418	335	271	289	262	216	164	121	71	44	19	11	2	2	.
PEL-EN-LE-FRITH. (.)	10383	M.	5250	733	638	568	526	495	406	264	271	275	274	220	178	164	129	92	46	25	5	.	.
		F.	5133	678	620	582	521	483	400	327	282	282	212	188	213	153	107	69	33	22	5	.	.
42 HAYFIELD.																							
SOP. (W. H.)	23550	M.	10769	1432	1253	1185	1121	1004	797	697	640	579	491	453	392	341	220	137	51	19	5	2	.
		F.	12781	1535	1341	1271	1355	1256	1079	856	708	745	685	587	437	372	230	151	78	24	7	.	.
FIELD. (W.)	12734	M.	6274	804	765	974	641	552	454	408	344	344	287	263	192	183	131	108	45	14	3	.	.
		F.	6520	850	894	790	642	581	496	441	384	368	319	276	200	198	127	84	40	17	6	2	.

Table 4.—MALE AND FEMALE CHILDREN *at each Year of Age* under 5 in the NORTH-MIDLAND DIVISION and its REGISTRATION COUNTIES.

REGISTRATION COUNTY.	TOTAL UNDER 5 YEARS. Persons.		TOTAL UNDER 5 YEARS. Males and Females.	Under 1 Year.	1–	2–	3–	4–
VII. NORTH-MIDLAND COUNTIES.	229852	M.	114511	24295	22104	22792	22769	22461
		F.	115341	24543	22367	23159	22013	22859
28 LEICESTERSHIRE	46322	M.	22929	4974	4480	4522	4556	4397
		F.	23393	5000	4579	4698	4574	4482
29 RUTLANDSHIRE	2854	M.	1456	315	279	282	284	296
		F.	1398	283	290	279	272	274
30 LINCOLNSHIRE	62123	M.	31127	6389	5934	6250	6365	6189
		F.	30996	6371	6019	6286	6026	6294
31 NOTTINGHAMSHIRE	61779	M.	30692	6546	5995	5980	6087	6084
		F.	31087	6020	5940	6136	6178	6213
32 DERBYSHIRE	56774	M.	28307	5971	5506	5758	5497	5575
		F.	28467	6009	5539	5760	5563	5596

Table 5.—Male and Female Children *at each Year of Age* under 5 in Registration Districts.

Registration District.	Total under 5 Years. Persons.	Males and Females.		Under 1 Year.	1–	2–	3–	4–
28 LEICESTERSHIRE.								
400 LUTTERWORTH - -	1580	M. -	782	168	143	162	160	149
		F. -	798	158	139	181	143	177
401 MARKET HARBOROUGH	2067	M. -	1064	219	209	222	211	203
		F. -	1003	226	172	224	189	192
402 BILLESDON - -	1278	M. -	636	119	138	125	145	109
		F.	642	124	129	121	122	146
403 BLABY - -	3372	M. -	1660	366	313	337	340	315
		F. -	1712	370	349	344	351	289
404 HINCKLEY - -	2555	M.	1196	268	223	227	239	239
		F. -	1359	267	266	286	268	272
405 MARKET BOSWORTH -	2200	M. -	1136	240	226	209	235	226
		F. -	1064	224	191	232	229	188
406 ASHLEY-DE-LA-ZOUCH -	5112	M. -	2546	634	479	509	617	507
		F.	2566	472	555	515	537	487
407 LOUGHBOROUGH -	3896	M. -	1914	408	382	360	374	390
		F. -	1982	438	413	399	379	353
408 BARROW-UPON-SOAR -	4320	M. -	2118	466	390	438	419	405
		F. -	2202	472	372	451	443	464
409 LEICESTER - -	17270	M. -	8536	1910	1706	1645	1673	1596
		F.	8734	2029	1732	1682	1656	1644
410 MELTON MOWBRAY -	2672	M. -	1341	281	271	288	243	258
		F. -	1331	280	261	263	257	270
29 RUTLANDSHIRE.								
411 OAKHAM - - -	1365	M. -	682	150	113	141	136	142
		F.	683	138	146	127	133	140
412 UPPINGHAM - - -	1489	M. -	774	165	166	141	148	154
		F. -	715	145	145	152	139	134
30 LINCOLNSHIRE.								
413 STAMFORD -	2251	M. -	1134	234	227	205	237	231
		F. -	1117	229	217	221	215	235
414 BOURN - -	2508	M. -	1274	248	220	280	256	270
		F. -	1234	255	243	236	240	260
415 SPALDING - -	2999	M. -	1524	308	300	296	313	307
		F. -	1475	288	279	284	319	305
416 HOLBEACH - -	2719	M. -	1319	276	243	233	267	309
		F. -	1400	292	255	325	268	260
417 BOSTON -	5028	M. -	2486	505	460	491	533	497
		F. -	2542	501	509	543	491	498
418 SLEAFORD - - -	3331	M. -	1654	355	335	302	340	322
		F. -	1677	318	328	340	333	358
419 GRANTHAM - - -	4551	M.	2314	475	446	487	453	454
		F. -	2237	484	442	462	427	422
420 LINCOLN - - -	8756	M. -	4356	804	836	915	840	871
		F. -	4400	987	828	912	832	891
421 HORNCASTLE - -	2634	M. -	1300	242	251	271	280	266
		F. -	1334	284	270	252	250	278

Registration District.	Total under 5 Years. Persons.	Males and Females.		Under 1 Year.	1–	2–	3–
30 LINCOLNSHIRE —*cont.*							
422 SPILSBY - - -	3506	M. -	1763	356	351	363	3
		F. -	1743	343	367	333	3
423 LOUTH - - - -	4307	M. -	2233	462	409	450	4
		F. -	2074	382	408	436	3
424 CAISTOR -	9466	M. -	4749	996	893	908	10
		F. -	4717	973	915	951	9
425 GLANFORD BRIGG - -	5805	M. -	2924	604	537	642	5
		F. -	2881	608	637	689	5
426 GAINSBOROUGH - -	4262	M. -	2097	435	427	407	4
		F. -	2165	477	421	402	4
31 NOTTINGHAMSHIRE.							
427 EAST RETFORD -	3105	M. -	1604	358	277	338	31
		F. -	1501	316	295	361	31
428 WORKSOP -	4399	M. -	2130	471	418	413	40
		F. -	2269	454	422	455	46
429 MANSFIELD - -	6953	M. -	3455	690	705	653	71
		F. -	3498	744	644	718	68
430 BASFORD - - -	18630	M. -	9300	2046	1824	1846	18
		F. -	9330	2001	1763	1826	190
431 NOTTINGHAM -	20217	M. -	10001	2238	2002	1869	192
		F. -	10216	2219	1985	1961	200
432 SOUTHWELL - -	2494	M. -	1226	247	212	246	27
		F. -	1268	266	239	258	23
433 NEWARK - - -	4096	M. -	2014	419	376	414	39
		F. -	2082	432	407	438	41
434 BINGHAM -	1885	M. -	962	179	181	204	197
		F. -	923	189	185	179	176
32 DERBYSHIRE.							
435 SHARDLOW - -	6620	M. -	3236	717	592	664	613
		F. -	3384	709	610	715	656
436 DERBY -	11400	M. -	5847	1214	1137	1141	1079
		F. -	5753	1230	1161	1133	1154
437 BELPER -	8584	M. -	4362	897	857	874	873
		F. -	4222	898	818	842	858
438 ASHBORNE - -	2608	M. -	1319	256	251	247	287
		F. -	1289	251	266	240	261
439 CHESTERFIELD -	16470	M. -	8266	1729	1591	1710	1595
		F. -	8204	1758	1568	1689	1530
440 BAKEWELL - -	3952	M. -	1985	406	388	404	406
		F.	1967	417	398	361	401
441 CHAPEL-EN-LE-FRITH -	2519	M. -	1256	269	254	261	230
		F. -	1263	241	252	278	239
442 HAYFIELD - - -	4621	M. -	2236	473	485	457	416
		F. -	2385	505	468	502	454

Table 7.—Condition as to Marriage and Ages of Males and Females in the North-Midland Division and its Registration Counties.

Registration County.		All Ages.	Under 15 years.	15–	20–	25–	35–	45–	55–	65 and upwards.
VII. NORTH-MIDLAND COUNTIES.										
Unmarried	Males	409120	308700	80612	60068	31785	10000	6600	3800	2949
	Females	483096	306342	76545	45446	26219	11691	6986	4446	3421
Married	Males	289084	.	471	17649	79390	72236	56140	38824	24124
	Females	289796	.	2304	27344	84590	72322	53169	33488	16779
Widowed	Males	29307	.	9	202	1754	3078	4466	6187	13611
	Females	54340	.	15	262	2466	5535	9366	13160	23696
28 LEICESTERSHIRE.										
Unmarried	Males	95110	60199	15748	9519	5460	1859	1193	752	479
	Females	98563	61326	15725	9618	6188	2561	1442	876	697
Married	Males	57815	.	114	3932	16435	14677	11061	7653	4543
	Females	58337	.	381	5586	17489	14443	10617	6679	3192
Widowed	Males	5858		1	37	342	588	863	1260	2747
	Females	11038	.	2	53	506	1183	1906	2729	4657
29 RUTLAND.										
Unmarried	Males	7180	4224	1248	751	509	199	110	77	62
	Females	6751	4041	1030	664	485	233	145	69	72
Married	Males	3867	.	2	143	829	940	834	666	447
	Females	3878	.	12	225	940	967	811	594	329
Widowed	Males	472	.	.	1	12	31	57	89	282
	Females	859			4	24	61	131	205	451
30 LINCOLNSHIRE.										
Unmarried	Males	141660	85208	23379	15414	9511	3514	1843	1210	991
	Females	133832	83828	21076	12380	7694	3335	1874	1302	1049
Married	Males	81603		58	3634	20106	20428	16183	12446	8748
	Females	81240	.	476	6328	21721	20405	15455	10707	6153
Widowed	Males	8447	.	2	30	417	829	1176	1748	4239
	Females	16279	.	3	71	629	1475	2501	3681	7919
31 NOTTINGHAMSHIRE.										
Unmarried	Males	128848	80208	20015	13611	8227	2778	1537	900	672
	Females	129796	81560	21095	12520	7335	3162	1930	1137	856
Married	Males	78842	.	190	5644	22715	19482	15002	9828	5891
	Females	79254	.	798	8495	23887	19484	14050	8484	4056
Widowed	Males	7681	.	3	71	488	864	1231	1678	3443
	Females	14222		7	75	725	1575	2572	3550	5918
32 DERBYSHIRE.										
Unmarried	Males	119834	73797	18822	12985	8028	2649	1487	881	685
	Females	114215	74023	17610	10264	6314	2000	1398	1062	747
Married	Males	66907	.	167	4296	19508	17300	12970	8231	4405
	Females	67087	.	637	6715	20403	17023	12236	7024	3049
Widowed	Males	6869	.	3	57	495	766	1139	1512	2897
	Females	12102	.	5	57	582	1241	2256	3196	4768

Note.—In a few cases, persons described as "Married" were stated to be under 15 years of age. These have been classed with Married persons aged "15 and under 20 years."

[T]able 8.—Condition as to Marriage and Ages of Males and Females in Registration Districts.

[REG]ISTRATION [D]ISTRICT.		All Ages.	Under 15 Years.	15-	20-	25-	35-	45-	55-	65 and upw[ds].
[LE]ICESTER-[S]HIRE.										
[LUTT]ERWORTH:										
[UNM]ARRIED	M.	3819	2273	681	394	238	80	66	48	30
	F.	3831	2256	557	358	318	145	95	67	44
[MAR]RIED	M.	2448	.	1	83	460	488	558	519	339
	F.	2442	.	5	128	513	507	580	412	237
[WID]OWED	M.	291	.	.	1	7	13	35	69	166
	F.	525	.	.	1	13	36	57	126	292
[MAR]KET HARBO[RO]UGH:										
[UNM]ARRIED	M.	4789	2928	742	510	322	126	69	54	38
	F.	4826	2862	754	524	371	136	82	61	46
[MAR]RIED	M.	2823	.	2	124	635	602	570	456	341
	F.	2819	.	14	181	724	679	563	417	241
[WID]OWED	M.	340	.	.	1	15	27	42	82	178
	F.	602	.	.	.	22	41	105	154	280
[BILL]ESDON:										
[UN]MARRIED	M.	3176	1726	460	401	332	123	74	40	20
	F.	2937	1723	446	218	253	99	62	35	32
[MAR]RIED	M.	1730	.	4	60	442	455	363	262	144
	F.	1695	.	5	122	472	439	347	214	96
[WI]DOWED	M.	231	.	.	.	9	26	38	55	103
	F.	295	.	.	.	15	25	52	70	133
[BLAB]Y:										
[UN]MARRIED	M.	6541	4183	1182	621	324	115	39	49	28
	F.	6511	4153	911	637	414	178	86	39	33
[MAR]RIED	M.	3929	.	8	246	1138	1003	710	501	323
	F.	3911	.	16	353	1205	986	653	470	228
[WI]DOWED	M.	377	.	.	2	15	43	48	82	185
	F.	584	.	.	7	24	47	75	142	289
[HIN]CKLEY:										
[UN]MARRIED	M.	4860	3253	789	360	237	74	53	41	37
	F.	5300	3457	830	486	292	107	61	54	28
[MA]RRIED	M.	3096	.	1	227	829	678	599	476	286
	F.	3149	.	21	307	883	714	627	336	261
[WI]DOWED	M.	401	.	.	4	17	36	68	76	200
	F.	586	.	.	6	15	51	89	143	282
[MAR]KET BOS[WO]RTH:										
[UN]MARRIED	M.	4498	2886	700	448	245	80	50	36	53
	F.	4101	2828	520	321	213	94	57	23	45
[MA]RRIED	M.	2618	.	7	150	649	519	521	401	271
	F.	2601	.	17	228	710	592	494	362	198
[WI]DOWED	M.	289	.	.	.	11	17	40	64	150
	F.	511	.	.	5	16	38	75	118	259
[ASH]BY-DE-LA-[Z]OUCH:										
[UN]MARRIED	M.	10529	6637	1765	1051	569	196	131	82	48
	F.	9722	6722	1415	797	438	165	95	80	32
[MA]RRIED	M.	5796	.	9	334	1681	1397	1142	773	460
	F.	5812	.	39	549	1693	1453	1086	668	324
[WI]DOWED	M.	683	.	.	2	36	72	93	148	332
	F.	993	.	.	3	45	101	159	244	440
[LOU]GHBOROUGH:										
[UN]MARRIED	M.	7987	5185	1375	740	306	129	83	46	33
	F.	8476	5272	1418	799	451	237	142	86	71
[MA]RRIED	M.	4920	.	14	334	1312	1133	998	685	453
	F.	4975	.	35	472	1417	1155	901	624	311
[W]IDOWED	M.	578	.	.	2	33	57	98	108	280
	F.	938	.	1	3	50	104	150	212	418
[BAR]ROW UPON [SO]AR:										
[UN]MARRIED	M.	8488	5062	1389	715	378	149	82	66	45
	F.	8787	5799	1273	774	439	232	141	61	48
[MA]RRIED	M.	5020	.	9	321	1366	1256	974	684	410
	F.	5098	.	37	435	1465	1323	941	611	286
[W]IDOWED	M.	512	.	.	7	31	42	72	107	253
	F.	962	.	1	3	49	96	165	220	428
[LEI]CESTER:										
[UN]MARRIED	M.	34226	21846	5688	3501	1898	586	344	183	120
	F.	38118	22706	6768	4078	2540	987	500	309	235
[MA]RRIED	M.	21803	.	37	1881	7070	5514	3853	2321	1107
	F.	22227	.	174	2627	7432	5668	3630	1965	771
[W]IDOWED	M.	1693	.	1	15	158	208	276	368	665
	F.	4311	.	.	24	236	588	850	1102	1502
[MEL]TON MOWBRAY:										
[UN]MARRIED	M.	6199	3596	977	682	522	196	112	84	36
	F.	5894	3588	845	597	461	161	131	63	48
[M]ARRIED	M.	3617	.	2	172	844	859	775	569	416
	F.	3608	.	18	284	925	867	705	510	299
[W]IDOWED	M.	482	.	.	3	10	45	62	101	231
	F.	[illegible]	.	.	5	21	56	110	198	[illegible]

Registration District.		All Ages.	Under 15 Years.	15-	20-	25-	35-	45-	55-	[65 and] u[pwds].
29 RUTLAND.										
411 OAKHAM:										
Unmarried	M.	3343	1900	542	376	229	112	50	42	
	F.	3271	1905	497	317	221	117	85	34	
Married	M.	1865	.	2	69	402	453	410	313	
	F.	1847	.	5	118	432	482	364	273	
Widowed	M.	235	.	.	1	7	17	23	40	
	F.	419	.	.	1	12	30	78	91	
412 UPPINGHAM:										
Unmarried	M.	3837	2264	706	375	231	87	69	35	
	F.	3480	2046	542	347	257	116	80	35	
Married	M.	2004	.	.	74	424	406	418	353	
	F.	2031	.	7	107	508	485	417	321	
Widowed	M.	237	.	.	.	5	14	34	40	
	F.	340	.	.	3	12	31	53	114	
30 LINCOLNSHIRE.										
413 STAMFORD:										
Unmarried	M.	5474	3244	857	583	394	140	61	45	
	F.	5012	3254	823	618	426	194	69	70	
Married	M.	3031	.	.	135	708	706	585	416	
	F.	3076	.	11	207	788	770	648	372	
Widowed	M.	386	.	.	1	13	51	84	78	
	F.	765	.	.	.	24	71	141	173	
414 BOURN:										
Unmarried	M.	5765	3582	938	546	358	151	83	53	
	F.	5576	3552	845	497	345	138	92	65	
Married	M.	3241	.	2	95	687	787	686	568	
	F.	3238	.	7	179	798	805	668	493	
Widowed	M.	307	.	1	1	17	30	46	91	
	F.	703	.	.	3	19	51	84	150	
415 SPALDING:										
Unmarried	M.	7003	4382	1189	659	417	140	94	66	
	F.	6642	4263	1028	611	367	176	94	61	
Married	M.	3954	.	4	139	913	939	783	668	
	F.	4009	.	17	237	936	1061	772	605	
Widowed	M.	486	.	.	3	19	43	34	99	
	F.	867	.	.	5	28	50	123	192	
416 HOLBEACH:										
Unmarried	M.	5780	3737	931	[illegible]	294	140	61	48	
	F.	5512	3801	738	425	254	107	54	37	
Married	M.	3458	.	1	120	813	866	631	568	
	F.	3470	.	12	244	921	872	620	520	
Widowed	M.	374	.	.	1	19	20	48	89	
	F.	658	.	.	1	25	53	89	144	
417 BOSTON:										
Unmarried	M.	11660	7200	1883	1122	754	368	177	108	
	F.	11655	7137	1878	1148	734	289	200	153	
Married	M.	6827	.	4	275	1550	1681	1298	1121	
	F.	6898	.	37	454	1896	1759	1251	1000	
Widowed	M.	769	.	.	2	37	61	109	165	
	F.	1685	.	.	6	55	154	264	352	
418 SLEAFORD:										
Unmarried	M.	8122	4730	1392	937	579	240	117	[illegible]	
	F.	7524	4815	1156	684	450	174	110	54	
Married	M.	4640	.	2	135	928	1083	928	730	
	F.	4334	.	16	274	1051	1092	898	628	
Widowed	M.	309	.	.	1	24	37	72	168	
	F.	891	.	.	2	22	77	118	218	
419 GRANTHAM:										
Unmarried	M.	10257	6232	1667	1095	710	275	124	[illegible]	
	F.	9919	6186	1558	1000	602	258	149	[illegible]	
Married	M.	5834	.	5	279	1464	1455	1197	[illegible]	
	F.	5871	.	35	436	1530	1437	1153	78[illegible]	
Widowed	M.	[illegible]	.	.	3	30	68	80	[illegible]	
	F.	1134	.	.	7	42	91	197	251	
420 LINCOLN:										
Unmarried	M.	19858	11634	3152	2301	1527	612	306	184	
	F.	18702	11867	2937	1758	1113	642	245	18[illegible]	
Married	M.	11404	.	5	513	3068	3152	2209	149[illegible]	
	F.	11364	.	71	829	3347	3034	2041	180[illegible]	
Widowed	M.	1011	.	.	3	63	140	162	194	
	F.	2173	.	1	8	101	205	355	58[illegible]	
421 HORNCASTLE:										
Unmarried	M.	6451	3808	1125	657	442	166	103	8[illegible]	
	F.	6314	3660	1022	608	425	168	161	7[illegible]	
Married	M.	3787	.	3	133	790	873	807	66[illegible]	
	F.	3702	.	18	257	884	904	796	56[illegible]	
Widowed	M.	451	.	.	3	13	50	80	8[illegible]	
	F.	723	.	.	1	12	63	107	15[illegible]	

Table 8 *continued.*—Condition as to Marriage and Ages of Males and Females in Registration Districts.

Registration District.		All Ages.	Under 15 Years.	15–	20–	25–	35–	45–	55–	65 and upwds.
30 LINCOLNSHIRE—*cont.*										
422 SPILSBY:										
Unmarried	M.	8451	5249	1461	785	498	206	127	103	62
	F.	7999	5000	1284	711	467	224	157	81	75
Married	M.	4932	.	4	171	1039	1137	1082	843	656
	F.	4925	.	21	302	1163	1238	992	767	452
Widowed	M.	609	.	.	3	22	37	69	110	205
	F.	1044	.	.	6	23	60	137	248	570
423 LOUTH:										
Unmarried	M.	10188	6249	1697	1070	635	238	147	87	65
	F.	9913	6192	1615	978	599	255	169	107	87
Married	M.	5869	.	2	202	1216	1474	1207	1063	705
	F.	5917	.	21	387	1443	1495	1240	872	559
Widowed	M.	693	.	.	2	24	39	77	127	334
	F.	1362	.	.	2	54	131	209	304	662
424 CAISTOR:										
Unmarried	M.	21528	12150	4146	2821	1522	463	202	130	94
	F.	18372	12180	2902	1613	869	332	178	103	75
Married	M.	12241	.	13	753	3711	3105	2251	1537	871
	F.	11753	.	116	1322	3613	2880	2022	1210	592
Widowed	M.	991	.	1	7	61	136	165	180	432
	F.	2014	.	2	23	146	271	343	445	785
425 GLANFORD BRIGG:										
Unmarried	M.	12184	7774	1867	1260	749	214	136	84	80
	F.	11554	7676	1796	946	602	214	147	84	89
Married	M.	7220	.	7	379	1708	1799	1388	1109	740
	F.	7242	.	60	699	1967	1769	1384	941	522
Widowed	M.	736	.	.	4	43	88	94	145	362
	F.	1254	.	.	6	48	99	199	254	648
426 GAINSBOROUGH:										
Unmarried	M.	8931	5307	1484	1082	637	212	102	47	60
	F.	8538	5610	1295	736	441	178	100	87	73
Married	M.	5468	.	3	305	1423	1331	1001	824	581
	F.	5441	.	32	306	1531	1283	968	694	421
Widowed	M.	504	.	.	2	30	51	77	110	294
	F.	1006	.	.	2	30	99	144	209	531
31 NOTTINGHAMSHIRE.										
427 EAST RETFORD:										
Unmarried	M.	6844	4133	1173	696	485	158	112	56	61
	F.	6894	4221	1075	668	461	192	114	76	99
Married	M.	4110	.	3	186	920	969	802	676	488
	F.	4121	.	22	313	1044	1016	793	575	358
Widowed	M.	475	.	.	.	20	36	70	94	255
	F.	817	.	.	.	28	77	133	184	395
428 WORKSOP:										
Unmarried	M.	9055	5599	1349	920	695	230	134	80	48
	F.	8346	5838	1094	612	406	172	98	70	69
Married	M.	4873	.	7	275	1325	1262	992	634	378
	F.	4911	.	60	452	1446	1265	825	577	286
Widowed	M.	525	.	.	7	24	63	80	119	232
	F.	812	.	.	8	36	83	112	176	399
429 MANSFIELD:										
Unmarried	M.	14277	9042	2266	1356	917	322	174	104	96
	F.	12568	8943	1804	1020	520	180	155	85	60
Married	M.	7885	.	11	553	2365	1966	1504	939	547
	F.	7894	.	64	859	2339	1979	1405	838	380
Widowed	M.	843	.	.	4	38	99	146	177	379
	F.	1191	.	.	7	45	109	194	302	534
430 BASFORD:										
Unmarried	M.	36871	23848	5824	3755	2071	629	354	229	184
	F.	33199	23819	4718	2424	1204	498	263	179	124
Married	M.	21155	.	61	1639	6610	5262	3764	2411	1348
	F.	21028	.	253	2579	6649	5068	3490	2068	926
Widowed	M.	1972	.	1	27	132	250	306	407	829
	F.	2715	.	.	11	128	291	490	680	1112
431 NOTTINGHAM:										
Unmarried	M.	42577	25855	7142	4856	2898	989	473	238	128
	F.	49366	27042	9306	5969	3706	1022	958	478	290
Married	M.	29093	.	92	2381	9044	7342	5509	3130	1590
	F.	29090	.	310	3422	9596	7438	5163	2616	1045
Widowed	M.	2474	.	1	27	202	331	461	506	946
	F.	6163	.	7	42	420	801	1304	1461	2128
432 SOUTHWELL:										
Unmarried	M.	5805	3494	915	685	373	164	111	85	68
	F.	5950	3557	931	546	441	169	137	88	78
Married	M.	3628	.	2	129	720	808	748	671	550
	F.	3807	.	9	221	828	823	750	618	360
Widowed	M.	483	.	.	2	15	23	45	91	304
	F.	878	.	.	1	25	77	97	183	495

Registration District.		All Ages.	Under 15 Years.	15–	20–	25–	35–	45–	55
31 NOTTINGHAMSHIRE—*cont.*									
433 NEWARK:									
Unmarried	M.	9129	5559	1547	1009	581	184	119	7[illegible]
	F.	8975	5567	1445	867	732	238	136	10[illegible]
Married	M.	5411	.	9	289	1283	1296	1124	83[illegible]
	F.	5412	.	38	469	1378	1274	1047	70[illegible]
Widowed	M.	574	.	1	2	19	38	99	10[illegible]
	F.	1119	.	.	7	25	95	178	26[illegible]
434 BINGHAM:									
Unmarried	M.	4290	2681	699	424	257	102	60	33
	F.	4187	2570	628	416	268	123	71	60
Married	M.	2687	.	5	132	552	577	589	465
	F.	2691	.	12	180	611	626	577	430
Widowed	M.	335	.	.	2	18	24	37	64
	F.	531	.	.	1	18	39	64	101
32 DERBYSHIRE.									
435 SHARDLOW:									
Unmarried	M.	13630	8590	2250	1489	796	231	117	81
	F.	13204	8642	2934	1181	678	288	189	143
Married	M.	7794	.	3	553	2261	1961	1393	981
	F.	7883	.	69	747	2410	1899	1381	871
Widowed	M.	783	.	2	5	39	71	118	152
	F.	1369	.	.	5	76	101	237	315
436 DERBY:									
Unmarried	M.	23311	14291	3617	2773	1725	515	231	94
	F.	23251	14678	3820	2286	1273	562	322	171
Married	M.	14161	.	23	941	4769	3835	2562	1360
	F.	14128	.	119	1552	4746	3629	2398	1219
Widowed	M.	1209	.	.	20	136	163	219	262
	F.	2571	.	.	19	135	290	518	720
437 BELPER:									
Unmarried	M.	18018	11500	2916	1702	992	358	249	151
	F.	16813	11277	2518	1391	822	339	223	142
Married	M.	10167	.	30	685	2709	2511	2054	1384
	F.	10210	.	104	1088	2797	2532	1972	1150
Widowed	M.	1181	.	.	7	69	93	183	261
	F.	1805	.	.	7	70	168	280	468
438 ASHBORNE:									
Unmarried	M.	6105	3600	1016	623	438	161	116	67
	F.	6184	3597	997	662	436	185	115	106
Married	M.	3224	.	3	139	720	722	708	558
	F.	3248	.	11	207	833	818	649	472
Widowed	M.	430	.	.	1	20	34	65	96
	F.	804	.	.	.	30	72	118	196
439 CHESTERFIELD:									
Unmarried	M.	33020	20883	4833	3445	2286	731	395	231
	F.	27669	20505	3756	1676	934	330	218	148
Married	M.	17027	.	25	1198	5508	4525	3253	1558
	F.	16970	.	265	1946	5471	4287	2907	1920
Widowed	M.	1678	.	.	17	154	239	305	375
	F.	2370	.	3	17	116	246	439	643
440 BAKEWELL:									
Unmarried	M.	9118	5391	1381	1028	712	261	166	119
	F.	9330	5370	1483	1032	703	310	192	156
Married	M.	5135	.	6	271	1223	1283	1024	841
	F.	5189	.	15	308	1378	1507	1022	716
Widowed	M.	656	.	1	3	20	57	107	142
	F.	1103	.	.	1	42	113	193	294
441 CHAPEL-EN-LE-FRITH:									
Unmarried	M.	5341	3429	957	738	477	154	90	58
	F.	6197	3453	1031	723	520	213	133	85
Married	M.	3218	.	2	151	836	880	698	430
	F.	3164	.	25	258	923	841	613	381
Widowed	M.	333	.	.	.	19	46	56	74
	F.	631	.	.	3	37	61	132	175
442 HAYFIELD:									
Unmarried	M.	10191	6113	1753	1192	624	238	121	81
	F.	11507	6501	1971	1273	948	381	297	111
Married	M.	6191	.	9	380	1684	1808	1278	839
	F.	6345	.	26	519	1845	1809	1289	896
Widowed	M.	601	.	.	4	38	66	95	150
	F.	1449	.	.	5	70	190	341	402

ble 9.—CONDITION as to MARRIAGE and AGES* of MALES and FEMALES in each URBAN SANITARY DISTRIC of which the POPULATION EXCEEDS 50,000 PERSONS.

BAN SANITARY DISTRICT.		ALL AGES.	Under 15 Years.	15–	20–	25–	35–	45–	55–	65 and upw^{ds}.
STER:										
UNMARRIED	M. -	34226	21846	5688	3501	1898	686	344	183	120
	F. -	38118	22706	6768	4073	2540	967	590	309	235
MARRIED	M. -	21803	.	57	1681	7070	5514	3853	2321	1107
	F. -	22227		174	2527	7432	5068	3890	1996	771
WIDOWED	M. -	1691	.	1	15	158	208	276	368	663
	F. -	4311	.	.	24	236	588	859	1102	1502
INGHAM:										
UNMARRIED	M. -	50721	31219	8420	5643	3322	1113	542	287	175
	F. -	57505	32476	10655	6669	4045	1767	1034	529	330
MARRIED	M. -	34025	.	111	2797	10603	8631	6375	3641	1867
	F. -	34551	.	362	4042	11178	8722	5975	3064	1210
WIDOWED	M. -	2387	.	2	33	235	381	527	563	1128
	F. -	6886	.	7	43	455	684	1443	1626	2427

URBAN SANITARY DISTRICT.		ALL AGES.	Under 15 Years.	15–	20–	25–	35–	45–	55–
DERBY:									
UNMARRIED	M. -	24113	14877	3697	2818	1759	533	243	163
	F. -	23910	13247	3881	2307	1280	562	330	163
MARRIED	M. -	14600	.	23	991	4038	3961	2022	1358
	F. -	14504	.	128	1618	4931	3755	2445	1223
WIDOWED	M. -	1320	.	.	20	133	169	221	294
	F. -	2685	.	.	19	145	300	326	745

Table 10.—OCCUPATIONS of MALES and FEMALES in the NORTH-MIDLAND DIVISION and its REGISTRATION COUNTIES, and in each URBAN SANITARY DISTRICT of which the POPULATION exceeds 50,000 Persons.

OCCUPATIONS.	NORTH-MIDLAND COUNTIES.		REGISTRATION COUNTIES. 28. LEICESTERSHIRE.		29. RUTLANDSHIRE.		30. LINCOLNSHIRE.		31. NOTTINGHAMSHIRE.	
	Males.	Females.	Males.	Females.	Males.	Females.	Males.	Females.	Males.	Females.
TOTAL	810473	827392	158763	167878	11619	11488	231719	231351	215371	223271
I. PROFESSIONAL CLASS.										
1. PERSONS ENGAGED IN THE GENERAL OR LOCAL GOVERNMENT OF THE COUNTRY.										
1. *National Government.*										
Peer, M.P., Privy Councillor (not otherwise described)	27	.	7	.	3	.	6	.	6	.
Civil Service (officers and clerks)	723	192	127	46	8	7	254	50	163	29
Civil Service (messengers, &c.)	806	35	157	5	19	.	288	14	172	7
Prison Officer, &c.	78	14	21	4	.	.	18	5	14	2
2. *Local Government.*										
Police	1416	.	272	.	18	1	390	.	401	.
Municipal, Parish, Union, District, Officer	569	171	130	38	7	2	153	37	150	54
Other Local or County Official	418	.	106	.	17	.	105	.	92	.
3. *East Indian and Colonial Service.*										
East Indian and Colonial Service	3	.	.	.	.	.	1	.	1	.
2. PERSONS ENGAGED IN THE DEFENCE OF THE COUNTRY.										
1. *Army (at Home).*										
Army Officer (effective or retired)	163	.	50	.	4	.	37	.	36	.
Soldier and Non-commissioned Officer	565	.	205	.	3	.	131	.	58	.
Militia, Yeomanry, Volunteers	471	.	56	.	3	.	98	.	130	.
Army Pensioner	323	1	80	.	3	.	94	1	84	.
2. *Navy (ashore or in port).*										
Navy Officer (effective or retired)	31	.	6	.	3	.	8	.	10	.
Seaman, R.N.	93	.	1	.	.	.	87	.	3	.
Royal Marines (officers and men)	11	.	2	.	1	.	3	.	3	.
Navy Pensioner	74	.	19	.	.	.	34	.	15	.
3. PERSONS ENGAGED IN PROFESSIONAL OCCUPATIONS (WITH THEIR IMMEDIATE SUBORDINATES).										
1. *Clerical Profession.*										
Clergyman (Established Church)	1672	.	324	.	55	.	673	.	341	.
Roman Catholic Priest	113	.	50	.	1	.	23	.	21	.
Minister, Priest, of other religious bodies	578	.	119	.	7	.	182	.	114	.
Missionary, Scripture Reader, Itinerant Preacher	158	90	99	28	1	2	32	11	51	27
Nun, Sister of Charity	.	98	.	8	.	.	.	.	.	47
Theological Student	120	.	6	.	.	.	62	.	34	.
Church, Chapel, Cemetery—Officer, Servant	342	46	76	6	5	1	97	21	[illegible]	16
2. *Legal Profession.*										
Barrister, Solicitor	630	.	128	.	9	.	187	.	175	.
Law Student	38	.	3	.	.	.	13	.	8	.
Law Clerk, and others connected with Law	1163	3	220	.	10	.	363	.	300	3
3. *Medical Profession.*										
Physician, Surgeon, General Practitioner	798	1	140	.	19	.	248	.	199	.
Dentist	139	.	26	.	.	.	27	.	60	.
Medical Student, Assistant	163	1	30	1	2	.	41	.	33	.
Midwife	.	168	.	61	.	.	.	21	.	49
Subordinate Medical Service	162	1974	32	428	.	43	37	865	38	417
4. *Teachers.*										
Schoolmaster	2521	6264	485	1324	67	24	760	1763	611	1627
Teacher, Professor, Lecturer	174	1165	46	293	3	38	82	580	43	177
School Service, and others concerned in Teaching	83	48	18	10	1	9	13	7	35	12
5. *Literary and Scientific Persons.*										
Author, Editor, Journalist	73	7	17	4	.	.	21	.	17	1
Reporter, Short-hand Writer	108	.	19	.	.	.	32	.	33	.
Persons engaged in Scientific Pursuits	24	.	4	.	.	.	6	.	3	.
Literary, Scientific, Institution, Service, &c.	18	8	6	3	.	.	2	1	6	2
6. *Engineers and Surveyors.*										
Civil Engineer	271	.	43	.	1	.	71	.	64	.
Mining Engineer	139	.	12	.	.	.	7	.	46	.
Land, House, Ship, Surveyor	297	.	41	.	2	.	80	.	62	.
7. *Artists.*										
Painter (artist)	179	41	31	6	1	.	[illegible]	14	88	14
Engraver (artist)	25	1	3	1	.	.	3	.	8	.
Sculptor	22	.	4	.	1	.	5	.	6	.
Architect	246	.	76	.	1	.	71	.	99	.
Musician, Music Master	670	[illegible]	154	108	7	6	195	128	191	200
Art Student	40	24	5	2	.	3	17	4	14	9
Photographer	254	[illegible]	47	13	2	.	81	14	[illegible]	12
Actor	116	[illegible]	28	20	1	.	31	37	30	16
Art, Music, Theatre, Service	40	4	11	.	.	.	8	.	11	2

NOTE.—Persons returned as engaged in more than one occupation have been referred to the one that appeared to be of most importance; or, if there was no difference in this respect, to the one first given by the person in his or her return. In some cases special rules have been followed: *e.g.*, "Clergyman and Schoolmaster" in combination has always been referred to "Schoolmaster"; a Member of Parliament or Peer engaged in any branch of commerce or industry has always been referred to this latter, not to "Peer, M.P."

The numbers returned under any heading include Labourers, Apprentices, and Assistants, as well as Masters, but not Clerks, Messengers, Errand boys, Porters or Watchmen, for which occupations there are special headings. Civil, Military, and Naval Clerks, Law, Bank, Insurance, and Railway Clerks, and Government and Railway Porters, are, however, exceptions to this rule. Many young persons, being Apprentices or Assistants, have therefore been referred to occupations usually followed by adults. Women also, chiefly widows or orphans carrying on the business of their deceased husbands or fathers, will sometimes be found under occupations commonly followed by men only.

Persons returned as *retired* from any business have not been referred to that business. Inmates of workhouses have been referred to their trades, unless their age or infirmities showed that they were past work. But persons who might be supposed to be only temporarily separated from their usual employment, such as Prisoners, and Patients in General Hospitals, have been classed under their usual occupations.

Table 10 *continued.*—OCCUPATIONS of MALES and FEMALES in the NORTH-MIDLAND DIVISION and its REGISTRATION COUNTIES, and in each URBAN SANITARY DISTRICT of which the POPULATION exceeds 50,000 PERSONS.

OCCUPATIONS.	NORTH-MIDLAND COUNTIES.		REGISTRATION COUNTIES.							
			28. LEICESTERSHIRE.		29. RUTLANDSHIRE.		30. LINCOLNSHIRE.		31. NOTTINGHAMSHIRE.	
	Males.	Females.	Males.	Females.	Males.	Females.	Males.	Females.	Males.	Females.
8. *Persons engaged in Exhibitions, Shows, Games, &c.*										
Performer, Showman, Exhibition, Service	132	36	20	12	.	.	74	20	26	2
Billiard, Cricket, & other Games, Service	158	3	25	1	2	.	38	1	64	.
II. DOMESTIC CLASS.										
4. PERSONS ENGAGED IN DOMESTIC OFFICES OR SERVICES.										
1. *Domestic Service.*										
Domestic Coachman, Groom	5287	.	1126	.	276	.	2124	.	393	.
Domestic Gardener	3538	1	1293	.	147	.	1008	1	1376	.
Domestic Indoor Servant	3922	65832	990	11730	141	1481	904	23393	620	15582
Lodge, Gate, Park, Keeper (not Government)	37	33	3	3	2	4	9	8	7	7
Inn, Hotel, Servant	1186	1348	218	307	15	18	305	338	418	370
College, Club, Service	44	16	9	3	.	.	6	3	18	6
2. *Other Service.*										
Office Keeper (not Government)	45	68	13	12	.	.	11	7	3	23
Cook (not domestic)	36	57	8	5	1	2	3	1	6	24
Charwoman	.	5118	.	1061	.	56	.	1606	.	1305
Washing and Bathing Service	93	6511	20	1593	1	155	11	1693	23	1777
Hospital and Institution Service	159	421	38	118	1	1	49	102	48	102
Others engaged in Service	32	15	2	5	.	.	7	1	12	3
III. COMMERCIAL CLASS.										
5. PERSONS ENGAGED IN COMMERCIAL OCCUPATIONS.										
1. *Merchants and Agents.*										
Merchant	166	.	94	.	1	.	61	.	43	.
Broker, Agent, Factor	1243	38	325	10	9	2	220	12	429	8
Auctioneer, Appraiser, Valuer, House Agent	574	3	113	1	6	.	180	.	151	2
Accountant	384	.	91	.	1	.	97	.	109	.
Salesman, Buyer (not otherwise described)	46	37	9	5	.	2	9	8	14	14
Commercial Traveller	1410	.	392	.	11	.	334	.	522	.
Commercial Clerk	6191	182	1284	54	33	7	1183	22	2007	60
Officer of Commercial Company, Guild, Society, &c.	9	.	1	.	.	.	2	.	3	.
2. *Dealers in Money.*										
Banker	41	.	7	.	3	.	21	.	7	.
Bank Service	593	3	124	.	5	.	184	2	143	1
Bill Discounter, Bill Broker, Finance Agent	9	.	4	.	.	.	.	.	4	.
3. *Persons occupied in Insurance.*										
Life, House, Ship, &c., Insurance Service	528	2	117	.	1	.	114	.	153	2
6. PERSONS ENGAGED IN CONVEYANCE OF MEN, GOODS, AND MESSAGES.										
1. *On Railways.*										
Railway Engine Driver, Stoker	1565	.	351	.	2	.	237	.	47	.
Railway Guard	752	.	100	.	1	.	102	.	202	.
Pointsman, Level Crossing Man	392	14	79	1	5	.	171	9	133	2
Other Railway Officials and Servants	7508	22	1168	3	24	.	1813	8	1754	5
2. *On Roads.*										
Toll Collector, Turnpike Gate Keeper	43	33	7	9	.	.	8	5	12	5
Omnibus, Coach, Cab, Owner—Livery Stable Keeper	240	3	38	1	.	.	45	1	69	3
Cabman, Flyman, Coachman (not domestic)	593	.	91	.	7	.	84	.	238	.
Carman, Carrier, Carter, Haulier	4247	52	892	20	37	2	826	7	1839	18
Tramway Companies' Service	137	.	48	.	.	.	1	.	89	.
Wheel Chair Proprietor, Attendant, &c.	13		.	.	.				.	.
3. *On Canals, Rivers and Seas.*										
Inland Navigation Service	135	3	32	1	.	.	33	2	46	.
Bargeman, Lighterman, Waterman	958	3	173	5	.	.	364	.	358	.
Navigation Service (on shore)	103	6	1	.	1	.	92	6	2	.
Seaman (Merchant Service)	1348	.	22	.	.	.	1256	.	38	.
Pilot	45	.	.	.	.	.	45	.	.	.
Ship Steward, Cook	251	3	1	.	.	.	244	3	3	.
Boatman on Seas	15	.	.	.	.	.	15	.	.	.
Harbour, Dock, Wharf, Lighthouse, Service	363	.	14	.	.	.	334	.	9	.
4. *In Storage.*										
Warehouseman (not Manchester)	959	350	342	210	1	.	44	6	474	94
Meter, Weigher	20	.	3	.	.	.	12	.	5	.
5. *In conveying Messages, Porterage, &c.*										
Messenger, Porter, Watchman (not Railway nor Government)	4853	285	1107	83	55	1	1234	7	1465	188
Telegraph, Telephone, Service	400	84	43	13	6	2	81	16	104	28

Table 10 *continued*.—Occupations of Males and Females in the North-Midland Division and its Registration Counties, and in each Urban Sanitary District of which the Population exceeds 50,000 Persons.

Occupations.	North-Midland Counties.		Registration Counties. 28. Leicestershire.		29. Rutlandshire.		30. Lincolnshire.		31. Nottinghamshire.	
	Males.	Females.	Males.	Females.	Males.	Females.	Males.	Females.	Males.	Females.
IV. AGRICULTURAL CLASS.										
7. Persons engaged in Agriculture.										
1. *In Fields and Pastures.*										
Farmer, Grazier	21580	1811	2294	289	402	42	9470	578	3413	298
Farmer's, Grazier's—Son, Grandson, Brother, Nephew*	6316	.	896	.	152	.	2625	.	1060	.
Farm Bailiff	2014	.	234	.	32	.	1161	.	426	.
Agricultural Labourer, Farm Servant, Cottager	78309	1862	12758	207	2501	31	42057	990	13312	293
Shepherd	2629	.	513	.	160	.	1593	.	206	.
Land Drainage Service (not in towns)	121	.	27	.	10	.	25	.	51	.
Agricultural Machine—Proprietor, Attendant	789	7	85	.	18	1	547	6	125	.
Agricultural Student, Pupil	80	.	13	.	2	.	48	.	11	.
Others engaged in, or connected with, Agriculture	14	1	2	.	.	.	9	.	3	1
2. *In Woods.*										
Woodman	647	.	52	.	20	.	238	.	215	.
3. *In Gardens.*										
Nurseryman, Seedsman, Florist	395	17	70	10	5	.	111	3	[illegible]	3
Gardener (not domestic)	1989	107	252	12	28	2	623	55	600	27
8. Persons engaged about Animals.										
1. *About Animals.*										
Horse Proprietor, Breeder, Dealer	178	.	32	.	1	.	73	.	48	.
Groom, Horse-keeper, Horse-breaker	2708	.	664	.	70	.	850	.	800	.
Veterinary Surgeon, Farrier	374	.	61	.	4	.	162	.	79	.
Cattle, Sheep, Pig—Dealer, Salesman	639	1	117	.	13	.	276	.	124	1
Drover	208	.	40	.	4	.	103	.	34	.
Gamekeeper	946	.	147	.	41	.	284	.	293	.
Dog, Bird, Animal—Keeper, Dealer	56	7	5	2	2	.	39	5	6	.
Vermin destroyer	115	.	8	.	2	.	83	.	10	.
Fisherman	4368	5	.	.	.	.	4352	5	13	.
Knacker, Catsmeat Dealer, &c., &c.	15	.	3	.	.	.	3	.	4	.
V. INDUSTRIAL CLASS.										
9. Persons working and dealing in Books, Prints, and Maps.										
1. *Books.*										
Publisher, Bookseller, Librarian	311	69	75	16	4	1	71	18	107	16
Music—Publisher, Seller, Printer	30	15	5	10	.	.	6	.	6	4
Bookbinder	275	174	62	43	1	.	39	4	98	85
Printer	2396	77	494	15	10	.	498	5	863	13
Newspaper Agent, News Room Keeper	161	62	36	19	.	.	27	2	61	26
Others	1	.	.	.	.	.	.	.	1	.
2. *Prints and Maps.*										
Lithographer, Lithographic Printer	296	5	56	.	.	.	2	.	182	5
Copper Plate and Steel Plate Printer	9	.	.	.	.	.	.	.	1	.
Map and Print—Colourer, Seller	1	.	.	.	.	.	.	.	1	.
10. Persons working and dealing in Machines and Implements.										
1. *Machines.*										
Engine, Machine, Maker	1654	9	230	1	1	.	470	1	432	7
Millwright	339	.	27	.	5	.	101	.	11	.
Fitter, Turner (Engine and Machine)	4709	.	405	.	6	.	1125	.	1115	.
Boiler Maker	1341	.	90	.	.	.	445	.	207	.
Spinning and Weaving Machine Maker	2446	11	460	2	.	.	28	.	1653	.
Agricultural Machine and Implement Maker	466	3	28	.	.	.	150	3	85	.
Domestic Machinery—Maker, Dealer	11	.	1	.	.	.	7	.	2	.
2. *Tools and Implements.*										
Tool Maker, Dealer	168	2	9	1	.	.	11	.	34	1
Cutler, Scissors Maker	178	6	42	4	.	.	34	.	37	2
File Maker	48	1	2	.	.	.	1	.	5	1
Saw Maker	41	.	5	.	.	.	8	.	10	.
Pin Maker	1	1	.	.	.	.	.	.	.	.
Needle Maker	390	55	232	13	.	.	.	.	151	.
Steel Pen Maker	.	3	.	.	.	.	.	.	.	.
Pencil Maker (Wood)	.	.	.	.	.	.	.	.	.	.
Domestic Implement Maker	26	.	.	.	2	.	6	.	.	.
3. *Watches and Philosophical Instruments.*										
Watch Maker, Clock Maker	556	18	165	5	7	1	283	8	212	1
Philosophical Instrument Maker, Optician	49	3	5	.	.	.	7	.	15	3
Electrical Apparatus Maker	103	.	15	.	.	.	.	.	28	.
Weighing and Measuring Apparatus Maker	16	.	2	.	.	.	2	.	7	.

* [illegible]

Table 10 *continued.*—OCCUPATIONS of MALES and FEMALES in the NORTH MIDLAND DIVISION and its REGISTRATION COUNTIES, and in each URBAN SANITARY DISTRICT of which the POPULATION exceeds 50,000 PERSONS.

OCCUPATIONS.	NORTH-MIDLAND COUNTIES.		REGISTRATION COUNTIES. 28. LEICESTERSHIRE.		29. RUTLANDSHIRE.		30. LINCOLNSHIRE		31. NOTTINGHAMSHIRE.	
	Males.	Females.	Males.	Females.	Males.	Females.	Males.	Females.	Males.	Females.
4. Surgical Instruments.										
Surgical Instrument Maker	106	46	2	.	.	.	1	.	31	18
5. Arms and Ordnance.										
Gunsmith, Gun Manufacturer	78	3	9	.	1	.	43	1	11	1
Ordnance Manufacturer	.	.	.	.	.	.	.	.	.	.
Sword, Bayonet—Maker, Cutler	1	.	.	.	.	.	.	.	.	.
Others	1	.	.	.	.	.	.	.	1	.
6. Musical Instruments.										
Musical Instrument Maker, Dealer	153	4	45	.	1	.	36	.	54	4
7. Type, Dies, Medals, Coins.										
Type Cutter, Founder	2	.	.	.	.	.	1	.	1	.
Die, Seal, Coin, Medal, Maker	136	2	47	.	.	.	4	1	80	1
8. Tackle for Sports and Games.										
Toy Maker, Dealer	24	40	2	5	.	1	7	8	11	10
Fishing Rod, Tackle, Maker, Dealer	28	1	1	.	.	.	.	1	15	.
Apparatus for other Games, Maker, Dealer	7	.	1	.	1	.	.	.	2	.
11. PERSONS WORKING AND DEALING IN HOUSES, FURNITURE, AND DECORATIONS.										
1. Houses.										
Builder	1769	9	398	.	30	1	651	3	485	4
Carpenter, Joiner	13185	7	2589	1	208	1	3958	3	3435	1
Bricklayer	8824	4	2365	2	89	.	2487	1	2608	1
Mason	4105	4	382	1	100	.	724	2	1009	1
Slater, Tiler	541	2	32	1	9	1	149	.	140	.
Plasterer, Whitewasher	974	1	206	.	5	.	150	1	308	.
Paperhanger	92	8	9	1	.	.	24	4	48	3
Plumber	2059	17	347	1	36	1	535	5	650	8
Painter, Glazier	4296	19	912	3	37	.	947	3	1265	7
2. Furniture and Fittings.										
Cabinet Maker, Upholsterer	1821	204	377	42	18	2	518	39	585	66
French Polisher	165	40	32	5	.	.	28	4	78	9
Furniture Broker, Dealer	186	43	38	18	1	.	27	13	76	6
Locksmith, Bellhanger	66	.	19	.	.	.	13	.	12	.
Gas Fitter	453	1	135	.	2	.	93	.	107	1
House and Shop Fittings—Maker, Dealer	65	2	29	1	.	.	6	.	19	1
Funeral Furniture Maker, Undertaker	23	3	3	1	.	.	1	.	10	.
Others	.	.	.	.	.	.	.	.	.	.
3. House Decorations.										
Wood Carver	52	.	17	.	1	.	9	.	21	.
Carver, Gilder	202	7	41	1	.	.	30	2	93	1
Dealer in Works of Art	27	3	3	1	.	.	6	.	12	.
Figure, Image—Maker, Dealer	14	.	5	.	.	.	8	.	.	.
Animal, Bird, &c., Preserver, Naturalist	30	.	8	.	.	.	7	.	11	.
Artificial Flower Maker	3	8	.	3	.	.	1	.	2	5
12. PERSONS WORKING AND DEALING IN CARRIAGES AND HARNESS.										
1. Carriages.										
Coachmaker	1202	13	231	1	8	.	304	4	309	.
Railway Carriage, Railway Wagon, Maker	702	17	41	.	.	.	11	.	96	.
Wheelwright	2831	10	443	4	47	.	1185	6	640	.
Bicycle, Tricycle—Maker, Dealer	49	.	9	.	.	.	1	.	37	.
Others	122	4	39	1	.	.	12	.	55	3
2. Harness.										
Saddler, Harness, Whip, Maker	1265	20	219	4	24	1	432	7	347	5
13. PERSONS WORKING AND DEALING IN SHIPS AND BOATS.										
1. Hull.										
Ship, Boat, Barge, Builder	177	3	15	1	.	.	121	1	24	.
Shipwright, Ship Carpenter (ashore)	387	.	1	.	.	.	377	.	3	.
2. Masts, Rigging, &c.										
Mast, Yard, Oar, Block, Maker	53	.	.	.	.	.	53	.	.	.
Ship Rigger, Chandler, Fitter	12	.	.	.	.	.	12	.	.	.
Sail Maker	150	1	1	1	.	.	137	.	5	.

Table 10 *continued*.—Occupations of Males and Females in the North-midland Division and its Registration Counties, and in each Urban Sanitary District of which the Population exceeds 50,000 Persons.

Occupations.	North-Midland Counties.		Registration Counties. 28. Leicestershire.		29. Rutland-shire.		30. Lincolnshire.		31. Nottinghamshire.	
	Males.	Females.	Males.	Females.	Males.	Females.	Males.	Females.	Males.	Females.
14. Persons working and dealing in Chemicals and Compounds.										
1. *Colouring Matter.*										
Dye, Paint, Manufacture	75	2	1	.	.	.	.	.	5	1
Ink, Blacking, Colouring Substance, Manufacture	102	2	3	.	.	.	.	.	12	1
2. *Explosives.*										
Gunpowder, Guncotton, Explosive Substance, Manufacture	8	1	.	.	.	.	.	.	1	1
Fusee, Fireworks, Explosive Article, Manufacture	5	1	1	1	.	.	.	.	3	.
3. *Drugs and other Chemicals and Compounds.*										
Chemist, Druggist	1287	36	221	2	11	.	460	13	348	12
Manufacturing Chemist	156	25	15	1	.	.	26	1	49	3
Alkali Manufacture	6	.	.	.	.	.	3	.	1	.
Drysalter	13	.	8	.	.	.	.	.	4	.
15. Persons working and dealing in Tobacco and Pipes.										
1. *Tobacco and Pipes.*										
Tobacco Manufacturer, Tobacconist	539	1448	199	507	.	.	79	165	175	605
Tobacco Pipe, Snuff Box, &c., Maker	31	24	6	5	.	.	5	4	16	10
16. Persons working and dealing in Food and Lodging.										
1. *Board and Lodging.*										
Innkeeper, Hotel Keeper, Publican	3681	813	785	173	51	19	939	227	993	179
Lodging, Boarding House, Keeper	130	917	19	139	2	1	38	259	16	178
Coffee, Eating House, Keeper	119	79	31	78	.	.	28	16	32	29
2. *Spirituous Drinks.*										
Hop—Merchant, Dealer	9	.	3	.	.	.	.	.	1	.
Maltster	1502	7	134	3	9	.	532	1	711	2
Brewer	1308	15	234	1	20	.	401	4	408	2
Beerseller. Ale, Porter, Cider, Dealer	607	151	144	35	6	4	112	34	202	38
Cellarman	150	.	38	.	1	.	31	.	51	.
Wine, Spirit—Merchant, Agent	274	16	50	4	4	.	96	4	72	3
3. *Food.*										
Milkseller, Dairyman	755	177	166	55	1	1	229	34	275	67
Cheesemonger, Butterman	30	20	7	7	.	.	2	2	9	5
Butcher, Meat Salesman	6740	204	1188	86	96	3	1642	55	1613	69
Provision Curer, Dealer	624	240	184	52	.	3	78	16	202	99
Poulterer, Game Dealer	264	32	15	2	1	1	155	17	22	8
Fishmonger	1047	88	146	6	5	1	479	44	286	24
Corn, Flour, Seed—Merchant, Dealer	385	42	68	11	2	.	189	18	102	.
Corn Miller	1894	10	268	1	33	.	938	7	446	.
Baker	3642	294	949	68	109	3	1138	102	940	55
Confectioner, Pastrycook	714	469	179	95	6	8	179	106	206	93
Greengrocer, Fruiterer	927	253	161	69	5	3	235	66	246	54
Mustard, Vinegar, Spice, Pickle—Maker, Dealer	16	5	.	.	.	1	4	.	11	1
Sugar Refiner	50	7	9	1	.	.	11	.	17	.
Grocer. Tea, Coffee, Chocolate—Maker, Dealer	6744	1933	1178	429	65	32	2036	532	1806	489
Ginger Beer, Mineral Water—Manufacturer, Dealer	213	1	41	.	3	.	68	.	41	.
Others dealing in Food	.	1	.	1	.	.	.	.	.	.
17. Persons working and dealing in Textile Fabrics.										
1. *Wool and Worsted.*										
Woolstapler	73	1	46	.	.	.	5	.	14	.
Woollen Cloth Manufacture	511	465	358	357	.	.	11	2	74	42
Wool, Woollen goods—Dyer, Printer	54	.	44	.	.	.	1	.	4	.
Worsted, Stuff, Manufacture	307	634	286	808	.	.	2	.	7	5
Flannel Manufacture	2	1	1	1	.	.	.	.	.	.
Blanket Manufacture	.	2	.	.	.	.	.	.	.	1
Fuller	.	.	.	.	.	.	.	.	.	.
Cloth, Worsted, Stuff, Flannel, Blanket, Dealer	20	4	9	.	.	.	3	3	5	.
Others	6	31	1	.	.	.	.	.	2	20
2. *Silk.*										
Silk, Silk goods, Manufacture	817	3035	33	34	.	.	3	132	340	906
Silk Dyer, Printer	89	.	6	.	.	.	.	.	30	.
Ribbon Manufacture	24	15	3	13	.	.	.	.	3	1
Crape, Gauze, Manufacture	.	.	.	.	.	.	.	.	.	.
Silk Merchant, Dealer	37	7	3	.	.	.	12	.	20	7

Table 10 *continued*.—OCCUPATIONS of MALES and FEMALES in the NORTH-MIDLAND DIVISION and its REGISTRATION COUNTIES, and in each URBAN SANITARY DISTRICT of which the POPULATION exceeds 50,000 PERSONS.

OCCUPATIONS.	NORTH-MIDLAND COUNTIES.		REGISTRATION COUNTIES. 28. LEICESTERSHIRE.		29. RUTLANDSHIRE.		30. LINCOLNSHIRE.		31. NOTTINGHAMSHIRE.	
	Males.	Females.	Males.	Females.	Males.	Females.	Males.	Females.	Males.	Females.
3. Cotton and Flax										
Cotton, Cotton goods, Manufacture	5105	11147	173	330	1	.	4	5	706	2571
Cotton, Calico—Printer, Dyer, Bleacher	2013	287	29	2	.	.	3	.	37	4
Cotton, Calico—Warehouseman, Dealer	21	3	.	.	.	.	.	.	14	1
Flax, Linen—Manufacturer, Dealer	51	20	2	.	.	.	28	6	11	6
Lace Manufacturer, Dealer	10121	14565	38	161	.	.	5	21	8905	13323
Fustian Manufacturer, Dealer	.	163	.	.	.	.	.	1	.	162
Tape Manufacturer, Dealer	84	154	6	41	.	.	.	.	1	.
Thread Manufacturer, Dealer	13	6	6	.	.	.	1	.	3	1
4. Hemp and other Fibrous Materials.										
Hemp, Jute, Cocoa Fibre, Manufacture	6	17	.	.	.	.	6	17	.	.
Rope, Twine, Cord—Maker, Dealer	720	23	96	3	1	.	426	8	115	8
Mat Maker, Seller	12	1	1	.	.	.	10	.	1	.
Net Maker	18	32	.	1	2	.	4	26	5	3
Canvas, Sailcloth, Manufacture	.	.	.	.	.	.	.	.	.	.
Sacking, Sack, Bag—Maker, Dealer	17	19	1	.	.	.	8	13	6	1
Others working and dealing in Hemp	17	6	9	1	.	1	.	1	3	1
5. Mixed or Unspecified Materials.										
Weaver (undefined)	113	97	64	37	.	.	3	2	18	15
Dyer, Printer, Scourer, Bleacher, Calenderer (undefined)	1283	165	331	26	.	.	38	10	787	122
Factory hand (Textile, undefined)	383	2403	97	694	.	.	.	49	125	936
Felt Manufacture	.	7	.	7	.	.	.	.	.	.
Carpet, Rug, Manufacture	47	16	10	4	.	.	27	9	4	2
Manchester Warehouseman	4	.	2	.	.	.	.	.	1	.
Draper, Linen Draper, Mercer	2786	908	506	213	37	7	975	294	652	210
Fancy Goods (Textile), Manufacturer, Worker, Dealer	72	636	22	378	.	76	10	51	30	88
Trimming Maker, Dealer	445	252	244	15	.	.	1	.	61	194
Embroiderer	5	471	.	13	.	1	.	1	4	121
Others	20	.	4	.	.	.	.	.	14	.
18. PERSONS WORKING AND DEALING IN DRESS.										
1. Dress.										
Hatter, Hat Manufacture (not straw)	285	83	146	40	.	.	28	4	61	38
Straw—Hat, Bonnet, Plait, Manufacture	6	153	.	41	.	5	1	55	5	31
Tailor	6379	1613	1288	575	99	6	1978	182	1725	400
Milliner, Dressmaker, Staymaker	140	21301	71	4677	2	279	13	6031	40	5988
Shawl Manufacture	63	33	3	1	.	.	.	1	53	17
Shirt Maker, Seamstress	43	6770	16	2015	.	28	2	574	21	3212
Hosiery Manufacture	18501	19554	9388	12206	.	3	9	12	7817	6238
Hosier, Haberdasher	910	239	399	121	2	.	35	16	411	72
Glover, Glove Maker	142	376	77	294	.	.	2	7	35	40
Button Maker, Dealer	7	7	7	7	.	.	.	.	.	.
Shoe, Boot—Maker, Dealer	19302	5505	12001	4711	156	3	2555	98	2685	304
Patten, Clog, Maker	120	2	2	.	.	.	2	.	17	1
Wig Maker, Hairdresser	814	32	184	11	9	1	230	6	239	0
Umbrella, Parasol, Stick—Maker, Dealer	83	24	20	6	.	.	14	5	28	9
Accoutrement Maker	.	.	.	.	.	.	.	.	.	.
Old Clothes Dealer, and others	8	52	.	15	1	1	2	11	3	14
19. PERSONS WORKING AND DEALING IN VARIOUS ANIMAL SUBSTANCES.										
1. In Grease, Gut, Bone, Horn, Ivory, and Whalebone.										
Tallow Chandler. Candle, Grease, Manufacture	143	3	53	.	.	.	36	.	40	2
Soap Boiler, Maker	31	3	3	.	.	.	12	3	8	.
Glue, Size, Gelatine, Isinglass—Maker, Dealer	29	16	4	1	.	.	5	11	19	6
Manure Manufacture	142	.	11	.	.	.	103	.	23	.
Bone, Horn, Ivory, Tortoise-shell—Worker, Dealer	28	.	15	.	.	.	1	.	11	.
Comb Maker	14	.	.	.	.	.	1	.	2	.
Others	4	1	.	.	.	.	.	.	4	1
2. In Skins.										
Furrier, Skinner	324	37	25	3	1	.	121	25	147	7
Tanner, Fellmonger	476	12	48	.	20	.	157	2	111	5
Currier	880	76	244	4	2	.	153	2	874	64
Leather Goods, Portmanteau, Bag, Strap, &c.—Maker, Dealer	35	10	11	1	.	.	4	1	10	8
Parchment, Vellum—Maker, Dealer	51	4	2	1	3	1	14	2	7	.
3. In Hair and Feathers.										
Hair, Bristle—Worker, Dealer	4	2	3	1	.	.	1	.	.	.
Brush, Broom, Maker	282	56	84	9	.	.	39	.	91	18
Quill, Feather—Dresser, Dealer	8	46	2	9	.	.	4	25	.	9

Table 10 *continued*.—Occupations of Males and Females in the North-Midland Division and its Registration Counties, and in each Urban Sanitary District of which the Population exceeds 50,000 Persons.

Occupations.	North-Midland Counties.		Registration Counties. 28. Leicestershire.		29. Rutlandshire.		30. Lincolnshire.		31. Nottinghamshire.	
	Males.	Females.	Males.	Females.	Males.	Females.	Males.	Females.	Males.	Females.
20. Persons working and dealing in various Vegetable Substances.										
1. *In Oils, Gums, and Resins.*										
Oil Miller, Oil Cake—Maker, Dealer	244	2	6	.	.	.	206	1	29	
Oil and Colourman	19	1	2	.	.	.	2	.	3	.
Floor Cloth, Oil Cloth, Manufacture	.	.	.	.	.	.	.	.	.	.
Japanner	2	5	.	2	.	.	.	.	1	1
India Rubber, Gutta Percha—Worker, Dealer	1342	608	925	488	.	.	2	1	116	30
Waterproof Goods—Maker, Dealer	67	1	2	.	.	.	2	1	4	.
Others	6	2	.	.	.	.	1	.	.	.
2. *In Cane, Rush, and Straw.*										
Willow, Cane, Rush—Worker, Dealer, Basketmaker	789	64	169	17	4	.	168	13	226	19
Hay, Straw (not plait), Chaff—Cutter, Dealer	90	1	18	.	.	.	16	1	29	.
Thatcher	37	.	9	.	4	.	16	.	.	.
3. *In Wood and Bark.*										
Timber Wood—Merchant, Dealer	617	22	185	4	7	.	182	4	190	12
Sawyer	1374	.	241	.	18	.	349	.	411	.
Lath, Wooden Fence, Hurdle, Maker	60	2	7	.	.	.	31	2	19	.
Wood Turner, Box Maker	655	79	151	7	.	.	65	.	212	61
Cooper, Hoop Maker, Bender	448	8	55	.	3	.	170	2	88	.
Cork, Bark—Cutter, Worker, Dealer	42	1	8	.	.	.	9	1	15	.
Others	31	4	1	.	.	.	3	.	16	.
4. *In Paper.*										
Paper Manufacture	591	298	15	23	.	.	4	6	136	18
Envelope Maker	.	6	.	.	.	.	.	.	.	.
Stationer, Law Stationer	221	127	40	28	1	5	48	20	89	43
Card, Pattern Card, Maker	.	14	.	3	.	.	.	.	.	9
Paper Stainer	19	38	.	.	.	.	1	.	8	24
Paper Box, Paper Bag, Maker	183	819	33	267	.	.	.	1	140	415
Ticket, Label, Writer	17	12	4	1	.	.	3	6	9	3
Others	115	22	23	1	1	.	29	.	34	13
21. Persons working and dealing in various Mineral Substances.										
1. *Miners.*										
Coal Miner	40039	57	3699	1	.	.	13	.	18918	41
Ironstone Miner	818	.	115	.	1	.	589	.	41	.
Copper Miner	1	.	.	.	.	.	.	.	1	.
Tin Miner	.	.	.	.	.	.	.	.	.	.
Lead Miner	873	1	.	.	.	.	.	.	2	.
Miner in other, or undefined, Minerals	235	.	7	.	.	.	1	.	162	.
Mine Service	208	3	17	.	.	.	2	.	84	.
2. *Coal, Coal Gas, &c.*										
Coal Merchant, Dealer	1661	64	820	12	17	1	394	11	582	24
Coalheaver	474	.	111	.	17	.	225	.	73	.
Coke, Charcoal, Peat—Cutter, Burner, Dealer	181	.	.	.	.	.	1	.	13	.
Gas Works Service	1036	.	226	.	8	.	171	.	364	.
3. *Stone, Clay, and Road Making.*										
Stone Quarrier	3385	.	1587	.	1	.	137	.	201	.
Stone Cutter, Dresser, Dealer	673	.	140	.	3	.	23	.	74	.
Slate Quarrier	21	.	20	.	.	.	.	.	.	.
Slate Worker, Dealer	10	.	4	.	.	.	3	.	2	.
Limeburner	488	4	102	.	3	.	45	1	66	1
Clay, Sand, Gravel, Chalk—Labourer, Dealer	132	4	82	2	.	.	11	.	9	1
Fossil, Coprolite—Digger, Dealer	.	.	.	.	.	.	.	.	.	.
Well Sinker, Borer	57	.	6	.	.	.	14	.	13	.
Plaster, Cement, Manufacture	212	1	84	.	.	.	20	.	85	1
Brick, Tile—Maker, Burner, Dealer	4142	42	1158	31	57	.	1348	4	1017	3
Paviour	215	.	50	.	.	.	36	.	94	.
Road Contractor, Surveyor, Inspector	79	.	10	.	1	.	29	.	21	.
Road Labourer	806	.	136	.	17	.	231	.	186	.
Railway Contractor	104	.	11	.	.	.	25	.	15	.
Platelayer	2014	.	362	.	63	.	677	.	490	.
Railway Labourer, Navvy	4670	.	1123	.	105	.	1485	.	990	.
Others	81	14	17	1	.	.	.	.	3	2
4. *Earthenware and Glass.*										
Earthenware, China, Porcelain, Manufacture	1087	366	379	116	.	.	18	.	94	14
Glass Manufacture	43	2	5	.	.	.	6	.	12	2
Earthenware, China, Glass, Dealer	149	75	50	11	1	.	37	21	51	15
5. *Salt.*										
Salt Maker, Dealer	12	1	5	.	.	.	.	.	4	.

Table 10 *continued*.—OCCUPATIONS of MALES and FEMALES in the NORTH-MIDLAND DIVISION and its REGISTRATION COUNTIES, and in each URBAN SANITARY DISTRICT of which the POPULATION exceeds 50,000 PERSONS.

OCCUPATIONS.	NORTH-MIDLAND COUNTIES.		REGISTRATION COUNTIES. 28. LEICESTERSHIRE.		29. RUTLANDSHIRE.		30. LINCOLNSHIRE.		31. NOTTINGHAMSHIRE.	
	Males.	Females.	Males.	Females.	Males.	Females.	Males.	Females.	Males.	Females.
6. Water.										
Waterworks Service	101	1	25	-	1	-	22	-	22	-
Others	13	-	-	-	-	-	13	-	-	-
7. Precious Metals and Jewellery.										
Goldsmith, Silversmith, Jeweller	225	32	68	8	1	-	59	3	46	7
Gold, Silver, Beater	3	-	-	-	-	-	2	-	-	-
Lapidary	10	-	-	-	-	-	1	-	-	-
Others	-	4	-	-	-	-	-	-	-	2
8. Iron and Steel.										
Blacksmith	7649	15	1100	5	105	-	2498	5	1873	3
Whitesmith	340	1	45	-	3	-	94	-	147	1
Nail Manufacture	722	23	75	9	-	-	83	2	55	2
Anchor, Chain, Manufacture	11	-	-	-	-	-	3	-	2	-
Other Iron and Steel Manufactures	11088	8	588	-	1	-	2506	2	2360	3
Ironmonger, Hardware Dealer, Merchant	825	40	181	7	17	-	305	11	200	15
9. Copper.										
Copper, Copper goods—Manufacturer, Worker, Dealer	95	-	8	-	-	-	22	-	26	-
10. Tin and Zinc.										
Tin, Tin Plate, Tin goods—Manufacturer, Worker, Dealer	739	9	99	-	7	-	224	1	160	5
Zinc, Zinc Goods—Manufacturer, Worker, Dealer	3	-	-	-	-	-	-	-	1	-
11. Lead.										
Lead, Leaden goods—Manufacturer, Worker, Dealer	99	1	-	-	-	-	-	-	-	-
12. In Other, Mixed, or Unspecified, Metals.										
Metal Refiner, Worker, Turner, Dealer	68	-	8	-	-	-	9	-	9	-
Brass, Bronze, Manufacture. Brazier	664	6	75	1	-	-	145	1	218	2
Metal Burnisher, Lacquerer	2	4	-	-	-	-	1	-	1	1
White Metal, Plated Ware, Manufacture. Pewterer	6	1	-	-	-	-	-	-	3	1
Wire Maker, Worker, Weaver, Drawer	240	41	8	1	-	-	27	3	21	-
Bolt, Nut, Rivet, Screw, Staple, Maker	150	-	5	-	-	-	40	-	39	-
Lamp, Lantern, Candlestick, Maker	9	-	2	-	-	-	-	-	2	-
Clasp, Buckle, Hinge, Maker	-	-	-	-	-	-	-	-	-	-
Fancy Chain, Gilt Toy, Maker	7	-	-	-	-	-	7	-	-	-
Others	3	1	-	-	-	-	-	-	-	1
22. PERSONS WORKING AND DEALING IN GENERAL OR UNSPECIFIED COMMODITIES.										
1. Makers and Dealers (General or Undefined).										
General Shopkeeper, Dealer	1449	1320	322	319	11	10	385	251	483	485
Pawnbroker	286	22	85	3	-	-	46	4	119	9
Costermonger, Huckster, Street Seller	2189	647	408	132	17	5	641	183	389	172
Manufacturer, Manager, Superintendent (undefined)	267	33	81	18	2	-	40	4	78	4
Contractor (undefined)	149	-	20	-	-	-	49	-	46	-
2. Mechanics and Labourers (General or Undefined).										
General Labourer	39130	127	4732	17	426	-	10147	51	7995	35
Engine Driver, Stoker, Fireman (not railway, marine, nor agricultural)	4070	-	632	-	13	-	717	-	1756	-
Artisan, Mechanic (undefined)	1686	177	303	124	4	2	330	3	450	33
Apprentice (undefined)	168	22	41	6	-	-	43	5	39	7
Factory Labourer (undefined)	924	138	203	108	2	-	116	6	158	17
Machinist, Machine Worker (undefined)	367	1058	50	671	4	1	97	37	91	323
23. PERSONS WORKING AND DEALING IN REFUSE MATTERS.										
1. Refuse Matters.										
Town Drainage Service	58	-	3	-	-	-	4	-	46	-
Chimney Sweep, Soot Merchant	589	5	132	-	11	-	131	2	208	3
Scavenger, Crossing Sweeper	76	-	18	-	-	-	18	-	23	-
Rag Gatherer, Dealer	165	30	21	7	-	-	43	2	21	7
VI. UNOCCUPIED CLASS.										
24. PERSONS WITHOUT SPECIFIED OCCUPATIONS										
Persons returned by Property, Rank, &c., and not by special occupation	133311	510332	37541	94813	2957	7587	57180	157625	49683	129504
Children under 5 years of age	114511	116341	22929	23893	1456	1398	31127	30996	30662	31087

Table 10 *continued.*—Occupations of Males and Females in the North-Midland Division and its Registration Counties, and in each Urban Sanitary District of which the Population exceeds 50,000 Persons.

Occupations.	Registration County.		Urban Sanitary Districts.					
	32. DERBYSHIRE.		LEICESTER.		NOTTINGHAM.		DERBY.	
	Males.	Females.	Males.	Females.	Males.	Females.	Males.	Females.
TOTAL	193110	193404	57720	64656	87633	98942	40038	41135
I. PROFESSIONAL CLASS.								
1. Persons engaged in the General or Local Government of the Country.								
1. *National Government.*								
Peer, M.P., Privy Councillor (not otherwise described)	5	.	.	.	.	.	1	.
Civil Service (officers and clerks)	171	60	56	1	87	4	74	1
Civil Service (messengers, &c.)	170	9	60	.	77	1	53	.
Prison Officer, &c.	25	3	14	3	14	2	23	3
2. *Local Government.*								
Police	323	.	125	.	209	.	100	.
Municipal, Parish, Union, District, Officer	129	40	38	14	74	40	34	2
Other Local or County Official	96	.	26	.	43	.	12	.
3. *East Indian and Colonial Service.*								
East Indian and Colonial Service	1	.	.	.	.	.	.	.
2. Persons engaged in the Defence of the Country.								
1. *Army (at Home).*								
Army Officer (effective or retired)	41	.	3	.	4	.	8	.
Soldier and Non-Commissioned Officer	168	.	24	.	30	.	15	.
Militia, Yeomanry, Volunteers	178	.	8	.	9	.	22	.
Army Pensioner	61	.	32	.	46	.	22	.
2. *Navy (ashore or in port).*								
Navy Officer (effective or retired)	6	.	1	.	2	.	1	.
Seaman, R.N.	.	.	1	.	3	.	.	.
Royal Marines (officers and men)	2	.	1	.	3	.	1	.
Navy Pensioner	6	.	10	.	13	.	1	.
3. Persons engaged in Professional Occupations (with their immediate Subordinates).								
1. *Clerical Profession.*								
Clergyman (Established Church)	279	.	39	.	67	.	35	.
Roman Catholic Priest	18	.	7	.	13	.	3	.
Minister, Priest, of other religious bodies	146	.	40	.	52	.	25	.
Missionary, Scripture Reader, Itinerant Preacher	46	23	8	24	28	15	11	8
Nun, Sister of Charity	.	40	.	1	.	42	.	23
Theological Student	24	.	1	.	28	.	1	.
Church, Chapel, Cemetery—Officer, Servant	73	8	27	3	50	4	12	5
2. *Legal Profession.*								
Barrister, Solicitor	131	.	43	.	107	.	34	.
Law Student	14	.	2	.	4	.	2	.
Law Clerk, and others connected with Law	201	.	115	.	218	3	74	.
3. *Medical Profession.*								
Physician, Surgeon, General Practitioner	203	1	52	.	88	.	38	1
Dentist	36	.	20	.	44	.	24	.
Medical Student, Assistant	47	.	9	1	12	.	15	.
Midwife	.	47	.	15	.	24	.	10
Subordinate Medical Service	53	221	22	203	22	208	16	76
4. *Teachers.*								
Schoolmaster	618	1406	153	528	229	714	106	354
Teacher, Professor, Lecturer	50	128	16	87	26	61	18	24
School Service, and others concerned in Teaching	18	10	13	6	27	5	8	6
5. *Literary and Scientific Persons.*								
Author, Editor, Journalist	17	2	12	2	12	1	9	2
Reporter, Short-hand Writer	24	.	11	.	23	.	9	.
Persons engaged in Scientific Pursuits	8	.	3	.	4	.	1	.
Literary, Scientific, Institution, Service, &c.	4	2	1	1	6	2	2	.
6. *Engineers and Surveyors.*								
Civil Engineer	92	.	10	.	37	.	47	.
Mining Engineer	74	.	1	.	9	.	12	.
Land, House, Ship, Surveyor	112	.	16	.	26	.	47	.
7. *Artists.*								
Painter (artist)	43	7	21	5	65	12	24	4
Engraver (artist)	11	.	2	.	7	.	4	.
Sculptor	7	.	4	.	5	.	1	.
Architect	99	.	56	.	72	.	44	.
Musician, Music Master	123	79	112	73	137	158	55	37
Art Student	10	6	3	1	11	9	4	4
Photographer	31	8	37	8	54	11	.	.
Actor	28	19	25	17	26	13	7	.
Art, Music, Theatre, Service	10	1	9	.	9	3	7	.

Table 10 *continued.*—OCCUPATIONS of MALES and FEMALES in the NORTH-MIDLAND DIVISION and its REGISTRATION COUNTIES, and in each URBAN SANITARY DISTRICT of which the POPULATION exceeds 50,000 PERSONS.

OCCUPATIONS.	REGISTRATION COUNTY.		URBAN SANITARY DISTRICTS.					
	32. DERBYSHIRE.		LEICESTER.		NOTTINGHAM.		DERBY.	
	Males.	Females.	Males.	Females.	Males.	Females.	Males.	Females.
8. *Persons engaged in Exhibitions, Shows, Games, &c.*								
Performer, Showman, Exhibition, Service	18	2	17	11	18	1	12	1
Billiard, Cricket, & other Games, Service	29	1	19	.	39	.	9	.
II. DOMESTIC CLASS.								
4. PERSONS ENGAGED IN DOMESTIC OFFICES OR SERVICES.								
1. *Domestic Service.*								
Domestic Coachman, Groom	768	.	116	.	221	.	112	.
Domestic Gardener	1154	.	246	.	323	.	166	.
Domestic Indoor Servant	631	13628	132	3583	115	6060	84	2701
Lodge, Gate, Park, Keeper (not Government)	13	10	1	.	3	1	.	2
Inn, Hotel, Servant	229	315	130	190	312	228	71	115
College, Club, Service	11	4	8	3	17	6	6	.
2. *Other Service.*								
Office Keeper (not Government)	13	26	10	6	6	19	5	13
Cook (not domestic)	18	25	3	5	4	16	17	9
Charwoman	.	1006	.	442	.	569	.	233
Washing and Bathing Service	38	1203	10	680	14	848	5	307
Hospital and Institution Service	14	98	19	83	64	88	5	43
Others engaged in Service	11	6	2	2	8	1	3	.
III. COMMERCIAL CLASS.								
5. PERSONS ENGAGED IN COMMERCIAL OCCUPATIONS.								
1. *Merchants and Agents.*								
Merchant	87	.	9	.	30	.	3	.
Broker, Agent, Factor	269	6	199	6	315	6	97	3
Auctioneer, Appraiser, Valuer, House Agent	124	.	45	1	78	2	31	.
Accountant	86	.	81	.	67	.	39	.
Salesman, Buyer (not otherwise described)	13	8	9	4	13	14	6	3
Commercial Traveller	251	.	298	.	417	.	116	.
Commercial Clerk	1684	40	834	41	1306	40	631	24
Officer of Commercial Company, Guild, Society, &c.	3	.	1	.	.	.	2	.
2. *Dealers in Money.*								
Banker	8	.	1	.	3	.	1	.
Bank Service	137	.	74	.	85	.	42	.
Bill Discounter, Bill Broker, Finance Agent	1	.	5	.	4	.	.	.
3. *Persons occupied in Insurance.*								
Life, House, Ship, &c., Insurance Service	143	.	66	.	96	.	34	.
6. PERSONS ENGAGED IN CONVEYANCE OF MEN, GOODS, AND MESSAGES.								
1. *On Railways.*								
Railway Engine Driver, Stoker	628	.	97	.	202	.	344	.
Railway Guard	347	.	40	.	116	.	126	.
Pointsman, Level Crossing Man	204	2	29	.	88	.	51	.
Other Railway Officials and Servants	2882	6	474	2	705	3	1400	4
2. *On Roads.*								
Toll Collector, Turnpike Gate Keeper	16	14	2	.	2	.	1	1
Omnibus, Coach, Cab, Owner—Livery Stable Keeper	58	.	30	1	56	3	32	.
Cabman, Flyman, Coachman (not domestic)	178	.	65	.	188	.	86	.
Carman, Carrier, Carter, Haulier	1153	5	396	.	752	.	328	3
Tramway Companies' Service	29	.	46	.	69	.	24	.
Wheel Chair Proprietor, Attendant, &c.	13	.	.	.	.	.	.	.
3. *On Canals, Rivers and Seas.*								
Inland Navigation Service	34	.	2	.	9	.	2	.
Bargeman, Lighterman, Waterman	150	.	38	.	51	.	29	.
Navigation Service (on shore)	7	.	.	.	1	.	.	.
Seaman (Merchant Service)	32	.	10	.	24	.	9	.
Pilot	.	.	.	.	.	.	.	.
Ship Steward, Cook	3	.	1	.	3	.	.	.
Boatman on Seas	.	.	.	.	.	.	.	.
Harbour, Dock, Wharf, Lighthouse, Service	6	.	5	.	3	.	.	.
4. *In Storage.*								
Warehouseman (not Manchester)	98	40	271	194	431	67	33	17
Meter, Weigher	2	.	2	.	8	.	1	.
5. *In conveying Messages, Porterage, &c.*								
Messenger, Porter, Watchman (not Railway nor Government)	991	8	738	65	1074	168	473	2
Telegraph, Telephone Service	166	35	24	.	50	11	91	2

Table 10 *continued*.—OCCUPATIONS of MALES and FEMALES in the NORTH-MIDLAND DIVISION and its REGISTRATION COUNTIES, and in each URBAN SANITARY DISTRICT of which the POPULATION exceeds 50,000 PERSONS.

OCCUPATIONS.	REGISTRATION COUNTY.		URBAN SANITARY DISTRICTS.					
	32. DERBYSHIRE.		LEICESTER.		NOTTINGHAM.		DERBY.	
	Males.	Females.	Males.	Females.	Males.	Females.	Males.	Females.
IV. AGRICULTURAL CLASS.								
7. PERSONS ENGAGED IN AGRICULTURE.								
1. *In Fields and Pastures.*								
Farmer, Grazier	5211	609	42	1	78	3	27	1
Farmer's, Grazier's—Son, Grandson, Brother, Nephew*	1589	.	5	.	15	.	4	.
Farm Bailiff	161	.	1	.	9	.	6	.
Agricultural Labourer, Farm Servant, Cottager	7672	341	287	4	473	7	155	5
Shepherd	65	.	3	.	2	.	1	.
Land Drainage Service (not in towns)	8	.	.	.	.	.	.	.
Agricultural Machine—Proprietor, Attendant	14	.	1	.	4	.	.	.
Agricultural Student, Pupil	6	.	.	.	.	.	.	.
Others engaged in, or connected with, Agriculture	.	.	.	.	.	1	.	.
2. *In Woods.*								
Woodman	122	.	1	.	1	.	1	.
3. *In Gardens.*								
Nurseryman, Seedsman, Florist	116	1	17	2	33	3	6	1
Gardener (not domestic)	478	11	26	3	214	4	19	1
8. PERSONS ENGAGED ABOUT ANIMALS.								
1. *About Animals.*								
Horse Proprietor, Breeder, Dealer	24	.	13	.	27	.	8	.
Groom, Horse-keeper, Horse-breaker	318	.	236	.	344	.	121	.
Veterinary Surgeon, Farrier	69	.	13	.	19	.	13	.
Cattle, Sheep, Pig—Dealer, Salesman	109	.	31	.	26	1	27	.
Drover	27	.	13	.	13	.	17	.
Gamekeeper	179	.	1	.	5	.	1	.
Dog, Bird, Animal—Keeper, Dealer	4	.	2	.	1	.	2	.
Vermin destroyer	12	.	.	.	1	.	.	.
Fisherman	1	.	.	.	4	.	.	.
Knacker, Catsmeat Dealer, &c., &c.	3	.	2	.	2	.	2	.
V. INDUSTRIAL CLASS.								
9. PERSONS WORKING AND DEALING IN BOOKS, PRINTS, AND MAPS.								
1. *Books.*								
Publisher, Bookseller, Librarian	54	24	59	12	79	2	27	8
Music—Publisher, Seller, Printer	13	1	3	9	4	4	6	1
Bookbinder	75	62	52	41	93	64	62	61
Printer	601	46	324	13	717	10	379	44
Newspaper Agent, News Room Keeper	37	15	10	10	29	20	10	10
Others	.	.	.	.	1	.	.	.
2. *Prints and Maps.*								
Lithographer, Lithographic Printer	87	.	56	.	177	5	46	.
Copper Plate and Steel Plate Printer	8	.	.	.	1	.	8	.
Map and Print—Colourer, Seller	.	.	.	.	.	.	.	.
10. PERSONS WORKING AND DEALING IN MACHINES AND IMPLEMENTS.								
1. *Machines.*								
Engine, Machine, Maker	521	.	119	1	318	4	250	.
Millwright	125	.	9	.	20	.	50	.
Fitter, Turner (Engine and Machine)	2057	.	248	.	742	.	1359	.
Boiler Maker	580	.	44	.	105	.	374	.
Spinning and Weaving Machine Maker	309	9	293	1	1498	.	35	.
Agricultural Machine and Implement Maker	253	.	9	.	.	.	6	.
Domestic Machinery—Maker, Dealer	1	.	.	.	1	.	1	.
2. *Tools and Implements.*								
Tool Maker, Dealer	134	.	7	1	27	1	11	.
Cutler, Scissors Maker	65	.	25	4	17	2	7	.
File Maker	40	.	1	.	2	.	4	.
Saw Maker	18	.	5	.	9	.	8	.
Pin Maker	1	1	.	.	.	.	.	.
Needle Maker	7	.	93	11	89	6	.	.
Steel Pen Maker	.	2	.	.	.	.	.	.
Pencil Maker (Wood)	.	.	.	.	.	.	.	2
Domestic Implement Maker	18	.	.	.	.	.	.	.
3. *Watches and Philosophical Instruments.*								
Watch Maker, Clock Maker	189	3	80	2	117	.	67	2
Philosophical Instrument Maker, Optician	22	.	5	.	12	3	15	.
Electrical Apparatus Maker	60	.	15	.	17	.	46	.
Weighing and Measuring Apparatus Maker	5	.	2	.	6	.	4	.

* Only male relatives living with the farmer or grazier, and therefore presumably [illegible]

Table 10 *continued.*—OCCUPATIONS of MALES and FEMALES in the NORTH-MIDLAND DIVISION and its REGISTRATION COUNTIES, and in each URBAN SANITARY DISTRICT of which the POPULATION exceeds 50,000 PERSONS.

OCCUPATIONS.	REGISTRATION COUNTY.		URBAN SANITARY DISTRICTS.					
	32. DERBYSHIRE.		LEICESTER.		NOTTINGHAM.		DERBY.	
	Males.	Females.	Males.	Females.	Males.	Females.	Males.	Females.
4. Surgical Instruments.								
Surgical Instrument Maker	72	28	2	.	21	18	37	25
5. Arms and Ordnance.								
Gunsmith, Gun Manufacturer	11	1	4	.	5	.	9	1
Ordnance Manufacturer	.	.	.	.	.	.	.	.
Sword, Bayonet—Maker, Cutler	1	.	.	.	.	.	.	.
Others	.	.	.	.	1	.	.	.
6. Musical Instruments.								
Musical Instrument Maker, Dealer	10	.	32	.	35	4	8	.
7. Type, Dies, Medals, Coins.								
Type Cutter, Founder	.	.	.	.	1	.	.	.
Die, Seal, Coin, Medal, Maker	8	.	27	.	54	1	.	.
8. Tackle for Sports and Games.								
Toy Maker, Dealer	4	16	.	2	10	5	3	8
Fishing Rod, Tackle, Maker, Dealer	12	.	1	.	12	.	8	.
Apparatus for other Games, Maker, Dealer	3	.	1	.	2	.	1	.
11. PERSONS WORKING AND DEALING IN HOUSES, FURNITURE, AND DECORATIONS.								
1. Houses.								
Builder	262	1	140	.	288	2	97	.
Carpenter, Joiner	2968	1	985	.	1701	1	808	.
Bricklayer	1325	.	925	2	1410	1	515	.
Mason	1864	.	195	.	438	1	193	.
Slater, Tiler	182	.	45	1	128	.	49	.
Plasterer, Whitewasher	305	.	121	.	231	.	95	.
Paperhanger	71	.	5	1	46	3	3	.
Plumber	491	4	163	1	428	5	174	2
Painter, Glazier	1155	6	504	1	817	2	511	.
2. Furniture and Fittings.								
Cabinet Maker, Upholsterer	323	50	258	30	437	46	134	34
French Polisher	27	22	34	4	64	8	21	17
Furniture Broker, Dealer	44	11	24	8	59	4	26	7
Locksmith, Bellhanger	22	.	14	.	9	.	16	.
Gas Fitter	116	.	110	.	58	1	88	.
House and Shop Fittings—Maker, Dealer	12	.	28	1	16	1	7	.
Funeral Furniture Maker, Undertaker	9	2	3	1	10	.	7	2
Others	.	.	.	.	.	.	.	.
3. House Decorations.								
Wood Carver	4	.	15	.	14	.	3	.
Carver, Gilder	36	3	38	.	79	1	29	3
Dealer in Works of Art	6	2	1	.	11	.	4	1
Figure, Image—Maker, Dealer	1	.	5	.	.	.	.	.
Animal, Bird, &c., Preserver, Naturalist	4	.	6	.	4	.	1	.
Artificial Flower Maker	.	.	.	2	2	4	.	.
12. PERSONS WORKING AND DEALING IN CARRIAGES AND HARNESS.								
1. Carriages.								
Coachmaker	354	8	131	1	194	.	275	.
Railway Carriage, Railway Wagon, Maker	644	17	10	.	23	.	344	17
Wheelwright	536	.	92	.	160	.	100	.
Bicycle, Tricycle—Maker, Dealer	2	.	5	.	15	.	2	.
Others	16	.	18	1	36	3	4	.
2. Harness.								
Saddler, Harness, Whip, Maker	248	3	71	2	177	2	52	.
13. PERSONS WORKING AND DEALING IN SHIPS AND BOATS.								
1. Hull.								
Ship, Boat, Barge, Builder	17	1	9	1	14	.	6	.
Shipwright, Ship Carpenter (ashore)	6	.	.	.	1	.	2	.
2. Masts, Rigging, &c.								
Mast, Yard, Oar, Block, Maker	.	.	.	.	.	.	.	.
[illegible]	7	.	.	1	4	.	3	.

Table 10 *continued*.—Occupations of Males and Females in the North-midland Division and its Registration Counties, and in each Urban Sanitary District of which the Population exceeds 50,000 Persons.

Occupations.	Registration County.		Urban Sanitary Districts.					
	32. DERBYSHIRE.		LEICESTER.		NOTTING-HAM.		DERBY.	
	Males.	Females.	Males.	Females.	Males.	Females.	Males.	Females.
14. Persons working and dealing in Chemicals and Compounds.								
1. *Colouring Matter.*								
Dye, Paint, Manufacture	69	1	1	.	5	1	9	.
Ink, Blacking, Colouring Substance, Manufacture	87	1	3	.	10	1	63	1
2. *Explosives.*								
Gunpowder, Guncotton, Explosive Substance, Manufacture	7	.	.	.	.	.	1	.
Fuses, Fireworks, Explosive Article, Manufacture	1	.	.	.	.	.	.	.
3. *Drugs and other Chemicals and Compounds.*								
Chemist, Druggist	247	9	138	2	195	6	57	4
Manufacturing Chemist	66	20	11	1	15	.	16	1
Alkali Manufacture	2	.	.	.	1	.	.	.
Drysalter	1	.	6	.	4	.	1	.
15. Persons working and dealing in Tobacco and Pipes.								
1. *Tobacco and Pipes.*								
Tobacco Manufacturer, Tobacconist	86	81	181	468	152	636	27	17
Tobacco Pipe, Snuff Box, &c., Maker	4	5	3	4	12	6	.	4
16. Persons working and Dealing in Food and Lodging.								
1. *Board and Lodging.*								
Innkeeper, Hotel Keeper, Publican	869	215	264	48	416	72	217	44
Lodging, Boarding House, Keeper	55	340	7	101	10	128	7	76
Coffee, Eating House, Keeper	28	10	21	7	22	23	16	7
2. *Spirituous Drinks.*								
Hop—Merchant, Dealer	5	.	3	.	1	.	4	.
Maltster	116	1	42	1	133	.	63	.
Brewer	245	8	81	.	224	1	95	1
Beerseller, Ale, Porter, Cider, Dealer	143	40	88	16	169	19	24	7
Cellarman	29	.	30	.	46	.	16	.
Wine, Spirit—Merchant, Agent	52	5	19	2	47	1	16	1
3. *Food.*								
Milkseller, Dairyman	84	30	115	29	196	38	35	17
Cheesemonger, Butterman	12	6	5	2	2	3	5	3
Butcher, Meat Salesman	1203	41	463	18	787	40	315	11
Provision Curer, Dealer	162	70	118	38	149	73	69	34
Poulterer, Game Dealer	11	4	13	1	14	2	7	2
Fishmonger	112	13	104	6	199	23	51	7
Corn, Flour, Seed—Merchant, Dealer	44	4	39	6	47	4	15	.
Corn Miller	207	2	62	.	65	.	47	.
Baker	506	66	378	18	553	35	207	11
Confectioner, Pastrycook	144	159	139	62	156	64	69	75
Greengrocer, Fruiterer	280	81	107	51	149	36	76	40
Mustard, Vinegar, Spice, Pickle—Maker, Dealer	1	3	.	.	.	.	.	.
Sugar Refiner	13	6	7	.	14	.	7	5
Grocer, Tea, Coffee, Chocolate—Maker, Dealer	1640	471	498	151	778	210	384	71
Ginger Beer, Mineral Water—Manufacturer, Dealer	60	1	27	.	26	.	26	1
Others dealing in Food	.	.	.	.	.	.	.	.
17. Persons working and dealing in Textile Fabrics.								
1. *Wool and Worsted.*								
Woolstapler	8	1	43	.	14	.	5	1
Woollen Cloth Manufacture	63	64	303	327	53	38	1	29
Wool, Woollen goods—Dyer, Printer	8	.	43	.	4	.	1	.
Worsted, Stuff, Manufacture	12	21	243	586	5	5	4	10
Flannel Manufacture	1	.	.	1	.	.	1	.
Blanket Manufacture	.	1	.	.	.	1	.	.
Fuller	.	.	.	.	.	.	.	.
Cloth, Worsted, Stuff, Flannel, Blanket, Dealer	3	1	7	.	4	.	.	.
Others		11	.	.	2	2	.	.
2. *Silk.*								
Silk, Silk goods, Manufacture	441	1863	23	108	216	657	239	1486
Silk Dyer, Printer	45	.	6	.	34	.	45	.
Ribbon Manufacture	18	1	3	6	3	.	18	1
Crape, Gauze, Manufacture	.	.	.	.	.	.	.	.
Silk Merchant, Dealer	2	.	2	.	19	.	2	.

Table 10 *continued*.—OCCUPATIONS of MALES and FEMALES in the NORTH-MIDLAND DIVISION and its REGISTRATION COUNTIES, and in each URBAN SANITARY DISTRICT of which the POPULATION exceeds 50,000 PERSONS.

OCCUPATIONS.	REGISTRATION COUNTY.		URBAN SANITARY DISTRICTS.					
	32. DERBYSHIRE.		LEICESTER.		NOTTINGHAM.		DERBY.	
	Males.	Females.	Males.	Females.	Males.	Females.	Males.	Females.
3. Cotton and Flax.								
Cotton, Cotton goods, Manufacture	4221	8241	70	131	[illegible]	1581	36	279
Cotton, Calico—Printer, Dyer, Bleacher	1924	261	22	2	10	4	13	.
Cotton, Calico—Warehouseman, Dealer	7	2	.	.	10	.	.	.
Flax, Linen—Manufacturer, Dealer	10	8	2	.	4	.	.	.
Lace Manufacturer, Dealer	1173	1060	11	23	8138	12383	184	273
Fustian Manufacturer, Dealer	.	.	.	.	.	.	.	.
Tape Manufacturer, Dealer	77	118	1	4	.	.	.	.
Thread Manufacturer, Dealer	3	5	2	.	2	1	1	5
4. Hemp and other Fibrous Materials.								
Hemp, Jute, Cocoa Fibre, Manufacture	.	.	.	.	.	.	.	.
Rope, Twine, Cord—Maker, Dealer	84	4	57	2	63	2	12	1
Mat Maker, Seller	.	1	1	.	1	.	.	.
Net Maker	7	3	.	.	.	3	6	2
Canvas, Sailcloth, Manufacture	.	.	.	.	.	.	.	.
Sacking, Sack, Bag—Maker, Dealer	2	5	.	.	2	1	.	1
Others working and dealing in Hemp	5	2	3	.	2	.	5	2
5. Mixed or Unspecified Materials.								
Weaver (undefined)	28	43	58	18	16	9	20	23
Dyer, Printer, Scourer, Bleacher, Calenderer (undefined)	127	7	236	14	757	119	56	3
Factory hand (Textile, undefined)	167	814	71	431	66	442	63	310
Felt Manufacture	.	.	.	7	.	.	.	.
Carpet, Rug, Manufacture	6	1	10	1	4	1	3	1
Manchester Warehouseman	1	.	1	.	.	.	.	.
Draper, Linen Draper, Mercer	616	184	276	110	820	128	181	64
Fancy Goods (Textile), Manufacturer, Worker, Dealer	10	45	26	301	13	85	2	12
Trimming Maker, Dealer	139	43	232	5	57	167	134	28
Embroiderer	1	335	.	8	3	52	.	5
Others	2	.	1	.	13	.	.	.
18. PERSONS WORKING AND DEALING IN DRESS.								
1. Dress.								
Hatter, Hat Manufacture (not straw)	50	11	128	32	58	35	18	2
Straw—Hat, Bonnet, Plait, Manufacture	.	21	.	91	5	13	.	10
Tailor	1289	450	561	448	938	319	443	336
Milliner, Dressmaker, Staymaker	14	4323	16	1963	36	2938	2	1238
Shawl Manufacture	7	14	3	1	2	1	1	.
Shirt Maker, Seamstress	4	941	5	509	11	1196	2	161
Hosiery Manufacture	1187	1088	3121	5214	3314	3409	50	715
Hosier, Haberdasher	63	30	270	94	291	51	21	17
Glover, Glove Maker	8	125	70	175	52	24	.	2
Button Maker, Dealer	.	.	7	5	.	.	.	.
Shoe, Boot—Maker, Dealer	1962	389	9172	3583	1480	221	324	262
Patten, Clog, Maker	89	1	1	.	13	1	7	.
Wig Maker, Hairdresser	152	5	119	9	171	5	63	5
Umbrella, Parasol, Stick—Maker, Dealer	21	4	17	3	21	9	6	.
Accoutrement Maker	.	.	.	.	.	.	.	.
Old Clothes Dealer, and others	2	11	.	10	3	13	.	8
19. PERSONS WORKING AND DEALING IN VARIOUS ANIMAL SUBSTANCES.								
1. In Grease, Gut, Bone, Horn, Ivory, and Whalebone.								
Tallow Chandler, Candle, Grease, Manufacture	54	1	20	.	23	1	10	
Soap Boiler, Maker	8	.	1	.	8	.	4	
Glue, Size, Gelatine, Isinglass—Maker, Dealer	1	.	.	1	11	5	.	.
Manure Manufacture	6	.	4	.	7	.	1	.
Bone, Horn, Ivory, Tortoise-shell—Worker, Dealer	1	.	9	.	1	.	.	.
Comb Maker	11	.	.	.	1	.	1	.
Others	.	.	.	.	4	1	.	.
2. In Skins.								
Furrier, Skinner	30	2	6	3	139	5	3	2
Tanner, Fellmonger	140	5	10	.	60	4	19	.
Currier	116	6	163	2	338	6	19	5
Leather Goods, Portmanteau, Bag, Strap, &c.—Maker, Dealer	10	.	9	1	18	6	2	.
Parchment, Vellum—Maker, Dealer	5	.	2	.	7	.	5	.
3. In Hair and Feathers.								
Hair, Bristle—Worker, Dealer	.	1	.	.	.	.	.	1
Brush, Broom, Maker	8	28	44	1	44	14	45	23
Quill, Feather—Dresser, Dealer	.	3	2	9	.	9	.	3

Table 10 *continued*.—Occupations of Males and Females in the North-Midland Division and its Registration Counties, and in each Urban Sanitary District of which the Population exceeds 50,000 Persons.

Occupations.	Registration County.		Urban Sanitary Districts.					
	32. DERBYSHIRE.		LEICESTER.		NOTTINGHAM.		DERBY.	
	Males.	Females.	Males.	Females.	Males.	Females.	Males.	Females.
20. Persons working and dealing in various Vegetable Substances.								
1. *In Oils, Gums, and Resins.*								
Oil Miller, Oil Cake—Maker, Dealer	3	1	4	.	20	.	.	.
Oil and Colourman	3	1	.	.	.	.	2	1
Floor Cloth, Oil Cloth, Manufacture	.	.	.	.	.	.	.	.
Japanner	1	2	.	2	1	1	1	2
India Rubber, Gutta Percha—Worker, Dealer	239	89	757	196	70	19	276	57
Waterproof Goods—Maker, Dealer	59	.	2	.	1	.	.	.
Others	5	2	.	.	.	.	5	.
2. *In Cane, Rush, and Straw.*								
Willow, Cane, Rush—Worker, Dealer, Basketmaker	213	15	80	15	138	12	47	9
Hay, Straw (not plait), Chaff—Cutter, Dealer	27	.	8	.	34	.	10	.
Thatcher	8	.	1	.	.	.	.	.
3. *In Wood and Bark.*								
Timber, Wood—Merchant, Dealer	133	2	59	3	125	7	73	1
Sawyer	355		83	.	180	.	130	.
Lath, Wooden Fence, Hurdle, Maker	3	.	5	.	18	.	2	.
Wood Turner, Box Maker	227	11	101	7	113	60	75	4
Cooper, Hoop Maker, Bender	132	1	26	.	36	.	64	.
Cork, Bark—Cutter, Worker, Dealer	10	.	8	.	14	.	10	.
Others	11	4	.	.	.	.	.	.
4. *In Paper.*								
Paper Manufacture	436	251	14	18	88	9	16	26
Envelope Maker	.	6	.	.	.	.	.	6
Stationer, Law Stationer	41	31	30	20	69	33	17	11
Card, Pattern Card, Maker	.	2	.	3	.	9	.	1
Paper Stainer	15	8	.	.	2	22	4	1
Paper Box, Paper Bag, Maker	10	136	31	210	139	415	1	40
Ticket, Label, Writer	1	2	4	1	9	3	1	.
Others	28	8	10	1	24	12	9	.
21. Persons working and dealing in various Mineral Substances.								
1. *Miners.*								
Coal Miner	17409	15	17	.	2301	9	63	.
Ironstone Miner	72	.	1	.	2	.	3	.
Copper Miner	.	.	.	.	.	.	.	.
Tin Miner	.	.	.	.	.	.	.	.
Lead Miner	871	1	.	.	.		.	.
Miner in other, or undefined, Minerals	50	.	1	.	1	.	2	.
Mine Service	105	3	4	.	16	.	4	2
2. *Coal, Coal Gas, &c.*								
Coal Merchant, Dealer	342	16	106	3	389	17	111	3
Coalheaver	48	.	45	.	57	.	10	.
Coke, Charcoal, Peat—Cutter, Burner, Dealer	167	.	.	.	.	.	1	.
Gas Works Service	267	.	138	.	269	.	111	.
3. *Stone, Clay, and Road Making.*								
Stone Quarrier	1389	.	8	.	58	.	6	.
Stone Cutter, Dresser, Dealer	436	.	14	.	39	.	24	.
Slate Quarrier	1	.	.	.	.	.	.	.
Slate Worker, Dealer	1	.	2	.	2	.	1	.
Limeburner	272	2	7	.	15	1	.	.
Clay, Sand, Gravel, Chalk—Labourer, Dealer	30	1	3		4	.	1	1
Fossil, Coprolite—Digger, Dealer	.	.	.	.	.	.	.	.
Well Sinker, Borer	24	.	1	.	1	.	2	.
Plaster, Cement, Manufacture	73	.	1	.	10	.	37	.
Brick, Tile—Maker, Burner, Dealer	562	4	741	2	348	.	154	1
Paviour	35	.	40	.	79	.	25	.
Road Contractor, Surveyor, Inspector	18	.	3	.	9	.	3	.
Road Labourer	237	.	32	.	49	.	29	.
Railway Contractor	53	.	.	.	8	.	40	.
Platelayer	429	.	20	.	93	.	39	.
Railway Labourer, Navvy	1017	.	102	.	305	.	383	.
Others	61	11	.	1	.	2	27	4
4. *Earthenware and Glass.*								
Earthenware, China, Porcelain, Manufacture	566	237	9		47	2	102	107
Glass Manufacture	20	.	5	.	7	2	2	.
Earthenware, China, Glass, Dealer	30	18	17	6	30	10	11	8
5. *Salt.*								
Salt Maker, Dealer	3	1	3	.	.	.	.	.

Table 10 *continued.*—OCCUPATIONS of MALES and FEMALES in the NORTH-MIDLAND DIVISION and its REGISTRATION COUNTIES, and in each URBAN SANITARY DISTRICT of which the POPULATION exceeds 50,000 PERSONS.

OCCUPATIONS.	REGISTRATION COUNTY.		URBAN SANITARY DISTRICTS.					
	32. DERBYSHIRE.		LEICESTER.		NOTTINGHAM.		DERBY.	
	Males.	Females.	Males.	Females.	Males.	Females.	Males.	Females.
6. Water.								
Waterworks Service	31	1	12	.	11	.	14	.
Others	.	.	.	.	.	.	.	.
7. Precious Metals and Jewellery.								
Goldsmith, Silversmith, Jeweller	68	14	37	6	82	7	40	5
Gold, Silver, Beater	.	.	.	.	.	.	.	.
Lapidary	9	.	.	.	.	.	1	.
Others	.	.	.	.	.	3	.	.
8. Iron and Steel.								
Blacksmith	2078	2	231	.	668	1	638	.
Whitesmith	51	.	21	.	71	.	23	.
Nail Manufacture	612	15	50	2	21	.	27	3
Anchor, Chain, Manufacture	8	.	.	.	1	.	5	.
Other Iron and Steel Manufactures	5623	1	387	.	1122	2	2087	.
Ironmonger. Hardware Dealer, Merchant	148	7	81	3	115	7	50	1
9. Copper.								
Copper, Copper goods—Manufacturer, Worker, Dealer	39	.	6	.	21	.	35	.
10. Tin and Zinc.								
Tin, Tin Plate, Tin goods—Manufacturer, Worker, Dealer	210	3	41	.	139	4	84	1
Zinc, Zinc Goods—Manufacturer, Worker, Dealer	2	.	.	.	.	.	.	.
11. Lead.								
Lead, Leaden goods—Manufacturer, Worker, Dealer	39	1	.	.	.	.	42	.
12. In Other, Mixed, or Unspecified, Metals.								
Metal Refiner, Worker, Turner, Dealer	42	.	6	.	4	.	26	.
Brass, Bronze, Manufacture. Brazier	226	2	40	.	181	2	160	1
Metal Burnisher, Lacquerer	.	3	.	.	1	1	.	3
White Metal, Plated Ware, Manufacture. Pewterer	8	.	.	.	3	1	1	.
Wire Maker, Worker, Weaver, Drawer	184	37	5	1	10	.	7	33
Bolt, Nut, Rivet, Screw, Staple, Maker	66	.	3	.	36	.	55	.
Lamp, Lantern, Candlestick, Maker	5	.	3	.	2	.	3	.
Clasp, Buckle, Hinge, Maker	.	.	.	.	.	.	.	.
Fancy Chain, Gilt Toy, Maker	.	.	.	.	.	.	.	.
Others	3	.	.	.	.	.	.	.
22. PERSONS WORKING AND DEALING IN GENERAL OR UNSPECIFIED COMMODITIES.								
1. Makers and Dealers (General or Undefined).								
General Shopkeeper, Dealer	248	245	173	191	812	328	88	88
Pawnbroker	46	6	70	3	83	7	15	1
Costermonger, Huckster, Street Seller	624	155	168	53	337	98	119	47
Manufacturer, Manager, Superintendent (undefined)	66	7	49	15	60	3	37	4
Contractor (undefined)	35	.	12	.	20	.	10	.
2. Mechanics and Labourers (General or Undefined).								
General Labourer	8830	24	1298	12	2830	9	2173	6
Engine Driver, Stoker, Fireman (not railway, marine, nor agricultural)	1452	.	256	.	400	.	200	.
Artizan, Mechanic (undefined)	599	10	146	110	226	19	250	6
Apprentice (undefined)	45	4	20	5	21	8	19	3
Factory Labourer (undefined)	445	7	137	90	91	8	68	5
Machinist, Machine Worker (undefined)	125	26	18	668	75	294	79	1
23. PERSONS WORKING AND DEALING IN REFUSE MATTERS.								
1. Refuse Matters.								
Town Drainage Service	5	.	2	.	45	.	3	.
Chimney Sweep, Soot Merchant	107	.	51	.	104	3	30	.
Scavenger, Crossing Sweeper	17	.	16	.	10	.	8	.
Rag Gatherer, Dealer	20	14	9	3	4	4	3	7
VI. UNOCCUPIED CLASS.								
24. PERSONS WITHOUT SPECIFIED OCCUPATIONS								
Persons returned by Property, Rank, &c., and not by special occupation	45941	121213	13414	32379	19631	50034	9273	26213
Children under 5 years of age	28307	28467	8536	8784	12068	12281	5862	5986

Table 11.—BIRTH-PLACES of MALES and FEMALES enumerated in COUNTIES, and in each URBAN SANITARY DISTRICT of which the POPULATION EXCEEDS 50,000 PERSONS.

WHERE BORN.	WHERE ENUMERATED.									
	NORTH-MIDLAND COUNTIES.		COUNTIES.*							
			LEICESTERSHIRE.		RUTLANDSHIRE.		LINCOLNSHIRE.		NOTTINGHAMSHIRE.	
	Males.	Females.	Males.	Females.	Males.	Females.	Males.	Females.	Males.	Females.
TOTAL OF INHABITANTS	825146	841194	155881	165377	10764	10670	285219	284700	190778	201037
LONDON	9019	9350	1885	2229	208	225	3126	2584	2006	2328
MIDDLESEX (*Intra-metropolitan*)	7124	7559	1563	1821	165	186	2286	1987	1658	1928
SURREY (*Intra-metropolitan*)	1034	1033	218	236	21	28	330	310	239	235
KENT (*Intra-metropolitan*)	861	758	104	172	22	11	510	287	109	165
SOUTH-EASTERN COUNTIES	5689	5956	1172	1357	148	122	1857	1746	1251	1391
SURREY (*Extra-metropolitan*)	870	869	201	223	32	17	224	238	217	190
KENT (*Extra-metropolitan*)	1769	1941	336	384	47	34	769	639	353	440
SUSSEX	818	887	137	188	26	28	278	255	204	212
HAMPSHIRE	1496	1633	339	390	22	30	419	423	345	389
BERKSHIRE	736	676	179	172	21	19	167	158	152	151
SOUTH-MIDLAND COUNTIES	23027	22676	6952	7810	662	984	6750	6578	4086	3770
MIDDLESEX (*Ex.-metropolitan*)	632	742	148	174	14	91	182	166	191	222
HERTFORDSHIRE	1217	1051	231	221	20	28	337	293	350	233
BUCKINGHAMSHIRE	1623	1356	458	417	28	37	186	168	280	263
OXFORDSHIRE	1250	1107	414	425	25	21	186	166	254	209
NORTHAMPTONSHIRE	9370	10475	4363	5204	440	690	2151	2426	1146	1158
HUNTINGDONSHIRE	2008	1974	874	303	60	88	871	866	415	417
BEDFORDSHIRE	3160	2457	657	624	34	20	597	435	778	603
CAMBRIDGESHIRE	3847	3514	407	442	43	70	2340	2058	672	602
EASTERN COUNTIES	9712	8335	1164	1187	120	124	5200	4149	1568	1530
ESSEX	2134	1900	330	332	24	28	1154	932	296	310
SUFFOLK	2347	1829	296	304	27	30	916	625	450	394
NORFOLK	5231	4606	538	551	69	66	3130	2592	822	826
SOUTH-WESTERN COUNTIES	5558	5530	1027	1032	88	101	1280	1273	1447	1502
WILTSHIRE	939	896	200	181	17	22	165	168	175	204
DORSETSHIRE	647	574	156	119	10	11	160	148	140	135
DEVONSHIRE	1665	1775	313	380	16	23	502	521	438	488
CORNWALL	622	717	103	117	17	23	162	178	125	148
SOMERSETSHIRE	1685	1568	255	235	28	22	291	263	571	527
WEST-MIDLAND COUNTIES	29368	30768	7298	8406	152	145	1697	1740	5462	5628
GLOUCESTERSHIRE	2816	2504	659	608	34	26	293	254	779	723
HEREFORDSHIRE	589	639	146	159	7	15	84	53	124	148
SHROPSHIRE	1764	1824	250	301	13	11	132	181	495	475
STAFFORDSHIRE	13032	13990	1692	2009	35	38	454	485	2062	2170
WORCESTERSHIRE	2610	2536	561	616	13	12	265	292	439	474
WARWICKSHIRE	8557	9275	3990	4713	50	43	469	475	1543	1638
NORTH-MIDLAND COUNTIES	688956	704409	130524	137388	8946	8668	200808	202789	163765	173131
LEICESTERSHIRE	135778	141873	120887	126243	539	686	1554	1753	6892	6907
RUTLANDSHIRE	10643	10511	1415	1766	7532	6966	1081	1164	318	426
LINCOLNSHIRE	205746	209398	2045	2634	715	817	192541	193899	8020	9620
NOTTINGHAMSHIRE	158064	162578	3063	3380	79	99	4862	5188	139680	144417
DERBYSHIRE	178725	179754	3114	3356	61	60	770	885	9355	11761
NORTH-WESTERN COUNTIES	12253	12747	1190	1201	129	38	1477	1367	2105	2129
CHESHIRE	4535	5088	250	261	30	9	260	249	424	476
LANCASHIRE	7718	7659	940	940	99	29	1217	1118	1681	1653
YORKSHIRE	22371	24161	1472	1545	105	97	8067	8616	4859	5304
NORTHERN COUNTIES	2447	2594	385	453	31	16	682	708	502	606
DURHAM	1092	1214	137	162	8	6	316	372	238	277
NORTHUMBERLAND	680	726	106	132	8	4	223	211	138	177
CUMBERLAND	454	432	81	82	13	5	161	84	96	111
WESTMORLAND	221	222	61	77	2	1	42	41	30	41
MONMOUTHSHIRE AND WALES	1729	1948	347	423	18	29	295	273	397	421
MONMOUTHSHIRE	325	317	64	64	2	4	51	48	83	74
GLAMORGANSHIRE	349	349	72	84	3	4	70	49	86	89
CARMARTHENSHIRE	71	78	11	15	.	1	15	13	16	20
PEMBROKESHIRE	100	134	22	38	2	1	36	25	26	19
CARDIGANSHIRE	30	40	6	7	1	1	7	18	5	6
BRECKNOCKSHIRE	70	82	11	18	.	2	7	6	14	12
RADNORSHIRE	41	55	12	19	.	.	1	6	10	8
MONTGOMERYSHIRE	125	171	29	39	5	7	9	13	26	38
FLINTSHIRE	138	157	12	20	2	1	19	20	31	30
DENBIGHSHIRE	113	135	22	27	2	3	14	14	33	19
MERIONETHSHIRE	28	28	11	10	.	1	5	3	4	4
CARNARVONSHIRE	65	60	18	30	.	.	18	7	5	6
ANGLESEY	40	41	8	2	1	1	12	14	3	9
WALES (*County not stated*)	234	391	54	60	.	3	41	59	55	87
ENGLAND (*County not stated*)	1630	1362	270	270	4	3	707	451	300	342
OTHER PARTS OF BRITISH EMPIRE	10455	9191	1821	1750	125	89	2044	1761	2182	2213
ISLANDS in the BRITISH SEAS	206	267	32	51	2	2	51	51	55	79
SCOTLAND	2850	2477	349	487	50	44	621	580	713	687
IRELAND	6230	5106	967	889	55	30	1100	821	1151	1104
BRITISH COLONIES or DEPENDENCIES	1175	1341	273	323	18	13	272	309	268	368
FOREIGN COUNTRIES	2837	2087	347	313	27	28	1207	644	834	715
British Subjects	996	1030	155	166	11	6	189	202	421	441
Foreigners	1841	1057	192	147	16	22	1018	442	413	274
AT SEA	95	80	27	13	1	1	22	21	14	27
British Subjects	95	80	27	13	1	1	22	21	14	27
Foreigners	.	.	.	.	.	.	.	.	.	.

* The Counties proper, and not the Registration Counties, are referred to in this Table.

Table 11 *continued.*—BIRTH-PLACES of MALES and FEMALES enumerated in COUNTIES, and in each URBAN SANITARY DISTRICT of which the POPULATION EXCEEDS 50,000 PERSONS.

WHERE BORN.	WHERE ENUMERATED.							
	COUNTY.		URBAN SANITARY DISTRICTS.					
	DERBYSHIRE.		LEICESTER.		NOTTINGHAM.		DERBY.	
	Males.	Females.	Males.	Females.	Males.	Females.	Males.	Females.
TOTAL OF INHABITANTS	232504	229410	57720	64656	87633	98942	40033	41135
LONDON	1794	1984	1006	1055	1305	1501	681	692
MIDDLESEX (*Intra-metropolitan*)	1453	1637	818	849	1073	1241	559	509
SURREY (*Intra-metropolitan*)	226	224	128	116	159	147	89	77
KENT (*Intra-metropolitan*)	116	123	60	90	73	113	33	46
SOUTH-EASTERN COUNTIES	1261	1340	442	550	674	758	379	387
SURREY (*Extra-metropolitan*)	196	189	77	92	117	100	45	39
KENT (*Extra-metropolitan*)	324	415	125	172	195	263	106	119
SUSSEX	173	157	50	75	120	109	45	51
HAMPSHIRE	351	401	136	148	189	215	115	124
BERKSHIRE	217	181	54	63	53	71	68	54
SOUTH-MIDLAND COUNTIES	4577	3534	3122	3664	1969	1978	1145	992
MIDDLESEX (*Extra-metropolitan*)	117	158	50	57	111	128	37	60
HERTFORDSHIRE	279	216	83	73	173	148	32	75
BUCKINGHAMSHIRE	373	469	166	189	143	144	141	111
OXFORDSHIRE	371	280	135	165	132	112	106	71
NORTHAMPTONSHIRE	1270	988	2096	2509	570	631	320	296
HUNTINGDONSHIRE	388	300	128	144	183	218	105	91
BEDFORDSHIRE	1094	775	272	294	333	273	223	203
CAMBRIDGESHIRE	485	342	192	233	322	328	112	86
EASTERN COUNTIES	1660	1345	478	499	750	806	346	336
ESSEX	330	298	131	143	157	168	84	101
SUFFOLK	658	476	100	117	248	224	105	88
NORFOLK	672	571	247	239	345	414	157	147
SOUTH-WESTERN COUNTIES	1716	1622	403	424	896	985	565	529
WILTSHIRE	382	381	74	60	88	101	174	132
DORSETSHIRE	181	166	51	36	61	72	37	34
DEVONSHIRE	396	423	136	152	284	335	134	155
CORNWALL	217	231	36	53	54	74	29	31
SOMERSETSHIRE	540	461	106	118	409	413	191	177
WEST-MIDLAND COUNTIES	14759	14849	3383	3788	2884	3271	3925	3924
GLOUCESTERSHIRE	1051	863	314	296	464	441	359	296
HEREFORDSHIRE	228	224	47	51	71	77	64	76
SHROPSHIRE	874	856	97	102	128	148	195	175
STAFFORDSHIRE	8789	9288	738	795	994	1240	1896	2072
WORCESTERSHIRE	1312	1212	260	313	267	285	407	387
WARWICKSHIRE	2505	2406	1927	2231	960	1080	1009	916
NORTH-MIDLAND COUNTIES	184913	182433	46052	51878	73344	83575	29105	30844
LEICESTERSHIRE	6406	6284	43003	48296	3697	4258	1303	1517
RUTLANDSHIRE	277	249	534	738	140	224	76	83
LINCOLNSHIRE	2426	2328	754	902	2537	3594	516	510
NOTTINGHAMSHIRE	10380	9830	1047	1128	62746	69306	1441	1457
DERBYSHIRE	165425	163742	714	814	4895	6193	25769	27277
NORTH-WESTERN COUNTIES	7352	8012	577	572	1274	1311	1100	983
CHESHIRE	3571	4093	113	103	250	301	373	318
LANCASHIRE	3781	3919	464	469	1024	1010	727	665
YORKSHIRE	7868	8599	770	749	1849	1905	1020	966
NORTHERN COUNTIES	847	811	161	193	266	327	185	151
DURHAM	393	397	61	70	128	153	61	61
NORTHUMBERLAND	205	202	41	57	70	97	51	37
CUMBERLAND	163	150	32	33	52	57	46	36
WESTMORLAND	86	62	27	33	16	20	27	17
MONMOUTHSHIRE AND WALES	672	802	128	148	207	246	223	224
MONMOUTHSHIRE	125	129	18	22	53	51	56	60
GLAMORGANSHIRE	118	123	32	32	59	62	56	47
CARMARTHENSHIRE	39	29	6	2	6	6	5	7
PEMBROKESHIRE	24	51	8	16	14	5	11	21
CARDIGANSHIRE	11	8	4	2	2	3	1	.
BRECKNOCKSHIRE	38	44	6	5	8	9	9	11
RADNORSHIRE	18	22	3	9	6	4	8	8
MONTGOMERYSHIRE	66	74	9	11	12	17	15	15
FLINTSHIRE	74	86	2	8	9	10	7	12
DENBIGHSHIRE	42	72	8	4	14	7	18	10
MERIONETHSHIRE	8	10	2	1	2	2	1	.
CARNARVONSHIRE	24	27	12	9	3	3	10	10
ANGLESEY	21	15	2	1	.	2	6	4
WALES (*County not stated*)	84	112	16	26	19	59	28	19
ENGLAND (*County not stated*)	349	296	88	73	150	241	72	62
OTHER PARTS OF BRITISH EMPIRE	4283	3378	905	911	1351	1453	1136	950
ISLANDS IN THE BRITISH SEAS	60	84	17	23	40	46	21	21
SCOTLAND	917	699	294	233	427	393	295	210
IRELAND	2957	2262	453	495	736	801	677	589
BRITISH COLONIES OR DEPENDENCIES	349	333	141	160	148	213	143	130
FOREIGN COUNTRIES	422	387	197	146	707	568	140	92
British Subjects	220	215	86	86	360	366	65	48
Foreigners	202	172	111	60	347	202	75	44
AT SEA	31	18	14	6	7	17	11	3
British Subjects	31	18	14	6	7	17	11	3
Foreigners	.	.	.	.	.	.	.	.

Table 12.—Distribution of the enumerated Natives of Counties.

Where Enumerated.	Where Born.											
	NORTH-MIDLAND COUNTIES.		LEICESTERSHIRE.		RUTLANDSHIRE.		LINCOLNSHIRE.		NOTTINGHAMSHIRE.		DERBYSHIRE.	
	Males.	Females.	Males.	Females.	Males.	Females.	Males.	Females.	Males.	Females.	Males.	Females.
TOTAL ENUMERATED NATIVES OF EACH COUNTY	857157	881163	163660	169242	14170	14436	263863	273274	188446	192780	227024	231425
LONDON	19900	21666	4204	4163	672	842	8054	9676	3949	3925	3021	3060
Middlesex (*Intra-metropolitan*)	13747	15256	2958	2918	526	646	5580	6844	2699	2742	1984	2106
Surrey (*Intra-metropolitan*)	4831	5137	977	1014	113	161	1956	2248	965	968	820	746
Kent (*Intra-metropolitan*)	1322	1273	269	231	33	35	518	584	285	215	217	208
SOUTH-EASTERN COUNTIES	9201	8726	2040	1776	338	352	3316	3597	1826	1584	1681	1417
Surrey (*Extra-metropolitan*)	1979	2416	472	542	89	108	772	1028	332	377	314	358
Kent (*Extra-metropolitan*)	2292	2002	440	305	87	84	912	856	430	386	423	307
Sussex	1641	2110	379	402	70	84	909	877	323	397	282	350
Hampshire	2586	1574	509	311	61	56	801	389	601	331	524	298
Berkshire	703	624	150	166	31	22	222	289	142	93	158	114
SOUTH-MIDLAND COUNTIES	13326	15416	3391	3917	1067	1317	6099	7161	1429	1587	1340	1434
Middlesex (*Extra-metropolitan*)	1982	2599	408	485	87	99	782	1095	425	454	287	375
Hertfordshire	887	1046	183	207	50	63	408	464	136	167	110	145
Buckinghamshire	616	663	178	198	32	38	187	175	88	78	186	114
Oxfordshire	480	519	144	165	19	20	152	142	90	101	75	85
Northamptonshire	6071	5915	2018	2387	746	859	2518	2766	380	436	419	458
Huntingdonshire	666	926	80	80	12	96	433	623	63	77	48	48
Bedfordshire	895	1024	241	275	37	39	290	375	138	152	184	188
Cambridgeshire	1729	1284	154	170	54	92	1329	1514	111	122	81	96
EASTERN COUNTIES	4054	4280	672	639	119	130	2175	2429	520	566	568	516
Essex	1822	1810	376	342	60	76	789	840	298	300	299	232
Suffolk	672	708	125	118	29	13	304	373	100	94	114	110
Norfolk	1560	1762	171	179	30	41	1082	1216	122	172	155	154
SOUTH-WESTERN COUNTIES	2429	2379	566	529	66	77	712	776	543	461	542	537
Wiltshire	349	385	84	92	16	17	99	114	78	80	72	82
Dorsetshire	370	243	88	50	5	9	131	108	77	47	75	35
Devonshire	602	809	198	197	24	24	271	275	221	189	188	193
Cornwall	200	192	37	47	3	2	65	72	46	28	49	52
Somersetshire	602	690	159	148	18	25	146	207	121	185	158	175
WEST-MIDLAND COUNTIES	24291	25083	9342	9173	376	422	2466	2585	3156	3217	8951	9686
Gloucestershire	1820	1579	342	398	46	47	283	398	296	310	353	417
Herefordshire	282	227	75	61	11	8	74	56	42	37	74	65
Shropshire	672	693	247	194	6	18	142	142	92	118	178	222
Staffordshire	11299	11175	3303	2807	123	106	729	697	1181	1087	6013	6424
Worcestershire	1733	1752	627	578	35	39	289	318	296	307	492	510
Warwickshire	8985	9666	4748	5075	155	204	949	980	1292	1358	1841	2049
NORTH-MIDLAND COUNTIES	688956	704409	135778	141873	10643	10511	205746	209398	158064	162873	178725	179754
Leicestershire	130524	137388	120887	126348	1415	1796	2045	2634	3063	3382	3114	3556
Rutlandshire	8946	8668	539	686	7352	6997	715	917	79	96	61	60
Lincolnshire	200808	202789	1554	1753	1081	1164	192541	193992	4302	5138	770	885
Nottinghamshire	169765	175181	6392	6907	518	426	8020	9628	139098	144417	9855	11761
Derbyshire	184913	182433	6406	6284	277	245	3423	2328	10388	9836	165425	163742
NORTH-WESTERN COUNTIES	29001	32901	2976	2974	221	240	5766	6744	4686	4993	15352	17950
Cheshire	6468	7772	528	486	30	36	723	854	627	729	4560	5667
Lancashire	22533	25129	2448	2488	191	204	5043	5890	4059	4264	10792	12283
YORKSHIRE	59766	61106	3637	3344	537	453	27293	29052	13112	12622	15187	15635
NORTHERN COUNTIES	4426	3660	545	428	86	54	1800	1494	826	687	1169	997
Durham	3003	2329	310	225	59	21	1296	1021	536	427	799	627
Northumberland	832	782	129	126	10	4	358	331	159	143	176	178
Cumberland	430	394	88	62	8	17	193	103	93	78	145	140
Westmoreland	152	155	18	15	9	16	38	39	38	39	49	52
MONMOUTHSHIRE AND WALES	1807	1537	509	427	45	38	436	362	329	271	488	439
Monmouthshire	283	251	61	62	10	14	96	67	61	47	85	61
Glamorganshire	505	472	108	91	17	6	159	111	84	96	187	115
Carmarthenshire	62	56	13	16	1	3	14	13	16	10	18	14
Pembrokeshire	137	57	42	18	4	1	47	25	27	7	17	6
Cardiganshire	24	20	3	4	1		8	5	7	4	5	3
Brecknockshire	62	53	15	11		3	14	18	11	5	22	13
Radnorshire	22	21	5	16			6	4	6	2	5	5
Montgomeryshire	73	55	13	9		1	14	14	20	10	26	21
Flintshire	153	177	42	53		2	27	24	17	36	67	68
Denbighshire	166	178	51	58	3	4	40	34	29	21	48	66
Merionethshire	64	39	19	12	5	3	18	5	9	6	19	13
Carnarvonshire	215	127	134	87	4	1	21	36	25	34	31	45
Anglesey	41	27	3	7		1	8	8	17	2	13	9

Table 14.—NUMBER AND AGES of MALES and FEMALES returned as BLIND or BLIND FROM BIRTH in the NORTH-MIDLAND DIVISION and its REGISTRATION COUNTIES.

Registration County.	All Ages. Both Sexes.	All Ages. Males and Females.	0–	5–	15–	20–	25–	45–	65 and upwards.
VII. NORTH MIDLAND COUNTIES.	1429	M. 733	19	58	28	33	148	208	239
		F. 696	20	51	30	24	107	155	309
28 LEICESTERSHIRE	297	M. 152	3	9	3	6	24	49	58
		F. 145	4	8	3	3	25	35	67
29 RUTLANDSHIRE	19	M. 10	.	1	.	.	2	5	2
		F. 9	.	.	1	.	.	4	4
30 LINCOLNSHIRE	415	M. 202	6	14	4	7	38	61	72
		F. 213	5	7	5	4	28	50	114
31 NOTTINGHAMSHIRE	400	M. 210	5	25	16	16	47	45	56
		F. 190	6	24	15	11	36	33	65
32 DERBYSHIRE	298	M. 159	5	9	5	4	37	48	51
		F. 139	5	12	6	6	18	33	59

Table 15.—NUMBER and AGES of MALES and FEMALES returned as BLIND in the NORTH-MIDLAND DIVISION and its REGISTRATION COUNTIES.

Registration County.	All Ages. Both Sexes.	All Ages. Males and Females.	0–	5–	15–	20–	25–	45–	65 and upwards.
VII. NORTH MIDLAND COUNTIES.	1300	M. 673	13	40	25	24	135	201	235
		F. 627	10	38	27	17	87	144	304
28 LEICESTERSHIRE	268	M. 139	2	7	2	3	20	47	58
		F. 129	2	5	1	2	21	33	65
29 RUTLANDSHIRE	17	M. 8	.	.	.	.	1	5	2
		F. 9	.	.	1	.	.	4	4
30 LINCOLNSHIRE	374	M. 183	4	6	3	6	35	59	70
		F. 191	1	5	5	3	22	43	112
31 NOTTINGHAMSHIRE	358	M. 189	3	20	15	12	42	43	54
		F. 169	2	21	14	9	27	32	64
32 DERBYSHIRE	283	M. 154	4	7	5	3	37	47	51
		F. 129	5	7	6	3	17	32	59

Table 16.—NUMBER and AGES of MALES and FEMALES returned as BLIND FROM BIRTH in the NORTH-MIDLAND DIVISION and its REGISTRATION COUNTIES.

Registration County.	All Ages. Both Sexes.	All Ages. Males and Females.	0–	5–	15–	20–	25–	45–	65 and upwards.
VII. NORTH MIDLAND COUNTIES.	129	M. 60	6	18	3	9	13	7	4
		F. 69	10	13	3	7	20	11	5
28 LEICESTERSHIRE	29	M. 13	1	2	1	3	4	2	.
		F. 16	2	3	2	1	4	2	2
29 RUTLANDSHIRE	2	M. 2	.	1	.	.	1	.	.
		F. .	.	.	.	.	.	.	.
30 LINCOLNSHIRE	41	M. 19	2	8	1	1	3	2	2
		F. 22	4	2	.	1	6	7	2
31 NOTTINGHAMSHIRE	42	M. 21	2	5	1	4	5	2	2
		F. 21	4	3	1	2	9	1	1
32 DERBYSHIRE	15	M. 5	1	2	.	1	.	1	.
		F. 10	.	5	.	3	1	1	.

Table 17.—NUMBER and AGES of MALES and FEMALES returned as DEAF AND DUMB in the NORTH-MIDLAND DIVISION and its REGISTRATION COUNTIES.

Registration County.	All Ages. Both Sexes.	All Ages. Males and Females.	0–	5–	15–	20–	25–	45–	65 and upwards.
VII. NORTH MIDLAND COUNTIES.	705	M. 395	18	76	49	49	119	64	20
		F. 310	10	44	34	32	108	63	19
28 LEICESTERSHIRE	114	M. 64	7	11	7	4	18	13	4
		F. 50	.	10	5	11	10	12	2
29 RUTLANDSHIRE	6	M. 2	.	.	.	.	1	1	.
		F. 4	1	.	.	.	2	1	.
30 LINCOLNSHIRE	205	M. 112	3	17	16	14	40	14	8
		F. 93	3	11	9	9	38	16	7
31 NOTTINGHAMSHIRE	171	M. 96	4	25	8	17	26	14	2
		F. 75	5	12	6	8	29	13	6
32 DERBYSHIRE	209	M. 121	4	23	18	14	34	22	6
		F. 88	3	11	14	6	29	21	4

Table 18.—NUMBER and AGES of MALES and FEMALES returned as IDIOTS or IMBECILES, and LUNATICS in the NORTH-MIDLAND DIVISION and its REGISTRATION COUNTIES.

REGISTRATION COUNTY.	ALL AGES. Both Sexes.	ALL AGES. Males and Females.	0–	5–	15–	20–	25–	45–	65 and upwards.
VII. NORTH MID-LAND COUNTIES.	3921	M. 2008	17	167	132	167	706	581	238
		F. 1913	15	112	100	150	702	578	256
28 LEICESTERSHIRE	1042	M. - 618	2	44	34	41	217	203	77
		F. - 424	3	25	22	29	180	110	55
29 RUTLANDSHIRE	19	M. - 10	.	.	.	3	7	.	.
		F. - 9	.	2	1	.	4	2	.
30 LINCOLNSHIRE	1248	M. - 604	5	43	44	48	219	171	74
		F. - 644	4	30	85	49	218	213	97
31 NOTTINGHAMSHIRE	1171	M. - 556	7	46	34	47	202	156	65
		F. - 615	2	34	29	49	220	195	86
32 DERBYSHIRE	441	M. - 220	3	35	20	28	61	51	22
		F. - 221	6	21	13	23	82	58	18

Table 19.—NUMBER and AGES of MALES and FEMALES returned as IDIOTS or IMBECILES in the NORTH-MIDLAND DIVISION and its REGISTRATION COUNTIES.

REGISTRATION COUNTY.	ALL AGES. Both Sexes.	ALL AGES. Males and Females.	0–	5–	15–	20–	25–	45–	65 and upwards.
VII. NORTH MID-LAND COUNTIES.	2039	M. 1005	16	161	116	114	323	188	87
		F. 1034	15	108	81	117	364	242	107
28 LEICESTERSHIRE	438	M. - 213	2	40	21	17	68	48	17
		F. - 225	3	23	19	22	80	43	27
29 RUTLANDSHIRE	17	M. - 8	.	.	.	2	6	.	.
		F. - 9	.	2	1	.	4	2	.
30 LINCOLNSHIRE	852	M. - 324	4	42	41	39	120	55	23
		F. - 328	4	30	38	40	110	86	28
31 NOTTINGHAMSHIRE	550	M. - 272	7	44	34	33	79	46	29
		F. - 278	5	33	18	33	93	62	37
32 DERBYSHIRE	382	M. 188	3	35	20	23	50	39	18
		F. 194	6	21	13	22	68	49	15

Table 20.—NUMBER and AGES of MALES and FEMALES returned as LUNATICS in the NORTH-MIDLAND DIVISION and its REGISTRATION COUNTIES.

REGISTRATION COUNTY.	ALL AGES. Both Sexes.	ALL AGES. Males and Females.	0–	5–	15–	20–	25–	45–	65 and upwards.
VII. NORTH MID-LAND COUNTIES.	1882	M. 1003	1	6	16	53	383	393	151
		F. 879	.	4	19	33	338	336	149
28 LEICESTERSHIRE	604	M. - 405	.	4	13	24	149	155	60
		F. - 199	.	3	3	7	91	67	28
29 RUTLANDSHIRE	2	M. - 2	.	.	.	1	1	.	.
		F. - .	.	.	.	.	.	.	.
30 LINCOLNSHIRE	596	M. - 280	1	1	8	6	99	116	51
		F. - 316	.	.	5	9	106	127	69
31 NOTTINGHAMSHIRE	621	M. - 284	.	1	.	14	123	110	36
		F. - 337	.	1	11	16	127	133	40
32 DERBYSHIRE	59	M. - 32	.	.	.	5	11	12	4
		F. - 27	.	.	.	1	14	9	3

Table 21.—Number of the Blind, of the Deaf and Dumb, of Idiots or Imbeciles, and of Lunatics in the North-Midland Division and its Registration Counties and Districts.

Registration County and District.	Blind.			Deaf and Dumb.	Mentally Deranged.		
	From Birth.	Others.	Total.		Idiots.	Lunatics.	Total.
VII. NORTH-MIDLAND COUNTIES.	129	1300	1429	705	2039	1882	3921
28 LEICESTERSHIRE -	29	268	297	114	438	604	1042
29 RUTLANDSHIRE -	2	17	19	6	17	2	19
30 LINCOLNSHIRE -	41	374	415	205	652	596	1248
31 NOTTINGHAMSHIRE	45	358	400	171	550	621	1171
32 DERBYSHIRE -	15	283	298	209	382	59	441
28 LEICESTERSHIRE.							
400 LUTTERWORTH - -	3	14	17	9	15	1	16
401 MARKET HARBOROUGH	4	13	17	2	21	1	22
402 BILLESDON - -	.	11	11	5	22	388	410
403 BLABY - - -	1	12	13	13	24	.	24
404 HINCKLEY -	2	17	19	8	17	.	17
405 MARKET BOSWORTH -	1	9	10	6	18	1	19
406 ASHBY-DE-LA-ZOUCH -	2	28	30	10	29	3	32
407 LOUGHBOROUGH -	3	24	27	13	30	1	31
408 BARROW-UPON-SOAR -	2	22	24	10	32	2	34
409 LEICESTER -	10	91	101	31	202	206	408
410 MELTON MOWBRAY -	1	27	28	7	28	1	29
29 RUTLANDSHIRE.							
411 OAKHAM - -	1	7	8	6	8	1	9
412 UPPINGHAM - -	1	10	11	.	9	1	10

Registration County and District.	Blind.			Deaf and Dumb.	Mentally Deranged.		
	From Birth.	Others.	Total.		Idiots.	Lunatics.	Total.
30 LINCOLNSHIRE.							
413 STAMFORD -	2	14	16	7	25	3	2
414 BOURN - - -	3	14	17	8	16	1	1
415 SPALDING -	1	20	21	11	47	4	5
416 HOLBEACH -	.	10	10	9	13	2	1
417 BOSTON - - -	3	45	48	24	61	3	6
418 SLEAFORD -	1	26	27	9	50	3	5
419 GRANTHAM - -	5	23	28	16	50	3	3
420 LINCOLN - -	7	41	48	28	174	556	73
421 HORNCASTLE - -	2	16	18	15	41	3	4
422 SPILSBY - -	2	32	34	10	44	5	4
423 LOUTH - - -	5	36	41	12	38	3	4
424 CAISTOR - -	7	37	44	20	58	6	6
425 GLANFORD BRIGG -	2	36	38	11	80	2	8
426 GAINSBOROUGH -	1	24	25	25	26	1	2
31 NOTTINGHAMSHIRE.							
427 EAST RETFORD - -	3	22	25	9	44	3	47
428 WORKSOP - -	1	25	26	12	38	2	40
429 MANSFIELD -	2	31	33	11	41	2	43
430 BASFORD - -	9	68	77	47	112	9	121
431 NOTTINGHAM -	20	172	192	64	247	597	844
432 SOUTHWELL -	4	17	21	6	19	3	22
433 NEWARK - - -	2	15	17	13	35	3	38
434 BINGHAM - -	1	8	9	9	14	2	16
32 DERBYSHIRE.							
435 SHARDLOW - -	1	31	32	11	40	2	42
436 DERBY -	4	47	51	34	29	.	29
437 BELPER -	4	56	60	47	80	14	94
438 ASHBORNE -	1	20	21	12	27	1	28
439 CHESTERFIELD -	1	68	69	48	93	1	94
440 BAKEWELL - -	2	18	20	27	47	1	48
441 CHAPEL-EN-LE-FRITH -	1	16	17	14	14	40	54
442 HAYFIELD -	1	27	28	16	32	.	32

AGES,

CONDITION AS TO MARRIAGE,

OCCUPATIONS, AND BIRTH-PLACES

OF THE PEOPLE:

WITH THE

NUMBERS AND AGES OF THE BLIND, DEAF AND DUMB, IDIOTS OR IMBECILES, AND LUNATICS.

DIVISION VIII.—NORTH-WESTERN COUNTIES;

CHESHIRE,
LANCASHIRE.

TABLES IN DIVISION VIII.—NORTH-WESTERN COUNTIES.

AGES.

Table.

1.—Ages of Males and Females in the North-Western Division and its Registration Counties.

2.—Ages of Males and Females in Registration Districts.

3.—Ages of Males and Females in Registration Sub-Districts.

4.—Male and Female Children at *each Year of Age* under 5 in the North-Western Division and its Registration Counties.

5.—Male and Female Children at *each Year of Age* under 5 in Registration Districts.

6.—Ages of Males and Females in Sanitary Districts.

CONDITION AS TO MARRIAGE.

7.—Condition as to Marriage and Ages of Males and Females in the North-Western Division and its Registration Counties.

8.—Condition as to Marriage and Ages of Males and Females in Registration Districts.

9.—Condition as to Marriage and Ages of Males and Females in each Urban Sanitary District of which the Population exceeds 50,000 persons.

OCCUPATIONS.

10.—Occupations of Males and Females in the North-Western Division and its Registration Counties, and in each Urban Sanitary District of which the Population exceeds 50,000 Persons.

BIRTH-PLACES.

11.—Birth-Places of Males and Females enumerated in Counties, and in each Urban Sanitary District of which the Population exceeds 50,000 Persons.

12.—Distribution of the enumerated Natives of Counties.

13.—Number and Country of Birth of Foreigners enumerated in Counties, and in each Urban Sanitary District of which the Population exceeds 50,000 Persons.

THE BLIND, DEAF AND DUMB, IDIOTS OR IMBECILES, AND LUNATICS.

14.—Number and Ages of Males and Females returned as Blind or Blind from Birth in the North-Western Division and its Registration Counties.

15.—Number and Ages of Males and Females returned as Blind in the North-Western Division and its Registration Counties.

16.—Number and Ages of Males and Females returned as Blind from Birth in the North-Western Division and its Registration Counties.

17.—Number and Ages of Males and Females returned as Deaf and Dumb in the North-Western Division and its Registration Counties.

18.—Number and Ages of Males and Females returned as Idiots or Imbeciles, and Lunatics in the North-Western Division and its Registration Counties.

19.—Number and Ages of Males and Females returned as Idiots or Imbeciles in the North-Western Division and its Registration Counties.

20.—Number and Ages of Males and Females returned as Lunatics in the North-Western Division and its Registration Counties.

21.—Number of the Blind, of the Deaf and Dumb, of Idiots or Imbeciles, and of Lunatics, in the North-Western Division and its Registration Counties and Districts.

AGES.

DIVISION VIII.—NORTH-WESTERN COUNTIES.

Table 1.—AGES of MALES and FEMALES in the NORTH-WESTERN DIVISION and its REGISTRATION COUNTIE

REGISTRATION COUNTY.	ALL AGES. Persons.	ALL AGES. Males and Females.	Under 5* Years.	5–	10–	15–	20–	25–	30–	35–	40–	45–	50–	55–	60–	65–	70–	75–	80–	85–	90–	95–
I.-NORTH ESTERN OUNTIES.	4108184	M. 1986673	284219	246167	215407	193884	184021	166671	141903	122073	110736	84630	73756	53070	45652	27742	17625	8628	3375	803	150	23
		F. 2121511	287120	249185	218828	207108	204902	181489	152040	132238	120507	94863	83618	61024	54172	33378	22130	11240	4910	1315	278	69
HESHIRE -	622365	M. 301768	42155	37474	33904	30528	26406	23148	19670	17577	16458	13147	11767	9258	8179	5408	3915	1890	801	221	48	8
		F. 320597	42075	37836	34068	31402	30072	25876	21533	19269	17608	14644	13258	9960	9037	5030	4201	2240	1026	303	70	17
ANCASHIRE -	3485819	M. 1684905	242064	208693	181443	163356	158155	145423	122233	105095	84338	71483	61989	44712	37482	22334	14010	6808	2574	582	113	15
		F. 1800914	245065	211849	184780	175616	174890	165613	130516	112978	102899	80219	70360	51994	45133	27448	17688	9000	3393	1015	208	52

te.—Registration Counties consist of groups of Registration Districts, which are generally co-extensive with the Poor Law Unions. Those Regis ricts which extend into two or more counties are included in that Registration County in which the principal town of the District or the greater part dation is located. The boundaries of Registration Counties, therefore, differ more or less from the boundaries of Counties. For such differences in Divisio Vol. II., Table 11.
For the number of Children at each Year of Age under 5, see Table 4.
Each of these Males was stated to be 100 years of age. Two of these Females were stated to be 100 years of age, two 101, one 104, one 105, and one 106 years

Table 2.—AGES of MALES and FEMALES in REGISTRATION DISTRICTS.

REGISTRATION DISTRICT.	ALL AGES. Persons.	ALL AGES. Males and Females.	Under 5* Years.	5–	10–	15–	20–	25–	30–	35–	40–	45–	50–	55–	60–	65–	70–	75–	80–	85–	90–	95–
3 CHESHIRE.																						
STOCKPORT - -	117157	M. - 54135	7526	6496	6210	6370	4656	4163	3666	3202	3022	2334	2171	1630	1458	907	578	252	107	29	7	.
		F. - 63022	7664	6882	6340	6282	6343	5403	4457	3965	3376	3022	2754	2022	1761	1095	707	356	152	37	8	1
MACCLESFIELD -	62013	M. - 28970	3788	5473	3182	2960	2334	1968	1709	1495	1521	1355	1408	1146	1054	727	471	254	94	24	4	1
		F. - 33043	4019	3594	3168	5220	3077	2604	2203	1937	1899	1658	1598	1236	1117	738	479	292	79	28	5	5
ALTRINCHAM	58899	M. - 27393	3730	3434	3093	2582	2385	1984	1818	1593	1497	1221	1080	985	798	513	371	217	94	35	1	.
		F. - 31506	3765	3408	3149	3252	3288	2763	2175	1927	1745	1495	1270	1026	871	557	422	255	110	28	10	1
RUNCORN - -	34023	M. - 17445	2540	2214	1901	1735	1660	1310	1186	988	911	723	649	512	441	290	208	97	48	14	2	1
		F. - 16578	2442	2102	1866	1631	1381	1179	1014	956	857	735	630	469	437	316	220	124	64	22	2	1
NORTHWICH -	44046	M. - 22579	3335	2002	2573	2344	1972	1691	1351	1281	1111	976	865	686	549	404	294	164	62	23	3	1
		F. - 21467	3260	2896	2608	1888	1757	1520	1338	1236	1070	932	815	614	571	430	270	147	78	22	3	1
CONGLETON -	38010	M. - 18589	2605	2437	2118	1904	1586	1265	1043	963	988	901	770	586	604	397	271	158	63	17	1	.
		F. - 19421	2480	2458	2131	2039	1719	1460	1167	1078	1037	880	847	623	386	385	295	134	69	17	6	.
NANTWICH - -	61566	M. - 31062	4292	4011	3405	3250	2700	2273	1928	1733	1881	1370	1174	966	818	647	373	227	102	55	8	1
		F. - 30504	4350	3974	3640	2947	2582	2170	1877	1745	1613	1354	1173	911	847	546	385	232	105	34	9	1
CHESTER - -	75297	M. - 37252	4656	4408	4471	3887	3282	2775	2305	2171	2093	1609	1460	1158	973	752	516	266	133	26	11	1
		F. - 38045	4873	4509	4297	3629	3270	2704	2442	2237	2053	1683	1635	1252	1102	864	673	351	159	56	16	[illegible]
WIRRAL -	27928	M. - 13853	1805	1062	1612	1828	1241	1080	707	778	669	523	406	304	357	221	177	87	26	7	2	1
		F. - 14075	1754	1548	1472	1478	1434	1186	978	871	702	582	552	429	370	288	205	101	49	18	3	.
BIRKENHEAD -	103496	M. - 50490	7473	6347	5273	4559	4604	4319	3866	3373	3055	2175	1604	1266	1120	534	357	168	72	20	4	[illegible]
		F. - 52956	7428	6276	5389	5211	5207	4638	3882	3318	3006	2245	1054	1341	1315	761	545	240	134	41	8	[illegible]
LANCASHIRE.																						
LIVERPOOL - -	210164	M. - 104290	12464	10987	9878	9733	10384	9041	8579	7596	7410	5055	4350	2762	2701	1308	709	277	116	22	8	[illegible]
		F. - 105874	12694	10824	10110	10143	11134	9817	8152	7132	7191	5148	4573	2898	3100	1690	971	463	267	46	7	[illegible]
TOXTETH PARK -	117028	M. - 55341	8370	6014	5717	4902	5090	4899	4246	3672	3338	2330	2017	1319	1148	654	412	169	67	15	.	[illegible]
		F. - 61687	8492	7131	5905	5618	5906	5580	4847	4082	2641	2632	2322	1605	1601	921	625	297	140	39	12	[illegible]
WEST DERBY -	359273	M. - 174164	28409	22135	18463	16030	16227	15334	13029	11689	10182	7260	5968	3934	3478	1975	1160	589	221	51	11	.
		F. - 185109	29438	22139	18821	17367	17631	16515	13908	12209	10676	7838	6722	4089	4309	2606	1723	845	380	118	17	[illegible]
PRESCOT - -	117960	M. - 60932	8396	7948	6508	5731	5861	5471	4474	3655	3254	2440	2067	1417	1186	729	469	238	66	20	5	.
		F. - 57028	8340	7826	6346	5282	4885	4511	3873	3261	2959	2315	2037	1377	1251	822	522	257	120	26	7	1
ORMSKIRK - -	83212	M. - 38380	5505	4714	4335	3871	3455	3024	2506	2162	1938	1553	1430	1190	1032	777	497	280	120	27	5	.
		F. - 44832	5471	4893	4402	4609	4563	3609	3139	2653	2537	2033	1780	1479	1405	962	629	362	149	46	9	1
WIGAN - -	139918	M. 70460	10969	9479	7332	6958	6828	5788	4523	4043	3398	2732	2397	1844	1434	887	551	250	101	23	4	.
		F. - 69458	10991	8501	7266	7050	6333	5429	4444	3826	3372	2702	2419	1913	1512	920	606	288	149	20	10	1
WARRINGTON -	70218	M. - 36084	5492	4746	3965	3634	3479	3118	2580	2055	1973	1373	1200	891	761	387	277	133	69	10	5	1
		F. - 34134	5624	4606	3897	3149	3029	2688	2232	1948	1761	1379	1179	848	707	435	321	127	73	18	5	1
LEIGH - -	56318	M. - 27655	4218	3678	3026	2788	2620	2268	1867	1501	1437	1115	956	694	601	420	283	148	43	10	4	.
		F. - 28663	4363	3748	3101	2892	2024	2213	1787	1569	1339	1204	1000	818	717	468	276	161	72	11	2	.
BOLTON -	192405	M. - 91985	13550	11861	10271	9404	8475	7718	6297	5443	4784	3828	3392	2512	1070	1238	765	386	113	27	2	.
		F. - 100420	13764	12145	10736	9303	9732	8533	7035	6075	5613	4453	3899	2941	2344	1480	979	481	180	54	4	2
BURY - -	129608	M. - 61645	8632	7607	6577	6326	5780	5254	4336	3702	3309	2651	2322	1863	1464	906	501	281	87	23	5	.
		F. - 67963	8745	7751	6941	6748	6620	6017	4856	4225	3808	3132	2770	2187	1763	1112	691	374	154	30	10	1
BARTON UPON IRWELL - -	72815	M. - 33973	4904	4468	3975	3821	3001	2654	2359	2150	1783	1404	1278	913	742	503	304	149	40	14	2	.
		F. - 38842	4924	4486	4187	4087	3028	3246	2823	2326	2119	1693	1454	1155	947	654	410	211	98	20	1	.

ote.—The Registration Districts of Division VIII. are co-extensive with the Poor Law Unions of the same name, with the following exception:—Chester) comprises the three Poor Law Unions of Chester, Tarvin, and Hawarden.
or the Parishes comprised in each Registration District, see Vol. II., Division VIII., Table 4.
he Districts are arranged topographically under the Registration Counties, and are numbered consecutively, commencing with the Metropolitan D ision I.
For the Number of Children at each Year of Age under 5, see Table 5.

Table 2 *continued*.—Ages of Males and Females in Registration Districts.

Registration District.	All Ages. Persons.	Males and Females.	Under 5 Years.	5-	10-	15-	20-	25-	30-	35-	40-	45-	50-	55-	60-	65-	70-	75-	80-	85-	90-	95-
34 LANCASHIRE —*cont.*																						
464 CHORLTON	258226	M.-122027	17359	14698	12947	11784	11958	11421	9449	8023	6803	5061	4326	2994	2479	1415	851	389	140	29	2	.
		F.-136199	17696	15080	13126	13361	14097	12854	10575	8881	7774	6108	5247	3817	3269	2023	1292	648	294	67	19	1
465 SALFORD	181526	M.- 87199	12234	11239	9521	8415	7968	7626	6712	5694	4979	3650	2885	2042	1565	812	532	223	97	20	2	1
		F.- 94327	13882	11393	9552	8768	8602	8572	7298	6278	5535	4097	3447	2372	2193	1281	843	432	161	39	10	1
466 MANCHESTER	148794	M.- 72005	8978	8458	7360	7056	6942	6405	5588	4756	4555	3177	2954	1823	1587	780	502	187	60	12	4	1
		F.- 76789	10148	8713	7479	7261	7898	6765	5666	4983	4779	3600	3415	2141	2115	1003	687	278	119	30	7	3
467 PRESTWICH	121287	M.- 58321	8547	7332	6043	5488	5204	6129	4410	3718	3301	2490	2070	1536	1372	767	529	256	95	21	4	.
		F.- 62966	8718	7193	6260	6128	6169	6555	4620	3928	3571	2891	2587	1773	1622	946	677	346	137	33	12	2
468 ASHTON UNDER LYNE	154526	M.- 73205	10252	9286	8102	7438	6489	5947	5029	4383	4013	3160	2922	2107	1746	1160	769	308	112	29	2	1
		F.- 81321	10341	9426	8324	7932	7565	6796	5720	5149	4871	3893	3436	2681	2173	1459	1008	450	166	41	11	1
469 OLDHAM	168461	M.- 81008	11294	9728	8700	8194	7635	7231	5928	5037	4490	3601	3183	2278	1761	1063	619	281	78	22	2	2
		F.- 87453	11572	10187	9080	8723	8643	7528	6161	5362	5155	4162	3567	2677	2047	1259	772	371	148	33	5	3
470 ROCHDALE	121912	M.- 57305	7411	6999	6381	5946	5256	4717	3944	3389	3260	2683	2400	1798	1411	895	483	226	83	18	5	.
		F.- 64607	7608	7087	6586	6428	6383	5719	4688	4097	3843	3182	2853	2234	1693	1002	653	317	130	38	6	1
471 HASLINGDEN	98293	M.- 48464	6517	5502	4808	4631	4404	3853	3125	2733	2382	1948	1789	1574	1087	652	373	206	64	14	4	.
		F.- 49829	6483	5687	5148	5082	4920	4371	3637	3075	2785	2221	1987	1591	1248	762	422	236	79	17	2	1
472 BURNLEY	118334	M.- 57319	8268	6974	6164	5774	5859	4876	4163	3578	3046	2401	2130	1662	1273	798	517	232	92	16	1	.
		F.- 61015	8564	7260	6253	6031	5698	5423	4477	3760	3233	2635	2270	1789	1451	878	572	279	109	28	4	1
473 CLITHEROE	23502	M.- 11831	1487	1432	1374	1280	1041	933	726	650	599	500	457	419	390	235	160	89	47	7	4	1
		F.- 11671	1518	1299	1209	1084	1105	987	803	677	604	500	490	411	388	262	176	104	48	10	2	.
474 BLACKBURN	175954	M.- 83617	12247	10930	9480	8466	8035	6979	5750	4867	4571	3591	3067	2107	1788	1104	685	337	132	26	6	2
		F.- 92337	12198	10785	9696	9271	9469	8020	6563	5767	5101	4136	2524	2606	2073	1284	824	393	166	46	4	1
475 CHORLEY	47730	M.- 23044	3377	2967	2573	2342	2699	1706	1485	1236	1187	903	825	720	599	419	352	159	102	15	6	1
		F.- 24686	3469	3010	2608	2448	2340	1921	1643	1475	1266	987	935	824	684	434	346	184	71	25	5	.
476 PRESTON	129180	M.- 60325	8230	7364	6875	6496	5462	4634	3884	3492	3413	2689	2297	1739	1584	972	702	345	150	83	7	.
		F.- 68855	8463	7434	6968	6940	6846	5707	4853	4371	4157	3318	2933	2251	1897	1178	844	428	184	56	9	4
477 FYLDE	40910	M.- 19318	2643	2378	2231	1984	1691	1383	1216	1115	1071	782	672	622	550	382	293	151	68	14	1	1
		F.- 21592	2646	2395	2121	2096	1938	1634	1539	1361	1241	1036	936	749	681	425	317	176	62	32	4	1
478 GARSTANG	12375	M.- 6374	834	736	772	749	544	463	353	315	283	243	266	234	213	165	105	86	29	9	.	.
		F.- 6001	837	759	627	587	497	446	391	316	278	288	250	291	162	135	112	86	22	4	2	1
479 LANCASTER	40838	M.- 20262	2770	2287	2204	2014	1975	1716	1440	1124	1053	853	789	641	580	341	255	136	47	19	3	.
		F.- 20576	2733	2313	2119	2057	1925	1662	1410	1191	1091	962	881	711	574	414	305	159	78	21	9	1
480 LUNESDALE	7132	M.- 3568	430	437	387	387	320	250	193	168	147	176	157	139	115	95	62	43	20	11	2	.
		F.- 3564	467	411	371	350	338	284	211	187	172	155	144	130	108	103	70	39	13	4	1	2
481 ULVERSTON	43681	M.- 22229	3274	2909	2506	1975	1923	1747	1475	1325	1162	890	802	651	602	396	298	185	76	23	5	.
		F.- 21452	3329	2849	2331	1838	1755	1690	1354	1232	1050	936	768	688	584	462	310	172	83	40	11	1
482 BARROW IN FURNESS	47259	M.- 25575	3948	3166	2358	2183	3738	2774	2311	1794	1527	955	701	447	343	173	97	30	12	2	2	.
		F.- 21684	3963	3135	2362	1868	1990	1913	1695	1422	1114	704	573	599	288	172	105	46	22	5	1	.

Table 3.—Ages of Males and Females in Registration Sub-Districts.

Registration Sub-District.	All Ages. Persons.	Males and Females.	Under 5 Years.	5-	10-	15-	20-	25-	30-	35-	40-	45-	50-	55-	60-	65-	70-	75-	80-	85-	90-	95-
33 CHESHIRE.																						
443 STOCKPORT.																						
1 Marple	6598	M.- 2985	344	348	349	[illegible]	250	236	181	178	164	141	123	100	88	79	37	17	14	4	.	.
		F.- 3613	429	378	360	404	383	297	222	215	204	176	158	128	107	66	43	31	8	4	.	.
2 Hyde	24739	M.- 11470	1089	1462	1375	1090	897	962	742	731	578	498	422	315	320	178	125	54	25	2	2	.
		F.- 13269	1706	1538	1387	1239	1219	1118	901	903	755	626	585	442	356	261	139	61	38	8	1	1
3 Heaton Norris, (R.)	25904	M.- 11859	1679	1384	1404	1214	1029	988	807	681	666	496	492	334	272	173	96	41	10	3	1	.
		F.- 14045	1698	1512	1429	1476	1545	1293	1019	824	777	642	615	426	369	193	134	69	21	6	1	.
4 Stockport First (W.H.R.)	32006	M.- 14825	2007	1684	1646	1446	1282	1262	1060	846	893	661	613	489	411	262	178	73	24	5	2	.
		F.- 17181	2009	1813	1642	1698	1696	1519	1270	1089	1072	849	769	546	529	303	215	102	48	9	4	.
5 Stockport Second, (R.)	13449	M.- 6236	803	783	680	636	528	546	421	376	363	273	265	161	158	92	53	23	13	2	.	.
		F.- 7213	903	794	751	683	765	604	498	455	441	304	321	247	180	118	88	37	23	2	1	.
6 Cheadle (H².L.)	8074	M.- 3716	493	441	481	375	278	283	265	231	199	140	161	122	110	69	50	21	15	1	1	.
		F.- 4358	517	437	457	447	423	362	318	277	241	218	185	153	124	76	59	29	6	6	1	.
7 Hazelgrove	6387	M.- 3044	441	395	318	383	288	227	210	139	161	125	95	104	93	63	45	28	6	3	1	.
		F.- 3343	432	408	349	340	325	266	231	192	186	147	121	105	97	76	29	27	8	2	.	.
444 MACCLESFIELD.																						
1 Prestbury	4893	M.- 2370	324	236	231	236	201	186	157	127	133	95	119	75	79	62	50	16	7	6	.	.
		F.- 2523	356	326	239	232	207	225	166	153	134	88	96	87	91	51	31	27	11	3	.	1
2 Bollington	10424	M.- 4817	686	619	536	494	380	342	297	257	241	222	210	202	144	96	55	28	11	3	.	.
		F.- 5607	702	591	562	564	524	448	368	326	324	301	268	195	180	119	87	39	7	2	.	.
3 Rainow	3402	M.- 1698	254	195	163	182	142	121	110	74	93	87	67	60	58	33	33	13	11	1	1	.
		F.- 1704	326	209	175	151	140	148	122	84	96	79	74	63	47	41	19	21	4	3	.	.
4 East Macclesfield (R.)	10656	M.- 4932	638	561	622	523	372	326	256	243	259	223	247	201	196	126	73	58	11	5	1	1
		F.- 5724	720	649	556	590	516	460	377	364	291	286	295	201	178	124	68	41	11	8	.	1
5 West Macclesfield (W.H.L.B.)	17963	M.- 8315	999	957	917	802	633	560	478	450	464	418	432	345	332	229	171	84	25	8	2	.
		F.- 9648	1067	949	876	922	904	771	652	566	626	512	521	416	375	237	137	86	24	5	1	.
6 Sutton	7195	M.- 3294	469	418	335	292	281	210	190	194	169	136	163	132	116	98	54	37	9	.	.	.
		F.- 3901	486	423	337	353	327	328	263	237	235	207	177	138	140	92	74	48	11	3	2	3
7 Gawsworth	2797	M.- 1389	153	163	137	197	136	84	71	73	70	59	67	54	44	29	20	17	12	1	.	.
		F.- 1408	178	180	168	149	119	96	78	75	63	62	55	55	41	37	34	12	4	4	1	.
8 Alderley	4683	M.- 2165	271	264	241	240	189	163	140	105	101	95	97	76	85	54	15	21	8	.	.	.
		F.- 2518	284	274	257	250	301	227	176	142	130	123	113	84	65	37	29	18	7	.	1	.

Note. For the Parishes comprised in each Registration Sub-District, *see* Vol. II., Division VIII., Table 4.
(W.) denotes that a Workhouse and (WS.) that a Workhouse School belonging to the District is situated within the Sub-district; (w.) denotes a Wo
and (ws.) a Workhouse School not belonging to the District, (H.) a Hospital or Infirmary, (L.) a Lunatic Asylum, (P.) a Prison or Convict Establishment
certified Reformatory or Industrial School, (B.) Barracks, &c., (S.) H.M. Ships. A figure appended to any of these letters denotes the number of Instituti
similar class situated within the Sub-district. The names of the Institutions thus indicated, and the number of inmates enumerated therein, will b
in Vol. II., Division VIII., Table 6.

Table 3 *continued*.—AGES of MALES and FEMALES in REGISTRATION SUB-DISTRICTS.

REGISTRATION SUB-DISTRICT.	ALL AGES. Persons.	ALL AGES. Males and Females.	Under 5 Years.	5-	10-	15-	20-	25-	30-	35-	40-	45-	50-	55-	60-	65-	70-	75-	80-	85-	90-	95
33 CHESHIRE —*cont.*																						
445 ALTRINCHAM.																						
WILMSLOW. (L.)	10315	M. - 4885	633	633	582	448	411	313	300	255	269	208	225	191	178	97	74	48	25	6	1	
		F. - 5430	691	596	527	559	525	426	382	331	303	261	245	210	161	92	72	45	18	4	1	
ALTRINCHAM. (H^2.R.)	32611	M. - 14465	2095	1879	1644	1362	1185	1039	978	881	821	643	548	465	375	241	179	99	30	13	.	
		F. - 18146	2091	1907	1751	1837	2018	1677	1327	1122	1029	860	692	538	477	292	224	140	57	14	4	
HALE	7008	M. - 3065	497	488	464	385	308	278	242	238	193	187	159	135	113	82	51	34	10	3	4	
		F. - 3943	474	455	431	408	341	267	251	233	210	194	181	134	104	73	53	27	14	5	2	
KNUTSFORD. (W.P.)	8065	M. - 4078	511	434	422	387	391	334	289	224	227	188	146	154	137	93	67	38	23	13	.	
		F. - 3987	509	439	401	403	364	353	235	241	203	178	152	144	129	100	63	34	21	3	3	
446 RUNCORN.																						
BUDWORTH	4420	M. - 2270	275	258	223	251	248	178	125	116	114	114	100	70	75	54	38	18	10	4	1	
		F. - 2150	268	263	251	248	109	131	116	100	115	109	104	78	62	44	23	19	13	7	.	
DARESBURY. (W.)	3103	M. - 1656	216	200	187	196	195	116	100	78	76	59	73	49	37	33	39	16	7	1	.	
		F. - 1447	202	149	171	147	140	99	77	85	77	94	58	36	50	31	39	10	9	2	.	
RUNCORN	19203	M. - 9874	1517	1293	1071	951	910	798	720	581	544	388	323	276	227	126	80	42	23	4	.	
		F. - 9329	1507	1290	1015	801	736	703	696	549	498	422	339	266	226	155	109	66	23	10	2	
FRODSHAM	7297	M. - 3645	541	463	440	337	313	218	241	215	177	162	133	117	102	77	51	23	8	5	1	
		F. - 3652	465	490	429	356	306	246	215	222	167	160	159	119	119	89	58	30	14	3	-	
447 NORTHWICH.																						
WEAVERHAM	7947	M. - 4048	571	486	433	413	378	286	223	236	235	178	177	117	118	82	67	30	10	6	1	
		F. - 3899	549	473	461	354	340	286	254	215	209	158	155	103	128	105	51	33	19	4	1	
NORTHWICH. (W.)	17024	M. - 8784	1286	1089	1007	914	777	682	528	500	407	372	346	278	213	152	120	64	23	6	.	
		F. - 8240	1252	1093	958	693	698	604	505	487	410	373	334	250	229	164	102	52	29	7	.	
OVER	13018	M. - 6683	1052	928	781	672	547	486	419	384	322	282	232	192	144	108	69	42	16	5	2	
		F. - 6335	1050	941	816	349	479	433	398	367	305	265	221	166	127	95	75	38	20	3	1	
MIDDLEWICH	6057	M. - 3064	416	389	358	345	270	227	181	161	147	144	110	90	74	58	58	28	13	6	.	
		F. - 2993	400	389	373	298	259	198	181	167	146	136	105	93	87	66	42	24	10	8	1	
448 CONGLETON.																						
CHURCH HULME	2974	M. - 1557	217	172	181	191	148	97	79	86	83	69	69	34	45	40	23	17	4	2	.	
		F. - 1417	178	163	181	164	120	105	83	82	78	43	72	47	32	31	24	9	4	1	.	
CONGLETON. (W.H.)	19544	M. - 9186	1277	1271	1068	880	711	644	527	465	491	416	407	289	301	200	128	64	30	6	1	
		F. - 10358	1316	1306	1687	1114	961	761	640	562	552	481	455	335	318	197	155	65	41	9	3	
SANDBACH. (W.R.)	15492	M. - 7846	1111	994	869	833	677	524	409	412	414	376	204	263	258	157	110	77	29	9	.	
		F. - 7646	996	939	863	761	638	594	444	434	407	356	320	241	236	157	113	60	24	7	3	
449 NANTWICH.																						
WYBUNBURY.* (H.)	37203	M. - 19104	2738	2609	2138	1982	1769	1504	1275	1151	1068	883	602	522	403	246	142	81	37	14	3	
		F. - 18099	2816	2530	2228	1623	1427	1299	1180	1076	1037	811	646	459	398	244	157	101	30	15	2	
NANTWICH. (W.)	11146	M. - 5469	735	671	631	577	453	359	320	280	298	246	216	183	171	141	96	54	28	13	1	
		F. - 5677	607	680	661	600	557	419	310	305	259	238	232	199	204	128	86	48	27	3	2	
BUNBURY	7338	M. - 3556	429	433	416	376	327	232	192	161	184	147	103	148	134	77	72	54	18	1	3	
		F. - 3782	477	456	445	353	339	246	213	217	185	164	168	138	134	99	78	44	17	6	3	
WRENBURY	5879	M. - 2933	390	398	312	315	241	178	141	141	136	145	113	103	108	83	63	38	19	7	3	
		F. - 2946	360	338	315	311	259	215	174	147	132	141	127	115	111	75	64	39	11	10	2	
450 CHESTER.																						
TATTENHALL	11186	M. - 5478	735	631	692	579	444	335	288	290	279	232	222	204	190	134	112	62	38	10	1	
		F. - 5708	724	708	663	580	476	306	316	328	282	233	237	186	174	164	123	72	34	8	2	
CHESTER CASTLE (W.P.R.B.)	22625	M. - 11196	1518	1300	1270	1209	1041	887	750	618	635	500	419	318	286	198	120	56	30	2	.	
		F. - 11429	1439	1336	1318	1106	1038	860	759	640	659	517	400	309	347	220	189	81	46	19	6	
CHESTER CATHEDRAL (W.H.L.B.)	25791	M. - 12352	1507	1455	1432	1265	1150	993	798	744	680	503	507	386	304	241	159	93	30	10	5	
		F. - 13439	1600	1426	1389	1460	1259	1071	918	837	764	598	560	466	407	284	233	125	81	20	6	
HAWARDEN. (W.)	15695	M. - 8226	1136	1103	1067	834	647	560	469	489	490	374	312	250	193	179	124	55	26	4	5	
		F. - 7469	1110	1089	937	543	506	477	454	432	388	335	339	241	234	196	129	73	25	9	2	
451 WIRRAL.																						
NESTON	6510	M. - 3174	460	423	393	327	255	231	172	154	143	130	151	102	88	54	49	24	11	4	2	
		F. - 3336	448	425	362	331	313	227	188	203	171	161	136	114	90	63	59	31	15	8	1	
EASTHAM. (W.R^2.S^*.)	14564	M. - 7435	930	808	840	1160	700	607	454	442	304	271	218	208	186	102	91	42	9	1	.	
		F. - 7129	852	787	713	747	765	669	532	444	368	280	273	207	194	123	100	45	22	7	1	
WOODCHURCH. (H.)	6854	M. - 3244	505	431	379	341	286	242	171	182	162	122	127	84	81	65	37	21	6	2	.	
		F. - 3610	454	436	397	395	356	309	258	224	163	151	143	108	86	52	46	23	12	3	1	
452 BIRKENHEAD.																						
BIRKENHEAD. (H^4.R.)	51610	M. - 26723	3869	3209	2687	2494	2563	2423	2111	1833	1699	1210	892	647	600	296	135	50	24	9	1	
		F. - 24887	3797	3143	2621	2151	2187	2049	1770	1579	1515	1128	1025	633	628	287	219	93	57	20	4	
TRANMERE. (W.W.S.)	30624	M. - 13740	2164	1841	1505	1234	1181	1083	967	850	738	528	400	365	325	228	135	76	30	8	2	
		F. - 16884	2169	1886	1698	1861	1897	1568	1282	1036	969	663	587	483	415	286	190	98	47	15	3	
WALLASEY. (R^3.B^2.)	21192	M. - 10027	1470	1297	1081	961	860	813	787	690	598	437	342	244	196	130	87	42	18	3	1	
		F. - 11165	1472	1246	1091	1199	1178	1030	830	703	622	464	362	275	278	188	136	56	30	6	1	
4 LANCASHIRE.																						
453 LIVERPOOL.																						
ST. MARTIN	70606	M. - 36476	5013	4348	3593	3860	3380	3195	2908	2668	2608	1744	1433	819	776	286	171	30	28	2	4	
		F. - 34130	5069	4141	3582	2871	3927	2732	2671	2343	2362	1555	1390	835	877	325	203	80	53	9	3	
HOWARD STREET. (H.)	15382	M. - 7649	879	826	768	771	779	721	547	489	558	382	349	209	247	75	30	15	4	2	2	
		F. - 7733	923	821	759	711	756	609	554	483	597	412	408	213	295	95	54	24	15	4	-	
DALE STREET. (H.P.)	19937	M. - 10192	1120	948	836	885	1077	1026	932	772	760	482	491	280	309	133	90	22	10	2	.	
		F. - 9745	1139	939	941	939	952	806	705	640	779	546	463	280	320	148	94	27	22	4	.	
ST. GEORGE	6644	M. - 3452	278	285	489	363	410	391	284	243	207	151	127	87	71	42	18	4	2	.	.	
		F. - 3192	279	259	349	433	386	290	238	239	163	157	136	75	78	41	32	22	6	1	.	
ST. THOMAS. (H.S.)	18910	M. - 9564	1035	909	792	901	1052	1029	829	748	690	453	386	271	335	114	65	22	9	3	.	
		F. - 9346	1096	987	859	876	972	815	733	669	634	445	400	285	267	149	96	52	17	1	1	
MOUNT PLEASANT. (W.H^6.L.R.)	41997	M. - 18323	1946	1840	1730	1746	1842	1716	1314	1264	1175	900	757	607	608	438	248	131	51	10	.	
		F. - 23674	2067	1829	1987	2809	3005	2264	1818	1523	1429	1148	1016	797	907	587	360	203	118	23	3	
ISLINGTON. (H.R.)	36688	M. - 18634	2193	1831	1676	1796	1844	1863	1673	1412	1408	943	816	480	435	220	87	33	12	3	2	
		F. - 18054	2121	1848	1662	1705	2036	1801	1433	1232	1221	885	769	413	455	254	132	55	6	4	.	

ae of the Wybunbury Sub-District was altered to Crewe on 14th July 1881.

Table 3 *continued*.—Ages of Males and Females in Registration Sub-Districts.

Registration Sub-District.	All Ages. Persons.	All Ages. Males and Females.	Under 5 Years.	5–	10–	15–	20–	25–	30–	35–	40–	45–	50–	55–	60–	65–	70–	75–	80–	85–	90–	95–
34 LANCASHIRE —*cont.*																						
454 TOXTETH PARK.																						
1 Toxteth Park. (W. W.H².R².)	117028	M. - 55341	8370	6014	5717	4962	5090	4899	4240	3672	3338	2330	2017	1319	1148	654	412	169	67	15	.	
		F. - 61687	8492	7131	5905	5618	5906	5580	4647	4082	3641	2692	2322	1665	1061	921	825	297	149	39	12	
455 WEST DERBY.																						
1 Everton. (W².H.R⁵.B.)	109812	M. - 53855	8250	6856	6018	5210	4829	4671	3940	3548	3118	2228	1872	1224	1002	591	308	141	46	6	1	.
		F. - 55057	8236	7034	6859	4906	4942	4771	4136	3750	3301	2456	2168	1429	1311	770	513	230	100	27	1	
2 Kirkdale. (W8.H.P. R.B.)	58145	M. - 29679	4629	3942	3114	2514	2725	2674	2370	2072	1814	1518	1002	596	612	244	153	60	20	7	.	.
		F. - 28466	4544	3744	3027	2449	2401	2493	2213	1903	1659	1222	1003	627	682	280	196	73	48	12	1	
3 Walton. (W.H.P.B.)	48023	M. - 23648	3524	2859	2160	1984	2332	2268	1802	1669	1474	964	807	554	641	368	239	133	58	8	4	.
		F. - 24375	3624	2768	2303	2354	2450	2245	1899	1696	1549	962	802	582	874	402	283	176	71	26	6	
4 Crosby. (R.)	10717	M. - 4644	630	587	592	510	430	338	286	285	239	190	187	130	99	58	43	30	9	1	.	.
		F. - 6073	647	591	586	680	819	583	416	418	334	265	235	160	158	89	85	40	14	5	.	.
5 Litherland	8990	M. - 3871	582	528	398	332	381	303	277	244	227	148	135	100	86	65	38	20	12	4	1	.
		F. - 5119	589	665	480	583	625	617	387	328	269	180	180	126	121	69	48	28	12	7	.	.
6 West Derby Municipal. (R².)	67727	M. - 32967	5183	4080	3407	3086	3100	3028	2541	2243	1862	1346	1111	703	634	361	167	90	32	8	3	.
		F. - 34760	5113	4121	3516	3122	3177	3151	2644	2281	2067	1504	1262	918	866	515	301	134	61	13	3	1
7 West Derby Rural. (L.R.)	33474	M. - 14912	2113	1905	1774	1444	1344	1131	1026	904	838	672	514	374	364	177	136	65	27	12	9	.
		F. - 18562	2226	1955	1019	2130	1993	1618	1339	1198	1010	756	669	326	502	326	210	114	48	16	5	1
8 Wavertree	22385	M. - 10588	1648	1399	1006	980	1022	921	778	734	690	395	358	253	240	122	76	50	17	5	.	.
		F. - 11797	1559	1361	1151	1135	1233	1137	954	738	678	491	413	327	256	167	113	42	27	12	1	1
456 PRESCOT.																						
1 Hale	2941	M. - 1498	205	182	156	138	155	118	110	72	82	69	61	33	46	23	24	18	4	1	1	.
		F. - 1443	199	181	160	160	121	87	97	98	76	66	67	44	42	30	24	12	.	.	.	.
2 Much Woolton. (H.)	5700	M. - 2621	383	349	262	288	230	211	185	162	136	110	87	75	71	48	30	16	8	.	.	.
		F. - 3079	368	356	283	310	293	283	221	195	191	139	135	98	96	67	41	29	10	2	2	.
3 Huyton	5937	M. - 2765	347	315	299	308	304	268	177	165	148	117	103	64	76	54	31	19	5	1	.	.
		F. - 3172	374	343	313	338	340	308	297	196	174	148	114	117	83	64	32	23	11	1	1	.
4 Farnworth. (H.)	27686	M. - 14900	2435	1941	1582	1196	1388	1474	1206	1015	861	590	455	292	218	126	79	45	6	4	2	.
		F. - 12786	2295	1848	1490	1141	1061	1003	894	761	655	508	390	247	220	131	78	43	17	5	1	.
5 Prescot. (W.)	15070	M. - 7604	1112	1006	888	723	640	593	510	422	408	315	275	227	209	160	96	52	23	6	1	.
		F. - 7466	1177	973	835	632	628	667	493	451	382	303	284	199	233	142	108	46	33	8	1	.
6 St. Helens. (H.L.)	56872	M. - 29531	4619	3926	3168	2870	2928	2678	2157	1709	1515	1160	1025	671	618	390	191	71	19	8	1	.
		F. - 27341	4628	3865	3078	2552	2323	2147	1855	1489	1410	1090	909	631	545	358	222	92	47	7	2	1
7 Rainford	3745	M. - 2004	295	227	213	251	218	189	135	119	105	79	61	35	49	23	15	18	1	.	.	.
		F. - 1741	299	260	187	150	123	146	122	91	72	66	58	41	42	39	10	12	2	3	.	.
457 ORMSKIRK.																						
1 Bickerstaffe	3536	M. - 1892	233	221	210	215	227	173	118	91	91	71	68	49	39	42	21	13	5	2	.	.
		F. - 1644	251	226	184	174	142	118	112	78	73	64	69	47	47	30	15	16	8	1	.	.
2 Aughton. (H.)	5045	M. - 2713	421	351	272	228	206	216	161	140	122	110	126	81	82	51	44	24	9	.	.	.
		F. 2332	390	354	297	360	281	251	192	148	145	105	101	98	76	59	53	23	8	9	3	.
3 Halsall	2116	M. - 1111	137	128	140	137	112	77	65	49	58	43	45	19	27	24	17	9	5	1	.	.
		F. - 1005	164	129	119	103	88	68	62	41	52	36	32	31	22	28	18	8	4	.	.	.
4 Formby. (H.R.)	13163	M. - 5820	915	713	787	624	439	558	385	242	263	216	221	170	140	116	72	36	20	2	1	.
		F. - 7343	840	754	752	833	775	678	518	457	387	297	275	218	240	147	90	53	18	5	1	1
5 North Meols. (H³.)	33763	M. - 14064	1956	1703	1617	1340	1191	1125	927	824	754	631	490	430	423	290	178	115	41	14	1	.
		F. - 19699	1974	1732	1746	2109	2207	1856	1407	1273	1188	974	842	680	606	469	200	167	81	15	3	.
6 Tarleton	3668	M. - 1904	272	229	197	184	187	148	111	103	91	83	70	74	56	49	33	9	9	4	.	.
		F. - 1764	267	260	172	187	138	138	105	89	86	59	66	67	62	38	29	16	13	2	.	.
7 Scarisbrick	4522	M. - 2281	325	265	236	251	199	199	154	128	117	68	87	65	59	50	34	27	12	2	2	.
		F. 2241	325	291	244	201	208	148	141	140	108	97	90	67	67	53	33	21	10	7	.	.
8 Ormskirk. (W.)	6651	M. - 3297	421	410	351	332	288	261	207	179	102	128	119	121	111	77	67	23	17	2	1	.
		F. - 3354	440	418	341	326	297	223	210	176	193	167	143	107	131	69	54	27	18	3	1	.
9 Lathom	10148	M. - 5298	821	604	555	540	546	442	378	306	250	203	203	121	95	72	41	24	15	.	.	.
		F. 4850	836	745	618	376	417	347	323	257	272	194	168	124	104	69	38	31	9	4	2	1
458 WIGAN.																						
1 Standish	8135	M. - 4204	628	593	478	426	384	311	225	234	201	172	149	116	101	73	44	25	8	4	1	.
		F. 3931	606	553	480	375	321	258	235	201	191	155	133	136	92	80	41	27	27	5	.	.
2 Aspull	13533	M. - 6942	1014	932	789	709	710	544	446	386	320	250	267	173	133	84	69	33	12	2	.	.
		F. 6591	1144	985	804	822	587	479	393	375	305	234	198	174	127	82	58	34	11	4	.	.
3 Wigan. (W.H².)	48194	M. - 23508	3500	2987	2648	2284	2283	2012	1690	1383	1250	941	838	590	522	275	179	59	38	11	2	.
		F. - 24686	3594	3076	2715	2673	2422	1988	1631	1405	1306	1040	930	705	544	314	208	76	59	5	2	1
4 Hindley	33360	M. - 17026	2681	2358	1836	1618	1848	1421	1219	1006	794	650	522	426	275	185	114	44	13	3	.	.
		F. - 16334	2740	2357	1946	1581	1428	1296	1073	854	790	599	526	404	320	177	118	62	27	6	1	.
5 Pemberton. (H.)	18606	M. - 9252	1497	1371	1078	921	841	722	567	503	406	349	298	261	195	127	74	44	9	1	.	.
		F. - 9354	1485	1290	1130	977	852	741	578	514	401	343	326	242	196	133	79	48	10	4	5	.
6 Upholland	8266	M. - 4277	648	646	487	421	401	353	267	254	185	171	165	117	105	82	43	23	13	1	.	.
		F. - 3989	638	534	449	371	364	300	230	215	172	150	166	121	120	89	48	22	7	4	1	.
7 Ashton in Makerfield. (H.)	9824	M. - 5251	797	692	607	602	664	425	379	279	242	198	180	165	103	61	38	28	8	1	1	.
		F. - 4573	724	701	592	457	389	337	304	292	213	172	153	131	113	85	56	10	8	2	1	.

Table 3 *continued.*—AGES of MALES and FEMALES in REGISTRATION SUB-DISTRICTS.

REGISTRATION SUB-DISTRICT.	ALL AGES. Persons.	ALL AGES. Males and Females.	Under 5 Years.	5-	10-	15-	20-	25-	30-	35-	40-	45-	50-	55-	60-	65-	70-	75-	80-	85-	90-	95-
LANCASHIRE —cont.																						
WARRINGTON.																						
EWTON IN MAKERFIELD. (L.R.)	16443	M. - 8748	1314	1155	940	918	806	779	680	476	485	339	291	191	172	98	70	21	12	1	.	.
		F. - 7695	1308	1128	875	611	606	610	553	420	383	331	251	212	184	108	60	34	11	1	1	.
INWICK	1761	M. - 891	115	99	90	88	99	79	66	48	42	33	41	30	27	16	16	8	5	.	1	.
		F. - 870	124	109	108	88	69	67	47	43	46	46	37	42	24	16	19	4	2	2	.	.
NKEY	3364	M. - 1738	247	223	224	186	172	129	110	84	81	98	67	49	31	23	21	13	6	1	1	.
		F. - 1626	237	226	234	169	121	106	90	80	88	65	61	48	41	22	20	3	5	1	.	.
ARRINGTON. (W.WS.H².B.)	40957	M. - 20883	3248	2795	2311	2082	2031	1828	1427	1241	1180	762	684	503	360	199	137	69	32	5	2	.
		F. - 20074	3377	2649	2205	1947	1894	1563	1312	1153	1064	762	690	490	430	229	164	38	30	10	2	.
ATCHFORD	5566	M. - 2714	404	349	269	266	264	215	215	146	133	120	97	87	77	33	20	12	7	.	.	.
		F. - 2852	423	358	281	261	255	264	189	168	142	121	110	79	85	41	43	18	12	2	2	.
IXTON	2127	M. - 1110	166	125	131	99	107	83	82	65	46	51	46	31	34	16	13	10	7	3	1	.
		F. - 1017	155	139	104	90	84	78	61	66	42	54	30	31	33	19	16	9	4	2	.	.
460 LEIGH.																						
OWTON	7092	M. - 3437	493	441	393	359	301	251	211	175	186	150	115	112	89	64	51	27	6	4	1	.
		F. - 3655	499	473	434	399	297	266	207	188	203	168	130	114	136	69	41	21	7	3	.	.
ULCHETH	12182	M. - 5935	877	750	672	612	579	442	371	346	284	247	231	187	147	94	69	34	11	5	3	.
		F. - 6247	915	769	693	603	557	471	360	378	351	229	214	236	166	116	84	56	26	5	1	.
ESTLEIGH	14488	M. - 7084	1081	954	721	710	704	599	495	386	273	280	246	171	151	108	73	30	6	4	.	.
		F. - 7404	1140	953	798	749	718	624	451	428	373	290	266	196	187	135	49	26	18	.	.	.
THERTON. (W.)	22536	M. - 11199	1787	1528	1230	1102	1045	976	790	594	564	432	362	244	214	152	96	57	20	6	.	.
		F. - 11337	1800	1551	1178	1139	1052	852	769	685	610	457	391	282	238	148	102	78	21	3	1	.
461 BOLTON.																						
ARNWORTH. (W.)	27961	M. - 13304	2027	1736	1518	1301	1198	1065	874	785	691	647	501	345	317	198	116	70	22	5	.	.
		F. - 14657	2035	1794	1571	1468	1400	1156	1023	868	854	694	606	304	312	215	149	80	30	9	1	.
ULTON. (R.)	13701	M. - 6711	1024	921	857	726	609	493	483	403	305	278	219	138	123	83	50	24	9	5	.	.
		F. - 6990	943	908	848	703	606	562	445	426	369	280	265	175	144	102	78	36	15	3	.	.
WESTHOUGHTON	9197	M. - 4590	745	602	531	445	404	379	292	241	210	190	156	131	123	63	44	24	6	3	1	.
		F. - 4607	701	633	525	429	393	369	299	266	230	181	169	141	120	88	45	21	11	1	.	.
HALLIWELL	14012	M. - 6617	1047	874	761	680	655	504	481	380	326	298	206	182	123	69	53	25	6	2	.	.
		F. - 7395	1018	884	793	727	742	633	556	472	386	335	275	209	146	112	61	36	6	2	2	.
HORWICH	4543	M. - 2190	322	254	245	201	190	185	134	128	109	84	96	75	62	55	27	15	5	.	.	.
		F. - 2353	306	299	222	215	213	201	158	154	119	98	92	86	75	60	28	18	5	4	.	.
TONGE WITH HAULGH	10067	M. - 4745	682	570	503	464	425	427	333	285	220	193	208	136	110	95	56	26	11	1	.	.
		F. - 5322	682	611	560	522	528	490	414	314	236	221	219	179	144	97	50	39	11	3	1	.
TURTON	6514	M. - 3071	431	388	354	338	306	261	200	148	163	127	109	92	62	43	28	10	9	2	.	.
		F. - 3443	489	378	361	368	355	290	230	207	191	166	147	108	75	59	39	22	9	2	.	.
EDGEWORTH	2474	M. - 1287	187	180	176	131	116	88	90	61	57	48	40	40	28	23	10	10	1	1	.	.
		F. - 1187	167	153	131	110	113	99	94	75	56	40	48	29	31	20	13	4	3	1	.	.
SHARPLES	6225	M. - 2981	460	397	341	311	262	231	188	170	155	115	115	88	47	41	33	17	7	1	.	.
		F. - 3244	421	359	329	354	310	284	233	192	208	150	142	88	71	45	31	16	9	2	.	.
LITTLE BOLTON	41937	M. - 19878	2923	2516	2078	1980	1851	1867	1435	1222	1079	816	705	554	412	220	146	64	7	3	.	.
		F. - 22059	3110	2643	2279	2186	2131	1953	1611	1327	1296	934	808	675	525	267	198	75	39	12	.	.
BOLTON EASTERN. (H.)	25919	M. - 12193	1684	1588	1365	1308	1183	1047	828	758	667	560	484	307	269	157	85	47	20	1	.	.
		F. - 13726	1831	1569	1418	1451	1383	1195	917	854	816	634	520	380	329	198	134	64	27	6	.	.
BOLTON WESTERN. (W.)	19775	M. - 9541	1365	1234	1000	965	820	850	699	556	559	413	330	272	301	127	76	31	11	5	.	.
		F. - 10234	1304	1239	1120	989	988	861	706	605	588	478	308	326	265	141	87	47	21	5	.	.
LEVER	10080	M. - 4877	712	651	542	539	458	331	370	206	242	224	155	132	98	64	32	23	2	.	1	.
		F. - 5203	717	677	579	510	460	450	350	325	273	242	183	151	107	81	96	23	4	4	.	.
462 BURY.																						
HOLCOMBE	9707	M. - 4557	627	577	486	493	397	387	334	256	246	196	161	138	118	74	37	28	6	1	.	.
		F. - 5150	647	554	549	517	514	452	371	325	319	217	188	173	137	92	55	26	9	2	3	.
TOTTINGTON LOWER END	6894	M. - 3361	497	452	390	331	285	255	223	221	169	137	126	86	85	44	33	22	1	2	2	.
		F. - 3533	480	447	406	366	300	286	247	216	189	143	129	102	87	58	40	19	6	2	1	.
WALMERSLEY	5130	M. - 2480	337	297	272	264	230	221	206	140	130	115	95	73	53	34	20	18	5	1	.	.
		F. - 2650	375	304	262	238	264	228	180	154	133	142	106	80	81	39	27	19	9	1	.	.
BIRTLE. (W.)	3953	M. - 2018	255	218	178	181	166	154	143	108	104	89	99	92	91	63	36	20	1	2	.	.
		F. - 1935	210	200	182	168	169	164	158	119	109	101	97	72	70	45	36	24	7	3	1	.
HEYWOOD. (H.)	21088	M. - 9788	1330	1202	1074	1038	872	817	665	561	582	463	301	334	232	151	77	35	15	2	.	.
		F. - 11300	1244	1230	1185	1208	1076	1011	820	733	648	524	513	303	317	192	110	61	27	7	2	.
SOUTH BURY	18067	M. - 8505	1198	947	896	807	733	753	618	579	514	388	340	259	208	133	79	41	11	1	.	.
		F. - 9562	1215	1036	925	922	985	858	605	629	574	487	398	269	253	160	110	51	25	5	.	.
NORTH BURY. (B.)	22411	M. - 10524	1486	1358	1144	1050	979	909	782	654	565	435	391	320	211	127	78	81	9	3	2	.
		F. - 11887	1581	1299	1164	1173	1162	1092	847	719	710	568	473	419	295	182	96	69	31	6	1	.
ELTON. (B.)	13370	M. - 6508	925	802	635	693	700	616	433	388	322	237	215	178	148	92	43	30	8	4	.	.
		F. - 6862	972	833	693	686	628	634	477	330	380	280	265	213	183	99	96	36	12	6	.	.
RADCLIFFE	15863	M. - 7615	1125	955	807	828	714	670	549	476	385	341	253	192	162	85	46	19	6	2	.	.
		F. - 8248	1130	1034	852	774	808	728	612	524	444	381	221	255	155	109	76	31	11	3	.	.
PILKINGTON	13125	M. - 6289	833	799	695	640	627	481	423	379	322	280	251	191	161	108	52	31	15	5	1	.
		F. - 6836	891	815	723	701	634	564	440	418	391	309	280	212	185	130	75	38	17	4	2	.
463 BARTON UPON IRWELL.																						
WORSLEY. (WB.L.)	23785	M. - 11632	1743	1670	1519	1147	1054	908	768	670	518	434	414	268	214	162	82	37	17	.	1	.
		F. - 12153	1704	1655	1502	1166	1073	922	814	750	619	521	430	340	278	185	116	54	23	5	1	.
BARTON. (W.)	25994	M. - 11909	1706	1500	1302	1121	1006	916	810	736	662	518	450	358	208	190	135	72	20	7	1	.
		F. - 14085	1781	1586	1437	1477	1410	1158	1018	836	789	646	560	434	370	204	165	73	43	8	.	.
STRETFORD	23036	M. - 10432	1355	1292	1154	1053	941	860	781	724	603	482	414	287	220	145	87	40	12	7	.	.
		F. - 12604	[illegible]	1245	1228	1444	1445	1106	991	791	713	526	464	361	304	215	129	84	32	7	.	.

Table 3 *continued*.—Ages of Males and Females in Registration Sub-Districts.

Registration Sub-District.	All Ages. Persons.	All Ages. Males and Females.	Under 5 Years.	5–	10–	15–	20–	25–	30–	35–	40–	45–	50–	55–	60–	65–	70–	75–	80–	85–	90–	95–
34 LANCASHIRE —*cont.*																						
464. CHORLTON.																						
1 Didsbury. (W.)	19067	M. - 8224	1082	949	905	712	785	645	559	569	478	353	330	260	274	194	150	74	21	3	.	
		F. - 10843	1066	994	918	1141	1373	1119	864	698	563	482	460	313	292	239	183	104	58	11	4	
2 Ardwick. (H.P.R.)	93230	M. - 45528	6839	5597	4827	4441	4535	4236	3500	2971	2520	1828	1496	1043	847	420	260	113	46	8	.	
		F. - 47702	7039	5962	4750	4363	4449	4256	3600	3153	2761	2064	1710	1244	1027	610	342	160	82	15	5	
3 Chorlton upon Medlock. (W.H.R.)	55598	M. - 25404	3225	2821	2707	2475	2630	2600	2047	1675	1404	1052	960	684	546	338	207	92	28	4	1	
		F. - 30194	3289	2830	2784	3195	3466	3048	2356	1983	1700	1441	1274	914	787	523	350	160	66	16	3	
4 Hulme (B.)	90331	M. - 42871	6213	5130	4436	4156	4250	4040	3343	2818	2401	1830	1540	1007	810	460	254	110	45	7	1	
		F. - 47460	6302	5294	4674	4662	4818	4411	3857	3027	2736	2121	1854	1546	1163	687	412	204	88	25	7	
465 SALFORD.																						
1 Pendleton. (W.H.)	48408	M. - 22912	3594	3099	2462	2221	2381	1943	1725	1473	1216	935	775	556	375	221	161	64	27	4	.	
		F. - 25496	3691	3031	2584	2468	2456	2205	1890	1628	1433	1077	948	645	556	346	244	122	48	11	3	
2 Broughton	31534	M. - 14589	2258	1774	1522	1419	1357	1407	1187	948	792	680	452	360	247	133	75	20	18	4	.	
		F. - 16945	2244	1835	1568	1570	1905	1810	1449	1087	946	681	607	431	349	230	138	63	22	6	2	
3 Greengate. (H.)	31869	M. - 15260	2284	1870	1666	1489	1429	1381	1072	977	893	659	576	374	309	180	79	43	12	2	2	
		F. - 16609	2211	1863	1677	1504	1523	1979	1321	1076	1023	830	663	429	465	252	157	75	34	7	1	
4 Regent Road. (W.H.B.)	69715	M. - 34429	5148	4487	3871	3256	3041	2895	2728	2299	2078	1470	1082	752	634	308	227	95	40	10	.	
		F. - 35286	5236	4814	3728	3128	2988	2918	2638	2482	2133	1500	1234	867	823	454	306	172	57	15	4	
466 MANCHESTER.																						
1 Ancoats. (H.)	47980	M. - 22949	3410	2825	2463	2306	2098	1909	1709	1460	1290	940	916	548	482	206	134	44	10	2	2	
		F. - 25031	3273	2966	2509	2427	2309	2142	1769	1531	1576	1177	1159	728	715	820	201	90	44	11	2	
2 Deansgate. (H*.)	15114	M. - 7549	795	744	606	670	764	711	694	561	546	391	370	219	217	108	65	22	3	.	.	.
		F. - 7565	908	772	678	698	818	603	598	495	523	357	340	218	223	109	82	42	8	4	1	.
3 Market Street. (W.H.)	26569	M. - 12857	1879	1860	1301	1220	1327	1184	1010	890	765	605	635	364	317	183	133	50	13	2	.	.
		F. - 13712	1689	1381	1173	1374	1575	1319	1029	944	814	640	696	407	374	198	129	39	28	1	2	.
4 St. George	59131	M. - 28650	4188	3820	2930	2770	2713	2550	2166	1855	1751	1292	1133	702	571	288	170	71	25	8	2	1
		F. - 30481	4276	3604	3119	2772	2933	2611	2279	1963	1886	1420	1320	783	893	349	225	107	39	14	2	1
467 PRESTWICH.																						
1 Newton. (H.)	55318	M. - 27138	4407	3751	2972	2572	2318	2369	2017	1693	1498	1084	901	639	436	241	147	57	24	7	2	.
		F. - 28180	4424	3865	2969	2605	2525	2327	2020	1746	1603	1124	1089	761	589	303	208	102	53	11	4	
2 Cheetham. (W.w.H.P.)	33875	M. - 15881	1880	1651	1498	1515	1565	1452	1264	1042	913	752	606	457	538	320	238	126	50	9	2	.
		F. - 17994	1963	1618	1599	1892	2050	1765	1348	1105	1019	791	787	540	609	375	202	141	76	17	5	.
3 Failsworth. (H.)	11378	M. - 5550	870	718	604	541	498	477	384	313	316	223	189	178	113	78	48	32	5	3	.	.
		F. - 5828	985	707	651	538	533	488	402	348	251	266	220	151	123	70	66	35	5	2	2	.
4 Blackley. (H.R.)	10885	M. - 5220	831	683	609	506	412	447	384	322	283	208	177	113	120	50	42	15	8	1	.	.
		F. - 5665	849	694	585	523	530	458	451	338	316	237	217	132	134	83	52	34	10	1	1	.
5 Prestwich. (L.)	9831	M. - 4632	569	520	400	364	411	401	361	347	291	232	197	149	145	69	54	24	8	1	.	.
		F. 5199	547	509	456	475	531	517	309	371	352	283	288	189	107	106	59	34	13	2	.	.
468 ASHTON UNDER LYNE.																						
1 Knott Lanes	8478	M. - 4134	600	505	501	439	350	358	256	247	206	160	166	119	95	65	32	19	7			.
		F. - 4344	654	534	493	411	388	367	289	267	253	183	134	140	123	68	46	26	7	2	1	.
2 Ashton Town. (W.H.)	36399	M. - 17167	2371	2052	1791	1714	1546	1488	1166	1013	1031	767	729	508	426	316	205	81	34	9	.	.
		F. - 19232	2203	2047	1913	1830	1867	1672	1417	1225	1183	944	824	664	557	362	220	119	54	11	1	.
3 Audenshaw	19832	M. - 9581	1389	1227	1073	941	838	757	697	593	483	425	395	268	220	133	81	39	15	5	1	1
		F. - 10251	1339	1251	1074	988	933	839	711	663	629	468	406	310	272	179	97	56	23	9	4	1
4 Denton	12711	M. - 6124	866	824	765	696	537	456	423	370	331	237	270	167	139	77	65	31	8	3	.	.
		F. - 6587	845	823	726	681	570	525	455	457	351	296	243	179	149	114	70	37	14	4	2	.
5 Newton	8732	M. - 4060	580	556	451	393	319	327	311	230	235	188	157	126	102	67	38	13	4	.	.	.
		F. 4672	622	562	453	444	394	385	342	310	279	226	179	178	121	104	61	23	5	3	.	.
6 Dukinfield	29675	M. - 13802	2039	1706	1589	1425	1234	1049	934	782	744	583	509	394	323	216	117	58	18	5	1	.
		F. - 15873	2050	1836	1587	1555	1435	1340	1078	972	962	791	701	555	448	267	207	66	30	3	1	.
7 Hartshead. (B.)	21855	M. - 10468	1395	1357	1123	1142	962	881	712	626	593	453	410	286	231	151	94	31	10	2	.	.
		F. - 11387	1449	1291	1120	1116	1165	929	819	713	664	580	504	353	364	185	105	68	13	3	1	.
8 Mottram	7046	M. - 2807	473	446	425	357	334	300	243	220	210	172	158	117	98	74	37	29	6	1	.	.
		F. - 4240	497	517	425	448	486	334	273	254	276	104	188	148	87	86	46	28	12	2	1	.
9 Stayley	8898	M. - 4172	590	520	444	421	369	367	285	262	210	169	178	122	109	71	40	15	6	4	.	.
		F. - 4726	643	565	481	480	417	375	345	288	274	256	207	152	112	94	50	28	8	2	.	.
469 OLDHAM.																						
1 Oldham below Town. (W.H[3].)	66535	M. - 32278	4557	3756	3351	3150	3084	3011	2466	2062	1845	1444	1286	869	689	365	217	106	32	11	1	2
		F. - 34257	4468	4074	3479	3466	3536	3931	2466	2058	2001	1697	1410	1011	776	451	205	139	64	18	4	9
2 Oldham above Town	44808	M. - 21258	2929	2579	2337	2163	1954	1826	1555	1367	1190	966	828	600	478	286	154	51	22	3	.	.
		F. - 23550	3063	2598	2425	2345	2207	2348	1671	1516	1446	1162	996	726	576	340	208	107	31	2	1	.
3 Chadderton	24153	M. - 11749	1723	1491	1264	1239	1151	1038	810	661	613	498	443	319	226	134	90	39	8	4	.	.
		F. - 12404	1815	1548	1380	1223	1161	1069	841	719	695	577	475	316	264	162	91	51	16	4	.	.
4 Middleton	10726	M. - 5157	649	613	577	497	456	498	373	293	290	239	206	172	136	118	80	39	11	.	.	.
		F. - 5569	698	634	609	541	526	410	406	370	301	276	245	217	131	111	87	26	17	4	.	.
5 Royton	12442	M. - 5956	788	710	645	628	586	562	403	383	311	252	214	197	146	78	36	30	2	4	1	.
		F. - 6486	855	734	678	628	622	500	486	394	374	267	265	233	180	103	66	28	9	3	.	1
6 Crompton	9797	M. - 4610	648	579	526	517	424	386	321	281	241	204	176	121	85	42	33	22	3	.	.	.
		F. - 5187	684	602	567	539	499	410	351	308	338	253	176	172	120	92	55	20	11	2	.	.

Table 3 *continued*.—AGES of MALES and FEMALES in REGISTRATION SUB-DISTRICTS.

REGISTRATION SUB-DISTRICT.	ALL AGES. Persons.	Males and Females.	Under 5 Years.	5-	10-	15-	20-	25-	30-	35-	40-	45-	50-	55-	60-	65-	70-	75-	80-	85-	90-
34 LANCASHIRE —*cont.*																					
470. ROCHDALE.																					
1 Butterworth Freehold side	3574	M. - 1673	229	197	189	169	139	131	146	97	101	75	50	54	42	27	16	4	6	.	1
		F. - 1901	232	238	186	171	163	189	140	132	104	97	68	67	67	35	16	15	8	3	.
2 Butterworth Lordship side	4837	M. - 2315	270	264	268	231	235	192	163	128	132	112	106	74	87	48	23	11	3	.	1
		F. - 2522	287	269	280	249	285	214	169	151	176	114	118	88	82	88	26	18	7	1	.
3 Castleton further (H.)	16540	M. - 7745	1064	988	873	852	694	603	536	439	483	319	316	228	191	108	60	28	10	1	.
		F. - 8795	1039	992	881	888	842	760	645	550	520	411	401	384	219	139	88	46	17	3	1
4 Castleton nearer	18732	M. - 8673	1136	1070	886	818	798	777	588	553	524	424	377	283	227	109	66	23	9	5	1
		F. - 10059	1138	1069	1000	984	1033	925	751	654	626	531	447	352	253	152	99	38	18	5	.
5 Spotland nearer side	12290	M. - 5736	789	720	626	578	517	475	363	382	322	292	284	206	138	94	38	22	10	.	.
		F. - 6554	763	657	631	672	638	594	455	421	403	346	317	241	182	106	67	24	8	3	1
6 Spotland further side	7006	M. - 3380	424	390	368	303	322	267	214	191	187	174	158	116	87	66	30	22	4	3	.
		F. - 3626	410	419	390	359	346	307	205	209	205	203	154	125	57	70	42	21	13	2	.
7 Wardleworth (H.)	19711	M. - 9123	1138	1115	1082	952	814	725	640	516	326	461	358	259	218	138	79	27	16	4	1
		F. - 10588	1241	1132	1063	1088	1070	944	748	663	620	634	469	338	293	143	107	43	23	8	1
8 Wuerdle. (W.)	10487	M. - 4994	586	627	591	461	419	389	320	298	252	248	200	183	139	139	70	38	14	2	.
		F. - 5493	625	622	582	504	507	484	414	329	317	268	245	197	107	112	75	51	15	7	1
9 Blatchinworth	7891	M. - 3730	466	442	420	418	358	324	264	226	203	140	154	126	79	55	28	13	4	3	1
		F. - 4161	518	468	444	420	410	361	308	239	214	182	181	142	88	61	46	20	8	1	.
10 Whitworth	20844	M. - 9936	1319	1208	1072	1104	970	829	702	609	550	438	400	265	238	123	68	33	7	1	.
		F. - 10908	1449	1235	1139	1093	1134	946	795	689	640	405	453	320	255	146	88	41	18	5	2
471 HASLINGDEN.																					
1 Newchurch	28261	M. - 13473	1903	1586	1443	1457	1309	1307	911	761	684	581	580	429	301	195	96	62	12	2	1
		F. - 14788	1899	1676	1518	1547	1456	1308	1029	849	829	659	721	486	339	193	118	70	16	3	.
2 Rossendale. (W.)	16130	M. - 7758	1116	926	865	708	738	614	458	474	365	348	311	254	222	125	67	37	15	5	.
		F. - 8372	1103	937	879	876	834	720	560	521	436	376	333	301	221	145	69	39	18	3	1
3 Burnfield	4936	M. - 2376	355	316	268	210	202	192	174	149	128	99	78	69	59	37	27	11	6	1	.
		F. - 2560	346	320	264	234	224	220	207	172	131	106	86	77	73	38	30	16	7	.	.
4 Haslingden	14531	M. - 6893	974	871	707	634	658	568	508	402	368	311	263	198	169	95	66	42	12	1	2
		F. - 7638	959	888	801	752	778	639	613	487	443	336	268	224	188	125	60	31	11	5	.
5 Accrington	31435	M. - 14964	2169	1838	1523	1482	1497	1272	1080	947	817	626	583	424	336	200	123	54	19	5	1
		F. - 16471	2185	1871	1686	1674	1668	1486	1228	1036	941	744	679	503	371	261	146	80	27	6	1
472 BURNLEY.																					
1 Burnley. (W.H.B.)	69053	M. - 33525	4839	4055	3566	3359	3173	2847	2481	2159	1862	1436	1222	930	717	403	295	120	56	6	.
		F. - 35528	5021	4265	3946	3531	3467	3136	2647	2204	1999	1535	1342	963	828	453	332	145	72	10	1
2 Padiham	13984	M. - 6782	940	821	772	655	632	582	486	395	366	289	293	204	132	103	60	35	13	3	1
		F. - 7202	942	824	740	667	709	638	535	415	400	342	302	228	182	135	61	36	16	5	2
3 Colne. (L.)	33934	M. - 16333	2298	2030	1762	1708	1506	1392	1138	978	791	650	584	501	390	260	132	71	16	7	.
		F. - 17601	2517	2077	1800	1767	1753	1598	1238	1092	800	729	606	551	414	277	164	95	19	13	1
4 Pendle	1363	M. - 679	91	63	64	52	49	55	58	46	27	26	31	22	34	25	12	6	7	.	.
		F. - 684	84	94	87	46	69	51	37	49	34	29	26	27	27	13	12	3	2	.	.
473 CLITHEROE.																					
1 Gisburn	2348	M. - 1224	133	145	138	126	124	85	73	57	57	38	56	60	55	39	20	12	6	.	.
		F. - 1124	139	139	118	104	84	101	76	57	59	30	40	52	42	33	24	12	5	.	.
2 Slaidburn	1662	M. - 867	84	120	105	85	84	54	47	51	35	41	33	38	38	30	12	7	3	.	.
		F. - 795	116	95	89	63	58	73	49	39	40	45	41	28	25	22	7	4	1	3	.
3 Chipping	3205	M. - 1860	169	156	296	300	144	164	92	101	79	82	72	58	67	37	22	19	3	2	.
		F. - 1345	158	176	141	125	124	77	82	67	73	75	59	47	48	34	33	15	10	.	1
4 Clitheroe. (W.)	13099	M. - 6326	897	822	671	618	528	512	414	358	338	273	236	220	170	100	90	46	24	4	4
		F. 6773	913	736	720	687	687	541	477	409	353	332	264	228	170	140	87	52	22	5	1
5 Whalley	3188	M. - 1554	204	187	164	151	161	118	98	83	90	66	60	40	64	29	16	11	12	1	.
		F. - 1634	193	154	141	137	172	145	119	105	79	99	86	61	38	33	25	21	10	3	.
474 BLACKBURN.																					
Billington	1997	M. - 1009	110	124	93	93	84	100	74	62	49	53	48	30	38	24	11	11	5	.	.
		F. - 988	138	108	95	76	98	84	73	57	50	47	32	40	31	19	17	11	1	2	.
Harwood	17752	M. - 8617	1213	1102	1010	858	857	718	579	484	443	400	308	222	165	119	84	40	9	3	.
		F. - 9135	1209	1104	1032	1026	904	778	601	560	469	402	353	257	183	134	77	36	14	2	1
Mellor	2272	M. - 1116	134	125	132	111	88	70	95	62	57	43	49	58	49	34	21	15	11	1	.
		F. - 1156	132	128	101	116	110	87	79	81	60	56	56	46	37	28	24	10	2	3	.
Blackburn. (W. H.)	91958	M. - 43453	6488	5255	4783	4304	4229	3616	3051	2564	2442	1803	1638	1176	940	546	318	163	67	12	3
		F. - 48505	6561	5459	4966	5076	5155	4281	3502	3003	2728	2237	1913	1371	1098	630	402	204	88	26	3
Oswaldtwisle	17066	M. - 8241	1182	978	941	928	827	698	542	474	426	327	291	225	170	121	64	33	10	2	.
		F. - 8815	1313	1023	966	873	996	715	612	560	506	354	326	268	199	113	92	33	15	6	.
Darwen	33555	M. - 15836	2277	2064	1853	1628	1437	1356	1138	911	872	681	547	356	305	188	113	56	16	5	3
		F. - 17719	2304	2184	1993	1866	1699	1554	1258	1148	966	761	616	440	364	258	152	72	33	5	.
Witton	11364	M. - 5345	848	711	588	546	513	431	316	310	280	224	193	130	118	72	41	19	14	3	.
		F. - 6019	841	689	634	632	597	521	408	357	313	278	225	183	163	82	50	27	3	2	.

Table 3 *continued*.—Ages of Males and Females in Registration Sub-Districts.

Registration Sub-District.	All Ages. Persons.	Males and Females.	Under 5 Years.	5–	10–	15–	20–	25–	30–	35–	40–	45–	50–	55–	60–	65–	70–	75–	80–	85–	90–	95–
34 LANCASHIRE —*cont.*																						
475 CHORLEY.																						
1 Brindle	5720	M. - 2820	407	344	328	294	254	193	176	148	132	125	106	105	64	57	48	28	11	4	1	.
		F. - 2900	370	334	307	291	275	232	164	172	158	113	119	108	96	48	49	27	9	2	1	.
2 Leyland	9300	M. - 4887	617	613	470	468	392	337	267	236	207	182	152	148	151	87	76	51	20	2	2	.
		F. - 4813	683	500	400	469	465	377	331	276	249	204	172	172	122	120	82	47	15	7	2	.
3 Rivington	4920	M. - 2396	348	368	300	269	208	147	121	121	144	96	96	61	38	29	24	15	5	.	.	.
		F. - 2524	366	316	297	291	226	175	138	170	142	112	80	71	57	30	33	14	4	1	1	.
4 Chorley. (W.)	22796	M. - 10901	1659	1435	1210	1072	958	844	697	610	570	409	376	309	255	169	161	77	48	8	3	1
		F. - 11895	1710	1474	1278	1177	1124	946	803	717	599	471	468	362	326	181	144	70	29	14	1	.
5 Croston	5094	M. - 2540	346	307	259	230	232	185	174	126	134	91	95	97	91	68	43	18	14	1	.	.
		F. - 2554	370	328	236	220	250	191	177	140	123	97	96	111	83	55	38	26	14	1	.	.
476 PRESTON.																						
1 Longton	6574	M. - 3251	406	418	334	361	267	226	193	178	174	156	105	105	83	69	68	34	13	5	1	.
		F. - 3323	409	422	364	329	298	245	225	196	182	153	118	89	94	80	62	34	18	3	1	1
2 Trinity. (P.)	31960	M. - 14851	2103	1861	1705	1670	1544	1089	949	862	808	718	578	445	331	233	145	66	22	7	2	.
		F. - 17109	2084	1822	1784	1829	1721	1395	1159	1102	1050	851	753	573	430	250	168	83	36	17	2	.
3 St. Peter. (H.)	33968	M. - 15571	2276	2071	1866	1612	1336	1176	1025	921	863	657	561	409	378	194	132	61	50	3	.	.
		F. - 18397	2517	2117	1908	1780	1749	1408	1361	1168	1106	800	730	548	492	250	181	88	32	5	2	1
4 St. John	27792	M. - 12564	1722	1542	1419	1250	1107	1054	826	787	771	517	484	358	317	198	135	54	26	3	.	.
		F. - 15228	1737	1540	1503	1608	1630	1336	1090	959	952	712	688	485	403	269	197	88	39	11	1	1
5 Walton-le-Dale	10096	M. - 4674	662	569	558	540	428	362	262	228	243	225	160	125	135	72	62	30	14	1	1	.
		F. - 5422	679	601	559	575	526	459	347	332	338	242	217	171	153	91	75	42	12	2	.	1
6 Alston. (W.)	6365	M. - 3108	419	380	380	328	269	218	187	159	165	141	126	100	91	62	43	27	9	4	.	.
		F. - 3257	387	394	373	293	319	253	197	208	184	155	128	130	78	72	47	26	10	2	1	.
7 Broughton. (W.L.B.)	12405	M. - 6306	642	583	563	729	714	509	422	357	389	275	283	197	224	180	117	73	36	10	3	.
		F. - 6099	656	529	477	520	663	551	474	406	345	343	299	207	241	168	114	67	37	16	2	.
477 FYLDE.																						
1 Kirkham. (W.)	9946	M. - 4713	643	590	541	512	425	331	247	231	227	189	167	155	164	103	97	52	24	5	.	1
		F. - 5233	612	592	522	507	508	421	364	333	299	229	222	185	168	109	90	42	15	12	3	.
2 Lytham. (H.)	5617	M. - 2453	339	333	336	224	207	195	152	125	120	81	75	82	65	48	37	23	11	3	.	.
		F. - 3164	348	367	302	344	314	303	248	171	150	155	128	117	105	78	46	36	13	5	.	.
3 Poulton-le-Fylde. (B.)	25347	M. - 12152	1661	1446	1354	1248	1050	1007	817	759	664	492	430	385	321	231	159	78	33	6	1	.
		F. - 13195	1685	1500	1297	1245	1116	1119	926	807	702	652	580	447	408	258	181	104	34	15	1	1
478 GARSTANG.																						
1 Stalmine	3358	M. - 1725	251	214	216	171	160	105	91	72	83	62	59	71	59	43	39	22	5	2	.	.
		F. - 1633	247	210	185	166	125	109	102	79	74	63	80	51	53	32	31	19	6	.	1	.
2 St. Michael	3184	M. - 1671	204	175	180	211	151	137	92	80	69	69	71	62	60	39	31	25	11	4	.	.
		F. - 1513	196	182	153	163	138	124	100	64	56	81	58	66	36	34	23	27	7	1	.	1
3 Garstang. (W.R.)	5833	M. - 2978	379	344	376	361	233	211	170	163	131	112	130	101	94	58	35	39	13	3	.	.
		F. - 2855	394	367	292	258	234	213	183	173	148	144	112	84	73	60	58	40	9	3	1	.
479 LANCASTER.																						
1 Ellel	3818	M. - 2014	264	233	230	218	190	145	120	112	102	77	92	51	76	39	26	26	7	6	.	.
		F. - 1804	228	208	204	201	173	129	100	94	101	88	85	56	50	32	26	19	5	6	1	.
2 Heaton	5181	M. - 2409	334	267	251	248	235	181	150	111	108	103	115	99	78	41	55	22	6	4	1	.
		F. - 2772	333	208	283	292	267	210	169	132	159	152	142	110	102	60	38	21	11	1	1	1
3 Lancaster. (W.H.L.P.B.)	26182	M. - 12968	1738	1402	1450	1297	1273	1141	965	768	710	560	481	406	353	206	135	60	26	5	2	.
		F. - 13214	1729	1477	1341	1330	1253	1102	942	797	595	562	551	460	346	262	196	99	51	13	6	.
4 Warton	5657	M. - 2871	440	385	273	251	277	248	215	143	133	113	101	88	73	55	39	28	8	4	.	.
		F. - 2786	463	330	291	234	230	221	199	168	138	100	105	85	76	70	45	20	11	1	1	.
480 LUNESDALE.																						
1 Caton	2501	M. - 1260	177	163	142	136	112	88	60	72	50	60	53	46	33	33	16	9	7	2	1	.
		F. - 1241	175	139	111	119	129	107	87	63	58	49	53	44	39	35	16	13	2	1	.	1
2 Wray. (W.)	2046	M. - 1003	104	165	107	98	94	63	68	52	45	47	48	45	33	28	24	19	15	6	.	.
		F. - 1043	132	120	109	103	85	87	48	70	55	45	39	44	29	27	34	10	4	2	.	.
3 Tunstal	771	M. - 359	39	41	38	40	35	24	18	19	16	22	13	18	12	4	9	2	3	1	1	.
		F. - 412	50	44	50	45	42	25	28	20	23	19	13	11	16	15	8	3	2	.	.	.
4 Arkholme	1814	M. - 946	110	128	130	104	79	73	47	45	36	47	43	35	37	30	13	13	4	2	.	.
		F. 868	104	108	101	83	82	65	46	44	36	42	38	31	24	26	14	13	5	1	1	1
481 ULVERSTON.																						
1 Cartmel	5600	M. - 2671	345	318	353	285	184	173	144	131	163	106	123	106	103	67	58	12	16	5	.	.
		F. - 2929	343	312	259	302	276	237	174	169	152	143	134	118	92	92	62	27	23	10	4	.
2 Colton	3464	M. - 1774	238	218	194	208	130	105	113	90	87	67	73	52	82	46	37	30	3	2	1	.
		F. - 1690	215	203	191	154	146	116	101	96	76	86	66	68	64	46	39	17	6	2	1	.
3 Ulverston. (W.H.)	12244	M. - 6094	922	788	696	488	527	509	442	376	299	235	191	198	163	91	79	56	24	8	2	.
		F. - 6150	946	779	654	585	519	516	386	374	294	247	199	199	159	125	85	49	23	13	4	.
4 Dalton	15778	M. - 8365	1334	1200	927	640	789	738	590	561	452	317	278	179	161	98	53	38	15	2	1	.
		F. - 7413	1406	1144	843	499	548	592	409	419	303	289	247	189	147	112	84	31	12	9	1	1
5 West Broughton	3224	M. - 1646	206	199	167	172	148	111	102	74	86	79	70	63	55	49	34	21	9	2	1	.
		F. - 1578	217	192	186	138	131	88	106	83	78	79	52	57	47	49	32	25	14	8	1	.
6 Hawkshead	3371	M. - 1679	229	191	191	177	147	112	84	93	85	86	62	63	48	46	55	28	9	4	.	.
		F. - 1692	210	210	198	160	135	141	88	91	87	92	69	59	55	39	28	23	5	3	.	.
482 BARROW IN FURNESS.																						
1 Barrow in Furness. (W. H.)	47259	M. - 25575	3948	3160	2868	2183	2758	2774	2311	1794	1527	966	701	447	343	173	97	30	12	2	2	.
		F. - 21684	3953	3155	2362	1868	1906	1913	1696	1422	1114	704	573	399	288	172	105	46	22	5	1	.

Table 4.—MALE and FEMALE CHILDREN *at each Year of Age* under 5 in the NORTH-WESTERN DIVISION and its REGISTRATION COUNTIES.

REGISTRATION COUNTY.	TOTAL UNDER 5 YEARS. Persons.	TOTAL UNDER 5 YEARS. Males and Females.	Under 1 Year.	1–	2–	3–	4–
VIII. NORTH-WESTERN COUNTIES.	571349	M. - 284219 F. - 287130	61088 61573	55369 55974	56826 57277	55823 56586	54414 55720
33 CHESHIRE	84230	M. - 42155 F. - 42075	8848 8879	8254 8093	8523 8333	8303 8371	8227 8399
34 LANCASHIRE	487119	M. - 242064 F. - 245055	53140 52694	47115 47881	48302 48944	47320 48215	46187 47321

Table 5.—MALE and FEMALE CHILDREN *at each Year of Age* under 5 in REGISTRATION DISTRICTS.

REGISTRATION DISTRICT.	Total under 5 Years. Persons.	Total under 5 Years. Males and Females.	Under 1 Year.	1–	2–	3–	4–
33 CHESHIRE.							
STOCKPORT	15220	M. - 7526 F. - 7694	1594 1630	1460 1442	1487 1535	1476 1515	1509 1572
MACCLESFIELD	7807	M. - 3788 F. - 4019	780 838	741 755	784 757	738 816	766 853
ALTRINCHAM	7501	M. - 3736 F. - 3765	771 743	734 741	738 720	765 792	728 769
RUNCORN	4991	M. - 2549 F. - 2442	546 520	489 485	534 507	488 464	495 478
NORTHWICH	6595	M. - 3335 F. - 3260	669 700	690 638	683 659	676 668	617 595
CONGLETON	5095	M. - 2605 F. - 2490	554 549	511 436	505 509	513 506	522 490
NANTWICH	8642	M. - 4292 F. - 4350	887 964	847 830	885 839	863 865	810 852
CHESTER	9839	M. - 4966 F. - 4873	1061 999	969 964	987 940	971 990	977 980
WIRRAL	3649	M. - 1895 F. - 1754	402 362	361 337	367 370	367 343	378 342
BIRKENHEAD	14901	M. - 7473 F. - 7428	1605 1574	1461 1465	1553 1497	1448 1422	1426 1470
34 LANCASHIRE.							
LIVERPOOL	25158	M. - 12464 F. - 12694	2893 2900	2333 2412	2533 2526	2426 2449	2279 2407
TOXTETH PARK	16862	M. - 8370 F. - 8492	1971 1859	1672 1660	1574 1729	1606 1629	1547 1615
WEST DERBY	52847	M. - 26409 F. - 26438	5952 5896	5289 5180	5231 5248	5028 5176	4909 5138
PRESCOT	18736	M. - 9396 F. - 9340	2023 1966	1814 1849	1953 1965	1980 1848	1726 1812
ORMSKIRK	10976	M. - 5505 F. - 5471	1171 1124	1018 1093	1121 1127	1165 1087	1030 1040
WIGAN	21960	M. - 10969 F. - 10991	2414 2367	2131 2162	2198 2119	2102 2146	2124 2198
WARRINGTON	11116	M. - 5492 F. - 5624	1206 1209	1061 1113	1089 1102	1059 1082	1077 1118
LEIGH	8581	M. - 4218 F. 4363	955 958	787 835	842 880	769 836	865 854

REGISTRATION DISTRICT.	Total under 5 Years. Persons.	Total under 5 Years. Males and Females.	Under 1 Year.	1–	2–
34 LANCASHIRE—*cont.*					
461 BOLTON	27323	M. - 13559 F. - 13764	2937 2910	2642 2757	2635 2689
462 BURY	17377	M. - 8632 F. - 8745	1820 1908	1722 1660	1707 1689
463 BARTON UPON IRWELL	9818	M. - 4894 F. - 4924	1023 1097	934 941	941 965
464 CHORLTON	35055	M. - 17359 F. - 17696	3707 3855	3396 3362	3500 3493
465 SALFORD	26666	M. - 13284 F. - 13382	3003 2953	2502 2581	2659 2716
466 MANCHESTER	20126	M. - 9978 F. - 10148	2226 2333	1911 1975	2050 1996
467 PRESTWICH	17265	M. - 8547 F. - 8718	1907 1908	1696 1674	1651 1703
468 ASHTON UNDER LYNE	20593	M. - 10252 F. - 10341	2202 2208	2041 1952	1980 2062
469 OLDHAM	22867	M. - 11294 F. - 11573	2454 2407	2224 2283	2255 2328
470 ROCHDALE	15079	M. 7411 F. - 7668	1497 1594	1428 1387	1524 1574
471 HASLINGDEN	13010	M. - 6517 F. 6493	1386 1307	1289 1244	1288 1364
472 BURNLEY	16832	M. - 8268 F. - 8564	1848 1837	1621 1733	1625 1742
473 CLITHEROE	3005	M. - 1487 F. - 1518	324 279	314 299	278 308
474 BLACKBURN	24445	M. - 12247 F. - 12198	2703 2603	2309 2446	2525 2430
475 CHORLEY	6846	M. - 3377 F. - 3469	709 732	663 656	700 736
476 PRESTON	16683	M. - 8230 F. - 8453	1806 1857	1618 1674	1597 1726
477 FYLDE	5288	M. - 2643 F. - 2645	583 562	524 504	530 548
478 GARSTANG	1671	M. - 834 F. - 837	184 157	164 166	174 178
479 LANCASTER	5529	M. - 2776 F. 2753	588 561	558 559	579 562
480 LUNESDALE	891	M. - 430 F. - 461	97 87	90 91	74 92
481 ULVERSTON	6603	M. - 3274 F. - 3329	673 671	618 675	689 647
482 BARROW IN FURNESS	7901	M. - 3948 F. - 3953	818 839	748 758	810 810

Table 7.—CONDITION as to MARRIAGE and AGES of MALES and FEMALES in the NORTH-WESTERN DIVISION and its REGISTRATION COUNTIES.

REGISTRATION COUNTY.		ALL AGES.	Under 15 Years.	15–	20–	25–	35–	45–	55–	65 and upwards
VIII.—NORTH-WESTERN COUNTIES.										
UNMARRIED	Males	1232915	745793	194067	139422	95207	31062	14223	7899	4642
	Females	1260448	755143	201600	134818	93484	37088	19898	11588	6829
MARRIED	Males	687030	.	1196	44651	209930	192758	181201	75400	31804
	Females	699903	.	5457	69231	229456	191659	122046	61526	20624
WIDOWED	Males	66728	.	21	548	5537	9643	12872	16323	21979
	Females	161064	.	51	913	10596	24088	36537	42982	45895
33 CHESHIRE.										
UNMARRIED	Males	187595	113593	30358	20878	13812	4769	2367	1409	910
	Females	193314	113079	30742	20723	14710	6237	3470	2066	1367
MARRIED	Males	103358	.	170	6017	28333	27896	20719	13448	6775
	Females	104597	.	743	9247	51468	27801	19725	10564	4408
WIDOWED	Males	10815	.	.	71	673	1370	1838	2571	4292
	Females	22776	.	7	102	1231	2860	4764	5967	7905
34 LANCASHIRE.										
UNMARRIED	Males	1045320	632200	164209	119944	81395	26293	11866	6490	3725
	Females	1067134	641164	170858	114095	78774	30851	16428	9522	5462
MARRIED	Males	583672	.	1026	38634	181597	164862	170672	61952	25029
	Females	595492		4714	59984	197988	163798	102318	50962	16128
WIDOWED	Males	55913	.	21	477	4864	8278	11034	13752	17687
	Females	138288	.	44	811	9367	21228	31833	37015	37990

Note.—In a few cases persons described as "Married" were stated to be under 15 years of age. These have been classed with Married persons aged "15 and under 20 years."

Table 8.—CONDITION as to MARRIAGE and AGES of MALES and FEMALES in REGISTRATION DISTRICTS

REGISTRATION DISTRICT.		ALL AGES.	Under 15 Years.	15–	20–	25–	35–	45–	55–	65 and upwds.
33 CHESHIRE.										
443 STOCKPORT:										
UNMARRIED	M.	32135	20262	6317	3251	1992	673	334	192	114
	F.	37453	20825	8140	4478	3092	1400	773	418	227
MARRIED	M.	10016	.	53	1389	6025	5502	3315	2397	1035
	F.	10580	.	140	1847	6550	5535	3840	1961	269
WIDOWED	M.	1984	.	.	16	142	240	356	490	722
	F.	4980	.	2	18	269	696	1154	1301	1459
444 MACCLESFIELD:										
UNMARRIED	M.	17172	10443	2934	1656	1038	450	325	204	122
	F.	19744	10770	3134	2170	1808	864	497	300	192
MARRIED	M.	10483	.	35	668	2578	2436	2210	1652	895
	F.	10781	.	86	808	2967	2727	2236	1326	547
WIDOWED	M.	1345	.	.	10	61	130	213	343	538
	F.	2318	.	.	9	127	245	523	727	887
445 ALTRINCHAM:										
UNMARRIED	M.	17142	10263	2577	1964	1357	476	232	166	127
	F.	20120	10318	3205	2596	2089	838	507	300	202
MARRIED	M.	9216	.	5	483	2494	2499	1910	1318	641
	F.	9201	.	46	681	2758	2450	1853	1012	401
WIDOWED	M.	1085	.	.	8	41	115	159	239	463
	F.	2188	.	1	8	121	287	403	685	760
446 RUNCORN:										
UNMARRIED	M.	11037	6664	1726	1257	846	274	130	82	58
	F.	9654	6500	1501	752	459	191	138	71	42
MARRIED	M.	5801	.	9	406	1602	1579	1130	734	381
	F.	5820	.	50	626	1673	1507	1196	601	282
WIDOWED	M.	697	.	.	3	45	80	112	137	221
	F.	1104	.	.	3	56	115	211	264	455
447 NORTHWICH:										
UNMARRIED	M.	14100	8816	2329	1446	872	305	162	105	65
	F.	12620	8704	1802	949	580	211	131	85	58
MARRIED	M.	7720	.	15	521	2114	1091	1568	949	571
	F.	[illegible]	.	86	772	2222	1385	1428	816	410
WIDOWED	M.	750	.	.	5	[illegible]	96	111	183	311
	F.	1154	.	.	6	86	180	188	290	464

REGISTRATION DISTRICT.		ALL AGES.	Under 15 Years.	15–	20–	25–	35–	45–
33 CHESHIRE—*cont.*								
448 CONGLETON:								
UNMARRIED	M.	11537	7160	1895	1163	894	264	163
	F.	11685	7079	1996	1168	705	289	161
MARRIED	M.	6316	.	2	377	1580	1698	1345
	F.	6446	.	43	546	1767	1694	1290
WIDOWED	M.	736	.	.	6	36	79	173
	F.	1290	.	1	6	65	132	267
449 NANTWICH:								
UNMARRIED	M.	19422	11798	3290	2181	1316	423	218
	F.	18066	11973	2885	1610	921	323	187
MARRIED	M.	10509	.	10	601	2818	2852	2172
	F.	10675	.	33	962	3048	2861	2027
WIDOWED	M.	1041	.	.	8	67	130	157
	F.	1733	.	2	10	78	174	313
450 CHESTER:								
UNMARRIED	M.	23850	13925	3880	2728	1925	708	357
	F.	22887	13689	3509	2297	1077	739	407
MARRIED	M.	12037	.	7	550	3067	3280	2484
	F.	12137	.	69	974	3406	3241	2540
WIDOWED	M.	1365	.	.	4	88	177	228
	F.	3021	.	1	8	168	360	582
451 WIRRAL:								
UNMARRIED	M.	9223	5169	1823	1038	744	232	114
	F.	9020	4874	1463	1126	865	328	194
MARRIED	M.	4200	.	5	202	1102	1160	844
	F.	4124	.	20	302	1261	1116	763
WIDOWED	M.	430	.	.	1	31	46	61
	F.	931	.	.	6	46	129	177
452 BIRKENHEAD:								
UNMARRIED	M.	31977	19093	4637	3724	3028	984	323
	F.	32035	19033	5068	3554	2454	987	475
MARRIED	M.	16091	.	22	870	5043	5211	3828
	F.	17060	.	143	1646	5208	4765	2978
WIDOWED	M.	1592	.	.	10	113	253	318
	F.	3851	.	.	28	218	602	908

Table 8 *continued.*—CONDITION as to MARRIAGE and AGES of MALES and FEMALES in REGISTRATION DISTRICTS.

REGISTRATION DISTRICT.		ALL AGES.	Under 15 Years.	15-	20-	25-	35-	45-	55-	65 and upwds.
LANCASHIRE.										
LIVERPOOL:										
UNMARRIED	M.	64468	33320	9664	8238	7920	3108	1312	577	224
	F.	57907	33637	9694	6774	4390	1682	935	562	323
MARRIED	M.	35662	.	66	2116	10250	11023	7119	3733	1254
	F.	35998	.	440	4246	12082	10374	5752	2460	653
WIDOWED	M.	4606	.	9	80	811	700	906	1163	804
	F.	11889	.	11	112	1017	2297	3034	3076	2372
TOXTETH PARK:										
UNMARRIED	M.	34348	21001	4836	4008	3030	865	297	151	61
	F.	30497	21828	5411	3776	2698	1046	485	315	206
MARRIED	M.	19166	.	26	1077	5087	5841	3820	1664	751
	F.	20640	.	207	2185	7284	5800	3252	1497	421
WIDOWED	M.	1827	.	.	5	149	304	480	452	487
	F.	5574	.	.	33	454	877	1277	1514	1419
WEST DERBY:										
UNMARRIED	M.	110135	67027	15963	12964	9489	2890	1998	458	266
	F.	100005	67308	16767	11929	7611	2939	1564	917	569
MARRIED	M.	68583	.	66	3224	18415	18064	10971	5657	2186
	F.	61304	.	576	5507	21618	17431	9647	4232	1293
WIDOWED	M.	5496	.	1	39	420	927	1177	1287	1556
	F.	14800	.	4	104	1084	2515	3349	3900	3835
PRESCOT:										
UNMARRIED	M.	30623	23862	5703	4480	3480	1203	524	257	124
	F.	34271	23512	5068	2563	1662	636	366	206	144
MARRIED	M.	19454	.	26	1360	6295	5413	3631	1905	819
	F.	18669	.	218	2204	6486	5099	3240	1550	572
WIDOWED	M.	1856	.	2	22	170	287	352	441	561
	F.	3388	.	1	22	222	485	746	873	1039
ORMSKIRK:										
UNMARRIED	M.	24334	14654	3853	2760	1831	644	321	237	144
	F.	28329	14766	4510	3387	2848	1270	758	484	306
MARRIED	M.	12638	.	18	700	3599	3279	2426	1626	990
	F.	12972	.	60	1161	3890	3412	2315	1448	647
WIDOWED	M.	1408	.	.	5	103	177	245	299	582
	F.	3531	.	.	15	210	478	740	892	1196
WIGAN:										
UNMARRIED	M.	45580	28380	6933	5124	3233	1003	470	282	146
	F.	42713	28458	6875	3847	2017	714	378	258	166
MARRIED	M.	22583	.	34	1683	7182	6113	4194	2409	968
	F.	22715	.	174	2462	7583	5908	3864	2050	674
WIDOWED	M.	2297	.	1	21	196	325	456	587	711
	F.	4050	.	1	24	273	576	876	1117	1163
WARRINGTON:										
UNMARRIED	M.	23275	14203	3613	2676	1757	598	343	141	84
	F.	20406	14127	3049	1720	880	327	199	129	85
MARRIED	M.	11733	.	20	797	3836	3307	2112	1193	468
	F.	11633	.	96	1361	3939	3072	1930	983	312
WIDOWED	M.	1076	.	1	6	100	163	218	258	330
	F.	2005	.	1	8	141	310	429	533	583
LEIGH:										
UNMARRIED	M.	17313	10917	2771	1893	1048	334	160	94	96
	F.	17371	11210	2814	1594	905	364	205	162	114
MARRIED	M.	9423	.	12	720	3000	2467	1753	1010	466
	F.	9537	.	78	1021	2980	2836	1624	873	316
WIDOWED	M.	819	.	.	16	87	117	183	191	355
	F.	1755	.	.	9	103	208	375	500	560
BOLTON:										
UNMARRIED	M.	57081	35691	9368	6316	3673	1005	638	302	188
	F.	60747	36645	9818	6860	4471	1633	803	467	241
MARRIED	M.	32051	.	38	2137	10116	8831	5106	3459	1364
	F.	32553	.	172	3331	10646	9046	5835	2892	928
WIDOWED	M.	2853	.	.	29	280	391	516	721	979
	F.	7120	.	3	32	451	1009	1678	1926	2021
BURY:										
UNMARRIED	M.	37566	22816	6278	4223	2678	804	408	218	141
	F.	40428	23437	6623	4587	3230	1260	687	390	192
MARRIED	M.	22030	.	47	1482	6764	5991	4213	2578	964
	F.	22491	.	123	1924	7343	6172	4092	2154	683
WIDOWED	M.	2040	.	.	15	168	276	352	531	698
	F.	5046	.	2	18	300	681	1123	1416	1506
BARTON UPON IRWELL:										
UNMARRIED	M.	21199	13337	2307	2307	1435	411	208	124	70
	F.	24120	13597	4029	2857	2012	781	420	274	150
MARRIED	M.	11719	.	14	686	3527	3340	2279	1289	507
	F.	11934	.	56	1053	3886	3358	2123	1080	378
WIDOWED	M.	1064	.	.	6	81	156	195	242	384
	F.	2788	.	2	18	171	309	604	748	876
CHORLTON:										
UNMARRIED	M.	75310	44912	11723	9288	6544	1742	683	298	146
	F.	80886	45902	13612	9874	7053	2643	1443	812	467
MARRIED	M.	42885	.	56	2672	13974	12459	7900	4212	1503
	F.	43959	.	346	4404	15506	12140	7227	3296	971
WIDOWED	M.	3852	.	.	30	362	625	804	963	1078
	F.	[illegible]	[illegible]	[illegible]	[illegible]	860	1863	2685	2978	2916

REGISTRATION DISTRICT.		ALL AGES.	Under 15 Years.	15-	20-	25-	35-	45-	55-
34 LANCASHIRE —cont.									
465 SALFORD:									
UNMARRIED	M.	53606	34035	8350	5743	3676	1088	439	18
	F.	54787	34297	8478	5402	3786	1409	743	37
MARRIED	M.	31006	.	64	2134	10393	9140	5548	279
	F.	31859	.	309	6450	11296	9018	6069	617
WIDOWED	M.	2583	.	1	31	263	445	548	62
	F.	7682	.	1	80	546	1326	1748	201
466 MANCHESTER:									
UNMARRIED	M.	43580	25703	6083	5028	3533	1614	563	26
	F.	42867	26340	6093	4556	2961	1103	876	29
MARRIED	M.	25857	.	71	1884	8256	7327	4962	253
	F.	26231	.	273	3025	8879	7268	4412	193
WIDOWED	M.	2569	.	2	30	205	480	634	62
	F.	7661	.	3	54	651	1391	2027	209
467 PRESTWICH:									
UNMARRIED	M.	32795	21922	5455	3926	2763	856	416	22
	F.	37324	22171	5978	4160	2874	1066	509	36
MARRIED	M.	20472	.	32	1265	6608	5884	3735	214
	F.	20624	.	143	2850	7026	5780	3518	166
WIDOWED	M.	2144	.	1	13	173	279	416	54
	F.	5018	.	2	19	275	763	1161	136
468 ASHTON UNDER LYNE:									
UNMARRIED	M.	43990	27700	7379	4625	2614	860	441	24
	F.	47619	28091	7754	5022	3471	1656	907	47
MARRIED	M.	25866	.	59	1842	8144	7158	5187	302
	F.	27274	.	184	2513	8070	7474	5036	256
WIDOWED	M.	2549	.	.	22	218	328	454	58
	F.	6428	.	1	30	348	890	1388	181
469 OLDHAM:									
UNMARRIED	M.	48475	29722	8126	5468	3262	1019	480	26
	F.	50552	30840	8510	5468	3273	1293	647	34
MARRIED	M.	30009	.	66	2130	9663	8144	5782	314
	F.	30551	.	219	3134	10027	8291	5330	262
WIDOWED	M.	2624	.	2	37	234	364	488	62
	F.	6350	.	4	30	387	933	1632	175
470 ROCHDALE:									
UNMARRIED	M.	34342	20791	5909	3876	2306	722	366	24
	F.	38073	21341	6334	4567	3339	1208	739	33
MARRIED	M.	21173	.	36	1381	6222	5708	4370	248
	F.	21738	.	94	1798	6818	5963	4187	222
WIDOWED	M.	1790	.	1	19	133	219	347	48
	F.	4790	.	.	18	240	679	1109	136
471 HASLINGDEN:									
UNMARRIED	M.	27440	16826	4395	3120	1804	540	283	17
	F.	29710	17328	4983	3409	2402	864	394	22
MARRIED	M.	16567	.	34	1245	5077	4399	3181	180
	F.	16808	.	99	1571	5428	4539	3066	162
WIDOWED	M.	1446	.	2	20	97	176	263	3
	F.	3311	.	1	10	178	467	748	37
472 BURNLEY:									
UNMARRIED	M.	34634	21406	5700	3578	2449	856	424	2
	F.	36296	22077	5527	3743	2597	1032	474	2
MARRIED	M.	20650	.	64	1767	6445	5612	3770	22
	F.	20886	.	203	2227	6033	5442	3567	194
WIDOWED	M.	1845	.	1	14	145	256	337	4
	F.	3844	.	1	28	265	519	864	10
473 CLITHEROE:									
UNMARRIED	M.	7614	4298	1263	836	637	230	148	7
	F.	7156	4026	1067	825	622	238	185	11
MARRIED	M.	3722	.	16	202	988	962	717	5
	F.	3717	.	21	278	1081	908	733	4
WIDOWED	M.	465	.	1	5	36	51	92	1
	F.	796	.	.	2	37	75	162	1
474 BLACKBURN:									
UNMARRIED	M.	51100	32036	8300	6625	3184	1003	463	2
	F.	55826	32709	9408	6463	4281	1588	791	3
MARRIED	M.	29720	.	77	2378	9311	8075	6684	2
	F.	30336	.	210	2072	9888	8375	5413	20
WIDOWED	M.	2707	.	1	32	240	306	511	6
	F.	6176	.	1	34	414	906	1466	10
475 CHORLEY:									
UNMARRIED	M.	14541	8911	2330	1861	930	541	155	1
	F.	16420	9087	2412	1089	1207	406	248	1
MARRIED	M.	7638	.	12	532	2163	1974	1452	97
	F.	7725	.	36	646	2282	2082	1461	8
WIDOWED	M.	863	.	.	6	58	108	121	1
	F.	1532	.	.	6	75	163	283	4
476 PRESTON:									
UNMARRIED	M.	37338	22469	6427	3953	2605	906	497	2
	F.	41800	22865	6804	4892	3511	1776	905	51
MARRIED	M.	20747	.	62	1436	5821	5641	4101	247
	F.	21528	.	134	1925	6437	5930	4495	221
WIDOWED	M.	2240	.	1	17	172	268	388	58
	F.	6447	.	2	29	312	802	1251	141

Table 8 *continued*.—Condition as to Marriage and Ages of Males and Females in Registration Districts.

Registration District.		All Ages.	Under 15 Years.	15–	20–	25–	35–	45–	55–	65 and upw.ds
34 LANCASHIRE —*cont.*										
477 FYLDE:										
Unmarried	M.	12098	7252	1980	1347	910	303	120	101	80
	F.	13302	7165	2083	1497	1319	590	368	209	141
Married	M.	6498	.	4	335	1791	1761	1203	903	501
	F.	6629	.	43	474	1957	1779	1244	788	344
Widowed	M.	727	.	.	9	48	62	111	168	328
	F.	1061	.	.	7	96	233	360	433	532
478 GARSTANG:										
Unmarried	M.	4217	2339	743	464	309	137	77	83	65
	F.	3745	2223	578	368	298	111	78	48	40
Married	M.	1886	.	.	80	480	441	379	305	201
	F.	1882	.	9	126	535	444	402	242	136
Widowed	M.	271	.	.	.	17	20	47	59	128
	F.	374	.	.	3	16	39	38	72	186
479 LANCASTER:										
Unmarried	M.	12019	7267	2010	1575	1159	408	239	156	105
	F.	12637	7185	2016	1360	996	480	247	200	157
Married	M.	6628	.	4	398	1941	1692	1277	902	414
	F.	6516	.	41	570	1988	1659	1282	723	293
Widowed	M.	715	.	.	2	55	87	126	163	282
	F.	1423	.	.	5	78	143	304	336	557
34 LANCASHIRE —*cont.*										
480 LUNESDALE:										
Unmarried	M.	2329	1254	387	279	194	75	40	51	[illegible]
	F.	2265	1243	340	272	216	76	42	37	[illegible]
Married	M.	1093	.	.	41	248	247	254	176	[illegible]
	F.	1082	.	4	65	271	273	225	146	[illegible]
Widowed	M.	146	.	.	.	4	13	30	27	[illegible]
	F.	217	.	.	1	8	20	32	55	[illegible]
481 ULVERSTON:										
Unmarried	M.	14430	8691	1973	1594	1178	426	259	165	[illegible]
	F.	12999	8500	1785	1132	814	318	188	134	[illegible]
Married	M.	7024	.	5	326	1909	1663	1307	916	[illegible]
	F.	7057	.	53	617	2159	1822	1269	767	[illegible]
Widowed	M.	775	.	.	3	45	98	128	172	[illegible]
	F.	1396	.	.	6	71	142	245	361	[illegible]
482 BARROW IN FURNESS:										
Unmarried	M.	16446	9466	2178	2200	1849	486	174	69	[illegible]
	F.	12838	9450	1795	907	483	102	54	35	[illegible]
Married	M.	8515	.	6	584	3183	2702	1340	579	[illegible]
	F.	7960	.	73	982	3046	2204	1031	440	[illegible]
Widowed	M.	614	.	.	4	88	133	142	142	[illegible]
	F.	896	.	.	17	78	170	192	212	[illegible]

Table 9.—Condition as to Marriage and Ages of Males and Females in each Urban Sanitary District of which the Population exceeds 50,000 Persons.

Urban Sanitary District.		All Ages.	Under 15 Years.	15–	20–	25–	35–	45–	55–	65 and upw.ds
STOCKPORT:										
Unmarried	M.	16052	10020	2696	1623	1048	333	174	98	60
	F.	18303	10410	2095	2138	1464	660	355	188	93
Married	M.	10436	.	32	777	3183	2738	1999	1216	490
	F.	10795	.	96	1089	3487	2858	1992	1009	314
Widowed	M.	1079	.	.	10	78	131	210	284	366
	F.	2868	.	2	10	175	468	686	797	732
BIRKENHEAD:										
Unmarried	M.	26085	15496	3820	3073	2491	781	255	107	65
	F.	25904	15456	4034	2853	1909	792	380	230	157
Married	M.	13943	.	20	718	4101	4226	2632	1558	588
	F.	13836	.	117	1328	4702	3963	2295	1169	361
Widowed	M.	1246		.	9	99	217	243	312	366
	F.	3093		.	21	201	495	757	764	855
LIVERPOOL:										
Unmarried	M.	169589	98130	24972	20307	16801	2793	2228	959	390
	F.	156796	98738	24425	15518	10219	3823	2061	1271	741
Married	M.	93924	.	143	5471	28458	28026	17878	9019	3229
	F.	97602	.	1061	11081	33705	27642	15320	6483	1760
Widowed	M.	9383	.	2	65	818	1710	2190	2398	2181
	F.	26714	.	12	219	2147	4796	6555	7078	5907
ST. HELENS:										
Unmarried	M.	19336	11858	2872	2157	1368	854	240	101	37
	F.	16459	11680	2476	1146	673	228	132	78	46
Married	M.	9541	.	17	765	3204	2504	1781	875	335
	F.	9555	.	119	1189	3243	2460	1601	695	248
Widowed	M.	860	.	2	17	89	143	182	209	218
	F.	1592	.	1	18	122	237	368	407	444
BOLTON:										
Unmarried	M.	30688	19053	5091	3481	2046	534	278	137	63
	F.	33215	20047	5427	3712	2456	848	394	240	111
Married	M.	17753	.	21	1160	3767	4973	3294	1865	675
	F.	18052	.	108	1724	6029	5094	3082	1579	436
Widowed	M.	1524	.	.	12	128	235	305	382	462
	F.	4185	.	1	17	277	638	1033	1175	1044
BURY:										
Unmarried	M.	14815	9084	2368	1029	1140	360	173	89	72
	F.	16187	9384	2025	1845	1268	540	310	142	73
Married	M.	8913	.	13	601	2775	2470	1637	1039	373
	F.	9154	.	52	826	3030	2488	1630	864	244
Widowed	M.	865	.	.	5	69	126	162	221	281
	F.	2179	.	1	7	146	298	476	608	646
SALFORD:										
Unmarried	M.	51915	32995	8065	5547	3564	1054	424	180	86
	F.	53091	33199	8209	6246	3682	1436	724	372	229
Married	M.	30160	.	62	2069	10109	8612	5402	2712	894
	F.	31008	.	284	3361	11031	8803	4911	2036	530
Widowed	M.	2538	.	1	28	263	487	539	607	659
	F.	7526	.	1	48	545	1305	1718	1958	1951
MANCHESTER:										
Unmarried	M.	100121	58853	15909	12212	8693	2694	1071	487	22
	F.	102341	60066	16768	11541	7979	3005	1622	900	460
Married	M.	58021	.	112	3983	18773	16571	10061	5638	1068
	F.	59153	.	542	6525	20118	16107	9914	4460	1132
Widowed	M.	5333	.	2	55	466	948	1201	1326	1335
	F.	16445	.	4	106	1336	2888	4225	4810	3382
OLDHAM:										
Unmarried	M.	31880	19506	5260	3582	2218	747	318	166	39
	F.	33173	20068	5047	3659	2206	878	402	206	57
Married	M.	19965	.	81	1435	6480	5440	3863	2034	[illegible]
	F.	20344	.	160	2142	6686	5492	3714	1696	454
Widowed	M.	1687	.	2	21	160	267	323	436	473
	F.	4290	.	4	32	264	651	1059	1189	1091
ROCHDALE:										
Unmarried	M.	19003	11723	3208	2085	1249	389	182	116	48
	F.	21580	11896	3645	2639	1914	740	457	198	81
Married	M.	11360	.	26	768	3508	3236	2472	1424	638
	F.	12404	.	57	1010	3939	3390	2390	1254	358
Widowed	M.	1022	.	.	15	75	144	215	264	309
	F.	2927	.	.	12	151	436	706	853	785
BURNLEY:										
Unmarried	M.	17188	10599	2775	1764	1226	477	209	101	37
	F.	17893	11060	2898	1782	1233	484	234	137	66
Married	M.	10336	.	41	951	3279	2862	1829	1025	345
	F.	10456	.	119	1200	3593	2784	1715	871	224
Widowed	M.	874	.	1	9	76	144	182	198	264
	F.	2004	.	.	16	160	325	462	639	512
BLACKBURN:										
Unmarried	M.	29905	18807	4817	3282	1859	595	272	168	105
	F.	32935	19067	6620	3936	2576	975	492	211	107
Married	M.	17613	.	48	1456	5466	4600	3353	1760	672
	F.	18026	.	129	1816	6504	4923	3264	1558	436
Widowed	M.	1615	.	1	24	145	210	315	430	489
	F.	3860	.	.	21	280	565	929	1060	1015
PRESTON:										
Unmarried	M.	26930	17011	4612	2863	1603	568	269	140	78
	F.	31655	17549	5282	3672	2701	1264	608	327	162
Married	M.	15838	.	47	1215	4567	4392	3080	1792	760
	F.	16525	.	117	1371	5086	4803	3022	1588	463
Widowed	M.	1406	.	1	15	121	201	288	371	489
	F.	4193	.	2	26	248	842	1025	1106	1143

Table 10.—OCCUPATIONS of MALES and FEMALES in the NORTH-WESTERN DIVISION and its REGISTRATION COUNTIES, and in each URBAN SANITARY DISTRICT of which the POPULATION exceeds 50,000 PERSONS.

OCCUPATIONS.	NORTH-WESTERN COUNTIES.		REGISTRATION COUNTIES. 33. CHESHIRE.		34. LANCASHIRE.		URBAN SANITARY DISTRICTS. STOCKPORT.		BIRKENHEAD.	
	Males.	Females.	Males.	Females.	Males.	Females.	Males.	Females.	Males.	Females.
TOTAL	1986073	2121511	301768	320597	1684305	1800914	27507	31866	41174	42832
I. PROFESSIONAL CLASS.										
1. PERSONS ENGAGED IN THE GENERAL OR LOCAL GOVERNMENT OF THE COUNTRY.										
1. *National Government.*										
Peer, M.P., Privy Councillor (not otherwise described)	2	.	1	.	1	.	.	.	.	.
Civil Service (officers and clerks)	2156	224	328	60	1828	164	16	1	90	5
Civil Service (messengers, &c.)	2324	26	363	10	1961	16	54	.	65	.
Prison Officer, &c.	256	89	38	5	218	84	.	.	1	.
2. *Local Government.*										
Police	4780	.	594	.	4186	.	55	.	143	.
Municipal, Parish, Union, District, Officer	2035	516	338	61	1697	455	40	7	53	9
Other Local or County Official	630	.	152	.	478	.	7	.	18	.
3. *East Indian and Colonial Service.*										
East Indian and Colonial Service	6	.	.	.	6	.	.	.	.	.
2. PERSONS ENGAGED IN THE DEFENCE OF THE COUNTRY.										
1. *Army (at Home).*										
Army Officer (effective or retired)	295	.	83	.	212	.	2	.	9	.
Soldier and Non-commissioned Officer	3503	.	328	.	3175	.	4	.	16	.
Militia, Yeomanry, Volunteers	1649	.	289	.	1360	.	2	.	6	.
Army Pensioner	1055	2	148	.	907	2	24	.	19	.
2. *Navy (ashore or in port).*										
Navy Officer (effective or retired)	91	.	49	.	42	.	.	.	22	.
Seaman, R.N.	450	.	376	.	74	.	.	.	38	.
Royal Marines (officers and men)	169	.	97	.	72	.	.	.	6	.
Navy Pensioner	192	.	58	.	134	.	1	.	35	.
3. PERSONS ENGAGED IN PROFESSIONAL OCCUPATIONS (WITH THEIR IMMEDIATE SUBORDINATES).										
1. *Clerical Profession.*										
Clergyman (Established Church)	1618	.	414	.	1204	.	9	.	37	.
Roman Catholic Priest	570	.	50	.	520	.	6	.	8	.
Minister, Priest, of other religious bodies	1149	.	256	.	893	.	10	.	30	.
Missionary, Scripture Reader, Itinerant Preacher	389	207	52	28	337	179	4	.	8	9
Nun, Sister of Charity	.	369	.	22	.	347	.	5	.	10
Theological Student	380	.	86	.	294	.	1	.	60	.
Church, Chapel, Cemetery—Officer, Servant	827	132	115	26	712	106	10	3	10	2
2. *Legal Profession.*										
Barrister, Solicitor	1629	.	306	.	1323	.	16	.	62	.
Law Student	135	.	24	.	111	.	.	.	1	.
Law Clerk, and others connected with Law	2995	1	480		2515	1	45	.	65	.
3. *Medical Profession.*										
Physician, Surgeon, General Practitioner	1852	2	312	.	1540	2	24	.	40	.
Dentist	616	.	80	.	536	.	10	.	13	.
Medical Student, Assistant	695	7	94	1	601	6	9	.	9	.
Midwife	.	573	.	81	.	492	.	5	.	11
Subordinate Medical Service	363	2886	51	415	312	2471	15	48	4	75
4. *Teachers.*										
Schoolmaster	5487	13211	972	2645	4515	10566	59	104	97	438
Teacher, Professor, Lecturer	705	2208	106	308	599	1900	12	2	26	71
School Service, and others concerned in Teaching	295	116	43	15	252	100	6	2	8	1
5. *Literary and Scientific Persons.*										
Author, Editor, Journalist	277	20	38	3	239	17	4	.	9	1
Reporter, Short-hand Writer	341	1	46	1	295	.	5	.	12	.
Persons engaged in Scientific Pursuits	237	2	35	.	202	2	.	.	1	.
Literary, Scientific, Institution, Service, &c.	89	8	7	.	82	8	1	.	1	.
6. *Engineers and Surveyors.*										
Civil Engineer	1039	.	209	.	830	.	10	.	58	.
Mining Engineer	321	.	44	.	277	.	.	.	2	.
Land, House, Ship, Surveyor	734	.	109	.	625	.	8	.	13	.
7. *Artists.*										
Painter (artist)	624	184	82	41	542	143	8	.	19	11
Engraver (artist)	349	2	12	.	337	2	.	.	3	.
Sculptor	79	.	10	.	69	.	1	.	1	.
Architect	1039	.	201	.	838	.	9	.	48	.
Musician, Music Master	2294	1544	210	216	2084	1328	34	18	20	53
Art Student	229	86	44	13	185	73	3	.	10	3
Photographer	726	180	107	15	619	165	8	.	13	5
Actor	400	376	30	24	370	352	13	9	4	3
Art, Music, Theatre, Service	140	22	18	1	122	21	3	.	3	.

NOTE.—Persons returned as engaged in more than one occupation have been referred to the one that appeared to be of most importance; or, if there was no difference in this respect, to the one first given by the person in his or her return. In some cases special rules have been followed: *e.g.*, "Clergyman and Schoolmaster" in combination has always been referred to "Schoolmaster"; a Member of Parliament or Peer engaged in any branch of commerce or industry has always been referred to this latter, not to "Peer, M.P."

The numbers returned under any heading include Labourers, Apprentices, and Assistants, as well as Masters, but not Clerks, Messengers, Errand boys, Porters, or Watchmen, for which occupations there are special headings. Civil, Military, and Naval Clerks, Law, Bank, Insurance, and Railway Clerks, and Government and Railway Porters are, however, exceptions to this rule. Many young persons, being Apprentices or Assistants, have therefore been referred to occupations usually followed by adults. Women also, chiefly widows or orphans carrying on the business of their deceased husbands or fathers, will sometimes be found under occupations commonly followed by men only.

Persons returned as *retired* from any business have not been referred to that business. Inmates of workhouses have been referred to their trades, unless their age or infirmities showed that they were past work. But persons who might be supposed to be only temporarily separated from their usual employment, such as Prisoners, and Patients in General Hospitals, have been classed under their usual occupations.

In some cases, for convenience of space, the male designation, *e.g.*, "Schoolmaster," alone is given, instead of "Schoolmaster, Schoolmistress."

Table 10 *continued*.—Occupations of Males and Females in the North-western Division and its Registration Counties, and in each Urban Sanitary District of which the Population exceeds 50,000 Persons.

Occupations.	North-Western Counties.		Registration Counties. 33. Cheshire.		Registration Counties. 34. Lancashire.		Urban Sanitary Districts. Stockport.		Urban Sanitary Districts. Birkenhead.	
	Males.	Females.	Males.	Females.	Males.	Females.	Males.	Females.	Males.	Females.
8. *Persons engaged in Exhibitions, Shows, Games, &c.*										
Performer, Showman, Exhibition, Service	221	87	7	3	214	84	1	1	2	1
Billiard, Cricket, & other Games, Service	564	7	60	1	504	6	3	.	9	.
II. DOMESTIC CLASS.										
4. Persons engaged in Domestic Offices or Services.										
1. *Domestic Service.*										
Domestic Coachman, Groom	5899	.	1760	.	4139	.	62	.	152	.
Domestic Gardener	9543	3	3345	2	6198	1	118	.	312	.
Domestic Indoor Servant	2808	146161	751	32172	2058	113989	18	1447	33	5230
Lodge, Gate, Park, Keeper (not Government)	312	99	56	26	256	73	13	2	5	.
Inn, Hotel, Servant	4464	4461	468	506	3996	3955	47	28	105	83
College, Club, Service	306	78	30	12	276	66	6	4	3	1
2. *Other Service.*										
Office Keeper (not Government)	254	931	14	36	240	895	.	7	6	5
Cook (not domestic)	264	200	5	44	259	156	.	10	.	12
Charwoman	.	15075	.	2110	.	12965	.	367	.	371
Washing and Bathing Service	231	14744	22	2917	208	11827	6	224	1	381
Hospital and Institution Service	554	1349	103	191	451	1158	7	13	3	22
Others engaged in Service	226	100	18	2	208	98	6	.	2	2
III. COMMERCIAL CLASS.										
5. Persons engaged in Commercial Occupations.										
1. *Merchants and Agents.*										
Merchant	2489	8	564	1	1925	7	11	.	171	.
Broker, Agent, Factor	7744	125	1473	6	6271	119	81	2	463	.
Auctioneer, Appraiser, Valuer, House Agent	1758	15	300	.	1458	15	33	.	48	.
Accountant	1653	3	353	.	1300	3	18	.	94	.
Salesman, Buyer (not otherwise described)	1430	469	117	23	1313	446	15	4	15	7
Commercial Traveller	6294	.	683	.	5611	.	128	.	84	.
Commercial Clerk	38184	818	4755	102	33429	716	405	12	1440	20
Officer of Commercial Company, Guild, Society, &c.	42	.	4	.	38	.	.	.	2	.
2. *Dealers in Money.*										
Banker	66	.	20	.	46	.	.	.	4	.
Bank Service	1855	4	388	.	1467	4	19	.	78	.
Bill Discounter, Bill Broker, Finance Agent	84	.	8	.	76	.	1	.	1	.
3. *Persons occupied in Insurance.*										
Life, House, Ship, &c., Insurance Service	3794	39	483	6	3312	33	37	1	146	1
6. Persons engaged in Conveyance of Men, Goods, and Messages.										
1. *On Railways.*										
Railway Engine Driver, Stoker	4196	.	777	.	3418	.	63	.	80	.
Railway Guard	1482	.	279	.	1203	.	37	.	48	.
Pointsman, Level Crossing Man	1822	12	306	3	1516	9	31	.	37	.
Other Railway Officials and Servants	17112	62	3073	17	14039	45	340	3	552	1
2. *On Roads.*										
Toll Collector, Turnpike Gate Keeper	107	38	37	10	70	28	.	.	1	1
Omnibus, Coach, Cab, Owner—Livery Stable Keeper	865	42	142	6	723	36	15	2	25	2
Cabman, Flyman, Coachman (not domestic)	4328	.	424	.	3904	.	40	.	107	.
Carman, Carrier, Carter, Haulier	28658	102	2343	20	26315	82	480	.	435	3
Tramway Companies' Service	739	.	78	.	661	.	.	.	39	.
Wheel Chair Proprietor, Attendant, &c.	38	.	.	.	38	.	.	.	.	.
3. *On Canals, Rivers and Seas.*										
Inland Navigation Service	607	4	337	1	270	3	4	.	9	.
Bargeman, Lighterman, Waterman	5864	137	2341	52	3323	85	10	.	372	1
Navigation Service (on shore)	410	6	97	4	313	2	.	.	57	1
Seaman (Merchant Service)	16356	.	2857	.	13499	.	6	.	1898	.
Pilot	357	.	95	.	262	.	.	.	86	.
Ship Steward, Cook	1908	133	308	18	1600	115	.	.	.	.
Boatman on Seas	33	.	.	.	33	.	1	.	248	16
Harbour, Dock, Wharf, Lighthouse, Service	7269	24	1857	1	15412	23	1	.	1341	1
4. *In Storage.*										
Warehouseman (not Manchester)	8955	406	407	11	8548	396	98	6	118	.
Meter, Weigher	211	.	14	.	197	.	.	.	5	.
5. *In conveying Messages, Porterage, &c.*										
Messenger, Porter, Watchman (not Railway nor Government)	22960	185	2316	20	20644	165	301	5	559	1
Telegraph, Telephone, Service	1245	402	179	50	1066	352	26	1	86	14

Table 10 *continued.*—OCCUPATIONS of MALES and FEMALES in the NORTH-WESTERN DIVISION and its REGISTRATION COUNTIES, and in each URBAN SANITARY DISTRICT of which the POPULATION exceeds 50,000 PERSONS.

OCCUPATIONS.	NORTH-WESTERN COUNTIES.		REGISTRATION COUNTIES. 33. CHESHIRE.		REGISTRATION COUNTIES. 34. LANCASHIRE.		URBAN SANITARY DISTRICTS. STOCKPORT.		URBAN SANITARY DISTRICTS. BIRKENHEAD.	
	Males.	Females.	Males.	Females.	Males.	Females.	Males.	Females.	Males.	Females.
IV. AGRICULTURAL CLASS.										
7. PERSONS ENGAGED IN AGRICULTURE.										
1. *In Fields and Pastures.*										
Farmer, Grazier	21110	2479	8287	854	14823	1625	24	2	27	2
Farmer's, Grazier's—Son, Grandson, Brother, Nephew*	8345	.	2820	.	5525	.	11	.	6	.
Farm Bailiff	862	.	272	.	590	.	5	.	5	.
Agricultural Labourer, Farm Servant, Cottager	42844	2896	16558	887	26286	2009	283	8	137	12
Shepherd	189	.	74	.	115	.	.	.	.	.
Land Drainage Service (not in towns)	103	.	42	.	61	.	.	.	.	.
Agricultural Machine—Proprietor, Attendant	52	.	22	.	30	.	1	.	.	.
Agricultural Student, Pupil	24	.	8	.	16	.	.	.	.	.
Others engaged in, or connected with, Agriculture	25	3	9	.	16	3	.	.	2	.
2. *In Woods.*										
Woodman	303	.	83	.	220	.	.	.	.	.
3. *In Gardens.*										
Nurseryman, Seedsman, Florist	544	65	256	36	288	29	10	.	21	.
Gardener (not domestic)	3891	151	1104	78	2797	73	35	.	12	.
8. PERSONS ENGAGED ABOUT ANIMALS.										
1. *About Animals.*										
Horse Proprietor, Breeder, Dealer	232	.	43	.	189	.	1	.	4	.
Groom, Horse-keeper, Horse-breaker	4157	2	750	.	3407	2	31	.	94	.
Veterinary Surgeon, Farrier	751	.	109	.	642	.	8	.	12	.
Cattle, Sheep, Pig—Dealer, Salesman	396	2	172	.	424	2	3	.	6	.
Drover	237	.	33	.	204	.	5	.	4	.
Gamekeeper	875	.	331	.	544	.	2	.	.	.
Dog, Bird, Animal—Keeper, Dealer	113	25	12	2	101	23	2	.	2	.
Vermin destroyer	54	.	23	.	31	.	.	.	.	.
Fisherman	1599	77	328	6	1271	71	.	.	46	.
Knacker, Catsmeat Dealer, &c., &c.	24	1	3	.	21	1	2	.	1	.
V. INDUSTRIAL CLASS.										
9. PERSONS WORKING AND DEALING IN BOOKS, PRINTS, AND MAPS.										
1. *Books.*										
Publisher, Bookseller, Librarian	962	170	124	25	838	145	13	2	16	6
Music—Publisher, Seller, Printer	123	30	22	4	101	26	3	.	7	.
Bookbinder	944	1270	70	30	874	1240	12	4	15	11
Printer	7580	551	621	59	6966	492	106	1	115	1
Newspaper Agent, News Room Keeper	754	246	80	26	674	220	17	1	5	7
Others	2	.	.	.	2	.	.	.	.	.
2. *Prints and Maps.*										
Lithographer, Lithographic Printer	917	44	54	2	863	42	9	1	11	1
Copper Plate and Steal Plate Printer	26	2	3	.	23	2	.	.	.	.
Map and Print—Colourer, Seller	28	17	7	3	21	14	.	.	.	1
10. PERSONS WORKING AND DEALING IN MACHINES AND IMPLEMENTS.										
1. *Machines.*										
Engine, Machine, Maker	8994	78	1804	7	7190	71	93	1	303	.
Millwright	1944	.	250	.	1694	.	38	.	15	.
Fitter, Turner (Engine and Machine)	14068	.	2679	.	11389	.	113	.	490	.
Boiler Maker	7316	.	1796	.	5520	.	56	.	774	.
Spinning and Weaving Machine Maker	9127	513	515	15	8612	498	133	3	.	.
Agricultural Machine and Implement Maker	218	2	37	.	181	2	.	.	2	.
Domestic Machinery—Maker, Dealer	61	2	4	.	57	2	3	.	1	.
2. *Tools and Implements.*										
Tool Maker, Dealer	805	3	30	.	775	3	2	.	4	.
Cutler, Scissors Maker	230	9	35	2	195	7	7	.	2	.
File Maker	1093	27	77	1	1026	26	17	.	30	1
Saw Maker	156	.	10	.	146	.	1	.	4	.
Pin Maker	12	6	1	1	11	5	1	.	.	.
Needle Maker	5	1	.	.	5	1	.	.	.	.
Steel Pen Maker	.	3	.	.	.	3	.	.	.	.
Pencil Maker (Wood)	.	.	.	.	.	.	.	.	.	.
Domestic Implement Maker	15	4	1	.	14	4	.	.	.	.
3. *Watches and Philosophical Instruments.*										
Watch Maker, Clock Maker	3362	83	324	4	3038	79	31	1	70	.
Philosophical Instrument Maker, Optician	226	7	22	.	204	7	.	.	5	.
Electrical Apparatus Maker	285	2	36	.	248	2	26	.	4	.
Weighing and Measuring Apparatus Maker	301	5	14	.	287	5	3	.	1	.

* Only *male* relations living with the farmer or grazier, and, therefore, presumably engaged in agriculture, are included above.

Table 10 *continued.*—Occupations of Males and Females in the North-western Division and its Registration Counties, and in each Urban Sanitary District of which the Population exceeds 50,000 Persons.

Occupations.	North-Western Counties.		Registration Counties. 33. Cheshire.		Registration Counties. 34. Lancashire.		Urban Sanitary Districts. Stockport.		Urban Sanitary Districts. Birkenhead.	
	Males.	Females.	Males.	Females.	Males.	Females.	Males.	Females.	Males.	Females.
4. *Surgical Instruments.*										
Surgical Instrument Maker	53	4	6	.	47	4	.	.	.	.
5. *Arms and Ordnance.*										
Gunsmith, Gun Manufacturer	136	.	23	.	113	.	3	.	9	.
Ordnance Manufacturer	1	.	.	.	1	.	.	.	.	.
Sword, Bayonet—Maker, Cutler	.	.	.	.	.	.	.	.	.	.
Others	1	.	.	.	1	.	.	.	.	.
6. *Musical Instruments.*										
Musical Instrument Maker, Dealer	663	8	61	.	602	9	5	.	10	.
7. *Type, Dies, Medals, Coins.*										
Type Cutter, Founder	56	3	6	3	49	.	1	.	.	.
Die, Seal, Coin, Medal, Maker	115	1	6	.	109	1	3	.	1	.
8. *Tackle for Sports and Games.*										
Toy Maker, Dealer	135	139	9	16	126	123	1	1	1	5
Fishing Rod, Tackle, Maker, Dealer	22	1	.	.	22	1	.	.	.	.
Apparatus for other Games, Maker, Dealer	57	9	13	.	44	9	6	.	.	.
11. Persons working and dealing in Houses, Furniture, and Decorations.										
1. *Houses.*										
Builder	2788	10	529	1	2259	9	29	.	87	.
Carpenter, Joiner	36070	32	6452	2	29618	30	410	.	987	1
Bricklayer	14258	11	3202	2	11056	9	306	.	331	.
Mason	14700	10	1605	4	13095	6	109	1	252	.
Slater, Tiler	2346	4	325	.	2021	4	51	.	33	.
Plasterer, Whitewasher	5175	9	694	.	4481	9	45	.	160	.
Paperhanger	707	5	49	.	658	5	11	.	7	.
Plumber	7787	48	1151	14	6636	34	110	1	237	1
Painter, Glazier	16098	50	2333	7	13765	43	325	.	484	1
2. *Furniture and Fittings.*										
Cabinet Maker, Upholsterer	6805	1320	780	142	6025	1178	77	14	110	46
French Polisher	1104	252	90	4	1014	248	15	.	23	1
Furniture Broker, Dealer	882	305	103	29	779	276	21	5	21	3
Locksmith, Bellhanger	306	2	20	.	286	2	3	.	4	.
Gas Fitter	1144	.	173	.	971	.	14	.	65	.
House and Shop Fittings—Maker, Dealer	403	26	38	.	365	26	5	.	14	.
Funeral Furniture Maker, Undertaker	231	57	25	1	206	56	2	.	4	.
Others	2	2	.	.	2	2	.	.	.	.
3. *House Decorations.*										
Wood Carver	331	1	23	1	308	.	1	.	5	.
Carver, Gilder	1034	43	70	6	964	37	8	.	21	5
Dealer in Works of Art	141	12	12	.	129	12	.	.	3	.
Figure, Image—Maker, Dealer	47	1	8	.	39	1	.	.	.	.
Animal, Bird, &c., Preserver, Naturalist	59	6	7	.	52	6	1	.	1	.
Artificial Flower Maker	43	252	2	4	41	248	.	.	1	1
12. Persons working and dealing in Carriages and Harness.										
1. *Carriages.*										
Coachmaker	3134	18	368	3	2766	15	18	.	75	1
Railway Carriage, Railway Wagon, Maker	1283	4	107	.	1176	4	.	.	5	.
Wheelwright	4685	11	1024	2	3661	9	43	.	50	.
Bicycle, Tricycle—Maker, Dealer	30	1	3	.	27	1	.	.	.	.
Others	269	7	56	.	213	7	.	.	10	.
2. *Harness.*										
Saddler, Harness, Whip, Maker	1912	52	371	13	1541	39	30	.	33	.
13. Persons working and dealing in Ships and Boats.										
1. *Hull.*										
Ship, Boat, Barge, Builder	3349	6	616	2	2733	4	.	.	403	2
Shipwright, Ship Carpenter (ashore)	3801	.	830	.	2971	.	1	.	363	.
2. *Masts, Rigging, &c.*										
Mast, Yard, Oar, Block, Maker	284	.	31	.	253	.	.	.	17	.
Ship Rigger, Chandler, Fitter	909	7	85	.	824	7	.	.	61	.
Sail Maker	895	1	118	.	777	1	.	.	35	.

Table 10 *continued.*—OCCUPATIONS of MALES and FEMALES in the NORTH-WESTERN DIVISION and its REGISTRATION COUNTIES, and in each URBAN SANITARY DISTRICT of which the POPULATION exceeds 50,000 PERSONS.

OCCUPATIONS.	NORTH-WESTERN COUNTIES.		REGISTRATION COUNTIES.				URBAN SANITARY DISTRICTS.			
			33. CHESHIRE.		34. LANCASHIRE.		STOCKPORT.		BIRKENHEAD.	
	Males.	Females.	Males.	Females.	Males.	Females.	Males.	Females.	Males.	Females.
14. PERSONS WORKING AND DEALING IN CHEMICALS AND COMPOUNDS.										
1. *Colouring Matter.*										
Dye, Paint, Manufacture	313	38	28	1	285	37	6	-	14	1
Ink, Blacking, Colouring Substance, Manufacture	169	42	12	1	157	41	5	1	1	-
2. *Explosives.*										
Gunpowder, Guncotten, Explosive Substance, Manufacture	72	6	5	-	67	6	-	-	-	-
Fusee, Fireworks, Explosive Article, Manufacture	88	156	-	-	88	156	-	-	-	-
3. *Drugs and other Chemicals and Compounds.*										
Chemist, Druggist	2906	138	425	13	2481	125	48	6	74	1
Manufacturing Chemist	4625	127	1272	7	3353	120	12	-	5	-
Alkali Manufacture	1799	5	78	-	1721	5	1	-	-	-
Drysalter	341	52	23	-	318	52	2	-	2	-
15. PERSONS WORKING AND DEALING IN TOBACCO AND PIPES.										
1. *Tobacco and Pipes.*										
Tobacco Manufacturer, Tobacconist	1534	2413	247	154	1287	2259	86	60	17	25
Tobacco Pipe, Snuff Box, &c., Maker	328	127	31	10	297	117	10	4	5	-
16. PERSONS WORKING AND DEALING IN FOOD AND LODGING.										
1. *Board and Lodging.*										
Innkeeper, Hotel Keeper, Publican	7474	1715	1196	337	6278	1378	120	30	142	25
Lodging, Boarding House, Keeper	619	6119	43	592	576	5527	5	73	3	99
Coffee, Eating House, Keeper	630	371	60	61	570	310	8	7	12	4
2. *Spirituous Drinks.*										
Hop—Merchant, Dealer	14	-	4	-	10	-	-	-	-	-
Maltster	154	-	16	-	138	-	1	-	-	-
Brewer	2720	63	351	12	2369	51	58	3	34	-
Beerseller, Ale, Porter, Cider, Dealer	3314	1022	300	120	3014	902	64	20	33	20
Cellarman	684	55	46	1	638	54	4	-	18	1
Wine, Spirit—Merchant, Agent	1066	49	214	9	852	40	11	-	56	3
3. *Food.*										
Milkseller, Dairyman	2446	680	302	114	2144	566	50	11	77	23
Cheesemonger, Butterman	93	10	30	2	63	8	6	-	2	-
Butcher, Meat Salesman	11109	793	1889	114	9220	679	191	37	305	19
Provision Curer, Dealer	4197	2588	633	380	3564	2208	163	102	134	27
Poulterer, Game Dealer	434	130	36	21	388	109	2	-	14	4
Fishmonger	1923	675	188	57	1735	618	39	7	19	7
Corn, Flour, Seed—Merchant, Dealer	1353	80	234	8	1119	72	25	-	66	2
Corn Miller	2334	26	537	5	1797	21	22	-	10	-
Baker	7599	950	1258	116	6341	834	148	15	237	21
Confectioner, Pastrycook	1999	4039	247	502	1752	3537	47	80	33	84
Greengrocer, Fruiterer	3538	1287	429	154	3109	1133	104	20	58	42
Mustard, Vinegar, Spice, Pickle—Maker, Dealer	86	74	9	1	77	73	-	-	-	-
Sugar Refiner	852	23	22	2	830	21	2	-	5	-
Grocer, Tea, Coffee, Chocolate—Maker, Dealer	16316	4616	2531	695	13785	3921	261	32	296	75
Ginger Beer, Mineral Water—Manufacturer, Dealer	894	64	67	12	827	52	10	1	16	6
Others dealing in Food	9	-	-	-	9	-	-	-	-	-
17. PERSONS WORKING AND DEALING IN TEXTILE FABRICS.										
1. *Wool and Worsted.*										
Woolstapler	196	2	26	-	170	2	5	-	3	-
Woollen Cloth Manufacture	5570	5791	37	7	5533	5784	12	1	4	1
Wool, Woollen goods—Dyer, Printer	424	19	2	-	422	19	1	-	-	-
Worsted, Stuff, Manufacture	697	898	9	16	688	882	1	4	-	1
Flannel Manufacture	151	40	2	-	149	40	-	-	1	-
Blanket Manufacture	11	66	-	-	11	66	-	-	-	-
Fuller	1172	1	-	-	1172	1	-	-	-	-
Cloth, Worsted, Stuff, Flannel, Blanket, Dealer	351	14	20	2	331	12	2	-	-	2
Others	6	15	1	9	5	6	1	3	-	-
2. *Silk.*										
Silk, Silk goods, Manufacture	8444	15875	5054	9023	3390	6852	38	78	1	-
Silk Dyer, Printer	590	10	318	2	272	8	1	-	-	-
Ribbon Manufacture	82	18	63	9	19	9	-	-	-	-
Crape, Gauze, Manufacture	23	81	19	38	4	43	-	-	-	-
Silk Merchant, Dealer	340	14	84	1	256	13	4	-	1	-

Table 10 *continued*.—Occupations of Males and Females in the North-western Division and its Registration Counties, and in each Urban Sanitary District of which the Population exceeds 50,000 Persons.

Occupations.	North-Western Counties.		Registration Counties. 33. Cheshire.		Registration Counties. 34. Lancashire.		Urban Sanitary Districts. Stockport.		Urban Sanitary Districts. Birkenhead.	
	Males.	Females.	Males.	Females.	Males.	Females.	Males.	Females.	Males.	Females.
3. Cotton and Flax										
Cotton, Cotton goods, Manufacture	159681	265121	8902	15322	150779	249799	3963	7567	6	9
Cotton, Calico—Printer, Dyer, Bleacher	19674	3615	1296	120	18378	3495	263	30	.	.
Cotton, Calico—Warehouseman, Dealer	2838	344	374	9	2464	335	61	9	39	.
Flax, Linen—Manufacturer, Dealer	662	2352	52	122	610	2230	16	66	4	.
Lace Manufacturer, Dealer	115	153	17	29	98	124	2	3	.	.
Fustian Manufacturer, Dealer	2502	4774	772	1271	1730	3503	2	1	.	.
Tape Manufacturer, Dealer	428	238	8	2	420	236	1	1	.	.
Thread Manufacturer, Dealer	251	1165	140	269	111	896	119	224	.	.
4. Hemp and other Fibrous Materials.										
Hemp, Jute, Cocoa Fibre, Manufacture	209	837	12	5	197	832	9	6	1	.
Rope, Twine, Cord—Maker, Dealer	2190	463	230	39	1960	424	111	34	8	.
Mat Maker, Seller	219	72	5	.	214	72	.	.	.	.
Net Maker	14	24	3	1	11	23	.	.	.	.
Canvas, Sailcloth, Manufacture	35	26	.	.	35	26	.	.	.	.
Sacking Sack, Bag—Maker, Dealer	74	397	5	5	69	392	.	1	9	.
Others working and dealing in Hemp	41	40	2	.	39	40	1	.	.	.
5. Mixed or Unspecified Materials.										
Weaver (undefined)	216	835	18	53	198	786	4	21	1	.
Dyer, Printer, Scourer, Bleacher, Calenderer (undefined)	2719	327	154	91	2585	236	118	71	9	3
Factory hand (Textile, undefined)	1909	2484	55	104	1854	2380	18	39	.	2
Felt Manufacture	194	6	9	.	185	6	.	.	1	.
Carpet, Rug, Manufacture	619	296	32	3	587	293	2	1	8	.
Manchester Warehouseman	697	4	62	3	635	1	1	1	.	.
Draper, Linen Draper, Mercer	7263	3804	1026	437	0237	3367	90	70	157	91
Fancy Goods (Textile), Manufacturer, Worker, Dealer	165	1127	8	60	157	1067	1	14	1	13
Trimming Maker, Dealer	179	1421	35	117	144	1304	1	5	.	.
Embroiderer	9	413	.	7	9	406	.	.	.	1
Others	24	6	1	.	23	6	.	.	.	.
18. Persons working and dealing in Dress.										
1. Dress.										
Hatter, Hat Manufacture (not straw)	7364	5910	3124	2302	4240	3608	1642	1225	14	6
Straw—Hat, Bonnet, Plait, Manufacture	24	160	.	24	24	136	.	.	.	1
Tailor	15883	6436	2328	1091	13357	5345	289	147	262	32
Milliner, Dressmaker, Staymaker	290	47256	28	7186	262	40040	9	548	1	1266
Shawl Manufacture	10	4	.	.	10	4	.	.	.	.
Shirt Maker, Seamstress	162	12732	7	1037	155	11695	2	142	.	186
Hosiery Manufacture	41	187	3	9	38	178	.	2	.	1
Hosier, Haberdasher	464	337	62	74	402	263	7	14	4	2
Glover, Glove Maker	28	21	5	2	23	19	1	.	.	.
Button Maker, Dealer	93	94	4	6	89	88	1	.	.	.
Shoe, Boot—Maker, Dealer	16018	1855	3769	509	12249	1346	300	13	297	35
Patten, Clog, Maker	4619	27	474	.	4145	27	89	.	6	.
Wig Maker, Hairdresser	2382	83	288	3	2094	80	39	.	63	.
Umbrella, Parasol, Stick—Maker, Dealer	588	829	30	8	558	821	8	2	2	1
Accoutrement Maker	1	3	.	.	1	3	.	.	.	.
Old Clothes Dealer, and others	166	292	12	14	154	278	1	4	6	2
19. Persons working and dealing in various Animal Substances.										
1. In Grease, Gut, Bone, Horn, Ivory, and Whalebone.										
Tallow Chandler, Candle, Grease, Manufacture	557	59	189	15	368	44	6	.	10	1
Soap Boiler, Maker	642	167	69	.	573	167	3	.	3	.
Glue, Size, Gelatine, Isinglass—Maker, Dealer	60	10	8	5	52	5	3	.	1	2
Manure Manufacture	106	5	54	1	52	4	.	.	4	.
Bone, Horn, Ivory, Tortoise-shell—Worker, Dealer	103	3	23	1	80		4	.	1	.
Comb Maker	24	2	.	.	24	2	.	.	.	.
Others	44	6	.	.	44	6	.	.	.	.
2. In Skins.										
Furrier, Skinner	346	111	38	3	308	108	7	.	2	2
Tanner, Fellmonger	1593	9	342	4	1251	5	22	2	22	.
Currier	1289	51	202	7	1087	44	38	1	13	1
Leather Goods, Portmanteau, Bag, Strap, &c.—Maker, Dealer	423	85	27	.	396	85	17	.	2	.
Parchment, Vellum—Maker, Dealer	1	1	.	.	1	1	.	.	.	.
3. In Hair and Feathers.										
Hair, Bristle—Worker, Dealer	52	62	2	1	50	61	.	.	.	.
Brush, Broom, Maker	1418	323	106	20	1312	303	29	14	3	1
Quill, Feather—Dresser, Dealer	54	235	4	14	50	221	.	9	2	.

Table 10 *continued*.—OCCUPATIONS of MALES and FEMALES in the NORTH-WESTERN DIVISION and its REGISTRATION COUNTIES, and in each URBAN SANITARY DISTRICT of which the POPULATION exceeds 50,000 PERSONS.

OCCUPATIONS.	NORTH-WESTERN COUNTIES.		REGISTRATION COUNTIES. 33. CHESHIRE.		REGISTRATION COUNTIES. 34. LANCASHIRE.		URBAN SANITARY DISTRICTS. STOCKPORT.		URBAN SANITARY DISTRICTS. BIRKENHEAD.	
	Males.	Females.	Males.	Females.	Males.	Females.	Males.	Females.	Males.	Females.
20. PERSONS WORKING AND DEALING IN VARIOUS VEGETABLE SUBSTANCES.										
1. *In Oils, Gums, and Resins.*										
Oil Miller, Oil Cake—Maker, Dealer	761	26	161	1	600	25	12	.	10	.
Oil and Colourman	100	12	17	2	83	10	1	.	8	1
Floor Cloth, Oil Cloth, Manufacture	280	2	4	.	276	2	.	.	.	.
Japanner	89	49	2	1	87	48	1	.	.	.
India Rubber, Gutta Percha—Worker, Dealer	676	318	15	5	661	313	5	.	1	2
Waterproof Goods—Maker, Dealer	461	108	18	.	443	108	1	.	2	.
Others	27	3	2	.	25	3	.	.	.	.
2. *In Cane, Rush, and Straw.*										
Willow, Cane, Rush—Worker, Dealer, Basketmaker	1635	212	214	12	1421	200	48	3	6	2
Hay, Straw (not plait), Chaff—Cutter, Dealer	383	15	91	4	292	11	2	.	8	2
Thatcher	17	.	9	.	8	.	.	.	.	.
3. *In Wood and Bark.*										
Timber, Wood—Merchant, Dealer	1379	57	164	5	1215	52	25	.	40	5
Sawyer	3068	.	509	.	2559	.	35	.	66	.
Lath, Wooden Fence, Hurdle, Maker	272	2	20	.	252	2	12	.	2	.
Wood Turner, Box Maker	2098	464	162	24	1936	440	67	18	8	.
Cooper, Hoop Maker, Bender	3160	19	334	3	2826	16	18	.	25	1
Cork, Bark—Cutter, Worker, Dealer	310	31	81	11	229	20	.	.	7	.
Others	11	3	3	2	8	1	2	2	.	.
4. *In Paper.*										
Paper Manufacture	2775	1542	105	55	2670	1487	11	1	3	.
Envelope Maker	4	156	.	.	4	156	.	.	.	.
Stationer, Law Stationer	1182	873	155	86	1027	787	8	6	30	25
Card, Pattern Card, Maker	569	31	13	3	556	28	4	.	.	1
Paper Stainer	500	108	25	31	475	77	5	.	.	.
Paper Box, Paper Bag, Maker	81	1156	2	34	79	1122	.	6	.	1
Ticket, Label, Writer	96	48	3	1	93	47	.	1	.	.
Others	269	6	40	1	229	5	8	.	8	.
21. PERSONS WORKING AND DEALING IN VARIOUS MINERAL SUBSTANCES.										
1. *Miners.*										
Coal Miner	63478	1246	3921	2	59557	1244	36	.	15	.
Ironstone Miner	3756	3	14	.	3742	3	1	.	.	.
Copper Miner	81	.	7	.	74	.	.	.	4	.
Tin Miner	6	.	.	.	6	.	.	.	.	.
Lead Miner	55	.	23	.	32	.	.	.	2	.
Miner in other, or undefined, Minerals	403	2	292	1	111	1	.	.	11	1
Mine Service	566	8	52	1	514	7	.	.	6	.
2. *Coal, Coal Gas, &c.*										
Coal Merchant, Dealer	3978	254	713	22	3265	232	111	4	198	1
Coalheaver	1726	.	231	.	1495	.	23	.	76	.
Coke, Charcoal, Peat—Cutter, Burner, Dealer	308	14	7	8	301	6	.	.	1	8
Gas Works Service	3631	.	374	.	3257	.	64	.	75	.
3. *Stone, Clay, and Road Making.*										
Stone Quarrier	5156	.	483	.	4673	.	2	.	51	.
Stone Cutter, Dresser, Dealer	573	.	77	.	496	.	4	.	9	.
Slate Quarrier	397	.	1	.	396	.	.	.	.	.
Slate Worker, Dealer	87	.	24	.	63	.	.	.	3	.
Limeburner	147	.	33	.	114	.	2	.	2	.
Clay, Sand, Gravel, Chalk—Labourer, Dealer	199	13	36	4	163	9	5	.	.	.
Fossil, Coprolite—Digger, Dealer	.	1	.	.	.	1	.	.	.	.
Well Sinker, Borer	236	.	20	.	216	.	.	.	4	.
Plaster, Cement, Manufacture	67	5	9	.	58	5	.	.	3	.
Brick, Tile—Maker, Burner, Dealer	7947	87	1842	5	6105	82	143	.	163	.
Paviour	1836	.	176	.	1660	.	42	.	22	.
Road Contractor, Surveyor, Inspector	93	.	20	.	73	.	.	.	2	.
Road Labourer	1567	.	307	.	1260	.	15	.	37	.
Railway Contractor	165	.	38	.	127	.	3	.	1	.
Platelayer	2971	.	717	.	2254	.	65	.	21	.
Railway Labourer, Navvy	4760	.	810	.	3950	.	92	.	47	.
Others	53	27	.	1	53	26	.	.	.	.
4. *Earthenware and Glass.*										
Earthenware, China, Porcelain, Manufacture	641	65	158	13	483	52	1	1	2	1
Glass Manufacture	5244	781	39	2	5205	779	1	.	18	1
Earthenware, China, Glass, Dealer	701	383	100	56	601	327	23	3	9	6
5. *Salt.*										
Salt Maker, Dealer	2322	49	2195	38	127	11		.	15	1

Table 10 *continued*.—OCCUPATIONS of MALES and FEMALES in the NORTH-WESTERN DIVISION and its REGISTRATION COUNTIES, and in each URBAN SANITARY DISTRICT of which the POPULATION exceeds 50,000 PERSONS.

OCCUPATIONS.	NORTH-WESTERN COUNTIES.		REGISTRATION COUNTIES. 33. CHESHIRE.		34. LANCASHIRE.		URBAN SANITARY DISTRICTS. STOCKPORT.		BIRKENHEAD.	
	Males.	Females.	Males.	Females.	Males.	Females.	Males.	Females.	Males.	Females.
6. Water.										
Waterworks Service	511	.	60	.	451	.	12	.	18	.
Others	12	.	.	.	12	.	.	.	.	.
7. Precious Metals and Jewellery.										
Goldsmith, Silversmith, Jeweller	768	96	88	13	680	83	2	1	22	3
Gold, Silver, Beater	67	.	.	.	67	.	.	.	.	.
Lapidary	2	1	.	.	2	1	.	.	.	.
Others	32	198	1	1	31	197	.	.	.	.
8. Iron and Steel.										
Blacksmith	15306	22	2520	7	12786	15	136	1	339	.
Whitesmith	1184	4	172	.	1012	4	7	.	52	.
Nail Manufacture	728	105	70	.	658	105	8	.	1	.
Anchor, Chain, Manufacture	233	1	106	1	127	.	2	.	2	.
Other Iron and Steel Manufactures	43378	60	4183	4	39195	56	386	.	1019	.
Ironmonger. Hardware Dealer, Merchant	1917	190	319	18	1598	172	36	1	70	5
9. Copper.										
Copper, Copper goods—Manufacturer, Worker, Dealer	1621	1	380	.	1241	1	3	.	64	.
10. Tin and Zinc.										
Tin, Tin Plate, Tin goods—Manufacturer, Worker, Dealer	3903	41	364	5	3489	36	74	1	32	2
Zinc, Zinc Goods—Manufacturer, Worker, Dealer	53	.	4	.	49	.	.	.	2	.
11. Lead.										
Lead, Leaden goods—Manufacturer, Worker, Dealer	214	28	103	28	111	.	2	.	3	.
12. In Other, Mixed, or Unspecified, Metals.										
Metal Refiner, Worker, Turner, Dealer	360	7	36	.	324	7	7	.	17	.
Brass, Bronze, Manufacture. Brasier	2875	23	235	.	2640	23	60	.	56	.
Metal Burnisher, Lacquerer	9	28	.	1	9	27	.	.	.	1
White Metal, Plated Ware, Manufacture. Pewterer	45	3	1	.	44	3	.	.	.	.
Wire Maker, Worker, Weaver, Drawer	1975	79	92	2	1883	77	8	.	1	.
Bolt, Nut, Rivet, Screw, Staple, Maker	1343	44	38	.	1305	44	8	.	7	.
Lamp, Lantern, Candlestick, Maker	40	6	4	1	36	5	.	.	.	.
Clasp, Buckle, Hinge, Maker	202	5	.	.	202	5	.	.	.	.
Fancy Chain, Gilt Toy, Maker	7	.	.	.	7	.	.	.	.	.
Others	128	3	2	.	126	3	.	.	.	.
22. PERSONS WORKING AND DEALING IN GENERAL OR UNSPECIFIED COMMODITIES.										
1. Makers and Dealers (General or Undefined).										
General Shopkeeper, Dealer	3230	5212	457	598	2773	4614	59	82	78	123
Pawnbroker	2041	322	184	40	1857	282	34	19	55	4
Costermonger, Huckster, Street Seller	4781	4736	604	374	4177	4362	148	85	33	24
Manufacturer, Manager, Superintendent (undefined)	1161	73	125	6	1036	67	5	.	44	1
Contractor (undefined)	567	3	61	.	506	3	1	.	17	.
2. Mechanics and Labourers (General or Undefined).										
General Labourer	89388	336	14637	37	74751	299	1101	2	2499	7
Engine Driver, Stoker, Fireman (not railway, marine, nor agricultural)	13758	.	1628	.	12110	.	193	.	266	.
Artizan, Mechanic (undefined)	6245	277	462	24	5783	253	89	.	76	4
Apprentice (undefined)	882	120	111	9	771	111	1	.	24	2
Factory Labourer (undefined)	3555	442	233	23	3322	419	21	.	88	.
Machinist, Machine Worker (undefined)	748	337	74	131	674	206	13	7	29	14
23. PERSONS WORKING AND DEALING IN REFUSE MATTERS.										
1. Refuse Matters.										
Town Drainage Service	300	.	28	.	272	.	7	.	4	.
Chimney Sweep, Soot Merchant	614	2	103	2	511	.	15	.	16	.
Scavenger, Crossing Sweeper	722	2	47	.	675	2	12	.	10	.
Rag Gatherer, Dealer	310	330	31	20	279	310	5	16	1	2
VI. UNOCCUPIED CLASS.										
24. PERSONS WITHOUT SPECIFIED OCCUPATIONS										
Persons returned by Property, Rank, &c., and not by special occupation	449847	1173171	73803	189068	376044	984103	5704	14638	9883	27441
Children under 5 years of age	284215	287130	42155	42075	242064	245055	3824	3818	6081	6013

Table 10 *continued*.—OCCUPATIONS of MALES and FEMALES in the NORTH-WESTERN DIVISION and its REGISTRATION COUNTIES, and in each URBAN SANITARY DISTRICT of which the POPULATION exceeds 50,000 PERSONS.

OCCUPATIONS.	URBAN SANITARY DISTRICTS.									
	LIVERPOOL.		ST. HELENS.		BOLTON.		BURY.		SALFORD.	
	Males.	Females.	Males.	Females.	Males.	Females.	Males.	Females.	Males.	Females.
TOTAL	271996	280512	29797	27606	49902	56452	24693	27520	84610	91625
I. PROFESSIONAL CLASS.										
1. PERSONS ENGAGED IN THE GENERAL OR LOCAL GOVERNMENT OF THE COUNTRY.										
1. *National Government.*										
Peer, M.P., Privy Councillor (not otherwise described)	.	.	.	.	.	.	.	.	.	.
Civil Service (officers and clerks)	885	35	3	2	23	1	10	2	66	4
Civil Service (messengers, &c.)	584	1	22	.	53	.	27	.	126	1
Prison Officer, &c.	56	6	.	.	.	.	.	.	16	.
2. *Local Government.*										
Police	1126	.	55	.	115	.	42	.	299	.
Municipal, Parish, Union, District, Officer	258	109	22	.	54	3	36	7	114	23
Other Local or County Official	56	.	8	.	12	.	9	.	38	.
3. *East Indian and Colonial Service.*										
East Indian and Colonial Service	.	.	.	.	.	.	.	.	.	.
2. PERSONS ENGAGED IN THE DEFENCE OF THE COUNTRY.										
1. *Army (at Home).*										
Army Officer (effective or retired)	23	.	.	.	.	.	4	.	21	.
Soldier and Non-Commissioned Officer	231	.	6	.	6	.	4	.	701	.
Militia, Yeomanry, Volunteers	43	.	10	.	5	.	69	.	10	.
Army Pensioner	252	1	10	.	12	.	15	.	118	.
2. *Navy (ashore or in port).*										
Navy Officer (effective or retired)	10	.	.	.	.	.	.	.	.	.
Seaman, R.N.	49	.	1	.	.	.	.	.	3	.
Royal Marines (officers and men)	83	.	.	.	1	.	.	.	.	.
Navy Pensioner	68	.	2	.	2	.	.	.	2	.
3. PERSONS ENGAGED IN PROFESSIONAL OCCUPATIONS (WITH THEIR IMMEDIATE SUBORDINATES).										
1. *Clerical Profession.*										
Clergyman (Established Church)	130	.	14	.	22	.	15	.	48	.
Roman Catholic Priest	98	.	12	.	9	.	4	.	20	.
Minister, Priest, of other religious bodies	101	.	9	.	27	.	17	.	33	.
Missionary, Scripture Reader, Itinerant Preacher	103	56	2	1	7	17	2	3	30	12
Nun, Sister of Charity	.	106	.	28	.	35	.	.	.	6
Theological Student	26	.	.	.	3	.	1	.	19	.
Church, Chapel, Cemetery—Officer, Servant	48	29	4	1	34	1	9	2	31	4
2. *Legal Profession.*										
Barrister, Solicitor	119	.	12	.	41	.	12	.	76	.
Law Student	11	.	1	.	3	.	1	.	5	.
Law Clerk, and others connected with Law	383	1	33	.	76	.	48	.	144	.
3. *Medical Profession.*										
Physician, Surgeon, General Practitioner	322	.	15	.	38	.	20	.	72	.
Dentist	116	.	5	.	29	.	13	.	41	.
Medical Student, Assistant	100	.	8	.	22	.	10	.	19	.
Midwife	.	143	.	6	.	17	.	4	.	35
Subordinate Medical Service	39	592	3	10	8	60	6	32	25	131
4. *Teachers.*										
Schoolmaster	522	1709	58	207	153	300	75	121	191	574
Teacher, Professor, Lecturer	165	373	2	7	8	31	2	15	33	110
School Service, and others concerned in Teaching	57	33	2	.	11	1	3	.	20	8
5. *Literary and Scientific Persons.*										
Author, Editor, Journalist	58	3	1	.	5	.	2	.	15	4
Reporter, Short-hand Writer	57	.	4	.	10	.	6	.	31	.
Persons engaged in Scientific Pursuits	31	.	17	.	2	.	4	.	21	.
Literary, Scientific, Institution, Service, &c.	48	3	1	.	.	.	.	.	2	.
6. *Engineers and Surveyors.*										
Civil Engineer	141	.	6	.	13	.	10	.	63	.
Mining Engineer	10	.	13	.	3	.	2	.	9	.
Land, House, Ship, Surveyor	69	.	20	.	25	.	8	.	39	.
7. *Artists.*										
Painter (artist)	150	23	1	.	15	2	8	1	34	11
Engraver (artist)	28	.	.	.	3	.	3	.	49	1
Sculptor	24	.	.	.	.	.	1	.	8	.
Architect	103	.	1	.	38	.	17	.	47	.
Musician, Music Master	800	381	20	14	42	41	30	9	96	68
Art Student	23	10	3	.	12	1	3	.	12	6
Photographer	154	63	3	.	10	3	9	1	38	6
Actor	89	100	7	12	14	6	15	8	13	4
Art, Music, Theatre, Service	33	7	1	.	.	.	4	.	8	3

Table 10 *continued.*—Occupations of Males and Females in the North-western Division and its Registration Counties, and in each Urban Sanitary District of which the Population exceeds 50,000 Persons.

Occupations.	Urban Sanitary Districts.									
	LIVERPOOL.		ST. HELENS.		BOLTON.		BURY.		SALFORD.	
	Males.	Females.	Males.	Females.	Males.	Females.	Males.	Females.	Males.	Females.
8. *Persons engaged in Exhibitions, Shows, Games, &c.*										
Performer, Showman, Exhibition, Service	48	18	.	.	1	2	5	1	9	1
Billiard, Cricket, & other Games, Service	103	.	5	.	13	.	8	.	46	.
II. DOMESTIC CLASS.										
4. Persons engaged in Domestic Offices or Services.										
1. *Domestic Service.*										
Domestic Coachman, Groom - - - -	587	.	19	.	58	.	69	.	525	.
Domestic Gardener - - - -	292	.	14	.	96	.	82	.	384	.
Domestic Indoor Servant - - - -	245	22870	18	1774	27	1909	20	1013	131	5661
Lodge, Gate, Park, Keeper (not Government) - - - - -	31	2	1	.	.	1	2	1	24	6
Inn, Hotel, Servant - - - - -	1418	1048	32	33	56	107	28	52	226	231
College, Club, Service - - -	45	5	1	.	3	1	11	5	14	9
2. *Other Service.*										
Office Keeper (not Government) -	131	360	.	3	7	30	3	3	2	95
Cook (not domestic) - - -	105	20	.	.	1	2	.	1	23	9
Charwoman - - - - -	.	3597	.	112	.	399	.	170	.	891
Washing and Bathing Service - -	52	2277	1	76	3	228	3	91	11	706
Hospital and Institution Service - -	91	357	26	35	1	10	1	.	12	32
Others engaged in Service - -	82	13	.	.	2	.	.	1	11	15
III. COMMERCIAL CLASS.										
5. Persons engaged in Commercial Occupations.										
1. *Merchants and Agents.*										
Merchant - - - - - -	407	3	2	.	2	.	3	.	137	2
Broker, Agent, Factor - - - - -	1325	28	36	.	136	5	53	.	423	9
Auctioneer, Appraiser, Valuer, House Agent - - - - -	205	3	16	.	35	1	15	.	85	1
Accountant - - - - - -	298	1	13	.	34	.	10	.	60	.
Salesman, Buyer (not otherwise described)	84	115	1	2	4	5	2	.	181	26
Commercial Traveller - - - -	1006	.	26	.	113	.	53	.	388	.
Commercial Clerk - - - -	9278	223	357	3	590	16	352	3	3223	52
Officer of Commercial Company, Guild, Society, &c. - - - -	10	.	.	.	.	.	3	.	.	.
2. *Dealers in Money.*										
Banker - - - - - -	12	.	.	.	.	.	1	.	3	.
Bank Service - - - - -	206	3	10	.	36	.	33	.	85	.
Bill Discounter, Bill Broker, Finance Agent - - - - -	24	.		.	2	.	.	.	6	.
3. *Persons occupied in Insurance.*										
Life, House, Ship, &c., Insurance Service	735	10	52	.	99	1	50	1	127	2
6. Persons engaged in Conveyance of Men, Goods, and Messages.										
1. *On Railways.*										
Railway Engine Driver, Stoker - -	540	.	108	.	34	.	56	.	181	.
Railway Guard - - - - -	175	.	13	.	30	.	13	.	31	.
Pointsman, Level Crossing Man - -	127	.	21	1	53	.	13	.	79	.
Other Railway Officials and Servants -	2871	7	183	1	201	.	103	.	1081	7
2. *On Roads.*										
Toll Collector, Turnpike Gate Keeper -	1	.	.	.	.	.	.	.	5	.
Omnibus, Coach, Cab, Owner—Livery Stable Keeper - - - - -	226	18	3	1	10	.	11	.	19	.
Cabman, Flyman, Coachman (not domestic) - - - - -	1021	.	54	.	81	.	54	.	161	.
Carman, Carrier, Carter, Haulier -	6607	83	315	3	751	1	435	.	1907	.
Tramway Companies' Service - -	245	.	8	.	84	.	.	.	104	.
Wheel Chair Proprietor, Attendant, &c. -	.	.	.	.	.	.	.	.	.	.
3. *On Canals, Rivers and Seas.*										
Inland Navigation Service - -	26	.	2	1	.	.	.	.	16	.
Bargeman, Lighterman, Waterman -	1066	12	7	.	4	.	1	.	120	1
Navigation Service (on shore) - -	107	.	.	.	1	.	.	.	17	.
Seaman (Merchant Service) - - -	10778	.	4	.	11	.	3	.	29	.
Pilot - - - - - - -	198	.	.	.	.	.	.	.	.	.
Ship Steward, Cook - - -	7294	81	1	.	1	.	.	.	.	.
Boatman on Seas - - - - -	2	.	.	.	.	.	.	.	.	.
Harbour, Dock, Wharf, Lighthouse, Service	13287	23	4	.	.	.	1	.	2	.
4. *In Storage.*										
Warehouseman (not Manchester) -	1538	182	15	.	51	6	7	2	1336	31
Meter, Weigher - - - -	139	.	9	.	2	.	5	.	2	.
5. *In conveying Messages, Porterage, &c.*										
Messenger, Porter, Watchman (not Railway nor Government) - -	7803	27	153	3	355	.	134	.	1825	28
Telegraph, Telephone Service - -	245	74	8	1	90	.	16	.	96	36

Table 10 *continued*.—OCCUPATIONS of MALES and FEMALES in the NORTH-WESTERN DIVISION and its REGISTRATION COUNTIES, and in each URBAN SANITARY DISTRICT of which the POPULATION exceeds 50,000 PERSONS.

OCCUPATIONS.	URBAN SANITARY DISTRICTS.									
	LIVERPOOL.		ST. HELENS.		BOLTON.		BURY.		SALFORD.	
	Males.	Females.	Males.	Females.	Males.	Females.	Males.	Females.	Males.	Females.
IV. AGRICULTURAL CLASS.										
7. PERSONS ENGAGED IN AGRICULTURE.										
1. *In Fields and Pastures.*										
Farmer, Grazier	82	11	44	9	20	1	37	1	26	7
Farmer's, Grazier's—Son, Grandson, Brother, Nephew*	23	.	14	.	4	.	11	.	6	.
Farm Bailiff	3	.	4	.	.	.	5	.	7	.
Agricultural Labourer, Farm Servant, Cottager	267	29	120	10	78	4	176	5	214	5
Shepherd	6	.	.	.	.	.	.	.	2	.
Land Drainage Service (not in towns)	.	.	.	.	2	.	.	.	.	.
Agricultural Machine—Proprietor, Attendant	.	.	.	.	.	.	.	.	1	.
Agricultural Student, Pupil	1	.	.	.	.	.	.	.	1	.
Others engaged in, or connected with, Agriculture	.	.	.	.	.	.	.	.	1	.
2. *In Woods.*										
Woodman	.	.	.	.	.	.	.	.	.	.
3. *In Gardens.*										
Nurseryman, Seedsman, Florist	31	11	1	.	1	.	3	.	12	4
Gardener (not domestic)	58	1	35	.	60	.	9	.	19	2
8. PERSONS ENGAGED ABOUT ANIMALS.										
1. *About Animals.*										
Horse Proprietor, Breeder, Dealer	73	.	3	.	1	.	.	.	20	.
Groom, Horse-keeper, Horse-breaker	690	2	21	.	68	.	36	.	308	.
Veterinary Surgeon, Farrier	174	.	6	.	26	.	14	.	25	.
Cattle, Sheep, Pig—Dealer, Salesman	71	.	2	.	5	.	8	.	75	.
Drover	55	.	.	.	2	.	2	.	57	.
Gamekeeper	9	.	1	.	.	.	2	.	.	.
Dog, Bird, Animal—Keeper, Dealer	18	3	2	.	1	1	1	1	2	2
Vermin destroyer	2	.	.	.	.	.	.	.	.	.
Fisherman	77	.	.	.	.	.	.	.	.	.
Knacker, Catsmeat Dealer, &c., &c.	6	.	1	.	1	.	1	.	.	.
V. INDUSTRIAL CLASS.										
9. PERSONS WORKING AND DEALING IN BOOKS, PRINTS, AND MAPS.										
1. *Books.*										
Publisher, Bookseller, Librarian	168	28	6	1	31	4	9	2	64	5
Music—Publisher, Seller, Printer	17	12	.	.	4	2	.	.	8	1
Bookbinder	261	554	3	3	25	18	13	2	121	202
Printer	1894	70	36	.	202	2	85	.	808	105
Newspaper Agent, News Room Keeper	120	49	3	1	35	8	10	2	34	18
Others	.	.	.	.	.	.	.	.	.	.
2. *Prints and Maps.*										
Lithographer, Lithographic Printer	248	3	.	.	8	.	2	.	114	10
Copper Plate and Steel Plate Printer	6	.	.	.	2	.	.	.	2	1
Map and Print—Colourer, Seller	6	8	.	.	.	.	.	.	10	1
10. PERSONS WORKING AND DEALING IN MACHINES AND IMPLEMENTS.										
1. *Machines.*										
Engine, Machine, Maker	1048	9	53	1	230	1	168	.	459	11
Millwright	174	.	19	.	216	.	51	.	141	.
Fitter, Turner (Engine and Machine)	1665	.	203	.	478	.	376	.	689	.
Boiler Maker	2036	.	78	.	164	.	82	.	110	.
Spinning and Weaving Machine Maker	1	2	.	.	666	110	272	4	413	35
Agricultural Machine and Implement Maker	6	.	.	.	5	.	.	.	5	1
Domestic Machinery—Maker, Dealer	6	.	.	.	4	.	2	.	4	.
2. *Tools and Implements.*										
Tool Maker, Dealer	36	1	6	.	16	.	6	.	74	1
Cutler, Scissors Maker	53	2	1	.	2	1	5	.	16	.
File Maker	28	.	8	.	20	.	7	.	17	2
Saw Maker	33	.	.	.	4	.	.	.	13	.
Pin Maker	.	1	.	.	.	.	.	.	1	.
Needle Maker	1	.	.	.	.	.	.	.	1	.
Steel Pen Maker	.	1	.	.	.	.	.	.	.	1
Pencil Maker (Wood)	.	.	.	.	.	.	.	.	.	.
Domestic Implement Maker	6	2	.	.	.	.	.	.	4	.
3. *Watches and Philosophical Instruments.*										
Watch Maker, Clock Maker	852	16	81	5	51	.	28	.	101	2
Philosophical Instrument Maker, Optician	111	4	.	.	3	.	.	.	9	.
Electrical Apparatus Maker	44	1	2	.	20	.	.	.	38	.
Weighing and Measuring Apparatus Maker	60	1	1	.	1	.	.	.	26	2

* Only *male* relations living with the farmer or grazier, and, therefore, presumably engaged in agriculture are included above.

Table 10 *continued.*—Occupations of Males and Females in the North-western Division and its Registration Counties, and in each Urban Sanitary District of which the Population exceeds 50,000 Persons.

Occupations.	Urban Sanitary Districts.									
	Liverpool.		St. Helens.		Bolton.		Bury.		Salford.	
	Males.	Females.	Males.	Females.	Males.	Females.	Males.	Females.	Males.	Females.
4. *Surgical Instruments.*										
Surgical Instrument Maker	18	1	.	.	2	.	.	.	8	1
5. *Arms and Ordnance.*										
Gunsmith, Gun Manufacturer	22	.	.	.	2	.	.	.	8	.
Ordnance Manufacturer	.	.	.	.	.	.	.	.	.	.
Sword, Bayonet—Maker, Cutler	.	.	.	.	.	.	.	.	.	.
Others	.	.	.	.	.	.	.	.	.	.
6. *Musical Instruments.*										
Musical Instrument Maker, Dealer	172	3	.	1	6	.	1		56	1
7. *Type, Dies, Medals, Coins.*										
Type Cutter, Founder	1	.	.	.	1	.	.		8	.
Die, Seal, Coin, Medal, Maker	14	1	.	.	9	.	.	.	22	.
8. *Tackle for Sports and Games.*										
Toy Maker, Dealer	24	32	.	.	1	4	1	2	17	6
Fishing Rod, Tackle, Maker, Dealer	5	1	.	.	1	.	.	.	.	.
Apparatus for other Games, Maker, Dealer	11	.	.	.	.	.	.	.	5	1
11. Persons working and dealing in Houses, Furniture, and Decorations.										
1. *Houses.*										
Builder	403	2	31	.	33	.	26	1	125	.
Carpenter, Joiner	5597	4	435	.	884	.	431	.	1814	2
Bricklayer	1915	.	304	.	404	.	184	.	657	1
Mason	1501	.	119	.	466	1	218	.	470	.
Slater, Tiler	282	1	28	.	99	.	41	.	107	.
Plasterer, Whitewasher	1294	4	33	.	103	.	31	.	209	1
Paperhanger	368	2	.	.	6	.	.	.	67	.
Plumber	1616	2	93	1	169	1	81	.	468	1
Painter, Glazier	3136	8	124	.	484	1	137	.	903	1
2. *Furniture and Fittings.*										
Cabinet Maker, Upholsterer	1353	453	23	1	205	12	84	6	347	192
French Polisher	309	51	1	.	24	6	12	2	90	23
Furniture Broker, Dealer	181	66	5	1	33	11	9	2	52	22
Locksmith, Bellhanger	85	1	.	.	22	.	2	.	30	.
Gas Fitter	348	.	25	.	41	.	4	.	48	.
House and Shop Fittings—Maker, Dealer	132	4	.	.	10	1	3	.	33	3
Funeral Furniture Maker, Undertaker	30	9	1	1	15	2	.	.	16	11
Others	2	.	.	.	.	.	.	.	.	1
3. *House Decorations.*										
Wood Carver	89	.	.	.	4	.	1	.	13	.
Carver, Gilder	281	6	1	.	25	1	6	.	111	3
Dealer in Works of Art	27	5	.	.	2	.	1	.	9	1
Figure, Image—Maker, Dealer	26	1	.	.	.	.	.	.	3	.
Animal, Bird, &c., Preserver, Naturalist	14	6	.	.	.	.	.	.	4	.
Artificial Flower Maker	3	26	.	.	.	.	.	.	1	51
12. Persons working and dealing in Carriages and Harness.										
1. *Carriages.*										
Coachmaker	716	5	13	.	77	.	40	.	310	.
Railway Carriage, Railway Wagon, Maker	16	.	2	1	.	.	38	.	4	.
Wheelwright	515	1	68	.	86	.	65	.	159	1
Bicycle, Tricycle—Maker, Dealer	10	.	.	.	.	.	.	.	3	.
Others	12	1	5	.	2	.	5	.	6	.
2. *Harness.*										
Saddler, Harness, Whip, Maker	316	11	18	.	48	.	31	.	110	1
13. Persons working and dealing in Ships and Boats.										
1. *Hull.*										
Ship, Boat, Barge, Builder	1087	1	1	.	3	.	.	.	13	1
Shipwright, Ship Carpenter (ashore)	2141	.	12	.	.	.	.	.	5	.
2. *Masts, Rigging, &c.*										
Mast, Yard, Oar, Block, Maker	227	.	1	.	.	.	.	.	.	.
Ship Rigger, Chandler, Fitter	735	7	.	.	.	.	.	.	.	.
Sail Maker	651	1	6	.	.	.	.	.	5	.

Table 10 *continued.*—OCCUPATIONS of MALES and FEMALES in the NORTH-WESTERN DIVISION and its REGISTRATION COUNTIES, and in each URBAN SANITARY DISTRICT of which the POPULATION exceeds 50,000 PERSONS.

OCCUPATIONS.	URBAN SANITARY DISTRICTS.									
	LIVERPOOL.		ST. HELENS.		BOLTON.		BURY.		SALFORD.	
	Males.	Females.	Males.	Females.	Males.	Females.	Males.	Females.	Males.	Females.
14. PERSONS WORKING AND DEALING IN CHEMICALS AND COMPOUNDS.										
1. *Colouring Matter.*										
Dye, Paint, Manufacture	72	35	.	.	4	.	10	.	61	.
Ink, Blacking, Colouring Substance, Manufacture	36	24	.	.	2	.	2	.	11	3
2. *Explosives.*										
Gunpowder, Guncotton, Explosive Substance, Manufacture	1	.	.	3	.	.	.	.	.	.
Fusee, Fireworks, Explosive Article, Manufacture	8	34	.	7	.	.	.	.	1	1
3. *Drugs and other Chemicals and Compounds.*										
Chemist, Druggist	533	32	36	2	68	3	28	4	113	7
Manufacturing Chemist	246	59	1024	.	26	1	26	.	71	12
Alkali Manufacture	10	.	67	1	5	.	.	.	1	.
Drysalter	38	10	2	.	3	.	10	5	24	2
15. PERSONS WORKING AND DEALING IN TOBACCO AND PIPES.										
1. *Tobacco and Pipes.*										
Tobacco Manufacturer, Tobacconist	512	1597	13	1	92	86	13	13	66	40
Tobacco Pipe, Snuff Box, &c., Maker	60	29	1	.	5	3	1	.	3	1
16. PERSONS WORKING AND DEALING IN FOOD AND LODGING.										
1. *Board and Lodging.*										
Innkeeper, Hotel Keeper, Publican	1739	290	123	27	117	27	74	17	156	29
Lodging, Boarding House, Keeper	188	1214	3	49	9	79	10	41	5	121
Coffee, Eating House, Keeper	183	87	6	2	14	7	10	7	24	16
2. *Spirituous Drinks.*										
Hop—Merchant, Dealer	1	.	.	.	1	.	.	.	2	.
Maltster	10	.	.	.	.	.	.	.	1	.
Brewer	339	4	41	1	135	4	30	.	174	1
Beerseller. Ale, Porter, Cider, Dealer	79	38	32	15	177	41	64	11	224	57
Cellarman	298	51	3	1	4	.	7	.	51	.
Wine, Spirit—Merchant, Agent	280	8	4	.	8	3	2	.	37	1
3. *Food.*										
Milkseller, Dairyman	719	217	25	11	13	5	18	3	166	45
Cheesemonger, Butterman	10	1	.	.	2	1	.	.	7	.
Butcher, Meat Salesman	1809	155	113	12	298	40	145	19	554	32
Provision Curer, Dealer	744	311	61	28	196	177	31	24	294	205
Poulterer, Game Dealer	132	44	2	.	8	4	1	.	48	4
Fishmonger	306	219	15	4	54	20	27	2	130	16
Corn, Flour, Seed—Merchant, Dealer	440	20	5	.	23	4	7	1	82	7
Corn Miller	463	9	6	.	22	.	9	.	74	.
Baker	1792	119	51	4	207	36	55	14	389	49
Confectioner, Pastrycook	357	806	14	58	66	86	48	37	93	100
Greengrocer, Fruiterer	525	330	27	14	115	38	62	13	160	49
Mustard, Vinegar, Spice, Pickle—Maker, Dealer	21	35	.	.	1	.	.	.	8	8
Sugar Refiner	632	6	3	2	5	.	2	.	14	2
Grocer. Tea, Coffee, Chocolate—Maker, Dealer	1965	324	236	87	412	105	175	94	601	107
Ginger Beer, Mineral Water—Manufacturer, Dealer	175	14	21	2	33	2	11	1	44	1
Others dealing in Food	.	.	3	.	.	.	.	.	.	.
17. PERSONS WORKING AND DEALING IN TEXTILE FABRICS.										
1. *Wool and Worsted.*										
Woolstapler	26	.	.	.	4	.	4	.	1	.
Woollen Cloth Manufacture	25	5	.	.	6	14	416	539	51	14
Wool, Woollen goods—Dyer, Printer	3	.	.	.	1	.	15	.	13	.
Worsted, Stuff, Manufacture	8	2	.	.	2	3	5	11	28	139
Flannel Manufacture	3	.	.	.	.	.	1	.	1	.
Blanket Manufacture	.	.	.	.	4	40	.	16	.	.
Fuller	.	.	.	.	.	.	30	.	.	.
Cloth, Worsted, Stuff, Flannel, Blanket, Dealer	13	2	.	.	4	1	14	.	36	.
Others	2	.	.	.	.	.	1	.	.	.
2. *Silk.*										
Silk, Silk goods, Manufacture	9	10	.	2	1	3	13	32	267	695
Silk Dyer, Printer	2	.	.	.	2	.	5	.	17	1
Ribbon Manufacture	2	1	.	.	.	.	.	.	1	2
Crape, Gauze, Manufacture	.	.	.	.	.	.	.	.	2	.
Silk Merchant, Dealer	17	2	.	.	45	.	1	2	15	2

Table 10 *continued.*—Occupations of Males and Females in the North-western Division and its Registration Counties, and in each Urban Sanitary District of which the Population exceeds 50,000 Persons.

Occupations.	Urban Sanitary Districts.									
	Liverpool.		St. Helens.		Bolton.		Bury.		Salford.	
	Males.	Females.	Males.	Females.	Males.	Females.	Males.	Females.	Males.	Females.
3. Cotton and Flax										
Cotton, Cotton goods, Manufacture	30	318	1	6	8495	19630	2030	6294	2087	8387
Cotton, Calico—Printer, Dyer, Bleacher	5	3	.	.	1909	366	474	55	1775	209
Cotton, Calico—Warehouseman, Dealer	365	32	.	.	195	87	29	31	216	21
Flax, Linen—Manufacturer, Dealer	6	10	.	.	10	13	3	6	243	997
Lace Manufacturer, Dealer	11	41	.	.	1	.	1	.	10	19
Fustian Manufacturer, Dealer	1	1	.	1	.	.	32	146	301	423
Tape Manufacturer, Dealer	.	1	.	.	7	5	.	7	2	28
Thread Manufacturer, Dealer	.	.	.	.	4	22	1	.	7	54
4. Hemp and other Fibrous Materials.										
Hemp, Jute, Cocoa Fibre, Manufacture	8	7	.	.	2	1	.	.	11	5
Rope, Twine, Cord—Maker, Dealer	287	113	20	.	91	3	30	2	108	43
Mat Maker, Seller	82	13	.	.	1	.	.	.	2	3
Net Maker	1	1	.	.	1	.	.	.	.	4
Canvas, Sailcloth, Manufacture	2	2	3	.	1	.	.	.	9	.
Sacking, Sack, Bag—Maker, Dealer	26	263	.	4	1	3	.	2	3	9
Others working and dealing in Hemp	6	25	.	.	4	.	.	.	1	.
5. Mixed or Unspecified Materials.										
Weaver (undefined)	10	24	.	.	6	.	1	11	12	6
Dyer, Printer, Scourer, Bleacher, Calenderer (undefined)	102	78	1	.	11	9	119	.	1104	22
Factory hand (Textile, undefined)	4	33	.	8	14	72	139	.	382	384
Felt Manufacture	.	.	.	.	2	.	1	2	1	.
Carpet, Rug, Manufacture	27	6	.	.	2	.	3	.	19	1
Manchester Warehouseman	1	.	.	.	.	.	1	.	52	.
Draper, Linen Draper, Mercer	1448	637	70	27	231	82	124	44	214	161
Fancy Goods (Textile), Manufacturer, Worker, Dealer	14	69	.	1	.	12	.	3	18	184
Trimming Maker, Dealer	9	32	1	.	.	1	6	50	30	358
Embroiderer	1	15	.	.	.	14	.	.	.	52
Others	2	.	.	.	.	.	.	.	17	.
18. Persons working and dealing in Dress.										
1. Dress.										
Hatter, Hat Manufacture (not straw)	109	120	6	.	24	2	306	361	70	107
Straw—Hat, Bonnet, Plait, Manufacture	9	38	.	2	.	6	.	2	1	11
Tailor	2891	1439	109	73	450	70	172	58	632	368
Milliner, Dressmaker, Staymaker	16	9461	3	637	3	903	4	576	18	2222
Shawl Manufacture	1	.	.	.	.	.	.	.	.	1
Shirt Maker, Seamstress	18	2676	.	74	3	221	.	101	18	1063
Hosiery Manufacture	3	8	.	.	1	8	1	3	2	.
Hosier, Haberdasher	101	85	4	1	11	7	4	6	19	8
Glover, Glove Maker	5	5	.	.	.	.	1	.	3	2
Button Maker, Dealer	2	1	.	.	.	.	.	.	4	3
Shoe, Boot—Maker, Dealer	2624	386	135	8	287	32	143	10	651	87
Patten, Clog, Maker	94	3	75	.	283	2	143	.	104	1
Wig Maker, Hairdresser	550	37	25	.	57	1	31	1	102	2
Umbrella, Parasol, Stick—Maker, Dealer	62	32	3	1	9	11	5	3	51	110
Accoutrement Maker	.	2	.	.	.	.	.	.	.	1
Old Clothes Dealer, and others	79	124	2	2	6	10	.	2	1	9
19. Persons working and dealing in various Animal Substances.										
1. In Grease, Gut, Bone, Horn, Ivory, and Whalebone.										
Tallow Chandler, Candle, Grease, Manufacture	132	34	5	1	16	1	7	.	15	1
Soap Boiler, Maker	105	121	6	.	.	.	1	.	55	.
Glue, Size, Gelatine, Isinglass—Maker, Dealer	1	1	.	.	1	.	1	.	4	1
Manure Manufacture	2	3	3	.	2	.	.	.	4	.
Bone, Horn, Ivory, Tortoise-shell—Worker, Dealer	2	2	.	.	1	.	.	.	10	.
Comb Maker	1	1	.	.	6	.	.	.	1	.
Others	9	2	.	.	1	.	.	.	1	.
2. In Skins.										
Furrier, Skinner	37	16	3	.	3	1	2	1	30	15
Tanner, Fellmonger	92	1	15	.	84	.	44	.	47	2
Currier	110	6	6	.	92	4	39	3	67	3
Leather Goods, Portmanteau, Bag, Strap, &c.—Maker, Dealer	42	27	.	.	23	1	7	.	38	10
Parchment, Vellum—Maker, Dealer	1	.	.	.	.	.	.	.	.	.
3. In Hair and Feathers.										
Hair, Bristle—Worker, Dealer	20	30	.	1	.	.	.	.	4	3
Brush, Broom, Maker	177	64	1	.	70	22	18	.	90	11
Quill, Feather—Dresser, Dealer	10	68	.	.	.	1	4	2	2	8

Table 10 *continued*.—OCCUPATIONS of MALES and FEMALES in the NORTH-WESTERN DIVISION and its REGISTRATION COUNTIES, and in each URBAN SANITARY DISTRICT of which the POPULATION exceeds 50,000 PERSONS.

OCCUPATIONS.	URBAN SANITARY DISTRICTS.									
	LIVERPOOL.		ST. HELENS.		BOLTON.		BURY.		SALFORD.	
	Males.	Females.	Males.	Females.	Males.	Females.	Males.	Females.	Males.	Females.
20. PERSONS WORKING AND DEALING IN VARIOUS VEGETABLE SUBSTANCES.										
1. *In Oils, Gums, and Resins.*										
Oil Miller, Oil Cake—Maker, Dealer	265	6	4	.	5	.	4	.	38	1
Oil and Colourman	39	1	.	.	2	.	.	.	6	1
Floor Cloth, Oil Cloth, Manufacture	11	2	1	.	2	.	2	.	25	.
Japanner	14	7	.	.	.	.	.	.	6	3
India Rubber, Gutta Percha—Worker, Dealer	63	55	.	.	3	8	2	.	38	20
Waterproof Goods—Maker, Dealer	25	2	57	5	9	2	4	.	60	7
Others	1	.	.	.	.	.	.	.	5	2
2. *In Cane, Rush, and Straw.*										
Willow, Cane, Rush—Worker, Dealer, Basketmaker	149	47	5	1	68	3	8	1	21	7
Hay, Straw (not plait), Chaff—Cutter, Dealer	54	5	4	.	18	2	2	.	11	1
Thatcher	.	.	.	.	.	.	.	.	.	.
3. *In Wood and Bark.*										
Timber, Wood—Merchant, Dealer	289	25	10	.	46	.	13	.	80	2
Sawyer	423	.	40	.	73	.	48	.	174	.
Lath, Wooden Fence, Hurdle, Maker	70	.	1	.	8	.	5	.	10	.
Wood Turner, Box Maker	300	41	5	.	45	1	26	.	99	11
Cooper, Hoop Maker, Bender	1317	5	114	.	37	.	10	.	81	2
Cork, Bark—Cutter, Worker, Dealer	105	8	.	.	6	.	.	.	10	1
Others	1	.	.	.	.	.	.	.	.	.
4. *In Paper.*										
Paper Manufacture	48	82	.	1	68	30	322	217	225	107
Envelope Maker	1	28	.	.	.	.	.	.	.	11
Stationer, Law Stationer	208	240	7	5	17	14	6	6	89	77
Card, Pattern Card, Maker	12	1	.	.	.	.	1	.	115	8
Paper Stainer	5	4	1	.	.	.	.	.	13	27
Paper Box, Paper Bag, Maker	8	237	.	1	6	64	.	3	7	138
Ticket, Label, Writer	34	10	2	.	.	4	1	.	10	4
Others	40	1	3	.	19	.	2	.	5	.
21. PERSONS WORKING AND DEALING IN VARIOUS MINERAL SUBSTANCES.										
1. *Miners.*										
Coal Miner	85	2	2949	98	580	1	147	2	637	.
Ironstone Miner	1	.	.	.	.	.	.	.	3	.
Copper Miner	6	.	1	.	.	.	.	.	1	.
Tin Miner	1	.	.	.	.	.	.	.	.	.
Lead Miner	6	.	.	.	.	.	.	.	.	.
Miner in other, or undefined, Minerals	16	.	2	.	1	.	.	.	1	.
Mine Service	21	.	14	.	6	.	3	.	4	.
2. *Coal, Coal Gas, &c.*										
Coal Merchant, Dealer	552	78	13	3	116	5	42	8	194	18
Coalheaver	622	.	2	.	24	.	28	.	135	.
Coke, Charcoal, Peat—Cutter, Burner, Dealer	8	.	.	.	.	1	.	.	.	1
Gas Works Service	428	.	36	.	141	.	73	.	306	.
3. *Stone, Clay, and Road Making.*										
Stone Quarrier	172	.	.	.	38	.	51	.	3	.
Stone Cutter, Dresser, Dealer	62	.	2	.	5	.	8	.	18	.
Slate Quarrier	3	.	.	.	.	.	.	.	.	.
Slate Worker, Dealer	12	.	.	.	2	.	1	.	3	.
Limeburner	7	.	4	.	1	.	.	.	3	.
Clay, Sand, Gravel, Chalk—Labourer, Dealer	6	3	6	.	4	.	8	.	.	.
Fossil, Coprolite—Digger, Dealer	.	.	.	.	.	.	.	.	.	.
Well Sinker, Borer	4	.	4	.	3	.	1	.	15	.
Plaster, Cement, Manufacture	8	.	1	.	.	.	.	.	6	3
Brick, Tile—Maker, Burner, Dealer	488	2	140	4	213	.	114	.	348	7
Paviour	352	.	13	.	64	.	30	.	126	.
Road Contractor, Surveyor, Inspector	6	.	2	.	.	.	.	.	3	.
Road Labourer	271	.	12	.	39	.	7	.	62	.
Railway Contractor	7	.	1	.	4	.	.	.	6	.
Platelayer	120	.	61	.	28	.	13	.	46	.
Railway Labourer, Navvy	292	.	42	.	76	.	89	.	229	.
Others	6	1	4	.	.	.	.	.	6	.
4. *Earthenware and Glass.*										
Earthenware, China, Porcelain, Manufacture	17	8	79	6	2	.	1	.	13	2
Glass Manufacture	119	23	3163	601	32	.	1	.	777	2
Earthenware, China, Glass, Dealer	131	82	3	8	22	10	10	5	27	16
5. *Salt.*										
Salt Maker, Dealer	66	3	2	.	2	.	1	.	4	.

Table 10 *continued.*—OCCUPATIONS of MALES and FEMALES in the NORTH-WESTERN DIVISION and its REGISTRATION COUNTIES, and in each URBAN SANITARY DISTRICT of which the POPULATION exceeds 50,000 PERSONS.

OCCUPATIONS.	URBAN SANITARY DISTRICTS.									
	LIVERPOOL.		ST. HELENS.		BOLTON.		BURY.		SALFORD.	
	Males.	Females.	Males.	Females.	Males.	Females.	Males.	Females.	Males.	Females.
6. Water.										
Waterworks Service	62	.	2	.	17	.	8	.	29	.
Others	7	.	.	.	.	.	.	.	.	.
7. Precious Metals and Jewellery.										
Goldsmith, Silversmith, Jeweller	192	20	.	.	13	3	5	1	60	5
Gold, Silver, Beater	18	.	.	.	.	.	.	.	26	.
Lapidary	1	.	.	.	.	.	.	.	.	.
Others	1	5	.	.	.	1	.	.	1	4
8. Iron and Steel.										
Blacksmith	1748	1	241	.	386	2	273	.	570	1
Whitesmith	460	1	4	.	29	.	2	.	86	.
Nail Manufacture	41	1	7	1	8	.	.	.	24	17
Anchor, Chain, Manufacture	19	.	1	.	.	.	.	.	28	.
Other Iron and Steel Manufactures	2207	8	311	1	3450	9	1596	.	2723	3
Ironmonger, Hardware Dealer, Merchant	302	22	21	6	50	11	29	3	76	15
9. Copper.										
Copper, Copper goods—Manufacturer, Worker, Dealer	277	.	256	.	5	.	14	.	312	.
10. Tin and Zinc.										
Tin, Tin Plate, Tin goods—Manufacturer, Worker, Dealer	704	6	22	2	116	3	99	2	148	.
Zinc, Zinc Goods—Manufacturer, Worker, Dealer	28	.	.	.	.	.	.	.	4	.
11. Lead.										
Lead, Leaden goods—Manufacturer, Worker, Dealer	24	.	3	.	.	.	.	.	8	.
12. In Other, Mixed, or Unspecified, Metals.										
Metal Refiner, Worker, Turner, Dealer	58	2	3	.	13	.	7	.	59	1
Brass, Bronze, Manufacture, Brazier	740	3	6	1	118	1	64	1	366	3
Metal Burnisher, Lacquerer	2	5	.	.	.	1	.	.	.	3
White Metal, Plated Ware, Manufacture, Pewterer	13	.	.	.	.	.	.	.	1	.
Wire Maker, Worker, Weaver, Drawer	79	3	3	.	16	.	.	.	114	14
Bolt, Nut, Rivet, Screw, Staple, Maker	48	7	11	.	17	.	37	.	55	2
Lamp, Lantern, Candlestick, Maker	12	2	2	.	.	.	.	.	.	.
Clasp, Buckle, Hinge, Maker	1	.	.	.	.	.	.	.	.	.
Fancy Chain, Gilt Toy, Maker	.	.	.	.	1	.	.	.	4	.
Others	3	.	.	.	.	.	.	.	2	.
22. PERSONS WORKING AND DEALING IN GENERAL OR UNSPECIFIED COMMODITIES.										
1. Makers and Dealers (General or Undefined).										
General Shopkeeper, Dealer	704	1327	30	85	91	144	22	42	178	271
Pawnbroker	666	30	25	3	77	9	26	16	136	17
Costermonger, Huckster, Street Seller	533	1935	23	12	145	111	73	42	272	130
Manufacturer, Manager, Superintendent (undefined)	256	14	37	.	29	.	0	.	80	1
Contractor (undefined)	47	1	6	.	10	.	9	.	26	.
2. Mechanics and Labourers (General or Undefined).										
General Labourer	17548	107	3174	14	1519	3	918	1	3461	8
Engine Driver, Stoker, Fireman (not railway, marine, nor agricultural)	1062	.	268	.	388	.	206	.	544	.
Artizan, Mechanic (undefined)	824	62	73	.	152	4	90	.	784	39
Apprentice (undefined)	159	31	2	3	6	1	1	.	34	10
Factory Labourer (undefined)	396	162	34	4	45	5	16	4	507	49
Machinist, Machine Worker (undefined)	83	.	4	1	11	2	7	.	82	13
23. PERSONS WORKING AND DEALING IN REFUSE MATTERS.										
1. Refuse Matters.										
Town Drainage Service	22	.	8	.	15	.	6	.	23	.
Chimney Sweep, Soot Merchant	96	.	7	.	21	.	9	.	20	.
Scavenger, Crossing Sweeper	132	.	5	.	6	.	10	.	63	1
Rag Gatherer, Dealer	15	47	4	1	27	26	4	3	3	2
VI. UNOCCUPIED CLASS.										
24. PERSONS WITHOUT SPECIFIED OCCUPATIONS										
Persons returned by Property, Rank, &c., and not by special occupation	62071	177766	7247	18623	10641	28474	5109	18962	19569	50940
Children under 5 years of age	35173	38408	4656	4808	7261	7591	3430	3664	12090	12946

Table 10 *continued*.—OCCUPATIONS of MALES and FEMALES in the NORTH-WESTERN DIVISION and its REGISTRATION COUNTIES, and in each URBAN SANITARY DISTRICT of which the POPULATION exceeds 50,000 Persons.

OCCUPATIONS.	URBAN SANITARY DISTRICTS.											
	MANCHESTER.		OLDHAM.		ROCHDALE.		BURNLEY.		BLACKBURN.		PRESTON.	
	Males.	Females.	Males.	Females.	Males.	Females.	Males.	Females.	Males.	Females.	Males.	Females.
TOTAL	163475	177939	53536	57837	31985	35381	28208	30353	49133	54881	46264	52273
I. PROFESSIONAL CLASS.												
1. PERSONS ENGAGED IN THE GENERAL OR LOCAL GOVERNMENT OF THE COUNTRY.												
1. *National Government.*												
Peer, M.P., Privy Councillor (not otherwise described)	.	.	.	.	.	.	.	.	.	.	.	.
Civil Service (officers and clerks)	184	15	21	3	25	.	8	.	24	.	48	.
Civil Service (messengers, &c.)	261	1	42	.	28	.	22	1	35	.	60	.
Prison Officer, &c.	29	17	.	.	.	.	.	.	.	.	25	6
2. *Local Government.*												
Police	779	.	99	.	65	.	38	.	104	.	120	.
Municipal, Parish, Union, District, Officer	171	13	49	5	46	1	31	.	43	6	27	.
Other Local or County Official	29	.	8	.	13	.	9	.	14	.	20	.
3. *East Indian and Colonial Service.*												
East Indian and Colonial Service	.	.	.	.	.	.	.	.	.	.	.	.
2. PERSONS ENGAGED IN THE DEFENCE OF THE COUNTRY.												
1. *Army (at Home).*												
Army Officer (effective or retired)	18	.	.	.	.	.	7	.	1	.	5	.
Soldier and Non-Commissioned Officer	411	.	8	.	5	.	134	.	11	.	18	.
Militia, Yeomanry, Volunteers	7	.	1	.	1	.	34	.	5	.	19	.
Army Pensioner	106	.	9	.	13	.	13	.	20	.	67	.
2. *Navy (ashore or in port).*												
Navy Officer (effective or retired)	2	.	.	.	.	.	.	.	1	.	.	.
Seaman, R.N.	3	.	.	.	.	.	.	.	1	.	.	.
Royal Marines (officers and men)	2	.	.	.	.	.	.	.	.	.	.	.
Navy Pensioner	8	.	2	.	1	.	3	.	.	.	5	.
3. PERSONS ENGAGED IN PROFESSIONAL OCCUPATIONS (WITH THEIR IMMEDIATE SUBORDINATES).												
1. *Clerical Profession.*												
Clergyman (Established Church)	76	.	19	.	16	.	10	.	26	.	29	.
Roman Catholic Priest	42	.	5	.	7	.	2	.	10	.	27	.
Minister, Priest, of other religious bodies	58	.	25	.	24	.	15	.	17	.	26	.
Missionary, Scripture Reader, Itinerant Preacher	39	29	8	9	3	2	6	2	3	3	4	17
Nun, Sister of Charity	.	21	.	.	.	7	.	1	.	43	.	.
Theological Student	9	.	3	.	3	.	2	.	1	.	2	.
Church, Chapel, Cemetery—Officer, Servant	66	18	18	2	16	4	19	2	37	1	24	1
2. *Legal Profession.*												
Barrister, Solicitor	97	.	26	.	30	.	11	.	28	.	38	.
Law Student	13	.	.	.	.	.	.	.	1	.	3	.
Law Clerk, and others connected with Law	366	.	64	.	65	.	36	.	83	.	95	.
3. *Medical Profession.*												
Physician, Surgeon, General Practitioner	172	1	38	.	32	.	23	.	36	.	43	.
Dentist	103	.	17	.	14	.	6	.	5	.	16	.
Medical Student, Assistant	99	2	17	.	7	.	8	.	18	.	14	.
Midwife	.	57	.	13	.	6	.	3	.	5	.	4
Subordinate Medical Service	51	316	17	67	8	42	9	34	18	39	12	71
4. *Teachers.*												
Schoolmaster	356	1084	115	286	110	195	82	113	142	300	162	315
Teacher, Professor, Lecturer	104	238	13	15	3	7	8	5	4	14	11	29
School Service, and others concerned in Teaching	24	20	13	.	3	1	4	.	7	.	6	.
5. *Literary and Scientific Persons.*												
Author, Editor, Journalist	24	6	2	1	1	1	2	.	3	.	7	.
Reporter, Short-hand Writer	29	.	9	.	2	.	4	.	8	.	15	.
Persons engaged in Scientific Pursuits	20	1	3	.	1	.	.	.	1	.	1	.
Literary, Scientific, Institution, Service, &c.	8	2	.	.	.	.	.	.	.	.	.	.
6. *Engineers and Surveyors.*												
Civil Engineer	197	.	8	.	8	.	2	.	11	.	26	.
Mining Engineer	10	.	9	.	1	.	1	.	1	.	2	.
Land, House, Ship, Surveyor	43	.	16	.	16	.	12	.	19	.	22	.
7. *Artists.*												
Painter (artist)	101	23	15	3	8	2	9	3	4	2	10	.
Engraver (artist)	137	1	.	.	.	.	.	.	1	.	.	.
Sculptor	14	.	.	.	.	.	.	.	2	.	2	.
Architect	99	.	36	.	13	.	14	.	19	.	18	.
Musician, Music Master	448	201	58	18	82	18	45	14	46	17	78	43
Art Student	19	11	4	.	6	1	.	.	1	.	3	1
Photographer	88	23	18	.	11	3	9	.	20	7	18	8
Actor	82	94	13	13	4	4	8	5	11	9	16	16
Art, Music, Theatre, Service	28	6	2	.	4	.	6	.	2	.	4	.

Table 10 *continued*.—Occupations of Males and Females in the North-western Division and its Registration Counties, and in each Urban Sanitary District of which the Population exceeds 50,000 Persons.

Occupations.	Urban Sanitary Districts.											
	Manchester.		Oldham.		Rochdale.		Burnley.		Blackburn.		Preston.	
	Males.	Females.	Males.	Females.	Males.	Females.	Males.	Females.	Males.	Females.	Males.	Females.
8. *Persons engaged in Exhibitions, Shows, Games, &c.*												
Performer, Showman, Exhibition, Service	37	17	12	3	4	.	7	1	7	8	3	.
Billiard, Cricket, & other Games, Service	126	1	11	2	5	.	7	.	13	1	13	.
II. DOMESTIC CLASS.												
4. Persons engaged in Domestic Offices or Services.												
1. *Domestic Service.*												
Domestic Coachman, Groom	219	.	90	.	46	.	28	.	58	.	41	.
Domestic Gardener	203	.	46	.	46	.	10	.	32	.	29	.
Domestic Indoor Servant	128	11469	18	1849	29	1807	23	1008	35	2675	37	2380
Lodge, Gate, Park, Keeper (not Government)	26	7	19	4	15	4	.	.	3	2	5	1
Inn, Hotel, Servant	258	948	71	52	40	40	27	25	37	78	45	85
College, Club, Service	48	8	8	2	7	3	4	.	15	6	9	4
2. *Other Service.*												
Office Keeper (not Government)	31	204	4	15	2	3	3	2	4	16	2	17
Cook (not domestic)	78	66	1	1	1	1	1	5	.	2	.	8
Charwoman	.	2209	.	325	.	337	.	124	.	237	.	304
Washing and Bathing Service	32	1381	3	175	3	104	3	93	3	135	3	193
Hospital and Institution Service	44	155	4	17	.	5	.	3	1	11	1	22
Others engaged in Service	53	32	8	2	.	1	.	.	1	.	4	.
III. COMMERCIAL CLASS.												
5. Persons engaged in Commercial Occupations.												
1. *Merchants and Agents.*												
Merchant	382	1	4	.	1	.	1	.	1	.	5	.
Broker, Agent, Factor	383	43	162	.	112	3	53	.	118	3	103	3
Auctioneer, Appraiser, Valuer, House Agent	202	2	39	.	27	.	21	.	34	2	53	1
Accountant	146	19	31	.	16	.	10	.	30	.	24	.
Salesman, Buyer (not otherwise described)	521	153	9	6	8	1	1	.	1	10	2	1
Commercial Traveller	1452	.	78	.	96	.	58	.	128	.	134	.
Commercial Clerk	4872	171	745	8	415	6	209	4	368	7	530	8
Officer of Commercial Company, Guild, Society, &c.	7	.	1	.	2	.	4	.	1	.	1	.
2. *Dealers in Money.*												
Banker	4	.	.	.	2	.	.	.	.	.	.	.
Bank Service	154	.	43	.	30	.	13	1	29	.	33	.
Bill Discounter, Bill Broker, Finance Agent	19	.	1	.	1	.	1	.	2	.	2	.
3. *Persons occupied in Insurance.*												
Life, House, Ship, &c., Insurance Service	372	5	83	.	51	.	60	.	138	2	73	.
6. Persons engaged in Conveyance of Men, Goods, and Messages.												
1. *On Railways.*												
Railway Engine Driver, Stoker	122	.	15	.	4	.	15	.	78	.	185	.
Railway Guard	183	.	12	.	6	.	2	.	34	.	62	.
Pointsman, Level Crossing Man	80	.	20	.	18	.	18	.	38	.	43	.
Other Railway Officials and Servants	2039	11	207	.	166	.	96	1	256	1	392	1
2. *On Roads.*												
Toll Collector, Turnpike Gate Keeper	5	.	1	1	1	2	.	.	.	.	1	.
Omnibus, Coach, Cab, Owner—Livery Stable Keeper	83	2	13	.	19	2	3	.	6	2	20	.
Cabman, Flyman, Coachman (not domestic)	591	.	83	.	105	.	46	.	72	.	131	.
Carman, Carrier, Carter, Haulier	3906	2	871	.	511	.	346	1	655	1	449	.
Tramway Companies' Service	85	.	5	.	.	.	2	.	.	.	3	.
Wheel Chair Proprietor, Attendant, &c.	1	.	.	.	.	.	.	.	.	.	.	.
3. *On Canals, Rivers and Seas.*												
Inland Navigation Service	24	.	.	.	4	.	7	.	5	1	8	.
Bargeman, Lighterman, Waterman	318	3	12	.	15	.	59	1	46	1	30	.
Navigation Service (on shore)	17	.	.	.	.	.	.	.	.	.	2	.
Seaman (Merchant Service)	61	.	4	.	3	.	1	.	5	.	52	.
Pilot	.	.	.	.	.	.	.	.	.	.	.	.
Ship Steward, Cook	9	.	1	.	.	.	.	.	1	.	2	.
Boatman on Seas	.	.	.	.	.	.	.	.	.	.	.	.
Harbour, Dock, Wharf, Lighthouse, Service	38	.	1	.	5	.	.	.	1	.	11	.
4. *In Storage.*												
Warehouseman (not Manchester)	3485	133	132	.	88	9	1	.	2	3	2	.
Meter, Weigher	2	.	.	.	1	.	.	.	2	.	.	.
5. *In conveying Messages, Porterage, &c.*												
Messenger, Porter, Watchman (not Railway nor Government)	4301	67	265	1	180	.	98	.	251	.	423	2
Telegraph, Telephone, Service	109	70	3	1	7	.	8	1	14	.	30	1

Table 10 *continued*.—OCCUPATIONS of MALES and FEMALES in the NORTH-WESTERN DIVISION and its REGISTRATION COUNTIES, and in each URBAN SANITARY DISTRICT of which the POPULATION exceeds 50,000 PERSONS.

OCCUPATIONS.	URBAN SANITARY DISTRICTS.											
	MANCHESTER.		OLDHAM.		ROCHDALE.		BURNLEY.		BLACKBURN.		PRESTON.	
	Males.	Females.	Males.	Females.	Males.	Females.	Males.	Females.	Males.	Females.	Males.	Females.
IV. AGRICULTURAL CLASS.												
7. PERSONS ENGAGED IN AGRICULTURE.												
1. *In Fields and Pastures.*												
Farmer, Grazier	28	2	85	7	72	10	30	2	124	11	39	1
Farmer's, Grazier's—Son, Grandson, Brother, Nephew*	4	.	16	.	18	.	9	.	26	.	6	.
Farm Bailiff	.	.	2	.	3	.	3	.	2	.	5	.
Agricultural Labourer, Farm Servant, Cottager	146	8	128	8	116	8	63	1	161	19	207	8
Shepherd	.	.	.	.	.	.	.	.	.	.	1	.
Land Drainage Service (not in towns)	.	.	.	.	.	.	2	.	.	.	2	.
Agricultural Machine—Proprietor, Attendant	.	.	.	.	.	.	.	.	.	.	.	.
Agricultural Student, Pupil	.	.	.	.	1	.	.	.	.	.	1	.
Others engaged in, or connected with, Agriculture	1	.	.	.	.	.	.	.	.	.	.	.
2. *In Woods.*												
Woodman	2	.	.	.	.	.	.	.	.	.	.	.
3. *In Gardens.*												
Nurseryman, Seedsman, Florist	14	3	1	.	4	.	.	.	2	.	12	1
Gardener (not domestic)	48	1	26	.	87	.	51	1	85	.	232	4
8. PERSONS ENGAGED ABOUT ANIMALS.												
1. *About Animals.*												
Horse Proprietor, Breeder, Dealer	27	.	5	.	2	.	7	.	1	.	4	.
Groom, Horse-keeper, Horse-breaker	528	.	78	.	58	.	25	.	61	.	79	.
Veterinary Surgeon, Farrier	101	.	26	.	22	.	3	.	7	.	10	.
Cattle, Sheep, Pig—Dealer, Salesman	24	1	3	.	3	.	9	.	4	.	17	.
Drover	12	.	2	.	2	.	1	.	.	.	8	.
Gamekeeper	2	.	1	.	.	.	3	.	2	.	3	.
Dog, Bird, Animal—Keeper, Dealer	14	6	.	.	1	.	1	.	4	.	3	.
Vermin destroyer	5	.	.	.	.	.	.	.	.	.	1	.
Fisherman	3	.	.	.	.	.	7	.	.	.	7	.
Knacker, Catsmeat Dealer, &c., &c.	2	.	.	.	.	.	.	.	1	.	.	.
V. INDUSTRIAL CLASS.												
9. PERSONS WORKING AND DEALING IN BOOKS, PRINTS, AND MAPS.												
1. *Books.*												
Publisher, Bookseller, Librarian	140	44	19	6	24	4	11	2	13	2	29	8
Music—Publisher, Seller, Printer	22	3	1	.	4	.	2	.	4	3	3	.
Bookbinder	176	288	12	18	14	13	13	2	19	1	17	11
Printer	1376	160	174	2	121	12	63	2	100	3	198	2
Newspaper Agent, News Room Keeper	101	53	20	14	19	4	13	1	25	9	21	5
Others	.	.	.	.	.	.	.	.	.	.	.	.
2. *Prints and Maps.*												
Lithographer, Lithographic Printer	290	21	2	1	9	3	1	.	5	.	23	1
Copper Plate and Steel Plate Printer	8	1	.	.	.	.	.	.	1	.	.	.
Map and Print—Colourer, Seller	1	4	.	.	.	.	.	.	.	.	1	.
10. PERSONS WORKING AND DEALING IN MACHINES AND IMPLEMENTS.												
1. *Machines.*												
Engine, Machine, Maker	823	18	767	4	362	1	114	.	205	2	216	1
Millwright	140	.	124	.	58	.	16	.	51	.	61	.
Fitter, Turner (Engine and Machine)	1513	.	771	.	649	.	112	.	260	.	352	.
Boiler Maker	516	.	57	.	80	.	45	.	71	.	139	.
Spinning and Weaving Machine Maker	869	79	861	111	409	.	371	.	350	2	526	4
Agricultural Machine and Implement Maker	16	1	1	.	1	.	.	.	.	.	3	.
Domestic Machinery—Maker, Dealer	17	.	4	.	2	.	1	.	2	.	.	.
2. *Tools and Implements.*												
Tool Maker, Dealer	101	1	56	.	4	.	3	.	3	.	4	.
Cutler, Scissors Maker	56	2	5	2	3	.	2	.	5	.	7	.
File Maker	135	10	60	2	16	.	10	.	4	.	13	.
Saw Maker	29	.	5	.	3	.	2	.	2	.	7	.
Pin Maker	.	.	.	.	.	.	.	.	.	.	.	.
Needle Maker	2	.	1	.	.	.	.	.	.	.	.	.
Steel Pen Maker	.	1	.	.	.	.	.	.	.	.	.	.
Pencil Maker (Wood)	.	.	.	.	.	.	.	.	.	.	.	.
Domestic Implement Maker	1	2	.	.	.	.	.	.	1	.	1	.
3. *Watches and Philosophical Instruments.*												
Watch Maker, Clock Maker	273	6	64	3	51	1	34	1	54	1	67	.
Philosophical Instrument Maker, Optician	34	1	1	.	1	.	.	.	1	.	1	1
Electrical Apparatus Maker	58	.	.	.	1	.	1	.	5	.	16	.
Weighing and Measuring Apparatus Maker	48	1	74	.	6	.	2	1	3	.	3	.

* Only *male* relations living with the farmer or grazier, and, therefore, presumably engaged in agriculture, are included above.

Table 10 *continued*.—Occupations of Males and Females in the North-Western Division and its Registration Counties, and in each Urban Sanitary District of which the Population exceeds 50,000 Persons.

Occupations.	Urban Sanitary Districts.											
	Manchester.		Oldham.		Rochdale.		Burnley.		Blackburn.		Preston.	
	Males.	Females.	Males.	Females.	Males.	Females.	Males.	Females.	Males.	Females.	Males.	Females.
4. Surgical Instruments.												
Surgical Instrument Maker	7	2	.	.	.	.	1	.	.	.	1	.
5. Arms and Ordnance.												
Gunsmith, Gun Manufacturer	29	.	.	.	.	.	.	.	2	.	8	.
Ordnance Manufacturer	.	.	.	.	.	.	.	.	.	.	.	.
Sword, Bayonet—Maker, Cutler	.	.	.	.	.	.	.	.	.	.	.	.
Others	.	.	.	.	.	.	.	.	.	.	.	.
6. Musical Instruments.												
Musical Instrument Maker, Dealer	158	3	8	.	12	.	6	.	8	.	10	.
7. Type, Dies, Medals, Coins.												
Type Cutter, Founder	12	.	1	.	.	.	1	.	.	.	.	.
Die, Seal, Coin, Medal, Maker	39	.	.	.	1	.	.	.	.	.	.	.
8. Tackle for Sports and Games.												
Toy Maker, Dealer	53	40	.	.	1	.	.	.	1	4	1	7
Fishing Rod, Tackle, Maker, Dealer	4	.	1	.	.	.	.	.	3	.	1	.
Apparatus for other Games, Maker, Dealer	20	5	.	.	3	1	2	.	.	.	.	.
11. Persons working and dealing in Houses, Furniture, and Decorations.												
1. Houses.												
Builder	228	1	54	.	30	.	22	.	77	.	39	.
Carpenter, Joiner	3597	12	739	2	491	.	396	.	776	2	300	1
Bricklayer	1280	2	289	.	159	1	54	.	260	1	340	1
Mason	909	.	296	.	208	1	455	.	609	1	275	.
Slater, Tiler	295	.	71	.	48	.	24	.	130	.	116	1
Plasterer, Whitewasher	410	2	132	.	91	1	67	.	148	.	249	.
Paperhanger	116	2	3	.	5	.	1	.	4	1	5	.
Plumber	1017	9	133	2	109	.	84	1	143	1	189	.
Painter, Glazier	2114	13	328	2	314	1	187	.	313	.	421	.
2. Furniture and Fittings.												
Cabinet Maker, Upholsterer	1336	295	68	3	129	13	102	4	233	13	220	30
French Polisher	277	101	31	18	20	2	12	1	24	4	21	3
Furniture Broker, Dealer	157	81	23	6	18	4	13	1	25	3	40	10
Locksmith, Bellhanger	40	.	3	.	2	.	2	.	1	.	5	.
Gas Fitter	86	.	31	.	19	.	12	.	7	.	27	.
House and Shop Fittings—Maker, Dealer	87	12	6	.	1	3	.	.	6	.	4	.
Funeral Furniture Maker, Undertaker	65	18	14	1	9	1	.	.	3	.	5	.
Others	.	1	.	.	.	.	.	.	.	.	.	.
3. House Decorations.												
Wood Carver	105	.	2	.	5	.	4	.	7	.	4	.
Carver, Gilder	281	17	4	.	12	1	8	1	23	1	56	2
Dealer in Works of Art	87	2	.	1	.	.	1	.	7	.	3	.
Figure, Image—Maker, Dealer	8	.	.	.	1	.	.	.	.	.	.	.
Animal, Bird, &c., Preserver, Naturalist	9	.	2	.	.	.	.	.	2	.	1	.
Artificial Flower Maker	22	140	1	1	2	2	.	1	3	1	.	.
12. Persons working and dealing in Carriages and Harness.												
1. Carriages.												
Coachmaker	536	4	40	1	87	.	44	.	38	.	114	.
Railway Carriage, Railway Wagon, Maker	68	1	1	.	.	.	4	.	2	.	4	.
Wheelwright	277	1	70	.	61	.	47	.	68	.	73	.
Bicycle, Tricycle—Maker, Dealer	8	1	.	.	.	.	.	.	.	.	.	.
Others	35	4	2	.	2	1	1	.	.	.	4	.
2. Harness.												
Saddler, Harness, Whip, Maker	230	13	40	.	34	.	19	.	38	.	53	.
13. Persons working and dealing in Ships and Boats.												
1. Hull.												
Ship, Boat, Barge, Builder	20	.	6	.	2	.	19	.	4	.	29	.
Shipwright, Ship Carpenter (ashore)	22	.	.	.	1	.	3	.	3	.	30	.
2. Masts, Rigging, &c.												
Mast, Yard, Oar, Block, Maker	3	.	.	.	.	.	.	.	.	.	.	.
Ship Rigger, Chandler, Fitter	1	.	.	.	.	.	.	.	.	.	.	.
Sail Maker	5	.	.	.	.	.	.	.	.	.	6	.

Table 10 *continued.*—OCCUPATIONS of MALES and FEMALES in the NORTH-WESTERN DIVISION and its REGISTRATION COUNTIES, and in each URBAN SANITARY DISTRICT of which the POPULATION exceeds 50,000 PERSONS.

OCCUPATIONS.	URBAN SANITARY DISTRICTS.											
	MANCHESTER.		OLDHAM.		ROCHDALE.		BURNLEY.		BLACKBURN.		PRESTON.	
	Males.	Females.	Males.	Females.	Males.	Females.	Males.	Females.	Males.	Females.	Males.	Females.
14. PERSONS WORKING AND DEALING IN CHEMICALS AND COMPOUNDS.												
1. *Colouring Matter.*												
Dye, Paint, Manufacture	28	.	1	.	1	.	1	.	1	.	.	.
Ink, Blacking, Colouring Substance, Manufacture	68	30	.	.	.	.	.	.	3	.	1	.
2. *Explosives.*												
Gunpowder, Guncotton, Explosive Substance, Manufacture	1	.	.	.	.	.	.	.	.	.	.	.
Fusee, Fireworks, Explosive Article, Manufacture	8	18	.	.	.	.	.	.	.	.	.	.
3. *Drugs and other Chemicals and Compounds.*												
Chemist, Druggist	305	21	68	6	42	.	38	2	67	3	96	1
Manufacturing Chemist	155	12	6	3	7	1	1	.	25	.	4	.
Alkali Manufacture	3	.	1	.	.	.	.	2	.	.	.	.
Drysalter	61	21	4	.	11	1	7	.	6	.	11	.
15. PERSONS WORKING AND DEALING IN TOBACCO AND PIPES.												
1. *Tobacco and Pipes.*												
Tobacco Manufacturer, Tobacconist	216	340	13	3	20	3	15	3	23	12	49	35
Tobacco Pipe, Snuff Box, &c., Maker	36	61	3	1	3	4	.	.	3	3	3	1
16. PERSONS WORKING AND DEALING IN FOOD AND LODGING.												
1. *Board and Lodging.*												
Innkeeper, Hotel Keeper, Publican	531	143	211	31	125	31	67	20	210	60	220	50
Lodging, Boarding House, Keeper	84	664	6	46	3	21	7	60	6	121	7	160
Coffee, Eating House, Keeper	108	59	17	14	19	13	12	1	13	5	11	6
2. *Spirituous Drinks.*												
Hop—Merchant, Dealer	1	.	.	.	.	.	.	.	.	.	1	.
Maltster	1	.	.	.	9	.	3	.	5	.	42	.
Brewer	246	9	60	2	34	3	36	.	112	2	125	1
Beerseller. Ale, Porter, Cider, Dealer	701	239	93	25	97	25	51	14	116	36	128	26
Cellarman	125	.	6	1	6	.	7	.	12	.	9	.
Wine, Spirit—Merchant, Agent	88	2	12	2	16	.	11	.	12	.	13	1
3. *Food.*												
Milkseller, Dairyman	351	100	21	.	.	1	1	.	3	1	37	7
Cheesemonger, Butterman	17	3	.	.	.	.	.	.	.	.	6	1
Butcher, Meat Salesman	1047	84	277	26	220	17	164	9	240	21	311	28
Provision Curer, Dealer	595	506	74	16	61	20	11	3	80	26	236	223
Poulterer, Game Dealer	70	32	5	2	5	1	2	.	4	1	14	2
Fishmonger	313	76	54	12	35	5	27	1	115	10	90	7
Corn, Flour, Seed—Merchant, Dealer	80	7	5	2	24	1	5	.	14	.	44	3
Corn Miller	99	1	25	1	109	4	40	1	140	.	61	1
Baker	908	103	50	27	60	19	84	15	113	22	443	37
Confectioner, Pastrycook	318	334	58	116	33	126	40	37	82	180	67	127
Greengrocer, Fruiterer	541	218	106	21	58	29	55	4	86	34	80	35
Mustard, Vinegar, Spice, Pickle—Maker, Dealer	7	22	1	.	1	.	1	.	3	.	1	.
Sugar Refiner	28	6	1	.	2	.	1	.	.	.	3	.
Grocer, Tea, Coffee, Chocolate—Maker, Dealer	1093	171	511	139	350	97	371	116	586	184	377	84
Ginger Beer, Mineral Water—Manufacturer, Dealer	148	7	19	.	20	2	9	.	30	3	23	2
Others dealing in Food	.	.	.	.	.	.	.	.	.	.	.	.
17. PERSONS WORKING AND DEALING IN TEXTILE FABRICS.												
1. *Wool and Worsted.*												
Woolstapler	3	.	.	.	44	.	.	.	.	.	3	.
Woollen Cloth Manufacture	52	28	9	11	1802	2245	3	5	4	8	1	2
Wool, Woollen goods—Dyer, Printer	18	3	.	.	46	.	1	.	.	.	.	.
Worsted, Stuff, Manufacture	36	110	1	2	13	13	3	4	.	5	5	29
Flannel Manufacture	2	.	.	.	68	14	.	.	1	.	.	.
Blanket Manufacture	2	3	.	.	.	.	.	.	.	.	.	.
Fuller	.	.	.	.	180	.	1	.	.	.	.	.
Cloth, Worsted, Stuff, Flannel, Blanket, Dealer	62	.	3	1	40	2	6	.	10	.	5	.
Others	.	.	.	.	.	.	.	.	.	.	.	.
2. *Silk.*												
Silk, Silk goods, Manufacture	391	950	34	70	533	347	.	2	4	4	4	5
Silk Dyer, Printer	77	4	.	.	25	.	2	1	1	.	.	.
Ribbon Manufacture	9	1	.	.	.	.	.	.	.	.	.	.
Crape, Gauze, Manufacture	.	1	.	.	.	1	.	.	.	.	.	.
Silk Merchant, Dealer	39	4	11	.	2	.	1	.	2	.	.	.

Table 10 *continued*.—Occupations of Males and Females in the North-western Division and its Registration Counties, and in each Urban Sanitary District of which the Population exceeds 50,000 Persons.

Occupations.	Urban Sanitary Districts.											
	Manchester.		Oldham.		Rochdale.		Burnley.		Blackburn.		Preston.	
	Males.	Females.	Males.	Females.	Males.	Females.	Males.	Females.	Males.	Females.	Males.	Females.
3. Cotton and Flax												
Cotton, Cotton goods, Manufacture	4136	12544	12583	16366	5042	8039	7787	9023	14458	20274	9023	16886
Cotton, Calico—Printer, Dyer, Bleacher	2027	260	11	2	61	6	48	7	28	1	12	3
Cotton, Calico—Warehouseman, Dealer	277	146	121	2	108	4	25	1	20	5	7	.
Flax, Linen—Manufacturer, Dealer	46	79	2	1	1	.	20	24	1	.	14	280
Lace Manufacturer, Dealer	23	29	.	6	.	1	.	1	.	1	.	2
Fustian Manufacturer, Dealer	403	410	12	60	17	24	.	.	1	1	1	.
Tape Manufacturer, Dealer	9	56	1	.	.	1	33	.	92	1	49	.
Thread Manufacturer, Dealer	32	109	1	.	.	.	.	.	.	.	.	.
4. Hemp and other Fibrous Materials.												
Hemp, Jute, Cocoa Fibre, Manufacture	18	7	.	.	.	3	3	1	.	.	.	.
Rope, Twine, Cord—Maker, Dealer	129	36	52	5	60	2	23	2	78	1	75	2
Mat Maker, Seller	26	19	.	.	1	.	1	.	.	.	2	.
Net Maker	4	14	.	.	.	.	.	.	.	.	1	.
Canvas, Sailcloth, Manufacture	3	2	.	.	.	.	.	.	.	.	2	.
Sacking, Sack, Bag—Maker, Dealer	4	48	1	1	1	2	.	.	.	.	.	.
Others working and dealing in Hemp	14	6	.	.	.	.	.	1	1	1	.	2
5. Mixed or Unspecified Materials.												
Weaver (undefined)	57	104	.	.	16	83	.	.	.	104	.	188
Dyer, Printer, Scourer, Bleacher, Calenderer (undefined)	631	46	10	9	62	6	9	2	2	1	7	2
Factory hand (Textile, undefined)	457	613	1	5	166	269	7	.	3	26	9	103
Felt Manufacture	1	.	.	.	.	.	.	.	.	.	.	.
Carpet, Rug, Manufacture	47	35	1	1	203	196	5	.	4	.	3	1
Manchester Warehouseman	284	1	.	.	.	.	.	.	.	.	1	.
Draper, Linen Draper, Mercer	656	609	150	93	168	83	103	52	266	81	262	151
Fancy Goods (Textile), Manufacturer, Worker, Dealer	53	401	2	5	.	18	2	8	.	10	.	11
Trimming Maker, Dealer	52	738	.	.	.	.	.	.	.	.	.	.
Embroiderer	5	237	.	.	.	2	.	1	.	1	.	1
Others	1	2	.	.	.	.	.	.	.	.	.	4
18. Persons working and dealing in Dress.												
1. Dress.												
Hatter, Hat Manufacture (not straw)	207	415	34	53	21	5	9	1	20	4	34	6
Straw—Hat, Bonnet, Plait, Manufacture	8	33	1	7	.	4	.	1	1	1	.	2
Tailor	2816	1767	310	141	310	53	239	47	442	64	526	66
Milliner, Dressmaker, Staymaker	119	5781	4	966	.	722	4	534	5	949	4	1169
Shawl Manufacture	2	1	.	1	.	1	.	.	.	.	.	.
Shirt Maker, Seamstress	53	4153	1	119	4	60	3	82	1	75	3	202
Hosiery Manufacture	6	3	.	1	4	26	3	18	5	20	.	20
Hosier, Haberdasher	83	66	10	8	12	8	7	1	6	2	26	11
Glover, Glove Maker	4	7	1	1	.	.	.	.	.	.	1	.
Button Maker, Dealer	62	69	.	.	.	.	.	.	.	.	.	.
Shoe, Boot—Maker, Dealer	2138	337	282	18	181	14	157	15	312	27	406	43
Patten, Clog, Maker	297	3	190	2	195	.	122	.	208	3	191	.
Wig Maker, Hairdresser	356	16	62	2	36	2	34	2	77	1	83	.
Umbrella, Parasol, Stick—Maker, Dealer	322	606	6	2	8	3	7	.	4	4	13	.
Accoutrement Maker	.	.	.	.	.	.	.	.	.	.	.	4
Old Clothes Dealer, and others	28	45	1	4	5	17	1	1	6	8	6	16
19. Persons working and dealing in various Animal Substances.												
1. In Grease, Gut, Bone, Horn, Ivory, and Whalebone.												
Tallow Chandler, Candle, Grease, Manufacture	31	1	10	.	9	.	6	.	18	1	12	.
Soap Boiler, Maker	26	2	2	.	3	.	1	1	3	.	6	.
Glue, Size, Gelatine, Isinglass—Maker, Dealer	6	1	.	.	3	.	1	.	.	.	2	.
Manure Manufacture	5	.	.	.	3	.	.	.	3	.	.	.
Bone, Horn, Ivory, Tortoise-shell—Worker, Dealer	45	.	.	.	.	.	.	.	.	.	.	.
Comb Maker	2	1	.	.	2	.	1	.	.	.	.	.
Others	6	1	.	.	6	.	.	.	1	.	1	.
2. In Skins.												
Furrier, Skinner	37	66	.	1	3	1	1	.	2	.	2	.
Tanner, Fellmonger	70	.	.	.	24	.	14	.	8	.	24	.
Currier	122	6	29	.	50	3	23	4	30	1	48	.
Leather Goods, Portmanteau, Bag, Strap, &c.—Maker, Dealer	116	27	16	1	13	1	2	.	6	.	8	.
Parchment, Vellum—Maker, Dealer	.	.	.	.	.	.	.	.	.	.	.	.
3. In Hair and Feathers.												
Hair, Bristle—Worker, Dealer	18	19										
Brush, Broom, Maker	317	115	69	28	18	4	51	.	92	8	76	14
Quill, Feather—Dresser, Dealer	15	97	.	1	1	2	.	.	.	3	1	.

Table 10 *continued.*—OCCUPATIONS of MALES and FEMALES in the NORTH-WESTERN DIVISION and its REGISTRATION COUNTIES, and in each URBAN SANITARY DISTRICT of which the POPULATION exceeds 50,000 PERSONS.

OCCUPATIONS.	URBAN SANITARY DISTRICTS.											
	MANCHESTER.		OLDHAM.		ROCHDALE.		BURNLEY.		BLACKBURN.		PRESTON.	
	Males.	Females.	Males.	Females.	Males.	Females.	Males.	Females.	Males.	Females.	Males.	Females.
20. PERSONS WORKING AND DEALING IN VARIOUS VEGETABLE SUBSTANCES.												
1. *In Oils, Gums, and Resins.*												
Oil Miller, Oil Cake—Maker, Dealer	55	8	4	.	2	.	6	.	8	.	9	2
Oil and Colourman	15	3	1	.	1	.	.	.	.	.	1	2
Floor Cloth, Oil Cloth, Manufacture	38	.	.	.	.	.	.	.	.	.	1	.
Japanner	23	27	11	4	.	.	.	.	.	.	.	.
India Rubber, Gutta Percha—Worker, Dealer	276	176	5	.	1	.	1	.	10	.	2	1
Waterproof Goods—Maker, Dealer	189	68	3	.	1	.	1	.	3	.	1	.
Others	1	1	.	.	.	.	.	.	.	.	1	.
2. *In Cane, Rush, and Straw.*												
Willow, Cane, Rush—Worker, Dealer, Basketmaker	122	32	128	2	26	9	13	.	9	4	88	9
Hay, Straw (not plait), Chaff—Cutter, Dealer	23	1	9	.	1	.	4	.	12	.	12	.
Thatcher	.	.	.	.	.	.	.	.	.	.	.	.
3. *In Wood and Bark.*												
Timber, Wood—Merchant, Dealer	170	14	16	.	14	1	6	.	12	.	18	.
Sawyer	362	.	72	.	44	.	43	.	65	.	107	.
Lath, Wooden Fence, Hurdle, Maker	66	1	6	.	6	.	2	.	5	.	4	.
Wood Turner, Box Maker	313	62	164	3	46	1	14	.	71	.	134	2
Cooper, Hoop Maker, Bender	284	3	15	.	14	.	14	.	34	.	46	.
Cork, Bark—Cutter, Worker, Dealer	48	6	3	1	.	.	1	.	28	.	9	.
Others	6	.	.	.	.	.	.	.	.	.	.	.
4. *In Paper.*												
Paper Manufacture	103	187	15	1	15	8	46	16	70	26	6	1
Envelope Maker	.	23	.	.	.	.	.	.	.	.	.	.
Stationer, Law Stationer	181	160	18	11	8	3	5	1	20	9	17	.
Card, Pattern Card, Maker	302	40	.	.	8	.	.	.	.	.	.	19
Paper Stainer	20	20	.	.	.	.	.	.	30	.	.	.
Paper Box, Paper Bag, Maker	30	436	1	17	1	1	6	14	1	85	.	1
Ticket, Label, Writer	30	68	.	.	.	.	.	.	3	.	.	.
Others	50	4	8	.	9	.	6	.	8	1	5	.
21. PERSONS WORKING AND DEALING IN VARIOUS MINERAL SUBSTANCES.												
1. *Miners.*												
Coal Miner	212	7	966	.	220	1	1550	4	158	1	26	.
Ironstone Miner	1	.	3	.	.	.	.	.	.	.	.	.
Copper Miner	.	.	.	.	.	.	4	.	.	.	1	.
Tin Miner	.	.	.	.	.	.	.	.	.	.	.	.
Lead Miner	.	.	1	.	.	.	3	.	.	.	.	.
Miner in other, or undefined, Minerals	3	.	.	.	2	.	.	.	1	.	.	.
Mine Service	4	.	13	.	5	.	14	.	.	.	3	.
2. *Coal, Coal Gas, &c.*												
Coal Merchant, Dealer	312	27	108	3	65	.	32	.	126	1	121	8
Coalheaver	149	.	17	.	5	.	15	.	65	.	48	.
Coke, Charcoal, Peat—Cutter, Burner, Dealer	2	.	2	.	2	.	100	1	1	.	.	.
Gas Works Service	581	.	107	.	67	.	50	.	75	.	111	.
3. *Stone, Clay, and Road Making.*												
Stone Quarrier	12	.	15	.	23	.	45	.	113	.	10	.
Stone Cutter, Dresser, Dealer	41	.	5	.	9	.	13	.	15	.	14	.
Slate Quarrier	.	.	.	.	.	.	.	.	.	.	.	.
Slate Worker, Dealer	6	.	1	.	1	.	.	.	3	.	1	.
Limeburner	4	.	2	.	.	.	.	.	1	.	4	.
Clay, Sand, Gravel, Chalk—Labourer, Dealer	16	1	5	.	4	.	2	.	4	.	2	.
Fossil, Coprolite—Digger, Dealer	.	.	.	.	.	.	.	.	.	.	.	.
Well Sinker, Borer	9	.	3	.	3	.	2	.	.	.	.	.
Plaster, Cement, Manufacture	7	.	.	.	1	.	2	.	2	.	1	1
Brick, Tile—Maker, Burner, Dealer	585	5	254	.	76	.	115	.	191	1	273	.
Paviour	236	.	41	.	23	.	14	.	33	.	58	.
Road Contractor, Surveyor, Inspector	8	.	5	.	.	.	3	.	1	.	1	.
Road Labourer	110	.	12	.	11	.	21	.	43	.	11	.
Railway Contractor	3	.	.	.	.	.	.	.	2	.	6	.
Platelayer	73	.	16	.	18	.	14	.	30	.	42	.
Railway Labourer, Navvy	335	.	77	.	31	.	29	.	81	.	125	.
Others	19	7	.	.	3	2	.	1	2	.	.	.
4. *Earthenware and Glass.*												
Earthenware, China, Porcelain, Manufacture	34	7	3	.	4	.	7	.	5	1	8	3
Glass Manufacture	811	61	1	.	.	.	.	.	1	.	1	.
Earthenware, China, Glass, Dealer	111	78	19	5	12	6	10	2	15	5	34	13
5. *Salt.*												
Salt Maker, Dealer	5	2	2	1	.	.	1	.	3	.	7	.

Table 10 *continued*.—OCCUPATIONS of MALES and FEMALES in the NORTH-WESTERN DIVISION and its REGISTRATION COUNTIES, and in each URBAN SANITARY DISTRICT of which the POPULATION exceeds 50,000 PERSONS.

OCCUPATIONS.	URBAN SANITARY DISTRICTS.											
	MANCHESTER.		OLDHAM.		ROCHDALE.		BURNLEY.		BLACKBURN.		PRESTON.	
	Males.	Females.	Males.	Females.	Males.	Females.	Males.	Females.	Males.	Females.	Males.	Females.
6. *Water.*												
Waterworks Service	40	.	2	.	5	.	4	.	11	.	8	.
Others	2	.	.	.	.	.	.	.	.	.	.	.
7. *Precious Metals and Jewellery.*												
Goldsmith, Silversmith, Jeweller	168	12	11	2	13	.	6	.	8	2	15	.
Gold, Silver, Beater	18	.	.	.	.	.	.	.	.	.	.	.
Lapidary	1	1	.	.	.	.	.	.	.	.	.	.
Others	3	17	.	.	.	.	.	.	1	.	17	123
8. *Iron and Steel.*												
Blacksmith	1147	3	336	.	254	1	259	.	361	.	327	.
Whitesmith	106	1	17	.	14	.	4	.	19	.	27	.
Nail Manufacture	39	6	17	1	9	.	3	.	6	.	23	.
Anchor, Chain, Manufacture	18	.	8	.	3	.	3	.	.	.	.	.
Other Iron and Steel Manufactures	4268	12	3594	6	1075	4	533	.	1087	.	880	.
Ironmonger, Hardware Dealer, Merchant	197	35	41	8	39	3	28	.	57	3	56	1
9. *Copper.*												
Copper, Copper goods—Manufacturer, Worker, Dealer	129	.	1	.	4	.	.	.	8	.	3	.
10. *Tin and Zinc.*												
Tin, Tin Plate, Tin goods—Manufacturer, Worker, Dealer	581	10	213	1	80	1	57	1	113	1	154	.
Zinc, Zinc Goods—Manufacturer, Worker, Dealer	6	.	.	.	.	.	.	.	.	.	.	.
11. *Lead.*												
Lead, Leaden goods—Manufacturer, Worker, Dealer	23	.	2	.	.	.	.	.	1	.	.	.
12. *In Other, Mixed, or Unspecified, Metals.*												
Metal Refiner, Worker, Turner, Dealer	64	4	10	.	2	.	1	.	.	.	1	.
Brass, Bronze, Manufacture. Brazier	438	9	162	.	45	1	15	.	45	.	35	.
Metal Burnisher, Lacquerer	3	16	1	.	.	.	.	.	.	.	.	.
White Metal, Plated Ware, Manufacture, Pewterer	15	1	5	.	.	.	.	.	.	.	.	.
Wire Maker, Worker, Weaver, Drawer	297	36	7	1	12	.	.	.	15	.	43	3
Bolt, Nut, Rivet, Screw, Staple, Maker	206	1	177	1	19	.	44	.	38	1	60	.
Lamp, Lantern, Candlestick, Maker	6	.	.	.	.	.	.	.	.	.	.	.
Clasp, Buckle, Hinge, Maker	.	.	.	.	.	.	.	.	.	.	.	.
Fancy Chain, Gilt Toy, Maker	2	.	.	.	.	.	.	.	.	.	.	.
Others	27	2	.	.	6	.	.	.	.	.	1	.
22. PERSONS WORKING AND DEALING IN GENERAL OR UNSPECIFIED COMMODITIES.												
1. *Makers and Dealers (General or Undefined).*												
General Shopkeeper, Dealer	389	732	88	115	57	50	30	29	71	48	110	169
Pawnbroker	244	69	57	8	13	12	11	6	41	3	73	5
Costermonger, Huckster, Street Seller	1088	905	87	48	119	89	115	44	213	74	166	80
Manufacturer, Manager, Superintendent (undefined)	128	29	21	1	16	.	3	.	10	.	5	1
Contractor (undefined)	48	.	18	.	11	.	8	.	8	.	12	.
2. *Mechanics and Labourers (General or Undefined).*												
General Labourer	6360	25	1948	9	776	.	858	5	1730	.	1763	3
Engine Driver, Stoker, Fireman (not railway, marine, nor agricultural)	721	.	495	.	219	.	199	.	291	.	288	.
Artizan, Mechanic (undefined)	1286	98	322	7	63	.	17	.	53	.	46	10
Apprentice (undefined)	167	19	20	4	7	1	7	.	7	.	16	.
Factory Labourer (undefined)	1055	87	24	.	25	1	5	1	18	3	19	.
Machinist, Machine Worker (undefined)	168	17	28	.	26	13	10	14	8	44	7	46
23. PERSONS WORKING AND DEALING IN REFUSE MATTERS.												
1. *Refuse Matters.*												
Town Drainage Service	42	.	13	.	12	.	4	.	29	.	23	.
Chimney Sweep, Soot Merchant	75	.	17	.	24	.	11	.	15	.	14	.
Scavenger, Crossing Sweeper	269	.	39	.	26	1	37	.	18	.	17	.
Rag Gatherer, Dealer	47	152	2	7	11	7	2	.	13	4	21	6
VI. UNOCCUPIED CLASS.												
24. PERSONS WITHOUT SPECIFIED OCCUPATIONS												
Persons returned by Property, Rank, &c., and not by special occupation	35184	95131	10437	28427	6228	16914	5484	13391	9431	21248	9882	21355
Children under 5 years of age	22681	23241	7486	7351	4196	4258	4139	4308	7383	7225	6865	6550

Table 11.—BIRTH-PLACES of MALES and FEMALES enumerated in COUNTIES, and in each URBAN SANITARY DISTRICT of which the POPULATION EXCEEDS 50,000 PERSONS.

WHERE BORN.	WHERE ENUMERATED.											
	NORTH-WESTERN COUNTIES.		COUNTIES.* CHESHIRE.		COUNTIES.* LANCASHIRE.		URBAN SANITARY DISTRICTS. STOCKPORT.		URBAN SANITARY DISTRICTS. BIRKENHEAD.		URBAN SANITARY DISTRICTS. LIVERPOOL.	
	Males.	Females.	Males.	Females.	Males.	Females.	Males.	Females.	Males.	Females.	Males.	Females.
TOTAL OF INHABITANTS	1981052	2117426	311188	332849	1669864	1784377	27567	31986	41174	42832	271996	280512
LONDON	15527	16809	2445	2718	13082	14091	200	211	595	611	3634	3664
MIDDLESEX (*Intra-metropolitan*)	12871	14884	1994	2233	10877	11861	168	173	477	473	3152	3246
SURREY (*Intra-metropolitan*)	1740	1804	295	321	1445	1378	25	31	99	76	320	260
KENT (*Intra-metropolitan*)	916	1031	156	164	760	867	9	7	49	56	162	158
SOUTH-EASTERN COUNTIES	8934	9737	1704	1783	7230	7934	89	125	439	414	1737	1695
SURREY (*Extra-metropolitan*)	1122	1139	253	257	869	882	7	15	52	40	158	178
KENT (*Extra-metropolitan*)	2687	3047	458	516	2179	2531	36	43	125	16	337	541
SUSSEX	1191	1224	231	211	960	1013	12	12	58	41	244	225
HAMPSHIRE	3016	3328	568	622	2448	2704	20	36	182	217	634	611
BERKSHIRE	968	1061	194	177	774	824	14	19	32	28	157	140
SOUTH-MIDLAND COUNTIES	12630	12600	2367	2377	10263	10223	121	131	254	257	1257	1188
MIDDLESEX (*Ex.-metropolitan*)	954	921	140	156	814	765	9	8	31	46	186	160
HERTFORDSHIRE	744	788	150	185	594	603	13	15	16	18	91	101
BUCKINGHAMSHIRE	2040	1828	786	657	1254	1171	23	16	27	14	144	145
OXFORDSHIRE	1525	1507	257	262	1268	1245	8	9	37	44	179	150
NORTHAMPTONSHIRE	2655	2742	522	552	2133	2190	27	26	65	63	308	279
HUNTINGDONSHIRE	890	906	100	115	790	791	9	19	14	12	65	69
BEDFORDSHIRE	1107	1061	211	195	896	866	14	18	25	14	110	136
CAMBRIDGESHIRE	2715	2847	201	255	2514	2592	17	29	30	52	178	157
EASTERN COUNTIES	7991	8233	1041	1114	6950	7119	69	66	209	188	941	914
ESSEX	1753	1780	305	313	1448	1467	11	17	33	62	260	274
SUFFOLK	2471	2507	297	321	2174	2186	23	22	45	45	245	250
NORFOLK	3767	3946	439	480	3328	3466	35	27	101	81	436	390
SOUTH-WESTERN COUNTIES	16326	17670	2278	2479	14048	15191	135	160	718	739	3160	3407
WILTSHIRE	1463	1487	256	280	1207	1207	24	20	50	52	224	203
DORSETSHIRE	1665	1658	266	298	1399	1360	17	24	59	61	228	231
DEVONSHIRE	5074	5310	808	826	4266	4484	31	29	353	301	1380	1456
CORNWALL	4681	5378	415	478	4266	4900	25	57	127	151	609	736
SOMERSETSHIRE	3508	3837	538	597	2970	3240	38	31	149	174	719	781
WEST-MIDLAND COUNTIES	57223	71361	14209	18182	43014	53179	714	1048	1678	1968	7470	8063
GLOUCESTERSHIRE	5332	5768	836	952	4496	4816	66	68	192	299	1099	1160
HEREFORDSHIRE	1831	2350	383	476	1448	1874	13	27	71	85	392	395
SHROPSHIRE	12830	19625	3971	5317	8859	14308	108	234	644	790	2146	2485
STAFFORDSHIRE	24388	29477	6917	9005	17471	20472	352	515	415	504	1956	2086
WORCESTERSHIRE	4532	5101	745	910	3787	4191	37	78	117	147	555	551
WARWICKSHIRE	8330	9140	1377	1522	6953	7618	121	126	239	229	1412	1476
NORTH-MIDLAND COUNTIES	29001	32901	6468	7772	22533	25129	749	910	394	418	2430	2189
LEICESTERSHIRE	2976	2974	528	486	2448	2488	66	56	73	63	408	353
RUTLANDSHIRE	231	240	30	36	191	204	3	3	3	7	29	24
LINCOLNSHIRE	5795	6744	723	854	5043	5890	77	73	28	111	585	591
NOTTINGHAMSHIRE	4686	4993	627	729	4059	4264	76	101	75	88	820	337
DERBYSHIRE	15382	17950	4560	5607	10792	12283	528	675	150	149	788	704
NORTH-WESTERN COUNTIES	1540280	1638169	247193	258701	1293087	1379468	23020	26039	26548	27898	175674	186560
CHESHIRE	266696	278337	213190	219129	53506	59208	17120	19319	20598	21012	7953	8289
LANCASHIRE	1273584	1359832	34003	39572	1239581	1320260	5900	6720	5950	6886	167721	178271
YORKSHIRE	59434	64799	5119	6187	54315	58612	479	605	723	643	4575	4134
NORTHERN COUNTIES	24177	28714	1935	2398	22242	26316	133	142	716	791	4499	5069
DURHAM	4308	4696	391	476	3917	4220	36	30	115	130	558	549
NORTHUMBERLAND	2628	2806	316	341	2312	2465	21	18	105	86	505	456
CUMBERLAND	10335	13142	942	1196	9393	11946	54	68	423	488	2625	3336
WESTMORLAND	6906	8070	286	385	6620	7685	22	26	73	87	811	729
MONMOUTHSHIRE AND WALES	29991	41777	6972	10499	23019	31278	131	233	2174	2697	10123	11440
MONMOUTHSHIRE	1241	1533	170	208	1071	1325	16	14	49	40	231	255
GLAMORGANSHIRE	1299	1640	185	257	1114	1383	9	9	61	92	367	393
CARMARTHENSHIRE	358	329	78	80	280	249	3	3	23	28	113	93
PEMBROKESHIRE	881	947	150	169	731	778	5	6	74	63	325	320
CARDIGANSHIRE	638	643	102	107	536	536	4	3	41	28	238	240
BRECKNOCKSHIRE	238	304	31	45	207	259	3	1	8	7	58	56
RADNORSHIRE	220	384	48	73	172	311	3	7	3	8	33	47
MONTGOMERYSHIRE	1865	2943	466	753	1399	2190	13	22	148	202	562	718
FLINTSHIRE	6628	9247	2245	3502	4383	5745	27	29	522	629	1676	1827
DENBIGHSHIRE	6171	8823	1737	2849	4434	5974	20	57	421	545	1879	1867
MERIONETHSHIRE	926	1324	224	314	702	1010	1	7	77	74	431	454
CARNARVONSHIRE	2530	3697	459	707	2071	2990	0	13	207	265	1256	1476
ANGLESEY	2714	3578	442	645	2272	2933	0	22	210	312	1482	1759
WALES (*County not stated*)	4282	6685	635	996	3647	5595	15	34	330	402	1412	1936
ENGLAND (*County not stated*)	3929	3535	450	417	3479	3118	58	23	69	69	767	739
OTHER PARTS OF BRITISH EMPIRE	158942	161036	17228	17040	141714	143996	1592	2214	5945	5868	49131	48762
ISLANDS in the BRITISH SEAS	4482	5832	478	754	4004	5078	17	38	239	337	2057	2260
SCOTLAND	32151	31550	3883	3986	28268	27564	130	141	1673	1641	10621	9813
IRELAND	117396	118569	12108	11807	105288	107062	1400	1953	3699	3700	35199	35778
BRITISH COLONIES OR DEPENDENCIES	4913	5085	759	793	4154	4292	45	81	334	190	1254	911
FOREIGN COUNTRIES	16312	9632	1729	1129	14583	8503	70	66	696	258	6517	2581
British Subjects	5212	3988	524	536	4688	3452	25	26	189	143	1519	724
Foreigners	11100	5644	1205	593	9895	5051	45	40	507	115	4998	1857
AT SEA	355	453	50	53	305	400	7	7	16	13	81	107
British Subjects	353	450	49	53	304	397	7	7	16	13	80	105
Foreigners	2	3	1	..	1	3	..	..	..	..	1	2

Table 11 *continued*.—BIRTH-PLACES of MALES and FEMALES enumerated in COUNTIES, and in each URBAN SANITARY DISTRICT of which the POPULATION EXCEEDS 50,000 PERSONS.

WHERE BORN.	WHERE ENUMERATED.									
	URBAN SANITARY DISTRICTS.									
	ST. HELENS.		BOLTON.		BURY.		SALFORD.		MAN-CHESTER.	
	Males.	Females.	Males.	Females.	Males.	Females.	Males.	Females.	Males.	Females.
TOTAL OF INHABITANTS	29797	27606	49962	55452	24693	27520	84610	91625	163475	177939
LONDON	112	108	230	268	96	110	989	999	2232	2230
MIDDLESEX (*Intra-metropolitan*)	91	95	167	198	79	85	811	820	1904	1919
SURREY (*Intra-metropolitan*)	12	5	41	40	10	14	115	100	223	173
KENT (*Intra-metropolitan*)	9	8	22	30	7	11	63	79	105	138
SOUTH-EASTERN COUNTIES	68	73	113	142	89	104	541	612	932	1069
SURREY (*Extra-metropolitan*)	5	5	24	11	10	7	53	62	124	131
KENT (*Extra-metropolitan*)	25	26	34	44	33	36	187	208	301	340
SUSSEX	17	7	9	24	7	14	69	76	125	139
HAMPSHIRE	12	27	35	48	30	38	194	216	391	343
BERKSHIRE	9	8	11	15	9	9	33	50	91	116
SOUTH-MIDLAND COUNTIES	111	56	149	140	120	125	589	641	1822	1210
MIDDLESEX (*Ex.-metropolitan*)	6	2	10	7	7	7	62	68	145	127
HERTFORDSHIRE	4	5	6	9	9	6	47	51	85	74
BUCKINGHAMSHIRE	11	6	15	14	11	3	70	64	158	134
OXFORDSHIRE	24	11	27	18	10	15	61	66	187	134
NORTHAMPTONSHIRE	38	25	42	47	18	30	134	177	317	294
HUNTINGDONSHIRE	3	3	9	9	16	12	40	29	93	102
BEDFORDSHIRE	15	4	14	8	19	18	68	64	112	94
CAMBRIDGESHIRE	10	.	26	28	30	32	107	127	275	237
EASTERN COUNTIES	41	24	148	132	122	140	419	411	715	756
ESSEX	11	9	21	22	14	21	110	97	169	187
SUFFOLK	20	11	42	47	35	39	139	111	182	201
NORFOLK	10	4	85	63	73	80	177	203	364	368
SOUTH-WESTERN COUNTIES	151	134	197	211	103	111	665	678	1115	1268
WILTSHIRE	6	9	26	19	10	8	108	93	164	151
DORSETSHIRE	7	4	40	32	8	14	53	52	118	118
DEVONSHIRE	35	28	68	77	25	27	231	230	380	447
CORNWALL	33	28	32	44	29	35	90	115	144	171
SOMERSETSHIRE	70	64	31	39	31	27	183	188	309	381
WEST-MIDLAND COUNTIES	792	687	774	1025	339	564	2968	3748	5545	7230
GLOUCESTERSHIRE	102	66	71	75	23	39	354	279	568	661
HEREFORDSHIRE	32	22	17	33	12	14	111	149	173	220
SHROPSHIRE	144	124	147	320	71	176	632	1033	1018	1744
STAFFORDSHIRE	304	271	391	416	133	195	1180	1427	2089	2778
WORCESTERSHIRE	62	60	71	83	39	58	212	259	414	486
WARWICKSHIRE	148	138	77	98	62	83	579	601	1283	1341
NORTH-MIDLAND COUNTIES	147	99	379	460	222	264	1848	2056	4707	5021
LEICESTERSHIRE	33	18	37	53	18	32	209	178	472	485
RUTLANDSHIRE	3	2	1	2	.	2	11	17	31	29
LINCOLNSHIRE	28	22	68	106	27	47	446	560	1108	1268
NOTTINGHAMSHIRE	36	23	71	79	46	40	353	383	878	915
DERBYSHIRE	50	36	202	221	131	144	830	918	2158	2323
NORTH-WESTERN COUNTIES	23843	23247	43612	47846	21315	23414	63010	66988	118303	127539
CHESHIRE	712	580	761	943	489	594	3642	3893	7220	7959
LANCASHIRE	23131	22667	42851	46903	20826	22820	59368	63095	111083	119580
YORKSHIRE	275	244	903	1023	653	763	2934	3022	6018	6338
NORTHERN COUNTIES	265	240	331	469	155	196	904	1073	1665	1862
DURHAM	110	106	73	84	36	41	234	223	416	431
NORTHUMBERLAND	94	56	38	32	22	30	156	182	284	303
CUMBERLAND	41	59	155	238	61	64	359	435	662	783
WESTMORLAND	20	19	65	114	36	61	165	233	303	345
MONMOUTHSHIRE AND WALES	407	341	263	448	99	234	1050	1565	1892	3138
MONMOUTHSHIRE	9	6	9	10	2	7	66	69	90	119
GLAMORGANSHIRE	25	17	17	18	5	10	75	84	66	115
CARMARTHENSHIRE	7	1	7	2	3	.	8	9	29	19
PEMBROKESHIRE	6	4	9	10	4	7	24	25	39	68
CARDIGANSHIRE	5	3	1	4	2	6	21	16	52	59
BRECKNOCKSHIRE	.	3	1	6	.	1	12	18	17	23
RADNORSHIRE	.	.	6	2	.	3	9	10	28	42
MONTGOMERYSHIRE	10	9	36	50	8	15	86	148	138	251
FLINTSHIRE	125	118	61	91	23	60	179	290	380	687
DENBIGHSHIRE	54	43	45	98	23	60	267	389	363	603
MERIONETHSHIRE	3	3	6	13	4	5	26	47	59	92
CARNARVONSHIRE	19	18	23	60	8	18	84	125	122	254
ANGLESEY	29	20	9	18	4	4	37	53	95	154
WALES (*County not stated*)	115	97	53	72	13	38	185	263	414	749
ENGLAND (*County not stated*)	158	109	40	38	16	5	220	222	433	426
OTHER PARTS OF BRITISH EMPIRE	3365	2214	2677	3119	1283	1424	7936	9154	15534	17827
ISLANDS IN THE BRITISH SEAS	16	25	47	86	16	20	122	175	297	405
SCOTLAND	343	323	470	420	145	131	1500	1364	3231	2858
IRELAND	2983	1883	2093	2535	1071	1144	5861	7123	11533	14033
BRITISH COLONIES OR DEPENDENCIES	23	19	67	78	51	69	453	492	473	531
FOREIGN COUNTRIES	61	29	135	123	76	65	517	429	3027	1972
British Subjects	30	18	69	56	19	27	245	202	1241	953
Foreigners	31	11	66	67	57	38	272	227	1786	1019
AT SEA	1	1	11	8	5	1	20	27	35	53
British Subjects	1	1	11	8	5	1	20	27	35	53
Foreigners	.	.	.	.	.	.	.	.	.	.

Table 11 *continued*.—BIRTH-PLACES of MALES and FEMALES enumerated in COUNTIES, and in each URBAN SANITARY DISTRICT of which the POPULATION EXCEEDS 50,000 PERSONS.

WHERE BORN.	WHERE ENUMERATED.									
	URBAN SANITARY DISTRICTS.									
	OLDHAM.		ROCHDALE.		BURNLEY.		BLACKBURN.		PRESTON.	
	Males.	Females.	Males.	Females.	Males.	Females.	Males.	Females.	Males.	Females.
TOTAL OF INHABITANTS	53536	57807	31985	36881	28398	30353	49183	54881	44264	52273
LONDON	228	233	133	171	120	111	163	207	231	263
MIDDLESEX (*Intra-metropolitan*)	194	201	97	136	102	90	130	172	187	220
SURREY (*Intra-metropolitan*)	16	21	23	22	10	12	16	10	29	22
KENT (*Intra-metropolitan*)	18	11	13	13	8	9	17	19	15	21
SOUTH-EASTERN COUNTIES	121	133	81	86	122	113	88	127	149	208
SURREY (*Extra-metropolitan*)	11	12	7	7	9	8	7	7	15	15
KENT (*Extra-metropolitan*)	54	53	27	28	38	39	25	40	62	75
SUSSEX	16	19	11	15	13	12	8	17	15	16
HAMPSHIRE	40	40	26	24	54	47	38	50	52	85
BERKSHIRE	16	11	10	12	9	7	10	13	5	17
SOUTH-MIDLAND COUNTIES	298	307	179	203	127	146	145	166	188	223
MIDDLESEX (*Ex.-metropolitan*)	18	12	4	9	6	4	6	15	17	16
HERTFORDSHIRE	12	15	8	12	18	15	7	8	6	6
BUCKINGHAMSHIRE	49	61	8	4	13	14	44	38	50	61
OXFORDSHIRE	40	53	13	10	4	9	19	19	21	39
NORTHAMPTONSHIRE	90	74	35	50	27	28	21	29	47	50
HUNTINGDONSHIRE	21	11	30	44	18	13	13	9	10	9
BEDFORDSHIRE	15	21	9	12	12	12	13	12	18	25
CAMBRIDGESHIRE	53	61	72	62	43	51	22	36	19	17
EASTERN COUNTIES	230	216	150	165	121	145	111	150	115	140
ESSEX	22	34	21	24	14	16	11	36	37	40
SUFFOLK	133	109	46	57	34	24	29	34	25	29
NORFOLK	75	73	83	84	83	105	71	80	53	71
SOUTH-WESTERN COUNTIES	298	335	136	181	724	792	147	198	119	147
WILTSHIRE	25	20	17	24	16	15	21	25	12	13
DORSETSHIRE	120	134	17	10	10	12	17	15	17	19
DEVONSHIRE	49	43	27	36	150	182	57	53	33	48
CORNWALL	33	63	40	60	518	606	26	64	23	19
SOMERSETSHIRE	71	75	35	42	30	27	26	41	34	48
WEST-MIDLAND COUNTIES	977	1323	417	784	231	388	335	631	406	599
GLOUCESTERSHIRE	108	116	44	52	28	33	52	44	44	39
HEREFORDSHIRE	18	37	11	49	12	16	11	11	21	30
SHROPSHIRE	163	308	93	286	42	125	61	285	63	170
STAFFORDSHIRE	402	571	165	243	82	126	110	182	140	208
WORCESTERSHIRE	100	93	52	67	12	21	41	41	57	57
WARWICKSHIRE	186	198	52	87	55	67	55	68	81	95
NORTH-MIDLAND COUNTIES	1031	1112	243	421	235	270	221	288	183	215
LEICESTERSHIRE	70	39	22	27	25	17	23	26	23	30
RUTLANDSHIRE	1	4	2	7	1	2	11	12	1	3
LINCOLNSHIRE	218	199	67	128	72	82	54	74	46	61
NOTTINGHAMSHIRE	130	151	48	76	28	31	37	49	48	44
DERBYSHIRE	612	699	104	183	109	138	97	127	65	77
NORTH-WESTERN COUNTIES	43265	46224	27092	30344	22432	23718	43913	47910	39091	45149
CHESHIRE	1974	1896	490	653	293	324	357	448	291	386
LANCASHIRE	41291	44328	26602	29691	22139	23394	43556	47462	38800	44763
YORKSHIRE	3820	4065	1759	2014	2457	2551	1182	1294	677	819
NORTHERN COUNTIES	296	333	156	241	404	503	335	536	622	1001
DURHAM	103	105	59	67	179	196	51	59	63	78
NORTHUMBERLAND	36	41	16	25	33	39	34	43	41	50
CUMBERLAND	115	146	55	99	115	165	136	216	224	387
WESTMORLAND	42	41	26	50	77	103	114	218	294	486
MONMOUTHSHIRE AND WALES	208	454	161	366	84	147	90	229	123	265
MONMOUTHSHIRE	9	21	18	20	8	20	13	23	16	43
GLAMORGANSHIRE	14	17	5	16	9	12	8	14	9	26
CARMARTHENSHIRE	1	5	4	.	1	3	2	.	1	5
PEMBROKESHIRE	7	8	10	16	4	2	1	4	9	12
CARDIGANSHIRE	5	8	6	8	3	2	.	2	1	1
BRECKNOCKSHIRE	3	4	2	1	.	2	2	4	4	3
RADNORSHIRE	4	12	3	18	.	.	2	2	3	7
MONTGOMERYSHIRE	17	28	19	38	3	6	4	24	9	22
FLINTSHIRE	37	32	26	56	18	34	23	35	17	38
DENBIGHSHIRE	27	102	26	70	16	24	11	48	18	24
MERIONETHSHIRE	5	12	1	11	.	5	1	3	1	1
CARNARVONSHIRE	23	28	6	37	2	10	2	7	9	12
ANGLESEY	6	12	3	9	.	5	2	6	5	7
WALES (*County not stated*)	50	115	32	66	21	22	21	57	21	64
ENGLAND (*County not stated*)	84	101	40	28	22	27	42	34	22	16
OTHER PARTS OF BRITISH EMPIRE	2503	2809	1336	1771	1275	1397	2240	3001	2223	3099
ISLANDS IN THE BRITISH SEAS	18	40	12	23	20	25	17	32	23	33
SCOTLAND	305	327	194	225	170	193	359	446	346	381
IRELAND	2110	2352	1085	1466	1030	1109	1795	2437	1743	2506
BRITISH COLONIES OR DEPENDENCIES	70	90	45	57	55	70	69	86	111	179
FOREIGN COUNTRIES	171	151	95	99	40	41	119	101	111	117
British Subjects	72	77	39	56	15	20	48	43	40	51
Foreigners	99	74	56	43	25	21	71	58	71	66
AT SEA	12	9	7	7	4	4	2	9	4	12
British Subjects	12	9	7	7	4	4	2	9	4	12
Foreigners	.	.	.	.	.	.	.	.	.	.

Table 12.—Distribution of the enumerated Natives of Counties.

Where enumerated.	Where Born.					
	North-Western Counties.		Cheshire.		Lancashire.	
	Males.	Females.	Males.	Females.	Males.	Females.
TOTAL ENUMERATED NATIVES OF EACH COUNTY	1673071	1767071	298738	309851	1374833	1457220
LONDON	17157	16962	2977	3100	14180	13862
Middlesex (*Intra-metropolitan*)	11368	11418	1994	2086	9372	9332
Surrey (*Intra-metropolitan*)	4563	4369	772	780	3791	3589
Kent (*Intra-metropolitan*)	1228	1175	211	234	1017	941
SOUTH-EASTERN COUNTIES	9170	6998	1684	1542	7486	5456
Surrey (*Extra-metropolitan*)	1636	1824	315	400	1321	1424
Kent (*Extra-metropolitan*)	2486	1602	427	322	2059	1280
Sussex	1214	1459	258	349	956	1110
Hampshire	3272	1647	539	362	2733	1285
Berkshire	562	466	145	109	417	357
SOUTH-MIDLAND COUNTIES	4429	4183	1002	923	3427	3260
Middlesex (*Extra-metropolitan*)	1588	1688	333	341	1255	1347
Hertfordshire	509	460	124	123	385	337
Buckinghamshire	483	418	128	114	355	304
Oxfordshire	371	330	93	72	278	258
Northamptonshire	744	646	177	145	567	501
Huntingdonshire	82	73	14	15	68	58
Bedfordshire	283	299	60	60	223	239
Cambridgeshire	369	269	73	53	296	216
EASTERN COUNTIES	2642	2448	523	416	2119	2027
Essex	1671	1465	326	246	1345	1219
Suffolk	465	363	79	68	386	295
Norfolk	506	615	118	102	388	513
SOUTH-WESTERN COUNTIES	3936	3235	760	720	3176	2515
Wiltshire	381	384	72	98	309	286
Dorsetshire	651	239	109	59	542	180
Devonshire	1631	1246	325	265	1306	981
Cornwall	519	366	87	59	432	307
Somersetshire	754	1000	167	239	587	761
WEST-MIDLAND COUNTIES	23587	23565	11125	10574	12462	12991
Gloucestershire	1608	1835	296	365	1312	1470
Herefordshire	409	418	105	107	304	311
Shropshire	3100	3490	1776	1975	1324	1515
Staffordshire	12422	11480	7568	6718	4854	4762
Worcestershire	1429	1664	355	394	1074	1270
Warwickshire	4619	4678	1025	1015	3594	3663
NORTH-MIDLAND COUNTIES	12253	12747	4535	5088	7718	7659
Leicestershire	1190	1201	250	261	940	940
Rutlandshire	129	38	30	9	99	29
Lincolnshire	1477	1367	260	249	1217	1118
Nottinghamshire	2105	2129	424	476	1681	1653
Derbyshire	7352	8012	3571	4093	3781	3919
NORTH-WESTERN COUNTIES	1540280	1638169	266696	278337	1273584	1359832
Cheshire	247193	258701	213190	219129	34003	39572
Lancashire	1293087	1379468	53506	59208	1239581	1320260
YORKSHIRE	35007	35917	4780	4797	30227	31120
NORTHERN COUNTIES	14069	12325	1302	1138	12767	11187
Durham	5812	4362	675	500	5137	3862
Northumberland	1751	1434	208	195	1543	1239
Cumberland	3984	3610	326	291	3658	3319
Westmorland	2522	2919	93	152	2429	2767
MONMOUTHSHIRE AND WALES	10541	10527	3354	3216	7187	7311
Monmouthshire	507	435	114	107	393	328
Glamorganshire	1351	1043	247	170	1104	873
Carmarthenshire	161	106	35	21	126	85
Pembrokeshire	236	173	49	37	187	136
Cardiganshire	119	107	27	18	92	89
Brecknockshire	115	77	31	22	84	55
Radnorshire	45	49	10	12	35	37
Montgomeryshire	346	376	126	131	220	245
Flintshire	2828	3068	864	942	1964	2126
Denbighshire	2445	2592	1207	1219	1238	1373
Merionethshire	287	307	101	87	186	220
Carnarvonshire	1314	1508	350	341	964	1167
Anglesey	787	686	193	109	594	577

Table 14.—NUMBER and AGES of MALES and FEMALES returned as BLIND or BLIND FROM BIRTH in the NORTH-WESTERN DIVISION and its REGISTRATION COUNTIES.

REGISTRATION COUNTY.	ALL AGES.		0–	5–	15–	20–	25–	45–	65 and upwards.
	Both Sexes.	Males and Females.							
VIII. NORTH-WESTERN COUNTIES.	3004	M. 1628	49	161	101	111	452	448	306
		F. 1376	55	132	58	73	294	367	397
33 CHESHIRE	450	M. 248	10	18	8	12	55	75	70
		F. 202	6	17	6	12	36	48	77
34 LANCASHIRE	2554	M. 1380	39	143	93	99	397	373	236
		F. 1174	40	115	53	60	258	319	320

Table 15.—NUMBER and AGES of MALES and FEMALES returned as BLIND in the NORTH-WESTERN DIVISION and its REGISTRATION COUNTIES.

REGISTRATION COUNTY.	ALL AGES.		0–	5–	15–	20–	25–	45–	65 and upwards.
	Both Sexes.	Males and Females.							
VIII. NORTH-WESTERN COUNTIES.	2687	M. 1455	26	123	78	86	406	431	305
		F. 1232	31	99	41	63	263	347	388
33 CHESHIRE	408	M. 223	3	13	7	9	48	73	70
		F. 185	6	15	3	12	29	46	74
34 LANCASHIRE	2279	M. 1232	23	110	71	77	358	358	235
		F. 1047	25	84	38	51	234	301	314

Table 16.—NUMBER and AGES of MALES and FEMALES returned as BLIND FROM BIRTH in the NORTH-WESTERN DIVISION and its REGISTRATION COUNTIES.

REGISTRATION COUNTY.	ALL AGES.		0–	5–	15–	20–	25–	45–	65 and upwards.
	Both Sexes.	Males and Females.							
VIII. NORTH-WESTERN COUNTIES.	317	M. 173	23	38	23	25	46	17	1
		F. 144	24	33	17	10	31	20	9
33 CHESHIRE	42	M. 25	7	5	1	3	7	2	.
		F. 17	.	2	2	1	7	2	3
34 LANCASHIRE	275	M. 148	16	33	22	22	39	15	1
		F. 127	24	31	15	9	24	18	6

Table 17.—NUMBER and AGES of MALES and FEMALES returned as DEAF AND DUMB in the NORTH-WESTERN DIVISION and its REGISTRATION COUNTIES.

REGISTRATION COUNTY.	ALL AGES.		0–	5–	15–	20–	25–	45–	65 and upwards.
	Both Sexes.	Males and Females.							
VIII. NORTH-WESTERN COUNTIES.	1872	M. 995	40	298	92	114	293	130	28
		F. 877	26	256	90	107	273	96	29
33 CHESHIRE	268	M. 139	2	34	16	13	49	17	8
		F. 129	3	26	14	21	45	17	3
34 LANCASHIRE	1604	M. 856	38	264	76	101	244	113	20
		F. 748	23	230	76	86	228	79	26

Table 18.—Number and Ages of Males and Females returned as Idiots or Imbeciles, and Lunatics in the North-western Division and its Registration Counties.

Registration County.	All Ages.		0–	5–	15–	20–	25–	45–	65– and upwards.
	Both Sexes	Males and Females.							
VIII. NORTH-WESTERN COUNTIES.	11198	M. 5338	34	457	394	470	2206	1404	373
		F. 5860	28	329	318	395	2314	1893	583
33 CHESHIRE - - - -	2008	M. 961	5	57	39	73	413	277	87
		F. - 1057	2	38	49	61	434	340	133
34 LANCASHIRE - - - -	9190	M. - 4387	29	400	355	397	1793	1127	286
		F. - 4803	26	291	269	334	1880	1553	450

Table 19.—Number and Ages of Males and Females returned as Idiots or Imbeciles in the North-western Division and its Registration Counties.

Registration County.	All Ages.		0–	5–	15–	20–	25–	45–	65– and upwards.
	Both Sexes	Males and Females.							
VIII. NORTH-WESTERN COUNTIES.	4467	M. 2287	33	445	327	277	691	349	165
		F. 2180	26	318	252	235	720	418	211
33 CHESHIRE - - - -	758	M. - 376	5	65	35	50	120	78	33
		F. - 382	2	38	36	35	148	78	45
34 LANCASHIRE - - - -	3709	M. - 1911	28	390	292	227	571	271	132
		F. - 1798	24	280	216	200	572	340	166

Table 20.—Number and Ages of Males and Females returned as Lunatics in the North-western Division and its Registration Counties.

Registration County.	All Ages.		0–	5–	10–	15–	20–	25–	65– and upwards.
	Both Sexes	Males and Females.							
VIII. NORTH-WESTERN COUNTIES.	6731	M. 3051	1	12	67	193	1515	1055	208
		F. 3680	2	11	66	160	1594	1475	372
33 CHESHIRE - - -	1250	M. - 575	.	2	4	23	298	199	54
		F. 675	.	.	13	26	286	262	88
34 LANCASHIRE - - -	5481	M. - 2476	1	10	63	170	1222	856	154
		F. - 3005	2	11	53	134	1308	1213	284

Table 21.—NUMBER of the BLIND, of the DEAF AND DUMB, of IDIOTS or IMBECILES, and of LUNATICS in the NORTH-WESTERN DIVISION and its REGISTRATION COUNTIES and DISTRICTS.

Registration County and District.	Blind.			Deaf and Dumb.	Mentally Deranged.		
	From Birth.	Others.	Total.		Idiots.	Lunatics.	Total.
VIII. NORTH-WESTERN COUNTIES.	317	2687	3004	1872	4467	6731	11198
33 CHESHIRE	42	418	460	268	758	1250	2008
34 LANCASHIRE	275	2279	2554	1604	3709	5487	9196
33 CHESHIRE.							
443 STOCKPORT	15	77	92	62	173	170	343
444 MACCLESFIELD	5	55	60	29	141	573	714
445 ALTRINCHAM	5	28	33	31	55	12	67
446 RUNCORN	..	21	21	25	40	2	42
447 NORTHWICH	1	30	31	21	66	1	67
448 CONGLETON	2	29	31	13	48	1	49
449 NANTWICH	5	45	50	26	59	2	61
450 CHESTER	4	56	60	32	118	475	593
451 WIRRAL	1	13	14	5	10	2	12
452 BIRKENHEAD	4	54	58	34	48	12	60
34 LANCASHIRE.							
453 LIVERPOOL	16	311	327	161	82	48	130
454 TOXTETH PARK	17	61	78	46	148	15	163
455 WEST DERBY	47	189	236	128	187	74	261
456 PRESCOT	8	58	66	41	180	651	831
457 ORMSKIRK	2	36	38	26	72	2	74
458 WIGAN	14	92	106	75	186	6	192
459 WARRINGTON	1	38	39	23	99	188	287
460 LEIGH	1	25	26	28	65	2	67
461 BOLTON	9	122	131	73	125	93	218
462 BURY	6	61	67	47	143	81	224
463 BARTON-UPON-IRWELL	23	108	131	180	39	42	81
464 CHORLTON	14	135	149	106	259	16	275
465 SALFORD	11	128	139	66	131	69	200
466 MANCHESTER	15	106	121	72	60	7	67
467 PRESTWICH	4	86	90	46	190	1470	1660
468 ASHTON-UNDER-LYNE	10	94	104	66	109	86	195
469 OLDHAM	10	118	128	74	228	20	248
470 ROCHDALE	9	62	71	62	67	114	181
471 HASLINGDEN	7	49	56	35	122	5	127
472 BURNLEY	6	62	68	46	107	3	110
473 CLITHEROE	1	18	19	9	28	14	42
474 BLACKBURN	11	89	100	58	169	77	246
475 CHORLEY	1	23	24	31	86	2	88
476 PRESTON	71	97	168	40	150	1331	1481
477 FYLDE	..	19	19	7	26	1	27
478 GARSTANG	..	2	2	8	23	2	25
479 LANCASTER	13	29	42	22	547	1057	1604
480 LUNESDALE	..	5	5	2	15	3	18
481 ULVERSTON	5	40	45	11	49	1	50
482 BARROW-IN-FURNESS	3	16	19	10	17	1	18

AGES,

CONDITION AS TO MARRIAGE,

OCCUPATIONS, AND BIRTH-PLACES

OF THE PEOPLE:

WITH THE

NUMBERS AND AGES OF THE BLIND, DEAF AND DUMB, IDIOTS OR IMBECILES, AND LUNATICS.

DIVISION IX.—YORKSHIRE;

WEST RIDING,
EAST RIDING (with YORK),
NORTH RIDING.

TABLES IN DIVISION IX.—YORKSHIRE.

AGES.

CONDITION AS TO MARRIAGE.

OCCUPATIONS.

BIRTH-PLACES.

THE BLIND, DEAF AND DUMB, IDIOTS OR IMBECILES, AND LUNATICS.

AGES.

DIVISION IX.—YORKSHIRE.

Table 1.—AGES of MALES and FEMALES in the YORKSHIRE DIVISION and its REGISTRATION RIDINGS.

REGISTRATION RIDING.	ALL AGES. Persons.	ALL AGES. Males and Females.	Under 5* Years.	5–	10–	15–	20–	25–	30–	35–	40–	45–	50–	55–	60–	65–	70–	75–	80–	85–	90–	95–	100 and up†
IX.—YORKSHIRE.	2894759	M. 1423925	201574	175719	156966	141414	126334	115578	97704	86638	77449	62030	54319	42429	35054	23887	14908	7898	3305	875	131	20	
		F. 1470834	263124	179122	156186	143043	135353	119079	99665	88238	80070	65594	56774	45497	38748	26378	17503	9779	4807	1241	285	42	
35 WEST RIDING	2197999	M. 1075334	153231	133254	118278	106874	95845	88280	73933	65908	58190	46942	40973	31801	25050	17019	10335	5372	2064	509	68	9	
		F. 1122665	154602	136235	119023	109609	104173	93310	76563	68188	61056	50071	43613	31398	28655	18994	12265	6611	2621	738	158	23	
36 EAST RIDING (with YORK)	362375	M. 179394	24661	21186	19154	17962	16001	14258	12323	10864	9644	7825	6909	5544	5099	3572	2374	1239	586	163	26	3	
		F. 182981	24781	21948	19028	17538	16395	14329	12424	10796	9800	8028	7082	5907	5397	4000	2882	1694	829	243	71	7	
37 NORTH RIDING	334385	M. 168197	23682	21879	18634	16578	14478	13040	11448	9808	9115	7263	6497	5084	4605	3296	2199	1287	655	203	39	8	
		F. 166188	23741	20939	18135	16101	14485	12340	10678	9254	8284	6895	6078	5207	4096	3384	2416	1474	757	260	56	9	

Note.—The Registration Ridings of Yorkshire consist of groups of Registration Districts, which are generally co-extensive with the Poor Law Unions. The Registration Districts which extend into two or more Ridings are included in that Registration Riding in which the principal town of the District or the greatest part of the population is located. The boundaries of the Registration Ridings therefore, differ more or less from the boundaries of the Ridings proper. For such differences in Division IX., see Vol. II., Table 11.

* For the Number of Children at each Year of Age under 5, see Table 4.

† One of these Males was stated to be 100, one 101, and one 103 years of age. Four of these Females were stated to be 100, and two 101 years of age.

TABLE 2.—AGES of MALES and FEMALES in REGISTRATION DISTRICTS.

REGISTRATION DISTRICT.	ALL AGES. Persons.	ALL AGES. Males and Females.	Under 5* Years.	5–	10–	15–	20–	25–	30–	35–	40–	45–	50–	55–	60–	65–	70–	75–	80–	85–	90–	95–	100 and up
35 WEST RIDING.																							
483 SEDBERGH	4079	M. - 2074	260	241	223	232	135	145	112	121	104	74	77	95	69	75	54	35	19	2	.	.	
		F. - 2005	250	215	207	195	169	148	114	111	93	78	94	80	78	71	54	31	8	.	1	.	
484 SETTLE	13800	M. - 6848	937	754	756	721	588	513	405	350	306	284	304	256	239	176	142	72	29	13	3	.	
		F. - 6952	874	836	688	674	704	556	452	384	338	293	254	244	240	160	123	69	36	18	.	.	
485 SKIPTON	37120	M. - 18081	2492	2123	1870	1802	1656	1386	1213	999	895	750	774	675	585	380	246	138	66	21	1	.	
		F. - 19039	2452	2192	1980	1851	1851	1586	1355	1115	962	874	808	662	516	386	267	110	56	18	3	.	
486 PATELEY BRIDGE	8944	M. - 4536	618	576	479	452	390	325	235	205	233	211	196	198	163	122	67	39	24	4	1	.	
		F. - 4408	509	513	494	413	364	323	202	275	216	188	208	170	126	99	59	40	33	12	3	.	
487 RIPON	16447	M. - 7879	1023	932	872	793	626	540	481	329	421	363	349	298	265	234	149	88	42	11	1	.	
		F. - 8568	958	983	859	888	798	644	529	494	411	385	391	315	312	216	161	94	58	26	5	1	
488 GREAT OUSEBURN	11955	M. - 5928	778	740	646	593	500	384	322	291	289	261	216	241	208	158	134	73	30	11	3	.	
		F. - 6027	758	745	668	539	515	382	362	339	288	256	202	212	191	180	135	76	47	16	5	1	
489 KNARESBOROUGH	22635	M. - 10440	1332	1236	1348	1040	789	746	589	865	544	466	448	423	330	259	158	85	54	12	2	1	
		F. - 12195	1350	1242	1199	1316	1225	969	795	736	679	589	541	449	381	301	212	118	52	15	5	1	
490 WETHERBY	16194	M. - 8046	981	920	1103	809	645	514	420	410	411	350	357	298	301	312	153	107	38	9	.	.	
		F. - 8148	995	935	850	753	679	599	406	473	440	439	321	290	287	242	183	96	55	20	4	.	
491 WHARFEDALE	46705	M. - 22626	3193	2714	2655	2164	1856	1790	1445	1373	1209	1004	893	756	632	444	274	139	65	18	2	.	
		F. - 24079	3113	2855	2441	2415	2414	2044	1602	1514	1275	1076	926	758	674	401	253	167	74	11	6	.	
492 KEIGHLEY	61121	M. - 29054	3841	3567	3230	3054	2581	2288	1848	1665	1589	1339	1246	967	822	503	290	143	71	13	.	.	
		F. - 32067	3950	3535	3292	3255	3280	2795	2163	1972	1859	1577	1345	1098	814	537	312	183	77	12	.	2	
493 TODMORDEN	35527	M. - 17095	2268	1901	1721	1597	1616	1418	1271	1005	968	807	652	594	406	318	182	78	28	2	1	.	
		F. - 18432	2176	1885	1736	1778	1801	1624	1394	1207	1073	938	790	690	568	393	236	97	33	10	1	.	
494 SADDLEWORTH	22299	M. - 10693	1358	1269	1178	1092	950	834	705	621	386	536	470	380	305	215	106	64	16	5	.	.	
		F. - 11606	1302	1335	1190	1192	1070	958	768	665	649	600	487	392	335	246	110	86	25	1	2	.	
495 HUDDERSFIELD	156512	M. - 75377	10022	9108	8479	7624	6939	6186	5003	4322	4059	3390	2940	2449	2026	1244	865	433	172	38	6	.	
		F. - 81136	10017	9322	8535	8354	8128	6895	5553	4905	4501	3707	3203	2645	2179	1461	978	460	188	44	7	2	
496 HALIFAX	170440	M. - 81074	10859	9867	8974	8188	7288	6632	5326	4872	4474	3616	3230	2622	2146	1400	807	375	129	34	3	2	
		F. - 89366	11122	10107	8957	8963	8465	7741	6287	5545	5219	4296	3652	3029	2535	1681	1009	520	190	46	10	2	
497 BRADFORD	311582	M. 146727	20401	18231	16314	16916	12084	11803	9997	9101	8229	6581	5710	4424	3509	2229	1364	646	223	53	6	2	
		F. 164855	20947	18444	16357	10333	16449	14460	11581	10294	9634	7970	6698	5180	4186	2532	1519	771	309	79	16	2	
498 HUNSLET	58215	M. - 28893	4520	3716	3148	2806	2466	2506	2062	1859	1616	1173	1037	786	539	331	195	100	32	1	.	.	
		F. - 29322	4670	3814	3196	2616	2470	2471	2006	1792	1592	1265	1061	831	650	411	265	145	36	16	3	1	
499 HOLBECK	24051	M. - 11642	1680	1489	1298	1113	970	943	802	767	666	498	440	351	243	176	101	43	16	4	1	.	
		F. - 12409	1815	1603	1289	1172	1081	978	838	792	662	558	458	384	326	213	148	72	17	2	1	.	

Note.—The Registration Districts of Division IX. are co-extensive with the Poor Law Unions of the same name, with the following exceptions—The Bradford District (497) comprises the two Poor Law Unions of Bradford and North Bierley; the Wortley District (507) comprises the two Unions of Wortley and Penistone; and the Helmsley District (530) comprises the two Unions of Helmsley and Kirkby Moorside. The Hull District (521) is an Incorporation under a Local Act.

For the Parishes comprised in each Registration District, see Vol. II., Division IX., Table 4.

The Districts are arranged topographically under the Registration Counties, and are numbered consecutively, commencing with the Metropolitan Division.

* For the Number of Children at each Year of Age under 5, see Table 5.

Table 2 *continued*.—Ages of Males and Females in Registration Districts.

Registration District.	All Ages. Persons.	All Ages. Males and Females.	Under 5 Years.	5-	10-	15-	20-	25-	30-	35-	40-	45-	50-	55-	60-	65-	70-	75-	80-	85-	90-	95-	100 and upw^{ds}
35 WEST RIDING —cont.																							
500 BRAMLEY	54400	M. - 26961	3878	3381	2851	2757	2457	2306	1862	1682	1450	1195	1016	703	583	365	221	113	41	12	.	.	.
		F. - 27439	3970	3433	2949	2595	2439	2323	1886	1611	1537	1258	1103	809	680	411	241	131	41	15	5	.	.
501 LEEDS	190847	M. - 91460	13843	11082	9733	8668	8159	7958	6545	6074	5362	4021	3587	2530	2116	1340	760	338	118	20	5	1	.
		F. - 99387	13217	11335	10202	10079	9726	8677	6909	6222	5731	4467	3946	2835	2511	1611	1064	533	198	46	13	5	.
502 DEWSBURY	153712	M. - 73701	10591	9267	8349	7812	6728	6043	4852	4467	4118	3242	2695	2047	1551	981	555	284	101	13	3	.	.
		F. - 80011	10842	9695	8577	8808	7975	6792	5382	4877	4503	3553	3066	2292	1758	1099	693	382	111	32	5	.	.
503 WAKEFIELD	89113	M. - 45283	6981	5812	4906	4281	4129	3856	3228	2889	2396	1834	1574	1174	965	605	396	214	70	18	5	.	.
		F. - 43830	6863	5747	4708	3976	3822	3585	3010	2656	2358	1776	1528	1190	991	688	456	275	106	27	11	2	.
504 PONTEFRACT	47876	M. - 24944	3944	3191	2727	2460	2258	2120	1801	1498	1230	971	838	599	534	390	228	129	42	13	.	1	.
		F. - 22932	3765	3348	2596	1869	1804	1857	1580	1323	1133	918	748	579	567	364	270	158	70	25	8	.	.
505 HEMSWORTH	11106	M. - 5935	814	640	708	576	598	480	426	340	297	270	237	151	165	91	64	30	22	4	.	.	.
		F. - 5171	754	683	616	443	435	383	339	303	258	205	204	150	125	117	78	44	25	8	1	.	.
506 BARNSLEY	78611	M. - 41083	6418	5291	4465	3924	3846	3632	3028	2505	2083	1622	1393	953	802	557	332	154	59	16	.	1	.
		F. - 37528	6324	5557	4234	3082	3046	2972	2507	2159	1855	1482	1277	909	758	556	313	170	69	10	2	.	.
507 WORTLEY	52258	M. - 26953	4061	3383	2904	2736	2458	2228	1813	1548	1586	1129	961	764	656	403	234	134	54	21	.	.	.
		F. - 25305	4078	3463	3014	2145	1074	1845	1668	1471	1295	1089	944	774	627	412	261	159	58	19	6	1	.
508 ECCLESALL BIERLOW	114418	M. - 56123	8102	6829	5997	5533	5057	4523	4083	3542	3036	2392	1918	1465	1201	728	487	218	80	19	3	.	.
		F. - 58295	8166	7061	6332	6440	5026	4988	4048	3656	3177	2339	2111	1690	1416	885	588	321	112	15	3	1	.
509 SHEFFIELD	183135	M. - 92945	13542	11580	9893	8875	8246	8171	6992	6296	5440	4156	3415	2382	1806	1135	625	266	94	24	5	.	.
		F. - 90190	13804	11086	9763	8356	7763	7230	6274	5482	5038	4145	3300	2401	2010	1228	822	392	137	41	6	1	.
510 ROTHERHAM	75515	M. - 38880	6231	5331	4356	3709	3382	3181	2756	2439	1935	1578	1333	940	787	509	296	177	46	13	1	.	.
		F. - 36635	6195	5391	4205	2985	2865	2759	2454	2216	1817	1480	1228	957	853	575	348	200	78	25	4	.	.
511 DONCASTER	53872	M. - 27056	3737	3346	2922	2607	2422	2101	1791	1602	1423	1230	1050	859	706	549	399	230	94	26	2	.	.
		F. - 26816	3727	3234	3044	2464	2279	2027	1731	1580	1445	1148	1052	890	771	530	419	236	117	47	8	2	.
512 THORNE	16181	M. - 8044	1029	987	964	768	602	466	424	405	417	365	373	347	306	245	142	125	72	19	8	.	.
		F. - 8137	994	994	945	759	581	512	437	423	418	414	380	331	299	254	177	123	60	28	7	1	.
513 GOOLE	19558	M. - 9802	1429	1185	1013	983	848	769	622	563	510	455	387	294	274	208	147	84	25	12	2	1	.
		F. - 9756	1371	1207	1059	891	794	720	609	517	541	441	384	330	311	213	137	102	48	15	6	.	.
514 SELBY	15815	M. - 7809	1043	978	896	782	620	509	449	407	395	333	344	288	269	197	140	98	46	11	.	.	.
		F. - 8006	1011	978	910	769	653	556	471	409	403	385	360	301	263	210	143	117	50	14	5	2	.
515 TADCASTER	23955	M. - 12342	1804	1496	1332	1304	1057	900	799	646	603	497	463	421	357	277	161	102	44	17	2	.	.
		F. - 11613	1701	1813	1319	942	920	882	691	652	589	493	454	395	338	250	171	124	47	21	2	.	.
36 EAST RIDING (with York).																							
516 YORK	76605	M. - 38001	4996	4268	4076	3995	3802	3162	2580	2223	2041	1623	1468	1118	1058	772	521	246	112	29	4	1	1
		F. - 38604	4868	4329	3941	3855	3685	3169	2628	2298	2064	1798	1511	1291	1124	880	614	370	166	55	19	.	.
517 POCKLINGTON	15461	M. - 7979	1001	860	870	1000	681	496	407	412	350	351	379	330	296	226	161	89	46	19	2	.	.
		F. - 7482	944	922	881	740	632	408	435	356	395	329	328	293	271	192	127	91	56	16	5	1	.
518 HOWDEN	13287	M. - 6869	813	815	874	801	523	440	349	335	325	309	303	282	260	169	141	80	35	13	2	.	.
		F. - 6418	859	764	705	580	523	376	381	336	304	288	285	290	232	163	149	88	35	14	3	2	1
519 BEVERLEY	23460	M. - 11730	1565	1872	1187	1218	1040	850	718	629	626	534	476	393	386	282	230	112	53	17	2	.	.
		F. - 11730	1521	1426	1277	1053	907	843	728	688	651	510	484	398	418	328	256	151	71	14	6	.	.
520 SCULCOATES	99868	M. - 48696	7406	6081	5346	4401	4103	4029	3640	3104	2672	2057	1715	1324	1141	796	499	231	121	21	5	1	.
		F. - 51172	7312	6414	5380	4671	4566	4152	3694	3146	2772	2157	1858	1468	1348	968	681	366	161	61	14	2	1
521 HULL	78222	M. - 38402	5292	4521	3873	3407	3430	3427	3027	2691	2234	1735	1419	1091	966	573	355	180	87	20	3	1	.
		F. - 39820	5470	4673	3914	3728	3813	3443	2894	2481	2238	1725	1519	1185	1078	734	475	252	135	84	5	1	.
522 PATRINGTON	8758	M. - 4355	555	482	448	440	386	275	236	224	202	203	205	200	198	133	74	59	24	9	2	.	.
		F. - 4403	505	540	463	422	378	288	240	235	216	200	192	177	163	125	91	68	38	8	1	.	.
523 SKIRLAUGH	9795	M. - 4852	618	568	494	558	440	314	271	256	277	215	193	179	160	112	89	87	23	10	2	.	.
		F. - 4943	688	643	510	480	412	330	279	276	203	207	173	170	158	128	106	74	32	8	5	.	.
524 DRIFFIELD	20067	M. - 10275	1336	1245	1121	1155	922	726	585	515	501	444	429	334	357	270	169	100	49	16	2	.	.
		F. - 9792	1418	1227	1065	896	823	672	594	519	473	425	401	327	325	256	195	102	66	12	7	.	.
525 BRIDLINGTON	16762	M. - 8145	1080	974	865	894	674	539	510	435	410	384	318	293	282	230	155	75	39	9	2	.	.
		F. - 8617	1136	1004	892	904	706	608	551	475	424	391	331	299	292	226	188	102	60	21	6	7	.
37 NORTH RIDING.																							
526 SCARBOROUGH	43265	M. - 20009	2694	2475	2280	1986	1623	1487	1231	1087	1068	906	777	724	666	442	288	150	92	30	3	.	.
		F. - 23256	2696	2385	2255	2445	2331	1881	1699	1306	1274	1118	965	826	790	546	401	241	116	34	7	8	.
527 MALTON	23031	M. - 11622	1533	1389	1265	1325	988	771	682	602	581	486	473	402	387	315	202	139	61	19	4	.	.
		F. - 11409	1554	1348	1261	1148	1063	844	687	606	516	496	421	411	369	292	222	127	71	34	1	.	.
528 EASINGWOLD	9533	M. - 4897	619	544	527	609	443	319	259	204	226	207	205	180	197	153	104	69	39	11	1	1	.
		F. - 4636	580	558	506	478	402	301	239	248	212	205	197	184	165	129	111	70	37	13	.	.	.
529 THIRSK	12848	M. - 6317	892	801	646	632	519	409	353	330	318	293	270	220	192	170	181	90	44	15	2	.	.
		F. - 6531	900	774	726	677	496	465	385	359	289	309	261	235	201	177	131	85	44	14	2	1	.
530 HELMSLEY	11433	M. - 5974	732	684	723	701	496	391	305	286	310	258	228	221	211	166	126	82	40	14	.	.	.
		F. - 5459	698	688	626	573	460	330	283	262	308	237	224	196	207	140	106	73	39	10	4	.	.
531 PIÇKERING	10678	M. - 5424	730	694	632	532	384	354	300	269	288	250	238	195	215	158	99	55	21	8	1	.	.
		F. - 5254	727	700	609	467	409	339	312	305	288	212	215	180	195	128	99	54	22	12	1	.	.
532 WHITBY	26474	M. - 12834	1791	1638	1488	1188	1047	960	794	708	650	567	582	442	418	277	208	99	65	13	4	.	.
		F. - 13640	1853	1619	1437	1345	1191	985	796	739	674	615	582	461	466	327	254	183	84	32	4	2	1
533 GUISBROUGH	43126	M. - 22392	3505	3114	2388	1954	1875	1825	1736	1482	1232	888	762	572	480	301	169	98	39	21	.	3	.
		F. - 20734	3484	3052	2484	1830	1703	1604	1475	1103	971	766	622	530	432	303	192	102	47	15	5	.	1
534 MIDDLESBROUGH	89853	M. - 47744	7053	6140	4996	4346	4420	4396	3948	3288	2841	2036	1624	943	753	431	289	117	52	13	6	1	1
		F. - 42109	7137	6167	4878	3968	3613	3261	2998	2510	2208	1529	1287	918	748	436	248	114	58	29	6	.	1
535 STOKESLEY	12009	M. - 5975	758	741	677	627	477	413	332	301	234	258	279	224	194	159	112	77	40	8	4	.	.
		F. - 6034	772	715	631	628	572	427	336	276	276	264	244	235	199	155	109	82	46	10	7	.	.
536 NORTHALLERTON	11884	M. - 5989	798	736	679	629	507	403	340	297	278	233	261	222	202	164	112	73	40	6	5	.	.
		F. - 5895	822	643	621	508	513	445	368	309	298	238	227	245	170	142	114	67	53	12	2	.	.
537 BEDALE	8270	M. - 4133	559	470	479	425	332	252	246	193	185	188	164	164	157	129	97	49	27	10	7	1	.
		F. - 4137	486	460	439	396	363	299	243	210	211	179	177	170	161	136	79	72	43	11	3	.	.
538 LEYBURN	8324	M. - 4066	512	433	515	438	341	266	214	160	175	182	161	173	182	135	87	53	25	11	1	.	.
		F. - 4258	500	403	419	401	373	312	235	264	202	184	159	191	190	146	108	58	23	6	5	1	.
539 AYSGARTH	5482	M. - 2793	360	315	335	254	248	216	183	142	169	180	107	121	114	74	52	30	13	9	1	.	.
		F. - 2689	332	285	280	271	242	197	159	149	121	136	131	109	95	80	51	23	20	5	2	1	.
540 REETH	4717	M. - 2370	291	309	279	227	198	154	157	155	143	107	90	79	67	54	34	16	9	1	.	.	.
		F. - 2347	308	293	229	207	194	155	168	132	131	97	91	78	92	69	56	26	16	3	2	.	.
541 RICHMOND	13458	M. - 6658	885	799	777	704	580	424	383	362	317	274	256	222	220	170	139	90	48	14	2	2	.
		F. - 6800	800	764	734	681	615	545	417	336	327	290	276	253	216	178	157	97	38	20	5	1	.

Table 3.—AGES of MALES and FEMALES in REGISTRATION SUB-DISTRICTS.

REGISTRATION SUB-DISTRICT.	ALL AGES. Persons.	ALL AGES. Males and Females.	Under 5 Years.	5-	10-	15-	20-	25-	30-	35-	40-	45-	50-	55-	60-	65-	70-	75-	80-	85-	90-	95-	100 and upw^ds^.
35 WEST RIDING.																							
483 SEDBERGH.																							
1 SEDBERGH. (W.)	2268	M. - 1151	139	122	145	138	79	84	88	55	61	40	39	44	32	40	24	16	10	.	.	.	.
		F. - 1117	141	124	112	122	99	78	70	59	60	42	47	38	40	35	27	16	7	.	.	.	.
2 GARSDALE	602	M. - 307	51	48	31	23	12	21	15	23	10	11	9	22	5	8	9	4	3	.	.	.	.
		F. - 295	51	54	42	21	16	35	16	21	9	12	15	9	8	7	6	3	.	.	.	.	.
3 DENT	1209	M. - 616	70	71	47	52	44	40	36	45	27	23	20	29	32	20	21	15	6	2	.	.	.
		F. - 593	68	67	55	54	54	45	28	31	24	22	33	38	24	29	21	13	1	.	1	.	.
484 SETTLE.																							
1 BENTHAM. (L.)	5438	M. - 2634	390	324	275	232	135	182	180	163	127	119	107	96	108	68	64	31	7	4	2	.	.
		F. - 2804	386	364	321	228	274	208	164	178	143	121	90	100	96	65	42	28	13	10	.	.	.
2 SETTLE. (W.)	5598	M. - 2786	384	298	323	324	252	223	165	182	110	101	130	100	75	56	53	25	19	5	1	.	.
		F. - 2812	384	296	245	290	305	247	196	146	132	196	102	69	80	69	56	24	11	6	.	.	.
3 LONG PRESTON	1620	M. - 883	101	72	92	77	86	77	52	32	37	46	46	32	30	25	18	5	1	4	.	.	.
		F. - 737	85	101	70	76	86	53	62	36	32	23	40	26	38	22	12	12	7	4	.	.	.
4 KIRKBY MALHAM	762	M. - 386	44	35	49	30	38	16	25	22	20	12	14	20	19	10	12	8	2	.	.	.	.
		F. - 376	32	47	33	54	27	33	21	20	24	18	16	14	13	11	6	4	3	.	.	.	.
5 ARNCLIFFE	353	M. - 180	26	22	17	19	17	15	13	11	12	5	7	8	7	7	5	3	.	.	.	.	.
		F. - 173	17	28	16	26	19	15	9	8	7	6	8	6	5	2	7	1	2	.	.	.	.
485 SKIPTON.																							
1 KETTLEWELL	854	M. - 446	68	55	48	44	30	32	29	15	24	16	23	28	16	11	8	5	3	.	.	.	.
		F. - 408	42	47	29	38	39	32	24	20	25	20	22	18	15	14	12	3	5	1	.	.	.
2 GARGRAVE	2117	M. - 1004	148	118	98	110	90	63	62	43	46	46	50	36	39	20	10	9	1	3	.	.	.
		F. - 1113	134	114	131	117	119	98	75	60	67	42	58	37	27	16	13	7	8	2	.	.	.
3 BARNOLDSWICK	7290	M. - 3391	521	417	397	393	358	258	246	198	147	119	133	122	115	97	41	26	15	4	.	.	.
		F. - 3899	491	443	378	378	380	315	263	206	189	147	158	127	78	72	47	21	8	.	.	.	.
4 KILDWICK	8923	M. - 4286	536	492	424	421	371	337	275	267	213	183	207	173	140	117	73	40	13	3	1	.	.
		F. - 4637	563	537	461	434	428	380	348	259	250	263	183	168	156	110	76	21	15	1	.	.	.
5 SKIPTON. (W.)	12772	M. - 6154	834	760	649	590	504	507	436	319	304	271	229	185	180	98	75	35	20	7	.	.	.
		F. - 6618	889	760	682	680	686	539	476	401	333	308	256	207	164	106	77	38	12	5	.	.	.
6 ADDINGHAM	3262	M. - 1640	191	148	154	169	131	127	103	90	111	80	85	83	68	47	28	17	7	1	.	.	.
		F. - 1622	200	182	194	183	151	182	113	69	78	62	88	87	54	36	29	16	3	1	1	.	.
7 GRASSINGTON	1902	M. - 960	141	133	105	60	64	62	61	64	56	44	47	42	29	20	12	6	7	4	.	.	.
		F. - 942	130	169	104	71	68	64	57	74	57	32	45	48	29	32	19	10	7	6	2	.	.
486 PATELEY BRIDGE.																							
1 RAMSGILL	936	M. - 489	53	51	46	51	40	44	26	23	34	25	12	10	25	19	9	4	4	.	1	.	.
		F. - 447	56	32	47	45	45	24	23	34	25	20	17	15	15	21	12	4	4	1	1	.	.
2 PATELEY BRIDGE (W.)	3750	M. - 1915	203	268	209	194	167	142	102	96	80	98	77	74	43	40	31	14	11	1	.	.	.
		F. - 1835	276	232	222	189	136	141	106	119	88	83	82	58	41	38	21	21	12	1	2	.	.
3 THORNTHWAITE	1625	M. - 820	111	107	74	77	65	51	41	40	48	37	38	46	39	21	16	9	3	.	.	.	.
		F. - 805	97	83	85	63	63	48	55	54	49	28	40	30	37	12	16	13	6	3	.	.	.
4 DACRE BANKS	2633	M. - 1312	188	150	150	130	122	88	64	52	64	51	69	57	56	38	17	12	6	3	.	.	.
		F. - 1321	171	151	139	139	120	110	78	72	54	57	66	61	33	28	16	11	8	7	.	.	.
487 RIPON.																							
1 RIPON. (W.)	10402	M. - 4831	639	592	557	471	374	328	309	241	206	225	214	181	154	123	72	56	23	6	.	.	.
		F. - 5671	623	632	573	602	541	411	363	328	275	237	233	202	200	121	90	62	40	17	1	.	.
2 KIRKBY MALZEARD	2831	M. - 1419	171	153	156	128	111	92	75	77	71	65	77	57	57	58	37	16	15	2	1	.	.
		F. - 1412	184	162	139	138	121	98	84	60	76	70	75	53	59	42	29	17	8	4	2	1	.
3 WATH	1625	M. - 831	107	96	85	101	64	67	44	40	47	34	27	31	29	23	27	5	4	.	.	.	.
		F. - 794	102	106	80	77	62	58	41	52	30	41	40	39	21	28	12	7	6	2	.	.	.
4 DISHFORTH	1589	M. - 798	106	91	74	95	77	55	53	31	37	39	31	29	25	30	13	11	.	5	.	.	.
		F. - 791	104	82	67	71	74	77	41	34	30	37	43	31	28	25	30	8	4	3	2	.	.
488 GREAT OUSEBURN.																							
1 BOROUGHBRIDGE	4942	M. - 2455	329	314	277	248	208	168	137	104	120	101	97	90	86	65	49	28	10	4	1	.	.
		F. - 2487	309	311	272	238	191	168	166	158	112	101	132	87	65	73	56	31	17	8	3	.	.
2 WHIXLEY. (W.)	3778	M. - 1875	236	223	213	210	158	97	101	87	89	91	76	58	62	50	48	31	13	5	1	.	1
		F. - 1903	236	233	211	160	180	109	108	88	97	91	91	63	76	61	47	28	20	2	1	1	.
3 POPPLETON. (L.[2])	3235	M. - 1598	213	208	158	135	134	120	91	100	71	69	73	59	60	43	37	13	7	2	1	.	.
		F. - 1637	213	201	185	143	144	105	98	113	79	64	68	62	50	46	32	17	10	6	1	.	.
489 KNARESBOROUGH.																							
1 KNARESBOROUGH. (W.)	8497	M. - 4025	593	479	438	389	259	291	215	207	235	185	213	175	129	118	78	35	27	9	1	1	.
		F. - 4472	539	405	462	420	462	313	274	231	252	244	206	161	153	120	104	53	21	7	1	1	.
2 HARROGATE. (H.[2])	14138	M. - 6415	829	757	904	651	490	452	374	358	309	221	255	248	201	141	82	50	29	3	1	.	.
		F. - 7723	811	747	737	887	823	676	521	505	423	345	335	288	228	181	108	65	31	8	4	.	.
490 WETHERBY.																							
1 WETHERBY. (W.)	7274	M. - 3614	482	424	384	348	317	225	198	195	175	164	176	130	134	104	79	57	22	2	.	.	.
		F. - 3660	478	430	391	308	294	277	227	198	191	186	143	118	141	102	82	68	28	12	1	.	.
2 BOSTON. (R.)	8920	M. - 4432	499	496	719	462	328	289	231	215	236	188	181	168	167	108	74	50	16	7	.	.	.
		F. - 4488	517	505	459	445	385	322	269	275	240	244	178	172	146	140	101	43	27	8	3	.	.
491 WHARFEDALE.																							
1 HORSFORTH. (H.[2], R.)	11799	M. - 5894	784	674	863	575	446	431	359	369	329	270	231	181	167	105	71	28	7	4	.	.	.
		F. - 5905	760	752	583	583	551	536	437	382	295	282	214	171	161	105	61	42	12	7	1	.	.
2 FEWSTON. (W.)	2927	M. - 1502	191	172	169	143	118	103	92	88	76	73	74	55	51	37	26	18	11	4	1	.	.
		F. - 1425	200	179	147	119	130	102	89	103	72	62	62	45	44	34	24	13	6	.	2	.	.
3 OTLEY. (H.[2])	15616	M. - 7270	1030	881	738	631	579	624	519	431	392	308	301	251	200	150	86	45	25	8	.	.	.
		F. - 8346	1045	926	869	857	889	724	595	520	433	370	322	285	254	136	86	59	25	3	1	.	.
4 YEADON	16363	M. - 7960	1138	967	885	815	722	632	475	465	412	358	287	269	214	142	91	48	22	2	1	.	.
		F. - 8403	1108	998	902	866	834	682	341	509	475	392	328	257	215	136	85	58	29	1	2	.	.

Note.—For the Parishes comprised in each Registration Sub-district, see Vol. II., Division IX., Table 4.
(W.) denotes that a Workhouse and (W.S.) that a Workhouse School belonging to the District is situated within the Sub-district. (w.) denotes a Workhouse and (w.s.) a Workhouse School not belonging to the District, (H.) a Hospital or Infirmary, (L.) a Lunatic Asylum, (P.) a Prison or Convict Establishment, (R.) a Certified Reformatory or Industrial School, (B.) Barracks, &c., (S.) H.M. Ships. A figure appended to any of these letters denotes the number of Institutions of a similar class situated within the Sub-district. The names of the Institutions thus indicated, and the number of inmates enumerated therein, will be found in Vol. II., Division IX., Table 6.

Table 3 *continued*.—Ages of Males and Females in Registration Sub-Districts.

Registration Sub-District.	All Ages. Persons.	All Ages. Males and Females.	Under 5 Years.	5-	10-	15-	20-	25-	30-	35-	40-	45-	50-	55-	60-	65-	70-	75-	80-	85-	90-	95-
35 WEST RIDING —cont.																						
492 KEIGHLEY.																						
1 Bingley	20703	M. - 9721	1387	1211	1091	1013	867	714	638	548	520	480	431	297	268	173	96	43	19	3	.	.
		F. - 10992	1364	1209	1135	1124	1093	944	752	685	651	528	454	372	282	191	104	68	30	4	.	2
2 Keighley. (W. H.)	35545	M. - 18017	2089	1901	1785	1691	1440	1303	1017	882	870	722	673	517	456	248	158	68	40	8	.	.
		F. - 17528	2164	1962	1782	1780	1829	1549	1185	1079	1007	885	739	588	427	271	156	88	39	7	.	.
3 Haworth	6873	M. - 3326	415	365	384	360	274	268	183	186	190	167	142	153	146	82	36	32	12	2	.	.
		F. - 3547	422	364	375	351	367	311	226	208	201	164	152	138	105	75	52	27	8	1	.	.
493 TODMORDEN.																						
1 Hebden Bridge	12314	M. - 5887	881	677	596	536	358	460	377	342	341	278	221	224	198	114	85	36	15	1	.	.
		F. - 6427	733	820	591	641	612	670	470	420	378	323	290	285	225	140	90	37	17	3	.	.
2 Todmorden. (W. H.)	23213	M. - 11208	1465	1314	1125	1061	1068	929	894	763	627	529	487	370	300	190	98	40	13	1	1	.
		F. - 12005	1446	1265	1145	1137	1189	1054	924	787	695	615	506	425	343	253	140	60	16	6	1	.
494 SADDLEWORTH.																						
1 Delph	10461	M. - 5052	692	624	555	508	426	394	328	292	288	250	225	165	130	90	45	30	7	2	.	.
		F. - 5409	737	665	556	612	469	436	361	311	303	278	238	176	146	111	57	37	11	.	1	.
2 Upper Mill. (W.)	11838	M. - 5641	696	645	623	587	524	440	377	320	303	286	245	197	166	116	61	34	9	3	.	.
		F. - 6197	765	670	634	683	581	522	417	354	346	322	249	222	170	135	53	49	14	1	1	.
495 HUDDERSFIELD.																						
1 Slaithwaite	8964	M. - 4352	561	490	494	420	421	352	297	246	224	188	207	143	137	84	44	33	8	2	1	.
		F. - 4612	523	518	518	488	467	366	307	283	230	214	203	156	147	85	86	26	5	1	.	.
2 Honley. (W. H.)	13583	M. - 6420	773	761	698	681	558	496	309	290	356	335	272	244	165	122	98	53	23	3	2	.
		F. - 7163	836	717	769	698	668	590	517	426	472	375	305	268	188	138	106	51	27	1	2	.
3 Holmfirth	9583	M. - 4713	646	532	519	491	430	371	308	252	238	203	246	169	150	79	67	34	7	2	1	.
		F. - 4870	615	618	608	487	462	482	297	300	238	210	206	144	146	104	65	28	19	5	.	.
4 Newmill	5752	M. - 2838	431	369	317	289	264	228	189	[illegible]	161	116	[illegible]	86	88	53	34	23	7	.	.	.
		F. - 2914	402	336	351	342	268	235	176	158	140	120	118	70	62	64	34	23	6	2	.	.
5 Kirkburton	12275	M. - 5996	806	789	634	661	495	404	363	322	311	[illegible]	231	[illegible]	196	130	55	40	20	9	.	.
		F. - 6279	840	784	[illegible]	650	546	470	[illegible]	371	348	270	233	196	180	131	75	51	11	7	3	.
6 Almondbury	14591	M. - 6962	921	890	814	708	682	573	467	387	398	298	298	227	148	108	94	38	15	7	.	.
		F. - 7629	979	921	790	776	723	612	542	473	437	346	290	243	197	117	111	38	20	4	.	1
7 Kirkheaton	14576	M. - 7206	998	867	856	718	682	572	467	370	358	326	267	256	204	118	109	44	17	6	.	.
		F. - 7370	944	893	802	738	738	609	489	403	385	331	295	253	180	129	78	54	14	2	1	1
8 Huddersfield. (H².)	42234	M. - 19960	2552	2340	2147	1963	1860	1813	1408	1236	1127	948	892	696	611	283	184	73	41	6	2	.
		F. - 22274	2512	2380	2124	2369	2516	2045	1668	1322	1274	1010	900	727	629	463	270	114	51	12	.	.
9 Lockwood. (W.)	14751	M. - 7161	971	885	830	719	619	594	589	430	410	320	248	204	199	120	85	43	16	1	.	.
		F. - 7590	966	890	825	760	706	616	564	480	425	330	285	230	214	120	79	37	19	4	1	.
10 Golcar	20205	M. - 9770	1364	1206	1148	1034	933	828	635	543	522	429	324	278	197	147	67	43	18	2	.	.
		F. - 10435	1404	1265	1167	1050	1034	923	712	629	543	471	380	319	229	161	93	37	16	6	.	.
496 HALIFAX.																						
1 Rastrick	8542	M. - 4111	652	539	425	436	367	329	292	282	212	182	142	124	90	62	27	16	6	1	.	1
		F. - 4431	567	531	491	454	405	369	327	262	248	217	165	131	115	83	39	16	9	1	1	.
2 Brighouse	15683	M. - 7544	1039	954	811	778	680	619	568	466	416	356	289	216	176	96	62	29	9	4	1	.
		F. - 8139	1131	1000	842	846	746	717	558	470	393	379	340	275	185	116	86	40	11	4	3	.
3 Southowram. (H. R.)	8813	M. - 4976	616	578	518	452	540	348	296	232	235	183	148	128	87	66	40	13	2	.	.	.
		F. - 4837	630	576	479	469	396	375	289	270	268	200	166	131	120	85	58	25	6	2	.	1
4 Halifax. (W. H. B.)	54038	M. - 25195	3178	2948	2678	2428	2363	2141	1725	1604	1478	1231	1107	847	670	443	265	105	36	12	.	1
		F. - 28843	3267	3026	2777	2896	2041	2060	2048	1832	1746	1423	1272	984	835	554	327	173	78	17	2	1
5 Elland	17940	M. - 8523	1137	1009	1017	902	802	673	585	524	449	360	309	236	216	142	79	40	17	.	.	.
		F. - 9417	1221	1096	961	968	877	773	686	571	547	441	346	297	276	180	104	51	21	6	1	.
6 Ripponden	6679	M. - 3218	392	434	417	347	272	239	190	178	165	134	119	121	71	69	43	18	7	3	.	.
		F. - 3461	472	444	411	344	310	265	236	190	209	153	147	101	78	66	41	23	9	1	1	.
7 Sowerby	16846	M. - 8104	1081	1053	886	842	738	637	530	473	448	338	297	288	236	158	91	40	16	3	.	.
		F. - 8742	1181	981	815	876	830	749	667	558	480	437	329	310	290	164	98	63	12	4	.	.
8 Luddenden	6053	M. - 2827	388	333	290	281	264	202	198	160	152	111	107	93	105	76	33	28	3	3	.	.
		F. - 3226	359	368	320	328	296	285	237	221	172	137	126	131	118	70	35	18	7	2	1	.
9 Ovenden	12874	M. - 6232	827	729	694	622	515	546	426	323	388	295	256	201	191	124	61	34	14	6	.	.
		F. - 6642	848	787	658	656	560	578	445	415	419	312	271	236	198	137	68	45	9	6	.	.
10 Northowram	22972	M. - 11044	1531	1346	1229	1108	1018	808	716	636	581	490	437	392	305	171	100	52	20	2	2	.
		F. - 11928	1532	1365	1203	1106	1109	1010	805	727	735	597	480	427	310	226	140	64	28	3	1	.
497 BRADFORD.																						
1 Cleckheaton	17464	M. - 8475	1195	1063	969	914	798	648	561	538	454	360	321	225	180	140	66	34	14	1	.	.
		F. - 8989	1242	1075	1000	937	872	721	619	508	502	412	331	280	226	133	68	43	18	9	1	.
2 Drighlington	9845	M. - 4839	629	620	578	540	448	360	275	261	261	232	194	166	119	75	43	28	7	1	.	.
		F. - 4996	662	654	535	480	464	416	258	281	279	246	234	156	109	71	48	29	8	1	.	1
3 North Bierley	15620	M. - 7439	1061	872	780	781	778	604	475	462	395	346	264	265	186	112	78	33	10	2	.	.
		F. - 8181	1036	937	822	829	777	722	562	543	474	306	348	285	214	122	91	46	13	3	.	.
4 Bowling	28738	M. - 13643	1941	1720	1467	1488	1240	1132	972	852	780	608	612	377	278	193	84	69	8	7	.	.
		F. - 15095	1901	1708	1558	1502	1493	1311	1080	966	864	772	605	472	353	196	129	56	26	8	.	.
5 Bradford, East End. (H. R. R.)	52892	M. - 25853	3656	3131	2700	2496	2235	2181	1814	1675	1523	1132	978	672	517	315	191	70	42	5	.	.
		F. - 27439	3945	3110	3815	2749	2536	2352	2029	1768	1619	1306	1045	795	669	384	215	90	52	11	3	.
6 Bradford, West End (H².)	18143	M. - 8390	1070	948	888	795	777	718	626	557	627	387	356	263	242	134	68	40	14	.	.	.
		F. - 9753	1060	992	896	1080	1090	927	749	616	623	444	454	270	305	126	70	47	23	3	.	.
7 Horton. (W.)	83349	M. - 37815	5580	4837	4291	3818	3263	3020	2563	2371	2148	1672	1435	1117	829	512	319	151	47	12	.	.
		F. - 45534	5452	4868	4119	4700	4891	4240	3338	2812	2709	2108	1872	1451	1090	689	433	197	101	24	3	.
8 Thornton. (W.)	16713	M. - 8203	1064	1005	875	913	718	623	509	429	416	366	357	289	272	170	104	58	22	10	3	1
		F. - 8510	1033	966	914	877	786	721	560	518	474	445	374	281	213	169	84	53	16	6	1	.
9 Wilsden	6651	M. - 3078	415	352	397	344	268	239	253	182	145	138	137	104	98	64	29	13	6	4	.	.
		F. - 3573	489	399	385	386	349	307	258	202	209	179	134	128	94	64	40	19	11	5	.	.
10 Shipley. (H.)	18200	M. - 8455	1168	1110	1035	934	685	655	543	484	454	332	324	224	191	122	69	41	10	2	1	1
		F. - 9745	1217	1074	1037	1088	1012	860	616	582	595	409	359	280	245	137	65	53	12	3	.	1
11 Idle	20412	M. - 9789	1464	1212	1150	916	831	721	657	622	527	434	372	317	235	181	94	45	19	3	.	.
		F. - 10623	1427	1294	1173	977	977	848	690	714	586	489	441	348	265	180	124	69	23	8	1	.
12 Calverley	8206	M. - 3852	506	430	438	386	330	303	235	236	215	186	148	154	112	77	46	25	8	3	1	.
		F. - 4354	502	487	438	461	411	383	301	282	236	217	175	159	138	100	44	23	4	1	.	.
13 Pudsey	15459	M. - 7386	1002	993	817	757	613	599	441	490	470	321	314	251	217	184	79	48	16	3	1	.
		F. - 8073	1026	882	866	808	730	652	556	530	463	405	296	271	256	170	90	44	22	2	1	.

Table 3 *continued*.—AGES of MALES and FEMALES in REGISTRATION SUB-DISTRICTS.

REGISTRATION SUB-DISTRICT.	ALL AGES. Persons.	ALL AGES. Males and Females.	Under 5 Years.	5–	10–	15–	20–	25–	30–	35–	40–	45–	50–	55–	60–	65–	70–	75–	80–	85–	90–	95–	100 and upw^ds^.
35 WEST RIDING —*cont.*																							
498 HUNSLET.																							
1 HUNSLET. (W.)	46942	M. - 23297	3687	2995	2308	2242	2013	2069	1680	1530	1291	967	836	618	410	259	139	72	22	.	.	.	.
		F. - 23655	3791	3003	2534	2129	2048	2035	1641	1470	1300	1041	859	669	516	327	180	105	26	9	1	1	.
2 WHITKIRK	5034	M. - 2550	409	331	268	240	224	192	174	155	145	97	96	68	70	33	28	13	2	1	.	.	.
		F. - 2484	379	352	276	200	169	202	156	147	135	105	88	74	76	35	41	23	8	4	1	.	1
3 ROTHWELL	6239	M. - 3056	474	387	372	324	229	245	208	173	180	119	105	100	50	39	38	15	8	.	.	.	.
		F. - 3183	530	459	384	278	253	234	203	175	157	119	114	88	68	46	44	15	4	3	1	.	.
499 HOLBECK.																							
1 HOLBECK. (W.)	24051	M. - 11642	1680	1490	1298	1113	970	963	862	767	666	498	440	321	243	176	101	43	16	4	1	.	.
		F. - 12409	1815	1603	1289	1172	1081	978	838	792	692	558	458	384	326	213	148	72	17	2	1	.	.
500 BRAMLEY.																							
1 BRAMLEY	11055	M. - 5578	763	665	583	530	484	377	371	330	237	240	211	175	187	83	53	31	16	4	.	.	.
		F. - 5477	740	696	622	565	486	477	408	340	328	259	218	196	145	93	53	33	11	4	2	.	.
2 GILDERSOME	3470	M. - 1741	240	212	241	201	149	122	101	107	85	80	67	40	35	25	13	8	6	.	.	.	.
		F. - 1729	256	225	204	177	153	139	101	106	83	78	68	50	38	23	17	8	2	1	.	.	.
3 WORTLEY. (W. P.)	39875	M. - 19842	2866	2484	2027	2017	1829	1807	1390	1215	1068	873	736	672	411	257	156	74	20	8	.	.	.
		F. - 20033	2974	2514	2123	1868	1798	1707	1377	1165	1120	921	817	564	407	295	171	93	28	10	3	.	.
501 LEEDS.																							
1 SOUTH-EAST LEEDS. (H.)	30368	M. - 14994	2192	1855	1663	1463	1271	1224	1070	963	910	704	609	415	331	165	101	51	15	2	.	.	.
		F. - 15374	2322	1944	1669	1531	1354	1286	1019	961	901	743	609	482	355	203	132	71	26	5	1	1	.
2 NORTH LEEDS. (W. W S. H. R. R.)	55849	M. - 28010	4104	3437	2859	2539	2577	2520	1905	1867	1640	1202	1108	713	686	434	223	94	33	6	3	.	.
		F. - 27839	4105	3384	3017	2608	2467	2383	1860	1767	1632	1222	1039	726	701	419	263	115	37	14	1	2	.
3 WEST LEEDS. (H^2^.)	73592	M. - 34653	4710	4039	3718	3394	3182	3074	2530	2546	2048	1496	1323	981	745	513	301	129	50	8	.	1	.
		F. - 38939	4897	4189	3831	4173	4055	3508	2826	2509	2234	1780	1602	1227	1014	689	447	253	88	19	7	2	.
4 KIRKSTALL	19158	M. - 8718	1304	1072	938	773	744	748	611	579	474	378	348	242	242	141	74	37	11	1	1	.	.
		F. - 10420	1263	1166	1076	1087	1114	958	748	617	596	415	379	318	278	177	130	60	22	6	1	.	.
5 CHAPELTOWN. (H.)	11600	M. - 5185	788	679	560	509	415	392	339	329	281	241	193	178	142	87	61	27	9	3	1	.	.
		F. - 6415	752	673	609	680	736	603	447	378	378	268	257	197	166	123	84	54	25	2	3	.	.
502 DEWSBURY.																							
1 MORLEY	15011	M. - 7274	1124	985	805	719	646	628	490	457	396	332	250	172	129	71	45	24	11	1	.	.	.
		F. - 7737	1195	1003	889	802	734	638	517	430	410	346	286	194	130	77	45	34	8	1	.	.	.
2 BATLEY. (H.)	27505	M. - 12907	1868	1689	1491	1291	1141	1041	929	833	756	545	424	310	244	164	84	44	20	2	1	.	.
		F. - 14598	1904	1807	1375	1569	1477	1260	1016	973	840	607	516	371	289	177	93	56	18	2	.	.	.
3 GOMERSAL	13453	M. - 6302	906	721	668	638	564	527	400	372	343	285	246	197	146	100	77	40	15	1	1	.	.
		F. - 7151	921	806	734	733	719	631	479	414	401	308	304	212	194	132	76	39	14	4	.	.	.
4 LIVERSEDGE	22039	M. - 10697	1516	1301	1233	1135	983	835	682	614	600	483	379	336	264	166	36	51	13	.	.	.	.
		F. - 11342	1034	1369	1200	1226	1006	902	762	665	650	511	458	397	271	179	113	61	13	4	1	.	.
5 MIRFIELD. (R.)	15872	M. - 7695	1055	964	954	893	750	633	468	448	398	332	268	221	151	97	42	24	5	2	1	.	.
		F. - 8177	1058	978	889	872	790	707	577	477	474	352	319	247	172	115	82	46	12	3	.	.	.
6 DEWSBURY. (W. H.)	29637	M. - 14179	1962	1786	1521	1473	1284	1170	974	900	830	682	553	400	324	179	88	37	13	3	.	.	.
		F. - 15458	2037	1719	1573	1611	1655	1361	1077	983	901	758	612	419	347	191	121	57	16	9	1	.	.
7 SOOTHILL	10395	M. - 5059	725	687	547	584	471	428	316	310	311	212	182	152	70	75	39	23	10	.	.	.	.
		F. - 5336	764	685	576	560	514	430	327	242	304	247	183	148	105	73	60	23	14	2	.	.	.
8 OSSETT	10957	M. - 5232	744	658	629	591	433	401	307	363	266	230	209	148	127	85	40	25	17	3	.	.	.
		F. - 5725	711	668	638	622	678	403	345	326	318	247	223	205	183	95	66	43	7	6	1	.	.
9 THORNHILL	8843	M. - 4356	677	546	502	476	423	362	287	230	219	161	178	111	87	44	39	16	3	1	.	.	.
		F. - 4487	668	610	503	499	442	370	282	249	198	177	165	129	78	52	30	23	9	1	2	.	.
503 WAKEFIELD.																							
1 BRETTON	5812	M. - 2956	424	393	343	323	261	205	187	166	126	117	108	91	88	55	40	23	7	2	1	.	.
		F. - 2856	433	407	345	261	248	182	173	162	130	115	96	90	79	52	32	24	8	6	1	.	.
2 SANDAL	22580	M. - 11767	2004	1609	1280	1058	1030	1075	833	606	602	401	342	226	182	111	77	38	18	5	2	.	.
		F. - 10813	1932	1684	1197	750	867	937	771	676	530	336	325	232	180	113	93	45	27	2	2	.	.
3 STANLEY. (W. H. L.)	13431	M. - 6870	974	827	735	606	545	554	494	464	385	315	270	222	183	120	87	43	11	2	.	.	.
		F. - 6561	979	838	698	508	490	532	434	440	418	274	267	234	169	125	99	47	14	1	.	.	.
4 WAKEFIELD. (H. P.)	22173	M. - 10994	1483	1226	1080	1037	1096	1041	821	741	658	482	417	297	272	152	97	58	11	3	1	.	.
		F. - 11179	1496	1178	1130	1238	1124	967	775	704	640	406	422	314	298	219	137	74	36	7	5	.	.
5 HORBURY	5050	M. - 2384	391	304	273	248	206	171	139	127	134	85	99	79	47	38	22	11	7	3	.	.	.
		F. - 2666	337	341	308	320	230	184	155	137	151	113	102	95	51	39	25	19	6	2	1	.	.
6 ALVERTHORPE	10486	M. - 5298	885	751	542	518	478	433	340	279	265	185	162	148	114	79	34	23	6	2	1	.	.
		F. - 5188	845	643	573	521	457	416	373	289	220	234	171	141	111	87	60	39	8	5	1	.	.
7 ARDSLEY	9575	M. - 5014	810	692	538	491	509	372	348	306	226	220	183	114	81	50	39	16	10	1	.	.	.
		F. - 4561	832	656	527	378	346	357	317	242	225	208	145	104	93	55	30	27	12	4	1	2	.
504 PONTEFRACT.																							
1 KNOTTINGLEY	9875	M. - 5002	787	617	584	434	419	369	310	306	203	204	182	132	171	120	84	37	15	3	.	.	.
		F. - 4873	714	642	531	418	420	353	309	254	229	213	107	158	140	123	96	47	19	9	1	.	.
2 WHITLEY	2462	M. - 1277	182	134	118	169	118	92	84	69	57	59	40	42	33	31	21	12	4	3	.	.	.
		F. - 1185	167	159	112	109	100	97	67	71	64	40	44	25	47	19	25	17	6	2	1	.	.
3 PONTEFRACT. (W. B.)	15784	M. - 8227	1284	996	897	847	792	717	608	523	433	322	279	204	156	98	64	46	15	6	.	1	.
		F. - 7557	1217	1104	842	628	617	633	552	432	357	318	228	181	171	93	68	61	26	10	3	.	.
4 CASTLEFORD	19785	M. - 10468	1749	1414	1128	1010	929	912	802	680	537	386	325	220	174	111	58	34	8	1	.	.	.
		F. - 9317	1867	1443	1111	716	667	774	602	546	483	338	279	211	209	129	63	53	19	4	3	.	.
505 HEMSWORTH.																							
1 HEMSWORTH. (W.)	11106	M. - 5935	814	640	706	578	593	440	426	540	297	270	237	151	168	91	84	50	22	4	.	.	.
		F. - 5171	754	683	616	443	435	388	330	303	258	205	204	150	125	117	78	44	25	5	1	.	.
506 BARNSLEY.																							
1 DARTON	7078	M. - 3796	573	495	428	366	353	318	296	240	192	141	130	88	59	61	37	17	8	4	.	.	.
		F. - 3282	585	516	391	236	225	230	248	191	164	130	126	88	55	52	28	15	4	1	.	.	.
2 BARNSLEY. (W. H^2^.)	41474	M. - 21168	3227	2656	2268	1930	1913	1842	1574	1318	1114	855	768	520	454	318	202	101	38	6	.	.	.
		F. - 20306	3261	2834	2222	1844	1808	1671	1347	1177	1001	814	585	544	496	343	178	98	41	10	2	.	.
3 DARFIELD	21087	M. - 11342	1855	1482	1324	1102	1135	1036	844	641	553	454	348	232	198	129	65	20	16	4	.	.	.
		F. - 9745	1884	1542	1118	710	726	741	645	556	492	372	329	221	196	104	79	39	16	5	.	.	.
4 WORSBROUGH	8972	M. - 4777	763	658	550	467	445	416	314	306	224	172	147	115	101	49	28	10	3	2	.	1	.
		F. - 4195	826	645	593	282	287	330	269	233	198	166	138	116	91	57	25	18	8	2	.	.	.

Table 3 *continued*.—Ages of Males and Females in Registration Sub-Districts.

Registration Sub-District.	All Ages. Persons.	All Ages. Males and Females.	Under 5 Years.	5–	10–	15–	20–	25–	30–	35–	40–	45–	50–	55–	60–	65–	70–	75–	80–	85–	90–	95–
35 WEST RIDING —*cont.*																						
507 WORTLEY.																						
1 Cawthorne	5162	M. - 2693	381	343	286	294	200	201	175	129	148	108	91	83	75	54	37	18	9	1	.	.
		F. 2469	422	358	302	166	195	166	159	126	125	93	86	88	64	49	31	29	8	3	.	.
2 High Hoyland	3226	M. - 1592	238	183	176	156	144	115	91	80	90	76	58	47	51	36	22	23	7	1	.	.
		F. 1634	204	181	184	174	137	124	105	92	97	77	69	59	44	36	24	16	8	3	1	.
3 Penistone. (W.)	8285	M. 4366	677	547	464	424	404	389	295	223	203	177	182	124	121	80	34	23	8	6	.	.
		F. 3919	635	545	491	347	316	296	249	206	174	179	146	111	35	81	47	28	6	.	1	1
4 Wortley	3259	M. - 1734	260	226	202	192	177	144	119	89	78	79	56	39	34	19	9	6	3	3	.	.
		F. - 1525	283	253	188	131	114	75	108	80	65	67	52	47	31	17	11	6	3	.	.	.
5 Ecclesfield. (W. L.)	21156	M. - 10812	1621	1347	1158	1061	969	906	765	688	610	442	389	320	244	141	37	41	17	7	.	.
		F. - 10344	1684	1336	1151	792	787	814	729	660	640	472	424	311	282	163	96	56	27	9	3	.
6 Bradfield (R[2].)	11170	M. - 5756	874	737	708	610	604	474	368	330	257	248	185	151	131	87	46	24	10	4	.	.
		F. - 5414	870	773	698	835	495	370	323	229	294	201	167	158	121	87	52	30	6	4	1	.
508 ECCLESALL BIERLOW.																						
1 Nether Hallam. (R.B.)	38967	M. - 19271	2914	2429	2112	1946	1848	1607	1465	1296	1048	774	645	454	348	204	114	53	23	4	.	.
		F. - 19696	2972	2593	2229	1956	1834	1588	1400	1188	1024	768	669	527	489	236	162	77	29	4	2	.
2 Upper Hallam	4058	M. - 1918	301	250	211	177	163	144	106	113	94	87	74	69	56	39	18	16	9	2	.	.
		F. - 2140	284	255	238	232	227	165	142	112	101	71	82	62	61	50	31	15	11	1	.	.
3 Norton	3855	M. - 1951	296	258	207	169	158	147	134	117	97	91	66	61	61	39	34	23	.	.	.	.
		F. - 1904	259	256	207	171	148	147	132	115	102	93	69	66	66	35	17	16	4	.	1	.
4 Ecclesall Bierlow. (W. H.)	67538	M. - 31983	4597	3892	3467	3247	2898	2625	2329	2016	1802	1380	1134	901	738	416	321	126	48	18	3	.
		F. - 35555	4671	3957	3658	4081	3717	3088	2374	2341	1950	1407	1291	1035	850	565	378	218	88	10	.	1
509 SHEFFIELD.																						
1 West Sheffield. (H[3].)	14957	M. - 7478	914	815	808	726	721	661	575	454	470	392	328	244	182	109	49	24	7	.	.	.
		F. - 7479	904	817	735	875	782	566	486	486	442	377	332	232	224	123	70	46	11	4	.	.
2 North Sheffield. (W. H.)	38982	M. - 19549	2636	2382	2075	1829	1809	1685	1424	1306	1206	912	828	487	434	281	153	64	22	5	1	.
		F. - 19433	2828	2404	2069	1971	1698	1628	1287	1132	1137	936	714	554	482	302	223	103	32	12	1	.
3 South Sheffield	17919	M. - 8889	1235	1041	929	938	780	796	683	593	537	419	329	242	212	108	62	25	8	2	.	.
		F. - 9030	1223	1057	910	952	915	751	631	554	497	439	383	264	214	136	78	33	8	4	1	.
4 Sheffield Park	19048	M. - 9978	1526	1182	1028	926	994	916	761	668	562	411	379	276	183	123	83	30	13	7	.	.
		F. - 9070	1567	1298	1064	918	924	836	677	575	535	422	345	276	211	135	102	58	26	4	2	1
5 Brightside. (W.)	56719	M. - 29118	4418	3723	3055	2699	2930	2618	2225	1996	1694	1301	992	710	521	331	176	76	26	4	2	.
		F. - 27601	4328	3876	3037	2317	2310	2283	1983	1719	1527	1266	1022	667	548	352	232	93	41	10	.	.
6 Attercliffe	26965	M. - 13871	2165	1875	1604	1396	1115	1160	1043	1034	794	554	422	305	307	123	74	81	15	4	2	.
		F. - 13094	2351	1988	1529	1030	916	1011	958	826	756	527	410	316	258	135	82	30	12	5	1	.
7 Handsworth	7645	M. - 4062	648	562	436	402	388	336	263	246	196	187	137	118	61	60	28	10	5	2	.	.
		F. 3583	608	549	421	293	273	243	242	210	194	158	114	92	76	45	36	15	7	2	1	.
510 ROTHERHAM.																						
1 Beighton	5608	M. - 2958	460	409	316	281	260	236	206	163	155	115	100	81	56	45	21	20	6	.	.	.
		F. - 2650	461	428	305	167	195	200	187	148	124	116	79	68	65	58	28	16	8	2	.	.
2 Rotherham. (W. H.)	21186	M. - 10864	1809	1409	1158	974	950	844	785	681	579	457	409	259	237	158	87	68	14	3	.	.
		F. - 10322	1601	1335	1168	991	936	811	721	651	533	452	387	297	230	159	121	77	20	14	.	.
3 Kimberworth. (L.)	30083	M. - 15284	2569	2197	1743	1529	1331	1314	1110	970	766	622	463	365	289	171	106	56	18	5	.	.
		F. - 14349	2583	2231	1671	1098	1042	1071	945	884	725	561	481	369	318	213	101	61	21	3	1	.
4 Wath	16120	M. - 8333	1411	1155	893	814	723	695	577	537	381	328	274	180	168	96	59	33	4	4	1	.
		F. 7787	1378	1220	963	609	590	588	535	468	363	297	243	173	177	115	73	30	12	4	3	.
5 Maltby	2568	M. - 1241	162	161	126	111	98	92	79	58	61	66	57	55	37	39	23	20	5	1	.	.
		F. - 1327	172	177	158	120	102	89	66	65	72	64	58	50	54	35	25	10	8	2	.	.
511 DONCASTER.																						
1 Tickhill. (R.)	11549	M. - 5860	847	770	633	345	530	486	386	360	276	258	221	157	144	116	88	56	16	5	1	.
		F. - 5689	878	775	639	455	435	406	408	334	295	236	215	185	140	117	78	68	26	12	2	.
2 Barnbrough	10237	M. - 5300	770	706	593	529	455	443	382	309	250	239	184	140	120	83	54	35	17	3	.	.
		F. 4937	829	654	575	432	402	379	288	283	265	212	161	150	117	79	58	32	16	3	2	.
3 Doncaster. (W. H.)	21139	M. - 10445	1375	1213	1138	1001	1004	834	704	638	609	499	400	348	266	184	116	73	31	5	.	.
		F. - 10694	1315	1156	1191	1068	1009	834	722	632	604	460	478	354	312	237	159	80	45	16	2	.
4 Campsall	4913	M. - 2427	310	289	265	222	204	182	160	153	124	94	104	97	81	76	44	35	9	5	.	.
		F. - 2486	331	299	296	219	177	190	138	154	129	94	91	88	92	82	57	27	14	9	.	.
5 Bawtry	6034	M. - 3024	435	362	291	307	224	216	179	161	159	146	132	108	96	90	57	31	21	8	1	.
		F. - 3010	379	350	343	290	232	218	175	158	152	146	107	119	110	73	67	39	10	7	2	1
512 THORNE.																						
1 Epworth	4253	M. - 2112	265	248	242	206	149	124	101	119	105	95	116	93	78	79	39	21	23	6	3	.
		F. - 2141	231	258	264	206	145	127	123	118	114	106	109	88	88	69	38	35	12	7	2	.
2 Thorne. (W.)	7076	M. - 3532	442	432	429	337	268	214	189	162	178	147	140	164	124	109	68	77	30	11	4	.
		F. - 3544	465	399	389	321	255	232	192	166	188	171	165	157	129	128	91	69	38	16	4	1
3 Crowle	4852	M. - 2400	322	287	253	225	185	128	154	125	134	123	108	99	104	57	37	27	19	2	1	.
		F. 2452	233	337	292	232	181	153	122	139	138	137	106	88	91	59	48	29	10	5	1	.
513 GOOLE.																						
1 Swinefleet	3908	M. - 1983	275	234	224	246	169	114	92	85	88	91	91	71	71	61	33	30	9	4	2	1
		F. - 1925	242	235	207	190	144	111	86	100	117	84	94	83	79	68	38	27	17	4	4	.
2 Goole. (W. H.)	11680	M. - 5943	906	739	595	545	534	521	422	378	334	272	192	161	135	93	79	27	7	3	.	.
		F. - 5737	853	784	639	531	466	463	414	314	312	268	193	158	139	103	81	43	17	8	1	.
3 Snaith	3970	M. - 1876	239	212	198	182	161	154	108	100	90	92	104	62	68	52	35	27	9	5	.	.
		F. 2094	273	249	213	170	182	154	109	103	112	89	97	89	93	62	48	52	14	5	1	.
514 SELBY.																						
1 Carlton	2223	M. - 1096	168	133	127	103	73	80	50	54	69	43	55	38	43	36	33	12	10	3	.	.
		F. - 1127	141	137	120	99	85	74	67	61	66	60	54	46	41	40	22	23	8	1	2	.
2 Selby. (W.)	10243	M. - 5017	685	631	582	613	405	333	307	275	256	228	211	170	164	110	78	54	23	4	.	.
		F. - 5226	653	655	613	590	434	363	319	277	264	245	237	177	158	125	95	68	30	9	3	1
3 Riccall	3549	M. - 1896	214	214	187	166	142	116	92	78	70	64	78	82	62	51	31	32	13	4	.	.
		F. - 1653	217	186	177	186	154	110	95	71	83	80	69	78	64	45	28	20	12	4	.	1

Table 3 *continued.*—AGES of MALES and FEMALES in REGISTRATION SUB-DISTRICTS.

REGISTRATION SUB-DISTRICT.	ALL AGES. Persons.	Males and Females.	Under 5 Years.	5–	10–	15–	20–	25–	30–	35–	40–	45–	50–	55–	60–	65–	70–	75–	80–	85–	90–	95–	100 and upw.
35 WEST RIDING —*cont.*																							
515. TADCASTER.																							
1 ABERFORD	14097	M. 7316	1133	917	813	751	616	580	610	384	368	284	260	232	178	134	74	54	22	6	.	.	.
		F. 6781	1007	1083	802	528	602	627	439	404	337	286	236	210	168	183	89	63	21	7	1	.	.
2 TADCASTER (W.)	4300	M. 2200	305	240	232	233	195	152	130	117	111	93	85	92	76	61	40	20	10	6	2	.	.
		F. 2100	279	248	212	168	193	161	118	119	114	85	88	85	76	63	35	24	11	3	.	.	.
3 APPLETON ROEBUCK	5548	M. 2826	366	339	287	320	246	238	159	146	124	120	118	97	105	82	47	28	12	3	.	.	.
		F. 2722	415	332	306	228	234	194	144	129	138	122	139	100	94	84	47	29	15	11	1	.	.
36 EAST RIDING (With YORK).																							
516 YORK.																							
1 SKELTON	1501	M. 768	99	79	81	87	78	63	43	33	37	32	40	29	27	25	8	12	4	1	.	.	.
		F. 733	93	96	84	63	60	51	39	44	30	41	28	23	26	16	19	10	3	1	.	.	.
2 BOOTHAM (W. L[2]. R.)	17358	M. 8102	981	864	1005	844	632	619	543	475	460	366	320	287	275	220	146	65	33	6	.	1	.
		F. 9256	918	883	842	1053	970	802	636	579	572	450	366	347	322	241	162	112	33	13	5	.	.
3 MICKLEGATE	19190	M. 9185	1207	1113	966	882	850	772	659	560	532	418	383	303	215	162	113	51	17	8	3	.	.
		F. 10005	1230	1091	985	1042	967	804	729	599	528	501	407	340	271	226	160	85	44	18	4	.	.
4 WALMGATE. (H. L[2]. P. R. B[3].)	31415	M. 16274	2224	1829	1655	1667	1866	1478	1126	979	878	615	554	396	415	236	180	83	35	10	.	.	1
		F. 15141	2160	1831	1864	1348	1329	1263	1018	902	789	602	587	467	403	317	198	127	40	18	5	.	.
5 ESCRICK	2714	M. 1418	226	147	128	108	141	107	86	68	54	47	57	35	30	34	26	14	9	.	.	.	.
		F. 1296	194	163	124	140	138	96	88	64	71	49	42	55	39	24	25	10	4	1	3	.	.
6 DUNNINGTON	2726	M. 1391	157	153	150	186	119	76	78	62	61	77	64	56	49	52	22	10	8	2	.	.	.
		F. 1335	163	180	157	120	113	83	66	61	60	72	55	48	48	38	39	21	7	8	.	.	.
7 FLAXTON	1781	M. 963	130	102	113	131	89	60	45	37	40	41	44	22	33	23	17	11	6	2	1	.	.
		F. 838	111	106	85	91	72	30	46	44	42	43	36	31	26	18	19	7	9	1	2	.	.
517 POCKLINGTON.																							
1 EAST STAMFORD BRIDGE	4043	M. 2161	267	222	240	272	198	133	93	111	103	105	100	80	76	65	45	25	12	4	1	.	.
		F. 1882	251	237	215	185	165	117	106	105	98	80	84	67	75	37	25	26	13	6	1	.	.
2 POCKLINGTON (W.)	6583	M. 3351	423	370	374	415	271	218	172	176	144	144	157	148	134	95	71	36	18	6	1	.	.
		F. 3232	398	395	388	313	262	218	184	133	179	141	146	124	97	89	63	30	19	7	4	1	.
3 MARKET WEIGHTON	4835	M. 2467	311	268	286	313	212	150	142	125	108	102	122	109	86	68	45	28	13	9	.	.	.
		F. 2368	295	290	278	242	185	133	146	113	118	108	98	102	99	66	30	29	24	3	.	.	.
518 HOWDEN.																							
1 HOLME. (R.)	1893	M. 1092	100	112	200	210	79	49	48	49	45	39	38	34	34	23	20	13	7	2	.	.	.
		F. 801	108	100	99	75	74	29	36	40	35	28	25	40	30	24	12	14	9	2	1	.	.
2 BUBWITH	1748	M. 903	132	99	100	119	79	64	47	35	43	34	44	39	23	24	17	9	2	4	1	.	.
		F. 845	131	104	96	74	72	51	40	45	38	38	44	37	21	19	17	6	10	2	.	.	.
3 HOWDEN (W.)	5722	M. 2865	322	330	340	276	239	189	133	140	149	146	143	130	124	64	63	37	21	5	1	.	.
		F. 2857	358	318	315	259	227	172	163	146	142	143	189	130	118	70	82	40	21	3	1	2	.
4 NEWPORT	3924	M. 2009	259	254	234	196	144	136	120	111	100	90	80	79	72	58	39	21	5	2	.	.	.
		F. 1915	268	242	195	181	150	124	123	106	88	70	77	92	63	52	68	19	15	3	1	.	1
519 BEVERLEY.																							
1 SOUTH CAVE	3707	M. 1890	228	213	201	194	175	151	123	103	102	96	83	59	53	50	31	23	10	4	1	.	.
		F. 1817	245	216	224	159	136	127	107	108	105	82	75	52	55	54	31	27	10	1	1	.	.
2 BEVERLEY (W. H. L. B.)	15509	M. 7557	1047	930	731	732	617	581	473	443	408	357	294	267	258	160	156	67	36	9	1	.	.
		F. 7952	1030	943	829	689	629	588	514	477	436	334	329	281	300	224	184	102	51	10	5	.	.
3 LOCKINGTON	2833	M. 1521	191	155	174	187	163	108	78	74	84	64	61	60	57	35	29	17	3	3	.	.	.
		F. 1312	172	181	153	135	99	88	67	72	74	57	53	45	34	36	26	10	8	2	.	.	.
4 LEVEN	1411	M. 762	99	74	61	105	85	40	46	49	32	37	38	17	18	17	14	5	4	1	.	.	.
		F. 649	74	84	71	70	52	40	40	31	30	37	27	20	23	14	15	12	2	1	.	.	.
520 SCULCOATES.																							
1 SUTTON	11561	M. 5845	953	754	847	547	490	454	439	396	308	295	206	164	113	88	48	17	15	1	.	.	.
		F. 5796	873	756	636	504	458	427	481	357	279	223	229	170	133	86	65	32	10	5	3	.	.
2 COTTINGHAM	6562	M. 3058	446	415	311	209	245	232	207	172	160	149	129	86	93	72	39	14	12	6	1	.	.
		F. 3504	435	420	398	341	350	288	209	212	181	161	125	97	106	66	35	35	18	7	.	.	.
3 FERRIBY	1798	M. 838	110	84	78	98	85	50	51	51	44	40	22	28	36	20	17	6	5	1	.	.	.
		F. 968	102	112	100	106	92	76	72	53	53	43	33	48	25	18	19	8	8	1	1	.	.
4 HESSLE	11605	M. 5627	906	756	579	484	451	454	438	353	325	237	183	149	118	94	54	26	18	2	2	.	.
		F. 5978	914	849	684	515	476	486	455	362	344	227	165	132	143	108	64	36	13	5	1	1	.
5 HEDON	2030	M. 957	127	116	119	79	82	54	47	65	48	37	48	38	26	34	20	12	5	3	1	.	.
		F. 1073	136	125	120	92	92	37	66	67	43	43	44	47	38	27	34	16	13	5	1	1	.
6 DRYPOOL. (H. L. P. R. S[1].)	20899	M. 10983	1637	1345	1269	994	977	963	584	680	637	483	360	268	214	152	73	33	8	1	1	1	.
		F. 9916	1630	1356	1049	798	801	772	770	651	522	421	341	279	228	148	86	43	14	6	1	.	.
7 EAST SCULCOATES	13136	M. 6460	944	763	683	637	566	580	426	419	351	340	258	171	174	108	67	43	17	3	.	.	.
		F. 6676	931	798	698	583	565	520	411	376	383	323	255	231	216	162	129	65	32	9	1	.	.
8 WEST SCULCOATES (W. H. R.)	32289	M. 14938	2283	1848	1683	1298	1207	1294	1150	962	709	606	514	420	307	228	181	78	41	4	.	.	.
		F. 17351	2203	1998	1889	1732	1713	1609	1280	1088	967	716	677	400	468	351	229	131	53	23	6	.	1
521 HULL.																							
1 HUMBER	6616	M. 3183	320	321	287	280	317	251	248	238	225	180	162	118	117	80	27	21	6	3	.	1	.
		F. 3433	352	342	301	309	334	296	240	219	187	171	166	117	112	76	82	43	19	6	1	.	.
2 ST. MARY	4136	M. 2083	231	222	217	202	172	178	145	165	135	100	108	64	69	57	24	6	6	.	.	.	.
		F. 2053	274	210	221	202	168	151	121	148	125	89	101	68	64	39	40	19	10	3	.	.	.
3 MYTON (W. H. L.)	67470	M. 33136	4741	3978	3369	3015	2941	2308	2039	2298	1874	1456	1140	909	780	467	384	151	73	17	3	.	.
		F. 34334	4844	4121	3302	3157	3311	2906	2533	2116	1226	1463	1252	1090	897	619	353	226	106	23	4	1	.
522 PATRINGTON.																							
1 PATRINGTON (W.)	8758	M. 4355	553	482	448	440	386	275	236	224	292	203	205	200	198	133	74	59	24	9	2	.	.
		F. 4403	565	540	463	422	378	288	240	235	218	200	192	177	163	123	91	68	33	8	1	.	.

Table 3 *continued*.—Ages of Males and Females in Registration Sub-Districts.

Registration Sub-District.	All Ages. Persons.		Males and Females.	Under 5 Years.	5-	10-	15-	20-	25-	30-	35-	40-	45-	50-	55-	60-	65-	70-	75-	80-	85-	90-	95-	100 and upw.
36 EAST RIDING —cont.																								
523 SKIRLAUGH.																								
1 Humbleton	1264	M.	650	71	74	64	95	63	40	31	34	38	30	24	19	21	21	11	8	4	2	.	.	.
		F.	614	98	73	64	58	47	40	35	35	28	31	23	22	12	22	15	7	8	1	1	.	.
2 Skirlaugh (W.)	2246	M.	1143	149	146	104	117	110	76	64	55	66	41	58	46	46	17	17	19	9	4	.	.	.
		F.	1103	164	159	115	103	82	88	63	53	60	45	42	34	37	20	19	17	8	.	2	.	.
3 Aldbrough	1469	M.	735	77	81	69	81	69	44	30	37	40	40	32	38	23	14	19	9	3	1	.	.	.
		F.	734	91	101	89	73	55	32	34	45	34	32	27	27	20	24	19	11	7	2	2	.	.
4 Hornsea	3234	M.	1486	107	170	142	155	125	101	93	83	85	72	56	51	50	48	26	22	4	1	2	.	.
		F.	1748	238	208	172	171	172	118	101	102	100	70	61	57	66	45	40	24	10	3	.	.	.
5 Brandesburton	1582	M.	838	129	89	91	110	73	53	53	47	39	32	29	25	29	18	16	9	3	2	.	.	.
		F.	744	107	108	70	73	56	52	44	41	41	20	20	30	19	17	13	15	3	2	.	.	.
524 DRIFFIELD.																								
1 Foston	2856	M.	1473	199	165	130	159	142	115	92	70	68	58	65	40	53	31	34	20	8	4	1	.	.
		F.	1383	206	183	133	117	110	115	81	71	55	64	54	50	50	37	35	17	7	1	.	.	.
2 Driffield (W. H.)	9153	M.	4505	614	570	530	421	359	293	230	240	237	193	194	137	175	126	80	45	24	8	.	.	.
		F.	4648	640	574	507	431	385	310	230	236	240	208	202	150	164	127	100	46	30	5	3	.	.
3 Bainton	3820	M.	2039	236	221	244	264	191	153	102	93	103	96	90	73	62	53	20	17	8	3	1	.	.
		F.	1781	255	208	198	172	165	124	101	102	84	78	64	62	48	54	23	25	11	5	2	.	.
4 Langtoft	4238	M.	2258	286	289	217	311	230	165	132	112	93	87	80	75	67	60	96	18	9	1	.	.	.
		F.	1980	317	269	227	178	183	123	122	101	94	75	81	65	61	38	37	14	18	1	2	.	.
525 BRIDLINGTON.																								
1 Skipsea	1800	M.	992	107	98	103	140	114	74	59	48	45	54	28	39	31	16	20	11	4	1	.	.	.
		F.	808	118	93	91	91	61	60	52	47	44	40	33	26	15	18	15	7	4	.	1	.	.
2 Bridlington (W. H².)	11026	M.	5129	688	634	533	483	375	338	330	281	278	250	225	188	187	164	100	47	28	8	1	.	.
		F.	5897	727	661	604	617	509	403	380	333	292	290	233	208	221	155	128	71	45	18	4	1	.
Hunmanby	3036	M.	2024	285	242	220	260	185	127	115	106	87	70	63	66	64	59	35	17	7	.	1	.	.
		F.	1012	299	250	197	196	145	145	113	95	88	61	65	65	56	53	45	24	11	3	1	.	.
37 NORTH RIDING.																								
526 SCARBOROUGH.																								
1 Filey	4189	M.	1985	280	244	227	192	146	130	122	102	94	92	87	68	75	60	30	15	11	4	.	.	.
		F.	2204	282	246	257	218	162	142	146	107	138	88	89	89	67	56	42	18	10	6	.	.	.
2 Scarborough (W.H³.B.)	32616	M.	14633	1963	1829	1671	1370	1167	1118	943	813	811	660	579	518	476	310	207	105	64	20	5	.	.
		F.	17983	1973	1742	1645	1919	1878	1485	1281	1137	991	893	753	621	620	420	312	190	66	23	7	3	.
3 Hutton-Bushell	4980	M.	2601	340	294	300	313	239	175	135	133	126	125	90	111	92	46	37	24	13	5	.	.	.
		F.	2379	329	236	285	260	198	156	138	118	117	108	93	98	60	51	40	23	15	4	.	.	.
4 Sherburn	1480	M.	790	111	108	82	102	71	58	33	34	37	31	21	27	24	26	14	6	4	1	.	.	.
		F.	690	109	101	68	58	63	48	34	34	28	29	30	27	23	19	7	10	1	1	.	.	.
527 MALTON.																								
1 Rillington	4169	M.	2160	263	231	221	298	202	156	137	113	98	99	85	81	69	51	33	25	5	3	1	.	.
		F.	2009	309	272	234	193	165	144	104	95	92	94	56	69	70	44	35	20	9	4	.	.	.
2 Westow	2648	M.	1364	164	182	149	170	118	98	83	78	68	96	58	41	44	33	21	15	5	1	.	.	.
		F.	1284	190	163	132	115	98	91	68	71	67	59	60	49	27	33	22	19	6	4	.	.	.
3 Malton (W.)	10545	M.	5146	780	639	545	484	422	381	307	277	282	229	218	167	158	125	92	55	27	7	1	.	.
		F.	5399	720	611	588	571	509	429	368	300	241	222	196	166	166	119	93	52	28	20	1	.	.
4 Hovingham	1993	M.	1010	117	107	119	124	90	51	52	52	53	30	41	42	42	46	28	11	9	4	1	.	.
		F.	983	112	110	104	72	90	60	52	48	38	38	44	48	47	29	22	15	10	2	.	.	.
5 Bulmer (R.)	3676	M.	1922	229	236	231	249	156	106	103	82	82	81	71	71	74	58	41	33	15	4	1	.	.
		F.	1754	223	192	203	145	141	120	106	91	78	83	76	79	59	67	50	21	18	4	.	.	.
528 EASINGWOLD.																								
1 Stillington	2526	M.	1332	163	142	131	194	129	90	74	41	69	60	52	50	46	43	23	26	7	3	.	.	.
		F.	1194	150	139	141	121	101	70	60	70	56	50	49	49	35	41	24	24	7	4	.	.	.
2 Easingwold (W.)	5330	M.	2696	340	312	301	290	232	165	143	119	132	116	121	78	124	83	63	31	26	8	.	1	.
		F.	2634	341	325	280	249	224	175	132	130	130	122	113	107	102	65	69	41	22	7	.	.	.
3 Coxwold	1677	M.	809	116	90	95	116	82	64	42	44	35	31	32	32	28	25	18	12	6	.	1	.	.
		F.	868	95	94	85	103	74	56	47	48	26	33	35	28	28	23	18	5	8	2	.	.	.
529 THIRSK.																								
1 Topcliffe	1734	M.	864	117	112	101	98	72	52	37	37	39	40	31	29	35	22	24	10	7	1	.	.	.
		F.	870	110	106	111	90	71	67	43	32	48	32	38	31	26	20	19	18	8	3	.	.	.
2 Pickhill	1382	M.	659	97	79	62	58	59	48	28	30	34	31	28	27	19	17	16	10	4	2	.	.	.
		F.	723	94	86	67	67	48	52	49	32	32	27	29	21	29	25	22	10	6	1	1	.	.
3 Thirsk (W.)	6745	M.	3242	467	412	328	308	260	209	194	182	188	151	150	96	92	88	58	53	19	9	1	.	.
		F.	3503	501	414	369	336	268	241	216	215	164	162	143	122	107	92	67	48	23	8	1	1	.
4 Sutton	1247	M.	638	79	87	73	64	40	32	45	39	25	37	22	26	26	20	18	9	7	2	.	.	.
		F.	609	77	62	63	62	40	57	33	29	27	33	23	27	25	19	8	3	4	2	.	.	.
5 Knayton	1740	M.	899	122	111	79	94	88	68	49	42	54	34	38	43	20	23	17	8	7	1	1	.	.
		F.	841	118	106	86	104	72	59	44	44	28	55	28	34	14	21	15	11	3	.	.	.	.
530 HELMSLEY.																								
1 Helmsley (W.)	3961	M.	2079	255	249	244	261	190	120	102	95	100	93	77	73	75	56	48	28	20	2	.	.	.
		F.	1882	250	248	215	206	154	110	90	101	104	88	77	68	80	50	37	19	15	3	1	.	.
2 Oswaldkirk	1958	M.	1072	116	111	142	149	79	87	50	50	50	30	47	37	39	38	23	18	3	5	.	.	.
		F.	886	114	101	104	87	79	58	50	26	50	43	40	29	38	31	22	8	6	1	1	.	.
3 Kirkby Moorside (W.)	5514	M.	2823	361	338	337	291	227	184	158	141	180	155	104	111	97	74	55	56	17	7	.	.	.
		F.	2691	334	333	309	290	227	162	143	125	154	128	107	101	102	59	47	46	18	6	2	.	.

Table 3 *continued.*—AGES of MALES and FEMALES in REGISTRATION SUB-DISTRICTS.

REGISTRATION SUB-DISTRICT.	ALL AGES. Persons.		ALL AGES. Males and Females.	Under 5 Years.	5-	10-	15-	20-	25-	30-	35-	40-	45-	50-	55-	60-	65-	70-	75-	80-	85-	90-	95-	100 and upw^ds.
37 NORTH RIDING—*cont.*																								
531 PICKERING.																								
1 Lastingham	1473	M.	739	84	38	85	66	58	50	38	40	48	35	36	36	37	19	8	9	6	1	.	.	.
		F.	784	108	36	85	62	50	44	48	43	38	22	39	25	33	18	9	4	4	2	.	.	.
2 Pickering. (W.)	5199	M.	2654	306	338	317	231	177	160	162	128	139	119	117	88	99	75	46	23	8	2	1	.	.
		F.	2545	355	334	306	215	186	171	175	180	140	106	96	72	91	55	46	28	7	5	.	.	.
3 Sinnington	1034	M.	501	57	66	49	49	33	34	27	25	22	30	21	26	21	12	14	7	3	.	.	.	.
		F.	533	76	71	53	38	40	36	26	26	24	22	24	23	22	18	7	1	4	1	.	.	.
4 Allerston	2462	M.	1275	155	173	159	140	94	85	89	65	64	54	51	39	47	43	30	14	3	4	1	.	.
		F.	1187	150	142	142	114	98	71	78	69	65	64	45	50	40	31	27	22	3	4	.	.	.
5 Lockton	506	M.	256	38	30	22	27	17	16	14	11	20	12	13	6	11	9	5	2	1	1	.	.	.
		F.	250	38	37	23	18	29	17	10	17	17	8	11	6	9	6	10	1	2	.	.	.	.
532 WHITBY.																								
1 Egton	4920	M.	2543	365	330	308	266	214	158	138	137	128	111	113	96	61	51	44	14	7	2	2	.	.
		F.	2377	358	313	237	211	196	156	128	120	115	101	87	85	82	51	48	32	12	1	.	.	1
2 Whitby. (W.)	16806	M.	7830	1102	967	843	712	603	630	508	446	380	339	338	263	268	168	133	67	47	8	2	.	.
		F.	8976	1180	1019	880	894	809	688	517	502	448	414	396	300	313	219	180	122	57	26	3	2	.
3 Lythe	4748	M.	2461	326	306	287	210	230	173	148	125	133	118	111	85	89	58	31	18	11	3	.	.	.
		F.	2287	310	287	264	240	137	142	141	110	111	100	99	76	71	57	31	29	15	5	1	.	.
533 GUISBROUGH.																								
1 Lofthouse. (H^3.)	11982	M.	6399	994	910	640	583	538	553	510	446	361	249	199	147	128	77	82	29	8	6	.	.	.
		F.	5583	1050	848	689	446	416	435	409	316	260	185	163	129	98	75	50	18	13	3	.	.	1
2 Marske. (H^3.)	22071	M.	11299	1899	1543	1215	988	931	912	907	752	621	461	397	272	193	136	75	40	15	11	.	1	.
		F.	10772	1742	1552	1242	888	920	849	775	623	527	405	325	271	221	163	96	51	23	6	2	.	.
3 Guisbrough. (W. H.)	7336	M.	3831	524	566	428	328	303	315	270	241	215	145	139	116	77	59	38	20	5	2	.	1	.
		F.	3505	580	527	416	311	356	264	237	187	153	132	107	98	78	43	33	23	7	3	1	.	.
4 Danby	1737	M.	863	108	105	103	85	83	47	49	44	38	33	36	37	32	29	14	9	11	2	.	1	.
		F.	874	112	125	107	86	87	65	82	37	31	44	27	32	35	22	13	10	4	3	2	.	.
534 MIDDLESBROUGH.																								
1 Middlesbrough. (W. H^4. R.)	56568	M.	29508	4337	3776	3142	2638	2626	2671	2458	2047	1802	1282	1015	622	480	254	171	72	35	8	2	1	.
		F.	27060	4432	3883	3165	2637	2393	2098	1934	1596	1456	982	841	595	478	293	168	73	37	17	2	.	.
2 Ormesby. (H.)	21785	M.	12068	1759	1513	1185	1121	1247	1189	987	814	728	480	408	213	178	109	36	26	8	5	2	.	1
		F.	9717	1778	1484	1114	825	794	780	708	593	483	330	237	206	157	88	44	22	13	7	2	.	.
3 Thornaby	11480	M.	6168	917	851	669	687	547	536	503	427	351	255	201	108	86	68	52	19	9	.	2	.	.
		F.	5312	927	800	599	601	436	463	356	318	209	211	149	117	113	55	36	13	8	5	2	.	1
535 STOKESLEY.																								
1 Stokesley. (W.)	9349	M.	4652	580	577	521	460	373	326	260	234	219	209	213	185	160	123	85	66	23	7	1	.	.
		F.	4697	583	559	538	492	447	336	267	202	213	199	189	150	152	114	90	64	34	9	6	.	.
2 Hutton	2660	M.	1323	178	164	156	137	104	87	72	67	75	49	66	39	34	36	27	11	17	1	3	.	.
		F.	1337	189	156	148	136	125	91	69	56	63	65	55	46	47	41	19	18	12	1	1	.	.
536 NORTHALLERTON.																								
1 Appleton upon Wiske	2499	M.	1285	160	160	132	165	114	79	72	46	62	59	53	50	44	33	24	16	12	2	2	.	.
		F.	1214	152	119	120	117	116	104	70	37	62	65	46	69	42	37	22	18	13	4	1	.	.
2 Northallerton. (W. H. P.)	9385	M.	4704	638	578	547	464	393	324	274	251	216	174	208	172	158	131	88	57	28	4	1	.	.
		F.	4681	670	524	501	481	397	341	288	252	234	193	181	186	123	116	92	40	40	8	1	.	.
537 BEDALE.																								
1 Bedale. (W.)	5550	M.	2756	367	312	314	298	219	167	160	137	118	123	103	113	108	86	69	31	21	8	6	1	.
		F.	2794	346	315	298	258	236	200	167	138	132	118	112	125	113	93	55	50	26	6	3	.	.
2 Masham	2720	M.	1377	192	158	165	127	113	86	85	56	67	60	61	61	49	43	38	18	6	2	1	.	.
		F.	1343	136	145	141	138	127	99	76	72	79	61	65	45	48	43	24	22	17	5	.	.	.
538 LEYBURN.																								
1 Middleham	3513	M.	1732	211	183	219	193	147	108	90	65	80	77	60	71	78	58	45	26	16	5	.	.	.
		F.	1781	207	223	197	163	135	127	93	108	81	78	65	73	90	69	48	21	7	3	3	.	.
2 Leyburn. (W.)	4811	M.	2334	301	252	296	245	194	158	124	98	95	105	101	102	104	77	42	27	9	6	1	.	.
		F.	2477	293	270	232	238	238	185	142	140	121	106	94	118	100	77	53	37	16	3	2	1	.
539 AYSGARTH.																								
1 Askrigg. (W.)	2969	M.	1509	186	170	205	126	131	93	78	83	57	74	58	74	65	48	26	10	10	3	1	.	.
		F.	1460	173	134	156	151	131	108	82	81	71	70	78	65	57	48	31	19	15	5	.	.	.
2 Hawes	2513	M.	1284	174	145	130	128	117	123	85	59	52	56	49	47	49	26	26	11	3	4	.	.	.
		F.	1229	159	151	130	120	111	89	77	68	50	66	53	44	38	33	29	13	5	.	2	1	.
540 REETH.																								
1 Muker	2002	M.	1008	130	122	124	89	83	66	68	87	63	30	43	36	34	24	16	9	5	.	.	.	.
		F.	994	123	123	92	96	91	67	72	56	45	40	37	34	39	34	20	12	6	1	.	.	.
2 Reeth. (W.)	2715	M.	1362	161	187	155	138	115	88	89	68	80	68	47	43	33	30	18	7	4	1	.	.	.
		F.	1353	185	170	137	111	133	88	96	76	86	51	54	44	53	35	36	14	10	2	2	.	.
541 RICHMOND.																								
1 Richmond. (W. B.)	7387	M.	3562	469	445	388	380	330	231	212	191	160	144	146	120	113	88	63	45	22	7	1	1	.
		F.	3825	500	417	430	392	363	323	240	190	184	180	101	126	102	86	73	53	21	7	1	1	.
2 Catterick. (H.)	2946	M.	1510	194	157	206	189	124	81	71	81	63	57	55	86	52	44	40	24	12	6	1	.	.
		F.	1436	100	171	144	134	122	106	79	67	56	71	58	57	52	54	36	18	9	7	2	.	.
3 Newsham	1183	M.	597	75	67	72	56	51	34	41	25	29	33	27	19	18	13	14	13	6	3	.	1	.
		F.	586	74	69	57	67	44	47	29	29	26	30	29	12	23	19	10	11	6	3	2	.	.
4 Aldbrough	1942	M.	989	127	130	111	79	75	78	59	65	59	40	38	27	37	25	22	8	8	1	.	.	.
		F.	953	126	113	103	88	85	69	63	50	59	39	28	38	40	19	18	19	2	3	.	.	.

Table 4.—MALE and FEMALE CHILDREN *at each Year of Age* under 5 in the YORKSHIRE DIVISION and its REGISTRATION RIDINGS.

REGISTRATION RIDING.	TOTAL UNDER 5 YEARS. Persons.	TOTAL UNDER 5 YEARS. Males and Females.	Under 1 Year.	1–	2–	3–	4–
IX YORKSHIRE -	404698	M. - 201574	43335	39189	39755	39737	39558
		F. 203124	43656	39265	40268	40094	39841
35 WEST RIDING - - -	307833	M. - 153231	33073	30042	30034	30130	29952
		F. - 154602	33474	30018	30501	30312	30297
36 EAST RIDING (WITH YORK) -	49442	M. - 24661	5280	4749	4856	4957	4819
		F. - 24781	5213	4773	4910	5040	4845
37 NORTH RIDING - - -	47423	M. - 23682	4982	4398	4845	4650	4807
		F. - 23741	4969	4474	4857	4742	4699

Table 5.—MALE and FEMALE CHILDREN *at each Year of Age* under 5 in REGISTRATION DISTRICTS.

REGISTRATION DISTRICT.	Total under 5 Years. Persons.	Total under 5 Years. Males and Females.	Under 1 Year.	1–	2–	3–	4–
35 WEST RIDING.							
483 SEDBERGH - - -	520	M. - 260	59	46	51	51	53
		F. - 260	61	43	52	53	51
484 SETTLE - - -	1811	M. - 937	197	224	197	152	167
		F. - 874	193	194	165	201	161
485 SKIPTON - - -	4944	M. - 2492	506	512	510	481	483
		F. - 2452	513	497	473	478	490
486 PATELEY BRIDGE -	1217	M. - 618	123	121	123	123	128
		F. - 599	132	122	126	107	112
487 RIPON - -	2021	M. - 1023	216	202	220	200	191
		F. - 998	219	193	191	206	189
488 GREAT OUSEBURN -	1536	M. - 778	142	166	156	173	141
		F. - 758	155	142	137	159	165
489 KNARESBOROUGH -	2682	M. - 1332	274	256	256	298	210
		F. - 1350	282	249	279	260	280
490 WETHERBY - -	1976	M. - 981	208	197	195	177	204
		F. - 995	194	159	212	202	198
491 WHARFEDALE -	6306	M. - 3193	682	641	637	606	627
		F. 3113	677	638	600	596	602
492 KEIGHLEY - - -	7791	M. - 3841	744	782	728	794	793
		F. 3950	820	797	775	776	782
493 TODMORDEN -	4444	M. - 2266	475	463	440	456	424
		F. - 2178	485	401	412	430	450
494 SADDLEWORTH -	2860	M. - 1358	286	276	266	244	286
		F. - 1502	325	288	298	311	282
495 HUDDERSFIELD -	20839	M. - 10022	2171	1918	1937	1998	1998
		F. - 10817	2119	1924	2037	1975	1964
496 HALIFAX -	21981	M. - 10859	2361	2103	2187	2063	2145
		F. - 11122	2437	2079	2195	2187	2224
497 BRADFORD -	41438	M. - 20491	4321	3996	3944	4015	4016
		F. - 20947	4465	4037	4153	4172	4120
498 HUNSLET -	9190	M. - 4520	1011	870	912	874	844
		F. - 4670	1061	893	922	900	892
499 HOLBECK -	3496	M. - 1686	369	340	327	309	335
		F. - 1810	385	356	364	333	377
500 BRAMLEY -	7848	M. - 3878	830	774	762	746	767
		F. - 3970	862	761	799	778	770
501 LEEDS -	26260	M. - 13043	2866	2587	2565	2489	2542
		F. - 13217	2956	2578	2592	2870	2521
502 DEWSBURY -	21433	M. - 10691	2298	1992	2105	2142	2054
		F. - 10842	2255	2126	2136	2130	2165
503 WAKEFIELD - -	13794	M. - 6931	1520	1531	1556	1375	1349
		F. - 6863	1499	1308	1347	1416	1293
504 PONTEFRACT -	7729	M. - 3944	869	778	775	767	755
		F. - 3785	867	713	775	749	721
505 HEMSWORTH - -	1568	M. - 814	168	165	162	163	156
		F. - 754	151	151	146	151	155
506 BARNSLEY -	12942	M. - 6418	1345	1301	1194	1307	1271
		F. - 6524	1376	1255	1302	1250	1341
507 WORTLEY - -	8129	M. - 4451	840	774	808	798	836
		F. - 4678	931	779	780	776	812
508 ECCLESALL BIERLOW -	16288	M. - 8102	1755	1662	1579	1508	1534
		F. - 8186	1798	1587	1587	1583	1631
509 SHEFFIELD - -	27346	M. - 13542	3002	2050	2621	2701	2868
		F. - 13804	3057	2780	2640	2678	2634
510 ROTHERHAM - -	12426	M. - 6231	1305	1223	1189	1262	1282
		F. 6195	1310	1254	1185	1241	1205
511 DONCASTER -	7464	M. - 3737	822	697	775	732	711
		F. - 3727	856	726	723	726	696
512 THORNE -	2023	M. - 1029	201	187	220	214	207
		F. - 994	218	193	205	187	191
513 GOOLE -	2791	M. - 1420	310	287	276	286	261
		F. 1371	279	268	294	260	270
514 SELBY - - -	2056	M. - 1045	222	186	209	198	230
		F. - 1011	217	186	228	172	206
515 TADCASTER - - -	3565	M. - 1804	383	328	363	355	375
		F. - 1761	349	345	362	300	347
36 EAST RIDING (with YORK).							
516 YORK - - - -	9864	M. - 4996	1124	985	964	1002	9
		F. - 4868	1031	916	1007	905	9
517 POCKLINGTON - -	1945	M. - 1001	238	183	188	206	1
		F. - 944	203	179	185	212	1
518 HOWDEN - - -	1672	M. - 813	161	143	178	163	1
		F. - 859	188	165	169	178	1
519 BEVERLEY - - -	3086	M. - 1565	320	304	305	304	3
		F. - 1521	308	323	272	323	3
520 SCULCOATES -	14718	M. - 7406	1540	1474	1458	1464	14
		F. - 7312	1525	1432	1416	1494	14
521 HULL - - -	10762	M. - 5292	1118	1030	1037	1074	10
		F. - 5470	1172	1076	1073	1128	10
522 PATRINGTON - -	1120	M. - 555	128	100	100	150	1
		F. - 565	123	104	138	108	[illegible]
523 SKIRLAUGH - -	1306	M. - 618	143	108	122	122	1
		F. - 688	150	128	130	146	
524 DRIFFIELD - - -	2753	M. - 1335	273	230	287	233	2
		F. - 1418	290	269	269	294	2
525 BRIDLINGTON -	2216	M. - 1080	240	212	219	204	2
		F. - 1136	259	190	247	262	2
37 NORTH RIDING.							
526 SCARBOROUGH -	5387	M. - 2694	565	502	565	545	51
		F. 2693	548	538	532	537	5
527 MALTON -	3087	M. - 1523	319	254	306	318	3
		F. 1564	326	284	326	310	3
528 EASINGWOLD -	1265	M. - 619	120	128	126	113	1
		F. - 650	126	106	126	131	1
529 THIRSK - -	1782	M. - 882	171	182	172	177	1
		F. 900	175	183	196	169	17
530 HELMSLEY - -	1430	M. - 732	162	136	144	144	14
		F. - 698	153	137	140	138	1
531 PICKERING - -	1457	M. - 730	141	150	158	132	1
		F. - 727	148	141	143	128	1
532 WHITBY -	3644	M. - 1791	419	328	352	333	3
		F. - 1853	394	347	378	354	3
533 GUISBROUGH -	6989	M. - 3505	725	641	708	683	7
		F. 3484	728	645	693	700	7
534 MIDDLESBROUGH -	14190	M. - 7053	1538	1261	1436	1395	14
		F. 7137	1522	1289	1478	1432	14
535 STOKESLEY - -	1530	M. - 758	164	129	155	149	1
		F. 772	149	150	168	161	1
536 NORTHALLERTON -	1620	M. - 798	174	135	178	151	1
		F. 822	158	160	171	171	1
537 BEDALE - -	1044	M. - 559	89	114	120	127	1
		F. 485	111	88	94	91	10
538 LEYBURN - -	1012	M. - 512	90	106	111	100	10
		F. - 500	99	97	109	91	10
539 AYSGARTH - -	692	M. - 360	69	70	85	65	7
		F. - 332	86	69	80	56	6
540 REETH - - -	599	M. - 291	56	50	69	69	5
		F. - 308	70	62	68	68	5
541 RICHMOND - - -	1755	M. - 865	185	184	174	182	1
		F. - 890	176	178	174	187	1

Table 7.—CONDITION as to MARRIAGE and AGES of MALES and FEMALES in the YORKSHIRE DIVISION and its REGISTRATION RIDINGS.

REGISTRATION RIDING.		All Ages.	Under 15 Years.	15–	20–	25–	35–	45–	55–	65 and upwards.
IX.—YORKSHIRE.										
UNMARRIED	Males	876094	583369	140763	96370	63139	21582	10071	6611	4149
	Females	864467	538482	138701	85787	56469	21470	11546	7140	4922
MARRIED	Males	500077	.	642	29671	146724	136373	96897	60405	29275
	Females	505144	.	4820	42038	157726	133870	90754	56153	19288
WIDOWED	Males	40854	.	9	283	3390	6192	8461	10977	17603
	Females	101225	.	22	528	5449	12968	20068	26954	35236
35 WEST RIDING.										
UNMARRIED	Males	658784	404763	100372	71918	45781	15104	7563	4504	2996
	Females	659870	469860	106477	63531	43767	16388	8860	5025	3082
MARRIED	Males	381802	.	496	23094	113825	104864	73947	44982	20094
	Females	386302	.	3116	37580	127985	105610	69821	37172	13088
WIDOWED	Males	34658	.	6	283	2607	4630	6415	8175	12593
	Females	76698	.	11	382	4171	10176	15963	20846	25204
36 EAST RIDING (with YORK).										
UNMARRIED	Males	110321	65001	17862	12546	8500	3137	1614	1008	653
	Females	105683	65757	16861	10060	6670	2737	1016	1137	905
MARRIED	Males	62881	.	99	3124	17677	16622	12085	8191	4783
	Females	63715	.	668	6246	19343	16292	11145	6774	3243
WIDOWED	Males	6192	.	2	31	464	749	1036	1444	2128
	Females	13635	.	9	87	740	1567	2549	3393	5488
37 NORTH RIDING.										
UNMARRIED	Males	107889	63596	16529	11306	8908	3341	1804	1009	797
	Females	99164	62815	15563	9196	6032	2345	1370	978	865
MARRIED	Males	55304	.	47	2553	15222	14887	10806	7322	4408
	Females	55127	.	536	5230	16448	13968	9788	6207	2950
WIDOWED	Males	6004	.	2	19	358	753	1031	1358	2483
	Females	10897	.	2	50	538	1225	1816	2713	4544

Note.—In a few cases, persons described as "Married" were stated to be under 15 years of age. These have been classed with the married persons aged "15 and under 20 years."

Table 8.—Condition as to Marriage and Ages of Males and Females in Registration Districts.

Registration District.		All Ages.	Under 15 Years.	15–	20–	25–	35–	45–	55–	65 and upw^{ds}.
35 WEST RIDING.										
488 SEDBERGH:										
Unmarried	M.	1829	724	232	114	128	46	31	24	27
	F.	1212	683	192	123	95	53	23	25	20
Married	M.	637	.	1	21	127	168	101	122	97
	F.	637	.	5	46	161	139	122	101	66
Widowed	M.	111	.	.	.	2	11	19	18	61
	F.	156	.	.	2	6	12	25	32	79
484 SETTLE:										
Unmarried	M.	4361	2447	710	482	368	120	107	78	60
	F.	4336	2398	667	528	371	144	92	75	61
Married	M.	2167	.	2	105	533	508	430	349	221
	F.	2138	.	7	175	619	535	380	284	138
Widowed	M.	310	.	.	1	17	28	42	68	154
	F.	460	.	.	1	18	43	75	125	216
485 SKIPTON:										
Unmarried	M.	11107	6485	1798	1266	834	347	224	156	89
	F.	11566	6624	1816	1398	977	399	223	116	113
Married	M.	6164	.	9	393	1723	1477	1202	923	437
	F.	6190	.	35	549	1901	1554	1175	715	261
Widowed	M.	720	.	.	8	42	70	107	152	316
	F.	1283	.	.	4	63	142	284	346	444
486 PATELEY BRIDGE:										
Unmarried	M.	2887	1678	452	325	210	84	55	49	33
	F.	2616	1611	408	246	181	87	47	23	13
Married	M.	1463	.	.	64	337	347	311	263	137
	F.	1467	.	5	115	305	380	290	192	90
Widowed	M.	196	.	.	1	7	13	41	47	87
	F.	325	.	.	3	9	24	56	81	152
487 RIPON:										
Unmarried	M.	4654	2827	791	522	384	143	81	56	50
	F.	5196	2840	872	611	448	177	94	90	64
Married	M.	2679	.	4	101	620	636	574	461	293
	F.	2688	.	16	187	695	671	558	381	186
Widowed	M.	346	.	.	3	17	31	57	56	182
	F.	684	.	.	.	30	57	129	156	312
488 GREAT OUSEBURN:										
Unmarried	M.	3685	2166	395	424	277	96	47	56	52
	F.	3609	2171	528	372	255	123	65	42	44
Married	M.	2017	.	.	76	440	463	425	346	264
	F.	2012	.	11	141	477	403	418	281	191
Widowed	M.	226	.	.	.	6	21	32	53	114
	F.	415	.	.	2	12	31	65	80	225
489 KNARESBOROUGH:										
Unmarried	M.	6436	3910	1084	649	439	177	95	87	45
	F.	7594	3791	1305	981	744	341	208	129	94
Married	M.	3587	.	6	140	874	904	781	556	326
	F.	3639	.	13	241	903	971	749	455	217
Widowed	M.	417	.	.	.	19	28	58	110	202
	F.	962	.	.	3	47	100	172	246	393
490 WETHERBY:										
Unmarried	M.	5145	3004	867	548	402	137	106	65	56
	F.	4916	2780	746	500	450	201	116	62	67
Married	M.	2562	.	1	96	523	692	555	450	295
	F.	2570	.	7	178	619	657	540	361	208
Widowed	M.	330	.	.	1	8	32	48	84	168
	F.	662	.	.	1	20	55	161	154	325
491 WHARFEDALE:										
Unmarried	M.	13976	8502	2153	1438	1041	345	216	126	95
	F.	14717	8409	2374	1761	1340	480	246	146	82
Married	M.	7861	.	10	414	2141	2141	1502	1082	511
	F.	7866	.	41	650	2378	2142	1470	877	301
Widowed	M.	789	.	1	4	53	96	119	180	336
	F.	1503	.	.	3	88	188	286	409	529
492 KEIGHLEY:										
Unmarried	M.	17677	10638	3040	1925	1130	428	257	175	82
	F.	19282	10777	3208	2402	1723	639	336	190	109
Married	M.	10808	.	13	652	2913	2712	2130	1842	531
	F.	10560	.	47	881	3146	2909	2106	1125	346
Widowed	M.	1074	.	1	5	81	110	189	272	407
	F.	2125	.	.	6	94	283	460	397	668

Registration District.		All Ages.	Under 15 Years.	15–	20–	25–	35–	45–	55–	65 and upw^{ds}.
35 WEST RIDING—*cont.*										
493 TODMORDEN:										
Unmarried	M.	10245	5878	1586	1175	825	309	173	123	7
	F.	10975	5790	1737	1291	1090	441	278	190	10
Married	M.	6247	.	11	435	1825	1674	1196	798	30
	F.	6263	.	41	507	1933	1692	1180	690	23
Widowed	M.	663	.	.	6	80	89	90	160	2[illegible]
	F.	1334	.	.	3	56	167	270	328	44
494 SADDLEWORTH:										
Unmarried	M.	6509	3805	1085	718	475	172	120	84	4
	F.	6972	4027	1172	758	553	191	145	84	4
Married	M.	3826	.	10	228	1044	992	858	601	21
	F.	3872	.	22	303	1134	1064	791	478	15
Widowed	M.	359	.	.	4	20	43	53	100	1[illegible]
	F.	762	.	1	9	39	82	151	195	27
495 HUDDERSFIELD:										
Unmarried	M.	46185	27009	7001	5441	3299	975	506	381	203
	F.	48490	27924	8254	5878	3810	1378	658	377	211
Married	M.	20687	.	28	1475	7788	7391	5344	2450	1518
	F.	26869	.	99	2234	8330	7335	5106	2774	181
Widowed	M.	2555	.	.	23	192	300	420	635	979
	F.	5771	.	1	18	302	683	1148	1673	1933
496 HALIFAX:										
Unmarried	M.	49189	29730	8158	5576	3406	1120	530	392	240
	F.	52916	30136	8842	6078	4464	1723	826	614	258
Married	M.	29327	.	31	1694	8578	7964	5816	2767	1341
	F.	29750	.	121	2349	9262	8103	5686	3166	1063
Widowed	M.	2558	.	1	18	174	322	461	613	960
	F.	6700	.	.	28	302	988	1436	1884	2112
497 BRADFORD:										
Unmarried	M.	88333	56038	14031	9484	5572	1798	790	423	235
	F.	97295	56248	16582	11283	7940	2885	1413	718	276
Married	M.	53892	.	76	3467	15751	14990	10654	6320	2621
	F.	56575	.	350	5103	17339	15352	10554	5298	1579
Widowed	M.	4512	.	.	35	387	562	838	1133	1557
	F.	11986	.	1	63	762	1741	2701	3350	3367
498 HUNSLET:										
Unmarried	M.	17355	11354	2782	1680	974	302	135	54	33
	F.	16869	11680	2526	1212	690	244	131	81	36
Married	M.	10767	.	18	774	3318	3044	1928	1068	419
	F.	10891	.	82	1240	3562	2906	1813	906	275
Widowed	M.	771	.	.	8	76	128	152	250	207
	F.	1522	.	1	12	116	248	382	504	307
499 HOLBECK:										
Unmarried	M.	6965	4458	1109	673	446	136	72	24	14
	F.	7058	4707	1137	618	318	148	71	42	19
Married	M.	4826	.	4	284	1350	1237	795	457	191
	F.	4831	.	35	457	1433	1176	751	336	165
Widowed	M.	381	.	.	2	26	60	73	38	136
	F.	976	.	.	5	65	131	196	273	220
500 BRAMLEY:										
Unmarried	M.	16127	10110	2742	1707	975	289	126	72	48
	F.	15683	10354	2520	1418	836	204	148	98	45
Married	M.	10071	.	15	687	3119	2747	1931	1142	433
	F.	10142	.	75	1016	3290	2875	1871	647	269
Widowed	M.	763	.	.	5	76	94	152	163	97
	F.	1614	.	.	5	104	265	342	444	559
501 LEEDS:										
Unmarried	M.	55501	33858	8620	6097	4387	1379	666	387	167
	F.	58264	34754	9762	6250	4267	1622	387	466	282
Married	M.	32863	.	48	2046	9911	9649	6502	3736	144
	F.	33490	.	316	3428	10876	9235	5855	2862	91
Widowed	M.	3096	.	.	14	205	508	640	753	97
	F.	7638	.	1	87	449	1096	1691	2085	227
502 DEWSBURY:										
Unmarried	M.	44722	28207	7779	4690	2409	754	390	178	9
	F.	47377	29014	8354	5219	3002	968	469	243	10
Married	M.	26011	.	84	1816	8215	7359	6215	2926	114
	F.	27553	.	148	2725	8562	7645	5039	2586	74
Widowed	M.	2008	.	1	28	181	272	402	494	66
	F.	5081	.	1	31	310	769	1111	1401	190

Table 8 *continued.*—CONDITION as to MARRIAGE and AGES of MALES and FEMALES in REGISTRATION DISTRICTS.

Registration District.		All Ages.	Under 15 Years.	15–	20–	25–	35–	45–	55–	65 and upwds.
35 WEST RIDING —*cont.*										
503 WAKEFIELD:										
Unmarried	M.	28310	17649	4260	3119	2016	696	324	166	96
	F.	25893	17378	3827	2164	1386	342	278	159	139
Married	M.	15620	.	20	1098	4072	4501	2810	1683	721
	F.	16479	.	147	1646	5114	4132	2585	1362	403
Widowed	M.	1344	.	1	9	91	183	274	290	491
	F.	2515	.	2	17	132	335	441	560	933
504 PONTEFRACT:										
Unmarried	M.	13097	9302	2446	1720	1134	400	183	98	83
	F.	13254	9709	1783	877	513	191	106	98	37
Married	M.	8320	.	14	528	2727	2221	1506	875	449
	F.	8332	.	116	922	2802	2128	1324	758	282
Widowed	M.	737	.	.	1	60	107	120	183	266
	F.	1336	.	.	3	72	137	256	336	558
505 HEMSWORTH:										
Unmarried	M.	3863	2162	575	514	374	109	65	48	16
	F.	3133	2053	409	258	138	73	64	33	35
Married	M.	1875	.	8	84	513	504	407	220	144
	F.	1774	.	14	161	611	468	328	184	108
Widowed	M.	197	.	.	.	15	23	35	48	77
	F.	264	.	.	5	13	20	37	58	130
506 BARNSLEY:										
Unmarried	M.	26957	16174	3902	2841	1959	631	312	144	94
	F.	21680	16295	2862	1344	683	253	124	84	58
Married	M.	13842	.	32	985	4594	3794	2450	1360	627
	F.	12900	.	220	1600	4690	3533	2220	1121	416
Widowed	M.	1184	.	.	19	107	163	233	253	398
	F.	1682	.	.	12	109	238	406	523	687
507 WORTLEY:										
Unmarried	M.	17507	10428	2728	1988	1415	464	235	161	90
	F.	15111	10557	2053	1075	737	312	156	102	79
Married	M.	8618	.	8	464	2547	2330	1713	1065	488
	F.	8632	.	92	806	2695	2250	1555	875	295
Widowed	M.	828	.	.	6	79	111	144	194	294
	F.	1542	.	.	9	81	204	292	424	548
508 ECCLESALL BIERLOW:										
Unmarried	M.	33620	20928	5508	3735	2222	612	256	151	88
	F.	35208	21579	6218	3651	2208	805	357	220	140
Married	M.	19916	.	24	1309	6210	3938	3642	2164	881
	F.	20210	.	321	2215	6682	5486	3302	1736	556
Widowed	M.	1678	.	1	13	123	250	352	371	568
	F.	3877	.	1	36	104	342	709	1060	1229
509 SHEFFIELD:										
Unmarried	M.	56678	35615	8826	5026	4222	1511	870	868	134
	F.	50468	35555	7980	3715	1962	678	540	298	120
Married	M.	53287	.	49	2302	10653	9696	6240	3126	1211
	F.	53362	.	465	4613	11183	8835	5617	2493	748
Widowed	M.	2980	.	.	17	275	538	655	688	894
	F.	6379	.	1	35	396	987	1473	1710	1759
510 ROTHERHAM:										
Unmarried	M.	24525	15798	3604	2529	1568	562	214	121	49
	F.	21271	15701	2895	1390	782	250	122	105	70
Married	M.	13278	.	15	847	4265	3702	2479	1378	593
	F.	13317	.	179	1462	4385	3363	2366	1170	408
Widowed	M.	1077	.	.	9	74	179	210	228	389
	F.	2047	.	1	19	96	278	381	535	746
511 DONCASTER:										
Unmarried	M.	16548	10005	2600	1805	1179	422	216	137	94
	F.	15508	10095	2382	1368	868	376	212	159	138
Married	M.	9524	.	7	521	2654	2477	1905	1216	744
	F.	9484	.	82	904	2823	2454	1665	1056	500
Widowed	M.	984	.	.	6	80	126	159	212	422
	F.	1824	.	.	7	67	126	323	453	790
512 THORNE:										
Unmarried	M.	4733	2569	767	480	276	113	60	46	31
	F.	4560	2933	749	375	232	107	85	55	53
Married	M.	2946	.	1	122	601	670	633	536	374
	F.	2940	.	10	204	706	630	613	432	279
Widowed	M.	365	.	.	.	13	39	45	71	208
	F.	628	.	.	2	11	44	96	137	338
35 WEST RIDING —*cont.*										
513 GOOLE:										
Unmarried	M.	3955	3020	982	625	366	116	71	41	34
	F.	3423	2607	850	427	210	102	90	47	30
Married	M.	3628	.	1	222	1093	932	722	485	203
	F.	[illegible]	.	41	358	1080	882	650	425	190
Widowed	M.	319	.	.	1	22	35	49	62	150
	F.	707	.	.	9	30	74	115	188	361
514 SELBY:										
Unmarried	M.	4629	2910	775	407	346	132	70	59	40
	F.	4080	2809	747	440	316	108	77	46	48
Married	M.	2663	.	7	120	503	636	564	415	296
	F.	2681	.	24	200	683	638	545	378	195
Widowed	M.	317	.	.	3	19	22	46	62	150
	F.	639	.	.	4	28	66	103	140	258
515 TADCASTER:										
Unmarried	M.	7823	4632	1298	856	586	131	112	75	62
	F.	6867	4693	908	565	388	171	100	60	14
Married	M.	4048	.	6	193	1142	1011	773	390	383
	F.	4001	.	36	302	1151	1014	733	486	217
Widowed	M.	474	.	.	8	30	45	71	113	261
	F.	745	.	.	2	51	36	114	185	354
36 EAST RIDING (With YORK).										
516 YORK:										
Unmarried	M.	24138	13940	3979	3152	2065	766	378	268	162
	F.	23048	13136	3751	2484	1812	758	496	382	277
Married	M.	12636	.	16	640	3564	3342	2488	1608	972
	F.	12702	.	102	1188	3846	3289	2288	1319	690
Widowed	M.	1317	.	.	4	83	156	227	295	552
	F.	2854	.	2	13	137	339	527	714	1131
517 POCKLINGTON:										
Unmarried	M.	5178	2731	1009	589	401	173	138	82	[illegible]
	F.	4475	2747	728	452	284	111	71	56	[illegible]
Married	M.	2442	.	.	89	486	580	530	462	[illegible]
	F.	2462	.	12	176	609	588	511	379	[illegible]
Widowed	M.	359	.	.	3	15	86	55	88	[illegible]
	F.	545	.	.	4	16	52	73	129	[illegible]
518 HOWDEN:										
Unmarried	M.	4521	2502	709	430	295	132	71	46	[illegible]
	F.	3714	2328	575	348	213	97	57	51	[illegible]
Married	M.	2328	.	3	84	470	496	467	423	[illegible]
	F.	2234	.	14	174	525	514	455	374	[illegible]
Widowed	M.	300	.	.	.	15	32	44	73	[illegible]
	F.	470	.	.	1	19	20	61	106	[illegible]
519 BEVERLEY:										
Unmarried	M.	7343	4124	1214	863	588	231	135	161	[illegible]
	F.	6841	4224	1019	582	408	223	117	89	[illegible]
Married	M.	3070	.	4	177	955	1020	916	530	[illegible]
	F.	4600	.	34	321	1062	1029	756	513	[illegible]
Widowed	M.	418	.	.	.	25	44	59	98	[illegible]
	F.	889	.	.	4	31	87	191	214	[illegible]
520 SCULCOATES:										
Unmarried	M.	29230	18623	4770	2973	1979	624	250	124	[illegible]
	F.	20225	19106	4463	2582	1027	643	348	250	[illegible]
Married	M.	18008	.	33	1123	5571	4851	3268	2000	[illegible]
	F.	18351	.	203	1961	5591	4818	3005	1665	[illegible]
Widowed	M.	1410	.	1	7	119	201	236	332	[illegible]
	F.	3508	.	.	23	203	427	662	931	[illegible]
521 HULL:										
Unmarried	M.	22801	13686	3469	2390	1872	721	320	160	[illegible]
	F.	21867	14057	3491	2050	1296	424	277	185	[illegible]
Married	M.	14310	.	38	919	4477	3308	2582	1579	[illegible]
	F.	14698	.	230	1692	4835	3823	2343	1271	[illegible]
Widowed	M.	1291	.	.	11	105	296	243	300	[illegible]
	F.	3265	.	7	31	248	462	722	822	[illegible]
522 PATRINGTON:										
Unmarried	M.	2592	1485	430	326	168	78	38	36	[illegible]
	F.	2583	1548	409	247	154	69	40	46	[illegible]
Married	M.	1568	.	1	61	354	333	347	308	[illegible]
	F.	1526	.	13	130	340	351	319	230	[illegible]
Widowed	M.	197	.	.	.	5	17	25	54	[illegible]
	F.	204	.	.	1	13	11	31	70	[illegible]

Table 8 *continued.*—CONDITION as to MARRIAGE and AGES of MALES and FEMALES in REGISTRATION DISTRICTS.

Registration District.		All Ages	Under 15 Years.	15-	20-	25-	35-	45-	55-	65 and upw^ds.
36 EAST RIDING (With York)—*cont.*										
523 SKIRLAUGH:										
Unmarried	M.	3039	1660	558	367	230	184	59	34	27
	F.	3014	1847	463	291	208	100	46	24	35
Married	M.	1617	.	.	71	349	418	325	263	191
	F.	1697	.	17	120	390	412	296	115	100
Widowed	M.	176	.	.	2	6	11	30	42	85
	F.	322	.	.	1	11	27	35	80	168
524 DRIFFIELD:										
Unmarried	M.	6588	3701	1152	779	408	160	116	70	56
	F.	5685	3710	668	328	323	108	60	40	48
Married	M.	3362	.	3	142	709	827	707	524	380
	F.	3418	.	28	200	915	818	663	442	251
Widowed	M.	375	.	.	1	17	23	50	68	100
	F.	694	.	.	6	25	59	98	168	339
525 BRIDLINGTON:										
Unmarried	M.	5122	2919	802	589	377	150	104	69	52
	F.	5191	3032	889	506	365	174	96	70	60
Married	M.	2722	.	2	112	663	668	518	485	324
	F.	2722	.	15	192	762	672	510	362	205
Widowed	M.	301	.	.	3	9	27	48	71	143
	F.	704	.	.	4	32	53	117	159	338
37 NORTH RIDING.										
526 SCARBOROUGH:										
Unmarried	M.	12305	7449	1983	1298	907	207	179	125	70
	F.	14134	7383	2431	1707	1319	608	351	219	186
Married	M.	6850	.	3	325	1773	1785	1375	1169	618
	F.	7225	.	34	814	2019	1832	1302	910	420
Widowed	M.	714	.	.	3	30	73	129	150	317
	F.	1807	.	.	16	101	223	846	481	742
527 MALTON:										
Unmarried	M.	7473	4187	1324	893	570	235	154	83	87
	F.	6963	4163	1125	729	493	194	121	85	59
Married	M.	3679	.	1	184	865	985	723	605	426
	F.	3671	.	21	271	1007	860	709	517	286
Widowed	M.	470	.	.	1	18	43	82	101	225
	F.	769	.	.	3	31	68	87	178	402
528 EASINGWOLD:										
Unmarried	M.	3197	1680	609	390	247	102	71	46	42
	F.	2733	1650	459	287	194	93	55	27	28
Married	M.	1436	.	.	53	320	314	318	268	223
	F.	1488	.	14	115	334	347	306	226	143
Widowed	M.	204	.	.	.	11	14	23	43	118
	F.	368	.	.	.	12	20	41	96	189
529 THIRSK:										
Unmarried	M.	5084	2325	632	443	286	114	81	54	51
	F.	4004	2406	664	367	284	113	77	50	46
Married	M.	2053	.	.	76	467	512	453	298	247
	F.	2038	.	13	129	567	496	411	266	163
Widowed	M.	280	.	.	.	15	22	29	60	154
	F.	489	.	.	.	9	36	82	120	242
530 HELMSLEY:										
Unmarried	M.	3968	2139	701	440	351	156	74	56	57
	F.	3512	2007	565	529	191	96	64	39	30
Married	M.	1723	.	.	56	336	425	374	313	220
	F.	1732	.	8	139	411	425	349	260	140
Widowed	M.	283	.	.	1	11	21	38	62	131
	F.	415	.	.	1	11	40	48	104	202
531 PICKERING:										
Unmarried	M.	3422	2056	538	326	254	109	68	57	29
	F.	3151	2036	457	301	177	74	37	46	29
Married	M.	1741	.	.	80	391	438	369	294	169
	F.	1767	.	19	107	459	465	345	250	131
Widowed	M.	281	.	.	.	9	10	51	59	123
	F.	336	.	.	1	15	34	45	85	150
532 WHITBY:										
Unmarried	M.	8040	4862	1185	875	613	268	150	91	56
	F.	8055	4909	1311	867	513	187	121	96	117
Married	M.	4277	.	3	172	1112	1087	874	845	334
	F.	4425	.	34	377	1220	1101	883	530	272
Widowed	M.	517	.	.	.	29	63	75	124	226
	F.	1162	.	.	7	38	125	103	301	408

Registration District.		All Ages.	Under 15 Years.	15-	20-	25-	35-	45-	55-	65 and upw^ds.
37 NORTH RIDING—*cont.*										
533 GUISBROUGH:										
Unmarried	M.	14814	6005	1943	1467	1111	422	202	97	
	F.	12586	8070	1708	872	482	162	74	60	
Married	M.	7423	.	11	406	2396	2187	1816	758	8[illegible]
	F.	7408	.	122	623	2680	1640	1180	660	2[illegible]
Widowed	M.	655	.	.	2	52	105	132	146	2[illegible]
	F.	950	.	.	7	72	123	154	234	3[illegible]
534 MIDDLESBROUGH:										
Unmarried	M.	30306	18180	4821	3480	2923	1069	416	139	[illegible]
	F.	24687	18182	3727	1669	768	188	82	49	[illegible]
Married	M.	15061	.	25	350	5292	4002	2351	1305	4[illegible]
	F.	15384	.	234	1924	5536	4210	2287	1073	3[illegible]
Widowed	M.	1237	.	.	16	129	258	293	252	2[illegible]
	F.	2038	.	2	20	165	325	447	544	5[illegible]
535 STOKESLEY:										
Unmarried	M.	3788	2176	626	420	277	178	74	50	
	F.	3680	2168	614	404	258	77	51	56	[illegible]
Married	M.	1944	.	1	57	460	440	428	307	24[illegible]
	F.	1939	.	14	168	488	444	307	283	14[illegible]
Widowed	M.	243	.	.	.	8	28	55	61	11[illegible]
	F.	415	.	.	.	17	31	60	95	21[illegible]
536 NORTHALLERTON:										
Unmarried	M.	3809	2213	628	436	262	106	69	48	66
	F.	3565	2086	392	380	258	112	59	50	33
Married	M.	1943	.	.	71	477	446	407	316	227
	F.	1903	.	6	182	532	452	347	290	144
Widowed	M.	237	.	1	.	10	24	27	60	115
	F.	427	.	.	1	18	41	79	73	218
537 BEDALE:										
Unmarried	M.	2578	1508	424	281	192	68	48	30	32
	F.	2452	1384	360	272	206	67	51	40	42
Married	M.	1351	.	1	50	299	297	277	245	182
	F.	1387	.	6	88	324	321	265	234	119
Widowed	M.	204	.	.	1	6	18	27	46	103
	F.	348	.	.	3	12	33	40	77	183
538 LEYBURN:										
Unmarried	M.	2619	1462	497	305	120	66	58	40	31
	F.	2603	1412	317	297	241	110	54	40	43
Married	M.	1281	.	1	36	254	252	265	278	195
	F.	1307	.	4	76	297	311	242	237	141
Widowed	M.	166	.	.	.	6	17	20	37	86
	F.	346	.	.	1	9	35	47	93	161
539 AYSGARTH:										
Unmarried	M.	1840	1010	254	222	193	66	44	28	23
	F.	1669	837	269	179	140	81	39	33	31
Married	M.	828	.	.	26	188	175	178	173	88
	F.	826	.	2	62	211	174	200	119	58
Widowed	M.	125	.	.	.	9	10	15	34	
	F.	154	.	.	1	5	15	28	62	53
540 REETH:										
Unmarried	M.	1506	879	227	178	145	87	44	19	16
	F.	1419	836	201	134	129	65	31	16	13
Married	M.	669	.	.	19	161	199	138	94	58
	F.	664	.	6	63	189	177	109	82	43
Widowed	M.	106	.	.	1	5	12	15	33	46
	F.	264	.	.	1	5	21	48	72	117
541 RICHMOND:										
Unmarried	M.	4351	2441	702	516	363	138	81	46	64
	F.	4280	2388	673	471	394	123	103	75	59
Married	M.	2005	.	1	64	492	515	419	313	281
	F.	2033	.	8	141	550	494	386	270	184
Widowed	M.	302	.	1	.	12	26	40	83	140
	F.	481	.	.	3	18	46	77	104	223

Table 9.—CONDITION as to MARRIAGE and AGES of MALES and FEMALES in each URBAN SANITARY DISTRICT of which the POPULATION EXCEEDS 50,000 PERSONS.

URBAN SANITARY DISTRICT.		ALL AGES.	Under 15 Years.	15-	20-	25-	35-	45-	55-	65 and upwds.
UDDERSFIELD:										
UNMARRIED	M.	23368	14200	3372	2800	1758	472	253	146	87
	F.	25404	14359	4394	3287	2025	738	317	199	105
MARRIED	M.	14150	.	15	801	4278	3877	2779	1081	719
	F.	14803	.	62	1256	4609	3921	2652	1361	462
WIDOWED	M.	1219	.	.	13	102	167	199	309	429
	F.	3177	.	.	11	180	412	656	924	994
HALIFAX:										
UNMARRIED	M.	20683	12458	3337	2840	1502	508	260	179	90
	F.	22758	12716	3702	2715	2031	794	381	234	135
MARRIED	M.	12849	.	14	765	3760	3495	2614	1587	608
	F.	13103	.	53	1101	4161	3686	2461	1313	418
WIDOWED	M.	1102	.	1	8	67	149	218	271	388
	F.	3095	.	.	13	151	476	689	853	919
BRADFORD:-										
UNMARRIED	M.	51379	32029	8467	5491	3485	1137	461	243	116
	F.	57820	32731	9873	6917	5005	1796	886	448	156
MARRIED	M.	31281	.	45	2018	9333	8918	6113	3443	1369
	F.	32514	.	212	3109	10464	9028	5998	2892	821
WIDOWED	M.	2548	.	.	20	258	353	506	639	787
	F.	7487	.	1	45	527	1175	1772	2083	1884
LEEDS:										
UNMARRIED	M.	90528	56173	14311	9686	6402	2019	941	463	238
	F.	92165	57714	15147	9071	5850	2203	1168	644	367
MARRIED	M.	54735	.	81	3599	16009	15673	10348	5326	2299
	F.	56027	.	48	5612	18228	15118	9738	4787	1472
WIDOWED	M.	4786	.	.	24	368	767	972	1152	1503
	F.	11483	.	2	88	705	1627	2502	3156	3430
SHEFFIELD:										
UNMARRIED	M.	85965	63230	13618	9211	6177	2072	891	493	204
	F.	82092	64502	13617	7150	4012	1423	689	411	261
MARRIED	M.	50831	.	71	3471	16174	14754	9449	5008	1954
	F.	51258	.	641	5974	17117	13737	8516	4048	1225
WIDOWED	M.	4482	.	1	28	388	792	959	1010	1284
	F.	9929	.	2	63	568	1491	2208	2716	2872
KINGSTON UPON HULL:										
UNMARRIED	M.	45212	28138	6821	4738	3400	1207	522	266	120
	F.	43556	28423	6832	3912	2346	892	525	331	295
MARRIED	M.	28135	.	67	1844	8871	7798	5070	3060	1425
	F.	28826	.	400	3312	9563	7458	5039	2484	943
WIDOWED	M.	2309	.	1	18	207	366	427	569	811
	F.	6112	.	7	49	419	841	1178	1563	2055
MIDDLESBROUGH:										
UNMARRIED	M.	18493	11162	2568	2018	1718	662	246	89	40
	F.	15719	11376	2403	1141	525	130	45	29	20
MARRIED	M.	9901	.	12	555	3306	3049	1845	834	300
	F.	9636	.	139	1106	3319	2583	1446	671	193
WIDOWED	M.	781	.	.	4	75	167	173	176	186
	F.	1354	.	2	10	196	215	303	357	361

Table 10.—Occupations of Males and Females in the Yorkshire Division and its Registration Ridings, and in each Urban Sanitary District of which the Population exceeds 50,000 Persons.

Occupations.	Yorkshire.		Registration Ridings. 35. West Riding.		36. East Riding.		37. North Riding.		Urban Sanitary District. Huddersfield.	
	Males.	Females.	Males.	Females.	Males.	Females.	Males.	Females.	Males.	Females.
TOTAL	1425925	1470834	1075334	1122665	178394	182981	169197	165188	38957	42884
I. PROFESSIONAL CLASS.										
1. Persons engaged in the General or Local Government of the Country.										
1. *National Government.*										
Peer, M.P., Privy Councillor (not otherwise described)	9	.	3	.	1	.	5	.	.	.
Civil Service (officers and clerks)	1204	217	609	124	360	29	145	64	31	3
Civil Service (messengers, &c.)	1336	28	928	17	243	3	165	8	48	.
Prison Officer, &c.	187	47	138	36	39	8	10	3	1	.
2. *Local Government.*										
Police	2840	.	2136	.	411	.	293	.	93	.
Municipal, Parish, Union, District, Officer	1196	221	907	165	152	33	137	33	53	6
Other Local or County Official	480	.	327	.	54	.	90	.	10	.
3. *East Indian and Colonial Service.*										
East Indian and Colonial Service	3	.	1	.	1	.	.	.	.	.
2. Persons engaged in the Defence of the Country.										
1. *Army (at Home).*										
Army Officer (effective or retired)	339	.	156	.	130	.	53	.	4	.
Soldier and Non-commissioned Officer	3036	.	1948	.	1844	.	144	.	5	.
Militia, Yeomanry, Volunteers	525	.	379	.	85	.	61	.	3	.
Army Pensioner	554	4	371	4	120	.	63	.	3	.
2. *Navy (ashore or in port).*										
Navy Officer (effective or retired)	70	.	15	.	37	.	18	.	1	.
Seaman, R.N.	167	.	10	.	112	.	45	.	.	.
Royal Marines (officers and men)	25	.	9	.	12	.	4	.	.	.
Navy Pensioner	147	.	40	.	78	.	29	.	1	.
3. Persons engaged in Professional Occupations (with their immediate Subordinates).										
1. *Clerical Profession.*										
Clergyman (Established Church)	1678	.	1029	.	307	.	342	.	27	.
Roman Catholic Priest	151	.	98	.	24	.	29	.	2	.
Minister, Priest, of other religious bodies	1024	.	747	.	144	.	133	.	29	.
Missionary, Scripture Reader, Itinerant Preacher	265	125	182	87	47	17	36	21	10	1
Nun, Sister of Charity	.	232	.	134	.	80	.	18	.	.
Theological Student	249	.	164	.	74	.	11	.	3	.
Church, Chapel, Cemetery—Officer, Servant	577	115	459	90	74	17	44	8	26	2
2. *Legal Profession.*										
Barrister, Solicitor	1171	.	790	.	229	.	152	.	44	.
Law Student	76	.	45	.	20	.	11	.	1	.
Law Clerk, and others connected with Law	2071	1	1502	1	383	.	186	.	82	.
3. *Medical Profession.*										
Physician, Surgeon, General Practitioner	1250	1	863	1	192	.	195	.	41	.
Dentist	373	.	286	.	65	.	22	.	22	.
Medical Student, Assistant	482	1	379	.	47	.	56	1	13	.
Midwife	.	172	.	148	.	14	.	10	.	3
Subordinate Medical Service	234	2015	186	1242	34	539	15	234	9	42
4. *Teachers.*										
Schoolmaster	4830	9235	3552	6969	618	1264	660	1002	116	288
Teacher, Professor, Lecturer	408	1788	287	989	74	437	47	362	21	88
School Service, and others concerned in Teaching	245	96	214	78	16	15	15	3	15	2
5. *Literary and Scientific Persons.*										
Author, Editor, Journalist	142	6	98	3	26	1	18	2	6	.
Reporter, Short-hand Writer	219	.	151	.	38	.	30	.	10	.
Persons engaged in Scientific Pursuits	92	2	39	.	8	1	25	1	.	.
Literary, Scientific, Institution, Service, &c.	40	7	19	2	21	1	.	4	.	.
6. *Engineers and Surveyors.*										
Civil Engineer	578	.	386	.	107	.	85	.	14	.
Mining Engineer	243	.	211	.	2	.	30	.	1	.
Land, House, Ship, Surveyor	418	.	324	.	51	.	43	.	19	.
7. *Artists.*										
Painter (artist)	368	58	269	40	55	7	44	11	14	1
Engraver (artist)	158	7	134	7	20	.	4	.	5	1
Sculptor	97	2	67	.	13	1	7	1	13	.
Architect	696	.	525	.	113	.	58	.	27	.
Musician, Music Master	1381	962	1045	742	219	148	117	72	53	34
Art Student	126	22	103	17	18	2	5	3	2	1
Photographer	457	85	313	34	73	20	71	11	18	3
Actor	187	202	142	138	22	18	23	46	1	.
Art, Music, Theatre, Service	73	15	64	12	5	2	6	1	2	.

Note.—Persons returned as engaged in more than one occupation have been referred to the one that appeared to be of most importance; or, if there was no difference in this respect, to the one first given by the person in his or her return. In some cases special rules have been followed: *e.g.*, "Clergyman and Schoolmaster" in combination has always been referred to "Schoolmaster"; a Member of Parliament or Peer engaged in any branch of commerce or industry has always been referred to this latter, not to "Peer, M.P."

The numbers returned under any heading include Labourers, Apprentices, and Assistants, as well as Masters, but not Clerks, Messengers, Errand boys, Porters, or Watchmen, for which occupations there are special headings. Civil, Military, and Naval Clerks, Law, Bank, Insurance, and Railway Clerks, and Government and Railway Porters are, however, exceptions to this rule. Many young persons, being Apprentices or Assistants, have therefore been referred to occupations usually followed by adults. Women also, chiefly widows or orphans carrying on the business of their deceased husbands or fathers, will sometimes be found under occupations commonly followed by men only.

Persons returned as *retired* from any business have not been referred to that business. Inmates of workhouses have been referred to their trades, unless their age or infirmities showed that they were past work. But persons who might be supposed to be only temporarily separated from their usual employment, such as Prisoners, and Patients in General Hospitals, have been classed under their usual occupations.

In some cases, for convenience of space, the male designation, *e.g.*, "Schoolmaster," alone is given, instead of "Schoolmaster, Schoolmistress."

Table 10 *continued*.—OCCUPATIONS of MALES and FEMALES in the YORKSHIRE DIVISION and its REGISTRATION RIDINGS, and in each URBAN SANITARY DISTRICT of which the POPULATION exceeds 50,000 PERSONS.

OCCUPATIONS.	YORKSHIRE.		REGISTRATION RIDINGS. 35. WEST RIDING.		36. EAST RIDING.		37. NORTH RIDING.		URBAN SANITARY DISTRICT. HUDDERSFIELD.	
	Males.	Females.	Males.	Females.	Males.	Females.	Males.	Females.	Males.	Females.
8. Persons engaged in Exhibitions, Shows, Games, &c.										
Performer, Showman, Exhibition, Service	150	30	122	56	15	2	13	1	21	14
Billiard, Cricket, & other Games, Service	299	12	208	10	50	2	41	.	16	2
II. DOMESTIC CLASS.										
4. PERSONS ENGAGED IN DOMESTIC OFFICES OR SERVICES.										
1. Domestic Service.										
Domestic Coachman, Groom	5032	.	4018	.	1003	.	821	.	164	.
Domestic Gardener	4211	.	2962	.	636	.	613	.	98	.
Domestic Indoor Servant	2492	99029	1552	64461	457	18358	503	16210	52	2465
Lodge, Gate, Park, Keeper (not Government)	102	45	74	34	10	4	18	7	2	1
Inn, Hotel, Servant	2133	1594	1492	1175	383	238	256	181	74	68
College, Club, Service	135	56	107	54	10	1	18	1	15	5
2. Other Service.										
Office Keeper (not Government)	132	276	112	183	15	78	5	15	2	1
Cook (not domestic)	51	117	37	108	6	7	8	2	1	6
Charwoman	.	9087	.	6663	.	1454	.	970	.	294
Washing and Bathing Service	151	6970	114	4337	17	1615	20	1018	9	169
Hospital and Institution Service	293	748	187	492	98	209	8	47	4	23
Others engaged in Service	70	7	58	7	10	.	2	.	3	2
III. COMMERCIAL CLASS.										
5. PERSONS ENGAGED IN COMMERCIAL OCCUPATIONS.										
1. Merchants and Agents.										
Merchant	372	.	227	.	117	.	28	.	26	.
Broker, Agent, Factor	2962	68	1887	52	455	12	220	4	84	3
Auctioneer, Appraiser, Valuer, House Agent	1043	5	699	4	161	1	183	.	25	.
Accountant	785	.	565	.	99	.	121	.	31	.
Salesman, Buyer (not otherwise described)	148	142	139	120	8	12	1	10	8	7
Commercial Traveller	3802	.	3149	.	464	.	189	.	265	.
Commercial Clerk	15546	298	11819	218	2592	42	1125	36	543	11
Officer of Commercial Company, Guild, Society, &c.	18	.	14	.	4	.	.	.	1	.
2. Dealers in Money.										
Banker	51	.	24	.	14	.	13	.	.	.
Bank Service	1063	2	749	2	165	.	149	.	44	1
Bill Discounter, Bill Broker, Finance Agent	64	.	47		12	.	5	.	1	.
3. Persons occupied in Insurance.										
Life, House, Ship, &c., Insurance Service	1691	30	1411	18	170	8	110	4	68	.
6. PERSONS ENGAGED IN CONVEYANCE OF MEN, GOODS, AND MESSAGES.										
1. On Railways.										
Railway Engine Driver, Stoker	2900	.	2041	.	443	.	416	.	31	.
Railway Guard	1378	.	981	.	230	.	167	.	11	.
Pointsman, Level Crossing Man	873	17	691	7	119	4	62	6	27	.
Other Railway Officials and Servants	12092	28	8637	17	2280	9	1175	2	240	1
2. On Roads.										
Toll Collector, Turnpike Gate Keeper	60	19	42	14	11	4	7	1	1	.
Omnibus, Coach, Cab, Owner—Livery Stable Keeper	584	15	387	7	95	7	102	1	13	.
Cabman, Flyman, Coachman (not domestic)	1704	.	1304	.	261	.	139	.	67	.
Carman, Carrier, Carter, Haulier	14019	58	12331	35	1043	12	645	11	552	1
Tramway Companies' Service	256	.	202	.	41	.	13	.	.	.
Wheel Chair Proprietor, Attendant, &c.	13	.	8	.	.	.	5	.	.	.
3. On Canals, Rivers and Seas.										
Inland Navigation Service	310	6	275	4	30	2	5	.	6	1
Bargeman, Lighterman, Waterman	3406	14	2170	10	1231	4	75	.	44	.
Navigation Service (on shore)	236	12	38	4	133	4	65	4	2	.
Seaman (Merchant Service)	5835	.	1020	.	3628	.	1797	.	15	.
Pilot	121	.	2	.	78	.	41	.	.	.
Ship Steward, Cook	420	27	38	2	286	24	96	1	.	.
Boatman on Seas	26	.	5	.	10	.	11	.	2	.
Harbour, Dock, Wharf, Lighthouse, Service	2710	8	347	5	2159	2	204	1	.	.
4. In Storage.										
Warehouseman (not Manchester)	2604	561	2386	558	160	3	58	.	240	11
Meter, Weigher	99	.	55	.	38	.	6	.	.	.
5. In conveying Messages, Porterage, &c.										
Messenger, Porter, Watchman (not Railway nor Government)	9299	144	7004	131	1583	8	622	5	374	2
Telegraph, Telephone, Service	846	134	624	87	140	24	82	23	17	6

Table 10 *continued.*—OCCUPATIONS of MALES and FEMALES in the YORKSHIRE DIVISION and IN exceeds 50,000 RIDINGS, and in each URBAN SANITARY DISTRICT of which the POPULATION REGISTRATION PERSONS.

OCCUPATIONS.	YORKSHIRE.		REGISTRATION RIDINGS. 35. WEST RIDING.		36. EAST RIDING.		37. NORTH RIDING.		URBAN SANITARY DISTRICT. HUDDERSFIELD.	
	Males.	Females.	Males.	Females.	Males.	Females.	Males.	Females.	Males.	Females.
IV. AGRICULTURAL CLASS.										
7. PERSONS ENGAGED IN AGRICULTURE.										
1. *In Fields and Pastures.*										
Farmer, Grazier	25252	2215	15638	1370	3485	224	6169	621	254	24
Farmer's, Grazier's—Son, Grandson, Brother, Nephew*	8339	.	4326	.	1298	.	2715	.	25	.
Farm Bailiff	1815	.	747	.	585	.	483	.	0	.
Agricultural Labourer, Farm Servant, Cottager	58738	3123	28805	1892	15100	530	14833	701	324	11
Shepherd	1391	.	332	.	869	.	310	.	1	.
Land Drainage Service (not in towns)	221	.	110	.	37	.	74	.	.	.
Agricultural Machine—Proprietor, Attendant	282	8	133	4	100	2	49	2	.	.
Agricultural Student, Pupil	55	.	26	.	10	.	29	.	.	.
Others engaged in, or connected with, Agriculture	59	1	37	1	15	.	7	.	2	.
2. *In Woods.*										
Woodman	740	.	422	.	78	.	340	.	1	.
3. *In Gardens.*										
Nurseryman, Seedsman, Florist	408	24	271	13	74	8	63	3	11	1
Gardener (not domestic)	6008	142	4132	81	1166	44	711	17	114	1
8. PERSONS ENGAGED ABOUT ANIMALS.										
1. *About Animals.*										
Horse Proprietor, Breeder, Dealer	296	.	163	.	87	.	46	.	2	.
Groom, Horse-keeper, Horse-breaker	3227	2	1914	.	693	2	710	.	77	.
Veterinary Surgeon, Farrier	370	.	242	.	49	.	80	.	16	.
Cattle, Sheep, Pig—Dealer, Salesman	768	3	419	3	181	.	168	.	8	.
Drover	139	.	87	.	24	.	28	.	1	.
Gamekeeper	1197	.	619	.	176	.	402	.	2	.
Dog, Bird, Animal—Keeper, Dealer	62	13	42	12	9	.	11	1	2	.
Vermin destroyer	109	1	37	1	29	.	43	.	.	.
Fisherman	3233	28	23	3	1995	8	1215	17	.	.
Knacker, Catsmeat Dealer, &c., &c.	19	1	14	1	2	.	3	.	.	.
V. INDUSTRIAL CLASS.										
9. PERSONS WORKING AND DEALING IN BOOKS, PRINTS, AND MAPS.										
1. *Books.*										
Publisher, Bookseller, Librarian	628	105	429	71	119	14	80	20	22	4
Music—Publisher, Seller, Printer	109	10	88	8	18	2	3	.	6	1
Bookbinder	612	495	475	419	119	61	27	15	39	32
Printer	4193	225	3185	177	690	45	320	3	179	23
Newspaper Agent, News Room Keeper	442	95	386	85	33	6	23	4	18	6
Others	2	1	2	1	.	.	.	.	.	.
2. *Prints and Maps.*										
Lithographer, Lithographic Printer	721	48	621	48	84	.	16	.	25	2
Copper Plate and Steel Plate Printer	12	.	11	.	1	.	.	.	1	.
Map and Print—Colourer, Seller	13	9	9	.	4	3	.	.	1	.
10. PERSONS WORKING AND DEALING IN MACHINES AND IMPLEMENTS.										
1. *Machines.*										
Engine, Machine, Maker	6274	41	5328	32	535	7	318	2	159	4
Millwright	1261	.	1038	.	129	.	76	.	42	.
Fitter, Turner (Engine and Machine)	8915	.	6954	.	1212	.	749	.	114	.
Boiler Maker	3539	.	2223	.	790	.	526	.	43	.
Spinning and Weaving Machine Maker	7165	108	7149	108	13	.	3	.	521	23
Agricultural Machine and Implement Maker	851	11	759	7	46	4	46	.	.	.
Domestic Machinery—Maker, Dealer	51	5	48	5	1	.	2	.	1	.
2. *Tools and Implements.*										
Tool Maker, Dealer	2964	76	2906	75	52	1	6	.	3	.
Cutler, Scissors Maker	15001	1509	14940	1509	33	.	23	.	3	.
File Maker	5609	1150	5606	1150	3	.	.	.	.	.
Saw Maker	1303	87	1280	87	17	.	6	.	2	.
Pin Maker	11	9	11	9	.	.	.	.	1	.
Needle Maker	7	17	7	17	.	.	.	.	.	.
Steel Pen Maker	2	3	2	3	.	.	.	.	.	.
Pencil Maker (Wood)	.	.	.	.	.	.	.	.	.	.
Domestic Implement Maker	342	235	339	235	.	.	3	.	1	.
3. *Watches and Philosophical Instruments.*										
Watch Maker, Clock Maker	1417	13	965	12	253	1	199	.	48	.
Philosophical Instrument Maker, Optician	231	33	163	33	58	.	10	.	1	.
Electrical Apparatus Maker	123	1	111	1	7	.	5	.	13	.
Weighing and Measuring Apparatus Maker	209	14	194	14	11	.	4	.	2	.

* Only male relatives living with the farmer or grazier, and therefore presumably engaged in agriculture, are included above.

Table 10 *continued.*—OCCUPATIONS of MALES and FEMALES in the YORKSHIRE DIVISION and its REGISTRATION RIDINGS, and in each URBAN SANITARY DISTRICT of which the POPULATION exceeds 50,000 PERSONS.

OCCUPATIONS.	YORKSHIRE.		REGISTRATION RIDINGS. 35. WEST RIDING.		36. EAST RIDING.		37. NORTH RIDING.		URBAN SANITARY DISTRICT. HUDDERSFIELD.	
	Males.	Females.	Males.	Females.	Males.	Females.	Males.	Females.	Males.	Females.
4. Surgical Instruments.										
Surgical Instrument Maker	260	51	238	45	22	6	.	.	1	.
5. Arms and Ordnance.										
Gunsmith, Gun Manufacturer	130	3	68	2	45	1	17	.	8	.
Ordnance Manufacturer	.	.	.	.	.	.	.	.	.	.
Sword, Bayonet—Maker, Cutler	12	.	12	.	.	.	.	.	.	.
Others	.	.	.	.	.	.	.	.	.	.
6. Musical Instruments.										
Musical Instrument Maker, Dealer	601	13	443	9	146	3	12	1	86	.
7. Type, Dies, Medals, Coins.										
Type Cutter, Founder	122	22	121	22	.	.	1	.	4	.
Die, Seal, Coin, Medal, Maker	156	4	154	3	1	.	1	1	.	.
8. Tackle for Sports and Games.										
Toy Maker, Dealer	70	73	55	43	14	20	1	10	.	.
Fishing Rod, Tackle, Maker, Dealer	5	1	4	.	1	1	.	.	.	.
Apparatus for other Games, Maker, Dealer	82	2	80	1	1	.	1	1	.	.
11. PERSONS WORKING AND DEALING IN HOUSES, FURNITURE, AND DECORATIONS.										
1. Houses.										
Builder	1863	5	1280	2	396	2	287	1	35	
Carpenter, Joiner	23246	32	16168	25	3976	4	3112	3	706	.
Bricklayer	9950	6	5907	4	2671	.	1372	2	63	.
Mason	17791	16	15836	15	731	1	1224	.	1065	.
Slater, Tiler	1183	1	986	1	111	.	86	.	30	.
Plasterer, Whitewasher	2924	6	2647	4	159	.	118	2	176	.
Paperhanger	249	38	152	37	87	1	10	.	3	.
Plumber	4282	26	3315	16	576	5	371	5	175	.
Painter, Glazier	8202	36	5991	31	1383	3	828	2	387	1
2. Furniture and Fittings.										
Cabinet Maker, Upholsterer	6011	704	4721	570	848	99	442	35	190	15
French Polisher	527	333	408	323	98	10	21	.	31	5
Furniture Broker, Dealer	508	96	396	74	89	16	23	6	4	3
Locksmith, Bellhanger	78	4	60	1	11	3	6	.	1	.
Gas Fitter	573	95	415	95	106	.	52	.	15	1
House and Shop Fittings—Maker, Dealer	113	.	101	.	8	.	4	.	3	.
Funeral Furniture Maker, Undertaker	34	2	26	2	3	.	5	.	.	.
Others	.	.	.	.	.	.	.	.	.	.
3. House Decorations.										
Wood Carver	306	2	233	2	66	.	7	.	19	.
Carver, Gilder	561	31	425	26	89	1	47	4	25	2
Dealer in Works of Art	48	8	39	1	6	3	3	4	.	.
Figure, Image—Maker, Dealer	33	3	17	3	15	.	1	.	1	.
Animal, Bird, &c., Preserver, Naturalist	68	.	42	.	10	.	16	.	1	.
Artificial Flower Maker	12	28	11	22	1	6	.	.	.	.
12. PERSONS WORKING AND DEALING IN CARRIAGES AND HARNESS.										
1. Carriages.										
Coachmaker	1646	10	1182	7	337	3	127	.	63	.
Railway Carriage, Railway Wagon, Maker	1537	2	1309	2	228	.	.	.	8	.
Wheelwright	2468	11	1908	8	408	3	152	.	88	.
Bicycle, Tricycle—Maker, Dealer	29	.	29	.	.	.	.	.	.	.
Others	389	11	281	11	17	.	91	.	7	.
2. Harness.										
Saddler, Harness, Whip, Maker	1537	27	906	20	290	4	351	3	48	.
13. PERSONS WORKING AND DEALING IN SHIPS AND BOATS.										
1. Hull.										
Ship, Boat, Barge, Builder	1541	2	146	.	679	1	817	1	2	.
Shipwright, Ship Carpenter (ashore)	1508	.	279	.	757	.	472	.	1	.
2. Masts, Rigging, &c.										
Mast, Yard, Oar, Block, Maker	140	.	11	.	99	.	30	.	.	.
Ship Rigger, Chandler, Fitter	89	2	8	.	58	2	23	.	.	.
Sail Maker	324	1	64	.	196	.	64	1	1	.

Table 10 *continued*.—Occupations of Males and Females in the Yorkshire Division and its Registration Ridings, and in each Urban Sanitary District of which the Population exceeds 50,000 Persons.

Occupations.	Yorkshire.		Registration Ridings. 35. West Riding.		36. East Riding.		37. North Riding.		Urban Sanitary District. Huddersfield.	
	Males.	Females.	Males.	Females.	Males.	Females.	Males.	Females.	Males.	Females.
14. Persons working and dealing in Chemicals and Compounds.										
1. *Colouring Matter.*										
Dye, Paint, Manufacture	393	60	165	10	228	50	.	.	20	1
Ink, Blacking, Colouring Substance, Manufacture	56	22	41	4	14	18	1	.	8	.
2. *Explosives.*										
Gunpowder, Guncotton, Explosive Substance, Manufacture	14	6	10	6	.	.	4	.	.	.
Fuses, Fireworks, Explosive Article, Manufacture	91	133	74	101	16	32	1	.	3	1
3. *Drugs and other Chemicals and Compounds.*										
Chemist, Druggist	2076	69	1387	54	463	7	226	8	68	1
Manufacturing Chemist	940	161	804	66	94	92	42	3	80	3
Alkali Manufacture	16	1	16	1		.	.		.	.
Drysalter	280	13	229	8	48	5	3	.	21	.
15. Persons working and dealing in Tobacco and Pipes.										
1. *Tobacco and Pipes.*										
Tobacco Manufacturer, Tobacconist	855	738	692	674	114	47	49	17	71	71
Tobacco Pipe, Snuff Box, &c., Maker	152	44	113	38	29	3	10	3	6	.
16. Persons working and dealing in Food and Lodging.										
1. *Board and Lodging.*										
Innkeeper, Hotel Keeper, Publican	5766	973	4170	687	822	133	774	153	174	30
Lodging, Boarding House, Keeper	367	3240	172	1526	75	851	120	863	5	73
Coffee, Eating House, Keeper	349	156	246	108	71	21	32	27	17	9
2. *Spirituous Drinks.*										
Hop—Merchant, Dealer	12	.	10	.	1	.	1	.	.	.
Maltster	1527	5	1366	4	121	1	46	.	19	.
Brewer	2318	42	1912	36	253	6	151	.	87	2
Beerseller. Ale, Porter, Cider, Dealer	1160	261	994	217	119	29	47	15	47	13
Cellarman	352	40	281	39	42	1	29	.	23	.
Wine, Spirit—Merchant, Agent	591	31	392	18	128	5	71	8	19	.
3. *Food.*										
Milkseller, Dairyman	1797	281	1394	212	276	48	127	21	68	6
Cheesemonger, Butterman	124	25	102	17	4	4	18	4	3	2
Butcher, Meat Salesman	9631	271	7110	202	1367	45	1154	24	261	7
Provision Curer, Dealer	1300	510	943	382	276	102	81	26	37	7
Poulterer, Game Dealer	255	45	161	24	57	10	37	11	1	.
Fishmonger	1616	162	963	64	471	45	182	53	50	5
Corn, Flour, Seed—Merchant, Dealer	702	54	354	28	264	19	84	7	15	1
Corn Miller	2550	17	1670	9	467	4	413	4	42	.
Baker	1685	488	1208	415	308	44	169	29	60	33
Confectioner, Pastrycook	1471	1624	912	1357	447	154	112	113	48	63
Greengrocer, Fruiterer	3030	570	2454	428	344	89	232	53	114	22
Mustard, Vinegar, Spice, Pickle—Maker, Dealer	76	117	72	116	3	.	1	1	.	.
Sugar Refiner	74	17	49	14	18	.	7	3	1	2
Grocer. Tea, Coffee, Chocolate—Maker, Dealer	13448	3547	10087	2729	1728	469	1633	349	392	95
Ginger Beer, Mineral Water—Manufacturer, Dealer	431	31	318	24	63	3	50	4	29	2
Others dealing in Food	1	.	1	.	.	.	.	.	.	.
17. Persons working and dealing in Textile Fabrics.										
1. *Wool and Worsted.*										
Woolstapler	1369	2	1354	2	11	.	4	.	109	.
Woollen Cloth Manufacture	42637	43374	42602	43360	23	9	12	5	958	4724
Wool, Woollen goods—Dyer, Printer	1919	12	1916	12	1	.	2	.	236	.
Worsted, Stuff, Manufacture	34056	61446	34047	61438	5	5	4	3	794	926
Flannel Manufacture	193	221	193	221	.	.	.	.	1	8
Blanket Manufacture	1141	1221	1141	1221		.	.	.	.	.
Fuller	1133	9	1133	9	.	.	.	.	32	2
Cloth, Worsted, Stuff, Flannel, Blanket, Dealer	4309	9	4292	9	13	.	4	.	288	.
Others	361	424	360	424	1	.	.	.	18	11
2. *Silk.*										
Silk, Silk goods, Manufacture	2003	3384	2001	3377	2				80	122
Silk Dyer, Printer	125	6	124	6	1	.	.	.	4	1
Ribbon Manufacture	2	6	2	5	.	.	.	.	.	.
Crape, Gauze, Manufacture	1	1	1	1	.	.	.	1	.	.
Silk Merchant, Dealer	61	6	52	6	2	1	.	.	4	1

Table 10 *continued*.—OCCUPATIONS of MALES and FEMALES in the YORKSHIRE DIVISION and its REGISTRATION RIDINGS, and in each URBAN SANITARY DISTRICT of which the POPULATION exceeds 50,000 PERSONS.

OCCUPATIONS.	YORKSHIRE.		REGISTRATION RIDINGS. 35. WEST RIDING.		36. EAST RIDING.		37. NORTH RIDING.		URBAN SANITARY DISTRICT. HUDDERSFIELD.	
	Males.	Females.	Males.	Females.	Males.	Females.	Males.	Females.	Males.	Females.
3. Cotton and Flax										
Cotton, Cotton goods, Manufacture	18820	20753	18508	20207	247	532	5	13	963	1001
Cotton, Calico—Printer, Dyer, Bleacher	745	12	744	12	.	.	1	.	110	9
Cotton, Calico—Warehouseman, Dealer	190	12	187	12	2	.	1	.	28	2
Flax, Linen—Manufacturer, Dealer	2557	4785	2280	4580	125	101	152	104	3	1
Lace Manufacturer, Dealer	58	84	53	69	4	11	1	4	.	.
Fustian Manufacturer, Dealer	507	171	507	170	.	.	.	1	3	.
Tape Manufacturer, Dealer	5	50	5	50	.	.	.	.	.	.
Thread Manufacturer, Dealer	44	103	42	103	.	1	2	.	.	2
4. Hemp and other Fibrous Materials.										
Hemp, Jute, Cocoa Fibre, Manufacture	124	48	78	39	32	9	14	.	2	.
Rope, Twine, Cord—Maker, Dealer	1152	277	789	257	291	18	72	2	41	2
Mat Maker, Seller	40	27	27	12	11	15	2	.	1	.
Net Maker	15	74	4	1	8	54	3	19	.	.
Canvas, Sailcloth, Manufacture	38	61	16	43	1	3	21	16	1	.
Sacking, Sack, Bag—Maker, Dealer	81	103	54	78	22	20	5	3	.	.
Others working and dealing in Hemp	19	4	14	4	4	.	1	.	1	.
5. Mixed or Unspecified Materials.										
Weaver (undefined)	1070	933	1049	929	11	2	10	2	307	36
Dyer, Printer, Scourer, Bleacher, Calenderer (undefined)	5229	175	5135	140	57	27	37	8	249	8
Factory hand (Textile, undefined)	2996	1711	2961	1661	10	36	25	14	94	45
Felt Manufacture	91	10	91	10	.	.	.	.	2	.
Carpet, Rug, Manufacture	3160	1488	3126	1485	30	2	4	1	82	141
Manchester Warehouseman	11	.	11	.	.	.	.	.	.	.
Draper, Linen Draper, Mercer	5684	1680	4020	1288	823	251	841	141	206	52
Fancy Goods (Textile), Manufacturer, Worker, Dealer	249	364	234	238	10	66	5	60	19	10
Trimming Maker, Dealer	12	14	12	11	.	3	.	.	3	.
Embroiderer	4	23	4	20	.	1	.	2	.	1
Others	157	30	156	30	1	.	.	.	5	1
18. PERSONS WORKING AND DEALING IN DRESS.										
1. Dress.										
Hatter, Hat Manufacture (not straw)	552	759	453	740	65	16	34	3	19	2
Straw—Hat, Bonnet, Plait, Manufacture	8	161	7	113	.	34	1	14	2	4
Tailor	13094	4336	9243	3984	1989	284	1862	68	418	187
Milliner, Dressmaker, Staymaker	285	34599	857	24542	17	5429	16	4628	11	972
Shawl Manufacture	116	343	116	342	.	1	.	.	6	13
Shirt Maker, Seamstress	15	3757	11	2742	2	683	2	332	.	194
Hosiery Manufacture	28	198	22	106	2	4	4	85	3	3
Hosier, Haberdasher	371	241	270	177	73	47	28	17	21	4
Glover, Glove Maker	7	21	4	7	1	9	2	5	.	1
Button Maker, Dealer	69	93	69	93	.	.	.	.	.	.
Shoe, Boot—Maker, Dealer	16755	1876	12743	1679	2031	116	1981	81	304	18
Patten, Clog, Maker	1441	8	1367	8	23	.	51	.	71	.
Wig Maker, Hairdresser	1707	63	1282	52	268	6	157	5	67	5
Umbrella, Parasol, Stick—Maker, Dealer	265	431	235	418	23	12	7	1	11	.
Accoutrement Maker	3	.	3	.	.	.	.	.	.	.
Old Clothes Dealer, and others	50	164	36	121	11	33	3	10	3	4
19. PERSONS WORKING AND DEALING IN VARIOUS ANIMAL SUBSTANCES.										
1. In Grease, Gut, Bone, Horn, Ivory, and Whalebone.										
Tallow Chandler, Candle, Grease, Manufacture	347	12	256	7	54	1	37	4	8	1
Soap Boiler, Maker	327	31	315	30	9	1	3	.	2	4
Glue, Size, Gelatine, Isinglass—Maker, Dealer	90	6	79	4	10	1	1	.	.	.
Manure Manufacture	107	3	37	2	59	1	11	.	.	.
Bone, Horn, Ivory, Tortoise-shell—Worker, Dealer	252	55	245	54	6	.	1	1	.	.
Comb Maker	316	130	202	95	114	35	.	.	2	.
Others	8	2	8	2	.	.	.	.	1	.
2. In Skins.										
Furrier, Skinner	271	98	243	83	17	14	11	1	10	6
Tanner, Fellmonger	2052	12	1384	6	553	5	115	1	3	.
Currier	3263	148	2977	143	157	5	129	.	85	2
Leather Goods, Portmanteau, Bag, Strap, &c.—Maker, Dealer	330	146	298	146	28	1	4	.	12	.
Parchment, Vellum—Maker, Dealer	1	1	1	1	.	.	.	.	.	.
3. In Hair and Feathers.										
Hair, Bristle—Worker, Dealer	88	128	81	125	7	2	.	1	.	1
Brush, Broom, Maker	979	299	796	231	166	62	18	6	24	1
Quill, Feather—Dresser, Dealer	16	59	6	48	9	7	1	4	.	1

Table 10 *continued.*—Occupations of Males and Females in the Yorkshire Division and its Registration Ridings, and in each Urban Sanitary District of which the Population exceeds 50,000 Persons.

Occupations.	YORKSHIRE.		Registration Ridings.						Urban Sanitary District.	
			35. WEST RIDING.		36. EAST RIDING.		37. NORTH RIDING.		HUDDERSFIELD.	
	Males.	Females.	Males.	Females.	Males.	Females.	Males.	Females.	Males.	Females.
20. Persons working and dealing in various Vegetable Substances.										
1. In Oils, Gums, and Resins.										
Oil Miller, Oil Cake—Maker, Dealer	1670	5	298	2	1365	3	9	.	16	.
Oil and Colourman	34	7	20	5	14	2	.	.	2	1
Floor Cloth, Oil Cloth, Manufacture	47	4	44	3	1	1	2	.	.	.
Japanner	27	49	25	49	2	.	.	.	.	.
India Rubber, Gutta Percha—Worker, Dealer	68	11	60	11	7	.	1	.	9	.
Waterproof Goods—Maker, Dealer	55	4	43	3	7	1	5	.	4	.
Others	45	.	28	.	17	.	.	.	.	.
2. In Cane, Rush, and Straw.										
Willow, Cane, Rush—Worker, Dealer, Basketmaker	716	56	536	41	123	12	57	3	19	.
Hay, Straw (not plait), Chaff—Cutter, Dealer	361	4	304	4	42	.	15	.	6	.
Thatcher	2	.	1	.	.	.	1	.	.	.
3. In Wood and Bark.										
Timber, Wood—Merchant, Dealer	1112	16	762	12	245	2	105	2	40	.
Sawyer	2028	.	1421	.	443	.	164	.	48	.
Lath, Wooden Fence, Hurdle, Maker	178	1	32	.	136	.	10	1	1	.
Wood Turner, Box Maker	1883	102	1649	99	178	9	56	.	38	.
Cooper, Hoop Maker, Bender	1397	8	719	8	588	.	90	.	18	1
Cork, Bark—Cutter, Worker, Dealer	125	24	61	22	57	2	7	.	6	.
Others	38	1	24	1	.	.	14	.	.	.
4. In Paper.										
Paper Manufacture	879	638	787	580	33	30	59	28	6	4
Envelope Maker	1	4	1	3	.	1	.	.	.	.
Stationer, Law Stationer	627	290	467	230	106	35	55	25	19	5
Card, Pattern Card, Maker	132	28	138	28	.	.	.	.	5	2
Paper Stainer	238	8	226	8	12	.	.	.	.	.
Paper Box, Paper Bag, Maker	41	388	33	327	8	30	.	11	1	2
Ticket, Label, Writer	39	50	31	48	6	2	2	.	.	1
Others	204	10	159	9	28	.	17	1	12	1
21. Persons working and dealing in various Mineral Substances.										
1. Miners.										
Coal Miner	55774	138	55680	138	22	.	72	.	193	.
Ironstone Miner	8192	11	789	2	6	.	7397	9	1	.
Copper Miner	4	.	2	.	1	.	1	.	.	.
Tin Miner	6	.	6	.	.	.	.	.	.	.
Lead Miner	1008	4	261	.	.	.	742	4	.	.
Miner in other, or undefined, Minerals	247	6	151	.	31	3	65	1	8	.
Mine Service	672	.	626	.	8	.	39	.	2	.
2. Coal, Coal Gas, &c.										
Coal Merchant, Dealer	2578	89	1967	73	428	12	183	4	87	2
Coalheaver	748	.	342	.	331	.	75	.	15	.
Coke, Charcoal, Peat—Cutter, Burner, Dealer	477	19	472	18	4	1	1	.	1	.
Gas Works Service	2478	.	2089	.	234	.	155	.	92	.
3. Stone, Clay, and Road Making.										
Stone Quarrier	8700	.	8121	.	20	.	559	.	148	.
Stone Cutter, Dresser, Dealer	1831	.	1761	.	36	.	34	.	80	.
Slate Quarrier	21	.	11	.	.	.	10	.	1	.
Slate Worker, Dealer	51	9	30	7	14	2	7	.	1	.
Limeburner	292	3	256	3	9	.	27	.	.	.
Clay, Sand, Gravel, Chalk—Labourer, Dealer	341	3	326	3	10	.	5	.	17	.
Fossil, Coprolite—Digger, Dealer	1	.	.	.	.	.	1	.	.	.
Well Sinker, Borer	188	.	132	.	13	.	43	.	.	.
Plaster, Cement, Manufacture	148	1	50	1	90	.	8	.	5	.
Brick, Tile—Maker, Burner, Dealer	4330	36	3449	25	493	5	378	6	122	.
Paviour	570	.	497	.	61	.	12	.	14	.
Road Contractor, Surveyor, Inspector	155	.	130	.	5	.	20	.	.	.
Road Labourer	1441	.	1194	.	71	.	176	.	64	.
Railway Contractor	157	.	122	.	25	.	10	.	13	.
Platelayer	2807	.	1921	.	262	.	624	.	21	.
Railway Labourer, Navvy	5004	.	3676	.	790	.	529	.	64	.
Others	45	140	45	138	.	1	.	1	.	.
4. Earthenware and Glass.										
Earthenware, China, Porcelain, Manufacture	1638	353	1455	298	33	.	150	55	40	.
Glass Manufacture	3853	168	3439	152	312	9	102	2	2	.
Earthenware, China, Glass, Dealer	428	185	327	137	56	7	45	31	15	5
5. Salt.										
Salt Maker, Dealer	30	2	29	2	1	.	.	.	1	.

Table 10 *continued.*—OCCUPATIONS of MALES and FEMALES in the YORKSHIRE DIVISION and its REGISTRATION RIDINGS, and in each URBAN SANITARY DISTRICT of which the POPULATION exceeds 50,000 PERSONS.

OCCUPATIONS.	YORKSHIRE.		REGISTRATION RIDINGS. 35. WEST RIDING.		36. EAST RIDING.		37. NORTH RIDING.		URBAN SANITARY DISTRICT. HUDDERSFIELD.	
	Males.	Females.	Males.	Females.	Males.	Females.	Males.	Females.	Males.	Females.
6. *Water.*										
Waterworks Service	356	2	314	2	21	.	20	.	4	.
Others	5	.	3	.	1	.	1	.	.	.
7. *Precious Metals and Jewellery.*										
Goldsmith, Silversmith, Jeweller	2433	345	2289	334	95	10	49	1	24	.
Gold, Silver, Beater	11	.	11	.	.	.	.	.	.	.
Lapidary	983	19	13	2	2	.	968	17	.	.
Others	65	872	63	870	.	2	.	.	.	.
8. *Iron and Steel.*										
Blacksmith	13338	32	9475	20	1871	7	1992	5	243	.
Whitesmith	1340	8	901	7	312	.	127	1	93	1
Nail Manufacture	835	293	781	289	20	1	34	3	8	.
Anchor, Chain, Manufacture	46	1	32	1	7	.	7	.	.	.
Other Iron and Steel Manufactures	41493	104	30202	78	1372	2	9829	24	323	.
Ironmonger. Hardware Dealer, Merchant	1319	93	928	76	203	6	188	11	60	2
9. *Copper.*										
Copper, Copper goods—Manufacturer, Worker, Dealer	157	.	111	.	39	.	7	.	.	.
10. *Tin and Zinc.*										
Tin, Tin Plate, Tin goods—Manufacturer, Worker, Dealer	2087	77	1659	73	369	4	169	.	71	1
Zinc, Zinc Goods—Manufacturer, Worker, Dealer	10	.	10	.	.	.	.	.	1	.
11. *Lead.*										
Lead, Leaden goods—Manufacturer, Worker, Dealer	143	14	100	5	24	9	19	.	7	.
12. *In Other, Mixed, or Unspecified, Metals.*										
Metal Refiner, Worker, Turner, Dealer	327	83	312	83	5	.	10	.	.	.
Brass, Bronze, Manufacture. Brazier	2229	40	1944	38	236	1	50	1	74	.
Metal Burnisher, Lacquerer	4	51	4	50	.	.	.	1	.	.
White Metal, Plated Ware, Manufacture, Pewterer	1238	247	1235	247	2	.	1	.	.	.
Wire Maker, Worker, Weaver, Drawer	2433	128	2358	123	39	5	36	.	25	1
Bolt, Nut, Rivet, Screw, Staple, Maker	511	107	453	107	19	.	39	.	1	.
Lamp, Lantern, Candlestick, Maker	63	5	61	5	2	.	.	.	.	.
Clasp, Buckle, Hinge, Maker	3	12	3	12	.	.	.	.	.	.
Fancy Chain, Gilt Toy, Maker	3	.	3	.	.	.	.	.	.	.
Others	79	3	79	3	.	.	.	.	1	.
22. PERSONS WORKING AND DEALING IN GENERAL OR UNSPECIFIED COMMODITIES.										
1. *Makers and Dealers (General or Undefined).*										
General Shopkeeper, Dealer	1893	1981	1302	1505	353	299	237	177	73	77
Pawnbroker	892	93	757	49	98	38	37	6	13	3
Costermonger, Huckster, Street Seller	3659	1761	2788	1336	469	287	402	138	176	106
Manufacturer, Manager, Superintendent (undefined)	1082	23	897	22	139	.	46	1	41	1
Contractor (undefined)	367	2	276	1	36	1	55	.	6	.
2. *Mechanics and Labourers (General or Undefined).*										
General Labourer	44462	160	28320	119	8616	25	7516	16	929	3
Engine Driver, Stoker, Fireman (not railway, marine, nor agricultural)	10674	.	8510	.	891	.	1273	.	331	.
Artisan, Mechanic (undefined)	4182	459	3931	445	165	8	86	6	221	10
Apprentice (undefined)	347	24	236	22	73	2	38	.	5	3
Factory Labourer (undefined)	1877	535	1623	487	129	39	125	9	29	5
Machinist, Machine Worker (undefined)	329	408	255	408	53	.	21	.	2	.
23. PERSONS WORKING AND DEALING IN REFUSE MATTERS.										
1. *Refuse Matters.*										
Town Drainage Service	202	.	167	.	13	.	22	.	4	.
Chimney Sweep, Soot Merchant	737	4	545	2	114	1	78	1	23	.
Scavenger, Crossing Sweeper	313	9	263	8	30	1	30	.	15	.
Rag Gatherer, Dealer	396	330	343	315	30	17	23	7	9	40
VI. UNOCCUPIED CLASS.										
24. PERSONS WITHOUT SPECIFIED OCCUPATIONS										
Persons returned by Property, Rank, &c., and not by special occupation	330710	804633	243190	672297	44383	120932	43137	111404	8776	24725
Children under 5 years of age	201574	203124	153231	154602	24661	24781	23682	23741	5167	5136

Table 10 *continued*.—OCCUPATIONS of MALES and FEMALES in the YORKSHIRE DIVISION and its REGISTRATION RIDINGS, and in each URBAN SANITARY DISTRICT of which the POPULATION exceeds 50,000 PERSONS.

OCCUPATIONS.	URBAN SANITARY DISTRICTS.											
	HALIFAX.		BRADFORD.		LEEDS.		SHEFFIELD.		KINGSTON UPON HULL.		MIDDLESBROUGH.	
	Males.	Females.	Males.	Females.	Males.	Females.	Males.	Females.	Males.	Females.	Males.	Females.
TOTAL - - -	34634	38296	85211	97821	149844	159275	141208	143210	75746	78494	29175	26759
I. PROFESSIONAL CLASS.												
1. PERSONS ENGAGED IN THE GENERAL OR LOCAL GOVERNMENT OF THE COUNTRY.												
1. *National Government.*												
Peer, M.P., Privy Councillor (not otherwise described)	.	.	.	.	.	.	.	.	.	.	.	.
Civil Service (officers and clerks)	35	1	51	.	134	12	75	10	226	7	30	11
Civil Service (messengers, &c.)	38	.	103	.	171	2	121	2	115	.	28	.
Prison Officer, &c.	.	.	.	2	30	7	.	.	22	5	.	.
2. *Local Government.*												
Police	77	.	222	.	378	.	351	.	213	.	59	.
Municipal, Parish, Union, District, Officer	39	3	72	12	170	30	85	19	76	12	82	4
Other Local or County Official	11	.	13	.	32	.	51	.	16	.	6	.
3. *East Indian and Colonial Service.*												
East Indian and Colonial Service	.	.	.	.	.	.	.	.	1	.	.	.
2. PERSONS ENGAGED IN THE DEFENCE OF THE COUNTRY.												
1. *Army (at Home).*												
Army Officer (effective or retired)	11	.	16	.	20	.	34	.	7	.	1	.
Soldier and Non-Commissioned Officer	254	.	270	.	400	.	772	.	7	.	4	.
Militia, Yeomanry, Volunteers	15	.	3	.	8	.	5	.	3	.	3	.
Army Pensioner	44	.	50	1	87	2	43	1	48	.	12	.
2. *Navy (ashore or in port).*												
Navy Officer (effective or retired)	.	.	1	.	2	.	4	.	15	.	.	.
Seaman, R.N.	.	.	1	.	3	.	1	.	64	.	3	.
Royal Marines (officers and men)	1	.	1	.	2	.	1	.	4	.	1	.
Navy Pensioner	1	.	2	.	10	.	4	.	62	.	2	.
3. PERSONS ENGAGED IN PROFESSIONAL OCCUPATIONS (WITH THEIR IMMEDIATE SUBORDINATES).												
1. *Clerical Profession.*												
Clergyman (Established Church)	19	.	53	.	126	.	68	.	32	.	13	.
Roman Catholic Priest	3	.	6	.	17	.	11	.	5	.	6	.
Minister, Priest, of other religious bodies	22	.	53	.	109	.	80	.	56	.	18	.
Missionary, Scripture Reader, Itinerant Preacher	8	4	20	10	35	30	38	16	24	10	12	4
Nun, Sister of Charity	.	.	.	9	.	16	.	12	.	20	.	8
Theological Student	3	.	13	.	67	.	17	.	.	.	1	.
Church, Chapel, Cemetery—Officer, Servant	17	2	47	6	57	12	39	9	27	8	3	.
2. *Legal Profession.*												
Barrister, Solicitor	35	.	62	.	115	.	88	.	57	.	16	.
Law Student	.	.	4	.	10	.	7	.	5	.	1	.
Law Clerk, and others connected with Law	72	1	132	.	254	.	245	.	171	.	29	.
3. *Medical Profession.*												
Physician, Surgeon, General Practitioner	31	.	72	.	133	.	116	1	71	.	23	.
Dentist	21	.	56	.	40	.	44	.	37	.	9	.
Medical Student, Assistant	11	.	23	.	81	.	65	.	18	.	6	1
Midwife	.	3	.	22	.	20	.	43	.	9	.	8
Subordinate Medical Service	11	58	24	145	36	246	30	182	21	253	7	11
4. *Teachers.*												
Schoolmaster	109	226	216	629	504	1243	363	848	214	518	78	181
Teacher, Professor, Lecturer	12	53	33	43	70	59	34	80	42	103	8	15
School Service, and others concerned in Teaching	3	2	25	10	34	9	39	7	8	2	3	.
5. *Literary and Scientific Persons.*												
Author, Editor, Journalist	3	.	21	.	19	2	17	.	12	.	2	.
Reporter, Short-hand Writer	8	.	9	.	27	.	33	.	17	.	14	.
Persons engaged in Scientific Pursuits	5	.	5	.	10	.	24	.	6	.	6	.
Literary, Scientific, Institution, Service, &c.	.	.	4	.	4	.	4	.	3	.	.	.
6. *Engineers and Surveyors.*												
Civil Engineer	8	.	31	.	117	.	54	.	61	.	33	.
Mining Engineer	.	.	5	.	19	.	21	.	.	.	1	.
Land, House, Ship, Surveyor	11	.	41	.	56	.	31	.	22	.	8	.
7. *Artists.*												
Painter (artist)	12	.	35	7	73	11	59	8	29	6	4	4
Engraver (artist)	2	.	7	.	80	.	56	5	10	.	1	.
Sculptor	.	.	5	.	14	.	11	.	5	.	.	.
Architect	30	.	57	.	94	.	63	.	39	.	10	.
Musician, Music Master	63	32	140	96	197	138	183	179	116	99	32	16
Art Student	7	.	15	3	22	4	23	5	9	2	1	1
Photographer	8	3	58	14	61	16	39	11	35	7	6	8
Actor	4	5	19	20	25	40	25	15	15	14	10	33
Art, Music, Theatre, Service	3	.	16	5	25	5	12	1	4	1	4	1

Table 10 *continued.*—OCCUPATIONS of MALES and FEMALES in the YORKSHIRE DIVISION and its REGISTRATION RIDINGS, and in each URBAN SANITARY DISTRICT of which the POPULATION exceeds 50,000 PERSONS.

OCCUPATIONS.	URBAN SANITARY DISTRICTS.											
	HALIFAX.		BRADFORD.		LEEDS.		SHEFFIELD.		KINGSTON UPON HULL.		MIDDLESBROUGH.	
	Males.	Females.	Males.	Females.	Males.	Females.	Males.	Females.	Males.	Females.	Males.	Females.
8. *Persons engaged in Exhibitions, Shows, Games, &c.*												
Performer, Showman, Exhibition, Service	3	4	11	2	23	9	19	9	12	1	8	1
Billiard, Cricket, & other Games, Service	8	.	39	.	48	1	28	1	29	2	14	.
II. DOMESTIC CLASS.												
4. PERSONS ENGAGED IN DOMESTIC OFFICES OR SERVICES.												
1. *Domestic Service.*												
Domestic Coachman, Groom	159	.	188	.	498	.	352	.	166	.	33	.
Domestic Gardener	142	.	47	.	254	.	170	.	61	.	82	.
Domestic Indoor Servant	51	1884	50	4303	141	9636	106	10073	43	6032	18	1788
Lodge, Gate, Park, Keeper (not Government)	3	1	15	.	9	4	9	2	6	.	2	.
Inn, Hotel, Servant	62	64	243	145	341	247	254	179	185	134	44	34
College, Club, Service	2	3	14	5	30	8	9	10	7	.	9	1
2. *Other Service.*												
Office Keeper (not Government)	13	8	17	32	26	66	16	32	10	54	2	10
Cook (not domestic)	.	8	9	42	14	35	4	1	3	4	.	1
Charwoman	.	332	.	820	.	1247	.	1282	.	823	.	62
Washing and Bathing Service	9	179	21	484	26	838	6	630	9	744	3	89
Hospital and Institution Service	1	16	9	39	16	100	12	78	19	72	2	10
Others engaged in Service	1	1	6	.	32	3	6	1	8	.	.	.
III. COMMERCIAL CLASS.												
5. PERSONS ENGAGED IN COMMERCIAL OCCUPATIONS.												
1. *Merchants and Agents.*												
Merchant	9	.	69	.	32	.	46	.	79	.	8	.
Broker, Agent, Factor	76	7	293	4	421	17	235	11	290	11	60	.
Auctioneer, Appraiser, Valuer, House Agent	17	.	62	2	110	2	97	.	57	.	31	.
Accountant	36	.	59	.	85	.	121	.	54	.	49	.
Salesman, Buyer (not otherwise described)	2	.	28	18	67	52	22	17	5	8	1	3
Commercial Traveller	108	.	879	.	920	.	479	.	255	.	58	.
Commercial Clerk	480	8	1547	21	2446	77	2217	48	1787	30	544	15
Officer of Commercial Company, Guild, Society, &c.	.	.	3	.	.	.	3	.	3	.	.	.
2. *Dealers in Money.*												
Banker	1	.	2	.	5	.	.	.	4	.	.	.
Bank Service	46	.	71	.	132	.	122	.	55	.	24	.
Bill Discounter, Bill Broker, Finance Agent	.	.	4	.	15	.	16	.	12	.	3	.
3. *Persons occupied in Insurance.*												
Life, House, Ship, &c., Insurance Service	66	.	177	2	332	6	209	3	85	7	28	.
6. PERSONS ENGAGED IN CONVEYANCE OF MEN, GOODS, AND MESSAGES.												
1. *On Railways.*												
Railway Engine Driver, Stoker	4	.	199	.	541	.	263	.	94	.	212	.
Railway Guard	5	.	124	.	262	.	116	.	95	.	97	.
Pointsman, Level Crossing Man	5	.	33	.	86	.	70	.	59	.	10	.
Other Railway Officials and Servants	197	1	678	2	1643	4	848	1	1102	3	183	.
2. *On Roads.*												
Toll Collector, Turnpike Gate Keeper	.	.	.	.	1	.	4	1	2	.	.	.
Omnibus, Coach, Cab, Owner—Livery Stable Keeper	19	.	64	3	83	2	51	1	39	2	14	.
Cabman, Flyman, Coachman (not domestic)	48	.	157	.	277	.	312	.	151	.	19	.
Carman, Carrier, Carter, Haulier	602	1	1476	3	2177	3	3054	9	556	3	67	.
Tramway Companies' Service	1	.	.	.	78	.	80	.	35	.	13	.
Wheel Chair Proprietor, Attendant, &c.	.	.	1	.	.	.	.	.	.	.	.	.
3. *On Canals, Rivers and Seas.*												
Inland Navigation Service	4	.	1	.	15	1	10	.	20	1	5	.
Bargeman, Lighterman, Waterman	7	.	20	.	218	1	35	.	1010	2	42	.
Navigation Service (on shore)	.	.	1	.	.	.	1	.	104	3	7	.
Seaman (Merchant Service)	6	.	13	.	46	.	22	.	2742	.	987	.
Pilot	.	.	.	.	.	.	.	.	74	.	22	.
Ship Steward, Cook	3	.	1	.	.	.	1	.	278	24	57	1
Boatman on Seas	1	.	2	.	.	.	.	.	1	.	.	.
Harbour, Dock, Wharf, Lighthouse, Service	1	.	1	.	14	1	7	.	2004	2	159	1
4. *In Storage.*												
Warehouseman (not Manchester)	153	1	559	13	413	18	165	401	120	2	19	.
Meter, Weigher	.	.	1	.	15	.	11	.	26	.	2	.
5. *In conveying Messages, Porterage, &c.*												
Messenger, Porter, Watchman (not Railway nor Government)	300	10	903	6	1374	45	1817	56	1068	6	178	1
Telegraph, Telephone, Service	37	2	85	2	189	34	70	3	55	10	21	3

Table 10 *continued*.—Occupations of Males and Females in the Yorkshire Division and its Registration Ridings, and in each Urban Sanitary District of which the Population exceeds 50,000 Persons.

Occupations.	Urban Sanitary Districts.											
	HALIFAX.		BRAD-FORD.		LEEDS.		SHEF-FIELD.		KINGSTON UPON HULL.		MIDDLES-BROUGH.	
	Males.	Females.	Males.	Females.	Males.	Females.	Males.	Females.	Males.	Females.	Males.	Females.
IV. Agricultural Class.												
7. Persons engaged in Agriculture.												
1. *In Fields and Pastures.*												
Farmer, Grazier	58	8	108	8	253	25	177	14	110	10	16	.
Farmer's, Grazier's—Son, Grandson, Brother, Nephew*	10	.	25	.	68	.	61	.	6	.	6	.
Farm Bailiff	1	.	6	.	20	.	11	.	1	.	.	.
Agricultural Labourer, Farm Servant, Cottager	142	17	258	6	757	16	480	6	249	18	55	18
Shepherd	1	.	2	.	3	.	2	.	1	.	.	.
Land Drainage Service (not in towns)	.	.	.	.	1	.	.	.	1	.	.	.
Agricultural Machine—Proprietor, Attendant	.	.	.	.	12	.	3	.	.	.	.	.
Agricultural Student, Pupil	.	.	.	.	1	.	.	.	.	.	1	.
Others engaged in, or connected with, Agriculture	.	.	1	.	12	.	1	.	3	.	.	.
2. *In Woods.*												
Woodman	.	.	2	.	11	.	3	.	2	.	.	.
3. *In Gardens.*												
Nurseryman, Seedsman, Florist	15	.	9	1	33	2	17	2	17	5	.	.
Gardener (not domestic)	40	1	232	1	567	8	411	1	104	1	12	.
8. Persons engaged about Animals.												
1. *About Animals.*												
Horse Proprietor, Breeder, Dealer	3	.	14	.	57	.	15	.	30	.	1	.
Groom, Horse-keeper, Horse-breaker	42	.	160	.	294	.	314	.	92	.	8	.
Veterinary Surgeon, Farrier	9	.	15	.	26	.	22	.	9	.	4	.
Cattle, Sheep, Pig—Dealer, Salesman	6	.	13	.	26	1	19	.	35	.	5	.
Drover	2	.	6	.	18	.	9	.	6	.	1	.
Gamekeeper	1	.	1	.	4	.	7	.	2	.	.	.
Dog, Bird, Animal—Keeper, Dealer	.	.	3	.	6	.	4	4	4	.	.	.
Vermin destroyer	.	.	.	.	1	.	1	.	3	.	.	.
Fisherman	.	.	1	.	1	.	.	.	1578	1	70	.
Knacker, Catsmeat Dealer, &c., &c.	.	.	1	.	2	.	7	1	2	.	2	.
V. Industrial Class.												
9. Persons working and dealing in Books, Prints, and Maps.												
1. *Books.*												
Publisher, Bookseller, Librarian	19	10	57	10	106	6	58	17	59	9	10	.
Music—Publisher, Seller, Printer	8	1	3	.	18	4	7	1	10	1	.	.
Bookbinder	41	41	70	64	180	157	47	95	66	44	15	14
Printer	159	7	410	83	980	46	492	46	366	88	105	2
Newspaper Agent, News Room Keeper	14	3	55	5	95	14	74	33	16	2	7	1
Others	.	.	.	.	.	.	.	.	.	.	.	.
2. *Prints and Maps.*												
Lithographer, Lithographic Printer	11	2	199	34	220	6	81	2	45	.	8	.
Copper Plate and Steel Plate Printer	1	.	2	.	2	.	5	.	.	.	.	.
Map and Print—Colourer, Seller	3	.	.	.	2	.	3	.	.	.	.	.
10. Persons working and dealing in Machines and Implements.												
1. *Machines.*												
Engine, Machine, Maker	188	2	865	.	2098	16	616	2	433	4	151	.
Millwright	44	.	60	.	282	.	97	.	78	.	13	.
Fitter, Turner (Engine and Machine)	237	.	484	.	2281	.	985	.	687	.	874	.
Boiler Maker	301	.	139	.	688	.	275	.	678	.	366	.
Spinning and Weaving Machine Maker	365	22	1035	12	1090	24	45	.	11	.	.	.
Agricultural Machine and Implement Maker	2	.	2	.	61	1	369	5	7	3	1	.
Domestic Machinery—Maker, Dealer	2	.	6	.	11	.	11	4	1	.	2	.
2. *Tools and Implements.*												
Tool Maker, Dealer	116	.	15	.	861	1	2087	71	7	1	2	.
Cutler, Scissors Maker	4	.	25	3	34	.	13823	1467	18	.	7	.
File Maker	1	.	16	.	74	6	4612	1029	8	.	.	.
Saw Maker	5	.	20	1	14	.	1151	86	14	.	2	.
Pin Maker	.	.	.	.	5	3	1	.	.	.	.	.
Needle Maker	1	.	.	.	.	.	3	17	.	.	.	.
Steel Pen Maker	.	.	.	.	1	1	1	2	.	.	.	.
Pencil Maker (Wood)	.	.	.	.	.	.	.	.	.	.	.	.
Domestic Implement Maker	4	.	12	.	40	4	227	229	.	.	3	.
3. *Watches and Philosophical Instruments.*												
Watch Maker, Clock Maker	44	1	107	2	184	.	144	1	119	.	38	.
Philosophical Instrument Maker, Optician	11	.	3	.	20	.	188	33	15	.	8	.
Electrical Apparatus Maker	40	.	14	.	17	.	15	.	1	.	2	.
Weighing and Measuring Apparatus Maker	3	.	17	.	81	.	100	14	9	.	4	.

* Only male relatives living with the farmer or grazier, and therefore presumably engaged in agriculture, are included above.

Table 10 *continued*.—OCCUPATIONS of MALES and FEMALES in the YORKSHIRE DIVISION and its REGISTRATION RIDINGS, and in each URBAN SANITARY DISTRICT of which the POPULATION exceeds 50,000 PERSONS.

OCCUPATIONS.	URBAN SANITARY DISTRICTS.											
	HALIFAX.		BRADFORD.		LEEDS.		SHEFFIELD.		KINGSTON UPON HULL.		MIDDLESBROUGH.	
	Males.	Females.	Males.	Females.	Males.	Females.	Males.	Females.	Males.	Females.	Males.	Females.
4. Surgical Instruments.												
Surgical Instrument Maker	2	.	1	1	13	5	211	30	2	6	.	.
5. Arms and Ordnance.												
Gunsmith, Gun Manufacturer	3	.	5	.	10	.	27	2	12	.	2	.
Ordnance Manufacturer	.	.	.	.	.	.	.	.	.	.	.	.
Sword, Bayonet—Maker, Cutler	.	.	.	.	.	.	12	.	.	.	.	.
Others	.	.	.	.	.	.	.	.	.	.	.	.
6. Musical Instruments.												
Musical Instrument Maker, Dealer	46	2	30	.	98	5	74	1	92	2	6	.
7. Type, Dies, Medals, Coins.												
Type Cutter, Founder	1	.	.	.	12	.	100	21	.	.	.	.
Die, Seal, Coin, Medal, Maker	.	.	4	.	8	3	127	.	1	.	1	.
8. Tackle for Sports and Games.												
Toy Maker, Dealer	1	.	8	6	20	16	7	12	9	14	.	4
Fishing Rod, Tackle, Maker, Dealer	.	.	.	.	.	.	3	.	1	1	.	.
Apparatus for other Games, Maker, Dealer	1	.	2	.	14	.	55	1	.	.	1	1
11. PERSONS WORKING AND DEALING IN HOUSES, FURNITURE, AND DECORATIONS.												
1. Houses.												
Builder	33	.	110	.	202	1	215	.	115	.	47	.
Carpenter, Joiner	513	.	1536	.	2244	5	1757	11	1546	2	379	.
Bricklayer	59	.	248	.	1717	1	1397	9	1096	.	341	1
Mason	722	.	1204	.	1232	9	1273	.	332	.	74	.
Slater, Tiler	53	.	96	.	168	.	216	.	64	.	35	.
Plasterer, Whitewasher	168	.	405	.	328	2	315	1	51	.	21	2
Paperhanger	4	2	19	.	44	6	44	23	59	1	.	.
Plumber	173	.	415	2	667	3	383	2	300	1	72	.
Painter, Glazier	245	.	730	.	1264	8	795	7	671	2	187	1
2. Furniture and Fittings.												
Cabinet Maker, Upholsterer	245	18	442	51	808	146	721	257	413	57	70	7
French Polisher	42	4	65	9	81	133	84	150	59	.	7	.
Furniture Broker, Dealer	40	3	51	6	117	14	68	26	67	12	7	2
Locksmith, Bellhanger	8	.	8	.	19	.	18	1	9	2	.	.
Gas Fitter	10	.	17	.	47	93	142	1	49	.	14	.
House and Shop Fittings—Maker, Dealer	8	.	20	.	38	.	21	.	5	.	2	.
Funeral Furniture Maker, Undertaker	3	.	2	.	8	1	7	.	3	.	2	.
Others	.	.	.	.	.	.	.	.	.	.	.	.
3. House Decorations.												
Wood Carver	19	.	39	.	51	.	67	2	27	.	3	.
Carver, Gilder	24	.	57	3	152	10	92	9	46	1	14	4
Dealer in Works of Art	1	.	6	.	13	1	6	.	4	3	1	.
Figure, Image—Maker, Dealer	2	.	3	3	7	.	3	.	7	.	.	.
Animal, Bird, &c., Preserver, Naturalist	2	.	4	.	11	.	3	.	4	.	4	.
Artificial Flower Maker	.	.	1	1	3	8	4	3	.	2	.	.
12. PERSONS WORKING AND DEALING IN CARRIAGES AND HARNESS.												
1. Carriages.												
Coachmaker	32	.	119	.	246	3	208	3	109	.	17	.
Railway Carriage, Railway Wagon, Maker	1	.	18	.	37	.	679	1	3	.	.	.
Wheelwright	49	1	121	.	263	1	189	2	66	.	2	.
Bicycle, Tricycle—Maker, Dealer	.	.	.	.	12	.	12	.	.	.	.	.
Others	15	.	21	.	49	11	9	.	3	.	7	.
2. Harness.												
Saddler, Harness, Whip, Maker	33	1	75	.	170	7	107	7	64	.	18	1
13. PERSONS WORKING AND DEALING IN SHIPS AND BOATS.												
1. Hull.												
Ship, Boat, Barge, Builder	3	.	2	.	16	.	.	.	561	.	402	.
Shipwright, Ship Carpenter (ashore)	.	.	.	.	15	.	3	.	696	.	223	.
2. Masts, Rigging, &c.												
Mast, Yard, Oar, Block, Maker	.	.	.	.	.	.	.	.	94	.	8	.
Ship Rigger, Chandler, Fitter	1	.	.	.	.	.	.	.	55	2	9	.
Sail Maker	.	.	2	.	14	.	3	.	173	.	15	.

Table 10 *continued*.—OCCUPATIONS of MALES and FEMALES in the YORKSHIRE DIVISION and its REGISTRATION RIDINGS, and in each URBAN SANITARY DISTRICT of which the POPULATION exceeds 50,000 PERSONS.

OCCUPATIONS.	URBAN SANITARY DISTRICTS.											
	HALIFAX.		BRADFORD.		LEEDS.		SHEFFIELD.		KINGSTON UPON HULL.		MIDDLESBROUGH.	
	Males.	Females.	Males	Females.	Males.	Females.	Males.	Females.	Males.	Females.	Males.	Females.
14. PERSONS WORKING AND DEALING IN CHEMICALS AND COMPOUNDS.												
1. *Colouring Matter.*												
Dye, Paint, Manufacture	17	1	10	.	50	5	3	.	211	50	.	.
Ink, Blacking, Colouring Substance, Manufacture	.	.	2	.	8	.	.	.	12	18	.	.
2. *Explosives.*												
Gunpowder, Guncotton, Explosive Substance, Manufacture	.	.	.	.	.	.	.	.	.	.	.	.
Fusee, Fireworks, Explosive Article, Manufacture	.	.	.	.	26	36	.	1	6	6	.	.
3. *Drugs and other Chemicals and Compounds.*												
Chemist, Druggist	48	1	140	9	305	15	238	6	194	3	28	.
Manufacturing Chemist	25	.	28	18	133	14	42	20	58	32	25	2
Alkali Manufacture	.	.	2	.	1	1	3	.	.	.	.	.
Drysalter	12	.	18	2	79	5	16	1	43	5	2	.
15. PERSONS WORKING AND DEALING IN TOBACCO AND PIPES.												
1. *Tobacco and Pipes.*												
Tobacco Manufacturer, Tobacconist	58	39	66	36	225	174	101	285	67	28	15	12
Tobacco Pipe, Snuff Box, &c., Maker	14	.	10	5	26	11	15	11	18	3	5	3
16. PERSONS WORKING AND DEALING IN FOOD AND LODGING.												
1. *Board and Lodging.*												
Innkeeper, Hotel Keeper, Publican	123	21	289	26	555	73	578	99	335	28	82	15
Lodging, Boarding House, Keeper	10	27	13	220	30	308	6	200	36	480	5	62
Coffee, Eating House, Keeper	10	2	42	10	50	21	50	15	53	13	8	5
2. *Spirituous Drinks.*												
Hop—Merchant, Dealer	.	.	1	.	7	.	.	.	1	.	.	.
Maltster	14	.	82	.	248	1	31	1	44	.	2	.
Brewer	49	2	158	1	444	4	274	6	103	4	10	.
Beerseller. Ale, Porter, Cider, Dealer	79	11	132	27	126	21	172	34	80	17	24	5
Cellarman	20	.	46	3	72	7	62	11	27	.	7	.
Wine, Spirit—Merchant, Agent	28	3	41	2	63	1	64	2	80	.	8	1
3. *Food.*												
Milkseller, Dairyman	34	.	163	19	321	81	235	48	131	20	35	2
Cheesemonger, Butterman	9	.	12	3	31	5	6	5	1	1	4	1
Butcher, Meat Salesman	204	10	650	27	1108	43	963	50	653	19	211	7
Provision Curer, Dealer	13	6	81	18	254	91	216	183	150	33	23	6
Poulterer, Game Dealer	2	.	71	1	52	6	27	7	25	5	5	.
Fishmonger	44	4	142	12	208	14	155	12	367	39	25	8
Corn, Flour, Seed—Merchant, Dealer	11	1	18	1	75	13	21	.	139	10	9	.
Corn Miller	34	.	35	.	229	.	88	1	107	1	5	.
Baker	79	13	119	45	181	54	183	40	199	24	36	2
Confectioner, Pastrycook	40	82	106	161	175	262	195	232	110	65	22	18
Greengrocer, Fruiterer	138	18	310	54	431	109	270	85	258	63	67	24
Mustard, Vinegar, Spice, Pickle—Maker, Dealer	3	7	4	6	14	31	8	48	2	.	1	.
Sugar Refiner	2	.	4	1	7	3	11	5	16	.	4	.
Grocer. Tea, Coffee, Chocolate—Maker, Dealer	409	100	1080	342	1436	363	1110	292	774	251	298	38
Ginger Beer, Mineral Water—Manufacturer, Dealer	9	.	32	1	42	7	50	4	31	2	7	.
Others dealing in Food	.	.	.	.	.	.	.	.	.	.	.	.
17. PERSONS WORKING AND DEALING IN TEXTILE FABRICS.												
1. *Wool and Worsted.*												
Woolstapler	185	.	478	1	135	1	.	.	2	.	.	.
Woollen Cloth Manufacture	777	633	1100	998	5457	6782	20	4	9	7	.	1
Wool, Woollen goods—Dyer, Printer	73	4	166	2	363	1	1	.	1	.	1	.
Worsted, Stuff, Manufacture	2181	5136	10242	29817	847	953	1	3	4	5	.	.
Flannel Manufacture	1	.	3	.	2	1	.	.	.	.	.	.
Blanket Manufacture	3	2	1	2	58	114	.	.	.	.	.	.
Fuller	.	.	3	.	46	1	.	.	.	.	.	.
Cloth, Worsted, Stuff, Flannel, Blanket, Dealer	105	1	2048	1	770	5	13	.	2	.	.	.
Others	4	5	41	116	1	2	1	.	1	.	.	.
2. *Silk.*												
Silk, Silk goods, Manufacture	173	310	434	1170	17	50	1	7	2	4	.	.
Silk Dyer, Printer	1	.	47	.	4	.	.	.	.	.	.	.
Ribbon Manufacture	.	.	1	1	.	.	.	.	.	.	.	.
Crape, Gauze, Manufacture	.	.	.	.	1	.	.	1	.	.	.	.
Silk Merchant, Dealer	2	.	16	.	4	.	.	.	3	.	.	.

Table 10 *continued.*—OCCUPATIONS of MALES and FEMALES in the YORKSHIRE DIVISION and its REGISTRATION RIDINGS, and in each URBAN SANITARY DISTRICT of which the POPULATION exceeds 50,000 Persons.

OCCUPATIONS.	URBAN SANITARY DISTRICTS											
	HALIFAX.		BRADFORD.		LEEDS.		SHEFFIELD.		KINGSTON UPON HULL.		MIDDLESBROUGH.	
	Males.	Females.	Males.	Females.	Males.	Females.	Males.	Females.	Males.	Females.	Males.	Females.
3. Cotton and Flax												
Cotton, Cotton goods, Manufacture	1659	1323	914	887	63	347	8	12	248	525	1	7
Cotton, Calico—Printer, Dyer, Bleacher	64	1	186	.	11	.	.	.	.	.	.	.
Cotton, Calico—Warehouseman, Dealer	13	1	18	.	17	2	.	.	2	.	1	.
Flax, Linen—Manufacturer, Dealer	69	184	12	4	792	2709	3	1	39	71	1	1
Lace Manufacturer, Dealer	2	2	37	8	7	17	6	20	1	6	.	.
Fustian Manufacturer, Dealer	.	.	.	.	.	.	.	.	.	.	.	1
Tape Manufacturer, Dealer	1	.	.	.	.	4	2	43	.	.	.	.
Thread Manufacturer, Dealer	.	1	1	2	8	33	.	.	.	1	.	.
4. Hemp and other Fibrous Materials.												
Hemp, Jute, Cocoa Fibre, Manufacture	7	3	1	.	5	1	2	17	28	9	.	.
Rope, Twine, Cord—Maker, Dealer	93	1	41	3	63	47	28	2	168	15	3	.
Mat Maker, Seller	.	.	.	1	1	1	5	.	10	15	.	.
Net Maker	.	.	.	.	.	1	1	.	7	52	.	.
Canvas, Sailcloth, Manufacture	.	1	1	.	8	41	.	.	1	2	1	.
Sacking, Sack, Bag—Maker, Dealer	.	7	13	10	13	35	.	5	11	16	.	.
Others working and dealing in Hemp	.	.	3	2	2	2	.	.	4	.	.	.
5. Mixed or Unspecified Materials.												
Weaver (undefined)	55	10	88	144	31	266	2	7	5	.	2	.
Dyer, Printer, Scourer, Bleacher, Calenderer (undefined)	763	5	1506	48	707	19	23	19	34	20	4	3
Factory hand (Textile, undefined)	234	27	359	463	210	529	1	8	9	30	.	.
Felt Manufacture	1	.	1	.	66	10	.	.	.	.	.	.
Carpet, Rug, Manufacture	1055	834	25	14	116	45	14	4	17	2	2	1
Manchester Warehouseman	.	.	.	.	7	.	1	.	.	.	.	.
Draper, Linen Draper, Mercer	174	47	407	142	776	262	330	247	395	141	121	28
Fancy Goods (Textile), Manufacturer, Worker, Dealer	16	21	13	31	11	38	9	23	7	34	.	4
Trimming Maker, Dealer	.	1	.	1	5	4	.	1	.	3	.	.
Embroiderer	.	.	3	6	1	10	.	.	.	1	.	.
Others	19	.	89	5	7	22	.	.	.	.	.	.
18. PERSONS WORKING AND DEALING IN DRESS.												
1. Dress.												
Hatter, Hat Manufacture (not straw)	15	4	30	9	184	255	80	3	42	12	15	2
Straw—Hat, Bonnet, Plait, Manufacture	.	3	.	8	5	19	.	21	.	19	1	2
Tailor	810	67	867	129	2148	2740	953	252	718	234	254	33
Milliner, Dressmaker, Staymaker	9	925	13	2571	31	4001	56	3359	6	2513	5	647
Shawl Manufacture	.	.	.	2	2	2	.	.	.	.	.	.
Shirt Maker, Seamstress	.	138	2	204	3	361	2	340	.	401	.	37
Hosiery Manufacture	.	1	3	10	2	14	2	5	1	.	1	.
Hosier, Haberdasher	22	7	33	20	66	16	50	81	42	24	4	7
Glover, Glove Maker	.	1	1	.	1	2	.	1	.	1	.	.
Button Maker, Dealer	.	.	.	2	2	.	66	90	.	.	.	.
Shoe, Boot—Maker, Dealer	489	82	763	61	4692	1135	1113	103	810	74	197	14
Patten, Clog, Maker	198	1	197	2	88	1	93	1	13	.	3	.
Wig Maker, Hairdresser	75	.	174	12	244	6	185	22	150	8	41	.
Umbrella, Parasol, Stick—Maker, Dealer	8	1	27	4	17	5	68	131	10	7	.	.
Accoutrement Maker	1	.	1	.	.	.	.	.	.	.	.	.
Old Clothes Dealer, and others	.	4	13	16	7	59	71	40	7	31	3	4
19. PERSONS WORKING AND DEALING IN VARIOUS ANIMAL SUBSTANCES.												
1. In Grease, Gut, Bone, Horn, Ivory, and Whalebone.												
Tallow Chandler, Candle, Grease, Manufacture	11	.	20	.	30	2	16	3	32	.	3	4
Soap Boiler, Maker	4	.	51	18	48	2	3	.	7	1	1	.
Glue, Size, Gelatine, Isinglass—Maker, Dealer	2	.	2	.	32	.	.	2	4	1	.	.
Manure Manufacture	.	.	1	.	12	.	4	.	11	1	.	.
Bone, Horn, Ivory, Tortoise-shell—Worker, Dealer	.	.	3	1	1	.	233	49	.	.	.	.
Comb Maker	1	.	8	2	3	1	184	91	.	.	.	.
Others	.	.	2	.	2	2	3	.	.	.	.	.
2. In Skins.												
Furrier, Skinner	1	1	5	4	187	52	20	8	8	2	1	.
Tanner, Fellmonger	9	.	14	.	872	5	48	.	166	3	2	.
Currier	57	2	68	.	1539	123	104	1	51	1	10	.
Leather Goods, Portmanteau, Bag, Strap, &c.—Maker, Dealer	31	23	16	4	73	7	94	165	24	1	2	.
Parchment, Vellum—Maker, Dealer	.	.	.	1	.	.	.	.	.	.	.	.
3. In Hair and Feathers.												
Hair, Bristle—Worker, Dealer	1	.	11	1	7	3	54	118	6	1	.	.
Brush, Broom, Maker	121	67	129	10	271	80	121	56	121	57	1	1
Quill, Feather—Dresser, Dealer	.	5	.	4	5	29	.	2	7	7	.	.

Table 10 *continued*.—OCCUPATIONS of MALES and FEMALES in the YORKSHIRE DIVISION and its REGISTRATION RIDINGS, and in each URBAN SANITARY DISTRICT of which the POPULATION exceeds 50,000 PERSONS.

OCCUPATIONS.	URBAN SANITARY DISTRICTS.											
	HALIFAX.		BRADFORD.		LEEDS.		SHEFFIELD.		KINGSTON UPON HULL.		MIDDLESBROUGH.	
	Males.	Females.	Males.	Females.	Males.	Females.	Males.	Females.	Males.	Females.	Males.	Females.
20. PERSONS WORKING AND DEALING IN VARIOUS VEGETABLE SUBSTANCES.												
1. *In Oils, Gums, and Resins.*												
Oil Miller, Oil Cake—Maker, Dealer	7	.	12	.	98	.	9	1	1199	1	4	.
Oil and Colourman	2	.	3	2	3	1	2	1	13	2	.	.
Floor Cloth, Oil Cloth, Manufacture	24	1	1	.	2	2	1	.	.	1	.	.
Japanner	1	2	2	.	2	4	7	35	2	.	.	.
India Rubber, Gutta Percha—Worker, Dealer	12	5	1	.	11	4	6	1	3	.	1	.
Waterproof Goods—Maker, Dealer	4	.	12	.	6	1	2	2	6	1	.	.
Others	.	.	.	.	.	.	5	.	16	.	.	.
2. *In Cane, Rush, and Straw.*												
Willow, Cane, Rush—Worker, Dealer, Basketmaker	12	1	66	5	61	13	41	6	74	8	6	.
Hay, Straw (not plait), Chaff—Cutter, Dealer	13	.	28	.	66	1	53	1	18	.	2	.
Thatcher	.	.	.	.	.	.	.	.	.	.	.	.
3. *In Wood and Bark.*												
Timber, Wood—Merchant, Dealer	39	.	114	3	157	4	123	8	164	1	23	2
Sawyer	59	.	258	.	262	.	164	.	304	.	37	.
Lath, Wooden Fence, Hurdle, Maker	8	.	12	.	10	.	4	.	133	.	5	.
Wood Turner, Box Maker	60	4	190	18	239	40	250	13	106	9	8	.
Cooper, Hoop Maker, Bender	31	.	47	1	165	.	206	2	517	.	15	.
Cork, Bark—Cutter, Worker, Dealer	10	14	4	.	19	1	13	1	33	1	2	.
Others	.	.	.	.	2	.	3	.	.	.	1	.
4. *In Paper.*												
Paper Manufacture	6	.	47	23	136	40	21	23	28	30	2	.
Envelope Maker	.	.	.	.	1	3	.	.	.	1	.	.
Stationer, Law Stationer	22	6	58	28	143	81	63	65	47	17	18	11
Card, Pattern Card, Maker	21	2	19	10	6	1	.	1	.	.	.	.
Paper Stainer	.	.	2	.	219	7	.	1	12	.	.	.
Paper Box, Paper Bag, Maker	1	33	14	81	6	126	6	73	8	46	.	6
Ticket, Label, Writer	.	7	7	4	13	10	6	5	5	1	.	.
Others	9	.	20	.	32	2	19	1	17	.	4	.
21. PERSONS WORKING AND DEALING IN VARIOUS MINERAL SUBSTANCES.												
1. *Miners.*												
Coal Miner	107	.	377	.	3013	6	1893	1	12	.	4	.
Ironstone Miner	.	.	77	.	158	.	4	.	3	.	2	.
Copper Miner	.	.	.	.	1	.	.	.	1	.	.	.
Tin Miner	.	.	.	.	.	.	.	.	.	.	.	.
Lead Miner	.	.	1	.	1	.	6	.	.	.	.	.
Miner in other, or undefined, Minerals	8	.	12	.	40	.	1	.	30	6	16	.
Mine Service	3	.	3	.	39	.	23	.	.	.	1	.
2. *Coal, Coal Gas, &c.*												
Coal Merchant, Dealer	92	7	389	9	297	16	254	9	221	3	74	.
Coalheaver	13	.	62	.	78	.	55	.	238	.	21	.
Coke, Charcoal, Peat—Cutter, Burner, Dealer	1	.	17	.	20	1	85	12	1	1	.	.
Gas Works Service	129	.	284	.	439	.	381	.	113	.	47	.
3. *Stone, Clay, and Road Making.*												
Stone Quarrier	212	.	485	.	361	.	196	.	3	.	3	.
Stone Cutter, Dresser, Dealer	102	.	113	.	117	.	67	.	24	.	1	.
Slate Quarrier	.	.	2	.	.	.	2	.	.	.	.	.
Slate Worker, Dealer	1	.	.	.	16	7	1	.	13	2	3	.
Limeburner	1	.	1	.	3	.	2	.	1	.	.	.
Clay, Sand, Gravel, Chalk—Labourer, Dealer	33	.	3	.	25	2	4	.	.	.	.	.
Fossil, Coprolite—Digger, Dealer	.	.	.	.	.	.	.	.	.	.	.	.
Well Sinker, Borer	2	.	20	.	16	.	5	.	4	.	.	.
Plaster, Cement, Manufacture	8	.	2	.	8	1	4	.	46	.	.	1
Brick, Tile—Maker, Burner, Dealer	164	1	177	.	1037	7	322	.	84	1	38	.
Paviour	51	.	100	.	184	.	76	.	25	.	3	.
Road Contractor, Surveyor, Inspector	4	.	5	.	4	.	12	.	.	.	1	.
Road Labourer	30	.	77	.	118	.	90	.	10	.	6	.
Railway Contractor	2	.	1	.	25	.	8	.	3	.	.	.
Platelayer	17	.	81	.	260	.	64	.	45	.	84	.
Railway Labourer, Navvy	104	.	150	.	471	.	175	.	265	.	35	.
Others	.	.	.	.	1	.	15	119	.	1	.	.
4. *Earthenware and Glass.*												
Earthenware, China, Porcelain, Manufacture	34	1	16	.	345	56	125	1	9	.	64	27
Glass Manufacture	2	.	14	.	488	12	139	14	10	.	4	.
Earthenware, China, Glass, Dealer	15	4	43	16	66	38	44	28	20	7	10	2
5. *Salt.*												
Salt Maker, Dealer	.	.	3	2	8	.	4	.	.	.	.	.

Table 10 *continued*.—OCCUPATIONS of MALES and FEMALES in the YORKSHIRE DIVISION and its REGISTRATION RIDINGS, and in each URBAN SANITARY DISTRICT of which the POPULATION exceeds 50,000 PERSONS.

OCCUPATIONS.	URBAN SANITARY DISTRICTS.											
	HALIFAX.		BRADFORD.		LEEDS.		SHEFFIELD.		KINGSTON UPON HULL.		MIDDLESBROUGH.	
	Males.	Females.	Males.	Females.	Males.	Females.	Males.	Females.	Males.	Females.	Males.	Females.
6. Water.												
Waterworks Service	8	.	17	.	31	1	46	.	6	.	9	.
Others	.	.	.	.	1	.	.	.	1	.	.	.
7. Precious Metals and Jewellery.												
Goldsmith, Silversmith, Jeweller	15	.	38	14	121	21	1946	273	50	7	10	.
Gold, Silver, Beater	.	.	.	.	7	.	4	.	.	.	.	.
Lapidary	1	.	2	.	2	2	.	.	1	.	.	.
Others	.	2	.	.	.	.	62	864	.	2	.	.
8. Iron and Steel.												
Blacksmith	211	.	371	.	1274	1	1573	4	608	2	872	2
Whitesmith	39	1	107	.	199	1	95	3	102	.	7	.
Nail Manufacture	4	.	11	.	202	243	24	18	7	.	9	3
Anchor, Chain, Manufacture	.	.	.	.	9	.	5	.	1	.	.	.
Other Iron and Steel Manufactures	431	1	1549	.	6329	2	9620	37	831	2	4907	16
Ironmonger. Hardware Dealer, Merchant	34	2	75	3	184	5	150	20	74	4	30	.
9. Copper.												
Copper, Copper goods—Manufacturer, Worker, Dealer	7	.	7	.	54	.	14	.	31	.	7	.
10. Tin and Zinc.												
Tin, Tin Plate, Tin goods—Manufacturer, Worker, Dealer	76	1	180	1	326	16	172	53	191	2	26	.
Zinc, Zinc Goods—Manufacturer, Worker, Dealer	1	.	.	.	1	.	.	.	.	.	.	.
11. Lead.												
Lead, Leaden goods—Manufacturer, Worker, Dealer	1	.	.	.	10	.	31	5	20	9	.	.
12. In Other, Mixed, or Unspecified, Metals.												
Metal Refiner, Worker, Turner, Dealer	.	.	1	.	17	.	251	83	4	.	6	.
Brass, Bronze, Manufacture. Brazier	180	1	121	1	322	6	473	23	186	1	30	1
Metal Burnisher, Lacquerer	.	1	.	.	.	1	4	43	.	.	.	.
White Metal, Plated Ware, Manufacture. Pewterer	.	.	1	.	.	.	1193	245	1	.	.	.
Wire Maker, Worker, Weaver, Drawer	546	54	22	3	78	4	519	16	13	4	81	.
Bolt, Nut, Rivet, Screw, Staple, Maker	16	.	26	.	159	14	127	90	6	.	30	.
Lamp, Lantern, Candlestick, Maker	.	.	1	.	4	1	37	3	1	.	.	.
Clasp, Buckle, Hinge, Maker	.	.	.	.	.	.	3	11	.	.	.	.
Fancy Chain, Gilt Toy, Maker	.	.	.	.	.	.	2	.	.	.	.	.
Others	.	.	.	.	1	1	68	2	.	.	.	.
22. PERSONS WORKING AND DEALING IN GENERAL OR UNSPECIFIED COMMODITIES.												
1. Makers and Dealers (General or Undefined).												
General Shopkeeper, Dealer	43	73	101	143	255	272	154	287	180	173	41	30
Pawnbroker	28	.	71	4	180	17	288	9	68	37	15	2
Costermonger, Huckster, Street Seller	147	63	849	155	515	281	351	228	278	175	78	34
Manufacturer, Manager, Superintendent (undefined)	64	1	152	1	115	11	129	2	96	.	20	.
Contractor (undefined)	20	.	25	.	43	.	26	.	17	1	18	.
2. Mechanics and Labourers (General or Undefined).												
General Labourer	672	1	1718	6	4439	16	3925	10	4600	15	2286	1
Engine Driver, Stoker, Fireman (not railway, marine, nor agricultural)	242	.	758	.	1117	.	1100	.	356	.	462	.
Artizan, Mechanic (undefined)	309	7	638	38	919	49	448	118	112	5	34	4
Apprentice (undefined)	14	.	16	1	48	3	21	3	37	1	3	.
Factory Labourer (undefined)	105	7	109	4	218	31	534	397	94	82	40	4
Machinist, Machine Worker (undefined)	12	.	20	62	69	329	34	.	39	.	3	.
23. PERSONS WORKING AND DEALING IN REFUSE MATTERS.												
1. Refuse Matters.												
Town Drainage Service	7	.	21	.	93	.	10	.	11	.	2	.
Chimney Sweep, Soot Merchant	21	.	71	.	93	1	84	.	61	1	13	.
Scavenger, Crossing Sweeper	24	.	40	.	53	.	51	4	22	.	6	.
Rag Gatherer, Dealer	9	5	33	40	50	63	9	2	18	11	7	1
VI. UNOCCUPIED CLASS.												
24. PERSONS WITHOUT SPECIFIED OCCUPATIONS												
Persons returned by Property, Rank, &c. and not by special occupation	6863	20678	18026	48280	34502	95974	32349	93991	18162	51865	7135	18239
Children under 5 years of age	4080	4634	12047	12341	21728	22267	20602	21009	10980	11070	4506	4395

Table 11.—BIRTH-PLACES of MALES and FEMALES enumerated in YORKSHIRE, and in each URBAN SANITARY DISTRICT of which the POPULATION EXCEEDS 50,000 PERSONS.

WHERE BORN.	WHERE ENUMERATED.							
	YORKSHIRE.*		URBAN SANITARY DISTRICTS.					
			HUDDERSFIELD.		HALIFAX.		BRADFORD.	
	Males.	Females.	Males.	Females.	Males.	Females.	Males.	Females.
TOTAL OF INHABITANTS	1420001	1466563	38957	42844	34634	38996	85211	97821
LONDON	10796	11499	164	191	257	275	666	785
MIDDLESEX (*Intra-metropolitan*)	8638	9376	128	158	223	215	535	662
SURREY (*Intra-metropolitan*)	1283	1276	21	19	21	39	95	81
KENT (*Intra-metropolitan*)	875	847	15	14	13	21	36	42
SOUTH-EASTERN COUNTIES	7851	7318	92	111	135	172	317	434
SURREY (*Extra-metropolitan*)	908	909	6	13	22	17	51	56
KENT (*Extra-metropolitan*)	2471	2297	39	36	40	57	111	158
SUSSEX	1068	1065	11	15	22	35	82	66
HAMPSHIRE	1975	2087	23	32	38	49	97	113
BERKSHIRE	929	860	13	15	13	14	26	41
SOUTH-MIDLAND COUNTIES	15544	13173	150	204	275	321	817	971
MIDDLESEX (*Extra-metropolitan*)	729	708	10	13	12	12	39	74
HERTFORDSHIRE	1027	898	15	18	23	20	52	62
BUCKINGHAMSHIRE	1511	1091	6	14	52	53	77	68
OXFORDSHIRE	1573	1337	26	28	22	30	40	67
NORTHAMPTONSHIRE	3657	3283	29	46	51	71	100	237
HUNTINGDONSHIRE	1382	1240	7	14	23	35	111	132
BEDFORDSHIRE	2110	1646	27	29	50	49	115	91
CAMBRIDGESHIRE	3572	3000	30	42	42	51	184	240
EASTERN COUNTIES	17621	14559	181	233	291	363	1276	1421
ESSEX	2511	1858	34	34	28	48	105	109
SUFFOLK	4718	3704	54	62	115	126	456	467
NORFOLK	10392	8997	93	137	148	189	715	845
SOUTH-WESTERN COUNTIES	9554	9552	136	149	175	241	677	775
WILTSHIRE	1323	1251	20	20	15	37	86	89
DORSETSHIRE	880	764	17	11	9	13	37	39
DEVONSHIRE	3128	3214	44	58	54	72	267	290
CORNWALL	1999	2118	18	21	18	30	56	81
SOMERSETSHIRE	2224	2205	37	39	79	89	231	276
WEST-MIDLAND COUNTIES	28767	27993	328	525	440	620	1082	1536
GLOUCESTERSHIRE	3711	3263	75	76	56	79	175	100
HEREFORDSHIRE	891	952	16	36	15	32	95	131
SHROPSHIRE	3008	3465	40	133	40	103	109	217
STAFFORDSHIRE	12344	11618	97	141	82	111	205	375
WORCESTERSHIRE	3548	3459	26	59	128	156	189	267
WARWICKSHIRE	5265	5238	74	80	119	139	309	356
NORTH-MIDLAND COUNTIES	59766	61106	469	760	478	694	1512	2095
LEICESTERSHIRE	3637	3344	33	53	76	108	242	287
RUTLANDSHIRE	537	453	6	6	5	12	30	43
LINCOLNSHIRE	27293	29052	206	364	213	337	640	1020
NOTTINGHAMSHIRE	13112	12622	108	154	68	99	314	363
DERBYSHIRE	15187	15635	116	183	116	138	280	382
NORTH-WESTERN COUNTIES	35007	35917	1265	1335	1360	1615	3071	3574
CHESHIRE	4780	4797	201	224	158	240	292	336
LANCASHIRE	30227	31120	1064	1111	1202	1375	2779	3238
YORKSHIRE	1153327	1205193	34522	37775	29256	32415	69715	78420
NORTHERN COUNTIES	25290	28691	235	258	214	299	936	1310
DURHAM	16572	18722	96	112	85	136	450	662
NORTHUMBERLAND	4168	4772	48	62	34	48	129	194
CUMBERLAND	2319	2634	33	54	30	48	170	223
WESTMORLAND	2231	2563	58	60	65	67	187	231
MONMOUTHSHIRE AND WALES	4821	5123	60	156	63	142	135	293
MONMOUTHSHIRE	983	913	5	9	10	15	30	56
GLAMORGANSHIRE	856	806	8	7	10	19	19	26
CARMARTHENSHIRE	135	106	3	3	1	3	6	2
PEMBROKESHIRE	235	247	3	9	7	8	20	29
CARDIGANSHIRE	104	73	.	.	.	4	3	6
BRECKNOCKSHIRE	185	100	3	1	2	6	3	6
RADNORSHIRE	63	93	.	4	1	5	3	8
MONTGOMERYSHIRE	186	319	6	18	6	20	14	26
FLINTSHIRE	314	397	7	19	4	15	6	23
DENBIGHSHIRE	403	415	8	31	9	18	7	33
MERIONETHSHIRE	41	56	1	2	.	.	2	2
CARNARVONSHIRE	121	187	5	13	2	8	1	13
ANGLESEY	90	94	.	7	2	3	2	5
WALES (*County not stated*)	1135	1253	11	33	9	24	18	60
ENGLAND (*County not stated*)	2497	2251	36	25	40	34	84	125
OTHER PARTS OF BRITISH EMPIRE	42692	38993	1174	993	1550	1701	4238	5587
ISLANDS IN THE BRITISH SEAS	435	664	10	28	12	18	83	70
SCOTLAND	9903	9483	302	272	229	237	848	847
IRELAND	30264	26614	808	636	1233	1361	3336	4478
BRITISH COLONIES OR DEPENDENCIES	2090	2231	54	57	76	85	171	192
FOREIGN COUNTIES	6804	5043	140	95	92	101	672	489
British Subjects	1965	1804	40	47	38	61	306	233
Foreigners	4839	3239	100	48	54	50	367	256
AT SEA	164	153	5	4	8	3	13	6
British Subjects	160	152	5	4	8	3	13	6
Foreigners	4	1	.	.	.	.	.	.

* The County *proper*, and not the Registration County, is referred to in this Table.

Table 11 *continued*.—BIRTH-PLACES of MALES and FEMALES enumerated in YORKSHIRE, and in each URBAN SANITARY DISTRICT of which the POPULATION EXCEEDS 50,000 PERSONS.

WHERE BORN.	WHERE ENUMERATED.							
	URBAN SANITARY DISTRICTS.							
	LEEDS.		SHEFFIELD.		KINGSTON UPON HULL.		MIDDLESBROUGH.	
	Males.	Females.	Males.	Females.	Males.	Females.	Males.	Females.
TOTAL OF INHABITANTS	149844	159275	141298	143210	75746	78494	29175	26759
LONDON	1585	1642	1435	1487	1492	1338	405	355
MIDDLESEX (*Intra-metropolitan*)	1292	1355	1161	1214	1187	1076	298	271
SURREY (*Intra-metropolitan*)	188	188	154	162	150	148	62	39
KENT (*Intra-metropolitan*)	105	99	120	111	156	114	45	45
SOUTH-EASTERN COUNTIES	793	834	724	722	1000	892	278	223
SURREY (*Extra-metropolitan*)	125	115	69	79	79	77	18	19
KENT (*Extra-metropolitan*)	249	241	233	211	504	476	124	97
SUSSEX	113	139	101	99	114	101	35	29
HAMPSHIRE	216	258	252	200	244	193	79	58
BERKSHIRE	85	81	79	73	59	45	22	20
SOUTH-MIDLAND COUNTIES	1890	1640	2171	1656	998	791	324	272
MIDDLESEX (*Extra-metropolitan*)	95	87	56	71	48	52	19	25
HERTFORDSHIRE	107	87	85	78	45	35	25	17
BUCKINGHAMSHIRE	134	99	216	135	94	55	27	20
OXFORDSHIRE	189	173	180	147	81	48	30	22
NORTHAMPTONSHIRE	600	501	503	467	183	160	37	44
HUNTINGDONSHIRE	151	156	220	179	78	53	24	10
BEDFORDSHIRE	266	234	283	188	65	45	32	26
CAMBRIDGESHIRE	348	303	538	391	334	343	130	108
EASTERN COUNTIES	1660	1507	1221	967	2167	1911	862	624
ESSEX	221	195	186	148	257	169	71	60
SUFFOLK	514	432	247	171	326	240	220	158
NORFOLK	925	880	788	648	1584	1502	571	406
SOUTH-WESTERN COUNTIES	736	853	698	675	871	920	268	196
WILTSHIRE	103	112	109	114	89	68	71	38
DORSETSHIRE	85	63	71	61	60	46	17	18
DEVONSHIRE	228	288	277	250	514	602	97	71
CORNWALL	88	122	59	70	133	109	31	20
SOMERSETSHIRE	232	268	182	180	105	95	52	49
WEST-MIDLAND COUNTIES	2292	2544	5101	4725	639	665	1234	981
GLOUCESTERSHIRE	396	431	386	312	142	157	133	73
HEREFORDSHIRE	87	78	79	65	17	36	22	23
SHROPSHIRE	222	343	511	478	43	69	96	53
STAFFORDSHIRE	770	876	1952	1841	192	176	651	546
WORCESTERSHIRE	295	286	467	452	63	63	216	164
WARWICKSHIRE	522	530	1706	1577	182	174	122	102
NORTH-MIDLAND COUNTIES	3552	3820	16885	16178	6764	7952	586	487
LEICESTERSHIRE	398	376	748	623	137	137	45	32
RUTLANDSHIRE	68	33	103	83	20	25	2	3
LINCOLNSHIRE	1620	1932	4703	4293	5754	6965	401	[illegible]
NOTTINGHAMSHIRE	714	732	4897	4337	656	633	55	56
DERBYSHIRE	752	748	6434	6842	197	192	83	80
NORTH-WESTERN COUNTIES	3651	3581	3241	3058	1522	1347	574	436
CHESHIRE	453	443	631	512	241	207	68	50
LANCASHIRE	3198	3138	2610	2546	1281	1140	506	386
YORKSHIRE	123139	132310	103826	108880	54706	58284	15358	15296
NORTHERN COUNTIES	2067	2378	709	577	889	898	4623	4858
DURHAM	1109	1314	355	291	485	501	3650	3910
NORTHUMBERLAND	529	584	203	158	276	303	621	649
CUMBERLAND	262	299	105	90	88	67	285	258
WESTMORLAND	167	181	46	38	40	27	67	41
MONMOUTHSHIRE AND WALES	320	407	360	346	193	184	885	795
MONMOUTHSHIRE	63	64	74	63	33	35	194	177
GLAMORGANSHIRE	54	55	92	56	44	34	210	192
CARMARTHENSHIRE	12	9	16	11	9	1	27	30
PEMBROKESHIRE	14	22	22	15	30	24	24	21
CARDIGANSHIRE	4	7	1	4	13	1	25	12
BRECKNOCKSHIRE	11	17	13	10	4	10	40	38
RADNORSHIRE	3	4	8	3	3	2	6	5
MONTGOMERYSHIRE	18	37	29	23	3	7	3	7
FLINTSHIRE	25	40	25	16	9	16	8	4
DENBIGHSHIRE	31	32	85	39	7	8	10	3
MERIONETHSHIRE	2	4	3	5	2	2	2	1
CARNARVONSHIRE	10	19	15	14	1	7	14	8
ANGLESEY	8	13	5	13	5	5	5	1
WALES (*County not stated*)	65	84	61	81	30	32	317	296
ENGLAND (*County not stated*)	258	206	234	168	178	145	81	78
OTHER PARTS OF BRITISH EMPIRE	6452	6388	3979	3273	2567	2158	3341	1999
ISLANDS IN THE BRITISH SEAS	40	83	41	74	63	60	16	7
SCOTLAND	1398	1256	867	727	1003	810	907	847
IRELAND	4780	4761	2782	2224	1322	1148	2371	1315
BRITISH COLONIES OR DEPENDENCIES	234	288	289	248	179	140	47	30
FOREIGN COUNTRIES	1424	1147	684	471	1814	987	350	155
British Subjects	235	202	220	202	314	237	91	59
Foreigners	1189	945	464	269	1500	750	259	96
AT SEA	25	18	20	27	16	22	6	4
British Subjects	25	18	19	27	15	22	4	4
Foreigners	.	.	1	.	1	.	2	.

Table 12.—Distribution of the enumerated Natives of Yorkshire.

Where Enumerated.	Where born. YORKSHIRE. Males.	Where born. YORKSHIRE. Females.
TOTAL ENUMERATED NATIVES OF YORKSHIRE	1815767	1869158
LONDON	16409	15814
Middlesex (*Intra-metropolitan*)	10972	10608
Surrey (*Intra-metropolitan*)	4214	4111
Kent (*Intra-metropolitan*)	1223	1095
SOUTH-EASTERN COUNTIES	7851	6619
Surrey (*Extra-metropolitan*)	1549	1613
Kent (*Extra-metropolitan*)	2257	1590
Sussex	1273	1577
Hampshire	2192	1451
Berkshire	580	388
SOUTH-MIDLAND COUNTIES	4981	4811
Middlesex (*Extra-metropolitan*)	1545	1648
Hertfordshire	560	472
Buckinghamshire	388	338
Oxfordshire	356	365
Northamptonshire	1063	974
Huntingdonshire	192	197
Bedfordshire	360	350
Cambridgeshire	518	476
EASTERN COUNTIES	3454	3044
Essex	1613	1303
Suffolk	664	577
Norfolk	1177	1164
SOUTH-WESTERN COUNTIES	2852	2406
Wiltshire	357	312
Dorsetshire	509	212
Devonshire	1065	916
Cornwall	292	236
Somersetshire	630	730
WEST-MIDLAND COUNTIES	8584	8618
Gloucestershire	1179	1239
Herefordshire	196	219
Shropshire	561	529
Staffordshire	2888	2778
Worcestershire	1090	1113
Warwickshire	2670	2749
NORTH-MIDLAND COUNTIES	22371	24161
Leicestershire	1402	1590
Rutlandshire	105	97
Lincolnshire	8067	8616
Nottinghamshire	4850	5304
Derbyshire	7868	8509
NORTH-WESTERN COUNTIES	59434	64799
Cheshire	5119	6187
Lancashire	54315	58612
YORKSHIRE	1153327	1205193
NORTHERN COUNTIES	34532	32008
Durham	28249	22861
Northumberland	3545	3540
Cumberland	1825	1210
Westmorland	1303	1397
MONMOUTHSHIRE AND WALES	1972	1685
Monmouthshire	315	283
Glamorganshire	719	530
Carmarthenshire	61	41
Pembrokeshire	82	61
Cardiganshire	27	24
Brecknockshire	53	38
Radnorshire	9	12
Montgomeryshire	101	89
Flintshire	173	210
Denbighshire	182	198
Merionethshire	50	46
Carnarvonshire	161	157
Anglesey	40	38

Table 14.—Number and Ages of Males and Females returned as Blind or Blind from Birth in the Yorkshire Division and its Registration Ridings.

Registration Riding.	All Ages.		0–	5–	15–	20–	25–	45–	65 and upwards.
	Both Sexes.	Males and Females.							
IX. YORKSHIRE	2294	M. 1234	37	122	69	53	299	322	332
		F. 1060	50	108	46	51	188	248	379
35 WEST RIDING -	1602	M. - 860	29	88	36	41	213	227	226
		F. 742	38	75	21	36	144	186	240
36 EAST RIDING - -	407	M. - 206	5	29	24	6	46	44	51
		F. - 201	7	25	21	9	29	36	74
37 NORTH RIDING -	285	M. - 168	2	5	9	6	40	51	55
		F. - 117	5	3	4	4	10	26	65

Table 15.—Number and Ages of Males and Females returned as Blind in the Yorkshire Division and its Registration Ridings.

Registration Riding.	All Ages.		0–	5–	15–	20–	25–	45–	65 and upwards.
	Both Sexes.	Males and Females.							
IX. YORKSHIRE -	2071	M. 1125	18	92	57	49	268	311	330
		F. 946	35	70	37	39	154	237	374
35 WEST RIDING - -	1439	M. - 779	15	66	26	38	189	220	225
		F. - 660	26	50	15	29	121	181	238
36 EAST RIDING - - -	368	M. - 185	1	21	22	6	42	42	51
		F. - 183	7	18	19	6	25	34	74
37 NORTH RIDING - -	264	M. 161	2	5	9	5	37	49	54
		F. - 103	2	2	3	4	8	22	62

Table 16.—Number and Ages of Males and Females returned as Blind from Birth in the Yorkshire Division and its Registration Ridings.

Registration Riding.	All Ages.		0–	5–	15–	20–	25–	45–	65 and upwards.
	Both Sexes.	Males and Females.							
IX. YORKSHIRE -	223	M. 109	19	30	12	4	31	11	2
		F. 114	15	33	9	12	29	11	5
35 WEST RIDING -	163	M. - 81	14	22	10	3	24	7	1
		F. - 82	12	25	6	9	23	5	2
36 EAST RIDING - -	39	M. - 21	5	8	2	.	4	2	.
		F. - 18	.	7	2	3	4	2	.
37 NORTH RIDING -	21	M. - 7	.	.	.	1	3	2	1
		F. - 14	3	1	1	.	2	4	3

Table 17.—Number and Ages of Males and Females returned as Deaf and Dumb in the Yorkshire Division and its Registration Ridings.

Registration Riding.	All Ages.		0–	5–	15–	20–	25–	45–	65 and upwards.
	Both Sexes.	Males and Females.							
IX. YORKSHIRE -	1481	M. 787	21	240	79	85	224	107	31
		F. 694	26	206	67	56	213	94	32
35 WEST RIDING - -	1197	M. - 627	14	211	58	64	173	80	27
		F. - 570	20	185	52	42	173	78	20
36 EAST RIDING -	163	M. - 91	4	15	14	11	29	16	2
		F. - 72	4	11	10	9	21	9	8
37 NORTH RIDING - -	121	M. - 69	3	14	7	10	22	11	2
		F. - 52	2	10	5	5	19	7	4

Table 18.—NUMBER and AGES of MALES and FEMALES returned as IDIOTS or IMBECILES and LUNATICS in the YORKSHIRE DIVISION and its REGISTRATION RIDINGS.

REGISTRATION RIDING.	ALL AGES.		0–	5–	15–	20–	25–	45–	65 and upwards.
	Both Sexes.	Males and Females.							
IX. YORKSHIRE -	6765	M. 3246 F. 3519	30 11	231 163	221 163	271 255	1318 1431	935 1145	240 351
35 WEST RIDING - -	4784	M. - 2299 F. - 2485	27 10	179 119	155 119	201 187	948 1069	659 763	130 218
36 EAST RIDING - -	1674	M. - 794 F. 880	2 .	26 24	45 32	50 53	325 308	250 343	96 120
37 NORTH RIDING - -	307	M. 153 F. 154	1 1	26 20	21 12	20 15	45 54	26 39	14 13

Table 19.—NUMBER and AGES of MALES and FEMALES returned as IDIOTS or IMBECILES in the YORKSHIRE DIVISION and its REGISTRATION RIDINGS.

REGISTRATION RIDING.	ALL AGES.		0–	5–	15–	20–	25–	45–	65 and upwards.
	Both Sexes.	Males and Females.							
IX. YORKSHIRE -	2903	M. 1414 F. 1489	29 10	220 153	193 140	188 177	471 591	241 321	72 97
35 WEST RIDING - - -	2255	M. - 1094 F. - 1161	27 9	172 113	142 101	146 139	365 477	193 248	49 74
36 EAST RIDING - -	365	M. - 174 F. - 191	1 .	22 22	30 27	33 23	63 65	26 42	9 12
37 NORTH RIDING - -	283	M. - 146 F. - 137	1 1	26 18	21 12	10 15	43 49	22 31	14 11

Table 20.—NUMBER and AGES of MALES and FEMALES returned as LUNATICS in the YORKSHIRE DIVISION and its REGISTRATION RIDINGS.

REGISTRATION RIDING.	ALL AGES.		0–	5–	15–	20–	25–	45–	65 and upwards.
	Both Sexes.	Males and Females.							
IX. YORKSHIRE -	3862	M. 1832 F. 2030	1 1	11 10	28 23	83 78	847 840	694 824	168 254
35 WEST RIDING - - -	2529	M. - 1205 F. - 1324	. 1	7 6	13 18	55 48	583 592	466 515	81 144
36 EAST RIDING - -	1309	M. - 620 F. 689	1 .	4 2	15 5	27 30	262 243	224 301	87 108
37 NORTH RIDING - -	24	M. 7 F. 17	. .	. 2	. .	1 .	2 5	4 8	. 2

Table 21.—Number of the Blind, of the Deaf and Dumb, of Idiots or Imbeciles, and of Lunatics in the Yorkshire Division and its Registration Ridings and Districts.

Registration Riding and District.	Blind.			Deaf and Dumb.	Mentally Deranged.		
	From Birth.	Others.	Total.		Idiots.	Lunatics.	Total.
IX. YORKSHIRE.	223	2071	2294	1481	2903	3862	6765
35 WEST RIDING	163	1439	1602	1197	2255	2529	4784
36 EAST RIDING	39	368	407	163	365	1309	1674
37 NORTH RIDING	21	264	285	121	283	24	307
35 WEST RIDING.							
483 SEDBERGH	.	3	3	2	12	3	15
484 SETTLE	.	7	7	11	19	5	24
485 SKIPTON		20	20	13	29	5	34
486 PATELEY BRIDGE	.	6	6	7	14	.	14
487 RIPON	1	15	16	5	22	2	24
488 GREAT OUSEBURN	.	11	11	9	26	23	49
489 KNARESBOROUGH	1	8	9	6	12	1	13
490 WETHERBY	2	16	18	104	11	5	16
491 WHARFEDALE	4	27	31	23	31	1	32
492 KEIGHLEY	1	45	46	29	55	10	65
493 TODMORDEN	.	14	14	15	56	7	63
494 SADDLEWORTH	2	10	12	11	16	.	16
495 HUDDERSFIELD	11	85	96	63	134	16	150
496 HALIFAX	10	92	102	85	97	68	165
497 BRADFORD	23	217	240	121	390	34	424
498 HUNSLET	3	37	40	19	23	2	25
499 HOLBECK	1	19	20	14	23	1	24
500 BRAMLEY	4	18	22	27	35	1	36
501 LEEDS	20	159	179	97	94	29	123
502 DEWSBURY	14	75	89	60	99	16	115
503 WAKEFIELD	8	62	70	51	269	1187	1456
504 PONTEFRACT	7	28	35	19	47	2	49
505 HEMSWORTH	1	3	4	6	16	.	16
506 BARNSLEY	4	36	40	38	78	4	82
507 WORTLEY	4	50	54	30	239	1023	1262
508 ECCLESALL BIERLOW	13	94	107	46	99	22	121
509 SHEFFIELD	11	132	143	93	111	24	135
510 ROTHERHAM	5	44	49	20	73	19	92
511 DONCASTER	3	51	54	126	41	12	53
512 THORNE	3	13	16	15	16	4	20
513 GOOLE	2	14	16	7	17	1	18
514 SELBY	3	14	17	7	28	1	29
515 TADCASTER	2	14	16	9	23	1	24
36 EAST RIDING.							
516 YORK	16	127	143	27	83	921	1004
517 POCKLINGTON	.	11	11	9	21	3	24
518 HOWDEN	1	11	12	9	12	.	12
519 BEVERLEY	1	18	19	13	65	225	290
520 SCULCOATES	8	88	96	41	48	17	65
521 HULL	6	67	73	41	75	142	217
522 PATRINGTON	.	11	11	7	9	.	9
523 SKIRLAUGH	2	8	10	4	11	.	11
524 DRIFFIELD	1	17	18	6	30	.	30
525 BRIDLINGTON	4	10	14	6	11	1	12
37 NORTH RIDING.							
526 SCARBOROUGH	2	39	41	10	35	3	38
527 MALTON	2	22	24	6	24	2	26
528 EASINGWOLD	1	10	11	8	5	5	10
529 THIRSK	.	12	12	6	11	.	11
530 HELMSLEY	.	6	6	.	22	.	22
531 PICKERING	.	11	11	6	18	2	20
532 WHITBY	2	24	26	5	16	2	18
533 GUISBROUGH	1	20	21	5	17	1	18
534 MIDDLESBROUGH	9	53	62	26	38	5	43
535 STOKESLEY	1	18	19	5	16	.	16
536 NORTHALLERTON	.	10	10	5	21	.	21
537 BEDALE	2	7	9	2	12	.	12
538 LEYBURN	.	8	8	10	17	.	17
539 AYSGARTH	.	7	7	8	9	1	10
540 REETH	.	3	3	2	7	1	8
541 RICHMOND	1	14	15	8	15	2	17

AGES,

CONDITION AS TO MARRIAGE, OCCUPATIONS, AND BIRTH-PLACES OF THE PEOPLE:

WITH THE

NUMBERS AND AGES OF THE BLIND, DEAF AND DUMB, IDIOTS OR IMBECILES, AND LUNATICS.

DIVISION X.—NORTHERN COUNTIES:

DURHAM,
NORTHUMBERLAND,
CUMBERLAND,
WESTMORLAND.

TABLES IN DIVISION X.—NORTHERN COUNTIES.

AGES.

Table.

1.—Ages of Males and Females in the Northern Division and its *Registration* Counties.

2.—Ages of Males and Females in Registration Districts.

3.—Ages of Males and Females in Registration Sub-Districts.

4.—Male and Female Children at *each Year of Age* under 5 in the Northern Division and its Registration Counties.

5.—Male and Female Children at *each Year of Age* under 5 in Registration Districts.

6.—Ages of Males and Females in Sanitary Districts.

CONDITION AS TO MARRIAGE.

7.—Condition as to Marriage and Ages of Males and Females in the Northern Division and its Registration Counties.

8.—Condition as to Marriage and Ages of Males and Females in Registration Districts.

9.—Condition as to Marriage and Ages of Males and Females in each Urban Sanitary District of which the Population exceeds 50,000 Persons.

OCCUPATIONS.

10.—Occupations of Males and Females in the Northern Division and its Registration Counties, and in each Urban Sanitary District of which the Population exceeds 50,000 Persons.

BIRTH-PLACES.

11.—Birth-places of Males and Females enumerated in Counties, and in each Urban Sanitary District of which the Population exceeds 50,000 Persons.

12.—Distribution of the enumerated Natives of Counties.

13.—Number and Country of Birth of Foreigners enumerated in Counties, and in each Urban Sanitary District of which the Population exceeds 50,000 Persons.

THE BLIND, DEAF AND DUMB, IDIOTS OR IMBECILES, AND LUNATICS.

14.—Number and Ages of Males and Females returned as Blind or Blind from Birth in the Northern Division and its Registration Counties.

15.—Number and Ages of Males and Females returned as Blind in the Northern Division and its Registration Counties.

16.—Number and Ages of Males and Females returned as Blind from Birth in the Northern Division and its Registration Counties.

17.—Number and Ages of Males and Females returned as Deaf and Dumb in the Northern Division and its Registration Counties.

18.—Number and Ages of Males and Females returned as Idiots or Imbeciles, and Lunatics in the Northern Division and its Registration Counties.

19.—Number and Ages of Males and Females returned as Idiots or Imbeciles in the Northern Division and its Registration Counties.

20.—Number and Ages of Males and Females returned as Lunatics in the Northern Division and its Registration Counties.

21.—Number of the Blind, of the Deaf and Dumb, of Idiots or Imbeciles, and of Lunatics in the Northern Division and its Registration Counties and Districts.

AGES.

DIVISION X.—NORTHERN COUNTIES.

Table 1.—Ages of Males and Females in the Northern Division and its Registration Counties.

Registration County.	All Ages. Persons.	All Ages. Males and Females.		Under 5* Years.	5–	10–	15–	20–	25–	30–	35–	40–	45–	50–	55–	60–	65–	70–	75–	80–	85–	90–	95–	100† and upw^ds.
X.—NORTHERN COUNTIES	1624213	M.	820029	119242	106118	90278	81954	73246	66358	56362	49362	43199	34447	29147	22424	19385	12573	8424	4517	2005	550	114	23	8
		F.	804184	118511	105403	89297	78781	71272	61835	52154	45039	40902	33829	29070	23047	20439	14331	9862	5645	2716	879	200	40	19
38 DURHAM - -	875166	M.	447816	67140	59845	49387	44724	40243	36683	31408	27296	23689	18559	15420	11380	9576	6117	3868	1933	806	191	45	12	5
		F.	427350	66410	59164	48766	43963	37289	32752	27613	24356	21336	17294	14689	11128	9858	6458	4282	2444	1104	344	71	18	2
39 NORTHUMBERLAND - -	429086	M.	215882	30599	27268	23577	21558	19275	17424	14674	13266	11467	9343	7893	6262	5358	3573	2358	1297	546	172	33	8	1
		F.	213204	30363	27114	23387	21548	19986	16902	14422	12555	11454	9582	8201	6684	5801	4264	2987	1710	862	289	72	11	4
40 CUMBERLAND -	250647	M.	124746	17440	15505	13664	12510	11168	10018	8307	7108	6508	5162	4605	3681	3384	2414	1682	913	495	145	25	2	1
		F.	125901	17527	15312	13432	12022	11130	9684	8057	7206	6439	5490	4864	4037	3798	2817	2014	1147	579	195	43	8	2
41 WESTMORLAND	64314	M.	31585	4135	4000	3650	3182	2560	2233	1963	1692	1585	1383	1229	1101	1067	769	516	374	158	42	11	1	1
		F.	32729	4202	3825	3662	3248	2867	2407	2062	1822	1673	1462	1316	1138	984	792	599	338	171	51	14	3	2

Note.—Registration Counties consist of groups of Registration Districts, which are generally co-extensive with the Poor Law Unions. Those Registration Districts which extend into two or more counties, are included in that Registration County in which the principal town of the District, or the greater part of the population, is located. The boundaries of Registration Counties, therefore, differ more or less from the boundaries of Counties. For such differences in Division X., see Vol. II., Table 11.

* For the number of Children at each Year of Age under 5, see Table 4.

† Two of these Males were stated to be 100, two 101, three 102, and one 103 years of age. Seven of these Females were stated to be 100, two 102, and one 110 years of age.

Table 2.—Ages of Males and Females in Registration Districts.

Registration District.	All Ages. Persons.	All Ages. Males and Females.		Under 5* Years.	5–	10–	15–	20–	25–	30–	35–	40–	45–	50–	55–	60–	65–	70–	75–	80–	85–	90–	95–	100 and upw^ds.
38 DURHAM.																								
542 DARLINGTON -	47676	M. -	23519	3474	3166	2582	2299	2018	1824	1599	1407	1286	1004	808	633	578	343	292	128	68	14	1	.	.
		F. -	24157	3426	3047	2688	2616	2202	1851	1511	1384	1242	990	889	658	617	419	307	175	101	26	11	2	.
543 STOCKTON -	68312	M. -	35588	5156	4490	3653	3293	3322	3220	2781	2360	2050	1500	1235	801	706	462	314	149	72	19	4	1	.
		F. -	32724	5195	4544	3696	3075	2893	2611	2283	1904	1624	1321	1018	798	728	471	292	182	81	25	3	2	.
544 HARTLEPOOL -	48613	M. -	24868	3851	3254	2673	2434	2162	2049	1803	1549	1381	1070	810	624	542	322	197	93	38	13	1	1	1
		F. -	23745	3687	3297	2487	2487	2156	1825	1508	1385	1199	953	797	607	540	324	224	108	38	17	4	2	.
545 AUCKLAND - -	83572	M. -	43555	6440	5938	4984	4504	3860	3556	2927	2575	2224	1806	1532	1131	893	573	335	182	71	15	5	3	1
		F. -	40017	6400	5894	4964	3851	3379	3007	2580	2202	1989	1556	1304	965	825	548	306	203	84	22	7	1	.
546 TEESDALE - -	20777	M. -	10305	1331	1262	1275	1109	866	696	554	533	505	498	396	363	327	251	169	103	54	8	5	.	.
		F. -	10472	1299	1259	1189	1138	971	757	555	580	514	462	425	381	318	249	177	122	58	26	2	.	.
547 WEARDALE -	17542	M. -	9035	1157	1109	1029	1015	844	692	606	515	465	401	336	274	242	179	102	42	21	4	3	.	.
		F.	8507	1197	1117	1057	862	711	647	515	441	439	357	307	272	226	172	102	52	26	6	1	.	.
548 LANCHESTER -	57861	M. -	30842	4580	4034	3482	3304	3098	2523	2036	1704	1514	1215	1096	781	632	380	235	126	49	9	3	.	1
		F. -	27019	4511	4121	3218	2669	2290	1905	1671	1425	1245	1055	947	651	572	339	214	112	58	12	1	2	.
549 DURHAM -	64321	M. -	33092	4807	4407	3746	3381	3016	2703	2254	1936	1637	1357	1215	860	770	474	254	158	61	18	5	3	.
		F. -	31229	4748	4356	3646	3212	2781	2330	1916	1734	1456	1266	1124	812	705	450	328	191	87	29	6	2	.
550 EASINGTON -	41098	M. -	21208	3227	3062	2392	2166	1886	1862	1364	1196	1057	863	724	513	431	287	192	93	32	9	.	2	.
		F. -	19890	3261	3030	2433	1824	1656	1450	1177	1002	989	795	664	495	429	302	198	126	37	15	5	.	.
551 HOUGHTON-LE-SPRING -	34145	M. -	17724	2765	2801	2027	1817	1626	1394	1160	1081	833	669	582	466	387	257	160	109	31	14	4	.	1
		F. -	16421	2698	2335	1898	1515	1373	1228	1031	875	752	629	557	485	409	235	185	96	38	22	.	.	.
552 CHESTER-LE-STREET -	43352	M. -	22630	3388	2989	2606	2429	2086	1769	1443	1324	1062	898	766	624	514	332	235	108	45	10	.	.	1
		F. -	20722	3278	3038	2446	1955	1761	1528	1267	1134	940	848	713	583	488	334	195	133	67	13	2	1	.
553 SUNDERLAND -	139288	M. -	69146	10397	9199	7526	6868	6111	5730	4970	4282	3758	2625	2346	1721	1402	941	565	282	105	24	4	.	.
		F. -	70142	10336	9184	7442	7141	6376	5715	4598	4132	3634	2903	2486	1901	1727	1180	772	415	185	55	11	.	1
554 SOUTH SHIELDS -	103199	M. -	53027	8256	6918	5605	4921	4789	4498	4063	3466	3050	2291	1756	1278	923	612	341	156	75	19	4	1	.
		F. -	50172	8120	689	5609	4727	4508	3908	3448	3063	2709	2023	1684	1189	1039	675	409	239	125	37	8	2	1
555 GATESHEAD - -	105410	M. -	53277	8260	7126	5807	5184	4564	4367	3844	3368	2847	2161	1818	1311	1139	724	447	204	84	15	6	1	.
		F. -	52133	8205	7033	5998	4891	4432	3990	3605	3045	2694	2146	1824	1343	1235	760	573	288	118	39	10	4	.
39 NORTHUMBERLAND.																								
556 NEWCASTLE UPON TYNE -	150252	M. -	73572	10823	9189	7723	7049	6711	6407	5367	4846	4182	3272	2575	1937	1580	991	568	300	111	34	6	1	.
		F. -	76680	10739	9181	8004	7871	7629	6269	5235	4604	4133	3571	2818	2127	1814	1297	879	437	214	69	13	5	1
557 TYNEMOUTH -	114197	M. -	58264	8637	7624	6397	5867	5223	4813	4097	3627	3038	2465	2119	1607	1232	787	541	232	123	26	8	1	.
		F. -	55933	8402	7589	6189	5315	4807	4234	3637	3153	2901	2413	1955	1894	1406	971	619	376	179	64	14	2	3

Note.—The Registration Districts of Division X. are co-extensive with the Poor Law Unions of the same name, with the following exception:—Stockton District (543) comprises the two Poor Law Unions of Stockton and Sedgefield.

For the Parishes comprised in each Registration District, see Vol. II., Division X., Table 4.

The Districts are arranged topographically under the Registration Counties, and are numbered consecutively, commencing with the Metropolitan Districts, Division I.

* For the Number of Children at each Year of Age under 5, see Table 5.

Table 2 *continued.*—Ages of Males and Females in Registration Districts.

Registration District.	All Ages. Persons.		All Ages. Males and Females.	Under 5 Years.	5–	10–	15–	20–	25–	30–	35–	40–	45–	50–	55–	60–	65–	70–	75–	80–	85–	90–	95–
39 NORTHUMBERLAND—*cont.*																							
558 CASTLE WARD	10720	M.	9979	1323	1230	1186	1086	841	698	640	617	543	423	377	303	276	179	136	77	30	12	2	.
		F.	9741	1334	1200	1031	980	891	719	667	509	500	409	375	299	268	196	152	83	50	8	10	.
559 HEXHAM	34086	M.	16901	2223	2081	1920	1766	1503	1277	1010	962	873	740	649	520	512	350	253	151	65	26	2	1
		F.	17185	2262	2042	1805	1752	1614	1322	1087	940	868	734	703	692	488	434	277	171	65	42	16	.
560 HALTWHISTLE	7962	M.	4001	672	471	452	407	342	308	251	198	209	183	151	126	118	79	63	47	24	9	2	.
		F.	3961	546	439	425	404	339	295	249	218	210	187	142	113	82	83	65	45	24	4	1	.
561 BELLINGHAM	6107	M.	3022	372	364	307	260	241	206	187	192	141	164	123	110	115	105	71	46	13	11	1	.
		F.	3085	359	346	349	285	241	247	188	173	160	166	137	104	112	88	57	29	28	6	1	.
562 MORPETH	36077	M.	18444	2666	2454	2041	1943	1600	1369	1177	1119	892	791	651	540	463	317	212	128	51	15	3	2
		F.	17633	2659	2453	2036	1569	1428	1248	1153	982	910	746	623	521	512	336	227	152	63	21	3	.
563 ALNWICK	21318	M.	10410	1382	1254	1119	1119	905	765	689	572	515	426	411	384	338	251	171	99	38	8	3	1
		F.	10908	1296	1250	1113	1067	983	846	736	585	584	468	455	392	373	294	228	134	85	22	5	2
564 BELFORD	5737	M.	2727	334	328	323	304	280	195	163	115	138	108	122	117	90	70	86	20	12	5	2	.
		F.	3010	333	317	294	325	305	231	208	158	133	157	125	124	90	72	61	44	28	10	1	1
565 BERWICK	21048	M.	10106	1387	1245	1156	1060	880	702	629	543	501	414	381	310	327	240	157	112	31	14	2	.
		F.	10942	1349	1247	1134	1043	905	807	673	645	618	504	468	405	399	267	247	189	76	22	3	1
566 GLENDALE	10933	M.	5195	626	626	621	581	460	367	296	283	283	222	196	177	176	130	96	42	27	11	1	.
		F.	5738	645	647	628	590	530	451	367	310	317	276	257	187	177	146	118	60	28	12	2	.
567 ROTHBURY	6709	M.	3261	382	393	352	327	320	238	189	192	172	140	136	125	124	77	60	44	18	1	1	2
		F.	3448	419	369	379	376	314	233	222	193	160	182	143	126	93	100	67	46	24	9	3	.
40 CUMBERLAND																							
568 ALSTON	4621	M.	2253	269	274	271	245	183	169	130	131	118	112	118	80	60	42	24	11	6	3	1	.
		F.	2368	265	253	266	245	196	164	121	137	134	124	113	90	84	70	29	32	11	4	.	.
569 PENRITH	23242	M.	11525	1466	1482	1276	1245	968	796	647	653	543	484	439	446	381	306	206	119	71	26	1	.
		F.	11717	1430	1516	1233	1173	1092	885	728	652	584	515	459	451	379	288	235	154	68	30	4	1
570 BRAMPTON	10665	M.	5854	632	614	621	573	468	349	355	291	255	208	217	202	157	137	111	73	40	10	1	.
		F.	5211	569	572	532	522	504	387	337	317	249	244	220	201	179	126	111	60	43	12	5	.
571 LONGTOWN	7711	M.	3916	465	470	408	409	342	238	249	202	188	174	176	141	139	121	100	47	26	12	3	.
		F.	3795	460	415	413	377	326	287	228	221	191	181	152	137	123	104	100	45	25	5	3	1
572 CARLISLE	52762	M.	25255	3454	2932	2770	2609	2231	2068	1685	1451	1340	1063	980	782	674	478	345	193	110	24	5	.
		F.	27507	3403	3047	2768	2729	2376	2362	1867	1622	1478	1252	1108	997	896	621	443	234	114	43	10	.
573 WIGTON	23440	M.	11481	1520	1363	1282	1204	908	824	698	594	643	486	446	371	386	315	218	140	76	12	7	1
		F.	11959	1512	1385	1276	1101	1020	891	720	665	574	539	530	437	418	350	252	169	75	29	4	3
574 COCKERMOUTH	56789	M.	28473	4190	3825	3043	2820	2747	2430	1900	1603	1501	1160	989	807	750	472	332	168	91	35	4	.
		F.	28316	4267	3648	3074	3093	2420	2124	1780	1530	1420	1200	1068	861	830	615	429	228	120	34	8	1
575 WHITEHAVEN	59292	M.	30100	4601	3691	3338	2952	2761	2581	2153	1827	1603	1202	1026	677	671	414	272	121	53	14	1	1
		F.	29192	4605	3917	3250	2718	2505	2160	1587	1680	1524	1214	1001	788	743	522	351	185	95	37	8	1
576 BOOTLE	12225	M.	6389	952	808	855	653	560	528	480	356	311	257	214	169	159	129	74	41	22	9	2	.
		F.	5836	978	729	667	559	481	434	389	322	275	221	204	165	144	121	64	40	22	1	1	1
41 WESTMORLAND.																							
577 EAST WARD	14615	M.	7276	913	930	812	697	537	502	443	369	363	331	327	282	282	191	127	67	45	14	3	.
		F.	7339	984	789	781	666	625	529	469	378	396	382	312	253	221	188	145	79	47	12	6	1
578 WEST WARD	8225	M.	4195	509	507	507	412	380	281	259	229	193	189	182	137	157	103	79	59	27	6	3	.
		F.	4030	494	478	446	387	337	305	221	207	194	213	185	150	138	123	77	53	24	6	2	.
579 KENDAL	41574	M.	20114	2713	2563	2331	2053	1862	1450	1270	1097	960	952	720	682	628	470	310	228	86	22	5	1
		F.	21460	2734	2528	2435	2168	1905	1863	1872	1237	1064	918	819	735	625	481	377	264	100	33	6	2

Table 3.—Ages of Males and Females in Registration Sub-Districts.

Registration Sub-District.	All Ages. Persons.		All Ages. Males and Females.	Under 5 Years.	5–	10–	15–	20–	25–	30–	35–	40–	45–	50–	55–	60–	65–	70–	75–	80–	85–	90–	95–
38 DURHAM.																							
542 DARLINGTON.																							
1 Darlington (W. H². L.)	40244	M.	19778	2889	2874	2141	1919	1713	1584	1378	1184	1085	831	704	629	472	288	242	98	54	12	1	.
		F.	20466	2873	2537	2257	2237	1925	1566	1293	1169	1062	845	761	563	528	346	261	141	77	19	9	2
2 Aycliffe	7432	M.	3741	605	492	441	380	360	240	221	223	201	173	104	104	100	56	50	30	14	2	.	.
		F.	3691	553	520	426	379	277	285	218	215	180	145	128	105	94	73	46	34	24	7	2	.
543 STOCKTON.																							
1 Stockton (W. H.)	51209	M.	26674	3848	3364	2717	2468	2538	2461	2143	1792	1539	1111	983	568	492	315	223	95	46	13	2	1
		F.	24535	3901	3374	2737	2387	2214	1977	1748	1646	1204	963	756	575	533	343	203	127	52	21	3	1
2 Sedgefield (W. L.)	17103	M.	8914	1308	1126	938	808	786	739	638	568	611	589	302	243	214	147	91	54	26	6	2	.
		F.	8189	1204	1170	959	718	679	634	518	468	420	358	288	221	195	129	89	65	29	4	.	1
544 HARTLEPOOL.																							
1 Hartlepool (W. H. R.)	48613	M.	24868	3831	3254	2073	2434	2162	2049	1803	1549	1381	1070	810	624	542	322	197	98	38	13	1	1
		F.	23745	3687	3297	2487	2487	2156	1825	1608	1385	1199	963	797	607	540	324	224	108	38	17	4	5
545 AUCKLAND.																							
1 Bishop Auckland (W.)	58148	M.	30350	4427	4189	3497	3142	2731	2513	2035	1796	1572	1301	1032	759	614	396	216	114	46	12	5	2
		F.	27798	4471	4091	3437	2701	2341	2111	1802	1552	1294	1115	914	636	508	358	208	127	55	15	2	.
2 Hamsterley	25424	M.	13205	2013	1709	1487	1362	1129	1043	892	779	652	505	600	372	279	177	119	68	25	3	.	1
		F.	12219	1989	1603	1627	1150	1038	896	748	650	695	441	396	327	259	190	98	76	29	7	6	1

Note. For the Parishes comprised in each Registration Sub-District, see Vol. II., Division X., Table 4.
(W.) denotes that a Workhouse, and (W S.) that a Workhouse School belonging to the District is situated within the Sub-District; (w.) denotes a w[illegible] house, and (w s.) a Workhouse School not belonging to the District; (H.) a Hospital or Infirmary, (L.) a Lunatic Asylum, (P.) a Prison or Convict Establishm[illegible] (R.) a certified Reformatory or Industrial School, (B.) Barracks, &c., (S.) H.M. Ships. A figure appended to any of these letters denotes the number of Institutio[illegible] a similar class situated within the Sub-District. The names of the institutions thus indicated, and the number of inmates enumerated therein, will be foun[illegible] Vol. II., Division X., Table 6.

Table 3 *continued*.—AGES of MALES and FEMALES in REGISTRATION SUB-DISTRICTS.

REGISTRATION SUB-DISTRICT.	ALL AGES. Persons.	ALL AGES. Males and Females.	Under 5 Years.	5–	10–	15–	20–	25–	30–	35–	40–	45–	50–	55–	60–	65–	70–	75–	80–	85–	90–	95–	100 and upwds.
38 DURHAM—*cont.*																							
546 TEESDALE.																							
1 Staindrop	5817	M. - 2920	413	375	396	318	209	161	164	167	130	155	104	87	80	74	55	32	12	1	.	.	.
		F. - 2897	389	379	341	297	276	185	163	164	134	119	96	97	69	65	49	36	27	16	2	.	.
2 Barnard Castle. (W.)	8064	M. - 3881	471	493	467	411	301	253	189	191	183	202	106	148	165	113	70	44	24	5	3	.	.
		F. - 4183	499	490	483	481	391	318	217	234	213	188	160	163	165	94	72	47	16	5	.	.	.
3 Middleton	6896	M. - 3504	447	396	412	380	356	282	201	175	183	161	136	128	92	64	44	27	18	3	.	.	.
		F. - 3392	411	390	365	410	304	254	175	182	167	147	160	121	94	90	56	40	15	11	.	.	.
547 WEARDALE.																							
1 St. John	3960	M. - 1991	245	225	242	216	184	135	138	127	102	99	67	74	58	40	33	7	3	1	1	.	.
		F. - 1969	234	239	236	202	179	150	120	102	105	91	83	80	56	49	25	11	7	.	.	.	.
2 Stanhope. (W.)	5687	M. - 2937	375	380	342	316	268	217	200	155	152	129	148	88	66	81	34	13	7	.	2	.	.
		F. - 2750	361	327	340	292	258	220	171	156	137	118	106	87	63	62	34	23	12	.	.	.	.
3 Wolsingham	7895	M. - 4107	537	504	446	484	402	340	272	233	211	173	126	112	119	78	35	22	11	3	.	.	.
		F. - 3788	602	551	481	368	294	277	224	183	197	151	118	105	101	61	43	18	7	6	1	.	.
548 LANCHESTER.																							
1 Tanfield	18203	M. - 9608	1500	1281	1116	1026	881	737	614	549	472	401	320	265	208	108	63	48	16	4	.	.	.
		F. - 8595	1435	1354	1065	824	701	680	524	451	357	335	281	220	197	103	56	37	18	1	.	1	.
2 Lanchester. (W. H.)	39658	M. - 21234	3080	2763	2367	2278	2217	1786	1422	1215	1042	814	778	516	424	252	172	78	33	5	3	.	1
		F. - 18424	3076	2767	2153	1845	1589	1316	1147	974	848	720	666	425	375	238	158	75	41	11	1	1	.
549 DURHAM.																							
1 St. Oswald. (W. H. P.)	44989	M. - 23474	3415	3101	2643	2450	2202	1961	1647	1420	1188	951	816	557	520	299	169	98	30	12	3	2	.
		F. - 21515	3424	3092	2539	2181	1846	1619	1368	1254	1010	838	756	522	435	262	189	115	52	18	4	1	.
2 St. Nicholas. (H. B.)	19332	M. - 9618	1392	1306	1103	931	814	742	607	516	449	408	399	303	250	176	125	60	81	6	2	1	.
		F. - 9714	1314	1364	1107	1031	935	711	558	530	446	438	368	290	270	188	139	76	35	11	2	1	.
550 EASINGTON.																							
1 Easington. (W. H.)	41098	M. - 21208	3287	3062	2392	2166	1886	1662	1364	1186	1057	865	724	513	451	287	192	93	32	9	.	2	.
		F. - 19890	3261	3036	2433	1824	1656	1450	1177	1003	989	795	654	495	429	302	198	128	37	15	3	.	.
551 HOUGHTON-LE-SPRING.																							
1 Houghton-le-Spring. (W.)	17590	M. - 8968	1592	1153	1034	928	785	707	630	518	469	346	300	226	205	141	89	65	15	3	1	.	.
		F. - 8422	1329	1221	961	803	693	640	544	452	339	325	282	264	221	127	94	52	26	9	.	.	.
2 Hetton-le-Hole	16755	M. - 8756	1373	1238	993	889	841	687	660	513	374	323	282	240	182	116	71	46	18	6	3	.	1
		F. - 7999	1369	1164	937	712	680	588	487	423	373	304	275	231	188	108	91	44	12	13	.	.	.
552 CHESTER-LE-STREET.																							
1 Chester-le-Street. (W.)	23279	M. - 12147	1824	1629	1408	1304	1138	970	804	704	561	438	386	324	272	173	131	63	18	4	.	.	.
		F. - 11132	1800	1610	1272	1056	975	847	708	572	490	438	367	293	258	212	100	69	47	9	.	.	.
2 Harraton	20073	M. - 10483	1584	1366	1290	1125	950	799	639	620	691	461	380	300	242	159	104	46	27	6	.	.	1
		F. - 9590	1476	1438	1174	893	786	681	553	562	430	410	346	290	230	122	86	64	28	4	3	1	.
553 SUNDERLAND.																							
1 North Bishop Wearmouth. (W. H².)	38734	M. - 19697	2973	2639	2235	1978	1670	1604	1465	1260	1034	762	571	503	396	277	161	63	38	12	1	.	.
		F. - 19037	3032	2681	2069	1775	1567	1475	1284	1124	996	770	648	408	427	316	219	88	47	13	3	.	1
2 South Bishop Wearmouth. (H. R².)	48372	M. - 22722	3502	3109	2425	2221	2024	1865	1537	1390	1299	924	816	540	612	318	192	104	27	5	2	.	.
		F. - 25650	3440	3026	2592	2937	2640	2202	1694	1501	1317	1070	919	698	619	464	259	158	78	23	4	.	.
3 East Sunderland (R. B. S.)	9341	M. - 5205	658	527	531	501	546	474	422	378	335	237	184	131	109	70	65	33	11	2	.	.	.
		F. - 4136	569	650	442	366	356	326	274	247	228	181	138	124	134	83	78	43	16	2	2	.	.
4 West Sunderland	6483	M. - 3224	418	373	337	308	297	290	242	172	210	155	152	87	90	52	20	16	3	.	1	.	.
		F. - 3259	448	399	338	538	300	255	192	180	192	141	136	98	99	65	37	27	12	2	1	.	.
5 Monk Wearmouth	36358	M. - 18298	2854	2551	1948	1859	1574	1497	1308	1112	920	747	625	480	386	224	137	68	31	5	.	.	.
		F. - 18060	2847	2478	2061	1721	1515	1457	1153	1080	991	741	645	483	448	262	182	99	32	15	1	.	.
554 SOUTH SHIELDS.																							
1 Westoe. (W. H². R.)	57770	M. - 28083	4735	3968	3173	2548	2201	2141	1966	1695	1470	1167	931	747	544	339	340	102	50	11	2	1	.
		F. - 29687	4683	3935	3269	2848	2810	2359	2060	1774	1669	1214	1010	772	657	460	292	170	91	25	6	2	1
2 South Shields. (H².)	45430	M. - 24944	3501	2959	2432	2373	2588	2357	2102	1771	1580	1124	825	531	379	232	101	64	25	8	2	.	.
		F. - 20486	3537	2964	2359	1879	1698	1540	1398	1289	1140	809	624	417	392	215	117	69	34	12	2	.	.
555 GATESHEAD.																							
1 Heworth	17138	M. - 8846	1344	1181	944	919	742	699	639	572	470	379	296	215	194	139	72	28	10	2	1	.	.
		F. - 8292	1348	1141	1009	752	649	605	546	457	428	352	296	222	217	119	84	43	15	8	.	1	.
2 Gateshead. (W. H. R.)	65041	M. - 32611	5147	4361	3549	3117	2750	2706	2421	2134	1796	1296	1134	778	628	381	236	117	50	7	1	.	.
		F. - 32430	5048	4295	3637	3041	2860	2569	2275	1954	1734	1323	1144	810	723	442	344	161	75	18	4	3	.
3 Whickham. (L.)	7976	M. - 4019	645	549	427	373	332	323	289	232	213	167	125	115	99	67	49	14	8	1	1	.	.
		F. - 3957	626	561	485	362	314	285	242	222	186	151	132	107	113	79	40	34	10	4	4	.	.
4 Winlaton	15255	M. - 7801	1124	1038	887	775	740	630	495	440	368	319	263	262	218	187	88	45	16	5	3	1	.
		F. - 7454	1183	1036	867	736	639	531	442	412	346	323	252	204	182	139	96	60	15	9	2	.	.
39 NORTHUMBERLAND.																							
556 NEWCASTLE UPON TYNE.																							
1 Westgate. (W.)	66358	M. - 32664	4896	4199	3409	3093	3003	2873	2305	2167	1790	1351	1052	877	683	430	262	136	48	18	4	.	.
		F. - 33694	4805	4061	3485	3358	3186	2862	2373	2070	1607	1430	1263	942	826	553	419	215	97	26	3	6	.
2 St. Andrew. (H². B.)	18731	M. - 8759	1077	954	873	846	966	835	607	630	493	413	324	251	240	134	80	60	17	7	1	1	.
		F. - 9972	1123	972	889	1229	1192	873	661	586	535	488	403	294	257	220	134	69	35	12	.	.	.
3 St. Nicholas. (H².)	10028	M. - 5401	559	619	490	526	522	518	491	391	355	301	255	175	130	94	47	18	8	2	.	.	.
		F. - 4627	660	628	472	507	493	363	300	272	257	240	189	137	120	93	50	26	8	9	3	.	1
4 All Saints. (H². P. R.)	24424	M. - 12198	1696	1456	1326	1221	1091	1080	847	808	719	575	461	313	271	183	95	43	13	3	1	.	.
		F. - 12226	1770	1457	1356	1186	1086	965	806	726	681	588	486	335	314	226	157	69	41	13	5	.	.
5 Byker	30711	M. - 14550	2395	2302	1626	1368	1139	1187	1057	892	825	632	483	521	256	150	84	45	25	6	.	.	.
		F. - 16161	2391	2143	1803	1641	1672	1446	1005	950	823	635	477	599	289	206	119	58	33		2	.	.

Table 3 *continued*.—Ages of Males and Females in Registration Sub-Districts.

Registration Sub-District.	All Ages. Persons.	All Ages. Males and Females.	Under 5 Years.	5–	10–	15–	20–	25–	30–	35–	40–	45–	50–	55–	60–	65–	70–	75–	80–	85–	90–	95–	100 and upwards.
39 NORTHUMBERLAND—*cont.*																							
557 TYNEMOUTH.																							
1 Wallsend	13737	M. - 7194	1120	965	749	712	638	586	529	604	424	310	226	159	119	79	50	17	7				
		F. - 6543	1126	965	763	560	600	465	432	396	326	271	221	155	135	111	48	52	14	8	2		
2 North Shields (R. S.)	20651	M. - 11103	1335	1204	1177	1116	1035	1069	884	771	631	519	480	209	266	167	88	31	21	3	1	1	
		F. - 9548	1382	1214	983	964	860	763	625	530	505	413	320	323	204	176	103	73	34	12	2	1	
3 Tynemouth (W. H. R. B.)	25713	M. - 11699	1837	1608	1357	1002	924	871	759	624	631	484	454	361	287	174	135	70	35	8	2		
		F. - 14914	1717	1618	1418	1492	1414	1131	935	818	749	627	583	484	428	281	187	114	63	22	3		
4 Longbenton (H.)	19126	M. - 10068	1550	1346	1039	951	902	808	761	672	625	402	349	276	190	158	78	37	23	3	1		
		F. - 9078	1490	1296	1065	818	664	673	639	526	477	393	238	265	183	144	93	56	18	7	1	1	1
5 Earsdon	13989	M. - 7451	1147	1016	858	792	713	620	480	436	332	308	240	196	137	87	47	29	14	4	1		
		F. - 6538	1047	1038	802	562	494	492	395	356	310	290	245	174	138	91	65	31	18	7	3		
6 Blyth (H.)	20971	M. - 10759	1639	1433	1217	1094	1011	859	684	620	493	433	364	317	233	153	125	48	23	8	3		
		F. - 10212	1640	1436	1158	918	876	729	611	552	535	419	362	313	258	168	133	70	32	18	3		1
558 CASTLE WARD.																							
1 Ponteland (W. L. R.)	10429	M. - 5219	682	623	648	603	413	334	320	328	294	234	218	152	159	87	59	43	18	4	1		
		F. 5210	668	595	544	557	523	380	355	310	265	227	208	163	141	99	79	48	36	4	8		
2 Stamfordham	9291	M. - 4760	841	695	541	483	428	384	320	259	249	180	159	151	117	92	77	34	12	8	1		
		F. 4531	636	665	487	423	368	339	312	259	235	182	167	130	127	97	73	35	14	4	2		
559 HEXHAM.																							
1 Bywell	11752	M. - 6064	837	842	661	636	564	463	372	374	311	239	211	143	144	94	78	40	15	8			
		F. - 5688	876	765	620	536	518	447	358	306	259	230	214	136	134	122	76	62	8	9	2		
2 Hexham (W.)	10216	M. - 4839	632	561	645	492	402	358	295	264	238	216	177	178	174	123	84	62	26	10	2		
		F. - 5377	616	675	523	577	542	423	346	303	287	230	242	190	176	143	101	58	23	13	10		
3 Allendale	6395	M. - 3164	587	347	400	334	283	228	165	164	176	163	143	94	106	73	60	30	8	3			
		F. 3231	406	363	334	358	314	212	202	166	160	153	144	136	95	77	54	30	15	9	3		
4 Chollerton	5723	M. - 2834	349	341	314	283	254	226	178	166	148	122	118	105	88	66	41	19	16	6		1	
		F. - 2889	354	343	328	281	240	249	181	165	162	121	103	110	81	72	46	31	19	11	1		
560 HALTWHISTLE.																							
1 Haltwhistle (W.)	7902	M. 4001	572	471	462	407	342	308	251	198	209	183	151	126	115	70	63	47	26	9	2		1
		F. 3901	546	489	425	494	339	295	249	218	210	167	142	113	82	63	65	46	24	4	1		
561 BELLINGHAM.																							
1 Bellingham (W.)	3226	M. - 1597	191	192	168	116	127	113	112	113	70	82	61	55	60	57	38	27	10	4	1		
		F. - 1629	214	189	172	160	126	118	102	87	83	81	69	52	68	44	36	18	14	4	1		
2 Kirkwhelpington	2881	M. - 1425	181	172	180	134	114	92	75	79	71	82	62	55	60	48	33	18	8	7			
		F. 1456	175	168	177	125	115	129	68	86	67	74	68	52	44	44	21	11	14	2			
562 MORPETH.																							
1 Morpeth (W. L. P.)	8568	M. - 4148	528	455	468	413	320	390	233	236	246	189	168	148	142	100	76	42	25	5	2	1	
		F. 4420	517	488	436	436	404	622	291	279	242	199	182	160	181	117	82	59	25	10			
2 Bedlington	27509	M. - 14296	2138	2006	1573	1530	1260	1060	924	833	644	602	483	392	321	217	138	86	28	10	1	1	
		F. - 13213	2142	1985	1610	1134	1024	928	862	708	608	547	441	361	331	219	140	93	35	11	3		
563 ALNWICK.																							
1 Warkworth	8218	M. - 4071	534	492	433	431	359	290	287	222	182	178	167	151	122	92	67	39	18	1	2		
		F. 4147	510	525	444	395	362	316	282	201	220	174	185	140	128	109	83	41	34	6	3		
2 Alnwick (W. H.)	7447	M. - 3566	474	440	402	390	274	240	232	188	192	159	134	122	118	88	56	42	11	8		1	
		F. - 3881	448	415	398	375	388	292	259	227	214	147	178	125	156	117	84	63	33	10	2		
3 Embleton	5653	M. - 2773	354	322	284	298	272	226	150	182	141	94	110	111	98	71	48	18	9	4	1		
		F. 2880	338	310	271	287	233	238	195	157	150	147	112	118	89	68	61	30	18	6		2	
564 BELFORD.																							
1 Belford (W.)	5737	M. - 2727	334	328	323	304	290	195	163	115	138	103	122	117	90	70	36	29	12	5	2		
		F. - 3010	333	317	294	325	306	231	208	153	133	157	125	124	90	72	61	44	28	10	1	1	
565 BERWICK.																							
1 Islandshire	3079	M. - 1477	182	200	183	130	139	104	86	77	62	68	32	54	47	36	22	16	7	2			
		F. 1602	211	199	163	184	140	115	103	89	79	61	73	58	64	33	22	16	9	3			
2 Berwick upon Tweed (W. H. B.)	14599	M. 7020	983	873	780	730	615	438	448	394	361	282	280	108	228	156	98	79	17	11			
		F. 7579	946	841	778	700	596	557	462	430	430	355	324	291	265	192	182	102	58	16	3	1	
3 Norhamshire	3370	M. - 1609	222	172	204	180	135	100	95	72	78	64	50	64	52	48	37	17	7	1	2		
		F. - 1761	192	216	193	179	160	135	108	106	79	88	71	56	60	42	43	21	9	3			
566 GLENDALE.																							
1 Ford	5521	M. - 2592	297	319	320	300	210	184	144	142	134	116	90	91	87	71	40	15	19	4			
		F. 2929	339	333	334	290	270	225	193	156	159	133	130	96	92	72	58	25	11	4	1		
2 Wooler (W.)	5412	M. - 2603	329	306	301	281	240	173	151	141	149	106	93	86	89	59	50	27	8	7	1		
		F. 2809	306	314	294	251	260	226	174	154	158	143	127	82	35	74	60	35	17	8	1		
567 ROTHBURY.																							
1 Rothbury (W.)	5119	M. - 2460	292	292	246	255	235	175	140	147	130	110	104	106	95	60	35	35	10	1	1	1	
		F. - 2659	317	274	294	265	253	183	156	149	124	148	121	105	71	78	37	38	19	6	3		
2 Elsdon	1590	M. 801	99	101	88	72	85	88	49	46	42	30	32	19	39	17	16	9	6			1	
		F. 789	102	95	85	91	61	50	66	44	36	34	23	23	22	22	20	8	3	3			
40 CUMBERLAND.																							
568 ALSTON.																							
1 Alston (W.)	4621	M. - 2233	269	274	271	248	183	169	130	131	118	112	118	86	60	42	24	11	6	3	1		
		F. 2388	265	283	266	245	196	164	121	137	134	124	113	90	84	79	29	32	11	4			
569 PENRITH.																							
1 Penrith (W. H.)	12803	M. - 6101	811	741	891	830	510	424	357	376	286	256	220	239	193	172	110	61	34	14	1		
		F. - 6702	823	764	717	654	639	507	419	363	338	288	270	272	209	184	134	93	30	17	3		
2 Greystoke	4675	M. - 2393	275	288	253	270	209	167	137	112	127	98	101	91	92	71	51	33	15	3			
		F. - 2282	271	251	224	252	199	189	126	124	117	109	99	76	82	53	56	24	25	5			
3 Kirkoswald	5764	M. - 3031	380	403	332	345	249	205	153	168	150	140	112	118	106	63	45	38	22	9			
		F. - 2733	336	301	292	267	254	189	183	165	141	118	129	103	88	71	46	37	13	8	1	1	

Table 3 *continued*.—AGES of MALES and FEMALES in REGISTRATION SUB-DISTRICTS.

REGISTRATION SUB-DISTRICT.	ALL AGES. Persons.	Males and Females.	Under 5 Years.	5-	10-	15-	20-	25-	30-	35-	40-	45-	50-	55-	60-	65-	70-	75-	80-	85-	90-	95-	100 and upw^ds.
40 CUMBERLAND —*cont.*																							
570 BRAMPTON.																							
1 HAYTON	2413	M. - 1232	138	140	126	142	117	82	89	72	41	56	53	52	37	24	39	9	12	4	.	.	.
		F. - 1181	141	112	109	113	109	97	88	65	57	45	63	46	51	32	28	12	10	2	.	.	.
2 BRAMPTON. (W.)	5710	M. - 2906	376	358	349	301	241	225	197	138	131	190	167	93	76	69	45	38	13	4	1	.	.
		F. - 2813	329	335	305	265	261	208	179	184	127	142	109	107	83	57	58	32	23	6	2	.	1
3 WALTON	2433	M. - 1216	121	116	146	130	110	82	69	61	60	52	57	57	44	42	23	23	15	2	.	.	.
		F. - 1217	119	125	118	144	134	82	79	68	95	57	48	48	46	35	25	16	10	4	3	.	.
571 LONGTOWN.																							
1 HIGH LONGTOWN	2357	M. - 1240	137	121	131	138	115	81	79	73	74	64	45	44	44	30	29	19	10	4	2	.	.
		F. - 1117	140	119	106	117	103	86	60	65	64	47	44	44	82	30	34	9	11	2	2	1	1
2 LOW LONGTOWN. (W.)	5354	M. - 2676	328	356	277	271	227	157	170	129	114	110	131	97	95	87	71	25	16	8	1	.	.
		F. - 2678	340	296	307	240	233	171	128	156	127	134	108	93	91	74	66	36	14	3	1	.	.
572 CARLISLE.																							
1 WETHERAL	4033	M. - 1924	260	238	202	185	127	130	121	125	103	103	82	66	58	37	34	22	13	2	1	.	.
		F. - 2109	231	276	227	211	185	148	134	150	109	102	71	59	79	53	43	28	9	5	2	.	.
2 ST. CUTHBERT. (W. WS. L. P.)	17276	M. - 8557	1202	961	896	828	812	753	629	485	485	307	311	246	218	147	110	69	38	8	2	.	.
		F. - 8719	1115	974	846	806	783	795	614	523	520	397	379	305	262	187	121	66	27	12	1	.	.
3 ST. MARY. (H². B.)	22233	M. - 10439	1450	1285	1168	1129	954	869	672	622	534	409	425	306	252	169	109	52	28	5	2	.	.
		F. - 11794	1510	1307	1221	1221	1153	1029	808	668	613	528	400	388	303	236	164	84	40	12	4	.	.
4 STANWIX. (H. R.)	4110	M. - 1931	234	234	258	215	149	131	120	90	97	77	73	65	66	38	48	24	19	4	.	.	.
		F. - 2179	238	217	203	211	168	178	151	132	108	101	107	86	80	57	58	27	22	4	1	.	.
5 BURGH	1360	M. - 641	67	57	78	69	68	44	40	33	29	33	20	26	20	33	15	10	4	.	.	.	.
		F. - 719	58	64	63	68	78	67	37	40	35	28	33	31	41	32	16	13	8	5	1	.	.
6 DALSTON	3750	M. - 1763	235	217	198	183	126	127	103	87	98	74	69	74	90	54	29	16	8	6	.	.	.
		F. - 1987	251	209	205	217	177	145	128	100	104	96	68	68	86	56	42	22	8	5	1	.	.
573 WIGTON.																							
1 WIGTON. (W.)	9116	M. - 4310	565	494	424	466	349	340	251	205	238	193	183	145	153	132	82	48	30	8	3	1	.
		F. - 4806	560	525	514	472	437	366	279	288	219	234	222	181	175	152	106	73	37	13	3	.	.
2 ABBEY HOLME. (H.)	9970	M. - 4959	682	623	675	504	395	344	313	275	284	198	184	140	156	114	83	57	32	3	3	.	.
		F. - 5011	675	617	567	429	408	379	310	295	247	199	215	178	162	134	95	71	28	10	1	1	.
3 CALDBECK	4354	M. - 2212	273	236	283	234	164	140	134	114	121	95	79	86	80	69	53	35	14	1	1	.	.
		F. - 2142	277	243	205	200	175	146	131	132	108	105	102	78	81	64	51	25	10	6	.	2	.
574 COCKERMOUTH.																							
1 KESWICK	6937	M. - 3261	412	369	350	320	278	240	195	171	191	155	124	130	130	74	61	31	20	9	1	.	.
		F. - 3676	414	400	368	416	344	208	233	196	197	153	158	146	134	101	73	41	21	11	3	.	.
2 COCKERMOUTH. (W.)	10964	M. - 5307	748	864	588	477	429	410	311	272	251	232	205	188	203	142	90	50	33	12	2	.	.
		F. - 5657	767	646	585	512	471	390	367	319	263	271	249	214	228	163	114	50	36	10	2	.	.
3 WORKINGTON	20840	M. - 10862	1628	1360	1132	971	1179	1087	795	653	574	427	327	245	203	113	96	43	16	10	.	.	.
		F. - 9978	1688	1394	1106	850	820	789	650	502	518	376	325	244	248	160	101	79	31	10	1	1	.
4 MARYPORT. (W.)	18048	M. - 9043	1402	1232	973	852	861	698	596	507	485	352	333	244	214	143	85	44	22	4	1	.	.
		F. - 9005	1403	1208	1015	825	779	677	530	484	442	460	306	277	220	151	141	67	35	3	2	.	.
575 WHITEHAVEN.																							
1 HARRINGTON	15455	M. - 8133	1284	1005	911	758	738	698	607	469	459	306	248	179	157	111	86	39	23	4	.	1	.
		F. - 7322	1286	1067	875	624	573	513	564	410	374	272	219	169	151	123	81	37	24	8	2	.	.
2 WHITEHAVEN. (H.)	13374	M. - 6512	918	826	694	684	557	575	481	442	357	285	227	147	170	112	67	25	10	4	1	.	.
		F. - 6862	978	826	695	635	573	540	468	420	385	316	255	210	222	164	86	52	26	10	1	.	.
3 ST. BEES. (W.)	16906	M. - 8399	792	723	640	551	488	438	342	292	240	219	207	139	181	86	65	36	13	1	.	.	.
		F. - 8507	790	680	578	543	521	417	343	306	269	238	209	178	161	113	85	46	23	6	2	.	.
4 EGREMONT	19557	M. - 10056	1507	1287	1093	1039	1008	870	723	624	553	392	344	212	193	105	74	21	7	5	.	.	1
		F. - 9501	1541	1344	1108	891	838	690	582	544	496	388	318	231	209	132	99	51	22	13	3	1	.
576 BOOTLE.																							
1 MUNCASTER	2655	M. - 1379	158	140	156	158	140	101	86	62	66	63	57	60	38	44	22	13	1	8	.	.	.
		F. - 1276	183	139	127	140	91	102	89	67	68	53	50	46	41	43	17	13	9	.	.	1	.
2 BOOTLE. (W.)	9670	M. - 5110	794	662	409	406	420	427	404	294	245	194	157	109	121	85	52	28	21	1	2	.	.
		F. - 4560	793	590	540	419	390	352	300	255	207	165	154	119	103	81	47	27	13	1	1	.	.
41 WESTMORLAND.																							
577 EAST WARD.																							
1 APPLEBY	5548	M. - 2740	334	358	324	246	214	195	171	139	142	123	118	103	92	86	46	31	14	3	2	.	.
		F. - 2808	407	273	287	263	248	217	185	140	153	117	133	100	86	71	63	30	15	8	.	1	.
2 KIRKBY STEPHEN. (W.)	5665	M. - 2856	350	363	300	282	201	182	161	157	169	145	126	104	125	79	61	39	20	7	1	.	.
		F. - 2809	343	322	311	275	251	194	191	144	149	145	110	103	81	87	44	35	19	1	4	.	.
3 ORTON	3302	M. - 1680	209	219	188	169	122	125	111	73	81	64	83	75	62	46	21	17	11	4	.	.	.
		F. - 1622	234	194	183	155	120	118	93	89	93	70	69	60	54	30	36	14	13	3	2	.	.
578 WEST WARD.																							
1 MORLAND (W.)	4266	M. - 2223	278	274	264	210	190	142	136	112	100	109	94	71	87	51	48	31	20	5	1	.	.
		F. - 2043	257	238	231	201	158	158	117	113	100	111	80	77	74	51	46	26	12	4	1	.	.
2 LOWTHER	3959	M. - 1972	231	233	243	202	170	139	114	117	93	80	88	66	70	37	31	28	7	1	2	.	.
		F. - 1987	227	240	218	186	179	147	104	94	94	102	105	73	74	72	33	27	12	2	1	.	.
579 KENDAL.																							
1 AMBLESIDE	10442	M. - 4955	609	611	585	517	395	396	285	279	254	227	207	191	152	102	69	52	17	7	.	.	.
		F. - 5487	670	623	549	515	541	458	371	320	300	255	220	189	177	114	96	58	21	6	3	1	.
2 GRAYRIGG	3920	M. - 2007	268	262	251	221	197	131	115	98	87	78	71	68	63	47	21	17	12	1	1	.	.
		F. - 1913	250	247	240	205	180	142	103	92	89	94	83	53	40	31	24	19	8	4	.	.	.
3 KIRKBY LONSDALE	6607	M. - 3164	471	400	366	323	256	197	214	157	162	127	102	103	103	75	55	33	17	1	2	.	.
		F. - 3443	431	388	423	304	268	254	210	172	160	141	127	129	85	79	58	33	20	7	2	.	.
4 KENDAL. (W. H. P.)	13983	M. - 6651	919	898	764	649	547	505	438	337	313	251	213	206	197	140	92	68	17	8	.	.	.
		F. - 7332	996	897	783	736	653	570	491	403	384	290	260	235	214	154	129	58	29	11	1	.	2
5 MILNTHORPE. (W.)	6622	M. - 3337	446	392	365	343	268	221	218	176	143	149	127	114	115	97	73	38	23	5	2	1	1
		F. - 3285	417	403	378	318	263	250	197	190	151	138	123	129	100	103	70	58	22	5	.	1	.

Table 4.—MALE and FEMALE CHILDREN *at each Year of Age* under 5 in the NORTHERN DIVISION and its REGISTRATION COUNTIES.

REGISTRATION COUNTY.	TOTAL UNDER 5 YEARS. Persons.	Males and Females.		Under 1 Year.	1–	2–	3–	4–
X. NORTHERN COUNTIES.	237753	M.	119242	25602	22760	23841	23580	23469
		F.	118511	25391	22558	23656	23454	23452
38 DURHAM	133568	M.	67149	14337	12750	13534	13259	13269
		F.	66419	14370	12498	13204	13160	13187
39 NORTHUMBERLAND	60872	M.	30509	6608	5875	5981	6049	6016
		F.	30363	6419	5837	6091	5977	6039
40 CUMBERLAND	34976	M.	17449	3784	3332	3512	3481	3340
		F.	17527	3711	3369	3549	3486	3412
41 WESTMORLAND	8337	M.	4135	873	803	834	791	834
		F.	4202	891	854	812	831	814

Table 5.—MALE and FEMALE CHILDREN *at each Year of Age* under 5 in REGISTRATION DISTRICTS.

REGISTRATION DISTRICT.	Total under 5 Years. Persons.	Males and Females.		Under 1 Year.	1–	2–	3–	4–
38 DURHAM.								
542 DARLINGTON	6900	M.	3474	726	633	707	687	721
		F.	3426	703	621	683	719	700
543 STOCKTON	10351	M.	5156	1016	1001	1141	974	1030
		F.	5195	1140	975	978	1030	1072
544 HARTLEPOOL	7538	M.	3851	830	733	781	767	740
		F.	3687	786	730	701	725	745
545 AUCKLAND	12900	M.	6440	1421	1171	1284	1285	1279
		F.	6460	1434	1219	1229	1255	1323
546 TEESDALE	2630	M.	1331	296	236	255	267	277
		F.	1299	256	221	261	271	290
547 WEARDALE	2354	M.	1157	238	220	261	259	239
		F.	1197	256	199	269	242	231
548 LANCHESTER	9091	M.	4580	1004	845	961	884	886
		F.	4511	967	804	895	894	951
549 DURHAM	9555	M.	4807	1023	942	958	955	929
		F.	4748	1031	863	961	957	936
550 EASINGTON	6548	M.	3287	683	616	664	663	661
		F.	3261	716	634	600	675	621
551 HOUGHTON-LE-SPRING	5463	M.	2765	607	520	552	538	539
		F.	2698	620	516	546	485	531
552 CHESTER-LE-STREET	6664	M.	3388	717	586	670	694	721
		F.	3276	728	617	683	635	632
553 SUNDERLAND	20733	M.	10397	2207	2048	2086	2085	1971
		F.	10336	2198	2019	2056	2064	2009
554 SOUTH SHIELDS	16376	M.	8256	1796	1576	1691	1602	1591
		F.	8120	1820	1522	1672	1563	1543
555 GATESHEAD	16465	M.	8260	1779	1614	1583	1599	1685
		F.	8205	1715	1558	1681	1655	1596
39 NORTHUMBERLAND.								
556 NEWCASTLE UPON TYNE	21362	M.	10623	2317	2143	2023	2108	2032
		F.	10739	2287	2110	2166	2074	2102
557 TYNEMOUTH	17039	M.	8637	1915	1607	1698	1688	1729
		F.	8402	1826	1588	1619	1689	1680
558 CASTLE WARD	2657	M.	1323	288	248	262	254	291
		F.	1334	277	269	248	274	266
559 HEXHAM	4477	M.	2225	451	458	422	456	438
		F.	2252	453	444	440	456	459
560 HALTWHISTLE	1118	M.	572	121	117	111	115	108
		F.	546	121	111	95	113	106
561 BELLINGHAM	761	M.	372	79	74	75	72	72
		F.	389	81	73	77	88	70
39 NORTHUMBERLAND—*cont.*								
562 MORPETH	5325	M.	2666	585	491	510	549	531
		F.	2659	579	471	525	515	569
563 ALNWICK	2658	M.	1362	305	256	279	274	248
		F.	1296	252	222	309	246	268
564 BELFORD	667	M.	334	78	65	57	58	76
		F.	333	64	68	80	56	66
565 BERWICK	2736	M.	1387	286	240	313	264	284
		F.	1349	280	273	300	245	251
566 GLENDALE	1271	M.	626	134	111	129	133	119
		F.	645	113	130	133	143	126
567 ROTHBURY	801	M.	382	69	65	82	78	88
		F.	419	86	78	99	80	76
40 CUMBERLAND.								
568 ALSTON	534	M.	269	62	49	49	54	55
		F.	265	46	48	51	63	57
569 PENRITH	2896	M.	1466	342	273	292	284	275
		F.	1430	290	297	300	281	263
570 BRAMPTON	1221	M.	632	148	106	135	121	122
		F.	589	125	109	130	100	125
571 LONGTOWN	945	M.	465	104	80	90	93	98
		F.	480	89	88	102	96	105
572 CARLISLE	6857	M.	3454	739	665	707	699	644
		F.	3403	730	663	709	634	667
573 WIGTON	3032	M.	1520	313	305	303	300	285
		F.	1512	305	282	333	290	293
574 COCKERMOUTH	8457	M.	4190	894	848	851	811	788
		F.	4267	933	794	829	881	830
575 WHITEHAVEN	9106	M.	4501	959	837	889	923	893
		F.	4605	1010	872	898	946	884
576 BOOTLE	1928	M.	952	223	169	196	188	178
		F.	976	184	216	202	186	188
41 WESTMORLAND.								
577 EAST WARD	1897	M.	913	197	178	176	165	197
		F.	984	204	212	192	193	183
578 WEST WARD	993	M.	509	104	94	111	92	108
		F.	484	98	85	100	99	101
579 KENDAL	5447	M.	2713	572	533	545	584	529
		F.	2734	589	547	520	548	530

Table 7.—CONDITION as to MARRIAGE and AGES OF MALES and FEMALES in the NORTHERN DIVISION and its REGISTRATION COUNTIES.

REGISTRATION COUNTY.		ALL AGES.	Under 15 Years.	15–	20–	25–	35–	45–	55–	65 and upwards.
X. NORTHERN COUNTIES.										
UNMARRIED	Males	[illegible]	[illegible]	81610	58233	43401	14654	7285	4115	2885
	Females	480821	313218	75042	42244	26101	9661	6197	4126	3537
MARRIED	Males	260467	.	341	14861	78581	74832	51294	31371	15797
	Females	269081	.	3224	28674	84962	70254	46099	25261	10677
WIDOWED	Males	26941	.	3	162	1928	3678	5015	6323	9832
	Females	54282	.	16	354	2326	6696	10603	14099	19589
38 DURHAM.										
UNMARRIED	Males	286100	175881	44500	30991	21536	7215	3323	1618	1036
	Females	251326	174339	39730	19435	10156	3446	1968	1271	975
MARRIED	Males	143324	.	322	9155	45515	41720	27992	16238	7482
	Females	149918	.	2216	17645	48596	38871	24812	12833	4945
WIDOWED	Males	13392	.	2	97	1040	2030	2664	3100	4459
	Females	26106	.	11	209	1613	3375	5203	6892	8803
39 NORTHUMBERLAND.										
UNMARRIED	Males	138614	81354	21485	15824	11670	4124	2086	1246	825
	Females	131784	80864	20800	13125	8704	3345	2189	1411	1296
MARRIED	Males	69754	.	72	3411	19885	19627	13805	8603	4351
	Females	70231	.	694	6756	21820	18666	12365	6944	2986
WIDOWED	Males	7514	.	1	40	543	1009	1345	1771	2812
	Females	16189	.	4	105	800	1998	3220	4130	5923
40 CUMBERLAND.										
UNMARRIED	Males	81473	46818	12470	9254	7288	2645	1401	950	761
	Females	77072	45321	11757	7493	5481	2332	1566	1128	974
MARRIED	Males	38608	.	40	1897	10765	10439	7489	4980	2998
	Females	39142	.	265	3604	11824	10212	6091	4247	1899
WIDOWED	Males	4665	.	.	17	277	532	786	1135	1918
	Females	9687	.	.	33	436	1101	1777	2508	3832
41 WESTMORLAND.										
UNMARRIED	Males	20434	11785	3155	2164	1712	670	384	301	263
	Females	20689	11689	3159	2191	1760	738	454	316	292
MARRIED	Males	9781	.	7	388	2416	2446	2008	1550	966
	Females	9790	.	49	669	2723	2535	1931	1237	647
WIDOWED	Males	1370	.	.	8	68	114	220	317	643
	Females	2300	.	.	7	77	229	394	569	1031

Note.—In a few cases, persons described as "Married" were stated to be under 15 years of age. These have been classed with married persons aged "15 and under 20 years."

Table 8.—Condition as to Marriage and Ages of Males and Females in Registration Districts.

Registration District.	Condition	Sex	All Ages.	Under 15 Years	15–	20–	25–	35–	45–	55–	65– and upw^{ds}.
38 DURHAM.											
542 DARLINGTON:	Unmarried	M.	14959	9222	2291	1626	1126	361	176	97	60
		F.	14826	9156	2862	1455	887	308	202	148	108
	Married	M.	7787	.	8	385	2237	2210	1406	955	406
		F.	7857	.	54	744	2407	2159	1393	709	351
	Widowed	M.	773	.	.	2	60	122	140	139	290
		F.	1474	.	.	3	68	179	284	358	582
543 STOCKTON:	Unmarried	M.	22931	13299	3280	2667	2206	835	384	165	106
		F.	19422	13435	2980	1538	898	288	154	102	32
	Married	M.	11569	.	13	626	3699	3412	2114	1135	570
		F.	11464	.	145	1342	3865	3015	1817	910	374
	Widowed	M.	1057	.	.	9	96	168	237	207	345
		F.	1838	.	.	13	121	230	368	506	600
544 HARTLEPOOL:	Unmarried	M.	15798	9778	2492	1693	1234	461	152	77	41
		F.	13870	9471	2383	1100	534	152	76	57	35
	Married	M.	8842	.	12	466	2567	2405	1554	928	400
		F.	8504	.	102	978	2865	2235	1401	724	259
	Widowed	M.	729	.	.	3	61	124	154	161	225
		F.	1371	.	.	18	94	197	273	366	423
545 AUCKLAND:	Unmarried	M.	27824	17362	4180	2834	1874	660	347	160	107
		F.	23679	17318	3580	1510	715	213	127	66	50
	Married	M.	14439	.	24	1015	4516	3942	2709	1665	678
		F.	14399	.	271	1852	4763	3615	2320	1188	460
	Widowed	M.	1292	.	.	11	98	197	282	309	406
		F.	2039	.	.	17	139	263	413	536	671
546 TEESDALE:	Unmarried	M.	6728	3868	1106	747	564	193	113	71	66
		F.	6560	3747	1114	758	475	194	107	97	78
	Married	M.	3148	.	3	119	667	801	708	519	320
		F.	3106	.	24	229	814	844	646	412	197
	Widowed	M.	431	.	.	.	19	44	73	100	195
		F.	786	.	.	4	23	56	124	190	358
547 WEARDALE:	Unmarried	M.	5959	3255	1014	728	536	185	98	69	38
		F.	5187	3371	837	468	290	101	47	28	25
	Married	M.	2721	.	1	118	786	756	559	565	197
		F.	2728	.	25	241	850	718	481	290	123
	Widowed	M.	355	.	.	3	25	39	80	92	116
		F.	612	.	.	2	22	61	136	160	211
548 LANCHESTER:	Unmarried	M.	20311	12056	3295	2509	1585	515	279	140	83
		F.	16320	11850	2529	1136	467	161	88	50	38
	Married	M.	9477	.	9	585	2909	2617	1850	1073	424
		F.	9406	.	139	1148	3041	2365	1658	805	206
	Widowed	M.	854	.	.	4	65	136	182	191	276
		F.	1283	.	1	6	58	140	276	368	434
549 DURHAM:	Unmarried	M.	21175	12960	3898	2328	1567	476	253	135	88
		F.	18508	12750	3018	1440	765	265	180	97	84
	Married	M.	10933	.	13	682	3313	2956	2160	1260	550
		F.	10891	.	193	1317	3368	2754	1878	989	392
	Widowed	M.	984	.	.	6	77	141	159	236	365
		F.	1730	.	1	15	115	221	332	431	617
550 EASINGTON:	Unmarried	M.	13610	8741	2155	1401	814	245	132	59	43
		F.	11670	8724	1694	714	312	105	60	38	28
	Married	M.	7093	.	11	479	2175	1920	1320	745	393
		F.	7084	.	129	923	2232	1752	1181	592	275
	Widowed	M.	555	.	.	6	37	78	115	140	179
		F.	1136	.	1	18	83	134	218	299	382
551 HOUGHTON-LE-SPRING:	Unmarried	M.	11156	7183	1803	1149	640	193	98	44	46
		F.	9457	6981	1402	580	307	96	63	50	28
	Married	M.	5054	.	14	474	1376	1606	1044	688	332
		F.	6033	.	113	831	1902	1442	958	389	198
	Widowed	M.	534	.	.	3	38	65	109	121	159
		F.	981	.	.	12	50	90	195	255	350
552 CHESTER-LE-STREET:	Unmarried	M.	14404	8938	2418	1598	916	317	143	69	50
		F.	12093	8760	1796	795	436	129	80	50	47
	Married	M.	7465	.	11	504	2261	1967	1402	892	438
		F.	7518	.	158	955	2304	1820	1284	709	283
	Widowed	M.	701	.	.	14	45	102	120	177	243
		F.	1116	.	1	11	55	125	197	312	415
553 SUNDERLAND:	Unmarried	M.	43518	27122	6831	4081	3235	1053	390	188	118
		F.	40491	26912	6782	3499	1917	657	358	210	157
	Married	M.	23632	.	26	1516	7295	6689	4400	2568	1148
		F.	24490	.	355	2830	8060	6417	3061	2055	783
	Widowed	M.	1996	.	1	14	170	318	381	457	655
		F.	5100	.	4	38	334	692	1050	1363	1879
38 DURHAM—*cont.*											
554 SOUTH SHIELDS:	Unmarried	M.	33709	20779	4806	3644	2830	948	390	149	7
		F.	28766	20028	4444	2038	913	321	163	120	7
	Married	M.	17830	.	25	1134	5628	5316	3587	1718	66
		F.	18264	.	283	2238	6205	4940	2842	1311	43
	Widowed	M.	1488	.	.	11	113	252	300	339	47
		F.	3202	.	.	32	238	502	852	797	98
555 GATESHEAD:	Unmarried	M.	33727	21103	5141	3501	2409	832	348	186	11
		F.	30566	21236	4663	2405	1240	461	263	163	13
	Married	M.	17906	.	42	1052	5651	5184	3300	1853	89
		F.	18119	.	226	2008	6050	4802	2902	1484	56
	Widowed	M.	1644	.	1	11	151	249	322	411	48
		F.	3448	.	3	19	265	476	715	931	109
39 NORTHUMBERLAND.											
556 NEWCASTLE UPON TYNE.	Unmarried	M.	40306	27535	7068	5330	4072	1844	672	289	15
		F.	45800	27924	7397	4942	3006	1034	633	332	312
	Married	M.	24849	.	41	1367	7618	7288	4763	2670	1102
		F.	26016	.	272	2641	8156	6865	4198	2071	723
	Widowed	M.	2417	.	.	14	174	306	612	563	753
		F.	5964	.	2	48	342	818	1338	1538	1880
557 TYNEMOUTH:	Unmarried	M.	37192	22658	6641	4148	2014	970	503	241	117
		F.	32804	22160	5068	2606	1361	469	292	186	172
	Married	M.	19506	.	26	1062	6832	6442	3760	2184	1094
		F.	19570	.	245	2164	6279	5126	3246	1807	708
	Widowed	M.	1772	.	.	13	164	253	331	414	597
		F.	4059	.	2	38	231	560	831	1107	1320
558 CASTLE WARD:	Unmarried	M.	6522	3739	1085	708	510	224	115	74	69
		F.	6025	3665	962	609	445	179	128	81	61
	Married	M.	3092	.	1	133	805	895	614	425	219
		F.	3090	.	18	280	915	820	568	330	164
	Widowed	M.	365	.	.	2	23	41	71	80	149
		F.	626	.	.	2	26	70	108	136	284
559 HEXHAM:	Unmarried	M.	11125	6226	1765	1301	965	402	214	146	112
		F.	10774	6108	1709	1181	892	350	229	179	131
	Married	M.	5063	.	.	201	1274	1346	1066	706	464
		F.	5114	.	43	426	1475	1363	966	678	323
	Widowed	M.	717	.	.	1	46	85	109	186	289
		F.	1297	.	.	7	42	155	242	326	531
560 HALTWHISTLE:	Unmarried	M.	2717	1495	407	297	270	98	63	45	44
		F.	2538	1466	392	257	209	96	47	23	38
	Married	M.	1133	.	.	46	282	291	248	165	108
		F.	1130	.	12	82	366	315	215	107	69
	Widowed	M.	151	.	.	.	7	20	23	31	70
		F.	238	.	.	.	5	17	47	53	118
561 BELLINGHAM:	Unmarried	M.	2027	1043	250	223	211	100	83	65	51
		F.	2036	1084	282	169	198	94	83	55	42
	Married	M.	834	.	.	18	173	221	176	131	115
		F.	824	.	3	43	230	205	175	110	66
	Widowed	M.	161	.	.	.	8	12	28	28	85
		F.	225	.	.	.	7	24	34	51	109
562 MORPETH:	Unmarried	M.	11983	7171	1940	1386	877	314	168	123	[illegible]
		F.	10664	7148	1494	875	545	253	138	120	96
	Married	M.	5868	.	3	289	1619	1821	1101	735	605
		F.	5891	.	66	647	1815	1526	1032	634	271
	Widowed	M.	618	.	.	5	50	78	98	140	254
		F.	1078	.	.	6	41	113	204	279	453
563 ALNWICK:	Unmarried	M.	6752	3735	1119	801	621	206	128	87	65
		F.	6830	3659	1044	776	642	255	169	145	140
	Married	M.	3168	.	.	103	782	831	641	518	313
		F.	3189	.	13	204	905	818	613	402	234
	Widowed	M.	470	.	.	1	31	50	68	117	233
		F.	889	.	.	3	25	96	141	218	346
564 BELFORD:	Unmarried	M.	1785	885	304	225	158	48	28	21	16
		F.	1945	944	324	266	193	86	64	28	41
	Married	M.	839	.	.	25	193	109	184	161	77
		F.	847	.	1	39	241	180	192	136	58
	Widowed	M.	103	.	.	.	7	6	18	25	63
		F.	218	.	.	.	5	21	26	50	119

Table 8 *continued.*—CONDITION as to MARRIAGE and AGES of MALES and FEMALES in REGISTRATION DISTRICTS.

REGISTRATION DISTRICT.		ALL AGES.	Under 15 Years.	15–	20–	25–	35–	45–	55–	65 and upw[d].
39 NORTHUMBERLAND—*cont.*										
565 BERWICK:										
UNMARRIED	M.	6574	3788	1058	777	533	198	92	76	56
	F.	6752	3780	1029	694	585	266	188	128	137
MARRIED	M.	7117	.	1	109	780	806	651	470	293
	F.	5197	.	14	208	845	873	618	424	215
WIDOWED	M.	415	.	1	3	16	40	52	101	202
	F.	935	.	.	3	50	124	108	247	403
566 GLENDALE:										
UNMARRIED	M.	3456	1872	581	411	306	122	75	48	41
	F.	3621	1920	576	458	409	177	135	76	70
MARRIED	M.	1554	.	.	89	339	485	322	258	161
	F.	1629	.	4	72	366	412	361	203	111
WIDOWED	M.	185	.	.	.	7	9	23	47	99
	F.	388	.	.	.	13	38	97	61	179
567 ROTHBURY:										
UNMARRIED	M.	2195	1107	327	299	231	109	55	37	30
	F.	2300	1167	373	264	219	97	73	59	48
MARRIED	M.	926	.	.	20	188	250	199	178	91
	F.	934	.	3	50	233	234	227	122	65
WIDOWED	M.	140	.	.	1	8	14	22	34	61
	F.	214	.	.	.	3	22	25	38	126
40 CUMBERLAND.										
568 ALSTON:										
UNMARRIED	M.	1562	814	244	169	161	78	48	31	17
	F.	1467	814	241	154	118	65	44	20	11
MARRIED	M.	614	.	1	14	185	161	165	88	50
	F.	633	.	4	42	162	184	140	79	22
WIDOWED	M.	77	.	.	.	3	10	17	27	20
	F.	268	.	.	.	5	22	53	75	113
569 PENRITH:										
UNMARRIED	M.	7587	4174	1244	892	643	270	163	134	125
	F.	7253	3979	1160	838	614	268	169	117	107
MARRIED	M.	3473	.	1	136	780	886	696	595	379
	F.	3526	.	13	252	938	893	690	464	236
WIDOWED	M.	465	.	.	.	20	40	72	108	225
	F.	938	.	.	2	41	84	145	229	437
570 BRAMPTON:										
UNMARRIED	M.	3637	1887	572	427	381	184	92	73	81
	F.	3312	1693	516	397	335	163	90	38	70
MARRIED	M.	1460	.	1	41	353	361	306	251	177
	F.	1475	.	6	107	378	375	308	214	89
WIDOWED	M.	237	.	.	.	10	21	27	65	114
	F.	424	.	.	.	13	38	68	108	199
571 LONGTOWN:										
UNMARRIED	M.	2731	1349	467	318	283	140	96	71	72
	F.	2533	1358	372	280	225	129	103	61	65
MARRIED	M.	983	.	2	29	194	233	222	164	139
	F.	960	.	5	54	251	261	186	144	39
WIDOWED	M.	262	.	.	.	10	17	32	45	98
	F.	272	.	.	2	9	22	44	55	140
40 CUMBERLAND—*cont.*										
572 CARLISLE:										
UNMARRIED	M.	16135	9216	2604	1813	1451	484	296	158	133
	F.	16887	9215	2689	1858	1609	646	482	512	232
MARRIED	M.	8982	.	5	413	2253	2200	1578	1046	387
	F.	8514	.	40	735	2085	2145	1427	912	400
WIDOWED	M.	1038	.	.	5	64	113	169	252	435
	F.	[illegible]	.	.	8	115	916	401	669	883
573 WIGTON:										
UNMARRIED	M.	7461	4155	1261	785	671	273	168	102	106
	F.	7406	4173	1092	779	845	283	190	142	122
MARRIED	M.	3540	.	8	123	832	929	701	645	416
	F.	3544	.	9	240	980	890	714	478	283
WIDOWED	M.	480	.	.	.	19	44	68	107	247
	F.	1009	.	.	1	36	86	174	235	477
574 COCKERMOUTH:										
UNMARRIED	M.	18348	10858	2697	2222	1628	576	209	153	105
	F.	17122	10989	2535	1476	992	398	290	210	223
MARRIED	M.	9053	.	13	520	2681	2457	1698	1116	618
	F.	9191	.	68	938	2826	2389	1584	950	442
WIDOWED	M.	1082	.	.	5	71	131	188	258	379
	F.	2003	.	.	6	92	223	355	551	776
575 WHITEHAVEN:										
UNMARRIED	M.	19723	11770	2940	2219	1715	575	264	141	79
	F.	17528	11778	2608	1433	848	351	217	164	129
MARRIED	M.	9432	.	12	335	2955	2715	1783	982	490
	F.	9534	.	105	1057	3088	2586	1549	810	339
WIDOWED	M.	923	.	.	7	64	140	181	225	308
	F.	2130	.	.	15	111	267	449	557	731
576 BOOTLE:										
UNMARRIED	M.	4229	2415	651	474	374	145	74	57	43
	F.	3364	2372	544	278	195	64	42	44	25
MARRIED	M.	1951	.	2	86	532	506	304	228	142
	F.	1935	.	15	199	634	480	323	176	99
WIDOWED	M.	209	.	.	.	16	18	37	48	92
	F.	337	.	.	4	14	44	60	89	126
41 WESTMORLAND.										
577 EAST WARD:										
UNMARRIED	M.	4696	2655	685	454	410	195	111	88	85
	F.	4488	2554	683	402	358	163	115	70	83
MARRIED	M.	2286	.	2	81	523	554	486	384	226
	F.	2232	.	10	162	625	554	455	272	156
WIDOWED	M.	344	.	.	2	12	23	92	92	153
	F.	510	.	.	1	17	56	74	132	239
578 WEST WARD:										
UNMARRIED	M.	2779	1523	412	317	270	113	61	45	38
	F.	2515	1408	378	283	213	79	64	43	45
MARRIED	M.	1241	.	.	42	234	289	280	209	167
	F.	1223	.	9	52	306	298	294	174	91
WIDOWED	M.	175	.	.	1	7	20	30	40	77
	F.	292	.	.	2	6	24	40	71	149
579 KENDAL:										
UNMARRIED	M.	12939	7607	2048	1393	1032	362	212	168	137
	F.	13836	7727	2138	1443	1187	496	275	203	184
MARRIED	M.	6304	.	5	265	1639	1023	1242	957	573
	F.	6335	.	30	455	1794	1683	1182	791	400
WIDOWED	M.	851	.	.	5	49	71	128	185	413
	F.	1439	.	.	4	54	142	280	366	643

Table 9.—CONDITION as to MARRIAGE and AGES of MALES and FEMALES in each URBAN SANITARY DISTRICT of which the POPULATION EXCEEDS 50,000 PERSONS.

URBAN SANITARY DISTRICT.		ALL AGES.	Under 15 Years.	15–	20–	25–	35–	45–	55–	65 and upw[d].
SUNDERLAND:										
UNMARRIED	M.	35737	22359	5550	3717	2643	860	340	165	103
	F.	34227	22352	5838	3100	1750	609	337	197	144
MARRIED	M.	19711	.	30	1249	6044	5579	3631	2200	978
	F.	20550	.	288	2328	6776	5379	3358	1750	669
WIDOWED	M.	1685	.	1	10	143	253	323	394	561
	F.	4632	.	4	36	294	636	958	1206	1498
SOUTH SHIELDS:										
UNMARRIED	M.	17964	11262	2615	1828	1422	516	203	80	38
	F.	16092	11216	2594	1275	671	199	118	78	40
MARRIED	M.	9625	.	15	583	2955	2815	1847	1010	400
	F.	10281	.	148	1215	3478	2727	1633	801	283
WIDOWED	M.	784	.	.	5	52	131	162	179	255
	F.	2128	.	.	21	174	329	425	523	656
GATESHEAD:										
UNMARRIED	M.	20724	13198	3109	2073	1487	483	202	104	64
	F.	19117	13126	2939	1579	832	340	163	98	85
MARRIED	M.	11260	.	33	748	3609	3826	2052	1068	464
	F.	11433	.	129	1281	3929	3097	1850	842	306
WIDOWED	M.	1011	.	.	4	97	158	287	260	285
	F.	2262	.	3	10	130	325	486	623	679
NEWCASTLE-ON-TYNE:										
UNMARRIED	M.	44756	26518	6750	5175	3962	1317	571	278	154
	F.	44368	26932	7398	4825	2932	1069	642	328	388
MARRIED	M.	24004	.	40	1325	7356	7037	4608	2577	1066
	F.	24069	.	264	2556	7869	6429	4060	1993	698
WIDOWED	M.	2341	.	.	14	167	388	492	546	734
	F.	5834	.	2	44	332	797	1315	1505	1845

TABLE 10.—OCCUPATIONS of MALES and FEMALES in the NORTHERN DIVISION and its REGISTRATION COUNTIES, and in each URBAN SANITARY DISTRICT of which the POPULATION exceeds 50,000 PERSONS.

OCCUPATIONS.	NORTHERN COUNTIES.		REGISTRATION COUNTIES.							
			38. DURHAM.		39. NORTHUMBERLAND.		40. CUMBERLAND.		41. WESTMORLAND.	
	Males.	Females.	Males.	Females.	Males.	Females.	Males.	Females.	Males.	Females.
TOTAL	820029	804184	447818	427350	215882	218204	124746	125901	31583	32729
I. PROFESSIONAL CLASS.										
1. PERSONS ENGAGED IN THE GENERAL OR LOCAL GOVERNMENT OF THE COUNTRY.										
1. *National Government.*										
Peer, M.P., Privy Councillor (not otherwise described)	11	.	6	.	3	.	1	.	1	.
Civil Service (officers and clerks)	808	153	338	51	289	49	140	39	41	14
Civil Service (messengers, &c.)	769	42	314	11	246	21	154	8	55	2
Prison Officer, &c.	80	21	30	6	35	10	10	4	5	1
2. *Local Government.*										
Police	1590	.	832	.	508	.	203	.	47	.
Municipal, Parish, Union, District, Officer	599	107	281	43	191	37	102	22	25	5
Other Local or County Official	246	.	96	.	76	.	50	.	24	.
3. *East Indian and Colonial Service.*										
East Indian and Colonial Service	.	.	.	.	.	.	.	.	.	.
2. PERSONS ENGAGED IN THE DEFENCE OF THE COUNTRY.										
1. *Army (at Home).*										
Army Officer (effective or retired)	133	.	41	.	54	.	30	.	8	.
Soldier and Non-commissioned Officer	1054	.	287	.	519	.	243	.	5	.
Militia, Yeomanry, Volunteers	227	.	92	.	58	.	63	.	14	.
Army Pensioner	263	.	102	.	89	1	62	2	10	.
2. *Navy (ashore or in port).*										
Navy Officer (effective or retired)	39	.	14	.	19	.	5	.	1	.
Seaman, R.N.	219	.	70	.	145	.	4	.	.	.
Royal Marines (officers and men)	3	.	1	.	2	.	.	.	.	.
Navy Pensioner	77	.	50	.	17	.	10	.	.	.
3. PERSONS ENGAGED IN PROFESSIONAL OCCUPATIONS (WITH THEIR IMMEDIATE SUBORDINATES).										
1. *Clerical Profession.*										
Clergyman (Established Church)	934	.	383	.	298	.	219	.	104	.
Roman Catholic Priest	136	.	66	.	49	.	19	.	2	.
Minister, Priest, of other religious bodies	548	3	240	.	181	.	88	.	28	.
Missionary, Scripture Reader, Itinerant Preacher	178	83	88	51	47	20	38	11	5	2
Nun, Sister of Charity	.	76	.	27	.	43	.	6	.	.
Theological Student	148	.	52	.	10	.	32	.	4	.
Church, Chapel, Cemetery—Officer, Servant	141	60	69	33	43	24	27	3	2	.
2. *Legal Profession.*										
Barrister, Solicitor	602	.	270	.	181	.	117	.	34	.
Law Student	57	.	31	.	17	.	6	.	3	.
Law Clerk, and others connected with Law	967	1	404	.	305	1	195	.	63	.
3. *Medical Profession.*										
Physician, Surgeon, General Practitioner	759	2	362	.	238	.	119	.	40	2
Dentist	121	.	46	.	47	.	23	.	5	.
Medical Student, Assistant	304	1	156	.	115	1	19	.	14	.
Midwife	.	42	.	22	.	16	.	4	.	.
Subordinate Medical Service	95	758	53	318	26	261	15	136	1	43
4. *Teachers.*										
Schoolmaster	2638	4780	1302	2346	718	1321	471	836	147	277
Teacher, Professor, Lecturer	227	579	97	309	83	154	35	83	12	33
School Service, and others concerned in Teaching	117	43	70	25	28	11	15	6	4	1
5. *Literary and Scientific Persons.*										
Author, Editor, Journalist	94	14	41	4	34	9	11	1	8	.
Reporter, Short-hand Writer	118	1	60	.	35	1	20	.	3	.
Persons engaged in Scientific Pursuits	70	.	41	.	16	.	12	.	1	.
Literary, Scientific, Institution, Service, &c.	46	2	30	2	11	.	5	.	.	.
6. *Engineers and Surveyors.*										
Civil Engineer	352	.	138	.	143	.	66	.	5	.
Mining Engineer	446	.	267	.	108	.	68	.	3	.
Land, House, Ship, Surveyor	156	.	82	.	43	.	19	.	12	.
7. *Artists.*										
Painter (artist)	153	30	55	8	60	16	28	3	10	3
Engraver (artist)	27	1	9	.	14	.	3	1	1	.
Sculptor	34	.	17	.	12	.	4	.	1	.
Architect	336	.	154	.	101	.	52	.	29	.
Musician, Music Master	524	348	249	167	168	108	89	61	18	12
Art Student	25	15	9	2	12	6	1	2	3	5
Photographer	233	75	92	37	87	21	37	17	17	.
Actor	140	106	78	48	40	45	22	12	.	.
Art, Music, Theatre, Service	45	10	24	4	14	6	7	.	.	.

NOTE.—Persons returned as engaged in more than one occupation have been referred to the one that appeared to be of most importance; or, if there was no difference in this respect, to the one first given by the person in his or her return. In some cases special rules have been followed: *e.g.*, "Clergyman and Schoolmaster" in combination has always been referred to "Schoolmaster"; a Member of Parliament or Peer engaged in any branch of commerce or industry has always been referred to this latter, not to "Peer, M.P."

The numbers returned under any heading include Labourers, Apprentices, and Assistants, as well as Masters, but not Clerks, Messengers, Errand boys, Porters, or Watchmen, for which occupations there are special headings. Civil, Military, and Naval Clerks, Law, Bank, Insurance, and Railway Clerks, and Government and Railway Porters, are, however, exceptions to this rule. Many young persons, being Apprentices or Assistants, have therefore been referred to occupations usually followed by adults. Women also, chiefly widows or orphans carrying on the business of their deceased husbands or fathers, will sometimes be found under occupations commonly followed by men only.

Persons returned *as retired* from any business have not been referred to that business. Inmates of workhouses have been referred to their trades, unless their age or infirmities showed that they were past work. But persons who might be supposed to be only temporarily separated from their usual employment, such as Prisoners, and Patients in General Hospitals, have been classed under their usual occupations.

In some cases, for convenience of space, the male designation, *e.g.*, "Schoolmaster," alone is given, instead of "Schoolmaster, Schoolmistress."

Table 10 *continued.*—OCCUPATIONS of MALES and FEMALES in the NORTHERN DIVISION and its REGISTRATION COUNTIES, and in each URBAN SANITARY DISTRICT of which the POPULATION exceeds 50,000 PERSONS.

OCCUPATIONS.	NORTHERN COUNTIES.		REGISTRATION COUNTIES. 38. DURHAM.		39. NORTHUMBERLAND.		40. CUMBERLAND.		41. WESTMORLAND.	
	Males.	Females.	Males.	Females.	Males.	Females.	Males.	Females.	Males.	Females.
8. *Persons engaged in Exhibitions, Shows, Games, &c.*										
Performer, Showman, Exhibition, Service	92	23	66	16	39	3	8	3		
Billiard, Cricket, & other Games, Service	115	5	38	3	34	1	29	1	3	.
II. DOMESTIC CLASS.										
4. PERSONS ENGAGED IN DOMESTIC OFFICES OR SERVICES.										
1. *Domestic Service.*										
Domestic Coachman, Groom	2408	.	827	.	923	.	450	.	208	.
Domestic Gardener	2979	11	1095	2	1048	6	484	.	352	.
Domestic Indoor Servant	1304	63880	461	28057	444	10968	286	12171	113	3683
Lodge, Gate, Park, Keeper (not Government)	89	44	46	14	34	15	8	11	1	4
Inn, Hotel, Servant	1215	833	511	319	484	248	159	206	61	60
College, Club, Service	43	17	19	11	20	2	3	2	1	2
2. *Other Service.*										
Office Keeper (not Government)	54	193	29	99	24	67	1	26	.	1
Cook (not domestic)	18	103	7	41	10	47	.	12	1	3
Charwoman	.	3285	.	1053	.	1056	.	938	.	238
Washing and Bathing Service	56	8447	22	1505	27	1171	5	531	2	240
Hospital and Institution Service	127	332	79	136	19	121	28	57	1	19
Others engaged in Service	39	7	15	4	18	3	4	.	2	
III. COMMERCIAL CLASS.										
5. PERSONS ENGAGED IN COMMERCIAL OCCUPATIONS.										
1. *Merchants and Agents.*										
Merchant	293	4	180	.	167	4	24	.	2	.
Broker, Agent, Factor	1649	22	744	14	752	7	131	1	22	.
Auctioneer, Appraiser, Valuer, House Agent	507	2	276	1	188	1	104	.	29	.
Accountant	715	.	372	.	208	.	129	.	6	.
Salesman, Buyer (not otherwise described)	32	164	22	84	13	62	1	15	1	3
Commercial Traveller	1366	.	609	.	710	.	202	.	45	.
Commercial Clerk	7508	220	3890	101	2852	96	709	17	117	6
Officer of Commercial Company, Guild, Society, &c.	18	.	5	.	9	.	4	.	.	.
2. *Dealers in Money.*										
Banker	38	.	10	.	13	.	11	.	4	.
Bank Service	632	4	227	.	223	3	140	1	38	.
Bill Discounter, Bill Broker, Finance Agent	18	.	10	.	8	.	.	.	.	.
3. *Persons occupied in Insurance.*										
Life, House, Ship, &c., Insurance Service	718	6	393	2	284	3	30	.	11	1
6. PERSONS ENGAGED IN CONVEYANCE OF MEN, GOODS, AND MESSAGES.										
1. *On Railways.*										
Railway Engine Driver, Stoker	2763	.	1645	.	270	.	771	.	77	.
Railway Guard	1115	.	594	.	224	.	268	.	29	.
Pointsman, Level Crossing Man	330	13	209	1	30	4	71	5	20	3
Other Railway Officials and Servants	6594	42	3264	22	1667	16	1340	3	323	1
2. *On Roads.*										
Toll Collector, Turnpike Gate Keeper	66	27	12	2	37	19	15	5	2	1
Omnibus, Coach, Cab, Owner—Livery Stable Keeper	178	6	85	3	62	2	16	.	10	1
Cabman, Flyman, Coachman (not domestic)	550	.	220	.	177	.	95	.	40	.
Carman, Carrier, Carter, Haulier	6134	20	2847	5	2414	4	735	10	138	1
Tramway Companies' Service	83	.	51	.	30	.	1	.	1	.
Wheel Chair Proprietor, Attendant, &c.	.	1	.	1	.	.	.	.	.	.
3. *On Canals, Rivers and Seas.*										
Inland Navigation Service	37	4	18	3	9	.	.	.	10	1
Bargeman, Lighterman, Waterman	2091	2	941	1	1035	1	15	.	30	.
Navigation Service (on shore)	389	16	208	4	155	5	25	7	1	.
Seaman (Merchant Service)	14653	.	9273	.	4818	.	845	.	17	.
Pilot	629	.	529	.	96	.	4	.	.	.
Ship Steward, Cook	536	27	308	6	216	18	10	3	2	.
Boatman on Seas	15	.	15	.	.	.	.	.	.	.
Harbour, Dock, Wharf, Lighthouse, Service	1901	1	781	1	745	.	375	.	.	.
4. *In Storage.*										
Warehouseman (not Manchester)	462	18	198	7	172	8	66	3	26	.
Meter, Weigher	95	.	63	.	23	.	9	.	.	.
5. *In conveying Messages, Porterage, &c.*										
Messenger, Porter, Watchman (not Railway nor Government)	3258	59	1518	16	1223	31	424	11	90	1
Telegraph, Telephone, Service	565	88	258	28	211	38	80	13	16	9

Table 10 *continued.*—Occupations of Males and Females in the Northern Division and its Registration Counties, and in each Urban Sanitary District of which the Population exceeds 50,000 Persons.

Occupations	Northern Counties.		Registration Counties.							
			38. Durham.		39. Northumberland.		40. Cumberland.		41. Westmorland.	
	Males.	Females.	Males.	Females.	Males.	Females.	Males.	Females.	Males.	Females.
IV. AGRICULTURAL CLASS.										
7. Persons engaged in Agriculture.										
1. *In Fields and Pastures.*										
Farmer, Grazier	13136	1367	3347	363	2756	292	4654	502	2379	210
Farmer's, Grazier's—Son, Grandson, Brother, Nephew*	6414	.	1422	.	1376	.	2486	.	1130	.
Farm Bailiff	898	.	304	.	363	.	150	.	81	.
Agricultural Labourer, Farm Servant, Cottager	26596	5795	6674	1183	8349	3361	8579	1059	2994	192
Shepherd	1677	.	117	.	1274	.	209	.	77	.
Land Drainage Service (not in towns)	323	.	146	.	141	.	31	.	5	.
Agricultural Machine—Proprietor, Attendant	89	.	32	.	51	.	4	.	2	.
Agricultural Student, Pupil	34	.	9	.	17	.	5	.	3	.
Others engaged in, or connected with, Agriculture	10	.	2	.	3	.	4	.	1	.
2. *In Woods.*										
Woodman	790	.	226	.	381	.	115	.	68	
3. *In Gardens.*										
Nurseryman, Seedsman, Florist	185	7	50	3	51	.	63	2	21	2
Gardener (not domestic)	1660	112	661	32	436	50	449	28	114	2
8. Persons engaged about Animals.										
1. *About Animals.*										
Horse Proprietor, Breeder, Dealer	128	.	62	.	33	.	30	.	3	.
Groom, Horse-keeper, Horse-breaker	1606	.	843	.	464	.	235	.	64	.
Veterinary Surgeon, Farrier	230	.	105	.	66	.	42	.	17	.
Cattle, Sheep, Pig—Dealer, Salesman	296	1	64	.	131	1	82	.	19	.
Drover	88	.	19	.	42	.	23	.	4	.
Gamekeeper	896	.	215	.	383	.	210	.	88	.
Dog, Bird, Animal—Keeper, Dealer	18	8	2	6	6	2	10	.	.	.
Vermin destroyer	97	.	15	.	55	.	18	.	9	.
Fisherman	1856	41	329	4	1366	36	148	1	13	.
Knacker, Catsmeat Dealer, &c., &c.	9	.	1	.	8	.	.	.	.	.
V. INDUSTRIAL CLASS.										
9. Persons working and dealing in Books, Prints, and Maps.										
1. *Books.*										
Publisher, Bookseller, Librarian	329	54	118	14	139	23	59	9	15	8
Music—Publisher, Seller, Printer	25	14	5	5	16	4	2	2	2	3
Bookbinder	247	238	107	90	94	96	35	45	11	1
Printer	2146	89	940	25	753	47	378	17	75	.
Newspaper Agent, News Room Keeper	204	56	104	29	84	22	13	5	3	.
Others	.	.	.	.	.	.	.	.	.	.
2. *Prints and Maps.*										
Lithographer, Lithographic Printer	161	2	46	2	55	.	53	.	3	.
Copper Plate and Steel Plate Printer	7	.	3	.	2	.	2	.	.	.
Map and Print—Colourer, Seller	.	2	.	1	.	1	.	.	.	.
10. Persons working and dealing in Machines and Implements.										
1. *Machines.*										
Engine, Machine, Maker	3599	11	2062	4	1354	6	156	1	27	.
Millwright	703	.	317	.	238	.	128	.	20	.
Fitter, Turner (Engine and Machine)	8593	.	5522	.	2418	.	613	.	40	.
Boiler Maker	4545	.	3227	.	1125	.	192	.	1	.
Spinning and Weaving Machine Maker	72	8	10	.	.	.	19	4	43	4
Agricultural Machine and Implement Maker	180	.	65	.	61	.	51	.	3	.
Domestic Machinery—Maker, Dealer	19	.	8	.	7	.	2	.	2	.
2. *Tools and Implements.*										
Tool Maker, Dealer	69	1	31	.	17	1	16	.	5	.
Cutler, Scissors Maker	61	.	34	.	19	.	6	.	2	.
File Maker	120	.	67	.	48	.	5	.	.	.
Saw Maker	38	.	18	.	16	.	4	.	.	.
Pin Maker	3	1	2	1	1	.	.	.	.	.
Needle Maker	1	.	1	.	.	.	.	.	.	.
Steel Pen Maker	1	1	.	.	1	1	.	.	.	.
Pencil Maker (Wood)	108	9	.	.	1	.	107	9	.	.
Domestic Implement Maker	2	.	2	.	.	.	.	.	.	.
3. *Watches and Philosophical Instruments.*										
Watch Maker, Clock Maker	867	11	374	6	248	5	193	.	52	.
Philosophical Instrument Maker, Optician	100	7	76	7	24	.	.	.	.	.
Electrical Apparatus Maker	60	5	30	4	23	1	3	.	4	.
Weighing and Measuring Apparatus Maker	35	.	20	.	14	.	1	.	.	.

* Only male relatives living with the farmer or grazier, and therefore presumably engaged in agriculture, are included above.

Table 10 *continued*.—OCCUPATIONS of MALES and FEMALES in the NORTHERN DIVISION and its REGISTRATION COUNTIES, and in each URBAN SANITARY DISTRICT of which the POPULATION exceeds 50,000 PERSONS.

OCCUPATIONS.	NORTHERN COUNTIES.		REGISTRATION COUNTIES. 38. DURHAM.		39. NORTHUMBERLAND.		40. CUMBERLAND.		41. WESTMORLAND.	
	Males.	Females.	Males.	Females.	Males.	Females.	Males.	Females.	Males.	Females.
4. Surgical Instruments.										
Surgical Instrument Maker	7	.	3	.	4	.	.	.	.	.
5. Arms and Ordnance.										
Gunsmith, Gun Manufacturer	75	1	12	.	54	1	6	.	3	.
Ordnance Manufacturer	98	.	1	.	89	.	.	.	.	.
Sword, Bayonet—Maker, Cutler	.	.	.	.	.	.	.	.	.	.
Others	1	.	.	.	1	.	.	.	.	.
6. Musical Instruments.										
Musical Instrument Maker, Dealer	143	6	39	4	39	.	18	1	7	.
7. Type, Dies, Medals, Coins.										
Type Cutter, Founder	5	.	1	.	2	.	2	.	.	.
Die, Seal, Coin, Medal, Maker	9	4	5	.	4	4	.	.	.	.
8. Tackle for Sports and Games.										
Toy Maker, Dealer	24	39	11	15	11	14	.	6	2	4
Fishing Rod, Tackle, Maker, Dealer	22	6	2	.	5	1	8	4	7	1
Apparatus for other Games, Maker, Dealer	3	2	1	2	2	.	.	.	.	.
11. PERSONS WORKING AND DEALING IN HOUSES, FURNITURE, AND DECORATIONS.										
1. Houses.										
Builder	1291	5	573	2	358	2	290	1	70	.
Carpenter, Joiner	14797	8	7642	2	3887	4	2547	1	721	1
Bricklayer	3571	3	2309	2	860	1	392	.	10	.
Mason	9363	6	4269	4	2590	2	1798	.	706	.
Slater, Tiler	776	2	316	.	323	2	109	.	28	.
Plasterer, Whitewasher	1044	.	313	.	373	.	274	.	84	.
Paperhanger	58	6	33	2	21	3	2	.	.	1
Plumber	2321	12	1166	6	761	4	281	1	113	1
Painter, Glazier	4124	18	2115	5	1317	11	537	2	155	.
2. Furniture and Fittings.										
Cabinet Maker, Upholsterer	2152	231	891	93	887	96	270	27	104	15
French Polisher	239	31	100	20	110	9	28	2	1	.
Furniture Broker, Dealer	124	46	85	22	32	13	5	10	2	1
Locksmith, Bellhanger	15	.	5	.	6	.	4	.	.	.
Gas Fitter	170	.	105	.	32	.	30	.	3	.
House and Shop Fittings—Maker, Dealer	32	.	10	.	15	.	7	.	.	.
Funeral Furniture Maker, Undertaker	22	5	11	1	10	3	1	.	.	.
Others	.	.	.	.	.	.	.	.	.	.
3. House Decorations.										
Wood Carver	95	.	36	.	45	.	12	.	2	.
Carver, Gilder	259	4	110	1	121	3	23	.	5	.
Dealer in Works of Art	17	1	6	1	8	.	3	.	.	.
Figure, Image—Maker, Dealer	14	1	5	.	8	1	.	.	1	.
Animal, Bird, &c., Preserver, Naturalist	17	1	7	1	5	.	4	.	1	.
Artificial Flower Maker	3	4	1	3	1	.	1	.	.	1
12. PERSONS WORKING AND DEALING IN CARRIAGES AND HARNESS.										
1. Carriages.										
Coachmaker	717	3	224	1	281	1	164	1	48	.
Railway Carriage, Railway Wagon, Maker	144	.	119	.	14	.	10	.	1	.
Wheelwright	113	1	54	.	27	.	21	.	11	1
Bicycle, Tricycle—Maker, Dealer	13	.	1	.	11	.	1	.	.	.
Others	583	.	378	.	166	.	35	.	4	.
2. Harness.										
Saddler, Harness, Whip, Maker	773	11	319	5	240	2	156	1	53	3
13. PERSONS WORKING AND DEALING IN SHIPS AND BOATS.										
1. Hull.										
Ship, Boat, Barge, Builder	10503	16	7069	10	3177	6	257	.	10	.
Shipwright, Ship Carpenter (ashore)	4500	.	3204	.	993	.	303	.	.	.
2. Masts, Rigging, &c.										
Mast, Yard, Oar, Block, Maker	260	.	195	.	50	.	15	.	.	.
Ship Rigger, Chandler, Fitter	312	6	192	3	105	3	15	.	.	.
Sail Maker	509	3	289	.	175	3	45	.	.	.

Table 10 *continued.*—OCCUPATIONS of MALES and FEMALES in the NORTHERN DIVISION and its REGISTRATION COUNTIES, and in each URBAN SANITARY DISTRICT of which the POPULATION exceeds 50,000 PERSONS.

OCCUPATIONS.	NORTHERN COUNTIES.		REGISTRATION COUNTIES. 38. DURHAM.		39. NORTHUMBERLAND.		40. CUMBERLAND.		41. WESTMORLAND.	
	Males.	Females.	Males.	Females.	Males.	Females.	Males.	Females.	Males.	Females.
14. PERSONS WORKING AND DEALING IN CHEMICALS AND COMPOUNDS.										
1. *Colouring Matter.*										
Dye, Paint, Manufacture	57	150	22	33	28	115	4	.	3	2
Ink, Blacking, Colouring Substance, Manufacture	25	5	19	5	5	.	1	.	.	.
2. *Explosives.*										
Gunpowder, Guncotton, Explosive Substance, Manufacture	58	4	1	.	1	.	.	.	56	4
Fusee, Fireworks, Explosive Article, Manufacture	10	10	2	.	8	9	.	.	.	1
3. *Drugs and other Chemicals and Compounds.*										
Chemist, Druggist	1013	27	465	14	324	8	185	5	39	.
Manufacturing Chemist	2940	36	2527	31	369	4	43	1	1	.
Alkali Manufacture	140	1	125	.	14	1	1	.	.	.
Drysalter	31	2	11	1	14	1	2	.	4	.
15. PERSONS WORKING AND DEALING IN TOBACCO AND PIPES.										
1. *Tobacco and Pipes.*										
Tobacco Manufacturer, Tobacconist	467	411	167	136	184	207	66	44	50	24
Tobacco Pipe, Snuff Box, &c., Maker	135	27	78	9	49	16	6	1	2	1
16. PERSONS WORKING AND DEALING IN FOOD AND LODGING.										
1. *Board and Lodging.*										
Innkeeper, Hotel Keeper, Publican	3351	929	1663	365	882	269	628	247	178	48
Lodging, Boarding House, Keeper	158	2103	78	779	44	769	26	445	10	119
Coffee, Eating House, Keeper	119	115	63	41	46	53	9	9	1	12
2. *Spirituous Drinks.*										
Hop—Merchant, Dealer	4	.	.	.	2	.	2	.	.	.
Maltster	138	.	59	.	30	.	34	.	15	.
Brewer	687	16	275	9	231	6	131	1	60	.
Beerseller. Ale, Porter, Cider, Dealer	271	125	162	69	93	28	11	23	5	5
Cellarman	168	18	78	1	75	16	14	1	1	.
Wine, Spirit—Merchant, Agent	386	31	129	9	136	10	98	10	23	2
3. *Food.*										
Milkseller, Dairyman	516	306	229	126	281	150	46	29	4	1
Cheesemonger, Butterman	36	11	16	3	17	5	1	3	2	.
Butcher, Meat Salesman	4778	147	2693	65	1409	40	534	36	142	7
Provision Curer, Dealer	792	435	327	155	345	227	103	44	17	9
Poulterer, Game Dealer	67	35	24	7	29	25	12	2	2	1
Fishmonger	409	178	191	86	155	81	50	9	13	2
Corn, Flour, Seed—Merchant, Dealer	349	20	122	6	148	12	54	1	25	1
Corn Miller	1069	23	375	7	304	7	312	6	78	3
Baker	1087	293	336	42	439	43	275	154	37	54
Confectioner, Pastrycook	493	886	272	369	161	245	48	221	12	51
Greengrocer, Fruiterer	1001	306	665	150	288	116	39	33	9	6
Mustard, Vinegar, Spice, Pickle—Maker, Dealer	13	4	5	2	8	2	.	.	.	.
Sugar Refiner	14	1	10	1	3	.	1	.	.	.
Grocer. Tea, Coffee, Chocolate—Maker, Dealer	7724	2093	4171	843	1990	392	1280	538	283	150
Ginger Beer, Mineral Water—Manufacturer, Dealer	228	21	122	12	65	8	38	1	3	.
Others dealing in Food	1	.	.	.	1	.	.	.	.	.
17. PERSONS WORKING AND DEALING IN TEXTILE FABRICS.										
1. *Wool and Worsted.*										
Woolstapler	48	6	18	6	9	.	6	.	15	.
Woollen Cloth Manufacture	740	606	99	62	79	17	225	256	337	271
Wool, Woollen goods—Dyer, Printer	47	1	2	.	4	.	8	.	33	1
Worsted, Stuff, Manufacture	111	333	71	296	.	2	.	1	40	34
Flannel Manufacture	.	.	.	.	.	.	.	.	.	.
Blanket Manufacture	.	.	.	.	.	.	.	.	.	.
Fuller	5	.	.	.	.	.	2	.	3	.
Cloth, Worsted, Stuff, Flannel, Blanket, Dealer	14	.	4	.	8	.	1	.	1	.
Others	.	.	.	.	.	.	.	.	.	.
2. *Silk.*										
Silk, Silk goods, Manufacture	10	13	5	2	2	4	3	6	.	1
Silk Dyer, Printer	4	.	.	.	1	.	1	.	2	.
Ribbon Manufacture	.	.	.	.	.	.	.	.	.	.
Crape, Gauze, Manufacture	.	.	.	.	.	.	.	.	.	.
Silk Merchant, Dealer	5	2	4	2	1	.	.	.	.	.

Table 10 *continued.*—OCCUPATIONS of MALES and FEMALES in the NORTHERN DIVISION and its REGISTRATION COUNTIES, and in each URBAN SANITARY DISTRICT of which the POPULATION exceeds 50,000 PERSONS.

OCCUPATIONS.	NORTHERN COUNTIES.		REGISTRATION COUNTIES. 38. DURHAM.		39. NORTHUMBERLAND.		40. CUMBERLAND.		41. WESTMORLAND.	
	Males.	Females.	Males.	Females.	Males.	Females.	Males.	Females.	Males.	Females.
3. Cotton and Flax										
Cotton, Cotton goods, Manufacture	[illegible]	1900	9	58	4	16	697	1797	9	5
Cotton, Calico—Printer, Dyer, Bleacher	217	23	2	.	.	.	215	23	.	.
Cotton, Calico—Warehouseman, Dealer	5	1	2	1	1	.	3	.	.	.
Flax, Linen—Manufacturer, Dealer	186	239	81	96	11	3	87	131	7	9
Lace Manufacturer, Dealer	3	15	1	8	1	6	.	2	1	.
Fustian Manufacturer, Dealer	.	.	.	.	.	.	.	.	.	.
Tape Manufacturer, Dealer	.	.	.	.	.	.	.	.	.	.
Thread Manufacturer, Dealer	72	212	2	9	.	2	70	201	.	.
4. Hemp and other Fibrous Materials.										
Hemp, Jute, Cocoa Fibre, Manufacture	75	87	3	17	3	2	2	2	68	66
Rope, Twine, Cord—Maker, Dealer	626	257	289	160	246	66	59	1	26	1
Mat Maker, Seller	38	5	13	2	13	3	8	.	2	.
Net Maker	2	14	.	3	1	9	1	2	.	.
Canvas, Sailcloth, Manufacture	65	35	31	14	24	7	10	14	.	.
Sacking, Sack, Bag—Maker, Dealer	5	28	2	4	3	23	.	1	.	.
Others working and dealing in Hemp	1	.	.	.	1	.	.	.	.	.
5. Mixed or Unspecified Materials.										
Weaver (undefined)	98	52	25	19	7	3	60	17	6	13
Dyer, Printer, Scourer, Bleacher, Calenderer (undefined)	188	60	53	29	65	28	65	12	5	.
Factory hand (Textile, undefined)	63	245	4	83	2	14	52	62	5	86
Felt Manufacture	2	5	1	.	1	5	.	.	.	.
Carpet, Rug, Manufacture	298	93	175	51	12	1	14	1	97	30
Manchester Warehouseman	5	.	1	.	2	.	2	.	.	.
Draper, Linen Draper, Mercer	4039	761	1747	402	1355	254	773	76	164	29
Fancy Goods (Textile), Manufacturer, Worker, Dealer	43	139	16	44	19	51	7	29	1	15
Trimming Maker, Dealer	.	6	.	2	.	1	.	3	.	.
Embroiderer	.	2	.	.	.	.	.	2	.	.
Others	.	8	.	.	.	.	.	.	.	8
18. PERSONS WORKING AND DEALING IN DRESS.										
1. Dress.										
Hatter, Hat Manufacture (not straw)	307	148	109	45	97	20	183	82	8	.
Straw—Hat, Bonnet, Plait, Manufacture	5	107	1	48	4	38	.	17	.	4
Tailor	7345	482	3063	230	2406	185	1473	57	403	11
Milliner, Dressmaker, Staymaker	31	20670	12	10087	8	5755	7	3521	4	907
Shawl Manufacture	.	3	.	1	.	2	.	.	.	.
Shirt Maker, Seamstress	2	1917	2	759	.	678	.	411	.	69
Hosiery Manufacture	11	70	4	33	2	19	4	10	1	14
Hosier, Haberdasher	146	115	43	60	45	20	50	24	7	2
Glover, Glove Maker	10	15	1	2	8	13	1	.	.	.
Button Maker, Dealer	2	.	.	.	7	.	.	.	1	.
Shoe, Boot—Maker, Dealer	6777	464	2894	138	2268	197	1175	39	442	80
Patten, Clog, Maker	537	11	92	4	69	.	331	7	45	.
Wig Maker, Hairdresser	744	15	405	6	219	7	105	1	15	1
Umbrella, Parasol, Stick—Maker, Dealer	40	9	24	4	15	3	6	2	4	.
Accoutrement Maker	.	.	.	.	.	.	.	.	.	.
Old Clothes Dealer, and others	36	64	17	36	16	9	2	8	1	1
19. PERSONS WORKING AND DEALING IN VARIOUS ANIMAL SUBSTANCES.										
1. In Grease, Gut, Bone, Horn, Ivory, and Whalebone.										
Tallow Chandler, Candle, Grease, Manufacture	191	10	115	4	51	5	20	1	6	.
Soap Boiler, Maker	24	1	2	.	22	1	.	.	.	.
Glue, Size, Gelatine, Isinglass—Maker, Dealer	2	10	.	9	2	1	.	.	.	.
Manure Manufacture	141	17	13	2	102	12	24	3	2	.
Bone, Horn, Ivory, Tortoise-shell—Worker, Dealer	5	2	.	.	2	2	3	.	.	.
Comb Maker	5	3	.	1	1	.	.	.	4	2
Others	6	.	2	.	4	.	.	.	.	.
2. In Skins.										
Furrier, Skinner	145	63	11	10	59	49	60	4	15	.
Tanner, Fellmonger	437	3	99	1	168	2	141	.	29	.
Currier	599	12	160	4	263	5	118	3	49	.
Leather Goods, Portmanteau, Bag, Strap, &c.—Maker, Dealer	63	3	9	.	44	2	5	.	5	1
Parchment, Vellum—Maker, Dealer	.	.	.	.	.	.	.	.	.	.
3. In Hair and Feathers.										
Hair, Bristle—Worker, Dealer	2	2	1	.	1	2	.	.	.	.
Brush, Broom, Maker	203	27	68	11	113	14	7	.	15	2
Quill, Feather—Dresser, Dealer	6	9	3	2	3	6	.	1	.	.

Table 10 *continued*.—OCCUPATIONS of MALES and FEMALES in the NORTHERN DIVISION and its REGISTRATION COUNTIES, and in each URBAN SANITARY DISTRICT of which the POPULATION exceeds 50,000 PERSONS.

OCCUPATIONS.	NORTHERN COUNTIES.		REGISTRATION COUNTIES. 38. DURHAM.		39. NORTHUMBERLAND.		40. CUMBERLAND.		41. WESTMORLAND.	
	Males.	Females.	Males.	Females.	Males.	Females.	Males.	Females.	Males.	Females.
20. PERSONS WORKING AND DEALING IN VARIOUS VEGETABLE SUBSTANCES.										
1. In Oils, Gums, and Resins.										
Oil Miller, Oil Cake—Maker, Dealer	80	2	33	3	42	.	1	.	4	.
Oil and Colourman	24	1	15	1	9	.	.	.	.	.
Floor Cloth, Oil Cloth, Manufacture	16	1	13	.	2	1	.	.	1	.
Japanner	17	1	.	.	17	1	.	.	.	.
India Rubber, Gutta Percha—Worker, Dealer	13	1	2	.	11	1	.	.	.	.
Waterproof Goods—Maker, Dealer	29	2	1	.	28	2	.	.	.	.
Others	9	1	3	1	.	.	6	.	.	.
2. In Cane, Rush, and Straw.										
Willow, Cane, Rush—Worker, Dealer, Basketmaker	183	18	56	9	60	1	44	8	23	.
Hay, Straw (not plait), Chaff—Cutter, Dealer	85	1	62	.	17	.	5	1	1	.
Thatcher	7	.	1	.	5	.	.	.	1	.
3. In Wood and Bark.										
Timber, Wood—Merchant, Dealer	622	15	390	9	140	5	74	.	18	1
Sawyer	1460	.	811	.	369	.	204	.	76	.
Lath, Wooden Fence, Hurdle, Maker	79	1	46	1	25	.	6	.	2	.
Wood Turner, Box Maker	615	20	107	1	63	14	160	2	285	3
Cooper, Hoop Maker, Bender	1506	4	918	1	391	2	103	1	94	.
Cork, Bark—Cutter, Worker, Dealer	112	4	33	.	58	3	17	1	4	.
Others	10	1	10	.	.	1	.	.	.	.
4. In Paper.										
Paper Manufacture	659	500	401	354	79	61	57	37	122	48
Envelope Maker	2	3	.	1	.	1	1	1	1	.
Stationer, Law Stationer	310	130	129	56	129	36	43	26	9	12
Card, Pattern Card, Maker	1	.	.	.	.	.	1	.	.	.
Paper Stainer	37	6	1	.	36	.	.	6	.	.
Paper Box, Paper Bag, Maker	2	48	1	16	1	14	.	16	.	2
Ticket, Label, Writer	21	2	4	.	16	2	1	.	.	.
Others	109	.	65	.	43	.	11	.	.	.
21. PERSONS WORKING AND DEALING IN VARIOUS MINERAL SUBSTANCES.										
1. Miners.										
Coal Miner	91424	250	65398	117	20734	18	5278	115	14	.
Ironstone Miner	5826	13	279	.	67	.	5478	13	2	.
Copper Miner	12	.	3	.	.	.	8	.	1	.
Tin Miner	3	.	2	.	.	.	1	.	.	.
Lead Miner	2901	.	1448	.	644	.	645	.	164	.
Miner in other, or undefined, Minerals	172	.	98	.	38	.	33	.	3	.
Mine Service	448	5	262	.	101	5	77	.	8	.
2. Coal, Coal Gas, &c.										
Coal Merchant, Dealer	781	94	408	14	217	11	110	69	46	.
Coalheaver	1297	.	866	.	378	.	44	.	9	.
Coke, Charcoal, Peat—Cutter, Burner, Dealer	3042	4	2797	3	179	.	65	1	1	.
Gas Works Service	823	.	474	.	184	.	126	.	39	.
3. Stone, Clay, and Road Making.										
Stone Quarrier	3185	.	1968	.	638	.	505	.	74	.
Stone Cutter, Dresser, Dealer	217	.	72	.	74	.	43	.	28	.
Slate Quarrier	204	.	2	.	1	.	84	.	117	.
Slate Worker, Dealer	28	1	10	.	9	.	7	1	2	.
Limeburner	113	.	65	.	21	.	20	.	7	.
Clay, Sand, Gravel, Chalk—Labourer, Dealer	36	4	11	2	18	.	5	2	1	.
Fossil, Coprolite—Digger, Dealer	.	.	.	.	.	.	.	.	.	.
Well Sinker, Borer	99	.	44	.	9	.	46	.	.	.
Plaster, Cement, Manufacture	254	5	180	5	71	.	3	.	.	.
Brick, Tile—Maker, Burner, Dealer	2406	112	1523	78	639	21	297	13	7	.
Paviour	168	.	60	.	80	.	25	.	3	.
Road Contractor, Surveyor, Inspector	86	.	15	.	48	.	20	.	3	.
Road Labourer	734	.	331	.	262	.	117	.	24	.
Railway Contractor	71	.	26	.	18	.	21	.	6	.
Platelayer	2464	.	1424	.	504	.	427	.	109	.
Railway Labourer, Navvy	2111	.	728	.	407	.	633	.	343	.
Others	34	9	3	3	.	1	30	3	1	2
4. Earthenware and Glass.										
Earthenware, China, Porcelain, Manufacture	932	397	496	141	392	253	39	2	5	1
Glass Manufacture	3043	172	2732	152	308	20	1	.	2	.
Earthenware, China, Glass, Dealer	166	89	61	29	64	28	37	24	4	8
5. Salt.										
Salt Maker, Dealer	12	1	3	1	8	.	1	.	.	.

Table 10 *continued*.—OCCUPATIONS of MALES and FEMALES in the NORTHERN DIVISION and its REGISTRATION COUNTIES, and in each URBAN SANITARY DISTRICT of which the POPULATION exceeds 50,000 PERSONS.

OCCUPATIONS.	NORTHERN COUNTIES.		REGISTRATION COUNTIES. 38. DURHAM.		39. NORTHUMBERLAND.		40. CUMBERLAND.		41. WESTMORLAND.	
	Males.	Females.	Males.	Females.	Males.	Females.	Males.	Females.	Males.	Females.
6. Water.										
Waterworks Service	137	2	70	1	47	1	8	.	6	.
Others	4	.	.	.	3	.	1	.	.	.
7. Precious Metals and Jewellery.										
Goldsmith, Silversmith, Jeweller	236	22	113	10	87	7	31	3	5	2
Gold, Silver, Beater	5	.	1	.	4	.	.	.	.	.
Lapidary	11	3	11	1	.	2	.	.	.	.
Others	3	1	2	.	1	1	.	.	.	.
8. Iron and Steel.										
Blacksmith	11655	15	7007	7	2873	5	1503	1	272	2
Whitesmith	367	.	168	.	154	.	33	.	12	.
Nail Manufacture	246	13	107	10	34	2	88	1	17	.
Anchor, Chain, Manufacture	573	2	427	2	141	.	4	.	1	.
Other Iron and Steel Manufactures	23313	22	17567	20	2507	1	3196	1	53	.
Ironmonger. Hardware Dealer, Merchant	869	57	344	19	296	22	192	10	37	6
9. Copper.										
Copper, Copper goods—Manufacturer, Worker, Dealer	666	2	468	2	196	.	5	.	.	.
10. Tin and Zinc.										
Tin, Tin Plate, Tin goods—Manufacturer, Worker, Dealer	867	85	386	2	241	4	237	39	33	.
Zinc, Zinc Goods—Manufacturer, Worker, Dealer	67	.	1	.	2	.	64	.	.	.
11. Lead.										
Lead, Leaden goods—Manufacturer, Worker, Dealer	651	37	291	22	320	15	35	.	5	.
12. In Other, Mixed, or Unspecified, Metals.										
Metal Refiner, Worker, Turner, Dealer	360	.	255	.	103	.	2	.	.	.
Brass, Bronze, Manufacture. Brazier	1186	4	754	2	404	2	25	.	3	.
Metal Burnisher, Lacquerer	3	.	3	.	.	.	.	.	.	.
White Metal, Plated Ware, Manufacture. Pewterer	1	.	1	.	.	.	.	.	.	.
Wire Maker, Worker, Weaver, Drawer	214	24	121	10	84	12	9	2	.	.
Bolt, Nut, Rivet, Screw, Staple, Maker	198	7	156	4	20	.	22	3	.	.
Lamp, Lantern, Candlestick, Maker	21	.	11	.	10	.	.	.	.	.
Clasp, Buckle, Hinge, Maker	7	.	7	.	.	.	.	.	.	.
Fancy Chain, Gilt Toy, Maker	7	1	7	.	.	1	.	.	.	.
Others	5	.	4	.	1	.	.	.	.	.
22. PERSONS WORKING AND DEALING IN GENERAL OR UNSPECIFIED COMMODITIES.										
1. Makers and Dealers (General or Undefined).										
General Shopkeeper, Dealer	858	1254	459	661	238	472	122	84	39	37
Pawnbroker	276	140	160	79	83	55	30	14	3	1
Costermonger, Huckster, Street Seller	1744	1450	882	624	506	553	274	232	82	41
Manufacturer, Manager, Superintendent (undefined)	317	10	187	1	97	8	30	1	3	.
Contractor (undefined)	253	1	157	1	59	.	33	.	4	.
2. Mechanics and Labourers (General or Undefined).										
General Labourer	36413	301	21440	108	8597	40	4077	148	1390	5
Engine Driver, Stoker, Fireman (not railway, marine, nor agricultural)	7272	.	4622	.	1514	.	1086	.	50	.
Artisan, Mechanic (undefined)	2275	64	1489	15	577	23	174	25	35	1
Apprentice (undefined)	268	7	189	6	64	1	11	.	4	.
Factory Labourer (undefined)	814	266	385	72	243	48	170	145	16	.
Machinist, Machine Worker (undefined)	247	153	170	84	70	11	7	15	.	43
23. PERSONS WORKING AND DEALING IN REFUSE MATTERS.										
1. Refuse Matters.										
Town Drainage Service	78	.	34	.	32	.	22	.	.	.
Chimney Sweep, Soot Merchant	222	4	95	3	97	1	24	.	6	.
Scavenger, Crossing Sweeper	74	2	30	.	19	2	23	.	2	.
Rag Gatherer, Dealer	66	64	34	19	7	32	19	13	6	.
VI. UNOCCUPIED CLASS.										
24. PERSONS WITHOUT SPECIFIED OCCUPATIONS										
Persons returned by Property, Rank, &c., and not by special occupation	203962	552995	111225	304771	52818	146094	31390	81188	8529	21012
Children under 5 years of age	119242	118511	67149	66419	30509	30363	17449	17527	4135	4202

TABLE 10 *continued*.—OCCUPATIONS of MALES and FEMALES in the NORTHERN DIVISION and its REGISTRATION COUNTIES, and in each URBAN SANITARY DISTRICT of which the POPULATION exceeds 50,000 PERSONS.

OCCUPATIONS.	URBAN SANITARY DISTRICTS.							
	SUNDERLAND.		SOUTH SHIELDS.		GATESHEAD.		NEWCASTLE-UPON-TYNE.	
	Males.	Females.	Males.	Females.	Males.	Females.	Males.	Females.
TOTAL - - -	57153	59415	28373	28502	32091	32812	71100	74259
I. PROFESSIONAL CLASS.								
1. PERSONS ENGAGED IN THE GENERAL OR LOCAL GOVERNMENT OF THE COUNTRY.								
1. *National Government.*								
Peer, M.P., Privy Councillor (not otherwise described)	.	.	.	.	.	.	1	.
Civil Service (officers and clerks) - -	76	3	45	1	36	3	103	4
Civil Service (messengers, &c.) - -	48	2	23	.	41	.	93	.
Prison Officer, &c. - - - -	.	.	.	.	1	.	17	7
2. *Local Government.*								
Police - - - - -	145	.	79	.	67	.	244	.
Municipal, Parish, Union, District, Officer	47	2	26	.	17	6	74	7
Other Local or County Official - -	18	.	8	.	7	.	19	.
3. *East Indian and Colonial Service.*								
East Indian and Colonial Service - -	.	.	.	.	.	.	.	.
2. PERSONS ENGAGED IN THE DEFENCE OF THE COUNTRY.								
1. *Army (at Home).*								
Army Officer (effective or retired) - -	10	.	1	.	2	.	24	.
Soldier and Non-Commissioned Officer -	168	.	.	.	10	.	276	.
Militia, Yeomanry, Volunteers -	7	.	.	.	4	.	8	.
Army Pensioner - - - -	16	.	5	.	17	.	50	.
2. *Navy (ashore or in port).*								
Navy Officer (effective or retired) - -	6	.	.	.	2	.	3	.
Seaman, R.N. - - - -	32	.	5	.	2	.	5	.
Royal Marines (officers and men)	.	.	1	.	.	.	2	.
Navy Pensioner - - - -	16	.	6	.	2	.	4	.
3. PERSONS ENGAGED IN PROFESSIONAL OCCUPATIONS (WITH THEIR IMMEDIATE SUBORDINATES).								
1. *Clerical Profession.*								
Clergyman (Established Church) - -	31	.	16	.	18	.	36	.
Roman Catholic Priest - - -	9	.	3	.	2	.	18	.
Minister, Priest, of other religious bodies	42	.	15	.	18	.	48	.
Missionary, Scripture Reader, Itinerant Preacher - - - - -	19	8	4	3	6	4	24	16
Nun, Sister of Charity - - -	.	17	.	.	.	.	.	37
Theological Student - - - -	19	.	1	.	1	.	4	.
Church, Chapel, Cemetery—Officer, Servant - - - - -	5	13	6	3	8	4	18	13
2. *Legal Profession.*								
Barrister, Solicitor - - - -	62	.	23	.	14	.	76	.
Law Student - - - - -	8	.	1	.	1	.	12	.
Law Clerk, and others connected with Law - - - - -	67	.	39	.	34	.	165	1
3. *Medical Profession.*								
Physician, Surgeon, General Practitioner	54	.	18	.	24	.	86	.
Dentist - - - - - -	15	.	2	.	6	.	33	.
Medical Student, Assistant - -	24	.	10	.	13	.	66	.
Midwife - - - - -	.	.	.	6	.	5	.	10
Subordinate Medical Service - -	10	92	3	52	3	30	15	175
4. *Teachers.*								
Schoolmaster - - - - -	125	323	97	310	86	242	177	499
Teacher, Professor, Lecturer - -	19	74	8	13	12	16	49	59
School Service, and others concerned in Teaching - - - - -	7	1	5	.	9	3	13	2
5. *Literary and Scientific Persons.*								
Author, Editor, Journalist - -	11	.	1	1	4	1	23	3
Reporter, Short-hand Writer - -	14	.	9	.	5	.	25	.
Persons engaged in Scientific Pursuits -	2	.	10	.	5	.	13	.
Literary, Scientific, Institution, Service, &c. - - - - -	4	1	2	.	12	.	8	.
6. *Engineers and Surveyors.*								
Civil Engineer - - - -	19	.	9	.	20	.	86	.
Mining Engineer - - - -	16	.	2	.	5	.	38	.
Land, House, Ship, Surveyor - -	9	.	3	.	10	.	17	.
7. *Artists.*								
Painter (artist) - - - -	13	3	12	1	9	2	43	12
Engraver (artist) - - - -	2	.	.	.	3	.	12	.
Sculptor - - - - - -	4	.	.	.	4	.	2	.
Architect - - - - -	32	.	16	.	17	.	68	.
Musician, Music Master - - -	64	36	34	22	26	17	122	69
Art Student - - - -	.	.	6	.	.	.	7	6
Photographer - - - - -	22	2	14	3	10	26	57	18
Actor - - - - - -	11	4	17	13	1	1	31	37
Art, Music, Theatre, Service - -	2	1	5	1	3	.	12	6

Table 10 *continued*.—OCCUPATIONS of MALES and FEMALES in the NORTHERN DIVISION and its REGISTRATION COUNTIES, and in each URBAN SANITARY DISTRICT of which the POPULATION exceeds 50,000 PERSONS.

OCCUPATIONS.	URBAN SANITARY DISTRICTS.							
	SUNDERLAND.		SOUTH SHIELDS.		GATESHEAD.		NEWCASTLE-UPON-TYNE.	
	Males.	Females.	Males.	Females.	Males.	Females.	Males.	Females.
8. *Persons engaged in Exhibitions, Shows, Games, &c.*								
Performer, Showman, Exhibition, Service	2	.	15	5	2	.	21	3
Billiard, Cricket, & other Games, Service	13	1	4	.	5	.	25	1
II. DOMESTIC CLASS.								
4. PERSONS ENGAGED IN DOMESTIC OFFICES OR SERVICES.								
1. *Domestic Service.*								
Domestic Coachman, Groom	115	.	14	.	56	.	240	.
Domestic Gardener	105	.	13	.	53	.	175	4
Domestic Indoor Servant	40	4402	7	1878	20	1972	101	7144
Lodge, Gate, Park, Keeper (not Government)	2	.	2	.	2	.	13	1
Inn, Hotel, Servant	143	47	82	81	79	21	371	138
College, Club, Service	7	7	.	1	1	.	19	1
2. *Other Service.*								
Office Keeper (not Government)	9	41	2	9	2	4	18	40
Cook (not domestic)	.	3	.	4	1	5	10	38
Charwoman	.	236	.	85	.	115	.	585
Washing and Bathing Service	5	347	1	123	1	128	11	516
Hospital and Institution Service	14	22	.	5	.	8	16	87
Others engaged in Service	.	.	3	4	2	.	9	2
III. COMMERCIAL CLASS.								
5. PERSONS ENGAGED IN COMMERCIAL OCCUPATIONS.								
1. *Merchants and Agents.*								
Merchant	19	.	6	.	29	.	96	.
Broker, Agent, Factor	224	5	75	2	127	.	485	1
Auctioneer, Appraiser, Valuer, House Agent	55	1	23	.	29	.	76	1
Accountant	87	.	15	.	54	.	146	.
Salesman, Buyer (not otherwise described)	3	19	2	16	4	15	10	44
Commercial Traveller	129	.	30	.	107	.	559	.
Commercial Clerk	723	18	307	8	703	20	1928	65
Officer of Commercial Company, Guild, Society, &c.	1	.	.	.	.	.	7	.
2. *Dealers in Money.*								
Banker	2	.	2	.	.	.	4	.
Bank Service	36	.	18	.	17	.	116	1
Bill Discounter, Bill Broker, Finance Agent	7	.	2	.	1	.	8	.
3. *Persons occupied in Insurance.*								
Life, House, Ship, &c., Insurance Service	80	.	20	.	52	.	133	2
6. PERSONS ENGAGED IN CONVEYANCE OF MEN, GOODS, AND MESSAGES.								
1. *On Railways.*								
Railway Engine Driver, Stoker	97	.	41	.	202	.	92	.
Railway Guard	43	.	23	.	83	.	138	.
Pointsman, Level Crossing Man	9	.	13	.	10	.	21	.
Other Railway Officials and Servants	232	1	167	2	357	11	753	10
2. *On Roads.*								
Toll Collector, Turnpike Gate Keeper	3	.	1	.	2	.	18	3
Omnibus, Coach, Cab, Owner—Livery Stable Keeper	16	1	6	1	5	.	32	1
Cabman, Flyman, Coachman (not domestic)	64	.	17	.	30	.	137	.
Carman, Carrier, Carter, Haulier	603	.	334	1	414	.	1301	1
Tramway Companies' Service	44	.	.	.	3	.	26	.
Wheel Chair Proprietor, Attendant, &c.	.	.	.	.	.	.	.	.
3. *On Canals, Rivers and Seas.*								
Inland Navigation Service	2	.	1	.	.	2	5	.
Bargeman, Lighterman, Waterman	189	1	237	.	96	.	829	1
Navigation Service (on shore)	110	1	34	.	6	1	80	1
Seaman (Merchant Service)	3317	.	3289	.	140	.	1014	.
Pilot	143	.	204	.	.	.	7	.
Ship Steward, Cook	91	1	143	4	2	.	54	10
Boatman on Seas	.	.	15	.	.	.	.	.
Harbour, Dock, Wharf, Lighthouse, Service	178	.	243	.	9	.	405	.
4. *In Storage.*								
Warehouseman (not Manchester)	42	1	5	.	46	.	150	1
Meter, Weigher	3	.	11	.	17	.	12	.
5. *In conveying Messages, Porterage, &c.*								
Messenger, Porter, Watchman (not Railway nor Government)	352	8	176	2	272	2	840	24
Telegraph, Telephone, Service	38	3	73	1	47	6	155	21

Table 10 *continued*.—OCCUPATIONS of MALES and FEMALES in the NORTHERN DIVISION and its REGISTRATION COUNTIES, and in each URBAN SANITARY DISTRICT of which the POPULATION exceeds 50,000 PERSONS.

OCCUPATIONS.	URBAN SANITARY DISTRICTS.							
	SUNDERLAND.		SOUTH SHIELDS.		GATESHEAD.		NEWCASTLE-UPON-TYNE.	
	Males.	Females.	Males.	Females.	Males.	Females.	Males.	Females.
IV. AGRICULTURAL CLASS.								
7. PERSONS ENGAGED IN AGRICULTURE.								
1. *In Fields and Pastures.*								
Farmer, Grazier	27	3	10	.	19	1	27	1
Farmer's, Grazier's—Son, Grandson, Brother, Nephew*	8	.	.	.	3	.	6	.
Farm Bailiff	1	.	1	.	2	.	5	.
Agricultural Labourer, Farm Servant, Cottager	119	48	33	16	80	92	151	36
Shepherd	.	.	1	.	.	.	6	.
Land Drainage Service (not in towns)	.	.	.	.	.	.	.	.
Agricultural Machine—Proprietor, Attendant	1	.	.	.	1	.	1	.
Agricultural Student, Pupil	.	.	3	.	1	.	2	.
Others engaged in, or connected with, Agriculture	.	.	.	.	.	.	1	.
2. *In Woods.*								
Woodman	2	.	.	.	2	.	6	.
3. *In Gardens.*								
Nurseryman, Seedsman, Florist	5	.	1	.	13	.	11	.
Gardener (not domestic)	71	4	23	.	56	1	49	7
8. PERSONS ENGAGED ABOUT ANIMALS.								
1. *About Animals.*								
Horse Proprietor, Breeder, Dealer	4	.	1	.	17	.	21	.
Groom, Horse-keeper, Horse-breaker	55	.	25	.	31	.	171	.
Veterinary Surgeon, Farrier	12	.	2	.	17	.	34	.
Cattle, Sheep, Pig—Dealer, Salesman	2	.	.	.	3	.	56	1
Drover	1	.	.	.	4	.	28	.
Gamekeeper	1	.	.	.	2	.	8	.
Dog, Bird, Animal—Keeper, Dealer	.	.	.	.	.	.	2	.
Vermin destroyer	.	.	.	.	2	.	.	.
Fisherman	95	1	19	2	.	1	18	.
Knacker, Catsmeat Dealer, &c., &c.	.	.	.	.	1	.	3	.
V. INDUSTRIAL CLASS.								
9. PERSONS WORKING AND DEALING IN BOOKS, PRINTS AND MAPS.								
1. *Books.*								
Publisher, Bookseller, Librarian	22	3	9	1	13	2	63	11
Music—Publisher, Seller, Printer	3	.	.	.	2	.	13	3
Bookbinder	19	10	2	3	30	38	89	93
Printer	205	2	75	.	150	6	330	34
Newspaper Agent, News Room Keeper	15	5	17	6	16	4	58	16
Others	.	.	.	.	.	.	.	.
2. *Prints and Maps.*								
Lithographer, Lithographic Printer	9	.	3	.	16	1	59	.
Copper Plate and Steel Plate Printer	1	.	.	.	1	.	2	.
Map and Print—Colourer, Seller	.	.	.	.	.	1	.	.
10. PERSONS WORKING AND DEALING IN MACHINES AND IMPLEMENTS.								
1. *Machines.*								
Engine, Machine, Maker	413	.	171	2	333	2	999	6
Millwright	29	.	7	.	84	.	94	.
Fitter, Turner (Engine and Machine)	1018	.	315	.	1105	.	1662	.
Boiler Maker	653	.	271	.	370	.	767	.
Spinning and Weaving Machine Maker	1	.	.	.	.	.	.	.
Agricultural Machine and Implement Maker	.	.	4	.	2	.	4	.
Domestic Machinery—Maker, Dealer	.	.	.	.	.	.	6	.
2. *Tools and Implements.*								
Tool Maker, Dealer	3	.	.	.	5	.	13	1
Cutler, Scissors Maker	6	.	2	.	9	.	14	.
File Maker	28	.	.	.	4	.	21	.
Saw Maker	5	.	1	.	.	.	12	.
Pin Maker	.	1	1	.	1	.	.	.
Needle Maker	1	.	.	.	.	.	.	.
Steel Pen Maker	.	.	.	.	.	.	1	1
Pencil Maker (Wood)	.	.	.	.	.	.	.	.
Domestic Implement Maker	.	.	.	.	.	.	.	.
3. *Watches and Philosophical Instruments.*								
Watch Maker, Clock Maker	62	2	31	.	32	.	114	3
Philosophical Instrument Maker, Optician	44	.	14	.	5	1	19	.
Electrical Apparatus Maker	4	.	1	.	8	4	17	1
Weighing and Measuring Apparatus Maker	.	.	.	.	9	.	13	.

* Only male relatives living with the farmer or grazier, and therefore presumably engaged in agriculture, are included above.

Table 10 *continued*.—OCCUPATIONS of MALES and FEMALES in the NORTHERN DIVISION and its REGISTRATION COUNTIES, and in each URBAN SANITARY DISTRICT of which the POPULATION exceeds 50,000 PERSONS.

OCCUPATIONS.	URBAN SANITARY DISTRICTS.							
	SUNDERLAND.		SOUTH SHIELDS.		GATESHEAD.		NEWCASTLE-UPON-TYNE.	
	Males.	Females.	Males.	Females.	Males.	Females.	Males.	Females.
4. Surgical Instruments.								
Surgical Instrument Maker	.	.	.	.	1	.	4	.
5. Arms and Ordnance.								
Gunsmith, Gun Manufacturer	2	.	.	.	1	.	45	1
Ordnance Manufacturer	.	.	.	.	.	.	4	.
Sword, Bayonet—Maker, Cutler	.	.	.	.	.	.	.	.
Others	.	.	.	.	.	.	1	.
6. Musical Instruments.								
Musical Instrument Maker, Dealer	9	.	.	.	5	.	35	.
7. Type, Dies, Medals, Coins.								
Type Cutter, Founder	.	.	1	.	.	.	2	.
Die, Seal, Coin, Medal, Maker	.	.	1	.	2	.	4	4
8. Tackle for Sports and Games.								
Toy Maker, Dealer	1	2	.	.	2	2	9	12
Fishing Rod, Tackle, Maker, Dealer	.	.	.	.	.	.	1	.
Apparatus for other Games, Maker, Dealer	.	.	.	.	.	.	.	.
11. PERSONS WORKING AND DEALING IN HOUSES, FURNITURE, AND DECORATIONS.								
1. Houses.								
Builder	93	.	64	1	53	.	181	1
Carpenter, Joiner	1217	.	572	.	693	3	[illegible]	1
Bricklayer	333	.	189	.	212	.	[illegible]	.
Mason	564	.	267	2	236	.	[illegible]	2
Slater, Tiler	86	.	29	.	33	.	165	.
Plasterer, Whitewasher	40	.	33	.	55	.	[illegible]	.
Paperhanger	17	2	3	.	4	.	[illegible]	1
Plumber	251	3	113	.	164	.	[illegible]	1
Painter, Glazier	601	1	189	.	230	1	[illegible]	7
2. Furniture and Fittings.								
Cabinet Maker, Upholsterer	246	28	54	3	64	15	[illegible]	80
French Polisher	36	17	4	.	13	.	[illegible]	6
Furniture Broker, Dealer	28	6	11	1	9	10	[illegible]	8
Locksmith, Bellhanger	2	.	.	.	2	.	[illegible]	.
Gas Fitter	15	.	10	.	8	.	17	.
House and Shop Fittings—Maker, Dealer	1	.	1	.	1	.	12	.
Funeral Furniture Maker, Undertaker	8	1	.	.	5	.	[illegible]	6
Others	.	.	.	.	.	.	.	.
3. House Decorations.								
Wood Carver	18	.	3	.	1	.	32	.
Carver, Gilder	45	.	15	.	7	.	85	3
Dealer in Works of Art	2	.	1	.	.	.	8	1
Figure, Image—Maker, Dealer	1	.	.	.	.	.	5	.
Animal, Bird, &c., Preserver, Naturalist	1	1	.	.	.	.	3	.
Artificial Flower Maker	1	3	.	.	.	.	.	.
12. PERSONS WORKING AND DEALING IN CARRIAGES AND HARNESS.								
1. Carriages.								
Coachmaker	25	.	5	.	27	.	201	1
Railway Carriage, Railway Wagon, Maker	5	.	.	.	5	.	7	.
Wheelwright	3	.	4	.	7	.	21	.
Bicycle, Tricycle—Maker, Dealer	.	.	1	.	.	.	14	.
Others	31	.	24	.	25	.	53	.
2. Harness.								
Saddler, Harness, Whip, Maker	35	.	9	.	45	.	197	.
13. PERSONS WORKING AND DEALING IN SHIPS AND BOATS.								
1. Hull.								
Ship, Boat, Barge, Builder	2356	8	439	1	41	.	510	1
Shipwright, Ship Carpenter (ashore)	1054	.	504	.	32	.	185	.
2. Masts, Rigging, &c.								
Mast, Yard, Oar, Block, Maker	89	.	48	.	1	.	11	3
Ship Rigger, Chandler, Fitter	74	.	43	2	3	.	17	2
Sail Maker	146	.	80	.	1	.	74	.

Table 10 *continued.*—Occupations of Males and Females in the Northern Division and its Registration Counties, and in each Urban Sanitary District of which the Population exceeds 50,000 Persons.

Occupations.	Urban Sanitary Districts.							
	Sunderland.		South Shields.		Gateshead.		Newcastle-upon-Tyne.	
	Males.	Females.	Males.	Females.	Males.	Females.	Males.	Females.
14. Persons working and dealing in Chemicals and Compounds.								
1. *Colouring Matter.*								
Dye, Paint, Manufacture	5	1	6	2	.	7	21	36
Ink, Blacking, Colouring Substance, Manufacture	1	.	.	.	1	.	2	.
2. *Explosives.*								
Gunpowder, Guncotton, Explosive Substance, Manufacture	.	.	.	.	.	.	.	.
Fusee, Fireworks, Explosive Article, Manufacture	.	.	.	.	1	.	5	9
3. *Drugs and other Chemicals and Compounds.*								
Chemist, Druggist	103	1	35	1	57	5	162	8
Manufacturing Chemist	15	.	401	1	443	3	91	4
Alkali Manufacture	.	.	99	.	6	.	7	1
Drysalter	2	.	.	.	3	.	9	1
15. Persons working and dealing in Tobacco and Pipes.								
1. *Tobacco and Pipes.*								
Tobacco Manufacturer, Tobacconist	66	7	18	5	27	83	113	185
Tobacco Pipe, Snuff Box, &c., Maker	11	3	6	.	42	5	17	7
16. Persons working and Dealing in Food and Lodging.								
1. *Board and Lodging.*								
Innkeeper, Hotel Keeper, Publican	182	42	113	20	102	23	304	98
Lodging, Boarding House, Keeper	16	165	12	86	8	67	21	376
Coffee, Eating House, Keeper	12	14	9	2	7	4	85	43
2. *Spirituous Drinks.*								
Hop—Merchant, Dealer	.	.	.	.	.	.	1	.
Maltster	9	.	.	.	10	.	10	.
Brewer	66	3	21	1	29	1	111	5
Beerseller. Ale, Porter, Cider, Dealer	32	21	10	6	10	2	56	20
Cellarman	23	.	5	1	15	.	54	15
Wine, Spirit—Merchant, Agent	29	2	5	.	10	.	89	.
3. *Food.*								
Milkseller, Dairyman	28	16	14	10	29	9	157	78
Cheesemonger, Butterman	2	1	3	.	5	.	17	3
Butcher, Meat Salesman	475	6	230	7	226	4	615	17
Provision Curer, Dealer	67	20	29	21	103	82	257	182
Poulterer, Game Dealer	3	2	2	.	2	1	18	17
Fishmonger	45	41	20	15	7	6	67	29
Corn, Flour, Seed—Merchant, Dealer	13	1	1	1	27	1	92	6
Corn Miller	52	.	2	.	31	.	97	2
Baker	89	7	59	4	52	2	200	16
Confectioner, Pastrycook	39	90	25	26	22	31	112	126
Greengrocer, Fruiterer	93	35	34	16	37	15	167	75
Mustard, Vinegar, Spice, Pickle—Maker, Dealer	.	.	.	.	2	.	8	2
Sugar Refiner	1	.	.	.	.	.	2	.
Grocer. Tea, Coffee, Chocolate—Maker, Dealer	616	146	291	83	284	56	737	138
Ginger Beer, Mineral Water—Manufacturer, Dealer	17	4	13	.	13	4	44	8
Others dealing in Food	.	.	.	.	.	.	1	.
17. Persons working and dealing in Textile Fabrics.								
1. *Wool and Worsted.*								
Woolstapler	.	.	.	.	1	.	.	.
Woollen Cloth Manufacture	5	3	.	.	.	.	2	.
Wool, Woollen goods—Dyer, Printer	.	.	.	.	.	.	6	2
Worsted, Stuff, Manufacture	.	.	.	.	.	.	2	.
Flannel Manufacture	.	.	.	.	.	.	.	1
Blanket Manufacture	.	.	.	.	.	.	.	.
Fuller	.	.	.	.	.	.	.	.
Cloth, Worsted, Stuff, Flannel, Blanket, Dealer	.	.	.	.	.	.	5	.
Others	.	.	.	.	.	.	.	.
2. *Silk.*								
Silk, Silk goods, Manufacture	2	.	.	.	.	1	.	3
Silk Dyer, Printer	.	.	.	.	.	.	1	.
Ribbon Manufacture	.	.	.	.	.	.	.	.
Crape, Gauze, Manufacture	.	.	.	.	.	.	.	.
Silk Merchant, Dealer	1	1	.	.	.	.	1	.

Table 10 *continued*.—OCCUPATIONS of MALES and FEMALES in the NORTHERN DIVISION and its REGISTRATION COUNTIES, and in each URBAN SANITARY DISTRICT of which the POPULATION exceeds 50,000 PERSONS.

OCCUPATIONS.	URBAN SANITARY DISTRICTS.							
	SUNDERLAND.		SOUTH SHIELDS.		GATESHEAD.		NEWCASTLE-UPON-TYNE.	
	Males.	Females.	Males.	Females.	Males.	Females.	Males.	Females.
3. Cotton and Flax								
Cotton, Cotton goods, Manufacture	.	3	.	2	2	.	6	12
Cotton, Calico—Printer, Dyer, Bleacher	.	.	.	.	1	.	.	.
Cotton, Calico—Warehouseman, Dealer	.	.	.	1	.	.	1	.
Flax, Linen—Manufacturer, Dealer	3	.	1	.	1	1	8	3
Lace Manufacturer, Dealer	.	.	.	.	.	1	1	2
Fustian Manufacturer, Dealer	.	.	.	.	.	.	.	.
Tape Manufacturer, Dealer	.	.	.	.	.	.	.	.
Thread Manufacturer, Dealer	.	.	.	.	.	.	.	.
4. Hemp and other Fibrous Materials.								
Hemp, Jute, Cocoa Fibre, Manufacture	1	5	.	2	1	.	2	1
Rope, Twine, Cord—Maker, Dealer	145	65	17	.	51	91	75	23
Mat Maker, Seller	2	.	.	.	2	.	9	1
Net Maker	.	.	.	.	.	.	.	.
Canvas, Sailcloth, Manufacture	14	1	.	.	4	7	21	7
Sacking, Sack, Bag—Maker, Dealer	.	2	.	.	1	1	1	23
Others working and dealing in Hemp	.	.	.	.	.	.	1	.
5. Mixed or Unspecified Materials.								
Weaver (undefined)	3	1	1	4	3	6	4	3
Dyer, Printer, Scourer, Bleacher, Calenderer (undefined)	29	10	1	.	3	1	25	13
Factory hand (Textile, undefined)	1	1	1	.	.	9	.	2
Felt Manufacture	.	.	.	.	.	.	1	5
Carpet, Rug, Manufacture	1	.	.	.	.	1	9	1
Manchester Warehouseman	1	.	.	.	.	.	2	.
Draper, Linen Draper, Mercer	372	81	129	36	166	38	767	140
Fancy Goods (Textile), Manufacturer, Worker, Dealer	3	10	.	2	1	4	16	35
Trimming Maker, Dealer	.	.	.	.	.	2	.	1
Embroiderer	.	.	.	.	.	.	.	.
Others	.	.	.	.	.	.	.	.
18. PERSONS WORKING AND DEALING IN DRESS.								
1. Dress.								
Hatter, Hat Manufacture (not straw)	24	6	5	5	30	25	72	18
Straw—Hat, Bonnet, Plait, Manufacture	.	12	.	11	.	5	4	18
Tailor	523	89	210	22	326	26	1069	159
Milliner, Dressmaker, Staymaker	3	1462	1	748	1	853	3	2201
Shawl Manufacture	.	1	.	.	.	.	.	2
Shirt Maker, Seamstress	.	212	.	78	1	81	.	366
Hosiery Manufacture	.	20	.	5	1	.	1	9
Hosier, Haberdasher	7	18	2	8	7	8	32	14
Glover, Glove Maker	.	.	.	.	.	.	1	1
Button Maker, Dealer	.	.	.	.	.	.	.	.
Shoe, Boot—Maker, Dealer	394	23	171	12	208	24	1113	136
Patten, Clog, Maker	15	.	5	.	14	.	23	.
Wig Maker, Hairdresser	93	.	29	.	55	.	140	4
Umbrella, Parasol, Stick—Maker, Dealer	7	.	3	1	5	1	10	3
Accoutrement Maker	.	.	.	.	.	.	.	.
Old Clothes Dealer, and others	.	18	3	5	1	2	14	5
19. PERSONS WORKING AND DEALING IN VARIOUS ANIMAL SUBSTANCES.								
1. In Grease, Gut, Bone, Horn, Ivory, and Whalebone.								
Tallow Chandler. Candle, Grease, Manufacture	16	.	15	1	17	.	24	5
Soap Boiler, Maker	.	.	.	.	.	.	21	1
Glue, Size, Gelatine, Isinglass—Maker, Dealer	.	.	.	.	.	9	3	1
Manure Manufacture	.	.	.	.	7	.	68	9
Bone, Horn, Ivory, Tortoise-shell—Worker, Dealer	.	.	.	.	.	.	2	2
Comb Maker	.	.	.	.	.	.	.	.
Others	.	.	.	.	2	.	2	.
2. In Skins.								
Furrier, Skinner	3	.	.	.	.	10	40	47
Tanner, Fellmonger	2	.	.	.	5	.	107	2
Currier	11	1	6	.	26	8	241	5
Leather Goods, Portmanteau, Bag, Strap, &c.—Maker, Dealer	1	.	2	.	5	.	36	2
Parchment, Vellum—Maker, Dealer	.	.	.	.	.	.	.	.
3. In Hair and Feathers.								
Hair, Bristle—Worker, Dealer	.	.	.	.	.	.	1	3
Brush, Broom, Maker	7	8	1	.	10	1	111	14
Quill, Feather—Dresser, Dealer	3	1	.	.	.	1	3	4

Table 10 *continued*.—Occupations of Males and Females in the Northern Division and its Registration Counties, and in each Urban Sanitary District of which the Population exceeds 50,000 Persons.

Occupations.	Urban Sanitary Districts.							
	Sunderland.		South Shields.		Gateshead.		Newcastle-upon-Tyne.	
	Males.	Females.	Males.	Females.	Males.	Females.	Males.	Females.
20. Persons working and dealing in various Vegetable Substances.								
1. *In Oils, Gums, and Resins.*								
Oil Miller, Oil Cake—Maker, Dealer	7	.	3	.	12	.	23	.
Oil and Colourman	4	.	.	.	4	.	7	.
Floor Cloth, Oil Cloth, Manufacture	2	.	.	.	1	.	1	.
Japanner	.	.	.	.	.	.	17	.
India Rubber, Gutta Percha—Worker, Dealer	1	.	.	.	1	.	7	1
Waterproof Goods—Maker, Dealer	1	.	.	.	.	.	25	.
Others	.	.	1	.	.	.	.	.
2. *In Cane, Rush, and Straw.*								
Willow, Cane, Rush—Worker, Dealer, Basketmaker	8	2	4	.	13	1	29	1
Hay, Straw (not plait), Chaff—Cutter, Dealer	10	.	1	.	2	.	9	.
Thatcher	.	.	.	.	.	.	.	.
3. *In Wood and Bark.*								
Timber Wood—Merchant, Dealer	84	3	34	.	10	1	60	2
Sawyer	173	.	59	.	82	.	200	.
Lath, Wooden Fence, Hurdle, Maker	3	.	5	.	10	1	17	.
Wood Turner, Box Maker	23	.	7	.	5	1	48	14
Cooper, Hoop Maker, Bender	59	.	139	.	195	1	195	1
Cork, Bark—Cutter, Worker, Dealer	14	.	.	.	14	.	48	1
Others	.	.	.	.	.	.	.	.
4. *In Paper.*								
Paper Manufacture	69	52	.	3	24	19	14	3
Envelope Maker	.	.	.	.	.	1	.	1
Stationer, Law Stationer	80	8	5	4	19	12	92	22
Card, Pattern Card, Maker	.	.	.	.	.	.	.	.
Paper Stainer	.	.	.	.	1	.	36	.
Paper Box, Paper Bag, Maker	1	.	.	.	.	.	1	14
Ticket, Label, Writer	3	.	.	.	1	.	18	2
Others	29	.	6	.	4	.	29	.
21. Persons working and dealing in various Mineral Substances.								
1. *Miners.*								
Coal Miner	1108	2	602	.	851	3	471	.
Ironstone Miner	3	.	1	.	2	.	2	.
Copper Miner	.	.	.	.	.	.	.	.
Tin Miner	.	.	.	.	.	.	.	.
Lead Miner	1	.	.	.	1	.	1	.
Miner in other, or undefined, Minerals	1	.	1	.	76	.	10	.
Mine Service	12	.	5	.	15	.	19	2
2. *Coal, Coal Gas, &c.*								
Coal Merchant, Dealer	86	3	82	.	65	3	134	5
Coalheaver	283	.	279	.	6	.	18	.
Coke, Charcoal, Peat—Cutter, Burner, Dealer	5	.	.	.	10	.	9	.
Gas Works Service	63	.	22	.	46	.	92	.
3. *Stone, Clay, and Road Making.*								
Stone Quarrier	45	.	48	.	108	.	84	.
Stone Cutter, Dresser, Dealer	10	.	10	.	15	.	24	.
Slate Quarrier	.	.	.	.	2	.	.	.
Slate Worker, Dealer	1	.	1	.	1	.	6	.
Limeburner	19	.	1	.	2	.	2	.
Clay, Sand, Gravel, Chalk—Labourer, Dealer	.	.	1	.	4	1	3	.
Fossil, Coprolite—Digger, Dealer	.	.	.	.	.	.	.	.
Well Sinker, Borer	.	.	.	.	.	.	.	.
Plaster, Cement, Manufacture	25	.	.	.	85	1	25	.
Brick, Tile—Maker, Burner, Dealer	74	4	42	5	81	1	137	2
Paviour	22	.	7	.	6	.	61	.
Road Contractor, Surveyor, Inspector	.	.	1	.	.	.	2	.
Road Labourer	34	.	15	.	15	.	60	.
Railway Contractor	.	.	1	.	6	.	6	.
Platelayer	51	.	57	.	56	.	96	.
Railway Labourer, Navvy	31	.	29	.	108	.	95	.
Others	.	.	.	.	.	2	.	.
4. *Earthenware and Glass.*								
Earthenware, China, Porcelain, Manufacture	91	39	4	.	62	16	319	224
Glass Manufacture	1035	33	481	67	582	41	270	19
Earthenware, China, Glass, Dealer	12	5	4	4	3	2	32	12
5. *Salt.*								
Salt Maker, Dealer	1	.	1	1	.	.	.	.

Table 10 *continued*.—OCCUPATIONS of MALES and FEMALES in the NORTHERN DIVISION and its REGISTRATION COUNTIES, and in each URBAN SANITARY DISTRICT of which the POPULATION exceeds 50,000 PERSONS.

OCCUPATIONS.	URBAN SANITARY DISTRICTS.							
	SUNDERLAND.		SOUTH SHIELDS.		GATESHEAD.		NEWCASTLE-UPON-TYNE.	
	Males.	Females.	Males.	Females.	Males.	Females.	Males.	Females.
6. Water.								
Waterworks Service	5	.	9	.	7	.	24	.
Others	.	.	.	.	.	.	3	.
7. Precious Metals and Jewellery.								
Goldsmith, Silversmith, Jeweller	34	1	8	.	11	1	71	4
Gold, Silver, Beater	.	.	.	.	.	.	4	.
Lapidary	2	.	.	.	.	.	.	3
Others	.	.	.	.	.	.	.	.
8. Iron and Steel.								
Blacksmith	1039	.	391	.	603	1	913	.
Whitesmith	26	.	2	.	25	.	127	.
Nail Manufacture	1	.	1	.	19	9	14	2
Anchor, Chain, Manufacture	147	1	3	.	199	1	88	.
Other Iron and Steel Manufactures	1214	4	291	.	1797	2	1658	.
Ironmonger, Hardware Dealer, Merchant	72	2	26	1	38	4	154	12
9. Copper.								
Copper, Copper goods—Manufacturer, Worker, Dealer	50	.	8	.	67	.	73	.
10. Tin and Zinc.								
Tin, Tin Plate, Tin goods—Manufacturer, Worker, Dealer	58	2	20	.	65	.	140	1
Zinc, Zinc Goods—Manufacturer, Worker, Dealer	.	.	.	.	.	.	2	.
11. Lead.								
Lead, Leaden goods—Manufacturer, Worker, Dealer	1	.	5	.	27	20	138	8
12. In Other, Mixed, or Unspecified, Metals.								
Metal Refiner, Worker, Turner, Dealer	31	.	17	.	85	.	75	.
Brass, Bronze, Manufacture, Brazier	220	.	34	.	196	.	352	2
Metal Burnisher, Lacquerer	.	.	1	.	.	.	.	.
White Metal, Plated Ware, Manufacture, Pewterer	.	.	.	.	1	.	.	.
Wire Maker, Worker, Weaver, Drawer	15	1	4	.	61	7	81	12
Bolt, Nut, Rivet, Screw, Staple, Maker	9	.	2	.	37	3	13	.
Lamp, Lantern, Candlestick, Maker	3	.	.	.	1	.	8	.
Clasp, Buckle, Hinge, Maker	1	.	.	.	.	.	.	.
Fancy Chain, Gilt Toy, Maker	.	.	.	.	.	.	.	1
Others	1	.	.	.	3	.	1	.
22. PERSONS WORKING AND DEALING IN GENERAL OR UNSPECIFIED COMMODITIES.								
1. Makers and Dealers (General or Undefined).								
General Shopkeeper, Dealer	74	157	38	69	44	82	103	262
Pawnbroker	48	24	19	17	15	13	62	47
Costermonger, Huckster, Street Seller	125	142	22	36	80	133	171	256
Manufacturer, Manager, Superintendent (undefined)	31	.	7	.	36	.	52	3
Contractor (undefined)	24	.	15	.	23	.	30	.
2. Mechanics and Labourers (General or Undefined).								
General Labourer	2788	14	1677	14	1881	17	3273	19
Engine Driver, Stoker, Fireman (not railway, marine, nor agricultural)	376	.	268	.	308	.	305	.
Artizan, Mechanic (undefined)	224	.	82	3	144	5	276	17
Apprentice (undefined)	43	3	9	1	18	1	25	.
Factory Labourer (undefined)	58	5	33	6	115	28	169	34
Machinist, Machine Worker (undefined)	21	4	4	.	74	29	58	1
23. PERSONS WORKING AND DEALING IN REFUSE MATTERS.								
1. Refuse Matters.								
Town Drainage Service	6	.	.	.	4	.	9	.
Chimney Sweep, Soot Merchant	23	1	7	.	14	.	45	.
Scavenger, Crossing Sweeper	9	.	2	.	3	.	4	1
Rag Gatherer, Dealer	2	2	2	2	4	2	3	28
VI. UNOCCUPIED CLASS.								
24. PERSONS WITHOUT SPECIFIED OCCUPATIONS								
Persons returned by Property, Rank, &c., and not by special occupation	14426	41561	8961	20099	8301	22841	16985	47901
Children under 5 years of age	8582	8014	4511	4377	5209	5098	10231	10336

Table 11.—Birth-Places of Males and Females enumerated in Counties, and in each Urban Sanitary District of which the Population exceeds 50,000 Persons.

Where Born.	Where Enumerated.									
	Northern Counties.		Counties.*							
			Durham.		Northumberland.		Cumberland.		Westmorland.	
	Males.	Females.	Males.	Females.	Males.	Females.	Males.	Females.	Males.	Females.
TOTAL OF INHABITANTS	816116	800066	443973	423285	215882	218204	124746	125901	31515	32676
LONDON	5629	5385	3064	2819	1881	1787	522	582	162	247
Middlesex (*Intra-metropolitan*)	4483	4308	2436	2236	1483	1383	431	483	133	204
Surrey (*Intra-metropolitan*)	567	586	293	304	201	189	49	66	24	34
Kent (*Intra-metropolitan*)	579	491	335	277	197	173	42	33	5	9
SOUTH-EASTERN COUNTIES	4548	3537	2916	2068	1157	987	362	356	113	126
Surrey (*Extra-metropolitan*)	361	332	204	182	96	94	44	36	17	20
Kent (*Extra-metropolitan*)	1868	1361	1212	836	507	350	113	113	36	32
Sussex	742	494	486	257	173	150	50	54	24	33
Hampshire	1330	1115	884	670	318	308	106	111	22	31
Berkshire	247	235	130	123	63	60	44	42	14	10
SOUTH-MIDLAND COUNTIES	2735	2275	1773	1403	549	475	270	266	143	131
Middlesex (*Ex-metropolitan*)	254	246	151	132	73	71	23	25	7	18
Hertfordshire	192	192	106	96	54	55	28	22	18	18
Buckinghamshire	307	255	172	142	75	53	40	38	20	17
Oxfordshire	287	250	163	128	54	62	51	44	19	16
Northamptonshire	456	382	273	227	82	79	61	57	40	28
Huntingdonshire	201	148	154	108	25	25	11	11	11	4
Bedfordshire	369	263	256	177	71	36	27	38	15	12
Cambridgeshire	669	539	504	390	115	98	34	31	16	20
EASTERN COUNTIES	10856	7703	8043	5589	2558	1846	188	188	67	80
Essex	2070	1366	1536	988	459	394	57	58	18	28
Suffolk	2247	1316	1755	1149	415	290	51	50	26	27
Norfolk	6539	4821	4752	3452	1684	1262	80	80	23	27
SOUTH-WESTERN COUNTIES	8377	7112	4717	3965	1720	1470	1811	1535	129	142
Wiltshire	365	357	253	263	78	84	44	49	10	21
Dorsetshire	393	325	229	170	109	90	29	36	26	29
Devonshire	2711	2334	1434	1231	672	603	567	463	38	37
Cornwall	3633	3192	1916	1721	693	548	1064	903	20	20
Somersetshire	1195	904	885	640	168	145	107	84	35	35
WEST-MIDLAND COUNTIES	8855	7409	6220	5032	1428	1307	1009	786	198	284
Gloucestershire	1152	901	725	570	296	214	153	110	48	67
Herefordshire	216	211	117	167	58	49	30	36	11	19
Shropshire	585	736	617	476	186	122	109	91	24	47
Staffordshire	4281	3598	3216	2631	390	557	422	333	53	77
Worcestershire	1263	970	916	724	160	128	116	85	31	33
Warwickshire	1098	933	629	524	258	237	179	131	32	41
NORTH-MIDLAND COUNTIES	4426	3660	3003	2329	832	782	439	394	152	155
Leicestershire	545	428	310	225	169	126	98	62	13	15
Rutlandshire	86	54	59	29	10	4	8	11	9	10
Lincolnshire	1800	1494	1299	1021	358	381	105	103	38	39
Nottinghamshire	826	687	536	427	159	143	93	78	36	39
Derbyshire	1169	997	799	627	176	178	145	140	49	52
NORTH-WESTERN COUNTIES	14069	12325	5812	4362	1751	1434	3984	3610	2522	2919
Cheshire	1302	1138	675	500	208	195	326	291	93	152
Lancashire	12767	11187	5137	3862	1543	1239	3658	3319	2429	2767
YORKSHIRE	34532	32008	28299	25861	3545	3540	1325	1210	1363	1397
NORTHERN COUNTIES	636665	653903	335131	338845	177218	185828	98543	103006	25773	26224
Durham	308922	315876	292084	298034	15390	15789	1145	1120	303	233
Northumberland	193978	200633	35042	36144	157189	162597	1649	1754	98	138
Cumberland	106333	110430	6753	5973	4378	4224	93438	97990	1764	2262
Westmorland	27432	26965	1252	1094	261	218	2311	2142	23608	23601
MONMOUTHSHIRE AND WALES	5033	4037	3810	3009	478	377	695	557	50	94
Monmouthshire	835	728	674	586	63	51	91	77	7	14
Glamorganshire	1019	896	753	623	101	92	161	142	4	9
Carmarthenshire	125	99	84	80	10	8	30	10	1	1
Pembrokeshire	193	138	116	81	56	37	23	10	4	4
Cardiganshire	93	30	48	23	19	3	24	2	2	2
Brecknockshire	148	125	117	99	18	12	17	17	1	.
Radnorshire	36	28	20	18	3	2	6	8	2	5
Montgomeryshire	60	54	33	25	7	11	17	13	3	5
Flintshire	593	446	481	352	37	25	68	51	7	14
Denbighshire	340	265	270	194	23	22	36	32	5	17
Merionethshire	33	25	22	16	7	2	4	4	.	3
Carnarvonshire	124	76	55	33	36	12	30	25	3	6
Anglesey	119	83	44	34	22	6	51	42	2	1
Wales (*County not stated*)	1321	1675	1003	845	51	94	138	123	9	13
ENGLAND (*County not stated*)	1981	1750	1005	909	512	431	435	387	29	23
OTHER PARTS OF BRITISH EMPIRE	72732	56560	37108	25848	19926	17081	14943	12838	755	793
Islands in the British Seas	881	742	164	135	117	101	586	492	14	14
SCOTLAND	32059	29320	13478	11236	12153	11260	5922	6265	506	539
IRELAND	38490	25227	22546	13918	7195	5294	8255	5838	194	177
British Colonies or Dependencies	1302	1271	920	559	461	426	180	223	41	63
FOREIGN COUNTRIES	5566	2308	3020	1200	2288	882	202	166	56	60
British Subjects	1554	1100	960	615	466	358	96	96	32	31
Foreigners	4012	1208	2060	585	1822	524	106	70	24	29
AT SEA	112	94	52	46	39	27	18	20	3	1
British Subjects	112	93	52	46	39	26	18	20	3	1
Foreigners	.	1	.	.	.	1	.	.	.	.

* The Counties *proper*, and not the Registration Counties, are referred to in this Table.

Table 11 *continued.*—BIRTH-PLACES of MALES and FEMALES enumerated in COUNTIES, and in each URBAN SANITARY DISTRICT of which the POPULATION exceeds 50,000 PERSONS.

WHERE BORN.	WHERE ENUMERATED. URBAN SANITARY DISTRICTS. SUNDERLAND.		SOUTH SHIELDS.		GATESHEAD.		NEWCASTLE-ON-TYNE.	
	Males.	Females.	Males.	Females.	Males.	Females.	Males.	Females.
TOTAL OF INHABITANTS	57133	59415	28373	28502	32991	32812	71100	74359
LONDON	690	713	440	289	299	252	1013	979
MIDDLESEX (*Intra-metropolitan*)	524	554	373	246	234	208	794	776
SURREY (*Intra-metropolitan*)	67	79	25	21	38	34	127	117
KENT (*Intra-metropolitan*)	99	80	42	22	27	10	92	86
SOUTH-EASTERN-COUNTIES	797	512	118	234	189	174	446	431
SURREY (*Extra-metropolitan*)	34	26	24	8	9	10	44	44
KENT (*Extra-metropolitan*)	271	203	199	94	112	99	188	175
SUSSEX	163	70	57	30	14	11	60	63
HAMPSHIRE	309	191	126	94	45	46	115	122
BERKSHIRE	20	22	10	8	8	8	39	27
SOUTH-MIDLAND COUNTIES	201	177	90	67	78	70	288	269
MIDDLESEX (*Extra-metropolitan*)	29	20	16	4	6	7	43	47
HERTFORDSHIRE	17	11	7	5	5	9	22	39
BUCKINGHAMSHIRE	15	18	6	2	16	7	46	38
OXFORDSHIRE	25	22	7	8	4	1	35	32
NORTHAMPTONSHIRE	31	27	9	10	13	14	40	40
HUNTINGDONSHIRE	13	4	7	11	3	4	15	13
BEDFORDSHIRE	16	16	11	5	3	9	36	10
CAMBRIDGESHIRE	55	60	27	22	29	19	51	50
EASTERN COUNTIES	983	683	954	678	411	337	861	697
ESSEX	217	121	149	72	82	67	130	87
SUFFOLK	216	159	155	64	78	75	138	129
NORFOLK	550	403	650	542	251	195	593	481
SOUTH-WESTERN COUNTIES	555	463	262	180	174	191	396	450
WILTSHIRE	45	24	16	10	9	24	37	41
DORSETSHIRE	55	33	33	18	5	13	39	37
DEVONSHIRE	149	157	131	86	61	81	168	209
CORNWALL	207	175	57	38	76	62	82	98
SOMERSETSHIRE	99	74	25	28	23	11	70	65
WEST-MIDLAND COUNTIES	615	492	159	167	420	348	627	607
GLOUCESTERSHIRE	92	79	45	35	39	42	110	100
HEREFORDSHIRE	12	14	1	4	7	4	17	21
SHROPSHIRE	38	31	16	12	66	63	45	44
STAFFORDSHIRE	286	239	62	77	191	142	213	223
WORCESTERSHIRE	92	43	5	11	51	33	80	52
WARWICKSHIRE	95	86	30	28	66	64	162	167
NORTH-MIDLAND COUNTIES	323	336	162	131	136	94	371	386
LEICESTERSHIRE	24	27	19	9	15	11	58	65
RUTLANDSHIRE	3	2	-	4	5	1	3	-
LINCOLNSHIRE	165	174	98	81	62	41	163	185
NOTTINGHAMSHIRE	65	70	29	18	23	16	81	73
DERBYSHIRE	66	63	16	19	31	25	66	63
NORTH-WESTERN COUNTIES	708	568	340	252	322	266	774	742
CHESHIRE	100	63	45	41	38	31	83	93
LANCASHIRE	608	505	295	211	284	235	691	649
YORKSHIRE	2154	2003	719	575	916	67	1974	1931
NORTHERN COUNTIES	43558	48841	20738	23483	26288	27031	55093	60063
DURHAM	38945	43980	17102	19259	18470	18843	6631	8772
NORTHUMBERLAND	3966	4295	3301	3927	7000	7434	46577	49578
CUMBERLAND	580	509	311	273	780	703	1781	1594
WESTMORLAND	68	57	24	24	38	51	104	119
MONMOUTHSHIRE AND WALES	335	174	131	60	86	90	160	154
MONMOUTHSHIRE	35	30	10	7	18	10	18	22
GLAMORGANSHIRE	48	48	28	16	20	19	34	40
CARMARTHENSHIRE	6	5	3	1	3	3	5	5
PEMBROKESHIRE	18	18	15	5	4	6	16	11
CARDIGANSHIRE	8	1	15	8	-	1	10	-
BRECKNOCKSHIRE	3	-	-	-	2	2	7	5
RADNORSHIRE	1	-	-	-	2	1	1	1
MONTGOMERYSHIRE	3	1	2	1	2	2	2	7
FLINTSHIRE	18	16	10	9	7	4	7	7
DENBIGHSHIRE	14	4	2	-	5	4	8	10
MERIONETHSHIRE	1	1	4	1	1	-	3	1
CARNARVONSHIRE	9	2	21	2	-	-	14	8
ANGLESEY	2	1	5	2	1	5	5	1
WALES (*County not stated*)	76	47	16	13	21	24	30	36
ENGLAND (*County not stated*)	117	122	75	65	105	101	206	181
OTHER PARTS OF BRITISH EMPIRE	5418	4022	3100	2170	3416	2905	7886	6851
ISLANDS in the BRITISH SEAS	17	18	37	18	4	11	40	52
SCOTLAND	2637	2077	1704	1365	1554	1450	4609	4123
IRELAND	2652	1815	1290	761	1796	1371	3029	2466
BRITISH COLONIES or DEPENDENCIES	112	112	69	26	62	73	208	210
FOREIGN COUNTRIES	770	293	781	145	141	82	986	508
British Subjects	255	125	135	72	59	45	289	182
Foreigners	515	168	646	73	82	37	697	326
AT SEA	9	16	4	6	10	4	19	10
British Subjects	9	16	4	6	10	4	19	9
Foreigners	-	-	-	-	-	-	-	1

Table 12.—DISTRIBUTION of the enumerated NATIVES of COUNTIES.

WHERE ENUMERATED.	WHERE BORN.									
	NORTHERN COUNTIES.		DURHAM.		NORTHUMBERLAND.		CUMBERLAND.		WESTMORLAND.	
	Males.	Females.	Males.	Females.	Males.	Females.	Males.	Females.	Males.	Females.
TOTAL ENUMERATED NATIVES OF EACH COUNTY	715500	739286	342801	351437	210208	217683	124018	130880	38473	39286
LONDON	10291	10021	4029	4041	3817	3961	1815	1546	630	473
MIDDLESEX (*Intra-metropolitan*)	6917	6843	2572	2657	2623	2721	1282	1093	440	373
SURREY (*Intra-metropolitan*)	2540	2368	1065	1000	895	933	433	359	147	76
KENT (*Intra-metropolitan*)	834	810	392	384	299	308	100	94	43	24
SOUTH-EASTERN COUNTIES	5264	4492	2719	2064	1576	1442	706	718	263	268
SURREY (*Extra-metropolitan*)	828	976	344	382	254	323	155	211	75	67
KENT (*Extra-metropolitan*)	1780	1236	939	627	510	390	211	146	65	63
SUSSEX	702	787	294	279	219	266	125	166	64	76
HAMPSHIRE	1720	1272	992	761	514	376	136	147	43	43
BERKSHIRE	234	221	98	65	79	84	40	58	16	14
SOUTH-MIDLAND COUNTIES	1988	1957	774	745	683	651	362	382	169	179
MIDDLESEX (*Ex-metropolitan*)	882	890	335	342	331	320	138	137	58	62
HERTFORDSHIRE	213	228	72	79	72	73	47	46	22	28
BUCKINGHAMSHIRE	133	148	56	51	43	42	23	35	12	29
OXFORDSHIRE	135	132	50	58	63	81	22	24	10	19
NORTHAMPTONSHIRE	278	284	98	101	72	79	61	77	43	27
HUNTINGDONSHIRE	47	43	22	13	14	18	8	9	3	3
BEDFORDSHIRE	89	119	34	43	33	40	14	17	8	8
CAMBRIDGESHIRE	211	122	107	56	66	57	25	17	13	12
EASTERN COUNTIES	2322	2312	1265	1193	739	741	219	195	99	83
ESSEX	1298	1073	710	550	403	349	128	122	57	52
SUFFOLK	341	430	183	241	115	147	32	32	11	10
NORFOLK	683	709	372	402	221	245	59	41	31	21
SOUTH-WESTERN COUNTIES	1677	1490	771	634	515	476	302	280	89	100
WILTSHIRE	183	158	69	69	74	56	28	22	12	11
DORSETSHIRE	233	136	102	65	87	44	24	21	26	6
DEVONSHIRE	637	577	298	219	204	206	109	109	26	43
CORNWALL	301	237	169	118	68	79	68	46	5	3
SOMERSETSHIRE	323	382	142	163	82	100	73	82	20	37
WEST-MIDLAND COUNTIES	3348	3573	1409	1485	940	1048	686	75[illegible]	313	290
GLOUCESTERSHIRE	577	739	234	335	108	103	112	158	43	51
HEREFORDSHIRE	79	94	24	24	19	17	21	33	15	20
SHROPSHIRE	243	260	84	74	50	71	61	73	4[illegible]	37
STAFFORDSHIRE	1226	1174	571	559	327	324	224	208	104	83
WORCESTERSHIRE	373	453	157	200	94	136	86	84	36	33
WARWICKSHIRE	850	853	319	298	282	395	182	189	67	66
NORTH-MIDLAND COUNTIES	2447	2594	1092	1214	680	726	454	432	221	222
LEICESTERSHIRE	385	453	137	162	106	132	81	82	61	77
RUTLANDSHIRE	31	16	8	6	8	4	13	5	2	1
LINCOLNSHIRE	682	708	316	372	223	211	101	84	42	41
NOTTINGHAMSHIRE	502	606	238	277	138	177	96	111	39	41
DERBYSHIRE	847	811	393	397	205	202	163	150	30	62
NORTH-WESTERN COUNTIES	24177	28714	4308	4696	2628	2806	10335	13142	6906	8070
CHESHIRE	1935	2398	391	476	316	341	942	1196	286	268
LANCASHIRE	22242	26316	3917	4220	2312	2465	9392	11946	6620	7685
YORKSHIRE	25290	28691	16572	18722	4168	4772	2319	2634	2231	2563
NORTHERN COUNTIES	636665	653903	308922	315876	193978	200633	106333	110439	27432	26955
DURHAM	335131	338845	292084	295634	35042	36144	6753	5973	1252	1064
NORTHUMBERLAND	177218	185828	13390	15789	157180	162597	4378	4224	261	218
CUMBERLAND	98543	103206	1145	1129	1640	1754	93488	97980	2311	2142
WESTMORLAND	25773	26224	303	383	98	138	1764	2252	23608	23501
MONMOUTHSHIRE AND WALES	2031	1639	940	767	484	427	487	362	120	83
MONMOUTHSHIRE	373	242	187	130	90	63	67	37	29	12
GLAMORGANSHIRE	949	772	473	397	256	231	188	120	37	24
CARMARTHENSHIRE	62	37	23	12	18	10	19	13	2	2
PEMBROKESHIRE	111	46	26	12	20	16	39	16	.	2
CARDIGANSHIRE	20	10	9	4	5	1	4	4	2	1
BRECKNOCKSHIRE	39	38	26	19	7	7	5	9	1	3
RADNORSHIRE	7	6	2	4	3	2	2	.	.	.
MONTGOMERYSHIRE	48	33	14	10	10	3	18	15	6	5
FLINTSHIRE	151	169	91	77	19	32	29	49	12	11
DENBIGHSHIRE	112	167	47	74	24	35	31	45	10	15
MERIONETHSHIRE	26	25	3	7	4	6	11	9	2	3
CARNARVONSHIRE	79	76	23	21	9	19	33	30	14	6
ANGLESEY	54	18	10	.	13	2	26	15	5	1

Table 14.—Number and Ages of Males and Females returned as Blind or Blind from Birth in the Northern Division and its Registration Counties.

Registration County.	All Ages. Both Sexes.	All Ages. Males and Females.	0–	5–	15–	20–	25–	45–	65 and upwards.
X. NORTHERN COUNTIES.	1259	M. 723	18	54	27	29	184	210	201
		F. 536	8	37	18	27	76	120	250
38 DURHAM	612	M. 352	8	28	13	17	96	107	83
		F. 260	7	18	10	9	32	65	119
39 NORTHUMBERLAND	356	M. 199	8	16	10	7	51	56	51
		F. 157	1	14	8	12	26	32	64
40 CUMBERLAND	232	M. 137	1	7	4	5	28	35	57
		F. 95	.	4	.	6	15	18	52
41 WESTMORLAND	59	M. 35	1	3	.	.	9	12	10
		F. 24	.	1	.	.	3	5	15

Table 15.—Number and Ages of Males and Females retuined as Blind in the Northern Division and its Registration Counties.

Registration County.	All Ages. Both Sexes.	All Ages. Males and Females.	0–	5–	15–	20–	25–	45–	65 and upwards.
X. NORTHERN COUNTIES.	1147	M. 666	9	37	21	29	170	200	200
		F. 481	3	24	13	24	61	110	246
38 DURHAM	565	M. 326	4	20	11	17	88	103	83
		F. 239	3	13	6	9	29	61	118
39 NORTHUMBERLAND	316	M. 178	4	11	6	7	47	53	50
		F. 138	.	9	7	11	21	27	63
40 CUMBERLAND	215	M. 131	1	5	4	5	26	33	57
		F. 84	.	1	.	4	10	18	51
41 WESTMORLAND	51	M. 31	.	1	.	.	9	11	10
		F. 20	.	1	.	.	1	4	14

Table 16.—Number and Ages of Males and Females returned as Blind from Birth in the Northern Division and its Registration Counties.

Registration County.	All Ages. Both Sexes.	All Ages. Males and Females.	0–	5–	15–	20–	25–	45–	65 and upwards.
X. NORTHERN COUNTIES.	112	M. 57	9	17	6	.	14	10	1
		F. 55	5	13	5	3	15	10	4
38 DURHAM	47	M. 26	4	8	2	.	8	4	.
		F. 21	4	5	4	.	3	4	1
39 NORTHUMBERLAND	40	M. 21	4	5	4	.	4	3	1
		F. 19	1	5	1	1	5	5	1
40 CUMBERLAND	17	M. 6	.	2	.	.	2	2	.
		F. 11	.	3	.	2	5	.	1
41 WESTMORLAND	8	M. 4	1	2	.	.	.	1	.
		F. 4	.	.	.	.	2	1	1

Table 17.—Number and Ages of Males and Females returned as Deaf and Dumb in the Northern Division and its Registration Counties.

Registration County.	All Ages. Both Sexes.	All Ages. Males and Females.	0–	5–	15–	20–	25–	45–	65 and upwards.
X. NORTHERN COUNTIES.	770	M. 403	16	108	50	54	115	46	14
		F. 367	10	114	38	47	105	37	16
38 DURHAM	355	M. 185	10	45	26	25	57	17	5
		F. 170	9	47	21	25	49	13	6
39 NORTHUMBERLAND	269	M. 146	2	54	15	15	36	20	4
		F. 123	.	53	11	8	32	14	5
40 CUMBERLAND	113	M. 55	3	8	6	12	14	9	3
		F. 58	.	13	4	9	20	8	4
41 WESTMORLAND	33	M. 17	1	1	3	2	8	.	2
		F. 16	1	1	2	5	4	2	1

Table 18.—NUMBER and AGES of MALES and FEMALES returned as IDIOTS or IMBECILES, and LUNATICS in the NORTHERN DIVISION and its REGISTRATION COUNTIES.

REGISTRATION COUNTY.	ALL AGES. Both Sexes.	ALL AGES. Males and Females.	0–	5–	15–	20–	25–	45–	65 and upwards.
X. NORTHERN COUNTIES.	3596	M. 1854	12	103	110	163	771	530	165
		F. 1742	3	100	88	113	677	572	189
38 DURHAM	1712	M. - 899	3	47	57	87	378	242	85
		F. - 813	1	60	50	65	317	245	75
39 NORTHUMBERLAND	1140	M. - 587	6	36	36	50	246	165	48
		F. - 553	2	27	20	36	228	186	54
40 CUMBERLAND	647	M. - 323	2	17	13	21	120	114	27
		F. - 324	.	7	11	10	118	130	48
41 WESTMORLAND	97	M. - 45	1	3	4	6	18	9	5
		F. - 52	.	6	7	3	14	11	12

Table 19.—NUMBER and AGES of MALES and FEMALES returned as IDIOTS or IMBECILES in the NORTHERN DIVISION and its REGISTRATION COUNTIES.

REGISTRATION COUNTY.	ALL AGES. Both Sexes.	ALL AGES. Males and Females.	0–	5–	15–	20–	25–	45–	65 and upwards.
X. NORTHERN COUNTIES.	1394	M. 696	12	102	96	96	223	117	50
		F. 698	3	99	77	72	236	149	62
38 DURHAM	614	M. - 292	5	47	50	46	83	37	26
		F. - 322	1	59	42	39	101	59	21
39 NORTHUMBERLAND	486	M. - 258	6	36	32	29	87	50	18
		F. - 228	2	27	18	25	80	52	24
40 CUMBERLAND	209	M. - 106	2	16	10	16	38	22	2
		F. - 103	.	7	10	6	43	28	9
41 WESTMORLAND	85	M. - 40	1	3	4	5	15	8	4
		F. - 45	.	6	7	2	13	10	8

Table 20.—NUMBER and AGES of MALES and FEMALES returned as LUNATICS in the NORTHERN DIVISION and its REGISTRATION COUNTIES.

REGISTRATION COUNTY.	ALL AGES. Both Sexes.	ALL AGES. Males and Females.	0–	5–	15–	20–	25–	45–	65 and upwards.
X. NORTHERN COUNTIES.	2202	M. 1158	.	1	14	67	548	413	115
		F. 1044	.	1	11	41	441	423	127
38 DURHAM	1098	M. - 607	.	.	7	41	295	205	59
		F. - 491	.	1	8	26	216	156	54
39 NORTHUMBERLAND	654	M. - 329	.	.	4	21	159	115	30
		F. - 325	.	.	2	11	148	134	30
40 CUMBERLAND	438	M. - 217	.	1	3	5	91	92	25
		F. - 221	.	.	1	4	75	102	39
41 WESTMORLAND	13	M. - 6	.	.	.	.	3	1	1
		F. - 7	.	.	.	.	2	1	4

Table 21.—NUMBER of the BLIND, of the DEAF and DUMB, of IDIOTS or IMBECILES, and of LUNATI
in the NORTHERN DIVISION and its REGISTRATION COUNTIES and DISTRICTS.

REGISTRATION COUNTY AND DISTRICT.	Blind.			Deaf and Dumb.	Mentally Deranged.		
	From Birth.	Others.	Total.		Idiots.	Lunatics.	Total.
X. NORTHERN COUNTIES.	112	1147	1259	770	1394	2202	3596
38 DURHAM - -	47	565	612	355	614	1098	1712
39 NORTHUMBERLAND	40	316	356	269	486	654	1140
40 CUMBERLAND -	17	215	232	113	209	438	647
41 WESTMORLAND -	8	51	59	33	85	12	97
38 DURHAM.							
542 DARLINGTON - -	2	27	29	14	36	34	70
543 STOCKTON -	2	50	52	29	65	909	974
544 HARTLEPOOL - -	3	30	33	13	29	3	32
545 AUCKLAND - -	1	45	46	33	39	3	42
546 TEESDALE - -	.	22	22	8	44	7	51
547 WEARDALE - -	.	17	17	8	11	1	12
548 LANCHESTER - -	3	25	28	30	39	2	41
549 DURHAM - -	3	45	48	34	40	4	44
550 EASINGTON - -	3	32	35	18	20	1	21
551 HOUGHTON-LE-SPRING	1	17	18	14	19	1	20
552 CHESTER-LE-STREET -	4	32	36	18	33	4	37
553 SUNDERLAND - -	14	102	116	51	102	72	174
554 SOUTH SHIELDS -	6	53	59	45	62	7	69
555 GATESHEAD - -	5	68	73	40	75	50	125

REGISTRATION COUNTY AND DISTRICT.	Blind.			Deaf and Dumb.	Me Der
	From Birth.	Others.	Total.		Idiots.
39 NORTHUMBERLAND.					
556 NEWCASTLE - UPON - TYNE -	21	132	153	148	135
557 TYNEMOUTH - -	11	83	94	44	80
558 CASTLE WARD -	.	10	10	12	22
559 HEXHAM - -	1	19	20	19	39
560 HALTWHISTLE - -	1	5	6	4	12
561 BELLINGHAM - -	.	3	3	1	12
562 MORPETH - -	2	18	20	17	65
563 ALNWICK - -	2	16	18	5	34
564 BELFORD - -	1	7	8	1	7
565 BERWICK - -	1	14	15	6	53
566 GLENDALE - -	.	4	4	5	26
567 ROTHBURY - -	.	5	5	7	11
40 CUMBERLAND.					
568 ALSTON - - -	1	7	8	6	6
569 PENRITH - -	1	19	20	12	25
570 BRAMPTON - -	1	8	9	11	18
571 LONGTOWN -	1	7	8	1	4
572 CARLISLE -	4	53	57	30	42
573 WIGTON - -	.	26	26	9	27
574 COCKERMOUTH -	5	40	45	23	41
575 WHITEHAVEN - -	4	44	48	19	44
576 BOOTLE - -	.	11	11	2	7
41 WESTMORLAND.					
577 EAST WARD - -	1	9	10	8	21
578 WEST WARD - -	6	7	13	2	8
579 KENDAL - -	1	35	36	23	56

AGES,

CONDITION AS TO MARRIAGE,

OCCUPATIONS, AND BIRTH-PLACES

OF THE PEOPLE:

WITH THE

NUMBERS AND AGES OF THE BLIND, DEAF AND DUMB, IDIOTS OR IMBECILES, AND LUNATICS.

DIVISION XI.—MONMOUTHSHIRE AND WALES.

MONMOUTHSHIRE.

GLAMORGANSHIRE.
CARMARTHENSHIRE.
PEMBROKESHIRE.
CARDIGANSHIRE.
BRECKNOCKSHIRE.
RADNORSHIRE.
MONTGOMERYSHIRE.
FLINTSHIRE.
DENBIGHSHIRE.
MERIONETHSHIRE.
CARNARVONSHIRE.
ANGLESEY.

TABLES IN DIVISION XI.—MONMOUTHSHIRE AND WALES.

AGES.

Table.

1.—Ages of Males and Females in the Welsh Division and its Registration Counties.

2.—Ages of Males and Females in Registration Districts.

3.—Ages of Males and Females in Registration Sub-Districts.

4.—Male and Female Children at *each Year of Age* under 5 in the Welsh Division and its Registration Counties.

5.—Male and Female Children at *each Year of Age* under 5 in Registration Districts.

6.—Ages of Males and Females in Sanitary Districts.

CONDITION AS TO MARRIAGE.

7.—Condition as to Marriage and Ages of Males and Females in the Welsh Division and its Registration Counties.

8.—Condition as to Marriage and Ages of Males and Females in Registration Districts.

9.—Condition as to Marriage and Ages of Males and Females in each Urban Sanitary District of which the Population exceeds 50,000 Persons.

OCCUPATIONS.

10.—Occupations of Males and Females in the Welsh Division and its Registration Counties, and in each Urban Sanitary District of which the Population exceeds 50,000 Persons.

BIRTH-PLACES.

11.—Birth-places of Males and Females enumerated in Counties, and in each Urban Sanitary District of which the Population exceeds 50,000 Persons.

12.—Distribution of the enumerated Natives of Counties.

13.—Number and Country of Birth of Foreigners enumerated in Counties, and in each Urban Sanitary District of which the Population exceeds 50,000 Persons.

THE BLIND, DEAF AND DUMB, IDIOTS OR IMBECILES, AND LUNATICS.

14.—Number and Ages of Males and Females returned as Blind or Blind from Birth in the Welsh Division and its Registration Counties.

15.—Number and Ages of Males and Females returned as Blind in the Welsh Division and its Registration Counties.

16.—Number and Ages of Males and Females returned as Blind from Birth in the Welsh Division and its Registration Counties.

17.—Number and Ages of Males and Females returned as Deaf and Dumb in the Welsh Division and its Registration Counties.

18.—Number and Ages of Males and Females returned as Idiots or Imbeciles, and Lunatics in the Welsh Division and its Registration Counties.

19.—Number and Ages of Males and Females returned as Idiots or Imbeciles in the Welsh Division and its Registration Counties.

20.—Number and Ages of Males and Females returned as Lunatics in the Welsh Division and its Registration Counties.

21.—Number of the Blind, of the Deaf and Dumb, of Idiots or Imbeciles, and of Lunatics in the Welsh Division and its Registration Counties and Districts.

AGES.

DIVISION XI.—MONMOUTHSHIRE AND WALES.

Table 1.—AGES of MALES and FEMALES in the WELSH DIVISION and its REGISTRATION COUNTIES.

REGISTRATION COUNTY.	ALL AGES. Persons.		ALL AGES. Males and Females.	Under 5* Years.	5–	10–	15–	20–	25–	30–	35–	40–	45–	50–	55–	60–	65–	70–	75–	80–	85–	90–	95–	100 and up
.—MONMOUTHSHIRE AND WALES.	1577559	M.	789074	106165	98897	89280	81250	69143	60420	61286	44595	39932	33695	30668	24922	22294	15709	10977	6405	3143	1079	229	39	
		F.	788483	106016	98118	87656	75260	66056	67947	60265	44760	40625	35232	31803	25738	23594	17607	12869	7963	4241	1596	423	118	
MONMOUTHSHIRE.	234332	M.	119965	16220	15345	13397	12829	10282	9079	7924	6699	6270	5129	4739	3740	3438	2310	1592	902	394	181	33	6	
		F.	114367	16364	15341	13131	10470	9380	8269	7102	6342	5903	4044	4654	3507	3325	2325	1620	929	464	179	43	12	
SOUTH WALES	881117	M.	438814	60805	56072	49764	45515	39748	33824	28950	24811	21762	18167	16470	12987	11416	7683	5450	3122	1636	530	117	24	
		F.	442303	60824	55405	49078	43523	39249	33204	28472	24986	22095	19283	17083	13623	12442	9140	6739	4134	2270	863	220	69	
NORTH WALES	462110	M.	230295	29340	27480	26138	23386	19113	16526	14403	13065	11906	10409	9423	8215	7440	5510	3935	2371	1113	418	79	9	
		F.	231815	29328	27232	25447	21257	18318	16484	14621	13432	12627	11095	9766	8098	7827	6142	4500	2900	1567	554	160	87	
…UTH WALES.																								
…MORGANSHIRE	518383	M.	256128	37379	33772	28804	27301	25715	22623	19236	16218	13695	10875	9649	7094	5853	3654	2261	1236	626	187	40	9	
		F.	262255	37817	33630	28596	24792	22798	19661	16760	14565	12443	10534	9042	6806	5861	3976	2625	1610	846	297	87	25	
…MARTHENSHIRE	111255	M.	53489	7580	7328	6545	5594	4433	3598	3178	2785	2420	2141	1977	1623	1492	1153	834	489	258	88	17	5	
		F.	57766	7464	7037	6541	5781	5290	4166	3756	3085	2815	2454	2204	1864	1702	1383	1145	685	369	168	47	15	
…BROKESHIRE	83679	M.	40085	5357	4890	4805	4376	3450	2588	2114	1633	1940	1729	1588	1437	1371	990	733	482	256	92	24	5	
		F.	43584	5325	4878	4592	4377	3841	3069	2535	2412	2243	1974	1876	1612	1608	1230	925	589	328	135	27	16	
…DIGANSHIRE	95137	M.	42717	5673	5654	5489	4690	3078	2806	2195	1972	1922	1821	1786	1519	1303	1177	925	558	289	90	22	3	
		F.	52420	5679	5581	5379	5034	4318	3684	3302	3040	2811	2565	2417	2040	2058	1681	1308	831	473	167	40	11	
…CKNOCKSHIRE	54140	M.	26991	3457	3298	3013	2724	2229	1889	1676	1450	1368	1170	1174	979	872	660	512	306	155	51	12	2	
		F.	27149	3408	3239	3086	2636	2241	1969	1624	1416	1351	1295	1155	974	916	717	545	306	180	74	17	3	
…NORSHIRE	18523	M.	9404	1159	1129	1098	986	842	626	560	503	426	421	402	335	325	249	198	121	52	22	2	.	
		F.	9119	1141	1104	1094	903	761	655	505	468	482	391	382	327	307	253	191	113	68	22	2	.	
…RTH WALES.																								
…TGOMERYSHIRE	76196	M.	38295	4724	4690	4584	4038	3110	2499	2058	2003	1901	1792	1632	1359	1336	993	801	455	202	80	17		
		F.	37901	4776	4706	4284	3876	3026	2422	2174	1938	2014	1760	1601	1352	1315	1076	810	505	326	98	36	6	
…NTSHIRE	45774	M.	23217	3061	2948	2641	2398	1875	1710	1513	1392	1275	1910	920	759	705	468	277	170	74	23	2	1	
		F.	22557	2985	2992	2724	1898	1533	1476	1366	1363	1251	1046	949	820	744	530	390	284	146	50	8	3	
…BIGHSHIRE	112940	M.	56501	7808	6894	6466	5918	4616	4021	3605	3174	2935	2576	2360	2026	1791	1218	882	514	236	86	14	1	
		F.	56439	7280	6820	6396	5179	4356	4046	3530	3245	3075	2692	2401	2083	1845	1388	1015	633	302	104	20	9	
…RIONETHSHIRE	68278	M.	34350	4405	4162	3681	3238	3068	2503	2342	2196	1763	1551	1292	1128	993	792	597	336	161	58	10	3	
		F.	33928	4486	4116	3804	2964	2678	2451	2221	2010	1841	1527	1307	1157	1055	876	661	435	223	78	35	6	
…ARVONSHIRE	123781	M.	60742	7704	7020	6921	6090	5088	4530	3850	3427	3108	2689	2440	2233	1918	1828	1008	641	305	111	25	.	
		F.	63039	7711	6756	6184	5898	5341	4836	4147	3837	3585	3082	2667	2417	2118	1721	1184	766	356	162	30	10	
…LESEY	35141	M.	17190	2043	1965	1845	1704	1350	1208	1038	893	858	791	764	700	694	505	370	235	135	60	11	4	
		F.	17951	2090	1903	1755	1652	1389	1252	1183	1039	911	898	841	779	758	651	446	277	184	62	22	3	

…ote.—Registration Counties consist of groups of Registration Districts, which are generally co-extensive with the Poor Law Unions. Those Registrati… …tricts which extend into two or more counties are included in that Registration County in which the principal town of the District or the greater part of t… …ulation is located. The boundaries of Registration Counties, therefore, differ more or less from the boundaries of counties. For such differences in Division X… Vol. II., Table 11.

* For the number of Children at each Year of Age under 5, see Table 4.

† Four of these Males were stated to be 100, three 101, and one 103 years of age. Seven of these Females were stated to be 100, one 101, three 102, two 103, thr… …, and two 105 years of age.

Table 2.—AGES of MALES and FEMALES in REGISTRATION DISTRICTS.

REGISTRATION DISTRICT.	ALL AGES. Persons.		ALL AGES. Males and Females.	Under 5*	5–	10–	15–	20–	25–	30–	35–	40–	45–	50–	55–	60–	65–	70–	75–	80–	85–	90–	95–	100 and up
… MONMOUTHSHIRE.																								
CHEPSTOW	18701	M.	9461	1226	1137	1096	898	787	646	561	500	488	429	439	352	353	246	187	88	58	12	5	1	
		F.	9240	1206	1158	1030	893	694	631	554	473	561	414	407	389	346	255	194	92	39	26	6	1	
MONMOUTH	30345	M.	15377	2042	2034	1888	1580	1126	931	851	778	779	657	656	594	533	395	295	178	61	33	6	2	
		F.	14968	2027	2000	1703	1282	1086	1013	866	797	756	708	696	634	534	373	308	188	86	41	11	4	
ABERGAVENNY	23571	M.	11879	1494	1382	1325	1166	933	803	820	722	661	548	515	381	380	301	189	104	48	18	2	2	
		F.	11692	1555	1447	1261	1024	1002	835	744	702	631	571	484	417	387	281	191	104	61	16	8	1	
BEDWELTY	55840	M.	29793	3958	3832	3252	3194	2898	2463	2088	1686	1583	1245	1089	881	756	472	273	144	69	16	3		
		F.	26047	4084	3816	3028	2406	2060	1867	1649	1448	1280	1091	972	756	656	442	264	135	64	20	6	3	
PONTYPOOL	35338	M.	18258	2494	2405	2112	1921	1665	1345	1131	938	910	764	733	545	535	315	228	147	67	23	8	1	
		F.	17080	2503	2406	2039	1581	1376	1188	1007	909	867	699	750	518	473	329	251	145	69	21	3	1	
NEWPORT	70542	M.	35197	5006	4545	3744	3500	3113	2831	2467	2075	1849	1486	1318	1005	872	587	419	241	100	20	10	.	
		F.	35345	4989	4514	4070	3484	3151	2725	2342	2018	1808	1461	1345	953	939	651	412	268	115	55	9	2	

…ote.—The Registration Districts of Division XI. are co-extensive with the Poor Law Unions of the same name, with the following exception:—Anglesey Distri… …) comprises the two Poor Law Unions of Anglesey and Holyhead.

…or the Parishes comprised in each Registration District, see Vol. II., Division XI., Table 4.

…he Districts are arranged topographically under the Registration Counties, and are numbered consecutively, commencing with the Metropolitan District… …ision I.

* For the Number of Children at each Year of Age under 5 see Table 5.

Table 2 *continued*.—Ages of Males and Females in Registration Districts.

Registration District.	All Ages. Persons.	All Ages. Males and Females.	Under 5 Years	5–	10–	15–	20–	25–	30–	35–	40–	45–	50–	55–	60–	65–	70–	75–	80–	85–	90–	95–
43. SOUTH WALES.																						
GLAMORGANSHIRE.																						
586 CARDIFF	106164	M. - 54128	7436	6326	5510	5384	5332	4980	4127	3684	3035	2398	1926	1434	1093	678	486	235	141	42	8	3
		F. - 52036	7581	6223	5462	5406	5332	4404	3610	3143	2679	2244	1830	1315	1166	659	454	298	151	59	16	4
587 PONTYPRIDD	93493	M. - 50675	7141	6318	5202	5121	5632	4784	3906	3108	2513	1983	1656	1206	920	573	333	167	84	22	4	1
		F. - 42818	6817	6154	5065	3934	3778	3399	2954	2504	2016	1663	1425	1048	788	523	332	188	111	28	10	1
588 MERTHYR TYDFIL	101441	M. - 52430	6657	6662	5892	5660	5036	4210	3641	3139	2725	2122	2002	1516	1329	800	449	223	91	27	7	2
		F. - 49011	7045	6721	5716	4742	4106	3622	3145	2753	2398	2107	1940	1463	1276	890	560	267	165	67	26	3
589 BRIDGEND	38920	M. - 20054	2708	2497	2186	1991	1821	1577	1402	1215	1002	812	785	646	561	350	241	168	91	32	9	1
		F. - 18866	2666	2520	2113	1738	1598	1397	1234	1193	867	801	745	683	512	389	287	174	81	37	13	5
590 NEATH	52077	M. - 26219	3806	3508	3085	2782	2317	2035	1759	1516	1306	1034	973	733	616	400	234	115	60	19	1	.
		F. - 25858	3755	3553	3025	2586	2286	1826	1649	1475	1270	1091	839	772	639	479	287	181	89	29	7	1
591 PONTARDAWE	20185	M. - 10116	1581	1466	1255	1084	849	736	626	519	411	405	327	284	227	168	101	66	39	14	2	1
		F. - 10069	1520	1474	1210	993	802	759	604	543	462	403	357	254	216	198	134	91	47	17	4	2
592 SWANSEA	95001	M. - 47207	7044	6255	5235	4828	4358	3936	3476	2814	2423	1891	1664	1101	948	520	375	187	94	20	7	1
		F. - 47794	7058	6255	5375	4851	4427	3827	3100	2728	2465	1866	1607	1177	1100	692	458	300	160	40	11	8
593 GOWER	11102	M. - 5239	756	740	602	541	380	363	299	302	256	250	216	164	160	116	106	75	26	11	2	.
		F. - 5863	781	736	614	542	464	427	334	316	287	254	232	244	161	141	104	91	42	16	.	1
CARMARTHENSHIRE.																						
594 LLANELLY	44616	M. - 22034	3341	3140	2680	2347	1862	1587	1433	1177	1055	862	721	512	444	380	234	124	64	14	3	3
		F. - 22582	3385	3128	2686	2248	1934	1666	1483	1226	1109	984	772	574	483	392	310	165	95	35	11	3
595 LLANDOVERY	12765	M. - 6106	738	772	796	647	484	363	330	281	278	261	258	257	235	167	116	85	35	14	2	.
		F. - 6659	763	740	669	702	652	469	461	350	349	243	271	259	248	188	168	120	63	28	10	5
596 LLANDILOFAWR	18799	M. - 9032	1303	1278	1081	924	658	585	513	462	378	370	312	258	264	227	175	100	60	21	3	.
		F. - 9767	1222	1213	1062	914	851	707	641	515	460	455	349	353	291	263	207	140	76	35	9	4
597 CARMARTHEN	35075	M. - 16317	2201	2130	1878	1676	1328	1063	902	785	780	648	686	596	549	429	309	180	99	39	9	2
		F. - 18758	2104	1956	1924	1817	1795	1424	1181	989	937	816	812	698	680	665	475	260	135	70	17	3
PEMBROKESHIRE.																						
598 NARBERTH	19541	M. - 9149	1285	1196	1174	946	661	557	500	414	404	355	355	323	364	241	165	118	63	30	8	1
		F. - 10392	1280	1173	1090	948	913	747	561	547	511	468	441	399	482	338	241	151	91	42	12	6
599 PEMBROKE	30347	M. - 14780	2005	1814	1713	1609	1373	909	828	741	769	664	585	482	447	314	226	110	68	21	6	2
		F. - 15567	1930	1771	1636	1668	1401	1130	958	872	829	715	648	551	600	384	259	186	82	41	8	2
600 HAVERFORDWEST	33791	M. - 16156	2087	1880	1918	1816	1416	1032	786	778	774	710	648	622	560	455	332	134	136	41	10	2
		F. - 17635	2115	1934	1866	1761	1527	1192	1015	893	985	735	787	662	676	512	425	253	155	52	7	7
CARDIGANSHIRE.																						
601 CARDIGAN	17615	M. - 7583	1030	1011	968	768	506	384	401	366	349	326	310	286	276	256	181	113	69	16	7	1
		F. - 10032	1008	989	960	900	776	713	660	622	681	513	463	409	451	316	323	180	110	47	9	2
602 NEWCASTLE IN EMLYN	19014	M. - 8643	1150	1132	1079	818	609	528	458	386	342	365	388	301	327	246	227	121	53	25	8	.
		F. - 10371	1121	1106	1028	979	894	735	644	556	512	529	484	391	418	337	283	193	107	36	7	1
603 LAMPETER	10087	M. - 4671	615	570	545	481	328	309	276	194	224	225	185	155	171	129	85	60	36	16	2	.
		F. - 5416	634	657	602	530	443	373	343	317	281	269	221	215	171	171	125	75	41	15	2	3
604 ABERAYRON	12543	M. - 5278	736	730	740	522	322	258	219	222	223	221	237	190	205	180	120	96	41	18	2	1
		F. - 7265	776	759	710	651	540	487	465	412	403	386	373	308	310	260	180	112	77	19	10	1
605 ABERYSTWITH	25606	M. - 11852	1518	1551	1526	1400	904	745	583	618	556	498	526	423	378	251	185	105	60	16	.	1
		F. - 13754	1501	1490	1531	1440	1215	873	800	895	752	668	642	486	601	337	258	174	90	35	11	4
606 TREGARON	10272	M. - 4690	629	640	591	501	319	278	258	204	228	186	186	164	147	135	117	59	40	6	3	.
		F. - 5582	638	646	558	534	450	403	370	289	282	380	234	221	207	166	123	85	48	15	1	.
BRECKNOCKSHIRE.																						
607 BUILTH	8182	M. - 4015	538	565	448	384	299	264	253	221	186	172	176	154	136	102	93	40	22	10	4	.
		F. - 4167	553	488	497	434	360	322	240	206	190	177	173	161	168	106	79	41	23	16	4	1
608 BRECKNOCK	17178	M. - 8578	1014	998	984	870	785	607	527	453	483	368	341	316	258	208	148	104	56	16	4	.
		F. - 8600	991	928	870	800	755	636	508	463	428	438	396	290	303	206	177	96	90	23	6	.
609 CRICKHOWELL	18558	M. - 9370	1286	1218	991	881	781	681	590	512	488	507	423	319	284	212	160	85	45	13	1	2
		F. - 9188	1251	1223	1065	818	690	638	549	485	470	410	377	330	312	250	158	85	58	13	6	1
610 HAY	10222	M. - 5028	619	577	590	480	364	337	306	284	262	235	236	190	184	138	111	68	33	13	5	.
		F. - 5194	633	620	554	484	486	363	318	253	264	240	210	193	193	175	131	84	30	16	1	1
RADNORSHIRE.																						
611 KNIGHTON	11782	M. - 6057	731	696	715	635	549	411	343	320	272	276	277	221	221	148	120	76	35	8	1	.
		F. - 5725	697	710	697	674	472	402	383	302	263	255	258	208	190	162	109	76	41	14	2	.
612 RHAYADER	6741	M. - 3347	428	433	383	361	294	216	217	183	163	145	125	114	104	100	76	45	17	14	1	.
		F. - 3394	444	394	397	328	288	253	202	166	160	136	124	118	117	101	82	37	27	8	.	.
44. NORTH WALES.																						
MONTGOMERYSHIRE.																						
613 MACHYNLLETH	12517	M. - 6080	737	738	737	653	466	398	320	310	302	293	256	233	212	180	183	76	31	9	1	.
		F. - 6437	728	757	751	637	549	426	363	305	353	325	269	260	228	188	159	83	42	11	13	.
614 NEWTOWN	25439	M. - 12732	1713	1574	1609	1356	1028	845	701	696	573	584	512	390	358	331	228	147	58	30	7	.
		F. - 12707	1724	1651	1406	1279	1069	810	720	668	685	537	511	399	401	333	253	152	103	31	13	3
615 FORDEN	18281	M. - 9445	1094	1162	1077	984	788	656	502	476	500	442	413	355	374	242	194	104	53	18	2	.
		F. - 8836	1111	1082	1001	791	692	570	515	474	496	386	393	339	312	262	172	136	67	34	3	.
616 LLANFYLLIN	19959	M. - 10038	1180	1221	1161	1045	804	600	635	521	517	493	407	381	394	276	235	128	60	23	7	.
		F. - 9921	1213	1216	1152	968	716	616	556	496	530	402	428	384	374	298	226	134	114	22	7	3
FLINTSHIRE.																						
617 HOLYWELL	45774	M. - 23217	3081	2843	2641	2398	1875	1710	1513	1392	1275	1010	920	759	705	468	277	170	74	23	2	1
		F. - 22557	2983	2992	2724	1908	1593	1475	1366	1363	1251	1046	949	820	744	580	390	284	146	50	8	3
DENBIGHSHIRE.																						
618 WREXHAM	55158	M. - 28325	3867	3578	3306	3051	2380	2088	1834	1611	1513	1277	1121	900	740	477	318	159	80	30	1	.
		F. - 26833	3926	3633	3242	2246	1885	1896	1711	1529	1508	1265	1074	879	769	553	369	227	100	32	8	1
619 RUTHIN	14215	M. - 7160	856	766	812	805	602	463	391	343	371	341	326	312	278	207	141	97	42	14	3	.
		F. - 7055	801	803	844	658	554	481	397	390	347	321	347	356	261	209	149	123	47	18	6	3
620 ST. ASAPH	29458	M. - 13935	1671	1561	1637	1383	1007	935	904	795	756	656	621	583	534	345	281	160	74	28	4	.
		F. - 15523	1695	1617	1660	1522	1316	1163	985	915	846	779	724	614	575	471	329	195	94	33	10	2
621 LLANRWST	14109	M. - 7081	914	799	717	679	627	535	476	426	356	302	292	281	239	189	142	98	40	14	6	1
		F. - 7028	858	776	730	713	601	508	436	411	374	327	256	264	240	175	178	88	52	21	4	3

Table 2 *continued*.—AGES of MALES and FEMALES in REGISTRATION DISTRICTS.

GISTRATION DISTRICT.	ALL AGES. Persons.	ALL AGES. Males and Females.	Under 5 Years.	5–	10–	15–	20–	25–	30–	35–	40–	45–	50–	55–	60–	65–	70–	75–	80–	85–	90–	95–	100 and upw^ds.
. NORTH .LES—*cont.*																							
ONETHSHIRE.																							
ŁWEN - -	16533	M. - 8438	1012	1023	952	833	715	571	505	480	402	387	359	387	285	229	180	98	45	14	3	.	1
		F. - 8295	1077	1080	947	710	658	543	518	417	462	370	387	322	281	239	182	121	43	28	8	1	1
.A - -	6740	M. - 3498	318	362	350	358	373	236	220	216	199	190	127	126	125	102	77	53	10	8	2	1	.
		F. - 3242	386	360	330	278	272	224	196	191	176	168	141	98	118	89	72	60	36	16	5	3	1
LGELLY - -	15180	M. - 7273	971	889	893	678	533	407	481	484	388	333	287	227	215	172	137	94	47	18	3	1	.
		F. - 7907	949	927	899	710	598	577	498	486	426	381	296	288	264	236	174	113	55	18	7	1	.
STINIOG -	29525	M. - 15141	2104	1688	1570	1376	1447	1239	1129	1016	774	652	519	428	368	280	183	91	47	18	2	1	.
		F. - 14384	2075	1740	1602	1263	1145	1107	1014	916	777	608	483	451	392	312	233	141	84	16	15	1	.
ARVONSHIRE.																							
LLHELI - -	22911	M. - 11161	1462	1288	1229	1087	919	738	647	628	531	489	428	447	395	388	254	164	82	30	7	.	.
		F. - 11750	1410	1218	1126	1016	987	823	737	726	659	553	490	563	455	391	292	183	92	47	6	1	.
RNARVON -	43997	M. - 22058	2984	2693	2481	2228	1921	1726	1471	1345	1146	901	814	704	607	462	302	199	87	29	8	.	.
		F. - 21939	2923	2475	2327	2056	1741	1758	1504	1384	1255	998	851	722	672	514	362	251	110	42	8	1	.
NGOR - -	38512	M. - 18792	2278	2051	2219	1934	1507	1410	1190	1003	979	893	821	742	646	503	318	202	93	38	5	.	1
		F. - 19720	2251	2093	2056	1853	1694	1408	1296	1151	1084	1037	876	795	671	589	378	251	113	50	12	6	1
NWAY - -	18361	M. - 8731	1120	999	892	891	741	652	542	451	452	406	386	340	270	197	154	76	45	14	5	.	.
		F. - 9630	1122	959	975	978	919	737	610	576	537	494	470	344	320	236	152	101	41	17	4	2	.
ANGLESEY.																							
GLESEY - -	35141	M. - 17190	2048	1965	1848	1704	1850	1208	1035	898	856	791	764	700	694	593	370	255	135	60	11	4	.
		F. - 17951	2090	1903	1755	1653	1389	1252	1183	1039	911	898	841	779	750	551	440	277	154	62	22	3	.

Table 3.—AGES of MALES and FEMALES in REGISTRATION SUB-DISTRICTS.

REGISTRATION SUB-DISTRICT.	ALL AGES. Persons.	ALL AGES. Males and Females.	Under 5 Years.	5–	10–	15–	20–	25–	30–	35–	40–	45–	50–	55–	60–	65–	70–	75–	80–	85–	90–	95–	100 and upw^ds.
MONMOUTH-SHIRE.																							
80 CHEPSTOW.																							
RE NEWTON - -	5541	M. - 2906	328	351	363	260	244	193	175	140	164	147	132	111	103	78	62	34	15	4	.	.	.
		F. - 2635	382	331	320	221	183	173	145	132	107	128	115	94	98	58	47	25	14	10	2	.	.
EPSTOW. (W.) -	7168	M. - 3517	480	423	384	349	254	265	215	198	162	146	166	114	142	96	74	22	23	4	2	1	.
		F. 3651	439	439	367	332	298	268	253	184	219	151	166	127	145	100	85	36	31	9	1	.	1
NNEY - -	5992	M. - 3038	418	363	348	289	239	188	171	165	182	136	141	129	106	72	51	32	20	4	3	.	.
		F. - 2954	365	388	343	250	211	190	156	157	185	135	126	108	105	97	62	31	14	7	3	1	.
80 MONMOUTH.																							
LEFORD -	14887	M. - 7652	1071	1097	974	816	569	467	387	376	397	302	305	262	226	161	128	68	19	12	4	1	.
		F. - 7235	1124	1084	835	590	403	462	403	396	359	333	331	231	266	171	122	85	43	19	6	2	.
NGESTOW -	4920	M. - 2500	304	304	281	227	202	144	146	184	125	132	116	98	107	87	50	39	17	6	.	1	.
		F. - 2420	304	300	293	208	151	153	147	125	134	107	120	86	99	53	68	33	10	3	3	.	.
NMOUTH, (W. H.) -	6358	M. - 3126	382	330	397	331	230	201	180	156	151	159	130	111	110	77	65	36	15	9	1	.	.
		F. - 3232	364	383	332	346	295	257	189	167	171	164	142	127	114	62	73	35	19	9	2	1	.
ELLICK - -	4175	M. - 2099	285	253	236	266	128	119	123	112	106	84	104	88	90	70	52	35	10	6	.	.	.
		F. - 2076	235	253	243	168	157	141	127	109	92	104	103	90	75	81	45	29	15	8	.	1	.
2 ABERGAVENNY.																							
ANARTH - -	1717	M. - 843	104	83	105	81	59	45	51	44	49	37	47	26	45	29	19	10	7	3	.	.	.
		F. - 874	80	100	80	89	86	67	48	57	43	40	37	46	27	31	27	12	4	.	.	.	.
ANVIHANGEL - -	1675	M. - 874	108	87	90	93	62	62	54	51	46	46	34	37	34	28	23	8	8	2	1	.	.
		F. - 801	98	96	100	80	68	64	41	49	43	42	27	31	25	21	10	7	4	.	.	1	.
ERGAVENNY. (W. L.)	10730	M. - 5217	637	504	541	465	390	397	402	342	238	246	234	171	176	126	92	65	20	11	.	.	.
		F. - 5513	674	591	531	491	521	421	401	324	304	272	250	206	178	136	97	56	42	13	6	.	.
AENAVON. (H.) -	9449	M. - 4945	825	623	589	527	422	359	310	285	278	219	200	147	134	118	55	21	13	3	1	2	.
		F. - 4504	703	680	550	364	382	293	254	272	241	217	170	134	127	93	48	30	11	3	2	.	.
583 BEDWELTY.																							
ERYSTRUTH - -	18672	M. - 9950	1396	1376	1042	1098	943	865	666	576	481	398	347	291	219	126	74	31	17	4	.	.	.
		F. - 8722	1473	1389	1011	798	641	595	568	451	418	335	324	250	188	135	66	42	24	7	1	1	.
EDEGAR. (W.) -	34685	M. - 18597	2294	2286	2054	1882	1774	1515	1345	1039	1026	793	703	556	503	318	179	101	36	11	3	.	.
		F. - 16088	2415	2277	1892	1401	1327	1181	1019	897	792	698	610	467	488	276	179	51	33	9	4	2	.
CK BEDWELTY -	2483	M. - 1246	168	171	156	114	81	83	77	71	76	54	49	34	34	29	20	12	7	1	.	.	.
		F. - 1237	196	170	125	117	92	91	62	70	75	58	38	39	30	31	19	12	7	4	1	.	.
84 PONTYPOOL.																							
NTYPOOL. (R.) -	25297	M. - 13048	1796	1753	1577	1489	1121	959	813	662	653	542	531	362	368	207	135	76	36	14	3	1	.
		F. - 12249	1863	1781	1494	1069	955	817	720	641	620	487	541	341	340	221	169	93	36	12	3	1	1
ANGIBBY. (W.) -	6310	M. - 3322	463	436	347	346	302	276	216	170	165	129	120	102	90	55	53	35	10	4	3	.	.
		F. - 2988	422	423	339	261	268	230	184	174	143	135	121	89	67	50	45	19	14	4	.	.	.
K. (P.) - -	3731	M. - 1888	235	216	188	206	142	116	102	106	92	93	82	81	77	53	41	36	21	3	2	.	.
		F. - 1843	218	202	208	171	153	141	94	94	104	77	88	85	66	52	37	28	19	5	.	.	.

te.—For the Parishes comprised in each Registration Sub-District, see Vol. II., Division XI., Table 4.
.) denotes that a Workhouse, and (WS.) that a Workhouse School belonging to the District is situated within the Sub-District; (w.) denotes a Workhouse, ws.) a Workhouse School not belonging to the District; (H.) a Hospital or Infirmary; (L.) a Lunatic Asylum; (P.) a Prison or Convict Establishment; a certified Reformatory or Industrial School; (B.) Barracks, &c.; (S.) H.M. Ships. A figure appended to any of these letters denotes the number of institutions similar class situated within the Sub-District. The names of the institutions thus indicated, and the number of inmates enumerated therein, will be found in II., Division XI., Table 6.

Table 3 *continued.*—AGES of MALES and FEMALES in REGISTRATION SUB-DISTRICTS.

REGISTRATION SUB-DISTRICT.	ALL AGES. Persons.	ALL AGES. Males and Females.	Under 5 Years.	5-	10-	15-	20-	25-	30-	35-	40-	45-	50-	55-	60-	65-	70-	75-	80-	85-	90-
42. *MONMOUTHSHIRE*—cont.																					
585 NEWPORT.																					
1 Caerleon. (WS.)	10709	M. - 5157	742	698	603	472	340	348	329	280	290	206	213	192	156	129	78	51	21	7	2
		F. - 5552	757	723	653	546	418	419	383	343	294	216	189	175	163	135	76	55	22	9	2
2 Newport. (W. H.[3] B.)	33932	M. - 16848	2396	2013	1617	1089	1636	1548	1321	1032	901	713	617	436	403	215	164	80	41	11	1
		F. - 17084	2362	2022	1828	1746	1790	1398	1199	973	867	633	686	430	460	267	134	103	46	18	6
3 St. Woollos - -	12811	M. - 6475	934	892	747	645	551	460	414	358	291	291	261	197	158	132	89	51	18	4	2
		F. - 6336	953	886	742	586	489	476	373	340	313	270	238	178	176	133	85	52	26	10	1
4 Mynyddyslwyn -	13090	M. - 6717	984	956	777	604	593	495	408	395	397	276	227	180	155	111	88	59	20	7	6
		F. - 6373	917	883	822	607	509	434	407	350	334	276	237	170	160	116	67	56	21	18	.
43. SOUTH WALES.																					
GLAMORGANSHIRE.																					
586 CARDIFF.																					
1 Whitchurch -	6474	M. - 3311	430	417	379	373	261	221	211	181	173	165	118	118	90	86	49	31	17	5	.
		F. - 3163	449	428	374	286	256	195	188	167	140	178	128	104	104	67	43	31	19	15	.
2 Cardiff. (W. WS. H.[3] P. R. B.)	94566	M. - 48299	6733	5618	4861	4767	4845	4582	3765	3297	2756	2115	1705	1208	908	515	326	173	97	28	7
		F. - 46267	6827	5514	4858	4831	4831	4046	3278	2858	2424	1950	1588	1115	979	519	373	231	104	42	15
3 St. Nicholas - -	5024	M. - 2518	273	291	289	254	216	187	151	126	166	118	103	113	96	77	51	31	27	9	1
		F. - 2506	309	281	260	289	245	163	144	118	115	110	114	96	83	73	38	36	38	7	1
587 PONTYPRIDD.																					
1 Pontypridd - -	30250	M. - 16146	2173	2011	1702	1617	1792	1422	1190	983	844	637	548	421	341	223	126	74	31	9	2
		F. - 14104	2179	2066	1659	1298	1253	1042	948	817	698	559	502	395	293	204	158	76	40	9	3
2 Llantrisaint. (W.) -	19197	M. - 10059	1430	1328	1109	977	904	848	754	595	490	496	383	264	225	150	94	56	31	5	1
		F. - 9138	1396	1283	1144	850	726	663	610	543	434	389	334	252	218	134	79	55	40	7	6
3 Ystradyfodwg -	44046	M. - 24470	3539	2979	2391	2527	2936	2514	1962	1531	1170	940	725	521	354	200	114	77	22	8	1
		F. - 19576	3342	2895	2262	1791	1819	1604	1376	1144	884	745	589	411	270	190	96	57	25	7	1
588 MERTHYR TYDFIL.																					
1 Gelligaer - -	11592	M. - 6201	855	752	686	680	611	518	425	372	317	241	247	176	153	92	42	27	6	2	.
		F. - 5391	807	759	671	537	463	381	331	305	253	221	194	138	136	68	38	25	15	7	2
2 Lower Merthyr Tydfil. (W.)	23904	M. - 12033	1616	1552	1362	1261	1076	906	848	689	608	465	455	351	318	227	134	61	32	8	3
		F. - 11871	1669	1570	1334	1136	972	911	771	657	508	499	464	336	342	272	173	78	47	19	7
3 Upper Merthyr Tydfil. (H.[3])	27808	M. - 14472	1849	1747	1530	1576	1480	1193	1034	838	768	609	567	408	430	218	125	58	31	10	2
		F. - 13336	1834	1788	1500	1329	1185	941	871	743	633	559	592	413	380	268	186	70	43	26	6
4 Aberdare. (WS.)	38137	M. - 19724	2687	2811	2515	2083	1809	1593	1334	1240	972	808	733	581	428	263	148	77	22	7	2
		F. - 18413	2718	2304	2211	1744	1506	1380	1172	1048	899	828	690	547	417	294	192	114	60	21	11
589 BRIDGEND.																					
1 Maesteg - -	18215	M. - 9762	1380	1266	1057	1015	671	837	603	596	462	335	370	271	198	138	90	45	26	7	5
		F. - 8453	1333	1284	985	755	692	623	547	487	398	312	300	228	177	153	85	53	22	13	4
2 Cowbridge -	6185	M. - 2966	357	322	310	314	209	198	179	171	139	166	130	118	114	70	57	55	30	11	2
		F. - 3219	375	340	359	331	301	236	168	165	135	176	132	108	111	81	76	54	25	11	5
3 Bridgend. (W. L.) -	14540	M. - 7346	971	906	738	882	641	542	530	449	401	312	285	262	246	182	94	68	33	14	3
		F. - 7194	952	896	775	652	606	538	499	451	326	313	311	266	224	155	116	67	34	13	4
590 NEATH.																					
1 Margam - -	18326	M. - 9272	1359	1281	1006	1024	823	679	598	480	445	350	368	274	232	159	72	38	15	8	1
		F. - 9054	1276	1281	1069	915	819	665	546	474	432	372	321	300	252	100	108	59	33	12	1
2 Neath. (W. L. R.) -	21548	M. - 10768	1519	1385	1201	1133	972	895	769	671	576	446	381	278	252	150	90	41	25	5	.
		F. - 10780	1562	1442	1284	1079	976	762	726	650	563	464	328	304	257	201	114	74	29	11	3
3 Ystradyfellte -	3916	M. - 1996	285	232	209	207	184	186	116	103	89	79	84	72	51	36	22	14	8	1	.
		F. - 1920	281	274	227	161	177	127	125	94	95	72	61	41	34	45	22	20	10	2	2
4 Cadoxton - -	8297	M. - 4193	648	590	527	439	338	273	286	252	196	160	150	109	80	64	46	22	14	6	.
		F. - 4104	635	686	505	451	324	272	252	248	180	183	129	98	96	73	43	28	17	4	1
591 PONTARDAWE.																					
1 Pontardawe. (W.) -	20185	M. - 10116	1531	1406	1255	1084	849	730	626	519	411	405	327	294	227	168	101	66	33	14	2
		F. - 10069	1520	1474	1210	995	899	759	604	543	462	408	337	254	210	198	134	91	47	17	4
592 SWANSEA.																					
1 Llandilotalybont. (W.)	11936	M. - 5778	839	872	741	652	471	418	397	325	230	225	183	118	96	61	50	28	17	3	1
		F. - 5658	893	842	717	494	437	402	349	293	278	225	185	123	120	71	67	48	23	5	1
2 Llangafelach -	25153	M. - 12820	2040	1787	1491	1387	1181	1069	909	728	610	463	417	289	205	122	76	33	13	2	2
		F. - 12333	1951	1752	1470	1241	1028	962	812	662	630	479	416	298	250	185	100	71	32	10	2
3 Swansea. (W. H.[2] P.) -	50120	M. - 24285	3445	2907	2482	2357	2298	2100	1668	1496	1430	1063	904	587	574	280	209	115	58	15	3
		F. - 25835	3584	3049	2704	2763	2641	2177	1707	1540	1367	1120	956	637	648	370	262	152	88	27	7
4 Llansamlet -	8392	M. - 4324	661	699	514	452	408	340	307	265	193	159	160	97	73	48	40	11	6	.	1
		F. 4068	680	612	484	353	321	296	262	233	170	151	140	119	82	68	39	34	17	7	1
593 GOWER.																					
1 Gower Eastern. (B.)	8248	M. - 3890	584	593	468	368	281	282	234	229	171	160	134	115	99	68	52	40	13	6	.
		F. - 4358	634	584	460	428	364	317	299	232	216	186	155	140	100	95	64	44	32	7	.
2 Gower Western. (W.)	2854	M. - 1409	172	147	136	138	99	81	65	73	79	70	82	40	61	48	54	35	13	5	2
		F. - 1445	147	152	154	118	100	110	85	84	71	74	88	55	61	46	40	47	19	9	.
CARMARTHENSHIRE.																					
594 LLANELLY.																					
1 Loughor - -	7481	M. - 3705	584	567	437	395	340	268	254	220	163	155	116	73	68	69	33	20	9	3	1
		F. - 3776	557	557	469	379	334	268	244	208	195	182	135	65	68	57	46	24	17	6	2
2 Llanelly. (W. H.) -	23933	M. - 11847	1738	1623	1402	1235	1140	944	777	812	610	463	395	275	241	154	120	43	27	3	1
		F. - 12086	1778	1679	1446	1224	1120	807	823	657	611	494	413	318	245	200	146	73	30	11	4
3 Pembrey - - -	8173	M. - 3958	626	630	508	396	262	223	251	212	187	168	130	93	94	69	43	35	17	3	1
		F. - 4215	640	657	457	395	332	300	278	233	131	218	146	123	109	80	76	44	22	10	1
4 Llannon - -	4969	M. - 2464	383	329	353	271	212	152	151	124	95	96	78	71	41	47	38	26	11	3	.
		F. - 2505	387	336	314	251	208	191	138	123	112	90	82	68	61	55	43	24	17	9	4

Table 3 *continued*.—AGES of MALES and FEMALES in REGISTRATION SUB-DISTRICTS.

REGISTRATION SUB-DISTRICT.	ALL AGES. Persons.	Males and Females.	Under 5 Years.	5–	10–	15–	20–	25–	30–	35–	40–	45–	50–	55–	60–	65–	70–	75–	80–	85–	90–	95–	100 and upw.
OUTH WALES —*cont.*																							
RMARTHEN-HIRE—cont.																							
LLANDOVERY.																							
NDDAUSAINT	647	M. - 325	27	42	36	36	22	25	16	10	9	16	17	18	17	11	8	6	4	1	.	.	.
		F. - 322	28	19	32	44	35	21	23	19	10	12	11	19	17	10	3	8	5	2	.	1	.
NGADOCK	1911	M. - 909	115	114	119	93	70	52	61	39	30	32	45	37	31	32	15	19	7	1	.	.	.
		F. - 1002	112	116	110	107	104	60	70	51	38	43	37	37	32	31	26	17	6	9	3	.	.
NSADWRN	1502	M. - 707	88	94	89	71	39	45	27	28	33	35	30	27	35	17	16	8	3	2	.	.	.
		F. - 795	79	97	71	99	84	56	48	38	36	32	33	29	34	22	18	14	12	2	1	2	.
NDINGAT. (W.)	3416	M. - 1635	176	196	244	216	151	91	74	80	79	76	64	64	60	48	24	15	6	4	1	.	.
		F. - 1781	198	197	192	181	173	119	135	90	75	79	71	56	74	36	44	34	19	7	.	2	.
NPAIRARYBRYN	1281	M. - 615	83	73	71	67	55	42	30	31	26	33	28	22	23	18	10	8	3	1	.	.	.
		F. - 666	88	68	69	77	70	52	44	29	33	21	30	21	19	16	14	13	4	2	1	.	.
NWRTYD	942	M. - 455	62	80	51	40	28	32	34	26	24	21	17	15	13	9	8	8	6	1	.	.	.
		F. - 487	62	61	52	50	45	30	35	38	22	16	19	19	17	10	8	3	2	.	1	.	.
TOWY	1087	M. - 512	61	65	71	45	39	29	36	30	25	20	20	19	16	15	9	7	2	.	.	.	.
		F. - 575	76	67	44	61	49	51	39	35	29	13	29	20	16	10	19	8	5	1	4	.	.
WIL-CAYO	1979	M. - 948	124	120	121	77	78	43	52	47	43	34	40	45	41	22	28	14	5	4	1	.	.
		F. - 1031	120	120	99	98	92	77	62	61	57	31	41	39	39	22	21	23	10	5	.	.	.
LLANDILOFAWR.																							
LLEY	1783	M. - 856	110	118	120	101	59	56	51	41	36	32	39	32	29	27	12	9	5	1	.	.	.
		F. - 927	124	113	104	80	85	59	65	42	46	42	37	26	27	25	16	13	11	3	.	.	.
ANFYNYDD	1169	M. - 559	63	68	68	53	35	37	27	39	24	26	25	26	22	24	16	8	4	3	.	.	.
		F. - 610	61	58	53	61	63	50	42	30	29	27	26	38	25	12	20	11	.	3	1	.	.
ANGATHEN	2506	M. - 1137	144	153	138	137	85	50	64	53	51	59	40	40	39	30	26	12	11	7	.	.	.
		F. - 1369	151	145	155	130	128	82	58	64	60	57	54	44	51	38	30	24	17	8	2	.	.
ANDILO. (W.)	4511	M. - 2084	279	273	231	191	150	136	120	107	98	97	71	87	78	61	43	36	16	4	.	.	.
		F. - 2427	241	266	248	251	235	106	151	125	109	114	98	91	87	81	55	46	21	4	2	1	.
LANFEGIE	8830	M. - 4396	707	684	637	442	319	306	250	251	174	156	150	113	96	85	78	35	24	6	3	.	.
		F. - 4434	646	622	597	383	360	320	274	258	216	185	134	164	101	107	86	46	27	17	4	3	.
97 CARMARTHEN.																							
LANGENDEIRNE	8549	M. - 3989	589	551	509	381	303	290	204	179	157	156	165	146	126	105	71	33	26	6	3	1	.
		F. - 4560	584	484	493	437	484	307	294	223	221	187	175	138	175	120	165	61	28	25	7	2	.
T. CLEARS	6181	M. - 2840	364	463	346	283	206	140	150	135	128	113	124	110	103	102	60	34	16	12	2	.	.
		F. - 3341	366	342	330	324	288	270	206	184	159	144	139	142	134	117	98	53	31	13	8	.	.
ARMARTHEN (W.H.L. P.B.)	12872	M. - 5950	743	702	683	648	547	408	356	314	283	261	254	215	192	143	94	63	28	12	3	.	.
		F. - 6922	667	694	687	743	711	499	443	386	357	316	341	290	257	212	172	89	43	21	1	1	2
ONWIL	7473	M. - 3538	526	483	441	384	279	216	192	157	141	118	143	115	123	78	84	42	29	9	1	1	.
		F. - 3935	493	426	434	413	360	298	238	196	190	160	157	128	114	116	100	57	33	12	1	.	.
PEMBROKE-SHIRE.																							
598 NARBERTH.																							
LANBOIDY	3447	M. - 1609	217	197	203	155	128	110	97	80	67	72	70	65	66	31	26	15	14	5	1	.	.
		F. - 1838	237	206	165	161	169	140	107	95	58	87	80	73	66	57	35	28	14	8	2	2	.
LANDISSILIO	3334	M. - 1550	265	203	200	142	103	91	89	69	68	63	69	56	51	33	17	14	7	4	.	1	.
		F. - 1784	225	208	198	149	168	139	95	93	97	83	73	68	62	43	44	17	22	5	2	2	1
AMROTH	3084	M. - 1454	207	186	182	154	107	89	84	48	73	45	54	54	67	38	24	25	9	6	1	.	.
		F. - 1630	218	185	178	128	146	103	95	90	87	63	58	66	72	52	34	29	11	11	1	.	.
NARBERTH	3383	M. - 1565	185	212	209	175	91	95	90	79	64	51	60	52	78	48	29	21	8	7	1	.	.
		F. - 1818	210	178	175	186	176	132	100	93	71	82	86	85	87	66	44	30	12	5	.	1	.
SLEBECH. (W.)	2483	M. - 1145	141	138	144	122	88	54	54	62	55	40	38	43	46	30	34	18	9	5	2	.	.
		F. - 1338	149	131	140	126	122	94	68	77	71	60	55	49	62	40	42	25	18	4	4	.	.
BEGELLY	3810	M. - 1826	269	234	235	197	144	108	86	76	79	74	64	53	63	52	33	25	6	3	3	.	.
		F. - 1984	241	264	234	188	133	130	96	160	97	93	80	74	83	80	42	22	14	9	3	1	.
599 PEMBROKE																							
TENBY. (H.[2] B.[2])	10342	M. - 4586	630	583	537	447	373	291	261	252	249	173	183	164	167	118	76	47	25	7	1	.	.
		F. - 5756	631	613	566	641	577	440	397	326	286	264	223	190	215	146	166	87	29	15	5	2	.
PEMBROKE. (W.B.[2] S.[2])	15689	M. - 7989	1028	936	879	945	823	539	450	379	416	300	313	260	236	156	116	48	33	12	5	3	.
		F. - 7700	1005	889	819	827	662	548	346	429	413	356	342	282	231	183	128	74	42	22	2	.	.
ROOSE	4317	M. - 2205	347	295	297	217	171	149	117	110	97	101	87	68	48	40	34	15	10	2	.	.	.
		F. - 2112	294	269	257	200	162	142	116	177	130	93	83	79	54	51	25	24	11	4	1	.	.
HAVERFORDWEST.																							
MILFORD. (B[2]. S.)	9507	M. - 5066	648	518	582	567	544	411	294	289	290	215	196	174	126	119	63	42	40	7	.	.	.
		F. - 4441	635	527	476	412	380	309	237	262	231	199	179	147	152	113	84	61	27	18	1	.	.
HAVERFORDWEST. (W.H.)	10755	M. - 5008	600	565	623	635	425	309	221	236	216	218	220	182	199	122	118	57	42	15	4	1	.
		F. - 5747	599	598	615	663	522	383	338	296	285	271	260	231	198	171	143	73	55	16	3	1	.
ST. DAVIDS	6282	M. - 2888	393	360	343	294	221	148	118	116	138	140	111	128	110	98	72	43	26	12	2	1	.
		F. - 3414	382	374	358	328	293	218	215	206	171	148	160	136	137	104	94	54	28	7	.	3	.
FISHGUARD	7247	M. - 3214	426	437	400	320	226	164	153	172	130	137	121	138	125	96	79	52	27	7	4	.	.
		F. - 4033	480	435	417	358	332	284	225	228	216	175	177	148	188	124	104	69	45	11	3	3	.
CARDIGAN-SHIRE.																							
601 CARDIGAN.																							
NEWPORT	5219	M. - 2170	292	287	311	198	129	89	117	116	92	101	88	101	72	63	63	31	17	7	.	.	.
		F. - 3049	293	309	309	300	227	192	177	194	164	188	144	121	135	83	104	60	24	12	1	2	.
CARDIGAN. (W.)	8705	M. - 3828	381	514	455	396	291	216	200	175	183	161	150	114	140	117	79	58	31	4	3	1	.
		F. - 4877	502	473	448	416	391	335	343	294	295	237	218	201	218	155	147	87	50	24	4	.	.
LLANDYGWYDD	3691	M. - 1585	207	219	192	174	86	83	84	75	74	64	63	71	63	56	38	24	11	5	4	.	.
		F. - 2106	213	207	203	184	158	136	140	134	122	88	101	87	98	68	72	33	27	11	4	.	.
602 NEWCASTLE IN EMLYN.																							
KENARTH. (W.)	8233	M. - 3800	532	529	471	395	280	245	213	153	150	163	147	117	144	103	86	31	28	11	2	.	.
		F. - 4433	547	498	461	427	387	385	260	225	205	216	184	161	151	122	117	80	48	15	2	1	.
PENBRYN	4547	M. - 2030	257	279	257	230	128	111	93	98	70	91	86	67	78	65	67	37	11	6	4	.	.
		F. - 2517	232	251	241	235	196	173	153	155	122	142	128	193	119	97	74	46	32	11	2	.	.
LLANDYSSIL	6234	M. - 2813	361	344	351	293	237	190	152	117	122	111	105	117	110	78	74	33	14	8	2	.	.
		F. - 3421	342	357	326	317	311	232	231	170	185	171	172	127	148	118	102	66	27	10	3	.	.

Table 3 *continued*.—AGES of MALES AND FEMALES in REGISTRATION SUB-DISTRICTS.

REGISTRATION SUB-DISTRICT.	ALL AGES. Persons.		Males and Females.	Under 5 Years.	5–	10–	15–	20–	25–	30–	35–	40–	45–	50–	55–	60–	65–	70–	75–	80–	85–	90–	95–
43 SOUTH WALES—*cont.*																							
CARDIGANSHIRE—cont.																							
603 LAMPETER.																							
1 LLANYBYTHER	2690	M.	1244	187	176	137	124	77	96	67	51	61	61	40	48	39	28	20	17	12	4	.	.
		F.	1446	186	153	163	140	108	109	80	87	80	62	54	60	41	42	41	19	10	3	2	.
2 PENCARREG	2600	M.	1188	158	153	160	111	86	61	78	42	46	71	54	38	50	46	22	19	9	8	1	.
		F.	1412	157	152	171	125	110	96	78	76	75	83	72	50	44	47	26	27	11	2	.	1
3 LAMPETER. (W.)	2938	M.	1392	165	151	138	150	162	107	93	62	77	58	53	38	60	27	23	14	10	3	.	.
		F.	1546	175	169	161	169	153	103	107	90	68	66	54	58	52	44	35	16	10	8	.	2
4 LLANWENOG	1859	M.	847	111	116	115	90	63	55	35	39	40	35	33	31	22	38	20	10	6	1	1	.
		F.	1012	116	117	97	96	72	65	78	58	58	38	41	38	34	58	23	11	16	2	.	.
604 ABERAYRON.																							
1 LLANDISILIO	5934	M.	2477	330	358	347	232	163	117	96	165	97	96	109	95	92	94	69	53	13	4	.	1
		F.	3457	393	360	398	308	284	230	236	207	174	189	171	154	139	123	88	46	28	7	7	.
2 LLANSAINTFFRAID. (W.)	6022	M.	2801	397	372	393	283	152	141	123	117	126	125	128	95	113	86	61	43	28	9	2	.
		F.	3308	383	390	402	343	276	257	246	205	229	197	202	154	151	135	96	63	40	12	3	1
605 ABERYSTWITH.																							
1 LLANRHYSTYD	3128	M.	1419	156	181	192	149	90	93	75	62	81	53	67	54	52	34	33	25	9	4	.	.
		F.	1709	180	179	207	177	153	119	86	108	77	88	81	65	63	45	34	28	11	7	1	.
2 ABERYSTWITH. (W.H.B.)	10271	M.	4608	531	548	875	677	371	283	218	263	217	224	197	161	154	169	74	41	21	9	.	.
		F.	5663	574	540	896	645	664	406	353	358	340	277	371	202	186	127	116	59	36	4	3	2
3 GENEURGLYNN	4527	M.	2132	288	310	274	246	130	117	95	101	99	85	104	84	61	46	40	24	15	.	.	1
		F.	2395	264	283	286	230	169	172	139	157	126	123	112	94	85	65	46	43	22	6	2	1
4 RHEIDOL	7880	M.	3698	508	512	485	428	298	255	195	192	139	136	158	124	111	62	42	16	15	2	.	.
		F.	3882	483	484	402	388	329	276	222	212	209	178	178	132	167	110	63	44	21	18	5	1
606 TREGARON.																							
1 GWNNWS	3314	M.	1556	183	216	209	213	121	100	79	55	74	70	65	56	47	33	23	8	8	.	.	.
		F.	1758	204	225	189	180	127	125	98	101	86	91	77	66	61	42	38	23	11	4	.	.
2 LLANGEITHO	3187	M.	1433	203	185	166	122	91	85	86	69	70	62	53	58	43	55	41	33	16	3	.	.
		F.	1754	196	165	165	160	148	117	120	101	87	92	78	75	62	51	37	44	13	4	.	.
3 TREGARON. (W.)	3771	M.	1701	241	233	216	166	107	93	98	80	78	64	68	56	55	47	53	18	16	2	3	.
		F.	2070	239	220	194	194	178	161	146	96	109	117	79	79	84	67	48	2	10	7	1	.
BRECKNOCKSHIRE.																							
607 BUILTH.																							
1 ABERGWESSIN	2679	M.	1294	159	159	144	138	103	98	79	60	65	40	65	55	33	39	30	17	1	6	2	.
		F.	1385	164	169	168	142	128	85	80	71	69	64	63	43	37	46	31	10	7	11	2	1
2 COLWYN	1847	M.	959	120	127	122	99	80	49	54	46	38	47	45	32	36	21	19	11	10	2	1	.
		F.	888	114	117	120	92	59	67	53	41	41	35	34	43	21	10	16	11	6	2	.	.
3 BUILTH. (W.)	3666	M.	1762	259	219	182	147	118	125	120	115	83	76	65	67	67	42	44	21	11	2	1	.
		F.	1904	255	202	209	200	173	170	116	98	80	78	76	75	50	50	32	20	10	3	2	.
608 BRECKNOCK.																							
1 MERTHYR-CYNOG	1371	M.	685	82	83	78	84	51	53	41	35	32	26	23	26	17	19	12	15	7	1	.	.
		F.	686	84	78	94	72	61	51	38	32	41	30	19	23	21	13	12	10	4	3	.	.
2 DEVYNNOCK	3727	M.	1805	215	230	200	197	158	126	125	82	87	73	74	74	53	43	31	22	15	5	1	.
		F.	1922	217	227	220	200	167	122	118	163	90	101	95	60	63	46	30	25	21	4	4	.
3 BRECKNOCK. (W.H.P.B.)	7987	M.	4024	474	459	475	478	403	302	230	234	200	171	138	136	120	71	57	41	23	4	2	.
		F.	3963	464	391	396	420	367	333	245	221	195	182	196	142	154	81	65	39	34	7	.	.
4 PENKELLY	1456	M.	747	73	89	82	65	66	44	50	34	35	41	44	36	27	30	20	5	5	1	.	.
		F.	709	78	83	90	78	47	64	39	41	26	48	35	14	26	25	18	9	3	4	1	.
5 LLANGORSE	2637	M.	1317	170	137	143	146	107	88	75	68	69	57	62	44	41	45	28	21	5	4	1	.
		F.	1320	148	140	170	124	113	101	68	86	78	77	51	51	30	41	23	13	4	5	1	.
609 CRICKHOWELL.																							
1 CWMDU	857	M.	455	77	50	46	34	28	20	27	29	22	17	23	15	20	21	14	7	3	3	.	.
		F.	402	60	53	58	43	26	46	24	30	21	22	18	17	23	18	12	5	5	2	.	.
2 LLANGUNIDER	3625	M.	1810	263	242	208	104	133	149	121	168	95	73	79	56	47	33	24	10	9	1	.	1
		F.	1815	295	285	204	185	137	123	106	193	95	63	60	62	59	59	29	16	6	4	1	.
3 LLANGATTOCK. (W.)	4731	M.	2411	313	338	251	235	236	162	147	125	130	104	97	67	80	54	36	27	15	4	.	.
		F.	2320	316	342	266	198	174	174	126	129	115	98	94	78	87	57	43	17	12	4	.	.
4 LLANELLY	6979	M.	3605	494	455	378	341	318	285	230	187	192	150	171	137	90	64	61	28	12	2	.	.
		F.	3374	449	457	403	285	254	218	237	165	179	162	140	129	97	79	51	31	25	7	2	.
5 CRICKHOWELL	2266	M.	1079	139	133	108	107	76	56	65	63	49	53	53	50	38	40	25	13	8	3	1	1
		F.	1187	122	116	144	134	99	82	56	63	63	65	36	44	46	37	23	16	10	2	3	1
610 HAY.																							
1 TALGARTH	2513	M.	1256	183	142	123	119	73	106	84	58	74	63	47	46	51	30	27	21	8	3	1	.
		F.	1257	167	141	127	112	116	76	75	60	59	63	42	50	45	43	31	19	16	6	.	.
2 CLYRO	3113	M.	1571	181	184	188	179	134	93	85	76	79	72	74	65	32	43	34	18	9	4	.	.
		F.	1542	174	191	186	171	113	99	91	65	69	86	70	54	52	54	32	21	7	7	.	.
3 HAY. (W.)	4596	M.	2201	275	251	274	191	152	138	137	132	110	98	114	79	91	56	50	29	16	6	2	.
		F.	2395	292	288	241	201	207	178	152	119	132	91	98	89	96	78	68	44	16	3	1	1
RADNORSHIRE.																							
611 KNIGHTON.																							
1 PRESTEIGNE	2336	M.	1142	132	138	130	108	82	66	78	62	52	62	62	32	49	42	23	22	5	2	.	.
		F.	1194	132	163	144	113	88	86	68	64	60	48	56	86	47	35	22	16	14	2	.	.
2 KNIGHTON. (W.)	5724	M.	2940	344	326	344	321	281	212	154	154	128	127	135	115	163	75	58	34	15	3	1	.
		F.	2784	342	322	326	234	235	189	147	153	140	122	133	103	88	80	56	35	20	8	1	.
3 LLANBISTER	3722	M.	1975	253	232	241	211	136	133	111	104	82	87	80	74	69	32	39	20	15	3	.	.
		F.	1747	223	226	237	177	149	127	88	85	63	85	69	63	55	37	31	25	7	4	1	.

Table 3 *continued.*—AGES of MALES and FEMALES in REGISTRATION SUB-DISTRICTS.

REGISTRATION SUB-DISTRICT.	ALL AGES. Persons.	ALL AGES. Males and Females.		Under 5 Years.	5–	10–	15–	20–	25–	30–	35–	40–	45–	50–	55–	60–	65–	70–	75–	80–	85–	90–	95–	100 and upw
13. SOUTH ALES—*cont.*																								
ONORSHIRE—cont.																								
12 RHAYADER.																								
AYADER	3439	M.	1696	214	200	182	140	180	112	107	82	65	71	77	54	52	40	41	23	11	8	.	.	.
		F.	1743	220	191	205	168	147	130	96	88	80	70	67	60	63	54	40	23	18	5	.	.	.
NTMEL. (W. H.)	3302	M.	1651	214	224	201	152	114	103	110	91	88	74	48	60	52	51	34	22	6	6	1	.	.
		F.	1651	215	203	192	161	142	123	106	78	89	66	57	59	54	47	33	14	9	3	.	.	.
14. NORTH WALES.																								
ONTGOMERY-SHIRE.																								
MACHYNLLETH.																								
CHYNLLETH. (W.)	4307	M.	2076	270	271	272	210	153	118	112	108	108	99	90	79	75	44	33	30	11	3	.	.	.
		F.	2231	276	278	267	205	154	140	141	116	126	115	80	75	61	69	42	33	16	4	5	.	.
NNAL	4713	M.	2290	266	267	246	230	215	179	118	115	107	115	87	93	76	60	63	22	9	1	1	.	.
		F.	2424	264	245	250	254	240	170	139	107	134	135	102	98	87	75	68	23	15	6	4	.	.
ROWEN	3497	M.	1715	202	195	219	193	128	101	90	87	87	93	79	62	61	46	37	35	11	5	.	.	.
		F.	1782	188	234	205	178	155	107	103	82	93	75	87	77	60	44	49	27	11	2	5	.	.
614 NEWTOWN.																								
PER LLANIDLOES	3830	M.	1913	263	247	250	198	131	110	86	128	87	94	84	57	57	49	33	13	7	4	1	.	.
		F.	1983	247	280	216	194	169	123	106	122	103	94	82	52	56	54	37	17	22	5	4	.	.
WER LLANIDLOES	4471	M.	2236	317	328	287	203	167	144	139	134	104	101	79	54	47	53	34	24	12	6	3	.	.
		F.	2235	361	314	259	202	141	132	148	126	113	84	87	48	70	60	48	22	17	5	3	.	.
ANWNOG. (W.)	4720	M.	2392	317	304	340	234	185	142	127	117	100	99	98	71	72	72	53	35	16	9	1	.	.
		F.	2328	321	311	281	227	185	145	117	117	111	96	90	91	70	54	62	56	11	11	1	1	.
ERRY	2601	M.	1339	178	169	188	158	97	87	67	69	60	54	59	62	39	36	28	20	1	4	2	.	.
		F.	1262	177	189	186	115	90	65	76	64	55	51	54	40	43	31	21	17	5	3	.	1	.
EWTOWN. (H.)	7170	M.	3495	476	335	377	401	327	253	212	171	164	161	148	99	118	98	64	33	18	5	.	.	.
		F.	3675	466	390	342	418	376	274	208	183	185	177	140	137	129	104	69	43	34	5	5	1	.
REGYNON	2581	M.	1357	162	150	181	182	121	100	70	77	88	56	49	55	26	33	37	22	4	2	.	.	.
		F.	1224	162	157	147	123	108	71	70	51	68	55	40	41	33	30	26	17	14	2	.	.	.
615 FORDEN.																								
MONTGOMERY	5721	M.	2932	347	379	329	291	240	206	132	144	151	148	128	128	115	80	64	42	15	3	1	.	.
		F.	2789	345	355	302	268	214	171	160	145	164	113	121	116	93	79	39	48	25	13	.	.	.
CHIRBURY. (W.)	5712	M.	3042	374	383	359	237	247	210	182	163	169	137	118	92	117	78	69	26	20	9	1	.	.
		F.	2670	372	365	296	205	198	178	151	131	143	111	128	107	78	87	44	45	21	10	.	.	.
WELSHPOOL. (H. B.)	6848	M.	3471	373	400	395	396	301	240	188	189	198	157	167	145	142	79	61	36	18	6	.	.	.
		F.	3377	304	382	403	318	280	221	198	198	139	162	144	122	141	86	65	43	23	11	3	.	.
616 LLANFYLLIN.																								
LANFAIR	5587	M.	2808	332	358	328	304	216	167	162	152	129	136	133	84	100	79	68	40	19	8	.	.	.
		F.	2779	342	338	331	286	194	172	156	140	131	127	133	98	96	71	73	45	33	3	1	.	.
LANSAINTFFRAID. (W.)	9583	M.	4786	587	571	561	401	375	263	228	244	261	251	212	186	203	158	116	62	21	11	6	.	.
		F.	4797	563	581	549	408	361	301	261	242	271	257	190	179	194	149	100	61	53	12	5	1	.
LLANRHAIADR	4780	M.	2444	290	292	272	250	213	170	145	125	136	103	112	111	86	86	56	29	26	4	2	.	.
		F.	2336	308	289	272	221	101	143	139	114	128	108	106	87	84	73	53	36	28	7	1	2	.
FLINTSHIRE.																								
617 HOLYWELL.																								
WHITFORD	8437	M.	4212	512	535	451	444	349	313	278	248	209	198	173	153	144	106	49	37	15	5	1	.	.
		F.	4225	510	573	370	330	253	253	260	234	206	183	200	187	142	118	79	74	26	12	5	1	.
HOLYWELL. (W.)	11566	M.	5778	780	691	639	568	487	446	390	325	310	249	235	210	204	142	87	44	18	5	.	.	.
		F.	5788	731	743	655	485	458	397	346	365	317	282	234	228	222	139	132	73	36	13	2	.	.
FLINT	11162	M.	5743	813	757	633	584	452	429	379	362	316	246	210	183	187	95	67	38	18	7	1	1	.
		F.	5419	774	705	629	470	359	348	341	378	285	246	231	190	170	102	77	65	38	10	.	1	.
MOLD. (H. B.)	14609	M.	7484	997	970	918	892	587	523	406	402	443	317	302	213	200	125	74	51	28	6	.	.	.
		F.	7125	970	971	870	664	468	477	419	446	443	335	284	220	210	171	102	72	46	15	1	1	.
DENBIGHSHIRE.																								
618 WREXHAM.																								
HOLT	6616	M.	3211	434	401	379	304	222	194	200	154	160	141	131	154	121	90	56	36	13	15	.	.	.
		F.	3405	437	396	371	369	272	210	104	183	135	161	156	113	121	88	64	45	24	6	1	.	.
RUABON. (H.)	15485	M.	8046	1067	1059	1025	902	630	555	475	447	437	361	327	246	208	134	78	50	21	6	.	.	.
		F.	7439	1098	1045	894	514	477	494	428	448	416	383	311	201	224	181	101	90	32	11	1	.	.
WREXHAM. (W. H. B.)	33057	M.	17068	2366	2100	1806	1845	1519	1339	1169	1010	916	775	663	500	411	253	184	73	40	9	1	.	.
		F.	15989	2391	2193	1077	1303	1136	1192	1089	898	897	721	607	475	424	264	104	92	53	16	7	1	.
619 RUTHIN.																								
LLANARMON	2714	M.	1404	196	165	172	159	109	85	67	75	81	55	41	59	52	33	14	14	7	.	.	.	.
		F.	1310	168	149	168	118	108	83	73	64	66	63	57	62	42	31	19	22	14	1	.	2	.
RUTHIN. (W. P.)	4038	M.	1946	242	134	227	209	149	133	113	107	99	92	85	93	73	49	47	28	11	2	1	.	.
		F.	2092	244	238	211	189	159	163	127	115	99	97	100	103	83	58	44	32	14	4	3	1	.
LLANELIDAN	2418	M.	1199	136	133	114	141	97	80	82	48	61	66	49	48	48	34	33	23	8	7	1	.	.
		F.	1219	131	161	136	110	101	82	54	68	58	62	58	53	40	39	30	26	7	5	.	.	.
GYFFYLLIOG	1189	M.	621	57	69	83	68	67	39	33	26	39	28	26	23	21	20	14	9	2	1	.	.	.
		F.	568	63	59	76	58	48	24	27	38	35	19	21	24	29	18	13	13	3	2	1	.	.
LLANRHAIADR	2379	M.	1238	133	121	155	165	115	80	60	50	65	58	60	47	48	41	21	20	6	2	1	.	.
		F.	1141	131	113	145	113	74	87	73	64	59	48	60	55	40	34	20	17	8	4	2	.	.
LLANDYRNOG	1477	M.	752	92	74	67	73	65	46	36	37	27	45	42	42	36	30	22	3	8	2	.	.	.
		F.	725	64	83	65	70	66	48	43	43	32	32	42	39	27	29	23	13	1	2	.	.	.
620 ST. ASAPH.																								
ST. ASAPH. (W. H.)	14230	M.	6579	809	779	818	647	457	452	440	334	347	310	284	265	259	156	114	82	34	11	2	.	.
		F.	7651	805	748	805	809	697	504	487	411	413	398	306	289	273	242	141	99	43	15	4	2	.
ABERGELE	6004	M.	2897	340	321	318	294	202	189	188	178	133	130	122	138	108	91	78	47	16	5	2	.	.
		F.	3107	368	360	303	246	242	222	205	185	166	148	141	142	124	97	81	47	21	6	3	.	.
DENBIGH. (H. L.)	9224	M.	4459	516	471	501	442	348	294	276	283	276	210	215	180	172	99	89	51	24	12	.	.	.
		F.	4765	522	514	492	507	377	347	291	319	267	233	217	173	173	132	107	43	36	12	3	.	.

Table 3 *continued*.—Ages of Males and Females in Registration Sub-Districts.

Registration Sub-District.	All Ages. Persons.		All Ages. Males and Females.	Under 5 Years.	5-	10-	15-	20-	25-	30-	35-	40-	45-	50-	55-	60-	65-	70-	75-	80-	85-	90-	95-
44. NORTH WALES—*cont.*																							
***DENBIGHSHIRE*—cont.**																							
621 LLANRWST.																							
1 Llanrwst. (W.)	7367	M.	3665	497	425	363	345	316	256	219	205	184	157	158	132	126	110	79	59	21	11	3	.
		F.	3702	440	405	395	376	311	266	222	213	183	180	141	140	129	103	98	47	34	10	2	2
2 Bettwsycoed	3649	M.	1828	210	191	184	187	176	153	144	121	88	80	71	52	62	46	34	15	11	1	1	1
		F.	1821	237	200	190	180	155	182	132	97	106	88	64	48	63	37	46	24	10	4	.	.
3 Ysbytty	3093	M.	1588	207	183	170	147	136	127	113	99	93	65	63	47	51	33	29	24	8	2	2	.
		F.	1505	181	171	165	151	135	110	85	101	86	50	51	60	46	35	54	17	8	7	2	1
MERIONETHSHIRE.																							
622 CORWEN.																							
1 Corwen. (W.)	8068	M.	4037	467	502	432	410	361	270	245	251	184	187	165	160	136	116	76	61	27	7	.	.
		F.	4031	522	531	470	338	318	253	264	187	216	166	169	148	130	113	81	71	24	18	5	1
2 Llangollen. (H.)	8765	M.	4401	545	521	520	423	354	301	268	265	218	186	194	101	150	113	104	37	21	7	3	.
		F.	4364	555	549	477	372	340	299	249	230	246	204	218	174	148	126	101	60	24	10	3	.
623 BALA.																							
1 Bala. (W.)	6740	M.	3498	318	362	350	356	373	256	229	210	199	199	127	126	125	102	77	53	10	8	2	1
		F.	3242	385	300	356	275	272	224	196	191	176	168	141	98	118	89	72	66	36	10	5	3
624 DOLGELLY.																							
1 Talyllyn	6437	M.	3239	468	413	371	291	234	232	211	223	178	155	108	91	82	65	53	46	11	4	3	.
		F.	3198	428	423	409	271	225	221	191	194	179	148	111	100	101	68	62	34	26	5	2	.
2 Barmouth. (W.)	8743	M.	4034	503	476	432	322	290	265	270	261	210	178	179	136	133	107	104	48	36	14	.	1
		F.	4709	621	504	400	445	373	350	307	292	247	233	186	186	163	168	112	79	29	13	5	1
625 FESTINIOG.																							
1 Llanfihangelytraethau. (W.)	5094	M.	2482	320	324	277	239	228	153	158	161	110	113	83	80	72	49	37	22	14	4	.	.
		F.	2612	385	325	305	207	181	181	175	145	164	120	85	84	80	60	43	33	28	7	4	.
2 Festiniog. (H.)	16115	M.	8132	1080	958	792	735	834	783	673	593	450	333	250	189	181	130	74	29	19	6	2	1
		F.	6983	1083	844	791	590	584	680	613	448	357	290	219	195	161	134	85	57	32	4	5	.
3 Tremadoc	9316	M.	4527	668	606	601	382	385	303	298	282	214	206	184	158	115	110	72	40	14	8	.	.
		F.	4789	607	580	506	460	380	346	326	323	256	193	179	172	131	118	105	51	24	5	6	1
CARNARVONSHIRE.																							
626 PWLLHELI.																							
1 Criccieth	6865	M.	3371	462	381	356	338	306	225	218	196	162	135	110	118	108	103	75	47	19	8	2	.
		F.	3494	443	379	345	328	273	243	227	230	190	168	124	154	117	111	90	40	19	13	.	.
2 Pwllheli. (W.)	7228	M.	3500	478	419	389	313	284	230	201	201	158	159	147	143	115	104	67	43	34	6	.	.
		F.	3728	446	410	345	311	320	267	237	227	218	176	148	156	149	134	80	61	29	11	2	1
3 Aberdaron	3618	M.	1813	208	187	222	181	111	100	101	104	98	90	75	82	80	72	36	37	11	8	3	.
		F.	1805	197	155	176	139	147	125	104	112	108	91	97	101	74	70	50	31	17	9	2	.
4 Nevin	5200	M.	2477	314	296	203	255	218	160	127	127	113	106	96	102	92	85	56	37	18	11	2	.
		F.	2723	324	274	260	258	247	193	165	157	143	118	121	142	115	76	72	31	27	14	2	.
627 CARNARVON.																							
1 Llandwrog	13456	M.	6901	987	857	772	661	590	660	408	475	348	255	212	187	177	143	75	60	33	7	4	.
		F.	6555	996	790	724	586	456	524	473	419	360	265	214	220	182	137	98	78	25	8	2	1
2 Llanrug. (H.)	14794	M.	7542	1028	937	891	785	610	672	483	427	384	305	291	259	228	157	92	70	20	9	.	.
		F.	7252	1061	839	816	636	546	647	482	461	406	343	291	234	225	182	119	71	38	13	3	.
3 Carnarvon. (W. P. B.)	12253	M.	5929	703	646	637	657	506	487	391	354	328	264	245	186	151	118	94	39	16	6	3	.
		F.	6324	769	645	604	678	614	550	432	394	380	298	266	196	199	145	102	68	32	16	3	.
4 Llanidan	3494	M.	1686	216	263	181	125	125	97	99	87	86	77	86	72	59	46	41	30	18	7	1	.
		F.	1808	222	203	183	156	126	131	117	119	103	92	70	72	66	60	43	34	15	6	.	.
628 BANGOR.																							
1 Beaumaris. (R. B.)	12781	M.	6227	730	658	654	653	431	439	338	304	290	266	264	253	243	216	147	90	50	18	3	.
		F.	6554	720	679	629	608	560	434	433	353	330	337	303	293	258	247	166	107	52	33	8	3
2 Bangor. (W. H.[2])	14957	M.	7165	850	798	764	717	640	509	493	361	406	334	329	274	229	176	92	67	23	12	.	.
		F.	7792	853	809	831	777	703	617	507	469	439	309	347	318	252	201	134	77	39	20	2	3
3 Llanllechid	10774	M.	5400	698	615	601	514	436	411	359	308	283	293	228	215	174	141	70	40	20	8	2	.
		F.	5374	673	605	596	468	481	412	356	339	315	301	226	187	161	132	78	67	22	3	2	.
629 CONWAY.																							
1 Conway. (W.)	5127	M.	2552	323	274	289	265	218	212	158	142	142	114	107	93	76	58	44	24	7	3	2	.
		F.	2575	311	241	249	247	246	217	180	157	149	142	117	108	82	64	45	26	10	5	2	.
2 Creuddyn	11560	M.	5347	713	624	677	541	452	581	337	268	275	252	240	207	168	106	91	34	30	8	3	.
		F.	6213	714	628	631	637	614	518	396	381	342	318	304	202	200	151	85	62	20	10	1	1
3 Llechwedd-Isaf	1674	M.	832	84	101	86	85	71	59	46	41	35	40	39	40	26	33	19	18	8	3	.	.
		F.	842	97	81	95	89	59	52	54	38	46	38	49	37	38	21	22	13	11	2	1	1
ANGLESEY.																							
630 ANGLESEY.																							
1 Llangefni	4891	M.	2820	258	266	259	220	164	134	145	117	127	91	105	93	114	88	61	48	20	10	3	.
		F.	2071	290	267	237	245	195	102	170	159	132	117	124	108	137	84	70	44	17	10	2	1
2 Bryngwran	5069	M.	2472	298	297	258	253	197	154	127	132	108	104	110	101	107	87	58	30	30	9	2	.
		F.	2597	282	273	278	234	203	194	138	157	122	135	124	113	99	88	72	45	30	11	1	.
3 Llandyfrydog	4025	M.	1950	232	206	201	214	147	118	104	93	90	98	92	85	91	60	59	32	18	11	3	.
		F.	2075	227	210	179	205	147	130	134	120	121	109	90	78	89	80	76	37	25	6	2	.
4 Amlwch. (W. H.)	6198	M.	2825	332	334	339	270	199	176	107	142	167	146	133	154	116	82	65	39	26	4	1	2
		F.	3373	347	370	330	317	253	208	216	178	185	218	161	163	142	105	82	55	39	8	11	1
5 Llanddausaint. (W.)	4827	M.	2439	297	265	282	256	179	177	137	109	103	111	96	109	112	78	69	52	24	12	1	2
		F.	2388	277	241	227	220	202	174	163	127	111	98	111	119	98	83	68	45	14	8	4	.
6 Holyhead. (H.)	10131	M.	5184	633	578	526	461	484	442	415	300	273	243	228	178	154	112	88	44	20	14	1	.
		F.	4947	687	542	498	481	389	375	362	300	280	221	222	198	185	113	80	51	31	19	2	1

Table 4.—MALE and FEMALE CHILDREN at *each Year of Age* under 5 in the WELSH DIVISION and its REGISTRATION COUNTIES.

REGISTRATION COUNTY.	TOTAL UNDER 5 YEARS. Persons.	Males and Females.	Under 1 Year	1–	2–	3–	4–
XI.—MONMOUTHSHIRE AND WALES.	212181	M. - 106165 F. - 106016	21919 21985	19971 20103	21560 21484	21432 21350	21274 21094
42. MONMOUTHSHIRE	32584	M. - 16220 F. 16364	3385 3349	2989 3120	3252 3317	3348 3334	3222 3246
43. SOUTH WALES.							
GLAMORGAN -	74696	M. - 37379 F. - 37317	7907 7962	7087 7147	7403 7539	7450 7304	7462 7365
CARMARTHEN -	15034	M. - 7580 F. 7454	1534 1531	1452 1415	1533 1448	1517 1551	1542 1489
PEMBROKE - - -	10682	M. 5357 F. - 5325	1108 1083	1032 997	1095 1117	1024 1069	1098 1059
CARDIGAN - - -	11352	M. 5678 F. - 5679	1088 1104	1031 1014	1159 1165	1150 1180	1185 1176
BRECKNOCK -	6865	M. 3457 F. 3408	722 718	613 683	738 649	680 678	690 760
RADNOR -	2300	M. - 1159 F. - 1141	218 232	205 228	265 224	238 237	243 220
44. NORTH WALES.							
MONTGOMERY - -	9500	M. - 4724 F. - 4776	925 943	881 898	970 1001	992 996	956 937
FLINT - - -	6046	M. - 3061 F. 2985	624 608	550 673	628 583	618 598	611 624
DENBIGH - -	14588	M. 7308 F. 7290	1516 1457	1563 1392	1427 1545	1474 1458	1528 1448
MERIONETH - - -	8891	M. - 4405 F. 4486	883 903	847 866	911 868	911 976	855 873
CARNARVON - - -	15395	M. - 7704 F. 7711	1597 1638	1465 1446	1648 1577	1597 1588	1493 1462
ANGLESEY - - -	4138	M. 2048 F. 2090	411 433	388 396	436 421	433 436	380 435

Table 5.—MALE and FEMALE CHILDREN at *each Year of Age* under 5 in REGISTRATION DISTRICTS.

REGISTRATION DISTRICT.	Total under 5 Years. Persons.	Males and Females.	Under 1 Year.	1–	2–	3–	4–
42. MOMMOUTHSHIRE.							
580 CHEPSTOW - -	2432	M. - 1226 F. - 1206	271 248	226 207	244 214	243 270	242 233
581 MONMOUTH -	4069	M. - 2042 F. - 2027	389 395	379 392	418 422	456 406	400 412
582 ABERGAVENNY - -	3049	M. - 1494 F. - 1555	295 320	299 295	297 303	285 323	318 314
583 BEDWELTY - - -	8042	M. - 3958 F. - 4084	854 821	700 762	777 832	809 818	816 851
584 PONTYPOOL - -	4997	M. - 2494 F. - 2503	506 501	461 493	527 505	514 504	492 500
585 NEWPORT - - -	9995	M. - 5006 F. - 4989	1073 1034	924 986	1019 1037	1026 1002	964 936
43. SOUTH WALES.							
GLAMORGANSHIRE.							
586 CARDIFF - -	15017	M. - 7436 F. - 7581	1511 1613	1483 1554	1453 1493	1539 1496	1450 1425
587 PONTYPRIDD - -	14058	M. - 7141 F. - 6917	1589 1510	1338 1289	1385 1394	1400 1349	1419 1375
588 MERTHYR TYDFIL -	14002	M. - 6957 F. - 7045	1469 1497	1281 1278	1395 1465	1418 1388	1394 1417
589 BRIDGEND - -	5308	M. - 2708 F. - 2600	556 536	501 517	594 531	544 539	513 537
590 NEATH - -	7561	M. - 3806 F. - 3755	792 782	751 709	735 714	763 768	765 782
591 PONTARDAWE - -	3051	M. - 1531 F. - 1520	331 290	268 290	313 324	284 303	335 313

REGISTRATION DISTRICT.	Total under 5 Years. Persons.	Males and Females.	Under 1 Year.	1–	2–	3–
43. SOUTH WALES—*cont.*						
GLAMORGANSHIRE—cont.						
592 SWANSEA -	14102	M. - 7044 F. - 7058	1521 1579	1293 1324	1464 1484	1330 1304
593 GOWER - - -	1537	M. 756 F. - 781	138 155	152 186	144 134	162 157
CARMARTHENSHIRE.						
594 LLANELLY -	6706	M. - 3341 F. - 3365	719 785	616 654	669 636	672 703
595 LLANDOVERY	1498	M. 735 F. - 763	142 142	152 146	131 139	160 147
596 LLANDILOFAWR - -	2530	M. - 1308 F. - 1222	232 249	270 219	234 248	265 263
597 CARMARTHEN - -	4305	M. - 2201 F. - 2104	486 435	414 397	479 425	426 438
PEMBROKESHIRE.						
598 NARBERTH	2565	M. - 1285 F. - 1280	258 254	235 210	270 280	[illegible] 251
599 PEMBROKE - -	3935	M. - 2005 F. - 1930	441 387	397 387	397 404	[illegible] [illegible]
600 HAVERFORDWEST -	4182	M. - 2067 F. - 2115	409 442	400 400	428 433	[illegible] [illegible]
CARDIGANSHIRE.						
601 CARDIGAN - -	2038	M. - 1030 F. - 1008	196 215	194 182	245 208	[illegible] [illegible]
602 NEWCASTLE IN EMLYN	2271	M. - 1150 F. - 1121	232 213	230 200	228 231	[illegible] [illegible]

Table 5 *continued*.—Male and Female Children at *each Year of Age* under 5 in Registration District

Registration District.	Total under 5 Years: Persons.	Total under 5 Years: Males and Females.	Under 1 Year.	1–	2–	3–	4–
43. SOUTH WALES—*cont.*							
CARDIGANSHIRE—cont.							
603 LAMPETER	1249	M. 615	118	135	104	128	130
		F. 634	119	128	125	129	135
604 ABERAYRON	1512	M. 736	151	141	154	138	164
		F. 776	172	146	156	146	158
605 ABERYSTWITH	3014	M. 1513	305	275	301	302	330
		F. 1501	321	242	314	325	299
606 TREGARON	1268	M. 629	116	126	127	132	128
		F. 639	124	119	131	127	138
BRECKNOCKSHIRE.							
607 BUILTH	1071	M. 538	112	89	121	100	116
		F. 533	110	107	90	102	115
608 BRECKNOCK	2005	M. 1014	215	196	225	194	184
		F. 991	208	150	187	214	223
609 CRICKHOWELL	2537	M. 1286	274	220	264	268	260
		F. 1251	262	210	255	243	281
610 HAY	1252	M. 619	121	108	128	123	139
		F. 633	128	127	108	119	141
RADNORSHIRE.							
611 KNIGHTON	1428	M. 731	134	127	165	151	154
		F. 697	136	144	135	150	132
612 RHAYADER	872	M. 428	84	78	90	87	89
		F. 444	96	84	89	87	88
44. NORTH WALES.							
MONTGOMERYSHIRE.							
613 MACHYNLLETH	1465	M. 737	132	150	143	171	141
		F. 728	130	138	155	148	157
614 NEWTON	3437	M. 1713	338	311	376	333	361
		F. 1724	334	326	370	367	327
615 FORDEN	2205	M. 1094	220	202	233	211	218
		F. 1111	221	210	232	236	212
616 LLANFYLLIN	2393	M. 1180	225	218	224	277	236
		F. 1213	263	224	244	241	241

Registration District.	Total under 5 Years: Persons.	Total under 5 Years: Males and Females.	Under 1 Year.	1–	2–	3–
44. NORTH WALES—*cont.*						
FLINTSHIRE.						
617 HOLYWELL	6046	M. 3061	624	580	628	618
		F. 2985	608	572	583	598
DENBIGHSHIRE.						
618 WREXHAM	7783	M. 3857	798	713	774	775
		F. 3926	776	787	863	780
619 RUTHIN	1657	M. 856	190	162	155	160
		F. 801	152	152	152	179
620 ST. ASAPH	3366	M. 1671	354	317	312	340
		F. 1695	348	336	361	306
621 LLANRWST	1772	M. 914	179	171	188	199
		F. 858	181	167	179	173
MERIONETHSHIRE.						
622 CORWEN	2089	M. 1012	196	180	217	222
		F. 1077	237	204	198	232
623 BALA	703	M. 318	67	55	70	68
		F. 385	86	73	78	71
624 DOLGELLY	1920	M. 971	178	197	194	221
		F. 949	187	173	192	195
625 FESTINIOG	4179	M. 2104	442	413	430	462
		F. 2075	398	416	400	478
CARNARVONSHIRE.						
626 PWLLHELI	2872	M. 1462	278	287	321	304
		F. 1410	307	242	298	283
627 CARNARVON	5862	M. 2934	627	530	594	625
		F. 2928	587	558	585	608
628 BANGOR	4529	M. 2278	462	434	494	427
		F. 2251	563	421	461	474
629 CONWAY	2242	M. 1120	230	208	233	243
		F. 1122	241	227	233	223
ANGLESEY.						
630 ANGLESEY	4138	M. 2048	411	388	436	483
		F. 2090	402	398	421	486

TABLE 7.—CONDITION as to MARRIAGE and AGES of MALES and FEMALES in the WELSH DIVISION and REGISTRATION COUNTIES.

REGISTRATION COUNTY.		ALL AGES.	Under 15 Years.	15–	20–	25–	35–	45–	55–
XI. MONMOUTHSHIRE AND WALES.									
UNMARRIED	Males	561612	294301	80869	56133	46434	14031	7425	4678
	Females	467154	201730	73551	44671	50509	11642	6775	4532
MARRIED	Males	258345	.	326	12832	68365	66883	51976	30796
	Females	260792	.	1713	21956	74855	67078	49254	30160
WIDOWED	Males	29717	.	5	176	1886	3892	4952	6742
	Females	60539	.	16	329	3088	6656	10706	14640
42. MONMOUTHSHIRE.									
UNMARRIED	Males	76126	44962	12269	8338	5980	2087	1209	762
	Females	66585	44636	10198	5697	3291	1142	636	432
MARRIED	Males	36422	.	68	1026	10760	10324	7935	5320
	Females	36483	.	271	3632	11687	10167	7368	4203
WIDOWED	Males	4417	.	1	18	253	558	744	1076
	Females	8361	.	1	60	443	936	1579	2102
43. SOUTH WALES.									
GLAMORGANSHIRE.									
UNMARRIED	Males	169036	99955	27173	20024	13676	4443	2026	1118
	Females	148106	99539	23895	13192	7073	2175	1079	640
MARRIED	Males	88429	.	126	5605	27409	24122	16677	9883
	Females	87295	.	887	9466	23287	22569	15075	7857
WIDOWED	Males	8671	.	2	36	774	1348	1721	1946
	Females	16854	.	12	140	1101	2264	3429	4160
CARMARTHENSHIRE.									
UNMARRIED	Males	34311	21454	5568	3480	2168	762	431	256
	Females	35496	20832	5708	3013	2655	1009	594	396
MARRIED	Males	17276	.	26	926	4496	4204	3371	2455
	Females	17738	.	72	1358	5037	4422	3319	2171
WIDOWED	Males	1863	.	.	21	115	189	296	404
	Females	4533	.	1	10	230	469	745	999
PEMBROKESHIRE.									
UNMARRIED	Males	23164	15052	4357	2807	1685	578	294	222
	Females	26648	14795	4323	2953	2310	969	699	423
MARRIED	Males	13254	.	13	639	2549	3132	2794	2230
	Females	13396	.	53	890	3256	3310	2682	1978
WIDOWED	Males	1667	.	.	4	66	165	229	306
	Females	3550	.	1	8	138	367	569	619
CARDIGANSHIRE.									
UNMARRIED	Males	27896	16786	4581	2637	2019	783	532	324
	Females	32528	16630	5002	3611	3316	1591	1036	730
MARRIED	Males	12966	.	9	439	2590	2977	2827	2274
	Females	14731	.	32	694	3479	3727	3214	2204
WIDOWED	Males	1865	.	.	2	86	134	248	424
	Females	5161	.	.	18	191	533	832	1164
BRECKNOCKSHIRE.									
UNMARRIED	Males	17192	9768	2718	1936	1521	534	320	222
	Females	16178	9753	2596	1620	1167	415	267	183
MARRIED	Males	8629	.	6	301	1975	2149	1834	1362
	Females	8737	.	40	615	2326	2176	1772	1158
WIDOWED	Males	1176	.	.	2	69	127	196	267
	Females	2847	.	.	6	100	178	381	554

Note.—In a few cases, persons described as "Married" were stated to be under 15 years of age. These have been classed with married persons aged "15 an 20 years."

le 7 *continued*.—CONDITION as to MARRIAGE and AGES of MALES and FEMALES in the WELSH DIVISION and its REGISTRATION COUNTIES.

REGISTRATION COUNTY.		ALL AGES.	Under 15 Years.	15–	20–	25–	35–	45–	55–	65 and upwards.
3. SOUTH WALES—*cont.*										
RADNORSHIRE.										
IED -	Males - -	6266	3320	934	750	600	244	148	116	78
	Females - -	5053	3339	387	534	426	165	108	76	63
D -	Males - -	2765	.	2	91	569	630	631	447	270
	Females - -	2777	.	10	182	706	680	567	393	251
ID - -	Males - -	383	.	.	2	17	46	44	97	188
	Females - -	684	.	.	5	26	65	93	165	358
44. NORTH WALES.										
MONTGOMERYSHIRE.										
RIED - -	Males -	24734	13968	4025	2731	2134	816	474	323	229
	Females -	22730	13766	3629	2267	1013	618	361	248	238
ID - -	Males - -	11808	.	9	381	2853	2931	2638	1997	1011
	Females - -	12051	.	47	752	2909	3100	2501	1695	1067
ED -	Males -	1693	.	.	4	79	157	270	378	814
	Females - -	3131	.	.	7	115	234	499	724	1552
FLINTSHIRE.										
RIED - -	Males - -	14840	8046	2389	1507	1317	450	215	158	78
	Females - -	12964	8701	1867	1016	727	291	178	115	70
ED -	Males -	7579	.	9	276	1847	2124	1590	1099	634
	Females - -	7625	.	40	567	2043	2129	1529	924	453
WED -	Males -	789	.	.	2	59	93	125	207	303
	Females -	1968	.	1	10	71	194	288	525	879
DENBIGHSHIRE.										
RRIED -	Males - -	35556	20428	5899	3888	3055	1033	564	380	260
	Females - -	33217	20306	5104	3089	2855	928	553	374	309
IED - -	Males - -	18593	.	18	722	4453	4868	4007	2850	1670
	Females -	18673	.	75	1249	5045	4925	3761	2422	1196
OWED - -	Males - -	2347	.	1	6	118	268	365	577	1012
	Females - -	4549	.		18	178	467	779	1132	1975
MERIONETHSHIRE.										
ARRIED -	Males -	21816	12248	3231	2848	2081	841	390	228	149
	Females - -	19970	12406	2918	1878	1442	572	308	239	250
RRIED - -	Males - -	11154	.	6	409	2739	2969	2240	1622	1169
	Females -	11208	.	40	787	3107	3006	2131	1380	839
OWED -	Males - -	1380	.	1	11	85	149	213	281	640
	Females - -	2626	.	.	8	123	273	395	600	1257
CARNARVONSHIRE.										
ARRIED - -	Males - -	37713	21741	6062	4303	3280	1153	593	408	278
	Females - -	36841	20931	5794	5834	3140	1386	802	519	435
RIED - -	Males - -	20406	.	28	873	4061	5087	4151	3180	2126
	Females - -	20940	.	104	1481	5395	5412	4100	2724	1524
OWED - -	Males - -	2623	.	.	12	139	295	394	563	1220
	Females - -	5258	.	.	26	248	574	847	1292	2271
ANGLESEY.										
ARRIED -	Males - -	10371	5858	1698	1100	908	324	209	161	113
	Females - -	10224	5748	1622	1007	805	387	244	164	157
RIED - -	Males - -	6020	.	6	244	1297	1357	1233	1067	816
	Females - -	6080	.	30	373	1468	1446	1220	951	584
OWED - -	Males - -	799	.	.	6	33	70	113	166	411
	Females - -	1647	.	.	9	74	117	275	404	768

Table 8.—Condition as to Marriage and Ages of Males and Females in Registration Districts.

Registration District.		All Ages.	Under 15 Years.	15–	20–	25–	35–	45–	55–	65 and upw^ds.
42. MONMOUTH-SHIRE.										
580 CHEPSTOW:										
Unmarried	M.	5809	3409	896	624	485	165	100	82	58
	F.	5374	3384	793	400	355	140	80	68	45
Married	M.	3211		2	112	700	703	714	532	340
	F.	3166	.	10	202	807	825	640	430	243
Widowed	M.	381	.	.	1	13	30	54	93	190
	F.	700	.	.	2	23	60	101	163	346
581 MONMOUTH:										
Unmarried	M.	9770	5904	1574	968	659	245	145	118	97
	F.	8560	5730	1206	734	406	201	121	80	84
Married	M.	5053	.	6	154	1039	1264	1091	841	538
	F.	5153	.	17	327	1349	1267	1106	721	375
Widowed	M.	554	.	.	4	24	48	70	128	274
	F.	1150	.	.	5	43	85	177	278	562
582 ABERGAVENNY:										
Unmarried	M.	7483	4211	1156	790	648	270	185	107	76
	F.	6763	4263	1008	662	423	172	122	60	53
Married	M.	3947	.	10	152	1022	1057	793	523	390
	F.	4236	.	16	330	1116	1060	762	501	233
Widowed	M.	499	.	.	1	10	56	85	140	198
	F.	893	.	.	1	40	92	171	213	376
583 BEDWELTY:										
Unmarried	M.	19210	11022	3166	2204	1603	597	338	188	92
	F.	15004	10928	2311	996	513	131	62	38	25
Married	M.	9429	.	28	598	2851	2494	1792	1146	520
	F.	9293	.	95	1059	2910	2389	1621	890	338
Widowed	M.	1154	.	.	6	97	178	214	303	359
	F.	1750	.	.	14	93	208	380	484	571
584 PONTYPOOL:										
Unmarried	M.	11767	7011	1982	1280	865	286	153	107	83
	F.	9033	6948	1477	827	387	133	62	49	50
Married	M.	5800	.	9	285	1583	1478	1248	829	438
	F.	6048	.	54	542	1744	1493	1162	652	409
Widowed	M.	631	.	.	.	28	89	91	144	274
	F.	1201	.	.	7	64	159	225	290	435
585 NEWPORT:										
Unmarried	M.	22677	13295	3486	2482	1730	524	288	160	112
	F.	20849	13573	3404	1088	1117	356	189	128	94
Married	M.	11928	.	13	625	3496	3243	2297	1449	790
	F.	11889	.	79	1172	3770	3124	2092	1005	557
Widowed	M.	1198	.	1	6	72	157	219	268	475
	F.	2607	.	1	31	180	341	525	669	860
43. SOUTH WALES.										
GLAMORGANSHIRE.										
586 CARDIFF:										
Unmarried	M.	33068	19272	5360	4176	3195	675	364	192	105
	F.	30502	19269	3197	3230	1739	513	280	153	84
Married	M.	18874	.	25	1130	5780	5432	3639	1962	912
	F.	18247	.	208	2052	6030	4800	3687	1513	857
Widowed	M.	1836	.	.	16	142	232	307	373	516
	F.	3287	.	1	41	225	504	701	815	1000
587 PONTYPRIDD:										
Unmarried	M.	32087	18661	5097	4402	2917	878	425	192	115
	F.	24798	18136	3698	1732	750	190	84	59	65
Married	M.	16360		23	1213	5591	4446	2864	1584	637
	F.	15801	.	229	2010	5391	4030	2501	1202	429
Widowed	M.	1628	.	1	17	182	296	360	359	432
	F.	2309	.	7	27	192	300	503	581	609
588 MERTHYR TYDFIL:										
Unmarried	M.	33332	19611	5568	3933	2606	925	409	260	120
	F.	28243	19462	4567	2341	1226	336	143	78	71
Married	M.	17137	.	31	1079	5681	4615	3306	2094	930
	F.	16976	.	174	1745	5313	4321	3092	1680	645
Widowed	M.	1961	.	1	24	164	323	418	451	540
	F.	3780	.	1	20	228	435	812	961	1292
589 BRIDGEND:										
Unmarried	M.	12833	7310	1980	1506	1130	410	233	156	93
	F.	11182	7209	1701	1081	671	231	110	72	67
Married	M.	6454	.	5	310	1707	1704	1241	874	523
	F.	6404	.	37	559	1898	1399	1196	707	408
Widowed	M.	707	.	.	8	52	94	123	177	218
	F.	1280	.	.	3	62	130	238	336	511
590 NEATH:										
Unmarried	M.	16606	10317	2772	1781	1141	377	180	107	51
	F.	15404	10333	2496	1359	726	205	113	58	54
Married	M.	8632	.	10	560	2574	2315	1661	1053	489
	F.	8666	.	88	929	2647	2255	1494	898	355
Widowed	M.	891	.	.	6	77	130	170	188	314
	F.	1788	.	2	8	102	234	323	455	664

Registration District.		All Ages.	Under 15 Years.	15–	20–	25–	35–	45–	5
43. SOUTH WALES—*cont.*									
GLAMORGANSHIRE—cont.									
591 PONTARDAWE:									
Unmarried	M.	6517	4252	1078	623	340	99	62	
	F.	6053	4204	960	477	203	76	25	
Married	M.	3267	.	6	222	994	782	611	4
	F.	3306		23	319	1037	841	591	3
Widowed	M.	332	.	.	4	22	49	59	
	F.	710	.	1	5	48	58	126	1
592 SWANSEA:									
Unmarried	M.	30031	18534	4804	3340	2128	691	312	14
	F.	28486	18088	4732	2672	1411	449	258	11
Married	M.	15887	.	24	1004	5163	4577	2953	164
	F.	16082	.	119	1721	5381	4271	2749	131
Widowed	M.	1289	.	.	14	121	190	260	26
	F.	5276	.	.	34	225	473	656	80
593 GOWER:									
Unmarried	M.	3264	2008	499	293	218	84	30	2
	F.	3523	2131	533	341	267	111	57	4
Married	M.	1818	.	2	87	429	448	388	25
	F.	1860	.	5	122	520	452	365	22
Widowed	M.	217	.	.	.	14	20	28	4
	F.	415	.	.	1	24	40	70	9
CARMARTHENSHIRE.									
594 LLANELLY:									
Unmarried	M.	14228	9161	2336	1407	786	223	128	40
	F.	13702	9179	2207	1258	619	236	129	8
Married	M.	7153	.	11	459	2178	1926	1332	771
	F.	7325	.	40	726	2332	1875	1303	64
Widowed	M.	651	.	.	7	54	83	122	13
	F.	1465	.	1	15	98	184	274	830
595 LLANDOVERY:									
Unmarried	M.	3014	2303	646	469	308	114	71	48
	F.	4121	2172	692	536	434	128	71	47
Married	M.	1633	.	1	72	382	432	419	362
	F.	1971	.	16	114	464	482	379	337
Widowed	M.	230	.	.	3	11	23	29	60
	F.	567	.	.	2	22	51	70	103
596 LLANDILOFAWR:									
Unmarried	M.	5759	3672	925	524	389	[illegible]	64	68
	F.	5930	3497	910	663	501	167	114	65
Married	M.	2945	.	1	132	718	711	570	434
	F.	3009	.	4	158	817	753	572	404
Widowed	M.	328	.	.	2	10	27	44	65
	F.	778	.	.	.	30	55	119	185
597 CARMARTHEN:									
Unmarried	M.	10413	6318	1693	1056	711	303	188	111
	F.	11602	5984	1809	1461	1101	478	280	212
Married	M.	5239	.	15	263	1220	1135	1049	887
	F.	5433	.	18	380	1424	1272	1085	788
Widowed	M.	665	.	.	9	34	56	97	137
	F.	1723	.	.	2	80	170	233	381
PEMBROKESHIRE.									
598 NARBERTH:									
Unmarried	M.	5812	3658	942	526	377	139	97	61
	F.	6423	3543	942	727	587	240	158	114
Married	M.	2956	.	3	134	660	642	505	548
	F.	3080	.	8	186	696	750	627	492
Widowed	M.	351	.	.	1	20	37	48	88
	F.	889	.	.	.	25	59	126	225
599 PEMBROKE:									
Unmarried	M.	9258	5532	1606	1130	617	190	72	62
	F.	9366	5337	1641	1034	707	280	169	116
Married	M.	4947	.	3	242	1188	1249	1098	745
	F.	5015	.	26	332	1331	1270	998	676
Widowed	M.	575	.	.	1	22	64	88	134
	F.	1156	.	1	8	51	142	194	258
600 HAVERFORDWEST:									
Unmarried	M.	10091	5865	1809	1151	691	247	158	96
	F.	10829	5915	1740	1102	916	431	284	183
Married	M.	5351	.	7	283	1101	1241	1111	944
	F.	5301	.	21	332	1220	1269	1087	810
Widowed	M.	711	.	.	2	26	64	92	130
	F.	1605	.	.	3	62	193	239	335
CARDIGANSHIRE.									
601 CARDIGAN:									
Unmarried	M.	4838	2500	704	410	329	147	88	51
	F.	6037	2957	897	668	640	392	214	173
Married	M.	2286	.	4	86	438	548	516	438
	F.	2905	.	3	105	687	753	601	463
Widowed	M.	369	.	.	1	18	20	37	74
	F.	1090	.	.	8	46	118	181	224

Table 8 *continued.*—CONDITION as to MARRIAGE and AGES of MALES and FEMALES in REGISTRATION DISTRICTS.

REGISTRATION DISTRICT.		ALL AGES.	Under 15 Years.	15–	20–	25–	35–	45–	55–	65 and upw^ds.
43. SOUTH WALES—*cont.*										
ARDIGANSHIRE—cont.										
NEWCASTLE IN EMLYN:										
UNMARRIED	M.	5613	3331	917	536	399	145	108	79	57
	F.	6548	3256	969	736	700	330	243	152	163
MARRIED	M.	2663	.	1	103	576	538	542	468	427
	F.	2835	.	19	155	646	645	621	440	318
WIDOWED	M.	377	.	.	.	9	27	63	92	196
	F.	988	.	.	3	38	93	149	217	493
LAMPETER:										
UNMARRIED	M.	3033	1730	489	345	368	93	56	38	29
	F.	3424	1823	528	353	346	186	96	69	43
MARRIED	M.	1438	.	1	43	307	316	330	240	201
	F.	1516	.	2	87	357	383	326	215	143
WIDOWED	M.	194	.	.	.	10	9	28	48	99
	F.	476	.	.	3	13	49	68	99	244
ABERAYRON:										
UNMARRIED	M.	3454	2206	522	281	202	91	77	43	32
	F.	4448	2245	649	468	454	244	163	128	92
MARRIED	M.	1579	.	.	41	266	343	353	302	274
	F.	2051	.	2	72	489	489	462	313	224
WIDOWED	M.	245	.	.	.	9	11	28	60	147
	F.	771	.	.	.	29	82	134	177	348
5 ABERYSTWITH:										
UNMARRIED	M.	7829	4590	1397	771	580	202	136	82	71
	F.	8528	4322	1427	1000	803	337	190	141	103
MARRIED	M.	3544	.	3	132	718	923	812	598	358
	F.	3905	.	13	212	913	1098	962	638	240
WIDOWED	M.	479	.	.	1	30	49	76	121	202
	F.	1326	.	.	3	37	152	238	318	558
06 TREGARON:										
UNMARRIED	M.	3123	1860	601	283	241	105	72	40	19
	F.	3553	1837	532	380	373	182	130	67	46
MARRIED	M.	1336	.	.	34	285	309	274	232	222
	F.	1519	.	2	63	387	369	322	232	154
WIDOWED	M.	211	.	.	.	10	18	26	39	118
	F.	510	.	.	1	13	39	82	129	246
BRECKNOCKSHIRE.										
607 BUILTH:										
UNMARRIED	M.	2620	1497	364	257	244	101	55	48	42
	F.	2646	1518	430	280	223	74	54	32	35
MARRIED	M.	1226	.	.	42	268	286	205	205	157
	F.	1232	.	4	80	333	298	247	165	105
WIDOWED	M.	169	.	.	.	5	20	24	39	81
	F.	289	.	.	.	15	23	40	72	130
608 BRECKNOCK:										
UNMARRIED	M.	5612	2996	968	707	629	178	101	76	59
	F.	6233	2990	989	690	453	172	108	74	58
MARRIED	M.	2633	.	2	76	684	674	663	423	311
	F.	2655	.	11	164	678	668	594	339	200
WIDOWED	M.	333	.	.	2	21	26	45	75	164
	F.	712	.	.	1	33	50	131	130	317
609 CRICKHOWELL:										
UNMARRIED	M.	5832	3405	678	638	452	106	108	57	48
	F.	5218	3539	800	419	246	88	68	34	34
MARRIED	M.	3108	.	3	143	787	784	631	455	305
	F.	3170	.	18	269	899	801	591	406	186
WIDOWED	M.	430	.	.	.	32	50	86	91	171
	F.	800	.	.	2	43	79	138	202	337
610 HAY:										
UNMARRIED	M.	3128	1786	488	324	296	91	61	43	39
	F.	3078	1807	477	331	245	81	47	43	47
MARRIED	M.	1602	.	1	40	336	405	372	279	229
	F.	1670	.	7	102	416	408	340	243	154
WIDOWED	M.	238	.	.	.	11	31	35	62	99
	F.	440	.	.	3	10	24	63	106	246
RADNORSHIRE.										
611 KNIGHTON:										
UNMARRIED	M.	4025	2142	634	484	379	152	102	84	48
	F.	3511	2104	362	362	246	98	64	45	30
MARRIED	M.	1782	.	1	63	384	410	423	294	227
	F.	1775	.	12	108	442	433	380	246	151
WIDOWED	M.	250	.	.	2	11	30	28	64	115
	F.	439	.	.	4	17	29	69	107	213
612 RHAYADER:										
UNMARRIED	M.	2231	1244	300	266	221	92	46	32	30
	F.	2147	1235	325	232	180	67	44	31	33
MARRIED	M.	973	.	1	28	205	229	208	153	149
	F.	1002	.	4	36	266	243	187	147	100
WIDOWED	M.	143	.	.	.	6	15	16	33	73
	F.	245	.	.	1	9	26	29	58	122

REGISTRATION DISTRICT.		ALL AGES.	Under 15 Years.	15–	20–	25–	35–	45–	55–
44. NORTH WALES.									
MONTGOMERYSHIRE.									
613 MACHYNLLETH:									
UNMARRIED	M.	3006	2207	652	441	340	112	58	51
	F.	3839	2218	634	430	292	105	66	57
MARRIED	M.	1883	.	1	55	367	470	447	319
	F.	1980	.	3	118	488	509	416	270
WIDOWED	M.	201	.	.	.	10	30	46	79
	F.	618	.	.	1	29	44	112	161
614 NEWTOWN:									
UNMARRIED	M.	8368	4896	1351	883	673	260	150	84
	F.	7781	4775	1259	779	486	206	128	72
MARRIED	M.	3850	.	5	142	844	984	844	570
	F.	3923	.	20	286	1000	1006	793	504
WIDOWED	M.	314	.	.	3	29	45	82	95
	F.	1003	.	.	4	44	88	147	224
615 FORDEN:									
UNMARRIED	M.	6048	3333	984	686	646	222	116	96
	F.	5718	3194	778	506	391	148	83	52
MARRIED	M.	2985	.	.	101	594	723	670	535
	F.	2943	.	13	186	673	773	692	446
WIDOWED	M.	412	.	.	1	18	40	69	98
	F.	675	.	.	1	21	49	104	153
616 LLANFYLLIN:									
UNMARRIED	M.	6412	3502	1042	721	589	232	152	89
	F.	5901	3581	958	553	443	159	84	67
MARRIED	M.	3150	.	3	83	553	774	725	580
	F.	3185	.	11	162	708	812	700	475
WIDOWED	M.	470	.	.	.	13	42	73	106
	F.	835	.	.	1	21	65	136	106
FLINTSHIRE.									
617 HOLYWELL:									
UNMARRIED	M.	14849	8645	2389	1597	1317	450	215	156
	F.	12964	8701	1857	1016	727	291	178	115
MARRIED	M.	7679	.	9	276	1847	2124	1590	1069
	F.	7626	.	40	507	2043	2129	1529	924
WIDOWED	M.	789	.	.	2	59	93	125	207
	F.	1868	.	1	10	71	194	288	525
DENBIGHSHIRE.									
618 WREXHAM:									
UNMARRIED	M.	17976	10745	3039	1946	1367	426	213	151
	F.	15596	10801	2195	1152	797	295	186	97
MARRIED	M.	9342	.	12	429	2403	2570	2002	1234
	F.	9316	.	51	723	2725	2526	1829	1025
WIDOWED	M.	1008	.	.	5	62	128	183	255
	F.	1921	.	.	10	85	217	344	526
619 RUTHIN:									
UNMARRIED	M.	4453	2424	805	532	382	123	72	61
	F.	4104	2408	655	430	318	130	74	63
MARRIED	M.	2352	.	.	70	457	561	647	450
	F.	2328	.	3	122	645	560	499	402
WIDOWED	M.	353	.	.	.	15	30	48	79
	F.	683	.	.	2	17	47	95	142
620 ST. ASAPH:									
UNMARRIED	M.	8671	4809	1379	865	828	335	177	126
	F.	9337	4612	1547	1057	920	360	244	166
MARRIED	M.	4623	.	3	141	987	1147	1012	836
	F.	4746	.	15	253	1168	1241	1020	690
WIDOWED	M.	641	.	1	1	24	69	88	156
	F.	1441	.	.	6	58	160	239	333
621 LLANRWST:									
UNMARRIED	M.	4457	2430	676	645	478	149	102	43
	F.	4180	2364	707	450	322	143	69	58
MARRIED	M.	2261	.	3	82	516	590	446	340
	F.	2264	.	6	151	607	599	413	365
WIDOWED	M.	343	.	.	.	17	41	46	87
	F.	564	.	.	.	18	43	161	131
MERIONETHSHIRE.									
622 CORWEN:									
UNMARRIED	M.	6308	2987	883	622	469	184	106	61
	F.	4939	3104	704	462	348	126	74	52
MARRIED	M.	2753	.	.	30	589	673	668	501
	F.	2797	.	6	175	690	680	590	403
WIDOWED	M.	377	.	.	3	16	31	52	80
	F.	659	.	.	1	12	64	93	148
623 BALA:									
UNMARRIED	M.	2333	1036	356	350	279	152	78	57
	F.	1940	1101	273	214	189	74	42	34
MARRIED	M.	1002	.	.	23	109	243	222	169
	F.	1006	.	2	36	222	274	222	135
WIDOWED	M.	166	.	.	.	7	9	26	25
	F.	276	.	.	2	9	13	45	47

Table 8 *continued.*—CONDITION as to MARRIAGE and AGES of MALES and FEMALES in REGISTRATION DISTRICTS.

REGISTRATION DISTRICT.		ALL AGES.	Under 15 Years.	15–	20–	25–	35–	45–	55–	65 and upw^{ds}.
44 NORTH WALES—*cont.*										
MERIONETHSHIRE—cont.										
24 DOLGELLY:										
UNMARRIED	M.	4474	2663	660	434	383	169	64	40	32
	F.	4704	2775	711	444	356	156	100	63	80
MARRIED	M.	2503	.	3	79	676	678	520	345	302
	F.	2564	.	5	153	689	698	487	317	220
WIDOWED	M.	296	.	1	.	19	25	36	57	158
	F.	639	.	.	1	31	65	90	150	304
26 FESTINIOG:										
UNMARRIED	M.	9701	5562	1373	1222	960	336	142	76	46
	F.	8573	5426	1230	738	556	216	92	63	68
MARRIED	M.	4889	.	3	217	1376	1370	930	607	587
	F.	4920	.	33	408	1500	1350	832	525	288
WIDOWED	M.	551	.	.	8	48	84	99	119	198
	F.	1082	.	.	4	71	127	167	255	458
CARNARVONSHIRE.										
6 PWLLHELI:										
UNMARRIED	M.	7034	3974	1082	736	597	295	149	108	73
	F.	6986	3764	1000	715	635	343	230	102	147
MARRIED	M.	3585	.	5	160	758	822	706	633	501
	F.	3770	.	16	267	896	948	669	599	370
WIDOWED	M.	542	.	.	3	25	42	62	101	309
	F.	994	.	.	5	36	94	144	247	469
7 CARNARVON:										
UNMARRIED	M.	15864	8108	2212	1562	1230	385	185	112	70
	F.	13646	7730	2001	1145	969	396	194	118	93
MARRIED	M.	7291	.	10	353	1914	1966	1372	904	664
	F.	7518	.	65	582	2204	2032	1380	806	459
WIDOWED	M.	905	.	.	4	53	120	168	208	363
	F.	1775	.	.	14	69	211	256	470	736
44 NORTH WALES—*cont.*										
CARNARVONSHIRE—cont.										
628 BANGOR:										
UNMARRIED	M.	11413	6648	1878	1263	1007	386	176	126	[illegible]
	F.	11832	6400	1829	1244	956	388	237	149	[illegible]
MARRIED	M.	6573	.	6	241	1561	1657	1422	1076	[illegible]
	F.	6698	.	24	444	1725	1668	1396	926	[illegible]
WIDOWED	M.	806	.	.	5	41	89	116	184	[illegible]
	F.	1090	.	.	6	81	179	261	394	[illegible]
629 CONWAY:										
UNMARRIED	M.	5402	3111	896	622	446	137	83	62	[illegible]
	F.	5877	3047	964	730	581	269	147	90	[illegible]
MARRIED	M.	2967	.	1	117	728	722	651	475	[illegible]
	F.	2954	.	9	188	773	764	656	395	[illegible]
WIDOWED	M.	372	.	.	2	30	44	58	73	[illegible]
	F.	799	.	.	1	43	90	167	181	[illegible]
ANGLESEY.										
630 ANGLESEY:										
UNMARRIED	M.	10371	5858	1098	1100	908	324	209	161	[illegible]
	F.	10224	5748	1622	1007	695	387	244	164	[illegible]
MARRIED	M.	6020	.	6	244	1297	1357	1233	1067	[illegible]
	F.	6080	.	30	375	1466	1446	1220	961	[illegible]
WIDOWED	M.	789	.	.	6	35	70	113	186	[illegible]
	F.	1647	.	.	9	74	117	276	404	[illegible]

Table 9.—CONDITION as to MARRIAGE and AGES of MALES and FEMALES in each URBAN SANITARY DISTRICT of which the POPULATION EXCEEDS 50,000 PERSONS.

URBAN SANITARY DISTRICT.		ALL AGES.	Under 15 Years.	15–	20–	25–	35–	45–	55–	65 and upw^{ds}.
CARDIFF:										
UNMARRIED	M.	26222	14941	4163	3868	2510	752	269	137	73
	F.	23481	14879	4016	2514	1324	386	206	108	52
MARRIED	M.	14014	.	21	928	4760	4388	2853	1412	562
	F.	14344	.	175	1686	4934	3821	2318	1082	330
WIDOWED	M.	1180	.	.	14	110	188	247	273	348
	F.	2020	.	.	35	203	408	588	664	721
YSTRADYFODWG:										
UNMARRIED	M.	19978	11294	3126	2811	1846	534	236	92	40
	F.	14207	10754	2467	880	347	86	33	15	25
MARRIED	M.	9901	.	17	842	3676	2720	1632	822	262
	F.	9485	.	154	1337	3413	2340	1371	613	187
WIDOWED	M.	908	.	1	16	130	192	204	188	183
	F.	1113	.	6	20	121	153	248	278	287
SWANSEA:										
UNMARRIED	M.	20306	12215	3185	2381	1582	523	246	118	56
	F.	19746	12481	3406	2600	1075	351	208	124	93
MARRIED	M.	11002	.	17	672	3531	3068	2084	1171	469
	F.	11175	.	92	1211	3742	2970	1921	918	328
WIDOWED	M.	918	.	.	10	89	155	183	184	296
	F.	2454	.	.	24	177	376	510	615	753

Table 10.—OCCUPATIONS of MALES and FEMALES in the WELSH DIVISION and its REGISTRATION COUNTIES, and in each URBAN SANITARY DISTRICT of which the POPULATION exceeds 50,000 PERSONS.

OCCUPATIONS.	MONMOUTHSHIRE AND WALES.		REGISTRATION COUNTIES. 42. MONMOUTHSHIRE.		43. SOUTH WALES.		44. NORTH WALES.	
	Males.	Females.	Males.	Females.	Males.	Females.	Males.	Females.
TOTAL	789074	788485	119966	114567	438814	442103	230296	231815
I. PROFESSIONAL CLASS.								
1. PERSONS ENGAGED IN THE GENERAL OR LOCAL GOVERNMENT OF THE COUNTRY.								
1. *National Government.*								
Peer, M.P., Privy Councillor (not otherwise described)	11	.	.	.	7	.	4	.
Civil Service (officers and clerks)	968	101	174	20	664	70	230	62
Civil Service (messengers, &c.)	787	90	105	8	411	54	271	28
Prison Officer, &c.	63	21	10	5	40	13	13	3
2. *Local Government.*								
Police	1178	.	196	.	696	.	286	.
Municipal, Parish, Union, District, Officer	726	108	98	21	383	49	245	38
Other Local or County Official	446	.	54	.	236	.	156	.
3. *East Indian and Colonial Service.*								
East Indian and Colonial Service	.	.	.	.	.	.	.	.
2. PERSONS ENGAGED IN THE DEFENCE OF THE COUNTRY.								
1. *Army (at Home).*								
Army Officer (effective or retired)	247	.	29	.	148	.	70	.
Soldier and Non-commissioned Officer	1529	.	77	.	1245	.	207	.
Militia, Yeomanry, Volunteers	783	.	42	.	347	.	394	.
Army Pensioner	225	.	38	.	132	.	55	.
2. *Navy (ashore or in port).*								
Navy Officer (effective or retired)	63	.	1	.	48	.	14	.
Seaman, R.N.	184	.	3	.	158	.	23	.
Royal Marines (officers and men)	26	.	3	.	22	.	1	.
Navy Pensioner	150	.	8	.	119	.	23	.
3. PERSONS ENGAGED IN PROFESSIONAL OCCUPATIONS (WITH THEIR IMMEDIATE SUBORDINATES).								
1. *Clerical Profession.*								
Clergyman (Established Church)	1434	.	206	.	723	.	505	.
Roman Catholic Priest	81	.	16	.	35	.	31	.
Minister, Priest, of other religious bodies	1862	.	199	.	1040	.	623	.
Missionary, Scripture Reader, Itinerant Preacher	120	35	22	12	55	21	43	2
Nun, Sister of Charity	.	45	.	10	.	10	.	25
Theological Student	494	.	46	.	213	.	235	.
Church, Chapel, Cemetery—Officer, Servant	146	124	22	19	66	68	58	37
2. *Legal Profession.*								
Barrister, Solicitor	618	.	94	.	341	.	183	.
Law Student	70	.	15	.	42	.	13	.
Law Clerk, and others connected with Law	948	2	114	.	539	2	295	.
3. *Medical Profession.*								
Physician, Surgeon, General Practitioner	698	.	99	.	353	.	246	.
Dentist	89	.	12	.	40	.	37	.
Medical Student, Assistant	284	1	22	.	142	.	120	1
Midwife	.	266	.	38	.	136	.	92
Subordinate Medical Service	69	510	9	95	43	253	17	162
4. *Teachers.*								
Schoolmaster	2845	4470	297	838	1590	2583	958	1049
Teacher, Professor, Lecturer	184	625	22	103	86	304	76	218
School Service, and others concerned in Teaching	77	41	14	11	40	21	23	9
5. *Literary and Scientific Persons.*								
Author, Editor, Journalist	63	7	2	1	38	3	23	3
Reporter, Short-hand Writer	74	1	17	.	35	1	22	.
Persons engaged in Scientific Pursuits	69	1	6	.	48	.	15	1
Literary, Scientific, Institution, Service, &c.	17	3	2	1	14	1	1	1
6. *Engineers and Surveyors.*								
Civil Engineer	394	.	68	.	216	.	110	.
Mining Engineer	365	.	62	.	234	.	69	.
Land, House, Ship, Surveyor	206	.	30	.	122	.	54	.
7. *Artists.*								
Painter (artist)	131	18	9	2	58	8	64	8
Engraver (artist)	14	.	.	.	12	.	2	.
Sculptor	63	.	13	.	46	.	3	.
Architect	169	.	26	.	82	.	61	.
Musician, Music Master	395	232	64	39	228	140	103	53
Art Student	10	12	.	.	5	9	5	3
Photographer	181	34	29	8	99	12	53	14
Actor	64	51	14	17	49	34	1	.
Art, Music, Theatre, Service	15	5	7	2	7	3	1	.

NOTE.—Persons returned as engaged in more than one occupation have been referred to the one that appeared to be of most importance; or, if there was no difference in this respect, to the one first given by the person in his or her return. In some cases special rules have been followed: *e.g.*, "Clergyman and Schoolmaster" in combination has always been referred to "Schoolmaster"; a Member of Parliament or Peer engaged in any branch of commerce or industry has always been referred to this latter, not to "Peer, M.P."

The numbers returned under any heading include Labourers, Apprentices, and Assistants, as well as Masters, but not Clerks, Messengers, Errand boys, Porters, or Watchmen, for which occupations there are special headings. Civil, Military, and Naval Clerks, Law, Bank, Insurance, and Railway Clerks, and Government and Railway Porters are, however, exceptions to this rule. Many young persons, being Apprentices or Assistants, have therefore been referred to occupations usually followed by adults. Women also, chiefly widows or orphans carrying on the business of their deceased husbands or fathers, will sometimes be found under occupations commonly followed by men only.

Persons returned as *retired* from any business have not been referred to that business. Inmates of workhouses have been referred to their trades, unless their age or infirmities showed that they were past work. But persons who might be supposed to be only temporarily separated from their usual employment, such as Prisoners, and Patients in General Hospitals, have been classed under their usual occupations.

[illegible]le designation, *e.g.*, "Schoolmaster," alone is given, instead of "Schoolmaster, Schoolmistress."

Table 10 *continued*.—Occupations of Males and Females in the Welsh Division and its Registration Counties, and in each Urban Sanitary District of which the Population exceeds 50,000 Persons.

Occupations.	Monmouthshire and Wales.		Registration Counties. 42. Monmouthshire.		43. South Wales.		44. North Wales.	
	Males.	Females.	Males.	Females.	Males.	Females.	Males.	Females.
6. *Persons engaged in Exhibitions, Shows, Games, &c.*								
Performer, Showman, Exhibition, Service	49	34	10	8	14	12	25	14
Billiard, Cricket, & other Games, Service	140	.	22	.	72	.	46	.
II. DOMESTIC CLASS.								
4. Persons engaged in Domestic Offices or Services.								
1. *Domestic Service.*								
Domestic Coachman, Groom	2375	.	349	.	1043	.	990	.
Domestic Gardener	3917	7	573	.	1791	5	1553	2
Domestic Indoor Servant	1841	74758	237	9083	888	40363	716	25312
Lodge, Gate, Park, Keeper (not Government)	55	78	8	10	34	28	13	40
Inn, Hotel, Servant	704	1570	112	223	310	883	282	464
College, Club, Service	34	4	.	.	29	4	5	.
2. *Other Service.*								
Office Keeper (not Government)	26	126	4	23	14	91	8	12
Cook (not domestic)	15	52	.	5	13	29	2	18
Charwoman	.	5014	.	663	.	2955	.	1398
Washing and Bathing Service	25	6353	1	1075	13	3711	11	1567
Hospital and Institution Service	124	254	27	47	81	134	16	73
Others engaged in Service	87	6	5	1	14	4	8	1
III. COMMERCIAL CLASS.								
5. Persons engaged in Commercial Occupations.								
1. *Merchants and Agents.*								
Merchant	272	10	35	.	180	7	87	3
Broker, Agent, Factor	1065	7	214	2	590	4	272	1
Auctioneer, Appraiser, Valuer, House Agent	509	.	82	.	272	.	155	.
Accountant	854	2	138	.	565	2	161	.
Salesman, Buyer (not otherwise described)	13	16	3	3	8	5	1	8
Commercial Traveller	1096	.	158	.	709	.	229	.
Commercial Clerk	4598	109	770	21	2849	50	979	38
Officer of Commercial Company, Guild, Society, &c.	6	.	1	.	5	.	.	.
2. *Dealers in Money.*								
Banker	35	.	5	.	14	.	16	.
Bank Service	625	2	89	1	321	1	235	.
Bill Discounter, Bill Broker, Finance Agent	19	.	2	.	12	.	5	.
3. *Persons occupied in Insurance.*								
Life, House, Ship, &c., Insurance Service	561	2	99	.	338	1	124	1
6. Persons engaged in Conveyance of Men, Goods, and Messages.								
1. *On Railways.*								
Railway Engine Driver, Stoker	1958	.	585	.	1128	.	257	.
Railway Guard	900	.	257	.	560	.	83	.
Pointsman, Level Crossing Man	326	10	58	.	188	6	80	4
Other Railway Officials and Servants	3541	10	1204	2	3205	5	1132	3
2. *On Roads.*								
Toll Collector, Turnpike Gate Keeper	80	132	10	12	51	73	19	47
Omnibus, Coach, Cab, Owner—Livery Stable Keeper	177	5	18	.	102	2	59	3
Cabman, Flyman, Coachman (not domestic)	725	.	78	.	424	.	223	.
Carman, Carrier, Carter, Haulier	7390	77	1397	15	4744	34	1258	28
Tramway Companies' Service	78	2	6	.	65	3	7	.
Wheel Chair Proprietor, Attendant, &c.	2	1	.	.	.	1	2	.
3. *On Canals, Rivers and Seas.*								
Inland Navigation Service	134	1	14	.	101	.	19	1
Bargeman, Lighterman, Waterman	579	8	69	.	411	3	108	6
Navigation Service (on shore)	133	3	16	.	88	2	29	1
Seaman (Merchant Service)	12215	.	1636	.	7601	.	2978	.
Pilot	502	.	56	.	347	.	99	.
Ship Steward, Cook	548	20	93	1	364	4	91	15
Boatman on Seas	83	.	.	.	27	.	61	.
Harbour, Dock, Wharf, Lighthouse, Service	2296	5	574	.	1523	3	199	.
4. *In Storage.*								
Warehouseman (not Manchester)	222	11	34	2	142	4	46	5
Meter, Weigher	249	.	65	.	174	.	10	.
5. *In conveying Messages, Porterage, &c.*								
Messenger, Porter, Watchman (not Railway nor Government)	2077	47	484	11	1218	30	395	6
Telegraph, Telephone, Service	408	88	40	17	297	49	71	20

Table 10 *continued*.—OCCUPATIONS of MALES and FEMALES in the WELSH DIVISION and its REGISTRATION COUNTIES, and in each URBAN SANITARY DISTRICT of which the POPULATION exceeds 50,000 PERSONS.

OCCUPATIONS.	MONMOUTH-SHIRE AND WALES.		REGISTRATION COUNTIES.					
			42. MON-MOUTHSHIRE.		43. SOUTH WALES.		44. NORTH WALES.	
	Males.	Females.	Males.	Females.	Males.	Females.	Males.	Females.
IV. AGRICULTURAL CLASS.								
7. PERSONS ENGAGED IN AGRICULTURE.								
1. *In Fields and Pastures.*								
Farmer, Grazier	32289	5621	2198	313	16530	2918	13561	2390
Farmer's, Grazier's—Son, Grandson, Brother, Nephew*	15010	.	1035	.	7968	.	6009	.
Farm Bailiff	1184	.	232	.	480	.	472	.
Agricultural Labourer, Farm Servant, Cottager	45680	4986	4784	217	20152	3600	20744	1169
Shepherd	941	.	111	.	488	.	342	.
Land Drainage Service (not in towns)	132	.	21	.	48	.	63	.
Agricultural Machine—Proprietor, Attendant	104	.	15	.	20	.	69	.
Agricultural Student, Pupil	26	.	7	.	8	.	11	.
Others engaged in, or connected with, Agriculture	10	.	1	.	7	.	2	.
2. *In Woods.*								
Woodman	776	.	336	.	271	.	169	.
3. *In Gardens.*								
Nurseryman, Seedsman, Florist	132	16	22	3	62	6	48	7
Gardener (not domestic)	1112	88	373	3	383	76	356	[illegible]
8. PERSONS ENGAGED ABOUT ANIMALS.								
1. *About Animals.*								
Horse Proprietor, Breeder, Dealer	104	.	14	.	47	.	43	.
Groom, Horse-keeper, Horse-breaker	1672	2	275	1	951	.	446	1
Veterinary Surgeon, Farrier	231	.	38	.	119	.	76	.
Cattle, Sheep, Pig—Dealer, Salesman	476	7	51	.	236	6	189	1
Drover	48	.	1	.	28	.	19	.
Gamekeeper	1096	.	74	.	396	.	627	.
Dog, Bird, Animal—Keeper, Dealer	13	11	.	3	8	3	5	5
Vermin destroyer	83	.	4	.	35	.	44	.
Fisherman	895	86	60	.	555	82	280	4
Knacker, Catsmeat Dealer, &c., &c.	6	.	1	.	5	.	.	.
V. INDUSTRIAL CLASS.								
9. PERSONS WORKING AND DEALING IN BOOKS, PRINTS, AND MAPS.								
1. *Books.*								
Publisher, Bookseller, Librarian	311	70	30	12	153	28	128	30
Music—Publisher, Seller, Printer	18	7	3	2	10	3	5	2
Bookbinder	147	65	15	7	90	46	42	12
Printer	1440	44	191	5	733	25	516	14
Newspaper Agent, News Room Keeper	90	18	21	2	45	10	24	6
Others	.	1	.	.	.	1	.	.
2. *Prints and Maps.*								
Lithographer, Lithographic Printer	37	.	11	.	18	.	8	.
Copper Plate and Steel Plate Printer	3	.	.	.	3	.	.	.
Map and Print—Colourer, Seller	.	2	.	1	.	.	.	1
10. PERSONS WORKING AND DEALING IN MACHINES AND IMPLEMENTS.								
1. *Machines.*								
Engine, Machine, Maker	823	8	220	2	527	4	76	2
Millwright	203	.	55	.	101	.	47	.
Fitter, Turner (Engine and Machine)	3125	.	849	.	1909	.	367	.
Boiler Maker	1326	.	295	.	894	.	137	.
Spinning and Weaving Machine Maker	5	.	.	.	1	.	4	.
Agricultural Machine and Implement Maker	97	2	11	.	63	1	23	1
Domestic Machinery—Maker, Dealer	4	.	1	.	3	.	.	.
2. *Tools and Implements.*								
Tool Maker, Dealer	16	.	7	.	7	.	2	.
Cutler, Scissors Maker	33	.	7	.	18	.	8	.
File Maker	21	.	6	.	15	.	.	.
Saw Maker	19	.	2	.	8	.	9	.
Pin Maker	1	.	.	.	1	.	.	.
Needle Maker	3	.	.	.	3	.	.	.
Steel Pen Maker	4	.	1	.	3	.	.	.
Pencil Maker (Wood)	.	.	.	.	.	.	.	.
Domestic Implement Maker	2	.	.	.	2	.	.	.
3. *Watches and Philosophical Instruments.*								
Watch Maker, Clock Maker	732	9	97	.	372	4	263	5
Philosophical Instrument Maker, Optician	29	.	7	.	18	.	4	.
Electrical Apparatus Maker	31	.	6	.	24	.	1	.
Weighing and Measuring Apparatus Maker	27	.	14	.	13	.	.	.

the farmer or grazier, and, therefore, presumably engaged in agriculture, are included above.

Table 10 *continued.*—Occupations of Males and Females in the Welsh Division and its Registration Counties, and in each Urban Sanitary District of which the Population exceeds 50,000 Persons.

Occupations.	Monmouthshire and Wales.		Registration Counties. 42. Monmouthshire.		43. South Wales.		44. North Wales.	
	Males.	Females.	Males.	Females.	Males.	Females.	Males.	Females.
4. Surgical Instruments.								
Surgical Instrument Maker	1	.	.	.	1	.	.	.
5. Arms and Ordnance.								
Gunsmith, Gun Manufacturer	25	.	2	.	10	.	13	.
Ordnance Manufacturer	.	.	.	.	.	.	.	.
Sword, Bayonet—Maker, Cutler	.	.	.	.	.	.	.	.
Others	2	.	.	.	2	.	.	.
6. Musical Instruments.								
Musical Instrument Maker, Dealer	52	1	17	.	28	1	7	.
7. Type, Dies, Medals, Coins.								
Type Cutter, Founder	.	.	.	.	.	.	.	.
Die, Seal, Coin, Medal, Maker	9	.	6	.	3	.	.	.
8. Tackle for Sports and Games.								
Toy Maker, Dealer	19	55	4	6	8	27	7	22
Fishing Rod, Tackle, Maker, Dealer	9	1	1	.	6	.	2	1
Apparatus for other Games, Maker, Dealer	6	.	2	.	4	.	.	.
11. Persons working and dealing in Houses, Furniture, and Decorations.								
1. Houses.								
Builder	1074	4	162	2	595	.	317	2
Carpenter, Joiner	13303	5	1541	1	7608	4	4154	.
Bricklayer	1278	6	130	3	283	1	865	2
Mason	11627	10	1699	.	7016	5	2812	5
Slater, Tiler	670	1	113	.	133	.	324	1
Plasterer, Whitewasher	1746	3	295	2	868	.	583	1
Paperhanger	42	12	11	1	10	4	21	7
Plumber	805	3	72	2	443	.	283	1
Painter, Glazier	2811	14	404	4	1510	10	897	.
2. Furniture and Fittings.								
Cabinet Maker, Upholsterer	1028	97	95	21	670	57	263	19
French Polisher	70	1	9	1	46	.	15	.
Furniture Broker, Dealer	64	6	15	2	41	2	8	2
Locksmith, Bellhanger	34	.	10	.	19	.	5	.
Gas Fitter	246	2	58	.	142	.	46	2
House and Shop Fittings—Maker, Dealer	12	1	.	.	8	1	4	.
Funeral Furniture Maker, Undertaker	43	1	18	1	25	.	.	.
Others	.	.	.	.	.	.	.	.
3. House Decorations.								
Wood Carver	17	.	1	.	10	.	6	.
Carver, Gilder	73	2	7	1	44	1	23	.
Dealer in Works of Art	9	3	1	.	4	2	4	1
Figure, Image—Maker, Dealer	6	.	1	.	5	.	.	.
Animal, Bird, &c., Preserver, Naturalist	15	1	3	.	8	1	4	.
Artificial Flower Maker	5	5	1	2	3	3	1	.
12. Persons working and dealing in Carriages and Harness.								
1. Carriages.								
Coachmaker	466	4	67	1	263	2	136	1
Railway Carriage, Railway Wagon, Maker	217	1	39	.	157	1	21	.
Wheelwright	1169	2	194	.	472	.	503	2
Bicycle, Tricycle—Maker, Dealer	4	.	.	.	4	.	.	.
Others	73	1	5	.	65	1	3	.
2. Harness.								
Saddler, Harness, Whip, Maker	923	10	106	3	488	4	329	3
13. Persons working and dealing in Ships and Boats.								
1. Hull.								
Ship, Boat, Barge, Builder	593	4	36	.	512	4	45	.
Shipwright, Ship Carpenter (ashore)	2346	.	151	.	1821	.	374	.
2. Masts, Rigging, &c.								
Mast, Yard, Oar, Block, Maker	75	.	11	.	51	.	13	.
Ship Rigger, Chandler, Fitter	352	1	33	.	295	1	24	.
Sail Maker	286	1	27	.	189	1	70	.

Table 10 *continued*.—OCCUPATIONS of MALES and FEMALES in the WELSH DIVISION and its REGISTRATION COUNTIES, and in each URBAN SANITARY DISTRICT of which the POPULATION exceeds 50,000 PERSONS.

OCCUPATIONS.	MONMOUTHSHIRE AND WALES.		REGISTRATION COUNTIES. 42. MONMOUTHSHIRE.		43. SOUTH WALES.		44. NORTH WALES.	
	Males.	Females.	Males.	Females.	Males.	Females.	Males.	Females.
14. PERSONS WORKING AND DEALING IN CHEMICALS AND COMPOUNDS.								
1. *Colouring Matter.*								
Dye, Paint, Manufacture	30	10	1	.	28	16	1	.
Ink, Blacking, Colouring Substance, Manufacture	4	.	2	.	2	.	.	.
2. *Explosives.*								
Gunpowder, Guncotton, Explosive Substance, Manufacture	48	2	.	.	40	2		.
Fuses, Fireworks, Explosive Article, Manufacture	11	25	.	4	8	12	3	9
3. *Drugs and other Chemicals and Compounds.*								
Chemist, Druggist	899	25	104	1	519	15	276	9
Manufacturing Chemist	924	15	58	.	226	15	640	.
Alkali Manufacture	47	.	7	.	24	.	16	.
Drysalter	.	.	.	.	.	.	.	.
15. PERSONS WORKING AND DEALING IN TOBACCO AND PIPES.								
1. *Tobacco and Pipes.*								
Tobacco Manufacturer, Tobacconist	98	55	19	15	37	33	42	7
Tobacco Pipe, Snuff Box, &c., Maker	29	22	6	12	13	9	10	1
16. PERSONS WORKING AND DEALING IN FOOD AND LODGING.								
1. *Board and Lodging.*								
Innkeeper, Hotel Keeper, Publican	2748	1742	619	222	2142	1023	987	497
Lodging, Boarding House, Keeper	208	2091	19	183	102	893	87	1015
Coffee, Eating House, Keeper	88	121	20	21	50	62	18	38
2. *Spirituous Drinks.*								
Hop—Merchant, Dealer	1	1	.	.	.	1	1	.
Maltster	362	9	79	1	178	4	105	4
Brewer	655	36	131	6	391	19	233	11
Beerseller. Ale, Porter, Cider, Dealer	115	69	31	26	78	52	6	11
Cellarman	121	3	22	.	81	1	18	2
Wine, Spirit—Merchant, Agent	173	29	23	4	75	20	75	5
3. *Food.*								
Milkseller, Dairyman	349	314	76	26	219	238	54	50
Cheesemonger, Butterman	98	63	.	1	54	26	39	37
Butcher, Meat Salesman	3525	237	517	21	1774	167	1234	49
Provision Curer, Dealer	212	101	24	5	116	42	72	54
Poulterer, Game Dealer	89	93	1	.	39	54	49	39
Fishmonger	966	116	54	13	133	74	79	29
Corn, Flour, Seed—Merchant, Dealer	294	68	32	6	123	16	139	46
Corn Miller	1633	67	169	2	727	50	737	15
Baker	1426	617	313	43	712	383	401	191
Confectioner, Pastrycook	330	498	59	55	196	251	75	192
Greengrocer, Fruiterer	522	666	87	109	349	460	86	97
Mustard, Vinegar, Spice, Pickle—Maker, Dealer	4	1	.	.	4	.	.	1
Sugar Refiner	40	14	7	3	26	9	7	2
Grocer. Tea, Coffee, Chocolate—Maker, Dealer	6461	2498	1077	260	3547	1406	1837	832
Ginger Beer, Mineral Water—Manufacturer, Dealer	168	80	13	5	43	11	112	14
Others dealing in Food	.	.	.	.	.	.	.	.
17. PERSONS WORKING AND DEALING IN TEXTILE FABRICS.								
1. *Wool and Worsted.*								
Woolstapler	50	4	3	.	24	3	23	1
Woollen Cloth Manufacture	2525	756	41	13	1542	243	942	500
Wool, Woollen goods—Dyer, Printer	14	6	.	2	5	4	9	.
Worsted, Stuff, Manufacture	5	3	.	1	4	.	1	2
Flannel Manufacture	294	196	12	7	79	15	203	173
Blanket Manufacture	.	.	.	.	.	.	.	.
Fuller	89	5	.	.	8	4	81	1
Cloth, Worsted, Stuff, Flannel, Blanket, Dealer	24	19	1	6	16	9	7	4
Others	7	70	1	.	.	8	6	62
2. *Silk.*								
Silk, Silk goods, Manufacture	9	11	2	4	6	4	1	2
Silk Dyer, Printer	2	3	.	.	1	3	1	.
Ribbon Manufacture	.	.	.	.	.	.	.	.
Crape, Gauze, Manufacture	.	.	.	.	.	.	.	.
Silk Merchant, Dealer	3	1	.	.	3	.	.	1

Table 10 *continued*.—OCCUPATIONS of MALES and FEMALES in the WELSH DIVISION and its REGISTRATION COUNTIES, and in each URBAN SANITARY DISTRICT of which the POPULATION exceeds 50,000 PERSONS.

OCCUPATIONS.	MONMOUTHSHIRE AND WALES.		REGISTRATION COUNTIES. 42. MONMOUTHSHIRE.		43. SOUTH WALES.		44. NORTH WALES.	
	Males.	Females.	Males.	Females.	Males.	Females.	Males.	Females.
3. Cotton and Flax								
Cotton, Cotton goods, Manufacture	33	47	15	3	6	36	12	8
Cotton, Calico—Printer, Dyer, Bleacher	1	.	.	.	1	.	.	.
Cotton, Calico—Warehouseman, Dealer	4	.	.	.	1	.	3	.
Flax, Linen—Manufacturer, Dealer	3	.	.	.	2	.	1	.
Lace Manufacturer, Dealer	1	22	.	3	.	17	1	2
Fustian Manufacturer, Dealer	.	2	.	.	.	1	.	1
Tape Manufacturer, Dealer	.	.	.	.	.	.	.	.
Thread Manufacturer, Dealer	.	.	.	.	.	.	.	.
4. Hemp and other Fibrous Materials.								
Hemp, Jute, Cocoa Fibre, Manufacture	1	.	.	.	.	.	1	.
Rope, Twine, Cord—Maker, Dealer	113	5	17	1	67	.	29	4
Mat Maker, Seller	18	118	2	1	7	8	9	109
Net Maker	5	7	.	.	1	6	4	1
Canvas, Sailcloth, Manufacture	1	.	.	.	1	.	.	.
Sacking, Sack, Bag—Maker, Dealer	6	5	2	1	4	4	.	.
Others working and dealing in Hemp	4	.	1	.	3	.	.	.
6. Mixed or Unspecified Materials.								
Weaver (undefined)	198	66	9	.	129	15	60	51
Dyer, Printer, Scourer, Bleacher, Calenderer (undefined)	46	25	7	2	31	21	8	2
Factory hand (Textile, undefined)	81	44	2	2	13	9	66	33
Felt Manufacture	6	1	2	.	4	1	.	.
Carpet, Rug, Manufacture	10	3	7	1	2	1	1	1
Manchester Warehouseman	1	1	.	.	.	1	1	.
Draper, Linen Draper, Mercer	3709	1262	367	228	2138	743	1204	201
Fancy Goods (Textile), Manufacturer, Worker, Dealer	28	166	3	26	13	75	12	65
Trimming Maker, Dealer	1	3	1	1	.	2	.	.
Embroiderer	.	1	.	.	.	1	.	.
Others	2	.	.	.	1	.	1	.
18. PERSONS WORKING AND DEALING IN DRESS.								
1. Dress.								
Hatter, Hat Manufacture (not straw)	83	18	20	2	40	12	23	4
Straw—Hat, Bonnet, Plait, Manufacture	3	49	.	9	2	32	1	8
Tailor	6764	540	633	194	3775	319	2356	27
Milliner, Dressmaker, Staymaker	20	22759	3	2726	11	13494	6	6539
Shawl Manufacture	2	3	1	.	1	.	.	3
Shirt Maker, Seamstress	2	1437	.	258	1	873	1	306
Hosiery Manufacture	6	1063	.	4	4	939	2	120
Hosier, Haberdasher	59	52	3	2	43	37	13	13
Glover, Glove Maker	12	19	.	1	6	18	6	.
Button Maker, Dealer	.	.	.	.	.	.	.	.
Shoe, Boot—Maker, Dealer	7899	330	1164	74	4249	179	2486	77
Patten, Clog, Maker	415	5	7	.	264	2	144	3
Wig Maker, Hairdresser	467	12	87	5	276	4	104	3
Umbrella, Parasol, Stick—Maker, Dealer	48	12	8	2	24	9	16	1
Accoutrement Maker	.	.	.	.	.	.	.	.
Old Clothes Dealer, and others	5	9	1	5	4	3	.	1
19. PERSONS WORKING AND DEALING IN VARIOUS ANIMAL SUBSTANCES.								
1. In Grease, Gut, Bone, Horn, Ivory, and Whalebone.								
Tallow Chandler, Candle, Grease, Manufacture	105	7	17	.	56	6	32	1
Soap Boiler, Maker	2	.	.	.	.	.	2	.
Glue, Size, Gelatine, Isinglass—Maker, Dealer	.	.	.	.	.	.	.	.
Manure Manufacture	12	4	2	.	10	4	.	.
Bone, Horn, Ivory, Tortoise-shell—Worker, Dealer	1	.	.	.	1	.	.	.
Comb Maker	.	.	.	.	.	.	.	.
Others	1	.	.	.	1	.	.	.
2. In Skins.								
Furrier, Skinner	195	3	9	.	52	1	134	2
Tanner, Fellmonger	365	5	37	.	203	.	125	5
Currier	334	15	27	1	165	6	142	8
Leather Goods, Portmanteau, Bag, Strap, &c.—Maker, Dealer	19	.	2	.	13	.	4	.
Parchment, Vellum—Maker, Dealer	.	.	.	.	.	.	.	.
3. In Hair and Feathers.								
Hair, Bristle—Worker, Dealer	.	1	.	1	.	.	.	.
Brush, Broom, Maker	50	17	12	1	21	14	17	2
Quill, Feather—Dresser, Dealer	.	13	.	.	.	8	.	5

Table 10 *continued.*—OCCUPATIONS of MALES and FEMALES in the WELSH DIVISION and its REGISTRATION COUNTIES, and in each URBAN SANITARY DISTRICT of which the POPULATION exceeds 50,000 PERSONS.

OCCUPATIONS.	MONMOUTHSHIRE AND WALES.		REGISTRATION COUNTIES. 42. MONMOUTHSHIRE.		43. SOUTH WALES.		44. NORTH WALES.	
	Males.	Females.	Males.	Females.	Males.	Females.	Males.	Females.
20. PERSONS WORKING AND DEALING IN VARIOUS VEGETABLE SUBSTANCES.								
1. *In Oils, Gums, and Resins.*								
Oil Miller, Oil Cake—Maker, Dealer	40	4	8	1	27	1	5	2
Oil and Colourman	5	2	.	.	2	1	3	1
Floor Cloth, Oil Cloth, Manufacture	3	.	.	.	2	.	1	.
Japanner	.	25	.	.	.	24	.	1
India Rubber, Gutta Percha—Worker, Dealer	14	.	2	.	10	.	2	.
Waterproof Goods—Maker, Dealer	10	2	.	.	9	2	1	.
Others	.	.	.	.	.	.	.	.
2. *In Cane, Rush, and Straw.*								
Willow, Cane, Rush—Worker, Dealer, Basketmaker	209	42	62	6	159	29	88	7
Hay, Straw (not plait), Chaff—Cutter, Dealer	154	4	44	1	96	1	14	2
Thatcher	59	.	2	.	52	.	5	.
3. *In Wood and Bark.*								
Timber, Wood—Merchant, Dealer	533	6	124	3	300	3	109	.
Sawyer	1676	.	247	.	998	.	431	.
Lath, Wooden Fence, Hurdle, Maker	113	1	31	1	56	.	26	.
Wood Turner, Box Maker	180	7	79	1	71	1	30	5
Cooper, Hoop Maker, Bender	628	5	117	2	328	2	183	1
Cork, Bark—Cutter, Worker, Dealer	10	3	1	3	9	.	.	.
Others	4	3	.	1	2	2	2	.
4. *In Paper.*								
Paper Manufacture	260	171	25	4	105	52	130	115
Envelope Maker	.	.	.	.	.	.	.	.
Stationer, Law Stationer	139	122	22	33	77	65	40	24
Card, Pattern Card, Maker	.	3	.	.	.	3	.	.
Paper Stainer	.	.	.	.	.	.	.	.
Paper Box, Paper Bag, Maker	2	10	.	1	2	9	.	.
Ticket, Label, Writer	1	4	.	.	1	.	.	4
Others	65	3	14	.	34	1	17	2
21. PERSONS WORKING AND DEALING IN VARIOUS MINERAL SUBSTANCES.								
1. *Miners.*								
Coal Miner	72190	846	17656	280	46794	507	7740	59
Ironstone Miner	958	25	396	2	516	23	46	.
Copper Miner	422	14	.	.	50	.	372	14
Tin Miner	51	.	3	.	46	.	2	.
Lead Miner	5394	181	2	.	1815	165	3577	16
Miner in other, or undefined, Minerals	176	.	4	.	45	.	127	.
Mine Service	731	6	128	3	500	3	103	.
2. *Coal, Coal Gas, &c.*								
Coal Merchant, Dealer	1209	117	147	14	708	66	354	37
Coalheaver	1463	.	167	.	1208	.	88	.
Coke, Charcoal, Peat—Cutter, Burner, Dealer	493	63	180	37	291	26	22	.
Gas Works Service	507	.	115	.	273	.	119	.
3. *Stone, Clay, and Road Making.*								
Stone Quarrier	3401	.	332	.	1130	.	1939	.
Stone Cutter, Dresser, Dealer	542	.	103	.	225	.	214	.
Slate Quarrier	13717	.	1	.	140	.	13576	.
Slate Worker, Dealer	561	1	.	.	58	.	503	1
Limeburner	323	12	48	3	141	8	134	1
Clay, Sand, Gravel, Chalk—Labourer, Dealer	128	31	41	6	55	25	32	.
Fossil, Coprolite—Digger, Dealer	.	.	.	.	.	.	.	.
Well Sinker, Borer	235	.	61	.	157	.	17	.
Plaster, Cement, Manufacture	34	5	.	.	7	5	27	.
Brick, Tile—Maker, Burner, Dealer	1586	522	218	157	603	363	765	2
Paviour	12	.	.	.	7	.	5	.
Road Contractor, Surveyor, Inspector	108	.	12	.	72	.	24	.
Road Labourer	977	.	140	.	555	.	282	.
Railway Contractor	75	.	20	.	40	.	15	.
Platelayer	2720	.	452	.	1514	.	754	.
Railway Labourer, Navvy	2588	.	575	.	1371	.	642	.
Others	6	24	.	1	6	6	.	17
4. *Earthenware and Glass.*								
Earthenware, China, Porcelain, Manufacture	322	57	23	3	163	44	136	10
Glass Manufacture	19	2	2	.	15	2	2	.
Earthenware, China, Glass, Dealer	172	121	23	22	90	71	59	28
5. *Salt.*								
Salt Maker, Dealer	6	2	4	.	1	.	1	2

Table 10 *continued*.—Occupations of Males and Females in the Welsh Division and its Registration Counties, and in each Urban Sanitary District of which the Population exceeds 50,000 Persons.

Occupations.	Monmouthshire and Wales.		Registration Counties. 42. Monmouthshire.		43. South Wales.		44. North Wales.	
	Males.	Females.	Males.	Females.	Males.	Females.	Males.	Females.
6. Water.								
Waterworks Service	78	2	13	.	38	.	27	2
Others	4	.	.	.	2	.	2	.
7. Precious Metals and Jewellery.								
Goldsmith, Silversmith, Jeweller	139	22	17	4	96	11	26	7
Gold, Silver, Beater	.	.	.	.	.	.	.	.
Lapidary	8	1	.	.	6	1	2	.
Others	99	2	3	.	94	2	3	.
8. Iron and Steel.								
Blacksmith	9339	20	1537	3	5519	8	2283	9
Whitesmith	68	.	21	.	11	.	36	.
Nail Manufacture	361	8	161	.	89	5	111	3
Anchor, Chain, Manufacture	106	1	20	.	86	1	.	.
Other Iron and Steel Manufactures	15613	365	6449	137	8573	226	591	2
Ironmonger, Hardware Dealer, Merchant	923	47	133	14	532	17	258	16
9. Copper.								
Copper, Copper goods—Manufacturer, Worker, Dealer	2487	32	14	.	2347	20	126	12
10. Tin and Zinc.								
Tin, Tin Plate, Tin goods—Manufacturer, Worker, Dealer	13411	3185	2497	552	10610	2591	304	42
Zinc, Zinc Goods—Manufacturer, Worker, Dealer	639	1	.	.	606	1	33	.
11. Lead.								
Lead, Leaden goods—Manufacturer, Worker, Dealer	600	2	.	.	280	2	290	.
12. In Other, Mixed, or Unspecified, Metals.								
Metal Refiner, Worker, Turner, Dealer	195	.	12	.	177	.	6	.
Brass, Bronze, Manufacture. Brazier	118	.	14	.	76	.	28	.
Metal Burnisher, Lacquerer	3	.	2	.	1	.	.	.
White Metal, Plated Ware, Manufacture, Pewterer	16	.	7	.	9	.	.	.
Wire Maker, Worker, Weaver, Drawer	175	2	105	1	41	1	29	.
Bolt, Nut, Rivet, Screw, Staple, Maker	101	23	70	22	27	1	4	.
Lamp, Lantern, Candlestick, Maker	15	.	8	.	12	.	.	.
Clasp, Buckle, Hinge, Maker	.	.	.	.	.	.	.	.
Fancy Chain, Gilt Toy, Maker	.	.	.	.	.	.	.	.
Others	9	.	3	.	6	.	.	.
22. Persons working and dealing in General or Unspecified Commodities.								
1. Makers and Dealers (General or Undefined).								
General Shopkeeper, Dealer	1112	1177	121	128	530	505	461	544
Pawnbroker	202	35	55	9	134	24	13	2
Costermonger, Huckster, Street Seller	1103	869	117	95	561	520	425	254
Manufacturer, Manager, Superintendent (undefined)	304	9	53	1	192	6	60	2
Contractor (undefined)	365	2	87	2	220	.	58	.
2. Mechanics and Labourers (General or Undefined).								
General Labourer	42647	411	7734	107	22277	268	12636	36
Engine Driver, Stoker, Fireman (not railway, marine, nor agricultural)	7077	.	1481	.	4506	.	1090	.
Artisan, Mechanic (undefined)	1305	12	235	2	846	4	224	6
Apprentice (undefined)	95	30	14	6	53	20	28	4
Factory Labourer (undefined)	616	121	254	50	645	52	117	19
Machinist, Machine Worker (undefined)	138	59	41	11	70	30	27	18
23. Persons working and dealing in Refuse Matters.								
1. Refuse Matters.								
Town Drainage Service	44	.	4	.	26	.	14	.
Chimney Sweep, Soot Merchant	145	1	30	.	84	1	31	.
Scavenger, Crossing Sweeper	56	7	10	6	29	1	17	.
Rag Gatherer, Dealer	67	43	15	4	42	28	10	13
VI. UNOCCUPIED CLASS.								
24. Persons without Specified Occupations								
Persons returned by Property, Rank, &c., and not by special occupation	193270	527686	28877	78525	107937	294345	56456	154816
Children under 5 years of age	106165	106016	16220	16364	60605	60324	29340	29328

Table 10 *continued*.—OCCUPATIONS of MALES and FEMALES in the WELSH DIVISION and its REGISTRATION COUNTIES, and in each URBAN SANITARY DISTRICT of which the POPULATION exceeds 50,000 PERSONS.

OCCUPATIONS.	REGISTRATION COUNTIES.									
	GLAMORGANSHIRE.		CARMARTHENSHIRE.		PEMBROKESHIRE.		CARDIGANSHIRE.		BRECKNOCKSHIRE.	
	Males.	Females.	Males.	Females.	Males.	Females.	Males.	Females.	Males.	Females.
TOTAL	256128	252255	53489	57766	40085	48604	42717	52420	26901	27149
I. PROFESSIONAL CLASS.										
1. PERSONS ENGAGED IN THE GENERAL OR LOCAL GOVERNMENT OF THE COUNTRY.										
1. *National Government.*										
Peer, M.P., Privy Councillor (not otherwise described)	2	.	1	.	2	.	1	.	.	.
Civil Service (officers and clerks)	230	23	60	9	97	17	47	9	16	11
Civil Service (messengers, &c.)	126	16	58	6	69	3	54	28	30	1
Prison Officer, &c.	28	10	8	2	.	.	.	.	4	1
2. *Local Government.*										
Police	444	.	67	.	83	.	46	.	41	.
Municipal, Parish, Union, District, Officer	171	16	54	9	40	5	60	6	42	10
Other Local or County Official	95	.	31	.	28	.	41	.	28	.
3. *East Indian and Colonial Service.*										
East Indian and Colonial Service	.	.	.	.	.	.	.	.	.	.
2. PERSONS ENGAGED IN THE DEFENCE OF THE COUNTRY.										
1. *Army (at Home).*										
Army Officer (effective or retired)	34	.	9	.	74	.	15	.	24	.
Soldier and Non-Commissioned Officer	215	.	2	.	924	.	7	.	96	.
Militia, Yeomanry, Volunteers	54	.	33	.	48	.	26	.	155	.
Army Pensioner	71	.	11	.	32	.	7	.	11	.
2. *Navy (ashore or in port).*										
Navy Officer (effective or retired)	12	.	3	.	31	.	2	.	.	.
Seaman, R.N.	32	.	8	.	95	.	23	.	.	.
Royal Marines (officers and men)	4	.	2	.	16	.	.	.	.	.
Navy Pensioner	42	.	4	.	59	.	11	.	3	.
3. PERSONS ENGAGED IN PROFESSIONAL OCCUPATIONS (WITH THEIR IMMEDIATE SUBORDINATES).										
1. *Clerical Profession.*										
Clergyman (Established Church)	265	.	94	.	122	.	120	.	89	.
Roman Catholic Priest	26	.	2	.	2	.	2	.	3	.
Minister, Priest, of other religious bodies	527	.	162	.	101	.	151	.	77	.
Missionary, Scripture Reader, Itinerant Preacher	34	18	3	1	5	.	10	.	2	3
Nun, Sister of Charity	.	9	.	1	.	.	.	.	.	.
Theological Student	81	.	30	.	28	.	29	.	36	.
Church, Chapel, Cemetery—Officer, Servant	36	32	7	16	6	9	6	8	11	3
2. *Legal Profession.*										
Barrister, Solicitor	178	.	47	.	43	.	36	.	29	.
Law Student	23	.	5	.	5	.	5	.	4	.
Law Clerk, and others connected with Law	304	.	61	1	65	.	60	1	36	.
3. *Medical Profession.*										
Physician, Surgeon, General Practitioner	193	.	45	.	36	.	36	.	28	.
Dentist	28	.	3	.	4	.	3	.	4	.
Medical Student, Assistant	83	.	23	.	11	.	17	.	8	.
Midwife	.	66	.	22	.	13	.	17	.	16
Subordinate Medical Service	37	164	8	32	1	22	.	12	2	16
4. *Teachers.*										
Schoolmaster	771	1802	260	245	182	211	243	122	97	148
Teacher, Professor, Lecturer	57	156	13	27	6	50	17	35	11	27
School Service, and others concerned in Teaching	30	10	4	.	1	.	1	2	3	.
5. *Literary and Scientific Persons.*										
Author, Editor, Journalist	23	3	3	.	7	.	5	.	1	.
Reporter, Short-hand Writer	24	1	5	.	3	.	3	.	.	.
Persons engaged in Scientific Pursuits	45	.	1	.	2	.	.	.	.	.
Literary, Scientific, Institution, Service, &c.	13	1	1	.	.	.	.	.	.	.
6. *Engineers and Surveyors.*										
Civil Engineer	181	.	18	.	14	.	4	.	8	.
Mining Engineer	193	.	17	.	3	.	16	.	3	.
Land, House, Ship, Surveyor	78	.	21	.	3	.	10	.	7	.
7. *Artists.*										
Painter (artist)	31	6	1	1	2	1	2	.	1	.
Engraver (artist)	8	.	.	.	.	.	3	.	1	.
Sculptor	25	.	6	.	2	.	3	.	3	.
Architect	60	.	7	.	4	.	5	.	5	.
Musician, Music Master	170	99	21	14	10	12	12	7	15	6
Art Student	3	9	1	.	.	.	.	.	.	.
Photographer	60	7	11	.	15	4	8	1	4	.
Actor	47	32	2	2	.	.	.	.	.	.
Art, Music, Theatre, Service	6	3	1	.	.	.	.	.	.	.

Table 10 *continued*.—OCCUPATIONS of MALES and FEMALES in the WELSH DIVISION and its REGISTRATION COUNTIES, and in each URBAN SANITARY DISTRICT of which the POPULATION exceeds 50,000 PERSONS.

OCCUPATIONS.	REGISTRATION COUNTIES.									
	GLAMORGANSHIRE.		CARMARTHENSHIRE.		PEMBROKESHIRE.		CARDIGANSHIRE.		BRECKNOCKSHIRE.	
	Males.	Females.	Males.	Females.	Males.	Females.	Males.	Females.	Males.	Females.
8. *Persons engaged in Exhibitions, Shows, Games, &c.*										
Performer, Showman, Exhibition, Service	11	16	1	2	1	.	.	.	1	.
Billiard, Cricket, & other Games, Service	46	.	7	.	10	.	6	.	3	.
II. DOMESTIC CLASS.										
4. PERSONS ENGAGED IN DOMESTIC OFFICES OR SERVICES.										
1. *Domestic Service.*										
Domestic Coachman, Groom	377	.	135	.	190	.	148	.	143	.
Domestic Gardener	991	8	190	1	184	.	121	1	249	.
Domestic Indoor Servant	321	25024	119	5543	193	4021	113	5722	91	3028
Lodge, Gate, Park, Keeper (not Government)	27	13	.	4	2	4	1	1	8	5
Inn, Hotel, Servant	190	575	26	86	27	74	25	68	28	57
College, Club, Service	15	4	.	.	1	.	13	.	.	.
2. *Other Service.*										
Office Keeper (not Government)	10	76	.	5	3	8	.	2	1	5
Cook (not domestic)	13	22	.	2	.	5	1	.	.	.
Charwoman	.	1160	.	467	.	284	.	782	.	201
Washing and Bathing Service	10	2076	.	378	.	579	1	321	2	276
Hospital and Institution Service	58	108	21	8	2	11	.	1	.	10
Others engaged in Service	10	3	.	.	1	1	2	.	1	.
III. COMMERCIAL CLASS.										
5. PERSONS ENGAGED IN COMMERCIAL OCCUPATIONS.										
1. *Merchants and Agents.*										
Merchant	72	2	23	1	28	1	25	3	1	.
Broker, Agent, Factor	498	2	52	2	22	.	10	.	15	.
Auctioneer, Appraiser, Valuer, House Agent	145	.	31	.	30	.	30	.	31	.
Accountant	433	.	67	.	19	2	16	.	18	.
Salesman, Buyer (not otherwise described)	3	4	.	.	.	.	.	.	.	1
Commercial Traveller	532	.	79	.	37	.	32	.	26	.
Commercial Clerk	2338	35	234	1	124	4	78	7	63	1
Officer of Commercial Company, Guild, Society, &c.	8	.	1	.	.	.	.	.	1	.
2. *Dealers in Money.*										
Banker	5	.	2	.	1	.	1	.	5	.
Bank Service	160	.	41	.	42	1	39	.	34	.
Bill Discounter, Bill Broker, Finance Agent	10	.	2	.	.	.	.	.	.	.
3. *Persons occupied in Insurance.*										
Life, House, Ship, &c., Insurance Service	239	1	27	.	16	.	18	.	20	.
6. PERSONS ENGAGED IN CONVEYANCE OF MEN, GOODS, AND MESSAGES.										
1. *On Railways.*										
Railway Engine Driver, Stoker	871	.	109	.	54	.	21	.	67	.
Railway Guard	462	.	39	.	29	.	7	.	33	.
Pointsman, Level Crossing Man	119	1	35	3	17	.	1	.	8	.
Other Railway Officials and Servants	2350	8	334	.	155	.	72	.	244	.
2. *On Roads.*										
Toll Collector, Turnpike Gate Keeper	20	25	13	18	8	5	7	9	5	12
Omnibus, Coach, Cab, Owner—Livery Stable Keeper	74	1	4	.	17	1	5	.	2	.
Cabman, Flyman, Coachman (not domestic)	333	.	17	.	38	.	23	.	10	.
Carman, Carrier, Carter, Haulier	3996	15	302	9	73	3	115	4	238	1
Tramway Companies' Service	63	2	.	.	.	.	.	.	2	.
Wheel Chair Proprietor, Attendant, &c.	.	.	.	.	.	1	.	.	.	.
3. *On Canals, Rivers and Seas.*										
Inland Navigation Service	93	.	.	.	1	.	.	.	7	.
Bargeman, Lighterman, Waterman	359	.	7	.	38	2	3	.	5	.
Navigation Service (on shore)	78	.	5	.	4	.	1	2	.	.
Seaman (Merchant Service)	5433	.	316	.	1182	.	883	.	3	.
Pilot	293	.	35	.	14	.	6	.	.	.
Ship Steward, Cook	310	2	8	.	45	1	1	.	.	.
Boatman on Seas	2	.	.	.	13	.	12	.	.	1
Harbour, Dock, Wharf, Lighthouse, Service	1353	3	35	.	132	.	3	.	.	.
4. *In Storage.*										
Warehouseman (not Manchester)	121	4	10	.	1	.	7	.	2	.
Meter, Weigher	161	.	5	.	1	.	.	.	7	.
5. *In conveying Messages, Porterage, &c.*										
Messenger, Porter, Watchman (not Railway nor Government)	337	20	97	2	94	5	23	2	53	1
Telegraph, Telephone, Service	343	74	15	6	20	4	5	5	9	.

Table 10 *continued.*—OCCUPATIONS of MALES and FEMALES in the WELSH DIVISION and i REGISTRATION COUNTIES, and in each URBAN SANITARY DISTRICT of which the POPULATIO exceeds 50,000 PERSONS.

OCCUPATIONS.	REGISTRATION COUNTIES.									
	GLAMORGANSHIRE.		CARMARTHENSHIRE.		PEMBROKESHIRE.		CARDIGANSHIRE.		BRECKNOCKSHIRE.	
	Males.	Females.	Males.	Females.	Males.	Females.	Males.	Females.	Males.	Femal
IV. AGRICULTURAL CLASS.										
7. PERSONS ENGAGED IN AGRICULTURE.										
1. *In Fields and Pastures.*										
Farmer, Grazier	2853	410	3798	651	2483	464	4480	1001	1938	201
Farmer's, Grazier's—Son, Grandson, Brother, Nephew*	1399	.	1709	.	985	.	2155	.	1002	.
Farm Bailiff	177	.	65	.	44	.	64	.	86	.
Agricultural Labourer, Farm Servant, Cottager	4275	400	3242	387	3807	741	4696	1285	2561	13
Shepherd	98	.	20	.	16	.	131	.	147	
Land Drainage Service (not in towns)	4	.	13	.	3	.	8	.	11	
Agricultural Machine—Proprietor, Attendant	3	.	.	.	.	.	5	.	9	
Agricultural Student, Pupil	1	.	1	.	1	.	.	.	3	
Others engaged in, or connected with, Agriculture	2	.	3	.	2	.	.	.	.	
2. *In Woods.*										
Woodman	147	.	31	.	14	.	80	.	44	
3. *In Gardens.*										
Nurseryman, Seedsman, Florist	20	2	18	.	4	.	14	.	5	
Gardener (not domestic)	226	38	40	6	66	9	37	19	6	
8. PERSONS ENGAGED ABOUT ANIMALS.										
1. *About Animals.*										
Horse Proprietor, Breeder, Dealer	19	.	7	.	2	.	18	.	7	
Groom, Horse-keeper, Horse-breaker	619	.	80	.	111	.	71	.	62	
Veterinary Surgeon, Farrier	69	.	9	.	8	.	11	.	15	
Cattle, Sheep, Pig—Dealer, Salesman	81	3	56	2	13	.	67	1	10	
Drover	17	.	4	.	3	.	5	.	1	
Gamekeeper	119	.	62	.	46	.	63	.	72	
Dog, Bird, Animal—Keeper, Dealer	6	.	.	.	1	1	1	2	.	
Vermin destroyer	5	.	8	.	6	.	8	.	7	
Fisherman	171	18	104	20	231	41	63	3	5	
Knacker, Catsmeat Dealer, &c., &c.	5	.	.	.	.	.	.	.	.	
V. INDUSTRIAL CLASS.										
9. PERSONS WORKING AND DEALING IN BOOKS, PRINTS, AND MAPS.										
1. *Books.*										
Publisher, Bookseller, Librarian	99	15	15	5	20	3	13	2	4	
Music—Publisher, Seller, Printer	8	2	.	.	1	1	.	.	1	
Bookbinder	55	44	17	1	5	1	10	.	3	
Printer	458	11	110	9	57	2	41	3	31	
Newspaper Agent, News Room Keeper	58	7	1	2	2	.	.	.	1	
Others	.	.	.	.	.	.	.	.	.	
2. *Prints and Maps.*										
Lithographer, Lithographic Printer	18	.	.	.	.	.	.	.	.	
Copper Plate and Steel Plate Printer	1	.	.	.	.	.	2	.	.	
Map and Print—Colourer, Seller	.	.	.	.	.	.	.	.	.	
10. PERSONS WORKING AND DEALING IN MACHINES AND IMPLEMENTS.										
1. *Machines.*										
Engine, Machine, Maker	453	4	34	.	17	.	12	.	10	
Millwright	59	.	15	.	9	.	8	.	5	
Fitter, Turner (Engine and Machine)	1585	.	154	.	100	.	42	.	42	
Boiler Maker	765	.	45	.	56	.	3	.	25	
Spinning and Weaving Machine Maker	1	.	.	.	.	.	.	.	.	
Agricultural Machine and Implement Maker	5	.	30	.	1	.	1	1	14	
Domestic Machinery—Maker, Dealer	2	.	.	.	.	.	.	.	1	
2. *Tools and Implements.*										
Tool Maker, Dealer	3	.	.	.	.	.	.	.	4	
Cutler, Scissors Maker	15	.	.	.	2	.	.	.	.	
File Maker	15	.	.	.	.	.	.	.	.	
Saw Maker	4	.	1	.	.	.	2	.	1	
Pin Maker	.	.	.	.	.	.	1	.	.	
Needle Maker	2	.	.	.	.	.	1	.	.	
Steel Pen Maker	3	.	.	.	.	.	.	.	.	
Pencil Maker (Wood)	.	.	.	.	.	.	.	.	.	
Domestic Implement Maker	.	.	2	.	.	.	.	.	.	
3. *Watches and Philosophical Instruments.*										
Watch Maker, Clock Maker	201	3	44	.	50	.	37	.	28	
Philosophical Instrument Maker, Optician	15	.	.	.	1	.	1	.	1	
Electrical Apparatus Maker	22	.	.	.	2	.	.	.	.	
Weighing and Measuring Apparatus Maker	12	.	1	.	.	.	.	.	.	

…with the farmer or grazier, and therefore presumably engaged in agriculture are included above.

Table 10 *continued*.—Occupations of Males and Females in the Welsh Division and its Registration Counties, and in each Urban Sanitary District of which the Population exceeds 50,000 Persons.

Occupations.	Registration Counties.									
	Glamorganshire.		Carmarthenshire.		Pembrokeshire.		Cardiganshire.		Brecknockshire.	
	Males.	Females.	Males.	Females.	Males.	Females.	Males.	Females.	Males.	Females.
4. Surgical Instruments.										
Surgical Instrument Maker	1		.	.	.	.	.	.	.	.
5. Arms and Ordnance.										
Gunsmith, Gun Manufacturer	6	.	1	.	1	.	1	.	1	.
Ordnance Manufacturer	.	.	.	.	.	.	.	.	.	.
Sword, Bayonet—Maker, Cutler	.	.	.	.	.	.	.	.	.	.
Others	2	.	.	.	.	.	.	.	.	.
6. Musical Instruments.										
Musical Instrument Maker, Dealer	21	1	.	.	6	.	.	.	1	.
7. Type, Dies, Medals, Coins.										
Type Cutter, Founder	.	.	.	.	.	.	.	.	.	.
Die, Seal, Coin, Medal, Maker	3	.	.	.	.	.	.	.	.	.
8. Tackle for Sports and Games.										
Toy Maker, Dealer	6	19	1	4	1	1	.	2	.	1
Fishing Rod, Tackle, Maker, Dealer	2	.	.	.	.	.	.	.	4	.
Apparatus for other Games, Maker, Dealer	2	.	.	.	.	.	2	.	.	.
11. Persons working and dealing in Houses, Furniture, and Decorations.										
1. Houses.										
Builder	332	.	61	.	121	.	40	.	23	.
Carpenter, Joiner	3061	.	927		1013	2	1060	2	440	.
Bricklayer	227	1	11	.	8	.	3	.	19	.
Mason	4194	3	735	.	751	1	720	1	432	.
Slater, Tiler	47	.	8	.	24	.	35	.	19	.
Plasterer, Whitewasher	646	.	63	.	82	.	39	.	83	.
Paperhanger	9	3	1	1	.	.	.	.	.	.
Plumber	319	.	38	.	39	.	10	.	26	.
Painter, Glazier	1082	3	122	1	93	2	97	1	93	1
2. Furniture and Fittings.										
Cabinet Maker, Upholsterer	290	41	139	2	137	8	88	2	16	4
French Polisher	41	.	2	.	2	.	1	.	.	.
Furniture Broker, Dealer	38	2	.	.	.	.	.	.	2	.
Locksmith, Bellhanger	13	.	2	.	3	.	.	.	1	.
Gas Fitter	112	.	4	.	10	.	4	.	10	.
House and Shop Fittings—Maker, Dealer	8	1	.	.	.	.	.	.	.	.
Funeral Furniture Maker, Undertaker	23	.	.	.	.	.	1	.	1	.
Others	.	.	.	.	.	.	.	.	.	.
3. House Decorations.										
Wood Carver	19	.	.	.	.	.	.	.	.	.
Carver, Gilder	37	.	8	.	2	1	1	.	1	.
Dealer in Works of Art	3	1	.	.	.	.	1	1	.	.
Figure, Image—Maker, Dealer	5	.	.	.	.	.	.	.	.	.
Animal, Bird, &c., Preserver, Naturalist	6	.	1	.	.	1	1	.	.	.
Artificial Flower Maker	3	3	.	.	.	.	.	.	.	.
12. Persons working and dealing in Carriages and Harness.										
1. Carriages.										
Coachmaker	142	1	20	.	44	.	42	1	15	.
Railway Carriage, Railway Wagon, Maker	146	1	5	.	2	.	.	.	4	.
Wheelwright	258	.	33	.	39	.	13	.	92	.
Bicycle, Tricycle—Maker, Dealer	4	.	.	.	.	.	.	.	.	.
Others	63	1	1	.	.	.	.	.	1	.
2. Harness.										
Saddler, Harness, Whip, Maker	235	2	54	2	67	.	75	.	43	.
13. Persons working and dealing in Ships and Boats.										
1. Hull.										
Ship, Boat, Barge, Builder	162	2	9	.	324	1	16	1	1	.
Shipwright, Ship Carpenter (ashore)	848		85	.	853	.	84	.	1	.
2. Masts, Rigging, &c.										
Mast, Yard, Oar, Block, Maker	44	.	1	.	3	.	2	.	.	.
Ship Rigger, Chandler, Fitter	323	1	3	.	68	.	1	.	.	.
Sail Maker	145	1	10	.	22	.	12	.	.	.

Table 10 *continued*.—OCCUPATIONS of MALES and FEMALES in the WELSH DIVISION and REGISTRATION COUNTIES, and in each URBAN SANITARY DISTRICT of which the POPULATI[ON] exceeds 50,000 PERSONS.

OCCUPATIONS.	REGISTRATION COUNTIES.									
	GLAMORGANSHIRE.		CARMARTHENSHIRE.		PEMBROKESHIRE.		CARDIGANSHIRE.		BRECKNOCKSHIRE.	
	Males.	Females.	Males.	Females.	Males.	Females.	Males.	Females.	Males.	Fema[les].
14. PERSONS WORKING AND DEALING IN CHEMICALS AND COMPOUNDS.										
1. *Colouring Matter.*										
Dye, Paint, Manufacture	10	2	18	8	.	.	.	.	.	
Ink, Blacking, Colouring Substance, Manufacture	2	.	.	.	.	.	.	.	.	
2. *Explosives.*										
Gunpowder, Guncotton, Explosive Substance, Manufacture	38	2	2	.	.	.	.	.	.	
Fusee, Fireworks, Explosive Article, Manufacture	7	12	1	.	.	.	.	.	.	
3. *Drugs and other Chemicals and Compounds.*										
Chemist, Druggist	277	11	77	1	63	1	66	1	27	
Manufacturing Chemist	149	6	57	6	7	3	7	.	6	
Alkali Manufacture	32	.	2	.	.	.	.	.	.	
Drysalter	.	.	.	.	.	.	.	.	.	
15. PERSONS WORKING AND DEALING IN TOBACCO AND PIPES.										
1. *Tobacco and Pipes.*										
Tobacco Manufacturer, Tobacconist	35	31	.	.	1	.	.	1	.	
Tobacco Pipe, Snuff Box, &c., Maker	13	9	.	.	.	.	.	.	.	
16. PERSONS WORKING AND DEALING IN FOOD AND LODGING.										
1. *Board and Lodging.*										
Innkeeper, Hotel Keeper, Publican	1313	410	263	193	170	138	174	175	180	
Lodging, Boarding House, Keeper	52	402	6	70	23	129	8	171	4	
Coffee, Eating House, Keeper	43	43	3	6	1	4	.	2	3	
2. *Spirituous Drinks.*										
Hop—Merchant, Dealer	.	.	.	.	.	1	.	.	.	
Maltster	79	.	23	1	21	1	29	1	17	
Brewer	210	9	56	2	8	3	5	1	11	
Beerseller, Ale, Porter, Cider, Dealer	64	28	3	5	.	1	1	1	6	
Cellarman	65	1	13	.	.	.	2	.	.	
Wine, Spirit—Merchant, Agent	39	2	7	7	16	8	4	.	9	
3. *Food.*										
Milkseller, Dairyman	171	161	10	30	21	28	7	14	6	
Cheesemonger, Butterman	24	9	19	10	3	5	7	1	.	
Butcher, Meat Salesman	1010	122	247	13	216	13	164	9	103	
Provision Curer, Dealer	80	6	3	6	9	2	20	28	4	
Poulterer, Game Dealer	6	14	10	16	14	9	4	14	2	
Fishmonger	98	35	8	12	14	17	8	9	4	
Corn, Flour, Seed—Merchant, Dealer	69	6	20	2	6	2	17	5	5	
Corn Miller	196	4	111	11	119	6	109	23	98	
Baker	516	129	21	39	91	71	24	124	31	
Confectioner, Pastrycook	158	113	11	48	7	29	9	31	10	
Greengrocer, Fruiterer	397	364	13	27	8	20	5	15	16	
Mustard, Vinegar, Spice, Pickle—Maker, Dealer	4	.	.	.	.	.	.	.	.	
Sugar Refiner	22	6	2	1	2	2	.	.	.	
Grocer, Tea, Coffee, Chocolate—Maker, Dealer	2409	625	346	216	262	239	249	294	222	1
Ginger Beer, Mineral Water—Manufacturer, Dealer	26	9	4	2	6	.	4	.	3	
Others dealing in Food	.	.	.	.	.	.	.	.	.	
17. PERSONS WORKING AND DEALING IN TEXTILE FABRICS.										
1. *Wool and Worsted.*										
Woolstapler	8	.	3	.	2	.	4	1	4	
Woollen Cloth Manufacture	817	67	420	41	164	8	561	126	72	
Wool, Woollen goods—Dyer, Printer	2	.	.	1	1	.	.	3	2	
Worsted, Stuff, Manufacture	3	.	.	.	1	.	.	.	.	
Flannel Manufacture	37	7	26	8	2	.	14	5	.	
Blanket Manufacture	.	.	.	.	.	.	.	.	.	
Fuller	.	1	2	.	.	.	6	3	.	
Cloth, Worsted, Stuff, Flannel, Blanket, Dealer	12	7	1	1	1	.	.	1	2	
Others	.	6	.	.	.	.	.	2	.	
2. *Silk.*										
Silk, Silk goods, Manufacture	6	4	.	.	.	.	.	.	.	
Silk Dyer, Printer	1	3	.	.	.	.	.	.	.	
Ribbon Manufacture	.	.	.	.	.	.	.	.	.	
Crape, Gauze, Manufacture	.	.	.	.	.	.	.	.	.	
Silk Merchant, Dealer	3	.	.	.	.	.	.	.	.	

Table 10 *continued.*—Occupations of Males and Females in the Welsh Division and its Registration Counties, and in each Urban Sanitary District of which the Population exceeds 50,000 Persons.

Occupations.	Registration Counties.									
	GLAMORGANSHIRE.		CARMARTHENSHIRE.		PEMBROKESHIRE.		CARDIGANSHIRE.		BRECKNOCKSHIRE.	
	Males.	Females.	Males.	Females.	Males.	Females.	Males.	Females.	Males.	Females.
3. Cotton and Flax										
Cotton, Cotton goods, Manufacture	.	5	3	11	1	1	1	16	1	1
Cotton, Calico—Printer, Dyer, Bleacher	1	.	.	.	.	.	.	.	.	.
Cotton, Calico—Warehouseman, Dealer	.	.	.	.	1	.	.	.	.	.
Flax, Linen—Manufacturer, Dealer	1	.	.	.	.	.	.	.	.	.
Lace Manufacturer, Dealer	.	13	.	.	.	.	.	4	.	.
Fustian Manufacturer, Dealer	.	1	.	.	.	.	.	.	.	.
Tape Manufacturer, Dealer	.	.	.	.	.	.	.	.	.	.
Thread Manufacturer, Dealer	.	.	.	.	.	.	.	.	.	.
4. Hemp and other Fibrous Materials.										
Hemp, Jute, Cocoa Fibre, Manufacture	.	.	.	.	.	.	.	.	.	.
Rope, Twine, Cord—Maker, Dealer	32	.	27	.	2	.	6	.	.	.
Mat Maker, Seller	6	5	1	1	.	1	.	1	.	.
Net Maker	.	1	.	.	.	3	.	2	.	.
Canvas, Sailcloth, Manufacture	1	.	.	.	.	.	.	.	.	.
Sacking, Sack, Bag—Maker, Dealer	4	3	.	1	.	.	.	.	.	.
Others working and dealing in Hemp	3	.	.	.	.	.	.	.	.	.
5. Mixed or Unspecified Materials.										
Weaver (undefined)	69	8	25	3	11	1	19	2	4	.
Dyer, Printer, Scourer, Bleacher, Calenderer (undefined)	27	18	1	1	1	.	1	2	.	.
Factory hand (Textile, undefined)	4	5	8	.	.	.	1	1	.	5
Felt Manufacture	4	1	.	.	.	.	.	.	.	.
Carpet, Rug, Manufacture	2	1	.	.	.	.	.	.	.	.
Manchester Warehouseman	.	1	.	.	.	.	.	.	.	.
Draper, Linen Draper, Mercer	1150	473	314	70	262	75	255	47	114	61
Fancy Goods (Textile), Manufacturer, Worker, Dealer	11	40	.	4	.	14	2	8	.	.
Trimming Maker, Dealer	.	2	.	.	.	.	.	.	.	.
Embroiderer	.	.	.	.	.	1	.	.	.	.
Others	1	.	.	.	.	.	.	.	.	.
18. Persons working and dealing in Dress.										
1. Dress.										
Hatter, Hat Manufacture (not straw)	25	3	9	1	4	1	2	7	.	.
Straw—Hat, Bonnet, Plait, Manufacture	.	10	1	2	1	18	.	1	.	1
Tailor	1798	275	562	10	479	10	574	9	267	11
Milliner, Dressmaker, Staymaker	9	7825	.	1860	.	1506	2	1712	.	677
Shawl Manufacture	1	.	.	.	.	.	.	.	.	.
Shirt Maker, Seamstress	1	462	.	101	.	117	.	124	.	48
Hosiery Manufacture	.	30	1	42	.	51	3	796	.	.
Hosier, Haberdasher	31	4	2	26	.	.	8	4	2	.
Glover, Glove Maker	.	9	1	6	3	2	2	1	.	.
Button Maker, Dealer	.	.	.	.	.	.	.	.	.	.
Shoe, Boot—Maker, Dealer	2251	118	554	12	393	18	528	4	390	23
Patten, Clog, Maker	30	1	47	.	68	.	90	1	12	.
Wig Maker, Hairdresser	232	2	14	.	14	1	11	1	16	.
Umbrella, Parasol, Stick—Maker, Dealer	17	8	2	1	.	.	2	.	3	.
Accoutrement Maker	.	.	.	.	.	.	.	.	.	.
Old Clothes Dealer, and others	3	3	1	.	.	.	.	.	.	.
19. Persons working and dealing in various Animal Substances.										
1. In Grease, Gut, Bone, Horn, Ivory, and Whalebone.										
Tallow Chandler, Candle, Grease, Manufacture	36	5	7	1	4	.	3	.	7	.
Soap Boiler, Maker	.	.	.	.	.	.	.	.	.	.
Glue, Size, Gelatine, Isinglass—Maker, Dealer	.	.	.	.	.	.	.	.	.	.
Manure Manufacture	5	4	2	.	.	.	1	.	2	.
Bone, Horn, Ivory, Tortoise-shell—Worker, Dealer	1	.	.	.	.	.	.	.	.	.
Comb Maker	.	.	.	.	.	.	.	.	.	.
Others	1	.	.	.	.	.	.	.	.	.
2. In Skins.										
Furrier, Skinner	27	.	4	.	5	.	4	1	7	.
Tanner, Fellmonger	62	.	31	.	28	.	49	.	24	.
Currier	57	2	37	3	26	.	29	1	12	.
Leather Goods, Portmanteau, Bag, Strap, &c.—Maker, Dealer	11	.	1	.	.	.	.	.	1	.
Parchment, Vellum—Maker, Dealer	.	.	.	.	.	.	.	.	.	.
3. In Hair and Feathers.										
Hair, Bristle—Worker, Dealer	.	.	.	.	.	.	.	.	.	.
Brush, Broom, Maker	16	3	1	6	1	1	3	4	.	.
Quill, Feather—Dresser, Dealer	.	6	.	.	.	.	.	2	.	.

Table 10 *continued*.—OCCUPATIONS of MALES and FEMALES in the WELSH DIVISION and its REGISTRATION COUNTIES, and in each URBAN SANITARY DISTRICT of which the POPULATION exceeds 50,000 PERSONS.

OCCUPATIONS	REGISTRATION COUNTIES.									
	GLAMORGANSHIRE.		CARMARTHENSHIRE.		PEMBROKESHIRE.		CARDIGANSHIRE.		BRECKNOCKSHIRE.	
	Males.	Females.	Males.	Females.	Males.	Females.	Males.	Females.	Males.	Females.
20. PERSONS WORKING AND DEALING IN VARIOUS VEGETABLE SUBSTANCES.										
1. *In Oils, Gums, and Resins.*										
Oil Miller, Oil Cake—Maker, Dealer	17	1	8	.	2	.	.	.	.	.
Oil and Colourman	1	.	1	.	.	1	.	.	.	.
Floor Cloth, Oil Cloth, Manufacture	2	.	.	.	.	.	.	.	.	.
Japanner	.	24	.	.	.	.	.	.	.	.
India Rubber, Gutta Percha—Worker, Dealer	8	.	.	.	2	.	.	.	.	.
Waterproof Goods—Maker, Dealer	9	2	.	.	.	.	.	.	.	.
Others	.	.	.	.	.	.	.	.	.	.
2. *In Cane, Rush, and Straw.*										
Willow, Cane, Rush—Worker, Dealer, Basketmaker	114	17	15	4	8	2	5	3	13	2
Hay, Straw (not plait), Chaff—Cutter, Dealer	86	1	7	.	1	.	.	.	3	.
Thatcher	33	.	3	.	10	.	3	.	.	.
3. *In Wood and Bark.*										
Timber, Wood—Merchant, Dealer	185	3	30	.	17	.	24	.	52	.
Sawyer	641	.	103	.	82	.	45	.	98	.
Lath, Wooden Fence, Hurdle, Maker	86	.	3	.	5	.	3	.	7	.
Wood Turner, Box Maker	41	.	8	.	6	1	14	.	2	.
Cooper, Hoop Maker, Bender	111	1	56	.	64	1	49	.	20	.
Cork, Bark—Cutter, Worker, Dealer	7	.	.	.	2	.	.	.	.	.
Others	2	1	.	1	.	.	.	.	.	.
4. *In Paper.*										
Paper Manufacture	82	38	.	.	6	6	.	.	17	8
Envelope Maker	.	.	.	.	.	.	.	.	.	.
Stationer, Law Stationer	50	30	16	11	3	.	5	3	2	19
Card, Pattern Card, Maker	.	.	.	.	.	3	.	.	.	.
Paper Stainer	.	.	.	.	.	.	.	.	.	.
Paper Box, Paper Bag, Maker	1	9	1	.	.	.	.	.	.	.
Ticket, Label, Writer	1	.	.	.	.	.	.	.	.	.
Others	24	.	3	.	2	.	1	1	4	.
21. PERSONS WORKING AND DEALING IN VARIOUS MINERAL SUBSTANCES.										
1. *Miners.*										
Coal Miner	44435	429	2036	.	477	31	32	.	2002	47
Ironstone Miner	464	18	12	.	2	.	1	.	37	5
Copper Miner	29	.	2	.	2	.	14	.	.	.
Tin Miner	86	.	6	.	4	.	.	.	.	.
Lead Miner	10	.	115	19	3	.	1678	151	1	.
Miner in other, or undefined, Minerals	39	.	2	.	3	.	.	.	1	.
Mine Service	393	1	58	1	8	.	36	.	4	1
2. *Coal, Coal Gas, &c.*										
Coal Merchant, Dealer	531	49	49	8	21	3	45	4	45	2
Coalheaver	1101	.	73	.	6	.	3	.	23	.
Coke, Charcoal, Peat—Cutter, Burner, Dealer	274	23	15	1	.	1	1	1	1	.
Gas Works Service	210	.	23	.	15	.	4	.	12	.
3. *Stone, Clay, and Road Making.*										
Stone Quarrier	765	.	73	.	76	.	31	.	180	.
Stone Cutter, Dresser, Dealer	111	.	39	.	20	.	46	.	13	.
Slate Quarrier	41	.	4	.	22	.	67	.	1	.
Slate Worker, Dealer	25	.	5	.	11	.	16	.	1	.
Limeburner	74	7	43	.	10	.	2	.	12	1
Clay, Sand, Gravel, Chalk—Labourer, Dealer	47	25	6	.	1	.	.	.	1	.
Fossil, Coprolite—Digger, Dealer	.	.	.	.	.	.	.	.	.	.
Well Sinker, Borer	152	.	4	.	.	.	.	.	1	.
Plaster, Cement, Manufacture	7	5	.	.	.	.	.	.	.	.
Brick, Tile—Maker, Burner, Dealer	443	297	105	27	7	.	16	.	31	39
Paviour	6	.	.	.	.	.	.	.	1	.
Road Contractor, Surveyor, Inspector	31	.	12	.	9	.	10	.	9	.
Road Labourer	229	.	91	.	63	.	69	.	72	.
Railway Contractor	35	.	1	.	1	.	1	.	2	.
Platelayer	1108	.	161	.	38	.	34	.	146	.
Railway Labourer, Navvy	827	.	301	.	88	.	28	.	101	.
Others	3	6	1	.	.	.	.	.	.	.
4. *Earthenware and Glass.*										
Earthenware, China, Porcelain, Manufacture	107	5	52	39	.	.	3	.	.	.
Glass Manufacture	12	2	1	.	1	.	.	.	1	.
Earthenware, China, Glass, Dealer	58	36	8	13	8	3	10	6	4	5
5. *Salt.*										
Salt Maker, Dealer	1	.	.	.	.	.	.	.	.	.

Table 10 *continued.*—Occupations of Males and Females in the Welsh Division and its Registration Counties, and in each Urban Sanitary District of which the Population exceeds 50,000 Persons.

Occupations.	Registration Counties.									
	GLAMORGANSHIRE.		CARMARTHENSHIRE.		PEMBROKESHIRE.		CARDIGANSHIRE.		BRECKNOCKSHIRE.	
	Males.*	Females.	Males.	Females.	Males.	Females.	Males.	Females.	Males.	Females.
6. *Water.*										
Waterworks Service	8	.	2	.	1	.	1	.	6	.
Others	3	.	.	.	.	.	.	.	.	.
7. *Precious Metals and Jewellery.*										
Goldsmith, Silversmith, Jeweller	61	7	10	.	6	1	15	3	4	.
Gold, Silver, Beater	.	.	.	.	.	.	.	.	.	.
Lapidary	.	.	.	.	.	.	.	.	.	.
Others	88	2	8	.	.	.	6	1	.	.
8. *Iron and Steel.*										
Blacksmith	3325	4	663	3	640	.	488	1	308	.
Whitesmith	5	.	.	.	3	.	2	.	1	.
Nail Manufacture	60	5	6	.	.	.	.	.	.	.
Anchor, Chain, Manufacture	86	1	.	.	.	.	.	.	21	.
Other Iron and Steel Manufactures	7700	210	540	5	31	4	51	.	244	7
Ironmonger. Hardware Dealer, Merchant	315	5	73	2	65	2	27	4	36	4
9. *Copper.*										
Copper, Copper goods—Manufacturer, Worker, Dealer	1891	17	446	5	9	.	.	.	1	.
10. *Tin and Zinc.*										
Tin, Tin Plate, Tin goods—Manufacturer, Worker, Dealer	7354	1839	3119	751	32	.	23	.	78	1
Zinc, Zinc Goods—Manufacturer, Worker, Dealer	805	1	1	.	.	.	.	.	.	.
11. *Lead.*										
Lead, Leaden goods—Manufacturer, Worker, Dealer	75	.	203	2	1	.	1	.	.	.
12. *In Other, Mixed, or Unspecified, Metals.*										
Metal Refiner, Worker, Turner, Dealer	177	.	.	.	.	.	.	.	.	.
Brass, Bronze, Manufacture. Brazier	60	.	12	.	2	.	.	.	.	.
Metal Burnisher, Lacquerer	1	.	.	.	.	.	.	.	.	.
White Metal, Plated Ware, Manufacture. Pewterer	2	.	4	.	1	.	.	.	.	.
Wire Maker, Worker, Weaver, Drawer	30	1	1	.	1	.	.	.	2	.
Bolt, Nut, Rivet, Screw, Staple, Maker	27	1	.	.	.	.	2	.	1	.
Lamp, Lantern, Candlestick, Maker	12	.	.	.	.	.	.	.	.	.
Clasp, Buckle, Hinge, Maker	.	.	.	.	.	.	.	.	.	.
Fancy Chain, Gilt Toy, Maker	.	.	.	.	.	.	.	.	.	.
Others	6	.	.	.	.	.	.	.	.	.
22. Persons working and dealing in General or Unspecified Commodities.										
1. *Makers and Dealers (General or Undefined).*										
General Shopkeeper, Dealer	293	256	56	80	45	53	88	91	36	18
Pawnbroker	127	24	3	.	1	.	.	.	3	.
Costermonger, Huckster, Street Seller	335	373	55	47	49	20	45	21	64	55
Manufacturer, Manager, Superintendent (undefined)	164	4	5	.	7	1	8	.	6	1
Contractor (undefined)	190	.	5	.	3	.	1	.	11	.
2. *Mechanics and Labourers (General or Undefined).*										
General Labourer	14870	111	2009	23	2307	17	1343	100	1247	14
Engine Driver, Stoker, Fireman (not railway, marine, nor agricultural)	3878	.	432	.	90	.	28	.	77	.
Artisan, Mechanic (undefined)	746	3	31	1	31	.	31	.	7	.
Apprentice (undefined)	35	12	9	1	8	2	.	1	.	4
Factory Labourer (undefined)	438	48	42	6	28	.	23	2	14	1
Machinist, Machine Worker (undefined)	52	34	3	.	4	4	3	1	7	.
23. Persons working and dealing in Refuse Matters.										
1. *Refuse Matters.*										
Town Drainage Service	22	.	.	.	3	.	1	.	.	.
Chimney Sweep, Soot Merchant	40	.	8	.	5	.	2	.	.	1
Scavenger, Crossing Sweeper	19	.	5	1	2	.	3	.	7	.
Rag Gatherer, Dealer	28	10	8	18	3	.	1	.	2	.
VI. UNOCCUPIED CLASS.										
24. Persons without Specified Occupations										
Persons returned by Property, Rank, &c., and not by special occupation	61361	171393	14725	37704	10600	28017	12221	33085	6687	18139
Children under 5 years of age	37379	37317	7580	7454	5357	5325	5878	5679	3457	3408

Table 10 *continued*.—OCCUPATIONS of MALES and FEMALES in the WELSH DIVISION and its REGISTRATION COUNTIES, and in each URBAN SANITARY DISTRICT of which the POPULATION exceeds 50,000 PERSONS.

OCCUPATIONS.	REGISTRATION COUNTIES.									
	RADNORSHIRE.		MONTGOMERYSHIRE.		FLINTSHIRE.		DENBIGHSHIRE.		MERIONETHSHIRE.	
	Males.	Females.	Males.	Females.	Males.	Females.	Males.	Females.	Males.	Females.
TOTAL	9404	9119	38296	37901	23217	23357	56591	56439	34350	33023
I. PROFESSIONAL CLASS.										
1. PERSONS ENGAGED IN THE GENERAL OR LOCAL GOVERNMENT OF THE COUNTRY.										
1. *National Government.*										
Peer, M.P., Privy Councillor (not otherwise described)	1	.	.	.	1	.	1	.	.	.
Civil Service (officers and clerks)	5	1	54	13	17	11	38	21	26	7
Civil Service (messengers, &c.)	9	.	51	5	25	1	66	6	38	6
Prison Officer, &c.	.	.	.	.	.	1	5	1	.	.
2. *Local Government.*										
Police	13	.	42	.	27	.	84	.	39	.
Municipal, Parish, Union, District, Officer	16	3	30	6	20	3	68	11	38	7
Other Local or County Official	13	.	27	.	14	.	42	.	27	.
3. *East Indian and Colonial Service.*										
East Indian and Colonial Service	.	.	.	.	.	.	.	.	.	.
2. PERSONS ENGAGED IN THE DEFENCE OF THE COUNTRY.										
1. *Army (at Home).*										
Army Officer (effective or retired)	2	.	12	.	3	.	33	.	6	.
Soldier and Non-Commissioned Officer	1	.	7	.	5	.	171	.	2	.
Militia, Yeomanry, Volunteers	1	.	106	.	32	.	187	.	3	.
Army Pensioner	.	.	13	.	7	.	13	.	5	.
2. *Navy (ashore or in port).*										
Navy Officer (effective or retired)	.	.	.	.	.	.	3	.	.	.
Seaman, R.N.	.	.	.	.	.	.	2	.	1	.
Royal Marines (officers and men)	.	.	.	.	.	.	1	.	.	.
Navy Pensioner	.	.	1	.	.	.	2	.	.	.
3. PERSONS ENGAGED IN PROFESSIONAL OCCUPATIONS (WITH THEIR IMMEDIATE SUBORDINATES).										
1. *Clerical Profession.*										
Clergyman (Established Church)	33	.	98	.	38	.	130	.	64	.
Roman Catholic Priest	.	.	10	.	9	.	6	.	.	.
Minister, Priest, of other religious bodies	22	.	100	.	30	.	120	.	104	.
Missionary, Scripture Reader, Itinerant Preacher	1	.	.	.	1	.	13	1	11	.
Nun, Sister of Charity	.	.	.	.	.	25	.	.	.	.
Theological Student	.	.	85	.	4	.	59	.	72	.
Church, Chapel, Cemetery—Officer, Servant	.	.	7	1	4	2	18	10	4	
2. *Legal Profession.*										
Barrister, Solicitor	8		30	.	13	.	58	.	27	.
Law Student	.	.	1		2	.	5	.	3	.
Law Clerk, and others connected with Law	13	.	50	.	29	.	104	.	34	.
3. *Medical Profession.*										
Physician, Surgeon, General Practitioner	15	.	40	.	15	.	58	.	41	.
Dentist	.	.	.	.	.	.	14	.	7	.
Medical Student, Assistant	.	.	21	.	8	.	25	1	21	.
Midwife	.	2	.	15	.	11	.	38	.	8
Subordinate Medical Service	.	7	5	33	.	9	4	32	3	25
4. *Teachers.*										
Schoolmaster	37	55	142	162	101	118	321	329	164	120
Teacher, Professor, Lecturer	2	9	10	28	14	8	28	77	9	28
School Service, and others concerned in Teaching	1	.	2	2	5	.	5	3	3	1
5. *Literary and Scientific Persons.*										
Author, Editor, Journalist	.	.	3	2	.	.	7	1	1	.
Reporter, Short-hand Writer	.	.	3	.	1	.	11	.	2	.
Persons engaged in Scientific Pursuits	.	.	.	.	10	.	5	1	.	.
Literary, Scientific, Institution, Service, &c.	.	.	.	.	.	.	1	1	.	.
6. *Engineers and Surveyors.*										
Civil Engineer	1	.	9	.	10	.	30	.	21	.
Mining Engineer	2	.	11	.	14	.	28	.	4	.
Land, House, Ship, Surveyor	3	.	16	.	4	.	18	.	6	.
7. *Artists.*										
Painter (artist)	1	.	1	.	.	.	29	1	5	2
Engraver (artist)	.	.	.	.	.	.	.	.	1	.
Sculptor	.	.	1	.	1	.	.	.	1	.
Architect	1	.	4	.	2	.	21	.	8	.
Musician, Music Master	.	2	16	8	8	6	32	13	10	2
Art Student	.	.	1	.	1	.	1	3	1	.
Photographer	1	.	4	1	3	.	14	3	10	.
Actor	.	.	.	.	.	.	1	.	.	.
Art, Music, Theatre, Service	.	.	.	.	1	.	.	.	.	.

Table 10 *continued.*—OCCUPATIONS of MALES and FEMALES in the WELSH DIVISION and its REGISTRATION COUNTIES, and in each URBAN SANITARY DISTRICT of which the POPULATION exceeds 50,000 PERSONS.

OCCUPATIONS.	REGISTRATION COUNTIES.									
	RADNORSHIRE.		MONTGOMERYSHIRE.		FLINTSHIRE.		DENBIGHSHIRE.		MERIONETHSHIRE.	
	Males.	Females.	Males.	Females.	Males.	Females.	Males.	Females.	Males.	Females.
8. *Persons engaged in Exhibitions, Shows, Games, &c.*										
Performer, Showman, Exhibition, Service	.	.	8	9	13	4	2	.	1	.
Billiard, Cricket, & other Games, Service	.	.	4	.	3	.	20	.	3	.
II. DOMESTIC CLASS.										
4. PERSONS ENGAGED IN DOMESTIC OFFICES OR SERVICES.										
1. *Domestic Service.*										
Domestic Coachman, Groom	48	.	182	.	82	.	368	.	95	.
Domestic Gardener	76	.	264	.	161	1	452	1	216	.
Domestic Indoor Servant	61	1125	135	4329	68	1841	232	6164	94	3856
Lodge, Gate, Park, Keeper (not Government)	1	1	1	7	1	8	5	13	.	7
Inn, Hotel, Servant	16	23	53	68	14	39	86	130	32	78
College, Club, Service	.	.	.	.	1	.	1	.	.	.
2. *Other Service.*										
Office Keeper (not Government)	.	.	2	1	.	2	1	3	2	.
Cook (not domestic)	.	.	2	2	.	.	.	4	.	2
Charwoman	.	121	.	267	.	157	.	294	.	182
Washing and Bathing Service	.	83	2	279	1	96	6	420	.	186
Hospital and Institution Service	.	1	1	7	.	3	11	40	.	4
Others engaged in Service	.	.	.	.	.	1	1	.	3	.
III. COMMERCIAL CLASS.										
5. PERSONS ENGAGED IN COMMERCIAL OCCUPATIONS.										
1. *Merchants and Agents.*										
Merchant	1	.	5	.	2	.	10	.	22	.
Broker, Agent, Factor	2	.	38	1	45	.	47	.	51	.
Auctioneer, Appraiser, Valuer, House Agent	5	.	86	.	9	.	55	.	16	.
Accountant	2	.	23	.	12	.	43	.	19	.
Salesman, Buyer (not otherwise described)	.	.	.	.	.	.	.	.	.	.
Commercial Traveller	3	.	14	.	18	.	70	.	23	2
Commercial Clerk	12	2	113	2	127	1	322	10	120	4
Officer of Commercial Company, Guild, Society, &c.	.	.	.	.	.	.	.	.	.	.
2. *Dealers in Money.*										
Banker	.	.	4	.	1	.	.	.	1	.
Bank Service	7	.	30	.	20	.	53	.	46	.
Bill Discounter, Bill Broker, Finance Agent	.	.	.	.	2	.	3	.	.	.
3. *Persons occupied in Insurance.*										
Life, House, Ship, &c., Insurance Service	.	.	9	.	13	1	45	.	14	.
6. PERSONS ENGAGED IN CONVEYANCE OF MEN, GOODS, AND MESSAGES.										
1. *On Railways.*										
Railway Engine Driver, Stoker	1	.	36	.	6	.	61	.	46	.
Railway Guard	.	.	10	.	.	.	18	.	19	.
Pointsman, Level Crossing Man	8	.	10	.	4	.	88	3	11	.
Other Railway Officials and Servants	50	.	144	.	92	.	285	.	184	.
2. *On Roads.*										
Toll Collector, Turnpike Gate Keeper	.	4	3	16	3	15	2	6	4	4
Omnibus, Coach, Cab, Owner—Livery Stable Keeper	.	.	1	.	3	.	12	1	1	.
Cabman, Flyman, Coachman (not domestic)	3	.	13	.	7	.	59	.	18	.
Carman, Carrier, Carter, Haulier	13	2	133	4	162	6	294	6	165	1
Tramway Companies' Service	.	.	.	.	2	.	3	.	1	.
Wheel Chair Proprietor, Attendant, &c.	.	.	.	.	.	.	1	.	.	.
3. *On Canals, Rivers and Seas.*										
Inland Navigation Service	.	.	11	.	2	.	1	.	3	.
Bargeman, Lighterman, Waterman	.	.	28	.	4	.	1	.	42	6
Navigation Service (on shore)	.	.	1	.	3	.	6	.	6	.
Seaman (Merchant Service)	2	.	59	.	240	.	61	.	233	.
Pilot	.	.	3	.	21	.	1	.	6	.
Ship Steward, Cook	.	.	.	.	6	1	2	.	3	.
Boatman on Seas	.	.	.	.	.	.	3	.	.	.
Harbour, Dock, Wharf, Lighthouse, Service	.	.	2	.	46	.	.	.	34	.
4. *In Storage.*										
Warehouseman (not Manchester)	1	.	24	3	3	.	6	.	5	2
Meter, Weigher	.	.	.	.	5	.	1	.	2	.
5. *In conveying Messages, Porterage, &c.*										
Messenger, Porter, Watchman (not Railway nor Government)	14	.	67	1	41	.	130	4	30	.
Telegraph, Telephone, Service	3	1	8	.	3	1	14	6	5	2

Table 10 *continued.*—OCCUPATIONS of MALES and FEMALES in the WELSH DIVISION and its REGISTRATION COUNTIES, and in each URBAN SANITARY DISTRICT of which the POPULATION exceeds 50,000 PERSONS.

OCCUPATIONS.	REGISTRATION COUNTIES.									
	RADNOR-SHIRE.		MONT-GOMERY-SHIRE.		FLINT-SHIRE.		DENBIGH-SHIRE.		ME-RIONETH-SHIRE.	
	Males.	Females.	Males.	Females.	Males.	Females.	Males.	Females.	Males.	Females.
IV. AGRICULTURAL CLASS.										
7. PERSONS ENGAGED IN AGRICULTURE.										
1. *In Fields and Pastures.*										
Farmer, Grazier	998	101	3357	467	609	117	2698	435	2474	414
Farmer's, Grazier's—Son, Grandson, Brother, Nephew*	556	.	1770	.	250	.	1139	.	1176	.
Farm Bailiff	44	.	133	.	53	.	137	.	52	.
Agricultural Labourer, Farm Servant, Cottager	1611	41	5073	209	1196	71	4867	239	2343	318
Shepherd	76	.	105	.	10		80	.	84	.
Land Drainage Service (not in towns)	9	.	41	.	10		5	.	7	.
Agricultural Machine—Proprietor, Attendant	3	.	19	.	1	.	16	.	6	.
Agricultural Student, Pupil	2	.	3	.	.	.	4	.	3	.
Others engaged in, or connected with, Agriculture	.	.	.	.	.	.	1	.	1	.
2. *In Woods.*										
Woodman	5	.	40	.	21	.	43	.	34	.
3. *In Gardens.*										
Nurseryman, Seedsman, Florist	1	.	5	1	3	.	13	5	5	.
Gardener (not domestic)	8	.	34	2	2	.	244	3	1	.
8. PERSONS ENGAGED ABOUT ANIMALS.										
1. *About Animals.*										
Horse Proprietor, Breeder, Dealer	.	.	21	.	5	.	6	.	3	.
Groom, Horse-keeper, Horse-breaker	18	.	94	.	44	.	130	.	48	.
Veterinary Surgeon, Farrier	7	.	18	.	3	.	19	.	14	.
Cattle, Sheep, Pig—Dealer, Salesman	1	.	37	.	15	1	41	.	15	.
Drover	4	.	8	.	.	.	2	.	4	.
Gamekeeper	33	.	110	.	48	.	176	.	113	.
Dog, Bird, Animal—Keeper, Dealer	.	.	.	.	.	2	2	2	.	.
Vermin destroyer	3	.	11	.	1	.	17	.	6	.
Fisherman	1	.	8	.	30	3	22	.	8	.
Knacker, Catsmeat Dealer, &c., &c.	.	.	.	.	.	.	.	.	.	.
V. INDUSTRIAL CLASS.										
9. PERSONS WORKING AND DEALING IN BOOKS, PRINTS, AND MAPS.										
1. *Books.*										
Publisher, Bookseller, Librarian	2	.	12	2	3	.	32	7	25	2
Music—Publisher, Seller, Printer	.	.	.	.	.	.	2	2	.	.
Bookbinder	.	.	5	1	.	2	17	7	6	1
Printer	6	.	50	1	47	8	147	3	74	1
Newspaper Agent, News Room Keeper	3	1	2	1	2	2	9	3	1	.
Others	.	.	.	.	.	.	.	.	.	.
2. *Prints and Maps.*										
Lithographer, Lithographic Printer	.	.	.	.	.	.	2	.	.	.
Copper Plate and Steel Plate Printer	.	.	.	.	.	.	.	.	.	.
Map and Print—Colourer, Seller	.	.	.	.	.	1	.	.	.	.
10. PERSONS WORKING AND DEALING IN MACHINES AND IMPLEMENTS.										
1. *Machines.*										
Engine, Machine, Maker	1	.	14	.	8	2	25	.	5	.
Millwright	5	.	7	.	9	.	10	.	3	.
Fitter, Turner (Engine and Machine)	.	.	21	.	67	.	94	.	49	.
Boiler Maker	.	.	1	.	17	.	43	.	1	.
Spinning and Weaving Machine Maker	.	.	3	.	1	.	.	.	.	.
Agricultural Machine and Implement Maker	12	.	12	.	.	.	11	1	.	.
Domestic Machinery—Maker, Dealer	.	.	.	.	.	.	.	.	.	.
2. *Tools and Implements.*										
Tool Maker, Dealer	.	.	.	.	.	.	2	.	.	.
Cutler, Scissors Maker	1	.	3	.	1	.	2	.	1	.
File Maker	.	.	.	.	.	.	.	.	.	.
Saw Maker	.	.	.	.	.	.	1	.	5	.
Pin Maker	.	.	.	.	.	.	.	.	.	.
Needle Maker	.	.	.	.	.	.	.	.	.	.
Steel Pen Maker	.	.	.	.	.	.	.	.	.	.
Pencil Maker (Wood)	.	.	.	.	.	.	.	.	.	.
Domestic Implement Maker	.	.	.	.	.	.	.	.	.	.
3. *Watches and Philosophical Instruments.*										
Watch Maker, Clock Maker	12	1	30	1	14	.	56	2	43	.
Philosophical Instrument Maker, Optician	.	.	1	.	1	.	1	.	.	.
Electrical Apparatus Maker	.	.	1	.	.	.	.	.	.	.
Weighing and Measuring Apparatus Maker	.	.	.	.	.	.	.	.	.	.

* [illegible]ith the farmer or grazier, and therefore presumably engaged in agriculture, are included above.

Table 10 *continued.*—Occupations of Males and Females in the Welsh Division and its Registration Counties, and in each Urban Sanitary District of which the Population exceeds 50,000 Persons.

Occupations.	Registration Counties.									
	Radnorshire.		Montgomeryshire.		Flintshire.		Denbighshire.		Merionethshire.	
	Males.	Females.	Males.	Females.	Males.	Females.	Males.	Females.	Males.	Females.
4. Surgical Instruments.										
Surgical Instrument Maker	.		.		.	.	.	.	.	.
5. Arms and Ordnance.										
Gunsmith, Gun Manufacturer	.		8	.	.	.	4	.	.	.
Ordnance Manufacturer	.		.		.	.	.	.	.	.
Sword, Bayonet—Maker, Cutler	.	.	.	.	.	.	.	.	.	.
Others	.	.	.	.	.	.	.	.	.	.
6. Musical Instruments.										
Musical Instrument Maker, Dealer	.	.	.		1	.	2	.	.	.
7. Type, Dies, Medals, Coins.										
Type Cutter, Founder	.	.	.	.	.	.	.	.	.	.
Die, Seal, Coin, Medal, Maker	.	.	.	.	.	.	.	.	.	.
8. Tackle for Sports and Games.										
Toy Maker, Dealer	.	.	1	4	.	2	4	5	1	6
Fishing Rod, Tackle, Maker, Dealer	.	.	.	.	.	.	2	.	.	1
Apparatus for other Games, Maker, Dealer	.	.	.	.	.	.	.	.	.	.
11. Persons working and dealing in Houses, Furniture, and Decorations.										
1. Houses.										
Builder	18	.	81	1	25	.	71	1	48	.
Carpenter, Joiner	198	.	606	.	230	.	938	.	650	.
Bricklayer	15	.	248	.	156	3	339	.	42	.
Mason	175	.	366	2	165	2	535	.	552	.
Slater, Tiler	.	.	16	.	56	1	100	.	49	.
Plasterer, Whitewasher	5	.	31	.	83	.	166	.	91	.
Paperhanger	.	.	1	.	8	.	11	.	.	.
Plumber	11	.	33	1	34	.	108	.	33	.
Painter, Glazier	23	.	148	.	63	.	216	.	104	.
2. Furniture and Fittings.										
Cabinet Maker, Upholsterer	10	.	43	2	12	2	49	7	28	3
French Polisher	.	.	1	.	8	.	4	.	1	.
Furniture Broker, Dealer	1	.	.	.	1	.	5	2	.	.
Locksmith, Bellhanger	.	.	.	.	1	.	2	.	.	.
Gas Fitter	2	.	6	.	3	2	23	.	1	.
House and Shop Fittings—Maker, Dealer	.	.	.	.	3	.	.	.	.	.
Funeral Furniture Maker, Undertaker	.	.	.	.	.	.	.	.	.	.
Others	.	.	.	.	.	.	.	.	.	.
3. House Decorations.										
Wood Carver	.	.	1	.	.	.	3	.	2	.
Carver, Gilder	.	.	.	.	1	.	11	.	3	.
Dealer in Works of Art	.	.	.	.	.	.	3	1	.	.
Figure, Image—Maker, Dealer	.	.	.	.	.	.	.	.	.	.
Animal, Bird, &c., Preserver, Naturalist	.	.	.	.	.	.	1	.	1	.
Artificial Flower Maker	.	.	.	.	.	.	1	.	.	.
12. Persons working and dealing in Carriages and Harness.										
1. Carriages.										
Coachmaker	.	.	16	.	.	.	54	1	15	.
Railway Carriage, Railway Wagon, Maker	1	.	2	.	7	.	10	.	2	.
Wheelwright	37	.	191	.	48	.	180	1	40	.
Bicycle, Tricycle—Maker, Dealer	.	.	.	.	.	.	.	.	.	.
Others	.	.	.	.	1	.	1	.	.	.
2. Harness.										
Saddler, Harness, Whip, Maker	14	.	69	1	31	.	94	1	37	.
13. Persons working and dealing in Ships and Boats.										
1. Hull.										
Ship, Boat, Barge, Builder	.	.	2	.	4	.	3	.	11	.
Shipwright, Ship Carpenter (ashore)	.	.	13	.	48	.	20	.	50	.
2. Masts, Rigging, &c.										
Mast, Yard, Oar, Block, Maker	1	.	.	.	.	.	.	.	.	.
Ship Rigger, Chandler, Fitter	.	.	.	.	4	.	.	.	5	.
Sail Maker	.	.	3	.	9	.	1	.	7	.
									20	.

Table 10 *continued*.—OCCUPATIONS of MALES and FEMALES in the WELSH DIVISION and its REGISTRATION COUNTIES, and in each URBAN SANITARY DISTRICT of which the POPULATION exceeds 50,000 PERSONS.

OCCUPATIONS.	REGISTRATION COUNTIES.									
	RADNORSHIRE.		MONTGOMERYSHIRE.		FLINTSHIRE.		DENBIGHSHIRE.		MERIONETHSHIRE.	
	Males.	Females.	Males.	Females.	Males.	Females.	Males.	Females.	Males.	Females.
14. PERSONS WORKING AND DEALING IN CHEMICALS AND COMPOUNDS.										
1. *Colouring Matter.*										
Dye, Paint, Manufacture	.	.	.	.	1	.	.	.	.	.
Ink, Blacking, Colouring Substance, Manufacture	.	.	.	.	.	.	.	.	.	.
2. *Explosives.*										
Gunpowder, Guncotton, Explosive Substance, Manufacture	.	.	.	.	.	.	3	.	3	.
Fusee, Fireworks, Explosive Article, Manufacture	.	.	1	.	.	.	2	9	.	.
3. *Drugs and other Chemicals and Compounds.*										
Chemist, Druggist	9	.	46	1	21	.	70	1	29	.
Manufacturing Chemist	.	.	.	.	617	.	20	.	3	.
Alkali Manufacture	.	.	.	.	16	.	.	.	.	.
Drysalter	.	.	.	.	.	.	.	.	.	.
15. PERSONS WORKING AND DEALING IN TOBACCO AND PIPES.										
1. *Tobacco and Pipes.*										
Tobacco Manufacturer, Tobacconist	1	.	1	1	.	.	6	7	3	2
Tobacco Pipe, Snuff Box, &c., Maker	.	.	.	.	.	.	9	1	.	.
16. PERSONS WORKING AND DEALING IN FOOD AND LODGING.										
1. *Board and Lodging.*										
Innkeeper, Hotel Keeper, Publican	42	22	167	84	123	64	284	109	132	50
Lodging, Boarding House, Keeper	9	18	8	60	3	48	28	271	7	166
Coffee, Eating House, Keeper	.	.	1	4	3	4	3	14	1	5
2. *Spirituous Drinks.*										
Hop—Merchant, Dealer	.	.	1	.	.	.	.	.	.	.
Maltster	9	1	43	3	11	.	33	1	10	.
Brewer	1	.	89	.	27	.	115	4	19	3
Beerseller, Ale, Porter, Cider, Dealer	4	1	.	1	3	2	3	6	1	.
Cellarman	1	.	1	.	.	1	11	.	.	.
Wine, Spirit—Merchant, Agent	.	1	16	1	1	.	31	2	3	.
3. *Food.*										
Milkseller, Dairyman	4	1	4	1	5	9	21	14	2	5
Cheesemonger, Butterman	1	.	2	1	3	.	6	5	15	1
Butcher, Meat Salesman	34	3	172	8	96	4	344	15	129	3
Provision Curer, Dealer	.	.	8	6	4	1	27	18	5	3
Poulterer, Game Dealer	2	.	8	5	4	4	10	8	3	2
Fishmonger	1	.	6	1	10	3	25	6	3	2
Corn, Flour, Seed—Merchant, Dealer	6	.	12	2	4	.	22	5	25	8
Corn Miller	35	3	192	7	60	1	178	1	106	3
Baker	29	4	31	36	30	20	107	44	43	84
Confectioner, Pastrycook	1	7	2	28	9	11	25	40	7	21
Greengrocer, Fruiterer	.	.	8	9	8	10	33	19	10	11
Mustard, Vinegar, Spice, Pickle—Maker, Dealer	.	.	.	.	.	1	.	.	.	.
Sugar Refiner	.	.	1	.	.	.	2	1	.	.
Grocer, Tea, Coffee, Chocolate—Maker, Dealer	68	26	396	177	251	97	540	163	214	93
Ginger Beer, Mineral Water—Manufacturer, Dealer	.	.	3	1	1	.	85	13	8	.
Others dealing in Food	.	.	.	.	.	.	.	.	.	.
17. PERSONS WORKING AND DEALING IN TEXTILE FABRICS.										
1. *Wool and Worsted.*										
Woolstapler	3	2	10	.	.	.	2	.	.	.
Woollen Cloth Manufacture	8	1	530	438	27	9	30	1	219	33
Wool, Woollen goods—Dyer, Printer	.	.	8	.	1	.	.	.	.	.
Worsted, Stuff, Manufacture	.	.	.	.	.	1	1	.	.	.
Flannel Manufacture	.	.	142	162	11	11	4	.	43	.
Blanket Manufacture	.	.	.	.	.	.	.	.	.	.
Fuller	.	.	42	1	.	.	4	.	24	.
Cloth, Worsted, Stuff, Flannel, Blanket, Dealer	.	.	7	2	.	2	.	.	.	.
Others	.	.	2	6	.	54	.	.	.	2
2. *Silk.*										
Silk, Silk goods, Manufacture	.	.	.	.	.	.	.	3	1	.
Silk Dyer, Printer	.	.	.	.	.	.	1	.	.	.
Ribbon Manufacture	.	.	.	.	.	.	.	.	.	.
Crape, Gauze, Manufacture	.	.	.	.	.	.	.	.	.	.
...erchant, Dealer	.	.	.	.	.	.	.	1	.	.

Table 10 *continued*.—OCCUPATIONS of MALES and FEMALES in the WELSH DIVISION and its REGISTRATION COUNTIES, and in each URBAN SANITARY DISTRICT of which the POPULATION exceeds 50,000 PERSONS.

OCCUPATIONS.	REGISTRATION COUNTIES.									
	RADNORSHIRE.		MONTGOMERYSHIRE.		FLINTSHIRE.		DENBIGHSHIRE.		MERIONETHSHIRE.	
	Males.	Females.	Males.	Females.	Males.	Females.	Males.	Females.	Males.	Females.
3. Cotton and Flax										
Cotton, Cotton goods, Manufacture	.	9	1	4	.	3	4	1	2	.
Cotton, Calico—Printer, Dyer, Bleacher	.	.	.	.	.	.	.	.	.	.
Cotton, Calico—Warehouseman, Dealer	.	.	.	.	.	.	.	.	.	.
Flax, Linen—Manufacturer, Dealer	1	.	.	.	.	1	1	.	.	.
Lace Manufacturer, Dealer	.	.	.	.	.	1	.	.	.	.
Fustian Manufacturer, Dealer	.	.	.	.	.	.	.	.	.	.
Tape Manufacturer, Dealer	.	.	.	.	.	.	.	.	.	.
Thread Manufacturer, Dealer	.	.	.	.	.	.	.	.	.	.
4. Hemp and other Fibrous Materials.										
Hemp, Jute, Cocoa Fibre, Manufacture	.	.	1	.	.	.	.	.	.	.
Rope, Twine, Cord—Maker, Dealer	.	.	14	1	3	1	3	.	.	.
Mat Maker, Seller	.	.	.	.	.	.	3	.	.	.
Net Maker	1	.	1	.	.	.	.	.	.	.
Canvas, Sailcloth, Manufacture	.	.	.	.	.	.	.	.	.	.
Sacking, Sack, Bag—Maker, Dealer	.	.	.	.	.	.	.	.	.	.
Others working and dealing in Hemp	.	.	.	.	.	.	.	.	.	.
5. Mixed or Unspecified Materials.										
Weaver (undefined)	1	1	12	43	1	5	2	.	20	2
Dyer, Printer, Scourer, Bleacher, Calenderer (undefined)	1	.	2	1	.	.	5	.	.	.
Factory hand (Textile, undefined)	.	.	8	14	.	18	.	.	53	.
Felt Manufacture	.	.	.	.	.	.	.	.	.	.
Carpet, Rug, Manufacture	.	.	.	1	.	.	.	.	.	.
Manchester Warehouseman	.	.	.	.	.	.	.	.	.	.
Draper, Linen Draper, Mercer	43	17	211	57	111	25	285	45	194	48
Fancy Goods (Textile), Manufacturer, Worker, Dealer	.	1	1	9	2	.	4	29	1	3
Trimming Maker, Dealer	.	.	.	.	.	.	.	.	.	.
Embroiderer	.	.	.	.	.	.	.	.	.	.
Others	.	.	1	.	.	.	.	.	.	.
18. PERSONS WORKING AND DEALING IN DRESS.										
1. Dress.										
Hatter, Hat Manufacture (not straw)	.	.	2	.	1	1	12	.	.	.
Straw—Hat, Bonnet, Plait, Manufacture	.	.	.	1	.	2	.	3	1	.
Tailor	100	4	400	5	143	2	560	7	331	1
Milliner, Dressmaker, Staymaker	.	214	.	903	.	548	2	1438	.	817
Shawl Manufacture	.	.	.	3	.	.	.	.	.	.
Shirt Maker, Seamstress	.	21	.	53	1	28	.	78	.	44
Hosiery Manufacture	.	11	1	27	.	2	.	8	.	37
Hosier, Haberdasher	.	.	1	2	4	1	4	6	1	.
Glover, Glove Maker	.	.	1	.	.	.	4	.	.	.
Button Maker, Dealer	.	.	.	.	.	.	.	.	.	.
Shoe, Boot—Maker, Dealer	155	4	500	15	186	5	632	26	353	7
Patten, Clog, Maker	8	.	23	1	11	1	34	1	14	.
Wig Maker, Hairdresser	5	.	16	.	11	.	88	.	11	2
Umbrella, Parasol, Stick—Maker, Dealer	.	.	2	.	1	.	8	.	.	.
Accoutrement Maker	.	.	.	.	.	.	.	.	.	.
Old Clothes Dealer, and others	.	.	.	.	.	.	.	.	.	.
19. PERSONS WORKING AND DEALING IN VARIOUS ANIMAL SUBSTANCES.										
1. In Grease, Gut, Bone, Horn, Ivory, and Whalebone.										
Tallow Chandler, Candle, Grease, Manufacture	.	.	.	.	7	.	7	1	5	.
Soap Boiler, Maker	.	.	.	.	2	.	.	.	.	.
Glue, Size, Gelatine, Isinglass—Maker, Dealer	.	.	.	.	.	.	.	.	.	.
Manure Manufacture	.	.	.	.	.	.	.	.	.	.
Bone, Horn, Ivory, Tortoise-shell—Worker, Dealer	.	.	.	.	.	.	.	.	.	.
Comb Maker	.	.	.	.	.	.	.	.	.	.
Others	.	.	.	.	.	.	.	.	.	.
2. In Skins.										
Furrier, Skinner	3	.	31	.	1	.	67	1	32	1
Tanner, Fellmonger	9	.	32	1	9	.	27	.	22	3
Currier	4	.	26	2	7	1	62	2	22	.
Leather Goods, Portmanteau, Bag, Strap, &c.—Maker, Dealer	.	.	.	.	.	.	2	.	1	.
Parchment, Vellum—Maker, Dealer	.	.	.	.	.	.	.	.	.	.
3. In Hair and Feathers.										
Hair, Bristle—Worker, Dealer	.	.	.	.	.	.	.	.	.	.
Brush, Broom, Maker	.	.	.	.	.	.	13	2	.	.
Quill, Feather—Dresser, Dealer	.	.	.	2	.	.	.	2	.	1

Table 10 *continued*.—OCCUPATIONS of MALES and FEMALES in the WELSH DIVISION and its REGISTRATION COUNTIES, and in each URBAN SANITARY DISTRICT of which the POPULATION exceeds 50,000 PERSONS.

OCCUPATIONS.	REGISTRATION COUNTIES.									
	RADNORSHIRE.		MONTGOMERYSHIRE.		FLINTSHIRE.		DENBIGHSHIRE.		MERIONETHSHIRE.	
	Males.	Females.	Males.	Females.	Males.	Females.	Males.	Females.	Males.	Females.
20. PERSONS WORKING AND DEALING IN VARIOUS VEGETABLE SUBSTANCES.										
1. *In Oils, Gums, and Resins.*										
Oil Miller, Oil Cake—Maker, Dealer	.	.	.	1	4	1	.	.	.	.
Oil and Colourman	.	.	.	.	1	.	1	1	.	.
Floor Cloth, Oil Cloth, Manufacture	.	.	.	.	.	.	1	.	.	.
Japanner	.	.	.	.	.	.	.	.	.	1
India Rubber, Gutta Percha—Worker, Dealer	.	.	.	.	1	.	1	.	.	.
Waterproof Goods—Maker, Dealer	.	.	.	.	1	.	.	.	.	.
Others	.	.	.	.	.	.	.	.	.	.
2. *In Cane, Rush, and Straw.*										
Willow, Cane, Rush—Worker, Dealer, Basketmaker	4	.	22	1	3	.	30	2	9	1
Hay, Straw (not plait), Chaff—Cutter, Dealer	.	.	1	.	1	1	2	.	.	.
Thatcher	3	.	.	.	2	.	3	.	.	.
3. *In Wood and Bark.*										
Timber, Wood—Merchant, Dealer	2	.	26	.	14	.	26	.	18	.
Sawyer	31	.	120	.	66	.	119	.	56	.
Lath, Wooden Fence, Hurdle, Maker	3	.	4	.	3	.	6	.	5	.
Wood Turner, Box Maker	.	.	8	5	.	.	9	.	7	.
Cooper, Hoop Maker, Bender	6	.	32	.	90	1	35	.	8	.
Cork, Bark—Cutter, Worker, Dealer	.	.	.	.	.	.	.	.	.	.
Others	.	.	.	.	.	.	2	.	.	.
4. *In Paper.*										
Paper Manufacture	.	.	.	.	108	78	22	32	.	1
Envelope Maker	.	.	.	.	.	.	.	.	.	.
Stationer, Law Stationer	1	2	1	3	7	1	15	9	4	4
Card, Pattern Card, Maker	.	.	.	.	.	.	.	.	.	.
Paper Stainer	.	.	.	.	.	.	.	.	.	.
Paper Box, Paper Bag, Maker	.	.	.	.	.	.	.	.	.	.
Ticket, Label Writer	.	.	.	4	.	.	.	.	.	.
Others	.	.	3	1	2	.	7	1	1	.
21. PERSONS WORKING AND DEALING IN VARIOUS MINERAL SUBSTANCES.										
1. *Miners.*										
Coal Miner	2	.	17	1	2268	8	5366	50	70	.
Ironstone Miner	.	.	.	.	3	.	38	.	2	.
Copper Miner	3	.	4	.	.	.	2	.	51	.
Tin Miner	.	.	.	.	.	.	.	.	1	.
Lead Miner	8	.	1212	10	1006	2	1072	.	53	.
Miner in other, or undefined, Minerals	.	.	32	.	4	.	15	.	20	.
Mine Service	1	.	18	.	34	.	43	.	6	.
2. *Coal, Coal Gas, &c.*										
Coal Merchant, Dealer	17	.	56	3	23	5	59	6	58	5
Coalheaver	2	.	5	.	16	.	37	.	3	.
Coke, Charcoal, Peat—Cutter, Burner, Dealer	.	.	.	.	9	.	12	.	.	.
Gas Works Service	4	.	17	.	18	.	34	.	10	.
3. *Stone, Clay, and Road Making.*										
Stone Quarrier	5	.	26	.	100	.	334	.	284	.
Stone Cutter, Dresser, Dealer	2	.	18	.	20	.	48	.	52	.
Slate Quarrier	5	.	265	.	.	.	621	.	4205	.
Slate Worker, Dealer	.	.	13	.	.	.	13	.	160	.
Limeburner	.	.	17	.	22	.	48	.	18	.
Clay, Sand, Gravel, Chalk—Labourer, Dealer	.	.	.	.	4	.	11	.	15	.
Fossil, Coprolite—Digger, Dealer	.	.	.	.	.	.	.	.	.	.
Well Sinker, Borer	.	.	4	.	2	.	10	.	.	.
Plaster, Cement, Manufacture	.	.	.	.	26	.	1	.	.	.
Brick, Tile—Maker, Burner, Dealer	1	.	53	.	173	.	425	2	69	.
Paviour	.	.	.	.	.	.	5	.	.	.
Road Contractor, Surveyor, Inspector	1	.	5	.	3	.	9	.	3	.
Road Labourer	31	.	89	.	25	.	63	.	35	.
Railway Contractor	.	.	4	.	.	.	2	.	5	.
Platelayer	32	.	79	.	89	.	178	.	135	.
Railway Labourer, Navvy	36	.	53	.	24	.	72	.	349	.
Others	.	.	.	.	.	1	.	1	.	4
4. *Earthenware and Glass.*										
Earthenware, China, Porcelain, Manufacture	1	.	1	.	19	.	72	7	21	1
Glass Manufacture	.	.	.	.	1	.	1	.	.	.
Earthenware, China, Glass, Dealer	2	3	11	6	1	5	13	6	15	5
5. *Salt.*										
Salt Maker, Dealer	.	.	.	.	.	.	1	2	.	.

Table 10 *continued*.—OCCUPATIONS of MALES and FEMALES in the WELSH DIVISION and its REGISTRATION COUNTIES, and in each URBAN SANITARY DISTRICT of which the POPULATION exceeds 50,000 PERSONS.

OCCUPATIONS.	REGISTRATION COUNTIES.									
	RADNORSHIRE.		MONTGOMERYSHIRE.		FLINTSHIRE.		DENBIGHSHIRE.		MERIONETHSHIRE.	
	Males.	Females.	Males.	Females.	Males.	Females.	Males.	Females.	Males.	Females.
6. *Water.*										
Waterworks Service	.	.	9	.	1	1	12	.	2	.
Others	.	.	.	.	1	.	.	.	.	.
7. *Precious Metals and Jewellery.*										
Goldsmith, Silversmith, Jeweller	.	.	2	3	1	.	12	.	2	
Gold, Silver, Beater	.	.	.	.	.	.	.	.		.
Lapidary	.	.	.	.	.	.	.	.		.
Others	.	.	.	.	2	.	.	.		.
8. *Iron and Steel.*										
Blacksmith	93	.	406	2	246	3	573	1	317	2
Whitesmith	.	.	4	.	2	.	28	.	1	.
Nail Manufacture	2	.	17	1	10	.	37	2	12	.
Anchor, Chain, Manufacture	.	.	.	.	.	.	.	.	.	.
Other Iron and Steel Manufactures	2	.	48	.	96	.	326	1	65	1
Ironmonger, Hardware Dealer, Merchant	16	.	61	4	26	.	59	1	20	1
9. *Copper.*										
Copper, Copper goods—Manufacturer, Worker, Dealer	.	.	.	.	98	1	1	.	.	.
10. *Tin and Zinc.*										
Tin, Tin Plate, Tin goods—Manufacturer, Worker, Dealer	4	.	31	1	113	39	59	1	26	1
Zinc, Zinc Goods—Manufacturer, Worker, Dealer	.	.	.	.	.	.	33	.	.	.
11. *Lead.*										
Lead, Leaden goods—Manufacturer, Worker, Dealer	.	.	.	.	276		4	.	.	.
12. *In Other, Mixed, or Unspecified, Metals.*										
Metal Refiner, Worker, Turner, Dealer	.	.	.	.	6	.	.	.	.	.
Brass, Bronze, Manufacture. Brazier	2	.	.	.	17	.	3	.	1	.
Metal Burnisher, Lacquerer	.	.	.	.	.	.	.	.	.	.
White Metal, Plated Ware, Manufacture, Pewterer	.	.	.	.	.	.	.	.	.	.
Wire Maker, Worker, Weaver, Drawer	.	.	3	.	21	.	3	.	.	.
Bolt, Nut, Rivet, Screw, Staple, Maker	.	.	.	.	1	.	.	.	2	.
Lamp, Lantern, Candlestick, Maker	.	.	.	.	.	.	.	.	.	.
Clasp, Buckle, Hinge, Maker	.	.	.	.	.	.	.	.	.	.
Fancy Chain, Gilt Toy, Maker	.	.	.	.	.	.	.	.	.	.
Others	.	.	.	.	.	.	.	.	.	.
22. PERSONS WORKING AND DEALING IN GENERAL OR UNSPECIFIED COMMODITIES.										
1. *Makers and Dealers (General or Undefined).*										
General Shopkeeper, Dealer	14	7	62	50	40	34	91	110	71	79
Pawnbroker	.	.	1	1	3	1	4	.	.	.
Costermonger, Huckster, Street Seller	13	4	77	31	41	47	122	86	46	21
Manufacturer, Manager, Superintendent (undefined)	2	.	12	1	10		12	.	19	.
Contractor (undefined)	1	.	4	.	10	.	19	.	11	.
2. *Mechanics and Labourers (General or Undefined).*										
General Labourer	462	3	2048	4	1716	5	3947	3	1613	6
Engine Driver, Stoker, Fireman (not railway, marine, nor agricultural)	3		85	.	269	.	407	.	89	.
Artizan, Mechanic (undefined)	.	.	22	.	42	3	37	1	38	.
Apprentice (undefined)	1	.	4	.	4	1	13	2	3	.
Factory Labourer (undefined)	1	.	17	5	9	2	28	12	25	2
Machinist, Machine Worker (undefined)	1	1	6	2	5	2	4	9	5	4
23. PERSONS WORKING AND DEALING IN REFUSE MATTERS.										
1. *Refuse Matters.*										
Town Drainage Service	.	.	13	.	.	.	.	.	.	.
Chimney Sweep, Soot Merchant	5	.	7	.	1	.	13	.	2	.
Scavenger, Crossing Sweeper	1	.	1	.	.	.	4	.	1	.
Rag Gatherer, Dealer	.	.	2	7	1	.	4	1	1	.
VI. UNOCCUPIED CLASS.										
24. PERSONS WITHOUT SPECIFIED OCCUPATIONS										
Persons returned by Property, Rank, &c., and not by special occupation	2443	6007	9786	24713	5653	15729	13593	38003	8213	22094
Children under 5 years of age	1159	1141	4724	4776	3051	2885	7308	7280	4405	4486

Table 10 *continued*.—OCCUPATIONS of MALES and FEMALES in the WELSH DIVISION and its REGISTRATION COUNTIES, and in each URBAN SANITARY DISTRICT of which the POPULATION exceeds 50,000 PERSONS.

OCCUPATIONS.	REGISTRATION COUNTIES.				URBAN SANITARY DISTRICTS.					
	CARNARVONSHIRE.		ANGLESEY.		CARDIFF.		YSTRADYFODWG.		SWANSEA.	
	Males.	Females.	Males.	Females.	Males.	Females.	Males.	Females.	Males.	Females.
TOTAL	66742	63039	17190	17991	42816	40145	30877	24755	32232	33375
I. PROFESSIONAL CLASS.										
1. PERSONS ENGAGED IN THE GENERAL OR LOCAL GOVERNMENT OF THE COUNTRY.										
1. *National Government.*										
Peer, M.P., Privy Councillor (not otherwise described)	1		1	.	.	.	.	.	.	.
Civil Service (officers and clerks)	75	9	20	1	143	6	5	.	80	1
Civil Service (messengers, &c.)	64	5	27	5	46	.	8	.	38	1
Prison Officer, &c.	8	1	.	.	14	4	.	.	13	3
2. *Local Government.*										
Police	76	.	19	.	118	.	34	.	71	.
Municipal, Parish, Union, District, Officer	63	3	17	8	35	3	9	.	24	2
Other Local or County Official	38	.	8	.	9	.	1	.	11	.
3. *East Indian and Colonial Service.*										
East Indian and Colonial Service	.	.	.	.	.	.	.	.	.	.
2. PERSONS ENGAGED IN THE DEFENCE OF THE COUNTRY.										
1. *Army (at Home).*										
Army Officer (effective or retired)	11	.	5	.	14	.	.	.	.	.
Soldier and Non-Commissioned Officer	10	.	12	.	167	.	8	.	23	.
Militia, Yeomanry, Volunteers	64	.	2	.	35	.	.	.	18	.
Army Pensioner	17	.	3	.	27	.	.	.	18	.
2. *Navy (ashore or in port).*										
Navy Officer (effective or retired)	7	.	4	.	.	.	.	.	1	.
Seaman, R.N.	7	.	13	.	4	.	.	.	3	.
Royal Marines (officers and men)	.	.	.	.	2	.	.	.	.	.
Navy Pensioner	19	.	8	.	13	.	.	.	13	.
3. PERSONS ENGAGED IN PROFESSIONAL OCCUPATIONS (WITH THEIR IMMEDIATE SUBORDINATES).										
1. *Clerical Profession.*										
Clergyman (Established Church)	135		40	.	23		10	.	20	.
Roman Catholic Priest	5	.	1	.	10		.	.	5	.
Minister, Priest, of other religious bodies	188	.	63	.	41		60	.	56	.
Missionary, Scripture Reader, Itinerant Preacher	16	1	2	.	9	4	.	3	5	1
Nun, Sister of Charity	.	.	.	.	.	5	.	.	.	.
Theological Student	18	.	2	.	8	.	11	.	9	.
Church, Chapel, Cemetery—Officer, Servant	16	7	9	12	11	10	2	.	8	4
2. *Legal Profession.*										
Barrister, Solicitor	50		7	.	38	.	.	.	32	.
Law Student	2	.	.	.	5	.	.	.	4	.
Law Clerk, and others connected with Law	70	.	8		84	.	6	.	80	
3. *Medical Profession.*										
Physician, Surgeon, General Practitioner	75	.	17	.	43	.	15	.	27	.
Dentist	16	.	.	.	7	.	.	.	12	.
Medical Student, Assistant	36	.	9	.	3	.	16	.	15	.
Midwife	.	24	.	6	.	.	.	12	.	5
Subordinate Medical Service	4	51	1	12	15	59	4	.	4	47
4. *Teachers.*										
Schoolmaster	363	258	67	56	92	310	62	133	101	291
Teacher, Professor, Lecturer	14	60	1	8	11	23	.	2	6	25
School Service, and others concerned in Teaching	6	1	2	2	3	3	2	.	5	2
5. *Literary and Scientific Persons.*										
Author, Editor, Journalist	19	.	2		11				5	1
Reporter, Short-hand Writer	5		.	.	11			.	5	.
Persons engaged in Scientific Pursuits	.		.		5		.	.	27	.
Literary, Scientific, Institution, Service, &c.	.		.	.	4		.	.	6	1
6. *Engineers and Surveyors.*										
Civil Engineer	35	.	5		59	.	1	.	35	.
Mining Engineer	8	.	4	.	78	.	19	.	18	.
Land, House, Ship, Surveyor	19		.	.	16	.	3	.	20	.
7. *Artists.*										
Painter (artist)	28	5	1	.	11	2	.	.	3	1
Engraver (artist)	1	.	.	.	5	.	.	.	3	.
Sculptor	.	.	.	.	5	.	3	.	3	.
Architect	24	.	2	.	27	.	3	.	8	.
Musician, Music Master	30	21	7	3	46	58	13	5	41	27
Art Student	1	.	.	.	2	6	.	.	.	2
Photographer	18	9	4	1	23	1	2	.	19	5
Actor	.	.	.	.	31	16	2	3	9	6
Art, Music, Theatre, Service	.	.	.	.	3	.	.	.	1	.

Table 10 *continued*.—OCCUPATIONS of MALES and FEMALES in the WELSH DIVISION and its REGISTRATION COUNTIES, and in each URBAN SANITARY DISTRICT of which the POPULATION exceeds 50,000 PERSONS.

OCCUPATIONS.	REGISTRATION COUNTIES.				URBAN SANITARY DISTRICTS.					
	CARNARVONSHIRE.		ANGLESEY.		CARDIFF.		YSTRADYFODWG.		SWANSEA.	
	Males.	Females.	Males.	Females.	Males.	Females.	Males.	Females.	Males.	Females.
8. Persons engaged in Exhibitions, Shows, Games, &c.										
Performer, Showman, Exhibition, Service	1	1	·	·	2	5	·	·	4	1
Billiard, Cricket, & other Games, Service	10	·	·	·	26	·	3	·	8	·
II. DOMESTIC CLASS.										
4. PERSONS ENGAGED IN DOMESTIC OFFICES OR SERVICES.										
1. Domestic Service.										
Domestic Coachman, Groom	228	·	35	·	23	·	8	·	35	·
Domestic Gardener	444	·	16	·	161	·	22	·	86	·
Domestic Indoor Servant	168	7674	29	1549	35	3649	9	1508	31	3161
Lodge, Gate, Park, Keeper (not Government)	5	5	1	·	6	·	·	·	10	8
Inn, Hotel, Servant	77	136	20	23	75	167	11	35	42	133
College, Club, Service	3	·	·	·	9	·	·	·	4	2
2. Other Service.										
Office Keeper (not Government)	3	5	·	·	9	30	·	·	3	20
Cook (not domestic)	·	7	·	3	7	8	·	4	5	6
Charwoman	·	376	·	120	·	280	·	·	·	208
Washing and Bathing Service	3	492	·	115	6	544	·	26	2	338
Hospital and Institution Service	3	16	1	3	5	19	·	132	7	16
Others engaged in Service	4	·	·	·	7	·	·	1	3	·
III. COMMERCIAL CLASS.										
5. PERSONS ENGAGED IN COMMERCIAL OCCUPATIONS.										
1. Merchants and Agents.										
Merchant	35	3	13	·	27	·	6	·	22	1
Broker, Agent, Factor	84	·	7	·	183	2	12	·	130	·
Auctioneer, Appraiser, Valuer, House Agent	32	·	7	·	34	·	9	·	28	·
Accountant	54	·	10	·	133	·	7	·	101	·
Salesman, Buyer (not otherwise described)	1	6	·	·	7	3	·	·	2	·
Commercial Traveller	96	·	8	·	203	·	17	·	146	·
Commercial Clerk	253	15	38	2	892	13	99	1	556	8
Officer of Commercial Company, Guild, Society, &c.	·	·	·	·	2	·	·	·	·	·
2. Dealers in Money.										
Banker	10	·	·	·	1	·	·	·	1	·
Bank Service	61	·	17	·	35	·	·	·	33	·
Bill Discounter, Bill Broker, Finance Agent	·	·	·	·	2	·	·	·	5	·
3. Persons occupied in Insurance.										
Life, House, Ship, &c., Insurance Service	36	·	7	·	55	·	21	·	66	1
6. PERSONS ENGAGED IN CONVEYANCE OF MEN, GOODS, AND MESSAGES.										
1. On Railways.										
Railway Engine Driver, Stoker	65	·	43	·	241	·	41	·	154	·
Railway Guard	24	·	12	·	145	·	23	·	66	·
Pointsman, Level Crossing Man	12	1	5	·	8	·	8	·	32	·
Other Railway Officials and Servants	253	2	174	1	571	·	173	·	303	2
2. On Roads.										
Toll Collector, Turnpike Gate Keeper	7	6	·	·	·	·	·	·	13	·
Omnibus, Coach, Cab, Owner—Livery Stable Keeper	31	1	11	1	45	·	·	·	16	1
Cabman, Flyman, Coachman (not domestic)	113	·	13	·	190	·	7	·	74	·
Carman, Carrier, Carter, Haulier	417	6	87	2	275	2	716	·	329	·
Tramway Companies' Service	1	·	·	·	33	·	·	·	16	·
Wheel Chair Proprietor, Attendant, &c.	1	·	·	·	·	·	·	·	·	·
3. On Canals, Rivers and Seas.										
Inland Navigation Service	2	1	·	·	10	·	·	·	15	·
Bargeman, Lighterman, Waterman	31	·	2	·	91	·	·	·	34	·
Navigation Service (on shore)	10	1	3	·	38	·	·	·	17	·
Seaman (Merchant Service)	1213	·	1168	·	3510	·	3	·	1145	·
Pilot	40	·	28	·	169	·	·	·	56	·
Ship Steward, Cook	19	2	61	12	241	1	·	·	41	·
Boatman on Seas	27	·	31	·	·	·	·	·	·	·
Harbour, Dock, Wharf, Lighthouse, Service	70	·	47	·	646	1	·	·	514	1
4. In Storage.										
Warehouseman (not Manchester)	8	·	·	·	82	3	1	·	82	·
Meter, Weigher	1	·	1	·	33	·	9	·	23	·
5. In conveying Messages, Porterage, &c.										
Messenger, Porter, Watchman (not Railway nor Government)	98	1	30	·	352	6	15	1	286	·
Telegraph, Telephone, Service	31	3	10	3	91	13	18	2	49	3

Table 10 *continued.*—OCCUPATIONS of MALES and FEMALES in the WELSH DIVISION and its REGISTRATION COUNTIES, and in each URBAN SANITARY DISTRICT of which the POPULATION exceeds 50,000 PERSONS.

OCCUPATIONS.	REGISTRATION COUNTIES.				URBAN SANITARY DISTRICTS.					
	CARNARVONSHIRE.		ANGLESEY.		CARDIFF.		YSTRADYFODWG.		SWANSEA.	
	Males.	Females.	Males.	Females.	Males.	Females.	Males.	Females.	Males.	Females.
IV. AGRICULTURAL CLASS.										
7. PERSONS ENGAGED IN AGRICULTURE.										
1. *In Fields and Pastures.*										
Farmer, Grazier	2925	649	1448	308	20	1	50	4	10	1
Farmer's, Grazier's—Son, Grandson, Brother, Nephew*	1108	.	557	.	3	.	23	.	2	.
Farm Bailiff	68	.	29	.	4	.	6	.	3	.
Agricultural Labourer, Farm Servant, Cottager	4602	260	2233	82	177	6	68	3	51	8
Shepherd	53	.	1	.	2	.	9	.	.	.
Land Drainage Service (not in towns)	.	.	.	.	.	.	.	.	.	.
Agricultural Machine—Proprietor, Attendant	19	.	8	.	.	.	.	.	.	.
Agricultural Student, Pupil	1	.	.	.	.	.	.	.	.	.
Others engaged in, or connected with, Agriculture	.	.	.	.	.	.	.	.	.	.
2. *In Woods.*										
Woodman	31	.	.	.	1	.	.	.	.	.
3. *In Gardens.*										
Nurseryman, Seedsman, Florist	21	1	1	.	10	.	.	.	3	2
Gardener (not domestic)	22	4	53	.	68	10	.	.	4	2
8. PERSONS ENGAGED ABOUT ANIMALS.										
1. *About Animals.*										
Horse Proprietor, Breeder, Dealer	1	.	7	.	.	.	.	.	2	.
Groom, Horse-keeper, Horse-breaker	83	1	51	.	96	.	86	.	42	.
Veterinary Surgeon, Farrier	12	.	10	.	9	.	9	.	12	.
Cattle, Sheep, Pig—Dealer, Salesman	41	.	40	.	18	.	2	.	12	.
Drover	.	.	2	.	7	.	.	.	.	.
Gamekeeper	137	.	43	.	2	.	.	.	.	.
Dog, Bird, Animal—Keeper, Dealer	2	1	1	.	4	.	.	.	.	.
Vermin destroyer	6	.	3	.	.	.	.	.	.	.
Fisherman	160	1	52	.	16	.	.	.	15	.
Knacker, Catsmeat Dealer, &c., &c.	.	.	.	.	3	.	.	.	.	.
V. INDUSTRIAL CLASS.										
9. PERSONS WORKING AND DEALING IN BOOKS, PRINTS, AND MAPS.										
1. *Books.*										
Publisher, Bookseller, Librarian	49	15	5	4	21	6	10	1	23	4
Music—Publisher, Seller, Printer	3	.	.	.	2	2	.	.	3	.
Bookbinder	14	1	.	.	23	32	.	.	14	5
Printer	179	1	10	.	220	6	13	.	96	.
Newspaper Agent, News Room Keeper	10	.	.	.	17	1	2	.	7	1
Others	.	.	.	.	.	.	.	.	.	.
2. *Prints and Maps.*										
Lithographer, Lithographic Printer	6	.	.	.	14	.	.	.	3	.
Copper Plate and Steel Plate Printer	.	.	.	.	.	.	.	.	1	.
Map and Print—Colourer, Seller	.	.	.	.	.	.	.	.	.	.
10. PERSONS WORKING AND DEALING IN MACHINES AND IMPLEMENTS.										
1. *Machines.*										
Engine, Machine, Maker	30	.	4	.	175	2	20	1	83	.
Millwright	15	.	3	.	10	.	1	.	4	.
Fitter, Turner (Engine and Machine)	87	.	49	.	390	.	78	.	260	.
Boiler Maker	21	.	54	.	348	.	27	.	154	.
Spinning and Weaving Machine Maker	.	.	.	.	.	.	.	.	.	.
Agricultural Machine and Implement Maker	.	.	.	.	1	.	.	.	1	.
Domestic Machinery—Maker, Dealer	.	.	.	.	2	.	.	.	.	.
2. *Tools and Implements.*										
Tool Maker, Dealer	.	.	.	.	1	.	.	.	1	.
Cutler, Scissors Maker	1	.	.	.	7	.	.	.	1	.
File Maker	.	.	.	.	11	.	.	.	.	.
Saw Maker	2	.	.	.	3	.	.	.	.	.
Pin Maker	.	.	.	.	.	.	.	.	.	.
Needle Maker	.	.	.	.	.	.	.	.	.	.
Steel Pen Maker	.	.	.	.	2	.	.	.	.	.
Pencil Maker (Wood)	.	.	.	.	.	.	.	.	.	.
Domestic Implement Maker	.	.	.	.	.	.	.	.	.	.
3. *Watches and Philosophical Instruments.*										
Watch Maker, Clock Maker	93	2	18	.	59	.	16	.	41	2
Philosophical Instrument Maker, Optician	1	.	.	.	10	.	.	.	4	.
Electrical Apparatus Maker	.	.	.	.	7	.	3	.	7	.
Weighing and Measuring Apparatus Maker	.	.	.	.	6	.	.	.	6	.

* [illegible] … and therefore presumably engaged in agriculture, are included above.

Table 10 *continued*. — Occupations of Males and Females in the Welsh Division and its Registration Counties, and in each Urban Sanitary District of which the Population exceeds 50,000 Persons.

Occupations.	Registration Counties.				Urban Sanitary Districts.					
	Carnarvonshire.		Anglesey.		Cardiff.		Ystradyfodwg.		Swansea.	
	Males.	Females.	Males.	Females.	Males.	Females.	Males.	Females.	Males.	Females.
4. Surgical Instruments.										
Surgical Instrument Maker	.		.		1	.	.	.	.	.
5. Arms and Ordnance.										
Gunsmith, Gun Manufacturer	3	.	.	.	4	.	.	.	3	.
Ordnance Manufacturer	.	.	.	.	.	.	.	.	.	.
Sword, Bayonet—Maker, Cutler	.	.	.	.	.	.	.	.	.	.
Others	.	.	.	.	1	.	.	.	1	.
6. Musical Instruments.										
Musical Instrument Maker, Dealer	3	.	1	.	10	1	.	.	6	.
7. Type, Dies, Medals, Coins.										
Type Cutter, Founder	.	.	.	.	.	.	.	.	.	.
Die, Seal, Coin, Medal, Maker	.	.	.	.	.	.	2	.	.	.
8. Tackle for Sports and Games.										
Toy Maker, Dealer	1	5	.	.	1	3	.	.	1	6
Fishing Rod, Tackle, Maker, Dealer	.	.	.	.	2	.	.	.	.	.
Apparatus for other Games, Maker, Dealer	.	.	.	.	2	.	.	.	.	.
11. Persons working and dealing in Houses, Furniture, and Decorations.										
1. Houses.										
Builder	79	.	13	.	116	.	23	.	30	.
Carpenter, Joiner	1259	.	421	.	1110	.	269	.	587	.
Bricklayer	68	.	13	.	104	.	10	.	24	.
Mason	983	1	221	.	903	1	391	1	644	.
Slater, Tiler	93	.	10	.	4	.	1	.	.	.
Plasterer, Whitewasher	229	1	33	.	214	.	47	.	78	.
Paperhanger	7	4	.	3	7	.	.	.	.	7
Plumber	72	.	4	.	103	.	6	.	120	.
Painter, Glazier	319	.	47	.	427	.	47	.	236	3
2. Furniture and Fittings.										
Cabinet Maker, Upholsterer	113	6	18	.	98	12	9	.	80	23
French Polisher	6	.	.	.	10	.	.	.	15	.
Furniture Broker, Dealer	2	.	.	.	14	1	.	.	11	.
Locksmith, Bellhanger	2	.	.	.	6	.	.	.	2	.
Gas Fitter	11	.	2	.	57	.	2	.	16	.
House and Shop Fittings—Maker, Dealer	1	.	.	.	5	.	.	.	3	1
Funeral Furniture Maker, Undertaker	.	.	.	.	8	.	2	.	8	.
Others	.	.	.	.	.	.	.	.	.	.
3. House Decorations.										
Wood Carver	.	.	.	.	6	.	.	.	3	.
Carver, Gilder	5	.	2	.	15	.	1	.	13	.
Dealer in Works of Art	1	.	.	.	2	.	.	.	1	.
Figure, Image—Maker, Dealer	.	.	.	.	1	.	.	.	1	1
Animal, Bird, &c., Preserver, Naturalist	2	.	.	.	3	.	.	.	.	.
Artificial Flower Maker	.	.	.	.	1	.	.	.	1	2
12. Persons working and dealing in Carriages and Harness.										
1. Carriages.										
Coachmaker	51	.	.	.	66	1	.	.	41	.
Railway Carriage, Railway Wagon, Maker	.	.	.	.	44	.	8	1	35	.
Wheelwright	39	1	5	.	62	.	4	.	51	.
Bicycle, Tricycle—Maker, Dealer	.	.	.	.	.	.	.	.	.	.
Others	1	.	.	.	30	.	8	.	3	.
2. Harness.										
Saddler, Harness, Whip, Maker	69	.	30	1	39	.	25	.	26	.
13. Persons working and dealing in Ships and Boats.										
1. Hull.										
Ship, Boat, Barge, Builder	21	.	5	.	81	.	.	.	82	.
Shipwright, Ship Carpenter (ashore)	186	.	59	.	496	.	.	.	209	.
2. Masts, Rigging, &c.										
Mast, Yard, Oar, Block, Maker	7	.	1	.	16	.	.	.	87	.
Ship Rigger, Chandler, Fitter	6	.	7	.	116	.	.	.	88	1
Sail Maker	24	.	13	.	72	1	.	.	65	.

Table 10 *continued*.—OCCUPATIONS of MALES and FEMALES in the WELSH DIVISION and its REGISTRATION COUNTIES, and in each URBAN SANITARY DISTRICT of which the POPULATION exceeds 50,000 PERSONS.

OCCUPATIONS.	REGISTRATION COUNTIES.				URBAN SANITARY DISTRICTS.					
	CARNARVONSHIRE.		ANGLESEY.		CARDIFF.		YSTRADYFODWG.		SWANSEA.	
	Males.	Females.	Males.	Females.	Males.	Females.	Males.	Females.	Males.	Females.
14. PERSONS WORKING AND DEALING IN CHEMICALS AND COMPOUNDS.										
1. *Colouring Matter.*										
Dye, Paint, Manufacture	.	.	.	.	6	1	.	.	3	.
Ink, Blacking, Colouring Substance, Manufacture	.	.	.	.	.	.	.	.	.	
2. *Explosives.*										
Gunpowder, Guncotton, Explosive Substance, Manufacture	3	.	.	.	.	.	.	.	2	.
Fuses, Fireworks, Explosive Article, Manufacture	.	.	.	.	.	.	.	.	4	12
3. *Drugs and other Chemicals and Compounds.*										
Chemist, Druggist	84	4	32	3	70	4	13	.	66	.
Manufacturing Chemist	.	.	.	.	11	.	1	.	38	.
Alkali Manufacture	.	.	.	.	5	.	.	.	5	.
Drysalter	.	.	.	.	.	.	.	.	.	.
15. PERSONS WORKING AND DEALING IN TOBACCO AND PIPES.										
1. *Tobacco and Pipes.*										
Tobacco Manufacturer, Tobacconist	7	.	25	3	12	13	2	.	9	8
Tobacco Pipe, Snuff Box, &c., Maker	1	.	.	.	.	1	.	.	4	4
16. PERSONS WORKING AND DEALING IN FOOD AND LODGING.										
1. *Board and Lodging.*										
Innkeeper, Hotel Keeper, Publican	219	125	62	60	214	38	81	17	215	56
Lodging, Boarding House, Keeper	40	426	1	35	38	120	1	55	5	86
Coffee, Eating House, Keeper	7	9	3	2	22	18	2	1	8	9
2. *Spirituous Drinks.*										
Hop—Merchant, Dealer	.	.	.	.	.	.	.	.	.	.
Maltster	5	.	3	.	11	.	.	.	13	.
Brewer	25	2	8	2	59	1	17	.	29	.
Beerseller. Ale, Porter, Cider, Dealer	.	2	.	.	16	3	1	.	14	2
Cellarman	4	1	2	.	29	.	2	.	15	.
Wine, Spirit—Merchant, Agent	24	2	.	.	15	.	.	.	14	2
3. *Food.*										
Milkseller, Dairyman	14	17	1	4	79	26	7	2	30	25
Cheesemonger, Butterman	10	11	3	19	6	.	7	.	5	5
Butcher, Meat Salesman	358	12	105	5	251	11	83	1	153	45
Provision Curer, Dealer	23	15	5	8	37	.	2	.	16	4
Poulterer, Game Dealer	16	18	8	4	3	4	.	.	2	5
Fishmonger	32	14	3	2	37	8	6	.	13	14
Corn, Flour, Seed—Merchant, Dealer	66	28	20	3	23	1	.	.	20	1
Corn Miller	159	1	42	2	67	1	.	.	15	.
Baker	151	38	30	17	348	22	16	10	130	12
Confectioner, Pastrycook	83	70	3	28	48	36	7	4	49	24
Greengrocer, Fruiterer	17	45	19	3	86	46	30	15	62	80
Mustard, Vinegar, Spice, Pickle—Maker, Dealer	.	.	.	.	3	.	.	.	.	.
Sugar Refiner	4	1	.	.	8	2	1	.	3	2
Grocer. Tea, Coffee, Chocolate—Maker, Dealer	356	237	80	63	586	92	295	22	355	133
Ginger Beer, Mineral Water—Manufacturer, Dealer	13	.	2		8	3		.	3	5
Others dealing in Food	.	.	.	.	.	.	.	.	.	.
17. PERSONS WORKING AND DEALING IN TEXTILE FABRICS.										
1. *Wool and Worsted.*										
Woolstapler	2	1	.	.	.	.	.	.	1	.
Woollen Cloth Manufacture	88	4	48	.	6	1	4	1	30	1
Wool, Woollen goods—Dyer, Printer	.	.	.	.	1	.	.	.	.	.
Worsted, Stuff, Manufacture	.	1	.	.	1	.	.	.	2	.
Flannel Manufacture	3	.	.	.	.	.	.	1	4	1
Blanket Manufacture	.	.	.	.	.	.	.	.	.	.
Fuller	8	.	3	.	.	.	.	.	.	.
Cloth, Worsted, Stuff, Flannel, Blanket, Dealer	.	.	.	.	4	1	1	.	.	.
Others	.	.	.	.	.	.	.	.	.	.
2. *Silk.*										
Silk, Silk goods, Manufacture	.	.	.	.	.	2	.	.	1	.
Silk Dyer, Printer	.	.	.	.	.	.	.	.	.	.
Ribbon Manufacture	.	.	.	.	.	.	.	.	.	.
Crape, Gauze, Manufacture	.	.	.	.	.	.	.	.	.	.
Silk Merchant, Dealer	.	.	.	.	3	.	.	.	.	.

Table 10 *continued*.—Occupations of Males and Females in the Welsh Division and its Registration Counties, and in each Urban Sanitary District of which the Population exceeds 50,000 Persons.

Occupations.	Registration Counties.				Urban Sanitary Districts.					
	Carnarvonshire.		Anglesey.		Cardiff.		Ystradyfodwg.		Swansea.	
	Males.	Females.	Males.	Females.	Males.	Females.	Males.	Females.	Males.	Females.
3. Cotton and Flax										
Cotton, Cotton goods, Manufacture	5	.	.	.	.	1	.	.	.	2
Cotton, Calico—Printer, Dyer, Bleacher	.	.	.	.	1	.	.	.	.	.
Cotton, Calico—Warehouseman, Dealer	3	.	.	.	.	.	.	.	.	.
Flax, Linen—Manufacturer, Dealer	1	.	.	.	.	.	.	.	.	.
Lace Manufacturer, Dealer	.	1	.	.	.	8	.	.	.	4
Fustian Manufacturer, Dealer	.	.	.	.	.	.	.	.	.	.
Tape Manufacturer, Dealer	.	.	.	.	.	.	.	.	.	.
Thread Manufacturer, Dealer	.	.	.	.	.	.	.	.	.	.
4. Hemp and other Fibrous Materials.										
Hemp, Jute, Cocoa Fibre, Manufacture	.	.	.	.	.	.	.	.	.	.
Rope, Twine, Cord—Maker, Dealer	7	2	2	.	20	.	1	.	3	.
Mat Maker, Seller	6	109	.	.	4	1	.	.	1	.
Net Maker	2	1	1	.	.	.	.	.	.	1
Canvas, Sailcloth, Manufacture	.	.	.	.	.	.	.	.	1	.
Sacking, Sack, Bag—Maker, Dealer	.	.	.	.	6	1	.	.	.	1
Others working and dealing in Hemp	.	.	.	.	.	.	.	.	.	.
5. Mixed or Unspecified Materials.										
Weaver (undefined)	23	1	2	.	3	1	2	1	15	4
Dyer, Printer, Scourer, Bleacher, Calenderer (undefined)	1	1	.	.	16	14	.	.	4	2
Factory hand (Textile, undefined)	5	1	.	.	1	2	1	.	.	.
Felt Manufacture	.	.	.	.	1	.	.	.	.	.
Carpet, Rug, Manufacture	1	.	.	.	.	.	.	.	2	.
Manchester Warehouseman	.	.	1	.	.	.	.	.	.	.
Draper, Linen Draper, Mercer	344	84	56	32	296	127	92	26	236	114
Fancy Goods (Textile), Manufacturer, Worker, Dealer	4	22	.	2	5	15	.	.	5	12
Trimming Maker, Dealer	.	.	.	.	.	.	.	.	.	2
Embroiderer	.	.	.	.	.	.	.	.	.	.
Others	.	.	.	.	.	.	.	.	.	.
18. Persons working and dealing in Dress.										
1. Dress.										
Hatter, Hat Manufacture (not straw)	6	3	2	.	12	1	.	.	6	.
Straw—Hat, Bonnet, Plait, Manufacture	.	2	.	.	.	2	.	1	.	3
Tailor	691	11	223	1	385	144	174	7	295	69
Milliner, Dressmaker, Staymaker	1	2187	3	645	1	1268	1	632	.	1280
Shawl Manufacture	.	.	.	.	.	.	.	.	.	.
Shirt Maker, Seamstress	.	81	.	24	1	164	.	10	.	84
Hosiery Manufacture	.	34	1	12	.	4	.	2	.	2
Hosier, Haberdasher	3	4	.	.	9	2	5	.	7	1
Glover, Glove Maker	1	.	.	.	.	.	.	1	.	2
Button Maker, Dealer	.	.	.	.	.	.	.	.	.	.
Shoe, Boot—Maker, Dealer	610	16	208	8	359	27	176	1	284	20
Patten, Clog, Maker	40	.	22	.	1	.	.	.	9	.
Wig Maker, Hairdresser	27	.	6	1	17	1	22	.	51	.
Umbrella, Parasol, Stick—Maker, Dealer	9	.	.	1	6	4	.	.	7	2
Accoutrement Maker	.	.	.	.	.	.	.	.	.	.
Old Clothes Dealer, and others	.	1	.	.	.	2	.	.	.	.
19. Persons working and dealing in various Animal Substances.										
1. In Grease, Gut, Bone, Horn, Ivory, and Whalebone.										
Tallow Chandler, Candle, Grease, Manufacture	10	.	3	.	6	.	2	.	9	2
Soap Boiler, Maker	.	.	.	.	.	.	.	.	.	.
Glue, Size, Gelatine, Isinglass—Maker, Dealer	.	.	.	.	.	.	.	.	.	.
Manure Manufacture	.	.	.	.	1	.	.	.	4	4
Bone, Horn, Ivory, Tortoise-shell—Worker, Dealer	.	.	.	.	.	.	.	.	.	.
Comb Maker	.	.	.	.	.	.	.	.	.	.
Others	.	.	.	.	.	.	.	.	1	.
2. In Skins.										
Furrier, Skinner	3	.	.	.	2	.	2	.	6	.
Tanner, Fellmonger	24	1	11	.	11	.	.	.	20	.
Currier	19	.	6	3	18	.	.	.	12	1
Leather Goods, Portmanteau, Bag, Strap, &c.—Maker, Dealer	.	.	1	.	7	.	.	.	2	.
Parchment, Vellum—Maker, Dealer	.	.	.	.	.	.	.	.	.	.
3. In Hair and Feathers.										
Hair, Bristle—Worker, Dealer	.	.	.	.	.	.	.	.	.	.
Brush, Broom, Maker	1	.	3	.	6	.	.	.	6	3
Quill, Feather—Dresser, Dealer	.	.	.	.	.	4	.	.	.	1

Table 10 *continued.*—OCCUPATIONS of MALES and FEMALES in the WELSH DIVISION and its REGISTRATION COUNTIES, and in each URBAN SANITARY DISTRICT of which the POPULATION exceeds 50,000 PERSONS.

OCCUPATIONS.	REGISTRATION COUNTIES.				URBAN SANITARY DISTRICTS.					
	CARNARVONSHIRE.		ANGLESEY.		CARDIFF.		YSTRADYFODWG.		SWANSEA.	
	Males.	Females.	Males.	Females.	Males.	Females.	Males.	Females.	Males.	Females.
20. PERSONS WORKING AND DEALING IN VARIOUS VEGETABLE SUBSTANCES.										
1. *In Oils, Gums, and Resins.*										
Oil Miller, Oil Cake—Maker, Dealer	1	.	.	.	5	.	.	.	2	1
Oil and Colourman	1	.	.	.	.	.	.	.	.	.
Floor Cloth, Oil Cloth, Manufacture	.	.	.	.	2	.	.	.	.	.
Japanner	.	.	.	.	.	.	.	.	.	.
India Rubber, Gutta Percha—Worker, Dealer	.	.	.	.	5	.	.	.	3	.
Waterproof Goods—Maker, Dealer	.	.	.	.	2	1	.	.	6	.
Others	.	.	.	.	.	.	.	.	.	.
2. *In Cane, Rush, and Straw.*										
Willow, Cane, Rush—Worker, Dealer, Basketmaker	13	2	5	1	39	1	.	.	44	11
Hay, Straw (not plait), Chaff—Cutter, Dealer	6	1	4	.	18	.	10	.	13	.
Thatcher	.	.	.	.	1	.	.	.	.	.
3. *In Wood and Bark.*										
Timber, Wood—Merchant, Dealer	17	.	8	.	77	1	7	.	27	2
Sawyer	68	.	12	.	136	.	63	.	125	.
Lath, Wooden Fence, Hurdle, Maker	8	.	.	.	19	.	.	.	10	.
Wood Turner, Box Maker	4	.	2	.	19	.	2	.	12	.
Cooper, Hoop Maker, Bender	12	.	6	.	29	1	1	.	43	.
Cork, Bark—Cutter, Worker, Dealer	.	.	.	.	3	.	.	.	4	.
Others	.	.	.	.	.	.	.	.	1	1
4. *In Paper.*										
Paper Manufacture	.	4	.	.	40	33	1	.	.	.
Envelope Maker	.	.	.	.	.	.	.	.	.	.
Stationer, Law Stationer	12	6	1	1	20	16	1	.	18	5
Card, Pattern Card, Maker	.	.	.	.	.	.	.	.	.	.
Paper Stainer	.	.	.	.	.	.	.	.	.	.
Paper Box, Paper Bag, Maker	.	.	.	.	.	8	.	.	1	.
Ticket, Label, Writer	.	.	.	.	.	.	.	.	1	.
Others	4	.	.	.	8	.	1	.	7	.
21. PERSONS WORKING AND DEALING IN VARIOUS MINERAL SUBSTANCES.										
1. *Miners.*										
Coal Miner	12	.	7	.	59	.	14142	98	319	1
Ironstone Miner	2	.	1	.	3	.	2	.	3	.
Copper Miner	50	.	265	14	1	.	2	.	11	.
Tin Miner	1	.	.	.	.	.	.	.	4	.
Lead Miner	227	4	7	.	1	.	3	.	1	.
Miner in other, or undefined, Minerals	42	.	5	.	.	.	7	.	4	.
Mine Service	3	.	.	.	47	.	72	.	27	.
2. *Coal, Coal Gas, &c.*										
Coal Merchant, Dealer	118	15	40	1	156	2	.	.	162	4
Coalheaver	9	.	24	.	639	.	25	.	91	.
Coke, Charcoal, Peat—Cutter, Burner, Dealer	.	.	1	.	.	1	86	7	8	.
Gas Works Service	34	.	6	.	52	.	13	.	27	.
3. *Stone, Clay, and Road Making.*										
Stone Quarrier	1184	.	11	.	6	.	95	.	11	.
Stone Cutter, Dresser, Dealer	68	.	8	.	25	1	2	.	3	.
Slate Quarrier	8408	.	17	.	.	.	1	.	20	.
Slate Worker, Dealer	310	1	1	.	12	.	.	.	7	.
Limeburner	28	1	1	.	7	.	1	.	3	.
Clay, Sand, Gravel, Chalk—Labourer, Dealer	1	.	1	.	1	.	.	.	9	.
Fossil, Coprolite—Digger, Dealer	.	.	.	.	.	.	.	.	.	.
Well Sinker, Borer	.	.	1	.	.	.	34	.	.	.
Plaster, Cement, Manufacture	.	.	.	.	5	.	.	.	1	.
Brick, Tile—Maker, Burner, Dealer	45	.	.	.	53	.	16	17	32	.
Paviour	.	.	.	.	6	.	.	.	1	.
Road Contractor, Surveyor, Inspector	4	.	.	.	.	.	.	.	.	.
Road Labourer	84	.	5	.	23	.	36	.	13	.
Railway Contractor	4	.	.	.	7	.	1	.	7	.
Platelayer	207	.	66	.	102	.	81	.	49	.
Railway Labourer, Navvy	112	.	32	.	118	.	25	.	101	.
Others	.	11	.	.	.	.	.	.	4	.
4. *Earthenware and Glass.*										
Earthenware, China, Porcelain, Manufacture	14	1	9	1	4	.	.	1	33	.
Glass Manufacture	.	.	.	.	4	.	.	.	2	.
Earthenware, China, Glass, Dealer	20	6	1	1	17	9	1	4	12	4
5. *Salt.*										
Salt Maker, Dealer	.	.	.	.	1	.	.	.	.	.

Table 10 *continued.*—OCCUPATIONS of MALES and FEMALES in the WELSH DIVISION and its REGISTRATION COUNTIES, and in each URBAN SANITARY DISTRICT of which the POPULATION exceeds 50,000 PERSONS.

OCCUPATIONS.	REGISTRATION COUNTIES.				URBAN SANITARY DISTRICTS.					
	CAR-NARVON-SHIRE.		ANGLESEY.		CARDIFF.		YSTRADY-FODWG.		SWANSEA.	
	Males.	Females.	Males.	Females.	Males.	Females.	Males.	Females.	Males.	Females.
6. *Water.*										
Waterworks Service	2	.	1	1	7	.	4	.	2	.
Others	1	.	.	.	.	.	.	.	1	.
7. *Precious Metals and Jewellery.*										
Goldsmith, Silversmith, Jeweller	8	4	1	.	25	2	.	.	17	.
Gold, Silver, Beater	.	.	.	.	.	.	.	.	.	.
Lapidary	2	.	.	.	.	.	.	.	.	.
Others	.	.	1	.	.	.	.	.	30	2
8. *Iron and Steel.*										
Blacksmith	582	1	159	.	532	.	298	2	396	.
Whitesmith	3	.	.	.	3	.	.	.	2	.
Nail Manufacture	23	.	12	.	9	.	1	.	12	4
Anchor, Chain, Manufacture	.	.	.	.	3	.	.	.	4	.
Other Iron and Steel Manufactures	39	.	25	.	208	.	36	.	622	1
Ironmonger. Hardware Dealer, Merchant	75	10	17	.	70	2	17	.	62	.
9. *Copper.*										
Copper, Copper goods—Manufacturer, Worker, Dealer	2	.	25	11	95	.	.	.	1397	13
10. *Tin and Zinc.*										
Tin, Tin Plate, Tin goods—Manufacturer, Worker, Dealer	51	.	24	.	37	.	11	.	933	216
Zinc, Zinc Goods—Manufacturer, Worker, Dealer	.	.	.	.	1	.	.	.	317	.
11. *Lead.*										
Lead, Leaden goods—Manufacturer, Worker, Dealer	.	.	.	.	1	.	.	.	50	.
12. *In Other, Mixed, or Unspecified, Metals.*										
Metal Refiner, Worker, Turner, Dealer	.	.	.	.	1	.	.	.	59	.
Brass, Bronze, Manufacture. Brazier	6	.	1	.	24	.	.	.	16	.
Metal Burnisher, Lacquerer	.	.	.	.	.	.	.	.	1	.
White Metal, Plated Ware, Manufacture. Pewterer	.	.	.	.	.	.	.	.	2	.
Wire Maker, Worker, Weaver, Drawer	1	.	1	.	26	.	.	.	2	.
Bolt, Nut, Rivet, Screw, Staple, Maker	1	.	.	.	6	.	.	.	8	.
Lamp, Lantern, Candlestick, Maker	.	.	.	.	.	.	3	.	1	.
Clasp, Buckle, Hinge, Maker	.	.	.	.	.	.	.	.	.	.
Fancy Chain, Gilt Toy, Maker	.	.	.	.	.	.	.	.	.	.
Others	.	.	.	.	.	.	.	.	1	.
22. PERSONS WORKING AND DEALING IN GENERAL OR UNSPECIFIED COMMODITIES.										
1. *Makers and Dealers (General or Undefined).*										
General Shopkeeper, Dealer	138	185	59	113	96	81	18	15	56	37
Pawnbroker	5	.	.	.	35	8	9	1	46	4
Costermonger, Huckster, Street Seller	113	57	26	12	87	160	24	2	47	48
Manufacturer, Manager, Superintendent (undefined)	9	1	5	.	54	4	2	.	30	.
Contractor (undefined)	12	.	2	.	18	.	29	.	30	.
2. *Mechanics and Labourers (General or Undefined).*										
General Labourer	2868	12	1144	6	3732	20	785	5	2753	9
Engine Driver, Stoker, Fireman (not railway, marine, nor agricultural)	264	.	36	.	338	.	564	.	340	.
Artizan, Mechanic (undefined)	54	2	14	.	222	.	49	.	81	1
Apprentice (undefined)	3	1	1	.	15	4	5	6	1	.
Factory Labourer (undefined)	32	.	6	.	138	1	17	.	55	6
Machinist, Machine Worker (undefined)	7	1	2	.	24	13	3	2	6	1
23. PERSONS WORKING AND DEALING IN REFUSE MATTERS.										
1. *Refuse Matters.*										
Town Drainage Service	1	.	.	.	7	.	6	.	3	.
Chimney Sweep, Soot Merchant	7	.	1	.	24	.	2	.	10	.
Scavenger, Crossing Sweeper	11	.	.	.	5	.	3	.	3	.
Rag Gatherer, Dealer	2	5	.	.	5	2	5	2	7	4
VI. UNOCCUPIED CLASS.										
24. PERSONS WITHOUT SPECIFIED OCCUPATIONS										
Persons returned by Property, Rank, &c., and not by special occupation	14868	41317	4123	13360	9679	26560	5953	17668	7849	21706
Children under 5 years of age	7794	7711	2048	2090	5919	5972	4424	4341	4742	4782

Table 11.—BIRTH-PLACES of MALES and FEMALES enumerated in COUNTIES, and in each URBAN SANITARY DISTRICT of which the POPULATION EXCEEDS 50,000 PERSONS.

WHERE BORN.	WHERE ENUMERATED.									
	MONMOUTHSHIRE AND WALES.		COUNTIES.*							
			MONMOUTHSHIRE.		GLAMORGANSHIRE.		CARMARTHENSHIRE.		PEMBROKESHIRE.	
	Males.	Females.	Males.	Females.	Males.	Females.	Males.	Females.	Males.	Females.
TOTAL OF INHABITANTS	786322	785458	108262	103005	262579	248854	59709	65155	43449	48375
LONDON	4656	4727	711	728	1819	1775	193	195	568	443
Middlesex (*Intra-metropolitan*)	3764	3852	605	622	1491	1448	155	167	332	258
Surrey (*Intra-metropolitan*)	479	455	67	55	188	207	23	17	80	39
Kent (*Intra-metropolitan*)	413	420	39	51	140	120	15	11	156	148
SOUTH-EASTERN COUNTIES	3927	3598	675	621	1627	1346	162	155	604	457
Surrey (*Extra-metropolitan*)	402	397	67	77	146	135	20	20	42	20
Kent (*Extra-metropolitan*)	1062	990	169	152	371	326	40	33	251	202
Sussex	547	498	101	89	218	170	35	29	59	50
Hampshire	1315	1218	206	205	603	502	45	52	211	151
Berkshire	601	495	132	98	289	204	22	21	41	34
SOUTH-MIDLAND COUNTIES	2380	1965	418	385	884	673	106	80	191	123
Middlesex (*Ex.-metropolitan*)	332	296	48	54	125	104	16	16	52	34
Hertfordshire	242	190	37	24	77	77	17	7	21	13
Buckinghamshire	311	222	56	41	128	79	11	5	23	6
Oxfordshire	619	480	138	102	270	190	25	27	23	19
Northamptonshire	406	320	69	71	117	85	12	18	28	28
Huntingdonshire	71	66	13	8	18	12	4	1	8	2
Bedfordshire	179	149	21	30	68	59	5	5	14	7
Cambridgeshire	221	200	36	35	81	67	16	6	25	14
EASTERN COUNTIES	1576	1271	223	203	581	451	67	43	200	137
Essex	611	513	80	80	230	194	30	17	73	64
Suffolk	424	373	65	64	150	134	14	12	62	31
Norfolk	541	385	78	59	201	123	23	14	65	42
SOUTH-WESTERN COUNTIES	32844	25358	8087	5981	21384	16519	563	419	868	697
Wiltshire	4097	2581	1481	890	2185	1381	81	44	82	53
Dorsetshire	1497	1109	345	226	887	560	37	37	54	47
Devonshire	8919	7097	1442	1116	6458	5068	166	123	567	308
Cornwall	3948	3706	362	336	2860	2759	115	81	154	121
Somersetshire	14383	10865	4457	3413	8994	6651	174	134	211	168
WEST-MIDLAND COUNTIES	29854	27141	9597	8480	9237	7644	495	424	451	407
Gloucestershire	11818	10308	4994	4427	5696	4866	197	151	215	191
Herefordshire	6526	6559	2904	2580	1503	1068	80	68	44	64
Shropshire	5795	5767	389	337	393	302	51	61	35	23
Staffordshire	2895	2697	478	485	644	592	77	74	67	44
Worcestershire	1476	1313	446	379	472	400	45	33	32	37
Warwickshire	1542	1497	294	272	523	416	45	37	58	48
NORTH-MIDLAND COUNTIES	1807	1537	283	251	505	412	62	50	137	57
Leicestershire	509	427	61	62	108	91	13	10	42	18
Rutlandshire	45	38	10	14	17	5	1	3	4	1
Lincolnshire	436	362	66	67	159	111	14	13	47	25
Nottinghamshire	329	271	61	47	84	90	16	10	27	7
Derbyshire	488	439	85	61	137	115	18	14	17	6
NORTH-WESTERN COUNTIES	10541	10527	507	435	1351	1043	161	106	236	173
Cheshire	3354	3216	114	107	247	170	35	21	49	37
Lancashire	7187	7311	393	328	1104	873	126	85	187	136
YORKSHIRE	1972	1685	315	233	719	589	61	41	82	61
NORTHERN COUNTIES	2031	1639	373	242	949	772	62	37	111	46
Durham	940	767	187	130	473	397	23	12	26	12
Northumberland	484	427	90	63	256	231	18	10	26	16
Cumberland	487	382	67	37	183	120	19	13	59	16
Westmorland	120	83	29	12	37	24	2	2	-	2
MONMOUTHSHIRE AND WALES	671425	690288	82454	82325	211429	210269	57318	63211	38835	45085
Monmouthshire	81825	82361	69327	69976	10323	10137	335	325	119	138
Glamorganshire	172720	177237	4772	4810	162900	167789	2366	2486	597	662
Carmarthenshire	69612	74199	1127	1003	14304	13297	50651	55887	1303	1597
Pembrokeshire	47736	52894	895	869	8275	7023	1828	2041	33833	41841
Cardiganshire	38070	43356	979	702	5124	3848	1517	1871	590	396
Brecknockshire	30204	29952	3860	3774	5804	6235	334	363	55	53
Radnorshire	12795	11766	784	565	973	643	22	42	14	15
Montgomeryshire	32462	31145	282	238	1522	986	52	31	37	26
Flintshire	33814	32618	86	50	232	155	24	14	35	14
Denbighshire	49810	48154	66	52	265	166	42	30	25	14
Merionethshire	23510	23864	43	28	293	161	24	16	24	6
Carnarvonshire	50668	53407	80	57	293	198	33	30	83	22
Anglesey	26321	27482	31	25	203	130	16	12	49	13
Wales (*County not stated*)	2078	1913	182	176	918	757	67	63	71	88
ENGLAND (*County not stated*)	665	404	255	142	298	183	7	6	15	5
OTHER PARTS OF BRITISH EMPIRE	18016	13449	3595	2736	8913	6377	382	321	1039	622
Islands in the British Seas	497	442	86	64	362	205	10	7	29	22
SCOTLAND	3278	2162	481	246	1309	710	148	91	200	105
IRELAND	13095	9777	2930	2282	6832	5126	196	166	669	322
British Colonies or Dependencies	1146	1068	148	148	510	336	28	57	141	173
FOREIGN COUNTRIES	4562	1793	750	251	2859	822	70	63	109	56
British Subjects	1109	914	161	144	588	365	29	26	31	28
Foreigners	3453	879	589	107	2271	457	41	37	78	28
AT SEA	66	76	19	12	24	29	-	4	3	6
British Subjects	65	76	19	12	23	29	-	4	3	6
Foreigners	1	-	-	-	1	-	-	-	-	-

roper, and not the Registration Counties are referred to in this Table.

Table 11 *continued.*—Birth-places of Males and Females enumerated in Counties, and in each Urban Sanitary District of which the Population exceeds 50,000 Persons.

Where Born.	Where enumerated.											
	Counties.											
	Cardigan-shire.		Breck-nock-shire.		Radnor-shire.		Mont-gomery-shire.		Flint-shire.		Den-bigh-shire.	
	Males.	Females.	Males.	Fe-males.	Males.	Fe-males.	Males.	Fe-males.	Males.	Fe-males.	Males.	Fe-males.
TOTAL OF INHABITANTS	31575	38695	28861	28885	11939	11589	33004	32714	40409	40178	56428	55312
LONDON	159	187	180	171	60	162	122	162	171	242	229	270
Middlesex (*Intra-metropolitan*)	141	159	143	151	50	89	103	143	141	208	196	233
Surrey (*Intra-metropolitan*)	10	18	29	14	4	7	14	11	25	26	19	23
Kent (*Intra-metropolitan*)	8	11	8	6	6	6	5	8	5	13	14	14
SOUTH-EASTERN COUNTIES	61	70	138	153	42	48	77	94	123	143	183	219
Surrey (*Extra-metropolitan*)	6	8	27	26	5	16	8	21	17	24	21	21
Kent (*Extra-metropolitan*)	14	24	31	32	15	8	20	23	34	20	37	69
Sussex	9	10	18	30	4	7	18	16	15	18	26	30
Hampshire	21	16	36	46	10	15	19	22	37	44	54	72
Berkshire	11	12	27	18	8	5	12	12	20	30	25	27
SOUTH-MIDLAND COUNTIES	54	38	119	107	42	37	68	60	123	132	158	150
Middlesex (*Extra-metropolitan*)	2	9	20	13	1	2	12	9	9	11	25	17
Hertfordshire	3	2	16	16	6	6	1	6	14	13	19	14
Buckinghamshire	11	7	14	11	2	4	8	7	14	12	14	20
Oxfordshire	15	8	33	22	17	10	13	18	28	26	27	34
Northamptonshire	16	7	23	14	4	6	21	12	30	32	34	30
Huntingdonshire	1	2	2	10	4	3	2	2	8	4	8	9
Bedfordshire	2	1	7	10	2	-	9	1	7	13	18	11
Cambridgeshire	4	2	5	10	4	8	2	10	13	15	13	15
EASTERN COUNTIES	36	27	70	52	15	25	35	32	51	68	102	104
Essex	12	5	24	25	6	13	13	13	15	21	24	36
Suffolk	9	8	13	8	3	6	9	10	15	19	38	35
Norfolk	15	11	33	19	6	8	13	9	21	28	40	33
SOUTH-WESTERN COUNTIES	139	148	621	471	66	65	145	144	227	232	251	238
Wiltshire	15	14	127	81	14	15	20	16	12	14	32	29
Dorsetshire	9	3	38	25	7	9	7	12	47	41	35	27
Devonshire	29	41	121	92	12	11	41	37	60	63	78	79
Cornwall	62	68	26	33	12	9	47	38	54	58	74	84
Somersetshire	24	22	309	231	21	21	30	41	54	56	36	39
WEST-MIDLAND COUNTIES	225	311	1675	1385	1348	1319	2050	2107	1414	1597	2416	2336
Gloucestershire	48	76	319	244	45	55	54	60	65	64	89	60
Herefordshire	24	30	950	844	713	668	77	93	24	36	50	40
Shropshire	74	65	167	128	460	450	1640	1671	556	766	1070	1482
Staffordshire	34	47	71	60	44	57	147	140	451	478	490	495
Worcestershire	19	28	101	62	57	57	70	56	79	84	83	99
Warwickshire	26	42	67	40	20	34	53	87	139	187	134	140
NORTH-MIDLAND COUNTIES	24	20	62	53	22	21	73	55	153	177	166	178
Leicestershire	8	4	15	11	5	10	13	9	42	58	51	53
Rutlandshire	1	-	-	3	-	-	-	1	-	2	3	4
Lincolnshire	8	9	14	18	6	4	14	14	27	24	40	34
Nottinghamshire	7	4	11	8	6	2	20	10	17	30	29	21
Derbyshire	5	3	22	13	5	5	26	21	67	63	43	66
NORTH-WESTERN COUNTIES	119	107	115	77	45	49	346	376	2828	3068	2445	2592
Cheshire	27	18	31	22	10	12	126	133	864	942	1207	1219
Lancashire	92	89	84	55	35	37	220	243	1964	2126	1238	1373
YORKSHIRE	27	24	52	38	9	12	101	89	173	210	182	198
NORTHERN COUNTIES	20	10	39	38	7	6	48	33	151	169	112	167
Durham	9	4	26	19	2	4	14	10	91	77	47	74
Northumberland	5	1	7	7	3	2	10	3	19	32	24	35
Cumberland	4	4	5	9	2	-	18	15	29	46	31	48
Westmorland	2	1	1	3	-	-	6	5	12	11	10	13
MONMOUTHSHIRE AND WALES	30523	37581	25295	25964	10214	9835	29652	29331	33748	33118	49218	47913
Monmouthshire	61	73	1365	1442	47	65	28	35	59	59	66	37
Glamorganshire	205	227	1335	1510	62	56	80	84	96	112	81	67
Carmarthenshire	761	893	1049	1256	50	48	35	41	46	31	58	52
Pembrokeshire	513	678	169	200	9	27	30	22	28	39	26	27
Cardiganshire	28151	34352	385	368	35	61	341	435	93	41	124	84
Brecknockshire	78	64	19526	19801	463	620	39	55	10	14	36	30
Radnorshire	38	46	1141	1167	9259	8793	407	458	15	14	26	34
Montgomeryshire	317	288	160	134	248	222	27415	28896	168	225	881	855
Flintshire	40	31	28	13	4	8	99	74	29567	28116	2845	2793
Denbighshire	52	33	26	15	16	11	462	477	2961	3497	42151	40489
Merionethshire	139	135	29	20	9	7	587	626	156	226	1371	1664
Carnarvonshire	69	57	36	12	3	3	83	72	366	487	1134	1313
Anglesey	33	25	11	10	2	-	36	21	180	235	266	305
Wales (*County not stated*)	86	70	36	27	23	19	60	49	74	79	163	163
ENGLAND (*County not stated*)	4	4	14	7	4	3	5	3	15	16	13	13
OTHER PARTS OF BRITISH EMPIRE	142	117	439	331	57	46	252	195	1053	914	870	825
Islands in the British Seas	3	8	4	4	-	-	5	5	16	28	9	22
SCOTLAND	55	54	116	87	22	21	113	77	161	202	266	284
IRELAND	65	38	263	181	28	19	117	82	788	608	528	445
British Colonies or Dependencies	19	17	56	59	7	6	17	31	80	70	67	74
FOREIGN COUNTRIES	40	47	41	35	8	21	28	33	177	88	78	104
British Subjects	17	29	17	13	5	13	15	18	36	44	47	62
Foreigners	23	18	24	22	3	8	13	15	141	44	31	42
AT SEA	2	4	1	3	-	-	2	-	2	4	5	5
British Subjects	2	4	1	3	-	-	2	-	2	4	5	5
Foreigners	-	-	-	-	-	-	-	-	-	-	-	-

Table 11 *continued.*—BIRTH-PLACES of MALES and FEMALES enumerated in COUNTIES, and in each URBAN SANITARY DISTRICT of which the POPULATION EXCEEDS 50,000 PERSONS.

WHERE BORN.	WHERE ENUMERATED.											
	COUNTIES.						URBAN SANITARY DISTRICTS.					
	MERIONETH-SHIRE.		CARNARVON-SHIRE.		ANGLESEY.		CARDIFF.		YSTRADYFODWG.		SWANSEA.	
	Males.	Females.	Males.	Females.	Males.	Females.	Males.	Females.	Males.	Females.	Males.	Females.
TOTAL OF INHABITANTS	26269	25769	58735	60614	25103	26313	42316	40445	30877	24755	32222	33375
LONDON	66	117	215	232	163	103	766	709	70	48	397	390
MIDDLESEX (*Intra-metropolitan*)	55	102	182	195	150	85	623	587	52	40	321	320
SURREY (*Intra-metropolitan*)	11	9	24	19	5	10	81	81	11	6	43	45
KENT (*Intra-metropolitan*)	.	6	9	18	8	8	62	54	7	2	33	25
SOUTH-EASTERN COUNTIES	41	45	116	163	78	84	681	546	70	47	277	254
SURREY (*Extra-metropolitan*)	4	7	11	15	8	13	48	51	5	4	31	29
KENT (*Extra-metropolitan*)	8	8	43	50	19	34	157	123	13	10	94	74
SUSSEX	9	14	16	16	19	12	98	59	6	.	46	47
HAMPSHIRE	10	11	38	61	28	21	292	239	31	26	72	71
BERKSHIRE	10	5	10	21	4	4	86	74	15	7	34	33
SOUTH-MIDLAND COUNTIES	60	34	99	130	58	36	263	223	56	18	179	142
MIDDLESEX (*Extra-metropolitan*)	11	5	9	18	2	5	49	41	8	.	19	23
HERTFORDSHIRE	4	3	11	12	15	6	31	28	5	4	16	14
BUCKINGHAMSHIRE	2	3	23	23	5	4	36	25	15	4	25	17
OXFORDSHIRE	10	4	13	19	7	5	77	65	12	4	50	36
NORTHAMPTONSHIRE	18	12	19	35	14	7	29	28	4	2	25	23
HUNTINGDONSHIRE	4	1	2	6	.	.	1	5	.	.	6	3
BEDFORDSHIRE	7	3	10	7	9	2	12	12	11	4	19	14
CAMBRIDGESHIRE	4	3	12	10	6	7	28	21	6	.	19	12
EASTERN COUNTIES	30	33	99	61	67	35	211	162	15	12	131	79
ESSEX	11	10	46	12	47	20	75	65	3	4	66	42
SUFFOLK	9	14	27	23	10	9	52	43	8	8	23	21
NORFOLK	10	9	26	26	10	6	84	54	4	.	42	16
SOUTH-WESTERN COUNTIES	97	91	266	262	130	91	6728	5951	1961	1074	3346	2908
WILTSHIRE	14	9	19	33	15	2	646	527	254	99	144	117
DORSETSHIRE	12	5	13	15	5	2	294	281	104	60	85	60
DEVONSHIRE	38	33	74	74	48	45	2009	1732	312	157	1681	1488
CORNWALL	10	15	125	91	47	31	573	634	234	195	694	625
SOMERSETSHIRE	23	29	35	49	15	11	3206	2777	1057	563	742	618
WEST-MIDLAND COUNTIES	317	301	493	701	136	129	3124	2924	865	530	1220	1172
GLOUCESTERSHIRE	28	25	60	72	8	11	2357	2186	574	338	737	753
HEREFORDSHIRE	35	13	24	40	10	14	270	251	142	83	109	123
SHROPSHIRE	145	164	151	232	40	40	69	72	37	22	67	52
STAFFORDSHIRE	46	33	120	163	26	24	134	153	61	49	115	89
WORCESTERSHIRE	28	31	33	44	11	12	121	124	32	19	68	66
WARWICKSHIRE	35	35	105	150	41	28	173	138	19	19	124	89
NORTH-MIDLAND COUNTIES	64	39	215	197	41	27	151	125	25	15	118	100
LEICESTERSHIRE	19	12	134	87	3	7	35	29	2	3	31	28
RUTLANDSHIRE	5	3	4	1	.	1	5	.	.	.	6	3
LINCOLNSHIRE	12	5	21	30	8	8	57	39	9	2	22	23
NOTTINGHAMSHIRE	9	6	25	34	17	2	22	20	5	4	18	23
DERBYSHIRE	19	13	31	45	13	9	32	37	9	6	41	29
NORTH-WESTERN COUNTIES	287	307	1314	1508	787	686	484	403	73	35	313	225
CHESHIRE	101	87	350	341	193	109	86	66	11	5	56	36
LANCASHIRE	186	220	964	1167	594	577	398	337	62	30	257	189
YORKSHIRE	50	45	161	157	40	38	303	197	45	19	96	100
NORTHERN COUNTIES	26	25	79	76	54	18	431	312	30	34	137	111
DURHAM	9	7	23	21	10	.	212	150	21	25	70	53
NORTHUMBERLAND	4	6	9	19	13	9	139	117	2	3	34	38
CUMBERLAND	11	9	33	30	26	15	70	41	6	4	29	18
WESTMORLAND	2	3	14	6	5	1	10	4	1	2	4	2
MONMOUTHSHIRE AND WALES	24920	24542	54797	56364	23022	24750	24084	26026	27306	22730	24020	26713
MONMOUTHSHIRE	40	28	47	43	19	11	1919	2368	2234	1818	458	506
GLAMORGANSHIRE	85	64	118	88	53	22	19910	21334	17194	15973	19829	22191
CARMARTHENSHIRE	61	41	46	59	21	15	440	443	2468	1582	1594	1958
PEMBROKESHIRE	18	28	79	61	33	39	870	961	1229	819	1222	1294
CARDIGANSHIRE	439	404	225	144	67	23	422	320	1712	972	355	309
BRECKNOCKSHIRE	25	18	30	19	5	6	206	288	1215	873	201	235
RADNORSHIRE	8	5	8	13	3	2	46	59	200	112	44	27
MONTGOMERYSHIRE	1101	979	244	223	25	42	45	39	687	401	42	22
FLINTSHIRE	197	122	578	524	139	109	21	15	30	13	60	45
DENBIGHSHIRE	1549	1289	2039	1913	156	173	31	23	47	17	26	26
MERIONETHSHIRE	19659	19408	1148	1266	84	105	15	7	90	41	13	6
CARNARVONSHIRE	1332	1806	46173	48145	998	1255	48	35	56	30	24	22
ANGLESEY	382	243	3741	3864	21391	22689	22	23	41	16	18	22
WALES (*County not stated*)	44	51	321	332	53	49	89	112	103	63	64	50
ENGLAND (*County not stated*)	8	3	20	15	7	4	113	92	39	21	27	17
OTHER PARTS OF BRITISH EMPIRE	178	123	650	580	446	262	3166	2519	246	120	1437	961
ISLANDS in the BRITISH SEAS	4	11	18	30	51	46	156	120	5	4	35	23
SCOTLAND	64	48	261	182	102	49	538	248	37	17	258	133
IRELAND	95	41	313	308	273	153	2211	2048	182	80	1084	740
BRITISH COLONIES OR DEPENDENCIES	15	23	58	60	20	14	261	103	22	19	60	60
FOREIGN COUNTRIES	125	60	207	166	70	47	1797	253	74	52	521	196
British Subjects	14	22	120	112	29	38	181	96	42	28	205	113
Foreigners	111	38	87	54	41	9	1616	157	32	24	316	83
AT SEA	.	4	4	2	4	3	14	10	2	.	3	7
British Subjects	.	4	4	2	4	3	14	10	2	.	2	7
Foreigners	.	.	.	.	.	.	.	.	.	.	1	.

Table 12.—Distribution of the enumerated Natives of Counties.

Where enumerated.	Where born.									
	Monmouthshire and Wales.		Monmouthshire.		Glamorganshire.		Carmarthenshire.		Pembrokeshire.	
	Males.	Females.	Males.	Females.	Males.	Females.	Males.	Females.	Males.	Females.
TOTAL ENUMERATED NATIVES OF EACH COUNTY	763286	804928	95259	99186	184069	191084	72271	76964	53009	59229
LONDON	11829	16216	1736	2762	1869	2427	818	784	1246	1586
Middlesex (*Intra-metropolitan*)	8500	11962	1187	2008	1308	1760	612	581	885	1129
Surrey (*Intra-metropolitan*)	2656	3278	427	594	425	513	169	163	234	295
Kent (*Intra-metropolitan*)	673	986	122	160	136	154	37	40	127	162
SOUTH-EASTERN COUNTIES	4835	5696	853	990	933	969	243	253	980	1019
Surrey (*Extra-metropolitan*)	868	1389	184	259	182	231	48	65	89	144
Kent (*Extra-metropolitan*)	1334	1348	184	183	211	220	56	58	411	359
Sussex	663	1105	128	205	123	192	43	65	67	124
Hampshire	1495	1363	255	252	311	228	72	46	325	337
Berkshire	475	491	102	91	106	98	24	19	90	55
SOUTH-MIDLAND COUNTIES	2059	2782	354	535	367	439	133	131	186	286
Middlesex (*Ex.-metropolitan*)	854	1304	155	264	166	211	56	67	74	142
Hertfordshire	196	281	30	48	30	35	10	10	24	35
Buckinghamshire	216	244	38	35	27	84	18	15	20	21
Oxfordshire	257	339	48	70	51	71	7	9	16	27
Northamptonshire	309	283	45	52	57	36	26	13	28	26
Huntingdonshire	22	42	3	16	2	10	1	4	3	7
Bedfordshire	105	163	19	23	14	22	8	8	12	18
Cambridgeshire	100	105	16	18	21	20	7	4	9	11
EASTERN COUNTIES	1219	1303	216	230	275	267	59	59	169	180
Essex	873	890	168	179	190	189	48	40	108	105
Suffolk	160	210	23	22	45	35	6	11	19	23
Norfolk	186	203	25	29	40	43	5	8	42	42
SOUTH-WESTERN COUNTIES	6151	6823	1685	2067	1910	2099	268	253	632	773
Wiltshire	888	1001	366	429	253	250	24	34	53	64
Dorsetshire	335	331	75	74	93	83	23	17	35	53
Devonshire	1701	1677	312	292	537	539	77	79	261	306
Cornwall	881	485	81	67	188	154	66	24	134	63
Somersetshire	2346	3329	851	1205	839	1073	78	118	149	287
WEST-MIDLAND COUNTIES	24194	28935	5206	6750	2472	3286	549	673	701	1025
Gloucestershire	5201	7866	2423	3623	1347	1363	252	362	258	650
Herefordshire	4022	4984	1162	1475	182	248	60	64	60	63
Shropshire	6766	7668	147	168	99	107	34	92	55	61
Staffordshire	4512	4175	619	570	325	365	70	73	80	96
Worcestershire	1336	1520	353	376	192	205	52	57	40	59
Warwickshire	2357	2772	505	538	327	398	81	75	99	96
NORTH-MIDLAND COUNTIES	1729	1948	325	317	349	349	71	78	100	134
Leicestershire	347	423	64	64	72	84	11	15	23	38
Rutlandshire	18	29	2	4	3	4		1	2	1
Lincolnshire	295	273	51	46	70	49	15	13	26	25
Nottinghamshire	397	421	83	74	86	89	16	20	25	19
Derbyshire	672	803	125	129	118	123	29	29	24	51
NORTH-WESTERN COUNTIES	29991	41777	1241	1533	1299	1640	358	329	881	947
Cheshire	6972	10499	170	208	185	257	78	80	150	169
Lancashire	23019	31278	1071	1325	1114	1383	280	249	731	778
YORKSHIRE	4821	5123	983	913	856	805	135	106	285	247
NORTHERN COUNTIES	5033	4037	855	728	1019	866	125	99	193	138
Durham	3810	3009	674	586	753	623	84	80	110	81
Northumberland	478	377	83	51	101	92	10	8	56	37
Cumberland	695	557	91	77	161	142	30	10	23	16
Westmorland	50	94	7	14	4	9	1	1	4	4
MONMOUTHSHIRE AND WALES	671425	690288	81825	82361	172720	177937	69512	74199	47736	52894
Monmouthshire	82454	82325	69327	69076	4772	4810	1127	1003	895	869
Glamorganshire	211429	210269	10323	10137	162900	167739	14804	13297	8275	7023
Carmarthenshire	57318	63211	385	329	2366	2486	50651	55887	1828	2041
Pembrokeshire	38835	43085	119	138	597	662	1303	1597	35833	41841
Cardiganshire	30623	37581	61	73	205	227	761	893	513	678
Brecknockshire	26296	25964	1365	1442	1335	1510	1049	1255	169	200
Radnorshire	10214	9835	47	63	52	56	50	48	9	27
Montgomeryshire	23652	23331	28	35	80	94	35	41	30	21
Flintshire	33748	33118	58	53	96	112	48	31	38	39
Denbighshire	49218	47913	56	37	81	67	58	82	26	27
Merionethshire	24920	24542	40	26	85	64	61	41	18	28
Carnarvonshire	54797	56304	47	43	118	88	66	39	79	61
Anglesey	23022	24750	19	11	33	22	31	15	33	39

Table 12 *continued*.—DISTRIBUTION of the enumerated NATIVES of COUNTIES.

WHERE ENUMERATED.	WHERE BORN.									
	CARDIGAN-SHIRE.		BRECK-NOCK-SHIRE.		RADNOR-SHIRE.		MONT-GOMERY-SHIRE.		FLINT-SHIRE.	
	Males.	Females.	Males.	Females.	Males.	Females.	Males.	Females.	Males.	Females.
TOTAL ENUMERATED NATIVES OF EACH COUNTY	41007	46056	32846	33351	16878	16916	40349	41479	43893	44602
LONDON	1176	1176	487	713	270	388	629	1022	373	373
MIDDLESEX (*Intra-metropolitan*)	907	891	355	550	193	282	454	809	255	270
SURREY (*Intra-metropolitan*)	235	247	108	122	67	91	146	171	100	83
KENT (*Intra-metropolitan*)	34	38	24	41	10	15	29	42	18	20
SOUTH-EASTERN COUNTIES	165	137	201	259	77	130	194	306	185	179
SURREY (*Extra-metropolitan*)	33	37	43	70	17	37	45	100	30	57
KENT (*Extra-metropolitan*)	48	30	49	56	9	23	48	64	48	35
SUSSEX	23	28	27	57	20	33	46	64	34	33
HAMPSHIRE	52	32	54	43	17	18	33	46	61	34
BERKSHIRE	25	9	28	23	14	19	22	32	12	20
SOUTH-MIDLAND COUNTIES	98	95	108	158	67	87	110	210	87	114
MIDDLESEX (*Ex.-metropolitan*)	43	52	40	66	20	29	46	85	44	34
HERTFORDSHIRE	9	8	17	15	11	19	12	31	10	10
BUCKINGHAMSHIRE	3	8	11	11	6	6	9	17	7	14
OXFORDSHIRE	17	8	22	25	19	11	13	24	4	16
NORTHAMPTONSHIRE	10	6	12	24	8	17	20	26	13	15
HUNTINGDONSHIRE	.	.	1	2	.	1	3	1	2	.
BEDFORDSHIRE	10	7	1	8	1	1	4	15	5	14
CAMBRIDGESHIRE	6	6	4	7	2	3	3	12	2	2
EASTERN COUNTIES	59	29	55	49	13	33	43	51	43	41
ESSEX	35	24	42	30	8	21	35	29	25	22
SUFFOLK	10	3	10	16	1	3	3	16	10	10
NORFOLK	14	2	3	3	4	9	5	6	8	9
SOUTH-WESTERN COUNTIES	210	96	169	200	67	84	86	91	107	85
WILTSHIRE	8	5	40	43	15	15	20	20	11	10
DORSETSHIRE	11	9	11	7	10	11	18	13	8	13
DEVONSHIRE	53	29	38	40	17	22	20	27	39	24
CORNWALL	81	12	7	9	5	1	7	6	34	13
SOMERSETSHIRE	57	41	73	101	20	35	21	25	15	25
WEST-MIDLAND COUNTIES	364	341	981	1340	3325	3868	4599	5167	1611	1549
GLOUCESTERSHIRE	95	99	214	312	78	144	63	98	20	47
HEREFORDSHIRE	34	37	386	620	1933	2179	107	123	14	11
SHROPSHIRE	69	64	83	90	789	888	3330	3720	601	669
STAFFORDSHIRE	57	38	88	64	253	254	732	744	744	611
WORCESTERSHIRE	22	26	90	98	142	197	110	125	57	63
WARWICKSHIRE	87	79	120	156	130	206	257	357	175	148
NORTH-MIDLAND COUNTIES	30	40	70	82	41	55	125	171	138	157
LEICESTERSHIRE	6	7	11	18	12	19	29	39	12	20
RUTLANDSHIRE	1	1	.	2	.	.	5	7	2	1
LINCOLNSHIRE	7	18	7	6	1	6	9	13	19	20
NOTTINGHAMSHIRE	5	6	14	12	10	8	26	38	31	30
DERBYSHIRE	11	8	38	44	18	22	56	74	74	86
NORTH-WESTERN COUNTIES	638	643	238	304	220	384	1865	2943	6628	9247
CHESHIRE	102	107	31	45	48	73	466	753	2245	3502
LANCASHIRE	536	536	207	259	172	311	1399	2190	4383	5745
YORKSHIRE	104	73	185	166	63	93	186	319	314	397
NORTHERN COUNTIES	93	30	148	128	30	28	60	54	593	442
DURHAM	48	23	117	99	20	18	33	25	481	352
NORTHUMBERLAND	19	3	13	12	3	2	7	11	37	25
CUMBERLAND	24	2	17	17	5	3	17	13	68	51
WESTMORLAND	2	2	1	.	2	5	3	5	7	14
MONMOUTHSHIRE AND WALES	38070	43396	30204	29952	12705	11766	32452	31145	33814	32018
MONMOUTHSHIRE	979	702	3800	3774	784	565	282	238	86	50
GLAMORGANSHIRE	5124	3642	5804	6239	978	643	1522	986	232	155
CARMARTHENSHIRE	1517	1871	354	363	29	42	52	31	24	14
PEMBROKESHIRE	590	596	55	53	14	15	37	26	35	14
CARDIGANSHIRE	28151	34962	78	64	38	45	317	288	40	51
BRECKNOCKSHIRE	365	368	19625	19801	1141	1157	160	134	28	13
RADNOCKSHIRE	35	61	463	320	9259	8793	248	222	4	3
MONTGOMERYSHIRE	341	438	39	55	407	458	27415	26896	99	74
FLINTSHIRE	93	41	10	14	15	14	103	226	29507	28116
DENBIGHSHIRE	124	84	36	30	26	34	861	855	2845	2798
MERIONETHSHIRE	439	464	25	18	8	5	1101	979	197	122
CARNARVONSHIRE	225	144	30	19	8	13	244	223	578	524
ANGLESEY	67	23	5	6	3	2	25	42	139	109

Table 12 *continued*.—DISTRIBUTION of the enumerated NATIVES of COUNTIES.

WHERE ENUMERATED.	WHERE BORN.									
	DENBIGH-SHIRE.		MERIONETH-SHIRE.		CARNARVONSHIRE.		ANGLESEY.		WALES. (County not stated.)	
	Males.	Females.	Males.	Females.	Males.	Females.	Males.	Females.	Males.	Females.
TOTAL ENUMERATED NATIVES OF EACH COUNTY	59943	61043	25227	25898	54628	58613	29842	31880	14065	18627
LONDON	508	604	221	337	354	430	186	250	1954	3364
Middlesex (*Intra-metropolitan*)	381	439	169	263	263	315	133	192	1398	2463
Surrey (*Intra-metropolitan*)	110	135	48	62	74	85	43	41	470	676
Kent (*Intra-metropolitan*)	17	30	4	12	17	30	12	17	86	225
SOUTH-EASTERN COUNTIES	190	225	74	76	154	192	81	99	555	862
Surrey (*Extra-metropolitan*)	52	67	20	26	32	67	8	21	98	202
Kent (*Extra-metropolitan*)	41	38	31	18	44	41	28	28	134	196
Sussex	19	37	5	14	19	42	12	15	97	195
Hampshire	58	51	16	10	49	28	31	30	161	208
Berkshire	20	32	2	8	10	14	4	5	67	61
SOUTH-MIDLAND COUNTIES	123	142	38	51	75	100	39	39	274	395
Middlesex (*Ex-metropolitan*)	38	50	19	25	24	46	10	15	120	217
Hertfordshire	8	15	3	4	4	12	1	4	27	36
Buckinghamshire	26	23	6	4	8	8	8	4	29	44
Oxfordshire	16	11	6	4	13	13	4	7	21	34
Northamptonshire	16	21	1	8	9	17	10	3	54	31
Huntingdonshire	.	.	.	2	2	.	1	1	4	5
Bedfordshire	13	18	1	2	4	2	3	1	10	17
Cambridgeshire	6	4	2	2	11	2	2	3	9	11
EASTERN COUNTIES	45	49	20	16	59	46	31	30	132	223
Essex	30	28	11	12	47	29	27	22	90	160
Suffolk	8	8	2	4	3	12	3	6	17	31
Norfolk	7	13	7	.	9	5	1	2	10	32
SOUTH-WESTERN COUNTIES	110	106	59	29	177	67	118	49	553	824
Wiltshire	17	22	3	6	5	3	4	4	69	106
Dorsetshire	8	8	2	3	5	1	2	1	34	38
Devonshire	54	33	15	6	50	26	49	28	179	235
Cornwall	13	13	25	4	101	8	50	11	89	100
Somersetshire	18	30	14	10	16	29	13	5	182	345
WEST-MIDLAND COUNTIES	2130	2325	277	293	301	351	131	135	1547	1832
Gloucestershire	49	79	10	16	37	43	13	17	243	414
Herefordshire	24	22	8	13	10	5	2	6	40	68
Shropshire	1198	1309	155	171	78	97	24	22	124	170
Staffordshire	625	532	50	42	83	88	53	50	728	649
Worcestershire	73	78	13	18	23	24	8	4	152	190
Warwickshire	161	215	41	34	65	93	32	36	260	341
NORTH-MIDLAND COUNTIES	113	135	28	28	65	60	40	41	234	301
Leicestershire	22	27	11	10	18	20	3	2	54	60
Rutlandshire	2	3	.	1	.	.	1	1	.	3
Lincolnshire	14	14	5	3	18	7	12	14	41	39
Nottinghamshire	33	19	4	4	5	6	3	9	55	87
Derbyshire	42	72	8	10	24	27	21	15	84	112
NORTH-WESTERN COUNTIES	6171	8623	926	1324	2530	3697	2714	3578	4282	6585
Cheshire	1737	2649	224	314	459	797	442	645	635	990
Lancashire	4434	5974	702	1010	2071	2900	2272	2933	3647	5595
YORKSHIRE	403	415	41	55	121	187	60	94	1135	1253
NORTHERN COUNTIES	340	265	33	25	124	76	119	83	1321	1075
Durham	276	194	22	16	55	33	44	34	1093	845
Northumberland	23	22	7	2	36	12	22	6	81	94
Cumberland	36	32	4	4	30	25	51	42	138	123
Westmorland	5	17	.	3	3	6	2	1	9	13
MONMOUTHSHIRE AND WALES	49810	48154	23510	23664	50668	53407	26321	27482	2078	1913
Monmouthshire	66	52	43	28	80	57	31	25	182	176
Glamorganshire	265	166	293	161	293	198	203	130	918	757
Carmarthenshire	42	30	24	16	33	30	16	12	67	63
Pembrokeshire	26	14	24	6	83	22	49	13	71	88
Cardiganshire	52	33	139	135	69	57	33	25	66	70
Brecknockshire	26	15	29	20	36	12	11	10	36	27
Radnorshire	16	11	3	7	3	3	2	.	23	19
Montgomeryshire	462	472	537	625	83	72	96	21	60	40
Flintshire	2961	3497	166	225	368	487	180	235	74	79
Denbighshire	42151	40489	1371	1664	1134	1313	266	305	163	163
Merionethshire	1549	1289	19669	19406	1332	1806	362	248	44	51
Carnarvonshire	2039	1913	1148	1266	46173	48145	3741	3664	321	322
Anglesey	156	173	84	105	993	1265	21391	22699	53	49

Table 14.—NUMBER and AGES of MALES and FEMALES returned as BLIND or BLIND FROM BIRTH in the WELSH DIVISION and its REGISTRATION COUNTIES.

REGISTRATION COUNTY.	ALL AGES. Both Sexes.	ALL AGES. Males and Females.	0–	5–	15–	20–	25–	45–	65 and upwards.
XI. MONMOUTHSHIRE AND WALES.	1597	M. 927 F. 670	15 6	41 39	20 22	32 20	168 83	266 135	385 365
42 MONMOUTHSHIRE	254	M. 155 F. 99	1 2	4 6	2 3	4 3	27 14	49 27	68 44
43 SOUTH WALES	884	M. 488 F. 396	9 3	27 20	15 12	19 12	94 48	132 81	192 220
44 NORTH WALES	459	M. 284 F. 175	5 1	10 13	3 7	9 5	47 21	85 27	125 101

Table 15.—NUMBER and AGES of MALES and FEMALES returned as BLIND in the WELSH DIVISION and its REGISTRATION COUNTIES.

REGISTRATION COUNTY.	ALL AGES. Both Sexes.	ALL AGES. Males and Females.	0–	5–	15–	20–	25–	45–	65 and upwards.
XI. MONMOUTHSHIRE AND WALES.	1515	M. 888 F. 627	10 3	32 24	13 18	30 15	158 76	260 129	385 362
42 MONMOUTHSHIRE	242	M. 151 F. 91	1 .	3 2	. 2	3 2	27 14	49 27	68 44
43 SOUTH WALES	847	M. 469 F. 378	8 2	23 15	11 10	19 9	89 46	127 77	192 219
44 NORTH WALES	436	M. 268 F. 158	1 1	6 7	2 6	8 4	42 16	84 25	125 99

Table 16.—NUMBER and AGES of MALES and FEMALES returned as BLIND FROM BIRTH in the WELSH DIVISION and its REGISTRATION COUNTIES.

REGISTRATION COUNTY.	ALL AGES. Both Sexes.	ALL AGES. Males and Females.	0–	5–	15–	20–	25–	45–	65 and upwards.
XI. MONMOUTHSHIRE AND WALES.	82	M. 39 F. 43	5 3	9 15	7 4	2 5	10 7	6 6	. 3
42 MONMOUTHSHIRE	12	M. 4 F. 8	. 2	1 4	2 1	1 1	. .	. .	. .
43 SOUTH WALES	37	M. 19 F. 18	1 1	4 5	4 2	. 3	5 2	5 4	. 1
44 NORTH WALES	33	M. 16 F. 17	4 .	4 6	1 1	1 1	5 5	1 2	. 2

Table 17.—NUMBER and AGES of MALES and FEMALES returned as DEAF AND DUMB in the WELSH DIVISION and its REGISTRATION COUNTIES.

REGISTRATION COUNTY.	ALL AGES. Both Sexes.	ALL AGES. Males and Females.	0–	5–	15–	20–	25–	45–	65 and upwards.
XI. MONMOUTHSHIRE AND WALES.	834	M. 449 F. 385	23 16	103 94	65 44	37 44	116 107	84 58	21 21
42 MONMOUTHSHIRE	98	M. 48 F. 50	4 3	13 11	8 3	2 8	13 16	7 8	1 1
43 SOUTH WALES	493	M. 259 F. 234	8 10	71 63	40 31	25 23	61 58	42 38	13 12
44 NORTH WALES	243	M. 142 F. 101	11 3	19 21	17 10	10 13	42 33	35 13	8 8

Table 18.—Number and Ages of Males and Females returned as Idiots or Imbeciles, and Lunatics in the Welsh Division and its Registration Counties.

Registration County.	All Ages.		0–	5–	15–	20–	25–	45–	65 and upwards.
	Both Sexes.	Males and Females.							
XI. MONMOUTHSHIRE AND WALES.	4294	M. 2081	11	135	149	172	851	566	197
		F. 2213	12	104	114	126	820	728	309
42 MONMOUTHSHIRE	829	M. 408	3	18	21	33	162	120	51
		F. 421	4	24	20	20	147	139	67
43 SOUTH WALES	2261	M. 1096	6	76	78	96	453	301	86
		F. 1165	5	58	64	67	426	396	149
44 NORTH WALES	1204	M. 577	2	41	50	43	236	145	60
		F. 627	3	22	30	39	247	193	93

Table 19.—Number and Ages of Males and Females returned as Idiots or Imbeciles in the Welsh Division and its Registration Counties.

Registration County.	All Ages.		0–	5–	15–	20–	25–	45–	65 and upwards.
	Both Sexes.	Males and Females.							
XI. MONMOUTHSHIRE AND WALES.	2030	M. 1019	10	128	132	105	356	200	88
		F. 1011	10	94	92	85	371	235	124
42 MONMOUTHSHIRE	296	M. 143	3	17	17	17	53	27	9
		F. 153	4	20	18	14	54	31	12
43 SOUTH WALES	987	M. 494	5	71	71	54	163	93	37
		F. 493	4	55	48	41	161	122	62
44 NORTH WALES	747	M. 382	2	40	44	34	140	80	42
		F. 365	2	19	26	30	156	82	50

Table 20.—Number and Ages of Males and Females returned as Lunatics in the Welsh Division and its Registration Counties.

Registration County.	All Ages.		0–	5–	15–	20–	25–	45–	65 and upwards.
	Both Sexes.	Males and Females.							
XI. MONMOUTHSHIRE AND WALES.	2264	M. 1062	1	7	17	67	495	366	109
		F. 1202	2	10	22	41	449	493	185
42 MONMOUTHSHIRE	533	M. 265	.	1	4	16	109	93	42
		F. 268	.	4	2	6	93	108	55
43 SOUTH WALES	1274	M. 602	1	5	7	42	290	208	49
		F. 672	1	3	16	26	265	274	87
44 NORTH WALES	457	M. 195	.	1	6	9	96	65	18
		F. 262	1	3	4	9	91	111	43

Table 21.—NUMBER of the BLIND, of the DEAF and DUMB, of IDIOTS or IMBECILES, and of LUNATICS in the WELSH DIVISION and its REGISTRATION COUNTIES and DISTRICTS.

Registration County and District.	Blind.			Deaf and Dumb.	Mentally Deranged.		
	From Birth.	Others.	Total.		Idiots.	Lunatics.	Total.
XI. MONMOUTHSHIRE AND WALES	82	1515	1597	834	2030	2264	4294
42 MONMOUTHSHIRE	12	242	254	98	296	533	829
43 SOUTH WALES	37	847	884	403	987	1274	2261
GLAMORGANSHIRE	26	450	476	270	382	688	1070
CARMARTHENSHIRE	3	113	116	66	234	494	728
PEMBROKESHIRE	1	90	91	49	102	32	134
CARDIGANSHIRE	3	117	120	61	173	44	217
BRECKNOCKSHIRE	3	60	63	33	57	11	68
RADNORSHIRE	1	17	18	14	39	5	44
44 NORTH WALES	33	426	459	243	747	457	1204
MONTGOMERYSHIRE	3	84	87	31	105	18	123
FLINTSHIRE	7	51	58	20	40	7	47
DENBIGHSHIRE	6	94	100	61	247	370	617
MERIONETHSHIRE	7	61	68	37	111	19	130
CARNARVONSHIRE	7	106	113	59	175	34	209
ANGLESEY	3	30	33	26	69	9	78
42 MONMOUTHSHIRE.							
580 CHEPSTOW	2	18	20	9	33	1	34
581 MONMOUTH	6	42	48	20	47	12	59
582 ABERGAVENNY	1	24	25	6	77	496	573
583 BEDWELTY	1	50	51	20	39	7	46
584 PONTYPOOL	1	40	41	13	43	13	56
585 NEWPORT	1	68	69	30	57	4	61

Registration County and District.	Blind.			Deaf and Dumb.	Mentally Deranged.		
	From Birth.	Others.	Total.		Idiots.	Lunatics.	Total.
43 SOUTH WALES							
586 CARDIFF	7	89	96	62	70	7	[illegible]
587 PONTYPRIDD	5	44	49	27	46	8	[illegible]
588 MERTHYR TYDFIL	1	102	103	37	55	10	[illegible]
589 BRIDGEND	.	38	38	19	70	567	[illegible]
590 NEATH	5	52	57	22	52	70	[illegible]
591 PONTARDAWE	2	26	28	6	14	2	[illegible]
592 SWANSEA	5	88	93	82	61	13	[illegible]
593 GOWER	1	11	12	5	12	2	[illegible]
594 LLANELLY	1	29	30	22	30	8	[illegible]
595 LLANDOVERY	.	15	15	9	18	4	[illegible]
596 LLANDILOFAWR	.	19	19	18	27	13	[illegible]
597 CARMARTHEN	2	50	52	17	159	460	[illegible]
598 NARBERTH	.	23	23	17	34	10	[illegible]
599 PEMBROKE	.	26	26	10	25	5	[illegible]
600 HAVERFORDWEST	1	41	42	22	43	17	[illegible]
601 CARDIGAN	2	25	27	7	18	6	[illegible]
602 NEWCASTLE-IN-EMLYN	1	20	21	17	39	12	[illegible]
603 LAMPETER	.	13	13	4	13	5	[illegible]
604 ABERAYRON	.	20	20	14	31	9	[illegible]
605 ABERYSTWITH	.	29	29	12	46	4	[illegible]
606 TREGARON	.	16	16	7	26	8	[illegible]
607 BUILTH	1	5	6	2	16	1	[illegible]
608 BRECKNOCK	1	17	18	14	13	1	[illegible]
609 CRICKHOWELL	.	23	23	12	26	7	[illegible]
610 HAY	1	15	16	5	8	2	[illegible]
611 KNIGHTON	1	9	10	9	17	3	[illegible]
612 RHAYADER	.	8	8	5	22	2	[illegible]
44 NORTH WALES							
613 MACHYNLLETH	.	8	8	6	9	6	[illegible]
614 NEWTOWN	1	20	21	6	33	8	[illegible]
615 FORDEN	2	31	33	13	32	4	[illegible]
616 LLANFYLLIN	.	25	25	6	31	.	[illegible]
617 HOLYWELL	7	51	58	20	40	7	[illegible]
618 WREXHAM	2	39	41	31	62	1	[illegible]
619 RUTHIN	1	14	15	6	18	5	[illegible]
620 ST. ASAPH	3	31	34	15	138	363	[illegible]
621 LLANRWST	.	10	10	9	28	11	[illegible]
622 CORWEN	1	10	11	11	29	5	[illegible]
623 BALA	3	7	10	5	12	.	[illegible]
624 DOLGELLY	.	12	12	3	31	5	[illegible]
625 FESTINIOG	3	32	35	18	39	9	[illegible]
626 PWLLHELI	1	24	25	10	56	7	[illegible]
627 CARNARVON	4	43	47	21	50	6	[illegible]
628 BANGOR	1	27	28	23	38	9	[illegible]
629 CONWAY	1	12	13	3	22	12	[illegible]
630 ANGLESEY	3	30	33	26	69	9	[illegible]

INDEX TO VOLUME III.

SUMMARY TABLES.—ENGLAND AND WALES.

DIVISIONAL AND COUNTY TABLES.

LONDON: Printed by EYRE and SPOTTISWOODE,
Printers to the Queen's most Excellent Majesty.
For Her Majesty's Stationery Office.

ERRATA.

VOLUME I.

Page			Inh. Houses.	Persons.	Males.	Females.
vii	Table iv, England and Wales, 1871 -	*for* -	2,444,433	12,059,843	5,953,458	6,106,385
		read -	2,444,747	12,062,269	5,954,825	6,107,444
,,	,, England, 1871 -	*for* -	2,277,648	11,270,415	5,561,591	5,708,824
		read -	2,277,732	11,271,305	5,562,277	5,709,028
,,	,, Wales, 1871 -	*for* -	166,785	789,428	391,867	397,561
		read	167.015	790,964	392,548	398,416
viii	,, Lincolnshire, Northern Division, 1871	*for* -	26,193	117,785	58,169	59,616
		read -	26,193	118,265	58,659	59,626
,,	,, Staffordshire, Northern Division, 1871	*for* -	24,110	119,807	60,572	59,235
		read	24,194	120,217	60,788	59,429
ix	,, Carnarvonshire, 1871 - -	*for*	17,197	78,581	39,287	39,294
		read	17,418	80,102	39,957	40,145
,,	,, Radnorshire, 1871 - -	*for* -	3,439	18,495	9,620	8,875
		read -	3,448	18,510	9,631	8,879
xii	Table v, Stockton, Parliamentary Boro', 1881	*for* -	10,072	55,457	29,095	26,362
		read -	10,073	55,460	29,097	26,368

Page		Inh. Houses.	Population.		Inh. Houses.	Population.
xvii & xviii	Total of Exeter diocese, *for* - -	106,274	603,211	*read*	105,761	600,616
xvii & xxi	,, Truro diocese, *for* -	69,803	340,766	*read*	70,316	333,361

Page		Population.		Population.
xvii	,, ecclesiastical provinces of Canterbury and York, *for* - -	26,116,230	*read*	26,115,699
,,	,, province of York, *for* - - -	8,655,794	*read*	8,655,263
xvii & xxiii	,, Sodor and Man diocese, *for* - - - -	54,089	*read*	53,558

246 *Cancel* Mile End New Town, Mile End Old Town, and Ratcliff, with figures relating thereto, and *insert* the following after Staple Inn :—

	Inhabited Houses.	Families or Separate Occupiers.	Population.	Poor Law Union in which situate.
Stepney ancient parish :—				
Mile End New Town - - - -	1,273	2,254	10,673	Whitechapel, 17.
Mile End Old Town - - -	14,039	24,598	105,613	Mile End Old Town, 20
Ratcliff -	2,125	3,719	16,107	Stepney, 19.

251 & 252 The two ecclesiastical parishes under Mile End New Town, the eleven under Mile End Old Town, and the four under Ratcliff, should be arranged alphabetically under Stepney, to follow Stanwell on page 254.

370 & 371 *Cancel* Battersea (p. 370) and Penge (p. 371), and *substitute* the following :—

		Inhabited Houses.	Families or Separate Occupiers.	Population.	Poor Law Union in which situate.
370	Battersea ancient parish :—				
	Battersea - - -	14,605	23,148	107,262	Wandsworth, 25.
	Penge - - -	2,839	3,597	18,650	Croydon, 38.

372 & 376 The three ecclesiastical parishes under Penge (p. 376) should be inserted under Battersea (p. 372).

385 " Dean, West, near Chichester." " Dean, West, near Eastbourne." Transpose the figures against these two places.

387 Walberton, Warbleton. Transpose the figures and Poor Law Union names against these two places.

VOLUME II.

Page

xxi Table vii, " England and Wales "—seventh column of figures—*for* 3,362,173 *read* 3,262,173

42 Alresford, *for* 42 37*w* *read* (under area column) 42,637*w*.

Page		Area.	Houses, 1881. Inhabd.	Uninhabd.	Buildg.	Population, 1881. Males.	Females.	Persons.	Population, 1871.
284	Blandford, Rural, *for* - -	—	2,151	78	9	4,998	5,051	10,049	—
	read - -	—	2,141	78	9	4,960	5,022	9,982	—
286	*For* Dorchester, Rural - -	115,082	3,613	239	3	8,567	8,756	17,323	19,152
	substitute { Cerne, Rural -	45,771	1,478	127	1	3,257	3,239	6,496	7,620
	substitute { Dorchester, Rural	69,311	2,135	112	2	5,310	5,517	10,827	11,532
292	Weymouth, Rural, *for* - -	—	1,784	103	18	4,008	4,171	8,179	—
	read - -	—	1,794	103	18	4,046	4,200	8,246	—

353 Birmingham, Urban, Edgbaston parish, under " Registration County " column, *for* " Warwick " *substitute* Worcester.

Page		Area.	Houses, 1881. Inhabd.	Uninhabd.	Buildg.	Population, 1881. Males.	Females.	Persons.	Population. 1871.
423	Boston, Rural, *for* - -	—	5,411	339	16	12,332	12,131	24,463	—
	read - -	—	5,412	339	16	12,337	12,132	24,469	—
425	Horncastle, Rural, *for* -	—	3,732	218	1	8,444	8,256	16,700	—
	read -	—	3,731	218	1	8,439	8,255	16,694	—
606	Sunderland, Urban—								
	Monkwearmouth, *for*	—	1,390	72	2	4,190	4,165	8,355	—
	read -	—	1,389	72	2	4,188	4,161	8,349	—
	Total, *for* - -	—	16,088	1,150	88	57,133	59,415	116,548	—
	read - -	—	16,087	1,150	88	57,131	59,411	116,542	—
652	Anglesey, Rural, *for* - -	113,514	6,169	464	35	12,006	13,004	25,010	26,532
		60,913	2,328	165	17	7,127	8,055	15,182	16,322

VOLUME III.*

Page.

x Total females, age 65, *for* "65308" *read* "653082."

xv (Order 18-1), Shoe, Boot—Maker, &c., *for* "18088 males, all ages," *read* "180884."

xvi (Order 20-1), Oil Miller, &c., age 65, *read* "3 females."

xvii (Order 24), Persons without Specified Occupations, males under 5 years, *for* "1757651," *read* "1757657;" males 5-, *for* "2649514," *read* "2649595;" males 15-, *for* "124012," *read* "124006;" males 20-, *for* "32171," *read* "32090."

xix Glass Manufacture, *for* "92 females" *read* "1692."

" Glazier, Painter, *for* "4 females" *read* "454."

xxix Russia, *for* "639, Total males," *read* "2639."

xliv Holland (Order 22-2), Artizan, Mechanic, &c., *for* "3 males" *read* "13."

xlix (Order 16), Lodging, Boarding House Keeper, *read* "3 females."

l (Order 22), General Shopkeeper, *read* "1 female."

" (Order 22), Costermonger, &c., *read* "3 females."

" (Order 23), Rag-Gatherer, &c., *read* "4 females."

7 Wandsworth, sub-district (25-3), *for* "128004 persons" *read* "28004."

9 Kent, Widowed females, age 55, *for* "53" *read* "2953."

10 St. Giles, district (11), age 15, unmarried, *for* "318 females" *read* "2318."

12 Middlesex (Order 3-4), School service, &c., *for* "43 females" *read* "143."

" " (Order 3-5), Author, Editor, &c., *for* "86 females" *read* "166."

" " (Order 3-5), Literary, Scientific Services, &c., *for* "1 female" *read* "41."

15 Kent (Order 10-6), Musical Instrument Maker, *read* "1 female."

" " (Order 10-7), Die, Seal, &c., Maker, *read* "1 female."

16 Surrey (Order 17-2), Silk Manufacturer, *for* "8 males" *read* "88."

" " (Order 17-2), Silk Dyer, &c., *for* "5 males" *read* "58."

" " (Order 17-2), Ribbon Manufacture, *read* "6 males."

27 Table 19, age 5, Surrey, *read* "46 females."

31 " 2, age 100, Kingston district (39), *read* "1 female."

33 Kingsclere, district (111), age 90, *read* "2 females."

43 Alresford (Rural), age 25, *read* "214 females."

" Brighton (Urban), *for* "0350 Total females" *read* "60350."

49 Worthing (Urban), age 60, *read* "127 males."

61 Sussex (Order 17-3), Cotton Manufacture, *read* "2 females."

62 " (Order 20-1), India Rubber, &c., worker, *read* "1 female.

65 Southampton (Order 6-3), Seaman, Merchant Service, *for* "683 males" *read* "1683."

73 Berkshire, Females born in London, *for* "505" *read* "5505."

82 Bicester, district (151), age 85, *read* "8 males."

99 Oxfordshire (Order 6-5), Telegraph service, *for* "1 female" *read* "11."

102 Hertfordshire (Order 17-2), Silk Merchant, &c., *read* "4 males."

" Buckinghamshire (Order 17-2), Silk Merchant, *for* "5 males" *read* "1."

109 Bedfordshire (Order 13-1), Ship, Boat, &c., Builder, *read* "10 males."

125 Table I. Heading line, *read* "45" in blank square.

127 Chelmsford, sub-district (192-2), age 85, *read* "9 males."

131 Fincham, sub-district (238-3), age 60, *read* "99 males, and 105 females."

137 Stow, district (208), Widowed females, age 20, *read* "1."

140 Eastern Division (Order 3-1), Theological Student, *for* "5 males" *read* "50."

147 Essex (Order 21-8), Other Iron and Steel Manufactures, *for* "288 males" *read* "1288."

" Eastern Division (Order 21-12), Wire Maker, Worker, &c., *for* "62 males" *read* "162."

" " " (Order 22-2), Engine Driver, &c., *for* "901 males" *read* "1901."

149 West Ham (Order 6-5), Telegraph Service, *read* "16 females."

150 Norwich (Order 10-2), Domestic Implement Maker, *read* "2 males."

151 West Ham (Order 10-5), Gunsmith, &c., *for* "7 males" *read* "17."

" " " (Order 13-2), Sail Maker, *read* "1 female."

152 Norwich (Order 14-3), Chemist, Druggist, *read* "2 females."

153 West Ham (Order 19-1), Tallow Chandler, &c., *read* "4 females."

154 Norwich (Order 21-2), Coal Merchant, *read* "4 females."

161 Table 20. Suffolk, Females, all ages, *for* "88" *read* "388."

178 Axminster (Rural), age 100, *read* "1 female."

185 Dorsetshire, age 65, widowed females, *read* "3498."

188 Truro, district (297), Widowed females, all ages, *for* "166" *read* "2166."

193 Wiltshire (Order 13-1), Ship, Boat, &c., Builder, *read* "11 males."

199 Plymouth (Order 6-5), Messenger, Porter, &c., *for* "1 female," *read* "14."

" " " Telegraph service, *read* "2 females."

200 " (Order 10-3), Weighing Apparatus Maker, *read* "1 male."

203 Cornwall (Order 19-2), Leather Goods, &c., Maker, *read* "1 male."

205 Bath (Order 24), Persons returned by Property, &c., *for* "16184 females" *read* "16148."

216 Ledbury, district (337), Age 10, *for* "56 males and 72 females" *read* "756" and "672" respectively.

* The errata in Vol. III. were almost entirely due to accidents in the process of printing.

VOLUME III.

Page.

227 Bromsgrove (Rural), Age 5, *for* "76 males and 94 females" *read* "676" and "694" respectively.

,, Bulkington (Urban), Age 90, *read* "1 female."

,, Note to Bristol, Age 85, *for* "6 males" *read* "64."

230 Newcastle under Lyme (Rural), *for* "663 persons" *read* "5663."

248 Warwickshire (Order 6-4), Meter, Weigher, *read* "9 males."

250 ,, (Order 11-1), Paperhanger, *read* "4 females."

251 Wolverhampton (Order 17-2), Silk Manufacture, *read* "1 female."

255 Walsall, *for* "29936 total males" *read* "29336."

,, Aston Manor (Order 3-1), Church, &c., Officer, *read* "1 female."

260 ,, (Order 17-3), Cotton Manufacture, *read* "9 females."

262 Walsall (Order 24), Persons returned by Property, &c., *for* "7814 males" *read* "7214."

272 Table 21, Hereford district (339), Total mentally deranged, *for* "304" *read* "430."

277 Table 1, Rutlandshire, Age 95, *read* "2 females," and Nottinghamshire, Age 100, *read* "2 males."

294 Lincolnshire (Order 3-1), Nun, Sister of Charity, *read* "3 females."

296 Nottinghamshire (Order 10-2), Needle Maker, *read* "42 females."

298 ,, (Order 16-3), Corn, Flour, &c., Merchant, *read* "9 females."

302 Derby (Order 3-7), Photographer, *read* "22 males and 5 females."

,, ,, (Order 3-7), Actor, *read* "4 females."

305 ,, (Order 11-1), Painter, Glazier, *read* "2 females."

,, ,, (Order 12-1), Coachmaker, *read* "6 females."

306 Derbyshire (Order 17-1), Others working in Wool, &c., *read* "3 males."

307 Nottingham (Order 19-2), Carrier, *for* "6 females" *read* "56."

,, Derbyshire (Order 19-3), Brush, Broom, Maker, *for* "8 males" *read* "68."

321 Islington, sub-district (453-7), Age 80, *for* "6 females" *read* "36."

323 In heading line, *read* "5" in blank square.

340 North-Western Counties (Order 6-3), Harbour, Dock, &c., Service, *for* "7269 males" *read* "17269."

344 Lancashire (Order 19-1), Bone, Horn, &c., Worker, *read* "2 females."

353 St. Helens (Order 21-3), Stone Quarrier, *read* "1 male."

354 Bury (Order 24), Persons returned by Property, &c., *for* "18968 females" *read* "13164."

,, Salford (Order 24), Persons returned by Property, &c., *for* "19568 males" *read* "18968."

360 Preston (Order 17-3), Cotton dealer, &c., *read* "3 females."

,, ,, (Order 17-4), Sacking, &c., maker, *read* "1 female."

,, Burnley (Order 19-3), Brush, Broom, Maker, *read* "5 females."

368 Salford, Total females, *read* "227."

384 Skirlaugh, district (523), Age 4, *read* "143 females."

393 Note to Todmorden, Age 4, *for* "21 females" *read* "321."

398 Stokesley, district (535), Age 65, unmarried males, *read* "47."

,, Aysgarth, district (539), Age 65, widowed males, *read* "63."

399 Leeds, Age 15, married females, *for* "48" *read* "485."

404 Huddersfield (Order 17-1), Woollen Cloth Manufacture, *for* "958 males" *read* "4958."

,, East Riding (Order 17-2), Silk Manufacture, *read* "7 females."

415 Leeds (Order 21-12), White Metal, &c., Manufacture, *read* "7 males."

425 Table 2, South Shields district (554), Age 5, *for* "689 females" *read* "6899."

427 Byker, sub-district (556-5), Age 85, *read* "10 females."

431 Alnwick and Canongate (Urban), Age 15, *for* "346 males" *read* "343."

432 Houghton-le-Spring (Rural), Age 5, *read* "2020 males."

434 Workington (Urban), Age 85, *read* "4 males."

443 Westmorland (Order 18-1), Hatter, &c., *read* "1 female."

464 Holywell, district (617), Age 15, *read* "1898 females."

468 Tregaron, sub-district (606-3), Age 75, *for* "2 females" *read* "32."

487 North Wales (Order 14-2), Gunpowder, &c., Manufacture, *read* "8 males."

491 Pembrokeshire (Order 3-7), Art Student, *read* "1 male."

496 Brecknockshire (Order 18-1), Hosiery manufacture, *read* "9 females," and Hosier, Haberdasher, *read* "3 females."

499 Merionethshire (Order 3-1), Church Officer, &c., *read* "5 females."

500 ,, (Order 4-2), Office Keeper, *read* "1 female."

506 ,, (Order 21-10), Tin, &c., Manufacture, *read* "1 female."

507 Swansea (Order 3-7), Art, Music, &c., service, *read* "3 females."

508 ,, (Order 6-2), Toll Collector, &c., *read* "1 female."

CENSUS OF ENGLAND AND WALES.

(43 & 44 VICT. c. 37.)

1881.

Volume III.

AGES,
CONDITION AS TO MARRIAGE,
OCCUPATIONS,
AND
BIRTH-PLACES
OF THE PEOPLE.

Presented to both Houses of Parliament by Command of Her Majesty.

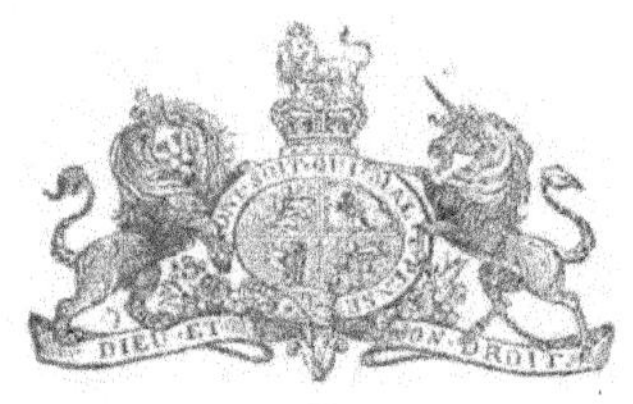

LONDON:
PRINTED BY EYRE AND SPOTTISWOODE.

To be purchased, either directly or through any Bookseller, from any of the following Agents, viz.,
Messrs. HANSARD and SON, 13, Great Queen Street, W.C., and 32, Abingdon Street, Westminster;
Messrs. EYRE and SPOTTISWOODE, East Harding Street, Fleet Street, and Sale Office, House of Lords;
Messrs. ADAM and CHARLES BLACK, of Edinburgh;
Messrs. ALEXANDER THOM and Co., or Messrs. HODGES, FIGGIS, and Co., of Dublin.

1883.

CENSUS OF ENGLAND AND WALES.

(43 & 44 VICT. c. 37.)

1881.

Vol. IV.

GENERAL REPORT.

Presented to both Houses of Parliament by Command of Her Majesty.

LONDON:
PRINTED BY EYRE AND SPOTTISWOODE.

To be purchased, either directly or through any Bookseller, from any of the following Agents, viz.,
Messrs. HANSARD & SON, 13, Great Queen Street, W.C., and 32, Abingdon Street, Westminster;
Messrs. EYRE & SPOTTISWOODE, East Harding Street, Fleet Street, and Sale Office, House of Lords;
Messrs. ADAM & CHARLES BLACK, of Edinburgh;
Messrs. ALEXANDER THOM & Co., or Messrs. HODGES, FIGGIS, & Co., of Dublin.

1883.

CENSUS OF ENGLAND AND WALES.

(43 & 44 Vict. c. 37.)

1881.

VOLUME IV.

GENERAL REPORT.

Presented to both Houses of Parliament by Command of Her Majesty.

LONDON:
PRINTED BY EYRE AND SPOTTISWOODE.

To be purchased, either directly or through any Bookseller, from any of the following Agents, viz.,
Messrs. HANSARD and SON, 13, Great Queen Street, W.C., and 32, Abingdon Street, Westminster;
Messrs. EYRE and SPOTTISWOODE, East Harding Street, Fleet Street, and Sale Office, House of Lords;
Messrs. ADAM and CHARLES BLACK, of Edinburgh;
Messrs. ALEXANDER THOM and Co., or Messrs. HODGES, FIGGIS, and Co., of Dublin.

1883.

TABLE OF CONTENTS.

REPORT.

APPENDIX A.

ENGLAND AND WALES.

Population, Houses, &c.

Sex and Age.

Conjugal Condition.

BIRTH-PLACES.

UNITED KINGDOM.

BRITISH EMPIRE.

APPENDIX B.

CENSUS OF 1881.

REPORT

TO

THE RIGHT HONOURABLE
SIR CHARLES WENTWORTH DILKE, BART., M.P.,
PRESIDENT OF THE LOCAL GOVERNMENT BOARD, &c.

Census Office, London,
August, 1883.

SIR,

AT no period earlier than the commencement of the present century was it possible to form any trustworthy estimate as to the number of persons inhabiting this country; for all computations founded on domesday books, on subsidy rolls, on payments of poll or hearth tax, and the like, however ingenious they might be, involved of necessity so large an intermixture of guesswork as to deprive their results of any very substantial value. Uncertainty of estimates of population before this century.

No proposal to ascertain the number of the population by systematic enumeration appears to have been made until the middle of the last century. On March 30th, 1753, Mr. Thomas Potter,* who sat as member for St. Germans in the House of Commons, brought in a Bill "for taking and registering an annual account of the " total number of the people, and of the total number of marriages, births, and deaths; " and also of the total number of the poor receiving alms from every parish and " extra-parochial place in Great Britain." This Bill apparently had the support of the ministry of the day; for among those whose names appear on the back are Mr. George Greville, a Lord of the Treasury; Lord Barrington, a Lord of the Admiralty; and Mr. Charles Yorke, the Lord Advocate for Scotland.† First proposal to have a census in 1753.

Accustomed as we are at the present time to such enumerations, the alarm with which the proposal was received, and the virulence of language with which it was combated, cannot but excite our surprise. "I did not believe," said its chief opponent‡ in the Commons, "that there was any set of men, or, indeed, any individual " of the human species, so presumptuous and so abandoned as to make the proposal " we have just heard. . . . . I hold this project to be totally subversive of the " last remains of English liberty. . . . . . The new Bill will direct the imposition of " new taxes, and indeed the addition of a very few words will make it the most effectual " engine of rapacity and oppression that was ever used against an injured people. " . . . . Moreover, an annual register of our people will acquaint our enemies abroad " with our weakness." Another opponent, Mr. Matthew Ridley, stated that he knew by letters from the town he represented, Newcastle-upon-Tyne, and from other parts, that "the people looked on the proposal as ominous, and feared lest some public misfortune or an epidemical distemper should follow the numbering." It was further urged that the scheme was costly and impracticable; that it was an imitation of French policy, borrowed from our natural enemies; and that it would not only be a basis for new taxation, but for a conscription. Nor was this latter fear probably without some justification. For Mr. George Greville, a Lord of the Treasury, in supporting the Bill, said that "it will be extremely useful at all times for many " useful purposes; and in the case of a long war, it will be absolutely necessary. " For the usual methods of raising recruits for our army would not then be sufficient. " We should be obliged to have recourse to that of obliging each parish to furnish a " certain number." The Bill, thus supported, passed through all its stages in the Proposal for census in 1753 opposed and rejected.

* Mr. Potter was son of the Archbishop of Canterbury, and a barrister of the Middle Temple.

† Besides these three ministers, the following members backed the Bill: Lord Hillsborough, Lord Dupplin, Mr. Oswald.

‡ Viz., Mr. Thornton, member for the city of York.

Commons by large majorities, but was thrown out on the second reading in the House of Lords.

Census again proposed in 1800.

Nearly half a century passed away before the proposal was renewed; but when the new Bill was introduced, in November 1800, into the House of Commons, it had the advantage of a great change which had apparently occurred in public opinion on the subject of population. The old fear that the number of the people was falling off, and that an enumeration would betray the inability of the country to furnish a due supply of soldiers for the army, had given place to a new and opposite form of alarm, namely, that the people were increasing so rapidly as to outstrip the means of subsistence. Among the causes which may be supposed to have brought about this change of opinion, probably the most powerful was the great dearth which prevailed in the country at the time when the Bill was brought forward, much of the time of both Houses of Parliament being occupied in the year 1800 in discussions on "the present high price of provisions;" while a second cause that may fairly be assumed to have had some influence in the matter, was the attention excited by Malthus's great work, of which the first edition was published anonymously in 1798, and taught its readers that there were other aspects of the question of population than the military one.

First census taken 1801.

The Population Bill was brought in by Mr. Abbot, member for Helston, on November 20th, 1800, and passed through all its stages without opposition. The enumeration was made on March 10th in the following year, and has been repeated ever since, without omission, in the first year of each successive decennium.

The recent census was, therefore, the ninth enumeration of the inhabitants of this country.

Method used in the first four enumerations.

The first four enumerations, namely, those of 1801, 1811, 1821, and 1831, were made by the agency of the overseers of the poor; this being the only or the best machinery available at those dates for the purpose. These overseers collected information concerning the inhabitants of their respective parishes by personal inquiry, no schedules being supplied, as at present, to the householders themselves, and, on the basis of the information thus collected, framed answers to printed questions addressed to them concerning the numbers and occupations of the persons living in their parishes.

As no small proportion of the overseers must have been utterly unfitted for the work, there can be little doubt that the answers returned by them must often have been excessively imperfect and inaccurate. Moreover, as the collection of the requisite data was by no means to be completed by them, as now, in the course of a single day, but to be carried on day after day until completion, there must almost unavoidably have been not only many omissions but many double entries, the same individual being present, and therefore enumerated, on different days in different parishes.

Fortunately, however, in enumerations made on a very large scale and by a very large number of enumerators, the opposite inaccuracies of omission and of double entry will always balance each other pretty closely; and we may therefore assume with much confidence that, though the returns made by the overseers in the earlier censuses for individual parishes or other small areas may not improbably have often been extremely inaccurate, yet the total summing up of the results for the country as a whole was not far off the mark; and it is to these totals for the whole country, and not to those for the smaller areas, that after the lapse of so many years the main interest attaches.

The present system introduced in 1841.

In 1841, when the time for the fifth decennial census arrived, the enumeration was carried out by a new machinery. Four years previously the Registration Act had come into force; and, for the purposes of this Act, the whole country had been mapped out into a number of districts,* each with a superintendent registrar, and these districts again divided into sub-districts, each with a resident registrar, whose duty it was to keep account of the births and deaths in his sub-district; while, presiding over the whole system, was the Registrar-General with a staff of assistants in London. It was obvious that such an organisation as this, extending as it did throughout all parts of the country, was well adapted to furnish the framework of the machinery for the work of enumeration; and the business was therefore taken out of the hands of the parochial overseers and entrusted to this new body of local registrars.

* The districts coincided in all but a few exceptional cases with the poor law unions which had been constituted in 1834. Strictly speaking, therefore, the mapping out of the country into districts was made on account of the new Poor Law, not on account of the Registration Act as stated in the text.

Simultaneously with this change, other important alterations were introduced. The overseers, as already mentioned, had collected the requisite information as to the inhabitants of their parishes in any chance way that might seem best to them, and the process of collection had occupied them for an indefinite period. But now each individual householder was furnished with a schedule in which himself to enter the required particulars as to his household, and the particulars which he was called on to supply related to all persons sleeping or present in his house on a certain fixed night, an alteration which greatly diminished the chance of omission or of double entry. The schedules were distributed and collected by special enumerators, each registrar's sub-district being parcelled out by him for this purpose into a number of small sub-divisions or enumeration districts, each of such size that a single person could conveniently visit all the houses within its boundaries in the course of an ordinary day's work. The schedules, when returned by the householders, were copied by the enumerators into enumeration books, which, after examination and revision by the registrar, were submitted to the superintendent, and, having received his approval and countersign, were forwarded for final tabulation to certain commissioners appointed by the Act to carry out the census.

This new method of enumeration was found to answer so well that it has been continued on each subsequent occasion, the only change in the machinery of any importance being that the place of the commissioners specially named in the Census Act has been taken by the Registrar-General and members of his permanent staff, selected by him for the purpose.

Number of persons employed in the enumeration of 1881.

The number of enumerators employed in 1881 in distributing, collecting, and copying the householders' schedules was 34,711. To these must be added 2,175 registrars and 630 superintendent registrars, making altogether an organised army of 37,516 persons engaged in the local collection of the necessary particulars. The central body, by whom the huge mass of details thus collected had to be sifted, abstracted, and tabulated, consisted of the Registrar-General and 55 members of the staff of the General Register Office and of 96 additional clerks.

The enumerators received but scanty remuneration for services which were by no means light or simple; and it is out of the question to expect that an army of men, each of whom is expected to do the work of a fairly adequate clerk while he is paid at a far lower rate, can be raised for a temporary purpose, and that no difficulty shall occur with any of them. It is satisfactory, however, to be able to state that, disregarding a few exceptional cases, the enumerators performed their part, within the limits of their capacity, quite as well as could reasonably be expected. There were often, it is true, omissions and inaccuracies which had to be set right afterwards by supplementary inquiries; but such omissions and inaccuracies are the unavoidable incidents of every census, and we have no reason to believe that they were more frequent on the present than on preceding occasions. Indeed, although the difficulty of taking an account of the population necessarily becomes greater and greater at each succeeding decennial period, owing to the rapid growth of the people and the ever-increasing complexity of the areas of local administration, yet it is probable that, owing to the gradual dying out of the prejudices which hung about the earlier censuses, and to the increased experience of the local officials in the process of enumeration, each successive census has been more accurately taken than that which preceded it.

Deficiencies in the local returns as regards boundaries.

The point in which the enumeration books, as forwarded to the central office by the registrars after local revision, were found to be most deficient, and to show the most serious amount of inaccuracy, was the matter of boundaries. England and Wales have been parcelled out at various times in a multiplicity of ways for diverse purposes; and it has often happened that, when a new parcelling out for some special purpose has been in hand, those entrusted with it have laid out their new areas without any, or with insufficient, regard to pre-existing areas of administration. The boundaries of civil and of ecclesiastical parishes, of municipal and of parliamentary boroughs, of urban and rural sanitary districts, of registration counties and counties in the ordinary sense, not to mention numerous other sub-divisions of the country, overlap and intersect each other with such complexity, that the enumerators and the local registrars in a vast number of cases failed altogether to unravel their intricacy. Nor is this to be wondered at, seeing that often no official or authoritative statement of the exact boundary of an area was procurable. This was more especially, but by no means solely, the case with the ecclesiastical districts, the boundaries of which we found to be often very uncertain, and subject of dispute between neighbouring incumbents. In these, and in all other similar cases, we laboriously investigated the evidence set before us, and finally adopted that conclusion which seemed most warrantable. These difficulties must, of necessity, have presented themselves to the compilers of former censuses, but the difficulties increase each census with the formation of new areas. One great addition to the labour on this occasion was caused by the institution in the preceding decade of sanitary districts. The rural sanitary districts, coinciding as they do generally either with entire registration areas or with the parts of such areas as remain after subtraction of any urban sanitary district within their limits, involved but little additional expenditure of time and labour; but the urban sanitary districts, nearly a thousand in number, with areas defined very frequently without any apparent regard to other administrative areas, added very materially to the toil of our work, and to the time required for its accomplishment.

We may illustrate this bewildering confusion of boundaries by a few examples taken almost at random.

The urban sanitary district of Mossley comprises parts of four registration sub-districts, parts of four parishes, parts of two unions, and parts of three counties, namely, Cheshire, Lancashire, and Yorkshire, but only parts of two registration counties, namely, Lancashire and Yorkshire.

The municipal city of York, which, together with the Ainsty, is included for parliamentary purposes in the North Riding, is included for registration purposes in the East Riding, and for all other purposes in the West Riding, while the parliamentary city of York, extending beyond the municipal limits, is partly in the North and partly in the East Riding.

The parliamentary borough of Stoke-upon-Trent consists of parts of six civil parishes and parts of four unions, and contains four municipal boroughs.

Halifax registration district contains one rural sanitary district and 19 entire urban sanitary districts with part of one other. The boundaries of 13 of these 19 districts do not correspond to any parish boundaries. For instance, the parish of Northowram is thus divided: one part constitutes the urban sanitary district of Northowram, a second part constitutes a portion of the urban sanitary district of Halifax, and a third part forms a portion of Queensbury urban sanitary district, the other portion of which is not only in another parish but in another registration district.

Bury registration district includes one rural sanitary district, and four entire urban sanitary districts with parts of three others. There are in this registration district 12 civil parishes or townships, and of these only two are not divided for registration purposes, the other 10 being split up so as to have portions in two, three, or more registration sub-districts. Moreover, each of six of the parishes contributes parts to two or more sanitary districts.

The parish of Ashton-under-Lyne, at the date of the census, contributed parts to no fewer than six urban sanitary districts, and to one rural sanitary district. It also comprised three registration sub-districts and part of a fourth.

The registration district of Crickhowel contains one rural sanitary district, one entire urban sanitary district and parts of three others. The remaining part of each of these three is not only in a different registration district, but in a different county.

Number and kinds of areas dealt with.

These examples will suffice to show how complicated were the boundaries of the areas with which we had to deal, and it will be readily understood how enormously this complexity added to the difficulties and labour of our task, difficulties and labour which, under any circumstances, could not but be great, seeing how numerous were the areas of which account was necessarily to be taken.

Those areas were as follows:—

1 England and Wales.
1 England.
1 Wales.
1 North Wales.
1 South Wales.
52 Counties.
95 Parliamentary counties or divisions of counties.
198 Parliamentary boroughs,
243 Municipal boroughs.
752 Wards of municipal boroughs.
830 Hundreds.
715 Petty and special sessional divisions.
616 Lieutenancy sub-divisions.
7 Cinque Ports and ancient towns (parent ports).
23 Additional members of Cinque Ports and ancient towns.

14,926 Civil parishes.
34 Ecclesiastical provinces and dioceses.
136 Separate constituent parts of such dioceses.
6,958 Ecclesiastical parishes that are neither entire mother parishes nor conterminous with civil parishes.
9,107 Separate constituent parts of such ecclesiastical parishes.
11 Registration divisions.
57 Registration counties.
630 Registration districts.
2,175 Registration sub-districts.
966 Urban sanitary districts.
578 Rural sanitary districts.
184 Various metropolitan areas not included above.

Various meanings of the term "population."

Before proceeding to discuss the results of the recent enumeration, there is a question which it will be well to answer distinctly, so as to prevent any possible misapprehension. What is meant by the population of a given place or area? In different countries different answers would have to be given to this question. In some countries those persons only are considered to belong to the population of a place who habitually reside therein, that is to say, who constitute its fixed or permanent inhabitants. In countries where the number of regularly domiciled inhabitants determines many financial arrangements relating to the amount of payments to be made by and to a community, and also is the foundation on which numerous details of municipal and general administration are based, doubtless this definition of the term "population" is that which best answers the purpose. It involves, however, an elaborate arrangement by which, when an enumeration is made, strict account is taken in each area, not only of the strangers from without who may be temporarily present, but also of those habitual inhabitants who are temporarily absent from their homes. It presents, moreover, the inconvenience, that not only is it difficult to define what constitutes temporary absence or habitual residence, but that a considerable number of persons are without fixed domicile at all, while others have more than one place of residence, to any one of which they may be referred with equal propriety.

A second answer to the question, what is meant by the population of a place, is the signification attached to the term in this country. According to it, the population of a given place or area consists of all those persons who are actually present within its boundaries at a certain fixed moment, and that moment in the recent enumeration was 12 p.m., 3rd April, 1881. All persons who were actually present in a place at that moment, were they natives or foreigners, strangers or habitual residents, were they lodged in houses or ships, or sleeping under a hedge, were alike counted as units in its population, and, besides such persons, no one else was reckoned in. The only exception to the rule was in the case of those few persons who might chance to be passing through the place in railway or other vehicles, and who for manifest reasons could not be taken into account. Such persons, on arriving at their destination in the morning, were counted as belonging to the population of the place to which they then came.

In short, then, by the population of a place is meant in this country its *actual* and not its *resident* population. For the main purposes to which the census in this country is subservient, it is this actual population of which it is most important to take account. Births, marriages, and deaths are registered in the places where they actually occur, without regard to the question whether the persons concerned were residents or strangers, and must therefore, in order to get true rates, be compared with the actual rather than with the resident population. It may, however, be observed, that, seeing that the enumeration is taken both at an hour in the day and at a season of the year when persons are mostly in their own homes, in all probability actual and resident population are very nearly identical, so far as regards their total amounts. Some absentees, of course, there will be and some strangers, but the two will balance each other with sufficient accuracy for all practical uses. Should there be in any instance reason to suspect that this is not the case, that is to say, should there have been any unusual cause for temporary congestion or the contrary in a given locality at the date of the census, the fact is recorded in a foot-note.

I.—NUMBER OF THE POPULATION AND RATES OF INCREASE.*

1.—*England and Wales.*

Total population of England and Wales on April 3, 1881.

The total number of persons returned as living in England and Wales on the night of the third of April 1881, was 25,974,439.

This was an increase of 3,262,173, or of 14·36 per cent., upon the numbers living at the previous census of 1871, and was almost exactly equivalent to the addition of another London with all its inhabitants to the population.

The rate of increase was higher than in any decennium since 1831–41, when it was 14·52. In the two succeeding decades (1841–51 and 1851–61) the rate fell, first to 12·65 and then to 11·93; but in 1861–71 the rate again rose to 13·19, and, as already noted, still further advanced to 14·36 in the decade ending in 1881. (*See* Appendix A, Table 2.)

Causes of the high rate of increase.

The rate of increase in the aggregate population of England and Wales is almost entirely determined by two factors, namely, the birth-rate and the death-rate; for, in comparison with these, emigration and immigration have but an insignificant effect. The rapid growth of the past decennium was due to the fact that the birth-rate was unusually high, while the death-rate was still more unusually low. That is to say, the additions were somewhat above the average, while the losses were far below it.

Intercensal Periods.	Mean Annual Birth-Rate.	Mean Annual Death-Rate.
1841–51	32·61	22·33
1851–61	34·15	22·25
1861–71	35·24	22·50
1871–81	35·35	21·27

The higher birth-rate in 1871–81, as compared with the preceding decade, implies the addition of 26,778 extra members to the community, while the lower death-rate implies the survival of 299,423 persons who with the previous rate of mortality would have died.

The natural increment.

The difference between the total number of births and the total number of deaths in the ten years, or "the natural increment of the people," amounted to 3,426,480, or to an increase of 15·09 per cent. upon the population at the beginning of the period; and as the actual increase, as determined by enumeration, was 14·36 per cent., the combined effects of all other movements of the population, including emigration and immigration, resulted in a loss of no more than 0·73 per cent. in the whole period.

How closely the growth of the population is determined by the "natural increment," and in what small degree comparatively it is affected by other causes, is seen in the following table, which gives the population and the rate of increase for three successive decennial periods, as they would have been if determined simply by the natural increment, and as they were found actually to be on enumeration:—

Census Years.	Population.		Excess of "Natural Increment" Population over "Enumerated" Population.	Increase* per cent. in previous Decade.		Excess of Natural Increment Rate over Enumeration Rate.	Census Years.
	As determined by "Natural Increment" only.	As actually enumerated.		As determined by "Natural Increment" only.	As determined by Actual Enumeration.		
1861	20,188,335	20,066,224	122,111	12·61	11·93	0·68	1861
1871	22,791,234	22,712,266	78,968	13·58	13·19	0·39	1871
1881	26,138,746	25,974,439	164,307	15·09	14·36	0·73	1881

* The rates of increase in this table refer to the intervals between the several censuses, without correction for the very slight inequalities of the periods.

* The tables relating to the Areas, Houses, and Population, male and female, of Counties, Parliamentary Divisions and Boroughs, Municipal Boroughs and Wards, Hundreds, Petty Sessional Divisions, Lieutenancy Sub-divisions, Civil Parishes, Ecclesiastical Provinces, Dioceses and Parishes, will be found in Vol. I., which has an index at p. 555.

The tables relating to the Areas, Houses, and Population, male and female, of Registration Counties, Districts, and Sub-districts with their component parts, as also of Sanitary Districts, Public Institutions, &c., will be found in Vol. II., which has an index at p. 685.

For comparative tables of successive Censuses, see Appendix to this Report, Tables 6, 7, and 9.

The slight excess of the "natural increment" population apparent at each period is due to emigration, or rather to the difference between the number of emigrants and the number of immigrants, using these terms in a somewhat wide sense to embrace all additions and all losses other than by births and deaths.* Neither the number of emigrants nor the number of immigrants can be told with more than vaguely approximative accuracy. The difference between the two, however, as shown in the above table, amounted in the past decade to 164,307, the balance, as in each of the two preceding decennia, being on the side of the emigrants.

Period in which the population doubles itself.

In the course of the last half century the population of England and Wales has increased 86·9 per cent. Supposing a similar rate of increase to be maintained, the population just enumerated would be doubled in the year 1936. Such a supposition, is, however, purely hypothetical, and we have scarcely more reason to assume that the rate of the last fifty years will be maintained for fifty-five years to come, than that a similar rate prevailed in former periods; and how far that was from being the case is shown by the fact that on such an hypothesis a single pair of persons living in the year A.D. 572 would have produced the whole of the present population of England and Wales.

Probable population in 1891.

The chances of great miscalculation are lessened if we confine our calculation to what will be the case at the next Decennial Census. What will be the population in 1891? We have no means of knowing; all we can do is to say what it will be on certain different hypotheses, one perhaps as probable as another. Thus if we assume that the rate of growth in the decade preceding the Census of 1891 will be the same as it was in the decade preceding the Census of 1881, the population that will be enumerated in 1891 will be 29,705,155. But the rate of increase has been rising in each decade since 1861, though in diminishing proportion. If we suppose that the series will be continued regularly in the decade ending in 1891, the population at the date of the next census will be 29,988,993.

Again, seeing how little the population as actually enumerated differs usually from the population as determined by "natural increment," we may proceed on another plan. What has been the "natural increment" growth in the two years that have already elapsed since the Census of 1881? We learn from the Registrar-General's Reports that, in the two years 1881–82, it has been 2·942 per cent. If this rate be maintained, the population in 1891, as determined by natural increment, will be 30,026,290; and the actual population, on the supposition that the loss by emigration will have been in the same proportion as it was in the decade preceding 1881, will be 29,837,545. Lastly, as all these manners of guessing are practically on an equality, we might take the mean of their results, which would give a probable population of 29,843,898 at the Census in 1891. It actually was 29,001,018

2. *Counties.*

Rates of increase or decrease in counties.

The increase of the population was by no means equably spread over the whole of the country. In 251 of the 630 districts, and in 985 of the 2,175 sub-districts, into which the country is divided for registration purposes, there was an actual falling off in the number of inhabitants. Even when larger aggregates, such as counties, are taken, there are some in which the population declined, while in the remainder the rates of increase were excessively unequal. In the following list those counties in which the population increased are arranged in the order of their rates of increase:—

* "Emigrant" as used above includes: (1) Emigrants proper; (2) Persons gone abroad as travellers, &c.; (3) Persons who removed from England to other parts of the United Kingdom; (4) Any persons who died in the decade, but whose deaths were not registered at the date of the census; (5) Any excess of English or Welsh persons in army, navy, or merchant service, abroad, over similar persons at previous census. "Immigrant," of course, is used to include the opposites of these groups. The Table of Emigrants at page 105 includes most of Group 1, and also many of Group 2. As regards Group 5, there was an excess of 3,642 persons in 1881 as compared with 1871. Of the other groups no numerical account whatsoever can be given.

REGISTRATION COUNTIES in which the POPULATION INCREASED in the past DECADE.

	Per cent.		Per cent.
Middlesex (*extra-metropolitan*)	43·8	Northamptonshire	11·6
Surrey (*metropolitan*)	32·1	Middlesex (*metropolitan*)	11·5
Glamorganshire	27·7	Carnarvonshire	11·1
Kent (*metropolitan*)	26·5	Merionethshire	11·0
Durham	26·3	Berkshire	10·2
Surrey (*extra-metropolitan*)	26·2	Carmarthenshire	9·7
Essex	25·3	Hampshire	9·6
Nottinghamshire	23·4	Lincolnshire	8·2
Lancashire	22·3	Gloucestershire	7·4
Derbyshire	19·0	Denbighshire	7·4
Leicestershire	18·6	Monmouthshire	6·7
Yorkshire (W.R.)	18·5	Flintshire	5·2
„ (E.R.)	18·2	Hertfordshire	4·0
„ (N.R.)	17·7	Bedfordshire	1·8
Sussex	17·4	Suffolk	1·8
Warwickshire	15·9	Somersetshire	1·7
Cheshire	15·3	Norfolk	1·6
Staffordshire	14·8	Oxfordshire	1·2
Worcestershire	14·0	Wiltshire	1·0
Cumberland	13·8	Buckinghamshire	0·6
Kent (*extra-metropolitan*)	12·6	Devonshire	0·4
Northumberland	12·3	Anglesey	0·04

In each of the 13 remaining counties the population declined. They are arranged in the following list in the order of their rates of decrease.

REGISTRATION COUNTIES in which the POPULATION DECREASED in the past DECADE.

	Per cent.		Per cent.
Cornwall	8·9	Dorsetshire	2·1
Huntingdonshire	8·3	Rutlandshire	1·6
Radnorshire	6·2	Westmorland	1·3
Brecknockshire	4·9	Cambridgeshire	0·5
Herefordshire	3·1	Shropshire	0·5
Cardiganshire	2·8	Pembrokeshire	0·2
Montgomeryshire	2·8		

3. *Urban and Rural Districts.*

Urban and rural population.

The inhabitants of the country may be divided for practical purposes into an urban and a rural population. Such a division can, however, only be roughly approximative; in the first place, because the terms urban and rural themselves have no very precise meaning, and, secondly, because many places which must indisputably be reckoned as urban have no distinct boundaries.

The method of division usually adopted is to select those registration districts and sub-districts in which are situated the chief towns, and to consider the inhabitants of these as representing the urban population, while the inhabitants of all the other districts and sub-districts are considered to be of rural character.

The urban population, as thus determined, consists of the inhabitants of the chief towns and their immediate neighbourhood, while the rural population includes the inhabitants of the smaller towns as well as of the strictly country parishes.*

* These are the urban and rural populations of the Registrar-General's Reports.

Adopting this method of dividing the population, we have the following results:—

—	Area in Acres.	Years.	Population enumerated.	Increase in preceding Decennium.	Increase per cent. in preceding Decennium.
England and Wales	37,239,351	1851	17,927,609	—	—
		1861	20,066,224	2,138,615	11·93
		1871	22,712,266	2,646,042	13·19
		1881	25,974,439	3,262,173	14·36
Town Population, *i.e.*, inhabitants of the districts and sub-districts which include the chief towns.	3,171,565	1851	9,155,964	—	—
		1861	10,933,234	1,777,270	19·41
		1871	12,910,647	1,977,413	18·09
		1881	15,445,296	2,534,649	19·63
Country Population, *i.e.*, inhabitants of the remainder of England and Wales which comprises the smaller towns and the country parishes.	34,067,786	1851	8,771,645	—	—
		1861	9,132,990	361,345	4·12
		1871	9,801,619	668,629	7·32
		1881	10,529,143	727,524	7·42

The urban population, therefore, using the term in the sense of the inhabitants of the chief towns only or their immediate neighbourhood, stood at the census of 1881, to the remaining or rural population, in the proportion of 147 to 100; the proportion in 1871 having been 132 to 100. This change in the proportions was not due to any decrease of growth in the rural population, which fully maintained the rate of increase attained in the previous decade, but to a considerable rise in the rate of growth of the urban population, this rate having mounted from 18·09 per cent. in the previous ten years to 19·63 in the decade just concluded.

The rural population, however, as determined by this method, includes the inhabitants of a very large number of places which, though not of sufficient magnitude to rank as "chief towns," are yet of such a size that their inhabitants can scarcely be considered as living under rural conditions. It would be highly desirable to ascertain, at any rate approximately, what was the number of the urban population, if the term be extended so as to include this class of persons.

Urban and Rural Sanitary Districts.

The recent division of the country into sanitary areas, some of which are styled Urban and the rest Rural Sanitary Districts, furnishes the best available basis for such a calculation.

At the time of the late census there were 966 urban sanitary districts, besides the 39 districts within the jurisdiction of the Metropolitan Board of Works (cf. Vol. II., Table 2.) The aggregate population of these 1,005 districts was 17,636,646, while the population of the remaining or rural sanitary districts amounted to only 8,337,793. The proportion, therefore, of persons living in places, which for one reason or another were considered to be of sufficient importance to exercise urban powers, to persons living elsewhere, was 212 to 100, or somewhat more than two to one.

Assuming these districts to represent the urban element and the remainder to represent the rural element in the population, the following would be an approximate account of the distribution of the people of England and Wales:—

Urban Sanitary Districts, with Populations of—	Number of Districts.	Aggregate Population, 1881.	Per-centage of Population of England and Wales, 1881.
250,000 and upwards	6*	5,722,677	22·0
100,000—250,000	14	1,976,498	7·6
50,000—100,000	27	1,796,149	6·9
20,000— 50,000	98	2,958,177	11·4
10,000— 20,000	158	2,172,630	8·4
3,000— 10,000	469	2,648,321	10·2
Under 3,000	195	362,194	1·4
Total **Urban** Population	967	17,636,646	67·9
Total **Rural** Population	—	8,337,793	32·1
England and Wales	—	25,974,439	100·0

* This includes the entire District of the Metropolitan Board of Works, which is here reckoned as a single urban sanitary district.

The urban sanitary districts are of such recent creation, and were often constructed with so little reference to previously existing boundaries, that it is impossible in many cases to ascertain what was the precise population at the date of previous censuses, and thus to calculate the comparative growths of the urban and rural elements in the country. If, however, we assume that the rate of growth has been the same for the total aggregates as for those parts for which the necessary data are procurable, the following figures will represent the respective growths of the present* urban and rural populations:—

—	Population,			Per-centage of Population of England and Wales.		
	1861.	1871.	1881.	1861.	1871.	1881.
Urban Population - -	12,696,520	14,929,283	17,636,646	63·3	65·7	67·9
Rural Population - -	7,369,704	7,782,983	8,337,793	36·7	34·3	32·1
England and Wales - -	20,066,224	22,712,266	25,974,439	100·0	100·0	100·0

The figures in this table show the increasing predominance of the urban as compared with the rural element. In 1861 there were 172 dwellers in towns to 100 dwellers in rural districts; but in 1871 the number had risen to 192, and in 1881 had reached 212.

4. *Municipal and Parliamentary Boroughs.*

Municipal boroughs.

The municipal boroughs (*see* Vol. I., Summary Table VI.) in England and Wales numbered 243 at the date of the census. Their aggregate population amounted to 8,412,121 persons; so that 32·4 per cent. of the total inhabitants of England and Wales were in enjoyment of such privileges and advantages as are derivable from municipal government. The population of Municipal boroughs had increased since 1871 by 27·3 per cent.; while the population living outside municipal boundaries had increased only by 9·0 per cent. This greater rate of increase in the municipal population was partly due to greater growth within the limits of the former boroughs, partly to the extension of their boundaries, and partly to the incorporation of 19 new boroughs in the course of the decennium.† The boroughs varied greatly in population, the smallest being Hedon in the East Riding of Yorkshire, with a population of 966, and the largest being Liverpool, with a population of 552,508.

Parliamentary boroughs.

There are 198 Parliamentary boroughs (*see* Vol. I., Summary Table V.) in England and Wales, neither their number nor their boundaries having been changed in the past ten years. It may be interesting to show here in one view the growth of these boroughs as an aggregate during the past 30 years:—

Year of Enumeration.	Number of Parliamentary Boroughs.	Enumerated Population.		
		In Parliamentary Boroughs.	Outside Parliamentary Boroughs.	Total.
1851	200	7,438,679	10,488,930	17,927,609
1861	200	8,638,569	11,427,655	20,066,224
1871	198	10,649,997*	12,062,269*	22,712,266
1881	198	12,285,537	13,688,902	25,974,439

* Between 1861 and 1871 there were considerable changes of electoral areas which affected the figures for that period.

* It must be remembered that many of the districts, which are at present urban, would not have been sufficiently populous to rank as urban in 1871, and still less in 1861. The urban population for 1861 and 1871, as given in the table, is therefore overstated.

† Namely, Accrington, Birkenhead, Blackpool, Burslem, Burton-upon-Trent, Bury, Cheltenham, Conway, Crewe, Heywood, Hyde, Jarrow, Leamington, Luton, Over Darwen, Peterborough, St. Ives, Stoke-upon-Trent, Taunton.

INCREASE in THREE successive DECADES.

1851–61	- - -	1,199,890	938,725	2,138,615
1861–71	- - -	2,011,428*	634,614*	2,646,042
1871–81	- - -	1,635,540	1,626,633	3,262,173

INCREASE per Cent. in THREE successive DECADES.

1851–61	- - -	16·1	8·9	11·9
1861–71	- - -	23·3*	5·6*	13·2
1871–81	- - -	15·4	13·5	14·4

* Between 1861 and 1871 there were considerable changes of electoral areas which affected the figures for that period.

5. *London and the other Great Towns.*

The population of the 20 great English towns, included in the weekly return of the Registrar General at the date of the recent census,* amounted to 7,580,319, showing an increase of 16·9 per cent. upon the numbers enumerated in 1871. The 20 great towns.

The rate of increase varied very widely in the different towns, but in one only was there no increase at all. This exception was Manchester, where the population was found to have slightly fallen, in consequence, probably, of the conversion of dwelling-houses into warehouses and offices. With this, however, must be taken into consideration the fact that the closely adjoining town of Salford showed an increase of no less than 41·2 per cent. Taking the two continuous towns together, there was an increase of 8·8 per cent.

THE 20 TOWNS, in the ORDER of their RATES of INCREASE in the past DECENNIUM.

Town.	Increase per cent. 1871–81.	Increase per cent. 1861–71.	Increase per cent. 1861–81.
Salford - - - -	41·2	21·8	72·0
Oldham - - -	34·8	14·2	53·9
Nottingham* - -	34·2	13·9	52·8
Leicester - - - -	28·5	39·9	79·8
Hull - -	26·5	24·8	57·9
Bradford* - - -	24·4	37·3	70·8
Leeds - - - -	19·3	25·1	49·2
Sheffield - - - -	18·6	29·6	53·6
Sunderland - - -	18·6	20·5	42·9
London - - - -	17·3	16·1	36·1
Birmingham - - -	16·6	16·1	35·4
Brighton* - - - -	16·3	17·5	36·6
Bristol - - - -	13·3	18·5	34·3
Newcastle-upon-Tyne - -	13·2	17·7	33·2
Portsmouth -	12·7	19·8	35·0
Liverpool - -	12·0	11·1	24·5
Wolverhampton - -	10·9	12·2	24·5
Norwich - -	9·3	7·3	17·3
Plymouth - - -	7·3	9·8	17·9
Manchester - - - -	–2·8 (*Decrease*)	3·7	0·8

* The municipal boundaries of Brighton, Nottingham, and Bradford were extended during the decade 1871–81, but all the rates of increase given in the above table relate to the populations of the extended areas.

The increase of the 19 provincial towns in the above list was 16·5 per cent. during the last decade, while that of London was 17·3 per cent. In the previous decennium (1861–71) the respective rates had been 16·1 for London, and 17·2 for the provincial towns. Thus London has increased in a somewhat higher ratio, and the 19 provincial towns in a somewhat lower ratio, than was the case in the preceding decennium.

The population of London was 3,816,483, and by itself somewhat exceeded the aggregate population of the 19 great provincial towns, which amounted to 3,763,836. London.

No fewer than 562,223 persons were added to the inhabitants of the metropolis in the course of the decade, a number exceeding the entire population of the largest of the provincial towns.

The population of London has almost exactly doubled itself in the course of 41 years, whereas the population of the rest of England and Wales has taken 57 years to

* Since the date of the census, eight other towns have been added to the list.

multiply in an equal degree. The metropolis has thus been gaining in its proportions as compared with the country at large; and, whereas at the beginning of the century out of nine inhabitants of England and Wales one lived in London, the proportion has now risen to one out of seven.*

Year of Enumeration.	Population of England and Wales and in London at the Nine Enumerations.		
	England and Wales.	London.	Persons in London to 100 in England and Wales.
1801 - -	8,892,536	958,863	10·78
1811 - -	10,164,256	1,138,815	11·20
1821 - -	12,000,236	1,378,947	11·49
1831 - -	13,896,797	1,654,994	11·91
1841 - -	15,914,148	1,948,417	12·24
1851 - -	17,927,609	2,362,236	13·18
1861 - -	20,066,224	2,803,989	13·97
1871 - -	22,712,266	3,254,260	14·33
1881 -	25,974,439	3,816,483	14·69

The increase of population in the last, as also in the preceding, decade was entirely peripheral. In the centre of London is a compact area, consisting of ten registration districts, in which, owing to the substitution of business premises for dwelling-houses, the resident population has for a long period been undergoing diminution. The inhabitants of this Central Area decreased by 7·8 per cent. in the course of the past ten years, having also diminished by 5·8 per cent. in the preceding decade.

Districts in Central Area.*	Decrease per cent.			Districts in Central Area.*	Decrease per cent.		
	1861–71.	1871–81.	1861–81.		1861–71.	1871–81.	1861–81.
St. George Hanover Square	0·0	4·2	4·2	Holborn - -	2·5	7·1	9·4
Westminster - -	3·0	9·1	11·8	London City -	33·0	32·3	54·6
Marylebone - -	1·5	2·7	4·2	Shoreditch - -	1·7	0·5	2·1
St. Giles - - -	1·0	15·6	16·1	Whitechapel	3·0	6·8	9·6
Strand - -	14·3	18·8	30·4	St. George-in-the-East	1·7	1·9	3·5

* The number of "inhabited houses" in this Central Area has diminished by 6,655 in the last 10 years, while the number of "uninhabited houses," that is, of houses not occupied at night, has increased by 3,055. In other words, 6,655 houses previously used as dwellings have been replaced by 3,055 houses, not used for any but business purposes.

Round this Central Area, and constituting the rest of Inner London, is a circle of districts, all of which have undergone more or less rapid increase, the growth, speaking generally, being greater the further the district is from the centre. The population in this circle increased 27·7 per cent. in the past ten years, and 28·4 per cent. in the preceding decade.

Other Districts of Inner London.	Increase per cent.			Other Districts of Inner London.	Increase per cent.		
	1861–71.	1871–81.	1861–81.		1861–71.	1871–81.	1861–81.
Kensington -	48·8	24·5	85·3	St. Saviour, Southwark.	0·7	11·5	12·2
Fulham - -	64·9	74·0	186·7	St. Olave, Southwark.	20·1	10·0	32·1
Chelsea - -	11·5	24·6	38·9	Lambeth -	28·6	21·8	56·6
Hampstead -	69·0	40·8	137·9	Wandsworth -	77·6	68·3	198·9
Pancras - -	11·4	6·7	18·8	Camberwell -	55·7	67·6	161·0
Islington - -	37·6	32·3	82·1	Greenwich -	17·0	30·4	52·6
Hackney -	50·0	49·2	123·9	Lewisham -	61·2	42·2	129·3
Bethnal Green -	14·3	5·7	20·8	Woolwich* -	*–2·8	10·2	7·1
Stepney -	2·0	1·5	3·5				
Mile End Old Town	27·5	13·3	44·5				
Poplar - -	46·9	34·5	97·6				

* Woolwich District forms an exception to the otherwise general rule, that those districts which increased in the past decade also increased in the preceding decade.

Nor does this represent the entire growth of the metropolis. For outside this circle of districts is still further an outer ring, not included within the limits of Inner London, but only separated from it by an arbitrary line, in which the growth has been even more rapid; its population having increased no less than 50·5 per cent. in the past decennium, and 50·8 in the preceding one.

* More precisely, the proportions were 1 : 9·3 in 1801, and 1 : 6·8 in 1881.

The growth of Greater London, that is of Inner London together with this outer ring, amounted to 22·7 per cent in the past decade, and to 47·9 per cent. in the past twenty years.

The following Table will serve to give a summary view of the changes of population described above as having occurred in the several constituent parts of Greater London :—

—	Population in			Rates of Increase or Decrease per cent.		
	1861.	1871.	1881.	1861–71.	1871–81.	1861–81.
Central Area	1,011,297	952,880	878,556	− 5·8	− 7·8	−13·1
Rest of Inner London	1,792,692	2,301,380	2,937,927	+28·4	+27·7	+63·9
Inner or Registration London*	2,803,989	3,254,260	3,816,483	+16·1	+17·3	+36·1
Outer Ring	418,731	631,381	950,178	+50·8	+50·5	+126·9
Greater London	3,222,720	3,885,641	4,766,661	+20·6	+22·7	+47·9

* Inner or Registration London is the London of the Registrar-General's Reports, and is practically conterminous with the District of the Metropolitan Board of Works. Greater London consists of the Metropolitan and City Police Districts.

II.—DENSITY OF THE POPULATION AND HABITATIONS.*

1. *Density and Proximity.*

The density of the population may be expressed equally well in several ways. We may either give the average number of persons to a square mile or other convenient unit of space, or the amount of space available on an average for each person, or, lastly, we may state the distance which would separate each individual from his next neighbour on any side, if the whole population were spread uniformly over the surface of the country. Modes of expressing density.

At the date of the census there were, on an average, 446 occupants to a square mile; each person, on an average, had 1·43 acres, and if the population had been uniformly distributed, the distance between any two neighbouring individuals would have been 90 yards.

According to the most recent returns to which we have access, there are but two European States in which the density of the population is so great as this. These countries are Saxony and Belgium, in which in 1880 there were 514 and 485 inhabitants respectively to the square mile.

The gradual increase of density of population in this country, at each successive census, is shown in the following table :— Gradual increase of density.

Date of Census.	Persons per Square Mile.	Acres per Person.	Proximity in Yards.
1801	153	4·19	153
1811	175	3·66	143
1821	206	3·10	132
1831	239	2·68	122
1841	274	2·34	114
1851	308	2·08	108
1861	345	1·86	102
1871	390	1·64	96
1881	446	1·43	90

The density of population varied, of course, enormously in different parts of England and Wales (cf. Appendix A., Table 32.) Limiting ourselves to areas of the size of counties, and excluding the metropolitan counties, we find at one end of the scale Westmorland and five Welsh counties, in which mountainous parts there were from 54 to 102 persons to a square mile, and at the other end of the scale, Durham, Warwickshire, West Riding of Yorkshire, Staffordshire, and Lancashire, with from 732 to 1,706 persons to a square mile.

* For references to tables see foot-note to page 6.

2. *Habitations.*

Number of houses.

The total number of houses in England and Wales at the date of the census was 5,264,609. Of these, 46,414 were in process of building, 386,676 were built but uninhabited, while the remaining 4,831,519 were inhabited. Of the houses reckoned as uninhabited, very many, especially in towns, were occupied in the daytime, being used as offices or warehouses; but such occupation does not amount to habitation as here understood, those houses alone being reckoned as inhabited in which, to use the terms of the Census Act, some person or persons abode on the night of Sunday, the 3rd day of April.

Proportion of houses to population.

To each inhabited house there were, on an average, 5·38 inhabitants. In 1871 the proportion was 5·33; so that it would appear that the houses had not increased in the interval since 1871 in equal proportion with the population. The difference, however, was extremely small. The population increased 14·4 per cent., while the inhabited houses increased 13·4 per cent., and even this small difference was probably not attributable to any falling off in the amount of house accommodation, but to the fact that a larger proportion of the population was living in towns, where the individual houses are, as a rule, much larger than in rural villages and accommodate more persons.

Even in our great towns, notwithstanding the ever-increasing inflow of migrants from without, no material change occurred in the course of the decade in the proportion borne by houses to population, as will be seen in the following table, which gives the ratios in 1871 and 1881 for London and all municipal towns with more than 100,000 inhabitants:—

Towns.	Persons per House.		Towns.	Persons per House.		Towns.	Persons per House.	
	1871.	1881.		1871.	1881.		1871.	1881.
London	7·79	7·85	Bradford	4·96	4·89	Leicester	4·81	4·90
Liverpool	6·29	5·99	Nottingham	4·84	4·84	Sunderland	7·70	7·24
Birmingham	5·02	5·12	Salford	5·22	5·15	Oldham	4·94	4·94
Manchester	5·23	5·09	Hull	4·85	4·76	Brighton	6·23	6·20
Leeds	4·64	4·76	Newcastle	7·80	7·17	Blackburn	5·20	5·18
Sheffield	4·95	4·96	Portsmouth	5·95	5·64	Bolton	5·09	5·04
Bristol	6·63	6·45						

Persons enumerated on board vessels.

In addition to the persons enumerated as sleeping in houses, including under that title not only private dwellings, but hospitals, workhouses, prisons, barracks, and other public institutions, each of which was reckoned as a single dwelling, there were 77,868 persons living on the water, either in harbours, or on rivers, creeks, and canals (*see* Vol. II., Summary Table IV.). Of these 9,876 were on board Her Majesty's ships, and 58,514 were on merchant sea-going vessels. There remain 8,978 persons, of whom 6,225 were males and 2,753 were females, who formed the population of barges and boats on canals and rivers. It appears from a comparison of former returns, that this floating population on our canals and rivers has been progressively decreasing, as indeed might have been anticipated. In 1851, the number returned as living on boats and barges was 12,562; in 1861 it had fallen to 11,915; in 1871 it had still farther decreased to 10,976; and lastly, in 1881, was reduced to 8,978. This 8,978 represents only such bargemen, lightermen, and watermen as slept on board on the night of the census, and it may be noted that taking all persons following this occupation, whether they slept on board or on shore, there was no falling off in numbers in 1881 as compared with 1871, though the diminution had been considerable in each of the two preceding intercensal periods. The number of persons returned as thus occupied in 1851 was 35,120; in 1861 it fell to 31,428; in 1871 to 29,864; but in 1881 it remained practically unchanged, being 30,223.

Vagrant population.

Besides the inhabitants of houses and the population on the water there is always a considerable vagrant population, consisting of travellers in caravans, of shelterers in barns and sheds, and of homeless persons in the open air. Of these, 10,924 were enumerated in 1881; but such persons are, of course, likely to escape the enumerator, so that probably the number returned is considerably below the mark. As, however, this defect would apply in equal measure to the returns of this class of persons in former enumerations, we may use the figures without much hesitation for the purposes of comparison. In 1861 this vagrant class numbered 11,444 persons; in 1871 the number fell to 10,383; and in 1881, as we have seen, it was 10,924. This vagrant class, therefore, did not increase in the same ratio as the population (*see* Vol. II., Summary Table V.).

III. SEXES.*

Of the 25,974,439 persons enumerated, 12,639,902 were males and 13,334,537 were females. This gives an excess of 694,635 females over males, an excess which would, however, be reduced to 547,095 if the English and Welsh members of the army, navy, and merchant service abroad were included in the reckoning. Proportion of male and females.

To each 100 males enumerated in England and Wales there were 105·5 females. A similar preponderance of females exists in almost all European countries, there being but two of them, namely, Greece and Bulgaria, in which the males are in the majority, and two, namely Belgium and Italy, in which the sexes almost exactly balance each other numerically.

This almost universal preponderance of females in the populations of Europe is the more curious, inasmuch as it is a law, to which, so far as we are aware, there is no exception, that the male births in a community invariably outnumber the female births. The physiological explanation of this fact is not yet ascertained with any certainty. But there are some reasons for believing that one at any rate of the causes that determine the sex of an infant is the relative ages of its father and mother, the offspring having a tendency to be of the same sex as its elder parent. As a general rule, the father is the elder parent, and thus it would follow that males would predominate among the offspring. In England and Wales the proportion of males to females among infants born in the years 1871 to 1880 was 103·8 of the former to 100 of the latter sex; and, though the ratio is not exactly the same in every country, yet in all, as before said, the rule holds good that more boys are born than girls. This original predominance of the male sex is, however, soon lost, and the relative proportions of the sexes inverted, as we shall have occasion presently to show at greater length, by the much higher death-rate of the males. Preponderance of females.

The proportion of females to males has been slightly but steadily increasing in England and Wales since 1851, having been in the last four successive censuses 104·2, 105·3, 105·4, and 105·5. Gradual increase of proportion of females.

The actual rate of increase in the last ten years was 14·30 per cent. for males, and 14·43 for females. But the "natural increment" of the males, that is to say, the number of male births *minus* the number of male deaths, was 1,704,435, or 15·4 per cent. of the male population in 1871, while the "natural increment" of the females was 1,722,045, or only 14·8 per cent. of the female population. From this it follows that the 164,307 persons who, as before (p. 7) pointed out, constituted the balance of emigrants over immigrants, consisted of 123,467 males and 40,840 females, and that the slight increase in the proportion of females in the enumerated population was entirely due to this excess of male emigrants. Had there been neither emigration nor immigration, the proportion of females to 100 males would have been 104·8, and not 105·5 as it was in fact.

———	Males.	Females.
Persons enumerated in 1871 - - - - -	11,058,934	11,653,332
Births *minus* deaths (April 1871—April 1881) - -	1,704,435	1,722,045
Population in 1881 by "natural increment" only - - -	12,763,369	13,375,377
Population enumerated in 1881 - - - - -	12,639,902	13,334,537
Difference, or excess of emigrants over immigrants* -	**123,467**	**40,840**

* For interpretation of the terms Emigrant and Immigrant, see foot-note, p. 7.

The relative proportions of the sexes differed very considerably in the different counties, and in nine of them the males were actually more numerous than the females. Moreover, the differences presented by the counties in this matter were clearly not due to accidental or temporary conditions, but were brought about by some tolerably persistent cause; for the order in which the counties stand, when classed by the Differences between counties in regard to proportion of sexes.

* For reference to tables, see foot-note to p. 6.

relative proportions of females in their populations, has been almost the same for several successive censuses. In the last five enumerations Cardiganshire has invariably stood at one end of the list, while at the other, or close to it, as invariably have come Glamorganshire, Monmouthshire, and Durham. This is not to be explained by any differences in the proportions of boy-births to girl-births; for, though such differences do in fact exist between different counties, yet they are too inconstant and too slight to have any very appreciable influence in the matter, and, moreover, these differences in the births do not tally with the differences in the population (*see* Appendix A., Table 17.). In Cardiganshire, for instance, the proportion of girls to boys in the births has been, on the whole, rather lower than in the country at large, and yet this is the county in which the population has always contained the highest proportion of females. The true explanation is doubtlessly to be found in the differences between counties in regard to occupations. Males and females congregate respectively in those parts that offer them the best chance of employment. It is obvious that the high proportion of males in Durham, Monmouthshire, Glamorganshire, Staffordshire, and Derbyshire is due to the mining industries of those counties. On the other hand, the high proportion of females in London with the adjoining parts of Surrey and Middlesex, as also in Sussex, is clearly due to the flocking in of young women to serve as domestic servants, dressmakers, shop assistants, &c.; while in Bedfordshire the still greater excess of the female sex is to be attributed to the strawplaiting and lacemaking carried on extensively in that county. But it must be confessed that such obvious explanations are not forthcoming in all cases. There is no obvious reason, for instance, why Cardiganshire should always, census after census, have a higher proportion of females than any other county. Still, it cannot be doubted that in this, and in other similar cases, close examination of the occupation tables for the two sexes, aided by local knowledge, would show that here as elsewhere the proportions of the two sexes are mainly determined by the amount of employment open to them respectively.

Changes in the proportions of the sexes at successive age-periods.

The proportion of males to females at the time of birth is, as was mentioned before, 103·8 of the former to 100 of the latter. This numerical advantage is, however, soon lost by the males, owing to their much higher death-rate. It has vanished, as may be seen in the age-tables, by the end of the first year of life; and at each subsequent age-period, with one exception, the females in this country outnumber the males, and in increasing proportions.

The exceptional period in which the females are equalled or slightly outnumbered by the males is the 10 and under 15 years age-period. We have elsewhere expressed our belief that the number of girls living at this age is somewhat understated in our tables, owing to many girls who are under 15 representing themselves to be above that age in order to get more readily into domestic service. But this cannot be the full explanation of the matter; for a somewhat similar change in the relative proportions of the sexes at this age-period is noticeable in the census returns of other countries, for instance, in Germany, in France, in Italy, and in Greece, and must, therefore, be due to some influence or agency common to them all. The probable cause is the critical change that occurs about this period in the female organisation.

In the next age-period, 15 and under 20, the enumerated females are again slightly in excess of the enumerated males. This at first seems strange, inasmuch as this age-period is one in which common experience teaches that the risk to female life is comparatively high. The explanation is to be found in the absence of those young men from the enumeration, who are serving abroad in the army and navy. When these are taken into account, the males are still, as in the immediately preceding age-period, slightly the more numerous.

In every age-period after this the females are the more numerous, and the excess is greater than can be accounted for by the absence of men serving in the army and navy. In any comparison, however, of the relative proportion of the sexes at any one of these age-periods, it must be remembered that considerable uncertainty exists on account of the great amount of misstatement of age on the part of women; and that the general consequence of such misstatement is to increase the apparent proportion of females to males at the earlier periods, and to diminish the proportion at the later periods. This misstatement of age is, however, a matter of which we shall have to speak again (pp. 18–19).

IV.—AGES.*

So long as we were dealing with the mere numbers of houses and of persons, male and female, present at the date of the census in each of the multitudinous areas into which the country is divided, we were on sure ground. Here and there an individual travelling all night, and not going to any house in the morning, may possibly have escaped enumeration, and here and there a house lying close to a doubtful boundary line may possibly have been reckoned as belonging to the wrong area; but such omissions and inaccuracies must have been so rare that they may be utterly disregarded, and for all practical purposes the figures in the first two volumes, which relate simply to the numbers of houses and of inhabitants, may be accepted as strictly accurate. But no sooner do we pass to the question of ages, or of occupations, or of other particulars dealt with in the third volume, than we find ourselves on very uncertain ground, and must proceed with much care and circumspection. Untrustworthy character the return as to ages &c.

As regards ages, there can be no doubt that the returns made by individuals are in a very considerable proportion of cases more or less inaccurate.

In the first place, very many persons, especially among the illiterate classes, do not know what their precise age may be. They keep their date of birth in mind for the earlier part of their life, up to 20 years or so, but after this they lose reckoning, and can only make an approximative statement. Such persons have a strong tendency to return their age as some exact multiple of 10; 30, 40, 50, 60, &c., as the case may be, though in reality they may be a year or two on one or the other side of that precise age. There is also a similar tendency, though in a far less degree, to return the unknown age as 35, 45, 55, or other uneven multiple of five. In consequence of Various causes of misstatem of age. Tendency use round numbers.

Age as Returned.	Number of Deaths.	Age as Returned.	Number of Deaths.	Age as Returned.	Number of Deaths.	Age as Returned.	Number of Deaths.
0	71,888	30	2,762	60	3,394	90	693
1	27,908	31	1,960	61	2,113	91	387
2	14,983	32	2,410	62	2,578	92	384
3	9,524	33	2,331	63	2,770	93	312
4	6,731	34	2,332	64	2,742	94	197
5	4,713	35	2,420	65	2,891	95	189
6	3,433	36	2,207	66	3,016	96	138
7	2,837	37	2,276	67	3,031	97	110
8	2,337	38	2,286	68	2,700	98	76
9	2,120	39	1,970	69	2,247	99	43
10	1,815	40	2,965	70	3,348	100	37
11	1,667	41	1,736	71	2,361	101	13
12	1,640	42	2,334	72	3,236	102	16
13	1,663	43	1,882	73	2,892	103	11
14	1,899	44	2,075	74	2,886	104	12
15	1,816	45	2,560	75	3,081	105	7
16	2,175	46	1,976	76	2,818	106	4
17	2,303	47	1,997	77	3,243	107	3
18	2,511	48	2,173	78	2,812	108 and upwards	2
19	2,643	49	1,897	79	2,071		
20	2,663	50	2,716	80	2,810		
21	2,800	51	1,701	81	1,852		
22	2,867	52	2,168	82	2,263	Unknown	874
23	2,747	53	1,977	83	1,843		
24	2,738	54	1,985	84	2,167		
25	2,607	55	2,391	85	1,770		
26	2,584	56	2,341	86	1,468		
27	2,580	57	2,116	87	1,234	Total -	335,956
28	2,542	58	2,110	88	1,195		
29	2,235	59	1,932	89	661		

* The tables relating to Ages are in Vol. III., which has an index at p. 526. Ages are given, with distinction of sex, for Registration Counties, Districts, and Sub-Districts, as also for Sanitary Districts, in Tables 1–6 of each Divisional Part. Ages in combination with civil or conjugal condition are given for Registration Divisions, Counties, and Districts in Tables 7, 8, and 9 of each Divisional Part.

this, when the ages of a considerable number of persons, as returned by themselves or their friends, are abstracted by single years, there is always found to be a marked excess for the years that terminate the decades, and a less marked, but distinctly recognisable, excess for the years that terminate the intervening quinquennia. This may be well seen in the First Annual Report of the Registrar-General, in which the deaths registered in England and Wales in the twelve months from July 1837 to June 1838 were abstracted by single years of age, and with the results shown in the Table on p. 17.

It will be noticed in this Table that at the ages of 10 and 20 there is very little, if any, apparent excess in the deaths as registered, but that after this period, during which alone the exact age is pretty certain to be retained in memory, there is a very great excess at each year that is a multiple of ten, and a small excess at most of the intervening multiples of five. When ages are abstracted, as in the census returns, by quinquennia instead of by single years, this tendency to return the age as a round number is of course less apparent. Still it exists, and the result of it must be that the figures for the successive quinquennia of life are alternately too high and too low, accordingly as they include or do not include a year of which the unit figure, or, to use a convenient French term, of which the *millésime* is 0.

In consequence of this tendency to round numbers, which has long been fully recognised, it is better to group the ages by decennial periods, and to arrange these so as to have the year which is an exact multiple of ten in the middle. The excess in such year and the deficiencies on either side of it will then counterbalance each other.

Confusion between year of life and years completed.

A second cause of erroneous statement as to age is the confusion made by many persons between the year of age in which they are living and the number of years they have completed; for instance, between "in the 21st year of life" and "21 years old."

The ages of children under five were abstracted at the Census Office by single years; and there can be no doubt that, owing to this confusion as to the proper mode of expression, the number of infants enumerated as under one year of age is very considerably below the mark, very many infants having been returned as one year old who really were only ten or nine, or even fewer, months of age. The returns of children in the second, third, fourth, and fifth years of life respectively are also probably far from correct; but here the amount of error will not be so great as in the first year, for, though a certain number in each case will have been pushed on a year beyond their proper place, yet this loss will have been more or less fully compensated by gain from the year below. The total number for the whole quinquennium will almost certainly be understated, because some children in the fifth year of life will have been returned as five years old.

Tendency of old persons to overstate their age.

A third cause of inaccuracy in the age-returns is the tendency of old persons, when uncertain as to their exact age, to exaggeration. In consequence of this tendency, very little trust should be put in the quinquennial or even the decennial totals after 85; and it is safer to make one single group in which all persons of 85 years and upwards shall be included. Not impossibly, nor indeed improbably, some few of the 141 persons who were stated to have completed their 100th year of life at the date of the census may have been entitled to centenarian honours; but the results of such inquiries as those made by Mr. Thoms show that it is extremely rare for human life to be prolonged to this extent, and it can scarcely be doubted that comparatively few of the cases would bear strict investigation.

Wilful misstatement of age by girls and women.

There remains yet another form of inaccuracy in the age-returns, which differs from those as yet mentioned in being of a wilful character. Many persons, and notably many women, desirous of being thought to be younger than they really are, return themselves as under 25 or as under 30 when their true age is even considerably beyond these limits.

On the other hand, we find reason to believe from careful examination of the age-tables that a not inconsiderable number of girls who are not yet fifteen return themselves as being of that or of more advanced age, probably with the view of getting more readily taken as servants. In consequence of this, the number of girls of the 10–15 years period of life, as given in our tables, is too low. Probably a similar overstatement of age on the part of many young women occurs in the next age-period, 15–20 years of age, and with a similar object. This age-period, however, receiving a certain number from below that do not rightly belong to it, and losing above a certain number that should rightly be retained, counterbalances its losses by its gains, and is therefore probably not very incorrect as regards the total assigned to it. But not so the next age-period, 20 and under 25 years of age. Young women under 20, as already explained, often state themselves to be over that age, while many others, who are 25 or more, state themselves to be under 25; so that this age-period receives at both ends without any counterbalancing loss, and thus the total of women returned as in this period of life comes to be very much too high.

That something of this kind occurs can be shown very easily and very conclusively. The young women in the 20 and under 25 years age-period who are alive at the date of any census are, of course, the survivors of the girls who were in the 10 and under 15 years age-period at the date of the preceding decennial census; and should therefore, owing to the deaths in the intervening ten years, be considerably fewer in number than the girls of whom they are the remainder. But, as a matter of fact, it is found, on examining the age-tables of successive censuses, that invariably the young women aged 20 and under 25 are considerably more numerous than were the girls aged 10 and under 15 ten years earlier.

Date of Census.	Girls enumerated as 10 and under 15 years of age at each Census.	Women enumerated as 20 and under 25 years of age 10 Years later.	Calculated Survivors of the Girls in Col. 2 after 10 Years on the Basis of the English Life Table.
1841	851,736	871,152	795,459
1851	949,362	969,283	886,634
1861	1,045,287	1,052,843	976,221
1871	1,203,469	1,215,872	1,123,951

It will be seen in this table that in 1841, to take a single example, there were 851,736 girls who returned their ages as between 10 and 15; but that in 1851 the survivors of these, who, according to the English life table, should have been 795,459, were, according to the returns, 871,152, or actually more numerous than the girls of whom they were the surviving remainder after a lapse of ten years! Death has apparently increased their number instead of diminishing it! Now, emigration and immigration cannot be supposed to affect the number of girls and women at these ages in any appreciable degree, and such slight effect as they may have would be to diminish rather than to increase the number of apparent survivors. There can, therefore, be no other explanation than that either the number of the girls was understated or that the number of young women was overstated; and, as we have already said, a close investigation of the figures has led us to the conclusion that both these explanations are true; but that the overstatement of the number of young women is very much greater than the understatement of the girls.

To what extent this falsification of the ages of girls and women prevails cannot be stated, and therefore no full correction can be made for it. Its effect is, however, somewhat reduced by making the age-periods under which the population is tabulated consist of decennia, rather than of quinquennia or other shorter periods. The age may then be not inconsiderably understated, and yet the person be kept within the group to which he or she properly belongs.

Such are the main causes that affect the accuracy of the age-returns, and that probably affect them very seriously. These causes, we should say, were fully recognised by our predecessors in former census reports. We have, however, thought it advisable to restate them at some length, lest incautious use should be made of the results of the enumeration. The age-figures, and especially those of the female sex, must be looked on as being at best simply approximative; and the shorter the age-period, the greater must be the margin allowed for misstatement.

The graduated age table.

It is convenient, however, for many purposes to have an estimate, even though no more than roughly approximative, of the number of persons living at each year of life. It has been shown already that the mode in which persons return their ages does not allow of this estimate being made by direct abstraction from the enumeration books. A more correct estimate can really be made by taking the numbers returned for longer periods of life, quinquennia for instance or still better decennia, and dividing these out to the individual years by interpolation. The series of figures thus obtained will, of course, present a much greater regularity than actually exists, but will be sufficiently close to the truth for all practical purposes, and at any rate will be much closer to the truth than any series founded on direct abstraction for single years of life. We have, therefore, constructed such a graduated table (Appendix A.,

Tables 10 and 11) by the method of differences. In this table the totals agree with the enumerated totals, raised to the middle of the year 1881, for the following life-periods:—

0 and under	5 years.		45 and under	55 years.	
5	,,	10 ,,	55	,,	65 ,,
10	,,	15 ,,	65	,,	75 ,,
15	,,	25 ,,	75	,,	85 ,,
25	,,	35 ,,	85	,,	95 ,,
35	,,	45 ,,	95 and upwards.		

The totals for each age-period, excepting the first, have been apportioned to the several years within that period by interpolation. But the first age-period (0 and under 5 years) has been dealt with on another plan, the enumerated total for this period of life having been divided out to the several years within it in proportions determined by calculation from the registers of births and deaths; and, inasmuch as the birth-rates and death-rates of children showed considerable fluctuations in the successive years 1876–1881, the series of figures for this first quinquennium of life is also necessarily very irregular. It has already been mentioned that, according to such estimate as we can form, the total for this first age-period is itself considerably understated. But notwithstanding this, we have retained the total in our graduated table without correction, because the same cause which leads to the understatement of the number of children living under five years of age will lead also to a similar understatement of the numbers dying at that period of life; and consequently a correction of the living total would interfere with the calculation of death-rates, which is one of the main uses of the age-tables.

Taking the graduated table as our basis, we may estimate the numbers living at several important periods of life as follows:—

Children under school-age.

The number of infants and young children who were not as yet of school-age at the date of the census, but all the survivors of whom will have to be taken into account by school managers when three years shall have elapsed from that date, was 2,192,871.

School-age.

The children of school-age, that is 3 and under 13 years of age, numbered 6,218,305, and of these 3,101,095 were males, and 3,117,210 were females.

Minors and persons of full age.

The number of young persons legally under age, that is who had not yet completed their twenty-first year, was 12,590,909. Of these 6,283,344 were males, and 6,307,565 were females.

The number of persons of legal age was 13,618,367. Of these 6,546,579 were males, and 7,071,788 were females.

Recruiting age.

The number of males of recruiting ages, that is of from 19 to 25 years of age, was 1,407,348, being 15·9 per cent. more than the number of corresponding ages in 1871.

Reproductive age.

The number of females of reproductive ages, which we may roughly consider as from 15 to 45 years, was 6,009,746; and of these, as may be estimated from another table (Vol. III., Summary Table 3), 2,953,078 had been married, and still had living husbands. The number of males of corresponding ages was 5,779,931.

Age-distribution of the population.

The age-distribution of the population, that is to say, the proportion of persons living at each successive period of life to the total population, underwent very little alteration in the interval between 1871 and 1881 (cf. Appendix A., Table 15). Some slight changes, however, occurred; and these may be summed up generally by saying that the proportion of persons under 25 years of age increased, while the proportion of persons over that age diminished, and, of course, to a corresponding extent. Here are the figures for three successive censuses:—

Changes in age-distribution at successive censuses.

PERSONS UNDER and OVER 25 YEARS of AGE per MILLION of POPULATION.

Date.	Under 25.	25 and upwards.
1861	543,807	456,193
1871	545,397	454,603
1881	552,237	447,763

This change was due to two main causes: firstly, to the fact that the birth-rate had been gradually increasing for many years; and, secondly, to the fact that the death-rate had been declining among persons under 25, while it had slightly increased in the aggregate of persons over that age. There had thus been an ever-increasing proportion of young members added to the community, and of this increasing addition a larger proportion survived. The following table gives the birth and death rates in three successive inter-censal periods:—

Decennial Period.	Mean Annual Birth-Rate* per 1,000 living.	Mean Annual Death-Rate per 1,000 living at the respective Ages.	
		Under 25.	25 and upwards.
1851–60	34·1	22·00	22·37
1861–70	35·1	21·99	22·92
1871–80	35·3	19·78	23·09

* The birth-rates in this table relate to periods of ten years commencing in January, and, therefore, differ slightly from those shown on page 6, which are for the intercensal periods commencing in April. The former periods are used in this table because deaths in combination with age are only abstracted for complete years beginning with January.

The age-distribution differed much in the two sexes; and, as is shown in the following table, the proportion of young males to males of all ages was much higher than the proportion of young females to all females. Differer age-distri tion of i and fem

MALES and FEMALES UNDER and OVER 25 YEARS of AGE per MILLION living of EACH SEX in 1881.

(*Army, Navy, Marines, and Merchant Seamen, at Home and Abroad, included.*)

Sex.	Under 25.	25 and upwards.
Males - - -	560,969	439,031
Females - - -	542,573	457,427

To this difference between the sexes, which is one that repeats itself each census, three causes contribute. In the first place, the number of male births, that is, the number of young males added each year to the community, is always considerably higher than the number of female births; secondly, more males than females disappear by emigration, a loss which chiefly affects the middle periods of life; thirdly and lastly, female life is of longer duration than male life, so that there is an accumulation of females at the later ages.

Age-distribution differed also very considerably in different localities, and notably in towns as compared with rural districts. (*See* Vol. III., Summary Table 2.) In towns there is always an abnormal proportion of adults in the prime or working period of life, who are drawn from without by the higher wages; and this excess of persons of reproductive ages again, as a rule, entails an abnormal proportion of young children; so that in towns the proportion of aged persons to the total population comes to be much lower than elsewhere. There is also, as has been pointed out on an earlier page, a great difference between town and country in the proportionate numbers of males and females in their respective populations; and combining this difference as to sex-proportions with the difference as to age-distribution, we have the results given in the following table:— Differe age-dist tion in and cou

The NUMBERS of MALES and FEMALES at each GROUP of AGES per MILLION PERSONS of ALL AGES in URBAN and RURAL DISTRICTS respectively.

AGES.	URBAN DISTRICTS.			RURAL DISTRICTS.			FEMALES to 100 Males.	
	PERSONS.	Males.	Females.	PERSONS.	Males.	Females.	Urban Districts.	Rural Districts.
All ages	1,000,000	480,085	519,915	1,000,000	500,471	499,529	108	100
0—	136,214	67,903	68,311	134,151	67,173	66,978	101	100
5—	118,604	58,930	59,674	126,607	63,476	63,131	101	99
10—	104,484	51,646	52,838	114,847	58,932	55,915	102	95
15—	99,278	47,529	51,749	95,506	51,575	43,931	109	85
20—	94,602	44,247	50,355	79,128	39,816	39,312	114	99
25—	155,034	74,080	80,954	127,030	61,769	65,261	109	106
35—	116,976	56,131	60,845	105,266	51,325	53,941	108	105
45—	82,219	38,553	43,666	86,760	42,376	44,384	113	105
55—	54,482	24,905	29,577	68,747	33,979	34,768	119	102
65—	28,042	12,160	15,882	42,922	21,040	21,882	131	104
75—	8,997	3,637	5,360	16,720	8,021	8,699	147	108
85 and upwards	1,068	364	704	2,316	989	1,327	193	134

NOTE.—London and the Urban Sanitary Districts are taken in this Table to represent the Urban Districts, and the remainder of England and Wales constitutes the Rural Districts.

The main points of contrast disclosed in this table between urban and rural population, are as follows. In the towns there is a great excess of adults between 20 and 45 years of age, and a deficiency in the proportion of persons of more advanced age. This excess of adults of reproductive ages causes a high birth-rate, and in consequence the proportion of children under five years of age is somewhat higher in the towns than in the country. That it is not even higher than the table shows it to be is to be attributed to two causes: firstly, a very large proportion of the excess of adults in the towns, though of reproductive ages, consists of unmarried shopmen and apprentices or of young women in domestic service; and, secondly, the mortality of young children is very much higher in towns than in the country. So great, indeed, is the difference in this respect, that though the proportion of children in the first age-period (0 and under 5 years) is, as we have seen, slightly higher in the towns, the position is reversed in the next age-period (5 and under 10 years), and still more decidedly in the next but one (10 and under 15 years), the proportion of young persons of these ages being much higher in the rural than in the urban population.

Passing from the columns headed "Persons" to the columns of "Males" and "Females," we find the following further contrasts:—The proportion of females to males is much higher in the towns than in the country, being in the former 108·3, and in the latter only 99·8 to 100. This difference is very decided in the third age-period, 10 and under 15 years of age, but becomes still more strongly marked in the next period, 15 and under 20 years of age, when the females in the towns are to the males as 109 to 100, whereas in the country they are only in the proportion of 85 to 100. This is due to the extensive migration of girls from the country to the towns to supply the demand for domestic servants. In the succeeding age-period, 20 and under 25 years, the disproportionate preponderance of females in the towns still continues, but is less strongly marked. The influx of young males has begun, and soon assumes such magnitude that in the next two periods, 25 and under 35 and 35 and under 45 years of age, the proportion of females to males is not much higher in the urban than in the rural communities. After this age the excessive proportion of females in towns again manifests itself, and the contrast between town and country in this respect continues henceforth to become more and more exaggerated with each successive age-period. Why this should be the case is not very apparent. It may be that aged women find life in towns more suited to their tastes, whereas old men prefer the quiet retirement of the country; and it may also be, and probably is, the case, that there are many more occupations open in towns to old women than to old men.

This question of age and sex distribution is not a matter of mere curiosity, but of much practical importance in vital statistics; for as the death-rates differ very greatly at different ages and in the two sexes, when an attempt is made to compare the healthiness of one locality with that of another locality, or the healthiness of one trade with that of another trade, it is not enough to take the general death-rates of the two as the basis of comparison, unless it has been first ascertained that the age and sex distribution in the two is the same, or sufficiently near for all practical purposes.

If we take the mean (1871–80) death-rates in England and Wales at each age-period as a standard, the death-rate in an urban population, as constituted above, would be 20·40 per 1,000, while the death-rate in the rural population would be 22·83. Such would be their respective death-rates on the hypothesis that the urban districts and the rural districts were equally healthy. We know, however, as a matter of fact, that urban death-rates, instead of being lower than rural death-rates, are much higher. The difference of healthiness, therefore, between the two is much greater than the difference between their death-rates.

V.—CONDITION AS TO MARRIAGE OR CIVIL CONDITION.*

Number of husbands of wives.

According to the returns the number of husbands in the population was 4,376,898, while the number of wives was 4,437,962. The wives, therefore, outnumbered the husbands by 61,064. This excess represents those wives whose husbands were out of the country, with probably some intermixture of women who, though they returned themselves as wives, had no strict title to that designation.

Fertility wives.

Of the enumerated wives 2,943,186 had not completed their 45th year, which, disregarding occasional exceptions, we may consider to be the limit of the reproductive period in women. The average annual number of legitimate births registered in the three years 1880, 1881, 1882, was 841,851, so that the average annual fertility of wives of reproductive ages was in the proportion of 286 births to 1,000 wives. The returns for 1871, when dealt with on the same method, give an annual fertility of 292 births to 1,000 wives, that is, give practically an identical result. We may therefore assume with much confidence that the proportion mentioned represents with close accuracy the annual fertility of wives in this country.

Illegitimate unions.

The women of reproductive ages, 15 to 45 years, were divided in 1881 into unmarried, wives, and widows in the following proportions: unmarried, 2,865,253; wives, 2,943,186; widows, 181,178. The unmarried and the widows together numbered 3,046,431. Now the average annual number of illegitimate births registered in the three years 1880, 1881, 1882, was 42,916; and, if we assume that the illegitimate unions are on the average neither more nor less productive than the legitimate unions, the total number of unmarried women and widows under 45 years of age, who were living in illegitimate union, would be 150,056, or one woman in 20 of corresponding age and condition.

Probably, however, the above assumption is not correct. It is very likely that among the women who contract illegitimate unions there is a larger proportion of young women than among wives of reproductive ages; and, if this be the case, the average fertility of illegitimate would be higher than that of legitimate unions. This would to some extent reduce our estimate of 150,056.

Proportion married to adult population.

The proportion of married persons to the adult population (15 and upwards) declined, though not very considerably, in the interval between the censuses of 1871 and 1881. In the case of the husbands the decline in the proportion was 0·98 per cent.; in the case of the wives it was 1·14 per cent. The decline in the proportions of the married was almost entirely confined to the earlier periods of life; among males affecting exclusively, and among females affecting mainly, those who were under 25 years of age. (*See* Appendix A., Table 23.)

The falling off in the proportion of married persons to the adult population was not due to any unusual mortality among this class, for had it been so there would have been an increase in the proportion of widowers and of widows; whereas, in fact, the contrary was the case, and the proportion of both showed a decline, though in the

---

* The tables relating to Conjugal Condition are in Vol. III., which has an index at p. 526. The Conjugal Condition is given for Registration Divisions, Counties, and Districts, and for the large Urban Sanitary Districts, in Tables 7, 8, and 9 of each Divisional Part.

case of the widows the decline was very slight. (*See* Appendix A., Table 22.) The true explanation is furnished by the fall in the annual marriage-rate, which, having averaged 16·4 persons married to 1,000 living in the five years immediately preceding the census of 1871, fell to 15·3 in the quinquennium ending with 1880. It is true, that if we take the entire decades instead of their second quinquennia, the difference in the rates was not quite so great. But even then the difference was considerable, the rate for 1861–70 having been 16·6, while for 1871–80 it was 16·2.

Relative ages of husbands and wives.

The average age (1871–80) of men when they marry or re-marry is 27·9 years, the average age of the women is 25·7 years. But the average age of all the enumerated husbands was 43·1, and that of all the enumerated wives was 40·7. The difference between the ages of the husband and wife had thus apparently increased from 2·2 to 2·4 years.

This seems strange; for the natural expectation would have been that the very opposite change would occur, and that the mean ages of husbands and wives would have become nearer to each other rather than have diverged more widely. For those marriages which would have been earliest dissolved by the death of one of the pair would, speaking generally, have been those in which one of the couple was much older than the other; so that the marriages with wide age-divergence would, on the whole, be more rapidly eliminated from the reckoning than the marriages between persons of more equal ages. The only explanation of the apparent inconsistency which we can suggest is the fact, of which, indeed, there is abundant other proof, that women are more given to understate their ages than are men; and that their propensity to do so increases as they become older. The great majority of women who marry are under 25 years of age at the time of marriage, and have no temptation at that period of life to understate their age. But as they become older this propensity develops itself.

Proportions of unmarried in different counties.

The relative proportions of married and unmarried persons in the population varied much in different parts. To examine into these variations in a satisfactory manner would require very extensive study of county peculiarities. A cursory examination, however, of the tables in which the proportions are given for each county shows that in mining parts, such as Durham, Monmouthshire, and Glamorganshire, to which large numbers of young men are attracted from without, the proportion of unmarried males is high; whereas, in the absence of any special occupation for unmarried females, the proportion of these is low. The proportion of unmarried females is also low, as a general rule, in purely agricultural counties, such as Cambridgeshire, Suffolk, Norfolk, or Lincolnshire, owing to the migration of young women into counties where there is a greater demand for domestic servants; such counties, for instance, as Sussex with its watering places, or the suburban parts of the counties of Middlesex and Surrey, which thus come to have a high ratio of unmarried amongst their female population. (*See* Appendix A., Tables 25 and 32.)

Difference between town and country districts as regards conjugal condition.

There does not appear to be much difference between urban and rural populations as regards their conjugal or civil condition. The proportions of married and of unmarried, whether males or females, are pretty nearly the same in both. This, at least, is the case if we take the entire population, without distinction of age. But if, instead of so doing, we break up the populations into age-groups, and see how many married there are in proportion to the number living in each of such age-groups, we find some points of contrast between town and country. In the towns there is a higher proportion of married, both males and females, in the earlier age-periods, probably because wages are higher in the towns, and marriages are consequently contracted at an earlier time of life; whereas in the later age-periods the proportion of married is higher in the country than in the town, the differences at these later age-periods being chiefly, though not entirely, due to the excessive numbers of widowers and widows living in the town as compared with the country. Why the widowed should be in such high proportion in the towns is not very apparent. In part it is probably a necessary accompaniment of the earlier marriages; in part due to the considerably higher death-rate of the towns; and partly, perhaps, it may be attributable to the social life of towns being more congenial and better suited to widowers and widows than the retirement and solitude of the country. Be the explanation what it may, the following table shows that the proportion of widowed persons is higher in the town than in the country at every age-period:—

The Numbers Unmarried, Married, and Widowed to 1,000 Persons enumerated at each Group of Ages in Urban and Rural Districts respectively.

Ages.	Males.						Females.						Ages.
	Unmarried.		Married.		Widowed.		Unmarried.		Married.		Widowed.		
	Urban.	Rural.	Urban.	Rural.	Urban.	Rural.	Urban.	Rural.	Urban.	Rural.	Urban.	Rural.	
All Ages	612	613	357	349	31	38	586	588	333	334	81	78	All Ages.
0—	1,000	1,000	—	—	—	—	1,000	1,000	—	—	—	—	0—
15—	991	997	6	3	0	0	970	983	30	17	—	—	15—
20—	757	787	241	211	2	2	648	703	347	294	5	3	20—
25—	307	307	678	680	15	13	286	319	683	659	31	22	25—
35—	129	132	832	837	39	31	151	171	749	760	100	69	35—
45—	87	92	835	846	78	62	119	128	670	733	211	139	45—
55—	73	77	733	804	154	119	112	113	509	632	379	255	55—
65 and upwards	69	66	579	615	352	319	116	98	253	368	631	534	65 and upwards.

Note.—The proportions in this table for urban districts relate to London and the 46 urban sanitary districts with populations above 50,000; the rural districts are represented by the 3rd, 4th, and 5th Registration Divisions, exclusive of the principal towns.

VI.—OCCUPATIONS.*

1. *Method of Tabulation and its Difficulties.*

The most laborious, the most costly, and, after all, perhaps the least satisfactory part of the Census, is that which is concerned with the occupations of the people. It is well that those who may purpose to make use of the tables relating to these occupations should be fully aware of the difficulties that beset such a tabulation, so that they may form a just estimate as to the degree of accuracy to be fairly expected in so complex a matter. Difficultie in tabulat occupatio

In the first place, the number of distinct manufactures and industries in such a country as this is enormous. Moreover, most of these manufactures and industries are sub-divided with great minuteness; and each group of artizans whose operations are confined to one of these minute sub-divisions is known by a special designation, or not infrequently by several different designations in different localities. These designations in a large proportion of cases give no indication whatsoever as to the character of the business to those who are not possessed of some special acquaintance with technical terms. Here, for instance, are a hundred,—all names of occupations in current use, and yet such that in all probability an ordinary educated man would know at most but one or two of them, and often would not know a single one. Moreover, in those cases where The vast number o occupatio Curious names of occupatio

* The tables relating to Occupations are in Vol. III., which has an index at p. 526. Occupations are given in combination with Ages and Sexes, for all England and Wales, in Summary Tables 4, 5, 6; and for each Registration Division and County, as also for the large Urban Sanitary Districts, in Table 10 of each Divisional Part. The Occupations of European Foreigners, distinguishing Country and Sex, are in Summary Table 13; and the Occupations of the Blind and the Deaf and Dumb in Summary Tables 17, 18, 19.

he might fancy that the term gave some clue, he would find on inquiry that the supposed clue was completely misleading.

All-rounder.
Barker.
Bat-printer.
Baubler.
Bear breaker.
Beatster.
Blabber.
Black picker.
Block minder.
Bomb setter.
Branner.
Brazil maker.
Budget trimmer.
Bull-dog burner.
Bullet pitcher.
Busheller.
Butt woman.
Buttoner-up.
Camberel maker.
Can breaker.
Carriage straightener.
Cheeker.
Chevener.
Churer.
Clapper carrier.
Combwright.
Coney cutter.
Crowder.
Crutter.
Cullet picker.
Cut looker.
Cut-jack maker.
Dasher.
Dirt refiner.
Doctor maker.
Dog minder.
Doler.
Duler.
Egger.
Fagotter.
Faster.
Firebeater.
Flat keeper.
Floker.
Foot maker.
Forwarder.
Gin maker.
Glan rider.
Grafter.
Hackneyman.
Hawk-boy.
Horse marine.
Hoveller.
Idle back maker.
Impression maker.
Iron bolster maker.
Keel bulley.
Lasher.
Learman.
Lurer.
Maidenmaker.
Marbler.
Moleskin shaver.
Muck roller.
Notch turner.
Off-bearer.
Oliver man.
Orange raiser.
Painted-front maker.
Paste fitter.
Patent turner.
Peas maker.
Piano puncher.
Ponty sticker.
Ransacker.
Riffler maker.
Sad-iron maker.
Sand badger.
Scratch brusher.
Shore woman.
Sparable cutter.
Spitch dealer.
Spittle maker.
Spragger.
Sprigger.
Swift builder.
Tawer.
Temple maker.
Tharme maker.
Thimble picker.
Thurler.
Tingle maker.
Toother.
Townsman.
Trowler.
Walk flatter.
Westernman.
Wheel glutter.
Whim driver.
Whitster.

Dictionary of names of occupations.

The abstracting clerks could not, of course, be expected to know the meaning of such names as these, and consequently it was necessary to make a dictionary for their use, instructing them how to deal with each name that might occur. It was found that the dictionary in use for past censuses, and which had been constructed, we believe, chiefly on the basis of the directories of London and other large towns, had become obsolete. A great many terms that occurred in it had ceased any longer to be used, and, what was of more importance, several thousands that are now used had no place in it at all. Under these circumstances we determined to make a new dictionary of the names of occupations,—a work, it need hardly be said, of very great labour, especially as we could lay no claim to special knowledge in the matter of trades. With this view we sent out circulars to leading manufacturers, asking for information as to the designations used in their branches of industry, and the information thus collected we supplemented by searches through trade directories, and especially by a preliminary examination of the enumeration books from the chief industrial centres. By these means we eventually collected together between eleven and twelve thousand different occupations having each its name.*

Classification of occupations.

The names thus collected by us we grouped into some 400 headings under which they were to be abstracted; and these headings were again grouped in sub-orders, orders, and classes, these larger groupings being taken with some modifications from the Census of 1871.

* The dictionary of occupations used in previous censuses contained almost exactly 7,000 names. The great change in the nomenclature of occupations that appears to have occurred since the former dictionary was compiled is partly due to new branches of industry having sprung up, and greater sub-division having been made; but probably also in great part to the fact that many of the names in current use are scarcely more than nick-names, which have but short lives, but which nevertheless it was necessary for our purposes to take into account as being actually used in the schedules.

We have mentioned that in some cases there are several names for one and the same occupation. This, of course, was of no importance, except that it added very slightly to the number of names of occupations with which we had to deal; but a much more serious matter was the fact that, again and again, one and the same name is used for totally different occupations. By Clothier is meant in some parts a Cloth-maker, whereas in other parts it means Clothes-dealer. By Bricksetter is in some parts meant a Bricklayer, whilst in most parts it means a man who performs certain operations in Brickmaking. By Bank Manager is ordinarily meant the manager of a money bank, but in mining parts it is also occasionally used for the man who superintends the operations at the pit's mouth. By Drummer may either be meant a Musician or a Blacksmith's hammerman; by Muffin-maker, either a man who makes the eatable that bears that name, or the man who makes what is known as a muffin in China manufacture. An Engineer may be either a maker or a driver of engines. A Collar maker may be a Seamstress or a Harness-maker. A Bookcase-maker may be a Cabinet-maker or a Bookbinder, and so on. In these instances the confusion is only between two occupations; but there are other cases, much more numerous and much more troublesome, in which a common name is used for some branch of perhaps half a dozen or even more different trades. There are Spinners, Weavers, Warpers, Winders, &c. in Cotton, Silk, Wool, and Flax Factories alike; and when an operative is returned simply under one of these or similar designations, without further specification, it is impossible to say to which of the several manufactures he should be assigned. Still more general names are such as Backer, Baller, Bender, Binder, Bleacher, Blocker, Blower, Bluer, Boxer, Brusher, Burnisher;—a list which by no means exhausts this one initial letter, and, if made complete, would be found to comprise some hundreds of similarly vague designations. Now an operative, not recognising the importance of greater precision, and perhaps in ignorance of the existence in other branches of industry of a designation identical with his own, very commonly returns himself by one of these general terms without further specification. In order, as far as possible, to prevent this, a special circular was sent to the persons engaged in local enumeration, calling their attention to the matter, and requesting them to see that in all cases the occupation should be described in a sufficiently specific manner. This, doubtless, had the effect of reducing the number of vague returns very considerably. Still, out of an army of thirty-five thousand enumerators, there could not but be a certain proportion of unintelligent or careless men, and the requisite precision of statement as to occupations was far from being universally observed. Thus, there are still in the tables of occupations such headings as "Miner (undefined)," "Weaver (undefined)," "Factory hand, textile (undefined)," "Artisan, Mechanic (undefined)," and the like. In estimating, therefore, the precise numbers of persons employed in any manufacture, the existence of these vague headings must not be lost sight of, and due allowance must be made for them. For instance, under Cotton Manufacture are given 487,777 persons employed; but there are also 21,145 returned as "Factory labourer (undefined)," 13,514 as "Factory hand, textile (undefined)," and 4,841 as "Weaver (undefined)"; and an unknown proportion of each of these was engaged in cotton manufacture. Still it will be seen that the number of these undefined Factory hands is but very small in proportion to the number known to be engaged in the Cotton Manufacture; and as, moreover, even of this small number only a part were Cotton hands, we may neglect, as practically unimportant, the slight understatement of the Cotton industry caused by the vague returns. So also in the case of Miners. There were, it is true, some two thousand men who were returned simply as Miners, without the kind of mineral being specified, but the men returned as miners of specified kinds were nearly half a million in number, so that the omission of any precise statement as to the 2,000 miners may be disregarded.

Names common several o pations.

Vaguene in stating specific occupatic

Another very great difficulty which occurs in tabulating occupations is this. The number of headings cannot, of course, be unlimited; there clearly cannot be one for every distinct occupation. Now, group these occupations as one may, it is practically impossible to devise such headings that a given occupation shall invariably fall naturally under one special heading and under no other. An example will make this plainer. There is a heading "Cutler and Scissors Maker," and there is a heading "Bone, Horn, Ivory, Tortoiseshell, Worker." Now, to which is a man who returns himself as "Knife-scale Maker" to be assigned? By knife-scales are meant the pieces, usually of horn or ivory or bone, that form the sides of the handle. So, again, there is a heading "Tool Maker," and a heading "Wood Turner." To which of these is the man who makes wooden hafts for tools to be assigned? In all such cases as these, and they

Cross di sions in sificatior

were extremely numerous, we were obliged to make arbitrary rules, and in the instances quoted we laid down the rule that the makers of handles and hafts for tools and cutlery were to be considered as tool makers and cutlers.

Rules as to persons with multiple occupations.

Then, again, came the question of how to deal with the numerous persons who return themselves as following more than one occupation. The general rules we laid down were, firstly, that a mechanical handicraft or constructive occupation should invariably be preferred to a mere shop-keeping occupation; secondly, that, if one of the diverse occupations seemed of more importance than the others, it should be selected; and, thirdly, that in default of such apparent difference the occupation first mentioned should be taken, on the ground that a person would be likely to mention his main business first. In some cases of multiple occupations we made special rules. For instance, a considerable number of clergymen are schoolmasters. How should "Clergyman, Schoolmaster," be dealt with? In this case we decided that Schoolmaster should be taken, on the ground that it was possible to ascertain pretty closely from other sources how many Clergymen there were, but there were not the same facilities in the case of Schoolmasters. So again, and on similar grounds, Members of Parliament engaged in any branch of commerce or industry were to be assigned to such branch, rather than to the heading "Legislator."

Rule as to persons to be included under any heading.

Another question to be settled was this: who should be considered as engaged in any stated occupation? For instance, was an apprentice to be so considered, or a person who returned himself as "retired" from any business, or as "out of employ," or the like? The rules we adopted were these: Apprentices, Journeymen, and Assistants were to be classed under the occupation to which they were apprenticed or in which they assisted; but Messengers, Errand Boys, Porters, and Watchmen (excepting Railway or Government) were not to be so classed, but to go to a special heading provided for them.* As regards persons "retired" from any business, we found ourselves in some doubt. In the Census of 1871 such persons had been considered as following the business from which they had really retired, and were abstracted accordingly. To depart from this former practice would, of course, interfere in some measure with the ready comparison of the returns for 1881 with those of 1871. But, on the other hand, it was known that a very inconsiderable proportion of persons who had retired from business made mention of their former occupation in their schedules, and that, consequently, if such persons were included, the return made by us under any occupation would be neither of persons actually so occupied, nor yet of these together with those who had retired from the trade, a large proportion of the latter being omitted. We found by careful examination of the enumeration books for an entire county, including a large town, that, had we included the "retired," as was done in 1871, the persons returned by us under any heading would on an average have been about 2 per cent. more than they are actually. On the whole, seeing that the difference was so small, we thought it best altogether to omit those who had retired from business; and we also excluded, as having almost certainly retired, all Patients in Lunatic Asylums and all Inmates of Workhouses over 60 years of age. Paupers under this age, Patients in General Hospitals, and Prisoners with stated occupations, were abstracted by their occupations, as being possibly only temporarily debarred from them; and the same rule was applied to persons "out of employ" from any stated handicraft.

It will thus be seen, without going into further details, that the tabulation of occupations required a very complex system of rules, and was not an operation that could be carried out by any chance clerk in an off-hand manner.

Few of us can in any way realize what is meant by a million, still less what is meant by twenty-six millions. But let any one try to realize to himself what is meant by sorting out twenty-six millions of persons according to their sexes, their ages, and their occupations, the very names of which are themselves a bewildering puzzle, and to sort these from enumeration books in which the handwriting is often very obscure. Let a person, we say, try to realize this, and he will, we think, admit that the task is not only one of gigantic dimensions, but one in which strict and unfailing accuracy is practically unattainable. We made every effort to secure as great accuracy as was possible under the circumstances, but we are bound to state that the margin that must be allowed for error is very considerable. Where the heading is something very definite, such as Baker, Butcher, Tailor, and the like, the abstracting clerk is not likely to have been much

* This rule as to apprentices will explain how it is that under occupations which are only carried on by adults, young lads or mere children will sometimes be found classified. But it also cannot be doubted that in some cases there has been a magnifying of office on the part of the lad or girl. When, for instance, we see boys under 15 returned as railway guards, or as authors or journalists, we cannot but think and hope that such is the explanation.

perplexed, and the figures given are doubtless fairly accurate, but in the case of complex businesses the figures must be regarded as only approximative.

We have thought it our duty to set forth as clearly as we could, and without any attempt at disguise, the difficulties that we met with, as also must have done our predecessors, in carrying out this part of the Census, and the consequent uncertainty that necessarily attaches to much of the tabulation. Having discharged ourselves of this duty, we shall now proceed to discuss the results.

The six classes.

The 400 and odd headings under which occupations in combination with ages were abstracted have been arranged by us, as was previously mentioned, in sub-orders, orders, and classes, much after the same plan as that followed in 1871, though with some not inconsiderable modifications. The largest groups, or the classes, are six in number,—the Professional, the Domestic, the Commercial, the Agricultural, the Industrial, and the Unoccupied class,—in which latter we have included all children under five years of age. The names of these classes must not be interpreted too literally, nor must the lines of demarcation between them be supposed to be very definite. Still, for general purposes, and disregarding minute details, this division into classes is not without use. It will be found, for instance, that if counties or other areas be compared with each other in regard to the per-centage of their populations that is included in each of these six classes, a very tolerable idea may be got of their general character. We have accordingly added some columns in Appendix A., Table 32, showing these proportions for each county, as well as for the whole country.

The goodness, however, of a classification depends on the purpose to which the classification is to be applied; and, as different classifiers may have different aims in view, we have, in addition to the table which gives the classified arrangement for the whole country, and those which give it for each division, county, and large urban sanitary authority, also given an alphabetically arranged list of the headings, with the numbers of persons, males and females, belonging to them severally; so that every one may have facilities for grouping the occupations in such way as seems best to him (*see* Vol. III., Summary Table VI.).

In such remarks as we shall ourselves make on the results of the tabulation, we shall not attempt to deal with all the headings, nor shall we confine ourselves strictly to the classification in our tables; but we shall select such headings, and group them in such combinations, as may seem suitable.

Comparison of figures 1881 with those for 1871.

From time to time we shall have occasion to compare the figures for 1881 with those for 1871; and in most of such cases it will be necessary to correct the returns for 1871, on account of persons "retired" from any business having been included in the returns for that Census, and not so included in the present Census. The correction which we shall apply can, of course, be only a rough one, and will consist in a deduction of two per cent. from the totals of 1871; this ratio having been found, as previously mentioned, to be approximately correct on examination of the enumeration books of a large county. For instance, in 1871, the returns gave 468,142 persons engaged in Cotton Manufacture; this, by a deduction of 2 per cent., becomes 458,779; and this latter number we shall consider to be the true return, for comparison with that of 1881, and shall speak of it as the "corrected" number. Other corrections will also have to be made by us on account of differences in the methods of tabulation adopted on the two occasions. The comparison can rarely be exact, and consequently too much stress must not be laid upon minute differences.

2. *Female as compared with Male Occupations.*

Relative numbers of the two sexes employed.

The total number of males returned as engaged in some definite occupation was 7,783,646, being 71·5 per cent. of all the enumerated males aged five years and upwards. The total number of females similarly occupied was 3,403,918, or only 29·4 per cent. of all females aged five years and upwards. It must be remembered, however, that a very large number of wives and daughters assist their husbands or fathers in business, and also that the most important of all female occupations, and that which employs the largest number, is altogether omitted from the reckoning, namely, the rearing of children and the management of domestic life. To make the comparison at all a fair one, we should take into account the existence of the 4,437,962 wives;* and, were we to do so, the proportion of occupied women would be much the same as that of occupied men. Although, in by far the greatest

* Some of these wives will, of course, have had specified occupations of their own, and so in the proposed calculation would be counted twice. But, on the other hand, daughters or nieces assisting their fathers or uncles in business will be omitted, as also widows employed in domestic duties.

Employments in which females predominate.

number of industries, the men employed largely outnumber the females, yet there are a considerable number of occupations in which the reverse is the case, and the female workers predominate. The following is a list of these :—

—	Females.	Males.	—	Females.	Males.
Subordinate Medical Service (including Midwives and Nurses).	37,821	1,972	Lace manufacture -	32,785	11,359
Teacher - - -	123,995	47,836	Fustian manufacture - -	5,176	3,011
Actor, Actress - - -	2,368	2,197	Tape manufacture - -	1,159	732
Domestic Service -	1,258,285	244,391	Thread manufacture - -	1,672	498
Washing, Charing, and other Service.	287,017	14,117	Hemp, Jute, Cocoa Fibre, manufacture.	2,297	1,181
Bookbinding - -	10,592	9,505	Net-maker - -	1,481	252
Pin manufacture - -	495	234	Sacking, Sack, Bag, manufacture	1,594	575
Steel-pen manufacture -	2,503	220	Trimming, Embroidery, Fancy Goods (textile), manufacture.	13,384	3,109
Toy-making, selling -	1,233	1,099	Straw-plait, Straw-hat, &c., manufacture.	27,983	3,001
Artificial Flower manufacture -	4,461	720	Milliner, Dressmaker, Staymaker	357,995	2,937
Fusee, Fireworks, and Explosive Articles, manufacture.	1,887	950	Shirt-maker, Seamstress -	81,865	1,379
Lodging-house, Boarding-house, keeping.	32,890	4,486	Shawl manufacture - -	408	208
Pastry-cook, Confectioner -	13,051	12,483	Hosiery manufacture -	21,510	18,862
Woollen Cloth manufacture -	58,501	57,307	Glove-maker, Glover -	13,261	2,263
Worsted, Stuff, manufacture -	63,801	35,436	Button-maker - - -	4,121	2,286
Blanket manufacture -	1,374	1,313	Old Clothes dealer - -	1,663	639
Silk, Silk goods, manufacture -	39,694	17,655	Hair, Bristle, worker - -	1,743	893
Ribbon manufacture - -	1,186	878	Quill, Feather, worker - -	2,089	429
Crape, Gauze, manufacture -	1,006	176	Japanner - - -	1,539	1,359
Cotton, Cotton goods, manufacture.	302,367	185,410	Envelope maker - - -	1,933	175
Flax, Linen, manufacture -	7,853	4,212	Paper-bag, Paper-box maker -	8,718	1,187
			Metal Burnisher, Lacquerer -	2,209	478
			Fancy Chain, Gilt-toy, maker -	700	342

With some exceptions, the occupations in which more women than men were engaged in 1881 are the same occupations in which the female workers were the more numerous in 1871. But it will be seen hereafter that, in many industries in which both sexes are engaged, there has been a tendency to employ an increased proportion of female labour.

Summary of female occupations.

The following gives, in small compass, a general summary of the occupations among which female workers were divided, and the numbers employed in each :—

Teaching - - - - - - -	123,995
Nursing and similar offices - - -	37,821
Lodging-house keeping - - - -	32,890
Domestic service - - - -	1,258,285
Laundry and other services - - - -	287,017
Agricultural labour - - - - -	64,171
Textile manufactures - - - -	590,624
Dressmaking - - - - -	616,425
All other industries - - - - -	392,690
Total females aged five years and upwards specially occupied	3,403,918

3. *Professional Class.*

PROFESSIONAL CLASS.

The Professional class, as given in the tables of occupations, numbered 647,075 persons, or 2·5 per cent. of the entire population at all ages. It is, however, a most heterogeneous class, including the highest State Dignitaries as well as the street mountebank. Moreover, many of the headings that are comprised in the class are such that the figures attached to them are but of little value. Such, for instance, are the headings "Artists," and "Literary and Scientific Persons;" in both of which cases the boundary is very vague that separates those who are really entitled to the designation from those who assume it undeservedly. Who can say how many of the 7,962 persons who were returned as Artist Painters were really such, and how many were house decorators, who had magnified their office? We shall, therefore, pass over a good many of the headings without comment.

Civil Service.

The Civil Service employed 50,245 persons, consisting of 25,568 officers and clerks, 21,180 office keepers, messengers, porters, and letter carriers, and 3,497 prison officers.

Of these 50,245 persons, 45,892 were males, and 4,353 were females. These figures are exclusive of dockyard and other artificers in Government establishments, who have been classed by the character of their craft, and therefore they are not comparable with the figures in the 1871 Census, when such artificers were included amongst civil servants.

Police.

The Police numbered 32,508, being about 17 per cent. in excess of the corrected total in 1871. The increase in the police force was, therefore, proportionally rather greater than that of the population. One policeman sufficed on an average to maintain order among 799 of the population.

Army.

The Soldiers, as given in the Occupation Table, are those soldiers only who were present in England and Wales at the date of the Census, and numbered 87,168, in which total are included those persons who returned themselves as in the Yeomanry, Militia, and other similar services outside the Regular Army, and also 8,572 pensioners. By special returns, however, we are enabled to give separate tables (*see* Appendix A., Tables 37 and 40) showing the number and ages of the entire regular army at home and abroad. It comprised 186,428 persons, of whom 9,222 were commissioned officers, and 177,206 were non-commissioned officers and men. Of the entire body, 128,856 were of English or Welsh birth; 15,177 were Scotch; 39,471 were Irish; and the remaining 2,924 were of foreign or colonial birth.

The Royal Navy.

The total number of officers and men in the Royal Navy returned as being in this country at the date of the Census, excluding 8,910 pensioners, was 20,732. To these must be added 23,668 who were serving out of the country at that date, making a total of 44,400 officers and men in the service. This is exclusive of the Marines, of whom 7,720 were enumerated in this country, while 5,464 were serving out of the country, making together a total of 13,184 officers and men. Table 40 in the Appendix gives the ages of persons serving in the Navy and Marines, whether at home or abroad.

Clerical Profession.

The Clergy of the Established Church number 21,663 in the table. But it must be remembered that many Clergymen are schoolmasters, and in such case they were classed as Teachers, not as Clergymen. Judging from the Clergy List, the real number of Clergymen at the time of the Census was not far short of 24,000. The Roman Catholic Priests numbered 2,089, against 1,620 in 1871. They had therefore increased by 29 per cent. The Ministers of other religious communities numbered 9,734, against 9,334 returned in 1871, an increase of 4 per cent. The Missionaries, Scripture Readers, and Itinerant Preachers, 4,625 in number, had increased by 42 per cent., and the Nuns and Sisters of Charity by more than 50 per cent. Taking the whole sub-order together the increase in the ten years was 14·7 per cent., or much the same as the increase of the population.

Legal Profession.

The Barristers and Solicitors together numbered 17,386, and were 12 per cent. more numerous than in 1871. The Law-students, 1,653 in number, had increased by 7 per cent.; and the Law-clerks, 24,602 in number, by 33 per cent. The whole legal profession, as thus constituted, included 43,641 persons, and had increased by 23 per cent.

Medical Profession.

The Medical Men on the official register in 1881 numbered 22,936; but the number of Physicians, Surgeons, and General Practitioners returned as being in England and Wales at the date of the Census was only 15,116. The balance consisted of Medical Men registered in England, but practising abroad, and of some who had died, but whose names had not been removed from the register, owing to no notice of death having been received. The number of Medical Practitioners enumerated in 1871 was 14,692; so that the increase in this group was less than 3 per cent. The increase of the Dentists was much greater. Of these there were 3,583 enumerated in 1881, and only 2,466 in 1871, a difference of 45 per cent. It is not improbable that the small apparent increase among the Medical Practitioners, and the large apparent increase among the Dentists, may be due to many, who since the passing of the Dentists' Act in 1878 style themselves Dentists, having preferred in 1871 to return themselves as Medical Practitioners, or, at any rate, under some other designation than Dentists. If the Medical Practitioners and the Dentists be taken together, the total was 17,158 in 1871, and 18,699 in 1881; an increase of close upon 9 per cent. Besides the 18,699 Medical Men and Dentists, there were also 6,056 Medical Students and Assistants, 2,646 Midwives, and 37,147 persons, most of whom were nurses, in the Subordinate Medical Service. The whole medical profession as thus constituted consisted of 64,548 persons; without reckoning the Chemists and Druggists, who numbered 19,000, or the Surgical Instrument makers, who numbered 1,511.

The large number of sick nurses included in this sub-order caused the Medical Profession to consist of many more females than males.

Schoolmasters and teachers.

The number of persons employed in general education, that is, the Schoolmasters and Schoolmistresses of all grades (including Professors, Lecturers, Tutors, Governesses, and Pupil Teachers), was 168,920, to whom should be added a further 2,911 engaged in subordinate school services, making a total of 171,831. Of these, 72 per cent. were women.

In 1871 the corrected total under the corresponding headings was 124,597, of whom 32,243 were males, and 92,354 were females. Thus the Teachers in the course of the decade had increased by 38 per cent., the male teachers by 48 per cent., and the female teachers by 34 per cent.

The results of this enormous increase in the number of teachers in diffusing elementary education cannot be stated with certainty, because the only available test we have of the spread of education is the increase in the proportion of persons who are able to sign their names in the register when they come to marry; and only few of the children who were at school in 1871, and none of those who were at school in 1881, are yet of marrying ages. Still it is worth noting that the educational efforts of late years, which of course date back far beyond the 1871 Census, have had the effect of reducing the proportion of persons who could not sign their names from 40 per cent. in the decade ending with 1850 to 20 per cent. in the decade ending with 1880.

Civil engineers, &c.

The Civil Engineers numbered 7,124, and were 35 per cent. in excess of the number returned in 1871. But it is by no means certain to us that the persons who returned themselves as Civil Engineers in 1881 precisely corresponded to those who did so in 1871; so that, though there was doubtless a great increase, it must be left uncertain what was its exact extent. The Mining Engineers, now for the first time taken out as distinct from the Mine Service, numbered 2,291; and the Surveyors, a somewhat vaguely-used term, numbered 5,394.

Musicians, &c.

Among artists and other persons who minister to our amusement, by far the most numerous were the Musicians. Of these, including all grades down to the street-organ player, 25,546 were enumerated, showing an increase of 38 per cent. upon the corrected total in 1871. The appliances of music were provided by 9,249 Musical Instrument Makers, who also had increased by 28 per cent. in the course of the decade, and by 1,440 Printers and Sellers of Musical Publications. Taking them all together, the persons who gain their livelihood by music amounted to 36,235, and had increased since 1871 by 37 per cent. This increase was the more remarkable, inasmuch as the growth of the same group had been 24 per cent. in the preceding intercensal period.

Actors, &c.

Nor was this great development confined to music. It extended to other forms of amusement. The Actors and Actresses, 4,565 in number, were 30 per cent. more numerous than in 1871; while the Persons engaged in Exhibitions or as Professionals in various games numbered 5,043, and had gone up more than 60 per cent. As regards the theatre, it is to be noted that whereas the Actors outnumbered the Actresses very considerably in 1871, the reverse was the case in 1881, there being 2,368 Actresses enumerated to 2,197 Actors.

Photographers.

The Photographers, as might be anticipated, had increased greatly. In 1871 the actual number given in the return was 4,715, which had increased in 1881 to 6,661, or more than 40 per cent.

4. *Domestic Class.*

Domestic Class.

The Domestic Class, as now constituted, differs very widely from the same class as constituted in the Census of 1871. It included at that time not only Domestic and other Servants, to which it has been restricted in the present Census, but also Innkeepers, Beersellers, and others whose business it is to provide board and lodging. These we have removed to the Industrial Class. We have also not taken Wives into account, inasmuch as to do so would in many cases involve reckoning the same woman twice over, once as Wife and again as Boarding-house Keeper or the like, when the wife has any specified occupation of her own. On the other hand, we have included in the class all persons engaged in Laundry-work, who in 1871 were classed with the Makers of Dress. The number of persons comprised in the class as now constituted was 1,803,810, and of these 86 per cent. were females.

The persons returned as Indoor Domestic Servants were no fewer than 1,286,668, and exceeded the next most numerous group, the Agricultural Labourers, by some 50 per cent. Out of every 22 persons in the population at all ages, one was an Indoor Domestic Servant. The proportion differed, of course, very largely in different parts. Speaking generally, it was lowest in mining and manufacturing parts, higher in agricultural districts, and highest in towns, especially in such towns as are the habitual resorts of the wealthier classes. Thus in London the proportion of Indoor Domestic Servants to the population was 1 to 15, in Brighton 1 to 11, and in Bath 1 to 9; in the Eastern Division, comprising the agricultural counties of Norfolk, Suffolk, and Essex, it was 1 to 21; and in the South-western Division, also mainly agricultural, 1 to 18; whereas in Staffordshire it was 1 to 28, in Lancashire 1 to 30, and in Durham 1 to 31.

Domestic indoor servants.

This occupation is practically monopolised by the female sex, who outnumbered the 56,262 males in the proportion of 22 to 1. Of females above 5 years of age, one in nine was an indoor servant. The occupation contrasts with most others in the age-distribution of those who follow it. Not far short of half of them were under 20 years of age; and of girls between 15 and 20 years of age no less than one in three was a domestic indoor servant. Such, at least, was the case according to the returns; but, as we have stated elsewhere, there is reason to believe that a considerable number of servant girls who are not yet 15 years old represent themselves as having reached that age, so as to be more readily taken into service.

The Indoor Domestic Servants in 1871 numbered 1,275,747;* so that the increase in this class of persons in the course of the decade was less than 1 per cent. As the population has increased more than 14 per cent., it is possible that the frequently heard complaint of householders as to the increasing difficulty in finding suitable servants may have a real foundation.

The above account refers simply to the Indoor Servants in private families; that is to say, it excludes Coachmen, Grooms, and Gardeners, who are dealt with in other paragraphs; neither does it include the 62,310 Inn Servants, nor the 92,474 Charwomen, nor the 180,078 persons engaged in Laundries. If all these and similar forms of service be included, the total number of servants, domestic or other, was no less than 1,803,810, as already stated.

5. *Commercial Class.*

In the Commercial Class are included not only the persons directly engaged in Commerce, that is to say, the Merchants, Bankers, and Insurers, with their Agents, Clerks, and Travellers, the Accountants and the Auctioneers, but also the persons engaged in Conveyance and Storage. The whole class as thus constituted comprised 980,128, or, in round numbers, a million persons. Of these, the first order, the persons directly engaged in commerce, numbered 316,865; and the second order, the persons engaged in conveyance and storage, numbered 663,263. But if we also take into consideration, as we shall do, those industries outside the class that are indirectly subservient to conveyance, we shall have a much larger total; conveyance and storage by themselves, as thus construed, occupying a million persons.

Commerci Class.

Among the headings in the Table relating to the Mercantile Class are some that are not very satisfactory. Such is "Merchant" itself. What constitutes a Merchant? Probably it would be said that the term applies to any wholesale dealer on a very large scale. But there are many large wholesale dealers who do not call themselves merchants, and many retail dealers who give themselves this designation. There are Wine and Spirit Merchants, Corn Merchants, Tea Merchants, Merchant Tailors, Rag Merchants, and the like, many of whom deal by retail. The rule adopted by us was, that whenever the nature of the goods in which the merchant dealt was stated, the individual should be classed by the character of his merchandise; but that when

Merchants

* No correction for "retired" has been made in this case in the 1871 total. For the great bulk of female servants retire by marriage, or by entering on other occupations, and would not return themselves, unless exceptionally, as "retired domestic servant."

the kind of goods was not stated, the simple return being "Merchant," without further specification, or when the name of the country only was given with which the merchant traded, *e.g.*, East India Merchant, he should be placed under the heading "Merchant." Of such persons the number was 10,359, whereas in 1871 the number placed under this heading was 15,936. Doubtlessly, the term Merchant must have been used with a less restricted signification in the tabulation of 1871 than on the present occasion.

Commercial Travellers.

That no such depression as these figures by themselves might be supposed to indicate really occurred in commerce may be inferred from the numbers returned under the less vague and indefinite heading "Commercial Traveller." Of these there were 35,478, or twice as many as in 1871. Among them were 878 European foreigners.

Commercial Clerks.

The Commercial Clerks numbered 181,457, and were also twice as many as were so classed in 1871, but the term was used in different ways on the two occasions. In 1871 the clerks in factories were placed to the account of the special manufacture in the office of which they were engaged. For instance, a clerk in a cotton warehouse was placed to Cotton Manufacture; but in 1881 all clerks, employed in any branch of commerce or industry, were assigned, not to that special branch, but to the general heading "Commercial Clerk." The heading was thus made to include all clerks excepting Civil Service, Army, Navy, Law, Bank, Insurance, and Railway Clerks. The returns, therefore, for 1881 and 1871 are not comparable. Of the 181,457 Commercial Clerks 3,327 were European foreigners, 1,795 being natives of the German Empire.

Merchants and Bankers, though their business keeps them in the daytime in towns, yet so often live outside that a comparison of the numbers present on the night of the Census in the respective great towns would hardly be of much interest. But it is otherwise with the Commercial Clerks as a rule, and we find that of the 181,457 enumerated, 116,520 were present in one or other of the 47 urban districts that had populations exceeding 50,000 persons. There were 60,605 in London, with 1,847 more in West Ham and 1,195 in Croydon, which in this respect may be looked on almost as parts of London, making together 63,647. Next to London came Liverpool with Birkenhead, where 10,961 clerks were enumerated. Then followed Manchester and Salford, together accounting for 7,324, Birmingham and Aston with 4,907, Leeds with 2,523, Sheffield with 2,265, Bristol with 2,253, Newcastle-on-Tyne with 1,993, Kingston-on-Hull with 1,817, Bradford with 1,568, and Nottingham with 1,346. In none of the other towns did the number reach 1,000.

Agents.

The Agents, Brokers, and Factors numbered 31,208, and were also vastly in excess of the number so returned in 1871; but these terms are used in so vague and indefinite a manner that not much importance can be attached to the returns.

Bankers.

The Bankers, together with the Bank Clerks and generally the Bank Service, numbered 16,055, and exceeded the corrected total for 1871 by 35 per cent.

Persons engaged in Insurance.

The increase was still greater among Persons engaged in Insurance. Of these, 15,068 were enumerated, whereas the number returned in 1871, after including 253 Underwriters and 11 Average Adjusters, was only 5,687, or not much more than one-third. This enormous apparent increase naturally leads us to suppose that the method of tabulation must have differed in 1871 from that pursued in 1881, but we can find no evidence that such was the case.

Accountants, Auctioneers, &c.

The Accountants numbered 11,606, and were 20 per cent. in excess of the corrected total in 1871; and, lastly, the Auctioneers, Valuers, House Agents, 10,075 in number, had increased apparently more than 60 per cent. Some small part of this apparent increase was due to the fact that in 1881 all Valuers were placed to this heading, whereas in 1871 some Valuers were classed by the commodities which they valued, Valuers of Mines, for instance, going to Mine Service, and Valuers of Timber and Wood to Timber Merchant. This change, however, can scarcely have had any very important effect on the figures, and, after all allowance for it, the growth under this heading must have been enormous.

Conveyance of goods and of passengers.

The number of persons engaged either directly in the Conveyance of Goods and Passengers, or in the industries that are subservient to such traffic, is enormous. The ramifications of these branches of industry are so wide and so complicated that it is impossible to follow them all out, and we must content ourselves with an estimate of the main contributories. The traffic may be either by road, by railway, or by water, and it will be convenient to estimate the three separately.

We will begin with Road traffic; and under it include the following trades and businesses:— Road traffic.

Road Contractor, Surveyor - - -	1,326	
Road Labourer - - -	10,947	
Turnpike-keeper - - - -	1,104	
Total engaged in making and keeping roads		13,377
Makers of Carriages and other Vehicles -	27,006	
Wheelwrights - - - -	28,732	
Saddlers, Harness makers - - -	23,866	
Total engaged in making vehicles and harness - - - -		79,604
Horse Proprietor, Breeder - -	2,233	
Groom, Horse-keeper, Breaker - -	40,863	
Domestic Coachman, Groom -	73,167	
Cabman, Flyman, Coachman (not dom.) -	30,492	
Omnibus, Cab, Livery-stable, &c., keeper -	6,787	
Carrier, Carter, Haulier - - -	125,342	
Tramway Service - - -	2,650	
Total engaged in driving or in care of horses - - - -		281,534
Total engaged in Road Traffic		374,515

Among the occupations that are included in the above reckoning is one that is dying out, namely, Turnpike-keeper. The number fell from 3,928 in 1871 to 1,104 in 1881. On the other hand, there are two that barely appeared in the returns for 1871, but had gained very largely in 1881, and, though as yet not of much importance, doubtlessly will make a much more considerable figure in 1891. These are Tramway service, the persons employed in which rose from 63 in 1871 to 2,650 in 1881; and the making of Bicycles and other Velocipedes, which occupied only 12 persons in 1871, but under which 1,072 were classed in 1881, chiefly at Coventry.

Let us now estimate in the same general way the persons engaged in Railway traffic and its ancillary industries. Railway traffic.

Railway Contractors - - -	1,182	
Railway Labourers - - - -	36,850	
Platelayers - - - -	21,997	
Total engaged in making and keeping railways - - - -		60,029
Railway Carriage-makers - -	7,570	
Locomotive Engine-makers - - -	?	
Total engaged in Carriage-making -		7,570
Guards - - - -	10,296	
Engine-drivers, Stokers - - -	22,856	
Pointsmen, Level-crossing Men - -	6,205	
Other Railway Officials and Servants - -	100,051	
Total engaged with trains or stations -		139,408
Total engaged in Railway Traffic -		207,007

We can give no estimate of the Locomotive Engine Makers, who are merged in the makers of engines of all kinds, nor of the Rail-makers, who are lumped with the iron and steel industries, nor of many other subsidiary trades that might otherwise be included.

Water traffic. There remains Traffic by Water, under which come—

Ship, Boat, Barge Builders - - -	21,741	
Shipwright, Ship-carpenter (ashore) - -	23,930	
Ship Riggers, Chandlers, Fitters - -	2,861	
Anchor, Chain Manufacturers - -	5,029	
Mast, Yard, Oar, Block, maker - -	1,419	
Sail-makers - - - - -	4,129	
Total engaged in making or equipping vessels		59,109
Seamen (Merchant Service) enumerated -	95,093	
Seamen (English and Welsh)* abroad -	63,330	
Bargemen, Lightermen, Watermen - -	30,223	
Boatmen on Seas - - - -	1,570	
Pilots - - - - -	2,991	
Ship Stewards, Cooks - - -	6,767	
Total seagoing persons - -		199,974
Navigation Service (on shore) -	4,697	
Harbour, Dock, Lighthouse Service - -	42,643	
Total of Shore Service - - -		47,340
Total engaged in Water Traffic -		306,423

The result of this necessarily imperfect estimate of the persons engaged directly or indirectly in the conveyance of goods and passengers is a total of 887,945; and if in addition to these we reckon in the 32,026 persons who were employed in storage, either as Warehousemen or as Weighers, and allow that about two-thirds of the 131,171 persons returned as Messengers, Porters, or Watchmen were occupied in porterage of goods, we have eventually a total of a million of the population employed in transport and its subsidiary industries.

6. *Agricultural Class.*

Agricultural Class. Under the various headings that are placed together to form the Agricultural Class 1,383,184 persons were enumerated; which number showed, as compared with the total in 1871, duly corrected for comparison, a decline of 8·2 per cent. The Agricultural Class, however, comprises not only those who may properly be called agricultural, as being engaged in cultivation, but also 104,560 persons engaged about animals, many of whom, and especially the Fishermen, are in no sense agricultural persons. The persons engaged in the cultivation of farm lands, including woods and gardens, numbered 1,278,624, and showed a decline since 1871 of 9·3 per cent.

Farmers. In 1871 there were 249,907 Farmers and Graziers enumerated in England and Wales. In 1881 the number had fallen to 223,943, a decline of 25,964, or of 10·39 per cent. It is true that in 1871 "retired farmers" were included in the reckoning, whereas this was not the case in 1881. But, as has been previously stated, the allowance to be made on this account is probably at the outside some two per cent.; so that the decline in the number of farmers was real and very considerable. Moreover, coincidently with this decline in the number of farmers, there was a notable increase in the number of farm bailiffs. In 1871 these had numbered 16,476, but in 1881 they had risen to 19,377, that is had increased nearly 18 per cent. These figures clearly point to the surrendering of farm-holdings by tenant farmers, and their cultivation by the owner himself or his bailiff.

Agricultural Labourers. As regards Agricultural Labourers, there was also doubtlessly a very considerable decline in the interval between the last two enumerations, but it is difficult to deal satisfactorily with this class, because of the confusion between agricultural and other labourers in the schedules. Special attention was called this time to the importance of carefully stating the exact kind of labour in the schedules, and, owing to this, the

* Only those Merchant Seamen abroad who were of English or Welsh birth are here reckoned in. The total number of Mariners abroad in Foreign-going British Merchant Vessels was 130,587.

returns of agricultural labourers were probably more complete in 1881 than on any previous occasion. At any rate we may be perfectly assured that the returns were fully as complete as in 1871, so that any apparent decline in the numbers of this class of persons will be, if anything, below and not above the mark, if we take care to allow the 2 per cent. already mentioned for the omission in 1881 of retired or superannuated labourers from the account. Now, in 1871 the Agricultural Labourers, the Indoor Farm Servants, the Shepherds, and the persons returned simply as Cottagers, amounted together to 981,988, or, after deduction of two per cent. for the superannuated, to 962,348, whereas in 1881 they numbered only 870,798. There was thus a decline of some 91,550, or of nearly 10 per cent., in this class of labourers. There was also a slight decline in another group of persons who may be regarded as an upper kind of farm labourers, namely, the sons, grandsons, and nephews of farmers, returned as living in the farmhouse and yet not stated to have had any definite occupation. These male relatives of farmers, who may be assumed to have been engaged in farm work, fell from 76,466 in 1871 to 75,197 in 1881.

This decline in the number of agricultural labourers was apparently not due to any falling off in the amount of land under cultivation; for it appears from the Agricultural Returns that though the total acreage of arable land in England and Wales fell from 14,946,179 in 1871 to 13,977,662 in 1881, yet this decline was much more than compensated by an increase in the permanent pasture from 11,376,298 to 13,471,238 acres; so that the acreage of arable and pasture land together had risen, from 26,322,477 in 1871 to 27,448,900 in 1881, an increase of 1,126,423 acres or of 4·28 per cent. To what extent the exchange of 968,517 acres of arable land for 2,094,940 acres of permanent pasture would affect the amount of labour required for cultivation is a question which we must leave to agricultural experts.

Some small indication, however, of a reason for the decline in the number of agricultural labourers is perhaps to be found in the fact that the Proprietors of, and Attendants on, Agricultural Machines, who only numbered 2,160 in 1871, had increased to 4,260 in 1881, that is to say, they had doubled in number in the course of the ten years. Machinery had taken the place of hand labour. In 1871 the ratio of agricultural labourers of one kind or other to cultivated land was 3·95 labourers to 100 acres; in 1881 the proportion of labourers to the same area was 3·45, that is to say, the labour had diminished by 12·7 per cent. for like areas of cultivation.

Although General Labourers are not grouped in the agricultural class, with which we are now more especially concerned, yet, inasmuch as there is admittedly a certain amount of confusion in the returns between general and agricultural labourer, it may be well to deal here with this group of workers, and it will be convenient to give a summary view of all such labourers as were abstracted separately. General Labourers.

	1871 (Corrected numbers).	1881.
Agricultural Labourers	962,348	870,798
General Labourers	506,273	559,769
Railway Navvies and Platelayers	44,169	58,847
Road Labourers	8,136	10,947
	1,520,926	1,500,361

There is a considerable increase under each heading, excepting the agricultural, the general labourers having increased 10·6 per cent., the railway labourers 33·2 per cent., and the road labourers 34·6 per cent. The whole mass of labourers put together, exclusive of labourers in more specialised occupations, was 1,520,926 in 1871, and was 1,500,361, or practically the same, in 1881. Thus the class of labourers had remained stationary, while the general population had increased by 14·36 per cent.

Had the labouring class increased in the same ratio as the general population there would have been 239,016 more of them than were actually enumerated. This number, therefore, may be supposed either to have emigrated or to have adopted more specialised kinds of work.

Passing from the cultivation of fields and pastures to that of gardens, we find some strange differences between the figures for 1871 and for 1881. The number of Market Gardeners had apparently gone down enormously, from 98,069 to 65,882, while the Gardeners

number of Nurserymen and Seedsmen had gone up, namely, from 5,495 to 7,755. If, however, we look to the heading "Domestic Gardener," we find that the number given in 1871 was 18,688, while the number returned in 1881 was 74,648. It is quite plain that there has been some confusion between Market Gardeners and Domestic Gardeners. In 1881, when a man returned himself simply as Gardener, he was taken, in the absence of any certainty, to be a Domestic Gardener, on the ground that this was likely to be the more numerous class. But our predecessors in 1871 took the contrary view, and considered the gardener undefined to be a Market Gardener. Clearly the only safe plan of comparison under these circumstances is to lump all Gardeners, market or domestic, together, and also with them to take in the Nurserymen and Seedsmen. These together in 1871 amounted to 122,252, or, after due deduction for the "retired," to 119,807, and had increased in 1881 to 148,285 or by 24 per cent.; so that garden cultivation, as measured by the number of persons employed in it, would appear to have grown at a much more rapid rate than the general population.

Fishermen.

The Fishermen, including 294 women, who were probably shrimp, cockle, or mussel gatherers, numbered 29,696. This tallies very nearly with the estimate formed by the Board of Trade, who calculated that the number of men and boys constantly employed in fishing and resident within the limits of the English and Welsh ports was 29,141 in 1881, in addition, however, to 12,519 other persons who, though not regular fishermen, were occasionally employed in fishing.

As compared with the corrected total for 1871, there was an increase of no less than 44 per cent. in the enumerated fishermen.

The produce of the industry of these fishermen, who were furnished with the implements of their craft by 1,733 Netmakers and 1,461 Tacklemakers, was distributed to the consumers by 17,906 Fishmongers; so that, disregarding the imported produce of foreign fishers, there was one seller to less than two catchers of fish. Neglecting, as insignificant in number, the few professional fishermen in inland waters, the fishermen are of course limited by the nature of their industry to the maritime districts. Their distribution, following the coast line, was as follows:—

Northumberland	1,402	Dorsetshire	370
Durham	327	Devonshire	1,826
North Riding	1,232	Cornwall	4,400
East Riding	2,003	Somersetshire	59
Lincolnshire	4,357	Gloucestershire	105
Norfolk	2,898	South Wales	637
Suffolk	2,763	North Wales	284
Essex	980	Cheshire	334
Kent	1,793	Lancashire	1,342
Sussex	1,473	Cumberland	149
Hampshire	527		

7. *Industrial Class.*

INDUSTRIAL CLASS.

The Industrial Class, speaking generally, is the class of Makers and of Shopkeepers. It includes all persons with specified occupations who were not referred to the Professional, Domestic, Commercial, or Agricultural Classes, and by itself outnumbers all these put together. It comprised in 1881 no fewer than 6,373,367 persons, or 24·5 per cent. of the entire population of all ages and both sexes, and 57·0 per cent. of the population with specified occupations. After carefully correcting the figures so as to render them as nearly comparable as possible, it appears that this class increased by somewhat less than 11 per cent. in the interval between the last two Censuses; or in a lower ratio than the general population.

It will be impossible to deal with all the headings and sub-divisions in this huge class. We shall, therefore, make a selection of the chief groups, and confine ourselves to these.

Industries subservient to production of Books, &c.

A fairly natural group of industries may be made by putting together those which are mainly subservient to the production of literature. There are, in the first place, the Authors. Of these no accurate account can be given. Writers of books, and especially of the best books, are scarcely likely to return themselves in the occupation column as Authors. There were, however, 3,434 persons, probably mostly Journalists, who returned themselves either as Author, Editor, or Journalist, to whom may be added 1,200 more who returned themselves as engaged in various scientific pursuits, and who would also be probably contributors to literature. The Journalists were furnished with their daily material by 2,677 Short-hand writers and Reporters; and the Authors had 1,083 persons to serve them in literary and scientific institutions. This gives us to begin with, 8,394 persons, as the direct or indirect contributors of literature, whom we borrow from the Professional Class.

The physical materials used by these persons are paper, which was derived from 18,629 persons employed in its manufacture, who in their turn received materials from 3,291 Rag-gatherers and dealers; steel pens, made by 2,723 persons, almost all women; pencils, made by 232 persons; and ink, the makers of which were not separately abstracted, but were included with the Makers of Blacking and other Colouring Matter. These goods were sold by 15,241 Stationers, who employed 2,108 persons, almost all women, merely to make envelopes. This second division of our group makes up in all 42,224 persons supplying writers with their materials.

Then come the Printers, numbering 61,290; besides 2,265 Engravers, 6,721 Lithographers, Copper or Steel-plate printers, and Map-makers. The type used by these printers was made by 1,169 Type founders and Cutters.

The printed matter was dealt with by 20,097 Bookbinders, and eventually distributed by 9,910 Publishers, Booksellers, and Librarians. If we also take into account 5,515 Newspaper Agents and News-room keepers, and 1,440 Sellers and Printers of Musical publications, with a few nondescripts, we have eventually a total of 159,094 persons contributing directly or indirectly to literature. Of course all the products of these persons were not literature. The Paper manufacture, for instance, supplied many other industries than the literary. But, on the other hand, there are numerous persons who contribute to fill our bookshelves who cannot be taken into the reckoning; so that the total may stand as a rough approximation.

Comparing the returns for the chief of the above-mentioned occupations in 1881 with those in 1871, we find, after due correction of the figures, that the Papermakers had increased 13·3 per cent., the Printers 39·6 per cent., the Binders 32·5 per cent., the Stationers 30·7 per cent., and the Publishers, Booksellers, and Librarians 7·7 per cent. In these industries there has been, as in many other handicrafts, a tendency to use female in place of male labour, doubtless on economical grounds. This is shown by the following statement of the proportion of females to 100 males employed in each industry in 1871 and in 1881:—

	1871.	1881.
Paper manufacture - -	65	80
Printer - - - - -	2	4
Bookbinder - - -	95	111
Stationer - - - -	34	53
Bookseller, Publisher, &c. - -	15	17

Even in the making of envelopes, which has always been a specially female occupation, the males have lost ground; for in 1871 there were 1,012 females to 100 males employed, whereas in 1881 the female proportion had risen to 1,105.

Makers of Machines and Implements.

The number of persons working and dealing in machines and implements was 267,976, who were almost exclusively males. Some of the smaller sub-divisions of this order have already been casually noticed, such as the Musical Instrument Makers, the Surgical Instrument Makers, and the Makers of Apparatus for Games. There remain, however, the three chief sub-orders, namely, the Machine Makers, the Toolmakers, and the makers of Clocks, Watches, and Philosophical Instruments.

Machinery Makers.

The makers of Machines of all kinds numbered 160,797, and, after due correction of the figures so as to make them comparable, showed an increase of 28 per cent. upon the return for 1871. The greatest increase was among the makers of Spinning and Weaving machinery, who were 19,896 in number, and almost exactly twice as many as in 1871. The makers of Agricultural Machines and Implements numbered 4,119, and had increased 16 per cent.; while the 6,940 Millwrights, the 26,170 Boiler-makers, the 64,663 Fitters and Turners, together with the 38,481 Makers of Engines and Machines other than spinning or weaving or agricultural, made up a total of 136,254, and showed an increase of 21 per cent. Of this last group of 136,254 persons, 25,864 were enumerated in Lancashire; 17,529 in London; 15,591 in the West Riding; 11,132 in Durham; 5,626 in Staffordshire; 5,141 in Northumberland; 3,596 in Warwickshire; and 3,283 in Derbyshire. Of the 19,896 Spinning and Weaving Machinery makers, 9,110 were enumerated in Lancashire; 7,257 in the West Riding; 1,653 in Nottinghamshire; 530 in Cheshire; 452 in Leicestershire; and 318 in Derbyshire.

Makers of Tools and Implements.

The Tool and Implement Makers numbered 48,556, and, as compared with the duly corrected total in 1871, showed an increase of scarcely more than 5 per cent. The chief sub-divisions under which they were grouped, and the number of persons in each sub-division, at the two Censuses, were as follows. The figures for 1871 have been corrected by a deduction of 2 per cent. for the retired.

	1871. (Corrected Numbers.)	1881.
Tool maker and dealer (undefined)	7,474	9,353
Cutler and Scissors maker	18,958	18,234
File maker	8,821	8,967
Saw maker	1,919	2,116
Pin maker	673	729
Needle maker	4,644	4,455
Steel-pen maker	1,741	2,723
Pencil maker	170	232
	44,400	46,809

It will be seen that though the smaller industries of Steel-pen, Pencil, and Pin making had increased, as also had the group as a whole, yet, under the chief heading of all, Cutler and Scissors maker, there had been a decline, as also under the heading of Needle maker.

The giant share of tool-making belongs to the West Riding, and especially to Sheffield. Of the 18,234 Cutlers and Scissors makers, no fewer than 16,449 were enumerated in this Riding, and of these 15,290 were in Sheffield. Similarly, of the 8,967 File makers, 6,756 were in this Riding, and of them 5,541 were in Sheffield; in this industry, however, Lancashire has a respectable share, 1,042 File makers having been enumerated in that county. Again, of the 2,116 Saw makers, there were 1,237 in Sheffield, and 130 others in the rest of the Riding. Altogether, of the 38,670 Cutlers, Scissors makers, File and Saw makers, and General Tool Makers and Dealers, who were enumerated in the country, no fewer than 27,553 were enumerated in the West Riding, and of these 24,206 were in Sheffield. The only other counties in which these tool-making industries can be said to be carried on, are Staffordshire, Warwickshire, and Lancashire, in which, respectively, 2,011, 2,783, and 2,168 such Tool makers and dealers were enumerated.

The manufactures of Needles, Pins, Steel-pens, and Pencils are carried on elsewhere. Of the 4,455 Needle makers, 2,394 were enumerated in Warwickshire, 1,555 in Worcestershire, 245 in Leicestershire, and 193 in Nottinghamshire, leaving only 68 scattered in other parts.

Of the 729 Pin makers, 406 were enumerated in Warwickshire, mostly in Birmingham and Aston, 180 were enumerated in Gloucestershire, in the Stroud district, and 51 in Worcestershire.

Of the 2,723 Steel-pen makers, 2,578 were enumerated in Birmingham and Aston, 75 in Worcestershire, and 30 in Staffordshire. This manufacture is almost exclusively in the hands of women, who outnumbered the men in the proportion of 1,138 women to 100 men.

The making of Pencils is carried on chiefly at Keswick, in Cumberland, in which county 116, or exactly half of the entire 232, were enumerated; of the remainder, 77 were enumerated in London, and 32 in Birmingham.

Makers of Clocks, Watches, and Scientific Instruments.

From Tools and Implements we pass on to instruments of greater delicacy and complexity, such as Clocks, Watches, Optical and Philosophical Instruments. The total number of persons returned in this sub-order was 32,064, almost exclusively of the male sex, and was about 22 per cent. in excess of the corrected total in 1871.

The most important heading in the sub-order is that of the Watch and Clock makers, who numbered 23,351, and had increased 12 per cent. Probably, in many cases, the Watchmakers are not distinguishable from Goldsmiths, Silversmiths, and Jewellers, who are not included in this sub-order, but numbered 24,715, and had increased 14·5 per cent., or much in the same ratio as the population. The Opticians and Philosophical Instrument makers, also doubtlessly often mixed up with the Watchmakers, numbered 3,605, and had risen by 13·5 per cent. The Makers of Electrical Apparatus, who in 1871 only numbered 428, had risen with the development of electrical science to 2,522 in 1881. The remaining heading in the sub-order, Makers of Measuring and Weighing Apparatus, included 2,586 persons, showing an apparent increase in the decade of not far from 50 per cent. The tabulation, however, under this heading was probably somewhat uncertain.

Makers of Guns and Weapons.

The Makers of Weapons comprised 8,227 persons, of whom 2,741 were Gunsmiths. The Gunsmiths had declined very considerably in number since 1871, when 11,576 were returned. This is the more noticeable, inasmuch as the Gamekeepers had slightly increased in the same period, having risen from 12,431 to 12,633. Probably the reduction in the number of Gunsmiths is to be explained by the decline in the export of small fire-arms from the United Kingdom, which fell from an annual mean of 469,207 in 1870–71 to a mean of 259,563 in 1880–81,—a decline of 45 per cent. Of the 7,741 persons returned as Gunsmiths, 4,408, or considerably more than half, were enumerated in Birmingham or Aston.

Building trades.

The number of persons employed in Building trades, using this general term to include Architects, Builders, Carpenters, Joiners, Bricklayers, Masons, Slaters, Tilers, Plasterers, Whitewashers, Paperhangers, Plumbers, Painters, and Glaziers, amounted to 673,636. But in order to make a comparison with 1871 we must also include 4,150 Paviours, as in the Census of 1871 Masons and Paviours were not distinguished. This gives us a total of 677,786 persons employed in these allied branches of industry. The number engaged in the same trades in 1871 was 571,217, which is reduced by correction for the "retired" to 559,793. The growth of the Building trades, as shown by the number of persons engaged, was thus 21 per cent. in the course of the ten years. These trades, therefore, had grown in higher proportion than the general population.

Of what this army of Builders may have done in the course of the ten years in the way of repairs, alterations, additions, and substitution of new houses for old houses no account can be given. But, as shown in the Summary Table (Vol. I., Table I.), taking the inhabited and uninhabited houses together, there were 697,733 more houses in 1881 than in 1871. There were, moreover, 46,414 houses in course of construction at the date of the Census in 1881 against 37,803 in 1871.

Stone, Slate, Cement, Brick, and Tile industries.

If the Building trades had thus increased, we should expect to find a corresponding growth in those trades which provide the Builder with his materials, namely, among the Stone and Slate quarriers and workers, the Cement and Plaster makers, and the Brick and Tile makers; and this anticipation is justified by the figures. The numbers engaged in these industries in 1871 was, after correction for the retired, 81,928; it had grown in 1881 to 105,544, that is, it had increased by 29 per cent., or even in a higher ratio than the Builders themselves.

Furnishing trades.

From the Building trades, and those who supply the Builders with their materials, we pass naturally to the Furnishing trades. Under this heading a vast number of trades might be classed. We shall take, however, the following as forming the group, Upholsterers, Cabinet Makers, French Polishers, Locksmiths, Bellhangers, Gas Fitters, House and Shop Fittings Makers and Dealers, Wood Carvers, Carvers and Gilders, Furniture Dealers, and Carpet and Rug Manufacturers. The total number of persons returned as engaged in these trades was 124,355, while the corrected number in 1871 was 106,108. The growth in these trades had, therefore, been at the rate of nearly 17 per cent., or again more rapid than that of the population.

The Carpet and Rug Manufacture had grown 23 per cent., and, as in the other textile manufactures, there had been a great increase in the proportion of female to male labour employed in it. In 1871 the proportion was 47 to 100, in 1881 it was 59 to 100.

China, Earthenware, and Glass manufacturers and dealers.

In the above account of the Furnishing industries we did not include the manufactures of Earthenware, China, and Glass, thinking it better to give the figures of these industries separately. The total workers and dealers in these articles numbered 74,407, showing an increase of 8 per cent. upon the corrected total for 1871. These industries, therefore, in contrast with the other Furnishing trades, do not appear to have grown in equal proportion with the population.

Putting out of the account the mere dealers in Glass and Earthenware, and confining ourselves to the Manufacturers, we find an increase of 5 per cent. in the Earthenware and China industry, and of 10 per cent. in the manufacture of Glass.

The Glass manufacture is almost monopolized by men, there being 19,938 men and only 1,692 women returned as engaged in it, or nearly twelve men to one woman. Not so the manufacture of China and Earthenware. Here the female sex has a considerable share, the males employed numbering 28,719, and the females 17,877.

The great bulk of the China and Earthenware Manufactures is carried on in Staffordshire; for of the 46,596 persons employed in these industries, no fewer than 36,230 were enumerated in this county.

The Glass manufacture is more widely distributed. For of the 21,630 persons engaged in it, 5,984 were enumerated in Lancashire, 3,591 in the West Riding, 2,884 in Durham, 2,769 in London, 2,089 in Worcestershire, 1,752 in Warwickshire, 1,151 in Staffordshire, and only 1,410 in all the other counties.

Carriage and Harness makers.

We have already incidentally spoken of Carriage and Harness makers, as also of Shipbuilders and Riggers, when we were dealing with the conveyance of goods. A few additional words are required, however, as to the comparison of the figures under these headings with those of 1871.

The Makers of Carriages and of Vehicles of all kinds, excepting bicycles, &c., numbered 62,236, and exceeded the corrected total in 1871 by 13·9 per cent. The Harness Makers numbered 23,866, and had increased by 5·8 per cent.

Ship Builders, &c.

The Ship and Boat Builders, including the Riggers, Fitters, Chandlers, Sailmakers, &c., numbered 54,080, whereas the uncorrected total in 1871 was only 45,164. The figures, however, are not comparable; for in 1871 the return did not include Shipwrights or others employed by the Government, who were classed on that occasion with "Government Messengers, Workmen," whereas in 1881 they were referred to their trade.

Purveyors of Food and Drink.

The Purveyors of Food form a very large class. They may be divided roughly into those who supply us with Animal Food, those who supply us with Bread and Vegetables, those who supply us with Groceries, and those who supply us with Spirituous or other Drinks.

The Purveyors of Animal Food, including 81,702 Butchers and Meat Salesmen, 3,591 Poulterers and Game Dealers, 17,906 Fishmongers, 16,584 Provision Curers and Dealers, 25,805 Milksellers, and 4,379 Buttermen and Cheesemongers, numbered in all 149,967, and exceeded the corrected total for 1871 by 15·4 per cent.

The Purveyors of Bread and Vegetables, including 23,462 Millers, 9,966 Corn or Flour Dealers, 71,032 Bakers, 25,534 Pastrycooks or Confectioners, and 29,614 Greengrocers and Fruiterers, numbered 159,608, and exceeded the corrected total for 1871 by 12·5 per cent.

The Dealers in Groceries, including 129,818 Grocers and Tea Dealers, 3,070 Sugar Refiners, and 1,509 Makers and Sellers of Mustard or other Condiments, numbered 134,397, and exceeded the corrected total for 1871 by 18·8 per cent.

The Purveyors of Spirituous Drinks, including 438 Hop Dealers, 9,531 Maltsters, 24,567 Brewers, 86,689 Innkeepers, Publicans, and Beersellers, together with 7,889 Wine or Spirit Merchants, and 6,044 Cellarmen, numbered 135,158, and showed, as compared with the corrected total for 1871, a decline of 5·8 per cent.

It thus appears that, while in each of the other great branches of food-supply there was a growth, fairly proportionate to the growth of the population, in the supply of spirituous drinks there was exceptionally a decline: The actual decline was, as shown, in the ratio of 5·8 per cent. But, if we take into consideration the growth of the population, it was much more, these trades having fallen off, for equal populations, no less than 17·7 per cent.

If to the above-mentioned Purveyors of Food be added 4,662 Makers and Dealers in Mineral Waters, 8,173 Coffee-house or Eating-house Keepers, and 30 nondescripts, we have a total of 591,995 persons engaged in purveying food; with whom are further grouped in the table 37,376 Keepers of Lodging or Boarding Houses, making the total in this order amount to 629,371 persons.

Tobacconists.

Many of those who deal in food also deal in tobacco; but the number of persons who were returned as dealing in this commodity, or in pipes and other smoking apparatus, was 22,175, or 34 per cent. more than the corrected total in 1871.

Makers of Textile Fabrics.

The persons returned as working and dealing in Textile fabrics numbered 1,053,648, or, in round numbers, a million.

Cotton Manufacture.

By far the most important of these industries is the Manufacture of Cotton and Cotton goods. The persons engaged in this manufacture, including 8,187 Fustian makers, 1,891 Tape makers, and 2,170 Thread makers, numbered in all 500,025; to whom are further to be added 26,682 Cotton printers, dyers, and bleachers, and 3,554 Cotton warehousemen and dealers. This makes up a grand total of 530,261 persons, without reckoning in the 82,362 Drapers or the 1,884 Manchester warehousemen, who deal in other goods besides cotton. Thus the cotton industries by themselves more than equal all the other textile industries put together.

The Cotton printers and dyers, as also the Cotton warehousemen and dealers, are chiefly males, but the Cotton manufacture itself employs very many more females than males, the number of the former being 310,374 and of the latter 189,651, or 164 females to 100 males. Moreover, the proportion of females to males has increased with successive Censuses. In 1861 there were 130 females employed to 100 males; in 1871 the female proportion rose to 148; and in 1881, as already mentioned, to 164. Not only has the proportion of females to males increased, but the absolute number of males has declined. The entire increase has been on the side of the women. Putting aside the printers and dyers, and the warehousemen and dealers, we have the following figures for three successive Censuses :—

Employed in Cotton Manufacture.	1861.	1871.	1881.
Males - - - -	202,540	192,881	189,651
Females - - -	264,166	286,258	310,374
Total - -	466,706	479,139	500,025

In 1871 the increase under the head of Cotton manufacture was 2·7 per cent. upon the total for 1861; and, if we correct the figures for 1871 by a deduction of two per cent. for the "retired" operatives, as previously explained, the increase in 1881 was 6·5 per cent. This manufacture, therefore, if measured by the number of persons employed, increased in the interval between 1871 and 1881 more rapidly than in the preceding decennium, but nevertheless did not grow in equal proportion to the population. According, however, to the returns of the Board of Trade, the increase, as measured by the declared quantity of Cotton goods exported from the United Kingdom between 1870-1 and 1880-1, was 39 per cent.

Of the 530,261 persons employed in Cotton industries, including again the printers and dyers and the Cotton warehousemen and dealers, no fewer than 432,146 were enumerated in Lancashire, 28.485 in Cheshire, 40,606 in the West Riding of Yorkshire, 14,854 in Derbyshire, and only 14,170 in all the other counties.

Linen Manufacture. The Manufacture of Linen forms but a small industry in this country, and an industry, moreover, that appears to be declining; for, whereas in 1871 the corrected number of persons employed in it amounted to 17,772, in 1881 there were but 12,065, showing a decline of 32 per cent. As in most other textile manufactures, the female outnumbered the male hands. There were 7,853 of the former to 4,212 of the latter. This manufacture is mainly carried on in the West Riding of Yorkshire and in Lancashire, where 6,860 and 2,840 persons respectively were enumerated as engaged in it.

Lace Manufacture. More important is the Lace industry. This employed 44,144 persons, of whom 32,785 were females. But this industry also seems to have declined, for the corrected number of persons engaged in it in 1871 was 48,383, the falling-off in the following decade being 8·8 per cent. The probable explanation of this decline is the gradual and increasing supersession of pillow-made or bone lace by lace bobbin-net, first made by hand-machines, but more recently by water-power or steam-power. This explanation of the matter is confirmed by the fact that the decline occurred in those counties where hand-made lace is made, namely, Bedfordshire, Devonshire, Buckinghamshire, and Northamptonshire, while in Nottinghamshire and the adjoining part of Derbyshire, where lace is made by machinery, there was an increase of no less than 36 per cent.

The following are the figures for each of the lace-making counties for the last three Censuses, the figures for 1861 and 1871 being uncorrected.

County.	1861.	1871.	1881.
Buckinghamshire - -	8,501	8,106	4,456
Northamptonshire - - -	8,221	6,404	3,232
Bedfordshire - - -	6,728	6,077	4,792
Devonshire - - - -	5,263	4,658	3,428
Nottinghamshire - -	16,712	16,620	22,228
Derbyshire - - - -	1,977	1,725	2,233

The substitution of machinery for hand labour further explains why the proportion of females to males employed in this industry declined in the decade 1871–1881, whereas in other textile manufactures the reverse was the case, and the proportion of female labour increased. In 1871 the females employed in Lace-making were 83 per cent., whereas in 1881 they were but 74 per cent., of the whole.

Hosiery Manufacture.

The Hosiery manufacture occupied 40,372 persons, and showed a slight decline as compared with 1871, when the corrected number was 41,197. This industry is almost confined to Leicestershire and Nottinghamshire, with the adjoining part of Derbyshire, there being also a small isolated factory in Cardiganshire. The figures for these counties are as follows:—

County	1861. (Uncorrected.)	1871. (Uncorrected.)	1881.
Leicestershire	22,276	20,286	21,594
Nottinghamshire	18,452	17,161	14,155
Derbyshire	2,960	2,286	2,275
Cardiganshire	515	819	799

In this manufacture, also, female labour appears to be supplanting male labour to a considerable extent. In 1871 there were 114 males employed to 100 females, but in 1881 the proportion was exactly inverted and there were 114 females to 100 males.

Woollen Manufactures.

Next in importance to Cotton among textile fabrics come Wool and Worsted. The workers and dealers in these substances, excluding those employed in the Carpet and Rug manufacture, of which we shall speak separately, numbered 233,256; and, comparing this total with the corrected total for 1871, it would appear that these great industries had slightly declined, viz., by 1·5 per cent., in the course of the decade.

Cloth Manufacture.

The Woollen Cloth manufacture occupied 115,808 persons, about 8 per cent. less than the corrected number in 1871. In 1871 the females employed in it were considerably outnumbered by the males, there being only 79 of the former to 100 of the latter. But in 1881 female labour had taken the place of male labour to such an extent that the males were slightly outnumbered, the proportion being 102 females to 100 males.

Cloth manufacture is mainly carried on in the West Riding of Yorkshire, where 85,962 persons employed in it were enumerated. Next came Lancashire with 11,317; Gloucestershire with 4,403; Wiltshire with 3,886; and Somersetshire with 1,881. The order was the same in 1871.

Worsted and Stuff Manufactures.

The Worsted and Stuff manufactures occupied 99,237 persons, which was almost exactly the same as the corrected total in 1871. In this industry the female outnumbered the male hands in much higher proportion than was the case in the Cloth manufacture. In the latter, as we have seen, there were 102 female hands to 100 male hands, but in the Worsted and Stuff manufacture the females were in the proportion of 180 to 100 males. As in other textile industries, they had partly superseded the males in the course of the decade; for in 1871 there were but 162 female to 100 male hands.

This manufacture is almost exclusively confined to the West Riding of Yorkshire, where 95,485 of the 99,237 were enumerated. Of the remainder, 1,570 were in Lancashire, and 894 in Leicestershire, leaving only 1,288 elsewhere.

Blanket and Flannel Manufactures.

The Blanket manufacture occupied 2,687 persons, whereas in 1871 only 1,845 persons were returned under it. Of the 2,687 persons engaged in this industry, 2,362 were enumerated in the West Riding and 220 in Oxfordshire against 1,681 and 125 respectively in 1871.

The Flannel manufacture had remained stationary during the decade, for in 1871 there were 1,158 and in 1881 there were 1,126 persons engaged therein.

Carpet Manufacture.

The Carpet and Rug Manufacture employed 13,985 persons, which was 23 per cent. in excess of the corrected number in 1871. This industry differs from other textile manufactures in having a larger number of male than of female workers, The males were 8,795, and the females only 5,190. Even here, however, a tendency to substitute female for male labour is apparent; for while in 1871 there were 47 women to 100 men in the business, in 1881 the female proportion had risen to 59.

The main seats of this manufacture are in Worcestershire and in the West Riding of Yorkshire; and it would appear from the following table that the increase in 1871–81 occurred exclusively in the former county.

—	1861. (Uncorrected.)	1871. (Uncorrected.)	1881.
Worcestershire - - -	1,673	3,590	6,659
West Riding of Yorkshire -	3,735	5,056	4,621
Other Counties - -	2,057	2,922	2,705

The persons employed in the manufacture of Silk and Silk goods, including Satin, Velvet, Ribbon, Crape, and Gauze, numbered 60,595. To these must be added 1,680 Silk Dyers or Printers, and 1,302 Silk Merchants, making a total of 63,577 returned as engaged in making or selling Silk goods. As compared with the corrected total for 1871, this showed a decline of 22·2 per cent. The decline was at the rate of 22·5 per cent. in the Silk, Satin, Velvet, and Crape manufactures; and of 31·9 per cent. in the Ribbon manufacture, under which small industry 2,064 persons were returned. The Silk Merchants declined 17·0 per cent. The Silk Dyers and Printers did not participate in the decline, but on the contrary increased by about 5·5 per cent. Coincidently with this decline in the persons employed in the Silk manufacture there was an even greater decline in the amount of raw silk imported into the country. This fell, in round numbers, from 14½ million pounds in the two years 1870 and 1871, to 6½ million pounds in 1880 and 1881,—a fall of 55 per cent. Silk Manufactures.

In the Silk and Ribbon manufactures, as in most other textile industries, the females employed largely outnumbered the males, there being 224 of the former to 100 of the latter. The proportion, moreover, of the females had increased; for in 1871 there were but 208 females to 100 males.

The counties which were the chief seats of the Silk manufacture, and the numbers of persons employed in each of such counties, were as follow; the returns for 1871 not being corrected for "retired."

County.	1871.	1881.
Cheshire - - -	17,768	14,206
Lancashire - - - -	15,920	10,317
Warwickshire - - -	13,444	9,109
West Riding of Yorkshire -	3,764	5,387
London - -	5,792	3,877
Staffordshire - - -	4,371	3,789
Essex - - -	3,032	2,803
Norfolk - -	2,602	2,623
Derbyshire -	4,000	2,323
Nottinghamshire	2,001	1,250
Suffolk - -	1,703	1,173
Somersetshire -	1,138	961
Wiltshire - -	802	670
Hertfordshire -	944	546
Gloucestershire	651	511
Other counties - - -	2,200	1,050
Total - -	80,132	60,595

It will be noticed that in the West Riding of Yorkshire there was a very considerable increase in the decade preceding the Census of 1881; that in Norfolk the number remained practically unaltered; but that in each of the other counties there was a large falling off. The increase in the West Riding was due to the establishment of a large factory at Bradford.

The Workers in Hemp and other fibrous materials numbered 22,471, the males employed in these rough textile industries outnumbering the females, of whom there were but 60 to 100 males. In some of the headings, however, that come into this Sub-order the female workers predominated. Thus of the 3,478 persons returned as engaged in the manufacture of Hemp, Jute, or Cocoa fibre, 2,297 were women; of the 1,733 Networkers, 1,481 were women; and so also were 1,594 of the 2,169 persons engaged in the manufacture or sale of Sacking and Sacks. Of the Hemp industries, Workers in Hemp, the largest is that of the Rope and Twine Makers. These numbered 11,751, mostly males, and, as compared with the corrected total of 1871, showed a slight increase. Ropemaking is carried on in all parts of the country; but the localities in which the numbers of workers were highest were, Lancashire 2,384, London 1,404, Dorsetshire 1,118, and the West Riding of Yorkshire 1,046; so that those four areas between them account for a full half of the Rope and Twine makers.

Persons working and dealing in Dress.

In treating of the great group of "Persons working and dealing in Dress" we shall depart from the table as printed, by omitting the 14,933 Hair-dressers and Wigmakers, and by including the 82,362 Drapers and Mercers. The group as thus constituted numbered a million, or, more exactly, 1,048,534 persons, of whom 404,096 were males, and 644,438 were females. As compared with the corrected returns for 1871, this great group taken as a whole had increased by only 7·1 per cent. There were, however, as we shall see, enormous differences in this respect between the several kinds of dress fabrication.

Milliners.

Among these workers in dress by far the most numerous were the Milliners, Dressmakers, and Staymakers. These together numbered 360,932 persons, almost exclusively women, and exceeded the corrected total for 1871 by 18·4 per cent.

Tailors.

The Tailors numbered 160,648, and exceeded the corrected total for 1871 by 9·4 per cent. Thus the Milliners, Dressmakers, and Staymakers had increased almost twice as much as the Tailors. There was one Milliner, &c. to every 37 females, and one Tailor to every 79 males. The proportion of females to males in this latter employment had considerably increased; in 1871 there was one tailoress to three tailors, whereas in 1881 there was one to two.

Seamstresses.

The Seamstresses and Shirtmakers numbered 83,244, and had grown since 1871 by only 5·2 per cent. It is true that there were also 7,524 women returned vaguely as Machine-workers or Machinists, and probably a large proportion of these were Seamstresses; but this cannot explain the small growth of this class of Needle-workers since 1871; for, in the Census of that date, the indefinite Machine-workers or Machinists were vastly more numerous, the females under this heading numbering no fewer than 20,971. The small growth, or actual decline, in the number of seamstresses is probably to be explained by the increased use of the sewing-machine; though it may also be true that many women are now returned as "tailoress" or as "milliner's assistant" who were formerly returned as "seamstress," the line of demarcation between these sewing industries being very vague.

Putting the three groups together as representing needle-workers we have a total of 604,824 persons, and an increase since 1871 of 14·0 per cent., or much the same as the increase of the population. The comparison, however, with 1871 is much vitiated by the large number of indefinite female machinists returned at that date.

Shoemakers.

The Boot and Shoe Makers, exclusive of 7,503 Patten and Clog Makers, numbered 216,556. They had slightly declined in number since 1871, when their corrected total was 219,213. If we look still further back to earlier Censuses, we find that there was an even greater decline in this industry in the interval between 1861 and 1871, so far as can be judged from the number of workers. Here are the figures, corrected for the retired, and for slight differences of classification:—

1851 - - -	235,447
1861 - - -	246,493
1871 - - -	219,213
1881 - - -	216,556

As boots and shoes are among the most indispensable of goods, it is highly improbable that their production should have declined, while the population increased by 14·36 per cent. The most probable explanation is that the use of machinery has gradually supplanted hand-work in this industry; and this accords with the fact that in Northamptonshire and Leicestershire, which are the chief, though not the only, seats of the manufacture of machine-made boots, the number of bootmakers increased enormously, namely, 34 per cent., in the interval between 1861 and 1871, and 41 per cent. in the interval between 1871 and 1881. The making of boots and shoes is mainly in the hands of male workers; but, as in many other industries so in this, there has been a great increase in the proportion of female labour. In 1871 the proportion was 13 females to 100 males; but in 1881 the proportion was 20 to 100.

Hatters.

The Hatters, excluding Straw-hat Makers, numbered 22,689, and were mostly men, Their increase since 1871 was under seven per cent.

Straw Plai Manufacture.

The makers of Straw Hats and Bonnets, and generally of Straw Plait, numbered 30,984, and showed a decline since 1871 of no less than 35 per cent. This industry had indeed shown signs of decay or of arrest in the preceding intercensal period, during which the numbers of persons employed in it remained stationary in spite of the growth of the population. This industry is practically monopolized by females, though a few males are engaged in it as agents and dealers. It is confined to a few counties; for of the 30,984 persons returned under it, 17,316 were enumerated in Bedfordshire, 7,882 in Hertfordshire, 1,741 in Buckinghamshire, 930 in Essex, 781 in Suffolk, and only 2,334 in the rest of England and Wales.

Notwithstanding the smallness of the increase in the number of Hatters, and the great decline in the Straw Plait manufacture, it appears from the returns of the Board of Trade that the export of hats of all kinds from the United Kingdom rose from 452,153 dozen in 1871 to 1,025,931 dozen in 1881.

Hosiery M nufacture.

The Hosiery manufacture employed 40,372 persons, more than half of whom were females; but of this manufacture we have spoken already, when dealing with Textile fabrics.

Glovers.

In previous Censuses, an attempt was made to divide the Glovers into those who made leather gloves and those who made gloves of other materials. But the distinction could not be made with any accuracy, as a large proportion of these workers return themselves simply as Glover, without specifying the material. We have therefore in this case, as in many others, abandoned a distinction which could not be made in a satisfactory manner. The Glovers of all kinds numbered 15,524, of whom 13,261, or 85 per cent., were females. The corrected total for 1871 was 22,590, so that this industry would appear to have declined no less than 31 per cent. How far this decline is to be explained by the use of sewing machines, and how far by increased importation of foreign-made gloves, we are unable to say. Of the 15,524 Glovers, 4,913 were enumerated in Somersetshire, 3,003 in Worcestershire, 2,180 in Dorsetshire, 1,533 in Oxfordshire, 1,242 in Devonshire, and 2,653 in the rest of England and Wales.

Drapers, Mercers, Hosiers, H berdashers, &c.

The Drapers, Mercers, Hosiers, and Haberdashers together amounted to 91,927, and as compared with 1871 showed an increase of 13·2 per cent.; that is to say, they had increased in nearly the same proportion as the population.

To the industries already mentioned must be further added 616 Shawl makers, 6,407 Button makers, 8,230 Umbrella, Parasol, and Stick makers, 600 Accoutrement makers, and 2,302 Old Clothes dealers and nondescripts, making up as before said a grand total of slightly over a million. The list of industries grouped under Dress might indeed be further extended. We might, for instance, have included the 2,421 Embroiderers, the 6,499 Trimming makers, and the 8,148 Furriers and Skinners. So also a very large proportion of the persons employed in the manufactures of Cotton, Woollen, Worsted, Linen, and Silk fabrics should be reckoned as ministering to dress. But all these we have excluded as only partly employed in the preparation of dress materials. Were it possible to make due allowance for these, in all probability it would be found that the number of persons occupied in clothing us could scarcely be less than a million and a half.

Miners and Mine Service.

The Miners of all kinds numbered 437,670, and with 2,291 Mining-engineers, and 3,602 persons engaged in Mine service, made up a total of 443,563.

The great bulk of the Miners were employed in the coal-fields; the Coal-miners by themselves numbering no fewer than 381,763, or 87 per cent. of the whole. Of these Coal-miners 65,515 were enumerated in Durham, 60,801 in Lancashire, 55,818 in the West Riding of Yorkshire, 44,864 in Glamorganshire, 37,514 in Staffordshire, 20,752 in Northumberland, 18,959 in Nottinghamshire, 17,424 in Derbyshire, 14,936 in Monmouthshire, 5,416 in Denbighshire, 5,393 in Cumberland, 5,079 in Somersetshire, and 29,292 in the remaining counties.

Next in numbers to the Coal-miners came the Ironstone miners, numbering 26,110, and mainly enumerated in the North Riding of Yorkshire, Cumberland, Lancashire, and Staffordshire. Then followed the Tin-miners, 12,402 in number, and almost entirely in Cornwall. After these, the Lead-miners, of whom 11,226 were returned, and who formed two main divisions, one in the Welsh counties of Cardigan, Montgomery, Flint, Denbigh and Carnarvon, in which five counties, 5,357, or nearly half the whole, were enumerated; the other in the Northern English counties of Derby, York, Durham, Northumberland, Cumberland, and Westmorland, which together accounted for 4,780 more. Of the remainder, 407 were in Cornwall, 302 in Shropshire, and 380 in all other parts.

The Copper-miners numbered only 4,067, and of these 3,505 were in Cornwall and Devonshire, 279 in the Isle of Anglesey, and only 283 in the other counties. Finally, there were 2,102 miners of other or unspecified minerals.

Comparing the figures for 1881 with the corrected figures for 1871, we find that the persons returned as working in mines had increased in the interval by 24 per cent. Unfortunately so large a number of miners were returned in 1871 without specification of the kind of mineral in which they worked, that it is impossible to make any accurate comparison of the numbers of each separate class of miners at the two periods. It is plain, however, that Coal-mining at any rate has increased very largely; for even if we consider that all the 38,712 undefined miners in 1871 were Coal-miners, which is highly improbable, and further make no deduction for the "retired" Coal-miners, we still have an increase of no less than 23 per cent. We may be sure, then, that Coal-mining, as measured by the number of persons employed, increased between 1871 and 1881 by fully 20 per cent.; and this tallies with the returns made by the Board of Trade, from which it appears that the output of Coal in 1881 was 31·4 per cent. more than in 1871.

We can also make some kind of comparison in the case of the Tin-miners, in the following way:—Cornwall is the only county in which there is any considerable number of Tin-miners; and the only other miners in this county are Copper-miners and a few Lead-miners. Now in 1871 the enumerated male Tin-miners in Cornwall numbered 10,393, and the enumerated male Copper and Lead miners numbered 3,513, while in the same county there were 7,315 male miners of undefined minerals. Dividing these latter, who must have been either tin, copper, or lead miners, between these groups in the proportions of their enumerated numbers, we have a total of 15,860 Tin-miners in Cornwall in 1871; and, correcting this for the "retired" by a deduction of 2 per cent., we have a total of 15,543 in 1871, to compare with the total of 10,253 in 1881. It thus appears that the Tin miners in Cornwall decreased by 34 per cent. or thereabouts in the interval between the two Censuses. The amount of tin produced in the United Kingdom also fell off, according to the Board of Trade returns, by 21 per cent. in the same interval.

Metal workers.

From the Miners we pass on naturally to the Workers in Metal, including under this general term those who smelt the ore, as well as those who deal with the metals thus extracted. The number of these Metal-workers is difficult of estimation, in more than a rough fashion,—so intricate are their ramifications, and so mixed up are they in many cases with workers in non-metallic industries. Putting together, however, all those headings in the Occupation Tables that relate to workers and dealers in metals, or in products that consist mainly of metal, we have a total of 760,411 persons; or, without affecting an accuracy that is of course impossible, of some three-quarters of a million. Treating the Occupation Returns of 1871 in the same way, we find, after correction for the retired, that the workers and dealers in metal had increased in the intercensal decade by about 15 per cent., or in a slightly higher ratio than the general population.

The Workers in metal might be divided into those who extract the metal from the ore, that is, the smelters, dressers, and the like; those who work the metal into comparatively coarse and simple forms, such as plates, rails, girders, or articles for rough usage; and those who construct articles of greater delicacy or complexity, such as machinery, tools, and watches. But, unfortunately, the excessively vague way in which a large proportion of the Metal-workers returned their occupation rendered this, and indeed any tabulation of them, very unsatisfactory. We found, for instance, that it was quite impossible to separate the Tin-smelters from the Tin-plate workers, or these from the Tinmen or Tinkers; the Copper-smelters from the Coppersmiths, and so on. We were obliged, therefore, to abandon these and many other distinctions which we had proposed to retain, and to lump all the Tin-workers together, as also the Copper-workers; and although in the case of Iron-workers we were able to separate a few well-marked industries, such as Nail-making and Anchor and Chain making, yet the great bulk of the Iron industries had to be thrown together under a single heading.

The makers of machines, tools, and metallic articles of greater delicacy, in which the form given by the workman vastly outweighs the material in importance, as a rule return their occupations in a clearer and more definite manner than the comparatively undifferentiated makers of coarser goods; and consequently of this higher class of metal workers we have been able to give better account. Putting these aside, we must deal with the others in a very summary manner.

The Workers and Dealers in Iron and Steel numbered 361,343; and only exceeded the corrected total in 1871 by some three per cent. Among them were 18,741 Nail-makers, and 5,029 Anchor and Chain makers. The Anchor and Chain makers remained much the same in number as in 1871; but the Nailmakers had fallen off by 18 per cent., probably owing to the increased use of wire and other foreign-made nails. Iron and Steel manufactures.

The Workers and Dealers in Copper numbered 7,348, and exceeded the corrected total in 1871 by 30 per cent. The Workers and Dealers in Tin numbered 36,923, and had increased by over 40 per cent. The Workers and Dealers in Zinc numbered 2,265, and had increased by 34 per cent. Finally, the Workers and Dealers in Lead, 2,460 in number, had fallen off by 27 per cent. Copper, Tin, Zinc, Lead manufactures.

Among the Workers and Dealers in Mixed or Unspecified Metals, the largest group is that of the Brass Workers, with whom may be grouped the Bronze Workers, and the Makers of Lamps, Candlesticks, and Chandeliers. These together amounted to 30,918, and exceeded the corrected total in 1871 by 36 per cent. The persons engaged in the White Metal, Electro-Plate, and Plated Ware manufactures, together with the Pewterers, numbered 5,629, and had increased very greatly, the uncorrected total returned under these headings in 1871 having been only 3,407. The Makers of Bolts, Nuts, Rivets, Screws, and Staples numbered 8,017, and had also increased very greatly, the uncorrected total in 1871 having been 5,726. The Burnishers and Lacquerers, who differ from most of the Metal-workers in being chiefly of the female sex, numbered 2,687, and had increased nearly 30 per cent. In the case of all these groups of Metal-workers, excepting the Iron-workers, the numbers are comparatively small, so that very small differences in the accuracy of the returns, or in the methods of tabulation, would seriously affect the comparison of the figures for the two Censuses. Still the rate of apparent increase or decrease is so great in each case that, when every allowance is made for possible inaccuracies, we may still feel assured that the changes agreed, if not in actual amount yet in direction, with those indicated. Workers and dealers in Mixed or Unspecified Metals.

8. *Unoccupied Class.*

There remain for brief consideration those persons who were returned without any specified occupation, constituting what we have styled the Unoccupied class. UNOCCUPIED CLASS.

In 1871 the class called the "Indefinite and Non-productive Class" comprised not only persons without specified occupations, but also the considerable body of persons whose occupations were described in the schedules in general or vague terms, such as General Labourer, Artisan, Apprentice, &c., or in terms the meaning of which was unknown. These latter we have removed to the Industrial class, and our *Unoccupied class comprises and is confined to all those persons who were returned by rank, property, &c., and not by occupation, including all children under five years of age.

The Class comprised 14,786,875 persons, or 57 per cent. of the entire population, the females in it being to the males in the proportion of rather more than two to one.

It included, in the first place, 8,936,851 children and young persons under 15 years of age, most of whom were simply unoccupied in the sense that they were as yet preparing for the various businesses of later life. Secondly, it included 532,441 others, who were 15 but under 20 years of age, and of whom also a large proportion were preparing for active life. Thirdly, it included 676,393 persons who were 65 years of age or more, and of whom a large number had been engaged in business, but had retired. Excluding these three classes of persons there remained 4,641,190 who were 20 but not yet 65 years of age, that is to say, who were in the working prime of life, and yet were without specified occupation. Of these, however, 4,458,908 were women; of whom by far the greater part were married and engaged in the management of domestic life, and who can only be called unoccupied, when that term is used in the limited sense that it bears in the Census Returns. Many more of these women, though unmarried, were also engaged in domestic duties, or were assisting their fathers or other near relatives in the details of business. Children and aged persons. Wives and other women engaged in domestic duties.

Of the 182,282 males in the working period of life (20–65) without specific occupation, a large number, doubtless, were busily engaged in avocations which were none the less serious or less important because not recognized in our classification. They were The male residue.

* By an inadvertence the old name of this class has been used in Vol. III., Summary Table 4.

managing their estates and property; directing charitable institutions; prosecuting literary or scientific researches; or engaged in other of the multifarious channels by which unpaid energy finds vent. If these were deducted from the 182,282 unoccupied males, and a further deduction were also made for those who were incapacitated for work by physical defects, the remainder, constituting the really idle portion of the community, would probably prove to be but very small.

VII. BIRTHPLACES OF THE POPULATION.*

1. *The General Composition of the Population.*

The following short summary shows the constituent parts of which the population of England and Wales, at the date of the Census, was made up; and also shows the proportions in which these several constituents contributed to the total.

Birthplace.	Persons enumerated in England and Wales.	Proportion to 100,000 Population.
England and Wales	24,855,822	95,694
Scotland	253,528	976
Ireland	562,374	2,165
Islands in British Seas	29,316	113
Colonies and Dependencies	94,399	363
Foreign parts:—		
British Subjects	56,373	217
Foreign Subjects	117,999	454
Ships at Sea	4,628	18
Total	25,974,439	100,000

2. *Natives of England and Wales.*

Births in excess of deaths in all counties.

It appears from the Reports of the Registrar-General that in every county of England and Wales, without exception, the births registered in the 10 years preceding the Census outnumbered the deaths; so that in every county, had there been no migration and no emigration, the population would have been greater in 1881 than at the previous enumeration. The rates of increase would, indeed, have been widely different. In those counties where the population contained a high proportion of married women of reproductive ages the increase would have been great; in such counties, for instance, as Staffordshire, Glamorganshire, and Durham, the growth due to this "natural increment" would have been over 20 per cent. Those counties, on the other hand, where the proportion of wives of reproductive ages was low would have shown but little increase; such, for instance, were Cornwall, Devonshire, and Herefordshire, among English counties, and Anglesey, Carnarvonshire, Pembrokeshire, and Cardiganshire, among Welsh counties, in none of which would the rate of growth have exceeded 11 per cent. Nevertheless, as before said, in every county without exception there would have been some, and a not inconsiderable, increase.

Counties that lose their natural increment.

As a matter of fact, we know that this was not the case. There were no fewer than 13 counties in which the population was found, on enumeration, to have diminished. These counties had not only lost all their natural increment, but something over and above this. There were 26 other counties in which the population had, it is true, increased, but in a lower ratio than would have been the case had there been no migration and no emigration. The actual increment in each of these counties was

* The tables relating to Birth-places are in Vol. III., which has an index at p. 526. Besides the tables relating to Foreigners (for which see foot-note to p. 56), the Summary Tables 7 and 8 give the country and county of birth of the population of England and Wales; while, in each Divisional Part, Table 11 gives the birth-places of the population of each county and large Urban Sanitary District, and Table 12 gives the distribution over the country of the natives of each county.

smaller than the natural increment. These 39 counties, therefore, had produced more men and women than they were able to retain, and had given off their surplus to other parts. Labour may be said to be one of their staple commodities, which they export to other counties or abroad.

There remain 11 counties, or 12, if we call London, with the extra-metropolitan parts of Middlesex and Surrey, a county, in which the actual growth as shown on enumeration was in excess of the natural growth. These counties which absorbed population from without were London, Sussex, Essex, Leicestershire, Nottinghamshire, Derbyshire, Cheshire, Lancashire, Yorkshire, Durham, Glamorganshire, and Carnarvonshire. Counties that absorb population from without.

A glance at the table in which the rates of increase, natural and actual, are given for each county, and a comparison with the columns in the same table that give the general character of the prevalent occupations, will show that, disregarding a few exceptions, the counties which export surplus population to other parts of the country are agricultural, while the counties that absorb population over and above their own native product are, as the list already given sufficiently indicates, mining, manufacturing, or commercial. The centres of industry, therefore, are fed with labour at the expense of the agricultural districts (*see* Appendix A., Table 32).

Notwithstanding, however, the very great disturbance produced in the natural distribution of the population by this constant migration from agricultural to industrial districts, or, speaking generally, from country to town, the native population shows, after all, stationary habits of a very decided character. Of the natives of England and Wales who were in the country at the time of the Census, no less than 75·19 per cent. were enumerated in their native counties. In 1871 the proportion of stationary natives, as we may call them, was 74·04 per cent., or nearly the same; so that it appears that the increased facilities of locomotion, and the extended knowledge among the working classes as to the conditions of life in parts outside their immediate localities, have not had the result that might have been anticipated, of leading to greater migration. Comparing the two sexes in this respect, it appears that women are on the whole rather more migratory than men, probably in consequence of the demand in towns for domestic servants from the country. At any rate, the proportion of stationary males was 75·9, and that of stationary females 74·5 per cent. of the enumerated of the corresponding sex (*see* Appendix A., Table 30). Amount of migration.

There were, as might be supposed, very great differences between different counties, in regard to the retention of their natives within their borders (*see* Appendix A., Table 32). In Lancashire more than 90 per cent. of the enumerated natives of the county were enumerated within the county itself; and in Yorkshire, Glamorganshire, Durham, and Carnarvonshire, severally, as well as in London, this was the case with over 80 per cent. These, it will be remembered, are among the counties that absorbed population from without; so that it appears that those industrial counties which attract immigrants from other parts also retain, as might be anticipated, a large proportion of their own natives. The counties, on the other hand, that retain the smallest proportions of their natives are the agricultural, as is shown by the following list of the counties in which the stationary proportion of the enumerated natives was less than 65 per cent. Difference between counties as to migration.

Rutlandshire	50·5	Berkshire	60·2
Radnorshire	53·4	Westmorland	60·6
Huntingdonshire	55·5	Hertfordshire	61·4
Brecknockshire	59·4	Shropshire	62·0
Buckinghamshire	59·6	Wiltshire	62·3
Oxfordshire	59·7	Cambridgeshire	63·3
Herefordshire	59·7	Dorsetshire	64·6

In what parts of the country did the natives of these counties, who migrated, and who formed from 35 to 50 per cent. of the whole, find a home?

It appears from the tables (Vol. III., Table 12 of each Divisional Part) which show the geographical distribution within the country of the enumerated natives of each county, that some 47 per cent., or nearly a half, of the migrants from these counties of greatest migration had gone but a very small distance from their birth-place, having simply moved into the adjoining county, into parishes therefore which were often as near to them as parishes in their own native county. Excluding these persons, who can scarcely be said to have left their native districts, there remain from 19 to 26 per cent. of the natives of these counties who had really left their place of birth, and had migrated into more distant parts. Of these the only general statement that can be made is that, as before stated, they had migrated into the industrial centres; the migration from one agricultural county into another of the same character, unless adjoining, being very limited in amount. Those, however, who are interested in the matter, and who wish to study the laws of migration in greater detail, will find materials for so doing in the tables already mentioned, which give the geographical distribution of the enumerated natives* of each county in England and Wales.

Besides those tables, which have been now given for the first time, there are also others, as in previous Census Reports, which may be said to be the inverse of those already mentioned. Those gave the distribution of the natives of each county; these (Vol. III., Table 11 of each Divisional Part) give the birth-places of the inhabitants of each county. As those tables served to measure the migration out of any given county, so these serve to measure the migration into it from without.

The two sets of tables show a considerable amount of parallelism. Those counties which are shown by the one to retain a large proportion of their natives are shown by the other to attract a large number of strangers from without; and those counties which retain but a small proportion of their natives, are shown to receive but few immigrants from other parts; the same causes which drive out their own natives preventing strangers from coming in. As a general rule, it will be found that the counties with the highest native element in their population are the agricultural, and that those with the lowest are the industrial and the metropolitan.

3. *Natives of Scotland and Ireland.*

The Scotch in England and Wales.

The natives of Scotland who were enumerated in England and Wales numbered 253,528, being in the proportion of 9·8 to 1,000 of the entire population. The number of natives of Scotland enumerated in their own country was 3,397,759, so that there was one Scotchman or Scotchwoman in England or Wales to 13·4 in Scotland.

The number of Scotch natives in this country in 1841 was only 103,768, but it increased progressively at each succeeding Census up to 1881. The number, moreover, increased more rapidly than did the population of England and Wales; so that there was a progressive rise in the proportion which the Scotch element bore to the general population. In 1841 this proportion was 6·5 per 1,000, and rose till in 1881 it was 9·8 per 1,000 (*see* Appendix A., Tables 26 and 27). The counties in which the Scotch element was highest were Northumberland, where it constituted 54 per 1,000 of the population; Cumberland, where it was 49; Durham, where it was 28; Westmorland and Lancashire, in each of which it was 16; Middlesex, where it was 13; and Cheshire, where it was 12, per 1,000 of the population. In no other county was the proportion so high as 10 to 1,000 (*see* Appendix A., Table 29).

Of the great towns those in which the natives of Scotland were most fully represented were, as might be expected from their proximity, the industrial towns on the Tyne and Wear. Thus, in Newcastle-upon-Tyne over six per cent. of the population were Scotch, and in South Shields, Gateshead, and Sunderland, from four to five per cent.; whereas in Liverpool and Birkenhead, which came next in order, the proportion was barely four per cent. Then followed Manchester, Salford, West Ham, London, Kingston-upon-Hull, Portsmouth, Southampton, and St. Helens, these towns exhausting the list of those in which the Scotch formed as much as one per cent. of the inhabitants.

If we examine the distribution of the natives of Scotland in this country by another plan, namely, by the proportion which such natives enumerated in each county bore to the total number of Scotch natives in the whole country, we find that of 1,000 Scotch persons enumerated in England and Wales 243 were enumerated in London with the extra-metropolitan parts of Middlesex, Surrey, and Kent, 220 in Lancashire, 97 in Durham, 92 in Northumberland, 76 in Yorkshire, 48 in Cumberland, 31 in Cheshire, and 23 in Hampshire, while in no other county was the proportion as high

* It must be carefully noted that the term in the text is "enumerated natives," that is to say, natives who were present in England and Wales at the time of the Census. Of the natives who had emigrated, in contradistinction to those who migrated within the country, we have no means of giving account.

as 20. Passing to the great towns, of 1,000 natives of Scotland enumerated in England and Wales 204 were enumerated in London or the closely adjoining town of West Ham, 94 in Liverpool or Birkenhead, 35 in Manchester or Salford, 46 in Newcastle-upon-Tyne or Gateshead, 19 in Sunderland, 12 in South Shields, and 10 in Leeds, while in no other of the great towns was the proportion as high as 10 out of the 1,000.

The Irish in England and Wales.

The natives of Ireland who were present in England and Wales at the date of the Census numbered 562,374, being in the proportion of 21·65 to 1,000 of the entire population. The natives of Ireland enumerated in their own country were, as shown in the Irish Census Report, 5,062,287; so that there were in England and Wales one ninth part as many Irishmen as in Ireland itself.

The number of Irish living in England and Wales in 1851 was 519,959, and in 1861 it had risen to 601,634; but at each Census since that date it was found to have fallen off. In 1871 it had fallen to 566,540, and in 1881, as already stated, to 562,374. It must be remembered, however, that the population of Ireland has itself declined very considerably. If this decline be taken into account it will be found that the Irish in England and Wales, when measured by their proportion to the Irish in their own country, have increased at each successive Census. In 1841 there were 36 Irish in this country to 1,000 in Ireland itself; in 1851 there were 80; in 1861 there were 105; in 1871 there were 107; and finally in 1881 the proportion had risen to 111 (*see* Appendix A., Tables 26 and 27).

The distribution of the Irish over the country was most unequal. In the purely agricultural counties their numbers were insignificant, while in the great manufacturing and mining counties they formed a not inconsiderable fraction of the population. Thus in Lancashire they formed 6·1 per cent., in Cumberland 5·6 per cent., in Durham 4·2 per cent., and in Cheshire 3·7 per cent. of the population; the proportion being also over 2 per cent. in Middlesex, Monmouthshire, Northumberland, and Glamorganshire. The proportion they bore to the population was lowest in the counties of Cardigan, Radnor, Norfolk, Huntingdon, Merioneth, Suffolk, Cambridge, Buckingham, Carmarthen, and Wilts; in no one of which was it as high as 0·3 per cent (*see* Appendix A., Table 29).

Passing from counties to towns, we find that in Liverpool the Irish formed 12·8, in Birkenhead 8·8, in St. Helens 8·5, in Manchester 7·5, and in Salford 7·4 per cent. of the population, these Lancashire and Cheshire towns being those in which the Irish element was strongest. Then followed in order Middlesbrough, Stockport, Cardiff, Gateshead, Preston, Bolton, Bradford, Bury, Blackburn, and Oldham, exhausting the list of great towns in which the Irish formed as much as 4 per cent. of the inhabitants. Of the aggregate inhabitants of London and of the 46 great towns each having a population exceeding 50,000 persons, 3·3 per cent. were natives of Ireland, while the proportion was only 1·5 per cent. in the rest of England and Wales.

Instead of considering, as we have hitherto done, the proportion borne by the natives of Ireland to the population of the several counties and towns, we may examine their local distribution in another way. Of each 1,000 natives of Ireland who were enumerated in this country, 378 were enumerated in Lancashire, 176 in London or the adjoining counties of Middlesex, Surrey, and Kent, 101 in Yorkshire, 65 in Durham, 42 in Cheshire, and over 20 in Cumberland, Staffordshire, Northumberland, Glamorganshire, and Hampshire respectively. With the exception of Hampshire, all these are mining or industrial counties, and the apparent exception presented by Hampshire is explicable by the comparatively large number of soldiers quartered in that county. Passing to the great towns, of 1,000 Irish enumerated in England and Wales 147 were enumerated in London or the adjoining town of West Ham, 139 in Liverpool or Birkenhead, 69 in Manchester or Salford, 17 in Leeds, 14 in Bradford, and 13 in Birmingham. In no other of the great towns was the proportion so high as 10 per 1,000.

Comparison of Scotch and Irish distribution in England and Wales.

If we compare the distribution of the natives of Scotland in this country with that of the natives of Ireland, we find, in the first place, that in both cases there is a very strong tendency to congregate in the industrial rather than in the agricultural parts, but that this tendency is somewhat less in the case of the Scotch than in the case of the Irish. Of 1,000 immigrant Scotch and 1,000 immigrant Irish, there were more Scotch than Irish in every one of the mainly agricultural counties, with the exceptions of Devonshire, Anglesey, Pembrokeshire, and Gloucestershire; each of which is either on the western coast, or at any rate more accessible from Ireland than from Scotland, through the ports of Plymouth, Holyhead, Milford, and Bristol. Secondly, we find that the distribution is considerably affected by the relative proximity to Ireland and Scotland respectively of the industrial centres. The Irish preferentially select Lancashire, Cheshire, Yorkshire, and the adjoining counties. The Scotch select the northern counties. The two areas overlap each other, doubtlessly, very considerably. Lancashire, Cheshire, Yorkshire, Northumberland, Cumberland, and Durham are easily accessible from either Scotland or Ireland. Still of these counties Lancashire and Cheshire are relatively more accessible from Ireland; and Northumberland, Cumberland, and Durham more accessible from Scotland. In correspondence with this, of 1,000 immigrants from each country, there were more Irish than Scotch in Lancashire and in Cheshire, and more Scotch than Irish in Northumberland, Cumberland, and Durham.

Of the other chief industrial counties, Glamorganshire, Monmouthshire, Staffordshire, and Warwickshire are proportionately more attractive to the Irish than to the Scotch; while, on the other hand, Middlesex, Surrey, Kent, and Essex, or in short London and its suburban environments, attract a larger proportion of the Scotch. Of 1,000 Scotchmen in this country, 261 were enumerated in these four counties, but only 185 out of 1,000 Irishmen.

DISTRIBUTION of NATIVES of SCOTLAND and IRELAND and of FOREIGNERS in COUNTIES, per 10,000 enumerated in ENGLAND and WALES.

COUNTIES IN WHICH ENUMERATED.	SCOTCH.	IRISH.	FOREIGNERS.	COUNTIES IN WHICH ENUMERATED.	SCOTCH.	IRISH.	FOREIGNERS.
Bedfordshire -	16	9	11	Oxfordshire -	23	10	20
Berkshire - -	41	26	34				
Buckinghamshire -	23	9	11	Rutlandshire -	4	2	3
Cambridgeshire -	16	9	15	Shropshire -	32	33	12
Cheshire - -	310	420	152	Somersetshire -	50	40	56
Cornwall - -	25	30	108	Staffordshire -	131	233	77
Cumberland -	481	251	15	Suffolk -	38	17	23
				Surrey - -	547	386	710
Derbyshire -	64	93	32	Sussex - -	108	64	157
Devonshire - -	110	111	98				
Dorsetshire -	28	25	20	Warwickshire -	115	171	140
Durham - -	975	654	224	Westmorland	41	7	4
				Wiltshire -	22	14	17
Essex - -	172	88	141	Worcestershire -	46	40	31
Gloucestershire -	92	95	96	Yorkshire - -	765	1,011	685
Hampshire - -	227	203	114				
Herefordshire -	16	10	9				
Hertfordshire -	37	14	23				
Huntingdonshire -	5	3	3				
Kent - -	340	283	314				
				Anglesey - -	6	8	4
Lancashire - -	2,204	3,775	1,267	Brecknockshire -	8	8	4
Leicestershire -	41	33	29	Cardiganshire -	4	2	3
Lincolnshire -	47	34	124	Carmarthenshire -	9	6	7
				Carnarvonshire -	17	11	12
Middlesex -	1,548	1,090	4,555	Denbighshire -	22	17	6
Monmouthshire -	27	93	59	Flintshire - -	16	25	16
				Glamorganshire -	80	213	231
Norfolk - -	41	18	27	Merionethshire -	4	2	13
Northamptonshire -	28	19	19	Montgomeryshire -	7	4	2
Northumberland -	923	222	199	Pembrokeshire -	12	18	9
Nottinghamshire -	54	40	58	Radnorshire -	2	1	1

NOTE.—This table may be read as follows:—Of 10,000 natives of Scotland enumerated in England and Wales, 16 were enumerated in Bedfordshire, 41 in Berkshire, &c. Of 10,000 natives of Ireland enumerated in England and Wales, 9 were enumerated in Bedfordshire, &c. &c. And similarly with the Foreigners.

DISTRIBUTION of NATIVES of SCOTLAND and IRELAND, and of FOREIGNERS, in the GREAT TOWNS of ENGLAND and WALES per 10,000 enumerated in the whole Country.

Towns in which Enumerated.	Scotch.	Irish.	Foreigners.	Towns in which Enumerated.	Scotch.	Irish.	Foreigners.
London - -	1,954	1,435	5,104	Bury - -	13	39	12
Croydon - -	30	18	77	Salford - -	113	231	84
Brighton -	32	20	104	Manchester -	240	455	431
Portsmouth - -	58	54	66	Oldham - -	25	79	29
Southampton -	27	14	43	Rochdale - -	17	45	18
Northampton -	7	8	12	Burnley - -	14	38	8
West Ham - -	88	36	137	Blackburn -	32	75	20
Ipswich - -	11	4	12	Preston - -	29	76	21
Norwich - -	13	6	17	Huddersfield -	23	26	21
Plymouth - -	18	25	47	Halifax - -	18	46	17
Bath - - -	12	12	32	Bradford - -	59	140	100
Bristol - -	45	57	98	Leeds - -	105	170	221
Wolverhampton -	15	30	21	Sheffield - -	63	89	102
Walsall - -	10	22	10	Kingston - upon-Hull.	72	44	241
West Bromwich -	4	7	9				
				Middlesbrough -	61	66	44
Birmingham -	66	126	186				
Aston Manor -	8	7	15	Sunderland -	186	79	92
Leicester - -	21	17	31	South Shields -	121	36	79
Nottingham -	32	27	110	Gateshead -	118	56	20
Derby - -	20	23	21	Newcastle-upon-Tyne.	344	98	129
Stockport - -	11	60	13	Cardiff - -	31	76	175
Birkenhead - -	131	132	83				
Liverpool - -	805	1,262	786	Ystradyfodwg -	2	5	11
St. Helens - -	25	87	8	Swansea - -	16	32	62
Bolton - -	35	82	23				
				TOTAL of 47 TOWNS	5,180	5,572	9,002

NOTE.—This table may be read as follows:—Of 10,000 natives of Scotland enumerated in England and Wales, 5,180 were enumerated in the 47 great towns, viz., 1,954 in London, 30 in Croydon, and so on.

4. *Natives of other parts of the British Empire.*

The population of England and Wales included 29,316 persons who were born in the Islands in the British seas, that is to say, in the Isle of Man or in the Channel Islands. This group of immigrants was 14·3 per cent. in excess of the 25,655 natives of these Islands enumerated in England and Wales in 1871. This increase is the more noticeable, inasmuch as the aggregate population enumerated in the Islands themselves had declined in the course of the decade from 144,638 to 141,260, that is, by 2·3 per cent. In 1841 the numbers of natives of these Islands who were enumerated in England and Wales was only 11,705; but the number has risen at each successive Census since that date. In 1881 there was one native of these Islands in England and Wales to 3·8 such natives in the Islands themselves. Natives of Isle of M[an] and Chan[nel] Islands.

The county which had the largest share of these islanders was Lancashire, closely connected with the Isle of Man, where 9,082 were enumerated, an additional 1,232 being in Cheshire. In Hampshire there were 2,122, and in Devonshire 1,336. In London, which is not only a port, but the centre of attraction to all immigrants, there were 5,397.

The natives of India and of other Dependencies and Colonies numbered 94,399. This element in our population has also increased with each successive Census, and in part, doubtlessly, because the Colonies and Dependencies have themselves increased in population and in extent. The increase, however, has been greater than can thus be explained. In 1841 the number returned was 17,248; in 1851 it rose to 33,688; in 1861 to 51,572; in 1871 to 70,812; and, finally in 1881, as before stated, to 94,399; the increase in the final decade being 33·3 per cent. Natives of Colonies [and] Dependencies.

To the foregoing may be added 4,628 persons born at sea, who were slightly more numerous than in 1871, when they numbered 4,395. Persons b[orn] at sea.

Casting up all the constituent parts of the population that have now been severally dealt with, we have a total of 25,800,067* persons who were either born in the United

* Persons born at sea are here reckoned as of British birth; but, as a matter of fact, a small proportion of them were Foreign subjects.

Kingdom or in some part of the British Empire, and this total formed 99·329 per cent. of the entire population of England and Wales, so that the foreign element was numerically insignificant.

5. *Natives of Foreign States.**

Persons born abroad.

The natives of Foreign States enumerated in England and Wales amounted altogether to 174,372, and constituted 0·671 per cent. of the aggregate population. This foreign element, as indeed each other constituent part of the population, with the single exception of the Irish, has increased uninterruptedly with each successive Census. The increase in the last intercensal period was 25 per cent., or much higher than the increase of the whole population. The same was the case in each preceding intercensal period; from which it would appear that this country presents ever-increasing attractions to foreigners. In 1841 there was one foreign-born person to 403 population; in 1851 one to 291; in 1861 one to 197; in 1871 one to 163; and finally in 1881 one to 149.

Foreigners by nationality as well as birth.

Of the 174,372 natives of Foreign States, 56,373 were British subjects, being either the children of British parents, born while their parents were sojourning abroad, or foreigners who had been naturalised. The remaining 117,999 were not only born abroad, but were Foreign subjects. This is the strictly foreign element in the population; and this element also, as the total of the foreign-born, has increased with each successive Census in somewhat higher proportion than the population itself. In 1851 there was one such foreign subject to 356 persons enumerated; in 1861 there was one to 239; in 1871 one to 226; and in 1881 one to 220; the increase in the last intercensal period having been 17·3 per cent.

Distribution of foreign subjects.

These foreign subjects, being mostly in this country for business purposes, were, as might be anticipated, almost exclusively enumerated in the towns. Fifty-one per cent. of the entire number, or more than a half, were enumerated in London, and 39 per cent. more in some or other of the 46 great provincial towns. The towns which, after London, contained the largest number of them were Liverpool, Manchester, Kingston-upon-Hull, Leeds, Birmingham, and Cardiff.

Natives of Europe, Asia, Africa, and America.

Of the 117,999 persons who were foreigners by nationality as well as by birth, 98,617 were born in Europe, 484 in Asia, 258 in Africa, 18,496 in America, and 144 in unstated countries. In addition to these there were 32 foreign subjects who were born at sea. The number of natives of Europe had increased since 1871 by 9·8 per cent.; those of Asia by 34·4 per cent.; and those of America by 85·5 per cent.; while the natives of Africa had fallen from 385 to 258. Of the Americans, the great bulk, namely 17,767, were natives of the United States, showing a great increase since 1871, when only 8,270 were enumerated. This contingent, however, of 17,767 persons, borrowed from the United States, is of course as nothing compared with the contribution made by this country to the population of those States; for no fewer than 745,928 persons of English or Welsh birth were enumerated in the United States in 1880.

Natives of European States.

The foreigners of European birth, enumerated in England and Wales, amounted in all to 98,617, the number in 1871 having been 89,829. This element in our population had, therefore, increased by nearly 10 per cent. A considerable proportion of these foreigners were sailors in our ports; and as the remainder consisted mainly not of permanent settlers but of persons sojourning temporarily with us for purposes of business, the proportion of males to females among them was naturally very great, there being 183 of the former to 100 of the latter.

The local distribution of these foreigners was governed by the same fact; for though there was no single county, either in England or in Wales, in which there were positively no European foreigners at all, yet the great bulk of them was found exclusively in the industrial centres. About 60 per cent. of the whole were enumerated in London and its immediate neighbourhood, 12 per cent. in Lancashire with the adjoining parts of Cheshire, nearly 7 per cent. in Yorkshire, and about 2 per cent. in Durham, Northumberland, and Glamorganshire, respectively. The details, however, of this distribution, both for all European foreigners collectively, and for the natives of each individual country, are given elsewhere. (Vol. III., Summary Table 11.)

Germans.

Of all the foreign European States by far the most fully represented in England and Wales was the German Empire, which contributed 37,301 persons to our population against 32,823 enumerated in 1871, showing an increase of 13·6 per cent.

* The following are the chief tables relating to Foreigners: Vol. III., Summary Tables 9, 10, 11, as also Table 13 in each Divisional Part, relate to their numbers and distribution; Summary Table 12 relates to their ages; and Summary Table 13 to their occupations. *See also* Appendix A. to this Report, Tables 26, 27, 29, and 42.

The chief occupations followed by these Germans were as follows:—

Teachers	2,048	Bakers	2,043
Musicians	880	Sugar Refiners	444
Servants	3,978	Tailors	1,719
Cooks (*not domestic*)	526	Milliners, Dressmakers, &c.	277
Merchants and Brokers	1,438	Shoemakers	603
Commercial Clerks and Travellers	2,091	Hairdressers	383
Seamen, &c.	1,860	Furriers	448
Watchmakers	886	Jewellers	261
Cabinet-makers	586	General Labourers	594
Butchers	743		

The French sojourners amongst us numbered 14,596 against 17,906 in 1871, when the number of French resident in England was temporarily increased in consequence of the German invasion, and had decreased by 18·5 per cent. They included the following:— French.

Teachers	1,647	Seamen	1,280
Roman Catholic Priests	119	Tailors	144
Sisters of Charity	269	Milliners, Dressmakers, &c.	648
Servants	1,592	Hairdressers, Wig Makers	126
Cooks (*not domestic*)	566	Jewellers	160
Merchants and Brokers	292		
Commercial Clerks and Travellers	455		

The Russians and Russian Poles numbered 14,468, there being 3,789 of the former and 10,679 of the latter. The numbers in 1871 were 2,513 and 7,056 respectively, or in all 9,569. The increase, therefore, in the course of the decade was 51·2 per cent. Their main occupations were as follows:— Russians and Poles.

Teachers	144	Cabinet-makers	168
Servants	172	Tobacconists	125
Merchants and Brokers	105	Hatters	151
Commercial Clerks and Travellers	347	Tailors	3,264
Seamen, &c.	529	Shoemakers	652
Painters, Glaziers	449	Hairdressers, Wig Makers	103
		Furriers	251

The enumerated natives of Italy amounted to 6,504 against 5,063 in 1871, having thus increased by 28·5 per cent. Amongst them were returned:— Italians.

Teachers	109	Carvers, Gilders	134
Musicians	1,240	Image Makers	245
Servants	510	Inn, Boarding, Lodging, Coffee-house Keepers	132
Cooks (*not domestic*)	130	Confectioners, Pastrycooks	198
Merchants and Brokers	109	Paviours, &c.	107
Commercial Clerks and Travellers	112	Street Sellers	356
Seamen, &c.	771	General Labourers	241
Cabinet-makers	78		

The natives of Holland numbered 5,357 against 6,258 in 1871, having decreased by 14·4 per cent. Among them were included:— Dutch.

Teachers	91	Tobacconists	634
Musicians	52	Tailors	245
Servants	188	Milliners, Dressmakers, &c.	73
Merchants and Brokers	140	Shoemakers	85
Commercial Clerks and Travellers	215	Jewellers	98
Seamen	405	General Shopkeepers	105
		Street Sellers	51

Swiss.

The natives of Switzerland numbered 4,089 against 3,226 in 1871, having therefore increased by 26·8 per cent. They included:—

Teachers	558	Watchmakers	61
Servants	1,329	Inn, Boarding, Lodging, Coffee-house Keepers	101
Cooks (*not domestic*)	121	Confectioners, Pastrycooks	182
Merchants and Brokers	117		
Commercial Clerks and Travellers	243		

Scandinavians.

The enumerated natives of Scandinavia numbered in all 7,917, namely 1,748 Danes, 3,203 Norwegians, and 2,966 Swedes. In 1871 the number had been 7,573. The increase therefore in the decade was 4·5 per cent. Among the enumerated were:—

Servants	371	Seamen, &c.	4,248
Merchants and Brokers	214	Tailors	266
Commercial Clerks and Travellers	300	General Labourers	143

Belgians.

The enumerated Belgians were 2,462, showing a decrease of 2·9 per cent. from the 2,535 enumerated in 1871. Amongst the enumerated were:—

Roman Catholic Priests	67	Commercial Clerks and Travellers	96
Sisters of Charity	37	Seamen	159
Teachers	125	Cabinet-makers	61
Painters (Artists)	41	Tobacconists	84
Musicians	51	Tailors	45
Servants	212	Milliners, Dressmakers, &c.	58
Cooks (*not domestic*)	39		
Merchants and Brokers	42		

Austrians and Hungarians.

The enumerated Austrians, including 441 Hungarians, were 2,809, against 1,802 in 1871, showing an increase of 55·9 per cent. Amongst the enumerated were:—

Teachers	84	Cabinet-makers	46
Musicians	38	Tailors	161
Servants	221	Shoemakers	40
Merchants and Brokers	126	Furriers	78
Commercial Clerks and Travellers	163	Salt Makers	77
Seamen, &c.	369	Jewellers	71
		General Labourers	79

Spaniards.

The Spaniards in the country numbered 1,433, against 1,484 in 1871; there was, therefore, a decrease of 3·4 per cent. in the decade. Of these 1,433 no fewer than 576 were Seamen, while of the remainder, 20 were Teachers, 54 Servants, 77 Merchants or Brokers, and 70 Commercial Clerks or Travellers.

Greeks, Turks, Portuguese, Roumanians, Servians.

The numbers of the natives of other European States were inconsiderable. There were 695 Greeks, including 255 Seamen and 112 Merchants and Brokers, with 45 Commercial Clerks and Travellers. There were 599 Turks, of whom 56 were Seamen and 158 Merchants or Brokers, with 37 Commercial Clerks and Travellers. There were 292 Portuguese, including 56 Seamen; and finally there were 91 Roumanians and 4 natives of Servia.

6. *Population of London.*

The population of London is so gigantic, and forms by itself so large a part of the entire population of the whole country, that it may be well to give a separate account of it. The tables we have already referred to will allow any one to make a similar analysis of the population of each county, and of each urban sanitary district having a population of as much as 50,000; excepting that in the case of these districts he will not be able to separate the natives of the district itself from the natives of the county in which it is situated.

BIRTH-PLACE TABLE of the POPULATION of LONDON.

BIRTH-PLACES.	Of 1,000 Persons Enumerated in London, the Number Born in each County &c.	Of 1,000 Enumerated Natives of each County &c., the Number Resident in London.
Total of inhabitants	1,000	147
London	629·36	804
Surrey (extra-metropolitan)	16·58	189
Kent (extra-metropolitan	25·02	136
Sussex	11·63	96
Hampshire	14·07	95
Berkshire	8·47	137
Middlesex (extra-metropolitan)	25·60	355
Hertfordshire	9·38	158
Buckinghamshire	7·15	124
Oxfordshire	5·86	100
Northamptonshire	4·60	59
Huntingdonshire	1·94	93
Bedfordshire	4·11	90
Cambridgeshire	6·57	109
Essex	24·25	168
Norfolk	13·97	120
Suffolk	13·10	90
Wiltshire	8·21	95
Dorsetshire	4·78	78
Devonshire	15·45	86
Cornwall	4·33	43
Somersetshire	11·40	79
Gloucestershire	8·94	56
Herefordshire	1·75	45
Shropshire	1·80	22
Staffordshire	3·35	13
Worcestershire	2·50	24
Warwickshire	6·63	36
Leicestershire	2·19	25
Rutlandshire	0·40	53
Lincolnshire	4·65	33
Nottinghamshire	2·06	21
Derbyshire	1·59	13
Cheshire	1·50	10
Lancashire	7·35	10
Yorkshire	8·44	12
Durham	2·11	12
Northumberland	2·04	18
Cumberland	0·88	13
Westmorland	0·29	14
Monmouthshire	1·18	23
England (county not stated)	4·85	244
Wales	6·17	17
Islands in the British Seas	1·41	184
Scotland	12·98	195
Ireland	21·17	144
British Colonies or Dependencies	6·95	281
British subjects born in Foreign Countries and at Sea	5·09	319
Foreigners:		
Europe:		
Russian Empire	2·29	602
German Empire	5·76	589
Holland	1·10	783
France	2·16	565
Italy	0·92	539
Other European States	2·21	417
Asia	0·06	502
Africa	0·02	380
America	1·22	253
Country not stated, and at Sea	0·02	494

The first column of figures gives the proportion of the population of London that was contributed by each county or other area. The second column of figures shows what proportion these several contributions bore to the total number of natives of such county or area enumerated in England and Wales. For instance, we learn that of the inhabitants of London 629 per 1,000 were London-born; and that of 1,000 London-born persons in the whole country 804 were living at the date of the Census in London itself. The English counties that contributed the largest proportion of immigrants to the population were, in the first place, the extra-metropolitan parts of Middlesex, Kent, and Surrey, which contributed between them 67 per 1,000; Essex, which gave 24; Devonshire, which gave 15; and Norfolk and Suffolk, which gave 14 and 13 per 1,000 respectively. The English counties that furnished the smallest contingents to the London population were Cumberland, Rutlandshire, and Westmorland.

The amounts of these contingents depended, of course, in great measure on the relative sizes of the counties. Cumberland, Rutlandshire, and Westmorland contributed few immigrants to London, partly because they were of small dimensions; and Devonshire contributed many, because of its own large size and population. But in the second column of figures the differences due to this cause are excluded, the figures indicating the proportion of the enumerated natives of each area that was resident in London. It becomes at once apparent that a most important factor in determining these proportions is proximity, and that the attraction of London is felt most strongly in the parts nearest to it. The counties that would head the list, were they arranged in the order of their *pro ratâ* contributions, would be Middlesex (extra-metropolitan), Surrey (extra-metropolitan), Essex, Hertfordshire, Berkshire, Kent (extra-metropolitan), and Buckinghamshire, being the counties closest at hand; while at the other end of the list would come, speaking generally, the counties that were farthest away. Doubtless there is also another factor, the effect of which is visible in the table, but is comparatively of little importance. The *pro ratâ* contributions of Cheshire and of Lancashire were only 10 per 1,000; of Yorkshire and of Durham only 12; of Derbyshire and of Staffordshire only 13. This was not merely because those counties were far off, for there were counties quite as far off that made larger, though still small, contributions. An additional cause was that the counties mentioned had attractions of their own; they were centres of industry, and retained a more than average proportion of their natives at home.

Neither Scotland nor Ireland contributed in any very material degree to the population of London; the natives of the former country constituting only 13 and of the latter country 21 per 1,000 of the inhabitants. These proportions were vastly exceeded in many of the great provincial towns. The subjects of Foreign States present in London were somewhat more numerous than the Scotch, but less numerous than the Irish, and formed about 16 per 1,000 of the entire population. Measured, however, by the proportions they bore to the total number of foreigners in the entire country, they were much more numerous than either the Scotch or the Irish; for, while of 1,000 Scotch and 1,000 Irish enumerated in England and Wales 195 and 144 respectively were enumerated in London, of 1,000 enumerated foreign subjects no less than 510 were found in the capital.

VIII.—INFIRMITIES.*

1. *The Blind.*

Gradual diminution in the proportionate numbers of the blind.

The total number of persons returned as afflicted by blindness was 22,832, being in the proportion of 879 to a million of the population, or one blind person in every 1,138. The proportion of the blind to the population has decreased with each successive enumeration since 1851, in which year account of them was taken for the first time; but the decrease in the decade ending in 1881 was much greater than in either of the preceding decennial intervals.

Year.	Number of Blind.	Blind per Million Persons enumerated.	Persons enumerated to one Blind Person.
1851 -	18,306	1,021	979
1861 -	19,352	964	1,037
1871	21,590	951	1,052
1881 - -	22,832	879	1,138

This decrease may be fairly attributed to the progressive improvement in the surgical treatment of affections of the eyes, and to the diminished prevalence among children of such diseases as small-pox, to which a not inconsiderable amount of blindness was formerly due. The extent of the decrease may be stated in the following form. Had blindness been as common an affliction in 1881 as it was in 1851, there would have been 26,523 blind persons in the country instead of 22,832, or 16·2 per cent. more than there actually were.

Blindness more common among males than females.

Of the blind, 12,048 were males and 10,784 were females, being in the proportion of 953 males and 809 females per million living of each sex. Thus one in every 1,049 males was blind, but only one out of every 1,237 females. In each of the four censuses in which account of the blind has been taken, the affliction has been found to be much more common among males than among females. This is what might

* The tables relating to persons suffering from Infirmities are in Vol. III., which has an index at p. 526. Summary Tables 14, 15, and 16 relate to their number, sex, and distribution; as also do Tables 14 to 21 in each Divisional Part. Summary Tables 17, 18, and 19 relate to their Occupations.

have been anticipated, considering the differences between the two sexes in regard to their occupations, their exposure to accidents, and their liability to disease. This natural anticipation is, moreover, confirmed by the statistics of most other countries concerning which we have the necessary data. It is curious, therefore, to note that in Ireland the contrary was found to be the case, both in 1881 and in previous enumerations; and, further, that in this respect Ireland agrees with Finland and the Scandinavian countries in the north of Europe, and differs from the southern parts of Europe. This is shown in the following table:—

BLIND per MILLION living of each Sex.

——	Males.	Females.
England and Wales	953	809
Scotland	865	827
Ireland	1,141	1,219
Denmark	776	793
Norway	1,313	1,411
Sweden	767	843
Finland	1,514	2,938
German Empire	884	881
Hungary	1,280	1,123
Holland	499	394
Belgium	982	641
France	948	726
Spain	1,242	1,011
Italy	1,106	925

NOTE.—The proportions in this table for foreign countries are taken from "Die Verbreitung der Blindheit, &c. in Bayern." By Dr. G. Mayr, 1877, p. 100.

The proportion of the blind to the population of the same time of life in England and Wales increases rapidly in the successive age-periods, as is shown in the following table; and at each age-period, excepting the last, the male proportion is considerably higher than the female. That the female rate is exceptionally higher than the male in the last age-period, 65 years and upwards, is to be explained, at any rate in part, by there being many more extremely old persons, say of 85 years and upwards, among the females than among the males. The apparent irregularity in the series of rates would probably disappear were it possible to subdivide this age-period into smaller sub-periods.* Ages of blind.

BLIND per MILLION of corresponding Ages.

Age-period.	1881.			1871.		
	PERSONS.	Males.	Females.	PERSONS.	Males.	Females.
0—	166	172	161	185	189	180
5—	288	312	263	306	345	267
15—	388	449	328	404	451	358
20—	422	491	359	451	518	390
25—	641	800	494	680	871	506
45—	1,625	1,947	1,336	1,720	2,002	1,459
65 and upwards	6,915	6,897	6,929	7,354	7,245	7,446
All ages	879	953	809	951	1,029	876

Among the 22,832 blind persons enumerated were 1,958 who, according to the returns (*see* Vol. III., Summary Table 14), had been "blind from birth." This term, however, must be interpreted as including not only those who literally answered such description, but those also who had lost their sight at a very early period of life; for it appears to be an excessively rare thing for an infant to be actually blind at the time of birth. It has been thought well to give a separate account, The bli[nd] from bi[rth].

* The mode in which the facts were abstracted in 1871 enables us to break up the age-period, 65 and upwards, into two sub-periods, 65 to 85, and 85 and upwards. The male blind-rate was 6,812 in the earlier sub-period, while the female rate was only 6,687. But in the later sub-period, 85 and upwards, the female rate was 25,810, and far above the male rate, which was 21,450. It would, therefore, appear that in very advanced life women are more likely than males to become blind.

(*see* Vol. III., Summary Table 18), of these persons who either never saw or lost their sight before their education began, because it is a matter of some interest to know what occupations are open to persons thus heavily weighted in the race of life. Here and there a person thus afflicted, compensating the want of vision by increased attention to the indications of the other senses, learns to follow occupations that at first seem incompatible with his or her condition. One such man, for instance, was returned as ostler in an inn, and another as engaged in sea fishing.* But, putting such exceptional cases aside, the occupations open to those who have been blind from infancy are very few. Among such of these blind as were 15 years of age and upwards, only 51 per cent. of the males and 19 per cent. of the females were returned as following any definite occupation, whereas out of the whole population of England and Wales of the corresponding age the proportion occupied was 94 per cent. for males and 37 per cent. for females. Of the 436 with definite occupations, 110 were musicians, including seven piano-tuners; basket-making gave employment to 95, brush and broom making to 25, mat-making to 23, and chair-caning to 14; the knitting of stockings or other hosiery occupied 44 persons, all women; 19 were agricultural or general labourers, and 18 were street hawkers, leaving only 88 engaged in all other specified occupations.

Occupations of the blind.

The table (Vol. III., Summary Table 17) which gives the occupations of the blind generally, irrespectively that is of the age at which the blindness occurred, shows a great variety of employments. This table, however, is not of much practical value, for the returns on which it is based did not allow of any separation between occupations carried on by blind persons and occupations followed by such persons previously to their loss of sight.

2. *The Deaf and Dumb.*

The deaf-mutes.

The term "deaf and dumb" is used in the census returns in its popular meaning, that is to say, as comprising not only such persons as are absolutely without hearing and without speech, but also those persons who, though they might be vaguely conscious of loud noises made close to their ears, have yet from their birth, or from early childhood, been so deficient in the sense of hearing as to be unable to acquire articulate speech in the ordinary way. The returns, moreover, doubtlessly include a considerable intermixture of persons who had at first sufficient hearing to acquire speech, but who became deaf before they had firm hold on the faculty of articulation, and in consequence lost it completely. Possibly also there may be a few persons in the returns who, though completely deaf from infancy or childhood, have yet been taught to articulate by the modern method of instruction.

The directions given to the clerks employed in the abstraction were to include all persons returned as "deaf and dumb" or as "dumb" only, and also those returned as "deaf" who were inmates of deaf and dumb institutions. All other persons returned only as "deaf" were to be omitted.

Probable omissions in the returns of deaf-mutes.

There is no reason to suppose that the returns of the deaf and dumb were vitiated, as were those of idiots and imbeciles, by distinctly wilful omissions. But there can be no doubt that here also many excusable omissions were made in the first age-period, that is among children under five years of age. Parents are often not aware of the deafness of their infants; and, even when an impartial observer would have no doubt as to the fact, the parent not unnaturally hopes on against hope, and will not publicly acknowledge as a fact what he as yet refuses to accept as a certainty even to himself.

Correction for omissions.

There are two modes of meeting this deficiency in the returns: either we might ignore altogether the first age-period, and confine ourselves to the statistics relating to persons over that age, a method which, though it would not serve for estimating the absolute numbers of deaf and dumb, would of course be sufficient, if adopted universally, for purposes of comparison between different countries or different parts of a country; or secondly, we might suppose that the proportion of deaf-mutes under five to all children of that age was the same as the proportion in the next age-period, 5 and under 15 years, in which the returns are probably fairly correct. This would enable us to estimate approximately the absolute number of deaf-mutes in the country, but requires us to admit, what is probably not the case, that deaf-mute children are as likely to live as other children, and also ignores the fact that some few children become deaf, and

* Special inquiry was made in each of these cases as to the accuracy of the return.

in consequence dumb, after their fifth year.* Still these two defects in the proposed method of estimation operate in different directions, and tend to neutralise each other; so that probably the method will give us a tolerable approximation to the actual facts. We shall, therefore, adopt this method.

The total number of deaf-mutes enumerated was 13,295; of whom only 498 were under five years of age, being in the proportion of 141 per million children at that age, whereas the proportion in the next age-period, 5 and under 15 years, was 590 per million. Correcting the numbers in the first age-period, so as to get this same proportion, we have 2,077 probable deaf-mutes under five years of age, and a total of 14,874 at all ages.

This is in the proportion of 573 deaf-mutes per million persons enumerated, or one in 1,746 persons. The proportion in 1871, after similar correction for the first age-period, was 572 deaf-mutes per million persons enumerated, or one in 1,748.

Probable improven in the country i respect of deaf-muti

It appears, therefore, that the proportion of the population suffering from deaf-mutism remained practically unaltered in the interval between the two last censuses. It by no means necessarily follows from this, that no improvement took place in regard to the infirmity in question in the course of the decade. Though at first it looks like a paradox, yet it is plainly true that an increased proportion of deaf-mutes to the total population might really betoken an improvement; for it might be due merely to increased longevity among the deaf-mutes as compared with the rest of the population. If to such supposed increased longevity there were also superadded a diminished production of fresh deaf-mutes, a double improvement would have been effected, and yet the rate might remain practically unaltered. Fewer deaf-mutes would have been added to the register at the one end, but fewer would have disappeared from it at the other. Now, an examination of the deaf-mute rates at successive age-periods leads to a belief that something of this kind actually occurred. Indeed the figures in the following table seem inexplicable on any other hypothesis:—

PROPORTIONS of DEAF-MUTES to POPULATION at successive Periods of Life.

[As enumerated and uncorrected.]

Age-Period.	Per million Persons living at each Age-Period.			
	1851.	1861.	1871.	1881.
0—	212	205	145	141
5—	818	799	625	590
15—	674	776	626	564
20—	632	647	611	593
25—	559	601	524	568
45—	497	603	511	534
65 and upwards	442	531	436	560

In each of the three censuses preceding that of 1881 the proportion of deaf-mutes per million population of the same age diminished gradually in the successive age-periods, the first age-period (0 and under 5 years) being disregarded for reasons already explained. This gradual diminution in the rate was, of course, a plain and indisputable proof that the condition of deaf-mutism was unfavourable to vitality; for, had it not been so, the proportion of deaf-mutes to the population would have remained constant or without decrease throughout. But the figures for the census of 1881 give a perfectly different result. Here there is no gradual decrease in the proportion of deaf-mutes with advancing age. The proportions fluctuate somewhat irregularly; but it is distinctly observable, in the first place, that the proportions have considerably increased, as compared with 1871, in the three later age-periods, a fact which can only be

* Not many, however. Inquiries instituted in 1840 and 1858 in Bavaria, into the age at which deaf-mutism occurred in 5,403 cases concerning which the necessary data were to be had, gave the following results per 1,000 cases:—

Congenital	799
Under 5 years	158
5 and under 10 years	35
10 years and upwards	8
	1,000

In Ireland, also, it was found at the recent census that 80 per cent. of the deaf-mutes were congenitally afflicted.

accounted for by increased survival of former deaf-mutes; and, in the second place, that the proportions have considerably diminished in the earlier age-periods, a fact which can only be explained by diminished introduction of fresh deaf-mutes during the last and penultimate decades.

The result of this double alteration has been that the unfavourable influence of deaf-mutism in regard to longevity, which was so conspicuous in the previous returns, has been completely masked.

Deaf-mutism in relation to sex. Of the corrected number of deaf-mutes in 1881, 8,043 were males and 6,831 were females, being in the proportion of one in 1,572 males and one in 1,952 females. Out of equal numbers living of each sex there would, therefore, be 124 male to 100 female deaf-mutes.* This is in accordance with the fact, which will again present itself when we come to speak of idiocy, that congenital defects are, as a rule, much more common among males than among females, as also very probably are those infantile diseases which tend to destroy the auditory apparatus.

Geographical distribution of deaf-mutism. As regards the distribution of deaf-mutism over the surface of the country, we have followed the same plan as will be described more fully when we come to deal with the statistics of idiocy, our object being to avoid the interference in the distribution caused by the presence in some parts of special asylums or institutions. With this view we have taken birth-place, and not the place of habitation, as our basis, and have calculated the proportion of deaf-mutes to the enumerated natives of each county. The proportions cannot be calculated with perfect accuracy, inasmuch as in nearly six per cent. of the cases the place of birth was not given. Moreover, as already pointed out, the returns of deaf and dumb in the earlier years of life are utterly untrustworthy. The figures, therefore, which we shall give will only represent the comparative, and not in any way the absolute, amounts of deaf-mutism among the natives of the several counties. The counties are arranged in order of prevalence of deaf-mutism; and the table may be read as follows: the same number of natives which in England and Wales gave 1,000 deaf-mutes gave in Anglesey 1,378, in Merionethshire 1,317, and so on.

PROPORTIONATE AMOUNTS OF DEAF-MUTISM amongst NATIVES of the several COUNTIES.

Anglesey	1,378	Wiltshire	984
Merionethshire	1,317	Northamptonshire	976
Cardiganshire	1,297	Shropshire	966
Herefordshire	1,200	Sussex	964
Middlesex	1,198	Carnarvonshire	962
Radnorshire	1,172	Lincolnshire	958
Flintshire	1,162	Buckinghamshire	945
Cornwall	1,160	Yorkshire	945
Westmorland	1,147	Norfolk	945
Carmarthenshire	1,141	Glamorganshire	945
Cambridgeshire	1,131	Lancashire	943
Warwickshire	1,129	Hampshire	941
Derbyshire	1,105	Cumberland	939
Gloucestershire	1,099	Somersetshire	935
Surrey	1,079	Cheshire	933
Pembrokeshire	1,075	Denbighshire	933
Suffolk	1,053	Monmouthshire	907
Worcestershire	1,036	Rutlandshire	899
Oxfordshire	1,030	Essex	891
Devonshire	1,028	Hertfordshire	867
Dorsetshire	1,028	Kent	853
Bedfordshire	1,024	Brecknockshire	808
Durham	1,016	Nottinghamshire	768
Northumberland	1,008	Leicestershire	731
Berkshire	1,006	Huntingdonshire	699
England and Wales	1,000	Montgomeryshire	556
Staffordshire	998		

* In the United States of America, according to the recent census returns, there were 117 male to 100 female deaf-mutes out of equal numbers of each sex.

The totals on which this table is based, that is the actual number of deaf-mutes born in the individual counties, are very small, much smaller than the totals on which the corresponding table of idiocy is based, and consequently much irregularity must be expected in the results. This much, however, seems to be tolerably plain, that deaf-mutism is much more common among the natives of the mountainous parts of England and Wales than elsewhere; for, though the county of Montgomery is at the bottom of the list, yet in the ten counties at the top are no fewer than six Welsh counties, and also Westmorland. In this respect deaf-mutism goes hand in hand with idiocy and imbecility, for these affections, as will be seen hereafter, are also disproportionately prevalent in the mountainous parts. The marked contrast, however, which is observable in the case of idiocy between the purely agricultural and the manufacturing or mining counties is not apparent in the case of deaf-mutism. It may possibly be that, were the data more abundant, this want of correspondence might disappear. But it must also be remembered that some 37* per cent. of the deaf-mutes owe their condition not to congenital deficiency, but to such diseases as scarlet fever and the like, and that these diseases are much more prevalent as a rule in the crowded industrial centres than in purely agricultural parts.

Occupa of deaf-mutes.

There are, of course, some occupations from which deaf-mutes are necessarily debarred by their infirmity. These, however, are but few, and most occupations can be pursued by them, though doubtlessly with some disadvantage as compared with those competitors who can hear and speak. The female deaf-mutes at any rate find apparently no great difficulty in getting employment; for 40 per cent. of those of them who were 15 years of age and upwards were returned as having some special occupation, whereas this was the case with only 37 per cent. of the general female population of the corresponding ages.† The male deaf-mutes, on the other hand, seem to be at a not inconsiderable disadvantage, for only 76 per cent. of those of them who had finished their fifteenth year were engaged in definite occupations, against 94 per cent. in the corresponding general male population.

The occupations for which deaf-mutes show preference, or which they find most suitable to their condition, are naturally such as can be followed by individuals independently and do not require frequent communication with fellow workers. Agricultural or general labour, shoemaking, and tailoring are the chief occupations of the men; while dressmaking and sewing, domestic service and charing, washing, and, in Lancashire, work in cotton mills, form the main occupations of the women. The following is a brief abstract of the chief occupations of these deaf-mutes:—

Males.	—	Females.	—
Agricultural or general labourer	823	Domestic servant, charwoman	339
Boot, shoe, clog, patten maker	530	Dressmaker, seamstress	654
Tailor	344	Washerwoman	158
Textile manufacture	162	Cotton manufacture	134
Carpenter, joiner	137	Tailoress	75
Mason, bricklayer	102		
Painter, glazier, plumber	91		
Cabinet-maker, upholsterer, French polisher.	96		
Printer, bookbinder	95		
Miner	89		
Iron and steel manufacture	76		
Blacksmith	55		
Harness maker	43		
All other occupations	1,188	All other occupations	366
Total employed	3,831	Total employed	1,776

* *See* Census Report, 1871, vol. iv., page lxii.

† The figures given above might seem to imply that female deaf-mutes find employment more readily than females not so afflicted. But probably the explanation is that a much smaller proportion of the deaf-mutes is married than of women generally; so that there is a larger proportion of these dependent for support on their own labour.

3.—*The Insane.*

Different forms of mental unsoundness.

Persons of unsound mind are variously returned in the schedules as lunatic, idiot, and imbecile.

No accurate line of demarcation can be drawn between the several conditions indicated by these terms. Speaking generally, however, the term idiot is applied in popular usage simply to those who suffer from congenital mental deficiency, and the term imbecile to persons who have fallen in later life into a state of chronic dementia. But it is certain that neither this nor any other definite distinction between the terms was rigorously observed in the schedules, and consequently no attempt has been made by us to separate imbeciles from idiots. The term lunatic also is used with some vagueness, and probably some persons suffering from congenital idiocy, and many more suffering from dementia, were returned under this name. Still, as a rule, the term lunatic is not used to include persons suffering from such affections, but is limited to those afflicted by more acute forms of mental disease. We have, therefore, separated the lunatics from the idiots and imbeciles; the division being desirable for practical purposes hereafter to be mentioned. Some term, however, was required by us which should stand for all kinds of mental unsoundness, and for convenience we have taken the term insanity to include them all.

Use of terms insane, lunatic, idiot, imbecile.

The insane.

The total number of persons returned as suffering from some or other form of insanity was 84,503, being in the proportion of 3,253 per million of the whole population, or one person of unsound mind in every 307.

Apparent increase of insanity.

In 1871 the proportion was 3,034 per million, or one insane person in every 329. Thus a not inconsiderable increase in the proportion of persons admitted to be insane occurred in the interval between the censuses of 1871 and 1881. Whether this apparent increase of insanity was a real increase, or whether it was explicable, as was thought to be the case with the similar apparent increase in the preceding intercensal period, 1861–71, by diminished unwillingness on the part of persons to admit the existence of insanity in their families, is a question to which answer must be sought outside the census returns. It may be noted, however, that the increase in the amount of admitted unsoundness of mind was entirely in the class returned as lunatics, that is as persons suffering from the comparatively acute forms of unsoundness, and not in the class returned as idiots or imbeciles, that is as persons suffering from congenital or chronic forms of unsoundness; and that it is in the case of these latter rather than of the former that concealment would be most possible; for the former, or lunatics, are mostly lodged in institutions, public or private, whose superintendents would have no motive for concealment, while of the idiots and imbeciles a much larger proportion remain at home with their families, and are included in the householders' schedules.

The increase not shared by the idiot and imbecile class.

Proportions of insane in each sex.

Of the 84,503 insane persons 39,789 were males and 44,714 were females, being in the proportions of 3,148 males and 3,353 females per million of the corresponding sex, or of one in every 318 males and one in every 298 females.*

In a certain sense, therefore, it is indisputably true that there is more insanity among females than among males, namely, in the sense that out of equal numbers living of each sex and at all ages there are more insane females living than insane males. But it must be clearly understood that this statement is by no means identical with another that is sometimes confounded with it, namely, that the proportion of females who are attacked by insanity is higher than the proportion of males similarly attacked. Not impossibly, nor improbably, the contrary is the case. It may very possibly be that mental disease attacks a larger proportion of males than of females, but that, owing to the enormously high death-rate of the male insane as compared with the female insane, the number of the latter living at any given moment comes to be greater than the number of the former. The male cases that occur are on this hypothesis more numerous, but are rapidly swept away by death, while the female cases, though fewer in number, live on and accumulate. This hypothesis squares with the figures in the following table; from which it appears that it is only in the last two age-periods, namely after 45 years of age, that the proportion of the female insane exceeds that of the male insane.

Comparative liability of each sex to insanity.

---

* In the United States of America the recent census gave proportions of 3,367 per million persons; 3,516 per million males, and 3,214 per million females.

NUMBER of INSANE, MALE and FEMALE, at successive AGE-PERIODS per MILLION of PERSONS enumerated of corresponding AGES and SEX.

AGES.	INSANE.					
	TOTAL.		LUNATIC.		IDIOT OR IMBECILE.	
	Males.	Females.	Males.	Females.	Males.	Females
0— - - -	159	103	3	3	156	100
5— - - -	993	700	28	27	965	673
15— - - -	2,034	1,634	293	302	1,741	1,332
20— - -	2,777	2,284	1,037	894	1,740	1,390
25— - -	4,854	4,729	3,298	3,117	1,556	1,612
45— - - -	6,519	7,822	5,029	5,965	1,490	1,857
65 and upwards -	6,946	8,864	4,776	6,137	2,170	2,727
All ages - -	3,148	3,353	1,874	2,107	1,274	1,246

According to the returns of the Lunacy Commissioners from 1872 to 1881 inclusively, the mean annual death-rate among the registered male insane was 11·94 per cent. of the average daily number on the register; while the death-rate of the females was only 8·13 per cent. The recovery rate of the males was 10·50 per cent., and that of the females 11·59 per cent. Thus the per-centage of the male cases of insanity that would annually disappear from the register, either by death or cure, or what for convenience we call shortly the discharge-rate, would be 22·44, while the per-centage of female cases that would disappear from the same causes would be only 19·72. Now, if we assume that these discharge-rates, which were true for such insane persons as were under the observation of the Lunacy Commissioners, were true for all insane persons, whether under observation or not, we can make a very simple calculation. There were at the date of the census, as we have seen, 3,148 male insane and 3,353 female insane persons per million living of each sex respectively. Of these, 706 males and 661 females would be discharged either by death or recovery in the course of the year ending on April 3rd, 1882. In order, therefore, to maintain the same proportionate numbers of insane in each sex (neglecting as insignificant the slight increase in the population during the year), there would have to be 706 new male cases of insanity per million males living, and 661 new female cases per million females living, or out of equal numbers living of each sex there would be 106·8 new male cases to 100 new female cases. These figures, therefore, may be taken as probably representing with approximate accuracy the comparative liability of the two sexes, irrespectively of age differences, to mental unsoundness.

Combi[illegible] of insa[illegible] with o[illegible] afflicti[illegible]

Among the 84,503 persons enumerated as insane, that is either as lunatics or as idiots or imbeciles, 461 were stated to be dumb, and 355 were stated to be blind; while 17 others were both dumb and blind (*see* Vol. III., Summary Table 15).

Lunati[illegible]

It has already been stated that though, speaking generally, neither idiots nor imbeciles are included among the persons returned as lunatics, yet the distinction has not been universally observed, and that a certain intermixture of congenital idiots, especially at the earlier age-periods, and a considerable intermixture of imbeciles, especially at the later age-periods, has almost certainly occurred. We may, however, take the group of lunatics, as a whole, to represent all other forms of insanity than idiocy or imbecility.

The total number of persons returned as lunatics was 51,786, or 1,994 per million of the population. The females were 28,102, and far in excess of the males, who only numbered 23,684. This excess, moreover, was not only absolute but relative; for there were 2,107 lunatic females and only 1,874 lunatic males per million living of the corresponding sex.

It has already been explained that a difference in the proportions of *existing* cases in the two sexes does not necessarily imply a corresponding difference in the proportions of *occurring* cases. It may be, and very possibly is, the case, that the difference would disappear, or be inverted, if the discharge-rates for the two sexes were taken into account. Unfortunately, we have not got the discharge-rates for lunatics as distinguished from the insane of all kinds. If, however, we assume the discharge-rates for the former to be the same as those for the latter, namely, 22·44 and 19·72 per cent. for males and females respectively, and make a similar calculation to that made in treating of the insane of all kinds, the result will be that the new male cases of lunacy exceed the new female cases, for equal numbers of each sex, in the proportion of 101·2 to 100.

It is only in the later periods of life, from the 45th year upwards, that the female lunatics are, proportionately to the numbers living, in excess of the males. There is one exception to this statement, for in the age-period 15 and under 20 years, the female rate of lunacy very slightly exceeds the male rate, there being 302 lunatic females and only 293 lunatic males per million living of similar age in each sex. This is also, as shown by the annual reports of the Registrar-General,* the age-period in which alone the female sex is equally disposed to suicide with the male sex; and again is an age-period in which the female death-rate exceptionally exceeds the male death-rate; and the explanation is doubtlessly in each case to be found in the critical changes that occur at this period of life in the female organisation.

Idiots and imbeciles.

It appears to be generally admitted that the system of dealing with the insane which has for some years past been adopted in London is the one which has most to recommend it, not only from a medical, but also from an economical point of view. By that system the idiots and imbeciles, or, in brief, the harmless insane, are kept apart from persons afflicted by more acute forms of insanity, and are dealt with by special methods and in special institutions, these harmless persons being themselves still further subdivided according to their ages. Although, therefore, no exact line of demarcation can be drawn between these two classes of the insane, we have nevertheless thought it expedient to give a separate account of those persons who have been returned as idiots or as imbeciles, so that possibly those concerned in the matter may be able to form some kind of estimate of the numbers with which they would have to deal should the system become general.

The total number of persons returned as idiots or imbeciles was 32,717, being in the proportion of one such person in every 794 of the population. The proportion in 1871 was one in 771, so that as regards this kind of mental unsoundness a diminution had apparently occurred in the course of the decade. As there is no reason to suppose that the returns made in 1881 as regards this kind of insanity were less truthful than those made on the previous occasion, it is fair to conclude that the apparent was also a real diminution.

Untrustworthy character of the returns.

But though the figures may be used for such purposes of comparison, it would be most unsafe to accept them as representing with even approximative accuracy the actual amount of idiocy or imbecility existing in the country. There can be no doubt whatsoever that the returns made by persons as to the mental capacity of their children or other relatives are far from trustworthy. In the earliest years of life this imperfection in the returns is unavoidable. It cannot be expected, for instance, that a mother will return her child, as yet only two or three years old, as an idiot, however much in her own heart she may believe or fear this to be the case; for to acknowledge it as such would be to abandon all hope. But when the child has reached such an age that no doubt as to its mental incapacity can any longer be entertained, concealment of the fact by omitting all mention of it in the schedule is no longer equally excusable; and yet it is certain that such omission is excessively common. We have taken much trouble to ascertain, so far as possible, to what extent the returns are vitiated by such *suppressio veri*.

Attempt to form a corrected estimate.

With this object we obtained from the managers of a large idiot asylum the addresses of the families of all those idiots who had been admitted into the institution in the year commencing with the day of the census. We then examined the schedules given in by these families, and found that in exactly half the cases of such of these indisputable idiots as were 5 but under 15 years of age, no mention whatsoever was made in the schedule as to the existence of any mental incapacity. We have no reason to suppose that the cases admitted into this institution were in any respect of exceptional character, or drawn from classes in which there would be any exceptional inclination to concealment; and consequently we are compelled to accept the conclusion that half the cases of undoubted idiocy or imbecility of children residing with their families, and from 5 to 15 years of age, altogether escape enumeration; and we cannot but suppose that the proportion of omissions would be still greater if it were possible to take into account not only such kinds of idiocy as render the sufferers fit for admission into an asylum, but idiocy of every degree. As regards idiots 15 years of age

* See 43rd Annual Report, p. xxviii.

and upwards, the number of cases which we were able to investigate after a similar fashion was too small to furnish a basis for estimating the probable omissions; but, so far as we could judge from the obtainable data, the omissions are not very numerous, and we shall therefore assume that the returns of idiots and imbeciles 15 years of age and upwards are sufficiently correct, and that the omissions only affect the returns under that age. Now, the total number of idiots and imbeciles enumerated as 5 but under 15 years of age was 4,870; but of these 1,361 were in asylums or institutions, where all idiots would be correctly returned. There remain 3,509 who were with relatives or friends, and this number must at least be doubled, as explained above. This gives us a total of 8,379 idiots, of 5 and under 15 years of age, being in the proportion of 1,409 to a million living at such ages. But the proportion of enumerated idiots in the next age-period, 15 and under 20 years, was 1,536 per million living at those ages, and it is impossible to admit that the proportion could be less in the earlier age-period than in the later; for at these ages the cases of idiocy are almost exclusively cases of congenital idiocy, or, at any rate, of idiocy beginning soon after birth, and consequently the proportion of living idiots to a million of the same ages cannot possibly increase with successive age-periods, unless it be true that idiot children live longer than sound children, which is, of course, not the case. It appears, therefore, that the correction made by us for omissions was insufficient, and the insufficiency finds its explanation in the fact already noted, that only idiots of such character as to be selected for admission into asylums were taken into account.

We must, therefore, make another correction, and this may be best done, though the correction will still be inadequate, by supposing that the proportion of idiots among children of 5 but under 15 years of age was the same as the proportion among young persons who were 15 but under 20. In all probability it was considerably higher, as idiot children are likely to die earlier than sane children; but at any rate we shall be within the mark if we only assume equality. This method gives us 9,136 idiots, of 5 but under 15 years of age, and, being equally applicable to idiots at the still earlier age-period, gives us 5,408 idiots under five years of age. Thus the total number of idiots and imbeciles at all ages may be estimated at 41,940, instead of 32,717, as enumerated, and this estimated total is doubtlessly still too low; for not only have we supposed that idiot children are as likely to live as other children, and that there were no omissions in the returns of idiots who were 15 and under 20 years of age, neither of which suppositions is likely to be true, but we have also necessarily taken no account of the great probability that some omissions are likely to have been made at the still later age-periods, owing to the want of any clear distinction between imbecile and lunatic, many harmless insane adults being returned under this latter designation.

Congenit idiocy mo common among m than fem

Persons returned as idiots or as imbeciles form two very distinct classes, which, however, the returns give us no means of accurately separating from each other. There are, firstly, those persons who, owing to defects either congenital or dating from early infancy, have never been of sound mind; and, secondly, there are those who have only become demented at a later period. As this latter form of imbecility rarely occurs in the earlier part of life, we may assume that the figures in our table for the first three age-periods, and perhaps for the fourth, relate mainly, if not exclusively, to cases of congenital or infantile idiocy; and, proceeding then to compare the figures for the two sexes with each other, we see that such congenital defect is, as are most congenital deficiencies, much more common among males than among females; for out of equal numbers living of each sex under 25 years of age, there were 133 male idiots enumerated to 100 female idiots.

Geograph distributi of idiocy imbecility

The distribution of idiots and imbeciles over the country is of course largely affected by the presence or absence of special institutions for their treatment or relief, and consequently very erroneous conclusions might possibly be drawn from the table which gives the proportion of such persons in each county to its total population. Although, therefore, we have given such a table (Vol. III., Summary Table 16) in accordance with previous usage, we have also attempted to construct another, which it appeared to us would be of more value, in which the birth-places are taken as the basis, and it is shown how many idiots and imbeciles there were to a million enumerated natives of each county. If, as there seems no reason to doubt, the omissions in the returns of the idiots and imbeciles were proportionately the same in all parts of the country, then this table would of course give us a strictly accurate account, not of the absolute, but of the proportionate, numbers of idiots and imbeciles among the natives of the several counties.

Unfortunately a difficulty presented itself which interfered with the satisfactory completion of this comparative table. We found that in the case of 12·7 per cent. of the enumerated idiots and imbeciles the place of birth was not stated, and this kind of omission was by no means equally common in all parts of the country, so that it could not be disregarded, like the other kind of omission, as affecting only the absolute and not the proportionate results. We were obliged, therefore, somewhat to modify our plan. So far as possible, that is in 87·3 per cent. of the cases, we took the birth-places, as stated in the schedules, for our basis; in the remaining 12·7 per cent. we made an assumption. The inmates of any county asylum with unstated birth-places were assumed to have been natives of that county, and a similar assumption was made in the case of workhouses and other purely local institutions. The inmates of the great asylums at Caterham and Leavesden were similarly assumed to have been born in London (though this was probably not true of a considerable proportion of them), and were distributed by us to the three metropolitan counties in the proportions in which the natives of such counties contributed to the population of London. When an institution received patients indifferently from all parts of the kingdom, those inmates whose birth-places were not stated were left out of account.

These assumptions can scarcely have interfered in any material degree with the accuracy of the table, except, indeed, as presently to be pointed out, in the case of the metropolitan counties. The results were very curious, as will be seen in the following table, in which the counties are ranged in the order of frequency of idiocy and imbecility among their natives. The figures attached to each county do not represent the actual number of idiots per million natives, a number which, as has been shown, it was impossible to give with any accuracy, but represent the proportional amount of native idiocy in the several counties as compared with each other or with the entire country. It may be read as follows: the same number of natives which in the case of the whole of England and Wales gave 1,000 idiots or imbeciles gave in the case of Herefordshire 1,437, in the case of Cardiganshire 1,351, and so on.

PROPORTIONATE AMOUNTS of IDIOCY amongst NATIVES of the several COUNTIES.

Herefordshire	1,437	Westmorland	1,015
Cardiganshire	1,351	Montgomeryshire	1,015
Merionethshire	1,339	Lincolnshire	1,014
Carnarvonshire	1,330	Sussex	1,005
Denbighshire	1,312	England and Wales	1,000
Gloucestershire	1,289	Devonshire	995
Wiltshire	1,280	Kent	992
Anglesey	1,253	Surrey	985
Somersetshire	1,210	Essex	981
Northamptonshire	1,199	Bedfordshire	977
Oxfordshire	1,182	Nottinghamshire	977
Radnorshire	1,168	Cheshire	968
Berkshire	1,154	Norfolk	932
Carmarthenshire	1,150	Northumberland	910
Middlesex	1,147	Staffordshire	904
Hampshire	1,131	Lancashire	899
Warwickshire	1,129	Yorkshire	890
Buckinghamshire	1,124	Monmouthshire	882
Shropshire	1,108	Derbyshire	875
Cambridgeshire	1,097	Huntingdonshire	873
Hertfordshire	1,090	Rutlandshire	845
Worcestershire	1,076	Cornwall	782
Dorsetshire	1,076	Brecknockshire	755
Suffolk	1,057	Glamorganshire	728
Pembrokeshire	1,056	Cumberland	720
Leicestershire	1,048	Durham	614
Flintshire	1,028		

The one great fact that stands out conspicuously in this table is the much greater comparative amount of idiocy and imbecility that exists among the natives of agricultural counties, and especially of such agricultural counties as are also mountainous, than among the natives of manufacturing and mining counties.

The former, as a rule, have proportional rates above the mean of the whole country; the latter, as a rule, have proportional rates below the average. There are some few apparent exceptions to this general statement. Thus there are one or two purely agricultural counties with low rates; but these are mostly very small counties, such as Huntingdonshire, Rutlandshire, and Brecknockshire, where the data on which the calculation is founded are so scanty as to furnish a very insecure basis. On the other hand, Middlesex, in spite of its mainly urban character, shows a rate considerably above the average; and it may be noted as tending to confirm the probability of a high rate of idiocy for this county, that it shows also an excessively high proportion in the table of deaf-mutism (cf., p. 64). There is, however, reason to suppose that the rate assigned to Middlesex in the idiocy table is unfairly high; for somewhat more than a fourth of the idiots and imbeciles whose birth-places were unknown were patients in the Caterham and Leavesden asylums, and all these were considered to be natives of London, and were distributed to the several metropolitan counties in accordance with the rule laid down by us and mentioned above. It is probable that many of these persons should have been assigned to other counties, in which case the proportion for Middlesex (and in a lesser degree those for Surrey and Kent) would have been lower than in the table. At any rate, the unfortunate deficiency of information as to the birth-places of the inmates of the Caterham and Leavesden Asylums makes the calculation as to the proportionate amounts of idiocy much less trustworthy in the case of the metropolitan counties than in that of the other counties. Another exception to the general rule is presented by Warwickshire, which county, notwithstanding its industrial character, shows a rate of idiocy far above the average of the country.

Disregarding, however, these apparent exceptions, the general rule is unmistakable: agricultural districts produce numerous idiots and imbeciles, industrial districts produce few. What may be the explanation of this marked contrast we can but conjecture. It may be that the industrial centres attract from the rural districts those who are comparatively strong in mind and body; and that the children born to these stronger parents are less liable to congenital deficiencies than the offspring of the comparatively feeble parents, mentally and physically, who are left behind; and it may also be that the varied interests and quickened mental activities which accompany the industrial life of urban communities maintain the brain in a healthier condition than does the comparatively monotonous existence of an agricultural labourer, so that fewer adults become demented in the towns than in the country. These, however, are questions of which the discussion hardly falls within our province.

Thus much as to the several infirmities, mental and physical, concerning which we were directed by the terms of the Census Act to make inquiry. We have given much time and space to their discussion; for we felt bound to point out, as clearly as we could, how very incomplete are the returns which relate to these afflictions, and more especially those which relate to idiocy and imbecility. We have done the best we could with these unsatisfactory data. We cannot, however, but express our decided opinion that statements made by persons as to the deficiencies, mental or bodily, of their children or other relatives are not worth the cost and labour of collection and tabulation. In the recent census in the United States of America the returns made by householders as to idiocy and lunacy were supplemented by a system of special inquiries by specially paid enumerators, and by correspondence with nearly 100,000 medical men.* It is possible that, with such an elaborate and costly machinery, returns might be obtained of fairly approximate accuracy; but without it the returns will never, in our judgment, be of much value.

4. *Sickness and other Infirmities.*

Hospitals.

The English Census did not embrace any inquiry as to the amount of other forms of sickness or infirmity existing in England and Wales. It may be noted, however, that 24,087 patients were enumerated in the General and Special Hospitals (*see* Vol. II., Summary Table III). The patients enumerated in Hospitals were 7,619 in 1851; 10,414 in 1861; and 19,585 in 1871. The proportion of these hospital inmates, to 100,000 of the enumerated population of England and Wales, was 42 in 1851; 52 in 1861; 86 in 1871; and 93 in 1881. It is scarcely necessary to point out that the proportion of patients in hospitals to the general population is a measure rather of the relative amount of hospital accommodation, at these four Censuses, than of the relative

* Compendium of the Census of the United States, 1880. Vol. ii., pp. 1660–61.

amount of sickness prevailing in the country. It is an undoubted fact that in recent years the amount of hospital accommodation has increased at a greater rate than the population, mainly through the erection of a large number of Cottage Hospitals, and of Hospitals for Infectious Diseases. The number of Hospitals included in the list of Public Institutions, published in the Registrar-General's Annual Report for 1871, was but 346, whereas it had increased to 691 in the Report for 1881.

Workhouses.

In addition, however, to the patients in Hospitals, a very considerable proportion of the sick are constantly under treatment in the Workhouse Infirmaries, which are the legal hospitals for paupers. We have, however, no means of ascertaining what proportion of in-door pauperism was due to sickness. The special or pauper inmates of Workhouses (including Workhouse Infirmaries, the Metropolitan Asylum Hospitals, and Pauper Schools) were 179,620 in 1881, against 120,978 in 1851; 125,722 in 1861; and 148,291 in 1871. The proportion of in-door paupers, to 100,000 of the population, was 676 in 1851; 627 in 1861; 652 in 1871; and rose to 692 in 1881. This increase in the number and proportion of in-door paupers was undoubtedly due, in great measure, to the action of Boards of Guardians in applying the "house-test."

Prisons and Reformatories.

From the bodily and mental infirmities which fill the Asylums for the Blind, the Deaf and Dumb, the Imbecile, and the Lunatic, and the Hospitals for the Sick, and that also supply the Workhouses with a large proportion of their inmates, it is no difficult transition to the moral infirmities which provide the inmates of Prisons. Recent anthropometrical investigations, moreover, clearly prove that the criminal classes suffer from distinct physical deficiencies. The number of prisoners enumerated in 1881 was 27,889, and was equal to 107 per 100,000 of the entire population. It is satisfactory to find that the proportion of prisoners has shown a steady decline since 1851. It was 132 in 1851; 130 in 1861; 127 in 1871; and, as above stated, further declined to 107 in 1881. In addition, however, to the inmates of Prisons, 16,856 boys and girls were enumerated in certified Reformatories and Industrial Schools; whereas the number so returned in 1871 did not exceed 10,598. This large increase in the number of young persons under detention in these Institutions was probably attributable in great measure to the increase of accommodation for such detention resulting from the operation of the Education Act of 1870, and the necessity for dealing with incorrigible truants and street waifs.

The decrease in the number of adult prisoners may, to some extent, be reasonably attributed to the remedial effect, upon the juvenile criminal classes, of the detention and individual training received in Reformatories and Industrial Schools.

—	Special Inmates of Institutions.				Number in 100,000 of the Population.			
	1851.	1861.	1871.	1881.	1851.	1861.	1871.	1881.
Total	167,593	186,577	246,476	303,069	935	930	1,085	1,167
Workhouses (including Pauper Schools)	120,978	125,722	148,291	179,620	676	627	652	692
Hospitals (General and Special)	7,619	10,414	19,585	24,087	42	52	86	93
Lunatic Asylums	15,243	24,345	39,246	54,617	85	121	173	210
Prisons	23,753	26,096	28,756	27,889	132	130	127	107
Reformatory and Industrial Schools	—	—	10,598	16,856	—	—	47	65

IX.—THE UNITED KINGDOM.*

1. *Population of the United Kingdom.*

So far we have dealt exclusively with the results of the Census in England and Wales, that is to say, in that portion of the United Kingdom in which alone the enumeration was carried out and the results tabulated under our immediate superintendence.† Having now concluded our report on those results, our proper task is finished. It will probably, however, be convenient that we should go somewhat beyond our strict province, and give a summary view of the numerical results of the Census as carried out in the United Kingdom as a whole, and still further as carried out in the entire British Empire.

The population of the United Kingdom of Great Britain and Ireland amounted to 34,884,848 persons; and if, in accordance with the usage of previous Censuses, we take into account the Islands in the British Seas, and also the natives of the United Kingdom who were serving abroad at the date of the Census in the Army, the Navy, and the Merchant Service, we have a total of 35,241,482 persons. This was 3,396,103 in excess of the population in 1871, the increase being equivalent to an average daily addition of 929 persons to the community throughout the decade, the similar daily increase in the preceding decade having been 692.

The decennial rate of increase was no less than 10·7 per cent., which was considerably higher than the rate of increase in any of the three preceding decades, in which it had been successively 2·5, 5·7 and 8·6 per cent.

This gradual rise of the rate of increase was due in the main, though not entirely, to the fact that the decrease of the population of Ireland, which in 1841–51 was at the rate of 19·8 per cent., has become less and less in each succeeding decennium. The decrease in this division of the Kingdom was, as already stated, no less than 19·8 per cent. in 1841–51; it fell in the next decade to 11·8 per cent.; in the next to 6·7 per cent.; and finally in the decade ending with the Census of 1881 to 4·4 per cent. The population of Ireland decreased in the whole interval between 1841 and 1881 by 3,021,761 persons, or 36·9 per cent. The decrease in the final decade was of 237,541 persons, or at the rate of 4·4 per cent.

To this loss of population in Ireland must be further added a loss of 2,894 persons in the population of the Channel Islands, which fell off 3·2 per cent. in the decade 1871–81, having previously remained almost stationary since 1851; before which date it had increased much more rapidly than the population of the rest of the United Kingdom.

The population of the Isle of Man also showed a slight decline. In 1871 it numbered 54,042 persons; but in 1881 the number had fallen to 53,558.

The increase, therefore, in the aggregate population of the United Kingdom and the Islands in the British Seas was entirely confined to Great Britain, that is to say, to England, Wales, and Scotland. In England and Wales the rate of increase was 14·4 per cent., and in Scotland 11·1 per cent.; and in each case the rate of increase was higher than it had been in any of the three preceding decades. The gains and losses in the respective sub-divisions were as follows:—

—	Increase.	Decrease.
England and Wales	3,262,173	—
Scotland	375,555	—
Ireland	—	237,541
Channel Islands	—	2,894
Isle of Man	—	484
Army, Navy, &c. Abroad	—	706
Total	3,637,728	241,625

Total increase = 3,396,103.

* For tables relating to the United Kingdom, and to natives of the United Kingdom who were abroad at the date of the Census, see Appendix A., Tables 33–46.

† The enumeration in the Isle of Man and in the Channel Islands was carried out under the directions of the authorities of those Islands. The results were tabulated under our superintendence, but were kept distinct from those of the English and Welsh Census, and published as a separate volume.

2. Natives of the United Kingdom abroad at the time of the Census.

Of the 34,884,848 persons forming the population of the United Kingdom (excluding the Islands in the British Seas, and the Army, Navy, and Merchant Seamen, abroad) 34,535,095 were born within its limits; while 349,753 were born abroad, namely, 145,863 in British Colonies or Dependencies, and 203,890 in Foreign States.

Against these 349,753 persons born out of the country who were in the United Kingdom at the time of the Census, must be put the natives of the United Kingdom who at that date were living abroad. The returns of these were necessarily somewhat imperfect. From those countries in which regular Censuses are taken accurate accounts were received by us. But the Consular or other returns from countries in which no such systematic enumerations are made could of course be only approximative estimates. As, however, the great bulk of our fellow countrymen abroad were in countries where regular Censuses are taken, the possible errors from mistaken estimates in other parts may be neglected as practically insignificant when merged in the grand total. There were, then, according to the returns received by us, 3,959,899 * natives of the United Kingdom living out of the country at the date of the Census. These, with the 34,535,095 who were enumerated in the country itself, make up a total of 38,494,994 persons born in the United Kingdom, and alive on April 4, 1881.

Of the 3,959,899 natives of the United Kingdom who were abroad, 89,798 were in India, and 988,934 were in some other of our colonies or dependencies, while the remaining 2,881,167 were in the dominions of foreign powers. Of these 2,881,167 persons, the great bulk, namely 2,772,169, were in the United States, and consisted of 745,978 natives of England and Wales, 170,136 natives of Scotland, and 1,854,571 natives of Ireland, while the precise nationality of the remaining 1,484 was not specified. The natives of England and Wales enumerated in the United States had increased in the interval between 1870 and 1880 by 19·3 per cent., and the natives of Scotland by 20·8 per cent., while, as might have been anticipated from the emigration returns, the natives of Ireland had slightly fallen off in number. As compared with the contingent furnished by the United Kingdom to the United States, the number of our fellow countrymen in any other foreign state, or in all other foreign states together, was quite insignificant. There were in all but 108,998 of these, of whom 36,447 were in France, 11,139 in the German Empire, 7,230 in Italy, and 5,007 in Russia, these four countries being those in which the British-born sojourners were most numerous.

X.—THE BRITISH EMPIRE.

The British Empire may be considered as consisting of three portions; firstly, the United Kingdom; secondly, British India and Ceylon; and, thirdly, all other British Possessions, Dependencies, and Colonies.

The population of the United Kingdom, as we have already seen, amounted in 1881 to 34,884,848 persons. The population of Ceylon and British India, exclusive of the Feudatory and Native States, was 206,837,886; while the inhabitants of the remaining Dependencies, Possessions, and Colonies, numbered 12,464,896. Thus the aggregate population of the whole Empire consisted of 254,187,630 persons, a total which would be increased to 304,005,549, and would fall very little short of the estimated population of the whole of Europe, were it thought proper to include in the British Empire the Feudatory and Native States of India with their 49,817,919 inhabitants (*See* Appendix A., Tables 47 and 48).

In 1871 the population of the British Empire, excluding these Indian States, was reckoned at 234,802,593† persons, so that the increase in the course of the decade 1871–81, whether by growth of former dependencies or by the addition of new dependencies, amounted to 19,385,037 persons, being in the ratio of 8·3 per cent.

---

* The natives of the United Kingdom serving in the Army, Navy, and Merchant Seamen abroad are included in this total.

† The figure given in the Census Report of 1871 was 234,762,593. To this, however, have to be added 40,000 as the mean estimated number of native Indians in British Columbia. See Census Report 1871, vol. iv. p. 162, foot-note.

The 19,385,037 persons who were added to the population were distributed as shown in the following Summary and Comparative Table:—

——	Population in 1871.	Population in 1881.	Increase.	Rate of Increase per cent.
UNITED KINGDOM - -	31,484,661	34,884,848	3,400,187	10·80
COLONIES, POSSESSIONS, DEPENDENCIES:—				
In Europe* -	320,851	327,805	6,954	2·17
In North America -	3,829,670	4,520,415	690,745	18·04
In West Indies and Central America.	1,088,596	1,243,861	155,265	14·26
In South America - -	194,294	254,532	60,238	31·00
In Africa - -	1,813,450	2,579,163	765,713	42·22
In Asia:—				
British India† - -	191,307,070	204,108,762	12,801,692	6·69
Ceylon - -	2,405,287	2,763,984	358,697	14·91
Straits and Other Settlements.	433,119	590,084	156,965	36·24
In Australasia - -	1,925,595	2,914,176	988,581	51·34
BRITISH EMPIRE - -	234,802,593	254,187,630	19,385,037	8·26

* Including the Islands in the British Seas.

† Aden and Perim are here included in order to facilitate comparison with the figures for 1871, when no separate return was made of the population of those places.

The territory occupied by the 254,187,630 inhabitants of the British Empire is estimated as consisting of slightly over eight millions of English square miles,—an area more than twice as large as Europe, larger than North America, almost half as large as Asia, and not very far short of one-sixth of the land surface of the earth. Of these eight millions of square miles, somewhat more than three and a half millions are in America, and form nearly a quarter of that continent; three millions more square miles are in Australasia; somewhat less than a million are in Asia; a quarter of a million are in Africa; while the portion that lies in Europe constitutes a very inconsiderable fraction of the whole, amounting to no more than 120,960 square miles, of which 120,537 form the United Kingdom.

We have the honour to be,

Sir,

Your most obedient Servants,

BRYDGES P. HENNIKER, Registrar General.

WILLIAM CLODE.

WILLIAM OGLE.

F. J. WILLIAMS, Secretary.

APPENDIX A.

GENERAL REPORT TABLES.

TABLE 1.—ENGLAND and WALES.—HOUSES and POPULATION at each successive Census.

DATE OF THE ENUMERATION.	HOUSES.			NUMBER of FAMILIES or SEPARATE OCCUPIERS.	POPULATION.*		
	Inhabited.	Uninhabited.	Building.		PERSONS.	Males.	Females.
1801, March 10th	1,575,923	57,476	Not returned.	1,896,723	8,892,536	4,254,735	4,637,801
1811, May 27th	1,797,504	51,020	16,207	2,142,147	10,164,256	4,873,605	5,290,651
1821, May 28th - -	2,088,156	69,707	19,274	2,493,423	12,000,236	5,850,319	6,149,917
1831, May 29th - -	2,481,544	119,915	24,759	2,911,874	13,896,797	6,771,196	7,125,601
1841, June 7th - -	2,943,945	173,247	27,444	Not returned.	15,914,148	7,777,586	8,136,562
1851, March 31st -	3,278,039	153,494	26,571	3,712,290	17,927,609	8,781,225	9,146,384
1861, April 8th	3,739,505	184,694	27,305	4,491,524	20,066,224	9,776,259	10,289,965
1871, April 3rd - -	4,259,117	261,345	37,803	5,049,016	22,712,266	11,058,934	11,653,332
1881, April 4th -	4,831,519	366,676	46,414	5,633,192	25,974,439	12,639,902	13,334,537

* The Army, Royal Navy, and Seamen belonging to registered vessels are not included in the numbers for the years prior to 1841; the Military at home were included with the general population for the first time in 1841; and persons on board vessels of the Royal Navy and Merchant Service in the harbours, creeks, and rivers of England and Wales were first included in 1851, 1861, 1871, and 1881.

TABLE 2.—ENGLAND and WALES.—INCREASE of the INHABITED HOUSES and POPULATION in each Intercensal Period.

INTERVAL BETWEEN THE ENUMERATIONS.	INHABITED HOUSES.		POPULATION.	
	Actual Increase.	Decennial rate of Increase per cent.	Actual Increase.	Decennial rate of Increase per cent.
1801—1811 = 10·212 years	221,581	13·77	1,271,720	14·30
1811—1821 = 10·004 " -	290,652	16·16	1,835,980	18·06
1821—1831 = 10·001 " -	393,388	18·84	1,896,561	15·80
1831—1841 = 10·026 " -	462,401	18·59	2,017,351	14·52*
1841—1851 = 9·812 " -	334,094	11·56	2,013,461	12·65*
1851—1861 = 10·023 " - -	461,466	14·05	2,138,615	11·93
1861—1871 = 9·985 "	519,612	13·92	2,646,042	13·19
1871—1881 = 10·004 " -	572,402	13·43	3,262,173	14·36
Increase in 80·067 years -	3,255,596	Total increase per cent. in 80·067 years 206·58	17,081,903	Total increase per cent. in 80·067 years 192·09

* In computing the rate of increase between 1831 and 1841, the Military returned in the latter year are excluded; and in computing the rate of increase between 1841 and 1851, the Seamen and others enumerated on board vessels in 1851 are excluded.

TABLE 3.—ENGLAND and WALES.—AVERAGE NUMBER of PERSONS to a FAMILY, PERSONS to an INHABITED HOUSE, FAMILIES to an INHABITED HOUSE, PERSONS to a SQUARE MILE, INHABITED HOUSES to a SQUARE MILE, and ACRES to an INHABITED HOUSE, at each successive Census.

Years.	Persons to a Family.	Persons to an Inhabited House.	Families to an Inhabited House.	Persons to a Square Mile.	Inhabited Houses to a Square Mile.	Acres to an Inhabited House.
1801	4·69	5·64	1·20	153	27·0	23·7
1811	4·74	5·65	1·19	174	30·8	20·8
1821	4·81	5·75	1.19	206	35·8	17·9
1831	4·77	5·60	1·17	238	42·6	15·0
1841	?	5·41	?	273	50·5	12·7
1851	4·83	5·47	1·13	307	56·2	11·4
1861	4·47	5·37	1·20	344	64·1	10·0
1871	4·50	5·33	1·19	390	73·0	8·8
1881	4·61	5·38	1·17	446	83·0	7·7

TABLE 4.—ENGLAND and WALES.—POPULATION, exclusive of the ARMY, NAVY, MARINES, and MERCHANT SEAMEN, serving abroad, estimated to the MIDDLE of each of the Years 1801 to 1881.

MIDDLE of the YEARS.	POPULATION (Estimated).			MIDDLE of the YEARS.	POPULATION (Estimated).		
	PERSONS.	Males.	Females.		PERSONS.	Males.	Females.
1801	9,060,993	4,404,490	4,656,503	1841	15,929,492	7,784,883	8,144,609
1802	9,129,636	4,441,131	4.688,505	1842	16,130,326	7,887,620	8,242,706
1803	9,234,649	4,494,127	4,740,522	1843	16,332,228	7,990,370	8,341,858
1804	9,366,826	4,559,230	4,807,596	1844	16,535,174	8,093,100	8,442,074
1805	9,513,111	4,631,137	4,881,974	1845	16,739,136	8,195,776	8,543,360
1806	9,656,119	4,700,476	4,955,643	1846	16,944,092	8,298,360	8,645,732
1807	9,794,594	4,768,221	5,026,373	1847	17,150,018	8,400,820	8,749,198
1808	9,924,001	4,831,985	5,092,016	1848	17,356,882	8,503,116	8,853,766
1809	10,056,421	4,895,182	5,161,239	1849	17,564,656	8,605,212	8,959,444
1810	10,185,578	4,957,559	5,228,019	1850	17,773,324	8,707,074	9,066,250
1811	10,322,592	5,025,212	5,297,380	1851	17,982,849	8,808,662	9,174,187
1812	10,479,871	5,103,251	5,376,620	1852	18,193,206	8,909,938	9,283,268
1813	10,649,743	5,191,211	5,458,532	1853	18,404,368	9,010,866	9,393,502
1814	10,820,112	5,280,331	5,539,781	1854	18,616,310	9,111,410	9,504,900
1815	11,004,012	5,375,916	5,628,096	1855	18,829,000	9,211,528	9,617,472
1816	11,196,156	5,474,848	5,721,308	1856	19,042,412	9,311,182	9,731,230
1817	11,377,841	5,568,195	5,809,646	1857	19,256,516	9,410,334	9,846,182
1818	11,555,054	5,659,313	5,895,741	1858	19,471,291	9,508,949	9,962,342
1819	11,723,379	5,747,842	5,975,537	1859	19,686,701	9,606,982	10,079,719
1820	11,903,722	5,843,289	6,060,433	1860	19,902,713	9,704,394	10,198,319
1821	12,105,614	5,946,821	6,158,793	1861	20,119,314	9,801,152	10,318,162
1822	12,320,360	6,050,929	6,269,431	1862	20,371,013	9,923,272	10,447,741
1823	12,529,518	6,153,157	6,376,361	1863	20,625,855	10,046,909	10,578,946
1824	12,720,736	6,246,003	6,474,733	1864	20,883,889	10,172,089	10,711,800
1825	12,903,059	6,333,955	6,569,104	1865	21,145,151	10,298,826	10,846,325
1826	13,074,286	6,417,196	6,657,090	1866	21,409,684	10,427,146	10,982,538
1827	13,247,277	6,500,546	6,746,731	1867	21,677,525	10,557,066	11,120,459
1828	13,438,474	6,591,959	6,846,515	1868	21,948,713	10,688,600	11,260,113
1829	13,625,045	6,681,424	6,943,621	1869	22,223,299	10,821,775	11,401,524
1830	13,805,041	6,767,221	7,037,820	1870	22,501,316	10,956,608	11,544,708
1831	13,994,460	6,859,085	7,135,375	1871	22,788,594	11,092,620	11,695,974
1832	14,164,696	6,943,932	7,220,764	1872	23,096,495	11,242,495	11,854,000
1833	14,328,471	7,023,322	7,305,149	1873	23,408,556	11,394,394	12,014,162
1834	14,520,297	7,116,031	7,404,266	1874	23,724,834	11,548,346	12,176,488
1835	14,724,063	7,213,625	7,510,438	1875	24,045,385	11,704,378	12,341,007
1836	14,928,477	7,310,074	7,618,403	1876	24,370,267	11,862,519	12,507,748
1837	15,103,778	7,392,191	7,711,587	1877	24,699,539	12,022,796	12,676,743
1838	15,287,699	7,479,021	7,808,678	1878	25,033,259	12,185,238	12,848,021
1839	15,514,255	7,586,593	7,927,662	1879	25,371,489	12,349,875	13,021,614
1840	15,730,813	7,689,301	8,041,512	1880	25,714,288	12,516,737	13,197,551
				1881	26,061,736	12,682,383	13,379,353

NOTE.—The Table has been deduced from the Estimated Population in the Middle of each Census Year. The Population for each year from 1801 to 1841 has been obtained from the probable increase deduced from the annual excess of *Baptisms* over Burials, and from the population enumerated at each Census. (*See* Census Report for 1851, Vol. I. p. xxix.) The population for each year from 1841 to 1861 is deduced from the ascertained rate of increase of males and females observed in the 20 years; and for the years 1861 to 1881 from the annual rate of increase prevailing in each of the last two Census decades.

TABLE 5.—ENGLAND and WALES.—STRENGTH of the ARMY, NAVY, MARINES, and MERCHANT SERVICE, abroad; the EXCESS of FEMALES over MALES at home and abroad, and over MALES at home; and the PROPORTION of FEMALES to every 1,000 MALES in ENGLAND and WALES, at each successive Census.

YEARS.	Men in the Army, Navy, Marines, and Merchant Service abroad.	Excess of Females over Males at home and abroad.	Excess of Females over Males at home.	Number of FEMALES to 1,000 MALES, *including* Army, Navy, Marines, and Merchant Service at home and abroad.	Number of FEMALES to 1,000 MALES, *excluding* Army, Mavy, Marines, and Merchant Service abroad.
1801 -	131,817	119,431	251,248*	1,026	1,057*
1811 -	145,136	126,773	271,909*	1,025	1,054*
1821 - -	84,688	127,170	211,858*	1,021	1,036*
1831 -	76,221	199,216	275,437*	1,029	1,040*
1841 - -	121,050	237,926	358,976	1,030	1,046
1851 -	126,561	238,598	365,159	1,027	1,042
1861 -	162,273	351,433	513,706	1,035	1,053
1871 -	143,898	450,500	594,398	1,040	1,054
1881	147,540	547,095	694,635	1,043	1,055

* The Army, Navy, and Seamen ashore were excluded from the population enumerated at the Censuses in 1801, 1811, 1821, and 1831; corrections have, however, been made for this fact in calculating the excess of females over males at home, and the proportion of females to males in the home population, at those Censuses.

TABLE 6.—ENGLAND AND WALES.—AREA and POPULATION of COUNTIES PROPER at each successive Census.

COUNTIES PROPER.	Area in Statute Acres.	PERSONS.								
		1801.	1811.	1821.	1831.	1841.	1851.	1861.	1871.	1881.
ENGLAND AND WALES	37,239,351	8,892,536	10,164,256	12,000,236	13,896,797	15,914,148*	17,927,609	20,066,224	22,712,266	25,974,439
BEDFORDSHIRE - -	294,983	63,393	70,213	84,052	95,483	107,936	124,478	135,287	146,257	149,473
BERKSHIRE -	462,210	110,480	119,430	132,639	146,234	161,759	170,065	176,256	196,475	218,363
BUCKINGHAMSHIRE - -	477,151	108,132	118,065	135,133	146,977	156,439	163,723	167,993	175,926	176,323
CAMBRIDGESHIRE -	524,935	89,346	101,109	122,387	143,955	164,459	185,405	176,033	186,906	185,594
CHESHIRE - - -	657,123	192,305	227,031	270,098	334,391	395,660	455,725	505,428	561,201	644,037
CORNWALL - - -	863,665	192,281	220,525	261,045	301,306	342,159	355,558	369,390	362,343	330,686
CUMBERLAND -	970,161	117,230	133,665	156,124	169,262	178,038	195,492	205,276	220,253	250,647
DERBYSHIRE	658,624	161,567	185,487	213,651	237,170	272,202	296,084	339,327	379,394	461,914
DEVONSHIRE -	1,655,208	340,308	382,778	438,417	493,908	532,959	567,098	584,373	601,374	603,595
DORSETSHIRE - -	627,265	114,452	124,718	144,930	159,385	175,054	184,207	188,789	195,774	191,028
DURHAM - -	647,592	149,384	165,293	193,511	239,256	307,963	390,997	508,666	685,089	867,258
ESSEX -	987,032	227,682	252,473	289,424	317,507	344,979	369,318	404,834	466,436	576,434
GLOUCESTERSHIRE	783,699	250,723	285,955	336,190	387,398	431,495	458,805	485,770	534,734	572,433
HAMPSHIRE -	1,037,764	219,290	246,514	282,897	313,976	354,682	405,370	481,815	544,447	593,470
HEREFORDSHIRE	532,918	88,436	93,526	102,669	110,617	113,272	115,489	123,650	125,370	121,062
HERTFORDSHIRE - -	405,141	97,393	111,225	129,731	142,844	156,660	167,298	173,280	192,226	203,069
HUNTINGDONSHIRE	229,515	37,568	42,208	48,946	53,192	58,549	64,183	64,250	63,708	59,491
KENT -	995,392	308,667	371,701	427,224	479,558	549,353	615,766	733,887	848,294	977,706
LANCASHIRE - -	1,208,154	673,486	828,499	1,052,948	1,336,854	1,667,054	2,031,236	2,429,440	2,819,495	3,454,441
LEICESTERSHIRE - -	511,907	130,082	150,559	174,571	197,003	215,867	230,308	237,412	269,311	321,258
LINCOLNSHIRE - -	1,767,879	208,625	237,634	283,058	317,465	362,602	407,222	412,246	436,599	469,919
MIDDLESEX	181,317	818,129	953,774	1,145,057	1,358,330	1,576,636	1,886,576	2,206,485	2,539,765	2,920,485
MONMOUTHSHIRE	370,350	45,568	62,105	75,801	98,126	134,368	157,418	174,633	195,448	211,267
NORFOLK	1,356,173	273,479	291,947	344,368	390,054	412,664	442,714	434,798	438,656	444,749
NORTHAMPTONSHIRE -	629,912	131,525	141,353	163,097	179,336	199,228	212,380	227,704	243,891	272,555
NORTHUMBERLAND - -	1,290,312	168,078	183,269	212,589	236,959	266,020	303,568	343,025	386,646	434,086
NOTTINGHAMSHIRE -	527,752	140,350	162,964	186,873	225,327	249,910	270,427	293,867	319,758	391,815
OXFORDSHIRE	483,621	111,977	120,376	138,224	153,526	163,127	170,439	170,944	177,928	179,559
RUTLANDSHIRE -	94,889	16,300	16,380	18,487	19,385	21,302	22,983	21,861	22,073	21,434
SHROPSHIRE -	844,565	169,248	184,973	198,311	213,518	225,820	229,341	241,021	248,111	248,014
SOMERSETSHIRE	1,049,812	273,577	302,836	355,789	403,795	435,599	443,916	444,873	463,339	469,109
STAFFORDSHIRE	748,433	242,693	294,540	345,972	409,480	509,472	608,716	746,943	858,326	981,013
SUFFOLK -	944,060	214,404	233,963	271,541	296,317	315,073	337,215	337,070	348,869	356,893
SURREY	485,129	268,233	323,851	399,417	486,434	584,036	683,082	831,093	1,091,635	1,436,899
SUSSEX -	933,269	159,471	190,343	233,328	272,644	300,075	336,844	363,735	417,456	490,505
WARWICKSHIRE	566,271	206,798	228,906	274,482	336,645	401,703	475,013	561,855	634,189	737,339
WESTMORLAND	500,906	40,805	45,922	51,359	55,041	56,454	58,287	60,817	65,010	64,191
WILTSHIRE -	866,677	183,820	191,853	219,574	237,244	256,280	254,221	249,311	257,177	258,965
WORCESTERSHIRE - -	472,453	146,441	168,982	194,074	222,655	248,460	276,926	307,397	338,837	380,283
YORKSHIRE, EAST RIDING -	750,828	111,192	133,975	154,643	168,891	194,936	220,983	240,227	268,466	315,460
,, NORTH ,,	1,361,664	158,927	170,127	188,178	192,206	204,701	215,214	245,154	293,278	346,260
,, WEST ,, -	1,770,359	589,014	681,974	831,074	1,010,869	1,192,422	1,361,798	1,548,229	1,874,611	2,224,844
WALES.										
ANGLESEY -	193,511	33,806	37,045	45,063	48,325	50,891	57,327	54,609	51,040	51,416
BRECKNOCKSHIRE	460,158	32,325	37,735	43,826	47,763	55,603	61,474	61,627	59,901	57,746
CARDIGANSHIRE -	443,387	42,956	50,260	57,784	64,780	68,766	70,796	72,245	73,441	70,270
CARMARTHENSHIRE -	594,405	67,317	77,217	90,239	100,740	106,326	110,632	111,796	115,710	124,864
CARNARVONSHIRE -	369,477	41,521	49,655	58,099	66,818	81,093	87,870	95,694	106,282	119,349
DENBIGHSHIRE -	425,038	60,299	64,249	76,428	82,665	88,478	92,583	100,778	104,941	111,740
FLINTSHIRE -	161,807	39,469	45,937	53,893	60,244	66,919	68,156	69,737	76,312	80,587
GLAMORGANSHIRE	516,959	70,879	85,067	102,073	126,612	171,188	231,849	317,752	397,859	511,433
MERIONETHSHIRE	384,717	29,506	30,854	34,382	35,315	39,332	38,843	38,963	46,598	52,038
MONTGOMERYSHIRE	495,089	48,184	52,184	60,245	66,844	69,607	67,335	66,919	67,623	65,718
PEMBROKESHIRE - -	391,181	56,280	60,615	73,788	81,425	88,044	94,140	96,278	91,998	91,824
RADNORSHIRE - -	276,552	19,135	20,417	22,533	24,743	25,458	24,716	25,382	25,430	23,528

* The population of England and Wales in 1841 included 5,016 persons (4,130 males and 886 females) travelling on railways and canals on the night of June 6th, 1841, and not apportioned to counties. At each Census subsequent to 1841 such persons have been enumerated at the places where they arrived or were found on the day of the Census.

TABLE 7.—ENGLAND AND WALES.—AREA and POPULATION of REGISTRATION DIVISIONS and COUNTIES at each successive CENSUS.*

REGISTRATION DIVISION AND COUNTY.	AREA in Statute Acres.	PERSONS.								
		1801.	1811.	1821.	1831.	1841.	1851.	1861.	1871.	1881.
ENGLAND AND WALES	37,239,351	8,892,536	10,164,256	12,000,236	13,896,797	15,914,148†	17,927,609	20,066,224	22,712,266	25,974,439
DIVISIONS.										
I.—LONDON	75,334	958,863	1,138,815	1,378,947	1,654,994	1,948,417	2,362,236	2,803,989	3,254,260	3,816,483
II.—SOUTH-EASTERN	3,994,502	876,608	1,006,312	1,169,908	1,318,774	1,477,761	1,625,831	1,844,961	2,165,179	2,487,076
III.—SOUTH-MIDLAND	3,238,579	707,581	788,648	921,869	1,030,845	1,141,847	1,235,065	1,296,393	1,443,722	1,596,259
IV.—EASTERN	3,136,622	696,223	756,202	879,121	974,815	1,040,616	1,113,982	1,142,562	1,218,728	1,343,524
V.—SOUTH-WESTERN	4,992,821	1,101,513	1,220,964	1,417,683	1,594,630	1,741,781	1,805,113	1,837,522	1,882,112	1,859,013
VI.—WEST-MIDLAND	3,965,966	1,102,844	1,252,699	1,446,360	1,671,484	1,918,839	2,148,978	2,449,334	2,721,918	3,029,504
VII.—NORTH-MIDLAND	3,535,223	652,357	746,889	869,095	988,024	1,111,611	1,216,001	1,289,419	1,407,145	1,637,865
VIII.—NORTH-WESTERN	1,951,126	873,283	1,064,035	1,331,737	1,678,985	2,068,796	2,492,587	2,940,418	3,389,044	4,108,184
IX.—YORKSHIRE -	3,726,829	854,309	981,279	1,170,054	1,370,490	1,594,244	1,801,728	2,040,882	2,444,709	2,894,759
X.—NORTHERN -	3,528,621	482,321	535,490	621,885	708,756	816,582	956,445	1,126,031	1,365,041	1,624,213
XI.—WELSH - -	5,093,728	586,634	672,923	793,577	905,000	1,048,638	1,169,643	1,294,713	1,420,408	1,577,559
I.—LONDON.										
MIDDLESEX (*Intra-metn.*)	31,499	746,718	869,634	1,045,711	1,245,184	1,444,999	1,745,601	2,030,814	2,286,568	2,550,556
SURREY (*Intra-metropn.*)	22,472	161,642	202,941	259,714	327,820	399,247	482,435	579,748	742,155	980,522
KENT (*Intra-metropn.*) -	21,363	50,503	66,240	73,522	81,990	104,171	134,200	193,427	225,537	285,405
II.—SOUTH-EASTERN.										
1. SURREY (*Extra-metropn.*)	453,028	105,627	120,192	138,044	156,292	182,257	196,413	261,498	365,279	461,054
2. KENT (*Extra-metropn.*) -	969,418	258,450	304,961	354,064	398,471	447,115	485,021	545,272	629,126	708,527
3. SUSSEX -	947,132	161,306	192,333	235,606	275,110	302,460	339,604	366,836	420,910	494,194
4. HAMPSHIRE	1,050,116	220,572	247,374	284,293	315,417	355,983	406,434	466,805	524,836	575,409
5. BERKSHIRE	574,808	130,653	141,452	157,901	173,484	189,946	198,859	204,550	225,028	247,892
III. SOUTH-MIDLAND.										
6. MIDDLESEX (*Extra-metn.*)	178,755	77,582	91,883	107,875	122,750	140,847	150,606	187,325	264,854	380,814
7. HERTFORDSHIRE	441,623	101,892	114,783	134,087	147,575	162,394	173,962	177,452	194,612	202,375
8. BUCKINGHAMSHIRE	410,176	95,827	105,276	120,330	130,982	138,248	143,655	147,207	155,007	155,869
9. OXFORDSHIRE -	489,727	112,453	120,819	138,985	153,992	163,569	170,980	172,125	179,397	181,570
10. NORTHAMPTONSHIRE	632,982	128,245	139,764	160,933	177,946	199,208	213,844	231,079	248,234	277,085
11. HUNTINGDONSHIRE -	204,473	34,704	38,864	45,983	50,463	55,565	60,319	59,137	58,031	58,228
12. BEDFORDSHIRE -	307,050	66,176	73,033	87,522	98,804	112,378	129,805	140,479	151,554	154,259
13. CAMBRIDGESHIRE - -	573,793	90,702	104,221	126,154	148,383	169,638	191,894	181,589	192,033	191,114
IV.—EASTERN.										
14. ESSEX - -	904,194	210,408	234,171	268,101	294,435	320,782	344,110	379,705	440,880	552,268
15. SUFFOLK -	925,884	214,690	233,726	271,136	296,238	314,710	336,156	335,409	347,210	353,545
16. NORFOLK	1,306,544	271,125	288,305	339,884	384,142	405,124	433,716	427,448	430,638	437,711
V.—SOUTH-WESTERN.										
17. WILTSHIRE	793,144	175,105	182,543	209,021	225,898	244,521	242,788	237,835	246,146	248,664
18. DORSETSHIRE	610,582	109,846	119,034	138,374	152,204	167,876	177,095	182,193	189,000	184,972
19. DEVONSHIRE -	1,643,390	337,785	381,398	437,559	492,935	532,308	569,072	589,278	606,102	608,400
20. CORNWALL	879,328	192,879	220,477	261,016	301,642	342,333	353,687	364,848	358,356	326,375
21. SOMERSETSHIRE	1,066,377	286,098	317,512	371,713	421,951	454,743	462,521	463,368	482,508	490,602

* The figures in this table for Censuses prior to 1881, with but few and unimportant exceptions (in which cases the necessary corrections for changes of boundaries could not be carried out), relate to the areas of the Registration Counties as constituted at the time of the Census in 1881.

† The population of England and Wales in 1841 included 5,016 persons (4,130 males and 886 females) travelling on railways and canals on the night of June 6th, 1841, and not apportioned to the counties. At each Census subsequent to 1841 such persons have been enumerated at the places where they arrived or were found on the day of the Census.

TABLE 7 (*continued*).—ENGLAND AND WALES.—AREA and POPULATION of REGISTRATION DIVISIONS and COUNTIES at each successive Census.

REGISTRATION DIVISION AND COUNTY.	AREA in Statute Acres.	PERSONS.								
		1801.	1811.	1821.	1831.	1841.	1851.	1861.	1871.	1881.
VI.—WEST-MIDLAND.										
22. Gloucestershire -	701,414	228,895	261,555	307,621	354,699	395,533	419,514	443,535	488,904	525,167
23. Herefordshire -	519,141	85,622	90,737	99,926	107,691	110,009	111,991	120,014	121,985	118,147
24. Shropshire - -	933,582	186,934	203,394	219,682	225,708	246,378	249,815	260,662	267,175	265,890
25. Staffordshire - -	766,668	253,544	307,586	361,250	424,643	523,382	630,079	769,089	877,280	1,006,758
26. Worcestershire	434,554	132,334	151,832	174,635	203,381	230,322	258,422	294,700	336,104	383,011
27. Warwickshire -	610,587	215,515	237,645	283,246	345,362	408,215	479,157	561,334	630,470	730,531
VII.—NORTH-MIDLAND.										
28. Leicestershire -	535,103	134,595	155,188	179,235	201,545	221,227	233,920	243,648	275,328	326,641
29. Rutlandshire -	107,352	18,311	18,177	20,435	21,363	23,151	24,272	23,479	23,385	23,007
30. Lincolnshire - -	1,731,716	205,340	233,628	277,514	311,903	356,280	400,242	404,157	428,075	463,061
31. Nottinghamshire	604,181	152,373	177,330	203,939	243,875	270,727	294,374	323,784	355,457	438,642
32. Derbyshire - -	556,869	141,538	162,571	187,972	209,338	240,276	261,193	294,351	324,900	386,514
VIII.—NORTH-WESTERN.										
33. Cheshire	643,745	190,031	223,940	264,450	318,039	370,187	425,286	475,052	589,785	622,365
34. Lancashire - -	1,307,381	683,252	840,095	1,067,287	1,360,946	1,698,609	2,067,301	2,465,366	2,849,259	3,485,819
IX.—YORKSHIRE.										
35. West Riding	1,776,884	579,866	671,360	820,304	998,157	1,180,825	1,344,620	1,530,491	1,854,119	2,197,999
36. East Riding (*with York*)	696,296	124,705	148,905	171,037	189,753	218,305	251,022	273,941	306,580	362,375
37. North Riding -	1,253,649	149,738	161,014	178,713	182,560	195,114	206,086	236,450	284,010	334,335
X.—NORTHERN.										
38. Durham -	765,075	156,135	172,634	201,662	247,363	315,915	398,998	516,784	693,012	875,166
39. Northumberland -	1,290,312	168,078	183,269	212,589	236,959	266,020	303,568	343,025	386,646	434,086
40. Cumberland - -	970,161	117,230	133,665	156,124	169,262	178,038	195,492	205,276	220,253	250,647
41. Westmorland - -	503,073	40,878	45,922	51,510	55,172	56,609	58,387	60,946	65,130	64,314
XI.—WELSH.										
42. Monmouthshire	427,848	54,750	72,927	88,639	112,686	151,021	177,130	196,977	219,708	234,332
43. South Wales:										
Glamorganshire	576,426	74,189	89,099	107,263	132,161	178,050	240,095	326,254	405,798	518,383
Carmarthenshire -	485,499	55,571	64,642	75,363	84,339	89,559	94,672	96,651	101,381	111,255
Pembrokeshire -	355,530	50,270	54,213	65,442	72,946	78,557	84,472	87,690	83,873	83,679
Cardiganshire -	594,883	61,290	70,067	81,765	90,690	96,002	97,614	97,401	97,869	95,137
Brecknockshire -	443,133	34,791	39,495	44,853	43,799	55,420	59.178	58,860	56,932	54,140
Radnorshire - -	221,252	13,171	14,176	15,782	17,401	18,282	18,554	19,648	19,754	18,523
44. North Wales:										
Montgomeryshire -	581,221	56,041	60,331	69,349	77,121	79,756	77,142	76,923	78,400	76,196
Flintshire - -	73,380	22,163	26,632	31,178	35,307	40,798	41,047	39,941	48,517	45,774
Denbighshire -	375,977	56,853	61,140	73,105	78,560	85,621	90,515	99,443	105,164	112,940
Merionethshire -	481,081	35,847	38,644	42,721	45,217	50,713	51,307	53,230	61,507	68,278
Carnarvonshire	354,416	48,006	53,447	63,669	72,475	86,753	94,674	103,538	111,378	123,781
Anglesey - -	123,082	25,692	28,110	34,448	37,298	38,106	43,243	38,157	35,127	35,141

Table 8.—ENGLAND AND WALES.—Increase per Cent. of the Population of Registration Divisions and Counties in each Intercensal Period.

Registration Divisions and Counties.	Increase per Cent.							
	1801 to 1811.	1811 to 1821.	1821 to 1831.	1831 to 1841.	1841 to 1851.	1851 to 1861.	1861 to 1871.	1871 to 1881.
ENGLAND AND WALES	14	18	16	15	13	12	13	14
I.—LONDON	19	21	20	18	21	19	16	17
II.—SOUTH-EASTERN COUNTIES	15	16	13	12	10	13	17	15
III.—SOUTH-MIDLAND COUNTIES	11	17	12	11	8	5	11	11
IV.—EASTERN COUNTIES	9	16	11	7	7	3	7	10
V.—SOUTH-WESTERN COUNTIES	11	16	12	9	4	2	2	−1
VI.—WEST-MIDLAND COUNTIES	14	15	16	15	12	14	11	11
VII.—NORTH-MIDLAND COUNTIES	14	16	14	13	9	6	9	16
VIII.—NORTH-WESTERN COUNTIES	22	25	26	23	20	18	15	21
IX.—YORKSHIRE	15	19	17	16	13	13	19	18
X.—NORTHERN COUNTIES	11	16	14	16	17	19	23	19
XI.—MONMOUTHSHIRE AND WALES	15	18	14	16	12	11	10	11
I.—LONDON.								
Middlesex (*Intra-Metropolitan*)	16	20	19	16	21	16	13	12
Surrey (*Intra-Metropolitan*)	26	28	26	22	21	20	28	32
Kent (*Intra-Metropolitan*)	31	11	12	27	29	44	17	27
II.—SOUTH-EASTERN COUNTIES.								
1 Surrey (*Extra-Metropolitan*)	14	15	13	17	8	33	40	26
2 Kent (*Extra-Metropolitan*)	18	16	13	12	8	12	15	18
3 Sussex	19	22	17	10	12	8	15	17
4 Hampshire	12	15	11	13	14	15	12	10
5 Berkshire	8	12	10	9	5	3	10	10
III.—SOUTH-MIDLAND COUNTIES.								
6 Middlesex (*Extra-Metropolitan*)	18	17	14	15	7	24	41	44
7 Hertfordshire	13	17	10	10	7	2	10	4
8 Buckinghamshire	10	14	9	6	4	2	5	1
9 Oxfordshire	7	15	11	6	4	1	4	1
10 Northamptonshire	9	15	11	12	7	8	7	12
11 Huntingdonshire	12	18	10	10	9	−2	−2	−8
12 Bedfordshire	10	20	18	14	16	8	8	2
13 Cambridgeshire	15	21	18	14	13	−5	6	−1
IV.—EASTERN COUNTIES.								
14 Essex	11	14	10	9	7	10	16	25
15 Suffolk	9	16	9	6	7	*Sta.*	4	2
16 Norfolk	6	18	13	5	7	−1	1	2
V.—SOUTH-WESTERN COUNTIES.								
17 Wiltshire	4	15	8	8	−1	−2	4	1
18 Dorsetshire	9	16	10	10	5	3	4	−2
19 Devonshire	13	15	13	8	7	4	3	*Sta.*
20 Cornwall	14	18	16	13	3	3	−2	−9
21 Somersetshire	11	17	14	8	2	*Sta.*	4	2

Note.—Wherever the *minus* sign (−) is used in this Table it denotes that, instead of increasing, the population decreased at the rate per cent. expressed by the figures before which it is placed. *Sta.* denotes that the population was stationary.

TABLE 8 (*continued*).—ENGLAND AND WALES.—INCREASE per CENT. of the POPULATION of REGISTRATION DIVISIONS and COUNTIES in each INTERCENSAL PERIOD.

REGISTRATION DIVISIONS AND COUNTIES.	INCREASE PER CENT.							
	1801 to 1811.	1811 to 1821.	1821 to 1831.	1831 to 1841.	1841 to 1851.	1851 to 1861.	1861 to 1871.	1871 to 1881.
VI.—WEST-MIDLAND COUNTIES.								
22 GLOUCESTERSHIRE - - -	14	18	15	12	6	6	10	7
23 HEREFORDSHIRE - - -	6	10	8	2	2	7	2	−3
24 SHROPSHIRE - - -	9	8	7	5	1	4	3	−1
25 STAFFORDSHIRE - -	21	17	18	24	19	22	14	15
26 WORCESTERSHIRE - -	15	15	16	13	12	14	14	14
27 WARWICKSHIRE - - -	10	19	22	18	17	17	12	16
VII.—NORTH-MIDLAND COUNTIES.								
28 LEICESTERSHIRE - -	15	15	12	10	7	3	13	19
29 RUTLANDSHIRE - - - -	−1	12	5	8	5	−3	*Sta.*	−2
30 LINCOLNSHIRE -	14	19	12	14	12	1	6	8
31 NOTTINGHAMSHIRE - - - -	16	15	20	11	9	10	10	23
32 DERBYSHIRE - - -	15	16	11	15	9	13	10	19
VIII.—NORTH-WESTERN COUNTIES.								
33 CHESHIRE - -	18	18	20	16	15	12	14	15
34 LANCASHIRE - -	23	27	28	25	22	19	16	22
IX.—YORKSHIRE.								
35 WEST RIDING - - -	16	22	22	18	14	14	21	19
36 EAST RIDING (*with York*) - - -	19	15	11	15	15	9	12	18
37 NORTH RIDING - - - -	8	11	2	7	6	15	20	18
X.—NORTHERN COUNTIES.								
38 DURHAM - -	11	17	23	28	26	30	34	26
39 NORTHUMBERLAND -	9	16	11	12	14	13	13	12
40 CUMBERLAND - - - -	14	17	8	5	10	5	7	14
41 WESTMORLAND -	12	12	7	3	3	4	7	−1
XI.—WELSH.								
42 MONMOUTHSHIRE -	33	22	27	34	17	11	12	7
43 SOUTH WALES:								
GLAMORGANSHIRE - -	20	20	23	35	35	36	24	28
CARMARTHENSHIRE - -	16	17	12	6	6	2	5	10
PEMBROKESHIRE - -	8	21	11	8	7	4	−4	*Sta.*
CARDIGANSHIRE -	14	17	11	6	2	*Sta.*	1	−3
BRECKNOCKSHIRE -	14	14	9	14	7	−1	−3	−5
RADNORSHIRE -	8	11	10	5	1	6	1	−6
44 NORTH WALES:								
MONTGOMERYSHIRE -	8	15	11	3	−3	*Sta.*	2	−3
FLINTSHIRE -	20	17	13	16	1	−3	9	5
DENBIGHSHIRE -	8	20	7	9	6	10	6	7
MERIONETHSHIRE -	8	11	6	12	1	4	16	11
CARNARVONSHIRE - - - -	16	19	14	20	9	9	8	11
ANGLESEY - - - -	9	23	8	2	13	−12	−8	*Sta.*

TABLE 9.—ENGLAND AND WALES.—POPULATION of LONDON, and of each URBAN SANITARY DISTRICT of which the Population in 1881 exceeded 50,000 Persons, at each successive CENSUS.

NOTE.—In many cases in which the Urban Sanitary District as now constituted includes parts of parishes or townships, it has been impossible to ascertain the precise population enumerated within its present boundaries at each Census. In such cases the population within these parts of parishes at each Census has been approximately estimated. All the figures in the following Table which include any such estimated numbers are printed in italics.

URBAN SANITARY DISTRICT.	POPULATION.								
	1801.	1811.	1821.	1831.	1841.	1851.	1861.	1871.	1881.
TOTAL - -	1,904,643	2,278,750	2,843,446	3,644,713	4,503,772	5,589,035	6,744,207	7,968,703	9,477,453
ASTON MANOR - -	*701*	*862*	*1,151*	*1,927*	2,896	6,426	16,337	33,948	53,842
BATH -	33,196	38,408	46,700	50,800	53,196	54,240	52,528	52,548	51,814
BIRKENHEAD -	*740*	*893*	*1,429*	*4,340*	*11,998*	*34,275*	51,649	65,971	84,006
BIRMINGHAM -	70,670	82,753	101,722	143,986	182,922	232,841	296,076	343,787	400,774
BLACKBURN	*14,374*	*17,557*	*25,709*	*31,321*	*41,268*	*52,187*	*71,065*	*85,579*	104,014
BOLTON	*19,541*	*26,786*	*34,465*	*45,414*	*54,514*	*65,302*	*76,480*	*92,203*	105,414
BRADFORD - -	13,738	16,593	26,941	44,198	67,398	104,652	107,155	147,101	183,032
BRIGHTON	*7,559*	*12,436*	*24,745*	*40,566*	*47,409*	*66,465*	*78,726*	92,469	107,546
BRISTOL	*61,153*	*71,433*	*85,108*	*104,408*	125,146	137,328	154,093	182,696	206,874
BURNLEY	*4,840*	*6,639*	*10,068*	*12,204*	*17,320*	*24,745*	*34,381*	40,858	58,751
BURY	*9,708*	*12,080*	*14,467*	*20,467*	*27,622*	*33,912*	*40,146*	*43,294*	52,213
CARDIFF	*2,824*	*3,471*	*4,742*	*7,545*	*11,442*	*20,258*	*41,422*	*57,363*	82,761
CROYDON	5,743	7,801	9,254	12,447	16,712	20,343	30,240	55,652	78,953
DERBY	*11,356*	*13,598*	*18,117*	*24,742*	*34,357*	*43,178*	*50,614*	*64,180*	81,168
GATESHEAD	*8,725*	*8,910*	*11,943*	*15,419*	20,123	25,568	33,587	48,627	65,803
HALIFAX	*16,913*	*18,104*	*23,822*	*30,926*	*39,639*	*48,019*	*51,937*	65,510	73,630
HUDDERSFIELD	14,871	19,085	25,173	34,621	44,865	53,941	60,944	70,253	81,841
HULL	*29,580*	*37,005*	*44,520*	*51,911*	67,308	84,690	97,661	121,892	154,240
IPSWICH	11,277	13,670	17,186	20,201	25,384	32,914	37,950	42,947	50,546
LEEDS	53,162	62,534	83,796	123,393	152,074	172,270	207,165	259,212	309,119
LEICESTER -	17,005	23,453	31,036	40,639	50,806	60,584	68,056	95,220	122,376
LIVERPOOL -	*82,295*	*104,104*	*136,354*	*201,751*	286,487	375,955	443,938	493,405	552,508
LONDON -	958,863	1,138,815	1,378,947	1,654,994	1,948,417	2,362,236	2,803,989	3,254,260	3,816,483
MANCHESTER -	75,281	89,068	126,066	182,016	235,507	303,382	338,722	351,189	341,414
MIDDLESBROUGH -	*412*	*396*	*437*	*568*	*5,917*	*8,109*	*19,286*	*39,552*	55,934
NEWCASTLE-UPON-TYNE -	33,048	32,573	41,794	53,613	70,337	87,784	109,108	128,443	145,359
NORTHAMPTON	7,020	8,427	10,793	15,351	21,242	26,657	32,813	41,168	51,881
NORWICH	36,854	36,256	50,288	61,116	62,344	68,713	74,891	80,386	87,842
NOTTINGHAM -	*36,406*	*44,846*	*53,473*	*76,490*	*87,219*	*98,911*	*122,095*	*136,876*	186,575
OLDHAM	12,024	16,690	21,662	32,381	42,595	52,820	72,333	82,633	111,343
PLYMOUTH	16,040	20,803	21,591	31,080	36,520	52,221	62,599	68,758	73,794
PORTSMOUTH	33,226	41,587	46,743	50,389	53,032	72,096	94,799	113,569	127,989
PRESTON -	*12,787*	*17,972*	*24,522*	*34,574*	*51,616*	*70,309*	*83,872*	*87,291*	96,537
ROCHDALE -	*12,996*	*16,350*	*21,127*	*27,899*	*34,004*	*41,513*	*53,308*	63,485	68,866
ST. HELENS -	*6,974*	*8,630*	*9,734*	*12,964*	*18,626*	*25,403*	*37,794*	45,134	57,403
SALFORD	*18,179*	*24,990*	*32,818*	*51,132*	68,386	85,108	102,449	124,801	176,235
SHEFFIELD	45,755	53,231	65,275	91,692	111,091	135,310	185,172	239,946	284,508
SOUTHAMPTON	7,913	9,617	13,353	19,324	27,744	35,305	46,960	53,741	60,051
SOUTH SHIELDS -	11,011	15,165	16,503	18,756	23,072	28,974	35,239	45,336	56,875
STOCKPORT	*49,772*	*24,996*	*31,399*	*40,603*	50,154	53,835	54,681	53,014	59,553
SUNDERLAND	*24,469*	*25,205*	*30,923*	*39,470*	*51,465*	*64,720*	*81,742*	98,278	116,548
SWANSEA	*9,378*	*11,227*	*13,997*	*18,467*	24,604	31,461	41,606	51,702	65,597
WALSALL -	*10,292*	*11,143*	*11,843*	*14,824*	*20,849*	*26,838*	*39,496*	*49,018*	58,795
WEST BROMWICH -	5,687	7,485	9,505	15,327	26,121	34,591	41,795	47,918	56,295
WEST HAM -	6,485	8,136	9,753	11,580	12,738	18,817	38,331	62,919	128,953
WOLVERHAMPTON	12,565	14,836	18,380	24,732	36,382	49,985	60,860	68,291	75,766
YSTRADYFODWG -	*1,235*	*1,779*	*2,142*	*2,145*	*2,702*	*3,824*	*8,097*	*23,950*	55,632

TABLE 10.—ENGLAND AND WALES.—ESTIMATED POPULATION LIVING (1) AT EACH YEAR OF AGE, and (2) AT AND ABOVE EACH YEAR OF AGE in the MIDDLE OF THE YEAR 1881, *including* the NATIVES of ENGLAND AND WALES serving abroad in the ARMY, NAVY, MARINES, and MERCHANT SERVICE.

—	ESTIMATED POPULATION at each Year of Age in the MIDDLE of the Year 1881.			POPULATION at and above the Ages in the first column.			—	ESTIMATED POPULATION at each Year of Age in the MIDDLE of the Year 1881.			POPULATION at and above the Ages in the first Column.		
x	P_x			Q_x			x	P_x			Q_x		
YEAR OF AGE.	PERSONS.	Males.	Females.	PERSONS.	Males.	Females.	YEAR OF AGE.	PERSONS.	Males.	Females.	PERSONS.	Males.	Females.
0—	786,457	393,311	393,146	26,209,276	12,829,923	13,379,353	55—	183,220	86,773	96,447	2,733,006	1,263,468	1,469,538
1—	711,318	354,367	356,951	25,420,819	12,433,612	12,987,207	56—	177,800	84,304	93,496	2,549,786	1,176,695	1,373,091
2—	693,096	345,616	347,480	24,709,501	12,079,245	12,630,256	57—	171,886	81,519	90,367	2,371,986	1,092,391	1,279,595
3—	670,723	333,864	336,859	24,016,405	11,733,629	12,282,776	58—	165,494	78,424	87,070	2,200,100	1,010,872	1,189,228
4—	669,103	333,406	335,697	23,345,682	11,399,765	11,945,917	59—	158,580	75,061	83,519	2,034,606	932,448	1,102,158
5—	662,687	329,922	332,765	22,676,579	11,066,359	11,610,220	60—	151,633	71,488	80,145	1,876,026	857,387	1,018,639
6—	646,912	322,132	324,780	22,013,892	10,736,437	11,277,455	61—	144,158	67,775	76,383	1,724,393	785,899	938,494
7—	631,295	314,554	316,741	21,366,980	10,414,305	10,952,675	62—	136,659	63,991	72,668	1,580,235	718,124	862,111
8—	615,987	307,196	308,791	20,735,685	10,099,751	10,635,934	63—	129,144	60,204	68,940	1,443,576	654,133	789,443
9—	601,092	300,046	301,046	20,119,698	9,792,555	10,327,143	64—	121,702	56,476	65,226	1,314,432	593,929	720,503
10—	585,780	293,005	292,775	19,518,606	9,492,509	10,026,097	65—	114,646	53,001	61,645	1,192,730	537,453	655,277
11—	573,048	286,298	286,750	18,932,826	9,199,504	9,733,322	66—	107,956	49,766	58,190	1,078,084	484,452	593,632
12—	560,678	280,672	280,006	18,359,778	8,913,206	9,446,572	67—	101,354	46,595	54,759	970,128	434,686	535,442
13—	549,698	275,852	273,846	17,799,100	8,632,534	9,166,566	68—	94,836	43,485	51,351	868,774	388,091	480,683
14—	539,944	271,521	268,423	17,249,402	8,356,682	8,892,720	69—	88,395	40,427	47,968	773,938	344,606	429,332
15—	532,586	267,577	265,009	16,709,458	8,085,161	8,624,297	70—	82,023	37,416	44,607	685,543	304,179	381,364
16—	526,198	263,637	262,561	16,176,872	7,817,584	8,359,288	71—	75,734	34,455	41,279	603,520	266,763	336,757
17—	519,534	259,322	260,212	15,650,674	7,553,947	8,096,727	72—	69,532	31,545	37,987	527,786	232,308	295,478
18—	512,303	254,605	257,698	15,131,140	7,294,625	7,836,515	73—	63,435	28,690	34,745	458,254	200,763	257,491
19—	504,262	249,480	254,782	14,618,837	7,040,020	7,578,817	74—	57,470	25,904	31,566	394,819	172,073	222,746
20—	495,208	243,961	251,247	14,114,575	6,790,540	7,324,035	75—	51,918	23,261	28,657	337,349	146,169	191,180
21—	484,980	238,072	246,908	13,619,367	6,546,579	7,072,788	76—	46,564	20,762	25,802	285,431	122,908	162,523
22—	473,481	231,851	241,630	13,134,387	6,308,507	6,825,880	77—	41,425	18,374	23,051	238,867	102,146	136,721
23—	460,661	225,355	235,306	12,660,906	6,076,656	6,584,250	78—	36,419	16,058	20,361	197,442	83,772	113,670
24—	446,495	218,629	227,866	12,200,245	5,851,301	6,348,944	79—	31,500	13,804	17,696	161,023	67,714	93,309
25—	434,474	212,347	222,127	11,753,750	5,632,672	6,121,078	80—	26,650	11,562	15,088	129,523	53,910	75,613
26—	423,159	206,703	216,456	11,319,276	5,420,325	5,898,951	81—	21,932	9,398	12,534	102,873	42,348	60,525
27—	412,002	201,190	210,812	10,896,117	5,213,622	5,682,495	82—	17,704	7,516	10,188	80,941	32,950	47,991
28—	401,094	195,818	205,276	10,484,115	5,012,432	5,471,683	83—	14,012	5,993	8,019	63,237	25,434	37,803
29—	390,486	190,587	199,899	10,083,021	4,816,614	5,266,407	84—	10,949	4,730	6,219	49,225	19,441	29,784
30—	380,155	185,503	194,652	9,692,535	4,626,027	5,066,508	85—	8,819	3,693	5,126	38,276	14,711	23,565
31—	370,101	180,560	189,541	9,312,380	4,440,524	4,871,856	86—	7,036	2,873	4,163	29,457	11,018	18,439
32—	360,386	175,763	184,623	8,942,279	4,259,964	4,682,315	87—	5,565	2,207	3,358	22,421	8,145	14,276
33—	350,978	171,103	179,875	8,581,893	4,084,201	4,497,692	88—	4,360	1,673	2,687	16,856	5,938	10,918
34—	341,870	166,580	175,290	8,230,915	3,913,098	4,317,817	89—	3,376	1,249	2,127	12,496	4,265	8,231
35—	333,167	162,266	170,901	7,889,045	3,746,518	4,142,527	90—	2,582	919	1,663	9,120	3,016	6,104
36—	324,829	158,149	166,680	7,555,878	3,584,252	3,971,626	91—	1,944	665	1,279	6,538	2,097	4,441
37—	316,671	154,113	162,558	7,231,049	3,426,103	3,804,946	92—	1,439	473	966	4,594	1,432	3,162
38—	308,652	150,130	158,522	6,914,378	3,271,990	3,642,388	93—	1,043	330	713	3,155	959	2,196
39—	300,723	146,169	154,554	6,605,726	3,121,860	3,483,866	94—	737	225	512	2,112	629	1,483
40—	292,844	142,204	150,640	6,305,003	2,975,691	3,329,312	95—	508	151	357	1,375	404	971
41—	284,977	136,208	148,769	6,012,159	2,833,487	3,178,672	96—	339	98	241	867	253	614
42—	277,089	134,160	142,929	5,726,182	2,696,270	3,030,903	97—	219	63	156	528	155	373
43—	269,157	130,044	139,113	5,449,093	2,561,119	2,887,974	98—	135	39	96	309	92	217
44—	261,155	125,846	135,310	5,179,936	2,431,075	2,748,861	99—	80	23	57	174	53	121
45—	252,993	121,619	131,374	4,918,781	2,305,230	2,613,551	100—	46	14	32	94	30	64
46—	244,751	117,439	127,312	4,665,788	2,183,611	2,482,177	101—	26	8	18	48	16	32
47—	236,627	113,320	123,307	4,421,037	2,066,172	2,354,865	102—	13	5	8	22	8	14
48—	228,631	109,240	119,391	4,184,410	1,952,852	2,231,558	103—	6	2	4	9	3	6
49—	220,811	105,212	115,599	3,955,779	1,843,612	2,112,167	104—	3	1	2	3	1	2
50—	213,273	101,316	111,957	3,734,968	1,738,400	1,996,568							
51—	206,336	97,847	108,489	3,521,695	1,637,084	1,884,611							
52—	199,943	94,733	105,210	3,315,359	1,539,237	1,776,122							
53—	193,958	91,829	102,129	3,115,416	1,444,504	1,670,912							
54—	188,452	89,207	99,245	2,921,458	1,352,675	1,568,783							

TABLE 11.—ENGLAND AND WALES.—ESTIMATED POPULATION LIVING (1) AT EACH YEAR OF AGE, and (2) AT AND ABOVE EACH YEAR OF AGE in the MIDDLE OF THE YEAR 1881, *excluding* the ARMY, NAVY, MARINES, and MERCHANT SEAMEN serving abroad.

—	Estimated Population at each Year of Age in the Middle of the Year 1881.			Population at and above the Ages in the first Column.			—	Estimated Population at each Year of Age in the Middle of the Year 1881.			Population at and above the Ages in the first Column.		
x	P_x			Q_x			x	P_x			Q_x		
Year of Age.	Persons.	Males.	Females.	Persons.	Males.	Females.	Year of Age.	Persons.	Males.	Females.	Persons.	Males.	Females.
0—	788,457	396,311	392,146	26,061,736	12,682,383	13,379,353	55—	183,014	86,567	96,447	2,731,881	1,262,343	1,469,538
1—	711,318	354,367	356,951	25,273,279	12,286,072	12,987,207	56—	177,625	84,129	93,496	2,548,867	1,175,776	1,373,091
2—	693,096	345,616	347,480	24,561,961	11,931,705	12,630,256	57—	171,738	81,371	90,367	2,371,242	1,091,647	1,279,595
3—	670,723	333,864	336,859	23,868,865	11,586,089	12,282,776	58—	165,372	78,302	87,070	2,199,504	1,010,276	1,189,228
4—	669,103	333,406	335,697	23,198,142	11,252,225	11,945,917	59—	158,578	74,959	83,619	2,034,132	931,974	1,102,158
5—	662,687	329,922	332,765	22,529,039	10,918,819	11,610,220	60—	151,450	71,405	80,045	1,875,554	857,015	1,018,539
6—	646,912	322,132	324,780	21,866,352	10,588,897	11,277,455	61—	144,091	67,708	76,383	1,724,104	785,610	938,494
7—	631,295	314,554	316,741	21,219,440	10,266,765	10,952,675	62—	136,605	63,937	72,668	1,580,013	717,902	862,111
8—	615,987	307,196	308,791	20,588,145	9,952,211	10,635,934	63—	129,101	60,161	68,940	1,443,408	653,965	789,443
9—	601,092	300,046	301,046	19,972,158	9,645,015	10,327,143	64—	121,669	56,443	65,226	1,314,307	593,804	720,503
10—	586,780	293,005	293,775	19,371,066	9,344,969	10,026,097	65—	114,620	52,975	61,645	1,192,638	537,361	655,277
11—	573,042	286,292	286,750	18,784,286	9,051,964	9,732,322	66—	107,936	49,746	58,190	1,078,018	484,386	593,632
12—	560,637	280,631	280,006	18,211,244	8,765,672	9,445,572	67—	101,340	46,581	54,759	970,082	434,640	535,442
13—	549,580	275,734	273,846	17,650,607	8,485,041	9,165,566	68—	94,825	43,474	51,351	868,742	388,059	480,683
14—	539,704	271,281	268,423	17,101,027	8,209,307	8,891,720	69—	88,388	40,420	47,968	773,917	344,585	429,332
15—	532,181	267,172	265,009	16,561,323	7,938,026	8,623,297	70—	82,017	37,410	44,607	685,529	304,165	381,364
16—	523,601	261,040	262,561	16,029,142	7,670,854	8,358,288	71—	75,730	34,451	41,279	603,512	266,755	336,757
17—	515,036	254,824	260,212	15,505,541	7,409,814	8,095,727	72—	69,530	31,543	37,987	527,782	232,304	295,478
18—	506,244	248,546	257,698	14,990,505	7,154,990	7,835,515	73—	63,434	28,689	34,745	458,252	200,761	257,491
19—	497,001	242,219	254,782	14,484,261	6,906,444	7,577,817	74—	57,469	25,903	31,566	394,818	172,072	222,746
20—	487,101	235,854	251,247	13,987,260	6,664,225	7,323,035	75—	51,918	23,261	28,657	337,349	146,169	191,180
21—	476,355	229,447	246,908	13,500,159	6,428,371	7,071,788	76—	46,564	20,762	25,802	285,431	122,908	162,523
22—	464,628	222,998	241,630	13,023,804	6,198,924	6,824,880	77—	41,425	18,374	23,051	238,867	102,146	136,721
23—	451,824	216,518	235,306	12,559,176	5,975,926	6,583,250	78—	36,419	16,058	20,361	197,442	83,772	113,670
24—	437,872	210,006	227,866	12,107,352	5,759,408	6,347,944	79—	31,500	13,804	17,696	161,023	67,714	93,309
25—	426,212	204,085	222,127	11,669,480	5,549,402	6,120,078	80—	26,650	11,562	15,088	129,523	53,910	75,613
26—	415,365	198,909	216,456	11,243,268	5,345,317	5,897,951	81—	21,932	9,398	12,534	102,873	42,348	60,525
27—	404,745	193,933	210,812	10,827,903	5,146,408	5,681,495	82—	17,704	7,516	10,188	80,941	32,950	47,991
28—	394,409	189,133	205,276	10,423,158	4,952,475	5,470,683	83—	14,012	5,993	8,019	63,237	25,434	37,803
29—	384,385	184,486	199,899	10,028,749	4,763,342	5,265,407	84—	10,949	4,730	6,219	49,225	19,441	29,784
30—	374,632	179,980	194,652	9,644,364	4,578,856	5,065,508	85—	8,819	3,693	5,126	38,276	14,711	23,565
31—	365,134	175,593	189,541	9,269,732	4,398,876	4,870,856	86—	7,036	2,873	4,163	29,457	11,018	18,439
32—	355,943	171,320	184,623	8,904,598	4,223,283	4,681,315	87—	5,565	2,207	3,358	22,421	8,145	14,276
33—	347,023	167,148	179,875	8,548,655	4,051,963	4,496,692	88—	4,360	1,673	2,687	16,856	5,938	10,918
34—	338,362	163,072	175,290	8,201,632	3,884,815	4,316,817	89—	3,376	1,249	2,127	12,496	4,265	8,231
35—	330,065	159,164	170,901	7,863,270	3,721,743	4,141,527	90—	2,582	919	1,663	9,120	3,016	6,104
36—	322,093	155,413	166,680	7,533,205	3,562,579	3,970,626	91—	1,944	665	1,279	6,538	2,097	4,441
37—	314,262	151,704	162,558	7,211,112	3,407,166	3,803,946	92—	1,439	473	966	4,594	1,432	3,162
38—	306,534	148,012	158,522	6,896,850	3,255,462	3,641,388	93—	1,043	330	713	3,155	959	2,196
39—	298,862	144,308	154,554	6,590,316	3,107,450	3,482,866	94—	737	225	512	2,112	629	1,483
40—	291,210	140,570	150,640	6,291,454	2,963,142	3,328,312	95—	508	151	357	1,375	404	971
41—	283,543	136,774	146,769	6,000,244	2,822,572	3,177,672	96—	339	98	241	867	253	614
42—	275,831	132,902	142,929	5,716,701	2,685,798	3,030,903	97—	219	63	156	528	155	373
43—	268,052	128,939	139,113	5,440,870	2,552,896	2,887,974	98—	136	39	96	309	92	217
44—	260,185	124,875	135,310	5,172,818	2,423,957	2,748,861	99—	80	23	57	174	53	121
45—	252,148	120,774	131,374	4,912,633	2,299,082	2,613,551	100—	46	14	32	94	30	64
46—	244,006	116,694	127,312	4,660,485	2,178,308	2,482,177	101—	26	8	18	48	16	32
47—	235,971	112,664	123,307	4,416,479	2,061,614	2,354,865	102—	13	5	8	22	8	14
48—	228,054	108,663	119,391	4,180,508	1,948,950	2,231,558	103—	6	2	4	9	3	6
49—	220,305	104,706	115,599	3,952,454	1,840,287	2,112,167	104—	3	1	2	3	1	2
50—	212,831	100,874	111,957	3,732,149	1,735,581	1,996,568							
51—	205,951	97,462	108,489	3,519,318	1,634,707	1,884,611							
52—	199,609	94,399	105,210	3,313,367	1,537,245	1,776,122							
53—	193,671	91,542	102,129	3,113,758	1,442,846	1,670,912							
54—	188,208	88,961	99,245	2,920,087	1,351,304	1,568,783							

TABLE 12.—ENGLAND AND WALES.—ESTIMATED POPULATION in QUINQUENNIAL, DECENNIAL, and VICENNIAL PERIODS OF AGE, at the MIDDLE of the YEARS 1871 and 1881, *including* the NATIVES of ENGLAND AND WALES serving abroad in the ARMY, NAVY, MARINES, and MERCHANT SERVICE.

YEARS OF AGE.	PERSONS.		MALES.		FEMALES.	
	1871.	1881.	1871.	1881.	1871.	1881.
ALL AGES -	22,926,710	26,209,276	11,237,021	12,829,923	11,689,689	13,379,353
0—	3,080,814	3,532,697	1,541,214	1,763,564	1,539,600	1,769,133
5—	2,714,932	3,157,973	1,354,995	1,573,850	1,359,937	1,584,123
10—	2,432,433	2,810,148	1,225,209	1,407,348	1,207,224	1,402,800
15—	2,208,046	2,594,883	1,098,193	1,294,621	1,109,854	1,300,262
20—	2,047,946	2,360,825	1,002,555	1,157,868	1,045,391	1,202,957
25—	1,821,660	2,061,215	885,465	1,006,645	936,195	1,054,570
30—	1,588,414	1,803,490	768,172	879,509	820,242	923,981
35—	1,383,877	1,584,042	667,862	770,827	716,015	813,215
40—	1,215,077	1,385,222	586,672	670,461	628,405	714,761
45—	1,084,221	1,188,813	524,378	566,830	559,843	616,983
50—	925,148	1,001,962	446,767	474,932	478,381	527,030
55—	749,417	857,080	360,739	406,081	388,678	450,999
60—	596,562	683,196	282,784	319,934	313,778	363,262
65—	453,576	507,187	211,884	233,274	241,692	273,913
70—	314,093	348,194	144,552	158,010	169,541	190,184
75—	185,686	207,826	83,541	92,259	102,145	115,567
80—	86,984	91,247	37,496	39,199	49,488	52,048
85—	28,907	29,156	11,555	11,695	17,352	17,461
90—	7,508	7,745	2,557	2,612	4,951	5,133
95 and upwards	1,409	1,375	432	404	977	971
0—	5,795,746	6,690,670	2,896,209	3,337,414	2,899,537	3,353,256
10—	4,640,479	5,405,031	2,323,401	2,701,969	2,317,078	2,703,062
20—	3,869,606	4,422,040	1,888,020	2,164,513	1,981,586	2,257,527
30—	2,972,291	3,387,532	1,436,034	1,650,336	1,536,257	1,737,196
40—	2,299,298	2,569,035	1,111,050	1,237,291	1,188,248	1,331,744
50—	1,674,565	1,859,042	807,506	881,013	867,059	978,029
60—	1,050,138	1,190,383	494,668	553,208	555,470	637,175
70—	499,779	556,020	228,093	250,269	271,686	305,751
80—	115,891	120,403	49,051	50,894	66,840	69,509
90 and upwards	8,917	9,120	2,989	3,016	5,928	6,104
0—	10,436,225	12,095,701	5,219,610	6,039,383	5,216,615	6,056,318
20—	6,841,897	7,809,572	3,324,054	3,814,849	3,517,843	3,994,723
40—	3,973,863	4,428,077	1,918,556	2,118,304	2,055,307	2,309,773
60—	1,549,917	1,746,403	722,761	803,477	827,156	942,926
80 and upwards	124,808	129,523	52,040	53,910	72,768	75,613

TABLE 13.—ENGLAND AND WALES.—ESTIMATED POPULATION in QUINQUENNIAL, DECENNIAL, and VICENNIAL PERIODS OF AGE at the MIDDLE of the YEARS 1871 and 1881, *excluding* the ARMY, NAVY, MARINES, and MERCHANT SEAMEN serving abroad.

YEARS OF AGE.	PERSONS.		MALES.		FEMALES.	
	1871.	1881.	1871.	1881.	1871.	1881.
ALL AGES	22,782,812	26,061,736	11,093,123	12,682,383	11,689,689	13,379,353
0—	3,080,814	3,532,697	1,541,214	1,763,564	1,539,600	1,769,133
5—	2,714,932	3,157,973	1,354,995	1,573,850	1,359,937	1,584,123
10—	2.431,768	2,809,743	1,224,544	1,406,943	1,207,224	1,402,800
15—	2,189,629	2,574,063	1,079,775	1,273,801	1,109,854	1,300,262
20—	2,008,543	2,317,780	963,152	1,114,823	1,045,391	1,202,957
25—	1,787,611	2,025,116	851,416	970,546	936,195	1,054,570
30—	1,563,339	1,781,094	743,097	857,113	820,242	923,981
35—	1,370,315	1,571,816	654,300	758,601	716,015	813,215
40—	1,208,826	1,378,821	580,421	664,060	628,405	714,761
45—	1,080,645	1,180,484	520,802	563,501	559,843	616,983
50—	923,290	1,000,268	444,909	473,238	478,381	527,030
55—	748,708	856,327	360,025	405,328	388,678	450,999
60—	596,315	682,916	282,537	319,654	313,778	363,262
65—	453,495	507,109	211,803	233,196	241,692	273,913
70—	314,093	348,180	144,552	157,996	169,541	190,184
75—	185,686	207,826	83,541	92,259	102,145	115,567
80—	86,984	91,247	37,496	39,199	49,488	52,048
85—	28,907	29,156	11,555	11,695	17,352	17,461
90—	7,508	7,745	2,557	2,612	4,951	5,133
95 and upwards	1,409	1,375	432	404	977	971
0—	5,795,746	6,690,670	2,896,209	3,337,414	2,899,537	3,353,256
10—	4,621,397	5,383,806	2,304,319	2,680,744	2,317,078	2,703,062
20—	3,796,154	4,342,896	1,814,568	2,085,369	1,981,586	2,257,527
30—	2,933,654	3,352,910	1,397,397	1,615,714	1,536,257	1,737,196
40—	2,289,471	2,559,305	1,101,223	1.227,561	1,188,248	1,331,744
50—	1,671,993	1,856,595	804,934	878,566	867,059	978,029
60—	1,049,810	1,190,025	494,340	552,850	555,470	637,175
70—	499,779	556,006	228,093	250,255	271,686	305,751
80—	115,891	120,403	49,051	50,894	66,840	69,509
90 and upwards	8,917	9,120	2,989	3,016	5,928	6,104
0—	10,417,143	12,074,476	5,200,528	6,018,158	5,216,615	6,056,318
20—	6,729,808	7,695,806	3,211,965	3,701,083	3,517,843	3,994,723
40—	3,961,464	4,415,900	1,906,157	2,106,127	2,055,307	2,309,773
60—	1,549,589	1,746,031	722,433	803,105	827,156	942,926
80 and upwards	124,808	129,523	52,040	53,910	72,768	75,613

TABLE 16.—ENGLAND AND WALES.—NUMBER of PERSONS, MALES and FEMALES, returned as LIVING at ELEVEN GROUPS of AGES, at each of the last FIVE CENSUSES.

	PERSONS.				
Census Years - -	1841.	1851.	1861.	1871.	1881.
Total Population -	14,995,138	17,927,609	20,066,224	22,712,266	25,974,439
Ages : 0—	3,775,944	4,440,466	5,044,848	5,777,802	6,668,260
10—	3,123,415	3,670,546	4,037,818	4,604,651	5,347,563
20— - - -	2,679,726	3,137,082	3,398,657	3,785,337	4,376,218
30— - -	1,940,548	2,364,685	2,611,320	2,901,348	3,286,868
40— -	1,443,939	1,767,608	2,064,967	2,282,843	2,550,725
50—	963,569	1,235,088	1,420,567	1,662,857	1,828,539
60— - -	653,817	808,829	932,812	1,063,923	1,230,091
70—	320,956	396,264	441,985	505,960	552,277
80— -	85,946	99,245	105,626	119,419	125,737
90—	7,070	7,581	7,423	7,966	8,020
100— - -	213	215	201	160	141
	MALES.				
Total Population - -	7,323,387	8,781,225	9,776,259	11,058,934	12,639,902
0—	1,882,415	2,226,981	2,527,867	2,887,283	3,326,236
10— -	1,563,163	1,837,231	2,017,819	2,305,483	2,670,499
20— -	1,259,068	1,494,800	1,594,497	1,795,195	2,093,632
30— - - - -	944,205	1,150,569	1,251,970	1,387,139	1,585,183
40— -	708,537	867,093	1,004,368	1,097,044	1,220,479
50— - -	466,897	600,996	691,196	801,695	867,756
60— -	309,030	378,880	441,074	500,045	572,104
70— - - - -	149,460	179,746	200,208	231,978	248,180
80— -	37,850	42,113	44,615	50,258	53,100
90— - - - -	2,690	2,738	2,590	2,773	2,689
100— - - -	72	78	55	41	44
	FEMALES.				
Total Population -	7,671,751	9,146,384	10,289,965	11,653,332	13,334,537
0— -	1,893,529	2,213,485	2,516,981	2,890,519	3,342,024
10— - - - -	1,560,252	1,833,315	2,019,999	2,299,168	2,677,064
20— - -	1,420,658	1,642,282	1,804,160	1,990,142	2,282,586
30— - -	996,338	1,214,116	1,359,350	1,514,209	1,701,685
40— -	735,402	900,515	1,060,599	1,185,799	1,330,246
50— - -	496,672	634,092	729,371	861,162	960,783
60— -	344,787	429,949	491,738	563,878	657,987
70— -	171,496	216,518	241,777	273,982	304,097
80— - -	48,096	57,132	61,011	69,161	72,637
90— - - - -	4,380	4,843	4,833	5,193	5,331
100— - -	141	137	146	119	97

Table 17.—ENGLAND AND WALES.—Females to 1,000 Males at each of the last Five Censuses in Registration Counties, arranged in order of the Proportions in 1881; and the Number of Female Births to 1,000 Male Births in each of the last Four Decades.

Registration County, &c.	Females to 1,000 Males at the Census in					Births of Females to 1,000 of Males Registered in the Decade			
	1841.	1851.	1861.	1871.	1881.	1841–50.	1851–60.	1861–70.	1871–80.
ENGLAND and WALES	1,046	1,042	1,053	1,054	1,055	954	956	960	963
Glamorganshire	947	919	944	936	948	943	950	956	958
Monmouthshire - -	911	919	950	930	953	938	951	960	967
Durham - -	1,022	988	965	941	954	943	946	952	954
Radnorshire -	972	950	909	944	970	898	929	967	957
Flintshire - -	973	975	997	967	972	919	954	931	950
York, North Riding -	1,031	1,015	1,013	967	976	956	958	958	957
Merionethshire -	1,024	1,021	1,023	999	988	941	943	965	965
Montgomeryshire - -	1,020	1,002	978	984	990	945	939	926	973
Staffordshire - -	975	965	981	988	994	954	956	965	966
Rutlandshire -	995	976	1,016	1,004	997	978	970	950	961
Lincolnshire - -	996	987	1,016	1,014	998	948	959	954	960
Shropshire	1,003	1,002	999	1,010	999	960	952	960	952
Denbighshire - - -	1,008	993	988	1,007	999	918	963	954	958
Essex - -	1,000	992	993	992	1,000	964	957	961	969
Derbyshire - -	1,014	1,013	1,002	1,005	1,003	953	953	962	964
Northamptonshire -	1,009	1,003	1,006	1,012	1,006	968	956	950	972
Brecknockshire -	989	973	986	998	1,006	930	946	946	957
Cumberland - -	1,063	1,031	1,046	1,019	1,009	947	960	948	957
Berkshire - -	1,006	1,008	1,027	1,022	1,010	973	971	969	966
Northumberland -	1,064	1,030	1,010	1,007	1,011	945	937	948	960
Herefordshire	997	987	972	1,005	1,019	938	960	963	962
York, East Riding -	1,053	1,043	1,042	1,025	1,020	951	950	954	971
Kent (Extra-Metropolitan)	1,005	1,002	986	1,010	1,021	949	953	955	959
Wiltshire - -	1,019	1,026	1,036	1,031	1,026	953	961	964	965
Buckinghamshire -	1,043	1,025	1,030	1,046	1,030	956	965	967	959
Cambridgeshire - -	1,019	1,005	1,043	1,036	1,035	948	954	955	968
Dorsetshire - -	1,094	1,063	1,054	1,042	1,036	955	951	967	960
Westmorland - -	1,001	1,004	981	971	1,036	949	945	958	975
Nottinghamshire -	1,045	1,036	1,065	1,051	1,037	952	960	965	960
Carnarvonshire - -	1,052	1,037	1,054	1,060	1,038	947	951	944	936
Oxfordshire - -	1,012	990	1,017	1,037	1,042	947	940	965	967
Huntingdonshire -	1,018	1,009	1,030	1,045	1,042	964	953	974	959
York, West Riding	1,010	1,009	1,033	1,027	1,044	955	960	957	965
Anglesey - -	1,086	1,042	1,062	1,0[illegible]0	1,044	976	922	942	944
Hampshire - -	1,028	1,006	986	1,007	1,045	951	955	963	961
Hertfordshire -	1,025	1,012	1,045	1,045	1,045	966	960	975	952
Suffolk - - -	1,045	1,029	1,043	1,040	1,047	952	937	960	966
Warwickshire - -	1,047	1,036	1,049	1,051	1,055	958	962	971	970
Leicestershire - -	1,040	1,035	1,052	1,051	1,057	949	948	957	967
Cheshire - - -	1,037	1,045	1,060	1,063	1,062	951	949	957	965
Norfolk - - -	1,075	1,058	1,081	1,079	1,067	951	943	950	953
Lancashire - -	1,046	1,049	1,071	1,076	1,069	955	955	960	966
Carmarthenshire -	1,098	1,080	1,094	1,097	1,080	946	955	948	939
Worcestershire - -	1,041	1,037	1,051	1,076	1,081	967	962	961	964
Pembrokeshire - -	1,158	1,132	1,069	1,125	1,088	959	960	964	963
Surrey (Extra-Metropolitan)	990	1,020	1,000	1,072	1,105	961	969	972	974
Middlesex do. do. -	1,009	1,054	1,084	1,100	1,108	964	967	968	970
Sussex - - -	1,030	1,031	1,078	1,091	1,110	948	956	961	962
Devonshire - -	1,113	1,105	1,092	1,110	1,116	958	952	956	957
Somersetshire - -	1,079	1,100	1,118	1,117	1,120	950	965	960	962
London - -	1,136	1,135	1,144	1,137	1,123	961	962	966	964
Bedfordshire - - -	1,069	1,076	1,115	1,118	1,125	937	959	960	979
Cornwall -	1,071	1,073	1,095	1,185	1,133	938	950	943	950
Gloucestershire - -	1,106	1,113	1,133	1,126	1,138	955	964	954	966
Cardiganshire - -	1,158	1,162	1,191	1,212	1,227	954	942	950	960

TABLE 18.—ENGLAND AND WALES.—FEMALES to 1,000 MALES at TWELVE GROUPS of AGES, at each of the last FIVE CENSUSES.

AGE PERIODS.	1841.	1851.	1861.	1871.	1881.
All Ages	1,046	1,042	1,053	1,054	1,055
0—	1,009	995	993	999	1,003
5—	999	993	998	1,004	1,007
10—	967	985	986	986	997
15—	1,030	1,012	1,018	1,010	1,008
20—	1,143	1,095	1,127	1,106	1,093
25—	1,084	1,085	1,117	1,102	1,083
35—	1,036	1,043	1,067	1,089	1,074
45—	1,051	1,040	1,055	1,075	1,103
55—	1,085	1,090	1,073	1,093	1,123
65—	1,152	1,169	1,164	1,154	1,186
75—	1,195	1,274	1,266	1,253	1,275
85—	1,437	1,508	1,583	1,601	1,602

TABLE 19.—ENGLAND AND WALES.—FEMALES to 1,000 MALES in LONDON and in each URBAN SANITARY DISTRICT having a POPULATION exceeding 50,000 PERSONS.

URBAN SANITARY DISTRICTS.	Females to 1,000 Males.	URBAN SANITARY DISTRICTS.	Females to 1,000 Males.	URBAN SANITARY DISTRICTS.	Females to 1,000 Males.
YSTRADYFODWG -	802	BIRKENHEAD - -	1,040	LEICESTER - -	1,120
MIDDLESBROUGH - -	917	NEWCASTLE-UPON-TYNE -	1,044	LONDON - - -	1,123
ST HELENS -	926	PORTSMOUTH - -	1,051	HALIFAX - -	1,126
CARDIFF -	956	NORTHAMPTON - -	1,055	NOTTINGHAM -	1,129
WEST HAM - -	971	BIRMINGHAM -	1,060	IPSWICH - -	1,130
WEST BROMWICH -	990	LEEDS - -	1,063	BRADFORD -	1,148
GATESHEAD - -	995	BURNLEY -	1,069	ROCHDALE - -	1,153
WOLVERHAMPTON - -	1,003	ASTON MANOR - -	1,079	STOCKPORT - -	1,160
WALSALL - -	1,004	OLDHAM - - -	1,080	NORWICH - - -	1,180
SOUTH SHIELDS - -	1,005	SALFORD - -	1,083	PRESTON - -	1,181
SHEFFIELD -	1,014	MANCHESTER - -	1,088	PLYMOUTH - - -	1,186
DERBY - -	1,028	HUDDERSFIELD - -	1,101	BRISTOL - -	1,208
LIVERPOOL - -	1,031	BOLTON - -	1,110	CROYDON - - -	1,242
KINGSTON-UPON-HULL - -	1,036	BURY - -	1,114	BRIGHTON - -	1,279
SWANSEA - - -	1,036	SOUTHAMPTON -	1,116	BATH - - -	1,465
SUNDERLAND - - -	1,040	BLACKBURN - - -	1,117		

TABLE 20.—ENGLAND AND WALES.—DISTRIBUTION by SEX and AGE of the POPULATION of REGISTRATION COUNTIES in 1881.

COUNTIES.	PROPORTION TO 100,000 PERSONS.													
	MALES.							FEMALES.						
	0—	5—	15—	25—	45—	65 and upwards.	All Ages.	All Ages.	0—	5—	15—	25—	45—	65 and upwards.
ENGLAND AND WALES -	6,767	11,437	9,165	12,472	6,760	2,082	48,663	51,337	6,788	11,461	9,605	13,455	7,514	2,514
LONDON - - -	6,514	10,158	9,114	13,613	6,252	1,447	47,098	52,902	6,509	10,433	10,633	15,535	7,542	2,244
SURREY (Extra-Met.) -	6,306	11,287	9,097	12,400	6,451	1,995	47,516	52,484	6,391	11,268	10,275	14,484	7,546	2,520
KENT (Extra-Met.) -	6,659	11,730	9,353	12,272	6,989	2,476	49,485	50,515	6,623	11,516	9,130	12,879	7,529	2,838
SUSSEX - - - -	6,379	11,478	8,571	11,526	6,882	2,564	47,400	52,600	6,408	11,227	9,923	13,918	8,107	3,017
HAMPSHIRE - -	6,467	11,264	9,208	12,215	7,240	2,495	48,889	51,111	6,471	11,171	9,283	13,263	8,017	2,886
BERKSHIRE - -	6,645	11,654	9,403	11,778	7,279	2,781	49,740	50,260	6,580	11,565	8,510	12,649	7,901	3,055
MIDDLESEX (Ex.-Met.)	6,824	12,008	8,502	12,253	6,063	1,781	47,431	52,569	6,811	11,619	10,196	14,266	7,198	2,479
HERTFORDSHIRE -	6,612	12,695	8,398	10,937	7,416	2,893	48,901	51,099	6,683	11,971	8,349	12,687	8,230	3,279
BUCKINGHAMSHIRE -	6,711	12,530	8,667	10,836	7,582	2,954	49,268	50,732	6,655	12,229	8,268	12,287	8,149	3,142
OXFORDSHIRE - -	6,502	12,102	8,848	10,813	7,604	3,042	48,966	51,034	6,557	11,862	8,676	12,329	8,316	3,274
NORTHAMPTONSHIRE -	6,857	11,802	9,228	11,873	7,441	2,585	49,846	50,154	6,977	11,790	8,568	12,246	7,840	2,804
HUNTINGDONSHIRE -	6,896	12,447	8,460	10,246	8,085	3,343	48,977	51,023	6,371	12,444	8,117	11,568	8,637	3,886
BEDFORDSHIRE -	6,440	12,069	8,304	10,407	7,128	2,700	47,048	52,952	6,510	11,931	9,623	13,414	8,488	2,982
CAMBRIDGESHIRE -	6,441	12,061	9,137	11,075	7,367	3,114	49,135	50,865	6,431	12,032	8,426	12,086	8,242	3,648
ESSEX - -	7,108	12,548	8,807	12,147	7,017	2,381	50,008	49,992	7,101	12,293	8,257	12,517	7,235	2,589
SUFFOLK - - -	6,665	12,640	8,813	10,477	7,706	3,355	48,856	51,144	6,636	11,998	8,565	11,904	8,433	3,908
NORFOLK -	6,364	11,382	8,772	10,612	7,849	3,410	48,389	51,611	6,349	11,350	8,855	12,220	8,911	3,917
WILTSHIRE - - -	6,583	12,053	8,913	10,906	7,781	3,134	49,370	50,630	6,603	11,896	8,287	11,885	8,523	3,436
DORSETSHIRE - -	6,307	11,473	9,255	11,351	7,642	3,179	49,107	50,893	6,281	11,386	8,804	12,198	8,606	3,649
DEVONSHIRE - -	6,034	11,095	9,099	10,590	7,362	3,060	47,249	52,751	5,965	11,033	9,786	13,034	8,990	3,913
CORNWALL - -	5,848	11,536	9,747	9,868	7,065	3,004	46,883	53,117	5,780	11,230	9,862	12,819	9,281	4,145
SOMERSETSHIRE -	6,394	11,812	8,479	10,437	7,087	2,956	47,165	52,835	6,378	11,699	9,428	12,850	8,681	3,799
GLOUCESTERSHIRE -	6,321	11,580	8,521	11,103	6,793	2,473	46,771	53,229	6,473	11,536	10,086	13,481	8,363	3,290
HEREFORDSHIRE -	6,066	11,900	8,744	11,303	8,351	3,182	49,536	50,464	6,085	11,709	8,465	11,945	8,565	3,695
SHROPSHIRE -	6,416	11,952	9,208	11,324	8,061	3,037	50,018	49,982	6,304	11,654	8,359	11,836	8,160	3,469
STAFFORDSHIRE -	7,454	12,367	9,548	12,388	6,644	1,747	50,148	49,852	7,533	12,382	9,061	12,247	6,871	1,958
WORCESTERSHIRE -	6,752	11,705	8,869	11,518	6,953	2,248	48,045	51,955	6,794	11,715	10,000	13,095	7,621	2,730
WARWICKSHIRE -	7,049	11,525	9,094	12,408	6,677	1,917	48,670	51,330	7,056	11,619	9,640	13,371	7,373	2,271
LEICESTERSHIRE -	7,026	11,410	8,985	11,865	6,947	2,378	48,665	51,335	7,162	11,634	9,802	12,987	7,424	2,616
RUTLANDSHIRE -	6,323	12,031	9,323	10,979	7,967	3,436	50,067	49,933	6,076	11,488	8,449	11,794	8,497	3,629
LINCOLNSHIRE - -	6,722	11,698	9,291	11,836	7,473	3,019	50,039	49,961	6,604	11,732	8,709	11,890	7,671	3,265
NOTTINGHAMSHIRE -	6,997	11,288	9,218	12,437	6,877	2,282	49,099	50,901	7,087	11,507	9,801	12,851	7,186	2,469
DERBYSHIRE - -	7,324	11,769	9,384	12,611	6,784	2,090	49,962	50,038	7,365	11,786	9,136	12,460	7,081	2,216
CHESHIRE - -	6,773	11,476	9,157	12,350	6,803	1,928	48,487	51,513	6,751	11,563	9,892	13,556	7,536	2,215
LANCASHIRE -	6,944	11,192	9,281	13,400	6,187	1,332	48,336	51,664	7,030	11,363	10,355	14,402	7,105	1,709
WEST RIDING - -	6,971	11,444	9,223	13,049	6,627	1,609	48,923	51,077	7,034	11,613	9,740	13,631	7,168	1,881
EAST RIDING - -	6,805	11,132	9,373	12,994	7,003	2,198	49,505	50,495	6,838	11,308	9,399	13,060	7,289	2,685
NORTH RIDING -	7,082	11,936	9,288	12,999	6,905	2,299	50,509	49,491	7,100	11,685	9,147	12,129	6,840	2,500
DURHAM - - -	7,673	12,424	9,708	13,604	6,277	1,483	51,169	48,831	7,589	12,331	9,056	12,119	6,054	1,682
NORTHUMBERLAND -	7,028	11,713	9,406	13,098	6,648	1,840	49,733	50,267	6,995	11,634	9,568	12,746	6,973	2,351
CUMBERLAND - -	6,962	11,637	9,447	12,744	6,715	2,265	49,770	50,230	6,993	11,488	9,237	12,621	7,276	2,715
WESTMORLAND - -	6,420	11,696	8,897	11,546	7,432	2,911	49,111	50,889	6,534	11,641	9,506	12,525	7,620	3,063
MONMOUTHSHIRE -	6,922	12,265	9,840	12,791	7,274	2,093	51,194	48,806	6,985	12,151	8,475	11,893	7,011	2,380
GLAMORGANSHIRE -	7,211	12,071	10,228	13,844	6,438	1,546	51,338	48,662	7,199	12,003	9,181	12,234	6,219	1,826
CARMARTHENSHIRE -	6,813	12,471	9,613	10,724	6,501	2,556	48,078	51,922	6,700	12,024	9,951	12,424	7,392	3,431
PEMBROKESHIRE -	6,402	11,586	9,346	10,247	7,320	3,003	47,903	52,097	6,364	11,317	9,821	12,260	8,449	3,886
CARDIGANSHIRE -	5,968	11,660	8,060	9,028	6,968	3,222	44,901	55,099	5,960	11,520	9,830	13,493	9,649	4,638
BRECKNOCKSHIRE -	6,385	11,657	9,148	11,776	7,748	3,140	49,854	50,146	6,295	11,720	9,008	11,747	7,961	3,415
RADNORSHIRE - -	6,257	12,023	9,604	11,413	8,006	3,466	50,769	49,231	6,160	11,867	8,983	11,121	7,596	3,504
MONTGOMERYSHIRE -	6,200	12,178	9,388	11,104	8,042	3,352	50,259	49,741	6,206	11,799	8,795	11,218	7,911	3,750
FLINTSHIRE - - -	6,687	12,199	9,335	12,868	7,415	2,217	50,721	49,279	6,521	12,488	7,495	11,917	7,775	3,083
DENBIGHSHIRE -	6,471	11,662	9,827	12,214	7,750	2,613	50,027	49,973	6,446	11,710	8,443	12,806	7,987	3,081
MERIONETHSHIRE -	6,451	11,487	9,235	12,983	7,285	2,868	50,309	49,691	6,570	11,600	8,258	12,483	7,396	3,392
CARNARVONSHIRE -	6,297	11,267	9,050	12,050	7,504	2,924	49,072	50,928	6,230	10,680	9,080	13,213	8,808	3,417
ANGLESEY - -	5,826	10,842	8,891	11,551	8,392	3,818	48,917	51,083	5,947	10,409	8,654	12,479	9,300	4,294

TABLE 21.—ENGLAND AND WALES.—UNMARRIED, MARRIED, and WIDOWED in 100,000 of EACH SEX at each of the LAST FOUR CENSUSES.

DATE OF CENSUS.	MALES.			FEMALES.		
	Unmarried.	Married.	Widowed.	Unmarried.	Married.	Widowed.
1851 - - -	62,505	33,692	3,803	59,799	32,971	7,237
1861 - - -	61,249	35,069	3,682	58,740	33,906	7,354
1871 - - -	61,284	35,115	3,601	58,573	33,883	7,544
1881	61,932	34,628	3,440	59,226	33,282	7,492

TABLE 22.—ENGLAND AND WALES.—UNMARRIED, MARRIED, and WIDOWED in 100,000 of EACH SEX aged 15 YEARS and UPWARDS at each of the LAST FOUR CENSUSES.

DATE OF CENSUS.	MALES.			FEMALES.		
	Unmarried.	Married.	Widowed.	Unmarried.	Married.	Widowed.
1851 - - -	41,103	52,924	5,973	38,539	50,399	11,062
1861 -	38,783	55,400	5,817	36,892	51,860	11,248
1871 - - -	38,402	55,869	5,729	36,136	52,234	11,630
1881 - -	39,180	55,324	5,496	36,738	51,638	11,624

TABLE 23.—ENGLAND AND WALES.—MARRIED PERSONS in 100,000 living at successive AGE-PERIODS, at each of the LAST FOUR CENSUSES.

AGES.	MALES.				FEMALES.			
	Census Years.				Census Years.			
	1851.	1861.	1871.	1881.	1851.	1861.	1871.	1881.
15 years and upwards -	52,924	55,400	55,869	55,324	50,399	51,860	52,234	51,638
15— -	439	529	549	462	2,516	3,049	3,155	2,535
20—	20,045	22,273	23,027	22,067	30,775	33,138	34,318	33,064
25—	62,736	66,648	66,833	66,851	64,261	66,684	67,567	68,147
35— -	79,498	82,110	82,585	82,572	75,720	76,272	76,240	76,498
45—	80,256	82,075	83,195	84,858	71,508	71,966	71,658	71,078
55— -	74,742	76,085	77,147	77,876	58,925	58,972	58,912	58,078
65 and upwards -	57,135	56,918	57,939	58,732	33,467	33,459	33,125	32,620

TABLE 24.—ENGLAND AND WALES.—UNMARRIED, MARRIED, and WIDOWED in 100,000 of EACH SEX living at successive AGE-PERIODS in 1881.

AGES.	MALES.			FEMALES.		
	Unmarried.	Married.	Widowed.	Unmarried.	Married.	Widowed.
All Ages - -	61,932	34,628	3,440	59,226	33,282	7,492
0— - -	37,408	—	—	35,548	—	—
15— - -	9,986	46	1	9,347	243	2
20— - -	6,839	1,942	20	6,067	3,015	36
25— - -	4,568	9,633	209	4,320	10,077	390
35— - -	1,546	9,263	409	1,753	8,736	931
45— - -	787	6,803	585	1,021	6,078	1,452
55— - -	474	4,452	791	663	3,535	1,888
65 and upwards -	324	2,489	1,425	507	1,598	2,793

TABLE 25.—ENGLAND AND WALES.—UNMARRIED, MARRIED, and WIDOWED in 100,000 of EACH SEX, in REGISTRATION COUNTIES, in 1881.

COUNTIES.	PROPORTION PER 100,000 OF EACH SEX.					
	MALES.			FEMALES.		
	Unmarried.	Married.	Widowed.	Unmarried.	Married.	Widowed.
ENGLAND AND WALES -	61,932	34,628	3,440	59,226	33,282	7,492
LONDON -	61,132	35,706	3,162	59,051	32,373	8,576
SURREY (Extra-Met.)	64,115	32,727	3,158	62,794	30,232	6,974
KENT (Extra-Met.)	62,641	33,870	3,489	59,910	33,144	6,946
SUSSEX - - -	62,119	34,144	3,737	61,496	31,209	7,295
HAMPSHIRE - -	62,511	33,997	3,492	58,499	33,766	7,735
BERKSHIRE - -	62,359	33,927	3,714	59,326	33,718	6,956
MIDDLESEX (Extra-Met.)	63,247	33,811	2,942	61,834	30,964	7,202
HERTFORDSHIRE -	62,236	33,861	3,903	60,079	32,641	7,280
BUCKINGHAMSHIRE	61,100	34,833	4,067	58,973	33,950	7,077
OXFORDSHIRE -	61,860	34,064	4,070	59,565	32,996	7,439
NORTHAMPTONSHIRE	60,551	35,671	3,778	57,906	35,502	6,592
HUNTINGDONSHIRE - -	60,191	35,708	4,101	57,269	34,685	8,046
BEDFORDSHIRE - -	59,959	36,230	3,811	59,938	32,772	7,290
CAMBRIDGESHIRE -	61,054	35,005	3,941	57,795	34,216	7,989
ESSEX	62,057	34,561	3,382	58,846	34,535	6,619
SUFFOLK	59,914	36,018	4,068	57,693	34,822	7,485
NORFOLK	58,883	37,167	3,950	56,663	35,277	8,060
WILTSHIRE -	61,033	35,015	3,952	58,279	34,418	7,303
DORSETSHIRE -	60,946	35,079	3,975	58,889	33,365	7,746
DEVONSHIRE	61,223	34,987	3,790	58,648	32,548	8,804
CORNWALL -	63,067	33,386	3,547	58,399	31,305	10,296
SOMERSETSHIRE -	60,987	35,408	3,610	59,514	32,203	8,283
GLOUCESTERSHIRE	61,149	35,356	3,495	60,061	31,915	8,024
HEREFORDSHIRE -	63,047	32,960	3,993	59,063	32,579	8,358
SHROPSHIRE -	63,234	32,836	3,930	59,536	33,010	7,454
STAFFORDSHIRE - -	62,887	34,025	3,088	59,385	34,444	6,171
WORCESTERSHIRE -	61,900	34,789	3,311	60,493	32,564	6,943
WARWICKSHIRE -	61,131	35,570	3,299	58,731	34,204	7,065
LEICESTERSHIRE - -	59,907	36,416	3,677	58,676	34,749	6,575
RUTLANDSHIRE -	62,331	33,571	4,098	58,766	33,757	7,477
LINCOLNSHIRE -	61,136	35,218	3,646	57,849	35,115	7,036
NOTTINGHAMSHIRE - -	59,826	36,608	3,566	58,133	35,497	6,370
DERBYSHIRE - -	61,796	34,647	3,557	59,056	34,687	6,257
CHESHIRE - -	62,165	34,251	3,584	60,299	32,597	7,104
LANCASHIRE - - -	62,041	34,641	3,318	59,255	33,066	7,679
WEST RIDING - -	61,263	35,514	3,223	58,760	34,409	6,831
EAST RIDING - -	61,496	35,052	3,452	57,728	34,821	7,451
NORTH RIDING -	63,765	32,686	3,549	60,031	33,372	6,597
DURHAM - -	63,887	33,122	2,991	58,810	35,081	6,109
NORTHUMBERLAND -	64,208	32,311	3,481	60,395	32,186	7,419
CUMBERLAND - -	65,311	30,949	3,740	61,216	31,090	7,694
WESTMORLAND - -	64,695	30,967	4,338	63,061	29,912	7,027
MONMOUTHSHIRE -	63,457	32,861	3,682	58,219	34,523	7,258
GLAMORGANSHIRE -	63,514	33,228	3,258	58,713	34,606	6,681
CARMARTHENSHIRE -	64,146	32,296	3,558	61,446	30,707	7,847
PEMBROKESHIRE -	62,776	33,065	4,159	61,128	30,729	8,143
CARDIGANSHIRE -	65,304	30,330	4,366	62,053	28,102	9,845
BRECKNOCKSHIRE -	63,695	31,970	4,335	59,578	32,145	8,277
RADNORSHIRE -	66,525	29,296	4,179	62,046	30,453	7,501
MONTGOMERYSHIRE	64,588	30,991	4,421	59,996	31,743	8,261
FLINTSHIRE -	63,958	32,644	3,398	57,472	33,803	8,725
DENBIGHSHIRE -	62,930	32,916	4,154	58,855	33,085	8,060
MERIONETHSHIRE - -	63,511	32,472	4,017	58,878	33,294	7,828
CARNARVONSHIRE - -	62,087	33,595	4,318	58,441	33,218	8,341
ANGLESEY - - -	60,332	35,020	4,648	56,955	33,870	9,175

TABLE 26.—NATIVES of ENGLAND AND WALES, SCOTLAND, IRELAND, and other PARTS, enumerated in ENGLAND AND WALES at each of the LAST FIVE CENSUSES.

—	PERSONS.				
	1841.	1851.	1861.	1871.	1881.
TOTAL ENUMERATED POPULATION	15,906,741	17,927,609	20,066,224	22,712,266	25,974,439
BORN IN ENGLAND AND WALES - -	15,441,530	17,165,656	19,120,052	21,692,165	24,855,822
„ OTHER PARTS - -	465,211	761,953	946,172	1,020,101	1,118,617
„ SCOTLAND - -	103,768	130,087	169,202	213,254	253,528
„ IRELAND - - -	290,891	519,959	601,634	566,540	562,374
„ ISLANDS IN THE BRITISH SEAS	11,705	13,753	18,423	25,655	29,316
„ COLONIES AND INDIA - -	17,248	33,688	51,572	70,812	94,399
„ FOREIGN PARTS	39,446	61,708	101,832	139,445	174,372
„ SHIPS AT SEA	2,153	2,758	3,509	4,395	4,628

NOTE.—The numbers in the column for 1841 in the above Table given as "born in Islands in the British Seas, Colonies, and India, and in Ships at Sea" were calculated from the corresponding numbers in 1851, 1861, and 1871; and 81,237 "not specified where born" have been distributed proportionally throughout the column.

TABLE 27.—NATIVES of ENGLAND AND WALES, SCOTLAND, IRELAND, and other PARTS, in 100,000 PERSONS enumerated in ENGLAND AND WALES at each of the LAST FIVE CENSUSES.

—	IN 100,000 PERSONS.				
	1841.	1851.	1861.	1871.	1881.
TOTAL ENUMERATED POPULATION -	100,000	100,000	100,000	100,000	100,000
BORN IN ENGLAND AND WALES - -	97,075	95,750	95,285	95,509	95,693
„ OTHER PARTS - -	2,925	4,250	4,715	4,491	4,307
„ SCOTLAND - -	652	726	843	939	976
„ IRELAND - -	1,829	2,900	2,999	2,493	2,166
„ ISLANDS IN THE BRITISH SEAS	74	77	92	114	113
„ COLONIES AND INDIA -	108	188	257	312	363
„ FOREIGN PARTS -	248	344	507	614	671
„ SHIPS AT SEA - -	14	15	17	19	18

TABLE 28.—NATIVES of ENGLAND AND WALES enumerated in SCOTLAND, IRELAND, the ISLANDS in THE BRITISH SEAS, and in the UNITED STATES, at each of the LAST FIVE CENSUSES.

WHERE ENUMERATED.	1841.	1851.	1861.	1871.	1881.
IN SCOTLAND - - -	37,796	46,791	56,032	70,482	91,823
IN IRELAND - -	21,552	34,454	50,936	67,599	69,382
IN ISLANDS IN BRITISH SEAS -	18,006	22,043	19,815	18,990	16,986
	77,354	103,288	126,783	157,071	178,191
IN UNITED STATES - -	?	314,106(1850)	483,423(1860)	626,440(1870)	745,978(1880)
TOTAL - -	—	417,394	610,206	783,511	924,169

TABLE 29.—ENGLAND AND WALES.—NATIVES of ENGLAND AND WALES, SCOTLAND, IRELAND, and other PARTS in 100,000 PERSONS enumerated in 1881 in each COUNTY.

COUNTIES.	OF 100,000 PERSONS ENUMERATED, THE NUMBERS BORN IN						
	England and Wales.	Scotland.	Ireland.	Islands in the British Seas.	Colonies and India.	Foreign Parts.	Ships at Sea.
ENGLAND AND WALES	95,694	976	2,165	113	363	671	18
ENGLAND.							
BEDFORDSHIRE	98,669	278	330	33	466	209	15
BERKSHIRE	97,845	479	674	71	551	367	13
BUCKINGHAMSHIRE	98,873	336	284	33	271	193	10
CAMBRIDGESHIRE	99,084	215	275	31	206	183	6
CHESHIRE	94,219	1,222	3,667	191	241	444	16
CORNWALL	98,268	194	512	122	285	604	15
CUMBERLAND	88,750	4,870	5,623	430	161	147	19
DERBYSHIRE	98,155	350	1,130	31	148	175	11
DEVONSHIRE	97,239	464	1,036	221	629	387	24
DORSETSHIRE	97,988	376	749	212	417	246	12
DURHAM	92,243	2,850	4,239	34	136	487	11
ESSEX	97,288	758	860	94	472	509	19
GLOUCESTERSHIRE	97,631	408	931	81	563	367	19
HAMPSHIRE	95,160	968	1,928	358	1,046	510	30
HEREFORDSHIRE	98,778	327	482	22	202	182	7
HERTFORDSHIRE	98,458	463	391	45	364	267	12
HUNTINGDONSHIRE	99,193	202	257	15	187	134	12
KENT	95,777	882	1,626	129	869	685	32
LANCASHIRE	91,042	1,616	6,147	263	244	668	20
LEICESTERSHIRE	98,671	322	578	26	186	205	12
LINCOLNSHIRE	98,786	256	409	22	124	394	9
MIDDLESEX	93,338	1,343	2,100	136	706	2,344	33
MONMOUTHSHIRE	96,515	320	2,470	66	140	474	15
NORFOLK	99,205	234	230	21	162	138	10
NORTHAMPTONSHIRE	98,943	262	394	25	205	162	9
NORTHUMBERLAND	90,730	5,394	2,877	50	204	730	15
NOTTINGHAMSHIRE	98,473	352	576	34	160	395	10
OXFORDSHIRE	98,783	324	313	51	276	242	11
RUTLANDSHIRE	98,734	439	397	19	145	257	9
SHROPSHIRE	98,584	327	750	27	176	126	10
SOMERSETSHIRE	98,357	273	484	83	511	279	13
STAFFORDSHIRE	97,998	339	1,335	22	109	187	10
SUFFOLK	99,049	267	271	24	219	162	8
SURREY	95,803	965	1,510	124	627	943	28
SUSSEX	97,142	558	729	115	728	708	20
WARWICKSHIRE	97,596	394	1,306	41	235	416	12
WESTMORLAND	97,401	1,628	578	44	162	181	6
WILTSHIRE	98,978	214	299	57	271	173	8
WORCESTERSHIRE	98,699	307	590	31	172	189	13
YORKSHIRE	96,749	672	1,970	38	150	410	11
WALES.							
ANGLESEY	98,380	294	829	189	66	228	14
BRECKNOCKSHIRE	98,527	352	769	14	199	132	7
CARDIGANSHIRE	99,498	155	147	16	51	124	9
CARMARTHENSHIRE	99,327	191	290	14	68	107	3
CARNARVONSHIRE	98,652	371	520	40	99	313	5
DENBIGHSHIRE	98,311	492	871	28	126	163	9
FLINTSHIRE	97,223	495	1,730	55	161	329	7
GLAMORGANSHIRE	96,281	395	2,338	91	165	720	10
MERIONETHSHIRE	99,058	215	261	29	73	356	8
MONTGOMERYSHIRE	99,224	289	303	15	73	93	3
PEMBROKESHIRE	98,001	332	1,079	56	342	180	10
RADNORSHIRE	99,439	183	200	—	55	123	—

Table 30.—ENGLAND AND WALES.—Amount of Migration from and into Counties Proper; with the Natural and Actual Increase or Decrease of Population in Registration Counties.

Counties.	Number Born in County out of 100,000 enumerated therein.		Number Resident in County out of 100,000 Natives thereof enumerated in England and Wales.		Increase or Decrease of Population, 1871–81.	
	Males.	Females.	Males.	Females.	Natural (Excess of Births over Deaths).	Actual (Increase or Decrease of Enumerated Population).
ENGLAND AND WALES	72,361	71,556	75,870	74,541	3,410,471	3,262,173
Bedfordshire - -	79,124	74,595	65,057	66,750	21,625	2,705
Berkshire -	66,614	63,595	63,061	57,551	32,342	22,864
Buckinghamshire -	75,993	72,742	61,053	58,139	22,394	862
Cambridgeshire -	79,269	77,087	65,032	61,618	26,093	−919
Cheshire - - -	68,508	65,834	71,364	70,721	81,789	82,580
Cornwall - - -	87,893	90,653	77,115	75,754	33,903	−31,981
Cumberland - - -	74,903	77,881	75,342	74,870	31,981	30,394
Derbyshire - -	71,149	71,375	72,867	70,754	60,714	61,614
Devonshire - - -	82,061	81,989	72,196	71,800	62,066	2,298
Dorsetshire - -	79,411	79,545	65,956	63,423	22,564	−4,028
Durham - - -	65,789	69,843	85,205	84,121	160,531	182,154
Essex - - -	65,193	64,313	70,188	65,484	75,274	111,388
Gloucestershire - - -	75,654	71,864	69,719	69,287	64,047	36,263
Hampshire - - -	67,568	69,076	72,858	70,533	70,673	50,573
Herefordshire - -	73,761	71,112	61,614	57,813	12,904	−3,838
Hertfordshire -	69,949	66,849	63,282	59,625	27,064	7,763
Huntingdonshire - -	76,712	71,475	58,060	53,163	7,352	−4,808
Kent - - -	67,610	66,527	74,430	71,260	136,142	139,269
Lancashire - - -	74,232	73,982	90,195	90,601	418,798	636,560
Leicestershire - - -	77,551	76,336	73,865	74,593	46,356	51,313
Lincolnshire - -	81,856	82,616	72,970	70,954	62,678	34,986
Middlesex - - -	62,157	59,827	74,721	73,427	330,565	379,948
Monmouthshire - -	64,036	67,935	72,777	70,550	36,349	14,624
Norfolk - - -	88,645	87,483	71,114	69,348	47,801	7,073
Northamptonshire - -	76,707	75,041	70,788	67,854	39,616	28,801
Northumberland - -	72,812	74,516	74,778	74,694	62,753	47,440
Nottinghamshire - -	73,216	71,836	74,124	74,911	61,047	83,185
Oxfordshire - - -	76,625	71,730	62,011	57,544	22,984	2,173
Rutlandshire -	70,160	64,724	53,296	47,839	2,840	−378
Shropshire - - -	79,452	77,216	64,443	59,603	33,174	−1,285
Somersetshire - -	79,315	75,396	66,696	65,021	57,800	8,094
Staffordshire - - -	76,412	77,423	78,241	76,201	176,831	129,478
Suffolk -	84,715	82,355	68,179	65,604	46,723	6,335
Surrey - -	52,526	49,546	74,768	72,273	187,431	334,142
Sussex - - -	73,183	66,659	74,958	72,438	58,884	73,284
Warwickshire - - -	71,004	69,661	74,776	74,067	104,753	100,061
Westmorland - -	74,910	71,921	61,363	59,820	8,682	−816
Wiltshire - - -	80,830	77,973	64,739	60,034	31,311	2,518
Worcestershire - - -	70,476	67,917	67,632	65,960	54,575	46,907
Yorkshire - - -	81,220	82,178	87,654	88,024	396,259	450,050
WALES.						
Anglesey - -	85,213	87,025	71,681	71,829	2,432	14
Brecknockshire - -	67,652	68,551	59,444	59,372	6,683	−2,792
Cardiganshire - -	89,156	90,353	68,649	75,912	8,582	−2,732
Carmarthenshire -	84,830	85,775	70,085	72,614	15,326	9,874
Carnarvonshire - -	78,612	79,429	84,523	82,140	11,188	12,403
Denbighshire - -	74,699	73,201	70,318	66,329	11,893	7,776
Flintshire - -	73,021	69,979	67,225	63,038	5,466	2,257
Glamorganshire - -	62,038	67,405	88,499	87,783	82,276	112,585
Merionethshire - - -	74,837	75,308	77,928	74,932	8,319	6,771
Montgomeryshire - -	83,066	82,216	67,945	64,842	8,961	−2,204
Pembrokeshire - -	82,471	86,493	67,598	70,643	9,198	−194
Radnorshire -	77,553	75,874	54,858	51,980	2,479	−1,231

Note.—The table may be read as follows:—Of 100,000 males enumerated in England and Wales, 72,361 were natives of the county in which they were enumerated; of 100,000 males enumerated in Bedfordshire, 79,124 were natives of that county; and so on for cols. 1 and 2. Of 100,000 male natives of England and Wales enumerated therein, 75,870 were enumerated in their native counties; of 100,000 male natives of Bedfordshire enumerated in England and Wales, 65,057 were enumerated in that county; and so on for cols. 3 and 4.

Table 31.—ENGLAND AND WALES.—Persons returned as Blind, Deaf and Dumb, and Insane, in 1,000,000 of the Population of each Registration County.

Registration County.	Blind.			Deaf and Dumb.	Insane.		
	From Birth.	Others.	Total.		Idiots.	Lunatics.	Total.
ENGLAND AND WALES	75	804	879	512	1,260	1,998	3,258
London - - -	66	776	842	517	545	1,036	1,581
Surrey (*Extra-Met.*) -	85	694	729	527	4,585	8,641	13,226
Kent (*Extra-Met.*) -	64	711	775	742	2,255	3,216	5,471
Sussex - - -	83	781	864	579	1,222	2,218	3,440
Hampshire - - -	66	789	855	450	1,425	2,219	3,644
Berkshire - - -	65	827	892	492	1,610	3,416	5,026
Middlesex (*Extra-Met.*) -	71	670	741	488	748	11.468	12,216
Hertfordshire -	84	840	924	618	5,090	6,216	11,306
Buckinghamshire -	96	943	1,039	507	1,713	2,399	4,112
Oxfordshire -	72	1,074	1,146	551	1,806	2,754	4,560
Northamptonshire -	72	791	863	448	1,606	2,996	4,602
Huntingdonshire - -	56	1,058	1,109	376	1,164	132	1,296
Bedfordshire -	91	732	823	512	1,977	5,413	7,390
Cambridgeshire - -	52	838	890	576	1,622	1,742	3,364
Essex - -	74	690	764	418	1,389	1,686	3,075
Suffolk - -	113	936	1,049	560	1,657	1,924	3,581
Norfolk - -	105	1,072	1,177	514	1,387	2,716	4,103
Wiltshire -	56	901	957	511	2,035	4,383	6,418
Dorsetshire - -	108	1,108	1,216	519	1,562	2,487	4,049
Devonshire -	104	1,158	1,262	615	1,376	1,837	3,213
Cornwall -	89	1,639	1,728	613	1,131	1,853	2,984
Somersetshire - -	98	1,041	1,139	532	1,767	1,877	3,644
Gloucestershire - -	137	1,146	1,283	630	1,758	2,523	4,281
Herefordshire - -	110	1,117	1,227	643	2,192	2,455	4,647
Shropshire - - -	109	974	1,083	489	1,730	2,028	3,758
Staffordshire - -	62	755	817	478	1,164	1,751	2,915
Worcestershire - -	70	1,014	1,084	786	1,269	1,893	3,162
Warwickshire -	88	692	780	508	1,515	1,744	3,259
Leicestershire -	89	820	909	349	1,341	1,849	3,190
Rutlandshire -	87	739	826	261	739	87	826
Lincolnshire - -	89	807	896	443	1,408	1,287	2,695
Nottinghamshire - -	96	816	912	390	1,254	1,416	2,670
Derbyshire - -	89	732	771	541	988	158	1,141
Cheshire - - -	67	656	723	431	1,218	2,008	3,226
Lancashire -	79	654	733	460	1,064	1,572	2,636
West Riding - -	74	655	729	545	1,026	1,151	2,177
East Riding - - -	108	1,015	1,123	450	1,007	3,613	4,620
North Riding -	63	789	852	362	846	72	918
Durham - - -	54	645	699	406	702	1,254	1,956
Northumberland - -	92	728	820	620	1,120	1,506	2,626
Cumberland - - -	68	858	926	451	834	1,747	2,581
Westmorland - -	124	793	917	513	1,321	187	1,508
Monmouthshire - -	51	1,033	1,084	418	1,268	2,275	3,538
Glamorganshire -	50	861	911	521	787	1,327	2,064
Carmarthenshire -	27	1,016	1,043	593	2,103	4,440	6,543
Pembrokeshire - -	12	1,075	1,087	586	1,219	382	1,601
Cardiganshire - - -	32	1,229	1,261	641	1,819	462	2,281
Brecknockshire -	55	1,109	1,164	610	1,053	203	1,256
Radnorshire - -	54	918	972	756	2,105	270	2,375
Montgomeryshire -	39	1,103	1,142	407	1,378	236	1,614
Flintshire -	153	1,114	1,267	634	874	153	1,027
Denbighshire - -	53	832	885	540	2,187	3,276	5,463
Merionethshire - -	103	893	996	542	1,626	278	1,904
Carnarvonshire -	57	856	913	477	1,413	275	1,688
Anglesey - -	85	854	939	740	1,964	256	2,220

TABLE 32.—ANALYSIS of CENSUS

REGISTRATION COUNTY, &c.	Persons per Square Mile.	Increase or Decrease per Cent. of Population 1871–81.		Females to 1,000 Males.	Age Distribution of 1,000 Persons enumerated.				Married Males and Females, in 1,000 of each Sex, aged 15 and under 45 years.		Per-centage of Population living in Urban and Rural Sanitary Districts.	
		Natural.	Actual.		0—	15—	45—	65—	Males.	Females.	Urban.	Rural.
1.	2.	3.	4.	5.	6.	7.	8.	9.	10.	11.	12.	13.
ENGLAND AND WALES	446	15·0	14·4	1,055	365	446	143	46	470	491	67·90	32·10
I.—LONDON.												
LONDON -	32,343	14·0	17·3	1,123	336	489	138	37	482	470	99·98	00·02
II.—SOUTH EASTERN.												
1. SURREY (*Extra-Met.*) -	651	16·0	26·2	1,105	352	463	140	45	430	423	53·90	46·10
2. KENT (*Extra-Met.*) -	468	15·5	12·6	1,021	365	437	145	53	445	486	59·20	40·80
3. SUSSEX	334	14·0	17·4	1,110	355	439	150	56	456	433	52·58	47·42
4. HAMPSHIRE - -	351	13·5	9·6	1,045	354	439	153	54	430	482	57·81	42·19
5. BERKSHIRE -	276	14·4	10·2	1,010	366	424	152	58	439	487	35·86	64·14
III.—SOUTH MIDLAND.												
6. MIDDLESEX (*Extra-Met.*)	1,365	16·5	43·8	1,108	373	451	133	43	486	458	81·92	18·08
7. HERTFORDSHIRE - -	293	13·9	4·0	1,045	379	403	156	62	463	472	29·14	70·86
8. BUCKINGHAMSHIRE -	243	14·4	0·6	1,030	381	401	157	61	471	496	20·65	79·35
9. OXFORDSHIRE	237	12·8	1·2	1,042	371	407	159	63	443	470	38·29	61·71
10. NORTHAMPTONSHIRE -	280	16·0	11·6	1,006	375	420	151	54	479	527	39·57	60·43
11. HUNTINGDONSHIRE	167	12·7	−8·3	1,042	377	384	167	72	464	499	34·44	65·56
12. BEDFORDSHIRE	321	14·3	1·8	1,125	370	417	156	57	500	453	31·19	68·81
13. CAMBRIDGESHIRE	213	13·6	−0·5	1,035	369	407	156	68	456	499	42·31	57·69
IV.—EASTERN.												
14. ESSEX - - -	391	17·1	25·3	1,000	390	417	143	50	483	536	52·16	47·84
15. SUFFOLK - -	244	13·5	1·8	1,047	373	396	161	70	473	508	34·80	65·20
16. NORFOLK	214	11·1	1·6	1,067	355	404	168	73	475	493	38·66	61·34
V.—SOUTH WESTERN.												
17. WILTSHIRE -	201	12·7	1·0	1,026	371	400	163	66	451	493	33·70	66·30
18. DORSETSHIRE -	194	11·9	−2·1	1,036	353	418	161	68	436	461	35·70	64·30
19. DEVONSHIRE	237	10·2	0·4	1,116	342	424	164	70	431	437	54·48	45·52
20. CORNWALL	238	9·5	−8·9	1,133	344	422	163	71	400	416	31·21	68·79
21. SOMERSETSHIRE	294	12·0	1·7	1,120	363	411	158	68	471	450	38·76	61·24
VI.—WEST MIDLAND.												
22. GLOUCESTERSHIRE	479	13·1	7·4	1,138	359	431	152	58	477	449	63·43	36·57
23. HEREFORDSHIRE - -	146	10·6	−3·1	1,019	358	404	169	69	399	454	26·80	73·20
24. SHROPSHIRE -	182	12·4	−0·5	999	365	408	162	65	402	465	32·09	67·91
25. STAFFORDSHIRE - -	840	20·2	14·8	994	397	433	133	37	483	546	76·69	23·31
26. WORCESTERSHIRE -	564	16·2	14·0	1,081	370	434	146	50	472	466	54·86	45·14
27. WARWICKSHIRE -	768	16·6	15·9	1,055	372	446	140	42	496	512	76·04	23·96
VII.—NORTH MIDLAND.												
28. LEICESTERSHIRE - -	391	16·8	18·6	1,057	372	434	144	50	507	514	54·47	45·53
29. RUTLANDSHIRE -	137	12·1	−1·6	997	359	405	165	71	411	460	00·00	100·00
30. LINCOLNSHIRE -	171	14·6	8·2	998	368	418	151	63	452	513	40·37	59·63
31. NOTTINGHAMSHIRE -	465	17·2	23·4	1,037	369	442	141	48	506	530	66·41	33·59
32. DERBYSHIRE - -	444	18·7	19·0	1,003	382	436	139	43	485	537	54·40	45·60
VIII.—NORTH WESTERN.												
33. CHESHIRE -	619	15·2	15·3	1,062	366	450	143	41	486	475	67·68	32·32
34. LANCASHIRE - -	1,706	14·7	22·3	1,069	365	472	133	30	488	500	90·00	10·00
IX. YORKSHIRE.												
35. WEST RIDING -	792	16·3	18·5	1,044	371	456	138	35	496	518	83·26	16·74
36. EAST RIDING - -	333	15·2	18·2	1,020	361	447	143	49	467	525	68·59	31·41
37. NORTH RIDING -	171	16·4	17·7	976	378	436	138	48	439	509	56·69	43·31
X.—NORTHERN.												
38. DURHAM	732	23·2	26·3	954	400	445	123	32	474	579	61·67	38·33
39. NORTHUMBERLAND -	215	16·2	12·3	1,011	374	448	136	42	440	495	66·30	33·70
40. CUMBERLAND -	165	14·5	13·8	1,009	371	439	140	50	416	475	49·97	50·03
41. WESTMORLAND -	82	13·3	−1·3	1,036	365	424	151	60	400	422	29·91	70·09
XI.—WELSH.												
42. MONMOUTHSHIRE	351	16·5	6·7	953	383	427	143	47	439	542	61·54	38·46
43. SOUTH WALES:												
GLAMORGANSHIRE -	576	20·3	27·7	948	385	454	127	34	459	551	68·05	31·95
CARMARTHENSHIRE -	147	15·1	9·7	1,080	380	421	139	60	439	437	30·42	69·58
PEMBROKESHIRE -	151	11·0	−0·2	1,088	357	416	158	69	411	406	34·79	65·21
CARDIGANSHIRE -	102	8·8	−2·8	1,227	351	404	166	79	370	357	14·22	85·78
BRECKNOCKSHIRE	78	11·7	−4·9	1,006	361	416	157	66	391	459	37·98	62·02
RADNORSHIRE - -	54	12·6	−6·2	970	363	411	156	70	334	421	9·29	90·71
44. NORTH WALES:												
MONTGOMERYSHIRE	84	11·4	−2·8	990	364	405	160	71	363	444	27·64	72·36
FLINTSHIRE - -	398	12·6	5·2	972	379	416	152	53	419	531	27·32	72·68
DENBIGHSHIRE	192	11·3	7·4	999	363	423	157	57	414	482	25·23	74·77
MERIONETHSHIRE -	91	13·5	11·0	988	361	429	147	63	404	491	37·38	62·62
CARNARVONSHIRE -	223	10·0	11·1	1,038	345	434	158	63	420	456	35·80	64·20
ANGLESEY - -	183	6·9	0·04	1,044	380	412	177	81	412	446	24·70	75·30

Statistics for Registration Counties.

Number Born in County of 1,000 enumerated therein.	Number Resident in County of 1,000 Natives thereof enumerated in England and Wales.	Comparative Amount of Idiocy and Imbecility among Natives of Counties.*	Comparative Amount of Deaf-Mutism among Natives of Counties.*	Persons engaged in each Class of Occupation of 1,000 persons enumerated.						Registration County, &c.
				Professional Class.	Domestic Class.	Commercial Class.	Agricultural Class.	Industrial Class.	Unoccupied Class.	
14.	15.	16.	17.	18.	19.	20.	21.	22.	23.	24.
—	—	1,000	1,000	25	69	38	53	245	570	ENGLAND AND WALES.
										I.—LONDON.
629	804	—*	—*	37	100	68	6	237	552	London.
										II.—SOUTH EASTERN.
478	627	985	1,079	50	123	34	51	158	584	1. Surrey (*Extra-Met.*)
720	727	992	853	44	86	32	78	168	592	2. Kent (*Extra-Met.*)
697	737	1,005	964	31	111	28	67	167	576	3. Sussex.
683	716	1,131	941	60	88	32	67	170	583	4. Hampshire.
651	602	1,154	1,006	32	94	20	111	166	577	5. Berkshire.
										III.—SOUTH MIDLAND.
357	480	1,147	1,198	36	113	43	30	169	609	6. Middlesex (*Ex.-Met.*)
684	614	1,090	867	23	85	19	108	191	574	7. Hertfordshire.
743	596	1,124	945	20	76	13	113	214	564	8. Buckinghamshire.
741	597	1,182	1,030	25	93	17	124	166	575	9. Oxfordshire.
759	693	1,199	976	20	60	22	92	243	563	10. Northamptonshire.
740	555	873	699	22	72	12	169	145	580	11. Huntingdonshire.
767	659	977	1,024	21	59	15	119	283	503	12. Bedfordshire.
782	633	1,097	1,131	22	76	18	156	133	595	13. Cambridgeshire.
										IV.—EASTERN.
648	678	981	891	27	64	43	89	172	605	14. Essex.
885	669	1,057	1,053	22	69	19	142	160	588	15. Suffolk.
880	705	932	945	21	69	22	133	177	578	16. Norfolk.
										V.—SOUTH WESTERN.
794	623	1,280	984	22	69	17	131	179	582	17. Wiltshire.
795	643	1,076	1,028	36	71	22	120	181	570	18. Dorsetshire.
820	720	995	1,028	47	84	28	86	183	572	19. Devonshire.
894	764	782	1,160	25	62	27	107	187	592	20. Cornwall.
772	658	1,210	935	24	84	25	90	206	571	21. Somersetshire.
										VI.—WEST MIDLAND.
736	695	1,289	1,099	27	88	35	58	221	571	23. Gloucestershire.
724	597	1,437	1,200	23	87	14	149	146	581	23. Herefordshire.
783	620	1,108	966	20	80	17	111	183	589	24. Shropshire.
760	772	904	998	15	47	25	28	288	597	25. Staffordshire.
692	668	1,076	1,036	21	75	28	60	249	567	26. Worcestershire.
703	744	1,129	1,129	18	57	35	37	297	556	27. Warwickshire.
										VII.—NORTH MIDLAND.
769	742	1,048	731	18	57	22	60	298	545	28. Leicestershire.
675	505	845	899	21	99	13	158	127	582	29. Rutlandshire.
822	719	1,014	958	10	69	20	143	150	599	30. Lincolnshire.
725	745	977	768	16	52	24	49	309	550	31. Nottinghamshire.
713	718	875	1,105	16	50	25	44	285	579	32. Derbyshire.
										VIII.—NORTH WESTERN.
671	710	968	933	19	72	45	50	256	558	33. Cheshire.
741	904	899	943	17	47	50	18	338	580	34. Lancashire.
										IX.—YORKSHIRE.
				16	40	29	28	331	556	35. West Riding.
817	878	890	945	26	68	49	73	190	594	36. East Riding.
				17	62	24	89	204	604	37. North Riding.
										X.—NORTHERN.
678	847	614	1,016	13	39	34	19	267	628	38. Durham.
737	747	910	1,008	18	59	44	50	231	598	39. Northumberland.
764	751	720	939	18	61	27	76	229	589	40. Cumberland.
734	606	1,015	1,147	19	78	18	117	180	588	41. Westmorland.
										XI.—WELSH.
659	716	882	907	16	53	36	43	255	597	42. Monmouthshire.
										43. South Wales:
646	881	728	945	15	50	43	22	277	593	Glamorganshire.
853	714	1,150	1,141	15	63	18	99	200	605	Carmarthenshire.
846	692	1,056	1,075	32	77	27	109	166	589	Pembrokeshire.
898	725	1,351	1,297	15	77	13	149	151	595	Cardiganshire.
681	594	755	808	22	76	17	119	181	585	Brecknockshire.
767	534	1,168	1,172	15	83	7	190	124	581	Radnorshire.
										44. North Wales:
826	664	1,015	556	17	73	11	158	168	578	Montgomeryshire.
715	651	1,028	1,162	15	54	21	55	252	603	Flintshire.
740	683	1,312	933	21	73	15	92	214	585	Denbighshire.
751	764	1,339	1,317	15	70	18	110	204	583	Merionethshire.
790	833	1,330	962	16	77	26	82	219	580	Carnarvonshire.
861	718	1,253	1,378	14	54	51	140	153	588	Anglesey.

* The Metropolitan portions of Surrey, Kent, and Middlesex are included in those Registration Counties as regards the distribution of Idiocy, Imbecility and Deaf Mutism.

TABLE 33.—UNITED KINGDOM.—AREA and POPULATION of the UNITED KINGDOM and of the ISLANDS in the BRITISH SEAS in 1881.

—	AREA of LAND* in ACRES.	ENUMERATED POPULATION in 1881.		
		PERSONS.	Males.	Females.
England and Wales	36,772,723	25,974,439	12,639,902	13,334,537
Scotland	19,084,659	3,735,573	1,799,475	1,936,098
Ireland	20,194,602	5,174,836	2,533,277	2,641,559
UNITED KINGDOM	76,051,984	34,884,848	16,972,654	17,912,194
Isle of Man	140,985	53,558	25,760	27,798
Channel Islands	48,322	87.702	40,321	47,381
Army, Navy, and Merchant Seamen abroad, being Natives of the United Kingdom	—	215,374	215,374	—
UNITED KINGDOM, &c.	76,241.291	35,241,482	17,254,109	17,987,373

* The Areas in this Table for the several parts of the United Kingdom are of land only; that is, exclusive of inland and tidal water and also of foreshore.

TABLE 34.—UNITED KINGDOM.—POPULATION of the UNITED KINGDOM, of the ISLE OF MAN, and of the CHANNEL ISLANDS, at each of the LAST SEVEN CENSUSES.

—	1821.	1831.	1841.	1851.	1861.	1871.	1881.
England and Wales	12,000,236	13,896,797	15,914,148	17,927,609	20,066,224	22,712,266	25,974,439
Scotland	2,091,521	2,364,386	2,620,184	2,888,742	3,062,294	3,360,018	3,735,573
Ireland	6,801,827	7,767,401	8,196,597	6,574,278	5,798,967	5,412,377	5,174,836
UNITED KINGDOM	20,893,584	24,028,584	26,730,929	27,390,629	28,927,485	31,484,661	34,884,848
Isle of Man	40,081	41,000	47,975	52,387	52,469	54,042	53,558
Channel Islands	49,427	62,710	76,065	90,739	90,978	90,596	87,702
Army, Navy, and Merchant Seamen abroad, being Natives of the United Kingdom*	289,095	260,191	202,954	212,194	250,356	216,080	215,374
UNITED KINGDOM, &c.	21,272,187	24,392,485	27,057,923	27,745,949	29,321,288	31,845,379	35,241,482

* The returns for 1821 and 1831 included the Army, Navy, and Merchant Seamen at home as well as abroad. The return for 1841 included men abroad and on board vessels in home ports, but not those on shore at home. The returns after that date were limited to men abroad.

TABLE 35.—UNITED KINGDOM.—INCREASE OR DECREASE of POPULATION in the UNITED KINGDOM in each INTERCENSAL PERIOD since 1821.

—	1821–31.	1831–41.	1841–51.	1851–61.	1861–71.	1871–81.
England and Wales	15·8	14·5	12·7	11·9	13·2	14·4
Scotland	13·0	10·8	10·2	6·0	9·7	11·1
Ireland	14·2	5·5	–19·8	–11·8	–6·7	–4·4
UNITED KINGDOM	15·0	11·2	2·5	5·6	8·8	10·8
Isle of Man	2·3	17·0	9·2	0·2	3·0	–0·9
Channel Islands	26·9	21·3	19·3	0·3	–0·4	–3·2
Army, Navy, and Merchant Seamen abroad, being Natives of the United Kingdom	—	—	—	18·0	–13·7	–0·3
UNITED KINGDOM, &c.	14·7	10·9	2·5	5·7	8·6	10·7

NOTE.—A minus sign signifies a decrease.

TABLE 36.—UNITED KINGDOM.—PER-CENTAGE of POPULATION residing in the several DIVISIONS of the UNITED KINGDOM at each of the LAST SEVEN CENSUSES.

—	1821.	1831.	1841.	1851.	1861.	1871.	1881.
England and Wales	57·4	57·9	59·5	65·5	69·4	72·1	74·5
Scotland	10·0	9·8	9·8	10·5	10·6	10·7	10·7
Ireland	32·6	32·3	30·7	24·0	20·0	17·2	14·8

TABLE 37.—UNITED KINGDOM.—NUMBER and NATIONALITY of the OFFICERS and MEN serving at HOME and ABROAD in the several BRANCHES of the BRITISH ARMY at the time of the CENSUS, 1881.

—	TOTAL OFFICERS AND MEN.	OFFICERS.				NON-COMMISSIONED OFFICERS AND MEN.			
		English.	Scotch.	Irish.	Others.	English.	Scotch.	Irish.	Others.
AT HOME.									
Staff at Head Quarters and Districts	1,260	342	84	229	4	411	44	140	6
Cavalry	10,934	395	47	75	8	8,385	877	1,117	30
Infantry	43,694	1,285	201	321	14	28,405	3,841	9,498	129
Brigade Depôts	11,332	442	63	136	4	6,873	1,011	2,766	37
Royal Artillery	16,300	461	49	102	2	11,619	1,078	2,889	100
Royal Artillery serving with Militia and Volunteers	298	41	5	7	1	171	13	59	1
Royal Engineers	3,024	54	14	14	—	2,364	217	332	29
" not attached to any Company	557	174	34	44	—	224	47	34	—
" Individual Members not doing duty at a Station	142	114	15	12	1	—	—	—	—
Army Service Corps	2,103	73	5	12	—	1,626	104	279	4
Army Hospital Corps	1,321	12	6	11	—	1,058	66	158	10
Hospitals and other Institutions, Branch of Service not stated	1,212	125	30	105	16	657	71	172	36
ARMY AT HOME	92,177	3,518	553	1,068	50	61,793	7,369	17,444	382
ABROAD.									
Staff	1,449	263	64	199	5	553	43	154	168
Do. Artillery	53	13	4	3	—	27	1	5	—
Cavalry	5,859	203	32	52	1	4,612	323	609	27
Infantry	65,986	1,557	240	417	31	42,342	5,260	16,001	138
Royal Artillery	15,464	393	52	77	1	11,029	970	2,827	115
Royal Engineers	1,859	164	31	41	1	1,251	139	215	17
Army Service Corps	573	6	2	2	—	431	26	105	1
Army Hospital Corps	894	27	7	26	—	583	51	192	8
West India Regiments	1,759	71	6	21	—	19	4	12	1,626
Royal Malta Fencible Artillery	355	—	—	—	21	1	—	1	332
ARMY ABROAD	94,251	2,697	438	838	60	60,848	6,817	20,121	2,432
TOTAL ARMY AT HOME AND ABROAD	186,428	6,215	991	1,906	110	122,641	14,186	37,565	2,814

TABLE 38.—UNITED KINGDOM.—NUMBER and NATIONALITY of the OFFICERS and MEN serving ABROAD in the ARMY, the ROYAL NAVY, and the ROYAL MARINES at the time of the CENSUS, 1881.

—	TOTAL.	BIRTH-PLACE.			
		England and Wales.	Scotland.	Ireland.	Other than the United Kingdom.
Army	94,251	63,545	7,255	20,959	2,492
Royal Navy	21,493	17,548	800	1,697	1,448
Royal Marines	3,612	3,117	212	241	42

TABLE 39.—UNITED KINGDOM.—NUMBER and NATIONALITY of MARINERS serving abroad in FOREIGN-TRADING BRITISH MERCHANT VESSELS, at the time of the CENSUS, 1881.

CAPACITIES.	ALL AGES.	NATIVES OF						Born at Sea.	Not stated.
		England.	Scotland.	Ireland.	Channel Islands and Isle of Man.	Colonies.	Foreign Parts.		
Masters - - -	6,206	3,868	1,226	343	146	387	202	8	26
Mates - - - -	11,424	6,978	2,720	605	255	408	363	20	75
Able and Ordinary Seamen -	52,715	19,720	5,260	3,572	970	3,345	19,711	26	111
Apprentices - -	4,816	3,398	997	175	50	138	49	8	1
Boys - - - -	1,455	1,008	151	104	23	68	96	3	2
Engineers, Firemen, and others.	44,033	23,712	10,224	3,619	685	2,808	2,815	41	129
TOTAL - -	120,649*	58,684	20,578	8,418	2,129	7,154	23,236	106	344

* This total excludes 9,938 Merchant Seamen (mainly employed in Home-trading vessels) who arrived in port within a month after the Census Day. Of these 9,938 Seamen 4,319 were stated to have been born in England and Wales, and adding a due proportion of the cases in which the birth-place was not specified, it may be estimated that 4,427 were of English or Welsh birth.

TABLE 40.—UNITED KINGDOM.—AGES of the ARMY, NAVY, MARINES, and MERCHANT SEAMEN in 1881.

——	All Ages.	0—	15—	20—	25—	45—	65—
Army - -	186,428	324	16,477	71,062	90,472	6,619	1,474
Navy - - -	44,400	—	10,863	13,227	19,495	815	—
Marines - -	13,184	9	1,494	4,791	6,792	96	2
Merchant Seamen - -	225,680	1,415	22,793	46,054	123,809	28,690	2,919

TABLE 41.—UNITED KINGDOM.—NUMBER and AGES of MARINERS serving abroad in FOREIGN-TRADING BRITISH MERCHANT VESSELS, at the time of the CENSUS, 1881.

CAPACITIES.	ALL AGES.	* Under 15.	15—	20—	25—	30—	35—	40—	45—	50—	55—	60—	65—	70 and upwards.	Not stated.
Masters -	6,206	—	—	48	732	1,321	1,353	1,047	834	511	236	64	26	8	26
Mates -	11,424	—	227	2,133	2,918	2,086	1,333	1,180	718	459	180	90	19	—	81
Able and Ordinary Seamen.	52,715	146	5,044	17,891	13,896	7,176	3,519	2,423	1,372	804	193	67	16	2	166
Apprentices - -	4,816	211	3,912	686	6	—	—	—	—	—	—	—	—	—	1
Boys - - -	1,455	150	1,159	123	7	1	—	—	—	—	—	—	—	—	15
Engineers, Firemen, and others.	44,033	106	1,806	8,430	10,968	8,696	6,149	4,055	1,963	989	473	162	48	8	180
TOTAL -	120,649*	613	12,148	29,311	28,527	19,280	12,354	8,705	4,887	2,763	1,082	383	109	18	469

* This total excludes 9,938 Merchant Seamen (mainly engaged in Home-trading vessels) who arrived in Port within a month after the Census Day. Trustworthy returns of the Ages of these Seamen were not obtainable.

EMIGRATION.

TABLE 42.—UNITED KINGDOM.—NUMBER and NATIONALITY of EMIGRANTS who left the UNITED KINGDOM for Places out of Europe during the Ten Years 1871 to 1880.

YEAR.	TOTAL NUMBER OF EMIGRANTS.	English.	Scotch.	Irish.	Foreigners.	Not distinguished.
1871 - - -	252,435	102,452	19,232	71,067	53,246	6,438
1872 -	295,213	118,190	19,541	72,763	79,023	5,696
1873 - -	310,612	123,343	21,310	83,692	72,198	10,069
1874 - -	241,014	116,490	20,286	60,496	38,465	5,277
1875 - -	173,809	84,540	14,686	41,449	31,347	1,787
1876 -	138,222	73,396	10,097	25,976	25,584	3,169
1877 - -	119,971	63,711	8,653	22,831	21,289	3,487
1878 -	147,663	72,323	11,087	29,492	31,697	3,064
1879 - -	217,163	104,275	18,703	41,296	49,480	3,409
1880 -	332,294	111,845	22,056	93,641	100,369	4,383
TOTAL -	2,228,396	970,565	165,651	542,703	502,698	46,779

NOTE.—It appears from the above table, derived from Returns furnished by the Board of Trade, that 2,228,396 Emigrants sailed from the Ports of the United Kingdom during the ten years 1871-80. But in order to judge more accurately of the extent to which Emigration has affected the Population, the following Table has been prepared, showing the number of Emigrants in the interval between the Censuses of 1871 and 1881. The Emigrants whose origin was not distinguished in the Returns have been distributed in the proportions of those whose birth-places were ascertained.

NUMBER and ORIGIN of EMIGRANTS from the UNITED KINGDOM between the CENSUSES of 1871 and 1881.

PERIODS.	TOTAL.	English.	Scotch.	Irish.	Foreigners.
Total - -	2,244,338	996,038	170,757	530,924	546,619
1871 (April 1st to Dec. 31st) - -	224,694	91,788	17,942	63,995	50,969
1872-80 - -	1,975,961	886,208	149,472	458,813	481,468
1881 (to March 31st) - -	43,683	18,042	3,343	8,116	14,182

It may be inferred from the official returns that the number of Emigrants from the United Kingdom was not less than—

717,913 in the interval of the Censuses 1831 and 1841;
1,692,063 ditto ditto 1841 and 1851;
2,249,355 ditto ditto 1851 and 1861;
1,976,577 ditto ditto 1861 and 1871;
2,244,338 ditto ditto 1871 and 1881.

The following is a comparison of the number of Emigrants of British and Foreign Extraction during each of the intervals between the last four Censuses:—

	Total.	English.	Scotch.	Irish.	Foreigners.
1851 (April 1st) to 1861 (April 7th) - -	2,249,355	640,316	182,954	1,231,308	194,777
1861 (April 8th) to 1871 (March 31st) -	1,976,577	649,742	158,226	866,626	301,983
1871 (April 1st) to 1881 (March 31st)	2,244,338	996,038	170,757	530,924	546,619

TABLE 43.—UNITED KINGDOM.—SUMMARY of RETURNS* relating to NATIVES of the UNITED KINGDOM residing in FOREIGN COUNTRIES at or about the time of the Census, 1881.

(For Details see Table 44.)

COUNTRY, &c.	PERSONS.	Males.	Females.
Total	2,881,167*	—	—
France	36,447	16,018	20,429
Switzerland	2,812	1,027	1,785
Spain	4,771	3,014	1,757
Portugal	1,798	920	878
Italy	7,230	3,445	3,785
Greece	566	285	281
Turkey in Europe	1,518	808	710
German Empire	11,139	?	?
Austria (including Hungary)	2,169	939	1,230
Belgium	3,789	1,410	2,379
Holland	480	197	283
Luxembourg	20	?	?
Denmark	298	177	121
Norway	518	286	232
Sweden	340	165	175
Russia	5,007	2,646	2,361
Bulgaria	59	44	15
Bosnia and Herzegovina	4	2	2
Eastern Roumelia	14	9	5
Roumania	416	232	184
Servia	13	9	4
Turkey in Asia	1,599	793	806
Persia	191	127	64
Arabia	7	7	—
China	2,352	1,585	767
Japan	1,105	754	351

COUNTRY, &c.	PERSONS.	Males.	Females.
Philippine Islands	211	171	40
Siam	99	81	18
Java	225	180	45
Borneo	126	93	33
Egypt	2,481	1,570	911
Barbary (Tripoli)	1,749	950	799
Morocco	661	318	343
Angola	75	74	1
Algeria	622	354	268
Canary Islands	142	75	67
Cape Verd Islands	89	60	29
Mozambique	48	42	6
Zanzibar	101	76	25
Madeira	438	189	249
United States	2,772,169	?	?
Central America	1,552	1,374	178
Panama	400	?	?
Cuba	654	371	283
Peru	2,000	?	?
Haiti	2,000	?	?
Dominican State	500	?	?
Chili	4,267	3,459	808
Uruguay	2,772	?	?
Guiana (Dutch)	1,566	969	597
Brazil	825	630	195
Navigation Islands	70	58	12
Tahiti	350	191	159
New Caledonia	313	177	136

TABLE 44.—UNITED KINGDOM.—ABSTRACT OF RETURNS* relating to NATIVES of the UNITED KINGDOM residing in FOREIGN COUNTRIES at or about the time of the Census, 1881.

COUNTRIES.	PERSONS.	Males.	Females.
FRANCE	36,447	16,018	20,429
DEPARTMENTS.			
Seine	12,636	5,299	7,337
Pas-de-Calais	5,704	2,590	3,114
Alpes-Maritimes	2,347	1,195	1,152
Seine-Inférieure	1,762	786	976
Nord	1,640	763	877
Basses-Pyrénées	1,622	676	946
Oise	1,188	779	409
Seine-et-Oise	943	399	544
Ille-et-Vilaine	859	288	571
Bouches-du-Rhône	666	325	341
Calvados	592	268	324
Gironde	554	230	324
Côtes-du-Nord	448	151	297
Manche	366	151	215
Somme	350	168	182
Var	338	52	286
Indre-et-Loire	263	78	185
Loire-Inférieure	244	148	96
Marne	259	132	127
Rhône	242	96	146

COUNTRIES.	PERSONS.	Males.	Females.
FRANCE—*continued.*			
Eure	227	118	109
Seine-et-Marne	217	81	136
Finistère	215	106	109
Maine-et-Loire	208	77	131
Aisne	136	61	75
Charente-Inférieure	124	18	106
Meurthe-et-Moselle	123	72	51
Hérault	120	64	56
Loiret	116	40	76
Loire	94	51	43
Charente	85	38	47
Sarthe	85	31	54
Haute-Garonne	73	19	54
Morbihan	71	20	51
Allier	69	35	34
Eure-et-Loir	68	21	47
Isère	66	31	35
Puy-de-Dôme	65	31	34
Corsica	64	42	22
Saône-et-Loire	61	32	29
Hautes-Pyrénées	59	34	25
Loir-et-Cher	58	21	37

* These Returns, which were received from the Foreign Office, probably include a small proportion of British subjects, who were not natives of the United Kingdom, as well as many children of natives of the United Kingdom, born while their parents were resident abroad.

TABLE 44 (*continued*).—UNITED KINGDOM.—ABSTRACT of RETURNS relating to NATIVES of the UNITED KINGDOM residing in FOREIGN COUNTRIES at or about the time of the Census, 1881.

COUNTRIES.	PERSONS.	Males.	Females.
FRANCE—*continued.*			
Orne	57	18	39
Ardennes	57	26	31
Dordogne	55	18	37
Yonne	51	20	31
Nièvre	49	23	26
Vienne	48	21	27
Gard	44	12	32
Haute-Vienne	43	19	24
Tarn	34	22	12
Doubs	33	17	16
Cher	33	9	24
Indre	31	12	19
Côte-d'Or	30	15	15
Drôme	30	17	13
Aube	29	13	16
Deux-Sèvres	28	8	20
Tarn-et-Garonne	27	6	21
Haute-Savoie	27	14	13
Lot-et-Garonne	25	6	19
Ain	25	9	16
Savoie	25	4	21
Mayenne	21	7	14
Aude	19	6	13
Landes	19	8	11
Meuse	18	8	10
Gers	16	6	10
Ardèche	13	7	6
Haute-Marne	13	1	12
Haute-Loire	12	3	9
Jura	12	3	9
Pyrénées-Orientales	12	3	9
Vaucluse	12	3	9
Haut-Rhin	9	2	7
Basses-Alpes	8	5	3
Ariège	8	7	1
Cantal	8	5	3
Aveyron	7	5	2
Vosges	7	4	3
Vendée	6	1	5
Lot	6	4	2
Haute-Saône	4	1	3
Corrèze	4	2	2
Lozère	3	—	3
Hautes-Alpes	2	1	1
Creuse	—	—	—
SWITZERLAND	2,812	1,027	1,785
CANTONS.			
Zurich	132	72	60
Berne	96	35	61
Lucerne	14	3	11
Uri	—	—	—
Schwyz	5	1	4
Unterwalden-le-Haut	—	—	—
Unterwalden-le-Bas	—	—	—
Glaris	2	2	—
Zeug	4	3	1
Fribourg	18	12	6
Soleure	14	11	3
Bâle-Ville	49	27	22
Bâle-Campagne	4	1	3
Schaffhouse	15	6	9
Appenzell Rh-Extér	6	3	3
Appenzell Rh-Intér	—	—	—
St. Gall	27	18	9
Grisons	248	103	145
Argovie	16	11	5
Thurgovie	11	4	7
Tessin	19	9	10
Vaud	1,414	438	976
Valais	1	1	—
Neuchâtel	199	69	130
Genève	518	198	320
SPAIN	4,771	3,014	1,757
PROVINCES.			
Alava	10	6	4
Albacete	1	1	—
Alicante	34	23	11
Almeria	64	47	17
Avila	2	1	1
Badajos	19	11	8
Baleares	16	11	5
Barcelona	370	230	140
Burgos	2	1	1
Cáceres	4	2	2
Cadiz	1,563	792	771
Canarias	71	39	32
Castellon	—	—	—
Ciudad-Real	12	9	3
Cordova	22	11	11
Coruña	97	72	25
Cuenca	—	—	—
Gerona	12	9	3
Granada	8	6	2
Guadalajara	6	6	—
Guipuzcoa	50	19	31
Huelva	273	219	54
Huesca	—	—	—
Jaen	115	80	35
Leon	3	2	1
Lérida	1	1	—
Logroño	5	4	1
Lugo	5	3	2
Madrid	215	111	104
Malaga	367	204	163
Murcia	239	209	30
Navarra	7	2	5
Orense	—	—	—
Oviedo	41	33	8
Palencia	1	—	1
Pontevedra	35	25	10
Salamanca	21	20	1
Santander	167	124	43
Segovia	4	4	—
Sevilla	266	166	100
Soria	—	—	—
Tarragona	15	9	6
Ternel	—	—	—
Toledo	1	1	—
Valencia	111	70	41
Valladolid	67	61	6
Vizcaya	442	365	77
Zamora	—	—	—
Zaragoza	7	5	2
PORTUGAL	1,798	920	878
DISTRICTS.			
Angra	1	—	1
Aveiro	10	4	6
Beja	3	3	—
Braga	19	7	12
Braganca	9	3	6
Coimbra	19	16	3
Evora	9	6	3
Faro	—	—	—
Funchal (Island of Madeira).	441	191	250
Horta	26	18	8
Lisbon	586	307	279
Oporto	495	248	247
Paula Delgada	72	48	24
Vianna	5	4	1
Villa Real	2	2	—
Santarem	2	2	—
Azores or Western Islands.	99	61	38

TABLE 44 (*continued*).—UNITED KINGDOM.—ABSTRACT of RETURNS relating to NATIVES of the UNITED KINGDOM residing in FOREIGN COUNTRIES at or about the time of the Census, 1881.

COUNTRIES.	PERSONS.	Males.	Females.
ITALY	7,230	3,445	3,785
PROVINCES.			
Alessandria	12	4	8
Ancona	25	13	12
Aquila	—	—	—
Arezzo	3	1	2
Ascoli Piceno	3	—	3
Avellino	3	2	1
Bari	22	15	7
Belluno	—	—	—
Benevento	1	1	—
Bergamo	20	10	10
Bologna	32	16	16
Brescia	10	3	7
Cagliari	66	51	15
Caltanisetta	20	14	6
Campobasso	—	—	—
Caserta	9	4	5
Catania	111	78	33
Catanzaro	7	5	2
Chieti	3	3	—
Como	46	17	29
Cosenza	—	—	—
Cremona	2	2	—
Cuneo	12	7	5
Ferrara	5	—	5
Firenze	1,073	325	748
Foggia	1	—	1
Forlì	4	1	3
Genova	741	386	355
Girgenti	124	110	14
Grosseto	5	1	4
Lecce	34	16	18
Livorna	402	236	166
Lucca	29	9	20
Macerata	2	—	2
Mantova	3	1	2
Massa Carrara	22	10	12
Messina	273	156	117
Milano	370	148	222
Modena	2	1	1
Napoli	823	390	433
Novara	69	37	32
Padova	—	—	—
Palermo	397	305	92
Parma	3	—	3
Pavia	1	—	1
Perugia	12	7	5
Pesaro Urbino	1	—	1
Piacenza	3	2	1
Pisa	73	33	40
Porto Maurizio	545	156	389
Potenza	2	1	1
Ravenna	—	—	—
Reggio (Calabria)	2	—	2
Reggio (Emilia)	4	—	4
Roma	1.266	550	716
Rovigo	4	1	3
Salerno	31	21	10
Sassari	37	31	6
Siena	36	9	27
Siracusa	24	18	6
Sondrio	—	—	—
Teramo	2	—	2
Torino	2	—	2
Trapani	175	61	114
Trevisa	21	13	8
Udine	—	—	—
Venezia	200	164	36
Verona	—	—	—
Vicenza	—	—	—
GREECE	566	285	281
Morea	58	25	33
Negropont	169	91	78
Ionian Islands	209	92	117
Syra	130	77	53

COUNTRIES.	PERSONS.	Males.	Females.
TURKEY IN EUROPE	1,518	808	710
Constantinople	1,206	638	568
Dardanelles	108	56	52
Adrianople	7	5	2
Epirus, Macedonia, Thessaly, &c.	180	100	80
Crete	15	7	8
Dedeagatch	2	2	—
GERMAN EMPIRE	11,139	?	?
Prussia	5,219	—	—
Bavaria	517	—	—
Saxony	1,246	—	—
Würtemberg	659	—	—
Baden	822	—	—
Hesse	274	—	—
Mecklenberg-Schwerin	96	—	—
Sachsen Weimar	102	—	—
Mecklenberg-Strelitz	9	—	—
Oldenburg	31	—	—
Brunswick	96	—	—
Sachsen-Meiningen	10	—	—
Sachsen-Altenberg	10	—	—
Sachsen-Coburg-Gotha	75	—	—
Anhalt	31	—	—
Schwarzburg-Sondershausen.	16	—	—
Schwarzburg-Rudolstadt.	3	—	—
Waldeck	13	—	—
Reuss (elder line)	5	—	—
Reuss (younger line)	7	—	—
Schaumburg-Lippe	5	—	—
Lippe	10	—	—
Lubeck	70	—	—
Bremen	389	—	—
Hamburg	1,273	—	—
Alsace-Lorraine	151	—	—
AUSTRIA AND HUNGARY	2,169	939	1,230
AUSTRIA PROPER.			
Lower Austria	942	407	535
Upper Austria	40	24	16
Salzburg	15	6	9
Styria	75	26	49
Carinthia	9	3	6
Carniola	4	2	2
Trieste, &c.	306	130	176
Goritz and Gradisca	18	8	10
Istria	12	5	7
Tyrol	62	23	39
Vorarlberg	12	8	4
Bohemia	251	112	139
Moravia	63	23	40
Silesia	27	12	15
Galicia	90	37	53
Bukowine	6	2	4
Dalmatia	15	9	6
HUNGARY.			
Hungary	195	86	109
Transylvania	8	7	1
Fiume (free city of)	5	2	3
Croatia and Slavonia	14	7	7

TABLE 44 (*continued*).—UNITED KINGDOM.—ABSTRACT of RETURNS relating to NATIVES of the UNITED KINGDOM residing in FOREIGN COUNTRIES at or about the time of the Census, 1881.

COUNTRIES.	PERSONS.	Males.	Females.
BELGIUM - -	3,789	1,410	2,379
PROVINCES.			
Anvers - -	780	334	446
Brabant - -	1,511	509	1,002
Flandre Occidentale -	697	254	443
Flandre Orientale -	318	118	200
Hainaut - -	164	69	95
Liege - -	207	82	125
Limbourg -	18	9	9
Luxembourg -	31	14	17
Namur -	63	21	42
HOLLAND -	480	197	283
LUXEMBOURG -	20	?	?
DENMARK - -	298	177	121
NORWAY -	518	286	232
SWEDEN -	340*	165	175
RUSSIA - -	5,007	2,646	2,361
Petersburg	1,711	849	862
Moscow -	660	318	342
Poland -	160	88	72
Ekaterinoslav	283	169	114
Vladimir -	136	74	62
Caucasus -	59	38	21
Odessa, Crimea, &c.	785	442	343
Courland -	123	108	15
Reval - -	30	22	8
Cronstadt -	76	42	34
Archangel -	44	19	25
Other Provinces -	940	477	463
BULGARIA -	59	44	15
Roustchouk	32	20	12
Varna	27	24	3
BOSNIA AND HERZEGOVINA -	4	2	2
EASTERN ROUMELIA	14	9	5
ROUMANIA - -	416	232	184
SERVIA -	13	9	4

COUNTRIES.	PERSONS.	Males.	Females.
ASIA.			
TURKEY IN ASIA -	1,599	793	806
Smyrna -	1,246	640	606
Trebizond - -	25	—	25
Vilayets of Van, Bitlis, and Hakkiari.	2	2	—
Scutari	7	4	3
Mossul	2	1	1
Vilayet of Khudavendikyar.	17	9	8
Damascus	61	29	32
Erzeroum -	3	3	—
Jerusalem	103	46	57
Beyrout - -	119	47	72
Anatolia	7	5	2
Aleppo	7	7	—
PERSIA -	191†	127	64
ARABIA	7	7	—
Yeddah	5	5	—
Eastern Oman	2	2	—
CHINA - -	2,352	1,585	767
Shanghai	1,044	692	352
Peking	64	39	25
Canton -	108	85	23
Ningpo	77	43	34
Amoy -	150	98	52
Hankow	104	80	24
Tientsin	147	92	55
Newchwang -	71	41	30
Foochow	186	138	48
Swatow	81	52	29
Tamsin - -	27	21	6
Kiukiang -	23	21	2
Wuhu - -	22	16	6
Pakhoi - -	6	6	—
Wenchow - -	13	9	4
Kiungchow -	7	7	—
Tchang -	18	14	4
Chefoo - - -	95	56	39
Chiukiang - -	46	31	15
Saigon (Cochin China)	20	16	4
Taiwan (Isle of Formosa).	43	28	15
JAPAN - - -	1,105	754	351
Hiogo and Osaka	238	176	62
Yokohama	561	365	196
Hakodat - -	24	14	10
Yedo - -	156	105	51
Nagasaki -	107	77	30
Residents at other places.	19	17	2
PHILIPPINE ISLANDS	211	171	40
SIAM - -	99	81	18
JAVA - -	225	180	45
BORNEO - -	126	93	33

* Including 223 persons (123 males and 100 females) who were returned as British-born.
† Exclusive of 754 British Indian subjects (505 males and 249 females).

TABLE 44 (*continued*).—UNITED KINGDOM.—ABSTRACT of RETURNS relating to NATIVES of the UNITED KINGDOM residing in FOREIGN COUNTRIES at or about the time of the Census, 1881.

Countries.	Persons.	Males.	Females.
AFRICA.			
EGYPT -	2,481	1,570	911
Alexandria -	694	406	288
Suez -	940	668	272
Port Said -	373	232	141
Cairo	474	264	210
BARBARY (TRIPOLI) -	1,749	950	799
MOROCCO -	661	318	343
ANGOLA -	75	74	1
ALGERIA -	622	354	268
CAPE VERD ISLANDS	89	60	29
CANARY ISLANDS	142	75	67
MOZAMBIQUE -	48	42	6
ZANZIBAR	101	76	25
MADEIRA -	438	189	249
AMERICA.			
UNITED STATES -	2,772,169*	?	?
MEXICO -	No return.		
CENTRAL AMERICA -	1,552	1,374	178
Guatemala -	176	126	50
St. Salvador -	34	28	6
Costa Rica -	1,238	1,134	104
Nicaragua	104	86	18

Countries.	Persons.	Males.	Females.
PANAMA -	400†	?	?
CUBA -	654	371	283
PERU -	2,000‡	?	?
HAITI -	2,000‡	?	?
DOMINICAN STATE	500‡	?	?
CHILI (1875) -	4,267	3,459	808
ARGENTINE REPUBLIC	No return.		
URUGUAY -	2,772§	?	?
GUIANA (DUTCH) -	1,566	969	597
BRAZIL -	825	630	195
Bahia	282	179	103
Sergipe -	22	15	7
Para Maranham and Amazonas.	95	80	15
Parniba -	25	22	3
Alagoas -	7	6	1
Ceara -	20	14	6
Rio Grande do Norte -	37	33	4
Rio Grande do Sul -	258	224	34
Santa Catharina	15	14	1
Parana -	55	35	20
Piauhy -	5	4	1
Espiritu Santo -	4	4	—
POLYNESIA.			
SANDWICH ISLANDS -	No return.		
NAVIGATION ISLANDS	70	58	12
TAHITI -	350	191	159
NEW CALEDONIA	313	177	136

* This number is derived from the Compendium of the United States Census, 1880.
† Estimated number, exclusive of about 1,000 Jamaica-born subjects. ‡ Estimated. § Including 1,280 in Monte Video.

Table 45.—UNITED KINGDOM.—Distribution of Natives of the United Kingdom* enumerated in the United States on 1st June 1880.

States and Territories.	England.	Wales.	Scotland.	Ireland.	United Kingdom (not otherwise specified).
Total	662,676	83,302	170,136	1,854,571	1,484
States.					
Alabama	935	69	426	2,966	11
Arkansas	1,176	99	229	2,432	1
California	24,657	1,920	6,465	62,962	55
Colorado	8,797	1,212	1,673	8,263	2
Connecticut	15,453	407	4,157	70,638	28
Delaware	1,433	51	285	5,791	1
Florida	866	23	216	652	8
Georgia	1,144	52	395	4,148	21
Illinois	56,318	3,694	15,645	117,343	202
Indiana	11,093	927	2,731	25,741	16
Iowa	22,519	3,031	6,885	44,061	91
Kansas	14,172	2,088	3,788	14,993	11
Kentucky	4,100	394	982	18,236	5
Louisiana	2,582	71	659	13,807	8
Maine	3,716	283	1,397	13,421	5
Maryland	5,231	924	2,645	21,865	13
Massachusetts	47,263	873	12,507	226,700	89
Michigan	43,202	830	10,731	43,413	64
Minnesota	8,495	1,103	2,964	25,942	47
Mississippi	1,047	12	303	2,753	5
Missouri	15,798	1,766	3,641	48,898	44
Nebraska	8,207	624	2,230	10,133	19
Nevada	4,146	315	671	5,191	15
New Hampshire	3,497	21	1,102	13,052	11
New Jersey	31,285	863	7,633	93,079	22
New York	116,362	7,223	28,066	499,445	263
North Carolina	738	12	408	611	5
Ohio	41,555	13,763	8,946	78,927	76
Oregon	2,896	165	1,129	3,659	64
Pennsylvania	80,102	29,447	20,735	236,505	76
Rhode Island	12,500	167	3,039	35,281	3
South Carolina	670	10	354	2,626	4
Tennessee	1,956	302	516	5,975	18
Texas	6,528	221	1,659	8,103	26
Vermont	2,253	514	1,006	11,657	4
Virginia	2,781	135	893	4,835	6
West Virginia	2,051	369	622	6,459	2
Wisconsin	24,916	5,352	5,770	41,907	112
Territories.					
Arizona	708	57	250	1,296	1
Dakota	2,311	205	940	4,104	—
District of Columbia	1,648	56	495	7,840	1
Idaho	1,594	641	253	981	9
Montana	1,249	246	324	2,408	2
New Mexico	339	28	110	795	—
Utah	19,654	2,390	3,201	1,321	13
Washington	1,653	193	628	2,243	4
Wyoming	1,080	154	432	1,093	1

* The figures in this table are derived from the Compendium of the Tenth Census of the United States, 1880.

Table 46.—UNITED KINGDOM.—Natives of the United Kingdom enumerated in the United States at each of the last Four Censuses.

Census Years.	United Kingdom (Total).	England.	Wales.	Scotland.	Ireland.	United Kingdom (Country not specified).
1850	1,364,986	278,675	29,868	70,550	961,719	24,174
1860	2,224,743	431,692	45,763	108,518	1,611,304	27,466
1870	2,626,241	550,924	74,533	140,835	1,855,827	4,122
1880	2,772,169	662,676	83,302	170,136	1,854,571	1,484

Table 47.—BRITISH EMPIRE.—Area and Population of the British Empire at the Census of 1881.

——	Area in Square Miles.	Population.
United Kingdom - - - - - -	120,537	34,884,848
Colonies and Dependencies -	7,951,735	219,302,782
British Empire - - -	8,072,272	254,187,630

Table 48.—Area and Population of the British Colonies and Dependencies.

——	Area in Square Miles.	Population.
TOTAL AREA and POPULATION of COLONIES and DEPENDENCIES* -	7,951,735	219,302,782
Europe - -	423	327,805
North America - -	3,510,611	4,520,415
West Indies and Central America -	20,564	1,243,861
South America -	79,664	254,532
Africa -	267,886	2,579,163
Asia -	896,717	207,462,830
Australasia - -	3,175,870	2,914,176
EUROPE -	423	327,805
Isle of Man -	227	53,558
Jersey - - -	45	52,445
Guernsey and adjacent Islands	31	35,257
Heligoland -	1	2,001
Gibraltar	2	23,991
Malta -	117	160,553
NORTH AMERICA -	3,510,611	4,520,415
Canada:		
Nova Scotia - -	20,907	440,572
New Brunswick -	27,174	321,233
Quebec -	188,688	1,359,027
Ontario - - - -	101,733	1,923,228
Manitoba - - -	123,200	65,954
British Columbia	341,305	49,459
Territories -	2,665,252	56,446
Prince Edward Island -	2,133	108,891
Newfoundland -	40,200	179,509
The Bermudas	19	16,096
WEST INDIES AND CENTRAL AMERICA	20,564	1,243,861
The Bahamas - -	5,390	43,521
Turks and Caicos Islands -	130	4,778
Jamaica -	4,193	580,804
British Honduras - -	7,562	27,452
The Leeward Islands, comprising—		
Antigua and Barbuda -	170	34,964
Montserrat - -	32	10,083
St. Christopher (or St. Kitts) -	68	29,137
Nevis - - -	50	11,864
Anguilla (or Snake Island) -	35	3,219
The Virgin Islands (Tortola, &c.)	94	5,287
Dominica - - -	291	28,211
The Windward Islands, comprising—		
Barbados	166	171,860
St. Lucia -	248	38,551
St. Vincent - - -	133	40,548
Grenada	133	42,403
Tobago - - -	114	18,051
Trinidad - -	1,755	153,128
SOUTH AMERICA - -	79,664	254,532
British Guiana - - -	76,000	253,118
The Falkland Islands -	3,664	1,414
AFRICA - - - -	267,886	2,579,163
Island of Ascension -	34	300
St. Helena -	47	5,059
West African Settlements, comprising—		
Sierra Leone	300	60,546
The Gambia -	69	14,150
The Gold Coast	6,000	400,000
Lagos -	73	75,270
Cape Colonies and Dependencies, comprising—		
Cape Colony, including British Kaffraria - -	241,900	811,450
Basutoland - -		128,176
Griqualand, West		49,101
Griqualand, East -		78,352
Transkei (part of) -		58,623
Dependencies - -		124,122
Natal - - - -	18,755	413,167
The Mauritius and Dependencies -	708	360,847
ASIA - - -	896,717	207,462,830
British India - -	870,016	204,073,902
Perim - - -	71	149
Aden - - -		34,711
Ceylon - -	25,365	2,763,984
The Straits Settlements, comprising—		
Singapore - -	224	139,208
Penang (or Prince of Wales' Islands, Province Wellesley), and the Dindings) - -	342	190,597
Malacca - -	640	93,579
Labuan and smaller islands	30	6,298
Hong Kong -	29	160,402
AUSTRALASIA - -	3,175,870	2,914,176
West Australia -	1,060,085	29,708
South Australia - -	903,690	279,865
Victoria - - -	87,884	862,346
New South Wales - -	316,320	751,468
Norfolk Island -	13	663
Queensland -	669,520	213,525
Tasmania -	26,215	115,705
New Zealand -	104,403	533,801
Fiji - -	7,740	127,095

* This is exclusive of the Feudatory and Native States of India, of which the area was 509,284 square miles, and the population was 49,817,919. It is also exclusive of the Island of Cyprus.

APPENDIX B.

An Act (43 & 44 Vict. cap. 37.) for taking the CENSUS of ENGLAND, passed 7th September 1880.

WHEREAS it is expedient to take the census of England in the year one thousand eight hundred and eighty-one:

Be it enacted by the Queen's most Excellent Majesty, by and with the advice and consent of the Lords Spiritual and Temporal, and Commons, in this present Parliament assembled, and by the authority of the same, as follows:

1. The Local Government Board shall have the care of superintending the taking of the census, and shall cause to be prepared and printed, for the use of the persons to be employed in taking it, such forms and instructions as the said Board shall deem necessary, and the Registrar General shall issue all such forms and instructions to the persons for whose use they shall be intended; and all the expenses which shall be incurred by authority of the said Board, with the consent of the Treasury, under this Act, shall be paid out of such moneys as shall be provided by Parliament for that purpose. Local Government Board to superintend the taking of the census.

2. Every registrar's sub-district in England shall be formed into enumerators divisions according to instructions to be prepared by or under the direction of the said Board, who shall cause a sufficient number of copies of such instructions to be sent to every registrar of births and deaths in England; and the registrars, with all convenient speed, shall divide the several sub-districts into enumerators divisions according to such instructions, and subject in each case to the revision of the superintendent registrar, and to the final revision and approval of the Registrar General. Registrars sub-districts to be formed into enumerators divisions.

3. The several registrars of births and deaths in England shall make and return to their respective superintendent registrars a list containing the names and places of abode of a sufficient number of persons, duly qualified according to instructions to be prepared by or under the direction of the said Board, to act as enumerators within their several sub-districts, and such persons, when approved of by the superintendent registrar, shall be appointed by him enumerators for taking the census, subject nevertheless to the approval of the Registrar General; and the registrar, with the approval of the superintendent registrar, shall assign a division to each enumerator, and shall distribute to the several enumerators in his sub-district the forms and instructions which shall have been issued for that purpose by the Registrar General, and shall personally ascertain that each enumerator thoroughly understands the manner in which the duties required of him are to be performed. Enumerators to be appointed.

4. Schedules shall be prepared by or under the direction of the said Board for the purpose of being filled up by or on behalf of the several occupiers of dwelling-houses as herein-after provided, with particulars of the name, sex, age, rank, profession or occupation, condition as to marriage, relation to head of family, and birthplace of every living person who abode in every house on the night of Sunday the third day of April one thousand eight hundred and eighty-one, and also whether any were blind, or deaf and dumb, or imbecile or lunatic; and the registrars in England shall in the course of the week ending on Saturday the second day of April in the said year one thousand eight hundred and eighty-one, leave or cause to be left at every dwelling-house within their respective sub-districts one or more of the said schedules for the occupier or occupiers thereof or of any part thereof, and upon every such schedule shall be plainly expressed that it is to be filled up by the occupier of such dwelling-house, (or where such dwelling-house is let or sublet in different stories or apartments, and occupied distinctly by different persons or families, by the occupier of each such distinct story or apartment,) and that the enumerator will collect all such schedules within his division on the Monday then next following. Householders schedules to be left at dwelling-houses.

Every occupier of any dwelling-house, or of any distinct story or apartment in any dwelling-house, with or for whom any such schedule shall have been left as aforesaid, shall fill up the said schedule to the best of his or her knowledge and belief, so far as relates to all persons dwelling in the house, story, or apartment occupied by him or her, and shall sign his or her name thereunto, and shall deliver the schedule so filled up, or cause the same to be delivered, to the enumerator when required so to do. Occupiers to fill up the schedules and sign and deliver them to the enumerator.

Every such occupier who shall wilfully refuse or without lawful excuse neglect to fill up the said schedule to the best of his or her knowledge and belief, or to sign and deliver the same as herein required, or who shall wilfully make, sign, or deliver, or cause to be made, signed, or delivered, any false return of all or any of the matters specified in the said schedule, shall forfeit a sum not more than five pounds nor less than twenty shillings. Penalty for neglect.

5. The enumerators shall visit every house in their respective divisions, and shall collect all the schedules so left within their division from house to house, so far as may be possible, on Monday the fourth day of April in the said year one thousand eight hundred and eighty-one, and shall complete such of the schedules as upon delivery thereof to them shall appear to be defective, and correct such as they shall find to be erroneous, and shall copy the schedules, when completed and corrected, into books to be provided them for that purpose, and shall add thereunto an account, according to the best information which they shall be able to obtain, of all the other persons living within their division who shall not be included in the schedules so collected by them. Schedules to be collected from house to house, and corrected if found to be erroneous.

Enumerators to take an account of houses, &c., and to distinguish the boundaries of parishes, boroughs, &c.

6. Every enumerator shall also take an account of the occupied houses, and of the houses then building and therefore uninhabited, and also of all other uninhabited houses within his division, and shall also take an account of all such particulars herein-before mentioned, and none others, according to the forms and instructions which may be issued under this Act; and in the book into which he shall have copied the householders schedules and other particulars, as herein-before directed, each enumerator shall distinguish the several civil parishes within his division, or such parts thereof as shall be within his division, and shall also distinguish those civil parishes or parts of civil parishes within his division which are within the limits of any city or borough returning or contributing to return a member or members to serve in Parliament, or of any incorporated city or borough, or of any urban sanitary district, or of any rural sanitary district, or of any ecclesiastical district or parish, or of any area prescribed in that behalf by the instructions, and shall deliver such book to the registrar of the sub-district, together with the householders schedules collected by him, and shall sign a form or declaration to the effect that the said book has been truly and faithfully filled up by him, and that to the best of his knowledge the same is correct, which form of declaration shall be prepared by or under the direction of the Local Government Board, and issued by the Registrar General with the forms and nstructions aforesaid.

Enumerators to deliver their books, with the householders schedules, to the registrar.

Registrars to verify the enumerators books.

7. The registrar to whom such enumerators books shall be delivered shall examine the same, and shall satisfy himself that the instructions in each case have been punctually fulfilled, and if not shall cause any defect or inaccuracy in the said book to be supplied so far as may be possible; and when the books shall have been made as accurate as is possible the registrar shall deliver them to the superintendent registrar of his sub-district, and thereafter shall transmit the householders schedules to the Registrar General.

Superintendent registrars to examine the enumerators books and return them to the Registrar General.

8. The superintendent registrar shall examine all the books which shall be so delivered to him, and shall satisfy himself how far the registrars have duly performed the duties required of them by this Act, and shall cause any inaccuracies which he shall discover in such books to be corrected so far as may be possible, and shall return on or before the second day of May one thousand eight hundred and eighty-one, or such other day as may be fixed by the Registrar General, all the said books to the Registrar General for the use of the Local Government Board.

An abstract of returns to be printed and laid before Parliament.

9. The said Board shall cause a detailed abstract to be made of the said returns; and also a preliminary abstract, which shall be printed and laid before both Houses of Parliament within three calendar months next after the first day of June in the year one thousand eight hundred and eighty-one, if Parliament be sitting, or if Parliament be not sitting, then within the first fourteen days of the session then next ensuing.

Masters, &c. of gaols, &c. to be appointed enumerators of the inmates thereof.

10. The master or keeper of every gaol, prison, or house of correction, workhouse, hospital, or lunatic asylum, and of every public or charitable institution, which shall be determined upon by the Registrar General, shall be the enumerator of the inmates thereof, and shall be bound to conform to such instructions as shall be sent to him by the authority of the said Board for obtaining the returns required by this Act, so far as may be practicable, with respect to such inmates.

Overseers, peace officers, and relieving officers of unions formed under 4 & 5 Will. 4. c. 76. bound to act as enumerators.

11. The overseers of the poor in every civil parish in England, and the constables or other peace officers for such civil parishes, and the relieving officers of any union or civil parish not in union having a board of guardians acting under the Poor Law Amendment Act, 1834, or the Acts amending the same, shall be bound to act as enumerators under this Act within their respective civil parishes and unions, if required so to act by the said Board; and where they shall so act shall be entitled to allowances as enumerators under the provisions of this Act; and every such overseer, relieving officer, constable, and other peace officer who shall refuse or wilfully neglect so to act, and duly to perform the duties required of the said enumerators by this Act, shall for every such offence forfeit a sum not more than ten pounds nor less than five pounds.

Returns of persons travelling, or on shipboard, or not in houses.

12. The Local Government Board shall obtain, by such ways and means as shall appear to them best adapted for the purpose, returns of the particulars required by this Act with respect to all persons who during the said night of Sunday the third day of April were travelling or on shipboard, or for any other reason were not abiding in any house of which account is to be taken by the enumerators and other persons as aforesaid, and shall include such returns in the abstract to be made by them as aforesaid.

Table of allowances to enumerators and others.

13. The said Board shall cause to be prepared a table of allowances to be made to the several enumerators, registrars, superintendent registrars, and other persons in England employed in the execution of this Act, and such table, when approved by the Treasury, shall be laid before both houses of Parliament on or before the first day of March one thousand eight hundred and eighty-one, if Parliament be sitting, or if Parliament be not sitting, then within the first fourteen days of the session then next ensuing.

Payments to be certified to the Registrar General.

14. The superintendent registrar of every district in England shall within one calendar month next after the taking of the census certify to the Registrar General the total amount of the allowances to which he, and the registrars, enumerators, and other persons in that district, are respectively entitled according to the said table.

Manner in which the payments shall be made to persons employed in execution of this Act in England.

15. The Treasury shall, through the Registrar General, pay to each superintendent registrar, out of the moneys provided by Parliament for that purpose, the whole amount of the allowances to which the said superintendent registrar, and the registrars, enumerators, and other persons in each district, are severally entitled according to the said table; and each superintendent registrar shall pay over to the registrars in his district the allowances to which they the said registrars are entitled, and shall also pay over or cause to be paid over to the enumerators and other persons in his district the allowances to which they are severally

entitled according to the said table; and the receipts to be given by the enumerators and other persons and registrars for payment of their said allowances shall be delivered to the superintendent registrar, who shall transmit the same, together with the receipt for his own allowance, to the Registrar General.

Provided that no such payment shall be made to any enumerator or other person who shall be required to act as an enumerator under this Act, but upon production of a certificate under the hand of the registrar that the duties required of such enumerator or other person acting as enumerator by this Act have been faithfully performed, and the like certificate shall be required under the hand of the superintendent registrar with respect to the registrar before any payment shall be made to the registrar, and the like certificate under the hand of the Registrar General with respect to the superintendent registrar before any payment shall be made to the superintendent registrar.

16. Every superintendent registrar and registrar, and every enumerator and other person who is bound under this Act if required to act as enumerator, making wilful default in any of the matters required of them respectively by this Act, or making any wilfully false declaration, shall for every such wilful default or false declaration forfeit a sum not exceeding five pounds nor less than two pounds. Penalty on persons for wilful default.

17. The enumerators and other persons employed in the execution of this Act shall be authorised to ask all such questions as shall be directed in any instructions to be prepared by or under the direction of the Local Government Board, which shall be necessary for obtaining the returns required by this Act; and every person refusing to answer or wilfully giving a false answer to such questions, or any of them, shall for every such refusal or wilfully false answer forfeit a sum not exceeding five pounds nor less than twenty shillings. Penalty for refusing information or giving false answers.

18. All penalties imposed by this Act shall be recovered in a summary manner before two justices of the peace having jurisdiction in the county or place where the offence is committed in the manner prescribed by law in this behalf. Recovery of penalties.

19. In this Act— Interpretation of terms.

The expression "civil parish" means a place for which a separate poor rate is or can be made, and has in the metropolis the same meaning as in the Metropolis Management Act, 1855. 18 & 19 Vict. c. 120.

The expression "dwelling-house" shall include all buildings and tenements of which the whole or any part shall be used for the purpose of human habitation.

The expression "Treasury" means the Commissioners of Her Majesty's Treasury.

20. This Act may be cited as the Census Act, 1880. Title of the Act.

LONDON: Printed by Eyre and Spottiswoode,
Printers to the Queen's most Excellent Majesty.
For Her Majesty's Stationery Office.

CENSUS OF ENGLAND AND WALES.

(43 & 44 VICT. c. 37.)

1881.

Vol. IV.

GENERAL REPORT.

Presented to both Houses of Parliament by Command of Her Majesty.

LONDON:
PRINTED BY EYRE AND SPOTTISWOODE.

To be purchased, either directly or through any Bookseller, from any of the following Agents, viz.,
Messrs. HANSARD & SON, 13, Great Queen Street, W.C., and 32, Abingdon Street, Westminster;
Messrs. EYRE & SPOTTISWOODE, East Harding Street, Fleet Street, and Sale Office, House of Lords;
Messrs. ADAM & CHARLES BLACK, of Edinburgh;
Messrs. ALEXANDER THOM & Co., or Messrs. HODGES, FIGGIS, & Co., of Dublin.

1883.

CENSUS—1881.

ISLANDS

IN THE

BRITISH SEAS.

ISLE OF MAN.

JERSEY.

GUERNSEY AND ADJACENT ISLANDS.

Presented to both Houses of Parliament by Command of Her Majesty.

LONDON:
PRINTED BY GEORGE E. B. EYRE AND WILLIAM SPOTTISWOODE.

To be purchased, either directly or through any Bookseller, from any of the following Agents, viz.,
Messrs. HANSARD, 13, Great Queen Street, W.C., and 32, Abingdon Street, Westminster;
Messrs. EYRE and SPOTTISWOODE, East Harding Street, Fleet Street, and Sale Office, House of Lords;
Messrs. ADAM and CHARLES BLACK, of Edinburgh;
Messrs. ALEXANDER THOM and Co., or Messrs. HODGES, FIGGIS, and Co., of Dublin.

1883.

CENSUS—1881.

ISLANDS

IN THE

BRITISH SEAS.

ISLE OF MAN.

JERSEY.

GUERNSEY AND ADJACENT ISLANDS.

Presented to both Houses of Parliament by Command of Her Majesty.

LONDON:
PRINTED BY GEORGE E. B. EYRE AND WILLIAM SPOTTISWOODE.

To be purchased, either directly or through any Bookseller, from any of the following Agents, viz.,
Messrs. HANSARD, 13, Great Queen Street, W.C., and 32, Abingdon Street, Westminster;
Messrs. EYRE and SPOTTISWOODE, East Harding Street, Fleet Street, and Sale Office, House of Lords;
Messrs. ADAM and CHARLES BLACK, of Edinburgh;
Messrs. ALEXANDER THOM and Co., or Messrs. HODGES, FIGGIS, and Co., of Dublin.

1883.

[C.—3643.] *Price 5d.*

TABLES

RELATING TO THE

ISLANDS IN THE BRITISH SEAS.

ISLE OF MAN.

TABLE 1.—AREA, HOUSES, and POPULATION in 1881, and at each of the SIX preceding CENSUSES.

Census Years.	Area in Statute Acres.	HOUSES.			POPULATION.			Increase of Population between the Censuses.	
		Inhabited.	Uninhabited.	Building.	PERSONS.	Males.	Females.	Number of Persons.	Rate per Cent.
- - -	145,325	6,627	279	49	40,081	19,158	20,923		
- -	,,	6,864	361	62	41,000	19,560	21,440	919	2·3
- - -	,,	7,978	370	56	47,975	23,011	24,964	6,975	17·0
- -	,,	8,613	434	62	52,387	24,915	27,472	4,412	9·2
- - -	,,	8,946	477	93	52,469	24,727	27,742	82	0·2
- -	,,	9,413	856	60	54,042	25,914	28,128	1,573	3·0
- - -	,,	9,425	1,018	112	54,089	26,291	27,798	47	0·1
CREASE IN 60 YEARS -	—	2,798	—	—	14,008	7,133	6,875	14,008	34·9

TABLE 2.—AREA, HOUSES, and POPULATION of CIVIL PARISHES in 1871 and 1881.

CIVIL PARISH.	Area in Statute Acres.	HOUSES 1871. Inhabited.	HOUSES 1871. Uninhabited.	HOUSES 1871. Building.	HOUSES 1881. Inhabited.	HOUSES 1881. Uninhabited.	HOUSES 1881. Building.	POPULATION Persons 1871.	POPULATION Persons 1881.	POPULATION Males 1871.	POPULATION Males 1881.	POPULATION Females 1871.	POPULATION Females 188
ick - - - - - -	10634w	515	55	1	470	46	4	2888	2626	1483	1385	1405	124
nan Parish—[1]													
German, Landward-part -	11679 w	333	34	–	316	24	8	1762	1691	891	867	871	82
Peel, Town - - -		524	12	3	565	18	8	3513	4360	1702	2426	1811	193
own - - - - - -	6585w	218	12	–	192	28	–	1123	990	548	498	575	49
hael - - - - -	8772w	254	17	2	281	29	2	1231	1101	596	536	635	56
augh - - - - -	6086w	232	23	–	225	14	2	1076	970	531	471	545	49
y - - - - - -	4721w	150	19	–	127	24	1	788	661	373	332	415	32
reas - - - - - -	7571w	356	33	–	324	45	–	1759	1482	854	710	905	77
ie - - - - - -	5801w	155	8	2	142	13	–	880	741	450	375	430	36
yre Parish—[2]													
Lezayre - - -	16277 w	338	23	1	304	37	3	1620	1486	788	737	832	74
Ramsey, Town, *part of* [a] - -		139	22	–	174	15	1	739	883	303	340	436	54
ghold Parish—[3]													
Maughold, Landward-part - -	9094 w	299	16	1	238	50	6	1432	1147	736	568	696	57
Ramsey, Town, *part of* [a] - -		546	68	6	551	34	10	3195	3142	1537	1492	1658	165
an - - - -	9423w	669	12	6	613	75	2	3740	3277	1911	1683	1829	159
chan Parish—[4]													
Conchan, Landward-part [b] - -	7880 w	293	27	–	286	27	1	1621	1508	747	697	874	81
Douglas, Town, *part of* [c] - -		1919	262	23	2266	272	47	12521	14977	5445	6720	7076	825
ldan Parish—[5]													
Douglas, Town, *part of* [c] - -	11454 w	138	19	–	106	19	1	1451	742	717	357	734	38
Braddan, Landward-part [d] -		401	33	1	349	53	–	2214	2071	1038	990	1176	108
nne - - - -	4250w	109	7	2	109	12	–	628	593	324	307	304	28
w Parish—[6]													
Malew, Landward-part [e] - -	12865 w	460	51	1	467	40	2	2467	2597	1290	1361	1177	123
Castletown, Town [f] - - -		439	65	6	429	70	4	2320	2243	1059	1016	1261	122
ry	4477w	262	23	2	251	24	–	1355	1274	659	626	696	64
en -	7456w	664	15	3	690	49	10	3719	3527	1932	1797	1787	173
Entire Civil Parishes:													
[1] German - - -	14679w	857	46	3	881	42	16	5275	6051	2593	3293	2682	275
[2] Lezayre - -	16277w	477	45	1	478	52	4	2359	2369	1091	1077	1268	129
[3] Maughold - - -	9094w	845	84	7	789	84	16	4627	4289	2273	2060	2354	222
[4] Conchan - -	7880w	2212	289	23	2552	299	48	14142	16485	6192	7417	7950	906
[5] Braddan - - -	11454w	539	52	1	455	72	1	3665	2813	1755	1347	1910	146
[6] Malew - - -	12865w	899	116	7	896	110	6	4787	4840	2349	2377	2438	246

ENERAL NOTES.—The areas of Parishes in the Isle of Man, which are reprinted from the Census Tables of 1871, were supplied
Ordnance Survey Department.
he above return of the population for 1881 includes 271 sailors and others, who on the night of the 3rd April 1881, were on board vess
e several harbours of the Island, and 1,256 fishermen (belonging to various parishes) who left the port of Peel, and 766 fishermen w
Rushen and other ports, during the month of March for the mackerel fishery at Kinsale. For details see Table 4.
e military in the barracks at Castletown, numbering with their families 31 persons, are also included in the above return.

he town of Ramsey is comprised partly in the parish of Lezayre and
in that of Maughold; the entire population is 4,025.
he return for the parish of Conchan, Landward-part, includes 52 persons
Douglas Industrial Home for Destitute Children.
he town of Douglas is comprised partly in the parish of Conchan and
in that of Braddan; the entire population is 15,719. The return for
art that is in Conchan parish includes 67 persons in the House of
stry, and 18 persons in the General Hospital and Dispensary. The
e of Industry is thus described in the enumeration book:—"This in-
" stitution is similar to an English workhouse, but is supported by volunt
" subscriptions, collections in churches, and interest on legacies."

[d] The return for the parish of Braddan, Landward-part, includes 185 p
sons in the General Lunatic Asylum.

[e] The return for the parish of Malew, Landward-part, includes 155 pers
in King William's College, a public school for boys.

[f] The return for the town of Castletown includes 38 persons in Castle Rus
Gaol, and 31 persons in military barracks.

R 6950. Wt. 545.

ISLE OF MAN—*continued.*

TABLE 3.—INHABITED HOUSES and POPULATION of such ECCLESIASTICAL DISTRICTS or PARISHES as are not entire Mother Parishes or that consist of more than one Civil Parish.

Ecclesiastical District or Parish.	Date of Formation.	Inhabited Houses.	Population.
ARBORY.			
Arbory, *part of*[1a]	—	251	1,274
BRADDAN.			
Braddan St. Brendan	—	349	2,071
Douglas St. George, *part of*[2b]	—	8	44
" St. Matthew, *part of*[3c]	1879	98	698
CONCHAN.			
Kirk-Onchan	—	344	1,773
Douglas St. Barnabas	1869	559	3,695
" St. George, *part of*[2b]	—	662	4,476
" St. Matthew, *part of*[3c]	1879	261	2,297
" St. Thomas	1872	726	4,244
LEZAYRE.			
Lezayre Kirk-Christ	—	366	1,812
Sulby St. Stephen	—	112	557
MAUGHOLD.			
St. Maughold	—	217	1,054
Ramsey St. Paul	1879	572	3,235
PATRICK.			
Kirk-Patrick	—	404	2,307
Dalby St. James	—	66	319
RUSHEN.			
Rushen Kirk-Christ	—	661	3,410
Arbory, *part of*[1a]	—	29	117
Entire Ecclesiastical Parishes:			
[1] Arbory	—	280	1,391
[2] Douglas St. George	—	670	4,520
[3] Douglas St. Matthew	1879	359	2,995

[a] The ecclesiastical parish of Arbory comprises the entire civil parish of that name and part of the civil parish of Rushen.
[b] The ecclesiastical parish of Douglas St. George comprises parts of the civil parishes of Braddan and Conchan.
[c] The ecclesiastical parish of Douglas St. Matthew comprises parts of the civil parishes of Braddan and Conchan.

TABLE 4.—NUMBER of PERSONS on board VESSELS in HARBOURS on the night of the 3rd April 1881, and of FISHERMEN who left the Ports of PEEL, RUSHEN, &c., for the Mackerel Fishery at KINSALE, during the month of March, all of whom were included among the General Population of PARISHES, &c.

Parish or Place.	Persons on board Vessels enumerated by Officers of H.M.'s Customs.		Fishermen at Kinsale specially enumerated.	Total Number of Persons.	Number of Vessels.
	On board British Vessels.	On board Foreign or Colonial Vessels.			
ISLE OF MAN	271	—	2,022	2,293	330
Patrick	—	—	231	231	330*
German, Landward part	—	—	99	99	
Peel, Town	25	—	531	556	
Marown	—	—	10	10	
Michael	—	—	50	50	
Ballaugh	—	—	30	30	
Jurby	—	—	25	25	
Andreas	—	—	40	40	
Bride	—	—	24	24	
Lezayre	—	—	10	10	
Maughold, Landward part	—	—	32	32	
Ramsey, Town (*the part in Maughold Parish*)	46	—	18	64	
Lonan	—	—	24	24	
Conchan, Landward part	—	—	9	9	
Douglas, Town (*the part in Conchan Parish*)	186	—	112	298	
Braddan, Landward part	—	—	19	19	
St. Anne	—	—	16	16	
Malew, Landward part	—	—	73	73	
Castletown, Town	6	—	54	60	
Arbory	—	—	98	98	
Rushen	8	—	522	530	

* Of these 330 vessels, 265 were fishing boats which left the various ports of the Island during the month of March for the mackerel fishery at Kinsale. 161 boats with 1,256 men started from the port of Peel, and 104 boats with 766 men from Rushen and other ports.

ISLE OF MAN—*continued.*

TABLE 5.—NUMBER of PERSONS in BARRACKS and in PUBLIC INSTITUTIONS.

PARISH.	NAME OF INSTITUTION.	TOTAL NUMBER OF INMATES, including Officers, &c.			NUMBER OF SPECIAL INMATES, such as Paupers, Patients, Lunatics, &c.		
		PERSONS.	Males.	Females.	PERSONS.	Males.	Females.
- -	House of Industry - -	67	41	26	65	40	25
	General Hospital and Dispensary -	18	5	13	14	4	10
	Douglas Industrial Home for Destitute Children - -	52	29	23	47	27	20
	General Lunatic Asylum - -	185	69	116	149	58	91
- - -	Military Barracks - -	31	28	3	24	24	—
	Gaol of Castle Rushen -	38	21	17	26	17	9

BLE 6.—NUMBER of BIRTHS and DEATHS registered in each of the Years 1871 to 1880.

—	1871.	1872.	1873.	1874.	1875.	1876.	1877.	1878.	1879.	1880.	Total in 10 Years.
- -	1,684	1,511	1,586	1,518	1,488	1,431	1,439	1,437	1,569	1,539	15,205
- -	1,200	1,039	1,122	1,040	1,308	1,058	1,129	1,174	1,122	1,180	11,872
of regis- Births Deaths -	484	472	464	478	180	376	310	263	447	359	3,833

This Table has been compiled from returns supplied by Mr. S. Harris, Registrar-General of the Isle of Man.

TABLE 7.—AGES of MALES and FEMALES.

	Persons.	Males.	Females.	Ages.	Persons.	Males.	Females.
-	54,089	26,291	27,798	35–	3,019	1,435	1,584
				40–	2,917	1,369	1,548
-	1,229	609	620	45–	2,424	1,086	1,338
-	1,233	633	600	50–	2,236	1,044	1,192
-	1,309	644	665	55–	1,881	863	1,018
-	1,253	630	623	60– -	1,902	888	1,014
-	1,369	665	704	65–	1,385	642	743
				70–	1,040	447	593
-	6,393	3,181	3,212	75–	616	278	338
-	6,364	3,192	3,172	80– -	304	121	183
-	6,206	3,183	3,023	85– -	107	48	59
-	5,704	2,949	2,755	90–	18	4	14
	4,712	2,285	2,427	95– -	2	–	2
	3,754	1,803	1,951	100 and upwards	1	1*	–
-	3,104	1,472	1,632				

* Stated to be aged 105.

TABLE 8.—AGES and CONDITION as to MARRIAGE of MALES and FEMALES.

—	All Ages.	Under 15 years.	15–	20–	25–	35–	45–	55–	65 and upwards.
d { Males	17,009	9,556	2,946	2,015	1,438	512	260	166	116
Females -	17,149	9,407	2,724	1,919	1,434	702	405	285	273
- { Males	8,234	–	3	267	1,786	2,165	1,734	1,350	929
Females -	8,086	–	31	500	2,040	2,135	1,673	1,109	598
- { Males -	1,048	–	–	3	51	127	136	235	496
Females	2,563	–	–	8	109	295	452	638	1,061
- { Males -	26,291	9,556	2,949	2,285	3,275	2,804	2,130	1,751	1,541
Females	27,798	9,407	2,755	2,427	3,583	3,132	2,530	2,032	1,932

ISLE OF MAN—*continued.*

TABLE 9.—OCCUPATIONS of MALES and FEMALES at DIFFERENT PERIODS of LIFE.

Ages of Males.								Occupations.	Ages of Females.							
Under 5 years.	5-	15-	20-	25-	45-	65 and upwards.	All Ages.		All Ages.	Under 5 years.	5-	15-	20-	25-	45-	65 and upwards.
3181	6675	2949	2285	6079	3881	1541	26291	TOTAL	27798	3312	6195	2755	2427	6715	4562	1832
								I. PROFESSIONAL CLASS.								
								1. PERSONS ENGAGED IN THE GENERAL OR LOCAL GOVERNMENT OF THE COUNTRY.								
								1. *National Government.*								
				3	3	1	7	Peer, M.P., Privy Councillor (not otherwise described)								
		4	4	15	17	4	44	Civil Service (officers and clerks)	3				1	1	1	
	9	6	3	6	2	1	27	Civil Service (messengers, &c.)	1				1			
				3	1		4	Prison Officer, &c.	2						2	
								2. *Local Government.*								
			2	32	7	1	42	Police								
				4	1	1	6	Municipal, Parish, Union, District, Officer								
					5	3	8	Other Local or County Official								
								3. *East Indian and Colonial Service.*								
								East Indian and Colonial Service								
								2. PERSONS ENGAGED IN THE DEFENCE OF THE COUNTRY.								
								1. *Army (at Home).*								
			1	7	13	10	31	Army Officer (effective or retired)								
		7	7	7	1	1	23	Soldier and Non-commissioned Officer								
				2	1	1	4	Militia, Yeomanry, Volunteers								
				4	22	5	31	Army Pensioner								
								2. *Navy (ashore or in port).*								
				1	2	2	5	Navy Officer (effective or retired)								
								Seaman, R.N.								
					3		3	Royal Marines (officers and men)								
				1	1		2	Navy Pensioner								
								3. PERSONS ENGAGED IN PROFESSIONAL OCCUPATIONS (WITH THEIR IMMEDIATE SUBORDINATES).								
								1. *Clerical Profession.*								
			3	16	23	6	48	Clergyman (Established Church)								
			1	1	1		3	Roman Catholic Priest								
			1	13	6		20	Minister, Priest, of other religious bodies								
			1	7	2	1	11	Missionary, Scripture Reader, Itinerant Preacher	4					3	1	
								Nun, Sister of Charity								
			4	1			5	Theological Student								
				1	2	2	5	Church, Chapel, Cemetery—Officer, Servant	1						1	
								2. *Legal Profession.*								
				28	10	6	44	Barrister, Solicitor								
		1	1				2	Law Student								
	4	8	5	4			21	Law Clerk, and others connected with Law								
								3. *Medical Profession.*								
				13	9	6	28	Physician, Surgeon, General Practitioner	1						1	
			1	1	1		3	Dentist								
		3	1	2			6	Medical Student, Assistant								
								Midwife	4					1	3	
								Subordinate Medical Service	40			2	5	14	12	7
								4. *Teachers.*								
	7	26	20	30	13	5	101	Schoolmaster	163		8	48	36	52	18	1
		2	3	4	6		15	Teacher, Professor, Lecturer	46			5	19	18	4	
								School Service, and others concerned in Teaching								
								5. *Literary and Scientific Persons.*								
			1	2	2		5	Author, Editor, Journalist								
		2	1				3	Reporter, Short-hand Writer								
								Persons engaged in Scientific Pursuits								
				2			2	Literary, Scientific, Institution, Service, &c.								
								6. *Engineers and Surveyors.*								
			1	2	2	1	6	Civil Engineer								
				1	4		5	Mining Engineer								
				2			2	Land, House, Ship, Surveyor								
								7. *Artists.*								
				3			3	Painter (artist)	2			1	1			
								Engraver (artist)								
								Sculptor								
				5			5	Architect								
				7	6	1	14	Musician, Music Master	14			2	3	8	1	
		1					1	Art Student	1					1		
	1	5	7	8	3		24	Photographer	1					1		
			1				1	Actor								
								Art, Music, Theatre, Service								

NOTE.—Persons returned as engaged in more than one occupation have been referred to the one that appeared to be of most importance; or, if there was no difference in this respect, to the one first given by the person in his or her return. In some cases special rules have been followed; *e.g.*, "Clergyman and Schoolmaster" in combination has always been referred to "Schoolmaster"; a Member of Parliament or Peer engaged in any branch of commerce or industry has always been referred to the latter, not to "Peer, M.P., &c."

The numbers returned under any heading include Labourers, Apprentices, and Assistants, as well as Masters, but not Clerks, Messengers, Errand boys, Porters, or Watchmen, for which occupations there are special headings. Civil, Military, and Naval Clerks, Law, Bank, Insurance, and Railway Clerks, and Government and Railway Porters, are, however, exceptions to this rule. Many young persons, being Apprentices or Assistants, have, therefore, been referred to occupations usually followed by adults. Women also, chiefly widows or orphans, carrying on the business of their deceased husbands or fathers, will sometimes be found under occupations commonly followed by men only.

Persons returned as *retired* from any business have not been referred to that business. Inmates of workhouses have been referred to their trades, unless their age or infirmities showed that they were past work. But persons who might be supposed to be only temporarily separated from their usual employment, such as Prisoners, and Patients in General Hospitals, have been classed under their usual occupations.

In some cases, for convenience of space, the male designation, *e.g.*, "Schoolmaster," alone is given, instead of "Schoolmaster, Schoolmistress."

ISLE OF MAN—*continued.*

TABLE 9.—OCCUPATIONS of MALES and FEMALES at DIFFERENT PERIODS of LIFE—*cont.*

Ages of Males.								Occupations.	Ages of Females.							
Under 5 years.	5-	15-	20-	25-	45-	65 and upwards.	All Ages.		All Ages.	Under 5 years.	5-	15-	20-	25-	45-	65 and upwards.
								8. *Persons engaged in Exhibitions, Shows, Games, &c.*								
.	.	.	.	.	.	.	.	Performer, Showman, Exhibition Service	.	.	.	.	.	.	.	.
.	1	1	2	2	1	1	8	Billiard, Cricket, and other Games, Service	.	.	.	.	.	.	.	.
								II. DOMESTIC CLASS.								
								4. PERSONS ENGAGED IN DOMESTIC OFFICES OR SERVICES.								
								1. *Domestic Service.*								
.	.	6	14	41	17	5	83	Domestic Coachman, Groom	.	.	.	.	.	.	.	.
.	2	12	15	74	70	35	208	Domestic Gardener	.	.	.	.	.	.	.	.
.	9	20	4	10	4	.	47	Domestic Indoor Servant	3487	.	215	1107	806	896	340	123
.	.	.	.	.	.	.	.	Lodge, Gate, Park, Keeper (not Government)	.	.	.	.	.	.	.	.
.	5	10	12	12	3	.	42	Inn, Hotel, Servant	67	.	.	14	22	20	.	1
.	.	.	.	1	.	.	1	College, Club, Service	.	.	.	.	.	.	.	.
								2. *Other Service.*								
.	.	.	.	.	.	.	.	Office Keeper (not Government)	2	.	.	.	.	1	1	.
.	.	.	1	.	.	.	1	Cook (not domestic)	.	.	.	.	.	.	.	.
.	.	.	.	.	.	.	.	Charwoman	211	.	.	.	5	81	97	28
.	.	.	.	2	1	.	3	Washing and Bathing Service	173	.	.	8	9	65	67	24
.	.	.	1	6	1	.	8	Hospital and Institution Service	7	.	.	.	.	6	1	.
.	.	.	.	.	1	.	1	Others engaged in Service	.	.	.	.	.	.	.	.
								III. COMMERCIAL CLASS.								
								5. PERSONS ENGAGED IN COMMERCIAL OCCUPATIONS.								
								1. *Merchants and Agents.*								
.	.	.	.	6	2	1	9	Merchant	1	.	.	.	.	1	.	.
.	.	.	3	28	11	2	44	Broker, Agent, Factor	.	.	.	.	.	.	.	.
.	.	1	.	3	9	2	15	Auctioneer, Appraiser, Valuer, House Agent	.	.	.	.	.	.	.	.
.	.	.	2	21	5	.	28	Accountant	.	.	.	.	.	.	.	.
.	.	.	.	1	.	1	2	Salesman, Buyer (not otherwise described)	7	.	.	.	3	4	.	.
.	.	.	4	16	4	.	24	Commercial Traveller	.	.	.	.	.	.	.	.
.	5	26	16	30	8	4	89	Commercial Clerk	7	.	1	1	.	3	.	.
.	.	.	.	.	.	.	.	Officer of Commercial Company, Guild, Society, &c.	.	.	.	.	.	.	.	.
								2. *Dealers in Money.*								
.	.	.	.	.	1	1	2	Banker	.	.	.	.	.	.	.	.
.	.	10	9	11	3	1	34	Bank Service	.	.	.	.	.	.	.	.
.	.	.	.	.	.	.	.	Bill Discounter, Bill Broker, Finance Agent	.	.	.	.	.	.	.	.
								3. *Persons occupied in Insurance.*								
.	.	.	.	8	2	.	10	Life, House, Ship, &c., Insurance Service	.	.	.	.	.	.	.	.
								6. PERSONS ENGAGED IN CONVEYANCE OF MEN, GOODS, AND MESSAGES.								
								1. *On Railways.*								
.	.	1	3	10	1	.	15	Railway Engine Driver, Stoker	.	.	.	.	.	.	.	.
.	.	.	.	5	2	.	7	Railway Guard	.	.	.	.	.	.	.	.
.	.	1	.	4	.	3	8	Pointsman, Level Crossing Man	3	.	.	.	.	1	1	1
.	2	18	11	35	8	.	80	Other Railway Officials and Servants	.	.	.	.	.	.	.	.
								2. *On Roads.*								
.	.	.	.	.	.	.	.	Toll Collector, Turnpike Gate Keeper	.	.	.	.	.	.	.	.
.	.	1	.	4	2	.	7	Omnibus, Coach, Cab, Owner—Livery Stable Keeper	1	.	.	.	.	1	.	.
.	.	2	1	2	2	.	7	Cabman, Flyman, Coachman (not domestic)	.	.	.	.	.	.	.	.
.	2	13	26	121	52	11	225	Carman, Carrier, Carter, Haulier	.	.	.	.	.	.	.	.
.	.	2	.	.	.	1	3	Tramway Companies' Service	.	.	.	.	.	.	.	.
.	.	.	.	.	.	.	.	Wheel Chair Proprietor, Attendant, &c.	.	.	.	.	.	.	.	.
								3. *On Canals, Rivers and Seas.*								
.	.	.	.	1	.	.	1	Inland Navigation Service	.	.	.	.	.	.	.	.
.	.	.	.	1	2	1	4	Bargeman, Lighterman, Waterman	.	.	.	.	.	.	.	.
.	.	.	.	2	3	1	6	Navigation Service (on shore)	.	.	.	.	.	.	.	.
.	.	68	94	334	182	51	729	Seaman (Merchant Service)	.	.	.	.	.	.	.	.
.	.	.	.	.	1	.	1	Pilot	.	.	.	.	.	.	.	.
.	1	9	6	10	1	.	27	Ship Steward, Cook	7	.	.	.	.	3	4	.
.	.	3	4	24	6	.	37	Boatman on Seas	.	.	.	.	.	.	.	.
.	.	.	4	28	24	1	57	Harbour, Dock, Wharf, Lighthouse, Service	.	.	.	.	.	.	.	.
								4. *In Storage.*								
.	.	.	.	1	5	.	6	Warehouseman (not Manchester)	.	.	.	.	.	.	.	.
.	.	.	.	.	.	.	.	Meter, Weigher	.	.	.	.	.	.	.	.
								5. *In conveying Messages, Porterage, &c.*								
.	39	36	8	17	12	3	115	Messenger, Porter, Watchman (not Railway nor Government)	3	.	2	.	.	.	1	.
.	.	2	2	2	1	.	7	Telegraph, Telephone, Service	6	.	1	.	2	2	1	.

ISLE OF MAN—*continued.*

TABLE 9.—OCCUPATIONS of MALES and FEMALES at DIFFERENT PERIODS of LIFE—*cont.*

Ages of Males.								Occupations.	Ages of Females.							
Under 5 years.	5-	15-	20-	25-	45-	65 and upwards.	All Ages.		All Ages.	Under 5 years.	5-	15-	20-	25-	45-	65 and upwards.
								IV. AGRICULTURAL CLASS.								
								7. PERSONS ENGAGED IN AGRICULTURE.								
								1. *In Fields and Pastures.*								
		1	20	359	500	181	1062	Farmer, Grazier	172			3	2	14	83	69
		167	132	233	25		557	Farmer's, Grazier's—Son, Grandson, Brother, Nephew*								
			1	11	9	1	22	Farm Bailiff								
	104	403	205	441	321	112	1586	Agricultural Labourer, Farm Servant, Cottager	153		6	17	11	37	64	18
		2		10	1	2	15	Shepherd								
								Land Drainage Service (not in towns)								
								Agricultural Machine — Proprietor, Attendant								
			1				1	Agricultural Student, Pupil								
								Others engaged in, or connected with, Agriculture								
								2. *In Woods.*								
								Woodman								
								3. *In Gardens.*								
		1	1	3	5	1	11	Nurseryman, Seedsman, Florist	1						1	
			1	4	2		7	Gardener (not domestic)								
								8. PERSONS ENGAGED ABOUT ANIMALS.								
								1. *About Animals.*								
					1	1	2	Horse Proprietor, Breeder, Dealer								
	1	1	5	6	1	1	15	Groom, Horse-keeper, Horse-breaker								
			3	3	6	2	14	Veterinary Surgeon, Farrier								
				1	1		2	Cattle, Sheep, Pig—Dealer, Salesman	1					1		
								Drover								
				2			2	Gamekeeper								
			1				1	Dog, Bird, Animal—Keeper, Dealer								
								Vermin Destroyer								
	138	554	539	1,041	311	50	2633	Fisherman								
								Knacker, Catsmeat Dealer, &c., &c.								
								V. INDUSTRIAL CLASS.								
								9. PERSONS WORKING AND DEALING IN BOOKS, PRINTS, AND MAPS.								
								1. *Books.*								
				5	4		9	Publisher, Bookseller, Librarian	4			2		1	1	
								Music—Publisher, Seller, Printer								
			1	2			3	Bookbinder	8			6		2		
	4	21	13	20	10		68	Printer								
				1			1	Newspaper Agent, News Room Keeper	1							1
								Others								
								2. *Prints and Maps.*								
			1				1	Lithographer, Lithographic Printer								
								Copper Plate, Steel Plate, Printer								
								Map, Print—Colourer, Seller								
								10. PERSONS WORKING AND DEALING IN MACHINES AND IMPLEMENTS.								
								1. *Machines.*								
				3	2		5	Engine, Machine, Maker								
		1	2	1	6	1	11	Millwright								
	1	4	3	12	5		25	Fitter, Turner (Engine and Machine)								
		2	3	5	1		11	Boiler Maker								
			1	1			2	Spinning and Weaving Machine Maker								
								Agricultural Machine and Implement Maker								
								Domestic Machinery—Maker, Dealer								
								2. *Tools and Implements.*								
								Tool Maker, Dealer								
		1		1	2		4	Cutler, Scissors Maker								
								File Maker								
								Saw Maker								
								Pin Maker								
								Needle Maker								
								Steel Pen Maker								
								Pencil Maker (Wood)								
								Domestic Implement Maker								
								3. *Watches and Philosophical Instruments.*								
		7	11	14	10		42	Watch Maker, Clock Maker	1					1		
								Philosophical Instrument Maker, Optician								
			1				1	Electrical Apparatus Maker								
				1			1	Weighing and Measuring Apparatus Maker								

* Only male relatives living with the farmer or grazier, and therefore presumably engaged in agriculture, are included above.

ISLE OF MAN—*continued.*

TABLE 9.—OCCUPATIONS of MALES and FEMALES at DIFFERENT PERIODS of LIFE—*cont.*

Males: Under 5 years.	Males: 5-	Males: 15-	Males: 20-	Males: 25-	Males: 45-	Males: 65 and upwards.	Males: All Ages.	OCCUPATIONS.	Females: All Ages.	Females: Under 5 years.	Females: 5-	Females: 15-	Females: 20-	Females: 25-	Females: 45-	Females: 65 and upwards.
								4. Surgical Instruments.								
.	.	.	.	.	1	.	1	Surgical Instrument Maker	.	.	.	.	.	.	.	.
								5. Arms and Ordnance.								
.	.	.	.	.	.	.	.	Gunsmith, Gun Manufacturer	.	.	.	.	.	.	.	.
.	.	.	.	.	.	.	.	Ordnance Manufacturer	.	.	.	.	.	.	.	.
.	.	.	.	.	.	.	.	Sword, Bayonet—Maker, Cutler	.	.	.	.	.	.	.	.
.	.	.	.	.	.	.	.	Others	.	.	.	.	.	.	.	.
								6. Musical Instruments.								
.	.	1	3	2	4	1	11	Musical Instrument Maker, Dealer	.	.	.	.	.	.	.	.
								7. Type, Dies, Medals, Coins.								
.	.	.	.	.	.	.	.	Type Cutter, Founder	.	.	.	.	.	.	.	.
.	.	.	.	.	.	.	.	Die, Seal, Coin, Medal, Maker	.	.	.	.	.	.	.	.
								8. Tackle for Sports and Games.								
.	.	.	.	.	.	.	.	Toy Maker, Dealer	1	.	.	.	.	.	1	.
.	.	.	.	.	.	.	.	Fishing Rod, Tackle, Maker, Dealer	.	.	.	.	.	.	.	.
.	.	.	.	.	.	.	.	Apparatus for other Games, Maker, Dealer	.	.	.	.	.	.	.	.
								11. PERSONS WORKING AND DEALING IN HOUSES, FURNITURE, AND DECORATIONS.								
								1. Houses.								
.	.	1	3	22	20	3	49	Builder	.	.	.	.	.	.	.	.
.	9	192	141	218	124	34	718	Carpenter, Joiner	.	.	.	.	.	.	.	.
.	.	.	2	1	.	.	3	Bricklayer	.	.	.	.	.	.	.	.
.	4	73	89	190	110	32	498	Mason	.	.	.	.	.	.	.	.
.	.	.	.	.	.	.	.	Slater, Tiler	.	.	.	.	.	.	.	.
.	.	21	22	33	12	1	89	Plasterer, Whitewasher	.	.	.	.	.	.	.	.
.	.	.	.	1	1	.	2	Paperhanger	.	.	.	.	.	.	.	.
.	3	21	9	18	3	.	54	Plumber	1	.	.	.	.	.	1	.
.	2	48	39	63	33	3	188	Painter, Glazier	.	.	.	.	.	.	.	.
								2. Furniture and Fittings.								
.	5	33	23	45	16	3	125	Cabinet Maker, Upholsterer	5	.	.	1	1	2	1	.
.	.	1	.	5	.	.	6	French Polisher	3	.	.	.	.	1	2	.
.	.	.	.	2	.	1	3	Furniture Broker, Dealer	.	.	.	.	.	.	.	.
.	.	.	.	1	.	.	1	Locksmith, Bellhanger	.	.	.	.	.	.	.	.
.	.	.	1	.	2	.	3	Gas Fitter	.	.	.	.	.	.	.	.
.	.	.	.	1	.	.	1	House and Shop Fittings—Maker, Dealer	.	.	.	.	.	.	.	.
.	.	.	.	.	.	.	.	Funeral Furniture Maker, Undertaker	.	.	.	.	.	.	.	.
.	.	.	.	.	.	.	.	Others	.	.	.	.	.	.	.	.
								3. House Decorations.								
.	.	.	.	.	1	.	1	Wood Carver	.	.	.	.	.	.	.	.
.	.	2	.	7	.	.	9	Carver, Gilder	.	.	.	.	.	.	.	.
.	.	.	.	.	.	.	.	Dealer in Works of Art	.	.	.	.	.	.	.	.
.	.	.	.	.	.	.	.	Figure, Image—Maker, Dealer	.	.	.	.	.	.	.	.
.	.	.	.	.	.	.	.	Animal, Bird, &c., Preserver, Naturalist	1	.	.	.	.	1	.	.
.	.	.	.	.	.	.	.	Artificial Flower Maker	.	.	.	.	.	.	.	.
								12. PERSONS WORKING AND DEALING IN CARRIAGES AND HARNESS.								
								1. Carriages.								
.	.	4	6	18	14	1	43	Coachmaker	1	.	.	.	.	.	.	1
.	.	.	.	.	.	.	.	Railway Carriage, Railway Wagon, Maker	.	.	.	.	.	.	.	.
.	.	1	.	.	1	1	3	Wheelwright	.	.	.	.	.	.	.	.
.	.	.	.	.	.	.	.	Bicycle, Tricycle—Maker, Dealer	.	.	.	.	.	.	.	.
.	.	1	1	2	2	1	7	Others	.	.	.	.	.	.	.	.
								2. Harness.								
.	3	10	5	13	10	5	46	Saddler, Harness, Whip, Maker	.	.	.	.	.	.	.	.
								13. PERSONS WORKING AND DEALING IN SHIPS AND BOATS.								
								1. Hull.								
.	1	2	.	15	2	1	21	Ship, Boat, Barge, Builder	.	.	.	.	.	.	.	.
.	.	17	12	38	25	6	98	Shipwright, Ship Carpenter (ashore)	.	.	.	.	.	.	.	.
								2. Masts, Rigging, &c.								
.	.	2	1	1	1	.	5	Mast, Yard, Oar, Block, Maker	.	.	.	.	.	.	.	.
.	.	.	.	2	3	.	5	Ship Rigger, Chandler, Fitter	.	.	.	.	.	.	.	.
.	2	10	7	10	4	2	35	Sail Maker	.	.	.	.	.	.	.	.

ISLE OF MAN—*continued.*

TABLE 9.—OCCUPATIONS of MALES and FEMALES at DIFFERENT PERIODS of LIFE—*cont.*

AGES OF MALES.								OCCUPATIONS.	AGES OF FEMALES.							
Under 5 years.	5–	15–	20–	25–	45–	65 and upwards.	All Ages.		All Ages.	Under 5 years.	5–	15–	20–	25–	45–	65 and upwards.
								14. PERSONS WORKING AND DEALING IN CHEMICALS AND COMPOUNDS.								
								1. *Colouring Matter.*								
.	.	.	.	1	1	.	2	Dye, Paint, Manufacture	1	.	.	.	.	1	.	.
.	.	.	.	.	.	.	.	Ink, Blacking, Colouring Substance, Manufacture	.	.	.	.	.	.	.	.
								2. *Explosives.*								
.	.	.	.	.	.	.	.	Gunpowder, Guncotton, Explosive Substance, Manufacture	.	.	.	.	.	.	.	.
.	.	.	.	.	1	.	1	Fusee, Fireworks, Explosive Article, Manufacture	.	.	.	.	.	.	.	.
								3. *Drugs and other Chemicals and Compounds.*								
.	2	6	8	20	6	1	43	Chemist, Druggist	2	.	.	.	1	1	.	.
.	1	1	.	4	3	.	9	Manufacturing Chemist	.	.	.	.	.	.	.	.
.	.	.	.	.	.	.	.	Alkali Manufacture	.	.	.	.	.	.	.	.
.	.	.	.	.	.	.	.	Drysalter	.	.	.	.	.	.	.	.
								15. PERSONS WORKING AND DEALING IN TOBACCO AND PIPES.								
								1. *Tobacco and Pipes.*								
.	6	6	2	18	5	2	39	Tobacco Manufacturer, Tobacconist	8	.	1	.	.	5	2	.
.	.	.	.	.	.	.	.	Tobacco Pipe, Snuff Box, &c., Maker	.	.	.	.	.	.	.	.
								16. PERSONS WORKING AND DEALING IN FOOD AND LODGING.								
								1. *Board and Lodging.*								
.	.	.	3	64	42	10	119	Innkeeper, Hotel Keeper, Publican	52	.	.	.	1	18	25	8
.	.	.	.	19	19	6	44	Lodging, Boarding, House Keeper	280	.	.	3	7	102	134	34
.	.	.	1	2	1	.	4	Coffee, Eating, House Keeper	4	.	.	2	1	1	.	.
								2. *Spirituous Drinks.*								
.	.	.	.	.	.	.	.	Hop—Merchant, Dealer	.	.	.	.	.	.	.	.
.	.	1	.	2	4	.	7	Maltster	.	.	.	.	.	.	.	.
.	.	1	2	12	7	1	23	Brewer	.	.	.	.	.	.	.	.
.	.	.	.	.	.	.	.	Beerseller, Ale, Porter, Cider, Dealer	.	.	.	.	.	.	.	.
.	.	.	.	1	2	.	3	Cellarman	.	.	.	.	.	.	.	.
.	.	3	.	6	6	1	16	Wine, Spirit—Merchant, Agent	.	.	.	.	.	.	.	.
								3. *Food.*								
.	.	.	3	3	5	2	13	Milkseller, Dairyman	46	.	1	8	10	14	9	4
.	.	.	.	.	.	.	.	Cheesemonger, Butterman	.	.	.	.	.	.	.	.
.	3	22	23	64	25	4	141	Butcher, Meat Salesman	5	.	.	.	.	2	2	1
.	.	1	.	7	6	2	15	Provision Curer, Dealer	30	.	.	.	.	13	11	6
.	.	1	.	2	4	.	7	Poulterer, Game Dealer	4	.	1	.	.	2	.	1
.	1	1	2	15	13	5	37	Fishmonger	7	.	.	.	.	1	5	1
.	.	6	2	10	5	3	26	Corn, Flour, Seed—Merchant, Dealer	6	.	.	1	.	3	2	.
.	2	12	8	30	22	8	82	Corn Miller	.	.	.	.	.	.	.	.
.	13	77	53	69	23	2	237	Baker	15	.	.	5	3	4	2	1
.	.	.	1	3	3	1	8	Confectioner, Pastrycook	49	.	.	11	11	16	11	.
.	.	1	1	8	2	2	14	Greengrocer, Fruiterer	24	.	.	1	4	12	6	1
.	.	.	.	.	.	.	.	Mustard, Vinegar, Spice, Pickle—Maker, Dealer	.	.	.	.	.	.	.	.
.	.	1	1	2	.	.	4	Sugar Refiner	2	.	.	.	.	1	1	.
.	6	57	26	90	32	13	224	Grocer, Tea, Coffee, Chocolate—Maker, Dealer	64	.	.	1	4	21	31	7
.	.	.	1	3	1	.	5	Ginger Beer, Mineral Water—Manufacturer, Dealer	.	.	.	.	.	.	.	.
.	.	.	.	.	.	.	.	Others dealing in Food	.	.	.	.	.	.	.	.
								17. PERSONS WORKING AND DEALING IN TEXTILE FABRICS.								
								1. *Wool and Worsted.*								
.	.	.	.	.	.	.	.	Woolstapler	.	.	.	.	.	.	.	.
.	5	6	3	16	19	11	60	Woollen Cloth Manufacture	16	.	.	1	.	6	4	5
.	.	.	.	2	3	.	5	Wool, Woollen Goods—Dyer, Printer	.	.	.	.	.	.	.	.
.	.	.	.	.	.	.	.	Worsted, Stuff, Manufacture	.	.	.	.	.	.	.	.
.	.	.	.	.	.	.	.	Flannel Manufacture	.	.	.	.	.	.	.	.
.	.	.	.	.	.	.	.	Blanket Manufacture	.	.	.	.	.	.	.	.
.	.	.	.	.	.	.	.	Fuller	.	.	.	.	.	.	.	.
.	.	.	.	.	.	.	.	Cloth, Worsted, Stuff, Flannel, Blanket, Dealer	.	.	.	.	.	.	.	.
.	.	.	.	.	1	2	3	Others	.	.	.	.	.	.	.	.
								2. *Silk.*								
.	.	.	.	.	.	.	.	Silk, Silk Goods, Manufacture	.	.	.	.	.	.	.	.
.	.	.	.	.	.	.	.	Silk Dyer, Printer	.	.	.	.	.	.	.	.
.	.	.	.	.	.	.	.	Ribbon Manufacture	.	.	.	.	.	.	.	.
.	.	.	.	.	.	.	.	Crape, Gauze, Manufacture	.	.	.	.	.	.	.	.
.	.	.	.	.	1	.	1	Silk Merchant, Dealer	.	.	.	.	.	.	.	.

ISLE OF MAN—*continued.*

TABLE 9.—OCCUPATIONS of MALES and FEMALES at DIFFERENT PERIODS of LIFE—*cont.*

Ages of Males.								Occupations.	Ages of Females.							
Under 5 years.	5–	15–	20–	25–	45–	65 and upwards.	All Ages.		All Ages.	Under 5 years.	5–	15–	20–	25–	45–	65 and upwards.
								3. Cotton and Flax.								
.	.	.	.	.	3	.	3	Cotton, Cotton Goods, Manufacture	3	.	.	1	.	2	.	.
.	.	.	.	.	.	.	.	Cotton, Calico—Printer, Dyer, Bleacher	.	.	.	.	.	.	.	.
.	.	.	.	.	.	.	.	Cotton, Calico—Warehouseman, Dealer	.	.	.	.	.	.	.	.
.	.	1	4	11	6	2	24	Flax, Linen—Manufacturer, Dealer	36	.	1	11	10	9	5	.
.	.	.	.	.	.	.	.	Lace Manufacturer, Dealer	2	.	.	.	.	.	2	.
.	.	.	.	.	.	.	.	Fustian Manufacturer, Dealer	.	.	.	.	.	.	.	.
.	.	.	.	.	.	.	.	Tape Manufacturer, Dealer	.	.	.	.	.	.	.	.
.	.	.	.	.	.	.	.	Thread Manufacturer, Dealer	.	.	.	.	.	.	.	.
								4. Hemp and other Fibrous Materials.								
.	.	.	.	.	.	.	.	Hemp, Jute, Cocoa Fibre, Manufacture	.	.	.	.	.	.	.	.
.	6	8	5	24	14	1	58	Rope, Twine, Cord—Maker, Dealer	6	.	.	2	2	2	.	.
.	.	.	.	.	.	.	.	Mat Maker, Seller	1	.	.	.	.	.	.	1
.	.	.	.	4	3	.	7	Net Maker	72	.	1	14	17	36	4	.
.	.	2	9	11	7	2	31	Canvas, Sailcloth, Manufacture	14	.	1	2	2	6	3	.
.	.	.	.	.	.	.	.	Sacking, Sack, Bag—Maker, Dealer	.	.	.	.	.	.	.	.
.	.	.	.	.	.	.	.	Others working and dealing in Hemp	.	.	.	.	.	.	.	.
								5. Mixed or Unspecified Materials.								
.	1	2	4	3	5	2	17	Weaver (undefined)	.	.	.	.	.	.	.	.
.	.	.	1	5	5	1	12	Dyer, Printer, Scourer, Bleacher, Calenderer (undefined)	.	.	.	.	.	.	.	.
.	.	.	.	2	.	.	2	Factory Hand (Textile, undefined)	.	.	.	.	.	.	.	.
.	.	.	.	.	.	.	.	Felt Manufacture	.	.	.	.	.	.	.	.
.	.	.	.	.	.	.	.	Carpet, Rug, Manufacture	.	.	.	.	.	.	.	.
.	.	.	.	1	.	.	1	Manchester Warehouseman	.	.	.	.	.	.	.	.
.	4	60	30	50	17	.	161	Draper, Linen Draper, Mercer	15	.	.	4	3	8	.	.
.	.	1	.	1	1	.	3	Fancy goods (Textile), Manufacturer, Worker, Dealer	6	.	.	1	.	3	2	.
.	.	.	.	.	.	.	.	Trimming Maker, Dealer	.	.	.	.	.	.	.	.
.	.	.	.	.	.	.	.	Embroiderer	.	.	.	.	.	.	.	.
.	.	.	.	.	.	.	.	Others	.	.	.	.	.	.	.	.
								18. PERSONS WORKING AND DEALING IN DRESS.								
								1. Dress.								
.	.	.	1	6	4	1	12	Hatter, Hat Manufacture (not straw)	4	.	.	.	.	1	2	1
.	.	.	.	.	.	.	.	Straw—Hat, Bonnet, Plait, Manufacture	1	.	.	1	.	.	.	.
.	6	65	60	113	91	30	365	Tailor	12	.	.	3	5	3	1	.
.	.	.	.	1	.	.	1	Milliner, Dressmaker, Staymaker	1315	.	34	428	309	389	132	23
.	.	.	.	.	.	.	.	Shawl Manufacture	.	.	.	.	.	.	.	.
.	.	.	.	.	.	.	.	Shirt Maker, Seamstress	106	.	1	3	11	34	43	14
.	.	.	.	.	.	.	.	Hosiery Manufacture	8	.	.	.	.	2	2	4
.	.	.	.	1	.	.	1	Hosier, Haberdasher	.	.	.	.	.	.	.	.
.	.	.	.	.	.	.	.	Glover, Glove Maker	.	.	.	.	.	.	.	.
.	.	.	.	.	.	.	.	Button Maker, Dealer	.	.	.	.	.	.	.	.
.	7	33	32	160	146	65	443	Shoe, Boot—Maker, Dealer	13	.	.	1	2	5	3	2
.	.	.	.	.	1	.	1	Patten, Clog, Maker	.	.	.	.	.	.	.	.
.	4	6	4	8	5	.	27	Wig Maker, Hairdresser	1	.	.	.	1	.	.	.
.	.	.	1	.	2	.	3	Umbrella, Parasol, Stick—Maker, Dealer	2	.	.	1	.	.	1	.
.	.	.	.	.	.	.	.	Accoutrement Maker	.	.	.	.	.	.	.	.
.	.	.	.	.	.	.	.	Old Clothes Dealer, and others	1	.	.	.	.	1	.	.
								19. PERSONS WORKING AND DEALING IN VARIOUS ANIMAL SUBSTANCES.								
								1. In Grease, Gut, Bone, Horn, Ivory, and Whalebone.								
.	.	.	.	3	3	.	6	Tallow Chandler, Candle, Grease, Manufacture	.	.	.	.	.	.	.	.
.	.	.	.	.	.	.	.	Soap Boiler, Maker	.	.	.	.	.	.	.	.
.	.	.	.	.	.	.	.	Glue, Size, Gelatine, Isinglass—Maker, Dealer	.	.	.	.	.	.	.	.
.	.	.	.	.	.	.	.	Manure Manufacture	.	.	.	.	.	.	.	.
.	.	.	.	.	.	.	.	Bone, Horn, Ivory, Tortoise-shell—Worker, Dealer	.	.	.	.	.	.	.	.
.	.	.	.	.	.	.	.	Comb Maker	.	.	.	.	.	.	.	.
.	.	.	.	.	.	.	.	Others	.	.	.	.	.	.	.	.
								2. In Skins.								
.	.	.	.	1	1	.	2	Furrier, Skinner	.	.	.	.	.	.	.	.
.	.	.	.	9	6	5	20	Tanner, Fellmonger	.	.	.	.	.	.	.	.
.	.	.	1	5	3	.	9	Currier	.	.	.	.	.	.	.	.
.	.	.	.	1	.	.	1	Leather goods, Portmanteau, Bag, Strap, &c.—Maker, Dealer	.	.	.	.	.	.	.	.
.	.	.	.	.	.	.	.	Parchment, Vellum—Maker, Dealer	.	.	.	.	.	.	.	.
								3. In Hair and Feathers.								
.	.	.	.	.	.	.	.	Hair, Bristle—Worker, Dealer	.	.	.	.	.	.	.	.
.	.	.	.	.	.	.	.	Brush, Broom, Maker	.	.	.	.	.	.	.	.
.	.	.	.	.	.	.	.	Quill, Feather—Dresser, Dealer	.	.	.	.	.	.	.	.

ISLE OF MAN—*continued.*

TABLE 9.—OCCUPATIONS of MALES and FEMALES at DIFFERENT PERIODS of LIFE—*cont.*

Ages of Males.								Occupations.	Ages of Females.							
Under 5 years.	5-	15-	20-	25-	45-	65 and upwards.	All Ages.		All Ages.	Under 5 years.	5-	15-	20-	25-	45-	65 and upwards.
								20. PERSONS WORKING AND DEALING IN VARIOUS VEGETABLE SUBSTANCES.								
								1. *In Oils, Gums, and Resins.*								
.	.	.	.	.	.	1	1	Oil Miller, Oil Cake—Maker, Dealer	.	.	.	.	.	.	.	.
.	.	.	.	.	.	.	.	Oil and Colourman	.	.	.	.	.	.	.	.
.	.	.	.	.	.	.	.	Floor Cloth, Oil Cloth, Manufacture	.	.	.	.	.	.	.	.
.	.	.	.	.	.	.	.	Japanner	.	.	.	.	.	.	.	.
.	.	.	.	.	.	.	.	India Rubber, Gutta Percha—Worker, Dealer	.	.	.	.	.	.	.	.
.	.	.	.	.	.	.	.	Waterproof Goods—Maker, Dealer	.	.	.	.	.	.	.	.
.	.	.	.	.	.	.	.	Others	.	.	.	.	.	.	.	.
								2. *In Cane, Rush, and Straw.*								
.	.	.	.	.	2	1	3	Willow, Cane, Rush—Worker, Dealer, Basket Maker	1	.	.	.	.	.	.	1
.	.	.	.	.	.	.	.	Hay, Straw (not plait), Chaff—Cutter, Dealer	.	.	.	.	.	.	.	.
.	.	.	.	.	.	.	.	Thatcher	.	.	.	.	.	.	.	.
								3. *In Wood and Bark.*								
.	.	.	.	5	4	.	9	Timber, Wood—Merchant, Dealer	.	.	.	.	.	.	.	.
.	.	.	1	9	11	4	25	Sawyer	.	.	.	.	.	.	.	.
.	.	.	.	2	2	1	5	Lath, Wooden Fence, Hurdle, Maker	.	.	.	.	.	.	.	.
.	.	1	.	4	.	.	5	Wood Turner, Box Maker	.	.	.	.	.	.	.	.
.	.	.	.	4	7	5	16	Cooper, Hoop Maker, Bender	.	.	.	.	.	.	.	.
.	.	.	.	1	.	.	1	Cork, Bark—Cutter, Worker, Dealer	.	.	.	.	.	.	.	.
.	.	.	.	.	.	.	.	Others	.	.	.	.	.	.	.	.
								4. *In Paper.*								
.	1	.	.	2	3	2	8	Paper Manufacture	.	.	.	.	.	.	.	.
.	.	.	.	.	.	.	.	Envelope Maker	.	.	.	.	.	.	.	.
.	.	2	.	2	.	.	4	Stationer, Law Stationer	9	.	.	1	.	5	3	.
.	.	.	.	.	.	.	.	Card, Pattern Card, Maker	.	.	.	.	.	.	.	.
.	.	.	.	.	.	.	.	Paper Stainer	.	.	.	.	.	.	.	.
.	.	.	.	.	.	.	.	Paper Box, Paper Bag, Maker	.	.	.	.	.	.	.	.
.	.	.	.	.	.	.	.	Ticket, Label, Writer	.	.	.	.	.	.	.	.
.	.	.	.	1	.	.	1	Others	.	.	.	.	.	.	.	.
								21. PERSONS WORKING AND DEALING IN VARIOUS MINERAL SUBSTANCES.								
								1. *Miners.*								
.	.	1	.	1	1	.	3	Coal Miner	.	.	.	.	.	.	.	.
.	.	.	.	2	1	.	3	Ironstone Miner	.	.	.	.	.	.	.	.
.	.	.	.	2	.	.	2	Copper Miner	.	.	.	.	.	.	.	.
.	.	.	.	.	.	.	.	Tin Miner	.	.	.	.	.	.	.	.
.	57	144	136	429	226	48	1040	Lead Miner	.	.	.	.	.	.	.	.
.	.	2	1	3	4	.	10	Miner in other, or undefined, Minerals	.	.	.	.	.	.	.	.
.	.	.	.	4	4	.	8	Mine Service	.	.	.	.	.	.	.	.
								2. *Coal, Coal Gas, &c.*								
.	.	.	.	4	8	2	14	Coal Merchant, Dealer	.	.	.	.	.	.	.	.
.	.	2	.	4	4	2	12	Coalheaver	.	.	.	.	.	.	.	.
.	.	.	.	.	.	.	.	Coke, Charcoal, Peat—Cutter, Burner, Dealer	.	.	.	.	.	.	.	.
.	1	1	.	8	3	.	13	Gas Works Service	.	.	.	.	.	.	.	.
								3. *Stone, Clay, and Road Making.*								
.	.	1	1	11	14	6	33	Stone Quarrier	.	.	.	.	.	.	.	.
.	1	8	4	9	3	1	26	Stone Cutter, Dresser, Dealer	.	.	.	.	.	.	.	.
.	.	.	.	.	.	.	.	Slate Quarrier	.	.	.	.	.	.	.	.
.	.	.	.	1	1	.	2	Slate Worker, Dealer	.	.	.	.	.	.	.	.
.	.	.	.	.	.	1	1	Limeburner	.	.	.	.	.	.	.	.
.	.	.	.	.	.	.	.	Clay, Sand, Gravel, Chalk—Labourer, Dealer	.	.	.	.	.	.	.	.
.	.	.	.	.	.	.	.	Fossil, Coprolite—Digger, Dealer	.	.	.	.	.	.	.	.
.	.	.	.	.	.	.	.	Well Sinker, Borer	.	.	.	.	.	.	.	.
.	.	.	.	.	.	.	.	Plaster, Cement, Manufacture	.	.	.	.	.	.	.	.
.	.	2	.	6	3	.	11	Brick, Tile—Maker, Burner, Dealer	.	.	.	.	.	.	.	.
.	.	.	.	.	.	.	.	Paviour	.	.	.	.	.	.	.	.
.	.	.	1	.	3	1	5	Road Contractor, Surveyor, Inspector	.	.	.	.	.	.	.	.
.	.	.	.	12	25	6	43	Road Labourer	.	.	.	.	.	.	.	.
.	.	.	.	.	.	.	.	Railway Contractor	.	.	.	.	.	.	.	.
.	.	.	3	19	4	.	26	Platelayer	.	.	.	.	.	.	.	.
.	.	1	2	7	5	.	15	Railway Labourer, Navvy	.	.	.	.	.	.	.	.
.	.	.	.	.	.	.	.	Others	.	.	.	.	.	.	.	.
								4. *Earthenware and Glass.*								
.	.	.	.	.	.	.	.	Earthenware, China, Porcelain, Manufacture	.	.	.	.	.	.	.	.
.	.	.	.	1	1	.	2	Glass Manufacture	.	.	.	.	.	.	.	.
.	.	.	1	1	2	1	5	Earthenware, China, Glass, Dealer	.	.	.	.	.	.	.	.
								5. *Salt.*								
.	.	.	.	.	1	.	1	Salt Maker, Dealer	.	.	.	.	.	.	.	.

ISLE OF MAN—*continued.*

TABLE 9.—OCCUPATIONS of MALES and FEMALES at DIFFERENT PERIODS of LIFE—*cont.*

AGES OF MALES.								OCCUPATIONS.	AGES OF FEMALES.							
Under 5 years.	5–	15–	20–	25–	45–	65 and upwards.	All Ages.		All Ages.	Under 5 years.	5–	15–	20–	25–	45–	65 and upwards.
								6. *Water.*								
.	.	.	.	2	.	.	2	Waterworks Service	.	.	.	.	.	.	.	.
.	.	.	.	.	.	.	.	Others	.	.	.	.	.	.	.	.
								7. *Precious Metals and Jewellery.*								
.	.	.	2	3	2	.	7	Goldsmith, Silversmith, Jeweller	.	.	.	.	.	.	.	.
.	.	.	.	.	.	.	.	Gold, Silver, Beater	.	.	.	.	.	.	.	.
.	.	.	.	.	.	.	.	Lapidary	.	.	.	.	.	.	.	.
.	.	.	.	.	.	.	.	Others	.	.	.	.	.	.	.	.
								8. *Iron and Steel.*								
.	4	50	46	93	61	17	271	Blacksmith	1	.	.	.	.	1	.	.
.	.	4	1	6	3	.	14	Whitesmith	.	.	.	.	.	.	.	.
.	.	.	.	.	1	5	6	Nail Manufacture	.	.	.	.	.	.	.	.
.	.	.	.	.	.	.	.	Anchor, Chain, Manufacture	.	.	.	.	.	.	.	.
.	2	5	1	9	8	1	26	Other Iron and Steel Manufactures	.	.	.	.	.	.	.	.
.	.	9	11	15	6	.	40	Ironmonger, Hardware Dealer, Merchant	4	.	.	.	1	2	.	1
								9. *Copper.*								
.	.	.	.	.	.	.	.	Copper, Copper goods—Manufacturer, Worker, Dealer	.	.	.	.	.	.	.	.
								10. *Tin and Zinc.*								
.	1	4	7	8	1	1	22	Tin, Tin Plate, Tin goods—Manufacturer, Worker, Dealer	.	.	.	.	.	.	.	.
.	.	.	.	.	.	.	.	Zinc, Zinc goods — Manufacturer, Worker, Dealer	.	.	.	.	.	.	.	.
								11. *Lead.*								
.	.	.	.	.	.	.	.	Lead, Leaden goods—Manufacturer, Worker, Dealer	6	.	.	.	.	.	5	1
								12. *In Other, Mixed, or Unspecified, Metals.*								
.	.	.	.	.	.	.	.	Metal Refiner, Worker, Turner, Dealer	.	.	.	.	.	.	.	.
.	.	.	.	3	2	.	5	Brass, Bronze, Manufacture. Brazier	.	.	.	.	.	.	.	.
.	.	.	.	.	.	.	.	Metal Burnisher, Lacquerer	.	.	.	.	.	.	.	.
.	.	.	.	.	.	.	.	White Metal, Plated Ware, Manufacture. Pewterer	.	.	.	.	.	.	.	.
.	.	.	.	.	.	1	1	Wire Maker, Worker, Weaver, Drawer	.	.	.	.	.	.	.	.
.	.	.	.	.	.	.	.	Bolt, Nut, Rivet, Screw, Staple, Maker	.	.	.	.	.	.	.	.
.	.	.	1	.	.	.	1	Lamp, Lantern, Candlestick, Maker	.	.	.	.	.	.	.	.
.	.	.	.	.	.	.	.	Clasp, Buckle, Hinge, Maker	.	.	.	.	.	.	.	.
.	.	.	.	.	.	.	.	Fancy Chain, Gilt Toy, Maker	.	.	.	.	.	.	.	.
.	.	.	.	.	.	.	.	Others	.	.	.	.	.	.	.	.
								22. PERSONS WORKING AND DEALING IN GENERAL OR UNSPECIFIED COMMODITIES.								
								1. *Makers and Dealers (General or Undefined).*								
.	1	4	4	12	14	4	39	General Shopkeeper, Dealer	95	.	.	8	10	31	36	10
.	.	.	.	.	1	.	1	Pawnbroker	1	.	.	1	.	.	.	.
.	.	2	2	6	7	4	21	Costermonger, Huckster, Street Seller	21	.	.	1	1	8	8	3
.	.	.	1	.	.	.	1	Manufacturer, Manager, Superintendent (undefined)	3	.	.	.	.	3	.	.
.	.	.	.	1	1	.	2	Contractor (undefined)	.	.	.	.	.	.	.	.
								2. *Mechanics and Labourers (General or Undefined).*								
.	15	62	75	256	233	78	719	General Labourer	54	.	.	3	2	17	23	9
.	.	2	8	32	16	2	60	Engine Driver, Stoker, Fireman (not railway, marine, nor agricultural)	.	.	.	.	.	.	.	.
.	.	3	7	8	2	2	22	Artizan, Mechanic (undefined)	.	.	.	.	.	.	.	.
.	1	2	.	.	.	.	3	Apprentice (undefined)	1	.	.	1	.	.	.	.
.	.	.	1	.	2	.	3	Factory Labourer (undefined)	2	.	.	.	.	1	1	.
.	.	.	.	2	1	1	4	Machinist, Machine Worker (undefined)	.	.	.	.	.	.	.	.
								23. PERSONS WORKING AND DEALING IN REFUSE MATTERS.								
								1. *Refuse Matters.*								
.	.	.	.	.	.	.	.	Town Drainage Service	.	.	.	.	.	.	.	.
.	2	.	1	.	4	.	7	Chimney Sweep, Soot Merchant	.	.	.	.	.	.	.	.
.	.	.	.	.	1	.	1	Scavenger, Crossing Sweeper	.	.	.	.	.	.	.	.
.	.	.	.	.	1	.	1	Rag Gatherer, Dealer	1	.	.	.	.	.	1	.
								VI. UNOCCUPIED CLASS.								
								24. PERSONS WITHOUT SPECIFIED OCCUPATIONS.								
3181	5858	349	55	177	801	427	10848	Persons returned by Property, Rank, &c., and not by special occupation	20758	3212	5021	1618	1081	4680	3827	1519

ISLE OF MAN—*continued.*

TABLE 10.—BIRTH-PLACES of PERSONS enumerated in the ISLE OF MAN.

Where Born.	Males.	Females.	Where Born.	Males.	Females.
Total enumerated	26,291	27,798	Foreign Parts (Foreign Subjects):		
			Denmark	—	2
			Norway	2	—
e of Man	22,592	23,392	Sweden	1	—
gland	2,328	2,869	Poland	4	—
les	113	70	Switzerland	1	1
otland	389	413	Germany	9	7
land	693	839	Holland	1	—
rsey	8	10	France	2	1
ernsey and adjacent Islands	2	2	Spain	1	—
tish Colonies and East Indies	70	114	Italy	1	1
rn at Sea (British Subjects)	1	9	America, United States	22	28
reign Parts (British Subjects)	51	40			

BLE 11.—NUMBER and AGES of MALES and FEMALES returned as "BLIND," as "DEAF AND DUMB," as "IDIOTS or IMBECILES," and as "LUNATICS," in the ISLE OF MAN.

Returned as	All Ages.			0–	5–	15–	20–	25–	45–	65 and upwards.
	Both Sexes.	Males and Females.								
nd	66	Males	37	—	3	1	—	7	8	18
		Females	29	—	1	1	—	3	7	17
f and Dumb	35	Males	24	—	5	1	3	9	5	1
		Females	11	1	5	1	—	2	1	1
atics	132	Males	44	—	—	1	—	25	15	3
		Females	88	—	—	1	3	26	40	18
ots or Imbeciles	57	Males	29	—	7	1	5	7	7	2
		Females	28	—	2	4	3	6	7	6

JERSEY.

ILE 1.—AREA, HOUSES, and POPULATION in 1881, and at each of the SIX preceding CENSUSES.

US YEARS.	AREA in Statute Acres.	HOUSES.			POPULATION.			Increase of Population between the Censuses.	
		In-habited.	Unin-habited.	Building.	PERSONS.	Males.	Females.	Number of Persons.	Rate per Cent.
- - -	28,717	4,053	41	28	28,600	13,056	15,544		
- - -	,,	4,990	115	50	36,582	17,006	19,576	7,982	27·9
- - -	,,	6,684	255	134	47,544	21,602	25,942	10,962	30·0
- - -	,,	7,918	333	69	57,020	26,238	30,782	9,476	19·9
- -	,,	8,338	367	46	55,613	24,843	30,770	−1,407	−2·5
- - -	,,	8,738	471	35	56,627	24,875	31,752	1,014	1·8
- -	,,	8,969	488	26	52,445	23,485	28,960	−4,182	−7·4
SE IN 60 YEARS	—	4,916	—	—	23,845	10,429	13,416	23,845	83·4

ie minus sign prefixed to certain figures in the column headed Increase of Population denotes a decrease instead of an increase in the population : shown.

population of Jersey amounted to 22,855 persons, viz., 10,312 males and 12,543 females; and in 1815 to 22,763 persons, viz., 10,496 males and s.

TABLE 2.—AREA, HOUSES, and POPULATION of CIVIL PARISHES in 1871 and 1881.

CIVIL PARISH.	Area in Statute Acres.	HOUSES.						POPULATION.					
		1871.			1881.			Persons.		Males.		Females.	
		Inhabited.	Uninhabited.	Building.	Inhabited.	Uninhabited.	Building.	1871.	1881.	1871.	1881.	1871.	1881.
- - - -	2125	4591	315	26	4649	305	7	30756	28020	13128	12160	17628	15860
b - - -	2296	638	28	1	677	23	2	3883	3890	1657	1785	2226	2105
t - - - -	1044	225	10	4	255	3	7	1445	1313	667	612	778	701
-	1935	391	17	–	412	19	4	2461	2385	1068	1095	1393	1290
e - - -	2455	507	28	1	528	53	–	3135	2913	1422	1424	1713	1489
- - -	3030	386	9	–	353	12	3	2149	2002	996	932	1153	1070
- -	2154	292	10	–	303	11	–	1699	1643	772	760	927	883
- - - - -	1602	167	6	–	196	7	–	1079	989	539	468	540	521
- - - -	3707	337	7	–	345	6	–	2247	2267	996	1059	1251	1208
- - -	2875	397	9	1	401	13	1	2524	2488	1178	1152	1346	1336
[f] - -	3157	414	19	–	443	14	2	2777	2192	1322	951	1455	1241
e - - - -	2337	393	13	2	407	22	–	2472	2343	1130	1087	1342	1256

L NOTES.—The areas are reprinted from the Census Tables of 1871.

ve return of the population for 1881 includes 211 sailors and others who, on the night of the 3rd April 1881, were on board vessels ral harbours of the Island. For details, see Table 4.

tary in barracks numbering, with their families, 853 persons, are also included in the above return.

rn for the parish of St. Helier includes 267 persons in the General d 47 in the Gaol and House of Correction, as well as the military milies in barracks, &c., 649 persons, and 164 persons on board e harbour.

rn for the parish of St. Saviour includes 127 persons in the Jersey lum.

rn for the parish of St. Martin includes 137 persons in the Jersey chool for boys, and 37 persons on board vessels in the harbour l on board H.M. Ship "Dasher").

[d] The return for the parish of St. Ouen includes 23 persons on board vessels in the harbour.

[e] The return for the parish of St. Peter includes the military and their families in barracks, 200 persons.

[f] The return for the parish of St. Brelade includes 11 persons in St. Aubin's Hospital, and 8 persons on board vessels in the harbour.

JERSEY—*continued.*

TABLE 3.—INHABITED HOUSES and POPULATION of such ECCLESIASTICAL DISTRICTS or PARISHES as are not entire Mother Parishes or that consist of more than one Civil Parish.

ECCLESIASTICAL DISTRICT OR PARISH.	Date of Formation.	HOUSES.			POPULATION.		
		Inhabited.	Uninhabited.	Building.	PERSONS.	Males.	Females.
ST. CLEMENT.							
St. Clement - - -	—	206	3	7	1,096	510	586
St. Luke, *part of* [1] *	1846	49	—	—	217	102	115
ST. HELIER.							
St. Helier	—	2,329	218	3	13,679	5,832	7,847
All Saints -	1868	788	31	4	4,450	1,906	2,544
St. Andrew -	1870	533	14	—	4,268	1,994	2,274
St. Luke, *part of* [1] *	1846	370	16	—	2,001	837	1,164
St. Simon -	1870	629	26	—	3,622	1,591	2,031
ST. SAVIOUR.							
St. Saviour -	—	506	18	—	3,026	1,424	1,602
St. Luke, *part of* [1] *	1846	171	5	2	864	361	503
Entire Ecclesiastical District:							
[1] St. Luke -	1846	590	21	2	3,082	1,300	1,782

* The ecclesiastical district of St. Luke comprises parts of the mother parishes of St. Clement, St. Helier, and St. Saviour.

TABLE 4.—NUMBER of PERSONS on board VESSELS in HARBOURS on the night of 3rd April 1881.

CIVIL PARISH.	Persons on board Vessels enumerated by the Officers of H.M.'s Customs.		Total Number of Persons.	Number of Vessels.
	On board British Vessels.	On board Foreign or Colonial Vessels.		
JERSEY -	201	10	211	33
St. Helier - - - - -	154	10	164	23
St. Martin - -	16	—	16	7
St. Ouen	23	—	23	1
St. Brelade	8	—	8	2

TABLE 5.—NUMBER of PERSONS in BARRACKS and on board H.M. SHIPS, and in PUBLIC INSTITUTIONS.

CIVIL PARISH.	NAME OF INSTITUTION.	TOTAL NUMBER OF INMATES, including Officers, &c.			NUMBER OF SPECIAL INMATES, such as Paupers, Patients, Lunatics, &c.		
		PERSONS.	Males.	Females.	PERSONS.	Males.	Females.
St. Helier - -	Fort Regent Barracks, Hospital, Military Prison, and Married Quarters -	467	406	61	385	385	—
	Elizabeth Castle and Old Married Quarters - - -	182	137	45	105	105	—
	Poor House and General Hospital -	267	122	145	259	119	140
	Her Majesty's Gaol and House of Correction - - - -	47	32	15	33	25	8
St. Saviour -	Jersey Lunatic Asylum -	127	48	79	107	40	67
St. Martin - -	H.M. Ship "Dasher" - - -	21	21	—	21	21	—
	Jersey Industrial School for Boys -	137	133	4	129	129	—
St. Peter - -	St. Peter's Barracks - - -	200	159	41	142	142	—
St. Brelade - -	St. Aubin's Fort - - -	4	2	2	1	1	—

JERSEY—*continued.*

ABLE 6.—NUMBER of BIRTHS and DEATHS registered in each of the Years 1871 to 1880.

—	1871.	1872.	1873.	1874.	1875.	1876.	1877.	1878.	1879.	1880.	Total in 10 Years.
- -	1,510	1,421	1,442	1,346	1,311	1,110	1,283	1,285	1,812	1,415	13,435
- -	1,268	1,301	1,051	1,081	1,299	947	1,316	1,062	1,099	1,147	11,571
of Regis- Births Deaths -	242	120	391	265	12	163	Defect –33	223	213	268	1,864

This table has been compiled from returns supplied by Colonel J. F. Murray, Government Secretary of Jersey.

TABLE 7.—AGES of MALES and FEMALES.

Persons.	Males.	Females.	Ages.	Persons.	Males.	Females.
52,445	23,485	28,960	35– -	3,323	1,443	1,880
1,170	584	586	40– -	3,117	1,277	1,840
999	520	479	45–	2,851	1,177	1,674
1,052	527	525	50–	2,778	1,128	1,650
1,064	531	533	55– -	2,213	922	1,291
1,017	503	514	60–	2,044	863	1,181
			65–	1,505	604	901
5,302	2,665	2,637	70–	1,007	401	606
5,113	2,528	2,584	75–	675	265	410
5,079	2,581	2,498	80– -	391	138	253
4,935	2,334	2,601	85–	110	33	77
4,549	1,910	2,639	90–	31	9	23
3,816	1,647	2,169	95–	9	3	6
3,596	1,557	2,039	100 and upwards	2	–	2*

* Both stated to be aged 100.

TABLE 8.—AGES and CONDITION as to MARRIAGE of MALES and FEMALES.

—	All Ages.	Under 15 years.	15–	20–	25–	35–	45–	55–	65 and upwards.
Males -	13,988	7,774	2,326	1,591	1,258	517	275	149	98
Females - -	16,277	7,719	2,544	1,977	1,645	920	723	409	340
Males -	8,538	–	8	316	1,895	2,124	1,865	1,391	939
Females - -	9,059	–	57	649	2,391	2,380	1,875	1,153	554
Males -	959	–	–	3	51	79	165	245	416
Females - -	3,624	–	–	13	172	420	725	910	1,388
Males -	23,485	7,774	2,334	1,910	3,204	2,720	2,305	1,785	1,453
Females - -	28,960*	7,719	2,601	2,639	4,208	3,720	3,324	2,472	2,277

JERSEY—*continued.*

TABLE 9.—OCCUPATIONS of MALES and FEMALES at DIFFERENT PERIODS of LIFE.

Ages of Males.								Occupations.	Ages of Females.							
Under 5 years.	5-	15-	20-	25-	45-	65 and upwards.	All Ages.		All Ages.	Under 5 years.	5-	15-	20-	25-	45-	65 and upwards.
2665	5109	2334	1910	5924	4090	1453	23485	TOTAL	28960	2637	5082	2601	2639	7928	5796	2277
								I. PROFESSIONAL CLASS.								
								1. PERSONS ENGAGED IN THE GENERAL OR LOCAL GOVERNMENT OF THE COUNTRY.								
								1. *National Government.*								
.	.	.	.	.	.	.	.	Peer, M.P., Privy Councillor (not otherwise described)	.	.	.	.	.	.	.	.
.	.	7	6	7	13	.	33	Civil Service (officers and clerks)	2	.	.	.	.	.	2	.
.	6	5	6	12	10	1	40	Civil Service (messengers, &c.)	.	.	.	.	.	.	.	.
.	.	.	.	3	3	.	6	Prison Officer, &c.	2	.	.	.	1	.	1	.
								2. *Local Government.*								
.	.	.	3	8	4	1	16	Police	.	.	.	.	.	.	.	.
.	.	.	1	6	5	8	20	Municipal, Parish, Union, District, Officer	.	.	.	.	.	.	.	.
.	.	.	.	3	7	2	12	Other Local or County Official	.	.	.	.	.	.	.	.
								3. *East Indian and Colonial Service.*								
.	.	.	1	.	.	.	1	East Indian and Colonial Service	.	.	.	.	.	.	.	.
								2. PERSONS ENGAGED IN THE DEFENCE OF THE COUNTRY.								
								1. *Army (at Home).*								
.	.	3	9	42	57	18	129	Army Officer (effective or retired)	.	.	.	.	.	.	.	.
.	8	207	166	288	4	1	674	Soldier and Non-commissioned Officer	.	.	.	.	.	.	.	.
.	.	4	3	9	7	.	23	Militia, Yeomanry, Volunteers	.	.	.	.	.	.	.	.
.	.	.	.	12	31	18	61	Army Pensioner	.	.	.	.	.	.	.	.
								2. *Navy (ashore or in port).*								
.	.	1	.	8	14	3	26	Navy Officer (effective or retired)	.	.	.	.	.	.	.	.
.	.	4	11	34	3	.	52	Seaman, R.N.	.	.	.	.	.	.	.	.
.	.	.	.	4	.	.	4	Royal Marines (officers and men)	.	.	.	.	.	.	.	.
.	.	.	.	12	24	5	41	Navy Pensioner	.	.	.	.	.	.	.	.
								3. PERSONS ENGAGED IN PROFESSIONAL OCCUPATIONS (WITH THEIR IMMEDIATE SUBORDINATES).								
								1. *Clerical Profession.*								
.	.	.	.	24	18	8	50	Clergyman (Established Church)	.	.	.	.	.	.	.	.
.	.	1	3	49	11	3	67	Roman Catholic Priest	.	.	.	.	.	.	.	.
.	.	.	2	9	6	.	17	Minister, Priest, of other religious bodies	.	.	.	.	.	.	.	.
.	.	.	.	1	3	.	4	Missionary, Scripture Reader, Itinerant Preacher	4	.	.	1	.	2	1	.
.	.	.	.	.	.	.	.	Nun, Sister of Charity	32	.	.	.	3	25	3	1
.	.	.	28	107	.	.	135	Theological Student	.	.	.	.	.	.	.	.
.	.	.	.	2	3	2	7	Church, Chapel, Cemetery—Officer, Servant	2	.	.	.	.	.	.	2
								2. *Legal Profession.*								
.	.	.	2	33	12	7	54	Barrister, Solicitor	.	.	.	.	.	.	.	.
.	.	1	.	.	.	.	1	Law Student	.	.	.	.	.	.	.	.
.	.	17	17	3	2	.	39	Law Clerk, and others connected with Law	.	.	.	.	.	.	.	.
								3. *Medical Profession.*								
.	.	.	2	26	19	8	55	Physician, Surgeon, General Practitioner	.	.	.	.	.	.	.	.
.	.	4	3	4	3	.	14	Dentist	.	.	.	.	.	.	.	.
.	.	3	5	.	.	.	8	Medical Student, Assistant	.	.	.	.	.	.	.	.
.	.	.	.	.	.	.	.	Midwife	10	.	.	.	.	2	2	6
.	.	.	1	2	2	.	5	Subordinate Medical Service	113	.	.	.	.	21	72	20
								4. *Teachers.*								
.	4	15	14	28	12	.	73	Schoolmaster	238	.	4	47	37	100	46	4
.	.	1	4	20	10	.	35	Teacher, Professor, Lecturer	115	.	.	14	28	55	15	3
.	.	.	.	.	.	.	.	School Service, and others concerned in Teaching	.	.	.	.	.	.	.	.
								5. *Literary and Scientific Persons.*								
.	.	.	.	3	1	.	4	Author, Editor, Journalist	1	.	.	.	.	1	.	.
.	.	.	.	1	1	.	2	Reporter, Short-hand Writer	.	.	.	.	.	.	.	.
.	1	.	.	1	.	1	3	Persons engaged in Scientific Pursuits	.	.	.	.	.	.	.	.
.	.	.	.	2	.	.	2	Literary, Scientific, Institution, Service, &c.	1	.	.	.	.	1	.	.
								6. *Engineers and Surveyors.*								
.	.	.	1	6	5	.	12	Civil Engineer	.	.	.	.	.	.	.	.
.	.	.	.	.	.	.	.	Mining Engineer	.	.	.	.	.	.	.	.
.	.	.	.	.	2	1	3	Land, House, Ship, Surveyor	.	.	.	.	.	.	.	.
								7. *Artists.*								
.	.	1	2	7	6	1	17	Painter (artist)	3	.	.	.	.	1	2	.
.	.	.	2	2	.	1	5	Engraver (artist)	.	.	.	.	.	.	.	.
.	.	.	.	1	2	.	3	Sculptor	.	.	.	.	.	.	.	.
.	.	.	1	2	2	1	6	Architect	.	.	.	.	.	.	.	.
.	2	5	6	18	14	2	47	Musician, Music Master	57	.	1	11	12	25	7	1
.	.	2	.	.	.	.	2	Art Student	1	.	.	.	1	.	.	.
.	1	1	6	12	8	.	28	Photographer	2	.	.	2	.	.	.	.
.	.	1	1	2	1	.	5	Actor	4	.	.	2	.	2	.	.
.	.	.	.	.	.	.	.	Art, Music, Theatre, Service	.	.	.	.	.	.	.	.

NOTE.—Persons returned as engaged in more than one occupation have been referred to the one that appeared to be of most importance; or, if there was no difference in this respect, to the one first given by the person in his or her return. In some cases special rules have been followed; *e.g.*, "Clergyman and Schoolmaster" in combination has always been referred to "Schoolmaster"; a Member of Parliament or Peer engaged in any branch of commerce or industry has always been referred to the latter, not to "Peer, M.P., &c."

The numbers returned under any heading include Labourers, Apprentices, and Assistants, as well as Masters, but not Clerks, Messengers, Errand boys, Porters, or Watchmen, for which occupations there are special headings. Civil, Military, and Naval Clerks, Law, Bank, Insurance, and Railway Clerks, and Government and Railway Porters, are, however, exceptions to this rule. Many young persons, being Apprentices or Assistants, have, therefore, been referred to occupations usually followed by adults. Women also, chiefly widows or orphans, carrying on the business of their deceased husbands or fathers, will sometimes be found under occupations commonly followed by men only.

Persons returned as *retired* from any business have not been referred to that business. Inmates of workhouses have been referred to their trades, unless their age or infirmities showed that they were past work. But persons who might be supposed to be only temporarily separated from their usual employment, such as Prisoners, and Patients in General Hospitals, have been classed under their usual occupations.

In some cases, for convenience of space, the male designation, *e.g.*, "Schoolmaster," alone is given, instead of "Schoolmaster, Schoolmistress."

JERSEY—*continued.*

TABLE 9.—OCCUPATIONS of MALES and FEMALES at DIFFERENT PERIODS of LIFE—*cont.*

Ages of Males.								Occupations.	Ages of Females.							
Under 5 years.	5-	15-	20-	25-	45-	65 and upwards.	All Ages.		All Ages.	Under 5 years.	5-	15-	20-	25-	45-	65 and upwards.
								8. *Persons engaged in Exhibitions, Shows, Games, &c.*								
.	.	.	.	.	.	.	.	Performer, Showman, Exhibition Service	.	.	.	.	.	.	.	.
.	.	2	1	2	.	.	5	Billiard, Cricket, and other Games, Service	.	.	.	.	.	.	.	.
								II. DOMESTIC CLASS.								
								4. PERSONS ENGAGED IN DOMESTIC OFFICES OR SERVICES.								
								1. *Domestic Service.*								
.	1	16	34	94	33	4	182	Domestic Coachman, Groom	.	.	.	.	.	.	.	.
.	7	31	35	128	113	23	337	Domestic Gardener	.	.	.	.	.	.	.	.
.	21	31	23	27	15	1	118	Domestic Indoor Servant	3081	.	164	810	696	887	436	88
.	.	.	.	.	.	1	1	Lodge, Gate, Park, Keeper (not Government)	1	.	.	.	.	1	.	.
.	2	13	15	27	4	1	62	Inn, Hotel, Servant	23	.	.	3	7	11	2	.
.	.	.	.	3	.	.	3	College, Club, Service	.	.	.	.	.	.	.	.
								2. *Other Service.*								
.	.	.	.	.	2	.	2	Office Keeper (not Government)	4	.	.	.	.	1	2	1
.	.	1	.	4	.	.	5	Cook (not domestic)	1	.	.	.	.	.	1	.
.	.	.	.	.	.	.	.	Charwoman	559	.	.	10	19	209	268	53
.	.	.	.	.	1	.	1	Washing and Bathing Service	773	.	11	54	87	283	280	58
.	.	.	.	10	6	1	17	Hospital and Institution Service	24	.	.	3	2	10	7	2
.	.	.	.	3	1	.	4	Others engaged in Service	.	.	.	.	.	.	.	.
								III. COMMERCIAL CLASS.								
								5. PERSONS ENGAGED IN COMMERCIAL OCCUPATIONS.								
								1. *Merchants and Agents.*								
.	.	2	3	36	35	9	85	Merchant	3	.	.	.	.	1	.	2
.	.	1	2	22	20	6	51	Broker, Agent, Factor	.	.	.	.	.	.	.	.
.	.	.	.	8	9	.	17	Auctioneer, Appraiser, Valuer, House Agent	.	.	.	.	.	.	.	.
.	.	.	1	12	4	1	18	Accountant	.	.	.	.	.	.	.	.
.	.	.	.	.	.	.	.	Salesman, Buyer (not otherwise described)	4	.	.	.	.	1	3	.
.	.	3	4	28	13	.	48	Commercial Traveller	.	.	.	.	.	.	.	.
.	2	42	42	69	22	3	180	Commercial Clerk	8	.	.	1	1	6	.	.
.	.	.	.	.	.	.	.	Officer of Commercial Company, Guild, Society, &c.	.	.	.	.	.	.	.	.
								2. *Dealers in Money.*								
.	.	.	.	4	3	1	8	Banker	.	.	.	.	.	.	.	.
.	.	3	6	17	4	2	32	Bank Service	.	.	.	.	.	.	.	.
.	.	.	.	.	1	.	1	Bill Discounter, Bill Broker, Finance Agent	.	.	.	.	.	.	.	.
								3. *Persons occupied in Insurance.*								
.	.	.	.	5	6	.	11	Life, House, Ship, &c., Insurance Service	.	.	.	.	.	.	.	.
								6. PERSONS ENGAGED IN CONVEYANCE OF MEN, GOODS, AND MESSAGES.								
								1. *On Railways.*								
.	.	.	.	6	.	.	6	Railway Engine Driver, Stoker	.	.	.	.	.	.	.	.
.	.	1	.	4	.	.	5	Railway Guard	.	.	.	.	.	.	.	.
.	.	.	.	.	4	1	5	Pointsman, Level Crossing Man	.	.	.	.	.	.	.	.
.	1	5	4	16	8	3	37	Other Railway Officials and Servants	.	.	.	.	.	.	.	.
								2. *On Roads.*								
.	.	.	.	.	.	.	.	Toll Collector, Turnpike Gate Keeper	.	.	.	.	.	.	.	.
.	.	.	2	10	18	1	31	Omnibus, Coach, Cab, Owner—Livery Stable Keeper	1	.	.	.	.	.	1	.
.	.	5	4	8	2	1	20	Cabman, Flyman, Coachman (not domestic)	.	.	.	.	.	.	.	.
.	2	18	30	69	54	1	174	Carman, Carrier, Carter, Haulier	.	.	.	.	.	.	.	.
.	.	.	.	.	.	.	.	Tramway Companies' Service	.	.	.	.	.	.	.	.
.	.	.	.	.	.	.	.	Wheel Chair Proprietor, Attendant, &c.	.	.	.	.	.	.	.	.
								3. *On Canals, Rivers and Seas.*								
.	.	.	.	.	.	.	.	Inland Navigation Service	.	.	.	.	.	.	.	.
.	.	.	1	4	3	.	8	Bargeman, Lighterman, Waterman	.	.	.	.	.	.	.	.
.	.	.	.	3	12	4	19	Navigation Service (on shore)	1	.	.	.	.	.	.	1
.	17	97	138	433	208	30	923	Seaman (Merchant Service)	.	.	.	.	.	.	.	.
.	.	.	1	9	1	4	15	Pilot	.	.	.	.	.	.	.	.
.	1	7	6	12	2	.	28	Ship Steward, Cook	9	.	.	.	.	8	1	.
.	.	1	.	2	4	1	8	Boatman on Seas	.	.	.	.	.	.	.	.
.	.	1	2	11	8	2	24	Harbour, Dock, Wharf, Lighthouse, Service	.	.	.	.	.	.	.	.
								4. *In Storage.*								
.	.	.	.	.	1	.	1	Warehouseman (not Manchester)	1	.	.	.	1	.	.	.
.	.	1	.	2	1	.	4	Meter, Weigher	.	.	.	.	.	.	.	.
								5. *In conveying Messages, Porterage, &c.*								
.	60	32	9	24	11	3	139	Messenger, Porter, Watchman (not Railway nor Government)	.	.	.	.	.	.	.	.
.	1	5	2	5	.	.	13	Telegraph, Telephone, Service	2	.	.	.	.	2	.	.

JERSEY—*continued*.

TABLE 9.—OCCUPATIONS of MALES and FEMALES at DIFFERENT PERIODS of LIFE—*cont.*

Ages of Males.								Occupations.	Ages of Females.							
Under 5 years.	5-	15-	20-	25-	45-	65 and upwards.	All Ages.		All Ages.	Under 5 years.	5-	15-	20-	25-	45-	65 and upwards.
								IV. AGRICULTURAL CLASS.								
								7. Persons engaged in Agriculture.								
								1. *In Fields and Pastures.*								
.	.	16	64	803	520	104	1507	Farmer, Grazier	200	.	.	3	4	58	45	90
.	.	177	143	140	9	.	469	Farmer's, Grazier's—Son, Grandson, Brother, Nephew*	.	.	.	.	.	.	.	.
.	.	.	.	4	1	.	5	Farm Bailiff	.	.	.	.	.	.	.	.
.	78	275	187	478	219	51	1286	Agricultural Labourer, Farm Servant, Cottager	272	.	5	29	44	126	67	11
.	.	.	.	.	.	.	.	Shepherd	.	.	.	.	.	.	.	.
.	.	.	.	.	.	.	.	Land Drainage Service (not in towns)	.	.	.	.	.	.	.	.
.	.	.	.	.	1	.	1	Agricultural Machine — Proprietor, Attendant	.	.	.	.	.	.	.	.
.	.	.	1	.	.	.	1	Agricultural Student, Pupil	.	.	.	.	.	.	.	.
.	.	.	1	1	1	.	3	Others engaged in, or connected with, Agriculture	.	.	.	.	.	.	.	.
								2. *In Woods.*								
.	.	.	.	.	.	.	.	Woodman	.	.	.	.	.	.	.	.
								3. *In Gardens.*								
.	.	2	2	8	11	3	26	Nurseryman, Seedsman, Florist	1	.	.	.	.	.	1	.
.	.	3	1	7	5	3	19	Gardener (not domestic)	3	.	.	1	.	1	1	.
								8. Persons engaged about Animals.								
								1. *About Animals.*								
.	.	.	.	2	.	.	2	Horse Proprietor, Breeder, Dealer	.	.	.	.	.	.	.	.
.	.	4	3	1	5	.	13	Groom, Horse-keeper, Horse-breaker	.	.	.	.	.	.	.	.
.	.	.	.	10	7	.	17	Veterinary Surgeon, Farrier	.	.	.	.	.	.	.	.
.	.	.	.	6	4	.	10	Cattle, Sheep, Pig—Dealer, Salesman	.	.	.	.	.	.	.	.
.	.	.	.	.	.	.	.	Drover	.	.	.	.	.	.	.	.
.	.	.	.	.	.	.	.	Gamekeeper	.	.	.	.	.	.	.	.
.	.	.	.	.	.	.	.	Dog, Bird, Animal—Keeper, Dealer	.	.	.	.	.	.	.	.
.	.	.	.	.	2	.	2	Vermin Destroyer	.	.	.	.	.	.	.	.
.	2	7	14	61	49	14	147	Fisherman	.	.	.	.	.	.	.	.
.	.	.	.	.	.	.	.	Knacker, Catsmeat Dealer, &c., &c.	.	.	.	.	.	.	.	.
								V. INDUSTRIAL CLASS.								
								9. Persons working and dealing in Books, Prints, and Maps.								
								1. *Books.*								
.	.	.	1	6	3	1	11	Publisher, Bookseller, Librarian	14	.	.	3	1	5	3	2
.	.	.	.	.	.	.	.	Music—Publisher, Seller, Printer	2	.	.	.	.	1	1	.
.	1	2	3	3	1	1	11	Bookbinder	1	.	.	.	.	1	.	.
.	16	15	17	29	13	2	92	Printer	.	.	.	.	.	.	.	.
.	.	.	.	2	.	.	2	Newspaper Agent, News Room Keeper	.	.	.	.	.	.	.	.
.	.	.	.	.	.	.	.	Others	.	.	.	.	.	.	.	.
								2. *Prints and Maps.*								
.	.	.	.	.	.	.	.	Lithographer, Lithographic Printer	.	.	.	.	.	.	.	.
.	.	.	.	.	.	.	.	Copper Plate, Steel Plate, Printer	.	.	.	.	.	.	.	.
.	.	.	.	.	.	.	.	Map, Print—Colourer, Seller	.	.	.	.	.	.	.	.
								10. Persons working and dealing in Machines and Implements.								
								1. *Machines.*								
.	.	1	1	5	1	.	8	Engine, Machine, Maker	.	.	.	.	.	.	.	.
.	.	.	1	1	.	.	2	Millwright	.	.	.	.	.	.	.	.
.	.	7	4	8	5	.	24	Fitter, Turner (Engine and Machine)	.	.	.	.	.	.	.	.
.	.	.	.	.	.	.	.	Boiler Maker	.	.	.	.	.	.	.	.
.	.	.	.	.	.	.	.	Spinning and Weaving Machine Maker	.	.	.	.	.	.	.	.
.	.	.	.	.	.	.	.	Agricultural Machine and Implement Maker	.	.	.	.	.	.	.	.
.	.	.	.	.	.	.	.	Domestic Machinery—Maker, Dealer	.	.	.	.	.	.	.	.
								2. *Tools and Implements.*								
.	.	.	.	.	.	.	.	Tool Maker, Dealer	.	.	.	.	.	.	.	.
.	.	1	.	2	1	1	5	Cutler, Scissors Maker	.	.	.	.	.	.	.	.
.	.	.	.	.	.	.	.	File Maker	.	.	.	.	.	.	.	.
.	.	.	.	.	.	.	.	Saw Maker	.	.	.	.	.	.	.	.
.	.	.	.	.	.	.	.	Pin Maker	.	.	.	.	.	.	.	.
.	.	.	.	.	.	.	.	Needle Maker	.	.	.	.	.	.	.	.
.	.	.	.	.	.	.	.	Steel Pen Maker	.	.	.	.	.	.	.	.
.	.	.	.	.	.	.	.	Pencil Maker (Wood)	.	.	.	.	.	.	.	.
.	.	.	.	.	.	.	.	Domestic Implement Maker	.	.	.	.	.	.	.	.
								3. *Watches and Philosophical Instruments.*								
.	3	10	6	23	8	3	53	Watch Maker, Clock Maker	1	.	.	.	1	.	.	.
.	.	1	.	1	2	.	4	Philosophical Instrument Maker, Optician	1	.	.	.	.	1	.	.
.	.	.	.	.	.	.	.	Electrical Apparatus Maker	.	.	.	.	.	.	.	.
.	.	.	.	.	2	.	2	Weighing and Measuring Apparatus Maker	.	.	.	.	.	.	.	.

* Only male relatives living with the farmer or grazier, and therefore presumably engaged in agriculture, are included above.

JERSEY—*continued.*

TABLE 9.—OCCUPATIONS of MALES and FEMALES at DIFFERENT PERIODS of LIFE—*cont.*

Males: Under 5 years	5-	15-	20-	25-	45-	65 and upwards	All Ages	OCCUPATIONS.	Females: All Ages	Under 5 years	5-	15-	20-	25-	45-	65 and upwards
								4. Surgical Instruments.								
.	.	.	.	.	1	.	1	Surgical Instrument Maker	.	.	.	.	.	.	.	.
								5. Arms and Ordnance.								
.	.	.	1	2	1	.	4	Gunsmith, Gun Manufacturer	.	.	.	.	.	.	.	.
.	.	.	.	.	.	.	.	Ordnance Manufacturer	.	.	.	.	.	.	.	.
.	.	.	.	.	.	.	.	Sword, Bayonet—Maker, Cutler	.	.	.	.	.	.	.	.
.	.	.	.	.	.	.	.	Others	.	.	.	.	.	.	.	.
								6. Musical Instruments.								
.	.	.	2	7	2	.	11	Musical Instrument Maker, Dealer	.	.	.	.	.	.	.	.
								7. Type, Dies, Medals, Coins.								
.	.	.	.	.	.	.	.	Type Cutter, Founder	.	.	.	.	.	.	.	.
.	.	.	.	.	.	.	.	Die, Seal, Coin, Medal, Maker	.	.	.	.	.	.	.	.
								8. Tackle for Sports and Games.								
.	.	.	.	.	1	.	1	Toy Maker, Dealer	5	.	1	1	.	2	.	1
.	.	.	.	.	.	.	.	Fishing Rod, Tackle, Maker, Dealer	.	.	.	.	.	.	.	.
.	.	.	1	.	.	.	1	Apparatus for other Games, Maker, Dealer	.	.	.	.	.	.	.	.
								11. PERSONS WORKING AND DEALING IN HOUSES, FURNITURE, AND DECORATIONS.								
								1. Houses.								
.	.	.	4	16	24	5	49	Builder	.	.	.	.	.	.	.	.
.	38	128	90	261	158	44	719	Carpenter, Joiner	.	.	.	.	.	.	.	.
.	1	3	.	4	8	1	17	Bricklayer	.	.	.	.	.	.	.	.
.	17	39	42	109	111	22	340	Mason	.	.	.	.	.	.	.	.
.	.	.	.	1	.	.	1	Slater, Tiler	.	.	.	.	.	.	.	.
.	19	63	52	107	43	9	293	Plasterer, Whitewasher	.	.	.	.	.	.	.	.
.	.	2	1	6	5	3	17	Paperhanger	.	.	.	.	.	.	.	.
.	5	13	6	15	7	2	48	Plumber	.	.	.	.	.	.	.	.
.	8	14	36	80	37	4	179	Painter, Glazier	.	.	.	.	.	.	.	.
								2. Furniture and Fittings.								
.	11	29	14	33	32	9	128	Cabinet Maker, Upholsterer	13	.	.	.	1	5	6	1
.	.	4	2	4	.	.	10	French Polisher	1	.	.	.	.	1	.	.
.	1	2	.	4	2	2	11	Furniture Broker, Dealer	9	.	.	.	.	3	4	2
.	1	.	1	4	2	.	8	Locksmith, Bellhanger	.	.	.	.	.	.	.	.
.	4	3	7	9	5	1	29	Gas Fitter	.	.	.	.	.	.	.	.
.	.	.	1	.	.	.	1	House and Shop Fittings—Maker, Dealer	.	.	.	.	.	.	.	.
.	.	2	.	5	2	2	11	Funeral Furniture Maker, Undertaker	.	.	.	.	.	.	.	.
.	.	.	.	.	.	.	.	Others	.	.	.	.	.	.	.	.
								3. House Decorations.								
.	.	.	.	1	1	.	2	Wood Carver	.	.	.	.	.	.	.	.
.	.	.	1	4	1	1	7	Carver, Gilder	.	.	.	.	.	.	.	.
.	.	.	1	3	.	.	4	Dealer in Works of Art	.	.	.	.	.	.	.	.
.	.	.	.	.	.	.	.	Figure, Image—Maker, Dealer	.	.	.	.	.	.	.	.
.	.	.	.	3	.	.	3	Animal, Bird, &c., Preserver, Naturalist	.	.	.	.	.	.	.	.
.	.	.	.	.	.	.	.	Artificial Flower Maker	.	.	.	.	.	.	.	.
								12. PERSONS WORKING AND DEALING IN CARRIAGES AND HARNESS.								
								1. Carriages.								
.	2	19	9	30	17	1	78	Coachmaker	2	.	.	.	.	1	1	.
.	.	.	.	.	.	.	.	Railway Carriage, Railway Waggon, Maker	.	.	.	.	.	.	.	.
.	2	6	6	8	5	2	29	Wheelwright	.	.	.	.	.	.	.	.
.	.	.	.	.	.	.	.	Bicycle, Tricycle—Maker, Dealer	.	.	.	.	.	.	.	.
.	.	.	.	.	.	.	.	Others	.	.	.	.	.	.	.	.
								2. Harness.								
.	2	13	7	15	6	2	45	Saddler, Harness, Whip, Maker	.	.	.	.	.	.	.	.
								13. PERSONS WORKING AND DEALING IN SHIPS AND BOATS.								
								1. Hull.								
.	.	.	1	8	9	6	24	Ship, Boat, Barge, Builder	.	.	.	.	.	.	.	.
.	.	8	18	93	45	14	178	Shipwright, Ship Carpenter (ashore)	.	.	.	.	.	.	.	.
								2. Masts, Rigging, &c.								
.	1	2	.	5	4	1	13	Mast, Yard, Oar, Block, Maker	.	.	.	.	.	.	.	.
.	1	.	.	2	5	.	8	Ship Rigger, Chandler, Fitter	.	.	.	.	.	.	.	.
.	2	8	6	13	11	1	41	Sail Maker	.	.	.	.	.	.	.	.

JERSEY—*continued.*

TABLE 9.—OCCUPATIONS of MALES and FEMALES at DIFFERENT PERIODS of LIFE—*cont.*

Ages of Males.								Occupations.	Ages of Females.							
Under 5 years.	5-	15-	20-	25-	45-	65 and upwards.	All Ages.		All Ages.	Under 5 years.	5-	15-	20-	25-	45-	65 and upwards.
								14. PERSONS WORKING AND DEALING IN CHEMICALS AND COMPOUNDS.								
								1. *Colouring Matter.*								
.	.	.	.	1	.	.	1	Dye, Paint, Manufacture	1	.	.	.	1	.	.	.
.	.	.	.	.	1	.	1	Ink, Blacking, Colouring Substance, Manufacture	.	.	.	.	.	.	.	.
								2. *Explosives.*								
.	.	.	.	.	.	.	.	Gunpowder, Guncotton, Explosive Substance, Manufacture	.	.	.	.	.	.	.	.
.	.	.	.	.	.	1	1	Fusee, Fireworks, Explosive Article, Manufacture	.	.	.	.	.	.	.	.
								3. *Drugs and other Chemicals and Compounds.*								
.	.	5	4	21	8	2	40	Chemist, Druggist	1	.	.	.	.	1	.	.
.	.	.	.	1	2	3	5	Manufacturing Chemist	1	.	.	.	.	1	.	.
.	.	.	.	.	.	.	.	Alkali Manufacture	.	.	.	.	.	.	.	.
.	.	.	.	.	.	.	.	Drysalter	.	.	.	.	.	.	.	.
								15. PERSONS WORKING AND DEALING IN TOBACCO AND PIPES.								
								1. *Tobacco and Pipes.*								
.	3	5	1	20	16	1	46	Tobacco Manufacturer, Tobacconist	5	.	.	.	1	2	1	1
.	.	.	.	.	.	.	.	Tobacco Pipe, Snuff Box, &c., Maker	.	.	.	.	.	.	.	.
								16. PERSONS WORKING AND DEALING IN FOOD AND LODGING.								
								1. *Board and Lodging.*								
.	.	.	4	77	61	14	152	Innkeeper, Hotel Keeper, Publican	64	.	1	.	1	25	34	3
.	.	.	.	.	4	4	8	Lodging, Boarding, House Keeper	151	.	.	1	3	54	73	20
.	.	.	.	8	3	.	11	Coffee, Eating, House Keeper	4	.	.	1	.	1	.	2
								2. *Spirituous Drinks.*								
.	.	.	.	.	.	.	.	Hop—Merchant, Dealer	.	.	.	.	.	.	.	.
.	.	.	.	2	2	.	4	Maltster	.	.	.	.	.	.	.	.
.	.	3	2	10	3	1	19	Brewer	.	.	.	.	.	.	.	.
.	.	.	.	.	.	.	.	Beerseller. Ale, Porter, Cider, Dealer	.	.	.	.	.	.	.	.
.	.	.	1	1	1	1	4	Cellarman	.	.	.	.	.	.	.	.
.	.	1	2	14	13	3	33	Wine, Spirit—Merchant, Agent	.	.	.	.	.	.	.	.
								3. *Food.*								
.	1	3	2	4	7	1	18	Milkseller, Dairyman	47	.	.	6	6	25	7	3
.	.	.	1	1	.	.	2	Cheesemonger, Butterman	7	.	.	.	.	1	6	.
.	10	35	18	53	48	5	169	Butcher, Meat Salesman	15	.	.	3	.	3	8	1
.	.	1	.	3	4	.	8	Provision Curer, Dealer	10	.	.	1	4	3	2	.
.	.	3	.	3	1	.	7	Poulterer, Game Dealer	1	.	.	.	.	.	.	1
.	.	.	2	4	1	.	7	Fishmonger	22	.	.	.	1	8	11	2
.	.	1	1	7	5	.	14	Corn, Flour, Seed—Merchant, Dealer	4	.	.	.	.	2	2	.
.	1	5	7	21	12	3	49	Corn Miller	.	.	.	.	.	.	.	.
.	13	39	18	67	41	6	184	Baker	21	.	.	2	2	4	11	2
.	1	6	4	10	4	4	29	Confectioner, Pastrycook	15	.	.	1	2	8	4	.
.	.	1	1	9	16	.	27	Greengrocer, Fruiterer	34	.	.	.	.	5	22	7
.	.	.	.	.	2	1	3	Mustard, Vinegar, Spice, Pickle—Maker, Dealer	.	.	.	.	.	.	.	.
.	.	.	.	1	.	.	1	Sugar Refiner	.	.	.	.	.	.	.	.
.	3	24	20	51	47	12	157	Grocer. Tea, Coffee, Chocolate—Maker, Dealer	154	.	2	14	15	57	56	10
.	.	2	2	5	.	1	10	Ginger Beer, Mineral Water—Manufacturer, Dealer	.	.	.	.	.	.	.	.
.	.	.	.	.	.	.	.	Others dealing in Food	.	.	.	.	.	.	.	.
								17. PERSONS WORKING AND DEALING IN TEXTILE FABRICS.								
								1. *Wool and Worsted.*								
.	.	.	.	1	.	.	1	Woolstapler	.	.	.	.	.	.	.	.
.	.	.	.	.	.	.	.	Woollen Cloth Manufacture	.	.	.	.	.	.	.	.
.	.	.	.	.	.	.	.	Wool, Woollen Goods—Dyer, Printer	.	.	.	.	.	.	.	.
.	.	.	.	.	.	.	.	Worsted, Stuff, Manufacture	1	.	.	.	.	.	1	.
.	.	.	.	.	.	.	.	Flannel Manufacture	.	.	.	.	.	.	.	.
.	.	.	.	.	.	.	.	Blanket Manufacture	.	.	.	.	.	.	.	.
.	.	.	.	.	.	.	.	Fuller	.	.	.	.	.	.	.	.
.	.	.	.	.	.	.	.	Cloth, Worsted, Stuff, Flannel, Blanket, Dealer	.	.	.	.	.	.	.	.
.	.	.	.	.	.	.	.	Others	.	.	.	.	.	.	.	.
								2. *Silk.*								
.	.	.	.	.	.	.	.	Silk, Silk Goods, Manufacture	.	.	.	.	.	.	.	.
.	.	.	.	.	.	.	.	Silk Dyer, Printer	.	.	.	.	.	.	.	.
.	.	.	.	.	.	.	.	Ribbon Manufacture	.	.	.	.	.	.	.	.
.	.	.	.	.	.	.	.	Crape, Gauze, Manufacture	.	.	.	.	.	.	.	.
.	.	.	.	.	1	.	1	Silk Merchant, Dealer	.	.	.	.	.	.	.	.

JERSEY—*continued.*

TABLE 9.—OCCUPATIONS of MALES and FEMALES at DIFFERENT PERIODS of LIFE—*cont.*

Ages of Males. Under 5 years.	5-	15-	20-	25-	45-	65 and upwards.	All Ages.	Occupations.	Ages of Females. All Ages.	Under 5 years.	5-	15-	20-	25-	45-	65 and upwards.
								3. *Cotton and Flax.*								
.	.	.	.	.	1	.	1	Cotton, Cotton Goods, Manufacture	.	.	.	.	.	.	.	.
.	.	.	.	.	.	.	.	Cotton, Calico—Printer, Dyer, Bleacher	.	.	.	.	.	.	.	.
.	.	.	.	.	.	.	.	Cotton, Calico—Warehouseman, Dealer	.	.	.	.	.	.	.	.
.	.	.	.	.	.	.	.	Flax, Linen—Manufacturer, Dealer	.	.	.	.	.	.	.	.
.	.	.	.	1	.	.	1	Lace Manufacturer, Dealer	4	.	.	.	.	2	1	1
.	.	.	.	.	.	.	.	Fustian Manufacturer, Dealer	.	.	.	.	.	.	.	.
.	.	.	.	.	.	.	.	Tape Manufacturer, Dealer	.	.	.	.	.	.	.	.
.	.	.	.	.	.	.	.	Thread Manufacturer, Dealer	.	.	.	.	.	.	.	.
								4. *Hemp and other Fibrous Materials.*								
.	.	.	.	.	.	.	.	Hemp, Jute, Cocoa Fibre, Manufacture	.	.	.	.	.	.	.	.
.	7	3	6	12	11	2	41	Rope, Twine, Cord—Maker, Dealer	1	.	.	.	.	.	1	.
.	.	.	.	.	.	.	.	Mat Maker, Seller	1	.	.	.	.	.	1	.
.	.	.	.	.	.	.	.	Net Maker	.	.	.	.	.	.	.	.
.	.	.	.	.	.	.	.	Canvas, Sailcloth, Manufacture	.	.	.	.	.	.	.	.
.	.	.	.	.	.	.	.	Sacking, Sack, Bag—Maker, Dealer	.	.	.	.	.	.	.	.
.	.	.	.	.	.	.	.	Others working and dealing in Hemp	.	.	.	.	.	.	.	.
								5. *Mixed or Unspecified Materials.*								
.	.	.	.	.	.	.	.	Weaver (undefined)	.	.	.	.	.	.	.	.
.	5	.	3	10	3	1	24	Dyer, Printer, Scourer, Bleacher, Calenderer (undefined)	2	.	.	1	.	.	1	.
.	.	.	.	.	.	.	.	Factory Hand (Textile, undefined)	.	.	.	.	.	.	.	.
.	.	.	.	.	.	.	.	Felt Manufacture	.	.	.	.	.	.	.	.
.	.	.	.	.	.	1	1	Carpet, Rug, Manufacture	2	.	.	.	1	1	.	.
.	.	.	.	.	.	.	.	Manchester Warehouseman	.	.	.	.	.	.	.	.
.	13	35	23	41	41	8	161	Draper, Linen Draper, Mercer	105	.	.	25	28	34	18	.
.	.	.	.	1	.	.	1	Fancy goods (Textile), Manufacturer, Worker, Dealer	15	.	.	3	5	3	3	1
.	.	.	.	.	.	.	.	Trimming Maker, Dealer	1	.	.	.	.	1	.	.
.	.	.	.	1	.	.	1	Embroiderer	1	.	.	.	.	1	.	.
.	.	.	.	.	.	.	.	Others	.	.	.	.	.	.	.	.
								18. PERSONS WORKING AND DEALING IN DRESS.								
								1. *Dress.*								
.	.	1	.	1	6	1	9	Hatter, Hat Manufacture (not straw)	3	.	.	1	.	1	1	.
.	.	.	.	.	.	.	.	Straw—Hat, Bonnet, Plait, Manufacture	.	.	.	.	.	.	.	.
.	22	51	38	65	46	23	245	Tailor	434	.	47	94	55	142	84	12
.	3	.	.	.	.	1	4	Milliner, Dressmaker, Staymaker	2283	.	103	498	434	809	384	55
.	.	.	.	.	.	.	.	Shawl Manufacture	.	.	.	.	.	.	.	.
.	.	.	.	.	1	.	1	Shirt Maker, Seamstress	146	.	2	12	11	44	63	14
.	.	.	.	.	.	.	.	Hosiery Manufacture	9	.	.	.	2	.	4	3
.	.	2	1	4	1	.	8	Hosier, Haberdasher	5	.	.	1	.	1	3	.
.	.	.	.	.	.	.	.	Glover, Glove Maker	1	.	.	.	.	.	.	1
.	.	.	.	.	.	.	.	Button Maker, Dealer	.	.	.	.	.	.	.	.
.	21	39	40	141	164	46	451	Shoe, Boot—Maker, Dealer	26	.	.	2	5	7	11	1
.	.	.	.	.	1	.	1	Patten, Clog, Maker	.	.	.	.	.	.	.	.
.	5	7	3	12	13	2	42	Wig Maker, Hairdresser	2	.	.	.	2	.	.	.
.	.	1	.	2	2	.	5	Umbrella, Parasol, Stick—Maker, Dealer	7	.	.	1	2	1	3	.
.	.	.	.	.	.	.	.	Accoutrement Maker	.	.	.	.	.	.	.	.
.	.	.	.	.	.	.	.	Old Clothes Dealer, and others	1	.	.	.	.	.	1	.
								19. PERSONS WORKING AND DEALING IN VARIOUS ANIMAL SUBSTANCES.								
								1. *In Grease, Gut, Bone, Horn, Ivory, and Whalebone.*								
.	.	.	.	.	1	.	1	Tallow Chandler, Candle, Grease, Manufacture	1	.	.	.	.	1	.	.
.	.	1	.	2	1	.	4	Soap Boiler, Maker	.	.	.	.	.	.	.	.
.	.	.	.	.	.	.	.	Glue, Size, Gelatine, Isinglass—Maker, Dealer	.	.	.	.	.	.	.	.
.	.	.	.	.	.	.	.	Manure Manufacture	.	.	.	.	.	.	.	.
.	.	.	.	.	.	.	.	Bone, Horn, Ivory, Tortoise-shell—Worker, Dealer	.	.	.	.	.	.	.	.
.	.	.	.	.	.	.	.	Comb Maker	.	.	.	.	.	.	.	.
.	.	.	.	.	.	.	.	Others	.	.	.	.	.	.	.	.
								2. *In Skins.*								
.	.	.	.	.	.	.	.	Furrier, Skinner	4	.	.	.	.	2	1	1
.	.	.	.	2	1	2	5	Tanner, Fellmonger	.	.	.	.	.	.	.	.
.	.	.	3	4	6	1	14	Currier	1	.	.	.	.	.	1	.
.	.	1	.	.	.	1	2	Leather goods, Portmanteau, Bag, Strap, &c.—Maker, Dealer	1	.	.	.	.	1	.	.
.	.	.	.	.	.	.	.	Parchment, Vellum—Maker, Dealer	.	.	.	.	.	.	.	.
								3. *In Hair and Feathers.*								
.	.	.	.	.	.	.	.	Hair, Bristle—Worker, Dealer	.	.	.	.	.	.	.	.
.	1	.	.	2	1	1	5	Brush, Broom, Maker	.	.	.	.	.	.	.	.
.	.	.	.	.	.	.	.	Quill, Feather—Dresser, Dealer	1	.	.	.	.	.	1	.

JERSEY—*continued.*

TABLE 9.—OCCUPATIONS of MALES and FEMALES at DIFFERENT PERIODS of LIFE—*cont.*

Males: Under 5 years.	Males: 5-	Males: 15-	Males: 20-	Males: 25-	Males: 45-	Males: 65 and upwards.	Males: All Ages.	OCCUPATIONS.	Females: All Ages.	Females: Under 5 years.	Females: 5-	Females: 15-	Females: 20-	Females: 25-	Females: 45-	Females: 65 and upwards.
								20. PERSONS WORKING AND DEALING IN VARIOUS VEGETABLE SUBSTANCES.								
								1. In Oils, Gums, and Resins.								
.	.	.	.	1	.	1	2	Oil Miller, Oil Cake—Maker, Dealer	.	.	.	.	.	.	.	.
.	.	.	.	.	.	.	.	Oil and Colourman	1	.	.	.	.	1	.	.
.	.	.	.	.	.	.	.	Floor Cloth, Oil Cloth, Manufacture	.	.	.	.	.	.	.	.
.	.	.	.	.	.	.	.	Japanner	.	.	.	.	.	.	.	.
.	.	.	.	.	.	.	.	India Rubber, Gutta Percha—Worker, Dealer	.	.	.	.	.	.	.	.
.	.	.	.	.	.	.	.	Waterproof Goods—Maker, Dealer	.	.	.	.	.	.	.	.
.	.	.	.	.	.	.	.	Others	.	.	.	.	.	.	.	.
								2. In Cane, Rush, and Straw.								
.	1	8	1	9	4	1	24	Willow, Cane, Rush—Worker, Dealer, Basket Maker	3	.	1	.	.	1	1	.
.	.	.	.	.	.	.	.	Hay, Straw (not plait), Chaff—Cutter, Dealer	.	.	.	.	.	.	.	.
.	.	4	2	6	9	2	23	Thatcher	.	.	.	.	.	.	.	.
								3. In Wood and Bark.								
.	1	2	2	3	6	3	17	Timber, Wood—Merchant, Dealer	2	.	.	.	.	.	2	.
.	1	1	1	7	3	3	16	Sawyer	.	.	.	.	.	.	.	.
.	.	1	1	3	1	.	6	Lath, Wooden Fence, Hurdle, Maker	.	.	.	.	.	.	.	.
.	.	.	.	1	.	.	1	Wood Turner, Box Maker	.	.	.	.	.	.	.	.
.	4	5	11	42	18	3	83	Cooper. Hoop Maker, Bender	.	.	.	.	.	.	.	.
.	.	.	.	1	.	.	1	Cork, Bark—Cutter, Worker, Dealer	.	.	.	.	.	.	.	.
.	.	.	.	.	.	.	.	Others	.	.	.	.	.	.	.	.
								4. In Paper.								
.	.	.	.	.	.	.	.	Paper Manufacture	.	.	.	.	.	.	.	.
.	.	.	.	.	.	.	.	Envelope Maker	.	.	.	.	.	.	.	.
.	.	1	.	3	2	.	6	Stationer, Law Stationer	9	.	.	1	3	3	2	.
.	.	.	.	.	.	.	.	Card, Pattern Card, Maker	.	.	.	.	.	.	.	.
.	.	.	.	.	.	.	.	Paper Stainer	.	.	.	.	.	.	.	.
.	.	.	.	.	.	.	.	Paper Box, Paper Bag, Maker	1	.	.	1	.	.	.	.
.	.	.	.	.	.	.	.	Ticket, Label, Writer	.	.	.	.	.	.	.	.
.	.	.	.	2	.	.	2	Others	.	.	.	.	.	.	.	.
								21. PERSONS WORKING AND DEALING IN VARIOUS MINERAL SUBSTANCES.								
								1. Miners.								
.	.	.	1	.	.	.	1	Coal Miner	.	.	.	.	.	.	.	.
.	.	.	.	.	.	.	.	Ironstone Miner	.	.	.	.	.	.	.	.
.	.	.	.	.	.	.	.	Copper Miner	.	.	.	.	.	.	.	.
.	.	.	.	.	.	.	.	Tin Miner	.	.	.	.	.	.	.	.
.	.	.	.	.	.	.	.	Lead Miner	.	.	.	.	.	.	.	.
.	.	.	.	1	.	.	1	Miner in other, or undefined, Minerals	.	.	.	.	.	.	.	.
.	.	.	.	.	1	.	1	Mine Service	.	.	.	.	.	.	.	.
								2. Coal, Coal Gas, &c.								
.	.	.	2	15	10	3	30	Coal Merchant, Dealer	1	.	.	.	.	.	1	.
.	1	.	1	1	3	.	6	Coalheaver	.	.	.	.	.	.	.	.
.	.	.	.	.	.	.	.	Coke, Charcoal, Peat—Cutter, Burner, Dealer	.	.	.	.	.	.	.	.
.	.	.	1	8	5	.	14	Gas Works Service	.	.	.	.	.	.	.	.
								3. Stone, Clay, and Road Making.								
.	1	6	8	30	19	4	68	Stone Quarrier	.	.	.	.	.	.	.	.
.	.	5	9	24	24	4	66	Stone Cutter, Dresser, Dealer	.	.	.	.	.	.	.	.
.	.	.	.	.	.	.	.	Slate Quarrier	.	.	.	.	.	.	.	.
.	.	.	.	.	.	.	.	Slate Worker, Dealer	.	.	.	.	.	.	.	.
.	.	.	.	.	.	.	.	Limeburner	.	.	.	.	.	.	.	.
.	.	.	.	2	1	1	4	Clay, Sand, Gravel, Chalk—Labourer, Dealer	.	.	.	.	.	.	.	.
.	.	.	.	.	.	.	.	Fossil, Coprolite—Digger, Dealer	.	.	.	.	.	.	.	.
.	.	1	.	1	2	.	4	Well Sinker, Borer	.	.	.	.	.	.	.	.
.	.	.	.	.	.	.	.	Plaster, Cement, Manufacture	.	.	.	.	.	.	.	.
.	7	7	9	12	9	5	49	Brick, Tile—Maker, Burner, Dealer	.	.	.	.	.	.	.	.
.	.	.	.	.	.	.	.	Paviour	.	.	.	.	.	.	.	.
.	.	.	.	.	.	1	1	Road Contractor, Surveyor, Inspector	.	.	.	.	.	.	.	.
.	.	.	.	6	5	2	13	Road Labourer	.	.	.	.	.	.	.	.
.	.	.	.	.	.	.	.	Railway Contractor	.	.	.	.	.	.	.	.
.	.	.	.	2	2	.	4	Platelayer	.	.	.	.	.	.	.	.
.	.	.	2	3	2	.	7	Railway Labourer, Navvy	.	.	.	.	.	.	.	.
.	.	.	.	.	.	.	.	Others	.	.	.	.	.	.	.	.
								4. Earthenware and Glass.								
.	.	.	1	.	.	.	1	Earthenware, China, Porcelain, Manufacture	.	.	.	.	.	.	.	.
.	.	.	.	.	.	.	.	Glass Manufacture	.	.	.	.	.	.	.	.
.	.	.	.	3	1	.	4	Earthenware, China, Glass, Dealer	.	.	.	.	.	.	.	.
								5. Salt.								
.	.	.	.	.	.	.	.	Salt Maker, Dealer	.	.	.	.	.	.	.	.

JERSEY—*continued.*

TABLE 9.—OCCUPATIONS of MALES and FEMALES at DIFFERENT PERIODS of LIFE—*cont.*

AGES OF MALES.								OCCUPATIONS.	AGES OF FEMALES.							
Under 5 years.	5-	15-	20-	25-	45-	65 and upwards.	All Ages.		All Ages.	Under 5 years.	5-	15-	20-	25-	45-	65 and upwards.
								6. Water.								
.	.	.	1	.	.	.	1	Waterworks Service	.	.	.	.	.	.	.	.
.	.	.	.	.	.	.	.	Others	.	.	.	.	.	.	.	.
								7. Precious Metals and Jewellery.								
.	2	5	3	9	2	3	24	Goldsmith, Silversmith, Jeweller	3	.	.	.	.	3	.	.
.	.	.	.	.	.	.	.	Gold, Silver, Beater	.	.	.	.	.	.	.	.
.	.	.	.	.	.	.	.	Lapidary	.	.	.	.	.	.	.	.
.	.	.	.	.	.	.	.	Others	.	.	.	.	.	.	.	.
								8. Iron and Steel.								
.	19	76	33	95	46	12	281	Blacksmith	.	.	.	.	.	.	.	.
.	.	1	.	.	2	.	3	Whitesmith	.	.	.	.	.	.	.	.
.	.	.	.	.	.	.	.	Nail Manufacture	.	.	.	.	.	.	.	.
.	.	.	.	.	.	.	.	Anchor, Chain, Manufacture	.	.	.	.	.	.	.	.
.	.	5	3	10	6	.	24	Other Iron and Steel Manufactures	.	.	.	.	.	.	.	.
.	.	2	3	14	8	2	32	Ironmonger, Hardware Dealer, Merchant	1	.	.	.	.	.	1	.
								9. Copper.								
.	.	.	.	3	5	1	9	Copper, Copper Goods—Manufacturer, Worker, Dealer	.	.	.	.	.	.	.	.
								10. Tin and Zinc.								
.	2	9	4	9	7	2	33	Tin, Tin Plate, Tin goods—Manufacturer, Worker, Dealer	1	.	.	.	.	1	.	.
.	.	.	.	.	.	.	.	Zinc, Zinc goods—Manufacturer, Worker, Dealer	.	.	.	.	.	.	.	.
								11. Lead.								
.	.	.	.	.	.	.	.	Lead, Leaden goods—Manufacturer, Worker, Dealer	.	.	.	.	.	.	.	.
								12. In Other, Mixed, or Unspecified, Metals.								
.	.	.	.	.	.	.	.	Metal Refiner, Worker, Turner, Dealer	.	.	.	.	.	.	.	.
.	.	.	.	.	.	.	.	Brass, Bronze, Manufacture. Brazier	.	.	.	.	.	.	.	.
.	.	.	.	.	.	.	.	Metal Burnisher, Lacquerer	.	.	.	.	.	.	.	.
.	.	.	.	.	.	.	.	White Metal, Plated Ware, Manufacture, Pewterer	1	.	.	1	.	.	.	.
.	.	.	.	.	2	.	2	Wire Maker, Worker, Weaver, Drawer	.	.	.	.	.	.	.	.
.	.	.	.	.	.	.	.	Bolt, Nut, Rivet, Screw, Staple, Maker	.	.	.	.	.	.	.	.
.	.	.	1	1	.	.	2	Lamp, Lantern, Candlestick, Maker	.	.	.	.	.	.	.	.
.	.	.	.	.	.	.	.	Clasp, Buckle, Hinge, Maker	.	.	.	.	.	.	.	.
.	.	.	.	.	.	.	.	Fancy Chain, Gilt Toy, Maker	.	.	.	.	.	.	.	.
.	.	.	.	.	.	.	.	Others	.	.	.	.	.	.	.	.
								22. PERSONS WORKING AND DEALING IN GENERAL OR UNSPECIFIED COMMODITIES.								
								1. Makers and Dealers (General or Undefined).								
.	2	9	12	14	9	3	49	General Shopkeeper, Dealer	74	.	1	13	14	24	18	4
.	.	.	1	1	1	2	5	Pawnbroker	1	.	.	.	.	1	.	.
.	1	3	2	6	3	1	16	Costermonger, Huckster, Street Seller	18	.	.	2	.	4	9	3
.	.	.	1	2	2	.	5	Manufacturer, Manager, Superintendent (undefined)	.	.	.	.	.	.	.	.
.	.	.	.	.	6	1	7	Contractor (undefined)	.	.	.	.	.	.	.	.
								2. Mechanics and Labourers (General or Undefined).								
.	17	84	72	318	282	54	827	General Labourer	73	.	1	6	4	31	23	8
.	.	.	.	12	1	.	13	Engine Driver, Stoker, Fireman (not railway, marine, nor agricultural)	.	.	.	.	.	.	.	.
.	.	1	.	2	.	.	3	Artizan, Mechanic (undefined)	.	.	.	.	.	.	.	.
.	6	6	1	.	.	.	13	Apprentice (undefined)	3	.	1	2	.	.	.	.
.	.	.	1	1	.	.	2	Factory Labourer (undefined)	.	.	.	.	.	.	.	.
.	.	.	.	1	.	1	2	Machinist, Machine Worker (undefined)	.	.	.	.	.	.	.	.
								23. PERSONS WORKING AND DEALING IN REFUSE MATTERS.								
								1. Refuse Matters.								
.	.	1	.	.	2	.	3	Town Drainage Service	.	.	.	.	.	.	.	.
.	3	1	1	5	2	1	12	Chimney Sweep, Soot Merchant	1	.	.	.	.	1	.	.
.	1	.	.	.	4	.	5	Scavenger, Crossing Sweeper	.	.	.	.	.	.	.	.
.	.	.	.	2	2	1	5	Rag Gatherer, Dealer	1	.	.	.	.	1	.	.
								VI. UNOCCUPIED CLASS.								
								24. PERSONS WITHOUT SPECIFIED OCCUPATIONS.								
2865	4582	332	81	294	511	587	9052	Persons returned by Property, Rank, &c., and not by special occupation	19646	2687	4737	915	1091	4776	3350	1842

JERSEY—*continued.*

TABLE 10.—BIRTH-PLACES of PERSONS enumerated in JERSEY.

Where Born.	Males.	Females.
Total enumerated	23,485	28,960
Jersey	16,399	21,080
England	3,393	3,646
Wales	19	29
Scotland	140	156
Ireland	581	682
Guernsey and adjacent Islands	332	543
Isle of Man	6	5
British Colonies and East Indies	313	518
Born at Sea (British Subjects)	17	15
Foreign Parts (British Subjects)	145	251

Where Born.	Males.	Females.
Foreign Parts (Foreign Subjects):		
Denmark	2	—
Norway	1	—
Poland	8	—
Austria	2	—
Hungary	1	—
Switzerland	2	7
Germany	36	14
Holland	6	3
Belgium	2	15
France	2,030	1,942
Portugal	1	—
Spain	3	2
Italy	20	7
Greece	1	—
Asia	1	2
America: United States	21	31
„ Other States, or State not specified	2	12
Born at Sea (Foreign Subjects)	1	—

TABLE 11.—NUMBER and AGES of MALES and FEMALES returned as "BLIND," as "DEAF AND DUMB," as "IDIOTS or IMBECILES," and as "LUNATICS" in JERSEY.

Returned as	All Ages.		0–	5–	15–	20–	25–	45–	65 and upwards.
	Both Sexes.	Males and Females.							
Blind	81	Males 30	1	2	1	—	5	7	14
		Females 51	—	1	—	1	6	16	27
Deaf and Dumb	35	Males 15	—	2	—	1	8	3	1
		Females 20	1	3	2	1	5	6	2
Lunatics	125	Males 46	—	—	—	1	19	20	6
		Females 79	—	—	—	3	28	37	11
Idiots or Imbeciles	86	Males 45	—	3	3	7	19	11	2
		Females 41	—	3	2	2	17	9	8

GUERNSEY AND ADJACENT ISLANDS.

ᴀBLE 1.—AREA, HOUSES, and POPULATION in 1881, and at each of the SIX preceding CENSUSES.

ɴsus Years.	Area in Statute Acres.	Houses.			Population.			Increase of Population between the Censuses.	
		Inhabited.	Uninhabited.	Building.	Persons.	Males.	Females.	Number of Persons.	Rate per Cent.
	19,605	3,083	107	21	20,827	9,519	11,308		
- -	"	3,804	321	114	26,128	11,983	14,145	5,301	25·5
- -	"	4,528	244	30	28,521	12,943	15,578	2,393	9·2
- -	"	5,319	328	72	33,719	15,701	18,018	5,198	18·2
- -	"	5,728	465	34	35,365	16,570	18,795	1,646	4·9
-	"	5,831	605	18	33,969	15,433	18,536	−1,396	−3·9
- - -	"	5,803	453	75	35,257	16,836	18,421	1,288	3·8
ᴇase in 60 Years	—	2,720	—	—	14,430	7,317	7,113	14,430	69·3

The minus sign prefixed to certain figures in the column headed Increase of Population denotes a decrease instead of an increase in the population nt shown.

ırn of the population of the Island of Alderney was made in 1821. In the returns of 1851 and 1861 there was a considerable increase of population, attributed to the Government works then in progress. In 1871 there was a decrease, which was attributed to the discontinuance of such works, a larger military force in the Islands of Guernsey and Alderney in 1861 than in 1851.

TABLE 2.—AREA, HOUSES, and POPULATION of CIVIL PARISHES in 1871 and 1881.

CIVIL PARISH.	Area in Statute Acres.	HOUSES.						POPULATION.					
		1871.			1881.			Persons.		Males.		Females.	
		Inhabited.	Uninhabited.	Building.	Inhabited.	Uninhabited.	Building.	1871.	1881.	1871.	1881.	1871.	1881.
GUERNSEY.													
Port [a]	1499	2540	201	7	2530	160	44	16166	16658	6731	7486	9435	9172
on [b]	1435	525	2	2	571	7	12	3038	3780	1497	1985	1541	1795
-	2088	497	13	2	550	16	7	2867	3477	1429	1759	1438	1718
w - - -	1203	229	8	—	224	9	2	1127	1141	528	532	599	609
ɪ [d] - - -	1799	411	23	4	436	33	9	2158	2311	986	1057	1172	1254
le Castro, or Catel [e] - -	2659	393	9	—	400	12	1	2173	2207	1046	1115	1127	1092
r - - -	1754	204	20	—	188	25	—	946	884	462	423	484	461
lu Bois	1662	230	14	3	229	9	—	1142	1171	544	581	598	590
- - -	1090	122	7	—	131	2	—	622	599	295	277	327	322
- - - -	816	85	3	—	84	3	—	354	379	167	185	187	194
ADJACENT ISLANDS.													
f - -	1962	464	292	—	353	174	—	2738	2048	1437	1144	1301	904
-	*320*	15	3	—	4	11	—	83	20	45	14	38	6
- -	*44*	1	1	—	2	—	—	4	4	2	3	2	1
ant - - - -	—	—	—	—	—	—	—	—	—	—	—	—	—
ᴄ - - -	*1035*	105	6		91	2	—	493	526	239	251	254	275
; - - - - -	*239*	9	3	—	9	—	—	53	45	22	20	31	25
- - - -	—	1	—	—	1	—	—	5	7	3	4	2	3

ʟ NOTES.—The areas of the Islands of Herm, Jethou, and Great and Little Sark, which are printed in script type, were supplied ṅance Survey Department. The areas which are printed in French type (*e.g.*, St. Peter Port, 1499) are reprinted from the bles of 1861.

ve return of the population for 1881 includes 250 sailors and others who, on the night of the 3rd April 1881, were on board vessels ral harbours of the Islands of Guernsey and Alderney. For details see Table 4.

itary in the various barracks, numbering, with their families, 1,331 persons, are also included in the above return.

ırn for the parish of St. Peter Port includes 286 persons in the ṙhouse, and lunatic asylum, 15 in an industrial home, and 12 in esides the military and their families, 654 persons, and 88 persons ssels in the harbour.

rn for the parish of St. Sampson includes 158 persons on board

rn for the parish of Vale includes the military and their families,

[d] The return for the parish of St. Martin includes the military and their families, 35 persons.

[e] The return for the parish of St. Mary de Castro includes 126 persons in the Country hospital, and the military and their families, 86 persons.

[f] The return for the island of Alderney includes the military and their families, 517 persons, and 6 persons on board vessels in harbour.

GUERNSEY AND ADJACENT ISLANDS—*continued.*

TABLE 3.—INHABITED HOUSES and POPULATION of such ECCLESIASTICAL DISTRICTS or PARISHES as are not entire Mother Parishes or that consist of more than one Civil Parish.

Ecclesiastical District or Parish.	Date of Formation.	Houses.			Population.		
		Inhabited.	Uninhabited	Building.	Persons.	Males.	Females.
St. Peter Port.							
St. Peter Port -	—	1,348	102	12	*9,027	4,023	5,004
Holy Trinity -	1858	589	47	3	3,654	1,597	2,057
St. John - - -	1841	599	22	29	4,001	1,883	2,118
St. Mary de Castro or Catel.							
St. Mary de Castro or Catel -	—	216	5	—	1,304	677	627
St. Matthew -	1855	184	7	1	903	438	465

* The population of the islets of Herm and Jethou amounting to 24 are included in the population of St. Peter Port, although not strictly belonging to any ecclesiastical parish. The rector of St. Peter Port states that he baptises children born there.

TABLE 4.—NUMBER of PERSONS on board VESSELS in HARBOURS on the night of 3rd April 1881.

Civil Parish.	Persons on board Vessels enumerated by Officers of H.M.'s Customs.		Total Number of Persons.	Number of Vessels.
	On board British Vessels.	On board Foreign or Colonial Vessels.		
GUERNSEY AND ADJACENT ISLANDS	239	11	250	49
St. Peter Port - -	81	7	88	14
St. Sampson - -	152	4	156	34
Alderney - - - - -	6	—	6	1

TABLE 5.—NUMBER of PERSONS in BARRACKS and in PUBLIC INSTITUTIONS.

Civil Parish.	Name of Institution.	Total Number of Inmates, including Officers, &c.			Number of Special Inmates, such as Paupers, Patients, Lunatics, &c.		
		Persons.	Males.	Females.	Persons.	Males.	Females.
St. Peter Port - -	Military and Families in Forts George, Belvidere, Castle Cornet, and Brehant Tower - - -	654	521	133	450	450	—
	Hospital of St. Peter Port (Hospital, Poor House, and Lunatic Asylum)	236	125	111	215	113	102
	Her Majesty's Prison - - - -	12	11	1	9	9	—
	Industrial Home - -	15	—	15	14	—	14
St. Michael in the Vale -	Military and Families in Forts Doyle, Le Marchant, and Crevelt -	39	19	20	7	7	—
St. Martin	Military and Families in Jerbourg -	35	14	21	9	9	—
St. Mary de Castro -	Military and Families in Forts Hommette, Le Crocq, Richmond - -	86	75	11	69	69	—
	Country Hospital - -	126	77	49	119	73	46
Alderney -	Military and Families - -	517	400	117	349	349	—

GUERNSEY AND ADJACENT ISLANDS—*continued.*

TABLE 6.—NUMBER of BIRTHS and DEATHS in each of the Years 1871 to 1880.

—	1871.	1872.	1873.	1874.	1875.	1876.	1877.	1878.	1879.	1880.	Total in 10 Years.
ıs - -	693	687	646	739	658	753	724	733	743	786	7,162
ıs -	688	683	572	811	780	686	632	609	778	723	6,962
ess of Regis-ered Births ver Deaths -	5	4	74	Defect −72	Defect −122	67	92	124	Defect −35	63	200

This table has been compiled from returns supplied by Colonel W. Bell, Government Secretary of Guernsey and the adjacent islands.

TABLE 7.—AGES of MALES and FEMALES.

ges.	Persons.	Males.	Females.	Ages.	Persons.	Males.	Females.
ıges -	35,257	16,836	18,421	35- -	2,115	1,029	1,086
	835	433	402	40-	1,939	907	1,032
	841	427	414	45-	1,690	783	907
	820	420	400	50-	1,572	703	869
-	767	375	392	55- -	1,400	608	792
	862	432	430	60-	1,322	576	746
				65-	1,047	456	591
r 5	4,125	2,087	2,038	70-	796	324	472
	3,580	1,786	1,794	75- -	484	207	277
	3,348	1,617	1,731	80-	266	94	172
	3,287	1,624	1,663	85- -	102	36	66
-	3,036	1,494	1,542	90- -	26	10	16
	2,770	1,360	1,410	95- -	8	3	5
	2,344	1,132	1,212	100 and upwards	–	–	–

TABLE 8.—AGES and CONDITION as to MARRIAGE of MALES and FEMALES.

—		All Ages.	Under 15 years.	15-	20-	25-	35-	45-	55-	65 an upward
ıarried	Males -	10,179	5,490	1,618	1,249	1,078	402	167	98	7
	Females -	10,452	5,563	1,622	1,061	885	467	202	285	27
ried -	Males -	6,016	–	6	241	1,393	1,484	1,230	954	70
	Females -	6,295	–	41	472	1,660	1,508	1,192	861	56
owed -	Males - -	641	–	–	4	21	50	89	132	84
	Females -	1,674	–	–	9	77	143	292	392	76
otal -	Males - -	16,836	5,490	1,624	1,494	2,492	1,936	1,486	1,184	1,1
	Females - -	18,421	5,563	1,663	1,542	2,622	2,118	1,776	1,538	1,5

GUERNSEY AND ADJACENT ISLANDS—*continued.*

TABLE 9.—OCCUPATIONS of MALES and FEMALES at DIFFERENT PERIODS of LIFE.

Ages of Males.								Occupations.	Ages of Females.							
Under 5 years.	5-	15-	20-	25-	45-	65 and upwards.	All Ages.		All Ages.	Under 5 years.	5-	15-	20-	25-	45-	65 and upwards.
2037	3403	1624	1494	4428	2670	1130	16636	TOTAL	18421	2038	3525	1663	1642	4740	3314	1599
								I. PROFESSIONAL CLASS.								
								1. PERSONS ENGAGED IN THE GENERAL OR LOCAL GOVERNMENT OF THE COUNTRY.								
								1. *National Government.*								
								Peer, M.P., Privy Councillor (not otherwise described)								
		2	5	7	10	4	26	Civil Service (officers and clerks)								
	5	3	2	12	11	2	33	Civil Service (messengers, &c.)	1						1	
				1	2		3	Prison Officer, &c.								
								2. *Local Government.*								
				4	4	1	9	Police								
				2		1	3	Municipal, Parish, Union, District, Officer								
					8	8	16	Other Local or County Official								
								3. *East Indian and Colonial Service.*								
		1	1	2			4	East Indian and Colonial Service								
								2. PERSONS ENGAGED IN THE DEFENCE OF THE COUNTRY.								
								1. *Army (at Home).*								
		1	7	41	27	10	86	Army Officer (effective or retired)								
		81	183	602	20		886	Soldier and Non-commissioned Officer								
		5	1	21	9		36	Militia, Yeomanry, Volunteers								
				20	24	10	54	Army Pensioner								
								2. *Navy (ashore or in port).*								
				3	5	3	11	Navy Officer (effective or retired)								
				1			1	Seaman, R.N.								
					2		2	Royal Marines (officers and men)								
				3	9	1	13	Navy Pensioner								
								3. PERSONS ENGAGED IN PROFESSIONAL OCCUPATIONS (WITH THEIR IMMEDIATE SUBORDINATES).								
								1. *Clerical Profession.*								
				5	16	4	25	Clergyman (Established Church)								
			1	4	4		9	Roman Catholic Priest								
			1	8	6	5	20	Minister, Priest, of other religious bodies								
					3		3	Missionary, Scripture Reader, Itinerant Preacher	1							1
								Nun, Sister of Charity	6					4	2	
				1			1	Theological Student								
					3		3	Church, Chapel, Cemetery—Officer, Servant	1							1
								2. *Legal Profession.*								
			2	13	10	2	27	Barrister, Solicitor								
								Law Student								
	2	1	1	1	1		6	Law Clerk, and others connected with Law								
								3. *Medical Profession.*								
				10	8	7	25	Physician, Surgeon, General Practitioner								
		1		2	1	1	5	Dentist								
			2	1			3	Medical Student, Assistant								
								Midwife	10					2	5	3
		1	1	1	2		5	Subordinate Medical Service	68				1	17	28	22
								4. *Teachers.*								
	1	11	6	13	6		37	Schoolmaster	141		5	46	26	48	12	4
		1		4	7	2	14	Teacher, Professor, Lecturer	82		1	11	19	46	5	
								School Service, and others concerned in Teaching								
								5. *Literary and Scientific Persons.*								
				3	1	1	5	Author, Editor, Journalist								
								Reporter, Short-hand Writer								
								Persons engaged in Scientific Pursuits								
								Literary, Scientific, Institution, Service, &c.								
								6. *Engineers and Surveyors.*								
		1		3			4	Civil Engineer								
								Mining Engineer								
				2			2	Land, House, Ship, Surveyor								
								7. *Artists.*								
			2		2		4	Painter (artist)	4			1	1	2		
								Engraver (artist)								
			1				1	Sculptor								
				1			1	Architect								
		6	4	16	3	5	34	Musician, Music Master	28			8	10	11	8	1
								Art Student								
		1	1	7	2	1	12	Photographer	9			2	1	3	3	
								Actor								
								Art, Music, Theatre, Service								

NOTE.—Persons returned as engaged in more than one occupation have been referred to the one that appeared to be of most importance; or, if there was no difference in this respect, to the one first given by the person in his or her return. In some cases special rules have been followed; *e.g.*, "Clergyman and Schoolmaster" in combination has always been referred to "Schoolmaster"; a Member of Parliament or Peer engaged in any branch of commerce or industry has always been referred to the latter, not to "Peer, M.P., &c."

The numbers returned under any heading include Labourers, Apprentices, and Assistants, as well as Masters, but not Clerks, Messengers, Errand boys, Porters, or Watchmen, for which occupations there are special headings. Civil, Military, and Naval Clerks, Law, Bank, Insurance, and Railway Clerks, and Government and Railway Porters, are, however, exceptions to this rule. Many young persons, being Apprentices or Assistants, have, therefore, been referred to occupations usually followed by adults. Women also, chiefly widows or orphans, carrying on the business of their deceased husbands or fathers, will sometimes be found under occupations commonly followed by men only.

Persons returned as *retired* from any business have not been referred to that business. Inmates of workhouses have been referred to their trades, unless their age or infirmities showed that they were past work. But persons who might be supposed to be only temporarily separated from their usual employment, such as Prisoners, and Patients in General Hospitals, have been classed under their usual occupations.

In some cases, for convenience of space, the male designation, *e.g.*, "Schoolmaster," alone is given, instead of "Schoolmaster, Schoolmistress."

GUERNSEY AND ADJACENT ISLANDS—*continued.*

TABLE 9.—OCCUPATIONS of MALES and FEMALES at DIFFERENT PERIODS of LIFE—*cont.*

Ages of Males. Under 5 years.	5-	15-	20-	25-	45-	65 and upwards.	All Ages.	OCCUPATIONS.	Ages of Females. All Ages.	Under 5 years.	5-	15-	20-	25-	45-	65 and upwards.
								8. *Persons engaged in Exhibitions, Shows, Games, &c.*								
.	.	.	.	.	.	.	.	Performer, Showman, Exhibition Service	.	.	.	.	.	.	.	.
.	.	.	1	.	.	.	1	Billiard, Cricket, and other Games, Service	.	.	.	.	.	.	.	.
								II. DOMESTIC CLASS.								
								4. PERSONS ENGAGED IN DOMESTIC OFFICES OR SERVICES.								
								1. *Domestic Service.*								
.	.	15	19	46	13	2	95	Domestic Coachman, Groom	.	.	.	.	.	.	.	.
.	15	68	39	115	71	36	344	Domestic Gardener	.	.	.	.	.	.	.	.
.	4	14	12	14	4	2	50	Domestic Indoor Servant	1775	.	111	586	437	434	167	40
.	.	.	.	.	.	.	.	Lodge, Gate, Park, Keeper (not Government)	.	.	.	.	.	.	.	.
.	2	4	6	3	2	.	16	Inn, Hotel, Servant	16	.	.	3	5	6	2	.
.	.	.	.	1	1	1	3	College, Club, Service	.	.	.	.	.	.	.	.
								2. *Other Service.*								
.	.	.	.	.	1	.	1	Office Keeper (not Government)	.	.	.	.	.	.	.	.
.	.	.	1	1	.	.	2	Cook (not domestic)	8	.	.	.	.	5	2	1
.	.	.	.	.	.	.	.	Charwoman	305	.	5	16	20	98	120	4
.	.	.	.	.	.	.	.	Washing and Bathing Service	410	.	6	38	44	157	146	5
.	.	.	.	3	.	1	4	Hospital and Institution Service	2	.	.	.	.	.	2	.
.	.	.	1	1	.	.	2	Others engaged in Service	1	.	.	.	.	.	.	1
								III. COMMERCIAL CLASS.								
								5. PERSONS ENGAGED IN COMMERCIAL OCCUPATIONS.								
								1. *Merchants and Agents.*								
.	.	.	3	13	10	6	31	Merchant	4	.	.	.	.	3	.	1
.	.	1	1	14	10	6	32	Broker, Agent, Factor	4	.	.	.	.	2	2	.
.	.	.	.	1	3	2	6	Auctioneer, Appraiser, Valuer, House Agent	.	.	.	.	.	.	.	.
.	.	.	.	2	1	1	4	Accountant	.	.	.	.	.	.	.	.
.	.	.	.	.	.	.	.	Salesman, Buyer (not otherwise described)	.	.	.	.	.	.	.	.
.	.	1	2	13	4	.	20	Commercial Traveller	.	.	.	.	.	.	.	.
.	2	11	12	27	7	1	60	Commercial Clerk	2	.	.	.	1	1	.	.
.	.	.	.	.	.	.	.	Officer of Commercial Company, Guild, Society, &c.	.	.	.	.	.	.	.	.
								2. *Dealers in Money.*								
.	.	.	.	2	.	.	2	Banker	.	.	.	.	.	.	.	.
.	.	2	4	4	3	.	13	Bank Service	.	.	.	.	.	.	.	.
.	.	.	.	.	.	.	.	Bill Discounter, Bill Broker, Finance Agent	.	.	.	.	.	.	.	.
								3. *Persons occupied in Insurance.*								
.	.	.	.	5	2	3	10	Life, House, Ship, &c., Insurance Service	.	.	.	.	.	.	.	.
								6. PERSONS ENGAGED IN CONVEYANCE OF MEN, GOODS, AND MESSAGES.								
								1. *On Railways.*								
.	.	.	.	1	.	.	1	Railway Engine Driver, Stoker	.	.	.	.	.	.	.	.
.	.	.	.	.	.	.	.	Railway Guard	.	.	.	.	.	.	.	.
.	.	.	.	.	.	.	.	Pointsman, Level Crossing Man	.	.	.	.	.	.	.	.
.	.	1	.	2	.	.	3	Other Railway Officials and Servants	.	.	.	.	.	.	.	.
								2. *On Roads.*								
.	.	.	.	.	.	.	.	Toll Collector, Turnpike Gate Keeper	.	.	.	.	.	.	.	.
.	.	1	.	4	6	.	11	Omnibus, Coach, Cab, Owner—Livery Stable Keeper	.	.	.	.	.	.	.	.
.	.	2	6	1	1	.	10	Cabman, Flyman, Coachman (not domestic)	.	.	.	.	.	.	.	.
.	4	32	23	86	38	7	200	Carman, Carrier, Carter, Haulier	.	.	.	.	.	.	.	.
.	1	.	.	1	1	.	3	Tramway Companies' Service	.	.	.	.	.	.	.	.
.	.	.	.	.	.	.	.	Wheel Chair Proprietor, Attendant, &c.	.	.	.	.	.	.	.	.
								3. *On Canals, Rivers and Seas.*								
.	.	.	.	.	.	.	.	Inland Navigation Service	.	.	.	.	.	.	.	.
.	.	.	.	.	1	1	2	Bargeman, Lighterman, Waterman	.	.	.	.	.	.	.	.
.	.	.	.	1	3	2	6	Navigation Service (on shore)	.	.	.	.	.	.	.	.
.	2	80	115	268	105	8	578	Seaman (Merchant Service)	.	.	.	.	.	.	.	.
.	.	2	2	13	12	6	35	Pilot	.	.	.	.	.	.	.	.
.	1	5	4	7	4	.	21	Ship Steward, Cook	.	.	.	.	.	.	.	.
.	.	2	2	2	5	1	12	Boatman on Seas	.	.	.	.	.	.	.	.
.	.	.	1	7	11	2	21	Harbour, Dock, Wharf, Lighthouse, Service	.	.	.	.	.	.	.	.
								4. *In Storage.*								
.	.	.	.	.	.	.	.	Warehouseman (not Manchester)	.	.	.	.	.	.	.	.
.	.	.	.	1	.	.	1	Meter, Weigher	.	.	.	.	.	.	.	.
								5. *In conveying Messages, Porterage, &c.*								
.	29	17	4	10	11	7	78	Messenger, Porter, Watchman (not Railway nor Government)	.	.	.	.	.	.	.	.
.	.	1	3	1	.	.	6	Telegraph, Telephone, Service	1	.	.	.	1	.	.	.

GUERNSEY AND ADJACENT ISLANDS—*continued.*

TABLE 9.—OCCUPATIONS of MALES and FEMALES at DIFFERENT PERIODS of LIFE—*cont.*

Ages of Males.								Occupations.	Ages of Females.							
Under 5 years.	5-	15-	20-	25-	45-	65 and upwards.	All Ages.		All Ages.	Under 5 years.	5-	15-	20-	25-	45-	65 and upwards.
								IV. AGRICULTURAL CLASS.								
								7. PERSONS ENGAGED IN AGRICULTURE.								
								1. *In Fields and Pastures.*								
.	.	3	26	318	387	169	903	Farmer, Grazier	40	.	.	.	.	5	24	11
.	.	116	84	111	5	.	316	Farmer's, Grazier's—Son, Grandson, Brother, Nephew*	.	.	.	.	.	.	.	.
.	.	.	.	3	.	.	3	Farm Bailiff	.	.	.	.	.	.	.	.
.	61	156	112	327	237	77	970	Agricultural Labourer, Farm Servant, Cottager	70	.	3	24	13	22	8	.
.	.	.	.	1	.	.	1	Shepherd	.	.	.	.	.	.	.	.
.	.	.	.	.	.	.	.	Land Drainage Service (not in towns)	.	.	.	.	.	.	.	.
.	.	.	.	.	.	.	.	Agricultural Machine — Proprietor, Attendant	.	.	.	.	.	.	.	.
.	.	.	.	.	.	.	.	Agricultural Student, Pupil	.	.	.	.	.	.	.	.
.	.	.	.	.	.	.	.	Others engaged in, or connected with, Agriculture	.	.	.	.	.	.	.	.
								2. *In Woods.*								
.	.	.	.	.	.	.	.	Woodman	.	.	.	.	.	.	.	.
								3. *In Gardens.*								
.	.	1	5	4	2	3	15	Nurseryman, Seedsman, Florist	2	.	.	.	1	.	.	1
.	.	2	1	5	6	5	19	Gardener (not domestic)	1	.	.	.	.	.	1	.
								8. PERSONS ENGAGED ABOUT ANIMALS.								
								1. *About Animals.*								
.	.	.	.	.	1	.	1	Horse Proprietor, Breeder, Dealer	.	.	.	.	.	.	.	.
.	.	2	.	1	2	.	5	Groom, Horse-keeper, Horse-breaker	.	.	.	.	.	.	.	.
.	.	.	1	2	2	.	5	Veterinary Surgeon, Farrier	.	.	.	.	.	.	.	.
.	.	.	.	5	1	.	6	Cattle, Sheep, Pig—Dealer, Salesman	.	.	.	.	.	.	.	.
.	.	.	.	.	.	.	.	Drover	.	.	.	.	.	.	.	.
.	.	.	.	2	.	.	2	Gamekeeper	.	.	.	.	.	.	.	.
.	.	.	.	.	1	.	1	Dog, Bird, Animal—Keeper, Dealer	2	.	.	.	.	2	.	.
.	.	.	.	.	.	.	.	Vermin Destroyer	.	.	.	.	.	.	.	.
.	4	30	35	108	66	28	271	Fisherman	.	.	.	.	.	.	.	.
.	.	.	.	.	.	.	.	Knacker, Catsmeat Dealer, &c., &c.	.	.	.	.	.	.	.	.
								V. INDUSTRIAL CLASS.								
								9. PERSONS WORKING AND DEALING IN BOOKS, PRINTS, AND MAPS.								
								1. *Books.*								
.	1	1	2	1	2	.	7	Publisher, Bookseller, Librarian	6	.	.	2	1	.	3	.
.	.	.	.	.	1	.	1	Music—Publisher, Seller, Printer	.	.	.	.	.	.	.	.
.	.	3	1	3	2	.	9	Bookbinder	.	.	.	.	.	.	.	.
.	5	14	17	21	5	3	65	Printer	1	.	.	1	.	.	.	.
.	.	.	.	.	.	.	.	Newspaper Agent, News Room Keeper	3	.	.	.	.	1	1	1
.	.	.	.	.	.	.	.	Others	.	.	.	.	.	.	.	.
								2. *Prints and Maps.*								
.	.	.	.	.	.	.	.	Lithographer, Lithographic Printer	.	.	.	.	.	.	.	.
.	.	.	.	.	.	.	.	Copper Plate, Steel Plate, Printer	.	.	.	.	.	.	.	.
.	.	.	.	.	.	.	.	Map, Print—Colourer, Seller	.	.	.	.	.	.	.	.
								10. PERSONS WORKING AND DEALING IN MACHINES AND IMPLEMENTS.								
								1. *Machines.*								
.	.	.	.	.	2	.	2	Engine, Machine, Maker	.	.	.	.	.	.	.	.
.	.	.	.	.	1	.	1	Millwright	.	.	.	.	.	.	.	.
.	.	1	2	5	.	.	8	Fitter, Turner (Engine and Machine)	.	.	.	.	.	.	.	.
.	.	.	.	.	.	.	.	Boiler Maker	.	.	.	.	.	.	.	.
.	.	.	.	.	.	.	.	Spinning and Weaving Machine Maker	.	.	.	.	.	.	.	.
.	.	.	.	.	.	.	.	Agricultural Machine and Implement Maker	.	.	.	.	.	.	.	.
.	.	.	.	.	.	.	.	Domestic Machinery—Maker, Dealer	.	.	.	.	.	.	.	.
								2. *Tools and Implements.*								
.	.	.	.	.	.	.	.	Tool Maker, Dealer	.	.	.	.	.	.	.	.
.	.	.	1	2	.	.	3	Cutler, Scissors Maker	.	.	.	.	.	.	.	.
.	.	.	.	.	.	.	.	File Maker	.	.	.	.	.	.	.	.
.	.	.	.	.	.	.	.	Saw Maker	.	.	.	.	.	.	.	.
.	.	.	.	.	.	.	.	Pin Maker	.	.	.	.	.	.	.	.
.	.	.	.	.	.	.	.	Needle Maker	.	.	.	.	.	.	.	.
.	.	.	.	.	.	.	.	Steel Pen Maker	.	.	.	.	.	.	.	.
.	.	.	.	.	.	.	.	Pencil Maker (Wood)	.	.	.	.	.	.	.	.
.	.	.	.	.	.	.	.	Domestic Implement Maker	.	.	.	.	.	.	.	.
								3. *Watches and Philosophical Instruments.*								
.	2	4	1	9	6	1	23	Watch Maker, Clock Maker	.	.	.	.	.	.	.	.
.	.	.	.	.	.	.	.	Philosophical Instrument Maker, Optician	.	.	.	.	.	.	.	.
.	.	.	.	.	.	.	.	Electrical Apparatus Maker	.	.	.	.	.	.	.	.
.	.	.	.	1	.	.	1	Weighing and Measuring Apparatus Maker	.	.	.	.	.	.	.	.

* Only male relatives living with the farmer or grazier, and therefore presumably engaged in agriculture are included above.

GUERNSEY AND ADJACENT ISLANDS—*continued.*

TABLE 9.—OCCUPATIONS of MALES and FEMALES at DIFFERENT PERIODS of LIFE—*cont.*

Ages of Males: Under 5 years.	5-	15-	20-	25-	45-	65 and upwards.	All Ages.	OCCUPATIONS.	Ages of Females: All Ages.	Under 5 years.	5-	15-	20-	25-	45-	65 and upwards.
								4. *Surgical Instruments.*								
.	.	.	.	.	.	.	.	Surgical Instrument Maker	.	.	.	.	.	.	.	.
								5. *Arms and Ordnance.*								
.	.	.	.	3	1	.	4	Gunsmith, Gun Manufacturer	.	.	.	.	.	.	.	.
.	.	.	.	.	.	.	.	Ordnance Manufacturer	.	.	.	.	.	.	.	.
.	.	.	.	.	.	.	.	Sword, Bayonet—Maker, Cutler	.	.	.	.	.	.	.	.
.	.	.	.	.	.	.	.	Others	.	.	.	.	.	.	.	.
								6. *Musical Instruments.*								
.	.	.	.	2	.	1	3	Musical Instrument Maker, Dealer	.	.	.	.	.	.	.	.
								7. *Type, Dies, Medals, Coins.*								
.	.	.	.	.	.	.	.	Type Cutter, Founder	.	.	.	.	.	.	.	.
.	.	.	.	.	.	.	.	Die, Seal, Coin, Medal, Maker	.	.	.	.	.	.	.	.
								8. *Tackle for Sports and Games.*								
.	.	.	.	.	.	.	.	Toy Maker, Dealer	1	.	.	.	.	.	1	.
.	.	.	.	.	.	.	.	Fishing Rod, Tackle, Maker, Dealer	.	.	.	.	.	.	.	.
.	.	.	.	.	.	.	.	Apparatus for other Games, Maker, Dealer	.	.	.	.	.	.	.	.
								11. PERSONS WORKING AND DEALING IN HOUSES, FURNITURE, AND DECORATIONS.								
								1. *Houses.*								
.	.	1	1	14	21	3	40	Builder	.	.	.	.	.	.	.	.
.	33	90	65	171	103	33	495	Carpenter, Joiner	.	.	.	.	.	.	.	.
.	.	2	1	6	5	1	15	Bricklayer	.	.	.	.	.	.	.	.
.	6	25	28	83	60	20	222	Mason	.	.	.	.	.	.	.	.
.	.	.	.	.	.	.	.	Slater, Tiler	.	.	.	.	.	.	.	.
.	7	19	18	79	41	19	183	Plasterer, Whitewasher	.	.	.	.	.	.	.	.
.	.	.	.	1	2	.	3	Paperhanger	.	.	.	.	.	.	.	.
.	4	4	4	8	5	1	26	Plumber	.	.	.	.	.	.	.	.
.	3	7	6	31	16	2	65	Painter, Glazier	.	.	.	.	.	.	.	.
								2. *Furniture and Fittings.*								
.	12	16	21	24	16	10	99	Cabinet Maker, Upholsterer	9	.	.	2	.	4	2	1
.	.	.	.	1	.	.	1	French Polisher	.	.	.	.	.	.	.	.
.	.	.	1	1	4	.	6	Furniture Broker, Dealer	.	.	.	.	.	.	.	.
.	1	.	2	1	.	.	4	Locksmith, Bellhanger	.	.	.	.	.	.	.	.
.	1	4	6	4	2	.	17	Gas Fitter	.	.	.	.	.	.	.	.
.	.	.	.	.	.	.	.	House and Shop Fittings—Maker, Dealer	.	.	.	.	.	.	.	.
.	.	.	.	.	.	.	.	Funeral Furniture Maker, Undertaker	.	.	.	.	.	.	.	.
.	.	.	.	.	.	.	.	Others	.	.	.	.	.	.	.	.
								3. *House Decorations.*								
.	.	.	.	1	.	.	1	Wood Carver	.	.	.	.	.	.	.	.
.	.	.	1	1	3	.	5	Carver, Gilder	1	.	.	.	.	.	1	.
.	.	.	.	.	.	.	.	Dealer in Works of Art	.	.	.	.	.	.	.	.
.	.	.	.	.	.	.	.	Figure, Image—Maker, Dealer	1	.	.	.	1	.	.	.
.	.	.	.	.	.	.	.	Animal, Bird, &c., Preserver, Naturalist	.	.	.	.	.	.	.	.
.	.	.	.	.	.	.	.	Artificial Flower Maker	.	.	.	.	.	.	.	.
								12. PERSONS WORKING AND DEALING IN CARRIAGES AND HARNESS.								
								1. *Carriages.*								
.	1	6	.	18	5	.	30	Coachmaker	.	.	.	.	.	.	.	.
.	.	.	.	.	.	.	.	Railway Carriage, Railway Waggon, Maker	.	.	.	.	.	.	.	.
.	1	9	1	5	5	.	21	Wheelwright	.	.	.	.	.	.	.	.
.	.	.	.	.	.	.	.	Bicycle, Tricycle—Maker, Dealer	.	.	.	.	.	.	.	.
.	.	.	.	.	.	.	.	Others	.	.	.	.	.	.	.	.
								2. *Harness.*								
.	1	5	3	7	6	.	22	Saddler, Harness, Whip, Maker	.	.	.	.	.	.	.	.
								13. PERSONS WORKING AND DEALING IN SHIPS AND BOATS.								
								1. *Hull.*								
.	.	2	.	3	3	.	8	Ship, Boat, Barge, Builder	.	.	.	.	.	.	.	.
.	.	4	8	63	36	5	116	Shipwright, Ship Carpenter (ashore)	.	.	.	.	.	.	.	.
								2. *Masts, Rigging, &c.*								
.	1	2	.	3	2	.	8	Mast, Yard, Oar, Block, Maker	.	.	.	.	.	.	.	.
.	.	1	.	3	3	2	9	Ship Rigger, Chandler, Fitter	.	.	.	.	.	.	.	.
.	3	8	3	9	2	3	28	Sail Maker	.	.	.	.	.	.	.	.

GUERNSEY AND ADJACENT ISLANDS—*continued.*

TABLE 9.—OCCUPATIONS of MALES and FEMALES at DIFFERENT PERIODS of LIFE—*cont.*

Ages of Males.								Occupations.	Ages of Females.							
Under 5 years.	5-	15-	20-	25-	45-	65 and upwards.	All Ages.		All Ages.	Under 5 years.	5-	15-	20-	25-	45-	65 and upwards.
								14. PERSONS WORKING AND DEALING IN CHEMICALS AND COMPOUNDS.								
								1. *Colouring Matter.*								
.	.	.	.	.	.	.	.	Dye, Paint, Manufacture	.	.	.	.	.	.	.	.
.	.	.	.	.	.	.	.	Ink, Blacking, Colouring Substance, Manufacture	.	.	.	.	.	.	.	.
								2. *Explosives.*								
.	.	.	.	.	1	.	1	Gunpowder, Guncotton, Explosive Substance, Manufacture	.	.	.	.	.	.	.	.
.	.	.	.	.	.	.	.	Fusee, Fireworks, Explosive Article, Manufacture	.	.	.	.	.	.	.	.
								3. *Drugs and other Chemicals and Compounds.*								
.	1	6	3	8	10	1	29	Chemist, Druggist	2	.	.	.	1	.	1	.
.	.	.	.	2	.	.	2	Manufacturing Chemist	.	.	.	.	.	.	.	.
.	.	.	.	.	.	.	.	Alkali Manufacture	.	.	.	.	.	.	.	.
.	.	.	.	.	.	.	.	Drysalter	.	.	.	.	.	.	.	.
								15. PERSONS WORKING AND DEALING IN TOBACCO AND PIPES.								
								1. *Tobacco and Pipes.*								
.	2	2	3	11	6	1	25	Tobacco Manufacturer, Tobacconist	3	.	.	1	.	1	1	.
.	.	.	.	.	.	.	.	Tobacco Pipe, Snuff Box, &c., Maker	.	.	.	.	.	.	.	.
								16. PERSONS WORKING AND DEALING IN FOOD AND LODGING.								
								1. *Board and Lodging.*								
.	.	.	.	11	20	4	35	Innkeeper, Hotel Keeper, Publican	20	.	.	.	.	5	11	4
.	.	.	.	2	4	3	9	Lodging, Boarding, House Keeper	83	.	.	1	.	27	43	12
.	.	.	.	2	1	.	3	Coffee, Eating, House Keeper	8	.	.	1	.	1	6	.
								2. *Spirituous Drinks.*								
.	.	.	.	.	.	.	.	Hop-Merchant, Dealer	.	.	.	.	.	.	.	.
.	.	.	.	.	.	1	1	Maltster	.	.	.	.	.	.	.	.
.	1	4	2	3	4	.	14	Brewer	.	.	.	.	.	.	.	.
.	.	.	.	1	.	.	1	Beerseller. Ale, Porter, Cider, Dealer	1	.	.	.	.	.	.	1
.	1	.	1	6	1	.	9	Cellarman	.	.	.	.	.	.	.	.
.	1	2	4	8	12	5	32	Wine, Spirit—Merchant, Agent	1	.	.	.	.	1	.	.
								3. *Food.*								
.	.	.	.	.	.	.	.	Milkseller, Dairyman	.	.	.	.	.	.	.	.
.	.	.	.	.	.	.	.	Cheesemonger, Butterman	.	.	.	.	.	.	.	.
.	1	6	18	30	15	6	76	Butcher, Meat Salesman	10	.	.	.	.	5	4	1
.	.	.	.	1	3	2	6	Provision Curer, Dealer	1	.	.	.	.	1	.	.
.	1	.	.	.	1	.	2	Poulterer, Game Dealer	1	.	.	.	.	.	.	1
.	.	.	.	1	.	.	1	Fishmonger	14	.	.	.	.	7	6	1
.	.	.	.	1	1	1	3	Corn, Flour, Seed—Merchant, Dealer	.	.	.	.	.	.	.	.
.	.	2	2	19	5	4	32	Corn Miller	.	.	.	.	.	.	.	.
.	6	11	22	49	28	6	122	Baker	10	.	.	2	.	2	3	4
.	1	2	.	10	2	1	16	Confectioner, Pastrycook	13	.	1	2	2	4	3	1
.	.	.	.	1	2	.	3	Greengrocer, Fruiterer	15	.	.	.	.	4	10	1
.	.	.	.	.	.	.	.	Mustard, Vinegar, Spice, Pickle—Maker, Dealer	.	.	.	.	.	.	.	.
.	.	.	.	.	.	.	.	Sugar Refiner	.	.	.	.	.	.	.	.
.	2	20	13	61	35	6	130	Grocer, Tea, Coffee, Chocolate—Maker, Dealer	114	.	2	9	4	38	46	15
.	.	.	.	3	.	.	3	Ginger Beer, Mineral Water—Manufacturer, Dealer	.	.	.	.	.	.	.	.
.	.	.	.	.	.	.	.	Others dealing in Food	.	.	.	.	.	.	.	.
								17. PERSONS WORKING AND DEALING IN TEXTILE FABRICS.								
								1. *Wool and Worsted.*								
.	.	.	.	.	.	.	.	Woolstapler	.	.	.	.	.	.	.	.
.	.	.	.	.	.	.	.	Woollen Cloth Manufacture	.	.	.	.	.	.	.	.
.	.	.	.	.	.	.	.	Wool, Woollen goods—Dyer, Printer	.	.	.	.	.	.	.	.
.	.	.	.	.	.	.	.	Worsted, Stuff, Manufacture	.	.	.	.	.	.	.	.
.	.	.	.	.	.	.	.	Flannel Manufacture	.	.	.	.	.	.	.	.
.	.	.	.	.	.	.	.	Blanket Manufacture	.	.	.	.	.	.	.	.
.	.	.	.	.	.	.	.	Fuller	.	.	.	.	.	.	.	.
.	.	.	.	.	.	.	.	Cloth, Worsted, Stuff, Flannel, Blanket, Dealer	.	.	.	.	.	.	.	.
.	.	.	.	.	.	.	.	Others	.	.	.	.	.	.	.	.
								2. *Silk.*								
.	.	.	.	.	.	.	.	Silk, Silk goods, Manufacture	.	.	.	.	.	.	.	.
.	.	.	.	.	.	.	.	Silk Dyer, Printer	.	.	.	.	.	.	.	.
.	.	.	.	.	.	.	.	Ribbon Manufacture	.	.	.	.	.	.	.	.
.	.	.	.	.	.	.	.	Crape, Gauze, Manufacture	.	.	.	.	.	.	.	.
.	.	.	.	.	1	.	1	Silk Merchant, Dealer	.	.	.	.	.	.	.	.

GUERNSEY AND ADJACENT ISLANDS—*continued.*

TABLE 9.—OCCUPATIONS of MALES and FEMALES at DIFFERENT PERIODS of LIFE—*cont.*

Ages of Males.								Occupations.	Ages of Females.							
Under 5 years.	5–	15–	20–	25–	45–	65 and upwards.	All Ages.		All Ages.	Under 5 years.	5–	15–	20–	25–	45–	65 and upwards.
								3. Cotton and Flax.								
.	.	.	.	.	.	.	.	Cotton, Cotton goods, Manufacture	.	.	.	.	.	.	.	.
.	.	.	.	.	1	.	1	Cotton, Calico—Printer, Dyer, Bleacher	.	.	.	.	.	.	.	.
.	.	.	.	.	.	.	.	Cotton, Calico—Warehouseman, Dealer	.	.	.	.	.	.	.	.
.	.	.	.	.	.	.	.	Flax, Linen—Manufacturer, Dealer	.	.	.	.	.	.	.	.
.	.	.	.	.	.	.	.	Lace Manufacturer, Dealer	.	.	.	.	.	.	.	.
.	.	.	.	.	.	.	.	Fustian Manufacturer, Dealer	.	.	.	.	.	.	.	.
.	.	.	.	.	.	.	.	Tape Manufacturer, Dealer	.	.	.	.	.	.	.	.
.	.	.	.	.	.	.	.	Thread Manufacturer, Dealer	.	.	.	.	.	.	.	.
								4. Hemp and other Fibrous Materials.								
.	.	.	.	.	.	.	.	Hemp, Jute, Cocoa Fibre, Manufacture	.	.	.	.	.	.	.	.
.	5	4	3	12	7	3	34	Rope, Twine, Cord—Maker, Dealer	.	.	.	.	.	.	.	.
.	.	.	.	.	.	.	.	Mat Maker, Seller	.	.	.	.	.	.	.	.
.	.	.	.	.	.	.	.	Net Maker	1	.	.	.	.	.	1	.
.	.	.	.	1	.	.	1	Canvas, Sailcloth, Manufacture	.	.	.	.	.	.	.	.
.	.	.	.	.	.	.	.	Sacking, Sack, Bag—Maker, Dealer	.	.	.	.	.	.	.	.
.	.	.	.	.	.	.	.	Others working and dealing in Hemp	.	.	.	.	.	.	.	.
								5. Mixed or Unspecified Materials.								
.	.	.	.	.	.	.	.	Weaver (undefined)	.	.	.	.	.	.	.	.
.	2	.	1	.	2	.	5	Dyer, Printer, Scourer, Bleacher, Calenderer (undefined)	1	.	.	.	.	1	.	.
.	.	1	.	.	.	.	1	Factory Hand (Textile, undefined)	.	.	.	.	.	.	.	.
.	.	.	.	.	.	.	.	Felt Manufacture	.	.	.	.	.	.	.	.
.	.	.	.	.	.	.	.	Carpet, Rug, Manufacture	.	.	.	.	.	.	.	.
.	.	.	.	.	.	.	.	Manchester Warehouseman	.	.	.	.	.	.	.	.
.	8	27	20	35	24	3	117	Draper, Linen Draper, Mercer	49	.	.	12	13	16	7	1
.	.	1	.	.	3	.	4	Fancy goods (Textile), Manufacturer, Worker, Dealer	7	.	.	.	1	2	1	3
.	.	.	.	.	.	.	.	Trimming Maker, Dealer	.	.	.	.	.	.	.	.
.	.	.	.	.	.	.	.	Embroiderer	1	.	.	.	.	.	1	.
.	.	.	.	.	.	.	.	Others	.	.	.	.	.	.	.	.
								18. PERSONS WORKING AND DEALING IN DRESS.								
								1. Dress.								
.	.	.	.	1	1	.	2	Hatter, Hat Manufacture (not straw)	1	.	.	.	.	1	.	.
.	.	.	.	.	.	.	.	Straw—Hat, Bonnet, Plait, Manufacture	.	.	.	.	.	.	.	.
.	5	22	21	52	37	17	154	Tailor	47	.	1	7	2	16	12	9
.	.	.	.	.	.	.	.	Milliner, Dressmaker, Staymaker	1085	.	61	280	175	357	173	39
.	.	.	.	.	.	.	.	Shawl Manufacture	.	.	.	.	.	.	.	.
.	.	.	.	.	.	.	.	Shirt Maker, Seamstress	97	.	1	5	5	27	35	24
.	.	.	.	.	.	.	.	Hosiery Manufacture	2	.	.	.	.	1	1	.
.	.	.	.	.	.	.	.	Hosier, Haberdasher	1	.	.	.	.	.	.	1
.	.	.	.	.	.	.	.	Glover, Glove Maker	3	.	.	.	.	1	.	1
.	.	.	.	.	.	.	.	Button Maker, Dealer	.	.	.	.	.	.	.	.
.	7	9	9	80	77	30	212	Shoe, Boot—Maker, Dealer	31	.	.	2	.	4	11	4
.	.	.	.	.	.	.	.	Patten, Clog, Maker	.	.	.	.	.	.	.	.
.	1	6	1	6	7	1	22	Wig Maker, Hairdresser	2	.	.	.	.	1	1	.
.	.	.	.	.	.	1	1	Umbrella, Parasol, Stick—Maker, Dealer	6	.	.	.	2	2	1	1
.	.	.	.	.	.	.	.	Accoutrement Maker	.	.	.	.	.	.	.	.
.	.	.	.	.	.	.	.	Old Clothes Dealer, and others	.	.	.	.	.	.	.	.
								19. PERSONS WORKING AND DEALING IN VARIOUS ANIMAL SUBSTANCES.								
								1. In Grease, Gut, Bone, Horn, Ivory, and Whalebone.								
.	.	.	.	1	.	.	1	Tallow Chandler, Candle, Grease, Manufacture	.	.	.	.	.	.	.	.
.	.	.	.	2	.	.	3	Soap Boiler, Maker	.	.	.	.	.	.	.	.
.	.	.	.	.	.	.	.	Glue, Size, Gelatine, Isinglass—Maker, Dealer	.	.	.	.	.	.	.	.
.	.	.	.	.	.	.	.	Manure Manufacture	.	.	.	.	.	.	.	.
.	.	.	.	.	.	.	.	Bone, Horn, Ivory, Tortoise-shell—Worker, Dealer	.	.	.	.	.	.	.	.
.	.	.	.	.	.	.	.	Comb Maker	.	.	.	.	.	.	.	.
.	.	.	.	.	.	.	.	Others	.	.	.	.	.	.	.	.
								2. In Skins.								
.	.	.	.	.	.	.	.	Furrier, Skinner	.	.	.	.	.	.	.	.
.	.	.	.	.	.	.	.	Tanner, Fellmonger	.	.	.	.	.	.	.	.
.	.	.	.	.	.	.	.	Currier	.	.	.	.	.	.	.	.
.	.	.	.	1	2	.	3	Leather Goods, Portmanteau, Bag, Strap, &c.—Maker, Dealer	.	.	.	.	.	.	.	.
.	.	.	.	.	.	.	.	Parchment, Vellum—Maker, Dealer	.	.	.	.	.	.	.	.
								3. In Hair and Feathers.								
.	.	.	.	1	.	.	1	Hair, Bristle—Worker, Dealer	.	.	.	.	.	.	.	.
.	.	.	.	.	.	.	.	Brush, Broom, Maker	.	.	.	.	.	.	.	.
.	.	.	.	.	.	.	.	Quill, Feather—Dresser, Dealer	.	.	.	.	.	.	.	.

GUERNSEY AND ADJACENT ISLANDS—*continued.*

TABLE 9.—OCCUPATIONS of MALES and FEMALES at DIFFERENT PERIODS of LIFE—*cont.*

Males: Under 5 years	5-	15-	20-	25-	45-	65 and upwards	All Ages	OCCUPATIONS	Females: All Ages	Under 5 years	5-	15-	20-	25-	45-	65 and upwards
								20. PERSONS WORKING AND DEALING IN VARIOUS VEGETABLE SUBSTANCES.								
								1. In Oils, Gums, and Resins.								
								Oil Miller, Oil Cake—Maker, Dealer								
								Oil and Colourman								
								Floor Cloth, Oil Cloth, Manufacture								
								Japanner								
								India Rubber, Gutta Percha—Worker, Dealer								
								Waterproof Goods—Maker, Dealer								
								Others								
								2. In Cane, Rush, and Straw.								
	3	2	2	5	1	1	14	Willow, Cane, Rush—Worker, Dealer, Basket Maker	1					1		
	1						1	Hay, Straw (not plait), Chaff—Cutter, Dealer								
			2	3	3	1	9	Thatcher								
								3. In Wood and Bark.								
		1	1			2	4	Timber, Wood—Merchant, Dealer								
		1	2	14	7	1	25	Sawyer								
				1		1	2	Lath, Wooden Fence, Hurdle, Maker								
			1		1		2	Wood Turner, Box Maker								
		1	1	5	6	2	15	Cooper, Hoop Maker, Bender								
								Cork, Bark—Cutter, Worker, Dealer								
								Others								
								4. In Paper.								
								Paper Manufacture								
								Envelope Maker								
	1	2	2	1			6	Stationer, Law Stationer	16				4	6	6	
								Card, Pattern Card, Maker								
								Paper Stainer								
								Paper Box, Paper Bag, Maker	2		1			1		
								Ticket, Label, Writer								
								Others								
								21. PERSONS WORKING AND DEALING IN VARIOUS MINERAL SUBSTANCES.								
								1. Miners.								
				1			1	Coal Miner								
								Ironstone Miner								
								Copper Miner								
								Tin Miner								
								Lead Miner								
				1			1	Miner in other, or undefined, Minerals								
								Mine Service								
								2. Coal, Coal Gas, &c.								
			2	6	4		12	Coal Merchant, Dealer	1					1		
		2		4	3		9	Coalheaver								
								Coke, Charcoal, Peat—Cutter, Burner, Dealer								
		1	2	7	4	1	15	Gas Works Service								
								3. Stone, Clay, and Road Making.								
	71	101	107	310	169	22	780	Stone Quarrier								
	41	121	97	144	56	9	468	Stone Cutter, Dresser, Dealer								
								Slate Quarrier								
				2		3	5	Slate Worker, Dealer								
					2		2	Limeburner								
								Clay, Sand, Gravel, Chalk—Labourer, Dealer								
								Fossil, Coprolite—Digger, Dealer								
								Well Sinker, Borer								
								Plaster, Cement, Manufacture								
	2	6	3	8	4	4	27	Brick, Tile—Maker, Burner, Dealer								
								Paviour								
						1	1	Road Contractor, Surveyor, Inspector								
	53	46	28	69	22	8	226	Road Labourer								
								Railway Contractor								
					2		2	Platelayer								
					2		2	Railway Labourer, Navvy								
								Others	1					1		
								4. Earthenware and Glass.								
								Earthenware, China, Porcelain, Manufacture								
								Glass Manufacture								
				6	2		8	Earthenware, China, Glass, Dealer	2			1		1		
								5. Salt.								
					1	1	2	Salt Maker, Dealer								

GUERNSEY AND ADJACENT ISLANDS—*continued.*

TABLE 9.—OCCUPATIONS of MALES and FEMALES at DIFFERENT PERIODS of LIFE—*cont.*

Ages of Males.								Occupations.	Ages of Females.							
Under 5 years.	5-	15-	20-	25-	45-	65 and upwards.	All Ages.		All Ages.	Under 5 years.	5-	15-	20-	25-	45-	65 and upwards.
								6. *Water.*								
.	.	.	.	.	.	.	.	Waterworks Service	.	.	.	.	.	.	.	.
.	.	.	.	.	.	.	.	Others	.	.	.	.	.	.	.	.
								7. *Precious Metals and Jewellery.*								
.	.	1	.	7	2	1	11	Goldsmith, Silversmith, Jeweller	1	.	.	.	.	.	1	.
.	.	.	.	.	.	.	.	Gold, Silver, Beater	.	.	.	.	.	.	.	.
.	.	.	.	.	.	.	.	Lapidary	.	.	.	.	.	.	.	.
.	.	.	.	.	.	.	.	Others	.	.	.	.	.	.	.	.
								8. *Iron and Steel.*								
.	13	23	29	60	36	9	170	Blacksmith	.	.	.	.	.	.	.	.
.	1	5	2	7	2	.	17	Whitesmith	.	.	.	.	.	.	.	.
.	.	.	.	1	.	.	1	Nail Manufacture	.	.	.	.	.	.	.	.
.	.	.	.	.	.	.	.	Anchor, Chain, Manufacture	.	.	.	.	.	.	.	.
.	.	1	2	6	8	.	17	Other Iron and Steel Manufactures	.	.	.	.	.	.	.	.
.	1	4	4	8	5	1	23	Ironmonger, Hardware Dealer, Merchant	1	.	.	.	.	1	.	.
								9. *Copper.*								
.	.	.	.	1	1	.	2	Copper, Copper goods—Manufacturer, Worker, Dealer	.	.	.	.	.	.	.	.
								10. *Tin and Zinc.*								
.	3	6	5	8	2	5	29	Tin, Tin plate, Tin goods—Manufacturer, Worker, Dealer	.	.	.	.	.	.	.	.
.	.	.	.	.	.	.	.	Zinc, Zinc goods — Manufacturer, Worker, Dealer	.	.	.	.	.	.	.	.
								11. *Lead.*								
.	.	.	.	.	.	.	.	Lead, Leaden goods—Manufacturer, Worker, Dealer	.	.	.	.	.	.	.	.
								12. *In Other, Mixed, or Unspecified, Metals.*								
.	.	.	.	.	1	.	1	Metal Refiner, Worker, Turner, Dealer	.	.	.	.	.	.	.	.
.	.	.	.	.	1	.	1	Brass, Bronze, Manufacture. Brazier	.	.	.	.	.	.	.	.
.	.	.	.	.	.	.	.	Metal Burnisher, Lacquerer	.	.	.	.	.	.	.	.
.	.	.	.	.	.	.	.	White Metal, Plated Ware, Manufacture. Pewterer	.	.	.	.	.	.	.	.
.	.	.	.	.	.	.	.	Wire Maker, Worker, Weaver, Drawer	.	.	.	.	.	.	.	.
.	.	.	.	.	.	.	.	Bolt, Nut, Rivet, Screw, Staple, Maker	.	.	.	.	.	.	.	.
.	.	1	.	.	.	.	1	Lamp, Lantern, Candlestick, Maker	.	.	.	.	.	.	.	.
.	.	.	.	.	.	.	.	Clasp, Buckle, Hinge, Maker	.	.	.	.	.	.	.	.
.	.	.	.	.	.	.	.	Fancy Chain, Gilt Toy, Maker	.	.	.	.	.	.	.	.
.	.	.	.	.	.	.	.	Others	.	.	.	.	.	.	.	.
								22. PERSONS WORKING AND DEALING IN GENERAL OR UNSPECIFIED COMMODITIES.								
								1. *Makers and Dealers (General or Undefined).*								
.	.	6	2	8	7	3	26	General Shopkeeper, Dealer	73	.	1	10	8	25	22	7
.	.	.	.	1	.	1	2	Pawnbroker	.	.	.	.	.	.	.	.
.	1	.	1	6	.	1	9	Costermonger, Huckster, Street Seller	6	.	.	1	.	2	1	2
.	.	2	1	3	1	1	8	Manufacturer, Manager, Superintendent (undefined)	1	.	.	.	.	.	.	1
.	.	.	.	.	1	.	1	Contractor (undefined)	.	.	.	.	.	.	.	.
								2. *Mechanics and Labourers (General or Undefined).*								
.	11	65	65	204	142	34	521	General Labourer	4	.	.	1	1	1	1	.
.	1	5	5	12	7	1	31	Engine Driver, Stoker, Fireman (not railway, marine, nor agricultural)	.	.	.	.	.	.	.	.
.	.	1	6	4	1	.	12	Artisan, Mechanic (undefined)	1	.	1	.	.	.	.	.
.	5	2	.	.	.	.	7	Apprentice (undefined)	4	.	3	1	.	.	.	.
.	.	4	.	3	1	.	8	Factory Labourer (undefined)	1	.	1	.	.	.	.	.
.	.	1	.	.	.	.	1	Machinist, Machine Worker (undefined)	.	.	.	.	.	.	.	.
								23. PERSONS WORKING AND DEALING IN REFUSE MATTERS.								
								1. *Refuse Matters.*								
.	.	.	.	.	.	.	.	Town Drainage Service	.	.	.	.	.	.	.	.
.	.	1	1	1	3	.	6	Chimney Sweep, Soot Merchant	.	.	.	.	.	.	.	.
.	.	.	.	1	2	.	3	Scavenger, Crossing Sweeper	.	.	.	.	.	.	.	.
.	.	.	.	1	1	1	3	Rag Gatherer, Dealer	.	.	.	.	.	.	.	.
								VI. UNOCCUPIED CLASS.								
								24. PERSONS WITHOUT SPECIFIED OCCUPATIONS.								
2087	2388	164	60	133	282	872	5986	Persons returned by Property, Rank, &c., and not by special occupation	13,661	2038	3322	592	742	3324	2357	1286
.	.	.	.	.	.	.	.	Children under 5 years of age	.	.	.	.	.	.	.	.

GUERNSEY AND ADJACENT ISLANDS—*continued.*

TABLE 10.—BIRTH-PLACES of PERSONS enumerated in GUERNSEY and ADJACENT ISLANDS.

Where Born.	Males.	Females.
Total enumerated	16,836	18,421
Guernsey and adjacent Islands -	13,262	14,403
England	2,131	2,314
Wales -	40	34
Scotland	89	69
Ireland -	223	305
Jersey - -	441	517
British Colonies and East Indies	143	241
Born at Sea (British Subjects)	5	4
Foreign Parts (British Subjects)	74	122

Where Born.	Males.	Females.
Foreign Parts (Foreign Subjects):		
Denmark -	1	—
Norway - -	4	—
Sweden	5	—
Russia - -	—	1
Switzerland	1	9
Germany - -	16	4
Belgium - -	9	2
France	360	369
Portugal -	3	—
Spain	1	2
Italy -	6	6
Africa -	1	—
America: United States	18	26
" Mexico -	1	—
" Brazil - -	2	—
" Other States, or State not specified -	1	—

TABLE 11.—NUMBER and AGES of MALES and FEMALES returned as "BLIND," as "DEAF AND DUMB," as "IDIOTS or IMBECILES," and as "LUNATICS" in GUERNSEY.

Returned as	All Ages.			0–	5–	15–	20–	25–	45–	65 and upwards.
	Both Sexes.	Males and Females.								
Blind -	48	Males -	28	—	3	—	1	5	3	16
		Females -	20	—	1	—	1	2	3	13
Deaf and Dumb -	18	Males	9		—	—	—	5	3	1
		Females -	9	1	3	1	—	2	3	—
Lunatics	47	Males	27	—	—	3	—	11	11	2
		Females	20	—	—	—	—	11	5	4
Idiots or Imbeciles -	43	Males	24	—	1	4	4	10	3	2
		Females -	19	—	1	3	—	7	5	3

LONDON:
Printed by GEORGE E. B. EYRE and WILLIAM SPOTTISWOODE,
Printers to the Queen's most Excellent Majesty.
For Her Majesty's Stationery Office.

CENSUS—1881.

ISLANDS

IN THE

BRITISH SEAS.

ISLE OF MAN.

JERSEY.

GUERNSEY AND ADJACENT ISLANDS.

Presented to both Houses of Parliament by Command of Her Majesty.

LONDON:
PRINTED BY GEORGE E. B. EYRE AND WILLIAM SPOTTISWOODE.

To be purchased, either directly or through any Bookseller, from any of the following Agents, viz.,
Messrs. HANSARD, 13, Great Queen Street, W.C., and 32, Abingdon Street, Westminster;
Messrs. EYRE and SPOTTISWOODE, East Harding Street, Fleet Street, and Sale Office, House of Lords;
Messrs. ADAM and CHARLES BLACK, of Edinburgh;
Messrs. ALEXANDER THOM and Co., or Messrs. HODGES, FIGGIS, and Co., of Dublin.

1883.

Milton Keynes UK
Ingram Content Group UK Ltd.
UKHW031913050224
437294UK00006B/322